D1223257

THE
CAMBRIDGE
DICTIONARY
OF
JUDAISM
AND
JEWISH CULTURE

The Cambridge Dictionary of Judaism and Jewish Culture is an authoritative and accessible reference work for a twenty-first-century audience. Its entries, written by eminent scholars, define the spiritual and intellectual concepts and the religious movements that distinguish Judaism and the Jewish experience. They cover central personalities and places, formative events, and enduring literary and cultural contributions, and they illuminate the lives of ordinary Jewish women and men. Essays explore Jewish history from ancient times to the present and consider all aspects of Judaism, including religious practices and rituals, legal teachings, legendary traditions, rationalism, mysticism, and messianism. This reference work differs from many others in its broad exploration of the Jewish experience beyond Judaism. Entries discuss secular and political movements and achievements and delineate Jewish endeavors in literature, art, music, theater, dance, film, broadcasting, sports, science, medicine, and ecology, among many other topics from the ancient Near East to the Internet.

Judith R. Baskin is Philip H. Knight Professor of Humanities and Associate Dean for Humanities in the College of Arts and Sciences at the University of Oregon. Her books include *Pharaoh's Counsellors: Job, Jethro, and Balaam in Rabbinic and Patristic Tradition* (1982) and *Midrashic Women: Formations of the Feminine in Rabbinic Literature* (2002). She is the editor of *Jewish Women in Historical Perspective* (1991; 2nd edition, 1998) and *Women of the Word: Jewish Women and Jewish Writing* (1994) and is coeditor of *The Cambridge Guide to Jewish History, Religion, and Culture* (with Kenneth Seeskin, 2010), which received the 2010 National Jewish Book Award for anthologies and collections.

THE CAMBRIDGE DICTIONARY OF JUDAISM AND JEWISH CULTURE

EDITOR:

Judith R. Baskin, *University of Oregon*

SUBEDITORS:

Glenda Abramson, *St. Cross College, Oxford University*: Literature

Zachary Braiterman, *Syracuse University*: Modern Jewish Thought

Joseph Dan, *Hebrew University of Jerusalem*: Mysticism

David Engel, *New York University*: Antisemitism; Holocaust

Isaiah Gafni, *Hebrew University of Jerusalem*: Rabbinic Judaism

Rela Mintz Geffen, *Baltimore Hebrew Institute, Towson University, Emerita*: Religious Life and Practice

Sara R. Horowitz, *York University*: Literature

Ephraim Kanarfogel, *Yeshiva University*: Medieval and Early Modern Europe

Carol Meyers, *Duke University*: Bible and Ancient Near East

Pamela S. Nadell, *American University*: Contemporary Religious Movements

Jonathan D. Sarna, *Brandeis University*: The Americas

Lawrence H. Schiffman, *Yeshiva University*: Second Temple Period

Jeffrey Shandler, *Rutgers University*: Popular Culture

Anita Shapira, *Tel Aviv University*: Modern Middle East; Israel

Norman Stillman, *University of Oklahoma*: The Muslim World

Steven J. Zipperstein, *Stanford University*: Europe, 1800 to the Present

THE
CAMBRIDGE
DICTIONARY
OF
JUDAISM
AND
JEWISH CULTURE

Edited by
JUDITH R. BASKIN
University of Oregon

CAMBRIDGE
UNIVERSITY PRESS

GUELPH HUMBER LIBRARY
205 Humber College Blvd
Toronto, ON   M9W 5L7

CAMBRIDGE UNIVERSITY PRESS
Cambridge, New York, Melbourne, Madrid, Cape Town,
Singapore, São Paulo, Delhi, Tokyo, Mexico City

Cambridge University Press
32 Avenue of the Americas, New York, NY 10013-2473, USA

www.cambridge.org
Information on this title: www.cambridge.org/9780521825979

© Judith R. Baskin 2011

This publication is in copyright. Subject to statutory exception
and to the provisions of relevant collective licensing agreements,
no reproduction of any part may take place without the written
permission of Cambridge University Press.

First published 2011

Printed in the United States of America

A catalog record for this publication is available from the British Library.

Library of Congress Cataloging in Publication data

The Cambridge dictionary of Judaism and Jewish culture / [edited by] Judith R. Baskin.
 p.   cm.
Includes bibliographical references and index.
ISBN 978-0-521-82597-9 (hardback)
1. Judaism – Dictionaries.   I. Baskin, Judith Reesa, 1950–   II. Title.
BM50.C26   2011
909′.04924 – dc22   2010047383

ISBN 978-0-521-82597-9 Hardback

Cambridge University Press has no responsibility for the persistence or accuracy of URLs for external
or third-party Internet Web sites referred to in this publication and does not guarantee that any content
on such Web sites is, or will remain, accurate or appropriate.

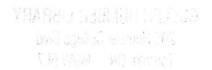

CONTENTS

PLATES AND MAPS

Plates

1   ASTARTE FIGURINES. Judah, Israelite period, 8th century–early 6th century BCE. The Israel Museum, Jerusalem. Accession numbers: 68.32.4, 64.67/3, 64.67/4 IAA 60–725, 80–2. Photo © The Israel Museum Jerusalem by Nahum Slapak. See ARCHEOLOGY, LAND OF ISRAEL: ANCIENT TIMES TO PERSIAN PERIOD; CANAAN, CANAANITES; ISRAELITES: MARRIAGE AND FAMILY; ISRAELITES: RELIGION; JUDAH, KINGDOM OF; and WOMEN, ANCIENT: BIBLICAL REPRESENTATIONS.

2   DEAD SEA SCROLL: The Community Rule (detail). Qumran, 1st century BCE–1st century CE. Parchment. The Shrine of the Book at the Israel Museum, Jerusalem. Accession number: 96.83/208A. Photo © The Israel Museum, Jerusalem. See ARCHEOLOGY, LAND OF ISRAEL: SECOND TEMPLE PERIOD; DEAD SEA SCROLLS; and QUMRAN.

3   SYNAGOGUE MOSAIC FLOOR (detail): The central shrine (possibly a Torah ark) and the menorahs, *shofars*, and incense shovels symbolize the Jerusalem Temple and expectation of messianic redemption. Beth Shean, Byzantine period, 6th century CE. The Israel Museum, Jerusalem. IAA Photo © The Israel Museum Jerusalem. See ART: LATE ANTIQUITY; BYZANTINE EMPIRE; DECAPOLIS CITIES; MENORAH; MESSIANISM: BIBLICAL AND SECOND TEMPLE ERAS; *SHOFAR*; and SYNAGOGUES, ANCIENT.

4   THE REGENSBURG PENTATEUCH: This depiction of Aaron the High Priest lighting the Tabernacle menorah, with Tabernacle implements, invokes a rebuilt Temple and future redemption. Regensburg, Bavaria, Germany, ca. 1300 CE. Pen and ink, tempera and gold leaf on vellum. The Israel Museum, Jerusalem. Accession number: B05.0009; 180/05. Photo © The Israel Museum Jerusalem by David Harris. See AARON; ART: MEDIEVAL MANUSCRIPT ILLUSTRATION; MENORAH; TABERNACLE; TEMPLE AND TEMPLE CULT; and TEMPLE, SECOND.

5   PASSOVER PLATE. Spain, ca. 1480. Earthenware. The Israel Museum, Jerusalem. Gift of Jakob Michael, New York, in memory of his wife, Erna Sondheimer-Michael. Accession number: B65.12.0483; 134/057. Photo © The Israel Museum Jerusalem by Nahum Slapak. See CEREMONIAL OBJECTS; PASSOVER; and SPAIN, CHRISTIAN.

6   BRIDAL CASKET (*cofanetto*) represents from right to left the three duties incumbent on Jewish women: *hallah* (putting aside a portion of the Sabbath dough); *niddah*; and *hadlakat ha-ner* (kindling Sabbath lights). North Italy, late 15th century. Cast and engraved silver, niello, partly gilt. The Israel Museum, Jerusalem. Gift of Astorre Mayer, Milan. Accession number: B51.04.0207; 131/030. Photo © The Israel Museum Jerusalem. See ITALY; *NIDDAH*; SABBATH; IMMERSION, RITUAL: WOMEN; MIKVEH; and WOMEN, ANCIENT: RABBINIC JUDAISM.

7   *MAHZOR CORFU*: Elijah sounding a *shofar* while leading the Messiah into Jerusalem. Corfu, Greece, 1709. Courtesy of The Library of The Jewish Theological Seminary. See ELIJAH:

Museum, NY/Art Resource, NY ART132848. See ART, AMERICAN: BEFORE 1940; and ART, AMERICAN: SINCE 1940; and NEW YORK CITY.

19 Leonard Baskin (1922–2000), THE ALTAR, 1977. Lindenwood: carved and laminated. Location: The Jewish Museum, New York City. Photo credit: © Estate of the artist. See ART, AMERICAN: SINCE 1940; and HOLOCAUST REPRESENTATION: ART.

20 Deborah Kass (b. 1952), SIX BLUE BARBRAS (THE JEWISH JACKIE SERIES), 1992. Screen print and acrylic on canvas. The Jewish Museum, New York City. Gift of Seth Cohen, 2004–10. Photo: Richard Goodbody, Inc. Photo credit: The Jewish Museum, NY/Art Resource, NY ART334071. See ART, AMERICAN: SINCE 1940; and CELEBRITIES.

21 Ephraim Moses Lilien (1874–1925), SKETCH FOR A CARPET (triptych; dedicated to Mr. and Mrs. David Wolffson): right: *GALUT* [exile], center: ALLEGORICAL WEDDING, left: LIBERATION, 1906. Oil and pencil on canvas. The Israel Museum, Jerusalem. Photo © The Israel Museum Jerusalem. Accession number: B88.0279. See ART, EUROPE: TWENTIETH CENTURY; and ART, ISRAELI.

22 Reuven Rubin (1893–1974), FIRST FRUITS (triptych): right: SERENITY (THE BEDOUINE); center: FRUIT OF THE LAND; left: THE SHEPHERD, 1923. Oil on canvas. Rubin Museum Collection, Tel Aviv. See ART, ISRAELI.

23 Itzhak Danziger (1916–1977), NIMROD, 1939. Nubian sandstone. The Israel Museum, Jerusalem. Gift of Dr. H. David Orgler, Zurich and Jerusalem. © Estate of the artist. Accession number: B81.0600. Photo © The Israel Museum Jerusalem by Nahum Slapak. See ART, ISRAELI.

24 Mordecai Ardon (1896–1992), AT THE GATES OF JERUSALEM (triptych): right: SIGN; center: LADDERS; left: ROCK, 1967. Oil on canvas. The Israel Museum, Jerusalem. Gift of the artist in honor of Israel's twentieth anniversary and the reunification of Jerusalem. © Estate of the artist. Accession number: B67.0546. Photo © The Israel Museum Jerusalem. See ART, ISRAELI.

Maps

Color plates follow page 336.

CONTRIBUTORS

Philip I. Ackerman-Lieberman, *Vanderbilt University*: **Masorah, Masoretes, Nagid**

Howard Tzvi Adelman, *Queen's University, Kingston, Ontario*: Ascarelli, Devorà; Modena, Leon; Sulam, Sarra Copia

Eliyana Adler, *United States Holocaust Museum*: Prostitutes, Prostitution: Modern Era

Reuben Aharoni, *The Ohio State University, Emeritus*: Yemen

Phyllis Cohen Albert, *Harvard University*: Antisemitism: France, 1789–1939; Emancipation: France; France: 1789–1939; France: Consistories (1806–1939); Jewish Studies: France (Nineteenth Century); Judaism, Reform: France; Synagogues: France; Zionism: France

Natalia Aleksiun-Madrzak, *New York University*: **Yizkor** Books

Elizabeth Shanks Alexander, *University of Virginia, Charlottesville*: Mishnah

Rebecca T. Alpert, *Temple University*: Judaism, Reconstructionist; Reconstructionist Rabbinical College

Ziva Amishai-Maisels, *Hebrew University of Jerusalem*: Holocaust Representation: Art

Joyce Antler, *Brandeis University*: Szold, Henrietta

Yaakov Ariel, *University of North Carolina, Chapel Hill*: Interfaith Dialogue: United States

Allan Arkush, *Binghamton University, SUNY*: Strauss, Leo; Zionism

Nehama Aschkenasy, *University of Connecticut, Stamford*: Literature, Hebrew: Women Writers, 1882–2010

Dianne N. Ashton, *Rowan University*: Philadelphia

Karen Auerbach, *University of Michigan*: Poland; Warsaw

Ilan Avisar, *Tel Aviv University*: Holocaust Representation: Film

Merle Lyn Bachman, *Spalding University*: Poetry, Yiddish

Gershon Bacon, *Bar-Ilan University*: **Agudat Israel**

Carol Bakhos, *University of California, Los Angeles*: Ishmael: Rabbinic Traditions; Rabbinic Literature: Midrash

Daphne Barak-Erez, *Tel Aviv University*: Israel, State of: Judicial System

Israel Bartal, *Hebrew University*: Council of Four Lands and Council of Lithuania

Judith R. Baskin, *University of Oregon*: Abortion; Abraham; Adoption; Adultery; **Agunah; Alphabet of Ben Sira**; Amos, Book of; Balaam; Beruriah; Betrothal; Brandeis, Louis Dembitz; Bride and Bridegroom; Chagall, Bella Rosenfeld; Death and Mourning; Divorce: Historical Development; Education, Girls: Medieval and Early Modern; Eve; Exilarch; Glückel of Hameln; Hagar; Hanukkah and Women; Hasidism, Europe: Women; Head Covering: Women; **Herem ha-Yishuv**; Immersion, Ritual: Women; Infertility; Isaac the Blind; Israel,

Land of; Israel, State of: Immigration before 1948; Jacob ben Asher; Jethro; JEWISH STUDIES; Job: Rabbinic Traditions; Jonas, Regina; Judaism; *Kallah* Months; *Ketubbah*; Leeser, Isaac; Lilith; Marriage, Levirate; Palestine; Purity and Impurity; *Rebbetzin*; Rossi, Azariah dei; Samuel ibn Naghrela ha-Nagid; Sanhedrin; *Simḥat Bat; Tikkun Olam*: Contemporary Understandings; Torah; Verbermacher, Hannah Rachel; Wengeroff, Pauline Epstein; Women: Early Modern Europe; Women: Middle Ages; Women, Modern: Britain and North America; Women: Pre- and Post-State Israel; Zephaniah

Samantha Baskind, *Cleveland State University*: Art, American: Before 1940; Art, American: Since 1940

Sigrid Bauschinger, *University of Massachusetts, Amherst*: Lasker-Shüler, Else

Diane Baxter, *University of Oregon*: Anthropology

Michael J. Bazyler, *Chapman University School of Law:* Holocaust Reparations and Restitution

Daniel Beer, *University College London*: Beilis Trial

Michael Beizer, *Hebrew University of Jerusalem*: Dubnow, Simon; Joint Distribution Committee; Saint Petersburg; Soviet Union: Jewish Movement, 1967–1989

Dean Phillip Bell, *Spertus Institute of Jewish Studies*: Conversion: Early Modern Period; Court Jews; Messianism: Early Modern

Elissa Bemporad, *Queens College, CUNY*: Belorussia

Mara H. Benjamin, *St. Olaf College*: Rosenzweig, Franz

Evelyn Rose Benson, *Independent Scholar*: Nursing: United States

Michael Berenbaum, *Sigi Ziering Institute*: Holocaust Representation: Television

Nancy E. Berg, *Washington University*: Memoir and Life Writing: Mizraḥi

David Berger, *Yeshiva University*: Middle Ages: Jewish–Christian Polemics

Wendy H. Bergoffen, *Mount Holyoke College*: Crime and Criminals: United States

Joel Berkowitz, *University of Wisconsin, Milwaukee*: Theater, Yiddish

Andrew Berns, *University of Pennsylvania*: Medicine

Paul F. Bessemer, *Hillel Foundation, University of Oregon*: Sabbateanism (Ottoman Empire and Turkey)

Henry Bial, *University of Kansas*: Television: United States

Asher D. Biemann, *University of Virginia*: Buber, Martin

Gideon Biger, *Tel Aviv University*: Israel, State of: Agricultural Settlements, 1878–1948

Ellen Birnbaum, *Independent Scholar*: Philo of Alexandria

Miriam Bodian, *University of Texas, Austin*: Amsterdam

Linda J. Borish, *Western Michigan University*: Sports, United States: Women

Olga Borovaya, *Stanford University*: Journalism, Ladino (Ottoman Empire)

Ra'anan Boustan, *University of California, Los Angeles*: Temple, Second

Steven R. Bowman, *University of Cincinnati*: Byzantine Empire

Zachary Braiterman, *Syracuse University*: Aesthetics; God; Rubenstein, Richard L.

Ross Brann, *Cornell University*: Dunash ben Labrat; Ibn Gabirol, Solomon; Poetry, Medieval: Muslim World

Michael Brenner, *Ludwig Maximilian University, Munich*: Graetz, Heinrich; Zunz, Leopold

Marc Brettler, *Brandeis University*: Aramaic; Bible: Prayer Language; Hebrew, Biblical; Psalms, Book of

Tobias Brinkmann, *Pennsylvania State University*: Chicago

Adriana M. Brodsky, *St. Mary's College of Maryland*: Argentina

Robert Brody, *Hebrew University of Jerusalem*: Gaon, Geonim, Geonic Academies; Hai ben Sherira; Pumbedita; Saboraim

Daniel M. Bronstein, *Congregation Beth Elohim, Brooklyn, New York*: Comedy and Comedians; United States: Military Chaplaincy

Judith Bronstein, *University of Haifa*: Middle Ages: Crusades

Emily Budick, *Hebrew University of Jerusalem*: Literature: United States (since 1900)

Stephen G. Burnett, *University of Nebraska, Lincoln*: Christian Hebraism; Reformation

Sean Burt, *University of Arizona*: Chronicles, Books of; Ezra and Nehemiah, Books of; Jacob; Jonah, Book of; Moses; Phoenicia, Phoenicians; Solomon

Lisa Rubenstein Calevi, *Independent Scholar*: Luzzatto, Samuel David; Mortara Affair

Eric Caplan, *McGill University*: Prayer Books: United States

Nina Caputo, *University of Florida*: Naḥmanides (Moses ben Naḥman)

Michael Carasik, *Independent Scholar*: Bible: Wisdom Literature; Ecclesiastes, Book of; Job, Book of; Proverbs, Book of

Shalom Carmy, *Yeshiva University*: Berkovits, Eliezer; Soloveitchik, Joseph B.: Religious Thought

Jerome A. Chanes, *Brandeis University*: Organizations: North America

Yael Chaver, *University of California at Berkeley*: Literature, Yiddish: The **Yishuv**

Robert Chazan, *New York University*: Middle Ages: Demography

Carmel U. Chiswick, *University of Illinois at Chicago, Emerita*: United States: Economic Life

Adina Cimet, *YIVO Institute for Jewish Research*: Mexico

Amos Cohen, *Independent Scholar*: Film: Europe (Post–World War II)

Beth B. Cohen, *California State University, Northridge*: Holocaust Survivors: United States

Judah M. Cohen, *Indiana University*: Music, Popular

Lisa Cohen, *Abraham Joshua Heschel High School, New York*: **Shtetl**; Women, Modern: Eastern Europe

Michael R. Cohen, *Tulane University*: Boston; Marshall, Louis; Straus Family; United States: Fraternal Societies; United States: Sephardim

John J. Collins, *Yale University*: Bel and the Dragon; Eschatology: Second Temple Period; Sibylline Oracles

Sandra Collins, *Byzantine Catholic Seminary*: Esther, Book of; Lamentations, Book of

Olivia Remie Constable, *Notre Dame University*: Benjamin of Tudela

David M. Crowe, *Elon University*: Auschwitz; Bełżec; Chełmno; Holocaust; Holocaust: Camps and Killing Centers; Holocaust Rescuers; Holocaust: Roma; **Kristallnacht**; Majdanek; Schindler, Oskar; Sobibór; Theresienstadt; Treblinka; Wannsee Conference

Joseph Dan, *Hebrew University of Jerusalem*: Abulafia, Abraham; **Adam Kadmon; Baal Shem; Bahir, Sefer ha-;** Breaking of the Vessels; Cordovero, Moses; **Devekut**; Dov Ber of Międzyrzecz; Dybbuk; **Ein Sof; Golem**; Kabbalah; Kabbalah, Lurianic; Luria, Isaac; Luzzatto, Moses Ḥayyim; Metatron; Moses de Leon; Mysticism: Ancient; Mysticism: **Hekhalot and Merkavah** Literature; Naḥman of Bratslav; Numerology (**Gematria**); Safed; Samael; Scholem, Gershom Gerhard; **Sefer Yetzirah; Sefirot; Tikkun Olam; Tzimtzum;** Zalman, Schneur ben Baruch, of Liady; *Zohar*

Robert Daum, *Vancouver School of Theology*: Tosefta

Marni Davis, *Georgia State University*: Banking and Banking Houses; Baron de Hirsch Fund

Sergio DellaPergola, *Hebrew University of Jerusalem and The Jewish People Policy Planning Institute*: Demography

David deSilva, *Ashland Theological Seminary*: Apocrypha

Elliot N. Dorff, *American Jewish University*: Capital Punishment; Courts; Ethics, Medical; Ethics, Sexual; **Halakhah**

Jean Duhaime, *University of Montreal*: Dualism: In Ancient Judaism

James D. G. Dunn, *Durham University*: New Testament

Aminadav Dykman, *Hebrew University of Jerusalem*: Hebrew, Translation into

Glenn Dynner, *Sarah Lawrence College*: Family and Marriage: Early Modern Period; Frank, Jacob, and Frankism; Ḥasidism: Europe

Marsha Bryan Edelman, *Gratz College*: Cantor, Cantorate: Contemporary; Music: Synagogue

Martin Edelman, *University at Albany, SUNY, Emeritus*: Israel, State of: Political Institutions; Israel, State of: Political Parties

Carl S. Ehrlich, *York University*: Archeology, Land of Israel: Ancient Times to Persian Period; Philistines

Susan Einbinder, *Hebrew Union College–Jewish Institute of Religion, Cincinnati*: Poetry, Medieval: Christian Europe

Ellen Eisenberg, *Willamette University*: United States: Agricultural Settlements

David Engel, *New York University*: Antisemitism

Marc Michael Epstein, *Vassar College*: Art: Medieval Manuscript Illustration

Harley Erdman, *University of Massachusetts, Amherst*: Theater: United States

Ruth Eshel, *University of Haifa*: Dance: Pre- and Post-State Israel

Anat Feinberg, *College of Jewish Studies, Heidelberg*: Theater: Europe

Shmuel Feiner, *Bar-Ilan University*: **Haskalah**

Marjorie N. Feld, *Babson College*: Social Work: United States; Wald, Lillian D.

Michael Feldberg, *The History Consultancy, LC*: Center for Jewish History

Jackie Feldman, *Ben-Gurion University*: Tourism

Steven Fine, *Yeshiva University*: Art: Late Antiquity; Synagogues, Ancient

Sylvia Barack Fishman, *Brandeis University*: Film: United States

K. E. Fleming, *New York University*: Balkans; Greece

Jerold C. Frakes, *University at Buffalo, SUNY*: Literature, Yiddish: Beginnings to 1700

Barry Freundel, *Baltimore Hebrew Institute, Towson University*: **Beit Din**; Confession of Sin; **Eruv**; Head Covering: Men; **Omer; Omer**, Counting of the; Shaving

Ken Frieden, *Syracuse University*: Literature, Yiddish: 1800 to Twenty-First Century

Harriet Pass Friedenreich, *Temple University*: Women, Modern: Central Europe

Kate Friedman, *Editorial Assistant*: Ahab; Almohads; Almoravids; Ark of the Covenant; Asher ben Jeḥiel; Ashkenaz, Ashkenazim; Baḥia ben Joseph ibn Pakuda; Bathsheba; Cain and Abel; Damascus Affair; Deborah; Eldad ha-Dani; Flood; Frankel, Zacharias; Hammurabi; Hezekiah; Hittites; Host, Desecration of; Jericho; Jonah ben Abraham Gerondi; Josiah; Judah ben Asher; Levinsohn, Isaac Baer; Lilienthal, Max; Nazirite; Newport, Rhode Island; Queen of Sheba; Radhanites; Red Heifer; Rehoboam; Ruth, Book of

Baruch Frydman-Kohl, *Beth Tzedec Congregation, Toronto*: Arama, Isaac; **Dina de-Malkhuta Dina**; Gersonides (Levi ben Gershon); Halevi, Judah; Thought, Medieval

Kirsten A. Fudeman, *University of Pittsburgh*: France: Middle Ages

Michael Galchinsky, *Georgia State University*: Human Rights

Alexandra Garbarini, *Williams College*: Holocaust Diaries

Rela Mintz Geffen, *Baltimore Hebrew Institute, Towson University, Emerita*: Bar Mitzvah; Bat Mitzvah; Circumcision; Confirmation; Consecration; Custom (**Minhag**); Judaism, Conservative; Judaism, Masorti; **Kittel**; Life-Cycle Rituals; Philanthropy; Synagogue Sisterhoods; United States: Community Center Movement

Mark H. Gelber, *Ben-Gurion University*: Literature: Central Europe

Dov Gera, *Ben-Gurion University*: Tobiads

Jane Gerber, *Graduate Center, CUNY*: Spain, Muslim

Nurit Gertz, *The Open University of Israel*: Film: Israel

Barry Gittlen, *Baltimore Hebrew Institute: Towson University*: Canaan, Canaanites

Carole Glauber, *Independent Scholar*: Photography

Edward Bernard Glick, *Temple University, Emeritus*: Israel, State of: Arab–Israeli Conflict, 1948–2010; Israel, State of: Diaspora Relations; Israel, State of: Founding of the Modern State; Israel, State of: Wars (1948)

Nora Glickman, *Queens College and the Graduate Center, CUNY*: Film: Latin America

Matthew Goff, *Florida State University*: Hasmonean Dynasty; Wisdom of Ben Sira, Book of

Motti Golani, *University of Haifa*: Israel, State of: Military and Paramilitary Bodies; Jerusalem, 1948–1967

Peter B. Golden, *Rutgers University*: Khazars

Simha Goldin, *Tel Aviv University*: Middle Ages: Childhood

Gabriel Goldstein, *Yeshiva University Museum:* Ceremonial Objects

Elaine Goodfriend, *California State University, Northridge*: Canaan, Canaanites; Egypt and Ancient Israel; Exodus, Book of; Mesopotamia and Ancient Israel; Near East, Ancient; Prostitutes, Prostitution: Hebrew Bible through Middle Ages

Rachel Gordan, *Harvard University*: **Ḥavurah** Movement; Jewish Theological Seminary of America; Judaism, Humanistic; Judaism, Progressive; Workmen's Circle; World Union for Progressive Judaism; Yeshiva University; Zionism: United States

Peter E. Gordon, *Harvard University*: Benjamin, Walter; Freud, Sigmund; Psychoanalysis

Alon Goshen-Gottstein, *Bet Morasha of Jerusalem*: Elisha ben Abuya

Evlyn Gould, *University of Oregon*: Dreyfus Affair

Lisa D. Grant, *Hebrew Union College–Jewish Institute of Religion, New York*: Education, North America: Adult

Alyssa M. Gray, *Hebrew Union College–Jewish Institute of Religion, New York*: Talmud, Jerusalem

Abigail Green, *Brasenose College, University of Oxford*: Montefiore, Moses Haim and Judith Barent Cohen

Deborah A. Green, *University of Oregon*: Anointment; Incense

Elizabeth E. Greenberg, *Independent Scholar*: Fashion

Gershon Greenberg, *American University*: Holocaust: Theological Responses

Yudit Kornberg Greenberg, *Rollins College*: Love

Rachel L. Greenblatt, *Harvard University*: Prague

Frederick E. Greenspahn, *Florida Atlantic University*: Bible; Bible: Modern Scholarship; Deuteronomy, Book of; Genesis, Book of

Leonard Greenspoon, *Creighton University*: Bible: Translations and Translators; Cities of Refuge; Ten Commandments

Michael Greenstein, *Independent Scholar*: Literature: Canada

Adam Gregerman, *Institute for Jewish and Christian Studies, Baltimore*: Hellenism; Jerusalem: Biblical and Rabbinic Sources; Pharisees; Sadducees

Grace Cohen Grossman, *Skirball Cultural Center, Los Angeles*: Museums

Samuel D. Gruber, *Jewish Heritage Research Center, Syracuse, New York*: Synagogues, Europe: Medieval to Eighteenth Century; Synagogues: Twentieth Century

Naomi Grunhaus, *Yeshiva University*: Kimḥi Family

Jeffrey S. Gurock, *Yeshiva University*: Sports and Americanization

Aviva Halamish, *The Open University of Israel*: Israel, State of: Youth Movements

Chaya T. Halberstam, *Indiana University*: Bible: Prophets and Prophecy; Law: Ancient Near East and Hebrew Bible

David J. Halperin, *University of North Carolina, Chapel Hill, Emeritus*: Shabbatai Zevi

Mark W. Hamilton, *Abilene Christian University*: Israelites: Kingship; Kings, Books of

Rachel S. Harris, *University of Illinois at Urbana-Champaign*: Holocaust Literature: Poetry; Literature, Hebrew: The *Yishuv*, 1880–1948; Poetry, Modern Hebrew

Steven Harvey, *Bar-Ilan University*: Science and Mathematics: Middle Ages and Early Modern Period

Rachel Havrelock, *University of Illinois at Chicago*: Israelites: Tribes; Joshua, Book of; Judges, Book of; Samuel, Books of

Kenneth Helphand, *University of Oregon*: Gardens; Israel, State of: Landscape Architecture

Marc Hirshman, *Hebrew University of Jerusalem*: *Epikoros*

Leah Hochman, *Hebrew Union College–Jewish Institute of Religion, Los Angeles*: Krochmal, Nachman; Maimon, Salomon; Mendelssohn, Moses

Brian Horowitz, *Tulane University*: Society for the Promotion of Enlightenment among the Jews of Russia (OPE)

Sara R. Horowitz, *York University*: Holocaust Literature; Holocaust Literature: Fiction; Wiesel, Elie

Thomas C. Hubka, *University of Wisconsin, Milwaukee*: Synagogues, Wooden

Tal Ilan, *Freie Universität, Berlin*: Talmud Study: Feminist Approaches; Women, Ancient: Rabbinic Judaism; Women, Ancient: Second Temple Period

Stanley Isser, *University at Albany, SUNY*: David

Andrew S. Jacobs, *Scripps College*: Church Fathers: Attitudes toward Jews and Judaism

Benjamin M. Jacobs, *University of Minnesota, Twin Cities*: Education, North America: Day Schools

Martin Jacobs, *Washington University*: Travel Writing: Middle Ages and Early Modern Period

Jenna Weissman Joselit, *George Washington University*: Menorah Association

Ava Fran Kahn, *California Studies Center, Berkeley*: Los Angeles; San Francisco; United States, Western

Ephraim Kanarfogel, *Yeshiva University*: Education, Boys: Medieval and Early Modern; Meir ben Barukh (Maharam) of Rothenburg; Middle Ages: *Ḥasidei Ashkenaz*; Tosafists

Dana Evan Kaplan, *Temple B'nai Israel, Albany, Georgia*: Judaism, Reform: North America

Edward K. Kaplan, *Brandeis University*: Heschel, Abraham Joshua

Gregory Kaplan, *Rice University*: Secularism

Jonathan Karp, *Binghamton University, SUNY*: Commerce: Modern Europe (1700–1900); Emancipation

Claire Katz, *Texas A&M University*: Levinas, Emmanuel

Martin Kavka, *Florida State University*: Messianism: Modern Approaches

Robert S. Kawashima, *University of Florida*: Bible: Narrative Literature

Ari Y. Kelman, *University of California, Davis*: Radio: United States

Mark Kligman, *Hebrew Union College–Jewish Institute of Religion, New York*: Music, Folk; Music, Religious

Sharon Koren, *Hebrew Union College–Jewish Institute of Religion, New York*: Mysticism, Women and; *Shekhinah*

Daniel P. Kotzin, *Medaille College*: Magnes, Judah L.

Carol Herselle Krinsky, *New York University*: Synagogues: Nineteenth Century

Robert Kugler, *Lewis and Clark College*: Alexandria, Ancient; *Aristeas, Letter of*; Egypt: Heracleopolis Papyri; Pseudepigrapha; Ptolemies

Jenny R. Labendz, *Jewish Theological Seminary*: Dietary Laws

Gail Labovitz, *American Jewish University*: Marriage and Marriage Customs

Matthew LaGrone, *University of Delaware*: Chosenness

Berel Lang, *Wesleyan University*: Levi, Primo

Ruth Langer, *Boston College*: Worship

Daniel J. Lasker, *Ben-Gurion University*: Karaism; Saadia ben Joseph Gaon

Aliza Lavie, *Bar-Ilan University*: Prayer: Women's Devotional

Eric Lawee, *York University*: Abravanel Family

Peter Lawson, *Open University, United Kingdom*: Poetry: Britain; Theater: Britain

Anson Laytner, *Seattle University*: China

Arlene Lazarowitz, *California State University, Long Beach*: United States: Political Involvement; United States Presidents

Oliver Leaman, *University of Kentucky*: Evil and Suffering

Jeffrey Lesser, *Emory University*: Brazil

Mark Leuchter, *Temple University*: Israelites: Religion; Temple and Temple Cult

Vladimir Levin, *Hebrew University of Jerusalem*: Chmelnitzki, Bogdan; Pogrom; Ukraine

Stephanie Wellen Levine, *Tufts University*: Ḥasidism: North America; Schneerson, Menachem Mendel

Avigdor Levy, *Brandeis University*: Mendes-Nasi Family; Ottoman Empire

Judith Lewin, *Union College*: Literature: Women Writers (Europe and North America)

Gideon Libson, *Hebrew University of Jerusalem*: Responsa Literature

Tatjana Lichtenstein, *University of Texas, Austin*: Czechoslovakia

Laura S. Lieber, *Duke University*: Poetry, Liturgical (*Piyyut*); Song of Songs, Book of

Yehiel Limor, *Tel Aviv University*: Journalism: Israel

Naomi Lindstrom, *University of Texas, Austin*: Latin America

Vivian Liska, *University of Antwerp*: Kafka, Franz; Literature: Contemporary Europe

Elizabeth Loentz, *University of Illinois, Chicago*: Pappenheim, Bertha

Steven M. Lowenstein, *American Jewish University*: Berlin

Anthony MacFarlane, MD, *Independent Scholar*: Caribbean; Jamaica

Shaul Magid, *Indiana University*: Antinomianism; Kook, Abraham Isaac

David Marc, *Syracuse University*: Broadcasting: Radio and Television; Sports, United States: Baseball; Sports, United States: Basketball; Sports, United States: Football; Sportscasters

Evyatar Marienberg, *University of North Carolina, Chapel Hill*: *Baraita de-Niddah*; Mikveh; *Niddah*

Steve Mason, *York University*: Josephus, Flavius

Mary McCune, *State University of New York, Oswego*: Organizations, Women's: North America

Keren McGinity, *University of Michigan*: Intermarriage: Historical Perspectives; Intermarriage: Twenty-First-Century United States

Rafael Medoff, *David S. Wyman Institute for Holocaust Studies*: Holocaust: United States Jewish Response

Esther Meir-Glitzenstein, *Ben-Gurion University*: Israel, State of: Jewish Immigration Post-1948

Yitzhak Y. Melamed, *Johns Hopkins University*: Crescas, Ḥasdai ben Abraham

Renée Levine Melammed, *Schechter Institute, Jerusalem*: Inquisition, Spanish

Adam Mendelsohn, *College of Charleston*: Australia; New Zealand; South Africa; United States: African American–Jewish Relations; United States: Civil Rights Movement

Amitai Mendelsohn, *Israel Museum, Jerusalem*: Art, Israeli

Ted Merwin, *Dickinson College*: Entertainment

Michael A. Meyer, *Hebrew Union College–Jewish Institute of Religion, Cincinnati, Emeritus*: Geiger, Abraham; Germany; Hebrew Union College–Jewish Institute of Religion; Judaism, Reform: Germany

Carol Meyers, *Duke University*: Adam; Bible: Ancestral Narratives; Bible: Music and Dance; Hannah; Illness and Disease: Bible and Ancient Near East; Israelites: Marriage and Family; Menorah; Miriam; Rebekah; Women, Ancient: Biblical Representations; Women, Ancient: Israelite

Eric M. Meyers, *Duke University*: Babylonian Exile; Daniel, Book of; Malachi, Book of; Zechariah, Book of; Zerubbabel

Deborah Dash Moore, *University of Michigan*: New York City; World War II: Impact on American Jews

Menachem Mor, *University of Haifa*: Jewish War, Second

Milton Moreland, *Rhodes College*: Archeology, Land of Israel: Second Temple Period

Samuel Morell, *Binghamton University, SUNY*: Karo, Joseph

Michael L. Morgan, *Indiana University*: Fackenheim, Emil Ludwig

Daniel Morris, *Purdue University*: Poetry: United States

Robin R. Mundill, *University of St Andrews; Glenalmond College*: England: Middle Ages

Yael Munk, *The Open University of Israel*: Film: Israel

Pamela S. Nadell, *American University*: Priesand, Sally; Rabbinic Ordination of Women

Allan Nadler, *Drew University*: Judaism, Orthodox: Ultra-Orthodox

Steven Nadler, *University of Wisconsin*: Spinoza, Baruch

Beth Alpert Nakhai, *University of Arizona*: Ammon; Beth El; Edom; Hazor; Hebron; Lachish; Moab; Samaria; Shechem; Shiloh

Alice Nakhimovsky, *Colgate University*: Literature: Russia and Soviet Union (in Russian)

Chaim Meir Neria, *University of Chicago, Divinity School*: *Musar* Movement; Talmud Study: Modern Approaches; Vilna Gaon, Elijah ben Solomon Zalman

Susan Niditch, *Amherst College*: Bible: Representations of War and Peace

Vered Noam, *Tel Aviv University*: **Megillat Ta'anit**

Thomas Nolden, *Wellesley College*: Literature: France

Julius Novick, *Purchase College, SUNY, Emeritus*: Theater, United States: Playwrights

Dalia Ofer, *Hebrew University of Jerusalem, Emerita*: Holocaust: Role of Gender

Adri K. Offenberg, *Bibliotheca Rosenthaliana, Amsterdam University, Retired*: Printing

Jess Olson, *Yeshiva University*: Frankfurt am Main; Friedländer, David; Hirsch, Samson Raphael

Ranen Omer-Sherman, *University of Miami*: Arabs: Representations in Israeli Literature; Literature: Graphic Novels; Oz, Amos; Yehoshua, A. B.

Aharon Oppenheimer, *Tel Aviv University*: Bar Kokhba

Michal Palgi, *University of Haifa and Emek Yezreel College*: Israel, State of: Kibbutz Movement

Avinoam J. Patt, *University of Hartford*: Displaced Persons

Moshe Pelli, *University of Central Florida*: Literature, Hebrew: **Haskalah**

William Plevan, *Princeton University*: Revelation

Eddy Portnoy, *Rutgers University*: Internet

Hannah S. Pressman, *University of Washington*: Memoir and Life Writing: Hebrew

Alon Raab, *University of California, Davis*: Israel, State of: Peace Movements; Sports: Israel

Moshe Rachmuth, *University of Oregon*: Bialik, Hayyim Nahman; Isaac; Joseph

Amnon Ramon, *Jerusalem Institute for Israel Studies*: Jerusalem: Since 1967

Randi Rashkover, *George Mason University*: Redemption; Theology

Lucia Raspe, *Goethe-Universität, Frankfurt am Main*: Cemeteries: Medieval and Early Modern Europe

Benjamin Ravid, *Brandeis University*: Venice

Martha A. Ravits, *University of Oregon*: Frank, Anne

Jonathan Ray, *Georgetown University*: **Conversos**/Crypto Jews; Spain, Christian

Uzi Rebhun, *Hebrew University of Jerusalem*: United States: Demography

Annette Yoshiko Reed, *University of Pennsylvania*: Christianity and Second Temple Judaism

Bernard Reich, *George Washington University*: Israel, State of: Wars (1956–1967)

Stefan C. Reif, *University of Cambridge*: Amram bar Sheshna; Genizah, Cairo

David M. Reis, *Bridgewater College*: Alexander the Great; Gnosticism; Ptolemies: Impact on Jewish Culture and Thought; Samaritans; Seleucids

Ira Robinson, *Concordia University*: Adler, Cyrus; Judaism, Orthodox: Modern Orthodox

Meri-Jane Rochelson, *Florida International University*: Zangwill, Israel

Leonard Rogoff, *Jewish Heritage Foundation of North Carolina*: United States, Southern

Freddie Rokem, *Tel Aviv University*: Theater: Israel

Lilach Rosenberg-Friedman, *Bar-Ilan University*: Hebrew: Modern Revival; Israel, State of: Military Roles of Women

Dale Rosengarten, *College of Charleston*: Charleston, South Carolina

Laurence Roth, *Susquehanna University*: Literature: Popular Fiction

Evie Levy Rotstein, *Hebrew Union College–Jewish Institute of Religion, New York*: Education, North America: Supplemental Schools

Adam Rovner, *University of Denver*: Literature, Hebrew: Israeli Fiction

Marsha L. Rozenblit, *University of Maryland*: Intermarriage: Modern Europe and United States; Vienna

Joshua Rubenstein, *Amnesty International and Davis Center, Harvard University*: Ehrenburg, Ilya; Jewish Anti-Fascist Committee; Trotsky, Leon

Jay Rubin, *Jewish Community Association of Austin*: Hillel Foundations

Marina Rustow, *Emory University*: Egypt: Middle Ages

Leonard V. Rutgers, *Utrecht University*: Catacombs

Yona Sabar, *University of California, Los Angeles*: Kurdistan

Angel Sáenz-Badillos, *Universidad Complutense, Madrid, and Real Colego Complutense, Harvard University*: Grammarians and Lexicographers

Jeffrey K. Salkin, *The Temple, Atlanta, Georgia*: Judaism: Jewish Renewal Movement

Rivanne Sandler, *University of Toronto, Emerita*: Iran; Iraq; Judeo-Persian Language and Literature

Marianne Sanua, *Florida Atlantic University*: Fraternities and Sororities: North America

Marc Saperstein, *Leo Baeck College, London*: Ethical Wills; Sermons

Jonathan D. Sarna, *Brandeis University*: Columbus, Christopher; Jewish Publication Society; United States: Civil War

Lawrence H. Schiffman, *Yeshiva University*: Dead Sea Scrolls

Jonathan Wyn Schofer, *Harvard University*: **Avot De Rabbi Natan**; Ethics, Rabbinic

Laura S. Schor, *Hunter College*: British Mandate over Palestine; Rothschild, Baroness Betty de; Rothschild Family

Daniel J. Schroeter, *University of Minnesota*: North Africa

Yechiel Y. Schur, *University of Pennsylvania*: Communal Organization: Medieval and Early Modern Eras; Councils and Synods: Medieval and Early Modern

Diane Tickton Schuster, *Claremont Graduate University*: Education, North America: Adult

Daniel R. Schwartz, *Hebrew University of Jerusalem*: Maccabees, Books of

Dov Schwartz, *Bar-Ilan University*: Thought, Early Modern

Marcus Mordechai Schwartz, *Jewish Theological Seminary*: **Mitzvah**; Rabbinic Ordination

Jan Schwarz, *University of Chicago*: Memoir and Life Writing: Yiddish

Ora Rodrigue Schwarzwald, *Bar-Ilan University*: Ladino; Literature, Ladino

Kenneth Seeskin, *Northwestern University*: Autonomy and Heteronomy; Maimonides, Moses (Moses ben Maimon); Reason

Alan F. Segal, *z"l*: Afterlife: Hebrew Bible and Second Temple Period; Messianism: Biblical and Second Temple Eras; Resurrection

Zohar Segev, *University of Haifa*: Silver, Abba Hillel

Jonathan Seidel, *University of Oregon*: Magic

Shlomo Sela, *Bar-Ilan University*: Abraham bar Ḥiyya; Astrology

Robert M. Seltzer, *Hunter College and the Graduate Center, CUNY*: Kaplan, Mordecai M.; Thought, Modern

Bülent Şenay, *Uludag University, Turkey*: Turkey

Arvi Sepp, *University of Antwerp*: Kafka, Franz

Jeffrey Shandler, *Rutgers University*: Celebrities

Joshua M. Shanes, *College of Charleston*: Bund; Galicia

David Shatz, *Yeshiva University*: Soloveitchik, Joseph B.

Shmuel Shepkaru, *University of Oklahoma*: Martyrdom

Rona Sheramy, *Association for Jewish Studies*: Holocaust Education: North America

Ira M. Sheskin, *University of Miami*: United States: South Florida

Avigdor Shinan, *Hebrew University of Jerusalem*: David: Post-Biblical Traditions; Elijah: Biblical and Post-Biblical Traditions; **Targum**; Torah Reading

Ephraim Shoham-Steiner, *Ben-Gurion University*: Pilgrimage

Marci Shore, *Yale University*: Bolshevism: Russian Empire and Soviet Union; Communism: Eastern Europe

Devorah Shubowitz, *Indiana University*: Film: Europe (Post–World War II)

Elizabeth Shulman, *Editorial Assistant*: Aaron; Abraham ben David of Posquières; Akiva ben Joseph; Arabia; Assyria; Babylon/Babylonia; Barak, Ehud; Begin, Menachem; Belgium; Blessing of the Moon; Covenant; Decapolis Cities; Denmark; Elisha; Film: Yiddish-Language; Firstborn Son, Redemption of (*Pidyon ha-Ben*); France, Contemporary; Galilee; *Haftarah; Havdalah*; Herod and Herodian Dynasty; Herzl, Theodor; Hillel; Judah, Kingdom of; *Kaddish; Kiddush; Kindertransport*; Leo Baeck Institute; Meir, Golda; Menasseh ben Israel; *Mezuzah*; Rabin, Yitzhak; Sharansky, Nathan; Sharon, Ariel; *Shofar*; Tabernacle; *Tallit; Tefillin*; Tel Aviv; United States: American Revolution; *Yahrzeit*; YIVO Institute for Jewish Research; *Yizkor*; Yom Ha-Atzma'ut; Yom Ha-Shoah or Yom Ha-Shoah Veha-Gevurah

Efraim Sicher, *Ben-Gurion University*: Literature: Britain

Laurence J. Silberstein, *Lehigh University*: Post-Zionism

Edward Silver, *Wellesley College*: Jeremiah, Book of; Joel, Book of

Larry Silver, *University of Pennsylvania*: Art, Europe: Nineteenth Century; Art, Europe: Twentieth Century

Shlomo Simonsohn, *Tel Aviv University, Emeritus*: Sicily

Helene J. Sinnreich, *Youngstown State University*: Holocaust: Ghettos

Alexei Sivertsev, *DePaul University*: Zealots

Robert Skloot, *University of Wisconsin*: Holocaust Representation: Drama

Mark Slobin, *Wesleyan University*: Cantor, Cantorate: Historical Development

Naomi Sokoloff, *University of Washington*: Agnon, S. Y.

Moshe Sokolow, *Yeshiva University*: Ibn Ezra, Abraham; Ibn Ezra, Moses

Benjamin D. Sommer, *Jewish Theological Seminary*: Habakkuk, Book of; Haggai, Book of; Hosea, Book of; Isaiah, Book of; Micah, Book of; Obadiah, Book of

Daniel Soyer, *Fordham University*: Journalism, Yiddish: North America; United States: Labor Movement

Nina Spiegel, *American University*: Dance: United States

David Starr, *Me'ah Hebrew College, Newton, Massachusetts*: Education, North America: Hebrew Colleges; Schechter, Solomon

Ilan Stavans, *Amherst College*: Literature: Latin America

Richard Stein, *University of Oregon, Emeritus*: Disraeli, Benjamin

Naomi Steinberg, *DePaul University*: Dinah; Leah; Rachel; Sarah; Tamar (Genesis 38); Tamar (2 Samuel)

Paul Steinberg, *Valley Beth Shalom, Encino, California*: Fast Days; Festivals; Firstborn, Fast of; Five Scrolls (*Ḥamesh Megillot*); *Hallel*; Ḥanukkah; High Holidays; New Years; Passover; Purim; Repentance; Rosh Ḥodesh; Shabbat ha-Gadol; Shavuot; Simḥat Torah; Sukkot; Tu B'Shevat

Günter Stemberger, *University of Vienna, Emeritus*: Rome, Roman Empire; Tannaim

Christopher M. Sterba, *San Francisco State University*: World War I: Impact on American Jews

Gregg Stern, *University of Massachusetts, Amherst*: France, Southern: Middle Ages

Michael Stern, *University of Oregon*: Literature: Scandinavia

Sacha Stern, *University College London*: Calendar

Kenneth Stow, *University of Haifa*: Ghetto; Italy

Marvin A. Sweeney, *Claremont School of Theology and Claremont Graduate University*: Ezekiel, Book of; Leviticus, Book of; Numbers, Book of

Susan L. Tananbaum, *Bowdoin College*: Britain: Early Modern and Modern

Magda Teter, *Wesleyan University*: Ritual Murder Accusation

Hava Tirosh-Samuelson, *Arizona State University*: Ecology; Ethics, Environmental; Israel, State of: Ecology

Michael Toch, *Hebrew University of Jerusalem*: Commerce: Medieval and Early Modern Europe; Money Lending: Medieval and Early Modern Europe

William Toll, *University of Oregon*: United States: Immigration

Emanuel Tov, *Hebrew University of Jerusalem*: Septuagint

Amram Tropper, *Hebrew University of Jerusalem*: **Avot**

Gerald Tulchinsky, *Queen's University, Kingston, Ontario*: Canada

Ellen M. Umansky, *Fairfield University*: Jewish Science; Judaism, Feminist

Christine Schmidt van der Zanden, *University of Maryland*: Holocaust Denial; Holocaust Documentation; Holocaust Resistance; Holocaust Trials

Sharon Vance, *Northern Kentucky University*: Judeo-Arabic Language and Literature

Kati Vörös, *University of Chicago*: Habsburg Empire; Hungary

Saul Wachs, *Gratz College*: Blessings; Blessings Before and After Meals

David A. Wacks, *University of Oregon*: Literature, Hebrew: Medieval Spain

Felicia Waldman, *University of Bucharest*: Romania

Barry Dov Walfish, *University of Toronto*: Biblical Commentary: Middle Ages to 1800; Encyclopedias; Rashi

Harold S. Wechsler, *New York University*: United States: Higher Education

Judith Romney Wegner, *Connecticut College*: Islam and Judaism

Shalva Weil, *Hebrew University of Jerusalem*: **Bene Israel**; Cochin Jews; Ethiopia; India; Tribes, Ten Lost

David Weinberg, *Wayne State University*: Urban Life

Robert Weinberg, *Swarthmore College*: Birobidjan

Dvora E. Weisberg, *Hebrew Union College–Jewish Institute of Religion, Los Angeles*: **Aggadah**; Amoraim; Rabbinic Hermeneutics

Kalman Weiser, *York University*: Journalism, Yiddish: Eastern Europe; Yiddish Dictionaries

Andrea L. Weiss, *Hebrew Union College–Jewish Institute of Religion, New York*: Bible: Poetry

Anton Weiss-Wendt, *Center for the Study of the Holocaust and Religious Minorities, Oslo, Norway*: Baltic States

Steven H. Werlin, *University of North Carolina, Chapel Hill*: Jewish War, First; Masada; Qumran

Libby K. White, *Baltimore Hebrew Institute, Towson University*: Bulgaria; Periodicals: Canada (English Language); Periodicals: United States (English Language); Vilna

Stephen J. Whitfield, *Brandeis University*: Journalism: United States (English Language)

Shohama Wiener, *Academy for Jewish Religion*: Academy for Jewish Religion

Barry Wimpfheimer, *Northwestern University*: Rabbinic Literature: Mishnah and Talmuds; Talmud, Babylonian

Ora Wiskind-Elper, *Lander Institute of Jewish Studies, Jerusalem*: Folktales

Diane Wolfthal, *Rice University*: Art: Illustrated Yiddish Books

Yaakov Yadgar, *Bar-Ilan University*: Judaism, Israeli Forms of

Bracha Yaniv, *Bar-Ilan University*: Ceremonial Objects: Islamic Lands

James E. Young, *University of Massachusetts, Amherst*: Holocaust Memorials

Michael Zank, *Boston University*: Atonement; Cohen, Hermann

Joshua Zimmerman, *Yeshiva University*: Marx, Karl

Steven J. Zipperstein, *Stanford University*: Aḥad Ha-Am; Pale of Settlement; Pinsker, Leon; Russia

Gary Phillip Zola, *Hebrew Union College-Jewish Institute of Religion, Cincinnati*: Summer Camping

PREFACE

The Cambridge Dictionary of Judaism and Jewish Culture is an authoritative reference work for a twenty-first-century audience. Its entries, written by eminent scholars, define the spiritual and intellectual concepts and the various religious movements that distinguish Judaism and the Jewish experience. Their subjects include central personalities, formative events, and enduring literary and cultural contributions. Essays outline Jewish history from ancient times to the present, and they also illuminate the daily lives of Jewish women and men in many eras and locations. Contributions discuss legal teachings and legendary traditions, and they explain the roles of rationalism, mysticism, and messianism within Jewish thought. The religious rituals and customs of Judaism – and the texts and contexts that explain, expand, and animate them – are a major focus as well. Many entries focus on geographic regions, countries, and cities, documenting the distinctive characteristics of Jewish life and cultural production in these specific places. Yet what makes this reference different from many others is that it also explores Jewish acitivities and contributions outside the religious boundaries of Judaism.

Articles in this dictionary explore Jewish secular and political movements, Jewish achievements beyond the confines of the traditional Jewish world, and the often disregarded lives of Jewish women. Discussions of numerous events of the modern era, including the Holocaust, Zionism, and the founding of the State of Israel, and Jewish involvement in numerous aspects of mainstream culture, demonstrate the inadequacy of defining Jews only from a religious viewpoint. Entries in this book consider manifestations of religious disaffection and secularism, as well as the impact of intellectual, social, and political tendencies in the larger societies of which Jews have been a part. Authoritative essays delineate Jewish expressions and achievements in a variety of languages and literatures and in the visual and lively arts. Readers of this compendium will find new and compelling approaches both to Judaism and to the intellectual and cultural development of the Jewish people.

The Cambridge Dictionary of Judaism and Jewish Culture reviews Jewish participation in a wide variety of areas, including journalism, literature, art, music, theater, dance, film, sports, travel, and other forms of popular culture from periodicals, radio, and television to the graphic novel and the Internet. Topics of interest include the involvement of Jews in medicine, politics, science and mathematics, ecology and the environmental movement, and the academic world of higher education. Authors of articles in this volume employ the insights of art history, cinema studies, musicology, social sciences, cultural studies, women's studies, and gender studies, in addition to more traditional approaches centered on historical, philosophical, literary, religious, and textual scholarship and analysis.

A one-volume dictionary of Judaism and the Jewish experience could never claim to be fully comprehensive, and this work is no exception. However, the sixteen subeditors have endeavored to provide coverage of topics ranging from the ancient Near East to Jewish demography in the twenty-first century. Most important, *The Cambridge Dictionary of Judaism and Jewish Culture* is designed for ease of use. Its articles are succinct, clearly written, and accessible to general readers.

In many cases, authors have suggested further reading from reliable and readily available primary and secondary sources in English for those who would like to explore a topic in more depth.

This volume would not have been possible without the contributions of the subeditors, who chose the subjects to be covered in their areas of expertise and who recommended colleagues as potential authors. I am grateful for their efforts in helping make this dictionary a reality. Most essential to this project's success, of course, are the hundreds of contributors whose entries reflect both cutting-edge scholarship and perceptive analysis. I am in their debt, as are all who make use of this book. Special thanks are due to my assistants over the years: Peter Calley, Noah Mullin, Moshe Rachmuth, Brianna Bridegum, Kate Friedman, Elizabeth Shulman, and Sara Waltemire. Without their much appreciated help, this volume would never have been completed.

I am most grateful for a very generous gift from the Harold and Arlene Schnitzer Care Foundation of Portland, Oregon, which made possible the inclusion of color plates. These images significantly enhance a number of the articles on art and ceremonial objects. Harold Schnitzer died on April 27, 2011, just a few months before the publication of this volume. His vision in establishing the Harold Schnitzer Family Program in Judaic Studies at the University of Oregon was typical of his many extraordinary acts of philanthropy. Certainly it transformed my life and I will always be grateful to Harold and his family for bringing me to Oregon in 2000 to head this exciting academic program and for their ongoing support of my academic endeavors. I know that Harold's memory will be a blessing for many generations to come. A research leave in 2007 and a sabbatical in 2009 allowed me to do essential work on this project. I am grateful to the University of Oregon and particularly the College of Arts and Sciences for providing me with these gifts of time. As always, I am deeply appreciative of the sustaining love and patience of my husband and children, Warren, Sam, and Shira Ginsberg; they help make the impossible possible.

HOW TO USE THIS BOOK

Entries in this volume are arranged alphabetically. Within each entry, asterisks (*) identify people, places, literary works, and concepts and movements for which separate articles exist. Often, in the course of an essay or at its conclusion, references to other relevant entries are indicated in UPPERCASE letters. Articles often refer to interesting and important individuals for whom there are no designated entries. A comprehensive **Index of Names** at the end of the volume directs readers to all the entries in which a particular person is mentioned. The **Contributors** listing at the beginning of the book identifies each author and the entry or entries she or he has written.

Some articles have been grouped by topic for the reader's convenience. For example, substantive entries about Jewish writers and writings in various times and places appear alphabetically under Literature. Similar groupings are found under Art, Bible, Film, Holocaust, Israel, State of, Journalism, Middle Ages, Music, Poetry, Sports, Theater, United States, and Women, among others. Articles related to one or more of these topics also stand alone, but cross-references direct readers to them.

The entries in this volume are relatively brief; none is longer than 3,000 words and most are far shorter. They are also highly focused, exploring specific subjects in some detail. In many ways, this book complements *The Cambridge Guide to Jewish History, Religion, and Culture* (ed. Judith R. Baskin and Kenneth Seeskin, 2010), whose far longer historical and thematic essays provide comprehensive overviews of particular eras and subjects. The entries in *The Dictionary* address in detail topics that essays in *The Guide* could only mention in passing. Together the two volumes provide in general and specific ways a sense of the immense richness and diversity of Judaism and the bountiful expressions of Jewish culture and creativity through the ages.

A NOTE ON TRANSLITERATION

Generally, the Hebrew letter *ḥet* is represented in this volume by **ḥ**, the Hebrew letter *khaf* by **kh**, and *tzadei* by **tz**. However, an effort has been made to balance the demands of consistency with those of familiarity. Thus, biblical names and places are spelled here as they are in *The Jewish Bible: Tanakh: The Holy Scriptures. The New Jewish Publication Society Translation according to the Hebrew Text* (1985). Similarly, the names of individuals from the eighteenth century on are spelled as they most commonly appear in English. The name Ḥayyim, for instance, may be spelled Chaim, Chayim, Haim, or Haym depending on the individual involved. Names of individuals have been standardized as much as possible across entries, although this occasionally leads to inconsistencies in transliteration within entries. Names of places in the State of Israel generally follow conventional English spellings. Transliterations of other languages, such as Arabic, Ladino, Russian, and Yiddish, usually respect the choices of the authors of specific entries.

ABBREVIATIONS

Abbreviations appear throughout the volume in the following categories:

CHRONOLOGY

b.	Born
BCE	Before the Common Era
CE	Common Era
ca.	Latin *circa* ("approximately")
d.	Died
fl.	Latin *floruit* ("was active")
r.	Reigned

BIBLICAL BOOKS (in the order in which they appear in the Hebrew Bible)

Gen	Genesis
Exod	Exodus
Lev	Leviticus
Num	Numbers
Deut	Deuteronomy
Josh	Joshua
Judg	Judges
Sam	Samuel
Kgs	Kings
Isa	Isaiah
Jer	Jeremiah
Ezek	Ezekiel
Hos	Hosea
Hab	Habbakuk
Hag	Haggai
Zech	Zechariah
Ps	Psalms
Prov	Proverbs
Song	Song of Songs
Lam	Lamentations
Eccl	Ecclesiastes
Dan	Daniel
Neh	Nehemiah
Chron	Chronicles

APOCRYPHAL BOOKS

Macc	Maccabees
Sira	Wisdom of Ben Sira

NEW TESTAMENT BOOKS

Matt	Matthew
Cor	Corinthians
Rev	Revelations

RABBINIC LITERATURE (these abbreviations precede the names of specific tractates of the Mishnah and Talmuds; a chart of these tractates appears in the entry MISHNAH: ORDERS AND TRACTATES)

b.	Hebrew *ben* ("son of")
BT	Babylonian Talmud
JT	Jerusalem Talmud
M.	Mishnah
R.	Rabbi
T.	Tosefta

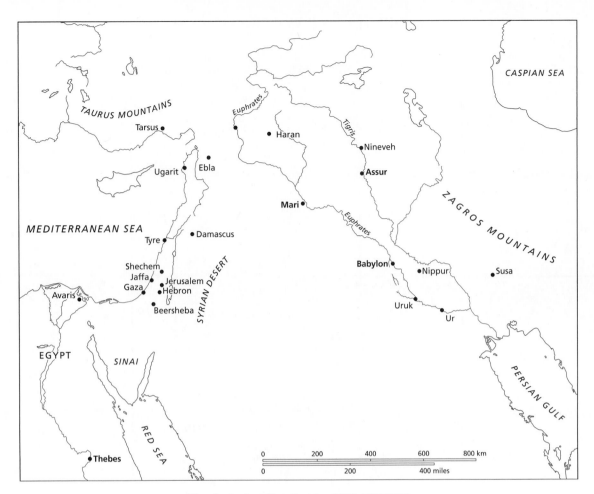

Map 1. Ancient Near East (ca. 2000–1800 BCE)

Map 2. Divided Monarchy (ca. 920–730 BCE)

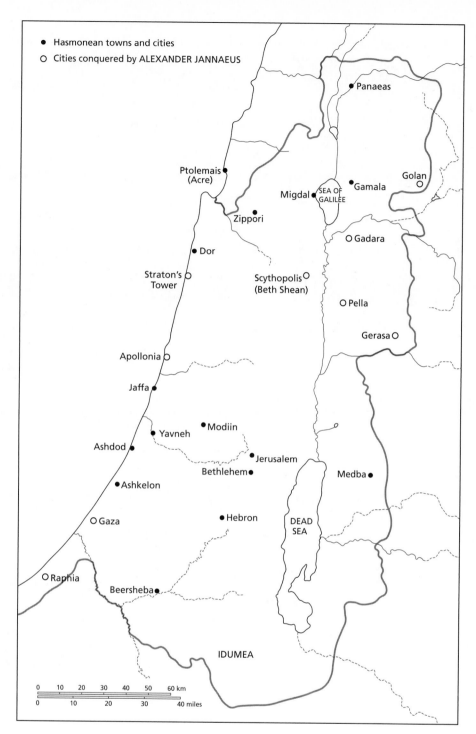

- Hasmonean towns and cities
- Cities conquered by ALEXANDER JANNAEUS

Panaeas

Ptolemais
(Acre)

Golan

Migdal • Gamala

SEA OF
GALILEE

Zippori

Dor

Gadara

Straton's
Tower

Scythopolis
(Beth Shean)

Pella

Gerasa

Apollonia

Jaffa

Modiin

Yavneh

Ashdod

Jerusalem

Bethlehem

Medba

Ashkelon

Gaza

Hebron

DEAD
SEA

Raphia

Beersheba

IDUMEA

0	10	20	30	40	50	60 km
0	10		20		30	40 miles

Map 3. Hasmonean Dynasty under Alexander Jannaeus (ca. 176–103 BCE)

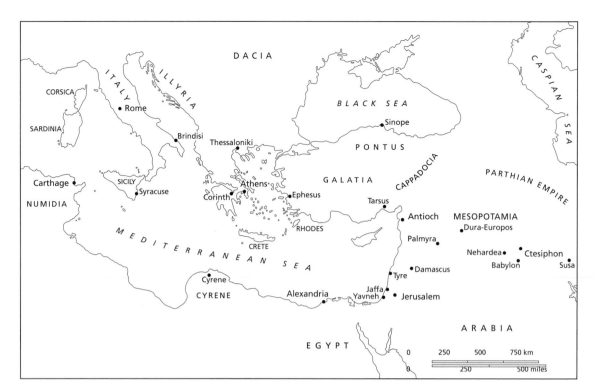

Map 4. The Mediterranean World in Late Antiquity (ca. 200 CE)

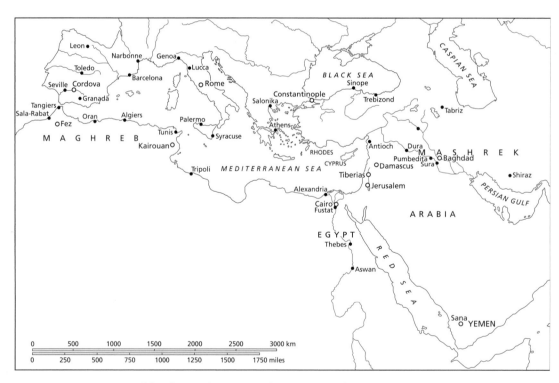

Map 5. Jewish Centers in the Geonic Period (750–1040 CE)

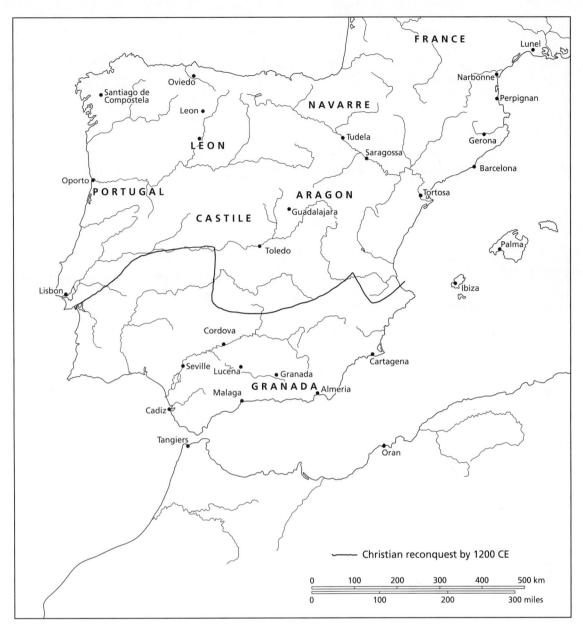

Map 6. Jewish Centers in Medieval Spain (ca. 1200)

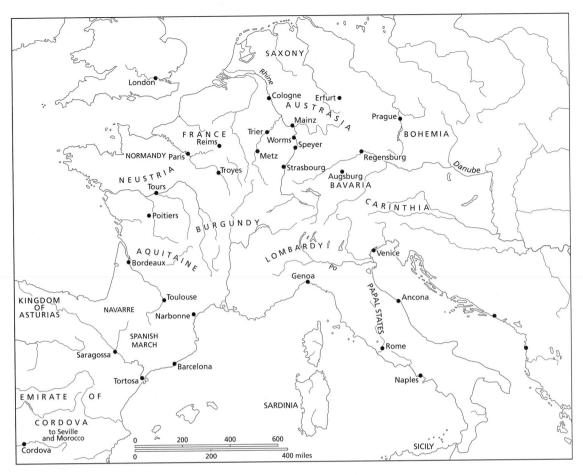

Map 7. Jewish Centers in Medieval Europe

Map 8. Jewish Centers in Early Modern Europe (17th century)

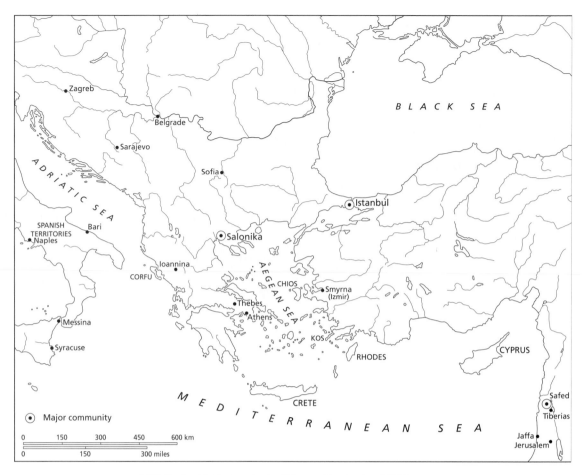

Map 9. Jewish Centers in the Ottoman Empire (ca. 1600)

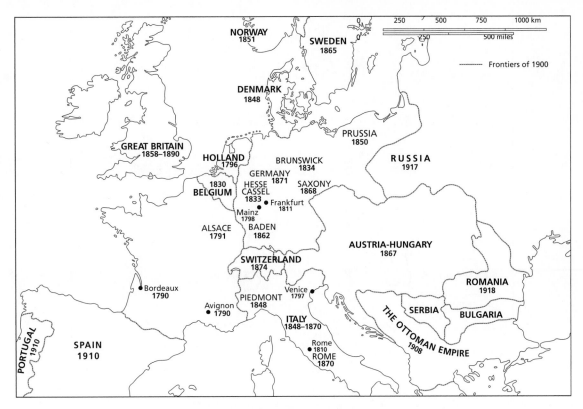

NORWAY
1851

SWEDEN
1865

DENMARK
1848

PRUSSIA
1850

GREAT BRITAIN
1858–1890

RUSSIA
1917

HOLLAND
1796

BRUNSWICK
1834

GERMANY
1871

BELGIUM
1830

HESSE
CASSEL
1833

SAXONY
1868

Frankfurt
1811

Mainz
1798

ALSACE
1791

BADEN
1862

AUSTRIA-HUNGARY
1867

SWITZERLAND
1874

Bordeaux
1790

Venice
1797

ROMANIA
1918

Avignon
1790

PIEDMONT
1848

SERBIA

BULGARIA

PORTUGAL
1910

ITALY
1848–1870

THE OTTOMAN EMPIRE
1908

SPAIN
1910

Rome
1810

ROME
1870

250   500   750   1000 km

250

500 miles

———— Frontiers of 1900

Map 10. Emancipation of European Jews

xliii

Map 11. Pale of Settlement (1791–1917)

xliv

Map 12. 1947 UN Partition Plan for Palestine

Map 13. State of Israel: Armistice Lines, 1949

Map 14. State of Israel and Occupied Territories, 1967

Aaron is the brother of *Moses and *Miriam; he speaks for Moses and performs signs on his behalf before the Exodus from *Egypt (Exod 4:10–17, 27–31; 7:19; 8:1; 8:12). Aaron is also the father of the levitical *priesthood (Exod 28:1); Leviticus 8–10 describes the ordination of Aaron and his sons as the priests (*kohanim*) of the *Tabernacle. Nadab and Abihu, two of Aaron's sons, die in the course of this event (Lev 10:1–3), apparently because they disobey God by incorporating foreign elements into the cultic service. Numbers 18 affirms the primacy of the priestly roles of Aaron and his direct descendants: They alone are responsible for maintaining the purity of the sanctuary (18:1), while the other members of the tribe of Levi are to provide support services and "do the work of the Tent of Meeting" (Num 18:2–7). Aaron sometimes challenges his brother's leadership. When Moses ascends Mount Sinai, Aaron stays behind and is persuaded to build the golden calf; he is spared, however, from the plague that strikes the idolaters (Exod 32). Numbers 12 relates that both Aaron and Miriam speak against Moses and challenge the unique nature of Moses' prophetic relationship with God. Both are verbally chastised by God, but only Miriam is punished with a skin affliction and a week's expulsion from the camp. Aaron, like Moses, is barred from entrance to *Canaan for his failure to sanctify God as commanded at the waters of Meribah (Num 20:1–13). Numbers 20:22–29 describes Aaron's death at Mt. Hor and the thirty days of communal mourning that follow. **See also DEUTERONOMY, BOOK OF; EGYPT AND ANCIENT ISRAEL; EXODUS, BOOK OF; INCENSE; LEVITICUS, BOOK OF; NUMBERS, BOOK OF; TEMPLE AND TEMPLE CULT; WORSHIP.**

ELIZABETH SHULMAN

Abarbanel: See ABRAVANEL

Abel: See ADAM; CAIN AND ABEL; EVE.

Abortion. Judaism respects the sanctity of life and of potential life and has generally prohibited abortion. When a pregnant woman's life was endangered, however, rabbinic and medieval authorities permitted abortion on the basis of Exodus 21:22–25. This text was understood to make a distinction between the actual human status of the pregnant woman and the potential human status of her fetus, which was not considered an independent entity before its birth (BT *Yevamot* 69b; BT *Ḥullin* 58a). Because the fetus is not an autonomous being, abortion is not regarded as murder. Once most of the child has emerged from the mother's body, M. *Ohalot* 7:6 rules that "it is not to be touched, for one [life] is not [to] be put aside for another." Moses *Maimonides wrote that when the mother's life was at risk the fetus should be regarded as a pursuer (*rodef*) attempting to kill her and be dealt with accordingly (*Mishneh Torah, Rotze'aḥ* 1:9).

Although most legal authorities permitted abortion when it was judged essential for a woman's physical or mental health, debate focused on permissible conditions and situations. Rabbi Jacob Emden (1697–1776), among others, permitted abortion "as long as the fetus has not emerged from the womb, even if not to save the mother's life, but only to save her from the harassment and great pain which the fetus causes her," ruling that abortion was permitted when a pregnancy resulted from *adultery or another prohibited sexual union (*She'elat Yavez* 1:43).

There is no monolithic attitude toward abortion in modern Judaism, and contemporary Jews hold diverse opinions. However, various movements have formulated denominational positions. All streams of Orthodox Judaism endorse the rabbinic position (based on Exod 21:22–25) that abortion is permitted when there is a high probability that the mother's life is at risk, whether for physical or psychological reasons (see JUDAISM, ORTHODOX: MODERN ORTHODOX; JUDAISM: ORTHODOX: ULTRA-ORTHODOX). However, most Orthodox legal authorities prohibit abortion when the fetus has a significant abnormality or a fatal genetic condition. One recent exception is Rabbi Eliezer Waldenberg (1915–2006), who allowed the first-trimester abortion of a fetus with a deformity that would cause it to suffer and permitted abortion up to the end of the second trimester of pregnancy of a fetus with a lethal defect such as Tay-Sachs disease (*Tzitz Eliezer* 9:51:3).

The position of Conservative Judaism, expressed in 1983, is that "an abortion is justifiable if a continuation of pregnancy might cause the mother severe physical or psychological harm, or when the fetus is judged by competent medical authorities to be severely defective." Conservative authorities, as well as some Orthodox rabbinic decision makers, would permit abortion when pregnancy resulted from rape or from illicit sexual relations such as adultery or incest (See JUDAISM, CONSERVATIVE).

Reform Judaism allows the option of abortion in all of the instances mentioned above, as well as for additional reasons in individual cases. In a 1967 statement approved at the 49th General Assembly, a lay policymaking body, the movement declared abortion permissible "under such circumstances as threatened disease or deformity of the embryo or fetus, threats to the physical and mental health of the mother, rape and incest and the social, economic and psychological factors that might warrant therapeutic termination of pregnancy." In a 1975 statement, passed at the 53rd General Assembly, Reform Judaism expressed confidence in the right and ability of a woman to exercise her ethical and religious judgment in making her own decision (See JUDAISM, REFORM: NORTH AMERICA).

In Israel, the 1977 penal code permits legal abortions by appropriately trained physicians in medical facilities that are "specifically and publicly recognized" as providers of abortions. A termination committee must approve abortion requests. Acceptable grounds include the following: a pregnant woman younger than seventeen, the legal age for marriage; physical, emotional, or psychological damage to the mother; a pregnancy resulting from irregular circumstances (rape, incest, pregnancy outside of marriage); and the probability that the fetus is severely disabled or otherwise unlikely to live a normal life. The committee approves almost all requests. Liberal political parties in Israel favor legalized abortions on the basis of a woman's right to choose; Orthodox political parties and other traditionally oriented and right-wing groups argue that, except for rare cases, abortion should not be permitted in a Jewish state.

For further reading, see ETHICS: MEDICAL; and R. Biale, *Women and Jewish Law* (1984); A. L. Mackler, *Life and Death Responsibilities in Jewish Biomedical Ethics* (2000); and D. Schiff, *Abortion in Judaism* (2002).   JUDITH R. BASKIN

Abraham is the ancestral father of the Jewish people through *Isaac, his son with his wife *Sarah, and of the Arabs through *Ishmael, his son with the Egyptian maidservant, *Hagar. Abraham's origins are in *Mesopotamia in Ur of the Chaldeans (Gen 11:28); later he settles with his father Terah, his wife Sarai, and his nephew Lot in Haran. According to Genesis 12, Abraham set out with his wife and nephew for the land of *Canaan in obedience to a divine mandate; there, *God promised, his progeny would become a great people. Abraham's relationship with God progresses through a series of *covenants in which Abraham's faith is tested in various ways. These covenants require transformations, including the change of name from Abram to Abraham (and Sarai to Sarah) and the institution of male *circumcision (*berit milah*) within Abraham's household (Gen 17). Abraham is characterized by his obedience to God's commands, yet he also questions divine decisions, as in his bargaining with God to save the inhabitants of Sodom and Gomorrah from destruction (Gen 18). Abraham is also portrayed as less than admirable in certain circumstances; one example is when he yields his wife Sarah to another man to save his own life (Gen 20).

Despite the divine promises of untold numbers of descendants who would inherit the land of Canaan, Abraham and his wife Sarah remain childless for many years, another test of Abraham's devotion to God. The less patient Sarah attempts to provide her husband with an heir by giving him her maidservant, Hagar (Gen 16); however, after Hagar conceives and gives birth to *Ishmael, tensions escalate within the household, ultimately leading to the expulsion of Hagar and her son (Gen 21). Finally, when Sarah is beyond the normal age of pregnancy, divine promises (Gen 18) are fulfilled with the birth of Isaac (Gen 21). This biblical motif of female *infertility overcome by divine intervention also appears in other narratives about the births of important figures such as *Jacob, *Joseph, and *Samuel.

Perhaps the greatest challenge to Abraham's faith is the divine commandment to sacrifice Isaac in Genesis 22. The binding of Isaac (*akedah*), a literary masterpiece of concision and terror, establishes indisputably both the depth of Abraham's devotion and the kind of faith that God demands. This biblical episode is followed by Sarah's death and Abraham's purchase of a family burial place at Machpelah (Gen 23). In his old age, Abraham marries Keturah (Gen 25) and fathers six more sons, although Isaac remains his sole heir (25:5–6).

Scholars who advocate some level of historicity to the figure of Abraham point out that place names associated with the Syro-Mesopotamian (Amorite) region that are found in Mesopotamian literature of the late second and early first millennium BCE correspond to names in Abraham's ancestry. Nevertheless, most would agree that the Genesis narratives about Abraham should be understood as ancestral narratives that developed over a long period of time and were shaped to express themes that were important to Israelite religion and culture. **See also** BIBLE: ANCESTRAL NARRATIVES; GENESIS, BOOK OF. Map 1   JUDITH R. BASKIN

Abraham bar Ḥiyya (ca. 1065–ca. 1140), mathematician, philosopher, and astrologer, was born in Barcelona and died in Provence. In an epistle he reports that he was held in high esteem by grandees and kings and that he was engrossed from youth in learning, dealing with, and teaching the so-called science of the stars. Bar Ḥiyya's reference to grandees and kings is borne out by his appellation, *Savasorda*, a corruption of *sahib al-shurta* (chief of the guard). Abraham Bar Ḥiyya's work has a scientific and encyclopedic character; it is written entirely in Hebrew, an indication that he developed his career principally among Jews.

His *Yesodei ha-Tevuna u-Migdal ha-'Emuna* (Foundations of Understanding and Tower of Faith) is the first medieval Hebrew encyclopaedia of science (it was edited by J. M. M. Vallicrosa in 1952). *Ḥibbur ha-Meshiḥah veha-Tishboret* (Treatise on Mensuration and Calculation) is a mathematical work intended for the use of landholders and judges (ed. M. Guttman [1913]). Bar Ḥiyya described *Surat ha-'Aretz* (The Shape of the Earth) as presenting the "shape of the configuration of the heavens and the earth, and the order of the motion visible in the skies and in the stars" (ed. Munster [1546]). He drew up a set of planetary tables called *Luḥot ha-Nasi* (Tables of the Prince), the canons of which appear in *Ḥeshbon Mahalakhot ha-Kokhavim* (Computation of the Motions of Stars; ed. J. M. M. Vallicrosa [1959]). As for the Jewish *calendar, Bar Ḥiyya wrote *Sefer ha-'Ibbur* (Book of Intercalation), which was in all likelihood the first Hebrew work of this type. This treatise also includes vigorous polemics and rich astronomical materials (ed. T. Philipowsky [1851]).

Megillat ha-Megalleh (Scroll of the Revealer) is devoted to foretelling the exact date of the coming of the *messiah, mainly by means of scriptural data (ed. J. Guttmann [1924]). Its fifth chapter, the largest in the entire work, includes a voluminous and impressive Jewish and universal astrological history. He also wrote a long, apologetic epistle to Rabbi Judah Barzilai of Barcelona, justifying the study and use of a specific astrological approach (ed. Z. Schwarz in *Festschrift Adolf Schwarz*, ed. S. Kraus [1917]), and see S. Sela, "Abraham Bar Ḥiyya's Astrological Work and Thought," *Jewish Studies Quarterly* 12 (2005): 1–31. Abraham Bar Ḥiyya expounded his Neoplatonic philosophy in *Hegyon ha-Nefesh ha-Atzuvah* (Meditation of the Sad Soul; ed. E. Freimann [1860]).

See also ASTROLOGY; SCIENCE AND MATHEMATICS: MIDDLE AGES AND EARLY MODERN PERIOD.
                                                                     SHLOMO SELA

Abraham ben David of Posquières (ca. 1125–1198), also known by the acronym Rabad, was a halakhic authority in southern *France. Born in Narbonne, Rabad received most of his talmudic education from Moses b. Joseph and Meshullam b. Jacob of Lunel. Rabad used some of his significant wealth, possibly acquired through dealings in textiles, to establish and direct an important school in Posquières. A number of his students, including his son *Isaac the Blind, went on to become major scholars. Rabad's commentaries on rabbinic texts and his *responsa were particularly influential. So, too, were his annotations (*hassagot*) to *Maimonides' *Mishneh Torah*; they were frequently published together, beginning in 1509. In his *hassagot*, Rabad expands and reconstructs many of Maimonides' halakhic arguments; he is critical of Maimonides both for excluding the references and explanations from earlier sources that informed his legal decisions and for some of his philosophical views. Rabad left no mystical writings, but is known to have transmitted kabbalistic teachings to his sons (see KABBALAH). **See also FRANCE, SOUTHERN: MIDDLE AGES; ISAAC THE BLIND; MONEYLENDING: MEDIEVAL AND EARLY MODERN EUROPE.** ELIZABETH SHULMAN

Abraham ibn Daud [ben David] (ca. 1110–1180) was a philosopher, historian, and astrologer in *Spain; he was probably born in Cordova and is said to have died as a martyr in Toledo. The first of three scholars known by the acronym Rabad, he is sometimes designated as Rabad I. Strongly influenced by the Muslim Aristotelians, al-Farabi and Avicenna, Ibn Daud was the first to introduce the Aristotelian system and form into Jewish philosophy in *Ha-Emunah ha-Ramah* (The Exalted Faith, trans. with commentary, N. M. Samuelson [1986]), written in Arabic around 1160. The original text is no longer extant, but two fourteenth-century Hebrew translations survive. Ibn Daud's philosophical impact was overshadowed by *Maimonides' *Guide of the Perplexed*, which appeared a few decades later. Ibn Daud's important Hebrew chronicle, *Sefer ha-Kabbalah* (Book of Tradition, trans. with commentary, G. D. Cohen [1967]), is a defense of the chain of rabbinic tradition against the *Karaites. This work, which has messianic undertones, includes the story of the "Four Captives," *Babylonian sages who established centers of learning in Spain, *North Africa, and *Egypt. **See also THOUGHT, MEDIEVAL.**

KATE FRIEDMAN

Abravanel (also Abarbanel) Family. Despite their claim to *Davidic descent, members of the Abravanel family first appear in history as eminent figures at a number of medieval courts in *Spain. In additional to prominent financier-politicians and Jewish communal leaders, the family produced two illustrious scholars, **Isaac** (1437–1509) and his eldest son **Judah** (ca. 1460–c. 1521), although only the former had a significant impact on later Jewish thought and literature.

ISAAC ABRAVANEL, born in Lisbon in 1437, spent most of his life in *Portugal; he moved to Spain in 1483, nine years before Spanish Jewry's 1492 expulsion. A leader of Spanish Jewry at the time, he chose departure from Spain over conversion to Christianity and lived the rest of his life in *Italy. Abravanel was one of late medieval and early modern Judaism's most prolific and versatile Hebrew scholars. His premier work is his commentary on the *Torah; he interpreted prophetic literature and the book of *Daniel as well. Abravanel's other writings are theological tomes, although they also often took the form of commentaries. His commentary on the *Passover *haggadah* is the best known example.

Isaac Abravanel's political thought included strong opposition to monarchy. His three lengthy messianic works contain much anti-Christian argumentation. Isaac Abravanel employed Renaissance methods and ideas in both his Iberian and Italian works, attracting the attention of a wide range of Jewish scholars and many Christians, some of whom translated excerpts into Latin.

JUDAH ABRAVANEL, Isaac's son, better known as Leone Ebreo, wrote the *Dialoghi d'amore* (Dialogues of Love), a Renaissance Neoplatonic tract whose original language is a matter of dispute. After its posthumous publication in Italian in 1535, it was translated into other languages, including French and Latin. The work comprises three dialogues on love between the characters Philo and Sophia. Its style and contents bear strong affinities to literary and intellectual currents associated with contemporaneous Florentine Neoplatonist trends. Its later readership included Giordano Bruno, *Spinoza, and Friedrich Schiller. Judah's wrenching Hebrew lament to a son living in Portugal as a forced convert to Christianity also survives.

Various Abravanels continued to hold eminent positions in *Sephardic *Diaspora communities during the sixteenth and seventeenth centuries. BENVENIDA (ca. 1473–after 1560) of Naples and later Ferarra, daughter of Jacob Abravanel (d. 1528), one of Isaac's two brothers, and wife of Isaac's son Samuel (d. 1547), was one of the most influential and wealthy Jewish women in early modern Italy. A supporter of the *messianic pretender David Reuveni (d. 1538), Benvenida had close ties with Eleanor of Toledo, who became the wife of Cosimo the Great of the Medici family. The Abravanel family's contemporary descendants live on several continents and many proudly identify with the family motto: "*Basta mi nombre que es Abravanel*" (It is enough that my name is Abravanel).

For further reading, see E. Lawee, *Isaac Abarbanel's Stance toward Tradition* (2001); and B. Netanyahu, *Don Isaac Abravanel* (5th ed., 1998). ERIC LAWEE

Abulafia, Abraham (1240–ca. 1291) was one of the greatest mystics among medieval Jewish *kabbalists. He developed an intensely individual type of mystical contemplation based on a mystical attitude toward language. Born in *Spain, Abulafia wandered in several countries, reaching Acre in 1260; he lived and taught in *Sicily, *Greece, and *Italy. Gershom *Scholem characterized his work as "ecstatic" or "prophetic" *kabbalah; indeed, Abulafia sometimes described himself as a "prophet," and the aim of his mystical contemplation was the achievement of *prophecy. Abulafia rejected the prevalent kabbalistic set of symbols describing the ten divine attributes, the *sefirot*, as personalized elements of the divine pleroma. To assist in achieving perception of the divine, he developed mystical methodologies, including some physical exercises, a rare element among Jewish mystics.

Abulafia was versed in rationalistic philosophy, but in *Sitrei Torah* (The Secrets of the Torah), a commentary he wrote on *Maimonides' *Guide of the Perplexed*, he attributes kabbalistic ideas to Maimonides. He wrote more than a score of treatises, among them a commentary on the divine name of seventy-two letters, *Sefer ha-Shem* (The Book of the Name); commentaries on the ancient *Sefer Yetzirah* (Book of Creation); and polemical works against his opponents (who included Solomon ben Adret). In 1280 Abulafia was sentenced to death in Rome after he attempted to meet the Pope, Nicholas III, to convince him to be more tolerant toward the Jews; he was saved by the Pope's death. Messianic elements became dominant in his activities in his last years, and he was accused of pretending to be the *Messiah.

Abulafia's writings influenced some of the Christian kabbalists of the late fifteenth and early sixteenth centuries, especially Pico della Mirandola and Johannes Reuchlin. Some of the *Safed kabbalists of the sixteenth century made use of his works, and several later Jewish mystics derived ideas from his writings.

For further reading, see G. Scholem, *Major Trends in Jewish Mysticism* (1954); M. Idel, *Mystical Experiences of Abraham Abulafia* (1988); and idem, *Language, Torah and Hermeneutics in Abraham Abulafia* (1989).   JOSEPH DAN

Academy for Jewish Religion (AJR),

with campuses in metropolitan New York (*www.ajrsem.org*) and Los Angeles, California (*www.ajrca.org*), trains and ordains rabbis and cantors to serve across denominations, as well as in unaffiliated synagogues and community organizations. AJR's flexible scheduling allows part-time extended study and attracts many mature and second-career students.

AJR was founded in 1956 as an independent rabbinical seminary after the nondenominational Jewish Institute of Religion merged with Hebrew Union College (Reform). AJR pioneered in promoting a pluralistic and spiritual view of Judaism, while its curriculum remained grounded in text and tradition. A cantorial school was added in 1992. In 2002, a campus was opened in Los Angeles, which currently operates independently of the New York campus while maintaining the same ethos.   SHOHAMA WIENER

Adam is the name of the first human being in the Eden narrative of Genesis 2–3. Because the Hebrew word *'adam* can be a collective noun meaning a generic "human being" (as in Gen 1:26–28), its use in Genesis 2:7 to describe the first human can be understood as denoting a genderless or androgynous being. When God divides the first human being by removing one "side" (rather than "rib"), both "woman" (*'ishah*) and "man" (*'ish*) are created as gendered beings (Gen 2:23). Throughout the narrative (except Gen 2:5) until the divine surgery, *'adam* is used with the definite article and should be understood as "*the* human." The proper name Adam appears unambiguously in 3:17, when Adam is told that he must undertake difficult labor to grow crops. Adam names his wife *Eve in 3:20; she gives birth to three sons, *Cain and Abel (Gen: 4:1-2), and Seth (Gen 4:25). The hard life of Israelite farmers, as well as the reunion of male and female in *marriage, is explained in this etiological narrative.   CAROL MEYERS

Adam Kadmon (literally "primordial man," *anthropos*) is a kabbalistic term that came to represent, in the *Kabbalah of the thirteenth century and later, the concept of the uppermost, hidden essence of the totality of divine powers – the pleroma – when it is conceived in anthropomorphic terms. It is a counterpart to the ancient term *shiur komah*, which expresses the concept of divinity in *hekhalot* *mysticism (both terms coexisted within the Kabbalah). The term became a potent mystical symbol in the *Zohar, and especially in the *Lurianic myth of the late sixteenth century, in

which it is described as the first emanation from the eternal divine light. *Adam Kadmon* often designates the highest stages in the divine hierarchy of powers and appears mostly in cosmogonic contexts. This concept expresses the kabbalistic perception of the different divine powers as limbs of an enormous, mystical anthropomorphic entity. For further reading, see G. Scholem, *Major Trends in Jewish Mysticism* (1954); and idem, *Kabbalah* (1974).   JOSEPH DAN

Adar is the twelfth month of the Jewish calendar; it is equivalent to February or March on the Gregorian calendar. In the process called intercalation, which maintains synchronization between the festivals and their appropriate seasons, a leap month is added to the calendar seven times in a nineteen-year cycle. In the years when this leap month is added, it follows Adar and is called Adar II (Adar Bet). In leap years the festival of *Purim (Adar 14) takes place in Adar II (M. *Megillah* 1:4). **See also CALENDAR and CALENDAR: MONTHS OF THE YEAR.**

Adler, Cyrus (1863–1940) was an academic administrator and communal leader. The first American-trained PhD in Semitics (1887), Adler was librarian of the Smithsonian Institution (1892) and its assistant secretary (1905). Adler helped found the *Jewish Publication Society of America (1888), the American Jewish Historical Society (1892), and the *American Jewish Committee (1906). In 1908 Adler became president of Dropsie College, an institution devoted to advanced Judaic and Semitic scholarship; in 1915, he succeeded *Solomon Schechter as president of the *Jewish Theological Seminary while retaining his presidency of Dropsie. He remained president of both institutions until his death. Adler helped found both the *Jewish Welfare Board and the *American Jewish Joint Distribution Committee and chaired the committee that produced the Jewish Publication Society translation of the Hebrew Bible (1917). In 1919, he represented the American Jewish Committee at the Versailles Peace Conference and participated in negotiations for an enlarged Jewish Agency for *Palestine. He went on to serve as president of its council and chair of its administrative committee (1930–31). **See also ORGANIZATIONS: NORTH AMERICA; UNITED STATES: MILITARY CHAPLAINCY.**

IRA ROBINSON

Adoption. Historically, there has been no process of adoption in Jewish law because identity in the traditional Jewish community is determined by lineage and bloodlines. A male whose birth father is of priestly descent is also a *priest, regardless of the status of the adoptive father; an adopted son cannot become a priest even if his adoptive father is of priestly descent. The status of the birth mother is also crucial: A child born of a Jewish mother is a Jew. However, a child born from an illicit sexual relationship such as incest or *adultery (i.e., the mother's husband is not the father of her child) is a *mamzer ("illegitimate") and is permanently limited in his or her standing and marital options in the traditional Jewish community.

An individual may be appointed a guardian (*apotropos*) who assumes permanent responsibility for a child's well-being, undertaking all obligations that natural parents have toward their offspring. Jewish tradition teaches that a person who raises an orphan is equivalent to a natural parent (BT *Sanhedrin* 19b and BT *Megillah* 13a). Legal sources addressing the guardian include BT *Ketubbot* 101b; *Maimonides, *Mishneh Torah, Ishut* 23:17–18; and *Karo, *Shulḥan Arukh, Even Ha-Ezer* 114 and *Hoshen Mishpat* 60:2–5; 207:20–21.

In contemporary Jewish life, adoption of children according to the laws of the country of residence occurs frequently; perhaps 3% of contemporary Jewish families are formed by adoption. Halakhic concerns focus on the child's Jewish status, because any uncertainty may affect the child's ability to marry into the traditional Jewish community. Adoptive parents are often advised to obtain documentation on the natural parents' backgrounds and marital status. Proof of the birth mother's Jewish status is also necessary should the child move to Israel and/or wish to be married there; it is also important to know if a Jewish father was of priestly descent. To avoid many of these complexities, potential adoptive parents may choose to adopt a Gentile infant who can then be formally converted to Judaism, although conversions of adopted children may also raise halakhic questions.

Until 1998, all adoptions in *Israel were handled by the Adoption Service of Israel's Ministry of Labor and Social Affairs and had to be approved by both secular and rabbinical courts. Court-sanctioned adoptions remove all family ties with the natural parents and create family ties with the adoptive parents equivalent to those between natural parents and their child. In recognition of *halakhah*, however, adoption does not affect the consequences of the blood relationship between the adoptee and his or her birth parents: Prohibitions and permissions regarding marriage and divorce based on the child's bloodlines continue to apply. Only Israeli citizens may adopt Israeli infants and the process is difficult. Few healthy Jewish infants are available and adoption requirements are stringent. Israeli legislation as of 1998 allows adoptions from other countries if arranged by private, licensed, nonprofit agencies. Foreign adoptees need not have Jewish parentage or be converted to Judaism after adoption. For further reading, see M. Gold, *And Hannah Wept: Infertility, Adoption, and the Jewish Couple* (1988); and S. K. Rosenberg, *Adoption and the Jewish Family* (1998).

JUDITH R. BASKIN

Adultery. In Judaism, adultery refers to sexual relations between a man, married or single, and a married woman (or a woman bound in some other way by *halakhah* to a particular man). A married man's sexual involvement with a single woman, Jewish or Gentile, although morally problematic, is not adulterous. This gender inequity reflects the patriarchal contexts of biblical and rabbinic Judaism, as well as the importance placed on purity of lineage; a man wanted to be sure that his wife's children were also his own. Fear of adultery led to rabbinic strictures on women's free movement beyond the home, the expectation that modest women would be veiled outside the house, and efforts to restrict women's contacts with men beyond the family circle.

In medieval Muslim environments Jewish religious and community ideals continued to dictate that women should remain at home. Although *marriages were often unhappy and *divorce was not uncommon, accusations of adultery against wives rarely appear in sources from this milieu. In Germany and elsewhere in Northern Europe, where women were far less sequestered than in the Muslim world, concern with adultery was more frequent. The *Ḥasidei Ashkenaz, the pietistic authors of the twelfth-century *Sefer Ḥasidim*

(Book of the Pious), are preoccupied with illicit encounters, whether real or imagined, in which Jewish men have sexual contact with single and married Jewish women (both minors and adults), Jewish and Christian maidservants, and other Christian women. These encounters are presented as temptations of everyday life, and the pietistic response is to set up as many barriers as possible to men's contacts with women, including women of their own families. The *responsa of R. *Meir of Rothenburg (d. 1293) contains a number of queries in which men accuse their wives of adultery, sometimes with Jews and sometimes with Gentiles; in at least one case a wife admits adultery. In almost every instance, R. Meir rejects the veracity of the evidence and rules against the right of the husband to divorce his wife without returning her *ketubbah* (contracted financial settlement), even in a case where a woman bore a child twelve months after her husband's departure on a business trip. R. Meir's evident motivations were to preserve the public sanctity of the family, to deter men from making false accusations in order to rid themselves of unloved wives without significant expense, and to discourage women from engaging in or pretending to engage in adulterous behavior to instigate a divorce to escape an unhappy marriage.

In *Spain and *Italy, sexual mores, particularly among wealthy acculturated Jews, were often far from halakhic ideals; archival records indicate that both men and women were involved in adulterous relationships. Accusations of adultery also figure in divorce cases in early modern and modern Eastern Europe, although here, too, they may have reflected other family tensions and anxieties (Freeze, 182).

The theme of adultery appears frequently in modern Jewish literature, often symbolizing social and historical crises affecting individuals and communities. Examples include I. J. Singer's *Yoshe Kalb* (Yiddish, 1932), set in a Ḥasidic court; I. B. Singer's short stories and novels; S. Y. Agnon's novel *Shira* (Hebrew, 1971), set in 1930s Palestine; the late-twentieth-century American novels of Saul Bellow and Philip Roth; and novels of Israeli writers Amos Oz (*My Michael*) and A. B. Yehoshua (*The Lover*), among others.

For further reading see Y. Assis, "Sexual Behaviour in Mediaeval Hispano-Jewish Society," in *Jewish History: Essays in Honour of Chimen Abramsky* (1988) 25–59; J. R. Baskin, "From Separation to Displacement: The Problem of Women in *Sefer Hasidim*," *AJS Review* 19 (1994): 1–18; D. Biale, *Eros and the Jews* (1992); C. Y. Freeze, *Jewish Marriage and Divorce in Imperial Russia* (2002); S. D. Goitein, *A Mediterranean Society*, vol. 3: *The Family* (1978); and A. Grossman, *Pious and Rebellious: Jewish Women in Medieval Europe* (2004).

JUDITH R. BASKIN

Aesthetics. Unlike *ethics and epistemology, the central role played by aesthetics in modern Jewish *thought remains little studied. Despite its low reputation (identified with pleasure, subjectivism, relativism, and pagan idolatry), aesthetics was central to the actual practice of modern Jewish thought, starting in the eighteenth century with Moses *Mendelssohn. Once the arbiters of Jewish law lost the political power to coerce communal conformity in the eighteenth and nineteenth centuries, the expression of Jewish life and thought (its conception of *God, law, ethics, and community) turned into a type of applied art. Understood broadly, aesthetics refers not just to the disinterested, autonomous study of art, poetry, and beauty. Rather, it calls for sustained attention to the full gamut of *aesthesis*, showing how sensation and sign organize subjects and objects into visual, sonic, and dramatic patterns. Viewed through a holistic prism, a fundamental connection is presumed between aesthetics, ethics, and truth. These signs and the patterns they shape are constituted by physical acts, mental images, and intellectual forms.

ARTISTIC REPRESENTATION: Modern Jewish intellectual history has been particularly unsympathetic to visual aesthetics. The notion that Judaism is fundamentally aniconic and hostile to visual expression reflects a German philosophical cliché in which *poetry and time were privileged over plastic art and space. This conception began with Lessing, Kant, and Hegel, but liberal German-Jewish historians and philosophers such as Heinrich *Graetz and Hermann *Cohen identified it with Judaism as well. It enters into the arts and theory of German modernism via Arnold Schoenberg and Theodor Adorno. However, the notion of an aniconic Judaism is out of step with Jewish scholarship of the twenty-first century. Historians of Jewish *art have convincingly demonstrated that the ban on idolatry in the second of the *Ten Commandments (Exod 20:4–5) applies only to graphic representation of God and the use of images in *worship and does not comprehensively prohibit all figurative expression. That Judaism lacks an extensive fine arts tradition has less to do with the second commandment than with political realities and social exclusions unique to Jewish history and to the practice of art in Christian Europe (see also entries under ART).

AESTHETICS AND RITUAL: The ritual act was the first and primary figure that preoccupied modern Jewish thought at its inception in the eighteenth and nineteenth centuries. Having lost its law-based, coercive character, "*Torah" became "ceremonial." As ceremony, the force of "law" is no longer legal. Its authority is as much, if not more, aesthetic as it is cognitive and moral. According to Mendelssohn (*Jerusalem*, *Philosophical Writings*), language is a system of signs, first oral and then written, that forms knowledge out of sense impression. The sign sets an object, phenomenon, or other characteristic apart from the surrounding mass of sense impressions into which it would otherwise vanish. Understood as a living script composed of visible signs, the ceremonial law points the mind to reflect on universal philosophical truths. For Cohen (*Religion of Reason*), Judaism is a pure pattern (*Gebild*). Despite his own excoriation of art, he compared the Mosaic law to the fine detail of Persian miniature painting. The notion that law constituted an allusive pattern for the cultivation of spiritual and ethical goods continued into the twentieth century in works by Franz *Rosenzweig (*The Star of Redemption*) and Abraham Joshua *Heschel (*Man Is Not Alone*; *God in Search of Man*). The Orthodox thinker Joseph *Soloveitchik (*Halakhic Man*; *The Halakhic Mind*) does not reject aesthetic rapture as much as he founds it on halakhic cognition, referring repeatedly to the beauty of *mitzvot* (commandments) and of the behavior of those who study and uphold them. For Soloveitchik, the value of *mitzvah* was not instrumental, but rather innate (*l'shma*), enjoying the same autonomy as a Modernist work of art.

GOD: As a figure of thought, *God was the subject of the most radical aestheticization in early-twentieth-century Jewish thought. Straining against the second commandment, Martin *Buber (*I and Thou*) and Franz Rosenzweig (*The Star of Redemption*) evoked the visual character of religious experience with words. The key word is *Gestalt*. For Buber, God is the Eternal You, eluding all the limited and limiting categories of language and instrumental reason. And yet, Buber made clear that the revelation of an evanescent, shapeless presence creates its own form in time and space: The living forms of God known through the history of religions are an index to a divine reality that transcends their own historical nature. These forms are the product of the human image-making power in response to *revelation and are subject to generation, decay, and regeneration in concrete human situations. For Rosenzweig, Jewish and Christian ritual practice constellate into a meta-cosmos, in which six figures (God, world, "man," creation, revelation, and *redemption) assemble into an integrated star-shaped figure. At the end of Rosenzweig's system, a now visible manifestation of God's face, a palpable image of absolute truth, confronts the soul at death's border and ushers it back into life. In short, despite the divine resistance to representation, some simulacral appearance (or discourse about such an appearance) is present in twentieth-century Jewish thought.

EMBODIMENT: Physical sensation and the physical body, and the images and ideas that shape them, are the heart and soul of aesthetics. In classical Jewish thought, God's presence is inseparable from *covenant and human community. Philosophically, modern Jewish thought's emphasis on peoplehood and bodies results from the decline of idealism and metaphysics in twentieth-century western philosophy. The body of Israel is a central figure from the work of Buber, Rosenzweig, and Leo Baeck to post-Holocaust thinkers (Richard *Rubenstein, Eliezer *Berkovits, Emil *Fackenheim, Arthur Cohen), and Michael Wyschogrod, Arthur Green, and *feminist thinkers (Judith Plaskow and Rachel Adler [see JUDAISM, FEMINIST]). Contemporary Jewish thought cannot be imagined apart from the creation of *personae*: the biblical *prophet, Judah *Halevi, the *Ḥasidic sage, the Israeli, the Jewish *woman.

The self-conscious attention to aesthetics in modern Jewish thought signals an increasingly expansive view of human culture and Jewish community, in tandem with an increasingly expansive view of human reason. For this tradition, committed to *reason, but not bound by it, aesthetics provides an embodied notion of human intelligence that is thoroughly imbricated in human sensation and imagination and, more broadly, in community, tradition, and politics. As an aesthetic practice, modern Jewish thought creates out of Judaism an image space from which to think about the interface among God, Torah, and Israel.

For further reading, see Z. Braiterman, *The Shape of Revelation: Aesthetics and Modern Jewish Thought* (2007); and THOUGHT, MODERN.   ZACHARY BRAITERMAN

Afterlife: Hebrew *Bible and *Second Temple Period.

Ancient Israelite thought made no strict distinction between body and soul; the idea that something of importance could survive death is not prominent in biblical writings. The Hebrew word *nefesh*, often translated as "soul," did not pertain to something that could be separated from the body. The word might be better translated as "person," because although *Adam is called a living soul, a corpse is described as a dead soul (Lev 21:11; Num 6:6). The life-sustaining essence of creatures was normally understood to be their blood, as the *dietary laws demonstrate. Yet the disappearance of breath was also observed as a characteristic of dying, abetting the idea of the spirit (*ruah*, "wind" or "breath") of the dead. No sense of reward or desirability was attached to the idea of becoming a spirit. According to various passages in the Hebrew Bible, the dead reside together in a dark and silent underworld called Sheol, in greatly attenuated form (Gen 37:36; 1 Sam 28:7–20). Sheol is not equivalent to heaven or hell; rather it is the grave itself, a place of weakness and estrangement from God.

Ancient Israelite society generally did not believe that there would be life after death. According to *Ecclesiastes 3:19, "For the fate of the son of man and the fate of the beasts is the same; as one dies, so dies the other. They all have the same breath, and man has no advantage over the beasts; for all is ephemeral." *Job 14:14 asks directly whether human beings live again after they die and answers that there is nothing else (14:20–22). Job 19:25–27, a passage that has suffered in transmission, is often read as a prediction of Job's *resurrection. However, the passage only affirms that Job wants to be vindicated while still alive in a heavenly court by a heavenly advocate or lawyer, as the logical outcome of his challenge to the justice of *God. In fact, the book of Job appears to argue against any simple pietistic notion of immortality.

Some intimations of immortality do appear in the Hebrew Bible. In the later prophetic books especially, the *Canaanite mythological battle between Death and *Baal is used as a metaphor for God's power. *Isaiah 25:8 says, "God will swallow up death forever." Isaiah 26 and *Ezekiel 37 speak of the restoration of the people as a resurrection of buried bones. Yet these verses do not imply the expectation of a literal resurrection; rather, resurrection is a metaphor for the people's national and spiritual rebirth under the influence of *prophecy. The first indubitable reference to physical resurrection in biblical literature comes from the visions in the book of *Daniel, which date to the period of the *Maccabean revolt. Daniel 12:2–3 states, "And many of those who sleep in the dust of the earth shall awake, some to everlasting life, and some to shame and everlasting contempt. And those who are wise shall shine like the brightness of the firmament; and those who turn many to righteousness, like the stars forever and ever." These verses do not articulate any general theory of immortality, only the resurrection of the many, which satisfies the Israelite concept of justice. Those who suffered and died while remaining true to God's *Torah will be vindicated. The reference to the saved as "those who sleep in the dust" may be a reinterpretation of Isaiah 26:19. Those who persecuted the righteous of God will also be resurrected so that they can be punished.

Second Temple Judaism evidently developed this doctrine of resurrection in response to the problem of righteous suffering and *martyrdom. Resurrection of this type, the most frequent type in Jewish thought, focuses on rebirth in this world at a time when present injustices have been righted and removed. Another aspect of the tradition of resurrection is the theme of ascension to the eternal, deathless heaven where the most deserving and righteous go. The story of the seven martyred sons in 2 Maccabees 7 clarifies the

importance of this idea (see MACCABEES, BOOKS OF). Several of the sons, who are tortured because they will not eat pork, report that after their short time of pain and suffering on earth they expect to be transported to heaven as an eternal reward for their martyrdom.

In none of these stories is the journey to heaven itself an important motif. However, the heavenly journey motif is central in I *Enoch and other *apocalyptic and *pseudepigraphical writings (see ESCHATOLOGY: SECOND TEMPLE PERIOD). In most cases, a journey to heaven is assumed to take place at death, for paradise and hell are both located in one of the several heavens. Great personages or mystics could undertake heavenly ascent during life by means of an ecstatic trance or other extracorporeal experiences. Mystical techniques appear in some Jewish *apocalyptic texts, and the resulting heavenly journey functions as verification for the eschatological beliefs of the community. Once a credible *prophet has visited heaven and seen the ultimate rewards there, he vividly communicates these notions of eternal life and compensation to the community.

In the first century CE, the concept of resurrection was very much debated. The *Sadducees rejected it entirely, but the *Pharisees accepted the idea, as did early Christians (see CHRISTIANITY AND SECOND TEMPLE JUDAISM). In ensuing centuries, resurrection became a general belief in both rabbinic Judaism and *Christianity. For further reading, see A. F. Segal, *Life After Death: A History of the Afterlife in Western Religion* (2004), and see also MYSTICISM: *HEKHALOT* AND *MERKAVAH* LITERATURE.   ALAN F. SEGAL

Aggadah (plural: *aggadot*; variant: *haggadah*; Aramaic: *aggad'ta*, from the Hebrew *nagad*, "to tell, relate") refers in the broadest sense to nonlegal rabbinic traditions. This term, in Hebrew and *Aramaic, appears in early rabbinic works as distinct from or in contrast to *Mishnah, *Talmud, and *halakhah. *Aggadah* describes a broad variety of literary forms. Much of *aggadah* can also be categorized as *midrash, exegesis of scripture. This type of *aggadah* seeks to explain the meaning of biblical verses, usually focusing on those portions of the *Bible that are nonlegal in nature. The term is also used to describe expansions of *biblical narratives: Rabbinic stories that focus on the lives of biblical characters are characterized as *aggadah*, even when they do not cite specific biblical verses. There is also a fair amount of aggadic material that is unrelated to the biblical text. Accounts of historical events, stories about rabbis, folktales, maxims, and ethical aphorisms – all of these fall under the rubric of *aggadah*. It is the wide variety of genres within *aggadah* that has led some scholars to assert that whatever cannot be categorized as *halakhah* should be considered *aggadah*.

Many *aggadot* may have originated in folk traditions, but the *versions* found in *rabbinic literature have been shaped and reworked by the Rabbis. The willingness not only to transmit stories but also to revise them to function in new contexts is evident when we compare multiple versions of the same story within a rabbinic work or in several rabbinic works. Although individual *Tannaim and *Amoraim are often credited with both halakhic and aggadic teachings, some Rabbis were associated primarily with *aggadah*. Several rabbinic texts identify individuals as *ba'alei aggadah*, "masters of *aggadah*." Popular affection for *aggadah* is evident in a story about two sages who came to a town to teach; the one who offered a halakhic lecture found himself alone, while crowds flocked to hear his colleague give an aggadic presentation (BT *Sotah* 40a). One tradition identifies *halakhah* as the "essence of *Torah" and *aggadah* as that which appeals to the heart (*Sifre Deuteronomy, Ha'azinu*).

Aggadah can be found in all the major works of classical rabbinic literature. Even "legal" texts like the *Mishnah and *Tosefta contain aggadic material. Although the Palestinian Amoraim are more closely associated with *aggadah* than their Babylonian counterparts, the Babylonian *Talmud contains significant amounts of *aggadah*. There are also works that are almost exclusively aggadic in nature; these include the major collections of amoraic midrash such as *Genesis Rabbah* and *Exodus Rabbah*.

Aggadah and *halakhah* were recognized as distinct by the early Rabbis but they should not be read in isolation in those texts in which both appear. The Mishnah, the most "legal" of rabbinic works, uses aggadic accounts of individuals' behavior to support or challenge legal rulings. *Aggadah* may serve to highlight a problem with a law or to commend behavior that goes beyond the letter of the law. A talmudic story is best understood in the context of the larger unit (*sugya*) of which it is a part, a unit that is likely to include legal material as well. Post-talmudic authorities often expressed discomfort with the fluidity and creativity of *aggadah* and with the willingness of creators and redactors to generate and preserve multiple meanings from a word or phrase without reaching a consensus. This discomfort began in the period of the *Geonim and led to a growing emphasis on *halakhah* and the publication of works that were wholly halakhic in nature, even when they were based on earlier texts that contained both *aggadah* and *halakhah*.

For further reading, see J. Heinemann, "The Nature of Aggadah," and J. Goldin, "The Freedom and Restraint of Haggadah," both in *Midrash and Literature*, ed. G. H. Hartman and S. Budick (1986); J. Rubenstein, *Talmudic Stories* (1999); G. Hasan-Rokem, *Web of Life: Folklore and Midrash in Rabbinic Literature* (2000); and A. Shinan, *The World of the Aggadah* (1990).   DVORA E. WEISBERG

Agnon, S. Y. (1888–1970) was the most celebrated Hebrew prose writer of the twentieth century and the recipient of the 1966 Nobel Prize for Literature. Agnon is renowned for fiction that combines thematic scrutiny of modern crisis with abundant echoes of traditional Jewish sources. He produced numerous novels and short stories, and his daughter Emuna Yaron has published many posthumous volumes of his work, including letters, sketches, legends, and the unfinished novel, *Shira* (1971).

Born Shmuel Yosef Czaczkes in *Galicia, he moved to *Palestine in 1907; he spent periods of his life in *Germany, but from 1924 on lived in *Jerusalem. Agnon's writing memorializes Buczacz, his hometown, and laments its destruction during the *Holocaust; he also recounts stories of Jewish life in Germany between the world wars (in, for example, *A Guest for the Night* [1938]) and portrays the *Yishuv in the early days of *Zionist settlement (importantly, in *Only Yesterday* [1945]). His art displays probing psychological realism; highly symbolic, dreamlike sequences; and elements of folktale and the picaresque. Yet these generically diverse narratives are all tied to a central concern with loss,

especially communal collapse, and *redemption. Agnon cultivated a distinct prose style, closer to rabbinic language than to modern spoken Hebrew. Notable for its musicality and allusive richness, his writing is also suffused with ironies. The author rebelled against Orthodoxy in his youth but later returned to it, along the way fashioning a sophisticated literary wit that slyly plays religious and secular perspectives against one another. As a young man Agnon also published in *Yiddish.

In his lifetime Agnon became an iconic figure. After his death, his house in Jerusalem became a museum; an Agnon archive was established at Israel's National Library, his picture appeared on Israeli currency, and streets are named after him throughout *Israel. He himself promoted his image as the master storyteller of modern Jewish upheaval and continuity. The name he invented for himself, Agnon, testifies to that self-construction. It is based on the title of an early story, "*Agunot*," which describes Jews who are both anchored in community and alienated from it.

      NAOMI SOKOLOFF

Agricultural Settlements: See BARON DE HIRSCH FUND; CANADA; FILM: LATIN AMERICA; ISRAEL: AGRICULTURAL SETTLEMENTS; LATIN AMERICA; UNITED STATES: AGRICULTURAL SETTLEMENTS

Agudat Israel (also *AGUDAS ISRAEL; AGUDAH*) is a worldwide movement of *Orthodox Jewry founded in 1912. Branches were established in most countries of Europe, as well as in the *United States and *British Mandate *Palestine. *Agudat Israel* reached its apogee of political achievement and institutional development in interwar Eastern Europe, electing representatives to national parliaments in *Poland, Latvia, and *Romania; to city councils and Jewish communal boards and boards administering educational systems; and to youth and workers' movements. The initiative for the founding of *Agudat Israel* (and several of its important ideologues) came from the separatist Orthodox community of *Germany, which tried to enlist Eastern European Orthodoxy and its leaders in the fight against *Zionism and *Reform Judaism. This effort coincided with the first steps by Orthodox Jews in Eastern Europe toward political organization. The supreme body of *Agudat Israel* is the *Kenessiah Gedolah*, the movement's grand assembly, first convened in 1923. In *Agudah*'s ideology, however, the movement is ultimately guided and legitimated by its Council of Torah Sages (*Moetzet Gedolei Ha-Torah*), which determines policy on all matters political, social, or educational. In the post-*Holocaust era, this doctrine of rabbinic authority, known as *Da'at Torah* (first popularized in the interwar period by rabbis and *Hasidic rebbes associated with *Agudat Israel* in Eastern Europe), became widespread in Orthodox Jewry. Another innovation adopted and developed by *Agudah* was the *Beis Yaakov* schools (see SCHENIRER, SARAH), offering formal religious education for young women. After World War II, *Israel and the *United States became the main centers for the movement. In Israel, *Agudat Israel* continues to function as a political party, offering a joint list of parliamentary candidates with another religious party, *Degel ha-Torah*, under the rubric "United Torah Judaism." In the eighteenth Knesset (elected 2009), United Torah Judaism won five seats. In the United States, *Agudah* serves as an effective lobbying group, uniting much of Ḥasidic and non-Ḥasidic non-Zionist Orthodoxy under its banner.   GERSHON BACON

Agunah. The designation *agunah* ("anchored" or "chained" woman) applies to women in several situations, including a married woman whose husband has disappeared but whose death cannot be proven for lack of physical remains or witnesses to his death. Such a woman may never remarry according to Jewish law. A woman whose estranged husband refuses to give her a *get* (divorce document), either out of malice or in an effort to extort funds from the woman or her family, is in a similar predicament, because *divorce has always been a prerogative restricted to men in Jewish law (*halakhah*). A third instance occurs in the case of the levirate widow (see MARRIAGE, LEVIRATE). Even though levirate marriages virtually never occur in the contemporary era, Orthodox Judaism (see JUDAISM, ORTHODOX) requires a childless widow to undergo the ceremony of *halitzah* to be free to remarry. If her brother-in-law refuses to cooperate or makes exorbitant financial demands, this woman may also find herself an *agunah*. Should an *agunah* make a civil marriage or become involved with a man outside of marriage, any children of this union will be considered illegitimate (*mamzerim*) according to *halakhah*. This is a permanent disability; the *mamzer* may only marry another Jew of similar "illegitimate" status. Contemporary Orthodox communities attempt to resolve the situation of the *agunah* on a case-by-case basis and by exerting pressure on the reluctant men involved, but many thousands of women remain in this situation of significant disability. In recent years, a number of Orthodox advocacy groups have been established to address the plight of the "chained woman."   JUDITH R. BASKIN

Ahab, king of *Israel in the ninth century BCE, succeeded his father Omri and ruled for twenty-two years (1 Kgs 16:29). He was a contemporary of the prophet *Elijah. Ahab's alliances with *Judah (to the south), *Phoenicia (to the north), and particularly with Tyre, through his marriage to Jezebel, the king's daughter, resulted in periods of significant economic prosperity. Ahab was killed in an effort to recover Ramoth-Gilead from the Arameans (1 Kgs 22) ca. 850 BCE and was succeeded by his son Ahaziah (1 Kgs 22:40). Despite his accomplishments, Ahab is admonished for doing "what was displeasing in the eyes of God, more than all who had preceded him" (1 Kgs 16:30 and 22:25–26), a reference to his support of Jezebel's introduction of widespread worship of *Baal (16:31–33). 1 *Kings 22 recounts how Jezebel arranged the death of the innocent Naboth so that Ahab could possess his vineyard. Confronted by Elijah, who predicted the disasters that would befall his house, Ahab repented (22:27–29), delaying the fulfillment of Elijah's prophesies. **Map 2**   KATE FRIEDMAN

Aḥad Ha-Am (1856–1927) is the pen name of Hebrew essayist and Zionist ideologue Asher Ginzberg; the name means "one of the people." An austere master of Hebrew prose, Aḥad Ha-Am wrote expositions on morality and politics in the vein of Herbert Spencer or the Russian populist intellectual Piotr Lavrov. These essays, mostly rather brief, remain among the most influential Hebrew works of their kind. Aḥad Ha-Am was also the father of "cultural *Zionism"; he believed that Jews must carve out for themselves a national state where, because of Jewish values more

fundamental than those of *theology, the requirements of decency would forever overshadow those of pragmatism. He was the founding editor of the most important Hebrew periodical of its time, *Ha-Shiloah*, and led a semi-secret group within the Zionist movement, the *B'nei Moshe*. Aḥad Ha-Am's best known essays include "The Truth from the Land of Israel" and "The Supremacy of Reason." He was one of the first important Zionists to call attention to the primacy of the Arab question. For further reading see RUSSIA; ZIONISM; and S. J. Zipperstein, *Elusive Prophet: Ahad Ha'am and the Origins of Zionism* (1993).   STEVEN J. ZIPPERSTEIN

Akedah **("Binding" of Isaac): See** ABRAHAM; ISAAC

Akiva ben Joseph (ca. 45–135 CE) was a third-generation *Tanna and one of the most influential rabbinic sages. Rabbinic tradition holds that he spent his early life as a shepherd and remained uneducated until the age of forty; subsequently he devoted himself to study with the support of his wife Rachel. Akiva developed a method of biblical *hermeneutics in which every word, sign, orthographic variation, and grammatical peculiarity had a significance that could be used to make *halakhic decisions (see RABBINIC HERMENEUTICS). He defended the holiness of the biblical book *Song of Songs, which he interpreted as an allegory of the relationship between *God and the people of Israel, and he supported its canonization. Akiva appears to have originated the organization of rabbinic legal teachings by subject matter, a method later used in the *Mishnah. Among his students were many of the leading fourth-generation Tannaim. An avid Jewish nationalist, Akiva traveled to *Rome in an attempt to reverse Domitian's legislation against Jews, and he is said to have been an enthusiastic supporter of *Bar Kokhba's revolt and of his messianic claims. Akiva was arrested for defying the Emperor Hadrian's decree against the study of *Torah and was one of the ten Rabbis martyred by the Romans at Caesarea. **See also** *AVOT DE RABBI NATAN*; **CAPITAL PUNISHMENT; FOLKTALES; JEWISH WAR, SECOND; MYSTICISM:** *HEKHALOT* **AND** *MERKAVAH* **LITERATURE; LOVE; MARTYRDOM; REDEMPTION; TRIBES, TEN LOST.**   ELIZABETH SHULMAN

Alexander the Great. The son of Philip II and Olympias, Alexander III (356–323 BCE) became king of Macedon in 336 after the assassination of his father. Seeking revenge on the Persians for their earlier wars against the Greeks, Alexander embarked on a ten-year campaign in which he conquered Asia Minor, the Levant, *Egypt, and *Mesopotamia while establishing footholds in Bactria and the Indus River valley. Between his victories over Darius III at Issus (333) and Gaugamela (331), Alexander marched through *Phoenicia to Egypt, where the oracle of Amon confirmed his claims of divine ancestry. Bolstered by his military victories and a growing confidence in his status as the son of Zeus, Alexander sought to incorporate the heritage of the Greeks into the cultures of the East. This emerging syncretism had a profound impact on Jewish life and would polarize later generations of Jews. Not surprisingly, Jewish literature treats Alexander in an ambivalent manner. Both 1 *Maccabees (1:1–8) and *Daniel (7:7; 8:5–7, 20–22; 11:3) highlight his military ruthlessness, with the latter text placing his empire within an apocalyptic framework. Yet *Josephus (*Antiquities* 11.321–347) and the Babylonian

*Talmud (*Yoma* 69a) describe Jews and *Samaritans contending with one another for Alexander's patronage. Josephus' longer account has Alexander visit *Jerusalem, where he offered sacrifices to the Jewish God and conferred economic privileges on the Jews after learning that their scripture (attributed anachronistically to *Daniel) prophesied his victory over the Persians. Still other talmudic sources (BT *Tamid* 32a–b) contain legendary stories about the king, a phenomenon that reflects late antiquity's interest in romanticizing Alexander's life. **See also HELLENISM; NEAR EAST, ANCIENT; PERSIA, ANCIENT; PTOLEMIES; SELEUCIDS.**

DAVID M. REIS

Alexandria, Ancient. Founded by *Alexander the Great in 331 BCE, Alexandria became the dominant city in the Mediterranean world. Its location at the Nile's outlet to the sea made it the point of departure to the wider world for the agricultural riches of *Egypt, while the *Ptolemies' passion for gathering great scholars and literature in the city made it the cultural capital of the *Hellenistic world. Thus, Alexandria was a magnet for émigrés from around the region, including Judeans who came there from the Levant, *Mesopotamia, and even Asia Minor.

In fact, Judeans appear to have been among the earliest settlers of Alexander's city; *Aramaic burial inscriptions have been found in the city's east necropolis from as early as the beginning of the third century BCE. If *Josephus is to be believed, Alexander himself settled some Judeans there (*War* 2.487; *Apion* 2.35); others may have arrived as slaves taken in war (*Letter of *Aristeas 12–13) or as economic immigrants from both outside of Egypt and from existing Jewish settlements in Egypt such as Elephantine. Although the evidence is ambiguous, Jews in Alexandria were apparently given the right to form a *politeuma*, which offered limited form of self-government (cf. *Letter of Aristeas* 310; *Corpus papyrorum judaicarum* 2.143), during the reign of Philometor (d. ca. 145 BCE). By the end of the Hellenistic period, *Philo reports that Jews in Egypt numbered around one million (*Against Flaccus* 43); even allowing for hyperbole, the Jewish population in Alexandria must have been considerable. Josephus (*Antiquities* 14.117) quotes the Greek geographer Strabo (d. ca. 24 CE) to the effect that the Jews were (favorably) quartered in a single portion of the city, although Philo's report that Jews were not confined to a single part of Alexandria during the disturbances in 38 CE seems to contradict this (*Against Flaccus* 54–56). In any case, by all accounts the period of Hellenistic rule over Alexandria was a mostly peaceful time when Jews prospered and experienced socioeconomic mobility, in large part through military service.

Roman hegemony brought unwelcome changes to Jews living in Alexandria. Almost immediately *Rome rescinded many privileges enjoyed by the Jews and instituted the *laographia* (a tax on native Egyptians and other non-Greeks) in 24/23 BCE. In 38 CE, Rome mismanaged a dispute that broke out between Jews and Greeks, and the ensuing rioting and violence continued on and off until 41, when Claudius issued an edict that stabilized Jewish rights in the city. An uneasy peace prevailed until 66 when Tiberius Alexander, Philo's apostate nephew, put down a revolt with force (*War* 3.487–498). Both violent interludes diminished Jewish prospects in Alexandria; further unrest broke out in 115, leading to the virtual destruction of the Jewish presence in the city in 117. Jews returned to live in the city in the fourth century CE, but only under tense conditions. In 415, violence against the Jews instigated by the Christian Patriarch of the city, Cyril of Alexandria, once more essentially ended the Jewish presence there. **See PTOLEMIES: IMPACT ON JEWISH CULTURE AND THOUGHT; SEPTUAGINT. Map 4**

ROBERT KUGLER

Algeria: See NORTH AFRICA

Aliyah: **See ISRAEL, STATE OF: IMMIGRATION entries; TORAH READING**

Alliance Israélite Universelle (AIU) is an organization formed in 1860 in *France to help Jews in other countries gain civil rights and *emancipation. Its establishment was prompted by outrage at the 1840 *Damascus blood libel and the 1858 *Mortara Affair. The AIU established a network of schools that extended from Morocco to *Iran, brought talented young men and women from their home communities to be trained as teachers in France, and provided academic, religious, and vocational training to tens of thousands of Jewish young people. Alliance schools provided late-nineteenth- and early-twentieth-century Jews of the Middle East and *North Africa with a modern education and fluency in French and other European languages, as well as technical skills. Through these advantages, Jews achieved a new and unprecedented mobility in the economic life of the Muslim world that was far out of proportion to their numbers or their traditional social status. For further reading, see ARGENTINA; FRANCE: 1789–1939; IRAN; IRAQ; NORTH AFRICA; and A. Rodrigue, *Images of Sephardi and Eastern Jewries in Transition: The Teachers of the Alliance Israélite Universelle, 1860–1939* (1993).

Almohads (Arabic: *al-Mowahhidum*) were a *North African Berber sectarian reform movement started by Muhammad ibn Tumart (d. 1128) at the beginning of the twelfth century. Tumart's successor, Abd al-Mumin (d. 1163), expanded the dynasty's political power to *Egypt and *Spain, and in 1170 the Almohads established Seville as their capital city. Intolerant of all non-Muslims, the Almohads offered Jews and Christians in Spain the choice of conversion, exile, or death; many Jews fled to Christian *Spain or more tolerant locations in the Muslim world. In 1212, an alliance of Castille, Aragon, Navarre, and *Portugal decisively stopped further Almohad expansion on the Iberian Peninsula. The impact of Almohad rule on Jews in *North Africa, where many adopted *Islam outwardly and practiced Judaism secretly, was devastating and long lasting. **Map 6**   KATE FRIEDMAN

Almoravids were a Berber dynasty from the southwest Sahara that adopted a fundamentalist form of *Islam in 1080 and established a capital at Marrakesh in Morocco. The Almoravids conquered parts of *North Africa. In 1086, Muslims in *Spain invited the Almoravids to help defend them against the invasion of Alfonso VI, the Christian king of Castile. The successful Almoravids remained in Muslim Spain, assuming power by 1090. Almoravid rulers appear to have been tolerant of Jews in both North Africa and in Spain, although the situation may have deteriorated somewhat by the mid-twelfth century in North Africa. Jewish soldiers, diplomats, and physicians commonly served Almoravid rulers. **Maps 5, 6**   KATE FRIEDMAN

Alphabet of Ben Sira is an anonymous midrashic work, probably composed in a Muslim country during the period of the *Geonim (possibly as early as the eighth century CE). This rather mysterious text, falsely attributed to the author of the *Wisdom of Ben Sira, consists of two collections of twenty-two proverbs; one collection is in *Aramaic and the other is in *Hebrew and both are arranged as alphabetic acrostics. Each proverb is followed by an *aggadic commentary. Many of the themes in these commentaries are bawdy, satirical, and often misogynistic. Among other folklore traditions, the *Alphabet* identifies *Lilith with the "first *Eve" and explains her refusal to submit to *Adam as a consequence of her equal creation with him in *Genesis 1.

A translation of parts of the *Alphabet* by N. Bronznick appears in *Rabbinic Fantasies: Imaginative Narratives from Classical Hebrew Literature*, ed. D. Stern and M. J. Mirsky (1990), 167–202. For a critical Hebrew edition of this text, see E. Yassif, *Sippurei Ben Sira* (1984).   JUDITH R. BASKIN

American Jewish Committee: See ORGANIZATIONS: NORTH AMERICA

American Jewish Congress: See ORGANIZATIONS: NORTH AMERICA

American Jewish Joint Distribution Committee: See JOINT DISTRIBUTION COMMITTEE

Amidah (Hebrew for "standing") is the central prayer of communal Jewish *worship; it is also known as "the prayer" or the Eighteen Benedictions (*shemoneh esrei*).

Ammon was an ancient region located east–west between the Jordan River and the Syro-Arabian desert, and north–south between the Jabbok (Wadi Zerqa) and Arnon (Wadi Mujib) rivers. Its precise boundaries fluctuated in response to shifting regional dynamics, including those with *Moab to the south and Israel to the west. Occupied as early as the Middle and Late Bronze Ages, Ammon is best known from Iron Age remains, found through the excavation of sites such as the Amman Citadel, Tall al-'Umayri, Tall Sahab, and Tall Jawa. In the Iron Age II, Ammon became a nation ruled from Rabbat Ammon. Ammonites were polytheistic; their chief god was Milcom. The economy was based on a mix of agriculture and animal husbandry.

The relationship between Ammon and the Israelites was complex. The Bible describes kinship (through *Abraham and Lot in *Gen 19:38 and through *Solomon and *Rehoboam in 1 *Kgs 14:21), as well as conflict (*Josh 13:8–10; *Judg 3:12–14, 10:7–9; 1 *Sam 11:1–11; 2 Sam 8:11–12, 11:1). Like Israel, Ammon suffered under the onslaught of the *Assyrian Empire. Beginning in the *Babylonian period, Ammon became home to a small population of Jews (Jer 40:10–15; for post-exilic conflict, see *Neh 2:19, 4:7–8); it was briefly part of the *Hasmonean Kingdom (1 *Macc 5:6–8). In later years its capital, renamed Philadelphia, numbered among the important cities of the *Decapolis, the group of ten Greco-Roman cities on the *Roman Empire's eastern frontier. **See also** ARCHEOLOGY, LAND OF ISRAEL: ANCIENT TIMES TO PERSIAN PERIOD. **Map 2**
                              BETH ALPERT NAKHAI

Amora, Amoraim (from *Aramaic and *Hebrew *amar*, "to say, speak") are rabbinic teachers from the formative periods of the Palestinian and Babylonian *Talmuds (the *Yerushalmi* and *Bavli*, respectively). The amoraic period begins with the completion of the *Mishnah and its introduction as the focus of rabbinic study and teaching (early third century CE). Scholars place the last of the Amoraim in the first half of the fifth century, with the period ending slightly earlier in *Palestine than in *Babylonia. Palestinian Amoraim are usually counted in five generations, whereas Babylonian Amoraim are assigned to six generations.

Although sages are generally associated either with Babylonia or Palestine, rabbis and students traveled between the two communities. The first of the Babylonian Amoraim, Rav, studied for many years in Palestine. R. Johanan, the first of the Palestinian Amoraim, was said to have studied with the prominent Babylonian sages, Rav and Samuel, and had many students from Babylonia. A small number of rabbis frequented both of the two centers, transmitting the teachings from one community to the other; the best known of these rabbis, known as *naḥutei* ("those who go down" [from the Land of Israel to Babylonia], from the Aramaic *naḥat*, "to go down"), were R. Zeira, Ulla, and Rabbah bar bar Ḥana.

The central figure among first-generation Palestinian Amoraim was R. Johanan b. Napaḥa. Johanan was one of the last students of Rabbi *Judah ha-Nasi. Johanan had many associates and students; the most prominent among them included Simon b. Lakish, who was also Johanan's brother-in-law; Eleazar b. Pedat; R. Ammi; and R. Assi. Another important figure in the early amoraic movement in Palestine was R. Joshua b. Levi, who studied with one of the last of the *Tannaim, Bar Kappara. R. Joshua b. Levi was particularly interested in *aggadah*. Important figures in subsequent generations included R. Jeremiah and R. Zeira. During this period, Palestinian Rabbis were increasingly associated with larger towns and cities, especially Tiberias, Sepphoris, Caesarea, and Lod. Students studied with Rabbis in small groups, often meeting in their homes. There appear to have been strong ties between Rabbis and the *Patriarch, who at times appointed Rabbis to communal positions.

The major Amoraim in the first generation in Babylonia were Rav and Samuel. Rav was the nephew of R. Ḥiyya, one of the last of the Tannaim; he studied with his uncle and R. Judah ha-Nasi in Palestine before returning to Babylonia. The Babylonian Talmud traces Rav's lineage back to a brother of King *David or to David himself. It places Rav on the level of the Tannaim; he alone among the Amoraim is permitted to contradict a Tanna. Rav's school was in Sura, whereas Samuel's was in Nehardea. The house of study in Sura was subsequently headed in the second and third generations by R. Huna, R. Ḥisda, and Rabbah. R. Judah, a student of Samuel, founded a school in *Pumbedita that was later headed by R. Joseph, Abbaye, and R. Zevid. In the fourth generation, Abbaye, a contemporary of Rava, taught in Mehoza. R. Pappa, a fifth-generation Amora, taught in Naresh. The major figures of the sixth and final generation of Babylonian Amoraim were Ravina and R. Ashi. These two Amoraim are traditionally associated with the completion of the Babylonian Talmud, although modern scholars now believe that the Bavli was in fact completed after the amoraic period by the *Saboraim or *Stammaim. As in Palestine, rabbinic schools in Babylonia in the amoraic period were small, often meeting in the home of the teacher. Structure within these schools was loose; students could leave one teacher and go to another. Babylonian Amoraim were apparently less involved in the synagogue than their Palestinian counterparts, but did give public lectures. The *Exilarch sometimes appointed Rabbis as judges, and others presided over informal courts.

The Palestinian and the Babylonian Talmuds contain many stories about the lives of the Amoraim, especially their interactions with their students and colleagues. These stories have been used to write biographical sketches of the Amoraim, but contemporary scholars have challenged the historicity of such material. However, some scholars are willing to use talmudic discussions to date Amoraim and to establish relationships between teachers and students, and, to some degree, to consider rabbinic pedigrees. The teachings of the Amoraim are found in the Palestinian and Babylonian Talmuds and in midrash collections on the *Torah (*Genesis Rabbah, Exodus Rabbah, Leviticus Rabbah, Numbers Rabbah*, and *Deuteronomy Rabbah*) and the *Writings (*Song of Songs Rabbah, Ruth Rabbah, Lamentations Rabbah, Ecclesiastes Rabbah*, and *Esther Rabbah*).

The Talmuds are heavily redacted documents so it is difficult to make definitive statements about amoraic style. Scholars have observed that statements attributed to earlier Amoraim are often in Hebrew, whereas those attributed to later Amoraim are usually in Aramaic. Statements of early generations of Amoraim frequently respond to, explain, or complement the Mishnah. The comments of later Amoraim are more likely to respond to earlier amoraic material. Although the Talmuds do record exchanges among Amoraim, much of the dialogic structure found in the Bavli is the result of redaction. A secondary use of the word *amora* denotes a "speaker" for a sage giving a lecture. The *amora* in this setting essentially functions as a translator or announcer for the lecturer, conveying his spoken softly words to the audience. Although this term, unlike the secondary use of *tanna*, is not derogatory, it describes a position that requires less learning or ability for original thought than the ability to repeat accurately what one hears.

For further reading, see *The Cambridge Companion to the Talmud and Rabbinic Literature*, ed. C. E. Fonrobert and M. Jaffee (2007); R. Kalmin, *The Sage in Jewish Society of Late Antiquity* (1999); L. Levine, *The Rabbinic Class of Roman Palestine in Late Antiquity* (1989); S. Schwartz, *Imperialism and Jewish Society 200 B.C.E. to 640 C.E.* (2001); and G. Bader, *Encyclopedia of Talmudic Sages* (1988).   DVORA E. WEISBERG

Amos, Book of. This biblical book, the third of the "Twelve Prophets," records prophecies attributed to Amos, a sheep breeder (Amos 1:1) and tender of sycamore trees (7:14), who came from the Judean village of Tekoa. Amos, whose prophetic career is dated around 750 BCE, was the first "classical" or "literary" prophet; that is, he is the first prophet whose words were collected and preserved in a book that carries his name (see BIBLE: PROPHETS AND PROPHECY; PROPHETS [*NEVI'IM*]; and PROPHETIC BOOKS). Although he was a native of the southern kingdom of *Judah, his active prophecy, probably of short duration, took place in *Beth El and *Samaria in the northern kingdom of *Israel. At some point in his life, Amos, who had no connection with professional prophetic guilds (7:14), was inspired to deliver a series of prophecies predicting the divine punishment and coming destruction both of neighboring peoples and of the Israelites themselves. Among Amos' themes is the unique bond that exists between God and the children of Israel, an intimacy that has preserved Israel since the Exodus from *Egypt. Yet he insisted that this special connection did not excuse the Israelites' sins; on the contrary, their punishments would be more severe because they had rejected this special relationship. This theme is clearly expressed in Amos 3:2: "You only have I know of all the families of the earth; therefore I will punish you for all of your iniquities." Contrary to popular expectations of a future time when Israel would be elevated above the other nations, Amos predicted a "day of the Lord" (5:18–20) that would bring divine wrath and terror on God's erring people. His oracles condemned a nation that had repudiated righteousness and tolerated the exploitation of the needy. Amos was especially critical of ritual that was not accompanied by ethical behavior (5:21–23), and he famously declaimed, "But let justice well up like water,/ Righteousness like an unfailing stream./ Did you offer sacrifice and oblation to Me/Those forty years in the wilderness,/ O House of Israel?" (5:24–25). His excoriation of the priestly cult infuriated the religious leadership. According to 7:10–13, Amaziah, the priest of Beth El, sought royal support to have Amos expelled from the kingdom of Israel. The final literary unit of the book of Amos (9:11–15) looks to a time of *redemption, rebuilding, and overwhelming fertility, when "the fallen booth of David" will be restored, when "the mountains shall drip wine," and Israel "nevermore to be uprooted/From the soil I have given them." Although many scholars believe that these verses are a later addition by an exilic or post-exilic editor, others maintain that they are part of the original book, arguing that promises of restoration of the Davidic monarchy and the establishment of a time of lasting peace and bounty were already long-standing traditions in Amos' time. For further reading, see BIBLE: REPRESENTATIONS OF WAR AND PEACE; and S. Paul, *Amos: A Commentary on the Book of Amos* (1991).   JUDITH R. BASKIN

Amram bar Sheshna (d. about 875), set himself up as an alternative *Gaon to Natronai b. Hilai, the head of the recognized academy in *Sura; he may have returned to head the mother institution after Natronai's death. Amram issued numerous *responsa on halakhic problems and talmudic interpretation, including one concerning the legal status of *tannaitic material outside the *Mishnah. His most famous responsum was sent to a Spanish community anxious to have an "order of prayers and benedictions for the whole year." His text, *Seder Rav Amram*, is generally considered the first *prayer book or *siddur*; it became so popular that it was often copied and adjusted throughout the Jewish world, thus losing much of its original format. **See also WORSHIP.**
                                                    STEFAN C. REIF

Amsterdam is the capital and largest city in the Netherlands. The pioneers of documented Jewish settlement in Amsterdam were New Christians (*conversos*), descendants of baptized Jews from *Portugal and *Spain, who migrated to Amsterdam in the 1590s. Amsterdam was then the commercial center of the Dutch Republic, recently formed in the wake of the Netherlanders' revolt against Spanish domination. New Christian merchants and their families were attracted by commercial opportunities and by Amsterdam's environment of religious toleration, established by the city's ruling regent class. By the early seventeenth century these émigrés practiced Judaism openly but discreetly and encountered no opposition from the civic authorities. Although their status remained unclear, they began organizing communal life, bringing an *Ashkenazi rabbi from *Germany to conduct worship and instruct the émigrés, who had been isolated from Jewish life for generations.

After a 1609 truce between the Netherlands and Spain, many more emigrants arrived. In 1639, when Spanish and Portuguese Jews numbered about one thousand, they united into a single and highly organized community. Rabbinic leadership was provided by *Sephardi rabbis from the Mediterranean area who made special efforts to bring the "re-judaizing" community into conformity with rabbinic law. Not everyone complied: Among those banned by the communal leadership for nonconformist views were Uriel da Costa and Baruch *Spinoza. *Ashkenazim fleeing *Central Europe came to Amsterdam during the Thirty Years War (1618–1648). Dependent at first on the Sephardim, they formed their own community in 1635; the two communities, which had deep cultural and socioeconomic differences, maintained strict separation up to modern times.

Given Amsterdam's commercial wealth and religious freedoms, the Amsterdam Sephardim emerged as one of the most powerful Jewish communities in seventeenth-century Europe. They provided leadership for the entire western Sephardi Diaspora, and the Amsterdam Sephardi community became a center of *printing, polemical writing, and intercommunal activity. However, by the eighteenth century, the Sephardim entered an irreversible process of economic decline and demographic stagnation; their population peaked at about 3,000 in the mid-eighteenth century. The Ashkenazim, initially a community of impoverished refugees, gained ascendancy; their numbers grew to about 10,000 in 1750 and continued to increase into the early twentieth century.

During the eighteenth and nineteenth centuries, *Haskalah, *emancipation, and assimilation took their particular course among the Jews of Amsterdam. By this time, neither Amsterdam nor its Jews played a leading role on the European scene, and the community experienced significant poverty. Conditions improved in the 1870s, with the growth of the diamond industry (and labor movement), and migrants came from the provinces and elsewhere. Amsterdam's Jewish population in 1900 was about 60,000; subsequently, emigration and a low birth rate led to declining numbers. Jewish community life in Amsterdam came to a halt in 1940 with the Nazi occupation. By the end of the war, 100,000 Dutch Jews had been deported and killed, and the Jewish quarter of Amsterdam was devastated. In the first decade of the twenty-first century, about 25,000 Jews live in Amsterdam of a total population of approximately 750,000. They mainly reside outside the historic Jewish quarter, which boasts the elegant 1665 Portuguese Synagogue and nearby Jewish Historical Museum, housed in a complex of four Ashkenazi synagogues from the seventeenth and eighteenth centuries.

For further reading, see SYNAGOGUES: MEDIEVAL TO EIGHTEENTH CENTURY; J. C. H. Blom, R. G. Fuks-Mansfeld, and I. Schoeffer, eds., *The History of the Jews in the Netherlands* (2002); and M. Bodian, *Hebrews of the Portuguese Nation: Conversos and Community in Early Modern Amsterdam* (1997). **Maps 8, 10**
                                                          MIRIAM BODIAN

Anointment. The Hebrew Bible describes the anointment of kings and priests with perfumed oil (a mixture of aromatic spices and olive oil) during installation rituals as an indication of divine *election. The term *"messiah" derives from the root, *mashaḥ*, "to anoint." Although only one spice, opalbalsam, was indigenous to the Land of *Israel, spices were available from foreign merchants traversing the area from south to north. Spices and perfume were a precious commodity, closely associated with royalty. *Solomon received precious spices from the *Queen of Sheba (1 Kgs 10:10); *Hezekiah displayed his cache of spices and fragrant oil to *Babylonian visitors (2 Kgs 20:13); and Asa was buried with "all kinds of spices mixed in an ointment pot" (2 Chron 16:14).

Anointment with perfumed oil after bathing was common. Naomi directed her widowed daughter-in-law, *Ruth, to bathe, anoint herself, and dress up in order to entice a potential husband (Ruth 3:3). After mourning his son's death, *David arose, bathed, and anointed himself (2 Sam 12:20). In the book of *Esther, maidens prepared to enter the king's bed chamber by bathing for "six months in oil of myrrh and six months in spices" (2:12). The close association between oil and love making is most dramatic in *Song of Songs, where the lover's oil is more pleasing than his name (1:3) and the beloved's hands are "dripping with myrrh" (5:5).

During the *Roman period scented oils were used at the public bathhouse, at home, at the market, and in burials. In addition to its use in anointment, oil was rubbed on the hands to remove odors, dripped or sprinkled on the floor before cleaning, and rubbed or inhaled medicinally (JT *Berakhot* 6:6 10d, T. *Shabbat* 5:9–10). Spices and oils were purchased from perfumers, who probably also served as apothecaries (T. *Shevuot* 5:12; BT *Ḥullin* 55b). Perfume was used to anoint corpses before burial and containers of perfume were sometimes buried with the deceased (M. *Berakhot* 8:6, M. *Shabbat* 23:5). **See also INCENSE.**
                                                          DEBORAH A. GREEN

Anthropology, literally "an account of man," is the comparative study of human societies and cultures. Jews played a significant role in the founding and development of cultural anthropology (defined as the study of contemporary cultures and societies and the study of human behavior that is learned rather than genetically transmitted) in the latter part of the nineteenth century. Among these early figures was Marcel Mauss (1872–1950), nephew of influential sociologist Emile Durkheim. His most influential work, *The Gift* (1925), explored religious, legal, economic, mythological, and other aspects of giving, receiving, and repaying in different cultures. Lucien Lévy-Bruhl (1857–1939) wrote a series of ethnological works on various aspects of preliterate culture. The German-born Franz Boas (1858–1942) is often considered the "father of American anthropology"; he came to the *United States in 1886 and became professor of anthropology at Columbia University (*New York City) in 1899. Boas did extensive field research in North America and helped make fieldwork a hallmark of anthropology. His theory of "historical particularism" stresses the biological and "psychic unity" of humans and explains cultural diversity by appeal to specific cultural histories and environments. He introduced the concept of cultural relativism, which holds that cultures cannot be evaluated on an evolutionary scale but should be examined in relation to the environment in which they are found. Boas, a prolific writer, spoke out forcefully against racism and intolerance and wrote and lectured widely in opposition to the Nazis. In his classic *Anthropology and Modern Life* (1928), he examined the topic of race and culture, demonstrating the fallacies of claims of racial and ethnic superiorities. His outstanding American students included Margaret Mead, Ruth Benedict, and many more, including many scholars of Jewish origin. Under the tutelage of Benedict, the Columbia University Research in Contemporary Cultures was inaugurated shortly after the end of World War II. A goal of this project was to encourage the study of changing and, in some cases, disappearing cultures. *Life is with People: The Jewish Little-Town of Eastern Europe* by Mark Zborowski and Elizabeth Herzog, was an outcome of this effort. Published in 1952, this book documented the religious rituals and daily observances of the vanished *shtetl culture of pre–WWII *Eastern Europe and was one of the first anthropological studies of Jews.

Jewish *psychoanalysts have been highly influential in the study of the interrelationships between culture and psychology and pivotal in the development of the culture and personality subfield of cultural anthropology. Of particular importance is the work of Geza Roheim (1891–1953), Abram Kardiner (1891–1981), Theodor Reik (1888–1969), and Erich Fromm (1900–1980).

Claude Lévi-Strauss (1908–2009) born in Brussels, was the most distinguished social anthropologist in twentieth-century *France. His most original and significant contribution is his theory of structural anthropology. Heavily influenced by linguistics, it assumes that the most effective way to understand human societies is to investigate the structures, rather than the content, of their organization. His book, *The Elementary Structures of Kinship* (1949), is regarded as one of the most important works on this topic.

Contemporary Jewish anthropologists in the United States include a number of influential women who have examined issues related to Jews and Jewish identity. Barbara Myerhoff (1935–1985), a renowned scholar, writer, and filmmaker, helped popularize anthropology with her works *Peyote Hunt* (1974), *Number Our Days* (1978), and the autobiographical film, *In Her Own Time* (1985). In the book and film, *Number Our Days,* Myerhoff explores the lives of poor, aged Jews in Venice, CA. Karen Brodkin's *How Jews Became White Folks and What That Says About Race in America* (1999) analyzes the interrelationships among Jewishness, gender, and class. Riv-Ellen Prell's *Fighting to Become Americans: Jews, Gender and the Anxiety of Assimilation* (1999) examines challenges to identity faced by Jewish women. Ruth Behar, writer, poet, and filmmaker, has written about the relationship between her Jewish identity and her anthropological work. Barbara Kirshenblatt-Gimblett's *Destination Culture* (1998) lays the foundation for studies of Jewish *museums, exhibits, and material culture. Other significant American anthropologists who addressed issues of Jewish interest include Melford Spiro (b. 1920), who has written extensively about the Israeli *kibbutz; Jack Kugelmass, who has written on various topics dealing with American Jews; and Jonathan Boyarin, whose collection *Thinking in Jewish* (1996) broke

new ground in applying theoretical issues to the study of Jewish communities.

In recent years, there has been increasing interest in examining the profound influence that Jews have had in the development of anthropology in the United States, France, and *Britain. Analysts assume that Jews' marginality and sometimes vulnerable positionality in their societies are what led many Jewish anthropologists to focus on issues of race, ethnicity, culture, nationalism, and identity. In the past, the silence surrounding this subject resulted from several factors, including *antisemitism. When anthropology was becoming established as an academic discipline, there was concern that its strong association with Jews could discredit its reputation. Some Jewish anthropologists downplayed their religious heritage in their pursuit of academic positions, at a time when there was broad discrimination in hiring practices. Additionally, Boasian anthropology was premised on the insignificance of race, ethnicity, and religion; the corollary was that the ethnic/religious identity of anthropologists was irrelevant. However, in recent years, anthropologists have acknowledged that they, like others, are influenced by their various heritages and that their backgrounds may affect their disciplinary choices and conclusions. Anthropology has become more reflective as scholars have become increasingly aware of how their own cultural and personal backgrounds have an impact on their work.

DIANE BAXTER

Antinomianism (*contra-nomos*) is a term that may refer to any religious movement claiming that fulfillment of the divine will does not need to conform to accepted religious norms or doctrine. Some forms of antinomianism suggest that the divine will can be fulfilled outside the law, and more radical branches argue that the divine will is fulfilled only through the abrogation of the law. It has been argued that the first real antinomian movement in Judaism rose with the apostle Paul in conjunction with the transition of Judaism to a religion of law in the first centuries of the Common Era. Paul's polemic, waged largely against the Jewish-Christian communities of his time, argued that Christ's death and resurrection overcame the need for the law or, more strongly, erase the law as a category of salvation. This is not to suggest that Christianity is a form of Jewish antinomianism. Jewish antinomianism would require that the law still serve as a category that is broken or overcome by another avenue of worship. Because Jewish law no longer functions as a category in Christianity, the term "antinomianism" would not apply (See CHRISTIANITY AND SECOND TEMPLE JUDAISM).

There have been numerous antinomian movements throughout Jewish history depending on how one understands the limits of the term. One could posit that the medieval *Karaite movement that rebelled against rabbinic authority was antinomian if we specify *nomos* (in this case, law) as being confined to the dictates of rabbinism. More common forms of antinomianism apply to movements or individuals who claim some direct access to God, making legal norms inapplicable. In Christianity, the famous 1637 dispute of Anne Hutchinson with the Massachusetts Bay Colony is a case in point. Hutchinson claimed that her immediate relation to God enabled her to circumvent church authority and practice in the name of true religion (see

David Hall, ed., *The Antinomianism Controversy 1636–1638: A Documentary History* [1990]).

Many Jewish forms of antinomianism are mixed with both *mysticism and *messianism. The anonymous late-fourteenth- or early-fifteenth-century books *Sefer Temunah* and *Sefer Peliah* are a case in point. Both argued that the law is particular to that historical epoch and would be overcome with the movement into a new era (although neither claimed such a move was imminent). Although these obscure works are not antinomian in practice, one might claim that they are antinomian is principle. The most famous case of antinomianism in Judaism is the false messiah *Shabbatai Zevi (1626–1676?) and the movement that grew around him. Shabbatei Zevi revealed himself as messiah in 1666, converted to *Islam under duress soon after, and lived the rest of his life under the protection of the *Ottoman Sultan. Some of his disciples argued that his conversion was a holy act whereby, as *messiah, he descended into the depths of the demonic to liberate the final holy sparks and bring about *redemption. The notion of "sin for the sake of heaven" (a rabbinic term deployed by the *Sabbateans) or, as Gershom *Scholem preferred, "redemption through sin," became the underlying principle of the Sabbatean movement. The idea that the Righteous One (as messiah) had to sin in order to redeem the world was expanded by radical Sabbateans such as Jacob *Frank (1726–1791) to suggest that the community must sin with the intention of completing redemption. This led to overt transgression and sexual promiscuity among his disciples. The Frankist movement essentially died out when most of his disciples converted to Christianity around 1759.

Moderate Sabbateanism, however, has a more complex history. Some have argued that some forms of *Ḥasidism, especially early Ḥasidism before 1815, contained certain Sabbatean and thus antinomian tendencies. Its focus on *devekut* (experiential cleaving to God) as the goal of the religious life and its encouragement of joyous worship instead of austere and uncompromising devotion to the law have led some to see Sabbatean strands in some early Ḥasidic communities. Alternatively, one could say that Reform Judaism (see JUDAISM, REFORM) and most non-Orthodox Judaisms that followed also contain some dimensions of antinomianism in that they posit that fulfilling the divine will requires activity that does not conform to the law and, in fact, may require abrogation of the law in certain circumstances. Support of gender equality, positive attitudes toward a range of sexual orientations and preferences, and an accepting stance toward non-Jews (including *intermarriage) can all be framed as antinomian in some form. These behaviors are quite different from the Frankist idea of sin as *mitzvah* (*commandment) but may be closer to a more moderate Sabbatean notion that changing times require a reformulation, sometimes radical, of the *nomos* of the tradition. This is not to suggest any direct historical link between Reform and Sabbateanism since such a link is tenuous at best. Rather, it is to say that Judaism, construed as a religion of *nomos*, at least from the rabbinic period on, always contained within it forces that questioned the exclusivity and even primacy of law and sought to provide alternative avenues of worship and practice beyond its bounds.

Recent scholarship includes S. Magid, *Hasidism on the Margin: Reconciliation, Antinomianism, and Messianism in Izbica/Radzin Hasidism* (2003); and E. R. Wolfson, *Venturing Beyond: Law and Morality in Kabbalistic Mysticism* (2006).

SHAUL MAGID

Antisemitism is a word that came into common usage during the 1880s in German-speaking Europe to signify activities aimed at ending what proponents believed was undue influence exercised by Jews over European cultural, social, economic, and political life. Although it is often asserted that German writer Wilhelm Marr (1819–1904) coined the term, no persuasive evidence has been adduced to this effect. The stem *antisemit-* was used in *Germany since 1860 as a characterization for statements asserting the inferiority of cultures belonging to the *Semitic language family, as compared to those employing an Indo-European language. That usage appears to have been current when a group called the *Antisemiten-Liga* (League of Antisemites) came into being under the leadership of Marr and Hector de Grousillier in September 1879. This small society was one of several such organizations, all founded more or less around the same time, that expressed dissatisfaction with the consequences of the provision of Germany's 1871 imperial constitution that had abolished all legal restrictions on Jews and Jewish communities. In November 1879, Heinrich von Treitschke, a leading German historian of his day, labeled these groups collectively as *Antisemitenvereine* (antisemitic associations), and the name caught on quickly.

People joined the *Antisemitenvereine* for many reasons: some because of religiously inspired notions about the proper role of Jews in Christian society, some because they identified Jews with *capitalism, and others because they thought that attacking Jews might bring them political advantage. In other words, no single set of ideas about Jews united them. "Antisemitism" thus originally meant little more than "acting like an antisemite" – that is, engaging in activities that the so-called antisemitic associations espoused. The widespread belief that the word conveyed opposition to alleged Jewish influence in society because of Jews' purported racial characteristics instead of their religious beliefs has no basis in fact.

The first antisemitic associations arose in Germany. Their earliest intervention in German politics was the presentation of the so-called Antisemites' Petition to Chancellor Bismarck in April 1881. The petition made four demands: restriction of Jewish immigration from other countries, a ban on the appointment of Jews to positions of authority, preservation of the Christian character of schools, and separate registration of Jews in official statistics. Although the document garnered more than 250,000 signatures, none of its demands was implemented. During the following decade several political parties were formed to ensure that the petition's goals were implemented through legislation. By any measure these parties were a failure: Their parliamentary representation never exceeded 4%, and in almost three decades of activity they managed to bring only seven bills to the Reichstag floor and none was enacted. Nevertheless, they attracted considerable public attention, both in Germany and beyond. In the early 1880s, groups espousing similar political platforms appeared in *Hungary, *Habsburg Austria, and *France. These groups, too, were soon labeled "antisemitic." In 1882, German, Austrian, and Hungarian activists convened an International Anti-Jewish Congress, which called for boycotting Jewish-owned newspapers, refusing membership in any organization of which Jews were members, and shunning Jews in social and economic life. The Congress signaled the beginning of a Europe-wide "antisemitic movement," although those who took part in it were not able to agree on a definition of the term.

Indeed, in popular usage the word's referents were already expanding. By mid-1882 Jewish newspapers in Germany were referring to the *pogroms in southern *Russia that had broken out the preceding year as "antisemitic" acts. The 1882 *ritual murder accusation in the Hungarian town of Tiszaeszlár was also widely given the same designation, as was the agitation in France conducted by journalist Édouard Drumont, especially after the publication of his 1886 book, *La France juive* (Jewish France). The basis for classifying these phenomena together with activities in the political sphere was evidently the belief that all of them challenged the notion that Jews could be integrated into European society in a way that would benefit society as a whole. In turn, that challenge was widely presumed to be rooted in the same sort of hostile attitudes and prejudices toward Jews that had been evident in medieval Christendom (and, according to some, in pre-Christian antiquity as well). Jewish observers quickly assimilated "antisemitism" to the traditional Jewish notion of *sin'at yisra'el* ("hatred of Israel"), according to which "Esau always hates Jacob" (*Genesis Rabbah* 78:9), and understood it as a well-known, age-old phenomenon. As a result, virtually any present or past act or expression by non-Jews that Jews found threatening was readily dubbed "antisemitic" and attributed to aggressive hatred. Moreover, by the end of the nineteenth century the word was widely used as a designation for the emotion itself, as well as for the broad range of behaviors, statements, and cultural artifacts that it was supposed to produce. In this way it came to point simultaneously to cause and effect. Such usage remains dominant in common parlance at the beginning of the twenty-first century.

From the early twentieth century, however, some observers, both Jewish and non-Jewish, noted that many actions or statements that Jews perceived as inimical to their collective security or interests might not stem from hatred or a desire to harm Jews. Instead, they could be the result of ordinary intergroup tensions in which the specific identity of the contending groups was secondary to the perception of differences between them. In consequence, analysts sought criteria for distinguishing phenomena that warranted the label "antisemitic" from those that did not, no matter how unwelcome Jews might find them. The task has proven daunting; twenty-first-century scholars have reached no more agreement than nineteenth-century self-proclaimed "antisemites" on how the term should be delimited and how "antisemitic" acts or utterances should be identified.

Since *World War II, efforts at refining usage of the term have generally posited the existence of a "special hatred" – distinct from normal xenophobic prejudices – that has generated stock images depicting Jews, the Jewish religion, or Jewish culture as inevitably harmful to the well-being of humankind. Scholars who have studied those images have done so largely under the impact of the *Holocaust, in the conviction that only a truly exceptional hatred could have motivated the Nazi regime in Germany to seek to kill every Jewish man, woman, and child within reach. They have

thus understood "antisemitism" as synonymous with a set of antagonistic beliefs about Jews both sufficiently powerful to arouse murderous impulses and sufficiently well known through familiar imagery to lend them widespread credence.

Much effort has gone into ascertaining how such beliefs have come about. Historians and social scientists have catalogued and classified the images through which hostile beliefs about Jews have been figured, examined when and where the images were created and deployed, and tried to explain why they have appeared more commonly in some times and places than in others. Psychologists have probed the mental processes that might make people accept such fanciful representations as true. No clear picture has emerged from their investigations, however. For example, psychological studies have not established that people who profess powerful hostility toward Jews display a fundamentally different emotional makeup from people who indicate powerful hostility toward other groups. Nor have they shown that acceptance of images presumably generated out of such powerful hostility necessarily indicates psychopathology. In other words, psychological methods have not demonstrated the existence of a special hatred toward Jews, marked by a unique mental configuration. Historical methods have similarly come up short. To begin with, historians have been unable to agree about when the purported special hatred that merits the label "antisemitism" first appeared. Opinions include the Greco-Roman era; the time of the separation between Judaism and Christianity; the high *Middle Ages in western Christendom (especially the twelfth and thirteenth centuries, when identifications of Jews with beasts and the devil initially surfaced in Christian anti-Jewish polemics), the later Middle Ages (when Jews were associated with witchcraft and sorcery); and the nineteenth century (when Jews were first branded incorrigible by virtue of their race). More significantly, however, they have not managed to identify which of the many hostile acts and utterances toward Jews were motivated by the ostensible special hatred, which by more mundane conflicts, and which by ordinary social processes.

Indeed, studies of the Nazi Holocaust have found that many who participated in mass killings of Jews did not display any particular animus toward their victims, but instead were driven by such commonplace emotions as the desire for self-aggrandizement, peer pressure, or deference to authority. Even those who conceived and ordered the murder campaign evidently responded more to general ideas about race, culture, and the biological basis of human behavior that circulated widely in Europe toward the end of the nineteenth century than to long-standing images of Jews allegedly born of special hatred. In short, the belief that it is possible to separate from the set of present and past activities that Jews have found threatening a subset motivated by an uncommon emotion that gave rise to the Holocaust appears to be illusory.

Another approach to determining what might constitute an "antisemitic" act or utterance takes into account that, after World War II, the label has generally been deemed pejorative; few wish to be known as "antisemites." As a result, some have proposed reserving the label "antisemitism" for expressions of hostility toward Jews that exceed the bounds of legitimate criticism. In this connection, efforts have been made to enumerate behaviors of this kind, including one by the European Union Monitoring Center on Racism and Xenophobia (later renamed the EU Agency for Fundamental Rights) in January 2005. The "Working Definition of Antisemitism" produced by this body notes that "contemporary examples of antisemitism... could include... calling for, aiding, or justifying the killing or harming of Jews in the name of a radical ideology or extremist view of religion; making mendacious, dehumanizing, demonizing, or stereotypical allegations about Jews as such or the power of Jews as a collective...; accusing Jews as a people of being responsible for real or imagined wrongdoing committed by a single Jewish person or group...; denying the fact, scope, mechanisms..., or intentionality of... the Holocaust; accusing Jews as a people, or *Israel as a state, of inventing or exaggerating the Holocaust; [and] accusing Jewish citizens of being more loyal to Israel, or to the alleged priorities of Jews worldwide, than to the interests of their own nations." The document also identifies certain attitudes and behaviors toward the State of Israel as "ways in which antisemitism manifests itself," including "denying the Jewish people their right to self-determination...; claiming that the existence of a state of Israel is a racist endeavor; applying double standards by requiring of it behavior not expected or demanded of any other democratic nation; using the symbols and images associated with classic antisemitism... to characterize Israel or Israelis; drawing comparisons of contemporary Israeli policy to that of the Nazis; [and] holding Jews collectively responsible for actions of the State of Israel." In contrast, it also notes that "criticism of Israel similar to that leveled against any other country cannot be regarded as antisemitic." (The document can be viewed at *http://eumc.europa.eu /eumc/material/pub/AS/AS-WorkingDefinition-draft.pdf*.)

This definition is a *prescriptive* statement about behaviors that might be regarded as socially unacceptable. According to the EU body it was prepared "to provide a practical guide for identifying incidents, collecting data, and supporting the implementation and enforcement of legislation dealing with antisemitism." Indeed, most of those using the term "antisemitism" since its introduction in the late nineteenth century have done so because they found it a useful vehicle for analyzing the relations between Jews and non-Jews in their day. As the character of those relations has changed, so have the meanings attached to the word. No single definition can be regarded as correct or incorrect; the test of the various definitions can be only the extent to which they aid or inhibit understanding of how Jews and non-Jews have interacted and continue to interact with one another.

DAVID ENGEL

Antisemitism: *France (1789–1939). Although the *emancipation decrees of 1790 and 1791 that emerged from the French Revolution should have quelled challenges to Jews' equal status in *France, resistance developed in the nineteenth century to their expression of lawful political rights. In several localities of eastern France there were attempts to prevent Jews from taking the civic oath, a requirement for citizenship. Similarly, the refusal of the new French republic to nationalize the debts of the formerly autonomous Jewish communities, although it did assume the debts of other communal groups, left the Jews with a financial disability that belied their equality. This discrimina-

tory situation, which lasted longest in the eastern provinces, disappeared only when those regions were annexed by *Germany after the Franco-Prussian War (1870). Another form of fiscal inequity was the lack of state funding for Jewish institutions until 1831, whereas Christian institutions had benefited from public funding from the time of Napoleon.

An old and humiliating symbol of Jewish disability that was retained throughout much of the nineteenth century was the special Jewish oath, known as an oath "*moré judaico*," which was frequently imposed on Jewish litigants and Jews taking political office. Such discriminatory treatment had no basis in French law and could easily have been eliminated by a simple order of the government's justice department. In fact, court decisions, beginning as early as 1826, ruled repeatedly that regular oaths were valid for Jews, although alternative forms were never actually repudiated. As the century wore on the oaths became generally less offensive than the degrading medieval practices that had survived into the early nineteenth century, but for those eager to see Jews treated on a par with others in France, any oath specific to Jews remained problematic. The refusal of some rabbis to administer *moré judaico* oaths, combined with legal challenges brought by attorney Adolphe Crémieux, resulted in a series of local court decisions and a ruling of the supreme appeals court in 1846 that rabbis could not be forced to preside over discriminatory oaths. Special Jewish oaths finally disappeared some time after the last known instance, which took place in Paris in 1872.

In 1840, when *ritual murder charges were lodged in Damascus against Jews of that city, the French consul endorsed the claims (see DAMASCUS AFFAIR). Foreign Minister Adolphe Thiers, motivated by his Middle East strategy, failed to condemn the consul's behavior, and some French Jews feared that it was a short step from their government's tacit approval of its consul's behavior to degradation of Jewish status at home. Adding to Jewish concerns about their public image at home was the fact that the French press reported the ritual murder story as credible. Again in 1860, the press accepted as fact another false accusation that Syrian Jews had massacred Christians. The climate of prejudice against Jews resulted in discriminatory hiring practices throughout the middle of the century. Such disabilities differed by region, but were especially significant in the teaching and judicial careers. In at least one case Jewish children were barred from enrolling in a public secondary school. Nor was France free of episodic virulent or even violent antisemitism. Attacks on Jews were most frequent in eastern France; they occurred in several locations at the time of the French Revolution and again during the revolutions of 1830 and 1848. In 1848 Jewish houses were pillaged in Alsace, some Jews fled to Switzerland, and the army was called out to restore order. In 1853 the Central Consistory (see FRANCE: CONSISTORIES [1806–1939]) concluded that it was useless to expect governmental assistance in response to the repeated threats menacing the Jews of Alsace.

From the 1830s through the 1850s, a series of Catholic publications vilified Jews, but the Consistories abstained from prosecution because they were afraid of defeat in court. In 1845 Catholic proselytizers enacted a deathbed conversion on Lazare Terquem, a member of a prominent Jewish family of Metz, and the Consistory proved powerless to prevent his burial in a Catholic cemetery. In 1859 a young rabbi, Elie-Aristide Astruc, broke with the Consistory's policy of silence and published a rebuttal to the popular Catholic conservative antisemitic journalist, Louis Veuillot. Much of the antisemitic literature before 1880 came from the left. Socialists, seeking an end to exploitation, discrimination, and the Catholic Church's temporal powers, attacked Judaism, which they considered the source of Christianity. With the Jewish banking families as mental models, socialists also made a facile equation of Jews with financial capitalism. Charles Fourier, Pierre Joseph Proudhon, and Alphonse Toussenel were among those who produced French socialist antisemitic writings. Preceding Marx's *On the Jewish Question*, Fourier introduced a full catalogue of charges against Jews, including usury, avarice, parasitism, deceit, betrayal, intolerance, and resistance to assimilation. It is thought that his hostility derived from competition with a rival utopian group, the Saint Simonians, which had attracted many Jews. Toussenel's 1845 *Les juifs rois de l'époque* added the charge that Jews were anti-nature and blamed *Rothschild's railroads for ruining the forests.

In the last two decades of the nineteenth century, right-wing, royalist, and Catholic political antisemitism was born. Building on traditional anti-Judaism, socialist stereotypes, and rejection of the Third Republic's universalism and anti-clericalism, it responded to the fact that Jews were active members of the movement to separate church and state, secularize schools, and institute civil divorce. Perhaps the success of Jewish mobility and integration also fueled the attacks, as political antisemitism fed on the socioeconomic and political dislocations caused by the new regime. One of the earliest evidences of antisemitism under the Third Republic was an 1881 article on German antisemitism in the influential *Revue du monde catholique*. In that same year Father Chabauty, a country priest, published *Les juifs, nos maîtres!* His theme was that Jewish leaders were organizing the Jewish nation and all secret societies against Christianity with the aim of obtaining Jewish dominion over the world. In 1883 Catholic antisemitic newspapers began to appear. *La Croix*, an inexpensive, popular antirepublican Catholic daily, took as its premise the concept that the French Revolution had been the work of Jews allied with Freemasons. This claim had enormous influence with the lower clergy and popular masses, although it was severely criticized by higher levels of the church.

The landmark antisemitic publication of the period was *La France juive* (1886) by Édouard Drumont. It portrayed Jews as materialistic, sordid, corrupt, and the primary cause of all France's misfortunes. Only Aryans, Drumont claimed, possessed notions of justice, the sentiment of good, and the idea of liberty. Ugly "Semites" were spies, traitors, criminals, and carriers of disease. *La France juive* quickly became not only the most widely read book in France but it also introduced a whole series of books and a journal by Drumont on the same theme. Within three years, in 1889, Drumont's ideas stimulated the formation of the French National Antisemitic League, and Adolphe Willette ran (unsuccessfully) for the Chamber of Deputies from Paris on an antisemitic ticket. Political antisemitism continued to gather momentum. In 1891 thirty-two deputies called for Jews to be expelled from France. The following year, with Jesuit support, Drumont founded *La Libre Parole*, a daily that immediately launched a

defamation campaign against Jewish army officers, accusing them of having plotted treason and of trafficking in secrets of the national defense. Drumont repeatedly fabricated and disseminated accusations that a "World Jewish Syndicate" aimed at world domination.

Antisemitic prejudice, albeit more discreetly stated, was found even in republican publications and in nonpolitical journals and romantic literature, especially drama. Although there were also philosemitic themes in such material, negative depictions of Jews included Jews as evil, conspiring, money-grubbing, foreign (oriental), wandering (*juif errant*), and inassimilable. Alphonse Daudet, Edmond de Goncourt, and Émile Zola (before his transformation into a leading Dreyfusard) are examples of popular writers who furthered negative stereotypes of Jews. Daudet even intervened to have Drumont's *La France juive* published after it had been rejected by several presses. It has been suggested that antisemitism sufficiently permeated society to serve as the glue uniting disparate factions into a single French national identity.

Yet in 1891 Rabbi Simon Debré represented the overconfidence of a faction of French Jewry when he wrote that this movement would die a rapid death. His view of France at the end of the century was that brotherhood and acceptance generally prevailed and that Drumont and his "meager following" had no influence on ideas and customs in France. Such optimistic perceptions changed by the mid-1890s. The 1895 *Dreyfus Affair was the best known milestone in French antisemitism before Vichy. When Alfred Dreyfus was falsely convicted of military treason and stripped of his commission, crowds throughout France rioted against Jews, pillaged and boycotted Jewish stores, and, in many cities, including Paris, rallied to cries of "death to the Jews." Despite clear proof of his innocence, the army did not reinstate Dreyfus until 1906, and it was only in 1995 that the French army officially declared him innocent.

Already in 1893, rebelling against the more conservative behavior of Jewish institutions, Isidore Singer founded a biweekly newspaper, *La Vraie Parole*, to provide a counterbalance to Drumont's *Libre Parole*. Through the intermediary of Chief Rabbi Zadoc Kahn, Edmond de Rothschild agreed to fund the paper when no other Jewish bankers would help (see ROTHSCHILD FAMILY). Long articles on the history of antisemitism did not, however, prove an effective means of combating *Libre Parole*, and *Vraie Parole* failed within a year.

By the time Dreyfus was reinstated, France was on the eve of *World War I, which brought with it consensus for a "union sacrée," or internal harmony and solidarity against external enemies. Despite the continued existence of nationalist right-wing factions, antisemitism remained quiescent through the 1920s, only to erupt with great force again in the following decade. Nevertheless the seeds were being laid for the next outbreak, including the appearance in 1920 and 1921 of the first French edition of what has become the essential and perennial antisemitic text, *The Protocols of the Elders of Zion* (see RUSSIA). By the eve of World War II a large and hostile literature had developed around the theses of this forgery. Political antisemitism was rare, but not unheard of. In 1923, within the Chamber of Deputies, Léon Blum was the recipient of an antisemitic insult; in his public response Blum asserted his pride in belonging to the Jewish "race."

The 1920s saw a flourishing of Jewish literature and culture, but at least one Jewish leader publicly expressed fear of so much public notice. Writing in a popular Jewish journal in 1925, and reacting especially to the burgeoning *Yiddish press, *theater, and *film, Jules Meyer titled his article, "They are talking too much about us." He called for a lower profile, warning that the currently hospitable atmosphere toward Jews could quickly disappear. Although it is doubtful that Jewish cultural production caused the eventual tragedies that befell a large part of the Jews in France, it is conceivable that the very nature of Jewish self-portrayal of the 1920s may have contributed to the sense of Jews as outsiders. Jewish characters in fiction by Jewish authors were frequently presented as "semitic" or "oriental," were often portrayed as torn between embracing and rejecting their Jewish heritage, and were sometimes involved in doomed mixed marriages.

Events around the world contributed in multiple ways to the evolution of a reinvigorated French antisemitism. The Paris Peace Conference of 1919 took up the issue of national minorities, and some French Jews, defending the notion, introduced a philosophy of multiculturalism into a France that was not prepared to accept such a premise or believe in an ethnic or national form of Judaism. *Zionism began also to attract adherents, thereby providing additional fodder for the suspicion of a lack of Jewish loyalty. As the world fell into a major economic crisis, Eastern European antisemitism and the imposition of immigration restrictions by the *United States stimulated the arrival of refugees, including Jews. The Jewish population of France doubled, from 150,000 to 300,000, in the twenty years that preceded World War II. Immigration, in turn, brought foreign antisemitism into France, stimulating public discussion and reaction. One example was the very public and dramatic trial in 1927 of Sholom Schwartzbard, a Ukrainian-born French citizen, for the 1926 murder of Ukrainian exile Simon Petlura. Schwartzbard was acquitted by the jury, which accepted the argument that he was rightfully avenging family members killed by Ukrainian nationalists under Petlura's command. France and the world were divided on the relative guilt of each man and there were repercussions. A *Ligue Internationale Contre l'Antisemitism* (LICA) was created in 1926, influenced by the model and teachings of Schwartzbard and extolling the creation of a new Jew, one who would not allow himself to be victimized or enslaved but would fight in his own defense and break the cycle of anti-Jewish hatred and violence.

The 1930s marked the return of political antisemitism, which went well beyond any prior manifestations. The responsible factors included the 1933 accession of Hitler to power in *Germany; economic depression; the 1936 emergence of a government by the "Popular Front," a coalition of socialists and communists under the leadership of Léon Blum; and the growing fear of war. It did not help the Jewish cause that Alexandre Stavinsky, a Jewish swindler with ties to several members of the government, was discovered to have been the embezzler whose schemes caused huge financial losses for many people. A riot in February 1934 portrayed Jews as stateless invaders, eternally inassimilable, who were corrupting the economic and political order, sapping France's economic strength, and leading the country into war.

Violence increased, with episodes of attacks in immigrant Jewish neighborhoods and businesses often orchestrated by the *Action Française* and other nationalist organizations. Anti-Jewish propaganda blossomed, with calls for a halt to immigration, rejection of refugees from Nazism, and proposals for legislation to make Jews second-class citizens. By the end of the 1930s there were approximately fifty antisemitic newspapers and magazines, with a total circulation in the millions. Numerous well-respected and prize-winning authors, including Louis-Ferdinand Céline and Jean Giradoux, wrote antisemitic literature. Although most of this material came from the right, the left and labor also occasionally disseminated anti-Jewish tracts. The way was being paved for the 1940 Vichy government law (*Statut des Juifs*), which initiated the loss of Jewish political and civil rights and culminated in the deportation and murder of nearly a quarter of the Jewish population living in France.

For further reading, see P. C. Albert, *The Modernization of French Jewry: Consistory and Community in the Nineteenth Century (1977)*; P. Birnbaum, *The Anti-Semitic Moment: A Tour of France in 1898* (2003); J. Frankel, *The Damascus Affair*, (1997); P. E. Hyman, *The Jews of Modern France* (1998); and M. Winock, *Nationalism, Antisemitism, and Fascism in France* (1998).   PHYLLIS COHEN ALBERT

Apocalyptic Writings: See AFTERLIFE: HEBREW BIBLE AND SECOND TEMPLE PERIOD; APOCRYPHA; DEAD SEA SCROLLS; ESCHATOLOGY: SECOND *TEMPLE PERIOD; PSEUDEPIGRAPHA

Apocrypha refers to a collection of Jewish texts written between the fourth century BCE and first century CE. The existence of this collection as a discrete corpus (distinguished from the many other para-biblical texts written during this period) reflects the reading practices of early *Christian communities. Many of these communities read some of these books alongside the Hebrew *Bible as their "Old Testament," as attested by fourth- and fifth-century codices of the *Septuagint (the Greek "Old Testament"). Others preferred to follow the stricter canon of the Hebrew Scriptures. The term "apocrypha" – Greek for "hidden things" – came to be applied to these books by communities that followed the latter practice.

CONTENTS: The limits of the collection are somewhat fluid owing to the slight variations in canon among Christian communions. The discussion here follows the broadest delineation of the collection, as found, for example, in modern printed editions of the *New Revised Standard Version of the Bible*. In most cases, the individual books that came to be included in the Apocrypha follow the pattern of classic texts of the Hebrew canon. They are discussed here according to major genres also found in the Hebrew Scriptures.

HISTORICAL WORKS: Several apocrypha resemble the historical books (e.g., 1 and 2 *Samuel). 1 Esdras, composed in *Aramaic or *Hebrew in the second or first century BCE, retells events recounted in 2 *Chronicles 35–36, *Ezra, and select chapters of *Nehemiah. It gives increased prominence to *Zerubbabel, who is victorious in the contest of the three bodyguards (a "wisdom" contest in which contestants were asked to identify the strongest force in the world) and takes over the role of Nehemiah. This revision may be an effort to affirm that the Davidic throne was indeed restored, in a sense, by the ascendancy of Zerubbabel, a descendant of *David.

1 *Maccabees, originally written in Hebrew, offers an account, written in a biblical idiom, of the tumultuous period of 175–141 BCE. Topics include the initiatives to refound *Jerusalem as a Greek city, the repression of the distinctive practices of *Judaism, and the revolutionary movement that led to the removal of the occupying forces and the establishment of the *Hasmonean dynasty. The approach taken by the author of this work, a supporter of the Hasmonean regime, is counterbalanced by 2 Maccabees, a work that covers much of the same period (through the death of Judas Maccabaeus), but is more keenly interested in the *theology of history revealed in these events. 2 Maccabees was originally composed in Greek, in the late second or early first century BCE, as an abridgement of a much longer work by Jason of Cyrene. Together, these writings provide a window into a crucial period in Jewish history and consciousness. 3 Maccabees, composed in Greek and set mainly in *Alexandria, *Egypt, acquired its title because it closely resembles the themes and events of 2 Maccabees 3–8 (an attack on the *Temple in Jerusalem, the subsequent repression of Judaism in *Ptolemaic Egypt, and God's miraculous deliverance), but it does not deal with the Maccabees and it is questionable whether it reflects historical events at all. Instead, it may be a work of historical fiction encouraging *Diaspora Jews to believe that *God is also attentive to their plight (See also MACCABEES, BOOKS OF).

PROPHETIC WRITINGS: The Apocrypha contains relatively little in the way of *prophetic literature, save for two books attached to the name and career of the prophet *Jeremiah and his scribe. Baruch, a composite work most of which was originally written in Hebrew, summarizes biblical traditions that were pertinent to life under Gentile domination. It consists of a liturgical confession of sin resembling *Daniel 9, a *wisdom poem celebrating *Torah as the path to life, a lament by *Jerusalem mourning for her children, and reaffirmations of prophetic texts of hope for their regathering. The Letter of Jeremiah, written in Hebrew and perhaps representing the oldest text in the Apocrypha, emphasizes the artificiality of idols and the foolishness of worshiping them; it may have attempted to insulate Diaspora Jews from the religious practices of their neighbors.

APOCALYPTIC LITERATURE: The post-prophetic period saw the rise of apocalypticism, a development of the prophetic and wisdom traditions whose literary legacy included visionary literature that is also intensely scribal in its interest in the Scriptures as a form of discerning a "word from the Lord." 4 Ezra (2 Esdras 3–14) is a witness to this ongoing development. Written near the close of the first century CE, this book places the devastation of Jerusalem and the ongoing success of *Rome in the context of the destruction of the First *Temple, giving assurance that God's justice will be manifested both in the *afterlife and in the forthcoming indictment and destruction of the Roman Empire. Despite all appearances, following the *Torah remains the only path to life.

WISDOM WRITINGS: In addition to historical and "prophetic" writings, there are important contributions to *wisdom and *prayer literature among the Apocrypha. The *Wisdom of Ben Sira preserves firsthand the "curriculum" of a Jewish sage who maintained a school in Jerusalem in the earliest decades of the second century BCE. His book, written on the eve of Judaism's confrontation with *Hellenism,

taught the sons of the Jerusalem elite that Torah observance remained the path to wisdom, honor, and national security. The Wisdom of Solomon, written in *Egypt in Greek during the early part of the first century CE, presents extended reflections on several themes: the postmortem vindication of the godly and their way of life, the role and nature of wisdom, the folly of Gentile religions, and God's providential care for God's people.

Several events in Israel's history provided poets with the inspiration to write liturgical literature of stunning beauty. The Prayer of Manasseh is inspired by the story of the repentance of *Judah's most wicked king (2 Chron 33:21–25) and supplies his lost confession (2 Chron 33:18–19). The story of the three young men in the furnace (Dan 3) attracts two liturgical pieces: a corporate confession of sin (The Prayer of Azariah), now placed on the lips of the exile Azariah, and a psalm of praise (The Song of the Three), sung by the youths from the midst of the flames. *Psalm 151 celebrates the election of David and his victory over Goliath.

NARRATIVES: In addition to wisdom and liturgical works, the Apocrypha contains several narratives. Tobit, written in *Aramaic perhaps in the third century BCE, tells the story of two pious Jewish families in the Diaspora, whose personal tragedies God resolves by means of a guardian angel and a fish. It is an important witness to Jewish ethical teachings and eschatological hopes, as well as the development of angelology and demonology. *Judith, written some time after the Maccabean revolution, tells the story of how God delivered his people "by the hand of a woman" and illuminates female roles, the acceptable use of deceit, and the persistence of *deuteronomistic theology. The story of *Esther is also retold, and substantially expanded, in the Apocrypha, this time with plentiful references to God, to distinctively Jewish practices, and to the causes of Jewish–Gentile tension. Similarly, two additional tales appear in the Greek version of Daniel: The first (Susanna) glorifies Daniel's wisdom and the second (*Bel and the Dragon) further criticizes and debunks Gentile religious practices especially known to Egypt (idolatry and zoolatry).

4 MACCABEES: Finally, the collection has come to include a thematic treatise known to the early church alternatively as "On the Supremacy of Reason" and 4 Maccabees. The author, writing from Asia Minor in perfect Greek in the later first century CE, presents the Torah-observant way of life as the God-given means by which to achieve the Greco-Roman ethical ideal of the mastery of the passions and consistency in virtue. The larger portion of this discourse focuses on the examples of the *martyrs from 166 BCE, whose story is first found in 2 Maccabees 6–7, as the supreme proof of the value of Torah's training in virtue, because it produces individuals who match the best ideals of the Greek philosopher-sage. This work is a testimony to how fully an author can acculturate without assimilating.

SIGNIFICANCE: The books of the Apocrypha do not appear to have been serious candidates for inclusion in the Hebrew Bible. One *rabbinic text declares that the Wisdom of Ben Sira "does not defile the hands" (T. *Yadayim* 2:13), meaning that it did not possess the sanctity of the canonical texts (and suggesting, indirectly, that its canonicity might have been discussed). Several Apocrypha books, however, were clearly held in high regard and exerted a significant influence on early Jewish circles. Substantial fragments of two copies of Ben Sira, five copies of Tobit, and one copy each of Psalm 151 and the Letter of Jeremiah were found among the caves near the Dead Sea, attesting to the reading and preservation of these texts by the community at *Qumran (see DEAD SEA SCROLLS). Rabbinic texts frequently quote Ben Sira with approval, although his words are not always attributed directly to him. The establishment of the Feast of Dedication (*Ḥanukkah) as a major festival of the Jewish liturgical *calendar attests to the impact not only of the events of the Maccabean revolt but also to the texts used to promote the observance of the festival among the Diaspora (e.g., 2 Maccabees).

The influence of the Apocrypha on Jewish *Christians, beginning with the founder of the early Christian movement, is even more remarkable. Ben Sira and Tobit have left a clear impression on the sayings attributed to Jesus in the synoptic gospels (see CHRISTIANITY AND SECOND TEMPLE JUDAISM; NEW TESTAMENT). To the extent that these sayings are authentic, Jesus is seen to have learned from these teachers (directly or indirectly) such "distinctive" religious and ethical tenets as the necessity of extending forgiveness to others if one hopes to be forgiven by God (Sira 28:1–4; Matt 6:12, 14–15, 18:23–35), the superiority of charity and almsgiving as the means by which to lay up treasure before God rather than allowing wealth to "rust" through hoarding (Sira 4:4–5, 29:1–12; Tobit 4:7–9; Matt 5:42, 6:19–21, 19:21; Luke 12:33, 18:22), and the danger of presuming God's forgiveness or favor on the basis of one's pious works (Sira 7:8–9; Luke 18:10–14). Similar influence can be discerned on James, who, like Ben Sira, removes God from temptation and human sin (James 1:13–14; Sira 15:11–12, 20) and cautions against the dangers of the tongue (James 3:6, 9–12; Sira 22:27, 28:12). The apocryphal literature also provided resources for Jewish Christian interpretation of the death of Jesus as an act of atonement in Jewish martyrological literature (2 Macc 6–7; 4 Macc).

The texts that comprise the Apocrypha are important historical sources for the later *Second Temple Period and the ongoing interpretation of Jewish tradition and sacred literature. The challenge of adapting to the new environment of *Hellenism while preserving a distinctive religious and cultural identity is a central theme throughout these books. These works also attest to major religious developments, including a clear articulation of a belief in *resurrection immortality, and the *afterlife, as well as to the ongoing renewal of dedication to Torah and its interpretation in the face of Gentile domination. The stories of the Apocrypha frequently appear in the history of western art, music, and literature.

For further reading, see D. A. deSilva, *Introducing the Apocrypha: Context, Message, and Significance* (2002); and B. M. Metzger, *An Introduction to the Apocrypha* (1957); **See also** ESCHATOLOGY: SECOND *TEMPLE PERIOD; DEAD SEA SCROLLS; PSEUDEPIGRAPHA.   DAVID A. deSILVA

Apostasy: See CONVERSION

Arab–Israeli Conflict: See BRITISH MANDATE OVER PALESTINE; ISRAEL, STATE OF: ARAB–ISRAELI CONFLICT, 1948–2010; Maps 12, 13, 14

Arab—Israeli Reconciliation: See BUBER, MARTIN; ISRAEL, STATE OF: PEACE MOVEMENT; MAGNES, JUDAH L.; SZOLD, HENRIETTA

Arabia refers to the peninsula west of *Mesopotamia that is bounded by the Red Sea, the Indian Ocean, the Persian Gulf, and the Gulf of Oman, and in the northeast by the Syrian desert. The *Roman province of Arabia, established by Emperor Trajan in 106 CE, contained the former Nabatean kingdom that occupied modern-day Jordan, parts of modern Syria and Saudi Arabia, and the Sinai peninsula (*Arabia Petraea*); the interior areas of southern modern Syria and northwestern modern Saudi Arabia (*Arabia Deserta*); and the regions bordering the Indian Ocean, including modern Yemen and Oman (*Arabia Felix*). Arabia remained under Roman/*Byzantine control into the seventh century and had both Jewish and *Christian populations, although the majority of inhabitants were polytheistic. During the sixth and seventh centuries CE, Arabia was subject to increasing cultural and religious influences from Sassanian *Iran to the east, as well as ongoing military competition between the Byzantine and Sassanian Empires for political control of the region.

Jews had a long history of residence in Arabia; Jewish communities spoke Arabic, were organized into clans and tribes like their Arab neighbors, and were generally assimilated into the surrounding culture. Medina, in particular, had a large Jewish population of farmers and artisans. Despite their overall acculturation, Jews were regarded as a separate group because of their distinctive religion and customs, yet were also seen as an ethnic community with kinship ties to the Arabs. According to biblical tradition, the Arabs were the descendants of *Abraham, through his son *Ishmael, and this belief also became central to Islam. It is generally accepted that Jewish religious practices, ethical concepts, and homiletic lore played a significant role in the formative traditions of Islam (see ISLAM AND JUDAISM).

Relations between Muhammed, the founder of Islam, and the Jewish tribes grew increasingly hostile during his years of residence in Medina (622–632),. Between 625 and 627, Muhammed and the adherents of the new religion expelled two of Medina's Jewish tribes and killed the men and enslaved the women and children of the third. In 628 Muhammed and his forces marched against the Jewish oases of Khaybar, Fadak, and Wadi al-Qura to the north and subdued them, establishing the precedent for later Islamic rule over all tolerated non-Muslim scriptural peoples. The Jews of these oases were allowed to remain in their homes and carry on their lives in return for the payment of tribute (see *DHIMMI*). When all of Arabia submitted to Muhammad and most Arabs accepted his new religion, the Jews and Christians of the peninsula became subjects of the new Islamic polity, the *Umma*, under these conditions. For further reading, see G. N. Newby, *A History of the Jews of Arabia* (1989). **Map 5**   ELIZABETH SHULMAN

Arabic: See ISLAM AND JUDAISM; JUDEO-ARABIC

Arabs in Israel: See DEMOGRAPHY; ISRAEL, STATE OF: POLITICAL PARTIES; ZIONISM

Arabs: Representations in Israeli Literature. Modern Hebrew *literature's preoccupation with the figure of the Arab is expressed in a staggering range of narratives that present a variety of responses, including envy, fear, regret, distrust, empathy, and frequently complex combinations of all of these. Literary responses to the Arab, especially after the 1948 war, reveal Israel's capacity for self-interrogation and for encountering uncomfortable truths. In the earliest waves of Jewish immigration (see BRITISH MANDATE OVER PALESTINE; ISRAEL, STATE OF: JEWISH IMMIGRATION BEFORE 1948), writers often presented a romanticized image of indigenous Arabs (particularly the Bedouin and rural peasantry), with some even fantasizing that both peoples shared Hebrew or biblical roots. Their literature deemphasized the likelihood of armed strife. An important exception is Yosef Haim Brenner (1881–1921), a prominent literary figure whose novel *Breakdown and Bereavement* (1920) pointed to inevitable conflict. Ironically, he himself was murdered by Arabs during the 1921 riots. Narratives written between the two world wars gradually turned away from the romantic view of Palestine toward pessimism.

Writers of the 1948 generation identified the treatment of the native Arab as the crux of the ideological crisis of *Zionism, and their works express a sense of loss and disillusionment, featuring protagonists conflicted by moral dilemmas. For example, in Benjamin Tammuz's "The Swimming Race" (1951) the anguished narrator recalls his childhood visit to a hospitable Arab village near Jaffa where he has now returned as a conquering soldier helpless to prevent the murder of the Arab who had been his friend. S. Yizhar (pen name of Yizhar Smilansky [1916–2006]) fought in Israel's War of Independence as an officer. Although Yizhar served as a member of the *Knesset for seventeen years, his most lasting impact on Israeli society may well be that of witness to the displacement of Palestine's native Arab population. Even before the war was over, he wrote his famous controversial novella, *Khirbet Khizeh*, which has had a powerful impact on Israelis ever since (it was only translated into English in 2008). The soldier-narrator (often identified as a surrogate for the author) recounts how he and his comrades receive orders to capture the Arab village of Khirbet Khizeh. Although the village appears peaceful, intelligence reports indicate that it has been infiltrated by enemy combatants. After some hesitation and debate, the soldiers assault the village, load its Arab residents onto trucks, and blow up their homes. At the time of its publication in 1949, there were calls for the work to be censored; however, over the years, *Khirbet Khizeh* has enjoyed tremendous popularity even among soldiers of Yizhar's generation for its honest portrayal of the moral complexities of Israel's War of Independence. Yizhar's *The Days of Ziklag* (1958) also portrays the brutality of war and, although sympathetic in its presentation of Israeli soldiers heroically defending a hilltop position against an Egyptian armored attack, is unsparing in depicting destruction of Arab villages (ISRAEL, STATE OF: WARS [1948]).

The early careers of both A. B. *Yehoshua (b. 1936) and Amos *Oz (b. 1939), two of Israel's most internationally acclaimed authors, include milestones in the historical representation of Israel's Arab minorities. Yehoshua's "Facing the Forest" (1963) is highly regarded not only for its representation of the figure of the Arab but also for its provocative portrayal of the troubled history of the landscape itself and the erasure of the past. In this story, a rootless and disaffected student accepts an appointment as a fire-watcher in a remote forest south of Jerusalem. There he encounters an aging Arab and a young girl who cares for him. The Arab is mute, his tongue having apparently been cut out during the 1948 War of Independence, although it remains unclear which side committed the atrocity. By the end of the story, the forest is burned, and the ghostly ruins of a Palestinian village are exposed. Oz's "Nomad and Viper" (1963) is a slyly subversive retelling of the biblical tale of *Dinah (whose ostensible rape leads to the massacre of the male inhabitants of Shechem). Geula, a troubled member of a young Negev *kibbutz, accuses a local Bedouin youth of rape. Juxtaposing the putative values (liberalism, egalitarianism, and democracy) embodied by the "civilized" rational society of the kibbutz members with those of the "savage" Bedouins, Oz's story brilliantly deconstructs the Zionist meta-discourse of enlightening and uplifting the indigenous population.

By the late twentieth century, writers had largely moved away from portraying the Arab as a distant, adversarial stranger and began to examine the complex identities of those living within Israel, often portraying the plight of the Arab citizen trapped between irreconcilable worlds. Yehoshua's *The Lover* (1977) is often singled out for its humane and appealing portrayal of the young Arab Israeli boy Na'im. Set before, during, and in the traumatic aftermath of the Yom Kippur War, the novel quietly insinuates that the neglect of Israel's Arab minority constitutes a growing crisis for the Jewish state. Na'im, a young mechanic, is struck by the disparity between his fluency in Hebrew, his education in Jewish literature and history, and the majority culture's abysmal ignorance of his people's language and culture. Because of his physical appearance he is often taken for a Jew and finds himself torn between belonging to his village and the opportunities he believes may await him in the Jewish society. Na'im falls in love at first sight with the daughter of his Jewish boss, and Yehoshua's poignant treatment of their transgressive romance is unforgettable.

Savyon Liebrecht's acclaimed short-story collection, *Apples from the Desert* (1986), includes narratives about the relations between Jewish Israelis and Arabs that are notable both for their social realism and psychological depth. In particular, three stories draw fascinating connections between the external politics of occupation and the relations between men and women. "A Room on the Roof" presents a classic scene of Jewish Israeli and Arab relationships – the former as employer and the latter as employee. When an Israeli woman's husband leaves the country she arranges for a crew of Arab workers to add a room to her house. At first an uneasy coexistence prevails, and there are hints of deeper bonds developing. Yet the woman vacillates between being a nurturer and a stern taskmaster to the men, and their tense relations are complicated further when she discovers that she is romantically attracted to one of them. By the conclusion, the woman's construction scheme is successfully completed, but the real "project" of the story – understanding and trust between disparate peoples – collapses. In "The Road to Cedar City," two families, Jewish Israeli and Palestinian, find themselves sharing a ride while vacationing in the United States, and the men of both families argue bitterly about politics and history. The Jewish woman, who is treated with aggressive male scorn by her husband and son, discovers that she feels solidarity with the Palestinians. In "Reserve Duty" (which appears only in the original Hebrew version of this collection) the commander of an Israel Defense Forces (IDF) unit investigating hostile action in an Arab village finds himself inexplicably drawn to crossing the barrier that separates the peoples and fantasizes about living in the village as a "native son."

Born in *Iraq in 1926, Sami Michael became involved in underground leftist activity against the repressive regime and escaped arrest by fleeing to *Iran, eventually reaching Israel in 1949. Michael considers Arabic language and culture to be intrinsic to his own identity. His novels exploring the interwoven lives of Jewish and Arab characters include *Trumpet in the Wadi* (1987), a tale combining pathos and high comedy in which a Russian Jewish immigrant courts a reticent Arab Israeli; *Victoria* (1993), an expansive family saga set largely in a single courtyard in Bagdad; and *Doves in Trafalgar* (2005), a sequel of sorts to Palestinian writer Ghassan Kanafani's "Returning to Haifa" (1969), in which a Palestinian couple fleeing the 1948 war is forced to abandon their child to a Jewish couple who survived the Holocaust.

Although primarily a novelist, David Grossman first came to international attention with *The Yellow Wind* (1987), a searing account of what he observed on the West Bank. This work and *Sleeping on a Wire: Conversations with Palestinians in Israel* (1992) are considered essential reading for any introduction to the Israel–Arab dispute, mediating between the complex collective myths and political animosities on both sides of the Palestinian–Israeli conflict. Grossman's *Smile of the Lamb* (1983), a memorably prescient novel set largely in a small Palestinian village, considers the moral cost incurred on occupier and occupied through the relationship of an idealistic soldier and an old Arab storyteller who regales the young man with richly mythic tales that create a tapestry of Palestinian life and culture until their friendship (like that of so many of the Jewish and Arab protagonists examined here) is destroyed by violence.

Sayed Kashua, an Arab citizen of Israel and native speaker of Palestinian Arabic, chooses to write his novels in Hebrew; in this he was preceded by Anton Shammas, whose novel *Arabesques* appeared in 1986. Born in 1975 in Tira, a northern village, Kashua writes for the daily newspaper *Ha'aretz* and lives in Jerusalem. Kashua's first novel, *Dancing Arabs* (2002), became a best-seller in Israel. Its anonymous Arab protagonist grows up in Tira and wins a scholarship to a Jewish high school. Like Yehoshua's Na'im, he experiences a taboo and ultimately hopeless love with a Jewish girl. After this and subsequent disappointments, he grows to despise himself, other Arabs (he even feels alienated from his family's proud history resisting the Jews), and the Israelis themselves. In his inherently stagnant life, the protagonist seems to embody the collective condition of Israel's Arab minority. *Let It Be Morning* (2005) was written in the wake of the Al-Aksa Intifada and reflects the author's sense of the worsening status of Israeli Palestinians within the dominant Jewish society. It is narrated by a Palestinian journalist with Israeli citizenship (a figure resembling Kashua) who reluctantly leaves *Tel Aviv and returns to the village where he grew up. There he is depressed by his sense of how little has changed. This novel, which also examines the rift between Israeli Arab and Palestinian identities, is especially striking in its depiction of a loyal village that wakes up one day, bewildered to find itself under siege by the Israeli army. Kashua's novels address the complex interplay among language, identity, and the Israeli Arab's growing sense of disenfranchisement in the twenty-first century.

Valuable resources include the anthology E. Ben-Ezer, ed., *Sleepwalkers & Other Stories* (1999); R. Domb, *The Arab in Hebrew Prose: 1911–1948* (1982); G. Ramras-Rauch, *The Arab in Israeli Literature* (1989); R. Feldhay Brenner, *Inextricably Bonded: Israeli Arab and Jewish Writers Re-Visioning Culture* (2003); and G. Z. Hochberg, *In Spite of Partition: Jews, Arabs, and the Limits of Separatist Imagination* (2007).

RANEN OMER-SHERMAN

Arama, Isaac (1420–1495), a rabbi in Castile and Aragon, was part of a movement of Jewish thinkers in *Spain (post–1391) who sought to reinvigorate Judaism by emphasizing faith as a willful act of fidelity to God extending beyond the limitations of reason. This movement also stressed spiritual closeness with the divine and ultimate salvation through classical Jewish practice of the commandments (*mitzvot). In advocating this linkage of faith and behavior, Arama sought to go beyond the concept of medieval Aristotelianism that correct belief was propositional and that ultimate happiness (Hebrew, *osher*; Greek, *eudaemia*) was available only to the philosophical elite. Arama identified six basic beliefs, but linked them to the embodied observance of the six biblical holy days by the entire community.

Arama, who accepted Aristotelian ethics and some ideas from *Kabbalah, argued against dissident Jewish intellectuals and disputed core Christian beliefs. However, he spoke respectfully of the culture of Christian faithfulness. His major work, *Akedat Yitzhak*, is a philosophical and exegetical commentary on the *Torah. He also composed commentaries on *Proverbs, studies on the *Five Scrolls, and a polemical essay, *Hazut Kashah* (Terrible Vision). After the 1492 expulsion from Spain, he spent the rest of his life in Naples. **See also BIBLICAL COMMENTARY: MIDDLE AGES TO 1800.**

BARUCH FRYDMAN-KOHL

Aramaic is an ancient *Semitic language, cognate to Biblical Hebrew. Approximately ten chapters of the Hebrew *Bible are in *Aramaic. Although *Hebrew was the main language spoken by the Judeans and Israelites throughout the biblical period, it was slowly replaced during and after the *Babylonian Exile by Aramaic, the dominant language of western Asia at that time. By the end of the biblical period (second century BCE), Aramaic had become the main Jewish spoken language and Hebrew was used in formal, liturgical, and written contexts rather than in everyday speech. This is reflected in the fact that most late biblical and early *rabbinic works are written in Hebrew, albeit a Hebrew that betrays significant Aramaic influence. Exactly when Hebrew ceased to be a spoken language is debated. Both Aramaic and Hebrew have consonantal writing systems that use the alphabet developed in *Phoenicia in the late second millennium BCE; they differ from Akkadian and Egyptian, which had much more complex writing systems. The Hebrew and Aramaic systems developed differently over time. The current script for the Bible is an Aramaic script borrowed during the *Babylonian Exile that displaced the earlier Hebrew script, sometimes called paleo-Hebrew.

The following biblical passages appear in Aramaic: two words in *Genesis 31:48, one verse in *Jeremiah 10:11, four chapters in *Ezra (4:8–6:18, 7:12–26), and six in *Daniel (2:4–7:28). The material in Daniel reflects a late author more comfortable in Aramaic. Some of the Ezra material purports to contain official documents of the *Persian chancellery, which would have been written in Aramaic, and it may have influenced the surrounding material, which is also in Aramaic. The verse in Jeremiah is aimed at a non-Jewish audience, and the words in Genesis are in Aramaic because they are spoken by Laban, an Aramean. MARC BRETTLER

Arbeter Ring: See WORKMEN'S CIRCLE

Archeology, Land of Israel: Ancient Times to Persian Period.

The Land of Israel is an amorphous entity, encompassing not only the geographical borders of the eponymous modern state but also a larger region that figures in some manner as the homeland of Israelite/Judean/Jewish history. The Land of Israel itself is concentrated in the region west of the Jordan River and is bounded by the mountains of Lebanon in the north and by the Red Sea in the south. However, its larger geographic matrix encompasses the whole of the ancient *Near East, from *Mesopotamia in the east in a northwesterly direction toward Anatolia and south/southwestward to *Egypt.

The discipline of archeology of the Land of Israel arose out of the field of biblical or Syro-Palestinian archeology, which itself is a subfield of archeology, a social science closely allied with *anthropology. Archeology seeks to understand the development of human society based on its material remains. In contrast to biblical archeology, archeology of the Land of Israel maintains both a broader temporal focus and more limited geographical boundaries.

Archeological excavation is a complex process involving specialists active both in the field and in the subsequent analysis of finds. In addition to the actual physical toil, which is performed by both hired laborers and "volunteers," who pay for the privilege of doing the dirty work, the fieldwork is overseen by a hierarchical structure of trained field archeologists. Because archeology is the science of destruction – one generally has to destroy one's evidence as one uncovers it – the careful and accurate recording of each find, architectural feature, and level is paramount. To have both horizontal and vertical control over the excavation and recording process, excavation is usually carried out in a grid-like pattern of excavation squares providing horizontal exposure, whereas the baulks (the unexcavated grid lines) between them provide vertical exposure. Specialists analyze the various types of material, faunal, and floral finds. In addition, various types of scientific analyses, including C^{14} analysis, thermoluminescence, and neutron activation, allow studies of the age and provenance of finds.

Most excavations in the Land of Israel are conducted at artificial mounds known as "tells" (from the Arabic) or "tels" (from the Hebrew), which may contain dozens of layers or levels of habitation. The two major sources of relative dating of an archeological site are stratigraphy, the isolation and comparison of the layers of habitation, and pottery chronology, the sequential analysis of the changing forms of pottery over time. Because the sequence of pottery development may also be dated on an approximate absolute scale, and because of pottery's ubiquity at archeological sites as of the middle of the Neolithic Age (9500–6400 BCE), pottery chronology serves as the most important tool in identifying and dating a site. Although there are a number of slightly differing schemes for dating and naming archeological periods, this article follows the conventions of the *New Encyclopedia of Archaeological Excavations in the Holy Land 5: Supplementary Volume* (2008).

The Land of Israel forms a geographical bridge between Africa and Asia. This fact has played a major role in determining the course of human habitation there. As a resource-poor link between the great river valley civilizations of Egypt and Mesopotamia, the Land of Israel has often been a pawn caught between these mighty geopolitical entities. Its location has also determined its economic importance as a conduit of trade to and from Egypt, Mesopotamia, Anatolia, Cyprus, and the *Arabian Peninsula.

As Africa's outlet to Asia, it is not surprising that the oldest evidence for hominids and early human beings (Neanderthals, Homo erectus, and Homo sapiens) outside of the African birthplace of humanity has been found at sites in the Land of Israel, including Ubeidiya in the Jordan Valley and the Carmel Caves. These remains date to the Paleolithic or "Old Stone" Age (from ca. 1,500,000 to 20,000 BCE). Human society was characterized during this extensive period by social organization into hunting and gathering societies. In addition there is evidence for the use of the rudimentary stone tools from which this age gets its name.

During the subsequent Epipaleolithic or Mesolithic ("Middle Stone") Age (20,000–9,500 BCE), we find the first evidence of the transition from hunter and gatherer societies to settled communities. A first tentative step in this direction was identified at the site of Ohalo II on the shores of the Sea of Galilee from the beginning of this period. During the last two millennia or so of the Epipaleolithic, the so-called Natufian period, evidence exists of the rise of more complex village communities.

However, it is during the Neolithic ("New Stone") Age (9500–6400 BCE) that the transition to settled village communities was completed. Society became more complex, which presumably entailed the division of labor and functions beyond a conjectured differentiation between gender roles. The first plants and animals were domesticated, and permanent dwellings were built. During the course of the Neolithic the technology of firing pottery was invented, which allowed for the safer storage and transportation of food products. Artistic expression and possibly religious belief are evidenced by plastered skulls with lifelike features found at *Jericho and throughout the Levant and by relatively large anthropomorphic figures made of straw overlaid with clay found at 'Ain Ghazal east of the Jordan River. At sites such as Çatalhöyük in Turkey, painted walls and statuary were found. The function of a stone tower uncovered at Jericho has not been satisfactorily explained.

As its name indicates, the Chalcolithic or "Copper-Stone" Age (6400–3600 BCE) is characterized by the introduction of metal working, in particular for luxury items. During this period one may identify the continuation of earlier social and technological processes. Characteristic of this age is the development of regional cultures. In the Golan Heights, basalt was worked into small altars(?) with human features. Walls painted with intricate geometric designs and fantastic creatures were found at Teleilat Ghassul in the Jordan Valley northeast of the Dead Sea. Beersheba in the south had a thriving industry in ivory carving and metallurgy. Burials appear in necropolises near the Mediterranean coast, where bones were interred secondarily – after the flesh had decomposed or been boiled off – in small clay containers; these containers often had the shape of a house. Round stone graves called *nawamis* are found in the Negev Desert. Uniquely formed pottery styles have been interpreted as conveying the importance of milk and a *dea nutrix* or nurturing mother goddess in the Chalcolithic cult. Arguably the most intriguing finds are those of En Gedi and Nahal Mishmar. A building found at En Gedi has been identified as a temple overlooking the Dead Sea. Nearby, in the Nahal Mishmar, a horde of hundreds of copper objects, including crowns, scepters, and mace heads, was found neatly wrapped in a cave. The presumption is that these were objects removed from the En Gedi temple for safekeeping, but never recovered.

The Early Bronze Age (3600–2000 BCE) was the first great urban age in the ancient Near East. Although the cities of the Land of Israel did not reach the size of those in other regions, they do represent a sizable advance over what existed previously. By the second phase of the Early Bronze Age, large walled cities had begun to spring up throughout the land. The presence of fortifications indicates both war between the cities and, as is known from Egyptian sources, invasions from outside the immediate region. The increasing complexity of society and its stratification are indicated in city quarters of differing size and quality and by the contrasts among cities, towns, and villages. Among the major sites are Arad in the Negev, Ai in the central hill country, Jericho in the Jordan Valley, and *Hazor and Megiddo in the north. At Megiddo a large temple complex with an open-air altar was uncovered. Burials were either in underground burial chambers or in charnel houses for the burial of bones; an example is the necropolis at Bab edh-Dhra' on the eastern shore of the Dead Sea.

After an intermediate period (2400/2300–2000 BCE), which some ascribe to the Early Bronze Age and some to the Middle Bronze Age, during which the urban culture collapsed, a new urban age was ushered in by the Middle Bronze Age (2000–1550 BCE). In effect, the Middle Bronze Age is continuous with the subsequent Late Bronze Age (1550–1200 BCE). The differentiation between the two is mainly historical and not archeological. Together they represent the heyday of *Canaanite culture. Metallurgy and pottery technology reached new heights. There is evidence of active foreign trade, particularly with Egypt. The so-called Execration Texts from Egypt indicate that it had political and economic designs on the Land of Israel and its produce. Cities, such as Dan, Hazor, Megiddo, Tel Batash/Timnah, and *Lachish, received massive fortifications, consisting in the main of thick mud brick walls. Also characteristic of Middle Bronze Age fortifications are the earthen ramparts that surrounded a number of the cities and determined their shape and extent in subsequent periods. More or less complete mud brick city gates have been excavated at Ashkelon and Dan. Temples and intricate ritual objects are found at major sites throughout the land. The end of this period is associated with the Egyptian campaigns to Canaan at the end of Egypt's Second Intermediate Period and beginning of its New Kingdom.

Egypt reasserted control over the Land of Israel during the Late Bronze Age (1550–1200 BCE). Cities shrank in size and number. No new fortifications were built, which raises the question whether the Middle Bronze fortifications remained in use or whether the Egyptians prohibited the fortification of their Canaanite vassals to maintain unfettered control. Although this period is viewed as the decline of Canaanite culture, there are two aspects that make it worthy of special attention. First, the Late Bronze Age is characterized by extensive international trade connections. One can find beautiful fragments of imported wares from *Egypt, *Syria, Cyprus, and the Mycenaean culture of the Aegean world in the Land of Israel from this period. Second, it was during this age that the alphabet, one of the greatest human inventions, was developed. It vastly simplified written communication and ultimately would lead to the prospect of universal literacy. Cultic (i.e., religious) finds from the Late Bronze Age provide insight into the richness of Canaanite practice and the Canaanite pantheon. A cache of just under four hundred cuneiform tablets dating to the mid-fourteenth century BCE was found at Tell el-Amarna in Egypt. In large part these tablets were sent from the rulers of the Canaanite city-states, including *Jerusalem, *Shechem, *Hazor, and others, to the Egyptian pharaoh. Hence, this is the first period for which one has hard and fast historical information from the Land of Israel. Ultimately, however, Bronze Age Canaanite culture was to fall victim to the general decline of civilization throughout the eastern Mediterranean world around 1200 BCE. Scholars have speculated that this cultural collapse was due to a combination of environmental, economic, and political factors.

Despite the decline in material culture, the Iron Age I (1200–1000 BCE) is a complex period. Egyptian control over the land of Israel came to an end. A few Canaanite cities in the valleys and lowlands – such as Gezer – managed to survive. After their arrival shortly after 1200 BCE, the *Philistines settled on the southwestern coastal strip of Canaan. In the central hill country, small agricultural villages began to take root; scholars see the eventual origin of the Israelites in this phenomenon. There are, however, no material remains that would allow one to identify the ethnicity of the village dwellers, so the identification of a settlement as Israelite rather than Canaanite is impossible. Nor is there any evidence for a massive invasion or influx of people as recounted in the biblical book of *Joshua.

The Iron Age II (1000–586 BCE) is characterized by the rise of small national states in the land of Israel and its immediate environs. The Philistines and associated "Sea Peoples" appear to have retained a city-state organization along the Mediterranean coast, whereas *Israel and *Judah formed small states centered around *Samaria and *Jerusalem. To the northwest, the *Phoenician coastal cities (Tyre and Sidon) were heirs to the Canaanite tradition. To the northeast, an Aramean state formed with Damascus as its capital city. East of the Jordan River the *Ammonites, *Moabites, and *Edomites formed states that rivaled the Israelite ones and yet were similar in many respects. Their languages were related, and their material culture and religious structures appear to have been similar.

Both Israelite and foreign inscriptions give insight into the life, economics, and history of the Israelites. In the Land of Israel itself, hundreds of tiny seals and seal impressions document the names in use among the Israelites. Important collections of *ostraca* (broken pieces of pottery with writing on them) have been found at Samaria, Lachish, and Arad. Monumental inscriptions have been found in Jerusalem and at Tel Dan. The inscription at Tel Dan, an *Aramaic inscription dating to the late ninth century, mentions the "house/dynasty of *David"; it is the first, albeit indirect, reference to David outside the *Bible. One of the major current controversies in the archeology of the Land of Israel is whether the archeological evidence supports the existence of a Davidic empire or whether it is more likely that David was a local chieftain whose exploits were exaggerated during the course of oral transmission.

Israelite cult centers, cultic objects, and inscriptions have been found from Tel Dan in the north to Tel Arad and Kuntillet 'Ajrud in the south. The preponderance of evidence suggests that religious life in ancient Israel tended much more toward the polytheistic than the Bible would indicate (**Plate 1**). Among the most impressive finds from this era are the tunnels built through bedrock to secure access to sources of water at Gibeon, Megiddo, Hazor, and Jerusalem. Graphic remains of the destructions of both Israel by the *Assyrians in 721 BCE and Judah by the *Babylonians in 586 BCE have also been discovered.

Although previous excavations tended to concentrate on the largest tells and architectural features, more recently work has been dedicated to uncovering the lives of the broad mass of common people living in poorer town quarters or in villages (P. J. King and L. E. Stager, *Life in Biblical Israel* [2001]). Moreover, although earlier generations of archeologists paid greater attention to reconstructing the lives of men, in recent years appreciable attention has been devoted to reconstructing the lives of women (see C. Meyers, *Discovering Eve: Ancient Israelite Women in Context* [1988]; and ISRAELITES: MARRIAGE AND FAMILY).

While the kingdom of Israel disappeared from history and its territory was transformed into the Assyrian province of Samaria, post-destruction Judah remained sparsely inhabited at sites such as Mizpah and Jerusalem. The *Persian conquest of Babylon in 539 BCE led to a small revival of life in Judah, but it would not be until the *Hellenistic period (332–37 BCE) that the material culture of the Land of Israel would begin to rival that of the Iron Age and it was not until the early *Roman period (37 BCE-132 CE) that it would be exceeded.

Among the many works dealing with the archeology of the land of Israel, E. Stern (ed.), *New Encyclopedia of Archaeological Excavations in the Holy Land* (4 volumes 1993 with supplement 2008), is the essential guide to individual sites. A broader cultural matrix is provided by E. M. Meyers, ed., *The Oxford Encyclopedia of Archaeology in the Near East* (1997). Synthetic introductions to the archeology of the land of Israel include A. Ben-Tor, ed., *The Archaeology of Ancient Israel* (1992); T. E. Levy, ed., *The Archaeology of Society in the Holy land* (1995); A. Mazar, *Archaeology of the Land of the Bible, 10,000–586 BCE* (1990, 1992); and E. Stern, *Archaeology of the Land of the Bible, Volume II: The Assyrian, Babylonian, and Persian Periods (732–332 B.C.E.)* (2001); information on the latest finds and analyses can be found in the *Bulletin of the American Schools of Oriental Research, Israel Exploration Journal, Near Eastern Archaeology* (formerly *Biblical Archaeologist*), and *Tel Aviv*. **Maps 1, 2**   CARL S. EHRLICH

Archeology, Land of Israel: *Second Temple Period.

Archeological artifacts that date from the end of the sixth century BCE to 70 CE, when the Second *Temple was destroyed, reveal a great deal about the culture of nascent Judaism in ancient *Judah-*Palestine. This period is divided according to the three dominant cultural influences in the eastern Mediterranean: *Persian (539–332 BCE), *Hellenistic (333–63 BCE), and early *Roman (63 BCE–70 CE).

Archeological remains from the Persian period are relatively sparse. Sites on the coast provide clear evidence for significant contact between the *Near East and the rest of the eastern Mediterranean world. In parts of *Samaria and *Galilee there was noteworthy contact with *Phoenicia to the north. Inland, in the hills of ancient Judah, the artifacts reveal a more isolated cultural setting. The area around *Jerusalem was not heavily affected by other cultures, other than the locally operated Persian administration. Persia did not overtly colonize this area, and thus there was not a major influx of new pottery styles and technology. Instead, excavations at Persian period sites have revealed many similarities to the earlier Iron Age (see ARCHEOLOGY, LAND OF ISRAEL: ANCIENT TIMES TO PERSIAN PERIOD). However, major differences are found in the number and size of the sites: The *Babylonians devastated much of the population in the region of Judah, and it took centuries before the number of residents equaled what it was before 586 BCE when the First *Temple was destroyed.

The history of the region can be reconstructed from both texts and archeological remains. Nearly fifty years after the Babylonian destruction of the First Temple, the Persian Empire reconstituted the province of Judah, calling it *Yehud. The rebuilding of the Jerusalem Temple began after Cyrus, the Achaemenid Persian ruler (559–530 BCE), allowed the exiled Judeans to return to Yehud. *Ezra-*Nehemiah is our best literary source for the period. It is likely that most of the Judeans who returned from Babylon resettled in and around Jerusalem and took up subsistence farming practices, without much interaction with the cosmopolitan settings that were found in many of the coastal cities.

The first seventy years of Persian rule were a period of stability and slow growth in and around Yehud and Samaria. After Artaxerxes I came to power in 465 BCE, Persia used Yehud as a staging ground for military incursions into *Egypt. The Persian military presence increased exponentially in the middle of the fifth century, as seen in the excavations of dozens of fortresses and military outposts, particularly in the region of the Judean hill country (*shephelah*) near Egypt. This was also the time of Ezra and Nehemiah, a period of social and religious reforms in Yehud, and the rebuilding of the walls of *Jerusalem. Although archeological evidence for Jerusalem in the Persian period is still scarce, excavations have revealed enough evidence to postulate a city of approximately 2,500 people.

During the period of the *Babylonian Exile many rural inhabitants remained in the region. Archeologists have found significant continuity in the material culture remains of people living in Judah-Yehud during the Neo-Babylonian and the Persian administrations. The major change in Yehud was not in pottery forms and building techniques, but in population size. Archeologist Oded Lipschits suggests that the population of the region dropped from 108,000 before the Babylonian destruction to less than 32,000 in the fourth century BCE. The majority of this population decline occurred in cities like Jerusalem. Small village sites were more abundant in the Persian period, suggesting a time of relative peace for the rural agriculturalists. Although pottery forms did not change significantly from the seventh to the fifth centuries, the impact of the Persian administration is evident in the large quantity of seal impressions and coins found in the region.

Along the Mediterranean coast the cultural situation was quite different. Many Persian military outposts and fortresses, used to guard coastal and inland routes, have been excavated. Cities like Shikmona, Ashdod, Ashkelon (with its massive dog cemetery), Gaza, Jaffa, Dor, and Acco prospered as ports for increased trade connections with the rest of the Mediterranean world. These cities had significant economic and cultural contacts with both the Persians and Greek city-states, as indicated by the Attic and Corinthian pottery found in almost every Persian period site in the Land of Israel, particularly in coastal areas. Many of the vessels would have been used in meals, particularly for mixing and drinking wine (decorated bell kraters, or large mixing bowls, and cups are found in large quantities).

When *Alexander the Great moved through Palestine in 332 BCE on his way to take control of Egypt, Greek influence was already a significant feature in Palestine – especially along the coast. Archeological evidence of Alexander's military and political occupation of the region is meager, because the transition from Persian to *Hellenistic rule was relatively peaceful. After Alexander's death in 323 BCE, as the Land of Israel made the transition from the rule of the *Ptolemies to that of the *Seleucids at the end of the third century BCE, many aspects of life remained the same. No major destruction layers have been found, an indication that the Hellenistic kingdoms did not destroy local cities as they vied for power in the region. Rather they wished to maintain the ongoing economic success achieved in the area through wine and olive oil production, as well as trade through the coastal cities. Although the Persian Empire built small administrative buildings around Yehud, its rulers did not significantly alter the landscape or introduce radically different cultural configurations. In contrast Hellenistic cities brought new customs, institutions, and ideas, including diverse forms of education (gymnasium), language (koine, Greek), religion (the heroes and gods of the new empire), and lifestyles (physical culture and public bathing).

In the south, Gaza became a major trade center, and new Nabatean outposts were built on the trade routes across the Negev from the Mediterranean coast to Petra. Further up the coast, port cities like Dor grew and prospered in the Hellenistic period as urban residents embraced Hellenism and international trade expanded. More than forty-five miles inland, the city of Marisa (Mareshah) was built in the region of Idumea. Excavations at Marisa have revealed a lively center of commerce, dove breeding, and olive oil production, with well-decorated homes stocked with imported dishes and wine amphora.

Other Hellenistic cities in the wider region include Gerasa and Philadelphia (*Ammon) in the Trans-Jordan – an area known as the *Decapolis. Nearer to the Sea of Galilee, Hellenistic settlements include the cities of Scythopolis (next to the ancient city of Beth Shean), Hippos, and Philoteria. Two excavated sites in northern *Galilee have revealed the extensive trade networks of this era. In the ongoing work at the site of Tel Kedesh, excavators have revealed a significant Phoenician outpost and administrative center. The discoveries of several thousand small stamped seals and a massive governmental building at the site reveal that the center was used throughout the Hellenistic era to control trade and commerce in the area. The presence of imported pottery from Greece, Italy, and Egypt illustrates the area's vast trade networks and diverse population. Approximately fifteen kilometers northeast of Tel Kedesh, the site of Tel Anafa became a wealthy center of trade in the middle of the Hellenistic period. With ties to the port city of Tyre, these sites reveal the increasingly cosmopolitan nature of the inland areas that had been sparsely populated during the Persian period (see also HELLENISM).

In the hills north of Jerusalem, Macedonian soldiers stationed in Samaria constructed large towers and introduced a Hellenistic temple; an inscription indicates that it was dedicated to Serapis and Isis. Nearby, the newly rebuilt city of *Shechem was located below the sacred *Samaritan Temple site on Mt. Gerizim. Excavations of its walled, sacred precinct revealed considerable building activities during the early second century BCE. Further north, in the regions of northern Samaria and Galilee, subsistence farmers lived on small farms and in villages. This northern area continued to have strong ties to *Phoenicia in the north until the period of the *Hasmonean revolt.

In the Hellenistic period, Jerusalem continued as a small, relatively poor city, devoted primarily to the work of the Temple. The city occupied only the Temple Mount and the area known as the City of David. Only later did the city grow and begin to add new neighborhoods to the southwest. Culturally, Jerusalem was insular, although the growing amount of imported pottery from the third to the second centuries BCE demonstrates increasing contact with wider Mediterranean trade networks. Excavations have also revealed signs of the local system of taxation in the form of more than one hundred stamped storage jars that bear the stamp YHD or YRSLM (for Yehud or Jerusalem). These jars were likely used for wine, wheat, or oil, paid as a tax to the Temple or the local administrator.

As this era progressed, the local population in the Land of Israel had to decide between maintaining their traditions or adopting Greek customs. Becoming an ally of the Greek administration could mean prosperity and luxurious lifestyles. For example, excavations at the site of Iraq el-Emir in Trans-Jordan have revealed the elaborate palace of the *Tobiads, a Jewish family that benefited from the decision to embrace Hellenism. Many wealthy Judeans, including residents of Jerusalem, made similar decisions. *Josephus and the authors of I and II *Maccabees report that in the early years of Seleucid control aristocratic families were drawn to Hellenism. The high priest Jason built a gymnasium in the city in 175 BCE. In 168 BCE, Antiochus IV – the Seleucid ruler – built the Acra, a new fortress for the foreign mercenary garrison he stationed in Jerusalem.

In contrast to the Tobiads and the Hellenized Judeans in the cities, supporters of more traditional Judean practices reacted violently to the introduction of Hellenism, particularly when Antiochus IV brought worship of Zeus into the Jerusalem Temple. In the archeological record, the Hasmonean revolt (also known as the Maccabean revolt) and its aftermath left a significant mark. Excavations in Jerusalem and surrounding regions show that there was a steady population growth and the construction of many new buildings.

Judeans increasingly moved into the region of Galilee and into coastal cities that were once dominated by Gentiles; archeological surveys date more than ninety-three new settlements to this period. Hasmonean outposts were established to protect the new settlements and trade routes, and many non-Judeans appear to have moved out of the region of Palestine, sometimes by force. Archeologists have found destruction layers at sites like Tel Kedesh, Dor, and Strato's Tower. The types of pottery that were used during the Hasmonean period also suggest that some Judeans were intentionally differentiating themselves from their more Hellenized and cosmopolitan neighbors around the region. Large quantities of a high-quality, imported type of pottery called Eastern Sigillata A have been found in all the regions surrounding the Hasmonean kingdom, but this ware is much less plentiful and is often absent in Hasmonean-controlled territory (A. M. Berlin). Similarly, pig bones are much rarer in Hasmonean sites, suggesting that Hasmonean Judeans avoided pork.

By 63 BCE the *Roman Empire had annexed the region. The Roman general Pompey began the transfer of power when he conquered the Seleucids, followed by *Herod who was appointed by the Emperor Augustus to oversee the remnants of the Hasmonean kingdom. Herod's impressive building projects were the primary means by which he controlled the economic climate of his small Roman tributary territory. His massive building program honored Rome and his patrons and also bolstered his comfort, political security, and personal pride. In the 20s BCE Herod undertook more than a dozen major building projects in Judea, with the Temple in Jerusalem as his crowning achievement. Herod appeased portions of the Judean population and bolstered his reputation in Rome by transforming the Temple and surrounding public spaces into a major cultic, economic, and tourist center.

From a very small population in the early Hellenistic period, Jerusalem grew steadily under the Hasmoneans, particularly throughout the early first century CE, into a city that on the surface looked very much like a typical Roman urban center. By the middle of the first century the size of the city's residential area was approximately 58 hectares. The growth of the residential area that occurred with the construction of the so-called second wall expanded the potential population of the city to approximately 25,000 people. With the addition of the so-called third wall, the population of the city may have doubled again just before the beginning of the war against Rome in 66 CE. Excavations of Jerusalem residences of the late Second Temple period demonstrate a high standard of living. Elite priestly families were no doubt the occupants of many of these private houses in Jerusalem, especially in the region of the upper city immediately surrounding the Temple. Although some homes are less elaborate than the private mansions near the Temple, items such as frescoes, mosaics, fine ceramic wares, glass objects, and well-made stepped, plastered pools (most likely Jewish *ritual baths), are commonly found and speak to significant economic prosperity.

In the middle of the first century CE, entering Jerusalem on any of the five roads that led into the city was similar to visiting any major Greek or Roman city of the age. Cemeteries, with monumental tomb structures, would have been seen outside of the walls. These were reminders of the great families and patrons of Jerusalem from the past two centuries, including the Hasmonean royal family and elite members of Jewish communities from Judea and the *Diaspora. A visitor to the city would certainly have noticed the large stone blocks that were constantly being pulled into the city from the nearby limestone quarries. Archeologists have revealed that major construction activities, including paving the roads and constructing new buildings in and around the Temple Mount, continued to be a feature of the city's urban scene throughout the decades before the destruction of the Second Temple in 70 CE.

*Herod's reconstruction of the Temple Mount dominated the urban landscape in Jerusalem. The extant sections of the retaining walls give us our primary clues about this massive building complex. The average stone in the walls was two to three meters in length and about three to five tons in weight. Some stones at the base of the walls were as long as ten to twelve meters. Josephus' descriptions of the Temple are the primary source for our knowledge of the components of the compound.

*Josephus clearly indicates that during and after the time of Herod the urban landscape also included a huge *stoa* or basilica building, grand palaces, many elite residences, a Roman theater, an amphitheater, a hippodrome, and the Roman military fortress (Antonia) that dominated a position next to the Temple. The walled city, ruled by either a Herodian client-king loyal to Rome or by one of thirteen different Roman governors, was tightly controlled. The Roman administration commanded garrisoned troops, held sway as the supreme judicial authority, and directed financial affairs on behalf of Rome.

Archeology has also shown that the local Judean population was highly concerned with ritual *purity. Evidence for ritual baths (*mikveh) and stone vessels that were used in Jewish purity rituals have been found throughout the region. Yet this interest in purity ritual was combined with typical signs of Roman culture. Private Roman-style baths (caldaria) have been found in several elite houses in the city, the Greek language was well known in Jerusalem, and typical Roman urban features were mixed into the landscape in a way that nearly defies any attempt to neatly separate and distinguish "Roman" and "Jewish" cultural features.

Archeologists have discovered similar patterns of social and cultural development throughout Judea and adjacent regions. Herod's new port city of Caesarea was a massive building project that used the newest Roman technology to alter the coastline and establish a Roman-style city, complete with a Roman temple, palace, theater, amphitheater, and hippodrome. Herod built additional Roman temples in Sebaste in Samaria, as well as the beautiful city of Panias in northern *Galilee. Herod Antipas followed his father's pattern and built two major Roman cities in Galilee. The excavations at Sepphoris have revealed a Roman-style city in the middle of a region that was still dominated by dozens of small agrarian villages. The existence of stone vessels and ritual baths in Sepphoris indicates that the residents were primarily Jewish. Antipas also built the city of Tiberias on the Sea of Galilee and moved his administrative headquarters there just before 20 CE. Excavations at the sites of Gamla and Jotapata (Yodefat) have provided a great deal of information about Jewish villages in the region during the late

*Second Temple period. The Roman army destroyed both villages before 70 CE, marking the end of the Second Temple period and the beginning of a new era of destruction, population shifts, and rebuilding efforts in Palestine.

For further reading, see A. M. Berlin, "Between Large Forces: Palestine in the Hellenistic Period," *Biblical Archaeologist* 60:1 (1997): 2–51; J. W. Betlyon, "A People Transformed: Palestine in the Persian Period," *Near Eastern Archaeology* 68:1–2 (2005): 4–58; M. A. Chancey and A. Porter, "The Archaeology of Roman Palestine," *Near Eastern Archaeology* 64:4 (2001): 164–201; O. Lipschits, "Demographic Changes in Judah between the Seventh and the Fifth Centuries B.C.E.," in *Judah and the Judeans in the Neo-Babylonian Period*, ed. O. Lipschits and J. Blenkinsopp (2003); and E. Stern, *Archaeology of the Land of the Bible II: The **Assyrian**, Babylonian, and Persian Periods (732–332 BCE)* (2001). Maps 3, 4   MILTON MORELAND

Argentina. Although a few Jews arrived in Argentina after it achieved independence from *Spain in the early nineteenth century, organized Jewish life dates to 1862, when a group of French and German Jews (later joined by a handful of Moroccan Jews) founded the *Congregación Israelita de la República Argentina* in Buenos Aires. By the end of the nineteenth century there was a significant Jewish presence, both in Buenos Aires and in the rest of the country (mostly in the center and north). An 1881 decree by Argentine president Julio A. Roca opened the door to "Israelite immigration," and the arrival of the *Wesser* in 1889, a ship carrying 816 Eastern European Jews, marked the beginning of a steady flow of *Ashkenazic immigrants. Heading mostly to the interior of the country, Jewish families settled in *agricultural settlements created with the aid of the Jewish Colonization Association (JCA), a philanthropic organization founded in Paris in 1891 by *Baron Maurice de Hirsch. By 1937, there were sixteen JCA colonies in the provinces of Buenos Aires, Santa Fé, La Pampa, Entre Ríos, and Santiago del Estero. Life in the colonies was initially hard, as the settlers had little knowledge of how to work the land. They faced adverse weather conditions and a bureaucratic organization that hindered their progress. Yet Jewish life flourished, and these communities maintained the *Yiddish language and a distinctive identity by founding libraries, theaters, Jewish schools, cemeteries, and many other Jewish cultural and political societies. Many of the immigrants' children and grandchildren, however, left the colonies to pursue academic and professional careers in larger cities.

In contrast to Ashkenazic immigration, which was aided by the JCA and other organizations created to help the newcomers, *Sephardic immigration was not organized. Moroccan Jews started moving into northern areas of Argentina from *Brazil in the late nineteenth century; by 1895 they had founded two communities (in Buenos Aires and in Santa Fé) and a cemetery (in Santa Fé.) Other Sephardic groups also settled in Buenos Aires and interior cities during the early years of the twentieth century. These Jews came mostly from the *Ottoman Empire (Rhodes, Smyrna, Constantinople, Aleppo, and Damascus), but Sephardim from *Bulgaria, *Italy, and *Jerusalem joined the community as well. A second wave of immigrants (mostly of Moroccan Jews) came to Argentina after the creation of Israel in 1948 (see NORTH AFRICA).

In the interior cities, Sephardim created their own communal institutions wherever they settled, usually separate from the Ashkenazim but not from other Sephardim. By contrast, each Sephardic group in Buenos Aires settled in a different part of the city, built its own synagogues, and founded philanthropic societies and cemeteries. During the first half of the twentieth century, these separate Sephardic communities seldom mixed with other Sephardic groups or with Ashkenazic Jews.

A whole host of Jewish institutions were created in Buenos Aires during the years of massive immigration. Among others, they included *Bikur Jolim*, a Jewish soup kitchen; SOPROTIMIS (Society for the Protection of Immigrants); the Jewish Anti-Tuberculosis League (the Sephardim organized their own); Jewish orphanages for girls and boys; a home for the elderly; a Jewish hospital; and the Argentine Zionist Federation. These organizations were financially supported by the various Jewish communities in Buenos Aires and in the rest of the country. As stated earlier, Sephardic Jews tended to use their own societies.

Jewish education was provided since the early years. For the JCA colonies, the *Alliance Israélite Universelle sent graduates from their schools in Morocco and the Ottoman Empire who taught both "Jewish" topics and the Argentine curriculum. The Argentine government, however, later took on the responsibility of teaching secular education, and Jewish education became optional after Argentine schools were done for the day. These *Talmudei Torah* were linked to religious congregations and were under the supervision of rabbis. After 1917, a debate emerged around what constituted Jewish education, and secular Jewish schools (led by leftist *Zionists) were created. In the first decade of the twenty-first century, there are about seventy educational institutions under a Central Committee of Jewish education (*Vaad Hajinuj*).

Jewish cultural life in Buenos Aires and in the cities in the interior of the country was varied. Certain neighborhoods in Buenos Aires, like *Once, Barracas, Flores, Villa Crespo*, had a high concentration of Jews. Yiddish *theater was very popular, and Argentina boasted various local theater companies and enjoyed visits from international troupes. Jewish writers (in Yiddish or Spanish) enjoyed a very active publishing scene and avid readers. Elie *Wiesel's original Yiddish version of his famous memoir *Night* (originally titled *And the World Kept Silent*), for example, was first published in 1956 in Buenos Aires as part of a collection of Polish Yiddish works edited by Mark Turkow, a renowned local editor and writer. Many Jewish newspapers and monthly/biweekly papers were available as well, both in Yiddish (*Yiddishe Tzaitung, Di Presse*, among several others) and in Spanish (*Mundo Israelita, Israel, La Luz*).

Various Jewish sports clubs, imbued with *Zionist ideology, sprang up in Buenos Aires and in some cities in the interior. *Sociedad Hebraica Argentina*, Macabi, and *Nautico Hacoaj* are some of the institutions that still provide sports, recreation, and cultural options for Jewish families.

Although Argentine Jewry did not split into Reform, Conservative, or Orthodox denominations, at the beginning of the twenty-first century Argentina has both Conservative synagogues (usually led by graduates from the *Seminario Rabínico Latinoamericano* founded by American Conservative rabbi Marshall Meyer in 1962) and Orthodox congregations. There were various attempts at centralizing Sephardic and Ashkenazic Jewish organizations during the first decades of the twentieth century, and in 1935, the *Delegación de Asociaciones Israelitas Argentinas* (DAIA) was created for that purpose. Although its role was briefly challenged during the late 1940s and 1950s by other groups, its legitimacy has been unquestioned since 1955. In 1931, in another centralizing move, the Ashkenazic community consolidated its social and philanthropic activities with the creation of the AMIA (*Asociación Mutual Israelita Argentina*), originally the Ashkenazic *Chevra Kadisha*. This organization's building (which also housed the DAIA and the Instituto (IWO) archive and library) was bombed in 1993, causing the deaths of eighty-five men and women. Today, most of the estimated 200,000 Argentine Jews live in the city of Buenos Aires.

For further reading, see H. Avni, *Argentina and the Jews: A History of Jewish Immigration* (1991); and V. Mirelman, *Jewish Buenos Aires, 1890–1930: In Search of an Identity* (1990); **See also LATIN AMERICA; FILM: LATIN AMERICA; and LITERATURE: LATIN AMERICA.**   ADRIANA M. BRODSKY

Aristeas, Letter of.

This Greek text, apparently written by an Alexandrian Jew, purports to describe the origins of the *Septuagint. According to the *Letter*, *Ptolemy II (reigned 281–246 BCE) was assembling a library of the world's great works in *Alexandria and believed that a translation of the Jewish *Torah should be included. To entice translators from the Land of *Israel, he freed Jewish prisoners of war (1–81). The *Letter* goes on to describe the *Temple in Jerusalem, defends the integrity of the Jewish law, and reports on the journey of seventy-two scribes to Alexandria. During a seven-day banquet the king learned of the high quality of the translators' religion by questioning them (83–300). Lastly, the *Letter* recounts the actual translation, accomplished in seventy-two days, and its approval by the Jewish community (301–21). Written some time in the second or first century BCE in Alexandria, the work likely aimed to situate Jewish *law favorably within the context of the other legal systems available in Ptolemaic *Egypt and to justify the translation of the *Torah for Jews of the Greek-speaking *Diaspora.   ROBERT KUGLER

Ark of the Covenant

(*aron ha-berit*) is the sacred chest, said to have been finely crafted of acacia wood (*shittim*) by Bezalel according to divine instructions (Exod 25:9–22) as a repository for "the pact which I shall give you" (25:16). Presumably this verse refers to the stone tablets on which the *Ten Commandments (Decalogue) were inscribed. Stored in the portable *Tabernacle (*mishkan*) used during the wilderness wanderings, the ark was overlaid with gold, had a gold cover (*kapporet*) adorned with cherubim (25:17–22), and was carried through the desert on gold-plated poles by *priests. According to Exodus 25:22, the ark was the location of divine communication to Israel. Other passages relate that the ark accompanied the *Israelites in the wilderness (Num 4:5–20), across the Jordan River (Josh 3:6–17), and into battle (Josh 6:4–14; 1 Sam 4:3–7; 2 Sam 11:11). When it was captured by the *Philistines (1 Sam 4: 11), the ark brought them only misfortunes and was ultimately returned (1 Sam 6:1–15). King *David brought the ark into *Jerusalem (2 Sam 6:1–17), and eventually it found a permanent home in *Solomon's *Temple (1 Kgs 8:1–9). The ark's known history ends when Jerusalem was captured by the *Babylonians in 586 BCE, but it has had an active afterlife in Jewish, Christian, and Muslim folklore traditions.   KATE FRIEDMAN

Aron Ha-Kodesh

(Holy Ark) is the repository in which the *Torah scrolls are placed in the *synagogue. **See also CEREMONIAL OBJECTS.**

Art, American: Before 1940.

The term "Jewish American art," like the more generalized term "Jewish art," is fraught with complications and variously understood. Critics debate whether Jewish American art need only be art made by a Jewish American, independent of content, or if both the artist's and the artwork's identity must be Jewish. Indeed, working in myriad styles and adopting both figuration and abstraction, some artists of Jewish origins address Jewishness and the more specific Jewish American experience, whereas others make art that is indistinguishable in theme and content from their Gentile counterparts. Whether a Jewish American artist should be defined sociologically or by subject matter remains an open question; in the discussion that follows Jewish American artists are accepted according to either criterion.

Jews did not participate in American visual art in a meaningful way until the nineteenth century. They were certainly free to do so, but religious constraints, as well as uneasiness about the respectability of a career in art, disappeared slowly. This hesitancy was sometimes the result of the prohibition against graven images in the second commandment of the biblical *Decalogue; for centuries, some Jews understood it as prohibiting the creation of visual art of any kind. However, close reading of the text shows that the commandment was directed against figuration used for idol worship and not other types of artistic expression.

In the nineteenth century, some Jewish American artists designed *ceremonial objects, which was considered religiously acceptable. For example, Myer Myers (1723–1795), an eighteenth-century silversmith, made both secular and religious objects for colonial merchants. He created *rimonim* (literally "pomegranates"; these were ornaments for the tops of the wooden rollers of Torah scrolls) for several synagogues, including *New York's Congregation Shearith Israel and the Jeshuat Israel Congregation in *Newport, Rhode Island. In the nineteenth century, a handful of Jews were painters. Wealthy patrons commissioned the brothers Joshua and John Canter (or Canterson) to paint their portraits. Theodore Sidney Moïse (1808–1885), Frederick E. Cohen (1818–1858), and Jacob Hart Lazarus (1822–1891) are other nineteenth-century Jewish portraitists of note.

Solomon Nunes Carvalho (1815–1897) is the best known artist from this period. In addition to making portraits of members of the Jewish community, he also painted allegorical portraits, including one of Abraham Lincoln (1865). Carvalho created a few biblical paintings and landscapes as well, but his fame rests on his work as a daguerreotypist for John C. Frémont's 1853 exploratory expedition through Kansas, Utah, and Colorado. Primarily known in his time as a printmaker, Max Rosenthal (1833–1919) was the official illustrator for the U.S. Military Commission during the Civil War. Later, Rosenthal painted *Jesus at Prayer* for a Protestant church in Baltimore, presenting Jesus with phylacteries on his forehead and right arm. The altarpiece was promptly rejected. Henry Mosler (1841–1920) began his career as an artist correspondent for *Harper's Weekly* during the Civil War. Like many non-Jewish artists, Mosler went to Europe for artistic training. He soon became a painter of genre scenes, frequently picturing peasant life in Brittany, France. His canvas *The Wedding Feast* (ca. 1892), which was exhibited at the Paris Salon, records Breton marriage customs.

The eminent sculptor Moses Jacob Ezekiel (1844–1917) made numerous portrait heads, including a bronze bust of Isaac Mayer *Wise (1899). The *B'nai B'rith commissioned Ezekiel's large marble Neoclassical group *Religious Liberty* for the Centennial Exhibition of 1876, and in 1888 he designed the seal for the recently established Jewish Publication Society of America. Ephraim Keyser (1850–1937) created commemorative sculptures, including President Chester Arthur's tomb at the Rural Cemetery in Albany, New York. Katherine M. Cohen (1859–1914) studied with the famous sculptor Augustus Saint-Gaudens and made portrait busts, as well as sculptures with Jewish themes such as *The Vision of Rabbi Ezra* and *The Israelite*. These early painters and sculptors worked independently and were not known to each other. They created in relatively divergent styles, following the same trends as the larger American artistic community. It was not until the twentieth century that Jewish American artists began interacting and taking art classes together.

Among the large influx of immigrants to the *United States between 1880 and 1920 were two million Jews. Mostly from poor communities in *Eastern Europe, these immigrants were eager to assimilate. The Educational Alliance, a settlement house on the Lower East Side of *New York City, where many immigrants went to learn American manners and customs, offered art classes starting in 1895; discontinued in 1905, the classes resumed in 1917. From the school's reopening until 1955, Russian immigrant Abbo Ostrowsky served as director. Many artists who later achieved great success studied at the Alliance, including sculptors Saul Baizerman (1899–1957) and Jo Davidson (1883–1952) and painters Peter Blume (1906–1992) and Philip Evergood (1901–1973). The Alliance sponsored art exhibitions as did other venues in New York that were identified with Jewish life. In 1912, the Ethical Culture Society's Madison House Settlement arranged a show of Jewish Russian immigrant artists, such as Samuel Halpert (1884–1930), in which Gentile artists also participated. The People's Art Guild held more than sixty exhibitions from 1915 to 1918. In May 1917, three hundred works by eighty-nine artists were exhibited at the *Forverts* Building, home of the *Yiddish daily newspaper, the *Forward*; more than half of the artists were Jewish. Well-known Jewish community leaders Stephen Wise, Judah *Magnes, and Jacob Schiff helped sponsor the exhibition. The Jewish Art Center, directed by artists Jennings Tofel (1891–1959) and Benjamin Kopman (1887–1965), held exhibitions focusing on Yiddish culture from 1925 to 1927.

In the early decades of the twentieth century some artists, such as Abraham Walkowitz (1878–1965), William Meyerowitz (1887–1981), and Jacob Epstein (1880–1959), began their careers by portraying the Lower East Side. The Gentile observer Hutchins Hapgood described East Side imagery in his book, *The Spirit of the Ghetto* (1902), as typically Jewish. Characterizing this work as "ghetto art," Hapgood named Epstein, Bernard Gussow (1881–1957), and

Nathaniel Loewenberg as exemplars of the mode. To illustrate Hapgood's evocation of the cultural and religious nature of the Jewish people, Epstein made fifty-two drawings and a cover design for the book. Epstein later became an expatriate, settling in London and gaining fame as a Modernist sculptor.

The photographer Alfred Stieglitz (1864–1946) championed Modernism in the 1910s. Although most of the artists whom Stieglitz supported were not Jewish, his coreligionists Max Weber (1881–1961) (**Plate 16**), an avant-garde painter and sculptor, and the Modernist Walkowitz, enjoyed his patronage. An underlying tone of antisemitism, or at least an intense nativism, pervaded some discussions of Modernism at this time; the conservative critic Royal Cortissoz described Modernism as "Ellis Island art." Certainly, Modernism was frequently associated with Jews, especially in Europe; Adolf Hitler later adopted this position.

In addition to taking many innovative pictures, Stieglitz nearly single-handedly legitimized *photography as a rightful counterpart to painting and sculpture. Moreover, Stieglitz mentored several important photographers in their own right, including Arnold Newman (1918–2006) and Paul Strand (1890–1976). In the 1930s, artist Ben Shahn (1898–1969) took documentary photographs for the Farm Security Administration, a government program enacted to chronicle the poverty and desperation in Dust Bowl America for urban Americans.

Often called "the father of modern photojournalism," Alfred Eisenstaedt (1898–1995) was one of the four original staff photographers at *Life* magazine. Working for *Life* for forty years starting in 1936, the prolific and self-taught Eisenstaedt took photos for approximately 2,500 assignments, and his work appeared on more than ninety covers. Eisenstaedt is especially known for his ability to capture the salient moment in rich detail, whether the character of an important figure or a slice of everyday life, such as the reactions of women purchasing undergarments in a department store. Also a photojournalist, Weegee (born Usher Fellig, 1899–1968) achieved fame chronicling crime and disaster; he specialized in capturing the effects of these tragedies on the people of New York, subsequently selling his images to newspapers and tabloids. Weegee's sensationalized, lurid, nocturnal pictures of bloody corpses, distraught tenement dwellers watching as their meager homes were engulfed in flames, car accidents, and additional agonies – as well as his other photographic subjects – number in the thousands; 5,000 negatives and around 15,000 prints were counted after his death, and more have been discovered since. In the latter half of the twentieth century, Jews continued to play a large role in photography, especially in the *fashion industry.

Many artists addressed political, social, and economic issues, especially during the Great Depression. It has been argued that traditions of social justice impelled Jewish artists to create imagery of the underdog. Although secular in theme, these works, influenced by the Jewish experience, would be recognized as Jewish American art even by critics who define the term in its strictest sense. Working as Social Realists in the thirties, the Soyer brothers (Raphael, 1899–1987; Moses, 1899–1974; and Isaac, 1902–1981) represented mundane details of life, including waiting in an unemployment line, with gentleness and compassion. Peter Blume, Ben Shahn (**Plate 18**), Mitchell Siporin (1910–1976), and Harry Sternberg (1904–2001) were more emphatic about their political commitments; Shahn made more than twenty images decrying the ethnically biased trial and executions of Italian American anarchists Nicola Sacco and Bartolomeo Vanzetti. William Gropper (1897–1977) expressed his political sympathies as a cartoonist for the left-wing publication *New Masses* and the Yiddish daily *Morning Freiheit*. The desire of several of these artists for social change encouraged them to find a like-minded community; some joined socialist or communist organizations, such as the John Reed Club.

In 1935, nine Jewish artists formed a group they dubbed "The Ten" (the tenth spot was reserved for a guest artist). Ben-Zion (1897–1987), Ilya Bolotowsky (1907–1981), Adolph Gottlieb (1903–1974); Louis Harris (1902–1970), Jack (Yankel) Kufeld (1907–1990), Marcus Rothkowitz (Mark Rothko, 1903–1970), Louis Schanker (1903–1981), Joseph Solman (1909–2008), and Nahum Tschacbasov (1899–1984), members of the original group, exhibited together for four years. That the artists shared a Jewish background is typically understood as a coincidence. No common style or theme pervades the group's work, but most members were committed to Modernist developments.

During the 1940s, Jack Levine (1915–2010) worked as a Social Realist, although he painted more satirically and expressionistically than practitioners of the mode in the 1930s. Beginning in 1940, Levine painted and made prints of biblical figures and stories in addition to his politically motivated art. Since his first biblical painting, *Planning Solomon's Temple,* Levine rendered hundreds more images inspired by the Bible's narrative. Often employing Hebrew labels to identify figures, Levine explained that his biblical works attempted to augment Jewish pictorial expression, which he felt was hampered by the second commandment. The Boston-born Levine began a lifelong friendship with Hyman Bloom (1913–2009) when the pair studied art together at a Jewish Community Center in their early teens. Bloom also retained the human figure in an increasingly abstract art world, painting secular and religious matter in brilliant colors. David Aronson (b. 1928), who like Levine, frequently painted biblical subjects, and Philip Guston (1913–1980), an abstract artist who moved to New England late in life to teach at Boston University, are associated with the Boston Expressionist school. After his arrival in Boston, Guston adopted Jewish themes – painted representationally – on a more consistent basis.

Clearly, all these artists have contributed to the rich field of Jewish American art in diverse fashions. They paved the way in the second half of the century for a more overt embrace of Jewishness, often rendered in an avant-garde manner, in the wake of the trauma of the Holocaust and the later rise in ethnic consciousness.

Recent research includes M. Baigell, *American Artists, Jewish Images* (2006); S. Baskind, *Raphael Soyer and the Search for Modern Jewish Art* (2004); idem, *Encyclopedia of Jewish American Artists* (2007); J. Gutmann, "Jewish Participation in the Visual Arts of Eighteenth- and Nineteenth-Century America," *American Jewish Archives* (April 1963): 21–57; N. Kleeblatt and S. Chevlowe, eds., *Painting a Place in America: Jewish Artists in New York, 1900–1945* (1991); M. Kozloff, *New York: Capital of Photography* (2002); and O. Soltes, *Fixing the World:*

Jewish American Painters in the Twentieth Century (2003); and see also PHOTOGRAPHY.   SAMANTHA BASKIND

Art, American: Since 1940. As painters, sculptors, printmakers, and photographers, as well as artists who engage in newer forms of visual expression such as video, conceptual, and performance art, Jewish American artists, considering their small numbers in the general population, have had an exceptionally large presence in the art world from the mid-twentieth century onward.

Several of the leading Abstract Expressionists were Jewish. Adolf Gottlieb (1903–1974), Philip Guston (1913–1980), Lee Krasner (1908–1984; **Plate 17**), Barnett Newman (1905–1970), and Mark Rothko (1903–1970) are among several Jewish artists who eschewed representation in the late 1940s and 1950s. The styles in which the artists worked are difficult to generalize, but they typically painted on large canvases and were interested in spontaneous expression. Although abstract, Newman's painting has been understood as shaped by his Jewish sensibilities, in part because of titles like *Covenant* and *The Name*, and also because, it has been argued, his knowledge of *Kabbalah (Jewish mysticism) influenced his "zip paintings," which can be read as symbolic of God and Creation. The only photographer aligned with the Abstract Expressionists was Aaron Siskind (1903–1991). Some second-generation Abstract Expressionists were Jewish. Helen Frankenthaler (b. 1928) and Morris Louis (1912–1962) stained unprimed canvases with thinned color that seems to float on and through the canvas, and over many years Jules Olitski (1922–2007) experimented with abstraction in several media. Currently, Tobi Kahn (b. 1952) paints abstract canvases that convey landscape through color. Clement Greenberg (1909–1994) and Harold Rosenberg (1906–1978), two of the major art critics who promulgated Abstract Expressionism in its beginnings, were Jewish.

Some artists who worked as Social Realists during the thirties turned their sensibilities toward the civil rights movement of the sixties. Raphael Soyer (1899–1987) made a lithograph titled *Amos on Racial Equality* (1960s), which quotes the biblical prophet Amos in Hebrew and English and depicts a white woman carrying a black infant. Ben Shahn's (1898–1969) lithograph *Thou Shalt Not Stand Idly By* (1965) portrays an oversized interracial handshake; the title comes from Leviticus 19:16 and is printed in Hebrew and in English at the top of the image. Artists of the next generation also engaged social issues. After the fact, R. B. Kitaj (1932–2007) – who made a large body of richly allegorical imagery representing Jewish concerns – commented on the integration of blacks into professional baseball with his painting *Amerika (Baseball)* (1983–4). Jewish–Black relations have become strained since the *civil rights movement, a situation cartoonist Art Spiegelman (b. 1948) tackled with his cover design of a black woman kissing a Ḥasidic man for a February 1993 issue of the *New Yorker*.

Two Jewish artists initiated the *feminist art movement. At the height of the women's liberation movement in 1971, Judy Chicago (b. 1939) and Miriam Schapiro (b. 1923) jointly founded the Feminist Art Program at the California Institute of the Arts. Chicago is especially known for her enormous multimedia installation, *The Dinner Party: A Symbol of Our Heritage* (1974–9). Made with more than 400 collaborators, *The Dinner Party* was created to raise awareness of forgotten women's history in a world that privileges men. Eleanor Antin (b. 1935), Audrey Flack (b. 1931), Barbara Kruger (b. 1945), and Nancy Spero (1926–2009) are other important feminist artists; Flack's photorealist paintings comment on stereotypes of femininity, and Kruger deconstructs power relations, often related to gender, in her photomontage images. Recent scholarship has argued that many of the early feminist artists were Jewish because as perennial outsiders and as the children or grandchildren of radical immigrants, fighting for justice and equality was their natural heritage.

In the sixties, seventies, and eighties, Jewish artists worked in diverse manners. Jim Dine (b. 1935) and Roy Lichtenstein (1923–1997) first adopted a Pop idiom during the sixties. Emerging into the public eye in the seventies, Philip Pearlstein (b. 1924) paints figures in a flat, unemotional style that treats the human form with the same objectivity as the inanimate objects surrounding the model. Also painting figuratively, Alex Katz (b. 1927) typically fills his large canvases with the flattened, simplified heads and shoulders of his sitters rendered in crisp color. Sol LeWitt (1928–2007) explored and wrote about Conceptual Art in addition to making Minimalist sculpture, and Jonathan Borofsky (b. 1942) continues to make multimedia site-specific installations using his own life as source material. In contrast, sculptor and Process artist Richard Serra (b. 1939) asserts that his focus on the physical qualities of materials and the act of creation leaves little room for expressions of the artist's personality. At the same time that LeWitt, Borofsky, and Serra experimented with avant-garde modes of artistic expression, they made works investigating or memorializing the *Holocaust.

Some artists who mostly worked within the mainstream for the majority of their careers became interested in Jewish matters late in life. Raphael Soyer illustrated two volumes of Isaac Bashevis Singer's memoirs (1978, 1981) and two short stories by Singer for the Limited Editions Club (1979). Larry Rivers (1923–2002) also illustrated a Singer story for the Limited Editions Club (1984) and painted an enormous three-paneled painting, *History of Matzah (The Story of the Jews)* (1982–4), tackling the nearly four millennia of Jewish experience. In his eighties, Harry Sternberg (1904–2001) worked on a series of prints, drawings, and paintings delineating Jewish prayer and study as part of his *Tallit Series* (1980s), named after the prayer shawl worn by observant Jews when they pray. Husband and wife William Meyerowitz (1887–1981) and Theresa Bernstein (1890?-2002) traveled to Israel thirteen times after 1948 and painted many images of the land after having previously pursued a more traditional American art trajectory. Chaim Gross began sculpting Jewish subjects in the 1960s. Although Shahn and Leonard Baskin (1922–2000) explored some Jewish topics early on, they more consistently embraced Jewish identity in the visual arts as they aged, notably with *Passover *haggadah* illustrations done in 1965 and 1974, respectively. Baskin's subject matter, both in his sculpture and his graphic images, frequently addressed biblical figures and Holocaust themes (**Plate 19**). Earlier in the century Saul Raskin (1878–1966) illustrated a *haggadah* with woodcuts (1941).

Several Jews worked as photojournalists, including Richard Avedon (1923–2004) and Irving Penn (1917–2009).

Avedon's career spanned sixty years, beginning as a fashion photographer for *Harper's Bazaar* in the 1940s when he was barely twenty years old. His pioneering pictures set standards for the fashion industry, and his subsequent portraits, most not taken on commission but as part of the artist's own project, chronicle the faces of major twentieth-century celebrities and public figures. Avedon shoots his portraits against a plain white background and without accoutrements in an effort to convey his sitters' personalities in an unidealized manner. Considered one of the most versatile photographers of the twentieth century, Penn produced more than one hundred covers for *Vogue* magazine, myriad fashion and advertising spreads for various magazines, and many other photographs in genres such as still life and portraiture.

Later in the century, photographers used the medium to varying ends. Popularly described as a photographer of misfits and freaks, Diane Arbus (1923–1971) is recognized for a body of black-and-white photographs that explore and question the fine line between normalcy and difference. In opposition to the suggested objectivity of documentary photography, Arbus's work is clearly subjective. Moreover, the America she depicts is disturbing and unsentimental, much like the vision presented earlier in the century by Weegee (Arnold Felig, 1899–1968) and Robert Frank (b. 1924). Indeed, Frank is best known for his book *The Americans* (1959), a Guggenheim-funded project that exposes the divisions and alienation of his era, as opposed to the sentimental and celebratory photographs of America more popular at that time. Frank's innovative style, the "snapshot aesthetic" – a then-unconventional style deliberately employing odd angles, occasional blurriness, and seemingly spontaneous scenes – influenced several important photographers in addition to Arbus; these include Lee Friedlander (b. 1934) and Garry Winogrand (1928–1984), two of the original street photographers.

The Holocaust has been a major preoccupation of later twentieth-century Jewish artists. One of Seymour Lipton's (1903–1986) last representational sculptures responded to news of Nazi persecution of the Jews. Titled *Let My People Go* (1942), based on a divine command in *Exodus, Lipton's sculpture portrays a bust of a pious Jewish male wearing a prayer shawl. Ben-Zion (1897–1987) was a poet who turned to painting because he felt that words could not adequately express the horrors of fascism and later the Shoah. Exhibited as a whole in 1946, the series *De Profundis (Out of the Depths): In Memory of the Massacred Jews of Nazi Europe* comprises seventeen Expressionistic works conveying the artist's distress at the events of the Holocaust; it pays homage to those who perished by Nazi hands. Leon Golub's (1922–2004) lithograph *Charnel House* (1946) and his *Burnt Man* series of the early 1950s describe murdered victims, also in an Expressionist fashion.

Interest in the Holocaust as a subject for art has only increased in the years since. Audrey Flack's photorealist canvas *World War II (Vanitas)* (1976–77) presents a still life in collage format, including a Jewish star from her key chain and a photograph of the 1945 liberation of Buchenwald taken by *Life* magazine photographer Margaret Bourke-White. Alice Lok Cahana (b. 1929), a survivor of concentration and labor camps, uses visual art to work through her memories of the Holocaust in semi-abstract mixed media collages.

Cahana's art, she explains, is her *kaddish for those who perished. The sculptor George Segal (1924–2000) symbolically employs the biblical figures *Eve, *Abraham, *Isaac, and Jesus in his *Holocaust Memorial* (1983), which overlooks the Pacific Ocean in San Francisco's Legion of Honor park. Another Holocaust sculpture group by Segal is in the permanent collection of the Jewish Museum in New York (1982). Judy Chicago's enormous installation *Holocaust Project: From Darkness into Light* (1985–93) is anchored by a 4 1/2 by 18-foot tapestry titled *The Fall*, which portrays the disintegration of rationality. More recently, Shimon Attie (b. 1957) worked on a series of projects in Europe collectively called "Sites Unseen" (1991–96). In several countries, Attie projected photographs onto or from public buildings, and in one case on a body of water, all using images from World War II. Although united by an interest in imaging the unthinkable, Holocaust works by Jewish American artists differ greatly in approach, conception, and style (**See also** HOLOCAUST REPRESENTATION: ART).

In the last decades of the twentieth century, Jewish identity became an increasing concern in the visual arts. New York City's Jewish Museum initially investigated this phenomenon in two exhibitions, the first in 1982 and the second four years later in 1986. The eighteen living artists in the premier show, *Jewish Themes/Contemporary American Artists*, and the twenty-four in the subsequent exhibition, *Jewish Themes/Contemporary American Artists II*, explored aspects of Jewishness in media ranging from video installation to painting. The coolness and impersonality of the movements preceding the eighties – Pop art and Minimalism, for example – were also eschewed in the art world in general, when pluralism and subjectivity became a focus of artists from all backgrounds. Indeed, the work in these two exhibitions investigated religious and cultural elements of Judaism, sometimes in an autobiographical manner. Hebrew text, Jewish literature, religious ritual, and explorations of the Holocaust can be found in the imagery of these artists, including Flack, Kitaj, and Archie Rand (b. 1949).

A decade later, the Jewish Museum mounted the exhibition *Too Jewish?: Challenging Traditional Identities*. Again paralleling a larger interest in multicultural difference by other marginalized groups, the eighteen artists in the show explored Jewish consciousness, while testing the viewer's and the art world's (dis)comfort with what was perceived by some as excessively conspicuous Jewishness. These highly assimilated younger artists portray vastly different concerns from those of their immigrant and first-generation predecessors. Long after Andy Warhol, Deborah Kass (b. 1952) appropriates Pop techniques and a fascination with celebrity in her portraits of Barbra Streisand (1992) and Sandy Koufax (1994). Titling her Streisand silkscreens *Jewish Jackies*, playing on Warhol's iconic silkscreens of Jackie Kennedy, Kass proffers the ethnic star while subverting American norms of beauty (**Plate 20**). Also influenced by Warhol, Adam Rolston's (b. 1962) *Untitled (Manischewitz American Matzos)* (1993) asserts ethnicity into a once "pure" American consumer culture. Dennis Kardon's installation *Jewish Noses* (1993–95) presents an array of noses sculpted from forty-nine Jewish models, destabilizing the notion that the Jew can be categorized as a monolithic type.

Just as Kardon demonstrates that the Jew's body cannot be homogenized, neither can Jewish American art. As this essay has described, Jewish American artists have worked in manifold fashions, partly and sometimes entirely influenced by larger trends, and at the same time making significant contributions in style and content.

For further reading, see Z. Amishai-Maisels, *Depiction and Interpretation: The Influence of the Holocaust on the Visual Arts* (1993); M. Baigell, *Jewish Artists in New York: The Holocaust Years* (2002); S. Baskind, *Raphael Soyer and the Search for Modern Jewish Art* (2004); idem, *Encyclopedia of Jewish American Artists* (2007); S. Goodman, *Jewish Themes/Contemporary American Artists* (1982); idem, *Jewish Themes/Contemporary American Artists II* (1986); N. Kleeblatt, *Too Jewish?: Challenging Traditional Identities* (1996); O. Soltes, *Fixing the World: Jewish American Painters in the Twentieth Century* (2003); and S. Zalkind, *Upstarts and Matriarchs: Jewish Women Artists and the Transformation of American Art* (2005); and **see PHOTOGRAPHY.**   SAMANTHA BASKIND

Art, Europe: Nineteenth Century.

To the extent that our modern concept of art is chiefly defined by paintings, modern Jewish art began in Europe in the early nineteenth century and flourished mostly in the German-speaking countries of Europe's center, while also extending outward to the margins of the continent. Even in their earliest creations, emerging out of the historical moment of the Jewish Enlightenment (*Haskalah) and political *emancipation, Jewish painters presented distinctly Jewish subjects as well as imagery suited for a wider audience. Most of their work was formulated in the same vividly descriptive naturalist mode that dominated nineteenth-century painting.

Indisputably, the first Jewish painter was Moritz *Oppenheim (1800–1882) who was active near Frankfurt am Main. Oppenheim accompanied other young German artists, self-styled "Nazarenes," to Rome, but his career was well supported back home by the *Rothschilds; they commissioned family portraits that led to other commissions of culturally significant figures, including the converts to Christianity Ludwig Börne and Heinrich Heine, as well as the Jewish emancipation advocate, Gabriel Riesser. Oppenheim also painted images of contemporaneous Jewish life, beginning with *Return of the Jewish Volunteer from the Wars of Liberation* (1833–34: Jewish Museum, New York). His 1850s genre series, *Scenes from Traditional Jewish Family Life*, represented *life-cycle events and *Sabbath rituals situated in both synagogue and home. These images became still more popular and widespread through subsequent reproduction as prints that were reissued in numerous editions.

The same pattern of the self-invention of the Jewish artist recurred in other locations. Following Oppenheim's lead, Isidor Kaufmann (1853–1921) capitalized on an urban nostalgia in *Vienna for images of traditional Jews of the Austro-Hungarian Empire. After making visits to traditional centers in Eastern Europe, Kaufmann forged an entire oeuvre of meticulously rendered genre studies; these included scenes of Talmud study, synagogue worship, and family rituals in spare domestic settings (**Plate 12**). More than Oppenheim, Kaufmann's art attempted to preserve images of a vanishing *shtetl life that was newly threatened by modernity. Kaufman also painted landscapes, portraits, and genre images with non-Jewish content.

The tragic early death of Maurycy Gottlieb (1856–1879) robbed the nineteenth century of a supremely talented Jewish artist. Born in Drohobycz in *Galicia, Gottlieb attempted the seemingly impossible task of forging a composite artistic identity as both a Pole and a Jew, when neither a Polish nor a Jewish state existed to mitigate tensions between those communities. Gottlieb took Rembrandt as an inspiration, apparently because the great Dutch artist had portrayed Jews sympathetically in historical scenes and portraits. Gottlieb developed both of these categories, producing numerous self-portraits in various historical guises. A massive unfinished *Christ before his Judges* (1877–79; Jewish Museum, Israel) shows a biblical scene of the Passion while nevertheless emphasizing the Jewish features and identity (with *tallit*) of Jesus; his *Christ Preaching at Capernaum* (1878–79; Museum Narodowe, Warsaw) reprises Rembrandt's etchings of Jesus preaching to Jew and Gentile alike. Among Gottlieb's projects was an uncompleted cycle to illustrate Shakespeare's *Merchant of Venice* in both small paintings and prints. Movingly, a scene made in his final year of life shows a Gottlieb self-portrait (with a self-conscious inscription in Hebrew) among *Jews Praying in the Synagogue on Yom Kippur* (1878; Tel Aviv Museum of Art).

The *Pale of Settlement continued to produce its share of Jewish painters in the waning nineteenth century. Recording the unhappy social tensions of the region, Maurycy Minkowski (1881–1930) produced works like *After the *Pogrom* (1905; Tel Aviv Museum of Art), a painting depicting the alienation and dislocation of a silent family gathering of sufferers. More overtly political and socially active, Samuel Hirszenberg (1865–1908), a native of Lodz, followed Gottlieb's path by training in Kraków and Munich. However, Hirszenberg used his art in response to tsarist *Russia's persecution of Jews with such works as *Wandering Jew* (1899; Israel Museum, Jerusalem) and *Exile* (1904; lost). The latter, a representation of refugees in the snow, quickly became a *Zionist icon. Hirszenberg's own Zionist sympathies were fulfilled when he immigrated to Palestine in 1907, assuming a teaching position at the new Bezalel Academy of Arts and Design in *Jerusalem.

In contrast to this politicized radicalism and Jewish identity, the major painter Camille Pissarro (1830–1903), born to a French *Sephardic family in the *Caribbean, in the Danish Virgin Islands, would not be recognizable as a Jewish painter from his themes. Pissarro, who would eventually marry a Catholic, professed to be a secular Modernist and a political radical – even an anarchist – who had no religion whatsoever. Nevertheless, he was identified by many contemporaries, especially Renoir, as a Jew. Pissarro, of course, is most closely associated with the Impressionist painting circle, with whom he exhibited in the 1870s and 1880s in Paris, but he expressly chose to live in the countryside around such villages as Pontoise and Eragny and to paint images of peasant life as well as rural landscapes. In his final decade he moved to the capital and painted street scenes of modern Paris. He is also remembered for his mentoring of younger artists, notably van Gogh and Gauguin.

One of the most famous and successful late-nineteenth-century Jewish artists, the Dutchman Josef Israëls (1824–1911), also drew on the precedent of Rembrandt for his somber interiors. However, Jewish subjects make up a relatively small portion of his sentimental domestic genre paintings, which chiefly depict poor-but-honest peasants and fishermen. Israëls was a member of The Hague School of painters, and his themes tend to feature deathbeds or frugal repasts, although sometimes his dignified picturesque subjects are given a Jewish character (*A Son of the Ancient Race*, ca. 1889; Jewish Museum, New York). His later work takes on more expressly Jewish subjects (*A Jewish Wedding*, 1903; Rijksmuseum, Amsterdam). Israëls remained a lifelong friend of his younger colleague, the Berlin Jewish painter, Max Liebermann (1847–1935).

Liebermann represents both the social and the artistic gains of Jewish painters over the course of the nineteenth century. Born to a prosperous manufacturing family in *Berlin, he was a member of a liberal and culturally active elite. Liebermann achieved fame and artistic leadership in his region for his translation of French Impressionist brushwork to Dutch genre themes and modern leisure subjects for German galleries. Like Oppenheim, he painted portraits; like Gottlieb he also produced self-portraits, albeit usually representing himself in dapper bourgeois suits. Liebermann seldom painted Jewish subjects, although he did feature the *Judengasse* of *Amsterdam in a series of works (1908). He was, however, embroiled in bitter antisemitic culture wars in the early twentieth century, when Kaiser Wilhelm led a new cultural chauvinism that tarred foreign, and, by extension, "Jewish" art, which was associated with "internationalism and cosmopolitanism." Nevertheless, Jewish museum curators and private collectors continued to avidly collect Liebermann's works. For further reading, see S. T. Goodman, ed., *The Emergence of Jewish Artists in Nineteenth-Century Europe* (2001).

LARRY SILVER

Art, Europe: Twentieth Century. Although nineteenth-century Jewish artists were relatively few in number and often beset by difficulties because of their religio-cultural heritage, the early twentieth century saw a considerable increase in opportunities in Jewish art across Europe. These possibilities were curtailed traumatically by the horrors of the *Holocaust. The story of Jewish artists in twentieth-century Europe involves discussion more of urban cultural centers and communities of artists than of isolated individuals. Their aesthetic innovations, particularly in Paris and *Saint Petersburg, often overlapped with new political movements, ranging from *Zionism to the Russian Revolution, as Jewish artists formed a cosmopolitan avant-garde in major centers.

Pre-*World War I *Berlin, where Jews were part of an emerging Modernism in all the arts, also percolated with a variety of political movements, including Zionism. Many Jewish artists joined the clarion call of Martin *Buber and others to foster a new cultural assertion of Jewish identity and advocacy for a Jewish state in *Palestine. Boris Schatz (1867–1932) would soon emigrate to found the Bezalel School of Arts and Crafts in *Jerusalem (1906). Some other leading Zionist artists used printmaking and publishing (especially the journal *East and West*) as their media of outreach. Ephraim Moses Lilien (1874–1925) designed Zionist graphic images with lettering in *Jugendstil*, the organic and flowing linear contemporary style, with an orientalist cast (**Plate 21**). Lesser Ury (1861–1931) emphasized muscular, dark isolated figures – *Jeremiah, *Moses – as heroic cultural leaders in his Zionist pastels, but (like Pissarro in

Paris or the Soyer brothers in *New York) he also recorded modern urban street life in the German capital. Inspired by Rembrandt and Josef Israëls, virtuoso printmaker Hermann Struck (1876–1944) made etchings and lithographs of picturesque observant Jews as well as landscapes, including scenes of Palestine, where he would eventually settle.

Struck also mentored a younger generation of German Jewish artists. Most prominent among those were Jacob Steinhardt (1887–1968, a later émigré to Israel) and Ludwig Meidner (1884–1966); both were closely associated with the jagged forms and acid colors of contemporary Expressionism. Steinhardt and Meidner produced apocalyptic landscapes and elongated suffering figures, even in urban settings; their work evoked pathos and an ominous foreboding in viewers.

Despite social barriers in the *Pale of Settlement, many talented Jewish artists emerged in *Russia, the location of Europe's largest Jewish population. At the turn of the twentieth century, Russian culture was discovering new cosmopolitan links through a movement known as *Mir Iskusstva* ("The World of Art") that was led from Saint Petersburg by Francophile Serge Diaghilev. Diaghilev and the influential *Ballets Russes* that he had founded eventually enjoyed great success after they left Russia for Paris. Diaghilev's chief designer of exotic costumes and spectacular sets was a Jewish painter, Leon Bakst (1866–1924); Bakst, whose work emphasized either Asiatic or ancient body-hugging garments, also participated in a contemporary aesthetic of nostalgic rediscovery of Slavic artistic roots in Russian art.

Against this movement, other Jewish artists sought to find their own visual heritage and establish a truly "Jewish" art, within a more sharply defined ethnic identity. Inspired by Semyon Ansky, ethnographer and playwright of *The Dybbuk*, this search for Jewish folk art led to documentation and study of the decorations of painted synagogues. (see SYNAGOGUES, WOODEN). Two young artists, Issachar Ryback (1897–1935) and El Lissitzky (1890–1941), who were particularly involved in this project, went on to exhibit graphics with Jewish motifs; Ryback also produced Cubist-inspired paintings of the buildings themselves. Lissitzky would later combine the stylized motifs of Jewish folk art with decorative Cubist angular forms in his 1917–19 *Had Gadya* illustrations (based on the song, "An Only Kid," from the Passover *haggadah*), which have been interpreted as an allegory of Jewish liberation from tsarist oppression (**Plate 13**).

Fusing all of these impulses, Marc Chagall (1887–1985), surely the most famous Jewish painter of the twentieth century, dominated Russian modern art. Chagall first studied in his beloved hometown of Vitebsk and then sought out Bakst in Saint Petersburg. Between 1910 and 1914, Chagall, like Bakst, moved to Paris, where he exhibited in leading salons. Some of Chagall's art displayed a nostalgic, yet magical representation of *shtetl* life with representative figures, such as his celebrated fiddlers on the roof, inflected by an arbitrary coloristic brilliance and Modernist simplification of forms. Chagall returned to Russia before the revolution, where a number of Jewish artists formed a Jewish Society for the Encouragement of the Arts in 1916; the society's logo was designed with traditional motifs and Hebrew script by Natan Altman (1889–1970), designer of *Jewish Graphics* (1913–14). In 1918 the Kultur Lige was formed as an organization of Jewish artists in Kiev; before he went on to work with the new State Jewish Theater in Moscow (1920), Chagall founded a short-lived Vitebsk art academy, where Lissitzky taught. There Chagall made celebrated murals, and Altman designed costumes and sets for the staging of *The *Dybbuk*.

Around the time of the revolution, Russian artists offered a powerful response, Suprematism, to the abstraction pioneered in Paris and Munich to serve as a radical break with representational art of the past. Altman and Lissitzky, who were particularly sympathetic to the secular goals of the Russian Revolution and to Lenin as its leader, adapted the new artistic forms to the new political era. Altman, who served as Director of Fine Arts of the People's Commissariat (1921), designed public spectacles of "agit-prop" (agitation and propaganda) to celebrate the new state in Palace Square, Saint Petersburg; he also made portraits of Lenin. Lissitzky, strongly influenced by the radical abstraction of Kasimir Malevich, developed formal designs, sometimes in three dimensions, that he called "Prouns" (acronym for "Project for the Affirmation of the New") and also created an abstract propaganda poster, "Beat the Whites with the Red Wedge" (1919). By 1922, however, most of these Jewish artists had emigrated to Berlin and largely abandoned their works with expressly Jewish content. Although Lissitzky and Altman returned to Russia, Ryback and Chagall remained in *France. Two avant-garde abstract sculptors, the brothers Naum Gabo (1890–1977) and Antoine Pevsner (1886–1962), exemplify Russia's increasing cosmopolitanism as well as the migrations of Jewish artists in the wake of the revolution. Pevsner, who was also a painter, studied in Kiev; he then traveled to Paris in the teens, where he was exposed to Cubism as well as the growing community of Jewish artists in the city. Both brothers left an innovative sculptural legacy of dynamic constructions in plastic, wood, and metal wires, often created for public projects. Pevsner's successful career was made in Paris after 1923, whereas Gabo settled in London after 1936.

The longest lasting community of émigré Jewish artists from Eastern Europe, who have come to be known as the "School of Paris," were active from the teens until the outbreak of World War II. Although Marc Chagall continued to paint his trademark colorful *shtetl* subjects, most of the others did not paint Jewish themes. For the most part Francophilic art historians have regarded this group as distinctive and creative artists but also as unassimilated and marginal. Emblematic of this group is Chaim Soutine (1894–1943), born in *Lithuania and a legendarily penniless recluse. His slashing brushwork and vibrant colors energize twisting representations of single figures, still lifes (often of butchered meat), and dynamic landscapes. He almost defiantly worked on neutral subjects with self-consciously modern forms. In similar fashion, Amadeo Modigliani (1884–1920), a portrait and figure painter, especially of female nudes, and a sculptor at times, used a distinctively elegant linear outline and simplified features. Arriving in Paris from northern *Italy, he created portraits of his close circle of fellow Jewish artists, including Soutine, whose early death from tuberculosis left a gaping void in the Paris community. Jules Pascin, born Julius Pincas in *Bulgaria in 1885, was also a leader among Jewish artists. His paintings popularized late Impressionist brushwork, and he was a prolific graphic artist with both watercolors and prints. Although his reputation has diminished, this prolific figure and portrait artist enjoyed considerable success with collectors in Europe as well as the United States (where he lived during World War I) before his suicide in 1930.

Paris also fostered several important Jewish sculptors, led by Jacques Lipchitz (1891–1973) from Bialystock and *Vilna, who, following Picasso's lead in the teens, became noted as the leading Cubist sculptor of heads and bodies in faceted components. His long productive career included a final phase in *New York City after World War II, where his powerful late bronze figures embodied mythic subjects and primal passions as if in allegorical commentary on a century filled with tragedy (**Plate 15**). Female artists also made their mark in Paris, led by Sonia Terk (1885–1979) from the Ukraine, wife of the pioneer color abstractionist Robert Delaunay, with whom she sometimes collaborated. In her own right, Terk produced significant collages and fiber works, textiles, and costumes (including work for the *Ballets Russes*). A creative force in multiple media, American-born Man Ray (Emmanuel Radnitsky, 1890–1976) made his main career in Paris, albeit with little acknowledgment of his Russian Jewish roots. His principal associations included Marcel Duchamp and the conceptually minded Dadaists, who challenged the premises and commodification of art with "found objects" and assemblages. Man Ray is also celebrated for his photo experimentation, including "rayographs," ordinary objects placed on exposed negative plates.

Many Jewish artists working in Paris were able to find safety in the United States during World War II; among them were Man Ray, Jacques Lipchitz, and, most notably, Marc Chagall. Chagall had already painted a memorable reaction to the Nazi persecution of German Jews in *White Crucifixion* (1938; Art Institute of Chicago); the painting presents Jesus on the cross, wearing a *tallit* loincloth, amid the flames of a chaotic *shtetl* *pogrom (**Plate 14**). These intimations of further tragedy would be echoed by several significant German-Jewish artists who were caught up in the tentacles of the *Holocaust (See HOLOCAUST REPRESENTATION: ART).

Jankel Adler (1895–1949) left Poland to study in Germany, and his career was similar to those of other leading German artists; however, with the Nazi ascent to power in 1933, he left his teaching job in Dusseldorf and eventually settled in London. His images partake of the arbitrary colors and geometrical simplifications of Paul Klee, but starkly depict expressly Jewish figures of rabbis or musicians. Charlotte Salomon (1917–1943) exemplifies the trauma and dislocation of World War II; she is an older, artist equivalent to Anne *Frank. Born and raised in a culturally rich and fashionable setting in Berlin, she escaped to safety in France in 1939, where she produced a vast series of 1,325 gouache paintings, *Life? Or Theater?* (1940–42; Joods Museum, Amsterdam), before she was deported to her death in *Auschwitz. These stark images of active figures in expansive spaces with explanatory texts recount the entire story of Salomon's tragically short lifetime. Surely the most poignant imagery was created by the mature artist Felix Nussbaum (1904–1944) of Osnabrück. His haunted and gaunt figures suggest loneliness, fear, and the anxiety of exiles or fugitives. Indeed, Nussbaum was interned early in the war and escaped, only to be recaptured and killed in Auschwitz. Nussbaum painted one self-portrait in which he displays his own Jewish identity card (1943; Kulturgeschichtliches Museum, Osnabrück). This haunting bust image presents the distraught artist wearing a hat and coat, complete with yellow badge, while standing outdoors against a high, gray, featureless wall. His last works present apocalyptic horrors.

One of the great losses to both art and literature during the war was Bruno Schulz (1892–1942), known as the "Polish *Kafka" for his disturbing short fiction. Equally disturbing are some two hundred ink drawings reminiscent of Goya, some of them illustrations of his fiction (*Sanatorium under the Sign of the Hourglass* [1937]). Many of these works show disorienting urban scenes in a German Expressionist idiom, often situating unequal encounters between the sexes, dominated by the power of *femmes fatales*. Schulz was shot by a Gestapo officer in his native Drohobycz and is buried in an unmarked grave in the local Jewish cemetery.

For further reading, see A. Kampf, *Chagall to Kitaj: Jewish Experience in 20th Century Art* (1990); E. Bilski, *Berlin Metropolis: Jews and the New Culture 1890–1918* (1999); S. T. Goodman, ed., *Russian Jewish Artists in a Century of Change 1890–1990* (1995); and K. Silver, *The Circle of Montparnasse: Jewish Artists in Paris, 1905–1945* (1985).

LARRY SILVER

Art: Illustrated Yiddish Books. Illustrated books written in *Yiddish, the vernacular language of *Ashkenazi Jews, had two golden ages, first in early modern Europe, especially sixteenth-century *Italy, and then in the *Soviet Union, from 1916 to 1923. Only a few scattered remnants survive from the earliest illuminated Yiddish manuscripts. A scene of a cat holding a mouse accompanies the *Passover song *"Ḥad Gadya,"* which was written in alternating stanzas of *Aramaic and Yiddish in an Italian *haggadah* of the fifteenth or sixteenth century. Decorative animals embellish a Yiddish translation of the *Torah and *haftarot (prophetic readings) from sixteenth-century Germany. Disembodied heads and pointing hands adorn the initial words of a *maḥzor* (festival *prayer book) completed with Yiddish instructions in Kraków in 1558–60; scenes illustrating a collection of Yiddish stories were produced in Germany beginning in 1580.

MANUSCRIPTS: The most important illustrated Yiddish manuscript is a book of customs (*Sefer Minhagim*), completed in northern Italy around the year 1503; it is profusely illustrated with drawings depicting Jewish holidays and life-cycle events, landscapes, animals, fantastic creatures, and scenes from Jewish history. These images are remarkable in their depiction of a wide range of Jewish holidays, which are generally constructed as joyous events. Although the text only briefly cites eating, dancing, and drinking, the drawings emphasize these aspects of festival celebration. Significantly, no rabbis are depicted, but women appear in a third of the scenes. They perform a wide range of ritual roles, and the images construct a complex, positive, and active spiritual role for women. For example, one drawing shows men and women standing on the same floor of the synagogue for *Rosh Ha-Shanah, not separated by a divider. Each individual holds an open *prayer book, suggesting general literacy. Because the artist was the Jewish scribe and not a trained illuminator, his remarkable images are strikingly unconventional. Independent and original, they suggest the multilayered richness of Jewish rituals.

PRINTED BOOKS: The production of profusely illustrated *printed Yiddish texts began in 1546, when the Christian humanist Christoph Froschauer published an edition of

Josippon in Zurich. This was a translation of *Sefer Josippon* (see JOSIPPON, BOOK OF*), a popular tenth-century Italian Hebrew work loosely based on the historical writings of *Josephus. Two other secular Yiddish texts, both heavily illustrated, were published in Verona in 1594–95: the chivalric romance *Paris un Viene* and a collection of fables called the *Kuh-Bukh*. In 1593 and 1600, two illustrated books of customs were published in *Venice. Although the later edition is more famous because of its finer illustrations, it is the earlier version that was repeatedly reprinted with very little variation well into the twentieth century. Reading the same books and viewing the same imagery helped shape Jewish collective memory and common identity in Europe. Yet these printed books, like the *Josippon*, inhabit the borders of Jewish life: Published by Christians and illustrated most probably by Christian artists, these books were written in Yiddish and produced for Jews. In short, they belong to both cultures.

MODERN ERA: In modern times, illustrated Yiddish books were produced in great numbers and variety, from children's books to avant-garde literature. Published in the major centers of Jewish book production, including *Warsaw, Kiev, Paris, and *New York, these books were mostly modest, inexpensive works. However, some were beautifully illustrated by superb Jewish artists of the twentieth century, such as El Lissitzky (1890–1941), Marc Chagall (1887–1985), Henryk Berlewi (1894–1967), and Louis Lozowick (1892–1973).

A renaissance in illustrated Yiddish books took place in *Russia over the years 1916–23, thanks to the Kultur Lige, an artists' collective in Kiev devoted to creating a Jewish national art. This movement of at least thirteen artists, which included Chagall and Lissitzky, illustrated more than fifty books. Chagall illustrated *Troyer*, a collection of poems by David Hofstein (1889–1952) expressing pain and sorrow over recent *pogroms in the *Ukraine. Lissitzky's *Ḥad Gadya*, published in 1917, is probably the most famous book the group produced. Pointing the way to Constructivism and combining Fauvist and Cubist elements with Yiddish writing, Lissitzky's colorful illustrations present an idealized vision of the *shtetl* (**Plate 13**). Other Yiddish books by Lissitzky show his brilliant typography, as in the cover of the book of poems *Achsen*. However, when the Kultur Lige dispersed, the second flowering of illustrated Yiddish books came to an end.

Recent research includes R. Apter-Gabriel, ed., *Tradition and Revolution: The Jewish Renaissance in Russian Avant-Garde Art 1921–1928* (1987), 61–70; and D. Wolfthal, *Picturing Yiddish: Gender, Identity, and Memory in Illustrated Yiddish Books of Renaissance Italy* (2004). **See also ART, EUROPE: TWENTIETH CENTURY.**   DIANE WOLFTHAL

Art, Israeli.

Art, Israeli. What is generally called Israeli art first appeared about fifty years before the 1948 founding of the State of *Israel. Its deeper roots go back to the emergence of Jewish artists in nineteenth-century Europe and to the early days of *Zionist activity. When the Russian-born sculptor Boris Schatz (1867–1932) approached Theodor *Herzl in 1903 about establishing an art school in Jerusalem, Herzl recognized the need for visual representation of the Zionist cause. In 1906 the Bezalel School of Arts and Crafts was created in Jerusalem, named after Bezalel ben Uri,

who built the *Tabernacle in the desert (Exod 31). Under Schatz's directorship and the influence of teachers such as Ephraim Moses Lilien (1874–1925) (**Plate 21**) and Ze'ev Raban (1890–1970) (**Plate 11**), the school developed a style that combined eastern and western imagery and patterns, Hebrew script, and biblical and Zionist themes. Its artists were mainly influenced by the popular Central European *Jugendstil* movement (the equivalent of French Art Nouveau). The objects made at Bezalel were mostly handicraft products and included Judaica artifacts, carpets, and souvenirs depicting biblical stories, the landscape of *Palestine, the holy sites, and portraits of Zionist leaders and Jewish pioneers.

The fusion of techniques and elements originating in *Persia, *Yemen, and Syria with western aesthetic values and Zionist and Jewish themes made the Bezalel style unique. Bezalel artifacts were displayed at major exhibitions in centers such as London and *New York. Schatz envisioned Bezalel as an artistic and cultural center in Palestine that would connect the Jewish people to their old–new land. As part of this vision, the school opened the first *museum in Palestine and collected works by Jewish artists, *archeological finds, and flora and fauna of the Holy Land. This museum was the basis for the collection of the Israel Museum in Jerusalem (inaugurated in 1965).

In the 1920s the prestige of the Bezalel School and style began to decline, and the school temporarily closed in 1929. It reopened in 1935 and has been the leading art school in Israel ever since. The Bezalel style, a turn-of-the-century, pre-Modernist idiom, was challenged by new trends animating the Zionist *Yishuv* especially after 1919, when the immigrant wave known as the Third Aliyah (1919–23) began arriving in the early *British Mandate era (see ISRAEL, STATE OF: IMMIGRATION BEFORE 1948). Intellectuals including poets such as H. N. *Bialik and Uri Zvi Greenberg and artists such as Reuven Rubin (1893–1974) (**Plate 22**), Arieh Lubin (1897–1980), Menahem Shemi (Schmidt) (1898–1951), Nahum Gutman (1898–1981), Ziona Tajar (1900–1988), and Yisrael (Feldman) Paldi (1893–1979) formed the core of a secular culture in *Tel Aviv, overshadowing the Jerusalem-based Bezalel School.

Some of these artists had acquired knowledge of the Modernist style of Picasso, Chagall, and others. These artists – especially Rubin and Gutman (who both studied at Bezalel in the first decade of the twentieth century, but later broke with the style taught there) – sought to create a new style, that of the "new Jew." Their Modernist vision opposed the old world of religion, Jewish customs, and nineteenth-century artistic values, including the academic realism and the *Jugendstil* manner favored at Bezalel. They depicted landscapes using bright palettes, flattened color surfaces, and simple forms, inspired by trends such as Naïve art, Fauvism, and Picasso's 1920s classicist style. Many works depicted idealized images of Arabs as strong men connected to the soil or as full-bodied, sensual women. For these artists, the Arab was a symbol of the close connection to land and body that was seen as the ideal for the "new Jew," in contrast with the image of the suffering, weak, and rootless diasporic Jew. Many artists portrayed *Tel Aviv (founded in 1909) and its people as young, energetic, and secular, free of the tribulations and hardship experienced in the homelands and religious background in which they were reared.

The outbreak of violent clashes between Arabs and Jews in 1929 had a marked effect on the young Jewish community in Palestine in general, and on the artistic realm in particular. Many artists changed their palettes and began painting in darker shades. Instead of landscapes, they focused on interiors. The École de Paris, a group of Parisian-based painters that included Chagall, Modigliani, and Pascin, and, especially, the Expressionistic art of Chaim Soutine, had a major influence on artists living in Palestine in the 1930s, many of whom traveled to Paris to study. This trend is seen most clearly in works by Moshe Mokady (1902–1975) and Haim Atar (1902–1953).

The 1930s also marked the beginning of abstract art, an important trend that was later to become the leading art movement in the young country. The most important artist working in this style was Yossef Zaritsky (1891–1985). Zaritsky, who arrived in Palestine from Kiev in 1923, moved away from themes of national or Jewish interest. His paintings, although rooted in the surrounding landscape, were attuned mainly to correlations between color and form, becoming more and more abstract over the years. In 1948, the year of the founding of the State of Israel and the end of the British Mandate, he founded the "New Horizons" group whose members were mostly abstract artists. This group was to be the leading Israeli art circle in the 1950s and into the 1960s, with Zaritsky as its authoritative leader. Zaritsky, Yehezkel Streichman (1906–1993), and Avigdor Stematzky (1908–1989), the prominent artists of the New Horizons group, scoffed at art that dealt directly with Jewish, national, or local themes using symbolic or narrative means. They were preoccupied with issues of color and form and saw themselves as the country's avant-garde Modernist group, aware of artistic trends in the international art world. They looked to Paris, especially to lyrical abstract artists such as Jean Fautrier, Alfred Manessier, and Georges Braque. The highly abstract art of the principal New Horizons members drove other abstract-oriented artists to develop an ideologically milder, more local approach. Semi-abstract efforts to capture the Israeli light and landscape can be seen in the works of Eliahu Gat (1919–1987), Michael Gross (1920–2004), and Ori Reisman (1924–1991).

The late 1930s and the 1940s saw the emergence of yet another force in Israeli art, which was in its essence opposed to the New Horizons group. An alliance of writers, poets, and artists – led by poet Yonatan Ratosh and dubbed, pejoratively at first, the "Canaanites" – sought a connection with the cultural realms of the ancient civilizations of the Middle East. This poetically resonant approach appropriated ancient history to create a unique cultural stance, opposed to the European heritage in general and to the old Jewish world in particular. The artists influenced by Canaanism drew their inspiration from ancient *Near Eastern visual cultures, from ancient *Egypt to *Mesopotamia. They believed that, in this way, the new Jews could reconnect with their origins in the region, overcome the negative influence of the millennia of exile, and construct a new identity based on and incorporating their ancient past. The most important example of this trend is Itzhak Danziger's (1916–1977) statue "Nimrod," from 1939 (Israel Museum, Jerusalem). The image of the biblical hunter (Gen 10:8–10), carved from red sandstone, is influenced chiefly by ancient Egyptian sculptures (**Plate 23**). The adolescent youth holding a slingshot behind his back and with a falcon perched on his shoulder is literally "of the land," connected to the soil by his very substance and to the fruit of the land by the shape of his eyes, which are modeled on wheat seeds. He generates a powerful impression of primal force, very much the opposite of the figure of the old European Jew (as depicted, for example, in Chagall's works). This powerful idol, a pre-Jewish hunter (who in the Jewish tradition was an enemy of *Abraham, the forefather of the Israelites), was created on the eve of the greatest tragedy in Jewish history, the *Holocaust. "Nimrod" became a symbol of the ideally formed Israeli youth – the Sabra.

In the 1950s, the formative years of Israel's statehood, the country faced complex issues and a growing military threat. In addition, it was only beginning to come to terms with the *Holocaust. Although overshadowed by the dominant abstract idiom of the New Horizons school, Social Realist artists such as Avraham Ofek (1935–1990), Ruth Schloss (b. 1922), and Naftali Bezem (b. 1924) engaged thematically with the *Arab–Israeli conflict, the hardships encountered by new immigrants, and the memory of the Holocaust. These artists worked in a realistic style, influenced by 1950s Italian Social Realists and by Mexican artists such as Diego Rivera, who sought to advance their social and political agendas through art. They were opposed to the idea of "art for art's sake," especially in the wake of World War II.

Other artists, such as Mordecai Ardon (1896–1992), Jakob Steinhardt (1887–1968), and Yosl Bergner (b. 1920), incorporated Jewish narratives and symbols in their art (Bezem's later work is very much of this kind). The most important artist in this context was Ardon, who had studied at the Bauhaus school in Weimar in the 1920s where he was a pupil of Paul Klee and Wassily Kandinsky. In his works, Ardon combined Modernist abstract ideas with Jewish themes, Hebrew script, and kabbalistic symbols (**Plate 24**) (and see KABBALAH).

Thus, in the 1950s and into the 1960s, two major opposing forces were active in the Israeli art world. On one side were artists inclined toward abstract trends, who thought art should not concern itself with national or symbolic issues or with the immediate political and social reality. On the other hand were artists who aimed to incorporate Jewish-identity themes in their work or who engaged with local, social, and political issues as a means of defining their artistic stance.

A number of artists found themselves between these major conflicting groups. They included the Russian-born Arie Aroch (1909–1974); a member of the New Horizons group, he was also influenced by other trends of modern art such as the child-like works of Paul Klee. In the 1960s he became influenced by Neo-Dada art and especially by Robert Rauschenberg, a major predecessor of Pop art who combined everyday objects in his works. Aroch's work throughout the 1960s and 1970s includes ready-made objects, texts, child-like scribbles, and elements related to his early childhood experiences in Kharkov, Russia (now *Ukraine). Some of his works incorporate Jewish elements such as the use of Yiddish text and Jewish iconography. This combination of Pop-oriented art style, themes from his personal memories, and Jewish motifs differentiated Aroch from the other artists in the New Horizons group and made him an important influence on a generation of young artists beginning to be active in the 1960s.

The hegemony of the New Horizons school and its abstract inclinations was challenged in the 1960s, and ultimately the group lost its dominant role as new and younger forces came to the foreground. Worldwide, abstract art was yielding to the return of the figure in Pop art and to its European equivalent, New Realism, both of which sought to connect art to everyday life. In 1961, artist Igael Tumarkin (b. 1933) returned to Israel from Europe, after working as assistant to the stage director in Bertolt Brecht's *Berlin theater troupe and spending time in Holland and Paris. Tumarkin's work combined everyday objects with traditional techniques of painting and sculpture, infused with a strong sense of political awareness. Many of his works of this period were figurative sculptures incorporating weapons and expressing a sense of violent urgency and a sharp antiwar message. After the victorious 1967 Six Day War, Tumarkin sculpted a human figure with guns emerging from his abdomen – one of the first examples of a new sort of political art that challenged the mainstream sense of post-war national euphoria.

Other young artists followed suit; between 1969 and 1973, artists such as Joshua Neustein (b. 1940), Avital Geva (b. 1941), and Micha Ullman (b. 1939) addressed the negative outcomes of war and the occupation of territories, whereas others, such as Michael Druks (b. 1940), explored the influence of mass culture on Israeli society. These were the first attempts at a political avant-garde art that was to flourish during the 1970s.

The Yom Kippur War of October 1973 is considered a turning point in Israeli history (see ISRAEL, STATE OF: ARAB-ISRAELI CONFLICT, 1948–2010). This war dealt a serious blow to the way Israeli society viewed the army and its political leadership, leading eventually to the first political shift of power in Israel's history in 1977. The war and the subsequent political and social changes had a profound influence on the Israeli art world. The dominant art scene became more political, confronting social matters and the continuing adverse effects of the occupation. Gender and the body became important and central themes in the work of young artists. Artistic media, influenced by international trends, shifted from the classical forms of painting and sculpture to environmental, performance, installation, and video art. Even artists engaged with more traditional Jewish and national themes began to employ avant-garde media such as performance art and open-air installations. Young artists engaged in conceptual art, with the creative process itself coming to the fore in works on paper and sculptures that unveiled the process of their own making. These artists' works dealt as much with artistic borders as with political ones and with the connection between these two realms. Some of the central artists of these years were Pinchas Cohen-Gan (b. 1945), Michal Naaman (b. 1951), Tamar Getter (b. 1953), Gideon Gechtman (1942–2008), Benni Efrat (b. 1936), and Motti Mizrachi (b. 1946).

Continuing the Pop-influenced trends of the 1960s, many artists of the 1970s and into the 1980s used crude materials to form a typically coarse surface, in works unconcerned with national or Jewish themes; rather, they explored "low," everyday experience. This style found its most definitive expression in the works of Raffi Lavie (1937–2007) who was also an important teacher and critic. Influenced by Arie Aroch and the powerful Expressionist drawings of Aviva Uri (1922–1989), he combined childlike scribbling and text with daily materials such as newspaper clippings on plywood to create a unique artistic idiom.

As in the international art scene, the 1980s were years when many Israeli conceptual artists of the 1970s and younger artists turned to figurative painting and sculpture and to photography; they tackled issues of otherness (whether national, ethnic, sexual, or gendered), engaging in political criticism and post-modern reflections. As in other art centers of the world, many of their works addressed internal artistic issues, incorporating quotes from art history and other cultural references. The Israeli art world became more pluralistic; prominent artists now took up issues that had previously been shunned, such as narrative works engaging with Jewish issues and the trauma of the Holocaust (often by artists who were the offspring of Holocaust survivors) or painting from nature.

Among them was Moshe Gershuni (b. 1936), who had been a conceptual artist in the 1970s, mostly addressing political issues. In the early 1980s Gershuni turned to Expressionistic works in the wake of a personal crisis and began exploring identity issues such as homoeroticism. This approach constituted a break with the conceptual aesthetics of the 1970s that had produced monochromatic, cerebral works. Gershuni's new paintings were full of color and bodily Expressionistic drama; at the same time, they evinced an interest in Jewish texts and symbols. They marked a new direction in Israeli art, providing painting with renewed legitimacy.

Young artists such as Larry Abramson (b. 1954), Yitzhak Livneh (b. 1952), Gabi Klasmer (b. 1950), and Joshua Borkovsky (b. 1952) became a central force in the painting revival, and painters of an earlier generation, such as abstract painter Moshe Kupferman (1926–2003), came to the foreground. Some artists engaged in realistic painting from observation, most notably Israel Hershberg (b. 1948). At the same time, artists such as Zibi Geva (b. 1951), David Reeb (b. 1952), and Arnon Ben-David (b. 1951) tackled political issues, offering sharp criticism of the mainstream Zionist ideals and addressing the 1982 Lebanon War and the First Intifada (1987–93). It was during these years that Menashe Kadishman (b. 1932), one of Israel's leading sculptors, created his major works dealing with the binding of *Isaac as a symbol of the horrors and futility of war. These were also the years when Arab artists such as Asim Abu-Shakra (1961–1990) began exhibiting in major art spaces in the country.

The 1990s saw the waning of the style dubbed "Want of Matter" (of which Raffi Lavie was the leading exponent), in favor of meticulous, highly polished works by young artists such as Hilla Lu-Lu Lin (b. 1964) and Nir Hod (b. 1970). Their concern with issues of personal versus collective identity and gender-related themes, with a strong emphasis on visual values, was evident in a wide array of artistic fields, from photography and painting to sculpture and video art. Young artists who became active in the mid-1990s and toward the end of the century, such as Sigalit Landau (b. 1969), Gil Marco Shani (b. 1968), Ohad Meromi (b. 1967), Yehudit Sasportas (b. 1969), and Gal Weinstein (b. 1970), have continued these trends. Their at times idiosyncratic and fantastic creations call to mind escapist realms and apocalyptic visions; in other cases, seemingly otherworldly works in fact allude to Israeli political and social reality, employing indirect, mythic undertones that can be understood both locally and universally. As elsewhere, video art and large-scale installations have become a prominent part of the Israeli artistic landscape. Many of these works are not only meticulously finished but also are spectacular, offering an overpowering visual experience.

The art made in Israel in the early-twenty-first century continues to display a perpetual tension between ideas and qualities unique to Israeli society, as well as international influences that erase national, cultural, and religious boundaries. Developments in the global art scene – the huge and ever growing scope and number of art fairs, biennials, and international exhibitions, and technological advances in communication, most notably the internet – afford young Israeli artists greater exposure to the latest trends and forms of art worldwide. The works of young Israeli artists exhibiting at major art centers abroad are charged with both Israeli and Jewish themes, alongside international, universal messages that can appeal to audiences everywhere. This tension, between the local and the international, between Jewish and Israeli issues and an overall human message, was and still is one of the driving forces of Israeli art.

For further reading, see G. Ofrat, *One Hundred Years of Art in Israel* (1988); D. Manor, *Art in Zion: The Genesis of National Art in Jewish Palestine* (2005); A. Barzel, ed., *Israele Arte e Vita, 1906–2006* (exhibition catalogue, Milan, 2006); and *60 Years of Art in Israel*, a joint project of six exhibitions and catalogues, each dedicated to a different decade of Israeli art from 1948 until 2008: *The First Decade: 1948–1958*, Museum of Art, Ein Harod (G. Ofrat and G. Bar Or); *The Second Decade: 1958–1968*, Ashdod Art Museum – Monart Center (Y. Fischer and T. Manor-Friedman); *The Third Decade: 1968–1978*, Tel Aviv Museum of Art (Curator: M. Omer); *The Fourth Decade: 1978–1988*, Haifa Museum of Art (Curator: I. Tenenbaum); *The Fifth Decade: 1988–1998*, Herzliya Museum of Contemporary Art (Curator: D. Rabina); and *The Sixth Decade: 1998–2008*, The Israel Museum, Jerusalem (Curators: A. Mendelsohn and E. Natan).   AMITAI MENDELSOHN

Art, Late Antiquity: In the Land of Israel and the Diaspora.
The surviving Jewish art that was created in the Roman and Persian worlds during late antiquity (ca. 200–700 CE) is preserved mainly in burial contexts and monumental *synagogue remains. The most important remains are the Jewish catacombs in *Rome and Beth Shearim in the *Galilee; more than 150 synagogues in the Land of Israel (including, for example, Capernaum, Kefar Baram, Hammath Tiberias B, Sepphoris, and Beth Alpha); and the *Diaspora synagogues at Dura Europos (*Syria), Sardis (Asia Minor), Ostia Antica (the port of *Rome), Hamman Lif (Tunisia), and elsewhere. References to ancient Jewish art appear in *rabbinic literature, which is often useful in providing contexts for interpreting the material evidence.

Late antique Jewish art was a minority art in which Jews generally used the same forms of visual communication as their non-Jewish neighbors. Thus, Jews in fourth and fifth century CE Rome buried their dead in catacombs that were indistinguishable from those of other Romans, and synagogue architecture reflected the places where Jews lived. The standard art of the Greco-Roman period was made "Jewish" through the adaptation of specific Roman imagery (such as the zodiac), the avoidance of art deemed to be "idolatrous," and the use of unique Jewish imagery. Jewish imagery includes *Torah shrines (by the third century called an "ark") and the symbolic representation of Torah shrines in synagogue mosaics, on carved architectural synagogue elements (e.g., Chorazin, Capernaum, Sardis), as catacomb decoration (Rome, Beth She'arim), and, in Rome, on oil lamps. In Rome and Sardis the Torah shrine is shown with its doors open so that scrolls may be seen within. In Palestine the doors are closed, with a hanging textile before the shrine (e.g., Hammath Tiberias B, Beth Alpha). By far the most widespread Jewish symbol was the seven-branched *menorah, a visual reminder of the Jerusalem *Temple (**Plate 3**). Menorahs appear flanking Torah shrines in Rome and in Palestine, on their own throughout the Roman world within synagogues and tombs, and in decorative contexts on jewelry, seals, oil lamps, and other artifacts. Three-dimensional menorahs have been discovered at sites including Hammath Tiberias A, Maon [Judah] and Sardis. Menorahs appear on Jewish seals from Sassanian *Persia. The menorah is often flanked by a palm frond bunch (*lulav* and *etrog*), an incense shovel (in Palestine), and other imagery.

Biblical representations first appear in the synagogue at Dura Europos in Syria (ca. 245 CE), where the wall paintings of biblical scenes appear in three registers. Dura is the most important single artifact of ancient Jewish art, providing the earliest biblically themed paintings in existence. Approximately 60% of these paintings are extant. The iconography interprets biblical themes through the prisms of both biblical interpretation and the local environment. Represented events include the discovery of *Moses by Pharaoh's daughter, crossing the Red Sea, the tribes encamped around the *Tabernacle, *Ezekiel's vision of the dry bones, and *Esther before King Ahashuerus. The painting technique is typical of the art of Dura and is stylistically of a piece with Persian and Roman art of Mesopotamia and the Syrian desert.

Biblical scenes appear in fifth- and sixth-century synagogue mosaics from Palestine; they include *Aaron before the Tabernacle, the first fruits and table for showbread in Sepphoris, the binding of *Isaac at Sepphoris and Beth Alpha, the angels' visit to *Abraham and *Sarah at Sepphoris, *Noah's ark at Gerasa, *Daniel in the lion's den at Na'aran and perhaps Khirbet Susiya, and *David playing the harp at Gaza. Rabbinic sources suggest the existence of wall paintings from as early as the third century. Hebrew characters also served as markers of Jewish identity within both Palestinian and *Diaspora contexts, although Greek inscriptions are often found as well.

Recent research includes R. Hachlili, *Ancient Jewish Art and Archaeology in the Land of Israel* (1988) and *Ancient Jewish Art and Archaeology in the Diaspora* (1998). S. Fine, *Art and Judaism in the Greco-Roman World: Toward a New Jewish Archaeology* (2005) details past scholarship and presents a comprehensive view of the extant literary and archaeological evidence. **See also SYNAGOGUES, ANCIENT.**
                                                                STEVEN FINE

Art: Medieval Manuscript Illustration.
Jewish books in both medieval *Sepharad and *Ashkenaz were always at risk. In 1242, six ox carts of Jewish manuscripts were burned in the Place de Grève in Paris, destroying nearly every Jewish book in the Île de France, a great center of Jewish manuscript production. Given such deliberate acts of

obliteration, as well as confiscations, censorship, and the vagaries of expulsions and migrations, it is not surprising that relatively few volumes have survived. Nevertheless, many of the major iconographic themes of Jewish illumination can be reconstructed from what remains.

Medieval Jewish manuscripts both in Sepharad and Ashkenaz fall very much within the general stylistic parameters of the surrounding cultures. Medieval Jews shared the same cultural milieu as their neighbors and made use of identical stylistic and iconographic elements. It is the analysis of how those raw elements were fashioned into something Jewish that distinguishes the study of Jewish manuscript illumination.

Narrative art existed among the Jews of late antiquity. The most notable examples are the wall paintings of the synagogue at Dura Europos in *Syria. However, the iconographic traditions represented there never made their way to Europe. During the early thirteenth century, concomitant with the emergence of Christian narrative art from monastic contexts into urban workshops, Jews in both Ashkenaz and Sepharad seem to have developed a renewed interest in narrative painting. By the early fourteenth century, the rebirth of figurative art in Jewish culture had reached its most articulated development (**Plate 4**).

The greatest creativity occurred within the realm of iconography. Medieval Jewish iconography is first and foremost concerned with the illustration of narrative themes in the Hebrew *Bible and other Jewish literature. These illustrations are sometimes fairly straightforward and literal depictions of the biblical stories – an illustration of the Israelites crossing the Sea of Reeds, for instance. However, these scenes are always filtered through the imagination of the authorship of each manuscript, whether patron or artist, who had to interpret in visual terms the usually narratologically sparse biblical episodes. Accordingly, illuminations often depict their subjects through a midrashic lens. Thus, the Sea of Reeds might be shown divided into twelve paths or the Israelites represented bearing arms, traditions found in rabbinic legends.

The depictions were sometimes part of a sequence, such as a series of images illustrating the narrative events leading up to the *Exodus from Egypt, but artists also represented discrete scenes from the text being illustrated. The choice to depict particular narratives or series of events often had an extratextual significance that was rooted in specific historical contexts. For example, most illustrations of the crossing of the Sea of Reeds appear in *haggadot, in manuscripts containing all or part of the Bible, or in *prayer books (which include the "Song at the Sea," Exod 15:1–18). Yet whoever determined the content of a book's illustrations had a myriad of scenes from which to choose. Thus, the choice to include an illumination of crossing the Sea of Reeds may have been for reasons specifically linked to the particular history of a given manuscript. Perhaps the name of the manuscript's patron was Moses, or the community in which the manuscript was illuminated had just gone through a particularly traumatic engagement with the surrounding culture from which it had emerged triumphant, like the Israelites from the Sea of Reeds.

Scholars are now beginning to analyze medieval Jewish illumination in the same ways they consider medieval illumination in general: as a repository of the larger cultural outlook and context of its creators, rather than as a striving toward some aesthetic ideal. Manuscript illumination provided a forum for Jews to express, often in occluded language, deeply held feelings that were theologically or politically dangerous to articulate explicitly. In their engagement with art, Jews reencountered and grappled with all the classical Jewish questions of self-definition, including their place in history, their relationship with *God and their neighbors, and their hopes for *redemption.

A comparison of illuminated fourteenth-century *haggadot* from *Spain and Ashkenaz demonstrates how these concerns were expressed in manuscript iconography. In medieval illuminated *haggadot* of the Sephardic realms, the text is accompanied by what we might call static or "iconic" illustrations: Figures representing various rabbis are displayed next to the words attributed to them, with a similar arrangement for the "Four Children." Illustrations of central elements of the *Passover ritual meal – matzah (unleavened bread) and maror (bitter herbs) – are depicted on the pages that contain the blessings to be recited over them. Yet in a series of Sephardic manuscripts from the fourteenth century, the text, with these iconic illustrations, is preceded by a series of narrative illuminations depicting selected events and incidents from the creation of the world until the Exodus from *Egypt, as well as images of ancient, contemporary, and future Passover celebrations. In the so-called *Golden Haggadah* (London, British Library, MS Add. 27210), illuminated in Catalonia, ca. 1320–30, the Genesis-to-Exodus sequence contains scenes that are deliberately selected and related to each other in terms of physical placement on each folio to emphasize particular aspects of history and theology. Close readings of the illuminations – not only in literal sequence but also in the way the eye is led across the page by apparently stylistic elements like strong verticals and horizontals, and in the way particular illuminations relate, thematically and in their physical disposition, to others that appear later in the sequence – attune us to the iconographic richness of this manuscript. It is evident that it was created as the result of intensive and concerted planning, thorough knowledge of the tradition, and meticulous attention to detail. The illuminations, which appear so similar to those in contemporary Christian manuscripts, are not only stylistically refined but also Jewishly sophisticated. Representations of the Exodus story remind us that the Rabbis understood that the Exodus was present in God's mind even before its first scriptural mention to *Abraham at the "Covenant of the Pieces" (Gen 15:7–21). *Rabbinic literature positions the events of Israelite slavery and *redemption as a part of the sacred destiny of the people who would become the Children of Israel, even from the moment of the creation of the world. The iconographic strategy of prefacing the *haggadah* and the depictions of the contemporary Passover with a sequence of narratives beginning with the Garden of Eden parallels this rabbinic tradition by demonstrating the centrality of the Exodus in the Jewish sacred story and by emphasizing that it was foreordained and inevitable.

In Ashkenazic *haggadot*, narrative illustration is less panoramic and more selective. Throughout the Middle Ages illustrations remained fairly limited and tended to be based on the narratives contained in the text of the *haggadah* itself, with illustrations based only on elements referred to explicitly in the text, like the Rabbis of B'nai B'rak, the "Four

Children," the labors of the Israelites, the plagues, and the drowning of the Egyptians. Illumination in Western and Central Europe opens up more in the aftermath of *printing, and the magnificent courtly manuscripts produced in the eighteenth century are testimony to great iconographic richness.

Yet distinctive emphases and agendas can be detected even in the apparently straightforward sequences of illumination in medieval Ashkenazic manuscripts. For instance, scholars have characterized the sequence of narrative illustrations in the earliest known surviving illuminated *haggadah*, the so-called *Birds' Head Haggadah* (Jerusalem, Israel Museum, MS 180/57), illuminated in Mainz, *Germany, around 1300, as "confused" and "disjointed." On closer examination, however, one notes that instead of a single linear narrative of the Exodus, the manuscript contains five fairly distinct groups of images, including (1) depictions of events that form a sort of prehistory of the Exodus, (2) images depicting the Exodus and the desert wandering narratives, (3) illustrations of the poem *"Dayenu"* ("It would have been enough!"), and (4) a cluster of illuminations revolving around the making of *matzah*. A fifth strand of iconography that runs through the manuscript, overlapping these other groups of images, depicts five different Passovers that are discussed in rabbinic and medieval literature. The first "Passover" in this group is represented by a series of events that the Rabbis understood to foreshadow the actual historical Exodus. Next are Passovers that occur in two historical eras: the very first, or Egyptian Passover, and the Passover of *Temple times. Next, the Passover of post-Temple times, up to and including the present day, is represented. Finally, the iconography depicts a Passover at the end of history, the Passover of Redemption.

If we expect a single, simple, continuous "story" in the sequence of illuminations of the *Birds' Head Haggadah*, we are bound to be disappointed. However, if we read the "five Passovers" as they intertwine with the Exodus prehistory, Exodus and desert wanderings, *"Dayenu,"* and *matzah*-baking sequences, we observe that together they form a complex, interlinked, and polyvalent narrative. The manuscript's iconography continually affirms its authorship's understanding that the tradition, although grounded in historical events, simultaneously transcends history and points toward *messianic redemption, a theme that pervades medieval Jewish visual culture as a whole, both in Ashkenaz and in Sepharad (**Plate 7**).

Although biblical narrative is the dominant source for images in medieval Jewish manuscripts, the closely related iconographic theme of eschatological redemption is often intertwined with biblical representations. Because the Jewish worldview was suffused with historical memory and eschatological hope, illuminations depicted scenes from history that incorporated future consolation: They looked back at a time when Jews possessed political and cultural sovereignty while simultaneously pointing to the restoration of that status. This dissonance between the reality of religious and political subjugation and the historical memories and future hopes of the Jewish people is what gives Jewish art its uniqueness – as far back as Dura Europos, and probably before.

Jewish illumination mirrors Jewish texts in making the connection between past redemptions and the great redemption yet to come, while also reflecting on the continuing persecution of Jews in an as-yet unredeemed world. A subtheme of eschatological imagination is that of fantasies of vindication. Just as the redemption would bring salvation for Jews, it would represent the downfall of their enemies. Such subversive and revolutionary ideas, which would not have gone over well with the majority culture, were veiled in symbolic images or indicated by the use of a politically pointed narrative iconography meant primarily for an internal Jewish audience. For instance, by commissioning images that represent Pharaoh and his courtiers in the garb of a contemporary monarch and his entourage, the patrons of one fourteenth-century Sephardic *haggadah* may have been expressing a rather explicit dream of subversion. By depicting the plagues afflicting some figures in contemporary dress and some in more "archaic" clothing, the patrons of an eighteenth-century Ashkenazic *haggadah* made the message somewhat more ambiguous. And by generalizing the figures so thoroughly that the landscape completely dominates, the patrons of yet another *haggadah*, a Moravian example of the eighteenth century, softened any explicit subversive message, while maintaining the implicit message of the plagues that strike enemies and spare God's chosen ones.

The embodiment of sacred narrative in manuscript art was one of the ways in which medieval Jews testified to the continuity of the *revelation at Sinai. Alongside their traditional modes of text commentary, medieval Jews could employ iconography as exegesis, using images as another mirror of revelation in history.

Recent research on Hebrew manuscript illustration includes M. M. Epstein, *Dreams of Subversion in Medieval Jewish Art and Literature* (1997); idem, *The Medieval Haggadah: Art, Narrative, and Religious Imagination* (2011); E. Frojmovic, ed., *Imagining the Self, Imagining the Other: Visual Representation and Jewish-Christian Dynamics in the Middle Ages and Early Modern Period* (2002); and K. Kogman-Appel, *Illuminated Haggadot from Medieval Spain* (2006).

MARC MICHAEL EPSTEIN

Ascarelli, Devorà (sixteenth century) was an Italian poet and translator of Hebrew liturgical texts. The only information about her is her thirty-one page book (1601 and 1609), perhaps the first published volume by a Jewish woman. Its dedication indicates that she was the wife of Joseph Ascarelli, a member of a Roman family associated with the leadership of *Rome's Catalan Jewish community. Ascarelli's book was apparently intended for use on *Yom Kippur; the liturgical pieces appear in both Hebrew and Italian. The volume is usually identified by its first selection, *L'abitacolo degli Oranti* (*Maon ha-Shoalim*, [The Abode of the Supplicants]), a rhymed translation of a liturgical poem for Yom Kippur by Moses Rieti of Perugia (1388–1459), from his *Mikdash Me'at* (*Il Tempio* [The Small Sanctuary], part 2, canto 2). Other prose translations include *Barekhi Nafshi*, or *Benedici il Signore o anima mia* (May God Bless My Soul), which is a prayer in the Roman rite by Rabbenu Bahia ben Joseph the Pious (eleventh century) of Saragossa; *La Grande Confessione* (The Great Confession) by Rabbenu Nissim, identified as the head of the *Babylonian Academy; and an *avodah* prayer for the Sephardic Yom Kippur service. Also included in the work are two original sonnets, *"Il Ritratto di Susanna"* (The Picture of Susannah), based on the story in the *Apocrypha of Susannah and the Elders, and "*Quanto è in me di Celeste*," (Whatever in Me Is of Heaven); as well as one anonymous short poem dedicated to Ascarelli: "*Ape, ingegnosa voli*," (Fly, Clever Bee).

HOWARD TZVI ADELMAN

Asher ben Jeḥiel (ca. 1250–1328), also known as the Rosh, was a halakhic authority, talmudist, and moralist. A pupil of *Meir ben Barukh of Rothenburg, he was seen as the leader of German Jewry after his teacher's imprisonment. He survived the Rindfleisch massacres of 1298, in which two hundred Jews were murdered. In 1303 he left *Germany with his family, probably to escape government persecution; he became the rabbi of Toledo, *Spain, in 1305. The Rosh introduced the *Ashkenazic approach to Talmud study to Spain and attempted a synthesis of Ashkenazic and *Sephardic practices and customs. He was opposed to philosophical studies and was a leader of those who opposed the writings of *Maimonides. His published works include *Piskei ha-Rosh*, commentaries on large parts of the *Mishnah and *Talmud, and *Orkhot Ḥayyim*, an ethical treatise written for his sons.

KATE FRIEDMAN

Asherah: See CANAAN, CANAANITES: CANAANITE MYTHOLOGY; and PLATE 1.

Ashkenaz, Ashkenazim; adj. Ashkenazi or Ashkenazic. Ashkenaz is a biblical place name mentioned in Genesis 10:3, Jeremiah 51:27, and 1 Chronicles 1:6. In the tenth century CE, Jews identified their settlements in *Germany (the Rhineland) with this location, and Jews in northern Europe became known as Ashkenazim. Over the course of the next six hundred years, Ashkenazim spread into other parts of Europe, settling particularly heavily in *Eastern Europe. Ashkenazim are differentiated from *Sephardim, Jews of Iberian descent, and *Mizraḥim, Jews of Middle Eastern descent. Each group developed distinctive liturgical customs (*nusakh*), rituals, and social practices, as well as differing Hebrew pronunciations, and vernacular languages, with numerous internal variations. See also YIDDISH; Maps 7, 8, 10, 11   KATE FRIEDMAN

Assyria was a Mesopotamian empire centered on the upper Tigris River in what is now *Iraq. Assyria's origins date back to at least the twentieth century BCE, and its name derives from its original capital city Assur. Over the centuries, Assyria had periods of political dominance and of subordination in its relations with neighboring peoples. *Babylon, to the south, and *Egypt were perennial rivals. The main language was a dialect of Akkadian, a *Semitic language; a great deal is known about Assyrian society and beliefs from cuneiform writing on clay tablets and from Assyrian art (see MESOPOTAMIA AND ANCIENT ISRAEL and NEAR EAST, ANCIENT).

In the Neo-Assyrian era (911–612 BCE), military power grew under Ashurnasirpal II; during his reign the northern kingdom of *Israel benefited from Assyria's defeat of the Arameans (2 Kgs 13:5). When the next Assyrian king, Shalmaneser III, attacked Ben-Hadad II of Damascus in 853 BCE, King *Ahab of Israel opposed his efforts, but his successor, Jehu, paid tribute to Assyria. Assyria declined during the late ninth and early eighth centuries BCE until Tiglath-Pileser II came into power in 745. He invaded Israel in 738 during the reign of Menahem, requiring a heavy tribute (2

Kgs 15:19). Ahaz, king of *Judah, allied with Assyria against Israel and *Syria, and Tiglath-Pileser occupied Damascus in 732 and deported its inhabitants to Assyria. Shalmaneser V succeeded Tiglath-Pileser II in 727, and King Hoshea of Israel allied with Egypt against Assyria in 725, which led to Shalmaneser V's invasion of Syria and *Samaria (Israel's capital). Shalmaneser V died in 722 while in Samaria, and Sargon II succeeded him, taking 27,000 Israelites into Assyrian captivity (see TRIBES, TEN LOST).

Judah remained loyal to Assyria until 701 when King *Hezekiah allied with Egypt against Sennacherib (702–681 BCE). In response Sennacherib sacked a number of cities in Judah, including *Lachish, and laid siege to *Jerusalem. However, before Jerusalem was captured, Sennacherib returned to Nineveh, his capital city, to put down a rebellion. Biblical writers interpret this unexpected rescue as a miracle effected by an angel (2 Kgs 19:35). An Assyrian version of these events, which are presented as a victory that yielded rich tribute from Hezekiah, is found on the clay hexagonal "Taylor prism," found in the ruins of ancient Nineveh in 1830 and now in the Oriental Institute in *Chicago. The Assyrian empire collapsed by the end of the seventh century BCE after its defeat by *Babylon in 612. **Map 1**

ELIZABETH SHULMAN

Astrology. Two Hebrew treatises with astrological themes, the *Baraita de-Shmuel* and *Baraita de-Mazzalot*, survive from the transition period between antiquity and the Middle Ages. Both draw on Hellenistic astrology and use Greek terminology. From the mid-eighth century to 1000, important Jewish astrologers who wrote in *Arabic include Mash'allah (d. ca. 815), Sahl ibn Bushr ibn Habib al-Yahd (fl. early ninth century), Ali ibn Dawud al-Yahd (fl. end of the ninth century), and Dunash ibn Tamim of Kairouan (fl. ca. 950).

During the twelfth century, many Jews were active in astrology. The fifth chapter of *Megillat ha-Megalleh* (Scroll of the Revealer) by *Abraham bar Ḥiyya (d. 1140) is an impressive Jewish and universal astrological history. Bar Ḥiyya also wrote a letter to Judah ben Barzilai, the leading rabbinic authority of Barcelona, setting forth a detailed halakhic defense of his version of astrology. The most prominent medieval Jewish expert on astrology was Abraham *ibn Ezra (1089–1167). His seventeen treatises address the main genres of Arabic astrology. Ibn Ezra also incorporated a significant astrological component into his biblical commentaries, thereby integrating astrological concepts into mainstream Jewish culture. Ibn Ezra's subsequent influence is evident in an epistle addressed to *Maimonides from southern France (see FRANCE, SOUTHERN: MIDDLE AGES).

Moses Maimonides (1135–1204) attacked the study of astrology, emphasizing its strong connection to star worship and its implied denial of free will. Nevertheless, scholarly astrology spread widely within Jewish society after Maimonides' death. Ibn Ezra's astrological treatises were transmitted as components of astrological compilations or collections. Hebrew translations of astrological texts, mainly from Arabic, grew in number in the thirteenth and particularly in the fourteenth centuries. Astrological sections appeared in some Hebrew encyclopedias of sciences and medieval rabbinic writings.

Like Ibn Ezra, *Gersonides (1288–1344) incorporated astrology into his biblical commentaries. He also wrote a prognostication for the 1345 conjunction of Saturn and Jupiter. The anthropocentric view that the celestial bodies were purposely created to emanate influences that perfect the sublunar world is a cornerstone of *The Wars of the Lord*, his great philosophical work.

For recent research, see S. Sela, "Abraham Bar Hiyya's Astrological Work and Thought," *Jewish Studies Quarterly* 12 (2005):1–31; idem, "Queries on Astrology Sent from Southern France," *Aleph* 4 (2004): 89–190; idem, *Abraham Ibn Ezra and the Rise of Medieval "Hebrew Science"* (2003); G. Freudenthal, "Maimonides' Stance on Astrology in Context: Cosmology, Physics, Medicine, and Providence," in *Moses Maimonides: Physician, Scientist, and Philospher*, ed. F. Rosner and S. Kottek (1993), 77–90; and T. Langermann, "Gersonides on Astrology," in *The Wars of the Lord*, trans. S. Feldman (1999), 3:506–19.   SHLOMO SELA

Astronomy: See SCIENCE AND MATHEMATICS: MIDDLE AGES AND EARLY MODERN PERIOD

Atonement. Rituals of atonement aim to restore cultic *purity and remove guilt. Many ancient communities shared the underlying belief that the gods, as guardians of law and order, were angered by transgression and required appeasement. In the *Torah (*Lev 16), one day of the year is set aside for the cultic system to be restored to its original purity and for the sins of the community to be "wiped away" or "covered" (the etymology of *kapper* is uncertain). On the Day of Atonement (*Yom Kippur), as practiced in *Second Temple *Jerusalem, the High Priest (cf. *Wisdom of Ben Sira 50) entered the Holy of Holies, the most sacred space in the *Temple, in his official vestments while the people (who had been fasting since nightfall) awaited his successful return. Celebration followed the solemn ritual observances; the *Mishnah (*Ta'anit* 4:8) mentions that when the Day of Atonement concluded, the young women of Jerusalem would dance in the vineyards in hopes of attracting a husband.

After the Second Temple's destruction (70 CE), the Rabbis found consolation in other means of atonement, such as acts of lovingkindness. Medieval spirituality focused on *repentance, forgiveness, and inner purification. The trope of *kol nidre,* chanted on the eve of Yom Kippur, is among the most haunting tunes of the liturgical year. Concluding a period of "ten days of repentance" (*asseret yemei teshuvah* [see HIGH HOLIDAYS]) that begins with Rosh Ha-Shanah, the New Year (see NEW YEARS), the mythological arc of Yom Kippur worship extends from the proclamation of divine kingship to the collective confession of guilt to the hope that God will move from the throne of judgment to the throne of mercy. Jewish tradition teaches that the heavenly books are opened, and each individual's name is inscribed for life or for death (hence the pious wish for a "benevolent inscription" [*hatimah tovah*]). Immediately after the heavenly gates are closed at sunset (*ne'ilah*), families traditionally begin to build the *sukkah* required for the celebration of the feast of *Sukkot (Tabernacles), which follows the *High Holidays and confirms that God has forgiven and that life has once again been granted and provided for.

The ethical-legal potential of the liturgical drama of atonement was first recognized by Hermann *Cohen (1842–1918), who saw the restoration of innocence and purity as a religious contribution to an ethical conception of the human being. The Jewish conception of atonement models what jurisprudence merely demands; namely, the transformation of the transgressor to a restored moral self. For Cohen, confession of wrong, repentance, and atonement can rehabilitate the individual who, by accepting guilt and punishment, begins a process of return to innocence and moral value. Mindful of the social and psychological dimensions of crime, modern legal scholars have also highlighted other elements of atonement, such as remorse and apology.

For further reading see S. Agnon, *Days of Awe* (1938; rep. 1995); and S. Bibas and R. A. Bierschbach, "Integrating Remorse and Apology into Criminal Procedure," *Yale Law Journal* 114/1 (2004): 85–148.   MICHAEL ZANK

Auschwitz (Oświęcim), a camp in Poland where the *Nazis murdered almost a million Jews, along with 70,000–75,000 Poles, 21,000 *Roma, and 15,000 Soviet prisoners of war. More than two-thirds of the Jewish victims were from *Hungary (438,000) and *Poland (300,000). Auschwitz was unique both for its size (25 square miles) and sense of permanency. In addition to its three major camps, Auschwitz I, II, and III, Auschwitz had a large network of *Nebenlager* or subcamps. Auschwitz I was the *Stammlager* (main camp) or concentration camp, Auschwitz II–Birkenau was the death camp, and Auschwitz III–Buna/Monowitz was the I. G. Farben complex in which slave labor manufactured synthetic rubber. There were four large gas chamber and crematorium complexes in Birkenau with plans for a fifth. There was a single gas chamber–crematorium at Auschwitz I. The *Theresienstadt "Czech" Family Camp and the Roma Family Camp were also located in Birkenau. Once prisoners arrived in Birkenau through the infamous arched rail entranceway, they were herded off the train cars and then forced to pass through a small line of SS physicians, who, with a gesture to the left or right, decided who would be gassed or who would live briefly as slave laborers. Those chosen for death were quickly marched to a nearby gas chamber–crematorium, where they were ordered to undress. As they entered the anteroom to the gas chambers, signs directed them *zu den Bäden* ("to the baths") and *zur Desinfektion* ("to disinfection"). If there was a backlog of victims or one of the gas chambers was not operating, some would be taken outside and shot. Once the gassings ended, SS physicians selected some bodies for dissection.

The SS forced a large contingent of inmates to work as *Kapos* (prisoner trustees), *Blockälteste* (block or barracks elders), and *Vorarbeiter* (workers' foremen) throughout the Auschwitz complex. In addition, they used inmate *Sonderkommandos* (special detachments) in Birkenau to remove the bodies from the gas chambers and burn them in the crematoria or nearby pits. Once the chambers were aired out, *Sonderkommandos* entered to look for gold and other hidden items among the bodies. After the bodies were cremated, the ashes were dumped in the Vistula River or in local streams or ponds. Bones were crushed and buried in nearby pits. Inmates sorted and stored the victims' food, clothing, and other personal items in special *Kanada* barracks. These goods were either stolen by the SS or sent to ethnic German colonists in Poland or Ukraine. When the Soviets entered Auschwitz in early 1945, they found 350,000 men's suits, more than 800,000 women's dresses and other personal items, children's clothing, and almost seven tons of human hair.

The SS conducted gruesome medical experiments at Auschwitz. Dr. Carl Clauberg performed sterilization experiments on inmates, and Dr. Josef Mengele experimented on twins, Roma children, dwarfs, and others. He worked closely with Berlin's prestigious Kaiser Wilhelm Institute for Anthropology, Human Genetics, and Eugenics, sending it copies of his research reports and human specimens. Dr. Miklos Nyiszli, a Jewish physician from Hungary who was forced to work as Mengele's assistant, described his work with Auschwitz's "angel of death" in his memoir, *Auschwitz: A Doctor's Eyewitness Account*.

The last major act of *Holocaust resistance took place in Auschwitz in the fall of 1944 when three hundred *Sonderkommandos*, who had just learned of Himmler's plans to close Auschwitz, blew up crematorium IV and fought the SS with hammers and axes. The SS killed 451 Jews during the uprising and executed others involved in the plot. Two weeks later, a smaller rebellion took place after a Jewish woman shot two SS guards. Himmler ordered the destruction of the crematoria at Auschwitz I and II after the October 7 rebellion. When the Soviet army liberated Auschwitz on January 17, 1945, all that remained of its once vast prisoner population were 7,000 sick or dying inmates.

See also HOLOCAUST; HOLOCAUST: CAMPS AND KILLING CENTERS; HOLOCAUST RESCUERS; HOLOCAUST TRIALS.

DAVID M. CROWE

Australia. Australian Jewry proudly traces its origins to the bedraggled Jewish convicts who were shipped in the First Fleet to the penal colony of New South Wales in 1788. More than three hundred Jews were among the chained prisoners transported to Australia between 1788 and 1830. The first Jewish free settlers began arriving in the 1820s and soon outnumbered the Jewish convict population. They began to organize regular religious services and the first communal institutions, closely modeled along Anglo-Jewish lines. Although some Jews scattered throughout the countryside, working as hoteliers, pub owners, shopkeepers, and tradesmen, most clustered in Sydney, Melbourne, and Hobart. The discovery of gold in 1851 brought substantial numbers of Jewish fortune seekers, and during the 1850s, the Australian Jewish population more than doubled in size to more than 5,000 in the early 1860s. Men made up roughly two-thirds of this early community.

Australia's remoteness limited the scale of Eastern European Jewish immigration from 1880s until the outbreak of World War I. Nonetheless, the new arrivals, disapproving of their acculturated and largely irreligious counterparts, created their own religious and cultural institutions, as well as the first *Zionist organizations. By 1914, well over half of the total Jewish population was native-born; the communal leadership was dominated by an Anglicized elite that also found success in politics, commerce, and cultural life. Acculturation and acceptance – strident

*antisemitism was all but absent until the late 1930s – ensured high rates of *intermarriage. The Australian government's acceptance of Jewish refugees from *Germany between 1936 and the outbreak of war – about 5,000 in 1939 alone – created a tide of hostility and xenophobia. Over time, the infusion of these outsiders revitalized Australian Jewish life, introducing the first Liberal synagogues and strengthening Orthodoxy, spurring Jewish education and philanthropic initiatives, providing Zionist activity with new life, and broadening and democratizing the communal leadership. These trends gained further momentum after the end of World War II as Australia initially welcomed the immigration of Jewish *displaced persons from Europe, most of whom settled in Sydney and Melbourne. Largely because of this influx, the Australian Jewish population doubled between 1933 and 1945 to more than 48,000. These numbers were bolstered by more than 23,000 additional Jewish refugees between 1946 and 1960.

In the post-war decades, Australian Jewish life was marked by rapid upward social mobility, suburbanization, professionalization, and embourgeoisement. Intermarriage rates, which had been of great concern in the 1920s, declined significantly in the 1950s and 1960s. Over the last four decades, the Jewish community has thrived as Australia has become increasingly multicultural and prosperous. It has also continued to attract significant numbers of Jewish immigrants, mostly *Russians, *South Africans, and *Israelis. Given the relatively small size of the total Jewish population and the residential clustering of immigrants, this influx has had a significant impact on the community. As of 1996 more than 9% of the Australian Jewish population of 106,000 was born in South Africa; ex-South Africans made up more than half of the Jewish community of Perth. These immigrants have helped sustain the post-war blossoming and diversification of Jewish life in Australia.

For further reading, see S. Rutland, *Edge of the Diaspora: Two Centuries of Jewish Settlement in Australia* (1997); and H. Rubinstein and W. D. Rubinstein, *The Jews in Australia: A Thematic History* (1991).

ADAM MENDELSOHN

Austria, Austro-Hungarian Empire: See HABSBURG EMPIRE; PRAGUE; VIENNA; Maps 8, 9

Autobiography See entries under MEMOIR AND LIFEWRITING

Autonomy and Heteronomy. The etymology of *autonomy* (*auto* + *nomos*) suggests the imposition of law on oneself; its opposite, *heteronomy* (*heteros* + *nomos*), is the imposition of law on (or from) another. In the history of philosophy, the distinction between the two is associated with Immanuel Kant (1724–1804). His basic insight is that the individual alone bears responsibility for her or his actions. To be responsible for oneself is in some sense to be master of oneself or, as Kant characterizes it, autonomous. Taking this idea to its logical extreme, Kant concludes that every moral agent is both an end *in* itself and a being capable of legislating morality *for* itself.

Suppose *God commands me to do something. Why I should obey? A reason often given is that my life will be uncomfortable if I do not. Yet the central question is not "What is it in my interest to do?" but "What am I obliged to do?" Kant's point is that obligation can only come from within: Neither God nor anyone else can create obligation *for me*. Rather than say, "Do this" and "Don't do that," as a person in authority, I must be allowed to see for myself what is right. Not to do so is heteronomous and therefore degrading.

The classic statement of autonomy reads, "The will is thus not merely subject to the law but is subject in such a way that it must be regarded also as legislating for itself and only on this account as being subject to the law (of which it can regard itself as the author)" (Kant, *Grounding of the Metaphysics of Morals*, 431). To say that I must be able to regard myself as the author of the law is not to say that I must be the author of the law in fact. I did not draft the Fifth Amendment to the U.S. Constitution; however, because it prohibits torture, it articulates a principle to which I am committed, and thus I have no trouble adopting it *as if* I were the author.

How is autonomy compatible with the idea of divine *commandment? According to Kant, I can obey God as long as my reason for doing so is that the commandment I have been given is morally valid; what I cannot do is obey blindly. Proponents of autonomy point out that the typical way for God to issue commandments is to enter into a *covenant or *berit*, an arrangement that requires the consent of both parties. Unlike Pharaoh, God does not simply say "Do this," but asks, "Will you pledge yourself to the claim that this ought to be done?" The difference is critical because only the latter approach respects the dignity of both parties.

Opponents of autonomy reply that if I must be able to regard myself as the author of the law, its status as God-given becomes irrelevant. If, for example, I can see on my own that murder is wrong, why do I need God to point it out? The answer is that, although God can serve as a moral teacher, God must still recognize that I am a moral agent.

Closely connected to the issue of autonomy is the question of whether God commands something because it is right or whether it is right because God commands it. Typically a proponent of autonomy will assert the former, an opponent the latter.

Thinkers who address this issue include I. Kant, *Grounding of the Metaphysics of Morals* (1785), H. *Cohen, *Religion of Reason out of the Sources of Judaism* (1919), and K. Seeskin, *Autonomy in Jewish Philosophy* (2001).

KENNETH SEESKIN

Av. Fifth month of the Jewish calendar; takes place in July or August of the Gregorian calendar. **See also CALENDAR; CALENDAR: MONTHS OF THE YEAR; AND TISHA B'AV.**

Avot (or *Pirkei Avot*; "Chapters of the Fathers" or "Ethics of the Fathers"), the sole nonlegal tractate in the *Mishnah, is found in the Order *Nezikin*. Its content is more closely akin to biblical *wisdom literature than to the legal materials comprising the bulk of the Mishnah. The tractate's timeless lessons and straightforward language have rendered the work highly popular beyond the learned few who have traditionally studied rabbinic legal literature. The custom of studying *Avot* on the *Sabbath, which spread from *geonic *Babylonia (see GAON; GEONIC ACADEMIES) to Jewish communities around the globe, enhanced the public profile of the work and led to its inclusion and mass circulation in the *prayer book. Over the centuries, *Avot* has inspired numerous commentaries and has been translated into many languages.

The first four of the tractate's five chapters are an anthology of wisdom sayings attributed to rabbinic (and proto-rabbinic) sages; the fifth is comprised of similarly nonlegal though mostly anonymous materials. The sayings in *Avot* highlight ethical precepts and establish study of *Torah and observance of its precepts as fundamental Jewish values. Typical is the saying, attributed to Simon the Righteous in 1:2, that the three pillars on which the world stands are Torah, worship, and deeds of lovingkindness.

The central structuring principle of chapters one through four is the chain of transmission that begins the tractate: "Moses received the Torah from Sinai and passed it on to Joshua, and Joshua to the elders, and the elders to the prophets, and the prophets passed it on to the Men of the Great Assembly" (*Avot* 1:1). This opening statement constructs the earliest stages of the transmission of the Torah in its fullest sense – that is, the Hebrew *Bible and extrabiblical oral traditions, from its initial reception on Mount Sinai until the early *Second Temple period. This chain of transmission explicitly structures the first two chapters of *Avot*, tracing the history of the Torah's transmission via a teacher–disciple schema from biblical times until the early *tannaitic period. Chapters three and four continue the chronological theme until the end of the tannaitic period, but are structured along generational lines rather than by a teacher–disciple pattern. *Avot*'s chain is not a straightforward reflection of historical reality but rather a rhetorical construct designed to establish the continuity of the rabbinic enterprise and thereby ground rabbinic teachings in the ancient past.

Avot was produced by rabbinic sages in third-century Roman *Palestine, and the Greco-Roman setting provides an illuminating backdrop for the tractate. For instance, *Avot*'s chain of transmission is a fine example of a *Hellenistic scholastic succession list; collections of sayings were also quite popular in Greco-Roman antiquity. In fact, the interspersing of attributed sayings (*chreiai* in Greek) within a succession list was apparently an ancient Greek practice. *Avot* thus reflects a rabbinic community that was embedded within the overarching cultural environment of the Greco-Roman Near East.

AMRAM TROPPER

Avot de Rabbi Natan. *(AdRN)*, "The Fathers According to Rabbi Nathan," is one of the minor tractates of the Babylonian *Talmud. The core of *AdRN* is made up of wisdom teachings found in Mishnah *Avot. Sometimes *AdRN* comments directly on the passages of *Avot* (like *gemara), and at other times we find additions and supplements (like the *Tosefta). *AdRN* may preserve the earlier phrasing of key passages. For example, in M. *Avot* the first saying is attributed to the "men of the Great Assembly": "Be deliberate in judgment, raise up many disciples, and make a fence for the Torah." In *AdRN* the order of items is different: The phrase "make a fence for the Torah" comes before "raise up many disciples." Judah Goldin suggested that such alternate versions may enable reconstruction of the original meaning.

The commentary can be extensive. In *AdRN*, the instruction to "make a fence" inspires an elaborate discussion of fences contributed to by eight figures or documents: *God, *Adam, the *Torah, *Moses, *Job, the *Prophets, the *Writings, and the Sages. The images of distance and boundary conveyed by a fence are also developed in several ways. The most basic fence establishes a standard for practice stricter than a given biblical commandment in order to guard against transgression. *AdRN* describes men distancing themselves from transgression or reining in their own desires. Long digressions are common; discussion of *Adam's fence includes midrashic traditions concerning the events in Eden.

AdRN raises several technical difficulties because it is not one text but a family of texts that includes several manuscripts and Cairo *Genizah fragments; their relationships are difficult to specify. Scholars have labeled the printed edition and similar manuscripts as "Version A," and another group as "Version B," but this division is contested. Similarly, the dating is hotly debated. *AdRN* initially appears to be a *tannaitic work, but scholars have long been aware that it was compiled over a much longer period. Menahem Kister's recent analysis makes clear that post-talmudic editing of the material is also extensive.

Scholars have highlighted various prominent literary and thematic features of *AdRN*. Jacob Neusner has discussed the emphasis on the narratives of sages, including edited compilations concerning Hillel and Shammai, Rabban Joḥanan ben Zakkai, R. Eliezer ben Hyrcanus, and R. *Akiva. Anthony Saldarini characterizes the text as distinctly "scholastic," presuming the context of a disciple circle that is comparable to Greco-Roman philosophical schools; Jonathan Schofer studies *AdRN* as a collection of *ethical literature that offers instruction in character and actions for rabbinic disciples. Judith R. Baskin analyzes AdRN version B as emphasizing *women's alterity and subordination, particularly through midrashic reflection on *Eve.

For further reading, see J. Goldin, *Studies in Midrash* (1988); M. Kister, *Studies in Abot de-Rabbi Nathan* ([Hebrew with English summary], 1998); J. Neusner, *Judaism and Story* (1992); A. Saldarini, *Scholastic Rabbinism* (1982); J. W. Schofer, *Making of a Sage* (2005); and J. R. Baskin, "She Extinguished the Light of the World," in *Current Trends in the Study of Midrash*, ed. C. Bakhos (2005).

JONATHAN WYN SCHOFER

Ayn Sof: See *EIN SOF*

B

Baal: See CANAAN, CANAANITE: CANAANITE MYTHOLOGY

Baal Shem, "Master of the Holy Name," is a term used in medieval and Early Modern times to denote a master of magical powers who employed holy names, divine or angelic, for supernatural purposes. The earliest citation for this term is an epistle of *Hai ben Sherira *Gaon of *Babylonia. The twelfth-century Judah the Pious of Regensburg, a major figure in the pietist *Ḥasidei Ashkenaz, described a certain Rabbi Joseph as a master of holy names who used his powers to move miraculously from place to place. Several scholars, poets, and halakhists were described by this title in the Middle Ages, but beginning in the sixteenth century it was most commonly applied to mystics, healers, and magicians in Central and Eastern Europe. Among them was R. Joel Baal Shem of Zamoscs, who is credited with treatises dealing with *magic and popular *medicine. The eighteenth-century Shmuel Jacob Ḥayyim Falk was known as the Baal Shem of London. R. Adam Baal Shem of Bingen, a seventeenth-century figure, was later described as the mysterious teacher of the founder of the Ḥasidic movement, R. Israel *Baal Shem Tov (the Besht). There is no real difference in meaning between the terms *baal shem* and *baal shem tov* ("Master of the Good Name"). **See also DOV BER OF MIĘDZYRZECZ; ETHICAL WILLS; FOLKTALES; ḤASIDISM, EUROPE; HESCHEL, ABRAHAM JOSHUA; KABBALAH; NAḤMAN BEN SIMḤA OF BRATZLAV; SCHNEUR ZALMAN BEN BARUCH OF LIADY; UKRAINE.** JOSEPH DAN

Baal Shem Tov, R. Israel Ben Eliezer (1698–1760), the charismatic founder of the Ḥasidic movement, was born in Międzybóż, Podolia (present-day *Ukraine); he is often known by the acronym, the Besht. As his title indicates, he was renowned among his followers as a healer and magician. The Besht was not a scholar in a traditional sense and had limited knowledge of mystical teachings, but he attracted others with his piety and his enthusiasm for ecstatic prayer. The Besht taught that connection with God (*devekut) is the goal of religious life for all Jews and that prayer should be characterized by joy and humility. He attracted many disciples, some of whom went on to found their own study centers and gather followers. **See also ḤASIDISM: EUROPE.**

Babylon/Babylonia was a Mesopotamian city-state between the Tigris and Euphrates rivers (modern-day Al Hillah, Babil Province, *Iraq). Initially a small town, by the seventeenth century BCE, Babylon had become the capital of *Hammurabi's empire; it was around this time that Marduk became its chief diety. Babylonian mythology, literature, legal writings, and social customs had a significant impact on ancient Israel.

Babylon and the kingdom of *Judah were closely involved in the middle centuries of the first millennium BCE. Although Babylon was besieged by *Assyria throughout the seventh century BCE, it finally broke free from Assyrian rule in 626 BCE under Nabopolassar. Nebuchadnezzar II (604–561 BCE) inherited the Neo-Babylonian Chaldean Empire and led successful military campaigns against Judah in 597 and 586 BCE. He dissolved the monarchy, destroyed the *Jerusalem *Temple, and exiled much of Judah's population to Babylon. The *Babylonian Exile was a crucial event in the history and future of the Jewish people; the immediate pain of dislocation is reflected in *Psalm 137 and *Lamentations. The biblical books of *Ezekiel and *Daniel have a Babylonian setting, whereas the books of *Ezra and *Nehemiah detail the return of some of the exiles' descendants to Jerusalem. Although the enforced exile was relatively short-lived, ending with the conquest of Babylon by Cyrus the Great of *Persia in 539 BCE, a large and important Jewish community remained in *Diaspora in Babylon for centuries to come. **See also MESOPOTAMIA AND ANCIENT ISRAEL; NEAR EAST, ANCIENT; IRAN; IRAQ; TALMUD, BABYLONIAN.** ELIZABETH SHULMAN

Babylonian Exile. The Neo-Babylonians under King Nebuchadnezzar completed their destruction of *Judah by capturing *Jerusalem in 586 BCE and taking many captives and deporting them to *Mesopotamia. This period of removal from the land is known as the "exilic period," and the captivity in Mesopotamia as the "Babylonian Exile." Among the most important captives and deportees were the elites of the Jerusalem establishment: the *priests and the ruling class. Among those who were exiled were deposed King Jehoiachin and his family in 597 BCE, along with military personnel and craftsmen (2 Kgs 24: 15–16), as well as other survivors including deserters (2 Kgs 25:11) in 586, and still others in 582 (Jer 52:30). The tragic impact of these events on the nation is reflected in *Psalm 137 and *Lamentations; it is not known how many remained in the land. The exilic experience produced surprising results in a very short time, partly because the Neo-Babylonian Kingdom was replaced by the *Persian Empire in 539 when Cyrus defeated King Nabonidus of Babylonia.

Among the accomplishments of the exilic era were the editing of the *Pentateuch and of the Former *Prophets, learning to worship in small groups without a *Temple, and integrating successfully into a new society far away from the homeland while maintaining a distinctive identity. When Cyrus the Great of Persia announced in 538 that it would be possible for the dispersed to return to the Land of Israel under the governor Sheshbazzar (Ezra 1:8; 5:14), not many of the exiles responded. A more significant return began under the leadership of the Persian-appointed governor *Zerubbabel (Hag 1:1, 14) in 520 BCE. The Babylonian Exile did not end even then, however, since many Jews chose to stay in Mesopotamia; that group formed the nucleus of the community that produced the Babylonian *Talmud a millennium later. The "period" of the exile came to a conclusion in 515 BCE when the Second *Temple was rededicated, nearly seventy years after the destruction of Jerusalem. The many Jews who chose to remain in their newly acquired places of residence made the *Diaspora a permanent feature of Jewish life. **See also EZRA AND NEHEMIAH, BOOKS OF; IRAQ; and YEHUD; Maps 1, 4, 5**   ERIC MEYERS

Babylonian Talmud: See TALMUD, BABYLONIAN

Baeck, Leo: See LEO BAECK INSTITUTE

Baghdad: See IRAQ; Map 5

Bahir, Sefer Ha- (The Book of Brilliance), also known as the Midrash of Rabbi Neḥunia ben ha-Kanah (after the name of the second-century sage to whom the first paragraph in the book is attributed), is the earliest work of the *Kabbalah. It was written around 1185 by an anonymous author, probably in *Provence or northern *Spain. It comprises about two hundred paragraphs, attributed to various talmudic sages, and written in imitation of classical *midrash. It is the first work to present the divine powers as made up of ten layers, one above the other (although the number three also plays a prominent part). These powers are often pictured as an upside-down tree, whose roots are high above and whose branches extend toward the world. Exegeses of the names and shapes of the letters of the alphabet characterize many sections of the book; *satan* and *Samael, the source and nature of evil, are central subjects, as is the process of creation. The two main elements that justify characterizing *Sefer ha-Bahir* as the first kabbalistic treatise are the layered image of the divine pleroma (*malei*, "fullness") and the feminine characterization of the seventh or tenth divine power (*Shekhinah), neither of which appears in any previous Jewish work.

The author of the work reinterpreted many biblical verses, midrashic statements, and especially ancient Hebrew esoteric and mystical works, including *Sefer Yetzirah* (Book of Creation) and *hekhalot* treatises. It is unclear whether he used unknown sources to formulate the concepts of the ten-power pleroma and the feminine nature of one of those powers or if these are his original contributions. It was from these concepts, however, that the kabbalistic image of the ten *sefirot* developed in the next several decades.

Gershom *Scholem described the *Bahir* as an eruption of mythical thought within rabbinic Judaism and attributed its unique features – the *sefirot*, the feminine *Shekhinah*, and the divine tree – to influence from *gnostic-type thought. He did not decide whether the gnostic sources were originally Jewish, secretly transmitted from generation to generation, or the result of non-Jewish teachings. Attempts to find some influence from the contemporaneous Cathar heresy in southern *France have not been successful. It is uncertain whether the school of kabbalists that appeared in Provence at the end of the twelfth century and the beginning of the thirteenth used the ideas of the *Bahir* or whether the school was an independent and strikingly similar phenomenon. These two sources – the *Bahir* and the Provençal teachings – were united in the kabbalistic school of Gerona in the first half of the thirteenth century, which laid the foundations for classical Kabbalah (see MYSTICISM: HEKHALOT AND MERKAVAH LITERATURE).

For further reading, see G. Scholem, *The Origins of the Kabbalah* (1987); J. Dan and R. Kiener, *The Early Kabbalah* (1986); D. Abrams, *The Book Bahir* (1994).   JOSEPH DAN

Baḥia ben Joseph ibn Pakuda was a rabbinic judge in eleventh-century Saragossa, in what was then Muslim *Spain. A major figure in medieval Jewish *thought, Baḥia was the author of the first Jewish ethical treatise, *Ḥovot ha-Levavot* (Duties of the Heart), written in Arabic around 1080 and translated into Hebrew by Judah ibn Tibbon between 1161 and 1180. Deeply influenced by Sufi mystical teachings, Baḥia's approach contrasted with that of his predecessors and contemporaries, who focused more on the physical performance of the laws (duties of the body) than on inner observance. His book of ten chapters is a manual for the ascension of the spiritual self in the service of God. In these ten "gates," Baḥia provides a philosophical and theological basis for the unity and existence of *God, much of which was borrowed from the philosophical proofs of the Muslim *Kalam* and *Neoplatonism (see THOUGHT, MEDIEVAL); he addressed topics including divine service, the complexity of trust in God, *repentance, moderate asceticism, the importance of study to conquer the evil inclination, love and gratitude to God, and other critical articles of faith. Baḥia also composed liturgical *piyyutim* (such as *Barekhi Nafshi*), a penitential prayer, and a more recently recovered manuscript called "Reflections of the Soul." *Ḥovot ha-Levavot* has enjoyed enduring popularity in Judaism as a devotional work. A recent scholarly study is D. Lobel, *Philosophy and Mysticism in Bahya ibn Paquda's "Duties of the Heart"* (2006).

KATE FRIEDMAN

Balaam is a complex biblical figure who first appears in *Numbers 22 as a seer who is invited by Balak, king of *Moab, to curse the Israelites. Balaam, "son of Beor," is presented as in communication with God, and he sets out on his mission with apparent divine permission. However, in a satirical interlude, not unlike Jonah's encounter with the whale (see COMEDY AND COMEDIANS; JONAH), God sends an angel to block Balaam's path; Balaam cannot see the angel, but his ass does and steps off the road. When Balaam beats his animal, the ass answers in human speech, and Balaam finally perceives the heavenly messenger, who reprimands Balaam but allows him to proceed. After Balaam arrives at his destination he attempts to curse Israel, but he utters blessings instead (Num 22–24). According to *Deuteronomy 23:4–7 and *Joshua 24:9–10, God turned Balaam's curses into blessings. Numbers 31:16 blames Balaam for the seduction of Israelite men into immorality and idolatry by Midianite women at Baal Peor (Num 25:1–9); when the Israelites take revenge against the Midianites, Balaam is listed among those who are killed (Num 31:8).

The primary difficulty Balaam posed to later commentators was the contrast between his prophetic powers and his moral depravity. Numbers 22–24 presents Balaam in relatively neutral terms but other Hebrew *Bible (Josh 13:22; Neh 13:2) and *New Testament references (Rev 2:4; Jude 1:11; 2 Peter 2:15–16) vilify him. Thus, the Balaam who emerges from biblical literature is a puzzling combination of evil actions and undoubted visionary and even magical abilities. Early Qu'ranic commentaries attribute similar qualities to Balaam. Balaam's prophecy of a star emerging from Jacob (Num 24:17) was a further complication because both Jews (see BAR KOKHBA) and Christians gave it messianic meaning. Christian biblical exegetes often linked Balaam's prediction with the star followed by the Magi in Matthew 2:1–12.

In *rabbinic literature, Balaam came to represent the personification of the malice that the nations of the world directed toward Israel. Throughout rabbinic literature, the wicked Balaam advises the kings of the nations on how to destroy Israel. The Rabbis affirm that Balaam had prophetic powers and the facility to bless and curse effectively, but he used these gifts for evil and sorcery. According to *Numbers Rabbah* 14:20, God bestowed these special abilities on Balaam so that the nations of the world should not say, "Had we possessed a prophet like Moses we [too] would have worshiped the Holy One, blessed be He."

The 1967 discovery at Deir 'Alla in Jordan of fragmentary inscriptions on plaster in a *Canaanite dialect (published in 1976 by J. Hoftsijizer and G. van der Kooij as *Aramaic Texts from Deir 'Alla*) has directed new attention to Balaam. These inscriptions, dated to approximately 800 BCE, record "The chastisements of the book of Balaam, the son of Be'or, the man who sees the gods." The inscriptions include a number of striking parallels to the narrative in Numbers and indicate that Balaam was a well-known seer in the larger Canaanite cultural context.

For further reading, see J. R. Baskin, *Pharaoh's Counsellors: Job, Jethro and Balaam in Rabbinic and Patristic Tradition* (1983); and G. H. van Kooten and J. van Ruiten, eds., *The Prestige of the Pagan Prophet: Balaam in Judaism, Early Christianity and Islam* (2008).   JUDITH R. BASKIN

Balfour Declaration. This November 2, 1917, statement by *Britain's Foreign Secretary, Arthur James Balfour, was made in a letter to Lord Walter *Rothschild, a prominent British Zionist leader. It was a result, at least in part, of material support provided to the Allied cause in *World War I by Jewish soldiers and by the notable contribution of Dr. Chaim *Weizmann (1874–1952), who aided the British war effort through his discovery of a process for producing acetone (a vital element in gunpowder). Weizmann, a Russian Jewish immigrant to Great Britain and a leader of the World Zionist Organization, gained access to the highest levels of the British government and helped secure this declaration: that "His Majesty's Government view with favor the establishment in *Palestine of a national home for the Jewish people, and will use their best endeavors to facilitate the achievement of this object, it being clearly understood that nothing shall be done which may prejudice the civil and religious rights of existing non-Jewish communities in Palestine, or the rights and political status enjoyed by Jews in any other country." This statement was the first recognition of Jewish national aspirations and of *Zionism as a political movement by one of the "Great Powers" and was greeted with enormous elation in many sectors of the world Jewish community. In 1922 the League of Nations recognized "the historical connection of the Jewish people with Palestine" and incorporated the Balfour Declaration into its "Mandate for Palestine," which it awarded to Britain. See also BRITISH MANDATE OVER PALESTINE; ISRAEL, STATE OF: FOUNDING OF THE MODERN STATE; ZIONISM.

Balkans. The Balkans, the region of Europe incorporating *Greece, the former Yugoslav republics, and *Bulgaria, has been home to a Jewish population for millennia. At its peak at the end of the nineteenth century, the Jewish population of the region numbered about 250,000.

The region's Jews fall into three broad categories: *Romaniote, *Ashkenazic, and *Sephardic. The Romaniote is the oldest but smallest group; they are "indigenous" Jews whose origins in the region lie in the *Roman period, in the centuries before and after the start of the Common Era. According to legend, many of these early Jews first came to the Balkans as Roman slaves, but sources on early Romaniote history are scarce and the actual time and circumstances of Jewish arrival are difficult to establish.

Ashkenazic Jews first arrived in the Middle Ages, over the course of the thirteenth and fourteenth centuries, in the wake of expulsions from *England, *France, and *Germany. A later wave of Ashkenazim came toward the end of the eighteenth century, after the partition of *Poland and *Lithuania. Most of the migrating Ashkenazim, from both the Middle Ages and the later period, settled in the northern Balkans (that is, today's *Romania and *Hungary) but some moved further south into the Balkan peninsula.

The *Sephardim are the third and largest group of Balkan Jews; they came to the region in waves after the decrees of Jewish expulsion from *Spain (1492) and *Portugal (1497). In terms of the distribution of Jewish communities in the region, the northern portion of the former Yugoslavia, now Slovenia and Croatia, was historically dominated by Ashkenazim and the southern areas, which are today Serbia and Montenegro, were a center for Sephardim, with about 70,000 total in the region in the early twentieth century.

Overwhelmingly, the Jewish history of the Balkans is an *Ottoman history. It was during the Ottoman period that Jews settled in the region in greatest numbers, and this is when they enjoyed their greatest economic, cultural, and spiritual prosperity. After the expulsions from the Iberian Peninsula at the end of the fifteenth century, the Ottoman Empire famously encouraged Jews to settle in newly conquered Ottoman lands, mainly in the Balkans. The Ottoman Empire provided an environment in which Jews were treated with a high degree of tolerance and granted a number of privileges. Of course, the degrees of "tolerance" and "privilege" are widely debated, as is the extent to which Ottoman lands were truly a place of peaceful religious cohabitation; however, it is widely accepted that, compared to contemporaneous regimes, the Ottomans provided a significantly persecution-free haven.

The relative comfort of Jewish life in the region is reflected in the fact that Western Jewish culture reached one of its cultural and economic peaks in the Ottoman Balkans. It is in the Ottoman Balkans that a rich *Ladino literary tradition developed, with Ladino *printing and a widely varied Ladino press that was disseminated throughout the region. Balkan Jews also developed a powerful and hugely learned Sephardic rabbinic establishment and created a far-flung and influential trade network that was largely sustained by Jewish merchants.

Jewish fortunes were largely propelled by the Ottoman context; with its demise, Jewish security went into decline. After *World War I and the dismantling of the Ottoman Empire, the Balkan territories were carved into numerous smaller states, with Bulgaria, Greece, and Macedonia battling to gain control of the region's most important city, Salonika, where the plurality of the population was Sephardic. Despite unsuccessful efforts in the interwar period to turn Salonika and its hinterland into an autonomous international zone, Jewish interests were swept away in the region's fierce commitment to nation-building.

With the arrival of *World War II, close to half of Balkan Jewry was deported. Only Bulgaria, a German ally, did not permit deportation of its Jewish citizens. This was in response to popular protests and after Bulgaria agreed to the deportation of non-native Jews in Bulgarian-occupied zones. Although Bulgaria's 50,000 Jews survived the war, virtually all emigrated to *Israel after the creation of the state in 1948. At the end of the first decade of the twenty-first century, there are well under ten thousand Jews in the Balkans, once home to one of the most prosperous and intellectually accomplished Jewish communities in history.

Recent research includes E. Benbassa and A. Rodrigue, *The Jews of the Balkans: The Judeo-Spanish Community, 15th–20th Centuries* (1995); P. B. Gordiejew, *Voices of Yugoslav Jewry* (1998); and S. Schwartz, *Sarajevo Rose: A Balkan Jewish Notebook* (2005). **Map 9**   K. E. FLEMING

Baltic States. Lithuania, Latvia, and Estonia emerged as separate geographic and political entities in 1918. Jewish settlement in Lithuania goes back to the fourteenth century; in 1388 local Jews, also known as Litvaks, received their first charter from the Grand Duke of Lithuania. By the second half of the eighteenth century, the Commonwealth of *Poland-Lithuania was home to the world's largest Jewish population. Between 1623 and 1796 Lithuanian Jews regulated their affairs through the *Council of Lithuania (*Va'ad Medinat Lita*). The rabbinic leader and talmudic scholar Elijah, the *Vilna Gaon (1720–1797), was instrumental in halting the spread of *Hasidism in Lithuania. The territories of the former Grand Duchy of Lithuania were incorporated into the Russian *Pale of Settlement after the third partition of Poland in 1795. By 1897 the Jewish population of Lithuania was 753,000, 14.4% of the total population. In the nineteenth century *Vilna (Vilnius), the capital city, was a preeminent center of Jewish learning, informally referred to as the "Jerusalem of Lithuania"; the first government-sponsored rabbinical seminary in the Russian Empire opened in Vilna in 1847. The *Musar movement, which was highly influential in the non-Hasidic *yeshivah* world of *Eastern Europe, originated in Lithuania. Lithuania may also be considered the cradle of modern Jewish politics. Both the largest Jewish socialist organization, the *Bund, and the religious *Zionist party, *Mizrahi, were founded in Vilna, in 1897 and 1902 respectively.

Jews in Latvia were fewer in number and less homogeneous. As a center of foreign trade, the city of Riga attracted Jewish merchants, who tended to be well educated and spoke German and Russian. In 1914 the Latvian Jewish population was 185,000. The first Jewish communities in present-day Estonia were founded by former Jewish soldiers (cantonists) in the 1860s. At its peak, the Estonian Jewish population numbered 5,500. During World War I, the Russian Army expelled 240,000 Baltic Jews on charges of disloyalty.

The proportion of Jews in the general population was highest in interwar Lithuania (7.5%), followed by 5.3% in Latvia; Jews were never more than 0.4% of the population in Estonia. All three countries enacted a limited cultural

autonomy for their Jewish minorities, most extensively in Estonia in 1925. The Lithuanian authorities were particularly eager to cultivate Jewish voters in an attempt to recover Vilnius from Poland. The descent into authoritarianism (in Lithuania in 1926, in Estonia and Latvia in 1934) increased economic pressure on the Jews, who had hitherto controlled a substantial share of industry and foreign trade. Simultaneously, the Baltic governments cracked down on local fascist parties, which had pursued antisemitic agendas. Anti-Jewish *pogroms had broken out during the struggle for Vilnius in 1919; they recurred in 1939 when the city was incorporated into Lithuania. The Soviet occupation and annexation of the Baltic States in the summer of 1940 enabled Jews to enter government service in large numbers. Jews constituted more than 10% (17% in Lithuania) of the individuals deported by Russian security forces from the Baltic States on June 14, 1941.

Up to 15,000 Latvian Jews and three-quarters of Estonian Jews managed to flee to Russia before the arrival of German troops in July and August 1941. Partially instigated, but sometimes spontaneous, a series of pogroms rolled over Lithuania and Latvia (but not Estonia). One of the best documented, as well as most vicious, massacres took place on June 27 in Kaunas. However, most of the killing in 1941 was carried out, under the auspices of the German Security Police, by the Arājs Commando in Latvia and the Hamann Commando in Lithuania. Staffed with Latvians and Lithuanians, these two units murdered approximately 22,000 Jews in Latvia and 39,000 Jews in Lithuania. The largest mass executions of Jews took place on October 29 at 9th Fort in Kaunas (ca. 10,000) and on November 8 and December 12 at Rumbula near Riga (25,000). Later during the war, Lithuanian, Latvian, and to a lesser extent Estonian police battalions participated in atrocities in *Belorussia (White Russia) and *Ukraine. The 963 Jews who stayed in Estonia were apprehended and executed by the Estonian Security Police acting on German orders. Estonia thus became the first country in Europe proclaimed "free of Jews" at the notorious *Wannsee Conference in January 1942. By that time close to 90% of Latvian Jews and 80% of Lithuanian Jews were dead as well.

The remaining Baltic Jews were confined to *ghettos, most of which were established in the autumn of 1941. The largest were in Vilnius, Kaunas, Šiauliai, Riga, Daugavpils, and Liepāja. In late 1941 and 1942, the Germans deported 22,000 German and *Czech Jews to ghettos in Latvia and Estonia. The ghetto population was gradually reduced, and the ghettos themselves were liquidated on Himmler's order of June 21, 1943. About 10,000 Jews from the Vilnius and Kaunas ghettos were deported to Estonia where they were imprisoned in nineteen forced labor camps, working in synthetic oil production and building defenses. Some 45% of camp inmates survived, having been shipped to Stutthof concentration camp in Poland in the summer of 1944. The last mass execution on Baltic soil, of 1,634 Jews, took place at Klooga camp near Tallinn on September 19, 1944. The death toll of Jews in Estonia in 1941–44 is estimated at 8,500, with a survival rate of 37%. In Latvia, at the same time, 65% of the pre-war Jewish population or 61,000 Jews perished. The death rate among Lithuanian Jews was the highest anywhere in Nazi-occupied Europe, reaching 95% or 195,000. The "Righteous Among the Nations" database contains the names of 693 Lithuanian, 103 Latvian, and 3 Estonian rescuers.

The Latvian Jewish community was the largest (36,592 in 1959) and most vital of the Soviet Baltic Republics. Riga became a center of the *Soviet Union Jewish movement; nine defendants in the 1970 Leningrad hijacking trial were from Riga. In the second decade of the twenty-first century, approximately 3,200 Jews are living in Lithuania, 9,800 in Latvia, and fewer than 2,000 in Estonia. Major Jewish cultural institutions include the Vilna Gaon Jewish State Museum (est. 1988) and the Jewish Museum in Riga (est. 1990). In 2006 a new *synagogue was unveiled in downtown Tallinn, Estonia.

For further reading, see E. Mendelsohn, *The Jews of East Central Europe* (1983); idem, *On Modern Jewish Politics* (1993); J. Šteimanis, *History of Latvian Jews* (2002); A. Ezergailis, *The Holocaust in Latvia* (1996); A. Nikzentaitis et al., eds., *The Vanished World of Lithuanian Jews* (2004); and A. Weiss-Wendt, *Murder without Hatred* (2009). **Maps 8, 11**

ANTON WEISS-WENDT

Banking and Banking Houses. Jews began taking up banking and *money lending during the medieval period in areas under Christian and Muslim rule. In Europe, Jews' occupational choices were limited by injunctions against Jewish participation in crafts and agriculture. Simultaneously, ecclesiastic rulings prohibited Christians from charging interest on loans, although many continued to do so. Jews thus came to rely on loan banking and currency exchange as a source of income, often as a supplement to other commercial enterprises. Both women and men were engaged in banking, mostly on a modest scale, making small amounts of capital available to local merchants, craftsmen, and farmers.

On a far grander scale, the *Central European "*Court Jews" of the Early Modern period were generally attached to a specific absolutist regime. These wealthy Jews were retained to manage the royal treasury, facilitate tax collection, fund a ruling monarch's military operations, and import luxury items for his court. Jewish experience with transferable capital, their international connections with commercially active Jewish communities in cities throughout the *Diaspora, and their literacy and multilingualism gave them a decisive advantage in this early developmental phase of global capitalism. Modern banking houses, defined as independent transnational financial institutions engaged in capital investment, commerce, and industry, without attachment to any government, emerged during the Napoleonic Wars of the early nineteenth century. The *Rothschild family is generally credited with having established the first modern Jewish banking house. Founded in the 1780s by Mayer Amschel Rothschild, a Frankfurt-based coin dealer, the company was tapped by the British government to fund its anti-Napoleonic efforts. The House of Rothschild opened branches in London, Naples, *Vienna, and Paris; each office was run by one of Mayer's five sons. They were at the forefront of the creation of the international bond market, which enabled capitalists to subsidize government loans. The bond market made new capital available for national projects and proved fantastically profitable for the Rothschilds.

Although Jews did not hold a monopoly on European banking in the nineteenth century, many of the era's most prominent banking houses were founded and run by Jews. In Germany, the Oppenheim, Bleichröder, Bischoffsheim, Mendelssohn, and Warburg families each established successful firms, financing industrial development (and especially railroad construction) on nearly every continent. In England, the Goldsmid family firm predated the Rothschilds, and Ernest Cassel and Moses *Montefiore collaborated and competed with Nathan Rothschild's London office. In *Russia, the Günzberg family of *Saint Petersburg established commercial banks in Kiev and Odessa, as well as in their home city. A few of these bankers were granted hereditary titles of nobility, attaining status and access to circles of power unimaginable for the vast majority of European Jewry.

Jewish financial services played a role in events across the Atlantic as well. Haym Salomon, a Polish immigrant and commission merchant in Great Britain's North American colonies, became a leading financier of the revolutionary cause. He helped the Continental Congress procure loans from *France and subscribed a great deal of his own capital to American nationalizing efforts. It is said that Salomon was never able to collect on those debts and died penniless.

In the nineteenth century, partly as a result of increased German Jewish immigration to the United States, American Jewish banking practices came to resemble the European model. The Seligman brothers, the Lehman brothers, August Belmont, Abraham Kuhn, and Solomon Loeb, all immigrants from *Central Europe, invested in nineteenth-century American industrial and commercial expansion. Although some of these bankers created their vast fortunes from nothing, others began their American careers with significant backing; Belmont, for instance, arrived in North America as an agent of the Rothschilds.

The social practices of these most prominent Jewish bankers varied. Endogamy, which had been practiced by Europe's Court Jews, from whom some nineteenth-century Jewish bankers were descended, was common. Many Jewish banking firms sought to increase their available capital by creating kin relationships with other Jewish houses, fortifying their connections to one another and creating an international and close-knit Jewish socioeconomic elite. Others, however, married out of the Jewish faith or converted to Christianity. *Philanthropy and advocacy were other common undertakings. Some Jewish bankers used their access to power to press for the *emancipation of Jewish communities from occupational and residential restrictions. They also used their personal fortunes to relieve poverty, fund the construction of *synagogues, and underwrite Jewish entrepreneurial endeavors.

Jewish bankers, in their roles both real and imagined, became central characters in European and American *antisemitic rhetoric. Their rapid accumulation of wealth engendered widespread resentment and fed long-standing Gentile suspicions of Jewish financial practices. The Rothschild name was frequently cited in the nineteenth century by those who saw Jews in positions of power as a threat to the public good. The family was collectively referred to as "King of the Jews" and despised by many as bankrollers of tyrants. The role of privately held Jewish banking houses declined in the early decades of the twentieth century, as governments increasingly relied on national or central banks.

For further reading, see S. W. Baron, A. Kahan et al., "Banking and Bankers," and "Moneylending," in *Economic History of the Jews,* ed. N. Gross (1975); M. Keil, "Public Roles of Jewish Women in Fourteenth and Fifteenth-Century Ashkenaz: Business, Community and Ritual," in C. Cluse, ed., *The Jews of Europe in the Middle Ages* (2004); N. Ferguson, *The House of Rothschild: Money's Prophets, 1798–1848* (1998); and **see also COMMERCE: MEDIEVAL AND EARLY MODERN EUROPE; COMMERCE: MODERN EUROPE (1700–1900);** and **UNITED STATES: ECONOMIC LIFE.**

MARNI DAVIS

Bar Kokhba. The Bar Kokhba Revolt, sometimes called the Second Jewish War, took place between 132–135/6 CE and was the final act of Jewish opposition to *Roman rule in the Land of Israel. A large number of rebels joined together under the leadership of Simon bar Koseva; he was also known, in writings of the *Church Fathers, by the *Aramaic term *Bar Kokhba,* "son of a star," based perhaps on messianic understandings of one of *Balaam's prophecies in Numbers 24:17. Bar Kokhba formed some sort of independent political entity for the rebellion's duration; it had ruling authorities, minted coins (secondary minting over Roman coins), and leased land. Roman victory was achieved only after the Emperor Hadrian sent his most senior general, Julius Severus, the governor of *Britain, to Judea, as well as army units from Pannonia (modern *Hungary).

No ancient literary or historical work provides a first-hand account of the revolt; rather, partial and separate pieces of evidence, sometimes contradictory and sometimes rhetorical, are found in *talmudic literature, the works of Roman historians, the writings of the Church Fathers, and in *Samaritan chronicles. Exceptional archaeological discoveries from this period include Bar Kokhba's letters, discovered in caves in the Judean desert. These caves, including tunnels and underground hideouts, were used throughout the revolt and served as a refuge for the rebels in the war's final days. Also important are numismatic finds, inscriptions on milestones and tombs, as well as research into Roman roads, the fortifications of Beitar, the last stronghold of the rebels, and the Roman camps around it.

According to the Roman historian Cassius Dio (d. ca. 230), in his book on the history of Rome, the direct cause of the rebellion was Emperor Hadrian's decision, when he passed through *Judea in 130 on his way to *Egypt, to reconstruct *Jerusalem as a pagan city with a temple to Jupiter. He also planned to change its name to Aelia Capitolina – Aelia after his own name, Hadrianus Publius Aelius, and Capitolina in honor of Jupiter, whose temple was located on the Capitoline hill at Rome. The revolt did not break out spontaneously; preparations took place over two years, while Hadrian was in the East.

Bar Kokhba himself was more than a simple army commander. His coins designate him *nasi,* and he also signed his letters with this title, whose meaning is near to "king." In fact, *nasi* may indicate a status above that of a king, for the prophet *Ezekiel uses this term for the king who will rule at the end of days. According to the Jerusalem *Talmud, when Rabbi *Akiva saw Bar Kokhba, he said, "This is the King *Messiah" (JT *Ta'anit* iv 68d). The attribution of messianic qualities to Bar Kokhba can be explained in two ways; the first possibility is that he was seen as an eschatological messiah; that is, a redeemer and savior with a divine and supernatural nature. The second, more realistic option is that "messiah" ("anointed one") is simply a title indicating the kingship of Bar Kokhba as an earthly general and leader. The facts that the revolt did not break out spontaneously, that Bar Kokhba's letters deal with small aspects of day-to-day life in different military units, and his style of leadership tilt the balance toward the second possibility. Decisive evidence for this explanation appears in a parallel passage to the reference from the Jerusalem Talmud cited earlier. After Rabbi Akiva's declaration that Bar Kokhba was the messiah, the *midrash compilation *Lamentations Rabbah* 2.4 relates, "And what did Bar Kokhba do? He received stone missiles on his knee and returned them and killed several people, and this is what Rabbi Akiva was talking about here." In other words, the *messianism of Bar Kokhba was expressed in his exceptional physical strength. Bar Kokhba did not belong to rabbinical circles, but it is clear from his letters that he took care to observe the commandments. He appears as an aggressive general and ruler, involved in the everyday life of his army units. Christian sources describe Bar Kokhba as a murderer and robber and at the same time credit him with supernatural miracles and deeds. It seems unlikely that this literature reflects authentic traditions; instead, it is intended to blacken his reputation and present him as a sort of anti-Christ.

Most of the evidence and finds relate to the area of Judea, where the main part of the Bar Kokhba revolt likely took place. This is reasonable, because the revolt broke out over Jerusalem and its main goal was to free Jerusalem from the Romans. Scholars are divided over whether the revolt also extended to *Galilee and perhaps even to Trans-Jordan. Similarly, there is debate over whether Jerusalem was conquered by the rebels, because almost no coins of the revolt have been discovered in Jerusalem. However, the contemporaneous historian Appian relates that the city fell into the hands of the rebels and the Roman army had to conquer it again.

The last rebel stronghold was Beitar, located eleven kilometers southwest of Jerusalem on the site of the present-day Arab village called Battir. Bar Kokhba's death there and the fall of the settlement after a siege marked the end of the revolt. The mound or tell next to the village is called Hirbet al-Yehud by the Arabs. An epilogue to the revolt was the attempt by Bar Kokhba's men in the area of Ein Gedi to flee and take refuge in the barely accessible caves found in the rock crevices around the wadis (dry river beds) descending from the Judean desert to the Dead Sea.

After the revolt, the Romans imposed repressive legislation on the Jews of the Land of Israel in general and on the area of Judea in particular. The reactions of the *Rabbis and the people varied: Some tried to carry out forbidden *commandments with modifications or in secret; others contravened the legislation in public and were ready to be killed. Some also left Judaism altogether. **See also ELISHA BEN ABUYA; JEWISH WAR, SECOND; MARTYDOM.**

AHARON OPPENHEIMER

Bar Mitzvah, literally "son of the commandments," refers to the legal coming of age of a Jewish boy at thirteen. Now an adult according to Jewish law, the boy has responsibility for his own transgressions and is obligated to fulfill all applicable commandments (*mitzvot). He may count in a quorum for communal worship (*minyan) and lead a congregation in prayer. To demonstrate the change in legal status, it became customary for boys to fulfill publicly a ritual obligation on behalf of a congregation. This usually involved a *Torah honor and/or reading from the Torah scroll. In some communities boys would also deliver learned speeches. Parents would generally follow the rite with a festive meal. These celebrations became so lavish in some communities that sumptuary laws were enacted by rabbis to limit spending. This *life-cycle ritual is so important in the mind of Jewish parents that it has been used as leverage to require a minimum of five years of religious *education by the Reform and Conservative movements (see JUDAISM entries). **See also BAT MITZVAH.**   RELA MINTZ GEFFEN

Baraita (Aramaic for "external") refers to a legal tradition from the era of the *Tannaim that is not preserved in the *Mishnah. Many *baraitot* are compiled in the *Tosefta; others appear in halakhic *midrash collections.

Baraita De-Niddah is a text mentioned by several medieval authors. In 1890, Chaim Horowitz published a manuscript that opened with the statement, "This is the *Baraita de-Niddah*," together with shorter, related texts he had found in print and in manuscripts. The long text published by Horowitz (*BdN/a*) is peculiar. It discusses at length possible consequences to descendants of couples who are not meticulous regarding the laws of the *niddah (the legislation pertaining to a husband's separation from his menstruating wife), as well as the rewards for those who are. *BdN/a* insists that strict observance of these laws will ensure clever, healthy, and beautiful sons, whereas negligence may result in offspring deficient in body and spirit. *BdN/a* also discusses ways in which the menstruating woman (*niddah*) transmits impurity via breath, nails, hair, saliva, touch, clothes, food, and the like. In many areas, *BdN/a* is more severe than the canonical talmudic literature; it tries to relate itself to an ancient authority by claiming links to the more rigorous teachings of the school of Shammai against the school of *Hillel, the tradition generally endorsed by talmudic literature.

Horowitz was unsure of the authenticity of the text and of its origins. In *Guide of the Perplexed* (3:47), Maimonides had declared that practices similar to those in *BdN/a* were non-Jewish. Horowitz finally opted for a rabbinic origin, concluding that *BdN/a* was composed around the fourth century CE in *Palestine. He based this attribution on the fact that all the sages mentioned were Palestinian and that the latest among them was Rabbi Tanḥuma of the fourth century. However, the language and the content of *BdN/a* strongly indicate that it is a later composition, likely from the later part of the first millennium CE. The core was probably composed in Palestine (which might explain its lack of *Aramaic and its fidelity to Palestinian sages) or at least by an author (or authors) with strong Palestinian ties, perhaps from other centers of Hebrew scholarship such as *Italy. Further research is necessary to ascertain *BdN/a*'s precise date and the location of its composition.

Some scholars have suggested that *BdN/a* was a direct influence on medieval authorities regarding the laws of *niddah*, but this cannot be proven. Except perhaps for some short quotations, this work was not widely accessible. Its direct impact was therefore, at best, limited. It is possible,

however, to say that the spirit of *BdN/a* – that severity with regard to the *niddah* is always the best approach – did influence later authors, even if they had never seen *Baraita de-Niddah* itself.

For further reading, see E. Marienberg, *La Baraita de-Niddah: Un texte juif pseudo-talmudique sur les lois religieuses au sujet de la menstruation, traduit de l'hébreu et présenté* (2011).
                                                EVYATAR MARIENBERG

Barak, Ehud (b. 1942 as Ehud Brog) served as Israel's tenth prime minister between 1999 and 2001. Born on Kibbutz Mishmar Hasharon, Barak changed his name when he joined the Israel Defense Forces in 1959. During a thirty-five-year military career, he served as commander of an elite unit, tank brigade commander, armored division commander, and head of the Military Intelligence Directorate; he is among Israel's most highly decorated soldiers. In 1991 he was appointed Chief of the General Staff. After his election as prime minister, Barak withdrew Israeli troops from Lebanon in 2000. In the same year, he undertook peace negotiations with the Palestine Liberation Organization, participating in the ultimately unsuccessful negotiations at Camp David under the leadership of President Bill Clinton. His party was defeated in elections held in 2001. Barak regained leadership of the Labor Party in 2007 and holds the role of Defense Minister in the coalition government elected in 2009.   ELIZABETH SHULMAN

Baron de Hirsch Fund, one of several philanthropic entities to facilitate the emigration of Eastern European Jews, was created by German financier and railroad magnate Baron Maurice de Hirsch (1831–1896). Founded in 1891, the organization focused on Jewish immigrants in *New York City, funding a range of Americanizing efforts, including English-language classes for children and adults, classes in hygiene for mothers, and technical and industrial training opportunities. The Fund is best remembered for its *agricultural colonies; it was the Baron's hope that Jewish immigrants would leave the crowded Lower East Side for rural climes and choose a life of farming over trade-oriented occupations. The Fund established a Jewish farming community and agricultural college in Woodbine, New Jersey, and organized dozens of Jewish farming associations in the Northeastern and Midwestern United States, as well as in *Argentina and *Canada. Few of these farming communities and associations lasted beyond a generation or two.
                                                        MARNI DAVIS

Baseball: See SPORTS, UNITED STATES: BASEBALL

Basketball: See SPORTS, UNITED STATES: BASKETBALL

Bat Mitzvah, literally "daughter of the commandment," refers to the legal age of twelve and a half, at which time a Jewish girl is considered an adult. Originally linked to puberty, it marked the moment when the responsibility for a girl's transgressions passed to her and when she became obligated to observe *commandments incumbent on Jewish women. No public ceremony was linked to this rite of passage until the early twentieth century in America when Rabbi Mordecai *Kaplan decided that the eldest of his four daughters should mark the occasion in his *synagogue. Since then Bat Mitzvah has become a parallel rite to *Bar Mitzvah in the more liberal movements of *Judaism, with girls having *Torah honors and leading the congregation in prayer. Among the Modern Orthodox, girls may give learned speeches at a festive meal or have a Torah honor in an all-women's service. Because few women had the opportunity to celebrate a public coming of age ceremony before the 1960s, adult Bat Mitzvah has been instituted in many Reform and Conservative synagogues. Often, after several years of study a group of women conduct the *Sabbath service for their congregation.   RELA MINTZ GEFFEN

Bathsheba was the daughter of Eliam (or Ammiel, 1 Chron 3:5) and wife of Uriah the Hittite. 2 Samuel 11–12 describes how King *David invited Bathsheba into a sexual relationship while her husband Uriah the Hittite was absent, fighting with David's army. Bathsheba conceived a child and David recalled Uriah to *Jerusalem, attempting to cover up the affair. When Uriah refused the opportunity to sleep at home, David engineered his death in battle. After David's marriage to Bathsheba, the *prophet Nathan delivered *God's rebuke through a parable about a wealthy man who took a poor man's sole ewe lamb; Nathan predicted that henceforth "the sword shall never depart from your House." Although David repented, his prayers that God spare the child conceived in adultery were unsuccessful. Bathsheba's second son is *Solomon, who is "favored" by God (2 Sam 11–12). 1 Kings 1:11–31 details Nathan's and Bathsheba's interventions with the dying David to ensure that Solomon would succeed to the throne rather than his half-brother Adonijah.   KATE FRIEDMAN

Bavli: See TALMUD, BABYLONIAN

Begin, Menachem (1913–1992). Born in Brest-Litovsk, *Poland, Begin attended a *Mizrachi (*Orthodox *Zionist) Hebrew school and then a Polish gymnasium (high school). He earned a law degree from Warsaw University in 1935. A leader of Betar, the youth movement associated with the Zionist Revisionist movement, Begin traveled extensively on the organization's behalf. In 1939 he became head of the Betar movement in Poland. At the start of *World War II, Begin was arrested and held in Russian prisons and labor camps until he was released under the Sikorski-Mayski Agreement. In 1941, he arrived in *Palestine and soon began working with Irgun Zvati Leumi (Etzel); by 1944 he was leading the organization's operations against the *British Mandate over Palestine. When the State of *Israel was established, Begin agreed to disband the Irgun and deploy its fighters and weapons to the Israel Defense Forces. This was accomplished, although not without conflict with the new Prime Minister David *Ben-Gurion. In August of 1948, Begin and other Irgun leaders formed the Ḥerut party. In 1965, Ḥerut and the Liberal Party were combined into the Gahal party with Begin as its leader. In June 1967, Begin joined the Government of National Unity and served as Minister without Portfolio for more than three years. In 1973, Begin agreed to Ariel *Sharon's plan to combine Gahal and other opposition parties to form the Likud party. In 1977, Likud became the largest party in the Knesset, and Begin became prime minister of the State of Israel. With the help of his cabinet, Begin negotiated the Camp David Accords and signed the Israel–Egypt Peace Treaty in 1979. He was later

awarded the Nobel Peace Prize for his role in the negotiations, although the Likud party was critical of his willingness to cede territory. In 1981, he ordered the destruction of Osirak, Iraq's nuclear reactor. He authorized the Israel Defense Forces to invade Lebanon in 1982, hoping for a short involvement that would force the Palestine Liberation Organization out of southern Lebanon. However, there was no quick victory, and support for the war waned, particularly after the Sabra and Shatila Massacre in 1982. Begin retired from politics in 1983 and was succeeded as prime minister by Yitzhak Shamir. **See also ISRAEL, STATE OF: FOUNDING OF THE MODERN STATE; ISRAEL, STATE OF: MILITARY AND PARAMILITARY BODIES; ISRAEL, STATE OF: POLITICAL PARTIES.**   ELIZABETH SHULMAN

Beilis Trial. The 1913 blood libel trial of Menaḥem Mendel Beilis (1874–1934) in Kiev was one of the most notorious episodes of *antisemitism in Imperial *Russia.

In March 1911 the body of a thirteen-year-old boy, Andrei Iushchinskii, was discovered in a cave. He had died from multiple stab wounds. A gang of thieves had committed the murder because they feared that the boy, their lookout, would report their activities to the police.

Mendel Beilis, a clerk at a brick factory on whose property Iushchinskii's body was found, was arrested on suspicion of the murder in July 1911. Beilis was identified as the "man with the black beard," whom witnesses claimed they saw with Iushchinskii. Beilis was brought to trial in September and October 1913. The indictment charged that he had committed the murder "out of religious fanaticism, for ritual purposes," to harvest the maximum possible quantity of blood from the body so that it might be consumed.

Beilis was indisputably the victim of a web of political intrigues among tsarist officials. Some sought to win favor with Nicholas II; others were responding to pressure from antisemitic journalists and rabble-rousers. Yet, there is little evidence of a deliberate conspiracy at the highest levels of the tsarist state. The prosecution's case rested on hearsay, dubious "expert" opinion about the Jews' blood-drinking proclivities, and a number of witnesses who were either rabid antisemites or deranged. The defense boasted some of the finest lawyers in late Imperial Russia, and they had no difficulty in proving Beilis's innocence and the guilt of the criminal band who had actually committed the murder. As the prosecution's case unraveled, even some leading antisemites spoke out against the trial as a farce besmirching Russia's reputation. Although the jury of mostly peasants acquitted Beilis of the crime, they upheld the prosecution's indictment that Iushchinskii had probably been killed to harvest his blood. Thus, the possibility was left open that some Jews, if not Beilis, did indeed commit *ritual murder to collect the blood of Christian children. After his acquittal, Beilis emigrated first to *Palestine and then, in 1920, to the *United States where he lived until his death. **See also RITUAL MURDER ACCUSATION.**

DANIEL BEER

Beit Din, literally, "house of law," is the Hebrew term for a court of law (see also COURTS). The plural form is *batei din*. Traditionally, *batei din* have been made up of rabbis or other scholars of Jewish law. In *Second Temple times, there was a supreme *beit din* of seventy-one sages called the *Sanhedrin, lesser Sanhedrin courts of twenty-three judges, and minor courts of three adjudicators. Today, one only finds courts of three. The contemporary courts generally convene on civil or family matters. In the past, criminal and capital crimes were handled in the larger twenty-three- and seventy-one-member courts. Even in rabbinic times, the courts of three could be staffed by people who were not rabbis. Since these courts dealt with less serious matters, the determination was made that the flow of commerce required available adjudication, which would be made easier by allowing laypeople to serve.

In contemporary Jewish life, cities with a large Jewish population both in *Israel and the *Diaspora have permanently constituted rabbinic courts. These courts are constituted as binding arbitration panels in places like the *United States and *Britain. Both litigants accept the decision of the court as determinative. In Israel, the authority of the courts is given by the government. Those who do not prefer to use a sitting court may use a method known by its acronym, pronounced *zabla*. Under this system, each litigant chooses one judge, and the two judges agree on the third. The parties then sign a binding arbitration agreement to accept this panel's decision.

Proceedings in a rabbinic court are usually much quicker (usually no more than one or two days) and generally much less expensive than those in secular courts. Although a litigant may have a representative *(to'ein)*, the participants generally are encouraged to speak, and rules of evidence are much looser than in secular courts. Independent evaluations have shown that these proceedings generally produce fair and equitable results. This is particularly true because a *beit din* can be empaneled to decide the case in a way that allows for each side to score a partial victory. The decision will reflect how well each side has made its case instead of simply determining that one litigant is the winner and the other the loser. For example, if it is appropriate, the *beit din* may allow for a 75/25 split of disputed property. This practice is called *peshara karov le'din*.　　　BARRY FREUNDEL

Belarus: See BELORUSSIA

Bel and the Dragon is an apocryphal addition to the book of *Daniel, found in the Greek *Bible and other versions; it consists of two stories. In the first, Daniel proves that the offerings given to the statue of Bel are consumed by the priests, not by the god, and he causes the sacred snake to burst by feeding it a lethal mixture. In the second story, Daniel is cast into the lions' den, as in Daniel 6, but *Habakkuk is transported from *Judea by the hair of his head to bring Daniel a stew. In the end, the king acknowledges the *God of Daniel.

These stories were composed in either *Hebrew or *Aramaic. There is a medieval Aramaic text, but its authenticity is disputed. The apocryphal work is not necessarily dependent on canonical Daniel, although it shares the motif of the lions' den. For further reading, see J. J. Collins, *Daniel: A Commentary on the Book of Daniel* (1993), 405–439.
　　　　　　　　　　　　　　　　　　　　　JOHN J. COLLINS

Belgium. The earliest written evidence of Jews in Belgium dates from 1261 when Duke Henry III ordered all Jews and usurers expelled from the Brabant province. Christian efforts at forced conversion in 1309 led to the murders of many Jews, but under the protection of Duke John II the

community was rebuilt and grew when expelled Jews from other areas of Europe began settling there. The medieval community was largely destroyed by persecutions prompted by the outbreak of the Black Death in 1348 and by *host desecration charges in 1370. In the sixteenth century, *conversos* from *Spain and *Portugal settled in Antwerp and played an important role in building the diamond, sugar, and banking industries. By the seventeenth century, Antwerp Jews held synagogue services in secret and were often visited by Jewish merchants from *Amsterdam.

After Belgium came under Austrian rule in 1713 many *Ashkenazi Jews settled there; subsequent French (1794–1814) and Dutch (1814–1830) rulers further enhanced the freedom and autonomy of Belgian Jews. When Belgium declared its independence in 1831, it instituted religious *emancipation, and the Jewish community flourished, particularly in Antwerp and Brussels. The Jewish population in Belgium numbered between 65,000 and 75,000 in 1940 when the country was invaded by *Nazi *Germany. Most were Jews from other European countries who had found refuge in Belgium after World War I. Non-Jews made unusual efforts to hide Jews during the German occupation; perhaps as many as 25,000 Jews were hidden in Belgian homes. At the same time, some Belgian officials actively cooperated with *Nazi directives to register, round up, and deport Jews. By the time Belgium was liberated from the *Nazis in September 1944, about 44% of its Jewish population had been deported to concentration camps, primarily *Auschwitz, and approximately 25,000 perished. After World War II, the Jewish community in Belgium slowly rebuilt, and the government remained supportive. At the end of the first decade of the twenty-first century, about 40,000 Jews live in Belgium; the largest communities are in Antwerp and Brussels.

For further reading, see D. Michman, *Belgium and the Holocaust: Jews, Belgians, Germans* (1998).

　　　　　　　　　　　　　　　　　　　　　ELIZABETH SHULMAN

Belorussia (BELARUS; WHITE RUSSIA). Referred to by Jews as Raysn (in *Yiddish), Belorussia was part of *Poland-*Lithuania from the fourteenth to the eighteenth century and was annexed to the *Russian Empire between 1772 and 1795. In 1920, eastern parts of Belorussia were brought under Soviet rule and became the Belorussian Soviet Socialist Republic (BSSR). The Republic of Belarus was established in 1991 after the collapse of the Union of Soviet Socialist Republics (USSR).

Jews first settled in the towns of Belorussia during the fourteenth century. The Lithuanian Grand Duke Vitautas granted charters to the Jews of Brest (Brisk) and Grodno as early as 1388 and 1389, respectively. The Jewish communities of Pinsk (1506) and Nowogrodek (1539) were among the first to be founded. In the eighteenth century, 40% of Lithuanian Jewry lived in the territory of Belorussia; the largest and most important communities were those of Minsk, Pinsk, and Shklov. During the nineteenth century Jews formed the majority of the population in the main cities of the region (52.3% in Minsk, 52.4% in Vitebsk, 74.2% in Pinsk, and 54.8% in Gomel). They engaged primarily in commerce, handicrafts, tax collection, lease-holding, small trade, and peddling; the vast majority were relatively impoverished.

Belorussia became an important center for Jewish religious scholarship. The first *yeshivot* were founded in Brest and Grodno at the end of the sixteenth century, and the distinguished talmudist I. Heilperin (1660–1746) taught in late-seventeenth-century Minsk. Two of the most celebrated *yeshivot* in Eastern Europe were located in Volozhin and Mir. At the end of the 1800s, Jeroham Judah Leib Perelman (1835–1896), known as the "great scholar of Minsk," taught in the *Blumkes kloyz*, one of the largest *yeshivot* in Minsk. Although the "*litvish*" (Lithuanian) tradition, which took a rational approach, was dominant, one of the fathers of *Hasidism, Schneur *Zalman of Liady, founded Habad Hasidism in Belorussia.

Jewish Enlightenment, the *Haskalah*, penetrated the larger urban centers of Belorussia in the mid-nineteenth century; by the end of the 1800s, modern Jewish political movements (in particular, the socialist *Bund and *Zionism) had emerged in Minsk, Bobruisk, Gomel, and Vitebsk. In 1902, the Second Conference of Russian Zionists was held in Minsk. Bundists and Labor Zionists established self-defense organizations in every town of the region to protect Jews during the wave of *pogroms, especially after the 1903 Gomel pogrom.

Under Soviet rule, the Jews of Belorussia were granted unprecedented political freedoms, civil rights, and opportunities for upward mobility. At the same time Jewish communities were disbanded and all Jewish political parties dismantled. The Jewish sections of the *Communist Party (*Evsektsiia*) systematically persecuted Jewish religious and Zionist groups, closing down *synagogues and pursuing religious leaders. They also supported the establishment of communist institutions with a Soviet orientation that functioned in the Yiddish language; these included schools, newspapers, clubs, theaters, and courts. Belorussia was the only republic in the USSR whose constitution guaranteed an official status to Yiddish as one of the state languages. However, Yiddish institutions were gradually closed down in the late 1930s and by the late 1940s had been liquidated.

In the eastern part of Belorussia, which was under Soviet rule, Jewish social and economic life remained unchanged, as Jews continued to engage in commerce and crafts. Unlike the Jews of Soviet Belorussia, the Jews of western Belorussia (under Polish rule) experienced social discrimination but enjoyed more cultural freedoms. They established the *Tarbut* network of Hebrew-language schools, as well as several Zionist youth movements (*Betar, Ha-Shomer ha-Tzair*, etc.). Jewish religious life continued to flourish here. In 1931, 9.7% of the total population of western Belorussia was Jewish. In September 1939, western Belorussia was annexed to the USSR. Religious activities and Zionist groups were liquidated, and the Hebrew-language schools were turned into Soviet Yiddish schools.

After the German invasion of the USSR in June 1941, the *Einsatzgruppen* B, under the command of General A. Nebe, and in collaboration with Lithuanian, *Ukrainian, and Belorussian nationalists, identified, concentrated, and killed the great majority of the Jews of Belorussia, as well as the thousands of German, Austrian, and Czech Jews who had been deported there. About 10,000 Jews succeeded in escaping from the Minsk ghetto (established on July 20, 1941), a proportion without parallel in the history of the

*Holocaust (H. Smolar, *The Minsk Ghetto: Soviet-Jewish Partisans against the Nazis* [1989]).

According to the 1959 census, there were 150,000 Jews living in the BSSR (1.9% of the total population); in 1970, the Jewish population was 148,011. With the emergence of the *Soviet Union Jewish revival movement in the 1970s and 1980s, many Jews became active in the struggle for the right to repatriate to *Israel, and thousands emigrated to Israel, North America, and *Germany. In 1999, there were 10,141 Jews living in the Republic of Belarus. **Map 11**

ELISSA BEMPORAD

Bełżec was one of three temporary *Nazi death camps (the others were *Sobibór and *Treblinka) that were established in response to a 1941 directive, *Aktion Reinhard*, an SS program designed to murder the remaining 2.3 million Jews in the General Government area of occupied *Poland. Located eighty-five miles southeast of Lublin, Bełżec was chosen for its remoteness, access to rail lines, and close proximity to Jewish populations in the General Government and occupied parts of the *Soviet Union. The Germans, who had built a small forced labor camp for Jews in Bełżec, began construction of the death camp in late 1941. Christian Wirth, Bełżec's commandant, constructed permanent gas chambers because he did not like bottled carbon monoxide gas and wanted to use diesel engines in his gas chambers.

Once the gassings began in late February 1942, Wirth did everything possible to delude the arriving victims into thinking that they were being sent to a forced labor camp in Germany. He also moved victims quickly to the gas chambers and counted on the confusion and shock of arrival to deter outbursts and protests. It normally took between twenty and thirty minutes to kill everyone in the gas chambers. After the chambers were cleared of carbon monoxide, the bodies were put in mass graves that were covered with small layers of dirt. Between February and December 1942, 600,000 Jews were murdered there. By the end of December 1942, the Germans had killed most of the Jews in the General Government and ordered Bełżec closed. The camp was demolished and converted into a farm to prevent the villagers from plundering the area. The farm was given to one of the camp's former Ukrainian guards. **See also HOLOCAUST; HOLOCAUST CAMPS AND KILLING CENTERS; HOLOCAUST MEMORIALS.**

DAVID M. CROWE

Ben-Gurion, David (1886–1973) was the central figure of the *Yishuv administration throughout the period of the *British Mandate and served as prime minister in *Israel's first decades (1948–54; 1955–63). Born David Green in *Poland into an ardently Zionist family, Ben-Gurion became a teacher in *Warsaw in 1904 where he joined the socialist Zionist organization, *Poalei Zion*; he immigrated to *Palestine in 1906 and worked on a collective agricultural settlement. Expelled from Palestine by the Ottomans in 1915 for his political activities, Ben-Gurion advocated for *Zionism in the United States. In 1919, after serving in the Jewish Legion, a unit of the British army created by Vladimir *Jabotinsky, he returned to Palestine, now under British rule. In the 1920s Ben-Gurion worked in Labor Zionist politics (see ISRAEL, STATE OF: POLITICAL PARTIES) and helped establish the Histadrut, the national federation of trade unions. As Secretary General of the Histadrut, Ben-Gurion oversaw the

Jewish economy in *British Mandate Palestine and represented the Histadrut in the World Zionist Organization and the Jewish Agency (both of which he chaired in 1935). Associated with Ben-Gurion in the *Yishuv* leadership and in his tumultuous years as Israel's leader, beginning in 1948, were other prominent figures such as Levi Eshkol (1895–1969), Golda *Meir (1898–1978), and Yitzhak Ben-Zvi (1884–1963). With these colleagues and others, Ben-Gurion built the institutions necessary for the new state, oversaw the settlement of hundreds of thousands of immigrants from Europe and the Middle East, and set the tone for Israel's relations with other countries. Revered as the "Father of the State of Israel," Ben-Gurion spent his retirement years at Kibbutz Sde Boker in the Negev, where he died in 1973. For a recent appraisal of Ben-Gurion and his larger context, see S. Aronson, *David Ben-Gurion and the Jewish Renaissance* (2010).

Bene Israel ("Children of Israel"), *India's largest Jewish community, numbered 28,000 before Indian independence in 1947. They claim that their ancestors were shipwrecked off the Konkan coast as early as 175 BCE. The survivors took up the occupation of oil pressing, but, as *shanwar telis* (Saturday oilmen), refrained from work on the Sabbath. When discovered by David Rahabi (possibly in the eighteenth century), the *Bene Israel* only remembered the *shema* prayer, which proclaims divine unity. They observed *dietary laws, *circumcision, and many Jewish *festivals, but their religious customs and beliefs were also influenced by local Hindu and Muslim practices.

From the eighteenth century on, the British enlisted members of the *Bene Israel* in their armies and encouraged them to move out of the villages to the metropolis of Bombay (today Mumbai) and to other urban centers in the Indian subcontinent. A relatively large number of *Bene Israel* community members pursued higher education and contributed to Indian cultural life. After the establishment of the State of *Israel in 1948, the majority began to emigrate there. In Israel, their Jewishness was questioned, but after a 1964 sit-down strike, Israel's chief rabbis recognized them as "full Jews." Today, more than 60,000 *Bene Israel* reside in Israel; 4,500 remain in India.

Studies include S. B. Isenberg, *India's Bene Israel: A Comprehensive Inquiry and Sourcebook* (1988); and S. Weil, "Bene Israel Rites and Routines," in idem, *India's Jewish Heritage: Ritual, Art and Life-Cycle* (2004).   SHALVA WEIL

Benjamin of Tudela (twelfth century). Very little is known about Benjamin ben Jonah of Tudela beyond the information found in his famous Hebrew travel narrative, *Sefer ha-Masa'ot* (The Book of Travels), which records his journey through Europe and the Islamic world ca. 1166–73. Benjamin's journey started in eastern *Spain, presumably his homeland, and took him through southern *France and *Italy, *Byzantium, *Syria, *Iraq, *Iran, *Arabia, and *Egypt. His account contains valuable observations about people and places along his route, especially about the Jewish communities that he encountered. For a modern edition with an English translation by M. N. Adler, see *The Itinerary of Benjamin of Tudela: Travels in the Middle Ages* (2004); and TRAVEL WRITING: MIDDLE AGES AND EARLY MODERN PERIOD.
OLIVIA REMIE CONSTABLE

Benjamin, Walter (1892–1940), a highly influential literary and cultural critic, was born into a prosperous and acculturated Jewish family in *Berlin. Benjamin was unsuccessful in gaining a *Habilitation* (post-PhD degree) in German literature at the University of Frankfurt with his study on *The Origin of German Tragic Drama*. His essay on Goethe's *Elective Affinities*, published in 1924, brought him his first public recognition, followed by speculative essays on such diverse topics as Proust, Baudelaire, and the theory of translation. Although early friendships with Theodor W. Adorno and Siegfried Kracauer eventually earned him a membership and modest salary from the Institute for Social Research, he remained by temperament a peripatetic and largely independent intellectual, publishing most of his essays in newspapers and literary journals. Benjamin maintained close personal ties with Gershom *Scholem, and some of his writings reveal an interest in the *messianic elements of the Jewish *mystical tradition. He was also drawn to the left-modernist playwright Bertolt Brecht, whose influence can be detected in works such as "The Author as Producer" (1934) and "The Work of Art in the Age of its Mechanical Reproducibility" (1935). In 1933 Benjamin moved to Paris and continued work on his monumental (and never completed) study of the Paris arcades. When the *Nazis invaded *France, Benjamin fled southward, hoping to reach Portugal via Spain. However, at Portbou, on the French border with Catalonia, his group of refugees met the Spanish police. Fearing capture by the Gestapo, Benjamin took an overdose of morphine and died. In one of his final works, "On the Concept of History" (later published by Adorno and Horkheimer in the *Zeitschrift für Sozialforschung*), Benjamin developed a dramatic and now-famous image of the angel of history as a traumatized figure blown forward in time, even while it gazes backward on the catastrophe called "progress." With their inimitable style of critical-revolutionary insight tinged by melancholy, Benjamin's various works continue to inspire new efforts in philosophy and in literary and cultural criticism. For further reading, see G. Scholem, *Walter Benjamin: The Story of a Friendship* (1981); and S. Buck-Morss, *The Dialectics of Seeing: Walter Benjamin's Arcades-Project* (1989).
PETER E. GORDON

Berit: See COVENANT

Berit Milah: See CIRCUMCISION

Berkovits, Eliezer (1908–1992), was a *Romanian-born rabbi and theologian who studied at the Orthodox Hildesheimer Rabbinical Seminary under Rabbi Yehiel Weinberg and at the University of *Berlin where he wrote his dissertation on Hume. Berkovits escaped *Germany in 1938. After serving in rabbinical positions in Leeds, Sydney, and *Boston, he taught philosophy at Hebrew Theological Seminary (*Chicago) until 1975. Subsequently he lived and worked in *Jerusalem. He also lectured widely in North America. Berkovits' theological contributions fall under three headings: critical, constructive, and *halakhic. Although he worked in all three areas throughout his career, his publications focused on different facets at various times.

Berkovits' criticism of non-Orthodox Jewish philosophies is primarily found in the studies contained in *Major Themes in Modern Philosophies of Judaism* (1974). He takes to task thinkers as varied as Hermann *Cohen, *Rosenzweig,

*Buber, *Kaplan, and *Heschel for failing to appreciate sufficiently the transcendence of *God. His own positive doctrine is found in *God, Man and History: A Jewish Interpretation* (1959), *Prayer* (1962), and *Man and God: Studies in Biblical Theology* (1969). He also wrote a book-length response to Toynbee's characterization of Judaism (*Judaism, Fossil or Ferment?* [1956]).

Berkovits' philosophical *Faith after the Holocaust* (1973) and the narrative *With God in Hell: Judaism in the Ghettos and Death Camps* (1979) comprise his major contribution to *Holocaust theology. One distinctive thesis is his claim that any theological justification or theodicy in response to evils like the *Holocaust can only be authentically made by persons who have experienced them, not by bystanders. It is for this reason that the testimony of those who endured the Holocaust is so important, and those who suffered and lost their faith cannot be judged. This caveat does not prevent Berkovits from also formulating a version of the free will defense as an interpretation of evil.

Conditions in Marriage and Divorce ([Hebrew] 1966), Berkovits' first halakhic book, is a conventional rabbinic argument for a radical conclusion: He argued that by making *marriage conditional on future compliance with arbitration, those marriages where one partner's recalcitrance prevents the execution of a halakhically valid *divorce can be annulled retroactively. Despite a letter of approbation from the venerable Rabbi Weinberg, this solution did not receive serious attention. Another book-length monograph is on causality in *halakhah.

Additional books on the method and content of *halakhah* include *Halakhah: Authority and Role* ([Hebrew] 1981) and a parallel English volume, *Not in Heaven*, as well as *Jewish Women in Time and Torah*. In these works, Berkovits strove to identify an unchanging, objective set of principles underlying biblical and rabbinic teaching. He argued that practical halakhic rulings must be measured against that standard and that, in some instances, established case law must be revised to conform to the higher principles. Notable examples are some laws distinguishing between men and *women regarding marriage and the performance of commandments, which Berkovits regarded as unjust, and the requirement of full commitment to Jewish practice as a condition of *conversion, which today may undermine the ideal of Jewish unity.   SHALOM CARMY

Berlin, founded in the thirteenth century, was the capital of Prussia (originally the Electorate of Brandenburg) until 1871 and then the capital of *Germany from 1871 to 1945 and from 1991 to the present. Jews, who first settled in Berlin and its vicinity in the late thirteenth century, were expelled several times, notably in 1510 and 1573. They were readmitted in 1671 under extremely strict economic and demographic restrictions, which favored the settlement of wealthy Jews.

In the late eighteenth century, Berlin was the site of the first major Jewish Enlightenment movement (*Haskalah), which was associated with Moses *Mendelssohn and his followers. After Mendelssohn's death in 1786, this movement went into a radical phase, lasting until about 1830, which was marked by the rejection of traditional Jewish practices, freer sexual mores, and the *conversion to Christianity of a considerable number of Berlin Jews, especially among the elite. After Prussian Jews were given most of the rights of citizens in 1812, the city was one of the centers of the fledgling Reform movement until the government closed the Reform Temple in 1823 (see JUDAISM, REFORM: GERMANY).

The Jewish population of Berlin, which hovered between three and four thousand until the 1820s, grew at an accelerated pace to 9,604 in 1849, 36,015 in 1871, and 90,013 in 1910. By that year there were also another 40,000 Jews in the wealthy western Berlin suburbs that were incorporated into Greater Berlin in 1920. In 1925 the Jewish population reached its highest point of 172,674 (more than 4% of the total Berlin population and nearly one-third of all the Jews of Germany). In the early twentieth century, the Jews of central Berlin, consisting to a considerable extent of recent *Eastern European immigrants, differed greatly from the wealthy and more acculturated Jews of the city's western sections near the Kurfürstendamm, a broad boulevard known for its fine shops, hotels, and restaurants.

The organized Jewish community had an extensive network of institutions, including more than a dozen large *synagogues. Some were *Orthodox, but most were Liberal (moderately Reform), including the Fasanenstrasse and Oranienburgerstrasse synagogues with several thousand seats each. Most of Germany's Jewish organizations had their headquarters in Berlin. However, a large percentage of the city's Jews rarely took part in religious activities; by the late 1920s the rate of *intermarriage in Berlin was just above one-quarter of all Jews marrying. In addition to their important contributions to the city's economy (especially in the clothing industry, department stores, the press, retail and wholesale *commerce, and the legal and medical professions), Jews played a major role in Berlin's thriving cultural life during the late nineteenth and twentieth centuries. Among numerous leading Jewish names in Berlin public life were the scientists Fritz Haber and Albert *Einstein, the painters Lesser Ury and Max Liebermann, the theater director Max Reinhardt, the statesman Walther Rathenau, the publishers Mosse and Ullstein, and the musicians Kurt Weill, Bruno Walter, and Otto Klemperer.

The situation of Berlin Jews deteriorated rapidly after the *Nazis gained power in 1933. The anonymity of the big city and the rich network of Jewish institutions helped cushion the blow, but more than half of Berlin's Jews departed by 1939. Between late 1941 and early 1943, most remaining Jews were deported to ghettos and extermination camps in *Poland from which few returned. A few thousand Jews were able to survive in hiding (see HOLOCAUST entries).

After World War II the community was reestablished by camp survivors and returnees from abroad, but the Jewish population numbered only a few thousand and was concentrated in West Berlin. Beginning in the mid-1990s, migration from the former *Soviet Union led to rapid growth; Berlin's Jewish population in 2008 numbered more than 12,000. The new Jewish *museum, the memorial to the victims of the *Holocaust (see HOLOCAUST MEMORIALS), and the Centrum Judaicum in the restored Oranienburgerstrasse synagogue building are among the signs of a revived Jewish presence in Berlin.   STEVEN M. LOWENSTEIN

Beruriah. According to rabbinic tradition, Beruriah was the wife of the second-century sage, R. Meir, and she is said to have been unusually learned. Certainly, a number of rabbinic passages portray a woman named Beruriah as demonstrating a profound knowledge of rabbinic biblical exegesis, a sophisticated ability to manipulate traditional texts, and a quick wit. Examples of her astuteness appear in BT *Pesaḥim* 62b, BT *Berakhot* 10a, and BT *'Eruvin* 53b-54a. Yet aggadic praises of Beruriah's supposed halakhic skills have something of an illusory quality because, except for one ruling in *Tosefta Kelim Bava Metzia* 1:6, no actual legal traditions attributed to her appear in rabbinic literature. This single ruling reappears in *Mishnah Kelim* 11:4, but this time with no reference to Beruriah. It seems that, over time, Beruriah's reputed scholarly expertise became a problem for *rabbinic Judaism. In a medieval reference she is shown to reap the tragic consequences of the "lightmindedness" inherent in women: The eleventh-century commentator Solomon ben Isaac (*Rashi) relates a tradition in his commentary on BT *Avodah Zarah* 18b that Beruriah was seduced by one of her husband's students and subsequently committed suicide.

Recent scholarship has shown that the Beruriah who appears in the Babylonian *Talmud is a literary construct with little historical reality. Nor can any credence be given to Rashi's account of her ignominious downfall. However, Tal Ilan has convincingly argued that the early *tannaitic Tosefta ruling attributed to someone named Beruriah must be taken as historical and that in many ways the Rabbis of the amoraic period were as amazed by this citation as modern readers. She suggests that the composition and preservation of the later Babylonian Talmud traditions about Beruriah, built around the faint historical memory of an actual woman capable of making subtle legal distinctions, reflect the Rabbis' astonishment at such a "wonder-woman." Others have suggested that the Beruriah narratives express rabbinic dubiousness over the possibility of a woman fitting into a male scholarly world in which her gender was bound to be a source of havoc. Rabbinic society insisted on sharply defined and controlled categories of being in which each gender had a particular set of roles and obligations; this is why later teachings downgraded and denigrated the contributions and character of the anomalous Beruriah. For further reading, see J. R. Baskin, *Midrashic Women* (2002); T. Ilan, *Integrating Women into Second Temple History* (1999); and WOMEN, ANCIENT: RABBINIC JUDAISM.   JUDITH R. BASKIN

Beth El ("house of God"), is a religious site located some twelve miles (19 km) north of *Jerusalem, on the border between Ephraim and Benjamin (Josh 16:1-4). Formerly named Luz, its biblical stature as a holy place was second in importance only to Jerusalem. God appeared there to *Abraham (Gen 12:8) and to *Jacob ("Jacob's ladder" in Gen 28:10-22). Later narratives continue to emphasize its importance as a site sacred to the Israelites. *Deborah (Judg 4:5) and the Israelites (Judg 20:18, 26) consulted God there. *Samuel included Beth El in his annual circuit (1 Sam 7:16). King *Jeroboam built sanctuaries there and at Dan, complete with "golden calves," so that the people of the northern kingdom of Israel would have places where they could worship God (1 Kgs 12:25-33). The Beth El sanctuary, often condemned (1 Kgs 13; Amos 3:14), was destroyed by King *Josiah (2 Kgs 23:15-18). **Map 2**

BETH ALPERT NAKHAI

Betrothal. The *Talmud, at BT *Ketubbot* 57a, presents three steps to *marriage: engagement (*shiddukhin*), betrothal (*'erusin / kiddushin*), and consummation (*nissu'in*). Betrothal, which constituted a legally binding marriage, was affirmed by the reading of the marriage contract (*ketubbah*), expressing the groom's obligations toward the bride. The engaged man then presented the *ketubbah* to his fiancée, along with an object of value, in the presence of two witnesses. The marriage was finalized through *nissu'in* (literally, "elevation"), also known as *ḥuppah*, when the bride was escorted to her husband's home and benedictions were recited. Often, *nissu'in* did not take place until a year after the betrothal.

The *ketubbah* (BT *Kiddushin* 2a), a rabbinic innovation, protected the wife's financial interests in case of *divorce or widowhood. Although the Babylonian Talmud implies that a woman must agree to her betrothal, from ancient to early modern times, young girls almost always entered into the marriages contracted for them by their parents or guardians. A financially independent adult woman, whether widowed, divorced, or previously unmarried, could usually negotiate her own marriage.

During the Middle Ages, it became usual for betrothal and marriage to take place at the same time. The combined betrothal/wedding ceremony became a public event, authorized and attended by community leaders and celebrated in a *synagogue or communal hall. The earlier ceremony of escorting the bride to the groom's home was replaced with the symbolic public *ḥuppah* ("marriage canopy"), under which the seven wedding benedictions were recited.

The combined betrothal/marriage was generally preceded by a period of engagement. At the engagement ceremony (*shiddukhin*) a legal document (*tenna'im* or "conditions"), fixing the terms of the marriage and defining the penalties and damages to be paid if one of the parties should wish to abandon the match, was signed. Sometimes the endorsement of the *tenna'im*, which had been negotiated previously, was also advanced to right before the wedding.

Betrothal is invoked throughout Jewish religious literature as a metaphor for the relationship between God and the people of Israel, as in Hosea 2: 21-22, which begins, "And I will betroth you forever."

For further reading, see M. Satlow, *Jewish Marriage in Antiquity* (2001); R. Biale, *Women and Jewish Law* (1984); and J. R. Baskin, "Medieval Jewish Models of Marriage," in *The Medieval Marriage Scene*, ed. S. Roush and C. Baskins (2005), 1-22.   JUDITH R. BASKIN

Bialik, Hayyim Nahman (1873-1934), "the national poet" of the *Zionist movement, was the most influential figure in moving Hebrew *poetry into a modern idiom. Also an essayist, story writer, editor, and translator, Bialik was born in Radi, a village in northern *Ukraine. After his father died when he was seven, Hayyim Nahman was raised by his paternal grandfather. Bialik's early childhood appears in his poetry at times as a lost paradise, as in *"Zohar"* (Radiance, 1901); other poems, however, recall poverty and pain, as in *"Shirati"* (My Song, 1901).

Bialik's first published poem, *"El ha-Tzippor"* (To the Bird, 1891), reflects a longing for Zion, which became a major subject in his later work. In 1897 he published *"Akhen Hatzir ha-Am"* (Surely the People Is Grass), which invokes prophetic language to condemn popular indifference to the

Zionist movement. After the 1903 Kishinev *pogrom he published "*Al ha-Shehitah*" (On the Slaughter) and "*Be-Ir ha-Harigah*" (In the City of Killing, 1904) in which he wrote, "The sun rose, the rye bloomed and the slaughterer slaughtered," contrasting the innocence of nature with the horror of the massacre. In addition to ideological poetry, Bialik also wrote lyrical poems, such as "*Zanah lo Zalzal*" (A Twig Fell, 1911), which includes these lines: "Alone I'll search in the dark and beat/ my head against my wall."

In 1924, Bialik immigrated to *Tel Aviv where he was received with adulation; the street where he settled was named after him the day he arrived. In Tel Aviv, Bialik wrote very little poetry, but edited, with Y. H. Ravnitsky, *Sefer ha-Aggadah* (The Book of Legends), an anthology of rabbinic *midrash rendered into modern Hebrew. In 1937 Bialik's widow, Manya, donated their home to the city of Tel Aviv. Bialik House continues to be open to the public and is often a venue for cultural events.   MOSHE RACHMUTH

Bible. The Hebrew Bible comprises twenty-four books (or thirty-nine, if originally combined books such as 1 and 2 *Samuel are counted separately) and is divided into three sections: "*Torah" (Five Books of Moses or Pentateuch), "*Prophets" (*Nevi'im*), and "*Writings" (*Ketuvim*). The entire collection is designated by the resulting acronym *Tanakh* (*TaNaKh*). Early *Christians, who also considered these books sacred, called them the "Old Testament" to set them apart from the distinctly Christian books that were called the "*New Testament." Many people today avoid the term "Old Testament," because they do not wish to imply that the Jewish *covenant ("testament") was replaced or supplemented by a newer one. However, a satisfactory alternative has not really been found: "Hebrew Bible" overlooks the fact that parts of *Daniel and *Ezra are in *Aramaic, whereas "First Testament" implies the existence of an additional collection of covenantal writings. In what follows, I use the word "Bible" or the term "Jewish Bible."

The Jewish Bible includes several different kinds of books. Some recount the history of ancient Israel, beginning with the creation of the world through the fall of the Israelite kingdoms and the exiles' eventual return from *Babylonia (*Genesis through *Kings, *Ezra, *Nehemiah, and *Chronicles). Other books contain *prophetic teachings; the three longest (*Isaiah, *Jeremiah, and *Ezekiel) are designated "Major Prophets," whereas the remaining twelve shorter books are called the "Minor Prophets" (or "Book of Twelve"). There are also three poetic books, two of which (*Psalms and *Lamentations) contain liturgical *poetry. The third (the *Song of Songs) is a collection of love poems that have traditionally been understood as an allegory; according to Jewish tradition, the book describes God's relationship with Israel, while Christian interpreters have understood it as portraying Christ's relationship with the Church. Three other books (*Proverbs, *Job, and *Ecclesiastes/Kohelet) belong to a genre termed *wisdom literature and explore ethical and philosophical issues. *Ruth and *Esther contain short stories; in each the eponymous heroine plays a crucial role in the continuing destiny of Israel. The first half of Daniel is also a narrative, but the book ends with a series of apocalyptic visions of dramatic events prophesied for the future. These categories are not always distinct; significant sections of Exodus-Deuteronomy contain law rather than

*narrative (see LAW: ANCIENT NEAR EAST and HEBREW BIBLE). The book of Job and much of prophetic literature are actually poetic and both Chronicles and Genesis include extensive genealogies as well as narratives.

Modern *biblical scholarship and theology take a variety of approaches to the Hebrew Bible. These include investigations of (1) the original text ("lower criticism"); (2) how biblical books were composed ("higher criticism"); (3) the meanings of individual words and constructions, typically in light of ancient Semitic languages and literatures; (4) the history of ancient Israel and its neighbors; (5) literary features of biblical literature; (6) the ideology of the Bible and its authors, including both its own religious teachings and topics that are of special interest today, such as attitudes toward women; (7) how the Bible has been interpreted over the centuries since it was written; and (8) contemporary religious messages that can be derived from the Bible.

This research has yielded significant insights into each genre of biblical literature. For example, contemporary scholarship agrees that the first eleven chapters of Genesis, often called the "Universal" or "Primordial History," are more mythlike than historical. Our understanding of them has been greatly illuminated by comparison with literature from other ancient societies that *archeologists have uncovered over the past century and a half.

Wisdom literature is also found in other ancient *Near Eastern cultures. Its pragmatic approach rests on the belief in a universal organizing principle called *hokhmah* ("wisdom"), which is described in several of the discourses that open the book of Proverbs. *Hokhmah* resembles the ancient Egyptian concept of *Ma'at*, which was sometimes personified as a goddess. The books of Ecclesiastes (Kohelet) and Job challenge Proverbs' view of life as not accurately reflecting the reality of human experience.

Biblical poetry also resembles that of other Near Eastern cultures. Since the eighteenth century, scholars have been particularly attuned to its use of parallelism, in which a single idea is repeated in successive lines using different words. This technique requires an extensive array of synonym pairs; similar word pairs also occur in poetic texts from the ancient Near Eastern city of Ugarit, demonstrating the genre's international character. Recent scholarship has identified other features in biblical poetry (see BIBLE: POETRY; CANAAN, CANAANITES).

The historically oriented sections of the Bible contain important artistic and religious features. For example, the accounts of *David and *Solomon (the "United Monarchy") do not present events in the order in which they actually occurred, but in a sequence that makes certain religious points. Narratives in Genesis also present the fathers and mothers of the Israelites in ways that foreshadow the later period of David. These characteristics have led some to question the reliability of the biblical accounts; many scholars think that the stories about everything before the time of David are at least exaggerated and probably intended to make Israelite history appear to have unfolded in a simplistically linear fashion. Although the Bible's account of the subsequent "Divided Monarchy" period reflects a southern (Judahite) point of view, with particular emphasis on the reign of the seventh-century king, *Josiah, it is considered generally reliable, particularly because much of its data are in accord with information preserved in *Assyrian and *Babylonian records.

The prophetic books are attributed to individual figures who lived between the eighth and sixth centuries; some books, such as *Isaiah and *Zechariah, include writings by authors from several different periods. The prophetic speeches that fill these books present theological interpretations of contemporary events, such as the Assyrian invasion of Israel, *Jerusalem's fall to the Babylonians, and the Judeans' return from exile. These interpretations, which rest on the prophets' individual understandings of what God expects, emphasize social justice and religious fidelity. The prophetic books also contain varying amounts of narrative; indeed, the entire book of *Jonah and the first half of Daniel, which Christian Bibles include among the prophets, are devoted entirely to stories. The books of Samuel and Kings contain narrative material about the prophets Nathan and *Elijah.

Although the books of the Bible were written at various times between the twelfth and second centuries BCE, their authors drew on earlier documents. This is obvious for books like Psalms and Proverbs, which are plainly collections (the headings scattered throughout them are later additions), as well as the prophetic books, with their numerous speeches. However, it is equally true of the Bible's legal passages, which incorporate earlier documents such as the Covenant Code (Exod 20:22–23:33), and of narrative works such as Genesis and Job.

The process whereby these books came to be considered sacred, "canonization," stretched over centuries. It is widely thought to have taken place in three stages, beginning with the Torah (Pentateuch) in the time of Ezra (fifth century BCE), then the Prophets (around the second century BCE), and finally the Writings (by the first century CE). However, the evidence for each stage is limited, and some scholars dispute this entire process. In their opinion, the three-part arrangement found in Jewish editions of the Bible reflects the books' different styles and levels of authority rather than the historical process through which they came to be considered holy.

The Christian Old Testament is based on a Jewish translation of the Hebrew Bible into Greek (the *Septuagint) that was begun in the third century BCE. The biblical books are arranged in a different order in the Septuagint, which also includes several books not found in "normative" Jewish Bibles. The Protestant Reformers of the sixteenth century removed these books, calling them "*Apocrypha" ("hidden"), a term that originated in the time of the *Church Father Jerome (fourth to fifth century CE).

The sequence of books in the Hebrew Bible also developed over centuries. This is clear because the Babylonian *Talmud (sixth century CE) lists the books in a different order from the one that prevails today. For example, only in the Middle Ages were the *Five Scrolls (the books of Song of Songs, Ruth, *Lamentations, Ecclesiastes, and Esther) grouped together and arranged in the sequence of the holidays on which each is read in the synagogue (*Passover, *Shavuot, *Tisha B'Av, *Sukkot, and *Purim, respectively).

The *Dead Sea Scrolls demonstrate that various versions of biblical books existed side by side in antiquity. That can also be seen by comparing passages that are preserved in more than one book of the Bible (for example, the books of Kings and Chronicles) or in the traditional Hebrew text

and various ancient translations. Some of these differences are as small as matters of spelling; however, others are more extensive. For example, a copy of the book of Samuel that was found among the Dead Sea Scrolls begins 1 Samuel 11 with a brief episode that is not included in our Bible but is mentioned by the first-century-CE historian *Josephus. Other differences have to do with the order in which passages are arranged (especially in *Jeremiah). Modern scholars compare these versions to determine how the different readings arose and which is most likely to be original.

The accepted Hebrew edition used today (Masoretic text) was established in medieval times by authorities known as *Masoretes. Over a period of centuries, they determined a standard consonantal text. In addition, they developed systems of vowels and accents, which also indicated punctuation and liturgical melody.

Useful introductory works include D. W. Baker and B. T. Arnold, *The Face of Old Testament Studies, A Survey of Contemporary Approaches* (1999); A. Berlin and M. Z. Brettler, eds., *The Jewish Study Bible* (2004); and D. N. Freedman et al., *Anchor Bible Dictionary* (1992). **See also BIBLE: LANGUAGES; BIBLE: MODERN SCHOLARSHIP; BIBLE: POETRY; BIBLE: PRAYER LANGUAGE; BIBLE: PROPHETS AND PROPHECY; BIBLE: TRANSLATIONS AND TRANSLATORS: ISRAELITE RELIGION; LAW: ANCIENT NEAR EAST AND HEBREW BIBLE; NEAR EAST, ANCIENT; TEMPLE AND TEMPLE CULT.**   FREDERICK E. GREENSPAHN

Bible: Ancestral Narratives. The narratives of *Genesis 12–50 comprise a series of interlocking family stories, tracing a line from *Abraham and *Sarah through *Isaac and *Rebekah to *Jacob with his four wives and twelve sons who are the eponymous ancestors of the twelve *Israelite tribes. Collateral lineages representing the peoples around ancient Israel are also accounted for: Abraham's nephew Lot is the ancestor of *Moabites and *Ammonites, Abraham's sons with his other wives (*Hagar and Keturah) are ancestors of Arabian peoples (see ARABIA), and Jacob's brother *Esau is the ancestor of the *Edomites. The dramatic sibling and co-wife rivalries of the tales signify the tensions within Israel and between Israel and its neighbors. Similarly, the theme of movement in and out of the "Promised Land" foreshadows later biblical narratives of departure to and Exodus from *Egypt and also of *exile to and return from *Babylon. However, the overarching theme is the idea, embodied in *covenantal promises, that all of the rivalries and movements are part of God's scheme to establish a people, Israel, in its own land.

Although the narratives have long been believed to be authentic historical accounts of the precursors of the *Israelites, the discrepancies between the "facts" of the story and what is known about the pre-Israelite period from *archeology and ancient *Near Eastern history have led to a reassessment. The ancestor narratives are now understood to be a complex amalgam of traditions. They represent ancient Israel's self-understanding of its past, formed many generations if not centuries after the period they purport to describe; they were formulated to serve the needs of the period(s) of their formation while drawing on remembered tales. Abraham may well be an authentic figure, for a place name in a tenth-century inscription is equivalent to "Abram" (or "Abiram") and perhaps reflects Abraham groups in the northern Negev. Similarly, the names of Abraham's ancestry correspond with place names in the Syro-Mesopotamian (Amorite) region that appear in *Mesopotamian literature of the late second and early first millennium BCE. However, the episodes attached to the ancestors are at best legendary rather than historical; they have been imagined and embellished by storytellers over long periods of time before reaching a final form that was essential to the shaping and expression of Israelite identity and culture.

The ancestor narratives notably present themes that serve the national and religious interests of Israelites; they also vividly convey the fathers and mothers of Israel as heroic yet flawed humans, thus capturing the attention and sympathies of their audiences. Although the society depicted is patrilineal, matriarchs as well as patriarchs struggle to achieve family goals and are active participants in the unfolding story of divine promise. In the first generation Abraham's unyielding faith and manipulation of Sarah stand out; in the second generation Rebekah's active agency in arranging her own marriage and in securing the prominence of her favored second son overshadows Isaac's passivity; and in the third generation Jacob and his wives are caught up in a web of trickery and deceptions that continues among their sons, propelling *Joseph and his brothers into Egypt and setting the scene for the Exodus story.   CAROL MEYERS

Bible: Languages. The vast majority of the Jewish Bible is written in *Hebrew; approximately ten chapters are in *Aramaic. Hebrew was the main language that the Judeans and Israelites spoke throughout the biblical period; it was slowly replaced by Aramaic during and after the *Babylonian Exile, since Aramaic was the language most commonly in use in western Asia. Over several centuries, Aramaic replaced Hebrew as the main Jewish spoken language, and by the end of the biblical period (second century BCE), Hebrew was used in formal, written contexts rather than in everyday speech. This is reflected in the fact that most late biblical and early rabbinic works are written in Hebrew, albeit a Hebrew that betrays significant Aramaic influence. Exactly when Hebrew ceased to be a spoken language is debated.

The main source of Biblical Hebrew is the Bible. We have a small number of inscriptions from the First *Temple period; there are more from the *Second Temple era, thanks especially to the *Dead Sea Scrolls. We also have some knowledge of pre-Biblical Hebrew from pre-Israelite *Canaanite tablets written in Akkadian, the language of *Mesopotamia; some gloss or explain an Akkadian word with a pre-Israelite Canaanite word. Given that we do not have original versions of any biblical text, and the final form of the Bible is postbiblical, these nonbiblical sources act as important controls as we try to understand the actual Hebrew of the biblical period. Akkadian, Hebrew, and Aramaic are also categorized as Semitic languages, one of the related language groups among Afro-Asiatic languages. "Semitic" is a linguistic category, coined in the nineteenth century; the word originates in the name "Shem," one of Noah's sons (Gen 9–11). Other ancient Semitic languages that are relevant to biblical literature are Amorite, Ugaritic, the Canaanite languages, and *Phoenician. Syriac, a descendant of Aramaic, became the literary language of early Christianity in the early centuries of the Common Era. Like Hebrew and Aramaic, these are

all considered Northwest Semitic languages, whereas Akkadian, the earliest attested Semitic language, is classified as an Eastern Semitic language; after the Muslim conquests in the beginning of the seventh century CE, Arabic, categorized as a West Semitic language, largely replaced Aramaic dialects.

The Bible contains several dialects, which are typically defined chronologically. Most biblical texts are written in Standard Biblical Hebrew, which is close to the Hebrew spoken in *Judah at the time of the destruction of the First Temple (586 BCE). A small number of earlier texts such as the Song of the Sea (Exod 15) and the Song of Deborah (Judg 5) are in Archaic Biblical Hebrew – these have certain old forms rarely found in other texts and show some similarity to Ugaritic, a language spoken in *Syria in the pre-biblical period. A sizable section of the Bible, including *Chronicles, *Ezra-*Nehemiah, *Daniel, *Esther, and *Ecclesiastes, is written in Late Biblical Hebrew, which shows similarities to both Aramaic and Rabbinic Hebrew. There are other ways of defining dialects as well; we know especially from inscriptions that the Hebrew of *Israel, the northern kingdom, differed slightly from that of Judah. The extent of northern Hebrew now found in the Bible is debated; it appears that much of it was normalized to Judean Hebrew. As in other languages, *poetry is different from prose: The former has many more rare and difficult words and has slightly different grammatical rules.

Both Aramaic and Hebrew are consonantal languages, having borrowed the alphabet developed in Phoenicia in the late second millennium BCE; they differ from Akkadian and Egyptian, which had much more complex writing systems – cuneiform in the case of Akkadian and hieroglyphics in the case of Egyptian. The fit between Hebrew and Phoenician consonantal sounds was not perfect, which explains why there are twenty-two letters in the Hebrew alphabet, but one of these letters is pronounced in two different ways. The Hebrew and Aramaic systems developed differently over time. The current script for the Bible is an Aramaic script that was borrowed during the Babylonian Exile and displaced the earlier Hebrew script, sometimes called Paleo-Hebrew. Both Hebrew and Aramaic eventually incorporated vowel letters; these were certain consonants that can indicate vowels. In the second half of the first millennium CE, various vowel systems written above or below the line were developed; the one ultimately adopted is called the Tiberian system, after the city Tiberias in the *Galilee in northern Israel. We have several transliterations of Hebrew into Akkadian or Greek from the biblical or early post-biblical period; these indicate that the vowel system now used for chanting the Bible is relatively accurate, but it does not date to the biblical period.

The following passages appear in Aramaic in the Bible: two words in *Genesis 31:48, one verse in *Jeremiah 10:11, four chapters in Ezra (4:8–6:18; 7:12–26), and six in Daniel (2:4–7:28). The material in Daniel reflects a late author more comfortable in Aramaic. Some of the Ezra material purports to contain official documents of the Persian chancellery, which would have been in Aramaic, and this may have influenced the surrounding material, which is also in Aramaic. The verse in Jeremiah is aimed at a non-Jewish audience, and the words in Genesis are spoken by Laban, an Aramean (explaining why they are in Aramaic).

Our present solid understanding of the structure of Hebrew began with medieval Jewish commentators and *grammarians; they understood Hebrew in relation to Arabic and Aramaic and tried to show in polemical contexts that the Bible rather than the Qur'an was written in the most beautiful pristine language. The discovery of how to decipher other Semitic languages in the last century and a half has also helped significantly to clarify many obscure words and grammatical structures of Biblical Hebrew.

MARC BRETTLER

Bible: Modern Scholarship refers to scholarly approaches that read the Bible as any other written text, without reliance on religious tradition or any preconceptions. Its origins are in the Protestant *Reformation and subsequently the Enlightenment, which regarded reason as the standard of measurement. This approach created the unfettered environment in which modern biblical scholarship has flourished in the various forms discussed in this entry.

BIBLICAL TEXT: Various editions of the Bible differ, raising questions as to which reflects the original text. Already in ancient times, Jewish tradition reported that the ancient *Temple housed three *Torah scrolls, each with its own distinctive readings. This textual diversity was confirmed by the *Dead Sea Scrolls, which include Hebrew manuscripts of numerous biblical books that are a thousand years older than previously known versions. Modern scholars have produced several critical editions of the Hebrew Bible, which display the relevant data from these different documents in a convenient format. The best known is the *Biblia Hebraica*, now entering its fifth edition; another is being produced at the Hebrew University in Jerusalem.

During the second century CE, one textual tradition became normative. At that time, Hebrew was written without vowels or punctuation, although certain consonants were sometimes used to mark vowels. Medieval scholars, known as *Masoretes, developed several systems for indicating vowels and punctuation; they also noted various textual oddities. The resulting texts, therefore, are called masoretic. The system now in use was developed in the *Galilee city of Tiberias between the sixth and ninth centuries.

Close attention to the text led to questions about the authorship of biblical books, a topic of interest since antiquity. The disunity of the *Pentateuch (the *Torah or Five Books of Moses) and the book of *Isaiah has prompted scrutiny, and multiple authorship for other books has also been suggested. For example, the last six verses of *Ecclesiastes are widely thought to be additions. The Dead Sea Scrolls also provide important insights into the process by which the book of *Psalms was put together.

Most modern scholars think that a redactor (R) wove the Pentateuch together from four discrete sources, labeled J, E, D, and P on the basis of various stylistic features. According to some scholars, these sources were themselves composite (hence J^1 and J^2, etc.); others have proposed the existence of additional sources (e.g., K, N, and H). The exact nature of each source and how they came to be combined are more speculative topics. Although J is usually thought to have been written near the time of *David, some scholars place it after the return from the *Babylonian Exile. The question of whether P (the "priestly source") preceded or followed D (*Deuteronomy) and H (the Holiness Code) is particularly contentious. One widespread theory holds that D originally introduced the books of *Joshua, *Samuel, and *Kings (the "Deuteronomistic History") but was later detached and placed at the end of the Pentateuch. Although these issues are still being debated, there is little argument about the composite origin of the Pentateuch and, probably, other biblical books.

Scholars also examine individual episodes within the Bible. By comparing different versions of the same story, they are able to trace the history of individual traditions over time.

IMPACT OF SCIENCE: Modern science has had a profound impact on our understanding of the Bible. Biblical credibility was severely damaged by Copernicus' discovery that the earth travels around the sun, Charles Lyell's determination that our world is millions of years old, and Charles Darwin's theory of evolution. However, the most dramatic impact has come from *archeology, which opened up vast repositories of information about Israel's ancient *Near Eastern environment, including both written and material finds. Excavations have yielded direct information from cultures previously known only from the Bible's critical accounts. These finds include texts written in ancient languages that were spoken during biblical times and are related to Biblical Hebrew, including Akkadian, the language of the *Assyrians and *Babylonians, and Ugaritic, from *Ugarit, a city that flourished north of Israel during the centuries preceding the emergence of the Israelite state. These texts cast light on many biblical passages. For example, Psalm 68:5 speaks of God as riding the '*aravot* (v. 5). Although that word appears to be the plural form of '*arava*, which means "desert," Ugaritic texts refer to the *Canaanite god Baal as a rider of the '*rpt* (like the original Bible, the Ugaritic texts do not indicate vowels). The Ugaritic word, which resembles the Hebrew '*aravot*, means "clouds"; that meaning fits Psalm 68:34, which speaks of God as riding in the sky (see also Deut 33:26 and Isa 19:1). It would appear that, to describe his God, the psalmist borrowed a phrase that the Canaanites used for their deity, Ba'al.

The records of nearby nations include numerous references to people and events mentioned in the Bible. Although most of these inscriptions are from the period of Israel's Divided Monarchy (930–586 BCE), the earliest comes from the Egyptian pharaoh Merneptah, who reigned near the end of the thirteenth century BCE. He claims to have decimated the people Israel, who were then living near the *Galilee. A monument erected by Mesha, who ruled over *Moab several centuries later, describes his confrontation with ancient Israel, an event that is mentioned in 2 Kings 3. Another monument from Tel Dan in northern Israel mentions two biblical kings, apparently Jehoram and Ahaziah.

Archeological evidence has raised questions about several biblical accounts, especially from early periods of Israelite history (these include the activities of the Patriarchs, the Exodus, and, most dramatically, the conquest), as well as the extent to which Israel differed from its neighbors. The Israelite nation emerged at the same time as several other groups. Canaan was then in disarray; Egypt, which had previously dominated the region, was in decline; and the Mesopotamian empires that would eventually replace it had not yet arrived. Scholars draw on social scientific theories about cultural development to understand the dynamics that contributed to Israel's social and political structures as well as to literary prophecy. This approach was pioneered in the nineteenth century, when biblical stories, such as that of Samson, were compared with mythological traditions from other cultures and the *Song of Songs was interpreted in the light of Palestinian wedding practices.

Recent dramatic developments in scholarship pertain to *Israelite religion. Archeological discoveries and a fuller understanding of how religion develops suggest that Israelite beliefs and practices were probably more diverse than what is represented in the Bible, with different practices in different regions and among different social classes. Monotheism apparently developed over time, as characteristics from several different deities were combined.

LITERARY ANALYSIS: Uncertainty about Israel's history has led to increased interest in the Bible's literary features, an approach with roots in the Middle Ages. Literary scholars usually look at the Bible holistically to understand the structure of such patently composite works as the book of Psalms and the Minor *Prophets (which Jewish tradition calls "the Book of the Twelve"). Close attention to repeated words (Leitwörter) and narrative patterns (type scenes) has illuminated the purpose and relationship of biblical passages. Scholars have also discovered standard formats; as a result, it is possible to categorize poems and appreciate the literary background of prophetic speeches. Several sections of the Bible mimic the structure of ancient vassal treaties, presenting God as Israel's overlord.

Sensitivity to the Bible's literary characteristics has also heightened awareness of its ideological premises. Some scholars consider the Bible's male orientation (androcentrism) to be inherently patriarchal, whereas others regard it as more supportive of women's concerns. The Bible's relevance to disabilities and environmental and Third World concerns has also attracted increasing attention.

CANON FORMATION AND HISTORY OF INTERPRETATION: Awareness of the complex history of biblical composition has led scholars to study how the Bible took shape (canon) and how it has been interpreted. In fact, the Bible was being interpreted even before it was complete; for example, later books, such as *Daniel and *Chronicles, interpret statements in earlier ones. Biblical interpretation became a thriving enterprise during the *Second Temple period. The Dead Sea Scrolls, discovered in 1948, provided a wealth of new material and sparked interest in other post-biblical Jewish works, such as the *Apocrypha and *Pseudepigrapha. Scholars now study the Bible's role within the religious communities that cherish it.

All this activity makes biblical studies a lively field, involving scholars from many different countries and traditions, who heatedly debate the early history of Israel and the history of the Bible as a whole. What is not in dispute is the fundamental notion that the Bible should be studied like any other work. That assumption is part of our contemporary culture, where nothing is immune from challenge and where consensus and certainty are often beyond our grasp; it is unlikely to give way in any but the most cloistered communities.

For further reading, see S. D. Sperling, B. A. Levine, and B. B. Levy, *Students of the Covenant: A History of Jewish Biblical Scholarship in North America* (1992); and J. H. Hayes, ed., *Dictionary of Biblical Interpretation* (1999).

FREDERICK E. GREENSPAHN

Bible: Music and Dance. *Genesis 4:21–22 attributes the invention of musical instruments to Jubal and song to Na'amah ("tuneful"), the seventh generation of naturally born humans. This is an indication that the *Israelites understood music to be a foundational part of their culture. Using biblical data and *archeological evidence, musicologists have identified four categories of musical instruments in the biblical period: (1) five different kinds of *idiophones* (e.g., rattles and bells), in which sound is produced by parts moving against other parts; (2) a dozen or so different *aerophones* (wind instruments); (3) nine different *chordophones* (stringed instruments); and (4) one *membranophone* (percussion instrument), the frame drum or *tōp*.

These instruments appear singly, such as the use of the *shofar (ram's horn) in military or religious contexts (e.g., Josh 6:4–5; Lev 25:9); they also appear in various combinations in religious (e.g., 2 Sam 6:5; Ps 81:2–3), prophetic (1 Sam 10:5), and secular (e.g., Gen 31:27; 1 Kgs 10:12; Isa 5:11–12) contexts. Many of these texts mention song and/or dance along with specific instruments. Song and dance without instruments are also mentioned in the Bible (e.g., Exod 32:18–20). Given the intrinsic connections among vocal expression, movement, and instrumentation, with traditional songs composed and performed using all three modes of musical expression, it is likely that some references to only one or two of these expressive forms might elliptically imply the presence of all three.

Vocal music appears in the biblical lament tradition (Jer 9:17, 21; Ezek 32:16; 2 Chron 35:25), in several texts indicating secular performance (Eccl 2:8; 2 Sam 19:36; and possibly Ezra 2:64 and Neh 7:67), and also in reference to *Temple singers (Ezra 2:41; Neh 7:44). Indeed, musical terminology appears (especially in superscriptions) so frequently in *Psalms that the psalms can be understood as songs sung or chanted for various personal or communal purposes, including thanksgiving, praise, lament, celebration, liturgy, and commemoration (perhaps with instruments, as in Psalm 61:1, and movement). Also, in light of biblical references using "song" (shirah) in reference to *poetry (e.g., Deut 31:19, 21, 30, 32:44), biblical poetry and teachings in general may be understood as chants or songs, since the oral transmission of tradition involves rhythmic recitation and poetic forms as memory aids.

Both women and men participated in communal events involving music. They also would have personally sung lullabies, love songs (such as the passages attributed to the female and male lovers in the *Song of Songs), laments, and prayers (the so-called Song of *Hannah in 1 Sam 2 is introduced as *prayer). Biblical references to female and male singers in secular contexts imply that women and men performed together publicly; Psalm 68:4 refers to "musicians" and "singers" (both masculine plural forms but possibly used inclusively) surrounding female drummers in a Temple procession. Single-gender professional ensembles may have been more common, based on representations in ancient art depicting ensembles of all men or all women. A number of passages (Exod 15:20–21; Judg 11:34; I Sam 18:6; cf. Jer 31:4; Judg 5:1) depict a musical tradition involving women who perform with drums, dance, and song to celebrate the victory of Israelites through divine intervention. These passages, along with archeological evidence for the frame drum as a woman's instrument, suggest that female musicians were part of the musical ensembles, at least those having drums, mentioned in the Bible.

For recent research, see J. Braun, *Music in Ancient Israel/Palestine: Archaeological, Written, and Comparative Sources* (2002).   CAROL MEYERS

Bible: Narrative Literature.

The corpus of "classical" narratives in the Hebrew *Bible consists of the *Torah (*Pentateuch) and the Former *Prophets (*Deuteronomistic History); that is, the books of *Genesis through 2 *Kings. Broadly speaking, they were written during ancient Israel's monarchical period (1000–586 BCE) in Classical Biblical Hebrew, although they originated in pre-monarchical and even pre-Israelite traditions, and continued to be supplemented and edited into the *Babylonian Exile and later (Friedman, 1987). The books of *Ruth, *Jonah, and the frame-story of *Job, although of relatively late provenance, still conserve (or affect) both the language and conventions of classical narrative. Such is not the case, however, with the books of *Chronicles, *Ezra-*Nehemiah, *Esther, and *Daniel, which belong to a recognizably post-classical literary culture. Narrative elements are also occasionally found in biblical *poetry (e.g., Exod 15 and Judg 5), but here other linguistic and poetic factors predominate. The following mostly literary observations restrict themselves to classical prose narrative.

Biblical narrative developed out of the narrative poetry of surrounding West Semitic ancient *Near Eastern cultures, traditions attested to in particular by *Ugaritic myths and epics, which date roughly to the latter half of the second millennium BCE. Thus, *Abraham stands in a long line of *Canaanite patriarchs, resembling such Ugaritic heroes as Danel and Keret. Like his predecessors, he is a prosperous and powerful warrior-ruler (Gen 14); to his great dismay he lacks a son; God therefore promises, in a prophetic annunciation, to grant him a son. This literary development is also suggested by evidence within the Bible itself. So-called archaic biblical poems such as *Exodus 15 and *Judges 5 likely constitute the oldest passages in the Bible, and in various ways their accompanying prose narratives (Exod 14 and Judg 4, respectively) recast these traditional poems in historicized form. Within this history of narrative, it was the particular achievement of Israelite writers to translate a poetic, possibly oral, tradition into the radically different medium of literary (written) prose. In fact, the Hebrew Bible contains what is arguably the first extended prose narrative composition in the history of literature (Friedman, 1998). The shift from traditional poetry to literary prose had profound consequences for narrative representation and accounts for biblical narrative's distinctively literary qualities within the ancient world (Auerbach).

The change in verbal medium is reflected in the language and style of biblical narrative. Classical prose is characterized by two strictly literary constructions: a preterite (past tense) that is restricted to narrative uses and a form of represented consciousness. More precisely, the so-called converted imperfect (*wayyiqtol*) form, which expresses completed action in third-person narration, appears to have been restricted to the written language. Conversely, the perfect tense (*qatal*) is used to describe past action only in direct speech. Second, the "presentative" (*hinnēh*) in third-person narration represents individual characters' private points of view. In this way, biblical narrative, like the modern novel, creates a dualism comprising objective facts about the narrative world and subjective facts residing in the minds of characters, thus achieving a strikingly early example of literary realism. It is the medium of literary prose that makes these novelistic effects possible.

Alongside such comparisons to modern literature, it must always be kept in mind that biblical narrative was composed upward of three millennia ago. Not surprisingly, ancient Israelite writers employed various narrative conventions that are no longer directly available to modern readers. Rather, they must be historically reconstructed on the basis of literary inferences drawn from the corpus itself (Alter). For example, biblical narrative, in contrast to most modern literature, is characterized by a pronounced use of repetition. At the level of prose style, this is especially visible in what Martin *Buber and Franz *Rosenzweig identified as the Bible's *Leitwortstil*: A "leading word" recurs within a scene or sequence of scenes, creating a cumulative thematic resonance. At the level of compositional form, repetition shapes both dialogue and type-scenes. Thus, a character nearly repeats what has just been reported by another character or what has just been recounted in narration. Or a set sequence of events (the annunciation of the birth of the hero, for example) is nearly repeated on several different occasions (Gen 18; Judg 13; 1 Sam 1). In both cases, the qualification "nearly" is crucial. For the deviation from pure repetition generally provides the key to discerning the specific point of an apparently redundant snippet of dialogue or the particular emphasis of a seemingly typical instance of a recurring scene. The marked presence of repetition is sometimes mistaken as evidence that biblical narrative is still essentially tied to oral tradition. Although it is entirely possible that the origins of biblical narrative are to be found in oral epics – a thesis associated in particular with the names Umberto Cassuto and Frank Moore Cross – the verbal maneuvers encountered in biblical narrative itself derive from the manipulation of a text. Writing enabled the biblical authors to play with and even against the inherited tradition. The art of biblical narrative ultimately resides in a post-traditional aesthetic principle, a "technique" that the Russian formalists referred to as "defamiliarization." In stark contrast, traditional storytellers (Ugaritic, Homeric, etc.), however perfected their craft, remained within familiar terrain.

Finally, one must consider the complex process of writing and redaction by which biblical narrative assumed its present form. According to the documentary hypothesis put forward by source criticism, the Pentateuch consists of four primary sources, which were combined in two principal stages by two different redactors, all over the course of several centuries. The documentary hypothesis (and related theories) continues to have its detractors but it remains the most convincing account of Pentateuchal composition, as well as an enduring achievement of nineteenth-century philology (see BIBLE: MODERN SCHOLARSHIP). Recognition of the literary artistry of biblical narratives provides corroborating evidence for the existence of underlying written sources.

For further reading, see R. E. Friedman, *Who Wrote the Bible?* (1987); idem, *The Hidden Book in the Bible* (1998); S. B. Parker, *The Pre-Biblical Narrative Tradition: Essays on the Ugaritic Poems Keret and Aqhat* (1989); E. Auerbach, *Mimesis* (1953), 3–23; R. S. Kawashima, *Biblical Narrative and the*

Death of the Rhapsode (2004); and R. Alter, *The Art of Biblical Narrative* (1981).   ROBERT S. KAWASHIMA

Bible: Poetry. The earliest example of biblical poetry appears in the account of creation in *Genesis 2: As soon as God forms woman, man begins to speak. He declares, "*This one* at last is bone of my bone, / and flesh of my flesh; / *this one* shall be called 'Woman' ('*ishah*)/ for from man ('*ish*) was *this one* taken" (2:23). In most contemporary versions of the *Bible, this verse is set apart from the surrounding prose narrative and laid out in poetic verse. But what distinguishing features mark this utterance as poetry?

In this example, distinguishing characteristics include the repetition of the phrase, "this one" (*zot*), at the beginning of two consecutive lines, a poetic device called *anaphora*. The word *zot* recurs a third time, in the Hebrew at the very end of the verse, which makes it an *inclusio*, a word or phrase that appears at the beginning and end of a passage, framing the poetic unit. The word pairs, "bone of my bone" and "flesh of my flesh," parallel one another semantically and grammatically; the words "woman" and "man," which are etymologically distinct in Hebrew but share a similar sound, create a word play. Thus, with this finely crafted verse, human speech is initiated in the elevated style that characterizes poetry.

Poetry constitutes approximately one-third of the Bible. The *Torah includes several lengthy poetic texts, including Genesis 49:2–27, *Exodus 15:1–18, and *Deuteronomy 32 and 33, as well as shorter poetic compositions such as Exodus 15:21, *Numbers 10:35–36, and isolated poetic verses (e.g., Gen 4:6–7, 24:60). In the books of *Joshua through *Kings (often known as the Former *Prophets), poems are interspersed throughout the narrative account of Israel's history (e.g., Judg 5; 1 Sam 2:1–10; 2 Sam 23:1–7). In most of the books that record the prophets' actual discourse (the so-called Latter Prophets), poetic verse predominates (with the exception of the books of *Jonah and *Ezekiel). The third division of biblical books, *Writings (*Ketuvim*), contains the largest amount of poetic material, mainly in the books of *Psalms, *Proverbs, *Job, *Song of Songs, and *Lamentations.

A survey of these poetic texts reveals a considerable diversity in poetic form, including celebratory songs to God (e.g., Exod 15:1–18), mournful dirges (e.g., 2 Sam 1:19–27), aphorisms (Proverbs), and love songs (Song of Songs). Within the Psalms alone are hymns of praise (e.g., Ps 145), psalms of thanksgiving (e.g., Ps 30), laments (e.g., Ps 6), and pedagogical teachings (e.g., Ps 1). The poetry of the prophets is equally varied, with prophecies of condemnation found alongside prophecies of comfort (e.g., Hosea 2).

The Bible itself lacks any definition of poetry or discussion of poetics. Although certain poetic passages are labeled as a "song" (*shirah*, Deut 31:30), "dirge" (*kinah*, 2 Sam 1:17), "psalm" (*mizmor*, Ps 68:1), or "song of praise" (*tehillah*, Ps 145:1), such classifications are not used consistently or comprehensively. Furthermore, the convention of visually distinguishing poetic passages through stichography (special spacing) evolved over time; the visual layout of poetic verse cannot be relied on as a decisive indicator of poetry in the Hebrew Bible. Nonetheless, certain central indicators have enabled scholars to gain a consensus as to what qualifies as biblical poetry.

Since the mid-eighteenth century, scholars have highlighted parallelism as a key characteristic of biblical poetry. In his influential work, *Lectures on the Sacred Poetry of the Hebrews* (originally published in 1778), Robert Lowth defined poetic parallelism as "a certain equality, resemblance, or parallelism, between the members of each period," and he distinguished between synonymous, antithetic, and synthetic parallelism. Although Lowth's understanding of parallelism dominated the field for many years, more recent studies have called attention to the nuances and complexities of biblical verse. Most notably, Adele Berlin has characterized parallelism as a multifaceted phenomenon, one that involves grammatical, lexical-semantic, and phonological aspects on the level of individual words, as well as of clauses and larger expanses of a text. Instead of drawing a stark contrast between synonymous and antithetical elements, Berlin asserts that parallelism achieves its effectiveness from the interplay of equivalence and contrast along these various aspects and levels. Take, for example, Exodus 15:11: "Who is like You, O YHWH, among the gods?/ Who is like You, mighty in holiness, / awesome in accomplishments, worker of wonders?" The opening words of the first two lines are nearly identical, which gives them the impression of synonymy; however, the second halves of these two lines differ both semantically and grammatically. The third line adds two phrases, "awesome in accomplishments" and "worker of wonders," that resemble the expression in the second line, "mighty in holiness," in structure and meaning (although with some differences), thus creating a chain of two-word divine descriptors that illustrate why God is beyond compare. This combination of equivalence and contrast on multiple levels animates the verse.

Another distinguishing feature of biblical poetry is an abundance of imagery and metaphor. One example is the well-known "YHWH is my shepherd" (Psalm 23:1); another is the depiction of wisdom as a "tree of life" (Proverbs 3:18). Biblical poetry also contains various forms of repetition and patterning, with many passages displaying an artful, clever recurrence of key words, sounds, and other elements. These features are evident in Genesis 2:23, discussed earlier. Scholars have long debated whether biblical poetry exhibits some sort of metrical system. Of late, many have concluded that, although biblical poetry does not contain conclusive evidence of meter, it does display a certain degree of rhythm or sound repetition and regularity. All of these literary devices also appear in biblical prose but they occur in poetry with greater frequency and intensity.

In addition, biblical poetry is marked by terseness. The parallel lines in each two- or three-part poetic unit tend to be short and concise. Because the language is dense and poetic elements are woven together, reading biblical poetry requires effort and skill. Yet precisely because of these features, deciphering the artistic, elevated discourse of biblical poetry yields rich rewards.

For further reading, see A. Berlin, *The Dynamics of Biblical Parallelism* (1985); and R. Alter, *The Art of Biblical Poetry* (1985).   ANDREA L. WEISS

Bible: Prayer Language. *Prayer, by which I mean speech to (or, in some cases, about) *God, is very common in the Hebrew *Bible. Some prayers are short: *Genesis 17:18, "O that Ishmael might live by Your favor!" is only four words long in Hebrew, whereas *Psalm 119, at 176 verses, is the longest biblical chapter. Most prayers are in *poetry and are found in the book of *Psalms, although approximately one hundred are in prose and are spread throughout the Bible.

Prose texts suggest that men and women could pray anywhere, although they also suggest that special prayers were often recited in a shrine or *Temple setting, where God was believed to be more proximate. There was no *siddur* or *prayer book in the biblical period, although there were certain typical forms in which prayers were recited. For example, petitionary prayers, whether in poetry or prose, typically began with an invocation of God and contained a request and a reason or reasons why God should heed the request. Such prose prayers were spontaneous in nature and were typically recited out loud (see *Hannah's prayer in 1 Sam 1:11). On special occasions, especially when commemorating a special event or offering significant petitions, the person might recite a ready-made poetic prayer in a religious setting in the belief that these special words would be especially efficacious. Upraised hands was the typical position of prayer in the biblical period.

We do not know exactly when people prayed. There is little indication of regular statutory prayer in the Bible, and the First *Temple has been called the "Sanctuary of Silence," although this is surely an exaggeration. There are no indications that the *amidah*, the central prayer of *rabbinic Judaism, was recited in the biblical period. Although the *shema*, the quintessential Jewish statement of divine unity, is biblical in origin (Deut 6:4–9), there is no intimation that it was used as a prayer in biblical times. The *synagogue likely developed late in the biblical period, several centuries after the *Babylonian Exile, but it is unknown what prayers, if any, might have been recited in the earliest synagogues (see WORSHIP).

Both prayer and animal sacrifice were seen as legitimate ways of serving deities in the ancient *Near East, including Israel. Exactly how these two means of *Israelite religion functioned together or side by side in the biblical period is unknown. Biblical theology assumes the efficacy of prayer; in the words of Psalm 145:18, "The LORD is near to all who call Him, to all who call Him with sincerity." It also assumes that disinterested praise of God is virtuous, as in Psalm 92:2: "It is good to praise the LORD, to sing hymns to Your name, O Most High." The Bible rarely sees prayer as more efficacious than sacrifice, however (see Ps 51:18), and biblical authors condemn the insincere prayer or prayers of the wicked that accompany insincere sacrifices (Isa 1:1–17). Many sections of the Bible insist on divine freedom; thus no prayer is automatically effective. Prayer became more important after the destruction of the Second Temple in 70 CE, but evidence indicates that it already served as an important religious expression throughout the biblical period.

MARC BRETTLER

Bible: Prophets and Prophecy.

The most frequent word used for "prophet" in the Hebrew *Bible is *navi*. Although its etymology is uncertain, the word has been linked to the verb *nabu* in the Mesopotamian language, Akkadian, which means "to call, proclaim." It remains unclear, however, whether the word *navi* would have been understood in the active sense as "one who proclaims [YHWH's message]" or in the passive sense as "one who is called [by YHWH]." In either case, these two connotations of *navi* most accurately define the prophet in the Hebrew Bible: one who is called by YHWH to proclaim the divine word to the Israelite or Judahite king and/or people. Predictions of the future were often part of the message that YHWH charged the prophet to deliver but they were not the main themes of biblical prophets. Rather, advocacy for social justice and exclusive YHWH-worship dominates prophetic discourse.

PROPHECY IN THE ANCIENT *NEAR EAST: The discovery of a vast collection of omen texts from ancient *Mesopotamia suggests that prediction of the future in the ancient Near East was frequently accomplished by interpreting omens and performing divination, whether by experts or laypeople. References to prophetic oracle giving can be found throughout the region, but the Mari letters (early second millenium BCE) and the Nineveh oracles (seventh century BCE) stand out as examples of prophetic activity that parallel ancient Israelite prophecy.

HISTORY OF PROPHECY IN ISRAEL: Although the biblical text suggests that *Moses and *Miriam were among the first prophets, it is likely that such language is a retrojection from a later time; understood loosely, however, as intermediaries between YHWH and the Israelite people, both could be seen as early prophets. The institution of prophecy most probably arose alongside the early monarchy, with (among others) the figures of Samuel and Nathan in 1 and 2 *Samuel functioning as prophetic advisors to *Saul and *David, respectively. The history of prophecy is divided into two eras: "pre-classical" (or "nonclassical") and "classical" prophecy. Pre-classical prophets functioned during the tenth and ninth centuries BCE. Narratives about them appear in the biblical histories, particularly the books of Samuel and *Kings, and they are depicted as miracle workers who worked alone or banded together in guilds; prophets rebuked the king when necessary, and they also responded to the requests of ordinary individuals. The charismatic figures of *Elijah and *Elisha are paradigmatic of the pre-classical prophet.

Although the figure of the pre-classical prophet undoubtedly persists beyond the ninth century, "classical" prophets, such as *Hosea, *Amos, *Isaiah, and *Jeremiah, appear for the first time in the eighth century BCE. They are distinguished by having entire biblical books (scrolls) devoted to their actions and prophetic message. Classical prophets are far less likely to be portrayed as wonder workers and instead are depicted delivering oracles, at times punctuating their message with a symbolic activity, such as Jeremiah's donning of a wooden yoke to represent submission to *Babylon (Jer 27).

There is much variation among prophets of both eras. Some prophets emerge as fringe figures from the periphery of society (e.g., Elijah; see 1 Kgs 18:13, which portrays the Israelite monarchy as actively persecuting prophets of YHWH); others are tied to central institutions such as the royal court (e.g., *Isaiah; see 2 Kgs 19, which depicts King *Hezekiah consulting with the prophet Isaiah). Some prophets, primarily from the periphery, excoriate the monarchy and demand radical reform, whereas central prophets are generally conservative, advising maintenance of the social order or a return to older social institutions. Prophets addressed both cultic concerns, such as worship, and political matters, such as whether to resist or surrender in an upcoming battle; some focused on the former (e.g., Hosea) and others the latter (e.g., Jeremiah). Prophets with different positions in society and diverging messages appear to have coexisted and competed with one another. 1 Kings 22 relates a story in which the kings of *Judah and *Israel consult numerous prophets before embarking on a military campaign: Several central royal prophets delivered one message, whereas a peripheral prophet, Micaiah ben Imlah, conveyed divergent and more ominous advice.

According to Jewish tradition, prophecy ended around 400 BCE, after the restoration of the Second *Temple and the re-inauguration of the dynastic *priesthood. Prophetic activity undoubtedly continued through the late ancient era, but for reasons that are unclear prophets were no longer perceived as significant enough for their work and words to be recorded for posterity.

PROPHETIC LITERATURE: The second section of the Hebrew *Bible, Nevi'im (*Prophets), contains the works attributed to the classical prophets, fifteen in all. The prophets do not seem to have written down their own words, but rather to have delivered them orally; at a later date, they were collected, written down, and edited into complete works that often include some biographical material and historical narrative. A narrative in the book of Jeremiah gestures toward this process as it depicts the prophet dictating his words to the scribe Baruch, who wrote the oracle on a scroll and delivered it to the king (Jeremiah 36). Few of the prophetic books are seamless; in addition to the mixing of genres exemplified by the book of Jeremiah, oracles from different time periods are often collected and placed side by side. The book of Isaiah, for example, contains the oracles of either two or three different prophets, with the most notable disruption occurring between chapters 39 and 40; the first thirty-nine chapters clearly address a nation on the brink of destruction, and the fortieth chapter begins with an oracle of comfort to a nation in exile.

Much of prophetic literature is written in elevated, poetic language and includes word play, complex extended metaphors, and visual-verbal punning in the accounts of visions. References to prophetic books as part of the sacred canon can be found as early as the second century BCE.

For further reading, see J. Blenkinsopp, A History of Prophecy in Israel (1983); and R. R. Wilson, Prophecy and Society in Ancient Israel (1980).   CHAYA HALBERSTAM

Bible: Representations of War and Peace.
The Hebrew *Bible is steeped in war. Like the foundation tales and national epics of many cultures, stories of Israelite heroes and accounts of historical eras are often seen in terms of military victory or defeat, alternating with much hoped for periods of stability and peace. Scholarship on war in the Hebrew Bible has addressed the historicity of various biblical war accounts, the military tactics and material culture of war in a comparative ancient *Near Eastern context, the worldviews implicit in biblical portrayals of war, and, more specifically, the theological and ethical implications of images of *God as divine warrior.

The Hebrew Bible, in fact, reveals a complex variety of ideologies of war; many, if not most, reflect, in Michael Walzer's terms, the desire "even in war ... to act or to seem to act morally" (Just and Unjust Wars: A Moral Argument with

Historical Illustrations [1977], 20). Even the shocking ideology of the mandated ḥerem was understood in religious terms. Ḥerem, translated in the biblical context as "ban" or "devotion to destruction," meant that when the Israelites achieved victory over the inhabitants of the land of Canaan during the conquest era they were required to sacrifice to God all that would normally be understood as the spoils of war; they were banned from benefiting from their victory in any way. This meant destroying not only the enemy's possessions, including their animals, but the enemy, including women and children, as well. This was justified as either a sacrifice vowed to God (Num 21:2–3, Deut 2:34–36; Josh 6:17–21; 8:2, 24–28; 11:11, 14; 1 Kgs 20:35–28) or as an execution of divine justice requiring the extirpation of the idolatrous "other" (Deut 7:2–5, 23–26). The ḥerem as God's justice can be turned against Israelites themselves should they break their covenant with God (Deut 13:12–18).

Another ideology, the bardic tradition, is preserved in traditional biblical narrative style and portrays war as men's honorable sport or a contest in which a code of fair play operates. Combatants expect to fight their equals, as shown by General Joab's words to the younger, inexperienced warrior, Asahel (2 Sam 2:21–22), and the reaction of Goliath to the youthful David (1 Sam 17:43). A degree of respect and reciprocity is evident among enemies (Judg 8:18–21).

The ideology of tricksterism was a war ideology of the oppressed, who used deception to defend themselves or prevail. No code governs the fighting, but the cause is always just from the perspective of the underdogs. Examples of warrior tricksters include Samson (Judg 14–15), Ehud (Judg 3:12–30), and Jael (Judg 4–5). The ideology of expediency accepts that "war is hell." Any degree of cruelty is permissible to defeat the enemy, and brutal aggression is regarded as the activity of kings, including David (2 Sam 5:7–8, 8:2). The Hebrew Bible offers no true ideology of pacifism, but a tendency toward peace is implied in the ideology of nonparticipation. Rooted in biblical miracle accounts, this ideology suggests that Israel need not fight; God will defend and rescue His people. "Nonparticipation" is reflected in 2 Chronicles 20, which describes a scene in which the Judeans led by their king, Jehoshaphat, admit helplessness, confess their sins, and pray. They turn themselves over to the power of God, who soundly routs the enemy, causing the various invading groups to destroy one another (2 Chron 20:23).

Matching these ideologies with the actual conduct of wars in biblical times or with specific biblical contributors is difficult. The ideology of the ban is described by a ninth-century BCE *Moabite king on his victory stele; he claims to have "devoted Israel to destruction." There is no reliable evidence that Israel actually established itself in the land via the ban or conducted wars in this way during the monarchy, but the motif of "devotion to destruction" does provide an important ideological framework for biblical tales of conquest. The ban is a leitmotif in narratives concerning kings *Saul (1 Sam 15) and *Ahab (1 Kgs 20) and an important symbol in late biblical poetry (Isaiah). The bardic ideology is biblically set in the days of Israel's early heroes, the judges, and the early kings. Although this heroic ideology of war contributes to an ancient Israelite epic genre, it may not reflect the ways in which wars were actually fought. The ideology of expediency seems to be the most rooted in the realities of ancient Near Eastern warfare. All the ideologies, however, reflect an ongoing Israelite interest in security, the justification for killing, and the role of war in Israel's history.

Reports of war in the Hebrew Bible are balanced by contemplations on peace. Implicit in the bardic ideology is the concern with limits and codes, and implicit in nonparticipation is the possibility of not fighting at all. Deuteronomy 20 offers a code of sorts in which the possibility is, at least, offered for the enemy's surrender and for sparing his life (20:10–11). Fruit-bearing trees are to be spared (20:19–20), and some degree of status is offered to the unfortunate women who become spoils of war (Deut 21:14). The speech of the hero Jephthah in Judges 11:4–28 provides a virtual "just war" argument for fighting the *Ammonites; he does not desire war, but is justified for defensive reasons to fight if necessary. Overt critiques of warring behavior are offered by the eighth-century-BCE prophet *Amos (1:6, 9, 11, 13; 2:1) and the poet of *Genesis 49. Several passages enjoin proper and reconciliatory treatment of the enemy (2 Kgs 6; 2 Chron 28:15). The priestly passage of Numbers 31 acknowledges that war, with its inevitable death, defiles the fighters, who then need to mark ritually the passage from war status to peace status, from defilement to wholeness.

Post-biblical Jewish thinkers of the *rabbinic period continued to reflect on biblical texts dealing with war and peace. Creative exegeses bring forth significant nuances and suggest developments in attitudes to war and peace. For example, interpretive traditions in *Sifre D'varim* 194–196 push the biblical passage describing divinely commanded war in Deuteronomy 20 in the direction of nonparticipation, whereas midrashic traditions in *Deuteronomy Rabbah* 5:14 have the effect of turning *Joshua, the biblical imposer of the ban, into a leader who always sues for peace before fighting.

For further reading, see S. Niditch, *War in the Hebrew Bible: A Study in the Ethics of Violence* (1993); and G. von Rad, *Holy War in Ancient Israel* (2000).   SUSAN NIDITCH

Bible: Translations and Translators.
The *Tanakh* or Jewish Bible is written primarily in Hebrew (with substantial portions of the books of *Ezra and *Daniel, plus phrases in *Genesis and *Jeremiah, in *Aramaic). However, whenever it has been perceived that large numbers of Jews were no longer well acquainted with Hebrew, translations into more readily understood languages have been undertaken. Such a situation is noted within the Hebrew Bible itself, as narrated in *Nehemiah 8. The scribe Ezra arrives in *Jerusalem in the mid-fifth century BCE with perhaps the earliest completed version of the *Torah (the Five Books of Moses) in Hebrew. The first language of the crowd that assembles at the Water Gate to hear him is Aramaic. Hence, translators, or we might say interpreters, provide a simultaneous rendering into Aramaic as Ezra reads the Torah in Hebrew.

The Hebrew word meaning "to translate," found in Nehemiah 8:8, also has the connotation of "to interpret," a reminder that even the most literal translation involves some degree of interpretation. The fact that an oral Aramaic translation/interpretation accompanied the reading of the Hebrew indicates that some translations, even written ones, were intended to accompany the Hebrew, rather than serve as independent versions. This may well have been the case

when Aramaic biblical translations, known as *Targumim*, were later recorded in writing.

The first written translation of the Hebrew Bible was in *Greek. This process took perhaps a century, beginning in *Alexandria, *Egypt, in the first quarter of the third century BCE. As related in the *Letter of *Aristeas* (written in the mid-second century BCE), *Ptolemy II Philadelphus, the ruler of Egypt, requested a version of the Jewish Law – that is, the Torah – in Greek, to be placed in his great library. Seventy-two elders were said to have been sent from Jerusalem by the High Priest to accomplish this task. Working as a committee, these individuals, chosen for their high morality as well as linguistic skills, completed their work in exactly seventy-two days.

Later retellings of this story by Jews such as *Philo and by Christians expanded on the "miraculous" aspects of the account. For the *Letter of Aristeas*, it was sufficient to record that the Jews of Alexandria accepted and acclaimed this Greek version much as the Israelites had done for the Hebrew text at Mount Sinai. To further strengthen the unique status of this text, which came to be known as the *Septuagint and to include the entire Hebrew Bible plus other materials now found in the *Apocrypha, a curse was put on anyone who would change as much as a letter of the Greek rendering.

It cannot be known with certainty exactly when and by whom the remainder of the Septuagint was produced. Many of its books follow the essentially literal approach taken by the translators of the Torah. Others diverge considerably. The reasons for these differences in approach are not known. Furthermore, the extent of the differences is difficult to chart because modern scholars are often uncertain about the nature of the Hebrew text available to the translators. For some books, it was very close to the *Masoretic text (the traditional text of the Hebrew Bible), although without vowels; for other books, it differed in length, order of material, and content. For some biblical books, Hebrew versions similar to what the Greek translators read have been found among the *Dead Sea Scrolls.

In spite of the view promoted by the *Letter of Aristeas* that the Greek should in no way be altered, many revisions were made, often to bring the Greek into closer alignment with the Hebrew then in use. Three revisers known by name are Aquila, Theodotion, and Symmachus, all of whom were Jews. Their work began in the first century BCE and may have continued until the third century CE.

When the great codices that we know as Alexandrinus, Vaticanus, and Sinaiticus were compiled within third- and fourth-century-CE Christian communities, some of the work of the revisers (for example, Theodotion's version of Daniel and Aquila's version of *Ecclesiastes) were included, thereby increasing the heterogeneous nature of the Septuagint. The Septuagint's adoption by early Christians as their Old Testament led to a diminution of its use among Jews, although Greek-speaking Jews continued to use a form of Aquila's version for many centuries.

For the most part, the Septuagint was intended to replace, rather than accompany, the Hebrew text, unlike the Aramaic versions in written or oral form. Although written *Targumim* did not develop until the first or second century CE in *Palestine and *Babylonia, several Aramaic versions of biblical texts have been found among the Dead Sea Scrolls.

Overall, the *Targumim* follow the Hebrew texts they are translating, but they are prone to substantial paraphrases and to tendencies such as the avoidance of anthropomorphisms relating to *God.

During the centuries that followed, Jews moved into many different lands with many different languages, typically producing one or more versions of the Hebrew Bible in the process. For Arabic-speaking Jews, the tenth-century translation prepared by *Saadia Gaon in Baghdad, the center of Jewish life in medieval *Iraq, is both representative and exemplary. Originally written in the Arabic language but with Hebrew characters (*Judeo-Arabic), Saadia's renderings reflected his view that, when confronted by substantial differences between the base text (here, the Hebrew Bible) and the language of the target audience (Arabic), one should place greater emphasis on what would be easiest for contemporary readers to understand. Thus, his version is often situated closer to the free rather than the literal "zone" on what might be called the "translation continuum."

On the European continent, there is an extensive history of translation of the Hebrew Bible into forms of German. Many of the earliest attempts display only rudimentary knowledge of either Hebrew or German. The *Judeo-German *Tzene-rene* from the mid-1600s, was promoted as a "woman's Bible," in keeping with the long-standing view that only women and children (and unlearned men, who were like women in their lack of an education in Hebrew) would need vernacular texts. At the end of the eighteenth century, Moses *Mendelssohn, a major Jewish Enlightenment (*Haskalah) figure, produced a version that combined the best German diction and styling of his day with a distinctively Jewish exegetical stance. Like Saadia's translation, his earliest German version was rendered in Hebrew letters. Mendelssohn was convinced that his work would allow Jews, as Jews, to learn German and to integrate into the German-speaking majority culture. As is often the case, this translator had social, cultural, and political, as well as theological aims in mind.

In very much the opposite direction, philosophers Martin *Buber and Franz *Rosenzweig collaborated on a German-language translation in the 1920s that privileged the Hebrew to such an extent that the result was very difficult to understand without recourse to the original. Their purpose, which has been shared by other translators, was to emphasize the essential foreignness of the biblical text in modern society. By the time Buber had completed this mammoth task, many potential readers had been lost in the *Holocaust. This loss of readership was even more true for the *Yiddish version that Yehoash (pen name of Solomon Bloomgarden [1879–1927]) labored over for decades.

For Jews in *Britain, the King James Version (KJV) of 1611 seemed to suffice as a translation until the end of the eighteenth century. Along with the introduction of English- and Spanish-language sermons and prayer books, the earliest English versions of the Bible for Jewish readers appeared in the late 1700s. At first, they consisted of little more than a page of the KJV facing a page of Hebrew, with a sprinkling of notes from Jewish exegetes, especially *Rashi. Over the next century, the Anglo-Jewish community produced lists of passages that needed to be modified, new renderings of specific books, and a few complete translations. Rarely parting company with KJV style, these versions are mostly distinguished by the increasing prominence of those who produced or sponsored them.

In America, Isaac *Leeser (1806–1868), rabbi, newspaper editor, and organizer, prepared a new English version, beginning with the Torah, in the 1840s. Although his style was at times criticized as wooden, his rendering, in successive editions, served the American Jewish community until the early part of the twentieth century. In 1917, the *Jewish Publication Society of America (JPS), under the editorship of Max Margolis (1866–1932), issued its English translation. It looked and sounded very much like the KJV; indeed, for the most part, it retained the wording of the KJV, through the Revised Version of 1885, except where Christological or other explicitly Christian renderings were found.

In the late 1950s, the JPS embarked on an ambitious new project that, under the editorship and leadership of Harry M. Orlinsky (1908–1992), culminated in *Tanakh: The Holy Scriptures, The New JPS Translation According to the Traditional Hebrew Text* (1985). Orlinsky championed an approach to translation that was initially termed "dynamic equivalence," but is now most often known as "functional equivalence." In this view, the most important goal of a translation is to reflect for contemporary audiences how a given word or phrase would have functioned for its ancient hearers or readers. The results are less literal than renderings that exemplify formal equivalence, in which the form of the original is maintained wherever possible. In 2006, JPS published *The Contemporary Torah: A Gender-Sensitive Adaptation of the JPS Translation*, edited by D. E. S. Stein.

At the beginning of the twenty-first century, there are a number of options, in addition to the JPS translations, for English-speaking Jews. They include the *ArtScroll Tanach*, whose target audience encompasses Orthodox Jews; its publisher, Mesorah, has also come out with editions of individual books of the Bible. Another version aimed at traditional Jews is Aryeh Kaplan's *The Living Torah*; his followers prepared three successive volumes, *The Living Nach*, which cover the remainder of the Hebrew Bible. Moreover, several Jewish scholars, following distinctive approaches to the biblical text, have come out with their own renderings of the Torah and other biblical materials. Among these works are the *Schocken Bible: The Five Books of Moses*, by Everett Fox; Richard E. Friedman, *Commentary on the Torah*; and Robert Alter, *The Five Books of Moses: A Translation with Commentary*.

Translations of the Bible are important indicators of how Jews have read and interpreted the text, and they, along with the translators responsible for them, should be valued and studied. At the same time, a Jewish translation should never be thought of as an end in itself but rather as a means to the highest possible familiarity with the Hebrew original. Thus, it is desirable that the Hebrew and the English (or other modern language) always appear together, so as to keep their proper relationship constantly in mind.

LEONARD GREENSPOON

Bible: Wisdom Literature. Wisdom literature is the technical name for the biblical genre exemplified by the books of *Proverbs, *Job, and *Ecclesiastes. The post-biblical books, *Wisdom of Ben Sira (also known as Ecclesiasticus) and Wisdom of Solomon, also fall into this category (see *APOCRYPHA). *Jeremiah 18:18 identifies the three categories of knowledge in the biblical era as priestly tradition, prophetic oracles, and wisdom: "Instruction shall not fail from the priest, nor counsel from the wise, nor oracle from the prophet." The source of wisdom is not divine, but human. The three biblical wisdom books were placed into the third section of the Hebrew Bible, the "Writings," because they were neither *Torah nor prophecy. As such, they are not read as part of the annual synagogue *Torah reading/*haftarah cycle, although Ecclesiastes is read on the *Sabbath that falls during *Sukkot, and scattered verses from all three books have found their way into the *liturgy.

The essence of wisdom literature is the application of human understanding to the question of how to live a prosperous, happy, and righteous life. In Proverbs, this question is answered by conveying moral teachings in short, memorable, sometimes thought-provoking maxims. Job and Ecclesiastes tackle darker, more troubling aspects of the human condition. The book of Job asks, "Why do bad things happen to good people?" or, as Jewish tradition frames this conundrum, *tzaddik v'ra lo* ("a righteous man who has it bad"). Ecclesiastes wonders whether true wisdom is attainable at all, at least amidst the illusory, ephemeral, material world, in the endless cycle of life "under the sun."

What all three works share is the conclusion that the ultimate source of human wisdom is the fear of *God: "The fear of the LORD is the beginning of knowledge" (Prov 1:7); "Fear of the Lord is wisdom; to shun evil is understanding" (Job 28:28); "The sum of the matter, when all is said and done: Revere God and observe His commandments!" (Eccl 12:13). It is the attitude behind these pronouncements that differs. In Proverbs, it is confident; in Ecclesiastes, the author comes to this position out of sophisticated resignation. The book of Job, more complicated still, oscillates between irony and a profound awareness of the gap between finite humanity and its infinite Creator.

Various passages elsewhere in the Bible have been linked to the wisdom tradition. It is likely that *Deuteronomy was quite influenced by it (compare Deut 1:15 with Exod 18:21). There are clearly some wisdom psalms as well, although there is no agreement on which ones they are. Yet Psalm 1 is certainly among them, suggesting that this tradition had a great deal to do with framing the book of *Psalms as a whole.

The Wisdom of Ben Sira, written at the beginning of the second century BCE, was originally written in Hebrew but survives completely only in Greek; about two-thirds of the original Hebrew text have now been discovered, partly in the Cairo *Genizah and partly among the *Dead Sea Scrolls. Unlike its predecessors, this book unites the maxims of wisdom teaching with a survey of Jewish history in the section beginning, "Let us now praise famous men" (44:1). Although Jewish tradition excluded Wisdom of Ben Sira from the biblical canon, and one opinion, cited in BT *Sanhedrin* 100b, declares that it is forbidden to read it, statements from the work appear elsewhere in the *Talmud, sometimes cited with the formula that introduces biblical quotations. The Greek translation of Ben Sira was made by the author's grandson, who immigrated to *Egypt where there was a large Greek-speaking Jewish community. The Wisdom of Solomon may have been composed in in *Alexandria, Egypt, in the first century CE, most likely in Greek. Here, too, traditional wisdom is combined with a description of God's actions in history.

The closest continuation of wisdom literature in *rabbinic writings is the *Mishnah tractate *Avot. It is sometimes known in English as "Ethics of the Fathers," but is more properly understood as "Basic Principles." Here the Rabbis offer their own guidance about how life is best lived (see ETHICS, RABBINIC). As in rabbinic literature in general, they understand every biblical reference to "wisdom" as a reference to *Torah – God's *revelation to the Jewish people as understood by its interpreters within the rabbinic tradition. Elsewhere in later *Judaism, one may trace the continuation of wisdom literature in medieval *thought; in the moralistic writings of the *Musar movement; and, via *Sefer Yetzirah*, in the theosophic and *mystical tradition.

MICHAEL CARASIK

Bible: Women: See entries under WOMEN

Biblical Commentary: Middle Ages to 1800. During the rabbinic period, the Sages produced a steady stream of *aggadic (nonlegal) commentary on the *Torah and other biblical books, interpreting the text in a creative, homiletical fashion that offered moral, didactic, and theological instruction. These works of *midrash were compiled into books arranged either as verse-by-verse commentaries (e.g., *Midrash Rabbah* on the *Torah and *Five Scrolls) or as collections of sermons (e.g., *Pesikta Rabbati* or *Pesikta de-Rav Kahana*).

It was not until the *Geonic period, when major Jewish centers flourished under Islamic rule, that commentaries as we know them began to be produced. They were preceded by grammatical treatises, paraphrases, and glossaries in *Judeo-Persian and *Judeo-Arabic, many of which were of *Karaite provenance. The earliest commentary that has survived more or less intact is *Pitron Shenem 'Asar* (Commentary on the Twelve [Minor Prophets]) by Daniel al-Kumisi, a Karaite communal leader and scholar, who immigrated from northern Persia to Jerusalem ca. 880 CE. Daniel's sophisticated exegetical work was a distinct departure from his *Rabbanite and Karaite predecessors; written in Hebrew, it was characterized by a strong philological sensibility, cohesive analysis, and sensitivity to the Bible's stylistic qualities (e.g., the use of metaphor or simile). Although not yet called so by name, this was the beginning of *peshat* or contextual interpretation.

A wealth of Judeo-Arabic commentary was produced in the tenth century. *Saadia Gaon (882–942) wrote translations and commentaries for many biblical books, as well as grammatical and lexicographical treatises. His extensive introductions discussed grammatical, exegetical, and philosophical issues and polemicized against the Karaites. He advocated interpreting the text according to its contextual meaning, unless common sense, experience, reason, or tradition demanded otherwise. Although his Karaite opponents advocated absolute freedom of interpretation, Saadia feared this approach would lead to religious anarchy and argued for maintaining a balance between freedom and the demands of tradition. This debate would reverberate in Jewish intellectual circles for many centuries.

A flourishing Karaite community in tenth-century *Jerusalem became a center of learning and inspiration for Karaites throughout the Middle East. There, the prolific exegete Japheth ben Eli, the only scholar to have translated and commented on the entire biblical corpus, wrote voluminous commentaries in the *peshat* tradition. These commentaries were influential among both Karaites and Rabbanites of succeeding generations, the latter gaining access to Japheth's work mainly through the mediation of Abraham *ibn Ezra.

In the tenth and eleventh centuries the intellectual and spiritual center of medieval Jewry shifted to Muslim *Spain where grammarians such as Menaḥem ben Saruk, *Dunash ben Labrat, and especially Judah Ḥayyuj and Jonah ibn Janah refined the study of biblical Hebrew *grammar and philology. By the time of Abraham ibn Ezra (1089–1164) this golden age was drawing to a close. Ibn Ezra, a prominent grammarian, biblical commentator, philosopher, and poet, left his homeland in 1140 for points east, bringing the sophisticated grammatical, exegetical, and philosophical learning of Muslim Spain to the European Jewish communities through which he passed (including *Italy, *France, and *England). His commentaries, based on a thorough knowledge of Hebrew grammar and lexicography, are grounded in reason and logic. Ibn Ezra believed that Scripture uses human language and conforms to the rules of grammar, syntax, and rhetoric. A steadfast opponent of the Karaites and loyal defender of the oral tradition, Ibn Ezra never accepted as *peshat* an interpretation that contradicted Jewish law. He incorporated his philosophical views into his commentaries, especially about creation and God's relationship with the land and people of Israel (see GRAMMARIANS AND LEXICOGRAPHERS; and THOUGHT, MEDIEVAL).

In the twelfth century, the *Kimḥi family emigrated from Spain to Narbonne, *Provence, joining a growing community of scholars who followed the intellectual traditions of Spanish Jewry. The grammarian and exegete, David Kimḥi (Radak; ca. 1160–1235), wrote commentaries on the Torah, *Prophets, *Psalms, *Proverbs, *Job, and *Chronicles. His grammatical works, *Mikhlol* and *Shorashim*, contain considerable material of exegetical value. His commentaries, which often relied on his predecessors, represent the best of the Spanish *peshat* tradition but also are sensitive to the midrashic tradition as exemplified in the commentaries of *Rashi (see later). He peppered his commentaries with philosophical ideas of the *Maimonidean rationalist school and also applied certain biblical prophecies and verses from Psalms to the Jews of his own day; many of his writings include prayers and hopes for the *messianic era and ultimate *redemption.

In the second half of the eleventh century another school of *peshat* exegesis began to develop in northern France, drawing on the work of anonymous glossators, or *poterim*. The founder of the school was Solomon ben Isaac, commonly known as *Rashi (1040–1105), who wrote commentaries on almost the entire biblical corpus as well as an indispensable commentary on the *Talmud. The majority of Rashi's Torah commentary is based on midrashic sources, but it also includes many grammatical and lexicographical comments as well as comments on aspects of daily life and geographical locations. Its genius lies in its clarity of language, felicity of expression, and skillful editing of its sources. Rashi's purpose in his commentaries is to explain the text in its context; he usually avoids midrashic comments that stray too far from the plain meaning of the text but does

use them on occasion for didactic or polemical purposes. His commentary has enjoyed unparalleled popularity and has been translated and commented on numerous times.

Rashi's students and younger contemporaries in the northern French *peshat* school of exegesis moved away from his approach, severely restricting midrashic elements and focusing on contextual exegesis. Thus, Joseph Kara (1050–1125) argued for understanding the text on its own terms without midrashic embellishment. Rashbam (Samuel ben Meir; ca. 1080–ca. 1160), Rashi's grandson, was the foremost figure of this school. He is best known for his Torah commentary (he also probably commented on most of the *Five Scrolls and possibly *Job) in which he shows himself to be a radical adherent of *peshat* interpretation, favoring it over rabbinic tradition when the two clashed. He distinguished between halakhic commentary, used to establish Jewish practice, and *peshat* commentary, used to determine the meaning of the text, claiming a legitimate role for both. Interested in grammar and style, Rashbam was remarkably sensitive to literary aspects of the text. Eliezer of Beaugency (mid-twelfth century), the third major exponent of the *peshat* school, commented on many books, although only his commentaries on the Latter *Prophets have survived. His style is paraphrastic, and he pays a great deal of attention to matters of redaction. Joseph Bekhor Shor (1130–1200), the last member of the school, was a transitional figure between the *peshat* school and the *Tosafists. His Torah commentary included midrashic material and *gematria*, the latter a feature it shared with those of the German pietists (*Ḥasidei Ashkenaz*) of the thirteenth century. Later generations mostly neglected the *peshat* school; its work was only rediscovered in the nineteenth century. In recent years it has been the subject of renewed interest and study.

The thirteenth century witnessed the maturation of the mystical trend in Judaism called the *Kabbalah (tradition), culminating in the production of the *Zohar*, which is generally attributed to *Moses de Leon and his circle. It is in the *Zohar* and other writings of Moses de Leon that one first encounters the acronym *pardes* (*pardes* is also word meaning "orchard" in Hebrew), referring to four levels of interpretation of the biblical text: *peshat, remez, derash*, and *sod*, or historical, philosophical, homiletical, and mystical. The kabbalists seem to have introduced the fourth level to validate the work of their predecessors and to claim pride of place for their innovative mode of interpretation. The mystic, Baḥia ben Asher (d. 1340), was one of the few medieval exegetes to use all four levels of interpretation in one commentary, although he was not yet familiar with the term *pardes*.

*Naḥmanides (Moses ben Naḥman; Ramban; 1194–1270), the preeminent figure of mid-thirteenth-century Spanish Jewry, was best known for his commentary on the Torah. This commentary marks a new stage in the history of biblical interpretation because it was influenced by both the Spanish and *Ashkenazic traditions. Although trained in grammar and philology, Naḥmanides found the grammatical approach of the Spanish school, exemplified by Abraham ibn Ezra, too narrow and limiting. Sympathetic to Rashi's selective use of midrashic material, he struck a balance between the two approaches, incorporating theology, ethics, history, and character analysis into a holistic approach that operates on several levels. Ramban, who is famous for his psychological insights and deep understanding of human nature, was also a genuine kabbalist, steeped in the mystical traditions of the Provençal school of Kabbalah, and he makes numerous allusions to esoteric meanings of various biblical texts. In addition, he was among the few medieval commentators who made use of typology, the method of ascribing long-term influence and significance to the deeds and actions of biblical figures, a theological notion articulated in the expression, *ma'aseh avot siman le-vanim* ("the deed of the ancestors is a sign for their children").

This period also produced a number of Aristotelian philosophers, who sought to harmonize their philosophical learning with the teachings of the Torah. The Provençal philosopher and biblical commentator, Levi ben Gershon (Ralbag, *Gersonides, 1280–1344), the greatest of these philosophers, was arguably the most original Jewish thinker of the late Middle Ages. His commentaries on the Torah, Former *Prophets, *Five Scrolls, and Job are laced with philosophical insights, but contain straightforward *peshat* interpretations as well.

Fifteenth-century Spain produced a number of prominent biblical scholars, including Isaac *Arama (ca. 1420–1494) whose commentary '*Akedat Yitzhak*, a fine example of philosophico-homiletical exegesis, has retained a loyal following to this day. His student Isaac Abarbanel (also spelled Abrabanel or *Abravanel; 1437–1508), was a statesman, philosopher, and master exegete who produced voluminous commentaries on the Torah, Prophets, and *Daniel, arranged in problem–solution fashion. His primary focus was *peshat*, but Abarbanel also incorporated *midrashim* that he found acceptable. Although his theology preferred faith over reason, as a Renaissance humanist he was open to new ideas and introduced much contemporary thought into his writing. His commentaries on *Samuel and *Kings are full of his ideas about monarchy, which, based on his personal experience, he did not hold in high esteem.

The Early Modern period (sixteenth to eighteenth centuries) was not an era of great innovation but it produced a number of commentaries of lasting importance. Obadiah Sforno (1475–1550), rabbi, physician, and Renaissance humanist, was the most famous Italian biblical commentator of the sixteenth century. His commentaries on the Torah and Psalms, written in the *peshat* tradition with a humanist sensibility, are still widely read. Ephraim Solomon ben Aaron of Luntshits (1550–1619), rabbi, preacher, and communal leader in *Prague, was the author of *Keli Yekar* (Precious Vessel), a very popular and insightful homiletical commentary on the Torah. The Moroccan rabbi, Hayyim ben Moses ibn Attar (1696–1743), was the author of the compendious Torah commentary *Or ha-Hayyim* (The Light of Life), which included elements of *peshat* interpretation, as well as psychological analyses of biblical characters and their motives, interpretations of rabbinic statements, moral instruction and admonition, mystical lore, halakhic discussions, and historical and personal reflections. In Jaworow, *Galicia, David Altschuler and his son Jehiel produced immensely popular commentaries on the Prophets and Writings, *Metzudat David* and *Metzudat Tziyyon*. All of these commentaries are included in various editions of the *Mikra'ot Gedolot*, the "Rabbinic Bible," which has been produced in countless editions since the early 1800s.

Toward the end of the eighteenth century, the *Haskalah (Jewish Enlightenment) was under way in *Berlin. Moses *Mendelssohn (1729–1786), its most famous proponent, produced a new edition of the Bible, called *Netivot ha-Shalom* (Paths of Peace), intended for the educated German-speaking Jewish laity. It featured a carefully edited Hebrew text, a German translation in Hebrew characters, and a commentary in Hebrew called the *Bi'ur* (commentary), culled mainly from medieval *peshat* commentators (Rashi, Ibn Ezra, Rashbam, Ramban), but also including new linguistic and literary insights. Mendelssohn was assisted in this enterprise by other scholars, including Naftali Herz Wessely (1725–1805) and Solomon Dubno (1738–1813). They went out of their way to include both halakhic and aggadic rabbinic interpretations, demonstrating their beauty and value to an audience that may have had little exposure to rabbinic literature. *Netivot ha-Shalom*, which went through many nineteenth-century editions, paved the way for more critical works incorporating the findings of contemporary non-Jewish scholarship.

For further reading, see A. Y. Finkel, *The Great Torah Commentators* (1990); M. Saebo, ed., *Hebrew Bible/ Old Testament: The History of its Interpretation*, vol. I/2: *The Middle Ages* (2000), vol. II: *From the Renaissance to the Enlightenment* (2008); and B. D. Walfish, "Medieval Jewish Interpretation," in *The Jewish Study Bible*, ed. A. Berlin and M. Z. Brettler (2003), 1876–1900.   BARRY DOV WALFISH

Birobidjan is a geographic territory in *Russia's Far East, adjacent to the Chinese border. In the late 1920s the *Soviet Union designated certain territory in this region as the national homeland of Soviet Jewry. The Kremlin hoped that Birobidjan, officially known as the Jewish Autonomous Region since 1934, would become the center of a Soviet Jewish culture rooted in *Yiddish and *communist values and would serve as an alternative to *Palestine as the center of Jewish state-building. Yiddish, the nationally designated language of Soviet Jewry, was seen as the key to the secularization of Jewish society and culture. The Soviet government tried to foster the region's specifically Jewish nature by setting up Yiddish schools, newspapers, and cultural institutions. Street signs, railway station signs, and postmarks appeared in both Yiddish and Russian, and the teaching of Yiddish was obligatory in schools where Russian was the language of instruction. However, given its remote location and inclement living conditions, Birobidjan never attracted many Jews; the government's campaign against Jewish culture and intellectuals after the mid-1930s also undermined efforts to realize Birobidjan's goal as a center of Soviet Jewish society. For further reading, see R. Weinberg, *Stalin's Forgotten Zion* (1998).   ROBERT WEINBERG

Blessing of the Moon (*kiddush levanah*) is a *blessing established by the *Tannaim to be recited on seeing the *New Moon. The new month (*Rosh Hodesh*) was based on the observation of the moon and was to be formally blessed by the head of the Jewish court (*Beit Din*). It has become customary in traditional Jewish practice to recite this blessing with a *minyan* at the conclusion of the *Sabbath. The blessing is to be recited between the third and fifteenth day of the month, ideally when the moon is visible.

ELIZABETH SHULMAN

Blessings. A *berakhah* (pl. *berakhot*), or liturgical benediction, is a Jewish *prayer that contains the words *barukh*

atah adonai (Blessed" or "Praised are You, O Ruler"). When this formula appears at the beginning of the *berakhah*, it is usually followed by the words, *eloheinu melekh ha-olam* ("Our God, King [or Sovereign] of the Universe [or Eternal Sovereign]").

A *berakhah* is the Jewish response to a sense of awe in the presence of a divine gift, which might be as simple as a piece of bread or as important as a major life-cycle event. The first three words of the formula, which appear only twice in the Hebrew *Bible, were universally accepted as normative by the third century CE. Some have connected the word *berakhah* with the word *berekh,* which means "knee," and see the act of blessing as related to kneeling or genuflecting as a symbol of devotion to *God.

Judaism validates the physical dimension of life and sees physical gratification as an appropriate experience for religious devotion. There are *berakhot* for smell, sight, hearing, touch, and taste. One interesting example calls for a *berakhah* when one is in a place where one feels a miracle was performed; because the individual makes that decision, it is clear that the perception of the miraculous is understood to be subjective.   SAUL WACHS

Blessings: Before and After Meals. These benedictions express long-standing Jewish traditions of offering thanksgiving. The *blessing (*berakhah*) that precedes any substantial meal (defined by many as including bread) is called *Birkat ha-Motzi.* It consists of the usual *petihah* or opening formula: "*Barukh atah Adonai Eloheinu melekh ha-olam*" ("Blessed" or "Praised are You Adonai, our God, King, or Sovereign of the Universe . . .") and ends with the words, "*ha-motzi lehem min ha-aretz*" ("who takes out" or "brings forth bread from the earth"). Most *berakhot* that are recited before eating describe God's act with the verb "*borei,*" which is understood as "creates." An example is " . . . *borei peri ha-gafen*" ("who creates the fruit of the vine . . ."), which is recited before drinking wine or grape juice. This verb is only used to describe *divine* creativity. Perhaps one reason why the *berakhah* for bread employs a different verb is that the production of bread involves a combination of human and divine activity.

*Psalm 104:15 notes the distinctiveness of bread: "bread sustains human life." Psalm 104:14 serves as a source for the text of the *berakhah*: "You cause grass to grow for cattle and plants for people to cultivate, *bringing forth bread from the earth.*" Therefore, the blessing offers a hidden *midrash or rabbinic interpretation. In Psalm 104:14, human labor produces the bread. In the *berakhah,* God brings forth the bread, a reminder that human beings have a partner in producing the food that they eat.

Finally, the *berakhah* before meals uses the verb *motzi* ("takes out" or "brings forth"). The infinitive form, *l'hotzi,* from which *motzi* derives, is most commonly used in the Hebrew *Bible in connection with the Exodus from *Egypt and recalls the gift of freedom. Use of this verb in the blessing before a meal evokes the many places in the Bible where its meaning is attached to the transition from slavery to freedom. The *commandment to recall the Exodus is mentioned more frequently than any other in the Hebrew Bible and is usually accompanied by an injunction to care for the poor. Thus, the verb *motzi* also reinforces the idea, embedded in every *berakhah,* of the commandment to share so that no one is without sustenance.

Birkat ha-Mazon (grace after meals) consists of a collection of *berakhot* and other texts. The mandate to recite *Birkat ha-Mazon* is considered to be biblical, which makes it unique among all liturgical benedictions. The proof-text is Deuteronomy 8:10: "When you have eaten your fill, you shall give thanks to the Lord your God for the good land which He has given you." It is striking that there is a mandate to give thanks *after* eating. The context in Deuteronomy 8:11–18 makes clear the danger that, in a state of satiation, one might be tempted to forget God and celebrate only human achievements. A shared sense of dependence on God is more likely to express itself in acts of generosity and responsibility.

Although shared meals and religious fellowship are very old, it is generally accepted that the first three *berakhot* of *Birkat ha-Mazon* stem from the period of the *Second Temple. Talmudic tradition, however, ascribes them to biblical figures (*Moses, *Joshua, *David, and *Solomon) and connects the texts with major events in their lives (Moses gave thanks for the food as the manna fell from heaven, etc.). It seems likely that the text in its current form developed in stages, with spontaneous formulations gradually incorporating fixed topics and then fixed phrases. The first *berakhah,* cast in universal language, thanks God for providing sustenance for all. The second *berakhah* speaks to the experience of the Jew and expresses thanks for the Land of *Israel, for freedom from bondage in Egypt, for the *berit* (*covenant) between God and Israel, the *Torah, life, and food. The third blessing, petitionary in nature, asks God's compassion for the Jewish people, *Jerusalem, and the *Temple and requests that no one go hungry or be dependent on the gifts of others. The fourth and final *berakhah,* understood to have been added after the destruction of the Temple in 70 CE, recapitulates some of the earlier themes, expressing the goodness of life and God's beneficence to all living creatures.

According to the Babylonian *Talmud (*Berakhot* 48b), this final blessing was added to the original three in gratitude for the burial of those who died at Beitar, the site of the final battle in the Second *Jewish War against *Rome (132–135 CE) (see also BAR KOKHBA). It is an expansion of a short *berakhah* to be recited when one hears good news. Its status as an addition to the original three blessings is reflected in the fact that it starts with a *petihah* or opening formula, an indication of a new beginning. A series of petitions follow that vary in different rites (that is, liturgies associated with specific Jewish communities). Each begins by calling God "*ha-Rahaman*" (the merciful one). They reiterate themes of sustenance, freedom, and *redemption.

It is customary for a guest to lead *Birkat ha-Mazon* and to invoke God's blessings on the host and hostess. As in other major Jewish prayers, the final theme is *shalom* (peace). When three or more people eat together, *Birkat ha-Mazon* is introduced by a formula stating that all that is enjoyed belongs to God and therefore it is appropriate to express thanks for these gifts. This section is more fluid than most parts of Jewish *worship, and some people have added petitions that invoke God's blessings on the host country, the State of *Israel, the governments that protect us, and on all who work for peace. At the end of the grace are a series of biblical verses that reiterate the Jewish belief that God cares for everyone. Thus, *Birkat ha-Mazon* concludes as it began, expressing appreciation for God's role in sustaining life.   SAUL WACHS

Blood Libel: See BEILIS TRIAL; RITUAL MURDER ACCUSATION

B'nai B'rith. See ORGANIZATIONS: NORTH AMERICA; UNITED STATES: FRATERNAL SOCIETIES

Bolshevism: *Russian Empire and *Soviet Union.

Bolshevism, the Marxist-Leninist revolutionary movement that took power in the Russian Empire, was frequently seen, especially by its opponents, as "Jewish." This connection contained elements of both truth and falsehood. Jews who became Bolsheviks frequently Russified their names and rejected any identification with either Judaism or Jewishness. Such a rejection was in harmony with the Bolshevik project. That is, Bolshevism, which promised racial blindness and equality for all, was receptive to Jews as individuals; the Bolshevik Revolution abolished the *Pale of Settlement, together with all residency and professional restrictions on Jews. However, Bolshevism was not, either in theory or in practice, receptive to Judaism, which it condemned together with all religions as an "opiate of the masses." Moreover, Bolshevik ideology demanded that national identities be abandoned in favor of Marxist internationalism (see MARX, KARL).

Jews in the Russian Empire who became *communists comprised a small minority of the overall Jewish population; likewise, communists of Jewish origin were never the majority of Bolshevik Party members, either before or after the Bolshevik Revolution. Yet Jews were overrepresented in the Bolshevik Party: In 1927, when Jews comprised 1.8% of the total Soviet population, communists of Jewish origin represented 4.3% of the membership of the Communist Party of the Soviet Union. Only 5% of Jewish Communist Party members in 1922 had been Bolsheviks before the 1917 Bolshevik Revolution. Before that event, most Jews active in the Russian left had been Mensheviks or *Bundists. After 1917, the Bolsheviks monopolized the Russian left, and options such as Menshevism and Bundism were effectively foreclosed.

More striking was Jewish overrepresentation in the upper ranks of the party leadership, especially during the early decades of the Soviet regime when Jews played a prominent role. Of twenty-one Central Committee members in August 1917, six – Lev Kamenev, Grigory Sokolnikov, Yakov Sverdlov, Leon Trotsky, Moisei Uritskii, and Grigory Zinoviev – were of Jewish origin. In January 1937, the 111 highest ranking officers in the Soviet secret police, the NKVD, included 42 Jews, 35 Russians, 8 Latvians, and 26 individuals of other nationalities. During the Stalinist purges, known as the "Terror," the ethnic balance shifted quickly. By July 1939, ethnic Russians filled 67% of the highest ranking positions in the Soviet NKVD, ethnic Ukrainians 12%, and Jews 4%. Soviet *Ukraine followed a not dissimilar model: In 1936, sixty of ninety ranking officers in the Ukrainian branch of the NKVD were Jews. By 1939 this number had fallen dramatically.

In 1918, "Jewish sections," or *Evsektsii*, were established within the Bolshevik Party, together with an administrative leadership, the Jewish Commissariat, or *Evkom*. The *Evsektsii*, which remained in existence until 1930, were intended to facilitate the integration of Russian Jews into the Soviet project. Practically speaking, the *Evsektsii* were charged with overseeing the destruction of traditional Jewish life, translating communism into *Yiddish, bolshevizing the Jewish proletariat, and reconstructing Jewish life in accordance with Lenin's *korenizatsiia* (indigenization) campaign and its slogan: "National in form, socialist in content." (Leninist policy on nationalities was predicated on the idea that, just as the proletarian dictatorship was a stage toward the eventual withering away of the state, so was the blossoming of national cultures a stage toward the eventual withering away of national differences.) Thus, the Bolshevik Party and the *Evsektsii*, in particular, promoted the *Yiddish press, Yiddish publishing, and Yiddish schools; the Moscow State Yiddish *Theater flourished. *Hebrew, conversely, was identified with the "bourgeois-clerical-*Zionist camp" and accordingly was persecuted. In 1928, the Soviet government approved the creation of an autonomous Jewish agricultural settlement in *Birobidjan, a remote region in the Soviet Far East distant from existing centers of Jewish settlement. In the following decade some 43,000 Jews settled in Birobidjan; of these, only 19,000 decided to remain. *Judaism was condemned in the Jewish Autonomous Region, while Yiddish culture was championed. The Yiddish novelist Dovid Bergelson dedicated his story "Barg-aruf" (Uphill) to Birobidjan, where it was published in 1936 (see LITERATURE, YIDDISH: 1800 TO TWENTY-FIRST CENTURY).

During World War II, Soviet authorities supported the establishment of the *Jewish Anti-Fascist Committee (JAC) whose chairman, Solomon Mikhoels, was also the director of the Moscow State Yiddish Theater. The purpose of the Committee was to disseminate pro-Soviet propaganda among Jewish communities abroad and in this way to garner Western political and financial support for Soviet war efforts against *Nazi Germany. Among the results of the Committee's work was the publication of the so-called Black Book, documenting both the *Holocaust and the Jewish resistance movement.

The role of Jews in the Soviet regime decreased significantly after the war. Solomon Mikhoels was murdered in 1948 on Stalin's orders. That same year Stalin initiated an antisemitic campaign against so-called rootless cosmopolitans, Soviet support for the new State of *Israel ended, and the Jewish Anti-Fascist Committee was disbanded. The Moscow State Yiddish Theater was liquidated in 1949. In August 1952, during the "Night of the Murdered Poets," thirteen JAC members, including prominent Yiddish writers and poets, were executed. By this time Jews had ceased to play a prominent role in the Bolshevik Party.

Scholarship on this topic includes B.-C. Pinchuk, *Shtetl Jews under Soviet Rule: Eastern Poland on the Eve of the Holocaust* (1990); S. Redlich, *War, Holocaust and Stalinism* (1995); Y. Slezkine, *The Jewish Century* (2004); and R. S. Wistrich, *Revolutionary Jews from Marx to Trotsky* (1976).

MARCI SHORE

Boston, a port city founded in 1630, is the capital of Massachusetts and the largest metropolitan area (approximately 4.5 million) in New England. Boston's Jewish community emerged much later than those in other major Eastern Seaboard cities; as a result, its character was quite different. Few Jews passed through Boston during the colonial era; there was neither an organized Jewish community nor a significant Jewish presence in Boston's port. Similarly, the German Jewish *immigration of the mid-nineteenth century had a limited impact on Boston. Only in the 1880s and 1890s, when Jewish immigration from *Eastern Europe to America intensified, did Boston's Jewish community grow significantly.

The first East European Jews to settle in Boston worked primarily in the textile and shoe industries. They first lived in the South End, but the North End soon became a center of Jewish life; Jews lived alongside other minorities and many social and religious organizations emerged. The Federation of Jewish Charities, established in Boston in 1895, is considered the first federated Jewish philanthropy in the United States. Many Jews later moved to Chelsea and Boston's West End, and then in large numbers to Dorchester and Roxbury. By 1917, Boston's Jewish population was approximately 75,000, making it the fifth largest Jewish community in the United States.

These immigration patterns shaped Boston's character in several ways. The battles between German and East European Jews that defined most other large cities were drastically reduced because there was no entrenched German Jewish elite. This lack of a German Jewish presence also meant that *Reform Judaism grew more slowly in Boston than it did elsewhere and that the debate over *Zionism in Boston was much less contentious than in other American Jewish communities. One estimate suggests that 90% of Boston's Jews supported Zionism, and Louis D. *Brandeis, one of America's leading Zionist voices, was a key leader of Boston's Jewish community.

Boston was a homogeneous city, and its Jews faced the same xenophobia as the city's other minorities. This initially made Boston a much less appealing place for new immigrants to settle. *Antisemitism was a significant concern, particularly during the 1930s, and anti-Jewish violence in the 1960s impelled many Jews to move to new Jewish suburban centers in Newton and Brookline.

According to the 2005 Boston Community Survey conducted by the Steinhardt Social Research Institute, the Greater Boston Jewish community numbered approximately 210,000 Jews, comprising 7.2% of the population. The community was well educated: 91% of Jewish adults aged twenty-five and older were college graduates, and 27% had advanced degrees. Boston's *intermarriage rate was 37%, nearly identical to that of *New York City, but below the national average. According to the survey, the overwhelming majority of Boston Jewish adults were connected to Judaism in some way – for example, 85% donated to Jewish organizations, and 74% identified with Judaism through religious practice. Nearly half of all Boston Jewish adults in 2005 belonged to a religious congregation.

For further reading, see J. Sarna, E. Smith, and S. Kosofsky, eds., *The Jews of Boston* (1995); and Steinhardt Social Research Institute, *The 2005 Boston Community Survey*.

MICHAEL R. COHEN

Brandeis, Louis Dembitz (1856–1941), American jurist and Zionist leader, was born in Louisville, Kentucky, but established his career in *Boston after graduating from Harvard Law School in 1876. President Woodrow Wilson appointed Brandeis, an outspoken reformer, to the Supreme Court in 1916, where he served until his retirement in 1939. He was the first Jew appointed to the court, and his confirmation was highly contentious. Brandeis was a supporter of *Zionism, and he played an important role in persuading Wilson to support the *Balfour Declaration, a British statement of support for an eventual Jewish homeland in *Palestine, despite opposition from the State Department and Wilson's other advisors. As leader of the Federation of American Zionists beginning in 1914, Brandeis was able to reconcile support for Zionism with living in America in a way that made the movement acceptable to many Jews who had no intention of moving to *Palestine. For a recent biography, see M. Urofsky, *Louis D. Brandeis: A Life* (2009); and **see UNITED STATES PRESIDENTS; and ZIONISM: UNITED STATES.**

Brazil. Although the Brazilian census of 1872 recorded no Jewish inhabitants in Brazil, perhaps two thousand Jews were settled there at that time. They made significant social and economic progress in the capital city, Rio de Janeiro, and established some communal institutions. Most Jews in late-nineteenth-century Brazil were the descendants of *Ladino-speaking *Sephardic *North Africans who settled in Belém do Pará, with a smaller group going to Rio de Janeiro. Many were merchants who had discovered that they could easily obtain Brazilian naturalization certificates and thus return to Morocco with a sense of security.

The first proposal for Jewish colonization of Brazil was formulated in 1881 but was never acted on. The Jewish Colonization Association formed two agricultural colonies in Rio Grande do Sul between 1904 and 1924. These Eastern European Jewish colonists numbered no more than a few thousand, yet were critical to orienting Jewish migration toward Brazil, especially after World War I. Jews made up about 45% to 50% of immigrants arriving in Brazil from *Eastern Europe after 1920. Between 1924 and 1934, Eastern European immigration to Brazil increased almost tenfold, and by the end of the 1930s the Jewish population of Brazil approached 60,000.

Eastern European Jews settled primarily in the states of São Paulo, Rio Grande do Sul, and Rio de Janeiro; they achieved a level of economic success matched only by immigrants from the Middle East and Japan. This combination of economic success and cultural difference made Jews particular targets of Brazilian nativists during the Great Depression. By 1934 immigration quotas had been established, and criticism of Jewish immigration became a regular component of political discourse. Beginning in 1935, Brazil began to deny visas to Jews, an indication that *antisemitism was common among Brazilian intellectuals and policymakers in the 1930s. However, Jewish immigration continued according to established patterns, largely because Jewish leaders in and out of Brazil were able to convince important politicians that refugees from German-speaking Europe could bring skills and capital. In 1938 more Jews entered Brazil than in any of the ten previous years.

Jewish settlement expanded in the 1950s when significant numbers of Middle Eastern Jews, notably from *Egypt and Syria, arrived after the Suez Crisis. According to the 2000 census, Brazil's Jewish population is 86,825; virtually all live in urban areas. Some Jewish organizations in Brazil place the number between 100,000 and 140,000.

The largest Jewish community is in São Paulo, Brazil's largest city, with 60,000 members in a population of 10.4 million. The second largest Jewish community is in Rio de Janeiro (25,000–30,000 Jews in a population of 5.85 million); the third is in Porto Alegre (in the southern state of Rio Grande do Sul) with about 10,000–12,000 Jews in a population of about 1.36 million. There are also communities in Belo Horizonte (5,000), Curitiba (3,000), Santos (1,500), Salvador (1,000), and Recife (1,000).

For further reading, see J. Lesser, *Welcoming the Undesirables: Brazil and the Jewish Question* (1995).

JEFFREY LESSER

Breaking of the Vessels (*shevirat ha-kelim*) is the central dramatic event in the detailed myth of the evolution of divine and earthly realms in *Lurianic *Kabbalah. The *Safed kabbalist, Moses *Cordovero, introduced the term *kelim* (vessels), a generation before Luria, to describe the structure of the divine *sefirot* as vessels into which divine essence is poured to form divine powers of specific character and function. This process may be perceived as an inverse presentation of the Aristotelian concepts of matter and form; here, the more divine element is the essence, the counterpart of formless matter. Luria transformed this theosophical conception into a mythical creation narrative: After the *tzimtzum*, the contraction of the infinite Godhead into itself, a line of divine light entered the empty space and began to form the vessels and to fill them with pure divine light, the essence. A catastrophe occurred when the created vessels could not contain the essence and shattered; their shards created the lower realms in which the universe later came into being. One of the explanations for this event is that the vessels contained within them the potential seeds of evil, which rebelled against the attempt to integrate them in the positive process of creation. After this shattering, the process of *tikkun*, mending the vessels, began. It will culminate in the eradication of evil and constitute the true, final, divine unity. For further reading, see G. Scholem, *Major Trends in Jewish Mysticism* (1955); and idem, *On the Kabbalah and Its Symbolism* (1965).

JOSEPH DAN

Bride and Bridegroom. Biblical prophets use bridal imagery to characterize both Israel's unfaithfulness to *God (e.g., *Jer 2:32) and Israel's future *redemption when "a sound of joy and gladness, the voice of bridegroom (*ḥatan*) and bride (*kallah*)" (Jer 33:11) will be heard in the land. *Isaiah 62:4–5 imagines both the redeemed people and the restored Land of *Israel as a beloved bride. This metaphorical association of *marriage with joy and prosperity, fertility, and national rebirth became a part of Jewish life and practice. The seven blessings (*sheva berakhot*) recited at traditional Jewish weddings (found in BT *Ketubbot* 7b–8a) incorporate Jeremiah's prophecies of a messianic future with the happiness of the present, praising God who creates "joy and gladness, groom and bride, mirth, glad song, pleasure, delight, love, brotherhood, peace, and companionship" and "who causes the groom to rejoice with his bride." According to BT *Berakhot* 6b, gladdening the bride and groom is considered a legal obligation. Amusing the bride and groom with singing, dancing, and joking became traditional ways of celebrating Jewish weddings.

The *Song of Songs uses the Hebrew word *kallah*, generally translated as "bride," as a term of endearment for the female beloved (4:6–12, 5:1). Traditionally Jews understood this biblical book as an allegory referring to the loving intimacy between God and Israel. Some Jewish traditions connected with the festival of *Shavuot, which is linked with the revelation of the *Torah at Mount Sinai, celebrate the metaphorical marriage between God and Israel. In *Sephardic communities, the Sabbath before Shavuot is called *Shabbat Kallah* (Sabbath of the Bride).

The theme of the *Torah as bride and Israel as bridegroom, with God serving as divine matchmaker, is also found in traditional rituals connected with the autumn festival of *Simḥat Torah: The reader of the final section of the Torah is called *ḥatan Torah* (bridegroom of the Torah), and the reader of the first section of Genesis is known as *ḥatan bereshit* (bridegroom of the beginning). In other traditions the *Sabbath is personified as Israel's bride. According to the midrash collection *Genesis Rabbah* 11:8, the Sabbath is the bridal partner of the Jewish people. The ceremony of *Kabbalat Shabbat* (Welcoming the Sabbath) began in the sixteenth-century community of *mystics in *Safed. There, Solomon ha-Levi Alkabetz (ca. 1500–1580) wrote the famous invocation to the Sabbath bride, "*Lekhah dodi likrat kallah, penei Shabbat nekabbelah*" (Go, my beloved, to meet the bride, let us receive the presence of the Sabbath), that is still a part of the Sabbath eve liturgy.

For further reading, see E. Ginsburg, *The Sabbath in the Classical Kabbalah* (1989); M. Idel, "Sexual Metaphors and Praxis in the Kabbalah," in *The Jewish Family*, ed. D. Kraemer (1989), 197–224; and B. A. Holdrege, "Bride of Israel," in *Rethinking Scripture*, ed. M. Levering (1989), 180–261.

JUDITH R. BASKIN

Britain: Early Modern and Modern. The modern history of Jews in the United Kingdom of Great Britain [*England, Scotland, and Wales] and Northern Ireland (UK) begins in the mid-seventeenth century when a number of *Converso* merchants, among them some crypto-Jews, settled in England (see also ENGLAND: MIDDLE AGES). In 1655, rabbi and scholar *Menasseh ben Israel traveled to England from *Amsterdam to promote the official recognition of Jews. In his *Hope of Israel*, he argued that Jews had to reside in England for the *messiah to come. Britain's ruler at that time, Oliver Cromwell, a devout Puritan influenced by both theological and mercantile considerations, was open to Jewish readmission and called the "Whitehall Conference" in December 1655 to consider whether and under what conditions it was lawful to admit Jews. Although millennarians supported readmission, merchants feared commercial competition; *antisemitic literature probably influenced public opinion as well. Rather than have a negative decision on record, Cromwell dismissed the gathering.

Despite the failure of formal readmission, the Jewish community grew. *Sephardic Jews established a *synagogue in Creechurch Lane in 1657 and a cemetery shortly thereafter. In 1701, when the old synagogue proved too small, the community opened Bevis Marks Synagogue; its interior strongly reflects the influence of the 1677 Amsterdam synagogue. British Jews elected a governing body after Cromwell's death (1658) and the restoration of the Stuarts to the throne (1660) and accompanied William of Orange to England in 1688, during the Glorious Revolution.

Although some tension existed between *Ashkenazim and *Sephardim, they lived in close proximity and worshiped together until the founding of the Ashkenazi Great Synagogue in Duke's Place (1690). Marriages between the two communities increased as Ashkenazim became wealthier. By the mid-eighteenth century, synagogues cooperated on a scheme of charitable relief for immigrant Jews. During this period, Jewish observance appears to have been lax and Jewish knowledge limited. Behavior among the wealthy reflected English morés.

In the eighteenth century, Jewish occupations varied widely. Although Jewish merchants and contractors helped provide supplies for the Seven Years War, Christian merchants succeeded in limiting Jews to 12 places (of 124) on the Royal Exchange. Jews depended on the Crown and Lord Mayor to maintain their position. Ashkenazim, largely from *Central Europe, became numerically dominant early in the eighteenth century, but power remained in the hands of the "more respectable" and acculturated Sephardim. Most Ashkenazim were poor and worked as hawkers, peddlers, and rag and used clothing sellers; a small percentage was involved in crime.

As early as 1746, the Sephardi and Ashkenazi synagogues appointed a standing Committee of Deputies to lobby for change in naturalization laws. The test case for English *emancipation occurred in 1753 with debates over the Naturalization Bill, known as the "Jew Bill." Most of England's 8,000 Jews were foreign born; they suffered from special taxes and could not hold land, vote for Parliament, hold public office, be Freemen of the City, or attend university. The bill enabled Parliament to naturalize professing Jews. Although Tories and London merchants campaigned against it, the bill passed in May 1753. In November, Parliament reassembled and in December 1754 it repealed the bill. Tories feared an influx of Jews but used the unpopular legislation in their political battle against the Whigs. Despite a tradition of asylum, England also harbored an opposition to foreigners; some believed it inappropriate to legitimize Jews and *Judaism in England, a Christian country. While acceptance of Jews increased, efforts at *conversion also continued. The London Society for the Promotion of Christianity among Jews (established 1809), the first missionary society devoted exclusively to converting Jews, was well funded, although largely unsuccessful.

Initially, most Jews lived in the City of London; after 1820 some began moving north and west, and important centers developed in provincial towns and cities. During the eighteenth century, small clusters of Jews settled especially in the south and east and, in the nineteenth century, in Manchester and Leeds. Several leading families, collectively dubbed "The Cousinhood," played key roles in business, religious, and charitable institutions. Their actions reflected the Jewish tradition of *philanthropy and the English ideal of personal service. Levi Barent Cohen (1747–1808) came to London from Amsterdam before 1778. Prominent in the Jewish community, Cohen served in all the offices of the Great Synagogue. *Rothschild family connections in England also date to the end of the eighteenth century. Lionel Louis Cohen (1832–1887) was a founder of the Jewish Board of Guardians (1859), which sought to systematize philanthropy, and of the United Synagogue (1870).

Despite setbacks, on the eve of the French Revolution, Jews in England had the most favorable status in Europe. Between the 1780s and 1810, when Prussian and French Jews were actively seeking civil rights, Britain's Jews remained relatively inactive. Jews began a more conscious campaign for the franchise after Catholic emancipation in 1829. Offices began opening to Jews in the 1830s, and bills to emancipate Jews passed in the Commons from 1833 on, but failed in the House of Lords. The Jewish Board of Deputies (founded 1760), an organization claiming to represent Jews in all political matters and led by Moses *Montefiore, increased its efforts to gain *emancipation beginning in 1845.

Starting in 1847, London repeatedly elected Lionel de Rothschild to Parliament, but the wording of the oath and opposition from the Lords prevented him from taking his seat. In 1858 the Jewish Relief Act gave each house of Parliament power to determine its oath, finally enabling Rothschild to be sworn in. Jews gained permission to attend Oxford and Cambridge in 1871 (all ancient universities barred non-Anglicans until 1854–56.) Benjamin *Disraeli, a convert to Christianity, first became prime minister in 1868; although he supported efforts to end Jewish disabilities, he voted against Jewish emancipation in 1850 and 1854.

From the late nineteenth century, Jewish *women played key roles in philanthropic endeavors, education, and the arts. Absorbing a Victorian ethos, privileged women established organizations and charities to aid the poor, acculturate immigrants, and provide respectable recreation. Lady Louisa Goldsmid and Mrs. Fanny Hertz helped open higher education to young women, and women, including Grace Aguilar (1816–1847) and Amy Levy (1861–1889) made important contributions to Anglo-Jewish literature (see LITERATURE: BRITAIN).

British Jews founded and developed several communal institutions during the eighteenth and nineteenth centuries, including schools, among them the Jews' Free School; an orphanage at Norwood; the *Jewish Chronicle* (1841), the oldest continuing Jewish publication; and Jews' College (1855), a seminary for training Anglo-Jewish "ministers." Synagogues grew in number, and so too did approaches to Judaism. The Reform movement schism in Britain dates from the 1830s when requests for limited reforms from a number of anglicized families went unheeded and the Goldsmid family left the Great Synagogue and joined the Reform congregation (see JUDAISM, REFORM). It was not until the beginning of the twentieth century that Claude Montefiore and Lily Montagu founded the Liberal Jewish Religious Union.

As the Jewish community in England was settling into its new status, Russian Jews faced increased antisemitism and severe economic restrictions. Between 1881 and 1914, approximately 250,000 Jews from Russia immigrated to England and 120,000 settled there. Those who chose to stay in England did so because of its tradition of asylum and the existence of a native Jewish community. Immigrants gravitated to the East End of London, Liverpool, and Manchester where there were other Jews, synagogues, and kosher butchers. Jewish immigrants were urban semi-skilled laborers; they included more women and children and tended to have higher literacy rates than other immigrant groups. Most entered the garment and furniture trades or became peddlers and hawkers of used clothes. Jews became pioneers in mass production of ready-made, inexpensive, stylish clothing in Britain.

British Jewry did not offer these newcomers an unqualified welcome. The Jewish Board of Deputies earmarked funds to send immigrants on to the *United States or to repatriate them, and community leaders sent notices to *Eastern Europe indicating that their cities could not absorb any more immigrants. About 1886–87, when restriction became an issue in Parliament, the Jewish community feared that a large influx of aliens might bring latent *antisemitism to the surface. British advocates of restriction argued that further immigration would lead to unsanitary and unhealthy neighborhoods, impede assimilation, decrease wages, and displace natives from home and work. Charles Booth, the famed social reformer, suggested that foreign Jews lacked "class loyalty and trade integrity." As early as 1884, the Jewish Board of Guardians responded by establishing a Sanitary Committee. Others, however, considered Jews temperate, industrious, if to a fault, and law abiding.

Still, demands for restriction on Jewish immigration increased and led to the 1903 Royal Commission. Some Jews, including members of the Jewish Board of Guardians, agreed that restriction would benefit England. The Royal Commission acknowledged the problem of overcrowding, but their investigation found less disease than anticipated, suggesting that neighborhoods were more sanitary than they appeared. With the dissent of Lord Rothschild and Sir Kenelm Digby, the Commission recommended restrictive legislation. Throughout 1904 and 1905, the *Jewish Chronicle* defended immigrants and the established Anglo-Jewish community responded by creating an extensive anglicization program. Schools, clubs, and organizations taught hygiene and English and tried to refine the immigrant masses. Despite the seriousness of these concerns, 1870 to 1914 was also a golden age for British Jews. A number of Jews held high office, and a few had the friendship and patronage of King Edward VII. Although Jews' entry to elevated social circles indicates a high level of integration, some argue that association with aristocracy aroused antisemitism.

At the outset of World War I, Parliament passed an Aliens Restriction Bill. Aliens were required to register with the police, and some 40,000 Germans were interned. The shops of many German-born British residents and those with German-sounding names, including many Jews, were attacked. In November 1917, the *Balfour Declaration, communicated by Foreign Secretary Arthur Balfour to Lord (Walter) Rothschild, stated support for a Jewish homeland in *Palestine while affirming the rights of non-Jews in Palestine and Jews living in other parts of the world. Shortly afterward, British troops supplanted the *Ottomans in Palestine, and in 1922 the *British Mandate to govern Palestine was officially affirmed by the League of Nations.

The rise of *Nazism challenged the Jewish community in numerous ways. Generally, European governments were hesitant to take action against *Germany's systematic disenfranchisement of its Jewish citizens. Great Britain decided not to support the 1933 boycott, claiming it would prove detrimental to Germany's Jews. Despite the fact that British Jewry underestimated the dimensions of Hitler's plans, they did offer rescue and relief to refugees. Early in 1933, British Jews formed the Jewish Refugees Committee, the Academic

Assistance Council, and the Central British Fund for World Jewish Relief, which guaranteed that no Jewish refugee would become a public charge. British concerns over mass unemployment and antisemitism would likely have limited immigration without the guarantees from the Jewish community. More virulent forms of antisemitism emerged during the 1930s when the British Union of Fascists, led by Sir Oswald Mosley, attacked Jews in East and North London.

Britain's refugee policy changed over time. Initially, Britain took small numbers of Jewish refugees. In 1938, they imposed visa requirements on German nationals and at the Evian Conference, the same year, offered neither refuge nor financial assistance to refugees. Churchill feared that Jews fleeing from Nazism would arouse antisemitism in Great Britain, and political factors eliminated Palestine from consideration as a haven. *Kristallnacht, German government-incited attacks on Jewish homes and businesses in November 1938, is seen by many as a turning point; whereas most countries became more restrictive, Britain became more liberal. One outstanding British effort, the 1938–39 *Kindertransport, saved approximately 10,000 children. In December 1942, the Chief Rabbi proclaimed a Week of Mourning and Prayer and held a service in Bevis Marks. Jews organized various mass meetings and met with the Foreign Secretary, Anthony Eden. On December 17, 1942, the government denounced the atrocities, and Parliament rose for a minute of silence, an unprecedented action. However, the Bermuda Conference (April 1943) convened by Britain and the United States failed to provide safe havens for Jews. Britain made small concessions to alter some of the restrictions of the 1939 *White Paper limiting immigration to Palestine, but by this time Jews could not get out of Europe.

During the war, significant information about Nazi atrocities was available. The *Jewish Chronicle* reported on ghettoization and the Final Solution. Although the Foreign Office considered Gerhardt Reigner's famous August 1942 telegram, which exposed Nazi plans for total elimination of the Jews, to be "a rather wild story," they forwarded it to the chairman of the British Section of the World Jewish Congress. In 1944, British Jews encouraged the government to respond to rescue proposals from *Hungary, but the government was suspicious. As the war continued, the Central Fund became inadequate, and by 1945 the government covered all resettlement expenses, a figure that declined as refugees became integrated into the economy.

Some scholars have criticized the British government for its policy with regard to *Palestine, the limited number of refugees that Britain accepted, and the refusal to bomb railway lines to *Auschwitz. They also see failure on the part of Jewish leaders because the community lacked cohesion, *Zionism caused some dissension, and there were not enough Jewish homes for refugee children. However, Anglo-Jewish leadership faced significant challenges: Churchill refused to authorize controversial policies, especially with regard to Palestine; antisemitism was on the increase; and the war effort itself always took priority in policy decisions. Seen in context, many argue that Anglo-Jewry's actions compared favorably with those of Jews in other countries.

During the years after World War II, many Jews began moving from exclusively Jewish communities into the suburbs and became increasingly acculturated. Approximately two-thirds of Great Britain's 350,000 Jews (as of 2001) live in London. There are large communities in North London, Manchester, Leeds, and Glasgow. London's Stamford Hill is home to a significant *Hasidic population. In the first decade of the twenty-first century, three organizations represent *Orthodox Jews: the United Synagogue, the largest group, with 35,000 families; the Union of Orthodox Hebrew Congregations, which has a large Hasidic contingent; and the Federation of Synagogues (founded in 1887 by Russian-Polish immigrants). On the left are the Reform Synagogues of Great Britain (founded in 1840) and the Union of Liberal and Progressive Synagogues (1902). By the 1960s, there was an important growth in support for Zionism and diminishing fears about charges of dual loyalty.

In recent years, inner city communities have largely disbanded; the overwhelming majority of Jews now live in the suburbs of London, Manchester, Leeds, and Glasgow. More important, however, is the decline of Jewish life in provincial cities and the centralization of Jews in London, accounting for 70% of British Jews by the mid-1990s. North London is home to a number of Jewish communal institutions, among them the Board of Deputies of British Jews, Jewish Care, the Jewish Museum, Progressive Judaism's Leo Baeck College, the Jews Free School, and Adler House, the seat of the Chief Rabbi and London's *Beit Din (Jewish *court). Although significant *intermarriage and falling birth rates have led to an absolute decline in the number of British Jews, Jewish schools have been very robust and ultra-Orthodox Judaism has seen substantial growth. **Map 10**

For further reading, see G. Alderman, *Modern British Jewry* (1992); E. C. Black, *The Social Politics of Anglo-Jewry, 1880–1920* (1988); D. Cesarani, ed., *The Making of Modern Anglo-Jewry* (1990); T. M. Endelman, *The Jews of Georgian England: 1714–1830* (1979); idem, *The Jews of Britain, 1656–2000* (2002); D. Feldman, *Englishmen and Jews: Social Relations and Political Culture, 1840–1914* (1994).   SUSAN L. TANANBAUM

British Mandate Over Palestine. The *Balfour Declaration of November 2, 1917, announced the policy of the British government, "favoring the establishment in *Palestine of a National Home for the Jewish people ... it being clearly understood that nothing shall be done which may prejudice the civil and religious rights of existing non-Jewish communities in Palestine." Issued during World War I, the Declaration had broad support from English Christian *Zionists who had been lobbying for greater British involvement in Palestine for decades. It also had strong support from a minority of British Jews, led by Dr. Chaim *Weizmann and the British *Rothschild family, and it soon garnered support from American Jews led by Justice Louis *Brandeis. The feelings of the *Arab population of Palestine, who made up 90% of its inhabitants, were only briefly considered. Zionists, Jews and Christians alike, generally assumed that Arabs would benefit economically and culturally from new investment in Palestine.

Six weeks after the publication of the Declaration, General Allenby established British rule in Palestine. Within a few months the *Ottoman forces that had patrolled the area for four hundred years were routed. A provisional military government, the Occupied Enemy Territory Administration (OETA), remained in place through the summer of 1920 when Sir Herbert Samuel, the first British High Commis-

sioner for Palestine, was appointed. Samuel had previously been the first Jewish member of the British Cabinet. The League of Nations officially affirmed the British Mandate to govern Palestine in 1922.

The history of the British Mandate in Palestine has three main story lines: the economic, political, and social development of the area by an influx of Jewish Europeans bringing human resources and capital investment; the establishment by the British of infrastructure in the areas of law, transportation, communications, public health, and the development of education and cultural life; and the growing opposition of the Arab population to these changes. These stories intersected in hopes for peaceful solution and in periodic violence.

PALESTINE'S JEWS AND MANDATORY RULE: The narrative of Jewish immigration to Palestine and their establishment of the *Yishuv, the Jewish community of Palestine, is a story of early successes. These include the development of the Jewish Agency, a public body for the purpose of advising and cooperating with the British administration of Palestine; the establishment of a unified response to increasing Arab hostilities; and ultimately the declaration of statehood. From the end of World War I, the Jewish population of Palestine, which had been stagnant for hundreds of years, began a steady growth, increasing from 55,000 in 1918 to nearly 600,000 in 1948. The proliferation of agricultural settlements, as well as industrial and commercial enterprises, accompanied the population growth. The revival of the *Hebrew language, a dream of early Zionists, became a reality in new Jewish schools funded largely by the Jewish Agency and in the new villages of Palestine, settled by enthusiastic pioneers. In 1925, the cornerstone of the Hebrew University was laid, demonstrating broad support by the world Jewish community for the revival of a homeland in Palestine (see entries under ISRAEL, STATE OF).

During the ensuing years of the Mandate, growth of the Jewish population of Palestine was fueled by *antisemitism in Europe. Economic investment was supported at first by Jews who agreed with the goals of political Zionism and later more broadly by those who saw Palestine as a refuge for Jews escaping *Nazi Germany. The British policy on immigration reflected the desires of Jews and the fears of Arabs. The British planned to allow limited immigration to show good will to their Jewish supporters while maintaining the status quo of an Arab majority. However, a significant stream of visitors, primarily Jews, decided to remain in Palestine, circumventing legal immigration throughout the years of the Mandate. The proportion of immigrants to population as a whole was without precedent. By the end of the 1930s, the Jewish population in Palestine had grown more than 400%. During the critical pre-war years of 1933–37, Palestine absorbed more Jews from Axis-dominated areas than any other country, including the *United States.

ARAB RESPONSES TO JEWISH IMMIGRATION: The Arab response to Jewish immigration was designed to pressure the British to change the immigration policy of the Balfour Declaration, which Arabs feared would lead to a Jewish majority in Palestine. As a result of Arab riots in 1921 and 1929 as well as the sustained boycotts and rioting in 1936–39, the British appointed commissions to study the situation and promulgated *White Papers (government policy statements). The White Paper of 1922 included the proviso that immigrants should not be a burden on the people of Palestine as a whole and that they should not deprive any section of the present population of employment. The White Paper of 1930 set forth more stringent controls on immigration and land transfer. Finally, the White Paper of 1939 limited Jewish immigration to 75,000 people within a five-year period, after which time future immigration would require Arab consent.

In April 1942, at a Zionist conference in *New York City, David *Ben-Gurion and his supporters overrode the pro-British gradualist policy of Chaim *Weizmann and promulgated the Biltmore Programme, an explicit call for a Jewish commonwealth in Palestine that would be open to all Jews. After the end of World War II, the Jewish leadership of Palestine expected a change in British policy that would admit the hundreds of thousands of European Jews who had survived the *Holocaust. Yet the British adhered to their White Paper policies. A Jewish resistance movement was created to facilitate illegal immigration. An Anglo-American Commission was sent to Palestine and Europe to look into the problem of Jewish *displaced persons. Tension mounted as British troops continued to resist immigration and Jewish forces continued to encourage hunger strikes by refugees. The sympathies of British troops stationed in Palestine were frequently with the Arabs. Hundreds of Palestinian Jews were interned on suspicion of illegal activities. In retaliation, British offices in the King David Hotel were blown up in July 1946. A year later the *Exodus*, a ship carrying 4,500 refugees, arrived in Haifa and was forced to return to Europe. Publicity about the ship caused an international outcry against Britain. Eager to relieve themselves of the burden of the Mandate, the British brought the Palestine problem to the United Nations in May 1947.

BRITISH ADMINISTRATION OF THE MANDATE: From the outset, British rule in Palestine faced significant challenges in meeting the basic needs of a civilian population that had suffered greatly from famine and disease during World War I. The British brought years of experience in colonial administration, and they were aided by growing financial support for the *Yishuv* from the world Jewish community. Thus, although Palestine was poor in every respect – a small population, little industry or commerce, and no natural resources – the British were able to make significant progress in many critical areas during their thirty-year rule. The British administration addressed lawlessness, disease, lack of communications, and the paucity of education or social services. It created a new police force to establish basic public security, with British officers commanding both Arab and Jewish members. The British also established a new system of justice, eliminating the ubiquitous *baksheesh* (general bribery and corruption) prevalent under the Ottomans.

The British speedily established civilian telephone, telegraph, and postal services and began to provide jobs for unemployed Palestinians, both Jews and Arabs. Likewise, the British expanded the railroad system and built roads passable by civilian cars. This work also provided employment for the local population. Public health was a serious problem all over the region. In Palestine there were few public hospitals, although there were several private hospitals funded by missionary societies and by Jewish philanthropic societies. The government set up a Department of Health to respond to widespread malaria and trachoma and to educate expectant mothers. The average death rate of 23.8 per thousand in 1922 fell to 12.3 in 1946; life expectancy rose about 16.5 years among Arabs and Jews. These efforts virtually eradicated plague and smallpox and reduced malaria considerably. A new water supply was inaugurated in 1936, making proper sanitation possible and reducing disease.

The British created a Department of Education and substantially increased the number of primary schools in towns and villages. Schools for Jewish children taught in Hebrew were primarily run by a Jewish Board of Education, funded by the Jewish Agency. Missionary schools continued to teach primarily Arab children. Government funding for public schools was also directed at Arab children, accommodating about half of those eligible. There were fewer schools for girls than boys and more schools in towns than in villages.

While making progress in each of these areas, the Mandatory government failed in one of its important objectives: "to place the country under such political, administrative and economic conditions as will secure … the development of self-governing institutions." The Jewish Agency worked with the Mandatory government to establish structures that would result in the creation of a Jewish national home, but the leadership of the Arab population resisted this idea. Although they appeared to collaborate with the British, they made it clear that the development of self-governing institutions must depend on majority rule. The British repeatedly rejected the principle of majority rule because that would have given the Arabs control over the government of Palestine.

In an effort to meet some of the demands of Arab notables, the British created new Islamic institutions. The Supreme Muslim Council (SMC) was given control over vast revenues that traditionally were distributed to religious and judicial institutions and schools and orphanages. The position of Grand Mufti of Jerusalem was created; the Grand Mufti was appointed by the High Commissioner to head the SMC. This led to opportunities for patronage appointments on a large scale. In addition, educated Arabs were given employment opportunities in the Mandatory government. Nevertheless, the peaceable demands by Arab leaders soon gave way to more aggressive expressions by people who resisted changes to their traditional way of life. These grievances included the purchase of land farmed by Arabs by Jewish farming cooperatives, the literacy requirement for obtaining employment in towns, rising prices for housing and essential needs, and increasing challenges to Arab men as their wives received public health education.

In May 1921 Orthodox Easter Sunday fell on May Day. A minor conflict in *Tel Aviv ignited serious riots and looting in Jaffa that spread to other parts of the country. Arabs attacked Jews at random and looted shops. It took a week to quell the riots and required the intervention of the Royal Air Force. A second major confrontation occurred in late August 1929 on the occasion of a religious fast by Jews commemorating the destruction of the Jerusalem *Temple (*Tisha B'Av). A procession of Jews marched to the Wailing Wall and demanded their rights to ownership of this holy site. A rumor spread that the Jews planned to seize the Dome of the Rock and Al-Aqsa mosque on the Temple Mount (*Haram al-Sharif*), and the ensuing violence spread to Hebron, Jaffa, Haifa, and *Safed. In the end, 133 Jews were murdered and 116 Arabs were killed, mostly by the military or police. Jews blamed the Arabs and the failure of the British to protect them; Arabs blamed the Jews and the pro-Jewish sentiments of the police. This violence deepened the chasm between Palestinian Arabs and Jews.

Despite continued hostility toward Jews, the British became the main object of Arab attacks beginning in 1933. In April 1936 the Arabs declared a general strike involving work stoppages and boycotts of British and Zionist parts of the economy. It lasted for six months. This was the beginning of a three-year armed revolt against the British that erupted all over Palestine. A British Royal Commission of Inquiry (the Peel Commission, 1936–37) was appointed to review the situation and concluded that the basic premise of the Mandate was unworkable. The commission proposed a partition of the land, giving the Jews those areas along the coast in which they were the majority, and the remainder to the Arabs. Jerusalem, Nazareth, and Bethlehem, centers of Christian pilgrimage, and Haifa, the only important port, were to remain under the British Mandate. In September 1937, four hundred delegates from all parts of the Arab world met near Damascus and resolved unanimously that Palestine was an integral part of the Arab fatherland. They demanded the annulment of the Balfour Declaration and the conclusion of an Anglo-Palestine treaty establishing an independent Palestine with safeguards for minorities. The Arab leadership continued to support this position long after the Mandate ended.

END OF THE MANDATE PERIOD: On November 29, 1947, thirty years after the Balfour Declaration, the United Nations voted to partition Palestine into three parts: a Jewish state along the Mediterranean, an Arab state inland, and the international city of Jerusalem. This vote confirmed the recognition by the world community of the rights of Jews and of Arabs to respective national homelands, but it did not change the belief of the Arabs of Palestine and the surrounding countries that they were losing their homeland to the Jews. Hostilities between the two sides intensified during the spring. On April 9, 1948, armed Jewish gangs destroyed the village of Deir Yassin, near Jerusalem, killing 250 Arabs. Four days later, a Jewish convoy of medical personnel proceeding up Mt. Scopus on the way to Hadassah Hospital was attacked and thirty-nine people were killed. On May 14, 1948, when the last British officials left Haifa, Ben-Gurion declared the establishment of the State of Israel.

Recent research includes A. J. Sherman, *Mandate Days: British Lives in Palestine, 1918–1948* (2001); N. Shepherd, *Ploughing the Sand: British Rule in Palestine, 1917–1948* (2000); A. Ayalon, *Reading Palestine: Printing and Literacy, 1900–1948* (2004); and R. Khalidi, *Palestinian Identity* (1997). **Map 12**

LAURA S. SCHOR

Broadcasting: Radio and Television.

Gugliemo Marconi's 1890 demonstration of a wireless telegraph is often cited as the beginning of the radio and television broadcasting industry. Over the next two decades, wireless transmission of a range of sounds, including voice and music, was achieved. Initially, key industry figures feared that mass broadcasting would taint their branch of engineering with the brush of low-brow amusement. However, surging interest after World War I opened the new medium for popular entertainment and retailing purposes and loosened arrangements

that had barred ethnic minorities from executive leadership positions in radio companies. As commercial broadcasting emerged as a part of American show business in the 1920s, doors were opened to the talents and creativity of immigrants and their children. Jewish Americans benefiting from these opportunities included David Sarnoff, William S. Paley, and Leonard Goldenson, the eventual leaders of companies that defined commercial broadcasting during the radio era and oversaw the diffusion of television as a technology, industry, and art.

David Sarnoff (1891–1971) was born near Russian Minsk (now part of *Belarus) and immigrated to America at the age of nine. He left school at fifteen and ultimately found employment at the American subsidiary of the British Marconi Company, which became the Radio Corporation of America (RCA) in 1914. Sarnoff's rise to power at RCA was furthered by his support of mass broadcasting and his proposal for a *network* of stations that would transmit a shared signal capable of reaching every radio in the United States. RCA formally launched the National Broadcasting Company (NBC) on New Year's Day, 1927, with two network services: NBC-Red, directed at the higher end of the cultural spectrum, and the Blue Network, which had no such pretension. Their overwhelming success led to Sarnoff's election to the RCA board of directors in 1928. In 1930, he became company president, a position he held until his retirement in 1968.

Under Sarnoff's leadership, RCA was arguably the most powerful commercial communications company in the world – dominant in research, development, and manufacture of communications technologies for industrial, military, and consumer use. RCA also shaped production, promotion, and distribution of American electronic entertainment media for much of the twentieth century through its subsidiaries and partnerships, including NBC (television and radio), RCA Victor (recorded music), and RKO Pictures (cinema).

Sarnoff internalized the patrician values of the radio industry's founders. He formed the NBC Symphony Orchestra and lured Arturo Toscanini from Italy to lead it, and he facilitated radio adaptations of classical dramas on NBC. Denied a naval commission during World War I, most likely because of *antisemitism, Sarnoff was commissioned as a U.S. Army officer in 1942; his work in coordinating Allied communications efforts in Europe won him promotion to the rank of brigadier general.

William S. Paley (1901–1990) was Sarnoff's chief rival in commercial broadcasting. The Chicago-born son of Samuel Paley, a Ukrainian Jewish immigrant who had founded the Congress Cigar Company, Paley studied the latest mass marketing techniques and theories at the Wharton School of Business and persuaded his father to use radio advertising, doubling Congress Cigar's retail sales during the mid-1920s. Paley entered the radio business in 1927 when the Columbia Phonograph Broadcasting System, a would-be competitor to NBC, came close to failing just months after its launch. Convincing his father to buy the operation, Paley assumed the presidency in 1928 and changed the network's name to the Columbia Broadcasting System (CBS). With an infusion of cash from Congress Cigar, he began to expand the fledgling network from its base in the Northeast, organizing a coast-to-coast string of affiliated stations.

Paley made CBS the equal of NBC, despite overwhelming competitive disadvantages. NBC operated two networks, each larger than CBS, and its parent, RCA, held so many radio patents that CBS had to buy much of its equipment from its main competitor. Paley established a Columbia Workshop for radio writers and launched a weekly series to produce their scripts on the air. The Columbia Artists Bureau gave representation to new performers and functioned as a casting resource for CBS programs. Paley recruited academics to develop methods of audience measurement that would reassure CBS advertisers about how effectively they were spending their money.

Paley's most daring long-term strategy was establishment of a radio news gathering organization at CBS. Sarnoff had chosen to ignore news programming at NBC, believing editorial decisions would inevitably lead to conflicts with advertisers, audience segments, and, worst of all, the federal government, which licensed broadcasting. In contrast, Paley understood broadcasting's capabilities, especially instantaneous speed and mass distribution, for journalism. During the 1930s, Paley built the world's first international commercial broadcast journalism enterprise, hiring proven newspaper reporters as on-air personalities, including Edward R. Murrow, William Shirer, and Eric Severeid. When World War II began, CBS was ready to report events from around the world before newspapers could go to press. By the late 1940s, as the introduction of television began, war reporting had created a public image for CBS that was second to none.

Paley raided some of the most popular comedy stars on NBC radio, such as George Burns and Gracie Allen, Jack Benny, and Red Skelton, offering them innovative deals at CBS, including ownership of their programs. While popular NBC television stars, such as Milton Berle and Sid Caesar, were saddled with impossible work schedules, Paley made every effort to accommodate CBS talent and paid market prices to performers appearing on *The Ed Sullivan Show*. This policy helped make the series and CBS a portal into American show business for international acts ranging from Moscow State Circus performers to the Beatles and the Rolling Stones. CBS leaped past NBC in the ratings during the television era, beating its old rival season after season for some thirty years. As CBS achieved dominance in television with its entertainment offerings, Paley turned away from the news division. Paley was a founder of the Museum of Television and Radio, which was renamed the William S. Paley Center for Media Arts in 2007.

The least known Jewish broadcasting mogul is Leonard H. Goldenson (1905–1999), the son of Russian immigrant shopkeepers in Scottdale, Pennsylvania. Goldenson attended Harvard and Harvard Law School in the early 1920s and did legal work for Paramount Pictures bankruptcy proceedings. Impressed with his work, Paramount officials offered him a full-time job with the studio's theater division, where he rose through the ranks to a leadership position. In 1948, a federal antitrust suit forced film studios to divest their theater holdings, and Goldenson became the head of the newly independent United Paramount Theaters (UPT).

While the Hollywood studio old guard was fighting the looming threat of television with air conditioning, drive-in theaters, and 3-D movies, Goldenson had already concluded that television would inevitably dominate American entertainment. U.S. network television was a four-company oligopoly in the late 1940s, and it appeared likely to become smaller, not larger. The Dumont Network, owned by a television manufacturer with no experience in radio, ultimately failed in 1955, and the American Broadcasting Company (ABC), which was formed in 1943, seemed destined for the same fate. Goldenson focused on taking over ABC, raising hundreds of millions of dollars by selling off more than half of UPT's 1,425 theaters. In 1951, he made ABC management a generous offer that saved the company. Government approval came two years later, with Goldenson heading the merged company.

Goldenson used his connections in Hollywood to create a working relationship that served both movies and television for decades and led to their lateral integration. Walt Disney, who was seeking capital to construct a theme park near Los Angeles, was an eager partner, breaking ranks with other studio heads to make the first deal to supply prime-time television programs for a broadcasting company. Goldenson's next deal, with Warner Brothers, had a pivotal impact in the transformation of television from a theater-based medium presenting live word-dependent teleplays into a film-based medium offering action series such as westerns and police shows with outdoor settings.

Between 1948 and 1978, Goldenson achieved parity with his competitors in sports, news, prime-time entertainment, and daytime entertainment; he built ABC into a prototype of the contemporary multimedia entertainment company, bringing music recording, publishing, and electronics companies under the corporate umbrella. Having bought control of ABC for $8 million in 1953, Goldenson authorized its sale in 1985 for $3.5 billion.

DAVID MARC

Buber, Martin (1878–1965), German Jewish philosopher, is best known for his book *I and Thou* (1922) and his philosophy of dialogue. Buber was a prolific writer on the Hebrew *Bible, *Ḥasidism, Jewish *thought, and *Zionism. He played a formative role in the German Jewish cultural renaissance between 1900 and 1938, in the development of cultural Zionism, and in Jewish–Arab relations. His early writings, especially *Daniel: Dialogues on Realization* (1913), influenced German literary expressionism. Forced to emigrate in 1938, Buber and his family settled in *Jerusalem, where he lived and taught until his death in 1965.

Born to an assimilated Jewish family in *Vienna, Buber grew up in the observant home of his grandfather, rabbinics scholar Salomon Buber (1827–1906), in Lemberg (Lvóv). He returned to Vienna in 1896 to study philosophy and art history. After extended visits at the universities of Leipzig (1897–99), Zurich (1899), and *Berlin (1899–1901), Buber graduated from the University of Vienna in 1904 with a doctoral dissertation on Nicholas of Cusa and Jakob Böhme (unpublished). An avid reader of Schopenhauer, Plato, Kant, Feuerbach, and, most importantly, Nietzsche, the young Buber was also influenced by his Berlin teachers Georg Simmel (1858–1918) and Wilhelm Dilthey (1833–1911). His lifelong friendships with Hugo von Hofmannsthal (1874–1929), Fritz Mauthner (1849–1923), and Gustav Landauer (1870–1919) attuned Buber to the fin-de-siècle "crisis of language" and the significance of the "spoken word."

As a student, Buber became active also in Zionism. With Chaim *Weizmann and others, he organized the culture-oriented Democratic Fraction in the spirit of *Aḥad Ha-Am (1856–1927). Buber's ideas of ethical nationalism and liberated Judaism (*Heruth: On Youth and Religion* [1919]) influenced the *Prague Circle led by Hugo Bergmann, Felix Weltsch, and others. In 1904 Buber began working on a series of popular German adaptations of Ḥasidic texts, *mysticism, and other *folklore, including *The Tales of Rabbi Nachman* (1906), *The Legend of the Baal-Shem* (1908), *Tales of the Hasidism* (completed in 1946), *Ecstatic Confessions* (1909), *Tschuang-Tse* (1910), and the Finnish national epic *Kalevala* (1914). Between 1906 and 1912, he edited the series *Die Gesellschaft*; from 1916 to 1924, the journal *Der Jude*; and from 1926 to 1930, *Die Kreatur* (with Joseph Wittig and Viktor von Weizäcker).

Simultaneously with Ferdinand Ebner (1882–1931), Hermann *Cohen (1842–1918), Franz *Rosenzweig (1886–1929), and Eugen Rosenstock-Huessy, Buber developed his dialogical philosophy around 1918, arguing that "I–You" and "I–It" are different modes not only of speech but also of being in and toward the world. He refined his conception in *Dialogue* (1929), *The Question to the Single One* (1936), and *Elements of the Interhuman* (1954). In 1925, based on the idea of "spokenness," Buber and Rosenzweig undertook a new translation of the Hebrew Bible into German, which was completed in 1961 (see BIBLE: TRANSLATIONS AND TRANSLATORS).

Between 1933 and 1938, Buber used his writings and directorship of the *Frankfurt *Freies jüdisches Lehrhaus* to promote a new "biblical humanism" as a form of intellectual resistance to *Nazism. From 1938 to 1951 he taught social thought at the Hebrew University of Jerusalem, writing on *anthropology (*The Problem of Man* [1942]) and political theory (*Paths in Utopia* [1947]). An ever controversial voice, Buber worked with Judah *Magnes toward *Arab–Jewish reconciliation (*A Land of Two Peoples: Martin Buber on Jews and Arabs*, ed. Paul Mendes-Flohr [1983]) and was among the first to advocate Israeli Jewish relations with post-war *Germany (*Genuine Dialogue and the Possibilities of Peace* [1953]). Important works on Buber include H. Kohn, *Martin Buber, sein Werk und seine Zeit* (1961); and P. Mendes-Flohr, *From Mysticism to Dialogue* (1989).

ASHER D. BIEMANN

Bulgaria. Jews have lived in Bulgaria since Imperial *Roman times, and there appears to have been Jewish influence on early Bulgarian Christianity. Before the fifteenth century, Bulgarian Jews followed the *Byzantine or *Romaniote rite; later, *Ashkenazic and *Sephardic Jews arrived with their own customs. Eventually the community was unified under a single rabbinate, adopting the Sephardic rite and the *Ladino language. In the fourteenth century, Bulgaria became a part of the *Ottoman Empire. Medieval Jews were traders and tax farmers and owned quarries and leather tanneries. The celebrated scholar Joseph *Karo wrote some of his *Bet Yosef* in Nikopol, where he established a *yeshivah. Bulgarian Jews were enthusiastic supporters of *Shabbetai Zevi, the seventeenth-century false messiah.

When Bulgaria became independent in 1878, equal rights were promised to Jews. However, discrimination persisted; Jews were barred from the military academy, the state bank, and the municipal service. In the mid-1930s Bulgarian Jews numbered almost 60,000. Most worked in commerce and were self-employed. The community was strongly pro-*Zionist. In the years before World War II, *antisemitism increased, and nationalist fascist organizations were active.

During World War II Bulgaria was allied with *Germany; it declared war on the Western Allies, but not on the *Soviet Union (USSR). An antisemitic "Law for the Defense of the Nation" was enacted. In 1941 German army units were stationed in the country, and Germany demanded the deportation of Bulgarian Jews. The government cooperated in the seizure of Jews living in Macedonia and Thrace, areas annexed by Bulgaria, and most of this population was murdered. However, a protest led by Dimeter Peshev, vice president of Parliament, delayed deportations of Jews from Bulgaria proper. Other parliamentarians, the Greek Orthodox Church, professional groups, and cultural figures joined the protest. Although cruel anti-Jewish measures were enforced, the Jews of Bulgaria proper did survive. These events took place during a period of uncertainty when the Germans had begun to lose the war and elements of Bulgarian society hoped to disengage from the German alliance. The sudden, mysterious death of King Boris was a complication; his role in negotiations about the fate of Bulgaria's Jews has never been clear. While secret talks went on with the West, the USSR declared war on Bulgaria and invaded the country. At the end of the war, Bulgaria was ruled by the communist Fatherland Front.

Under *communism Jews were allowed only limited contact with other Jewish communities. The Bulgarian Peoples' Courts did mete out severe punishment to those who had harmed Jews during the war. When the USSR threw its support to the UN Partition of *Palestine, Bulgaria followed suit and permitted emigration. Many Jews left for the newly established State of *Israel, resulting in a near disappearance of Jewish life. With the end of communism in 1990, the Shalom organization was created to reinvigorate and coordinate cultural activities. *B'nai B'rith and *Ḥabad both lent assistance. In 2007, there were two *synagogues in Bulgaria, in Sofia and in Plovdiv, supervised by a chief rabbi; a Jewish school and religious schools; camps; and organizations for children and young adults. About 5,000 Jews live in Bulgaria, mainly in Sofia, and relations with Israel are good. A bronze plaque adjacent to the Parliament building honors Gentiles who resisted the deportations. Prominent Jews who were born in Bulgaria include the painter Jules Pascin (1885–1930) and writer Elias Canetti (1905–1994), the 1981 Noble laureate for literature.

For further information, see M. Bar-Zohar, *Beyond Hitler's Grasp: The Heroic Rescue of Bulgaria's Jews* (1998); D. J. Elazar et al., ed., *Balkan Jewish Communities: Yugoslavia, Bulgaria, Greece, and Turkey* (1984); and T. Todorov, *Fragility of Goodness: Why Bulgaria's Jews Survived the Holocaust* (2001); and BALKANS; BYZANTINE EMPIRE; HOLOCAUST RESCUERS; OTTOMAN EMPIRE. **Maps 9, 10**   LIBBY K. WHITE

Bund. The General Union of Jewish Workers in *Lithuania, *Poland, and *Russia (*Der Algemeyner Yidisher Arbeter Bund in Lite, Poyln, un Rusland*) was a revolutionary *socialist party founded in *Vilna in October 1897, one year before the Russian Social Democratic Workers' Party, which it helped organize. Its founders included both workers and acculturated middle-class Jewish intellectuals who sought to build class consciousness among the emerging Jewish proletariat and to integrate these workers into the broader revolutionary movement in Russia. Although initially espousing *Marxist internationalism, by 1903 the group had become a leading advocate of Jewish national-cultural autonomy in Russia. Its successful organization of armed self-defense units against *pogroms and its unique blend of *Diaspora Jewish nationalism, Yiddishism, and struggle for Jewish workers' rights earned the Bund significant popularity, well beyond its chief political competitor, the *Zionists. Despite its turn toward Jewish nationalism, the secular Bund remained radically anticlerical as well as anti-Zionist. Its support of *Yiddish as the Jewish national language and its insistence that Jewish rights (individual and national) must be won where Jews lived, an ideology known as *doikeit* or "hereness," contrasted sharply with the Zionist veneration of *Hebrew and ultimate hopes for a Jewish political entity in *Palestine.

Bundist fortunes in interwar Europe varied greatly. In post-revolutionary Russia, Bundists who refused to join the Communist Party were quickly suppressed or murdered. In newly independent Poland, in contrast, the Bund enjoyed spectacular growth, developing a secular Yiddish school system (*Tsisho*), youth groups, sports clubs, libraries, cultural centers, vibrant Yiddish (and Polish) *journalism, and more. It rose to political prominence in the late 1930s, as violent Polish *antisemitism, economic ruin, and looming war pushed Polish Jews to support the radical party. Bundists were active in armed resistance to the Nazis during the *Holocaust, but most ultimately suffered the same destruction as their Polish brethren, as did their leaders caught in the *Soviet Union.

For further reading, see J. Jacobs, *Jewish Politics in Eastern Europe: The Bund at 100* (2001); and J. Frankel, *Prophecy and Politics: Socialism, Nationalism, and the Russian Jews, 1862–1917* (1981).   JOSHUA M. SHANES

Byzantine Empire. The Roman Emperor Constantine I dedicated his new capital, Nea Roma, also known as Constantinoupolis or I Polis (the City), in 330 CE, on the site of the ancient city of Byzantium, effectively dividing the *Roman Empire into western (Latin-speaking) and eastern (Greek-speaking) realms. In Greek *Hebrew sources, the city is called Kosta, usually read as Kushta.

During the eleven centuries of the Eastern Roman Empire (designated the Byzantine Empire by modern scholars), the degradation of Jews and *Judaism was codified and consequently perpetuated. From the fourth to the sixth century, *Church Fathers (both before and after the Council of Nicaea of 325 CE) developed their theological arguments against Judaism and emphasized the necessity for social barriers to exclude Jews from the emerging Christian society. The law codes of Theodosius II (438 CE) and Justinian I (534 CE) followed this imperative, mandating the exclusion of Jews from political, economic, judicial, educational, military, and social participation (with some exceptions, such

as the decurionate) in public life. Palestina (*Palestine/the Land of Israel) was Christianized by huge building projects (churches, monasteries, pilgrim hostels, etc.), and Christian claims were extended to all biblical sites. Palestina was further divided into three provinces, and Jews, their centers of population already relocated to the *Galilee, were restricted from living in the environs of *Jerusalem. Finally, the office of the *Patriarch of the Jews, since the second century CE the political representative of Jews in the Roman Empire and the religious center for the development of post-mishnaic Judaism, was abolished in 439. This act completed the fragmentation and isolation of Jews subsequent to the destruction of the Second *Temple in 70 CE. Some later emperors, from Justinian in the sixth century to Romanos Lekapenos in the tenth, and briefly John Vatatzes in the thirteenth century, forcibly baptized Jews.

Notwithstanding legal limitations and persecutions of Jews in the Byzantine Empire, Judaism remained a permitted religion in all official Roman law codes. The Orthodox Church, although subject to the emperor (who, as *Pontifex Maximus* was officially the head of the church), followed *New Testament sources and refused to accept forcibly baptized Jews. During periods of persecution in the ninth and tenth centuries, Byzantine Jews fled to the *Khazar Empire.

After the mid-tenth-century Byzantine *Crusades, Jewish communities, which had been depleted in numbers by conversion and emigration, began to flourish, attracting Arabic-speaking *Rabbanite and *Karaite immigrants. From the eleventh to fifteenth centuries, Jews, who were primarily urban, were fully integrated into the economy of the empire; they specialized in cloth manufacture, dyeing, and trade. After the fragmentation of the empire in the wake of the conquest of Constantinople in the Fourth Crusade of 1204, *Romaniote Jews (Greek-speaking Jews from the Byzantine Empire) played an important role in the various states that emerged in the Christian and Muslim *Balkans and Anatolia.

On the intellectual level, Byzantine Jews wrote *piyyutim* (see POETRY: LITURGICAL) and *midrashic works; these latter traditions were preserved by *Rashi and others. They contributed to the spread of *Kabbalah, especially in the Palaeologue period (1261–1453), and regularly experienced *messianic movements. From the twelfth century on, Romaniote and Karaite Jews studied and commented on Aristotelian philosophy, and numerous Byzantine commentaries on the *Bible and *halakhah are extant. Byzantine Jews also excelled in *medical studies. Shabbetai Donnolo of Oria in southern Italy (913–942) wrote the first "Western" pharmacopia, *Sefer Ha-Mirkakhot* (Book of Remedies). An anonymous contemporary wrote *Sefer Yosippon* (Book of *Josippon) a tenth-century history of the *Second Temple period; a later rendition (ca. 1356), by the Romaniote Judah ibn Mosconi, became the major inspiration for a nationalist Jewish identity until the twentieth century. In sum, Romaniote Jewry played a major role in transmitting Jewish memory and culture to contemporaneous and subsequent Jewish cultures. For further reading, see S. R. Bowman, *The Jews of Byzantium: 1204–1453* (1985). **Map 5**   STEVEN R. BOWMAN

C

Cain and Abel are the first two sons of *Adam and *Eve; their story unfolds in Genesis 4. First-born Cain, whose name is linked to his mother's statement that she "acquired" (*kaniti*) a son with God's help (4:1), is a farmer; Abel is a shepherd. When Cain's vegetable offering to *God is ignored while Abel's animal offering is favored, God warns Cain against giving in to sin. Nevertheless, the jealous Cain kills Abel. Confronted by God, he famously responds, "Am I my brother's keeper?" (4:9). Protectively marked by God and sentenced to wander the earth, Cain settles in the land of Nod, east of Eden. There he marries and becomes the father of *Enoch, for whom he names his newly founded city (4:16–17). The story makes clear that fratricide is a crime against self, God, and society. Cain and Abel's sibling rivalry also becomes an important motif in Jewish, Christian, and Muslim interpretive traditions and in folklore, art, and literature. For some scholars, the story reflects the conflict between wandering herdsmen and land-bound farmers.

KATE FRIEDMAN

Cairo Genizah: See GENIZAH

Calendar (**See also CALENDAR: MONTHS OF THE YEAR**). The biblical *festivals have always been at the center of the Jewish calendar. Enumerated in several passages in the *Torah (esp. Lev 23, Num 28–9, and Deut 16), these special days include *Passover (Pesaḥ or the Festival of Unleavened Bread; it is always first in the list, because it takes place in the first month of the year); the Festival of Weeks (*Shavuot); the Day of Remembrance (later known as *Rosh Ha-Shanah, the New Year); the Day of Atonement (*Yom Kippur); and Tabernacles (*Sukkot). Later additions include various fast days, such as the 9th of *Av (*Tisha B'Av, the anniversary of the destructions of the Jerusalem *Temples) and minor festivals such as *Purim (based on events recounted in the book of *Esther) and *Hanukkah. These minor festivals usually commemorate historical events of importance to all Jews or to specific Jewish communities. *Megillat Ta'anit* (ca. first century CE) provided an early calendar of such minor festivals. Many *fast days and minor festivals have fallen into oblivion over the centuries, but new ones continue to be instituted by various Jewish communities (these include fast days to commemorate the destruction of *Polish Jewry in 1648 and the Nazi *Holocaust and festivals such as the Israeli Day of Independence). Beginning in the Early Modern period, it has become customary for Jewish communities to publish annually a local Jewish calendar of such observances (known as a *luaḥ*).

The structure of the Jewish calendar and the way it is reckoned are not explained in the Hebrew *Bible; however, it is likely that the ancient Israelite calendar was lunar, as were all calendars of the ancient *Near East. The months probably began at the *new moon, with an average length of twenty-nine or thirty days. The year ordinarily consisted of twelve such lunar months, but occasionally a thirteenth month was added to maintain the ordained festivals in appropriate synchronization with the seasons. This practice of adding leap months is called intercalation. In the post-exilic period (from the sixth century BCE on), the Jews adopted the standard *Babylonian calendar, a lunar calendar that was used for official, imperial purposes throughout the *Persian and (later) *Hellenistic empires of the Near East. Babylonian month names have remained in use until today, although by the *Roman period, the Jewish calendar had acquired a separate identity of its own.

However, Jewish literary sources from the late Hellenistic and early Roman periods (late third century BCE to first century CE), including the books of *Enoch and Jubilees (see PSEUDEPIGRAPHA) and the *Dead Sea Scrolls, assume a dissident, nonlunar calendar. This calendar consisted of a fixed year of 364 days (with months of 30 or 31 days), with exactly 52 weeks; in this calendar the New Year and festivals recurred on the same day of the week every year. Since it is slightly shorter than the solar or seasonal year of approximately 365 1/4 days, this dissident calendar gradually drifts away from a correct alignment with the seasons. It also differs from the lunar Babylonian Jewish calendar in the lengths of years and months, its disjunction from the moon and seasons, and, most importantly, its dates for festivals. The extent to which it was actually used, for example at *Qumran, and its relevance to Qumran sectarianism remain unclear. However, the dissident calendar is the earliest calendar to be explicitly described in any Jewish source; its description in the Dead Sea Scrolls achieves a level of complexity and sophistication that was hardly matched in any other culture of the same period.

After the first century CE, the lunar calendar prevailed entirely, although Jewish communities in both *Palestine and the *Diaspora reckoned it in very different ways. Disagreements often arose as to when the month had begun, depending, for example, on when the new moon had first been sighted, and Passover might be celebrated in two different months, depending on whether a thirteenth, intercalated month had been added to the year. Although most Jewish authorities do not appear to have regarded this diversity as a problem, the *Rabbis opposed calendar diversity and claimed that only a designated rabbinic *court in Palestine had the right to determine new moons and decide about the year's intercalation. The *Mishnah, in tractate *Rosh Ha-Shanah*, describes in detail the procedure of this court: Whoever sighted the new moon traveled to the court and testified before it; the judges then delivered their verdict ("the month is sanctified!"). Subsequently, the news was disseminated to the communities of Palestine and – somehow or other – the Diaspora. It is unclear to what extent this procedure was actually observed. However, because they wished to enforce a united calendar among all Jewish communities, the Rabbis very gradually abandoned this empirical system in favor of a fixed calculation, which was finalized in the tenth century (largely by *Saadia Gaon in *Iraq). This fixed calendar was widely disseminated among all Jewish communities, thus establishing uniformity of practice across the Jewish world.

The complex and, in astronomical terms, remarkably accurate calculations that underlie the fixed calendar were expounded in a number of twelfth-century rabbinic monographs (for example the "Laws of Sanctification of the Month" in *Maimonides' *Mishneh Torah*), and they have regulated the Jewish lunar calendar ever since. The calendrical system consists of the computation of the *molad* (a medieval astronomical concept also known as the mean conjunction of the sun and moon) as the basis for determining the new moon; a lunar–solar cycle of nineteen years during which leap months are intercalated seven times (in years 3, 6, 8, 11, 14, 17, and 19); and additional rules that prevent the occurrence of certain festivals on certain days of the week. However, calendar diversity persisted well into the medieval period. Calendar disputes and differences between adherents of rabbinic Judaism, or *Rabbanites, are still attested in the tenth century (most famously the Saadia–Ben Meir controversy of the 920s) and may well have gone on for some centuries later. This calendar diversity sometimes resulted in disputing Jewish groups celebrating festivals on different dates. The *Karaites, in this period and later, rejected the rabbinic calendar altogether and relied, by and large, on the empirical observation of the new moons and seasons. This resulted in deviations not only from the Rabbanite calendar but also among Karaite communities themselves. Recently, the practice of new moon sighting has been revived in some circles in *Israel, in a *messianic expectation of its future restoration.

For further reading, see S. Stern, *Calendar and Community: A History of the Jewish Calendar: 2nd Century BCE to 10th Century CE* (2001); and J. VanderKam, *Calendars in the Dead Sea Scrolls: Measuring Time* (1998).   SACHA STERN

Calendar: Months of the Year (See also CALENDAR).

The months of the Jewish calendar, beginning with the spring, are as follows: Nissan, Iyar, Sivan, Tammuz, Av, Elul, Tishri, Heshvan, Kislev, Tevet, Shevat, and Adar. This ordering is based on *Exodus 12:2, which identifies the first day of the spring month of Nissan (March-April) as the start of the year; in fact, Jewish tradition designates four distinct new year observances throughout the conventional twelve-month cycle (M. *Rosh Ha-Shanah* 1:1) (see NEW YEARS).

A leap month is added to the calendar seven times in a nineteen-year cycle to maintain synchronization between the festivals and their appropriate seasons. This process is called intercalation and this is why the Jewish calendar is best described as "lunar–solar." In the seven years in which the additional month is added, the leap month follows the final winter month of Adar and is called Adar II (*Adar Bet*). In leap years the festival of *Purim (Adar 14) takes place in Adar II (M. *Megillah* 1:4). The names of the months have their origins in the months of the Babylonian calendar.

Canaan, Canaanites.

The neighboring civilizations of *Mesopotamia and *Egypt significantly influenced Israel's religious culture but the beliefs and practices of the native peoples of Canaan had an even greater impact. Although *Deuteronomy demands the extermination of the Canaanites (Deut 20:17) and other portions of the *Torah command their expulsion (Exod 23:27, 28; Num 33:53) they appear to have remained a significant minority and some individuals and clans certainly integrated into the people of Israel. While

*Israelite religion was unique in its imageless cult and the exclusive worship of one *God, many aspects of Israelite religion were held in common with West Semitic peoples in general and are discussed in this entry.

THE TEMPLE: One of *Solomon's greatest achievements was the construction of a monumental *Temple in *Jerusalem, which the Bible describes in great detail (1 Kgs 6–8). His architectural models, construction techniques, and even artistic detail followed Canaanite tradition. After a comparison of the various features of the Temple (as described in *Kings and *Chronicles) with archeological discoveries in Syria-Palestine, William Dever concluded, "We now have direct Bronze and Iron Age parallels for every single feature of the 'Solomonic Temple' as described in the Hebrew Bible, and the best parallels come from, and only from, the Canaanite-*Phoenician world of the fifteenth to ninth centuries BCE."

CULT TERMINOLOGY: The titles of functionaries at Israelite holy places are the same or similar to designations for servants at Canaanite shrines. Texts found at a site called Ugarit in modern *Syria, just north of the boundaries of biblical Canaan, dating to the thirteenth century BCE, indicate that their priests were called *khnm*, like the *kohanim* or *priests in the Bible; other servants in their temples are called *ytnm* and *kdshm*, like the *netinim* and *kadesh* mentioned in the Bible. (*Kadesh*, "holy ones," are condemned in Deuteronomy 23 and the books of Kings; some modern scholars, probably erroneously, believe the term refers to cultic male *prostitutes.) The offering of animals and other food commodities played as crucial a part in the religious life of Canaan as it did in Israel, and there is substantial overlap regarding the vocabulary of sacrifice (Hess, 104). Cuneiform texts from Emar, a city that flourished in northern Syria in the fourteenth and thirteenth centuries BCE, provide descriptions of rituals and religious festivals similar to those of ancient Israel.

CULTIC INSTALLATIONS: *MATZEVOT.* The Bible describes the early ancestors of Israel erecting stone pillars (*matzevot*) as an act of worship (Gen 28, 35:14; Exod 24) or to memorialize the dead or an important event (Gen 31:51, 35:20; 2 Sam 18:18). This practice seems to have been an accepted practice in later Israelite history as well. The prophet *Isaiah speaks positively about the erection of a *matzevah* for Israel's God (Isa 19:19), and the books of *Kings record the proliferation of these uncarved standing stones in the period of the monarchy (1 Kgs 14:23; 2 Kgs 17:10). The Torah commands Israelites to smash the standing pillars of the land of Canaan and prohibits the erection of new ones because of their association with the worship of other gods (Exod 34:13; Lev 26:1; Deut 16:22). In this case, *archeology confirms the rationale for the Torah's prohibition, as standing pillars have been found in hundreds of sites throughout Syria-Palestine from the fifth to the first millennium BCE, including some that are definitely Israelite.

BULL FIGURINES: The Bible presents the Israelites' worship of a bull in two crucial episodes, the story of the "golden calf" in Exodus 32 and in 1 Kings 12, when the newly crowned king of Israel, *Jeroboam, erects golden calves at *Beth El and *Dan. Archeologists have discovered a bronze bull, seven inches long by five inches high, in a worship site in northern Israel dating to the twelfth century BCE. Ugaritic mythological texts use the title "Bull" for the chief god of the city, El. The representation of a god as a bull seems to have been a traditional component of Canaanite worship incorporated into *Israelite religion in the northern kingdom of *Israel, despite its strong condemnation in the Torah.

COPPER SNAKES: Numbers 21 describes how *Moses manufactured a copper snake as an antidote to the plague of poisonous snakes that God sent against the people as punishment for their complaining. "Copper snake" in Hebrew is *nahash nehoshet*, a wonderful example of alliteration. 2 Kings 18:4 records the destruction of Moses' metal serpent by King *Hezekiah, who was prompted by the popular worship of the ancient icon. Archeological discoveries suggest that metal snakes played a role in the worship of Israel's neighbors. A copper snake was found at a cultic site at Timna, near the Red Sea, and because of the pottery nearby, it is thought to have been used by Midianites, the kin of Zipporah, Moses' wife. A bronze snake figurine was found at Tel Mevorakh, a cultic site in northern Israel that is dated to the Late Bronze Age, before the Israelites' appearance in the land.

CANAANITE MYTHOLOGY: The mythological and ritual texts found in the archives of Ugarit have shed light on the religious thought of the people of Syria-Palestine before the emergence of Israel, as well as on biblical references to Canaanite religion. The language of the tablets is a West Semitic dialect very close to biblical *Hebrew, and the literary style of the mythic texts is similar to biblical *poetry. The chief god at Ugarit was El, linguistically related to the Hebrew term for God, *Elohim*. El was an aged, wise, creator god and husband of the goddess Asherah. He is described as "the Kind" and "the Compassionate," as is Israel's God in Exodus 34:6. The divine assembly over which El presides is called the "sons of El," similar to the Bible's term for angels (Gen 6:1; Ps 29:1, 82:1, 89:7). El's home is a tent at the source of freshwater rivers. Israel's God is also at home in a tented dwelling, and several prophets describe the abundance of freshwater that will flow from Jerusalem in a future, ideal time (Ezek 47:1–12, Joel 4:18, Zech 14:8). Although the dominant name for Israel's God in the period after Moses is Yahweh, the book of Genesis reflects an era during which the God of the ancestors had many names, almost all compounded with the term "El" (El Shaddai in Gen 17:1, El Elyon in Gen 14:19, El Olam in Gen 21:33, and El Roi in Gen 16:13). These points of correspondence testify to the influence of the Canaanite god El on the emerging religion of Israel.

The other major god at Ugarit was Baal, which means "lord"; this designation is found in the Bible as the rival of Israel's God during the period of the monarchy. At Ugarit, Baal is a fertility god and is associated with storms. That some Israelites thought that Baal could bring rain is obvious in the description of the prophet *Elijah's contest with the devotees of Baal in 1 Kings 18. Israel's God was probably worshiped by the name Baal during the period of the early monarchy. Both Baal and Yahweh are called "Rider on the Clouds" (Ps 68:4), and both are victorious in their conflict with the sea (Gen 1; Ps 74, 89:10–11, 104).

The family of gods at Ugarit included three prominent goddesses: Asherah, Astarte, and Anat. Anat is mentioned in the Bible as a personal name and a place name (Judg 3:3, Josh 21:18, Neh 11:32), whereas Astarte is referred to as the "god of the Sidonians" (1 Kgs 11:5, 33). The plural form is used in combination with *baal* as a derisive term for prohibited gods (Judg 10:6, 1 Sam 7:4) but also as a term for the young of the flock (Deut 7:13, 28:4, 18, 51). Asherah at Ugarit was the wife of El and the mother of the gods. She is the most interesting of the three because of archeological finds in the Negev and Sinai regions of Israel that date to the eighth or seventh centuries BCE. At these two sites, inscriptions mention Asherah (or Asherata) alongside the God of Israel, leading some scholars to conjecture that popular religion in Israel considered Asherah the consort or "wife" of Yahweh (Hess, 283–90, Zevit, 350–80). Asherah is mentioned in the Bible both as a goddess (1 Kgs 18:19; 2 Kgs 13:6) and as the term for a pole or tree that was planted near altars and symbolized the goddess or a "tree of life" in general (Deut 16:21; Judg 6:25, etc.). The hundreds of pillar-based female figures with prominent breasts found at Israelite archeological sites are also associated by some scholars with the worship of Asherah, although others have connected them with concern for successful motherhood and lactation **(Plate 1)**. *Jeremiah castigates his fellow Jerusalemites for the worship of the "Queen of Heaven" (Jer 7:18, 44:18), but her identity is unclear.

It is evident that Israelite religion incorporated aspects of Canaanite religion in its description of Yahweh. At the same time, the distinctiveness of Israel's religion is obvious. The God of Israel is nowhere depicted in the Bible as a sexual creature, as are the gods of Ugarit; nor is Israel's deity a god who dies and comes back to life, as Baal does in a Ugaritic mythological text. The gods of Ugarit are personified powers of nature and are reliant on food and drink, in contrast to Israel's God who stands outside of nature and has no physical needs. Biblical Hebrew has no feminine word for goddess corresponding to the term "Elohim," as does Canaanite, with its title *elat* for the goddess Asherah. This suggests that the basic concept might be lacking. In addition to the relatively modest female figurines mentioned earlier, the near absence of male or other human representation in the archeological remains from seventh and sixth century BCE *Judah is striking. Further, scholars note the almost complete absence of the names of other gods in the personal names of the period. The Israelites' unique religious culture, with its worship of one God who tolerates no images, emerged in the centuries before Jerusalem's destruction in 586 BCE despite the enormous pressures exerted on this small nation not only by the great civilizations of the ancient Near East, but also by the indigenous peoples who lived among them.

For further reading, see M. D. Coogan, *Stories from Ancient Canaan* (1978); W. G. Dever, *What Did the Biblical Writers Know and When Did They Know It?* (2001); R. Hess, *Israelite Religions: An Archaeological and Biblical Survey* (2007); and Z. Zevit, *Religions of Ancient Israel* (2002), 256–60; and ARCHEOLOGY: ANCIENT TIMES TO PERSIAN PERIOD; NEAR EAST, ANCIENT. **Maps 1, 2**   ELAINE GOODFRIEND

Canaanites was the designation for a school of artists in the *Yishuv. **See ART, ISRAELI.**

Canada. When fourteen Jewish merchants gathered in Montreal in 1768 to form Shearith Israel congregation, nine years after the capitulation of New France to the British conquerors, they founded what would be a unique Jewish community different in important respects from its future counterpart in the *United States. As Quebec and other

North American territories remained British after the American Revolution and united as the Dominion of Canada in 1867, immigrants slowly came to perceive these differences. Canada evolved as a binational state under the British Crown, not an independent nation that imposed allegiance to a distinctive identity. This reality created the special political and social contexts in which the Canadian Jewish community evolved.

The Montreal settlers, who were followed in the mid-1800s by immigrants arriving in Toronto, Quebec City, Hamilton (Ontario), and Victoria (British Columbia), were mainly small merchants. Because Canada did not attract significant numbers of German Jews, the Reform movement had little influence. Canada's first Reform synagogue was founded in Hamilton in 1873. By century's end Canada's established communities were confronted with newly arrived East European immigrants. While some settled in existing communities, others were helped to move on; some homesteaded in Canada's western territories. These colonization projects, only a few of which lasted, as well as urban social services, were strongly supported for many years by the *Baron de Hirsch Foundation, the Jewish Colonization Association, the *Alliance Israélite Universelle, and British philanthropies.

The clothing industry was the major focus of Jewish industrialists, who usually started out as contractors for manufacturers; it was also a significant employer for men, women, and children immigrant workers. Piecework, low wages, crowded garrets in back alley slums, sexual harassment, and other features of the hated "sweating system" resulted in bitter and bloody strikes and lockouts in what amounted to open intra-communal warfare. Militant trade unions helped ameliorate some of these conditions, but agreements often broke down, and some employers moved production to rural areas to escape unionization.

*East European immigrants were often loyal to one or more of *Zionism, *communism, and *socialism. The Federation of Zionist Societies of Canada was formed in 1898 to advance the goal of establishing a Jewish state in *Palestine; Canadian Jews avidly raised money for the Jewish National Fund and other projects. Women were active through Hadassah (Hadassah-WIZO), Pioneer Women, and Mizrachi Women in campaigns targeting women's and children's projects (see ORGANIZATIONS, WOMEN'S: NORTH AMERICA). Zionism in its various formations became the normative form of Canadian Jewish identity, and the Federation of Zionist Societies of Canada and its successor, the Zionist Organization of Canada, served as the first pan-Canadian Jewish organization. During World War I, however, many Canadian Jews put the dire situation of Jews in Eastern Europe temporarily ahead of Zionism. Recent immigrants emphasized the need for a Canadian Jewish alliance or congress to organize immediate relief in *Russia and *Poland; with the establishment of the Canadian Jewish Congress in March 1919, such aid was mobilized. The Congress also addressed pressing domestic issues such as the confessional school question in the Province of Quebec, where Jews had second-class status, as well as the Canadian government's increasingly restrictive immigration policies. Although the organization lapsed for more than a decade, the Congress was reestablished in 1933 to confront *antisemitism at home, in conjunction with *B'nai B'rith,

and abroad, as well as the almost complete official blockage of Jewish immigration.

Antisemitism in French Canada was fueled by influential nationalists who saw Jews as posing unique dangers to Quebec's cultural survival in a secular, English-speaking continent. Antisemitism in English Canada was evident in restrictions on university enrollment, property purchases, and many aspects of social life. Once World War II began, the Congress also devoted enormous efforts to organizing chaplaincy and other services for Jewish members of the Canadian armed forces.

Beginning in 1948, when government immigration policy was liberalized, *Holocaust survivors arrived in significant numbers. Next to *Israel, Canada quickly became the second largest home per capita of such persons, generally known as "refugees" or "*displaced persons." Most were able to get on with their lives, some with significant material success, despite disturbing evidence of vestigial antisemitism in the 1950s and 1960s. Canadian Jewry also responded vigorously to the mounting threats to Israel's security in the 1960s and to help *Soviet "refuseniks" in the 1970s and imprisoned and abused Syrian Jews in the 1980s. Marches, visitations, demonstrations, fundraising, and delicate behind-the-scenes rescue accompanied these concerns. Meanwhile, as overt antisemitism in Canada diminished, Jews became increasingly accepted and integrated into the mainstream; by the late 1970s, it was no longer unusual for qualified Jews to be elevated to the highest levels in public service, the judiciary and other professions, the universities, and business. At the same time, the community enjoyed unprecedented prosperity.

By the last third of the twentieth century, Canadian Jewry had matured. Gone were the severe economic struggles of the early immigrants, although significant pockets of poverty remained, especially among the elderly. The sons and daughters of once embattled garment workers entered the professions, moved to the suburbs, and in many ways lived upscale lifestyles. The old radical left still survived, but had lost much of its feistiness and, increasingly, its membership. The *Yiddish press had declined (see JOURNALISM, YIDDISH: NORTH AMERICA), and an English-language weekly, the *Canadian Jewish News*, spoke for the community. The Zionist organizations, too, had faded as their relevancy seemed dubious in the context of a strong Israel. In terms of relationships between Jews and non-Jews, toleration – even warm acceptance – had replaced antisemitism. This was true in Quebec as well, where secular nationalism seemed to pose few problems for a community that now included significant numbers of Francophone Jews.

Although Canada's Jews were in large measure confident and secure at the beginning of the twenty-first century, living in an atmosphere of peace, freedom, opportunity, and official multiculturalism, deep complexities and far-reaching challenges remained. Many Jews were increasingly concerned with "identity" and "survival," as assimilation and out-marriage increased to alarming proportions. Many of these trends appeared parallel to similar Jewish concerns in the United States, but knowledgeable observers pointed to Canadian structural differences. One of these was the relatively high level of Jewish day school *education, which received significant public support in some provincial jurisdictions; this promised well for the persistence of Jewish identity in Canada. Concerns also included the possibility that renewed nationalist sentiment could result in Quebec's separation from Canada as well as fears of reemerging antisemitism from some newer immigrants.

For further reading, see G. Tulchinsky, *Canada's Jews: A People's Journey* (2008); I. Abella and H. Troper, *None Is Too Many: Canada and the Jews of Europe 1933–1948* (1982); F. Bialystok, *Delayed Impact: The Holocaust and the Canadian Jewish Community* (2001); and M. Weinfeld, *Like Everyone Else ... But Different: The Paradoxical Success of Canadian Jews* (2001); and LITERATURE: CANADA and PERIODICALS: CANADA.

GERALD TULCHINSKY

Cantor, Cantorate: Contemporary. At the beginning of the twenty-first century, a cantor is the music professional who leads Jewish worshipers in *synagogue *prayer (usually in tandem with a rabbi). However, the term is a relatively recent one, only used among *Ashkenazic Jews since the nineteenth century and borrowed from Christianity. *Reform Jews who were trying to modernize and raise the aesthetic level of Jewish religious services hoped they could find Jewish musicians who not only possessed beautiful voices but could also write stirring compositions to inspire both reverence and congregational participation. Although most of the men who filled the post fell short of this ideal, Cantor Salomon Sulzer (1804–1890), the first to be called by that title, set a high standard. Renowned for his beautiful voice (which drew non-Jews as well as his co-religionists to Vienna's Seitenstettengasse Shul), Sulzer published two volumes of new music covering the entire liturgical cycle. Some of his melodies (most famously, his settings of *"Shema Yisrael"* and *"Ki MiTziyon"*) remain in use in most Ashkenazic synagogues (see JUDAISM, REFORM entries).

The "cantor" exemplified by Sulzer was very different from the "*ḥazzan*" whose role and function were rejected by the Reform movement. Traditional *ḥazzanim* were well versed in the *nusakh* (melody) and cantillation (chanting) practices that had defined Ashkenazic worship for centuries; many had sung as boy soloists in the company of an older relative who would travel from town to town, presiding at services on *festivals and other special occasions. Knowledge of the texts and the laws governing Jewish ritual was one of the most important criterion for designation as a *ḥazzan* and most received a good Jewish education, although few had any formal training in music (see MUSIC, RELIGIOUS). In contrast, cantors were trained in newly established "cantorial schools" and received a thorough education in music theory, sight-singing, and composition, sometimes at the expense of some traditional aspects of Jewish studies.

The designation of the cantor as Jewish music professional par excellence is one more step in the evolution of a position that has undergone substantial change in the course of Jewish history. In the post-*Temple era any knowledgeable layman could function as a *shaliaḥ tzibbur*, a "representative of the community," who would lead a gathering of worshipers. As the liturgy evolved, it became customary to expect the officiant to compose and chant extemporaneous prayers. The first use of the term *"ḥazzan"* was actually pejorative, alluding to those who lengthened worship services with their elaborate displays of poetic and vocal prowess. These early *ḥazzanim* may have been asserting a liturgical role

for themselves among their many tasks. Those responsibilities might include arranging and exchanging *prayer books, *Torah scrolls, and other *synagogue accoutrements for the changing liturgical season; performing ritual *circumcisions; slaughtering animals to provide *kosher meat; and teaching children. In the nineteenth century cantors adopted more purely musical roles: selecting music for *worship services (or composing their own), overseeing the work of the organist and choral director, and of course engaging the congregation in song.

The use of the title "cantor" was initially limited to the Reform movement, with professionals in the more traditional movements preferring to be known as "*ḥazzanim*." Ironically, it was the *Orthodox performers of the "Golden Age of Ḥazzanut" who helped make the term "cantor" essentially an English translation for "*ḥazzan*." Throughout the first half of the twentieth century, Columbia and RCA Records issued a string of recordings by "Cantors" Joseph 'Yossele' Rosenblatt (d. 1933), Gershon Sirota (d. 1943), Moshe Koussevitzky (d. 1966), and a host of others chanting traditional "cantorial" music. In the twenty-first century, some individuals (especially those associated with the Conservative movement) still prefer to be known as "*ḥazzan*," but the term "cantor" has become synonymous with "Jewish music professional."

The contemporary cantorate has continued to evolve, both in the styles of music performed in synagogues and in the expectations of services to be rendered by the cantor. Today cantors serve a variety of functions beyond being the "voice of the community." They play an important role in selecting and presenting liturgical music, usually in collaboration with a rabbi and a congregational ritual committee that may advocate for changes in the music of the service, adding or subtracting instrumental accompaniment, choral singing, and preferred melodies in response to popular preferences. If the position of cantor has lost some autonomy in the musical realm, however, it has gained in other areas. Cantors are welcomed as chaplains who counsel the needy, visit the sick, and comfort the bereaved. They are also active in various educational enterprises, preparing children and adult *b'nei mitzvah* (see BAR MITZVAH; BAT MITZVAH), providing music instruction in the religious school, and contributing choral and other musical expertise to a host of other community programs. Some smaller congregations that cannot afford to engage multiple full-time professionals have cantors who double as religious school principals or as the synagogue's executive director.

The largest change in the modern cantorate has come with the acceptance of *women as cantors. In the 1940s and 1950s there were isolated instances of women performing as cantors (occasionally in congregations, but more often singing liturgical music on recordings and in concert settings). The Reform movement led the way with the formal ordination of female cantors in 1975; the Conservative movement followed in 1987. In the first decade of the twenty-first century, women constitute at least half of the student body in the various non-Orthodox cantorial training programs and, as their older male colleagues retire, will soon represent the majority of active Jewish music professionals. Female cantors have successfully performed much of the most famous cantorial repertoire of the past, but the growing presence of women in the cantorate, combined with changing preferences in ritual music, will likely inspire the creation of new liturgical compositions in years to come.

MARSHA BRYAN EDELMAN

Cantor, Cantorate: Historical Development.

Cantor is a term of Christian origin applied to the professional sacred singer of the Jewish *synagogue, termed "ḥazzan" in Hebrew. The latinate term indicates the intersection of modernity – the Jewish entry into civil European society around 1800 – with ancient traditions.

The ḥazzan emerged as a prominent figure around the ninth century CE as a singer or singer/composer of expressive hymns – *piyyutim (liturgical poetry) – based on earlier models of individuals who led the congregation in *prayer. Not mandated by Jewish law, the cantor was selected as an expressive spokesman by a communal prayer group; he was also called shaliaḥ tzibbur, the "messenger of the congregation," because he could amplify and direct the group's supplication. Part of this power originally rested on the injunction of ḥiddur mitzvah, the beautification of a sacred obligation, in this case prayer. Thus, the aesthetic element was crucial in a congregation's decision to engage a cantor (see also CEREMONIAL OBJECTS).

The cantor played a role in the liturgical experience of both *Ashkenazic and *Sephardic Jews. In nineteenth-century *Central Europe, powerful cantor-composers established new forms of composition, including choral settings. Salomon Sulzer in *Vienna (1804–1890; a friend of the composer Franz Schubert) and Louis Lewandowski in *Berlin (1823–1894) were among the most influential. In *Eastern Europe, cantors often began as apprentices, meshorerim, learning the repertoire and possibly music notation from senior figures. Operatic style shaped cantorial vocal and compositional style. In the late nineteenth century, top cantors became well-paid stars of synagogues and communities, moving internationally from congregation to congregation and recording their music for wide dissemination: Gershon Sirota (1874–1943) was the first such star. However, ordinary cantors had a difficult time making a living. The figure of the cantor appeared in early *films, most notably in *The Jazz Singer* of 1927, featuring the Broadway star Al Jolson, himself a cantor's son, as a singer torn between his father's cantorial heritage and the call of the theater (see FILM: UNITED STATES).

The burgeoning of American Jewish synagogue life after World War II led to the development of professional cantorate organizations staffed by graduates of the new training institutes of the Reform, Conservative, and Orthodox Judaisms. The cantor attained a co-clergy status with the rabbi in congregational life, greatly broadening the job description. In the 1970s and 1980s, the Reform and Conservative movements opened cantorial training and ordination to *women, a radically egalitarian move for a previously all-male profession. Cantors learned newer song styles based on American folk music, from singer-songwriters such as Debbie Friedman (1951–2011), and *Hasidic melodies from Shlomo Carlebach (1925–1994). The 1980s and 1990s saw a move away from the cantor's centrality, as congregants demanded more active participation in worship services or broke away from large synagogues to form egalitarian prayer groups without professional clergy. The cantorate has declined among *Ashkenazic Orthodox Jews, but continues unabated among smaller communities such as the Syrian Jews of Brooklyn, New York.   MARK SLOBIN

Capital Punishment is the state-sanctioned execution of individuals convicted of specific crimes. Capital punishment is mandated in the *Torah not just for murder (Exod 21:12), but for many other offenses. These other offenses include what most modern people would consider moral, ritual, and theological violations. For example, immorality in the forms of *adultery, incest, bestiality, and male *homosexuality brings the death penalty (Lev 20:10–21); so, too, does rape (Deut 22:25) and, for a woman, premarital intercourse (Deut 22:20–21). Similarly, striking (Exod 21:15) or even cursing one's parents (Exod 21:17; Lev 20:9) warrants death, as does being a "stubborn and rebellious son" (Deut 21:18–21). The Torah demands the death penalty for violating some ritual *commandments, such as working on the *Sabbath (Exod 31:14), worshiping *God in the *Tabernacle while drunk (Lev 10:9), and, if being "cut off from one's people" (koret) also means death, working or failing to fast on *Yom Kippur (Lev 23:28–30). Theological misdeeds that bring the death penalty include witchcraft (Exod 22:17); worshiping the sun, moon, stars (Deut 17:2–7), or foreign gods (Lev 20:2; Deut 13:7–12); blasphemy (Lev 24:10–16); and worshiping God in the wrong way (Lev 10:1–2; 22:9).

The Bible records two acceptable methods of capital punishment: stoning (eighteen cases cited in *Maimonides' *Mishneh Torah Sanhedrin* 15:10) and burning (two instances in Lev 20:14; 21:9). Hanging is reported in the Bible as a mode of execution used by non-Jews (e.g., *Egyptians [Gen 40:22]; *Philistines [2 Sam 21:6–12]; *Persians [Esther 7:9]); as a non-Jewish law to be applied in Israel (Ezra 6:11); or as an extralegal measure (Josh 8:29). After execution, every person found guilty of a capital offense was to be impaled on a stake (Deut 21:22), but the body had to be taken down by nightfall, "for an impaled body is an affront to God" (Deut 21:23).

RABBINIC LITERATURE: The *Mishnah and *Talmud report the following four modes of execution: stoning, burning, slaying, and strangling (M. *Sanhedrin* 7:1). In describing how these penalties were to be executed, the Rabbis invoked two general principles. The first was that God's command to "Love your neighbor as yourself" (Lev 19:18) also applies to those condemned to death; this requires that the condemned be given the most humane ("beautiful") death possible (BT *Sanhedrin* 45a, 52a; BT *Pesaḥim* 75a; BT *Ketubbot* 37a). The second principle was that judicial execution should leave the body externally unchanged, as much as possible, just as natural death does (BT *Sanhedrin* 52a; *Sifra* 7:9). This whole discussion, however, was probably academic, because the *Romans deprived the Rabbis of the right to carry out capital punishment "forty years before the destruction of the *Temple" in 70 CE (BT *Sanhedrin* 41a; JT *Sanhedrin* 1:18a).

More instructive for later times is a general rabbinic reticence to use capital punishment altogether. This reluctance is evident in the Rabbis' narrow interpretations of the laws that authorized the ultimate penalty, their invention of rules of evidence that were virtually impossible to satisfy, and the following reflections on the topic in M. *Makkot* 1:10: "A court that puts a person to death once in seven years is called a murderous court. Rabbi Eleazar ben Azariah says,

'Or even once in 70 years.' Rabbi Tarfon and Rabbi *Akiva said: 'If we had been on the court, no death sentence would ever have been passed.' Rabban Simeon ben Gamliel said: 'If so, they would have multiplied murderers in Israel'" (see TANNAIM).

POST-TALMUDIC TIMES: There are a few instances, primarily in Muslim *Spain, where Jewish courts were empowered to inflict the death penalty, not only for the offenses recorded in earlier law but also for actions considered dangerous to the Jewish community at the time, especially informing on Jews to the government (*Mishneh Torah, "Injury and Damage" 8:11; responsa of *Asher ben Jeḥiel, 17:1, 2; 32:4).

In modern *Israel, capital punishment for murder or other crimes has never been carried out and was officially abolished in 1954. The death penalty remains in force only for genocide, as in the case of Adolf Eichmann, and for treason committed in times of actual warfare. The mode of execution is hanging for civilians and shooting for soldiers.

For further reading, see H. H. Cohen and L. I. Rabinowitz, "Capital Punishment," *Encyclopedia Judaica* (1972) 5:142–147; and E. Spitz, "The Jewish Tradition and Capital Punishment," in *Contemporary Jewish Ethics and Morality: A Reader*, ed. E. N. Dorff and L. E. Newman (1995), 344–49.

ELLIOT N. DORFF

Caribbean. The earliest Jewish communities in the Caribbean were established by *Sephardic Jews, many of whom came to the New World as *conversos*. In some locations they established successful sugar plantations; in other areas they were heavily involved in trade, importing supplies and luxury items. The earliest place where Jews were allowed to settle as Jews and to enjoy full political rights was the Dutch community in Surinam, which had Jewish inhabitants as early as 1639. Jews were among Dutch settlers in northern *Brazil between 1630 and 1654. When the Portugese retook this area, these Jews went to various Dutch colonies in the Caribbean and to New Amsterdam (*New York). They had learned sugar production in Brazil, and this expertise was very useful in their later undertakings in Surinam and other parts of the Caribbean (including Martinique, Guadeloupe, Barbados, Cayenne, and Pomeroon). In 1685 King Louis XIV instituted the *Code Noir*, ordering Jews to leave all French possessions within three months. The community in Cayenne (French Guiana) left for Surinam and other areas where Jews had established themselves.

In time, Jewish communities were established in Cuba, *Jamaica, St. Thomas and St. Croix in the Virgin Islands (originally controlled by Denmark), St. Martin, St. Eustatius, St. Christopher, Nevis, Guadeloupe, Martinique, Barbados, Tobago, Curaçao and its dependencies (Aruba, Bonaire), Trinidad and Tobago, and Haiti. In *Latin America communities existed in Colombia (Baranquilla), Panama, Venezuela (Coro), Tucacas, and Surinam (*Joden Savanah* [Jewish Savannah] and Paramaribo). These communities went through stages of enrichment and later descended into poverty; they were in touch with each other and with the Sephardic communities of New York, *Philadelphia, London, and *Amsterdam. French Impressionist painter, Jacob-Abraham-Camille Pissarro (1830–1903) was born on St. Thomas to a Sephardic family (see ART, EUROPE: NINETEENTH CENTURY).

A number of these communities had sufficient wealth at various times to bring in rabbinic leaders from Europe. The congregation in Amsterdam sent out Torah scrolls to the new congregations as well as rabbis. The Portuguese synagogue in Curaçao was built in 1723 and is the oldest synagogue structure in the Caribbean. In the nineteenth century a *Reform congregation developed there, and a synagogue continues to function. However, these communities lacked the institutional structures that were in place in Europe and struggled to keep traditions intact in an atmosphere that did not lend itself to observance. At the beginning of the twenty-first century, four surviving congregations in *Jamaica, Surinam, Panama, and Curacao still have remnants of Portuguese traditions. The organization, Jewish Congregations in the Caribbean and Latin America, attempts to keep Judaism alive in the region.

The community in Surinam is particularly interesting. In the "Jewish Savannah" Jews owned sugar plantations and slaves. In a letter to Governor Frederici on March 7, 1794, Abraham Bueno de Mesquita, Moses Hoheb Brandon, and Samuel Haim de la Parra wrote, "Several among the Portuguese Jewish Nation, out of private affection, begot children with some of their slave females and mulattos. Out of particular love for the Jewish Religion, the boys were properly circumcised and the girls instructed by a teacher, as were their descendants. Some of these were manumitted at the request of their Patrons, and others, having them born out of wedlock, after manumission, were instructed by their mothers of whom they were born and took the names of Portuguese Jews" (Arbell). Notwithstanding the conflicts in Jewish status (the mothers were not Jewish) the *haskamot* (communal decisions) of 1754 established rules by which individuals of mixed race would be admitted to the synagogue as *congreganten* but not as *yehidim* (full-fledged members). In 1759, *Darkhe Yesharim* (Paths of the Righteous), a *siva* (brotherhood) of Jewish mulattos was established. Eventually (in 1794) they assimilated into the Jewish community.

In Curaçao, Jews initially had small plantations, but later moved to the city and established extensive trade connections. Their imports from Europe included instruments, machinery, building materials, boat supplies, comestibles, books, and sometimes arms and munitions. In exchange, they imported tobacco, lemon juice, indigo, ginger, vanilla, hides, cotton, coffee, cacao, sugar, silver, and gold from various colonies for export to Europe. The main markets for Curaçao Jewish merchants were the Spanish colonies in Venezuela and Colombia (see LATIN AMERICA). Although this trade was clandestine and considered illegal by the Spanish, it was permitted because it filled a need for goods.

Jewish activities in the Caribbean can be divided into three general areas of endeavor: plantations (from the mid-seventeenth century); commercial enterprises (eighteenth to mid-nineteenth centuries and subsequent settlements in liberated Spanish colonies); and, in the nineteenth and twentieth centuries, involvement in economic development on a national scale, including construction, roads, transportation, shipping, aeronautics, refineries, and industry coupled with international commerce and banking. These patterns persist in Baranquilla, Santo Domingo, Panama City, and Jamaica. Caribbean Jews remain active in sugar plantations, coffee growing, and cattle breeding in Panama and El Salvador. Curaçao is a commercial center, and Panama's Colón Free Trade Zone, one of the largest centers of contemporary Caribbean commerce, is mostly in Jewish hands. In agro-industries, such as edible oil extraction, tropical fruit extracts, canning, spices, and juices, Jewish involvement continues in Panama, Colombia, Venezuela, El Salvador, and Jamaica.

*Ashkenazic Jews did not come to the Caribbean in any numbers until the late eighteenth century, and they tended to follow the same occupational patterns as Sephardic Jews. Jews of Ashkenazic descent are active today in commerce and manufacturing. During World War II the Dominican Republic and Jamaica absorbed Jewish refugees. The Jewish community in Cuba, which numbered 15,000 in 1959, now has a population of around 1,500. Cuban-born anthropologist Ruth Behar has written about Cuban Jewish life (*An Island Called Home: Returning to Jewish Cuba* [2007]).

Recent research includes M. Arbell, *The Spanish-Portuguese Jewish Settlements in the Caribbean and the Guianas* (2002); R. Cohen, *Jews in Another Environment: Surinam in the Second Half of the Eighteenth Century* (1991); and A. Ben-Ur and R. Frankel, *Remnant Stones: The Jewish Cemeteries of Suriname: Epitaphs* (2009).   ANTHONY MACFARLANE

Caro, Joseph: See KARO, JOSEPH

Catacombs are subterranean cemeteries consisting of underground burial chambers and of long winding galleries that also were used for burial. Although Jews in *Roman times normally preferred to be buried in smaller family-type tombs known as *hypogea*, catacombs were used when conditions demanded the construction of large community cemeteries. This happened in Beth She'arim, near Haifa in modern Israel, where a series of Jewish catacombs have been brought to light dating from the second through fourth centuries CE. Similarly, several Jewish communities in *Rome created four large catacombs that were used exclusively by Jews. Recent radiocarbon dating of materials from the Jewish catacombs of Rome suggest that they predate Rome's more famous early Christian catacombs. This finding suggests that Jews may have invented this particular type of burial. Both the Beth She'arim and Rome catacombs contain many important funerary inscriptions and are important sources of information about Jewish life and artistic production in Roman times. Recent research includes L. Brink and D. Green, eds., *Commemorating the Dead: Texts and Artifacts in Context: Studies of Roman, Jewish and Christian Burials* (2008); and **see CEMETERIES, MEDIEVAL AND EARLY MODERN EUROPE.**   LEONARD V. RUTGERS

Celebrities have been an important new aspect of Jewish culture since the beginning of the twentieth century, in response to larger cultural innovations in mass media and public relations. Although sages and heroic figures have long been fixtures of Jewish *folklore and popular religion, Jewish celebrities are a modern phenomenon, both because of the fields in which they are recognized (including the arts, sciences, *sports and athletics, politics, *commerce, *philanthropy, and *crime) and because of new notions of Jewishness and of the Jewish presence in public culture generally. The inventory of Jewish celebrities includes those acclaimed for achievements that are generally thought of as separate from their Jewishness (for example, biologist Jonas Salk, who developed a widely used polio vaccine, or Olympic champion swimmer Mark Spitz); those whose achievements are regarded as related to their Jewishness (such as "star *cantors" or acclaimed authors who write *literature or *drama about Jewish life); and those whose Jewishness is regarded as being in a provocative relationship with their renown. Examples of this last kind of celebrity range from nineteenth-century British Prime Minister Benjamin *Disraeli, who, although baptized and a practicing Anglican, maintained a sense of Jewish identity, to chess champion Bobby Fisher, who became an outspoken antisemite in the final years of his life.

The interrelation of fame and Jewishness in celebrities' lives can be complex. Tenor Richard Tucker (1913–1975), whose career embraced both cantorial and operatic singing, was forthright in proclaiming his Jewishness and, at the same time, felt that it hindered his opera career. Public declarations of celebrities' Jewishness have sometimes engendered larger public conversations on the interrelation of identity and culture. The crowning of Bess Myerson (b. 1924) as Miss America in 1945, amid reports that she resisted pressure to change her last name to obscure her Jewish identity, became a landmark event in postwar American Jewish popular culture; so, too, did the refusals of baseball players Hank Greenberg and Sandy Koufax to play in World Series games that coincided with *Yom Kippur (see SPORTS, UNITED STATES: BASEBALL). All three had triumphed in nationwide competitions in which their being Jewish was essentially irrelevant but they had done so forthrightly as Jews. By publicly demonstrating the limits to which they would compromise their Jewishness for the sake of competition, they presented personal profiles in which being a Jew enhanced their status as American celebrities, adding their manifest respect for their ethnic and religious heritage to their roster of accomplishments.

Jewish entertainers are known for especially elaborate public profiles, what Richard Dyer terms "star texts" – an aggregation of their performances and their "private" lives (*Stars* [1979]). Some entertainers crafted elaborate false biographies to obscure their Jewishness (an early example is silent screen actress Theda Bara [1855–1955], née Theodesia Goodman); others, such as Al Jolson (1886–1950; né Asa Yoelson) and Fanny Brice (1891–1951; née Fania Borach) incorporated autobiography into their performances, blurring the line between on-stage and off-stage personas. These and other star texts of nationally renowned performers evince the dynamics and range of possibilities for positioning Jewishness in the forum of public culture.

At the same time, Jews have elevated figures to celebrity status within their own communities. For example, avid readers of acclaimed Yiddish writers followed their lives and work closely in the Yiddish press, reproduced their portraits on postcards, named schools after them, attended their funerals in mass numbers, and demonstrated other practices of modern celebrity culture. Only occasionally, however, has the renown of Yiddish writers extended beyond the confines of the Jewish world, and in most of those cases – Morris Rosenfeld (1862–1923), Sholem Asch, Isaac Bashevis Singer – the consequences have proved controversial within the Jewish community (see LITERATURE, YIDDISH: 1800 TO TWENTY-FIRST CENTURY).

Jewish celebrities occasionally figure in public discourses of morality. The exploits of infamous Jewish gangsters and spies have prompted larger discussions of Jewish ethics and patriotism, while Jewish performers who test the limits of public decency sometimes raise questions about Jews' sense of propriety. Conversely, some Jewish victims of antisemitism, especially during the *Holocaust, have become figures of renown and, as exemplified by author Elie *Wiesel, have used their celebrity stature to address larger moral issues.

Listing Jewish celebrities has become a fixture of popular culture in the form of books, websites, halls of fame, collectibles, and the like. As J. Hoberman and Jeffrey Shandler note in *Entertaining America: Jews, Movies and Broadcasting* (2003), this is not only a Jewish pastime but is also a pursuit common to both philo- and antisemites, who keep registers of famous politicians or actors of Jewish origin who use different names professionally. Jews and their admirers claim these inventories as evidence of Jewish accomplishment within a variety of cultural mainstreams but their detractors cite these achievements as indicative of organized Jewish intentions to exploit and deceive.

JEFFREY SHANDLER

Cemeteries, Medieval and Early Modern Europe.

Although no early medieval Jewish cemeteries have been preserved anywhere in Europe, single gravestones of the seventh through ninth centuries with *Hebrew inscriptions have been found outside their original contexts in both *Italy and *Spain. In southern Italy, remains unearthed at Venosa document the transition from the *catacombs of late antiquity to the individual graves characteristic of medieval Europe.

Historic Jewish cemeteries within the *Ashkenazic realm include those of Worms, home to the earliest gravestone preserved *in situ* (1077), *Prague (1439), and Kraków (sixteenth century). Often, gravestones were confiscated for building purposes when a medieval cemetery was destroyed. Some of these gravestones have since resurfaced, most notably so at Würzburg, where about 1,500 medieval headstones came to light in 1987. One cemetery that has been excavated is that of medieval York, where work was suspended when findings demonstrated the Jewishness of the site (see ENGLAND: MIDDLE AGES); another is the *Montjuich* (Jews' Mount) of medieval Barcelona.

One apparently early difference between Ashkenazic and *Sephardic grave culture is the position of grave markers. Sephardic Jews place slabs horizontally to cover the entire grave while grave markers are positioned in an upright position, usually above the deceased person's head in Ashkenazic tradition. When Jewish populations mixed in the wake of large-scale migrations, communities often maintained separate burial places. Notable cemeteries of the Sephardic Diaspora include Hamburg-Altona (1612) and Ouderkerk near *Amsterdam (1614). Elsewhere, for example at *Venice, the various traditions are represented side by side. Medieval epigraphs were short and uniformly in Hebrew; their phraseology often followed local and regional convention. Inscriptions became more expansive in early modernity, as gravestones became a vehicle of artistic expression. The vernacular began to make inroads among Sephardic Jews after 1492; western Ashkenazic Jews followed suit

about three centuries later. Among both groups, bilingual inscriptions remained the rule well into the nineteenth century.

The layout of cemeteries often reflected social hierarchies, with kinship as a key criterion. There were separate areas for *priestly families (*kohanim*), often situated near the entrance to accommodate *purity laws, as well as special locations for children, suicides, and *martyrs (*kedoshim*, later interpreted to include the victims of any sort of violent death). Burial near martyrs or great scholars appears to have been a privilege reminiscent of the Christian practice of burial *ad sanctos* ("near the saints"). Visits to the cemetery were part of communal custom, especially on *fast days; it was widely believed that prayers offered near the graves of the righteous would be especially efficacious. Time and again, rabbis cautioned against directing prayer to the deceased themselves.

Recent studies include A. Bar-Levav, "We Are Where We Are Not: The Cemetery in Jewish Culture, *Jewish Studies* 41 (2002); and C. Weissler, "Measuring Candles and Laying Wicks, in *Judaism in Practice*, ed. L. Fine (2001). A comprehensive, multilingual bibliography is F. Wiesemann, *Sepulcra judaica: Bibliographie zu jüdischen Friedhöfen und zu Sterben, Begräbnis und Trauer bei den Juden von der Zeit des Hellenismus bis zur Gegenwart* (2005).

LUCIA RASPE

Center for Jewish History.

This *New York City home to a number of major American Jewish cultural and scholarly organizations opened to the public in January 2000. Its founding partners include the American Jewish Historical Society, the American Sephardi Federation (with Sephardic House), the Leo Baeck Institute, the Yeshiva University Museum, and the YIVO Institute for Jewish Research. Several smaller organizations are also located at the Center, including the American Society for Jewish Music, the Primo Levi Foundation, the Association for Jewish Studies, and Gomez Foundation for Mill House. Occupying 120,000 square feet on W. 16th Street in Manhattan, it is the largest facility for the collection and preservation of original materials relating to modern Jewish history in the western hemisphere. Each institution or organization at the Center retains its independence, maintains its own holdings, and mounts its own programs. The partners also conduct joint programs and exhibitions.

MICHAEL FELDBERG

Central Europe

is a region of Europe whose boundaries are not clearly defined and are much disputed. For the purposes of Jewish history and culture, Central Europe encompasses German-speaking Europe (present-day *Germany and Austria) and areas that came under German or *Habsburg rule during the Early Modern period where German was one of the languages of officialdom and culture. Thus, Central Europe could also include *Hungary, the Czech Republic, Slovakia, and parts of *Poland. **Maps 8, 10**

Ceremonial Objects.

Many types of appurtenances have been crafted for use in ritual ceremonies. Some are essential to the ritual; others are used to beautify the religious practice. The precept of *ḥiddur mitzvah* ("beautification of the commandment"), requiring the performance of religious commandments in a beautiful way (BT *Shabbat* 133b), is based on Exodus 15:2, "This is my Lord and I will beautify Him." Jewish ceremonial objects often stylistically resemble secular or religious artifacts crafted of the same materials or having parallel functions in contemporaneous locales and eras, and they tend to incorporate local decorative motifs and approaches. In Islamic countries, where the consumption of alcohol was prohibited, Jewish ceremonial cups and goblets often followed Western models.

LIFE-CYCLE EVENTS: Decorated instruments (knives, shields, medicine bottles) are often used by the *mohel* performing ritual *circumcisions. Silver trays associated with the *pidyon ha-ben* (redemption of the *firstborn son) ceremony frequently depict the *akedah (the binding of *Isaac narrative of Genesis 22). Ceremonial objects associated with *marriage include the *huppah* (canopy) under which the ceremony takes place, special cups (often interlocking), rings, and ornamented *ketubbot (marriage contracts). Water vessels, combs, and nail-cleaning implements for use in ritually cleansing a corpse are often ornamented with inscriptions or images related to *death.

DOMESTIC RITUALS: Many decorated objects are associated with *Sabbath meals, including *kiddush cups and various objects related to the *hallah* (Sabbath loaves), including plates, knives, and covers. Special lamps or candlesticks are used for kindling the Sabbath lights; the star-shaped hanging oil lamp known as a *Judenstern* was popular before the modern period. Adorned plates, cups, candleholders, and spice containers are used in the *Havdalah* ceremony, which concludes the Sabbath. In *Ashkenazi communities, tower-shaped spice containers, echoing Central European architecture, are very common, as are fruit- and flower-shaped containers. Decorative containers, frequently of silver, are used to store the *etrog* on *Sukkot.

*Hanukkah lamps (*hanukkiyah/hanukkiyot*) are essential to the celebration of the holiday. The two basic types of Hanukkah lamps are (1) eight-branch candelabras resembling the seven-branched *menorah of the biblical *Tabernacle and *Temples and (2) bench-type lamps, with eight lights arranged along a slightly elevated horizontal surface, often with a decorative backplate (**Plates 10, 11**). Decorative vessels are also used for the foods of the *Passover seder. They include wine cups and decanters, *matzah* covers or bags, and special plates (often three-tiered) for the distinctive food items invoked during the ceremonial meal (**Plate 5**). Scrolls of the book of *Esther (*megillah*), read on *Purim, are often ornamented with decorative borders or illustrations and may be housed in ornamental cases. Also associated with Purim are decorative noisemakers and plates for sending gifts (*mishloah manot*).

*SYNAGOGUE: Early sources indicate that *Torah scrolls were ornamented and protected with appurtenances. The *Mishnah discusses "figured" wrappers that covered Torah scrolls (*Kelayim* 28:4). Today, most *Sephardi and *Mizrahi communities both house and read the scroll upright within a *tik*, a rigid, hinged case. A *tik* is mentioned in a document, dated 1075, found in the Cairo *Genizah and is first depicted in early-fourteenth-century Spanish *haggadot. A *tik* is generally crafted of wood or metal and is cylindrical or polygonal, often twelve-sided to symbolize the twelve *Israelite tribes. Many examples feature ornamentation typical of Islamic metalwork; lavish carved and gilded wood examples from *Italy and *North Africa are also known. Finials ornament the top or sides of the *tik*, and it is often draped with scarves that are used to cover the open scroll before it is read. The reader often uses a pointer (*yad*; literally "hand") to follow the text and to avoid directly touching the Torah scroll.

Scrolls in both Ashkenazi and Sephardi congregations are generally attached to carved or inlaid Torah staves called *atzei hayyim* ("trees of life"), and lengths of fabric are used as binders to hold the two sides of the scroll together. Torah binders were generally crafted of beautiful fabrics. In Italy and elsewhere, they were often made and dedicated by women. The Roman liturgy includes a prayer for "every daughter of Israel who makes a mantle or cover in honor of the Torah." It was customary among many Jews in *Central Europe to create Torah binders from swaddling cloths that wrapped a male infant at his circumcision. This type of binder, often known as a *wimpel*, has been understood as a physical link between the *covenantal relationship established through circumcision and the Torah. The swaddling cloths were embroidered or painted with an inscription specifying the child's name, birth date, and a blessing for his future cited from the circumcision liturgy. The *wimpel* was often presented when the boy was first brought to the synagogue.

In many communities, a length of fabric is rolled with the Torah to cover the outside of the area opened for reading. A textile cover may also be placed over an open scroll. A closed scroll is covered with a fabric mantle (*meil*) generally of velvet or fine silks. Extant full-skirted mantles from the seventeenth century on, featuring soft or rigid circular or oval tops with two holes for insertion of the staves, are known from Sephardi communities in Western Europe, the *Ottoman Empire, and the Americas. This form is portrayed in the *Sarajevo Haggadah* (Spain, thirteenth century). Early Ashkenazi mantles were flat, joined segments of fabric, resembling a pillow case, with spaces at the top for staves. A 1582 example of this type is found in *Prague, and similar mantles appear in the fourteenth-century German Ulm *mahzor* (*High Holiday and *festival *prayer book). Most Ashkenazi mantles feature a rigid oval top and a tight straight skirt, often decorated with dedicatory inscriptions and symbols such as crowns, lions, and the *Decalogue. A decorated fabric curtain known as a *parokhet* often hangs on the ark (*aron kodesh*) housing the Torah scrolls, evoking the covering of the biblical *Ark of the Covenant and the parokhet curtain that separated the Holy of Holies from the public spaces in the Jerusalem Temple.

Other Torah ornaments, generally crafted of metal, usually silver, are also frequently used. The Torah staves are topped with a crown (*keter*) or a pair of finials; many communities use both simultaneously. Torah crowns made out of jewelry to be used on *Simhat Torah are discussed in a *responsum by *Hai ben Sherira *Gaon (939–1038); the earliest extant crowns are sixteenth-century Italian examples. Torah finials are generally known as *rimonim* ("pomegranates") or sometimes as *tappuhim* ("apples"), suggesting their fruit shapes (**Plate 8**); in the Spanish and Portuguese communities of *Britain and the Americas they are also known as bells because of the bells attached to most examples. Other finials resemble towers, corresponding to the vertical form of the staves and often reflecting local architectural traditions. Crown-shaped finials are also known. First mentioned in twelfth-century texts, the earliest extant example of Torah finials are a late-fifteenth-century pair now in the cathedral of Palma de Mallorca. A shield (*tas*) is often suspended on a chain over the staves in front of the mantle. Torah shields were originally used to label the reading to which a scroll was turned, but were later used for purely decorative purposes. A pointer is usually suspended on a chain over one stave. Pointers were often made of silver, although carved ivory and wood examples are also known; they generally terminate in a hand shape, often with an extended finger. Inscribed, decorated shofars (rams' horns) were used in some communities on *Rosh Ha-Shanah.   GABRIEL GOLDSTEIN

Ceremonial Objects: Islamic Lands. Ceremonial objects for *synagogue use in Islamic lands focused on the *Torah scroll with the purpose of protecting it, honoring it, and decorating it. These objects, which developed over a long period of time and throughout vast geographical regions, differ from community to community in both materials and design. There are two general types of Torah scroll coverings. One is a textile covering consisting of a wrapper, a Torah binder, and a mantle, all made from precious materials and usually patterned. The scroll itself is wound together with the wrapper, whose length is about three meters and whose width is the height of the Torah scroll parchment. A long binder is girded over the wrapper, and the mantle is placed over all. This type of covering is common to *Sephardic communities in the *Balkans, *Italy, *Morocco, and *Algeria and to the Portuguese communities, located mainly in *Holland and *England. Although it is similar to that of *Ashkenazi communities in Europe, what distinguishes the textile Torah covering in the Sephardic communities is the wrapper, which is not found in Ashkenazic practice, and the opening, which is down the front of the mantle. In the Ashkenazi mantle, the openings are to the sides. While the Torah scroll is being read these three items are taken off, and the scroll is placed horizontally on a slightly tilted table.

The second type of Torah scroll covering is the cylindrical or faceted case of wood or metal that opens down the front. Known as a *tik*, this protective covering has three subtypes. The most ancient, characterized by a flat top and two rolling staves that emerge from it, is found mainly in the communities of *Yemen, eastern *Iran, and the Cochin and *Bene Israel* communities in *India. The second kind is distinguished by an onion-shaped crown attached to the top of the case. The crown is separated into two sides when the case is opened, and two diagonal staves are driven through it, on which two finials are placed. This subtype is common to the communities that follow the Babylonian tradition: *Iraq, *Kurdistan, western *Iran, and the dispersions of these communities. One example of this subtype is the Torah scroll of the Kurdish communities of western Iran, with four or six staves emerging above its crown. The third subtype is characterized by a coronet around the edges of the case's top, and the staves for rolling the scroll come out from its top. It is used by the communities of the eastern Mediterranean basin. All the Torah scroll cases are decorated or overlaid in precious materials, in vegetal or geometric patterns; on top of many cases a kerchief is placed or tied, a remnant of the ancient custom of wrapping the Torah scroll in a kerchief.

Another decorative object connected with the Torah scroll is the finial. Finials are placed above the Torah scroll and developed from the practice of decorating the tops of the scroll's rolling staves. At some point in time the decoration was separated from the stave tops, and a hollow rod was added to it. The rods were placed on top of the rolling staves in most communities, although in communities following the Babylonian tradition, they were placed on top of the slanted staves above the cases. Apparently the original decoration was ball-shaped, which accounts for its being named for a round fruit, the "apple" (*tappuah*) in Sephardic communities and the "pomegranate" (*rimon*) in all others. These names are still in use, but the ball-like shape has changed over time. In Yemen the finial became taller and taller, and then another elongated ball, reminiscent in shape of the crown of the actual pomegranate, was added to it. In Iraq the round shape was preserved, and bells were added to it. The ball shape was preserved in the finials of the Middle Eastern communities. Each community had its own form, expressed in the style, size, and shape of the ball and in the number of bells. The finials of the Sephardic *Diaspora developed in a different direction and were influenced by the architectural shape of the tower that is typical of non-Jewish ritual objects in Europe. This type is characterized by a semi-round base topped by a tower-like form (**Plate 8**).

Other important ceremonial objects are the Torah crown (*keter*) and Torah shield (*tas*) placed above and in front the Torah scroll in *Turkey; plaques for inviting a person to read the Torah in Iraqi Kurdish communities; and the pointer (*yad*), used in every Jewish community by all readers of the Torah scroll, to follow the text and avoid losing one's place.   BRACHA YANIV

Chabad: See ḤABAD

Chagall, Bella Rosenfeld (1895–1940), writer and wife of artist Marc Chagall (1887–1985; see ART, EUROPE: TWENTIETH CENTURY), was born in Vitebsk, White Russia (see BELORUSSIA), the youngest of eight children of Shmuel Noah and Alta Rosenfeld. Her parents, owners of a successful jewelry business, were members of the *Ḥasidic community and conducted their family life according to Jewish tradition. However, they also sought out secular education and opportunities for their children. Chagall, who was educated in Russian-language schools, became a student in the Faculty of Letters at the University of Moscow in her teens; she was particularly interested in theater and art, and as a university student she contributed articles to a Moscow newspaper. In 1909, while visiting friends in *Saint Petersburg, Bella met Marc Chagall; their attraction was instantaneous and they were soon engaged. Although both were from Vitebsk, their social worlds were far apart, and the Rosenfelds were unhappy with the engagement. The couple finally married in 1915, and their only child, Ida, was born the next year. In 1922, Marc Chagall moved his family to *France. Bella was a constant subject in her husband's art, often represented as a beloved bride. The Chagalls fled to the United States after the outbreak of World War II, arriving in *New York in 1941. Bella Chagall died in 1944 in the United States, apparently of a viral infection.

Bella Chagall's literary work included the editing and translation of her husband's 1922 autobiography from Russian into French (*Ma Vie*, 1931; English translation, *My Life*, 1960). Her major book, *Brenendike Likht* (*Burning Lights*, trans. N. Guterman [1946; reprinted 1996]), was written in

*Yiddish in France in 1939; it was published posthumously in English. Chagall said that her visits to Jewish communities in *Palestine in 1931 and *Vilna in 1935 prompted her to write in Yiddish, her "faltering mother tongue."

In *Brenendike Likht* Chagall arranges her reminiscences according to the *calendar and observances of the Jewish year. Writing in the voice of her childhood self, Basha, she places female experience at the center of her luminous narrative. Chagall's selective portrait of her well-to-do urban family – living among and employing Gentiles, successful in business, religiously active, and communally philanthropic – contrasts with contemporaneous depictions of the contained and impoverished Jewish life of the Eastern European *shtetl. A great part of the genius of *Brenendike Likht* is Chagall's ability to convey simultaneously the timelessness of traditional Jewish life and a dark foreboding prompted by the existential reality of Eastern European Jewry in the 1930s. A second posthumous autobiographical volume, *First Encounter*, was published in 1983. For recent scholarship, see J. R. Baskin, "Piety and Female Aspiration in the Memoirs of Pauline Epstein Wengeroff and Bella Rosenfeld Chagall," *Nashim* 7 (Spring 2004): 65–96; and **see also MEMOIR AND LIFEWRITING: YIDDISH.**   JUDITH R. BASKIN

Charleston, South Carolina, boasts one of the oldest Jewish communities in the *United States. Attracted by economic opportunities and by a degree of religious tolerance remarkable for the time, *Sephardic Jews began settling in the port town as early as the 1690s. In 1749, Charleston's Jews chartered Kahal Kadosh Beth Elohim, one of the first five Jewish congregations in America. By 1800 Charleston was home to the largest, wealthiest, and most cultured Jewish community in North America, with a population of upward of five hundred individuals, or one-fifth of all the Jews in the United States at that time.

Charleston produced the first movement to modernize *Judaism in America: the Reformed Society of Israelites founded in 1824. In 1840, in a dispute with traditionalists, the reform faction at Beth Elohim prevailed. With the blessing of Beth Elohim's popular minister, Gustavus Poznanski, a proposal to install an organ in the *synagogue was narrowly adopted. The traditionalists seceded and formed Shearit Israel, with its own burial ground.

Meanwhile, a new group of immigrants introduced another brand of Judaism to Charleston. These residents were mainly of modest means – peddlers, artisans, metalworkers, and bakers – and they gave the city's Jewish population a more foreign appearance. As early as 1852, a *minyan, or prayer group, began meeting under the leadership of Rabbi Hirsch Zvi Levine, himself recently arrived from *Poland. In 1855 the newcomers organized as Berith Shalome (now Brith Sholom) or "Covenant of Peace." This was the first *Ashkenazic congregation in South Carolina and one of the first in the American South (**see UNITED STATES, SOUTHERN**).

Between 1905 and 1912, Charleston's Jewish community, which had maintained itself for decades at around seven hundred people, doubled in size. At one time some forty stores on upper King Street were closed on Saturday, in observance of the Jewish *Sabbath. The men held prayer services above their stores. The women kept *kosher homes, training their African American employees to make potato

kugel and *gefilte* fish, and learning, in turn, to fix fried chicken and okra gumbo.

After *World War II, an expansion of military facilities, port development, and the growth of educational and medical institutions and tourism brought new prosperity to Charleston. The Jewish population tripled from about 2,000 in 1948 to approximately 6,500 in 2008. At the end of the first decade of the twenty-first century, Charleston supports three congregations: Brith Sholom Beth Israel (Orthodox), Emanu-El Synagogue (Conservative), and K. K. Beth Elohim (Reform), as well as a Hebrew day school, Addlestone Hebrew Academy. The College of Charleston's Jewish Studies Program has attracted the largest Jewish enrollment in the state, and its Jewish Heritage Collection, initiated in 1995, serves researchers from around the world.

For further reading, see S. Breibart, *Explorations in Charleston's Jewish History* (2005); J. W. Hagy, *This Happy Land: The Jews of Colonial and Antebellum Charleston* (1993); and T. Rosengarten and D. Rosengarten, eds., *A Portion of the People: Three Hundred Years of Southern Jewish Life* (2002).

            DALE ROSENGARTEN

Chełmno (German, Kulmhof) was the only fully operational death camp located within the *Nazi Third Reich. Himmler opened it in late 1941 to murder Jews and Roma (see HOLOCAUST: ROMA) in the Łódž *ghetto and the Warthegau district of Greater *Germany. The central camp was located in an old castle in the village of Chełmno, where the SS murdered the victims in special gas vans. The bodies were then taken about 2.5 miles to the *Waldlager* (forest camp) for burial and, later, cremation. The mass murders at Chełmno took place in several phases. The first was between December 1941 and March 1943. The camp was reopened in the summer of 1944 to kill the remaining Jews in Łódž and then closed. The Germans murdered 147,000 Jews and 5,000 Roma at Chełmno from 1941 to 1944. **See HOLOCAUST; HOLOCAUST CAMPS AND KILLING CENTERS.**

           DAVID M. CROWE

Chicago, a major city of the American Midwest, is located on Lake Michigan in the state of Illinois. Chicago's origins as a small town on the western frontier reach back only to the 1830s. The first Jews who settled there, shortly after 1840, hailed from the *Central European regions of Bavaria, Bohemia, and Posen. Between 1860 and 1900 no American city matched either Chicago's rapid growth, dynamism, and optimism or its social inequality and brutality. Most Jewish immigrants successfully participated in the city's rise, especially in the production and wholesale of various textiles. Early on, Jews were active in local politics and enjoyed much respect. During the *Civil War (see UNITED STATES: CIVIL WAR), Chicago Jews organized their own company under the wings of the 82nd Illinois Volunteer Regiment. The small Jewish community remained distinct from the diverse population of German-speaking immigrants. Yet individual Jews were among the leaders of the Chicago German community; some also occupied prominent positions in the Czech community.

Chicago was a new city without established Jewish and Christian elites and this may partially explain why it became a center of the radical (or "German") Reform movement. The Reform movement in Chicago owed much to David *Einhorn's theology; Cincinnati Reform leader, Rabbi Isaac

Mayer *Wise, was a fierce critic. Under the auspices of Rabbis Bernhard Felsenthal, and later Kaufmann Kohler and Emil G. Hirsch, Sinai Congregation (founded in 1861), which strongly influenced several other Chicago *synagogues, emerged as one of the most radical Reform congregations in America and beyond. Hannah Solomon, co-founder of the *National Council of Jewish Women, and Julius Rosenwald, philanthropist, Sears and Roebuck magnate, and NAACP co-founder, were members of Sinai. They and other established "German" Jews promoted social reforms and worked closely with Hull House founder Jane Addams and other Progressives (see JUDAISM, REFORM: NORTH AMERICA).

Between 1880 and 1890 the number of Chicago's inhabitants doubled from 500,000 to more than one million. In 1890, 80% of Chicagoans consisted of foreign-born immigrants and their American-born children. Many new Chicagoans were Jews from *Eastern Europe. The Jewish population increased from around 10,000 in 1880 to approximately 300,000 in 1925, making Chicago the city with the third largest Jewish population in the world, trailing only *New York and *Warsaw. Jewish immigrants settled on the Near Westside in the "ghetto" neighborhood around Maxwell Street, working in particular in textile factories and sweatshops. The area was famous for its *Yiddish theaters. Nobel Laureate Saul Bellow, who grew up in this neighborhood, created unique descriptions of the Chicago Jewish immigrant experience in his novels (see LITERATURE, UNITED STATES: SINCE 1900). Chicago was an early center of *Zionism; Chicagoan Leon Zolotkoff was the only American delegate at the First Zionist Congress in Basel in 1897.

By the 1920s Jews were leaving the "ghetto," many for Lawndale, a Westside neighborhood known in Yiddish as "Deutschland" (Germany) – an indication of the high degree of assimilation and social mobility associated with the mid-nineteenth-century arrivals from Central Europe. After the late 1940s Jews moved overwhelmingly to the northern suburbs or left Chicago for Sunbelt cities. Metropolitan Chicago remains one of the largest Jewish communities in the United States with an approximate population of 270,000. Chicago elected its first Jewish mayor, Rahm Emanuel, in 2011.

TOBIAS BRINKMANN

Childhood: See MIDDLE AGES: CHILDHOOD

China. There has been a continuous, if small, Jewish presence in China for well over a thousand years, and five distinct ripples of immigration can be identified. In the medieval period, Jews journeyed to Kaifeng and other cities via ancient trade routes. In the wake of the nineteenth-century opening of Chinese ports to foreigners in response to British coercion, *Mizraḥi (Baghdadi) Jews from *Iraq made their way to Hong Kong and Shanghai; at the turn of the twentieth century, Russian Jews traveled to Harbin and other northeast Chinese cities. A fourth settlement occurred during World War II when German, Austrian, and Polish Jews fled to Shanghai. At the beginning of the twenty-first century, there is a community of North American, European, and Israeli Jews who are employed in China. With the exception of the Harbin and latter Shanghai experiences when China provided a place of refuge, Jews have primarily come to China for economic opportunities.

KAIFENG: Jews traveled from West Asia over the Silk Road and by sea, probably in the Tang dynasty (618–907 CE). Some scholars think they may have arrived even earlier, during the later Han dynasty (25–220 CE), which would coincide with *Roman persecution in *Judea. By 960 CE, Jews were certainly established in Kaifeng, which was then called Bianliang and served as a capital of the Song dynasty. At this time, China was a center of civilization and trade. Jews also settled in major shipping cities, such as Guangzhou (a southern coast port with access to Southeast Asia and *Persia), Quanzhou (in Southeast Fujian), Ningpo, Yangzhou (a Grand Canal port near the sea on the Yangzi River), and Hangzhou (also on the Grand Canal; a city known to have had a *synagogue). There is also evidence of a Jewish presence inland along the Silk Road in such locations as Dandan Uiliq, Dunhuang, and Ningxia.

In 1163, a synagogue was built in Kaifeng, and the community lived close by on what were called the North and the South "Teaching Torah" lanes. The Jewish community prospered despite repeated disasters, such as fires and the flooding of the Yellow River, which frequently destroyed the synagogue. In the wake of each of these calamities, the community erected a stele to commemorate their rebuilding of the synagogue; there are four in total, from 1489, 1512, 1663, and 1679. These stelae, except that of 1663 (which is lost), are currently kept in the Kaifeng Municipal Museum. They relate how the Jews believed they entered China, their history in Kaifeng, their view of the development of their religion and their religious beliefs, and their practice of the mitzvot (*commandments), which was, for centuries, very traditional.

In his diary, Marco Polo describes meeting with Jews in China in 1286. He reported that Kublai Khan celebrated Jewish, Christian, and Muslim festivals. However, it was not until 1605 that the Jewish presence in China was really "discovered" by the West when a Kaifeng Jew named Ai Tian went to Beijing to take a civil service examination and serendipitously met Fr. Matteo Ricci, the first Jesuit priest to visit China. After this meeting, the Vatican sent other Jesuits to Kaifeng. The missionaries left excellent sketches and notes about what they observed, and they confirmed that the Jews of Kaifeng had exactly the same *Torah and observed the same religious observances as the Jews of Europe. Contact with Jesuits ended when China closed itself off from missionaries in 1723.

By the seventeenth century, all the Jewish coastal communities had disappeared, leaving only Kaifeng. It is not known whether Jews in these other areas assimilated, moved to Kaifeng, or left China altogether. As China entered a period of decline, so, too, did the Kaifeng community. The last rabbi passed away in 1810, leaving little Jewish knowledge in the community. By 1854 the synagogue had fallen into ruins, but the impoverished community lacked the means to restore it. Shortly thereafter, they were "rediscovered" by Protestant missionaries and other Western travelers. At the turn of the twentieth century, William Charles White, an Anglican bishop from Toronto, tried unsuccessfully to revive the community.

Kaifeng was a closed city from after the communist victory until the early 1980s when its Jews were once more "rediscovered" by journalists and Jewish tourists. These visitors noted that Jewish self-identity persisted, most notably in the form of insisting on being registered as Jews in their identity papers, but that Jewish customs and practices had become a faded memory. The interest of contemporary Jews in Kaifeng in becoming more actively Jewish has yet to be determined, because of the skittishness of the local authorities regarding foreign interference. In recent years, a young Kaifeng Jew studied in Israel and has returned home to serve his community. Regardless, the community's one thousand years of continuous existence in relative isolation from the larger Jewish world in a welcoming but culturally powerful host country is an extraordinary display of commitment to Jewish heritage and tradition.

HONG KONG AND SHANGHAI: There has been a Mizraḥi (Middle Eastern) Baghdadi Jewish presence in Shanghai and Hong Kong since the Opium Wars of the mid-nineteenth century when Britain forced China to open five port cities for trade. Baghdadi Jewish traders arrived in 1844. By 1862 they had a cemetery, and a synagogue was built by 1887. Some Kaifeng Jews visited Shanghai in 1851, and exchanges between the two Jewish communities culminated in a second visit in 1900 following the establishment by the Baghdadi community of a society to "rescue" their Kaifeng siblings from cultural oblivion.

By World War I, Shanghai had about seven hundred Jews, more than half of Mizraḥi origin. In 1932, nearly 40% of the Shanghai Stock Exchange's one hundred members were Mizraḥi Jews. They joined the city's finest clubs and financed some of Shanghai's finest colonial architecture, including the magnificent Children's Palace (formerly the Kadoorie estate), the art deco Peace Hotel (then the Cathay Hotel), Shanghai Mansions (a Sassoon building that later was used to process hundreds of Jewish refugees), and two synagogues, Bet Aharon and Ohel Rachel.

As in Shanghai, Hong Kong's first Jews initially came from *Iraq and *India and were British subjects. The Ohel Leah Synagogue was built by Jacob Sassoon in 1901–02. There were 80 Jews in Hong Kong in 1900 and 250 in the 1960s, split between those of *Ashkenazi and Mizraḥi origins. In the first decade of the twenty-first century, Hong Kong's Jewish population stands at about 3,500, with several synagogues, a Jewish day school, and an active community center.

HARBIN AND POINTS SOUTH: Russian Jews first came to Harbin in 1898. They were seeking better economic opportunities in the Russian concession in connection with the building of the Chinese Eastern Railroad. After the Russo-Japanese War, decommissioned Jewish soldiers joined these settlers; they were soon followed by refugees from the Russian *pogroms of 1905–07. By 1908, some 8,000 Jews lived in Harbin, and the central synagogue was built in 1909. The deprivations and persecution that Jews suffered during WW1, the Russian Revolution, and the White Russian counterrevolution led to further Jewish immigration to the Far East. Harbin's Jewish population, which grew to between 10,000 and 15,000, supported schools, newspapers, a library, *Zionist groups, and four synagogues.

However, the 1928 transfer of the railroad to the Chinese and escalating White Russian violence led many Jews to move south to Shanghai, Tianjin, and other southern Chinese cities. For example, in Tianjin the Jewish population reached five hundred to six hundred families between the wars. In 1945, the Soviet Army invaded Manchuria and occupied Harbin. The Soviet administration arrested prominent members of the Jewish community, returning many to the USSR. All Zionist and other Jewish organizations were

suspended. Between 1951 and 1953 most Jews from Harbin immigrated to *Israel; by 1962 the community had disappeared.

REFUGE IN SHANGHAI: Harbiners moved south to Shanghai, Tianjin, and elsewhere after the Japanese captured Manchuria in the early 1930s. Many settled in the French concession, where they ran their own stores and restaurants, read Russian newspapers, and enjoyed their own music, theater, and synagogue, the Ohel Moishe. By 1939, there were about 5,000 Russian Jews in Shanghai. They were mostly people of modest means, working in restaurants, coffee houses, bookstores, and other shops; many became bus drivers, although some were engineers, lawyers, or musicians. Others engaged in criminal activities, such as drug smuggling and *prostitution. However, between 1938 and 1941, an influx of refugees from *Nazi *Germany increased the Jewish population of Shanghai to an estimated 18,000. Thousands arrived in rags, without entry permits or any means of support.

Shanghai, despite its perilous political situation in the 1930s, was an attractive destination because it was a free transit port, with no requirements for visas or other documentation. Jewish refugees came in three waves. The first, in 1933–34, were mostly well-educated German Jews; their flight was not made in haste, and they were able to bring their financial resources to use to reestablish their professional lives in China. The second wave, during 1938–39, lasted until the Japanese and Western powers imposed restrictions on immigration. Up to 15,000 Jews came during this period, more than one thousand per month, mainly from Austria and Germany. Their rapid flight prevented them from taking more than minimal belongings. The last wave occurred in 1939, when a few thousand Jews escaped from *Poland after it was attacked by Germany. Traversing Siberia and Japan, they arrived in Shanghai penniless.

With help from Shanghai's Mizraḥi Jews, a refugee resettlement program was organized that opened schools, organized sports teams, published newspapers and magazines, and even started a band, scout troops, and football teams. It established seven synagogues, a Jewish school, four cemeteries, and a performance hall. After Pearl Harbor in 1941, the Japanese sent foreigners from the Allied nations to prison camps. But German and Austrian Jews were considered stateless refugees. Early in 1943, the Japanese promulgated a bulletin announcing the establishment of a "designated area" for "all refugees who had arrived after 1937." By May, nationless refugees were moved to designated locations by the military police "for security reasons." About 8,000 Jews were moved into the Hongkou "ghetto," joining the approximately 8,000 impoverished Jews already residing there in an area of less than two square kilometers. Although there was no barbed wire and only light patrols, adults needed officially approved passes to exit the area.

During World War II, approximately 24,000 Jews lived in Shanghai. Given the high population density in the Hongkou "ghetto," living conditions deteriorated rapidly. Some people begged on the street, whereas others worked in Chinese mills. Still, Shanghai was preferable to the alternative in Europe. This "ghetto" lasted from May 1943 until Japan's surrender in August 1945. When the civil war between the Chinese nationalists and communists resumed after World War II, an exodus of foreigners began almost immediately. Jews left for Israel, the *United States, *Canada, *Australia, and other countries. In 1948, about 10,000 Jews still lived in Shanghai; by 1953, only 450 remained. In 1976, there were only about ten Jews in Shanghai; the last remaining Jew died in 1982.

CONTEMPORARY PERIOD: In the 1980s, China began opening up to the West, and Jewish businesspersons were among the many Westerners who flocked to Shanghai, Guangzhou, and Beijing. In the first decade of the twenty-first century, the Jewish communities of China consist primarily of those in Hong Kong, with about 3,500; Shanghai, with about 1,000; and Beijing, with at least 200. The Jewish descendants in Kaifeng number perhaps one thousand. Hong Kong has a long-standing, permanent Jewish community as well as a transitory business one; the Shanghai and Beijing Jewish communities are mostly transitory. Except for Kaifeng Jews, Jews are not considered, nor do they consider themselves, to be citizens of China.

China's educated elite is fascinated by the similarities between the Jewish Diaspora and Overseas Chinese experiences and the resemblances between Chinese and Jewish cultures. Many are knowledgeable about the Jewish experiences in China and are proud of their country's role in providing a refuge for Jewish refugees from Nazism. *Jewish studies are flourishing in China, with formal programs at universities in Shandong, Shanghai, Beijing, Nanjing, Kaifeng, and Kunming.

The most important studies of the Kaifeng Jews are W. C. White, *Chinese Jews* (1966); M. Pollak, *Mandarins, Jews and Missionaries* (1998); Xu Xin, *The Jews of Kaifeng, China* (2003); and T. Weisz, *The Kaifeng Stone Inscriptions* (2006). See also M. Pollak, *The Jews of Dynastic China: A Critical Bibliography* (1993); J. Goldstein, ed., *The Jews of China* (2000); R. Malik, *From Kaifeng to Shanghai* (2000); and Pan Guang, *The Jews in China* (2002). On WWII Shangai, see D. Kranzler, *Japanese, Nazis and Jews* (1976); a number of memoirs have also appeared. Since 1986, the Sino-Judaic Institute has published a thrice-yearly journal, *Points East*, as well as intermittent scholarly publications; useful websites are www.sino-judaic.org and www.jewsofchina.org.

ANSON LAYTNER

Chmelnitzki (Khmel'nyts'kyi; also Chmielnicki), **Bogdan** (1595–1657), was the leader of the Cossack uprising of 1648 in *Ukraine. Chmelnitzki was from an Eastern Orthodox noble family that served in the Cossack units of the *Polish army, and he rose to a high position in the Chyhyryn Cossack regiments; he fled to Zaporizhian Sich, an independent Cossack republic in 1646 because of a personal dispute. There he was elected as *hetman* and initiated an uprising against Polish landlords. With the help of Crimean Tatars and the support of Ukrainian peasants, Chmelnitzki's Cossacks defeated the Polish regular forces. The outrage of the rebels was channeled toward Polish nobles, who possessed huge estates worked by Ukrainian serfs; Catholic priests, who persecuted the Eastern Orthodox Ukrainians; and Jews, who served as administrators and tax collectors for the Poles.

The Cossack armies captured the majority of fortified towns in the Ukraine; only the strongest towns in Ruś Czerwona withstood their onslaughts or succeeded in paying the attackers to move on. The rebels killed Poles and Jews,

while their Tatar allies took prisoners to sell in the markets of Crimea and Istanbul. The bloodiest massacres took place in Nemirov, Tulchin, and Bar in 1648, where Jewish residents were completely annihilated. Recent research by Shaul Stampfer (*Jewish History* 17) shows that approximately 20,000 Jews were killed by the Cossacks, whereas another 20,000 fled to cities that were not captured or abroad, as far as *Italy and *Holland.

The Peace of Zborov, concluded in August 1649 between Chmelnitzki and the Polish king, established a semi-independent hetmanate on both banks of the Dnieper, in which Jews were forbidden to live. However, under the treaty of Bila Tserkva in 1651, Jews were allowed to return to the Cossack territories. After an attempt to become an *Ottoman vassal, Chmelnitzki turned to Moscow and in 1654 concluded the Pereyaslav treaty, transferring Ukrainian lands to Russian protection. This brought *Russia into a war with Poland that ended in 1667 with the establishment of the Dnieper as the border between the two states. Until his death in 1657 Chmelnitzki remained the hetman and directed the Cossacks' military and diplomatic activities.

In Jewish tradition the atrocities committed by Chmelnitzki's Cossacks were called "the [evil] decrees of 1648–49," and they were remembered as among the most horrible events in Jewish history. The most influential of the six chronicles about these atrocities was Nathan Hanover's *Even Metzulah* (Abyss of Despair), which appeared in 1653. The 20th of *Sivan, the day of the massacre in Nemirov, was established as a fast day, and special prayers in memory of the victims were written. In the Ukrainian community, the legacy and mythologizing of the anti-Jewish violence of Chmelnitzki's Cossacks significantly influenced further waves of anti-Jewish violence from the eighteenth to the mid-twentieth century.

For further reading, see *Jewish History* 17 (May 2003), which is devoted to the Chmelnitzki massacres. Also see *Abyss of Despair*, trans. A. J. Mesch (1983); and J. Raba, *Between Remembrance and Denial* (1995).   VLADIMIR LEVIN

Chosenness, or the doctrine of election, is central to Jewish self-understanding. Its roots are biblical. In *Exodus 19, *God calls for Israel's fidelity to the *covenant. If Israel is faithful to the covenant, then Israel will be God's "treasure from among all peoples" (19:5). Elected from all the nations, Israel will become a "kingdom of *priests" (19:6), appointed to observe and guard the *Torah and its moral and ritual obligations. God's election of Israel is not attributed to any distinctive essential or numerical advantage but because "God loved you [Israel]" (Deut 7:8).

Medieval Jewish philosophers assumed the truth of chosenness, but divergent understandings of election were common. The two most enduring theories emerge from the writings of Judah *Halevi (1075?-1141) and Moses *Maimonides (1135–1204). Halevi held an almost biological understanding of election. God chose the Jews by reason of their special, native spiritual qualities, qualities absent in other peoples. In contrast, Maimonides denied that inherent factors played any role in election. He believed that anyone by dint of reason and belief could enter into the covenant. Maimonides had a much more positive view of *conversion than Halevi.

Baruch *Spinoza (1632–1677) presented the most thoroughgoing critique of the idea of chosenness. Excommunicated from his native *Amsterdam Jewish community, he was the first Jew to seriously challenge the concept of election. In the *Tractatus Theologico-Politicus*, Spinoza reversed the traditional hierarchy of election, suggesting that Israel, through its desire for a properly ordered society, chose God. In Spinoza's understanding, the covenant between God and Israel is of human design and made for distinctly human purposes.

Later, Reform *Judaism attempted to reinterpret chosenness as a universalist concept. Building on Isaiah 42:6, in which Israel is commanded to be "a light to the nations," Reform leaders such as Abraham *Geiger (1810–1874) in *Germany and Kaufmann Kohler (1843–1926) in America identified chosenness with mission. This mission charged Jews with the task of circulating the belief in ethical monotheism throughout the Gentile world. This ideal justified the *Diaspora with the insistence that the Jewish role among humanity can be fulfilled outside of the Land of *Israel. Reform Jews applied the concept of mission as well to the correspondence of Jewish ethics and the moral ideals of Christianity. By demonstrating the mutuality of ethical concern, they were able to make a rational claim for full civic and political equality.

Two of the most significant contemporary works on chosenness are M. Wyschogrod, *The Body of Faith* (1996), and D. Novak, *The Election of Israel* (1995). Wyschogrod accepts the idea that God chose Israel because of a special love even before it received the Torah. Although Novak agrees with Wyschogrod that God forms a singular relationship with the Jewish people, he argues that the Torah, which is the record of election, also establishes God's moral covenant with the rest of the world.

MATTHEW LAGRONE

Christian Hebraism was an intellectual movement whose adherents borrowed and adapted texts, ideas, and literary forms from Jewish literature to meet Christian cultural and religious needs. There were several important Christian scholars who learned and used *Hebrew during the Middle Ages, including Nicholas of Lyra (ca. 1270–1349) and Raymond Martini (1220–1284), and a number of others who learned Hebrew for biblical interpretation or missionary purposes, but they were isolated experts. Only in early modern Europe (1500–1750) can we speak of Christian Hebraism as a broad-based intellectual movement.

Both biblical humanism and the Protestant *Reformation (beginning in 1517) with its doctrine of *sola scriptura* (the belief that the Bible is the only source of religious authority) motivated large numbers of Christians to learn Hebrew so they could read the original text of the Old Testament. Greater interest in Hebrew learning encouraged *printers to produce substantial numbers of books on Hebrew for non-Jewish customers; similarly, rulers, patrons, and university authorities were convinced to create professorships in Hebrew. Jewish scholars such as Elijah Levita (1468–1549), Leon *Modena (1571–1648), and *Menasseh ben Israel (1604–1657) aided the growth of Christian Hebraism by tutoring Christian students in Hebrew and *Aramaic and by making Jewish books and manuscripts available to them. Christian Hebraism had a broader cultural and religious impact on Protestants because of the greater availability of Hebrew instruction in Protestant lands and its greater importance for Protestant theology, but a number of gifted Catholic Hebraists such as Egidio di Viterbo (1469–1532), Jean Morin (1591–1659), and Richard Simon (1638–1712) were also active throughout this period.

Christian Hebraists made accessible what they considered "useful" Jewish knowledge to other Christians. Their encounter with Judaism focused primarily on *Bible commentary (above all study of the exegetical writings of *Rashi, David *Kimhi, and Abraham *ibn Ezra), Christian *Kabbalah, the translation of Jewish classics into Latin and other European languages, and the study of living Judaism.

Christian Hebrew study involved close cooperation with Jews, especially in *Italy and the *Netherlands. The work of some Hebraists such as Johann Buxtorf (1564–1629) also began a scholarly reevaluation of Judaism and the place of Jews within European society that resulted in a more realistic assessment of both. Christian writers also used this new knowledge of Judaism to create better informed anti-Jewish polemical books such as Johann Andreas Eisenmenger's *Entdecktes Judentum* (1700).

For recent research, see P. Beitchman, *Alchemy of the Word: Cabala of the Renaissance* (1998); S. G. Burnett, *From Christian Hebraism to Jewish Studies* (1996); D. C. Klepper, *The Insight of Unbelievers: Nicholas of Lyra and Christian Reading of Jewish Text in the Later Middle Ages* (2007); P. T. Van Rooden, *Theology, Biblical Scholarship and Rabbinical Studies* (1989); and A. P. Coudert and J. S. Shoulson, eds., *Hebraica Veritas? Christian Hebraists and the Study of Judaism in Early Modern Europe* (2004).

STEPHEN G. BURNETT

Christianity and Second Temple Judaism. Among the significant events of the last century of the *Second Temple period was the emergence of the Jesus movement. The birth of Jesus can be dated around 6–4 BCE and his death around 30–33 CE. The earliest surviving writings by a follower of Jesus are the letters of Paul; they are dated to the 50s and 60s. The oldest written accounts of the life of Jesus (Gospels of Mark, Matthew, Luke, and John) and of the deeds of the first generation of his followers (Acts) date from after the destruction of the Second *Temple in 70 CE. These and other texts in the *New Testament preserve evidence that the Jesus movement originated as a movement within *Judaism, even as they also reflect its increasing appeal to Gentiles.

In research on Christianity, it was once common to treat Jesus and Paul as founders of a new "religion." Consistent with the theological training and institutional settings of most New Testament scholars, nineteenth- and early-twentieth-century studies often took for granted a supersessionist model of history. They read the origins of Christianity as the restoration of biblical piety from the alleged corruption of "late Judaism" (the older label for what is now termed "Second Temple Judaism"). In the wake of World War II and the *Holocaust, however, concerted efforts were made to shed such theological biases, and there has emerged a new understanding of Second Temple Judaism and Christian origins. In addition, the discovery of the *Dead Sea Scrolls brought new attention to noncanonical sources, exposing the rich variety in Jewish belief and practice in Second *Temple times. Scholars have increasingly understood the Jesus movement as one among many *apocalyptic and *messianic movements in Second Temple Judaism. Accordingly, they have read the New Testament literature as evidence both for the diversity of Second Temple Judaism and for the origins of Christianity.

Much about the historical Jesus remains debated. Was he a wisdom teacher, political revolutionary, or apocalyptic prophet? Did he see himself as the Messiah (Greek: *christos*)? Among the few points of consensus are that Jesus was a Jew, he was born of a Jewish mother, and he lived and died as a Jew in the Land of *Israel. For instance, *Josephus' account of Jewish history includes a passing reference to Jesus and depicts him as a wise man and wonder worker (*Antiquities* 18.63–64). Likewise, in the stories about his life in the Gospels, we find no hint that Jesus saw himself as anything other than a Jew. Even though the Gospels were written at a later time when some of Jesus' followers were developing a self-definition in distinction from their Jewish contemporaries, these texts preserve traditions about Jesus preaching in *synagogues, celebrating *Passover, interpreting Jewish writings, and debating halakhic issues with *Pharisees. Jesus is described as teaching by means of parables that recall, in form and content, the *meshalim* ("proverbs" or wise sayings) of Jewish *wisdom literature and rabbinic *midrash. Many of his parables concern the coming of the "kingdom of God." In this too, Jesus fits well with the Judaism of his time, an age of uncertainty and upheaval when many charismatic leaders warned of the impending "end of days." There are also some hints that Jesus understood his message as meant for Jews; according to the Gospel of Matthew, for instance, he initially instructed his followers to preach only to "the lost sheep of Israel" (10:6).

Jesus' Jewishness is also evident in the Sermon on the Mount (Matthew 5–7), a set of teachings that later Christians understood as exemplifying Jesus' break from Judaism. However, the statements attributed to Jesus include exhortations to observe the whole of the *Torah (5:17–20). Such statements shed an interesting perspective on his polemics against Pharisees (e.g., Matthew 23), raising the possibility that he and his followers were engaged in internal Jewish controversies akin to the debates among other sects in Second Temple times.

According to the Gospels and Book of Acts, the Jesus movement initially consisted of Jews who believed that Jesus was the messiah foretold in the Jewish Scriptures. It was centered in Jerusalem and led by Peter. Followers of Jesus frequented the Temple and preached their message in synagogues (e.g., Acts 3, 13; 17–18). Like members of other Jewish apocalyptic and messianic movements of the time, they supported their claims with biblical proof-texts, drawing on the writings of the prophets (see BIBLE: PROPHETS AND PROPHECY) in particular. Like other such groups, they met with resistance from other Jews who did not share their particular beliefs.

Those who believed in Jesus as messiah, however, faced an additional challenge in persuading other Jews since Jesus had been executed by the *Romans. Jesus' followers proclaimed that he had been resurrected (see RESURRECTION), and they developed an understanding of his death as inaugurating a series of end-time events that included his future return. Many of their fellow Jews seem to have met such claims with skepticism (cf. Matthew 28:15).

Some members of the Jesus movement understood the coming of the messiah as marking the inclusion of Gentiles in God's promises to Israel, consistent with biblical and Second Temple Jewish ideas about the ingathering of "the nations" at the end of time (e.g., Isa 2:2–4, 14:1–2, 19:18–25; Jer 3:17; Micah 4:1–5; 1 Enoch 90). The inclusion of Gentiles was promoted particularly by Saul/Paul, who was a Pharisee and possibly a student of R. Gamaliel the Elder (Acts 22:3). Although Paul was not a disciple of Jesus during his lifetime, he later came to believe that Jesus was the messiah. In his letters, he describes how a vision prompted him to change his name from Saul to Paul and to become the "messenger/envoy (Greek: *apostolos*) to the Gentiles" (Romans 11:13; Galatians 2:2). Paul argued that Gentiles could be saved through faith in Jesus, even apart from Torah observance (e.g., Romans 1–9; Galatians 1–3). He traveled throughout the Roman Empire spreading his message and founding communities.

However, others in the Jesus movement did not share Paul's approach to Gentile inclusion. Some appear to have believed that Gentiles could join the Jesus movement only if they first converted to Judaism. In the letters of Paul and Acts, we find references to those who required *circumcision of Gentile male converts (Galatians 2:12; Acts 15:1–5). Contestation surrounding the inclusion of Gentiles is also evinced by debates about observance of the *dietary laws. For instance, Jesus' brother James apparently believed that Jewish followers of Jesus had to maintain their ritual *purity through separation from Gentiles, particularly at meals (Galatians 2:11–14; cf. Acts 10:28; Colossians 2:21). Initially, Peter seems to have embraced a similar position – that Torah observance was incumbent on all members of the Jesus movement (Galatians 2:12; Acts 10–11) – and only later became convinced that circumcision was unnecessary for Gentile converts (Acts 15:6). According to the Book of Acts, Peter ruled that they need only avoid fornication, improperly slaughtered meat, and food offered to idols (15:20), thus voicing a view of Gentile salvation that resonates with later rabbinic traditions about the Noachide commandments (T. *Avodah Zarah* 8:4).

Scholars continue to debate whether Paul believed that the coming of the messiah had negated the need for ritual observances for Jews as well as Gentiles. Paul may have maintained the efficacy of Torah observance for Jews, even as he also believed that a separate path to salvation for Gentiles had been opened with the coming of Jesus. In any case, it may be significant that Paul continued to self-identify as a Jew and as a Pharisee (Galatians 2:15; Philippians 3:5; Acts 22:3, 26:4–5). Eventually, the Pauline Epistles would be interpreted in terms of Christian claims that Torah observance had been abrogated by the Gospels and that Israel had been superseded by the church. Paul's own position on such questions, however, is less clear.

After the deaths of James, Paul, and Peter, the Jesus movement became increasingly displaced from its original Galilean and Judean settings. In the wake of the *Bar Kokhba Revolt, the Jerusalem church waned in power. The communities founded by Paul and others elsewhere in the Roman Empire flourished, and the movement attracted more and more Gentile converts. In the New Testament literature, we can discern the first traces of a long process by which some believers in Jesus distinguished themselves first from other Jewish groups and then from "Judaism" more broadly.

Nevertheless, it is perhaps not coincidental that so many Second Temple Jewish writings were preserved and transmitted by late antique and medieval Christian scribes (e.g., *Apocrypha; *Pseudepigrapha; writings of *Philo and *Josephus). Nor should it be surprising that there are so many parallels to early Christian traditions in Second Temple Jewish literature. The Jesus movement's origins in Second Temple Judaism continued to resonate in Christian belief and practice, leaving open lines for contact, conflict, and competition between Christians and Jews for many centuries.

Recent research includes P. Fredriksen, *Jesus of Nazareth* (1999); J. G. Gager, *Reinventing Paul* (2002); A. J. Levine, *The Misunderstood Jew* (2004); and S. Westerholm, *Perspectives Old and New on Paul* (2004).   ANNETTE YOSHIKO REED

Christians, Christianity: See CHRISTIAN HEBRAISM; CHRISTIANITY AND SECOND TEMPLE JUDAISM; CHURCH FATHERS: ATTITUDES TOWARDS JEWS AND JUDAISM; INQUISITION, SPANISH; INTERFAITH DIALOGUE: UNITED STATES; NEW TESTAMENT; MIDDLE AGES: JEWISH - CHRISTIAN POLEMICS; REFORMATION

Chronicles is the final book in the *Writings section of the Hebrew *Bible. An account of history from creation to the downfall of *Babylon, it is also known by the titles "Events of the Days" (Hebrew, *Divrei Hayyamim*) or "Supplements" (Greek, *Paraleipomena*). Although it is now generally separated into two books (1 and 2 Chronicles), Chronicles was originally a single historical work composed in the post-exilic period, most likely in the fourth century BCE. It appears to have some relation to *Ezra-Nehemiah (which begins where Chronicles leaves off), but most likely was not written by the same author. The book opens with an extensive set of genealogies (1 Chron 1–9) starting with *Adam that focus on the descendants of *Judah, Benjamin, and Levi. Chronicles initiates the narrative proper with a brief condemnation of *Saul's reign (1 Chron 10) and continues with an account of *David's career (1 Chron 11–29) and *Solomon's reign and efforts to build the Jerusalem *Temple (2 Chron 1–9). The last major section is a history of the kingdom of *Judah, in which there are virtually no references to the northern kingdom of *Israel (2 Chron 10–36).

Chronicles makes extensive use of known written sources, including *Psalms and *Joshua. Most prominently, it contains lengthy near-verbatim passages from the books of *Samuel and *Kings or from precursors of those books. Notwithstanding its reliance on earlier texts, Chronicles tells a story all its own in which David, Israel's quintessential political and religious leader, becomes the central figure. In this version, which contains little of the intrigue and precariousness of the Samuel account, David ascends the throne to overwhelming popular acclaim, consciously designates his son Solomon as his heir, makes extensive preparations for the construction of the Temple, and presides over the establishment of the duties and rotations of priests, Levites, singers, and gatekeepers. Yet the David of Chronicles is not a flawless, one-dimensional character; he is also a leader capable of sin and *repentance. Among other notable divergences from Samuel and Kings are the recounting of *Hezekiah's extensive physical and spiritual preparations

for Sennacherib's siege, culminating in a celebration of the long-neglected *Passover festival, as well as the story of Manasseh's exile to *Assyria where he humbles himself for his transgressions (see also the *apocryphal Prayer of Manasseh).

The narrative related in Chronicles is not disconnected from the realia of the past, but it offers a vision of Israel's history that is deeply imaginative, perhaps utopian. In this account, the turbulent history of the northern kingdom is irrelevant, and Judah was always Israel's predominant tribe. Additionally, the central aspect of Israel's public life is and always has been centralized Temple *worship – not sacrifice alone, but also the liturgies of *prayer and *music. Although formally a history, Chronicles marks a break from its past and present contexts and deemphasizes corporate and generational responsibility for sin. Written in an era when *Persia and its Judean governors exercised control over Judah's political and religious institutions, Chronicles theologically liberates the cult, reclaiming it as Israel's own.   SEAN BURT

Church Fathers: Attitudes Toward Jews and Judaism. By the Middle Ages, mainstream churches throughout Europe and the Near East ("Catholic" and "Orthodox" Christians, respectively) understood their religion to be substantively different from *Judaism. When compiling the writings of authoritative early Church Fathers on whom they might rely for guidance, these medieval churches selected those authors who would bolster and reflect their sense of religious distinction.

Ineligible for this collection, therefore, were ancient Christian groups, now practically lost to history, who attempted to view Christianity and Judaism as continuous or even identical. These included the so-called Ebionites, who observed the *Torah and believed in Jesus as the *messiah; the readers of such texts as the *Clementine Homilies*, who rejected the anti-covenantal stance of the apostle Paul; or even urban Christians who found power and mystery in the rituals of the *High Holidays and *Passover well into the fourth century. It has even been argued that a great many so-called Christians and Jews throughout late antiquity viewed their practices and beliefs along a continuous spectrum, which was only broken apart by the polemical discourse of hardline Christian bishops and Jewish Rabbis.

For later Christians, however, the "fathers of the faith" who became authoritative were those who made suitable distinctions between Christianity and Judaism. Such voices, which appear early on, include Justin Martyr (d. ca. 165 CE). Writing in the Greek-speaking East, he laid down some of the fundamental patterns of "orthodox" Christian anti-Judaism that prevailed throughout the late ancient period. Justin was one of the earliest sources to look to a common Scripture (the Jewish *Tanakh*/Christian Old Testament) as a dividing line between Christian truth and Jewish falsity. Thus, Justin insisted that *Isaiah 7:14 speaks of a virgin birth; he and his younger contemporary Melito of Sardis (d. ca. 180 CE) also vigorously argued against Jewish literal observance of the "Law." Melito's Easter homily *On the Pascha* not only insisted that the Christian Easter had forever fulfilled and abnegated the Jewish Passover (an approach known as supersessionism) but also introduced the insidious accusation of Jewish deicide.

Stereotypes hardened. In the Christian imagination, Jews continually replayed their gospel roles: In treatises *adversus Iudaeos* (against the Jews) they were represented as deniers of the faith who must be refuted, like the *Pharisees, or as shadowy crowds calling for the death of Christian martyrs in chilling echoes of the Passion. At the same time, early Christian apologists appropriated Judaism's antiquity and authenticity in defending the new religion against accusations of novelty and illegitimacy by pagan detractors. Even though it was rejected, Judaism remained fundamental to Christianity because of what both religions shared: common Scriptures, common ritual patterns, and common beliefs in the singularity of divinity and the inexorable path of history.

The public promotion of Christianity throughout the Roman Empire after Constantine the Great (d. 337) added urgency to the desire among Christian leaders to distinguish the new faith from the old, but a deep ambivalence surrounding Judaism remained. By the fourth century, the otherness of Judaism had become so internalized that Christians who held insufficiently orthodox positions on Christological doctrine could be tarred as "Judaizers." Some Christians did indeed "judaize," deliberately introducing Jewish practices into Christian life and ritual. Well into the fifth century, some Christians still regularly consulted their Jewish neighbors to determine the date for Easter in relation to the date for Passover (they were frequently condemned as *quartodecimani* or *tessareskaidekatitai*, "fourteeners" who calculated Easter around the fourteenth day of the Jewish month of *Nissan). John Chrysostom's venomous sermons "Against the Judaizers" (delivered in 386–87) attacked Christians who frequented *synagogues at festival times; his condemnations speak both to the horror that "orthodox" leaders felt at the otherness of Judaism and the allure that Jewish customs retained for Christians.

Ambivalence persisted. The hymnist and preacher Ephrem (d. 373), who wrote in Syriac on the Roman/Persian border, regularly lambasted Jews in his public hymns as blind and reprobate and having committed deicide; however, he had close contact with Jewish informants when composing his prose commentaries. The ascetic scriptural scholar Jerome (d. 420), who migrated from *Rome to Bethlehem in the 380s, consulted with Jews in producing his biblical commentaries and his new translation of the Jewish Scriptures from Hebrew to Latin, even as he castigated them and preached their eternal exile from Jerusalem. Perhaps no one encapsulated more acutely the ambivalent attitude of the Church Fathers toward Jews as reviled yet desired than Jerome when he wrote, "If it is expedient to hate any people and to detest any nation, I have a notable hatred for the circumcised [Jews]. . . . Yet, can anyone object to me for having had a Jew as a teacher?" (Jerome, *Letter* 84.3)

There seem to have been few incidents of outright conflict between Jews and Christians, although fantasies of persecuting Jews lasted throughout antiquity. Only one account from the early fifth century, left by Bishop Severus of Minorca, describes what may have been the forced conversion of a Jewish community. Nonetheless, as the world became more Christianized, the place of Jews and Judaism (desired yet feared, necessary yet abominated) grew increasingly incongruous. If Christianity had "triumphed," some asked, why were there still Jews in the Christian world?

The brilliant Christian thinker Augustine (d. 430), notable for his innovative theologies, attempted to address this incongruity. Augustine maintained that Jews must exist in a Christian world as witnesses to the truth of the Scriptures and the God of creation; in their subordinated state, increasingly marginalized by Christian governing powers, they also testified to the fate of a people once divinely chosen who had rejected God's final *redemption. Although this position may have been mainly theoretical in Augustine's own days, his "witness theology" later became standardized doctrine toward the Jews in the Catholic West. It led eventually to a dual policy, combining limitations and marginalization with preservation of Jewish life and property; this compromise position lasted well beyond the medieval period. In the Orthodox East, the militant Christian authority of the *Byzantine Empire seemed poised to move in less tolerant directions, as when Emperor Heraclius (d. 641) attempted a forced conversion of Jews. The rise of a new monotheistic power, however, altered interreligious relations in the East, and the views of the Church Fathers on Jews and Judaism were ultimately appropriated to shape Christian responses to Muslims and *Islam.

For further reading, see A. H. Becker and A. Y. Reed, eds., *The Ways That Never Parted: Jews and Christians in Late Antiquity and the Early Middle Ages* (2007); D. Boyarin, *Border Lines: The Partition of Judaeo-Christianity* (2004); P. Fredriksen, *Augustine and the Jews: The Story of Christianity's Great Theologian and His Defense of Judaism* (2008); and A. L. Williams, *Adversus Judaeos: A Bird's-Eye View of Christian "Apologiae" until the Renaissance* (1935).   ANDREW S. JACOBS

Circumcision. Male circumcision is the first *commandment specific to Jews mentioned in the *Torah. In Genesis 17 *Abraham is commanded to circumcise himself and his older son *Ishmael and to circumcise *Isaac on the eighth day after birth. *Berit milah* (literally "*covenant of circumcision") may be the most universally observed commandment. Although mandated to occur on the eighth day, circumcision can be postponed for health reasons. The biblical text sees it as a physical sign of the covenant between God and the Jewish people rather than as a hygienic measure. Circumcision is traditionally performed as a home ceremony, by a *mohel*, a pious, observant Jew educated in the relevant Jewish law and in surgical techniques. *Blessings are recited, including one over wine, and a drop of wine is placed in the infant's mouth. The child is then given a formal Hebrew name. A festive meal follows, with special prayers incorporated into the blessings after the meal. Male *converts to Judaism undergo circumcision as part of the conversion rite. If they have already been circumcised, a symbolic drop of blood is drawn by a mohel. Although women are permitted to perform circumcisions, only the Reform and Conservative movements in North America have sponsored training programs that prepare both *mohalim* and *mohalot* (see JUDAISM entries).

Despite the antiquity and centrality of *berit milah* in Jewish tradition, twenty-first-century Judaism is facing increasing challenges to this practice. These challenges include Jewish feminist demands to eliminate male circumcision on the grounds of gender equity, growing attacks from the larger culture that routine male circumcision is a form of mutilation, and ongoing debates over whether circumcision offers sufficient hygienic and health advantages to justify the practice.

Recent research includes S. J. D. Cohen, *Why Aren't Jewish Women Circumcised?* (2005); L. Glick, *Marked in Your Flesh* (2005); I. G. Marcus, *The Jewish Life Cycle* (2004); and E. Wyner Mark, ed., *The Covenant of Circumcision* (2003).

RELA MINTZ GEFFEN

Cities of Refuge. Biblical law clearly distinguished between murder, which involves premeditation and predisposition, and other instances of the taking of human life, which would include manslaughter. However, as a practical matter, residents of ancient *Near Eastern societies, including biblical *Israel, were likely to take direct, immediate action to avenge the loss of kinfolk. Biblical law thus established six cities of refuge (from among the forty-eight assigned to the Levites), to which individuals could flee and find protection until it was determined whether theirs was a capital offense. If it was, they were handed over to the deceased's avenger. If not, they were to stay in the city of refuge until the death of the high *priest, whose blood, as it were, atoned for the admittedly accidental shedding of blood by the one who committed involuntary homicide.

The relevant legislation is found in *Numbers 35, *Deuteronomy 19, and *Joshua 20 (see also 1 Chron 6). Only the Joshua section lists the cities by name: Three are west of the Jordan River (in the "Promised Land"), and three are east of the Jordan (where two and a half of the tribes had settled). There are points of disagreement, as well as broad agreement, among these biblical passages. Modern scholars dispute the origins and precise means of implementing the laws.

LEONARD GREENSPOON

Civil Rights Movement: See UNITED STATES: CIVIL RIGHTS MOVEMENT

Cochin Jews. This community from Kerala, in southern *India, one of the smallest Jewish ethnic groups in the world, is divided into two caste-like subgroups. The "White" (Paradesi) Jews are the descendants of European and other Jews, who arrived on the Malabar coast from the sixteenth century on. The "Black" (Malabar) Jews may have arrived with King *Solomon's merchants. Local southern Indian Christian legends mention Jews in the first century CE. Documentary evidence of Jewish settlement on the southern Indian coast can be found in copperplates in ancient Tamil script, in which seventy-two privileges were bestowed on the Cochin Jewish leader Joseph Rabban and his descendants. Ezekiel Rahabi (1694–1771), a Paradesi, acted as the principal merchant for the Dutch East India Company.

The Jews lived in several congregations, including Ernakulam, Mala, Parur, Chennemangalam, and Cochin. There was no intermarriage between Paradesi and Malabari Jews. The community never experienced any *antisemitism from their Indian neighbors. The religious observances of the Cochin Jews conform in every way to other Jewish communities, although they incorporated some unique "Indian-style" customs. From the eighteenth century on, emissaries from the Holy Land began to visit Cochin. Urged on by *Zionist fervor, 2,400 Cochin Jews immigrated to *Israel in 1954, where they settled in *moshavim* (agricultural settlements). Today, 8,000 Cochin Jews live in Israel; less than 50 remain in Kerala.

Important studies of this community include N. Katz and E. S. Goldberg, *The Last Jews of Cochin: Jewish Identity in Hindu India* (1993); S. H. Hallegua, "The Marriage Customs of the Jewish Community of Cochin," and G. Hacco, "The Ritual Cycle of Cochin Jewish Holidays: A Malabari Perspective," both in *India's Jewish Heritage: Ritual, Art and Life-Cycle*, 2nd edition, ed. S. Weil (2004), 60–67, 68–77. SHALVA WEIL

Codes: See HALAKHAH; JACOB BEN ASHER; KARO, JOSEPH; MAIMONIDES

Cohen, Hermann (1842–1918), a Jewish thinker, was born in Coswig in the German principality of Anhalt. Cohen, who remains among the most creative and influential modern Jewish philosophers of religion, was educated by some of the greatest philological, historical, and philosophical scholars of mid-nineteenth-century *Germany. He attended the newly founded Jewish Theological Seminary in Breslau and later studied in *Berlin. Among his teachers were Heinrich *Graetz, Jacob Bernays, Zacharias *Frankel, August Boeckh, and Adolf Trendelenburg. His Berlin mentor H. Steinthal (1823–1899) combined a commitment to the philological ideal of the "recognition of what had once been known" with dedication to a linguistic and psychological penetration of Jewish textual and liturgical traditions. Steinthal and Cohen also shared intimate memories of the devotional practices of the small but sophisticated Jewish community of Anhalt, where Cohen's father was a *cantor and *melamed* (teacher).

After a number of studies in which he applied the innovative psycho-linguistic method of Steinthal and Moritz Lazarus to the origins of Greek philosophical and mythological ideas, Cohen turned his attention to Kant. In 1871, he published the first of three studies on the interpretation of Kant's philosophy (*Kants Theorie der Erfahrung* [2nd ed., 1885], *Kant's Begründung der Ethik* [1877], and *Kants Begründung der Ästhetik* [1889]). These works brought him to the attention of the Marburg philosopher and socialist pedagogue Friedrich Albert Lange, who brought him to teach in Marburg. Cohen succeeded to the chair in philosophy after Lange's death in 1876. Although Cohen established an international reputation as a founder of the distinctive Marburg school of neo-Kantianism, he never received a call to another university and was subjected to other indignities that increased as *antisemitism among academics increased. In 1903, Cohen became curator of the Berlin *Lehranstalt für die Wissenschaft des Judentums* and taught there intermittently on Bible and the philosophy of religion. In 1912, after his retirement from Marburg, Cohen moved to Berlin, continuing to teach at the *Lehranstalt* on a regular basis. As a public speaker Cohen represented the anti-*Zionist agenda of the major German Jewish cultural and political associations such as the *Central-Verein* and *Bnai Briss*.

Among Cohen's most significant philosophical publications are *Logik der reinen Erkenntnis* (1902), *Ethik des reinen Willens* (1904), and *Ästhetik des reinen Gefühls* (1912). Notable works on philosophy of religion include *Der Begriff der Religion im System der Philosophie* (1915) and *Die Religion der Vernunft aus den Quellen des Judentums* (1919). Only the latter has been translated into English: *Religion of Reason out of the Sources of Judaism*, transl. by S. Kaplan, with an introduction by Leo *Strauss, (1972). For Cohen's complete works, see *Werke*, published by the Hermann-Cohen-Archiv am Philosophischen Seminar der Universität Zürich, ed. H. Holzhey (1977ff).

A full appreciation of Hermann Cohen as a Jewish thinker has been hampered by the fact that posthumous publications of many of his writings, including the three volumes of Jewish writings (*Jüdische Schriften*, 1924), two volumes of essays on philosophical and political topics (*Schriften zur Philosophie und Zeitgeschichte*, 1928), and a 1935 edition of letters, appeared in a climate of extreme hostility toward the Jews. At that time, it seemed advisable to emphasize Cohen's German patriotism; this one-sided image led many students of Jewish thought to dismiss Cohen as naïvely assimilationist and needlessly anti-Zionist.

Until recently, scholars have asked if Cohen's philosophy of religion constituted a departure from his systematic philosophy or whether he continued to be committed to the method of critical idealism. Franz *Rosenzweig stated that, although Cohen believed he had maintained his system, he objectively broke through the "veil of idealism," driven by his living connection with the Jewish faith. Alexander Altmann countered that the concept of correlation prominent in *Religion of Reason* tied the doctrine of *God, as developed in the course of the history of Jewish religious *thought, to the doctrine of humankind and that Cohen succeeded in maintaining the Kantian connection between ethics and religion. Steven Schwarzschild went further, stating that Cohen's entire philosophy of religion was already contained in his systematic ethics. However, Cohen himself expressly conceded that not all problems of ethics can be worked out within the parameters of the law and that religion was necessary to accomplish the transformation of the self that is postulated, but not delivered, in the context of ethics. More recently, scholars such as Robert Gibbs (*Correlations in Rosenzweig and Levinas* [1992]) and Reinier Munk ("Alterity in Hermann Cohen's Critical Idealism," *Journal of Jewish Thought and Philosophy* 9 [1999]: 251–65) have drawn attention to the fact that Cohen was the first modern Jewish thinker to shift from a Cartesian type of self-constitution to an ethics of alterity when he grounded ethical self-consciousness in the principles of contractual law. Another recent debate concerns Cohen's aesthetic theory of liturgical performance. As Steven Kepnes points out, "Cohen places liturgy at the crucial bridge points between the self and the community, the self and God, and the self and its growth to moral autonomy" and thus generates what Kepnes calls a "liturgical self" (*Jewish Liturgical Reasoning* [2007], 45).

Recent comprehensive studies on Cohen in English are A. Poma, *The Critical Philosophy of Hermann Cohen*, trans. J. Denton (1997); and M. Zank, *The Idea of Atonement in the Philosophy of Hermann Cohen* (2000).　　MICHAEL ZANK

Columbus, Christopher (d. May 20, 1506) was an explorer who was thought by some to be of Jewish origin. Columbus began his 1492 voyage three days after the final expulsion of Jews from *Spain. On board his ship was a Jewish-born interpreter, Luis de Torres, who underwent baptism just before sailing. Columbus's writings mention Jews, and several sixteenth-century Jewish sources refer to his discoveries. Columbus's reputation grew in the nineteenth century, particularly in America, where he came to be seen as a symbol of national ideals. On the occasion of the 400th anniversary of his landing in the Americas (October 12, 1892), Jews highlighted their ties to the event. Two years later, the Hungarian scholar Meyer (Moritz) Kayserling published a book detailing Jewish participation in the voyages of Columbus and other New World explorers, hoping that this would counter *antisemitism. Subsequent research led some twentieth-century scholars to claim that Columbus himself was a secret Jew. The evidence, however, was weak, and current biographers scoff at such claims. Recent research includes F. Fernández-Armesto, *Columbus* (1991) and J. D. Sarna, "The Mythical Jewish Columbus and the History of America's Jews," *Studies in Jewish Civilization* 5 (1996): 81–95.　　JONATHAN D. SARNA

Comedy and Comedians. In the contemporary era comedy and Jews have become inextricably intertwined, and some have suggested that "even the word Jewish has become laden with humorous overtones" (Altman). Although the term "comedy" is derived from the Greek word *komedia* and referred in antiquity to a specific theatrical form, and humor and comedy are universal to humanity, in the modern world and particularly in the United States, Jewish writers, performers, and artists have played a preeminent role in shaping the comedy of the majority culture, far out of proportion to their small number in the population.

Jewish comedy emerges from a series of tensions: the dichotomy between self-deprecation and social criticism, distinctions between Jews and Gentiles, and conflict between the sacred and profane. Most observers of Jewish comedy agree that Jewish comedy is grounded in anxiety, but grasping the essence of Jewish comedy is more difficult. There is a long history of discussion about whether Jewish comedy is simply comedy written and performed by those who happen to be Jewish or if the Jewishness of Jewish comedy is determined by particularly "Jewish" content. Similarly, analysts debate whether the Jewishness of Jewish comedy stems from the methodology behind the humor and the manner of delivery of a joke or if the unique elements of Jewish comedy are a combination of all of the elements already mentioned.

In general, Jewish comedy may be defined as comedy that is generated and performed by Jews on Jewish subject matter and is strained through a bifurcated worldview; whereas Jewish comedy usually revolves around self-parody, it often involves a critique of the host or majority culture as well. In this regard, Jewish comedy can appeal to a culturally broad audience and is not directed solely toward a Jewish audience. Beyond these generalities, arguments persist over the definition of Jewish comedy. Among the most basic questions are who and what to include under the rubric of Jewish comedy.

Over the past century, Jewish comedy has been extremely diverse, located both in "high" and "low" cultural forms and encompassing both physical comedy and more cerebral forms of humor. Expressed through *literature and *graphic novels, Jewish comedy has also been featured in every modern *entertainment medium, including vaudeville, *theater, Broadway musicals, comic books, cartooning, animated film, *radio, *television, *film, the *internet, and even *museum exhibitions.

In the realm of performance alone, Jewish comedians and Jewish comedy can be further divided among several subcategories, including "sketch" comedy, the culturally Jewish-specific "Borscht Belt" mode of comedy, as well as the culturally neutral forms of "stand-up" comedy and "roasting." A short listing of the luminaries of American Jewish comics and comedians includes performers who began their careers on the stage and vaudeville and later crossed over to film and television, such as George Burns (1896–1996), Jack Benny (1894–1974), the Marx Brothers, and the Three Stooges, as well as mid-twentieth-century television comedy pioneers such as Milton Berle (1908–2002), Sid Caesar (b. 1922), and Carl Reiner (b. 1922). From vaudeville to the small screen, all of these comedians embedded particularly Jewish material in their work while also setting the standards for American comedy as a whole. Stand-up comedians such as Henny Youngman (1906–1998) and Shelley Berman (b. 1925), Borscht belters such as Buddy Hackett (1924–2003) and Jackie Mason (b. 1936), and insult comics like Don Rickles (b. 1926) have also performed explicitly Jewish comedy while becoming part and parcel of the broader American culture. Finally, writer/performers such as Mel Brooks (b. 1926) and Woody Allen (b. 1935) through late-twentieth/early-twenty-first-century writer/performers such as Garry Shandling (b. 1949), Jon Stewart (b. 1962), and Larry David (b. 1947) continue exploring and relating Jewish themes while also playing a decisive role in shaping American comedy in its totality. Modern Jewish comedy has also been an equal opportunity employer, with Jewish women – from Fanny Brice (1891–1951), Totie Fields (1930–1978), Belle Barth (1911–1971), and Sophie Tucker (1884–1966) to Joan Rivers (b. 1933), Gilda Radner (1946–1989), and Madeline Kahn (1942–1999) in the late twentieth century to Sarah Silverman (b. 1970) and Susie Essman (b. 1955) in the new millennium – playing a coequal role in the world of Jewish comedy in quality if not always in quantity.

In the literary world, Philip Roth (b. 1933) is widely regarded as among the greatest of American writers, but his writing maintains an identifiably Jewish sense of humor; other American literary figures whose writing transcends ethnic boundaries but still maintains a specifically Jewish comedic outlook include Bernard Malamud (1914–1986), Joseph Heller (1923–1999), Bruce Jay Friedman (b. 1930), Cynthia Ozick (b. 1928), and most recently Michael Chabon (b. 1963) (see LITERATURE: UNITED STATES). American Jewish comedy in written form has also been expressed via more popular vehicles such as *Mad* magazine, most especially in the work of Harvey Kurtzman, Will Elder, and Albert Feldstein, among many other contributors. Although *Mad* is most certainly not a Jewish journal, its influence on postwar American humor and popular culture cannot be denied. Even so debate continues over the sources and history of Jewish comedy.

A standard perspective has been that Jewish comedy is a modern phenomenon largely traceable to *Eastern European Jewry of the nineteenth century in particular and to modernizing Jewish communities in general. Eastern European Jewish humor was preserved and transmitted orally in *Yiddish through Jewish folk traditions, including the insult form. Writer Sholem Aleichem captured some of this sensibility in his short stories and novels (see LITERATURE,

YIDDISH: 1800 to TWENTY-FIRST CENTURY). Still others argue that Jewish humor can be traced back to biblical and rabbinic literatures; many scholars believe that the incident of *Balaam and his talking ass (Num 22) and parts of the book of *Jonah, among other biblical passages, were intended to be humorous. There is, however, wide agreement that modern Jewish forms of comedy such as the "sketch" format stem from the traditional Jewish ritual of the *purimshpiln* or *Purim show that played a role in the development of Yiddish theater (see THEATER, YIDDISH). The *shpil*, like its modern descendants, is an exercise in bifurcation, often satirizing the Jewish community while at the same time functioning as a nonviolent assault against antisemites as embodied through the biblical figure of Haman. Indeed, the *shpil* often targeted traditional sources of Jewish authority such as rabbis, venerated institutions such as the Jewish family, and Judaism in and of itself, just as targets of modern Jewish comedy include contemporary sources of authority, both individual and institutional, as well as general notions of civility. Likewise, stand-up comedy has often been linked to the *badkhan* and other such performers associated with Jewish weddings (see ENTERTAINMENT; MARRIAGE).

Most would agree that modern Jewish comedy generally expresses Jewish "otherness"; it reflects the marginality of Jews who are neither grounded in traditional Jewish society nor fully integrated into the majority culture. Taken a step further, Jewish comedy serves as a means for satirizing and critiquing the majority culture's relationship to the Jewish minority. In this sense, Jewish comedy is analogous to the comic forms of other minority cultures, most especially *African American comedy, which often melds "uplifting race pride" with "self-mockery" (Watkins). In fact, an additional topic of debate has been whether Jewish comedy is simply a manifestation of self-hatred. Because comedy in general and Jewish comedy in particular are about "making a scene," at times comedians cause embarrassment by exposing the "dirty laundry" of Jews. Such comedy is necessarily discomfiting, and the lines separating self-hatred and self-criticism can blur. Nevertheless, self-deprecation is at its heart self-criticism, which itself is a Jewish tradition preached explicitly by the Hebrew *prophets and other sages throughout Jewish history. Woody Allen, Mel Brooks, and Philip Roth are among the most notable Jewish comedians accused of self-hatred. Yet Jewish comedic expressions of self-criticism are generally interlaced with a critique of the majority culture and general standards of civility. Typically divorced from the traditional Jewish community and not fully part of the majority culture, purveyors of modern Jewish comedy offer a unique perspective on Jews and Gentiles alike and often act as social critics. This satiric role of the Jewish comedian stretches from the Marx Brothers to Lenny Bruce (1925–1966) and continues through the work of comics such as Sacha Baron Cohen (b. 1971). Thus, even while Jewish comedy skewers Jewish tradition, it is still part of Jewish tradition. And although Jewish comedy assaults the majority culture from the periphery of mainstream society, Jewish comedy has also become an essential piece and widely recognized slice of popular, North American culture.

For further reading, see S. Altman, *The Comic Image of the Jew* (1971); L. J. Epstein *The Haunted Smile* (2001); N. L. Kneeblatt, ed., *Too Jewish: Challenging Traditional*

Identities (1996); W. Novak and M. Waldoks, *The Big Book of Jewish Humor* (1985); H. D. Spalding, *Encyclopedia of Jewish Humor* (1969; rep. 2001); J. Telushkin, *Jewish Humor* (1992); and M. Watkins, *African American Humor* (2002); and **see** CELEBRITIES; ENTERTAINMENT.   DANIEL M. BRONSTEIN

Commandment, Commandments: See *MITZVAH, MITZVOT;* TEN COMMANDMENTS

Commerce: Medieval and Early Modern Europe. Commerce, the buying and selling of goods for profit, is usually seen with *money lending as the central occupation of Jews in medieval and early modern Europe. Although there is much truth in this view, there is also a good measure of exaggeration; moreover, the connection of Jews and Judaism with commercial activities in both learned opinion and the popular imagination has had a troubling history. In fact, it is impossible to quantify the Jewish share in the commerce or economy of the pre-modern era. In all periods and regions, sizable parts of the Jewish population made their living as craftsmen and craftswomen and as providers of menial and skilled services to the well-to-do and to community institutions These individuals were in the lower classes of Jewish society, estimated in some places to have made up as much as one third of the total population. Many people practiced several occupations side by side; most conspicuous, however, are commerce and credit.

Jews were involved in commerce throughout the medieval era. However, the significance of commercial activities as the most important form of livelihood was especially pronounced during the early Middle Ages and again in the Early Modern period. Between the twelfth and sixteenth centuries, money lending eclipsed commerce. Like money lending, commerce was not necessarily practiced by the greatest number of Jews, but its profits, as those of money lending, placed Jewish communities as a whole in the higher income brackets. This facilitated the comfortable standard of living characteristic of medieval European Jewry and enabled Jews to purchase from rulers the wide-ranging judicial and legal independence characteristic of Jewish status. However, because their livelihoods were so dependent on exchanges with the majority society, Jews were especially vulnerable to economic, political, and religious crises.

Until recently, Jews have been portrayed as long-distance traders who connected Christian Europe with the Middle East and Muslim *Spain. In late antiquity they did so alongside other Middle Eastern merchants, but from the eighth to the eleventh century, they were believed to have been on their own. According to this picture of early medieval trade, Jews were uniquely equipped to engage in long-distance trade by talmudic law, *communal organization, and family ties, as well as by the Diaspora experience and their special relationships with rulers. Many scholars have suggested that Jews possessed a veritable monopoly over commerce, particularly in the slave trade, because they were seen as the only ones capable, by virtue of their religious neutrality, to travel between the two monolithic blocs of Christianity and Islam. Such views, which reflected nineteenth- and twentieth-century polemics and apologetics, are now discarded. They assumed a system and purpose where none existed and disregarded the rich sources on non-Jewish merchants, conferring on the very few documented Jewish merchants a weight and influence incommensurate with their slight population numbers and very limited spatial distribution across Europe. Wide-ranging conclusions had been drawn from an exceedingly thin documentary basis in Latin. Taking Hebrew documents into account has resulted in a more convincing, if less glamorous, interpretation.

In the Hebrew record from *Ashkenaz, from the second half of the tenth century onward, commerce is the evident mainstay of Jewish livelihood in central and northern *France, as well as in western *Germany. This was succinctly stated by *Gershom ben Judah, "Light of the Exile" of Mainz, the foremost religious authority of his time (ca. 960–1028), who wrote, "Because their (the Jews') livelihood depends on their commerce/merchandise." Merchants moved often, but mostly along local circuits and well-known itineraries between inland markets. At times Jews traveled abroad, to and from *Hungary, *Poland, and possibly also *Russia. Even without intercontinental ventures, these merchants were hardy travelers; to be on the move was their normal condition, as one of them explained in a legal argument, "I wished to take to the road, like all other men." In their inventories, one finds very little of the glittering treasures of intercontinental commerce and nothing at all of the slave trade. A blend of staple goods and more costly merchandise – salt, wine, dyes, medicine, salted fish, cattle, hides and pelts, ready-made garments and textiles, including silk, gilded and copper vessels, and some precious metals – was bought, transported, and sold. The customers were bishops and priests, and in one case the treasurer of a bishop; affluent ladies, including a queen of Hungary (the only royalty mentioned in the sources); and magnates and counts: in short, the upper classes. In *Italy, the few Jewish merchants on the record definitely did not participate in the thriving overseas trade of their cities of domicile; they seem to have been engaged mostly in local ventures. The most important mercantile centers, such as *Venice and Genoa, did not allow Jewish residence at all, whereas the handful of Jews admitted to the bustling port of Amalfi were all textile artisans. In southern Europe, as in the north, Jewish trade appears more as an ordinary local and regional matter than as an intricate and far-flung system linking continents.

In this period, the rich sources of the Cairo *Genizah do reveal that a small but lively set of Jewish merchants from Muslim *Spain were actively involved in Middle Eastern trade. These Arabic-speaking traders were part of a network that was centered in Tunisia and *Egypt and also took in Muslim Spain and *Sicily. However, it did not connect and work in tandem with Jewish merchants from Christian lands in northern Europe or in Italy.

By the twelfth and thirteenth centuries, trade by Jews appears to have declined in northern Europe in favor of an ever increasing engagement in credit operations. In these regions, there is no evidence that Jews were barred from trade by the rising power of Christian merchant guilds, as has been assumed for a long time. Rather, they were pushed out of trade by a set of new circumstances that combined strong demographic growth, rapid urbanization, and the broad expansion of market ties. Under these booming economic conditions, the task of entrepreneur and merchant underwent a marked change, shifting from provisioning the aristocracy with exotic merchandise to organizing the production and handling of mass consumer goods. The servicing of such huge and growing systems – in size, complexity, and capital outlays far in excess of the earlier model – was beyond the resources of a numerically still tiny Ashkenazic Jewry.

The rising tide of religious enmity also played a role in making the traveling Jewish merchant into an endangered species. Conversely, the same set of circumstances made the sedentary handling and lending of money increasingly attractive and inevitable. In the south of Europe, Jewish trade activities, including maritime ventures, appear to have continued in some parts, at least initially. By the thirteenth century, however, Jews in eastern Spain were clearly blocked from participating in the expansion of Catalan overseas trade. In some islands of the Mediterranean, the Italian masters allowed an exception to their policy of exclusion back at home and employed native Jews as local agents.

By the later Middle Ages, the clientele of Jewish merchants and money lenders was no longer confined to the well-to-do and powerful. As Jews increasingly became professional pawnbrokers, a petty trade in forfeited pawned goods, mostly household objects and used garments, developed all over Europe. In the regions where Jews lived in the sixteenth century, mainly Italy, Germany, and increasingly *Eastern Europe, the medieval pattern of urban settlement changed into a much more dispersed pattern of habitation. In addition to Jewish communities in some large towns, such as Rome, Venice, or *Frankfurt, they were also found in a host of small towns and villages. As has been shown for Frankfurt and its surroundings, the Jews of the city supplied rural Jews carrying out petty itinerant trade with an increasing range of cheap goods of daily consumption – garments, metal vessels, and other household goods. In return, the rural Jews would supply their co-religionists of the urban center with foodstuffs, both for home consumption and for the market.

One outgrowth of these new demographic and economic structures were the Jewish cattle and horse dealers characteristic of the Early Modern period and, in some areas of Germany, even of the nineteenth century. Such regional networks formed the organizational basis for the commercial ventures of a new upper class of merchant Jews, some of whom also served as *Court Jews at the numerous capitals of early modern German principalities and Polish noble estates. They supplied rulers and courts with luxury goods and jewelry. During the frequent wars of the sixteenth and seventeenth centuries, they also provisioned armies with the essentials of grains, wine, horses, and horse fodder. After the expulsion from the Iberian Peninsula (1492–97), one larger part of the *Sephardic Diaspora found refuge in the *Ottoman Empire; some of these exiles worked in crafts, whereas others became an important part of the local merchant classes. Sephardic Jews who settled in the Netherlands, and later in *Britain and northern parts of Germany were wholly engaged in international commercial and financial ventures. Some went on to found small but important merchant settlements in the overseas colonies of European powers in the Americas. In stages, the commerce of Jews grew to be part of a modern world economy. On the way, it became even less of a "Jewish commerce" than it had ever been.

For further reading, see J. I. Israel, *Diasporas within a Diaspora: Jews, Crypto-Jews and the World Maritime Empires,* *1540–1740* (2002); M. Toch, "The Jews in Europe, 500–1050," in *The New Cambridge Medieval History of Europe*, ed. P. Fouracre (2005) 1: 547–570; idem, *The Economic History of Medieval European Jews*. Vol. I: *The Early Middle Ages* (forthcoming).

MICHAEL TOCH

Commerce: Modern Europe (1700–1900). The expulsions of Jews from *Spain and *Portugal in the 1490s established *Sephardi and *converso communities throughout the Mediterranean and Atlantic worlds. At a time of growing competition among northern Italian city-states for access to Levantine and Asian goods, these new Jewish communities were able to barter their services both as overland and seaborne traders.

In *Ashkenaz, however, the preceding century and a half of local *expulsions had effectively depleted the financial resources of *Central European Jews. The core of Jewish *money lending was now limited to pawn brokerage and related petty credit services, increasingly conducted in the countryside and as a sideline to the peddling, old clothes business, and livestock trading that would be characteristic of the so-called *Landjuden* well into the nineteenth century. This development helped create the conditions for the rise of Central European *Court Jews in the aftermath of the Thirty Years War. Court Jews combined financial services to the crown with the cheap provisioning of military supplies, including clothing and victuals, endeavors that drew directly on their links to rural Jewish traders. The interlocking relationship of court and country helped revitalize the German Jewish economy and expand Jewish settlement rights.

A quite different situation prevailed further east. In late-seventeenth-century *Poland, after the devastation caused by the *Chmelnitzki uprising and foreign invasions, Jewish economic ties with the nobility actually strengthened. Throughout the Early Modern era, Jews served as lessees of noble monopolies, particularly of grain and alcohol. This was "commerce" of a peculiar sort, far more rigorously managed and monopolistic than most of the activities of Jews in the Mediterranean and Central Europe. However, more conventional Polish Jewish merchants did play an important role in the river trade, shipping grains, timber, furs, and other raw materials to *Baltic ports such as Danzig throughout the eighteenth century. Although these Jews did not comprise the most powerful merchant stratum in the Baltic trade, they were significant at the secondary levels. Jews were also amply represented in the overland trade between Eastern and Central Europe, especially through fairs such as Leipzig and Breslau.

Although Jews in all of these areas did not constitute a single, integrated commercial network, the parallel activities of Jewish merchants in the *Balkans, Mediterranean, Atlantic-colonial, Baltic river, and east–west overland trade contributed to the growing impression in early modern Europe that Jews represented a commercial people par excellence. Jews themselves helped promote this image, since their reputation as economic assets helped them secure and expand settlement rights. In spite of these efforts, however, developments in the second half of the eighteenth and early nineteenth centuries contributed to a counter-image of the Jew as economically extraneous and in need of occupational reform.

This negative image not only drew on traditional *antisemitism but also reflected a downturn in Jews' economic fortunes for a variety of reasons. First, the fortunes of Court Jews declined in the face of an increasing rationalization of state finances and bureaucracy. Second, by the middle of the eighteenth century, centers of Atlantic trade, such as *Amsterdam and Hamburg, both with significant Jewish merchant populations, were eclipsed by London, which contained only a small Jewish commercial elite, thus limiting opportunities for expanded colonial trade. Third, late mercantilist policies favoring home production over imports hit Jews hard. Lastly, Jewish population expansion in *Eastern Europe, which peaked in the late nineteenth century, was already in evidence by the late eighteenth; at the same time, economic opportunities in these lands were extremely limited. Throughout Europe, Jewish communities could not cope with the increased obligations of poor relief. The phenomenon of itinerancy, evident for centuries, became more visible and urgent.

With the onset of modernity, poverty became a core feature of the so-called Jewish Problem, as well as an object of state policy and a matter of serious concern for Jewish reformers. Jews' overrepresentation in petty commerce and the perceived deficit among Jews of so-called productive laborers were frequently identified as sources of these social ills. At the same time, cultural and ideological changes during the eighteenth century reinforced hostility to Jewish commerce. The Enlightenment favored meritocratic over corporate values; insofar as Jews resembled a commercial estate they became associated with the backwardness of the *ancien régime*. Similarly, *emancipation along the *French Revolutionary model established a tacit (and sometimes overt) expectation that Jewish incorporation into the body politic would be met with Jews' proportionate integration into the general occupational structure. Their evident failure to shift out of commerce in large numbers thus became a rationale for many of the economic tensions that intermittently erupted throughout the nineteenth century.

Nineteenth-century industrialization accelerated the breakdown of a Jewish economy that for centuries had been weighted toward rural commerce. This was a far more gradual process than has often been assumed and one that was partly offset by Central European Jewish immigration to the Americas during the first half of the nineteenth century. Yet the overall effect was to exacerbate the economic dislocation already apparent, especially in Eastern Europe. Industrialization eroded long-standing Jewish niches in transport, tavern keeping, artisan crafts, and estate management, although some new fields did open up for Jews in the upper echelons of manufacturing and in some crafts.

Yet, even when industrialization was well under way by the end of the nineteenth century, and despite the profound transformation it brought to European economies, Jews still remained heavily overrepresented in commerce. This was a cause of initial hardship but ultimately proved to be an advantage. Although Jews were impoverished and temporarily enmeshed in working-class environments, their long commercial apprenticeship fueled the upward mobility they eventually achieved in many locales during the twentieth century.

For further reading, see J. Israel, *European Jewry in the Age of Mercantilism, 1550–1750* (1991); A. Kahan, *Essays in Jewish Social and Economic History* (1986); J. Karp, *The Politics of Jewish Commerce: Economic Thought and Emancipation in Europe, 1638–1848* (2008); and idem, "Economic History and Jewish Modernity – Ideological versus Structural Change," *Simon Dubnow Yearbook* 6 (2007), 249–68; **see also UNITED STATES: ECONOMIC LIFE.**   JONATHAN KARP

Communal Organization: Medieval and Early Modern Eras. Medieval and early modern Jews lived in various locations, but the structures of their community organizations were strikingly similar. As a minority group dominated by other religions, mainly Christianity and Islam, Jews retained cultural autonomy through an effective community organization (*kehillah*, pl. *kehillot*). The major *kehillot* throughout the Jewish *Diaspora were organized as autonomous units with extensive discretionary powers. The *kehillah* dictated many aspects of Jewish communal life by establishing religious institutions and by facilitating communication with the surrounding non-Jewish world. It solidified social relations and was instrumental in confronting the constant threat of *conversion.

Members of the *kehillah* established and maintained different religious institutions such as a *synagogue, a school, a ritual bath (*mikveh), a slaughterhouse, and other institutions essential for conducting Jewish life in accordance with *halakhah. The range of religious functions that each community provided depended on the size of the *kehillah*, available resources, and external conditions. Whereas small *kehillot*, numbering at times only a few Jewish families, provided the most basic religious facilities, large *kehillot* often operated several synagogues, a *yeshivah, a *beit din* (*court), and a *cemetery.

The synagogue was the central religious institution of the *kehillah*. Jews gathered there daily for communal *worship, and the synagogue also functioned as an assembly house for community discussions, announcements, and debates. In northern Europe, any member of the community could interrupt public prayer if she or he felt wronged by another community member; prayer was not resumed until the matter was settled (*'ikuv tefillah*). When members of the *kehillah* decided that someone had violated the norms of the community, the sacral act of excommunication (*ḥerem) took place in the synagogue.

The *kehillah* regularly collected money from community members to cover ordinary costs such as maintenance of religious institutions or payment of functionaries. It also disbursed special charitable funds to assist the needy with food and shelter, redeem prisoners, and provide dowries for poor *brides. Through mutual aid the *kehillah* cemented communal responsibility and reinforced Jewish values of *philanthropy and good deeds.

The *kehillah* also facilitated and governed interactions between Jews and non-Jews. Appointed Jewish representatives negotiated with non-Jewish authorities in all matters concerning community life, including permission to settle in a place, the construction of community buildings, and the protection of Jews. Non-Jewish authorities demanded that a representative body govern the life of Jews, and community leaders were recognized as that representative body. Jewish delegates also ensured the exact and timely payment of taxes owed to local non-Jewish authorities.

The leaders of the *kehillah*, who were often called *parnassim*, were ordinarily elected by the members of the community. The number of elected officials, the election process, the involvement of non-Jewish authorities in their appointment, and the social status of the officials varied from place to place. Depending on the size of the community, the number of *parnassim* varied from one to more than ten. Attempts to undermine the authority of community leaders were more common in *Spain than in northern Europe, which has led some scholars to assume that the election process in northern Europe gained broader approval and was thus more "democratic." In reality, the *parnassim* in most places normally came from affluent and influential families. In addition to the leaders of the community, other functionaries involved in governing the life of the *kehillah* included treasurers (*gizbarim*), the warden of the synagogue (*gabai*), messengers (*shelikhim*), and rabbinic leaders.

Rabbis played an important role in the *kehillot* by ensuring that Jews strictly followed the demands of *halakhah and by finding creative solutions to numerous problems that resulted from evolving needs. In fact, one area that involved particular creativity, especially in northern Europe, was the conceptualization of the legal authority of the *kehillah* over its members. Some authorities attributed it to the right of the people of the town (*benei ha-'ir* [T. *Bava Metzi'ah* 11:23]) to execute community decisions; others grounded it in the right of the court to confiscate property (*hefker beit din hefker* [T. *Shekalim* 1:3]). Like *parnassim*, rabbis were often challenged, and their appointments were based not only on erudition but also on community power struggles within the *kehillot*.

Members of the *kehillah* were technically those who were born in the place or, under certain circumstances, those who had relocated there permanently. In some localities only those who registered officially as permanent residents of the town and regularly paid taxes were permitted to remain. According to Jewish law, permanent members of the *kehillah* were given priority in liturgical matters such as the right to lead the community in prayer during the mourning period. Only adult males who were permanent residents could participate in the election of functionaries for the community. Sometimes economic interests restricted the possibility of becoming a member. For instance, to reduce economic competition among Jews, northern European communities limited the right of other Jews to settle permanently in certain areas (*herem ha-yishuv*).

Members of the *kehillah* supervised the normative behavior of Jews, arbitrated between rival parties, and levied and collected taxes. When certain individuals violated community norms or transgressed religious rules, the *kehillah* confronted such deviations by punishing the perpetrators. Depending on the severity of the offense, punishments ranged from fines to various corporal punishments. Excommunication was another common sanction. The excommunicant could not participate in the religious and social activities of the community until he or she repented. In extreme and rare cases a malefactor was handed over to the non-Jewish authorities. Through such sanctions the *kehillot* were able to establish and maintain their authority.

Despite the relative autonomy of *kehillot* in governing Jewish life, Jewish communities were largely interdependent. For example, representatives from large *kehillot* convened councils and rabbinic synods that, through binding ordinances (*takkanot*), addressed issues common to several communities. Additionally, the authority of some rabbinic figures contributed to the dominance of certain *kehillot* as centers of spiritual and halakhic instruction for Jews living in different locations.

By the middle of the eighteenth century the traditional autonomous *kehillah* began to decline and disintegrate, especially in Western Europe. The undermining of medieval social control, increasing mobility, and the gradual breakdown of social and legal boundaries between Jews and non-Jews undercut the traditional roles of the *kehillah* and paved the way for the appearance of new forms of community organization in modern times.

For further reading, see S. W. Baron, *The Jewish Community: Its History and Structure to the American Revolution* (1942); L. Finkelstein. *Jewish Self-Government in the Middle Ages* (1964); J. Katz, *Tradition and Crisis: Jewish Society at the End of the Middle Ages* (1961); and K. R. Stow, *Alienated Minority: The Jews of Medieval Latin Europe* (1994), 157–95.

YECHIEL Y. SCHUR

Communism: *Eastern Europe. Communism was one of a variety of revolutionary options available to East European Jews who rejected traditional Jewish life in favor of modern politics; these options included Herzlian *Zionism, Labor Zionism, Revisionist Zionism, and *Bundism. Although Jews who became communists never comprised more than a small minority of the Jewish population in any given country, Jews were overrepresented in East European communist movements and strikingly overrepresented among the leadership of these movements. On the non-Jewish political right, an antisemitic stereotype identified Jews with communism. The Polish term *żydokomuna*, roughly "Judeo-*Bolshevism," referred to a Jewish communist or, more broadly, to a Jewish Bolshevik conspiracy. Although non-Jews generally perceived communists of Jewish origin as Jews, these individuals saw themselves as internationalists who vehemently rejected any association with their Jewish backgrounds. Many changed their names; for instance, Polonizing or Magyarizing them. "A Jew who becomes a communist ceases to be a Jew," the saying went.

Rosa Luxemburg (1871–1919) famously said, "I have no special corner in my heart for the ghetto." Luxemburg and Adolf Warski (1868–1937), both Polish Jews, were leaders of the Social Democratic Party of *Poland and *Lithuania; Max Horwitz-Walecki (1877–1938) and Alfred Lampe (1900–1943) were important figures in the interwar Communist Party of *Poland; Béla Kun (1886–1937) was the founder of the Hungarian Communist Party and leader of the short-lived Hungarian Soviet Republic (see HUNGARY); Georg Lukács (1885–1971) was among the most important Marxist philosophers of the twentieth century.

During the interwar years, communist parties were illegal everywhere in Eastern Europe except *Czechoslovakia; these parties' small membership fluctuated, and available statistics on party membership are only approximate. According to the most reliable estimates, membership in the Communist Party of Poland oscillated between perhaps

5,000 and 30,000. Jews and other minorities (in particular ethnic Ukrainians and Belarusians) were overrepresented; between one-quarter and one-third of Polish communists were of Jewish origin. Even so, in a population of some three million Polish Jews, at most some 7,000 to 7,500 were communists in the interwar years. Many more Jews voted for Jewish political parties, and a plurality of Polish Jews voted for the pro-government party, the Non-Party Bloc for Cooperation with the Government.

Jews were also overrepresented among Romanian, Lithuanian, and Hungarian communists. In 1918–19, some two-thirds of the original fifteen members of the Hungarian Communist Party's Central Committee and three-quarters of two hundred high officials in Béla Kun's short-lived Hungarian Soviet Republic were Jews by birth. Throughout the interwar years, the Communist Parties of *Romania and Hungary remained small and illegal; each was estimated to have had some thousand members on the eve of World War II. Available statistics suggest that the composition of the Romanian Communist Party in 1933 was 26.58% ethnic Hungarian, 22.65% ethnic Romanian, and 18.12% ethnically Jewish at a time when there were approximately 757,000 Jews in Romania, or 4.2% of the population. According to the Lithuanian secret police, there were 1,120 Lithuanian Communist Party members in 1939; of these just over 30% were Jews. Jewish participation is estimated to have been proportionally even higher in communist youth movements.

When the Soviet Red Army invaded eastern Poland and incorporated these lands into the Belarusian and Ukrainian Soviet Republics in 1939, many Poles believed that local Jews welcomed the Red Army and collaborated with the Stalinist occupiers. Among the motivations cited for the *pogroms and massacres of Jews that occurred in Polish towns such as Jedwabne and Radziłów immediately following the German attack on the *Soviet Union (and the Red Army's retreat from these areas) was revenge for real or perceived Jewish collaboration with the Stalinist regime. During the twenty-one months of Soviet rule in eastern Poland, more than 300,000 Polish citizens, including large numbers of Polish Jews, were deported to labor camps in the Soviet interior. While the death rate in these labor camps was high, survival rates were much higher than in Nazi extermination camps, built after Nazi *Germany attacked the Soviet Union in June 1941. Thus, many Polish Jewish *Holocaust survivors owed their survival to having been sent to a Soviet camp or having fled into the Soviet interior; for this reason, many Jews who returned to Poland after the war were not hostile to either communism or the Soviet Union. It was among the macabre perversities of this period that being a victim of Stalinism could save one's life.

The arrival of the Red Army in Eastern Europe at the end of World War II was a much less ambiguous liberation for the Jews than it was for their Polish, Czech, Slovak, Hungarian, and Romanian fellow citizens. Two-thirds of the Hungarian Jewish population did not survive the Holocaust. Of the approximately 150,000 Jewish survivors, an estimated one-quarter voted for the communists in the 1945 elections. At this time Jews made up 1–2% of the Hungarian population, but comprised 14–15% of the Hungarian Communist Party membership. In 1945 it was very clear to East European Jews that it was Stalin who was responsible for

Hitler's defeat. This drew much Jewish support for communism, even as the postwar Hungarian and Romanian Communist Parties recruited (allegedly repentant) ex-fascists as members.

After the communist takeovers, communists of Jewish origin occupied high-profile positions in post-war Eastern Europe. These communist leaders included Rudolf Slánský, General Secretary of the Communist Party of Czechoslovakia (1901–52); Hilary Minc and Jakub Berman, two of a triumvirate of Stalinist leaders in post-war Poland; Ana Pauker, communist Romania's foreign minister and the unofficial leader of the post-war Romanian Communist Party; and four men at the top of the Hungarian Communist Party – Mátyás Rákosi, Ernő Gerő, Mihály Farkas, and József Révai. Most resented was the overrepresentation of Jews in the upper echelons of the Stalinist security apparatus. A post-war joke alluded to the composition of the Hungarian Communist Party leadership: "Why is there one Gentile in the Hungarian Politburo?" "They need someone to sign decrees on Shabbat." The paradox was that even at a moment when Jewish communists were so visible in the party leadership, the Communist Party was itself not free of *antisemitism. Within a short time, the revolution began to devour its young. Stalin's "anti-cosmopolitan" campaign, initiated in 1948, was directed against Jews. Eleven of the fourteen defendants in the 1952 Czechoslovak communist show trial were Jews, including Rudolf Slánský. They were charged, among other things, with Zionist conspiracy. All were found guilty; eight of the eleven executed were Jews.

In 1967 Poland, the outbreak of the Six Day War in *Israel became the pretext for purging the Polish military of officers of Jewish origin. In January 1968, communist authorities claimed that student demonstrations were incited by Zionist conspirators. The party-led antisemitic campaign that subsequently peaked in March 1968 popularized a theory of a Nazi-Zionist conspiracy, leading to the purging of the remaining Polish Jewish communists from their positions; some 13,000 Polish Jews left Poland after March 1968.

In *Die Judenfrage* (The Jewish Question), Karl *Marx had written, "The social emancipation of the Jew is the emancipation of society from Judaism." Marx here invoked Judaism to stand for bourgeois capitalist exploitation; like many others, he associated Jews with *money lending and the rise of capitalism. Marxism was hostile to Judaism in another sense as well: Judaism, like all religions, was condemned as an "opiate of the masses." The embrace of communism, sometimes analyzed in Freudian terms as an oedipal rebellion, was a rejection of Jewish identity.

A substantial literature has sought to explain the attraction of Jews to communism. One set of explanations points to the historical-political context. In interwar Eastern Europe, despite the fact that the East European states whose borders were drawn at Versailles were made to sign minority protection treaties, Jews and other ethnic minorities were discriminated against by the nationalist regimes under which they resided. Quotas in higher education, ghetto benches (segregation of Jewish university students in Poland in designated sections of lecture halls),economic boycotts, and antisemitic violence led to a desire among Jews for revolutionary change. Like *Zionism, communism was seen by many Jews as an antidote to traditional Jewish emasculation. Communism also promised racial blindness and equality for all. Moreover, in the manichean world of the 1930s, many believed that communists represented the most decisive opposition to the Nazis. Holocaust survivors have noted that in Nazi camps, the communists presented the most inspiring model of *resistance. In a situation for which no one was prepared, they were the best prepared: They were uncompromising, organized, disciplined, and schooled in conspiracy and resistance. Many survivors embraced the Communist Party as their liberator.

A second set of explanations probes deeper affinities between Marxism and traditional Jewish culture. Writers have pointed to the inherent "Jewishness" of communism, particularly the rationalism and moralism central to both Marxism and Jewish theology. Marxism can be understood as a secular Jewish *messianism wherein the proletariat plays the role of the messiah. Others have pointed to the parallels between talmudic learning and the text-based nature of the communist movement, particularly the focus on the study of Marxist writings. Isaac Deutscher, most famously, has described Jewish communists as models of the cosmopolitan "non-Jewish Jew." In Deutscher's reading, the essence of Jewish culture was the tradition of crossing boundaries, synthesizing diverse cultures, and transcending limitations. Victimized time and time again by religious intolerance and nationalist sentiments, Jews have longed for a universalist *Weltanschauung* (worldview). For Deutscher, communism was the quintessential universalist *Weltanschauung*.

For further reading, see E. Mendelsohn, *The Jews of East Central Europe between the World Wars* (1983); M. Shore, "Children of the Revolution: Communism, Zionism, and the Berman Brothers," *Jewish Social Studies* 10:3 (2004): 23–86; J. Schatz, *The Generation: The Rise and Fall of the Jewish Communists of Poland* (1991); M. Checinski, *Poland: Communism, Nationalism, Anti-Semitism* (1982); and I. Deutscher, "The Non-Jewish Jew," in *The Non-Jewish Jew and Other Essays,* ed. T. Deutscher (1968), 25–41.   MARCI SHORE

Community Center Movement: See UNITED STATES: COMMUNITY CENTER MOVEMENT

Confession of Sin. *Repentance, or *teshuvah*, is one of the major belief principles of *Judaism. If someone does something wrong, the capacity to apologize, to be granted *atonement, and to be given a second chance is always available. That process begins with confession, or *viddui*, of one's sins. The confession must detail precisely what one did, and it is preferable to make it while standing. The confession is not made to any human being, but rather is offered to *God. The one caveat is that if a sin against another person is involved, one must first seek forgiveness from that individual.

On *Yom Kippur, the Day of Atonement, there is a section in the liturgy called *viddui* that is recited several times. It lists many types of sins and reflects a public confession of the community's shortcomings. It is also the custom that those who are terminally ill recite a *viddui* so that they leave this world cleansed of the things that they have done wrong in this life.   BARRY FREUNDEL

Confirmation. Initiated by the Reform movement in nineteenth-century *Germany, confirmation is a ceremony marking the public commitment to Judaism of teenagers, usually between age sixteen and eighteen. In early-twentieth-century America most classical Reform congregations eliminated public celebration of *Bar Mitzvah in favor of confirmation. It was felt that thirteen was too early an age to assume adult responsibilities in the modern world and also that confirmation was preferable because it included girls and boys. Always a group ceremony, confirmation generally takes place on *Shavuot, the pilgrimage festival marking the *covenant between the Jewish people and *God at Mount Sinai. In the middle of the twentieth century the *Conservative movement instituted confirmation for girls. In recent decades, as individual B'nei Mitzvah have become the norm at Reform synagogues, confirmation has faded in importance. It has now become a way to encourage boys and girls to extend their religious educations and is similar to a Hebrew High School graduation. **See JUDAISM: REFORM entries.**

RELA MINTZ GEFFEN

Consecration. In medieval Europe it was customary to sweeten the first day of *Torah study for young boys by putting honey on letters and letting them lick it off. In early-twentieth-century America *Reform Judaism developed the consecration ceremony with a similar purpose in mind: to mark the significance of kindergarten or first-grade boys and girls beginning their religious studies. Consecration often takes place at a Friday night service and may include the recital of the *shema (affirmation of divine unity) by the children. Since a fixed time was never set for this ritual, some synagogues hold it on the autumn festival of *Simhat Torah, while others choose the late spring festival of *Shavuot. The children receive small replicas of Torahs or some other gift to mark this important moment. More recently some *Conservative *synagogues have introduced consecration with a short performance by the children during a *worship service; the children are presented with *prayer books inscribed for the occasion. For further reading, see I. Marcus, *Rituals of Childhood: Jewish Acculturation in Medieval Europe* (1996); and EDUCATION, BOYS: MEDIEVAL AND EARLY MODERN.   RELA MINTZ GEFFEN

Conservative Judaism: See JUDAISM, CONSERVATIVE

Conversion: Early Modern Period. Conversion away from Judaism to another religion, or apostasy, is discussed extensively in rabbinic and medieval literature, where various *halakhic and social issues are addressed. The reasons for early modern apostasy could vary widely. Some individuals were genuinely convinced by the religious tenets of *Christianity or *Islam. Others sought material or professional gain, since converts could pursue social and vocational opportunities that were closed to Jews; in some cases, Jews were offered financial incentives for conversion. Some apostates, however, were quickly disillusioned because they continued to be seen as Jews by their new co-religionists. In other cases, Jews were forcibly converted to Christianity, as in *Spain and *Portugal between the late fourteenth and early sixteenth centuries. Although some Jews successfully returned to Judaism later, significant numbers remained Christian. This situation led to complicated Jewish, Christian, and crypto-Jewish identities. In Spain, as elsewhere, some apostates maintained close affiliation with the Jewish community. One of the main charges associated with the expulsion of the Jews from Spain was the contention that Jews were corrupting apostates and attempting to bring them back to Judaism.

Apostasy has generally been seen as a relatively limited phenomenon until the assimilation and secularization of modernity, but there are examples in the Early Modern period of both high-profile conversions from Judaism and, at times, relatively large numbers of apostates. Although women could apostasize, before the eighteenth century they did so less frequently than men. The social background of apostates varied widely; some scholars have suggested that particular groups of Jews were more inclined to apostasy at certain times. For example, in early modern *Germany, many apostates were second-rank religious functionaries who were accorded little respect within the Jewish community.

Some apostates became well-known and vigorous opponents of Judaism and Jewish communities. These individuals wrote about alleged anti-Christian sentiment and actions engaged in by Jews, and they were frequently instrumental in censorship of Jewish writings, legal discrimination against Jews, coerced religious *disputations, and in some cases expulsions of Jews or attacks against them. In early modern Germany, for example, Johannes Pfefferkorn (1429–1563) was involved in instigating proceedings against Jewish books, whereas the sixteenth-century convert Anthonius Margaritha, who wrote about allegedly anti-Christian aspects of Judaism, was an influential source for many Christian scholars, including Martin Luther. Some converts taught *Hebrew to Renaissance and *Reformation Christians who had a growing interest in Hebrew and rabbinic writings; some collaborated on scholarly works. Although non-Jewish communities often encouraged Jewish apostasy, they generally looked very unfavorably at co-religionists who converted to Judaism. Such conversions could result in legal prosecution and at times attacks against Jewish communities.

For further reading, see E. Carlebach, *Divided Souls: Converts from Judaism in Germany, 1500–1750* (2001); S. L. Gilman, *Jewish Self-Hatred* (1986); and M. Teter, "Jewish Conversions to Catholicism in the Polish-Lithuanian Commonwealth of the Seventeenth and Eighteenth Centuries," *Jewish History* 17:3 (2003): 257–83. **See also INTERMARRIAGE.**   DEAN PHILLIP BELL

Conversos/ **Crypto-Jews.** Small numbers of Jews in *Spain voluntarily converted to Christianity throughout the Middle Ages. Although some, such as Pablo Christiani (thirteenth century) and Abner of Burgos (d. 1348), became polemicists against their former religion, the overall impact of such converts remained negligible. This paradigm changed drastically in 1391 when a combination of Christian religious fervor and anti-Jewish sentiment erupted in a wave of attacks on Jewish communities. These assaults resulted in the conversion of roughly one-third of Spanish Jewry, giving rise to an entire society of *conversos* (also called New Christians and Marranos), who occupied an ambiguous space between Christianity and Judaism for centuries.

Disagreement over the proper treatment of the Spanish *conversos* persisted throughout the fifteenth century. No social or religious mechanisms existed to facilitate their integration into Christian society or to prevent their contact with Iberian Jewry. As a result, the fate of the Jews became bound up with that of the *conversos* over the course of the fifteenth century. Intense missionary activity was aimed at those who remained Jewish, including the year-long *Disputation of Tortosa (1413–14), while restrictive legislation and outbreaks of violence were directed against those who had already converted. Suspicion that the New Christians engaged in the clandestine practice of Jewish rituals fueled debate over their integration into Christian society. Some Old Christians argued that baptism could not remove the "impurity" of Jewish blood, whereas others fought hard to allow *conversos* into guilds, universities, and governing institutions as the only reasonable course of action. The dilemma provoked the establishment of a new, royally controlled office of the *Inquisition in 1478 that sought to distinguish believing Christians from crypto-Jews.

Both Jews and *conversos* echoed this general ambivalence toward the *conversos'* religious identity. The dominant rabbinic stance was to view *conversos* as having been forcibly converted and thus still Jews, but popular Jewish attitudes toward them were often less positive. As for the *conversos* themselves, some wrote treatises defending the unity of the Christian faith and their right to be accepted as full members of Christian society. Others maintained close ties to the Jewish community and sought to practice Judaism to the extent that they were able. The activities of the Inquisition severely inhibited their public religious expression, relegating most crypto-Jewish practices to the home. As a result, *conversa* women assumed a prominent role in the preservation and transmission of Jewish rituals and beliefs. The Spanish Inquisition championed the Christian conviction that Jews actively encouraged heresy (judaizing) among the New Christians, and this belief became the major motivation for Ferdinand and Isabella's decision to expel the Jews of Spain in 1492.

In 1497, the Jews of *Portugal were forcibly converted by royal edict, greatly increasing the ranks of *converso* society. Many among this later wave of converts eventually fled to the *Ottoman Empire, *Amsterdam, and various Italian cities in order to return to Judaism. For those who remained in Iberia, contact with Jews and general knowledge of Judaism diminished sharply from the sixteenth century onward. Many *conversos* intermarried into Old Christian families and assumed positions of political, intellectual, and economic prominence. Although most eventually assimilated into Hispano-Christian society, some continued to emigrate and revert to Judaism in more hospitable lands. They brought with them a sense of cultural distinctiveness, combining pride in their Jewish heritage with Spanish notions of blood purity to form the basis of a new "nation" of former Christians within the Jewish world.

For further reading see R. L. Melammed, *Heretics or Daughters of Israel: The Crypto-Jewish Women of Castile* (1999); H. Beinart, *Conversos on Trial: The Inquisition in Ciudad Real* (1981); and M. Bodian, *Hebrews of the Portuguese Nation: Conversos and Community in Early Modern Amsterdam* (1997).

JONATHAN RAY

Cordovero, Moses (1522–1570) was the greatest kabbalist in sixteenth-century *Safed prior to Isaac *Luria, who may have been his disciple. Although his birthplace is unknown, it is clear that his family originated in *Spain. Cordovero was the disciple of Shlomo Alkabetz, one of the founders of the school of *Kabbalah in Safed, and he also collaborated with the leading legal scholar of the period, Joseph *Karo. Cordovero saw himself as continuing the classical Spanish Kabbalah; his main work is *Or Yakar* (Precious Light), a multi-volume commentary on the *Zohar. The work was preserved only in one manuscript (in Modena) and was printed for the first time in the last decades of the twentieth century in *Jerusalem.

In his twenties Cordovero wrote his best known and most influential work, *Pardes Rimonin* (An Orchard of Pomegranates [Kraka, 1592]). It is an impressive and systematic presentation of kabbalistic thought with each chapter elucidating a major subject. One large chapter provides an extensive dictionary of the *Zohar*'s kabbalistic terminology. Cordovero wrote many other monographs; they include *Tefilah le-Moshe* (The Prayer of Moses [Przemysl, 1892]); *Sefer Gerushin* (Book of Wanderings [Venice, 1587]), describing his wanderings in the Safed mountains in search of spiritual inspiration; and *Or Neerav* (Delight of Light [Venice, 1587]), a methodological introduction to the kabbalah (I. Robinson, *Moses Cordovero's Introduction to Kabbalah: An Annotated Translation of his Or Neerav* [1994]). Cordovero's *Tomer Devorah* (The Palm Tree of Deborah [Venice, 1589]) was the first attempt to construct a system of ethics based on kabbalistic concepts; it advocated imitation of the "ways of God" as epitomized in the characteristics of each *sefirah. This brief work served as a cornerstone for the literature of kabbalistic ethics, which flourished in the Middle East and Europe in the following centuries (L. Jacobs, *The Palm Tree of Deborah* [1960]).

Although he believed that he was presenting the teachings of the *Zohar, Cordovero's views were often original and innovative. He tried to reconcile the different kabbalistic systems of the past centuries with some of the main conceptions of rationalistic philosophy (see THOUGHT, MEDIEVAL), defining the system of the *sefirot* as the means for bridging the distance between the Godhead and the universe. His system emphasizes divine immanence in all parts of creation and the workings of the divine will in all divine and earthly realms. He attempted to establish a demythologized kabbalistic system by denying the concept of antagonistic dualism within the divine world and by minimizing the references to erotic processes that were characteristic of the *Zohar. Cordovero's kabbalistic system dominated the Safed Kabbalah, spread to *Italy and other centers in the second half of the sixteenth century, and was gradually replaced by Lurianic Kabbalah during the 1600s.

JOSEPH DAN

Council and Synod: Medieval and Early Modern.

Councils and synods (*kinus, kinusim* or *va'ad, ve'adim*) were two forms of intercommunal assemblies of representatives from different Jewish communities. Although no formal definition distinguished the two, the participants in councils were often lay community leaders, while the participants in synods were rabbinic figures who convened to discuss issues concerning religious ritual and practice. Both institutions provided authoritative guidance and met the current needs of Jews in medieval and early modern times.

References to assemblies of community leaders already appear in eleventh-century sources. A council held in Mainz circa 1307 raised funds for the resettlement in *Germany of Jewish refugees from *France. Jewish communities in Germany, *England, and *Spain convened regularly to allocate taxes, raise money, and, in times of crisis, reinstitute social and religious values. Two particularly famous councils were the *Council of Four Lands in Poland and the *Council of Lithuania, which were the central intercommunal institutions in these countries from the middle of the sixteenth century until the middle of the eighteenth century.

In modern times, with the growing integration of Jews into national states and the diminishing role of traditional modes of life, Jewish organizations of various kinds have assumed the traditional role of intercommunal councils. Nonetheless, the gathering of Jews to discuss issues central to modern Jewish identity such as *Zionism, *Israel–Diaspora relations, and Jewish identity shows that, despite the diversified nature of modern Jewish society, solidarity and shared values still are a characteristic of Jewish life.

Synods convened in different parts of Europe during the Middle Ages. The first known synod in northern France convened in Troyes (ca. 1150) and was followed by a series of other intercommunal rabbinic assemblies. Beginning at the end of the twelfth century, rabbis from the three important Jewish communities in the Rhineland – Speyer, Worms, and Mainz – assembled regularly and made various rulings, called *takkanot* (ordinances effecting changes in law and practice). Synods addressed various pressing issues such as informers, litigation in non-Jewish courts, and problems related to marital discord. The main sanction against anyone who did not follow the synods' ordinances was a ban of excommunication (*ḥerem), which was formally executed by the *communal organizations (*kehillot*).

Several synods convened in Spain and *Italy to reinforce religious principles or to issue particular ordinances; for example, a synod in Ferrara in 1554 issued regulations regarding the *printing of Hebrew books. During the modern period, *Reform Jews challenged the traditional role of synods by questioning the legitimacy of rabbinic authority. Subsequently, the ordinances of synods only obligated those who accepted rabbinic authority and, with the disintegration of the traditional Jewish *kehillah*, alternative means of sanction other than the ḥerem had to be used to enforce rabbinic regulations. For further reading, see L. Finkelstein, *Jewish Self-Government in the Middle Ages* (1964).

YECHIEL Y. SCHUR

Council of Four Lands (*Va'ad Arba Aratzot* [VDA]) and Council of Lithuania (*Va'ad Medinat Lita* [VML])

were federative, intercommunal Jewish self-governance organizations that functioned in the Polish-Lithuanian Kingdom from the second half of the sixteenth century until 1764. They were the largest and most developed of the supra-communal *councils in the medieval and early modern *Ashkenazi Diaspora. Made up of representatives of local communities who coordinated mutual interests and negotiated collectively with the authorities, these councils were similar to other corporate organizations representing ethnic and/or religious groups. The Jewish regional councils and the councils of the Polish-Lithuanian Kingdom paralleled to a great extent the regional parliaments of the Polish nobility (Polish, *Sejmiki*) and the kingdom's parliament (the *Sejm*).

The VDA and VML originated when the Polish monarchy attempted to regularize tax collection from Jewish communities and establish a centralized leadership. Parallel to these efforts, judicial bodies were established and recognized as intercommunal courts of law (initially at the Lublin Fair). In this way, a regular gathering of representatives of major communities was established to deal with tax issues and intercommunal disputes. The first known regulation of the VDA is from 1580. Although a hierarchical structure characterized the councils, there was no symmetry or uniformity in how Jewish communities were represented. Additionally, representation was subject to change, reflecting the relative strength of various communities at particular times.

The basic unit of the council was the individual community, each of which was led by a *kahal* (see COMMUNAL ORGANIZATION: MEDIEVAL AND EARLY MODERN ERAS). The strongest and wealthiest communities were called *Main Kehilla* and were represented in the *Va'ad Hagalil* (district council). The boundaries of each district usually followed those of the administrative divisions of the Polish-Lithuanian Kingdom. The district council would convene on market days, and its structure was similar to that of the local *kahal*. The district councils and the main communities were represented in a nonsymmetric manner in the Council of the Four Lands: The lands (Hebrew, *aratzot*) were Great and Little Poland, Volhynia, and Red Russia, although sometimes there were three lands and at times five. In 1717 the VDA comprised eighteen units (nine main communities and nine district councils), ostensibly representing the entire Jewish population under the Polish crown. In Lithuania the representation was even more restricted: Only representatives of the main communities participated regularly in the Council's assemblies. Initially, the three "Communities of Heads of Courts of Law" were Brisk, Grodno, and Pinsk; later Vilnius and Slutsk were added.

The VDA and VML were oligarchic organizations; for example, only 1% of the eligible voters in the local communities participated in the elections for the VDA representatives. The structure of both councils was similar to that of the local *kahal*: The community elder (Polish, *marszałek*) headed the council; the "trustee" (Polish, *wiernik*) attended to financial matters; the lobbyist (Pol: *syndyk generalnosci*) handled contacts with the authorities and influencing taxation issues; the assessors (Polish, *symplarzy*) determined the division of tax portions among the various communities; and the scribe managed the registration of regulations, decisions, and verdicts of the Council's court of law. The Councils' minute books (Heb., *pinkasim*) were binding documents that validated all their decisions and actions. The VML minute book from the years 1623–1765 has been preserved (published in 1925); the VDA books are lost, except for a few pages (reconstructed and published in 1945; second, expanded edition in 1990).

However, the Polish authorities never officially recognized the Councils as institutions of self-rule. The only function officially recognized by the authorities was organizing the collection of the poll tax from the Jews. The Councils maintained a direct connection with the Polish and Lithuanian treasuries, and they determined the internal division of the tax (which was subdivided into equal units of payment called portions [Hebrew, *skhumot*; Polish, *sympla*]). At times, Councils collected the tax directly and passed the revenues on to the royal treasury; other times the communities directly paid the treasury or the military units that were funded by the poll tax.

Unofficially, the two Councils fulfilled a variety of functions in the religious, cultural, and economic life of the Jewish population in the Polish-Lithuanian Commonwealth that were of common concern. The Councils made "supra-regulations" concerning morals and traditions, *commerce and financial activities, and *philanthrophy, which were supposed to be binding on every community. Their courts of law were the highest legal authority, although acceptance of their decisions and judgments was contingent on the agreement of the representatives of the main communities and the district councils. The Councils issued approbations to books and protected the rights of their authors, actively opposed religious heresy (as in the case of the *Frankist movement in the middle of the eighteenth century) and supported immigrants from *Eastern Europe who settled in *Palestine. Communities from abroad (such as *Amsterdam, Hamburg, and *Frankfurt) approached the VDA with requests for aid in settling their internal disputes.

The Councils, like the local Jewish community, were also financial organizations that borrowed monies (mainly from church institutions and religious orders) to fund their own activities. Their main effort was directed toward defending Jewish interests, beginning with protecting their financial interests and including fighting blood libels (see RITUAL MURDER ACCUSATION), a matter that became pivotal in the eighteenth century. In one case, the journey of a VDA emissary to Rome following a blood libel in 1756 entailed significant expenses, which made it necessary to impose a special tax on the Jewish population of the kingdom. The restricted authority of the Councils and their limited ability to influence the behavior of communities or individuals were at times in complete contradiction to their ideal image in the minds of the Jews of the Polish-Lithuanian Kingdom, who viewed them as a "miniature kingdom" and as a moral and rabbinical authority (**Map 8**).

Modern Jewish historiography has seen the intercommunal Councils as a manifestation of a pre-modern, national entity. Simon *Dubnow (1860 – 1941), the most prominent scholar of the Jewish-Russian school of history, favored the renewal of Jewish autonomy within the multinational empires in which most of the Jews resided before World War I. Dubnow, who published the VML minute book, saw the VDA and VML as links in the chain of Jewish self-rule and as models for the renewal of an array of parliaments that would represent Jewish communities throughout the empires in which they lived and manage their internal affairs. These trends, which were combined within a *Zionist worldview, were carried on in the research of the Jerusalemite historian, Israel Halpern (1910–1971). Recent research includes I. Bartal, *The Jews of Eastern Europe, 1772–1881* (2006); and G. D. Hundert, *Jews in Poland-Lithuania in the Eighteenth Century: A Genealogy of Modernity* (2004).   ISRAEL BARTAL

Counting the Omer: SEE OMER, COUNTING OF THE

Court Jews (*Hofjuden*). Some Jews served in important economic and administrative capacities at various princely and imperial courts throughout medieval Europe. With growing mercantilism and centralization of political power in the seventeenth century, the role of the Court Jew expanded, particularly in the many independent political entities of German-speaking *Central Europe. Court Jews in the Early Modern period worked to overhaul administrative and tax systems, develop industry, secure and deliver provisions for armies, and create uniform coinage. They also helped in a wide range of political endeavors, at times serving as diplomats and helping rulers secure new crowns or lands. The particular role of the Court Jew depended on the personality and resources of the specific individual, as well as the needs of the ruler and the conditions of the court and the region.

One particularly well-known Court Jew of the seventeenth century was Samuel Oppenheimer (1630–1703) who, among other things, supplied the garrisons for the Elector of the Palatinate and later helped organize the successful defense of *Vienna against the Turks. Although most Court Jews appear to have been men, we do have evidence of some women serving in this role. One example is the famed late-seventeenth- and early-eighteenth-century Esther Schulhoff Liebmann (ca. 1645–1714), who worked with her husband Jost (also known as Judah Berlin; ca. 1640–1701); she continued to serve in a variety of capacities at the Prussian court after his death.

Dispersed networks of contacts with other Jews and Jewish communities helped facilitate the work of Court Jews, who also interacted vigorously with the non-Jewish world around them. Court Jews were often granted special privileges to assist them in their work, including freedom of travel or exemption from Jewish communal regulations. Some scholars have seen the early modern Court Jew as a prototype of the secularized Jew of the modern period. In fact, most Court Jews appear to have continued traditional Jewish observance, and many maintained important connections with their Jewish communities, serving frequently as political defenders and economic supporters. Many Court Jews were learned in Jewish law and were patrons of Jewish scholarship.

Court Jews often formed family dynasties, marrying among themselves and serving regional rulers for generations. The position was not without inherent risks. Joseph Süss Oppenheimer (1698–1738), Court Jew for Duke Charles Alexander of Württemberg, was tried and executed shortly after the death of his benefactor for his harsh and unpopular policies; his tragic fate serves as a poignant reminder of the challenges facing even the most affluent and influential Court Jews in the pre-modern period.

A classic overview of the Court Jews is S. Stern, *The Court Jew: A Contribution to the History of the Period of Absolutism in Central Europe* (1950). Also valuable are J. Israel, *European Jewry in the Age of Mercantilism, 1550–1750* (3rd ed., 1998); and the various essays in V. B. Mann and R. I. Cohen, eds., *From Court Jews to the Rothschilds* (1996).

DEAN PHILLIP BELL

Courts (Hebrew *beit din, batai din* [pl.]; see also *BEIT DIN*). Ever since *Moses adjudicated cases among the *Israelites in the wilderness (Exod 18), courts have been a central way in which Jews have settled their disputes and determined guilt or innocence. The goal of such courts rings through the ages: "Justice, justice shall you pursue" (Deut 16:20).

Court procedures were instituted in the *Torah. To forestall collusion, at least two witnesses were required to establish a fact in court (Deut 17:6, 19:15). To emphasize its proscription of false testimony, the Torah includes this prohibition in the *Ten Commandments (Exod 20:13; see also Exod 23:1–2; Deut 5:17). Moreover, a 20% fine is levied against witnesses who knowingly lie in a civil case (Lev 5:20–26), and full retribution is required of those who testify falsely in a criminal case (Deut 19:15–21). A judge's acceptance of bribes is roundly condemned, "for bribes blind the clear-sighted and upset the pleas of those who are in the right" (Exod 23:8; Deut 16:19). Each person is to be judged for his or her own actions exclusively (Deut 24:16), despite widespread practices in ancient, medieval, and modern times that punish relatives for the crimes of family members. The Torah insists that neither rich nor poor may be favored: "You shall not be partial in judgment; hear out low and high alike. Fear no man, for judgment is God's" (Deut 1:17; see also Exod 23:2, 6). The alien, too, is to be treated fairly: "Decide justly between any man and a fellow Israelite or stranger" (Deut 1:16).

The Rabbis of the *Talmud and Middle Ages added many more procedural rules to ensure impartial treatment in judicial proceedings. For example, one litigant may not be required to stand while the other is sitting, both parties to the case must wear clothing of similar quality, judges must understand the languages spoken by the people before them, and witnesses may not be related to each other or to the litigants (M. *Sanhedrin* 3–4; BT *Sanhedrin* 17a; and *Maimonides' *Mishneh Torah*, "Laws of Courts" [*Sanhedrin*] 26:1–3).

Furthermore, the character of the judges must be beyond reproach. They must be "capable men who fear God, trustworthy men who spurn ill-gotten gain" (Exod 18:21), "tribal leaders, wise and experienced men" (Deut 1:15). In addition, "Rabbi Joḥanan said: 'None are to be appointed members of the court except men of stature, wisdom, good appearance, mature age, with a knowledge of sorcery [so they can determine who is violating the law by practicing it], and who are conversant with all the seventy languages of mankind in order that the court should have no need of an interpreter'" (BT *Sanhedrin* 17a).

JURISDICTION: The Torah (Deut 17:8–13) grants judges the authority not only to rule on specific cases but also to interpret and apply the law as they see fit in each generation. The Rabbis maintain that the phrase "in charge at the time" (17:9) indicates that one may not argue that current judges lack the authority of earlier judges but rather "Jerubaal [Gideon] in his generation is like Moses in his" (T. *Rosh Hashanah* 1:17; BT *Rosh Hashanah* 25a-b). Because the Torah forbids adding to or subtracting anything from its body of legislative rulings (Deut 4:2; 13:1), it was through judicial interpretation that Jewish law changed over time to meet the needs of new circumstances. In other words, "judge-made law" is standard operating procedure in this legal system.

*Mishnah *Sanhedrin* depicts a legal system that is competent to judge civil, criminal, and even capital cases and to carry out their judgments. Whether such a system existed under *Roman rule is questionable. Under Muslim and Christian rule, however, Jews were generally granted a measure of autonomy according to which their courts had authority, backed by the government, to adjudicate civil, criminal, and, in Muslim *Spain, apparently even capital cases on the condition that the Jewish community pay substantial taxes to the government (see CAPITAL PUNISHMENT). Jewish judicial autonomy weakened with political *emancipation; as Jews became citizens of the countries in which they lived, jurisdiction over civil and criminal cases was ceded to secular courts.

Jewish courts continue to function in the *Diaspora in matters of Jewish *marriage and *divorce. In all modern Jewish movements, rabbis and central courts issue rulings on the whole gamut of issues that arise in Jews' lives. They may also serve as mediation or arbitration panels if both disputants agree to abide by the court's decision.

For further reading, see E. N. Dorff and A. Rosett, *A Living Tree: The Roots and Growth of Jewish Law* (1988); M. Elon, *Jewish Law: History, Sources, Principles* (1994); and I. Goldstein, *Jewish Justice and Conciliation* (1981).   ELLIOT N. DORFF

Covenant (Hebrew, *berit*) is a formal alliance that may be concluded between individuals, nations, or, in the biblical context, between *God and an individual or between God and the *Israelites as a national entity (see also ISRAELITES: RELIGION; THEOLOGY). Comparisons with ancient *Near Eastern documents, such as treaties from the *Hittite Empire in the period 1500–1400 BCE and the Neo-*Assyrian era (750–610 BCE), demonstrate that biblical covenant forms that convey Israel's relationship with God follow contractual models that express a vassal king's exclusive relationship with his overlord (see MESOPOTAMIA).

Biblical covenants between *God and individuals or God and the people of Israel promise prosperity, fertility, and military victory in return for worship and obedience to divine *commandments; these covenants sometimes included ritual performance, such as animal sacrifice (Gen 9, 15:9–11), and are often accompanied by an external sign. Thus, the covenant between God and *Noah after the flood (Gen 9) obligates Noah and his sons to populate the earth, gives them stewardship over plants and animals, and forbids murder and the eating of meat that has not been drained of blood. It further ordains punishment for murder. In return, God promises never again to disrupt the natural order or to destroy life on earth by flood; the rainbow is the sign of this covenant. In Genesis 17, the covenant effects a change in the names of the ancestral couple and requires an alteration to the male body: Abram becomes Abraham (17:5) and Sarai becomes Sarah (17:15), and the commandment of *circumcision (*berit milah*) is henceforth ordained for all males within the Israelite community (17:9–14).

The covenant at Mount Sinai includes all of the children of Israel; in it, God promises to make the Israelites a kingdom of priests and a holy nation (Exod 19–24). National covenants, associated with spiritual renewal or revival, can be found throughout the Hebrew *Bible (Exod 19:8; Deut 29–30; Josh 24:24; 2 Sam 7; 2 Kgs 23:3; 2 Chron 15:8–15, 23:16, 34:31–32; Neh 10:29; Jer 50:5).

Biblical covenantal *theology, which develops from this treaty model, assumes that the divine–human relationship is predicated on human free will. Obedience to divine laws is the prerequisite to fulfillment of God's promises; failure to comply will lead to catastrophe on a national scale. Thus, disaster is interpreted as deserved divine punishment.

This theological approach is central to most biblical writings, including the prophetic books. Biblical wisdom literature, however, especially the books of *Job and *Ecclesiastes, as well as some later Jewish *thought, calls divine justice into question in cases of innocent suffering (**see also BIBLE: PROPHETS AND PROPHECY; BIBLE: WISDOM LITERATURE; CIRCUMCISION**).   ELIZABETH SHULMAN

Covering the Head: See HEAD COVERING, MEN; HEAD COVERING, WOMEN

Crescas, Ḥasdai ben Abraham (1340–1410), a native of *Spain, was one of the most important, and arguably the most incisive of medieval Jewish philosophers (see THOUGHT, MEDIEVAL). Educated in rabbinic, kabbalistic, and philosophical literatures, Crescas served briefly as a rabbi in Barcelona, and in 1389 he was appointed as rabbi of Saragossa, the capital city of Aragon. Two years later, in the fateful Iberian anti-Jewish riots of 1391, Crescas' only son was murdered. Crescas composed several books, some of which do not survive. His two major extant works are polemical in nature (see also MIDDLE AGES: JEWISH-CHRISTIAN POLEMICS). In both, he applies sharp and rigorous argumentation to refute what he considered to be major threats to the continuity of Jewish life and thought. His 1398 treatise, *The Refutation of Christian Principles*, written in Catalan, is a straightforward and pointed attack on the tenets of Christian theology. Crescas seems to have been in contact with contemporary scholastic philosophers whose style and ideas both exerted a crucial influence on his thought and helped sharpen his understanding and criticism of Christianity.

His major philosophical work, *Or ha-Shem* (The Light of the Lord), was written in Hebrew (the most developed extant manuscript is dated 1410, shortly before his death). In this work, Crescas employs a series of nuanced and subtle arguments against the foundations of Aristotelian physics and metaphysics. His aim is to reaffirm the autonomy of Jewish thought against the Maimonidean synthesis of Aristotelian (and Arabic) philosophy with the precepts of rabbinic *Judaism. Crescas expresses sincere admiration for *Maimonides, yet, he believed that the latter's claim that the innermost secrets of rabbinic thought, *ma'aseh bereshit* (account of creation) and *ma'aseh merkavah* (account of the chariot), are expressions of Aristotelian physics and metaphysics made Judaism servile to Aristotelianism. Crescas also expresses dissatisfaction with Maimonides' authoritarian style in the *Mishneh Torah*, where Maimonides avoids providing justifications for most of his rulings. To refute the foundations of Aristotelian physics and metaphysics, Crescas provides several powerful arguments showing that the Aristotelian rejection of actual infinity and the void is ill founded. His analysis of infinity is particularly impressive in its precision and boldness. Crescas also argues against the Aristotelian rejection of the plurality of worlds, expressing moderate support for the possibilities both of temporally successive and temporally coexisting (but spatially distinct) worlds.

The influences of *Kabbalah and Christian scholastic thought can be discerned in Crescas' acceptance of the kabbalistic doctrine of the infinity of divine attributes and the Christian doctrines of divine love and original sin. *Spinoza's discussions of the nature of infinity, extension, and divine attributes seem to be strongly indebted to Crescas' views. Crescas' philosophy also had a significant impact on subsequent Jewish thinkers. One of his students was Joseph Albo (1380–1444), the author of the popular philosophical work, *Sefer ha-Ikkarim* (The Book of Principles). Crescas also exerted considerable influence on the thought of Leone Ebreo (see ABRAVANEL FAMILY), the Florentine humanist Pico Della Mirandola, and Salomon *Maimon.

For further reading, see Crescas, *The Refutation of the Christian Principles*, tr. D. J. Lasker (1992); and W. Z. Harvey, *Physics and Metaphysics in Hasdai Crescas* (1998).

YITZHAK Y. MELAMED

Crime and Criminals: United States.
The arrival of more than two million *Eastern European Jewish immigrants at the turn of the twentieth century coincided with a period of rapid industrialization, urban overcrowding, and mass unemployment. In the ghettos of *New York, *Chicago, and *Boston, among other cities, these conditions created a fertile environment for organized crime. Like other newcomers to America, some Jewish immigrants and their children chose lives of crime as a way to escape poverty. They became pickpockets, gamblers, bootleggers, drug runners, and extortionists, with names like "Kid Twist," "Longy" Zwillman, and "Dopey" Benny. Criminals were part of the fabric of Jewish immigrant communities, with thieves, *prostitutes, and murderers living side by side with garment workers, shop owners, and future doctors, educators, and intellectuals.

Young Jewish gang members robbed pushcarts and extorted money from successful shop owners in their neighborhoods. Hoodlums preyed on other Jews and later turned their attention to weightier criminal endeavors, such as extorting money from unions, bootlegging during Prohibition, and executing witnesses. Crime provided these ghetto youth with a way to move up the economic ladder and become American. A few graduated to the upper echelon of organized crime. The gambler, Arnold Rothstein (1882–1928), was purportedly responsible for the "Black Sox" scandal of 1919 (fixing the outcome of the World Series [see SPORTS, UNITED STATES: BASEBALL]). Jewish women were also members of the underworld. Organized Jewish *prostitution, what some sensational journalists and reformers called the "white slave" trade, spanned the Atlantic, connecting major cities in Europe with those in the Americas. Prostitution offered Jewish women a means to assert independence from the restrictive customs of the older generation and Jewish tradition and to avoid sweatshop labor. Some women willingly entered the business, while others were coerced by young Jewish men ("cadets") who promised marriage or better opportunities.

New York Police Commissioner Theodore A. Bingham brought national attention to Jewish criminality on New York City's Lower East Side when he published an article in the *North American Review* (September 1908) in which he claimed that Jews were responsible for 50% of the city's crime. This negative publicity prompted members of the German Jewish community in New York to challenge Bingham's accusations, including the implication that Jews were inherently drawn to crime. To address the problem of Jewish crime and to repair the damage inflicted by these "black sheep" on American images of Jews and Jewish immigrants,

they helped establish the Society to Aid the Jewish Prisoner, the Hawthorne School to rehabilitate wayward Jewish youth, and the Kehilla, a communal organization that united major segments of the Jewish community into a loose confederation that functioned between 1908-1922 to address shared concerns.

Organized Jewish crime reached its peak in the 1920s, during the era of prohibition, but declined precipitously in the 1930s and 1940s. As the children and grandchildren of immigrants improved their economic standing and moved to urban residential and suburban neighborhoods, the great majority left the criminality of the ghettos behind. Jewish gangsters and criminals are primarily remembered as a product of the *urban social ills that afflicted the immigrant generation (also PROSTITUTES, PROSTITUTION: MODERN ERA).

For further reading, see A. Fried, *The Rise and Fall of the Jewish Gangster in America* (1993); R. Rubin, *Jewish Gangsters of Modern Literature* (1990); E. Bristow, *Prostitution and Prejudice: The Jewish Fight Against White Slavery, 1870–1939* (1983); and J. Joselit, *Our Gang: Jewish Crime and the New York Jewish Community, 1900–1940* (1983).   WENDY H. BERGOFFEN

Croatia: See BALKANS

Crusades: See MIDDLE AGES: CRUSADES

Custom (*minhag*). Although *Judaism is most often characterized as a religion of law, custom is a powerful factor both in individual and communal life. A *Yiddish folk maxim states, "*A minhag brecht a din*"; literally, a custom breaks a law. *Minhag* can refer to a traditional mode of practice handed down within a family or to the communal liturgical customs of an entire community, region, or form of Jewish practice (see COMMUNAL ORGANIZATION; COUNCIL AND SYNOD). Thus, one can find *prayer books that are clearly labeled as following the *minhag* of Rome or of *Amsterdam or of a defined movement within Judaism such as *Ḥasidism. In the nineteenth century pioneering *Reform Rabbi Isaac Mayer *Wise tried to create a "*minhag* America." There is great respect for the power of custom. In his proposals for the reconstruction of Judaism in the first half of the twentieth century, Mordecai *Kaplan suggested that the term *minhag*, which he translated as "folkways," replace *mitzvah* (commandment).   RELA MINTZ GEFFEN

Czechoslovakia. In 1918, after the collapse of the *Austro-Hungarian Empire in World War I (see HABSBURG EMPIRE), the Jews of the Austrian provinces of Bohemia, Moravia, and Silesia and of the northern regions of the kingdom of *Hungary, known as Slovakia and Subcarpathian Ruthenia, became residents of the newly established Czechoslovakia. The history of these Jewries in the twentieth century is one of simultaneous social, cultural, and political integration and separation (**Map 8**).

Interwar Czechoslovakia was a multinational state dominated by the Czechs and Slovaks, but inhabited by significant minority populations of Germans, Hungarians, Jews, Ruthenians (Ukrainians), and Poles. The majority of the country's Jews lived in Slovakia (136,737 [1930]) and Subcarpathian Ruthenia (102,542), whereas there were 117,551 Jews in the western provinces of Bohemia, Moravia, and Silesia. As a result of the post–World War I amalgamation of these culturally diverse territories, the Jews of Czechoslovakia belonged to a multitude of linguistic, national, social, and political communities. Jews in the western part of the country were urban and secular with pockets of social and religious traditionalism. In eastern regions, Jews lived in small towns and rural enclaves that were strongholds of Orthodoxy with some reformist (see JUDAISM, NEOLOG) and *Hasidic adherents as well. Although German and Czech were the dominant languages among the western Jews, those in Slovakia spoke German, Hungarian, Slovak, and *Yiddish. Among Jews in Subcarpathian Ruthenia, Yiddish was the dominant language. In the course of the interwar years, the state expanded the public school system, a process of particular importance in the eastern provinces, and more Jews were educated in Czech- and Slovak-language schools. This development might have facilitated a gradual cultural homogenization of the country's Jews. The Czechoslovak government's recognition of Jews as a national minority is often upheld by historians as a significant indication of the state's tolerant and forthcoming attitude, but there was, in fact, considerable resistance to this designation among Jews in both the acculturated western communities and in the more traditional eastern ones. Nevertheless, Jews held generally positive attitudes toward the state because of their relative socioeconomic prosperity, expanded educational opportunities, and absence of state-sponsored *antisemitism. In the course of the 1920s and 1930s, socioeconomic mobility in the western provinces facilitated the entry of some Jews into the country's cultural and economic elite.

Beginning in the fall of 1938, Czechoslovakia gradually dissolved. Its Jews, including thousands of Jewish refugees from *Germany and Austria, became subjects of three different states: Germany, independent Slovakia, and Hungary. Most of Bohemia, Moravia, and Silesia were incorporated into *Nazi Germany as the Protectorate of Bohemia and Moravia in March 1939. At the same time, an independent authoritarian Catholic Slovak state emerged in parts of Slovakia. Hungary annexed southern Slovakia and Subcarpathian Ruthenia. Thus, by 1939, the Jews of the western provinces were under direct German control and the Jews of Slovakia and Subcarpathian Ruthenia were in the hands of hostile and openly antisemitic German allies. Although every Jewish community was subject to the processes of material dispossession, social isolation, and degradation, their roads to deportation took different forms. Between 1938 and 1941, more than 25,000 Jews fled the Protectorate; deportations of the remaining Jewish population began in October 1941. Some were sent immediately to killing centers in the East but most were assembled in the transit camp *Theresienstadt. From there they were sent to ghettos and camps in *Poland, the *Baltic States, and the *Soviet Union and, from October 1942, to *Auschwitz (see also HOLOCAUST entries). In Slovakia, the local authorities rounded up and handed over the majority of the country's Jews to the Germans who sent them to Auschwitz, *Majdanek, and *Sobibór for immediate extermination in October 1942. After this first wave of deportations, the Slovak authorities stalled the deportation of the country's remaining Jews. They, as well as most Jews living under Hungarian control, remained out of reach of the Germans until late spring 1944 when the German army occupied first Hungary and then Slovakia in August 1944. In the course of the next six months, about a half-million Jews living in Hungary were deported to Auschwitz; these included 140,000

Jews from the former Czechoslovak territories of southern Slovakia and Subcarpathian Ruthenia. By spring 1945, 263,000 (74%) of the Jews living in the former Czechoslovak territories were dead. Paradoxically, however, more Jews had survived in Slovakia than in either the Protectorate or the territories occupied by Hungary. About 68% of the Jews of independent Slovakia perished, while approximately 85% of the Jews of the Protectorate and in southern Slovakia and Subcarpathian Ruthenia died in camps and on death marches. In all areas, however, the persecution and deportation of Jews depended on the cooperation and at times the initiative of local authorities who assisted the Germans in their genocidal policies.

When fighting ended in May 1945, Czechoslovak Jewry had been all but destroyed. In the former Protectorate, less than five thousand Jews had been able to evade deportation; half of these were Jews married to non-Jews. In Slovakia several thousand Jews survived the war in hiding. They were joined by returning refugees and by survivors making their way home from camps across *Central Europe. In the following years, almost 30,000 Jews emigrated from Czechoslovakia, leaving behind a community of about 20,000. As in the interwar period, the largest community was in *Prague; it had been diminished from its pre-war Jewish population of 35,000 to a mere 3,000 Jews, many of whom came from other parts of the country, including Slovakia. Further east, Bratislava and Košice became the centers for Jews in Slovakia; many Subcarpathian Jews moved to the western part of Czechoslovakia after the ceding of the country's easternmost region to the Soviet Union in 1945. In the wake of the war, the government was determined to reconstitute Czechoslovakia as a state for Czechs and Slovaks, devoid of the unwanted pre-war minorities. This policy resulted in the expulsion of Czechoslovakia's ethnic German and Hungarian citizens. Although Jews were not expelled, they were considered "foreigners," much like the despised Germans and Hungarians. This attitude was complicated not only by the restitution of Jewish property that had been confiscated during the Nazi regime but also by the reintegration of Jews into Czech and Slovak societies. The fact that many ordinary Czechs and Slovaks had benefited materially from the dispossession and deportation of Jews also fueled the hostility toward Jews in the post-war years.

After the establishment of the communist regime in Czechoslovakia in 1948, Jewish associational life was severely circumscribed, and only the formal religious community was permitted to continue its activities (see COMMUNISM). As public displays of Jewish identity or religious practice were stigmatized, Jews relocated their cultural activities to the private sphere where Jewish cultural and religious traditions could be cultivated among family and friends. At the same time, secularization and social integration characterized Jewish life in all parts of Czechoslovakia, leading to a decline in religious practice and an increase in marriages between Jews and non-Jews (see INTERMARRIAGE). During this era, as well, the sociocultural differences between Jews in the eastern and western parts of the country, which had been so prominent in the interwar period, diminished; in many ways Czechoslovak Jewry emerged as a relatively homogeneous community. As the state idealized cultural and social homogeneity, Jewish distinctiveness rested significantly in a remembrance of a recent past that differed dramatically from the memories of the non-Jewish population. Indeed, any public commemoration of the *Holocaust was suppressed throughout the communist period, although on a few occasions artists and activists broke the taboo. In the early communist period, some Jews achieved prominent positions in the new political and administrative elite; however, this trend was curbed when the Communist Party initiated purges of Jews from its membership in the early 1950s. Riding a wave of popular hostility toward Jews fed by an intense antisemitic propaganda campaign, the authorities prosecuted and imprisoned communist leaders and bureaucrats of Jewish origin, most vividly embodied in the Rudolf Slánský show trial in 1952. However, although state-sponsored *antisemitism became a staple of communist Czechoslovakia, especially after 1968, it is unclear to what extent it met with a favorable public response.

The collapse of communism in 1989 allowed for the reconstitution of Jewish religious and social institutions in Czechoslovakia. In the following years, a significant revival of Jewish communal life has occurred among the estimated fewer than 10,000 Jews living mainly in Prague, Brno, Bratislava, and Košice. Still, the processes of socio-cultural change that transformed Czech and Slovak Jews in the post-war period continue to shape Jewish life. This is evident in the secular Jewish culture that predominates and thrives in these communities. Indeed, even though Czechoslovakia itself was replaced in 1993 by two new states, Slovakia and the Czech Republic, Czech and Slovak Jews in some ways still constitute one community united by kinship ties and social circles shaped by their shared historical experience as Czechoslovak Jews.

For further reading, see H. J. Kieval, *Languages of Community: The Jewish Experience in the Czech Lands* (2000); T. Lichtenstein, "Making Jews at Home: Zionism and the Construction of Jewish Nationality in Interwar Czechoslovakia," *East European Jewish Affairs* 36:1 (2006): 49–71; H. Margolious Kovály, *Under a Cruel Star: A Life in Prague 1941–1968* (1997); L. Rothkirchen, *The Jews of Bohemia and Moravia: Facing the Holocaust* (2005); and A. Heitlinger, *In the Shadows of the Holocaust and Communism: Czech and Slovak Jews since 1945* (2006).

TATJANA LICHTENSTEIN

Czerniakow, Adam (1880–1942), was a leader of the *Warsaw ghetto Jewish council (*Judenrat*) and diarist. He committed suicide on July 23, 1942, rather than comply with Nazi orders to begin mass deportations of children and the elderly. **See HOLOCAUST; HOLOCAUST DIARIES; HOLOCAUST: GHETTOS; HOLOCAUST RESISTANCE**, etc.

D

Damascus Affair refers to an 1840 *ritual murder accusation in Syria, then under the rule of Muhammad Ali of *Egypt. The disappearance of an Italian monk and his Muslim servant was blamed on Jews due to Christian and Muslim hostility. On the basis of false accusations and the encouragement of the French consul, Egyptian governor Sherif Padia arrested and tortured a number of Jews, including community notables, some of whom died. The "Damascus Affair" outraged Jews worldwide and several governments, including that of *Austria-Hungary, attempted to intervene. French and English Jews sent a delegation (including Sir Moses *Montefiore) to Muhammad Ali that successfully led to the release and exoneration of the nine surviving prisoners. The delegation next traveled to the *Ottoman ruler, Sultan Majid, in Istanbul, who declared the blood libel accusation absurd. This event played a role in the eventual creation of the *Alliance Israélite Universelle in *France and a heightened Jewish recognition of the need for international cooperation. A recent analysis is J. Frankel, *The Damascus Affair, "Ritual Murder," Politics, and the Jews in 1840* (1997).   KATE FRIEDMAN

Dance: Hebrew Bible: See BIBLE: MUSIC AND DANCE

Dance: Pre- and Post-State Israel. Between the first Jewish immigration waves in 1882 and 1920, there was no artistic dance company in the *Yishuv*, the Jewish settlement in *Palestine, nor any aspirations to have one. The pioneers rejected classical ballet, the only artistic dance form historically practiced in Europe, as outdated and elitist. Only after World War I, with the emergence of a revolutionary modern dance in *Central Europe known as *Ausdruckstanz* ("dance of expression"), and the growing urban and cosmopolitan population in *Tel Aviv, could an artistic dance tradition begin. *Ausdruckstanz* flourished in the *Yishuv* from the 1920s until the second half of the 1950s.

In 1920 Baruch Agadati presented a modern dance recital in Neve Tzedek on the outskirts of Tel Aviv. Wishing to create "Hebrew Dance," he turned for inspiration to the dances of the *Yemenite, *Arab, and *Ḥasidic communities, combining western and Middle Eastern motifs. Two years later, Margalit Ornstein, who had immigrated from *Vienna, established the first dance studio in Tel Aviv; she taught Dalcroze eurythmics, Isadora Duncan's style, and Rudolph von Laban dance theories. Rina Nikova immigrated in 1924 from *Saint Petersburg and became ballerina in the Eretz Israeli Opera, founded that year by the conductor Mordechai Golinkin. In 1933, she established the Yemenite Company, in which young Yemenite girls performed theatrical dances on biblical themes based on traditional songs and dance. The company successfully toured Europe between 1936 and 1939. The early 1930s also saw the rise of a second generation of dancers. Among them were twins Yehudit and Shoshana Ornstein, Deborah Bertonoff, Dania Levin, and Yardena Cohen.

The rise of the *Nazis to power brought highly professional dancers to the *Yishuv*. Among them were Tille Rössler, who had been a principal teacher at Gret Palucca's school in Dresden, and the dancers Else Dublon, Paula Padani, and Katia Michaeli, who had danced in Mary Wigman's company. In 1935, at the peak of her artistic success as a notable dancer and creator in the *Ausdruckstanz* style in Central European modern dance, Gertrud Kraus decided to immigrate to Eretz Israel where she founded the Peoples' Dance Opera Company, which operated from 1941 to 1947. Despite opposition to classical ballet in the *Yishuv*, Valentina Archipova-Grossman from *Latvia founded a classic ballet studio in Haifa in 1936, training many teachers. In 1938, Mia Arbatova, a former ballerina at the Riga Opera, founded her ballet studio in Tel Aviv, where many choreographers and artists studied.

After World War II broke out, all cultural links to Europe were severed, and the dance artists in the *Yishuv* entered a period of cultural isolation that lasted into the early 1950s. By the end of the 1940s a third generation of dancers was performing. They included Naomi Aleskovsky, Rachel Nadav, Hilde Kesten, and Hassia Levi-Agron, who later founded the faculty of dance at the Jerusalem Academy of Music and Dance. Isolation during the war increased the need for cultural self-reliance. Side by side with universal themes about humankind and society, choreographers created dances inspired by the landscape of the country and based on biblical themes that connected modern and ancient Israel. When the State of *Israel was founded in 1948, however, artistic dance was not among the cultural endeavors supported by the government; it was still viewed as elitist, whereas folk dances were considered acceptably socialist.

The founding of Israel brought dancers from the United States such as Ruth Harris, Rina Shaham, and Rena Gluck. A visit by the American modern dancer Martha Graham in 1956, courtesy of the Baroness Bathsheba de *Rothschild, was a turning point. Dancers of the older generation were confused by her American modernist style, while many younger dancers signed up to study in Graham's school in *New York. During the transition period between European and American influence, Sara Levi Tanai founded Inbal Dance Theatre (1949), an artistic Yemenite dance group inspired by traditional culture. During the 1950s Noa Eshkol invented the Eshkol/Wachman Dance Notation system, and Dr. Moshe Feldenkrais created his system for improving movement ability.

In ensuing years there were a number of unsuccessful attempts to establish a professional modern dance company, including the Israeli Ballet Theatre founded by Kraus and the Lyric Theatre founded by Anna Sokolow. In 1964, Bathsheba de Rothschild founded the Batsheva Dance Company with Graham as artistic advisor. The 1970s saw the establishment of several dance companies, such as Bat-Dor (1967) by de Rothschild; the Israeli Ballet (1968) by Berta

124

Yamposky and Hillel Markman; the Kibbutz Contemporary Dance Company (1969), with artistic director Yehudit Arnon; and Koldmama (1978) by Moshe Efrati, originally employing both deaf and hearing dancers. Between 1964 and 1976, all professional dance activities in Israel took place in these companies. Israeli dancers' technical and teaching standards improved, and their tours placed Israeli dance on the global map. Batsheva and Bat-Dor, the leading companies, imported internationally known choreographers. Unfortunately, this practice limited opportunities for Israeli choreographers and local creativity diminished.

In the mid-1970s, modern dance in Israel began to show signs of weariness. The dramatic, thematic approach, as well as the movement idiom and artistic concepts, had become repetitive. At that time, several young female choreographers, who had studied abroad, brought American postmodern influences to Israel. Post-modern dance legitimized a revolt against the canons of modern American dance as performed by Israel's major dance companies. In 1981, Pina Bausch came to Israel with the Wuppertal Dance Theater for the first time, and the local dance community became familiar with the *Tanztheater* style. There was an immediate creative upsurge after Bausch's visit to Israel. The following year, Nava Zuckerman founded Tmu-Na Theater, and Oshra Elkayam founded Movement Theater. Fringe dance in Israel was enriched by more dancers and creators in the 1980s, including Mirali Sharon (who was among the few choreographers who created for Batsheva and Bat-Dor), Amir Kolben (the Ramle Dance Company [Tamar], later the Tamar-Jerusalem Company), and Barak Marshall Dance.

In recent decades, Israeli creators and dancers have worked both in established companies and in marginal, fringe frameworks. Among the most notable creators and companies are Ohad Naharin, an enormous influence on the young generation of Israeli choreographers, who created "gaga" – a training system for professional dancers and amateurs (Batsheva Dance Company). In 1998 Valery Panov established the Ashdod Ballet; all of its dancers are immigrants from the former *Soviet Union. The Beta Dance Troupe studies *Ethiopian dance and creates contemporary dance inspired by *folklore. Flamenco is very popular, and there are several prominent flamenco dancers such as Silvia Doran, Neta Sheazaf, and Michal Natan. In 1989, the Susan Dellal Center was founded in Neve Tzedek, directed by Yair Vardi. This central home of Israeli dance is only a few blocks from where Agadati gave his first recital in 1920.

Recent research includes R. Eshel, *Dancing with the Dream – The Development of Artistic Dance in Eretz-Israel 1920–1964* (1991); G. Manor, *Agadati – The Pioneer of the Modern Dance in Israel* (1986); Y. Cohen, *The Drum and the Dance* (1963); G. Manor, *The Life and Dance of Gertrud Kraus* (1978); R. Sharett, *A Queen without Palace: Mia Arbatova: Pioneer of Classical Ballet in Israel* (2005); G. Toledano, *The Story of A Company: Sara Levi Tanai and Inbal Dance Theatre* (2005); and R. Gluck, *Batsheva Dance Company 1964–1980: My Story* (2006).   RUTH ESHEL

Dance: United States. MODERN AND POST-MODERN DANCE: American Jews have had a significant impact on modern and post-modern dance in the United States as teachers, performers, choreographers, organizers, and activists. They were also heavily represented in the major twentieth-century dance companies. Solidified as a new art form in the 1930s, modern dance attempted to create an American dance style, based on the rhythms of American life.

Helen Tamiris (born Helen Becker; d. 1966), the daughter of Russian Jewish immigrants, was among the founders of American modern dance. In 1928, Tamiris was the first American dancer to tour Europe since Isadora Duncan. In addition to creating dances addressing race and social justice for her company, Tamiris also choreographed for Broadway. Other prominent American-born Jewish choreographers who also created their own troupes included *New York City natives Sophie Maslow (d. 2006), Lillian Shapero (d. 1988), and Anna Sokolow (d. 2000), as well as the younger Pearl Lang (d. 2009), born in Chicago. Before forging their own groups, each danced with the Martha Graham Company, which had a large number of Jewish dancers, including Robert Cohan, Stuart Hodes, Linda Margolis Hodes, and Bertram Ross.

New York City, the center of American modern dance in the early twentieth century, was also home to the recent influx of *Eastern European Jewish immigrants. The Henry Street Settlement House on the Lower East Side of New York City, founded by Lillian *Wald in 1893, and its theater, the Neighborhood Playhouse, established in 1915, provided an important entry into dance. Under the artistic directorship of sisters Alice and Irene Lewisohn, Henry Street offered a range of dance classes, including those of the Jewish teacher Blanche Talmud, whose students included many important American Jewish choreographers.

In the 1930s, the newly emerging modern dance milieu embraced radical leftist values. American Jewish dancers and choreographers were active in the formation of dance organizations that were dedicated to social change and to the idea that dance should be available to everyone. The New Dance Group was established in 1932 with the slogan, "Dance is a weapon in the class struggle." Jewish members of the group included Anna Sokolow, Sophie Maslow, Miriam Blecher, Nadia Chilkovsky, Eve Gentry, Hadassah Spira, Daniel Nagrin, Muriel Mannings, and Edna Ocko. In that same year, Anna Sokolow, Edith Segal, Nadia Chilkovsky, and Miriam Blecher founded the Workers Dance League. Helen Tamiris was vital in creating the Federal Dance Theater (FDT) that granted federal aid to dance during the Depression.

Throughout the first half of the twentieth century, Jewish modern dancers choreographed America, presenting visions of America's opportunity and social critiques of American society. Tamiris' *Walt Whitman Suite* (1934), Maslow's *Dust Bowl Ballads* (1941) and *Folksay* (1942), and Sokolow's *Rooms* (1955) are examples of this choreography. Jews also created works that responded to world events such as the rise of fascism. Sokolow's 1937 *Slaughter of the Innocents* (revised in 1943 and called *Madrid, 1937*), Maslow's *Women of Spain* (1938) choreographed with Jane Dudley, Tamiris' *Adelante* (1939), and Pauline Koner's *Tragic Fiesta* all addressed the Spanish Civil War. Most American Jewish choreographers did not focus on Jewish themes until after the *Holocaust. One exception was Benjamin Zemach, who arrived from Russia in 1927. His experiences in the Habima Theatre in Moscow, and especially his participation in the production of *The Dybbuk*, shaped his dance career in the United States that spanned New York and *Los Angeles. Zemach was at the forefront of what was then referred to as Jewish dance, as evident in his signature pieces *Ruth* and *Farewell to Queen Sabbath*, created between 1928 and 1932 in New York. Polishborn Nathan Vizonsky pioneered in this arena of Jewish dance in *Chicago, where he arrived in 1926. Other Jewish dancers working with Jewish themes in those years included Lillian Shapero, Lasar Galpern, Dvora Lapson, and Corinne Chochem.

In the 1940s, several Jewish dancers and choreographers arrived in the United States after escaping Nazi-occupied Europe. They included Fred Berk, Katya Delakova, Claudia Vall, Pola Nirenska, Trudy Goth, Truda Kashmann, and Hans Wierner (or Jan Veen). Judith Berg, known for her choreography and performance in the 1937 Polish film of *The Dybbuk*, and her husband, Felix Fibich – a performer, choreographer, and teacher dedicated to preserving Jewish gesture – arrived in 1950.

Through its dance division, the New York City 92nd Street Y played an important role in fostering modern dance as well as dance works based on Jewish themes. Fred Berk, a modern dancer from *Vienna, performed with his partner Katya Delakova at the 92nd Street Y and also established the Jewish Dance Guild there. After the 1948 establishment of *Israel, Berk worked to spread Israeli folk dance in America. He initiated the Jewish (later, Israeli) folk dance evenings at the Y in 1951 and an annual Israel Dance Festival in New York in 1952. In that year he was one of the founders of the Merry-Go-Rounders (with Doris Humphrey and Bonnie Bird), a children's dance performing group at the Y. Ruth Goodman, along with Danny Uziel, later led the Israeli dance sessions at the Y. Israeli-born Dani Dassa brought Israeli folk dance to Los Angeles, where he became a well-known teacher.

During and after the devastation of the *Holocaust, American Jewish choreographers showed increased interest in creating dances based on Jewish history, identity, and culture. Noted works created in these years included Anna Sokolow's *Kaddish* (1945) and Sophie Maslow's *The Village I Knew* (1950). *Jerusalem-born Hadassah Spira's *Shuvi Nafshi* (1947) was based on an excerpt from Psalm 116, "Return O My Soul." Pearl Lang's signature piece *Shirah* (1960) rests on a *Ḥasidic parable. Sokolow, Maslow, and Lang each also choreographed a version of S. Ansky's well-known play, *The Dybbuk*.

This attention to Jewish themes continued into the late twentieth and early twenty-first century and entered the arena of post-modern dance as well. This movement, which emerged in the 1960s, challenged modernism and the concept of what constitutes a dance. Interdisciplinary artist Meredith Monk investigated the horrors of World War II in her landmark *Quarry: An Opera* (1976); Jews in the Middle Ages and beyond in her film *Book of Days* (1988); and immigration in her film *Ellis Island* (1981). In the San Francisco Bay Area, Anna Halprin pioneered the arena of dance and healing, including dance in community rituals. She explored and questioned Jewish ritual and heritage in *Kadosh* (1971) and *The Grandfather Dance* (1994).

Maryland-based Liz Lerman established her crossgenerational and multidisciplinary company in 1976. Lerman investigates issues of social justice and aims to build community through dance. Harvard Law School commissioned *Small Dances about Big Ideas* (2005), a work on the

Nuremberg Trials and genocide. Lerman explores Jewish identity and tradition in works such as *The Good Jew?* (1991), *Shehechianu* (1997), *613 Radical Acts of Prayer* (2007), and *The Hallelujah Project* (2000). Since establishing her company in 1982, Carolyn Dorfman has created numerous modern dance works on Jewish history, memory, and experience, such as *Mayne Mentschen* (My People, 2001), *Odisea* (2005), and *The Legacy Project* (2008). David Dorfman created his company in 1985 and has choreographed dances such as *Dayeinu* (1992) that investigate Jewish identity. He and choreographers Dan Froot, Stuart Pimsler, David Gordon, and Danial Shapiro use comedy and techniques from vaudeville to challenge conceptions of Jewish men and masculinity.

Other American Jewish modern and post-modern choreographers who address, question, or critique their Jewish identity and background in the late twentieth and early twenty-first century include Tamar Rogoff, Risa Jaroslow, Victoria Marks, Amy Sue Rosen, Ellen Bromberg, Nina Haft, Beth Corning, Heidi Latsky, dance historians Judith Brin Ingber and Rebecca Rossen, and video artist Douglas Rosenberg. Arnie Zane (1948–1988), who created a company with African American choreographer Bill T. Jones, incorporated Jewish references into a few of his works.

Many modern and post-modern Jewish choreographers throughout the twentieth and early twenty-first century have felt a sense of the Jewish concept of *tikkun olam, "repairing the world," which they have expressed through social activism and their creations, regardless of whether they overtly addressed Jewish themes. Jewish choreographers who do not directly address their Jewish identity in their work, but who have expressed social messages, include Margaret Jenkins, Martha Clarke, and Los-Angeles-based modern dance pioneer, Bella Lewitsky (1916–2004).

Israeli-born choreographers who have played an important role in the United States include Ze'eva Cohen, who performed with the Anna Sokolow Dance Company before creating her own troupe and heading the Dance Program at Princeton University; Neta Pulvermacher, who formed the Neta Dance Company with peers in New York in 1986; and Zvi Gotheiner, who founded his troupe, ZviDance, in New York in 1989. Yemenite-born Israeli Margalit Oved, after performing in the Inbal Dance Company in Israel, taught in the dance program at UCLA and founded the Margalit Oved Dance Theater Company. Her son, Barak Marshall, choreographs in Israel and lectures at UCLA.

In the late twentieth and early twenty-first century, prominent non-Jewish dance companies have created works based on Jewish history and culture. One example is Paul Taylor's *Klezmer Bluegrass* (2005), commissioned by the Foundation for Jewish Culture (formerly the National Foundation for Jewish Culture) as part of *Celebrate 350: Jewish Life in America 1654–2004*. Pilobolus Dance Theatre's *A Selection* (1999), a collaboration with Maurice Sendak and Arthur Yorinks based on the Holocaust, is featured in the film *Last Dance*. In 2000, on the occasion of its fortieth anniversary, the Foundation for Jewish Culture commissioned Pilobolus Dance Theatre's *Davenen*.

BALLET: American Jews also played a role in the development of ballet. Impresario Lincoln Kirstein (1907–1996) founded the New York City Ballet together with choreographer George Balanchine. The renowned choreographer

Jerome Robbins (1918–1998) created numerous ballets for companies around the world during his tenure at the New York City Ballet. He also choreographed Broadway musicals and plays including *West Side Story* and *Fiddler on the Roof* (premiered 1964), based on the stories of Sholom Aleichem. His version of *The Dybbuk* premiered in 1974.

Allegra Kent (b. 1937) was a prominent dancer in the New York City Ballet for whom Balanchine created several roles. Other noted American Jewish ballet dancers include Muriel Bentley, Nora Kaye, Melissa Hayden, and Joanna Berman.

CHOREOGRAPHY: Leading Jewish choreographers include Eliot Feld, born in New York in 1942, who founded Ballet Tech (formerly known as the Eliot Feld Ballet) in 1974. That year, he explored his Jewish heritage in *Tzaddik* and *Sephardic Song*. In 1978, following in the social activist tradition of many American Jewish dancers, he opened a tuition-free ballet school for students in New York City's public schools. Canadian-born Julia Adams choreographed *Ketubah*, about a Jewish wedding, for the Houston Ballet in 2004.

Jewish choreographers in all dance forms in America have incorporated a range of approaches to Jewish themes including nostalgia, critique, and memorialization. They have choreographed on topics such as the Eastern European Jewish *shtetl, Jewish rituals and *life-cycle events, the Holocaust, the State of Israel, contemporary American Jewish life, questions of identity, and stereotypes of Jews.

For further reading, see E. Graff, *Stepping Left: Dance and Politics in New York City, 1928–1942* (1997); J. B. Ingber, *Victory Dances: The Story of Fred Berk, A Modern Day Jewish Dancing Master* (1985); N. Jackson, *Converging Movements: Modern Dance and Jewish Culture at the 92nd Street Y* (2000); R. Rossen, "The Jewish Man and His Dancing Shtick: Stock Characterization and Jewish Masculinity in Postmodern Dance," in *You Should See Yourself: Jewish Identity in Postmodern American Culture*, ed. V. Brook (2006), 137–53; C. Schlundt, *Tamiris: A Chronicle of Her Dance Career, 1927–1955* (1972); and N. S. Spiegel and L. Warren, *Anna Sokolow: The Rebellious Spirit* (1998).

NINA S. SPIEGEL

Daniel, Book of. In the Hebrew *Bible, the book of Daniel is in *Ketuvim* or *Writings; in the *Septuagint, Daniel is located in the *Prophets. Narrated in the third person, chapters 1–6 are set in the *Babylonian and *Persian courts; chapters 7–12 are a series of apocalyptic visions and revelations that are narrated in the first person. The first part of the book is replete with historical mistakes and anachronisms, whereas the second part may be set in the time of the *Maccabean revolt and Antiochus IV Epiphanes, which is probably the date for the composition of the whole book. Daniel 2:4–7:28 consists of five tales involving Jews and an apocalyptic vision; this section is written in *Aramaic and is the most important source for our knowledge of biblical Aramaic of the period (cf. Ezra 4:8–6: 18 and 7:12–26). The *Dead Sea Scrolls cite Daniel as authoritative scripture, and the "son of man" vision in 7:13 has played an important role in both Jewish and Christian *apocalyptic literature. In calculating the end of days (12:7, 11–12) the book is also most unusual, and chapter 12:2 is thought to contain the first explicit reference to *resurrection in the Hebrew Bible.

ERIC MEYERS

David, the second king of biblical Israel, was the youngest son of Jesse of Bethlehem in Judah; his life is depicted in heroic but not idealized terms in 1 *Samuel through 1 *Kings 2. David founded an independent state after the failure of his predecessor *Saul. He emerges in 1 Samuel 8–16 during the reign of Saul when Samuel, following divine direction, anoints him as the future king. The talented young David, "a musician and man of valor and a soldier and clever in speaking and handsome, and YHWH was with him" (16:21), is invited to Saul's court. In 1 Samuel 17, he accepts the *Philistine giant Goliath's challenge and kills him. The new hero becomes a successful military officer, befriends Saul's son Jonathan, and marries the king's daughter Michal. Jealous of David's growing popularity and fearing his ambition, Saul makes several attempts to kill him (18–20). 1 Samuel 21–26 recounts how David flees to the Judean highlands, becoming the head of an outlaw band. During this period he marries Abigail, the widow of Nabal, and takes another wife, Ahinoam. (Saul had annulled David's marriage to Michal.) Subsequently (27–30), David offers his services to Achish of the Philistine city of Gath; however, when the Philistines are about to engage Saul in battle they exclude David from their ranks, suspicious of his loyalty. Consequently, when Saul and his sons are defeated and die at Mt. Gilboa, David is absent.

David becomes the sole ruler after a successful war against the northern tribes; he captures *Jerusalem from the Jebusites, making it his capital, defeats the Philistines, and moves the *ark of the covenant to Jerusalem. A *prophet, Nathan, mediates a *covenant between YHWH and the king, under which an eternal dynasty is promised for David and his descendants (2 Sam 7).

David's decline is narrated in 2 Samuel 11–20 and 1 Kings 1–2. Nathan denounces his abuse of power in the seduction of *Bathsheba and the murder of her husband Uriah. A series of tragedies follow, including rape and murder within the royal family; the exile of David's son and chief heir, Absalom; and, after Absalom's return, his surprise *coup d'état* that sends David into flight across the Jordan. These disasters conclude with Absalom's defeat and death. 1 Kings 1–2 describes both an old and senile David, who is persuaded by Nathan and Bathsheba to name her son *Solomon king, and a politically ruthless David, who provides Solomon with pragmatic advice about the uses of power. Taken out of the chronological narrative and added in 2 Samuel 21–24 are uncomplimentary accounts of David's elimination of Saul's heirs and his responsibility for a plague, abridged notices about the great deeds of his warriors, and samples of poetry attributed to him (see BIBLE: POETRY).

In the Hebrew Bible and beyond, David is the paradigmatic ruler who follows YHWH's *commandments "except in the matter of Uriah the Hittite" (1 Kgs 15:5). From David's descendants would arise the ideal king ("a shoot from the stump of Jesse" [Isa 11:1] or "branch from David's line" [Jer 23:5]) to preside over a future Israelite state. This hope is based on the covenant of 2 Samuel 7:11–16 (expressed in poetic form in Psalm 89) and on the popular tradition of David as the king of Israel's golden age (ISRAELITES: KINGSHIP).

Critical scholarship at the beginning of the twenty-first century is divided on the nature of these texts and the question of their historicity. As a segment of the *Deuteronomic

History (Joshua through 2 Kings), the story of David did not take final written form until just before or during the *Babylonian Exile, four centuries or more after the events it depicts. Some scholars commonly called "minimalists" have argued that the lateness of the text and the sparseness of archeological evidence from the tenth century BCE call into question the entire narrative, which they maintain created a fictional past for the post-exilic Jewish community (e.g., T. L. Thompson, *Early History of the Israelite People* [1992]; P. Davies, *In Search of Ancient Israel* [1992]). The majority of scholars reject this approach, citing a reference to the "house of David" in a ninth-century inscription from Tel Dan, which implies the existence of a Judean dynasty founded by David, as well as other archeological evidence; they also argue for the early date of many of the sources used by the Deuteronomist (e.g., W. G. Dever, *What Did the Biblical Writers Know and When Did They Know It?* [2001]). Those who date sources to the reign of David or Solomon have argued that the story of David as king (or the "succession history") should be seen as an eyewitness or near-eyewitness account. Other arguments suggest that the narrative is a collection of prose and poetic elements, including abridged references to more extensive traditions, which reflect the long-term growth of Davidic romance, legend, and folklore. Such materials are less likely to reveal historical details (D. Gunn, *The Story of King David: Genre and Interpretation* [1978]; S. Isser, *The Sword of Goliath: David in Heroic Literature* [2003]). Between the minimalists and those who see the evidence as supporting the basic biblical narrative are scholars who suggest that the account of David's rule is historical but exaggerated (D. W. Jamieson-Drake, *Scribes and Schools in Monarchic Judah* [1991]).   STANLEY ISSER

David: Post-Biblical Traditions. The image of King David underwent a significant shift in post-biblical literature, mainly in *rabbinic sources (surprisingly, David is not a significant figure in the *apocryphal books of the Hebrew Bible). Rabbinic writings focus on David's spiritual qualities; the emphasis is on David as the "sweet singer of Israel" (2 Sam 23:1), the builder of the *Temple in *Jerusalem, and the founder of the Israelite monarchy. For the Rabbis, David is also the father of the future *messiah (if not the messiah himself) and someone whose virtues are equal to those of *Moses. In clear contradiction to the biblical account, rabbinic texts praise David as a modest man, a pious person who kept all the *commandments and who devoted himself to learning Torah and composing psalms. Supplementing the biblical narratives, which detail David's life only from his young adulthood (1 Sam 16), the Rabbis describe him as chosen by God in his mother's womb, as a young prophet, and as a gracious shepherd. They also attribute to David the composition of the entire book of *Psalms, because his name is mentioned in that book around ninety times.

However, rabbinic interpreters could not ignore the biblical record of David's less positive actions, especially the account about *Bathsheba and Uriah the Hittite (2 Sam 11–12). Therefore, they employed complicated exegetical techniques to justify David's acts, or alternatively, they admitted his sins but placed much more emphasis on his remorse, punishment, penitence, and God's forgiveness. Rabbinic treatment of David is marked by a general apologetic tendency to purge specific biblical protagonists of sin. This need to repair David's image was reinforced for the Rabbis by the fact that David was the alleged ancestor of the contemporaneous *patriarchate in *Babylonia and the *Land of Israel.

This positive portrayal persists in post-rabbinic literature. David is among the biblical guests who are said to visit each *sukkah* on the holiday of *Sukkot, and his tomb on Mount Zion in *Jerusalem is still a popular pilgrimage site. The image of "David, King of Israel" is indeed "alive and vigorous," as a famous Hebrew song affirms. For further reading, see A. Shinan, "King David of the Sages," in *From Bible to Midrash: Portrayals and Interpretative Practices*, ed. H. Trautner-Kromann (2005), 53–78.   AVIGDOR SHINAN

Day of *Atonement: See HIGH HOLIDAYS; YOM KIPPUR

Days of Awe: See HIGH HOLIDAYS

Dead Sea Scrolls. The term "Dead Sea Scrolls" designates the corpus of manuscripts discovered more than sixty years ago in the Judean Desert in caves along the shore of the Dead Sea. The main body of materials comes from *Qumran, located at the northern end of the Dead Sea, 13.7 km (8.5 miles) south of *Jericho, and was discovered between 1947 and 1956. Although archeologists have periodically returned to the site, very few scrolls have been discovered since those early years. In addition to the manuscripts found in the caves, archeological excavations of the plateau immediately below the caves have revealed a complex of residential buildings. Numismatic evidence and carbon-14 dating show that the complex flourished from around 100 BCE to 68 CE when it was destroyed in the unsuccessful Jewish revolt against *Rome (66–74 CE). Paleographic studies of the Hebrew writing on the scrolls and carbon-14 dating have dated a few scrolls to the third century BCE, most to the second and first centuries BCE, and some to the first century CE. This indicates that many older scrolls were brought to Qumran by those who used the buildings and hid their scrolls in the caves. The large clay food storage pots, in which some of the major scrolls were protected, are almost unique to Qumran. Cave 4 held shelves in antiquity on which scrolls were arranged. *Mikvaot* (ritual pools), pottery that could have served two hundred people at a time, scribal ink wells, and *tefillin* are some of the physical objects that might have been used by this Jewish group. Therefore, the majority of scholars link the library in the caves with the nearby community.

The scrolls were first unearthed in 1947 by Bedouin, and the Hebrew University of *Jerusalem acquired seven of the major scrolls from Cave 1. In 1965 the Shrine of the Book was constructed as a separate building in the Israel Museum to house these scrolls and others subsequently acquired by *Israel. As a result of Israel's War of Independence that broke out in May 1948, Qumran was in Jordanian territory until 1967. Because the Bedouin continued to find scrolls and bring them to the antiquities market, the Jordanians sent an archeological team into the desert to look for more scrolls and to excavate the residential buildings. Thus, scrolls of the Judean Desert found after 1948 eventually came to the Palestine Archaeological Museum (PAM) in East Jerusalem owned by Jordan. As a result of the 1967 Six Day War (see ISRAEL, STATE OF: WARS [1956–67]), the area of Qumran reverted once more to Israel, as did East Jerusalem. The PAM was renamed the Rockefeller Museum and still maintains some of the Dead Sea Scrolls in its collection. In addition, there are Dead Sea Scrolls in Amman (including the Copper Scroll), some fragments with private collectors, and small fragments of scrolls in libraries around the world.

The history of research on the scrolls began with an international team of scholars appointed by the Antiquities Department of Jordan. They worked in the PAM piecing together the numerous fragments, guided by the continuity of the text, the appearance of the parchment, the handwriting, and the shapes of the pieces. Their work came to a virtual standstill in 1960 when the funding ran out. After 1967, Israel controlled the museum but allowed the same scholars to continue to control access to the scrolls. The international team, composed exclusively of Protestant and Catholic scholars, withheld the scrolls from view and did not publish them in a timely fashion. Scholars clamored for open access, and in 1991, the Israel Antiquities Authority appointed a new editor-in-chief of the official scrolls publication series, *Discoveries in the Judean Desert* (Oxford University Press). Since then, the entire corpus of scrolls, even the tiniest fragments, has been published with plates and in translation. More recently, the scrolls have been digitally photographed and made available on the web.

The contents of the manuscripts may be categorized into three main, approximately equal, divisions: biblical books, apocryphal compositions, and sectarian documents.

BIBLE: Evidence of every book of the Hebrew *Bible (Old Testament) has been found with the exception of the book of *Esther. Although many of these texts are fragmentary, others are complete scrolls. Two Isaiah scrolls, one complete, and fragments of *Leviticus and *Samuel are among the most important finds. Biblical materials at Qumran come in three varieties: proto-Samaritan, a tradition similar to the earlier Hebrew text that served as the basis of the *Samaritan Torah; proto-Septuagintal, a Hebrew version similar to that which underlies the Greek translation known as the *Septuagint; and proto-Masoretic, the version that later developed into the *Masoretic text. The rabbinic authorities of the first century CE finalized the Masoretic version in an effort to standardize the Bible and eliminate any competing traditions. It is the version seen in the Hebrew Bibles in use today. The Qumran manuscripts have helped scholars reconstruct the process of standardization that took place in the Second Temple period.

*APOCRYPHA AND *PSEUDEPIGRAPHA: The apocryphal compositions are works that are similar to biblical texts but are not part of the biblical canon. They represent books that were being read generally in the Land of *Israel at the time that the Dead Sea Scrolls library was collected. Most of these books were previously unknown, whereas others were known only in Greek or Latin translations before the discovery of the Dead Sea Scrolls. Portions of *Ben Sira, Jubilees, *Enoch, and apocryphal *Daniel literature can now be read in the original Hebrew or *Aramaic.

SECTARIAN DOCUMENTS: The third division of texts has generated the most controversy. These are the documents of the sect that is usually identified with the residential buildings in the area of the Qumran caves. It was these people who produced a group of unique compositions embodying their own theology, law, eschatology, customs, prayers, hymns, and specific regulations outlining membership in their group. Many scholars have identified them

with the *Essenes, a group described by the Jewish historian *Josephus and the Jewish writer *Philo of Alexandria. Both spoke about a group who lived a spiritual existence in isolation; the Roman writer Pliny the Elder placed this group at a location near the Dead Sea north of Ein Gedi.

The documents of the Jewish sectarians come in a variety of genres. The "Rule of the Community" defined membership in the sect. Admission was governed by regulations specifying the duties of a member and his gradual acceptance into full membership by a series of steps, each of which was expressed through purity laws. As a member demonstrated his careful observance of the sectarian way of life, he passed into different stages of purity that allowed him access to the pure food of the community and then to the pure drinks. Similarly he progressed in the ranks of officialdom and in the ranks of the troops preparing for the eschatological battle. If, however, he was accused of backsliding, his ritual purity was diminished and penalties were imposed. The ultimate penalty was expulsion from the sect.

The "Damascus Document" (formerly known as the Zadokite Fragments) is a two-part work, made up of a hortatory "historical" introduction followed by a compilation of laws dealing with the *Sabbath, oaths and vows, courts and testimony, *purity and impurity, and relations with non-Jews and with the perceived enemies of the sect, as well as a large number of sectarian internal procedural regulations. This document was already known from medieval copies found some hundred years earlier in the Cairo *Genizah.

The "Scroll of the War of the Sons of Light against the Sons of Darkness" is a description of the eschatological war that was expected to end the conflict with the enemies of the sect. The scroll describes the forces that will be arrayed one against the other as the Sons of Light, the sectarians, battle their enemies, the Sons of Darkness or the forces of evil. After a great battle lasting forty years, the Sons of Light will be victorious, and then the End of Days will be ushered in by a great messianic banquet.

The "Temple Scroll" is a text based on the Bible but reformulated to express the views of its author. It describes an idealized, huge Temple that covers practically the entire city of Jerusalem and a reformed polity headed by a righteous king. This scroll might not have been composed by the Dead Sea sect, but it was found in their library and reflects their views on many areas of Jewish law.

*Prayer, liturgy, and *poetry are represented in numerous compositions from Qumran. The "Thanksgiving Scroll" expresses the theology of the sect; parts of it may have been written by the "teacher of righteousness," an early leader of the sect. The "Songs of the Sabbath Sacrifices" were prayers meant to be recited weekly in a cycle specific to each *Sabbath of the year. They are actually a form of early Jewish *mysticism. Other scrolls detail the liturgy that was recited on *new moons and other *festivals.

Although it is not surprising that this scripturally oriented sect produced commentaries on the Bible, their use of the biblical text was quite unusual. In Bible study sessions they produced legal rulings based on their understanding of biblical passages that often are in agreement with the priestly, Zadokite/*Sadducean approach to Jewish law known from *Second Temple times. There are also commentaries on the prophetic books, such as *Habakkuk, known as *pesharim*. The *pesharim* understand the prophetic books as pointing to contemporary events rather than referring to the time in which the prophets actually lived. In this way, the *pesharim* yield information about historic events in the Second Temple era.

Numerous texts explain the theology of the sect, which maintained that there is a very sharp line between good and evil, expressed in a very strong dualism. People belong to one of two groups – the Sons of Light or the Sons of Darkness – and even in heaven, the cosmic forces of good and evil do battle with one another. In the end of days God will wage war with Belial (leader of the forces of evil), while on earth the sectarians will vanquish all evildoers with the help of the angels. Those who participate in these battles must be ritually pure members of the sect. At the same time, the sect believed in complete predestination. Therefore, the pure and righteous Qumranites had been foreordained by God to be among those who would attain salvation and live to see the messianic era. Then the world would be governed by the messiahs of *Aaron and Israel.

The "Copper Scroll," the only manuscript not written on parchment or papyrus, is incised into a sheet of copper that was then rolled up. It describes hidden treasure, purportedly in the Judean Desert, but none of the objects it describes or their locations have ever been found. Its treasure lies rather in what can be learned about the history of the *Hebrew language from its vocabulary and philology.

With such a variety of texts representing more than nine hundred manuscripts, it would seem plausible that the identity of the sect could be delineated rather clearly. In fact, there is scholarly debate over whether the term "Essenes" applies to the sect and whether it actually dwelt at Qumran or placed the manuscripts in the adjacent caves. Some say that the sect was a celibate religious order, whereas others maintain that Qumran was the center of a group whose members lived in scattered locations throughout the Land of Israel and included married individuals as well.

The Dead Sea Scrolls are a missing link between the biblical period and the talmudic period in Judaism. As such, they provide a wealth of information about the evolution of Judaism in Second Temple times and the subsequent development of rabbinic *Judaism. They also illuminate the variegated nature of the Judaism that is the background for the development of *Christianity. The scrolls reveal how some Jewish religious concepts – for example, an intense, immediate *messianism – were translated into early Christianity. The scrolls have also contributed to the interpretation of certain *New Testament passages. In the scrolls there is evidence for various versions of the Hebrew Bible before the text took its final, standardized form. The scrolls refer to an array of legal issues that were being debated during Second Temple times; although they present the Essenes' approach to Jewish law, they also preserve much information about the *Pharisees and Sadducees, their authors' philosophical rivals.

Although the sectarian materials emphasize their disagreements with other Jews, these texts prove that many customs and practices of Judaism were already being widely observed before 70 CE (date of the destruction of the Second *Temple). These include the three daily prayer services, the wearing of *tefillin* (phylacteries), the recitation of the *shema, the form of the *festival prayers, the *blessings before and after meals, legal procedures in the *courts, *dietary laws,

the Sabbath, and purity regulations. At the same time, the scrolls demonstrate that, although Jews observed the basic religious laws commanded in the Bible, understanding of the specific details of these laws differed from sect to sect. This situation obtained until, in the aftermath of the destruction of the Temple, the ancient sects were either annihilated or consolidated into what became rabbinic Judaism.

Surveys of the Dead Sea Scrolls and their significance are found in L. H. Schiffman, *Reclaiming the Dead Sea Scrolls: The History of Judaism, the Background of Christianity, the Lost Library of Qumran* (1994); J. VanderKam and P. Flint, *The Meaning of the Dead Sea Scrolls* (2002); and *Encyclopedia of the Dead Sea Scrolls* (2000), ed. L. H. Schiffman and J. VanderKam, 2 vols. (2000). For the texts themselves, see G. Vermes, *The Complete Dead Sea Scrolls in English* (1997); and M. G. Abegg, P. Flint, and E. Ulrich, *The Dead Sea Scrolls Bible* (1999).

LAWRENCE H. SCHIFFMAN

Death and Mourning. Traditionally, deceased individuals have been cared for by members of a *hevrah kadisha* ("holy society") who prepare the body for burial according to Jewish practice. To preserve the modesty of the deceased, members of this group include both men and women. Participation in a *hevrah kadisha* is considered a great honor and a significant good deed. In some communities, Jewish funeral homes or non-Jewish funeral homes that follow Jewish burial traditions have replaced the *hevrah kadisha*.

Judaism encourages burial within twenty-four hours after death whenever possible, and certainly within three days. However, funerals do not take place on the *Sabbath, *Yom Kippur, or generally on the first day of *festivals. It is traditional for the deceased to be buried in a linen shroud; rabbinic authorities encourage the use of a simple wooden coffin (*aron*). Viewing the body before burial is contrary to Jewish tradition because it is considered disrespectful of the deceased. Funeral services include readings of *psalms and other biblical passages (often *Proverbs 31:10–31 for a woman) and a eulogy or eulogies by family members, friends, and/or the officiating clergy. Funeral services held at a *synagogue or funeral home conclude with the chanting of the memorial prayer, *El malei rahamim* ("God full of compassion"), which asks that the deceased find complete rest. At the cemetery, mourners shovel symbolic amounts of dirt on the coffin and recite the *kaddish*. Judaism has traditionally opposed cremation.

A seven-day intensive period of mourning, known as *shivah* (from the word "seven" in Hebrew) follows the funeral and burial. During these seven days the bereaved remain at home, away from daily activities and concerns. *Shivah* begins with mourners sharing a "meal of consolation" prepared by friends; this reminder of life's continuity initiates the healing process. Friends and relatives visit the house of mourning throughout *shivah*, offering condolences and sharing remembrances; callers often bring prepared food to relieve the bereaved of daily chores. Mourners are required by Jewish law to recite the *kaddish*; to make this possible, services with the required minimum of ten worshipers (*minyan) are held in the home. Although the *Sabbath counts as a day of mourning, *shivah* is suspended from sunset Friday to sunset Saturday, and mourners recite *kaddish* at synagogue services. Recognizing the demands of work and family, many contemporary liberal American Jewish communities reduce *shivah* observance to three days.

Traditional observances for mourners during the seven days of mourning include sitting on the floor or low furniture; rending garments; and abstention from bathing, cutting hair, shaving, wearing leather, using cosmetics, or sexual activity. In some homes mirrors are covered. *Shivah* ends on the morning of the seventh day. The twenty-three days after *shivah* complete the *shloshim* or thirty-day mourning period; during this time many mourners curtail activities and avoid celebrations. Those who are mourning a parent traditionally continue reciting the *kaddish* during communal worship for an additional ten months. See also ETHICS, MEDICAL; and *YAHRZEIT*. Useful sources include M. Lamm, *The Jewish Way in Death and Mourning* (1972); and R. L. Eisenberg, *The JPS Guide to Jewish Traditions* (2004).   JUDITH R. BASKIN

Deborah (Judg 4–5), from the tribe of Issachar or Ephraim, "wife of Lappidoth" or, alternatively, "woman of torches," was a *prophet, leader of Israel, and judge in the conquest and settlement period. Also named "mother in Israel" (5:7), she rendered her decisions in the hill country of Ephraim, beneath the "Palm of Deborah" (Judg 4:4). Deborah relayed God's commandment to the general Barak to take 10,000 men to confront the troops of Sisera, who was the general of King Jabin of *Canaan. At Barak's insistence, Deborah accompanied him into battle, although she warned him that he would be diminished through her presence, because "the Lord will deliver Sisera into the hands of a woman" (4:9). Indeed, the defeated Sisera fled to the tent of Jael, who offered him shelter and then killed him while he slept (4:17–22, 5:24–27). Deborah's military success was followed by forty years of tranquility (5:31). "Deborah's Song" (Judg 5), a poetic account following the narrative, is one of the earliest extant examples of Hebrew poetry (see BIBLE: POETRY) and is considered one of the most ancient biblical passages (possibly from the eleventh century BCE).

KATE FRIEDMAN

Decalogue: See TEN COMMANDMENTS

Decapolis Cities. In ancient times, these ten cities, located in modern-day Jordan and *Israel, controlled the trade route from *Arabia to *Syria. The cities traditionally include Philadelphia (Rabbath-Ammon), Raphana, Scythopolis (Beth Shean), Gadara (Umm Qais), Gerasa (Jerash), Hippos, Pella (Pehal), Kanatha (Qanawat), Dion, and Abilene, although Pliny the Elder's list substitutes Damascus for Abilene. During the *Hellenistic period, they became centers of Greek culture; each had the right of coinage, and many of their coins call their cities "autonomous," "free," or "sovereign." After the Roman conquest of 63 BCE, they came under the supervision of the *Roman governor of Syria. In the second century CE, the cities were absorbed into the Roman provinces of Syria, Palestina Secunda, and *Arabia. Although some of the cities were abandoned after the Umayyad Caliphate's conquest in 641 CE, others were inhabited well into the Islamic period.

ELIZABETH SHULMAN

Demography. When the State of Israel celebrated the sixtieth anniversary of its founding in 2008, its total population was 7.3 million. Of these, 5.5 million were Jews (with an additional 300,000 non-Jews, mostly immigrants from the republics of the former *Soviet Union [FSU] who entered Israel under the framework of the Law of Return as spouses or other relatives of Jewish immigrants); about 1.5 million were *Arabs, of whom 1.2 million were Muslims, 150,000 were Christians, and 120,000 were Druze; in addition there were some other small minorities. These figures relate to Israel's territory before the June 1967 Six Day War, plus East *Jerusalem, the Golan Heights, and the West Bank (the Jewish population figures include the approximately 275,000 Jewish residents of localities within the West Bank).

With Jewish population growth in Israel, world Jewry's distribution has become radically different from what it was in 1948. Some eleven million Jews were left in the world after World War II and the *Shoah, in contrast to the 16.5 million before the war. The recovery of Jewish population size was quite slow. It took thirteen years for the post-war Jewish population to grow by one million and another forty-seven years to add a second million. Over the last sixty years world Jewry grew overall by 15% percent, in contrast to a 173% increase in the global population. Consequently, despite their numerical increase, Jews were only 2 per 1,000 of the world's total population in 2008, whereas they constituted 4.5 per 1,000 in 1948. The fifteen largest Jewish communities in 2008, ranked from smallest to largest (all population figures approximate), were *Belgium (31,200), *Mexico (39,800), *Hungary (49,700), *South Africa (72,000), *Ukraine (80,000), *Brazil (96,500), *Australia (103,000), *Germany (118,000), *Argentina (194,500), *Russia (228,000), *Britain (297,000), *Canada (373,500), *France (491,500), *United States (5,275,000), and Israel (5,313,800).

Slow global Jewish population growth reflected several factors: relatively low fertility; growing rates of out-marriage of Jews with non-Jews, the majority of whose children grow up without being identified as Jews; and Jewish population aging. Two important consequences stem from these trends.

The first is that frequent out-marriages across the *Diaspora have increasingly blurred the frontiers of Jewish identification, while Jewish population definition and the effort to estimate its size have become more complex and less conclusive. The so-called core Jewish population includes those who are ready to define themselves as such in censuses and social surveys, with the addition of many others who do not readily declare their Jewish identity but have Jewish parents and do not hold an alternative religious identity. Further population belts around the core include persons of Jewish origin with a declared non-Jewish identity, all other non-Jewish members of nuclear households that contain a person of Jewish origin, and the many others who are eligible for the Law of Return, namely third-generation descendants and spouses. Today, these Jewishly connected non-Jews include many millions of people (see INTERMARRIAGE entries).

A second consequence is the significantly different patterns of Jewish population development in different regions of the world. Jewish demography has actually evolved along two different and contrasting tracks, one in Israel and the other across the Jewish Diaspora. In 2008, as noted, some 5.5 million Jews lived in Israel. This figure stands against the 650,000 Jews who lived in Israel on Independence Day in May 1948. This means a growth in the Jewish Israeli population by a factor of nearly 8.5, which is a unique feature internationally. About half of this total growth can be attributed to the balance of immigrants versus emigrants, whereas the other half reflected the balance of births and deaths. By contrast, the number of Diaspora Jews decreased from 10,850,000 in 1948 to 7,750,000 in 2008, a diminution of more than three million or nearly 30%. Part of this reduction reflects migration to Israel, but, especially during the most recent decades, it represents a growing deficit between Jewish birth rates and death rates that has emerged across the Jewish Diaspora as a consequence of low fertility, assimilation, and aging.

Jewish population distribution across major geographical regions also has changed significantly. The share found in the "Old World" – Europe, Africa, and Asia without Israel – diminished from 44% in 1948 to 30% in 1970 and 12% in 2008. The "New World" – including North and South America and Oceania – hosted 50% of world Jews in 1948 and in 1970, and 47% in 2008. Israel's share of the total Jewish population rose from 6% in 1948 to 20% in 1970, and 41% in 2008. The Jewish presence virtually disappeared from entire regions, such as *Eastern Europe and the *Balkans, the FSU in Europe and Asia, and Muslim countries in Asia and Africa. In these areas Jewish population diminished by 83 to 99% between 1948 and 2008. In *Latin America and *South Africa more moderate shrinkages occurred (approximately 25–30%). Moderate Jewish population increases occurred in Western Europe and North America (+8–11%), whereas Jews in Oceania had the highest increase (+188%). The other country with a major Jewish population increase was *Germany, where the number of Jews rose from 30,000 in 1989 to 120,000 in 2008. The main reason for these changes was international migration. There was a strong relationship between the number of Jews and their share of total population in a given country and measures of life quality and human development in the same country.

Family patterns, too, played a central role in Jewish population change. Against a current fertility rate of 2.7 children among Jewish women (regardless of marital status) in Israel, worldwide fertility stands at 1.5 Jewishly raised children. Low fertility results from later marriages, growing numbers of unmarried individuals, and increasing frequencies of divorce. Out-marriages of Jews with non-Jews generate further demographic erosion. Their frequency is quite low in *Mexico (10% or less) and rises to 20% in *Australia and South Africa; more than 30% in *Canada; more than 40% in *France, *Britain, and the larger communities in Latin America; more than 50% in the *United States; and 70–80% in the republics of the FSU – but is virtually nil in Israel. The results affect Jewish population composition by age groups. Declining percentages of children reflect low Jewish fertility levels plus those individuals lost to assimilation, while the percent of people aged sixty-five and over constantly grows. Thus, the share of the elderly among the Jewish population increased from 4% in 1948 to 12% in 2006 in Israel; from 10% in 1957 to 19% in 2001 in the United States; and from 8% in 1957 to 37% in 2002 in the Russian Republic.

The continuation of current demographic trends is likely to bring about further growth of Israel's share of the total identified Jewish population and a further shrinkage in the number of Jews in most other countries. At the same time, the faster demographic growth among Israel's Arabs

is expected to generate higher shares of Muslims among Israel's total population. In 2030, about 6.9 million Jews in Israel would constitute 49% of the total Jews in the world versus 41% in 2008, and 72% of Israel's total population versus 76% in 2008.   SERGIO DELLAPERGOLA

Denmark. The first known Jewish settlement in Denmark dates to the early seventeenth century when Christian IV permitted a small community of merchants to settle in the newly founded city of Glückstadt. They were promised protection and the right to hold private religious services and maintain their own cemetery. By the 1680s there were both *Sephardic and *Ashkenazic communities in Fredericia and Copenhagen. The 1,600 Jews in Denmark in 1780 were subject to social and economic restrictions, but they were not confined to ghettos. During the final decades of the century, many of these limitations eased, and Jews were permitted to join guilds, attend universities, own real estate, and establish schools. By the early nineteenth century Danish Jews were fully emancipated, and many became active participants in Denmark's economic and cultural life (see LITERATURE: SCANDINAVIA). The Great Synagogue of Copenhagen was completed in 1833.

In the early twentieth century, approximately three thousand Jewish immigrants settled in Denmark, seeking refuge from *Russia's pogroms and the Russo-Japanese War; restrictive legislation enacted in the 1920s prevented further immigration. In 1940, Denmark was occupied by *Nazi Germany as a "protectorate." Aware of Danish support for the Jewish population, the Nazis did not immediately institute anti-Jewish actions. However, as Danish anti-Nazi resistance increased, Werner Best, the German plenipotentiary in Denmark, issued orders that all Danish Jews be arrested and deported on October 1 and 2, 1943 (which coincided with *Rosh Ha-Shanah). A German diplomat made this information available to a Danish political leader, who in turn alerted the Danish resistance and the Jewish community. The result was that more than 7,000 Jews were able to flee by boat to Sweden with the significant support of their fellow Danes (see HOLOCAUST RESCUERS). Fewer than five hundred Danish Jews were arrested and deported to *Theresienstadt; of these, fifty-two, mostly elderly individuals, perished. The numbers were so small (less than 1% of Denmark's Jewish population and less than in any other country in occupied Europe) because Danish authorities were permitted to provide food and medicine to imprisoned Jews, as they did for all Danes in Nazi custody. Moreover, Danish political pressure and the regular presence of the Danish Red Cross persuaded the Nazis not to deport Danish Jews to extermination camps. After the war, Denmark remained sympathetic toward foreign Jews, allowing refugees from *Hungary and *Czechoslovakia to settle during the 1960s, as well as several thousand *Polish Jews between 1969 and 1972. In the early twenty-first century, there are approximately 7,000 Jews in Denmark; most live in and around Copenhagen. See also LITERATURE: SCANDINAVIA.

For further reading, see E. E. Werner, *A Conspiracy of Decency: The Rescue of the Danish Jews During World War II* (2004). **Map 10**   ELIZABETH SHULMAN

Deuteronomy, the fifth book of the Hebrew Bible and the final book of the *Torah (Pentateuch or Five Books of

Moses), refers to itself several times as *sefer ha-torah hazeh* ("this book of the law"). In modern times it is called *Devarim* ("words") or sometimes by its full opening phrase, *eleh devarim* ("these are the words"). The English name comes from *deuteronomion*, the ancient Greek translation of the book's ancient Hebrew name, *mishneh torah*. That phrase occurs in Deuteronomy 17:18 (and Josh 8:32), where it refers to a copy of the law; however, the Greek translators understood it as "second law," because the book purports to be *Moses' repetition of the laws the Israelites received while wandering in the wilderness (see LAW: ANCIENT NEAR EAST and HEBREW BIBLE).

The bulk of Deuteronomy comprises three speeches (1:3–4:43, 4:44–28:68, and 29–30) that Moses is said to have given before his death. They are followed by a poem (32) and a series of blessings (33); the book concludes with the report of Joshua's appointment and the death of Moses. In its overall structure, Deuteronomy resembles ancient *Near Eastern vassal treaties, which typically begin by naming the suzerain king and then recounting his beneficent deeds (cf. 1–4:40). After that, the vassal's obligations, which typically include loyalty and support for his overlord, are enumerated (cf. 4:4–26), followed by provisions for depositing the treaty document in a temple (cf. 31:26) and reading it periodically (31:10–13). Finally, the gods are invoked as witnesses (cf. 4:26, 30:19, 31:28, 32:1) and a series of blessings and curses proclaimed (cf. 28). The book's commandment to love God (6:5) comes from that context, in which similar terminology is used as a metaphor for loyalty.

It has been recognized since antiquity that Moses could not have written everything in Deuteronomy, especially its description of his death (34:5–12). By the Middle Ages, the authorship of other passages (e.g., 1:1 and 3:11) was also questioned. In 1805, Wilhelm deWette adopted an insight first articulated by several early *Church Fathers, who connected Deuteronomy with the book discovered in the Jerusalem *Temple during the reign of *Josiah, a king of *Judah (2 Kgs 22–23). This was the first time that a book was considered to be the repository of divine *revelation, an important development in the history of religion. Josiah's reliance on that book marks the beginning of the process of canonization; that is, a book's elevation to the status of Scripture. It also provides a firm date (ca. 621 BCE) for the appearance of a biblical book, which can then be used for assessing when other biblical books were written, depending on whether or not they were familiar with the ideas in Deuteronomy.

Although Deuteronomy claims to be a summary and repetition of earlier biblical books, its legal provisions differ from those found elsewhere. One of its key teachings is the call for worship to be centralized at "the place where God will set His name" (12:11, cf. 14:23, 16:2, 6, 11, and 26:2). According to 2 Kings 23, Josiah carried out that mandate by destroying all Judean places of worship outside of *Jerusalem. The restriction of worship to a single sanctuary had significant consequences, including making it impractical to treat animal slaughter as a religious ritual (compare Lev 17:3–4, cf. Deut 12:15). Deuteronomy's commitment to centralizing worship, therefore, led it to "secularize" activities that other books treated as sacred.

Deuteronomy also insists that all Israelites abide by restrictions that other books apply only to *priests, such as not shaving the corner of their beards or not eating animals that were killed by other animals or died of natural causes (Deut 14:1, 21; cf. Levi 21:5, 22:8). In this, it imputes to all Israelites the level of sanctity that other biblical traditions apply to priests alone. It also extends regulations beyond what earlier sources required. For example, female slaves are to be freed after six years' service just like males (Deut 15:12; cf. Exod 21:2–7), and whoever finds a lost animal must care for it until it is claimed (Deut 22:1–3; cf. Exod 23:4). Some scholars also believe that Deuteronomy's statements about the place where God will set His name shows heightened theological sophistication in comparison to other biblical books.

Although Deuteronomy insists that worship be centralized, it never names Jerusalem as God's chosen place. This has led many scholars to suspect that it actually originated in the northern kingdom. They support that hypothesis by noting several similarities between Deuteronomy and the northern prophet Hosea (cf. Deut 8:12–14, 11:28, and 12:2 with Hos 4:13 and 13:6, 14), for whom *love was also a major theme; its reference to Mount Gerizim and Mount Ebal (Deut 27), which are located in the north; and its dependence on the Pentateuch's E source, which is widely thought to have originated in the northern kingdom. If that is true, it is possible that Deuteronomy was brought to Jerusalem after Israel fell to the *Assyrians in 721 BCE and then hidden during the reign of the wicked king Manasseh. Some scholars think that it originated within the ancient *wisdom movement because several of its teachings resemble passages in *Proverbs (e.g., 1:12, 19:14, 25:13–16, and 23:22).

Deuteronomy has a distinctive, sermonic style that uses many standardized words and phrases. Similar features are found in other biblical books (most notably *Jeremiah), suggesting that they were edited by followers of the deuteronomic school. Deuteronomic influence is especially pronounced in *Joshua, *Judges, *Samuel, and *Kings, which are therefore called the "Deuteronomistic History." Some scholars believe that those books may once have constituted an independent corpus introduced by Deuteronomy. According to this line of thought, Deuteronomy 1–4:40 and 31–34 were added later, when Deuteronomy was detached from this collection and joined to the other books of the Pentateuch. For further reading, see J. H. Tigay, *The JPS Torah Commentary: Deuteronomy* (1996); and M. Weinfeld, *Deuteronomy and the Deuteronomic School* (1972).

FREDERICK E. GREENSPAHN

Devekut literally connotes "cleaving" or "clinging to." The verbal root *DVK* appears several times in biblical literature to denote proximity of an individual or the people of Israel to *God (Deut 4:4, 13:5, etc.). It was not used systematically in classical *rabbinic literature, but in medieval and modern Hebrew it became the central term (especially in the noun form, *devekut*) to describe communion with God. It was used by the Gerona kabbalists, especially *Naḥmanides, and later by Rabbi Isaac of Acre (died first half of the fourteenth century) and others in ways approaching the Christian meaning of *unio mystica*. The term also frequently appears in Jewish ethical works (*sifrut *musar*) to signify a supreme achievement of devotion. G.*Scholem maintained that descriptions of *devekut* in *kabbalistic literature do not denote a full union with God, but I. Tishby, M. Idel, and others have pointed out contexts in which the term is indeed used for supreme union. Scholem also maintained that the use of this term to indicate the initial, rather than final, state of a person's approach to God was introduced by early *Ḥasidic teachers in the late eighteenth century. However, there are examples of this usage in pre-Ḥasidic ethical literature. For further reading, see G. Scholem, *Major Trends in Jewish Mysticism* (1954); I. Tishby, *The Wisdom of the Zohar* (1989); and M. Idel, *Mystical Union and Monotheistic Faith*, ed. B. McGinn and M. Idel (1989).

JOSEPH DAN

Dhimmi: This Arabic term for "protected persons" referred to Jews and Christians and other tolerated minority groups in Muslim lands. As long as they submitted to Muslim supremacy as humble tribute (*jizya*) bearers, they were not only to be tolerated but were also entitled to the protection of the Muslim commonwealth. The rules governing the status of the *dhimmi* were enumerated in a document known as the Pact of Umar. This model treaty with a minority community was probably based on the capitulation agreement in 639 between the second caliph, Umar ibn al-Khattab, and the Greek Patriarch of Jerusalem, Sophronios; this document probably assumed its final form during the caliphate of Umar II (717–20). In addition to poll and land taxes, *dhimmis* were not to bear arms, ride horses, or use normal riding saddles on their mounts. They were not to build new synagogues or churches or repair old ones. They were not to pray too loudly or hold religious processions in Muslim streets. They were never to raise a hand against a Muslim and had to wear clothing that set them apart. See also ISLAM AND JUDAISM; N. Stillman, "The Jewish Experience in the Muslim World," in J. R. Baskin and K. Seeskin, eds., *The Cambridge Guide to Jewish History, Religion, and Culture* (2010), 85–112.

Diaspora, from the Greek word for "dispersion" or "scattering," refers to the geographical diffusion of the Jewish people over the ages and more generally to Jewish communities living outside the Land of *Israel. Since the destruction of their First *Temple and the exile of much of the population of the southern kingdom of *Judah to *Babylonia in 586 BCE, most Jews have lived in the Diaspora, as minority communities living among a range of cultures on every continent. Although the Hebrew word *galut* ("exile") has historically been seen as equivalent to "Diaspora," *golah* is a neutral alternative. In recent decades the Hebrew word *tefutsot* ("scattered") has been increasingly accepted. Thus, the Hebrew name for the Nahum Goldmann Museum of the Jewish Diaspora in *Tel Aviv is *Beit Ha-Tefutsot* (see also DEMOGRAPHY).

Dietary Laws (*kashrut*). Food that is permitted according to *halakhah* is referred to as *kosher* ("fit"); unfit food is considered *treif*, a *Yiddish word derived from the *Hebrew *terefah* ("torn"). The laws of *kashrut* are complex; they originate in biblical sources and were further developed over time. No overarching principle underlies the broad range of laws related to eating in the Hebrew *Bible and *rabbinic literature. Certain foods are prohibited outright: These include animals that do not have cloven hoofs or do not chew their cud (Deut 14:7–8); a variety of birds (Lev 11:13–19; Deut 14:7–8, 12–18); fish without fins and scales (Lev 11:9–12); and most insects (Lev 11:20–23). Permitted species are

referred to as "pure" (*tahor*) and prohibited species as either "impure" (*tamei*) or "abomination" (*sheketz*); no explanation is provided for these categorizations. Jewish writers from antiquity to modernity have offered their own rationales, often relating to hygiene or *ethics, but the Bible's intent is impossible to ascertain (see also ECOLOGY).

The Bible also prohibits the consumption of "pure" animals that have not been prepared properly. Specifically, biblical injunction forbids the consumption of carrion (*nevelah*) (Lev 17:15, 22:8; Deut 14:21); this prohibition became the basis for rabbinic laws of ritual slaughter (*shehitah*) as the only means of rendering meat permissible. Biblical law also prohibits consuming an animal killed by another animal (*terefah*, literally, "torn apart") (Exod 22:30; Lev 17:15, 22:8). Rabbinic tradition expanded this prohibition to include any animal that had a fatal injury or sickness at the time of ritual slaughter, and methods were developed to check for such conditions.

In addition to prohibiting numerous species, the Bible prohibits the consumption of specific parts of permitted animals, each part for its own reason. All blood is forbidden (Lev 3:17, 7:26–7, 17:10–14; Deut 12:16, 23) on the grounds that "the life of the flesh is in the blood" (Lev 17:11; cf. v. 14; Deut 12:23). In addition, animal fat called *ḥelev* may not be consumed (Lev 3:17, 7:23–25). The sciatic nerve (*gid ha-nasheh*) is forbidden in Genesis 32:33 in commemoration of the patriarch *Jacob's injury at the hands of the mysterious "man" who wrestled with him one night.

The rabbinic tradition is responsible for the broad application of the prohibition of boiling a kid in its mother's milk (Exod 23:19, 34:26; Deut 14:21). In rabbinic literature, "a kid" is taken to represent any meat and poultry (excluding fish and grasshoppers), "its mother's milk" includes any dairy product whatsoever, and "boiling" is equivalent to any form of cooking or consumption. Moreover the Rabbis established additional restrictions to prevent consuming meat and dairy together, such as not placing them on the same table. As Jewish tradition evolved through the medieval period, other laws of this sort were introduced or expanded. Today, most rabbinic authorities require waiting between one and six hours (depending on the community's *custom) before eating any dairy products after having eaten meat. Also common is using separate dishes, pots and pans, sponges, sinks, and the like for meat and dairy, with a great deal of variation in practice among communities and individual households. No explicit reason is given in the Bible or rabbinic tradition for separating meat and milk, but theories abound. Some believe it was a response to pagan ritual practices. Others hold that milk, like blood, was seen as a life source and that it was considered unethical to mix it with meat, which symbolizes death.

According to the dietary laws all produce is potentially permissible, but a number of unrelated biblical laws limit its consumption. The law of "mixed species" (*kilayim*) prohibits sowing a field or vineyard with different types of seeds (Lev 19:19; Deut 22:9–11). The rabbinic tradition elaborates on the status of the resultant produce, in certain cases forbidding its consumption. The biblical law of "uncircumcised" fruit (*orlah*) prohibits consuming fruit picked from a tree in the Land of *Israel within three years of its planting (Lev 19:23). According to rabbinic interpretation of "fourth-year planting" (*neta revai*), fruit in the fourth year of a tree's life may only be eaten in *Jerusalem unless it is "redeemed" (Lev 19:24); only in the fifth year is fruit permitted unconditionally (19:25). Traditional Jews in Israel continue to observe these laws.

Several dietary laws are related to the ancient *Temple cult and the biblical requirement of giving tithes to *priests and Levites (Num 18:21–24; Deut 14:22–29). It is not permitted to eat produce from the land of Israel from which the appropriate tithes have not been separated (tevel). Furthermore, food set apart for priests may not be eaten by those who are not priests (Lev 22:10–15; Num 18:8–19, 25–32). Today food separated as priestly tithes is simply discarded; there is no genealogical distinction among Jews with regard to dietary laws. Also related to the Temple cult is a law restricting the consumption of grains from the spring crop (hadash – literally, "new" grain) until after the offering of the *omer sacrifice in the Jerusalem Temple on the second day of *Passover (Lev 23:14). There is a difference of rabbinic opinion as to whether this law applies in the *Diaspora; traditional Jews in Israel wait until after the second day of Passover before consuming new grain.

A rabbinic injunction against consuming the wine, oil, milk, and bread of Gentiles (M. Avodah Zarah 2:3, 5–6) is based partly on suspicions about the potential admixture of forbidden substances into these products and partly on a general desire to avoid contact with Gentiles, as when drinking together. Subsequent Jewish tradition, as promulgated in the *Talmud, by medieval rabbinic authorities, and also in modern communities, has variously limited and expanded these and other such restrictions. Much of the permissiveness in this area among some medieval and modern communities stems from the conviction that contemporary Gentiles are not to be mistrusted or avoided in the way that their predecessors were. Still, many Jewish communities maintain a high level of restriction with regard to foods not prepared or supervised by Jews.

Helpful resources include S. Dresner and S. Siegel, Jewish Dietary Laws (1980); L. Stern, How to Keep Kosher: A Comprehensive Guide to Understanding Jewish Dietary Laws (2004); and see ECOLOGY.   JENNY R. LABENDZ

Dina de-Malkhuta Dina. This rule, "the law of the land is the law," declares that the laws of a country of residence are binding on Jewish inhabitants. This dictum, attributed to the third-century *Babylonian *Amora, Samuel, had important legal and political ramifications for the relationship of Jews with Gentiles throughout the *Middle Ages. It was applied to monetary, civil, and real estate laws of host countries, but not to ritual or personal status laws.

Samuel's principle appears several times in the Babylonian *Talmud (Gittin 10b, Nedarim 28b, Bava Kamma 113a, Bava Batra 44b) without legal sources or justification. Later rabbinic authorities sought grounding for it. An anonymous *geonic responsum (Babylonia, ninth to tenth century) cited *Nehemiah 9:37 as proof that obedience to temporal rulers is based on divine will (Teshuvot ha-Geonim, no. 66, ed. Assaf (1942). *Rashi saw the source in a generally recognized obligation to maintain social order (commentary on Gittin 10b). *Maimonides and Rashbam (France, twelfth century) rooted the principle in the notion of a political contract between residents and ruler (Mishneh Torah, "Theft" 5.18; on Bava Batra 54b). Rabbenu Nissim of Gerona (fourteenth

century) asserted that a sovereign has territorial hegemony over all residents (on Nedarim 28a). Rabbi Yom Tov ibn Asevilli (Ritva, fourteenth-century Seville) contended that there is a legal equivalence between non-Jewish monarchs and Jewish sovereigns (on Ketubbot 52b). The *Tosafists of Franco-Germany extended the scope of this rule beyond the decree of sovereigns to argue that even customary law was authoritative (on Bava Batra 55a). These explanations provided internal justification for non-Jewish legal authority and played an important role in post-medieval debates about political *emancipation and citizenship.

                                       BARUCH FRYDMAN-KOHL

Dinah, the daughter of *Jacob and *Leah, was born after her parents had six sons (Gen 30:21, 46:15). When Jacob was camped by the city of *Shechem, Dinah went to meet some of the local women. Shechem, the son of Hamor, the city's founder, saw Dinah and had sexual intercourse with her (modern interpreters disagree on whether the relationship was consensual). Shechem fell in love with Dinah and initiated marriage negotiations between Jacob and Hamor. A condition for the marriage was the *circumcision of the adult males in Hamor's community. Dinah's brothers Simeon and Levi took advantage of the circumcision and killed the Hamorite adult males when they were in a weakened state and, with their brothers, took their possessions, including the women and children.

Genesis 34 never indicates how Dinah felt about Shechem or the events that surround her. The text says, "Simeon and Levi . . . took Dinah out of Shechem's house," indicating Dinah and Shechem lived together for several days. Jacob accused Simeon and Levi of making Jacob and his household "odious to the inhabitants of the land," but they replied, "Should our sister be treated like a whore?" The biblical narrator appears to agree that the event brought disgrace to the family: Even if the sexual relationship was consensual, *Israelites must form unions with those inside their patrilineal group (endogamy) rather than those outside of it (exogamy). Dinah's story also illustrates male control of family honor as ideologically expressed in the virginity of unmarried women.   NAOMI STEINBERG

Displaced Persons or She'erit Hapletah ("surviving remnant"), emerged from the catastrophe of the *Holocaust to form a vibrant, active, and fiercely independent community that played a prominent role in diplomatic negotiations leading to the creation of the State of *Israel.

Immediately following the liberation of *Germany by the victorious Allied forces on May 8, 1945, the roads were filled with up to ten million forced laborers, prisoners of war (POWs), and other displaced persons (DPs) who desired to return home. According to statistics prepared by the United Nations Relief and Rehabilitation Administration (UNRRA), there were 1,488,007 DPs in Germany, *Austria, and *Italy immediately after the war; of these, 53,322 or 3.6 percent were Jews. Allied policy defined a displaced person "as any civilian who because of the war was living outside the borders of his or her country and who wanted to but could not return home or find a new home without assistance." Displaced persons were initially divided into categories by place of origin. At that time, Germany and Austria were divided into American, British, and Soviet zones of occupation, with a small area in the southwest of Germany as a French zone of occupation. The majority of the Jewish population, perhaps some 35,000 out of 50,000, was in the American zone of occupation in Germany, many of them around Munich.

Soon after liberation, Jewish survivors began to search for family members, although most found that few had survived. For those Jewish DPs who made the decision to remain in Germany, the majority chose to live in a DP camp (generally German military barracks, former POW and slave labor camps, tent cities, industrial housing, and the like); approximately 15,000 German Jewish survivors chose to rebuild their pre-war communities in German cities. Those survivors who remained in the camps faced deplorable conditions: poor accommodations, no plumbing, no clothing, rampant disease, continuing malnourishment, and a lack of any plan on the part of the American military. Of the approximately 50,000 Jewish survivors at the time of liberation, many thousands perished within the first weeks after liberation from complications arising from disease, starvation, and the poor camp conditions.

The Jewish survivors organized quickly among themselves to advocate for their needs. In the summer of 1945, the Central Committee of Liberated Jews formed in the American zone under the leadership of Samuel Gringauz and Zalman Grinberg, and the Central Committee of Liberated Jews was organized in the British zone, under the leadership of Josef Rosensaft. The reports of continuing deprivation and poor recovery support sent by the DPs and Jewish chaplains eventually prompted American officials to take a greater interest in their problems. President Truman dispatched Earl Harrison to survey conditions; in his scathing report to Truman, Harrison concluded that we are "treating the Jews as the Nazis treated them except that we do not exterminate them." He proposed that Jews, who until then had been forced to live with other national groups and former collaborators, be separated in their own camps. He also proposed that 100,000 immigration certificates to *Palestine be granted immediately to the Jewish DPs to resolve their refugee status. After Harrison's report, American authorities, under the leadership of General Eisenhower, worked to ameliorate conditions for Jewish DPs, moving Jews to separate camps and agreeing to the appointment of an Advisor for Jewish Affairs.

With the arrival of more than 100,000 Jews fleeing continued persecution and *antisemitism in *Eastern Europe, the Jewish DP population had reached 250,000 in Germany, Italy, and Austria by the beginning of 1947 (approximately 185,000 were in Germany, 45,000 in Austria, and 20,000 in Italy.) The surviving population had a highly youthful demographic: Reports and surveys consistently estimated that more than half the Jewish DPs, and sometimes as many as 80%, were between the ages of fifteen and thirty. In the absence of families, many survivors quickly created new families, as evidenced by the many weddings and the remarkable birthrate among the surviving population in the first year after liberation.

While still living in a transitional situation and hoping for the possibility of emigration, DPs succeeded in creating a dynamic community in hundreds of DP camps and communities across Germany, Italy, and Austria. With the assistance of representatives from UNRRA, the American Jewish Joint Distribution Committee, the Jewish Agency, and other organizations, schools were established throughout the DP camps. The largest camps, including Landsberg, Feldafing, and Föhrenwald in the American zone of Germany, and *Bergen-Belsen in the British zone, boasted an active social and cultural life, with a flourishing DP press, theaters, active *Zionist youth movements, athletic clubs, historical commissions, and *yeshivot testifying to the rebirth of Orthodox *Judaism. The DPs took an active role in representing their own political interests: Political parties (mostly Zionist in nature, with the exception of the Orthodox *Agudat Israel) administered camp committees and met at annual congresses of the She'erit Hapletah. The Zionist youth movements, with the assistance of emissaries from *Palestine, created a network of at least forty agricultural training farms throughout Germany on the estates of former Nazis, demonstrating their ardent desire for immigration to *Palestine.

The Harrison report linked the resolution of the Jewish DP situation with the situation in Palestine, thereby elevating the diplomatic implications of the Jewish DP political stance. International observers from the Anglo-American Committee of Inquiry and the United Nations deemed DP Zionist enthusiasm central to the resolution of the political conflict over Palestine. As their stay dragged on in Europe, DPs staged mass protests condemning the British blockade of Palestine and participated in the illegal immigration (aliyah bet) movement to Palestine, most noticeably in the Exodus Affair of 1947 (see BRITISH MANDATE OVER PALESTINE).

Eventually, the United Nations Special Committee on Palestine (UNSCOP) recommended that the problem of the 250,000 Jewish DPs be dealt with through the partition of Palestine. After the passage of the UN Partition Plan (November 29, 1947) and the creation of the State of Israel in May 1948 (see ISRAEL, STATE OF: FOUNDING OF THE MODERN STATE), approximately two-thirds of the DP population immigrated to the new state, with a sizable percentage of the younger segment fighting in the 1948 war. Most of the remainder went to the United States, which had only become a realistic immigration option after passage of the Displaced Persons Act in 1948 and the amended DP Act of 1950, which authorized 200,000 DPs (Jewish and non-Jewish) to enter the United States. By 1952, more than 80,000 Jewish DPs had immigrated to the United States under the terms of the DP Act and with the aid of Jewish agencies. Almost all of the DP camps were closed by 1952.

Studies of Jewish DPs in the American and British zones include Z. Mankowitz, Life Between Memory and Hope: The Survivors of the Holocaust in Occupied Germany (2002); and H. Lavsky, New Beginnings: Holocaust Survivors in Bergen-Belsen and the British Zone in Germany, 1945–1950 (2002). See also A. J. Patt, Finding Home and Homeland: Jewish Youth and Zionism after the Holocaust (2008); and A. Grossmann, Jews, Germans, and Allies: Close Encounters in Occupied Germany (2007). On post-war refugee diplomacy, see A. Kochavi, Post-Holocaust Politics: Britain, the United States, and Jewish Refugees, 1945–1948 (2000).   AVINOAM J. PATT

Disputations: See MIDDLE AGES: JEWISH-CHRISTIAN POLEMICS; NAHMANIDES

Disraeli, Benjamin (1804–1881) was a British politician and writer. Celebrated as a dandy, novelist (eighteen novels in all), wit, and vocal Member of Parliament, he served three times as Chancellor of the Exchequer and twice as Prime

Minister, in 1868 and again from 1874 to 1880. He is the only person of Jewish descent to have served as Britain's prime minister. Although converted in 1817, Disraeli was seen (and attacked) as a Jewish outsider. Yet he skillfully exploited his ethnicity, as in his claim that Judaism's "racial" heritage (as well as his own) created the foundation of enlightened modern thought. When he spoke in favor of the Jewish Disabilities Bill in 1847, he argued that Christianity is "completed Judaism."

With a group of "radical Tories" who criticized their party from within, Disraeli supported the Chartists in their 1839 protest. From 1843 he was associated with the "Young England" movement, promoting its romantic traditionalism (and an alliance of the aristocracy with the working class) in such novels as *Sybil: or the Two Nations* (1845), a critique of industrialism; *Coningsby* (1844); and *Tancred* (1847). The latter two works include a character named Sidonia, a wealthy and influential *Sephardic Jew whose political and historical wisdom echoes the views of the author.

As prime minister, Disraeli arranged the British purchase of the Suez Canal in 1875 and persuaded Queen Victoria to accept the title of Empress of India in 1876. He was named Earl of Beaconsfield and elevated to the House of Lords in 1878. Recent scholarship includes S. Weintraub, *Disraeli* (1993); T. M. Endelman and T. Kushner, eds., *Disraeli's Jewishness* (2002); and A. Kirsch, *Disraeli* (2008).

RICHARD STEIN

Divorce: Historical Development.

Biblical and rabbinic traditions view divorce, the legal termination of a *marriage, as a tragic event. BT *Gittin* 90b quotes the biblical prophet Malachi 2:13–14 in support of the assertion, "If a man divorces his first wife even the altar sheds tears." Nevertheless, marital breakdown is a reality, and both Israelite custom and rabbinic legislation (*halakhah) permitted the dissolution of marital bonds.

Details of how and why a marriage should be dissolved do not appear in the Hebrew *Bible. Deuteronomy 24:1–4, the single biblical legal text on divorce, considers only the particular circumstances in which a man seeks to remarry someone to whom he had previously been married. This case, as well as indirect information (e.g., the departure of the Levite's wife in Judges 19:2), suggests that women as well as men could terminate a marriage. Isaiah 50:1 mentions a bill of divorce, an indication that written documents may have been a part of some marriages and divorces, especially those of the well-to-do (see ISRAELITES: MARRIAGE AND FAMILY LIFE).

Tractate *Gittin* (Bills of Divorce) in the *Mishnah and *Talmud delineates the halakhic parameters of divorce. The salient feature of divorce in rabbinic *Judaism is its unilateral nature: Just as marriage is constructed as a man's acquisition of a wife, so divorce is understood as a man's dismissal of what he had acquired. A divorced woman receives her *get* (divorce document) from her former husband, but she cannot divorce him or be divorced from him if he is unwilling to end the marriage. In the contemporary era, this inequality continues to be a significant disability for women in Orthodox and Ultra-Orthodox communities (see *AGUNAH*; JUDAISM, ORTHODOX: MODERN ORTHODOX; JUDAISM, ORTHODOX: ULTRA-ORTHODOX).

In response to some of these inequities, rabbinic *halakhah* introduced various protections for women into the marriage process. To address women's economic vulnerability in case of divorce or widowhood, a husband was obligated to promise his wife a financial settlement in the *ketubbah* (marriage contract). Rabbinic requirements that a *get* be written with permanent ink on an enduring surface in a standard form, including the names of the man, the woman, and the date, shielded a woman against later claims that her divorce was not valid. Similarly, if a man canceled a *get* without informing his wife, his marriage could be annulled by the court; a man who falsely claimed he issued a *get* under duress could be subject to corporal punishment. These were protections for women against financial blackmail from ex-husbands, and they also were ways of guarding against children of a later marriage being declared illegitimate (*mamzerim*), a highly complicated and irrevocable status in *halakhah*. The need for such rulings is also indicative of a divorced woman's unequal and vulnerable status.

The Rabbis ruled that, although a husband may divorce his wife for vaguely defined "unseemly matters," he must divorce her if she commits a sexual transgression. If a wife is divorced for a sexual or religious infraction, including refusing conjugal relations, her husband is generally not obligated to make the promised *ketubbah* payment. Sometimes a woman would deliberately refuse to immerse in the *mikveh following her state of *niddah, precluding marital relations, to engineer a way out of an uncongenial marriage, even though this meant losing her financial settlement. R. *Meir ben Barukh of Rothenberg tried to combat this strategem in thirteenth-century *Ashkenaz by ruling that a *moredet*, a rebellious wife, had to give up not only her *ketubbah* but also all personal property and private wealth that she had inherited or acquired through her business undertakings.

The Talmud does allow certain conditions when a woman may request the rabbinic *court (*beit din) to compel her husband to divorce her; an example is a childless marriage (see INFERTILITY). By the period of the *Geonim, women were also successful in petitioning the court to compel a divorce if a husband had a repulsive physical condition or violated his marital obligations. Some authorities were sympathetic to women who claimed sexual incompatibility or spousal abuse.

Evidence from the Cairo *Genizah indicates that in medieval Muslim lands some Jews did not follow the unilateral rabbinic *ketubbah* issued in the husband's name, but used an alternate marriage contract originating in the Land of *Israel based on a statement of mutual obligations. These contracts defined marriage as a partnership and promised a wife the right to initiate divorce proceedings if she found herself unable to live with her husband; this *ketubbah* was unknown among Jews in Christian countries and did not survive in mainstream Jewish practice.

The medieval Jewish communities of *France and *Germany enacted important reforms in divorce law. R. *Gershom of Mainz (eleventh century) is credited with ruling that a man could not divorce his wife against her will, an indication of the high status of women in this milieu. A thirteenth-century innovation declared that divorce was a public matter requiring approval by community representatives as well as by the couple involved; this development protected women by making divorce more difficult to obtain.

For further reading, see R. Biale, *Women and Jewish Law* (1995); Z. W. Falk, *Jewish Matrimonial Law in the Middle Ages* (1966); M. Friedman, "Marriage as an Institution: Jewry under Islam," in *The Jewish Family: Metaphor and Memory*, ed. D. Kraemer (1989), 31–45; A. Grossman, *Pious and Rebellious: Jewish Women in Medieval Europe* (2004); J. R. Baskin, "Male Piety, Female Bodies: Men, Women, and Ritual Immersion in Medieval Ashkenaz," *Journal of Jewish Law* 17 (2007): 11–30.   JUDITH R. BASKIN

Documentary Hypothesis. See BIBLE: MODERN SCHOLARSHIP

Dov Ber of Międzyrzecz (d. 1772), known as the *Maggid* (preacher) of Międzyrzecz, was the best known and most influential disciple of Israel *Baal Shem Tov (the Besht), the founder of the *Ḥasidic movement. In 1760, after the Besht's death, Dov Ber established, in Międzyrzecz, Poland, the first Ḥasidic court, in which the foundations of a Ḥasidic community were outlined. His meeting with the Besht is described in *Shivḥei ha-Besht* (The Praises of the Besht [1815]), as an encounter between two mystics who dedicated themselves to the study of ancient Hebrew texts. The conduct of Dov Ber's court is described in the autobiography of the philosopher Salomon *Maimon, who spent time there in his youth. The *Maggid*, like his teacher, did not write books, but his sermons were collected by his disciples and published in several volumes, the best known of which is *Maggid devarav le-Yaakov* (Preaching to [the Sons] of Jacob [1781]). The unusual group of charismatic, inspiring leaders who came out of his court and established the network of Ḥasidic communities in the last decades of the eighteenth century included Elimelech of Lizhensk, Levi Isaac of Berdichev, Schneur ben Baruch *Zalman of Liady, and others. For further reading, see R. Shatz, *Hasidism as Mysticism* (1992).   JOSEPH DAN

Drama: See entries under THEATER

Dreyfus Affair is a landmark event in the histories of modern *France and of European *antisemitism. In 1894, Captain Alfred Dreyfus, a Jewish army officer, was falsely charged with treason. This sensational accusation and the guilty verdict of a closed-door military tribunal resulted in the formal court-martial and degradation of Dreyfus in 1896. Journals that appeared overnight enflamed public opinion, splitting the nation into pro- and anti-Dreyfusard camps and elevating disputes over Dreyfus's guilt into an international media affair. The Dreyfus Affair reinforced traditional distinctions in class and party that had divided French society since the end of the French Revolution and strengthened powerful affiliations among the military, the church, and the state. New social designations such as the "intellectual" and the "nationalist" emerged to define public spokespersons in the pro- and anti-Dreyfus camps.

Caught in the tense fray, the "Jew" became the stereotypical focal point for both sides. At once an exemplar for the defense of *les droits de l'homme* ("the rights of man") and a scapegoat for the ills of the Republic, including financial scandals, the "Jew" also became the centerpiece of new forms of antisemitic propaganda that combined past prejudices with new fears. After much public pressure to appeal the case, handwriting experts discounted clear evidence of forged documents, and a second guilty verdict was returned.

The victimized Dreyfus continued his solitary confinement on Devil's Island and was fully exonerated only in 1906.

Emmanuel *Levinas considered the Dreyfus Affair the "great psychological turning point" for modern *emancipated Jewry. Although the case ended in the triumph of morality, it also revealed the fragility of reason in modern democracies and suggested the need for a new vigilance among assimilated Jews in modern nations. The idea of the "Jew" that emerged during the Dreyfus Affair – an idea at once religious, ethnic, racial, and cultural – created new socio-political relationships for Jews, their supporters, and their enemies. Bernard Lazare, the "first Dreyfusard" and one of very few outspoken Jews to support Dreyfus's appeal, went on to battle Jewish poverty and oppression throughout *Eastern Europe. The writer Émile Zola, one of Dreyfus's most celebrated intellectual supporters, condemned government-sponsored discrimination; the Dreyfus Affair figures significantly in Marcel Proust's magisterial novel, *À la recherche du temps perdu* (1913–1927). Witnessing the degradation of Dreyfus, Theodore *Herzl conceived the *Zionist project in *Palestine as a response to what he believed was widespread and ineradicable European antisemitism. French leftist anarchists and right-wing reactionaries united in antisemitic nationalism with long-term and devastating effects (see ANTISEMITISM: FRANCE).

The Dreyfus Affair challenged the democratic culture of Western Europe, the limits of tolerance, and definitions of national identity. It helped shape legislation in France to separate state and religion that was signed into law in 1905. The French secular state that grew from this legislation maintains unique characteristics to the present day. Recent scholarship includes M. Winock, *Nationalism, Anti-Semitism, and Fascism in France* (1998); and R. Harris, *Dreyfus: Politics, Emotion, and the Scandal of the Century* (2010).   EVLYN GOULD

Dualism: In Ancient Judaism. The Latin *duo* (two) postulates two irreducible principles, one good and one evil, as the ultimate causes of the world and its constitutive elements. Ancient Judaism used dualistic language but never adopted a full dualistic system integrating cosmic, ethical, and temporal dimensions. The Hebrew *Bible contains dualistic elements, but no dualistic doctrine, because *God always remains the unchallenged authority. In the creation narrative, God alone acts: Light and darkness are opposed, but darkness is never considered an autonomous source of *evil (Gen 1:2–4; cf. Isa 45:7). On the ethical level, humankind is not divided between two camps, good and evil; rather, human beings are responsible for their own decisions (Deut 30:15–20; Ezek 18). In terms of temporality, good and evil presently coexist, but God is expected to bring every deed into judgment, to exterminate the wicked, and to grant happiness, *resurrection, or everlasting life to the righteous (Joel 1:15; Ps 112; Eccl 12:14; Dan 12:3).

Divine transcendence is never questioned in the *Dead Sea Scrolls. However, a "soft" dualism is developed, namely in the "Instruction on the Two Spirits" (1QS 3:13–4:26). According to this text, God "created humankind [...] and He has provided it with two spirits according to which to behave until the fixed time of His visitation." These spirits, truth and deceit, have their origins in light and darkness, respectively. Their leaders, a Prince of Light and an Angel of Darkness, extend their dominion over two separate groups of human beings (their "sons") and influence their behavior. At the time of God's visitation, the followers of each spirit will be either rewarded or punished, truth will rise up forever, and deceit will be totally destroyed. Similar ideas are found in the "War of the Sons of Light against the Sons of Darkness" (1QM) and in several additional texts.

Dualistic thinking appears in other writings of the *Second Temple period. The Ethiopic Apocalypse of *Enoch attributes the origin of evil to fallen angels; it describes the present time as a struggle between the cosmic powers, parallel to the one opposing the righteous and the wicked, until the final judgment (1 Enoch 6–16; 91–107). The Book of Jubilees (found in the *Pseudepigrapha) identifies the prince of the demons, Mastema, as responsible for both the problem of evil and the tension between Israel and the nations (Jubilees 17:15–18:13; 48:1–4, 9–19). The Testaments of the Twelve Patriarchs (also found in the Pseudepigrapha) implies a sharp division between the spirit of truth and the spirit of error: The Patriarchs teach their descendants an elaborated doctrine of the two ways, one led by the Angel of the Lord, the other by Belial, until the last days, when evil will be definitely eradicated (Testament of Judah 20:1–5; Testament of Dan. 6:1–10; Testament of Asher 1:3–9; Testament of Joseph 20:2). In ancient Judaism, dualistic terminology was a tool through which various groups elaborated worldviews to make sense of their own situation, legitimated their particular interpretation of the *Torah and their commitment to it, and nourished their hope to be finally vindicated by God.   JEAN DUHAIME

Dubnow, Simon (1860–1941), a self-taught Jewish historian, publicist, and ideologue was born in Mstislavl, *Belorussia. From 1880 until 1922 he lived in *Russia (mostly in *Saint Petersburg); subsequently he resided in *Berlin. In 1933 he moved to Riga, *Latvia, where he was murdered by the *Nazis during the liquidation of the Riga ghetto (see HOLOCAUST entries).

Dubnow was one of the founders of the Jewish Historico-Ethnographical Society and an editor (1909–18) of its quarterly *Yevreiskaya Starina*. From 1908 through 1914 he taught Jewish history at the Courses on Oriental (Jewish) Studies established by Baron David Guenzburg in Saint Petersburg and, from 1919, at the Jewish People's University. Dubnow's three-volume *History of Jews in Russia and Poland* (1916–20) influenced a generation of Jewish historians. His major work was the ten-volume *World History of the Jewish People* (1925–29). His memoirs-diary, *Kniga zhizny* (Book of my Life), is a valuable testimony of his era seen from a Jewish viewpoint.

Dubnow saw Jews as one people with one history that had developed in a succession of "hegemonic centers" (*Babylon, *Spain, *Poland, etc.). He developed a theory of Jewish ex-territorial autonomy, based on modernized democratic communities, as a tool for Jewish national survival in the *Diaspora. He founded the Jewish People's Party (1906)

with his autonomist political platform. Dubnow was ambivalent toward *Zionism, which he saw as an appealing but dangerous political adventure.   MICHAEL BEIZER

Dunash ben Labrat, tenth-century Hebrew *grammarian and poet, is commonly credited with introducing Arabic-style prosody, poetics, and themes to the Jews of tenth-century *Spain. Accordingly, he is regarded as the founder of the Andalusian school of Hebrew *poetry. Ben Labrat was born in Morocco (see NORTH AFRICA) and later studied in Baghdad under *Saadia Gaon, the communal leader and most important rabbinic intellectual of the period (see *IRAQ). By mid-century, Ben Labrat was drawn to Umayyad Cordoba and the circle around the influential Jewish courtier and communal leader Ḥasdai ibn Shaprut (see SPAIN, MUSLIM). There he managed to displace Ibn Shaprut's previous court-poet and secretary, Menaḥem ibn Saruk, and he went on to engage Ibn Saruk's students in a fierce debate over his Arabic-style Hebrew metrics as well as the introduction of comparative (i.e., Arabic) philology to the study of *Biblical Hebrew. Only thirteen of Dunash's poems have survived intact, and they include both liturgical and social compositions. See P. Cole, *The Dream of the Poem* (2007), 23–27.   ROSS BRANN

Dura Europos, the site of a late antique city in present-day Syria, contains the most important single artifact of ancient Jewish art. The walls of its synagogue (ca. 245 CE) are covered with the earliest surviving biblically themed paintings. **See ART: LATE ANTIQUITY; and SYNAGOGUES, ANCIENT.**

Dybbuk, "attachment," is a popular term, which is used mainly in *Yiddish, from the Hebrew root DVK. It indicates the entrance of a second soul to a person's body (often used in the form *dybbuk-ra*, an "evil affliction"). This belief originated in the concept of reincarnation of souls, which developed in *Kabbalah at the end of the twelfth century. The original term for this phenomenon was *ibbur*, another soul that was conceived within a person's body; the term *gilgul* referred to the transportation of a soul from body to body. Since the sixteenth century a score or more narratives have been written describing the procedure of extracting the intruding soul from the body it entered; many of these narratives were written by well-known scholars, including figures like Ḥayyim Vital, the great disciple of Isaac *Luria in sixteenth-century *Safed. In most cases the *dybbuk* is the soul of a sinner who was refused entrance to the treasury of souls (see G. Scholem, *On the Mystical Shape of the Godhead* [1991]).

This mystical tradition inspired S. Ansky's 1914 Yiddish play, "The Dybbuk or Between Two Worlds," which was extremely popular in the first half of the twentieth century. The 1937 film version, produced in *Warsaw and directed by Michał Waszyński, is considered a masterpiece of Yiddish *film (see THEATER, YIDDISH).   JOSEPH DAN

E

Eastern Europe. There is no generally accepted definition of the regions and countries that constitute Eastern Europe. For the purposes of Jewish history and culture as they are discussed in this volume, Eastern Europe refers to the pre-1917 Russian Empire, including the areas of *Poland and *Lithuania that became part of *Russia after the late-eighteenth-century partitions of Poland. In addition, this designation includes the Polish province of *Galicia and other parts of Poland that became part of the *Habsburg Empire after the first partition of Poland in 1772, as well as those parts of Poland that fell under Prussian control (see *Germany).

Ecclesiastes, a book in the *"Writings" section of the Hebrew *Bible is found in the collection of *Five Scrolls that follows the books of *Psalms, *Proverbs, and *Job. With Proverbs and Job, it comprises biblical "wisdom literature" (see BIBLE: WISDOM LITERATURE). Jewish tradition identified King *Solomon as the author, but the book attributes itself more ambiguously to "Kohelet son of *David, king in *Jerusalem" (1:1), and the book's language shows that it was written no earlier than the *Persian period. "Ecclesiastes" is simply Greek for *kohelet*, "one who convenes an assembly." Uniquely in the Hebrew Bible, this book is framed as a first-person description of one man's search for wisdom. The kingly persona enables the author to portray his search as aided by limitless wealth and power.

Yet the search is portrayed as futile. "There is nothing new under the sun" (1:9), and life can best be described with Kohelet's theme word, *hevel*. This is the word famously translated in the King James Version as "vanity"; it has also been understood as "futility" and "existential absurdity." However, its basic meaning in Biblical Hebrew is "vapor" or something that is ephemeral. Life, for Kohelet, offers nothing solid to be grasped. Rather, it is "utter illusion" – for "the race is not to the swift, nor the battle to the strong, neither yet bread to the wise, nor yet riches to men of understanding, nor yet favor to men of skill; but time and chance happen to them all" (9:11).

Despite its skeptical tone, Ecclesiastes is read in the synagogue on the *Sabbath that falls during *Sukkot, perhaps because of its essentially autumnal quality. Moreover, the words, "man has no superiority over beast, for they all are *hevel*" (3:19), are traditionally recited every morning – immediately followed by the assertion, "but we are your *covenant people." According to BT *Shabbat* 30b, the Rabbis wished to exclude Ecclesiastes from the Bible; indeed, the *midrash compilation *Leviticus Rabbah* points out that Kohelet's advice to follow one's own desires (11:9) directly contradicts Numbers 15:39, repeated twice a day as part of the third paragraph of the *shema*. Ultimately, the book was saved by its attribution in 1:1 to "the son of David, king in Jerusalem" and its conclusion, in 12:9–14, a later addition: "The sum of the matter, when all is said and done: Revere God and observe His commandments!"

In the twentieth century, author Ernest Hemingway drew on Ecclesiastes for his title, *The Sun Also Rises* (1:5), and folksinger Pete Seeger used its words for a twentieth-century popular song, "Turn, Turn, Turn" (based on 3:1–8). This modern usage was only fitting, because Ecclesiastes itself, as is characteristic of wisdom writings, drew on ancient *Near Eastern literature, most famously in the advice to "Let your clothes always be freshly washed, and your head never lack ointment. Enjoy happiness with a woman you love" (9:8–9), originally from the *Epic of Gilgamesh*. For further reading, see M. V. Fox, *A Time to Tear Down and a Time to Build Up: A Re-Reading of Ecclesiastes* (1999).   MICHAEL CARASIK

Ecclesiasticus: See WISDOM OF BEN SIRA

Ecology. The literary and religious sources of Judaism offer an abundance of theological principles about nature that support an ecological worldview. All are based on the belief that *God created the world and all its inhabitants.

BIBLICAL AND RABBINIC SOURCES: The creation narrative of Genesis 1–2:3 depicts creation of the material world as an act of ordering unordered chaos (*tohu va-vohu*). This act involves the separation of light from darkness, water above from water below, dry land from the seas, vegetation from animals, aquatic animals from air and land animals, and finally humans from other land animals. The final act of creation is the institution of the *Sabbath. In this narrative, created nature is not divine, nor is it identified with the Creator. However, one created being, the human, is presented as different from all others, because it was made in the "divine image" (*tzelem elohim*, 1:26). The meaning of this phrase has been much debated, but it is evident that it is creation in the divine image that empowers humans to have dominion over other created entities. Although the human species is privileged, the earth belongs to God, and humans do not have the right to exploit its natural resources.

This doctrine of creation, which recognizes the gulf between the Creator and the created world, facilitates an interest in the natural world. As Psalm 19:1 proclaims, "The heavens declare the glory of God/ and the firmament proclaims God's handiwork." Psalm 148 depicts all of creation praising God and God's commanding power over nature. In these and other psalms, awareness of nature's orderliness, regularity, and beauty always points to the divine Creator. Prophetic texts are rich with metaphors and similes from the plant world. In *Jeremiah the almond tree represents old age, the vine and the fig tree depict coming desolation and destruction, and the olive tree is a common reference for longevity. In one famous parable, fruit trees and vines serve humans by providing oil, fruit, and wine (Judg 9:8–13). Conversely, nature does God's bidding when it punishes the people of Israel when they sin; indeed, ungodly behavior leads to ecological punishment. God is the sole Creator who may sustain or destroy nature (Ps 29:5–6; Zech 11:1–3; Hab 3:5–8). Mostly the *Bible emphasizes divine care of all creatures: God provides food to all (Ps 147:9), is concerned about humans and beasts (Pss 104:14, 145:16), and extends care to all; and they turn to God in time of need (Pss 104: 21, 27, 147:9; Job 38:41).

The Rabbis taught that God "did not create a single thing that is useless. Even those creatures that may appear superfluous, such as serpents, scorpions, flies, fleas, or gnats, they too are part of the entirety of creation" (BT *Shabbat* 77b; *Genesis Rabbah* 10:7; *Exodus Rabbah* 10:1). Various rabbinic tales remind humans that the gnat was created first (BT *Sanhedrin* 38a). In daily prayers, the worshiper sanctifies nature by expressing gratitude to the Creator "who in goodness creates each day." The prayers recognize the daily changes in the rhythm of nature – morning, evening, and night – and acknowledge God's control of the natural world, as do the *blessings that Jews are required to utter when they witness a storm or observe a tree. The observant Jew blesses God for the natural functions of the human body and for the food that God provides for nourishment. It is the consecration of the natural order to God that endows all activities with proper religious meaning.

This sanctification of nature is evident in the rabbinic reinterpretation of the biblical pilgrimage *festivals. *Sukkot (Festival of Booths, Feast of Ingathering) celebrated the harvest of summer crops and the preparation of the fields for winter; Pesah (*Passover; Feast of the Unleavened Bread) began with the *New Moon of the month just preceding the hardening of the barley, and *Shavuot (Feast of Weeks, Pentecost) celebrated the barley harvest, when reaping began (Exod 34:22; Deut 16:10). These agrarian activities were given historical-religious meaning in the Bible, linking them to the wilderness experience, the Exodus from *Egypt, and the giving of the *Torah at Sinai, respectively. Sukkot in particular illustrates how the Rabbis reinterpreted the natural origins of the pilgrimage festivals after the destruction of the *Temple. The Rabbis elaborated the symbolic meaning of the *sukkah*, viewing it as a sacred home and the locus for the divine presence. They homiletically linked the four species associated with the festival – the citron (*etrog*) and the willow, myrtle, and palm that comprised the *lulav* – to parts of the human body, to types of people, to the three *patriarchs, the four matriarchs, and even to God. The festival of Sukkot concluded with another festival, *Shemini Atzeret (Eighth Day of Assembly), which included prayers to God to deliver rain.

Placing limits on human consumption of animals and regulating all food sources are major concerns of the Bible and its Holiness Code. The laws of Leviticus 11 and Deuteronomy 14 are part of an elaborate system of *purity and impurity that affected the *Temple and the *priesthood, as well as the lives of individual Israelites. In general, the Torah prohibits eating the meat of certain creatures that are classified as impure or unclean, ingesting the blood of any animals, consuming animal fat (*helev*), and eating meat of the carcass (*nevelah*) of dead animals and fowls. More particularly, the Bible spells out which animals are permitted and which are forbidden for human consumption. The differentiation between "clean" and "unclean" animals, which is the core of Jewish *dietary laws (*kashrut*), has generated significant discussion about their internal logic. Some scholars explained that the unclean animals were a threat to life, whereas others suggested that forbidden animals were those regarded as deities in neighboring cultures. Still others considered the

means of locomotion as the crucial classification principle. Yet it is also possible to understand the prohibition on consuming certain animals as ecologically motivated. The Bible permits the husbandry and consumption of ruminants, animals that make the most efficient use of vegetation. Other animals (the horse, mule, and camel), which were domesticated, could be kept by farmers for transportation and fieldwork, but not for consumption. The cow was used for work and for milk and meat, the sheep and goat for milk and meat only. Permitted aquatic animals must have fins and scale (i.e., fish) but frogs, toads, and newts were not to be eaten, perhaps because the biblical authors were aware that they are beneficial to the ecosystem and cut down on the mosquito population. Lobsters, oysters, and mussels are also forbidden, most likely because the coast of *Palestine is not suited for them. All birds of prey, including owls, were forbidden for human consumption, as well as all storks, ibises, herons, and species of bats. Because many of the forbidden species were common in the Land of *Israel, it is possible to view these prohibitions as extended environmental protection in the interest of maintaining ecological equilibrium.

Deuteronomy 22:6–7 is concerned with the lives of nonhuman animals. If one finds a nest on the ground or on a tree with young ones or eggs in it and "the mother [is] sitting upon the young or upon the eggs, you shall not take the mother with the young; you shall let the mother go, but the young you may take to yourself, that it may go well with you and that you may live long." By saving the mother, the law enables the species to continue to reproduce itself and avoid potential extinction. This law is elaborated in *Deuteronomy Rabbah* 6:5, BT *Hullin* 138b–142a, and *Sifre Deuteronomy* 227, specifying that the person who finds the nest is only allowed to take the nestlings if they are not fledged. This concern suggests a notion of the sustained use of resources.

Attentiveness to the needs of animals was also a major concern of rabbinic tradition. On the basis of Deuteronomy 22:6, the Rabbis articulated the general principle of *tza`ar baalei hayyim* (literally "distress of living creatures") that prohibits the affliction of needless suffering on animals. They considered this one of seven commandments given to the sons of Noah that are binding on all human beings. The obligation to release the ass from its burden (Exod 23:5) – that is, to assist the owner in unloading merchandise or materials from a beast of burden – and a similar obligation to come to the assistance of a fallen animal (Deut 22:4) are understood by rabbinic sources (BT *Bava Metzia* 32b) as duties rooted in the concern for the financial loss that would be suffered by the animal's master were the animal to collapse under the weight of the burden. Although human needs generally take precedence over the suffering of animals, there are cases in which the Rabbis privilege the needs of animals. Thus, Deuteronomy 1:15 is understood as forbidding a person to eat before his or her animals have been fed (BT *Berakhot* 41a; *Gittin* 62a). Similarly, one is permitted to buy animals only if one can provide assurance that they will be fed (JT *Yevamot* 15:3; *Ketubbot* 4:8). The medieval rabbinic leader, physician, and philosopher, Moses *Maimonides, codified these traditions and taught that the concern for animal welfare is linked to the cultivation of a moral human personality (*Guide of the Perplexed* 3:17).

RECENT DEVELOPMENTS: Since the 1970s, Jews have confronted the charge that the Judeo-Christian tradition is the primary cause of the current environmental crisis. This is said to be because Genesis 1:28 gives humans "dominion" over the earth and its inhabitants. Orthodox thinkers were the first to defend *Judaism, demonstrating that such readings of the Bible are based on misunderstandings of the text or attest ignorance of the post-biblical Jewish tradition. In the 1970s and 1980s Jews from all branches of modern *Judaism – Reform, Conservative, Reconstructionist, and Humanistic – began to reflect on ecological concerns in light of Jewish religious sources. Jewish voices are now a part of the well-established discourse on religion and ecology and the ecological wisdom of the Jewish tradition is widely recognized.

By the 1990s Jewish environmentalism had also begun to affect the organized Jewish community. In 1993 the Coalition on the Environment and Jewish Life (COEJL) was founded as an umbrella group of twenty-nine Jewish organizations with thirteen regional affiliates. COEJL has promoted environmental education, scholarship, advocacy, and action in efforts to deepen the Jewish community's commitment to the stewardship of creation and to mobilize Jewish life and learning to protect the Earth and all its inhabitants. COEJL emphasizes environmental justice; the prevention of harm; energy independence; equitable distribution of responsibility among individuals, corporations, governments, and nations; pollution prevention; proper treatment of nuclear waste; energy conservation; utility regulation; and the promotion of sustainable development. COEJL is part of a larger network of religious *interfaith organizations that attempt to shape environmental policies on municipal, state, and federal levels. In *Israel too, there are significant attempts to anchor environmentalism in the sources of Judaism.

In the early-twenty-first century, Jewish environmentalism continues to grow, especially on a grassroot level. Many communities now celebrate the festival of *Tu B'Shevat as a "Jewish Earth Day," and Jewish newspapers regularly report on environmental issues in connection with this festival. A growing body of scholarly literature makes it possible to teach college-level courses on Judaism and ecology. Awareness of environmental concerns has also led to the "greening" of Jewish institutions. Still, Jews have found that certain assumptions, widely taken for granted by secular environmentalists, conflict with Jewish tradition. For example, a Jewish environmental philosophy and ethics cannot be based on a simplistic version of pantheism that does not acknowledge anything beyond the world itself. From a Jewish perspective, "biocentrism" constitutes an idolatrous worship of nature. To speak from the sources of Judaism, one must affirm that God created the world and that divine *revelation is possible. It is precisely because humans are created with the capacity to transcend nature that they are commanded by God to protect the world. Therefore, a Jewish environmental philosophy and ethics cannot give up the primacy of the human species in the created order, notwithstanding the fact that some proponents of "deep ecology" now regard "species-ism" as an unacceptable view. In a view true to Jewish teaching, human beings must first love and respect themselves if they are going to be able to love and respect other species. Yet the love of one's fellow human beings goes hand in hand with human responsibility toward other species created by God. Similarly, Jewish environmentalism cannot simplistically preach zero popula-

tion growth. The obligation to procreate is unambiguously articulated in Genesis and has become a necessity after the *Holocaust. Of course, it is possible to interpret the injunction "to be fruitful and multiply and fill the earth" to mean "to reach the maximum population sustainable at an acceptable standard of living but do not exceed it."

The main challenges to Jewish environmentalism come from within. In Israel and in the United States, the religious sources of Judaism do not inform the identity of most Jews, and secular Jews do not appeal to them in their attempt to address environmental concerns. Jews who come to environmentalism from a Jewish religious commitment face other challenges because contemporary environmental philosophy and ethics are predominantly secular. Religiously committed Jews must become familiar with a vast literature whose worldview and philosophical assumptions not only conflict with the beliefs of Judaism but are also in some cases self-consciously "neo-pagan." This is especially evident in nature-based feminist spirituality that promotes goddess worship to overcome the deterioration of nature allegedly caused by the masculinist "Judeo-Christian tradition." Likewise, the biocentrism of "deep ecology" conflicts with the anthropocentric stance of Judaism, which is the basis of its ethics of stewardship and responsibility toward nature. Jews can develop a Jewish eco-theology for the twenty-first century, but doing so will require a significant reinterpretation of Judaism in light of contemporary science, especially the biological sciences, which are in the midst of a major transformation.

For further reading, see R. Aubrey, ed., *Judaism and Ecology* (1992); E. Bernstein, ed., *Ecology and the Jewish Spirit: Where Nature and the Sacred Meet* (1998); idem, *The Splendor of Creation: A Biblical Ecology* (2005); E. Eisenberg, *The Ecology of Eden* (1998); A. Elon, N. M. Hyman, and A. Waskow, eds., *Trees, Earth and Torah: A Tu B'Shevat Anthology* (1999); R. H. Isaacs, *The Jewish Sourcebook on the Environment and Ecology* (1998); H. Tirosh-Samuelson, ed., Judaism *and Ecology: Created World and Revealed Word* (2002); A. Waskow, ed., *Torah of the Earth: Exploring 4000 Years of Ecology in Jewish Thought* (2000); and M. D. Yaffe, ed., *Judaism and Environmental Ethics: A Reader* (2001). **See also ETHICS: ENVIRONMENTAL; ISRAEL, STATE OF: ECOLOGY.**

HAVA TIROSH-SAMUELSON

Edom refers to a region extending north–south between the Zered (Wadi el-Hesa at the southern border of Moab) and the Red Sea. Its eastern border was formed by the Aravah; to the west, Edom extended to the Arabian Desert. The "kings' highway" (Num 21:22) ran north–south. Edom first appears in *Egyptian records in the thirteenth century, when much of the population was pastoralist. Copper mining in the Aravah was also important. Not until the eighth–seventh centuries BCE were permanent settlements established, at sites such as the capital Buseirah and the port of Tall al-Kheleifeh. Agriculture sustained the northern part of the country.

According to the *Bible, Edom shared roots with Israel through *Isaac's son *Esau (Gen 25:29–30). Subsequent narratives reflect military tensions between Israel and Edom (obstacle to *Moses [Num 20:14–21]; conquest by *David [2 Sam 8:13–14; 1 Kgs 11:14–16] and Uzziah, [2 Kgs 14:7]; and independence under Jehoram [2 Kgs 8:20–22] and Ahaz

[2 Kgs 16:6]). The *prophets reflected this hostility. Even as Edom fell under the control of *Assyrians and *Babylonians, Edomites pushed west into the Negev Desert. They settled at sites such as Horvat `Uza and Horvat Qitmit, where sanctuaries to their god Qos have been uncovered. The Edomites/Idumeans were conquered by the *Hasmoneans in the late second century BCE and forcibly converted to Judaism. It was to them that the *Herodian dynasty, the *Roman client-rulers of Judea in the first centuries BCE and CE, traced their ancestry. In rabbinic writings, Edom is used as a euphemism for *Rome; in later Jewish texts, it refers to Christians and *Christianity. **Maps 2, 3**

BETH ALPERT NAKHAI

Education, Boys: Medieval and Early Modern.

Education in the medieval and Early Modern periods, as throughout Jewish history before the twentieth century, was gendered. This entry discusses education for males; female education is discussed in the following entry. In medieval *Ashkenaz (*Germany and northern *France), boys began *Torah study at age five or six with an initiation ceremony at the *synagogue, often on *Shavuot (see CONSECRATION). The child was instructed to recite certain letters and verses that were written on a honey-covered tablet; he would then eat the honey, symbolizing the Torah he would incorporate. Education took place in informal settings; fathers would hire a tutor for a specific period of time or to teach a particular skill or text. Beyond occasional calls for affluent parents to include the children of those without means, communities had no formal mechanism to ensure that every child was taught. More formal educational structures and arrangements were established in both *Spain and *Provence and in Muslim lands on the elementary and more advanced levels.

A child was typically taught to recognize the (Hebrew) letters and then to understand how they formed words before moving on to the weekly Torah (together with the *Aramaic *Targum and *Rashi's commentary) and *haftarah portions. More extensive biblical readings and eventually *Talmud study followed. At thirteen or so, the capable child might join a local study hall or travel to an academy. Tutors were usually senior students, who often lived in the homes of their employers. Jewish boys in Muslim environments were often taught the rudiments of secular studies as well. It is not clear how young men advanced from elementary to more advanced studies; economic factors probably prevented many from making this transition. Local study halls (usually in the synagogue) enabled men to engage in some form of daily morning and evening study before or after communal *worship. *Sefer Ḥasidim* advises that informal study ought to be commensurate with the abilities of the student and according to his interests and proclivities. Those who prefer to study Scripture or *midrash rather than the Talmud should do so, and the study of practical Jewish law should also be encouraged (see MIDDLE AGES: ḤASIDEI ASHKENAZ).

A document of uncertain provenance entitled *Sefer Ḥukkei ha-Torah* describes a possibly theoretical system of tutors and schools that advanced promising younger students to elite study halls. Passages in *Sefer Ḥasidim* and other *Tosafist works suggest that some students traveled to an academy to study Talmud around the age of thirteen. They brought

funds for their sustenance and probably returned home for the holidays; such students often wandered from *yeshivah to *yeshivah*. The leading academies were relatively small, and typically their students lodged in the home of the teacher, and perhaps in several surrounding dwellings as well. The dining area in the teacher's home was the place of learning. Although these conditions may have ensured that the students were of similar (high) ability, it remains unclear exactly what was being taught in the large number of non-Tosafist academies or study halls spread throughout medieval Ashkenaz.

Tosafist academies were centers of vigorous debate with many similarities to contemporaneous cathedral schools in France and Germany. Indeed, virtually all of the most important cathedral schools and masters in northern France, as well as the leading Tosafist academies, were within eighty miles of Paris in varying directions. Certainly, the rules and extent of debate differed somewhat in these institutions, but both the cathedral schools and the Tosafist academies featured charismatic teachers as well as students who could at times equal or best their teachers in their reasoning and argumentation.

Evidence for educational structures in Spain and Provence during the twelfth and thirteenth centuries suggests that the leading talmudic academies were somewhat larger and more formal institutions than in Ashkenaz; often they were supported by local communities or regions. Students in these schools did not challenge and debate their teachers to the same extent as in Ashkenaz. Unlike Tosafist literature, in which students are often cited for the questions that they raised and the responses that they offered, the extensive commentaries of the leading Spanish talmudists in the twelfth and thirteenth centuries (such as R. Meir Abulafia, *Naḥmanides, and R. Solomon ben Aderet [Rashba]) assign a much smaller role to students. It appears that the larger, more formal (and more supportive) academies in Spain were necessary to attract students to high-level talmudic study.

Recent research has demonstrated that Ashkenazic rabbinic scholars were also engaged in *biblical interpretation, in the writing and interpretation of *piyyut* (see POETRY, LITURGICAL), and in certain forms of *mysticism and rationalistic conception. However, it is evident that the educational paths available in Spain, Provence, and Muslim lands were far more variegated. In these lands, full-fledged philosophers, mystics, biblical exegetes, and *grammarians coexisted with talmudic scholars, and they often encouraged syntheses among these disciplines as well. These educational and curricular differences explain why the passions raised by the *Maimonidean controversy, for example, as well as the excesses that sometimes resulted from intense philosophical or mystical study, were barely felt in Ashkenazic lands.

In the Early Modern period, the extent to which talmudic studies should be blended with these other areas of intellectual inquiry remained a central question, especially as large-scale *expulsions and other tumultuous events brought Ashkenazic and Sephardic Jews together in new configurations and locales. Pre-modern Jewish communities took a greater interest in ensuring that as many of their sons as possible were provided with the rudiments of education. In the late fifteenth and early sixteenth centuries, R. Judah Loew, Maharal of *Prague, for example, proposed a form of educational revisionism, derived principally from a series of passages in *Avot*, that would match a boy's abilities and his age with the material to be studied.

For further reading, see E. Kanarfogel, *Jewish Education and Society in the High Middle Ages* (1991); I. Marcus, *Rituals of Childhood: Jewish Acculturation in Medieval Europe* (1996); and S. D. Goitein, *A Mediterranean Society* 3: *The Family* (1978); and **see MIDDLE AGES: CHILDHOOD.**

EPHRAIM KANARFOGEL

Education, Girls: Medieval and Early Modern. The majority of Jewish girls in Christian Europe were instructed at home. Mothers taught their daughters cooking, needlework, and household management, as well as the *dietary laws, practices related to domestic *Sabbath and *festival observances, and the *commandments relevant to marital and family life. *Sefer Ḥasidim* ordains that young women must learn practical commandments and halakhic rules, but goes on to warn that "an unmarried man should not teach a girl, not even if the father is present, for fear that he will be sexually aroused or she will be overcome by her passions." Rather a father should teach his daughter, and a husband should teach his wife (Bologna version, par. 313).

Most medieval Ashkenazi rabbis maintained that women should not be taught the complexities of Jewish law. Typical is the teaching in *Sefer Mitzvot Gadol*, written in the early thirteenth century by Moses of Coucy, explaining that although "a woman is exempt from both the commandment to learn Torah and to teach her son, even so, if she aids her son and husband in their efforts to learn, she shares their reward for the fulfillment of that commandment" (Positive Commandment 12). Both the talmudic opinion that women earn merit by enabling male scholarly attainments through their economic endeavors and domestic support (BT *Berakhot* 17a) and the view that a woman must be instructed in the laws that apply to her life are cited by R. Moses *Isserles as accepted practice in his glosses for Ashkenazic Jewry to the sixteenth-century law code, the *Shulḥan Arukh*.

R. Jacob ben Moses Moellin (d. 1427), the Maharil, a German Jewish authority of the fifteenth century, opposed any formal religious education for girls, either from books or a tutor. In a responsum he indicated that girls can learn what they have to know from observing their parents in the home, only resorting to the local rabbi in instances of uncertainty. He gives his reasons as the rabbinic fear that an instructed woman will come to bad ways because "women's minds are weak," as well as his observation that the women of his generation seem to be adequately "knowledgeable about the laws of salting and rinsing and taking out the nerve, and the laws of the menstruating woman, and so forth" purely on the basis of home teaching (responsum 57). Although few girls were taught Hebrew, this was not seen as an impediment to women's religious practice and prayer. The statement in *Sefer Ḥasidim* – "It is better that a person pray in whatever language [the person] understands" – reflects the halakhic mainstream in its assumption that prayers in the vernacular are acceptable (*Sefer Ḥasidim*, Bologna, par. 588; *Shulḥan Arukh, Oraḥ Ḥayyim* 101). Whether medieval Jewish women in Ashkenaz had access to written texts of vernacular prayers is unknown because no manuscripts of vernacular prayers are extant from the period before the invention of *printing (see PRAYER: WOMEN'S DEVOTIONAL;

WOMEN: EARLY MODERN EUROPE; WOMEN: MODERN CENTRAL EUROPE).

Education of girls may sometimes have gone beyond the minimum knowledge necessary to fulfill legal obligations. In his fourteenth-century *ethical will, Eleazar b. Samuel of Mainz, urges all his children to attend synagogue in the morning and evening and to occupy themselves a little afterward with "Torah, the *Psalms or with works of charity." He insists that his children "must not let the young of either sex go without instruction in the Torah." A few Jewish women from rabbinical families were educated beyond the norm for their sex. Some of these women of the scholarly elite led prayers for the other women of their communities; these women include the twelfth-century Dolce, the wife of R. Eleazar ben Judah of Worms (see MIDDLE AGES: *HASIDEI ASHKENAZ*) and Urania of Worms of the thirteenth century.

It should be emphasized that Jewish women in medieval and early modern Ashkenaz were literate in the vernacular and also had a significant degree of numeracy. These were skills that were essential for their extensive business undertakings (see MONEY LENDING: MEDIEVAL AND EARLY MODERN EUROPE).

S. D. Goitein, whose magisterial studies of the documents of the Cairo *Genizah have illuminated Jewish society in the medieval Muslim realm, writes that the education of Jewish girls in this milieu was neglected to a degree not found in other periods of Jewish history. Because traditional Jewish attitudes did not advocate significant female learning, efforts to give girls a substantive religious education were rare. Moses *Maimonides (d. 1204) opposed exposing girls to traditional texts because women had no halakhic obligation to study; moreover, he believed that women lacked the mental skills required for serious *Torah study. He wrote that women should never study rabbinic legal teachings (oral Torah) because they would turn "the words of Torah into frivolity." Although he discouraged fathers from teaching their daughters written Torah, "if he did so, it is not considered as if he taught her frivolity" (*Mishneh Torah*, "Study of Torah" 1:13). Maimonides' views remained influential, not only throughout the Middle Ages but also well into the modern period. Goitein believes that the education of most Jewish women in the Muslim milieu was extremely limited, that illiteracy in all languages was common, and that knowledge of Hebrew was usually confined, at best, to being able to recite a few prayers from memory. Moreover, in some regions such as *Yemen, he notes that women were not even taught to repeat prayers. However, there were exceptions in elite learned households, particularly when there were no sons (see KURDISTAN).

Prosperous parents of girls who wished their daughters to learn essential Hebrew prayers often hired private teachers, some of whom were women. They probably also hired female teachers to instruct their daughters in needlework and other domestic skills. Embroidery and other forms of needlework were extremely important accomplishments because married women at all levels of Jewish society were expected to earn income through their handiwork. Usually a wife was permitted to keep her earnings for private use, although clauses in some Genizah marriage agreements stipulate that she provide her own clothing out of her profits. Sometimes one tutor might teach a group of girls. A responsum of Maimonides refers to a blind male teacher in Alexandria who taught Hebrew prayers to young girls. Because he was blind, the girls could dispense with their veils when studying with him (*Responsa of R. Moses b. Maimon*, 4 vols. [Hebrew], ed. Joshua Blau [Jerusalem, 1957–86], vol. 2: 524–25, no. 276). Yet, even though women were not learned, Genizah writings reveal that they were anxious to further the educations of their sons, even when doing so entailed significant financial sacrifice; this was how a Jewish woman in the Muslim world could earn approbation in the eyes of her family and her society.

For further reading, see J. R. Baskin, "The Education of Jewish Girls in the Middle Ages in Muslim and Christian Milieus" [Hebrew], *Pe'amim: Studies in Oriental Jewry* 82 (2000): 1–17; S. D. Goitein, *A Mediterranean Society*, 5 volumes (1978–88); idem, *Jewish Education in Muslim Countries: New Sources from the Geniza* (1962; [Hebrew]); A. Grossman, *Pious and Rebellious: Jewish Women in Medieval Europe* (2004); and see also MIDDLE AGES: CHILDHOOD; WOMEN: MIDDLE AGES; WOMEN: EARLY MODERN EUROPE; WOMEN: MODERN CENTRAL EUROPE.   JUDITH R. BASKIN

Education, North America: Adult. Although study has traditionally been valued as an essential component of Jewish life, adult Jewish learning did not routinely occur outside of the *Orthodox community for most of the twentieth century. By the 1980s, however, more and more Jews began to realize that their Jewish educations had failed to keep pace with their high levels of general education. At that same time, Jewish communal leaders began to place greater priority on increasing adult Jewish literacy as a means of enhancing Jewish identity and ensuring the Jewish knowledge base of policymakers. Since then, adult Jewish study programs have proliferated. Adults are motivated to engage in Jewish study for diverse reasons, which might include learning how to be a more active participant in communal worship or a search for personal meaning. Some may be seeking a greater connection to community, whereas others may be inspired by a thirst for knowledge or the desire to become Jewish role models for their children or grandchildren.

Many models and venues for adult Jewish study have developed in response to these varying motivations. In North America, programs exist in *synagogues, through institutional sponsorship by *Federations and Jewish *Community Centers, through independent programs and retreat centers, through *interfaith institutional partnerships, in private homes and offices, and through organized tours to sites of Jewish interest. Approaches to study include lectures and scholar-in-residence programs, text study groups, skill-building programs (e.g., how-to-make-Shabbat workshops, adult *b'nai mitzvah* programs), Jewish literacy offerings (ranging from single-topic programs to ongoing courses), experiential learning programs (e.g., Jewish cooking classes, Torah "yoga," social action study-and-do projects), travel programs (in local Jewish communities and to *Israel), retreats, cultural activities (including film festivals, book groups, and museum and music events that have Jewish themes), and "journey" groups that focus on Jewish identity or life transitions (e.g., workshops on "telling your Jewish story" and Jewish childbirth preparation classes). In addition to classes that meet face to face, there are distance-learning classes (including degree programs in Jewish studies), online learning opportunities (both for

self-study and e-discussion), and private tutorials (including spiritual direction activities).

Recent research points to a number of trends. Overall, the more advanced an individual's general education, the greater the likelihood of involvement in Jewish adult education. In-married Jewish adults are more involved in learning than the intermarried; however, non-Jewish partners (especially wives) are frequent Jewish learners who see themselves as the key purveyors of Jewish tradition in the family. Married adults who reside with children are more likely to be involved in adult Jewish education (especially family education) than other groups (such as childless young adults, single parents, and elderly adults with no children). Jewish women are more likely to engage in study than men, particularly in longer term programs and adult *b'nai mitzvah* preparation. Even with this wide array of venues, most adult Jewish learning takes place in synagogues. Synagogue members are more likely to participate in Jewish educational programs than unaffiliated Jews.

Although long-term courses in Jewish literacy (such as the Florence Melton Adult Mini-School and *Me'ah*) have attracted large numbers, most Jewish adults prefer shorter term programs that do not require a lengthy time commitment. This is demonstrated in the popularity of retreat programs such as Limmud New York and the biannual *Aleph Kallah* that combine serious Jewish learning with spiritual, cultural, and social activities. Yet, at the same time, in communities where long-term programs have succeeded, many "alumni" seek ongoing Jewish learning opportunities. Moreover, advanced learners are a growing communal resource who can teach others what they have learned.

Adult Jewish learning is now a central part of the Jewish communal landscape but few leaders have clearly articulated its *goals*. What kinds of changes should adult Jewish learning activities promote? Should they enhance Jewish identity, build leadership skills, strengthen Jewish communal commitments, increase Jewish literacy, or change Jewish practice? How should teachers of Jewish adults negotiate between teaching *about* Judaism and teaching students how to lead a Jewish life? At the end of the first decade of the twenty-first century, there appears to be an unspoken consensus that increasing Jewish literacy and learning inherently and automatically leads to more meaningful involvement in Jewish practices, philanthropy, and communal life. Indeed, many communal leaders accept the Talmudic dictum that "study leads to action" (BT *Kiddushin* 40b). However, little consensus has been achieved on the purposes, curriculum, and instructional philosophy of adult Jewish learning.

For further reading, see *National Jewish Population Survey* (2003); L. Grant et al., *A Journey of Heart and Mind* (2004); D. Schuster and L. Grant, "Adult Jewish Learning," *Journal of Jewish Education* 71 (2005): 179–200; L. Grant, "Finding Her Right Place in the Synagogue," in R. Prell, ed., *Women Remaking American Judaism*, (2007), 279–301; and D. Schuster, *Jewish Lives, Jewish Learning* (2003).

     DIANE TICKTON SCHUSTER AND LISA D. GRANT

Education, North America: Day Schools. Jewish day schools are private, full-time early childhood, elementary, middle, and/or secondary schools that provide Jewish children with instruction in both Jewish studies and general studies subjects within an environment purposefully directed toward the cultivation of Jewish identity. Every Jewish educational institution that provides an all-day program is ostensibly a Jewish day school but each school is unique. Among contingent and highly variable factors with respect to the mission, curriculum, and organization of any particular Jewish day school are a number of questions about how Jewish identity is defined (religious? national? cultural? linguistic? secular?), how it is meant to be developed (didactically? cooperatively? constructivistically?), with what type of curricular emphasis (Jewish literacy? general academic competence?), which personnel (composition of student body? background of teachers?), what infrastructure (administrative arrangements? financial supports? facilities and resources? relationships to the community?), and, above all, for what purposes (knowledge acquisition? behavioral modification? values clarification?).

The range of Jewish day schools includes *Ḥasidic and Ḥaredi (*Ultra-Orthodox) *yeshivot* that focus on teaching classical Jewish texts almost exclusively; *Modern Orthodox schools that value a balance between Jewish and secular studies but maintain a distinctly religious tenor throughout the school program; Solomon Schechter (*Conservative) and *Reform movement schools that promote the dictates of their denominational movements while also placing considerable emphasis on a rigorous general education; and trans-denominational (or "community") schools that attempt to meet the needs of all members of the surrounding Jewish community regardless of religious affiliation. Indeed, Jewish day schools are as variegated as the Jewish community itself and represent the entire spectrum of Jewish life.

Modern (i.e., non-Ḥaredi) day schools typically offer a bifurcated "dual curriculum" in which the school program is divided proportionately between general (secular) studies and Jewish studies. The general studies curriculum consists of the subject areas commonly found in any public or private school, including language arts, mathematics, sciences, social studies, foreign languages, and fine arts. The Judaic studies curriculum consists of some of the very same subjects that have been taught in Jewish schools for centuries, such as the Hebrew *Bible, *rabbinic literature, *Hebrew language, Jewish law codes (see *HALAKHAH*), Jewish history, Judaism, and *prayer. Generally speaking, the aim of the dual curriculum is to provide students with an adequate knowledge base both in traditional Jewish culture and modern western culture. As parodied by the novelist Cynthia Ozick in *The Cannibal Galaxy* (1983), the dual curriculum is a "scheme of learning luminous enough for a royal prince or princess," providing "lordly civilization enmeshed with lordly civilization, King David's heel caught in Victor Hugo's lyre, the metaphysicians Maimonides and Pascal, Bialik and Keats, Gemara hooked to the fires of algebra" (57). More than providing the basic instructional arrangement of the day school, however, the dual curriculum fundamentally represents a particular vision of education. The ideal product of the Jewish day school is someone who can comfortably navigate life within both the Jewish community and society at large.

In this sense, the Jewish day school is an eminently modern construct, the product of eighteenth- and nineteenth-century *Haskalah* thinking about the necessity of Jews to adopt the social mores of the countries in which they live

while still maintaining their Jewish commitments. Including secular studies in the Jewish school program would effectively demonstrate to the surrounding society that Jews were willing, capable, and deserving of the rights and privileges of citizenship, while also affording Jewish children the knowledge, skills, and dispositions they needed for full participation in modern Jewish life. What is more, it would preclude Jewish children from having to receive their secular education in state-sponsored schools that were officially nonsectarian but essentially Christian in character. The first modern day schools offering a dual religious and secular program began cropping up in the early to mid-nineteenth century in Western and *Eastern Europe and eventually in North America. By the beginning of the twentieth century, however, the burgeoning day school movement was already in decline, particularly in the United States. Public schools were becoming increasingly secularized and pluralistic, and they were progressively more geared toward the integration of new arrivals, including masses of Jews, into American society. Furthermore, in contrast to tuition-based Jewish schools, public schools were free of charge, which was no small enticement to the financially strapped yet economically striving immigrant population. Although many Orthodox Jews continued to shy away from public schooling and instead developed an extensive system of *yeshivot*, liberal and secular Jews for the most part forsook the notion of day schooling and preferred to supplement their children's public school education with Jewish afternoon and/or weekend schools.

Community priorities shifted once again in the mid-twentieth century in the aftermath of the *Holocaust and the establishment of the State of *Israel. Intensive Jewish education came to be viewed as a crucial way to promote Jewish identity, by inspiring an affinity toward Jewish customs and peoplehood, and to ensure Jewish continuity by serving as a buttress against assimilation and *intermarriage. As a result, communities and philanthropists began investing heavily in the prospect of day schooling (by 2000, the combined annual budget of North American day schools was more than $2 billion). Other factors, such as the increasing affluence, prominence, and self-actualization of the Jewish community, along with the real or perceived decline of public education and supplementary Jewish schooling, combined to propel a massive expansion of the day school enterprise. Between 1940 and 1965, the number of day schools in North America grew from thirty-five to more than three hundred, and enrollment rose from approximately 7,700 to more than 65,000 students (A. I. Schiff, *The Jewish Day School in America* [1966]). By the turn of the twenty-first century, more than seven hundred North American day schools were enrolling more than 200,000 students, and day schools were operating in Israel, *Britain, *Mexico, *South Africa, *Australia, *Russia, *Germany, and elsewhere (see www.peje.org). Although the majority of day schools are Orthodox in affiliation, the largest upsurge of late has been among the non-Orthodox.

BENJAMIN M. JACOBS

Education, United States: Hebrew Colleges. These trans-denominational institutions, founded by local Jewish communities, were established to train teachers for Jewish supplementary schools in the *United States. Early examples include Gratz College in *Philadelphia (1887); Teachers

Institute of the *Jewish Theological Seminary in *New York City (1909); the Mizrachi Organization of America/ Rabbi Isaac Elchanan in New York (1917); and Baltimore Hebrew College, now the Baltimore Hebrew Institute of Towson University (1919). Within the next decade five "sister" entities appeared: Hebrew College of *Boston (1921), now in Newton, Massachusetts; the now defunct Teacher Training School of the Hebrew Institute of Pittsburgh (1923); the College of Jewish Studies (now Spertus) in *Chicago (1924); the Hebrew Teachers Seminary (today Siegel College of Jewish Studies) in Cleveland (1926); and the Teachers Institute for Women, later part of *Yeshiva University, in 1929. Two new schools were added after World War II: the Teachers Institute of the University of Judaism in *Los Angeles in 1947 and Stern College for Women of Yeshiva University in 1954.

The colleges, founded primarily by Hebraists, *Zionists, and legatees of the East European *Haskalah, involved new approaches to education as a vehicle for cultural and ethnic transmission. Committed to *Hebrew language and culture, they also continued the work of Eastern European institutions like the ḥeder metukan, modernized Hebrew-language schools introduced in *Russia in the early twentieth century. At the same time Hebrew colleges filled a gap in American Jewish life. The considerable energy that immigrants had expended in integration and acculturation and the establishment of ethnic social welfare institutions had not been matched by equal investment in Jewish educational institutions. This gap stemmed from a lack of funds, a shortage of rabbis and trained educators, and some degree of both popular disinterest and disagreement about what Jewish education should be. The establishment of a series of local Bureaus of Jewish Education after World War I created a momentum for routinizing and standardizing Jewish education, including building modern Talmud Torahs and some oversight of teacher training.

The American context was also important. The colleges deemphasized religious ideology and embraced the Jewish cultural heritage; this approach dovetailed with contemporaneous social ideologies of cultural pluralism and of progressivism, which saw rational organization as a key to solving the myriad challenges of modern life, including higher education. Samson Benderly, the head of the New York City Jewish Kehillah's Bureau of Jewish Education, inspired a whole generation of future Jewish educational leaders with this ethos. These men and women went on to found schools and *summer camps like Yavneh and played key roles in the emerging Hebrew college movement. Camp Yavneh in particular signaled the belief that culture must be actualized through living experience, in formal and informal contexts. These educators also believed that modernized culture required intellectual deliberation. New methodology was necessary to rethink and reengineer teacher training, write new textbooks, and build new schools.

Trends in post-war America have contributed to the reformulation of Hebrew college programs, if not their larger purposes. For example, the founding of *Israel and the declining interest in intensive Jewish supplementary education led to the weakening of Hebraism as an ideology and as an approach to Jewish education. At one time, the colleges were the one place where interested intellectuals could seriously pursue advanced academic Judaic studies. The

explosion of academic *Jewish studies challenged the Hebrew Colleges' mission in that regard, and they now place a new emphasis on *adult Jewish learning.

The surviving Hebrew Colleges maintain Jewish life even as they alter it, incorporating and responding to the modern tensions between ethnicity and religion, Jewish tradition and modern notions of pluralism. They value classical notions of what constitutes Jewish culture – for example, biblical and rabbinic texts – even as they welcome new genres such as Modern Hebrew *literature that serve to expand our notion of the Jewish cultural canon.   DAVID STARR

Education, United States: Supplemental Schools. An estimated 230,000 children in *Canada and the United States receive their Jewish education in supplementary schools. According to Jack Wertheimer's 2008 report, *A Census of Jewish Supplementary Schools in the United States: 2006–2007*, published by the Avi Chai Foundation, there are approximately 2,000–2,100 Jewish supplementary schools. The majority of these schools are supported by *synagogues: 57% are affiliated with the *Reform movement, 26% with the *Conservative movement, 4% community or pluralistic, 3% *Reconstructionist, and another 4% sponsored by the *Ḥabad movement.

The congregational school model that exists in the early twenty-first century is an adaptation of the Talmud Torahs founded in the early twentieth century by Jewish educator Samson Benderly and his disciples. They believed that religious education should be structured much like education in public schools where a standardized curriculum with textbooks was required. They envisioned a system supported by local bureaus of Jewish education that would train professional Jewish teachers and determine a unified vision. Although Benderly advocated for a communal, centralized Talmud Torah system, it never developed; as Jews moved to the suburbs they looked to *synagogues to provide Jewish education in a less centralized context. Thus, the transmission of Jewish culture and knowledge to American Jewish children in an afterschool and weekend context has remained primarily in the denominational domain.

Since the 1970s a great deal of discussion has centered around the impact of the congregational school on the Jewish lives of adults. Two separate studies published by Geoffrey Bock (1976) and Harold Himmelfarb (1975) concluded that supplemental Jewish learning, whether for 1,000 or 3,000 hours over a period of years, respectively, was ineffective in fostering Jewish identity or Jewish practice. The results of these studies propelled communities to focus on the Jewish day school to achieve these goals. Jewish *Federations throughout the country began to pour financial resources into both denominational and community day schools, leading to significant growth in the last three decades of the twentieth century. Despite this increase, however, a significant majority of children still participate in "supplementary" schools. This reality has generated communal attention and funding for congregation-based Jewish learning.

The field of Jewish supplementary education has experienced major shifts in the first decade of the twenty-first century, with a different set of expectations and a renewed sense of possibility. Educators realize that the acquisition of *prayer skills and a basic knowledge of holiday rituals are not sufficient. Innovative efforts focus on connecting Jewish learning to Jewish living, thereby providing students with a stronger sense of Jewish community; parents are asked to be active partners in the process.

In a monograph entitled "Redesigning Jewish Education for the 21st Century" (2007), the Jewish Education Service of North America outlined a strategy to maximize the reach and impact of Jewish supplementary education. The authors write that effective Jewish education must build on mutual commitment among students, their parents, educators, and a strong interconnected Jewish community of clergy and lay leadership; Jewish learning must also be relevant to the lives of the students, addressing their concerns and questions.   EVIE ROTSTEIN

Educational Alliance: See ART, AMERICAN TO 1940; DANCE: UNITED STATES

Egypt and Ancient Israel. Egypt appears to have had significant influence on ancient Israel: Some fundamental Israelite institutions seem to be based on Egyptian models, and important people in Israel's early history bear Egyptian names. Egypt's impact on Israel is also discernible in the areas of *wisdom literature and *poetry, as well as in religious architecture.

*MOSES AND AKHENATEN: Moses' requirement that Israel exclusively worship one *God has been linked to the religious reforms of Akhenaten, a fourteenth-century-BCE king of Egypt. In *Moses and Monotheism* (1939), Sigmund *Freud, the father of modern *psychoanalysis, famously portrays Moses as an Egyptian priest who, in an attempt to save Akhenaten's religious legacy, imposed the Pharaoh's severe monotheism on a mob of Semitic slaves, who then rebelled and murdered their liberator. Although most modern scholars dismiss Freud's reconstruction, some think it plausible that Moses' beliefs were somehow related to Akhenaten's exclusive worship of the sun disc, the Aten. Akhenaten introduced radical religious reform on taking the throne of Egypt in 1353 BCE. He changed his name, originally Amunhotep IV ("the god Amun is satisfied"), to Akhenaten ("effective for Aten"). With his wife Nefertiti, he prohibited the worship of gods other than the Aten or the sun disc, whom the royal couple praised as the sole creator deity. Names of other gods and even the word "gods" were chiseled out of existing inscriptions. However, the worship of other deities seems to have continued throughout Egypt, and Akhenaten's religious revolution mostly ended with his death. No reliable evidence exists that allows us to establish when Moses was born and died; however, it is plausible that his life-span coincided with that of Akhenaten or fell somewhat later, so a connection is possible. Although it is true that the monotheism attributed to Moses in biblical texts differs from that of the Pharaoh regarding the use of representational art (Aten was depicted as a sun with hands) and the divine nature of Akhenaten himself (the king was thought to be the incarnation of the sun god), monotheistic intolerance of other deities remains the defining factor of their respective religions. A notable remnant of this relationship may be the strong resemblance between *Psalm 104 and Akhenaten's "Hymn to Aten." On this topic, see W. Propp, *Exodus 19–24* (2006), 762–93.

PROVERBS 22:17–24:22 AND "INSTRUCTION OF AMENEMOPE": *Proverbs 22:17–24:22 is noteworthy for its affinity to the Egyptian "Instruction of Amenemope," a collection of wise sayings dating to the twelfth century BCE. Both begin with exhortations to listen to the guidance that follows, and both contain similar admonitions; for example, to avoid the company of angry men and to desist from removing landmarks or robbing the poor. A connection between the two wisdom collections is also suggested because the Egyptian instructions are divided into thirty units and Proverbs 22:20, according to one reconstruction of the difficult text, could be translated, "Have I not written for you thirty sayings?" However, the similarities between the two do not necessarily mean that the Israelite scribe adapted the "Instruction of Amenemope" for his Hebrew-speaking audience, but rather that Israelite wisdom was part of an international literary form. The *Bible acknowledges the standard of excellence set by Egypt's wisdom tradition (1 Kgs 5:10), so it would not be surprising if a scribe in *Jerusalem's royal court emulated his Egyptian counterpart (see BIBLE: WISDOM LITERATURE).

THE SONG OF SONGS AND EGYPTIAN LOVE POETRY: Although the *Song of Songs functions in the Jewish canon as an allegory for God's *covenantal relationship with Israel, its secular origins and intent are suggested by the sensual and erotic nature of the poetry, but even more so by its neglect of anything cultic or ritual. The name of the Israelite God appears only once, in 8:6, as a superlative way of describing human love as a blazing flame. Although ancient *Mesopotamia offers literature about love that is comparable to the Song of Songs, this love poetry, mostly of Sumerian origin, is embedded in "sacred marriage" texts that describe the mystical union of king and goddess during the festivities for the New Year. From Egypt, however, about fifty love poems survive, dating to the period 1300–1150 BCE. This group shares many characteristics with the Song of Songs, including the use of "sister" as a term of endearment and the focus on sensual pleasures and the sensual power of nature. In each case, the lovers are single, are sexually egalitarian, and show no hesitation regarding premarital sex; in addition, although the lovers praise each other's beauty, there is no real dialogue as they do not respond to each other's remarks. Michael Fox writes that these many similarities justify the supposition that the Song of Songs is at least indirectly dependent on the Egyptian model. He suggests that this literary type would have entered *Canaan in the Late Bronze Age (1550–1200 BCE), when Egypt controlled Canaan through a network of garrison towns and administrative centers. Although Jewish tradition dates the Song of Songs to the tenth-century-BCE reign of King *Solomon, modern scholars tend to attribute it to a much later date, possibly even as late as the *Hellenistic period. This long period of incubation can be accounted for if we assume, with Fox, that this kind of erotic and sensual poetry became incorporated into the popular literary tradition and blossomed as the Song of Songs centuries later. On this topic, see M. V. Fox, *The Song of Songs and the Ancient Egyptian Love Songs* (1985), 186–93.

EGYPTIAN PERSONAL NAMES IN THE BIBLE: Although many modern scholars challenge the Torah's claim that the people of Israel experienced a prolonged stay in the land of Egypt, the Egyptian origins of the names of several significant people in the book of Exodus suggest that at least some Israelites had sojourned there. It is likely that the names of Moses' siblings, *Aaron and *Miriam, have Egyptian origins. "Miriam" is related to the Egyptian root *mry*, and means "love" or "beloved," just like the name of a son of Levi, Merari, mentioned in Genesis 46:11 and Exodus 6:16. Assir is mentioned as a son of the Levite Korah in Exodus 6:24, and it is likely that his name is connected to the Egyptian Osiris or the Egyptian word *isr*, the term for a tamarisk tree. The name Hur, given to the leader who assisted Moses and Aaron in the battle with Amalek (Exod 17:10, 12), is probably related to the name of the Egyptian sky god, Horus. Phineas, the zealous grandson of Aaron in Numbers 25, has a name that in Egyptian means "the Nubian," perhaps because he had a dark complexion. The name of Israel's greatest prophet Moses is also thought to be derived from the Egyptian root *msi*, which means "born of." Names with this element were popular during the New Kingdom (1570–1070 BCE) and include Thutmose, Ramose, and Amenmose.

THE TENT OF MEETING AND ITS ACCESSORIES: James Hoffmeier has shown that Israel's portable sanctuary or *Tabernacle (*mishkan*) described in Exodus 25–30 was inspired by an Egyptian model and that a significant number of Hebrew terms related to the *mishkan* probably originated in Egypt. The Egyptian origin of these items and the terms for them attests to their antiquity, for it shows that they are rooted in Israel's experience in Egypt. For example, the wood used in the construction of the Tabernacle and its components – the ark, poles, planks, and altars – is from the acacia tree, which grew in dry regions such as the Sinai wilderness. This contrasts with the extensive amount of cedar, a wood imported from Lebanon, used for Solomon's *Temple (1 Kgs 5:22, 6). In addition, the Hebrew term for acacia, *shittim*, is a loan word from Egyptian. The extensive use of thin gold overlay in the Tabernacle was an art that was well developed in Egypt, and the word used in the *Torah for this practice, *pakh* (Exod 39:3) comes from Egyptian. The term for linen, the cloth used for the curtains in the Tabernacle and the priestly garments, is *shesh*, also of Egyptian origin. Portable shrines carried on poles, similar to the *Ark of the Covenant, are depicted in Egyptian art from the New Kingdom period, and one was found in the tomb of Tutankhamun. Thus, Egyptian technology and design played a significant role in the fashioning of the ark and Tabernacle, the focal points of Israel's early religious life.

For further reading, see J. K. Hoffmeier, *Ancient Israel in Sinai: The Evidence for the Authenticity of the Wilderness Tradition* (2005); and R. Hess, *Israelite Religions: An Archaeological and Biblical Survey* (2007). **Maps 1, 2**   ELAINE GOODFRIEND

Egypt: Heracleopolis Papyri. The Heracleopolis Papyri, also known as the "Jewish *Politeuma* Papyri" (*P. Polit. Iud.*), date from 144/3 to 133/2 BCE and provide a detailed snapshot of the daily life of Egyptian Jews living under the *Ptolemies. The papyri include citizen petitions to the officials (archons, politarchs, and elders) of a Jewish *politeuma*; that is, a self-governing community of resident aliens. The petitions address disputes regarding personal honor, marriage arrangements and dowries, the law of persons, and business transactions.

The petitions definitively establish that the Jews of Ptolemaic Egypt had the right to form *politeumata*. The uses of this term in association with Jews in documents known before publication of the papyri in 2001 were ambiguous in

their meaning (*Letter of* *Aristeas 310; *CIG* 5361–5362 [two inscriptions of the first century BCE from Berenice in Cyrenaica]). In contrast, there is no ambiguity in the case of the Heracleopolis papyri. The phrase "the *politeuma* of the *Ioudaioi*" (*P. Polit. Iud.* 8.5, 20.8–9), a *politeuma* member's explicit self-identification as a *Ioudaios* ("Jew/Judean"; 2.2, 4), and the wealth of theophoric names (e.g., Dorotheos [7.2, 26, 29, 38; 8.13, 38] and Theodotos [6.2, 41; 8.6, 37; 13.2; 17.2–3]) leave no doubt as to the ethnicity of the *politeuma* members.

That said, the legal reasoning reflected in the papyri indicates that the petitioners only lightly embraced the right granted by the Ptolemies to use ethnic *politeumata* to govern their corporate life according to their ancestral *law. Evidence of the petitioners' reliance on non-Jewish normative systems abounds. For example, the disputes regarding *marriage arrangements and dowries reflect Greek and Egyptian practices and omit the biblical *mohar* or "bride price" (*P. Polit. Iud.* 3–5; cf. Gen 34:12; Exod 22:16; 1 Sam 18:25). A petition requesting the return of an orphan to her proper guardian depends on Greek common law. Loans are made at the standard Ptolemaic business interest rate of 24% (*P. Polit. Iud.* 8; cf. Exod 22:24; Lev 5:35–38; Deut 23:20–21). A Jew eschews his own ethnic label for that of a *Perses tes epigones* ("Persian of the Succession/Younger Generation"), a fictive identity taken by poor credit risks to qualify for a loan in the early second century BCE (*P. Polit. Iud.* 8). According to Greek custom a woman is represented by a *kyrios* (6).

Still, close analysis of the legal reasoning in the papyri uncovers evidence that the petitioners also appealed to the *Torah when doing so could strengthen their legal arguments. For example, in *P. Polit. Iud.* 7 a guardian seeking the return of his ward under Greek common law cites his keeping of the levitical law concerning care for one's destitute kin (Lev 25:35–38) as evidence of his suitability as a guardian. Likewise, in *P. Polit. Iud.* 4, a petitioner contesting the giving of his fiancée by her father to another man, courted the woman according to Egyptian norms and made a pre-marital pact with her father typical of Greek practice. Yet the same petitioner invoked Numbers 30:3 to remind the father of the binding nature of his promise to give his daughter to him, and he cited Deuteronomy 24:1 to argue that the father had not issued the "customary writ of separation" necessary to free a woman from *betrothal to another man.

For further reading, see J. M. S. Cowey and K. Maresch, eds. *Urkunden des Politeuma der Juden von Herakleopolis (144/3–133/2 v. Chr.) (P. Polit. Iud.): Papyri aus Sammlungen von Heidelberg, Köln, München und Wien* (2001); and R. Kugler "Dispelling an Illusion of Otherness? A First Look at Juridical Practice in the Heracleopolis Papyri," in D. C. Harlow, M. Goff, K. M. Hogan, J. S. Kaminsky, eds, *The "Other" in Second Temple Judaism: Essays in Honor of John J. Collins* (2011).

ROBERT KUGLER

Egypt: Middle Ages. Egypt was an important place of medieval Jewish settlement and home to an innovative office of Jewish self-government. The chronicler Ibn 'Abd al-Ḥakam reports that at the time of the Arab-Islamic conquest of *Alexandria in 642, 40,000 Jews resided in the city. Although the actual figure was most likely a fraction of that, the report reflects the Jews' disproportionate urbanization compared both to the Coptic Christian population of Egypt and to the Jews of *Palestine and *Iraq, who would not urbanize until the ninth century. Therefore, the history of the Jews in medieval Egypt is found in cities and towns, especially Fustat, Alexandria, and the Nile Delta.

The Jewish community of early-tenth-century Egypt seems to have been capable of educating young men in biblical and *rabbinic literature, to judge by the philosopher, exegete, and halakhic scholar *Saadia ben Joseph, who would later serve as *Gaon of *Sura (928–42): he came from the town of Dilāṣ (Coptic Tilōj) in the southeastern Fayyūm and lived in Egypt until he was twenty-three. The tenth-century historian al-Masʿūdī corroborates this in reporting that the Abbasid governor of Egypt Aḥmad ibn Ṭulūn (868–905) staged a religious disputation between a Copt and his Jewish physician. A Jewish congregation also bought a church in Fustat from the Coptic patriarch Michael III (895–909), most likely to found a Babylonian-rite *synagogue to house the numerous Iraqis who had begun to migrate westward in pursuit of economic stability.

The most important center of Jewish population was Fustat, which had been founded as an Arab military garrison in 641–42. By the Fatimid period (969–1171) it was the largest population center in Egypt, and it continued to grow after the Fatimids founded Cairo (al-Madīna al-qāhira, "the city victorious") as their capital and built their palace compound just north of the city in 972. The Jewish population of Fustat at the turn of the millennium was about 4,000. The geographer al-Maqdisī (d. ca. 990) wrote that Fustat had displaced Baghdad as "the greatest glory of the Muslims" and the hub of world culture and commerce. The sense of living at the very center of civilization pervades the correspondence of both traders and administrators of the Jewish community during this period. The vast number of books preserved in fragments or as titles in book lists from the Cairo *Genizah attest to the Palestinian congregation's important role in Fustat's robust cultural life. The Genizah storage-room preserved some 280,000 folio pages or manuscripts, mainly from the eleventh through thirteenth centuries. About fifteen thousand are documents (letters, contracts, receipts, amulets, lists, accounts); the rest are fragments of literary manuscripts (*Bible and *Bible commentary, rabbinic literature, philosophical writings, *science, *poetry, and belles lettres).

Jews' political status under Fatimid rule was in principle governed by the same *dhimma* (pact of protection and submission) that governed the People of the Book elsewhere in Islamic-ruled territory. The *dhimmi* was required to pay the *jizya* tax and abide by various strictures of subordination in exchange for protection and religious tolerance. In practice, except for the years of anti-Christian and anti-Jewish edicts under al-Ḥākim (1009–21 and 1012–21, respectively), the Fatimids refrained from enforcing sumptuary laws and appointed Jews and Christians to high-ranking bureaucratic posts and as retainers at the court in Cairo.

The Jews, for their part, profited from the Fatimids' general liberality. Many Jews served the court not only in formal appointments but also in informal positions; for example, the *Karaite merchant and banker Abū Saʿd Abraham ben Yashar al-Tustarī, who purveyed luxury goods to the Fatimid court. Al-Tustarī provided the caliph al-Ẓāhir (1021–36) with a slave girl of Nubian, Abyssinian, or Sudanese origin named Raṣad, who bore the future caliph

al-Mustanṣir (1036–94); during her regency she maintained al-Tustarī as her financial manager. Al-Tustarī's brother Abū Naṣr, together with the Karaite Abū Naṣr David b. Isaac ha-Levi (a bureaucrat in the tax office), mediated between the Jewish community, *Rabbanite and Karaite alike, and the Fatimid administration. Jews benefited widely from the Fatimids' use of the petition as a means of rule: Anyone could petition the court for redress in personal or collective issues. That the Genizah also preserved petitions of Muslims and Christians suggests that Jewish courtiers used their co-religionists' petitions as models.

Although it remains unclear whether the Iraqi *yeshivot*, the Palestinian *yeshivah*, or some combination of forces governed Egypt's Jews in the tenth century, by century's end, all three were already engaging in stiff competition over the loyalty of long-distance merchants in Fustat, especially those engaged in the Mediterranean and Indian Ocean trade. Some Jews also chose to join the Karaites; the rabbinic leadership was well aware of the possibility of their doing so and worked actively to retain their loyalty.

Like most Mediterranean Jewish centers, Egypt housed three distinct Jewish communities: the Palestinian Rabbanites, the Iraqi Rabbanites, and Karaite. However, in Egypt, they introduced an important change to Jewish communal organization. Having worked together closely over the first Fatimid century (with Karaites becoming central players in rabbinic politics in both Egypt and *Syria), they founded a new leadership office called the *raʾīs al-yahūd* (head of the Jews) of the Fatimid empire. The first incumbents were a series of Egyptian notables, including Rabbanite physicians at the Fatimid court, but through the political marriage of David ben Daniel (1082–94) to the daughter of a Karaite notable, the office came to serve all three Jewish communities. It also filled a vacuum in Jewish leadership: The rabbinic academies (*yeshivot*) in Baghdad had closed after 1040, and the Palestinian *yeshivah* had disbanded after the Seljuk conquest of *Jerusalem in 1073 and reconstituted itself in Tyre and then Damascus; many Jews fled to Egypt after the Crusader conquest of Jerusalem in 1099. The Fustat Jews who created the new office therefore replaced the old centralized leadership offices in *Jerusalem and Baghdad and ultimately persuaded the Palestinian *yeshivah* itself to move to Fustat around 1127. As the Latin Crusader kingdoms took over the eastern Fatimid realm and the Jews concentrated their administration in Egypt, the old ecumenical structure of governance centered on the *yeshivot* in Palestine and Iraq now gave way to a local administration centered on Egypt and transcending the local interests of the congregation.

The strength of this centralized Jewish community emerged particularly clearly in its institutions of communal governance, such as care for the indigent. Although Fustat and Cairo are overrepresented in Genizah material attesting to poverty relief, the community also loomed large among Mediterranean Jews seeking aid, and many migrated there to benefit from the communal dole. Charity lists also include numerous converts to Judaism, some of whom, such as peasants hoping to better their lot in the city, may have converted to benefit from the extensive Jewish system of poor relief. The indigent benefited from private benefactors, fines, taxes, foundations, bequests, and occasional collections, which funded distributions of food, clothing, and outright grants of money and met exigencies such as the ransom of captives and books after the First Crusade of 1096.

The community's reputation attracted the poet Judah *Halevi (ca. 1085–1141) and the philosopher, physician, and jurist Moses *Maimonides (1138–1204). Although Halevi merely visited over a period of months on his way to Palestine, Maimonides settled in Fustat for good around 1166 and served the Ayyubid vizier al-Qāḍī al-Fāḍil as physician. He wrote two of his three major works, the *Mishneh Torah and the Guide of the Perplexed, in Fustat, and draft pages have surfaced in the Genizah in his own hand, in addition to numerous *responsa. Maimonides also served as ra'īs al-yahūd (1171–ca. 1177 and ca. 1195–1204), although he was forced out of office temporarily by Abū Zikrī Sar Shalom ben Nathanel ha-Levi.

During the Ayyubid period (1171–1250), the office of ra'īs al-yahūd continued to be held by a series of Maimonides' descendants. These included his son Abraham, also a physician at the Ayyubid court (1205–37); his grandson David (1238–1300); his great-grandson Joshua; and his great-great-grandson David. The dynasty came to an end in the 1370s when David b. Joshua (d. 1410) left Egypt for Aleppo, Syria, bringing a large library of *Judeo-Arabic manuscripts with him and adding important works to the already distinguished legacy of Maimonidean Sufism. Edward Pococke (1604–1691) and Robert Huntington (1637–1701), both chaplains to English merchants in Aleppo, eventually acquired and donated many of these manuscripts to the Bodleian Library in Oxford, England.

The Mamluk era (1250–1517) witnessed a progressive deepening of state and judicial interference in dhimmī affairs, although in large part this continued the previous pattern whereby Jews took the initiative in inviting government intervention in settling intracommunal disputes. After 1391, many Iberian Jews and *conversos fleeing forced conversions and anti-converso riots in *Spain migrated to Egypt. Over the course of the Mamluk period, the population of Fustat shifted northward to Cairo, and the population of Egypt generally declined; the Genizah materials accordingly become less numerous.

For further reading, see: M. R. Cohen, Jewish Self-Government in Medieval Egypt: The Origins of the Office of Head of the Jews, ca. 1065–1126 (1980); idem, Poverty and Charity in the Jewish Community of Medieval Egypt (2005); P. Fenton, "The Literary Legacy of David ben Joshua, Last of the Maimonidean Něgīdim," Jewish Quarterly Review 75 (1984): 1–56; S. D. Goitein, A Mediterranean Society: The Jewish Communities of the Arab World as Portrayed in the Documents of the Cairo Geniza, 6 vols (1967–93); G. Khan, Arabic Legal and Administrative Documents in the Cambridge Genizah Collections (1993); and M. Rustow, Heresy and the Politics of Community: The Jews of the Fatimid Caliphate (2008); see also MEMOIRS AND LIFEWRITING: MIZRAḤI. Map 5   MARINA RUSTOW

Ehrenburg, Ilya (1891–1967), poet, journalist, and writer, was born in Kiev. He joined the *Bolshevik underground and was arrested in 1908. Released from jail, he moved to Paris where he met Vladimir Lenin and also worked with Leon *Trotsky in *Vienna. Disillusioned with the Bolsheviks, he became a bohemian poet and journalist. Ehrenburg returned to Moscow in 1917 and barely survived the civil war. He went back to Europe in 1921 where he wrote his first novel, The Adventures of Julio Jurenito and His Disciples; one chapter foretells the *Holocaust.

During World War II, Ehrenburg was the most prominent journalist in Moscow, urging soldiers to fight the Germans and decrying *Nazi atrocities against the Jews. After Stalin's death in 1953, Ehrenburg became the leading liberal voice in the country. His memoirs, People, Years, Life (1960–65), were a major source of inspiration for Soviet Jewry. For further reading, see J. Rubenstein, Tangled Loyalties: The Life and Times of Ilya Ehrenburg (1999).   JOSHUA RUBENSTEIN

Einhorn, David (1808–1879), led the movement for "radical reform" in the development of Reform *Judaism in the *United States. **See CHICAGO; JUDAISM, REFORM: NORTH AMERICA.**

Ein Sof (or Ayn Sof) literally, "no end," is a term used in *Kabbalah to denote the most supreme divine entity, beyond the realm of the *sefirot, which cannot be described by any positive symbol. Ein Sof is an abbreviation of a long series of negative phrases like "no beginning," "no boundary," and "no measurement"; an accurate translation is "infinity." The concept was derived by early mystics, mainly from the circle in Gerona, *Spain, in the first half of the thirteenth century, who were familiar with Jewish rationalistic *thought; they used it as a counterpart of the Aristotelian conception of the First Cause or Unmoved Mover who is the original source of all movement without itself moving or being moved. Some kabbalists, as indicated in some sections of the *Zohar, identified Ein Sof with the first sefirah, Keter ("crown"), which is called ayin ("nothingness"), although it is really the essence and source of everything. For further reading, see G. Scholem, Kabbalah (1974); and I. Tishby, The Wisdom of the Zohar (1989).   JOSEPH DAN

Einsatzgruppen. During World War II *Nazi occupying forces in Eastern Europe made use of "special operation units" to kill various categories of "undesirable" civilians, including Jews, *Roma, and communists. Specially trained Einsatzgruppen were given principal responsibility for these mass murders in territories that fell under German control; they were aided by other units drawn from Himmler's paramilitary SS units, the Wehrmacht, and native collaborators throughout western Russia. These killings took on immense proportions, culminating in the slaughter of more than 33,000 Jews at Babi Yar, just outside of Kiev, on September 29–30, 1941. By the end of 1941, these units had gunned down between 500,000 to 800,000 Jews in mass executions. **See HOLOCAUST.**

Einstein, Albert (1879–1955), a theoretical physicist and recipient of the Nobel Prize for Physics in 1921, among many other awards, was one of the most important scientific figures of the twentieth century. Born in *Germany into a secular Jewish family and educated in Switzerland, he was forced to flee *Nazi Germany in 1933, ultimately emigrating to the United States where he became a citizen in 1940. Einstein spent the remainder of his career at the Institute for Advanced Studies at Princeton University. In 1952, after the death of Chaim *Weizmann, Prime Minister David *Ben-Gurion offered Einstein the ceremonial position of president of the State of *Israel. Einstein declined the position, writing, "All my life I have dealt with objective matters, hence I lack both the natural aptitude and the experience to deal properly with people and to exercise official function. I am the more distressed over these circumstances because my relationship with the Jewish people became my strongest human tie once I achieved complete clarity about our precarious position among the nations of the world" (W. Isaacson, *Einstein: His Life and Universe* [2007], 522). Einstein bequeathed his personal papers to the Hebrew University of Jerusalem. Together with Hebrew University, Princeton University Press is engaged in publishing *The Collected Papers of Albert Einstein*; it is anticipated that thirty volumes will ultimately appear.

Eldad ha-Dani was a traveler in the late ninth century CE who claimed to be a descendant of the lost Israelite tribe of Dan (see ISRAELITES: TRIBES; TRIBES, TWELVE). In the 880s Eldad appeared in the Jewish community of Kairouan in *North Africa and then in *Spain, relating tales in Biblical *Hebrew about his adventures and the other lost *Israelite tribes he had encountered. He also reported their quasi-halakhic ritual slaughter practices and *dietary regulations, which were similar to normative *halakhah. Many Jews believed his stories and found *messianic implications in his accounts of independent Jewish kingdoms. Although some rabbinic authorities, such as *Meir ben Barukh of Rothenburg and Abraham *ibn Ezra, were convinced that Eldad was an imposter, others cited his halakhic teachings without reservation. Modern scholarship continues to debate Eldad Ha-Dani's origins and authenticity. *Travel writings, attributed to him, which exist in several different medieval manuscript versions, were popular and influential; the first printed edition is from Mantua in 1480. An English translation appears in E. N. Adler, *Jewish Travellers* (1930). For a recent survey of scholarship, see D. J. Wasserstein, "Eldad ha-Dani and Prester John," in *Prester John, The Mongols and the Ten Lost Tribes*, ed. C. F. Buckingham and B. Hamilton (1995); **see also TRAVEL WRITING.**   KATE FRIEDMAN

Election: See CHOSENNESS

Elijah: Biblical and Post-Biblical Traditions. The *prophet Elijah, who is believed to have lived in the northern kingdom of *Israel in the ninth century BCE, stands out for his zealotry in support of monotheism and against idolatry. His sudden appearance on the biblical stage (1 Kgs 17:1), his miraculous ascent to heaven (2 Kgs 2:11), and the miracles that he performed (such as multiplying food [1 Kgs 17:10–16] and resurrecting the dead [1 Kgs 17:17–24]) add to his mysterious image. Elijah is also mentioned in *Malachi 3:23–24 as the prophet who will come at the end of days, before the "Day of the Lord," to call for *repentance. His confrontations with *Ahab, king of Israel, and his wife Jezebel (especially 1 Kgs 21) and a short furious letter, sent to one of the Judean kings (2 Chron 21:12–15), further strengthen his image as a warrior for the sake of heaven.

Elijah's biblical image underwent a drastic shift in post-biblical literature. Although Elijah still maintains his fiery persona in the *Wisdom of Ben Sira 47–48, written at the beginning of the second century BCE, in *rabbinic literature he is generally portrayed quite differently. On the one hand, the Rabbis condemn him for his jealousy; on the other, they portray him as a scholar of *Torah, who frequents their academies and participates in their discussions. He reveals

heavenly secrets to human beings and comes to the rescue of communities and individuals, wherever and whenever needed, appearing in a range of disguises (as an old man, a warrior, a harlot, a Roman minister, etc.). Elijah's transformation fits the general tendency of the Rabbis to portray biblical figures as part of their world and ways of life. It is also a rabbinic response to the bitter outcomes of the First and Second *Jewish Wars against *Rome, which were instigated by religious and nationalistic *zealots. The rabbinic portrayal of Elijah continued to develop in the generations to come: Elijah is a welcomed guest at every *circumcision ceremony, and the door is opened for him at every *Passover *seder* (and a cup of wine is left for him on the *seder* table). Most important, Jews have anticipated his arrival and his proclamation of the coming of the *messiah in every given moment (**Plate 7**), particularly at the Saturday evening *havdalah* ceremony, which marks the separation between the *Sabbath and ordinary days of the week. For further reading, see L. Ginzberg, *Legends of the Jews* (1956), index.

AVIGDOR SHINAN

Elisha was an Israelite *prophet who became *Elijah's attendant, disciple, and successor. In 1 Kings 19, God commanded Elijah to anoint Elisha as his successor. Elijah found Elisha plowing with twelve yoke of oxen and threw his mantle over him; Elisha slaughtered his oxen and followed Elijah. After Elijah was elevated to heaven (2 Kgs 2:11), the prophets of *Jericho declared that his spirit rested on Elisha. Elisha settled in *Samaria and held the office of prophet in the northern kingdom of *Israel for sixty years. A cycle of legends has been incorporated into 2 Kings describing his many miracles, including multiplying oil and food (2 Kgs 4), healing barrenness and leprosy (2 Kgs 5), and resurrecting the dead (2 Kgs 4, 13:20–21). Elisha continued Elijah's campaign against the house of *Ahab, ordering the anointing of Jehu, son of Jehoshaphat, as king of *Israel (2 Kgs 9) and charging him with the destruction of Ahab's family.

ELIZABETH SHULMAN

Elisha ben Abuya was a second-century-CE Rabbi who has caught the Jewish imagination from the rabbinic period to contemporary times. This interest stems from his image as a heretic and sinner: Talmudic sources accuse him of a range of misdeeds, including the murder of young Torah scholars (JT Ḥagigah 2,1), harlotry and desecration of the *Sabbath (BT Ḥagigah 15a), theological denial of retribution (BT *Kiddushin* 39b), and holding *dualistic beliefs (BT Ḥagigah 15a). These various reports have led to a number of historical conjectures about Elisha ben Abuya being an apostate, as well as efforts to identify his alternate religious identity. Possibilities include *Gnosticism, *Christianity, and *Persian *Dualism. Elisha ben Abuya is the only rabbinic figure about whom such reports are preserved in the *Talmud; rabbinic texts sometimes refer to him by the unique sobriquet, *aher*, "the other." This otherness has been a source of fascination for modern Jews in search of precedents for contemporary rebellion from traditional *Judaism and Jewish practice. In Milton Steinberg's 1939 historical novel, *As A Driven Leaf*, Elisha ben Abuya is imagined as a man so entranced by the intellectual freedom of Greco-Roman culture and the apparent possibility of achieving philosophical certainty that he not only abandons his faith but also betrays his beleaguered people.

Close examination of the rabbinic sources suggests there is little we can learn about a historical Elisha ben Abuya; he can only be considered as a literary exemplar. The key question, therefore, is what message the rabbinic story-tellers wished to convey by means of this figure. There is a strong distinction between *tannaitic traditions (up to the early third century) and the later *amoraic texts. The tannaitic materials treat Elisha ben Abuya as a legitimate member of the rabbinic class and show no awareness of his sin or heresy. Moreover, if there is any historical lesson to be derived from these traditions about him, it is that he died a *martyr's death. Subsequent amoraic sources completely rework his image and actions; the primary drive for this reworking is interpretative. An enigmatic expression, occurring in T. Ḥagigah 2, a passage that is essentially a parable, speaks of Elisha ben Abuya's having "entered the orchard and cut the shoots." This expression required explanation by later Rabbis, which in turn generated the host of reports about his sinful behavior. Once his sinful image had been established, succeeding editors employed his figure to work out theological issues that were of concern to them, specifically the power of Torah being put to the test in the case of a sinful sage (Babylonian Talmud) and the ideal relations between master and disciple (Jerusalem Talmud). Thus, the various stories told at this layer of the tradition have little to do with the historical man and reflect the ideological agenda of subsequent generations. Nineteenth- and twentieth-century reworkings of Elisha ben Abuya have continued the process of recasting his image in accordance with contemporary concerns. For a detailed analysis of these traditions, see A. Goshen-Gottstein, *The Sinner and the Amnesiac* (2000).   ALON GOSHEN-GOTTSTEIN

Elul is the sixth month of the Jewish calendar, equivalent to August and/ or September on the Gregorian calendar. Since Elul precedes Tishri, when the *High Holidays take place, it has traditionally been considered a time of *repentance. **See CALENDAR; CALENDAR: MONTHS OF THE YEAR.**

Emancipation refers here to the acquisition by Jews of the civil and political rights granted to the majority populations of modern nation-states. It was a process fraught with ambiguities and contradictions. Scholars disagree over whether Jewish emancipation is best understood as a single moment within the life of a given country or whether it proceeded in stages, with expansion of privileges and granting of legal equality, and culminating in full political rights. Moreover, no single model for achieving emancipation is paradigmatic. In *France, the French Revolution offers a case of a legislative assembly deliberating and eventually passing specific laws allowing for Jewish citizenship (see EMANCIPATION: FRANCE). In other areas, such as northern *Italy, the Rhineland, and southern *Germany, emancipation was imposed by foreign occupier. In the *Ottoman Empire, Jews obtained a high degree of formal equality through two governmental decrees (1856 and 1869) promulgated by a reformist bureaucracy. Jews in *North Africa received legal equality (in contravention of established Islamic law [see *DHIMMI* and ISLAM AND JUDAISM]) through the diplomatic pressure imposed by European colonial powers. In an extreme instance of colonialist interference, the French government declared Algerian Jews, but not Algerian Muslims, citizens of France in 1870.

In the *United States, Jewish emancipation required no special deliberation or legislation (with the exception of a few states): Jews simply benefited from the federal prohibition on religious criteria for exercising political rights. In *Britain, in contrast, Jewish disabilities were whittled away over the course of many decades; the last vestiges (the eligibility of Jews to be seated in Parliament or elected as Fellows of Oxford and Cambridge) were only legislated away between 1858 and 1871. Expectations directed at Jews also differed. In France it was tacitly assumed that Jewish citizens would undergo voluntary *régénération* (e.g., cultural assimilation, religious reform, occupational restructuring), whereas most German states of the Restoration and *Vormärz* periods passed laws requiring Jews to undertake such changes prior to and as a pre-condition for emancipation.

Jewish emancipation generally proceeded in three stages: an era of pre-emancipation amelioration of Jewish status, a classical era of Jewish emancipation, and a post-emancipation period. The pre-emancipation era began when Jews were granted expanded residential and occupational liberties in areas of northern Italy and Western Europe during the late sixteenth and early seventeenth centuries. The most explicit case was that of Livorno (Leghorn), established in the late sixteenth century as a Ligurian free port by the Grand Duke of Tuscany. The 1593 "Livornina" document granted Jews full religious freedom (and permitted *conversos* to revert to Judaism without fear of Inquisitorial prosecution), among other benefits. Livorno was a trading zone devoid of established guilds and Jews had a range of occupational choices, although the document encouraged Jewish merchant activity above all. The "Livornina" did stipulate a requirement for periodic renewal, a limitation compared with most classical emancipation laws; the Jewish population, however, was never expelled.

Britain's Jewish Naturalization Act or "Jew Bill" of 1753 has also been cited as a milestone on the path to emancipation. Yet even had the bill not undergone quick repeal, its narrow provisions would have benefited only a handful of individuals. More significant was the 1740 Plantation Act, which permitted Jews and dissenting Protestants to become naturalized British subjects (foregoing religious oaths offensive to either group) in return for seven years of residence in Britain's western hemisphere colonies. By comparison, Emperor Joseph II's 1782 Edict of Toleration, which historians have touted for advancing Jewish claims to legal equality in *Habsburg lands, was modest in its aims and inconsistent in application. It removed long-standing restrictions on Jewish dress and eliminated formal prohibitions on Jews' entry into Christian guilds. At the same time it subjected Jews to a series of regulations geared more to advancing the administrative prerogatives of the absolutist regime than Jewish equality. Nevertheless, the Edict of Toleration, along with such individual reforms as Louis XVI's 1784 revocation of the special body toll on Jews, attests to a fresh humanitarian spirit on the eve of the French Revolution.

If the French Revolution ushered in the period of classical emancipation, it was quickly followed by a phase of backtracking. Prussia, which had removed most restrictions on Jews in 1812, imposed new ones after 1816, establishing a multi-tiered policy with more onerous disabilities directed at Jews living in newly acquired and less Germanized territories like Posen. Other German states, notably, Württemberg, Bavaria, and Saxony, took severe measures to undercut Jewish status after the fall of Napoleon. Yet Germany's multiple sovereignties and the consequent patchwork character of Jewish rights made it a laboratory for Jewish adaptation to modernity during the first half of the nineteenth century. Especially in the western parts of the country, Jews had briefly enjoyed full citizenship status under French influence only to see it withdrawn. In subsequent decades they created a cultural dynamic to demonstrate their worthiness as citizens; this era saw the emergence of *Reform and *Modern Orthodox Judaism, as well as *Wissenschaft des Judentums, the movement to reexamine Judaism and Jewish history using modern academic tools.

The 1840s witnessed a shift in public opinion regarding the "Jewish Question," despite the failures of the 1848 Revolutions (emancipation in Prussia and Habsburg Austria, for instance, was reversed when the uprisings were put down). The increasingly liberal orientation of the middle class in *Central Europe strongly facilitated the goal of equalizing Jewish status on a local and regional level, and emancipation advanced with the fortunes of Austrian (1867) and German unification (partly in 1869 and finally in 1871).

The situation in the *Russian Empire, where the majority of world Jewry resided in the second half of the nineteenth century, was quite different. Traditions of natural law had barely penetrated, and rights were not part of the political vocabulary. Jews, like other peoples, were subjected to shifting policies based on imperial exigency alone. Catherine the Great's early benevolent example was not followed; the draconian policies of Nicholas I (1827–55) were followed by the more benign approach of Alexander II (1855–81). However, emancipation along western lines was entirely inconsistent with tsarist absolutism. Relief in Russia came only under the revolutionary regime headed by Alexander Kerensky in 1917. With the division of the empire after World War I, successor states like *Poland, *Lithuania, and *Latvia instituted formal equality for their Jewish subjects (although bitterly contesting the "minority group rights" written into their constitutions by foreign powers).

Although Russia was the last major case of Jewish emancipation, questions of Jewish status in European nations remained. In fact, in the post-emancipation period *antisemitism could be more demoralizing to Jews than previously, because it now occurred in a context in which legal redress had already been achieved. The *Dreyfus Affair in France and the outbreak of political party-based antisemitism in Germany and Austria during the 1870s and 1880s suggested ominously that formal emancipation was not quite the panacea that many Jews had assumed.

For further reading, see P. Birnbaum and I. Katznelson, eds., *Paths of Emancipation* (1995); J. Karp, *The Politics of Jewish Commerce: Economic Thought and Emancipation in Europe* (2008); and R. Mahler, *Jewish Emancipation: A Selection of Documents* (1941).   JONATHAN KARP

Emancipation, France. *Emancipation was bestowed on Jews residing in *France and French-held territories by the French Revolution. The fact that French Jews, in stages, if not all at once, acquired the rights and privileges accorded other Frenchmen determined the nature of the Jewish community that evolved during the nineteenth century. It also provided a model for Jews of *Central and *Eastern Europe, who aspired to similar status in their countries of residence. Four basic documents defined the emancipation of French Jews. The first two – the August 26, 1789, "Declaration of the Rights of Man and Citizen" and the subsequent constitution of the new republic – did not address the Jews directly, but implicitly granted Jews the same rights as other French people. Some National Assembly deputies, nevertheless, did seek to restrict Jews to "passive" citizenship, whereas "active" citizenship alone conferred the right to vote and hold office and was by law a prerogative determined solely by financial status. Despite the lack of grounds for discriminating in any way other than financial, the question, once open, festered during the remainder of the National Assembly sessions.

Fearful that they would find themselves reduced to second-class citizenship, Jews in southern France of *Sephardic origin and from the former Papal States, who were more likely to have the financial means to qualify for active citizenship and who were more culturally integrated into the fledgling nation, vigorously campaigned for legal recognition of their right to active citizenship. Their success was embedded in an emancipation decree of January 28, 1790, which applied only to them. It then became essential for the *Ashkenazim to seek an equivalent measure. On September 27, 1791, shortly before the dissolution of the National Assembly, with the support of Count Mirabeau, Count Clermont-Tonnerre, Abbé Grégoire, and attorney Jacques Godard (whose influence in revolutionary circles was considerable), deputy Adrien du Port made the definitive argument that led to full emancipation. Reasoning that freedom of worship does not permit any distinction in the political rights of citizens on the basis of their creed and that any other interpretation would be inconsistent with the new constitution, du Port demanded that a decree be passed granting all Jews of France the privileges of full citizens. His argument was persuasive and the proposition was enthusiastically accepted. For more on this topic, see P. E. Hyman, *The Jews of Modern France* (1998); and S. Schwarzfuchs, *Napoleon, the Jews and the Sanhedrin* (1979).   PHYLLIS COHEN ALBERT

Encyclopedias. In the nineteenth century, with the accumulation of scholarly literature generated by the German *Wissenschaft des Judentums movement, the need was felt for an encyclopedia on Jews and Judaism to summarize this emerging body of knowledge. However, none of the many European efforts came to fruition. The first successful venture, the twelve-volume *The Jewish Encyclopedia* (JE; New York, 1901–09), was produced in North America by European and North American scholars under managing editor Isidore Singer. Although generally considered a success, its coverage of modern Hebrew *literature and *Eastern European Jewry was poor. The Russian language *Evreiskaia entsiklopediia* (1909–1916), based on the JE and edited by Russian scholars, addressed these deficiencies.

In the 1920s, Jakob Klatzkin and Nahum Goldmann began planning a new encyclopedia in German, English, and Hebrew. The German version, called *Encyclopaedia Judaica* (EJ) and projected to total sixteen volumes, began appearing in *Berlin in 1928 under Klatzkin's editorship. Sadly the rise of the *Nazi regime in Germany put an end to the project, and the tenth volume, published in 1933, completing the letter "L," was the last one. Two volumes of the Hebrew version *Eshkol* were also published during this period, but the English version was postponed because of financial constraints. Many consider the EJ, with its high-quality entries and sumptuous production, to be the finest Jewish encyclopedia ever produced.

A project to produce a general encyclopedia in *Yiddish, with some Jewish content, was spearheaded by a committee at *YIVO, headed by Nachman Meisel and underwritten by the Simon *Dubnow Fund in the 1930s. Unfortunately World War II intervened, and the potential audience for such a work was all but eliminated. Still, five volumes of the *Algemeyne entsiqlopedye,* covering the first two letters of the alphabet, ultimately appeared (1934–44), as well as seven volumes of *Yidn,* the section devoted to Jewish subject matter (1939–66). Although the quality was uneven, this encyclopedia testified to the advances made by Yiddish as a medium for scholarly discussion. The four-volume *Jewish People Past and Present* (1946–55) incorporated a good deal of material from the *Yidn* volumes. The *Universal Jewish Encyclopedia,* published in ten volumes from 1939–43 and edited by Isaac Landman, aimed at a popular audience. Although some of the articles suffered from a lack of scholarly expertise, special attention was devoted to American Jewish history and biography and other topics not covered by the EJ, thus assuring its place among the important Judaic reference works of the twentieth century.

The founding of *Israel coincided with the launch of a major Hebrew encyclopedia, *Entsiqlopedyah ha-'Ivrit* (EI). This general encyclopedia, with about one-quarter Judaic content, was initiated in 1949 with a projected length of sixteen volumes. By the time it was completed in 1985 it extended to thirty-five volumes, including two supplementary volumes (1966, 1983) and an index volume (1985). Volume 6 was devoted entirely to the Land of Israel. Among its editors were Judah Kaufman (Even-Shemuel), Joseph Klausner, Ben-Zion Netanyahu, Isaiah Leibowitz, and Joshua Prawer. Despite some deficiencies, this encyclopedia is generally considered a major achievement of modern Israeli scholarship.

In the late 1950s Nahum Goldmann revived his plan to produce an English-language version of the EJ. A company with a large staff was established to produce an up-to-date English-language encyclopedia; it turned out to be, for the most part, an independent publication. Unique among such ventures, the entire work was to appear at one time. Despite difficulties, volumes two to sixteen of the *Encyclopaedia Judaica* were published in 1971; the index volume appeared in 1972. Large articles that missed the deadline were included at the end of Vol. 16. Publishing the entire encyclopedia at once meant that it was up-to-date but it suffered from numerous mistakes and typographical errors. Nonetheless, the English-language EJ has enjoyed tremendous success and acclaim. A number of yearbooks also appeared, with new or updated articles, summaries of current events, and necrologies; a 1982 Decennial Book summarized the previous ten years in Jewish life and letters. In 1997, a CD-Rom version, including material from all the yearbooks, was released.

In the first decade of the twenty-first century the publisher Thomson Gale undertook the publication of a new edition of the EJ, under the editorship of Michael Berenbaum

and Fred Skolnik. The new EJ, which appeared in January 2007 in print (twenty-two volumes) and online versions, is not a complete revision: Only a portion of the articles were revised or rewritten, at the discretion of the editors. Hundreds of new entries reflect new areas of interest and importance, such as women and aspects of popular culture. Critics have noted that the coverage is uneven, that some editors were more diligent in their work than others, and that the whole work was rushed to publication without correcting mistakes and typographical errors, many of which survive from the first edition. For better or for worse, this encyclopedia will be the primary point of entry to the world of Judaic scholarship for the foreseeable future.

Along with the multi-volume encyclopedias, a number of one-volume reference works have been published over the years. Worthy of mention are *The Standard Jewish Encyclopedia* (1959); *New Standard Jewish Encyclopedia* (1970), edited by Cecil Roth and based on the *EI,* widely considered the best one-volume Judaica reference work of its era; and the *Encyclopedic Dictionary of Judaica* (*Everyman's Judaica*) (1974) a spinoff of the English EJ, with 15,000 entries and many illustrations, intended as a quick-reference tool.

A number of important specialized dictionaries and encyclopedias have appeared since World War II. Among the most important are the nine-volume *Entsiqlopedyah miqra'it* (1965–88), summarizing the best of Israeli biblical scholarship; *Entsiqlopedyah talmudit* (1949-), twenty-seven volumes to date, an encyclopedia of the Talmud and rabbinic literature; *The Encyclopedia of Judaism,* edited by J. Neusner, A. Avery-Peck, and W. S. Green (1st ed., three volumes, 2000; 2nd ed., four volumes, 2005); *Encyclopedia of the Holocaust,* edited by I. Gutmann (1st ed., 1990); *Jewish Women: A Comprehensive Historical Encyclopedia,* edited by P. E. Hyman, D. Ofer, and A. Shalvi (CD-ROM; ed., 2006); *The Oxford Dictionary of the Jewish Religion,* edited by R. J. Z. Werblowsky and G. Wigoder (1997); and *The YIVO Encyclopedia of Jews in Eastern Europe,* edited by G. D. Hundert (two volumes, 2008).

For further reading, see S. Brisman, *Jewish Research Literature.* vol. 2: *A History and Guide to Judaic Encyclopedias and Lexicons* (1987); and T. Wiener, "Encyclopedias," *Encyclopaedia Judaica,* 2nd ed. (2007).   BARRY DOV WALFISH

Engagement: See BETROTHAL; MARRIAGE

England: Middle Ages. Jews lived in medieval England for more than two centuries; the first settlers arrived at what Hebrew sources referred to as the "Isles of the Sea" from the small French Jewish community of Rouen in the wake of William the Conqueror in 1066. England's Jews were summarily expelled in 1290. For a short period in the twelfth century, contemporary chroniclers commented that the Jews were accepted and "ministered much to the prosperity of this country." They were regularly granted royal charters from the reign of Henry I (1100–35) onward. Some of the richer Jews, like Aaron of Lincoln, lent money to members of high society and to the new Cistercian monasteries. Some monasteries, which had once taken loans from Jews, went on to buy up the encumbered mortgaged estates of Jewish debtors.

In 1189, at the coronation of Richard I in London where Jewish elders had gathered to pay their respects, a brawl ensued that turned into a massacre. Attacks on Jews spread northward over the next three months through Colchester,

Norwich, Thetford, and Stamford, ending tragically in 1190 at York with the infamous massacre occurring on *Shabbat ha-Gadol. Besieged in the castle of York and urged on by Rabbi Yom Tov of Joigny, the majority of the York Jews took their own lives rather than surrender to the Christian mob. In two years, more than four hundred Jews died. There can be no doubt that at York the massacre was premeditated and inflamed by the machinations of a monk and by Richard Malebisse, a local nobleman, who was indebted to the Jews.

Out of the embers of York came a government incentive to control and regulate England's Jewish communities. Beginning in 1194, Hubert Walter, the King's Justiciar and the father of English archives, set up *archae* or chests in which any written deed or agreement between Jew and Christian had henceforth to be deposited. The kings of England, who virtually owned the Jewish communities, could now control their *money lending. In return the Jews were frequently taxed and their debtors squeezed; this was particularly so under John (d. 1216) and Henry III (d. 1272). In the most infamous tallage or tax of 1210 a Jew had his teeth extracted day by day until he paid up. The greatest tallage came in 1240 and the last was collected in 1287. The Jewish community became known to subsequent historians as the "King's Milch Cow."

A view has prevailed that all medieval Jews were fabulously wealthy and that they became money lenders because Christians were forbidden from lending. In fact, many Christians lent money, and there were poorer Jews who found work as pawnbrokers, physicians (see MEDICINE), vintners, fishmongers, cheese mongers, goldsmiths, jewelers, soldiers, and even servants or wet nurses. Records of medieval English Jewry are particularly good because of the 1194 establishment of a separate government department, the Exchequer of the Jews. The Jewish Exchequer, which controlled other officials in the towns that had *archae*, regulated and recorded all Jewish lending and had two appointed Justices to try all legal cases involving Jews or their debtors. Much of its work was concerned with collecting the profits from Jewish money lending for the king. It has left behind a unique and unparalleled record of the lives of medieval England's Jews.

The Jew was also the target of specific legislation. In 1194 the Ordinances of the Jewry systematized how Jewish lending would be tolerated. In 1215, in accordance with the Fourth Lateran Council, Jews were compelled to wear badges with the sign of the *Ten Commandments. Subsequent legislation modified how Jews were to lend money and laid down exactly where they were to live. Earlier laws had limited the amount of interest that a Jewish creditor could charge to 43.5% per annum. By 1269, Jews were banned from lending money in return for rent charges and revenues from mortgages and, by 1271 from investing in property other than the houses in which they lived. Finally, in 1275, they were forbidden to lend money at interest, which led to some Jews advancing loans on wool or grain.

Hatred of Jews led to accusations of *ritual murder. The first was the case of William of Norwich in 1144. This was followed by accusations and arrests at Bury (1181), Gloucester (1186), Worcester (1192), and London (1244) and culminated in the cult of Little St. Hugh of Lincoln

in 1255. At least four shrines to Christian boys who had allegedly been crucified by Jews at Easter were ultimately established. Accusations of *host desecration and blasphemy followed. There were often local outbursts of anti-Jewish violence. In 1278–79, the Jewish community as a whole was accused of clipping the coinage and melting down silver into ingots. Many were tried and brought to the Tower of London where some 279 were hanged.

Although English Jewry looked to rabbinical authorities in *France and *Germany for legal guidance, over several generations Jews developed their own rituals, traditions, and customs. There is evidence of more than twenty-four private and public synagogues, several *mikvaot (ritual baths), and ten burial grounds. Certainly Jews celebrated the main Jewish *festivals – even when incarcerated in the Tower of London some Jewish prisoners paid bribes so that they might celebrate their sacred days. They also imported kosher wine. Elegies written by English Jews to the martyrs of massacres at Blois and York are extant. Most Jews were trilingual, but for those who were not, the *Passover *haggadah* was translated into French. Jewish communities were highly organized; the Northampton community, for example, possessed a communal seal and had rental income from houses it owned that paid for the upkeep of the *synagogue and the *cemetery.

Medieval Anglo-Jewry left behind epitaphs, graffiti, marriage contracts, and business deeds in Latin, French, and Hebrew. The community bred its own legal experts who wrote *responsa on various topics. Rabbi Moses of London wrote a treatise on punctuation (c. 1234) and Jacob of London on the "Tree of Life." Just before the 1290 expulsion, Meir of Norwich wrote a poem, "Put a Curse on My Enemy," describing the deteriorating conditions of Jewish life. On November 1, 1290, under Edward I, all Jews were expelled from England. They were not officially readmitted until 1656.

Important studies include C. Roth, *History of the Jews in England*, 3rd ed. (1978); R. B. Dobson, *The Jews of York and the Massacre of March 1190* (1974); P. Skinner, ed., *Jews in Medieval Britain: Historical, Literary and Archaeological Perspectives* (2003); R. R. Mundill, *England's Jewish Solution: Experiment and Expulsion 1262–1290* (1998); and idem, *The King's Jews: Money, Massacre and Exodus in Medieval England* (2010).

See also COMMERCE: MEDIEVAL AND EARLY MODERN EUROPE; FRANCE: MIDDLE AGES; FRANCE, SOUTHERN: MIDDLE AGES; and BRITAIN, EARLY MODERN AND MODERN; Map 8.   ROBIN R. MUNDILL

Enlightenment, Jewish: See HASKALAH

Enoch, Books of: See ESCHATOLOGY; PSEUDEPIGRAPHA; MYSTICISM: HEKHALOT AND MERKAVAH LITERATURE

Entertainment. "Love and marriage," according to the 1950s hit song of the same title by Jewish songwriter Sammy Cahn, "go together like a horse and carriage." The same could be said of Jews and the entertainment business in America. Jews have been so active in every field of American popular culture that one could hardly imagine American society without them. This has made Jews a ready target for antisemites, beginning with Henry Ford in the 1920s and continuing to the present day, who have accused them of "controlling" the entire entertainment and media industry. An article in *Time Magazine* (October 2, 1978) once estimated that 80% of the professional comedians in the United States were Jewish (see COMEDY AND COMEDIANS).

Vaudeville was the most popular form of entertainment beginning in the mid-nineteenth century in America, and there were many prominent Jewish vaudevillians, including Barney Bernard, Irving Kaufman, and Monroe Silver. These comedians used heavily accented routines, known as dialect humor, to poke fun at Jewish mannerisms. They were exceedingly popular among both Jews and non-Jews; Silver's 1913 landmark recording, "Cohen on the Telephone," was purportedly the first comedy recording to sell a million records.

By the turn of the twentieth century in *New York City, Jews had developed an entire theatrical culture of their own, known as the Second Avenue *Yiddish *Theater. On the eve of *World War I, two dozen Yiddish theaters were operating simultaneously in New York (including those that specialized in Yiddish-language vaudeville), with dozens of others scattered throughout the country. Jews flocked to classic plays, often translated into Yiddish from European languages, as well as to what were called *shund* (literally, "trash") – light entertainments from melodramas to operettas. Many of the most famous performers of the Yiddish stage, like Jacob Adler, Paul Muni, and Molly Picon, crossed over to Broadway in the 1920s and 1930s, in a move that was decried by Yiddish newspapers as going *avek tsu di goyim* – "off to the Gentiles." However, by the 1920s, comedians like Fanny Brice, Eddie Cantor, and George Jessel, all American-born children of Jewish immigrants, had risen to the heights of American popular culture. Much of their success derived from comic material that, although still relying to a large extent on Jewish stereotypes, presented Jews as more fully rounded human beings.

Harley Erdman has speculated that fully half of the entertainment business in New York was "in Jewish hands" at the turn of the twentieth century, meaning that Jewish producers, theater owners, and agents were as heavily involved in the theater as they would be in the *film industry in succeeding decades. The only comparable industry, in terms of the extent of Jewish participation, was the garment trade; it is not surprising, then, that many Jewish comedy routines revolved around clothing, including Brice's signature song, "Second-Hand Rose," and Cantor's much reprised vaudeville routine, "A Belt in the Back."

By the middle of the twentieth century, Jews had gravitated to *television comedy; Milton Berle, Jack Benny, and George Burns adapted their vaudeville and *radio routines to the new medium with great success, and Sid Caesar's *Show of Shows* relied on the comic genius of writers like Mel Brooks, Neil Simon, Larry Gelbart, and Carl Reiner for its brilliant skits. The 1950s and 1960s were the high-water mark of Jewish comedy as well; most stand-up comedians were Jewish, including Mort Sahl, Lenny Bruce, Woody Allen, Myron Cohen, Don Rickles, and the team of Mike Nichols and Elaine May.

Such overrepresentation of Jews in the cultural life of a society is not unprecedented. As Oscar Schorske has argued, cultural life in *Vienna in the last decade of the nineteenth century was in large part the product of middle-class, largely assimilated Jewish artists. Steven Beller has recently validated this claim through statistical analysis and extended it to show that Jews shaped Viennese culture for more than seventy years – from 1867 until the *Anschluss*, the 1938 political union of Austria and *Nazi Germany.

Historical reasons are often adduced for the rise of the Jewish entertainer. The role of clown or jester has deep roots; Jewish weddings, particularly as they developed in Eastern European tradition, were occasions for broad comedy. The *badkhan*, or master of ceremonies, developed in the thirteenth century out of the tradition of the Jewish *leyts*, or fool, who was a kind of medieval troubadour. The status of the Jew as perennial outsider in western Christian culture is also frequently cited as a reason for Jews having an ironic lens on human experience. It is argued that their very marginality gives them a desperate desire to belong to society, but also makes them despair of ever being able to do so. This tension leads to the construction of an absurdist philosophy that flouts reason and logic.

Such psychological theories for the preponderance of Jewish entertainers generally depend on an analysis of Jewish humor, which is often characterized as self-deprecating. This humor is typically explained as a Jewish mode of coping with powerlessness and vulnerability by turning their rage inward, on themselves. Literary scholar Sanford Pinsker sees Jews as "laughing through their tears," finding solace from their pain in a rueful sense of irony. In this way, the *schlemiel*, or "loser," became an important figure in Jewish literature; as John Limon has put it, the *schlemiel* "inhabits his defeats rather than just suffers them." He embodies the very idea of defeat, or perhaps he "seems to be standing up, even if unconsciously, for some other definition of success" (unpublished paper, 2007 Association for Jewish Studies Conference).

In a now classic study, folklorist Dan Ben-Amos pointed out that the idea that Jewish wit is based on self-criticism is comparatively recent in origin (*The "Myth" of Jewish Humor* [1973]). It originated in Sigmund *Freud's *Jokes and the Their Relation to the Unconscious* (1905), in which the founder of *psychoanalysis argued that "a number of the most apt jokes... have grown up in the soil of Jewish popular life," adding, "They are stories created by Jews and directed against Jewish characteristics." However, Ben-Amos argued that Jewish humor is much more complicated than Freud's thesis. He noted that Jews who moved away from traditional Jewish lifestyles most often used humor to denigrate other Jews who were less assimilated than they were, as a way of identifying with (and seeking acceptance by) the dominant culture. In addition, Ben-Amos adduced many examples of Jews using humor to put down other groups.

There are also sociological explanations for Jewish involvement in American entertainment. In *World of Our Fathers* (1976), his landmark study of life in the immigrant Jewish neighborhoods on the Lower East Side of New York, Irving Howe wrote that second-generation Jewish entertainers defined themselves through the process of moving out of the ghetto. It was precisely in their "cutting loose" and "breaking out" from life on the street that their work was shaped. This led to what Howe called the "almost hysterical frenzy" with which they worked, "their need to perform under the highest possible pressure, as if still heeding the Jewish folk view that for a Jew to succeed, he must do things twice as well, or as hard, as a Gentile."

In the first decade of the twenty-first century a majority of American Jews, at least according to some surveys, have increasingly come to define themselves in "secular" rather than religious ways. Many of them find a source of pride in the number of prominent Jews in entertainment since popular culture with Jewish themes (like Jewish food) provides a foundation for a nonreligious, secular Jewish identity. Books like Darryl Lyman's *Great Jews in Entertainment* (2005) and websites like www.jewwatch.com foster this kind of ethnic pride and also allow Jews to play parlor games about the possible Jewish origins of various celebrities. Film actor Ben Stiller may not always play overtly Jewish roles, but his humor still springs from Jewish stereotypes about the clumsy, clueless, Jewish man whose innate sweetness wins him the (usually non-Jewish) girl. Other popular Jewish comedians play in more complex ways with their Jewish identities. Sacha Baron Cohen pokes vulgar, gleeful fun at *antisemitism by impersonating antisemites, whereas Sarah Silverman's sexually explicit routines explode the myth of the "nice Jewish girl."

It is essential to recognize that Jews have achieved success in the entertainment business through collaborating with many non-Jews. In the early decades of the twentieth century, Jews often teamed up with individuals of Irish origin to create and perform vaudeville, theater, music, and film. The relationship between Jews and *African Americans in popular music has been especially tangled and controversial, with black and Jewish composers working together, borrowing from each other, and often profiting from each other's music.

Thus, the history of American Jews in entertainment is bound up with the history of other Americans as well. Look again at the song, "Love and Marriage," cited in the first sentence of this essay. Although Cahn wrote the lyrics, the music was written by Protestant musician Jimmy van Heusen (christened Chester Edward Babcock), and the song was made famous by Italian American singer Frank Sinatra. More than a half-century later, Jews continue to be heavily overrepresented in every realm of American popular culture, but they also continue to find success through collaboration with non-Jews of every background.

For further reading, see H. Erdman, *Staging the Jew* (1997); O. Schorske, *Fin-de-Siècle Vienna* (1980); S. Beller, *Vienna and the Jews: A Cultural History* (1989); S. Pinsker, *The Schlemiel as Metaphor* (1971); and D. Ben-Amos, *The "Myth" of Jewish Humor* (1973); and **see CELEBRITIES; COMEDY and COMEDIANS; RADIO; TELEVISION.**

TED MERWIN

Epikoros. Although the Greek loanword *philosophos* appears in numerous contexts in both *tannaitic and *amoraic texts, the only contemporary philosopher cited by name in rabbinic literature is the second-century-CE Oenomaus of Gadara. As for founders of philosophical schools, Epicurus (*epikoros*) is the only one who is mentioned. The meaning of *epikoros* differs significantly in the more than twenty rabbinic sources in which it appears. Judah Goldin believed that the word *epikoros* was eventually used in rabbinic literature to suggest any kind of heretic or unbeliever, similar to its usage in late antique Greco-Roman writings, but he insisted that its earliest appearances in the *Mishnah (*Sanhedrin* 10:1; *Avot* 2:14) reflected full awareness of the

Epicureans' denial of providence and their penchant for exhaustive argumentation. As Goldin noted, the most accurate manuscript of *Avot* reads, "know how to refute an Epicurean" ("A Philosophical Session in a Tannaite Academy," *Traditio* 21 [1965]; repr. in *Studies in Midrash and Related Literature* [1988]).

This association with argumentation appears in several Palestinian texts in which both the serpent in Eden (Gen 3) and the rebellious Korah (Num 16) are called *epikoros* (*Sifre Deuteronomy* 12; *Genesis Rabbah* 19; JT *Sanhedrin* 10:4, 27a). Hans Jürgen Becker has pointed out an apparent affinity between JT *Sanhedrin* 10:4, 27a, and *Josephus' usage of key Epicurean terms in his characterization of Korah ("Epikureer im Talmud Yerushalmi," in *The Talmud Yerushalmi and Greco-Roman Literature*, ed. P. Schäfer [1998]). J. Labendz has traced the evolution of the word *epikoros*, showing that over time it came to refer to anyone who demonstrated disrespect for *Torah or Torah scholars, and eventually, in the *stammaitic literature, denoted general irreverence ("'Know What to Answer the Epicurean': A Diachronic Study of the 'Apiqoros in Rabbinic Literature," *Hebrew Union College Annual* 74 [2003]). S. Lieberman pointed out that later rabbinic literature preserved a key technical term of the Epicurean school, *automaton*; this term had already appeared in the writings of Josephus ("How Much Greek in Jewish Palestine," in A. Altman ed., *Biblical and Other Studies* [1962]).

MARC HIRSHMAN

Eruv. Carrying any object, such as keys or a handkerchief, in a public domain is prohibited on the *Sabbath. In truth, most, if not all, of the world as presently constituted does not match the biblical definition of a public domain. Nonetheless, the Rabbis prohibited carrying in any open area. However, they allowed the construction of an *eruv* that would allow carrying within a specific enclosed area. The area in question must be surrounded with walls on all four sides; these can be actual walls or fences, cliffs, or even inclines such as riverbanks. Where nothing that passes as a wall exists, doorways can be installed. These are defined as two side posts and a crossbeam that crosses over them. Often, two telephone poles and an electric wire can serve this purpose with only slight modification. Once the area has been enclosed, communal food such as *matzah* (unleavened bread that will not go stale for a long time) is placed within the boundaries of the space that has been enclosed. This food is the actual *eruv*, a word that means "mixing" or "mixture." It is the communal *matzah* that joins all the households into one *eruv* structure. Once all of this has been done, carrying is then permitted within the boundaries that have been created.

BARRY FREUNDEL

Esau was the firstborn son of *Isaac and *Rebekah and the favorite of his father. Through the machinations of his mother and brother *Jacob, he was displaced and lost the rights and blessing due him (Gen 25, 27). Esau became the father of the Edomites. **See also BIBLE: ANCESTRAL NARRATIVES; EDOM; GENESIS; ROME, ROMAN EMPIRE.**

Eschatology: Second Temple Period. Eschatology, from the Greek word *eschatos* ("last"), refers to the final days of human history. Eschatological writings are found in the Hebrew *Bible, the *Apocrypha, and the pseudepigraphical books (see PSEUDEPIGRAPHA). After the *Babylonian

Exile, ca. 586 BCE, *prophets hoped for definitive restoration to the Land of Israel. *Haggai and *Zechariah hailed *Zerubbabel as a *messiah (anointed king) of the *Davidic line who would restore the kingship, but he disappeared abruptly from history. The oracles in *Isaiah 56–66 show increasing disillusionment with the political order and speak of a new heaven and new earth (65:17), where people would live longer happier lives, although they would still die. Many of the prophetic books contain passages added in the *Second Temple period predicting universal judgment on the Day of the Lord (*Joel) and even speaking of the defeat of death (Isaiah 25:8). Occasional passages speak of a messianic king (Jer 33:14–16; Zech 9). Many of these passages lack historical context and are difficult to date.

The rise of *apocalyptic literature in the *Hellenistic period marks a dramatic change in Jewish eschatology. The earliest examples are found in the books of Enoch (see *PSEUDEPIGRAPHA), which relate the *revelations that Enoch received when he ascended to heaven. There are accounts of remote regions at the ends of the earth, of the chambers where the dead await judgment, and of the place where *God will sit while judging the earth (*The Book of the Watchers*, 1 Enoch 1–36). Dated in the late third or early second century BCE, *The Book of the Watchers* may be the earliest Jewish text that speaks of a differentiated fate for the righteous and wicked after death. It seems to locate the final abode of the righteous on a transformed earth. *The Epistle of Enoch* (1 Enoch 91–104) promises the righteous that they will become companions to the host of heaven. The *Animal Apocalypse* (1 Enoch 85–90) and the *Apocalypse of Weeks* (1 Enoch 93:1–10 and 91:11–17) provide overviews of the course of history in the guise of prophecy, ending with a time of divine intervention and judgment. These apocalypses within the books of Enoch date from the time of the *Maccabees in the second century BCE.

Also from the time of the Maccabees is the canonical book of *Daniel, although the Aramaic stories in chapters 2–6 are somewhat older. Already in Daniel 2 we encounter Nebuchadnezzar's dream of a statue with metals of declining value (head of gold, feet of iron mixed with clay). Daniel interprets this statue to refer to a sequence of four kingdoms in declining order, after which the God of heaven will set up a kingdom that will never be destroyed. In Daniel 7, this vision is reworked. Instead of four metals, we now have four beasts rising from the sea, and the fourth is the most violent and terrible. It has ten horns and sprouts a little horn that makes war on the holy ones. Then "one like a son of man" appears on the clouds and approaches the Ancient of Days. The beasts are judged and condemned, and dominion is conferred on the "one like a son of man." An angel explains to Daniel that the beasts represent kingdoms, and eventually earthly dominion is given to "the people of the holy ones." The significance of this vision is made clearer in chapters 10–12, which relate an ongoing struggle between the prince of Israel, the archangel Michael, and the "princes" of the other nations. Eventually, Michael rises in victory. Chapter 11 describes a period of persecution at the end of history and explains that "some of the wise will fall," a reference to *martyrdom in the Maccabean era. In the end, however, there will be a *resurrection, and the wise will shine like the splendor of the firmament. This means that they will be exalted to the stars.

Neither Daniel nor the early Enoch apocalypses have any place for a human messiah. The "one like a son of man" is a heavenly figure, most probably the archangel Michael. This figure is further developed in the *Similitudes of Enoch* (1 Enoch 37–71), where he sits as judge on the throne of glory. In the *New Testament, Jesus is identified with the "son of man." In an addition to the *Similitudes*, Enoch seems to be so identified. In later Jewish tradition (3 Enoch), Enoch is enthroned in heaven as *Metatron, a kind of super-angel.

Messianic expectation plays a significant, but not dominant, role in the *Dead Sea Scrolls, which often refer to two messiahs, a priestly one descended from *Aaron and a royal one from the tribe of *Judah. It is probable that this messianic expectation developed in reaction to the *Hasmoneans, the dynasty initiated by the Maccabees, who made themselves both *kings and High *Priests. The Dead Sea Scrolls insist that the offices should be separate and contrast the Hasmonean kings with the messianic king in the *Psalms of Solomon* (first century BCE; see PSEUDEPIGRAPHA). The Scrolls also speak of angelic deliverers such as Michael.

The early apocalypses envision a judgment of the dead and promise the righteous eternal life with the angels. The idea of bodily *resurrection after death appears clearly in the story of the *martyrs in 2 *Maccabees 7. The authors of the Dead Sea Scrolls clearly envision reward and punishment after death, although whether they expect bodily resurrection is disputed. Rather, they claim to be participating already in angelic life. In the Hellenistic *Diaspora, especially in *Egypt, the standard expectation was immortality of the soul, at least in circles influenced by Greek philosophy (*Philo, Wisdom of Solomon [see APOCRYPHA]).

Several apocalyptic texts were written in the aftermath of the destruction of *Jerusalem. Some (4 Ezra, 2 Baruch [see PSEUDEPIGRAPHA]) make an attempt to synthesize different strands of expectation. Thus in 4 Ezra 7 the messiah will reign for four hundred years and then die, followed by a resurrection and judgment. Later visions in the book speak both of a Davidic messiah (chapters 11–12) and of a figure like the "son of man" who comes on the clouds (chapter 13), but this figure is also identified as the messiah. Jewish eschatological belief was never uniform and apocalyptic eschatology was not universally accepted, but its view of the last things has remained influential both in Judaism and in Christianity down to the present. For more on this topic, see J. J. Collins, *The Apocalyptic Imagination* (1998).

JOHN J. COLLINS

Essenes. One of many diverse groups of Jews during the late *Second Temple period, the Essenes are described by *Josephus and *Philo of Alexandria as a community that lived in isolation and practiced an ascetic lifestyle that emphasized purity and taught a variety of eschatological doctrines. The Roman writer Pliny the Elder placed this group at a location near the Dead Sea north of Ein Gedi. Many scholars identify the Essenes with the *Qumran community at the Dead Sea and connect them with the *Dead Sea Scrolls that were discovered nearby; others suggest that the designation may refer to several separatist communities. Debate continues as well over whether the sect was a celibate religious order or whether it also included married members. Also unresolved is the relationship between the

Essenes and the *Therapeutae* or "Healers," mentioned by Philo. Philo described them as a group of Alexandrian Jews, apparently including men and women, who lived a monastic life and attempted to observe all of the Mosaic commandments.

If the Qumran communitarians were, in fact, the Essenes, then they are distinguished from other contemporaneous sectarian groups by their *priestly identification. According to Dead Sea documents, the group separated from the mainstream priestly community when a High Priest not to their liking was appointed in Jerusalem. With their leader, the "Teacher of Righteousness," they established themselves in the Judean wilderness to create their own center of priestly purity. They believed that they would become the saving remnant of Israel, after the priests in Jerusalem were destroyed in an imminent apocalyptic upheaval. For further reading, see A. F. Segal, "The Second Temple Period," in *The Cambridge Guide to Jewish History, Religion, and Culture*, ed. J. R. Baskin and K. Seeskin (2010).

Esther, Book of (Hebrew, *Megillat Esther*). Part of the *Writings section of the Hebrew *Bible and one of the *Five Scrolls, this biblical book recounts the story of Esther (Hadassah) who, as the narrative begins, lives with her uncle Mordecai in the *Diaspora community of Susa in *Persia. Ahashuerus, the king (identified as Xerxes I, reigned 486–465 BCE) is described as throwing a six-month-long drinking party; during the festivities, he commands his queen, Vashti, to appear before the drunken revelers. She refuses; the king dismisses her and initiates an all-Persia contest to pick his next consort. Esther wins the king's favor, but conceals her Jewish identity from him. Meanwhile, the grand vizier Haman despises Esther's uncle Mordecai because Mordecai will not bow down to him. Haman dupes the weak Ahashuerus into issuing an edict that spells death for all the Jews. When Mordecai hears of it, he appeals to Esther to intervene, saying, "Maybe you have come to royal position for just such a time as this" (4:4). Esther prepares a banquet for the king and Haman. By chance, Ahashuerus discovers that Mordecai once foiled an assassination plot against the king, but was never properly rewarded. The king asks Haman what should be done to honor a loyal servant. Thinking the king is speaking of himself, Haman envisions an elaborate and reverential procession. The king orders it on Mordecai's behalf, to Haman's humiliation. At her banquet, Esther pleads for the Jews; Ahashuerus claims no memory of such a brutal decree. When Haman is identified as the engineer of the edict, the king leaves the room. Haman throws himself on Esther, begging for mercy. The king returns, is outraged at Haman's effrontery, and has Haman hanged. Esther and Mordecai convince the king that the Jews should be permitted to defend themselves (because no royal edict can be withdrawn). Thousands of Persians die as the Jews fight off their enemies. The Jewish festival of *Purim is based on these events.

Although Esther, a faithful Jewish woman living in the Diaspora, may be seen as symbolizing Israel – the underdog who overcomes – her story presents many historical and textual problems and is generally seen as fictional. Beginning with the *Rabbis, many scholars have claimed that Mordecai is the true hero and Esther is merely his agent. Some feminists have decried the way in which Esther uses her sexual appeal to gain access to power; for some, Vashti, the disposed queen who resists male authority, is the greater gender hero. The narrative lacks any mention of observance of Jewish *dietary laws, the *Temple, or the Land of Israel and expresses no anxiety over Esther's marriage to a Gentile. God-language is completely absent, appearing only obliquely in 4:13–15 where Mordecai claims that "relief and deliverance will rise for the Jews from another quarter." Disturbingly, the Esther narrative ends with horrific violence and vengeance. The *Septuagint (LXX, or Greek version of the Hebrew Bible) intentionally added material of a more devout and noticeably religious nature to correct these perceived deficiencies and softened the slaughter into a time of celebration and gift giving. Finally, Esther is the only biblical book not found among the *Dead Sea Scrolls, suggesting that this Jewish community of the first century BCE to the first century CE either did not know of *Megillat Esther* or felt that it was not a divinely revealed religious text. Helpful resources include A. Berlin, *JPS Commentary on Esther* (2001); and S. A. White, "Esther," in *The Women's Bible Commentary*, ed. C. Newsom and S. Ringe (1992); **see also FIVE SCROLLS.**   SANDRA COLLINS

Estonia: See BALTIC STATES

Ethical Monotheism: See GOD; JUDAISM: REFORM, NORTH AMERICA

Ethical Wills are a genre of Jewish literature in which the writer, in contemplation of death, articulates a legacy of spiritual values to bequeath to survivors. It may be considered a subcategory of Jewish ethical or conduct literature. The most common Hebrew term, *tzava'ah*, derived from the root meaning "to command," suggests instructions to the survivors. However, these instructions do not concern how to divide the material inheritance but rather how to live their lives in accordance with the values of the deceased. Some writers have used the term *musar* ("ethical admonition") to describe what they are writing. The literary roots of this genre are biblical, with a paradigm in *David's deathbed instructions to his son *Solomon (1 Kgs 2: 1–9), although some of these directives appear to be anything but "ethical." *Rabbinic literature also contains accounts of final summations of a sage's wisdom intended for his disciples or addressed to his children. A collection of such material is found in BT *Pesaḥim* 112a–b.

Medieval texts are more extensive. Some are explicitly addressed to a son (Eliezer the Great, Judah ibn Tibbon, *Naḥmanides, Joseph ibn Kaspi) or to all the writer's children (Eleazar ben Samuel of Mainz; Elijah de Veali) and other members of the family (*Vilna Gaon), providing counsel, guidance, and instruction drawn from the writer's experience. Others are general statements of the writer's wisdom and worldview, providing guidance addressed to no one in particular. Many contain important autobiographical and historical content, including in one case (Ibn Kaspi) a detailed educational curriculum for the writer's son to follow. *Tzava'at ha-Rivash*, containing instructions in spiritual living from R. Israel *Baal Shem Tov, was the first *Hasidic work of conduct literature to be published (1793). The classic collection of texts in this genre, *Jewish Ethical Wills* (1926), selected, translated, and edited by Israel Abrahams, seems to have popularized the English term. An extensive bibliography of 180 Hebrew *tzava'ot* was published by D. Wachstein in *Kiryat Sefer* 11–12 (1935–36).

In recent years, the ethical will has become fashionable as a genre that can be emulated. A collection of modern texts is J. Reimer and N. Stampfer, *Ethical Wills: A Modern Jewish Treasury* (1983); a revision, *So That Your Values Live On: Ethical Wills and How to Prepare Them*, appeared in 1991. This volume includes a text by the *Yiddish writer Sholom Aleichem (see LITERATURE: YIDDISH), instructing that he be buried among ordinary Jewish workers and requesting that members of his family come together and read one of his humorous stories on the anniversary of his death. There are also several texts from the *Holocaust period and many examples written by *women. Some *synagogues have instituted workshops encouraging members to study and then prepare texts that will be read by members of their family as an enduring statement of what they held important; these ethical wills are preserved in the records of the synagogue for reference after the death of the author.

MARC SAPERSTEIN

Ethics, Environmental.

The core of Jewish environmental ethics is the notion that human beings are responsible for the natural world. The ethics of responsibility follows from the dual aspect of creation: Human beings are created entities, yet Judaism teaches that humans care for nature through their creation in the "divine image." Jewish legislation (*halakhah*) about various aspects of nature constitutes sound conservation policy. Jewish environmental ethics stress the causal connection between the moral quality of human life and the vitality of *God's creation. The corruption of society is closely linked to the corruption of nature. Thus, the just allocation of nature's resources is a religious issue of the highest order. Parts of the land's produce – the corner of the field (*peah*), the gleanings of stalks (*leket*), the forgotten sheaf (*shikhekhah*), the separated fruits (*peret*), and the defective clusters (*olelot*) – are given to the poor, the hungry, the widow, and the orphan (Lev 19:9–10, 23:22; Deut 24:19–21; Ruth 2:2). The failure to treat other members of society with justice is integrally tied to the fate of the land.

Concerns about *ecology figure prominently in the writings of several modern Jewish thinkers. Samson Raphael *Hirsch (1808–1888), the founder of Modern Orthodoxy (see JUDAISM: MODERN ORTHODOXY), advocated the rabbinic ethics of responsibility toward nature. Supportive of Jewish civic and intellectual integration into the modern world, Hirsch noted the negative impact of exile on the Jewish people in that it removed them from involvement with nature. In his discussion of *Tu B'shevat, the Jewish festival that celebrates the *new year for trees, Hirsch declared that "Jewish law continually invites us to the observation of the laws and ways of nature, and is ever leading us from nature to the life of man and there teaching us to use the products of the soil for bringing to ripeness the still nobler blossoms and fruits of a free human life permeated with the idea of God." Hirsch had no qualms, however, in speaking about the human "conquest of nature" and referred to *God as "Creator, Lawgiver, and Controller of Nature."

The ethics of responsibility toward nature informs the thought of Joseph Dov *Soloveitchik (1903–1992), the spiritual leader of Modern Orthodoxy in the twentieth century. In his famous essay, "The Lonely Man of Faith," Soloveitchik interpreted the two creation narratives in the Bible as two paradigmatic human postures toward nature. The first narrative presents "the majestic man" (*Adam I) who celebrates the unique position of the human in creation. Adam I is creative, functionally oriented, and enamored of technology; his aim is to achieve a "dignified" existence by gaining mastery over nature. By contrast, the second creation narrative presents the "covenantal man" (Adam II), the human who was commanded "to till and tend" the earth. Adam II eschews power and control; he is a nonfunctional, receptive, submissive human type who achieves a redeemed existence by bringing all his actions under God's authority. The two postures exist simultaneously and remain permanently at war with one another within every religious Jew. Soloveitchik thus warned against the modern glorification of humanity (Adam I) that brought about the destruction of nature and pointed to religious commitment (Adam II) as the only response to our ecological and existential crisis.

Attempts to link moral consciousness to environmentalism characterized the Jewish environmental movement that emerged in the 1970s and 1980s when some of Abraham Joshua *Heschel's disciples followed his call to return to Jewish sources and created the *Jewish Renewal movement. This movement involves various strands and intellectual sources, but on the whole it has been very instrumental in putting ecological awareness on the map of Jewish consciousness. Some environmental activists, who were born Jews, found their way back to the sources of Judaism by recognizing their ecological wisdom. The organization, Shomrei Adamah (Keepers of the Earth), popularized the idea of Jewish environmentalism; revived nature-based Jewish rituals, such as the ritual meal for the minor holiday *Tu B'Shevat; and organized wilderness trips with a strong Jewish component.

The most significant ecological thinker in the Jewish Renewal movement is Arthur Waskow, who popularized the concept of "eco-kosher" to highlight the connection between human mistreatment of the natural world and social mistreatment of the marginal and the weak. His concern for ecology is part of a deep passion for justice, and his recommendations include the cultivation of self-control, moderation in material consumption, sustainable economic development, and communitarianism. Whereas Waskow's environmentalism is linked to Heschel's social activism and indebted to social ecology, another disciple of Heschel, Arthur Green, has attempted to anchor Jewish ecological thinking in *Kabbalah and *Hasidism, the other dimension of Heschel's legacy. Adopting the ontological schema of Kabbalah, Green maintains that all created entities are in some way an expression of God and are to some extent intrinsically related to each other. Contrary to those who hold that nature per se is not sacred in Judaism, Green blurs the distinction between Creator and the created by adopting the monistic and immanentist ontology of Kabbalah. He suggests that the world and the *Torah are both God's self-disclosure; each is a linguistic structure that requires decoding – an act that humans can accomplish because they are created in the image of God. From the privileged position of the human, Green derives an ethics of responsibility toward all creatures that acknowledges their diversity and insists on the need to defend those that are weakest and most threatened. For Green, a Jewish ecological ethics must be a *torat ḥayyim*, namely, a set of laws and instruction that truly enhances life.

For further reading, see J. Helfand, "The Earth is the Lord's: Judaism and Environmental Ethics," in *Religion and Environmental Crisis*, ed. E. C. Hargrove (1986), 38–52; A. Waskow, *Down to Earth Judaism: Food, Money, Sex, and the Rest of Life* (1995); idem, ed., *Torah of the Earth* (2000); and M. D. Yaffe, ed., *Judaism and Environmental Ethics: A Reader* (2001); **see also** ECOLOGY; ISRAEL, STATE OF: ECOLOGY.

HAVA TIROSH-SAMUELSON

Ethics, Medical. Modern medical progress has radically increased physicians' ability to produce, improve, and extend life. These advances raise many problematic ethical questions for Judaism that have generally not been addressed by previous generations of legal experts. Some Jewish ethicists maintain that if Jewish tradition does not address these specific topics, Jews should look elsewhere for guidance. This approach is honest, but denying Judaism the ability to offer guidance on crucial issues renders it irrelevant to much of life. Conversely, others would quote the rabbinic text, "Turn it over, and turn it over again, for everything is in it" (M. *Avot* 5:22), empowering Jewish tradition to provide direction on everything. However, this approach has the potential to distort the tradition by reading into it much that is not there. These opposing points of view have forced Jews to ask how Jewish teachings can be interpreted honestly and responsibly, yet still provide ethical guidance on contemporary medical concerns. Jews differ widely on how to do this, depending on which methodological approach they adopt. This accounts for the range of opinions on any given topic.

THE BEGINNING OF LIFE: Jewish texts depict children as a great blessing in life. God's first command is "be fruitful and multiply" (Gen 1:28). At the same time, *Sarah, *Rebekah, *Rachel, *Leah, and *Hannah all had trouble conceiving and bearing children, an indication that *infertility was understood as both a heartbreaking and common phenomenon. At the beginning of the twenty-first century, as large numbers of Jews extend their educations, many postpone marriage and attempts to have children until their late twenties or thirties. This is the primary reason why many Jewish couples encounter infertility problems. Rabbis have generally supported assisted reproductive techniques that use the husband's sperm and the wife's egg, but most Orthodox rabbis (see JUDAISM, ORTHODOX entries) forbid the use of donor gametes (sperm or eggs). The Conservative movement (see JUDAISM, CONSERVATIVE) permits the use of donor gametes, but only when the donor's identity is ultimately made known to the child or when the donor reveals not only his or her medical history but also hobbies, traits, and other facts that will help the child gain a sense of his or her genetic heritage and identity.

Sometimes couples want to prevent or abort pregnancies. On the basis of Exodus 21:22–25, the Rabbis distinguished between the status of a fetus and an infant. They ruled that, during the first forty days of gestation, the embryo is "merely liquid"; from the forty-first day to the moment of birth, the child is "like the thigh of its mother." The fetus becomes a full human being only at the moment of birth – specifically, when the head emerges from the vaginal canal or, in a breech birth, when most of the body emerges. This view of fetal development, combined with the strong Jewish mandate to heal, has led Jews across the spectrum to support embryonic stem cell research strongly, because this research uses embryos that would otherwise be discarded when they are five to eight days old and are thus still "merely liquid." All Jewish legal authorities generally allow birth control, with those forms that prevent conception in the first place preferred over methods that prevent implantation thereafter. At the same time, rabbis warn married couples not to wait too long to procreate, lest they encounter infertility problems.

*Abortion is required if the mother's life or health is at stake. It is permitted, but not required, when there is an elevated but not dire risk beyond that of a normal pregnancy (e.g., when the pregnant woman has diabetes). Some rabbis permit abortion when the fetus has a lethal or significantly disabling genetic disease or condition. Exactly what constitutes sufficient danger to the mother or fetus to justify abortion is a matter of debate. Otherwise abortion is forbidden in traditional Jewish approaches, not because it is an act of murder, but because it is seen as an act of injuring oneself, which one may not do to a divinely created body.

END OF LIFE: In Jewish law the general principle is that a person's death may not be hastened; however, the process of dying should not be prolonged. This distinction was much easier to discern in the past, but it remains the line that separates murder from medical aid. In applying this principle, some Orthodox rabbis require every possible intervention to save a person's life and maintenance of life support until the person dies. Others maintain that such intervention is not mandatory but should be continued once it has been initiated. Some suggest attaching a timer to the machine so that a new treatment may be chosen each time the timer is about to run out. Still other rabbis would allow both the withholding and withdrawing of machines and medications at the end of life, just as one does during any other time when an intervention is not for the patient's benefit.

Orthodox rabbis universally classify artificial nutrition and hydration as food and require it whenever the patient cannot eat independently. Conservative rabbis disagree on this definition: Some classify artificial nutrition and hydration as food, whereas others define it as medicine. The latter group permits physicians to withhold or remove artificial nutrition and hydration when they are no longer in the best interests of the patient. Rabbis permit and encourage Jews to donate their body parts for transplant after their deaths. In 1989, Israel's Chief Rabbinate allowed even heart transplants, the hardest donation to justify given the need to ensure that one is not taking a life to help another live.

DISTRIBUTION OF HEALTH CARE: Given its strong commitment to justice and its vision of members of a community as bound to each other, Jewish tradition advocates access to health care for everyone.

Useful resources include E. N. Dorff, *Matters of Life and Death: A Jewish Approach to Modern Medical Ethics* (1998); A. Steinberg, *Encyclopedia of Jewish Medical Ethics* (2003); and M. Washofsky, *Jewish Living: A Guide to Contemporary Reform Practice* (2001), chapter 6.			ELLIOT N. DORFF

Ethics, Rabbinic. The juxtaposition of "rabbinic" and "ethics" inspires comparative reflection, for late ancient rabbinic sources have no term equivalent to "ethics" in the range of meanings employed today. The notion of rabbinic ethics, moreover, is contested in modern contexts. Some consider ethics to be at the heart of *Judaism, perhaps its essence. This view appeared in formulations of "ethical monotheism" first voiced by theologians of Reform Judaism (see JUDAISM, REFORM), and it is found as well in the primacy that Emmanuel *Levinas attributed to ethics in his phenomenology. Others have assigned a higher value to Jewish law (*halakhah) and have questioned whether the category of ethics is appropriate for classical Judaism at all. Such positions often turn on very different understandings of what ethics entails.

In *Hellenistic philosophical schools, roughly contemporaneous with the late ancient Rabbis, ethics addressed the achievement of well-being or flourishing. Certain rabbinic anthologies show similar strong concerns with character, motivation, and ideal ways of living. These collections have often been labeled as ethical, and in many respects they represent the rabbinic inheritance of biblical and ancient *Near Eastern wisdom literature. The distinctive literary form in these anthologies is the short maxim: a dense, compact statement that is often attributed to a specific sage. These maxims are frequently elaborated through commentaries that include *midrash, narrative, and further maxims.

The entirety of rabbinic ethics is not encompassed in ethical anthologies, but they are a good starting point for the definition and study of ethics in rabbinic culture. Rabbinic ethical instruction is a form of *aggadah, or nonlegal teaching, that both presumes and orients a person to the law or halakhah. Ethical matters include the appropriate mental and emotional states that one should maintain while engaging in legally prescribed action, the ways that rabbinic practice transforms character in accord with specific ideals, and exemplary behavior that goes beyond legal requirements. Ethical instruction may be broad, with general calls to avoid sin and perform good deeds, or it may address specific virtues of character or intellect, particularly responses to others and matters of etiquette.

The most influential ethical anthology is Mishnah *Avot, and its earliest commentary is the family of texts known as *Avot de Rabbi Natan (AdRN). Two other ethical texts are Derekh Eretz Rabbah (DER) and Derekh Eretz Zuta (DEZ): the "large" and "small" collections concerning derekh eretz. This phrase literally means "way of the land" and has a number of quite divergent meanings, including worldly or business matters, sexual activity, etiquette, and supererogatory activity (actions that go beyond basic legal or ethical requirements). Both anthologies are made up of smaller manuals that probably circulated independently as guides for conduct. Commentary to large portions of DER and DEZ appears in Kallah Rabbati ("the large text concerning brides"). Kallah Rabbati differs from AdRN in its considerable use of *Aramaic and is closer in style to the Babylonian *Talmud. DEZ has also been associated with a midrashic anthology addressing ethical themes entitled Tanna Devei Eliyahu (Teachings of the School of Elijah); this work is divided into two texts known as Seder Eliyahu Rabbah (SER) and Seder Eliyahu Zuta (SEZ). The topics of scholastic behavior and virtue are also addressed throughout the Talmuds and in midrashic collections. For example, the Babylonian Talmud

emphasizes the importance of virtue in BT Makkot 23b–24b, and other literary units use vivid narratives to uphold modesty and respect for fellows (BT Eruvin 13b, BT Bava Metzia 59a–b).

Rabbis understood ethical cultivation as a communal activity within a scholastic setting that required the guidance of a teacher. Ethical writings often address interpersonal relationships within these contexts. Teachers of Torah must be careful with their words (M. Avot 1:11). Students are told, "Let your house be a meeting place for the sages, sit in the very dust of their feet, and drink with thirst their words" (M. Avot 1:4). Commentary to this maxim specifies the student's response to a sage: "For every word that emerges from your mouth, let him receive it upon himself in awe, fear, trembling, and shaking." The same text also describes *Moses' similar state when he received the *Torah at Sinai (AdRNA, chs. 1, 6). Ethical instruction often addresses the everyday life of students. A maxim instructs, "Appoint for yourself a teacher, acquire for yourself a fellow (ḥaver), and judge every man with the scales weighted in his favor" (M. Avot 1:6). Commentary on this saying asserts that fellows should eat together, worship together, read together, and sleep together if unmarried (AdRNA, ch. 8). Other teachings prescribe behavior at the dining table, when walking between houses, when entering others' homes, in the bath house, and at the toilet (DER, chs. 4–10). All social space offers the opportunity and responsibility to learn appropriate behavior from the sages.

Rabbinic communities emphasized the commandment to "be fertile and increase" (Gen 1:28) and deprecated celibacy; therefore, scholastic values existed alongside concerns with marital and family relationships. Many rabbinic norms concerning *marriage (see also ETHICS: SEXUAL) and *family appear in legal discussions. Two examples address the work a woman does for her husband (M. Ketubbot 5:5; BT Ketubbot 59b–61b) and the obligations of father to son and son to father (M. Kiddushin 1:7). The *ketubbah (marriage contract; BT Kiddushin 2a) delineates a husband's obligations toward his wife. The command of the Decalogue (*Ten Commandments) to honor one's parents is integrated into M. Peah 1:1 and BT Shabbat 127a. In ethical anthologies, the most notable treatments of family are chapter-length discussions of marriage and brides in DER, ch. 1, and Kallah Rabbati, ch. 1, 2. Other passages in ethical literature reveal the Rabbis' dependence on their wives, whether for practical needs or to fulfill ideals such as hospitality (AdRNA, chs. 6, 7; AdRNB, ch. 14). Some sources present wives as a distraction from study (M. Avot 1:5; AdRNA, ch. 7; AdRNB, ch. 15), revealing a tension between two realms of ethical concern – scholastic pursuits and marriage – that remains unresolved in rabbinic writings. At some points as well, ethical literature addresses fathers' relationships with their children, as in teachings that criticize Rabbis who marry off their daughters when they are too young (AdRNB, ch. 48).

For further reading, see J. W. Schofer, The Making of a Sage: A Study in Rabbinic Ethics (2005); idem, "Rabbinic Ethical Formation and the Formation of Rabbinic Ethical Compilations," in The Cambridge Companion to the Talmud and Rabbinic Literature, ed. C. Fonrobert and M. Jaffee (2007), 313–35; and D. Sperber, "Manuals of Rabbinic Conduct," in Scholars and Scholarship, ed. L. Landman (1990), 9–26.

JONATHAN WYN SCHOFER

Ethics, Sexual. The *Torah articulates two goals for sex that are expressed in these commandments: "Be fruitful and multiply" (Gen 1:28), and "he must not withhold from her food, clothing, or conjugal rights" (Exod 21:10). Thus, procreation and the mutual enjoyment and bonding of the couple are understood as two *independent* divine imperatives for sexuality within *marriage. Accordingly, a husband's duty to offer to engage in conjugal relations with his wife applies even when procreation is not likely – for example, when they are using birth control or after her menopause. Conversely, artificial techniques that insert the man's sperm into the woman's womb medically or that bring together sperm and eggs in a petri dish rather than through intercourse may be used to procreate. Judaism conceives of sex as a great gift of God that enhances intimacy between committed partners. Jewish law (*halakhah*) restricts sexual activity to private quarters, and it demands modesty in both clothing and speech.

MARITAL COMPANIONSHIP: According to Genesis 2:4ff., *Adam and *Eve, the progenitors of all humanity, were specifically created for each other, "for it is not good that a person be alone, . . . and therefore a man leaves his father and his mother and clings to his wife so that they become one flesh" (Gen 2:18, 24). One aspect of the basic human need for intimate companionship is its sexual expression. *Exodus 21:10 assumes the sexual desires of women, as well as those of men. The Torah and its later rabbinic interpreters structure the laws of marriage so that both spouses have rights to regular marital sex. Specifically, the couple is forbidden to engage in sexual relations during the wife's menstrual period and for seven days thereafter (see *NIDDAH); during the rest of the month the husband could refuse to engage in sex with his wife for no more than a maximum of one week. The one exception is for students, who are permitted to study Torah elsewhere for up to thirty days without their wives' permission. In general, however, the frequency of marital duties enjoined for men by Jewish law is as follows: "for men of independent means every day, for workmen twice weekly, for ass-drivers once a week, for camel-drivers once every thirty days, for sailors once every six months" (M. *Ketubbot* 5:6).

A husband also has rights to sex within marriage, although the Rabbis forbade him to force himself on his wife (BT *Eruvin* 100b). However, if a woman refuses to engage in conjugal relations with her husband, "he may reduce her marriage settlement by seven *denars* every week . . . until it reaches the full amount of her divorce settlement" (M. *Ketubbot* 5:7). He can then divorce her without repaying her *ketubbah* (the amount specified in his marriage contract) and marry someone else. Jewish law permits couples to have sexual relations in any way they wish (BT *Nedarim* 20b). Marital companionship is more than sexuality – it should extend over a wide scope of activities and topics of conversation. In the Jewish *marriage ceremony, the only explicit reference to the couple being married describes them as *re'im ha-ahuvim*, "the loving friends."

CHILDREN: The Rabbis determined that the command "be fruitful and multiply" is fulfilled when the couple has borne two children, specifically, a boy and a girl (M. *Yevamot* 6:6). However, based on Ecclesiastes 11:6, "Sow your seed in the morning, and do not hold back your hand in the evening," the Rabbis – interpreting "morning" as youth and "evening"

as later in life – maintained that a couple should have as many children as they can (BT *Yevamot* 62b). This imperative has become particularly important for the contemporary Jewish community, which is only 0.2% of the world's population, which lost six million members in the *Holocaust, and which, at the beginning of the twenty-first century, is not even reproducing itself.

If a couple cannot reproduce, however, the commandment to procreate does not apply (see INFERTILITY). Nevertheless, infertile couples may consider *adoption, converting the child to Judaism if he or she was not born to a Jewish woman. The Talmud states that adopting and raising children are equivalent to giving birth to them and that adoptive parents "follow the Lord at all times" (BT *Megillah* 13a; BT *Ketubbot* 50a). Couples suffering from *infertility may also consider using artificial reproductive techniques. Children, of course, are not only an obligation; they are a blessing. Indeed, the Bible is so filled with statements that define a blessed person as one with children (e.g., Gen 15:5; Deut 7:13; Ps 128) that infertile couples all too often feel like failures. The Jewish community must ensure that the tradition's positive attitude toward children does not translate into feelings of alienation for those who cannot produce them.

Marriage also provides the primary context for Jewish education. *Abraham, the Patriarch of the Jewish people, was already charged with teaching his children (Gen 18:19); the *commandment for each Jew to do likewise, which appears several times in the Torah, is enshrined in the first two paragraphs of the *shema* prayer (Deut 6:4–9, 11:13–21).

LEGITIMATE PARTNERS AND CONTEXTS FOR SEX: The Torah (Lev 18, 20) prohibits both incest and *adultery, and it defines the relationships that constitute incest. The Rabbis ban sexual relations between people in more distant family relationships as well (*sheniyyot*, "secondary relatives"; BT *Yevamot* 21a–b; *Mishneh Torah*, "Laws of Marriage" 1:6). Although the tradition frowns on sexual activity by single people, it does not punish it nearly as severely as incest or *adultery. It was precisely to prevent sex out of wedlock that Jewish parents into the twentieth century arranged for their teenaged children to marry. Extended periods of education have made such early marriages rare in the twenty-first century, and sexual activity among the unmarried has become much more common among Jews. Some modern commentators recognize this reality and stress the need for maturity and commitment before entering into a sexual relationship, a sense of responsibility towards one's sexual partner, and concern and respect for the sexual health of oneself and one's partner.

The Torah (Lev 18:22) prohibits homosexual sex by men, and the Rabbis forbade women from engaging in sexual activities with other women as well (*Sifra*, *Aharei Mot* 9:5; *Mishneh Torah*, "Laws of Forbidden Intercourse" 21:8). However, all denominations in modern Judaism except the Orthodox (see JUDAISM: ORTHODOX entries) have eliminated or limited these bans. Again, for liberal Jews, the emphasis is on the cultivation of mature and lasting relationships, respect for oneself and one's partner, and concern for maintaining sexual health.

Useful resources include S. Boteach, *Kosher Sex: A Recipe for Passion and Intimacy* (1998); E. N. Dorff, *Love Your

Neighbor and Yourself: A Jewish Approach to Modern Personal Ethics (2003); and D. Shneer and C. Aviv, eds., *Queer Jews* (2002).   ELLIOT N. DORFF

Ethiopia. Jews of Ethiopia are known as Beta Israel (House of Israel), Israelawi (Israelites), or Falasha. This last designation is derogatory, indicating their outsider status in Ethiopia. The Beta Israel lived in hundreds of villages in northwest Ethiopia, scattered throughout the provinces of Simien, Dembeya, Begemder, Tigray, Lasta, and Qwara. They spoke two principal local languages, Amharic and Tigrinya, mixed with some Agau, a Cushitic language. The Beta Israel were monotheistic, practicing a *Torah-based Judaism; unlike other Jewish communities, they did not observe the Oral Law (rabbinic *Judaism). They followed both the lunar and solar *calendar, observed a complex cycle of *fasts and *festivals, *circumcised their sons on the eighth day, and refrained from work on the *Sabbath. Their religious practices were influenced by Ethiopic Christians; many ritual elements, such as praying to *Jerusalem, the common liturgical language of Geez, and the longing for Zion, characterized both religious communities.

According to many authorities, the inhabitants of the kingdom of Aksum were Jewish before the advent of Christianity in the third to fourth century CE. A popular Ethiopian belief is that the Beta Israel are descendants of Israelite henchmen, who returned to Ethiopia with Menelik, the son of the union of King *Solomon and the *Queen of Sheba. Another theory is that they are descendants of the "lost" Israelite *tribe of Dan (see ISRAELITES: TRIBES; TRIBES, TWELVE).

Some suggest that the Beta Israel emerged as an identifiable Jewish group between the fourteenth and sixteenth centuries. Travelers, from *Eldad ha-Dani in the ninth century to *Benjamin of Tudela in the twelfth, reported the presence of Jews in Ethiopia. Documentary evidence of a Judaized group opposing the Ethiopian Orthodox Church is found in a royal chronicle from the reign of Emperor Amde Zion (1314–44). During the reigns of Emperors Ishaq (1413–38) and Susenyos (1607–32), there were reports of "Ayhud," who resisted conversion to Christianity. They were defeated, lost their rights to land (*rist*), and became a subjugated people, employed as blacksmiths, weavers, and potters and accused of possessing *buda*, or magical evil eye powers. An apparent rebellion in Woggera in the reign of Emperor Sarsa Dengel (1563–97) ended in the captivity, massacre, and enslavement of hundreds of Beta Israel. During the reign of Emperor Fasilades (1632–37), Gondar became the political capital of the empire, and the situation of the Beta Israel improved. They were employed in higher ranking professions, as carpenters and masons in the churches and royal castles; this practice was continued by Emperors Yohannes I and Iyasu I. Although the economic position of the Beta Israel subsequently deteriorated, they continued to work as craftsmen well into the twentieth century.

The encounter with the western world began in the nineteenth century. Protestant missionaries, from the London Society for Promoting Christianity among the Jews and from other European missions, succeeded in converting some Beta Israel while challenging their beliefs and religious practices, such as monasticism, sacrifices, and a strict code of *purity laws. In 1867, Joseph Halévy (1827–1917), a scholar of *Semitics from the Sorbonne in Paris, met with Beta Israel in Ethiopia and described their degenerate condition. The *Kifu-Qen*, or Great Famine, hit Ethiopia between 1888 and 1892, and many Beta Israel either starved to death or converted to Christianity. Dr. Jacques Faitlovitch (1881–1953), Halevy's student, left Paris for his first expedition to Ethiopia in 1904–05. He returned to *Palestine and Europe with two "Falasha" boys, Taamrat Emmanuel and Gete Hermias. During the next thirty years Dr. Faitlovitch brought twenty-five young men from Ethiopia and educated them in different Jewish communities in Palestine and Europe. He hoped they would return and educate their fellow Ethiopian Jews in the tenets of normative Judaism. In 1923, Dr. Faitlovitch established a "Falasha school" in Addis Ababa, which operated until the Italian occupation of Ethiopia in 1935–36.

There was no mass emigration from Ethiopia by the Beta Israel after the establishment of *Israel in 1948. In the 1950s, Emperor Haile Selassie allowed two groups of young Beta Israel pupils to study in a dormitory school in Israel, on condition that they return. In 1973 and then again in 1975, Israel's chief rabbis declared that the Beta Israel could be recognized as descendants of the tribe of Dan and return to their historic homeland, Israel. Before 1984, however, only a few hundred Beta Israel had managed to reach Israel. Finally, in 1984–85, the Israeli government, through Operation Moses airlifted 7,700 Beta Israel from refugee camps in the Sudan to Israel. An estimated 4,000 had died on the way to Sudan. Once knowledge of the airlift reached the press, the Sudanese government suddenly terminated it. Diplomatic relations were restored between Ethiopia and Israel in 1989 and Israel coordinated Operation Solomon in May 1991 in response to international pressure demanding the rescue and emigration of the Beta Israel. In Operation Solomon, 14,310 Jews were airlifted out of Ethiopia to Israel in thirty-six hours, as the fate of the Ethiopian government headed by Mengistu Haile Mariam hung in the balance. During the 1990s, other Beta Israel groups in Ethiopia began claiming the right to immigrate to Israel; in response there was an airlift of a few thousand Beta Israel from the remote area of Qwara. Thousands of "Felesmura," claiming descent from Beta Israel who had converted to Christianity beginning in the nineteenth century, have since migrated to Israel and converted to Judaism; more are still waiting in Ethiopia.

In 1986 Ethiopian Jews in Israel staged a strike opposite the offices of the Israeli Chief Rabbinate in Jerusalem, objecting to the symbolic conversion they had to undergo to be accepted as "full" Jews. Today, there are still obstacles in registering Ethiopian Jewish marriages. *Kessotch (Ethiopian priests) act as spiritual leaders for the older generation, alongside young Modern Orthodox (see JUDAISM: MODERN ORTHODOX) Ethiopian rabbis, who have been ordained in Israel. New immigrants from Ethiopia are entitled to subsidized public housing, free Hebrew instruction, an initial cash payment for absorption expenses, and special educational advantages. They serve in the Israel Defense Forces. The majority of Ethiopian Jewish adults in Israel live beneath the poverty line. The laws of ritual impurity observed in Ethiopia are being modified, and married women are encouraged to go out to work to assist with family income. The seven-generation kinship unit is beginning to break down, and the Ethiopian divorce rate (30%) is far higher than in the general population. However, members of the community have been increasingly successful in attaining high-ranking jobs in politics, the media, *sports, and education. In the first decade of the twenty-first century, there are 105,000 Jews of Ethiopian origin in Israel. Their average age is 20.1 compared to 30.5 in the general Jewish population. More than 20% of the Ethiopian Jewish community was born in Israel.

Important studies of this community include S. Kaplan, *The Beta Israel (Falasha) in Ethiopia* (1992); W. Leslau, *Falasha Anthology, Yale Judaic Series* 6 (1951); T. Parfitt and E. Trevisan-Semi, eds., *The Beta Israel in Ethiopia and Israel: Studies on the Ethiopian Jews* (1999); J. Quirin, *The Evolution of the Ethiopian Jews: A History of the Beta Israel (Falasha) to 1920* (1992); S. Weil, "Ethiopian Jewish Women: Trends and Transformations in the Context of Trans-National Change," *Nashim* 8 (2004): 73–86; and idem, "Religion, Blood and the Equality of Rights: The Case of the Ethiopian Jews in Israel," *International Journal on Minority and Group Rights* 4 (1997): 397–412.   SHALVA WEIL

EVE. The initial chapters of Genesis contain two versions of human creation. In the first, unnamed human creatures, male and female, are simultaneously created by God's word in the divine image and likeness (1:26-27), as the ultimate act of six days of creation. The second narrative describes how the Lord God formed a man from the dust of the earth, animated him with the breath of life, and placed him in the garden of Eden. Noticing the man's solitary state, the Lord God formed woman from his sleeping body. The man proclaims this female to be "Bone of my bones and flesh of my flesh/This one shall be called woman, for from man was she taken" (2:23). The man, who is not explicitly called *Adam until Genesis 3:17, names his wife Eve (Ḥavvah) after the couple leave the garden. The biblical writer connects her name with the word for life (hai), since "she was the mother of all the living" (3:20). In Genesis 3, Eve is persuaded by a being called "the serpent" to disobey God's command and to eat fruit from a forbidden tree, and she convinces Adam to do so as well. The result is the expulsion from Eden and the human burdens of frustration, suffering, and mortality. A further consequence of this narrative is the lasting Jewish and Christian association of Eve (and by analogy all women) with sexual seduction, moral weakness, and blame for the human condition. Eve bears three sons, *Cain and Abel (4:1-2) and Seth (4:25). For further reading, see J. R. Baskin, *Midrashic Women: Formations of the Feminine in Rabbinic Literature* (2002); and A. L. Lerner, *Eternally Eve: Images of Eve in the Hebrew Bible, the Midrash, and Modern Hebrew Poetry* (2007).

JUDITH R. BASKIN

Evil and Suffering are issues of constant significance in the Hebrew *Bible and its commentaries and in the various philosophical and theological reflections that have emerged within Jewish culture (see THEOLOGY; THOUGHT, MODERN). In the Bible there are a variety of approaches to the topic. *God creates a world that God repeatedly says is good or very good, but creatures in the form of *Adam and *Eve rebel and are expelled to live in a world that is full of difficulties and hardships. They might well be seen as having brought their sufferings on themselves. Yet, if God could have foreseen what they were to do, then how free

were they to make the choices that they made? The contrast between an omniscient, omnipotent, and benevolent deity and the sorts of things that happen in the world that God created is a major concern in a number of later biblical works, in particular *Job and *Psalms. In more optimistic passages from the latter book, the psalmist has confidence in God's support for the virtuous and punishment of the wicked, but in more gloomy verses he questions the ubiquity of divine justice. Throughout Job the role of God's justice in the world is thrown into doubt, and although Job himself is satisfied with God's appearance toward the end of the book, hardly anyone else is. It does not answer the central question of why existence is so difficult and painful, nor does God address the apparently arbitrary distribution of evil and suffering in the world.

A significant difficulty in Job is the absence of a clear doctrine of an *afterlife. Later Jewish writings address this omission to a large extent, perhaps in reaction to the emphasis on the next world in *Christianity. Thus, thinkers could argue that undeserved suffering in this life could be compensated by future and more enduring rewards in a world to come. *Saadia Gaon, for example, argues in his commentary on Job that it is only fair for God to reward the virtuous and punish the wicked, and if there is no evidence that this happens in this world, then it must happen in the next. Yet in Jewish thought and, in particular, the writings of Moses *Maimonides, this sort of approach did not find many supporters. It was often rejected as banal and as implying too great a resemblance between divine and human justice. Divine providence certainly flows through the universe, Maimonides argues, and it is up to us to acquire it and use it in positive ways, but precisely what it is apart from the functioning of the laws of nature is difficult to specify. Because Maimonides holds that there is no point of comparison between divine and human attributes, we cannot really think of God as like a king who is trying to provide assistance to his subjects; this would make God far too similar to his creatures. However, in popular Judaism a belief in the afterlife has become entrenched, and many *prayers in the liturgy refer to the next world and the *resurrection of the dead. Of course, this afterlife can be allegorized and understood to represent something like the survival of part of us in our descendants or those whom we influence. However, many Jews literally interpret these prayers and the texts on which they are based, and they locate the evil and suffering of this world within an acceptable religious context.

The idea that suffering is a test or a punishment for some crime has been popular with many commentators. Such an explanation makes individual and collective distress part of the divine plan and easier to accept. Over the course of Jewish history, however, it became increasingly difficult to see suffering in this way; it is difficult to see any religious rationale for a history so replete with persecution and murder. Some *mystics (see BREAKING OF THE VESSELS; KABBALAH) saw suffering and the prevalence of evil as prefiguring the coming of the *messiah; in their view, God would have to prevent the world from sinking into total darkness.

In modern times the debate has become heightened in response to the *Holocaust. Some have argued that it was just one disaster among the many that have occurred in

Jewish history and that it raises no new questions of why God allows such suffering to occur. Yeshayahu *Leibowitz suggests that the Holocaust was an extreme period of suffering not unlike in quality the many previous such disasters in Jewish history and therefore not calling for a radical change in *theology. Some, particularly from the Orthodox community, have suggested that Jews deserved punishment because of their lax performance of *halakhah, or that God has a plan but we do not know what it is, or that the face of God is sometimes hidden, allowing human beings who are capable of great evil to exercise that evil. To do otherwise would be to interfere in our freedom of action. Other modern theologians, such as Richard *Rubenstein, have suggested that after the Holocaust it is impossible to believe in a personal God who has a *covenant with the people of Israel. This is a radical view, which suggests that the Holocaust represents a break with history. The amount of suffering that it brought about means that an entirely different understanding in Jewish theology is necessary, not only of the role of evil but also of the divine role in the fate of the Jewish people. Others have supported the view that the Holocaust led directly to the creation of *Israel and so was not futile but rather represented a period of necessary suffering before the successful event that it brought about.

For further reading, see O. Leaman, *Evil and Suffering in Jewish Philosophy* (1995); Y. Leibowitz, *Judaism, the Jewish People and the State of Israel*, trans. E. Goldman (1992); R. L. Rubenstein, *After Auschwitz: History, Theology and Contemporary Judaism* (1966); and **see HOLOCAUST: THEOLOGICAL RESPONSES.**   OLIVER LEAMAN

Exile: Hebrew, *galut*. See BABYLONIAN EXILE; DIASPORA

Exilarch ("Head of the Exile"; Hebrew, *rosh ha-golah*; Aramaic, *resh galuta*), was a Parthian or Sassanian imperial designation for the head of all the Jews in the ancient community of exiles in *Babylon. The origins and development of this institution are obscure; rabbinic traditions about the Exilarch in Babylonia and the *Patriarch (*nasi*) in the land of Israel are closely linked: Both institutions descended from King *David and had access to non-Jewish rulers, great wealth, and the power to appoint judges. The exilarchate may predate the patriarchate, and it is possible that Patriarchs and those who told stories about them looked to Babylonia for a model of inherited Jewish leadership. The conquering Muslims reconfirmed the authority of the Exilarch (as they did with the Nestorian Christian *Catholicos*) over his co-religionists. The process of consolidating and centralizing Jewish authority under Muslim rule was facilitated when the *Sura and *Pumbedita academies relocated to Baghdad shortly after the city was established and the Exilarch became a regular courtier at the Abbasid court. **See also GAON AND GEONIC ACADEMIES; and IRAQ.**

Exodus, Book of is the second of the five books in the *Torah (Pentateuch), the first section of the Hebrew *Bible. The English name "Exodus" (departure) is derived from the Greek title for the book; Israel's departure from *Egypt is the central theme of the book. In Hebrew the book is called *Shemot*, "names," after its first significant word: "These are the *names* of the sons of Israel who came down to Egypt" (1:1). Exodus contains forty chapters, according to the medieval

Christian division, and eleven weekly portions (*parashot*; see TORAH READING) according to the traditional Jewish classification. Geographically, Exodus begins in Egypt and ends with the Israelites encamped around Mount Sinai, located either in the Sinai Peninsula or across the Gulf of Eilat in the mountains of *Arabia. Chronologically, Jewish tradition holds that only 129 years elapsed from the death of *Joseph (1:4) to the completion of the *Tabernacle (40:2), despite verses that give the impression of a longer period of time (12:40).

STRUCTURE AND CONTENTS: Although the story of Israel in Egypt continues from that told in the last chapters of *Genesis and the completion of the Tabernacle (*mishkan*) in the last chapter sets the stage for *Leviticus, the book of Exodus is an independent literary work with an introduction and conclusion. It is a complex narrative, interspersed with *laws, instructions for rituals, and exact specifications for the structure of the Tabernacle and its paraphernalia. The narrative sections contain irony, rich characterizations, and evocative literary links to other sections of the Hebrew *Bible. Three major divisions can be discerned in Exodus. The first section focuses on the enslavement and liberation of Israel (1–18), including the emergence of *Moses (Exodus 1–2); the revelation at the burning bush (3:1–6) and Moses' commissioning (3–7:13); the plague narrative (7:14–11:10); the Exodus itself and laws regarding the *Passover (12–13); the journey to Mount Sinai, with the dramatic crossing of the Reed Sea and the triumphant Israelite victory song (14–17); and *Jethro's visit and the organization of a judicial system (18). The middle section of Exodus concentrates on the *covenant at Mount Sinai (19–24). Distinct themes encompass the preparation for the covenant (19), the giving of the *Ten Commandments (20:1–14), legislation regarding proper *worship (20:15–24), the "Book of the Covenant" (21–23), and the covenant ratification ritual (24). The final division, Exodus 24–40, is devoted to the Tabernacle (*mishkan*). Central incidents include instructions for building the Tabernacle, its accessories, and garments for the priests (25–31); the episode of the *golden calf (32–34); and the Tabernacle's construction (35–40).

SIGNIFICANCE: Exodus introduces many of the events and institutions crucial for the subsequent development of the Israelite nation and *Israelite religion. Among them is the affirmation of Israel's nationhood in Exodus 1, in fulfillment of God's promises to the patriarchs (Gen 12:2, 13:16, etc.). In Exodus as well, a more complete perception of Israel's *God as YHWH, sovereign over nature and history, is achieved. In Genesis, Israel's deity was known by several names, including YHWH (usually translated "Lord"). In Exodus, YHWH becomes the chief name for God in the Hebrew Bible, specifically through the revelation to Moses (3:6), the ten plagues, and the *redemption of the Israelites from slavery.

Central to the book is the Exodus event itself: Through it, God demonstrates the power to liberate Israel from oppression, to intervene in human events, and to make human history the stage for the unfolding of the divine will. The Exodus is henceforth the basis of God's authority to command Israel's undivided allegiance (Exod 20:2) and marks the beginning of Israel's history as a free nation. Leviticus 23:4–8 declares that the first month of the *calendar is the spring month of Nissan, in remembrance of the Exodus. Similarly, Moses' mediation between God and the Israelite nation at Mount Sinai and his repeated defense of the people define the *prophetic role for the rest of Israelite history. Exodus also describes the establishment, at Sinai, of God's covenant, a contractual, legal relationship with the people of Israel, who attain a new status as a "kingdom of priests and a holy nation." Conditional to Israel's role as God's covenant partner is its adherence to divinely ordained law (see LAW: ANCIENT *NEAR EAST and HEBREW *BIBLE). Finally, God's presence among the people is established by the construction of the Tabernacle, a movable dwelling place for the deity. It allows Israel access to God for leadership, worship, and prophetic inspiration. At the same time, Exodus establishes a religious leadership: The Levites, the tribe of Moses and Aaron, are given charge of the Tabernacle as a reward for their zeal for Israel's God, and Aaron and his sons inaugurate a hereditary priesthood (kohanim; see ISRAELITES: RELIGION; TEMPLE AND TEMPLE CULT).

HISTORICITY: Whether the book of Exodus reflects historical reality is an issue hotly debated by modern scholars. Modern scholarship assumes that the book was written hundreds of years after the described events, with a theological rather than historical focus. It mentions no names of the pharaohs of the enslavement or Exodus eras and offers little in the way of an exact chronology of events. In Exodus 12:40, for example, Israel's stay in Egypt is 430 years; Genesis 15:13–16 mentions 400 years and four generations for the enslavement alone. Further, the number of Israelites who participated in the Exodus would have been more than two million souls, based on the Exodus statement that 600,000 adult males left Egypt (12:37). These numbers support the religious claim that Israel's God had the capability to "take one people out of the midst of another" (Deut 4:34), but the objective historian must greet these figures with skepticism. Folkloric elements, such as Moses' salvation in a reed basket in Exodus 2 (similar to a legend about the *Mesopotamian king Sargon), also suggest that caution is necessary when using the book as a historical record. Compounding these problems on the Egyptian side is the complete absence of any corroborating evidence for the presence and enslavement of Israel in Egypt or of their departure en masse.

Yet, although Egyptian texts do not mention the name "Israel," there is ample evidence for the presence of Asiatics – those who spoke *Semitic languages akin to Hebrew – in New Kingdom Egypt, and many of these were slaves. Egyptian texts mention the presence in *Egypt (and *Canaan) of Apiru/Habiru, a class of mercenaries and renegades, and because this term bears a similarity to "Hebrew," it offers tentative evidence of the presence in Egypt of those who would later constitute Israel. That some Israelites had their origins in Egypt is attested by the fact that several members of the tribe of Levi bear Egyptian names, including Moses, Phineas, Hophni, and Merari. Further, Egyptian historical texts speak of the expulsion of the Hyksos, a ruling class with Canaanite origins, back into *Canaan around the year 1550 BCE. This event, along with less significant departures of Canaanites, including runaway slaves, may have been condensed into the Torah's memory of a large-scale Exodus from Egypt.

Recent scholarship includes W. H. C. Propp, *Exodus 1–18* (1999); idem, *Exodus 19–40* (2006); and N. Sarna, *The Jewish Publication Society Torah Commentary: Exodus* (1991).

ELAINE GOODFRIEND

Ezekiel generally appears as the third book of the Major *Prophets (see BIBLE: PROPHETS AND PROPHECY) in the Hebrew *Bible, immediately following *Isaiah and *Jeremiah. However, some authorities consider it to be the second book and place Isaiah in the third position (BT *Bava Batra* 14b). The book presents the words of Ezekiel ben Buzi, a *priest of the Zadokite line, who was exiled to *Babylonia together with the king of *Judah, Jehoiachin ben Jehoiakim, by the Babylonian monarch, Nebuchadnezzar, in 597 BCE (2 Kgs 24:8–17). Rabbinic tradition raises questions about the canonical status of the book of Ezekiel because it frequently conflicts with legal statements found in the *Torah. R. Ḥanina ben Ḥezekiah reportedly burned three hundred barrels of oil while working nights to reconcile the interpretation of Ezekiel with that of the Torah so that Ezekiel might be accepted as a legitimate biblical prophet (BT *Shabbat* 13b; BT *Ḥagigah* 13a; BT *Menaḥot* 45a).

Ezekiel's exile to Babylonia prevented him from serving as a Zadokite priest in the *Jerusalem *Temple. During his thirtieth year (Ezek 1:1–3), the age when a Zadokite priest would normally begin Temple service (Num 4:3; cf. Num 8:23–25, which states that priestly service begins at age twenty-five), Ezekiel began his prophetic career by experiencing visions of *God. Because his inaugural vision took place during the fifth year of King Jehoiachin's exile (i.e., 592 BCE), his final vision of the restored Temple in the twenty-fifth year (Ezek 40:1) must have taken place when Ezekiel was fifty (Ezek 40:1), the age when a priest would normally retire from active service. His birth in 622 BCE would then correspond to the eighteenth year of *Josiah, king of Judah, who sought to restore the sanctity of the Jerusalem Temple at the center of a reunited Israel. Ezekiel's own career constituted a continuation and expansion of Josiah's program, even after the death of the king, the destruction of the Temple, and the exile of the people, until the holy Temple was reestablished at the center of a reunited twelve *tribes of Israel and a reconstituted and purified creation.

The book of Ezekiel consists of thirteen units, each introduced by a date formula and each presenting his visions and oracles. Filled with Temple imagery and priestly concepts, these units indicate that Ezekiel adapted his priestly identity and role in his prophetic career, even in a foreign and unclean land. Ezekiel is a watchman for the people; his priestly and prophetic task is to instruct them to sanctify themselves according to the divine will. He interprets the *Babylonian Exile and the destruction of the Temple as a process through which God purges the world in preparation for the reestablishment of a purified Temple with Israel at the center of a purified creation. Ezekiel 1–7 presents his inaugural vision of God borne through the heavens by four heavenly creatures (ḥayyot); they are identified in Ezekiel 9–10 as the cherubs (kerubim) who guard the *Ark of the Covenant placed in the Holy of Holies of the Jerusalem Temple. Ezekiel's divine vision is based on the imagery of the Ark of the Covenant, a symbolic representation of God's presence in the Temple that would be experienced by the High Priest when he entered the Holy of Holies to present the *Yom Kippur purification offering (Lev 16; cf. M. *Yoma*). On the basis of this vision, Ezekiel was commissioned as a prophet of God to speak to Israel once he returned to his home in Tel Aviv, a known site in Babylonia.

Ezekiel 8–19 presents the vision of God's departure from the Temple. Ezekiel once again sees the divine throne chariot hovering above Jerusalem as God commands heavenly figures, dressed in white linen like priests, to destroy the city as if it were the Yom Kippur purification offering. Indeed, those persons killed in the city are likened to the goat slaughtered for the offering, and those persons who survived to go into exile are likened to the goat released into the wilderness to carry away the sins of the people (Lev 16). Successive units of the book present Ezekiel's oracles concerning the punishment of Israel (20–23); symbolic actions concerning the destruction of Jerusalem and the punishment of neighboring nations (24–25); oracles concerning Tyre and its rulers (26–28); oracles concerning *Egypt (29:1–16; 29:17–30:19) and Pharaoh (30:20–26; 31; 32); and final oracles concerning the nations and Ezekiel's role as the watchman warning of impending punishment (32:17–33:20).

Ezekiel 33:21–39:20 presents a series of oracles concerned with the restoration of Israel, such as the rise of a new Davidic monarch, the reunification of the kingdoms of *Israel and *Judah, the *resurrection of the dead bones, and the purification of the land from the impurity caused by the corpses of the army of Gog defeated by Magog, a symbolic representation of the forces of evil in the world that must be overcome as part of the process of divine purification. With the purification of the land from death, Ezekiel 40–48 presents a final vision of the restoration of the Temple, the twelve *Israelite tribes, and creation at large. This vision of the restored Jerusalem Temple does not correspond to either the Temple of *Solomon or the Second *Temple; this prompted later commentators such as *Rashi and David *Kimhi (Radak; see also, BIBLICAL COMMENTARY: MIDDLE AGES TO 1800) to declare that Ezekiel's vision represents the Third Temple that is yet to come. Ezekiel's visions of punishment and restoration served as an important model for the development of the rabbinic *hekhalot* (palaces) and *merkavah* (chariot) teachings (see MYSTICISM: *HEKHALOT* AND *MERKAVAH* LITERATURE). His statement that God will become "a small sanctuary" (11:16) for the exiles is the basis for the development of the *synagogue. The modern city of *Tel Aviv was named for Ezekiel's home in Babylonia to symbolize the restoration of Israel.

Recommended reading includes M. A. Sweeney, "Ezekiel," *The Jewish Study Bible*, ed. A. Berlin and M. Brettler (2003); M. Greenberg, *Ezekiel 1–37*. Anchor Bible 22, 22A (1983, 1997); and J. D. Levenson, *Theology of the Program of Restoration of Ezekiel 40–48* (1976).

MARVIN A. SWEENEY

Ezra and Nehemiah are the titular protagonists of the biblical book of Ezra-Nehemiah (or, as is often the case in modern Bibles, the books of Ezra and Nehemiah). Included in the Writings section (see BIBLE), Ezra-Nehemiah is an account of the restoration of *Jerusalem after the Persian defeat of *Babylon (sixth to fifth centuries BCE). The initial part of the book recounts the first waves of returnees from Babylon and their efforts to rebuild the *Temple in response to the decree of Cyrus of *Persia (Ezra 1–6). After the completion of the Temple, the text introduces the priest and scribe Ezra who travels from Babylon on a commission from the Persian king to restore the Temple vessels and install a legal system. On arriving in *Jerusalem, Ezra discovers that some Judean men had married women from outside the community and he extracts a pledge from those who have done so to expel their wives and children (Ezra 7–10).

Following the book of Ezra, the book of Nehemiah opens with a first-person narration of the Israelite Nehemiah, a courtier in the palace of Persian king Artaxerxes I, who travels to *Judah to become its governor. Amid local resistance emblematized by Sanballat and Tobiah (possibly governors of *Samaria and *Ammon, respectively), he leads a project to refortify Jerusalem and, in response to popular outcry, relieves the debt belonging to struggling small farmers (Neh 1–7). At this point in the story, Ezra reappears and undertakes a public reading of the "Book of the Torah of Moses." The community responds with a public confession of penitence and a written agreement to maintain the Temple (Neh 8–10). The final chapters of Nehemiah (11–13) are an eclectic mix of lists and short narratives, including the dedication of the newly built wall and the reemergence of Nehemiah's story, in which he institutes Temple and tithe reforms and, like Ezra, condemns exogamous marriages.

As this summary of the book suggests, Ezra-Nehemiah is a complex text that interweaves earlier sources with original writing. These sources include narratives, such as the "Nehemiah Memorial" (Neh 1–7, 13), and extensive lists, including two nearly identical lists of returnees in Ezra 2 and Nehemiah 7. Ezra-Nehemiah employs these diverse sources to create a purposeful, if complicated, story. The people of Jerusalem, led by the former exiles, make a unified, deliberate, and comprehensive effort to restore the city and its religious and social institutions. This story is a profoundly theological retelling of history and, as such, reflects the postexilic community's understanding of itself as much as actual events. At times, the text resorts to creative and ambiguous chronology (Ezra 4 obscures the differences between the sixth and fifth centuries; the time frame of Ezra's activities is far from clear). Additionally, the notion that the exiled Judeans responded immediately and single-mindedly to Cyrus is tempered by archeological evidence that suggests that Jerusalem remained depopulated and desperately poor well into the fifth century and did not thrive until the *Hellenistic era. **See ARCHEOLOGY: ANCIENT TIMES THROUGH THE PERSIAN PERIOD; BABYLONIAN EXILE; RUTH, BOOK OF; SAMARITANS.**

SEAN BURT

F

Fackenheim, Emil Ludwig (1916–2003), philosopher and theologian, was born in Halle, Germany. He entered the *Hochschule für die Wissenschaft des Judentums* in 1935, studied at the University of Halle, and fled *Germany to *Britain in 1939, after several months of detention in Sachsenhausen. After a year at the University of Aberdeen and a lengthy period of incarceration as an enemy alien in Britain and *Canada, he continued his studies at the University of Toronto. He taught at the University of Toronto from 1948 until his retirement in 1982, when he moved to *Jerusalem.

Fackenheim's philosophical work on Kant, Schelling, and Hegel focused on the problem of faith and reason and especially on the way in which philosophical thought confronted the reality of transcendence. *The Religious Dimension in Hegel's Thought* (1968) discusses how Hegel's philosophical system understands and incorporates religion and the divine. His early essays on German Idealism were edited by John Burbidge and published as *The God Within: Kant, Schelling, and Historicity* (1996). Their central theme is the problem of the historicity of human existence and the claim to transcendence offered by philosophy.

His Jewish theological work defended the primacy of faith and revelation for a responsible understanding of Jewish existence and the relationship between freedom and tradition in modern Jewish life. Adapting the conception of *revelation articulated by *Buber and *Rosenzweig in the Weimar period, Fackenheim argued against secular rejections of religion and naturalistic interpretations of Judaism. His essays written between 1948 and 1967 are collected in *Quest for Past and Future* (1968).

In the late 1960s Fackenheim began to confront the horrors of *Nazi atrocities. His study of Hegel had shown him that even the most comprehensive philosophical thought could not adequately find a place for radical *evil, and his study of the *Holocaust convinced him that even Hegel, were he alive today, would not be a Hegelian, because no philosophical, theological, or social scientific thought could satisfactorily grasp the meaning or purpose in those events. Although Fackenheim became persuaded of the radical historicity of thought in the face of such evil, he nevertheless argued that opposition to the aims of Nazi criminality could be hermeneutically articulated. The result, for Jewish thought, was Fackenheim's statement of the 614th commandment: Jews are forbidden to grant Hitler any posthumous victories. His most developed defense and formulation of this imperative of opposition are expressed in *God's Presence in History* (1970).

During the 1970s Fackenheim elaborated this obligation to recover the past. *To Mend the World* (1983) provides his most philosophically sophisticated demonstration of the necessity of post-Holocaust Jewish existence, its possibility, and the conceptual contribution of Judaism to the very understanding of the process of "mending" that must follow radical historical ruptures. In that work, Fackenheim shows how a dialectical inquiry into the agency of the Nazi atrocities and into the responses of its victims exposes both the limitations of thought to comprehend the evil and the necessity of life to resist it. Fackenheim's essays and books written after 1983 continued to elaborate the character of Jewish life in a post-Holocaust world and to explore the implications of the Holocaust for Christians, Germans, and others. **See also, HOLOCAUST: THEOLOGICAL RESPONSES; and THOUGHT, MODERN.**   MICHAEL L. MORGAN

Family: See also ISRAELITES: MARRIAGE AND FAMILY LIFE; MIDDLE AGES: CHILDHOOD; entries under WOMEN

Family and Marriage: Early Modern Period. The premodern Jewish family is popularly imagined as consisting of an arranged but stable marital union that produced many children and maintained strong bonds with an extended family. Yet sources reveal that Jewish family size between 1500 and 1800 was on average relatively modest (4.4 in *Poland-Lithuania) and that deviations from traditional standards of married life did occur. Adulterous affairs (see ADULTERY), sexual liaisons with non-Jews, spousal abuse, male absence because of extensive travel for *yeshivah study or trade, and sexual dysfunction or impotence could result in marital breakdown and divorce. Women were particularly vulnerable in such cases, since Jewish law and custom usually proscribed their ability to initiate *divorce and prevented abandoned wives (*agunot) from remarrying. Yet traditional Jewish *marriage practices remained the norm and were never seriously challenged until the appearance of Jewish advocates of *Haskalah (Jewish Enlightenment) in the late eighteenth century.

Arranged marriages (age sixteen for women and eighteen for men) were considered the ideal, because it was assumed that young people possessed neither the ability to postpone sexual activity until a more mature age nor enough life experience to choose proper partners. For families of means, matchmaking strategies were dictated by considerations of *yihus*, familial prestige emanating from the scholarly accomplishments and, to a lesser extent, wealth of one's forebears and living relatives. *Betrothal negotiations were accompanied by an examination of the potential groom's talmudic expertise. Some young men of humble backgrounds managed to acquire *yihus* independently by earning a scholarly reputation, enabling them to marry daughters of wealthy families. After the wedding, a young married couple and their offspring might be fed and housed by the wife's or husband's parents for a period of two to eight years; this support, known as *kest*, enabled the couple to learn a trade or the groom to continue his studies. In reality, only parents with the economic means for a dowry and *kest* could afford *yihus*-based matches for their teenaged children.

After the *kest* period husband and wife typically both worked, with the wife functioning as a junior partner in the family economic enterprise. The stereotypical arrangement whereby the wife supported her husband financially while he studied all day was only practiced among certain elites.

Both *Ashkenazic and *Sephardic elite families used marriage strategies to create continental familial trade networks, as well as inheritable rabbinical posts for the families' scholars. The most successful families took on surnames, including Horowitz, Shapiro, Margaliot, and Landau, and formed a Jewish aristocracy based predominantly on *yihus,* wealth, and, most important, *Torah knowledge. Unlike non-Jewish markers of nobility like land and titles, Torah knowledge could not be automatically transferred; hence there was an added urgency to educate one's sons. When, as a child, the Polish/Moravian memoirist Phineas Katzenellenbogen was unable to explain a certain passage, his father shamed him by reciting each scholar in his ancestral line. The education of daughters was usually less formal and rigorous; their value on the marriage market was determined by their *yihus,* mercantile abilities (including knowledge of non-Jewish languages), and physical attractiveness. Daughters were also treated differently in their fathers' wills, receiving one-half of the male's portion in Ashkenazic society.

Early modern memoirists, like Leon *Modena (Italy, 1574–1648) and Ber of Bolechow (Poland, 1723–1805), evinced discomfort with arranged marriages and strove to marry women of their own choosing. Yet *Glückel of Hameln (Germany, 1646–1724), who was betrothed at age twelve and married at fourteen, praised her husband as a good provider, pious Jew, and a "good and true father" who "loved his wife and children beyond all measure." Whether he displayed his affection is doubtful, however, because contemporaneous Jewish child-rearing manuals discouraged such a display on the grounds that it would cause disobedience. There are some indications that deference and respect for authority began to break down in eighteenth-century *Eastern Europe. Lower infant mortality rates fueled rapid demographic expansion, resulting in growing numbers of young people and increased generational conflict. The emergence of *Hasidism was central in shaping the youth culture of the period. Although Hasidic leaders maintained the traditional value of *yihus* and even established dynasties, their traditionalist opponents' bans against marriage into Hasidic families had an impact on matchmaking. *Maskilim,* supporters of Jewish Enlightenment, attacked arranged marriages in principle and sometimes encouraged growing disenchantment with them. The Polish *maskil* Salomon *Maimon (ca. 1752–1800) effectively abandoned his wife to pursue secular studies in Germany. Yet most of Jewish society in this era continued to adhere to traditional familial practices.

GLENN DYNNER

Fashion. From the mid-nineteenth-century influx of *Central European Jews to the later mass *immigration of *Eastern Europeans, Jews played a fundamental role in the development of the nineteenth- and twentieth-century American fashion industry. In Europe, many Jews had been peddlers, tailors, seamstresses, and fabric merchants; this experience eased their entry into the trades concerned with the making and selling of clothing, as did extended family networks. Jews may also have been so successful in the fashion industry exactly because of their outsider status: They combined an entrepreneurial spirit and business acumen with a distinct understanding of how status and acceptance could be gained, or faked, through the clothes one wore.

Many Jews began as peddlers and then became dry goods merchants as they settled in towns and cities across the nation. The most successful developed larger retail establishments and department stores. At the same time, growing *urban environments encouraged the marketing of fashion. Merchants often became producers as well; others stayed entirely on the production side, as both workers and owners. The initial investment needed to start a garment-making business was low compared to other industries, allowing many workers eventually to become owners.

UNDERWEAR: American Jews were leaders in the manufacture of foundation garments, including corsets, hoopskirts, and cotton underclothes in the nineteenth century and the modern brassiere in the twentieth. In the late nineteenth century, the American corset industry was based largely in and around Bridgeport and New Haven, Connecticut, where a vibrant German Jewish community and sewing machine factories contributed to its development. Firms such as Strouse, Adler & Co. were pioneers in the mass manufacture of corsets, first operating as a "home industry" and later centralizing production in large-scale factories, while continuously developing new designs to appeal to fashionable American women.

The manufacture of hoopskirts in the 1850s and 1860s offered another niche industry in which American Jews were heavily involved. To create the full-skirted modes of the time, the hoopskirt was made by attaching fabric-covered metal hoops, which graduated in size from hip to ankle, to vertical strips of linen. This contraption allowed women to maintain a fashionable silhouette without the added weight and constriction of numerous layers of petticoats. Manufacturers such as Abraham J. Ash, Baruch Mordecai Garfunkel, Moses Garfunkel, and Abraham Isaac Trager were typical of the hoopskirt entrepreneurs who were often connected through religion and family. In the twentieth century, the brassiere, the girdle, and the slip would replace the corset and the hoopskirt as staples of a woman's wardrobe, driving an industry that accounted for an estimated annual earnings of $216 million by 1935. Jews continued to be at the forefront of the design and manufacture of these garments.

The modern-style bandeau brassiere (as an alternative to the corset) was developed in the 1920s, encouraged by the tube-shaped fashions of the time and a greater focus on ease of movement for increasingly active women. The Rosenthals at Maidenform, the Bienenfelds at Bestform, and the Garson family at Lovable were just a few of the companies pioneering bra design and manufacture. Technological advances, such as stretch fabrics and new fastenings to create a better fit, were particularly important and new marketing techniques and powerful advertising campaigns encouraged customer loyalty.

WOMEN'S WEAR: By the mid-nineteenth century, *New York City was the acknowledged American fashion center. A variety of factors, including the presence of small workshops that could change production quickly and a willing and able workforce, created a positive environment for the developing women's wear industry. As the end of the nineteenth century neared, 65% by value of women's garments in the United States were being produced in the lofts and tenements that dotted the cityscape (Soyer). By 1890 the garment industry was firmly entrenched around Broadway, between Canal Street and Ninth Street. Located close to the tenements of the Lower East Side, where piecework was done in so-called sweatshops, this area was a bustling center of both retailing and manufacturing. In the 1920s, the garment industry moved uptown, settling in newly constructed buildings along Seventh Avenue. Although the New York City garment district extends approximately from 30th Street to 42nd Street and from Sixth Avenue to Tenth Avenue, the most successful ready-to-wear designers and manufacturers had showrooms and design studios located in the buildings along a short stretch of this thoroughfare. From the 1920s through the 1960s, the majority of fashionable garments made for American women either originated on Seventh Avenue or were directly influenced by those that did.

The physical movement of the industry reflected changing attitudes toward American fashion as well. The fashion industry did not truly develop until the first decades of the twentieth century. Before then, American designers were generally not known or respected. American manufacturers relied on Europe – Paris, London, and *Vienna – for inspiration, and their products were seen as exact copies or close adaptations, rather than original ideas. However, even though inspiration may have come from Europe, Americans were fully able to produce and market high-quality fashions, both custom-made and ready-wear, and the 1910s and 1920s saw the emergence of a new class of designers, who garnered greater respect and customer loyalty; they included Max Meyer, Edward Mayer, Hattie Carnegie, Nettie Rosenstein, Miss E. M. A. Steinmetz, and Sally Milgrim.

Well-known and respected Seventh Avenue firms raised the bar for American fashion, but low- and mid-priced apparel companies disseminated it to the average American woman through adaptations of the latest styles from Paris and New York. Designers like Maurice Rentner and Nettie Rosenstein may have represented the highest quality and creativity that Seventh Avenue had to offer, but firms such as Leslie Fay (Fred Pomerantz), Puritan (Carl Rosen), and Jonathan Logan (David Schwartz) made up in volume what they lacked in originality or luxury. These men, and many others like them, were manufacturers and businessmen rather than designers and artists, but they were able to take luxurious fashions and adapt them to the American market.

MEN'S WEAR: Although men's wear is rarely subject to the fashion vagaries that affect the women's industry, nineteenth-century ideals of respectability and gentility played a powerful role in the development of the fashionable male in western societies. The relative stability of men's wear styles in the nineteenth and early twentieth centuries allowed for the development of regional centers of manufacture outside New York City, including Rochester, New York; Baltimore; and *Chicago. Firms based in these cities pioneered one of the major American contributions to men's fashions – the production of high-end ready-to-wear suits and coats.

Rochester, New York, especially, became an important hub of men's clothing production and fine tailoring. In the late 1840s and early 1850s, a handful of German Jewish and Anglo-Jewish immigrants and their families founded Rochester's ready-made men's wear industry. From Rochester's first such firm, Greentree and Wile (est. 1847), to those established later such as Hickey-Freeman,

Adler-Rochester, Stein-Bloch, and Michaels Stern, the city's manufacturers developed numerous systems to simplify and increase production. Although manufacturing was eventually consolidated in large-scale factories, where unskilled workers could be given specific tasks to perform on each garment (facilitating faster, less expensive production), these companies also employed many highly skilled tailors to maintain production standards. Of the owners of these firms, all but Jeremiah Hickey were Jewish; Hickey's partnership with Freeman represented a relatively rare pairing of Jew and non-Jew as co-owners of a clothing company.

In *Chicago, too, firms such as Hart, Schaffner & Marx and Kuppenheimer produced quality men's wear. Hart, Schaffner & Marx (founded 1887) was one of the largest and most important men's wear manufacturers in the country, because of the quality of their product and innovations such as standard pricing, selling from swatches rather than fabrics carried in weighty trunks, and advertising in the first national men's apparel magazine.

The men's ready-wear industry soon produced other types of clothing, such as sports and leisure attire. The so-called Ivy League look was made famous by J. Press of New Haven, Connecticut. Originally geared toward well-to-do college boys, his finely tailored clothing was gradually adopted by men of all ages who favored a traditional American style.

CALIFORNIA: The western United States, and California in particular (see UNITED STATES, WESTERN), became important to the American fashion industry in the early to mid-twentieth century when several distinct regional influences, including traditional western work wear, Hollywood glamour, and the casual southern Californian lifestyle, created a new fashion vernacular.

The needs of miners flocking to Gold Rush-era California supported an early industry that provided strong and durable work wear. The best known purveyor of such clothing, Levi Strauss, came from Bavaria to New York City in 1847, where his brothers owned a wholesale dry goods business. He eventually ended up in *San Francisco where he started his own firm, first selling and then manufacturing clothing. His partnership with Jacob Davis, a Jewish tailor originally from Latvia and the inventor of riveted denim overalls (patented 1873), resulted in the famed jeans still worn today. Although Levi Strauss & Co. initially manufactured functional work wear, its clothing styles became virtually ubiquitous as casual wear in the twentieth century.

A similar reinvention of traditional western work wear can be seen in the flashy outfits made for rodeo stars and performers and produced by three Eastern European Jewish immigrant entrepreneurs: Nathan Turk (born Teig), Rodeo Ben (Bernard Lichtenstein), and Nudie Cohn (born Nutya Kotlyrenko). They capitalized on the increasing popularity of the cowboy as a symbol of "rugged individualism" in American myth and popular *entertainment while introducing a "cowboy" style that combined fine tailoring with decorative embroidery (based on Central and Eastern European motifs), fringes, and rhinestones. Movie, music, and rodeo stars such as Gene Autry, Roy Rogers, Hank Williams, and Elvis Presley became loyal customers, projecting the ornate styles across the country.

Although work wear was being produced in California in the nineteenth century, a full-fledged garment industry geared toward "fashion" did not develop until the 1920s and

'30s. As Eastern European immigrants and garment workers from the East Coast moved to California after *World War I, they opened new firms, benefiting from the booming economy centered on real estate, oil, and the movie industry. At the same time, well-established firms moved away from producing work wear. In Los Angeles, Jewish manufacturers drew on the distinctive southern Californian lifestyle centered on the car, the beach, and outdoor recreational activity for design inspiration. They used comfortable and easy-wear fabrics like cotton, denim, and gingham, creating youthful and inexpensive sportswear that became emblematic of an emerging "American Style" and a mainstay of the ready-to-wear industry in the twentieth century.

Frederick Cole (born Cohn) focused his attention on knitting colorful and fashionable swimsuits that reflected the southern California lifestyle. The company, renamed Cole of California in 1941, transformed women's swimwear through important innovations. These included the lowered back and defined bust in the late 1920s; the introduction of Malatex (Cole's exclusive process of stitching rubberized thread through fabric) in the 1930s; the design of the two-piece "Swoon Suit," which laced up the sides of the trunk and featured a tie-bra; and exclusive contracts with Esther Williams and Christian Dior in the 1950s.

Originally based in New York City, the *film industry moved to *Los Angeles after World War I, and Hollywood became the center of world movie production and distribution. Several of the early studio heads were Jews who had worked in the garment industry. Understanding the appeal that fashion had for women, they featured glamorous clothing in their movies and entered into cross-marketing arrangements with Los Angeles' garment manufacturers, who were also predominantly Jewish. The studios would often invite manufacturers to see a film before it opened, encouraging them to produce affordable copies of the dresses in conjunction with the film's release. Many labels incorporated the words "Hollywood," "Movie," or "Film" into their names, further promoting the idea that anyone could feel as glamorous as a big-screen star. At the same time, Hollywood costume designers became known across America as their styles were adapted for the average woman. As in other areas of the clothing industry, many of the best known designers were Jewish. Adrian (Adrian Adolph Greenberg), Helen Rose, Edith Head, and Bernard Newman all had an enormous influence on American fashion in the mid-twentieth century.

ACCESSORIES: Accessories, including footwear, handbags, gloves, belts, hats, and jewelry, have always constituted a significant part of the fashion business, and Jews have played a vital role here as well. In the nineteenth and first half of the twentieth centuries, hats and gloves were considered essential for both men and women. The glove industry, centered in and around Gloversville, New York, was initially dominated by owners and workers of Anglo-Saxon origin. By the 1890s, however, Jews had become the significant ethnic group in this niche industry. German Jewish immigrants like Nathan Littauer entered the field in the 1850s and 1860s, opening the door for later waves of Eastern European immigrants. Well-known Gloversville firms included Bachner-Moses-Louis (producers of Bacmo and Elite gloves) and the S. Schrecker Glove Co. (today the Grandoe Corp.).

Both men and women wore hats outside the home until the mid-twentieth century. From high end to low, millinery formed an important part of the fashion trades and employed many Jewish immigrants. At the top, firms such as Bes Ben and John-Frederics were heralded for their innovative designs; cheaper brands like Betmar produced fashionable models at more reasonable prices. While the status of hats and gloves declined over the course of the twentieth century, the fortunes of shoes continued to rise. By the 1920s, shoe design became significantly linked to fashion; in the 1930s, Jewish-owned companies such as Delman and I. Miller became major trendsetters of the women's shoe industry. Similarly, handbag manufacturers have produced a broad range of products for an equally diverse clientele, from low-priced firms such as Garay, to more upscale makers like Koret, to luxury brands like Judith Leiber.

For further reading, see E. E. Greenberg, "Fashion," in P. Buhle, ed., *Jews and American Popular Culture* (2006); Yeshiva University Museum, *A Perfect Fit: The Garment Industry and American Jewry* (2005); M. Gottesman, *Hoopskirts and Huppas* (1999); H. Cobrin, *The Men's Clothing Industry: Colonial through Modern Times* (1970); H. George-Warren and M. Freedman, *How the West Was Worn* (2000); J. Farrell-Beck and C. Gau, *Uplift: The Bra in America* (2002); and D. Soyer, *A Coat of Many Colors* (2005).   ELIZABETH E. GREENBERG

Fast Days. Fast days (known as a *ta'anit* or *tzom*) are periods of self-denial for three purposes: (1) to achieve *atonement for one's sins, (2) to commemorate a sorrowful moment in history, or (3) to show gratitude to God. There are six statutory, public fasts on the Jewish *calendar. Only *Yom Kippur, the Day of Atonement, is obligated by the *Torah itself. The Fast of Esther (13th of *Adar) is alluded to in the book of *Esther, but was rabbinically mandated as a means of commemorating the three-day fast Esther ordered on account of Haman's decree (Esther 4:16). The other four fasts are the 9th of *Av (*Tisha B'Av), the 17th of *Tammuz, the Fast of Gedaliah, and the 10th of *Tevet, all of which are associated with the destruction of *Jerusalem and the *Temple. They were extrapolated by the Rabbis on the basis of *Zechariah 8:19, which refers to four fasts that will be transformed into days of joy during the *messianic age.

Public fasts fall into two categories: major and minor. Yom Kippur and Tisha B'Av are the two major fasts; they require a complete day of abstention from eating, drinking, bathing, sexual intercourse, and wearing leather shoes. The four minor fasts are observed from sunrise to sunset and require the same abstentions, excluding bathing. Except for Yom Kippur, fasts are prohibited on the *Sabbath and are moved to another day. The *Mishnah (*Ta'anit* 4:6) explains the significance of both Tisha B'Av and the 17th of Tammuz. Tisha B'Av primarily memorializes the destruction of both the First and Second Temples, yet many calamities throughout Jewish history, subsequent to the *Mishnah, have also become associated with that day. The 17th of Tammuz primarily memorializes the events that led to the destruction of the First Temple. The Fast of Gedaliah is held on the day after the two days of *Rosh Ha-Shanah, the 3rd of Tishri. It memorializes the assassination of Gedaliah ben Aḥikam, a righteous Jewish governor, after the Babylonian conquest of Jerusalem. His death destroyed any hope for Jewish self-government after the Babylonian siege. The 10th of Tevet memorializes the actual siege of Jerusalem in 586 BCE, connecting it to the destruction of the Temple.

Jewish law obligates Jews over the age of *Bar or *Bat Mitzvah to fast. However, certain exceptions are noted to the rules of self-denial, including for pregnant and nursing women, people who are ill, and those who are very delicate or feeble. Other common fasts are the Fast of the *Firstborn (14th of *Nissan), the fast of the *bride and groom on their wedding day, fasting on an anniversary of *death (*yahrzeit), and Yom Kippur Katan. This rarely observed fast, inspired by sixteenth-century *kabbalists, is held on the day before the *New Moon. There is also a prominent tradition of holding individual or communal fasts to protect against disasters, such as drought. Moreover, some pietists fast as a means to combat the inner evil inclination or as personal atonement for improper dreams, thoughts, or behavior. For further reading, see P. Steinberg, *Celebrating the Jewish Year: The Spring and Summer Holidays* (2009); and E. Ki Tov, *The Book of Our Heritage* (1979).   PAUL STEINBERG

Federations: See ORGANIZATIONS: NORTH AMERICA

Feminism: See JUDAISM, FEMINIST

Festivals. There are six biblically based holidays: *Passover (Pesaḥ), *Shavuot, *Rosh Ha-Shanah, *Yom Kippur, *Sukkot, and *Purim. Five are derived from the *Torah and Purim is based on the book of *Esther. Of the six, the *Bible only designates the agriculturally based festivals of Passover, Shavuot, and Sukkot with the term *ḥag* ("festival"; pl. *ḥagim*). These holidays are also distinguished as the three "Pilgrimage Festivals," or the *shalosh regalim,* when Israelites would travel to the *Temple in *Jerusalem to make a pilgrimage offering.

Since the end of the Temple era, rabbinic *Judaism expanded the character of the pilgrimage festivals from their original agricultural origins to attain profound historical and spiritual significance. Thus, Passover is the "Season of Our Freedom"; Sukkot is the "Season of Our Rejoicing"; and Shavuot, identified as the date of the *revelation at Mount Sinai, is the "Season of the Giving of the Torah." Elevating the status of these festivals helped ensure their relevance to Jews after the Temple was destroyed in 70 CE and the majority of Jews lived outside the Land of *Israel and were no longer involved in agricultural labor. Sukkot and Passover are observed for seven days in *Israel but for eight days outside of Israel. This is because of the two-day extension of sacred days in the *Diaspora. Shavuot is observed for one day in Israel and two in the Diaspora. The eighth day of Sukkot, *Shemini Atzeret, deemed a day of sacred assembly, is biblically ascribed its own sanctity. Whether Shemini Atzeret is its own holiday or an extension of Sukkot itself is debatable. In Israel and among Reform Jews in the Diaspora, Shemini Atzeret is combined with *Simḥat Torah; other Jews in the Diaspora observe Simḥat Torah separately on the following day. The pilgrimage festivals, as well as Shemini Atzeret and Simḥat Torah, each have unique observances, yet they all share the work restrictions that apply on the *Sabbath, with the exception of food preparation, transference of fire, and carrying. The first and last days of Sukkot and Passover have this sacred significance, whereas the intermediate days (*ḥol ha-mo'ed*) are categorized as semi-festivals and allow for various additional forms of work.

The holiest days of biblical origin are Rosh Ha-Shanah (the *New Year) and Yom Kippur (Day of Atonement). They frame the "Ten Days of Repentance," marked by intense self-reflection, prayer, and penitence. Rosh Ha-Shanah is observed for two days both in Israel and in the Diaspora; most of the observances of the pilgrimage festivals apply. Yom Kippur is the final day of *repentance and judgment, which the Torah describes as a day of spiritual purification. Consequently, Yom Kippur is a day of self-denial and fasting (see HIGH HOLIDAYS).

Although Purim is a biblically derived holiday, it does not share the same sanctity as the aforementioned festivals. Rather it is a minor festival, akin to *Ḥanukkah, a post-biblical holiday. Several other minor holidays of rabbinic origin include Hoshanah Rabbah (the seventh day of Sukkot), *Tu b'Shevat, Lag ba-*Omer, and, in modern times, *Yom Ha-Atzma'ut (Israel Independence Day) and Yom Yerushalayim (commemoration of the 1967 unification of Jerusalem). The celebration of the New Moon (*Rosh Ḥodesh), is also intended to be a semi-festival, as demonstrated by its liturgical additions.

Useful resources are P. Steinberg, *Celebrating the Jewish Year: The Spring and Summer Holidays* (2009); T. H. Gaster, *Festivals of the Jewish Year* (1952); and I. Klein, *A Guide to Religious Jewish Practice* (1979).   PAUL STEINBERG

Film: Europe (POST–WORLD WAR II). The *Nazi era and World War II had an overwhelming impact on the roles and images of Jews in European cinema. A significant number of Jewish directors and actors perished in the *Holocaust, and others joined the exodus from Europe in the 1930s and did all of their subsequent work in Hollywood, the center of the U.S. film industry. The substantial majority of post-war European films with Jewish content concern the *Holocaust. Documentaries on this subject depict Jews in radically different ways. The relatively early *Night and Fog* (*Nuit et Brouillard;* directed by Alain Resnais, 1955) presents Jews as a passive historical presence; while a narrator explains the horrors of the Holocaust, the corpses of murdered Jews appear on the screen. In contrast, the monumental *Shoah* (directed by Claude Lanzmann, 1985) contains no still footage of the past. Instead, the Jews in the film are survivors who bear witness by relating their own experiences. Rather than being asked for judgments, these interviewees simply relate their recollections of the events they lived through, overwhelming the audience with inexplicable horror.

The Garden of the Finzi-Continis (*Il giardino dei Finzi Contini;* directed by Vittorio de Sica, 1970), a joint Italian/West German production based on the novel by Italian author Giorgio Bassani (see LITERATURE: CONTEMPORARY EUROPE), won the Oscar for Best Foreign Language Film. Focused on Bassani's native Ferrara, the narrative chronicles the passivity, obliviousness, and resulting destruction of a wealthy Jewish family that barricades itself behind the walls of its villa until it is too late to escape Nazi deportation. A later Italian movie, *The Truce* (*La Tregua;* directed by Francesco Rosi, 1997), is based on Primo *Levi's 1963 memoir of the same title (also published in English as *The Reawakening*) and stars John Turturro. The film begins with powerful images of the Soviet liberation of *Auschwitz and chronicles the nine subsequent months of "Primo's" wanderings through Europe before he was finally able to return to his home in Turin.

Many recent European films include Jewish characters largely as the occasion for non-Jews to experience the Holocaust. In the Czech film, *Divided We Fall* (directed by Jan Hřebejk, 2000), a young Jewish man, David, hides while Gentile characters act out the roles of an enthusiastic Nazi collaborator, a man who intellectually opposes the Nazis but does nothing, and the heroic Marie who insists on concealing David and saving his life. David only acts at the end, after Marie falsely claims to be pregnant to explain her suspicious behavior to the authorities; because her husband is incapable, David must impregnate Marie. Rather than focusing on David, this climax serves as a metaphor for Europeans' impotence to stop the Holocaust. Similarly, in the French romantic comedy, *God Is Great and I'm Not* (*Dieu est grand, je suis toute petite*; directed by Pascale Bailly, 2001), Jews serve as a foil for a young woman to work through her psychological pain. Her story becomes a commentary on European *antisemitism in that the special status of Jews highlights the non-Jew's feelings of deep insignificance, which could lead to suicide or murder. Several German dramas such as *Aimée & Jaguar* (directed by Max Färberböck, 1999) and *Rosenstrasse* (directed by Margarethe von Trotta, 2003) suggest a kinship in love and oppression between Jews and Germans during the Holocaust. In *Aimée & Jaguar*, the Christian Lilly complains to her lesbian Jewish lover Felice about the façade of her life as a heterosexual married woman. The movie further equates their positions as targets of oppression by having Felice declare that Lilly is "no better or worse than any of us." Despite Felice's death in a concentration camp, the movie continues this theme by focusing primarily on Lilly, who identifies her suffering with that of Felice. *Rosenstrasse* develops the theme of Jewish and German kinship, when Ruth, a Holocaust survivor, must consider the implications of having been saved by a non-Jew. Early in the movie, Ruth prevents her daughter, Hannah, from marrying her non-Jewish lover. After Hannah learns that a non-Jewish woman, Lena, saved Ruth, she travels to Germany to meet her. Lena convinces Hannah to reconcile with her mother, who in turn reverses herself and approves Hannah's marriage.

Other Holocaust dramas, such as *Europa Europa* (Germany; directed by Agnieszka Holland, 1991), *Life Is Beautiful* (Italy; directed by Roberto Benigni, 1997), and *The Pianist* (France/Germany/Poland/UK; directed by Roman Polanski, 2002), present Jews as active protagonists. *Europa Europa* portrays a Jewish teenager, Solly, struggling to survive by integrating further and further into Nazi society. Although Solly could superficially be characterized as wanting to erase his Jewish identity, the movie instead conveys that he is only trying to survive, and he deserves no criticism. Unlike *God is Great*, *Europa Europa* counters negative images of Jews, specifically the stereotype that Jewish men desire non-Jewish women sexually. Here, instead, a Christian girl pursues Solly, who must flee because his circumcision would reveal him as a Jew. The movie dramatizes the classic struggle to be German on the outside while remaining Jewish on the inside, extending it to its absurd limit in a scene where the Jew serves as the example for a Nazi scientist's lesson on Aryan anatomy. The movie also questions the circumcised penis as defining Jewish identity. In the final scene when the war is over, Solly urinates in public, exposing his penis entirely as a functional organ.

In *Life Is Beautiful*, co-written, directed by, and starring Roberto Benigni, the main character is a happy-go-lucky man who spends the first half of the movie courting and marrying a non-Jewish woman; after their deportation to a Nazi work camp, he spends the second half of the film trying to shield his son from the Holocaust experience by convincing him that it is all a game. Controversial for its overtly humorous approach to the Nazi murder of European Jewry, *Life Is Beautiful* adapts the Aryan anatomy scene in *Europa Europa* for comical purposes. Here, the Jew masquerades as a fascist Italian school superintendent who lampoons the pseudo-science of Nazi doctrine throughout his demonstration. The twenty-first-century audience identifies with the main character in this scene, because he, like them, knows that the racial science of that time was nonsense.

The Pianist (2002), directed by Roman Polanski, who himself survived the Holocaust as a child in *Poland, portrays the experience of Polish Jewish pianist Wladyslaw Szpilman (played by Adrien Brody in an Oscar-winning performance). Along with its enormous violence and destruction, the implication of the Holocaust is that it kills not just musicians, but music itself. Although the silencing of Jewish voices is expressed by silencing the piano, in one scene Szpilman is saved when he plays for a Nazi officer and the universality of the music trumps the particularity of his Jewishness.

An interesting theme in French cinema is the representation of positive relationships between Jews and Arabs; an early example is *Madame Rosa* (directed by Moshé Mizrahi, 1977; Oscar for best foreign film, 1977), based on the 1975 novel *The Life before Us* (*La vie devant soi*) by Romain Gary (see LITERATURE: FRANCE). Simone Signoret (1921–1985; born Simone Kaminker) plays an aging prostitute and Auschwitz survivor who cares for the children of her younger colleagues, including the Arab Momo (Mohammed), who becomes her sole support and comfort as she faces death. A Jewish boy known as Momo (Moïse) plays a similar role in *Monsieur Ibrahim* (*Monsieur Ibrahim et les fleurs du Coran*; directed by François Dupeyron and starring Omar Sharif, 2003). Here, the orphaned Momo forms a close relationship with the Turkish grocer Monsieur Ibrahim, who becomes his surrogate father.

The 2003 German comedy *Go for Zucker* (*Alles auf Zucker*; directed by Dani Levy) is about estranged brothers in contemporary Germany who must reconcile and follow Jewish religious ritual if they are to inherit their deceased mother's estate. This immensely popular slapstick, "politically incorrect" film has been described as "the first German-Jewish comedy since World War II"; it has been lauded for portraying Jews in a non-Holocaust context and for reviving the German Jewish humor that once played a central role in German popular culture.

Another trend in European films with Jewish themes is historical sagas. The 1999 international co-production *Sunshine* (written and directed by István Szábo and starring Ralph Fiennes), traces the triumphs and tragedies of a Hungarian Jewish family, the Sonnenscheins, during the course of the twentieth century as they encounter Hungarian nationalism, the Holocaust, and the communist regime. *Sofie* (directed by Liv Ullman, 1992) is based on a portion of the 1932 Danish novel, *Mendel Philipsen and Sons* by Henri Nathansen (see LITERATURE: SCANDINAVIA). Its powerful and sympathetic portrait of a loyal Jewish daughter torn between her family's traditions and the new possibilities offered by late-nineteenth-century *emancipation is a sensitive portrayal of Jewish life in *Denmark. Among a number of other Scandinavian films with Jewish characters and themes are *Freud flyttar hemifrån* (Freud's Leaving Home) directed by Susanne Bier (1991); *God afton, herr Wallenberg* (Good Evening, Mr. Wallenberg), directed by Kjell Grede (1990); *Opphav ukjent* (Origin Unknown), directed by Nina Grünfield (2005); *Mendel*, directed by Alexander Røsler (1997); and *Kådisbellan* (The Slingshot), directed by Åke Sandgren (1993).

For further reading, see I. Avisar, *Screening the Holocaust: Cinema's Images of the Unimaginable* (1988); O. Bartov, *The "Jew" in Cinema: From "The Golem" to "Don't Touch My Holocaust"* (2005); M. Marcus, *Italian Film in the Shadow of Auschwitz* (2007); S. Taberner, "Philo-Semitism in Recent German Film: *Aimée and Jaguar, Rosenstrasse,* and *Das Wunder Von Bern,*" *German Life and Letters* 58:3 (2005): 357–72; and R. Wright, *The Visible Wall: Jews and Ethnic Outsiders in Swedish Film* (1998).

Amos Cohen and Devorah Shubowitz

Film: *Holocaust. See HOLOCAUST REPRESENTATION: FILM

Film: Israel. The history of Israeli film production is linked to the political and ideological changes that have taken place since the beginning of *Zionism. The first Zionist propaganda films, directed in *Palestine by Russian-born Jewish filmmakers who were acquainted with Soviet cinematic techniques, emphasized the value of working the land and overcoming its hardships. This approach accompanied the idea of the "New Jew" who, as opposed to his oppressed and persecuted ancestors in the *Diaspora, had returned to his historical homeland to reclaim it through physical labor. Most of these films were documentaries for raising funds in *Diaspora communities. The few fiction films directed soon after Israel's independence had similar themes, retracing the Zionist pioneers' heroic tales and focusing on the collective efforts of the new settlers to make the desert bloom. Baruch Dinar's feature film, *They Were Ten* (1960), embodies these heroic ideas: Set at the end of the nineteenth century, the film retraces the many challenges that a group of Zionist pioneers, composed of nine men and one woman, faced on their arrival in Palestine, as they encounter the hardships of tilling an arid land and dealing with the local Arab population.

This national heroic cinema did not last for long. During the 1960s, as a result of western influences and the development of individualization and bourgeois tendencies in Israeli society, Israeli cinema began to reject collective aspirations and depict a more individual society. Joseph Miloh's film, *He Walked in the Fields* (1967), demonstrates the changes that had taken place in the national ethos. Adapted from Moshe Shamir's novel written twenty years earlier, this film reveals the first breaches in the national narrative through the story of its protagonist Uri (played by the leading Israeli actor, Assi Dayan), who does not automatically support national goals; on the contrary, he is hesitant about the Zionist ideological engagements of building a country, laboring on the land, and taking part in defending it. However, in contrast to the kind of heroes who would follow, Uri finally makes the "right" choice and meets his death in a dangerous and heroic operation against the soldiers of the *British Mandate.

This moment of hesitation was soon translated into the narratives and iconography of the next movement of Israeli cinema – "Personal Cinema" (also known as the "New Sensitivity") – a unique and influential cinematic movement that appeared between the 1967 Six Day War and the 1973 Yom Kippur War (see ISRAEL, STATE OF: WARS). Personal cinema chose to detach from the heroic values of previous films and create new protagonists and new narratives supported by a new cinematic language largely influenced by western cinematic new waves. Like their predecessors in the national cinema movement, the heroes of personal cinema bear no traces of the Diaspora. Moreover, they convey the experience of a generation born in this land, who therefore consider Israel as their only lived experience. Shot according to the style of the French new wave, these films exhibit new heroes, devoid of any kind of past, with a predilection for defining a new and nonpolitical urban Israeli identity. This urban predominance reflects the protagonists' rejection of their parents' conception of labor and heroism, a conception that was still dominant in the heroic national cinema.

Uri Zohar's film, *Three Days and a Child* (1968), exemplifies this new trend. Based on the modernist 1965 novella by A. B. *Yehoshua, the film tells the story of a Jerusalem student who is asked to take care of the son of his *kibbutz ex-girlfriend for three days. His love–hate relationship with the boy is expressed throughout the film by the changes in his attitude toward the innocent child, alternating between warm love and care to a strong desire to kill him. The protagonist's attempt to reconstruct past values and memories through his contacts with his lost lover in the kibbutz fails. At the end of the film he acknowledges that, by relinquishing his past on the kibbutz, he is left with a purposeless urban life, with no memory or identity.

Personal cinema was not the only cinematic genre in Israel during the 1960s. These years were also marked by the appearance of a new popular cinema named after a Middle Eastern pastry, the *burekas* films. Most of this genre's characteristics can be detected in the famous precursor, *Sallah Shabbati,* directed in 1964 by the Hungarian Jewish satirist Ephraim Kishon. *Sallah Shabbati* tells the adventures of Sallah, a *Mizraḥi emigrant, and his large family, from their first day in bureaucratic Israel to his final triumph over its hegemonic system. As opposed to the New Jew incarnated in the *sabra* image, Sallah does not consider labor to be the highest value, refuses to contribute to any form of collectivity, and spends his time playing cards with his neighbor. Yet Sallah ends up a winner, leading his family to the new housing project, and all without having worked one single day in his new country. Kishon's popular comedy showed the deeply rooted gaps between the newcomers and the Israelis and the unwillingness of the former to overcome them. Although *Sallah Shabbati* is not a typical *burekas* film, it invented the basic parameters of the genre by revealing the flaws of the Zionist ideology, mainly the separations among different groups in Israeli society: Middle Eastern Jews vs. European Jews, the kibbutz vs. government temporary housing, and, finally, the highly motivated workers vs. those who refuse to turn work into a religion. The *burekas* genre repeated and developed most of these themes, especially the oppression of the poor by the rich that, in the Israeli context, was translated into the oppression of the Mizraḥi Jew by his European brother. Underestimated by local critics, these films gained a large popularity and contributed to the normalization of Israeli society. However, neither personal cinema nor *burekas* cinema, both of which reflected a natural reaction to the ideological national cinema, lasted long; both came to a sudden end with the outbreak of the Yom Kippur War in 1973, which was to be remembered as Israel's most traumatic war with far-reaching implications for the entire political system.

After some nostalgic youth films, Israeli cinema reinvented itself after 1977, when the right-wing Likud party attained power for the first time since the establishment of the state. Israeli filmmakers, who mostly belonged to the dethroned elites of the left, reacted by creating the first political films that openly criticized the ways in which Zionism chose to implement itself among the country's various populations: Ne'eman's *Paratroopers* (1977), Moshinson's *Wooden Gun* (1979), Wollman's *Hide and Seek* (1980), and Bukai's *Avanti Popolo* (1986), among others, denounce some of the acts committed in the name of Zionism since Israel's earliest days. Barabash's *Once We Were Dreamers* (1987) goes one step further, using the basic narrative structure of the canonical national film *They Were Ten* to return to the past and provide another perspective on the heroic Zionist narrative. Like the earlier film, *Once We Were Dreamers* tells the story of a group of pioneers and how they cope with the hardships of the land, as well as their many confrontations with its Arab inhabitants. However, it also focuses on the pioneers' inability to realize their dream and create a new form of society based on collectivity and equality; finally it presents their disappointment as they come to understand the gaps between their utopian vision and reality.

During the 1980s, other important films such as *Noa Is 17* (Yeshuron, 1982), *Rage and Glory* (Nesher, 1984), *Late Summer Blues* (Shor, 1987), and *Himo, King of Jerusalem* (Gutman, 1987) turn to the past and, like *Once We Were Dreamers*, reveal a crisis in the Zionist ideology. Adopting the point of view of the "other," these films depict various Israeli–Palestinian interactions, emphasizing a reversal of the roles of the parties involved. Whereas, the early national cinema had offered a picture of the Israeli willing to sacrifice him- or herself for the birth of the nation, in the 1980s it was the Palestinian who was allotted the same heroic role, with the same motivations. Ne'eman's *Fellow Traveler* (1983) and *Streets of Yesterday* (1989), Barabash's *Beyond the Walls* (1984), and Haim Buzaglo's *Fictive Marriage* (1988), among others, tell how the encounter between Israelis and Palestinians led to an assertion of the humanistic standpoint vis-à-vis those who once were enemies.

Israeli cinema gave up its political discourse during the 1990s, after the end of the first Intifada and the signing of the Oslo accords, and began to focus on the investigation of more personal narratives related to particular ethnic, gender, and age identities. Films such as *Life According to Agfa* (Dayan, 1992), *Lovesick on Nana Street* (Gabison, 1995), *Sh'chrur* (Hasfari, 1995) and *Walk on Water* (Fox, 2003) – all conveying the experience of specific identities in Israeli society and their feelings of internal exile – mark a new stage in Israeli cinema that became highly popular. The main difference between this cinema and the personal cinema of the 1960s, both of which deal with private experiences, is that these later films

are reflections of a general atmosphere of alienation, guilt, and disappointment in Zionism. While focusing on private lives, these films also continue the tendencies of the political cinema of the 1980s in daring to deconstruct the founding mythologies of the national historiography and so confronting them with a universal morality.

In the first decade of the twenty-first century, Israeli films once more have returned to the Israeli–Palestinian conflict, although with a profoundly different approach from the 1980s. Not only are the political realities very different but Israeli filmmakers are also more critical in their reflections on the harm caused to both sides by the Israeli occupation. Amos Gitai's *Kedma* (2001), for example, takes a revisionist approach to Israel's 1948 War of Independence in its depiction of Jewish refugees from European *antisemitism who expel Palestinians from their homes. Udi Aloni's *Forgiveness* (2006) takes place on the site of the massacred Palestinian village Dir Yassin where an Israeli psychiatric hospital has been established. In this multilayered site, *Holocaust survivors continue to relive their nightmares, and a young Israeli soldier, weighed down by his responsibility for the death of a Palestinian child, sinks into madness.

Beaufort (2007), directed by Yosef Cedar, focuses on actual events that took place during the Israeli military's evacuation from south Lebanon in 2000 and asks critical questions about some of the basic assumptions of the Israeli security police and its responsibility for superfluous casualties. Ari Folman's *Waltzing with Bashir* (2008) takes Israeli guilt one step further in its meditation on the trauma of the first Lebanon war in which Folman participated as an eighteen-year-old soldier. Folman made the radical decision to use animation for most of the film, but his animated world abruptly ends with documentary footage of the brutal attacks on the Sabra and Shatila Palestinian refugee camps. Although Israel was not directly involved in these massacres, they were enabled by the wartime situation. In a quite different tone, Eran Kolorin's debut film, *The Band's Visit* (2007), recounts the story of an Egyptian police band that becomes lost in Israel and ends up in a remote development town. This bittersweet comedy points out the similarities between the Egyptians and their Jewish hosts. Another film that returns to the Israeli–Palestinian conflict with a different approach is *Lemon Tree* (2008) directed by Eran Riklis. As in his previous movie, *The Syrian Bride* (2004), Riklis has chosen a Palestinian woman as his protagonist, hinting that changes in both Israeli and Palestinian attitudes will only come with a different, feminine approach.

For further reading, see N. Ben-Shaul, *Mythical Expressions of Siege in Israeli Films* (1977); N. Gertz, *Motion Fiction: Israeli Fiction in Film* (1993); N. Gertz and Y. Munk, "The Representation of the Israeli-Palestinian Conflict in Israeli Cinema," in *Encyclopedia of the Israeli-Palestinian Conflict*, ed. C. Rubenberg (forthcoming); A. Kronish and C. Safirman, *Israeli Film: A Reference Guide* (2003); and E. Shohat, *Israeli Cinema: East/West and the Politics of Representation* (1989).

NURIT GERTZ AND YAEL MUNK (Research for this chapter was supported by the Israel Science Foundation [ISF] (grant number 786/03) and by the Israeli-Palestinian Science Organization [IPSO])

Film: Latin America. Jews have been significantly involved in Latin American cinema as writers and directors (see also

LATIN AMERICA; LITERATURE: LATIN AMERICA). Many Latin American films with Jewish themes depict historical events. Films that emphasize the saga of *Sephardi Jews include *The Jew* (directed by Jom Tob Azulay, 1999), an exploration of the fate of seventeenth-century Jews who practiced their religion in secret under the threat of the Spanish *Inquisition. Azulay re-creates the trial and execution of the Brazilian playwright Antonio José da Silva, whose martyrdom became a symbol of freedom when *Brazil gained its independence from *Portugal in 1829. *The Longing: The Forgotten Jews of South America* (2007), a documentary directed by Gabriela Bohm, presents the struggles of a small group of South American crypto-Jews (see *CONVERSOS/ CRYPTO-JEWS*), who secretly maintained their faith until contemporary times. *Ladino, the Judeo-Spanish language, is preserved in *Like a Bride*, directed by Guita Schyfter (1974), a film that surveys the *Turkish immigration to *Mexico in the early twentieth century. It is a sensitive portrayal of the friendship between two Jewish girls and their families, one Sephardi, the other *Ashkenazi. This cinematic adaptation of Rosa Nissan's novel also explores interactions between conservatives and liberals and between *communist and *Zionist Jews in *Mexico, up to the late 1960s. Ruth Behar, a Cuban *anthropologist living in the United States, produced *Adío Kerida* (*Goodbye My Love*, 2002), a testimonial film in which she rediscovers her own Turkish and Polish roots in *Cuba (see also *CARIBBEAN*). Guita Schyfter's *The Labyrinth of Memory* (2007) contrasts Schyfter's journey to *Poland to find her own Jewish background with the voyage of a non-Jewish woman from Cuba to Mexico. Through interviews and mutual exchanges both women fill in gaps in their family histories and reconstruct their lives.

The immigration of Ashkenazi Jews to Latin America at the end of the nineteenth century and the beginning of the twentieth century is also a central cinematic theme. Films explore ethnic and religious conflicts and difficulties in achieving integration, not only between Jews and Gentiles but also between Sephardi and Ashkenazic Jews. The pioneering experience of Ashkenazic Jews who settled in *agricultural colonies in *Argentina purchased by the *Baron de Hirsch Fund is recorded in several documentaries featuring oral histories and archival footage. These films about the "Jewish Gauchos of the Pampas" include *Yiddishe Gauchos* (directed by Mark Freeman and Alison Brysk, 1989). *Legacy* (directed by Marcelo Trotta and Vivian Imar, 2001), which is narrated in Spanish and Yiddish, vividly recounts the struggles of the *Wesser*, the ship that brought the first Jewish immigrants to Argentina in 1889. Other Argentine and Chilean documentaries of this kind are *From Bessarabia to Entre Ríos* (Pedro Banchik, 1974); *7 Days in El Once* (Daniel Burman, 2001); *A Kiss to This Land* (Daniel Goldberg, 1995); *Chevel Katz and his Landsmen* (Alejandro Vagnenkos, 2005); *Jews in Chile: Emigrants in Time* (Cristian Leighton, 2002); and *Be a Patriot* (David Blaustein, 2007). A 1974 musical adaptation of Alberto Gerchunoff's stories, *The Jewish Gauchos of the Pampas* (first published in 1910), was directed by Juan José Jusid and was a major commercial success.

The somber subject of the Jewish "white slave trade" – the *prostitution traffic that took place from *Eastern Europe to Argentina between the late 1890s and the mid-1930s – is featured in *Naked Tango*, a 1990 American–Argentine co-production, directed by Leonard Schrader. This violent thriller is set in Buenos Aires against a background of tango dancing. Another film on this topic is *The Road South* (Juan Bautista Stagnaro, 1988), which follows the route described by French journalist Albert Londres in his 1927 *The Road to Buenos Aires*, a journalistic account of the tricks employed by traffickers to ensnare innocent girls in Europe and force them into prostitution in Argentina. "The Tragic Week" is the term that identifies a violent attack against Jews that took place in Buenos Aires during January 1919. *A Pogrom in Buenos Aires* (Herman Szwarcbart, 2007) examines the conflicts between the victims' recollections and the official accounts of the same events. This hunt, targeted against "rusos" (a term used for Jews) who were regarded as communists, was provoked by upper class youths. The documentary includes a Yiddish text by Pinie Wald, one of the victims, who was tortured by the police.

The *Holocaust is addressed in films like *Jews in Many Lands: Sosúa, a Heaven in the Caribbean* (1981), a documentary from the Dominican Republic about the resourcefulness of a group of Holocaust survivors who found shelter in that country, where they created a prosperous agricultural community. A personal account of the suffering of Jews hiding from the *Nazis during *World War II is depicted in *Under the World* (1986, Beda Docampo Feijóo and Juan B. Stagnaro). Filmed in Poland, with Argentine Spanish-speaking actors, it tells the story of a family who spent the war in inhuman conditions, hiding in a hole in a forest while being hunted by both Nazis and local Poles, and their final escape to Argentina. *Ana's Trip* (2007), directed by Alan Jais, from Chile, documents individual journeys back to sites of extermination. *Poor Butterfly* (Raúl de la Torre, 1986) is a fictional film that covers the turbulent period at the end of World War II, when the conservative government of Argentina was fighting communists and harboring Nazis. The film explores the pervasive antisemitism within Argentine society in its treatment of an assimilated Jewish woman married to a Catholic surgeon; she is murdered while attempting to reveal her father's secret list of Nazi war criminals hiding in Argentina.

Whereas Latin American cinema from the 1960s onward revealed the decline in Jewish cultural and religious values within a predominantly Catholic society, more recent films depict a rebirth of Jewish identity. This is particularly the case in Argentina, the largest Jewish community in Latin America and the country where Jewish cinema has been most prominent. The Proceso Years (1976–82) and their aftermath, marked by repressive military dictatorships, are featured in *The Friend* (Jeanine Meerapfel, 1988), a film that develops the long-standing bond between two childhood friends, a Jewish actress who sings *Yiddish songs while in exile, and the mother of a "*desaparecido*," in their futile search for her son. The women's desperate attempt to find justice prepares the ground for the future Madres de la Plaza de Mayo.

J/18 (2004) commemorates the 2004 bombing of the AMIA (Asociación Mutual Israelita Argentina) in Buenos Aires (see *ARGENTINA*). In it, ten Argentine filmmakers (Daniel Burman, Adrián Caetano, Lucía Cedrón, Alejandro Doria, Alberto Lecchi, Marcelo Schapces, Carlos Sorín, Juan B. Stagnaro, Mauricio Wainrot, and Adian Saer) explore the impact of the attack and attest to a resurgence of vitality in Argentine Jewish life. Their vignettes use diverse artistic forms: *photography, *dance, monologues, fictional dramatizations, and testimonial accounts. The Brazilian film *The Year My Parents Went on Vacation* (Cao Hamburger, 1980) takes place in 1970, and both the military dictatorship and sports (Pelé and the World Cup) play a part in it. Set in the Jewish neighborhood of Sao Paolo, it depicts the trauma of a twelve-year-old boy whose parents are involved in political conflict and forced to flee the country (see BRAZIL).

Assimilation to the local culture is apparent in the comedy, *My Mexican Shiva* (Alejandro Springall, 2007); it depicts the death of a Jewish patriarch, whose mourners include his Catholic ex-lover and his newly *Orthodox son, against a background of Mexican mariachi and klezmer *music. A touch of magical realism is introduced by two Yiddish-speaking Ḥasidic Jews – two spirits who observe the events – who pass judgment on the unfolding situations and ultimately intercede for the soul of the dead man. The subject of *intermarriage, present in many Latin American Jewish films, is poignantly depicted as a fragile relationship in *Poor Butterfly*. A more conciliatory view is offered in *Autumn Sun* (Eduardo Mignona, 1996); in this film the mixed couple searches for harmony in both religions and moves toward integration into mainstream society. At first, mutually suspicious of each other (the man pretends to be a Jew), the couple develops a positive relationship, enhanced by discussions about Jewish gastronomy and Yiddish expressions.

Jewishness as a secondary theme first appears in the 1948 production of *Rag Ball* (Leopoldo Torre Ríos) contrasting the Jewish privileging of mind over body. In *Assassination in the Senate of the Nation* (1984) Juan José Jusid focuses on the internal political corruption of Argentina during the 1920s. The gruesome depiction of the meat market acts as a metaphor for the exploitation by corrupted officials of the "polacas" (a term used at the time to describe Jewish prostitutes). In Suzana Amaral's 1986 production of *Hour of the Star*, adapted from a story by the renowned Brazilian novelist Clarice Lispector, the protagonist's origin and courageous character are suggested by her name, Macabea. *Nine Queens* (Fabián Belinksky, 2000), satirizes the speech and behavior of a secondary character, an elderly Jewish woman. In addition, memorable literary adaptations include Leopoldo Torre Nilsson's 1954 *Dias de Odio*, based on "Emma Zunz" by Jorge L. Borges, and his 1972 *Los siete locos*, based on Roberto Arlt's story of the same name.

Many Latin American films with Jewish themes take an autobiographical approach; this is particularly evident in the *auteur* films of Daniel Burman, an Argentine director, producer, and screenwriter who places issues of Jewishness at the center of his movies. Burman explores the development of Jewish identity in the *Diaspora, and his films have gradually departed from Jewish stereotypes. Although some of his themes such as the generation gap, identity conflicts, and assimilation were previously examined in other Latin American Jewish films, Burman also delves into wider Jewish urban experiences, responses to *homosexuality, and the effects of recurrent economic crises on the population of Argentina. The influence of Hollywood is most clearly seen in Burman's *Samy and I* (2000), in which the protagonist is inspired by Woody Allen's *schlemiel*. He is an aspiring writer who lives and struggles in Buenos Aires; the son of a domineering mother, he uses his own neurotic life as a model and becomes a great comedian, despite himself.

Burman's trilogy – *Waiting for the Messiah* (2000), *Lost Embrace* (2004), and *Family Law* (2006) – is given unity by Ariel, his anti-hero and alter ego. Played in all three films by the same actor, Ariel is a character drawn from the director's third-generation Argentine Jewish, middle-class background. In *Waiting for the Messiah*, which shows the painful effects of the financial crisis of the 1990s, Ariel's personal preoccupation with his Jewish identity is shared with that of a second protagonist, Santamaría. Both men go through serious personal losses before they can move on. Throughout the film, Burman's protagonist is attached to his inner circle and seeks opportunities to photograph Jewish celebrations (*bar mitzvahs, Jewish weddings, and other festivities) in his neighborhood of El Once, yet he feels displaced. Although the protagonist of *Lost Embrace* begins as a marginal figure unable to define himself as a Jew or to commit to any serious relationship, he finally reconciles with his long-lost father and with himself. In *Family Law* both father and son are lawyers; however, rather than follow his father's model, the protagonist defies him by marrying a Gentile woman and becoming a "normal" Argentine. The relationship between Ariel and his spouse represents an inversion of traditional roles, as he comes to accept women's economic independence and adapts himself to new social responsibilities, sharing parenting with his wife and performing domestic chores. *The Empty Nest* (2008), Burman's latest film, moves even farther away from Jewish issues, focusing on a couple's readjustments when their children leave their home and their country.

NORA GLICKMAN

Film: United States. In his 1988 book, *An Empire of their Own*, Neal Gabler famously suggested that the "Jews invented Hollywood" in its business, mechanical, logistical, and creative and artistic aspects, from its beginnings in nickelodeon theaters at the turn of the twentieth century. Such extensive Jewish involvement, and public reactions to it, had profound effects on images of Jews in American film.

The nascent film industry began with scientific inventors in several locations who experimented with "magic lantern" type moving pictures in the mid-1890s (i.e., America's Armet and Jenkins' Phantascope, Woodville Latham's Panoptikon and Latham Loop, and William Selig's Polyscope Company; France's Lumière Brothers' Cinématographe). Fascinated entrepreneurs, including many Jews in the United States and Europe, frustrated the efforts of Thomas Edison's company, the Edison Trust, which had purchased and renamed many products in an attempt to squelch competition. Most Jews first entered the growing industry as distributors, including Marcus Loew (1870–1927), Adoph Zuckor (1873–1976), and William Fox (1879–1952), who banded together to form the Moving Picture Exhibitors Association (MPEA); Carl Laemmle (1867–1939), a German Jewish immigrant who founded the Independent Motion Picture Company of America (IMP) and produced and distributed his own moving pictures; and others. By 1904, William Fox formed a distribution company, Warner Brothers founded the Duquesne Amusement Supply Company and toured Pennsylvania with *The Great Train Robbery*, and Carl Laemmle opened the Chicago Nickelodeon. Three years later Sigmund Lubin, a German Jewish immigrant, released *The Unwritten Law*, the first American documentary about a sensational murder story. For only five cents, at any time of the day, patrons of all ages and financial means could escape into a world of fantasy and *entertainment at nickelodeons that featured not only the short films that were their official rationale but also songs, live acts, and sometimes amateur nights. Almost immediately the Jews in the nascent film industry and their products were labeled "morally objectionable" and the "cause of social unrest and criminal behavior" by newspaper critics, who called for censorship.

Nevertheless, the industry thrived and grew, moving to California in the early decades of the twentieth century. William Selig (1864-1948) became the first West Coast filmmaker in 1909, and by 1912, when Warner Brothers Pictures opened its Los Angeles office, there were fifteen film companies in Hollywood. The Edison Trust (Motion Pictures Production Company, MPPC) tried to limit their expansion, but an antitrust suit brought by Fox, Paramount, and Universal broke its hold in 1915. That same year D. W. Griffith released the powerfully xenophobic, anti-ethnic immigrant film, *Birth of a Nation*, criticizing immigrants as crude interlopers threatening to swamp America and presenting the Ku Klux Klan as upright defenders of American values. Disproportionately led by Jews, and attracting many Jews on all levels of employment, the Hollywood motion picture industry developed rapidly.

Many early silent films sympathetically represented the struggles of poor immigrants. *The Jazz Singer* (1927), for example, often called the "first talkie" (although only the musical portions of the film had sound, and the dialogue was posted onscreen in silent-film-style placards), spotlighted the American spirit in the heart of a young Jewish immigrant. Al Jolson's Jack Robins personifies the immigrant struggle between Old World tribalism and piety and universalistic, individualistic striving. Robins is a talented Jewish youth who is torn between his *cantor father, who urges him to remain in the *synagogue and "not debase the voice God has given you," and his non-Jewish show business girlfriend who encourages him to abandon the synagogue, sing the jazz tunes he adores, and give his voice to the world.

Less positive Jewish film images in the following years included Jewish gangsters, played by actors like James Cagney, who spouted *Yiddish out of the sides of their mouths. More commonly, studio heads encouraged Jewish actors not to appear "too Jewish," to change their names, and to play mostly non-Jewish roles. Theda Bara, born Theodosia Burr Goodman in 1885, is just one example of a long line of renamed Jewish film stars; her name became synonymous with the expression "vamp," meaning a predatory femme fatale.

Critics attacked these portrayals of steamy sexual liaisons and savvy criminals as seductively dangerous, and many of the campaigns to rein in the "depravity" of these unsupervised entertainments were openly antisemitic. Jewish Hollywood studio heads such as Samuel Goldwyn (1882–1974), Jesse Lasky (1880–1958), and Louis B. Mayer (1885–1957) – later joined by Harry and Jack Warner (1881–1958; 1892–1978), Harry Cohn (1891–1958), Irving Thalberg (1899–1936), and David O. Selznick (1902–1965) – were denigrated as uneducated, crude, and vulgar autocrats. American Jewish leaders were mortified by the films and their detractors and joined in the chorus urging the Hollywood film industry either to govern itself or submit to outside censorship. After several groups jockeyed for power in

the creation of such codes in the 1920s, Postmaster General Will Hays joined together with the Catholic Legion of Decency, which had been lobbying against the "pernicious" Jewish influence, to create and implement the 1930 Motion Picture Codes. Automobile magnate Henry Ford financed an English translation of the 1905 Russian antisemitic tract, *The Protocols of the Elders of Zion*, in response to what he perceived as "Jewish Hollywood," charging that Jews were ruining the Christian youth of America through their control of popular entertainment. Among other charges, Ford's publications accused Jewish filmmakers of being motivated by communist sympathies. This accusation recurred decades later during the notorious 1950s U.S. House Un-American Activities Committeee hearings. Overtly Jewish content virtually disappeared from films after the creation of movie codes that prohibited or severely restricted representations of ethnicity. In response to an atmosphere of rising *antisemitism, films written, directed, or produced by Jews promoted a melting pot philosophy in which marriage across cultural boundaries (demographically few in number at that time) symbolized tolerance. *Intermarriage was also a practical step for men in the industry to accelerate American acceptance, as they acquired symbolic Christian status by marrying Christian women.

After Adolph Hitler became German Chancellor in 1933, *Nazi *Germany fired Jewish filmmakers, demanding that American film offices in Germany do likewise. In America, too, film companies were pressured not to articulate anti-Nazi sentiments. Catholic Hollywood reporter Joseph I. Breen, head of the Production Code Administration from 1934 on, saw the rise of the Nazis as useful in lessening Jewish influence in Hollywood. He wrote that Jews, "the scum of the earth, think of nothing but money-making and sexual indulgence." When Warner Brothers' 1937 film, *The Life of Emile Zola*, focused on the French antisemitic persecution of Captain Alfred Dreyfus (see DREYFUS AFFAIR) without ever uttering the words "Jew" or "antisemitism," Breen privately complained about the film's "propaganda." Some Hollywood figures formed the Hollywood Anti-Nazi League (HNL) in 1936. When fifty-eight individuals in the industry petitioned for an anti-Nazi boycott in 1938, Breen and others accused Jews of trying to drag America into a Jewish war as well as promoting communism. Nevertheless, some studios continued to promote anti-Nazi films – some dramas and some comic – which enjoyed box office success. Significantly, none of these films referred to Jews as victims of Nazi aggression. Filmmakers wishing to emphasize Jewish stories were forced to do so unobtrusively. Ernst Lubitsch (1892–1947), for example, directed Jack Benny and Carole Lombard in a brilliant black comedy, *To Be or Not to Be* (1942), a film about the invading Nazis taking over a *Warsaw theater, scarcely mentioning the Jewish dimension of the story.

Film performers over the decades have been disproportionately Jewish. During the years of massive immigration, Jewishness was played for laughs. Many Jewish film actors learned to perform in front of Jewish audiences in the *Yiddish *theater or in the Catskill Mountain resorts. Unusually successful was Molly Picon (1898–1992), who acted, sang, and danced for decades in Yiddish plays, musicals, and films and later was also in demand in English-language commercial plays and films. Gertrude Berg (1899–1966), whose radio and television portrayals of the wise Jewish matriarch

Molly Goldberg first aired in 1929, was similarly successful. In contrast, most performers who could find work on the nonsectarian stage and screen left Jewish venues behind. Paul Muni (1895–1967, Muni Weisenfreund), Judy Holliday (1922–1965, Judith Tuvim), and John Garfield (1913–1952, Jacob Julius Garfinkle) were among the many performers who began in Jewish environments and went on to wider careers. None of these particular performers denied their Jewishness; Garfield was especially active on behalf of Israel and in diverse Jewish causes, playing the fearless Jewish soldier Dave Goldman in Gentleman's Agreement (1947). Some, like Shelley Winters (born Shirley Schrift, 1920–2006), at first played generic young women's roles and then depicted Jewish women as she aged. Although Jack Benny (Benjamin Kubelsky, 1894–1974), George Burns (Nathan Birnbaum, 1896–1996), Milton Berle (Mendel Berlinger, 1908–2002), Eddie Cantor (Israel Iskowitz, 1892–1964), Sophie Tucker (Sophie Kalish, 1884–1966), Sid Caesar (b. 1922–), and Danny Kaye (David Daniel Kaminsky, 1913–1987) all started on vaudeville stages, they shaped American comedy as American comics. Fanny Brice (1891–1951, Fania Borach) discovered that Jewish humor did not always translate into new environments. Her radio audiences, beginning in 1937, liked her nonethnic "Baby Snooks" far more than her earlier Yiddish-accented characters.

Even Groucho (1890–1977), Chico (1887–1961), and Harpo Marx (1888–1964) encoded their Jewishness, with Chico and Harpo taking on vaguely ethnic, but not Jewish, mannerisms. In film after film, as the zany and clever Marx Brothers outwitted their antagonists, Jewish audiences understood the Jewish subtext, which was safely invisible to Christian audiences. Similarly, in his television hit, Your Show of Shows (1950–54), Sid Caesar portrayed many foreign characters, none of them specifically Jewish. His skits often encoded Jewish materials or perspectives in ways that would only be visible to Jews. In one skit, for example, non-Jewish businessmen all order items such as "bacon and raisin" and "ham hock sandwiches" for lunch – unlikely pork-based combinations that reflect what Jews might imagine that non-Jews would eat. Many of these performers, however, perceived a Jewish dimension to their work. Slapstick comic actor Jerry Lewis was seldom perceived as Jewish; he saw himself as a universal defender of the human spirit.

Overtly Jewish themes and concerns went underground during the 1930s and 1940s, finding expression in films that pleaded for tolerance but seldom mentioned Jews. Like the Broadway original shows on which many of these films were based, these films trumpeted the wrongheadedness of prejudice against persons of African American or Polynesian – but never Jewish – backgrounds. Playwright and Jewish activist Ben Hecht (1894–1964), author of numerous prize-winning and popular screenplays, wrote of his disgust at "the almost complete disappearance of the Jew from American fiction, stage, radio and movies" in his A Guide for the Bedeviled (1944).

After the Allied victory in World War II, overtly Jewish materials reappeared, at first in critiques of anti-Jewish prejudice. Gentleman's Agreement and Crossfire, both of which appeared in 1947, portray the evils of antisemitism. A romantic, sanitized version of the The Diary of Anne *Frank appeared in 1959, followed by the Holocaust drama,

Judgment at Nuremberg. In Exodus (1960), based on Leon Uris' sprawling historical novel about events leading up to the founding of *Israel, a handsome and masculine Paul Newman epitomizes the Jewish Israeli hero. The Pawnbroker, directed by Sidney Lumet (1924), painfully brought the Holocaust and its psychological aftermath to the commercial screen in 1965, daring to portray an unpleasant Jewish title character. In 1971, a melodic, earnestly didactic, and nostalgic version of the 1960s stage musical Fiddler on the Roof gave viewing audiences the Israeli actor Topol as an utterly likeable, wisecracking, and not-too-pious *Diaspora Jewish everyman. Hollywood's suppression of overt Jewishness had come to an end.

As open portrayals of Jews and Jewish themes appeared in film, television, and literature, satiric portrayals became the dominant trope. Exemplars of middle-class mores, Jews were the butt of cinematic critiques of consumerism. Filmmakers like Paul Mazursky (b. 1930) made fun of pretentious Jews preoccupied by their possessions, devoted to their own self-gratification, and oblivious to the suffering of others or to deeper concerns in life. In cinematic renditions of the works of Jerome Weidman (1913–1998) and Canada's Mordecai Richler (1931–2001), to cite two of many examples, Jewish men were depicted as ruthlessly ambitious and amoral businessmen. A more frequent caricature of Jewish men in American media, however, was of the fearful, inept, and overly intellectual nebbish. Both of these stereotypes were common in nineteenth-century antisemitic writings, but in twentieth-century America they were almost always produced by Jewish artists.

Liberated by the rise of multiculturalism, humorist filmmakers, such as Mel Brooks (Melvin Kaminsky, b. 1926), and stand-up comics like Alan King (Irwin Alan Kniburg, 1927–2004), Jackie Mason (Yacov Moshe Moaza, b. 1931), Joan Rivers (Joan Sandra Molinsky, b. 1933), and others found that overtly (and sometimes abrasive) Jewish humor was immensely salable; they began including Jewish materials in the language, plots, and references in their comic routines. Both types of Jewish men, the "hustler" and the "wimp," appear in Mel Brooks' original comedy, The Producers (1968), starring Zero Mostel (1915–1977) and Gene Wilder (b. 1933). Indeed, the transition from Mostel's hilarious but not specifically Jewish performance in the musical comedy film, A Funny Thing Happened on the Way to the Forum (1966) only two years earlier, to the edgy, transgressive Jewish humor of The Producers marks a shift in cultural paradigms.

The artistic image of the scrawny, neurotic Jewish male was indelibly fixed in twentieth-century western culture through the films of Woody Allen (Allen Stewart Konigsberg, b. 1935). Although his first hilarious films in the 1960s included few if any overtly Jewish materials, by the late 1970s Allen satirized the foibles of Jewish – and non-Jewish – families in Annie Hall (1977), as the obsessive Jew Alvy Singer travels to Chippewa Falls, Wisconsin, to encounter the healthy, bland American family of his non-Jewish girlfriend, complete with a "Jew-hater" grandmother and a sociopathic brother. Younger television-personalities-turned-film-stars, such as Adam Sandler (b. 1966), took the inclusion of often edgy and offensive Jewish references as a given. As a result, Yiddish words and Jewish *life-cycle symbols and events became part of the American cultural heritage. In marked contrast to the mid-twentieth-century image of Jews emulating a non-Jewish America, by the early twenty-first century non-Jewish Americans routinely used words like *chutzpah* (nerve), *shlep* (drag), *schlemiel* (unsuccessful person), *tchochkeh* (kitschy bric-a-brac), as well as saltier terms such as *tokhes* (rear end) and *putz* (penis), that had once been limited to Jewish environments.

Jewish men were often portrayed as sensitive and responsible, if overly anxious souls, but Jewish women characters were more savagely satirized. Novelists Herman Wouk (b. 1915) and Philip Roth (b. 1933) and filmmaker Woody Allen, among others, promulgated two negative stereotypical images of Jewish women: the overbearing Jewish mother and the spoiled Jewish daughter. In his 1955 novel, *Marjorie Morningstar*, Wouk introduced readers to the Jewish daughter, the "Shirley," as the ultimate bourgeois consumer who wanted a "big diamond engagement ring, a house in a good neighborhood, furniture, children, well-made clothes, furs," etc. In the hands of other writers and filmmakers, as well as popular culture and jokes, this spoiled and demanding Jewish girl became known as the "Jewish American Princess," the JAP. Brenda Patimkin, a similar character, is featured in Roth's 1959 novella "Goodbye Columbus" (film version, 1969; directed by Larry Peerce). Roth's 1969 novel *Portnoy's Complaint* (film version, 1972; directed by Ernest Lehman), contributed domineering Jewish mother Sophie Portnoy. Woody Allen developed the Jewish mother's power even further. In "Oedipus Wrecks," part of the 1989 trilogy, *New York Stories*, a Jewish mother's pudgy face fills the sky to better control her son's every move. Cinematic plots showed Jewish men saving themselves by escaping the clutches of Jewish mothers and daughters.

Interestingly, Jewish women have been involved in a range of films that offer nuanced and diverse pictures of Jews and Jewish life. Prominent among them is singer and filmmaker Barbra Streisand (b. 1942). In films like *Funny Girl* (1968), *The Way We Were* (1973), *Yentl* (1983), and *Prince of Tides* (1991), Streisand portrayed Jewish women as talented singers and comediennes, loving social activists, religious scholars, and committed healers. Streisand also made history by shortening neither her name nor her nose. Similarly, films featuring singer, actor, and performance artist Bette Midler (b. 1945) followed Streisand's lead in exhibiting, rather than playing down, her sassy mouth, her comic talents, her enterprise, and her intelligence. Director Joan Micklin Silver (b. 1935) created *Hester Street* (1974), lovingly based on Abraham Cahan's novella, "Yekl," and the romantic comedy, *Crossing Delancey* (1988), which turned feminist platitudes on their heads and slyly recommended that Jewish women look for sweet men who pray in the synagogue. *Sephardic Jews in *Britain – and the struggles of intelligent women without money – were the subjects of *The Governess* (1998), directed by and starring Minnie Driver. Harvey Fierstein's (b. 1954) wrenching *Torch Song Trilogy* (based on his stage play) depicted a Jewish homosexual yearning to be a devoted Jewish parent while earning a living as a drag queen singer (1988). In recent years, Orthodox Jews (see JUDAISM: ORTHODOX) have received detailed cinematic scrutiny in American films. Although sometimes flattering, as in Sidney Lumet's *A Stranger Among Us* (1992), their portrayals have also been uncomfortably critical, as in *A Price Above Rubies* (1998).

At the end of the first decade of the twenty-first century, Jews continue to be significantly involved in North American film production as writers, directors, producers, and actors, among other roles. Given the enormous diversity of these individuals, and the reality that their attitudes toward Judaism and Jewish life fall across a broad spectrum from positive and involved to negative and even self-hating, it is not surprising that both stereotypical and nonstereotypical portrayals of Jews continue to be presented in contemporary films.

For further reading, see N. Gabler, *An Empire of Their Own* (1988); J. Hoberman and J. Shandler, *Entertaining America: Jews, Movies, Broadcasting* (2003); S. Carr, *Hollywood and Antisemitism: A Cultural History Up to World War II* (2001); and F. Couvares, *Movie Censorship and America Culture* (1996).

SYLVIA BARACK FISHMAN

Film: Yiddish-Language. Cinematic versions of some of the Yiddish plays of Jacob Gordin, including *Mirele Efros* and *Hasa the Orphan* (see THEATER, YIDDISH), were produced in *Poland before *World War I; Poland remained a major production center for Yiddish-language films, both silent and "talkies," until the outbreak of World War II in 1939. During the 1920s, films in Yiddish were produced in the *Soviet Union, and Yiddish-language films were also made in the *United States during the 1920s and 1930s.

Silent films made in Poland in the 1920s for Yiddish-speaking audiences include the romance, *Tkies-Kaf* (The Hand Contract, 1924); *Der Lamedvovnik* (One of the Thirty-Six, 1927); and *In the Polish Woods* (1928). The 1932 Travelog series by Shaul and Itzhak Goskind, documentaries filmed in *Warsaw, Łódź, *Vilna, Lwów, Kraków, and Bialystok, offers invaluable portraits of Jewish life in Poland before the *Holocaust. Writer Joseph Green (1900–1996) was responsible for four of the most popular talkies of the 1930s: *Yidl mit'n Fidl* (dir. Green and Jan Nowina-Przybylski, 1936) and *Mammele* (dir. Green, 1938; both with Molly Picon); *Purim Shpiler* (dir. Green and Nowina-Przybylski, 1937); and *A Brivele der Mammen* (A Letter to Mama; dir. Green, 1938), which was the last Yiddish-language film made in Poland before World War II. Other films were based on works by Jewish writers and playwrights, including Jacob Gordin, Peretz Hirshbein, Sholem Aleichem, Sholom Secunda, Isidore Zolotarefsky, Dovid Pinski, and Sholem Asch (see LITERATURE, YIDDISH). *The Dybbuk* (directed by Michal Waszynski, 1937), based on the play by S. Ansky (see DYBBUK; and THEATER, YIDDISH), is among the most ambitious and best known motion pictures in Yiddish. Important Yiddish-language films made in the Soviet Union include *Der Mabul* (The Deluge, 1925) and what many consider the masterpiece of Soviet Yiddish cinema, *Yidishe Glikn* (Jewish Luck, dir. Alexander A. Granovsky,1925), based on a Sholem Aleichem character, Menaḥem Mendl. The film starred Solomon Mikhoels (ca. 1890–1949) of the Moscow State Yiddish Theater.

Yiddish films produced in the United States featured actors from *New York City's Artef and Yiddish Art Theaters, including Celia Adler, Leo Fuchs (known as the "Yiddish Fred Astaire"), Molly Picon, and Maurice Schwartz, and well-known *cantors such as Josef "Yossele" Rosenblatt, Moishe Oysher, Louis "Labele" Waldman, and Mordechai Hershman. Directors included Boris Thomashefsky (also a popular actor) and Henry Lynn. These motion pictures covered a range of genres, including drama, romance, and comedy. In *Uncle Moses* (dir. Sidney Goldin and Aubrey Scotto, 1932), written by and starring Maurice Schwartz, Asch's immigrant tale of a man redeemed by love takes place in a contemporary Depression-era setting. Schwartz also wrote, directed, and starred in *Tevye der Milkhiker* (Tevye the Milkman, 1939), based on two short stories by Sholem Aleichem. Other Yiddish films of this era were adaptations of theater standards such as Gordin's *Mirele Efros* (dir. Joseph Berne, 1938) and *Grine Felder* (Green Fields; dir. by Edgar G. Ulmer and Jacob Ben-Ami, 1937), based on the play by Peretz Hirschbein.

The genre known as *shund,* melodramatic and sentimental depictions of Jewish American immigrant life, was particularly popular with filmgoers. Examples include *Bar Mitzvah* (dir. Henry Lynn and Joseph Green, 1935), *Vu Iz Mayn Kind* (Where is My Child?; written and directed by Henry Lynn and starring Celia Adler, 1939), and *Hayntike Mames* (Mothers of Today; dir. Henry Lynn, 1939). *Hayntike Mames* includes the only motion picture performance by Esther Field, a *radio performer known as the "Yiddishe Mama." *Shund* films often dealt with the plight of Jewish mothers caught between the values of the Old World and the New and forced to mediate between their husbands and their Americanizing children.

The production of films in Yiddish came to an end in the 1940s, a result of the *Nazi destruction of the Yiddish-speaking communities of Europe and the waning of secular Yiddish-language culture in the United States. The National Center for Jewish Film, located at Brandeis University in Waltham, Massachusetts, preserves a significant library of Yiddish films and restores rare Yiddish film footage for rerelease on DVD. Valuable resources include J. Hoberman, *Bridge of Light: Yiddish Film between Two Worlds* (1991); and the film documentary, *The Yiddish Cinema* (USA, 1991; directed by Rich Pontius).   ELIZABETH SHULMAN

Firstborn Son, Fast of. A fasting period for every firstborn male begins at sunrise on the eve of *Passover (14th of Nissan). Halakhic authorities debate whether this minor fast should also include firstborn females (*Shulḥan Arukh, Oraḥ Ḥayyim* 470:1). The fast commemorates the tenth plague mentioned in *Exodus, when all Egyptian firstborn males were killed, while the firstborn sons of the Israelites were saved. Compared with other fast days, this one is lenient. One prevalent custom, which sidesteps the fast entirely, is to hold a special learning session called a *siyyum bekhorim* ("concluding study period for firstborn") during the morning. This custom stems from the Jewish tradition of eating a festive meal after completion of a special event, such as a *berit milah* (*circumcision), or the completion of an entire text or course of study. Therefore, eating at the *siyyum* effectively supersedes the requirement to complete the fast.   PAUL STEINBERG

Firstborn Son, Redemption of (PIDYON HA-BEN). This ritual originated in the biblical period when firstborn sons were to be consecrated to God to serve as priests (Num 3:12). When the *priesthood was assigned to the Levites (see ISRAELITES: RELIGION; TEMPLE AND TEMPLE CULT), firstborn sons in nonpriestly families were redeemed from the priesthood at the price of five shekels (Num 3:46–48). Biblical *commandments also required that firstborn

unclean animals be redeemed and that firstborn clean animals be sacrificed (Num 18:15–17). Redemption of firstborn sons is also explained as a commemoration of the slaying of the firstborn sons of the *Egyptians before the Exodus (Exod 13:15; Num 3:13). The redemption is to occur on the thirtieth day after birth, although it may be postponed if that day is a *Sabbath, *festival, or *fast day. The ritual includes the recitation of a *blessing followed by the *sheheḥeyanu* prayer of thanksgiving; the father redeems his infant by giving five silver coins of a specific minimum weight to a guest of high priestly descent (*kohen*). Often the coins are returned to the family as a gift. Redemption does not apply if the child was born by cesarean section or if the mother had a miscarriage or stillbirth after the first forty days of a previous pregnancy; this is because the biblical commandment refers specifically to the firstborn son's opening of the mother's womb (Num 3:12).   ELIZABETH SHULMAN

Five Scrolls (Ḥamesh Megillot) comprise the following books from the *Writings (*Ketuvim*) section of the Hebrew *Bible: *Song of Songs, *Ruth, *Lamentations, *Ecclesiastes, and *Esther. Although all of the ancient writings of the Bible were on scrolls, these five are specifically distinguished, most likely because they are read publicly and because of the role they play in the cycle of the year by their assignment to a particular *festival. Only Esther and Lamentations are read in both *Sephardic and *Ashkenazic communities, whereas the other three are primarily read in Ashkenazic communities.

Song of Songs (*Shir ha-Shirim*) is read on the *Sabbath that falls during *ḥol ha-mo'ed* (the intermediate days) of *Passover. Traditionally, the book has been understood allegorically, describing a loving, intimate relationship between *God and the Jewish people. The Rabbis drew deep meaning from the title, the Song (singular) of Songs (plural), and taught that it is a summary account of all the "songs" – the moments when God spoke to Israel, as, for example, at the splitting of the Reed Sea and at Mount Sinai. The vivid natural imagery of the language is also well suited to Passover's spring setting and themes of rebirth. The custom of reading Ruth on *Shavuot (on the second day of the festival in the *Diaspora) is derived from a medieval work called Tractate *Soferim* (Scribes). The book may be read on Shavuot because it has a strong agricultural association with the late spring barley harvest and because of its theme of persistent faith. Lamentations, *Eikhah* in Hebrew (literally, "alas"), is read on *Tisha B'Av, the fast day memorializing the destruction of both *Temples. The book is a collection of five poetic laments, each specifically bemoaning the *Babylonians' destruction of the First Temple in 586 BCE with vivid imagery and emotional expressiveness.

Ecclesiastes or *Kohelet* (the self-ascribed name of the author) is read on the Sabbath that falls during *ḥol ha-mo'ed* (the intermediate days) Sukkot. The most commonly understood correlation between Sukkot and Ecclesiastes is that both the holiday and the book speak to the transitory nature of existence. Just as Sukkot commemorates the fall harvest and the end of the agricultural year, so, too, Ecclesiastes has the autumnal tone of a wise elder looking back on life. The reading of Esther, commonly referred to simply as "the *Megillah*," is the central observance of *Purim. The observance of the commandment is exceptional because its reading is mandated both at night and the following morning. The holiday's customs and observances are based on the story's account of the heroism of Esther and Mordecai in the face of Haman's evil plot to destroy the Jews. Helpful resources include H. L. Ginsberg, *Five Megilloth and Jonah: A New Translation* (1969); and Shlomo Yosef Zevin, *The Festivals in Halakhah* (1999).   PAUL STEINBERG

Flood. Genesis 6:5–9:17 describes how *God destroyed human beings with water because of their violence and corruption; the sole survivors in a rudderless ark were the righteous Noah, who "walked with God" (6:9), and his immediate family, along with pairs of all living creatures (6:19) or, in an interpolated alternate version, seven pairs of all ritually clean creatures and one pair of all other beings (7:2–3). When the flood ended, Noah freed a raven and a dove to determine whether land had surfaced in addition to the ark's perch, Mt. Ararat. After he and his family emerged from the ark, Noah made an offering to God (8:20); in a *covenant sealed by a rainbow, God promised that never again would the order of nature be disturbed and all living things destroyed. In return, human beings, who were now given permission to eat animal meat under certain circumstances, were required to refrain from murder and to be fruitful and multiply (8:21–9:17). Many cultures have flood legends, and the biblical account clearly reflects similar themes and details found in older *Mesopotamian narrative cycles, including the *Epic of Gilgamesh*, which would have been well known in the biblical world. However, scholars have noted that, despite the common ancient *Near Eastern elements, the biblical flood story is unique in its emphasis on divine demands for human righteousness and ethical standards.   KATE FRIEDMAN

Folktales. Throughout history, in a variety of languages and dialects, Jews have told stories. As in all literate societies, Jewish narrative traditions pass from one generation to the next in oral or written form; storytellers choose and adapt elements from tales of the past, at times including material from non-Jewish sources. Some Jewish folktales are conservative and show minimal creative innovation; others exploit traditional themes and motifs to articulate a new ideology or worldview to their audience. Jewish folktales integrate symbols and other elements of Jewish tradition, including *life-cycle events, *festivals, historical circumstance, and textual allusions. They often deal with basic concepts such as divine providence, free choice, and moral responsibility, as well as the sufferings of the righteous and interrelationships between Jews and their Gentile neighbors. Every folktale has a particular socio-religious and cultural context and reflects the values, theological views, and moral ideas of a specific narrator.

One controversial issue is which genres of Jewish literary tradition in which periods should be considered folktales. Most scholars consider biblical *narratives, such as the *Abraham and *Joseph stories and the book of *Esther, to be folktales. The mention of "the tales that our fathers told us" (Judg 6:13) would suggest that oral narratives were used in the biblical period itself to preserve the collective memory of Jewish society. Inarguably, the figures, motifs, themes, plots, and literary forms that appear in the Hebrew *Bible are building blocks used in all later Jewish folktales. As for the rabbinic period, some scholars (Yassif; Hasan-Rokem) treat the parables and stories in the *Talmud and *midrash as folk creations; others (Fraenkel) argue that classic *aggadic stories, despite their use of folk motifs, are constructed literary creations that reflect social and spiritual rabbinic concerns.

Folk traditions evolved around figures such as *Hillel the Elder and Rabbi *Akiva and social roles such as the leader and the holy man. Later, these traditions served as models for biographical tales portraying famous personalities such as *Rashi and *Maimonides (*Shalshelet ha-Kabbalah*, late sixteenth century), Judah the Pious (*Mayse-Bukh*, *Yiddish, early seventeenth century; see MIDDLE AGES: *HASIDEI ASHKENAZ*), and Shalom Shabazi (*Yemen, seventeenth century). Hagiographic tales, or *shevahim*, developed in the seventeenth century around the legendary, mystical figure of Rabbi Isaac *Luria and soon became a widespread genre, particularly in the early nineteenth century with tales of *Hasidic masters, most prominently R. Israel *Baal Shem Tov.

Another popular genre of folktales is the moral story, often used as a didactic device inserted in a non-narrative context, as in *Sefer Ḥasidim* (*Ashkenaz, thirteenth century). Similarly, the medieval genre of *exemplum* seeks to reinforce normative cultural values such as sin and punishment, virtue and its rewards, and loyalty to the commandments. Other common genres of Jewish folktales are historical and martyr legends, fables and animal tales, wisdom tales, humorous anecdotes, and romantic and magic stories. Modern, stylized folktales, written in the nineteenth and twentieth centuries by authors such as I. L. Peretz and Sholem Aleichem, use the tools and themes of Jewish storytelling, often with a "subversive twist" to express a sense of fragmentation "in a world that had broken with tradition" (Roskies). Yet Jewish folktales remain a living aesthetic form, and Jews everywhere will doubtless continue to tell stories, to share, and to remember.

Recent research includes E. Yassif, *The Hebrew Folktale: History, Genre, Meaning* (1999); G. Hasan-Rokem, *Web of Life: Folklore and Midrash in Rabbinic Literature* (2000); Y. Fraenkel, *Sipur Ha'agadah* (2001); D. Ben-Amos and J. Mintz, *In Praise of the Baal Shem Tov. Shivhei Ha-Besht: The Earliest Collection of Legends about the Founder of Hasidism* (1994); and D. Roskies, *Against the Apocalypse* (1984).   ORA WISKIND ELPER

Football: See SPORTS, UNITED STATES: FOOTBALL

France: 1789–1939. About 40,000 Jews lived in France at the start of the French Revolution in 1789. The vast majority (about 80%) resided in the eastern provinces of Alsace and Lorraine. Another 5,000 lived in the south, in two major groupings: (1) *Sephardim who had settled as *conversos* in Bordeaux but eventually returned to Judaism and (2) Papal Jews, who had lived for centuries in the Papal States before the area was annexed by France. A small group of about five hundred Jews lived in Paris. Jewish urbanization and movement toward Paris began soon after the revolution and accelerated by 1835. In 1841 France's total Jewish population had increased to 70,000, of whom 8,000 resided in Paris. The second largest community, Bordeaux, numbered 3,000. Data for 1861 show the Paris Jewish population at 25,000, whereas the size of Bordeaux's community had remained stable. By 1880 the Jewish population in metropolitan France numbered 70,000. The figure would have been higher had the 1871 loss of Alsace-Lorraine to

*Germany not siphoned off that sizable community. However, a quarter of these Alsatian Jews migrated into remaining French territory to retain their citizenship. Some formed new communities in Vesoul, Lille, and Besançon; many more moved to Paris, boosting the Parisian Jewish population to 40,000. Paris thereafter remained home to the majority of the French Jewish population.

In 1914, on the eve of World War I, France had 150,000 Jews. Immigration from *Eastern Europe and the *Balkans had swelled the Parisian Jewish population to about 75,000, of whom half were immigrants. Immigration picked up again after the war and accelerated when the *United States closed its gates in 1924, and again after 1933 when the *Nazis came to power in Germany. In 1939 there were approximately 300,000–330,000 Jews in France; 180,000 of that number were in Paris, with immigrants comprising more than two-thirds of the population.

A growing contingent of Algerian Jews also supplemented France's Jewish population. At the time of the 1830 French conquest there were about 16,000 Algerian Jews. By 1851 there were 21,000, and in 1870, when Algerian Jews were granted French citizenship, there were 33,000 Jews. Despite migration to metropolitan France, the Jewish population in French Algeria continued to climb, and there were about 50,000 in 1880, 58,000 in 1900, and 102,000 in 1931.

The percentage of Jews in the total French population never increased beyond 1% and never reached great proportions, even in urban areas. Except for the city of Toul, in the eastern province of Lorraine, whose Jewish population in 1861 was more than 8% percent of the total, the Jewish population in urban areas rarely reached 5% and then only in eastern towns. The Jewish population density in Paris reached about 3% in 1914, which was never exceeded. By 1939 Paris housed the largest Jewish community in Western Europe and the third largest in the world after *New York and *Warsaw. A section of central Paris known affectionately as the *pletzel* (Yiddish for "little square") was home to numerous *synagogues, small prayer houses, Jewish bookstores, kosher restaurants, and bakeries, serving mainly the large immigrant population. That same neighborhood had been the Jewish quarter in the thirteenth century. A second major area of Jewish settlement opened in Belleville, an eastern section of Paris.

In the early nineteenth century, French-speaking Sephardim of southern France had higher socioeconomic status and were more integrated into French society than *Yiddish-speaking Jews of the eastern provinces. However, high levels of poverty among Jews everywhere continued until the 1870s. Among the first and most active Jewish institutions were the many charity boards developed to address this problem. In Paris the economic advancement of Jews occurred somewhat faster than that of non-Jews, but slower than is often imagined. Jews in eastern France had a lower socioeconomic status; in 1856 Alsatian Jews were said to have a greater proportion of indigents than either the Catholics or Protestants. Beginning with their *emancipation (see EMANCIPATION: FRANCE), Jewish leaders sought to "regenerate," or improve, the socioeconomic status of their constituents. A series of initiatives, both private and communal, created institutions that offered financial support to families, educated children, trained skilled workers, and sought to eradicate begging.

Several unsuccessful attempts were made at preparing Jews to enter agriculture, but this project never materialized.

By the 1880s, Parisian Jews were mainly in middle-class occupations, working as merchants, professionals, gardeners, hairdressers, and skilled artisans (including tailors, shoemakers, and hatters). Very few remained in unskilled labor. Yet most were barely making ends meet. As native-born Jews began to climb out of poverty, immigrants replaced them at the bottom of the ladder. A large contingent of these immigrants consisted of foreign students who flocked to Paris to receive the training Jews were unable to receive elsewhere. Entire families arrived with consequent financial difficulty, but found assistance from the many *landsmanschaften* (immigrant social and charitable societies). Several wealthy Jewish families founded *banking houses. The *Rothschilds, whose Paris house opened in 1812, were followed in the next decades by the Péreires, the Bambergers, the Reinachs, the Goudchauxes, and the Bischoffsheims. In addition to banking, new sectors opened to Jews. They developed railroads (Rothschilds, Pereires, Foulds), the tradition of inexpensive newspapers (Moïse Polydore Millaud), and a successful publishing house (Michel and Calmann Lévy). By the early twentieth century André Citroen had founded the famous auto company.

Nineteenth-century French Jews were visible in political life. In the 1830s, banker Benoît Fould became the first Jew elected to the Chamber of Deputies. He must have felt fairly secure, because he had the courage to publicly chastise Foreign Minister Adolphe Thiers in the Chamber for not condemning the support of French consul Ratti Menton for *ritual murder accusations against Jews in *Damascus in 1840. By 1842 Fould's son, Achille Fould, also a financier, and attorney Adolphe Crémieux had become the second and third French Jewish deputies. The 1848 Revolution produced a government that named the first two Jewish ministers: Crémieux as Justice Minister and the banker Michel Goudchaux as Finance Minister. Achille Fould subsequently became the third Jewish minister, holding the posts of Finance Minister and then Minister of Culture during the Second Empire. During the Third Republic, Crémieux again served as Justice Minister. Jewish presence and influence in government institutions reached their pinnacle during the Third Republic (1871–1940), when at least 171 Jews served as deputies, senators, ministers, army generals, prefects, and magistrates. Jews, including Camille Sée and Alfred Naquet, along with Protestants, energetically sought the separation of church and state, secularization of education, free public secondary school education for girls, and the institution of civil divorce. By 1905 these aims had all been achieved. In 1936, Léon Blum became the first Jewish prime minister (there have since been three others). Despite the fact that official notice was taken of Jewish identity in nineteenth-century personnel records, and although the government refrained from posting Jewish officials to certain strongholds of Catholicism where they would encounter opposition, and despite the travesty of justice during the *Dreyfus Affair, there were no longer significant obstacles to Jews' career advancement. Their presence in the army of the Third Republic was notable, with hundreds of Jewish military officers and twenty-five serving as generals. At times as much as 3% of the regular army corps were Jewish.

Ethnic solidarity, exhibited at local, national, and international levels, was a significant characteristic of French Jews between 1789 and 1939. Although there were some spectacular conversions among high-profile figures, neither the number of conversions nor the number of *intermarriages seriously affected the natural increase of Jewish population. On the local level Jews established many charitable institutions. On the national scale, communities intervened to defend or support those with whom they were bound in a nationwide hierarchical administrative system.

Internationally, beginning early in the post-emancipation period and increasingly throughout the nineteenth century, French Jews intervened to assist less fortunate Jews around the world. Such efforts were the result of both private and communal initiative. In the 1830s a "Lafayette Committee" brought Jews and Poles together over the issue of Polish Jewish emancipation, and cooperation between the groups continued during the 1848 revolution. In 1863, when an *Alliance Polonaise* was established, seven of the first thirty-one members were French Jews, including Crémieux, Adolphe Franck, Salomon Munk, and the Chief Rabbi of Paris, Lazare Isidor. French Jews notably intervened on behalf of Levantine Jewry. In response to the accusation of *ritual murder launched against Damascus Jews in 1840 (see DAMASCUS AFFAIR), Jews of that region and around the world turned to the Rothschilds and French Jews for help. In response, and with the indispensable assistance of Albert Cohn and Salomon Munk, Adolphe Crémieux (together with Sir Moses *Montefiore of England) undertook an international diplomatic mission. During a subsequent trip in 1854, Albert Cohn, on behalf of both the Rothschilds and the French Jewish *Consistory, obtained from Sultan Abdulmecid a promise that Jews in the *Ottoman Empire would be extended the same rights that had been negotiated by the French emperor for Christians.

From 1840, French Jews, as part of a process of extending the benefits of emancipation beyond their borders, began creating schools in lands where Jews lacked secular education and civil and political rights. Crémieux established Jewish schools during his trip to Egypt on behalf of the Damascus Jews. The Rothschilds, through the work of Albert Cohn, founded schools in *Jerusalem, Smyrna, *Alexandria, and Constantinople. In Jerusalem, the Rothschilds provided money to open a school, and the Consistory agreed to raise maintenance funds. In 1854 the Consistory considered initiating a project to bring young Ottoman Jews to Paris to be trained as teachers for those schools, but it was only when the *Alliance Israélite Universelle became involved that such a scheme materialized.

French Jews, sometimes working through the Alliance, repeatedly attempted to assist the Jews of *Romania. In 1866 Crémieux traveled there to seek alleviation of Jewish civil and political disabilities. In 1878, under pressure from French Jewry, the French delegation to the Congress of Berlin obtained minority rights recognition as a condition of Romanian independence. Similar provisions were again made after World War I in the Versailles treaty, but Romania failed to implement these agreements. In 1900, Bernard Lazare visited Romania and denounced the terrible fate of Romanian Jews in the French press. In the 1920s a *Conseil pour les droits des minorités juives* was still working to remedy the situation.

For further reading, see P. C. Albert, *The Modernization of French Jewry* (1977); P. Birnbaum, *The Jews of the Republic: A Political History of State Jews in France from Gambetta to Vichy* (1996); M. Graetz, *The Jews in Nineteenth Century France* (1996); P. E. Hyman, *The Jews of Modern France* (1998); N. L. Green, *The Pletzl of Paris: Jewish Immigrant Workers in the Belle Époque* (1986); L. M. Leff, *Sacred Bonds of Solidarity: The Rise of Jewish Internationalism in Nineteenth-Century France* (2006); N. Malinovich, *French and Jewish: Culture and the Politics of Identity in Early Twentieth-Century France* (2008); and D. H. Weinberg, *A Community on Trial: The Jews of Paris in the 1930s* (1977). **See also ANTISEMITISM: FRANCE (1789–1939); FRANCE: CONSISTORIES, 1806–1939; JEWISH STUDIES: FRANCE; JUDAISM, REFORM: FRANCE; LITERATURE: FRANCE; SYNAGOGUES: FRANCE; ZIONISM: FRANCE; Map 10.** PHYLLIS COHEN ALBERT

France: Consistories, 1806–1939. In the wake of the chaos that devastated religious institutions during the revolutionary period, a hierarchical administrative structure was introduced by imperial edict on March 17, 1808, changing forever the character of Jewish communities in *France. The resulting local and national "consistories" were at once a measure of equality and a symbol of disability. They were modeled after Napoleonic institutions for the Catholic and Protestant churches. The details of the Jewish consistories were hammered out in Paris between 1806 and 1808, in discussions between the government and an "assembly of Jewish notables" followed by a "*Sanhedrin" of Jewish leaders. The goal was to reassure the emperor that Jews would be good citizens, that Jewish law would not conflict with Napoleonic law and civic obligation, and that there would be a mechanism for supervising and controlling the Jews. Regional consistories, comprising both rabbis and laymen, were supervised by a Central Consistory in Paris. Their assigned tasks were to administer and police the Jewish population and *synagogues, but they expanded their purview to include self-protection, redefinition of Judaism as a religion, and modernization of the rabbinate. For financial reasons, as well as to control the outward appearance of Judaism, the consistories sought, and partially gained, suppression of alternative synagogues. Regional consistories existed not only on French territory but also in French-controlled areas of *Italy, *Germany, *Belgium, and Algeria (see NORTH AFRICA).

Catholic and Protestant churches benefited from state subsidies instituted by Napoleon, but financial aid to Jewish institutions lagged by a full generation. The inequality was corrected by a law signed by King Louis-Philippe on February 8, 1831, in response to Jewish pressure, and with the help of deputies Comte de Rambuteau and Jean Viennet. Synagogues and rabbis then became recipients of state aid, but the new legislation rapidly proved a mixed blessing. From 1808 to 1831 the consistories had been authorized to tax their members, but this prerogative was lost under the new funding law, although governmental subsidies were chronically and severely insufficient. Governing a largely impoverished population with increasingly expensive needs, the consistories and their constituent local communities struggled perpetually. They relied on traditional sources of funding, such as taxes on kosher food and private voluntary donations. Eventually local municipalities assumed a significant part of the burden of funding religious edifices. These revenues, combined with spottily collected membership fees, combined to keep the institutions operating, but they were always in financial peril.

In addition to policing Jews through the consistory system, Napoleon introduced several restrictive measures in 1808, later dubbed "the infamous decrees," which reinstated limitations on Jews' civil liberties in regard to residential rights and freedom to exercise trades and commerce. At the same time Jews were disadvantaged in regard to their options concerning conscription to military service. These disabilities were removed ten years later when the "infamous" laws were allowed to lapse.

As part of their responsibility for "improving" the Jewish population, the consistories also oversaw Jewish education. By 1821 twelve primary schools had been established for Jewish children. In 1820 the Central Consistory adopted as the official textbook on religion Samuel Cahen's *Précis élémentaire*, often referred to as a "catechism," by analogy with the Catholic texts whose question-and-answer format it imitated. An 1833 law mandated the creation of public primary schools, but did not require that municipal funding be made available for the Jewish schools. Public financial aid was therefore spotty. After they learned reading, writing, and arithmetic in the free primary schools, the children of the poor needed vocational training. Beginning in the 1820s societies emerged to encourage, place, and assist apprentices; Jewish trade schools were also established. Their advantage was that parents could be sure that their children would not be forced to violate Jewish religious requirements while learning their trades. These schools opened in Strasbourg (Alsace) in 1825, Mulhouse (Alsace) in 1842, and Paris in 1865.

The consistories lost much of their authority at the beginning of the twentieth century. In 1905, as a result of the efforts of anticlerical intellectuals, many of whom were Jews, a law was passed separating church and state. Along with other recognized religions, the Jewish religion lost its official status, and state financial support was withdrawn. The organization of the Jewish community of France now rested on the voluntary acceptance of a central authority. The Central Consistory transformed itself into an association, preserving its earlier framework as far as possible. Synagogues built with public subsidies were nationalized, but placed at the disposal of the successor religious associations. The path was now open for both *Reform and strictly *Orthodox Jewish movements to establish themselves alongside consistorial Judaism. For further reading, see P. C. Albert, *The Modernization of French Jewry: Consistory and Community in the Nineteenth Century* (1977); and JUDAISM, REFORM: FRANCE; SYNAGOGUES: FRANCE.

PHYLLIS COHEN ALBERT

France: Contemporary. After *World War II the Jewish population in France numbered around 180,000, including refugees from *Eastern Europe. During the war, more than 77,000 Jews who had been deported from France were murdered in *Nazi camps. Of these, one-third were French citizens, and more than 8,000 were children under the age of thirteen. However, more than three-quarters of the Jews who resided or had found refuge in France in 1939 managed to survive. This high survival rate was due to many factors, including dispersal of Jews in many localities, a minimal German police presence, and assistance from some non-Jews. The French government was slow to acknowledge the wartime Vichy regime's collaboration with the Nazis in these deportations; however, in early 2009, France's highest court issued a ruling recognizing the state's complicity in the deportation of tens of thousands of French and foreign Jews (see HOLOCAUST; HOLOCAUST RESCUERS).

Many refugees from elsewhere in Europe settled in France after World War II; by the early 1950s the Jewish population had reached 250,000. *Sephardi and *Mizraḥi Jews from *North Africa also immigrated to France in the postwar decades as the French colonial empire declined; by 1968 Jews of North African origin constituted the majority of French Jewry. Today, the Jewish population of France, approximately 600,000, is the largest in Europe. Significant communities are in Paris (375,000), Marseilles, Lyons, Toulouse, Nice, and Strasbourg. Contemporary French Jews face a constant and visible level of *antisemitism, some of which is generated by anti-*Israel sentiment; since the late 1970s there have been a number of attacks on Jewish sites and *synagogues, as well as on individuals. There is a high degree of assimilation and *intermarriage but also an active Jewish religious, educational, and cultural life. Communal organizations include the Consistoire Central Israélite de France et d'Algérie; the Conseil Representatif des Juifs de France; and Fonds Social Juif Unifié, which was founded in 1949 and is particularly involved in addressing social welfare needs. For further reading, see S. Zuccotti, *The Holocaust, the French, and the Jews* (1999); and P. E. Hyman, *The Jews of Modern France* (2000).

ELIZABETH SHULMAN

France: Middle Ages. The territory roughly corresponding to modern *France sheltered two very different cultural and linguistic territories in the Middle Ages: northern France and Occitania in the south (see FRANCE, SOUTHERN: MIDDLE AGES). This article deals primarily with northern French Jewish culture, often studied within the larger cultural entity of *Ashkenaz.

Jews settled in the area corresponding to modern France beginning in *Roman times. *Herod's son Archelaus, banished to Vienne (a Roman city in what is now southeastern France) from Judea in 6 CE, is the first Jewish settler in Gaul mentioned in written sources. His brother, Herod Antipas, was sent to Lyon in 39 CE. Emigration to Gaul probably increased after the destruction of the *Temple of Jerusalem in 70 CE and after the *Bar Kokhba rebellion of 132–35, with many of the settlers passing first through *Italy. The Jews of medieval France had strong ties to Jewish communities in the Rhineland (see GERMANY) and, between 1066 and 1290, with Jewish communities in *England.

Information about Jewish life and Jewish–Christian relations during early medieval times comes in part from canons issued by ecclesiastical councils. Common themes include the prohibition of marriage or conjugal relations between Christians and Jews (e.g., Orleans 533 CE, Clermont 535, Orleans 538); prohibitions against clerics or Christian laymen taking part in banquets given by Jews (e.g., Vannes 461–91, Orleans 538); and the establishment of guidelines regarding Christian slaves who fled to churches for protection from Jewish masters (e.g., Orleans 538, Orleans 541). The Council of Clermont (535) declared that Jews should not be placed as judges over Christians. Later councils, such as Paris (614) and Clichy (626–27), prohibited Jews from holding a public office or function. Similar prohibitions can be found in other legal sources from the same period. Also in the seventh century, King Dagobert is said to have led a forced conversion of Jews to Christianity (ca. 631–39) at the urging of Emperor Heraclius. In the ninth century, Agobard, archbishop of Lyon, participated in forced conversions of Jews to Christianity, even targeting large numbers of Jewish children. The imperial court intervened against Agobard to prevent forced conversions and protect the Jewish community. In later centuries, urban centers, such as Paris, Rouen, and Troyes, sheltered the largest northern French Jewish communities. Many smaller towns and villages were home to small Jewish communities or even to individual Jews or Jewish families. Although many Jews prospered, all were subject to episodes of persecution and violence. An unconfirmed act of anti-Jewish violence is reported to have taken place in Limoges or Le Mans at the end of the tenth century. Between 1007 and 1012, northern French Jewish communities were affected by the widespread persecutions of Jews that took place across northern Europe.

During the First *Crusade (1096–99), at least one major attack on French Jews took place, in Rouen; a description by the French cleric and memoirist Guibert of Nogent survives. Jews of all ages and both genders were put to the sword; others saved themselves by converting to Christianity. In 1171 in Blois, more than thirty Jews were falsely accused of the *ritual murder of a child and then burned en masse under Count Thibault V. Jews were also accused of the 1163 murder of Richard of Pontoise, who was later canonized as Richard of Paris. Little is known of the murder accusations reported to have been leveled against the Jews of Loches-sur-Indre, Janville, and Épernay during the 1160s and 1170s. In 1191–92, the execution of a Christian for murdering a Jew had disastrous consequences for the Jewish community of Brie-Comte-Robert or Bray-sur-Seine (the exact location of the incident is debated by scholars), where King Philip Augustus subsequently had as many as eighty Jews executed. In 1288 in Troyes, thirteen Jews were burned to death, apparently falsely accused of murdering a Christian. In the thirteenth century, beginning with the reign of Louis IX (1226–70), Jews were required to wear the *rouelle*, a round badge, on their clothing. During this era as well, copies of the *Talmud were seized and the so-called Talmud trial was held (1240). This was followed by a mass burning of Jewish books in Paris in 1242.

Jews living in northern France suffered various expulsions, some affecting larger territories than others. In 1182, King Philip Augustus expelled the Jews from the French royal domain but readmitted them in 1198. Other major expulsions occurred in 1306, 1394, and perhaps 1322. Also in the fourteenth century, popular responses to the Black Death included numerous attacks on Jews, with the most violent persecutions taking place in Dauphiné and Savoy. In the early Middle Ages the Jews practiced a variety of professions, including viticulture and *medicine; some worked in the administrations of bishops or kings. By the twelfth century, many northern French Jews were confined to earning their living through *money lending at interest.

Among the great intellectual and cultural figures of medieval Jewry in northern France are *Rashi (Rabbi

Solomon ben Isaac, 1040–1105); Joseph ben Simon Kara (1050/55–1120/30); Rashbam (Rabbi Samuel ben Meir, 1080–1160); Eleazer of Beaugency (mid-twelfth century); and Joseph ben Isaac Bekhor Shor (mid- to late-twelfth century). Although Jews were often criticized by Christian scholars, Jewish and Christian scholars sometimes collaborated; the Victorines of Paris, who focused on biblical exegesis, were particularly known for working with Jewish scholars. Most Jewish literature surviving from medieval France is in Hebrew. Nonetheless, Jews also recorded glosses, *poetry, and other short texts, as well as longer glossaries and a treatise on fever, written in Old French in Hebrew letters. Rashi's biblical and talmudic commentaries contain hundreds of glosses in Old French explaining difficult Hebrew and Aramaic terms. An elegy to the martyrs of Troyes is generally considered the most famous medieval Jewish literary work in Old French (see POETRY, MEDIEVAL: CHRISTIAN EUROPE).

Selected studies dealing with medieval French Jewry include E. Benbassa, *Histoire des Juifs de France* (1997); R. Chazan, *Medieval Jewry in Northern France* (1973); W. C. Jordan, *The French Monarchy and the Jews* (1989), and idem, *Ideology and Royal Power in Medieval France* (2001); K. A. Fudeman, *Vernacular Voices: Language and Identity in Medieval French Jewish Communities (2010);* and A. Linder, *The Jews in the Legal Sources of the Early Middle Ages* (1997). **Map 7**

KIRSTEN A. FUDEMAN

France, Southern: Middle Ages.

France, Southern: Middle Ages. Common descent and shared cultural patrimony led the Jews of medieval Occitania to regard themselves as belonging to a single region, extending across the counties of Roussillon, Languedoc, Comtat Venaissin, and Provence, which are today part of southern France. At times, Jews referred to this territory as *Provincia* [*Narbonnensis*] – after Narbonne, its ancient Roman center. Unfortunately, some have confused *Provincia* with Provence, a distinct major county of the region. In fact, beyond the words "this land," the Jews of Occitania never coined a definitive name for their territory, perhaps because it traversed the jurisdictions of many sovereigns, including, at times, the kingdoms of Aragon, Majorca, France, and *Sicily; the Duchy of Toulouse; and the Papal See. Successfully exploiting their central geographic position, the Occitan Jews absorbed and transmitted Jewish culture from communities to the south (Andalusia, Castile, Catalonia) and to the north (France and Germany), in addition to making their own significant contributions. Beginning in the twelfth century, perhaps a century after the birth of other medieval Jewish intellectual centers in Western Europe, Occitania was distinguished by more than 250 years of diversified achievement in Jewish legal scholarship, the study of Hebrew language and biblical *commentary, preaching, polemics, and *poetry (see MIDDLE AGES: JEWISH-CHRISTIAN POLEMICS; SERMONS).

Initially, the Jewish communities of Occitania seem to have been most closely connected to those of Catalonia. The first major work of rabbinic law from Occitania, *Sefer ha-'Eshkol* of Abraham ben Isaac, Av Beit Din of Narbonne (d. 1179), is a précis of *Sefer ha-'Ittim*, the work of Abraham's teacher, Judah ben Barzilai of Barcelona. A portion of another early Occitan legal work, *Ha-'Ittur* of Isaac ben Abba Mari of Marseilles (d. 1190), was commissioned by Sheshet ben Isaac Benveniste of Barcelona. The following generation of scholars, in contrast, viewed their academy at Lunel as distinct from Catalonia. This generation included Occitania's masters of the Jewish legal tradition, Zeraḥiah ha-Levi (Razah) and *Abraham ben David (Rabad) of Posquières (d. 1198). Royal France had begun to bring Occitania into its orbit by this time (see HALAKHAH).

Simultaneously with these legal innovations, a monumental Hebrew translation movement began in Occitania. Over five or six generations, Jewish translators made available a vast corpus of *Judeo-Arabic and *Arabic philosophical and scientific texts, creating a Hebrew philosophic culture that affected all other areas of creativity and formed a distinct communal identity. This philosophic transformation was catalyzed by the arrival, in the middle of the twelfth century, of a small but significant group of Jewish refugee scholars from Muslim *Spain, including Judah ibn Tibbon (d. 1190) and Joseph *Kimḥi. The intellectual elite of Occitan Jewry, such as Meshullam ben Jacob of Lunel and Rabad of Posquières, welcomed their colleagues and were receptive to their learning. *Maimonides' *Mishneh Torah, which reached Occitania not long after 1180, impressed scholars with its legal and philosophical innovations and eventually changed the landscape of Jewish legal studies in Occitania. However, this transformation took time. Rabad of Posquières, esteemed for his Talmud commentary, among other works, immediately wrote critically about the *Mishneh Torah* in ways that defined his image in coming generations. Although Jonathan ha-Kohen and his academy at Lunel corresponded with Maimonides regarding his legal and philosophic views, Occitania focused its legal study on the interpretation of the *Halakhot* of Isaac of Fez (d. 1103). This is evident from the legal writings of Jonathan ha-Kohen, at the turn of the twelfth century, and Meshullam ben Moses of Béziers, at the beginning of the thirteenth century. It was not until the middle of the thirteenth century that Meshullam's student, Meir ben Simon of Capestang, returned to the Babylonian *Talmud as his central text. At the end of the thirteenth century, Menaḥem ha-Meiri of Perpignan (d. 1315) wrote his encyclopedic anthology of Jewish legal interpretation organized around the *Mishnah and Talmud. In contrast, Meiri's contemporary, Manoaḥ of Narbonne, directed his legal commentary to the *Mishneh Torah*, as did David ben Samuel of Etoile in the next generation.

Maimonides' interpretation of the meaning of Jewish tradition also had a profound impact in Occitania. Samuel ibn Tibbon of Marseilles (d. 1232) was a major agent in the transmission of Maimonidean perspectives, both as a translator of Maimonides' *Guide of the Perplexed* from Arabic to Hebrew, completed in Arles in 1204, as well as a daring exponent of the philosophic interpretation of Scripture in Hebrew in the ensuing decades. Over the course of the thirteenth century, the diverse Maimonidean commitments of Occitan Jewry became well established, although not without controversy. The Jewish scholars of Occitania were at the center of much high-profile correspondence that included the leading scholars of neighboring Jewish communities; issues of debate included Maimonides' understanding of the *resurrection of the dead (before Maimonides' own death in 1204); Maimonidean teaching as a whole (in the 1230s); and the work of the Tibbonide stream of the philosophic interpretation of Scripture, in the wake

of Maimonidean influence (1304–06). In this final controversy, Meiri stood prominently against any condemnation of Occitan Jewish scholarship or restriction of the curriculum of Jewish philosophic study, despite his more moderate Maimonidean orientation (see THOUGHT, MEDIEVAL).

At the turn of the twelfth century, just as Maimonides' work had begun to arrive, the *Sefer ha-Bahir*, the first book of *Kabbalah, emerged in Occitania. Rabad of Posquières' son, *Isaac the Blind (d. 1235), is history's first known kabbalist. He claimed to have received secret kabbalistic teachings from his father, who received them from his father-in-law, Abraham ben Isaac – Av Beit Din of Narbonne (Rabi); there is some support for this line of transmission. However, for unclear reasons the history of Kabbalah in Occitania was brief. It is known that Occitania's ruling rabbinic elite, Meshullam ben Moses of Béziers and Meir ben Simon of Capestang, regarded the *Bahir* and the teaching of the ten *sefirot* as a polytheistic heresy utterly foreign to Judaism, and they presumably played a major role in successfully expelling Kabbalah from Occitania. In fact, in a letter to his former students, Moses ben Naḥman (*Naḥmanides) and Jonah of Girona, Isaac warned against the improper dissemination of Kabbalah in *Spain.

Throughout the thirteenth and into the first half of the fourteenth century, Occitan philosophic translation and interpretation produced the first and only full-fledged medieval Jewish philosophic culture in Hebrew. From the influential philosophic sermons of Jacob Anatoli (d. 1256) and the magisterial *aggadah* commentary of Isaac ben Jedaiah, in the first half of the thirteenth century, to philosophical Torah commentaries of Levi ben Gerson of Orange (*Gersonides) and Nissim ben Moses of Marseilles, in the first half of the fourteenth century, Occitan Jews reshaped the tradition of the Bible, Talmud, and Midrash in a philosophic mold. Gersonides' monumental *Wars of the Lord*, one of the most important works of Jewish philosophy in Hebrew, emerges from this context. The philosophic works of Occitan Jews range from the translations of Averroes into Hebrew by Moses ibn Tibbon (d. 1283), to the medical and astronomical treatises of Jacob ben Makhir ibn Tibbon (d. 1306), to the vast encyclopedia of philosophic learning and interpretation by Levi ben Abraham ben Ḥayyim. Meiri's dramatic designation of Christianity and Islam as "civilizing religions" must be situated in this late-thirteenth-century Jewish philosophic cultural matrix. The 1306 expulsion of Jews from sections of Occitania that were newly subservient to royal France did not quell philosophic engagement. Hebrew versions of Aristotles' *Ethics* and Plato's *Republic* by Samuel ben Judah of Marseilles, based on Averroes' commentaries, were produced subsequently. So, too, were the mathematical and astronomical works of Jedaiah ha-Penini and the philosophic Bible commentaries of Joseph ibn Kaspi, as well as the translations and commentaries on the works of Averroes by Kalonymus ben Kalonymus (d. 1328) and Todros Todrosi (see SCIENCE AND MATHEMATICS: MIDDLE AGES).

A large portion of the Occitan Jewish interpretive legacy became submerged or disappeared during the later Middle Ages and Early Modern period. It seems likely that the gradual dissolution of Occitan Jewish identity in the second half of the fourteenth century significantly contributed to this loss. Even today, the Occitan Jewish community's momentous cultivation of and acculturation to

Greco-Arabic scientific and philosophic teachings are under-appreciated.

For further reading, see I. Twersky, "Aspects of the Social and Cultural History of Provençal Jewry," *Journal of World History* 11 (1968): 185–207; and G. Stern, *Philosophy and Rabbinic Culture: Jewish Interpretation and Controversy in Medieval Languedoc* (2009). **Map 7**   GREGG STERN

Frank, Anne (1929–1945), who is known for the diary she kept while in hiding from the *Nazis with her family in *Amsterdam, was born in *Frankfurt, *Germany, the younger daughter of Edith and Otto Frank. When Hitler assumed power in 1933, the family fled to Holland where Otto Frank had a business. Anne attended Dutch schools until the German occupation of Holland in 1940 introduced anti-Jewish measures. When Anne's sister Margot received a "call up" notice in the summer of 1942, the family quickly moved into a hiding place above Otto Frank's offices on Prinsengracht Street, which Anne called "the Secret Annex" in her diary. Anne received the diary as a thirteenth birthday gift just weeks before the move. In hiding, she used her diary to express her adolescent musings, literary aspirations, and fears. In its pages she reveals that the civilian population knew of the concentration camps and describes round-ups of Jews in the streets below her windows. In March 1944, the family heard a radio broadcast in which the Dutch government in exile announced its intentions to publish civilian accounts of suffering after the war. Anne began to revise her diary in hopes of publication.

Anne's writing gives a lively account of adolescent resilience and psychological dramas during two years of duress. Her family shared its few rooms with the van Pels family (renamed Van Daan in the diary), whose son Peter became a love interest for Anne. Later, the girl was forced to share a bedroom with an uncongenial newcomer, Friedrich Pfeffer, a dentist. Anne's diary describes how hunger, confinement, and boredom magnified tensions among the sequestered Jews. Personal reflections on identity, her struggle for independence under constant adult scrutiny, and her dawning sexuality are recorded, along with the terrors of break-ins to the building and night-time bombings of Amsterdam. In August 1944, the family was betrayed by an anonymous informant, arrested by the Gestapo, and held at Westerbork detention camp in Holland before being transported to *Auschwitz. Anne and Margot were sent on to *Bergen-Belsen in Germany, where the sisters died of typhus just weeks before the Allied liberation in 1945. Of the eight occupants of the Secret Annex, only Otto Frank survived. On his return to Amsterdam, Frank received Anne's diary from Miep Gies, the family protector who had rescued it from the annex. Frank published an edited version of the diary in Europe, but it became a literary sensation only after the English translation appeared in America in 1952, with an introduction by Eleanor Roosevelt. Its popularity led to a Pulitzer-Prize-winning Broadway play (1955) adapted from the diary by Frances Goodrich and Albert Hackett and a Hollywood film version (1959) directed by George Stevens that won three Oscars (see HOLOCAUST REPRESENTATION: DRAMA; HOLOCAUST REPRESENTATION: FILM).

The diary was one of the first widely read *Holocaust documents, and it has been particularly inspiring to successive generations of young people worldwide. It also became a model of women's memoir writing in the era before feminist literary studies, and it helped open the floodgates for Holocaust literature to follow. The Anne Frank House in Amsterdam has been a museum since 1960 and receives as many as a million visitors a year; devoted to promoting tolerance and education, it supports research on the Holocaust and racism and sponsors international exhibits. In 1989 the Netherlands State Institute for War Documentation brought out a critical edition of the diary, edited by David Barnouw et al., which assembles three versions of the diary: the original, Anne's revised version, and Otto Frank's edited version. **See also HOLOCAUST DIARIES.**   MARTHA A. RAVITS

Frank, Jacob and Frankism. Jacob Frank (ca. 1726–1791) was the *messianic leader of a Polish Jewish group known for its *antinomian rituals, public challenges to rabbinic Judaism, and subsequent mass conversion to Catholicism. Born Jacob ben Judah Leib Frank in Podolia (the *Ukraine) in either Korolówka or Buczacz, Frank married in Salonica and joined a radical group known as "Dönmeh," crypto-Jewish Muslims who believed that *Shabbetai Zevi had been the messiah. In 1755, he returned to *Poland and sought out *Sabbatean leaders. On the night of January 27, 1756, in the town of Lanckoronie nad Zbruczem, Frank and some followers were discovered conducting antinomian rituals. Frank was permitted to return to *Ottoman territories, where he converted to *Islam. His followers, who admitted to ritualistic wife swapping, studying Sabbatean books, and holding Sabbatean beliefs, were placed under ban (*herem) by the Brody rabbinical assembly and the *Council of Four Lands. The rabbinic authorities asked Bishop Mikołaj Dembowski to condemn the Frankists and suggested they be burned at the stake. However, Bishop Dembowski sided with the Frankists, who presented themselves as anti-talmudists with trinitarian beliefs. They produced a manifesto that called for a public disputation on nine principles of their faith, several of which seemed to uphold Christian doctrine. A disputation between nineteen Frankists and forty rabbis was held in Kamieniec Podolski from June 20–28, 1757. The "anti-talmudists" were declared the winners, their rabbinic opponents were fined and flogged, and copies of the *Talmud were burned.

After Bishop Dembowski's death on November 9, 1757, deprived the Frankists of their main protector, persecutions were renewed with a vengeance. Many Frankists fled to *Turkey and joined up with Frank himself but Bishop Kajetan Sołtyk, who had orchestrated a *ritual murder trial in Żytomierz four years earlier, persuaded King Augustus III to bring the Frankists back to Poland in order to hold another public disputation. The Frankists, now regarded as potential converts to Christianity, promised to prove that Jews used Christian blood for ritual purposes. The disputation was held from July 17 to September 19, 1759, in Lwów, but owing to an intervention by the Vatican no decisive verdict was issued. On September 17, Frank was baptized in the Lwów cathedral, and three thousand of his followers subsequently converted as well. Frank began to travel in aristocratic circles with great pomp but the sincerity of his conversion was questioned, and the adulation of his followers aroused further suspicion. Frank was arrested on January 7, 1760, and secluded in a Czestochowa monastery for thirteen years. Freed by the Russians, who took the

Czestochowa fortress in 1772, Frank moved to Brünn (Brno) in Moravia and resumed his visits to aristocrat courts. After falling out of favor with Joseph II in 1786, Frank left the *Habsburg Empire and settled in Offenbach am Main. He died on December 10, 1791. His daughter Eva (1754–1816) assumed leadership of his Offenbach court, but most followers left for *Warsaw (see MYSTICISM, WOMEN AND).

The most famous compilation of Frank's teachings is *Zbiór słów pańskich* (The Collection of the Words of the Lord). For further reading, see essays in R. Elior, ed., *Ha-Ḥalom VeShivro: The Sabbatean Movement and Its Aftermath: Messianism Sabbatianism and Frankism* (2001).   GLENN DYNNER

Frankel, Zacharias (1801–1875), rabbi and historian,

is considered the founder of what ultimately became *Conservative Judaism. Born in *Prague, Frankel was the first Bohemian rabbi to complete university studies, graduating in Budapest in 1831. He served Jewish communities in Leitmeritz (Litomerice), Teplitz (Teplice), and Dresden, where he remained from 1836 to 1854; in 1843 he declined an invitation to serve as the Chief Rabbi of *Berlin.

In a time of religious ferment and pressure for reform among Jewish communities in German-speaking Europe, Frankel took a cautious middle ground and was resistant to demands for changes from the laity. He believed that reforms in Jewish practice were possible if they were based on historical precedent, but he broke with the nascent *Reform movement in 1845 when radical reformers supported the elimination of the Hebrew language from communal *worship. Despite opposition from both the liberal and traditional camps, Frankel promoted a "Positive-Historical" approach that supported the gradual "organic" evolution of *halakhah. He argued that historical study demonstrated that Jewish law had always changed over time in response to new circumstances. In 1854 Frankel became the first president of the Jüdisch-Theologisches Seminar in Breslau, which he led for twenty-one years. As part of his effort to bring modern scholarly approaches to the study of Jewish legal texts, Frankel edited the journal *Die Monatsschrift für Geschichte und Wissenschaft des Judentums* between 1851 and 1868.

Frankel was an active scholar with a particular interest in comparative exegesis; he also prepared critical introductions to various rabbinic works, including the *Mishnah and the Palestinian *Talmud, using modern scholarly methods.

    KATE FRIEDMAN

Frankfurt am Main, the largest city in the *German state

of Hesse, is home to a Jewish community that has existed almost continuously from medieval times into the twenty-first century. A free imperial city and coronation site for the Holy Roman Emperors until the early nineteenth century, Frankfurt was formally annexed by Prussia in 1866. Although evidence shows the city to be far older, detailed records of its Jewish community emerge by the thirteenth century. Buffeted during the medieval and Early Modern periods by anti-Jewish attacks (most prominently in 1241, 1349, and the Fettmilch Riots of 1616) and by disasters such as the fire of 1711, Frankfurt nevertheless grew to be a center of Jewish economic, cultural, and intellectual life. In the mid-fifteenth century, the community of around one hundred individuals maintained a *synagogue, ritual bath (*mikveh), "dance hall" (*Tanzhaus*), and a study hall. In 1462 the community was relocated to a newly created,

walled *Judengasse* (Jews' street) – one of very few classic "*ghettos" in *Central Europe. Although the ghetto signified increased restriction, its establishment also marked the beginning of a period of significant demographic and cultural growth. By 1798, when the ghetto was dismantled, Frankfurt's Jewish population had grown to five hundred families, the maximum number allowed by law. Frankfurt was a major center of Jewish learning, and its rabbinic personalities included Rabbi Isaiah ben Abraham ha-Levi Horowitz (ca. 1565–1630), author of *Shnei luḥot ha-brit*; Meir ben Jacob ha-Kohen Schiff (the MaHaRam Schiff, 1605–1631); Aaron Samuel ben Israel Koidonover (the MaHaR-ShaK, 1614–1676); his son, Zevi Hirsh (d. 1712); and Jacob Joshua ben Zevi Hirsch Falk (1680–1756), author of *P'nei Yehoshua*.

Frankfurt Jews were sustained largely by petty trade, both in the city itself and in the surrounding countryside. For many, work in *commerce replaced peddling as the primary Jewish occupation in the modern period. *Banking also emerged as a small but important economic sector; the *Rothschild family, beginning with patriarch Mayer Amschel, emerged as a prominent symbol of the economic life of Frankfurt Jewry.

The Jewish population of Frankfurt grew from 4,900 in 1848 to more than 22,000 by 1900. In the mid-nineteenth century, the city was a focal point of German Jewish denominational struggle. It was the birthplace of prominent reformer Abraham *Geiger and the location of the second of the three foundational *Reform congresses in 1845. Frankfurt was also home to the first *Orthodox community in Germany to legally sever itself from the official community, the *Israelitische Religionsgesellschaft* (IRG), led by Samson Raphael *Hirsch. Throughout this period, Frankfurt's Jewish infrastructure and culture blossomed; by the end of the century, it boasted many *synagogues, including multiple Reform synagogues (such as the Hauptsynagogue, built 1860) and the Orthodox Schützenstrasse Synagogue of the IRG (built 1853). The city was also home to Moritz Daniel *Oppenheim, a renowned painter of nineteenth-century German Jewry (see ART, EUROPE: NINETEENTH CENTURY).

In the twentieth century, Franz *Rosenzweig's *Freies Jüdisches Lehrhaus* (free Jewish learning center) made Frankfurt an important center of Jewish thought; its teachers included Martin *Buber, Gershom *Scholem, and Leo *Strauss. Also prominent in the flowering of Jewish intellectual creativity was the *Frankfurt Institut für Sozialforschung*, the Frankfurt School of Social Research, whose members included Theodor Adorno, Max Horkheimer, Herbert Marcuse, and Leo Löwenthal.

After 1933, the approximately 26,000 Jews of Frankfurt were besieged as the *Nazi regime consolidated power. Jewish institutional buildings were plundered during the *Kristallnacht* pogroms of November 1938; in the war years the community was destroyed through a combination of emigration (approximately 16,000 left) and mass deportation to concentration and death camps in *Poland. Around one hundred and fifty Jews and other individuals subject to racial restrictions survived to 1945.

At the beginning of the twenty-first century, Frankfurt is home to 7,000 Jews, one of the largest Jewish communities in Germany; many of its members are Jews from the former

*Soviet Union. The Westendsynagogue, built in 1910 and fully restored in 1994, is the central synagogue of Frankfurt and the city's sole surviving pre-war synagogue.

For further reading, see R. Gay, *The Jews of Germany: A Historical Portrait* (1992); R. Lieberles, *Religious Conflict in Social Context: The Resurgence of Orthodox Judaism in Frankfurt am Main, 1838–1877* (1985); and M. Brenner, *The Renaissance of Jewish Culture in Weimar Germany* (1996).   JESS OLSON

Fraternal Societies: See UNITED STATES: FRATERNAL SOCIETIES

Fraternities and Sororities: North America.

The terms "fraternity" and "sorority" – from the Latin *frater* (brother) and *soror* (sister) – may describe many social, charitable, service, professional, and honorary societies. In the *United States and *Canada these terms most commonly refer to organizations for college and university students that provide room, board, social life, and life-long networking after graduation. Known collectively as "the Greek system," such groups go back to the dawn of North American higher education. Phi Beta Kappa, founded in 1776 at the College of William and Mary, began as a social group but eventually evolved into a scholarship society. Others followed from the 1820s onward. By custom, the founding organization would take on a two- or three-letter Greek name representing a motto known only to initiated members. Subsequent chapters at other schools in turn received additional letter designations, usually in Greek alphabetical order; for example, the "Alpha" chapter of Delta Phi, the "Beta" chapter, and so forth. Ancient Hellenic and Roman ideals, language, and secret mottoes allowed young men and women to identify with the romance and glory of past civilizations and also to distinguish themselves from the "barbarians" in their midst. Over the course of the nineteenth century, Greek-letter societies spread across the United States and developed an extensive culture that included passwords, secret handshakes, insignias, special ceremonial robes, and often elaborate esoteric rituals with details and symbols borrowed from Freemasonry and ancient Greek, Roman, and Christian traditions. At least fifty national men's college fraternities and twelve national sororities were established by 1900. By the 1920s, just when Jewish students by the thousands were moving into higher education, Greek-letter societies dominated student life on scores of American campuses.

However, the mainstream Greek system was virtually closed to all but the most exceptional or hidden Jewish students, as it was to African American and Asian students and, in many cases, Roman Catholics as well. The strong and explicitly Christian content of the insignia and initiation rituals of many of the existing fraternities and sororities were enough to discourage Jewish membership. However, barriers of race and religion were also enforced by a "gentleman's agreement" or spelled out explicitly in the groups' constitutions and initiation rituals. In one Christian fraternity in the late 1920s, possession of one-eighth Jewish blood disqualified a student for membership. A Jewish student might try to hide his background and "pass" as a Gentile through various means, but this path was fraught with difficulty. As late as the early 1950s, "rushing booklets" at the University of Pennsylvania made the religions of entering students a matter of public record by publishing a P, a C, or an H after each freshman's name, indicating Protestant, Catholic,

or Hebrew, for the specific purpose of steering students to the right fraternity. The university also maintained two separate inter-fraternity councils, A for Gentiles and B for Jews.

Jewish college students reacted by forming their own Jewish Greek subsystem of college fraternities and sororities. These flourished in the United States and Canada, reaching virtually every state. This network also included a "sub-sub" system of fraternities and sororities for Jewish students attending professional schools. At its height in the late 1920s, there were as many as twenty multi-chapter undergraduate national groups for men and five for women. Many more chapters existed solely on the local level; it is estimated that these organizations had initiated as many as 250,000 male and female students by 1968. Pi Lambda Phi, founded at Yale University in 1895 by three Jewish students, was the first national college fraternity in this subsystem, although its aim was to be nonsectarian. Zeta Beta Tau was founded as a student *Zionist organization at the Jewish Theological Seminary in 1898 by Professor Richard J. H. Gottheil and by fourteen young men who combined rabbinics with study at several local New York universities. Known at first simply as "ZBT" – the letters of its Hebrew motto, "*Zion Bemishpat Tipadeh*" ("Zion shall with judgment be redeemed" [Isaiah 1:27]) – Zeta Beta Tau soon evolved into the premier Jewish Greek-letter society, catering to the wealthy sons of *Reform Jews of German origins. The younger sister of a ZBT member helped found Iota Alpha Pi, the first Jewish college sorority, at New York's Hunter College in 1903. In English letters "Iota" became "J"; thus members were known as "JAPs," and their publication was entitled *The J.A.P. Bulletin.* Alpha Epsilon Phi, which in many ways served as the female counterpart of ZBT, was founded six years later at Barnard College.

By the end of *World War I, the entire Jewish subsystem had been formed. The roll of men's national college social fraternities, in order of their founding, included Pi Lambda Phi (1895, Yale), Zeta Beta Tau (1898, JTS), Phi Epsilon Pi (1904, City College of New York), Sigma Alpha Mu, or the "Sammies" (1909, CCNY), Phi Sigma Delta (1910, Columbia), Tau Epsilon Phi (1910, Columbia), Tau Delta Phi (1910, CCNY), Beta Sigma Rho (1910, Cornell), Kappa Nu (1911, University of Rochester), Phi Beta Delta (1912, Columbia), Omicron Alpha Tau (1912, Cornell), Phi Alpha (1914, George Washington University), Alpha Epsilon Pi (1914, New York University), Alpha Mu Sigma (1914, Cooper Union), Sigma Omega Psi (1914, CCNY), Sigma Lambda Pi (1915, NYU), and Sigma Tau Phi (1918, University of Pennsylvania). Jewish women's sororities included Iota Alpha Pi (1903, Hunter College), Alpha Epsilon Phi (1909, Barnard), Phi Sigma Sigma (1913, Hunter), Sigma Delta Tau (1917, Cornell), and Delta Phi Epsilon (1917, NYU Law School). Jewish Greek-letter societies for professional students had been founded for medicine, Phi Delta Epsilon (1904, Cornell) and Phil Lambda Kappa (1907, University of Pennsylvania); for dentistry, Sigma Epsilon Delta (1901, New York College of Dentistry) and Alpha Omega (1909, University of Maryland); for law, Nu Beta Epsilon (1919), Tau Epsilon Rho (1920), and Lambda Alpha Phi (1919); for pharmacy, Alpha Zeta Omega (1919) and Rho Pi Phi (1919); for osteopathy, Lambda Omicron Gamma (1924); for optometry, Mu Sigma Pi, (1932); and for veterinary medicine, Sigma Iota Zeta (1933).

In the early years of the Jewish Greek system a clear hierarchy operated based on such factors as wealth, family origin (where one's parents came from in Europe and being born in the United States were important determinants), appearance, and athletic ability. Much intra-Jewish snobbery and discrimination were practiced when choosing and rejecting members. However, Jewish fraternities and sororities served important community functions by providing places for Jewish students to eat and sleep in small college towns where landlords and fellow students did not want to live with Jews. It was not uncommon for parents to cooperate in helping buy fraternity houses for this purpose. Because dating and eventual marriage were key parts of any social fraternity, the Jewish system served as a national matchmaking bureau, bringing Jewish students together, especially at annual conventions and house parties, and keeping the Jewish *intermarriage rate among college students unusually low. They were also an important factor in achieving upward mobility, because members would often go into business together and alumni would help recent graduates find good positions. It was not uncommon for entire firms to be dominated by members from a single fraternity.

The insularity of the separate Gentile and Jewish Greek systems began breaking down in the 1950s with the enactment of laws forbidding publicly supported educational institutions from discriminating on the basis of race or religion. The years of student protest on college campuses in the 1960s and early 1970s also had a negative impact on the Jewish Greek system. At least three-quarters of formerly all-Jewish fraternities had to merge or go out of business; those few that remain came to accept large numbers of non-Jews. In the 1980s and 1990s the Greek system as a whole, as well as its Jewish segment, enjoyed a modest revival. At the turn of the twenty-first century four of the men's groups and four of the women's groups continue to function. One fraternity, Alpha Epsilon Pi, specifically embraces a Jewish mission and aims to train young men for leadership in the Jewish community. Many of the others are reasserting their traditional Jewish identity, a trend that has been encouraged by the wider American Jewish community. However, it is doubtful that Jewish fraternities and sororities will ever be able, legally or practically, to return to the insularity they enjoyed in the first half of the twentieth century. For a recent study, see M. Sanua, *Going Greek: Jewish College Fraternities in the United States, 1895–1945* (2003).   MARIANNE SANUA

Freud, Sigmund (1856–1939), the founder of *psychoanalysis, was born into a Jewish family in Moravia, then a province of the *Austro-Hungarian Empire. When Freud was still young, his family moved to *Vienna; there he excelled in school and graduated from the University of Vienna School of Medicine. After a short period of study with Charcot at Salpêtrière Hospital in Paris (1885–86), Freud returned to Vienna where he married Martha Bernays and opened his own clinical office in neurology, specializing in the treatment of hysteria. With his colleague Josef Breuer he developed the therapeutic technique known as "*psychoanalysis," which he went on to refine in a rich body of clinical and theoretical writings. Freud's early career was deeply marked by ascendant political *antisemitism in Vienna. His earliest and most revolutionary work, *The Interpretation of Dreams* (1899), documents his own dreams

of his father Jakob's humiliation by antisemites. Although the early membership of the psychoanalytic movement was largely Jewish, Freud was a principled atheist and remained wholly convinced of the scientific character of psychoanalysis. His hopes that his disciple Carl Jung (a non-Jew) would help secure the movement's broader legitimacy were eventually frustrated when their relationship came to an end. In his later years, Freud suffered a painful cancer of the palate (causing a disfigurement hidden beneath his beard). He continued to revise his psychoanalytic theory and technique while also addressing more creative themes in *anthropology and the philosophy of history. With the *Nazi invasion of Austria, Freud sought refuge in London in 1938, where he composed his final and most speculative work, *Moses and Monotheism* (1939).   PETER E. GORDON

Friedländer, David (1750–1834), was a *Haskalah* figure, *Berlin Jewish communal leader, and writer and major participant in *emancipation debates of the late eighteenth century. Friedländer was born in Königsberg, Prussia, to a wealthy merchant family, and his controversial life illustrates the struggles of a transitional figure in the early emancipation period. Starting his business career in the early 1770s, Friedländer moved to Berlin, home to the blossoming *German Jewish enlightenment movement centered around Moses *Mendelssohn. Young and affluent, Friedländer quickly gained an influential presence as a *maskil* and a central role in the leadership of both the Berlin Jewish and mercantile communities. Although he believed deeply in the unique position of the Jewish people and religion, Friedländer, in contrast to Mendelssohn, advocated a critical attitude toward Jewish law and practice and believed that religious reform was key to Jewish social and moral improvement, and ultimately to political emancipation. He helped fund the Berlin Jewish *Freischule* (free community school and publisher) in 1778, a flagship *Haskalah* effort to reform Jewish society through enlightened education, and he prepared a *Lesebuch für jüdische Kinder*, a primer for Jewish children. Friedländer translated the traditional *prayer book into modern German and authored a number of ethical essays, which he viewed as crucial tools for the reform of German Jewry. He published repeatedly in the prestigious Enlightenment journal *Deutsche Monatschrift*, and his collected essays such as *Reden der Erbauung* (Edifying Discourses) attest to the depth of his religious and philosophical ideas.

After 1786 and the death of Moses Mendelssohn, Friedländer and the Berlin *Haskalah* movement entered a period of crisis. His close relationship to Mendelssohn, passionate interest in the intellectual enlightenment of German Jewry, and wealth and contacts in the highest strata of Berlin society made Friedländer the most credible heir to Mendelssohn. However, because he was more receptive to fundamental religious reform than his mentor, Friedländer attracted attacks from traditionalistists. Simultaneously, Friedrich Wilhelm II rebuffed the efforts of Friedländer and other elite Berlin Jews toward Jewish legal emancipation in 1790. Despairing of the future of both the maskilic project of reforming Judaism and of the possibility of Jews achieving civic equality, Friedländer authored a *Sendschrift* (open letter), signed by several prominent Prussian Jews, to liberal Protestant theologian Wilhelm Abraham

Teller, volunteering their conversion to liberal Protestantism in exchange for full political equality and citizenship. Although Friedländer understood conversion to mean simply nominal Protestantism based on antidoctrinal deism, the letter sparked heated debate across religious lines, enraging *maskilim*, traditionalists, and even some Christian thinkers. Although it had little impact on Friedländer's later commu-nal career, the letter significantly diminished his prestige as a leader of enlightened Jewish thought and has made him a figure of much controversy in modern Jewish history.

For further reading, see M. Meyer, *The Origins of the Modern Jew: Jewish Identity and European Culture in Germany, 1749–1824* (1967); and S. Lowenstein, *The Jewishness of David Friedländer and the Crisis of Berlin Jewry* (1994).   JESS OLSON

G

Galicia (*Yiddish, *Galitsye*) is a region in southeastern *Poland and northwestern *Ukraine. Part of the old Polish-Lithuanian Commonwealth, Galicia entered *Habsburg Austria as a result of the Polish partitions beginning in 1772 (both its borders and the name itself, *Galizien*, were Austrian constructions). The region remained the Habsburg Empire's largest crown land, or province, until the empire's collapse in 1918, at which time it ceased to exist as a political entity.

At the time of its annexation, Galicia included nearly 200,000 Jews; the Jewish population increased to 575,000 in 1869 (10.6% of the population) and 873,000 in 1910 (10.9%). Galicia was an ethnically divided territory. The western part was overwhelmingly Polish with a significant Jewish minority (~9%). In contrast, Poles constituted the elites in the east, but numbered only 20% population, which was about 13% Jewish and 65% "Ruthenian" (the Austrian designation of later-day Ukrainians). Jews typically cconstituted more than a quarter of the population of Galicia's two largest cities, Lemberg (Lwów) and Kraków, and formed either a majority or a plurality in scores of other towns, including Brody, Buczacz, Stanislau, Kolomea, and Drohobycz. As a result, Jews often played a critical role in elections.

*Yiddish speaking and overwhelmingly commercial in a Slavic, agrarian environment, Galician Jewry largely retained its traditional *Eastern European character throughout the nineteenth and twentieth centuries. *Hasidism, including the Belz, Sandz, and Czortkow dynasties, struck deep roots in Galicia but so too did the *Haskalah*, many of whose earliest luminaries hailed from Galicia, including Yehuda Mieses, Joseph Perl, and Nachman *Krochmal. Partially as a result of the *Haskalah*, progressive Jews gravitated toward *German culture during the first half of the nineteenth century. However, as Poles gained control of the province after 1868, Jewish acculturation among the elites shifted toward Polonization.

Galician Jewry experienced *emancipation differently from Jews in other regions of pre-partition Poland. Already in the 1780s, the enlightened Habsburg absolutist Joseph II began the process of breaking down Jewish communal autonomy and opening up previously forbidden occupational and residential opportunities. By 1867, all legal restrictions based on religion were abolished. As a result of these unique freedoms in Eastern Europe, a broad array of modern political and cultural movements, as well as a vibrant Jewish press, developed in Galicia. The first *Orthodox political party, *Mahsike Hadas*, was founded in Galicia in 1878. *Zionism and other forms of Jewish nationalism emerged early (beginning in 1883), partially as a reaction to *antisemitism but mostly because of the Habsburg Empire's hypernationalist atmosphere in the waning years of its existence. Jewish socialism likewise emerged early in Galicia; Jews organized their first labor strike in 1892, and a Galician version of the *Bund formed in 1905. Economically, Galicia was the least developed province in the empire. The

Jewish situation grew especially dire toward the end of the nineteenth century as Polish and Ukrainian agrarian cooperatives deliberately cut Jewish middlemen from the economy. Mass migration was one result; 120,000 Jews emigrated during the 1890s alone, mostly to the *United States.

After *World War I, Polish victories against the Ukrainians secured the incorporation of Galicia into the new Polish state. Interwar Jewish life reflected the general Jewish experience throughout Poland, with a vibrant political and cultural life but rapidly declining economic conditions. Galician Jews were disproportionately Polonized and far more politically moderate than other segments of interwar Polish Jewry. Its population suffered disproportionately under *Nazi occupation, particularly in eastern Galicia, and the communities for the most part did not reconstitute themselves after the *Holocaust.

Negative references to the *Galitsianer* (Yiddish for Galician Jew) as cunning, unlearned, coarse, or a religious fanatic are still heard in the early twenty-first century; these images were created by nineteenth-century Germanized Jews to highlight their own acculturation. In reality, in addition to its nineteenth-century Hasidic, rabbinic, and *Haskalah* celebrities, Galicia produced countless Zionist and socialist leaders as well as a cadre of literary and academic stars in the twentieth century, most notably S. Y. *Agnon, many of whose stories describe life in his hometown of Buczacz. **Map 8**

For further reading, see I. Bartal and A. Polonsky, eds., *Focusing on Galicia: Jews, Poles, and Ukrainians, 1772–1918*, Polin 12 (1999); S. Redlich, *Together and Apart in Brzezany: Poles, Jews, and Ukrainians, 1919–1945* (2002); and O. Bartov, *Erased: Vanishing Traces of Jewish Galicia in Present-Day Ukraine* (2007).   JOSHUA M. SHANES

Galilee   (Hebrew, ha-Galil) is an extensive hilly region in the northern part of *Israel bounded by the Mediterranean in the west and the Jordan rift valley in the east; the northern boundary is the base of Mount Hermon, and the southern boundaries extend to Mount Carmel and Mount Gilboa. The region of Galilee was separated from biblical *Israel by *Assyrian ruler Tiglath-Pileser III in 732 BCE, and it was only reunited with Judea by *Hasmonean king Aristobulus I in 104 BCE. The Galilee later became the largest of the three districts (with *Judea and *Samaria) under the rule of *Rome's client-kings, the *Herodian dynasty.

During the First *Jewish War against *Rome (66–73 CE), the Galilee joined the revolt under the military leadership of *Josephus. After a forty-seven-day siege, the fortified village of Yodefat was captured, and Josephus surrendered to Vespasian, the Roman general. Major Galilean cities in Roman times included Sepphoris, Panias, and Tiberias, which Herod Antipas (see HEROD AND HERODIAN DYNASTY) built on the shore of the Sea of Galilee (Lake Kinneret) in honor of his patron, the Emperor Tiberius (see ARCHEOLOGY, LAND OF ISRAEL: SECOND TEMPLE PERIOD). All of these cities, as well as the region's villages and towns, had diverse populations. In the second century CE, after the destruction of the *Jerusalem *Temple in 70 CE and the depredations of the Second *Jewish War, Galilee became the center of *rabbinic activity in the Land of Israel. In *Byzantine times, the region also had a large Christian population. Between the eighth and tenth centuries, after the region had come under Muslim rule, Tiberias became one of the centers of the textual and *grammatical activities of the *Masoretes. After the 1492 expulsion from *Spain the Galilean city of *Safed became a center of *halakhic scholarship (see HALAKHAH) and Jewish *mysticism.

Galut (Hebrew, "exile"): See DIASPORA

Gaon, Geonim, Geonic Academies. The Geonim were scholars and religious leaders who presided over Babylonian institutions known as the academies (*yeshivot*) of *Sura and *Pumbedita during the geonic period (approximately 550–1050 CE) in what is now *Iraq. The Geonim functioned alongside the *Exilarch (*Rosh Galut*), a secular political figure, as the leaders of Babylonian Jewry. The Babylonian academies were named after their original locations, although both had relocated to Baghdad by the turn of the tenth century. The academies were dedicated primarily to *Talmud study and the application of talmudic sources to legal decision making; they were also administrative centers for the Jewish population of much of Iraq and *Iran. As the most important institutions of higher learning in the Jewish world, they attracted students from great distances. Only a relatively small number attended year-round; many others studied in their home towns most of the year and came to the academies for concentrated study sessions during the *kallah* months of *Adar and *Elul. The senior members of the academy, under the direction of the Gaon, also wrote *responsa, legal answers to questions sent to them from distant communities, especially those located in Islamic lands.

There was also a Gaon who served as head of the central academy in the Land of *Israel, located in Tiberias for most of this period. Unlike his Babylonian colleagues, he appears to have dedicated more of his energies to communal politics and less to talmudic learning. Around the middle of the tenth century, the Tiberian academy relocated to *Jerusalem. The constitutional basis of the Palestinian school was the Jerusalem Talmud, and Palestinian practice differed from Babylonian on various points of law and ritual. For example, in the Palestinian rite, the *Torah was read in the synagogue according to a three-year cycle, whereas in the Babylonian rite, the Torah was read in its entirety in one year. Palestinians celebrated only the one biblically ordained day for each holiday, whereas the Babylonians celebrated two. During worship, Palestinians recited the *shema* prayer, the invocation of divine unity, while standing; Babylonians recited it while seated.

Despite differences of custom and legal interpretation, the three academies recognized one another's religious authority. At the time of the Muslim conquest of the Land of Israel in 635, the Palestinian academy's authority extended throughout *Italy and the territories of the *Byzantine Empire, whereas the Babylonian academies held sway in the *Sassanian lands. However, after the shift of the Islamic world's political, economic, and cultural center of gravity to Iraq, and the steady flow of Jews from the east into the Mediterranean region, the Palestinian *yeshivah* was increasingly overshadowed by Sura and Pumbedita. By the twelfth century, the Babylonian form of rabbinic Judaism had become dominant throughout the Jewish world, due in significant part to the activism, creativity, and intellectual quality of such influential Geonim of the ninth, tenth, and early eleventh centuries as *Amram bar Shesna (d. 875), *Saadia ben Joseph (d. 942), and *Hai ben Sherira (d. 1038). For further reading see R. Brody, *The Geonim of Babylonia and the Shaping of Medieval Jewish Culture* (1998). **Map 5**

ROBERT BRODY

Gardens. In Jewish tradition gardens are actual places, but they also have a range of symbolic meanings. Gardens on any scale, from single plants to encompassing all of creation, employ the immutable elements of nature – stone, water, plants, and climate – along with the various meanings we ascribe to nature's qualities. *Genesis 2:5–3:24 situates the story of creation in *gan eden* (the garden of Eden). This biblical garden, which has *Mesopotamian precedents, is a microcosm of creation. It is a peaceful and innocent place where humans talk with *God, yet it also contains the seeds of its own destruction. The garden of Eden contains everything that is pleasant to look at and good to eat (2:9), and human beings are commanded to tend it. It is an implicit commentary on the idea of gardens that the aesthetic qualities are noted first and then coupled with utility. This essential linkage of artistry and pragmatic function is fundamental to garden creation; not surprisingly, the garden of Eden story is central to western thinking about gardens and garden design.

The Hebrew *Bible also mentions palatial gardens, including the royal garden of Uzza, where kings Manasseh and Amon were buried (2 Kgs 21:18, 26), and the palace garden of Ahasuerus of Shushan (*Esther 1). *Ecclesiastes 2:4 describes the garden of *Solomon, "in which I planted every kind of fruit tree. I constructed pools of water, enough to irrigate a forest shooting up with trees." The larger landscape is also referred to as a garden; as Lot looks across the Jordan valley, he says it is "like the garden of the Lord" (Gen 13:10).

The biblical paradise (Hebrew *pardes*, from the Persian *paridaiza*, "walled garden") is modeled on actual Middle Eastern desert gardens and oases that are in dramatic contrast to their arid surroundings. These sites of abundant vegetation, flowing waters, and sensory delight were surely the prototypes for the *gan eden* tale. The multisensory richness and physical pleasures of the oasis serve as a physical and emotional respite from the surroundings and embody a state of being. All of these qualities are transposed to the beloved female of the book of *Song of Songs, in which the garden is the central metaphor and there are profound associations to women, the female body, and garden imagery. She – and her body, "a garden locked" – is a site of pleasure and comfort. The garden is a locale and a metaphor for the female beloved: "the garden, my sister, my bride." The woman, the "fountain of gardens," is the wellspring of all of the poem's emotions; the garden also symbolizes the relationship that grows between the lovers – they are both in the garden and they create the garden.

Although most modern commentators read the Song of Songs as a collection of ancient love poetry, Jewish interpreters throughout the ages have often understood it as an allegory of the love between God and the people Israel in which God is the lover and Israel the *bride. Mystical interpretations emphasize images of the *Shekhinah, the indwelling divine presence, as a female alter ego of an infinite and eternal male aspect of the divine (*Ein Sof). For Jewish mysticism, the reconciliation of the male and female lovers in the Song of Songs garden setting represents the ultimate unification of the separated elements of God (see KABBALAH; KABBALAH, LURIANIC.

The garden's qualities of pleasure, sensory richness, and life-sustaining properties are also evoked elsewhere in biblical literature and Jewish tradition; the Torah itself is referred to as a "Tree of Life" (Prov 3:18), and the psalms abound with descriptions of the fecundity of nature. The Jerusalem *Talmud quotes Rabbi Jose ben Bun to the effect that "it is forbidden to live in a town in which there is no greenery" (Kiddushin 4:12). The Jerusalem and Babylonian Talmuds offer practical garden advice and glimpses into late antique garden practice for both ornamental and agricultural gardens. The appearance of gardens can be extrapolated from discussions of specific plantings, irrigation practice, the use of tools, and even the dimensions of walls and fences and the distance between seedbeds.

In the modern era of *emancipation, gardens took on new significance with the development of Labor *Zionism, whose call for the return to the Land of Israel included the imperative of working the land (see ISRAEL, STATE OF: ECOLOGY). The Israelitische Gartenbauschule in Ahlem, *Germany, founded in 1893, was established to train workers in horticulture and agriculture. In 1930s *Eastern Europe Zionist organizations established haksharah (training farms) to prepare and train Jewish agricultural workers. Even during the horrors of the *Holocaust gardens emerged. The Toporol (Society to Encourage Agriculture among Jews), founded in 1933, planted gardens in the *ghettos of *Warsaw and Łódź.

In the Palestinian *Yishuv and, as of 1948, the State of *Israel, gardens and gardening were and continue to be of fundamental importance. Zionist theorists, notably A. D. *Gordon, extolled the value of hard labor and the relationship to the land for Jews historically alienated from such work. The agricultural school at Mikve Israel, founded in 1870, trained gardeners and garden designers and established a botanical garden; a similar program was later established at Jerusalem's Hebrew University. European immigrants founded a professional gardeners association and on virtually every *kibbutz there are gardeners trained in design and maintenance. Making the desert bloom and planting trees, the credo of the Jewish National Fund, embodied garden ideology applied on a national scale. At the popular and professional level a distinctive Israeli garden design has emerged that combines Jewish tradition with historic Mediterranean and desert design sensibilities. It is common in Israel and the *Diaspora to create biblical gardens, featuring plants mentioned in the *Bible. The most striking example in Israel is Neot Kedumim (Biblical Landscape Reserve), founded in 1984 by Nogah Haruveni, son of noted botanist and biblical scholar, Ephraim Haruveni.

For further reading, see K. Helphand, Defiant Gardens: Making Gardens in Wartime (2006); for rabbinic references, "Horticulture," Jewish Encyclopedia (1906); and see also ECOLOGY; ETHICS: ENVIRONMENTAL; ISRAEL, STATE OF: LANDSCAPE ARCHITECTURE.   KENNETH HELPHAND

Geiger, Abraham (1810–1874), religious reformer and Jewish scholar, was born in *Frankfurt am Main. Geiger had a traditional upbringing but his university studies led him to consider the role of *Judaism within modernity and the reforms that would be necessary to sustain its vitality. As a rabbi, successively in Wiesbaden, Breslau, Frankfurt, and *Berlin, he argued for a progressive Judaism, based especially on the biblical *prophets, that stressed a universal message of ethical monotheism. He was the leading intellectual among the Liberal rabbis of *Germany, influential among his colleagues and disciples both in Europe and America. His broad scholarship extended to such areas as the text of the Hebrew *Bible, *biblical commentary, and medieval Hebrew *poetry. He edited two scholarly periodicals and compiled a modified *prayer book that omitted references to the reinstitution of the sacrificial service. During the last two years of his life he taught at the Liberal seminary in Berlin. **See also JUDAISM, REFORM: GERMANY.**   MICHAEL A. MEYER

Gemara (Aramaic term for "study") refers to expansions, analyses, and legal rulings based on the *Mishnah that were formulated by generations of scholars known as *Amoraim. The scholars were located in both the *Galilee and *Babylonia in the third to the fifth centuries CE. Their discussions of the Mishnah brought in a range of content, both legal and homiletic, including much that was only loosely connected to the texts under discussion. Ultimately, through the redaction efforts of later generations of sages (see SABORAIM; STAM), the *Talmuds emerged, comprising Mishnah and gemara. The gemara of the Palestinian Talmud differs in content, arrangement, and length from the gemara of the Babylonian Talmud.

Gematria: See KABBALAH; NUMEROLOGY

Genesis, Book of is the first book of the Hebrew *Bible. In Hebrew it is called by its first word, bereshit, which means "in the beginning." The English name comes from the Greek word for "origin," which appears in an ancient translation for the Hebrew word toledot in Genesis 2:4. This name more accurately describes a book that discusses the beginnings of the universe, the human species, and the Israelite nation and tribes, as well as the origins of a host of specific phenomena, including the challenges of the human condition, the diversity of languages, and the origins of place names, such as *Babylon and Beersheba.

The *narratives of Genesis are woven together by genealogy; this is evident in the tenfold repetition of the phrase beginning eleh toledot ("these are the generations" or "story of...") at 2:4, 6:9, 10:1, 11:10, 11:27, 25:12, 25:19, 36:1, 36:9, and 37:2. The first eleven chapters are often called the "universal history," because they describe the creation of the world and of all living beings, the great *flood, and the division of humanity into nations that then spread out over the earth. After *God creates the world, which God repeatedly calls "good," things quickly go awry. First, *Adam and *Eve eat the forbidden fruit; then one of their sons kills the other (see CAIN AND ABEL); then general violent disorder ensues. *God responds by wiping out creation and starting over with a new family and a new *covenant, in which the initial arrangements are modified so as to accommodate the problems that arose earlier. Yet still things go poorly. After *Noah is mistreated by his son, his descendants defy God's will by constructing the Tower of Babel. So God again chooses a single family, through which the divine message will be spread.

The central founders of the *Israelites are *Abraham (12–25:18) and his grandson *Jacob (also called Israel; 25:19–36). They are linked by *Isaac, although he receives very little independent attention. Finally, the story of Jacob's son *Joseph (37–50) explains how the Israelites came to *Egypt, thereby setting the stage for the events recounted in the books of *Exodus through *Deuteronomy. Narratives about Abraham center on his faithfulness to God and his need for an heir. They culminate in Abraham's willingness to sacrifice his favorite son at God's command. Isaac's son Jacob, a consummate trickster, is eventually given the name Israel, in recognition of his struggle with God and to signal his role as father of the twelve tribes (see ISRAELITES: TRIBES; and TRIBES, TWELVE). By contrast, the story of Joseph contains little explicitly divine activity; however, the narrator makes it clear that human behavior is the vehicle through which God protects the Israelites from the famine that engulfs their homeland (45:5–8 and 50:20).

Although Genesis is the first of the "Five Books of Moses" (or *Pentateuch) it contains no internal evidence of having been written by *Moses. Already by medieval times, scholars had found several passages that could not have been written in his lifetime (12:6, 14:14, 36:31). By the seventeenth and eighteenth centuries, the book's repetitions, contradictions, and stylistic diversity were major factors in the development of the documentary hypothesis (see BIBLE: MODERN SCHOLARSHIP), which argued that the Pentateuch was woven together from several independent sources. The most common version of this theory posits four primary sources, designated as J, E, D, and P (although D is limited to the book of Deuteronomy). It is generally agreed that these sources were composed long after the events they describe and that they reflect the periods in which they were written. For example, God's announcement that Abraham's descendants will be enslaved for four centuries (15:13) points to their eventual escape from Egypt under Moses; similarly, divine promises to the patriarchs were fulfilled in the time of *David and *Solomon. The story of creation resonates with the construction of the *Tabernacle (Exod 25–40), which, in turn, foreshadows the building of the *Temple. Other passages allude to the rise of David's tribe *Judah (49:10) and *Jerusalem as David's capital city (14 and 22).

Over the past century and a half, scholars have found several ancient *Near Eastern texts that shed light on various biblical passages. Among the most notable are *Mesopotamian stories about creation and the *flood, which closely resemble the biblical accounts. In fact, the Babylonian flood story is so similar to the biblical account that it may actually have influenced it, while the Mesopotamian creation myth is reflected in the account of the Tower of Babel in Genesis 11. For a long time, scholars relied on similarities between several distinctive practices in the patriarchal accounts and customs attested in various Near Eastern cultures during the Middle Bronze Age (ca. 2000–1550 BCE) to determine when the patriarchs lived. However, on closer scrutiny, the parallels turned out to be less striking than first thought. As a result, the likely historical setting for these stories is no longer certain. Some scholars think that the patriarchs lived during the Late Bronze Age (ca. 1550–1150 BCE); others place the stories in the post-exilic period.

It has even been suggested that they are symbolic of Judean history after the sixth century BCE exile in Babylonia (see BABYLONIAN EXILE).

One argument for the antiquity of the patriarchal stories is the religion they describe, which includes practices that are very different from those endorsed in other biblical books. The most notable example is the concept of God, who is often indicated by compounds based on "El" (e.g., Ishmael and Israel), which was the name of a *Canaanite deity. Elsewhere, the patriarchs' God is identified in terms of relationship to the clan leader; that is, "God of Abraham" (26:24), "Fear of Isaac" (31:42), and "Mighty One of Jacob" (49:2).

For further reading, see N. M. Sarna, *The JPS Torah Commentary: Genesis* (1989); and C. Westermann, *Genesis: A Commentary* (1984–86); **see also ARCHEOLOGY, LAND OF ISRAEL: ANCIENT TIMES TO PERSIAN PERIOD; BIBLE; BIBLE: ANCESTRAL NARRATIVES; BIBLE: MODERN SCHOLARSHIP; BIBLE: NARRATIVE LITERATURE; CANAAN, CANAANITES; ISRAELITES: RELIGION; and NEAR EAST, ANCIENT.** FREDERICK E. GREENSPAHN

Genizah. This term, which is probably *Persian in origin and has linguistic precedents in the Hebrew *Bible, was used in early *rabbinic literature describing the dignified disposal place for a sacred text that could no longer be used or for a text regarded as heretical that contained some sacred content. Many Jewish communities adopted the principle (usually through burial or inaccessible storage). **GENIZAH, CAIRO.** This storage place, which was established during the Middle Ages in the Ben Ezra Synagogue in Cairo (Fustat), *Egypt, preserved about 210,000 fragmentary texts, amounting to a total of about half a million folios. The relatively stable history of its Ben Ezra Synagogue and Cairo's dry climate, as well as the presence of Jews in the same location for many centuries, led to this unique survival. Many documents in the Cairo Genizah date from about a thousand years ago; they are written in various languages, especially *Hebrew, Arabic, and *Aramaic, mainly on vellum and paper, but also on papyrus and cloth. Most of the Arabic documents are written in Hebrew characters, in a Jewish dialect designated as *Judeo-Arabic. There are also items in other languages that were unique to Jews, including *Judeo-Persian, Judeo-Greek (see BYZANTINE EMPIRE), Judeo-Spanish (see *LADINO), and *Judeo-German. *Synagogue officials in Cairo sold some of the texts in the second half of the nineteenth century to dealers, orientalists, scholars, and visitors. Famous libraries in *Saint Petersburg, *Paris, London, Oxford, *New York, and *Philadelphia acquired major collections but it was Solomon *Schechter, Reader in Talmudic and Rabbinic Literature at the University of Cambridge in *Britain from 1890 until 1902, who obtained communal permission to remove 140,000 items to Cambridge University Library in 1897.

Genizah fragments represent the most important discovery of new material for every aspect of scientific Hebrew and Jewish studies in the Middle Ages, particularly between the tenth and thirteenth centuries. As a result of the conservation, deciphering, and description done for more than a century, but particularly in recent years at Cambridge, previous ignorance has been dispelled and theories drastically modified. The daily lives of Jewish men and women in the eastern Mediterranean and their relationships with other groups, as well as various aspects of their literacy, have been intriguingly illuminated.

Among the various subjects that have benefited substantially from Genizah documents are the evolution of the vowel systems and *Masoretic methods that were designed to protect and transmit the text of the Hebrew *Bible; the development of synagogal lectionaries originating in *Babylon and the Land of *Israel; and translations and interpretations of the Hebrew Bible especially into Aramaic, Judeo-Arabic, and Greek. The literary history of such "sectarian" works as the Damascus Document, the *Wisdom of Ben Sira, and the Testament of Levi (see PSEUDEPIGRAPHA) is also known from *Qumran (see *DEAD SEA SCROLLS). Major advances have also been made in the textual and exegetical study of talmudic, midrashic, liturgical, and poetic literature and in the evolution of Jewish religious law. Forgotten works, prolific personalities, and unusual decisions have been discovered. Texts related to the *Karaite-Rabbanite controversy, the Fatimid Egyptian court (see EGYPT: MIDDLE AGES), and pre-Crusader *Palestine and an unexpectedly large range of writings on *mysticism, *magic, and *medicine have significantly increased our knowledge of medieval Jews and *Judaism and their larger environment. Recent scholarship includes S. Reif, *A Jewish Archive from Old Cairo* (2000); and S. D. Goitein, *A Mediterranean Society: The Jewish Communities of the Arab World as Portrayed in the Documents of the Cairo Geniza*, 6 vols. (1967–93).

Map 5   STEFAN C. REIF

Germany. The first references to Jewish communities in German lands (*Ashkenaz) come from the early fourth century. It is thought that Jews migrated northward from *Italy, settling especially along the Rhine and its tributaries. They were involved in *commerce in such towns as Cologne, Trier, Mainz, Metz, and Strasbourg. Their economic situation during the early centuries was comparatively good, and there are no recorded instances of persecution. By their own choice Jews in each city lived in a separate quarter. Jewish legal status varied according to the jurisdiction in which they lived; it was determined by charters of privilege and restriction that were issued by local nobles or higher clergy. Political authorities favored the granting of residence to Jews because of their commercial talents. They were allowed to bear arms and to adjudicate their own quarrels in accordance with Jewish law.

In the early medieval period, Jews in Germany were allowed to own both fields and vineyards. However, they were excluded from the craft guilds, which possessed a Christian character. By the late Middle Ages they were increasingly concentrated in *money lending, either dealing on a small scale with pawned objects or offering loans against the mortgage of land. Unlike prominent Jews in Muslim lands, medieval German Jews did not play any political roles (see, for example SPAIN, MUSLIM).

Jewish community institutions included one or more *synagogues, a *cemetery, a *mikveh (ritual bath), a hospital and inn for itinerants and the poor, and a bridal chamber for newly married couples. German Jews initially looked to the Land of *Israel for religious guidance and later to the academies in Babylonia (see GAON, GEONIM, GEONIC ACADEMIES). By the tenth century, German Jews were beginning to gain independence in matters of religion. Their

first significant talmudic scholar was Rabbi *Gershom ben Judah of Mainz (960–1028), whose influence stretched well beyond his city of residence. Questions were addressed to him from *France, Germany, and Italy. He was able to promulgate regulations (*takkanot*) for all of Ashkenazic Jewry; among the best known are his prohibitions of bigamy and of the *divorce of a wife against her will. German Jewry was thus developing its own religious customs, which needed to be reconciled with the dicta of the Babylonian *Talmud.

The most important religious figure of Ashkenazi Jewry was Rabbi Solomon ben Isaac (known by the acronym *Rashi; 1040–1105). Although he lived in Troyes in *France, Rashi spent many years as a student in Mainz and Worms. He deeply influenced German Jewry through his establishment of a correct text of the Talmud and his biblical and talmudic commentaries (see BIBLICAL COMMENTARY: FROM THE MIDDLE AGES TO 1800). In the twelfth and thirteenth centuries an ascetic and otherworldly form of pietism developed by the *Hasidei Ashkenaz* gained limited popularity in Germany (see MIDDLE AGES: *HASIDEI ASHKENAZ*). With the exception of *medicine, the learning and creativity of German Jewry were found almost exclusively in the religious realm, with great emphasis placed on male literacy (see EDUCATION, BOYS: MEDIEVAL).

The First *Crusade (1096) brought plunder and slaughter to German Jewish communities. As Crusaders traveled through Rhineland towns, they attacked the local Jews, claiming thereby to avenge the blood of Jesus with the blood of Israel. Some Jews converted to Christianity to escape their attackers, and others defended themselves or hid; still others chose self-inflicted death over conversion. After the First Crusade, Jewish life for a time returned to what it had been earlier. However, by the thirteenth century, the Jewish position was deteriorating, as manifested in false accusations of various kinds, popular outbreaks of hostility, and diminution of legal status. Charges of *ritual murder and *host desecration were leveled against Jews in various places; at the time of the Black Death, in 1348, Jews were accused of poisoning wells. By the middle of the thirteenth century they were required to wear distinctive garb, prohibited from bearing arms, and referred to as "chamber serfs," subject entirely to the arbitrary will of the emperor or his vassals. Although Jews were never expelled from German territory as a whole, between 1300 and 1500 it is estimated that there were as many 150 local expulsions. During these centuries many German Jews chose to migrate eastward, where *Poland offered economic opportunities and relatively greater safety.

During the sixteenth-century "wars of religion," German Jews supported the Holy Roman Emperor against the Protestant princes; this was because the emperors (and popes) represented stability and support of Jewish long-term interests in contrast to the caprice of local authorities. Moreover, by mid-century the Protestant leadership, especially Martin Luther, had shown itself hostile to the Jews (see REFORMATION). The leading German Jew of the period was Josel of Rosheim (1478–1554), who served all Jewish communities in the Holy Roman Empire as their representative and advocate before various levels of government.

A thin stratum of German Jews emerged from the Thirty Years War (1618–48) with considerable accumulated capital. During the next century and a half, these *Court Jews were able to gain positions of economic and, in some cases, political influence at the courts of the numerous petty states of *Central Europe. They not only lent money but also provided supplies for armies, luxury goods for the wealthy, and served as mint masters, coining the local currencies. Often gaining the rights and privileges of Christian merchants and participating in the life of the courts, they came to regard themselves as a Jewish aristocracy and, in some cases, became lax in observance and alienated from the Jewish community. Some were tragically torn personalities, many of whose children or grandchildren converted to Christianity.

With the notable exception of the long-established Jewish community of *Frankfurt am Main, most seventeenth-century German Jews lived in small rural communities where they engaged in various forms of peddling or acted as middlemen between farm and town. They continued to be subject to economic restrictions and special taxes. Some were penurious vagrants dependent on charity or criminal activities. For nearly all German Jews their religious lives and culture remained much as they had been in the past.

By the middle of the eighteenth century, however, contacts began to develop between Jews and representatives of the German Enlightenment. The most prominent Jewish enlightener, Moses *Mendelssohn (1729–1786) of *Berlin, gained a broad reputation as a popular philosopher and literary critic. Although challenged by non-Jews for choosing to remain an observant Jew and by Jews for weakening barriers protective of Judaism, especially through his German translation of the *Pentateuch, Mendelssohn persisted in his attempt to reconcile Judaism with the natural religion of reason. He became the model for an identity that was both German and Jewish (see THOUGHT, MODERN).

The nineteenth century in German Jewish history was characterized by a protracted struggle for political *emancipation in the various German states. After initial progress was made during the period of French domination at the beginning of the century, emancipation efforts faltered during the post-Napoleonic era only to revive at the time of the 1848 revolution; they again slipped backward in the 1850s. Finally, political equality for all Jews in Germany was achieved with the establishment of the Second Empire in 1871. Among Jewish advocates, the most prominent was the widely respected Gabriel Riesser (1806–1863), who served as a vice president of the Frankfurt National Assembly in 1848.

During these years German Jews rapidly acculturated, gaining mastery of the German language, whereas earlier they had spoken western *Yiddish; they increasingly gave their children a secular education. However, Jews did not integrate economically. Efforts to establish Jews in crafts or in farming failed as most chose to remain within the sphere of *commerce. The Frankfurt *Rothschild family soon became the most powerful banking house in Europe. Likewise in their social lives, German Jews remained separate from their non-Jewish environment, socializing with their co-religionists and marrying fellow Jews.

German Jews now began to define their Jewish identity strictly in religious terms even as they retained bonds of communal solidarity. To varying degrees they modified religious belief and practice to better harmonize with their new position within the modern world. A variety of religious positions appeared, each differing from the insular traditionalism of the past. Samson Raphael *Hirsch (1817–1894) became the proponent of a modern *Orthodoxy that allowed for cultural integration along with such synagogue innovations as the German edifying sermon and clerical garb. Other rabbis, such as Zacharias *Frankel (1801–1875), the first head of the first modern rabbinical seminary, established in Breslau in 1854, and Abraham *Geiger (1810–1874), the principal figure in the broadening movement for religious reform in Germany, were to varying degrees willing to move beyond the religious status quo. University-trained scholars began to examine Jewish tradition with the tools of critical scholarship, an approach that considered classical Jewish texts within their historical contexts. The most prominent of these scholars, who represented a new and very different elite of Jewish learning from the older rabbinical model, was Leopold *Zunz (1794–1886), the principal progenitor of what became known as *Wissenschaft des Judentums.

The second half of the nineteenth century witnessed the growth of the German Jewish population; by 1871, it stood at more than a half-million, 1.25% of the general population. The Jewish population continued to grow until World War I, although its proportion of the total German population declined. Toward the end of the century German Jewry was augmented by East European Jews fleeing deteriorating conditions in *Russia. During this period German Jews also gained in wealth and were increasingly concentrated in the larger cities, especially Berlin, where a large majority engaged in commerce and trade. As the community became increasingly bourgeois, Jewish *women confined their activity mostly to the domestic sphere, although some followed Jewish men into higher education. As Jewish identity became increasingly a matter of the home, the family, and Jewish social circles, women played a large role in maintaining it (see WOMEN, MODERN: CENTRAL EUROPE).

During the last decades of the nineteenth century, the growth of the Jewish population, its greater visibility in the large cities, and the increased penetration of Jews into German economic and cultural spheres precipitated an *antisemitic reaction. This was expressed in religious, ethnic, and racially motivated agitation. In 1893, to protect their interests, German Jews created a Central Association of German Citizens of the Jewish Faith; this became the largest Jewish organization and soon stood in opposition to the small minority of German Jews who were drawn to *Zionism.

During the Weimar period the general cultural productivity of German Jews reached an apogee. Jews played major roles as scientists, most prominently Albert *Einstein (1879–1955); in the visual and performing arts; and in cultural criticism. A specifically Jewish renaissance, marked especially by religious philosophers such as Martin *Buber (1878–1965) and Franz *Rosenzweig (1886–1929), reached the more actively Jewish among German Jews. However, the majority relegated Judaism to a small role at the edge of their consciousness as Germans, and an increasing number married non-Jews.

With the ascent of the *Nazi party and Hitler's rise to power in 1933, German Jewish wealth was gradually expropriated; Jews were driven from positions of cultural influence and deprived of political equality. The Nuremberg Laws of 1935 erased their status as citizens. On November 9,

1938, a major *pogrom, popularly known as *Kristallnacht, destroyed synagogues and Jewish businesses throughout Germany. Newly defined in racial terms, many Jews initially reasserted their Jewish identity, flocking to synagogues and adult education classes and joining the Zionist movement. However, in time, morale faltered as some were able to emigrate and others were frustrated by the immigration restrictions imposed by nearly all countries. At least 125,000 German Jews perished in the *Holocaust.

A new German Jewish community, composed of survivors, *displaced persons from other European countries, and some returnees, began to emerge after World War II. The majority lived in West Germany. Until the demise of the *Soviet Union, the community remained relatively small, estimated at 33,000 in 1988. However, beginning in the 1990s a large number of Russian Jews migrated to the newly united Germany, which offered them economic incentives. By 2004 the Jewish population had reached 118,000 and was continuing to grow. This new community lacks roots in Germany and has yet to connect with the heritage of prewar German Jewry. The principal comprehensive history of German Jewry, especially of the modern period, is M. A. Meyer and M. Brenner, eds., *German-Jewish History in Modern Times*, 4 vol. (1996–98). **Maps 7, 8, 10** MICHAEL A. MEYER

Gershom ben Judah of Mainz (960–1028), also known as the Ragmah, was the first great rabbinic authority of *Ashkenazic Jewry. The study house he established in Mainz educated generations of students who were able to spread rabbinic learning throughout areas of Jewish settlement in the German Rhineland and northern *France. Subsequent generations of scholars referred to him as *Rabbenu Gershom, meor ha-golah* ("Our Rabbi Gershom, Light of the Exile"). His halakhic authority was such that he was able to institute *takkanot* (singular, *takkanah*; alterations to Jewish law) that had long-lasting consequences for the Jews of Christian Europe. These included a ban on polygamy and the ruling that no woman could be divorced against her will (see DIVORCE: HISTORICAL DEVELOPMENT). He also liberalized rules pertaining to Jews who had converted to Christianity under pressure.

Gersonides (Levi ben Gershon; 1288–1344), born in southern *France, was a mathematician, scientist, biblical commentator, and philosopher. His biblical exegesis is full of philosophical ideas, but his main philosophical works were supercommentaries on Averroes' commentaries on Aristotle and *Milḥamot Ha-Shem* (Wars of the Eternal). This book criticizes *Maimonides for adopting a conservative position toward Aristotle in regard to certain questions of *science and religious tradition and for refusing to carry his philosophical agenda to its reasonable conclusion. Influenced by Averroes' acceptance of virtually all of Aristotelian science and metaphysics and his subsequent reinterpretation of the Qur'an, Gersonides took a philosophical and religious stance that was more radical than Maimonides yet more critical of Aristotle than was Averroes.

Gersonides argued against creation *ex nihilo*, but used astronomical observation to reject the Aristotelian position of the eternity of the world; instead, he claimed that science and Torah were most truthfully aligned by a version of the Platonic theory of creation from primordial matter. Gersonides rejected all previous resolutions of the tension between divine knowledge and human freedom by arguing that *God could not logically know the outcome of particular contingent events. Divine knowledge extended to general laws, but not to particular human actions that were unconditioned and freely chosen. Regarding miracles and prophecy, Gersonides developed positions that preserved divine perfection by distancing God from active engagement in the world.

At the same time, contrary to Averroes, Gersonides argued for individual immortality, contending that at the highest level of human intellect, when the individual knower attains some sort of conjunction with the divine Agent Intellect, the independent identities of the human and the divine are preserved. As with Abraham *ibn Ezra before him, Gersonides believed in *astrological determinacy, but contended that one may avoid one's astral destiny by the exercise of reason. He defended a version of specific divine providence for those who have acted in such a way as to merit divine attention. Despite those modified traditional positions, Gersonides' synthesis of science and religion was generally rejected by later Jewish thinkers. Indeed, his *magnum opus* was criticized as the "Wars against the Eternal" by Shem Tov ibn Shem Tov and others who adopted a more conservative outlook. In contrast, philosophers such as Joseph ibn Kaspi and Moses Narboni were more radical than Gersonides and closely identified with Averroism. Recent research includes extensive introductions in *The Wars of the Lord*, trans. S. Feldman, 3 vols. (1984–99); *Commentary on Song of Songs*, trans. and ed. M. Kellner (1998); R. Eisen, *Gersonides on Providence, Covenant, and the Jewish People* (1995); and **see THOUGHT, MEDIEVAL.** BARUCH FRYDMAN-KOHL

Get. Document certifying the legal dissolution of a Jewish marriage. **See DIVORCE: HISTORICAL DEVELOPMENT.**

Ghetto. Technically, the first ghetto was decreed in 1516 when *the political leadership of Venice, which had never wanted Jews to live permanently in the city, finally agreed to their fixed settlement on the condition that the Jews reside separately, on an island that was known as the "ghetto." This preexisting name recalled the metal foundry that once existed in this location (hence, *gettare*, "to throw the liquid"). There have been many other suggestions as to the name's origin, but this is probably the correct one. The era of the ghetto in *Italy ended in 1870 with the fall of the Papal State and its replacement by the Italian monarchy. Today, the term "ghetto" has been universalized to mean any area of urban crowding, often populated by a specific population group. It also has the connotation of a city area in a deteriorated condition, most of whose residents are poor. During the *Holocaust, ghettos were intentionally established in urban areas as sites where Jews were concentrated and confined. From there, the next move was deportation to a death or labor camp.

Venice was not the first place where Jews were required to live in a fixed area. There were such areas by the fifteenth century in *Spain and *Germany. Certainly, medieval cities always had Jewish quarters, where Jews lived separately by their own choice. This is evident in Geoffrey Chaucer's "Prioress's Tale," in which he writes about a Jew's quarter or street. Thus, even though Chaucer was writing in fourteenth-century *England where there were no Jews at all, he was well aware that in places where Jews did live, they lived in separate areas. The boundaries of such Jewish neighborhoods, however, were not totally fixed, nor were the areas necessarily surrounded by a wall with gates that could be locked, as came to be the case in Italy.

The age of ghettos began in earnest in 1555. In July of that year, Pope Paul IV ordered all of Rome's Jews to live in a specific quarter – it was, in fact, where most Jews already lived. Within a few months, walls and gates surrounded that area. We even know how much cement was used to create those barriers. The Jews were mystified. A similar order to live in one place had been issued eleven years earlier, but never enforced. However, Paul IV, obsessive on the subject of heresy, refused to allow Rome's Jews to live as they pleased. He also wanted to convert them and believed their enforced enclosure – they could go out by day to conduct business, which was now also restricted – would prompt conversions. His successors agreed. Even Sixtus V, in the later 1580s, who allowed Jews to live temporarily throughout the Papal State, insisted on maintaining their enclosure in the ghetto. Jews began to call the enclosed area, which heretofore they had called "the Jews' quarter," *nostro ghet.* This half-Hebrew/half-Italian pun translates as "our bill of *divorce," a document given to a divorced wife, and so the Jews saw themselves,

Another ghetto was established in Florence in 1569, perhaps to appease Pope Pius V. More ghettos followed, but neither rapidly nor consistently. In Leghorn (Livorno), the same Grand Dukes of Tuscany who maintained a ghetto in Florence encouraged Jews from the Levant to come and settle to promote commerce. These Jews never were ghettoized. A ghetto did not appear in Modena, near Bologna, until 1638. These variations reflect the interaction of the growing lay state with ecclesiastical powers. The process of enforced ghettoization was slow and delayed by negotiations, and by the seventeenth century the Jews knew how to hold their own, insisting on a central open square and adequate water facilities. In fact, from the first, the Jews in the Roman ghetto were concerned about public sanitation, toilet facilities, and even drainage and sewers. By the time the Roman ghetto was definitively abandoned in 1870, on the very day the Italian monarchy replaced the Papal State, conditions had become so bad and the squalor caused by overcrowding and inadequate services was so great that the Roman municipality razed the ghetto to the ground. Its buildings and precincts had become a health hazard. The last ghetto in Italy was established in Correggio (in the province of Reggio Emilia) in 1738, at a time when the rest of Europe was headed toward broadening Jewish rights.

Thus, the phenomenon of the ghetto may be seen as both an indication of modernity and a symbol of its absence. Its initial establishment occurred during the Protestant *Reformation of the sixteenth century, a moment of crisis for all of Europe. Old patterns, in which Jews could live openly, if with restrictions, were now deemed insufficient. Jews had always symbolized potential threats to Christian unity, and the ghetto demonstrated that those threats might be controlled by walling them off.

Conversely, the continuation of the ghetto in the eighteenth century signified resistance to modernity in all its forms. Advocacy of Jewish civil rights and *emancipation was a component of the evolution of European states into secular entities, unified through common laws and the devotion of their citizens, rather than social bodies held together by shared religious beliefs. Modernizers argued that isolating Jews in the ghetto encouraged a Jewish propensity for isolation and delayed the modernization of both the Jews and the state. This is why the closing of ghettos during Napoleon's short reign in Italy could not be sustained once conservative and reactionary forces regained ground. Resisting the perceived dangers of modernity and secularism to its own prerogatives, the Papal State maintained the ghetto for another seventy years, until its own demise.

Nor was Italy the only place where the ghetto came to symbolize competing forms of governance. In *Frankfurt am Main, in Germany, the emperor and city heads constantly disputed authority over the city's Jews, living in the *Judengasse* (Jewish street or neighborhood).

In addition to seeing the ghetto's establishment as a bill of divorce from the larger culture, Jews also developed positive views of their separation from the mainstream. The ghetto permitted development of a Jewish sacred space. Jews could regulate to some degree who came in and out, and they could establish methods of consensual, but in fact virtually obligatory, arbitration for resolving intra-Jewish disputes. This translated into real internal governance, more than Jews had previously enjoyed. The ghetto also allowed for hiding those marked out to be seized and taken into various "Houses of Converts"; this occurred when individuals were "offered" to the church by converted relatives. No wonder that, in a mixture of cynicism and optimism, the founding of the ghetto was often compared to the events of *Purim, a moment of salvation and rejoicing, of making the most of a difficult predicament. For further reading, see K. Stow, *Theater of Acculturation: The Roman Ghetto in the Sixteenth Century* (2001); and idem, *Jewish Life in Early Modern Rome: Challenge, Conversion, and Private Life* (2007).   KENNETH STOW

Ghettos, Holocaust Era: See HOLOCAUST: GHETTOS

Glückel of Hameln (also GLIKL HAMELN; GLIKL BAS JUDAH LEIB; 1646/7–1724) is the author of the earliest surviving memoir written by a Jewish woman. Her extensive account of her life, in *Judeo-German, was written to drive away the melancholy that followed her husband's death and to let her children know about their ancestry. Born into the prosperous *Court Jew milieu of *Central Europe, Glückel was well read in Judeo-German literature and had some knowledge of Hebrew and German as well. Her memorial notice characterizes her as "a learned woman" (*melumedet*), unusual praise in her time and place.

Glückel was betrothed at twelve and married at fourteen; she was the mother of fourteen children. She also worked with her husband in the jewelry business, and after his death, when she was forty-four, Glückel continued the business and arranged marriages for her children into distinguished families across Europe. She later remarried and suffered grave financial and emotional hardship when her second husband became bankrupt.

Glückel autobiography is imbued with a strong feeling of connectedness to the Jewish community and a palpable sense of religious conviction. In many ways it is an *ethical will, a genre with which she was well acquainted. However, in her recollections Glückel goes far beyond the limited boundaries of that literature. As N. Z. Davis (1995) has shown, her originality lies in her use of stories she culled from her voluminous reading and incorporated into her narrative to provide challenging moral and religious commentary on difficult events in her own life. Glückel profited from the new technology of *printing, which allowed her to be a reader, and her extensive and deeply engaged reading, together with her immense energy and strong sense of self, empowered her to express her feelings and her piety through writing.

As Davis points out, all translations of Glückel's memoirs, whether in German, French, Hebrew, or English, omit significant amounts of the actual text. Two English translations are *The Life of Glückel of Hameln, 1646–1724, Written by Herself*, trans. and ed. B. Z. Abrahams (1963; 2010); and *The Memoirs of Glückel of Hameln*, trans. M. Lowenthal (1932; 1977). For further reading, see N. Z. Davis, *Women on the Margins: Three Seventeenth-Century Lives* (1995), 5–62; and see LITERATURE: WOMEN WRITERS (EUROPE AND AMERICA); WOMEN: EARLY MODERN EUROPE; WOMEN, MODERN: CENTRAL EUROPE.   JUDITH R. BASKIN

Gnosticism. Derived from the Greek adjective *gnostikos* ("knowing" or "knowledgeable"), the term "Gnosticism" was coined by the Cambridge philosopher Henry More (1614–1687), who used it to describe both the specific Christian "heresy" found at Thyatira (Rev 2:18–29) at the end of the first century CE and the "false" religious practices found within the Catholic tradition. Gnosticism thereafter became a pejorative term in the study of early *Christianity to characterize various early Christian movements emphasizing salvation through knowledge (*gnosis*).

In Greek philosophy, *gnosis* represented a distinct form of understanding based on theoretical rather than practical knowledge (Plato, *Statesman* 258e). For Plato and other philosophers, a gnostic exercised the soul's intellectual faculties to apprehend truth or reality. Later *Hellenistic religions, including forms of post-biblical Judaism, regarded *gnosis* as a divine gift, reserved for a privileged few, that leads to an understanding of *God (Wisdom of Solomon 2:13; 15:3; *Philo, *On the Virtues* 215). It is this view of *gnosis* that may underlie the claim of a group within Paul's Corinthian community that their acquisition of knowledge made them a spiritual elite (1 Cor 2:13–15, 8:1).

Based on various early Christian sources, contemporary scholars suggest that Gnosticism included belief in a plurality of divine beings, with a distinction made between a transcendent God and other lesser divinities (including the creator god); cosmological and anthropological dualism; and a redeemer (often Jesus or Christ) who descends into the world to deliver a message of salvation. This redemptive message centered on the reality of the "unknown" God and the divine origin of the soul. Gnostics also appear to have believed in the separation of the spiritual and material elements at death and the post-mortem ascent of the soul. From a Christian standpoint, these teachings put gnostics in conflict with proto-orthodox writers who articulated an alternate set of beliefs grounded in an emerging "Rule of Faith."

Christian opponents of Gnosticism, including Justin Martyr, Irenaeus, Hippolytus, and Epiphanius, sought to clarify Christian "truth" by uncovering and ridiculing the various "errors" found among their rivals. They investigated the origins and development of gnostic thought, identifying the source of *gnosis*-based theologies in the teachings of Simon Magus, a *Samaritan arch-heretic who was said to have defiled the pristine character of the apostolic church (Acts 8:9–24). They then constructed genealogies that linked his false teachings to subsequent "gnostics" of the second century CE (e.g., Saturninus, Basilides, and Valentinus) whom they believed threatened the purity of authentic Christianity.

This model for understanding ancient Christian *gnosis* has exercised a strong hold on modern scholarship. Drawing on these ancient reports, scholars have assumed that the gnostic worldview coalesced into a distinct (heretical) religion called Gnosticism by the middle of the second century. In the late nineteenth century, Adolf von Harnack described Gnosticism as the "acute Hellenization of Christianity," because of its affinity for applying Greek philosophy to the Christian story. Subsequently, the "History of Religions" school challenged Harnack by claiming that Gnosticism's roots lay in the mythic world of *Babylonian, *Persian, and *Egyptian thought. For these researchers, Gnosticism was pre-Christian and non-Christian.

This conclusion coincided with the hypothesis that *Second Temple Jewish literature was the main source for Christian Gnosticism. Moritz Friedländer was the first to advance this position at the end of the nineteenth century, arguing for the existence of a pre-Christian Jewish Gnosticism by the early first century that developed among Hellenized Jewish communities of the *Diaspora. Heterodox scriptural interpretations from these Jewish groups directly inspired the forms of Christian Gnosticism found among the Ophites, Cainites, Sethians, and Melchizedekians. Friedländer supported this hypothesis on the basis of the writings of *Philo, who distinguished between true and false *gnosis* (*Sacrifices of Abel and Cain*, 2; *Posterity and Exile of Cain*, 52–53) and polemicized against *antinomian Jews who spiritualized scriptural meaning (*Migration of Abraham*, 86–93). Friedländer also surmised that this type of heterodox Judaism influenced Palestinian thought, prompting the Rabbis to criticize those who believed in the existence of two powers in heaven and to condemn the use of books circulating among (non-Christian) gnostic heretics to whom they referred as *minim* (*Ecclesiasates Rabbah* 1.8.4; BT *Shabbat* 116a).

Scholars continue to identify the Jewish contours of Gnosticism. The 1945 discovery of a library of gnostic literature from Nag Hammadi in Egypt has demonstrated that Friedländer's instincts were generally correct. These papyrus documents written in Coptic, approximately forty of which are relevant for the study of Gnosticism, have confirmed that Judaism left a deep imprint among the authors of these writings. The *Apocryphon of John* and the *Hypostasis of the Archons*, for example, display a sophisticated exegetical engagement with the Hebrew *Bible, particularly Genesis 1–8, and contain names (e.g., Yaldabaoth and Saklas) that probably originated within a Semitic linguistic milieu. At a broader level, Jewish *apocalyptic texts (e.g., 1 *Enoch and the writings from *Qumran) offer a framework for appreciating Gnosticism's interest in cosmic and social dualism. *Wisdom traditions, such as *Proverbs 8:22–31 and 1 Enoch 42, foreground the gnostic interest in the character of Wisdom (*Hokhmah* in Hebrew; *Sophia* in Greek), a divine emanation instrumental in gnostic salvation history. Jewish *merkavah* *mysticism contains cosmic imagery and descriptions of the soul's ascent that parallel ideas found in Sethian Gnosticism.

These investigations have sharpened the scholarly study of Gnosticism, yet it is important not to let these advances obscure the fact that virtually every aspect of Gnosticism remains under debate. Michael Williams has effectively demonstrated that the early Christian typologies cannot encompass the wide range of beliefs about the cosmos, the human condition, and salvation found in the Nag Hammadi sources, and he considers the term "Gnosticism" too damaged to continue as a scholarly category. Others prefer to retain "Gnosticism," but continue to dispute the precise relationship among Gnosticism, Judaism, and Christianity. On this point, Karen King has argued that investigations into Gnosticism's origins are ultimately fruitless, for they simply reproduce the tendentious modes of argumentation advanced by the ancient Christian polemicists and "essentialize" traditions that were fundamentally variegated and marked by hybridity.

For further reading, see K. King, *What Is Gnosticism?* (2003); G. Scholem, *Jewish Gnosticism, Merkabah Mysticism, and Talmudic Tradition* (1965); A. F. Segal, *Two Powers in Heaven* (1977); and M. Williams, *Rethinking "Gnosticism": An Argument for Dismantling a Dubious Category* (1996).

DAVID M. REIS

God. Discourse about God in modern Jewish *thought is caught in productive tension between the God of the philosophers and the God of *Abraham, *Isaac, and *Jacob. For Jewish thought, God is first and foremost a concept used to solve metaphysical, ontological, epistemological, and ethical quandaries. In the history of philosophy and metaphysics – first in late ancient Greece and then in the Greco-Roman world, Islamic East, and Christian West – God appears as an abstract principle (the Good beyond Being, First Cause, Prime Mover, necessary existent, Infinite Substance, a postulate of practical reason, *Geist*). In the history of *Judaism, God is a particular person (and only then a more universal, cosmic principle or potency) around whose *Torah and redemptive force the existence of Israel, God's people, revolves. Insofar as their thought is both "philosophical" and "Jewish," most modern Jewish thinkers refuse to choose between *reason and *revelation. Instead, they simultaneously embrace two competing and contradictory forms of theological expression. Even as God remains a formal figure of thought, a deep and abiding intimacy defines the image of God in modern Jewish thought (see also THEOLOGY).

In the so-called age of rationalism (exemplified by Descartes, *Spinoza, and Leibniz) the basic truths about God, in contrast to the particular mysteries unique to each historical religion, are universal and open to the exercise of human reason. God, as such, was the subject of natural theology. Baruch Spinoza (*Political-Theological Treatise* [1670]; *Ethics* [1677]) developed his conception of God according to a geometric method that drew on Cartesian rationalism. However, he rejected mind/body *dualism in favor of a radical monism that posits thought and extension as aspects of a single overarching, infinite substance, which he identified as "God" or "Nature." In his view, only the most basic theological truths in the *Bible, expressed as they are in the most primitive and philosophically inadequate form, are compatible with reason. Scripture is no longer revelation, but rather

a product of the human imagination. Not only the ideas of God that Scripture contains, but also the *laws purportedly revealed to *Moses and the political commonwealth based on that law are products of humans. For his part, Moses *Mendelssohn (*Jerusalem* [1783], *Morgenstunden* [1785], *Die Sache Gottes, An die Freunde Lessings* [1786]) followed Leibniz and Wolff against Spinoza, developing a dualistic *theology based on the contention that after (but not before) the initial act of creation God and world constitute separate substances. Mendelssohn agreed with Spinoza that truths about God are not specific to Judaism or to any other historical religion. However, unlike Spinoza, Mendelssohn affirmed the abiding reality of revelation. Revelation persists, not *qua* theological contents but as ceremonial law, which Mendelssohn embraced as a living, poetic form that points the mind to consider universal religious truths, including the existence of God and providence and the immortality of the soul.

The idea of God assumed pride of place in nineteenth-century liberal Judaism. As reformers, thinkers like Saul Ascher and Abraham *Geiger had no option but to refuse the notion that law constitutes the unique feature of Judaism. Against Spinoza and Mendelssohn, they considered the essence of Judaism to be its idea – namely, the idea of God that they equated with ethical monotheism (see JUDAISM, REFORM: GERMANY). Everything else (law, social constitution, etc.) represents the historical accident of mere form. Rejecting the classical enlightenment position that basic theological truths are universal, they located the origin of ethical monotheism not in the ideas of reason, but in the particular history of Judaism. Revelation is now inspiration. Reflecting the emergent historicism in German culture, the proponents of this scheme assumed that the Jews have a special genius for religion; their mission was to spread throughout the world, not as a national community, but as a *Diaspora community. The idea of ethical monotheism remains a constant element unique to Judaism (in distinction to *Christianity, whose theology was considered not as strictly monotheist, and *Islam, whose practice was considered not as strictly ethical). Although "the idea" takes on different form in different historical contexts, ethical monotheism remains the constant sine qua non without which there is no Judaism. The Modern Orthodox thinker Samson Raphael *Hirsch and the leader of Positive-Historical Judaism, Zacharias *Frankel, rejected the contention that the essence of Judaism is an "idea." The former saw law (i.e., ritual practice) and the latter saw peoplehood as components that were just as "essential" to Judaism as its God idea.

In contrast to the nineteenth century, the twentieth century was a heyday in modern Jewish theology, understood narrowly as a distinct discourse about God. The fresh currents in modern Jewish theology were made possible by a theoretical shift from the focus in nineteenth-century German Idealism on essence, idea, and spirit to an emphasis in phenomenology and existentialism on existence and relationship. A new model of reason embedded in lived human reality changed the discourse about God in western religious thought: God no longer appeared as a disembodied figure of thought or an object of historical development but took shape as a lived presence in the human here and now. Twentieth-century Jewish thought supported Kant's famous contention that the destruction of scholastic metaphysics (i.e., a dogmatic belief in God as an object of pure reason and theoretical knowledge) makes room for faith (i.e., belief in God as a postulate of practical reason, guiding human moral reason and action). Yet it did so with a warmth and intensity that escaped Kant.

In twentieth-century German Jewish thought, God was both a philosophical and intimate figure. As a philosophical figure, God forms part of a purely intellectualist program. For Hermann *Cohen, God is the guarantor of social ethics and a standard of intersubjective relationship (*Ethik des reinen Willens* [Religion of Reason]). For Martin *Buber (*I and Thou*) and for Franz *Rosenzweig (*The Star of Redemption*), God is a theoretical figure of thought in opposition to "world" and to "humans." At the same time, a profound intimacy supplemented the more philosophical discussion about God. The idea of God advanced in Cohen's "religion of reason" is associated with the lyrical poetry of *prayer, supplementing the idea of God in "philosophical ethics." The "holy" God shared by *ethics and religious piety (i.e., God as regulative, a moral archetype) grounds social ethics and the alleviation of suffering ("my concern for the neighbor"). The "good" God who is unique to religion *qua* religion, especially in the religion of lyric prayer, satisfies the individual's personal cry for *redemption from guilt and from the fear of *death (peace secured by *atonement). For Buber and Rosenzweig, revelation means not the revelation of reason as it does for Cohen, but the revelation of divine presence to a human being in his or her unique individuality and human wholeness. God speaks through human forms of dialogue, language, and *love.

American Jewish theology in the twentieth century was less philosophical (and less metaphysical) than Jewish thought in Germany. Against a transcendent, supernatural conception of God, Mordecai *Kaplan (*The Meaning of God in Modern Jewish Religion*) proposed faith in the cosmos and "enthusiasm for living." What Kaplan meant by God was the power within nature that makes for emergent salvation, social and human regeneration, righteousness, and freedom. Kaplan's rejection of the special privileges invoked by Jewish *chosenness and covenantal theology was meant to keep pace with modern science and democratic values. This emphasis on divine immanence was to become more influential in the 1980s and 1990s with the entry of *mysticism and *feminism into modern Jewish thought. Yet Kaplan's rationalism always seemed to fall short for most readers. In contrast, Abraham Joshua *Heschel and Joseph *Soloveitchik reworked the biblical image of a transcendent, personal God. For Heschel (*Man is Not Alone*; *God in Search of Man*) and Soloveitchik (*Lonely Man of Faith*; *Kol Dodi Dofek: Listen – My Beloved Knocks*; *Uvikashtem mi sham*), God is the covenantal partner of beloved Israel, who constitutes an answer to the experience of human wonder before existence (especially the alienated life of "modern man"). God gives meaning to the problem of human *suffering, but is the One before whom the human person always seems to fall short.

The post-Holocaust theology of Richard *Rubenstein (*After Auschwitz*), Eliezer *Berkovits (*Faith after the Holocaust; With God in Hell*), Emil *Fackenheim (*God's Presence in History; To Mend the World*), and Arthur Cohen (*The Tremendum*) challenged American Jewish theology in the late 1960s and 1970s. For these theologians, the scale and intensity of the *Holocaust called into question the goodness, justice, and perfection of God and more specific claims regarding God's

*covenant with Israel. Whether outside or inside the framework of covenantal theology, each thinker proposed different ways to think through the problem of God and Jewish intellectual history by abandoning ancient and modern forms of theodicy (just deserts in this world or the next, afflictions of love, vicarious atonement, messianic recompense, free will). They exhibited less willingness to uphold the justice and goodness of God against perceived human shortcomings. For them, the relationship between God and human beings was more morally fraught. The theology driving the work of Emmanuel *Levinas ("Loving Torah more than God"; "Useless Suffering") belongs to this stage in post-Holocaust thought. The commanding face of the other is more human than divine per se.

Since then, Jewish discourse about God has remained a mixed bag. In the Jewish theology that emerged in the late 1970s and 1980s, the embrace of mysticism and divine immanence accompanied a sharp move away from the rationalist philosophical tradition. Often skirting close to New Age theology, thinkers like Arthur Green, Zalman Schachter-Shalomi, Judith Plaskow, Marcia Falk, Neil Gilman, and Lawrence Kushner have yet to create a Jewish theology that is rigorously philosophical. In contrast, participants in the more narrowly rarified circles of academic Jewish philosophy tend to focus on historical studies. As a philosophical figure, God gives way to "texts" and to ethics, meaning, law, politics, and the body. All recent academic Jewish philosophy is in this respect a Straussian exercise (see STRAUSS, LEO), in which God has not yet dared come out into the open. **See also THOUGHT, MODERN.**

ZACHARY BRAITERMAN

Golden Calf: See AARON; CANAAN, CANAANITES; EXODUS

Golem. Two commentaries on the *Sefer Yetzirah*, both of them written in the first half of the thirteenth century in *Central Europe, describe in detail the creation of a human being out of earth and its animation through recitation of the Hebrew *alphabet. One is a work attributed to *Saadia Gaon, but actually written by a writer of the esoteric "Unique Cherub Circle"; the second is by Eleazar ben Judah of Worms (d. 1238), a leading figure in the *Ḥasidei Ashkenaz. In the first of these commentaries, as well as in several other contemporaneous sources, the creation of the *golem* is associated with *Abraham and Shem, who are said to have studied *Sefer Yetzirah* together. However, many scores of other commentaries on *Sefer Yetzirah*, from the tenth to the twentieth century, do not refer to such a practice. Gershom *Scholem, followed by Moshe Idel, understood *Sefer Yetzirah* itself to contain instructions for creating a *golem*, and they connected it to two paragraphs in Babylonian *Talmud *Sanhedrin* 65b. This connection was refuted in a detailed study by Peter Schaefer, who proved that there is no valid reference to this practice before the High Middle Ages. Beginning in the sixteenth century scattered narratives describe great sages who created such beings to serve them (the earliest, from the late fifteenth century, attributes this ability to Samuel ben Kalonymus, the father of Judah the Pious).

This legend inspired the 1909 fictional narrative by Judah Judel Rosenberg (1859–1935) about the creation of a *golem* by the sixteenth-century rabbi, Judah Loew, the Maharal of *Prague. This became a Jewish bestseller throughout the twentieth century, and many creative works, Jewish and non-Jewish, have been based on it. For further reading, see J. Dan, *The Unique Cherub Circle: A School of Mystics and Esoterics in Medieval Germany* (1999); G. Scholem, *On the Kabbalah and Its Symbolism* (1965); M. Idel, *Golem: Jewish Magical and Mystical Traditions on the Artificial Anthropoid* (1990); P. Schäfer, "The Magic of the Golem," *Journal of Jewish Studies* 46 (1995): 249–61.   JOSEPH DAN

Gordon, Aharon David (1856–1922) was the spiritual leader of Labor *Zionism. Settling in *Palestine in 1904, Gordon joined the agricultural movement to create a new kind of Jewish life and Jewish person. He believed that through physical productive labor, in accord with the divinely ordained rhythms of nature, humanity would become a partner with God in the process of creation. **See also GAR-DENS; ISRAEL, STATE OF: ECOLOGY.**

Graetz, Heinrich (1817–1891) was the best known nineteenth-century historian of the Jewish experience. Born in the Prussian province of Posen, he received a traditional Jewish education and attended a *yeshivah. He later came in close contact with the founder of *Modern Orthodoxy, Samson Raphael *Hirsch, and lived for a while in his house in Oldenburg. Their friendship fell apart, and Graetz went to study at the University of Breslau but could not obtain a doctorate there as a Jew. He thus submitted his thesis to the University of Jena. It dealt with Jewish *Gnosticism and was a thinly revealed polemic against contemporary religious reformers. Graetz became allied with Zacharias *Frankel and his Positive-Historical Judaism. In 1854, Graetz was appointed lecturer in Frankel's newly established Jewish Theological Seminary in Breslau. In 1846, he published his theoretical conception of Jewish history (*Construction der jüdischen Geschichte*); the first volume (it was actually the fourth volume) of his magisterial *Geschichte der Juden* (*History of the Jews*), which would total eleven volumes, appeared in 1853. Graetz's *History* has often been characterized as a "*Leidens- und Gelehrtengeschichte*," a history of suffering with regard to relations with the outside world and of intellectual achievements where it concerns internal Jewish history. The conservative German historian Heinrich von Treitschke accused Graetz of spreading anti-German and anti-Christian sentiments. Although these accusations stemmed from von Treitschke's own *antisemitism, Graetz was indeed a passionate and often emotional historian who, in addition to profoundly rejecting Jewish *mysticism, was very outspoken about any anti-Jewish sentiments. Graetz had sympathies for the renewed Jewish settlement in *Palestine but his writings should not be seen as a precursor of political *Zionism.   MICHAEL BRENNER

Grammarians and Lexicographers. Systematic interest in the grammar and meaning of Biblical *Hebrew started among ninth-century Jews living in Muslim lands. In Basora, Kufa, and later in Baghdad (see IRAQ), Muslim scholars created important centers of study of the Arabic language, particularly focused on the Qu'ran, its true readings, and its meaning. Jewish scholars learned from Arab grammarians how to use linguistic tools to analyze the sacred text and then began their own linguistic studies of *Hebrew. Two particular groups played an important role in these first grammatical approaches to the *Bible. The first were

the *Karaites, sectarians who rejected the oral tradition and based their religious life exclusively on the biblical text; the second were the *Masoretes, who maintained an orthodox position and devoted their efforts to preserving and transmitting the received text of the Scripture.

In Iraq, Jewish scholars initiated the scientific study of the Hebrew language. As with Arabic grammarians, Jewish tradition considered grammar to be a component of biblical exegesis. At the beginning of the tenth century, *Saadia Gaon translated the Bible into Arabic with a commentary. In doing so, he established the basis for the scientific study of the grammar and lexicon of Biblical Hebrew. Interest in this field spread quickly to *North Africa: Dunash ibn Tamim and Judah ben Kuraish were major scholars of biblical language. The latter promoted a comparative study of Hebrew vocabulary. Al-Fasi, a Karaite scholar born in the Maghreb, wrote a dictionary of Hebrew roots in *Judeo-Arabic at the middle of the tenth century. Soon thereafter, interest in Hebrew philology also developed in al-Andalus, Muslim *Spain. In the middle of the tenth century in Cordova, Menaḥem ben Saruk wrote the first Hebrew–Hebrew dictionary, explaining the meaning of most of the roots used in the Bible and creating an adequate linguistic terminology in Hebrew. The novelties and limitations of Menaḥem's dictionary, the *Maḥberet*, spurred passionate discussion on grammatical and lexical problems, led by *Dunash ben Labrat and the disciples of Menaḥem. These questions were not simply of academic interest; rather, they were crucial for understanding the Hebrew Bible and applying it to Jewish life. At the same time, Spanish Jews were also using Hebrew to write a new kind of Arabized poetry (see POETRY, MEDIEVAL: MUSLIM WORLD).

The study of Hebrew reached its peak at the end of the tenth century and during the first half of the eleventh century. Thanks to a deep reflection on Hebrew with the help of the grammatical works of the Arabs, first Judah Ḥayyuj and then Jonah ibn Janah a few years later provided the necessary instruments to identify and group the roots of the Bible in Hebrew, explain their flexion and uses, distinguish the linguistically correct forms from the incorrect ones, and interpret their senses. Ḥayyuj initiated the scientific study of Hebrew by applying the linguistic analyses of Arab grammarians to its roots and by overcoming all previous doubts and inadequacies. Ḥayyuj, who saw the language from a diachronic perspective, argued that there is no Hebrew verb with fewer than three letters. He believed that one of the main activities of the linguist is to discover the basic form that can explain all the other forms. Ibn Janah tried to complete and improve the work of Ḥayyuj, writing one of the most complete grammars of the epoch as well as a dictionary that was translated and used by many generations of scholars.

Jewish grammarians of the tenth and eleventh centuries played a decisive role in initiating the study of Semitic comparative grammar; because they were familiar with Arabic, Hebrew, and *Aramaic, they used linguistic comparison as a tool to study the Bible and its lexicon. Their contributions to the first comparative semitics were particularly important. Indeed, with the exception of some ideological reluctance found in the work of a few grammarians like Menaḥem, most medieval Jewish linguists compared Hebrew with Arabic and Aramaic. Saadia, Ben Kuraish, Ḥayyuj, and Ibn

Janah discussed the degree of affinity among the three languages in treatises on grammar and lexicography. At the end of the eleventh century, Isaac ibn Barūn made a detailed comparison between Hebrew and Arabic grammar and lexicology.

During the twelfth century, two Jews of Andalusian origin played an important role in the European diffusion of Hebrew grammar and lexicography. Abraham *ibn Ezra was a true linguist who not only transmitted the philological knowledge of the eleventh century to European Jews but also created his own grammatical system. David *Kimḥi systematized Hebrew grammar and wrote the most popular dictionary in Hebrew. European *conversos and Christian scholars in the Renaissance primarily used the books of David Kimḥi, while the Judeo-Arabic dictionary written by the last scholar of Arabic Muslim Granada, Saadia ibn Danan, remained almost unknown.

Recent scholarship includes A. Dotan, "Saadia Gaon – A Master Linguist," *Jewish Studies at the Turn of the Twentieth Century* (1999): 26–30; G. Kahn, *The Early Karaite Tradition of Hebrew Grammatical Thought* (2000); A. Maman, *Comparative Semitic Philology in the Middle Ages* (2004); and A. Sáenz-Badillos and J. Targarona, *Gramáticos hebreos de al-Andalus (siglos X-XIII), Filología y Biblia* (1988).

ANGEL SÁENZ-BADILLOS

Graphic Novels: See LITERATURE: GRAPHIC NOVELS

Gratz, Rebecca (1781–1869), was a *Philadelphia native who played a major role in establishing institutions that benefited women and children and served as models for many other communities. Gratz helped found the Philadelphia Orphan Asylum in 1815, and concerned about evangelical overtones in other charities, she opened the Female Hebrew Benevolent Association in 1819; it remains active in the early twenty-first century. In 1838 she founded and was superintendent of the first Hebrew Sunday School; it served both male and female students. Gratz assisted women in *Charleston, Savannah, and Baltimore in organizing similar schools, and Jewish Sunday Schools were also founded in many other places. Gratz established the Jewish Foster Home in 1855; it eventually became the Association for Jewish Children in Philadelphia. Gratz, who never married, devoted herself to the organizations she established and maintained literary correspondences with writers such as Washington Irving and Grace Aguilar (see LITERATURE: BRITAIN). For further reading, see D. Ashton, *Rebecca Gratz: Women and Judaism in Antebellum America* (1997); and see also ORGANIZATIONS, WOMEN'S: NORTH AMERICA; PHILADELPHIA.

Greece. The Jewish community in the region that today comprises Greece, one of the oldest and most influential in Europe, falls into three general groups – *Romaniotes, *Sephardim, and *Ashkenazim – although there is great diversity within each of these categories.

Broadly speaking, Romaniotes are those Jews who trace their origins in the region to the early *Roman period. Communities of Romaniotes were found most notably in Didimoticho, Halkis, Jannina, the Peloponnese, Salonika, Serres, and Verroia. Most Romaniote communities are thought to date from the first century of the Common Era, although there is evidence for the presence of Jews in the region

well before then. Romaniotes, then, are rightly considered "indigenous" and may indeed be one of the most continuous presences in a region that has experienced several waves of migration and invasion, particularly in the late medieval and Early Modern periods. Romaniote Jews today are particularly associated with the city of Jannina, in northwestern Greece. Before World War II, Jannina was Greece's largest Romaniote community, but today there are virtually no Jews left in that city. Romaniotes historically have spoken Greek; after the formation of the Greek nation-state they were, for the most part, more readily integrated into Greek society than other Greek Jews, largely because of their cultural "Greekness."

Sephardim are Jews originally from *Spain and *Portugal (and in smaller numbers from southern *France and northern *Italy) who left the Iberian peninsula in a series of waves following various decrees of mandatory conversion and expulsion. In Spain, the Alhambra Decree, or Edict of Expulsion of 1492, and a similar decree in 1497 in Portugal triggered migratory waves of Iberian Jews and Jewish converts (*conversos) toward *North Africa and southeastern Europe in search of religious freedom and freedom from the *Inquisition. In the wake of these migrations Salonika rose to prominence as the *Ottoman Jewish city par excellence and became the world Sephardic center from the sixteenth century through the start of World War II. Most people think of Greek Jews as these Sephardic descendants of the Iberian expulsions, who settled in Ottoman Salonika (Selanik) during the sixteenth century and formed a vibrant community that was destroyed during the *Holocaust. Although depicted as one group, the Sephardim have diverse origins in literally hundreds of different communities of southwest Europe.

Ashkenazim, *Central, and *East European Jews, made up the smallest portion of Greek Jewry. It is thought that some hundreds came to the *Balkans in the 1400s, after being ejected from the kingdom of Bavaria. Hungarian-speaking Jews settled in northern Greece, in Kavala, at around the same period. Another very small wave of Ashkenazim migrated to the region in the early nineteenth century in search of economic opportunities in Athens, newly established as the Greek capital. Although Romaniote Jews continue to maintain a separate identity, most other Greek Jews assimilated to one extent or another to Sephardic practice and rabbinic authority. This process was most clearly marked around Salonika, where the rabbinic establishment long held authority not only over most Jews in the immediate region but also across the Mediterranean Jewish world as a whole.

Such, in broad historical strokes, are the contours of Jewish presence in Greek lands. Yet in framing a category of "the Jews of Greece," it is important to remember that Greece did not emerge as a nation-state until the end of the Greek War of Independence (1821–33); at the time of its inception there were very few, if any, "Greek Jews." The city of Salonika, the largest Jewish community in the *Balkans, only became part of Greece in the wake of the Balkans wars of 1912–13, with annexation by Greece in 1912; the horrors of the *Holocaust came just thirty years later. So Greece has been home to a sizably significant Jewish population for only a small part of its two-century history. One of the greatest struggles faced by the region's Jews was the transition from being Ottoman imperial subjects to being Greek national citizens; the implications of integration into a largely Christian state were extremely complex. Since Greece's creation, there has been a constant friction between Greek Jews and a state that defines itself in largely Christian (Orthodox) terms.

At the end of the first decade of the twenty-first century, there are roughly 5,000 Jews in Greece. In contrast, on the eve of World War II, there were close to 80,000. More than 65,000 Jews from Greece were murdered in the course of the war, most in *Auschwitz-Birkenau. Of those who survived, more than half ultimately emigrated in the post-war period, most to *Israel or the *United States. Emigration to Israel, in particular, continues, although the Greek Jewish population is now stable. Today's community tends to be highly secularized; much of its group cultural practice consists of commemorating the Greek Jewish past and remembering the community of the pre-war period. As with a number of European countries where the Jewish population was all but eradicated, Jewish post-war consolidation has been largely juridical: In Greece, the Central Board of Jewish Communities (KIS, *Kentriko Israelitiko Symvoulio Ellados*) was estab-

lished as a legal state entity in 1945, largely to represent the community in its various legal battles over Jewish-owned properties stolen during the war. Today it serves as the Jewish community's corporate representative body vis-à-vis foreign entities and the Greek state, and it coordinates the activities of Greece's nine Jewish communities or congregations. Formal communities exist today in Athens, Thessaloniki, Larissa, Halkis, Volos, Corfu, Trikkala, Jannina, and Rhodes, but only those in Athens, Thessaloniki, and Larissa are large enough to support regular worship and other communal activities (**Maps 4, 9**).

For further reading, see S. Bowman, *Jewish Resistance in Wartime Greece* (2006); R. Dalven, *The Jews of Jannina* (1990); K. E. Fleming, *Greece – A Jewish History* (2007); A. Levy, *The Sephardim in the Ottoman Empire* (1994); M. Mazower, *Salonica: City of Ghosts* (2004); idem, *Inside Hitler's Greece: The Experience of Occupation, 1941–44* (1993); N. Stavroulakis, *The Jews of Greece* (1990); and **see also** BYZANTINE EMPIRE.

K. E. FLEMING

Gypsies: See HOLOCAUST: ROMA

H

Ḥabad (also Chabad): A formulation of Ḥasidism shaped by R. Schneur *Zalman of Liady (1745–1813), Ḥabad is an acronym for *ḥokhmah* ("wisdom"), *binah* ("understanding"), and *daat* ("knowledge"). Lubavitch Ḥasidism, the major branch of Ḥabad, emerged as a dynasty in 1813 when R. Dov Ber of Lubavitch (1773–1828), the son of R. Schneur Zalman, prevailed in a succession conflict. **See ḤASIDISM: EUROPE and ḤASIDISM: NORTH AMERICA.**

Habakkuk is the eighth of the twelve "minor" prophetic books (see BIBLE: PROPHETS AND PROPHECY; PROPHETS). Because it mentions Chaldeans (a biblical term for *Babylonians), scholars date the book after the rise of the neo-Babylonian Empire in the late seventh century BCE. This would make the author (about whom nothing else is known) a contemporary of *Jeremiah. Like Jeremiah, Habakkuk sees the Babylonians as divinely commissioned to punish *Judah, but Habakkuk emphasizes that they attribute their might to their own god. Consequently they will be punished for their treatment of Judah (cf. *Isaiah's attitude in 10:5–19). The first section (1–2) is a dialogue between *God and the prophet, who bemoans the *suffering of the innocent – whether at the hands of corrupt Judean leaders or of Babylonians is not clear. Similarities between the prophet's questions and those in *psalms of lament are noteworthy. The critique of idolatry at the end of chapter 2 (which displays knowledge of Babylonian attitudes towards cult statues) could be intended against Judean idolaters or against the Babylonians. The second section (3) is a psalm petitioning God to act and describing a theophany, a vision of God. Its imagery resembles that of *Exodus 19, *Deuteronomy 33.2, *Judges 5.4, Psalm 29, and Canaanite texts describing the theophany of the god *Baal.

A commentary on Habakkuk found at *Qumran identifies the Chaldeans with the Kittim or *Romans. *Rabbinic literature (*Seder Olam Rabbah* 20.5) maintains that Habakkuk lived in the time of King Manasseh, whereas the *Zohar* identifies him with the son of the Shunammite woman whom *Elisha saved in 1 Kings 4 (*Zohar* 1.7b). However, these dates are too early, because they precede the rise of neo-Babylonian power. Habakkuk 3 is read on the second day of the festival of *Shavuot because of its description of a theophany.

BENJAMIN D. SOMMER

Habsburg Empire. The history of East-Central European Jewry is closely bound up with that of the multinational Habsburg monarchy. In addition to *Austria, the monarchy also incorporated *Hungary and the *Czech lands (Bohemia and Moravia) in 1526. With the annexation of *Galicia (1772) and Bukovina (1775), the Habsburg monarchy came to include the largest Jewish population in Europe west of the *Russian Empire.

EARLY MODERN PERIOD: Before 1526 the only significant Jewish settlement under Habsburg rule was in *Vienna. In 1421 the flourishing medieval Jewish community of that city was destroyed, and it was renewed only in the sixteenth century. The Czech lands became the cultural and demographic center of Habsburg Jewry in the sixteenth and seventeenth centuries. The Jews of Bohemia were expelled from the royal cities in 1541, but they were allowed to remain in *Prague, and the rest spread out into small towns and villages. Moravian Jews lived in private towns ruled by magnate families. The reigns of Maximilian II (1564–76) and Rudolph II (1576–1612) created favorable conditions for the expansion of Jewish life in the Czech lands. Rudolph II gave the Jews of Prague new privileges, and the Jewish population of the city grew from a few dozen in 1564 to 3,000 by 1600. The most important cultural figure of this period was Rabbi Judah Loew ben Bezalel (the Maharal, ca. 1520–1609).

The Thirty Years War (1618–47) improved the position of Jews, as the Habsburgs needed them to finance military needs. The number of Jewish families who could settle in Vienna grew, and Ferdinand II (1619–37) extended the privileges of the Jews of Bohemia and Moravia in the 1620s. In Vienna, however, he ordered the Jews to move to a separate quarter (Leopoldstadt) in 1625. The end of the war saw a long-term negative turn in Habsburg Jewish policy. Leopold I (1658–1705) ordered the expulsion of the Jews from Vienna in 1669. The Jewish community was destroyed once again, and those expelled settled in Hungary, Moravia, and also *Berlin. Wealthy Jews were soon readmitted to Vienna, as the Habsburgs desperately needed money to finance their wars with *France and the *Ottoman Empire. The Jews, however, were not allowed to form an organized community and could hold prayer services only in private homes. The small Viennese community was dominated by the *Court Jews, who had a crucial role in managing Austrian state finances. Samuel Oppenheimer (1630–1703) became army contractor in 1672, and he provisioned the advancing Austrian troops against the Turks in Hungary in the 1680s. Oppenheimer was followed by Samson Wertheimer (1658–1724), who was also a scholar and philanthropist.

Charles VI (1711–1780) and his daughter Maria Theresa (1740–1780) considered the presence of Jews harmful for the monarchy, and they introduced a series of restrictive laws. In 1726/27 the infamous Familiants Laws limited the number of Jewish families that could legally reside in Bohemia and Moravia. Only one male member of each family could legally marry, and many young men had to leave as a result. Thirty thousand Moravian Jews settled in Hungary in the eighteenth century, where the Jewish population grew from 11,621 in 1735 to 80,775 in 1787. When the Habsburgs annexed Galicia in 1772, the Jewish population of the empire doubled overnight. A series of regulations and special taxes were introduced for the 200,000 Galician Jews, who lived in towns under the rule of Polish nobles and fulfilled important economic functions.

1780–1848: The reign of Joseph II (1780–90) marked the beginning of the transformation of internal Jewish life and the end of communal autonomy. The emperor's Jewish legislation was part of a larger system of reforms to modernize the state. Joseph II issued a series of Edicts of Tolerance for the Jews of the various provinces between 1781 and 1789. The emperor encouraged Jews to found factories and to take up handicrafts, agriculture, and professions like *medicine. Joseph II also forbade the use of *Yiddish and *Hebrew in public and commercial records (1781), abolished rabbinical judicial authority (1784), obliged Jews to adopt German-sounding personal and family names (1787), and introduced compulsory military service (1788). He urged Jews to set up government-supervised German-language elementary schools and declared secondary schools and institutions of higher learning open to Jews.

Germanization was also furthered by the spread of the *Haskalah, and German culture became the primary context of acculturation for Jews in the entire monarchy until the mid-nineteenth century. The German Jewish schools enjoyed the support of Ezekiel Landau (1713–1793), the conservative chief rabbi of Prague, and they became a permanent feature of Jewish cultural life in Bohemia and Moravia. The school system soon collapsed in Hungary and Galicia, but Germanization did continue in both provinces. Galician maskilim, among them Nachman *Krochmal (1785–1840) and Solomon Judah Leib Rapoport (1790–1867), furthered Germanization and opened schools (see LITERATURE, HEBREW: HASKALAH).

*Hasidism quickly gained popularity among Galician Jews and spread to Hungary through a massive wave of immigration in the first half of the nineteenth century. Religious reform also found supporters. Isaac Noah Mannheimer (1793–1865), who came to Vienna in 1826, introduced moderate ritual reforms (see JUDAISM, REFORM). Aaron Chorin (1766–1844) brought Reform Judaism to Hungary, where an organized and influential *Orthodox resistance also emerged. The *yeshivah established by Moses Sofer (the Hatam Sofer, 1762–1839) in Pressburg (Bratislava, Pozsony) became a major center for traditional learning.

The legal situation of Habsburg Jews did not change until the 1840s, despite their growing economic role and the increasing acculturation of a significant segment of Jewish society. It was primarily Jewish businessmen and financiers who contributed to the development of the modern capitalist economy in Bohemia, Moravia, and Austria from the last third of the eighteenth century, for which they received special privileges (see COMMERCE). The Eskeles and Arnstein families led the leading *banking house in Vienna; both the Jewish and non-Jewish elite frequented the famous salon of Fanny von Arnstein (1754–1818). Salomon Mayer *Rothschild (1774–1855) came to Vienna in 1816 and was ennobled six years later. Many members of the highly acculturated and ennobled Jewish families, however, converted to Christianity. In Hungary in the first half of the nineteenth century, Jews contributed to the expansion of agricultural production and trade as merchants, lease-holders, and petty traders on the estates of the nobility. The Hungarian parliament granted the Jews freedom of residence and the right to own urban real estate in 1840.

1848–1918: A new era began with the revolutions of 1848, which held the promise of freedom and equality. Many Jews participated in the revolution in Kraków, and they were especially prominent in Vienna, where Jews came

to study from every corner of the empire. Several Jews, such as Hermann Jellinek, Ignaz Kuranda, and Adolf Fishof, were among the leaders of the Vienna revolution. The Moravian chief rabbi, Samson Raphael *Hirsch (1847–51), also played an active role, and many Jews enthusiastically supported the Hungarian war of independence. In Bohemia, Moravia, and Hungary, however, there were also serious anti-Jewish disturbances. In the end it was the imperial constitution of Emperor Francis Joseph (1848–1916) that first granted legal equality to the Jews in March 1849. It was repealed in 1851, but the special residential restrictions and taxes, gradually abolished in the 1840s, were not reinstated, even though a fine was levied on the Jews of Hungary and Galicia and their right to own landed property was suspended between 1853 and 1860.

Habsburg Jews finally gained civic equality in 1867, the year of the compromise between Austria and Hungary. Hungary received almost full independence, and Galicia was granted autonomy within the Austrian half of the monarchy, which also included the Czech lands. During the second half of the nineteenth century there were increasing migrations of Hungarian, Bohemian, and Moravian Jews to the urban centers of Budapest, Prague, Brünn (Brno), and Vienna. The imperial capital also became a magnet for Galician Jews. Prague lost its leading position in Habsburg Jewish life (with 29,107 Jewish residents in 1910), and Vienna (with 175,318 Jews in 1910) became the center of Jewish culture and politics in the monarchy. Poverty forced masses of Jews to emigrate outside the monarchy, primarily to the *United States.

After 1867, following Jews in the more advanced parts of the empire, Jews in Galicia and Hungary entered *banking, industry, and the free professions. Jews were especially prominent in the creation of the modern economy and culture in Budapest, which had the largest Jewish population in the monarchy by 1910 (203,618). Jews also contributed to the emergence of modern science, culture, and literature in Vienna. Sigmund *Freud, Gustav Mahler, Karl Kraus, Arthur Schnitzler, and Stefan Zweig (see LITERATURE: CENTRAL EUROPE) were among the cultural innovators of the time.

Jewish life and politics in the post-1867 period were dominated by fierce national conflicts and the emergence of modern *antisemitism. The Jews were caught up in the Czech–German conflict in Bohemia and Moravia. Most Moravian Jews allied with the Germans culturally and politically. In Bohemia, however, the increasing Czech political pressure initiated a new phase of acculturation. A Czech Jewish movement emerged in the 1890s, and German Jewish schools were closed down. German Jewish culture did live on, however, as demonstrated by the life and work of Prague writers such as Franz *Kafka, Max Brod, and Franz Werfel.

In Galicia, dominated by the Polish nobility, Jews were affected by the political struggle between *Poles and *Ukrainians. Jews mainly allied with the Poles in politics, and both were loyal to Austria. Polish acculturation also accelerated after emancipation, especially in the urban centers of Krakow and Lemberg (L'viv, Lwów). Yiddish retained its primacy among the Jewish masses, but German culture also remained influential. Bukovina became a separate province in 1846; Jews comprised 13% of the population by 1910, which was the highest percentage in the monarchy. Bukovina was both a Hasidic stronghold and the home of a politically influential and Germanized urban Jewish elite among Germans, Romanians, and Ukrainians.

The Hungarian political elite put much pressure on the Jews and the nationalities to assimilate. Jews allied with the ruling Hungarians in politics, and by the early twentieth century 77% declared Hungarian as their mother tongue. In 1868 the Hungarian government convened a Jewish congress to define the organizational structure of the Jewish community. The congress aggravated the conflict between the Neolog (the followers of moderate Reform Judaism) and the Orthodox, which resulted in an institutional schism in 1871 (see JUDAISM, NEOLOG). No such separation happened anywhere else in the monarchy. The diverse Viennese community remained institutionally intact, served by rabbis like the liberal Adolf Jellinek (1821–93) and the conservative Moritz Güdemann (1835–1918).

Antisemitism emerged all over the empire in the 1880s, and its intensification in the 1890s disrupted acculturation and accelerated the development of Jewish politics. In 1886 Rabbi Samuel Bloch (1850–1923) founded the Austrian Israelite Union, a self-defense organization. Nationalist conflicts also contributed to the emergence of Jewish nationalism, which offered a third way for Jews caught between nationalities. The first organization to promote Jewish settlement in *Palestine was founded in Galicia in 1875, where Hovevei Zion ("Lovers of Zion") groups also started springing up in the 1890s. Jewish nationalism was the strongest in Galicia and Bukovina, where the whole spectrum of Jewish politics, from politically active Orthodoxy to socialism, flourished. The Zionist student organization Kadimah was founded in Vienna in 1882. Theodor *Herzl (1860–1904) formulated the program of political Zionism in Vienna, but most of the followers of the movement came from Eastern Europe. Bohemian Zionism emerged from the student Zionist organization, Bar Kokhba, which was founded in 1899 in Prague. The Hungarian Zionist societies convened their first congress in 1903, but *Zionism in Hungary was much weaker than in the Czech lands and Galicia.

The Jewish population of the Austro-Hungarian Empire numbered more than 2.2 million in 1910. The majority lived in Galicia and Hungary: 871,895 and 911,227, respectively. World War I (1914–18) brought much suffering for Habsburg Jews, 300,000 of whom fought in the imperial army. After the collapse of the monarchy in 1918, Jews had to adapt to the new political and national contexts of Austria, Czechoslovakia, Hungary, the *Balkans, *Romania, and Poland.

For further reading, see H. J. Kieval, *Languages of Community: The Jewish Experience in the Czech Lands* (2000); O. McCagg, Jr., *A History of Habsburg Jews, 1670–1918* (1992); R. S. Wistrich, *The Jews of Vienna in the Age of Franz Joseph* (1989); I. Bartal and A. Polonsky, eds., *Focusing on Galicia: Jews, Poles, and Ukrainians, 1772–1918, Polin: Studies in Polish Jewry* 12 (1999); and M. L. Rozenblit, *Reconstructing a National Identity: The Jews of Habsburg Austria during World War I* (2001). **Maps 8, 10**   KATI VÖRÖS

Haftarah (pl. *haftarot*) is a selection from the *Prophets section of the *Bible that is chanted or read in the *synagogue after the *Torah reading on *Sabbath and *festival mornings and on both the mornings and afternoons of the *fast days of *Yom Kippur and *Tisha B'Av. The *haftarah* is

usually read by the *maftir*, the final Torah reader; this reader may be a *Bar or *Bat Mitzvah. Special blessings introduce and conclude the *haftarah*, and it is chanted according to a system of cantillation (*trop*) that differs from that used for the Torah. The origins for this custom are unknown; some scholars believe the *haftarah* was added after 168 BCE when Torah reading was prohibited by Antiochus IV Epiphanes prior to the *Hasmonean era and that the word comes from Greek, meaning "addition." Others suggest that the *haftarah* was created as a response to Jewish sects who rejected the canonicity of the Prophets. Originally, there were no set *haftarot*, and the selection would be chosen by the final Torah reader. After the Torah was divided into weekly portions in rabbinic times, corresponding *haftarot* were chosen for each Torah portion, generally based on shared thematic elements with the Torah reading or the festival or fast day being observed (BT *Megillah* 29b). The *haftarot* do not include the Prophets section in its entirety, and the specific weekly *haftarah* may vary among different Jewish communities.   ELIZABETH SHULMAN

Hagar first appears in *Genesis 16 as *Sarah's *Egyptian maidservant. As a remedy for her *infertility, *Sarah (Sarai) asks *Abraham (Abram) to have intimate relations with Hagar; she assumes that if Hagar bears a child, that child will be seen as her own. When Hagar becomes pregnant, however, it soon becomes evident that "her mistress is lowered in her esteem" (16:4). Sarah responds by treating Hagar harshly and Hagar flees into the wilderness. There she encounters an angel of *God who tells her to return to Sarah and to submit to her harsh treatment. The angel promises that Hagar will have many offspring and that she will bear a son named *Ishmael. Hagar returns and gives birth but after Sarah bears *Isaac, she finds the presence of Hagar and her son in Abraham's household unbearable (Gen 21: 9ff). God tells a reluctant Abraham to accede to Sarah's request to expel Hagar and Ishmael. In the wilderness once more and fearing for her son's survival, Hagar again has an encounter with an angel of God, who reassures her that Ishmael will become a great nation. Genesis 21:21 relates that when Ishmael grew up, his mother obtained a wife for him from Egypt.

This problematic story seems to have several purposes. On an etiological level, it explains the paternal connection between Abraham and the Arab people, who are said to descend from Ishmael. It establishes the tradition of infertile wives (see INFERTILITY) who bear children only when God deems the moment propitious and emphasizes the necessity of faith in divine promises. The narrative also introduces the motif of the triumph of the younger son over the elder, another indication of God's direction of history. The biblical author paints an unpleasant portrait of Sarah, who demonstrates unjust harshness to Hagar and cruelly demands Hagar's expulsion. Missing is any significant concern about Hagar's lack of agency in becoming Abraham's sexual partner or her inability to protect her position in Abraham's household. This is because this story also introduces a polemic against exogamy and the dangers of foreign women to the destiny of Israel, which, at the very moment of its birth as a nation, was threatened with contamination from an outside source. This narrative is another example of how Genesis recounts a lineage and succession constantly in jeopardy and miraculously preserved by the intervention of God.   JUDITH R. BASKIN

Haggai is the tenth of the twelve minor prophetic books (see BIBLE: PROPHETS AND PROPHECY; PROPHETS). The prophet is named in 1:1 of the book and mentioned also in *Ezra 5:1 and 6:14. His message is dated to 520 BCE in the second year of Darius I, king of *Persia, and addressed to the high priest, Joshua, and the governor, *Zerubbabel. With soaring rhetoric Haggai exhorts the people of *Yehud, the community of returned Jewish exiles in *Jerusalem, to rebuild the *Temple, which has lain in ruins nearly seventy years; he explains that many of their difficulties in the post-exilic community arise from their failure to do so (1). Haggai goes on to promise the people future blessings when the Temple is repaired and rebuilt (2:1–9); he then seeks a ruling of the *priests on a matter of ritual *purity (2:10–14). He concludes with a messianic passage that designates Zerubbabel, a descendant of King *David, as the symbol of future hope, by calling him "signet" (2:23).

BENJAMIN D. SOMMER

Hai ben Sherira was one of the last and greatest of the Babylonian *Geonim (d. 1038). He succeeded his father as head of the *Pumbedita academy and for more than thirty years served as its head and as the most prominent scholar in the Jewish world. His surviving writings include more than a thousand *responsa on a wide range of talmudic and legal topics, two important legal monographs (on sales and judicial oaths), and a number of poems. His other writings, of which only fragments survive, include additional legal monographs and what may have been the first dictionary of *Hebrew and *Aramaic ever written.

ROBERT BRODY

Halakhah, the word used to refer to Jewish law, comes from the Hebrew root meaning "to walk" or "to go"; this indicates that Jewish law prescribes a path through life, detailing what an individual should and should not do, according to divine commandments (*mitzvot*) as they have been interpreted and applied by legal scholars throughout the ages.

Halakhah occupies a central place in Jewish identity. Although theological convictions define Jewish understandings of *God, humanity, the *environment, and the relationships among them, Judaism has never defined itself in terms of official creeds. Instead, the focus is on actions. At the same time, *Judaism, in general, and Jewish norms of conduct, in particular, are not defined exclusively by *halakhah*. Stories, proverbs, *prayers, *thought, history, and ethical and theological convictions all shape how Jews understand themselves and determine how they should act.

According to traditional count the *Torah contains 613 commandments (BT *Makkot* 23b; also *Yevamot* 47b, *Nedarim* 25a, *Shevu'ot* 29a). In addition, some biblical *narratives serve as models for human actions. *Abraham's purchase of the cave of Machpelah to bury *Sarah (Genesis 23) demonstrated how to acquire property; the marital negotiations between Abraham's servant and Laban in securing *Rebekah as a wife for *Isaac (Genesis 24:47–61) exemplified the legal expectations of both sides in a *marriage. These stories, and the fact that *Moses was judging cases (Exodus 18) before the *Decalogue was announced (Exodus 19–10), indicate that in addition to the stated commandments, there was also a long oral tradition of accepted social norms, a form of "common law" or *custom (*minhag*).

The first officially recognized collection of legal traditions is the *Mishnah, edited by Rabbi *Judah ha-Nasi ("president" or "prince") of the *Sanhedrin, in approximately 200 CE. Divided into six sections or orders (*sedarim*), and subdivided into sixty-three tractates (*masekhtot*), the Mishnah organizes Jewish law by topic and records the law as it was lived in response to both written and oral traditions. These traits made it the basis for all future discussions of *halakhah*, especially the *Jerusalem Talmud (c. 400 CE) and the more complete and authoritative *Babylonian Talmud (c. 500 CE). Both of these legal compilations discuss the basis in the Torah for the Mishnah's laws, define the parameters of its rulings, and apply them to new circumstances.

During the Middle Ages, Jewish law took two primary forms. The most important way in which Jewish law developed was through *responsa literature, or *teshuvot* – literally, "answers" to questions posed to rabbis. In addition to the responses to questions recorded in the Talmud, separate questions and their answers have been recorded in responsa from the early Middle Ages to our own time. The great advantage of this genre of literature is that a rabbi in one community could consult an expert in a given area of law and receive an answer responding to his specific case. This practice continues in the present, and now both the questions and answers are often communicated through phone conversations and e-mail, as well as in writing. The great disadvantage of this genre has been that until recently it was difficult to know about all the responsa written on a given topic. Now, however, there are computer programs that give access to more than 300,000 responsa up to the Early Modern period, and contemporary responsa are often available on the internet.

From time to time rabbis would write restatements of the law, or *codes, in which they tried to summarize some or all of Jewish law. The most famous and authoritative of these codes are *Maimonides' *Mishneh Torah* (1180), *Jacob ben Asher's *Arba'ah Turim* (the "Tur," d. 1340; printed 1475), and Joseph *Karo's *Shulḥan Arukh* (1565), with glosses by Moses *Isserles to indicate where the practices of Jews of northern Europe (*Ashkenazim) differed from those of the Jews of the Mediterranean basin (*Sephardim) that Karo had recorded. The codes have the advantage of summarizing the law in one place, but they cannot deal with the specifics of a particular case. Thus, they lead to a deductive kind of reasoning that is foreign to the case-based foundations of Jewish law in the Torah and Talmud and the casuistic mode of reasoning that characterizes the responsa.

In modern countries that maintain a separation of church and state, the laws of the country govern most areas of life. Religious laws of various denominations apply only to those who choose to abide by them and then only in matters of ritual and personal status matters such as *marriage and *divorce. Jewish law, however, is a complete legal system, with laws governing not only rituals and family law but also civil and criminal law. Thus, the Torah and all the subsequent iterations of *halakhah* mentioned here include norms defining how one can acquire or sell property, rent an apartment, and recover compensation for property damages or personal injuries, as well as the penalties for a variety of crimes. *Halakhah* also includes laws governing *court procedures to ensure that justice is done.

In earlier eras, Jews were generally granted internal autonomy over their own communities, as long as they paid taxes to the ruling power. This meant that Jewish law was enforced on Jews by Jewish authorities through a system of *communal organization that was backed by the government. Now that Jews are citizens of the countries in which they live, they are governed by the state in civil and criminal matters. This means that individual Jews must determine for themselves how much authority *halakhah* will have in other areas of their lives. This has led to great diversity in Jewish practice and in Jewish interpretations of the ongoing authority of *halakhah*. Orthodox, Conservative, Reconstructionist, and Reform *Judaisms differ on these issues, within denominations as well as with the other movements. For further reading about Jewish law and its development, see E. N. Dorff and A. Rosett, *A Living Tree: The Roots and Growth of Jewish Law* (1988); M. Elon, *Jewish Law: History, Sources, Principles*, 4 vols. (1994); and E. N. Dorff, *The Unfolding Tradition: Jewish Law after Sinai* (2005); **see also DINA DE-MALKHUTA DINA**.   ELLIOT N. DORFF

Halevi, Judah (ca. 1085–1141), was one of the most renowned and prolific Hebrew poets of medieval *Spain (see POETRY, MEDIEVAL: MUSLIM WORLD) and the author of the highly influential philosophical treatise *Kuzari*, written in *Judeo-Arabic. Halevi, a physician and communal leader, was born and lived most of his life in Toledo, then under Christian rule. In 1140 Halevi decided to leave Spain and spend the rest of his life in the Land of *Israel. Documents preserved in the Cairo *Genizah indicate that he spent time in *Egypt before leaving for the Land of Israel in May 1141; he apparently died there not long after his arrival.

Halevi initially began the *Kuzari*, also known as *The Book of Refutation and Proof in Defense of the Despised Faith*, to respond to the claims of *Karaism, but over a twenty-year period, the book developed into a complex discussion of religious, intellectual, and cultural issues. The framework of the work is a reported historical event – the conversion of the *Khazars to Judaism. In Halevi's version, the Khazar king is told in a dream that his intentions are worthy, but his actions are deficient. To discover the proper path of action, he calls a philosopher, an imam, a priest, and a rabbi to help him determine what to do. The philosopher's exposition of Aristotelian theory is identified as persuasive, but not what the king is seeking. The claims of *Islam and *Christianity are subsequently seen as derivative from the primary *revelation of *Torah, leading the king to focus on *Judaism. The remainder of the book is a dialogue between the king and the *ḥaver*, a representative of the Jewish tradition.

In the course of the discussion, the *ḥaver* differentiates between a propositional statement of belief arrived at through rational speculation (*it'aqad*) and faith (*iman*) derived through a prophetic experience. Ha-Levi does not negate the value of *reason and metaphysics and recognizes the importance of mathematics and logic. He acknowledges philosophy as a valuable process through which human beings can come to an advanced understanding of God and the world. Nonetheless, Aristotelian methodology is seen as ultimately deficient because human beings with their limited rational abilities are unable to determine absolute truth. Philosophy is accepted as an epistemological precursor to a higher stage of knowledge. However, the highest level of understanding is limited to members in a divine order (*al-'amr al-'ilâhî*); it is revealed through *prophecy and governs all of existence. Halevi argues that the revelation experienced by the Jewish people at Sinai was an historical event preserved by an unbroken tradition; it is anchored in the biological heritage of Israel and is kept vibrant through ritual behaviors and practices. This argument allows Halevi to defend Jewish particularity – the chosenness of individual *prophets, the people of Israel, the Land of Israel, the *Hebrew language, and the *commandments – as part of this supernatural order of being. The faithfulness of Jews to the prophetic tradition, their observance of revealed commandments, and the certainty of *messianic *redemption – despite the humiliation of present exile – convinces the king to accept Judaism as true.

Some paradoxes are evident. Although Halevi argues that only those born into Judaism can become prophets, his work is a narrative about conversion, and he affirms that the true religion is open to all who seek to join its adherents. In addition, Halevi is usually portrayed as an anti-Aristotelian thinker, but his sophisticated argumentation uses philosophy and recognizes its value, even if it has inferior status to the knowledge of God that comes through the revelation of the divine order that determines and defines existence.

For further reading, see R. P. Scheindlin, *The Song of the Distant Dove* (2007); A. Shear, *The Kuzari and the Shaping of Jewish Identity, 1167–1900* (2008); Y. Silman, *Philosopher and Prophet: Judah Halevi, the Kuzari, and the Evolution of His Thought* (1995); and B. S. Kogan, "Judah Halevi and His Use of Philosophy in the *Kuzari*," in *The Cambridge Companion to Medieval Jewish Philosophy*, ed. D.H. Frank and O. Leaman (2003); **see also THOUGHT, MEDIEVAL**.
BARUCH FRYDMAN-KOHL

Hallel, literally "praise," refers to *Psalms 113–118 and is recited in the *synagogue on *festivals and *Ḥanukkah. This particular grouping of psalms is also known as the "Egyptian *Hallel*" because it mentions the Exodus from *Egypt (Ps 114:1). These psalms were apparently sung as Jewish pilgrims brought *Passover offerings to the *Jerusalem *Temple. On the last six days of Passover and on *Rosh Hodesh (the *New Moon), a "half *hallel*" is recited, omitting the first halves of Psalms 115 and 116. Since the establishment of the State of *Israel, many congregations also recite *hallel* on Israel Independence Day; *hallel* is omitted on *Purim because the reading of the book of *Esther itself is deemed *hallel* (BT *Megillah* 14a). There is also a "daily *hallel*" (Pss 145–150) recited each morning and a "great *hallel*" (Ps 136) recited as part of the Passover *seder* and each *Sabbath morning.   PAUL STEINBERG

Hammurabi was a *Babylonian king who ruled for forty years in the seventeenth or sixteenth century BCE. A stele containing his legal rulings, the most extensive collection of laws recovered from Babylonian society, was discovered in 1901 and is now in the Louvre Museum in Paris. Hammurabi's code resembles biblical law, although it is more casuistic (case-oriented) and retributive and not as broadly applicable as Mosaic legislation. The code does not link religious service or ethical behavior to obedience to its precepts.

The majority of its laws regard property, personal damage, and human relationships, and the laws are flanked by a prologue and epilogue praising the righteousness of the king and invoking the Babylonian pantheon of deities. **See also LAW: ANCIENT *NEAR EAST and HEBREW *BIBLE. Map 1**

KATE FRIEDMAN

Hannah is the main character in the story of *Samuel's birth in 1 Samuel 1:1–2:21. The wife of Elhanan and co-wife of Peninah, she overcomes *infertility through a vow made at the *Shiloh shrine during her family's annual journey there to offer *sacrifices. In fervent *prayer she promises that, if she bears a son, the child will be dedicated to *God as a *Nazirite. Her prayer is answered, and when the son is weaned, she brings him to Shiloh to begin his life of service to God; she also offers a sacrifice in gratitude. This narrative of a woman overcoming barrenness conveys the importance of Samuel, who will play a leading role in Israel's transition to statehood. At the same time, it provides a poignant insight into the activities of a good woman, illuminates the pain of infertility, and reveals a woman's agency and autonomy in approaching God and securing divine help.

CAROL MEYERS

Hanukkah, literally "dedication," also known as *Hag Ha-Urim* or the Festival of Lights, is an eight-day holiday commemorating the rededication of the Second *Temple in the second century BCE. Hanukkah's great appeal lies in its unique symbols and its message of freedom from religious oppression. It takes place from 25 *Kislev to 2 *Tevet.

The earliest sources for Hanukkah are the First and Second Books of *Maccabees (ca. 100–125 BCE), which provide parallel accounts of the Maccabean history, from approximately 180–160 BCE. They recall a Jewish rebellion under the Maccabee family against the *Seleucid ruler Antiochus and his attempts to impose aspects of *Hellenism on the Jewish population in the Land of Israel. The Maccabees achieved several military victories over Antiochus's army, finally recapturing Jerusalem and cleansing and rededicating the Temple on the 25th of Kislev, 165 BCE, precisely three years to the day after Antiochus erected a statue of Zeus in the Temple. Hanukkah commemorates this triumphant moment and the eight days of celebration that followed, which was probably a correlation to the eight-day festival of *Sukkot (2 Macc 10:5–7).

Rather than emphasizing the military victories, rabbinic *Judaism focused on the survival of Jewish spiritual values. The *Talmud claims that when the Maccabees rededicated the Temple and rekindled its *menorah, one day's worth of oil miraculously lasted for eight days, representing God's presence in the victory (BT *Shabbat* 21b). Thus, oil and candles serve as significant Hanukkah emblems and are found in the practice of lighting the *hanukkiyah* or Hanukkah *menorah, beginning with one light on the first night and culminating in eight illuminations on the final night (in fact, there is always an additional ancillary light, the *shamash*, from which the other lights are kindled). It is customary to eat food fried in oil, such as potato pancakes (*latkes* in Yiddish) and fried doughnuts. A minor festival from a religious perspective, Hanukkah is intended to be a joyous occasion, with songs, games (e.g., the *dreidl*, a spinning top), sweets, and gift giving to children, especially monetary gifts (*gelt* in Yiddish). In recent times, particularly in North America, there has been an attempt to equate Hanukkah to Christmas because they occur at the same general time and to offer Jewish children a parallel experience. Of course, the holidays are completely different, and this comparison accentuates an inherent contradiction, because Hanukkah represents the historic Jewish insistence against assimilation.

For further reading, see Paul Steinberg, *Celebrating the Jewish Year: The Winter Holidays* (2007); Noam Zion and Barbara Spectre, eds., *A Different Light: The Hanukkah Book of Celebration* (2000); and Philip Goodman, *The Hanukkah Anthology* (1992).

PAUL STEINBERG

Hanukkah and Women. Several traditions tie women to the Hanukkah miracle. The book of Judith in the *Apocrypha, which describes how Judith of Bethulia killed the military commander Holofernes, is connected with the Maccabean victory because her act was believed to have taken place during the rebellion (see HASMONEAN DYNASTY; MACCABEES) that the festival commemorates. Similarly the heroism of Hannah, the mother of seven sons, who saw all her children slaughtered in one day for refusing to apostasize (2 Macc 7; 4 Macc 8–18), is linked with Hanukkah. The *Kitzur Shulhan Arukh* 139:3 preserves the following tradition about women's key role in the festival, apparently conflating the story of Judith with other literary elements: "It is permitted to do work during Hanukkah, but women observe the custom not to work while the Hanukkah lights are burning in the synagogue, and it is not proper to be lenient with them about it. Women are more scrupulous about it because the decree affected them severely, for they decreed that a maiden before her marriage must first have conjugal intercourse with the governor. Another reason for this is that the miracle was performed through a woman. The daughter of Johanan the High Priest was a very beautiful maiden and the cruel king requested that she lie with him. She told him that she would fulfill his request, and she fed him dishes made of cheese so that he would become thirsty and drink wine until he fell asleep, drunk. Thus it happened, and she cut off his head and brought it to Jerusalem. When their general saw that their king had been killed, they all fled. Therefore it is customary to eat dairy dishes on Hanukkah, in memory of the miracle performed by means of dairy foods."

Several customary practices in various Jewish communities during Hanukkah gave special attention to women and girls. These included bestowing special gifts on daughters and wives among Tunisian Jews, and women's gatherings that featured consumption of delicacies made with cheese, singing, and dancing in Eastern Europe.   JUDITH R. BASKIN

Haredi (pl. Haredim; literally, "Those who tremble" (in awe at the word of God [Isa 66:2 and 66:5])," is a term used to describe the most stringent forms of Orthodox Judaism. **See JUDAISM, ORTHODOX: ULTRA-ORTHODOX.**

Hasdai ibn Shaprut: See SPAIN, MUSLIM

Hasidei Ashkenaz: See MIDDLE AGES: HASIDEI ASHKENAZ

Hasidism: Europe. This pietistic movement, based on popularized forms of Jewish *mysticism, originated in the teachings of R. Israel ben Eliezer (ca. 1700–1750), known as the *Baal Shem Tov (or by the acronym, Besht) of Międzybóż, Podolia (present-day *Ukraine). The Besht and his disciples radically simplified the *Kabbalah and renounced asceticism, asserting that God should be worshiped with a joyful countenance. They held that uniquely endowed individuals known as *tzaddikim* ("righteous ones"; *rebbes* in *Yiddish) could achieve *devekut, the ecstatic state of supreme communion, even through apparently mundane activities, and then draw down divine bounty to benefit their followers. As Ḥasidism was forged into a mass movement by disciples like R. *Dov Ber, the "Great Maggid" (preacher) of Międzyrzecz, even ordinary Jews were said to be capable of attaining spiritual heights and receiving divine bounty by associating with a *tzaddik*. Ḥasidic courts and eventually dynasties emerged with distinctive teachings, modes of worship, songs and melodies (*niggunim*), dances, and political stances. After the partitions of *Poland-*Lithuania (1772, 1793, 1795) by *Russia, *Prussia, and *Austria, these dynasties exhibited pronounced regional characteristics as well.

Two related historical phenomena also led to Ḥasidism's emergence. The dissemination of printed kabbalistic works led to an increase in mystical praxis throughout the Jewish communities of the Polish-Lithuanian Commonwealth (see PRINTING). Elitist kabbalists known as *hasidim* established mystical cells, studied privileged kabbalistic texts, favored ascetic practices, and employed the kabbalistic liturgy of the sixteenth-century *Safed mystic Isaac *Luria (1534–1572). Itinerant mystical healers known as *baalei shem* ("Masters of God's Names") became increasingly prominent as well, performing exorcisms, selling amulets, and offering herbal remedies for illness, difficulty in childbirth, and so on. The Besht himself was famous as a *baal shem. However, he increasingly took on a more public role, conveying prayers to their destinations, attempting to stave off catastrophes like *ritual murder accusations, intervening in appointments of ritual slaughterers and *arrendas* (leases on manorial estates), and propounding his nonascetic *hasidism*. The expanded role of the *baal shem* evolved through his disciples into the role of *tzaddik*.

The second precursor to Ḥasidism was *Sabbateanism – the messianic mysticism of *Shabbetai Zevi, and later of Jacob *Frank, who appeared in Poland-Lithuania in 1755. Sabbateans embraced an increasingly antinomian doctrine, claiming that *God could be worshiped by committing sinful acts, including sexual deviance. The Besht and his disciples neutralized Sabbateanism's more radical *antinomianism and *apocalypticism. Because divine sparks were present in all things, they taught that God could be worshiped through mundane but licit activities like eating, drinking, singing, dancing, engaging in business, and even engaging in marital sexual intercourse, if accompanied by proper intention (*kavannah). The *tzaddik* replaced the messianic pretender. His authority was still charisma based, and he still demanded complete devotion, but he usually stopped short of making apocalyptic claims. However, several *tzaddikim* did tacitly accept messianic attributions; thus, three hundred Ḥasidim under the leadership of R. Menaḥem Mendel of Vitebsk did embark on a messianic-inspired journey to the Land of *Israel in 1777. However, most *tzaddikim* strove to provide their followers with temporary redemption in the here and now.

With the emergence of the *tzaddik* as a public leader by the end of the eighteenth century, Ḥasidism became a full-fledged movement. The *tzaddik* amalgamated several preexistent spiritual leadership roles: *baal shem*, rabbi, preacher (*maggid*), and judge. He established a court to which pilgrims would travel for inspiration, blessings, and miracles and granted followers personal audiences regardless of their social status. Pilgrims, who were disproportionately women and young men, approached the *tzaddik* with written requests for his divine intercession, accompanied by a fee known as "redemption money" (*pidyon*). The *tzaddik* was believed capable of miracles like healing, exorcisms, and guaranteeing business success or fertility. He demonstrated his attainment of *devekut* by performing standard Jewish rituals with extreme devotion, usually accompanied by convulsions and gesticulations. He was also revered for his mystical homiletics delivered in *Yiddish at the third meal (*seudat shlishit*) of the *Sabbath, after which disciples would rush to record the sermons in *Hebrew. The translations were compiled, circulated in manuscript form, and eventually published to promote the movement, inspire adherents, and, if the *tzaddik* was deceased, honor his memory. Visits to the graves of *tzaddikim* with written petitions for divine intercession also became standard practice.

R. Dov Ber, the Great Maggid of Międzyrzecz, was the most successful early *tzaddik*. Each of his own major disciples became a recognized *tzaddik* with his own court, regional jurisdiction, and distinctive style. So popular was R. Aaron of Karlin (d. 1772) that Ḥasidim in historical Lithuania became known as "Karliners." After R. Menaḥem Mendel of Vitebsk emigrated, his disciple R. Schneur *Zalman of Liady (1745–1813) assumed leadership in what is today northern *Belarus and propagated the systematic Ḥasidic formulation known as Ḥabad (an acronym for *hokhmah* [wisdom], *binah* [understanding], and *da'at* [knowledge]). R. Elimelekh of Lezajsk (1717–1786), who first set the *tzaddik* idea on a theoretical foundation, established the first Ḥasidic court in *Galicia (Austrian Poland). The Besht's great-grandson R. *Naḥman of Bratslav (1772–1810), whose allegorical tales are often considered the first works of modern Jewish literature, carried Ḥasidism southeastward into the Bratslav Palatinate. Among the most famous Ḥasidim in the more urbanized and industrialized region of Central Poland were R. Levi Isaac of Żelechów (later, of Berdyczów, 1740–1810), R. Israel "the Maggid" of Kozienice (1733/7–1815), and R. Jacob Isaac "the Seer" of Lublin (1745–1815). Several disciples of the Seer of Lublin, including R. Jacob Isaac "the Holy Jew" of Przysucha (1765–1814) and R. Simḥa Bunem of Przysucha (1766–1827), broke away and formed a more rationalistic, *Talmud-centered school of Ḥasidism. Yet other disciples of the Seer, including R. Meir of Opatów/Stopnica (1760–1831), rejected this internal reform and preserved the miracle-centered approach.

The first attempted bans against Ḥasidism, initiated by R. Elijah, the *Vilna Gaon (1720–1797), complained that Ḥasidim established separate prayer houses that employed the Lurianic liturgy; changed the prescribed times of *prayer; behaved flamboyantly during prayer, even turning somersaults; performed ritual slaughter with specially honed knives; neglected Torah study and disrespected Torah scholars; had Sabbatean ties; indulged in excessive merrymaking and pipe smoking; and followed greedy miracle-working *tzaddikim*. Subsequent bans followed the publication of the first Ḥasidic theology, *Toldot Ya'akov Yosef* (1780) and of R. Shneur Zalman of Liady's *Tanya* (1796). The latter inspired the publication of classic anti-Ḥasidic pamphlets like R. Israel

Loebel of Słuck's *Sefer Vikuaḥ* and R. David of Maków's *Zemir Arizim* (both published in 1798). Because the specific allegations of *mitnaggedim* (opponents of Ḥasidism) rarely constituted outright ritual infractions, it is likely that they were informed more by anxiety over the movement's popularization of privileged kabbalistic practices, successful institutionalization of magic and folk religion, and eventual displacement of non-Ḥasidic communal leaders. When the Vilna *kahal issued a *ḥerem (ban of excommunication) in October 1797, the Ḥasidim appealed successfully to the tsarist government, which had outlawed such bans in 1795. The resulting denunciations and counter-denunciations culminated in the arrest and brief imprisonment of R. Schneur Zalman of Liady in 1798 and 1801. Yet Ḥasidic congregations were explicitly permitted by the 1804 statute of Tsar Alexander I. Vigorous opposition gradually gave way to tolerance and accommodation, possibly as a result of the appearance of a common enemy: advocates of Enlightenment-based reform known as *maskilim*. Anti-Ḥasidism emerged as a central and defining feature of *Haskalah literature. Galician *maskilim* like Mendel Lefin and Joseph Perl were especially assertive, with the latter writing the famous Ḥasidic satire, *Revealer of Secrets*, in 1819. However, maskilic polemics did little to stem the spread of Ḥasidism, because absolutist Eastern European rulers ultimately preferred the political quietism of Ḥasidim to the potential radicalism of *maskilim*.

Notwithstanding their insularity, Ḥasidic communities were deeply affected by the partitions of Poland. In the Ukraine, Belarus, and Galicia, now ruled by absolutist Russia and *Habsburg Austria, *tzaddikim* emulated the regal style and hereditary-based succession patterns of their absolutist monarchs. R. Barukh of Międzybóż (d. 1811) established his own court, employed a jester, drove a carriage in regal display, and emphasized his hereditary descent from the Besht. Lubavitch Ḥasidism, despite its rationalistic and systematic approach to theology, first institutionalized a dynasty in 1813 when R. Schneur Zalman of Liady's son, R. Dov Ber of Lubavitch (1773–1828), prevailed in a succession conflict. Each of R. Mordecai of Chernobyl's (1770–1837) eight sons established his own royal court. R. Israel of Ruzhin (1797–1851) exceeded all in his regal behavior, basing his authority on his descent from the Great Maggid of Międzyrzecz and presiding over a luxurious court in a palace, funded by donations, *pidyonot*, and taxation of communities under his domain. The dangers of such visibility were revealed in 1838, when R. Israel was implicated in the deaths of two alleged informers against the Jewish community and imprisoned for nearly two years. R. Israel fled tsarist Russia in 1842, reestablishing his court in Sadigora, under Habsburg control.

In contrast, Ḥasidism in Central Poland emerged predominantly under constitutional regimes like the Napoleonic Duchy of *Warsaw and the "Congress" Kingdom of Poland; it was shaped by the region's economic liberalism and the industrial revolution. Polish *tzaddikim* were groomed, funded, and defended by the region's premier entrepreneurs, in particular a woman named Temerel Sonenberg-Bergson. These patrons preferred succession by star disciples rather than by sons and enabled the emergence of a more worldly Ḥasidic leadership. The multilingual R. Simḥa Bunem of Przysucha (1766–1813) was initially a lumber merchant and licensed pharmacist. R. Isaac Kalish

of Warka (1779–1848) became one of the premier lobbyists on behalf of Polish Jewry by capitalizing on constitutional guarantees. Even more insular *tzaddikim,* like R. Jacob Isaac, the Seer of Lublin (1745–1815); R. Jacob Isaac Rabinowicz, the Holy Jew of Przysucha (1766–1813); and R. Menaḥem Mendel of Kotsk (Kock, 1787–1859), eschewed the royal displays and the hereditary claims of *tzaddikim* who lived under absolutist rule. Although sons of Polish *tzaddikim* attempted to succeed their fathers, most followers gravitated to a premier disciple on their deaths. This regional distinctiveness waned with the incorporation of the kingdom of Poland into the Russian Empire in the wake of the failed Polish Insurrection of 1863. One of R. Menaḥem Mendel of Kotsk's disciples, R. Mordecai Leiner (1800–1854), broke away from the reclusive *tzaddik*, moved to Izbica, and established a dynasty known for radical teachings. On R. Menaḥem Mendel's death, another premier disciple, the scholarly R. Isaac Meir Alter (1789–1866), founded the Ger dynasty. When R. Isaac Meir died in 1866, R. Hanokh Henokh of Aleksander (1798–1870) assumed leadership. However, R. Isaac Meir's grandson, R. Judah Leib Alter (1847–1905), the *Sefat Emet,* eventually became the Gerer *tzaddik.*

After Polish independence in 1918, the Ger and Aleksander dynasties were the most popular ones. In this period, the Gerer *tzaddik* R. Abraham Mordecai Alter (1866–1948) helped form the political party *Agudat Israel (established in Katowice, 1912), which published a party newspaper, elected representatives to the Polish Sejm, and won control of many local educational and religious institutions. R. Abraham Mordecai was also unique in endorsing the *Beit Yaakov* school for Ḥasidic girls, whose education had until now been largely neglected, and in his relative toleration of *Zionism, which was vilified by other Ḥasidic leaders. The sixth Lubavitcher *tzaddik*, Joseph Isaac Schneerson (1880–1950), surreptitiously supplied underground *yeshivot* and abetted religious observance in the newly formed Soviet Union at the height of its antireligious campaign. R. Joseph Isaac later fled to Poland; he escaped from the *Warsaw ghetto to Riga, *Latvia, in 1940 and then to America with the assistance of a half-Jewish Nazi officer, *Abwehr* Major Ernst Bloch. One of the few other Ḥasidic leaders who survived the *Holocaust was Rabbi Joel Moshe Teitelbaum of Satmar (Satu Mare, *Romania/*Hungary; 1887–1979), who was rescued from the *Bergen-Belsen concentration camp through a transport arranged by Zionist leader Rudolf Kastner (1906–1957). Nevertheless, the Satmar *tzaddik* continued to condemn Zionism, which he believed had provoked the Holocaust by inciting God's destructive wrath.

Recent scholarship includes M. Rosman, *Founder of Hasidism* (1996); D. Assaf, *The Regal Way: The Life and Times of Rabbi Israel of Ruzhin* (2002); G. Dynner, *Men of Silk: The Hasidic Conquest of Polish Jewish Society* (2006); and G. Hundert, ed., *Essential Papers on Hasidism* (1991). **Map 11**

GLENN DYNNER

Ḥasidism, Europe: Women. The development of the pietistic/mystical movement Ḥasidism in eighteenth-century *Poland had a profound and lasting impact on *Eastern European Jewry. Ḥasidism brought no improvements for women's status, however, and in some ways intensified negative views of women already present in Jewish *mysticism and traditional *rabbinic Judaism. Yet, Ḥasidic tradition does preserve descriptions of daughters, mothers, and sisters of rabbinic leaders who are said to have themselves led Hasidic communities and to have adopted rigorous standards of personal piety. Among them was Sarah Frankel Sternberg (1838–1937), daughter of Rabbi Joshua Heschel Teumim Frankel and wife of the *tzaddik* Hayyim Samuel Sternberg of Chenciny, a disciple of the famed Seer of Lublin. After her husband's death, she is said to have functioned successfully as a *rebbe* in Chenciny and was highly regarded for her piety and asceticism. Her daughter, Hannah Brakhah, the wife of R. Elimelekh of Grodzinsk, was an active participant in the life of her husband's court. A. Rapoport-Albert has pointed out that there is little written documentation about these women and that their authority was based on their connection to revered male leaders.

The one apparent example of a woman who crossed gender boundaries to achieve religious leadership in a Hasidic sect with some success was the well-educated, pious, and wealthy Hannah Rachel *Verbermacher (1815–1888?), known as the Holy Maid of Ludmir. Verbermacher, who acquired a reputation for saintliness and miracle working, attracted both men and women to her "court," to whom she would lecture from behind a closed door. Reaction from the male Hasidic leaders of her region was uniformly negative, and pressure was successfully applied on Hannah to resume her rightful female role in marriage. Although her marriages were unsuccessful, they had the intended result of ending her career as a religious leader, at least in *Poland. Around 1860, Verbermacher moved to Jerusalem where she reestablished herself as a holy woman. Here, too, she attracted a following of Hasidic women and men, as well as *Sephardi and possibly some Muslim Arab women, and led gatherings at the Western Wall, the Tomb of Rachel, and her own study house.

Hasidism, with its emphasis on mystical transcendence and on male attendance on the rabbinic leader – the *tzaddik* or *rebbe* – to the exclusion of the family unit, contributed to the breakdown of Jewish social life in nineteenth-century Eastern Europe. Similar tensions between family responsibility and devotion to *Torah were also present among the non-Hasidic learned elite of this milieu, where wives tended to assume the responsibility for supporting their families while husbands were studying away from home. D. Biale has noted that the sexual asceticism of the homosocial Hasidic courts and rabbinic *yeshivot of the eighteenth and nineteenth centuries offered young men a welcome withdrawal from family tensions and the threats of modernity. However, attitudes toward human sexuality they found in these environments were often openly misogynistic, incorporating many demonic images of women from rabbinic, *kabbalistic, and Jewish *folklore traditions.

For further reading, see D. Biale, *Eros and the Jews* (1992); N. Deutsch, *The Maiden of Ludmir* (2003); and A. Rapoport-Albert. "On Women in Hasidism..." in *Jewish History*, ed. A. Rapoport-Albert and S. Zipperstein (1988), 495–525.

JUDITH R. BASKIN

Hasidism: North America. Before World War II, Hasidism was centered in *Eastern Europe with only a few thousand Hasidism living in *New York City and *Jerusalem. Since Hasidic culture was flourishing in Eastern Europe, and most Hasidic *rebbes* there strongly discouraged their

followers from emigrating, the overwhelming majority of Hasidim did not join early-twentieth-century waves of Jewish immigration to North America. For these reasons, only a small remnant of Eastern Europe's Hasidim survived the *Holocaust. The majority of these survivors emigrated either to *Israel or to the *United States. Many of the pre-war sects vanished, but some managed to set up new roots in North America. Members of sects whose leaders had perished in Europe often affiliated with one of these surviving groups.

Brooklyn, New York, is home to the major Hasidic communities in North America. Estimating population numbers for Hasidim as a whole and for specific sects is difficult; different writers come up with different figures. R. Eisenberg suggests that there are about 250,000 Hasidim in North America, 150,000 of whom live in Brooklyn alone. In Brooklyn, about 80,000 Hasidim live in Borough Park, 45,000 in Williamsburg, 15,000 in Crown Heights, and 10,000 in other neighborhoods like Flatbush. The rest of *New York City, Long Island, and New Jersey are home to about 25,000 Hasidim.

Rockland County, about forty miles north of New York City, includes some notable suburban Hasidic enclaves. A. L. Nadler has estimated the population size of several of these communities: Kiryas Joel, in Monroe, is home to about 10,000 Satmar Hasidim; Squaretown, near Spring Valley, has about 4,000 Skverer Hasidim; and Monsey has a range of Ultra-Orthodox Jews, including approximately 15,000 Hasidim, who come from Lubavitch, Satmar, Skverer, Belzer, Gerer, and other groups. Beyond the New York area, Hasidic enclaves can be found in *Los Angeles, *Chicago, Baltimore, Detroit, Cleveland, Miami, St. Louis, *Philadelphia, Pittsburgh, Denver, and *Boston. Eisenberg estimates that 20,000 Hasidim live in *Canada, predominantly in Montreal or Toronto. Satmar is the largest Hasidic group in North America, with approximately 50,000 members. Bobov and Lubavitch each claim about 20,000 to 25,000 adherents. Belzers, Gerers, Vishnitzers, Skverers, and other groups have fewer members.

The Lubavitcher Hasidim have created a Hasidic presence throughout North America (and, for that matter, the world), even where no full-fledged Hasidic communities exist. Lubavitchers, also known as *Habad (or Chabad) Hasidim ("Habad" is an acronym representing the Hebrew words *hokhmah* [wisdom], *binah* [understanding], and *da'at* [knowledge]), are the most socially activist of the major North American Hasidic sects. Their last rebbe, Menahem Mendel *Schneerson (d. 1994), emphasized outreach to secular Jews to help them learn about Judaism and ideally become more religiously observant. This outreach is highly unusual among Hasidic sects; most have little interest in influencing Jews outside their communities. Lubavitchers are centered in Crown Heights, Brooklyn, where they comprise the overwhelming majority of the neighborhood's Hasidim. However, many North American Lubavitchers live outside Crown Heights. It is typical for bright young Lubavitch couples to leave their communities and set up outreach centers, known as Habad houses, generally near colleges and universities, which offer classes, holiday celebrations, and other activities designed to teach other Jews about observant Judaism. They see themselves as emissaries of their *rebbe*, who felt passionately about this sort of outreach. Lubavitch now has emissary couples living in forty-five U.S.

states; they are also active in Canada and throughout the world.

The Satmar Ḥasidim, whose North American members live predominantly in Williamsburg, Brooklyn, and Kiryas Joel in Monroe, New York, differ radically from the Lubavitchers in some key ways. They are much more insular and generally avoid social contact with non-Ḥasidim. North American Satmars typically speak *Yiddish as their first language. Although many Lubavitchers are fluent in *Yiddish, English is their tongue of choice in North America. Lubavitchers are strongly *Zionist, whereas Satmars oppose the establishment of a Jewish state before the coming of the messiah. Satmar Ḥasidim – and, for that matter, many non-Lubavitch Jews – have also disdained the large, often vocal sector of Lubavitch society that believes their most recent *rebbe* will reveal himself as the *messiah. Lubavitchers themselves are divided about this issue; many are unsure about the messiah's identity, and some are certain that Schneerson will not be the messiah. However, because those who believe that he will be the messiah have often promoted their stance aggressively, Satmars and others sometimes see them as representing Lubavitch society. Tension between Lubavitch and Satmar has become well known and bitter.

Satmar Ḥasidim have enjoyed tremendous population growth since arriving in North America. In 1947, they numbered just a few hundred families; in the twenty-first century the group is far larger than it had been in pre-war Europe. A high birthrate and relatively low attrition help explain this remarkable success. The Bobover Ḥasidim, based in Borough Park, Brooklyn, and the Skverer Ḥasidim, centered in Squaretown (near Spring Valley, New York), have also seen impressive growth. Indeed, Ḥasidim in general seems poised to thrive in North America for generations to come.

Many outsiders assume that virtually all members of a given Ḥasidic group will think and behave in predictable ways but getting to know a range of Ḥasidim in depth will typically disprove that notion. S. W. Levine has written about her year spent among teenaged girls from Crown Heights' Lubavitch community. The girls included mainstream teens who combined a love of fun and partying with deep religious conviction; rebels who visited a strip club, experimented with drugs, and spent many hours commiserating together over their loss of faith; and a girl whose mystical focus was unusual even among her Ḥasidic peers. H. Winston's research uncovers unexpected rebellion among the Satmar Ḥasidim.

The Ḥasidic path of early marriage, large families, and strict rules for dress, diet, and religious ritual alienates some individuals, who then often choose to leave the community. These include unbelievers, gays, asexuals, and others. However, for most Ḥasidim, whose personalities mesh with their sect's expectations, life within their communities can be deeply fulfilling and infused with an overarching sense of meaning that sometimes eludes North Americans from more mainstream backgrounds.

For further reading, see R. Eisenberg, *Boychiks in the Hood: Travels in the Hasidic Underground* (1996); A. L. Nadler, *The Hasidim in America* (1994); S. W. Levine, *Mystics, Mavericks, and Merrymakers: An Intimate Journey among Hasidic Girls* (2004); and H. Winston, *Unchosen: The Hidden Lives of Hasidic Rebels* (2006).   STEPHANIE WELLEN LEVINE

Haskalah, the Jewish Enlightenment movement of the late eighteenth and nineteenth centuries, was the first organized Jewish endeavor to promote consciously and intentionally the modernization of the Jewish people. Led by engaged and critical intellectuals, the *maskilim*, the movement initiated a cultural revolution that reconstructed the face of Jewish *education, *literature, and popular thought, as well as Jewish roles in the larger society. *Haskalah* was part of the mosaic of the general European Enlightenment period, but it retained a unique Jewish character. It incorporated modern European values of the era, such as belief in human progress, criticism of earlier ideas and familiar beliefs, humanism, and an aspiration toward freedom, while also retaining a commitment to Jewish tradition. *Maskilim* were revolutionary in challenging the Jewish establishment and rabbinic leadership, but they valued Jewish collective identity and solidarity and rejected the option of assimilation.

The European Enlightenment was an eighteenth-century phenomenon. The Jewish Enlightenment, however, reached its climax in *Eastern Europe exactly halfway through the nineteenth century, in the era of nationalism and romanticism. *Haskalah* was a multifaceted movement, carried out by moderates and radicals, sensitive poets, profound philosophers (Moses *Mendelssohn, Nachman *Krochmal), ordinary teachers in provincial schoolhouses, critics of *Ḥasidism (Joseph Perl, Isaac Erter), linguists (Solomon Judah Rapoport), counter-*maskilim* who opposed rationalism (Samuel David *Luzzatto), socialist-inclined reformers with well-developed social sensitivities (Judah Leib Levine, Moses Leib Lilienblum), deists (David *Friedländer, Lazarus Bendavid, Judah Leib Mises), anticlericals (Judah Leib Gordon, Joshua Heschel Shorr), nationalists (Peretz Smolenskin, David Gordon), and conservatives (Samuel Joseph Fuenn, Eliezer Zweifel, Kalman Shulman). Yet, these individuals were united by the *Haskalah* process itself, a social-cultural stance against the rabbinic elite, a critical and liberal mentality, and membership in a communication network (most importantly, through letters and journals) that established a public forum for action. Moreover, there was an awareness of continuity that connected successive generations of *maskilim* from the eighteenth-century early *Haskalah* through the "*Berlin Haskalah" and to the *Habsburg and *Russian Empires in the late nineteenth century.

The *Haskalah* was not a consolidated and organized movement; rather it is best understood as a literary undertaking, linking writers, poets, journalists, publishers, students, doctors, and teachers who were committed to the unique project of modernizing Jews. This intellectual community imbued their historic endeavor, unprecedented in Jewish history, with utopian dimensions, as if they were redeemers bringing messianic perfection to the world. *Maskilim* were committed to educating younger generations for a life as active and recognized citizens who were part of European society and culture; they were impelled by values of tolerance and a love of humanity based on belief in a shared human nature, and they were convinced of the potential of every human being to fashion a respectable, productive, and ethical life.

EARLY *HASKALAH*: This phase of the movement began in the eighteenth century in various corners of European

Jewish society among traditionally educated young men who were curious about *science and philosophy and could not find intellectual satisfaction within the institutional boundaries of elite *Torah study. Social exclusion caused by their Jewishness increased their feelings of inferiority and cultural exclusion from the development of science and the broadening of knowledge in the surrounding culture. Such young men protested the neglect of Jewish scientific tradition and Jewish philosophy and the exclusive Jewish focus on the study of *Talmud and *Kabbalah.

The most well known and influential of these early reformers was the Berlin Jewish philosopher, Moses *Mendelssohn (1729–1786). He was the first modern Jewish humanist and the most outstanding Jewish liberal of the German Enlightenment; he was also the first modern Jewish philosopher to deal with the dilemmas of Jewish existence in the larger world. Mendelssohn was sensitive to what he saw as the insularity of the traditional Jewish community and its culture. One of his most important undertakings, a translation of the *Pentateuch to German (*Bi'ur*), was intended to draw Jews closer to mainstream society through inculcating knowledge of German; he hoped, as well, to distance Jews from understanding the Torah through either *Yiddish translations or German translations prepared by and for Christians. In his book *Jerusalem* (1783), he recommended that membership in the Jewish community be based on choice and will, and he advocated against enforcing religious allegiance and practice by coercion. In Mendelssohn's opinion, one should observe the commandments out of personal persuasion, not from the enforced pressure of the rabbinic authorities. Mendelssohn also demanded that the political state and Christian society show tolerance toward the Jewish minority and banish their own superstitions and hatreds.

In his religious thought, Mendelssohn taught that God can be recognized through the human ability to *reason, and he insisted that belief in a beneficent universal God was essential to humanist convictions. Mendelssohn also believed in the particularity of the divine *revelation to the Jews at Mount Sinai and in the unique obligations that stemmed from it: to uphold the commandments and to guard the historical inheritance and framework of Jewish national life. Nevertheless, Mendelssohn believed that God is first and foremost the creator of the world who desires the success and well-being of all created beings. By means of their intelligence, human beings can recognize God without revelation, the holy books, or the guidance of the assembly. Mendelsson was the first Jewish thinker to advocate values of religious tolerance of others for both Jews and Christians, to imagine a multicultural society in which religion and the state were separated, and to explain that Judaism contained equal measures of rationalism and tradition. Nevertheless, he was not the actual impetus behind the *Haskalah* movement, which became increasingly organized and institutionalized in the 1780s. Even so, the *maskilim* themselves, in every generation, saw him as their founder and inspiration.

PHASES OF *HASKALAH*: The history of the *Haskalah* as a cultural and social movement may be divided into five phases, spreading over one hundred and twenty years – from 1778 until the late decades of the nineteenth century. In the first phase, which was intense yet relatively short (1778–97), *maskilim* in Berlin and in Königsberg, in Prussia, burst on the scene and challenged the authority of the rabbinic

leadership. Their arguments and objectives were expressed in Naphtali Herz Wessely's "Words of Peace and Truth" written between 1782–84. Young people – private teachers and students in communities in Central, Western, and Eastern Europe – organized the activities of the *Haskalah* in this stage. These reformers sought unity through shared statements of principles, and they created literary vehicles to spread their ideas and formulate an alternative to the rabbis and communal leadership. The motivating spirit behind these initiatives was Isaac Euchel (1756–1804), a native of Copenhagen and a student of Kant at the University of Königsberg. In the latter part of 1782, he brought together a very small circle of reformers, the Society of the Friends of the Hebrew Language. The following year, Euchel and others edited and published the first periodical edition of the "The Gatherer" (*Ha-Me'assef*). By means of this printed periodical, the *Haskalah* spread from a concentrated group to a broader community from *Vilna to London. Several years earlier, in 1778, the Jewish Free School (*Freischule*), the first modern Jewish school, had been founded in Berlin. Its educational program was divided between Torah and secular subjects. As the young movement expanded, the Society for the Promotion of Goodness and Justice was formed in 1787 with the goal of organizing the *maskilim* into broadly defined frameworks and by field.

Toward the end of the 1790s, the *Haskalah* faded in Berlin; *Ha-Me'assef* was shut down in 1797, and activities declined as the *maskilim* failed to find many who sympathized with their proposed cultural renaissance of Hebrew literature. However, the *Haskalah* would not end here; its ideas, programs, and literary creations were reborn in communities in which the processes of modernization were relatively slow or had yet to begin.

In its second phase (1797–1824), the *Haskalah* flourished in Breslau, Dessau, Posen, *Prague, *Vilna, *Amsterdam, and London. Toward the end of this period, lively and militant *maskilim* founded a center of Jewish Enlightenment in Austrian *Galicia. There, they invested significant and sophisticated literary efforts in the struggle against *Hasidism, which was seen as the central obstacle to modernization of the Jews. Thus, *Haskalah* writings portrayed Hasidism as a worrisome deviation in Jewish history that perpetuated the ignorance of the multitudes, nurtured false faith, and inhibited the forward march of progress. *Maskilim* in Galicia repeatedly petitioned the Austrian state to impose measures to curb the success of the Hasidim and their expansion.

The third stage of the *Haskalah* movement was centered in *Russia and Congress *Poland. These regional movements had objectives similar to those of the Berlin *Haskalah*: *Maskilim* hoped to decrease communal autonomy, encourage a shift in Jewish occupations from financial brokerage to agriculture, mandate children to attend Jewish government schools, and implement laws regarding Jewish citizenship and army service obligations. The *Haskalah* movement in Russia consolidated in the reign of Tsar Nicholas I (1825–55), and activities were also organized in a number of communities in *Ukraine, in *Belorussia, and especially in *Lithuania. Isaac Baer *Levinsohn was considered the source of inspiration of the *Haskalah* in Russia; his programmatic "A Testimony in Israel" (1828) called for changes in education, economic life, and the position of the Jews vis-à-vis the state and non-Jewish society. The support of the *maskilim* in the 1840s for Russian government modernization programs in Jewish education alienated many Orthodox Jews who saw *Haskalah* as a threat and danger (see JUDAISM: ORTHODOX).

Jewish Enlightenment reached its peak in the second half of the nineteenth century, especially during the reign of Tsar Alexander II (1856–81). In these years the activities of the *maskilim* became an established part of the cultural milieu; Hebrew literature blossomed in a number of forms, and new journals in Hebrew, Yiddish, Polish, and Russian were developed. At this time a number of women (most prominently Miriam Markel-Mosessohn) began to take prominent roles in the movement, publishing newspaper articles, as well as songs, translations, and literary works. By the end of this fourth chapter, in 1881, *The Love of the Righteous*, the first part of an original Hebrew novel by Sarah Foner Menkin – and the first Hebrew fiction composed by a woman – had appeared.

Modern Hebrew literature was enriched during this fourth phase of the *Haskalah* with the emergence of novels, poetry, and textbooks and teaching guides for geography and history. Literary and ideological criticism by radical *maskilim* (especially Abraham Uri Kovner) insisted that literature should be mobilized to address the social problems and daily distresses of so many poor Jews; these appeals inspired some *maskilim* (Isaac Kaminer, Aaron Liberman, and others) to decry class differences and economic inequity. At the same time, in the 1860s and 1870s, Lilienblum and Judah Leib Gordon ran a cultural campaign ("Religion versus Life") against rabbinic authority. Their intent was to lighten the yoke of religious law that they believed caused significant daily difficulties to many Jews. Others, including Peretz Smolenskin, the editor of the journal "The Dawn" (*Ha-Shahar*), were concerned about the disintegration of Jewish unity and solidarity in the era of *emancipation. Warning of assimilation and the dangerous character of modern *antisemitism, they fostered a nationalist current in *Haskalah* (see LITERATURE, HEBREW: *HASKALAH*).

The fifth and last chapter of the *Haskalah* period took place in the last two decades of the nineteenth century. In this period, critical voices from within the movement and a post-*Haskalah* tendency that undermined the enterprise or, at least sought to move beyond it, strengthened. Many of the issues that were central to the *Haskalah*'s agenda had already been realized; for example, widespread acceptance of the necessity of Jewish enlightenment and professional education. Moreover, as a result of the *pogroms of the 1880s and the beginning of a Jewish nationalist movement, the urgent concerns of the Jewish public had changed. *Haskalah* was overwhelmed by new issues, including efforts to overcome skepticism about humankind's ability to construct a complete and just world free of injustice, evil, and oppression; the growth of a modern national consciousness; "the New Movement," a post-Enlightenment and revisionist protest against *Haskalah* literature championed by young authors; controversy surrounding emigration and *Zionism; increased involvement in social radicalism; and the spread of secularism. In the past, the ideas of the *Haskalah* had supplied the intellectual bridge that allowed a passage from tradition to modernity; by the end of the nineteenth century, only the old-fashioned and the second-rate still resisted the accomplishments of the Enlightenment era.

CONCLUSION: The *Haskalah* gave birth to the self-consciousness and identity of the modern Jew. With its prophetic optimism, it represented an historic turning point toward the challenges of a new era. The *Haskalah* movement was not the first attempt to introduce processes of modernization; rather it was the first to suggest an ideology that justified modernization, to mobilize common knowledge that would support it, and to suggest "road maps" and practical means of implementation in many areas of Jewish life. From a historical viewpoint, the *Haskalah* was a revolution that established precedents and templates for many trends in modern Jewish history that remain central to the lives of contemporary Jews. It shaped modern Jewish culture's receptivity to a series of concepts that encompassed a wide range of meanings. The journalist, the author, the publicist, the literary critic, and the teacher are just some of the modern types formed by the *Haskalah*. In addition, the *Haskalah* is also responsible for some central cultural creations: the modern Jewish school, teaching manuals, journals, the newspaper, the Hebrew novel, the renewal of the Hebrew language, and also for the introduction of the values of the general European Enlightenment, such as tolerance, humanism, freedom, and rational thought, into Jewish discourse. The *Haskalah* also produced a new German translation of the Hebrew Bible, updated Jewish *thought, and founded the *Wissenschaft des Judentums*, the scientific study of Jewish history and geography. Some of these contributions were restorative; that is, they returned neglected forms of culture to legitimacy and to significant places in the intellectual discourse of the time (an example is a rediscovery of rationalism in Jewish thought, particularly as exemplified by *Maimonides' *Guide of the Perplexed*).

As a cultural process, the *Haskalah* brought rejuvenation and a focus on the innovative and revolutionary to European Jewry. The first innovation was the *maskil*. These individuals represented a new type of intellectual, people of the modern Jewish spirit who maintained the spark of faith for teaching Torah and performing the commandments. They appeared in the guise of author, doctor, philosopher, student, newspaper editor, and publisher. In their celebration of the value of knowledge of the wider world and of human beings, in their cultivation of rationalist Jewish thinkers, in their criticism of deficiencies in Jewish society and the foolishness and false beliefs of Jewish piety, in their championing of an identity that combined the individual of general culture and the Jew, and in their project to renew Jewish culture and to create the modern public sphere – using journals, *poetry, *literature, and the establishment of a new Jewish library – we identify the growth of a modern Jewish intellectual elite that continues to exist in the present day.

For further reading, see S. Feiner, *The Jewish Enlightenment* (2004); S. Feiner and D. Sorkin, eds., *New Perspectives on the Haskalah* (2001); A. Altmann, *Moses Mendelssohn: A Biographical Study* (1973); D. Sorkin, *Moses Mendelssohn and the Religious Enlightenment* (1996); idem, *Orphans of Knowledge: The Berlin Haskalah and German Religious Thought* (2000); idem, *The Transformation of German Jewry, 1780–1840* (1987); S. Lowenstein, *The Berlin Jewish Community, Enlightenment, Family and Crisis, 1770–1830* (1994); N. S. Sinkoff, *Out of the Shtetl: Making Jews Modern in the Polish Borderlands* (2004); M. Stanislawski, *Tsar Nicholas I and the Jews* (1983); M. Wodzinski, *Haskalah*

and Hasidism in the Kingdom of Poland (2005); T. Cohen and S. Feiner, eds., *Voice of a Hebrew Maiden: Women's Writing of the Nineteenth Century Enlightenment Movement* (2006; [Hebrew]); and S. Feiner, *Haskalah and History: The Emergence of a Modern Jewish Historical Consciousness* (2002); **see also LITERATURE, HEBREW:** *HASKALAH.* **Map 9**   SHMUEL FEINER
(Translated by Kate Friedman)

Hasmonean Dynasty refers to the ruling family of the first independent Jewish state in the Land of Israel after the collapse of the Davidic kingdom in the sixth century BCE. The Hasmoneans ruled from 142 to 63 BCE. Beginning as rebels, they became High Priests and kings. Jewish sects, such as the *Essenes and the *Pharisees, emerged in the second and first centuries BCE, in part in response to Hasmonean rule. The Hasmonean dynastic rulers were descended from Mattathias, a Jew of priestly descent. *Josephus states that the term "Hasmonean" comes from the Greek name of Mattathias' great-grandfather, *Asamonaios* (Josephus, *Antiquities* 12.265); this name in turn may stem from a place name such as Heshmon or Hasmonah. Mattathias, who had five sons – John, Simon, Judah, Eleazar, and Jonathan (1 Macc 2:2–5) – began a rebellion in the town of Modein (seventeen miles northwest of *Jerusalem) against the *Seleucid king Antiochus IV Epiphanes (175–164 BCE) and his anti-Jewish policies. The onset of the uprising is associated with Mattathias' refusal to offer a pagan sacrifice (1 Macc 2:19–22; Josephus, *Antiquities* 12.268–78; cf. 2 Macc 8:1–7). After Mattathias died in 165 BCE, Judah the "*Maccabee" (the "hammer") assumed leadership of the revolt. Judah successively conducted several military campaigns against Seleucid forces in Palestine and oversaw the rededication of the *Temple in 164 BCE, which had become defiled with the installation of a foreign idol by Antiochus IV (1 Macc 1:54, 4:52; cf. 2 Macc 10:1–9).

After Judah was killed in battle at Elasa in 160 BCE, his brother Jonathan became leader of the movement, a position he held until 142 BCE. In this period King Demetrius I and Alexander Balas, who claimed to be the son of Antiochus IV, vied against one another for dominance within the Seleucid Empire. Both factions gave privileges to Jonathan in an effort to win his favor. From Demetrius he received the authority to muster an official army; this enabled him to occupy Jerusalem in 152 BCE, except for the Akra, a portion of the city controlled by a Seleucid garrison (1 Macc 10:6–8; Josephus, *Antiquities* 13.42). Alexander appointed Jonathan as High Priest, an office that subsequent Hasmonean rulers retained. Their retention of the *priesthood remained controversial throughout the Hasmonean period because the family was not from the Zadokite line. Anti-Hasmonean sentiment is evident in the *Dead Sea Scrolls, documents that are associated with a movement that flourished in the first half of the first century BCE. Members of this group expected the arrival of "the *messiahs of Aaron and Israel." This belief in two messiahs, one associated with the priestly *Aaron and the other with King *David, may be implicit criticism of the Hasmonean practice of having the same person hold the offices of king and High Priest.

Simon (142–135 BCE) succeeded Jonathan, who had been killed by Trypho, a pretender to the Seleucid throne. Simon formally declared the independence of Judah from the Seleucid Empire in 142 BCE (1 Macc 13:41). He also arranged the surrender of the Akra. Simon was murdered, along with two sons, while drunk at a banquet near *Jericho. His son John Hyrcanus I (135–104 BCE) then became high priest and ruler. Emboldened by the death of the Seleucid king Antiochus VII Sidetes in 129 BCE, who had attempted to besiege Jerusalem, Hyrcanus initiated numerous military campaigns and expanded Hasmonean military control of the Land of *Israel. Hyrcanus also conquered Idumea (*Edom) and required its inhabitants to convert to Judaism.

After a brief reign by Hyrcanus' son, Judah Aristobulus I (104–103 BCE), his other son Alexander Jannaeus (Jannai) ruled for nearly thirty years (103–76 BCE). His tenure as king was turbulent and chaotic. He launched wars against numerous cities in *Phoenicia, *Syria, *Moab, and elsewhere (Josephus, *Antiquities* 13.395–397). According to Josephus, the populace pelted Jannaeus with citrons (*etrogim*) during the *Sukkot festival, reflecting resentment over his status as High Priest (13.372–373). In response he had more than 6,000 Jews killed. This led to a bloody period of unrest and rebellion. In 88 BCE, opponents of Jannaeus, who were probably Pharisees, asked the Seleucid king Demetrius III Eukarios to intervene, although no lasting alliance was formed (13.376). Jannaeus had eight hundred of the rebels crucified and their families slaughtered while he watched, dining with his concubines (13.380–381).

On his death Jannaeus bequeathed power to his widow Salome Alexandra (76–67 BCE), the only Hasmonean queen. Unlike her husband, she had good relations with the Pharisees, who wielded a great deal of political power during her reign. A leading Pharisee of this period was Simon ben Shetah. Alexandra had two sons, Hyrcanus II and Aristobulus II. A war of succession broke out between them when their mother died. Aristobulus II, the younger son, won the struggle to be king, although Hyrcanus II had already been appointed as High Priest during his mother's reign. The tenure of Aristobulus II as king was brief, from 67 to 63 BCE, because *Rome eventually switched its favor from him to Hyrcanus II, whose claim to the throne was encouraged by his advisor Antipater (the father of *Herod the Great).

Hasmonean rule ended in 63 BCE when the Roman general Pompey conquered Judah. According to Josephus, when Pompey took Jerusalem, 12,000 Jews were massacred (*Antiquities* 14.70), and the general entered the Holy of Holies, the most sacred part of the *Temple compound, killing the priests while they offered sacrifices. Hyrcanus II remained High Priest from 63 to 40 BCE. The Parthians invaded Jerusalem in 40 BCE and cut off Hyrcanus II's ears, a blemish that prevented him from serving as High Priest (*Antiquities* 14.366). His son Antigonus briefly ruled as king under the Parthians from 40 to 37 BCE, at which point Herod the Great successfully occupied the land. Herod's reign, from 37 to 4 BCE as a client-king serving the *Roman Empire, brought an effective end to the Hasmonean dynasty as a political force in Israel. However, Herod the Great married a Hasmonean princess, Mariamne, with whom he had several sons. His grandson from this union, Agrippa, who ruled Judea from 10 BCE to 44 CE, was therefore a Hasmonean descendant. **Map 3**   MATTHEW GOFF

Havdalah (literally, "distinction") is a brief ceremony concluding the *Sabbath that marks the transition from a consecrated day to the ordinary days of the new week. It is traditionally a home ceremony, but is also used to conclude Saturday evening worship in many *synagogues. The *havdalah* service takes place after three stars are visible in the night sky; if for some reason it must be postponed, it may be observed as late as Tuesday evening. The ceremony includes *blessings over wine, spices, and the kindling of a braided *havdalah* candle with multiple wicks (often there are six) that are to be lit from at least two different flames. In addition, there is a central blessing that praises God who distinguishes between the holy and the mundane, light and darkness, Israel and the nations, and the Sabbath and the six days of work. A *havdalah* that closes a *festival on a weekday includes the blessing over the wine and the main benediction, but not the blessings for kindling light or spices. When a festival immediately follows the Sabbath, the Sabbath is concluded with a special *havdalah* that incorporates the *kiddush; the spices are not included, and festival candles are lit in place of the *havdalah* candle. It is customary to place the spices in a decorative container called a *besamim* box or *hadas*. The *havdalah* ceremony is often followed by the songs *Eliyahu ha-Navi* (*"Elijah the Prophet") and *Shavua Tov* ("A Good Week"). Communities observe varying practices regarding *havdalah;* they include looking at the light's reflections on one's fingernails and palms when the candle is lit, filling the wine cup until it overflows, extinguishing the candle in the wine cup, and dipping one's fingers in the wine to put drops on the forehead or in one's pockets.

ELIZABETH SHULMAN

Ḥavurah Movement. Although the concept of the *ḥavurah* ("fellowship group") originated in *Second Temple times among the *Pharisees and *Essenes, it was in the late 1960s that *ḥavurot* arose as gatherings for worship, study, and fellowship. *Ḥavurot* were seen as alternatives to established Jewish modes of worship that were perceived as formal, cold, and nonegalitarian. Generally, the younger generation preferred *ḥavurot* over their parents' more institutionalized *synagogue-based style of Judaism. The first *ḥavurah*, Ḥavurat Shalom, was organized in Somerville, Massachusetts, in 1968; among its founders were Zalman M. Schachter-Shalomi, a leader in the Jewish Renewal movement (see JUDAISM: JEWISH RENEWAL MOVEMENT), of which the *ḥavurah* was one manifestation, and Arthur Green, who later became president of the *Reconstructionist Rabbinical College. A second *ḥavurah* was started in *New York City in 1970, and other *ḥavurot* followed, often in university communities.

In accordance with the counterculture movement of the late 1960s, the search for cultural authenticity determined *ḥavurot* norms, which were often in sharp contrast to those of suburban synagogues. Instead of employing rabbis, *ḥavurot* emphasized equality of participants. Denominational labels were dropped, as *ḥavurot* stood in the vanguard of what became known as "post-denominational Judaism." *Ḥavurot* displayed several commitments, including maintaining small-sized groups, experimenting in worship, and striving toward spirituality and meaning in Jewish practice. *Ḥavurot* members believed that they could re-create Judaism in their own generation's image. *Ḥavurah* ideals permeated American Jewish life in the 1970s, in part because of the 1973 publication of *The Jewish Catalogue*, edited by Richard Siegel, Michael Strassfeld, and Sharon Strassfeld, a guide to

becoming "personally involved in aspects of Jewish ritual life, customs, cooking, crafts, and creation." This "hands-on" approach to Judaism was often accomplished institutionally as synagogues formed their own *ḥavurot*, thus satisfying their members' desires for more intimate prayer and study experiences.

In the 1980s *ḥavurot* entered the mainstream as hundreds were established throughout the United States and other countries. As Jonathan Sarna has noted, this rise of *ḥavurot* was part of a larger movement of revival within American Judaism that manifested, among other things, a quest for more Jewish knowledge as well as a desire to experience the spiritual dimensions of religious life. Often, study and socializing, rather than *worship, were the primary objectives of these *ḥavurot*. Crucial to understanding the role of the *ḥavurah* in American Judaism, as well as in American religious culture more generally, is an appreciation of the desire for Jewish survival these groups embodied. Coming as it did in the wake of the 1950s suburbanization of American Judaism, the *ḥavurah* movement was a rejection of a middle-class Judaism, seemingly constructed on Protestant models. As Riv-Ellen Prell has observed, *ḥavurah* members were not rejecting Judaism, "only their parents' version of it."

In the early twenty-first century, there are several hundred independent *ḥavurot*, primarily in the United States, but also in *Canada, *Israel, and European countries. Since 1974, an annual summer retreat has been sponsored by the National Havurah Committee, the organizing body of these fellowship groups. For further reading, see J. Sarna, *American Judaism* (2004); and R. Prell, *Prayer and Community: The Havurah in American Judaism* (1989).   RACHEL GORDAN

Hazor (Tell el-Kedah), the largest ancient site in Israel, is located in the Upper *Galilee at the western edge of the Jordan Valley. Settlement began in the Early Bronze Age. Mentioned in Syrian texts from the Middle Bronze (MB) Age, Hazor remained strategically important throughout the Late Bronze (LB) Age as well. During the MB/LB, this great walled city was home to a diverse population of *Canaanites and other Near Eastern peoples. A major destruction, occurring some time toward the end of the Late Bronze Age, ended Canaanite control. Although the Bible claims *Joshua and the Israelites (Josh 11:10–13) brought about this destruction, archeologists are less certain. The next major settlement at Hazor was *Israelite. *Solomon rebuilt the city, making it into an Israelite district capital (1 Kgs 9:15). A later king, perhaps *Ahab, also engaged in major building projects in Hazor. A highlight of Israelite Hazor was its monumental water system. The city was destroyed by the *Assyrian king Tiglath-Pileser III late in the eighth century BCE (2 Kgs 15:29). **Map 2**

BETH ALPERT NAKHAI

Ḥazzan: See CANTOR, CANTORATE: CONTEMPORARY; and CANTOR, CANTORATE: HISTORICAL DEVELOPMENT

Head Covering: Men. There is no legal requirement for a man to cover his head. Rabbinic literature tells the story of Rabbi Naḥman, whose mother was told at his birth that he would grow up to be a thief. To prevent that, she was advised to make sure that his head remained covered at all times. One day, after he had grown up and become a rabbi, he was teaching in a garden when a wind blew off his head covering. He proceeded to absent-mindedly reach across the fence and take fruit from someone else's yard (BT *Shabbat* 156b).

From this story, and the practice in many countries of men covering their heads, the idea developed that head covering was a sign of respect for God and God's commandments. Covering one's head, particularly while eating or praying, became a widespread and deeply ingrained male practice. In recent years, and especially after the founding of *Israel, the desire to wear a visible symbol of Jewishness has increased. For this reason, many observant men wear head coverings at all times.   BARRY FREUNDEL

Head Covering: Women. It was customary for respectable women in the ancient *Near East and in the Greco-Roman world to be veiled when they went outside the home. Married Jewish women followed this practiced as well, covering their hair as a sign of modesty (*tzniut*) and as an indication of their marital status. According to BT *Gittin* 90a–b, a woman who goes out in public with unfastened hair and uncovered shoulders must be divorced for her immodesty; BT *Ketubbot* 65a recalls a widow whose veil slipped during a court proceeding. She was perceived by other women as making sexual advances to their husbands and was chased out of town. Female hair covering was an absolute requirement in a society so highly conscious of sexuality and its dangers; nevertheless, it was a personal imposition and restriction from which men were glad to be exempt (*Genesis Rabbah* 17.8; M. *Sotah* 3:8).

Married women from various contemporary traditional communities cover their hair when they are in public. Different communities have different degrees of stringency; in some, women may wear wigs, and in others they might wear snoods, scarves, berets, or hats. Some women also cover their hair at home whenever a male other than their husband is present; others, including many Modern Orthodox women (see JUDAISM, ORTHODOX: MODERN ORTHODOX), have more moderate customs such as only covering the head during worship.   JUDITH R. BASKIN

Hebrew, Biblical. The vast majority of the Jewish *Bible is written in Hebrew; approximately ten chapters are in *Aramaic. Hebrew was the main language that the Judeans and Israelites spoke throughout the biblical period; it was slowly replaced by Aramaic during and after the exile in *Babylon, where Aramaic was the common language. Over several centuries, Aramaic replaced Hebrew as the main Jewish spoken language, and by the end of the biblical period (second century BCE), Hebrew was used in formal, written contexts, rather than in everyday speech. This is reflected in the fact that most late biblical and early *rabbinic works are written in Hebrew, albeit a Hebrew that betrays significant Aramaic influence. Exactly when Hebrew ceased to be a spoken language is debated.

The main source of Biblical Hebrew is the Bible. A small number of inscriptions from the First *Temple period survive; there are more from the Second *Temple era, found in the *Dead Sea Scrolls. We also have some knowledge of pre-Biblical Hebrew from pre-Israelite *Canaanite tablets written in Akkadian, the language of *Mesopotamia; these inscriptions sometimes gloss or explain an Akkadian word

with a pre-Israelite Canaanite word. Given that we do not have original versions of any biblical text and that the final form of the Bible is post-biblical, these nonbiblical sources act as important controls as we try to understand the actual Hebrew of the biblical period.

The Bible contains several dialects, which are typically defined chronologically. Most biblical texts are written in Standard Biblical Hebrew, which is close to the Hebrew spoken in *Judah at the time of the destruction of the First Temple (586 BCE). A small number of earlier texts such as the Song of the Sea (*Exodus 15) and the Song of *Deborah (*Judges 5) are in Archaic Biblical Hebrew – these have certain old forms rarely found in other texts and show some similarity to Ugaritic, a language spoken in *Syria in the pre-biblical period. A sizable section of the Bible, including *Chronicles, *Ezra–*Nehemiah, *Daniel, *Esther, and *Ecclesiastes, is written in Late Biblical Hebrew, which shows similarities to both Aramaic and rabbinic Hebrew. There are other ways of defining dialects as well. Inscriptions written in the Hebrew of *Israel, the northern kingdom, differ slightly from the Hebrew used in *Judah. The extent of northern Hebrew now found in the Bible is debated; it appears that much of it was normalized to Judean Hebrew. As in other languages, poetry (see BIBLE: POETRY) is different from prose: The former has many more rare and difficult words and has slightly different grammatical rules.

Both Aramaic and Hebrew are consonantal languages, having borrowed the alphabet developed in *Phoenicia in the late second millennium BCE; they differ from Akkadian and Egyptian, which had much more complex writing systems. The fit between Hebrew and Phoenician consonantal sounds was not perfect, which explains why there are twenty-two letters in the Hebrew alphabet, but one of these letters is pronounced in two different ways. The Hebrew and Aramaic systems developed differently over time. The current script for the Bible is an Aramaic script that was borrowed during the *Babylonian Exile and displaced the earlier Hebrew script, sometimes called paleo-Hebrew. Hebrew (and Aramaic) eventually incorporated vowel letters in the form of certain consonants that can indicate vowels. In the second half of the first millennium CE, various vowel systems written above or below the line were developed; the one ultimately adopted is called the Tiberian system, after the city of Tiberias in the *Galilee in northern Israel. We have several transliterations of Hebrew into Akkadian or Greek from the biblical or early post-biblical period; these indicate that the vowel system now used for chanting the Bible is relatively accurate, but it does not go all the way back to the biblical period.

Knowledge of the structure of Hebrew has developed over the centuries, beginning with medieval Jewish commentators and *grammarians. These scholars understood Hebrew in relation to Arabic and Aramaic and tried to show in polemical contexts that the Bible rather than the Qu'ran was written in the most beautiful pristine language. The discovery of other ancient Semitic languages in the last century and a half has also helped significantly to clarify many obscure words and grammatical structures of Biblical Hebrew.   MARC BRETTLER

Hebrew Literature: See LITERATURE, HEBREW entries

Hebrew: Modern Revival.

The revival of Hebrew as a spoken language is a unique and unprecedented phenomenon. Although Hebrew was the language of the ancient *Israelites and of most of the Hebrew *Bible, in post-exilic times it was rarely used in ordinary spoken discourse. Instead, Jews spoke the languages of the peoples among whom they lived, although they tended to write Jewish versions of those languages in Hebrew characters. Hebrew itself became the language of *prayer and study and was used by a male scholarly elite for legal writings (see HALAKHAH) and *biblical commentary. Hebrew was also a language for poetry – both for liturgical uses (see POETRY: LITURGICAL [PIYYUT]) and, in Muslim *Spain, for secular enjoyment as well (see POETRY, MEDIEVAL: MUSLIM WORLD).

The Hebrew language revival began in the latter part of the eighteenth century as part of the Jewish Enlightenment movement, *Haskalah (see LITERATURE, HEBREW: HASKALAH), in *Central Europe; it developed primarily in the second half of the nineteenth century in *Russia. The Haskalah revival of Hebrew had no initial connection to nationalist revival; rather it was part of the effort to demonstrate that the Jewish people had a cultural heritage and their own language and literary traditions. A major figure in the revival of Hebrew literature in this period was Mendele Mokher Seforim (Shalom Jacob Abramovich; 1835–1917; see also LITERATURE: YIDDISH, 1800 TO TWENTY-FIRST CENTURY). The second stage of Hebrew language revival is identified with political *Zionism and the establishment of Jewish life in the *Yishuv. The commitment to Hebrew, the language of the Jewish people in biblical times, as the language of a new Zionist society in *Palestine was implemented gradually, beginning with the First *Aliyah (1882–1903; see ISRAEL, STATE OF: JEWISH IMMIGRATION BEFORE 1948.

Eliezer (Perelman) Ben-Yehuda (1858–1922), who immigrated to Palestine in 1881, played the central role in transforming Hebrew into a modern language. Ben-Yehuda wrote a dictionary that expanded Hebrew vocabulary substantially, providing important words for transforming Hebrew into a spoken language and adapting the style of literary Hebrew for modern use. He also promoted spoken Hebrew through Hebrew language newspapers and he initiated activities to make Hebrew the daily language of Jewish life in Palestine. In 1890 Ben-Yehuda established the Committee of the Hebrew Language, now the Academy of the Hebrew Language, to modernize the Hebrew language while preserving its distinct qualities.

The national Hebrew education system that began in 1887 in Jaffa and in Jewish agricultural colonies was crucially important in the successful adoption of Hebrew in the Yishuv. Students were taught in Hebrew from a young age by trained Hebrew-speaking teachers. The Herzliyah Hebrew High School (known as the Gymnasia Ha-Ivrit Herzliyah) established in Jaffa in 1906, the Hebrew High School established in Jerusalem in 1908, and additional educational institutions in which studies were conducted in Hebrew all contributed to the fostering of a generation of people who spoke Hebrew as their mother tongue.

Nevertheless, at the beginning of the twentieth century, Hebrew was still a foreign language in many private houses and public places in the Yishuv. Further progress came with the pioneers of the Second Aliyah (1904–14), who understood that using Hebrew was a fundamental element of the nationalist revival and the formation of a new society in the Land of *Israel. The victory of Hebrew in the 1914 "War of the Languages," which occurred as a result of efforts to impose the Hebrew language on educational institutions, solidified its identity as the language of the Yishuv. In 1922, the *British Mandate government declared Hebrew an official language in Palestine together with English and Arabic, an important recognition of the national rights of the Yishuv. For further reading, see M. Brinker, "Hebrew Literature and Zionist History," Zmanim: A Historical Quarterly 105 (Winter 2009): 16–23; and E. Y. Kutscher, A History of the Hebrew Language (1981).   LILACH ROSENBERG-FRIEDMAN

Hebrew Poetry:
See BIBLE: POETRY; POETRY, LITURGICAL; POETRY, MEDIEVAL entries; POETRY: MODERN HEBREW

Hebrew Translation.

When considered as a mode of cultural communication with cultures other than one's own, translation was a major factor in the shaping of modern Jewish life. However, any attempt at providing an overall description of the role of translation in Jewish culture is highly problematic given the diversity of languages used by Jews. In many respects, the problem is similar to discussions about what is Jewish literature, a question for which there is no one satisfactory answer. Given the pivotal role of *Hebrew for all Jews, this essay offers a succinct description of the role of translation into that language.

The emergence of the Jewish Enlightenment, the *Haskalah, at the end of the eighteenth century marked the first time that translation came to occupy a pivotal position in Jewish culture as an ideologically motivated activity. Since one of the principal aims of the Enlightenment movement was to narrow the gap between Jewish life and the surrounding European cultures, it was only natural for translation to became a central vehicle for the realization of this ambitious endeavor. Early translators into Hebrew had to work within unique cultural conditions. The "cultural importation" of foreign literature was done under strict restrictions. In principle, no textual element contradicting Jewish faith was to enter the "vineyard of Israel." This dictum affected both the choice of texts for translation and the actual translation strategies. A central point in the ideology of the Haskalah was the glorification of the pure Hebrew of the *Bible (see HEBREW, BIBLICAL): In general, any text translated into Hebrew was considered automatically upgraded. This principle, however, was paired with a strong inner sense of the relative inferiority and the limited capabilities of Biblical Hebrew as a language.

Texts dealing with Jewish themes were the first choice for translators (e.g., the biblical plays of Racine); on a par with these texts were those considered to hold (moral) "usefulness" (toelet). Aesthetic considerations were rarely a reason for translation. Following European literary hierarchies, poetry and drama were translated much more often than prose. The quintessence of Hebrew translation strategy in this period may be described as an act of "Hebraizing" or "Judaizing" texts, with varying degrees of intensity. All texts were carefully expurgated of Gentile components. Hebrew nomenclature often replaced titles and names of protagonists (e.g., Ithiel ha-Kushi for Othello). The ideologically motivated linguistic purism of translators (as well as of the original authors) of the first generations of the *Haskalah* sustained an emphasis on the Bible as the supreme source for literary production. Notwithstanding a few major exceptions, most of the translations of this period are of little literary value. However, translation contributed a great deal to the revival and development of Modern Hebrew literature (see entries under LITERATURE, HEBREW), especially in the emergence of hitherto nonexistent genres, such as children's literature and ballads.

The subsequent history of translation into Hebrew up to the present follows three main lines of development. During the first phase a gradual enlargement and deepening of contact with foreign literatures developed. During the Enlightenment period the general orientation of Hebrew literature moved eastward, from German to Russian literature and toward the end of that era, stable publishing organs emerged. At this point, translators and publishers began a more or less systematic effort to introduce entire works, and even bodies of literature, into Hebrew. The particular history of Hebrew translations of Greek and Roman classics, undertaken around the middle of the nineteenth century, is a case in point. Finally, with the rise of *Zionism and the immigration of Hebraists to *Palestine (and the *United States), the normalization of translation into the Hebrew language commenced, with the adaptation of regular European translation norms. During this final period, the range of languages of origin grew steadily, with literature in English becoming a major source in the 1930s. This tendency toward Anglo-American writing (especially since the 1950s) resulted in a general change of translation policies and practices, which had previously been influenced by Russian culture.

Over the more than two centuries that have passed since the emergence of the *Haskalah*, translation has been central in fulfilling the ambitious project of bringing Jewish culture up to date with the rest of Europe. In this context, it was also a major agent in the continual process of Jewish *secularization. However, much of the initial gap (in terms of what remains to be translated into Hebrew) has still not been filled.

AMINADAV DYKMAN

Hebrew Union College-Jewish Institute of Religion (HUC-JIR).

Established in Cincinnati, Ohio, by Rabbi Isaac Mayer *Wise in 1875, this institution is the oldest rabbinical seminary in the *United States. In the early twenty-first century, HUC-JIR trains men and women to become *rabbis and *cantors and also has broadly based programs in advanced *Jewish studies, communal service, and Jewish *education at campuses in *Los Angeles, Cincinnati, *New York City, and *Jerusalem. More than sixty scholars are on the combined faculty. HUC-JIR publishes the journal *Hebrew Union College Annual*, as well as scholarly books through its Union for Reform Judaism (formerly Hebrew Union College) Press. Its principal library, located in Cincinnati, contains close to a half-million volumes of printed Judaica, plus more than six thousand manuscripts. In 1972, HUC-JIR became the first rabbinical seminary to ordain women as rabbis. Under its current president, Rabbi David Ellenson, it is strongly oriented to *Zionism, to high academic standards, and to pastoral education.

MICHAEL A. MEYER

Hebron, This city, 30 kilometers (19 miles) southeast of *Jerusalem, features in several biblical narratives. *Abraham settled "by the terebinths of Mamre at Hebron" and built an altar to *God (Gen 13:14–18). There, too, he was informed of the imminent birth of his son *Isaac (18:1–15), and nearby, he pled for Sodom (18:16–33). *Sarah died at "Kiriath-arba, which is Hebron" (23:1–2), and Abraham purchased a burial cave at Machpelah, from its *Hittite owners (23:3–20). Hebron was one of a coalition of Amorite cities conquered by *Joshua and the Israelites (Josh 10:1–11); it was allocated to the tribe of Judah (Josh 15:13). *David was anointed king over *Judah there and ruled from Hebron for seven and a half years (2 Sam 2:1–4). Hebron was fortified by *Rehoboam (2 Chron 11:5–12) and resettled in the post-exilic period (Neh 11:25). **Map 2**   BETH ALPERT NAKHAI

Hellenism (from *hellenes*, the word Greeks used to describe themselves) was the process of cultural diffusion, or hellenization, by which Greek culture mixed with native cultures in the Asian and North African regions ruled by *Alexander the Great of Macedon (d. 323) and his successors in the last three centuries BCE to create new "Greek-like" cultures. Its roots lie in the changed political and military circumstances of these lands that had formerly been under *Persian rule (although Greek culture had penetrated these areas even before Alexander). After his death, Alexander's generals (the *diadochi* or "successors") carved up conquered territories into new empires. Jews in the Land of Israel fell first under the political rule of the *Ptolemies, who were centered in *Egypt (323–198 BCE) and then of the *Seleucids of *Syria (198 BCE–ca. 165 CE). During this era, many Jews settled throughout the Hellenistic world, especially in cities like *Alexandria and Antioch, forming a significant Greek-speaking *Diaspora.

With these political changes came profound cultural changes, as conquered peoples, Jews among them, embraced the Greek language. In addition, the arrival of Greek troops and traders and the founding of Greek-style cities led to the spread of Greek forms of education and entertainment (gymnasiums, theaters), as well as literary styles and philosophical ideas. This merger of local and Greek cultures produced new ways of worshiping, governing, learning, and living. Jews, like others, faced remarkable challenges to traditional ways of life. The vibrancy and creativity of this foreign culture prompted complex responses of acceptance and resistance. Greek culture was appealing to many Jews, both in *Judea and the Diaspora; scholars no longer suppose Judaism in the Land of Israel to have been largely untouched by Hellenism. Most Jews welcomed some of these new cultural and political ideas, adapting them to fit their own needs. However, they were wary of other aspects of Hellenism, especially those that might clash with Jewish religious beliefs.

By the third century BCE, many Jews read Greek literature and had begun to use Greek for writing and translating Jewish texts. The *Septuagint translation of the *Bible was a response to the needs of Diaspora Jews who were unable to read *Hebrew. Many Jews adopted Greek names and eagerly moved into newly founded Greek cities in Judea and the Diaspora, where they interacted with and learned from Gentiles. They arbitrated disputes according to Hellenistic (non-Jewish) law; Jewish material remains (coins, monuments, tombs) contain Greek inscriptions and Hellenistic, and sometimes pagan, images. Jewish writers adapted Greek literary genres and philosophical ideas. For example, 4 *Maccabees and perhaps *Ecclesiastes were influenced by Stoicism; Ezekiel the Poet was influenced by Greek tragedies, and Demetrius by Greek histories. Some Jews (Aristobulous, Eupolemus) even argued that the greatest Greek thinkers were dependent on the religious and philosophical insights of biblical heroes. This paradoxical claim, seeking to find Jewish roots for Greek accomplishments, reflects an uncomfortable recognition of the depth of Hellenistic influence on contemporary Jewish thought. Even groups one might think were hostile to Hellenism were undeniably influenced by it. The *Hasmoneans, who violently defended traditional Jewish practices, nonetheless used Greek names, minted Greek-style coins, and adopted Greek titles and political structures. The conservative *Qumran community focused on topics formerly of little interest to Jews but reflective of Hellenistic thought, such as communal ownership, celibacy, and utopianism (see also PTOLEMIES: IMPACT ON JEWISH CULTURE AND THOUGHT).

However, only a few Jews unreservedly adopted all aspects of Greek life (1 Macc 1:43; 2 Macc 4:13). The emergence of a shared language and practices and of trends that minimized ethnic and cultural differences prompted a Jewish counterreaction, particularly against aspects of Hellenism that appeared to threaten Judaism and Jews' distinctive religious identities. Rituals that separated Jews from Gentiles, like *Sabbath observance, *circumcision, and *dietary restrictions, increased in prominence (1 Macc 1:60–63; 3 Macc 3:4; Joseph and Asenath 7:1; Jubilees 15:11; see APOCRYPHA; PSEUDEPIGRAPHA). Hellenistic idolatry and polytheism were harshly decried (Joseph and Asenath 7:3; Wisdom of Solomon 13–15). Jews excoriated Gentile sexual practices (e.g., homosexuality; Letter of *Aristeas 152). This counterreaction reinforced the boundaries between Jews and Gentiles at a time when such boundaries were being lowered. Ironically, some of the harshest attacks appear in texts written in Greek and influenced by Hellenistic rhetoric (e.g., Wisdom of Solomon), highlighting the tension between Jewish acceptance and rejection.

For further reading, see V. Tcherikover, *Hellenistic Civilization and the Jews* (1959); M. Hengel, *Judaism and Hellenism* (1974); J. Barclay, *Jews in the Mediterranean Diaspora* (1996); and L. Levine, *Judaism and Hellenism in Antiquity* (1998).

ADAM GREGERMAN

Ḥerem is a ban of excommunication. It was the ultimate sanction available to Jewish *communal organizations in the Middle Ages and Early Modern Period to discipline recalcitrant members of the community. Offenses could be in a range of areas, including business and civil matters and family disputes, as well as doctrinal disagreements (see *SPINOZA. BARUCH). Excommunicants were cut off from any contact with local and neighboring Jewish communities in all realms of life until they expressed remorse for their actions (and made compensation where appropriate).

Ḥerem ha-yishuv (literally, "ban on settlement") was a restriction on residence imposed by established medieval and early modern Jewish communities on other Jews, mainly for economic reasons. It appears to have originated in Rhineland Jewish settlements in the eleventh century, spread throughout Europe, and persisted as late as the eighteenth century in *Italy. The right to forbid other Jews from settlement in a particular location was understood to fall within the autonomy Jews were granted by regional authorities. Such communal controls restricting settlement of newcomers were also common among non-Jews. The ordinance protected the economic livelihood of Jewish residents by limiting competition and permitted a community to reject paupers and individuals of questionable moral character. Since the concept of closed communities conflicted with the Jewish value of hospitality, some leaders and scholars supported a ḥerem ha-yishuv only when it excluded violent men, informers, or other individuals perceived as problematic. A ḥezkat ha-yishuv ("right of settlement") could sometimes be acquired from the Jewish communal organization (kehillah) by purchase or hire, as well as by inheritance.

JUDITH R. BASKIN

Herod and Herodian Dynasty. Herod the Great (ca. 74 BCE–4 BCE) was a local ruler (or "client-king") in the Land of Israel put in place and supported by *Rome. He was the second son of Antipater II, a powerful courtier of Idumean origins (see EDOM), who served the *Hasmoneans and made alliances with various Roman leaders after 63 BCE. Herod was appointed tetrarch (the ruler of a portion of a province) of *Galilee at age twenty-five. Antigonus II Mattathias, also known as Antigonus the Hasmonean, seized control of *Jerusalem in 40 BCE, and Herod fled to Rome to ask for support in regaining control of Judea. He was appointed "King of the Jews" in 40 BCE by the Roman Senate, but did not recapture Jerusalem and defeat Antigonus until 37 BCE. This victory marked the end of the Hasmoneans and the beginning of the Herodian Dynasty, although Herod attempted to maintain both his family's link with the Hasmoneans and favor with his Jewish subjects by marrying Mariamne, a member of the royal family. Herod's kingdom comprised *Judea, *Samaria, *Galilee, Idumea, Batanea, and Parea. In 20 BCE, Herod began an extensive reconstruction of the Second *Temple; his many other building projects included the port city of Caesarea, Panias in Galilee, as well as many religious shrines and fortresses (see ARCHEOLOGY, LAND OF ISRAEL: SECOND TEMPLE PERIOD). Throughout his reign, Herod imposed heavy taxes and used brutal methods to maintain his power; he executed his wife Mariamne, three of his sons, a mother-in-law, and a brother-in-law, among many others.

After Herod's death in 4 BCE, Emperor Augustus apportioned a section of the kingdom to each of Herod's three surviving sons by various wives. Archelaus ruled briefly in Judea and Samaria, but was replaced by a Roman procurator in 6 CE. Herod Antipas, the Herod who figures in the *New Testament, became tetrarch of Galilee and Perea and ruled until 39 CE when he was exiled by Emperor Caligula; among other projects, he built Tiberias as his capital and the city of Sepphoris. Philip was appointed over the provinces between the Jordan and Damascus where he ruled until his death in 34 CE. Agrippa I (10 BCE–44 CE), a grandson of Herod through his son Aristobulus (whom Herod executed in ca. 7 BCE) and Berenice (daughter of Herod's sister Salome), succeeded his uncle Philip. He was subsequently given control over the territories of Herod Antipas and parts of Judea that had been ruled by Herod Archelaus. Agrippa's son Agrippa II (d. ca. 92 CE), the last of the dynasty, was educated at the court of Emperor Claudius in Rome. He was appointed ruler of the northern parts of his father's kingdom. **Maps 3, 4**

ELIZABETH SHULMAN

Herzl, Theodor (1860–1904) was the founder of modern political *Zionism. Born in Budapest, he moved to *Vienna with his family when he was eighteen; although he earned a doctorate in law from the University of Vienna, he focused his career on literature and journalism. Herzl was transformed by the vicious *antisemitism that was a feature of Vienna and by the onslaught of anti-Jewish feeling he observed during the *Dreyfus Affair in Paris, where he was a correspondent for Vienna's *Neue Freie Presse*. In his 1896 *Der Judenstaat* (The Jewish State), he argued that Jews must declare themselves a nation, leave Europe, and create a Jewish state in *Palestine. With virtually no knowledge of others who shared this goal, Herzl began to construct the necessary institutional framework for a Zionist entity. He founded *Die Welt*, a Zionist newspaper; called for an international Zionist congress to assemble in 1897; and undertook negotiations with the *Ottoman Empire, Great *Britain, and *Germany for a "charter" for a Jewish state. The First Zionist Congress, held in Basel, Switzerland, in August 1897, adopted the Basel Program, a statement of the goal of the Zionist movement to establish a home for the Jewish people in Palestine secured under public law. The Congress also established the World Zionist Organization, and elected Herzl president. Herzl convened the Zionist Congress yearly; during these meetings the Jewish National Fund was developed. Although world leaders were generally not receptive to his proposals, the British government offered Herzl the possibility of a large autonomous Jewish settlement in East Africa. In 1903, at the Sixth Zionist Congress, he proposed the Uganda Program as a temporary solution for Russian Jews seeking refuge. This proposal, which caused significant controversy within the movement, was ultimately rejected by the Seventh Zionist Congress in 1905 after Herzl's untimely death. In 1949, Herzl's remains were reinterred on Mount Herzl in *Jerusalem.

ELIZABETH SHULMAN

Heschel, Abraham Joshua (1907–1972), philosopher, theologian, and social activist, was born in *Warsaw and immigrated to the *United States in 1940. A descendant of distinguished Ḥasidic dynasties (see ḤASIDISM: EUROPE), he was named after his great-great-grandfather, Abraham Joshua Heschel, the *rebbe* of Apt (Opatow). A child prodigy who mastered *Bible and *Talmud, as well as Jewish *mysticism and Ḥasidic traditions, Heschel published talmudic commentaries (*novellae*) in a Warsaw Orthodox monthly when he was fifteen. He received rabbinic ordination at sixteen, but left Warsaw for the secular, *Yiddish-language Real-Gymnasium in *Vilna, Lithuania, to prepare for university study. In *Berlin, he earned a degree from the *Hochschule für die Wissenschaft des Judentums*, a liberal rabbinical institute, and completed a PhD in philosophy at Friedrich Wilhelm University in 1933, with a minor in the history of art. In the same year, a collection of Heschel's Yiddish poems, *Der Shem Hameforash: Mentsh* (God's Ineffable Name: Man), which anticipate his mature theological system, was published in Warsaw.

Heschel remained for several years in Berlin, teaching and writing book reviews and essays for the Berlin Jewish community newspaper. His second book, a biography of *Maimonides, appeared in 1935. Impressed by Heschel's learning and personal piety, Martin *Buber invited Heschel to replace him at the Central Organization for Jewish Adult Education in *Frankfurt where he taught at the *Jüdisches Lehrhaus*, founded by Buber and Franz *Rosenzweig. In October 1938, Heschel was expelled from *Germany, along with thousands of other Jews with Polish passports. He returned to Warsaw and taught at the Institute for Jewish Studies for one academic year; in July 1939 he left for London on a transit visa. Invited to join the faculty of the *Hebrew Union College, the *Reform rabbinical seminary in Cincinnati, Ohio, Heschel reached *New York City in March 1940. He learned two years later that his mother and two sisters had perished in the Warsaw ghetto. In the United States, Heschel initially taught at Hebrew Union College; in 1945 he joined the faculty of the *Jewish Theological Seminary of America, the Conservative seminary (see JUDAISM: CONSERVATIVE), in New York, where he remained as Professor of Jewish Ethics and Mysticism until his death. In December 1946 he married Sylvia Straus, a concert pianist; they had one daughter, Hannah Susannah, herself a Judaic scholar and activist.

A consummate literary stylist, Heschel elaborated a vivid *theology of divine presence, a "*God of pathos" emotionally concerned about human events. Heschel's writings uniquely explore the intellectual and experiential foundations of traditional Judaism, combining philosophical polemic and lyrical prose to express the passion of a personal faith. *The Earth is the Lord's: The Inner Life of the Jew in East Europe* (1950) memorializes the Yiddish-speaking culture destroyed in the *Holocaust. *The Sabbath: Its Meaning for Modern Man* (1951) both analyzes and evokes the sanctification of time, not space, as the cornerstone of Jewish spirituality and culture.

Heschel's international renown began with the publication of *Man Is Not Alone: A Philosophy of Religion* (1951), and he clarified his Jewish sources in the companion volume, *God in Search of Man: A Philosophy of Judaism* (1955), which guides readers toward religious insight and the ethical and spiritual meaning of Jewish observance. *Man's Quest for God* (1955; reprinted as *Quest for God*) challenges contemporary religion to regain contact with the living God through *prayer. An anthology of Heschel's writings, *Between God and Man* (1959; bibliography revised in 1975), with an introduction to Heschel's life and works by editor Fritz A. Rothschild, defines the coherence of Heschel's philosophy of religion. Heschel also published a Hebrew multi-volume study on the multiplicity of talmudic theologies, *Torah min ha-shamayim be-aspaklaryah shel ha-dorot* (1962, 1965, 1996); it was translated and edited by Gordon Tucker with Leonard Levin as *Heavenly Torah as Refracted through the Generations* (2004).

In the 1960s, Heschel became a public intellectual; the mass media recognized him as a prophetic figure. His book, *The Prophets* (1962), an expansion in English of his 1933 Berlin doctoral dissertation, presents his identification with those ancient Hebrew critics of moral complacency. Heschel spoke dramatically at national events such as White House Conferences on Children and Youth (1960) and on Aging (1962), and the first National Conference on Religion and Race (1963). As a theological consultant during the

Second Vatican Council in *Rome (1962–65), Heschel played a crucial role in the formulation of *Nostra Aetate* (In Our Times), the official document of the Roman Catholic Church that affirmed the autonomy of Judaism in its own right and rejected the mission to convert the Jews. Heschel was one of the first Americans to protest against the persecution of Jews in the *Soviet Union.

Heschel joined Martin Luther King, Jr., at the Selma–Montgomery *civil rights march of 1965 and became the first Jew to join the faculty of Union Theological Seminary (1965–66) in New York City as the Harry Emerson Fosdick Visiting Professor. Many of his speeches and essays on contemporary issues are collected in *The Insecurity of Freedom* (1966) and *Moral Grandeur and Spiritual Audacity* (1996). In *Who Is Man?* (1965), based on his 1963 Fred West Memorial Lectures at Stanford University, Heschel summarizes his biblical philosophy of human holiness in terms that reject atheistic existentialism.

The last years of Heschel's life were painful and intense. As a co-founder in 1965 of the antiwar organization, Clergy and Laity against the War in Vietnam, he participated in demonstrations, prayer meetings, and rallies. The 1967 war in which Israel was threatened with destruction by its Arab neighbors affected him deeply; his book, *Israel: An Echo of Eternity* (1969), attempts to explain to Christians the depth of Jewish attachment to the Holy Land. Despite a massive heart attack in 1969, Heschel continued to teach, write, and advance *interfaith dialogue and cooperation. In 1972, the last year of his life, he completed two books, *A Passion for Truth (1973)* and *Kotsk: In gerangl far emesdikayt* (Struggle for Integrity, 1973); both are about Heschel's heretofore implicit role model, the dissident and uncompromising Ḥasidic rebbe, R. Menaḥem Mendel of Kotzk, whom he compared to Søren Kierkegaard. His other model, the optimistic and generous *Baal Shem Tov, the founder of Ḥasidism, exemplified Heschel's faith in and love of God and humankind.

Abraham Joshua Heschel's charisma derived from historical experience as well as faith and religious learning. He embodied the complete Jew, a person possessing immense religious and secular learning yet capable of profound emotion. His insistence on humankind's moral responsibility included an agonizing awareness of the Nazi destruction of *Eastern European Jewry and the conviction that political action must advance God's involvement in human life.

Important works about Heschel and his thought include J. Merkle, *The Genesis of Faith: The Depth Theology of A. J. Heschel* (1985); H. Kasimow and B. Sherwin, eds., *No Religion Is an Island: A. J. Heschel and Interreligious Dialogue* (1991); E. K. Kaplan, *Holiness in Words: Abraham Joshua Heschel's Poetics of Piety* (1996); E. K. Kaplan and S. H. Dresner, *Abraham Joshua Heschel: Prophetic Witness* (1998); and E. K. Kaplan, *Spiritual Radical: Abraham Joshua Heschel in America, 1940–1972* (2007).

EDWARD K. KAPLAN

Ḥeshvan is the eighth month of the Jewish calendar, usually falling in October or November of the Gregorian calendar. It is sometimes called Mar Ḥeshvan, "bitter Ḥeshvan" because there are no holidays in this month. **See also CALENDAR; CALENDAR: MONTHS OF THE YEAR.**

Hezekiah was the thirteenth king of *Judah, who reigned for twenty-nine years beginning ca. 715 BCE,

succeeding his father, Ahaz (2 *Kgs 18:1–2). Praised as Judah's most God-fearing king (2 Kgs 18:5–7), Hezekiah repaired the *Temple, removed idolatrous elements from *Israelite religion, and expanded Judah's territory (2 Kgs 18:4). Hezekiah combined religious reform with political unification by centralizing worship in *Jerusalem. During his reign, Sennacherib of *Assyria invaded Judah, and Jerusalem was besieged until Hezekiah agreed to pay tribute. In anticipation of the possibility of a siege, the Gihon Spring had been diverted by underground tunnels into the Siloam pool within the Jerusalem city walls (2 Kgs 20:20; 2 Chron 32:2–4, 30). The Siloam inscription in "Hezekiah's tunnel," discovered in 1880 and now in Istanbul, records the meeting of two teams of stonecutters working from opposite directions and is dated to Hezekiah's reign. **See also ARCHEOLOGY: ANCIENT TIMES TO PERSIAN PERIOD; ISRAELITES: KINGSHIP; LACHISH. Map 2**   KATE FRIEDMAN

High Holidays (also High Holy Days) are the most hallowed period of the Jewish year. Spanning ten days from *Rosh Ha-Shanah (1st of *Tishri) until *Yom Kippur (10th of Tishri) and generally occurring between late August and early October according to the secular calendar, the High Holidays are a time of self-examination, judgment, and *prayer. Also known as the Ten Days of Repentance (*aseret yemei teshuvah*), they mark a holy season of spiritual renewal when human beings are to contemplate their relationship with God. The *Bible does not use the designation "High Holidays"; rather it is an English derivation from the term *yamim noraim* (literally, "Days of Awe"), coined by the fourteenth-century Ashkenazic authority, Jacob Moellin, known as the Maharil. In addition, the Bible does not refer to Rosh Ha-Shanah as the "Head of the Year," which is a rabbinic development. The Torah simply identifies Rosh Ha-Shanah as the first day of the seventh month, which should be observed as a sacred occasion with "loud blasts" (Lev 23:23–25). This description would eventually become the source for sounding the *shofar* (ram's horn). Some scholars, however, suggest that the sounding of the *shofar* was to indicate the arrival of *Sukkot, a pilgrimage *festival exactly two weeks later.

Around the time of the destruction of the Second *Temple in 70 CE, the day was named Rosh Ha-Shanah and was said to be a time when human beings are judged (M. *Rosh Ha-Shanah* 1:2). The three primary themes of the holiday – God's sovereignty, remembrance, and *shofarot* – were also established then. The theme of God's sovereignty is associated with the acceptance of God as creator and Rosh Ha-Shanah's designation as the "birthday" of creation. The theme of remembrance denotes God's special relationship to those individuals "remembered" and thus deemed worthy of fulfilled promises and reward. *Shofarot* recalls the ascribed biblical reading for Rosh Ha-Shanah (Gen 22) – the *akedah ("binding") – which tells of *Abraham sacrificing a ram instead of his son *Isaac and alludes to the divine promise that God would forgive Abraham's descendants if they sounded the *shofar*. Simultaneously, the Rabbis established connections between Rosh Ha-Shanah and Yom Kippur. Yom Kippur, a biblically mandated day of *atonement, expiation of sins, and purification, was related to Rosh Ha-Shanah when the Rabbis wrote, "All are judged on Rosh Ha-Shanah and the verdict is issued on Yom Kippur"

(T. *Rosh Ha-Shanah* 1:13). Thus, the concept of High Holidays or *yamim nora'im* was born.

The medieval codes of Jewish *halakhah (law) specify particular observances for the days between Rosh Ha-Shanah and Yom Kippur, which help maintain the proper spirit of the season. They include the recitation of additional *prayers and supplications (e.g., *avinu malkeinu* ["our father, our king"]) and fasting, most notably on the *Fast of Gedaliah (3rd of Tishri). The day before Yom Kippur has its own unique significance. Customs for the day include the controversial practice of *kaparot* ("expiatory offerings" – swinging and slaughtering a fowl as a form of atonement), reciting a confessional, and eating a large, festive meal prior to the Yom Kippur fast.

For further reading, see P. Steinberg, *Celebrating the Jewish Year: The Fall Holidays* (2007); T. H. Gaster, *Festivals of the Jewish Year* (1952); R. Hammer, *Entering the High Holidays: A Guide to Origins, Themes, and Prayers* (1998); and I. Klein, *A Guide to Religious Jewish Practice* (1979).   PAUL STEINBERG

Hillel, also known as Hillel the Elder (ca. 70 BCE–ca. 10 CE), was a leader of the *Pharisees during the reign of *Herod. He is among the most famous sages of the *Second Temple period, founder of a *tannaitic school (Beit Hillel [House of Hillel]), and ancestor of a dynasty of *Patriarchs who held office in the Land of Israel for the next few hundred years. He was born in *Babylon into a family claiming *Davidic lineage and studied there before moving to *Jerusalem. He was said to have paid for his schooling with his earnings from manual labor before his appointment as *Patriarch (*nasi*) and head of the *Sanhedrin. Hillel is usually linked with his contemporary, Shammai, who also led a group of disciples (Beit Shammai). Although their disagreements were generally minor, Hillel is regarded as a more lenient interpreter of *halakhah, and his rulings are usually favored. Hillel developed a system of *rabbinic hermeneutics with seven rules of biblical interpretation that were later expanded to thirteen rules by R. Ishmael ben Elisha. He also enacted the *prosbul*; this word, of Greek origin, refers to a legal strategy that eliminated the cancellation of debts in the biblically ordained sabbatical year (Deut 15:1–6). The *prosbul* allowed lenders to protect their investments and enabled the poor to obtain essential loans (BT *Gittin* 36a). When asked to explain the entire *Torah while standing on one foot, Hillel's classic response was, "What is hateful to you, do not do to your fellow; this is the whole Torah; the rest is commentary – go and study" (BT *Shabbat* 31a).   ELIZABETH SHULMAN

Hillel Foundations. Hillel: The Foundation for Jewish Campus Life is the principal organization serving Jewish college and university students in the *United States and *Canada. Founded in 1923 at the University of Illinois, Urbana-Champaign, Hillel began as a classic campus ministry designed to meet the spiritual needs of Jewish students studying away from home. The organization grew rapidly under the aegis of *B'nai B'rith and the leadership of historian Abram Sachar, expanding across the continent during the next several decades. Sachar would later serve as the founding president of Brandeis University.

The B'nai B'rith Hillel Foundations benefited from a pluralist religious framework engaging rabbis from multiple movements, a national-local partnership under the B'nai

B'rith banner, social restrictions to full Jewish participation in university life, and a virtual monopoly given the relatively low level of Jewish communal interest in university students. Hillels offered a proverbial "home away from home" in an overwhelming Christian environment, providing Jewish students with religious, social, cultural, and leadership opportunities. Hillels also pioneered serious university-level Jewish learning in the pre-*Jewish studies era. Hillel Foundations played a heroic role before, during, and after *World War II in helping rescue and resettle European Jewish faculty and university students. They emerged on more and more campuses as a result of the post-war GI Bill and the entry of increasing numbers of Jewish families into the middle class.

The countercultural forces unleashed in the 1960s had a profound impact on Jewish life on campus. Mainstream organized religious activities, identified as part of "the establishment," attracted fewer students. As discriminatory barriers fell, Jewish students attended elite colleges in larger numbers and participated more fully in every aspect of university life. B'nai B'rith, the principal funder, like other fraternal organizations, also fell on hard times as a result of changing social norms. Although a number of campus Hillel Foundations adapted to these major cultural changes and planted the seeds of organizational transformation, Hillel as a movement fell into a steep decline.

If Abram Sachar shaped and nurtured the organization during its formative stages, another future university president, Richard Joel, a former prosecutor and law school dean, dramatically reshaped and rejuvenated Hillel during the 1990s. Joel downplayed the "synagogue on campus" model and inspired a vision of campus communities engaging a wide variety of Jewish interest groups. He encouraged Hillels to focus less on membership numbers and more on increasing participation or "doing Jewish." He also urged Hillels to become less concerned with constructing buildings, even as new Centers for Jewish Life were opening from coast to coast, and urged that they connect with Jewish students in a range of campus and community settings. Joel's approach attracted large numbers of talented professionals from a variety of backgrounds into Hillel's salaried ranks at the local and national level. He spearheaded Hillel's independence from B'nai B'rith and attracted major funding from Jewish philanthropists, foundations, and federations.

In the early twenty-first century, Hillel has became a prototype of Jewish organizational transformation and renewal with a new national headquarters in Washington, DC; a growing presence in *Israel, the former *Soviet Union, and *Latin America; affiliates at virtually every major university in the United States with a significant Jewish student population; and signature programs and partnerships in the areas of Israel, community service, arts and culture, student engagement, Jewish learning, celebration, and global exchange.   JAY RUBIN

Hirsch, Samson Raphael (1808–1888) was an Orthodox rabbi (see JUDAISM, ORTHODOX: MODERN ORTHODOX), theologian, community leader, educator, and publisher. Hirsch was the leader for most of his life of the *Frankfurt am Main *Israelitische Religionsgesellschaft* (Israelite Religious Society [IRG], also known as *Adass Jeschurun*), and played a central role in articulating "Neo-Orthodoxy," a response to Jewish religious reform in mid-nineteenth-century *Germany. His *theology combined limited modernization of religious practice; strict fidelity to *halakhah; deep commitment to the German language, culture, and social integration; and, ultimately, separation of Orthodox communities from larger, *Reform-dominated official Jewish communities.

Born in 1808 in Hamburg, Hirsch received both a religious and Gymnasium education. The chief rabbi of Hamburg was Isaac Bernays (1792-1849) and the religious milieu he established there had a decisive impact on Hirsch's enthusiasm for the harmony of Orthodox belief and practice with limited modernization. Hirsch attended university at Bonn for a year in 1829–30, and along with classmate Abraham *Geiger, founded a university society for German Jewish students. Opting to pursue a rabbinical career, Hirsch studied in Mannheim under the tutelage of Rabbi Jacob Ettlinger, a preeminent German halakhist and early experimenter in Orthodox popular publication. In 1830, Hirsch accepted the position of district rabbi in Oldenburg, an auspicious beginning to an impressive rabbinic career that took him ultimately in 1851 to Frankfurt am Main via Aurich and Osnabruch in Hannover (1841) and Nikolsberg, Moravia (1846).

It was during Hirsch's early career that religious reform, a simmering issue in Jewish communities throughout the German territories, intensified, and Hirsch emerged as one of its most vocal foes (see JUDAISM, REFORM: GERMANY). His opposition was highly nuanced, however. He embraced many cosmetic modernizations favored by reformers; like Bernays, Hirsch adopted German clerical dress, emphasized decorum in religious worship, accepted some rearrangement of *synagogue interiors, and advocated the use of German in *sermons. He believed that intimate Jewish participation in German culture was wholly compatible with committed Orthodox belief. At the same time, Hirsch defended the centrality of the entirety of Jewish law in his earliest treatises, the *19 Letters* (1836) and *Horeb* (1837). The emergence of a sophisticated German Jewish reading public proved to be among Hirsch's most potent tools; he reached out to his readers through his monthly *Jeschurun* (launched in the fall of 1855), a journal of Orthodox thought and culture, in which he aimed at creating a full sense of the meaning of being an Orthodox Jew in German society. Topics covered in the journal included discussions of religious education, home life, engagement with German political and social issues, and, in serialized form, a comprehensive commentary on the *Torah, the Jewish *calendar, and ritual.

As head of the IRG, Hirsch's greatest legacy was a key component of his thought: that secession by the Orthodox minority from the official Jewish community was justified to preserve the standards of Orthodox practice. This secession was accomplished for the IRG in 1876, after lengthy debate in the Prussian parliament, in an act that set a significant precedent for the interaction of Orthodox and non-Orthodox communities in Germany and beyond.

For further reading, see N. Rosenbloom, *Tradition in an Age of Reform: The Religious Philosophy of Samson Raphael Hirsch* (1976); and R. Lieberles, *Religious Conflict in Social Context: The Resurgence of Orthodox Judaism in Frankfurt am Main, 1838–1877* (1985).   JESS OLSON

Hittites designates two different ancient peoples, one originating in Anatolia (modern *Turkey) and the other a *Canaanite nation said to be descended from *Noah's great-grandson, Heth (Gen 10:15); it is unclear whether there is any connection between the two groups. *Abraham purchased *Sarah's burial place, a field and cave in *Hebron, from Ephron the Hittite (Gen 23). *Esau married two Hittite women (Gen 26:34); King *David enlisted Uriah, a Hittite soldier (2 Sam 11); and *Solomon married Hittite women (1 Kgs 1:11). From *exile in *Babylon, *Ezekiel invoked Israel's Hittite (and Amorite) antecedents to remind the people of their lowly, idolatrous beginnings and to admonish their faithlessness (16:3).   KATE FRIEDMAN

Holland/Netherlands: See AMSTERDAM; ANNE FRANK; HOLOCAUST MEMORIALS; LITERATURE: CONTEMPORARY EUROPE; MENASSEH BEN ISRAEL

Holocaust comes from the word *holokauston,* the Greek translation of the Hebrew *olah,* which is used in the *Torah to denote sacrificial offerings that were totally consumed by fire. The English word "holocaust" was first used in the sense of genocidal murder by the *New York Times* in 1895 to describe a Turkish massacre of Armenians. Today, the term is most often used to describe the *Nazi persecution and murder of Jews throughout Europe between 1933 and 1945, although some have used it to describe other genocidal crimes as well. During World War II, some Jewish commentators used another Biblical *Hebrew word, *shoah* ("catastrophe," "disaster," "suffering,"), to describe the Nazi genocide of Europe's Jews, and this word continues to be used in this more specific designation.

The origins of the Holocaust lie deep in European history and can be traced to the growing body of anti-Jewish prejudice that evolved in the early centuries of *Christianity. Toward the end of the nineteenth century, a new form of anti-Jewish prejudice, *antisemitism, emerged that blended religious prejudice, traditional folklore, cultural stereotypes, and economic resentment with new pseudo-scientific theories about race. This "racial" antisemitism became one of the cornerstones of a political movement that developed in *Germany after World War I and was led by Adolf Hitler. However, antisemitism and its corollary prejudices alone could not have produced the Holocaust. It was the success of Hitler's National Socialist (Nazi) Party in German elections in the early 1930s that transformed these pernicious ideas into German public policy between 1933 and 1945. Historians have long argued about the intentions of Hitler and the Nazi Party regarding Germany's Jews. What is certain is that from the moment that Hitler became chancellor of Germany on January 30, 1933, he and his Nazi movement began to implement a broad policy to force Germany's half-million Jews out of the country.

Initially the term "Holocaust" was applied only to Jewish victims of Nazi persecution. In the past few decades, however, scholars have pointed to other genocidal victims of the Nazis, particularly the handicapped or disabled and the *Roma. In addition, gays, Polish Christians, Soviet POWs, and others were caught up in the growing net of Nazi persecution and death. However, for the Germans, the Jews were always the principal group of victims. Hitler considered them a threat to his dream of creating a pure Aryan world. From the Nazi perspective, the Jew's supposed "principal crime" was a lust for power. Drawing from the fictitious late-nineteenth-century tsarist document, *The Protocols of the Elders of Zion* (see RUSSIA), which claimed that there was a secret Jewish plot to take over the world, Hitler embraced the idea of an international Jewish conspiracy and linked it to Vladimir Lenin's seizure of power in Russia in late 1917. In the 1920s and 1930s, the Nazis, who blamed the Jews for everything that had gone awry in the aftermath of the German defeat in World War I, insisted on a connection between Jews and *Bolshevism, linking Germany's Jews with the hated and feared *Soviet Union.

DOMESTIC PHASE, 1933–1939: The Holocaust officially began on January 30, 1933, and ended with the defeat of Germany in the spring of 1945. The evolution of Nazi policy can best be understood by dividing the Holocaust into three distinct phases. The first is the German domestic phase, between 1933 and 1939, when the Nazis cautiously developed a series of policies designed to force as many Jews as possible to leave Germany. However, the Jewish question was secondary at this time to the German leadership's main efforts to consolidate their power and prepare Germany for a war of expansion that would give Hitler the *lebensraum* or "living space" he felt he needed to build his Thousand Year Reich. Nazi hostility toward the Jews remained controversial within the party until the "Night of the Long Knives" purge by the virulently antisemitic SA (*Sturmabteilung*) in the summer of 1934. By the fall of 1934, Hitler was secure enough in power to give his top leadership the authority they needed to pressure Germany's Jews to leave.

By 1935, German Jews, who had been stripped of most of their political, social, and economic rights, had little reason to stay in Germany. From Hitler's perspective, what was called for was a set of laws to define and legislate the diminished status of Jews in the Reich. The result was the Nuremberg Laws. Hastily written (and later expanded), they were passed by the Reichstag during the Party Days in Nuremberg in September 1935. There were three laws: the *Blutschutzgesetz* (Law for the Protection of German Blood and Honor), the *Reichsburgergesetz* (Reich Citizenship Law), and the *Ehegesundheitsgesetz* (Marital Health Law). These laws and their supplements defined who was Jewish and declared that Jews could only have rights in Germany as "subjects of the state." They also outlawed *marriage between Jews and non-Jews and created a mechanism to prevent such marriages.

However, the Nazi leadership was not successful in forcing large numbers of Jews to leave in the mid-1930s, partly because few countries were willing to open their doors during a worldwide economic depression. In addition, the uneven nature of Germany's anti-Jewish policies caused some Jews, who would lose everything if they left, to imagine that the worst of Germany's antisemitic persecution had passed. Moreover, there was a lull in the persecution of Jews, driven in large part by Germany's desire to show the world a civilized face while it hosted the 1936 Winter and Summer Olympics. However, once the Olympics ended, pent-up Nazi frustration with the Jews exploded into a growing crescendo of violence, which culminated in the *Kristallnacht* pogrom on November 9–10, 1938.

It is important to understand the psychology that drove much of Nazi policy regarding Germany's Jews. Once Hitler had consolidated his hold on power in 1934, he constantly gambled internationally to see what he could get away with. With the announcement of the reestablishment of the draft and German rearmament in 1935, the unchallenged occupation of the Rhineland, and the successful Olympics a year later, Hitler and his inner circle became more and more convinced of his genius. Emboldened by Hitler's international successes, particularly in 1938 when he took over *Austria and then later convinced the Western powers to give him part of *Czechoslovakia as well, some of his top followers such as Joseph Goebbels decided to respond disproportionately to the Paris murder of a lower level German diplomat, Ernst vom Rath, by a young Jew, Herschel Grynszpan, in early November 1938. The *Kristallnacht* pogrom that followed was a Nazi-sponsored riot that destroyed or damaged 1,500 synagogues and thousands of Jewish businesses and homes; scores of Jews were murdered as well. On November 16, the Gestapo rounded up 30,000 Jewish men and sent them to the Dachau concentration camp outside of Munich. *Kristallnacht*, which means "night of broken glass," was controversial in and outside of Germany; it infuriated some of Hitler's closest associates who were concerned about its impact on the German economy and the country's image abroad. However, Nazi leaders were in agreement when it came to assigning blame: The Jews were responsible for the pogrom, and Germany's Jewish community should be required to pay 1 billion *Reichsmarks* ($401 million) for the murder of vom Rath and the damages caused by the riot. *Kristallnacht* also represented a major turning point in German policy toward its Jews. On January 30, 1939, Hitler told the Reichstag that if Jewish financiers "once again" plunged Europe into war, the result would not be the bolshevization of the world, but the "annihilation of the Jewish race in Europe."

INVASION OF POLAND, 1939: The second phase of the Holocaust began with the German invasion of *Poland on September 1, 1939, which triggered the outbreak of World War II. From the Nazis' perspective, Poland consisted of two racially inferior groups: Jews and Polish Christians. As a nation, it stood in the way of Hitler's dreams of creating an Aryan-pure Europe. Once German troops moved into Poland, they, in league with the *Einsatzgruppen* (paramilitary mobile killing units), began to murder Polish political, educational, and religious leaders in an effort to destroy any sense of Polish nationhood. Poland itself was divided, with a little more than half of the country turned over to Germany's new ally, the Soviet Union. Western Poland was integrated into the Greater Reich, whereas what remained under German occupation was transformed into the General Government for the Occupied Areas of Poland. The General Government became Nazi Germany's dumping ground for persecuted minorities such as Jews and Roma. Five of the Germans' six death camps were opened in the General Government in 1942.

In the midst of the Nazi campaign against Poland's Christians, the Germans also began to develop policies toward Poland's Jews. Pre-war Poland had a Jewish population of 3.3–3.5 million. About two million Polish Jews were trapped in the German zone at the beginning of the war, and the rest found themselves under Soviet rule. Jews living in those parts of western Poland integrated directly into the Reich were forced into the territory of the General Government. At the end of September 1939, Reinhard Heydrich, the Chief of the Security Police and the SD and one of Heinrich Himmler's principal associates, ordered the creation of *Judenräte* (Jewish Councils) and *Ältestenräte* (Elders Councils) to act as liaisons between the SS and Jewish communities within the General Government to ensure that Poland's Jews obeyed German dictates. During the first year of the German occupation, the Nazis stripped Polish Jews of all of their property and rights, leaving them desperate and impoverished. In addition, the Jews in the General Government were forced into ghettos to isolate them from the rest of the Polish population. The ghetto system was designed to exploit Jews as slave labor, a policy intended to kill Poland's Jewish population (see HOLOCAUST: GHETTOS).

By the summer of 1940, Nazi leaders were frustrated by the fact that they had still not developed a policy to deal with the growing Jewish populations under their control. Nazi leaders developed two plans for shipping Europe's Jews to Madagascar, which had been taken over by the Germans after the conquest of *France in June 1940. By the end of the summer, however, the SS had lost interest in Madagascar and began to develop new ideas for dealing with the Third Reich's growing Jewish population.

In the fall of 1940, Hitler began to develop plans for the invasion of Soviet Union, a country he saw as the center of "Jewish Bolshevism." This German plan, Operation Barbarossa, envisioned a quick victory that would destroy Joseph Stalin's armed forces and give Germany control over the Soviet Union's vast economic resources. Russia would then become a prime Aryan breeding ground for Hitler's Thousand Year Reich. Stimulated by their track record of easy victories in other parts of Europe and by Hitler's growing sense of invincibility, the Germans planned an invasion that would really be an extermination, intended to eliminate not only Soviet Russia's hated *communist elite but also the country's five million Jews. Specially trained *Einsatzgruppen* were given principal responsibility for the initial mass murder of Jews in territories that fell under German control; they were aided by other units drawn from Himmler's paramilitary units, the *Wehrmacht*, and native collaborators throughout western Russia. By the end of 1941, these units had murdered between 500,000 to 800,000 Jews in mass executions. Those Jews not murdered on the spot were sent to new ghettos in occupied parts of the Soviet Union.

The initial successes of German forces in the Soviet Union triggered a new discussion about how to deal with Russia's Jews. After talks with Hitler in July 1941, Himmler told Rudolf Höss, the commandant of the *Auschwitz concentration camp, that the *Führer* had ordered the *Endlösung der Judenfrage* (Final Solution of the Jewish Question). He added that Höss, working closely with Adolf Eichmann, Himmler's specialist on Jewish deportations, was just the person to carry out Hitler's wishes. On July 31, 1941, *Reichsmarschall* Hermann Göring, who was still technically in charge of Germany's Jewish policies, signed a decree that many scholars think provided Heydrich with the authority to begin planning for the "Final Solution." Over the next six months, the SS experimented with various methods of murder, using Zyklon B at Auschwitz I and gas vans at Chełmno near Łódź The SS also began to recruit specialists from the earlier T-4 program in Germany, which had been developed to engage in mass murder of the handicapped and the disabled. These

"euthanasia" specialists in mass death and body disposal provided the SS with the expertise needed to develop the final stages of the Final Solution.

FINAL SOLUTION, 1942–45: By the end of 1941, the mass murder of Jews in Russia was common knowledge to most top-ranking government and Nazi party leaders. Consequently, Heydrich decided to call a meeting at an SS villa in Wannsee, a suburb outside of Berlin, to ensure coordination between the various government and party agencies involved in various aspects of the Final Solution. Initially planned for December 9, the *Wannsee Conference was postponed after the Japanese attack on Pearl Harbor two days earlier and rescheduled for January 20, 1942. By this date, plans for the implementation of the Final Solution were almost complete. Once the meeting began, Heydrich announced that the SS was now fully in charge of the "Jewish Question." His goal was to oversee the complete annihilation of Europe's eleven million Jews. He planned to use the Nuremberg Laws to determine who was Jewish, which prompted a discussion about *mischlinge* (individuals who were partly Jewish).

What followed was the mass movement of Jews from various parts of German-occupied Europe to the General Government, where five of Nazi Germany's six death camps were opened. The first was at *Chełmno (Kulmhof) in the Greater Reich near Łódź (Litzmannstadt). Three camps– *Bełżec, *Sobibór, and *Treblinka – were opened as part of *Aktion Reinhard* to murder the 2.3 million Jews now in the General Government. The SS opened *Majdanek in the suburbs of Lublin as both a death camp and forced labor camp. Yet it was Auschwitz, Hitler's "factory of death," that became the symbol of the Final Solution (see HOLOCAUST: CAMPS AND KILLING CENTERS).

Approximately half of the six million Jews murdered during the Holocaust met their fate in these death camps. The Germans and their collaborators murdered the rest in mass field killings, in ghettos and occupied communities, in forced or slave labor camps, or in transit to the "East." Estimates are that the Germans murdered 1.1 million Jews in Auschwitz, 874,000 in Treblinka, 600,000 at Bełżec, 250,000 at Sobibór, 147,000 at Chełmno, and 80,000 in Majdanek.

Initially, German policy focused on murdering all Jews in Europe. Jews were deported to death camps from all areas and regions occupied by the Nazis. However, there was a constant struggle between the SS and other organs of state about the efficacy of murdering Jewish slave laborers who had become an important part of the German war economy. Those Jews who managed to survive the mass killings of 1941–1943 generally did so as slave laborers working in unimaginably horrible conditions. Their survival was due in large part to efforts at spiritual resistance that helped Jewish workers and inmates maintain a sense of dignity and humanity (see HOLOCAUST RESISTANCE).

The Germans did everything possible to delude Jews into thinking that their transfers to death camps were moves to better living conditions in labor camps. Such policies worked to a point, but by the time that the Germans began to liquidate the major ghettos in the General Government, word had spread about the real purpose of the transports. It was in the midst of these transfers that some of the most heroic acts of resistance took place in Warsaw, Treblinka, Sobibór, and other ghettos and camps. The most famous of these Jewish uprisings was in the Warsaw ghetto between April 19 and May 16, 1943, when a handful of young Jewish rebels held out against several thousand crack German troops.

The Holocaust ended once Allied troops liberated the scattered death and concentration camps in what remained of German-occupied Europe in 1944 and 1945. The Red Army liberated Majdanek in July 1944 and Auschwitz in January 1945. By this time, the Germans had forced most Jews in the East to participate in death march to camps in the Greater Reich. When World War II ended on May 7–9, 1945, 3.3 million Jews were still alive in Europe out of a pre-war population of 9.5 million.

For further reading, see M. Berenbaum and A. J. Peck, eds., *The Holocaust and History: The Known, the Unknown, the Disputed, and the Reexamined* (1998); R. Breitman, *The Architect of Genocide: Himmler and the Final Solution* (1991); C. Browning, *The Origins of the Final Solution: The Evolution of Nazi Jewish Policy, September 1939–March 1942* (2004); D. M. Crowe, *The Holocaust: Roots, History, and Aftermath* (2008); *Encyclopedia of the Holocaust*, I. Gutman, editor in chief, 4 vols. (1990); and R. Hilberg, *The Destruction of the European Jews*, 3rd edition, 3 vols. (2003).   DAVID M. CROWE

Holocaust: Camps and Killing Centers.

Immediately following Adolf Hitler's elevation to power as Germany's chancellor on January 30, 1933, the *Nazi Party began to open concentration, forced labor, and other types of camps to incarcerate individuals deemed to be criminal, political, biological, or racial enemies of the state. Over the next twelve years, the Nazi government expanded this network to include *ghettos and death camps in which Jews throughout German-occupied Europe were incarcerated and murdered.

The Nazis opened Dachau, their first major concentration camp (*Konzentrationslager*), in the spring of 1933. Its first commandant, Theodor Eicke, developed a strict administrative system that became the model for similar camps throughout Nazi-occupied Europe. These camps were run by the SS (*Schutzstaffel;* "security squad") and its death's head units (*Totenkopfverbände*). The SS built crematoria at Dachau, but there is some controversy over whether a gas chamber was used there. Dachau was the site of some abhorrent military-related medical experiments by SS and *Luftwaffe* physicians who infected some inmates with malaria and subjected others to deadly high altitude and low temperature experiments. Others were forced to drink large quantities of seawater.

Initially, Jews were not sent in large numbers to concentration camps because German policy was intended to drive the Third Reich's half-million Jews out of the country by gradually depriving them of civil, economic, and political rights. This all changed after *Kristallnacht ("Crystal Night" or "Night of Broken Glass") on November 9–10, 1938. Soon after, the Gestapo (secret state police) rounded up 30,000 Jewish men and sent them to the Dachau, Buchenwald, and Sachsenhausen concentration camps. Germany had already occupied Austria in the spring of 1938 and opened the Mauthausen concentration camp. About a third of the 119,000 inmates who died there during the Holocaust were Jews. After the German takeover of what remained of *Czechoslovakia in the spring of 1939, the region was transformed into the Protectorate of Bohemia and Moravia and the SS began to persecute Czech Jews. In October 1941,

Reinhard Heydrich, the Protectorate's deputy *Reichsprotektor*, and Adolf Eichmann, one of Heinrich Himmler's top deportation specialists, decided to open a new camp north of Prague in the town of Terezín (Theresienstadt). This was initially a ghetto for elderly and privileged Reich Jews, but Eichmann later transformed it into a special "show" camp to dispel rumors about the "Final Solution."

To maintain this façade, Eichmann, who kept an office at Theresienstadt, allowed the ghetto's large community of scholars, writers, musicians, and artists a certain amount of creative freedom to study, write, and compose. In 1944, Joseph Goebbels' propaganda office produced a film, *Theresienstadt: Ein Dokumentarfilm aus dem jüdischen Siedlungsgebiet* (Documentary Film of the Jewish Resettlement), that was later shown to a visiting Red Cross delegation. Fifteen thousand children passed through Theresienstadt on their way to death camps in occupied Poland. Some of their art and poems has been published in *I Never Saw Another Butterfly*, edited by Hana Volavkova. More than 33,000 Jews died in Theresienstadt, and more than 87,000 were sent on to death camps.

The Germans and the Soviets conquered and divided *Poland in the fall of 1939. Two million Polish Jews were trapped in the German zone in the west, and 1.3–1.5 million came under Soviet control. After the integration of certain portions of western Poland into the Greater Reich, the Germans transformed what remained into a region they called the General Government. Five of Nazi Germany's six death camps were opened in the General Government in 1942 as part of the "Final Solution of the Jewish Question." The deadliest of these camps was *Auschwitz (Oświęcim) where the Germans murdered almost a million Jews, along with 70,000–75,000 Poles, 21,000 *Roma, and 15,000 Soviet POWs. More than two-thirds of the Jewish victims were from Hungary (438,000) and Poland (300,000). Auschwitz was unique both for its size (25 square miles) and sense of permanency. In addition to its three major camps, Auschwitz I, II, and III, Auschwitz had a large network of *Nebenlager* or subcamps. Auschwitz I was the *Stammlager* (main camp) or concentration camp, Auschwitz II–Birkenau was the death camp, and Auschwitz III–Buna/Monowitz was the I. G. Farben complex that used slave labor to manufacture synthetic rubber. *Chełmno (German, Kulmhof), not Auschwitz, was the only fully operational death camp in the Third Reich. Himmler opened it in late 1941 to murder Jews and Roma in the Łódź ghetto and the Warthegau district of Greater Germany. The Germans murdered 147,000 Jews and 5,000 Roma at Chełmno from 1941 to 1944. Unlike Chełmno, *Majdanek was a sprawling (676 acres) death and forced labor camp. It opened in the summer of 1941 as the Waffen-SS POW Camp Lublin and later as the Waffen-SS Concentration Camp Lublin. More than 360,000 of Majdanek's half-million prisoners would die there; 16% were Jews.

In late 1941, Himmler asked Odilo Globocnik, the Higher SS and Police Leader in the Lublin district, to develop *Aktion Reinhard*, an SS program designed to murder the remaining 2.3 million Jews in the General Government in three temporary death camps: *Bełżec, *Sobibór, and *Treblinka. Six hundred thousand Jews died in Bełżec between February and December 1942. Sobibór was located about sixty-five miles northeast of Lublin. Commandant Franz Stangl and his staff murdered 250,000 Jews between April 1942 and September 1943 before transforming it into a farm. The concentration camp Treblinka, located in a remote area northeast of Warsaw, was the deadliest of the *Aktion Reinhard* death camps. From July 1942 until early August 1943, the Germans murdered 874,000 Jews and several thousand Roma at Treblinka. The camp was shut down after an uprising on August 2, 1943. Although the SS shot many of the camp's remaining prisoners during the escape, the rebels were able to destroy part of the camp. Unfortunately, the brick gas chambers remained intact and were used for several more weeks before Treblinka was closed and totally demolished. Ten weeks later, a similar rebellion took place at Sobibór. Hundreds of Jewish inmates attacked their guards and escaped, although the SS later captured about half of them. Himmler ordered Sobibór closed and the site turned into a farm. He then initiated Operation *Erntefest* (Harvest Festival) to murder all of the Jews still alive in the Lublin district. On November 3, 1943, the SS and Order Police murdered 42,000 to 45,000 Jews in the Trawinki, Pontiatowa, and Majdanek forced labor camps.

The last major rebellion of the Holocaust took place in Auschwitz in the fall of 1944. On October 7, 1944, three hundred *Sonderkommandos*, who had just learned of Himmler's plans to close Auschwitz, blew up crematorium IV and fought the SS with hammers and axes. The SS killed 451 Jews during the uprising and executed others involved in the plot. Two weeks later, a smaller rebellion took place after a Jewish woman shot two SS guards. Himmler ordered the destruction of the crematoria at Auschwitz I and II after the October 7 rebellion. When the Soviet army liberated Auschwitz on January 17, 1945, all that remained of its once vast prisoner population were 7,000 sick or dying inmates.

For further reading, see M. T. Allen, *The Business of Genocide: The SS, Slave Labor, and the Concentration Camp* (2002); Y. Arad, *Belzec, Sobibor, Treblinka; The Operation Reinhard Death Camps* (1987); Auschwitz-Birkenau State Museum, *Auschwitz, 1940–1945*, 5 vols. (2000); D. Cesarani, *Becoming Eichmann: Rethinking the Life, Crimes, and Trial of a "Desk Murderer"* (2004); D. M. Crowe, *The Holocaust: Roots, History, and Aftermath* (2008); H. Langbein, *Against All Hope; Resistance in the Nazi Concentration Camps*, trans. H. Zohn (1994); L. Poliakov, *Harvest of Hate: The Nazi Program for the Destruction of the Jews of Europe* (1979); and W. Sofsky, *The Order of Terror: The Concentration Camp*, trans. W. Templer (1997).

DAVID M. CROWE

Holocaust Denial is the attempt to refute the fact that approximately 5.1 to 6 million Jews were targeted simply because they were Jews – deprived of their legal rights, employment, homes, and possessions; dehumanized; and systematically murdered by the *Nazi regime and its collaborators before and during World War II (1939–45). Holocaust denial is not a homogeneous ideology; those who deny the Holocaust have diverse motivations, and statements of denial can be made in many different ways. The Holocaust is refuted by a broad range of groups, from radical right-wing hate mongers, to "revisionists" seeking scholarly legitimacy, to radical Muslim groups desiring the destruction of *Israel.

The origins of Holocaust denial can be traced to the Nazi perpetrators themselves. Nazi policies to murder the Jews were cloaked in secrecy, and the Nazis attempted to cover up or eliminate evidence of their destructive aims even while the process was under way. Official Nazi language regarding the planning and the process of murdering Europe's Jews was shrouded in euphemism; terms like "special treatment" were used to signify murder by gassing. When defeat became inevitable the Nazis tried to erase evidence of their plans by destroying documentation and eliminating forensic evidence, such as the crematoria in *Auschwitz-Birkenau.

These Nazi attempts to hide their crimes deprived prosecutors, historians, and others of significant evidence that could have been used to re-create the events of the Holocaust in full. This missing documentation accounts for much of the historiographical debate on the Holocaust that has continued since the Germans were defeated. Even today, the exact number of Jews murdered remains elusive, and there is no extant documentation of a clear order by Hitler or anyone else to destroy European Jewry. These gaps in the historical record have led some to question whether the Nazis actually intended the deliberate elimination of Europe's Jews. These deniers often state that, although many Jews lost their lives during World War II, there was no official Nazi policy to murder the Jews and that the Jews who were killed were casualties of war.

Many deniers want their theories popularized, seeking attention in hopes of opening a "legitimate debate" on whether the Holocaust happened. They want to be considered scholars or historical "revisionists," allegedly using historical methodology to prompt reconsideration of generally accepted assumptions about an historical event. Yet, deniers stray far from accepted methodological approaches; for instance, by falsifying evidence or disregarding overwhelming evidence that counters their claims. They often focus on discrediting one piece of evidence in order to argue that the entire event never happened at all. Robert Faurisson, who denied the existence of gas chambers, and David Irving, who was deemed a Holocaust denier by a British court in 2000 after an unsuccessful libel case he brought against historian Deborah Lipstadt, are two prime examples of Holocaust deniers.

Deniers often begin their claims with the illogical credo that the Holocaust was a "hoax" and lapse into solipsism, basing their "proof" that the Holocaust did not happen on other deniers' false claims and unsubstantiated arguments. Because deniers present an irrational negation of a historical event, legitimate historians – who operate within the realm of accepted logic and methodology – have little ability to counter their claims. Holocaust deniers are often motivated by *antisemitism, racism, or particular political beliefs. Thus, some argue that the Holocaust is an invention of a "world Jewish conspiracy" to advance the interests of world Jewry and specifically *Israel. Often they use the denial or severe minimization of the Holocaust as a means of questioning Israel's legitimacy. Others negate the Holocaust because they are true believers in Nazi ideology and hope for its resurgence in the political realm, seeking to remove the "negative stigma" of claims of genocide against the Nazi regime. These deniers include radical right-wing groups, neo-Nazis, and others who believe that Nazism was an effective political philosophy.

Holocaust denial is prevalent on the internet, especially on sites based in the United States where the First Amendment guarantees freedom of speech. In contrast, in some countries like Germany and Austria, Holocaust denial is illegal, and those who would deny the Holocaust in public are subject to prosecution.

For further reading, see D. Lipstadt, *Denying the Holocaust: The Growing Assault on Truth and Memory* (1994); M. Shermer and A. Grobman, *Denying History: Who Says the Holocaust Never Happened and Why Do They Say It?* (2002); R. Evans, *Lying about Hitler: History, Holocaust, and the David Irving Trial* (2002); and R. J. van Pelt, *The Case for Auschwitz: Evidence from the Irving Trial* (2002).

CHRISTINE SCHMIDT VAN DER ZANDEN

Holocaust Diaries. Jewish men, women, and youth from throughout Europe wrote diaries during the years of the *Holocaust. Although we will never know precisely how many people kept diaries, the hundreds of diaries that have turned up since the war's end suggest that thousands likely existed. Diary writing was thus a widespread phenomenon that constituted one significant component of Jewish cultural responses to persecution by *Nazi Germany and its collaborators. Unlike *memoirs and post-war testimonies, diaries reveal Jewish victims' perceptions and self-understandings in the midst of their increasingly desperate situations.

Diaries reflect the diversity of European Jewry on the eve of World War II as well as their varied wartime circumstances. The most widely read Holocaust diary, that of Anne *Frank, illuminates the situation of those acculturated *Central and Western European Jews who understood that their lives were in danger and who had the means and opportunity to go into hiding. These individuals had little comprehension of what awaited them in *Poland should they be captured and deported. The well-known diaries of Adam *Czerniakow, Emanuel *Ringelblum, and Chaim Kaplan attest to the range of Polish Jewish identities during this period and offer a multifaceted portrait of life in the *Warsaw ghetto, from the Polonized engineer (Czerniakow) who worked on a daily basis to improve the situation of his co-religionists in his capacity as head of the Jewish Council in Nazi-occupied Warsaw; to the leftist *Poalei Zion* community activist and historian Ringelblum who spearheaded the creation of the *Oyneg Shabes* underground archive and played a leading role in the Warsaw ghetto uprising; to Kaplan, the Hebrew elementary school principal who made it his mission to chronicle with candor the unprecedented crisis confronting Polish Jews. The diary of Victor Klemperer meticulously describes the experience of a university professor and German Jewish convert to Protestantism who was never deported from Dresden because of his "privileged status" as the spouse of a non-Jewish German. What even this brief summary of a few of the best-known diaries reveals is the complexity of Jewish identities during the Holocaust. Many individuals underwent subtle or even radical transformations in their conceptions of what it meant to be Jewish and German – or Polish or French, etc. – as a result of the persecution they were experiencing and their realization that they were facing death. We are privy to their wartime struggles because of the deliberate efforts of Jews to document their experiences.

The heterogeneity of Jewish victims is also evident in the different motivations that compelled people to write diaries. Many Jews turned to diary writing because they sought to connect their present suffering to the deeply rooted Jewish literary tradition of writing in response to catastrophe. Jewish diary writing also confirms the transformation of Jewish cultural practices in the nineteenth and twentieth centuries as part of the process of Jewish acculturation to European societies, in which diary writing had become a means of autobiographical reflection, intellectual exploration, and historical documentation. Some individuals were prompted to bear witness to their wartime experiences in hopes that their diaries would furnish evidence in the pursuit of justice after the war and in the writing of history. And for individuals with relatives abroad, diaries became a vehicle for imparting information about the fate of their family members to be delivered at war's end.

The content of diaries was largely determined by the diarists' reasons for writing. As a result, the body of source materials grouped under the rubric "diaries" is quite varied in subject matter and style of writing. Diarists who sought to contribute evidence for future historians, such as Herman Kruk in the *Vilna ghetto, Philip Mechanicus in the Dutch transit camp Westerbork, David Sierakowiak in the Łódź ghetto, as well as Kaplan, Ringelblum, and Klemperer, described everything from daily efforts to procure food, family and social relations, Jewish leadership, educational and cultural activities, religious responses, and news and rumors about the war and the fates of other Jews. Some diaries focused on intimate thoughts and feelings, especially, although not exclusively, those written by adolescents. Some diaries were written anonymously and others were signed; some diaries were written by individuals acting independently, and others were written by individuals participating in underground group efforts to record Jewish experiences. Finally, some diaries were revised or edited by their writers, whereas others remained unedited.

Certain aspects of Jewish victims' experiences during the Holocaust barely register in diaries. The impossibility of procuring writing supplies, as well as the lack of privacy and hiding places, meant that few people wrote diaries in concentration and extermination camps. Anne Frank's diary is a perfect illustration of this lacuna in the evidence; her diary stops three days before her deportation from *Amsterdam, which means that we must turn to other sources for information about her experiences in Westerbork, *Auschwitz, and Bergen-Belsen. At the same time, there are some notable exceptions. Among them are the diaries and notes written by three Jewish men who worked in the gas chambers and crematoria in Auschwitz-Birkenau. The manuscripts had been buried on the grounds of the crematoria and were discovered after the war.

Even in ghettos and in hiding, writing a diary proved emotionally and physically difficult. Paper, writing instruments, and privacy were in short supply in those settings where staving off hunger and evading round-ups for forced labor or deportation took precedence. Moreover, diaries endangered the lives of diarists and their helpers. As a result, some individuals discontinued their diaries. Others wrote in guarded language or avoided certain topics altogether out of consideration for other people's lives.

Although Holocaust diaries, taken together, are not a complete chronicle of Jewish experiences and perceptions during the Holocaust, they nonetheless open up aspects of Holocaust history that are otherwise inaccessible. Diarists' interpretive efforts are also significant because they reveal many Jews' efforts to translate their experiences into language and transmit them to others. In so doing, diarists attempted to empower themselves within the tremendous constraints imposed on them. They tried to allay the fear that nothing would remain of their lives and their worlds by recording their experiences, hoping that doing so would be affirming to themselves as well as to future readers.

For further reading, see R. Feldhay Brenner, *Writing as Resistance: Four Women Confronting the Holocaust* (1997); A. Garbarini, *Numbered Days: Diaries and the Holocaust* (2006); S. Kassow, *Who Will Write Our History? Emanuel Ringelblum, the Warsaw Ghetto, and the Oyneg Shabes Archive* (2007); and A. Zapruder, *Salvaged Pages: Young Writers' Diaries of the Holocaust* (2002).   ALEXANDRA GARBARINI

Holocaust Documentation

Holocaust Documentation is the collective term for the written, visual, and tangible documents regarding the antecedents, events, and aftermath of the *Holocaust; that is, the systematic disenfranchisement, dehumanization, and murder of five to six million Jews by *Nazi Germany and its allies and collaborators during the World War II era.

It is often said that the Holocaust is one of the most well documented crimes in human history. Because the Holocaust affected nearly every level of European society that came under Nazi occupation or influence in the 1930s and 1940s, documentation about or related to the Holocaust was generated by many sources. Much Holocaust documentation has survived, although it is scattered around the world in myriad archives, libraries, personal collections, and other repositories. There is no way to measure accurately the amount of documentation generated about the Holocaust, nor is there any way to discern with close certainty the amount of Holocaust documentation that was destroyed during the war or after, whether purposefully, unwittingly, or due to the ravages of time.

TYPES OF DOCUMENTATION: Documentation related to the Holocaust was generated for various reasons. Jewish victims sometimes kept *diaries, took photographs, conducted correspondence, and kept other kinds of documentation as part of their daily existence. One of the most famous diaries is that of the young German girl, Anne *Frank, who kept a journal while hiding in *Amsterdam for two years before she was deported. Concentration camp prisoners were able to keep some records (these include manuscripts written and hidden by the members of the *Sonderkommando* in *Auschwitz-Birkenau or the photographs taken by the camp *resistance). Official Jewish authorities (Jewish community bodies, "Jewish Councils," etc.) and legal and illegal organizations (aid organizations inside and outside Nazi rule, underground organizations, etc.) created a significant amount of documentation as well.

There were some organized efforts to catalogue eyewitness accounts and other evidence during the Holocaust itself. One prime example of this is the so-called Ringelblum archive, or *Oyneg Shabes* (Joy of Sabbath) collection. In 1939, historian Emanuel *Ringelblum formed a group of clandestine archivists who gathered all sorts of records (testimony, photographs, poetry, essays, music) chronicling the horrific daily events of the *Warsaw ghetto. Within the confines of the *ghetto, the group buried the documentation in milk cans, which were only partially recovered after

the war. The Ringelblum archive remains one of the most valuable collections of primary source documentation about the Holocaust. Another famous example of the attempt to document the mass murder was the "Auschwitz Protocols," a manuscript compiled by escapees from Auschwitz-Birkenau in the spring of 1944 to inform the world about the genocide. Witnesses to the horror often recorded what they saw clandestinely in various art forms, including visual (drawings, paintings, and sketches in different media), musical (for example, concerts, musical scores), and literary forms (poetry and plays, for instance). Felix Nussbaum, David Olère, and Joseph Nassy drew and painted painful scenes from the camps and ghettos where they were imprisoned. Nussbaum did not survive Auschwitz, although his numerous works, which depict graphic images of life in the camp, did (see HOLOCAUST REPRESENTATION: ART).

In the post-Holocaust era many survivors wrote recollections and memoirs about their Holocaust experiences. In addition, extensive testimonial collections were created; one of the largest is the USC Shoah Foundation Institute, which holds tens of thousands of video testimonies. In the decades following the Holocaust, the survivors of many destroyed communities compiled so-called memorial books (*Yizkor* books) consisting of contemporary documents, recollections, photographs, lists of names of the victims, etc.

Perpetrators of the Holocaust and those who collaborated in its perpetration also created documentation for various reasons and in many forms. The German Nazi party and state organizations, including financial, medical, administrative, transportation, law enforcement, military, and terror agencies (SS, SD, Gestapo, etc.), created a plethora of documents. Reports of the *Einsatzgruppen*, the mobile killing squads that were responsible for the murder of hundreds of thousands of Jews in *Eastern Europe, were one of the most prominent types of such documents. In the course of disenfranchising, looting, deporting, and murdering Jews, the authorities and organizations of the collaborating and pro-Nazi European governments produced a large amount of visual and written documents. The diaries of prominent top Nazis have also survived, among them, those of Minister of Public Enlightenment and Propaganda Joseph Goebbels and of Hans Frank, "General Governor" of occupied *Poland. Many perpetrators were called to account in trials (see HOLOCAUST: TRIALS) in the post-Holocaust years. These trials not only necessitated gathering thousands of pages of documentary and visual evidence to build cases against the accused perpetrators but also resulted in the creation of an immense amount of new documents pertaining to the perpetrators (interrogations, testimonies, and so on).

A third group of Holocaust documentation was created by bystanders and rescuers. Such documents include eyewitness accounts; contemporary diaries; individuals' correspondence; and materials produced during and right after the Holocaust by neutral and allied governments, military authorities, diplomatic corps, and aid organizations.

Holocaust documentation not only includes visual (photography, film, and artistic images) and written materials (letters, notes, diaries, orders, laws, reports, correspondence, press articles, recollections, trial materials) but also tangible or material "documents" such as cattle cars, barbed wires, concentration camp buildings and facilities, and textiles such as yellow stars and concentration camp clothing.

ARCHIVES AND REPOSITORIES: The most extensive archives and repositories of Holocaust-related documentation can be found in the *United States (the most prominent are at the United States Holocaust Memorial Museum, National Archives and Records Administration, and the *YIVO – Institute for Jewish Research); *Israel (*Yad Vashem – The Holocaust Martyrs' and Heroes' Remembrance Authority, Central Zionist Archives, Ghetto Fighters' House, among others); and *Germany (*Bundesarchiv*, International Tracing Service, and archives in former concentration camps). The two largest archives are at the United States Holocaust Memorial Museum and Yad Vashem in Israel; both have specific and sustained plans and programs that seek out valuable and often neglected collections around the world to preserve and digitize. The archives in the former *Auschwitz concentration camp (Oświęcim, Poland) also hold a significant amount of documentation relevant to the Holocaust.

In addition to the specific collections, many documents (especially those created by administrative, military, and law enforcement agencies) can be found in various national, municipal, governmental, provincial, communal, military, and Christian ecclesiastical archives of European countries. Jewish communities across Europe also preserve Holocaust-related documents.

An increasing number of documentation collections are becoming available on the *internet (see, for example, the websites of the United States Holocaust Memorial Museum and Yad Vashem, as well as more specialized projects such as the Avalon Project at Yale University's website, which makes available a considerable amount of documentation from the Nuremberg trials). However, despite this growing trend in open access on the internet, documents are still often closed because of stringent data regulation laws and for political reasons, issues of state security, and economic reasons. This is especially true in the former Communist Bloc countries, where, despite the changes in the political system in recent decades, document collections are only slowly becoming open. Yet these kinds of restrictions on sensitive or potentially implicative documentation apply to a certain extent everywhere, as, for instance, with the Vatican archives and, until recently, the International Tracing Service collection of documents.

Lastly, there is no way to estimate accurately the amount of potentially millions of pages of documentation stored in the personal collections of individuals. In 2007–08, for example, the photo album of SS officer Karl Höcker, a member of the staff of Auschwitz-Birkenau, was found in a private collection, as was a previously unknown blueprint of the gas chambers of the Birkenau death camps. These examples show that, in the years to come, more and more documentation will probably be discovered, yielding further information about the events of the Holocaust.

For further reading, see the descriptions, finding aids, and archival inventories of the largest Holocaust-related archives: www.ushmm.org, www.its-arolsen.org, www.yadvashem.org, http://college.usc.edu/vhi/, and http://www.auschwitz-muzeum.oswiecim.pl/.

CHRISTINE SCHMIDT VAN DER ZANDEN

Holocaust Education: North America.

The Holocaust did not exist as a discrete topic of study in the years immediately following *World War II. Still, curricular materials used in the *Reform, *Conservative, and *Yiddish school systems discussed the Jewish experience under *Nazism in a manner that conformed to early post-war American Jews' ideals and values. Drawing on the patriotism, optimism, and anti-totalitarianism of the wider American culture, and the emphasis on Jewish strength and bravery that characterized *Zionist thought, early Holocaust education in the American Jewish community emphasized Jewish wartime heroism, especially the *Warsaw ghetto uprising and the rescue mission of Hannah Senesh.

The Holocaust began to move from the periphery to the mainstream of American culture and education in the 1960s. A wave of media events and scholarly debates, most notably the capture of Nazi war criminal Adolf Eichmann in 1960, brought the Holocaust into the public spotlight. The destruction of European Jewry became an event distinct from the general destruction of World War II. This reconceptualization filtered down into the Jewish and secular classroom, as educators felt the need to help their students understand events being discussed in newspapers, magazines, and the new medium of *television. In the politically and ideologically charged climate of the 1960s, teachers in the Reform and Conservative movements, which experienced the most dramatic growth in the post-war period, found lessons in the Holocaust relevant to the civil rights movement (see UNITED STATES: CIVIL RIGHTS MOVEMENT), the anti-war movement, and other issues facing American society. *Israel's victory in the Six Day War (1967), with its redemptive imagery of Jewish soldiers defending the Jewish state, emboldened teachers to examine the greatest period of Jewish victimization. The 1973 Yom Kippur War heightened feelings of isolation and vulnerability among Israelis and American Jews, reinforcing the view that one could not understand the importance of Israel without understanding the Jewish experience under Nazism.

The moral education and civic education movements of the late 1970s, closely tied to the national introspection arising out of the Vietnam War and Watergate scandal, played important roles in promoting Holocaust education in the wider American public. Advocates of civic education, oriented toward teaching tolerance and individual responsibility, adopted the Holocaust as an ideal case study for exploring citizens' duties in a democratic, nonracist society. Attention surrounding the 1978 television mini-series *Holocaust* further spurred calls for education in America's public schools, as politicians, teachers, clergy, artists, and others saw in the Holocaust lessons relevant to contemporary American society. Following Steven Spielberg's film *Schindler's List* (see HOLOCAUST REPRESENTATION: FILM) and the opening of the *United States Holocaust Museum (see HOLOCAUST MEMORIALS; MUSEUMS: Holocaust Museums and Memorials), both in 1993, several states passed legislation mandating Holocaust and genocide education in their public schools. By the end of the twentieth century, Jewish educators had come to see study of the Holocaust as critical to inculcating ethnic identity in their students, and teachers in public and private schools across the religious and political spectrum regarded Holocaust education as essential not only to teaching American and world history but also to conveying lessons that reinforced their community's values.

RONA SHERAMY

Holocaust: Ghettos. "Ghettos" in this context refers to the residential districts in which the Germans and their allies forcibly interned Jews as a means of congregating and separating them from the main population. Their function was to hold Jews until such time as they could be deported elsewhere for forced labor or to be killed. Typically, ghettos were located in a poor section of a city with inadequate facilities to house the imprisoned inhabitants; population density often ranged from five to eight persons per room. These crowded conditions, coupled with inadequate food supplies and poor quality housing, led to the rapid spread of disease and high mortality rates. Ghettos were usually found in cities; Jewish populations from surrounding rural areas were forced to relocate to the designated area. However, some ghettos were located in small towns and the countryside. The majority of these rural ghettos were eventually emptied or liquidated, and Jews who were not deported to labor camps or to their deaths were sent to urban ghettos.

There were a variety of ghettos during the Holocaust period, including those under the jurisdiction of the German government in Nazi-occupied Europe as well as ghettos controlled by German allies *Romania and Japan. The three major types were closed ghettos, open ghettos, and destruction ghettos. The closed ghetto had guarded walls or barbed wire fences. Jews were not permitted to leave, and the authorities controlled food supplies and other necessities. Open ghettos were not necessarily closed off with a wall or fence, but movement in and out was restricted. Often inmates in open ghettos obtained food supplies through local markets. The destruction ghettos were small (usually one or two buildings), sealed, temporary ghettos in which victims were held for a few days to a month before deportation or massacre. Often no food supplies or other necessities were permitted to enter.

Ghettos were generally ruled internally by a Jewish Council (*Judenrat*), which often had been formed earlier to serve as an intermediary between the German authorities and the larger Jewish population and continued in that role after the ghetto was formed. The Jewish Councils controlled the internal day-to-day functioning of the ghetto, which could include distributing food supplies, maintaining sanitation, providing medical care, and in some cases overseeing labor and production. In a few of the larger ghettos, the internal Jewish administration produced ghetto currency and stamps for internal postal service.

Nazi ghettos varied depending on regional geography and when they were set up. The first ghettos were established in Nazi-occupied *Poland by the September 21, 1939, order of Reinhard Heydrich, the Chief of the Security Police, which required the concentration of Jews into urban residential areas. The first ghetto was set up in Piotrków Trybunalski, following an October 8, 1939, order by Oberburgermeister Hans Drexel. Jews from the surrounding areas were brought to the ghetto in Piotrków Trybunalski, increasing its population to more than 25,000 people. The ghetto itself comprised 182 buildings with a total of 4,178 rooms. On average, this would have forced eight people to live in each room in the ghetto. In July 1943, the Piotrków Trybunalski ghetto was liquidated; a sign posted at the train station read *Pietrikau ist Judenrein* ("Piotrkow is clean of Jews").

The first major ghetto was the Litzmannstadt ghetto in occupied Łódź, Poland; on December 10, 1939, SS Brigadenführer Friedreich Übelhoer ordered its establishment, noting that "[t]he creation of the ghetto is of course only a transition measure. I reserve to myself the decision concerning the times and the means by which the ghetto and with it the city of Łódź will be cleansed of Jews."

As envisioned in Übelhoer's memorandum, the ghetto included a sealed-off ghetto area, as well as barracks of Jewish laborers elsewhere in the city; the latter part of this plan was short-lived. The Litzmannstadt ghetto was soon sealed, with more than 160,000 individuals within its barbed wire border, making it the second largest ghetto in Nazi-occupied Europe. Its Jewish Council was headed by the infamous Mordechai Chaim Rumkowski, who developed a system that attempted to divide resources equally among all ghetto residents. As the German authorities, particularly Hans Biebow, who was in charge of the ghetto, took a more direct hand in its administration, laborers received resources and those not engaged in labor were deported to death camps. Because of its transformation into a work camp, the Litzmannstadt ghetto survived the longest of all the Nazi ghettos; it was liquidated in 1944, and most of its inhabitants were sent to *Chełmno death camp.

The *Warsaw ghetto, with 400,000 Jews interned within its walls, was the largest in Nazi-occupied Europe. Its leader, Adam *Czerniakow, committed suicide on July 23, 1942, rather than comply with orders to begin mass deportations of children and the elderly. On April 19, 1943, resistance organizations in the Warsaw ghetto staged an uprising against deportations, which resulted in a six-week battle with the German authorities. The Warsaw ghetto fighters were eventually defeated and the remaining ghetto population deported to concentration camps. Other uprisings took place in the ghettos of Łachwa (probably the first ghetto rebellion) and Białystok. There were also resistance fighters in ghettos in *Vilna, Kovno, Kraków, and elsewhere.

Not all ghettos were controlled by the Germans. The *Romanians controlled a vast network of ghettos. In *China the Japanese established specific areas for Jewish residence within the International zone in Shanghai, where numerous European Jews were stranded after the bombing of Pearl Harbor and the entry of the United States into the war. The Jews themselves referred to their restricted area in Shanghai as the "Shanghai ghetto," but this was not a ghetto in the same sense as those in Europe.

Internal life in the ghettos depended on size and geography, as well as the German and Jewish leadership. The open or closed nature of a ghetto also often dictated the level of starvation in the ghetto. In all ghettos, however, there was an active underground dealing in black market goods and disseminating information.

A number of the larger ghettos also had educational, cultural, social, and religious activities. Many had schools, whether conducted openly or underground. Depending on the politics of the ghetto dwellers or the specific teachers, these schools ranged from traditional *yeshivot* to underground academic high schools (gymnasiums), complete with diplomas for graduates. Languages of instruction included *Yiddish, *Hebrew, and various European languages. Classes met in private homes, in special ghetto schools, and even, in ghettos where education was forbidden, inside a clothes closet.

Theater and musical performances were among ghetto cultural activities. Some of the larger ghettos mounted theatrical productions with sets and costumes; others were limited to traditional plays for the *Purim holiday or street theater. One famous example of a major theatrical undertaking was the children's opera, *Brundibár*, with music by Czech composer Hans Krása and libretto by Adolf Hoffmeister, performed fifty-five times by children of the *Theresienstadt ghetto in 1943 and 1944. Music varied from performances in concert halls, to jazz trios in ghetto cafes, to street minstrels composing satirical lyrics about ghetto life set to popular tunes. Socially, people gathered formally and informally. A number of pre-war youth organizations continued to function, meeting in special collective farms organized inside the ghetto perimeter or secretly in apartments. Informally, people chatted with neighbors in courtyards or crowded kitchens.

Religious observance varied, based on the backgrounds and affiliations of the inhabitants. Worship took place in private homes as well as in *synagogues. In some of the larger ghettos, multiple congregations from a variety of Jewish traditions held separate services. Christians of Jewish descent and their families, who were also interned in some ghettos, successfully petitioned the authorities to hold Christian services. *Sabbath, *High Holiday, and *festival observances took place in the ghettos, and *seders* were held during *Passover. *Matzah* was even baked and distributed for Passover, although much of the starving ghetto population opted for the more filling option of bread. Traditional rituals for *death and mourning, including the preparation of the dead for burial and recitation of memorial prayers, were among the most frequently held religious observances.

Important research includes I. Trunk, *Judenrat* (1975); G. Corni, *Hitler's Ghettos: Voices from a Beleaguered Society, 1939–1944* (2002); E. J. Sterling, ed., *Life in the Ghettos during the Holocaust* (2005); and *Ghettos 1939–1945: New Research and Perspectives on Definition, Daily Life, and Survival : Symposium Presentations at the United States Holocaust Memorial Museum* (2005).   Helene J. Sinnreich

Holocaust Literature.

A product of the encounter of the literary imagination with historical memory, *Holocaust literature is a term that has come to refer to a body of works that reconstruct, memorialize, and mediate a set of events whose horrors have been termed unspeakable and unrepresentable. Encompassing a range of genres, languages, styles, and perspectives, Holocaust literature utilizes narrative strategies and aesthetic techniques to convey complex aspects of life, loss, survival, death, and memory of the *Nazi genocide and to contend with its psychological, philosophical, and ethical ramifications.

Already during the war years, literature offered its writers a way to preserve, understand, and mourn the ongoing destruction of lives and communities and to resist the assault on their humanity. Through almost impossible conditions, with meager resources, and under the threat of death, literary production continued in ghettos, labor camps, and in hiding. Motivated in part by an imperative to preserve a record of Jewish lives and communities even as they were being destroyed, the writing asserts confidence in the writer's ability to capture ongoing events and communicate them to readers elsewhere or at a later time. The *Łódź Ghetto Chronicle*, published in the early 1940s, asserts, "The hand does not waver in writing this down. The hand is guided by a brain that reliably preserves all impressions of the eye and the ear." Fiction, poetry, plays, and journals written during the Holocaust offer glimpses of daily life under the shadow of death, detailing the effects on intimate relationships, family and community dynamics, and the writer's inner life.

Leyb Goldin's (1900–1944) 1941 short story, "Chronicle of a Single Day," for example, preserved as part of Emanuel *Ringelblum's *Oyneg Shabbes* project, imagines a dialogue between a starving ghetto inhabitant and his demanding stomach. Set in the *Warsaw ghetto where Goldin himself died, the story conveys the challenge that unlivable conditions posed not only to one's life but also to one's dignity and humanity. Rachel Auerbach's (1903–1976) eulogy for the murdered Jews of the Warsaw ghetto, "*Yizkor* 1943," written after the liquidation of the ghetto, which she narrowly escaped; Simcha Bunim Shayetitch's (1907–1944) 1942 epic "Lekh Lekho," composed just before his family's deportation from the Łódź ghetto; Itzhak Katzenelson's (1886–1944) "Song of the Murdered Jewish People"; and other wartime works use Jewish texts, images, and traditions to lament, to challenge *God, and to depict their utter desperation. The Hungarian poet Miklós Radnóti (1909–1944) left behind a notebook of poems that depict his experiences and anticipate his own murder during the forced marches at the end of the war. Among the most prolific poets is Abraham (Avrom) Sutzkever (1913–2010), whose sustained literary corpus encompasses the war years and continues in the sixty years after the war. In more than eighty poems composed in the *Vilna ghetto between 1941 and 1943, Sutzkever's modernist technique captures the desperate resistance of the ghetto to pervasive doom, bereavement, and suffering. In "The Lead Plates at the Rom Press" (1943), the plan of the ghetto underground to produce bullets from printing plates taken from the publisher of the definitive edition of the *Talmud becomes the springboard for reflecting on different kinds of Jewish *resistance: The "liquified bullets" produce ammunition charged with "the spirit" of Jewish learning and creativity that the metal once imprinted. Other poems anticipate the struggle with language and memory that the survivor will contend with after the war, as well as the gap between survivors and those who come after. In "Burnt Pearls," (1943) the poet contemplates the remains of an unrecognizable corpse and reflects on the impossible charge of the poet, whose "written word" must "substitute for my world." "How" (1943) imagines the poet on the day of liberation, rendered mute by the irreversible losses made permanent by the passage of time – "jammed locks." While at Starzysko Kamienna and other slave labor camps, Ilona Karmel (1925–2000) and her sister, Henia Karmel-Wolfe (1922–1984), composed poetry in Polish on the backs of stolen paper forms. Published in a volume shortly after their liberation, the poems depict the inner lives of slave laborers – "robots" whose rebellion is controlled with brutality but who nonetheless resist dehumanization; they anticipate the grief, rage, and pain of survival, the future "collapse in silence."

Written in the Jewish languages (*Yiddish, *Hebrew, *Ladino) as well as in the European languages spoken by the Jews victimized by the Holocaust, the variety of tongues in wartime literature convey the vast reach of the Nazi genocidal net and the different histories and cultures of its victims. Poignantly, this body of writing reveals the futile hopes of many writers who did not survive.

Although it is common to refer to a body of writing that encompasses both wartime and post-war works as Holocaust literature, the term itself has been a contentious one not only among literary scholars but also among writers of works commonly included under its rubric. Beginning in the post-war period, Holocaust literature has been variously defined to include only wartime literature, only literature by Jewish victims and survivors of the Nazi genocide, only works in Jewish languages, or only works by victims and survivors of Nazi concentration camps, or it has been described more expansively to include all of those, as well as works by writers without direct experience of the war but who engage it in their writing. In addition to debates about the scope of Holocaust literature, discussions have centered on the accountability of the literary imagination to historical fact, the ethics of producing aesthetic pleasure based on brutality and mass murder, the inadequacy of language to represent the extremities of suffering, and the appropriateness of particular genres, modes, approaches, and works. The German political philosopher Theodor Adorno's (1903–1969) statement, "To write poetry after Auschwitz is barbaric," has become a touchstone for a range of concerns about the propriety, function, and adequacy of literary production in the aftermath of the Nazi genocide. More than in other contexts, literature of the Holocaust has been viewed as weighted with an obligation to the past, to historicity, to memorialization, to ethics.

Struggling to understand the place of the literary imagination in mediating the Holocaust has been a topic not of critical debate alone. It permeates the very fabric of literary writing, from memoirs to post-war poetry and fiction. Much of this literature is characterized by a tension between what we might call the testimonial impulse and the sense that the experience of life and death in the Holocaust is essentially impossible to represent. French philosopher Maurice Blanchot (1907–2003) expresses this tension cogently: "The wish of all, in the camps . . . : know what has happened, do not forget, and at the same time never will you know." Two influential memoirs about surviving Auschwitz – Primo *Levi's (1919–1987) *Survival in Auschwitz* (1968) and Charlotte Delbo's (1913–1985) *Auschwitz and After* (1970) – illustrate this dynamic. Levi's memoir charts the Italian chemist's struggle to survive the harsh physical conditions of the concentration camp, as well as the Germans' deliberate brutality, aimed not only at murdering but also at dehumanizing its inmates and thoroughly crushing their spirits. He observes, "Our language lacks words to express this offense, the demolition of a man." At one moment, Levi spontaneously recollects, and feels compelled to say aloud, verses from Canto 26 of Dante's *Divine Comedy*. Levi's recitation of poetry in *Auschwitz becomes a point of resistance against his forced "demolition" and argues for the enduring place of poetry, even – or perhaps especially – in the face of extreme brutality. Levi's evocation of the Italian poet points to the very structure of the memoir, set up as a modern descent into Dante's inferno. The use of Dante as model and counterpoint anchors Levi to the European literary tradition, suggesting both the value and failure of Western humanistic culture.

Delbo's memoir exemplifies a similar tension. Deported to Auschwitz on a convoy of 230 non-Jewish French women imprisoned for anti-Nazi activities, Delbo wrote her memoir soon after her return to *France. It takes the form of a trilogy that experiments with the boundaries between prose memoir, poetry, and imagination. Impelled by the compulsion to make those who were not there understand the suffering at Auschwitz, she writes repeatedly, "Il faut donner à voir" – insisting that readers "see" what happened through her writing. At the same time, she insists on the incapacity of language to do the work she requires: "Words do not necessarily have the same meaning" for her as they do for her readership.

Poetry by Holocaust survivors indirectly addresses Adorno's statement about the writing of poetry after Auschwitz. Years later, Adorno conceded that his earlier conclusion "may have been wrong," as "perennial suffering has as much right to expression as the tortured have to scream." Yet Holocaust poetry offers more than a response to torment; it meditates in complex ways about ethics, philosophy, and memory and uses language in particular ways to convey what is otherwise inexpressible. Dan Pagis (1930–1986), for example, draws on Jewish sources – biblical figures, medieval Hebrew texts – to pose questions about human and divine nature and good and evil that are both particularly Jewish and universal. "Testimony" ironically contrasts perpetrators "created in the image" of God with incinerated victims, whose "different creator" becomes "omnipotent smoke." His most famous poem, "Written in Pencil in a Sealed Railway Car," drawing on the biblical instance of fraternal murder, poses as an artifact of the war – an incomplete message by a Jewish woman condemned to death. Paul Celan's (1920–1970) complex body of poems explore loss, good and evil, and theodicy. A series of poems, including "Psalm" and "Tenebrae," use traditional prayer forms to question the nature of God. His best known poem, *"Todesfuge"* (Death Fugue), juxtaposes the perpetrator culture – represented by an SS officer who "plays with his vipers" as he makes a game of killing Jews, by the "golden" haired Margarete, and by Death himself, depicted as "a master from Deutschland" – with the Jewish victims, who are represented by dying and dead Jews who "drink . . . and drink" the "black milk" and by "ashen" haired Shulamith.

Not all Holocaust poetry was written by those with personal experience of the Nazi genocide. Already during Hitler's rise to power and the promulgation of increasingly aggressive restrictions on the rights of Jews in Europe, writers elsewhere responded to the deteriorating situation. The shared language, family connections, and personal roots of Yiddish writers in North America made them particularly aware of the growing crisis in Eastern Europe. For example, the poetry of Jacob Glatstein (1896–1971) took a sharp turn in the late 1930s from an introspective and universal focus to a collective Jewish mandate, announcing in "Good Night, World" his return to "the ghetto" of Jewish culture, rejecting the cosmopolitan but "polluted cultures" and intellectual traditions of the West. A later poem, "The Dead Do Not Praise God," inverts the language of Psalms and posits the Holocaust as a radically negative revelation. Canadian poet A. M. Klein (1909–1972) composed dark epic poems, including the 1944 "The Hitleriad," which traces the failure of modernity in the endurance of *antisemitism. Kadya Molodowsky's (1894–1975) poetry mourns the ghetto victims, the lost faith in the *covenant, and the wounding of the *Yiddish language in the European catastrophe. They and others continue to struggle with the meaning of the Jewish God, covenant, and culture after the Holocaust.

In the post-war years and continuing into the twenty-first century, fiction writers have experimented with narrative styles and novelistic structures to explore the aftereffects of the Holocaust, and poets have pushed the capacity of language to convey the resonances of trauma and brutality. Holocaust literature probes the psychological, philosophical, and ethical challenges posed to Western culture. If cultural critic Walter *Benjamin imagines the "angel of history" turning his face to the past, which he sees as a "pile of debris," an irredeemable "single catastrophe which keeps piling wreckage upon wreckage," Holocaust literature has the capacity to bridge historical and geographic distance, bringing the events of the past unnervingly close while maintaining a space for reflection on the aftermath of catastrophe and destruction.

For further reading, see L. L. Langer, *The Holocaust and the Literary Imagination* (1975); A. Mintz, *Hurban: Responses to Catastrophe in Hebrew Literature* (1984); D. Roskies, *Against the Apocalypse: Responses to Catastrophe in Modern Jewish Culture* (1984); J. Young, *Writing and Rewriting the Holocaust: Narrative and the Consequences of Interpretation* (1988); S. R. Horowitz, *Voicing the Void: Muteness and Memory in Holocaust Fiction* (1997); H. Flanzbaum, *The Americanization of the Holocaust* (1999); M. Rothberg, *Traumatic Realism: The Demands of Holocaust Representation* (2000); S. Gubar, *Poetry after Auschwitz: Remembering What One Never Knew* (2003); and M. Hirsch and I. Kacandes, *Teaching the Representation of the Holocaust* (2004); see also HOLOCAUST LITERATURE: FICTION; HOLOCAUST LITERATURE: POETRY; HOLOCAUST REPRESENTATION: DRAMA.   SARA R. HOROWITZ

Holocaust Literature: Fiction. Fiction by survivors and refugees of Nazism develops literary strategies to mediate what cannot be narrated directly. Through a coalescence of fragmentary images; narratives that circle around events that are never fully articulated; the repeated destabilization of chronological, memorial, and other structures; and other techniques, Holocaust literature suggests the world of chaos, loss, randomness, and brutality that cannot be fully represented. Novels and stories respond to personal and collective trauma and bereavement, and they negotiate the complexities of memory as well as philosophical, ethical, psychological, and cultural crises in Western and Jewish cultures.

Ida Fink's (b. 1921) short stories, most notably in *A Scrap of Time* (1987), present narrative slivers that isolate small but revealing details that unfold the complexities of memory, victimization, and survival. Her writing focuses on moments of shocking realization – that one's future, one's intimate relationships, one's world has unraveled. In "A Spring Morning," a father awakens abruptly in the early morning, suddenly understanding that the "buzzing fly" of his dream was the sound of trucks sent to deport Jewish families, and "a terrible feeling of regret tore through

him...and he understood that he had overslept his life." Jacov Lind's (1927–2007) set of sardonic stories in *Soul of Wood* (1964) convey the chaotic but bureaucratized world of Nazi fascism that gives some the right to murder and denies others the right to live at all. In "Journey through the Night," a man on a night train to Paris must justify his desire to live to the cannibal who wants to eat him; in "Soul of Wood," the narrator notes, "Those who had no papers entitling them to live lined up to die." Jorge Semprun's (b. 1923) novel *The Long Journey* (1963) centers on the long train ride to *Buchenwald, using a series of interlocking flashbacks, "flash forwards," and shifting images of "inside" and "outside" to convey the impossibility of adequately transmitting his memories of the Nazi landscape of death to those without personal experience. To outsiders, the corpses left in the camp courtyard at liberation are horrifying but depersonalized signs of horror, whereas to survivors, they are "comrades," the "fraternal dead." Using the device of a found manuscript, Piotr Rawicz's (1919–1982) novel, *Blood from the Sky* (1961), presents the memoirs of a Ukrainian Jew fleeing from Nazi round-ups, commented on and retold by a not entirely sympathetic editor in Paris. The novel layers factual and imaginative detail, suggesting the limitations of historical accounts, the profound effects of brutality, and the legacy of despair.

In addition to treating the complexities of memory and narrative, fiction set in ghettos, labor camps, or situations of refuge conveys the experience of living and dying under Nazi atrocity and captures its brutal and dehumanizing face. Jurek Becker's (1937–1997) novel, *Jacob the Liar* (1969), gives a sense of the vulnerability and uncertainty of the Łódź ghetto, sealed off from the outside world without access to reliable information. Jacob "lies" to the news-hungry ghetto inhabitants, fabricating optimistic broadcasts from an imaginary (and forbidden) radio. The novel warns against false comforts that shield one from the harsh implications of the Holocaust. Other novels that detail life during the war include Tadeusz Borowski's (1922–1951) biting collection of short stories, *This Way for the Gas, Ladies and Gentlemen* (1948), which looks at the brutalizing effects of atrocity on the more privileged non-Jewish prisoners at Auschwitz, based on the author's own experiences there as a political prisoner. The 1972 Yiddish trilogy set in the Łódź ghetto, *The Tree of Life*, by Chava Rosenfarb (1923–2011) follows ten people from the creation through the destruction of the ghetto. The interwoven short stories, *Auschwitz: True Tales from a Grotesque Land* (1985), by Sara Nomberg-Przytyk (1915–1996) present a complex vision of human behavior among a group of women who face choices such as abortions and infanticide to save the lives of mothers. Ka.-Tezetnik is the pseudonym for Yehiel Dinur (1909–2001), a survivor who took his pen name from the German abbreviation for concentration camp. His novels, including *Salamandra* (1946) and *The House of Dolls* (1953), depict the humiliation and suffering of Holocaust victims and their fierce struggle to survive. Arnošt Lustig (1926–2011) wrote more than a dozen novels focusing on the possibility of human ethics and the survival of the human spirit under oppression. His best known works are *Diamonds in the Night* (1958) and *A Prayer for Katerina Horovitzova* (1964).

A number of works explore the challenges that the Holocaust poses to *Judaism, Jewish culture and history, and the concepts of *God and *covenant. Elie *Wiesel's (b. 1928) *Night* (1958) presents *Auschwitz through the memory of a religious young man's struggle not simply for physical survival, but with a God whose silence ruptures his faith in Jewish covenant and continuity. Wiesel's subsequent writing grapples with the nature of God, Jewish faith, and the possibilities of human ethics after the Holocaust. The Yiddish writer Chaim Grade (1910–1982) takes a different approach to theodicy (see EVIL AND SUFFERING). His novella "My Quarrel with Hersh Rasseyner" (1950) presents a dialogue between two Holocaust survivors, a secular and an Orthodox Jew, about the possibilities of faith – whether in the Jewish God or in Western secular values – after the Holocaust. André Schwarz-Bart's (1928–2006) epic novel, *The Last of the Just* (1959), integrates the Holocaust into the long history of European *antisemitism by following the destiny of a single Jewish family over the course of centuries. Using the legend of the *lamed-vav* (thirty-six) just men whose existence guarantees the perpetuation of the entire world, Schwarz-Bart moves from the massacre of Jews in the *Middle Ages to the Nazi genocide and the gassing of the final just man. The novel brings together Jewish and Christian tropes for suffering and *redemption, leaving unresolved the possibility of human or divine meaning after the Holocaust. Although these works engage with issues of Jewish meaning and culture, at their heart are also universal questions about the reconstruction of ethics and values after the Holocaust.

The experiences of children form a recurrent theme in Holocaust fiction. In fiction written from the perspective of a child or adolescent, or tracing the resonances of atrocity later in adulthood, the child serves as an emblem of the innocence of the victims, in the dual sense of being unknowing and undeserving of their harrowing destiny. Their confrontation with brutality during their formative years speaks to the shattering and recalibration for the survivor not only of the self but also of the world. The Hebrew writer Aharon Appelfeld (b. 1932) insists that literature and, indeed, all art forms of the Holocaust have their genesis in the spontaneous play of child victims like himself, who took in their experience not only psychologically but also bodily, absorbing it into their very being. He observes, "Children sucked the horrors, not through their minds, but through their skin, intuitively . . . ; they were not able to think, to re-think, to evaluate, to analyze. . . . It was inside their body, all the darkness and all the horror." Appelfeld's spare yet expressive fiction renders the inner life of children during the war (e.g., *Tzili: The Story of a Life*, 1983; *All Whom I have Loved*, 2007; *Laish*, 2009); the enduring but inexpressible trauma in adulthood (e.g., *The Immortal Bartfus*, 1983; *The Iron Tracks*, 1991); or the childlike illusions of the acculturated Jews of Europe (e.g., *Badenheim 1939*, 1975; *The Age of Wonders*, 1983). Jerzy Kosinski's (1933–1991) brutal story of a young boy abandoned to the harsh landscape and the extreme cruelty of strangers, *The Painted Bird* (1965), uses the muteness of the child as an emblem not only of trauma but also of the collapse of all systems of meaning. Imre Kertész (b. 1929; Nobel Prize in Literature, 2002) draws on autobiographical memory for *Fatelessness* (1975) and *Kaddish for a Child Not Born* (1990), novels that explore an adolescent attempt to come to terms with the random chaos of Nazi victimization and the residue of guilt and trauma after the war. For Georges Perec (1936–1982), whose mother was murdered in *Auschwitz,

the years spent in hiding are a blank, and the attempt to recover them form the basis of his 1975 experimental novel, *W., or the Memory of Childhood*. Harry Mulisch (1927–2010), son of an Austrian Nazi father and a Jewish mother whose family was deported from the Netherlands and murdered, probes the impact of unacknowledged childhood trauma in *The Assault* (1982). An anesthesiologist who has evaded the childhood memory of the deportation of his family comes to symbolize the way that refuted traumatic memory nonetheless resurfaces and shapes one's life. Similarly, Louis Begley's (b. 1933) *Wartime Lies* (1991) suggests the devastating aftereffects of the dissimulation, shame, and disconnection experienced by a child who was saved by assuming false identities during the war.

Although the Holocaust was perpetrated on European soil, North American writers, too, addressed the profound and disturbing issues it raised in the decades after the war. Jewish American fiction writers such as Saul Bellow (1915–2005; *Mr. Sammler's Planet*, 1970), Edward Lewis Wallant (1926–1962; *The Pawnbroker*, 1961), Philip Roth (b. 1933; *The Ghost Writer*, 1979), and Cynthia Ozick (b. 1928; *The Shawl*, 1989), and poets such as Irene Klepfisz (b. 1941), Anthony Hecht (1923–2004), Charles Reznikoff (1894–1976), and Shirley Kaufman (b. 1923) have used the Holocaust as a fulcrum for the exploration of antisemitism, contemporary racism, good and evil, the human condition, and the complexities of personal and collective memory. However, the integration of the Holocaust into belles lettres was not limited to Jewish writers. Writers and poets such as William Styron (1925–2006), Don DeLillo (b. 1936), W. D. Snodgrass (1926–2009), William Heyen (b. 1940), and Sylvia Plath (1932–1963) have used Holocaust imagery to examine issues ranging from moral responsibility to personal trauma.

Israeli literature, too, brought the Holocaust into the compass of the literary imagination. In the decades after World War II, writers who had been in the *Yishuv* (pre-state Israel) during the Nazi genocide explored the impact of the European catastrophe and the influx of war refugees on the development of Israeli identity and national memory and on the relationship to the Jewish past. Fiction writers include Haim Gouri (b. 1923; *The Chocolate Deal*, 1965), Yoram Kaniuk (b. 1930; *Adam Resurrected*, 1968), Yehuda Amichai (1924–2000; *Not of This Time, Not of This Place*, 1963), Hanoch Bartov (b. 1926; *The Brigade*, 1965), and Aharon Megged (b. 1920; "The Name," 1950).

Works by writers born after World War II sometimes come under the rubric of "second-generation" literature. Originally used to refer to writers who are direct descendants of Holocaust victims or survivors, second-generation literature may be conceptualized as a broader category of writing that reflects the repercussions of the genocide of the Jews of Europe for generations who come later. The category encompasses writing from Israel – such as David Grossman's (b. 1954) *See under Love* (1986), Michal Govrin's (b. 1950) *The Name* (1998), Nava Semel's (b. 1954) *Glass Hat* (1985) – and European writing, such as Henri Raczymow's (b. 1948) *Writing the Book of Esther* (1995), and Patrick Modiano's (b. 1945) *La Place de l'Étoile* (1968), and *Dora Bruder* (1997). A number of those works examine the Nazi genocide from the perspective of the perpetrator or explore the inheritance of the perpetrator culture, including

Martin Amis's *Time's Arrow* (1991), Jonathan Littell's *The Kindly Ones* (2006), W. G. Sebald's (1944–2001) *Austerlitz* (2001), and Bernhard Schlink's (b. 1944) *The Reader* (1999). North American second-generation literature includes Art Spiegelman's (b. 1948) graphic novel *MAUS* (1986, 1991), Anne Michael's (b. 1958) *Fugitive Pieces* (1996), Michael Chabon's (b. 1963) *The Final Solution* (2004), Thane Rosenbaum's (b. 1960) *Second Hand Smoke* (1999), Melvin Bukiet's (b. 1953) *After* (1997), Marcie Hershman's (b. 1951) *Tales of the Master Race* (1992), and Aryeh Lev Stollman's *The Far Euphrates* (1997).

Refracted by the prism of the literary imagination, Holocaust fiction mediates memory, narratives, and images of the Jewish catastrophe across cultures and generations. In his 1936 essay "The Storyteller," cultural critic Walter *Benjamin (1892–1940) draws a distinction between the modern historian, who is "bound to explain" the flow of human events by relating "an accurate concatenation of definite events," and the "historyteller" of an earlier era, whose narrative reveals the way these events "are embedded in the great inscrutable course of the world." Although Benjamin decries the degeneration of storytelling into the contemporary novel, Holocaust fiction may be said to exemplify some of the force and contextualizing power of the older storytelling mode, representing a past that, while receding in the distance, deeply marks contemporary culture.

SARA R. HOROWITZ

Holocaust Literature: Poetry. Poetic responses to the atrocities of the *Holocaust have been written from divergent perspectives, in a variety of languages, in many different countries, and by Jews and non-Jews. Some of this poetry was written by individuals who were victims or witnesses of *Nazi brutality. Other poets, without personal experience of the Holocaust, chose to imagine or evoke various elements of its dimensions in their works. There are also poems written by those who were active participants in the atrocities or who stood by as passive observers. There is no uniformity to Holocaust poetry in style or theme. Some poets depict death camps, systematic shootings, pit burnings, and partisan trench warfare; others evoke survival under oppression or life as refugees, or they portray the heroism of individuals in desperate situations. There are also those who record the world before and after these events, leaving a blank where the horrors of history were perpetrated.

Unlike historical writing or fiction, poetry is not necessarily concerned with accurate or realistic representations of actual events. Thus, the best Holocaust poetry succeeds in conveying instances of authentic experience or "fugitive pieces," in the phrase of Canadian poet and novelist, Anne Michaels. Lawrence Langer has claimed that "history imposes limitations on the supposed flexibility of artistic license." However, because poetry functions in the realm of art, representing emotion and transcending horror to create beauty, it is able to sidestep questions about the legitimacy of bearing witness to the Holocaust. As Berel Lang has noted, literature and art have the capacity to "occupy new vantage points and to invent new modes of representation."

The German critic Theodor Adorno claimed in 1949 that "after Auschwitz, to write poetry is barbaric," because he believed that using art in a world where culture and education had proven unable to prevent a descent into

atrocity would be a meaningless act. He asked, "How could poetic language itself be anything but superficial, irrelevant, marginal, in a world of such horror since language was incommensurate to express it?" (cited in Schiff, xix). Paul Antschel (1920–1970), known by the pen name Paul Celan, offered an alternative response, insisting that silence in the face of the evils of the Holocaust was tantamount to complicity. Instead he claimed there was a requirement to bear witness. Born to a German-speaking Jewish family in the culturally rich city of Czernowitz in Bukovina (then part of *Romania, now in *Ukraine), Celan was deported to a Nazi work camp. He was liberated in 1944, and after the war he lived in *France. His complex and powerful poem, "Todesfuge" (Death Fugue), in which death is personified as "a master from Germany," begins with these words: "Black milk of daybreak we drink it at evening/ we drink it at midday and morning we drink it at night/ we drink and we drink/ we shovel a grave in the air there you won't lie too cramped."

The German Jewish poet and dramatist Nelly Sachs (1891–1970) fled to Sweden with her mother in 1940 to avoid conscription to a forced labor camp. Sachs was a close friend of Paul Celan; her poignant representations of the Jewish people's destruction integrate biblical and *mystical imagery drawn from Jewish sources. Her well-known poem, "O The Chimneys," concludes, "O you chimneys,/ O you fingers/ And Israel's body as smoke through the air!" (trans. Michael Hamburger). In 1966, Sachs shared the Nobel Prize in Literature with S. Y. *Agnon, observing that he represented *Israel, whereas "I represent the tragedy of the Jewish people."

The themes of silence and political apathy in the face of Nazi persecution are conveyed in the poem, "First They Came," attributed to Pastor Martin Niemöller (1892–1984); it is a critique of the inactivity of German intellectuals following the Nazi rise to power and the purging of their chosen targets. Known in several versions, copies are inscribed at the United States Holocaust Memorial Museum in Washington, D.C., and the New England Holocaust Memorial in Boston, Massachusetts.

Many poems were written during the Holocaust by poets who did not survive; these include works by David Vogel (1891–1944), a Russian-born Hebrew poet, novelist, and diarist who was arrested by the Nazis and disappeared in 1944. Vogel's innovative poetry is based in the Expressionist and Impressionist movements of *Central European pre-war poetics. Shot and buried in 1944 during a Nazi death march, Miklós Radnóti was an illustrious poet from *Hungary. When his body was excavated from a mass grave, poems were found in a notebook in his jacket. These poems developed the themes that he had been using since 1936 when he wrote about the inevitability of violent death in the war sweeping Europe. His poetry draws on biblical prophets to convey his antifascist ideals. Anne Sexton (1928–1974) and W. H. Auden (1907–1973) are among modern non-Jewish poets who employed Holocaust imagery in specific poems, such as Auden's "Refugee Blues" and Sexton's "After Auschwitz." Czeslaw Milosz (1911–2004) addresses the Holocaust from an outsider's perspective in "A Poor Christian Looks at the Ghetto," on the 1943 destruction of the *Warsaw *ghetto, whereas "Daddy" by Sylvia Plath (1932–1963) reveals the extent to which Holocaust imagery has been reappropriated to convey other forms of horror or trauma. Serbo-Croat, Russian, Polish, and Hungarian poets who write in sympathy or even in response to their involvement as Holocaust perpetrators include Jerzy Ficowski, János Pilinszky, and Vasko Popa. The works of many of these poets have only recently become available in English translation.

Writing about the Holocaust has provided an opportunity for some non-Jewish writers to contest the behavior of contemporaneous regimes. Russian poet Yevgeny Yevtyshenko's famous "Babi Yar" (1961) denounced the massacre of more than 33,000 Jews over two days in Kiev, *Ukraine, during September 1941. In recalling this atrocity, Yevtyshenko was also calling attention to the persistence of *antisemitism in the post-war *Soviet Union. This politically radical poem was subsequently set to music by Russian composer Dmitri Shostakovich (1906–1975) in his *Symphony No. 13*. As the survivor generation gives way to a new generation of writers removed from direct experience with the historical events, poetry continues to engage with the horrors of human actions through evocative images of the Holocaust.

For further reading, see *Selected Poems and Prose of Paul Celan*, trans. J. Felstiner (2000); J. Felstiner, *Paul Celan: Poet, Survivor, and Jew* (2001); E. E. George, *Miklós Radnóti: The Complete Poetry* (1980); B. Lang, ed., *Writing and the Holocaust* (1988), 14; L. L. Langer, ed., *Art from the Ashes: A Holocaust Anthology* (1995); and H. Schiff, ed., *Holocaust Poetry* (1995); **see also HOLOCAUST LITERATURE.**   RACHEL S. HARRIS

Holocaust Memorials. In keeping with the iconoclastic tradition in Jewish art and culture, the first "memorials" to the *Holocaust period came not in stone, glass, or steel, but in narratives and in commemorative fast days. *Yizkor Bikher*, memorial volumes, remembered both the lives and destruction of European Jewish communities during World War II (1939–45) according to the most ancient Jewish memorial medium: the book. For a murdered people without graves, without even corpses to inter, these memorial books often came to serve as symbolic tombstones. Their scribes hoped that *Yizkor Bikher* would turn the site of reading into memorial space, thus making interior spaces and imagined gravesites the first sites for memory.

At the same time, traditional commemorative days on the Jewish calendar recalling ancient catastrophes, primarily the destructions of the First and Second *Temples of Jerusalem on *Tisha B'Av (9th day of Av), were enlarged by Jewish religious communities after the Holocaust to encompass the destruction of Europe's Jews during World War II. With the founding of *Israel in 1948, just three years after the liberation of the death camps, the religious explanations for catastrophe (e.g., divine punishment) attending the traditional fast days of the Ninth of Av or Tenth of Tevet came widely to be regarded as politically and philosophically untenable. The State of Israel thus created new remembrance days, such as *Yom Ha-Shoah veha-Gevurah (Holocaust and Heroism Remembrance Day).

During the period between 1948 and 1960, dozens of other institutional forms of remembrance were also generated at both state and local levels, in Israel, as well as in Europe and the Americas. Holocaust memorials would come to include *museums and monuments, the sites and remnants of destruction, as well as religious and secular commemorative days. In fact, the farther that events of *World War II and the Holocaust have receded into time, the more prominent its physical memorials have become.

Thousands of monuments, preserved ruins, plaques, museums, and study centers devoted to Holocaust remembrance now dot European, North and *Latin American, *Australian, and Israeli landscapes. They come in all shapes, forms, and aesthetic styles: from figurative statuary (see Nathan Rapoport's "Warsaw Ghetto Monument," 1948), to monolithic abstract sculpture (see Viktor Tolkin's "Majdanek" in Lublin, *Poland, 1969); from minimalist architecture (see Henri Pingusson's "Memorial to the Deported" in Paris, 1959) to deconstructivist architecture (see Peter Eisenman's "Memorial to the Murdered Jews of Europe" in *Berlin, 2005); from realized conceptual installation art (see Jochen Gerz and Esther Shalev-Gerz's vanishing "Memorial for Peace and against War and Fascism" in Harburg-Hamburg, 1986) and to unrealizable agit-prop proposals (see Horst Hoheisel's "Blow Up the Brandenburger Tor," for Berlin, 1995); to large national landscapes, such as the planting of six million trees in Israel's "Forest of the Six Million Martyrs," to the dozens of local "memorial gardens" installed on *synagogue properties and in town parks everywhere.

Depending on where these memorials are constructed and by whom, these sites remember the past according to a variety of national myths and ideals and religious and political needs. Some recall war dead, others political resistance, and still others mass murder. All reflect both the past experiences and current lives of their communities, as well as the state's memory of itself. At a more specific level, these memorials reflect the aesthetic temper of their time, their designers' training, and their physical locations in national memorial landscapes.

The reasons given for Holocaust memorials, as well as the kinds of memory they generate, are as various as the sites themselves. Some are built in response to traditional Jewish religious injunctions to remember, others according to a government's need to explain a nation's past to itself. Where the aim of some memorials is to educate the next generation and to inculcate in it a sense of shared experience and destiny, other memorials are conceived as expiations of guilt or as self-aggrandizement. Still others are intended to attract tourists. In addition to traditional Jewish memorial iconography, every political entity has its own institutional forms of remembrance. As a result, Holocaust memorials inevitably mix national and Jewish figures, political and religious imagery.

The very first material Holocaust memorials were the places of destruction themselves. Liberated by the Red Army in July 1944, the intact remains of the concentration camp at *Majdanek, just outside Lublin in Poland, were turned into the first memorial and museum of its kind. Early the next year, the Polish Committee of National Liberation conferred similar status on the ruins of Stutthof, the first concentration camp in Poland, and on the gargantuan complex at *Auschwitz-Birkenau, commonly regarded as the "epicenter" of the Holocaust. Still other death camps in Poland, destroyed by the Germans in their retreat, such as *Treblinka, *Chełmno, *Sobibor, and *Bełżec, were turned into shrines of national martyrdom. In Poland, countless other memorials in destroyed and abandoned Jewish cemeteries and at former sites of synagogues across the countryside commemorate the entirety of Polish destruction through the figure of its murdered Jewish part. They recall the mass murder of Jews in Poland as an intrinsic part of Poland's own national landscape of martyrdom, often through images of irreparable breaches and shattered vessels.

In *Germany, by contrast, memorials to this time often recall Jews by their absence and German victims by their political resistance. Yet between 1945 and 1989, German Holocaust memorials and their meanings depended completely on whether they were located in the Federal Republic (West Germany) or in the German Democratic Republic (socialist East Germany). What was officially regarded in the West as Germany's disastrous defeat was recalled in the East, at the behest of its Soviet liberators-turned-occupiers, as a communist victory over fascism and as the redemption of socialist martyrs in the founding of the German Democratic Republic. Post-war German governments in the East and West thus preserved the ruins of concentration camps in Germany – at *Dachau, *Bergen-Belsen, and *Buchenwald – to tell both the histories of these sites and to explain how each new state came into being.

After Germany's 1989 reunification and the subsequent return of the nation's capital to *Berlin, the new national Holocaust memorial in Berlin, a gargantuan, undulating field of stelae designed by Peter Eisenman, had to address Germany's double-edged memorial conundrum, even if it could not answer it: How does a nation remember a people murdered in its name? How does a nation reunite itself on the bedrock memory of its crimes? Indeed, these questions have spawned a genre of memorials in Germany that might be called counter-monuments: They challenge not just the conventional contours of the monuments but also the very premise of their being. Rather than finding consolation in their Holocaust memorials, contemporary German artists have attempted to formalize the irreparable void of Germany's lost and murdered Jews, a permanent hole in the heart of German culture. In addition to the more conventional and often still powerful sculptural and landscape designs located throughout German sites of destroyed synagogues, places of deportation, and concentration camps, new and contemporary memorials are built into the ground, disappear, or make absence their defining motif. Rather than attempting to resolve Germany's memorial conundrum in their designs, contemporary artists and architects, such as Jochen Gerz and Esther Shalev-Gerz, Horst Hoheisel and Hans Haacke, Renata Stih and Frieder Schnock, Sol LeWitt and Richard Serra, Daniel Libeskind, and Peter Eisenman, have striven for formal articulation of the questions themselves.

Outside of Poland and Germany, the best known site-specific Holocaust memorial in Europe is probably the Anne *Frank House in *Amsterdam. The house and annex at Prinsengracht 263, where Anne and her family hid from July 1942 until August 1944 when they were betrayed by Dutch collaborators to the Germans and sent to Auschwitz and Bergen-Belsen (where Anne died), have been preserved as a national shrine and museum to Anne *Frank, her acclaimed diary, and a universal vision of tolerance. The Anne Frank House reminds the Dutch that, even though they harbored her, they also betrayed her in the end, along with another 100,000 Dutch Jews. By reflecting back to the Dutch their own mixed record of resistance and neutrality, victimization and complicity, Anne Frank effectively became Holland's patron saint of Holocaust memory, an archetypal figure for all of *Holland's war memory.

In *Israel, where half of the 1948 Jewish population had survived the Holocaust, martyrs and heroes are often remembered side by side. Israel's national Holocaust remembrance day, *Yom Ha-Shoah Veha-Gevurah, commemorates both the mass murder of Europe's Jews and the heroism of ghetto fighters, all seemingly redeemed by the birth of the state. Whereas memorials and museums in Europe, especially those located at the sites of destruction, focus relentlessly on the annihilation of Jews and almost totally neglect the millennium of Jewish life in Europe before the war, those in Israel locate events in a historical continuum that includes Jewish life before and after the destruction. Israeli museums at kibbutzim, like Lohamei Hageta'ot (Ghetto Fighters), Tel Yitzhak, Givat Chaim, and Yad Mordechai, emphasize Jewish life before and during the Holocaust over the killing itself. With the ingathering of hundreds of thousands of new immigrants from the former *Soviet Union, Israel's memory of the Holocaust has also grown more plural and inclusive, as reflected in the redesign of *Yad Vashem, Israel's national Holocaust memorial museum.

Just as political, aesthetic, and religious coordinates determine the shape that Holocaust memory takes in Europe and Israel, so, too, is Holocaust memory in the *United States guided by distinctly American ideals and experiences, such as liberty, pluralism, and *immigration. Whether in *New York City's Museum of Jewish Heritage – A Living Memorial to the Holocaust (in lower Manhattan, within sight of the Statue of Liberty and Ellis Island), or on *Boston's Freedom Trail, or at Liberty State Park in New Jersey, or in the United States Holocaust Memorial Museum located just off the National Mall in Washington, D.C., or nestled in Miami's community of Latin American immigrants, American Holocaust memorials and museums enshrine not just the history of the Holocaust but also American democratic and egalitarian ideals. In such monuments, American memory itself is enlarged to include the histories of its immigrants and the memory of events on distant shores that drove these immigrants to America in the first place. Other Holocaust memorials are built in much smaller scales in American Jewish cemeteries, small town squares, and synagogue courtyards to reflect the sensibilities of particular survivor communities. *Landsmanschaftn organizations have built simple tombstone memorials in local Jewish cemeteries to honor members of their communities who were murdered during the Holocaust but whose graves remain unknown.

CONCEPTUALIZING MEMORIALS: Artists and architects of Holocaust memorials face many dilemmas: How to remember horribly real events in the abstract gestures of geometric forms? How to create a focal point for remembrance among ruins without desecrating the space itself? How to embody remembrance without seeming to displace it? Moreover, Holocaust memory is always "contested" as long as more than one group or individual remembers. Open competitions with competing memorial conceptions and designs make such competing memories especially palpable by throwing into relief the complex, nearly impossible questions for those attempting to conceive of such monuments.

These questions and others arose with the very first open competition for a memorial at Auschwitz-Birkenau in 1957. "The choice of a monument to commemorate Auschwitz has not been an easy task," the sculptor Henry Moore wrote as head of the internationally acclaimed design jury assembled for the Auschwitz competition. "Essentially, what has been attempted here has been the creation…of a monument to crime and ugliness, to murder and to horror. The crime was of such stupendous proportions that any work of art must be on an appropriate scale. But apart from this, is it in fact possible to create a work of art that can express the emotions engendered by Auschwitz?" (Henry Moore, pamphlet published at Auschwitz, 1958, n.p.).

As was clear to Moore in 1957 and to many critics and artists since then, public art in general and Holocaust memorials in particular tend to beg traditional art historical inquiry. Until recently, most discussions of Holocaust memorial spaces ignored the essentially public dimension of their performance, remaining either formally aestheticist or almost piously historical. So although it is true that a sculptor like Nathan Rapoport (designer of the Warsaw Ghetto Memorial) will never be regarded by art historians as highly as his contemporaries, Jacques Lipshitz and Henry Moore, neither can his work be dismissed solely on the basis of its popular appeal. Unabashedly figurative, heroic, and referential, his work seems to be doomed critically by precisely those qualities – public accessibility and historical referentiality – that make it monumental. Yet in fact, it may be just this social and political resonance in the public mind that finally constitutes the Holocaust memorial's aesthetic performance. Instead of stopping at formal questions or at issues of historical referentiality, students of Holocaust memorials now ask how memorial representations of history may finally weave themselves into the course of ongoing events.

As the meanings of Holocaust memorials necessarily evolve over time, depending on the needs and preoccupations of every new generation that visits them, so too have the aims of critical inquiry into Holocaust memorials evolved. No longer content to examine only these memorials' formal and aesthetic qualities or their historical referents, critics now also ask *how* public history of Jewish life and death is being shaped through these memorials and to what interpretive ends. Instead of concentrating on finished or monolithic Holocaust memory, visitors to Holocaust memorials increasingly look at the process by which public history and memory are constructed. They ask, Who creates this memory, under what circumstances, for which audience? Which events are remembered, which are forgotten, and how are they explained? What are these memorials' places in national and religious commemorative cycles? What is the contemporary architect's role in shaping public memory? What are the consequences of these memorials for both Jewish and other religious and national identities?

To this end, the life and texture of Holocaust memorials have been enlarged to include the times and places in which they were conceived, their literal construction amid historical and political realities, their finished forms in public spaces, their places in the constellation of national memory, their ever-evolving lives in the minds of their communities and of the Jewish people over time – and even their eventual destruction. With these dimensions in mind, it is important to understand how individual monuments create and rein-force particular memories of the Holocaust period as well as the ways events reenter political life shaped by monuments.

Over time, a new post-war generation will necessarily visit these memorials under new circumstances and invest them with new meanings. The result will be an evolution in these memorials' significance, generated in the new times and company in which they find themselves. Rather than fixing ideology and memory in hard and impermeable forms, as has traditionally been the goal in the creation of monuments, contemporary designers strive to open a space in the landscape that will open a space within visitors for memory. Holocaust memorials in this vein are thus designed to accommodate all the disparate and changing reasons, both present and future, that will impel people to visit these memorials in the first place.

For further reading, see M. Bohm-Duchen, ed., *After Auschwitz: Responses to the Holocaust in Contemporary Art* (1995); H. Gerth, *Materials on the Memorial to the Murdered Jews of Europe* (2005); A. Konneke, ed., *Das Harburger Mahnmal gegen Faschismus* (The Harburg Monument against Fascism; 1994); K. Frahm, *Denkmal für die ermordeten Juden Europas* (Memorial to the Murdered Jews of Europe; 2005); E. Linenthal, *Preserving Memory: The Struggle to Create America's Holocaust Museum* (1995); S. Milton, *In Fitting Memory: The Art and Politics of Holocaust Memorials* (1991); A. Rieth, *Monuments to the Victims of Tyranny* (1969); J. E. Young, *The Texture of Memory: Holocaust Memorials and Meaning* (1993); idem, *At Memory's Edge: After-Images of the Holocaust in Contemporary Art and Architecture* (2000); and idem, ed., *The Art of Memory: Holocaust Memorials in History* (1994).

JAMES E. YOUNG

Holocaust Reparations and Restitution. All genocides are accompanied by looting and theft, and the *Holocaust is no exception. Accurate figures of the current value of the thievery perpetrated by the *Nazi regime and its allies are difficult to determine, but the best estimate is that between $230 billion and $320 billion in today's dollars was stolen from Europe's Jewish population.

With the end of World War II, the Allies, led by the *United States, set out to return stolen land and property to both nations and individuals. The process was imperfect and came nowhere close to returning even a significant share of what had been misappropriated. One significant milestone was the Washington Accord, signed in 1946, by which Swiss banks agreed to return approximately one-half of the gold they had taken from Nazi Germany, knowing that it was stolen from the treasuries of conquered Europe. In the western zones of Germany, military governments enacted laws requiring the return of all properties that had been confiscated or transferred under Nazi duress.

Between 1933 and 1945, the Germans stole approximately 600,000 artworks from both museums and private collections throughout Europe. This included paintings, sculpture, objets d'art, and tapestries. When rare books, stamps, and coins and fine furniture are considered, the number of items stolen goes into the millions. According to records from the Nuremberg trials, 29,984 railroad cars were required to transport all the German-stolen art to Germany. The value of the art plundered during the Holocaust, which exceeded the total value of all artworks in the United States in 1945, is astounding: $2.5 billion in 1945 prices, or

$20.5 billion in 2008 dollars. The Nazi art confiscation program was the greatest displacement of art in human history.

The Allies, led by the United States, also undertook to return art and other cultural objects but the task was enormous. A dedicated team of art experts from the United States and the United Kingdom, known at the "Monuments Men" because they sought to minimize damage to European monuments and other architecture, attempted to track down Nazi-looted artworks. Hidden stashes of art and sculptures were located in salt mines, castles, and trains and returned to their countries of origin. For example, 60,000 artworks were returned to *France, with 45,000 returned largely to their Jewish owners. However, for a variety of reasons, the effort was only partially successful.

With the onset of the Cold War in the 1950s, the theft that had accompanied the Nazi genocide was largely forgotten. At the end of the occupation, the Federal Republic of *Germany did enact indemnification laws. In 1952, *Israel, along with representatives of American Jewry and the West German government, reached an agreement whereby Germany would provide $715 million in goods and services to the State of Israel as compensation for taking in survivors; $110 million would go to the newly created New York-based Claims Conference (formally known as the Conference on Jewish Material Claims against Germany) to pay for programs focusing on relief, rehabilitation, and resettlement of Holocaust survivors; and direct reparations would be made through the Claims Conference to selected survivors, with more than 250,000 survivors receiving lifetime pensions. By 2000, Germany had paid more than $60 billion to Holocaust survivors. Yet that indemnity has been limited, and additional categories of elderly individuals eligible for compensation have been added only in recent years.

A totally unexpected development took place at the end of the 1990s. Even as the number of remaining Holocaust victims was dwindling, the Cold War ended, the *human rights movement was born, government doors flew open, and *Holocaust representations in *film, *television, and *museums transfixed the public imagination. Thefts from Jewish victims also came into the spotlight, particularly in the United States. The U.S.-based Holocaust restitution movement, launched in the late 1990s against European corporations and governments for their wrongful wartime activities, yielded more than $8 billion in payouts as compensation for the monetary losses and other injuries suffered by Jews during World War II. The settlements were achieved with three sets of entities. One was with Swiss and other European banks for failure to return funds deposited with the banks by Jewish depositors and (in the case of the Swiss) for trading in looted Nazi gold. The second was with European insurance companies for failure to pay on life insurance and other policies purchased by Jewish policyholders. The third settlement was with German industry for exploiting Jewish and non-Jewish victims as forced laborers, which for the Jews meant extermination through work, and for other misdeeds in which German business participated during World War II.

A wholly separate component of the Holocaust restitution movement has been claims for the return of Nazi looted artworks to their pre-war Jewish owners or heirs. The most notable settlement occurred in 2006, with the conclusion of litigation by Maria Altmann (d. 2011), a survivor from *Austria who resided in Los Angeles, against Austria and its Belvedere Gallery for the return of five valuable paintings by the Austrian Modernist, Gustav Klimt. The paintings, which had belonged to Altmann's aunt and uncle, Ferdinand and Adele Bloch-Bauer, were confiscated by the Nazis in 1938 when Ferdinand fled Austria after the *Anschluss*. Altmann filed her suit in Los Angeles federal court after being denied relief by both a government claims commission in *Vienna and the Austrian courts. After the U.S. Supreme Court refused to dismiss the case and an Austrian arbitration panel unanimously ruled that the paintings belonged to Altmann and her fellow heirs, Austria shipped the Klimts to Los Angeles.

Although reparations paid to Holocaust survivors and heirs and the restitution of stolen Holocaust assets to survivors or heirs cannot come close to fully compensating the personal and material losses of the Holocaust, return of stolen property and payment of damages for pain and suffering can provide a small measure of justice to the Jewish victims of World War II.   MICHAEL J. BAZYLER

Holocaust Representation: Art. Although philosophers have concluded that it is neither possible nor warranted to portray an event as horrific as the *Holocaust, many artists of different religions and nationalities have felt the need to express their reaction to the attempted destruction of the Jews and the horrors of *Nazi persecution. These artists can be divided into several categories: camp and ghetto inmates, survivors, refugees, and those who were in hiding; Nazis who took photographs; partisans; liberators; non-participants in *Germany and abroad; and members of the second and third generations (children and grandchildren of survivors, refugees, and Nazis) (see HOLOCAUST DOCUMENTATION).

Art was produced in camps and ghettos under impossible conditions with improvised materials at the risk of the artists' lives. Such art was a form of spiritual resistance to Nazi dehumanization: it allowed artists to maintain a link with their former identities and gave them some measure of control in a situation of powerlessness. Art also affirmed life in another way. Jószef Szajna stated that the trace of himself that he left on paper would survive even if he perished. This explains the large number of self-portraits and inmate portraits whose purpose was to indicate that the models had existed, even if they died as nameless victims. Some wished to be remembered in an idealized fashion, but there are also realistic portrayals of the old and sick. Self-portraits by survivors created after the war reveal the traumas they underwent. On liberation from *Auschwitz in 1945, Halina Olomucki drew herself contemplating her skeletal body in a mirror and asking in shock, "Is this me?" Samuel Bak's haunting "Self-Portrait at the Age of Thirteen" (1946) depicts the boy-artist wide-eyed in horror, still seeing before him the hell he had survived.

However, the main goal of this art was to provide documentary evidence of the brutal acts of the Nazis and the inhuman conditions in which their victims were forced to live and die. The works illuminate details about daily life in the camps and ghettos that are not otherwise known: from the cattle cars, selections, brutal camp labor, and the miserable living conditions to the death marches, gas chambers, and corpses. Most artists chose naturalistic styles, seeing their works as reportage rather than art. Others chose to heighten reality expressionistically to convey how their experiences actually felt. For instance, in depicting the many-tiered bunk beds in Buchenwald, Boris Taslitzky realistically drew inmates lying in them, whereas Auguste Favier revealed their deeper meaning by setting living "skeletons" in front to suggest the enervation and slow death that characterized that camp. In *Theresienstadt, naturalism was the style artists produced for their Nazi overseers to help them create the fraud of the "model camp." In works they did in secret, they assumed the moral duty to expose the death that lay behind this façade.

Art also involved catharsis, the attempt to cleanse oneself of anger and pain. As survivors recuperated they repeated scenes from the camps with increasing expressionism until they felt freed from their terrible experiences. Some survivors continued to document the Holocaust, believing it was their duty to the dead to record their agony. Many others eventually returned to Holocaust themes, inspired by events such as the Eichmann *trial. Artists who were in hiding, such as Felix Nussbaum, expressed their subjective feelings of alienation and loneliness. Partisans depicted their fight against the Nazis, while documenting the deportations and ruins they observed. Army and professional photographers such as Margaret Bourke-White and Lee Miller documented these sights, and Corrado Cagli and Leon Golub repeatedly drew these images, both on the spot and after the war.

Refugees who had escaped to safe havens remained emotionally afflicted. Feeling guilty because they had escaped, they had an overwhelming desire to impart the truth about the Holocaust. Artists such as Marc Chagall, Jacques Lipchitz, and George Grosz created allegories of their own escape and wanderings. However, in the main, in their themes as well as in the myriad artistic styles and personal iconography they used to express their ideas, their art parallels that of other artists who had no direct contact with the Holocaust. Despite the diversity of these artists, they used similar stereotypes and symbols to depict and interpret the Holocaust. The aim of these representations was to encapsulate an experience into a single image that would resonate meaningfully for the spectator. Instead of portraying camp life, from 1933 on, these artists used the only information they had: Camps were surrounded by barbed wire fences. Ben Shahn (1939), Leonard Baskin (1952), Audrey Flack (1976–77), and George Segal (1982–83) all depicted inmates behind barbed wire. This image was so closely identified with the camps that photographers accompanying the liberators filmed the inmates in this way, thus moving the image from art into reality and reinforcing its documentary value. From 1945 on, even a single strand of barbed wire in front of a head or hand was enough to represent the camps, and soon a strand of barbed wire could conjure up this image by itself. Igael Tumarkin used such strands to give a Holocaust context to his abstract reliefs in the early 1960s, and Sigmar Polke's *Camp* (1982) portrays a barbed wire fence. This symbol could also be used in other contexts to suggest the Holocaust: in 1974–75 Marc Klionsky wrapped barbed wire around a Russian Jew to liken his imprisonment in *Russia to being in a concentration camp. Later artists, often inspired by visits to camp sites in Europe, used barbed wire or photographs of the fences to create camp installations, such as Pearl Hirschfield's *Shadows of Auschwitz* (1989) and Gerda Meyer-Bernstein's *Shrine* (1991), into which the public was invited to enter.

Another early symbol, the crematorium chimney, stood for the most idiosyncratic form of Holocaust murder: death in the gas chamber and burning corpses in the crematorium. The chimney was especially important in the art of survivors, such as Yehuda Bacon, Naftali Bezem, Samuel Bak, and Friedensreich Hundertwasser, whether or not they had seen them. In Hundertwasser's *Blood Garden – Houses with Yellow Smoke* (1962–63), chimneys belch yellow smoke that turns the blood-filled windows of the barracks black, as the life within them is burnt in the crematorium. R.B. Kitaj's *Passion 1940–1945: Girl/Plume* (1985) places a fragile girl in a chimney that recalls a coffin.

Other widespread Holocaust symbols also demanded only minimal knowledge from the spectators. Cattle cars and railroad lines were used to represent deportations; skeletally thin but living figures were identified immediately through the liberators' photographs as survivors; and children, sometimes accompanied by their mothers, were used to express the innocence of the Holocaust's victims.

The second generation developed different symbols, focusing on what they had encountered at home and subverted the methods of Nazi dehumanization – the numbers tattooed on their parents' arms and preserved camp uniforms – to memorialize their parents' identities. From 1979 on, Mindy Weisel and Haim Maor repeatedly used these numbers in various contexts, in 1992 Tatana Kellner used casts of her parents' arms that accent their camp numbers, and from 1995–98 Yosef Lemel created enormous photographs of the numbers on survivors' arms. Such artists also used family photographs and their parents' drawings and memoirs to express a feeling of loss and to preserve their parents' experiences.

The image that created the deepest, most lasting impression on artists, whether or not they had experienced the Holocaust, was the gruesome mound of skeletally thin corpses. This image also posed the greatest aesthetic and emotional problems. Witnesses depicted these corpses as individuals, and as with the photographs, most spectators avert their eyes from these works. Haunted by photographs of such images seen in news reports, artists sought to translate them into art. Pablo Picasso fragmented the corpses, softening the image to help spectators overcome their repugnance. In contrast, Jews usually decided not to base such works on photographs: their identification with the dead precluded them from using these corpses to create art about the Holocaust. Instead, they substituted other visual sources for these images or gave them other meanings. Thus Hyman Bloom based the corpses he painted on autopsies, Baskin called his serene corpses *Dead Men*, and Shahn used children's corpses from a Holocaust photograph in *Allegory* (1948) to depict victims of a tenement fire.

In the concluding decades of the twentieth century, it became obvious that the world had learned nothing from the past. Massacres and genocide proceeded apace and some even denied that the Holocaust had occurred. Clearly, semi-abstract and generalized works had not succeeded in forcing people to confront the Holocaust. Zoran Music and Robert Morris opted for a more striking use of this imagery to shock the spectator into renewed realization of the Holocaust's lessons, creating harsh images that evoke a gut-wrenching experience reminiscent of that caused by the original contact with the corpses. Several children of survivors adopted an opposite tactic, turning the dead into ghosts that haunt us in a gentler fashion. Natan Nuchi's life-sized skeletally thin corpses from 1985–95 are ethereal specters, haunting rather than shocking us. Aharon Gluska's seemingly innocent *Black Boxes* of 1992–93 lie scattered on the floor like minimalist sculptures. Standing beside them, we are shocked to discover that each box contains a camp photograph of an inmate whose hazy features are barely discernible through the black fabric, but whose eyes stare at us hauntingly.

Other artists identified with the Holocaust dead. First-generation artists Bezem and Tumarkin placed self-portraits among the corpses in the 1950s and 1960s, whereas second-generation artists explored what their own fate would have been. Yocheved Weinfeld portrayed herself in 1979 as an inmate, and from 1975 on, Haim Maor depicted himself naked, about to be shot and thrown into a pit. Their tendency to explore what their own fate would have been was reinforced by their parents seeing them as "memorial candles" or replacements for relatives who had perished in the Holocaust.

Other themes in nonwitness art had a shorter life-span. Refugees were a popular subject in the 1930s and 1940s, as artists either were or had seen refugees firsthand. Depictions of *resistance, especially of the *Warsaw ghetto uprising, are found during and after the war. Artists stressed that the fighters were Jewish by including a bearded man among them. Both refugees and partisans almost completely disappeared from art after 1948, being amalgamated into a new iconography concerning *Israel, which was understood as solving many of the problems raised by the Holocaust.

Artists, however, wished not only to *document* or *describe* events but also to *understand* them by putting them into symbolic or religious frameworks that would elucidate their significance. They developed archetypes to represent victims, partisans, and Nazis. This was already apparent in the works of Germans such as Otto Dix, Grosz, and John Heartfield who warned the public of the dangers inherent in Nazism in the 1920s, and of Chagall, Lipchitz, and Max Beckmann who did so in 1933 after Hitler's rise to power. *Job, the righteous man who unjustifiably lost his possessions, children, and health, became the archetype of the innocent Holocaust victims who were helpless before the evils that befell them. Ivan Mestrovic's emaciated *Job* (1945) accuses *God, while Nathan Rapoport's *Job* (1967), with a number on his arm, retains his faith despite everything. In contrast, artists took liberties to make the binding of *Isaac applicable to the Holocaust (**Plates 15 and 19**). In 1947, Mordecai Ardon portrayed *Sarah crying out against God because Isaac lies dead on the altar; in 1973 Frederick Terna, a survivor, had *Abraham kill himself rather than sacrifice his son; and in Segal's *The Holocaust* (1982–83), both Abraham and Isaac lie dead, linked by a final gesture. In such works, artists did not express unquestioning faith, but rather their anger against God for not saving His people.

Beginning in the 1930s, many artists such as Otto Pankok and Chagall also used the crucifixion, Christianity's major symbol, to warn Christians that they crucified Christ anew when they slaughtered his Jewish brothers (**see Plate 14**).

After the war this image was used to denounce the church for not doing enough to save the Jews.

Artists who tried to represent the Nazis realistically soon found that they had only expressed the "banality of evil." Instead they decided to reveal the Nazis' true nature by symbolizing them as monsters, Death, or Moloch. Solutions ranged from Paul Klee's *Voice from the Ether: And Thou Shalt Have Thy Fill!* (1939) to Grosz' *Cain* (1944) and Kitaj's maniacal *The National Socialist* (1980–81). After the war, some artists – such as Matta, Francis Bacon, and Maryan S. Maryan – comprehended that evil was not just a Nazi trait but was inherent in human nature, and they began to portray all men as monstrous.

Another level of understanding the Holocaust led to the affirmation of Jewish identity, even by artists who had previously disdained religion. In Germany in the 1930s, Ludwig Meidner began depicting Jews praying and signing his works in Hebrew. In New York in the 1940s, Jack Levine turned to the Bible and William Gropper began to portray Jews praying as a yearly memorial to the Holocaust victims. Shahn and Baskin added Hebrew and Yiddish inscriptions to their works, and Barnett Newman translated the titles of his abstract works from Hebrew into English. To those who knew Hebrew, these artists transmitted "hidden messages" that would be incomprehensible to the general public. Younger Jewish artists, including Kitaj, Jonathan Borofsky, Nancy Spero, and Judy Chicago, underwent an opposite process: lacking any religious background, the Holocaust became for them the epitome of Judaism. Others lost their faith, representing the absence of God and the inability of Judaism to be restored.

This difference in generations can also be seen in artists' reactions to the connection between Israel and the Holocaust. In the late 1940s, Chagall and Lipchitz saw the creation of the State as a solution to the survivors' plight. However, Israel's constant wars and the threats to its existence led artists such as Bak, Bezem, and Erich Brauer to see a new Holocaust in every conflict. Leftist artists applied similar generalizations to other conflicts. In 1951 Picasso adapted the image of Nazis shooting naked women and children to the Korean War, thus evoking instinctive sympathy for the North Koreans and hatred for the Americans. Matta's poster *Auschwitz 1941–1945 – Palestine 1948–1968* (1968) and Joan Snyder's *Women in the Camps* (1988) equate Israelis with the Nazis and Palestinians with the Jews, whereas Jörg Immendorff's *Café Deutschland* (1978) uses Holocaust imagery to stress the differences between East and West Germany. These examples raise moral issues. Applying the lessons of the Holocaust to contemporary events rightly warns how hatred and the immoral use of technology lead to genocide. However, applying Holocaust imagery to inherently different situations in order to elicit an unthinking response does not further these aims; it distorts the Holocaust's lessons. Moreover, the common use of these images diffuses their meaning: one forgets that the Holocaust was a singular event that occurred at a given time to a specific people, and this becomes part of the process leading to *Holocaust denial.

The inability of some artists to confront the Holocaust and its implications was clear already at the end of the war. From the late 1940s through the 1970s, a generation of West German artists withdrew into abstraction and refused to deal with the war period. At that time, many Jewish artists also turned to abstraction, although residual symbolism can be found in some of their works. For instance, Morris Louis's *Charred Journal: Firewritten* alludes to Nazi book-burning; flames and burning images appeared in the abstract works of Avigdor Arikha and Bak, whereas Jimmy Ernst used spiky forms that evoke barbed wire.

More recently, artists have stressed the persistence of memory despite attempts to forget. In the series *Shulamith and Margarete* (1981–83), Anselm Kiefer demonstrates that the ashes of Jewish victims will always shadow, underlie, and affect the German people. In 1991–93, Shimon Attie filled German sites with black and white "Jewish ghosts" by projecting pre-war photographs of Jews onto buildings they had inhabited in *Berlin and onto the trains and tracks of the Dresden station from which they had been deported to their deaths.

Works by younger artists can sometimes be offensive because they involve post-modernist irony and an analysis of the way people reinvent history for their own ends. Some artists raise ethical questions by glorifying the Nazis, eroticizing scenes of murder, and using dolls or Lego blocks to portray the Holocaust.

In conclusion, the Holocaust has become part of our collective memory and continues to be expressed in art both in traditional and nonconventional ways.

For further reading, see Z. Amishai-Maisels, *Depiction and Interpretation: The Influence of the Holocaust on the Visual Arts* (1993); D. Apel, *Memory Effects: The Holocaust and the Art of Secondary Witnessing* (2002); M. Baigell, *Jewish-American Artists and the Holocaust* (1997); J. Blatter and S. Milton, *Art of the Holocaust* (1981); B. Brutin, "The Inheritance: Responses to the Holocaust by 'Second Generation' Israeli Artists" (in Hebrew, 2005); M. S. Costanza, *The Living Witness* (1982); M. Novitch, L. Dawidowicz, and T. Freudenheim, *Spiritual Resistance: Art from the Concentration Camps 1940–1945* (1981); G. Green, *The Artists of Terezin* (1969); E. van Alphen, *Caught by History: Holocaust Effects in Contemporary Art, Literature, and Theory* (1997); and J. E. Young, *At Memory's Edge: After-Images of the Holocaust in Contemporary Art and Architecture* (2000). Important anthologies and exhibitions include M. Bohn-Duchen, ed., *After Auschwitz: Responses to the Holocaust in Contemporary Art* (1995); S. C. Feinstein, ed., *Absence/Presence: Critical Essays on the Artistic Memory of the Holocaust* (2005); S. C. Feinstein, ed. *Witness and Legacy: Contemporary Art about the Holocaust* (1995); K. Holtzman, ed., *Burnt Whole: Contemporary Artists Reflect on the Holocaust* (1994); S. Hornstein and F. Jacobowitz, eds., *Image and Remembrance: Representation and the Holocaust* (2003); S. Hornstein, L. Levitt, and L. J. Silberstein, eds., *Impossible Images: Contemporary Art after the Holocaust* (2003); and N.L. Kleeblatt, ed., *Mirroring Evil: Nazi Imagery/Recent Art* (2002).   Ziva Amishai-Maisels

Holocaust Representation: Drama.

Playwrights did not begin to describe and interpret the Holocaust experience until a decade after the end of World War II. The most influential and lasting effort was the 1956 adaptation of Anne *Frank's *Diary of a Young Girl* by two Hollywood screenwriters, Frances Goodrich and Albert Hackett. Otto Frank, Anne's father, the only survivor of the family, had given them permission to create a universal story from his daughter's journal. Their play became a kind of American urtext for the *Holocaust experience, one that was invisibly Jewish

and ultimately optimistic, two reasons for the play's seemingly inexhaustible popularity. The play, *The Diary of Anne Frank*, and its 1959 Hollywood film version have influenced all other dramatic representations of the Holocaust in the United States (see HOLOCAUST REPRESENTATION: FILM).

In Europe, plays on Holocaust themes departed from the upbeat tone and generally realistic form favored by American playwrights. An early example is the prize-winning one-act play, *Korczak and the Children* (1957), by Erwin Sylvanus, a German war veteran; it recounts the story of a Holocaust hero, the Polish Jewish doctor-educator Janusz Korczak, through a chronologically disrupted, allegorical meta-theatrical form. The impetus to depart from realism stemmed from the challenge of confronting the Holocaust in the countries where its devastation had occurred, together with the recognition that realism could not artistically portray the "concentrationary universe" in which millions of victims had been slaughtered.

The countries most affected by the Holocaust tended to produce plays reflecting localized cultural and political concerns; these changed over time with the emergence of new knowledge of atrocities and new assumptions about their causes and effects. Most controversial were dramatic efforts to account for the deaths of so many innocent victims and the shattering of deeply valued ethical assumptions about humanity. In *France, Charlotte Delbo, a non-Jewish survivor of *Auschwitz, wrote *Who Will Carry the Word?* (1974); this play attempts to identify and analyze Delbo's own complicated presence among compatriots who were themselves implicated in the betrayal and murder of innocent people. In plays like *The Workroom* (1979), Jean-Claude Grumberg has sought to assess France's complicity with the Holocaust's perpetrators and its legacy of *antisemitism. Among German-speaking writers, Rolf Hochhuth in *The Deputy* (1963), Peter Weiss in *The Investigation* (1965), and Thomas Bernhard in *Eve of Retirement* (1979), in styles ranging from documentary to the poetic, explore the nature and source of evil in *Nazism and German culture. Hochhuth's greatest condemnation is reserved for the Vatican's indifference to Jewish suffering.

The most problematic Holocaust dramas present Jews as accomplices to their own murder, an idea first raised by the historian Raul Hilberg in *The Destruction of the European Jews* (1961) and by the philosopher Hannah Arendt in *Eichmann in Jerusalem* (1963). Plays such as Harold and Edith Lieberman's *Throne of Straw* (1978), Joshua Sobol's *Ghetto* (1984), and Roy Kift's *Camp Comedy* (1996) depict the lethal moral conundrums faced by Jewish leaders (Mordechai Chaim Rumkowski in Łódź, Jacob Gens in *Vilna, Jacob Eppstein in *Theresienstadt, respectively) whose efforts to save as many Jews as possible from Nazi annihilation required the sacrifice of others. The critic Lawrence Langer has called their dilemma one of "choiceless choice."

The Liebermans and Kift make use of "Brechtian" or "epic theater" techniques to disrupt the audience's emotional involvement as a way to force engagement with the ethical "gray zone," evoked by Primo *Levi in his famous essay about Rumkowski (in *The Drowned and the Saved*, [1986]). Other playwrights link Jewish victims to the criminal behavior of their abusers more explicitly; for example, Robert Shaw in *The Man in the Glass Booth* (1969) and Rainer Werner Fassbinder in *Garbage, the City and Death* (1975).

In the dramatization by Christopher Hampton of the 1981 novella, *The Portage to San Cristobal of A. H.* by the brilliant critic George Steiner, the character of Hitler voices the deliberately provocative and unanswered argument that he was responsible for establishing the State of *Israel.

Since the 1970s, the theater of the Holocaust has been used to affirm the distinctive experiences of specific groups. Delbo's theatrical work, as well as that of her French colleague Lillian Atlan (*Mr. Fugue or Earth Sick*, 1967), has been studied and praised for its focus on the experience of women; Martin Sherman's *Bent* (1979), a "coming out play," has come to stand for the suffering of male homosexuals in the concentration camps. Yet the most important change among the second- and third-generation playwrights, aside from the dramatization of stories about the children and grandchildren of Holocaust victims, has been the proliferation of plays that produce theatrical effects through *comedy, once thought to be demeaning or destructive to the telling of an exclusively tragic Holocaust experience. Peter Barnes's *Laughter* (1978), Joan Schenkar's *The Last of Hitler* (1982), Roy Kift's *Camp Comedy* (1996), and Eugene Lion's *Sammy's Follies* (2006) all use humor to make the performances of their plays more transgressive of conventional theatrical forms and ethical assumptions. No writer has so consistently or outrageously employed mordant wit and outrageous farce than George Tabori (whose father was murdered in Auschwitz); his long career includes Holocaust-themed tragicomedies like *The Cannibals* (1968) and *Mein Kampf* (1986).

In fact, changes in Holocaust representation over sixty years can be gauged in the various ways that Anne Frank's story has been adjusted and adapted for the theater according to national need, historical pressure, aesthetic preference, and thematic focus. Wendy Kesselman's realistic updating of the original version in 1997, together with Bernard Kops' surrealistic "play for young people," *Dreams of Anne Frank* (1992); Bobby Box's puppet play *Anne Frank: Within & Without* (2006); and Enid Futterman and Michael Cohen's musical theater piece *Yours, Anne* (1985) are only a few examples of the ways one historical victim's story has been represented dramatically. *Yours, Anne* is also an example of the important use of music in many dramatic depictions of the Holocaust; others include the Liebermans' klezmer, Kift's cabaret, C. P. Taylor's pastiche of classical to schmaltz in *Good* (1981), and Nicholas Maw's 2002 full-length opera based on William Styron's 1982 novel, *Sophie's Choice*.

For further reading, see E. Isser, *Stages of Annihilation* (1997); C. Schumacher, ed., *Staging the Holocaust* (1998); R. Skloot, *The Darkness We Carry* (1988); idem, ed., *The Theatre of the Holocaust*, 2 vols. (1981, 1999); and N. Watts, ed., *A Terrible Truth*, 2 vols. (2003); and entries under **THEATER.**   ROBERT SKLOOT

Holocaust Representation: Film. The unimaginable horrors and the monumental scope of the mass murder of the concentration camp universe pose a special challenge to efforts of comprehension, expression, or representation. Any Holocaust text is constrained in its ability to provide a truthful account or to transmit the unique "unreality of the other planet" by the codes of its artistic form, by technical possibilities, and by the cultural norms and socio-political ideologies of its time. At the same time, the representation of the Holocaust is essential to inform and to enlighten, to pay homage to the victims and their sufferings, and to warn against the dangers of ideologies of hatred. Cinema has been a witness to the Holocaust in documentary images, a participant in the unfolding of the Holocaust in propaganda films, and a repository of collective memory in popular movies. Films have played a central part in how the *Shoah* has been understood and remembered, just as the subject of the Holocaust has played a role in the evolution of cinema as an art form and as a major medium of cultural discourse and social communication.

Cinema was already used for propaganda purposes during the earliest years of *Nazism. Film crews headed by the talented filmmaker Leni Riefenstahl documented the first national Nazi rallies. *Victory of Faith* (*Sieg des Glaubens*, 1934) about the 1933 Nuremberg party convention was followed by *Triumph of The Will* (*Triumph des Willens*, 1935), a film designed to transform ordinary viewers into impassioned Nazis through stunning spectacles, fiery speeches by Adolf Hitler, and a musical soundtrack based on national and party anthems, military marches, and Wagnerian themes. After the outbreak of the war, antisemitic German films such as *Jew Suss* (*Jud Süss*, 1940), about an eighteenth-century *Court Jew, and the pseudo-documentary *The Eternal Jew* (*Der ewige Jude*, 1940) revealed the Nazis' genocidal intentions as early as the fall of 1940, nearly a year before the actual systematic killing of the Jews began. Both of these extraordinary hate films were shown to German troops assigned to carry out the genocide programs (see ANTISEMITISM).

Hollywood wartime movies tried to warn the free world about the dangers of Nazism and the need to fight and win the war, but very few films addressed the predicament of the Jews. During the war years, the Jewish heads of the major Hollywood studios feared antisemitic backlashes and accusations of double loyalty or Jewish war mongering to help the Jews in Europe. Charles Chaplin's *The Great Dictator* (1940) was a remarkable exception, produced with the artist's own money and outside the studio system (Chaplin was not Jewish). The film satirizes Hitler and Nazi Germany, and it features Nazi persecution of a Jewish barber and his community. Chaplin plays both the great dictator and the Jewish barber; the movie ridicules racial theories when, in a mistaken identity plot twist at the end of the film, the fanatic followers of the dictator hail the barber as their leader. Although the shocking revelations of the magnitude of suffering and destruction at the end of the war prompted Chaplin to express regret for his humorous approach, his genius made *The Great Dictator* a classic film and a rare early treatment of the plight of the Jews in the Third Reich.

During World War II, photographic images, both moving and still, played a major role as sources of information and communication. Newsreels shown in movie theaters, as well as published photographs of barbed wires, watchtowers, barracks, chimneys, and smoke, informed millions of people about the Holocaust's horrors, and they continue to evoke the Nazis' network of concentration and death camps. The most graphic images of the Holocaust are those of the victims at the liberated concentration camps. The astounded commanders of the Allied forces ordered the filming of these terrible scenes so that they could be recorded, widely distributed, and also preserved as evidence of Nazi atrocities and mass murder. Photographs of emaciated living bodies and stacked corpses have become the ultimate images of genocide and dehumanization.

In the immediate post-war years, aspects of the Holocaust were portrayed in realistic dramas, which were motivated by the desire to inform, to remember, and to learn the lessons of the past while asserting a commitment to a better world. The idea of "a better world" took many political forms. In the communist regimes of *Eastern Europe, national cinemas treated the Nazi horrors as the crucible for the ideological triumph of Russian-inspired socialism. Such films include the Polish *Border Street* (dir. Alexander Ford, 1947) and *The Last Stage* (dir. Wanda Jakubowska, 1947). Post-war films, such as *The Great Promise* (dir. Josef Lejtes, 1946), *My Father's House* (dir. Herbert Kline, 1947), and *The Illegals* (dir. Meyer Levin, 1948), have a Zionist emphasis, showing survivors recovering from their traumas in what would soon become the State of *Israel. In the United States, Hollywood followed years of ignoring the Jewish genocide with films like *Gentleman's Agreement* (dir. Elia Kazan, 1947) and *Crossfire* (dir. Edward Dmytryk, 1947), which address the problem of antisemitism and the need to eradicate racism and prejudice from post-war American society. The first major American film on the Holocaust was *The Diary of *Anne Frank* (dir. George Stevens, 1959). Based on the published diary and the Broadway *theater version, the Hollywood production sentimentalizes the Holocaust, promoting shallow forms of optimism. Its final message is of hope; the legacy of the universalized Anne appears in her words that "in spite of everything" she believes in human goodness. Contemporary discomfort with the simplistic sentimentality of the Hollywood presentation of Anne Frank also applied to productions in other parts of the world in the 1950s, as they were usually dramas that celebrated heroic and self-justified national ideology. However, many of these films represented their locations realistically. *The Diary of Anne Frank* was filmed in a replica of the authentic attic and included exterior pictures of the original site in *Amsterdam. Gilo Potecorvo's *Kapo* (1959) was shot in camps in operation during the war years.

Alain Resnais' *Night And Fog* (*Nuit et Brouillard*, 1955) is an artistic reflection on the newsreel footage and documentary evidence of Nazi atrocities. In less than 30 minutes, this exemplary documentary features the horrors of the concentration camp universe, employing wartime images and pictures of *Auschwitz in the present. Its dualistic structure and double perspective serve two purposes. On the one hand, the film exposes details of the Holocaust: the daily routine, the infernal organization, and the victims' helplessness once they were caught up in the process of the extermination system. On the other hand, the brooding camera, as it films Auschwitz in the 1950s, accompanied by cryptic narration and probing flute melodies, expresses the anguished recognition that the images of the unimaginable cannot represent the universe of atrocities.

In the 1960s, Modernist existentialist attitudes generated visions that regarded the concentration camp universe as an incarnation of the human condition in general. Thus, the Holocaust was invoked to offer insights and metaphors for understanding the human predicament. Luchino Visconti's *The Damned* (1969), Bob Fosse's *Cabaret* (1972), Joseph Losey's *Mr. Klein* (*Monsieur Klein*, 1976), and H. J.

Syberberg's *Hitler – A Film from Germany* (*Hitler, ein Film aus Deuschland*, 1977) confront those aspects of Western civilization that created Nazism and the Holocaust. Ingmar Bergman (*Serpent's Egg*, 1977) and François Truffaut (*The Last Metro* [*Le dernier métro*], 1980) explore the complexity of character in light of the human experience under Nazi menace. American movies like *Judgment at Nuremberg* (dir. Stanley Kramer, 1961) and *The Pawnbroker* (dir. Sidney Lumet, 1965) address the ethical dimension of social behavior vis-à-vis injustice and racism.

In Europe, the critical attitudes of Modernism led to a new, harsh reckoning with the past. The 1960s Czech cinematic new wave produced a remarkable combination of humanistic realism, as in *The Shop on Main Street* (dir. Jan Kadar, 1965), and surrealistic Modernism inspired by Alfred Radok's *Distant Journey* (1950) in films like *Transport from Paradise* (Zbyněk Brynych, 1963), *Diamonds of the Night* (Jan Němec, 1964), and *The Fifth Horseman Is Fear* (Brynych, 1965). In *France, *The Sorrow and the Pity* (*Le chagrin et la pitié*; dir. Marcel Ophuls, 1969), a documentary on the conduct of French society during World War II, counters national traditions of heroic resistance with details of widespread collaboration and antisemitic actions. The film spurred a new wave of "retro" films that subvert the heroic historical narratives that had been fostered by French official institutions and political leaders since the end of the war. Louis Malle explores the character of a young collaborator in *Lacombe Lucien* (1973) and personal guilt over the treatment of Jews in *Goodbye Children* (*Au revoir les enfants*, 1987). Jewish filmmakers, recalling personal experiences from the war years, feature the plight of the Jews in occupied France in *Violins at the Ball* (*Les violons du bal*; dir. Michel Drach, 1974) and *Black Thursday* (*Les guichets du Louvre*; dir. Michel Mitrani, 1974).

In the 1970s, a young generation of German filmmakers created movies that tried to deal with the history of their country from the perspective of a personal confrontation with the burden of Nazism. These films include the self-pitying *Germany Pale Mother* (*Deutschland, bleiche Mutter*; dir. Helga Sanders Brahms, 1980), the subversive *Lili Marleen* (dir. R. W. Fassbinder, 1980), and the reclaiming of a German past in the film series *Homeland* (*Heimat*; dir. Edgar Reitz, 1980–84). Israeli filmmakers also began to examine the legacy of the Holocaust in the national psyche and the effects of the historical trauma on the political behavior of the Jewish state in *Operation Jonathan* (dir. Menahem Golan, 1978) and *Wooden Gun* (dir. Ilan Moshenson, 1979).

The completion of Claude Lanzmann's *Shoah* in 1985 marks the appearance of a canonical text in the discourse of the Holocaust as well as a unique film masterpiece. In more than nine hours of film, Lanzmann focuses on the core of the horrors: the death camps and the methods and details of the killing process. The film presents the Holocaust as a watershed historical event, a singular human experience, and a unique challenge to the possibilities of artistic expression. The dramatic content occurs in two levels – the excruciating accounts of the past and their painful recounting in the present – that interact with each other. Thus, the film explores a past whose scars inform a tormented presence. Although it appears to be a lean documentary, seemingly limited to interviews and images of the sites of the genocide, avoiding narration, music, or any sound effects, *Shoah* is a highly artistic text, rich with significant aesthetic decisions and a sophisticated Modernist poetics. Most remarkably, the film has no documentary historical photographs or archival footage from the war years, underscoring Lanzmann's conviction that the Holocaust's heart of darkness is beyond representation and that documentary images might suggest that there are images of the unimaginable and that the unrepresentable can be shown. In recent decades Lanzmann's cautious approach to the visual image as a record of reality has been replaced by a post-modern celebration of spectacle and the power of images. This challenge to the notion of grand narratives, together with the new technologies of computer and video, is evident in numerous works on multiple and diverse aspects of the Holocaust. Many members of the second generation have used inexpensive film production methods to explore their family roots and the special predicaments of their parent survivors. Several ambitious projects established large collections of video testimonies by tens of thousands of survivors.

The popularity of the Holocaust as a subject for cinematic imagination was underscored by the success of *Schindler's List* (1993; Academy Award for Best Picture, 1993). Steven Spielberg, the most popular filmmaker in the world, created an epic account of the struggle to survive in the infernal ghettoes, labor camps, and extermination centers of *Poland. The story focuses on Oskar *Schindler, a real person who used his position in the German economy and Nazi circles to save thousands of Jews. Spielberg's *Schindler's List* is a powerful realistic presentation, shot in black and white to match the newsreel images from the past. He offers the project as a work of a Modernist artist, burdened by the personal angst and tragic recognitions of a Jew in the post-Shoah modern world. Ultimately, *Schindler's List* is a post-modern media event and a post-modern text celebrating the preservation of life, capitalism, and the power of the cinematic medium.

Schindler's List marks a shift from the engagement with victimizers and victims to saviors and survivors. Postmodernism is also characterized by the withdrawal from anguished reflections on the tragic aspects of existence, as manifested in Roberto Benigni's Holocaust drama, *Life Is Beautiful* (*La Vita è bella* [1999]). Holocaust comedy, arguably an impossible oxymoron, became a popular option, with films like *Train of Life* (*Train de vie*; dir. Radu Mihaileanu, 1998) and *Jacob the Liar* (dir. Peter Kassovitz, 1999). Rather than irreverence or mockery, these works attempt to offer the life-enhancing vision of comedy in connection with the Holocaust. As such, they echo numerous post-*Shoah* films that celebrate human virtues and resistance under pressure. These include *Weapons of the Spirit* (*Les armes de l'esprit*; Pierre Sauvage, 1989), a documentary on Le Chambon-sur-Lignon, a small Protestant farming village in France that hid Jews, and *Triumph of the Spirit* (Robert Young, 1989) a dramatic film about an actual individual who survived Auschwitz by winning boxing matches. Claude Lanzmann's last film, *Sobibór, October 14, 1943, 4 P.M* (2001), recounts the heroic prisoners' revolt in Sobibór that put an end to the functioning of the death camp. A recent example of this genre is *Defiance* (Edward Zwick, 2008) about the four Bielski brothers who saved 1,200 Jews in a settlement in a Polish forest while waging a campaign of armed resistance (see HOLOCAUST RESISTANCE).

Filmmakers have found rich material and intense dramatic situations in the Holocaust. The chief historical and moral lessons of the event fall into the categories of victims, bystanders, and perpetrators. Holocaust films feature the victims' predicament and human suffering and resistance in the face of genocidal assaults, or they examine the conduct of bystanders that may range from collaboration to indifference to righteous action. Films dealing with perpetrators have established Nazism as the ultimate evil of human experience. Notable examples include Roman Polanski's exploration of the plight of the victim survivor in *The Pianist* (2002); Costa Gavras' investigation of the role and ethical dilemmas of bystanders in *Amen* (2002), an adaptation of Rolf Hochuth's celebrated play on the conduct of Pope Pius XII and the Catholic church during the Holocaust; and German director Oliver Hirschbiegel's spectacular presentation of the last days of Hitler and the Nazi regime in *Downfall* (*Der Untergang*; 2004).

The Shoah continues to fascinate filmmakers and viewers around the world. The extensive personalization of the Holocaust by numerous young filmmakers exploring their family roots is evident in historical sagas like Claude Lelouch's *Bolero* (*Les uns et les autres* [1981]) and István Szábo's *Sunshine* (1999), films that feature the unfolding of the twentieth century through the sagas of individual characters but also highlight the centrality of the Holocaust in modern experience. By 1960, fewer than 120 feature films about the Holocaust had been made, in a total of fourteen countries. In the 1990s alone, more than two hundred Holocaust movies were produced in thirty-one countries. Since 1980, many films dealing with the Holocaust have won the American Academy Awards (Oscar) in the categories of documentaries and foreign films; these include the 2008 Austrian/German foreign film, *The Counterfeiters* (*Die Fälscher*; dir. Stefan Ruzowitzky; 2007).

In the present age of multichannel telecommunication, television has become the site for many Holocaust films, with numerous channels showing dramatic material based on historical events and real life (see HOLOCAUST REPRESENTATION: TELEVISION). The Shoah continues to inspire a variety of films, including historical sagas; morality tales; dramas of adolescent crises, social prejudice, and political conflicts; and adventure fantasies. In most cases, filmmakers are sensitive to the imperatives of historical memory, the limits of representation, and the risks of vulgarization and trivialization – due in great part to the public discourse and critical discussion about adequate representations and their ethical implications that have been generated by the apparently unending stream of Holocaust movies.

For further reading, see I. Avisar, *Screening the Holocaust: Cinema's Images of the Unimaginable* (1988); L. Baron, *Projecting the Holocaust into the Present: The Changing Focus of Contemporary Holocaust Cinema* (2005); T. Haggith and J. Newman, eds., *Holocaust and the Moving Image: Representations in Film and Television since 1933* (2005); A. Insdorf, *Indelible Shadows: Film and the Holocaust* (2002); and J. Hirsch, *Afterimage: Film, Trauma, and the Holocaust* (2004).   ILAN AVISAR

Holocaust Representation: Television. The Holocaust was first communicated visually to 1940s American and British audiences in newsreels and popular photojournalist magazines such as *Look* and *Life*. Over the next six decades various documentary and fictionalized representations of the Holocaust appeared on *television. The visual image, most often black and white, has remained central to consciousness of the Holocaust.

The first dramatic invocations of the Holocaust usually depicted an individual story, often tangential to the Holocaust, in which the larger event loomed in the shadows. Although these storylines may have indicated an initial unwillingness to confront the magnitude of the topic, the reduction of a major subject to fit the small screen may also reflect the nature of television. Some television programs of this era sought to fit the Holocaust narrative into their own format. In 1953 Ralph Edwards used his popular program *This Is Your Life* to tell the story of one survivor, Hanna Bloch Kohner. The story echoed major American themes: innocent youth interrupted by the trauma of persecution and incarceration, and separation and loss crowned with a love story and the triumph of survival. In this episode Kohner was reunited with her brother who had been flown in secretly from *Israel.

Some prominent writers of 1950s television dramas were Jewish but the custom of the time permitted depictions of only one Jewish character and one African-American character per year, per series. Programs with overtly Jewish themes were only scheduled on Sunday mornings when religious broadcasting was offered as a public service. These annual Jewish-centered programs usually coincided with a major Jewish *holiday, and Jewish writers, directors, and producers used their skills to craft impressive work. Thus, *Judgment at Nuremberg* (1961) was presented on television before it became the classic movie; *The Diary of Anne *Frank* was broadcast in 1952 as a half-hour Sunday morning *Frontier of Faith* program, even before its Broadway appearance and only months after it had first appeared in English. This program included Anne's proclamation of faith in the future that made her story palatable to contemporary American sensibilities: "I still believe that people are really good at heart. I simply can't build up my hopes on a foundation consisting of confusion, misery, and death." It was another forty years before an ABC docudrama followed Anne into concentration camps at Westerbork and *Auschwitz and on the death marches to Bergen-Belsen, where she died during the typhus epidemic in March 1945, only weeks before its liberation. By then the Holocaust had become American culture's pardigmatic manifestation of *evil within the world.

Judgment at Nuremberg focused on the *United States and its Allies as judges of *Nazi war criminals; it did not refer to American indifference to the fate of Europe's Jews during the war. Its most memorable moment was a word that was not said: The American Gas Company, sponsor of *Playhouse 90*, forbade the word "gas," the modality of Nazi killing, to be spoken. Over the next decades, the nature of the event being depicted would frequently clash with those financing the new industry. Only in 1998, when the Holocaust had emerged as a paradigmatic, seemingly sacred event, would the networks broadcast Steven Spielberg's *Schindler's List* without commercial interruption. (The sponsor was the Ford Motor Company, whose founder Henry Ford had financed *antisemitic publications including the *Protocols of the Elders of Zion*. His descendants and his successors were not unmindful of this past as they undertook this "public service.")

A significant change in Holocaust consciousness was marked in 1961, sixteen years after the camps' liberation, when the trial of Adolf Eichmann (see HOLOCAUST TRIALS) brought an unprecedented number of journalists to *Jerusalem and television coverage was provided. As background for the trial a number of documentaries about the Holocaust were produced; daily news broadcasts brought the trial into America's homes. Israel, which did not yet have television (David *Ben-Gurion, Israel's founding prime minister was wary of its potential cultural and materialistic impact on the state), broadcast the trial on closed-circuit television as Israelis sat glued to their radios. If Nuremberg was a trial by documents, the Eichmann trial was a trial by survivors, who narrated the entire history of the Holocaust whether it had relevance to the defendant's deeds or not. Over the next decade some important films were produced, and the Holocaust slowly made its way out of the ghetto of Sunday morning television.

In 1977 the mini-series *Roots*, an African American family saga, was broadcast on American television with great success. One year later, NBC, newly confident that minority programming could attract a large viewership, broadcast the docudrama *Holocaust* over a four-night period; some 250 million Americans watched at least part of it. Despite historical and aesthetic criticisms of aspects of the mini-series, the Holocaust had become mainstream. Fears that the Holocaust would be forgotten disappeared, and the only issue remaining was whether it would be remembered appropriately, with due deference to the power of the event, or whether television would reduce its real human drama to soap opera. In *Germany, where it was seen by a younger generation who had not lived through these events, the mini-series *Holocaust* also had a great impact. In its wake, the German Parliament rescinded the statute of limitations for the prosecution of Nazi war criminals. In the United States, the broadcast of *Holocaust* created the climate that led to the creation of the Office of Special Investigations of the Department of Justice to bring Nazi war criminals to justice and the establishment of the President's Commission on the Holocaust, which subsequently recommended the creation of the United States Holocaust Memorial Museum. The mini-series coincided with the emergence of Holocaust courses and research on college and university campuses, which increased fiftyfold in the 1970s.

In the late 1980s, the mini-series, *War and Remembrance,* based on Herman Wouk's 1978 epic novel, was broadcast; this series was far more graphic in its treatment of the Holocaust than anything seen before. By then, television had entered the cable era, which segmented the television audience while permitting greater program diversity. Stories of resistance particularly fascinated American television networks. *Escape from *Sobibor* (1987) portrayed resistance in a death camp. Jon Avnet's mini-series *Uprising,* the narrative of the *Warsaw ghetto, was a far more graphic and nuanced representation than previous work. It was broadcast on the same night as the Emmy Awards and the seventh game of the World Series in 2001, just weeks after 9/11. The rescue of *Denmark's Jews was depicted on national television, and so, too, was the story of Raoul *Wallenberg in *Wallenberg: A Hero's Story* (1985). By the late twentieth century, topical shows routinely presented themes connected to the Holocaust. Thus, one of the episodes of *Brooklyn Bridge* (1991–93), a Jewish family drama set in the 1950s, was entitled the "Last Immigrant," about the arrival of a Holocaust survivor and family efforts to keep a young boy from learning the fate of Europe's Jews (1992).

The cable channel Home Box Office (HBO) has played a unique role in broadcasting documentaries, both its own creations – such as *One Survivor Remembers: The Gerda Weismann Klein Story* (1995), winner of an Oscar and an Emmy, and *Into the Arms of Strangers: Stories of the* *Kindertransport* (2000) – and serving as an outlet for the broadcast of documentaries created for other purposes, such as *The Long Way Home* (1997) or *Last Days* (1998), both Academy-Award-winning films. It also created *Conspiracy*, the Emmy-winning ninety-minute reenactment of the *Wannsee Conference. The History Channel has also paid significant attention to the Holocaust. Both cable and network channels routinely rebroadcast major theatrical films with Holocaust themes.

For many decades the Holocaust was considered a sacred event, off limits to comedy or comedians. *Hogan's Heroes* (1965–71), a television comedy about American prisoners of war and their foolish German captors, presumed the evil of the Nazi cause, but steered clear of the Holocaust. Jewish comedians, in particular, began to break this taboo, from Mel Brooks' *The Producers* (film [1968], Broadway musical [2001], and film [2005]) to Jerry Seinfeld's "Soup Nazi" episode (*Seinfeld*, 1995, season 7). Larry David's television comedy, *Curb Your Enthusiasm*, routinely evokes the Holocaust, whether he pits a Holocaust survivor against a contestant on a television show (2004) or shows the tattoos on a chef's arm, which he mistakes for tattoos of an *Auschwitz survivor (2002). David uses the Holocaust's very sacredness as a comedic tool: Nothing is out of bounds, nothing too holy to touch.

Through television, the film industry has the unique capacity to shape the perceptions of historical events for the nonscholarly and nonliterary public (Shandler). Danny Anker's television documentary, *Imaginary Witness: Hollywood and the Holocaust* (AMC 2004), explores this very basic issue and its uniquely American dimension. Because of its status as the paradigmatic manifestation of twentieth-century evil, the Holocaust is often used as a backdrop to other instances of mass murder and genocide. Thus, Elie *Wiesel was featured as a commentator on *The Day After* (1983), the story of the morrow of nuclear conflagration. Television commentators invoked the failure to bomb Auschwitz when Kosovo was bombed by NATO forces.

The proliferation of creative approaches to the Holocaust by men and women of greater and lesser talent and sensitivities in commercial contexts raises ongoing concern about the subject's trivialization and vulgarization. However, for the most part the Holocaust has been handled on television with respect and dignity; for many who have worked with this material, it has elicited some of their finest work. Because of the compelling nature of this event in human history, as well as the abundance of visual images and recorded testimony, the Holocaust is bound to continue to fascinate filmmakers and documentarians for decades to come. For further reading, see J. Shandler, *While America Watches: Televising the Holocaust* (1999).   MICHAEL BERENBAUM

Holocaust Rescuers. In the early 1960s, *Yad Vashem, Israel's *Holocaust memorial authority, began to recognize non-Jews who helped save Jews during the *Shoah. To date, Yad Vashem has recognized more than 22,000 individuals and one country, *Denmark, as "Righteous Gentiles" or "Righteous among the Nations." In this entry, rescuers are dealt with country by country; there are many more documented rescuers in these and other countries who are not mentioned here.

BULGARIA: There were about 50,000 Jews in *Bulgaria on the eve of World War II, and most would survive the Holocaust. A Nazi ally during most of the war, the Bulgarian government began to implement anti-Jewish legislation in 1941. However, there was widespread opposition to these policies, particularly to plans to deport Jews to *Poland. In the spring of 1943, Alexander Belev, the head of Bulgaria's Commissariat for Jewish Questions, decided to include Bulgarian Jews in transports of Jews from Bulgarian-occupied Macedonia and Thrace to fill his quota of 20,000. Metropolitan Kiril of the Bulgarian Orthodox Church in Plovdiv immediately asked King Boris III to halt the transports from Bulgaria proper and threatened to lie down on the city's railroad tracks to stop the deportations. Similar protests took place elsewhere in Bulgaria. As a result, Belev decided not to include Bulgarian Jews in the transports, but he did send the 11,500 Jews in Macedonia and Thrace to death camps in Poland. He also forced 19,000 Jews in the capital, Sofia, to move to twenty towns and villages throughout the country in May 1943. Metropolitan Kiril was among nineteen Bulgarians later named Righteous Gentiles.

DENMARK: There were about 7,500 Jews in Denmark in 1940. After the German occupation, the Danish government told the Germans that the "Jewish question" was off limits for discussion. This all changed in the fall of 1943 when Dr. Werner Best, Germany's new ambassador to Denmark, began to plan the round-up and deportation of Denmark's Jews for October 1–2. Georg Ferdinand Duckwitz, an attaché at the German legation in Copenhagen, informed Swedish, Jewish, and Danish underground leaders of Best's plans, which prompted a Danish national rescue effort in October 1943. The Danes were able to smuggle 7,220 Jews into Sweden, although another 461 Danish Jews were unable to escape Best's dragnet and were sent to *Theresienstadt. Duckwitz was named a Righteous Gentile in 1971.

FRANCE: *France was conquered by the Germans in the spring and early summer of 1940 and divided into two occupation zones. Northern France was under *Wehrmacht* control, whereas southern France was governed by the collaborationist Vichy government. More than half of France's 330,000–340,000 Jews were trapped in the Vichy zone. Huguenots in the Vichy hamlet of Le Chambon-sur-Lignon, guided by Pastor André Trocmé, hid three to five thousand Jews. Pastor Marc Donadille and his wife Francoise saved another eighty Jews in Alsace and sent another one hundred to Le Chambon.

In Lyon, Father Pierre Chaillet, a Jesuit priest who worked with the resistance movement, searched for orphaned Jewish children and placed them with French families who agreed to hide them. He was supported by Cardinal Archbishop of Lyon, Pierre-Marie Gerlier, and his advisor on Jewish affairs, Abbé Alexandre Glasburg. Abbé Glasburg was credited with saving 180 children in the Vénissieux detention camp from deportation. French Quakers, the YMCA, and the American Jewish *Joint Distribution Committee also played active roles in saving French Jews. Varian

Fry, an American journalist working with the American Emergency Rescue Committee, helped smuggle more than 2,000 refugees out of Marseilles before he was arrested and deported by the Vichy government in the fall of 1941. All of these French heroes, including Fry, were later recognized as Righteous Gentiles.

GERMANY: Father Bernhard Lichtenberg, a staunch critic of the Nazis as rector and later provost of St. Hedwig's Cathedral in *Berlin, became involved in efforts to stop the persecution of Jews soon after Hitler took power. Constantly watched and threatened by German authorities, he initiated daily public prayers for Jews and Christians and argued that Nazi teachings about the *Volk* were un-Christian. In 1941, the Gestapo arrested Lichtenberg and charged him with attacks against the state and Nazi party. During their search of his apartment, Gestapo agents found a copy of a sermon he planned to deliver that said that Nazi ideas were incompatible with Catholic teachings. He was convicted and sentenced to two years in prison for his religious activities. His bishop, Konrad von Preysing, convinced the Gestapo to allow Lichtenberg to regain his freedom after he completed his sentence in return for a promise not to preach until the war was over. Lichtenberg refused and was sent to a work camp where he was badly beaten. He died on the way to *Dachau in 1943.

*HUNGARY: The Hungarian government of Admiral Miklós Horthy, a Nazi ally, initially refused Germany's demand in 1942 that it deport its 725,000 Jews and 100,000 Jewish converts to Christianity to the East because, it argued, they were too important to the country's economy. This all changed when Germany occupied Hungary in the spring of 1944. Heinrich Himmler, the *Reichsführer SS* and principal architect of the "Final Solution," sent Adolf Eichmann, his deportation specialist, to Budapest to oversee the round-up and transport of Hungary's Jews to *Auschwitz. Eichmann, working closely with Hungarian officials, sent more than 437,000 Jews to Auschwitz between May 15 and July 8, where most were murdered.

Rescue efforts began almost immediately, led by the Jewish Agency of Palestine's Relief and Rescue Committee of Budapest (RRCB). Joel Brand, a controversial RRCB leader, held three meetings with Eichmann, who agreed to sell Brand one million Jews in a "goods for blood" deal that involved the transfer of ten thousand new trucks and various foodstuffs to the SS. News of Eichmann's offer quickly reached the Allies, who, in league with the international press, condemned the scheme as a "Gestapo plot" and "humanitarian blackmail." A number of diplomats in Budapest did everything possible to save Hungary's Jews. Swedish diplomats Per Anger, Carl Ivan Danielsson, and Raoul Wallenberg went to extraordinary efforts to help, as did Swiss diplomats Carl and Gerturd Lutz, Papal Nuncio Angelo Rotta, Italian diplomat Giorgio Perlasca, and Swiss International Red Cross representative Friedrich Born. Yad Vashem later named each of them Righteous Gentiles. The diplomats issued fake *Schutz* (protection) *briefe* or *Schutzpässe* (protection passes) to Hungarian Jews, which identified them as Swedish subjects awaiting repatriation. Wallenberg and Anger also rented thirty buildings in Budapest to house "Swedish" Jews awaiting transfer, declaring the buildings inviolable Swedish territory. Wallenberg, who was later arrested by the Soviets as an American spy and died in Soviet captivity, risked his life over and over to save as many Jews as possible.

LITHUANIA: The first major effort to help Jews in the early years of World War II came in the summer of 1940 after the Soviet Union conquered the *Baltic states of Estonia, Latvia, and Lithuania. There were 260,000 Jews in Lithuania at this time. In early August 1940, Jewish refugees in Lithuania flooded foreign legations seeking exit visas to *Palestine or the *United States. Jan Zwartendijk, the acting Dutch consul, worked closely with Japanese diplomat Sempo Sugihara to issue Dutch and Japanese transit visas to thousands of Jews for Dutch Curaçao via Japan. Although Zwartendijk's efforts were supported by his government, Sugihara was criticized by Japanese authorities for violating strict Japanese immigration guidelines. Regardless, their work saved the lives of thousands of Jews, which led to their recognition as Righteous among the Nations. The following year, Ona Simiate, a librarian at the University of Vilnius, began to do everything she could to help the city's Jews. She got permission to enter the Vilnius (*Vilna) ghetto after explaining that she needed to recover books checked out by former Jewish students. She tried to retrieve as many books as she could from the famed *YIVO Institute, hiding them outside the ghetto. She also brought food, medicines, and other supplies to Jewish friends there and helped hide Jews who escaped from the ghetto. The Germans arrested Simiate in 1944 and brutally tortured her. After friends at the university bribed the police to prevent her execution, she was sent to Dachau and then to France. Although she refused any recognition for her rescue efforts, Yad Vashem later declared her a Righteous among the Nations.

POLAND: Occupied *Poland was both Nazi Germany's racial laboratory and principal killing field during the Final Solution. The Germans not only murdered 90% of pre-war Poland's 3.3–3.5 million Jews but they also killed three million Christian Poles. To help a Jew meant death to any Gentile. To date, Yad Vashem has recognized more than 6,000 Christian Poles as Righteous among the Nations.

One of the most famous Righteous Gentiles was Irena Sendlerowa, a leader of Żegota or Council for the Aid to Jews, a Catholic–Jewish organization committed to doing everything possible to save Jews. Sendlerowa was responsible for hiding Jewish children outside the *Warsaw ghetto. She placed most of them in foster homes or hid them in Catholic convents and orphanages. Over time, she had about 3,000 Jews under her care. She worked closely with other Żegota leaders such as Julian and Halina Grobelny and Irena Schutz, who helped her obtain illegal documents from the city of Warsaw's Sanitary–Epidemiological Office that allowed daily access to the ghetto. Children were smuggled out through underground tunnels, taken briefly to "safe" apartments, and then placed with Polish families, who risked a great deal to help them. Żegota also worked with the Zionist Jewish Fighting Organization (*Żydowska Organizacja Bojowa*, or ZOB) to save adults, particularly those involved in daily work details outside of the ghetto. Żegota gave ZOB the addresses of safe houses for adults who escaped from the ghetto. Once in the safe houses, the escapees were given forged Aryan papers and then integrated into the local Polish population. Irena Sendlerowa, Julian and Halina Grobelny, and Irena Schutz were all declared Righteous Gentiles after the war.

For further reading, see A. L. Bauminger, *The Righteous Among the Nations*, trans. A. Oved (1990); P. Friedman, *Their Brothers' Keepers* (1978); M. Gilbert, *The Righteous: The Unsung Heroes of the Holocaust* (2003); and M. Paldiel, *The Path of the Righteous: Gentile Rescuers of Jews During the Holocaust* (1993); see also BELGIUM; KINDERTRANSPORT.

DAVID M. CROWE

Holocaust Resistance. During the *Holocaust, both Jews and non-Jews across Europe opposed the *Nazis and their collaborators in many different ways. The goals and motivations of those who participated in resistance varied greatly, and not all resistance focused specifically on ending the war against the Jews. In what follows, I distinguish between resistance to Nazism (for example, political resistance on the far left, such as that of the communist underground) and direct resistance to the Holocaust through acts that sought to mitigate or end the dehumanization, expropriation, and murder of the Jews.

Within the historiography and public consciousness of Holocaust resistance, the best known cases of resistance are organized acts of collective armed revolt, especially in the last days of certain ghettos in Eastern Europe (see HOLOCAUST: GHETTOS). Although these rebellions created reverberations around the world and are often cited as prime examples of Jewish heroism, more nuanced historiographical approaches have expanded the notion of resistance to include other acts. These include the valiant attempts by Jews to retain shreds of human dignity in the face of utter dehumanization in the camps and ghettos, escapes and attempts to escape, efforts to go into hiding, endeavors to preserve religious observance, the extension of Jewish cultural and educational activities, as well as Jewish rescue efforts.

Resistance during the Holocaust was widespread, even if it ultimately failed to prevent the mass murder of millions of Jews. That it was attempted at all within the brutal conditions of war-torn and occupied Europe is significant. Both Jews and non-Jews participated in Holocaust resistance, even though non-Jews caught assisting Jews were punished to varying degrees, including death. Jewish armed struggle was carried out by a dispersed, poorly armed, untrained population that was far outnumbered by powerful, well-equipped trained militaries and paramilitary apparatuses. Collective armed resistance, especially in the ghettos, was organized and implemented in the last moments before final liquidation. Unarmed resistance in its various forms was also carried out, often under the brutal conditions of starvation, violence, severe restrictions in movement, forced separation, and isolation.

ARMED RESISTANCE: Armed resistance was implemented for a variety of reasons; its end goal was not always to save lives or to ensure the survival of a particular Jewish community or individual. Often, it was carried out to avenge the murder of other Jews and to ensure that Jewish heroism and bravery in the face of death would be remembered by future generations. Jewish armed resistance was carried out in the ghettos of Eastern Europe, within the Nazi network of concentration and death camps, and among the partisan groups that fought in territories in Eastern Europe and the *Balkan states, as well as in pockets of Western Europe, such as *France.

Perhaps the most well-known examples of collective armed resistance were organized by Jewish civilians in the ghettos of Poland and the occupied Soviet Union. One renowned instance is the *Warsaw ghetto uprising of April–May 1943. Between July and September 1942 about 270,000 Jews were deported from the ghetto to the *Treblinka death camp. In spring 1943, rumors spread that the ghetto was about to be liquidated and that the remaining residents would be deported as well. Faced with this impending reality, and despite the fact that the ghetto residents had been forced to live for months in deplorable conditions, members of the *Zionist Jewish Fighting Organization (*Żydowska Organizacja Bojowa*) and other Jewish groups organized an armed attack against the German SS and police as they entered the ghetto to begin the deportations. The Germans, who far outnumbered the poorly armed Jewish fighters, were taken by surprise and forced to make an initial retreat. The major resistance lasted for a few days, with pockets of fighters holding out for a month. Although the Warsaw ghetto uprising did not prevent the liquidation of the ghetto or the murder of a majority of its residents, news of the conflict spread throughout Europe, encouraging other revolts.

In the *Vilna ghetto, the United Partisan Organization (*Fareynegte Partizaner Organizatsye*; FPO) organized resistance to the Germans. Although it did not succeed in organizing an armed revolt within the ghetto, the FPO smuggled out several hundred fighters to join the partisans in the nearby forests. The leader of the FPO, Abba Kovner, issued a call for armed struggle against the Nazis, and his partisan forces succeeded in mounting guerrilla-type attacks on German forces and local Polish and Lithuanian collaborators.

Armed resistance was particularly difficult to organize collectively within the Nazi network of camps. Prisoners were strictly guarded at all times, their movement was restricted, they were forced to work in abysmal conditions, and they were subject to the brutality of the guards. Collective activities or communications of any sort were strictly forbidden. Moreover, the policy of "collective punishment" reigned, further discouraging attempts to resist. Still, the few cases of organized armed resistance in the Nazi camp network were implemented by Jewish prisoners. Escapes from the camp also accompanied some of these revolts. The uprising in the *Treblinka death camp was organized several months in advance, and the prisoners gathered crude weapons (axes, hammers, and so on) to be used against the mostly Ukrainian guards to break out of the camp. Some six hundred prisoners took part in the revolt on August 2, 1943, and although most were brutally murdered, several dozen prisoners managed to escape in the aftermath. Several months later, in October 1943, rebelling prisoners in *Sobibór killed ten SS men and seized their weapons. As elsewhere, most of the rebels were murdered, but some managed to escape to join partisans and continue the fight. Jewish prisoners belonging to the *Sonderkommando* (a special detachment that was assigned to cremate the bodies of Jews who had been gassed) revolted in *Auschwitz-Birkenau on October 6–7, 1944. They succeeded in destroying one of the crematoria in Birkenau and killing several SS men. The SS identified a group of five women prisoners (four of them Jewish) who had supplied the *Sonderkommando* with explosives to carry out the destruction of the crematoria, and all were executed for their resistance.

In addition to armed resistance in the camps and ghettos, guerrilla partisan groups focused on sabotage against the Germans and revenge against collaborators. Sometimes as members of Gentile units and sometimes creating separate Jewish formations, Jews participated in partisan groups throughout Eastern Europe and the Balkans, as well as in France. Generally speaking, only able-bodied Jews already possessing weapons would be accepted by a partisan group. An exception was the Bielski partisan group in the forests of western *Belorussia, which also sought to provide safe haven for Jewish women, children, and the elderly in addition to fighting. The Bielski partisans rescued 1,200 Jews. Other partisan groups ran "family camps" that were protected by armed guards. An independent Jewish unit, the *Armée Juive* (Jewish army) in France, took revenge against traitors and sabotaged Germany military vehicles and transports. The non-Jewish partisan groups were not organized to prevent the genocide against the Jews, and in Eastern Europe, nationalist partisan groups were known to murder Jews.

UNARMED RESISTANCE: Unarmed resistance took many forms. Since a major Nazi goal was to dehumanize the Jews as well as to erase all traces of their presence, Jewish efforts to preserve human dignity and extend the legacy and memory of the Jewish people may be considered a form of Holocaust resistance. Attempts to maintain dignity and to preserve one's physical and spiritual existence by smuggling food, continuing religious observance, and organizing cultural events in secret have been characterized as *kiddush ha-ḥayyim* or "sanctification of life," a form of spiritual resistance. Other forms of unarmed resistance included the formation of underground, clandestine groups that helped prolong survival through the creation of a black market and the dissemination of information that spurred others to resist or raised morale. Finally, rescue efforts organized by Jewish and non-Jewish organizations and individuals across Europe saved many lives (see HOLOCAUST RESCUERS).

Spiritual and cultural resistance took many forms. The creation of Jewish schools, theaters, orchestras, and other cultural expressions (the Vilna ghetto had a particularly vibrant cultural life) maintained human dignity and preserved Jewish traditions. Conscientious attempts were made to preserve evidence of Jewish life and history: In the Warsaw ghetto, the clandestine *Oyneg Shabes* archives organized by Emanuel *Ringelblum collected contemporary materials, including eyewitness accounts, poetry, art, and underground newspaper clippings, and stored them in buried milk jugs so that the story of the Warsaw ghetto would survive its destruction. Underground ghetto newspapers published not only fiction and poems but also calls to resist.

Holocaust resistance also took the form of rescue. Individual and collective acts of rescue were implemented throughout Europe. Underground groups, consisting of both Jews and non-Jews, often relied on intricate and disparate networks that created and obtained false identity papers for Jews in hiding and ran smuggling operations to transport Jews to other countries. In France, for instance, the Jewish-organized and run Children's Aid Society (*Oeuvre de Secours aux Enfants*) focused predominantly on rescuing Jewish children by placing them in group homes, hiding them under assumed non-Jewish identities, and getting them out of

transports and internment camps. Likewise the Council for the Aid to Jews (Żegota), run by both Jews and Christians, hid thousands of Jewish children with non-Jewish families and in orphanages across Poland. Youth movements also assisted greatly in rescue initiatives, as did several Christian ecclesiastical organizations. Even though individual efforts to rescue Jews were not typical of the non-Jewish population during the Holocaust, significant numbers of Gentiles did risk their lives to save Jews.

Attempting escape from the confines of the ghetto or camp and placing one's child in the hands of strangers in the hope that he or she would survive can also be classified as individual acts of Holocaust resistance. So, too, those who dared to violate imposed curfews or compulsory wearing of the Jewish star or who sabotaged the work they were forced to perform were resisting. Most of these "small" acts of resistance will never be known because those who were caught doing them were usually immediately executed. Many Jewish leaders who refused to comply with Nazi orders were killed: One example is Moshe Jaffe (d. 1942), the last leader of the Minsk *Judenrat* (Jewish Council), who warned the Jews who had been gathered for deportation to flee. Others, such as Adam *Czerniakow (1880–1942), leader of the Warsaw *Judenrat*, committed suicide rather than give in to Nazi demands. Trying to inform the world about the realities of the Final Solution was also a form of resistance. The most famous case is that of two Slovakian Jews, Rudolf Vrba and Alfred Wetzler, who escaped from Auschwitz-Birkenau in April 1944 to share their extensive knowledge. Their report, along with other eyewitness accounts of mass murder, was sent to Switzerland through *Hungary and ended up in the world press.

For further reading, see N. Tec, *Defiance: The Bielski Partisans* (2008); Y. Gutman, *Fighters among the Ruins: Stories of Jewish Heroism during World War II* (1988); S. Krakowski, *The War of the Doomed: Jewish Armed Resistance in Poland, 1942–1944* (1984); Y. Arad, *Ghetto in Flames* (1983); I. Gutman, *The Jews of Warsaw, 1939–1943: Ghetto, Underground, Revolt* (1982); Y. Bauer, *They Chose Life: Jewish Resistance in the Holocaust* (1973); J. Rudavsky, *To Live with Hope, To Die with Dignity: Spiritual Resistance in the Ghettos and Camps* (1997); H. Langbein, *Against All Hope: Resistance in the Nazi Concentration Camps, 1938–1945* (1996); N. Levin, *Rescue and Resistance by Jewish Youth during the Holocaust* (1983); I. Trunk, *Judenrat: The Jewish Councils in Eastern Europe under Nazi Occupation* (1996); A. Latour, *The Jewish Resistance in France, 1940–1944* (1981); L. Lazare, *Rescue as Resistance: How Jewish Organizations Fought the Holocaust in France* (1996), S. D. Kassow, *Who Will Write Our History?: Emanuel Ringelblum, the Warsaw Ghetto, and the Oyneg Shabes Archive* (2007); and M. Paldiel, *The Path of the Righteous: Gentile Rescuers of Jews during the Holocaust* (1992).   CHRISTINE SCHMIDT VAN DER ZANDEN

Holocaust: Role of Gender. While it is evident that gender was subordinate to racism in the *Nazi determination to annihilate all Jews, asking questions about gender, listening to women's stories, and incorporating discussions of the different ways in which men and women experienced the Nazi onslaught have expanded knowledge of this tragic epoch in crucial ways.

Holocaust researchers only began considering gender as a social category in the historical narrative of the Holocaust in the 1980s. This approach originated with feminist scholars, including Joan Ringelheim and Sybil Milton, who sought to present a missing voice in Holocaust research. The main objective of the editors of the first anthology that considered gender, *Different Voices* (ed. C. Rittner and J. K. Roth, 1993), was to understand where women were during the Holocaust and how the particularities of their experiences compared and contrasted with those of men. The 1998 coedited volume, *Women in the Holocaust* (ed. D. Ofer and L. Weitzman), demonstrated that, although women's experiences during the Holocaust were not totally different from those of men, there were many instances where gender shaped an individual's ordeal. Thus, a complete accounting of the Holocaust could only be achieved by understanding what was unique to women and what was unique to men. As Joan Ringelheim wrote in her chapter in that book, both Jewish men and Jewish women experienced unrelieved suffering during the Holocaust, but their paths were not always the same: "Jewish women carried the burdens of sexual victimization, pregnancy, abortion, childbirth, killing of newborn babies in the camps to save the mothers, care of children, and many decisions about separation from children" (350).

In *Women in the Holocaust*, Ofer and Weitzman organized Jewish experiences of Nazi occupation into four categories that illuminate the continuity and rupture that each of the sexes experienced. The first category focused on the prewar roles and responsibilities of men and women. Before the war Jewish men and women in both Western and Eastern Europe lived in gender-specific worlds that endowed them with different spheres of knowledge, expertise, social networks, and opportunities. These socialization patterns would affect the different ways in which men and women confronted Nazi aggression. The second category looked at anticipatory reactions of men and women to the Nazi regime and occupation. Because most Jews believed that the Nazis would treat men and women differently and because they assumed that only men were in "real" danger, they devised gender-specific strategies to protect men through plans for migration, hiding, and escape.

The third category considered German policy and treatment of men and women. Even though they planned to eradicate all Jews, the Nazis, especially during the early war years, issued different regulations and work requirements for men and women that provided distinctive opportunities and diverse constraints. The final category examined the responses of Jewish men and women to Nazi persecution. As they tried to cope with the calamity they were facing, Jewish men and women responded to Nazi persecution by drawing on gender-specific skills and resources.

This approach required careful study of the several stages of the war and the different arenas in which Jews faced persecution and murder. It also required scrutiny of the historical backgrounds of the Jews in different European communities, as well as an examination of public and private patterns of behavior, social class, education, and age. When all of these factors were taken into account, this methodology demonstrated that gender as a category of analysis was a necessary component in any comprehensive interpretation of human behavior during the Holocaust.

In recent years, publications on women and their experiences in the Holocaust have increased, taking a number of disciplinary approaches. This scholarship has created a greater awareness of how to integrate and disseminate personal documentation such as letters, *diaries, and post-Holocaust memoirs and oral history into the record of the past, and it has demonstrated that the absence of women's experiences in earlier research resulted in an incomplete reconstruction of events and prevented a comprehensive understanding of the Holocaust.

1933–1939: In her 1998 study of Germany's Jews under Nazi rule between 1933 and 1939, Marion Kaplan described the turmoil that invaded daily life. Until 1937, most men were able to keep their businesses, although they confronted significant changes in their working environment and were disappointed by colleagues and former friends. Women, however, sensed hostility earlier and more directly in their daily activities, whether grocery shopping or taking young children to the park; if they were involved with women's organizations they were soon excluded. They were also aware of the difficult situation that their children faced at school. This is why many women concluded earlier than men that emigration was essential. They also understood the need to restrain their anxiety and rage, behaving carefully and calmly with children and establishing a pleasant atmosphere at home.

During the *pogrom of November 1938 (*Kristallnacht*), more than twenty thousand Jewish men were arrested while women witnessed the vandalizing of their homes. Women had to rescue their husbands, deal with the authorities, pull together immigration papers, and, where possible, extricate their families from increasingly certain disaster. If men emigrated from *Germany first, women were often left to take care of children and aged parents and to arrange for the departure of the rest of the family. Moreover, gender also played a role in who left Germany; by 1939, women, mostly elderly, were 57.5% of Germany's Jewish population. These women were far less likely to emigrate, and they died disproportionately in Hitler's camps.

EASTERN EUROPE: After the occupations that began with *Germany's 1939 invasion of *Poland, the condition of Jews in Eastern Europe was a continual process of degradation and humiliation. Jews were deprived of all rights and were ultimately isolated economically and socially in *ghettos that were characterized by poverty and want. Hunger and diseases often developed into epidemics, killing many people long before deportation. The majority of the Jews shared the suffering, although in different degrees; men and women experienced want in both different and similar manners. Men were the first to be sent to forced labor, which entailed much humiliation and cruelty. Ample documentation testifies to the physical harassment of men in both the forced labor camps and in labor brigades in the cities. Husbands and fathers who returned from forced labor camps were often unable to function normally as heads of families, and young men were unable to assist their parents. As Sara Horowitz writes in her chapter in Ofer and Weitzman's anthology, "The Nazi genocide destabilized the boundaries of the self, unmaking the gendered self." During the ghetto period, families were uprooted from their homes and forced to live in extremely crowded dwellings; often a few families shared one room, and all families in the apartment shared one kitchen and bathroom. Many families did not have a male provider because men were in military service or in forced labor camps or had fled to Soviet territories. Everyone believed that men confronted greater danger than women, so mothers encouraged their young sons to escape and wives encouraged their husbands to leave, at least for a while.

Women were often more daring in testing the boundaries between what was legal and illegal, believing their situation to be less vulnerable than that of men. They were often inventive in creating situations in which they could disguise themselves as non-Jews, a task that was easier for women. They pretended to be Polish domestic help in Jewish homes (when this was still allowed) and were willing to change their external characteristics, such as coloring their hair or wearing rustic dress. Young girls were smuggled out of the ghettos and did not hesitate to use feminine charm to pass through the gate.

In these situations, women expressed a sense of satisfaction that they were able to maneuver and support their families, defend their husbands, engage in smuggling, and approach the Jewish authorities – or even the Nazi rulers – to get information about what had happened to their men and arrange their release. The hostile public sphere became a major arena for women's activities to help their loved ones. Sources also describe families sitting around a dinner table to create a semblance of a regular meal despite the meager food and of an attempt to bake a birthday cake for a family member. These, too, were efforts to maintain family cohesion and normalcy against the forces of rupture. In this new situation where mother, father, and children had to work together to ensure survival of the family unit, women took on new, stronger roles. Ofer and Weitzman have suggested that such family strategies for survival should be seen as a manifestation of resistance by ordinary men and women who were unprepared and unable to join in armed resistance.

However, there was very little that women could actually do to improve their situations. Contemporaneous sources disclose the frustration of mothers who were unable to provide basic cleanliness or food for their families and who helplessly observed the deteriorating health of children and adults. They also tell of a growing number of mothers who deserted their children, leaving them on an orphanage doorstep or near a self-help institution. Some mothers were absolutely desperate and unable to endure their own and their child's suffering any longer; others hoped that their child's chance of survival might be improved by leaving them with an institution. However, children were also deserted when mothers tried to escape during the deportations. Some families made the difficult decision to entrust a child to a non-Jewish family, regarding separation as a lesser evil. There are only a few surviving testimonies of such deliberations between couples; often the decision had to be made by mothers who had already been left alone.

UNDERGROUND AND ARMED RESISTANCE: Women were part of the underground and armed resistance from its outset. In Eastern Europe, the youth movements were the cradle of underground activities. In a number of communities young women assumed leadership of the youth movements, because the danger for females was considered to be less. Only when men began returning in the winter of 1940 from Soviet territories did a new kind of dual leadership of young men and women emerge. Some women adapted to male roles, including physical work and later participation in fighting, whereas others took on female roles, such as nurturing refugee youngsters who were strangers in the community and children whose families had become impoverished or split up.

Youth movement leaders, among them many young women, turned the movements' soup kitchens in the ghettos into more than a supplementary source of food; they were also cultural and educational centers providing members with nurturing and warmth. Underground papers and memoirs record the maternal character of key leaders such as Zivia, of the *Dror he-Ḥalutz* movement, who eventually became the leader of the *Warsaw ghetto uprising together with Mordecai Anielewitz, Tema Schneiderman from Bialystok, and many others. Young women were sent as couriers or emissaries from one ghetto to another, passing underground papers, exchanging messages, and distributing educational materials. They also became deeply involved in the problems of daily living experienced by the members of the movements. The groups visited by the emissaries described these meetings as beacons of light that provided a sense of belonging to a larger body, strengthened local initiatives, and supplied spiritual encouragement. When the mass killings began in the East the female couriers passed along this information.

Female couriers were the first to contact the non-Jewish underground to get armaments and smuggle in parts of weapons that would be assembled in the ghetto when the idea of armed resistance was initially formulated. Leaders of the movement and of the armed resistance valued the contribution of the couriers, as well as of the other young women who participated in the actual fighting in Warsaw and in the smaller direct clashes in Bialystok and other ghettos. The groups of Jewish partisans that were formed from among members of the youth movements and the underground in the ghettos also valued the contibutions of young women. Although women's central roles in the youth movements and the Jewish resistance have been acknowledged, these young women have usually been called couriers rather than fighters. A number of female scholars have challenged how such women have been remembered, arguing that they have not received the heroic status to which they are entitled.

THE CAMPS: Research on women in Nazi camps is uneven and does not always distinguish among concentration camps, forced labor camps, and death camps. True, all were a particular hell for men and women alike. However, conditions were different in each type of camp and changed in different stages of the war (see HOLOCAUST CAMPS).

From the outset, research on women in the camps has stressed female socialization as a source for differences in female and male conduct and experience. It has claimed that each of the sexes developed coping mechanisms according to their distinctive cultural baggage. Women's caretaking and homemaking skills were assets that enhanced their chances of survival. Women bonded more than men, cherished family memories, exchanged recipes, and were more inclined than men to create a "surrogate family." Such small support groups, according to female and male survivors, made survival a little more likely. The composition of such "families" changed according to the situation. Sometimes they were made up of biological family members: mothers and daughters, fathers and sons. However, when relatives were absent, surrogate families comprised fellow prisoners, often individuals who shared something in common. Women paid more attention to personal hygiene than men; they kept their bodies and hair clean and mended their clothing. In *Theresienstadt, for example, women attempted to re-create their homes in their living spaces. In many camps women tried to prepare additional foods from what they were able to sneak from garbage cans or from the camp's kitchen. Some scholars have concluded that men suffered more from hunger and women more from filth and vermin. Similarly, scholars have held that pregnant women and women with young children were marked for immediate death.

Recent research on women in *Auschwitz by Na'ama Shik refutes a number of these contentions. On the basis of memoirs written in the first few years after World War II by women who survived Auschwitz, Shik claims that women fought for food, a major battleground for survival, as much as men did. In her opinion this fighting demonstrated that the daily reality of Auschwitz transcended lines of gender. In the same vein she dismisses the idea that women bonded more than men or that the formation of surrogate families was more common among women. Shik maintains as well that bitter and desperate struggles between female prisoners contradicted the theory of friendships between women. Such relationships, like those between men, were more likely when conditions of imprisonment improved or when prisoners had spent a longer time in the camp. It is probable that Shik's scholarship on Auschwitz will prompt further research that will concentrate on comparisons of the male and female experience and that will be "gender-oriented" in the full sense of the word.

For further reading, see S. K. Cohen, "The Experience of the Jewish Family in the Nazi Ghetto: Kovno – A Case Study," *Journal of Family History* 31(3) (2006): 268–88; J. T. Baumel, *Double Jeopardy: Gender and the Holocaust* (1998); M. A. Kaplan, *Between Dignity and Despair: Jewish Life in Nazi Germany* (1998); D. Ofer, "Her View through My Lens: Cecilia Slepak Studies Women in the Warsaw Ghetto," in *Gender, Place and Memory in Modern Jewish Experience*, ed. J. T. Baumel and T. Cohen (2003), 29–50; D. Ofer and L. Weitzman, eds., *Women in the Holocaust* (1998); L. Pine, "Gender and the Family," in *The Historiography of the Holocaust*, ed. D. Stone (2004): 364–82; E. Herzog, ed., *Life, Death and Sacrifice: Women and Family in the Holocaust* (2008), 41–68; C. Rittner and J. K. Roth, eds., *Different Voices: Women and the Holocaust* (1993); N. Tec, *Resilience and Courage: Women, Men, and the Holocaust* (2003); L. Weitzman, "The *Kashariyot* (Couriers) in the Jewish Resistance during the Holocaust," in *Jewish Women: A Comprehensive Historical Encyclopedia*, ed. P. Hyman and D. Ofer (2006, electronic resource); N. Shik, "'Here Mothers Are No Longer Mothers to Their Children': Mothers' and Daughters' Relations in Auchwitz-Birkenau," *Tel Aviv Yearbook for German History* 36 (2008): 108–27; idem, "Infinite Loneliness: Some Aspects of the Lives of Jewish Women in the Auschwitz Camps According to Testimonies and Autobiographies Written between 1945 and 1948," in *Lessons and Legacies* 8: *From Generation to Generation*, ed. D. L. Bergen (2008), 125–56.   DALIA OFER

Holocaust: Roma. The fates of the Roma (Gypsies) and the Jews during the *Holocaust are inextricably linked, although the nature of the prejudice against them, as well as *Nazi policies toward both groups, was quite different. The Nazis viewed the Roma as an itinerant criminal element who, like Jews, were racially inferior "asocials" with *artfremdes blut* ("foreign" or "alien blood").

There were a half-million Jews and 26,000 Roma in Germany when Adolf Hitler came to power in 1933. At first, the Nazis relied heavily on pre-1933 German laws to monitor the movements and behavior of the two principal German Roma groups, the Roma and the Sinti. In late 1935, they began to apply all three Nuremberg Laws to the Roma; these outlawed marriages and extramarital relations between Aryans and non-Aryans, excluded non-Aryans from full Reich citizenship, and required couples who wished to marry to obtain a certificate of fitness to determine if one of the applicants might "racially damage" the marriage. In 1936, the Nazis opened the Reich Center for Combating the Gypsy Nuisance in *Berlin and ordered the detention of all Roma nationwide in *Zigeunerlager* (Gypsy concentration camps). The same year, Dr. Robert Ritter's new Research Institute for Racial Hygiene and Population Biology began to gather data on the Roma and Sinti and other "asocials" to determine who was a "Gypsy." Ritter's team ranked Roma and Sinti according to blood purity and developed a detailed racial classification system for them. He concluded that 90% of Germany's Roma, like the Jews, were a mixture of various "oriental" races and suggested sterilizing Roma *mischlinge* (mixed-blooded Roma). His assistant, Eva Justin, concluded in her 1943 doctoral dissertation on *Zigeunermischlinge* who had been raised by non-Roma that the "Gypsy problem" differed from the "Jewish problem" because the "Gypsy breed" (*Zigeunerart*), unlike "Jewish intellectuals" (*jüdischen Intelligenz*), was not a threat to the Aryan race.

On December 8, 1938, *Reichsführer SS* Heinrich Himmler issued Nazi Germany's first major Roma decree, "Combating the Gypsy Plague." He ordered police to register all Roma and Sinti older than age six, as well as all others who lived a similar itinerant lifestyle. Roma were now required to carry identification papers that designated by color their specific racial status or lifestyle, and new restrictions were also placed on their occupations and travel. Foreign Roma were to be expelled from Germany. Reinhard Heydrich, Himmler's right-hand man, announced in 1939 that Hitler planned to deport all of Germany's Roma to *Poland during the next year. About 2,500 Austrian Roma were sent to Poland in the spring of 1940. The following year, the Germans deported almost 5,000 Roma to the Łódź ghetto. They were put in a separate section of the ghetto where disease was rampant. In late 1941, the Germans decided to close the Roma compound, shipping its remaining inmates to *Chełmno, where they were gassed.

Roma were also caught up in the web of mass killings by the *Einsatzgruppen* and *Wehrmacht* during the campaign in the Soviet Union from 1941–45. Otto Ohlendorf, the commander of Einsatzgruppe D, testified at his trial after the war that he saw no difference between Jews and Roma; he considered both as dire threats to *Wehrmacht* security in Russia. In late 1942, Himmler ordered that all Greater Reich *Zigeunermischlinge* be sent to *Auschwitz, although he thought that pure Roma such as the Sinti should be exempt from the decree because they provided a possible key to the origins of Aryanism, being originally from India. The first transports of German Roma were sent to Auschwitz in early 1943, where they were interned in the Gypsy Family Camp

(*Zigeunerlager* BIIe) in Auschwitz II-Birkenau, which ultimately housed 20,946 Roma.

Life in the Gypsy Family Camp was harsh and disease was rampant. Dr. Josef Mengele, the physician at BIIe, performed gruesome experiments on Roma children with *noma,* a disease that ate away the face, as well as on Roma twins. Himmler decided to close the Gypsy Family Camp in the spring of 1944, but hesitated after Roma inmates challenged SS units. Instead, the SS sent most of its inmates to labor camps in the Reich. On August 2–3, the SS rounded up Birkenau's remaining 2,897 Roma and gassed them, a tragedy memorialized by Roma each year as *Zigeunernacht* ("the night of the Roma").

There has been considerable debate over the number of Roma who died during the Holocaust. The best estimate is that hundreds of thousands were murdered and many more were persecuted by the Nazis and their allies throughout Europe. Many Roma were able to escape death because they lived in parts of Eastern Europe that did not come under German control until late in the war. Recent research includes D. M. Crowe, *The Holocaust: Roots, History, and Aftermath* (2008); G. Lewy, *The Nazi Persecution of the Gypsies* (2000); and G. Margalit, *Germany and Its Gypsies: A Post-Auschwitz Ordeal* (2002).   DAVID M. CROWE

Holocaust Survivors: United States.

In the Holocaust's immediate aftermath, many survivors looked to the *United States as a haven. At the time, however, restrictive immigration laws and fixed quotas, unchanged since the 1920s, did not allow their entry. When the deplorable conditions in the displaced persons camps became known and Jewish refugees' quick entry into *Palestine appeared unlikely, President Truman bowed to pressure and issued a directive in December 1945 that allowed 39,681 refugees, including 28,000 Jews, to enter the United States. In 1948, the Displaced Persons Act permitted entry to 205,000 *displaced persons (DPs). This law permitted the majority of those 140,000 Jewish survivors destined for America to reach this country in the immediate post-war period.

Within a national mood of lingering *antisemitism and nativism, Jewish leaders promised President Truman that they would help shoulder the burden of Jewish DPs so that none would become a public charge. To this end, a new Jewish agency, United Service for New Americans (USNA), was formed. USNA's goal was to work with local cooperating Jewish communal agencies around the nation to sponsor newcomers and ease their resettlement in as many locales as possible. Because of USNA's diligence, Jewish communities in nearly every state in the country were persuaded to accept a quota of refugees. From 1946 on, the media regularly captured the newcomers' stories, emphasizing the speed with which they became model citizens and blended easily into the fabric of American life with the help of their hosts. However, survivors have noted that the assistance they received often fell short of their expectations and needs. The reality of survivors' adjustment was far less seamless and their reception less warm than the contemporary media depicted.

Certainly, many survivors quickly became "self-sustaining." This was due in part, to the newcomers' determination. It also resulted from the withdrawal of financial support by communal agencies after a year's time.

Records reveal that, even as the refugees moved forward during this period, they were beset with illness, fought discrimination by employers, and perceived themselves as socially marginalized. A common theme in survivors' testimonies is bitter disappointment with the Jewish community in general and American relatives in particular who distanced themselves from the newcomers. During their early years in the United States many survivors tried to tell their American hosts about their recent pasts, but these attempts generally fell on deaf ears. It was only in "New American" groups that survivors could recall their Holocaust experiences with each other. These meetings also fueled the first Holocaust commemorations in the United States. In the late 1940s and early 1950s, survivors erected monuments, prepared *yizkor books (memorial volumes), and held memorial programs. Only in the 1980s, when a wave of oral history ventures, *museums, and other Holocaust education and memorial projects swept America did significant numbers of American Jews demonstrate a willingness to listen to survivors speak about their long-repressed wartime memories.

Some survivors have achieved spectacular success in America, both personally and financially. Many have become prominent advocates for Holocaust remembrance and education – speaking publicly, recording testimony, and writing about their experiences. At the same time, significant numbers live in dire poverty, at society's margins, largely ignored by mainstream American Jews. Recent research includes B. B. Cohen, *Case Closed: Holocaust Survivors in Post-War America* (2007).   BETH B. COHEN

Holocaust: Theological Responses.

The first religious responses to the *Holocaust were formulated by Ultra-Orthodox Jews (see JUDAISM, ORTHODOX: ULTRA-ORTHODOX). They formulated these responses so quickly because they drew on a spiritual tradition and metahistorical framework that allowed them to draw a line between themselves and the war and to objectify the catastrophe. As memory diffused the immediacy of the Holocaust and as Jewish life revived, Jewish thinkers outside the Ultra-Orthodox community, whose religious identities were tied to empirical historical reality, also attempted to respond. These initial responses may be understood according to seven central areas of concern: silence, divine presence, assimilation, "Amalek" (Israel's enemies), *suffering and *teshuvah* (*repentance), the Land of *Israel, and *redemption. Later responses as well, including those outside Ultra-Orthodoxy, lend themselves to alignment with these themes.

SILENCE: The very questions that at first silenced thinkers (How could *God let six million die? allow the righteous to suffer? or permit world history to be run by Hitler?) opened a path to answers. Some responded that, although answers could not be articulated in terms dictated by the horrible events, they could be provided by *Torah (Elhanan Wasserman, Baranowicz). Others taught that one could find answers deep within the self, with a leap to *God and God's wisdom (Shlomoh Zalman Unsdorfer, Bratislava). One could also remain silent in the present time, confident that redemption would come and bring wisdom and the language to express it (Shlomoh Zalman Ehrenreich, Simleul-Silvaniei, Transylvania). Such silence allowed Yehezkel

Sarna (*Jerusalem) to hear God's weeping, enabling him to cry and then to speak; it moved Ya'akov Mosheh Harlap (Jerusalem) to the truths of *Kabbalah (Jewish mystical teachings). After the war, silence in the face of the tribulations pressed Simhah Elberg (Shanghai) to conclude that Israel's very nature was that of suffering, beginning with the *akedah (binding) of *Isaac in Genesis 22 and carried forward to actual sacrifice. Although pious Jews were able to emulate *Abraham's silence before the looming tragedy of Isaac's sacrifice, Hayim Yisrael Tsimerman (*Tel Aviv) provided explanations for those who needed them. Meir Feuerverger-Meiri (Brussels) anticipated that in time, when they were no longer enveloped by catastrophe, Jews would be able to comprehend the events.

Outside Ultra-Orthodoxy were those who could not get beyond silence. Elie *Wiesel struggled to find answers but failed. Emil *Fackenheim (Toronto) and Arthur A. Cohen (New York) projected silence back onto wartime thinkers, believing that the very collapse of history and reason that defined the Holocaust made verbal articulation impossible.

DIVINE PRESENCE: One religious response to the Holocaust was the affirmation of God's presence. On the individual level, Kalonymous Kalman Shapiro (*Warsaw) spoke of diminishing human, finite pain through immersion into the presence of God, who suffered infinitely over Israel's tribulations. Aharon Rokeah (Belz) announced that God became present to enable him to flee Budapest for *Palestine and to serve as a vessel for the redemption of those left behind. Sarna held that God's presence was objectively real, ready to manifest itself once people no longer removed themselves from God. On a collective level, Unsdorfer (and Reuven Katz, Petah Tikvah) spoke of the divine presence in terms of punishing Israel to bring about the deconstruction of assimilation. After the war, Joseph *Soloveitchik (*Boston) wrote that God was present during the tragedy, insofar as He absented Himself to accommodate the human freedom to sin.

There were divergent views on this theme outside Ultra-Orthodoxy after the war. Martin *Buber spoke of the eclipse of God's presence, which precluded *revelation. Fackenheim identified a divine presence that existed from a perspective deep within Jewish victims and commanded the Jew to survive lest the world succumb to Hitler. At the other extreme, Richard *Rubenstein (Pittsburgh) and Alexander Donat (New York) found it impossible to discern any divine presence in *Auschwitz unless one wished to make God evil; they turned to the Jewish people and the principle of social justice for religious meaning. In between the two, Hans Jonas (New York) spoke of God's developing relationship to Israel, comprehended processionally. Most Ultra-Orthodox wartime thinkers thought in metahistorical rather than historical terms (Yehudah Layb Gersht in Lodz and Gedaliah Bublick in New York were exceptions). For example, Wasserman related the Nazi chaos to the failure of Jews to follow the commandments and spoke of catastrophic pains leading to the *Messiah's birth, and Harlap identified the Holocaust as the struggle between light and dark of the era of the Messiah, son of Joseph, which set the stage for the absolute light of the Messiah, son of David. After the war ended, Feuerverger-Meiri attributed the Holocaust to a total breakdown of faith in God as creator of the moral universe, which opened the door to unlimited murder. Yosef

Taytlboym (Monsey, New York) asserted that once Israel violated its oath not to rebel against its masters or precipitate the end of history or immigrate en masse to the land of Israel, God's oath not to let the nations overly oppress His nation no longer held (BT *Ketubbot* 111a). Tsevi Yehudah Kook (Jerusalem) interpreted the coincidence of the Holocaust and birth of the Jewish state as meaning God's termination of exilic history. Redemption began with Palestine's interwar restoration, and when Jews resisted alignment with the process, God severed them from the *Diaspora (i.e., through the Holocaust) to finalize the redemptive process. For Chief Sefardi Rabbi Hayim David Halevi (Tel Aviv), the Holocaust took place when humankind's naturally troublesome inclination combined with divine inducements to end the exile in time to prevent an Arab demographic takeover of the Land of Israel. Elazar Man Shakh (Benei Berak) introduced the notion that the Holocaust was God's measure-for-measure response to the debt to Him, which Israel compounded with its sins over all the generations.

Outside the Ultra-Orthodox camp, Yitzhak Greenberg (New York) outlined how God was the active *covenantal partner and Israel the passive one in the biblical era; the partnership, which had balanced out after the destruction of the Second *Temple, became a matter for Israel's initiative when no covenant under God could be discerned during the Holocaust. Leo Baeck (*Theresienstadt-London-Cincinnati) placed the Holocaust within the chain of destruction that followed from Israel's role as teacher of God's word to humanity. As a nation of moral right and light, however, Israel would survive its darkness. For Ignaz Maybaum (London), Israel was a suffering servant (*Isaiah 53) sent to the world to teach and rescue humankind from sin. He believed that God brought the crucifixion of the Holocaust to atone for human sin. For Eliezer Schweid (Jerusalem), the Holocaust and other destructions were tied to Israel's destiny and covenantal mission, to be fulfilled with the *Zionist state. Finally, Zalman Schachter (Philadelphia) took the radical position that the Holocaust served to purge a form of *Torah that had arrested Israel's growth from history and enabled construction of a new Torah, one with a universal message.

ASSIMILATION: For Ultra-Orthodox wartime thinkers, the metahistorical context evolved around assimilation, Amalek (Israel's enemies), *teshuvah* (repentance), and redemption. They were inclined to blame fellow Jews for the disaster, thereby keeping it within the covenantal framework of divine reward and punishment and indicating that Jews could also work to stop the calamity. Remaining within the metahistorical mindset, they targeted assimilation as a violation of the divinely set separation between Israel and the nations. Jewish assimilation had provoked God to respond in fury to restore Israel in its holiness, apart from the profane. The severity of divine rage depended on how deeply the holy and the profane had mixed together. Examples of violations included *intermarriage (Ehrenreich) and secularism in the Land of Israel (Mosheh Avigdor Amiel, Chief Ashkenazi rabbi, Tel Aviv). Speaking historically, Joseph Henkin (New York) contended that assimilation gave the enemy the opportunity to imagine that Jews were out to undermine Christianity and led to their decision to attack. After the war, Abraham Weinfeld (Monsey,

New York) blamed Jewish disasters throughout history on the adulteration of transcendentally anchored Torah wisdom with outside literature; he cited the Jewish Enlightenment (*Haskalah*) as the reason for the Holocaust.

AMALEK: The symbolic figure of biblical Amalek (Gen 36; Num 12–14; I Sam 15; I Chron 1:36) is emblematic in Jewish tradition of Israel's enemies throughout history. For wartime Ultra-Orthodox thinkers, Amalek represented the effort to attack Israel's God through His people, while (unknowingly) purging them of their sin. In this way, Amalek was understood as a divine instrument to force Israel back to its Torah-true self (Amiel). Wasserman also identified anti-Torah Jews (*communists, nationalists, assimilationists) with Amalek. Nevertheless, Amalek's service to Israel did not lessen his evil or protect him from eventual destruction by God (Shlomoh Zalman Shragai, Jerusalem). As the war climaxed, Amalek's instrumental status was set aside. Instead, Amalek became the epitome of Israel's metaphysical evil-other (Shalom Noah Brazovsky, Slonim-Jerusalem) and was to be hated absolutely (Bentsiyon Firer, Ulm). Determined to obliterate the people of Israel lest redemption come through them, Amalek would ultimately destroy himself because Israel's holy being was the source of all life. Later on, the philosopher Shalom Rosenberg (Jerusalem), unable to explain the absurd and absolute evil of the Holocaust, settled on the aggadic terminology of Satan (Amalek) who set out to annul the God of goodness and His chosen people. Amalek was not a subject of deliberation for the non-Orthodox.

SUFFERING AND *TESHUVAH* (REPENTANCE): There were varied interpretations of suffering. For some, it was punitive and intended to frighten Jews into doing *teshuvah* (Schneersohn). Wasserman focused on suffering's messianic implications; he observed that the onset of the Messiah involved birth pains – and the closer the birth, the greater the suffering. Katz identified suffering as collective sacrifice, by the strength of which God would fulfill His promise to restore the Land of Israel. *Musar* (moralistic) thinkers probed the moments before death and dying itself from an existential perspective. As with Hannah and her seven sons (HANUKKAH AND WOMEN) and the Ten Martyrs under Roman rule (see MARTYRDOM), the deaths of Holocaust victims were sacred moments when the soul of Torah escaped the inevitably sin-infected body and leaped in trust to God. The blending of suffering and *love between God and the martyrs was so intense that physical suffering was transcended (Ya'akov Lesin, America; Avraham Grodzensky, Lithuania; and Efrayim Sokolover and Hillel Vitkind, Palestine).

After the war, *Hasidic thinkers identified the sufferings-unto-death with the *akedah* (biblical binding of Isaac). The collective *akedah* of the nation atoned for sin, mended the universe, and displaced *tumah* (pollution) with the *kedushah* (holiness) of messianic redemption (Grinvald, Belz-Paris; and Brazovsky). Harlap believed that with each *akedah*-death, the body shattered and the soul ascended into the light of the Messiah, son of Joseph – as it blended into the universal illumination of the Messiah, son of David. Later on, Eliezer *Berkovits combined the *akedah* with the biblical motif of the suffering servant (Isaiah 53). Together, they reflected divine suffering over humankind's wickedness and Israel's pain and also atoned for that wickedness, thereby preventing world chaos and enabling history to go on.

There were also explanations for why the pious suffered: Whenever calamities occurred, the pious were the first victims. Or the sins were so great that punishment overflowed to the innocent. Or the trespasses outweighed the generation's merits, leading to global punishment. Or lastly, when Torah-failure became severe, God let the nations act for Him, and they made no distinction between the pious and non-pious (Tsimerman).

Ultra-Orthodox thinkers identified *teshuvah* as the primary means to alleviate suffering. For Sarna, it belonged to a higher triad where *hurban* (suffering), *teshuvah*, and *geulah* (redemption) implied one another. The suffering of the Holocaust was so overwhelming, he added, that God first had to open a place for *teshuvah* in the sufferer's heart to begin the process. In the view of Eliyahu Dessler (Gateshead, England), *teshuvah* failure had separated Israel from the objective reality of God's moral universe. As that reality comprehended life and order, the separation created the chaos of the Holocaust; new *teshuvah* would restore life to Israel. Schneersohn believed that the intention of exile was to induce *teshuvah* and qualify Israel for return to the Land of Israel. When this did not happen, God confronted the Jewish people with a choice between *teshuvah* or death – with *teshuvah* as a metaphysical certainty awaiting alignment with Israel's *teshuvah* in history. An exceptional position was voiced by Shragai, who confined *teshuvah* to God and His people, dismissing the idea that it evoked persecution from outside. After the war, Mordekhai Atiyah (Mexico City) identified *teshuvah* with *aliyah (immigration to the land of Israel), to which God would respond with redemption. The philosopher Emmanuel *Levinas gave precedence to the ethical imperative to draw from resources within the individual self and alleviate the suffering of the other, before any theological *teshuvah*.

LAND OF ISRAEL: At one end of the Ultra-Orthodox spectrum, Ehrenreich condemned any humanly initiated attempt at restoration, religious or secular, as a violation of divine authority. At the other, Yissakhar Taykhtahl (Munkacz-Budapest) interpreted the catastrophe as God's instruction that the moment had come to shut down the *Diaspora and move en masse to the Land of Israel. Between the two, Wasserman regarded settlement with adherence to the commandments of Torah as fulfilling a divine command, but settlement in secular terms as a trespass. The differences sharpened after the war. After Joel Teitelbaum (Monsey) blamed all Zionists for violating the oaths of BT *Ketubbot* 111a, his followers identified them with Amalek and Nazis. At the other extreme, Tsimerman and Kook blamed the Holocaust on the failure to recognize the flowering of the land during the interwar period as the revealed end to history and to align with it by restoring the land completely. Later on, Halevi alleged that Israel's failure to initiate return over the generations precluded miraculous intervention by God, leaving the inevitable return to the bitter impetus of a Hitler.

REDEMPTION: From within the war zone, the Ultra-Orthodox remained certain of the advent of redemption. Unable to comprehend or verbalize the path to it out of current historical conditions, they urged silence and called for prayer and pious action to bridge present and future (Ehrenreich, Unsdorfer). Some cognition became possible from beyond the areas of war, where the path to redemption was identified with Torah study (Eliezer Silver, Cincinnati), religious settlement (Shragai), and *teshuvah* (Schneersohn). After the war, Elberg could not see beyond the eclipse of world history brought about by Hitler. At the other extreme, Menahem Mendel *Schneersohn (Brooklyn) was convinced that his generation was the end of exile and beginning of redemption. According to Schneersohn, redemption was already in place in this world, God's residence was established, and all that remained was for the individual to perform *mitzvot* so as to manifest the messianic reality in daily life. In between these points of view, Atiyah sensed a universe throbbing with redemption, because so many holy sparks had been sifted from the *tumah* of exile with the catastrophe. Once all pious Jews ascended to the Land of *Israel, the process would be complete.

A non-Orthodox view was articulated by the philosopher Yehoyada Amir (Jerusalem), for whom global injustice constituted exile and righteous human actions coupled with divine support meant redemption. The Holocaust, therefore, was an imperative to remove injustice.

Many of the sources identified here have been gathered together and translated into English (*Wrestling with God: Jewish Theological Responses during and after the Holocaust*, ed. S. T. Katz, S. Biderman, and G. Greenberg [2007]); **see also THOUGHT, MODERN.**   GERSHON GREENBERG

Holocaust Trials. Post–World War II trials related to the *Holocaust can generally be grouped into three categories: the prosecution of perpetrators of the Holocaust immediately after the war through the present, trials related to *Holocaust denial and deniers, and trials associated with compensation and *restitution claims on behalf of victims of the Holocaust.

After World War II, both international and domestic courts made efforts to convict Axis perpetrators of war crimes. Trials that aimed to seek justice for the victims of war crimes began immediately after war's end in Europe, stemming from declarations agreed on by the Allies during the war. On January 13, 1942, representatives of nine countries signed the Inter-Allied Declaration, announcing their determination to prosecute Axis war criminals. The Moscow Declaration, signed by Britain, the United States, and the Soviet Union in October 1943, stated that at the time of the signing of an armistice ending the war, high-ranking German officials of the state and military accused of war crimes would be sent back for trial to the countries in which they committed the crimes. War criminals whose crimes could not be assigned to any national jurisdiction were to be tried and punished by the International Military Tribunal (IMT). Based in Nuremberg, the IMT was established in August 1946 by Britain, the Soviet Union, the United States, and France.

NUREMBERG TRIALS: U.S. Supreme Court Justice Robert H. Jackson grouped the defendants into four categories: major war criminals whose offenses had no particular geographic location; those responsible for war crimes against U.S. servicemen; those who could be prosecuted in line with the Moscow Declaration, in the country where the crimes were committed; and those accused of collaboration or treason against their own nation. Between October 18, 1945, and October 1, 1946, the IMT tried twenty-two "major" war criminals, accused under any of these four counts: crimes against peace, war crimes, crimes against humanity, or con-

spiring to commit any of the foregoing in a "common plan." Crimes against humanity were defined as "murder, extermination, enslavement, deportation...or persecutions on political, racial, or religious grounds."

The focus of the Nuremberg Trials was not on crimes against humanity in general or the murder of the Jews in particular: The perpetration of the Holocaust, the systematic murder of the Jews by the Nazis and their collaborators, was not on trial. Rather, the Nuremberg trials aimed to bring to justice those who had waged a war of pure aggression, thereby upsetting the international balance of peace. Concentration camps and killing centers figured prominently in the evidence presented in cases against the Nazis on trial, but the centrality of the camps to the Holocaust was not examined. Most of the prosecutors equalized the victims, failing to distinguish the Jews as a group who had been targeted by the Nazis in a singular, destructive way. Although the Nuremberg trials have become synonymous with the Holocaust because of the testimony and evidence brought forth, the trials did not actually present a judgment on the Holocaust as such.

Twelve of the accused were found guilty on all four counts and were sentenced to death; they included high-ranking Nazi leaders Hermann Göring, Hans Frank, and Alfred Rosenberg and the Nazi journalist and propagandist Julius Streicher. Another seven were given prison terms of varying lengths, including life imprisonment. Three defendants were acquitted. The United States conducted twelve other trials of high-ranking German officials under the aegis of the IMT, which were called the Subsequent Nuremberg Proceedings (December 1946–April 1949). These proceedings included the Doctors' (or Medical) case, the IG Farben case, the Krupp case, and the *Einsatzgruppen* case, among others.

OTHER POST–WWII TRIALS IN OCCUPIED GERMANY: In addition to the IMT, trials related to World War II crimes were held in the four zones of occupation by each Allied member state (United States, United Kingdom, France, and Soviet Union). The earliest trials in the occupation zones tended to focus on those responsible for the murder of Allied personnel; however, later trials included concentration camp guards and others who committed crimes against the Jews and other victims. In the framework of the so-called camp trials, military authorities of Allied member states tried perpetrators associated with major concentration camps; for example, the (Bergen)-Belsen trial (September–November 1945), the Ravensbrück trials (December 1946–July 1948), and the Dachau trials (November 1945–December 1947). In the Dachau trials, U.S. military authorities tried crimes committed in the Dachau, Flössenbürg, Mauthausen, Buchenwald, Mühldorf, and Nordhausen camps. *Auschwitz perpetrators were tried in the course of two trials. The first Auschwitz trial was held in Poland in November–December 1947 under Polish jurisdiction. (Polish authorities had already sentenced and executed camp commandant Rudolf Höss in the spring of 1947.) The second (or "Frankfurt") Auschwitz trial was conducted by a West German court between December 1963 and August 1965.

To implement the Allies' goal to "denazify" Germany, the Allied Control Council Law No. 10 was passed in December 1945, allowing for the reestablishment of the German court system. Crimes that were perpetrated by German nationals against other German nationals – for example, so-called euthanasia cases – were left to the jurisdiction of the new German tribunals. Both the German Federal Republic (West Germany) and the German Democratic Republic (East Germany) continued to try Nazi war criminals.

TRIALS ELSEWHERE IN EUROPE: In the immediate post-war years, efforts to call Nazi collaborators to account spread throughout Europe. From the murders of real or alleged collaborators without trial in *France to the conviction and execution of four former pro-Nazi prime ministers in *Hungary, from the tarring and feathering of women who slept with occupying Germans in *Holland, to the collective punishment of ethnic Germans in East Central Europe, this wave of reckoning took many forms. Many countries held national trials of both Germans and local collaborators. In countries under Soviet rule, trials conducted by so-called People's Courts served propagandistic purposes, removing those who were potential risks to the upcoming communist takeover. Nevertheless, the number of those convicted justly far exceeds those who were not. In France former high-ranking officials of the collaborating Vichy state, Paul Touvier (1994) and Maurice Papon (1997), were tried for collaboration and crimes against humanity; their trials helped bring the role of the collaborating French state into public discourse and urged the country to face its past. Similarly, the 1998 trial of Dinko Šakić, former camp commander of the Jasenovac concentration camp in Zagreb, triggered debate about Croatia's role in the Holocaust.

Like the Nuremberg trials, this national reckoning in the immediate post-war years did not focus on genocide committed against the Jews. However, cases in the following decades were crucial in revealing facts about the Holocaust.

EICHMANN TRIAL: The most significant trial was conducted in Jerusalem in 1961 against former SS Lieutenant Colonel Adolf Eichmann. Eichmann, who played a major role in the implementation of the Nazis' genocidal plans, had fled to *Argentina after the war where he remained in hiding. He was captured by Israeli Secret Service agents who brought him to Jerusalem to be tried in an Israeli court. Eichmann was convicted and executed in 1962, having been charged with fifteen counts, including crimes against humanity and crimes against the Jewish people. This trial helped thrust the Holocaust into wider public discourse.

*HOLOCAUST DENIAL: Trials against Holocaust deniers can be considered another category of Holocaust trials. Holocaust denial is considered illegal in several countries, including Germany and Austria. Ernst Zündel, a prominent Holocaust denier who, in the 1990s, published several relatively widely circulated pamphlets questioning the veracity of the Holocaust, was indicted and tried in *Canada in the 1980s and in Germany in 2005 on charges of inciting Holocaust denial. In 2007, Zündel was convicted and sentenced to five years in prison.

One of the most prominent denial trials was that of the unsuccessful libel case that David Irving brought against historian Deborah Lipstadt. In her book, *Denying the Holocaust*, Lipstadt had written that Irving was a dangerous Holocaust denier. Irving sued Lipstadt in 1996 for defamation of his reputation as a historian. The trial began on January 11, 2000, and ended on April 11 with a judgment in favor of Lipstadt. The judge deemed Irving a racist, an active Holocaust denier, and an antisemite. The trial, which called on a vast array of historical expertise to prove that Irving's methodology and claims were ahistorical and false, had a significant impact on the understanding of Holocaust denial and reinforced the importance of responsible scholarship in sustaining historical truth.

REPARATIONS AND RESTITUTION TRIALS: The bulk of the Holocaust-related reparations/restitution compensation process has been conducted based on laws passed by various national parliaments. In some cases, however, the claims have been settled in court. The first such case took place as early as 1949, when a Holocaust survivor sued a Dutch-American enterprise for the forcible transfer of his business during WWII. (Relief was granted.) The first class action suit, later a common form of litigation, was filed in 1985 in the United States by Holocaust survivors from Yugoslavia against a former Croatian official. (Their case was dismissed.) The main wave of such cases commenced in October 1996 when three class action lawsuits were filed in the United States against Swiss banks regarding their handling of assets of Holocaust victims. A similar class action lawsuit was filed against Ford Motor Co. in March 1998 regarding its involvement in Nazi slave labor during the Holocaust. Later French financial institutions, Austrian enterprises, the French railways, and the U.S. government were also sued with regard to their WWII or immediate post-war activities related to the Holocaust or the assets of Holocaust victims. Some cases were not admitted, some were denied, and those that were successful have resulted in settlements.

A special subgroup of such cases is that focusing on the restitution of Nazi-looted artworks. The first lawsuit of this kind was filed in the United States in August 1998. Probably the most well-known case is that involving five famous paintings of Austrian artist Gustav Klimt, restituted in 2006 after an arbitration panel decided in favor of the original owner against the Austrian government (see HOLOCAUST REPARATIONS AND RESTITUTION).

For further reading on Holocaust trials, see M. S. Bryant, *The Revenge of Power: US and West German "Euthanasia" Trials, 1945–1953* (2005); L. Douglas, *The Memory of Judgement: Making Law and History in the Trials of the Holocaust* (2005); D. Lipstadt, *History on Trial: My Day in Court with a Holocaust Denier* (2006); B. Ferencz, *Less than Slaves: Jewish Forced Labor and the Quest for Compensation* (2002); M. Bayzler and R. Alford, eds., *Holocaust Restitution: Perspectives on the Litigation and Its Legacy* (2006); G. Hausner, *Justice in Jerusalem* (1977); and I. Deák, J. T. Gross, and T. Judt, *The Politics of Retribution in Europe: World War II and its Aftermath* (2000).

CHRISTINE SCHMIDT VAN DER ZANDEN

Holocaust: United States Jewish Response.

American Jewry's response to *Nazism and the *Holocaust was rooted in long-standing traditions of Jewish communities assisting one another in times of hardship. However, it was also affected by organizational rivalries, Jewish leaders' fears of domestic *antisemitism, and the Jewish community's relationship with President Franklin D. Roosevelt (FDR).

FDR regarded the Nazi persecution of German Jews in the 1930s as an internal matter in which the United States should not intervene. Although dismayed by FDR's stance, American Jewish leaders hesitated to publicly challenge a president whose other policies they strongly supported. The

Jewish leadership also refrained from challenging the tight U.S. *immigration quotas, fearing that asking for admission of more refugees, especially during the Depression years, would cause *antisemitism or provoke even stricter anti-immigration laws.

One major defense organization, the *American Jewish Congress, staged anti-Hitler rallies and led a boycott of German goods. The other major defense group, the *American Jewish Committee, opposed such protests. The Congress represented ethnically assertive East European immigrants who favored an activist response when Jewish interests were threatened while the Committee was led by wealthy, acculturated Jews of German descent who preferred backstairs diplomacy to public agitation. American *Zionists sought creation of a Jewish national home in *British Mandate *Palestine to serve as a haven for European Jewish refugees. However, under Arab pressure, the British in the late 1930s began restricting Jewish immigration. At a U.S.-initiated international refugee conference in Evian, France, in 1938, the British refused to discuss Palestine, and the other participants reaffirmed their unwillingness to admit more refugees.

The Germans' mass murder of European Jewry, underway since mid-1941, was officially verified by the Allies in late 1942. Eight major U.S. Jewish organizations set aside their disagreements to establish a Joint Emergency Committee on European Jewish Affairs and sponsored rallies urging the Allies to find havens for refugees. The committee made little headway as the Roosevelt administration insisted that nothing could be done until the war was over. An Anglo-American conference on the refugee problem, held in Bermuda in the spring of 1943, failed to initiate meaningful steps to aid the Jews. The Bermuda debacle deeply frustrated the Jewish community, but fresh conflicts between Zionists and non-Zionists distracted Jewish leaders and undermined the community's political effectiveness. Several organizations sought to aid European Jewry through direct philanthropy. The American Jewish *Joint Distribution Committee sent funds to Europe for relief efforts and to facilitate emigration. An *Orthodox group, the *Va'ad ha-Hatzalah*, assisted endangered rabbis and their students. Meanwhile, a maverick political action committee known as the Bergson Group launched its own campaign for American action to rescue refugees. It sponsored more than two hundred newspaper advertisements, lobbied Washington, and organized rallies, including a march by four hundred rabbis to the White House in 1943. This effort won the endorsement of many celebrities, intellectuals, and political figures. Some mainstream Jewish leaders, who feared the Bergson Group's high-profile criticism of the Allies would cause antisemitism, urged U.S. officials to draft or deport Bergson and sought to persuade public figures to withdraw their support from the group.

The Bergson effort culminated with the introduction of a congressional resolution asking the president to create a government agency to rescue Jews from the Nazis. With the resolution nearing passage and under behind-the-scenes pressure from the Treasury Department, President Roosevelt decided, in early 1944, to establish the War Refugee Board. Financed by the Joint Distribution Committee and other Jewish groups, the War Refugee Board played a key role in rescuing some 200,000 Jews during the final fifteen months of the war. Scholarship on this topic includes D. S. Wyman, *The Abandonment of the Jews: America and the Holocaust 1941–1945* (1984); and D. S. Wyman and R. Medoff, *A Race Against Death: Peter Bergson, America, and the Holocaust* (2002).

RAFAEL MEDOFF

Holocaust, Women and: See HOLOCAUST: ROLE OF GENDER

Homosexuality: See ETHICS, SEXUAL

Hosea, Book of, is the first book of the Minor Prophets (see BIBLE: PROPHETS AND PROPHECY; and PROPHETIC BOOKS). According to its first verse, Hosea was written in the eighth century BCE. It is the only prophetic book wholly from the northern kingdom of *Israel (a few glosses from later Judean scribes notwithstanding). Hosea is the most passionate *prophet; in vivid anthropopathic terms he describes *God's love for the nation Israel as well as God's anger and disappointment.

The book divides into two main parts: chapters 1–3 and 4–14. Its language is often difficult, perhaps because the *Hebrew text has not been transmitted accurately, perhaps because it is written in a northern dialect of Hebrew that differs significantly from the southern dialect in which most of the *Bible is written. The first part focuses on YHWH's anger over Israel's frequent worship of the *Canaanite god Baal. The first and third chapters describe symbolic acts that God commands Hosea to perform. In the first chapter, Hosea marries a promiscuous woman and has several children with her; God directs the prophet to give the children names symbolizing God's rejection of Israel. In the third chapter, Hosea loves a promiscuous woman; she is forced to remain without her lovers and without a husband for many days as punishment. The second chapter interprets these actions: God is the husband, and Israel (or Israel's leaders) is the adulterous wife who goes astray by worshiping Baal and attributing prosperity to him. God rejects Israel and shames her, but eventually He takes her back out of extraordinary grace. These chapters do not mention main themes of classical prophecy such as the primacy of *ethics. Further, they may regard the leaders of Israel (the wife in the metaphor) rather than the populace (the children) as guilty. Consequently, some scholars date this section to the reign of *Ahab in the ninth century, when the royal court promoted the worship of Baal; if this is the case, the first three chapters of Hosea are essentially an example of pre-classical prophecy.

The second part (ch. 4–14) is more typical of classical prophecy; it refers to events from the last decades of the northern kingdom's existence in the eighth century. Here the marital metaphor disappears. Instead God is portrayed as a parent (whether a mother or father is not specified) and Israel as a disobedient child (ch. 11). As in Hosea 1–3, God's love ultimately overcomes God's anger. Nonetheless, frightening portrayals of divine anger are common in this section.

Hosea had a profound influence on later biblical literature. Chapters 1–3 are the first introduction of a *marriage metaphor for the relationship between YHWH and Israel; this metaphor is picked up in the prophecy of *Jeremiah, *Ezekiel, and Deutero-*Isaiah and also in *rabbinic and Jewish *mystical literature. The author(s) of *Deuteronomy was especially influenced by the *covenant ideology found throughout Hosea and borrows and reworks a great deal of vocabulary from Hosea.

BENJAMIN D. SOMMER

Host, Desecration of. In medieval and early modern Europe the libel that Jews desecrated the host (the communion wafer used in the Eucharist ritual and believed to be the body of Christ) was sometimes conflated with the *ritual murder accusation (blood libel). The Roman Catholic Church first recognized the doctrine of transubstantiation at the Fourth Lateran Council of 1215, and the first accusation occurred in 1243 at Beliz, *Germany, resulting in the murder of a number of Jews. After the *Reformation, during which this doctrine was challenged, accusations gradually diminished in Protestant areas. In many Catholic countries, however, they continued into the nineteenth century.

KATE FRIEDMAN

Human Rights. During the past two hundred years, Jews have played every possible role in the human rights drama, as victims, advocates, violators, and judges. For modern Jews, securing human rights played a constant part in Jewish political decision making, both in the world at large and in the State of *Israel. During and after the French Revolution, Jews did not merely embrace Enlightenment universalism; they were in many instances the occasion for its expression, and they often made the universal their particular contribution to world politics. Whether in their capacities as state officials, members of voluntary associations, or empowered individuals, Jews stood for and stood up for human rights.

In the first two decades after the *Holocaust, Jews made some of the earliest and most important contributions to the formation of the international human rights system. In 1945, the *American Jewish Committee (AJC) led a coalition of organizations that convinced national representatives at the San Francisco Conference that human rights should be a central component of the United Nations Charter. Raphael Lemkin, an international lawyer who was also a Polish Jew, coined the term "genocide"; his lobbying efforts almost singlehandedly achieved the General Assembly's adoption of the UN Genocide Convention in 1948. René Cassin, president of the *Alliance Israélite Universelle, played a key role in the drafting of the UN Universal Declaration of Human Rights, a founding document of the international human rights movement. Throughout the late twentieth and early twenty-first centuries, Jewish activists contributed to drafting and ratifying human rights treaties, monitoring states' compliance, lobbying states, establishing international tribunals, and creating coalitions with other human rights activists.

Jews could succeed in advocating for universal rights protections because their *suffering conferred moral standing on their cause, because they could plumb a rich religious and philosophical tradition to find support for a cosmopolitan and pluralist worldview, and because they nurtured generations of experienced organizers. Many Jews saw their activism as the natural outgrowth of core Jewish values like *tikkun olam (*repair of the world*), b'tzelem elohim (the belief that all human beings were created in God's image), and ger lo tilhaz (the command not to oppress the stranger). Not all Jews, however, sought, found, or emphasized the universalism in their tradition. For example, while human rights activists interpreted "Never Again" as an imperative to work on behalf of the rights of all people, *Zionists often interpreted the phrase as a clarion cry to enable Jews to defend their own rights by building up a Jewish state. Many Jewish activists found themselves living in the contact zone among commitments to international human rights, Jewish nationalism, and domestic pluralism.

Often, these activists were associated with Jewish nongovernmental organizations (NGOs) involved at the United Nations, in the *Soviet Union and its successor states, or in *Israel. At the international level these NGOs included the AJC, World Jewish Congress, the International Council of Jewish Women, *B'nai B'rith, *Agudat Israel, and the *World Union for Progressive Judaism. In Israel they included such groups as the Association for Civil Rights in Israel, B'Tselem, HaMoked, Rabbis for Human Rights, and Physicians for Human Rights-Israel. As members of a globally dispersed set of political communities, Jewish rights activists sometimes worked collaboratively, sometimes independently, and sometimes at cross-purposes.

*Diaspora activists embraced international human rights during the 1950s and 1960s but their enthusiasm began to decline in the mid-1960s. The primary reason was that the new UN majority, including the Communist Bloc, Arab states, and newly independent African and Asian states, began to use the human rights system not just to criticize but also to ostracize Israel. The General Assembly's infamous "Zionism=Racism" resolution of November 10, 1975, led to forty years of claims of Israeli rights violations by various UN bodies. The Commission on Human Rights adopted more resolutions condemning Israel than it did for any other state, including those that sponsored genocide. Jewish activists often struggled over whether to participate in human rights forums that were dedicated to worthy causes but were often commandeered by anti-Zionists for other purposes. Until May, 2000, when it was admitted to the Western European and Others Group, Israel was denied access to a UN regional group, through which committee assignments were allocated. It was the subject of two resolutions to expel it from the international community. The International Committee of the Red Cross prohibited its Israeli affiliate from using the Star of David as its identifying symbol.

Starting in the 1970s Jewish NGOs began to identify such behavior as a "new *antisemitism," designed to turn Israel into a pariah and to deny the Jewish people their right to self determination. Even in the face of international condemnations, however, Jewish activists continued to put the human rights system to use where there they perceived a need to protect a vulnerable part of the Diaspora (e.g., in *Ethiopia, *Iraq, or the *Soviet Union), or where, as in the cases of the genocides in Bosnia and Darfur, Jewish history demanded action on behalf of non-Jewish victims.

While anti-Zionist activities challenged Jewish human rights advocates from one side, Israel's sometimes questionable practices with regard to the rights of Palestinians and Israeli minorities challenged activists from the other. Human rights bodies, both in Israel and at the UN, found Israel in violation of some of its treaty obligations to protect Palestinians' and Israeli Arabs' rights. In the context of the first Palestinian intifadah (1987–89), such allegations spurred the development of a domestic human rights sector in Israel. Using legal petitions, public campaigns, official advocacy, site monitoring, and individual casework, Israeli activists argued, among other things, against the use of torture, punitive house demolitions, destruction of Palestinian olive groves, and arbitrary detentions. Jewish international activism declined after the Six Day War of 1967, but at the same time Israeli domestic activism increased.

Allegations of Israeli violations caused excruciating tensions for many activists. For example, in the late 1970s, activists in the American Jewish Committee responded to the Zionism=Racism resolution with ambivalence. In public, they mounted a substantial public defense of Israel's rights record. Privately, however, they helped establish the Association for Civil Rights in Israel, the state's first liberal-centrist rights organization. They sought to balance national and international interests carefully. Although Israel helped draft the statute of the International Criminal Court (est. 1998), the state nonetheless declined to ratify the treaty. The sticking point was a clause criminalizing a state's resettlement of its own civilians in territory it occupies. Israel interpreted this clause as the world community's attempt to restrain the West Bank settlement enterprise. Hence, it decided not to join a court designed, among other things, to punish the perpetrators of genocide.

Although Jewish activists stood in solidarity with Israel against its enemies, many continued working for a fairer and more effective human rights system. They did so because they believed it was better to struggle for human rights than to revert to a world of unquestioned state power; because they carried deep historical memories and had witnessed recent instances of Jewish suffering; because they sought to answer their tradition's call for universal justice; because they hoped to strengthen Israel's democracy; and because they believed that no one should ever again become the victim of genocide. For further reading, see M. Galchinsky, *Jews and Human Rights: Dancing at Three Weddings* (2007); **see also ISRAEL, STATE OF: PEACE MOVEMENTS.**

MICHAEL GALCHINSKY

Humanistic Judaism: See JUDAISM, HUMANISTIC

Hungary. The end of World War I marked the beginning of a new era in the history of Hungarian Jewry. The collapse of the multinational *Habsburg Austro-Hungarian monarchy was accompanied by two revolutions in Hungary. The liberal regime set up in October 1918 was replaced in March 1919 by a *communist government, and both had several prominent Jewish members. The communist regime became identified with "the Jews," even if it was opposed by most Hungarian Jews and their leaders. The overthrow of the communists in the summer of 1919 was followed by a year-long white terror, with deadly *antisemitic violence in more than fifty towns. Hungary lost vast territories (mostly inhabited by non-Hungarian nationalities) as a result of the 1920 peace settlement. Its Jewish population shrank from more than 900,000 in 1910 to 473,355 in 1920. Hungarian Jewry lost its most religious and least assimilated communities, along with 80% of its Orthodox *yeshivot. The majority of Jews now affiliated with Neolog Judaism (the Hungarian version of moderate reform; see JUDAISM: NEOLOG), and almost half of Hungarian Jews lived in Budapest.

*Antisemitism became a defining element in the ideology of the nationalistic reactionary regime of the interwar period, which defined Hungary as "Christian" in direct opposition to "Jewishness." A *numerus clausus* law in 1920 limited the number of Jews in institutions of higher learning to 5%,

their proportion within the general population. Many Jewish students were forced to attend universities abroad. The consolidating regime mitigated the law in 1928 for practical reasons, because it needed the support of the Jewish economic elite and was concerned about Hungary's image abroad. Both the Neolog and the Orthodox (see JUDAISM, ORTHODOX) leadership remained loyal to the regime, and the majority of Jews continued to follow the path of acculturation. There was a revival of Jewish cultural and organizational life and *Zionist activism in the second half of the 1920s, but no significant Jewish nationalist alternative emerged until the 1940s. There was also a proliferation of Jewish periodicals of all kinds in the 1920s and 1930s, and the Hungarian Jewish *Museum in Budapest became an important center of Jewish cultural activity from 1931.

The 1930s saw the further advance of antisemitism, the growing influence of fascistic extreme right groups, and Hungary's increasingly close relationship with *Nazi Germany. The Jews were gradually stripped of their civic equality, rights, and livelihood after 1938. The first and second so-called Jewish laws in 1938 and 1939 restricted the participation of Jews in the economy, limited their number in all professions and occupations, and narrowed their political and property rights. The third Jewish law of 1941 aimed at the social separation of Jews as an inferior and alien race, banning marriages and sexual relations between Jews and non-Jews. Jewish organizations responded by organizing aid to alleviate the devastating effects of the legislation. The Neolog, the Orthodox, and the Zionists worked together in the Protection Office of Hungarian Israelites from 1938. An active Jewish cultural life survived in Budapest under the aegis of the National Hungarian Israelite Educational Association into the 1940s.

After the annexation of much of the territory lost in 1920, with the help of Nazi Germany, the Jewish population of Hungary grew to more than 800,000. Jews were drafted to military labor service beginning in 1941, and 50,000 to 70,000 died in the cruel labor battalions during the war. After the German occupation in March 1944, the Hungarian government immediately introduced a series of restrictive and humiliating measures. Ghettoization started in April, and 437,000 Jews were deported to concentration camps by the Hungarian authorities within six weeks (see HOLOCAUST: CAMPS AND KILLING CENTERS; HOLOCAUST: GHETTOS). Regent Miklós Horthy (1868–1957) stopped the deportations in July, when only the Jews of Budapest remained. With the rise to power of the fascist Arrow Cross regime in October 1944, the Jews of Budapest were also ghettoized. Tens of thousands fell victim to mass shootings, death marches, illness, and hunger until their liberation in February 1945. It is estimated that 550,000 Jews in territories under Hungarian rule perished during the Holocaust.

Of the approximately 200,000 Hungarian Jews who survived the Holocaust, 144,000 lived in Budapest at the end of the war. Antisemitism remained strong and those Jews who returned had to face considerable resentment. There were several instances of bloody and deadly antisemitic violence in 1946. Many Jews joined the Communist Party, and *Zionism gained unprecedented popularity. However, Zionism was suppressed in 1949 after the communist takeover, and several prominent Jews were arrested in the anti-Zionist atmosphere of the early 1950s. The Orthodox and the Neolog were forced to merge under the leadership of the state-controlled administrative body of the National Representation of Hungarian Israelites in 1951. Many Jews lost their property and livelihood again as a result of liquidation of the private sector and nationalization. Jewish life was restricted to religious observance, and all forms of community life were suppressed. Only a few welfare institutions, one high school, and the rabbinical seminary in Budapest were permitted to remain open.

Around 60,000 to 75,000 Jews left Hungary during two waves of emigration in 1945–48 and 1956–57; many of them were Orthodox and Zionist. The overwhelming majority of remaining Jews lived in Budapest, and they were mostly highly assimilated.

With the general easing of the dictatorship in the 1980s, Jewish history and tradition, as well as the Holocaust, could be discussed with increasing openness in public lectures and publications. The first alternative secular Jewish organization, the Hungarian Jewish Cultural Association, was founded in 1988. Two Jewish publishers were established in 1989, a year that also saw a renaissance of Jewish communal and cultural activity. Two new Jewish high schools (Orthodox and Liberal) were founded in 1990. Democratic changes also brought about the resurgence of antisemitism; the process of coming to terms with Hungary's role in the Holocaust has been slow and controversial. The Holocaust Memorial Center (a museum and educational facility) was opened only in 2004. Jewish life has continued to expand in the form of various religious, Zionist, and secular cultural organizations, institutions, and publications. The present Jewish population of Hungary is estimated at between 60,000 and 150,000.

For further reading, see R. Patai, *The Jews of Hungary: History, Culture, Psychology* (1996); N. Katzburg, *Hungary and the Jews: Policy and Legislation, 1920–1942* (1981); R. L. Braham, *The Politics of Genocide: The Holocaust in Hungary* (1981); T. Cole, *Holocaust City: The Making of a Jewish Ghetto* (2003); and A. Szalai, ed., *In The Land of Hagar. The Jews of Hungary: History, Society and Culture* (2002). **Maps 8, 10**   Kati Vörös

Iberian Peninsula: See PORTUGAL; SPAIN, CHRISTIAN; SPAIN, MUSLIM; Map 6

Ibn Ezra is the patronymic shared by several scholars of the eleventh and twelfth centuries in Muslim *Spain. The most prominent among them were Moses and Abraham.

IBN EZRA, MOSES [BEN JACOB] (1070–1138) was a poet, philosopher, and author of a singular work on Hebrew prosody. Born in Granada, Moses had three brothers, who were also distinguished scholars, and was a relative of Abraham ibn Ezra, discussed later in this entry. Moses' book on poetics includes advice on rhetoric and literary creativity, a critique of other Andalusian poets, and autobiographical reflections. His own liturgical *poetry is well represented in the *Sephardic rite, particularly that of the *High Holidays; therefore, he is often called by the nickname *ha-Sallah*: composer of *selihot* (penitential prayers). In his philosophical discussions of creation, nature, and the individual as a microcosm, Moses displays the influence of the Islamic "Brethren of Purity" (*Ikhwan al-Safa*) and quotes liberally from their "Epistles" (*rasa'il*). Recent research includes M. Z. Cohen, "The Aesthetic Exegesis of Moses ibn Ezra," *Hebrew Bible/Old Testament* 1:2 (2000); and R. P. Scheindlin, "Moses ibn Ezra," in *The Literature of Al-Andalus*, ed. M. R. Menocal, R. P. Scheindlin, and M. Sells (2000).

IBN EZRA, ABRAHAM [BEN MEIR] (1093–1164) was a biblical exegete (see BIBLICAL COMMENTARY: MIDDLE AGES TO 1800), translator, *grammarian, *poet and literary critic, *astronomer, mathematician, and *astrologer. Born in Tudela, Abraham made a precarious living as a poet. He was an acquaintance of Judah *Halevi, whom he cites occasionally in his Bible commentary and who is reported to have become his father-in-law. Forced to flee Tudela in 1140 after the *Almohad invasion, his life of wandering took him to *France (Narbonne, Beziers, Rouen), *Italy (Rome, Lucca, Mantua, Verona), and even *England (London). Due to his constant penury, Abraham grew dejected, and the heterodox religious proclivities of his son Isaac (a passage in al-Harizi's *Takhemoni* implies that he converted to Islam) could only have deepened his despondency.

Ibn Ezra's biblical commentaries (extant for all but the Early *Prophets, *Jeremiah, *Ezekiel, *Proverbs, *Ezra, and *Chronicles; some in multiple editions) are noteworthy for their adherence to the simple sense of the text (*peshat*), determined by affinity to the rules of Hebrew grammar and syntax; he has disdain for those who rely unquestioningly on *aggadah*. He regularly cites works by earlier exegetes, particularly *Saadia Gaon, as well as several *Karaites, whom he largely derides. Abraham played a pivotal role in the transmission of the *grammatical and lexicographical discoveries of his predecessors, including Judah Hayyuj and Jonah ibn Janah, some of whose works he translated from Arabic into Hebrew. His poetry, both religious and secular, is notable for its linguistic and structural simplicity and is especially well represented among the *zemirot* recited traditionally on the

*Sabbath. Although he wrote only one philosophical work, the Neoplatonic *Hayy ben Mekitz*, he is considered a significant figure in medieval Jewish *thought.

For further reading, see I. Twersky and J. M. Harris, eds., *Rabbi Abraham ibn Ezra: Studies in the Writings of a Twelfth-Century Jewish Polymath*, (1993); N. Sarna, "Hebrew and Bible Studies in Medieval Spain," in *The Sephardi Heritage*, ed. R. D. Barnett (1971); and S. Sela and G. Freudenthal, "Abraham ibn Ezra's Scholarly Writings: A Chronological Listing," *Aleph* 6 (2006); **see also ASTROLOGY; BIBLICAL COMMENTARY: MIDDLE AGES TO 1800; GRAMMARIANS AND LEXICOGRAPHERS; POETRY, MEDIEVAL: MUSLIM WORLD.**
MOSHE SOKOLOW

Ibn Gabirol, Solomon, an eleventh-century *Hebrew grammarian and Neoplatonic philosopher from Malaga, *Spain, was arguably the most creative and perplexing of the Andalusian Hebrew poets. Ibn Gabirol composed highly idiosyncratic Arabic-style Hebrew poetry on social themes and a huge corpus of profound devotional lyrics and sublime liturgical poems for recitation in the *synagogue. Although ibn Gabirol found a place in the circles of several prominent members of the Jewish elite, his poetic output gives the impression that he was very much an alienated loner who was drawn to philosophical speculation and spiritual introspection. In both his meditative poetry and his philosophy, ibn Gabirol is preoccupied with the place of the soul, its imprisonment in the material world, and its longing to be reunited with God. Ibn Gabirol's poetic masterpiece, "Kingdom's Crown," devoted to God's majesty in relation to creation, is still recited in *Sephardi and *North African congregations on *Yom Kippur, the Day of Atonement. Resources include P. Cole, *Selected Poems of Solomon ibn Gabirol* (2001); and R. Loewe, *Ibn Gabirol* (1989); **see also POETRY, MEDIEVAL: MUSLIM WORLD; THOUGHT, MEDIEVAL.**
ROSS BRANN

Illness and Disease: Bible and Ancient Near East. An extensive medical literature appears among the documents of the ancient *Near East, and Israelite concepts of illness and healing can be gleaned from biblical texts. The concept of "illness" as a psychological and physical experience is more appropriate in considering biblical times than is "disease," which refers to a biological or mental condition itself. Diseases can sometimes be recognized in ancient texts, but more often they are obscured by imprecise descriptions or are mislabeled by traditional translations. A case in point is biblical "leprosy" (e.g., Lev 13; 2 Kgs 5), which is almost certainly not Hansen's disease as defined in contemporary medical practice.

Like peoples everywhere, Israelites and their neighbors were concerned with maintaining and recovering health. They had health care systems – strategies for preventing and curing illness – that can be understood by examining relevant texts as well as by considering the discoveries of osteo-archeologists (who subject human skeletal remains to paleopathological analysis) and medical anthropologists. The beliefs of the ancients about the etiology of illness and their concomitant concern for the suffering of afflicted individuals affected their approach to treatment or therapy. Many held what has been called a "utopian" position – that is, they believed that illness has a cause that can be understood by the patient and is thus potentially curable. In the Bible, this view is most directly stated in *Deuteronomy 28 (vv. 15, 20–22, 27–28, 35, 45, 59–62) where illness is said to come from God as punishment for disobeying God's *commandments (mitzvot). Because of the dominant biblical view that illness is related to sin, a number of *priestly texts also connect the idea of *purity, or rather impurity, with illness. Infirm Israelites would thus have been denied access to the *Temple precincts until they were properly purified (e.g., Lev 14). Another, "realist" model is exemplified by *Job, who cannot understand the cause of his afflictions, rejects the idea that they are punitive, and claims they are the result of divine purposes that are not arbitrary but cannot be comprehended.

Those who believed that illness was related to sin sought relief by consulting health care specialists, who included religious personnel (priests) or other practitioners of folk medicine. Or, they may have carried out familiar *prayers and procedures themselves. Communication with the deity and the application of remedies were regarded as essential aspects of treatment, which comprised three steps. The first step, petitionary, involved a set of prayers or rituals to confess sins, beseech forgiveness, and request healing (e.g., Pss 38 and 39). The second, perhaps most akin to modern medicine, might be termed therapeutic; it consisted of physical procedures or the application of "medicinal" substances (e.g., the remedy for snake bite in Num 21:5–9). The final step, thanksgiving, entailed obligatory prayers, purification rituals, or *sacrifices; being freed from illness required expressions of gratitude to the deity (e.g., Ps 107:17–22). Because the human being was considered a whole entity, restoration to health required a holistic approach, using both appeals and thanks to God, as well as physical procedures. For further reading, see H. Avalos, *Illness and Health Care in the Ancient Near East: The Role of the Temple in Greece, Mesopotamia, and Israel* (1995); **see also MEDICINE.**   CAROL MEYERS

Immersion, Ritual: See MIKVEH; PURITY

Immersion, Ritual: Women. Immersion for women following menstruation and childbirth is a rabbinic not a biblical requirement (see NIDDAH). The halakhic regulations appear particularly in BT *Niddah*, which discusses the practical consequences for male ritual purity of women's menstrual and nonmenstrual discharges. On the eighth "white day" following the cessation of menstrual flow, the wife must immerse in the *mikveh (ritual bath) before marital relations can resume. Jewish girls were traditionally taught to comply strictly and promptly with the regulations connected with the niddah (the menstruating woman). Immersion, which took place only after the body and hair had been thoroughly cleansed, had to be complete. *Halakhah demanded a single immersion, but three became customary. Postmenstrual and postpartum women usually visited the mikveh at night, often accompanied by other women.

In the first half of the twentieth century, the practice of female ritual ablution declined significantly in North America, even among nominally traditional families, despite Orthodox exhortations in sermons and written tracts on the spiritual and medical benefits of taharat ha-mishpaḥah (family purity regulations), as these laws came to be called. Factors militating against ritual immersion included disaffection of Americanized children of immigrants with their parents' Old World ways, the success of liberal forms of organized Judaism that did not advocate such ablutions, and the deterrent effect of ill-maintained and unhygienic mikvaot. Many Jewish feminist writers of the late twentieth century also condemned taharat ha-mishpaḥah regulations as archaic expressions of male anxiety about the biological processes of the female body that reinforced the predominant construction in rabbinic *Judaism of women as other and lesser than men (see WOMEN, ANCIENT: RABBINIC JUDAISM).

The 1980s and 1990s saw a resurgence in the numbers of Orthodox Jews and a new sympathy among non-Orthodox denominations for various previously discarded practices of traditional Judaism. In this era, positive new interpretations of ritual ablution developed, accompanied by construction of attractive modern mikvaot. Orthodox advocates of taharat ha-mishpaḥah regulations praised the ways in which they enhanced the sanctity of *marriage and human sexuality and extolled the feeling of personal renewal and rebirth that followed each immersion.

At the beginning of the twenty-first century, ritual ablution has become a symbolic expression of a new spiritual beginning for both women and men in all branches of North American Jewish practice beyond the domain of taharat ha-mishpaḥah. In addition to conversion to Judaism, rituals developed incorporating mikveh immersion as part of *Bar and *Bat Mitzvah; before Jewish *festivals; prior to *marriage; in cases of miscarriage, *infertility, and illness; and after *divorce, sexual assault, or other life-altering events. An indication of the probable long-term impact of this trend is the increased construction of mikva'ot by non-Orthodox communities.

For further reading, see R. Adler. "'In Your Blood, Live': Re-Visions of a Theology of Purity," in *Lifecycles* 2, ed. D. Orenstein and J. R. Litman (1997), 197–206; J. R. Baskin, "Women and Ritual Immersion in Medieval Ashkenaz," in *Judaism in Practice*, ed. L. Fine (2001), 131–42; and R. R. Wasserfall, ed., *Women and Water* (1999).

JUDITH R. BASKIN

Incense, a mixture of aromatic resinous spices laid atop burning coals, was used from the time of the First *Temple into the *rabbinic period. *Ketoret*, a special incense restricted to cultic uses, was lit in the Temple morning and evening and was used by the High Priest in the inner sanctum on *Yom Kippur, the Day of Atonement (Exod 30:34–38; Lev 16:12–13). Incense was also associated with the divine election of the priesthood; the insurrection of the Levite clan of Korah was resolved by a duel between Aaron and Korah in which the two priests burned incense before the Lord. Aaron's incense was accepted, but Korah and his followers were swallowed by the earth (Num 16).

The Hebrew *Bible refers to the use of incense to fumigate rooms, bedding, and clothing. The adulterous woman in *Proverbs tells her potential lover, "I have waved myrrh, aloes, and cinnamon [over] my bed" (7:17). The prophet *Ezekiel compares Israel's sins to those of an *adulterous wife and describes the banquet she lays out for her lovers (the foreign powers), drawing an analogy between the Temple incense and the incense burned at the feast (Ezek 23:41). From this reference, we may deduce that the Jerusalemites living in *Babylonia in the fifth and sixth centuries BCE lit incense as part of elaborate meals. No doubt, this practice accompanied the exiles when they returned to the vicinity of *Jerusalem.

Practices surrounding incense continue well into the rabbinic period. The substance lit was more akin to oil than to incense that is used today (JT *Berakhot* 6:6). Rabbinic legal texts refer to fumigation of clothing and lighting incense (*mugmar*) after festive meals (e.g., M. *Berakhot* 6:6; JT *Berakhot* 6:6 10d). In some cases, Rabbis went to great lengths to preserve the scent of incense on the *Sabbath, lighting it shortly before the Sabbath began (T. *Yom Tov/Beitzah* 2:14). There are also references to lighting incense in the privy (BT *Berakhot* 53a) and for the dead (T. *Niddah* 9:16; JT *Berakhot* 8:6 11d). A scent that is created to provide a pleasant odor, such as incense lit after meals, is blessed; however, scents for other purposes, such as covering another odor or idolatry, are not blessed (BT *Berakhot* 53a). Although it does not appear that the spices for *havdalah* (the ritual concluding the Sabbath) were ignited, it is likely that they were similar to those used in fumigants (M. *Berakhot* 8:5). **See also ANOINTMENT; ISRAELITES: RELIGION; TEMPLE AND TEMPLE CULT.**

DEBORAH A. GREEN

India. Linguistic evidence confirms the possibility of ancient Jewish settlement in India and commercial connections between India and the Land of Israel. The articles brought on King *Solomon's ships, mentioned in 1 Kings 10:11 and 10:22 (also 2 Chron 9:10, 9:21), such as *kofim* (apes) *tukim* (peacocks), and *almag* (sandalwood = *valgum*), were of Indian origin. Travelers' tales in the *Talmud mention trade with India, including ginger and iron. In *Esther 1:1, King Ahaseuerus' kingdom is said to stretch from Hoddu (generally, India) to Kush (generally, *Ethiopia). From the ninth century CE, Jewish merchantmen known as *Radhanites traded between the Middle East and South Asia. Jewish texts from the eleventh to the thirteenth centuries, discovered in the Cairo *Genizah, include documentation of trade in spices, pharmaceuticals, metals, gold, and silks between Arabic-speaking Jews and Hindu partners.

In the seventeenth century, Jewish merchant centers were established in Madras, Calicut, and elsewhere. During the nineteenth century, Jewish emissaries reached India in hopes of finding members of the Ten Lost *Tribes, who were exiled from the kingdom of *Israel by *Assyrian kings in the eighth century BCE. In the twentieth century, Indian Jews were not particularly active in the Indian freedom struggle against the British, who had acted for the most part as their benefactors. However, several individuals supported Mahatma Gandhi and the nationalists in pre-partition India. Some European refugees reached India before, during, and after *World War II.

There are three major Jewish communities in India: the *Bene Israel, the *Cochin Jews, and the "Baghdadis." These small communities, which, in their heyday before Indian independence in 1947, numbered only 28,000 in all, never suffered from *antisemitism. In recent years, other groups

such as the Shinlung or Bnei Menashe of the Indo-Burmese borderlands are claiming Israelite status and identifying as Jews. To date, nearly 1,000 members of these groups have converted to Judaism and live in *Israel.

The largest of India's Jewish communities is the *Bene Israel* ("Children of Israel"), who claim that they came from the "North," as early as 175 BCE. According to their legend, their ancestors were shipwrecked off the Konkan coast and lost all their holy books; they only remembered the *shema* prayer, which declared their faith in monotheism. The survivors were offered hospitality by local Hindus and took up the occupation of oil pressing as *Shanwar Telis* (Saturday Oilmen), because they refrained from work on the Jewish *Sabbath. The *Bene Israel* observed the Sabbath, *dietary laws, *circumcision, and many of the Jewish *festivals. From the eighteenth century on, under the influence of the British, they began to move out of the Konkan villages south of Bombay (today Mumbai). By the twentieth century, the majority of the *Bene Israel* had set up synagogues and communities in urban centers, such as Bombay, Pune, Ahmedabad, New Delhi, Karachi, and Aden.

The religious customs of the *Bene Israel* were unique. On *Yom Kippur (Day of Atonement), known as the the "Festival of the Closing of the Doors," the *Bene Israel*, influenced by local Hindu and Muslim customs, arrived in *synagogue before dawn so as to avoid contact with other people. Their folk customs included hair-shaving ceremonies for babies, *pilgrimages, and special ways of celebrating the festivals. An unusual feature of *Bene Israel* religious worship is the strong belief in *Eliyahu Ha-Navi* (*Elijah the prophet).

The *Bene Israel* community boasted a relatively large number of army and navy personnel, lawyers, professors, doctors, mayors, and authors, who contributed to the progress of India. After the establishment of the State of Israel in 1948, the majority emigrated to Israel. At first, they were not fully accepted by Israel's Chief Rabbis as Jews for *marriage purposes. In 1962, they staged a strike in Jerusalem claiming that they were "full Jews in every respect," and in 1964, they received official recognition.

Today, some 4,000 *Bene Israel* remain in India, largely in the Maharashtra region, and more than 60,000 live in Israel.

The miniscule community of Cochin Jews numbered 2,400 souls before 1948; less than fifty souls remain on the Malabar coast today. Some attribute the settlement of the Cochin Jews to King Solomon's merchantmen, although a popular south Indian Christian legend holds that Cochin Jewry arrived in India at the time of Thomas the Apostle in the first century. Documentary evidence of Jewish settlement in Kerala can be found in Cochin Jewish copperplates inscribed in an ancient Tamil script (dated 1000 CE). During the reign of Bhaskara Ravi Varman (962–1020 CE), the Jews were granted seventy-two privileges, including the right to use a day lamp, to erect a palanquin, to blow a trumpet, and to be exempt from and to collect certain taxes.

After Vasco de Gama's expedition to India, some European Jews (called *Paradesi*, meaning "foreigners," and sometimes referred to as "Whites") from *Spain, Holland, Aleppo, and *Germany settled in Cochin. A prominent member of that community was Ezekiel Rahabi (1694–1771), the principal merchant for the Dutch East India Company in Cochin. The Cochin Jews were dispersed in five major settlements in eight communities in Kerala: Cochin, Ernakulam,

Chendamanglam, Mala, and Parur. Among the unique customs of the Jews in all these communities is the Cochin Jewish wedding ceremony, in which the groom himself recites the benedictions.

The Cochin Jews were acclaimed in 1968 when Prime Minister Indira Ghandi celebrated the 400th anniversary of the *Paradesi* synagogue, established in 1568; the Indian government issued a commemorative stamp on the occasion. After the establishment of Israel, most of the Jews from Cochin, motivated by *Zionism, decided to emigrate. Eight thousand Malabar Jews live largely in *moshavim* (*agricultural settlements); some have also moved to the cities. In 2005, the Kerala government completed the restoration of the synagogue in the village of Chennamangalam in Kerala. An exhibition on the Jews of Chennamangalam before and after their immigration to Israel was inaugurated on the premises in 2006.

The "Baghdadi" Jews migrated from *Iraq and *Syria to two major urban centers, Calcutta and Bombay, from the eighteenth century on. These Jewish merchants and their dependents escaped deteriorating conditions in Iraq and the pogroms of Daud Pasha in the mid-nineteenth century. They were followed by other Jews, who established thriving businesses in the East, as far afield as Singapore, Hong Kong, and Shanghai. The Sassoon dynasty built prayer houses, synagogues, hospitals, libraries, and schools in India for the benefit of Jews and non-Jews alike. In Calcutta, as many as eight Baghdadi synagogues operated regularly, as well as several *Hebrew and *Judeo-Arabic printing presses, which translated holy texts into local vernacular and published original works. After the British withdrew from India in 1947, many of the Baghdadis decided to emigrate to England and other countries; several thousand went to Israel. Today, there are less than two hundred Jews of Iraqi origin left in India.

In 1992, Israel and India renewed diplomatic relations. Today, 50,000 Israelis, mainly backpackers, visit India each year. Hindu-Jewish studies are beginning to develop as a field of study and there is new interest in syncretic religious practices combining spirituality, meditation, and *mysticism.

Important studies include B. Holdrege, *Veda and Torah: Transcending the Textuality of Scripture* (1996); S. Weil, "Judaism-South Asia," in *Encyclopedia of Modern Asia*, ed. D. Levinson, K. Christensen, et al., 3: 284–286; S. Weil, "The Heritage and Legacy of Indian Jews," in idem (ed.), *India's Jewish Heritage: Ritual, Art and Life-Cycle* (2004), 8–21; H. Goodman, ed., *Between Jerusalem and Benares: Comparative Studies in Judaism and Hinduism* (1994); and N. Katz, R. Chakravarti, B. M. Sinha, and S. Weil, eds., *Indo-Judaic Studies in the Twenty-First Century: A Perspective from the Margin* (2007).
                                                    SHALVA WEIL

Infertility. The inability to beget or bear children has been seen as a great misfortune throughout Jewish history. In the Hebrew *Bible, fertility is strongly linked with divine blessing. The theme of the barren wife who becomes a joyful mother of children through *God's favor (Ps 113:9) is a motif in the stories of a number of ancient Israel's most important figures. Thus, three of the four matriarchs of *Genesis – *Sarah, *Rebekah, and *Rachel – suffered from infertility, as did *Hannah. The unexpected aspect of the births of *Isaac, *Jacob, *Joseph, and *Samuel emphasized their exceptionality and demonstrated God's role in Israel's destiny. At the same time, these narratives illuminate the unhappy state of the woman who did not fulfill her primary social role of bearing her husband's children.

Classical Jewish texts consider childlessness a grave misfortune for both men and women. For the Rabbis, procreation was a male expression of potency as opposed to the female role of bearing and giving birth to the fruit of male seed. The childless man is said to be "cut off" from contact with God (BT *Pesaḥim* 113b) or "already dead" (BT *Nedarim* 64b). Thus, a man's failure to procreate is understood to violate the biblical *commandment to be fruitful and multiply (Gen 1:28) but a woman's infertility does not (M. *Yevamot* 6:6; further elaborated in BT *Yevamot* 65b–66). After ten years of an infertile *marriage, a man "may no longer abstain" from procreation (M. *Yevamot* 6:6). This *mishnah* is based on Genesis 16:3, where, after ten years of living in the land of *Canaan, *Sarah [Sarai] accepted her infertility and arranged for *Hagar to be her surrogate (BT *Yevamot* 65b). Although T. *Yevamot* 8:5 states that a man in an unfertile marriage must *divorce his wife and return her marriage settlement (*ketubbah*), BT *Yevamot* 65a suggests taking a second wife as an alternative.

A wife who is divorced after ten years of a marriage without offspring is not automatically assumed to be at fault. According to M. *Yevamot* 6:6, "If he divorced her, she is permitted to marry another and the second husband may also live with her for ten years." However, a childless woman who does not become pregnant during ten years of a second marriage is presumed to be barren and must once again be divorced. The Rabbis rule that she may marry once more if her third husband already has children from a previous union (BT *Yevamot* 65a). The *Talmud also records instances of wives who successfully petitioned rabbinic *courts to compel reluctant husbands to divorce them after ten years of an infertile marriage. Even though they were not legally required to procreate, these women feared an impoverished old age without the support of offspring and wished to try to have children with another husband (BT *Yevamot* 65b).

Rabbinic *aggadah* generally deplores the dissolution of marriages, even when male procreation is at stake. Many passages present the childless marriage as a situation in which human needs and feelings should overrule legal prescriptions. Thus, aggadic *midrash about infertile couples, including the biblical patriarchs and matriarchs, stresses the efficacy of *prayer and the necessity of faith, while emphasizing that infertility is never more than a presumption (e.g., *Pesikta de Rav Kahana* 22:2 and *Song of Songs Rabbah* 1:1–2).

Rabbinic midrash also acknowledges the domestic suffering of childless women, because "it is children who assure a wife's position in her home" (*Genesis Rabbah* 71:5; see also *Genesis Rabbah* 45:4; *Pesikta Rabbati* 42:5). Although the Rabbis offer various explanations for infertility, they agree that only God can open the womb (BT *Ta'anit* 2a–b), even though human beings can play a role through prayer. Seven biblical barren women whose yearnings for children were ultimately satisfied through supplications to God became important rabbinic models of consolation and comfort: Sarah, Rebekah, *Leah, Rachel, the wife of Manoah (Samson's mother), and Hannah, as well as the personified *Israel in the time of *redemption (based on the characterization of Zion as a barren woman in *Isaiah 54:1).

In these traditions, the repeated fulfillment of the prayers of the childless points to the ultimate restoration of the people and Land of Israel (*Pesikta de Rav Kahana* 20.1).

The theme of forced divorce in cases of infertility appears in modern Yiddish and Hebrew *literature by authors such as I. B. Singer and Devorah Baron and is the focus of the Israeli *film *Kadosh* (directed by Amos Gitai, 1999); Yiddish writers sometimes invoked the trope of infertility as a metaphor for perceived Jewish passivity (I. L. Peretz).

Infertility is a growing human problem in twenty-first-century Jewish communities, partly because of later ages of marriage. All contemporary forms of *Judaism are supportive of most forms of reproductive technology, including in vitro fertilization. S. M. Kahn has documented how Orthodox Jews (see JUDAISM, ORTHODOX) in *Israel have created collaborations among rabbis, doctors, and medical support staff to ensure that fertility treatments are conducted according to *halakhah* (Jewish law).

For further reading, see J. R. Baskin, *Midrashic Women: Formations of the Feminine in Rabbinic Literature* (2002); J. Cohen, *"Be Fertile and Increase, Fill the Earth and Master It": The Ancient and Medieval Career of a Biblical Verse* (1989); M. Gold, *And Hannah Wept: Infertility, Adoption, and the Jewish Couple* (1993); and S. M. Kahn, *Reproducing Jews: A Cultural Account of Assisted Conception in Israel* (2000); **see also** ETHICS: **MEDICAL.**   JUDITH R. BASKIN

Inquisition, Spanish. The main concern of the Papal Inquisition, an intensive inquiry conducted outside the realm of normal legal procedure, was to discover and extirpate heretics within the Roman Catholic church. During the Middle Ages, temporary courts would be established in problematic locales to deal with suspected aberrations. The 1478 decision to request a Papal Bull and establish an inquisition in Spain (see SPAIN, CHRISTIAN) resulted from the forced conversion of tens of thousands of Jews beginning in 1391. Once baptized, these converts (*conversos*) had the rights and privileges due all Christians; this turn of events and the subsequent social, vocational, and economic successes of many *conversos* resulted in hostility and suspicions toward former Jews. Although the church attempted to educate these converts, Spanish society did not accept them as faithful Catholics; this lack of acceptance was exemplified by the discriminatory purity of blood (*limpieza de sangre*) laws passed in Toledo in 1449 (which eventually were universally accepted throughout Iberia) and by the term "New Christians."

The Spanish Inquisition was instituted in 1481 to discover and deal with *conversos* who were still loyal to Judaism. Its rationale was the presence of judaizers among the New Christians and their continued contacts with Jews. The first court was established in Seville, considered a hotbed of crypto-Jewish activity, and eventually twenty-one central and peripheral tribunals were set up throughout Castile and Aragon. By 1483, the National *Suprema*, or Council of the Supreme and General Inquisition, was established with Tomás de Torquemada as the Inquisitor General. A centralized bureaucracy was created in which each local court reported to the *Suprema*. Before the expulsion of Spain's remaining Jewish population in 1492, the inquisitorial court had limited jurisdiction over Jews. It could only charge those suspected of blasphemy against Christianity or Christian

beliefs, usury, proselytizing among Christians, magic, or sorcery, or those who aided or received relapsed Jewish converts to Christianity; technically, a Jew was forbidden to bear witness against a Christian. Between 1481 and 1550, the Inquisition mainly dealt with supposed crypto-Jews. Ninety-five percent of those tried during this stage were accused of judaizing; 1,500 of those convicted were burned at the stake. Unlike other temporal inquisitions, the Spanish Holy Tribunal, which coordinated inquisitorial activities, continued to function even after it had successfully dealt with this heresy. After 1550, it sought out other heretics, including Lutherans, Erasmian humanists, Christianized Moors, Moriscos, and pietists, and it also began to supervise the clergy.

Judaizers again became the main focus in the mid-seventeenth century, due to the arrival in Spain of numerous Portuguese *conversos*. Native Portuguese Jews, as well as Spanish exiles in *Portugal, had been forcibly converted to Catholicism in 1497, and the Portuguese Inquisition was established in 1536. When the two Iberian nations united in 1580 and borders were opened, numerous *conversos* who returned to Spain were suspect. Consequently, from 1630–1730, the Inquisition once again focused on judaizers, most of whom had Portuguese names; again, about 95% of those tried at this time were accused of judaizing and 250 were burned at the stake.

Technically only baptized Catholics were under the Inquisition's jurisdiction; however, all the *conversos* and their descendants, whether judaizers or not, had been baptized. The Jewish world has traditionally defined those who were tried and convicted as *martyrs, because accusations of Jewish beliefs and practices led to their deaths. Some historians doubt the sincerity of the Inquisition's motives, assuming that greed played a major role in its decision-making process. In fact, despite attempts to maintain uniformity, there were discrepancies in procedures over the years. For instance, the personality of a particular inquisitor or the make-up of a particular court might influence the outcome of a given trial; likewise, there were periods of religious fanaticism as well as periods of abatement that resulted in differing sentences for identical transgressions. Nevertheless, a study of court procedures reveals a sophisticated legal system striving for the utmost secrecy in order to conduct serious trials with a minimum of outside interference.

The Spanish Inquisition diverged from papal standards; before it began actual trials, the court declared a set grace period of one to three months during which confessions and testimonies were accepted. Although the Pope advocated unlimited accessibility to confession for every Catholic, the Spanish church believed this policy would impede the trial process. In addition, the prosecution withheld the names of witnesses from the defense to protect those witnesses. Lastly, although the Pope objected to including the testimony of "untrustworthy" servants, such testimony appears frequently in the Iberian records.The Spanish Inquisition was not officially abolished until the nineteenth century; it became the quintessential symbol of European religious intolerance and medieval ethnic *antisemitism. It continues to be a topic of interest in contemporary historical writing, literary works, and film.

For further reading, see E. Peters, *Inquisition* (1989); H. Beinart, *Conversos on Trial* (1981); W. Monter, *Frontiers of*

Heresy (1990); and M. Giles, ed., *Women in the Inquisition: Spain and the New World* (1999).

RENÉE LEVINE MELAMMED

Intercalation: See CALENDAR; CALENDAR: MONTHS OF THE YEAR.

Interfaith Dialogue: United States. The relationship between the Jewish community and other communities of faith, especially Protestants and Catholics, has stood at the center of the American Jewish experience. Already in colonial times Jews encountered more welcoming brands of Christianity than they had in Europe, often because of these groups' more literal reading of the Hebrew *Bible/ Old Testament. Yet negative stereotypes and civil restrictions persisted, and Jews struggled throughout the nineteenth and twentieth centuries to combat unfavorable images and gain full equality.

Interfaith dialogue, which began in the latter decades of the nineteenth century, helped Jews bring about fundamental changes in the relationship between the Jewish community and other religious groups. A special moment occurred in 1893, when the World Parliament of Religions (WPR) convened in *Chicago, bringing together representatives of Christianity, Judaism, and other faiths. The WPR offered Jewish religious leaders an opportunity to defend Judaism against what they considered to be unjustified views of the Jewish faith. Attempts at dialogue took a more organized form in the 1920s, when the rise of hate groups in America impelled Roman Catholic, Protestant, and Jewish activists to establish a Committee on Good Will; the 1928 creation of the National Council of Christians and Jews was a further advance. Although many of the issues discussed were not spiritual or theological, rabbis generally represented the Jewish community in dialogue with representatives of other faiths. Simultaneously, similar attempts were taking place in other English-speaking countries. This early dialogue points to a more open and tolerant atmosphere in the English-speaking world, especially in comparison to the deteriorating situation of Jews in continental Europe during the period. However, while the interfaith dialogue in America progressed, the 1920s and 1930s also saw the rise of virulent *antisemitic expressions in America. A number of Christian groups and individuals joined in attacking Jews, blaming them for the nation's problems. These included Protestant and Roman Catholic clergymen, such as the reactionary Protestant minister Gerald L. K. Smith and Father Charles Coughlin, a Catholic priest, who used his radio program as a vehicle to attack the Jews. During that precarious era, Jewish organizations institutionalized their involvement with interfaith relations, attempting to combat bigotry and improve relationships with other communities of faith.

For the most part, Jewish and non-Jewish participants in the dialogue have been representatives of liberal wings of their faith. Christian representatives in the dialogue were often sympathetic to Jewish feelings and opposed bigotry. However, mainstream churches in America still maintained that Judaism was not equal to Christianity and could not offer its members adequate moral guidelines and salvation for their souls. Not only conservative groups but also mainstream Christian churches continued their efforts at evangelizing Jews. In contrast, the Protestant theologian Reinhold Niebuhr was an early proponent of an attitude that recog-

nized Judaism as a legitimate religious tradition. Concluding in 1926 that Jews had high moral standards, Niebuhr militated against the propagation of the Christian gospel among the Jews (Reinhold Niebuhr, "The Rapprochement between Jews and Christians," *Christian Century*, January 7, 1926, 9–11). Until that time, most Protestant and Catholic theologians had followed the traditional Christian line, which claimed that, having rejected their *messiah, the Jews had lost their position as the chosen people and that God's promises to Israel were inherited by the Christian church. A number of Jewish thinkers also began to change their views on the relationship between Judaism and other faiths; few, however, followed Mordecai *Kaplan, who suggested that Jews give up their claim to be the *chosen people.

Interfaith relations burgeoned after *World War II. The spirit of tolerance created by the war, including the camaraderie that developed between Jewish and non-Jewish soldiers serving in the armed forces, as well as among Jewish, Protestant, and Catholic chaplains, helped change the relationships among the faith communities. The GI Bill helped hundreds of thousands of Jews obtain education and move to the middle class and the suburbs, a socioeconomic development that made Jews more acceptable to the white Christian elite. The Cold War also enhanced the atmosphere of interfaith reconciliation because the American struggle against *communism helped legitimize all varieties of religious expression, including Judaism. In the 1950s, Judaism became one of the three "public religions" in America. Dialogue between Jews and Christians intensified and took a variety of forms. The most remarkable interfaith activity took place in the context of the *civil rights movement, in which Jewish leaders and thinkers, including Abraham Joshua *Heschel, participated alongside Protestant and Catholic clergy in the struggle for civil rights for all Americans. Still, a sociological survey conducted at the initiative of the Anti-Defamation League in the early 1960s discovered that prejudices against Jews were still prevalent among the majority of Christians in America.

Interfaith relations in America improved in the wake of Vatican II, the Roman Catholic general council that convened between 1962 and 1965 and promoted reconciliation between the Roman Catholic Church and other faiths. Vatican II came out with an historical resolution on the relationship between Christians and Jews, asserting that "the Jews should not be presented as rejected or accused by God." This document also rejected the claim that the Jews as a people were responsible for the killing of Jesus. A number of American Protestant churches, as well as Christian ecumenical groups, followed Vatican II in issuing similar statements, often going much further theologically. Like their counterparts in Europe, American Christians were motivated, at least in part, by a sense of guilt over the historical role of Christian anti-Jewish accusations in contributing to the *Holocaust, the mass murder of Jews during World War II. Since the 1970s, a growing number of Protestant and Catholic theologians have come to characterize Judaism as a religious community in *covenant with *God, alongside Christianity. This outlook, which places Judaism on an equal spiritual and moral footing with Christianity, has become the province of Americans and other English-speaking countries more than of European and Third World Christians. The new climate of interfaith dialogue motivated a keen Christian attempt to eradicate prejudices and establish a new basis for a relationship among faiths.

In the 1960s and 1970s, Protestants and Catholics systematically examined textbooks used in their religious schools and removed passages that drew a negative portrait of the Jews. However, this effort does not mean that old accusations against Jews disappeared in Christian popular culture. Jews have continued to be portrayed as the slayers of Jesus or as the motivating cause behind his death in popular productions and films, such as *The Passion of the Christ* (2004). Yet the Catholic Church, as well as mainline Protestants churches, decided to shut down their missionary enterprises among Jews. Evangelizing the Jews remained the declared agenda of the more conservative Protestant churches that did not take part in the dialogue movement.

The atmosphere of reconciliation has developed further. An impressive development in recent decades has been the growing curiosity among Christian scholars about Jewish tradition, which is considered important because, among other things, it sheds light on the history of Christianity. Since the 1980s, *synagogues in America have become attractive to non-Jews, who in groups or as individuals have begun visiting Jewish services in relatively large numbers. Some have come at the invitation of Jewish friends, and others have come in search of a new community of faith. In the open market of religions in the first decade of the twenty-first century, Judaism has become an option that some American spiritual seekers, most of them from educated middle-class Christian backgrounds, have come to consider. *Conversions to and from Judaism as well as *intermarriages between Jews and non-Jews have also become common. Many Jews today share their lives with non-Jews, often maintaining Jewish or semi-Jewish households. Non-Jewish spouses often join synagogues. This new reality affects the relationship between Jews and Christians. For example, many mixed couples get married in ceremonies officiated by both Jewish and non-Jewish clergy.

Although interfaith relations in America have undergone huge transformations, Jewish observers have complained that old anti-Jewish sentiments have not been fully eradicated and have, at times, been replaced by anti-*Israel rhetoric. Since the 1970s, liberal Christian groups in America, including the National Council of Churches, have developed a strong commitment to movements of national liberation, viewing the Israelis as oppressors. Christian activists differ considerably in their relationship to the Arab–Israeli conflict. Although liberal theologians have been concerned about *Palestinian rights, conservative evangelicals have supported Israel ardently. Many evangelical Christians subscribe to a messianic hope in the second coming of Jesus and view the Jews as the object of biblical prophecies about the *messiah's arrival and Israel's restoration to its land.

Especially since the 1967 Six Day War, evangelical views of Israel have been very positive. At the same time, evangelical missions to the Jews have persisted and a movement consisting of Jews who have adopted evangelical Protestant beliefs while retaining a Jewish identity has emerged. Virtually all Jewish leaders object to evangelical missionary work but many Jews and evangelicals cooperated in supporting Israeli causes.

During the past forty years, interfaith relationships and dialogue in America have expanded to include Middle Eastern and Far Eastern religious communities. Establishing a good relationship with Muslims has become a major item on the Jewish interfaith agenda. For many Muslims, American Jews are associated with Israel, a country they often resent. However, in the wake of the September 11, 2001, attack on the World Trade Center, a number of Jewish leaders raised their voice against the vilification of *Islam and the harassment of Muslims. In contrast, Jewish American organizations have refrained from establishing relationships with new religious movements (NRMs), which they have viewed as "cults." However, non-mainstream Jewish leaders, such as Zalman Schachter, of the *Jewish Renewal movement, have been happy to dialogue with leaders of NRMs. Representing a Jewish movement of spiritual revival and return to tradition, Schachter and others have been interested in learning what attracts young Jews to alternative religious groups, as a means of revitalizing their own tradition.

Important books include Y. Ariel, *Evangelizing the Chosen People* (2000); M. Braybooke, *A History of the Council of Christians and Jews* (1991); H. Croner, ed., *More Stepping Stones to Jewish Christian Relations*, (1985); E. Feldman, *Dual Doctrines: The Jewish Encounter with Protestant America* (1990); A. Gilbert, *The Vatican Council and the Jews* (1968); and A. J. Rudin and M. R. Wilson, eds., *A Time to Speak: The Evangelical Jewish Encounter* (1987).　YAAKOV ARIEL

Intermarriage: Historical Perspectives. The classic biblical prohibition of Jewish–Gentile intermarriage is Deuteronomy 7:3–4: "You shall not intermarry with them: do not give your daughters to their sons or take their daughters for your sons. For they will turn your children away from me to worship other gods, and the Lord's anger will blaze forth against you and He will promptly wipe you out." As this statement makes clear, the primary motivation behind forbidding Israelite marriages with non-Israelites was the fear that the non-Israelite spouse would encourage worship of deities other than the Israelite God. This prohibition was strongly restated in the fifth century BCE, the period of return to *Jerusalem from the *Babylonian Exile. The leaders *Ezra and *Nehemiah insisted that Israelite men abandon their foreign wives and the children of those marriages as a sign of *repentance and allegiance to God (Ezra 10; Neh 13).

During the rabbinic period, the principle of matrilineal descent was established, according to which only the child of a Jewish mother was considered a Jew. Although there was dissent, with some rabbis ruling the child of a Jewish father and a Gentile mother Jewish, and others who considered the child of a Jewish mother and a Gentile father Gentile, this principle was nearly universally accepted until 1983 when the *Reform movement declared that, for Reform Jews, Jewish commitment and a Jewish upbringing, regardless of the *gender of the Jewish parent, determined the Jewishness of a child in an intermarried household.

Recent research includes S. D. Cohen, *The Beginnings of Jewishness* (1999).　KEREN MCGINITY

Intermarriage: Modern Europe and United States. Intermarriage, a *marriage between a Jew and a non-Jew, is a feature of modernity. Before the invention of the concept of civil marriage in the modern era, all marriages were conducted under religious auspices, and intermarriage in the technical sense did not take place. If Jews converted to Christianity, they could, as Christians, marry other Christians, and the reverse was also true, but such marriages were not intermarriages. Only when civil marriage made it possible for Jews and Christians to marry could intermarriage proper take place (see CONVERSION: EARLY MODERN PERIOD).

The earliest public discussion of intermarriage and its relationship to the process of assimilation and integration into the larger society took place in 1806 when Emperor Napoleon of *France convened the Assembly of Notables and asked the rabbis and Jewish lay leaders who assembled in Paris to answer twelve questions. Their answers became the guiding principles of a recently emancipated French Jewry. The questions were designed to prompt Jewish leaders to assert that they identified as Frenchmen and regarded French law as primary over Jewish law (see *HALAKHAH). Question three inquired if Jewish law permitted Jews to marry Christians, a form of marriage recently made possible by the introduction of civil marriage in France. Seeking the full assimilation of Jews, Napoleon wanted Jewish leaders to advocate intermarriage, but they refused to do so. Although they noted that Jews who intermarried would remain Jews and that their marriages would be valid under civil law, French Jewish leaders announced that they would not perform or encourage intermarriage. They advocated acculturation, but they drew the line at total assimilation.

In the nineteenth century, intermarriage between Jews and non-Jews was rare. Jews in Western and *Central Europe acculturated, adopting the culture and lifestyles of the societies in which they lived, but they nevertheless socialized with other Jews, with whom they shared business, family, and communal ties. The widespread practice of arranged marriage in the Jewish middle classes virtually guaranteed that Jews married other Jews. So, too, did the laws in countries like *Habsburg Austria, which permitted civil marriage but not civil intermarriage. In Austria a Jew could not marry a non-Jew unless one of them converted to the religion of the other or to a neutral category, "without religion," a step that inhibited intermarriage. In *Eastern Europe, where most Jews remained enmeshed in the traditional Jewish community, intermarriage was unknown. In the *United States, most Jews were recent immigrants from traditional backgrounds who almost never married outside the Jewish community.

Intermarriage grew in significance only in the twentieth century as a result of the spread of civil marriage, widespread assimilation, and the decline of *antisemitism. In the newly created *Soviet Union, for example, the introduction of civil marriage, governmental suppression of religious institutions, and pressure to assimilate led to growing rates of intermarriage between Jews and non-Jews. By the 1930s, about a quarter of those Soviet Jews who married, married Gentiles. Weimar *Germany also witnessed a rapid growth in intermarriage, probably caused by the decline of arranged marriage and the new practice of marrying for love. By 1930, about 25% of German Jews who married, married a non-Jew; the rate was about 33% in the larger cities. In the United States, however, Jews were still close to their immigrant origins, and thus, despite rapid Americanization, intermarriage rates remained insignificant before World War II. Only after several generations of Americanization did

Jews begin to marry non-Jews in substantial numbers. In the 1970s, about 25% of Jews who married, married non-Jews. By the 1990s, that figure had doubled to 52%, although it remained lower in cities with large Jewish populations.

Jewish communities in Europe, as in America, have long opposed intermarriage. Before World War II, most Jews who intermarried did not raise their children as Jews. In the postwar years, Jewish leaders, concerned about Jewish survival, tried to develop strategies both to discourage intermarriage and to encourage those who intermarried to remain Jews. More recently, many Jews who intermarry continue to identify as Jews and raise their children as such, although this presents problems in Jewish law when the non-Jewish parent is the mother. Although *Orthodox and *Conservative rabbis do not perform intermarriages, some Reform rabbis do so in the hope that intermarried couples will raise Jewish children (see DEMOGRAPHY).

For further reading, see Z. Gitelman, *A Century of Ambivalence: The Jews of Russia and the Soviet Union, 1881 to the Present* (1988); and M. Kaplan, *The Making of the Jewish Middle Class: Women, Family and Identity in Imperial Germany* (1991).

MARSHA L. ROZENBLIT

Intermarriage: Twenty-First-Century United States. The rising rates of intermarriage in twentieth- and early-twenty-first-century America seem, on the surface, to indicate the inevitability of total Jewish assimilation. Before 1940, the rate of Jews married to non-Jews was estimated to be between 2 and 3.2%; this rate doubled to approximately 6% between 1941 and 1960. It rose to 28% between 1970 and 1979 and then from 38% between 1980 and 1984 to 43% between 1985 and 1995. The proportion of intermarriage reached an all-time high of 52% according to the 2001 National Jewish Population Survey, the last year for which statistics are available (see UNITED STATES: DEMOGRAPHY).

Before the 1970s, most Jews who married non-Jews were men; in recent decades, Jewish women have married non-Jews at a rate nearly equal to that of Jewish men. Thus, the openness of American culture has also enabled Jewish women to blend into the mainstream, should they choose to do so. Research indicates that the parent's *gender plays a significant role in decisions to raise the offspring of an intermarriage as Jews. Intermarried Jewish women are far more likely than Jewish men to maintain religious and social ties to the Jewish community and to incorporate Jewish activities and Jewish education into their children's lives (Barack Fishman). This reconciliation between the selection of a Gentile husband and the maintenance of a Jewish self may reflect twentieth-century social changes that have empowered American women in terms of education, vocational options, and political rights. These transformations have also resulted in women's increased personal power within their most intimate relationships and may explain why Jewish women in intermarriages have increasingly asserted their Jewishness and a commitment to raise Jewish children (McGinity).

For further reading, see S. Barack Fishman, *Double or Nothing: Jewish Families and Mixed Marriage* (2004); E. Mayer, *Love & Tradition: Marriages between Jews and Christians* (1985); and K. R. McGinity, *Still Jewish: A History of Women and Intermarriage in America* (2009).

KEREN R. MCGINITY

Internet. It is all but impossible to determine when material with Jewish content was first posted on the internet. In addition to Jewish-oriented material on various online bulletin boards, which began their postings and discussions during the late 1980s, usenet groups such as *soc.culture.jewish*, began providing contributors and readers with serious reading lists and often incisive discussions during the early 1990s. These lists have continued to grow. Additionally, the Lubavitch *Hasidim, also known as *Habad, staked out an early presence on the internet thanks to the activities of Rabbi Yosef Kazen. Kazen was one of the first to post digitized versions of traditional Jewish texts online, doing so as early as the late 1980s.

With the advent of the World Wide Web in the early 1990s, the amount of material on the internet grew at an exponential pace. Specifically Jewish material grew as well, and aggregators of Jewish websites began to appear. These included Andrew Tannenbaum's "Judaism and Jewish Resources" site, which began in 1993 with less than ten links. By 2009, there were millions of Jewish-related sites, with denominational, commercial, educational, periodical, and personal content. Spanning an incredibly wide range, these sites deal with virtually any and every topic that can be connected to Judaism, ranging from the digital publication of many traditional texts to all manner of popular culture phenomena and everything in between. This material comes from a vast number of different locations, although most originate in *Israel and the *United States.

Specifically Jewish responses to internet use have varied according to community. From its inception, the vast majority of individual Jews have used the internet without reservation, but also without any ethnic or religious intent. However, Ultra-Orthodox Jews, also known as *Haredim, have taken issue with what they consider to be invasive issues mostly related to modesty. As a result, the Haredi community has taken steps to deal with the burgeoning use of the internet among its constituents. In early 2000, a group of prominent Haredi rabbis in Israel representing Hasidic, Lithuanian, *Sefardic, and *Mizrahi precincts, issued a ban on use of the internet. They argued, "The Internet is a danger 1,000 times greater [than television, which was banned in the 1970s], and is liable to bring ruin and destruction upon all of Israel." In spite of this most daunting claim, the rabbis did manage to issue a dispensation for business use, a fact that clearly underscores the understanding that the internet is an indispensable tool. However, the rabbis specifically noted in their halakhic document that even if the internet was required for business, it should, under no circumstances, be available in the home.

As the ability to control internet content via filters became more advanced, Haredim began to make use of a variety of such technologies, some of which were created for other religious fundamentalist groups that feared the open, uncensored universe of the internet, and others that were created specifically for themselves. Technologies created specifically for Haredi internet use included companies such as *Yeshivanet*, which, as an Ultra-Orthodox internet service provider (ISP), required customers to submit URLs (web addresses) to their staff to determine whether the site was morally acceptable before they would be given access to it. However, the vast majority of Haredi internet users tended toward the use of filtering companies, such as *TheJnet.com*, *Koshernet.com* in America, and the *Rimon* ISP in Israel. As use of the internet became indispensable for business and personal communications, certain Ultra-Orthodox courts, the Belz Hasidim among them, relented and, realizing that their adherents were using the internet regardless, decided to permit its use under strict supervision. One of the significant issues troubling the Ultra-Orthodox is the anonymity provided by the internet. This anonymity has resulted in a number of bulletin board discussion groups and blogs that openly deal with issues that Haredi communities would prefer to deal with privately or not at all.

Another precinct wherein Jewishness plays a role is in online virtual reality games. *Second Life*, which has millions of players, is the largest of these games in which players create an "avatar," or game piece, and interact in a world of their own invention. *Second Life* has multiple *synagogues, Jewish *museums, and many Jewish activities that its players engage on many levels.

Just as numerous aspects of human life have migrated in some way to the internet, *antisemitic websites can also be found there. Their presence became evident early in the twenty-first century on Google, a popular search engine, when the top result for the word "Jew" turned out to be *Jewwatch.com*, a notoriously antisemitic website. Concerned about these results, Google currently posts a notice that says, "We're disturbed about these results as well. Please read our note here." This link leads to an "offensive search results" document that explains how Google's search algorithms result in a large number of antisemitic results. To counter this problem, the website *Jewschool.com* organized a "google-bombing" of the Wikipedia entry for "Jew" in 2004. This was a grassroots movement that placed links to the Wikipedia entry on a large number of websites, causing it to outnumber the antisemitic sites and take the top spot in Google's search results. As the internet continues to grow at an exponential rate, it can be anticipated that the amount of Jewish material will also continue to expand.

EDDY PORTNOY

Iran. Jewish communities existed in Iran before the Arab Muslim conquest of the seventh century CE. Between 637–644 the heartland of Iran (*Persia) was slowly incorporated into the emerging Islamic hegemony over the Middle East, and *Islam replaced Zoroastrianism as the official state religion. The jurists of Islam developed the legal concept of *dhimma* (protection) for adherents of monotheistic faiths other than Islam. Jews were among these *dhimmi, "protected people," within the dominant Islamic system. They could practice their religion and preserve their identity as separate social and legal entities, albeit with certain restrictions.

Nevertheless, the history of the Jews of Iran is one of suppression, harassment, and persecution, interspersed with periods of tolerance and well-being. Jews and Muslims lived in distinct and separated communities. Jews earned a living as merchants, artisans, agriculturalists, weavers, and dyers, among other occupations associated with the medieval Islamic world. Increased urbanization and international trade during Arab Abbasid rule (758–1258), centered in Baghdad (see *IRAQ), led to the emergence of wealthy Jewish merchants in Iranian cities such as Ahvaz, Shiraz, Rayy, and Ardabil (Levy). By the tenth century, Jews lived in virtually every Iranian city. Under the Safavid dynasty (1501–1731), Shi'i Islam became the state religion. There was a prolonged period of intolerance (Shi'ism stresses Muslim purity vis-à-vis non-Muslim impurity), and Jews were isolated from Sunni countries and the centers of *Torah study, especially Baghdad.

There is a dearth of Jewish historical sources about the community in Iran. A seventeenth-century versified history by Baba'i ben Lotf of Kashan details the tribulations of the Jewish communities during the years 1613–60; an addendum adds information about the Jews of Kashan and Isfahan between 1729–30. It seems that, from the fourteenth century onward, Jews were an increasingly impoverished community. Iranian Jewish oral tradition transmits the vulnerability and miserable circumstances of the Jews in Iran, especially in the seventeenth and eighteenth centuries when the majority Shi'i culture was also in decline. At that time Jews were artisans, craftsmen, small-scale merchants, and wine makers; they also bought and sold all sorts of items and made and sold medicine and magic. Jewish women had access to households of the elite and specialized in selling potions to women.

The isolation of the Iranian Jewish community persisted until the political, social, and educational changes of the early twentieth century. Jews participated in the Constitutional Revolution of 1906. The *Alliance Israélite Universelle, which established modern Jewish educational facilities throughout the Middle East, opened a school in Tehran in 1898. The following year, a school for girls was established, as were evening classes for adults. Alliance schools were also opened in the cities of Hamadan and Shiraz. Jews were allowed to attend government schools established in the 1920s by the government of Reza Shah Pahlavi (1925–41). This shah opened the doors of society to Jews, and the government hired Jews with language skills and education in the expanding economy under the second Pahlavi shah (1941–79). At that time, the Jewish community had its own schools and social and cultural organizations, and religious life flourished. Courses in the Hebrew language were offered, cultural contacts with *Israel increased, and Israeli scholars were invited to lecture in synagogues in Iran. However, although many in the Jewish community prospered, the majority continued to live in miserable conditions; their main occupation was peddling.

The culture of Persian Jews was similar to the culture of Muslim Persians. Jewish women tended to be veiled, and there was separation of the sexes. During the Pahlavi age, modernized Jews became as differentiated from the bulk of the population as were westernized Muslims. In the Islamic Republic, established in 1979, the situation of the remaining Jewish community in Iran is once again highly problematic (see also JUDEO-PERSIAN).

Recent research includes P. Banooni and S. Simnegar, "History of Jews in Iran: 1500-Present," *Teruā: The History of Contemporary Iranian Jews, Center for Iranian Jewish Oral History* 1 (1996): 13–43; H. Levy, *Comprehensive History of The Jews of Iran: The Outset of the Diaspora* (1999); D. Menashri, *Education and the Making of Modern Iran* (1992); V. B. Moreen, *Iranian Jewry's Hour of Peril and Heroism: A Study of Babai ibn Lutf's Chronicle 1617–1662* (1987); and H. Sarshar, ed., *Esther's Children: A Portrait of Iranian Jews* (2002). **Map 5**

RIVANNE SANDLER

Iraq. Iraq was the location of a large Jewish community from the time of the *Babylonian Exile in the sixth century BCE. Founded by the second 'Abbāsid Caliph al-Manṣūr in the mid-eighth century CE as the Babylonian Empire's capital city, Baghdad– the capital of present-day Iraq – became the main crossroads for connecting trade routes and the political and cultural center of the Muslim world. Under the law of *dhimma (protection for subjects who adhere to monotheistic faiths other than Islam), Jews could practice their religion and preserve their identity as a separate social and legal entity, with certain restrictions. However, the experience of the Jewish minority was variable and highly dependent on the tolerance of the authorities and on the material and political circumstances of the Muslim majority.

Jews participated in the burgeoning urban and commercial life of the empire. A Jewish consortium in Baghdad in the early tenth century provided the 'Abbasid rulers with loans and other banking and mercantile services. Arab chronicles describe the vital services of these merchant-bankers. Jews pursued a broad range of occupations; many were merchants, artisans, agriculturalists, physicians, and government clerks. By the tenth century Arabic was the shared vernacular of Muslims and Jews.

Jewish intellectual life in Abbasid Iraq continued trends developed in earlier times. The Jewish Babylonian academies of Sura and *Pumbedita moved to Baghdad in the late ninth century, and Baghdad became an important political and intellectual center for world Jewry. *Responsa (legal opinions in response to written questions) were issued from Baghdad based on the customs and traditions of Baghdadi Jews. A fundamentally conservative community, the Jews of Baghdad passed on family traditions and communal customs from generation to generation. The Jewish quarter provided all the necessities of Jewish life.

The Jewish community suffered along with the majority population when the Mongols destroyed the Arab caliphate and much of Baghdad in 1258. By the first half of the fourteenth century the Jewish community in Baghdad was no longer a thriving community, and it experienced the general stagnation of subsequent centuries that affected both Muslims and non-Muslims.

Modernization and exposure to European culture came to the Baghdadi Jewish community when the first school of the *Alliance Israélite Universelle opened in December 1864. It offered coeducational training in language and skills that prepared Jews to meet the needs of the civil service and economy during the British Mandate in Iraq (1921–32). Educated Jews applied for posts of clerks and senior officers requiring knowledge of both Arabic and English. Many Jews were employed in the postal service, railroads, ports, customs, banking, and courts. The community prospered and underwent change. European dress gradually replaced traditional clothing, and modern Jewish women did not cover their faces in the street.

However, whether the authorities were Persians, Arabs, Mongols, or Turks, or even the more benign British who took over from the Turks in 1917, the Jewish community was vulnerable. In post–1932 independent Iraq there was a developing chasm between Jews and Muslims. *Zionist activities both inside and outside Iraq were viewed as problematic both by members of the Iraqi Jewish community and the authorities. *Nazi activity in Baghdad and Arab nationalism fueled the 1941 anti-Jewish *pogrom (farhud). The majority of Iraqi Jews were airlifted to *Israel during 1950–51.

For further reading, see J. Kraemer, *Humanism in the Renaissance of Islam: The Cultural Revival during the Buyid Age* (1986), 75–89; and G. S. Golany, *Babylonian Jewish Neighbourhood and Home Design* (1999). **Map 5**   RIVANNE SANDLER

Isaac was the second patriarch, second son of *Abraham and only son of *Sarah, husband of *Rebekah, and father of *Esau and *Jacob (*Genesis, mainly 21–2, 25:19–27). Isaac was born in accordance with God's promise to Abraham (18:10), when Abraham was one hundred years old and Sarah was ninety years old. Isaac plays a passive role in several crucial events in his life, particularly when God tests Abraham's faith by ordering him to sacrifice "his beloved son" (22:2). Isaac is also comforted after his mother's death when Abraham obtains Rebekah for him as a wife (24). Later in his life, Isaac misunderstands the divine plan for Abraham's descendants by preferring his older son Esau over the younger twin, Jacob (25:28). However, Jacob and Rebekah deceive the old and blind Isaac to obtain the blessing of the firstborn for Jacob (27:19). Isaac's weakness has led some modern interpreters to suggest that the three major figures among the patriarchs and matriarchs are Abraham, Rebekah, and Jacob.   MOSHE RACHMUTH

Isaac the Blind (c. 1160–1235), also known as *Sagi Nahor* (*Aramaic, "full of light") was a prominent early *kabbalist in southern *France and the first scholar known by name to devote himself fully to mystical studies. He was the son of the talmudist *Abraham b. David of Posquières (Rabad); little is known about his life or the extent of his blindness, but elements of his thought have been derived from his surviving writings and from traditions preserved by his disciples and their students. Isaac's extant works include a commentary on *Sefer Yetzirah* and fragments on communion with *God (*devekut), intention (*kavannah) in prayer, and mystical meanings of light and colors. His commentary on *Sefer Yetzirah* presents a complex and original vision of three levels within the Divine (*ein sof [infinity], *maḥashavah* [thought], and *dibbur* [speech]). The *sefirot* flow from the latter two and through *dibbur* constitute and animate the created world. Contemplation, through *Torah study and prayer, enables human beings to communicate with the upper realms. For further reading, see J. Dan and R. Keiner, *The Early Kabbalah* (1986).   JUDITH R. BASKIN

Isaiah is the first of the three major prophetic books (see BIBLE: PROPHETS AND PROPHECY; PROPHETS [NEVI'IM]) and one of the most popular books in later *Judaism. It is cited more than any other prophetic text in *rabbinic literature, and more *synagogue readings (*haftarot) are taken from Isaiah than from any other prophetic book, even though other prophetic books (*Jeremiah and *Kings) are longer. The book, which has sixty-six chapters, is a composite document, made up of contributions from several sources and time periods.

Chapters 1–39 are largely the product of Isaiah, son of Amotz, a prophet who lived in *Jerusalem during the eighth century BCE. Many modern scholars regard substantial sections of 1–39 as the product of scribes working as late as the *Persian and *Hellenistic periods. These scholars, how-

ever, take well-structured poems that make sense as they stand and divide them into a series of nearly unreadable fragments. In fact, most of these chapters can be understood in an eighth-century context, and only a few sections need to be dated later than the eighth century: Chapters 13–14 were reworked by scribes in the sixth century or later; 24–27 were added in the post-exilic era and reflect the beginnings of an apocalyptic worldview; 34–35 belong to the same corpus as 40–66 (see the later discussion); and 36–39 contain narratives about Isaiah and are similar though not identical to 2 Kings 18–22.

Isaiah's central idea is that only YHWH can be exalted; any attempt by earthly beings to achieve greatness constitutes a sin and will be corrected. Almost all the offenses criticized by Isaiah attest to this central idea. Isaiah objects to the creation of large agricultural estates in eighth-century *Judah and *Israel that impoverish small farmers and enrich wealthy landowners. The injustice resulting from the economic chasm between rich and poor is one of Isaiah's main concerns (1, 5, 10). Similarly, he objects to the creation of empires by *Egypt and *Assyria (although he sees Assyria as having a divinely ordained role to punish the errant Israelites); these empires were the geopolitical equivalent of the vast estates of the aristocrats. Isaiah's dislike for anything overweening extends as far as his condemnation of tall trees and large ships (ch. 2); in the perfect future, God's own mountain (the *Temple Mount) would be raised up so that it alone was elevated. Isaiah criticizes the abundant *sacrifices brought by the wealthy (ch. 1); although he is not opposed to sacrificial *worship as such, he regards the ostentatious offerings of the wealthy as ridiculous, because these offerings exemplify the hubris at the root of all sin. Human self-aggrandizement is most obvious in idolatry when people turn away from the one true deity to worship one supposedly manifest in an object fashioned by human hands.

Isaiah bitterly criticizes the Judeans, especially the wealthy, and predicts that they will undergo catastrophe. Nonetheless, he does not predict the nation's end: A remnant will endure and return to God. This remnant will include the city of Jerusalem, which Isaiah regards as inviolable; he predicts (wrongly, it turned out) that Jerusalem will be surrounded by foreign armies sent by God to punish Judah, but will never be conquered. Isaiah expects an era of universal peace to emerge, probably within the near future: All nations, including the Assyrians and Egyptians, will recognize the one true God and worship Him at altars in their own land. Great empires, now reduced to their proper size, will enjoy their own covenantal relationships with YHWH, much like the Israelites already did (ch. 19). Distinct ethnicities will not disappear in this future; indeed, tensions among nations might persist, but they will not be solved through violent conflict. Rather, nations will seek arbitration from YHWH at his Temple in Jerusalem, as a result of which warfare will disappear (2:1–4). The Judean king, a descendant of *David, will rule all Israel in perfect justice, issuing divine rulings to the nations and to Israel (ch. 9, 11). From this set of ideas, later Judaism would construct the idea of the *messiah and the messianic era.

Chapters 40–66 represent a different voice. As early as the Middle Ages, Abraham *ibn Ezra recognized that chapters 40 and following were written by a Judean exile in *Mesopotamia in the sixth century BCE, after the destruction of Jerusalem by the Babylonians. Similarly, Samuel David *Luzzato, who lived during the nineteenth century, maintained that chapters 40–66 were addressed to the Judean exiles in *Babylonia and were not published until some time after 586 BCE (although Luzzato maintained that the eighth-century Isaiah had written them). All modern scholars share ibn Ezra's perspective and believe that chapters 40–66 (and also 34–35) were composed during and after the *Babylonian Exile in the sixth century. Many regard chapters 40–55 (or, according to a more likely theory, 40–53) as having been written by a single prophet in the Babylonian Exile in the 530s BCE. For want of any other name, scholars refer to this prophet as Deutero-Isaiah or Second Isaiah. According to these scholars, chapters 56–66 (or, more likely, 54–56) were written by another prophet (called Trito-Isaiah or Third Isaiah) or a group of prophets, who lived a generation or two later in the Land of Israel. However, because a single poetic style and theology run through all these chapters, it is likely that all of 40–66 and also 34–35 were written by a single prophet who lived in the Babylonian Exile and who returned to the Land of Israel as soon as the Persian emperor Cyrus, who conquered Babylon in 539 BCE, allowed the Judean exiles to return (PERSIA, ANCIENT).

These chapters address a people who has experienced catastrophic losses – of land, *Temple, and king. The prophet reassures Judeans that the God of Israel is still powerful; this deity alone created the world and brings *redemption. The prophet refers to God using both masculine and feminine metaphors (42:13–14, 45:10, 49:14–15, and 66:13). Deutero-Isaiah anticipates a new era without looking forward to the renewal of the Davidic monarchy in the rebuilt Jerusalem: This prophet believes in a messianic era, but not in a personal messiah. In the early chapters of this corpus, Deutero-Isaiah predicts that the return to Zion under Cyrus will be accompanied by the arrival of an era of universal peace and recognition of Israel's God by all nations. In fact, the restoration did not have far-reaching effects. Judah became a relatively poor and insignificant province under Persian rule, not an independent kingdom that was the center of all humanity worshiping the one God. Few exiles availed themselves of the opportunity to return to Zion. Peace did not become the world's norm. Deutero-Isaiah continues to predict in chapters 49 and following that a larger scale ingathering of exiles will take place eventually and that the era of universal peace and monotheism will ultimately arrive.   BENJAMIN D. SOMMER

Ishmael is *Abraham's firstborn son; his mother is *Hagar, *Sarah's Egyptian maidservant (Gen 16). After the birth of her son *Isaac, Sarah demands that Abraham expel Ishmael and his mother (Gen 21:9) to protect Isaac's inheritance. God advises the distraught Abraham to agree to Sarah's wishes and promises that Ishmael, too, will become a great nation (21:13). God sustains Hagar and Ishmael in the wilderness of Paran (21:17–20) and his mother arranges a marriage for him with an Egyptian woman (21:21). When Abraham dies, Ishmael and Isaac bury him in the cave of Machpelah (25:9); Ishmael's descendants are listed in Genesis 25:12–18; he is seen in Jewish and Muslim traditions as the father of the Arab people. This identification first appears in Jubilees 20:13 (see PSEUDEPIGRAPHA).

RABBINIC TRADITIONS: Rabbinic literature portrays Ishmael as a beloved yet displaced offspring, *Isaac's sibling rival, and the Arab forefather of robbers who engage in sinful behavior. He is depicted both specifically as Isaac's adversary and more generally and generically as Israel's "other." A few *tannaitic and *amoraic sources characterize Ishmael's descendants as Arab; however, more often, he and his descendants are depicted as Israel's imagined antipode, much like *Esau and the children of Keturah, the wife of Abraham's old age.

Rabbinic *aggadah of the *amoraic period attests less to a sibling conflict (*Genesis Rabbah* 55:4 and 56:4 [see MIDRASH]) than an affirmation that the *covenant is maintained through Isaac, not Ishmael (*Genesis Rabbah* 46:2 and 47:5). For example, *Genesis Rabbah* 53:12 unequivocally states that Abraham's seed will be through Isaac. Furthermore, especially in amoraic literature, Ishmael is paired with Esau. To reiterate the chosen stature of Israel/*Jacob, both Ishmael and Esau are deemed unworthy issue (e.g., *Sifre Deuteronomy* 312 and 343; *Genesis Rabbah* 67:13; and BT *Ta'anit* 10b; see also BT *Shabbat* 145b; BT *Pesahim* 56a and 119b; and BT *Bava Kamma* 92b). The figure of Esau generally symbolizes *Rome (both imperial and Christian) or is portrayed as Jacob's nemesis throughout rabbinic literature but the elusive figure of Ishmael is multivalent (with the exception of some tannaitic and amoraic material [*Genesis Rabbah* 2:3, 66:4, 67:13; *Leviticus Rabbah* 36:5]). In *Genesis Rabbah* 53:12, Ishmael is said to represent anyone who does not believe in the world to come (see AFTERLIFE); in this way, the midrash emphasizes the covenantal primacy of Isaac by depicting Isaac and Ishmael as metaphors for orthodox and unorthodox theological tenets.

Since the medieval period, Ishmael has often, but not exclusively, symbolized *Islam. As Islam emerged as a hegemonic power in the Near East, the Rabbis drew on long-standing traditions associating Ishmaelites with Arabs and used Ishmael metonymically to refer to Islam. When Islam's genealogical and theological contentions became more widespread, it is reasonable to assume that rabbinic exegetes addressed these challenging socio-political and religious matters in much the same way as they had confronted foreign rule in the past. References to Ishmael after the rise of Islam, however, are not always about the Arabs or Islamic rule. As with rabbinic invocations of any biblical figure, each reference must be understood contextually, in light of philological, cultural, and historical concerns – that is, with textual and extratextual factors in mind. Thus, the diverse ways in which Ishmael appears in rabbinic literature strongly indicate that the Rabbis did not systematically set out to use him for one purpose. Although his marginal status is implicitly recognized, he is neither embraced nor disavowed. In many instances Ishmael represents non-Jews in general and is portrayed negatively, yet his treatment as a member of Abraham's household also yields neutral and positive depictions. For further reading, see C. Bakhos, *Ishmael on the Border: Rabbinic Portrayals of the First Arab* (2006).   CAROL BAKHOS

Islam and Judaism. Islam emerged in the *Arabian peninsula in the early seventh century CE. Islamic tradition teaches that the Prophet Muhammad (570–632 CE) brought "the [true] religion in God's eyes" (Qur'an 3:19) to the Arabs in the form of divine revelations conveyed to him over a twenty-two-year period by the angel Gabriel (*Jibrīl*), who appeared to Muhammad from time to time when he fell into a trance. These revelations, memorized by early believers known as the Prophet's "Companions," were collected into a scripture during the century after his death in 632 CE. That scripture calls itself the Qur'an (Q.2:185) and specifies the name of the new religion as Islam (Q.3:19). The name of the deity *Allah* (Q.1:1), like its biblical cognate *Elohim*, means simply "God." The word "islam," from the Semitic root s-l-m common to Arabic, *Hebrew, and *Aramaic (meaning "whole, complete, entire"), connotes *wholehearted* surrender or submission to God's will. The word *qur'an*, likewise from a root common to all three languages, means literally "recitation" or "proclamation" of God's word (cf. the Bible's use of the identical Hebrew root *k-r-'* in *Isaiah 40:6).

From the inception of Islam in the early seventh century, Muslims and Jews have enjoyed varying degrees of interaction and cross-fertilization. Extensive parallels between the core beliefs and practices of Judaism and Islam are evident both in the Qur'an itself and in the oral *ḥadīth* traditions that evolved to supplement the Muslim scripture. This is especially true of the "five pillars of Islam": daily declaration of strict monotheism, daily prayer at set times, giving of charity, fasting in repentance, and observance of pilgrimage. After Muhammad's death, his revelations were collected and edited into the Qur'an, and oral traditions evolved rapidly as the new religion spread eastward from *Arabia to *Syria, *Iraq, and *Iran and westward through *Egypt to the *North African region known as *al-Maghrib* ("the West"). Later, throughout the period that historians dubbed the European "Dark Ages," most of the world's Jews lived under the hegemony of Islam; thus, Jewish scholars from the tenth to thirteenth centuries, including luminaries like *Saadia Gaon, Judah *Halevi , Abraham *ibn Ezra, *Maimonides, and *Naḥmanides, participated in what was then arguably the world's most flourishing culture. Medieval Islamic *medicine, philosophy, and language arts left an imprint on intellectual and spiritual developments within Judaism, especially in the fields of Hebrew *grammar, Hebrew *poetry, *thought, and *mysticism.

In Muhammad's day, numerous religious groups inhabited the Arabian peninsula. These groups included pagan Arabs, for whom Mecca with its sacred Ka'ba shrine was the focal point of an annual pilgrimage; Arabic-speaking Jews (based 200 miles to the north in the city of Yathrib, later to be renamed Medina, but founded by Jews centuries earlier), and Christians (centered in Najran, 375 miles south of Mecca on the border with *Yemen). The concept of monotheism was not unknown in pre-Islamic Arabia, and Islam, like Judaism, explicitly rejects the Christian doctrine of the trinity (Q.4:171). Muhammad himself, whom the Qur'an portrays as "unlettered" (Q.7:157), may have absorbed Jewish and Christian religious folklore from oral traditions circulating in Arabia. The Qur'an names most of the major figures in the *Hebrew Bible and *New Testament, from *Adam and *Noah in Genesis, through the Hebrew patriarchs and Israelite *prophets, to John the Baptist, the Virgin Mary, and Jesus Christ – identifying all but Mary (the sole woman mentioned by name in the Qur'an) as prophets. In addition to Jews and Christians, the Qur'an also specifies Zoroastrians ("Magians," Q.22:17) and "Sabians" (Q.2:62, a group still

unidentified by scholars) as *ahl-al-kitāb*, "People of the Book" (Q.3:199), to whom God had sent earlier revelations – in particular the *Torah *(tawrāh)* and the Christian Gospel (*injīl* from Gk. *Evangelion*; Q.3:3). The Qur'an makes clear that *ahl-al-kitāb* are not subject to forcible conversion, but enjoy the protected (albeit inferior) legal status of *dhimmi, so long as they pay a special poll tax called *jizya* ("tribute") "until they are utterly subdued" (Q.9.29).

The Qur'an explicitly endorses the major doctrines of earlier scriptural religions (Judaism, Christianity, and Zoroastrianism), including divine creation, revelation, and salvation, and it appropriates for Muslims (Q.3:110) the doctrine of election or "*chosen peoplehood" – which the Torah bestows on the Israelites (Deut 7:7) and the *New Testament on Christians (1 Peter 2:9). Other doctrines adopted by Islam include (from Judaism) predestination, the day of judgment (Arabic *yawm al-din* from Hebrew *yom ha-din*) and divine retribution (reward and punishment), and (from Zoroastrianism via Christianity) eternal life spent either in paradise (Gk. *paradeisos* from Persian *pairidaeza*, "garden"; Arabic *jannat-'adn*, "Garden of Eden," from Hebrew *gan-'eden*), or burning in hell (Greek *gehenna* and Arabic *jahannum* from Hebrew *gehinnom*). Doctrines rejected by Islam include the Jewish teaching that the gift of prophecy ended with the prophet Malachi in the fourth century BCE (which led the Jews, contrary to Muhammad's initial expectations, to deny his prophethood) and the Christian teaching that Jesus of Nazareth was the long-awaited Jewish *"messiah" (Hebrew, *mashiaḥ*; Arabic *masiḥ*). The Qur'an (Q.3:45) specifies that one name of Jesus is *masih*, but the name lacks the theological significance of the Hebrew term *mashiaḥ*. In addition, Muslims (like Jews) reject the Christian belief in Jesus as the begotten "son of God" (Q.112:1–4) and sole savior of humankind; however, unlike Jews, Muslims do acknowledge him as a prophet. Two new doctrines propounded in the Qur'an are the divine appointment of Muhammad as both *nabi* (the Biblical Hebrew term for prophet) and *rasul* (translating *apostolos* [messenger], the New Testament Greek term for the twelve disciples of Jesus who preached his message) and the Qur'an's status as the sole authentic text of *al-Kitab*, God's "Book," which by definition supersedes the earlier revealed scriptural texts "corrupted" by Jews and Christians alike.

The Qur'an adopts (mostly by brief references) many biblical stories, including the six days of creation, the *Flood, and the near-sacrifice of *Abraham's son *Isaac (Gen 22); however, the Qur'an's version of the last episode (Q.37:101ff) omits the son's name (even though it names Isaac frequently elsewhere). Hence, most Muslims identify the intended victim with *Ishmael, portrayed both in the Hebrew Bible and in Jewish tradition as the ancestor of the Arabs through Ishmael's son Qedar. The Qur'an speaks of the miraculous dryland crossing of "the Sea" and of the covenant God made with the Israelites on "the mountain" (Q.20:77–80). In some places it recounts events not found in the Bible at all, but only in later *midrashic traditions; these include the story of Abraham smashing his father's idols, as well as certain details in the qur'anic version of the story of *Cain and Abel (Q. 5:30ff) and of *Joseph (Q.12:30–31). Most midrashic traditions antedate Islam, suggesting that they may underlie the qur'anic version, but sometimes the reverse is the case, as where the Qur'an antedates a late midrash with nonbiblical details of the *Queen of Sheba's visit to King *Solomon (Q.27:44).

The interchange of ideas between Jews and early Muslims reflects ongoing economic and social interaction between Jews and Arabs in the region, generated not only by geographic proximity but also by their common linguistic heritage from Mesopotamia; three Semitic languages still extant in Muhammad's time were Arabic, Hebrew, and Aramaic. Indeed, Aramaic would remain the common language of the entire region throughout the first millennium CE, facilitating communication among Jews, Christians, and Muslims beyond the confines of Arabia, where adherents of all three religions were already native Arabic speakers in Muhammad's day.

The socio-cultural intercourse between Jews and Muslims that continued throughout the Middle Ages, and in many countries until modern times, has been aptly characterized by historian Shlomo Dov Goitein as a "creative Jewish-Arab symbiosis." For more than a thousand years, Jews residing in the Middle East lived under the political hegemony of Islam, during successive Arab caliphates (seventh through thirteenth centuries) and later in the *Ottoman Empire (fourteenth through twentieth centuries) until 1917, when that empire's alignment with the losing side in World War I led to its demise. In the Middle Ages, the cross-fertilization of ideas between Jews and Muslims was extensive and mutually fruitful, both in the sphere of religion and in secular fields like medicine, science, philosophy, philology, and poetry. Yet the most extensive evidence of Judaism's influence on Islam undoubtedly appears in the theocratic legal systems that form an integral part of both religions to this day.

Of Islam's four surviving schools of jurisprudence, the closest to rabbinic (talmudic) Jewish law is the Ḥanafī system that flourished in the Iraqi cities of Kufa and Basra, located along the trade route of the Fertile Crescent. These cities were not far from the Jewish academies of Sura and *Pumbedita where the *Talmud was completed about the time of Muhammad's birth and continued to be studied throughout the formative centuries of Islam. We find extensive correspondences between talmudic *halakhah and Islamic sharī'a, both as theocratic systems and at the level of individual rules on specific topics. The numerous parallels reflect in part the legacy of a common ancestral Mesopotamian culture and in part the influence of the dominant surrounding Zoroastrian culture. However, abundant evidence in Islamic oral tradition – in the work of early Muslim jurists like Muḥammad Idrīs al-Shāfi'ī (767–820 CE) – and in halakhic rulings by Jewish jurists like Moses *Maimonides (1135–1204 CE) points to intellectual cross-fertilization in the thought processes of Rabbis on the one hand and Muslim religious scholars and jurists ('ulamā' and fuqahā') on the other.

At the systemic level, Muslim jurists analyzed uṣūl-al-fiqh, "The [Four] Roots of Jurisprudence" – namely, qur'an, sunna, ijmā', and qiyās (written scripture, oral tradition, juristic consensus, and argument by analogy). These four roots bear a close linguistic and conceptual correspondence to the main sources of talmudic law: mikra, mishnah, gemara ("divrei ha-kol"), and hekkesh (scripture, oral law, talmudic consensus, and argument by analogy). Moreover, as regards qiyās and hekkesh, I have proposed that the term qiyās itself was artificially constructed through a grammatical misreading of the root of the Hebrew talmudic term hekkesh by an Arab Muslim jurist unfamiliar with Hebrew or Aramaic grammar.

As for individual topics of the law, the greatest overlap between the two systems occurs in rules governing the status of *women, namely the laws of *marriage, *divorce, and inheritance. Thus, both systems permit polygyny in principle (although Judaism banned its practice in the lands of Christendom since about 1025 CE and in Israel in the early 1950s), whereas both forbid polyandry; in both systems, the groom acquires exclusive use of the bride's sexual and reproductive function by payment of a bride price (biblical mohar, Arabic mahr). Most jurisprudential concepts and much of the technical terminology are the same in both halakhah and sharī'a. Thus, the Islamic law term muqaddasah (from a Hebrew root not native to Arabic) is modeled on the halakhic term mekuddeshet, "betrothed woman" (from the Hebrew root k-d-sh signifying "set apart" or "sacred"), indicating that the bride's sexual function is reserved for her husband's sole use. In sharī'a as in halakhah, divorce is unilateral; technically, only the husband can release the wife, because both systems treat the husband's exclusive claim on the wife's biological function as a valuable property, which the husband alone can relinquish. (Incidentally, the same Hebrew root k-d-sh generated both the Arabic name for *Jerusalem, al-Quds, from the biblical term 'ir ha-kodesh, "the Holy City," and the Arabic name for the Jerusalem Temple, bayt-al-maqdis, transliterating its talmudic name, beit ha-mikdash, "the House of the Sanctuary.")

At the same time, much cultural influence flowed from Islam to Judaism. In early medieval times, Islam – the dominant surrounding culture for Jews living under successive caliphates and sultanates that extended from Mesopotamia to the Iberian peninsula – was the world's most advanced civilization. Relations between Muslims and Jews were far more harmonious than between Jews and Christians in medieval Europe. Some Jews in Arab lands reached high social positions; *Samuel ibn Naghrela (ha-*Nagid) was appointed vizier to the Muslim ruler in eleventh-century Granada (see SPAIN, MUSLIM), and *Maimonides was private physician to Sultan Saladin in Egypt. Arab scholarship informed much of Jewish intellectual life, including science and medicine as well as philological disciplines like philosophy, poetry, and grammar. Medieval Hebrew poetry like that of Abraham ibn Ezra modeled its rules of prosody on Arabic counterparts, and the Hebrew names of verb conjugations were adopted directly from the terminology of Arabic grammar. Maimonides, Naḥmanides, and other Jewish philosophers absorbed Aristotelian and Platonic worldviews conveyed to them by Arab philosophers, and *Hebrew translations mediated these philosophical ideas to scholars residing in Christendom; in particular, Maimonides influenced Thomas Aquinas, who refers to him as "Rabbi Moses" and displays familiarity with his philosophical work.

For further reading on the creative Jewish–Muslim symbiosis, see S. D. Goitein, Jews and Arabs: Their Contacts through the Ages (1955); R. Firestone, Journeys in Holy Lands: The Evolution of the Abraham-Ishmael Legends in Islamic Exegesis (1990); idem, Children of Abraham: An Introduction to Judaism for Muslims (2001); idem, An Introduction to Islam for Jews (2008); B. Lewis, The Jews of Islam (1984); N. A. Stillman, The Jews of Arab Lands (1979); idem, The Jews of Arab Lands in Modern Times (1991); S. M. Wasserstrom, Between Muslim and Jew: The Problem of Symbiosis under Early Islam (1995); J. R. Wegner, "Halakhah and Sharīʿa: Roots of Law and Norms of Conduct in Theocratic Systems," CCAR Journal: A Reform Jewish Quarterly (Fall 2000): 81–95; and idem, "The Status of Women in Jewish and Islamic Marriage and Divorce Law," Harvard Women's Law Journal 5 (1982): 1–33.

JUDITH ROMNEY WEGNER

Israel: See JACOB

Israel, Kingdom of

Israel, Kingdom of was founded ca. 931 BCE, when *Jeroboam led a secession of ten of the twelve Israelite tribes (see ISRAELITES: TRIBES; TRIBES, TWELVE) from the *United Monarchy and the sovereignty of Solomon's son *Rehoboam. The northern kingdom that Jeroboam established was larger, richer, and more populous than the remaining portion of Solomon's realm, which became the southern kingdom of *Judah. Jeroboam established his capital at *Shechem, but later moved the kingdom's center to Tirzah. He also erected shrines at Dan and *Beth El to replace the *Jerusalem *Temple. No consistent dynasty maintained power in Israel. The Omride dynasty (1 Kgs 16:24) established close ties with *Phoenicia when Omri's son *Ahab married Jezebel, daughter of the ruler of Sidon. Ahab, who ruled from 871–52 BCE, was a strong monarch but was killed in battle. Succeeding kings were generally less successful. Israel had to negotiate constantly between the competing powers of *Egypt and *Mesopotamia and in 722–721 BCE, *Assyria conquered the northern kingdom, and the population was sent into exile. From that point on, the ten tribes were lost to history (see TRIBES, TEN LOST). **Map 2**

Israel, Land of

Israel, Land of (Hebrew, Eretz Yisrael) refers to the geographical region of the Middle East with which the Jewish people have been connected since biblical times. It is a designation that transcends politics or political sovereignty or even exact boundaries; rather it expresses the deep historical and spiritual ties that Jews have maintained with the land that was promised to *Abraham and *Sarah and their descendants as part of the *covenant Abraham established with *God. The "Land of Israel" has long been linked with the promise of *messianic *redemption implicit in Jewish *theology and liturgy (see WORSHIP) and has been understood by many thinkers and *mystics as the only place in which Jews can live most fully as Jews (see THOUGHT, MEDIEVAL). *Diaspora Jews throughout the ages contrasted their exile (galut) among the nations with the enhanced holiness that would one day enhance their lives in Eretz Yisrael.

JUDITH R. BASKIN

Israel, State of: Agricultural Settlements, 1878 to 1948.

For nineteenth-century Zionists, founding successful agricultural settlements in the Land of Israel was a major objective. They were convinced that changes in traditional Jewish occupations were necessary to create a "normal" society and that "the return to the land" was one step toward this goal. Establishing agriculture settlements was also seen as a way to acquire large portions of land that would ultimately constitute the considerable territory needed for a permanent, independent state. The dispersion of these settlements all over the country, which could be accomplished by relatively few people settling on large tracts of land, was also intended to establish a widespread Jewish presence.

From 1878 onward, private individuals, mostly wealthy Jews; local and national organizations; and international societies were involved in establishing settlements in the Land of Israel (Hebrew, Eretz Israel). The first attempts were made by Jews already in *Ottoman Palestine who left urban life in Safed and Jerusalem and tried to live in new agricultural villages. In 1878 Jews from Safed established Gei Oni (Valley of my Strength), and Jerusalem Jews established Petach Tikva (Opening of Hope), east of Jaffa. Both settlements were abandoned after a short period, but they indicated the direction that some future settlers would follow. At the same time, local associations of the Lovers of Zion (Ḥovevei Zion) groups were formed among Jews in *Eastern Europe with the aim of establishing new agriculture settlements in Eretz Israel. Beginning in 1882, a wave of Jewish immigrants, known as the First Aliyah (*ISRAEL, STATE OF: IMMIGRATION BEFORE 1948) began to arrive in the Land of Israel. Settlers from among these immigrants established four agricultural settlements in 1882. Two of these were built on the sites of the former Jewish settlements – Petach Tikva and Rosh Pinna (Head of the Corner), the location of Gei Oni. The settlers also built the settlements of Zamarin, later Zichron Yaakov (Jacob's Memorial), and Rishon LeZion (First in Zion). Those new villages were not initially successful, and only the financial support of Baron Edmond James de *Rothschild (1845–1934) enabled them to survive. Rothschild changed the structure of these settlements by introducing viniculture; he sent agronomists who helped the settlers plant vineyards. He also built two great vineyards in Rishon LeZion and Zichron Yaakov, and a glass factory and a small settlement in Tantura to produce the bottles needed for marketing the wine. With the help of Rothschild, other settlements were built including Givat Ada', Metula' Meir Shpheya, and Mahanayim. At the same time, BILU (Beit Ya'akov Lekhu V'nelkha ["House of Jacob, Let us go up" (Isaiah 2:5)]), a Jewish student association, established Gedera in the south.

The Jewish settlers looked for large plots of land to establish villages, rather than farms. The deserted coastal plain and the valleys of Eretz Israel including the Jezreel, Jordan, and Harod valleys, were not occupied by the local Arabs. From the late nineteenth century through the mid-1930s, most Jewish settlements were established on those plains in which heavy machinery could be used, rather than in more hilly regions that were not suitable for modern agriculture.

In the 1890s, private individuals established two more villages, Rehovot and Hadera. Other villages were subsequently established, but in 1900 Baron de Rothschild halted his activities in Eretz Israel and transferred his authority to the Jewish Colonization Association (JCA). The JCA established several more settlements in the lower Galilee area (Kfar Tavor, Ilaniya, Yavne'el, Menahamiya, and Mizpe) and reorganized the older settlements to enable more efficient agricultural activities. Thus, by 1900, there were twenty Jewish agriculture settlements, from Metulla in the north to Beer Tuvia in the south, and from Tantura in the west to Yesud Hamala in the east, with a total of 5,500 occupants. They had about 221,000 dunams of cultivated land; of these, about 24,000 dunams were planted in grapes, 2,200 dunams in citrus, 3,300 dunams in olives, and 60,000 dunams in cereals, mainly wheat; about 700 dunams were in populated areas.

In 1897 Theodor *Herzl founded the World Zionist Organization (WZO). In the years before World War I, the WZO established the model of future agriculture activities in the Land of Israel by introducing the idea of "national land"; Jews from all over the *Diaspora would donate money to the Jewish National Fund (*Keren Kayemet Le-Yisrael*) for the purchase of land, which would be leased to Jews for the establishment of new villages on the national land. Thus, the first *kibbutz (collective settlement), Degania, was established on the shores of the Sea of Galilee in 1909, and the prototype of the moshav (cooperative settlement), Ein Ganim, was established in 1908 near Petach Tikva. Other villages were established in Ben Shemen, Hulda, and Merhavia, all supported by the WZO.

The Second Aliyah, a new wave of Jewish immigrants, entered *Eretz Israel* between 1905 and 1914. Although many settled in the cities (especially Jerusalem and Jaffa), some established new villages. In the years immediately before World War I, there were about forty-four Jewish agricultural settlements with 12,000 inhabitants. Of the 400,000 dunams in Jewish hands, 230,000 were cultivated land; of these, 142,000 dunams were in grains and 68,000 dunam were plantations – about 10,000 dunams of citrus groves, 14,000 dunam of grapes, and 45,000 dunams of almonds and olives.

After the 1920 establishment of the *British Mandate, Jewish immigration increased, with approximately 350,000 Jewish immigrants arriving between 1918 and 1947; the result was a Jewish population of 600,000 by 1947. During those years, the WZO, together with the private Jewish sector, established more than 250 new villages. The first priority was for Jews to settle on the ground according to the ideals of "the national land"; thus, Jews established new *kibbutzim* and *moshavim* where they worked the land through their own physical labor, creating the "new modern Jew." The private sector also established new settlements, mainly based on citrus planting (Netanya, Raanana, Tel Mond). Up to 1936 most of the new villages, national and private, were established in the plains. When a British Royal Commission recommended the partition of *Eretz Israel* between Jews and Arabs according to the population dispersion, the WZO established, from 1937 onward, new settlements that were designed to hold areas needed for the future Jewish state. Thus, settlements were established in the Upper Galilee (Hanita, Eylon, Mazuba), in the northern Negev (Negba, Revivim), the Hebron mountains (Etzion Bloc), and on Mount Carmel. By 1947 a chain of Jewish settlements marked the limit of the settled area in *Eretz Israel*, from Metulla in the north to Mashabei Sadeh in the south and from Kfar Darom in the southwest to Beit Ha'arava and Ein Gev in the east. On this topic, see G. Biger, *The Boundaries of Modern Palestine: 1840–1947* (1980); and I. Troen, *Imagining Zion: Dreams, Designs, and Realities in a Century of Jewish Settlement* (2003).   GIDEON BIGER

Israel, State of: Arab–Israeli Conflict, 1948–2010.

Between 1948 (see also ISRAEL, STATE OF: WARS [1948]) and 1967, the year of the *Six Day War (see ISRAEL, STATE OF: WARS [1956–1967]), Egypt controlled Gaza, and Jordan ruled East Jerusalem and the West Bank. Jordan allowed Arabs living in the West Bank to become Jordanian citizens; a majority of today's Jordanians are of Palestinian stock. Egypt did not allow the Gazans to become Egyptians or work in Egypt. It was only after Israel conquered these territories in June 1967 that Arabs, Muslims, and the world at large began calling for Palestinian independence. It was after that conquest as well that the Israeli religious and political right began agitating for "Greater Israel," an allusion to the imagined boundaries of biblical Israel and a euphemism for permanent control of the conquered territories by modern Israel.

In September 1967, at a meeting in Khartoum, the Arab states proclaimed the famous "Three Nos": "No peace with Israel, no recognition of Israel, no negotiations with it." The United Nations Security Council passed Resolution 242 in November 1967, which coupled "withdrawal of Israeli armed forces from territories occupied in the recent conflict" with "respect for and acknowledgment of the sovereignty, territorial integrity, and political independence of every State in the area and their right to live in peace within secure and recognized boundaries." The Arabs interpret Resolution 242 to mean that Israel must unconditionally leave all the land it captured. The Israelis counter that, if the UN wanted them to do that, it would have called for their withdrawal "from all the territories" or "from the territories," rather than "from territories." In addition, they note, except for Egypt and Jordan, the Palestinians and other Arabs have rejected their right to a sovereign and serene existence in the Middle East.

Next to the 1967 Six Day War, and, before that, Israel's War of Independence, the most cataclysmic event in the history of the Arab–Israel conflict was the outbreak of the 1973 Yom Kippur War. In a surprise attack, Egyptian forces crossed the Suez Canal, broke through Israel's supposedly impregnable Bar Lev Line, and for a time threatened to overwhelm and defeat Israel's fabled army. After many deaths and casualties, as well as huge equipment losses, the Israelis counterattacked and restored the political and military status quo ante. However, this return to the pre-1973 situation did not last long. President Anwar el Sadat of Egypt converted military defeat into political victory. Expelling the Soviet presence from Egypt, he flew to Jerusalem in 1977, met with Prime Minister Menahem Begin, addressed the Israeli Knesset (parliament), and offered to make peace with Israel. The result was the Egyptian–Israeli peace treaty of 1979, according to which Israel returned the Sinai Peninsula, which it had acquired in the Six Day War. President Sadat, who shared the Nobel Prize for Peace with Prime Minister Menahem *Begin, was assassinated in 1981 by Egyptians opposed to his accommodation with Israel. However, the peace between Egypt and Israel has continued to hold.

Realizing that conventional military confrontations were doing nothing to end the occupation of captured territories, the Palestinians escalated terrorist attacks within Israel in what is known as the "First Intifada" (1987–93). In 1993 Yasser Arafat, the first chairman of the Palestinian Authority, shook hands with Israeli prime minister Yitzhak Rabin on the White House lawn and, as part of the Oslo Accords, declared his readiness to make peace with the State of Israel. Arafat, who died in 2004, never made good on his pledge, but in 1994 King Hussein of Jordan became the second Arab ruler to make peace with Israel. This peace, too, has continued to hold.

At the end of the first decade of the twenty-first century, Israeli accommodation with the Palestinians in Gaza and the occupied West Bank remains elusive. In 2000, at a meeting hosted by U.S. President Bill Clinton in Camp David, Maryland, Arafat rejected Israeli Prime Minister Ehud *Barak's offer to return 95% of the occupied territories, including a portion of Jerusalem to be used, if Arafat wished, as the capital of the state of Palestine. Arafat responded by launching the Second Intifada, which still continues. In 2006, a year after Prime Minister Ariel *Sharon ordered Israel's unilateral withdrawal from the Gaza Strip and after the Palestinian radical group Hamas won elections in Gaza, one of its leaders, Khalid Mish'al, said, "We shall never recognize the legitimacy of a Zionist state."

The elimination of Israel resonates powerfully with many Palestinians, as well as Arabs and non-Arab Muslims elsewhere. For them Israel is illegitimate – not only because its nationalism conflicts with theirs but also because Israel's existence contradicts a prime geopolitical precept of Islam. Although most Muslims acknowledge that Jews held sovereignty in the area in antiquity, they believe that once a non-Muslim land is conquered, it forever belongs to the *ummah*, the universal community of Islam. Should the non-Muslim regain the land, this reconquest is temporary and will last only until Muslims have the strength to reconquer the territory. A signal example is the kingdom of Jerusalem, which the Christian Crusaders established in 1099 and the Muslims recaptured in its totality in 1291.

A 2003 Pew Research Center poll found that "by wide margins, Muslim populations [throughout the world] doubt that a way can be found for the State of Israel to exist so that the rights and needs of the Palestinian people are met. Eight out of ten residents of the Palestinian Authority express this opinion." In 2008 the Palestinian Center for Policy and Survey Research found that, by majorities ranging from two-thirds to more than three-fourths, Palestinians favored continued attacks on Israel, as well as the termination of peace negotiations.

There have been eight Arab–Israeli wars in seven decades: the 1948–49 War of Liberation (in which Israel won its renascent independence); the 1956 Suez Campaign (in which Britain and France sought to prevent Egypt from nationalizing the Suez Canal, Israel captured the Sinai peninsula, and then returned it to Egypt in response to American and UN pressure); the 1967 Six Day War (in which Syria lost the Golan Heights, Egypt lost the Gaza Strip and Sinai, and Jordan lost the West Bank); the 1968–70 War of Attrition (a limited conflict begun by Egyptian president Gamal Abdel Nasser, the Soviet Air Force, and the Palestine Liberation Organization to recapture the Sinai peninsula); the 1973 Yom Kippur War (which Israel won, but which laid the foundation for President Anwar El Sadat's visit to Jerusalem, the return of the Sinai, and the Israeli–Egyptian peace treaty); the 1982 First Lebanon War (in which Israel tried without success to seal off its northern border); the 2006 Second Lebanon War, a conflict in which a few thousand Hizbollah militants fought the Israeli Defense Forces (IDF) to a draw; and the Israeli incursion into Gaza in 2008. During its sixty years of statehood, Israel's paramilitary enemies in the Arab world have also mounted countless attacks against Israel and its citizens. Despite repeated IDF strikes, the severity of which are limited by Israel's fear of incurring negative world opinion and of causing huge civilian casualties, these enemies, most recently militants in Gaza, have continued to lob rockets and missiles into Israel at will.

On the eve of the 2007 Middle East conference in Annapolis, Maryland, Saeb Erekat, the chief Palestinian negotiator, said, "One of the more pressing problems is the Zionist regime's insistence on being recognized as a Jewish State, but the Palestinian Authority would never acknowledge Israel's Jewish identity." This is the nub of the Israeli–Arab conflict. Except for Egypt and Jordan, the Arab states do not recognize the right of Israel to exist as a sovereign entity in the Middle East. Until they alter that stance or, in the 2005 words of Iran president Mahmoud Ahmadinejad, "wipe the Zionist entity off the face of the earth," a resolution of the Israeli–Arab conflict remains elusive.

For further reading, see J. G. Granados, *The Birth of Israel: The Drama as I Saw It* (1948); E. B. Glick, *Between Israel and Death* (1974); J. B. Glubb, *A Soldier with the Arabs* (1957); M. B. Oren, *Six Days of War* (2002); and B. M. Rubin and J. C. Rubin, *Yasir Arafat: A Political Biography* (2003); **see also BRITISH MANDATE OVER PALESTINE; ISRAEL, STATE OF: FOUNDING OF THE MODERN STATE; ISRAEL, STATE OF: WARS. Maps 12, 13, 14**   EDWARD BERNARD GLICK

Israel, State of: Diaspora Relations. Most of the thirteen million Jews in the world at the end of the first decade of the twenty-first century live in Israel and North America. Thus, although the smaller Jewish communities in Europe and *Latin America play some role, Israeli Jews and North American Jews are the central players in the perpetual effort to define the parameters of Jewish partnership and Jewish peoplehood (see DEMOGRAPHY; and DIASPORA).

Menachem *Begin, Israel's most nationalistic prime minister, once wrote to an American Jew, "I believe with all my heart that *Eretz Yisrael* (the land of Israel) belongs to the whole Jewish people and not only to those who live in it." Mordecai M. *Kaplan, founder of *Reconstructionist Judaism, wrote constantly of the centrality of Israel, which he called "the hub of the Jewish people throughout the world." In the days of the *Yishuv*, Eliezer Rieger, a Hebrew educator, wrote, "*Eretz Yisrael* and the *golah* (Diaspora Jewry) are mutually indispensable. Without the *golah* to encompass it, *Eretz Yisrael* will become parochial, and without *Eretz Yisrael* as its center, the *golah* is apt to deteriorate. The Jewish settlement in *Eretz Yisrael* will be the *avant garde* of the Jewish people and it will have to bear the responsibility for world Judaism."

These references to the relationship between Israel and the Diaspora denote the transnational, multilingual, historical, cultural, and religious interconnections of the Jewish people, no matter where they live. They express a unity and a partnership that pre-date the rebirth of Israel as a sovereign state. With the exception of the links that Muslims have forged to the cities of Mecca and Medina in Saudi Arabia, Judaism is the world's most geocentric religion. Its belief system has always been tied to the Land of *Israel.

In its relationship with the Diaspora, Israel receives material, moral, and political support, whereas the Diaspora gains psychological, ethnic, and religious pride. On the personal level of Diaspora–Israel relations, there is aliyah (Jewish immigration to Israel). On the group level, there are AIPAC (the American Israel Public Affairs Committee), which is the preeminent foreign lobbying group for Israel, and the World Jewish Congress (WJC), which, under the leadership of its late president Nahum Goldmann, laid the groundwork for what later became the *reparations agreement between Israel and post-war *Germany. Both Israel and the Diaspora carry a shared memory of the *Holocaust, encompassing a shared guilt that they survived, a shared fear of its repetition, and a shared determination that they must do everything in their combined power to prevent its ever happening again.

Nevertheless, there is sometimes tension in the Israeli–Diaspora relationship. Most foreign Jews realize that, in matters like security, Israel must always be the senior partner. Yet even junior partners prefer to be consulted beforehand rather than merely being informed afterward, nor do they like the downgrading of their contribution to the common cause. It can be harmful to both partners when older Israelis forget and younger Israelis are not taught the vital role played by North America's Jews in Israel's birth and ascension into statehood. Many North American Jews, most of whom are non-*Orthodox or unaffiliated, are concerned about the absence of Jewish religious pluralism in Israel and with the "Who is a Jew?" and "Who is a rabbi?" debates. Criticism by North American Jews is often resented by Israelis, who reject censure by those not living in the Jewish state and not serving in its army. American Jews have been nurtured by the constitutional principle of separation of church and state and by the ability of congregants in all branches of *Judaism to live Jewishly in the United States in any way they wish. By contrast, Israelis, regardless of their secular or religious bent, live under a semi-fusion of synagogue and state, where Orthodoxy is the only legally recognized and government-funded branch of Judaism. This presents problems, for example, when a would-be Jewish *oleh* (immigrant to Israel) is married to a Gentile, has a non-Jewish mother, or belongs to one of Judaism's non-Orthodox branches.

Perhaps the greatest Israeli resentment is of avowed Zionists in the Diaspora who refuse to make *aliyah. The "ingathering of the exiles" is a sacred tenet of Zionism, but it has not been significantly heeded by Jews living in the affluent and democratic West. This raises the subsidiary question of who is the better, more Jewish, partner – the one who lives in Israel or the one who does not? Relatively few American Jews become Israelis; however, significant numbers worry about Israel, demonstrate for it, speak up for it, send money to it, visit it, and send their children for sojourns under organized programs like *Taglit*, also known as Birthright Israel. Some even fought for it and died for it in the War of Independence.

This Diaspora pattern has existed since antiquity. From the beginning of the Babylonian *Exile in 586 BCE to the Roman destruction of the Second *Temple in 70 BCE, most Jews, even when given an opportunity, did not return to the Holy Land. When King Cyrus of *Persia allowed *Ezra and *Nehemiah to lead exiles to rebuild the Jerusalem Temple, those who stayed behind vastly outnumbered those who went along – and the numerical importance of the ancient Diaspora was matched by its intellectual vigor.

If for no other reason than the demographic imbalance between itself and its neighbors, Israel wants immigrants from North America. However, Israel fails to fathom that human migration is generally not a pull but a push phenomenon; most people who are satisfied with their lot do not exchange their native land for another. Except for idealists, people do not move from a country with a higher living standard to one with a lower living standard. Those who did emigrate, such as the *North African Jews who came in 1948 and the *Russian Jews who came from the 1970s through the 1990s, were usually driven by economic necessity or political, racial, or religious persecution.

Until quite recently, conventional wisdom held that as memories of the Holocaust faded, as the reasons for Israel's multiple wars became obscure, and as issues like universalism, *environmentalism, and nuclear proliferation took their place, more and more contemporary American Jews would alter attitudes toward Israel and its policies. However, a 2008 Brandeis University study concluded that a large majority of American Jews continue to feel that "Israel is a 'very important' aspect of their Jewish identity." Although earlier surveys had reported that younger *Reform and unaffiliated Jews were less attached to Israel, the Brandeis study found "no significant decline...for the period extending from the early 1990s to the most recent years." Only time will tell whether programs like Birthright Israel will have an enduring effect in establishing long-lasting positive attitudes toward Israel among young Diaspora Jews.

For further reading, see M. Davis, ed., *With Eyes toward Zion* (1977); E. B. Glick, *The Triangular Connection: America, Israel, and American Jews* (1982); T. Sasson, C. Kadushin, and L. Saxe, *American Jewish Attachment to Israel* (2008); and E. Stock, *Partners & Pursestrings: A History of the United Israel Appeal* (1987).   EDWARD BERNARD GLICK

Israel, State of: Ecology. The view that nature can be a resource for the revival of the Jewish people is a cornerstone of *Zionism. This Jewish secular nationalist movement rejected the mostly *urban Jewish lifestyles of the *Diaspora and called on Jews to return to the Land of Israel to establish a new relationship with nature through agriculture and secular reinterpretations of Jewish religious practices. Zionism generated very rich ecological thought about the creative power of nature and the organic ties of the Jewish people to the Land of Israel. The most ecologically interesting Zionist thinker was Aharon David *Gordon (1856–1922), the spiritual leader of Labor Zionism. He was keenly aware of the crisis of modernity and the causal connection between technology and human alienation from nature. Gordon settled in *Palestine in 1904 and joined an agricultural settlement. He viewed human beings as creatures of nature, but warned that people are in constant danger of losing contact with the natural world. Thus, his goal was to create a new kind of Jewish life and Jewish person. For Gordon, the regeneration of humanity and the regeneration of the Jewish people would not come through *Torah study, but rather through physical productive labor.

Despite Gordon's warnings, Jewish settlement in *Palestine and the establishment of *Israel created significant environmental degradation due to intensive agriculture, massive urbanization, rapid population growth, industrialization, and the perpetual state of war. Recognition of the severity of the situation in early-twenty-first-century Israel has generated new ecological awareness and extensive environmental legislation to address the price nature has paid for Israel's success in "making the desert bloom." Israeli environmentalism is largely secular, although there are small groups that attempt to link environmental activism with Jewish sources. About ten major nonprofit Israeli organizations provide information about the environmental crisis, engage in legal action, create educational materials, and even sustain two political parties. The Heschel Center for Environmental Learning and Leadership sponsors educational programs and a forum called *Le-Ovdah U'Le-Shomrah* (To Till and to Tend [Gen 2:15]), devoted to integrating religious nationalism with an environmentalism grounded in Jewish tradition.

A closer look at environmentalism in Israel sheds light on the uneasy relationship between Judaism and ecology. In Israel the concern for the physical landscape and support of action in regard to air and water pollution, treatment of waste products, and conservation of coastal lines are most popular among secular Israelis who wish to improve their quality of life and create a healthy lifestyle. This popularity reflects contact with environmental movements in Europe and North America rather than with the Jewish tradition. Conversely, Israeli Jews who are anchored in the Jewish tradition tend to link their love of the Land of Israel to a certain religious nationalist vision – the so-called Greater Israel vision – rather than the preservation of nature. Even though the religious nationalist parties now promote outdoor activities for their constituents, these activities are not grounded in the values and sensibilities of the environmental movement and are sometimes inimical to it.

For further reading, see L. A. Hoffman, ed., *The Land of Israel: Jewish Perspectives* (1986); A. Tal, *Pollution in the Promised Land: An Environmental History of Israel* (2002); E. Schweid, *The Land of Israel: National Home or Land of Destiny*, trans. D. Greniman (1985); and Y. Zerubavel, "The Forest as National Icon: Literature, Politics, and the Archeology of Memory," *Israel Studies* 1 (Spring 1996): 60–99; **see also** ECOLOGY; ETHICS: ENVIRONMENTAL.

HAVA TIROSH-SAMUELSON

Israel, State of: Founding of the Modern State.

From late antiquity through the nineteenth century, there was always a Jewish presence in the Land of Israel. However, it was only with the growth of Jewish nationalist movements and European *antisemitism in the 1880s that Jews began to return in visible numbers and establish a Jewish entity in *Palestine that came to be known as the *Yishuv (settlement). In 1894 Alfred *Dreyfus, a French Jewish army officer falsely charged with spying for Germany, was convicted of treason. Theodor *Herzl, a Viennese Jewish journalist, covered the trial. Incensed by the antisemitism manifested at the proceedings and in *France at large, he published *Der Judenstaat* (The Jewish State) in 1896. This book put a political face on the Jewish longing for a homeland and urged the creation of a Jewish state, although not necessarily in Palestine. The following year, at a congress in Basel, Switzerland, Herzl and other Jewish leaders created the World Zionist Organization, which proclaimed that "*Zionism seeks a publicly recognized, legally secured home . . . in Palestine for the Jewish people."

The first of the "Great Powers" to recognize Zionism as a political movement was *Britain. On November 2, 1917, its Foreign Secretary, Arthur Balfour, without the acquiescence of the Arabs of either *Palestine or the rest of the Middle East, declared, "His Majesty's Government view with favor the establishment in Palestine of a national home for the Jewish people, and will use their best endeavors to facilitate the achievement of this object, it being clearly understood that nothing shall be done which may prejudice the civil and religious rights of existing non-Jewish communities in Palestine, or the rights and political status enjoyed by Jews in any other country." Later, France, *Italy, the *United States, and other nations accepted what is known as the *Balfour Declaration. In 1922 the League of Nations recognized "the historical connection of the Jewish people with Palestine" and incorporated the Balfour Declaration into the League's "Mandate for Palestine," which it awarded to Britain. This mandate gave Britain the right to govern Palestine, which Britain had conquered in 1917 from the Turks in the course of World War I, as well as the responsibility "for placing the country under such political, administrative, and economic conditions as will secure the establishment of the Jewish national home."

Palestine under the *British Mandate originally comprised all of what is now Israel, Jordan, and the West Bank. In 1922, however, the British detached all the territory lying to the east of the River Jordan and created the semiautonomous Emirate of Trans-Jordan for the Hashemite prince Abdullah I (the great-grandfather of the current Jordanian monarch, whose name is also Abdullah).

Palestine's Arabs and Arabs elsewhere rejected Britain's support of a Jewish home, but Palestine's Jews accepted it eagerly. As time passed, the Jews stopped calling for a Jewish homeland and instead demanded a Jewish state. They wanted increasing immigration into Palestine so that Jews could become the majority in the country. This prospect galvanized Palestinian nationalism. In a violent effort to force the British to convert Palestine into an Arab entity, Arabs engaged in massacres of Jews, the most notorious of which occurred in 1929 and between 1936 and 1939.

The contradictions within the Balfour Declaration and the irreconcilability of Arab and Jewish nationalisms were obvious from the very start of British mandatory governance. Nevertheless, London tried to achieve some reconciliation. In 1936 it sent to *Jerusalem the Peel Commission, named after its chairman, Earl Peel. It reported that "there is no common ground between . . . [the two communities]. . . . Neither Arab nor Jew has any sense of service to a single state"; it concluded that "the disease is so deep rooted that, in our firm conviction, the only hope of a cure lies in a surgical operation." The recommended surgery was a three-way partition of the territory into an Arab state, a Jewish state, and a British-controlled area. Nothing came of this proposal, however, because the Arabs responded with riots and new attacks on Palestine's Jews.

Shortly before the outbreak of *World War II, Britain jettisoned the last vestiges of its support for Zionism. In May 1939, the British government issued a *White Paper (a policy document) stating first that its objective was now "the establishment within ten years of an independent Palestine state." To accomplish this goal, Arabs were to be given "an increasing part in the government of their country." Second, between 1939 and 1944 Jewish immigration into Palestine was to be limited to a total of 75,000 persons. After that date, "no further Jewish immigration will be permitted unless the Arabs of Palestine are prepared to acquiesce in it." Third, the Palestine government would be granted "powers to prohibit and regulate [further private] transfer of land [from Palestinian Arabs to Palestinian Jews]."

The war forced Britain to postpone most of its announced reforms, but it strictly enforced the restrictions on Jewish immigration and land purchase detailed in the 1939 White Paper. Once the war was over, the struggle between the British, the Jews, and the Arabs resumed and accelerated. To their earlier demand for a Jewish state, the Zionists added the demand that the survivors of the *Holocaust be allowed to come to Palestine immediately. When the British balked, Jews sought to bring the refugees in illegally. The Royal Navy stopped the refugees whenever it could, sending them either back to Europe or to internment camps in Cyprus.

In 1946 Britain proposed to the United States the formation of an Anglo-American Committee of Inquiry on the Palestine Problem. Its report recommended "that 100,000 certificates be authorized immediately for the admission into Palestine of Jews who have been the victims of *Nazi and Fascist persecution...and that those certificates be awarded as far as possible in 1946." It also recommended that "Palestine be neither a Jewish state nor an Arab state." The Anglo-American report satisfied no one. The immigration certificates were never issued because London made their issuance contingent on the disarmament of both Jews and Arabs, as well as on Washington's sharing of the "additional military and financial responsibilities" involved in bringing the Jewish immigrants to Palestine. President Harry S. Truman refused to accept these conditions. Consequently, London continued to curb Jewish immigration into Palestine. In February 1947 the British proposed that "His Majesty's Government should administer a five-year trusteeship over Palestine, with the declared object of preparing the country for [bi-national] independence." This, too, was rejected by the Palestinian Arab and Palestinian Jewish communities.

On April 2, 1947, after thirty years of governing Palestine, Britain brought the problem to the United Nations. On November 29, 1947, the General Assembly recommended the partition of Palestine into a Jewish state, an Arab state, and a UN-administered *corpus separatum* for Jerusalem. The Jews of the Y*ishuv* accepted the partition, even though it did not grant them sovereignty over Jerusalem. As David *Ben-Gurion, Israel's founding prime minister, put it, "Better a Jewish State without Jerusalem than Jerusalem without a Jewish State."

General Sir Alan Gordon Cunningham, the last British High Commissioner, departed on May 14, 1948. On the same day, David Ben-Gurion declared Israel's independence as a Jewish and democratic state and appealed for peace: "We extend our hand to all neighboring states and their peoples in an offer of peace and good neighborliness, and appeal to them to establish bonds of cooperation and mutual help with the sovereign Jewish people settled in its own land. The State of Israel is prepared to do its share in common effort for the advancement of the entire Middle East." As one of its first acts, the temporary National Council of State unanimously passed an ordinance voiding the restrictions on Jewish immigration and land purchases contained in the 1939 British White Paper.

The Arabs rejected the partition plan and went to war against Palestine's Jews, who had by then become one-third of the population of the country. Although the Jews of the *Yishuv*, now called Israelis, beat back seven invading Arab armies, they were unable to seize the Old City of Jerusalem or the lands that later came to be known as the Gaza Strip and the West Bank. The present boundaries between Israel and the Palestinian territories are not international frontiers. They are the ceasefire lines delineating where the opposing armies stopped fighting in 1948 and 1949. **Maps 12, 13**

BERNARD EDWARD GLICK

Israel, State of: Immigration Before 1948.

*Palestine in the nineteenth century was essentially a poor and rural society that had long been a backwater of the *Ottoman Empire. The population was overwhelmingly Muslim Arab with a primarily urban Christian Arab merchant and professional class. There were fewer than 25,000 Jews in Palestine before 1880; some two-thirds lived in *Jerusalem, where they constituted a majority of the population. This community, which came to be called the "Old *Yishuv*," consisted of descendants of Jews who had remained in the area since earliest times, as well as a small stream of new immigrants, mainly *Orthodox Jews who sought to live a religious life and die in the Holy Land.

In the late nineteenth century, in response to the nascent political Zionist movement (see ZIONISM), there was a wave of immigration of Jews from *Russia and *Eastern Europe. This First *Aliyah (from the Hebrew word "to ascend") took place between 1882 and 1903 and brought 20,000 to 30,000 individuals to Palestine. Many arrived in groups organized by the Ḥovevei Zion (Lovers of Zion) and BILU (*Beit Ya'akov Lekhu V'nelkha*; "House of Jacob, Let us go up" [Isa 2:5]) – Zionist movements in *Russia and *Romania; others, mostly from *Galicia, arrived on their own. The new Jewish migration was diverse. Some people came primarily for religious reasons and joined existing Jewish communities, mainly in Jerusalem, but also in other "holy" cities such as *Safed, Tiberias (see GALILEE), and *Hebron. Others were drawn by Zionist ideology that sought the creation of a Jewish state as a response to *antisemitism in their native lands; some were motivated by socialist ideas and concepts. These new immigrants joined farm villages or established new *agricultural settlements, such as Rishon LeZion, Zichron Yaakov, and Rosh Pinna. In 1878, a group of Jews from Jerusalem founded a new town, Petach Tikva; the initial settlement was abandoned but was reestablished in 1882. The immigrants of the First Aliyah, which also included Middle Eastern (*Mizraḥi) Jews from *Yemen, faced many obstacles. Yet it was this immigration and the agricultural settlements they founded that revived modern Jewish life in the *Land of Israel.

As the movement of Jews from Europe to Palestine continued in the earliest years of the twentieth century, the Jewish population of the Holy Land grew in urban and rural areas. The Second Aliyah (1904–14) involved some 35,000 to 40,000 young pioneers, mostly from Russia. By *World War I (1914) there were some 85,000 Jews and 600,000 Arabs in Palestine. Successive waves of immigration to Palestine between 1919 and 1939 contributed to different aspects of the developing Jewish community and economy. The Third Aliyah, comprising some 35,000 immigrants who arrived between 1919 and 1923, mainly from Russia, strongly influenced the character and structure of the "New *Yishuv*." These pioneers laid the foundations for a comprehensive social and economic infrastructure; developed agriculture by establishing collective agricultural settlements, *kibbutzim* and *moshavim* (see ISRAEL, STATE OF: AGRICULTURAL SETTLEMENTS, 1878 TO 1948; ISRAEL, STATE OF: KIBBUTZ MOVEMENT); and provided the labor for the construction of housing and roads.

The influx between 1924 and 1932 of some 80,000 mainly middle-class immigrants from Poland, the Fourth Aliyah, was instrumental in developing and enriching urban life. These immigrants mostly settled in *Tel Aviv, Haifa, and Jerusalem, where they established small businesses, construction firms, and light industry. The Fifth Aliyah (1932–38) consisted of some 215,000 urban professionals and businesspeople from *Central Europe who were fleeing the *Nazi regime. During World War II (1939–45), immigration to Palestine continued both legally and illegally and totaled some 82,000. Between the end of World War II (1945) and the declaration of the State of Israel in May 1948, there were severe British restrictions on Jewish immigration (see BRITISH MANDATE; WHITE PAPER); nevertheless some 57,000 Jews arrived. After independence in 1948, the State of Israel allowed free immigration, and the flow of immigrants grew dramatically, including entire communities from some Muslim countries.

For further reading, see B. Reich, *A Brief History of Israel* (2008); idem, "The Founding of Modern Israel and the Arab-Israeli Conflict," in *The Cambridge Guide to Jewish History, Religion, and Culture*, ed. J. R. Baskin and K. Seeskin (2010); and H. M. Sachar, *A History of Israel: From the Rise of Zionism to Our Time*, 3rd ed. (2007); **see also related entries under ISRAEL, STATE OF.**   JUDITH R. BASKIN

Israel, State of: Immigration Post-1948.

Israel is a special case of a country built on immigration. The influx of a sizable Jewish population from other places has been a crucial element in fulfilling *Zionist aspirations and a major factor in ensuring the Jewishness of the state. Organizing the emigration of Jews from other countries and moving them to Israel, as well as struggling for the independence of the Jewish State, have been one of the main activities of Zionism as the national movement of the Jewish people.

Israel's 1948 Declaration of Independence states, "The State of Israel will be open for Jewish immigration and for the Ingathering of the Exiles," and this clause constitutes the underpinnings of Israeli immigration policy. Two main laws govern implementation of this policy: the Law of Return and the Citizenship Law. According to the Law of Return (July 5, 1950), every Jew is entitled to move to Israel and receive an "immigrant's certificate"; this certificate gives him or her the right to Israeli citizenship. These laws resulted in a unique immigration policy based on ethnic-religious classifications, rather than the demographic, economic, and social criteria that are standard in other countries. In keeping with this conception, Israel refers to immigrating Jews as *olim* ("ascenders" [singular: *oleh, olah*]) and to Jewish immigration to Israel as *aliyah* ("ascent"); these biblical terms, which are used in connection with the ancient returns from *Egypt and *Babylonia to the Land of Israel and the pilgrimage to the *Temple in *Jerusalem, imply elevation, exaltation,

and sanctity. Thus, *olim* are portrayed as ideological immigrants fulfilling their national purpose, even though most of the newcomers in the large waves of aliyah were in fact motivated by various push and pull factors and lacked more attractive migration options.

*Aliyah has been an ongoing process. From the establishment of the state (1948) until 2007, more than 3 million *olim* (3,090,000) arrived in Israel, especially in two huge waves: 700,000 between 1948 and 1951, and more than 950,000 between 1990 and 2000. There were smaller waves in 1955–57 (165,000 immigrants), 1961–64 (230,000), and 1972–73 (110,000). Most of the *olim* came from four regions: *Eastern Europe, the Middle East, *North Africa, and the former *Soviet Union.

Aliyah from Eastern Europe was part of the first mass wave in the early years of the state (1948–51), with some 330,000 Jewish immigrants; another 225,000 came in the 1960s and 1970s. The main wave of immigrants from the Middle East, some 240,000, also arrived in the early years. They were followed in the 1960s and 1970s by another 70,000 immigrants. The first wave included almost all the Jews of *Yemen and *Iraq, as well as Jews from *Iran, *Turkey, and *Egypt. Immigration from *North Africa (the Maghreb) was spread over three decades, during which some 400,000 *olim* came to Israel. The *Ethiopian *olim*, who numbered more than 60,000, came mainly in the early 1980s and early 1990s. The greatest number of immigrants in Israel are from the former Soviet Union and total 1.1 million; 150,000 arrived in the early 1970s, whereas 970,000 came in the 1990s and later.

CHRONOLOGICAL OVERVIEW OF ALIYAH: The first wave of mass aliyah started as soon as Israel gained its independence in May 1948 and ended in late 1951. During this time the population doubled, as some 700,000 Jews, half from Europe and half from Islamic countries, were added to the 650,000 Jewish residents of the state.

First came *Holocaust survivors, from the detention camps in Cyprus, from *displaced persons camps in *Germany, and from *Bulgaria (37,000), the *Balkans, *Poland (106,000), and *Romania (118,000). In 1949 and 1950, Jews arrived from Libya (31,000), from Yemen and Aden (50,000), and then from Iraq (125,000). In addition, some 45,000 *olim* came from French North Africa and more than 20,000 from Iran, along with thousands from dozens of other countries. In this wave of aliyah, four communities immigrated to Israel almost in their entirety: the Jews of Libya, Bulgaria, Yemen, and Iraq.

Unlike immigration to other countries, this wave of aliyah included a large number of children and elderly persons, as well as people who were ill, disabled, or in need of public support. Most of the immigrants had fairly little education, and few had Zionist backgrounds. Some came to Israel for ideological reasons, including those who had struggled against the *British Mandate authorities for the right to move to *Palestine, but the vast majority left their countries of origin because they no longer felt physically and economically secure. European immigrants comprised both refugees who did not want to or could not return to their countries of origin and Holocaust survivors in Eastern Europe who were worried about the rise of *communism and the nationalization of the private economy. Those from the Middle East and North Africa were escaping the physical threat of *pogroms, discriminatory economic and social policies, and the ramifications of the ongoing *Arab–Israeli conflict. They were drawn, too, by the hope of full equality in the Jewish state. At the time Israel was almost the only immigration option these Jews had, and its sophisticated immigration system facilitated the process. In Israel, various ideological explanations were given for aliyah from these two regions: The European *olim* were described as "remnants" and survivors, and their experience of the Holocaust proved that the Zionist solution was correct. The Jews of Islamic countries were said to have immigrated because of persecution and a religious-*messianic conception that identified the State of Israel with the messianic redemption.

Israel suffered from severe housing shortages while absorbing these *olim*, and for many months and sometimes years, tens of thousands of people, most of them from Islamic countries, lived in tents and shacks in temporary camps known as *ma'abarot*. This experience left severe scars on Israeli society. Despite these hardships, this wave of aliyah played a formative role in shaping Israeli society: It doubled the population; broadened the distribution of Jewish settlement by boosting the population of preexisting localities and establishing new localities throughout the country, including some three hundred *agricultural settlements; and determined the main outlines of Israeli society for decades to come.

The social and cultural traits of different immigrant groups, especially those from Islamic countries, evoked anxiety for the future development of a unified Israel's culture. For this reason the country adopted what was later termed a "melting pot" policy: Immigrants were strongly encouraged to drop the unique elements of their traditions and to adopt the *Ashkenazi culture that prevailed at the time. The melting pot policy applied to all *olim*, but especially those from Islamic countries, because their Arab culture was perceived as inferior and antiquated and was also identified with the Arab enemy. The policy extended to all aspects of the immigrants' lives: from forms of settlement and employment to personal hygiene, family planning, and education. The most dramatic fight in the history of immigrant absorption in Israel was waged in the 1950s over the education of immigrant children, particularly the Yemenites. What made this policy unique was its intensity and its all-encompassing nature. Criticism of the negative effects of this policy ultimately brought about its replacement by a more pluralistic absorption policy that recognized the rights of the various groups of *olim* to cultural autonomy. Demands for immediate change were dropped in favor of an expectation of slower change, gradual adoption of the values of Israeli society, and eventual integration into Israeli society.

The second wave of aliyah lasted two decades. It included the arrival of more than 400,000 Jews from North Africa, especially Morocco and Tunisia, and peaked in 1954–56 and 1961–64. The *olim* were motivated by apprehension regarding the French withdrawal from North Africa and the transfer of rule to Muslims belonging to nationalist movements, as well as by hopes of full equality and an improved financial status in Israel. During those years 150,000 Jews who had left Eastern Europe due to communist regimes also arrived in Israel. For about a decade (1951–61), Israel instituted a selective policy regarding aliyah from North Africa, which gave preference to young, healthy people and kept out families with elderly or ill members or large numbers of children. The rationale for this policy was the country's severe economic plight and a desire to have the North African *olim* carry out the national task of settling the periphery. Another explanation claims that the selective policy also reflected fear of the influence of North African Jews on Israeli society and culture, as well as a desire to absorb them gradually and perhaps even to keep them away from influential positions in central Israel.

Indeed, North African immigrants played a crucial role in building up the Israeli periphery. Some 70% were placed in *moshavim* and new towns ("development towns") established in the north and south in a policy known as "ship to village"; meanwhile, the *olim* from Eastern Europe settled mainly in preexisting localities in central Israel. For the first time in the history of Zionist settlement, *olim* were forced to live in certain places, and the new system of administration made it hard for them to move elsewhere, even though this effort ran counter to the Israeli policy of "blending the exiles."

The third wave of aliyah started in the 1970s with immigration from the *Soviet Union (150,000 *olim*) and peaked in the 1990s with the disintegration of the Soviet Union and the arrival of close to a million immigrants, most from the European republics (Russia and *Ukraine), with a minority from the Asian republics, especially Uzbekistan. The main motivation was the collapse of the regime and the crisis in the socioeconomic order of the former Soviet Union. Additional factors were entry restrictions imposed by destination countries in the western world and Israel's open-door policy. This wave was characterized by small families and relatively few children, as well as a high proportion of single-parent families. The newcomers' level of education was high compared with the receiving society in Israel; a sizable percentage of the *olim* were scientists, academics, and members of the liberal professions. For the first time in the history of aliyah, a significant percentage of the immigrants were non-Jews entitled to immigrate under the 1970 amendment to the Law of Return, which extended citizenship rights and benefits to non-Jewish family members of persons eligible for immigration. In the early 1990s, non-Jews accounted for about one-tenth of *olim*; by the late 1990s they accounted for around 40%.

In terms of culture, these immigrants proved thoroughly secular, with a strong and solid Russian identity and only a weak affinity for the Jewish collective. They were not willing to give up their Russian culture and were in no rush to adopt the local Israeli mores. For its part, Israeli society turned out to be less cohesive and more pluralistic than earlier. These circumstances led to tolerance for and legitimation of the sectorial political parties founded by the immigrants. After a decade, it was clear that the Russian-speaking *olim* had developed an Israeli identity based on a sense of belonging to the Jewish people, while also preserving Russian culture and forming a Russian community in Israel.

The Russian-speaking *olim* underwent "direct absorption," which included economic grants and limited intervention by the government. The geographical distribution of the immigrants was correlated with their educational and employment capital. Young people with needed professions settled on the outskirts of the metropolitan areas and in the leading peripheral cities; older and less educated segments of this population settled in poor neighborhoods and peripheral localities, where they found readily available and relatively cheap housing, as the Israeli government increased the construction of public housing in the periphery. This immigration boosted the Jewish population by about 20%, contributed to substantial economic growth, and even influenced local culture.

Concurrently with the Russian-speaking aliyah, close to 60,000 *olim* came from *Ethiopia, forming a relatively small but unique community within Israeli society. Some 16,000 arrived in the 1980s, and more than 40,000 came in the 1990s and later. Most arrived in two waves that are known as "Operation Moses" and "Operation Solomon." The Ethiopian immigration was delayed for many years, mainly because of doubt as to the Jewishness of the community members. Until they moved to Israel, most Ethiopian Jews were villagers in transition from the country to the city; most adults lacked even an elementary education. The Ethiopian Israelis are an especially young population group because of their high rate of fertility. Community members settled mainly in medium-sized cities in the central and southern regions, where they tend to be concentrated in certain neighborhoods.

A retrospective examination of the settlement patterns of immigrants in Israel shows substantial consistency over the sixty-year history of the state. A strong population with high human capital, generally of European origin, settled in the large and medium-sized cities of central Israel, especially on the coastal plain, whereas the less educated population, mainly from Asia and North Africa, was concentrated in the geographical and social periphery. The advantages of living in the central region rather than the periphery are manifested in a growing socioeconomic gap that typifies Israeli society in its sixth decade.   ESTHER MEIR-GLITZENSTEIN

Israel, State of: Judicial System.

The judicial system of Israel plays a prominent role in the life of the country, which is reflected in both legal and nonlegal discourse. Formally, the judiciary is one of Israel's three branches of government, together with the legislative (the *Knesset, the Israeli parliament) and the executive (the Israeli government) branches. The main principles regarding the powers and functions of the judiciary are stated in "Basic Law: Judicature," which establishes the judicial system's magistrate courts, district courts, and the Supreme Court. In addition, there are specialized tribunals vested with judicial power, such as religious courts, military courts, and labor courts. Judges are elected by a special committee comprising two ministers, one of whom is the Minister of Justice; two Knesset members; two representatives of the Bar Association; and three Justices of the Supreme Court; this committee enjoys substantive independence. The general structure and powers of the judicial system originate from laws enacted during the time of the *British Mandate in Palestine. When Israel was established, it decided to adopt a principle of continuity regarding the legal system that existed in Mandatory Palestine, subject to necessary changes. This principle was also applied to the judicial system (which from this point in time was no longer subject to the appellate jurisdiction of the British Privy Council).

The most important judicial institution in the country is the Supreme Court. Formally speaking, it is the last and final appellate instance in both criminal and civil affairs. In addition, it acts also as a court of first instance when it hears public law petitions in its capacity as the High Court of Justice. Over the years, the precedents of the Israeli Supreme Court have defined fundamental principles of the Israeli legal system, including a judicial-based unwritten bill of rights. This tradition owes much to justices with profound awareness of the importance of rights and democratic values (particularly, Simon Agranat, Haim Cohn, and Aharon Barak). These precedents have proved very important because Israel did not adopt a formal written constitution in its formative years, due to political disagreements. To fill this void, the Knesset decided to enact a series of basic laws, which would eventually be consolidated into a formal constitution. Gradually, the Supreme Court has abandoned, by way of interpretation, the legal tradition of legislative sovereignty and adopted the view that the basic laws can also serve as a basis for judicial review of legislation contradicting them. This move, as well as the Supreme Court's general activist policy of judicial review of government decisions, is controversial. In general, the Supreme Court is both valued for its contribution to public life in Israel and highly criticized as operating outside the legitimate boundaries of judicial decision making. The critics of the Supreme Court argue that, as an unelected institution, it should not interfere in decisions that reflect policymaking and democratic choices of the political majority. In contrast, supporters of the Court's legacy argue that its contribution is indispensable to the protection of human rights and the struggle against government corruption.   DAPHNE BARAK-EREZ

Israel, State of: Kibbutz Movement.

There are 267 kibbutz communities scattered throughout Israel, from the Lebanon border in the north to the Red Sea in the south. *Kibbutzim* (plural of kibbutz) members constitute 2.1% (120,000) of the Jewish population in Israel, yet their contribution to the national economy amounts to 40% in agriculture, 7% in industrial output, 9% in industrial export, and 10% in tourism.

The first kibbutz, Degania, was built by a communal *agricultural group in 1910. By 1930, there were 29 kibbutz communities; their number rose to 82 in 1940, 229 in 1960, and 267 in 2009. Their population sizes range from thirty to two thousand residents; the average is about four hundred. Most *kibbutzim* were formed by members of *Zionist *youth movements, from abroad or in Israel. A large proportion of kibbutz communities are located on or near Israel's borders.

Kibbutz ideology drew on Zionist, socialist, and humanist values. The founders' stated goals were to cultivate the land from the wild, to build a Jewish national entity in the Land of Israel, and to create a just society. The ideology and goals led to three formative principles: (1) equality among kibbutz members as well as among *kibbutzim*, from which stemmed other values, such as giving equal worth to all work and providing assistance within the kibbutz and among *kibbutzim*; (2) direct democracy, which meant that all members participate in decision making and there is rotation of officeholders; and (3) self-labor, which ensured there was no exploitation of cheap paid labor. This principle of not using outside labor has been preserved, on the whole, in the education branches of the movement but less so in areas of production.

Because of differences in their ideals, kibbutz communities formed different umbrella organizations. The first two, *Ha-Kibbutz ha-Meuḥad* and *Ha-Kibbutz ha-Artzi*, were established in 1927 and a third, Ḥever ha-Kevutzot, in 1929. A fourth movement, of religious *kibbutzim*, was formed in 1935. In 1951 from an ideological split in *Ha-Kibbutz ha-Meuḥad* and a merger with *Ḥever ha-Kevutzot* came a new movement, *Iḥud ha-Kevutzot Veha-Kibbutzim*. These movements reunited in 1980 to form the United Kibbutz Movement. Later, in 1999, they were joined by the Artzi movement to constitute the Kibbutz Movement, with 251 *kibbutzim*; the religious kibbutz movement, with 16 *kibbutzim*, remains separate.

KIBBUTZ ECONOMY: The kibbutz economy in the first half of the twentieth century was based primarily on agriculture. Not until the 1960s did the tempo of industrialization increase because of economic and demographic conditions that hampered agricultural development. This industrial growth produced debate about the way in which industry should be organized to preserve kibbutz values, leading to a unique organizational structure. By 1981, there were 320 kibbutz industrial plants, only 34% of which had been established before 1960. In the mid-1980s, Israel's economic crisis affected the *kibbutzim*, and many required governmental help to survive. This move, criticized by the Israeli public, had a demoralizing effect on kibbutz members. The *kibbutzim* began recovering economically only in the twenty-first century.

FAMILY AND EDUCATION: The traditional kibbutz community provided all major household services. Meals were cooked and served in the communal dining hall; clothes were cleaned, ironed, and mended in the communal laundry. Women and men were economically independent of each other and almost all women belonged to the work force, although there tended to be a gendered division of labor. Economic rewards were equally distributed, regardless of the nature of one's occupation. Yet these structural changes did not solve "the problem of the woman member" (meaning her inferior status).

Until the 1980s, children in most *kibbutzim* slept in children's houses, situated in the center of the kibbutz, where they led their own autonomous lives, had better living conditions than did the adults, and could be protected from outside attacks. Parents had a minimal role in their children's education, which was mostly overseen by carefully selected kibbutz educators. This revolutionary approach to child rearing, originally designed to liberate women from the major responsibilities of child care and to circumvent what was perceived as the damaging impact of traditional family structures, has now been abandoned in all *kibbutzim*. Children live with their parents, and increasingly family units have assumed many communal services and activities, preferring to prepare their own meals, purchase and launder their own clothing, and pursue independent social and leisure activities.

CULTURAL CONTRIBUTIONS: The *kibbutzim* had a great impact on the formation of Israeli culture. In 1937, the first art museum was opened at Kibbutz Ein-Harod, and forty museums and galleries have been opened in *kibbutzim* since then. In 1939, the kibbutz movement inaugurated two publishing houses (*Sifriat Ha-Poalim* and *Ha-Kibbutz Ha-Meuḥad*). Merged in 1999, the new press publishes Israeli literature, children's books, poetry, encyclopedias, and philosophy. Two teachers colleges were opened, the first in 1940 (Seminar ha-Kibbutzim), and the second in 1950 (Oranim), initially for kibbutz educators and later for any student. The kibbutz movement has its own choir (since 1957), orchestra (since 1970), theater (since 1964), and *dance group (since 1964); all of them perform in Israel and abroad. The kibbutz movement's contribution to Israeli folk dancing was enhanced by the inauguration in 1944 of the yearly folk dance convention at Kibbutz Dalia.

Kibbutz writers (like Amos *Oz), poets (like Nathan Yonatan), composers (like David Zehavi, Michael Wolpe), and painters and sculptors (like Shmulik Katz) are well known (see LITERATURE, POETRY, and ART entries).

CHANGES: Over the years, many changes have been introduced in the kibbutz way of life, stemming mainly from the combination of a weakening collective ideology, changes in the economic situation of *kibbutzim*, and transformations in Israeli society. *Kibbutzim* have adjusted, but at a cost. One area of change, which might be considered a form of integration with the surrounding society, is the use of paid labor in kibbutz production and education. This practice has undermined the important kibbutz value of self-labor. Similar in consequences was the decision to open the children's houses to nonkibbutz children, which weakened one of the most important channels for passing on kibbutz values to the next generation. The kibbutz movement has also legitimated and encouraged members' work outside the kibbutz, partnered with nonkibbutz investors in kibbutz enterprises, rented apartments to nonmembers, and built adjacent neighborhoods for people who did not follow its way of life. The kibbutz also has experienced a transition from direct to representative democracy. The main body representing direct democracy in the kibbutz is the general assembly of all members, which now meets less frequently and has been partially replaced by a council of elected members and board of directors.

Another major area of transformation has been the privatization of aspects of kibbutz life. The process actually started in the 1950s with a slow change from the distribution of consumption services according to need to an equal distribution of money to pay for these services, with little consideration of different individual needs (privatization in kibbutz jargon). A bigger step came at the end of the 1990s, when some *kibbutzim* started to privatize members' earnings; by 2009, about two-thirds of the *kibbutzim* did so. They are the "differential" or "new" *kibbutzim*; the other third remain "collective" *kibbutzim*. A few *kibbutzim* transferred ownership of houses to their members.

In the 1970s, groups of young people who thought the kibbutz should be more integrated into outside society began to found urban *kibbutzim*. Kibbutz Reshit was formed in Jerusalem in 1979, Kibbutz Migvan in Sderot and Kibbutz Tamuz in Bet-Shemesh in 1987, and Kibbutz Beit Israel also in Jerusalem in 1992. In addition, several communal groups have been formed. These communities are small, totaling 1,500–2,000 members, and earn their livelihood mainly from educational community activities.

FUTURE OF THE KIBBUTZ: *Kibbutzim* are slowly moving from a welfare to a market society. Members are more independent economically, and there are new forms of membership for their adult children, such as "a member with economic independence." This status allows full participation in kibbutz life but also economic independence with no rights over kibbutz property. At the beginning of the twenty-first century, mutual aid in the kibbutz is more limited, and trends of privatization of property are evident.

The future of the kibbutz movement will depend on the vision of its members, as well as on local and global economic and political processes that will affect strategic decisions that *kibbutzim* will have to make. Contemporary concerns include the need to find a new meaning and mission, the degree of commitment required of new members, and whether to limit the nonmember population so that members remain the majority. Observers wonder whether *kibbutzim* will be able to attract entrepreneurs who can develop new ventures that accord with the movement's meaning and mission. Will *kibbutzim* preserve the community's small size and maintain and develop a rural ecological environment? Will they be able to unite and formulate a common action program that will have a continuing impact on the larger society, or will they merge into neighboring towns (as some government officials have proposed)? These are only a few of the issues that will determine whether twenty-first-century *kibbutzim* will develop their own unique social economy by updating their communal social and economic way of life or whether they will become ordinary dormitory villages or suburban residential communities.

For further reading, see M. Palgi, "Social Dilemmas and their Solution," in *Wirtschaft, Demokratie und soziale Verantwortung*, ed. G. W. Wolfgang, P. Pasqualoni, and C. Burtscher (2004), 317–32; and H. Near, *The Kibbutz Movement: A History*, 2 vols. (1992, 1997).   MICHAL PALGI

Israel, State of: Landscape Architecture. The key to understanding landscape architecture in Israel is its location as an environmental crossroads. Located at the periphery of three continents, it is simultaneously a meeting place of civilizations. The physical environment is small, but of great diversity. *Garden designs of the Mediterranean, desert oasis gardens, and the Middle Eastern *bustan* all have exerted their influence, as well as garden types and landscape ideals brought by immigrants from more than eighty nations, especially those from *Central and *Eastern Europe. A language of distinct Israeli landscape design is evolving that speaks eloquently in stone, is frugal with water, uses indigenous and naturalized vegetation, is intimate in scale, and creates places that are intensively used. Landscape design has oscillated between an appreciation and preservation of the indigenous landscape and the desire for transformation and a "greening of the desert."

A professional tradition of landscape design began in the 1920s and 1930s with a wave of immigrant designers, largely from *Germany. These pioneers included Shlomo Oren-Weinberg, Itzhak Kutner, Meir Victor, Avraham Karavan, Yechiel Segal, and Haim Latte. Their designs were distinguished by social idealism, and they engaged in ideological debates over design principles, the nature of community, and the creation of a symbolic landscape. Their work set a tone and standard for subsequent design. Landmark projects included Haifa's Gan Benjamin by Yechiel Segal, Gan Ha'atzmaut in Tel Aviv by Avraham Karavan, and Ramat ha-Nadiv by Shlomo Oren-Weinberg. A gardeners' association was formed in the 1930s, followed by the Israel

Association of Landscape Architects in 1951; professional education for landscape architects was inaugurated at the Technion in Haifa in 1975.

The next era was dominated by the partnerships of Lippa Yahalom and Dan Zur, Zvi Miller and Moshe Blum, and Joseph Segal (son of Yechiel) and Zvi Dekal. Their collective work paralleled the establishment of the state and its accompanying mass immigration and construction. Most modern landscape design has been sponsored by the public sector, and there is little private garden tradition. The unique Israeli communal models of the *kibbutz and moshav evolved distinct garden forms, as did new development towns. In addition, landscape architects were instrumental in the design of national parks, college and university campuses, roads, landscape preservation, afforestation, and regional planning.

Yahalom and Zur, the 1998 winners of the Israel Prize, designed projects that became national icons, including the grave of David *Ben-Gurion in the Negev desert at S'de Boker and *Yad Vashem's Valley of the Destroyed Communities. After the Six Day War in 1967, attention turned to *Jerusalem, and the Jerusalem National Park, a greenbelt of open spaces encircling the Old City, was designed. In the 1970s, a younger generation, including Gideon Sarig and Shlomo Aronson, established their landscape architectural practices. Jerusalem's Haas-Sherover promenade is Aronson's signature work.

In sixty years, Israel transformed itself from a developing to a prosperous nation. Landscape designers now confront problems of density, affluence, and the preservation of a rapidly disappearing traditional agricultural and rural landscape. For further reading, see K. Helphand, *Dreaming Gardens: Landscape Architecture and the Making of Modern Israel* (2002).   KENNETH HELPHAND

Israel, State of: Military and Paramilitary Bodies. The modern *Zionist nationalist experience that emerged in Europe in the late nineteenth century resulted in various phenomena that had hitherto been foreign to contemporary Jewish culture. A prominent example was the use of force to achieve goals of the collective, in this case the new Jewish national community.

Zionism sought an organized military entity. At the same time, as a result of the many centuries during which Jews abstained from such activities, movement leaders had doubts about military and paramilitary projects and feared those engaged in them. During the first six decades of Zionism (1880s—1940s), the intensifying Jewish–Arab struggle in *Palestine, the *Holocaust, and the 1947–49 war over Palestine brought about a complete transformation in attitudes toward the use of force. This process continued into Israeli statehood as well. After a series of wars that Israel regarded as successful (the War of Independence, the Sinai campaign, and the Six Day War), the Israeli Defense Forces (IDF) emerged as one of the country's leading social and cultural forces (see ISRAEL, STATE OF: WARS (1948); (1956–1967).

EARLY HISTORY: During the late nineteenth and early twentieth centuries, Jewish "self-defense" organizations emerged in *Russia, foreshadowing the formation of such groups in Palestine during the last years of *Ottoman rule. In September 1907, young Eastern European immigrants who had recently arrived in Palestine established a clandestine group that aimed to replace the Palestinian Arabs working as guards in Jewish settlements with Jews and to contribute to Jewish security in the country as a whole. Group members gave themselves the name *Bar Giora*, after one of the most extreme *Zealots active during the end of the *Second Temple period. The group, which was limited to some twenty members, was led by Israel Shochat and Alexander Zaid. Its commitment to the security of the Jewish collective was unprecedented in Palestine at that time, as were the criteria for new members, which included physical fitness, height, horsemanship, gunmanship, and agricultural capabilities.

Also in 1907, members of *Bar Giora* joined a group of women who had begun an agricultural collective farm at Sejera in the Lower Galilee, led by Mania Wilbushewitcz. The meeting between Shochat and Wilbushewitcz resulted in marriage, as well as the establishment of *Ha-Shomer* in April 1909. As a clandestine paramilitary organization, *Ha-Shomer* was a community of families engaged in guarding and livestock herding. Its members were also connected to the political platform of the radical Zionist socialist party *Poalei Tziyon* (Workers of Zion). This connection and the organization's political subordination to the party were hallmarks of paramilitary organizations in Palestine's Jewish *Yishuv. In fact, *Ha-Shomer* intensified what had been *Bar Giora*'s linkage of agriculture and Jewish settlement; this connection became a major practical and symbolic motif of the paramilitary security organizations of the organized Jewish community in Palestine until 1948 and, to some degree, after 1948 as well.

Even so, Israel Shochat had difficulty relinquishing his personal control of the organization, which, in conjunction with the dramatic changes in Palestine after World War I, made *Ha-Shomer* irrelevant. The organization's golden age between 1909 and 1914 came to an end with the general paralysis that gripped Palestine during the war and Shochat's expulsion from the country by the Turks, ostensibly because he was a Russian citizen. Moreover, the Jewish leadership feared the influence of Shochat and his associates, who did not conceal their arrogance as the *Yishuv*'s exclusive bearers of arms before WWI and the British conquest of Palestine.

*BRITISH MANDATE PERIOD: The legalization of the *Yishuv* reflected in the *Balfour Declaration (November 1917) and the establishment of the Zionist Commission (April 1918) as the *Yishuv*'s representative to the British authorities in Palestine resulted in a major change in the self-perception of Palestine's Jewish community. The focal points of Zionism's alliance with Great Britain and the concrete political goal of a Jewish state were institutionalized in the Mandate over Palestine, which *Britain received from the League of Nations in 1922. A clear sign of Zionist–British cooperation was the enlistment of Jews in general, and Zionists in particular, in the British army. For the first time ever, Jewish soldiers serving in a modern formal military framework bore Jewish symbols and a Jewish flag. This initiative was devised by a rising Zionist leader, Ze'ev (Vladimir) Jabotinsky. After the establishment of the Zion Mule Corps Battalion in the spring of 1915, in which Yosef Trumpeldor served as a deputy battalion commander, the British established an additional three battalions: the 38th (Jewish immigrants from Russia), the 39th (Jewish immigrants from North America), the 40th (volunteers from Palestine), and the 42nd (reserves). The soldiers of these battalions, which collectively were known as the "Jewish" or the "Hebrew"

Legion, took part in the fighting during WWI in Palestine and its surroundings.

The British dismantled the battalions after the war, leaving only the 40th battalion. In 1920, the battalion was referred to as the "First Battalion of Judea" and was commanded by Lieutenant Colonel Eliezer Margolin. In May 1921, after a new wave of Jewish-Arab violence, the British dismantled the battalion out of concern that it might lose control over it. For many future leaders of the *Yishuv*, the *Jewish Legion provided a military training framework that enabled them to consolidate political strength and return to Palestine, from which some had been expelled during the war. This was true of David *Ben-Gurion, Itzhak Ben Zvi, Eliyahu Golomb, Dov Hoz, and many others.

Against this background, the newly formed workers' party *Aḥdut ha-Avodah* (Labor Unity), which resulted from the merger of *Poalei Tziyon* and a group of nonpartisan workers, established a new paramilitary body, the *Haganah*. The party's 1920 congress at Kinneret decided to take a different approach from the two earlier groups, *Bar Giora* and *Ha-Shomer*. The *Haganah* would not be a closed, elitist group but rather a national militia open to all Jews in Palestine, under the authority of the Zionist movement and the Jewish *Yishuv*. As early as December 1920, with the establishment of the General Federation of Jewish Workers in Palestine, *Aḥdut ha-Avodah* placed the *Haganah* under General Federation's authority. In August 1929, this authority was transferred to the newly established Jewish Agency for Palestine. All of these supervisory organizations were legal, and the *Haganah* was directed through a conscious political process by a national command that, from the 1930s onward, represented the political left and right wings of the Jewish *Yishuv*. Beginning in 1937, the national command was headed by a member of Mapai (*Mifleget Poalei Eretz Israel* [Palestine Workers Party], a merger of *Aḥdut ha-Avodah* and *Ha-Poel ha-Tzair*), which controlled the politics of the Zionist movement, the Jewish Agency, the organized Jewish *Yishuv*, and the State of Israel until the late 1970s. This structure ensured that the *Haganah* had no independent policy; rather, its policy was dictated by the civilian political institutions controlling it.

From the time the *Haganah* was established, some thought the organization should be run in cooperation with the Mandate authorities. Commanders in the field rejected this approach, warning that the *Yishuv* could not risk losing control of the organization if situations arose where British and Zionist interests were at odds. In the 1920s, the *Haganah* was a federation of local cells, each engaged in local security; however, when violence erupted in the summer of 1929, the *Haganah* failed to address it effectively. This failure, along with the widening schism between Jews and Arabs and the feeling that the establishment of a Jewish state was just around the corner (with the Peel Commission's partition plan of 1937), led *Yishuv* leaders to transfer the responsibility for regular security to the British. They then began to transform the *Haganah* into an organization capable of providing solutions to a wide variety of situations – ranging from opposing outbreaks of Arab violence to fighting against British operations that were not in Zionist interests. At the same time, the *Haganah* began preparing to become the conventional army of the soon-to-be established Jewish state.

The *Yishuv* took a disastrous detour from this course with its rebellion against the British *White Paper policy, from October 1945 through August 1946. During this period the *Haganah* engaged in guerilla actions and terrorist attacks, which were entrusted to the *Palmakh* (*Plugot Makhatz* [shock forces]), the organization's standing army since May 1941. These activities came at the expense of investment of resources and training in other *Haganah* forces, which were organized as field forces and other groupings. This emphasis caused some of the organizational and equipment difficulties faced by the *Haganah* at the outbreak of Israel's War of Independence in late 1947.

The error of the rebellion was counterbalanced by the well-organized enlistment of some 30,000 men and women of the *Yishuv* in the British army between 1939 and 1946. As a result of this mobilization, driven by the Jewish Agency in general and the director of its Political Department, Moshe Shertok (Sharett), in particular, recruits served in all branches of the imperial army. The high point of this process was reached in September 1944 with the establishment of the Jewish Fighting Brigade, all of whose soldiers and most of whose commanders were Jews, and which carried a Hebrew flag and symbols. Mass enlistment had three goals: to assist Britain in defending itself and defending Palestine, to provide direct and indirect assistance to European Jewry, and to ensure future political and military profit when the recruits returned to Palestine. Indeed, these veterans of the British army subsequently made a decisive contribution to the *Haganah* and the Israeli Defense Forces (IDF).

1948 AND AFTER: By the winter of 1947–48, the *Haganah* had an impressive military-organizational foundation. Even before the end of the Mandate and the establishment of the State of Israel, the organization had transformed itself from a semi-legal militia into a modern army. By April 1948, the *Haganah* was operating a framework of brigades that succeeded in defeating the Palestinians before Israel was even established (May 15, 1948). In accordance with the "National Structure Order" of November 1947, the *Haganah* built an army that was based on the field forces, which were organized in regional units; the *Palmakh*; and new recruits. By May 1948, this army had twelve brigades, a nucleus of assisting forces (air, naval, and artillery), second-line guard brigades, and service forces. The army was centrally controlled by the General Staff (which was established in 1939) headed by Yaakov Dostrovski (Dori), which itself worked directly with the Jewish Agency Executive and the People's Administration (established in April 1948), which soon became the Provisional Government of Israel. As a result the national command was neutralized and finally dismantled in May 1948.

The IDF was officially established on May 30, 1948, two weeks after the establishment of the state. In late 1948, the IDF consisted of close to one-sixth of all Jews in the country.

Ben-Gurion regarded the army's subordination to the elected government as a necessity. In his opinion, the primary danger came from the political left wing; he and his government were greatly troubled by the security activism of *Mapam* (*Mifleget ha-Poalim ha-Meukhedet* [United Workers Party]), which included the United Kibbutz Movement and *Ha-Shomer ha-Tzair*, and the party's decisive political influence on the *Palmakh*. However, it was the attempt of the

Etzel (*Irgun Tzvai Leumi* [National Military Organization]) to bring a shipment of weapons into Jerusalem in June 1948 that gave Ben-Gurion the opportunity he was waiting for to assert the government's authority over the military. The IDF's sinking of the *Altalena*, an *Etzel* weapons' ship, off the coast of Tel Aviv on June 22, 1948, ended attempts to carry out independent military or semi-military action within the borders of Israel.

From its inception, the IDF was also seen as a cultural tool central to the integration of immigrant soldiers into Israeli society. The army experience was conceived of as a "melting pot" that ensured acceptance into Israeli society and provided the necessary common denominator for all Jewish citizens. The IDF even engaged in typically civilian endeavors such as education, immigrant absorption, settlement, and agriculture. If Israel had not also possessed counterbalancing social forces, the army could have easily become a threat to Israeli democracy. One example that demonstrates this potential was the government's failed attempt to use the army to break the seamen's strike of 1951. Another was the General Staff's uncompromising position toward Levi Eshkol's government, which, in May–June 1967, was hesitant about accepting the generals' calls to go to war.

Israel's frequent wars have ensured that defense has remained the dominant line item in the government budget. This reality, in conjunction with other factors outlined earlier, has made the Chief of General Staff a major figure with significant political power. This has been especially true when the position has been filled by officers of exceptional charisma who are associated with particular political ideologies. The most prominent Chiefs of General Staff have been Moshe Dayan (1953–58) and Yitzhak *Rabin (1964–68). Israel's military success in the Sinai War (October–November 1956), the war for water sources in northern Israel (1964–67), and the Six Day War (June 1967) improved the prestige of the army in general and of its senior commanders in particular, often paving their way from the high command to the country's political leadership.

The Yom Kippur War in October 1973 decreased the prestige of the IDF, but did not affect its central place in Israeli society. The reemergence of the conflict within historic Palestine/ *Eretz Israel* (the First Lebanon War, in which the IDF invaded Lebanon in June 1982 to fight the Palestine Liberation Organization, and the two Intifadas of 1987 and 2000) intensified the army's policing duties. This resulted in an increase in criticism within Israel regarding the manner in which the army dealt with the civil uprising in the occupied territories. Still, the Second Lebanon War of July–August 2006 demonstrated that, despite such criticism, there is still a great willingness to serve in the IDF. It is clear that Israeli citizens across the political spectrum continue to regard it as the cornerstone of Israel's national existence.

THREAT OF SECESSIONISM: From the outset, the Jewish *Yishuv* regarded secessionism in general and independent military action in particular as an existential threat. That is why *Ha-Shomer* disappeared, and why separatism henceforth existed only on society's margins. Thus, *Ha-Shomer* veterans' "Secret Kibbutz" was suppressed in the 1920s, and *Haganah-B* (1931–37), led by Avraham Tehomi, was eventually reabsorbed into the *Haganah*. The same was true of the two separatist organizations *Etzel* and *Leḥi* (*Loḥamei Ḥerut Israel* [Fighters for the Freedom of Israel]).

The emergence of these last two groups stemmed from the secession of the large revisionist party from the Zionist movement in 1935. Young party members of the *Betar* movement (*Brit Yosef Trumpeldor* [Yosef Trumpeldor Convenant]) found their place in *Haganah-B*, and when this body was dismantled in 1937 they established *Etzel*. In 1940, Avraham Stern (Yair) and his supporters left this group to establish *Etzel b'Israel*, which later came to be known as *Leḥi*. Unlike the *Haganah*, which was militia-like in nature and semi-legal, *Etzel* and *Leḥi* operated as underground groups. They were characterized by deep secrecy, a small number of members who engaged in acts of terrorism against a strong central government (British), and a commander who also functioned as an independent military leader. Prominent commanders of *Etzel* included David Raziel (1937–41); Avraham Stern, who established and commanded *Leḥi* (1940–42); and Menaḥem *Begin (1943–48).

Beyond their independent military actions, which *Yishuv* leaders viewed as dangerous, their primary struggle was aimed at the British, whom the *Yishuv* had not defined as enemies. During two high points of Zionist–British cooperation, the Arab Revolt (1936–39) and World War II, the secessionist groups operated against the British. *Etzel* ceased operations against the British at the outbreak of the war but resumed them in 1944, when Begin concluded that the group had no purpose without an independent policy. They took this approach even as the Jewish–Arab war intensified in the winter of 1947–48; subsequently they refused to accept state authority in Jerusalem, which had not yet been incorporated into Israel. From its perspective, the organized *Yishuv* had good reason to use force against these groups during and after WWII. The State of Israel continued this policy, and those who did not agree to be disarmed willingly (like Begin and his followers) were later disarmed by force.

The Israeli government implemented the same policy against a number of other attempts at paramilitary secessionism during the 1950s (the *"Tzrifin* Underground" and the *Leḥi* veterans who assassinated Israel Kastner in 1957). Prime Minister Yitzhak Shamir, who had helped lead *Leḥi* (with Nathan Yelin-Mor and Israel Eldad) after Stern's death, decisively suppressed the Israeli settlers' Jewish underground in the occupied territories in 1984. In the summer of 2005, during Israel's unilateral disengagement from the Gaza Strip, it was also made clear that independent military action outside the framework of the IDF would not be tolerated. Contemporary observers wonder if Israeli society will continue to pass this test in the future. For further reading, see N. Bethell, *The Palestine Triangle* (1979); J. Haller, *The Birth of Israel, 1945–1949* (2003); E. Luttwak, *The Israeli Army* (1974); B. Morris, *Righteous Victims, A History of the Zionist–Arab Conflict, 1881–1999* (1999); and P. A. Pentland, *Zionist Military Preparations for Statehood Strategies, 1920–1948* (1976).

MOTTI GOLANI

Israel, State of: Military Roles of Women.

Israel is one of the few countries with a mandatory military draft for women. The 1949 Defense Service Law mandated the conscription of women to maximize available human resources for protecting the recently founded State of Israel and to take advantage of the army's role as a melting pot in which diverse individuals would be integrated into a united society.

The presence of women also strengthened the image of the Israeli Defense Forces (IDF) as an army of the people.

Women had served in Jewish defensive forces in the *Yishuv. They were members of *Ha-Shomer* (1909); participated in the *Haganah* (1920); were conscripted into the British army during World War II; and volunteered in the *Palmakh* (1941), where they trained in battle and fought in the *War of Independence (1948). Such activities fed a myth of gender equality in pre-Israel society. In fact, most women took on gender-related roles, and during the War of Independence, all women, including female fighters, were given jobs on the home front. Nevertheless, women's defense activities and the mandatory integration of women in the IDF contributed to the image of Israel as an egalitarian society.

The IDF, like all armies, is essentially a masculine institution, and its hierarchy and organizational structure create marked gender differences. In Israel, as elsewhere, the army is a central force in building a male-dominant society and in reproducing such hierarchy in civilian society. It is unclear, therefore, whether women's army service constitutes the implementation of gender equality or whether it actually intensifies gender inequality. For one thing, there are significant differences between male and female military obligations: Women serve two years, whereas men must serve for three years; most women are free from reserve duty; and it is relatively easy for women to receive exemption from service for religious reasons.

The IDF, established in May 1948, was modeled after the British military. Thus, the IDF Women's Corps was modeled after the Auxiliary Territorial Service (ATS), the women's branch of the British army. Since there is no Men's Corps in the IDF (the different corps are determined according to soldiers' training and responsibilities), the Women's Corps defined female soldiers by gender rather than military role. Furthermore, army policies from the 1950s until the 1980s prohibited female soldiers from combat roles and assigned them primarily to support positions or jobs perceived as feminine, such as clerical work, instruction, and social work. Women's lesser roles restricted their ability to advance to senior army ranks, reduced their presence among the people who make decisions and determine priorities, and relegated them to second-class membership in a male organization under male governance.

After the *Yom Kippur War (1973), because of a serious shortage in human resources, new professions became open to women, thereby freeing men for combat roles. Beginning in the mid-1970s, female soldiers demanded additional opportunities. Social changes in Israel during the 1980s affected the IDF as well, and the army allowed women access to various technical and instructional positions relating to combat professions (such as serving as instructors in the Military Infantry Corps).

In November 1995, Israel's Supreme Court made a precedent-setting and highly publicized ruling regarding the petition submitted by Alice Miller. In that decision, the High Court ruled that the IDF must allow women to volunteer for the Israeli Air Force Flight School. This paved the way for conscription of women for combat roles in the border police, the Cannon Corps, and the antiaircraft division and opened the prestigious naval course to women, among other changes. In 2001 the Women's Corps was dissolved and the Women's Affairs Advisory established. In January 2000 the Knesset amended the Defense Service Law, opening all army positions to women, including combat positions. From a practical perspective, however, this amendment has had complex repercussions. Only a small percentage of women in the IDF serve in positions that were once only open to men. These female soldiers sometimes adopt masculine behavior, and men sometimes tend to see these jobs as women's work.

Masculinity therefore remains an identifying mark of the IDF. Women are a minority in the army (they comprise one-third of soldiers in basic training and between one-fifth and one-third of junior officers); they can be excused from army duty for reasons including marriage, motherhood, conscience, and religion. The opposition of Israel's religious parties to religious women serving in the IDF is surprising because religious groups in the Yishuv encouraged female participation in defense activities and religious female fighters were integral in the War of Independence.

Women's military roles in Israel in the first decade of the twenty-first century reflect a two-sided phenomenon. On the one hand, there are female soldiers in the IDF who fulfill combat roles; on the other hand, the number of women who are excused from army service for religious reasons is growing. Is the IDF therefore an egalitarian army of the people? From the perspective of women and gender, the answer is complex. Not all Israeli Jewish women serve in the IDF, and most who do are in positions that support men.

The IDF is a central element in Israeli society, and it is a place where many men make valuable connections that enhance their roles in civilian life. Thus, women's mostly subordinate positions in the army have a negative impact on their post-military opportunities. As gender-related changes in Israeli society and public discourse penetrate the IDF, there may be a greater effort to implement egalitarian values in the military; such transformations would ultimately have an impact on Israeli civilian society as well.

For further reading, see D. Izraeli, "Gendering Military Service in the Israel Defense Forces," *Israel Social Science Research*, 12(1) (1997): 129–66; S. Cohen, *Israel and Its Army: From Cohesion to Confusion* (2008); O. Sasson-Levy, *Identities in Uniform: Masculinities and Femininities in the Israeli Military* (2006); L. Rosenberg-Friedman, "The Religious Women Fighters in Israel's War of Independence," *Nashim* 6 (2003): 119–47.   LILACH ROSENBERG-FRIEDMAN

Israel, State of: Peace Movement. The Israeli peace movement, a small, decentralized alliance of individuals and groups who represent diverse worldviews, goals, and approaches, is committed to a peaceful resolution of the conflict with the Arab nations and especially the *Palestinians. The movement originated among Jews and Palestinians in the late nineteenth and early twentieth centuries; participants included businessman Yosef Eliyahu Chelouche, who wrote in the Jewish and Arab press about mutual respect, truth and compassion, and a shared destiny. Farmers, workers, and intellectuals took up the call, notably thinker *Aḥad Ha-Am and educator Yitzhak Epstein, who warned Jews against mistreating their Palestinian neighbors. Meetings followed, as well as small joint organizations to encourage mutual understanding.

During the *British Mandate, Jews and Arabs played together in sports clubs; worked together on railroads, at post offices and bakeries, and as civil servants; in Jaffa's citrus orchards, they went on strike together against their common bosses. Several groups, such as the Palestinian Communist party, with Arab and Jewish members, and *Ha-Shomer ha-Tzair* (The Young Guard), encouraged class solidarity. The latter opposed the creation of an exclusively Jewish state and formed, in the midst of riots and rebellion in 1939, the Jewish-Arab Rapprochement and Co-operation Group, which shared a *Marxist internationalist perspective.

Berit Shalom (Covenant of Peace), founded in 1925, never included more than several dozen activists, but because it was composed of leading intellectuals and high-level government administrators, including Martin *Buber, Judah *Magnes, Arthur Rupin, Gershom *Scholem, and Henrietta *Szold, it exerted influence in the *Yishuv. The group, based on universal and Jewish *ethics with a strong pacifist influence, proposed a binational state in which Jews and Arabs would have identical political representation, despite accusations that it was unrealistic and defeatist. *Kedma Mizraḥa* (Forward to the East), led by educator David Yellin, emphasized the necessity of Israel's integration into the region, and *Ihud* (Unity) urged the creation of a Jewish spiritual center in the land. Both warned of the dangers of nationalism. *Ihud*'s publication, *Ner* (Candle), was a clear voice for reconciliation for more than two decades. All three organizations formed ties with Palestinian individuals and groups.

Another early peace advocate was Uri Avneri, a young soldier. Before the United Nations' partition plan, he called, with Jewish and Palestinian comrades, for the two national movements to form a progressive "Semitic federation" to join in the global anticolonial struggle. As editor of the muckraking *Ha-Olam ha-Zeh* weekly and as a Knesset member, Avneri has remained, for more than sixty years, a tireless worker for peace.

Even in the midst of the 1948 War of Independence, activists decried the treatment of the Palestinians. Afterward, peace groups focused on the injustices imposed on Arab citizens by the military rule in their townships (which lasted until 1966), called for the return of Palestinian refugees to their homes, and opposed military solutions, including the 1956 Sinai campaign. In the new state's patriotic atmosphere, several pacifists refused military service and were imprisoned. In the early 1950s, *Va'ad ha-Shalom ha-Yisraeli* (Israeli Peace Committee) advocated neutrality and collected a half-million signatures (one-third of the country's population) against nuclear armaments, but its ties with the USSR limited its impact and within three years it had disbanded. An important new project was founded in 1949 at Kibbutz Givat Haviva, which included educational programs for children and adults, research and curriculum development, and dialogue groups. In 1963 it became the Jewish-Arab Center for Peace and is still active today. The journal *New Outlook*, founded in 1957 by Simha Flapan, reached the Arab world with its English-language message of cooperation with the Palestinian people. During the late 1950s and early 1960s, activists and intellectuals, including Buber, World Jewish Congress President Nahum Goldmann, and, briefly, high-ranking officials, met with their Arab counterparts in Europe. In 1966, Abie Nathan, a former bombardier, flew a small, white-painted Piper plane, "Peace 1," to Egypt.

His request to meet with President Nasser was denied, but his courage captured the public's imagination. Just before the Yom Kippur War, Nathan's pirate radio station, "Voice of Peace," broadcast popular music and calls for peace from "somewhere in the Mediterranean." Nathan persisted for 20 years and brought toys and medical supplies to the children of Gaza and other war zones.

The Six Day War of 1967 (see ISRAEL: WARS) ushered in a national euphoria, but within days voices were raised against the immorality of the occupation. These came from the New Left group *Matzpen* (Compass), writer S. Yizhar, playwright Hanoch Levin, and philosopher and scientist Yeshayahu Leibowitz. Leibowitz's sharp tongue and warnings of the dangers of a continued occupation earned him many adherents. During the late 1960s, several peace groups arose from the global student revolt movement, including a group of high school students who refused to serve in the army. At a time when Israeli leaders denied the existence of a Palestinian nation, members of *Matzpen*, *Siah* (Dialogue) and the Israeli Black Panthers met with Palestinian radicals. The Panthers connected the treatment of the Palestinians with the lot of Mizrahi Jews, proposing that peace and equality for both groups must go together.

Soon, even members of the Zionist establishment advocated recognizing the Palestinians' right to self-determination. Prominent among them was Lova Eliav, former Secretary General of the Labor Party, who spoke of both Israelis' moral obligation and self-interest in bringing peace in his book, *Land of the Hart* (1970). Yaakov Arnon, former director of the Finance Ministry; retired generals Mati Peled and Meir Pa'il; and the historians Yaakov Talmon and Yehoshua Arieli joined Eliav and hundreds of activists in new groups such as the *Tenua Leshalom Vebitahon* (Movement for Peace and Security) to oppose the annexation of territories and to demand direct negotiation with any willing Arab leader or group.

The heavy casualties of the 1973 Yom Kippur War underlined the value of peace, and grassroots groups such as the Israeli Council for Israeli–Palestinian Peace emerged. The council's founders included respected military and political leaders, giving legitimacy to its call to recognize the PLO. They held secret meetings (described in Uri Avneri's memoir, *My Friend, the Enemy* [1986]) abroad with Palestinian officials, several of whom were assassinated. In 1986, the Knesset barred contact with "terrorists," leading to the imprisonment of several Israelis, including the peace pilot Nathan. Still, the meetings signaled that each side could be a partner for peace, and they established trust and respect that proved important in the coming years.

The peace movement gained force and numbers after the 1977 Likud election victory and Sadat's visit to Israel the same year. A letter signed by 348 combat soldiers and officers demanded that the government seize the opportunity for peace. Tens of thousands joined them, and *Shalom Achshav* (Peace Now) was born. Concentrating initially on peace with Egypt, the group gradually shifted focus, opposing the spread of settlements and encouraging negotiations with Palestinian leaders. *Shalom Achshav* grew rapidly because of its humanist Zionist ideology and adherence to the mainstream. Although it was slower to act (it took the group ten days to respond to the 1982 Sabra and Shatila massacres) than smaller, more radical groups, it was

instrumental in the mass demonstrations (the largest of which drew 400,000 in Tel Aviv) against the Israeli army's complicity. These demonstrations led to the forming of the Kahan committee and the censure of Defense Minister *Sharon. During a 1983 march in Jerusalem, member Emil Grunzweig was murdered by a right-wing activist. In the years of the First Intifada (1987–89,) *Shalom Achshav* staged protests involving more than 100,000 people and promoted educational activities.

Among the more active groups established at the time, *Yesh Gevul* (There Is a Limit) comprised hundreds of soldiers who were jailed for their refusal to serve in Lebanon and, later, in the territories. Their actions broadened the public debate about individual obedience and responsibility and influenced the government's withdrawal from Lebanon in 1987 and 2000. Protests were accompanied by Israeli–Palestinian cooperative efforts, including the establishment of the Jewish–Arab village *Neve Shalom/Wahat Al-Salam* (Oasis of Peace) and its School of Peace, co-publishing by *New Outlook* and the East Jerusalem paper *Al Fajr*, conferences on the sources of the conflict and possible solutions, the co-founding of the Alternative Information Center by Israeli and Palestinian activists, and the "Hands around Jerusalem" action by 30,000 Israelis and Palestinians.

During the 1980s groups from specific constituencies emerged, such as women agitating to bring the troops home from Lebanon (*Arba Imahot* [Four Mothers]). Although many women had important roles in Peace Now and other organizations, they had rarely been involved in the decision-making process of those groups. Activists such as Gila Svirsky and Yehudit Kirstein Keshet and *Nashim Beshahor* (Women in Black) challenged this exclusion. From the outbreak of the First Intifada, members of *Nashim Beshahor*, Jewish and Palestinian citizens of Israel, held weekly vigils dressed in black in dozens of locations. They demanded an end to the occupation and showed the importance of Jewish and Palestinian women working together. Although the group has gone through transformations, it has withstood continued harassment and is still active.

In the 1990s, other women's groups such as *Bat Shalom* (Daughter of Peace) and *Reshet* (Net) emerged and, in the following decade, the Coalition of Women for Peace and *Mahsom Watch* (Checkpoint Watch). Integrating feminist and pacifist concerns and practices, empowering women, challenging the "security" ideology, and demanding participation in peace negotiations, women's groups tended to be less hierarchical than the mixed groups and more flexible in their approach. *Bat Shalom*'s close work with a Palestinian women's peace group resulted in the Jerusalem Link. Established in 1994, the Jerusalem Link comprises two women's organizations: *Bat Shalom* on the Israeli side and the Jerusalem Center for Women on the Palestinian side, The two organizations share a set of political principles, which serve as the foundation for a cooperative model of coexistence. In the 1980s and '90s, Mizrahi activists, also feeling marginalized, formed their own groups: *Hamizrah leshalom* (East toward Peace) and *Hakeshet Ha-Democratit Ha-Mizrahit* (Mizrahi Democratic Rainbow) criticized Israeli society and pledged to form a bridge of peace.

The 1993 Oslo peace agreements and *Rabin's and Arafat's handshake ignited disagreements among activists about governmental actions and the peace accords. Paradoxically, at the time of its greatest success, the peace camp faltered and lost credibility. After Rabin's assassination at a 1995 peace rally and the escalating violence, new groups sought a broader approach and outreach. Victor Cygielman and Ziad Abu Zayyad formed *The Palestine-Israel Journal*, and the women's group *Profil Ḥadash* (New Profile) opposed the occupation and military ethos by supporting the "refuseniks," mounting art shows that questioned media and cultural images, and lobbying to stop military training in schools.

With the outbreak of the Second Intifada in 2000 and the collapse of the peace talks, many in the movement despaired, but large numbers of high school students as well as active and reserve soldiers joined *Yesh Gevul* and the newly formed *Haometz Lesarev* (Courage to Refuse) to oppose military service. Backed by members of an elite commando unit and pilots, the movement had popular support. Many of the soldiers were women, often arguing against serving in a patriarchal institution; others were Druze. Gradually, new groups focused on direct aid to Palestinians. Money, food, medical and legal assistance, and work harvesting olives and rebuilding demolished homes came from groups such as *Ta'ayush* (Life in Common) and *Yesh Din* (There is Justice), which petitioned the Israeli courts. Help standing up to bulldozers and bullets came from groups such as *Havad ha-Tziburi Neged Harisat Batim* (Israeli Committee against House Demolitions) and the mostly young *Anarchistim Neged Hacohma* (Anarchists against the Wall), whose protests with the villagers of Bil'in and Ni'ilin lasted several years. The Coalition of Women for a Just Peace, composed of Jewish and Arab women, waged civil disobedience against closures and checkpoints. Other activists broke through a Bethlehem checkpoint, performed street theater, and organized the children's journal *Ḥalonot* (Windows,) the Hand in Hand bicultural schools, the radio station "All for Peace," the Sulha dialogue groups, and the Bereaved Parents Circle, which brought together family members on both sides who had lost loved ones in the violence.

The Geneva Accords and *Hamifkad ha-Leumi* (People's Voice), efforts to revive the peace process by Israeli and Palestinian politicians and activists – including former Deputy Foreign Minister Yossi Beilin, former head of the Shin Bet Ami Ayalon, and Palestinian academic Sari Nusseibeh – proposed two states within the June 4, 1967 borders, with Jerusalem as a common capital. More than a quarter-million Israelis and 150,000 Palestinians signed on.

It is difficult to measure the direct impact of the peace movement, but its mass demonstrations and continuing dialogue and cooperation with the "enemy" have laid the foundation for the peace process and helped change perceptions on both sides. At the end of the first decade of the twenty-first century a majority of the Israeli public believes that a political settlement is necessary, and many support a two-state solution. This belief, however, has not been translated into political action. In its persistent work for a peaceful and just resolution, the movement has remained a counterbalance to violence and extremism and a beacon of hope.

For further reading, see M. Bar-On, *In Pursuit of Peace: A History of the Israeli Peace Movement* (1996); G. Feuerverger, *Oasis of Dreams* (2001); D. Gavron, *Holy Land Mosaic* (2008); T. Hermann, "The Israeli Peace Movement 1967–1998," in *Mobilizing for Peace*, ed. B. Kidron (2002); E. Kaufman et al., eds., *Bridging the Divide* (2006); D. Schulman, *Dark Hope: Working for Peace in Israel and Palestine* (2007); and G. Svirsky, "The Israeli Peace Movement since the Al-Aqsa Intifada," in *The New Intifada*, ed. R. Carey (2001). Recent film documentaries include *Citizen Nawi* (dir. N. Mossek, 2007); *Encounter Point* (dir. R. Avni and J. Bacha, 2006); and *My Terrorist* (dir. Y. Cohen, 2002).   ALON RAAB

Israel, State of: Political Institutions. Following the terms of the 1947 United Nations partition resolution, the Jewish community in Palestine (*Yishuv*) established the State of Israel on May 14, 1948. Simultaneous with the Declaration of Independence, a Provisional Government was established. It was to remain in office "pending the setting up of duly elected bodies of the State in accordance with a Constitution to be drawn up by a Constituent Assembly."

Nonetheless a written constitution did not emerge. The Constituent Assembly was elected immediately after implementation of the various cease-fire agreements that ended the *War of Independence. Because of internal divisions among the delegates, especially on the role that Jewish religious law (*halakhah*) would play in the new state, the Constituent Assembly never undertook the task for which it was called into existence. Yet, because its members derived their authority directly from the people, the Constituent Assembly was more representative than the Provisional Government, whose members were largely self-selected. The Provisional Government therefore dissolved itself and transferred its powers to the newly elected Constituent Assembly. That body in turn enacted the Transition Law under which it became the first *Knesset (parliament).

ISRAELI POLITICAL INSTITUTIONS: To this day, Israel functions without a formal, integrated written constitution. Its governing arrangements are an outgrowth of the political arrangements that have emerged since independence. At the formal level, the operative governmental structure of Israel can be described easily: Israel is a secular democracy, with a theoretically supreme parliament (the Knesset), a powerful cabinet (the government), a strong independent *judiciary, and a weak, largely ceremonial, president. The operational reality, however, is much more complex.

ISRAELI ELECTORAL SYSTEM: Israel is a parliamentary democracy whose single chamber assembly is elected every four years unless a Knesset majority calls for earlier elections. The 120 members of the Knesset are selected via a nationwide, proportional system. An Israeli votes for a list of candidates, not an individual representative. The voter cannot alter the list prepared by a political party (or the joint list of a group of parties) in any way: The list must be accepted or rejected as a whole. The entire country is treated as a single electoral district, and Knesset seats are allocated in proportion to the strength of the lists at the polls. Any list that receives 2% of the vote is guaranteed some representation in the Knesset. This 2% requirement is the lowest threshold of any democracy using a proportional election system. Moreover, it is easier to form a political party and submit an electoral list in Israel than in any other democratic nation. Only the signatures of 100 citizens and $10,000 are needed to register a new party. The signatures of 1,500 supporters are needed for a new party to submit a list of candidates to compete in a Knesset election.

The combination of electoral rules that facilitate the creation of new parties and electoral lists with the rule guaranteeing at least one seat in the Knesset to any list that receives 2% of the national vote means that Israeli citizens have an extremely wide choice at the polls. In the 2003 elections, for example, there were twenty-seven electoral lists on the ballot, and fifteen parties gained representation in the Knesset.

Citizen participation in Israeli elections is among the highest in the world. About 80% of the eligible voters typically cast ballots. This high turnout is probably due to the fact that the "security issue" has always been an important, salient factor to all Israelis. What the government does has a direct, immediate impact on their lives. Most Israelis are constantly discussing politics in their homes, their workplaces, their schools, and their cafes. Therefore, Israeli elections function in an environment in which an almost bewildering range of policy alternatives are part of a robust, wide-open debate.

THE KNESSET AND THE GOVERNMENT: In a parliamentary democracy like Israel, the people elect their representatives, and the parliament selects the cabinet, which functions as the executive agency. For a cabinet to be installed, the support of at least sixty-one members of the Knesset (a majority of the parliament) is required. Once selected by a Knesset majority, the government remains in office until the next election unless it loses its Knesset support.

Because the Israeli electoral system facilitates a multiparty system, no single party (or party list) has ever achieved a Knesset majority. Therefore, all Israeli governments have been coalitions comprising several parties. Most usually, the government coalition is cobbled together by the leader of the largest single Knesset party (the prime minister-designate) from among the eight to fifteen parties represented in that chamber. To form this coalition, the prime minister-designate must agree to support some of the programs favored by the smaller parties and to assign the administration of certain government ministries to the leaders of those parties. Forming a government involves intense bargaining, much compromise, and considerable skill.

Real, effective power resides in the government, not in the theoretically sovereign Knesset. As is all parliamentary democracies, as long as the government retains its Knesset majority, the cabinet makes all significant policies. The politics of coalition formation explains why governmental policy in Israel is invariably based on bargaining and compromise rather than on the dictates of a single individual or group. The opposition, the parties comprising the minority of the 120 Knesset members, can only criticize; they have no role in the actual policymaking process.

Within the government, all significant decisions require the support of a majority of the ministers comprising the cabinet. The prime minister sets the cabinet's agenda. Because the government's policies are themselves the product of internal bargaining among the coalition parties, the authority of a prime minister is determined by his or her effectiveness in dominating the cabinet and by the ultimate success of the government's policies. Still, on any given issue, the prime minister of the day can lose the support of the coalition partners and of the Knesset majority and be forced to resign or to call new elections.

In September 2000, for example, the Labor Party-led government of Ehud *Barak fell apart over the "security issue" when he failed to reach a comprehensive peace arrangement with the Palestinians. Prime Minister Barak lost his Knesset majority and was forced to call new elections in 2001. He lost that election to the leader of the Likud Party, Ariel *Sharon, who became prime minister when he formed a government based on a Likud-led majority coalition of parties in the Knesset.

THE PRESIDENT: Whereas the prime minister is the most important single policymaker in Israel, the president's role is largely honorific and symbolic. The president symbolizes the sovereign independence of the state, receives the credentials of foreign ambassadors, and makes annual speeches at state holidays. The president does wield some political power because he or she can grant pardons (although that is usually done only with the advice of the prime minister and the minister of justice); in addition, after a national election he or she can select the prime minister-designate (although Israeli law requires the president to go first to the leader of the political party with the most Knesset seats). In the highly politicized Israeli political culture, even these tasks turn the decision of who will be president into a political event.

The Knesset elects the president, by secret ballot, for a period of five years, and he or she may serve no more than two terms. The party that formed the government coalition seeks to control that election as an indication of its leading role in Israel. However, the secret ballot requires it to support an individual widely recognized as embodying the values of Israeli society, even if he or she is not a member of that party. For example, the first president of Israel, Chaim *Weizmann, was selected because of his long leadership of the Zionist movement, even though he was not a member of the then-dominant *Mapai* (Labor) Party. In 2007, Shimon *Peres, a former prime minister and a Noble Peace Prize laureate, was elected president of Israel.

THE CIVIL COURTS (see ISRAEL, STATE OF: JUDICIAL SYSTEM): Because overt partisan considerations are an inseparable element in the workings of the Knesset, the potential for arbitrary governmental policies is obvious. Given the rampant partisanship of their political system, Israelis value the utility of independent objective and impartial decisions. The civil judiciary is seen as the institutional repository of those values. The authority that accompanies such an assessment gives the Israeli civil judiciary, particularly the Supreme Court, considerable power.

The nonpolitical conception of the civil judiciary is evident in the judicial selection procedures. All members of the Israeli civil judiciary are selected by a nine-member Nominations Committee. The Nominations Committee is chaired by the minister of justice, and it contains one other minister selected by the government of the day, the chief justice of the Supreme Court and two other justices selected by members of that Court, two members of the Knesset selected by secret ballot, and two practicing advocates (lawyers) elected by the Israeli Chamber of Advocates (Bar Association). The Nomination Committee's decisions are by majority vote, and its selections are binding on the president of Israel, who makes the actual appointments. Once appointed, the judges both of the Supreme Court and the lower civil courts hold their offices until the mandatory retirement age of seventy.

The civil court system for handling general legal conflicts is three-tiered. The 29 Magistrates' Courts (with 357 judges) deal with minor criminal offenses and small monetary claims. The 5 District Courts (with 121 judges) hear appeals from the Magistrates' Courts and deal with serious criminal offenses and major civil law suits. The Supreme Court (with fourteen justices) hears appeals from the District Courts and from specialized tribunals like the Labor Court and Housing Court. Sitting as the High Court of Justice, the Supreme Court has original jurisdiction over petitions alleging that a governmental action exceeds its legal authority.

It is largely in its capacity as the High Court of Justice that the Supreme Court has assumed the role of protecting the rule of law. From the beginning of the state, the civil courts emphasized the importance of the rule of law and their adherence to those rules. Gradually they expanded their conception of the rule of law. By 1974, it was clear that the Israeli civil courts, especially the Supreme Court, were extending the rule of law to protect human rights.

ISRAEL'S PIECEMEAL CONSTITUTION: This judicial trend dovetailed with an increasing public concern for protecting individual rights against potential arbitrary governmental actions. The public's reaction was reflected in a sustained demand that Israel adopt a formal written constitution to regulate governmental procedures and powers and to enumerate individual rights. The Knesset responded by enacting "Basic Laws" that have codified existing practices and symbols. By 2007, eleven Basic Laws had been enacted: The Knesset (1958); Israel Lands (1960); President of the State (1974); Government (1968); State Economy (1976); Armed Forces (1976); Jerusalem, the Capital of Israel (1980); Judiciary (1984); State Comptroller (1988); Freedom of Occupation (1992); and Human Dignity and Freedom (1992). These Basic Laws do not yet comprise a complete, integrated modern constitution, because they do not specifically mention such vital individual freedoms as free speech, the freedom of religion, and the equal protection of the law. Although Supreme Court decisions have generally protected those vital rights, the Court itself lacks the *explicit* authority to declare laws unconstitutional (despite a famous 1995 decision claiming that power), so both the nature of those rights and the scope of the courts' authority are not yet legally entrenched.

MARTIN EDELMAN

Israel, State of: Political Parties.

Political parties in Israel, as in all democracies, are the key mechanisms linking the public to the governmental policymaking institutions. They help translate popular needs and demands into actual policies and programs and help hold elected rulers accountable to the people they govern. The combination of Israeli electoral and parliamentary rules (see ISRAEL, STATE OF: POLITICAL INSTITUTIONS) has produced a robust democracy: Groups representing *all* shades of political opinion are encouraged to seek representation in the Knesset, Israel's parliament. A bewildering array of political parties compete for popular support. This complicated situation, however, can be simplified because Israeli parties are highly centralized and disciplined entities. Therefore, Israeli political parties can be discussed in terms of four perennial ideological blocs: center-left; center-right; Jewish Orthodox; and Palestinian (Arab).

CENTER-LEFT POLITICAL PARTIES: Center-left political parties in Israel grew out of the Labor Zionist movement that dominated the politics of the country in the first quarter-century after independence. At that time, Labor Zionist politics was organized around the *Histadrut* labor union federation and led by the *Mapai* political party. *Mapai's* principal rival within *Histadrut* and Labor Zionist politics generally was *Mapam,* a more Marxist socialist party. The Israeli polity that emerged after independence was shaped by *Mapai's* leaders – David *Ben-Gurion, Moshe Sharett, Levi Eshkol, and Golda *Meir – and reflected the party's ideology: Israel developed a democratic socialist political economy and a foreign policy aligned with the western world. By 1968, *Mapai* had incorporated several of the smaller *Histadrut* parties into the Labor Party, while *Mapam* continued its separate existence (see GORDON, AHARON DAVID; and ZIONISM).

In the early-twenty-first century, the largest political party in the center-left bloc remains the Labor Party. Its original socialist ideology has evolved into a political program that supports a capitalist economy with strong social welfare programs. In the post–Cold War era, this party's foreign policy retains a strong orientation toward the United States, and its security policy emphasizes that a permanent peace with the Palestinians can only be based on *enforceable* agreements.

Mapam was frequently a junior partner in *Mapai*/Labor government coalitions and gradually modulated its Marxist ideology. In 1992, *Mapam* joined other center-left parties to form *Meretz.* In the first decade of the twenty-first century, *Meretz* emphasizes the need for social economic policies that benefit the lower classes, including Palestinian Israelis, and a security policy that recognizes that a permanent peace with Israel's Arab neighbors can only come about through political means. Therefore, *Meretz* always urges Israel to take the initiative in proposing such arrangements without in any way neglecting the importance of maintaining a strong Israeli defense.

During the last half of the twentieth century, Israel made the transition from a developing nation into an economically prosperous player in the global economy. A highly educated middle class emerged that traced its political orientation to their parents' membership in Labor Zionism. Many of these Israelis coalesced around *Shinui.* In the twenty-first century, this party's ideology is similar to the Labor Party's social welfare program and to *Meretz's* approach to national security issues. *Shinui* is distinguished by its insistence that Israeli governmental policy be based on a complete separation of religion and the state.

Every national election has been contested by small center-left parties that have split off from one of the larger entities or have formed to reflect a newly perceived neglected interest. In the 2006 elections the Pensioners Party won seven seats in the Knesset.

All center-left political parties are committed to the continued existence of Israel as a Jewish and democratic state. The former commitment, they believe, requires Israel to maintain a strong defense force. The latter commitment makes them strong proponents of the need to promote and protect individual human rights; they support the general thrust of Israeli Supreme Court opinions on these matters and favor efforts to adopt a written constitution that would entrench *human rights.

CENTER-RIGHT POLITICAL PARTIES: Center-right political parties have evolved from the General Zionist and Revisionist movements in the World Zionist Organization and the *Yishuv.* The General Zionists advocated free-market economic policies; the Revisionists favored a more nationalist, militant program for establishing a Jewish state in Palestine. After independence, these movements formed the core opposition to the socialist-labor policies advanced by *Mapai*/Labor governments. To overcome Labor Party dominance, the bulk of the center-right parties formed *Likud,* and under the leadership of Menachem *Begin formed the government after the 1977 elections. Since then, the parties of the center-right have led most Israeli government coalitions.

In the early twenty-first century, *Likud* remains a major factor in the center-right political bloc. It emphasizes a national security policy based on a strong Israeli military force in the face of continued Arab enmity to the Jewish state's very existence. *Likud's* suspicions of Arab intentions, however, have not prevented it from reaching agreements with the Arabs, such as the 1979 peace treaty with Egypt.

Precisely because *Likud* has been willing to reach mutually acceptable agreements with the Arabs, other right-wing parties have formed. Their core belief is that the Jewish people are historically entitled to all of *Eretz Yisrael* (the Land of Israel) and that the territory Israel occupied after the 1967 Six Day War is necessary for the security of the state. That is why they opposed the Israeli withdrawal from the Sinai required by the Israel–Egypt treaty. Similarly, they continue to oppose any agreement that would require further Israeli withdrawals. Moreover, these Israelis believe that the Arabs continue to seek the destruction of the Jewish state and that therefore no viable peace arrangements are possible. At the beginning of the twenty-first century, the National Union Party speaks for most of these Israeli Jews. In the 2006 elections, a subset of these right-wing Israelis representing recent immigrants from the former Soviet Union formed the *Yisrael Beiteinu* (Israel Is Our Home) party and won twelve seats in the Knesset.

In 2005, *Likud* Prime Minister Ariel *Sharon concluded that the nation's security could best be secured by unilaterally relinquishing Israel's control of the Gaza Strip. Because most center-right Israelis, including a majority of *Likud*, adamantly opposed this policy, Sharon formed a new party, *Kadima*. Despite Sharon's incapacitating stroke in early 2006, *Kadima* won the most seats in that year's Knesset election. *Kadima*, under the leadership of Prime Minister Ehud Olmert, formed a coalition government with Labor and other smaller parties, which turned the Gaza Strip over to the Palestinian National Authority.

All center-right Israeli political parties believe that only a strong military can sustain the continued existence of Israel as a Jewish state. They share a reluctance to negotiate with Israel's Arab neighbors whom they believe continue to seek the destruction of the Jewish state. Although these parties have frequently criticized particular Supreme Court decisions, they remain committed to rule of law principles that they seek to entrench in a written constitution.

RELIGIOUS PARTIES: The Zionist movement was predominantly secular, but a small minority of religious Jews came to believe that the human struggle to re-create a Jewish state in the biblical homeland was not incompatible with the commands of Jewish religious law (*halakhah).* This was the origin of the National Religious Party (NRP).

Orthodox Jews believe that divine commands are embodied in *halakhah*, and therefore its rules cannot be subordinated to secular law. They also believe that Israel, as the Jewish state, must be based on *halakhah*, for that is what

it means (to them) to be Jewish. Now, as in the past, the NRP is willing to cooperate with non-Orthodox Israelis in governing the state, but it is never willing to forego its ultimate objective of creating a polity governed by *halakhah*. Tthe NRP invariably objects to any policy that it believes violates *halakhah*.

In the twenty-first century, the NRP adheres to the belief that Jews are divinely commanded to retain control of all of *Eretz Yisrael*. Members of this party have taken the lead in establishing Israeli settlements in the territory occupied by Israel since 1967. This position has made it impossible for the NRP to join any government coalition formed by the center-left bloc or even *Kadima*. Instead, in the 2006 elections, the NRP formed a joint list with the right-wing National Union Party that won nine seats in the Knesset.

When the political Zionist movement emerged in the 1890s and began recruiting supporters in Europe and America it was opposed by the vast bulk of Orthodox Jews. They continued to believe that a Jewish state would emerge only from divine intervention. To counter the efforts of the Religious Zionists, these Jews organized the *Agudat Israel* movement. In the wake of the *Holocaust, the anti-Zionist rabbis who led *Agudat Israel* recognized the great utility of a Jewish state as a haven *and* the organization became non-Zionist, rather than anti-Zionist: While not actively participating in the creation of Israel, it ceased its opposition. Over time *Agudat Israel* realized the benefits of more active participation in Israeli politics and agreed to become a coalition partner in several Israeli governments. However, *Agudat Israel's* original reservations about an essentially secular government for the Jewish state mean that it continues to refuse a cabinet position.

Before the 1984 elections, Ovadia Yosef, the former *Sephardic Chief Rabbi of Israel, formed *Shas* to represent Orthodox Jews from Arabic-speaking lands. Approximately half of Jewish Israelis are from such areas. Rabbi Yosef claimed they faced discrimination from both the secular parties and the *Ashkenazi (European) religious parties. *Shas* was successful in using the political process to obtain resources for this population, and by 1992 it was the largest religious party in Israel.

Shas has always sought to participate fully in the political process. Its position on security matters – particularly Israeli retention of the occupied territories – has been more ambiguous than that of the NRP. That ideological position, plus the size of its Knesset delegation, has made *Shas* a key player in the cabinet coalition process. As an Orthodox party, *Shas* has sought to use its political power to expand the role of *halakhah* in government policy, and it has frequently taken the lead in opposing Supreme Court decisions to the contrary.

The religious parties are committed to the continued existence of Israel as a Jewish state. They are united in the belief that such a state, to be truly Jewish, must be governed by *halakhah*. They seek to increase the role of Orthodox Jewish religious practices in the laws and policies of the state. That is why they remain adamantly opposed to a written constitution. They fear that having a human-made document as the supreme law of the land would undermine the authority of *halakhah* in Israel.

PALESTINIAN PARTIES: Palestinian Israelis comprise approximately 20% of the Israeli population. They exercise the franchise at only a slightly lower rate than their fellow citizens. Yet, Arabs are isolated from the mainstream of Israeli life; their political effectiveness is limited by the Jewish nature of the state and by the state's omnipresent security concerns. Only one Palestinian Israeli has been appointed as a Supreme Court justice, and the first Arab cabinet minister (a member of the Labor Party) was appointed in 2007.

Although Palestinian Israelis vote for and are members of mainline parties like *Kadima*, Labor, *Likud*, and *Meretz*, most support Palestinian parties. The names of these organizations have changed over time, but they still represent four persistent orientations: the Israeli Arab, communist, nationalist, and Islamist streams. The members of the Israeli Arab stream accept their status as a minority group in the Jewish state. Their core demand is for full equal citizenship. Because Palestinian Israelis have never been accorded such treatment, their politics are frequently difficult to distinguish from that of the Arab parties. In the 2006 national elections, the United Arab/*Ta'al* joint list reflected this outlook; it won six seats in the Knesset. The members of the communist stream emphasize a class orientation to politics. They do not accept the ethnic (Jewish) character of Israel and seek its transformation into a completely secular democratic state. In the 2006 national election, this outlook was represented by *Ḥadash*; it won three seats in the Knesset. *Ḥadash*, which literally means "new" in Hebrew, is an acronym for The Democratic Front for Peace and Equality.

The members of the nationalist stream see themselves as sharing a common identity with the Palestinians in the West Bank, Gaza Strip, and abroad. Their core objective is the transformation of Israeli into a binational (Jewish/Palestinian) state. In the short term, they seek policies that would grant Palestinians autonomy within Israel. In the 2006 national election, this outlook was represented by Balad (its name is an acronym for National Democratic Assembly); it won three seats in the Knesset.

The members of the Islamist stream derive their values from the tenets of that religion. Their ultimate goal is to establish an Islamist society in what they perceive as an Arab land. To date, no party representing this stream has competed in an Israeli national election, although such parties have had some success in local elections in Palestinian towns and cities.

The Palestinian parties are marginalized by the operation of the Israeli political system. Obviously the goals of the parties representing the communist, nationalist, and Islamist streams make them impossible coalition partners for any mainline Israeli party. Yet, even the more moderate parties of the Israeli Arab stream have yet to be included in a coalition. Given Israel's security situation, the mainline parties have been unwilling to include parties representing the same national group as their country's enemies. Political marginalization has increased the anger of the Palestinian Israeli population.

The reality of Palestinian marginalization is a serious issue but it should be seen as part of a larger political context. Israel has been a vibrant democracy for more than sixty years but as with most democratic nations, it has its flaws.

MARTIN EDELMAN

Israel, State of: Sports: See SPORTS: ISRAEL

Israel, State of: Wars (1948). Israel has fought seven wars since its declaration of independence on May 14, 1948: the 1948 War of Liberation, the 1956 Suez War, the 1967 Six Day War, the 1968–70 War of Attrition, the 1973 Yom Kippur War, the 1982 First Lebanon War, and the 2006 Second Lebanon War. In these wars and in the terrorist attacks that have occurred in between and after them, 22,000 Israelis have died.

WAR OF INDEPENDENCE (also War of Liberation): Of these wars, the War of Independence is the most significant because it not only established Israel's sovereignty but it also expanded Israel's boundaries beyond those suggested by the November 29, 1947, United Nations partition resolution. This war is known in Israel as the War of Independence and in the Arab world as *al-Nakba* (the disaster or catastrophe). It began in May 1948 after the withdrawal of British forces and Israel's declaration of sovereignty, when armies of the Arab states of Egypt, Syria, Jordan, Iraq, and Lebanon, with assistance from other Arab quarters, entered Palestine and engaged in open warfare with the defense forces of the new state.

Palestine's 650,000 Jews (who constituted themselves as the *Yishuv) accepted the 1947 UN partition resolution recommending the partition of Palestine into a Jewish state, an Arab state, and an internationalized *Jerusalem enclave, to be governed by the world organization itself (see ISRAEL, STATE OF: FOUNDING OF THE MODERN STATE). Palestine's Arabs, who numbered approximately 1.3 million, did not; nor did the neighboring Arab states. Convinced that they would prevail, the Arab Higher Committee urged Palestine's Arabs to "fight for every inch of their country." The religious leaders of Cairo's Al-Azhar University called for a jihad against the Jews. The emir of Trans-Jordan, a country carved out of the League of Nations Mandate by the British in 1922, announced, "I will have the pleasure and honor to save Palestine." The Arabs of Palestine took up arms against the Jews of Palestine even before the expiration of the British *Mandate on May 15, 1948, and Trans-Jordan, Lebanon, Syria, Iraq, and Egypt sent their armies into Palestine.

Only after the newly declared State of Israel had lost 1% of its population of approximately 600,000 did it beat back the Palestinians and the foreign armies. The war ended in 1949 not with treaties of peace and of mutual recognition, but with UN-brokered armistice agreements, which merely took note of the lines on which the opposing military forces had stopped fighting each other. Although the Jews of the *Yishuv*, now called Israelis, beat back seven invading Arab armies, they were unable to seize the Old City of Jerusalem or the lands that later came to be known as the Gaza Strip and the West Bank. The present boundaries between Israel and the Palestinian territories are not international frontiers: They are the cease-fire lines delineating where fighting stopped in 1948 and 1949 (see JERUSALEM, 1948–1967).

In the armistices signed between Israel, Egypt, Lebanon, and Jordan (Iraq did not sign an armistice), Israel ceded the eastern portion of Jerusalem, as well as territory that had been allocated to the Palestinian state, to the control of Trans-Jordan, which changed its name to Jordan to signify that it was now on both sides of the Jordan River. The world began to refer to Jordanian Palestine as the West Bank. The area of Palestine extending out from the city of Gaza became a new entity known as the Gaza Strip. This geopolitical reality remained until the 1967 Six Day War, when Israel captured East Jerusalem and the West Bank from Jordan, the Gaza Strip from Egypt, and the Golan Heights from Syria.

What would the geopolitical reality be today if the Arabs had accepted partition? There would be no Palestinian refugees and no refugee camps. The original 400,000 Arabs and their progeny in the area assigned to Israel by the United Nations would be there today, unless they balked at being citizens of the Jewish state and moved to neighboring countries or emigrated from the region entirely. There would be no Gaza Strip, and Jerusalem would be a *corpus separatum*. Part of the *Galilee in the north of Israel, as well as the Mediterranean coast of the Negev region in the south, would be part of the post-partition Arab state.

Although there are no doubts about these facts, questions have been raised about whether and the extent to which the Israelis forced Arab Palestinians to flee. The principal proponents of the view that the Israelis did so are a group of Israelis known as the "New Historians." They include Professors Avi Shlaim, Uri Milstein, Ilan Pappé, and Benny Morris. Certainly, there were some expulsions and also killings of Palestinian Arabs during the 1948 war, but such actions were not official Israeli policy. Otherwise, the Near East Arabic Radio would not have made this broadcast: "It must not be forgotten that the Arab Higher Committee encouraged the refugees to flee from their homes in Jaffa, Haifa, and Jerusalem and that certain leaders have tried to make political capital out of their miserable situation." Nor would Great Britain's Sir Alexander Cadogan have told the United Nations Security Council that "the Arabs are those responsible for the latest developments [of Arab flight] in Haifa." Nor would the American Lebanese daily *Al-Hoda* have written, "Brotherly advice was given to the Arabs of Palestine urging them to leave their lands, homes, and property and to stay temporarily in neighboring, brotherly states, lest the guns of the invading Arab armies mow them down. The Palestine Arabs had no choice but to obey the 'advice' of the [Arab] League and to believe what Azzam Pasha and other responsible men in the League told them – that their withdrawal from their lands was only temporary and would end in a few days with the successful termination of the Arab 'punishment' action against Israel." Nor did all Palestinian Arabs leave; at the end of the first decade of the twenty-first century, one-fifth of Israel's 7.2 million citizens and one-tenth of the 120 members of its parliament are Arabs. It should also be noted that another consequence of the 1948 war was that some 500,000 Jews who lived in Egypt, Syria, Iraq, and North Africa were forced from their homes and places of employment. Most of them were absorbed into Israel (see ISRAEL, STATE OF: IMMIGRATION POST-1948).

For further reading, see T. N. Dupuy, *Elusive Victory: The Arab-Israeli Wars, 1947–1974*; J. C. Hurewitz, *The Struggle for Palestine* (1950); D. Joseph, *The Faithful City: The Siege of Jerusalem, 1948* (1960); E. Karsh, "1948, Israel, and the Palestinians – The True Story," *Commentary* (May 2008); B. Morris, *1948: A History of the First Arab-Israeli War* (2008); and idem, *1948 and After: Israel and the Palestinians* (1994).   EDWARD BERNARD GLICK

Israel, State of: Wars (1956–1967). In the mid-1950s, Egypt, under the nationalist leadership of President Gamal

Abdul Nasser, sought the ouster of Great Britain from the Suez Canal Zone and supported Arab independence movements in *North Africa, particularly Algeria's efforts to put an end to French colonial rule. In July 1956, Egypt nationalized the Suez Canal and other British and French properties in Egypt and supported anti-French rebels in North Africa, creating a congruence of interests between Israel and these two European countries. By late October 1956, Britain and France had agreed with Israel to launch a coordinated action against Nasser's Egypt. The arrangement, known as the Sinai Campaign, was that Israeli forces would invade the Sinai Peninsula, to be followed by an Anglo-French ultimatum to both Israel and Egypt to cease fire while Anglo-French troops seized the Canal, ostensibly to protect it. It was anticipated that this action would ensure the safety of the Suez Canal, lead to the ouster of Nasser, and reduce the threat to Israel from the most populous Arab state. On October 29, 1956, Israel invaded the Gaza Strip and the Sinai Peninsula to destroy hostile Egyptian military positions and, in a brief war, captured the Gaza Strip and much of the Sinai Peninsula. After a British and French ultimatum, British and French forces were interposed between Israel and Egypt along the Suez Canal, ostensibly to separate the combatants and provide security for the Canal.

Eventually Israel withdrew from all of the captured territory to the pre-war frontiers under the weight of United Nations resolutions, but especially because of pressure from the Eisenhower administration. The United Nations Emergency Force (UNEF) was created to patrol the Egyptian side of the Egypt–Israel armistice line, and it helped ensure quiet. The sea lanes through the Strait of Tiran from the Red Sea to the Israeli port of Eilat were opened to Israeli shipping.

The next decade was characterized by relative tranquility, especially along the Israel–Egypt border, although no appreciable progress was made toward resolving the issues of the Arab–Israeli conflict. In the mid-1960s a growing number of terrorist raids into Israel, together with Syrian artillery attacks into agricultural settlements in northern Israel, altered the situation. Tensions between Israel and the Arabs grew throughout the spring of 1967 and escalated rapidly during the month of May. On May 26, Nasser said that, if war with Israel should come, the battle would be a general one and "our basic objective will be to destroy Israel."

SIX DAY WAR: In mid-May 1967, Egypt proclaimed a state of emergency, mobilized its army, and moved troops across Sinai toward the border with Israel. The UN complied with Nasser's request that the UNEF be removed from the Egypt–Israel border, and contingents of the Egyptian armed forces and of the Palestine Liberation Organization (PLO or Fatah) took over the UNEF's positions. Thus, Egypt and Israel faced each other with no buffer, and Nasser then announced that the Strait of Tiran would be closed to Israeli shipping and to strategic cargoes bound for Eilat. Israel regarded these actions as acts of war. On May 30, Jordan entered into a defense pact with Syria and Egypt, and Iraqi troops were stationed along the Israel–Jordan border.

On June 5, 1967, Israel launched a preemptive strike against the Egyptian air force, destroying 286 of Egypt's 420 combat aircraft and killing one-third of Egypt's pilots. Later that morning, the ground war began. Columns of tanks and artillery blasted into the Sinai, and Egypt's army soon crumbled. Despite Egypt's reverses, Nasser convinced King Hussein of Jordan to join in the defense of Arab allies. Jordanian forces began shelling Israeli positions in Jerusalem. Israel responded by seizing the Old City of Jerusalem and making gains elsewhere in the West Bank. The next day Syria began shelling northern Israel. On June 10, 1967, Israel captured the Golan Heights. In six days, Israel had decisively defeated Egypt, Jordan, Syria, and their allies and had radically transformed the situation in the Middle East. Israel was now in control of territories stretching from the Golan Heights in the north to Sharm el-Sheikh in the Sinai Peninsula and from the Suez Canal to the Jordan River. The occupied territories included the Sinai Peninsula, the Gaza Strip, the West Bank (referred to by Israel as Judea and Samaria), the Golan Heights, and East Jerusalem.

The Six Day War of June 1967 was a major watershed in the history of Israel, of the Arab–Israeli conflict, and of the Middle East. It altered the geography of the region, changed military and political perceptions, and brought an intensified international effort to resolve the conflict. Israel's victory also inaugurated a period of security, euphoria, and economic growth. Initially there were hopes that the magnitude of the victory might contribute to the prospects for peace and concord with the Arabs. Israel adopted the position that it would not withdraw from those territories until there were negotiations with the Arab states leading to peace agreements that recognized Israel's right to exist and accepted Israel's permanent borders. Between 1949 and 1967, Israel had been prepared for peace with the Arab states on the basis of the 1949 armistice lines with minor modifications, but after the events of May and June 1967, stark new realities entered into these considerations, including religious and ideological claims to territory. The status of these territories has been the focus of the peace process ever since.

Israeli hopes for a change in Arab attitudes waned as a result of the Khartoum Arab Summit at the end of the summer of 1967. The Arab states agreed to unite their efforts "to eliminate the effects of the aggression" and to secure Israeli withdrawal from the occupied territories within the framework of "the main principles" to which they adhered: "No peace with Israel, no recognition of Israel, no negotiation with it, and adherence to the rights of the Palestinian people in their country." This agreement appeared to rule out any peaceful settlement of the Arab–Israeli conflict. The United Nations Security Council, on November 22, 1967, adopted a British-sponsored resolution (Resolution 242) that emphasized "the inadmissibility of the acquisition of territory by war and the need to work for a just and lasting peace in which every state in the area can live in security." Although wording of the resolution was deliberately ambiguous, it emphasized an exchange of territory for peace.

In the first decade after the 1967 war there were various efforts but little significant progress toward the achievement of peace. The Palestinians became more active in the conflict – initially gaining publicity and attention through terrorist acts against Israel, some of which were spectacular in nature. **Map 14**   BERNARD REICH

Israel, State of: Women. See WOMEN, MODERN: PALESTINE AND ISRAEL

Israel, State of: Youth Movements. About a dozen Jewish youth movements (YMs) functioned in the *Yishuv;* the most

prominent were *Ha-Tzofim* (Hebrew Scouts Federation), *Ha-Shomer ha-Tzair; Ha-Maḥanot ha-Olim, Ha-Noar ha-Oved, Benei Akiva,* Betar, *Ha-Tenua ha-Meuḥedet* (The United Movement), *Ezra,* and *Maccabi ha-Tzair* (Young Maccabi). Some YMs merged and split following changes in the political map.

All of these YMs, except for *Ha-Tzofim* (founded in Palestine in 1919 in accordance with the views of Baden-Powell, the founder of the world scout movement), were affiliated with political entities. They presented a blend, in various degrees, of the three archetypes of YMs: the German Free Movement (*Wandervogel*), the British Scouts, and the Soviet *Komsomol*. These groups were all inspired by the belief that youth activities play a central role in the personality development of the individual and that youth culture should be supported for its own sake. However, these movements also considered adolescence as preparing members for their adult lives, preferably on a *kibbutz.

YMs adhered to *Zionist ideology, in most cases to its socialist-Zionist versions. Thus, they conformed to the values of the *Yishuv* and the young state, including the negation of exile (*shelilat ha-galut*), striving to create a new Jew, and the love of *Eretz Yisrael* (the Land of *Israel). Re-creation of the Jewish past, with an emphasis on the heroic stories of Tel Hai and *Masada, also played an important role.

YM members were involved in outdoor activities such as scouting, sports, excursions, and camping, in addition to intellectual discourse (such as study of Jewish and world history, Zionism, and the history and geography of *Palestine). They held discussions on personal and intimate issues; worked to implement moral values and develop social identities; and were involved in various degrees of political activity.

Although great emphasis was put on ideology, young people were attracted to YMs primarily by the social framework they offered of togetherness, shared social adventures, and a sense of emotional closeness. These activities and feelings, and the experience of being leaders (*madrikhim*) of younger groups, left a long-lasting impression on YM members. All in all, the impact of the YMs on their members, both as young participants and continuing into adult life, was immense; their imprint on Israeli society as a whole far exceeds their numerical size.

After the *Holocaust, with the loss of European Jewry, Israel became the center of all the Zionist youth movements. However, as most of them were mission-oriented, the establishment of the state stripped them of many of their unique features, a change from which they never fully recovered. YM members considered themselves a self-recruited leadership and cohort. This attitude led to a special arrangement concluded in the 1940s that enabled YM graduates to keep their social framework intact when they joined the *Palmakh* so that, after completing military service, specific groups could settle together on a kibbutz. This arrangement was adopted, with the necessary adjustments, after the 1948 establishment of Israel within the framework of the NAḤAL (*Noar Ḥalutzi Loḥem* [Fighting Pioneering Youth]). This system also guaranteed a continuous supply of leaders to the YMs.

Ha-Shomer ha-Tzair (HH [The Young Guard]), the oldest and the archetype of Jewish YMs, was founded in the second decade of the twentieth century in *Galicia, *Poland; the first branches of HH in Palestine were established in 1929. From its inception, HH in Palestine was intended to be a reservoir of manpower for the *Kibbutz Artzi*, the umbrella organization of communal agricultural settlements established by HH graduates in 1927. HH had a singular educational ideology and principles that combined scouting, personal example, training of the individual, development of the personality, political education and involvement, and socialist Zionist fulfillment through kibbutz life.

The movement had a very clear structure, from the nuclear group to the local branch (*ken* [nest]). The educational process advanced through three levels, each with its own program adapted to the emotional needs and intellectual capacity of the age group. Each level had its emblem and badge; the Mature Emblem (at the age of seventeen) was awarded only after considerable deliberations to those who declared an intention to live on a kibbutz. HH had a slogan, "Be strong and of good courage"; "ten commandments" covering all spheres of the members' lives; a uniform – blue shirt secured with white laces rather than buttons; and military-like rituals including a flag, formal ceremonies of opening and closing each meeting, and a salute.

Until 1947, HH supported a binational state, and it had a strong Soviet orientation until the late 1950s. From 1948, HH was affiliated with *Mapam* (United Workers Party) and shared its triple slogan: "For Zionism, Socialism, and the Brotherhood of Nations." HH served as a point of reference for all Zionist YMs, either as a model for imitation or as a model against which alternative groups were formed.

Ha-Maḥanot ha-Olim (HHO [The Rising Camps]) was founded by groups of students at the Herzliya Gymnasium in Tel Aviv in 1926. In 1930, this youth movement adopted the name HHO. HHO's slogan was "We will rise and ascend," and its uniform was a blue shirt with buttons instead of laces. Affiliated with the *Kibbutz ha-Meuhad*, HHO viewed the kibbutz as the sole way to fulfill its values, which included an activist approach in security matters, a readiness to serve the country's needs, and objection to the partitioning of Palestine. After the split within the political party *Mapai* (1944), some HHO members united with the Gordonia movement to form *Ha-Tenua ha-Meuhedet*, affiliated with *Mapai* and *Hever ha-Kevutzot*. HHO itself was affiliated with *Ha-Tenua l'Aḥdut ha-Avodah*.

Ha-Noar ha-Oved (Working Youth), a movement for working teenagers, was established in 1926 by the *Histadrut* (General Federation of Jewish Labor) with the aim of meeting the cultural, social, and economic needs of working youth. The movement's slogan was "For work, defense, and peace," and its uniform was a blue shirt with red laces. Although most of its instructors came from *kibbutzim*, the movement did not insist that kibbutz life was the sole means to Zionist fulfillment.

Ha-Noar ha-Oved merged with *Habonim-Ha-Tenua ha-Meuhedet* in 1959 to form *Ha-Noar ha-Oved veha-Lomed* (Working and Studying Youth). Although it had no formal party affiliation, the movement was known to have ties with *Mapai* and then the Israel Labor Party.

Benei Akiva (BA [Sons of (Rabbi) *Akiva]), a religious Zionist youth movement, was founded in Jerusalem in 1929 and affiliated with *Ha-Poel ha-Mizraḥi*. BA's slogan *"Torah va-Avodah"* (Torah and Labor), reflected the fusion of *Orthodox observance of religious commandments and Zionist pioneering, to be best fulfilled in the kibbutz. The basic educational units of BA are separate for boys and girls but groups for older teenagers are mixed, with full and equal participation of girls, including military service in the NAḤAL.

Betar (acronym for *Berit* [Alliance] *Yosef Trumpeldor*), was founded in 1923 in Riga, *Latvia, and began its activity in Palestine in 1926. Betar adopted the ideology of the Revisionist Party (and after 1948 of the *Ḥerut* movement) of monistic Zionism and rejected any fusion with "alien" creeds (meaning mainly socialism, with a deep negation of class struggle). The movement's aim was the creation of a Jewish state with a Jewish majority on both sides of the Jordan River. Betar held to a strong emphasis of discipline, with preeminence of the nation over the individual, and had a hierarchical structure resembling a military organization. Betar's brown uniform, adopted in the early 1920s to symbolize the earth of *Eretz Israel*, was construed by its rivals after 1933 as tangible proof of its "fascist character."   AVIVA HALAMISH

Israelites: Kingship.

Kingship, or rule by a single person atop a hierarchy with near-exclusive control of legitimated violence in a delimited territory, began in the Near East toward the end of the fourth millennium BCE. Over the next two millennia, polities of varying sizes and power developed a set of governmental practices, including control of key cult offices, the use of the state military and taxation system, gift giving for controlling subordinates and foreign rivals, and the writing of chronicles, hymns, and other literary forms celebrating the king's successes. In visual and auditory media, kings presented themselves as builders, worshipers pleasing to the high gods, conquerors, sexually potent founders of dynasties, and guarantors of order and prosperity.

During the early first millennium BCE, Israelites adopted these practices. Their earliest known monarchs, *Saul and especially *David and *Solomon, self-consciously took on the trappings of contemporary rulers. Israelite monarchy developed through five discernible stages: (1) a pre-monarchic stage of tribal chieftains/*judges and the *Canaanite city-state kings left over from the Amarna period of the Late Bronze Age; (2) early monarchs; (3) consolidation, in the north by the dynasty founded by Omri, and in the south by *Hezekiah; (4) a period of vassalage to foreign powers; and (5) the end of the monarchy and substitution of hereditary governors (at first of the Davidic house in *Judah). The stages occurred as much as a century earlier in the northern kingdom of *Israel than in Judah. Although the Israelite monarchies lasted only about four centuries (ca. 1000–586 BCE), with a brief revival in the second century under the *Hasmoneans, the kings' careers stimulated the production of much of the *Bible, through which they have exerted continued influence.

In particular, 1 and 2 *Samuel, 1 and 2 *Kings, and 1 and 2 *Chronicles contain stories of the Israelite monarchs, sometimes reporting legends, but often drawing on authentic royal archives or chronicles. Several monarchs also appear in inscriptions from Israel, *Moab, *Egypt, and *Mesopotamia. Thus the Tel Dan inscription refers to the "king of the house of David" (i.e., a ninth-century ruler of Judah), while *Assyrian texts refer to the "house of Omri," or the northern kingdom of Israel (see ARCHEOLOGY: ANCIENT TIMES THROUGH THE PERSIAN PERIOD). Other Assyrian texts mention Jehu (by Shalmaneser III), Hezekiah (by Sennacherib), and Menahem (by Tiglath-Pileser III). More than 1,500 seal impressions on jars from eighth-century Judah designate the jars' contents as belonging "to the king." Remains of palaces and other monumental architecture survive from *Samaria, Jezreel, Ramat Rahel, and arguably *Jerusalem, indicating that Israelite rulers enjoyed revenues that allowed displays of power and artistic sensibility.

The Bible displays different attitudes toward kingship. The Deuteronomistic History (DH) contains stories warning of royal tyranny (Judg 9:8–15; 1 Sam 8; 1 Kgs 11–12, 21) and conflicts between kings and *prophets (1 Kgs 17; 2 Kgs 1). *Deuteronomy 17:14–20, apparently a late pre-exilic reflection on the history of the monarchy, allows for kingship but restricts the crown's control of the military, treasury, and diplomatic service (by limiting the king's harem). The DH judges all rulers of the northern kingdom deficient by definition because of their patronage of religious shrines in Dan and *Beth El, and most kings of Judah as equally unworthy. It does allow that Hezekiah and *Josiah were successful, on account of their support of cult centralization in Jerusalem. The Deuteronomists' view of kingship and cult, however, created a serious problem of theodicy, leading them to blame the death of the good king Josiah on his evil grandfather, Manasseh (2 Kgs 23:26–27).

The chronicler addresses the untimely death of Josiah, blaming Josiah himself for his death (2 Chron 35:22) and recasting Manasseh as a penitent king. He also revises the Deuteronomistic portrayal of Israelite kingship in other ways. Chronicles largely omits stories of the northern kingdom, together with tales of David's sexual predations and Solomon's tyrannies (compare 1 Chron 9 with 1 Kgs 11). Chronicles augments its source in Samuel–Kings with stories of the building and remodeling of the Jerusalem *Temple and the celebration of major *festivals by David (1 Chron 22–29), Hezekiah (2 Chron 29–31), and Josiah (2 Chron 35). These additions may draw on older sources, although interpretive processes also play a role.

The prophetic texts include stories of conflict between prophets and Israelite kings (e.g., *Isa 7; *Jer 36; cf. *Amos 7), as well as criticisms of foreign rulers (e.g., Isa 14; *Ezek 28–29, 31–32). Although the prophets do not condemn kingship per se, the post-exilic redactors of the prophetic books rarely envision the restoration of the monarchy (but see Amos 9:10–15; *Hag 2:20–23). Similarly, texts in the wisdom tradition (see BIBLE: WISDOM LITERATURE) are skeptical about royal power (see *Prov 23:1–3; *Eccl 4:13–16; 5:8–9), although they also help potential courtiers manage themselves in the palace and hope for royal diligence (Prov 31:1–9; cf. Ps 101).

Texts from the *Second Temple period, an era when most Jews lived under foreign occupation, deal with kingship in four ways. First, David and Solomon become models of piety and inspirations for potential rulers. David was the prophet and psalmist, to whom a *Dead Sea Scroll, 11QPs[a], attributed 4,050 hymns. Solomon's reputation for wisdom led to the pseudonymous ascriptions of Wisdom of Solomon and Psalms of Solomon to him. Second, texts from the second century BCE, such as Pseudo-Aristeas and the *Temple Scroll* (one of the Dead Sea Scrolls, which includes an

extensive *midrash on Deut 17:14–20), reflected on the duties and limits of the monarchy (cf. 1 *Macc 14:4–15; *Testament of Job*). Third, the foreign monarch becomes an object of mockery (as in *Esther or *Daniel 1–6) or obloquy (as in Dan 7–12, 2 Macc, and the *Qumran *Serekh* texts). Fourth, biblical texts about kings, especially David, become models for a coming messiah (especially in early *Christianity). Although *messianism in the Second Temple period took several forms and not all Jews expected a royal messiah, still the biblical traditions about kings developed into a major aspect of messianism during this period. In the near absence of a human Israelite king whom everyone thought legitimate, the biblical kings took on new life as models for what might yet be. Thus, the royal traditions of Israel did not disappear; instead they were transformed.

For further reading, see M. W. Hamilton, *The Body Royal: The Social Poetics of Kingship in Ancient Israel* (2005); and M. Bockmuehl and J. C. Paget, eds., *Redemption and Resistance: The Messianic Hopes of Jews and Christians in Antiquity* (2007).

MARK W. HAMILTON

Israelites: Marriage and Family.

The Hebrew *Bible focuses more on national concerns than on the lives of ordinary individuals, and it originated largely from the urban center of *Jerusalem, removed from the agrarian settlements in which most people lived. Consequently, it is an inadequate source of information about Israelite marriage and family life. Indeed, biblical evidence alone gives a skewed notion of people's daily lives and interactions, especially with respect to gender dynamics. However, the data produced by archeology, along with ethnographic information, allow for a better understanding of Israelite domestic life (**see also ARCHEOLOGY, LAND OF ISRAEL: ANCIENT TIMES TO PERSIAN PERIOD; and WOMEN, ANCIENT: ISRAELITE**).

*MARRIAGE: The Hebrew Bible does not define marriage nor does it even have a specific term for it. The union of a woman and man to form a family unit is typically expressed by saying that a man "takes a woman" as a wife (e.g., Gen 24:67, 25:1, 28:2). This phrase reflects the dominant patrilocal pattern in ancient Israel whereby a woman would leave her natal family and join that of her spouse, who literally took her into his domain, usually his parent's household (see later discussion). Marriage within one's kinship group (endogamy) helped maintain patrilineages and was preferred, although marriage between unrelated groups (exogamy) sometimes occurred, especially to secure alliances.

Most marriages, at least those of people with property, were likely arranged by one or both parents. Shechem's passion for *Dinah led him to ask his father to negotiate with *Jacob about marrying her (Gen 34:4, 8), and Samson's mother and father, despite their misgivings, secured a certain *Philistine woman for their son (Judg 14:1–4). The desires of marriageable offspring may have affected their parents' choices of mates for them, judging from the Samson narrative and the assertiveness of the Shunammite in the *Song of Songs. Yet love was hardly a prerequisite for marriage, especially if a bride was acquired sight unseen, although it sometimes followed (Gen 24:67). In most cases romantic considerations were probably secondary to concerns about family alliances and property exchanges, especially because the marital relationship focused on procreation and the carrying out of household tasks rather than on companionship.

The Hebrew Bible contains no hints about the average age of first marriage, but ethnographic data suggest an early age, corresponding to the onset of puberty. Pre-modern societies like ancient Israel had high infant mortality rates and short life-spans (an average of thirty to forty years), and a young marriage age was necessary to maintain if not increase the population. The need for the labor provided by offspring was of paramount importance. Israelite demographic concerns are expressed in biblical language mandating population growth (e.g., "Be fertile and increase" in Gen 1:28 and 9:1), which likely reflects early marriages. Even for elites, whose interests in arranging marriages lay in the preservation of family land holdings, early marriages would have been more effective in ensuring the production of heirs. Very little is known about the arrangements leading up to and culminating in the formation of a marital pair, with only a few biblical narratives providing clues. The so-called Courtship of Rebekah in Genesis 24 provides considerable information, but should be used cautiously, for Rebekah and her spouse-to-be *Isaac are hardly ordinary folk. They are part of the exalted origins, according to the biblical construction, of the people of Israel, and their families control substantial resources. It is uncertain that the elaborate exchange of goods preceding their marriage would have taken place for individuals with fewer possessions. Nonetheless, as for the elite families whose marital arrangements appear in many ancient *Near Eastern *law codes, financial matters were integral to the formation of most marital liaisons, with premarital transactions serving a variety of economic, legal, and social functions.

The family of the bride would have provided a dowry, which ordinarily comprised movable property such as clothing, jewelry, and household items or furnishings; brides from wealthier families might also bring animals and servants (Gen 24:59, 29:24, 29). The groom or his family could even supplement the dowry (Gen 24:53). Although sometimes husbands had access to it, the dowry theoretically belonged to the woman for the duration of the marriage and would have been her chief resource in the event of widowhood or divorce, especially if she had no sons or parents. The groom's family in turn provided a payment or betrothal gift (*mohar*) to the bride's family (Gen 34:12; Exod 22:16; 1 Sam 18:25). Sometimes called the "bride-price," it has been interpreted as evidence that women were purchased by men. The notion that women were thus "property" of their husbands is also suggested by the fact that the taking of a wife is sometimes, as is Boaz' union with *Ruth, indicated by the verb *kāna* (Ruth 4:10), which can mean "to buy" but also, more generally, "to acquire." Similarly, the word for "husband" (*baʿal*) often, but not always, means "master." However, the notion of buying a bride is now understood to be flawed. Rather, the betrothal gift provided partial compensation to a family for the loss of a daughter's labor. In addition, betrothal gifts and dowries together constituted exchanges of payments that helped ensure the viability of a new family unit. They created or intensified alliances between a woman's natal and marital families, thus increasing the likelihood that those families would assist each other in the event of illness or economic difficulties; such assistance would otherwise have

been unusual for a pre-modern society living in a marginal ecological zone.

Men may not have owned their wives, but they did have exclusive rights to their sexuality. This imbalance in favor of the male must be understood against the backdrop of the great importance of immovable property for Israelites as an agrarian people. The ownership of land was essential for survival, and the transmission of property across generations along the male line was a highly charged process. Embedded in the patrilineal principle was a deep concern that men be certain about the paternity of their offspring. A preponderance of the legal texts in the *Pentateuch dealing with sexuality and exhibiting what might be called a "double standard" are in fact ways of assuring that a man will not leave his land to someone else's child. For example, women are treated differentially in adultery texts depending on their marital status (Lev 20:10; Deut 22:22–28), and sex between an unmarried woman and a married man is not forbidden. Similarly, a bride's virginity is valued as an assurance that the groom will be the father of her first child (e.g., Deut 22:13–21). The institution known as *levirate marriage, in which a childless widow marries her deceased husband's brother, was also a product of the concern for inheritance in that the first son born of that liaison was considered the dead man's heir (Deut 25:5–10; cf. Gen 38 and Ruth). The instance in which Zelophehad's daughters are heirs in the absence of sons (Num 26:33, 27:1–11, 36:1–12) seems contrary to absolute principles of patrilineality, but the daughters are enjoined to marry within the clan and thus retain the property within their kinship group.

A woman's *infertility had a negative impact on the labor productivity of a farm family and the ability of offspring to care for aging adults; it also affected a man's strong concern for transmitting land to his biological heirs. Taking a second wife, a slave wife, or a concubine was a possible solution, although polygany was probably uncommon given the demographic reality of a shorter life-span for women. However, affluent or important people (such as the patriarchs) had multiple wives as a sign of their significance. Similarly, the sizable and perhaps legendary harems reported for some biblical monarchs (e.g., 2 Sam 3:2–5, 5:13, 12:8, 19:6; 1 Kgs 11:1–3, 20:1–5; 2 Chron 11:18–21) indicate the kings' high status and political power; they also reflect the practice of taking foreign brides to secure political alliances. However, for most people, monogamy was the norm if not the ideal.

The dissolution of marriage, like its establishment, is not laid out in any biblical text. The one legal passage (Deut 24:1–4) dealing with *divorce addresses only the particular circumstances, probably reflecting concerns about paternity, in which a man seeks to remarry someone to whom he had once been married. This case, as well as indirect information from biblical texts (e.g., the departure of the Levite's wife in Judg 19:2), suggests that women as well as men could terminate a marriage. One passage (Isa 50:1) mentions a bill of divorce (*sēper kĕrîtut*), which indicates that, although not mentioned in the Bible, a written document (*ketubbah*) may have accompanied some marriages, especially those of the well-to-do (cf. Mal 2:14).

FAMILY LIFE: For most Israelite women and men daily life was centered in the family household. Known in the Bible as the "father's house" (*beit ʾāv*), in accordance with the organization of society according to male lineages, the family household is designated "mother's house" (*beit 'ēm*) in several female-oriented texts (Gen 24:28; Ruth 1:8; Song 3:4, 8:2; cf. Prov 14:1), probably a consequence of the role of the senior woman of the household in managing most of its daily activities. The family household consisted of a senior marital pair, their sons and the spouses of married sons, any children born to those young couples, and unmarried daughters, although this exact configuration shifted as older members died and younger ones married. The Bible's ancestor narratives give the impression that families had numerous offspring (see BIBLE: ANCESTRAL NARRATIVES), but the reality as calculated from the size of excavated dwellings is that the average nuclear family had about four children. Sometimes displaced kin from other families, indentured servants, or other workers would be part of the household. The family household also included its material components, the most important one being its immovable property. A family's land, on which were situated its fields, orchards, vineyards, and gardens, was the patrimony (*naḥălâ*) of the senior male and also the source of the entire family's livelihood. The family's dwellings (two or three buildings, one for each of the marital pairs, sharing a courtyard), its tools and implements for growing crops and producing food and clothing, and even its animals further comprised the household. The family tomb or grave site was also considered part of its patrimony.

As the primary social unit of the Israelites, the household was the chief economic as well as reproductive unit. The various productive activities of family members were generally divided along gender lines, with certain tasks performed mainly by males and others carried out largely by females. This complementary and interdependent arrangement is the most efficient way for people to master the many requirements of a largely self-sufficient household. However, extenuating circumstances such as death or illness might mean that members of one gender would sometimes perform the other's work (see ILLNESS AND DISEASE: BIBLE AND ANCIENT NEAR EAST); periods of intensive labor, such as the need to harvest a crop quickly, might also mean transgressing gendered work patterns (see Ruth 2:2–9). In general, males were responsible for clearing fields and then carrying out the subsequent plowing, seeding, and harvesting. The major horticultural and viticultural procedures were largely male activities, with vegetable and herb gardens likely planted and tended by women. Various family members, especially older children, cared for animals; indeed, from an early age children became involved in the economic activities of their parents – girls with their mothers and boys with their fathers.

Women carried out most of the arduous and time-consuming procedures for transforming crops into edible and preservable form. The most important food source was grain, with bread or cereals providing about half of a person's daily caloric needs. Because the outer husks of grains are inedible and grain's nutritional components cannot be digested in raw form, a series of procedures – soaking or parching, grinding, and cooking (which involved collecting fuel and starting and maintaining fires) – were required to transform harvested and winnowed grains into food. It took a woman about three hours a day to process enough grain to feed the six members of a nuclear family unit. Additional work was required to prepare many other compo-

nents of a largely vegetarian diet. Some of the fruits, vegetables, legumes, and dairy products were consumed raw, but many were processed by churning, pickling, fermenting, drying, pressing, or roasting to produce cheese, capers, dates, olives, nuts, raisins, herbs, oil, and wine. Such foods could be kept for extended periods and thus provide sustenance long past the growing seasons. Because they were costly and also had to be consumed all at once, animals were rarely slaughtered for food except for special occasions or festivals in which several families might share the meat.

In addition to the work required for making edible foods, women also carried out a similarly tedious sequence of tasks – perhaps in the winter months when less time was required for food processing – to produce clothing and other textiles. Wool shorn from the animals had to be carded, spun, occasionally dyed, woven into cloth, and then sewn into garments. It is not clear, however, whether women or men or both fashioned leather goods, baskets, and other household implements, although it is likely that each gender made the items associated with their particular productive responsibilities.

Certain benefits accrued to the women who performed these onerous tasks. Considerable technological expertise was necessary for many household procedures, and mastering the requisite skills could be gratifying, as was the satisfaction of feeding and clothing one's family. Men would have experienced similar gratification from their productive labors, although the periodic failure of crops due to drought or pestilence all too often diminished that reward. Another positive feature of women's work was that, because many of the tasks (such as grinding or spinning) were done by neighboring women working together, it involved pleasurable social interaction; in contrast, male labor to produce field crops was more solitary. Women's daily social interaction also served the larger community in that it meant the formation of informal women's networks that aided communication among household units and fostered the mutual aid necessary for dealing with illness, death, and other family problems.

In addition to its economic functions, the family household was also the place where offspring were socialized and educated. For most children, education consisted of learning the technologies they would need as adults and also the values and stories of their families and their larger communities. Some of this information was instilled in children in the course of routine daily activities through the instructions and admonitions of their parents; other information was absorbed as children observed or participated in family and community religious and social events, which were often intertwined.

The discovery in domestic contexts of "cult corners" and objects known to have been used in religious rituals indicates that religion was another aspect of family life (see also ISRAELITES: RELIGION). Community or national shrines may have been the locus of seasonal festivals and periodic sacrificial events, as set forth in the Bible, but other practices took place in the household, perhaps even on a daily basis. Men probably placed small-scale food or drink offerings in miniature vessels in household shrines in the hopes of securing plentiful agricultural yields. Women used amulets and figurines as well as apotropaic lamps and shiny jewelry, and perhaps also made offerings, all to the end of protecting themselves and their families from evil spirits, securing their own fertility, and achieving safe childbirth, adequate lactation, and the viability of newborns (see MAGIC and **Plate 1**). Chants and prayers likely accompanied the ritual acts of both women and men, enhancing the household religious culture and helping family members feel they had some control over the vagaries of existence in ancient Israel (see BIBLE: PRAYER LANGUAGE).

For further reading, see D. Bloch, "Marriage and Family in Ancient Israel," in *Marriage and Family in the Biblical World*, ed. K. M. Campbell (2003); C. Meyers, *Discovering Eve: Ancient Israelite Women in Context* (1988); idem, *Households and Holiness: The Religious Culture of Israelite Women* (2005); L. G. Perdue, J. Blenkinsopp, J. J. Collins, and C. Meyers, *Families in Ancient Israel* (1997); and L. E. Stager, "The Archaeology of the Family in Ancient Israel," *Bulletin of the American Schools of Oriental Research* 260 (1985): 1–35.   CAROL MEYERS

Israelites: Religion. The term "Israelite religion" refers to the system of beliefs, practices, liturgical rites, and social institutions that characterized the life of ancient Israel from roughly 1200–450 BCE (after which time most scholars see Israelite religion developing into early *Judaism). Israelite religion is characterized by a binding relationship between the Israelite tribal league and its common deity, intermediaries such as *priests and *prophets who supervised and guided the ethical and cultic life of the people, and the sanctity of the *family/clan culture and its traditions of leadership. Despite these persistent features, Israelite religion was constantly evolving in response to events, the needs of a growing and shifting populace, disagreements concerning the proper identity of Israel's deity, and disputes between the leaders of disparate religious groups regarding the nature of divine will.

PRE-MONARCHIC PERIOD: The religion of early Israel in the pre-monarchic period (ca. 1200–1020 BCE) involved diverse groups of people forming larger clans and *tribes who lived in geographical proximity to each other and shared the same agricultural resources. They worshiped at religious shrines associated with their common ancestors that were staffed with regional priests who possessed family ties to the surrounding clans. Israelite villagers would regularly visit shrines to sacrifice and pray, to receive legal/ritual instruction, and to divine the will of the deity. The major deity of early Israel was El, as indicated by the very name of the nation, *yisra-el* (he who strives with El), but was also known as YHWH. Many scholars believe that the two names derive from two originally different deities in Israel's earliest period. El was the name of the father-head of the *Canaanite pantheon, and most scholars agree that there was very strong cultural and ideological interchange between early Israel and their Canaanite neighbors. YHWH, by contrast, was a deity worshiped in northwest *Arabia and was viewed as a warrior-storm deity, a feature that survives in early Israel's poetic and narrative traditions (Exod 15:3, 19:16–19; Ps 29, 68, 77:16–20; Hab 3). The YHWH cult in Israel traces its origins to *Moses (Exod 3), a figure revered in a variety of biblical texts as the founder of the national religion. The introduction of YHWH worship likely accompanied the integration of groups with ties to Moses' leadership into the Israelite social matrix, and the two deities were identified with each other at an early stage (Exod 6:3).

As the various clans came together over time to form a tribal league, YHWH emerged as the nation's primary deity. Diverse concepts of YHWH are evident in biblical *poetic and *narrative traditions, suggesting the spectrum of ideas concerning the role of this high deity in the religious life of Israel. In addition, both *archeology and biblical evidence indicate that other, lesser deities were worshiped alongside the primary ancestral deity. Clan-based Israelite religion included ritual communion with departed ancestors and agricultural and livestock seasonal festivals with mythic overtones; it boasted a vibrant fertility cult, replete with devotees to a variety of goddesses. The most prominent of these goddesses were apparently Asherah (the consort of El and, later, YHWH) and "Queen of Heaven." The identity of the "Queen of Heaven" is uncertain, but the cult of this deity was fostered in a family context in which women played a prominent role (see Jer 7:16–20, 44:15–19). The central position of women in early narrative and poetic traditions, such as *Miriam (Exod–Num) *Deborah and Jael (Judg 4–5), and *Hannah (1 Sam 1–2), point to the sacral female dimensions of early Israelite religion that survived for several centuries (**Plate 1**).

ROLE OF THE MONARCH: The transition to a monarchic society (ca. 1020–587 BCE) introduced dramatic changes in the fabric of Israelite religion. Kings in ancient *Near Eastern culture very often headed the religion of their kingdoms as chief priests; in some cases they were viewed as divine or pseudo-divine. Biblical texts reflecting this shift place limits on a king's ability to serve as the ultimate religious authority of his kingdom (Deut 17:14–20) or condemn kingship outright (1 Sam 8:11–18). However, for much of the monarchic period, kingship was conceived in terms of the establishment of a *covenantal tradition between YHWH and King *David (2 Sam 7). The establishment of a central *Temple and Temple cult in *Jerusalem under David's son *Solomon (1 Kgs 5–8) firmly bound religion to the royal line. Much of the poetry in the book of *Psalms derives from the religious world of the Jerusalem Temple, which was understood as the center of the sacred cosmos and the portal between the human and divine realms. Israel's kings were thus imbued with a sacred status and held important cultic responsibilities. After the schism between north and south in 922 BCE, similar characteristics are to be found among the kings of *Israel, the northern kingdom (Amos 7:12–13; see ISRAELITES: KINGSHIP).

ROLE OF PROPHETS: With the shift to monarchy, prophets emerge more distinctly as YHWH's human spokespersons, perhaps to keep the king in check and to maintain religious and ethical standards. Many biblical passages suggest that the prophetic role was primarily to inaugurate or legitimize kings when they came to power and chastise them if they fell short of their duties as a representative of the people. Prophets thus provided independent and direct access to divine will in response to royal and priestly practices; they mediated between the king and his royal court on the one hand and YHWH and his heavenly court on the other. Much of the Bible's prophetic tradition constitutes sharp criticism of abuses of power. A significant number of prophets also appear to have strong connections to the priests who had ties to the clan system of the pre-monarchic period; these were the rural Levites whose socio-religious influence had been challenged by the elite royal institutions. The prophetic critiques of the royal court and the Temple priesthood may have been spearheaded by these Levites (see, for example, the oracles of *Hosea), who argued that the influence of the monarchy had compromised the integrity of the nation's fidelity to YHWH and corrupted its venerable ritual and ethical institutions (see BIBLE: PROPHETS AND PROPHECY).

After the conquest and destruction of the northern kingdom between 734–721 BCE by the *Assyrian Empire, the prophetic critique became a central part of Israelite religion, adopted by the surviving royal court in Jerusalem and worked by its scribes into a system of state-sponsored religious and ethical instruction during the second half of the reign of King *Hezekiah (715–685 BCE). The fall of Israel demonstrated what YHWH required: allegiance to the ruling family in Jerusalem and deference to its Temple cult. Partly as a result of Jerusalem's survival against an Assyrian military campaign that devastated the surrounding Judean countryside in the year 701 BCE, the belief in Jerusalem's special divine status was amplified at this time. Nevertheless, the kingdom of *Judah remained under the political domination of Assyria for almost a century, and Assyrian culture invariably influenced state religion.

As Assyrian power waned in 627 BCE, the Deuteronomistic movement surfaced in Jerusalem to purge Assyrian influence and outdated clan-based practices from Israelite religion. This group was an amalgam of royal administrators and Levites active during the reign of King *Josiah (640–609 BCE); they likely produced the book of *Deuteronomy (presented as the farewell address of Moses from centuries earlier) and attempted to reform Israelite society according to its ideology and laws. This reform involved the elimination of the ancestral cult and the suppression of the worship of fertility goddesses, the centralization of all ritual activity in Jerusalem, and the uncompromised adherence of every Israelite to the laws in Deuteronomy, all of which were apparently sponsored by King Josiah himself. According to 2 Kings 22, the king's agents discovered a version of Deuteronomy in 622 BCE while cleaning the *Temple of foreign influence, and it is indeed at this time that a more literary and intellectual form of dedication surfaces in Israelite religion. Deuteronomy constantly stresses its status as a sacred book and intellectual curriculum for all Israelites (6:5–9, 31:9–13). During this time, written texts began to eclipse sacrifice and Temple ritual as the focus of Israelite religion and many earlier and contemporaneous prophetic works and historical traditions were redacted and published (see also TEMPLE AND TEMPLE CULT; and WORSHIP).

After Josiah's untimely death in 609 BCE, the radical nature of the Deuteronomic reform became the center of religious debate between the Levites and scribal administrators who supported it and the royal sages and Jerusalem priests who advocated a return to older ideas regarding sacred kingship and the mythic status of the Jerusalem Temple. The destruction of Jerusalem and the exile of its population into *Babylon in 587 BCE, however, ended this disagreement (see BABYLONIAN EXILE). Although a large number of people were taken captive into Mesopotamia, many more remained behind in the land, fleeing for the most part to the region immediately north of Judah to avoid military confrontation with the Babylonian army. These sur-

vivors continued to worship YHWH at traditional shrines and at the ruins of the Jerusalem Temple (Jer 41); by contrast, the exiled population faced different challenges.

During the exilic period (587–538 BCE), many religious changes emerged, including the understanding that YHWH was not just Israel's deity but the only existing deity (see Isa 44:6). Furthermore, the institution of the Temple, physically destroyed in 587 BCE, was developed by exilic writers such as the prophet *Ezekiel into the basis for a complex cosmology. Ezekiel wrote that the metaphysical, holy divine presence evacuated the physical shell of the Temple even before the Babylonians destroyed it, but that it would return from the heavens when the exile was over and reestablish itself in a rebuilt Jerusalem (Ezek 1; 40–48). Since geographical location no longer defined Jewish identity, many scholars view the exilic and post-exilic periods as the time when many behavioral norms such as *Sabbath observance and *dietary laws received greater attention as markers of communal/national identity. Finally, although members of the Davidic royal house survived into the exilic and post-exilic periods, none managed to reclaim a position of significant religious and political authority. Hence, the concept of a powerful, divinely sponsored king ruling from his throne in Jerusalem became an eschatological *messianic idea: a descendant of David who would eventually appear and restore the fortunes of the nation at some time in the distant future.

POST-EXILIC PERIOD: In the place of an autonomous king ruling from Jerusalem, the Jerusalem priesthood emerged in the post-exilic period as the major religious authorities for Jews throughout the *Persian world – restored to their rebuilt Temple (completed in 516 BCE) and promulgating a systematized collection of sacred Scripture as the highest code of Jewish law, with the support of the Persian empire (Ezra 7:25–26; Neh 8). This is when Israelite religion develops into early Judaism, characterized by a decline in prophecy, dominated by the Jerusalem priesthood and its ritual/liturgical system, and practiced by a variety of dissident sects that would debate the meaning of their common Israelite religious heritage for several centuries to come.

For further reading, see F. M. Cross Jr., *Canaanite Myth and Hebrew Epic* (1973); J. D. Levenson, *Sinai and Zion: An Entry into the Jewish Bible* (1985); Z. Zevit, *The Religions of Ancient Israel: A Synthesis of Parallactic Aproaches* (2001); S. Ackerman, *Warrior, Dancer, Seductress, Queen: Women in Judges and Biblical Israel* (1998); and M. S. Smith, *The Early History of God: Yahweh and the Other Deities in Ancient Israel* (2nd ed., 2002).
MARK LEUCHTER

Israelites: Tribes. According to the *Torah, the twelve tribes of Israel stem from *Jacob's twelve sons: Reuben, Simeon, Levi, Judah, Dan, Naphtali, Gad, Asher, Issachar, Zebulun, Joseph, and Benjamin. The fact that the twelve are conceived amidst a competition between two sisters, *Rachel and *Leah, works etiologically to explain why conflict sometimes arises among the tribes. Leah gives birth to Reuben, Simeon, Levi, Judah, Issachar, and Zebulun, as well as to a daughter, *Dinah. Leah also claims Gad and Asher, the sons of Zilpah, her servant and surrogate, as her descendants. Rachel similarly absorbs Dan and Naphtali, born to her servant Bilhah. After contending with prolonged barrenness, Rachel gives birth to Joseph and Benjamin. However, a dozen sons and one daughter may not be the extent of Jacob's family because he is recorded immigrating to *Egypt with sons and daughters (Gen 46:7, 46:15).

The notion of twelve tribes informs the organization of Israel's camp during the period of wandering in the wilderness. Clustered according to their ancestral mothers, the Leah tribes of Judah, Issachar, and Zebulun set up camp on the east end of the *Tabernacle (mishkan) and the Rachel tribes of Benjamin, Ephraim, and Manasseh camp on the west. To the south, the Leah tribes of Reuben and Simeon reside with Gad, a Zilpah tribe, and to the north the Zilpah tribe of Asher camps alongside the Bilhah tribes of Naphtali and Dan (Num 2). The tribe of Levi does not figure among the cardinal directions, but rather assumes a central position along the peripheries of the Tabernacle. The number twelve is maintained by the splitting of Joseph into the tribes of Ephraim and Manasseh, named for Joseph's sons.

The tribal structure determines the territorial allotments meted out by *Joshua after the conquest of the land (Josh 13–19). The tribal schisms mentioned in the book of *Judges are more or less bridged during the duration of the United Monarchy (see ISRAELITES: KINGSHIP), but after King *Solomon's death the country splits into the northern kingdom of *Israel and the southern kingdom of *Judah. When the northern kingdom falls to *Assyria, its constitutive tribes are lost. Judah withstands Assyrian incursion, but eventually falls at the hands of the *Babylonian Empire. A significant number of those exiled by the Babylonians return, rebuild the *Temple in *Jerusalem, and reconstitute the state of Judah under *Persian rule.

Despite the coherence of the biblical account, scholars doubt its historicity. The story of twelve sons born to rival wives was likely formulated to account for the social organization of the tribes. How then did the tribal structure come into being? The question can be approached through various development models proposed by scholars, as well as by examining biblical texts that represent a tribal confederation. The archeological record does not comport with the account of the Israelites coming from a distance to invade the east and west banks of the Jordan. Some suggest that the tribes formed during the Late Bronze Age when Egyptian power diminished, leaving a power vacuum in *Canaan (see ARCHEOLOGY: ANCIENT TIMES THROUGH THE PERSIAN PERIOD). A theory popularized by Norman Gottwald proposes that an egalitarian tribal system resulted from a peasant revolt that shook the Judean highlands. The archeologist and *Bible scholar Carol Meyers suggests that the Hebrew word shevet, commonly translated as tribe, more likely indicates a complex chiefdom that enabled equality in some spheres of life while operating hierarchically in others. Martin Noth analogizes the twelve tribes of Israel to the Greek league of twelve peoples that rallied around the sanctuary of Apollo at Delphi. He accounts for the number twelve as an attempt to have the social order mirror the cosmic order of a year, which is both a unit onto itself and a conglomerate of twelve months.

Most contemporary theories acknowledge a process in which families ensured their survival by banding together as a clan that in turn consolidated with other clans to form a tribe for purposes of self-protection (see ISRAELITES: MARRIAGE AND FAMILY). The tribe's founding is then often attributed to an eponymous ancestor as a means of confer-

ring historical legitimacy. Based on the repeated acknowledgment of the families that comprise the tribes (Num 1; 26), it seems that such a process led to both the rise of individual tribes and the stories of the twelve brothers. Tribal leadership, however, proved an insufficient bulwark against the encroachments of enemies such as the *Philistines. This prompted the institution of chieftains or judges. *Saul may well have begun as a chieftain whose early military successes led him to constitute a monarchical system. Although tribal affiliations competed with fealty to the king, the monarchy seems to have contributed to the erosion of tribal identity in favor of regional identity (see ISRAELITES: KINGSHIP).

The image of twelve tribes recurs in biblical poetry (see BIBLE: POETRY) such as Genesis 49, where Jacob's blessing of his sons provides glimpses into the unique characteristics of each tribe. Whereas in Genesis 49 the recipients of blessing are the twelve sons, even though the content of the blessings speaks to tribal realities, in Deuteronomy 33 Moses gathers the tribes around him before he dies to bless them like sons. Levi appears in the roster of Deuteronomy 33, and Joseph figures as a singular tribe while Simeon is omitted. Scholars suggest that the omission of Simeon reflects the historical absorption of the tribe of Simeon by Judah. *Deborah, the judge and *prophet, addresses ten groups in the victory song of Judges 5. Some are familiar tribes such as Ephraim, Benjamin, Zebulun, Issachar, Naphtali, Reuben, Dan, and Asher, and others are alternately named Machir and Gilead. Machir and Gilead are figures associated with the eastern half of the tribe of Manasseh (Num 26:29, 32:39–40; Deut 3:15; Josh 13:29-31 [where Machir is a synonym for the tribe of Manasseh]; Josh 17:1). The omission of Simeon, Judah, and Levi in Judges 5 is noteworthy because it implies a northern provenance, perhaps before the rise of the tribe of Judah or the unification of northern and southern tribes.

Biblical narrative records ritual acts in which the number twelve symbolically represents the tribes. Moses builds an altar with twelve pillars during the *revelation at Sinai (Exod 24:4), and Joshua sets up a twelve-stone memorial after the national crossing of the Jordan (Josh 4:5–8). Twelve precious stones are inlaid in four rows on the breastplate worn by the High Priest (Exod 28:15–21, 39:8–14). In his vision of a restored Israel, the prophet *Ezekiel sees the land parceled out in twelve equal portions for the tribes of Dan, Asher, Naphtali, Manasseh, Ephraim, Reuben, Judah, Benjamin, Simeon, Issachar, Zebulun, and Gad, with the *priests and Levites situated at a sacred center and the strangers among Israel enjoying equal citizenship and property rights (Ezek 47–48).

For further reading, see N. Gottwald, *The Tribes of Yahweh: A Sociology of the Religion of Liberated Israel 1250–1050 B.C.E* (1979); Z. Kallai, *Historical Geography of the Bible: The Tribal Territories of Israel* (1986); and C. Meyers, "Tribes and Tribulations: Retheorizing Earliest 'Israel,'" in *Tracking the Tribes of Yahweh: On the Trail of a Classic*, ed. R. Boer (2002).

RACHEL HAVRELOCK

Isserles, Moses (1520–1572), known as the Rema, was a prominent rabbi and halakhic scholar in Kraków, *Poland. His major works include *Darkhei Moshe* (Ways of Moses), a commentary on the fourteenth-century *Arba'ah Turim* of *Jacob ben Asher. Isserles admired the *Shulḥan Arukh* (Set Table) of his contemporary Joseph *Karo, but realized that because this code privileged *Sephardic practice it would not be useful for *Ashkenazic Jews. He remedied this problem by preparing a comprehensive commentary he called the *Mappah* (Tablecloth), which consisted of notes (*haggahot*) inserted in Karo's text indicating where Ashkenazic rulings differed from Sephardic ones and including Ashkenazic *customs (*minhagim*). These notes first appeared in print in the Kraków edition of the *Shulḥan Arukh* (1571), in Rashi type to distinguish them from Karo's text. Isserles' *Mappah* defended both the notion of codification, which had been resisted by Ashkenazic scholars, and Karo's arrangement of Jewish law, enabling the *Shulḥan Arukh* to become a standard work of Jewish law up to the present. For further reading, see M. Berger, "The Centrality of Talmud," in *The Cambridge Guide to Jewish History, Religion, and Culture*, ed. J. R. Baskin and K. Seeskin (2010); **see also HALAKHAH.**

JUDITH R. BASKIN

Italy. Jews have lived in Italy for more than two thousand years. The first-century-CE statesman and writer Cicero blamed them for favoring Julius Caesar in factional Roman politics. Italian Jews, unlike Jews elsewhere in Europe, cannot be viewed as newcomers who settled among an already existing population. Indeed, Italian Jews have always spoken and written the vernacular, eaten local foods, and dressed as others, as artistic evidence reveals. The roots of Italian Jewish acculturation are deep, and one may ask who actually acculturated to whom. Roman Jews, for example, today maintain a cuisine dating back to the fifteenth century, if not earlier, and this food is commonly considered Rome's authentic fare. However, Jews did differ from their Italian neighbors in religion. This created friction, including socially, but it did not lead to attacks as occurred north of the Alps. The single notable massacre was a judicial one, at Trent in 1475, following a *ritual murder accusation. This was in territory that was part of the German Empire, where both Jews and others spoke a German dialect. Tensions as a rule were acted out in organized, even negotiated, annual "ritual stonings." The aim was to hurt no one or no thing, while proclaiming the "proper" social order of Christian dominance.

Rome has always been the site of a large Jewish community, and so was the south of the Italian peninsula until about 1500. *Ashkenazi (German) Jews, who lived in the medieval Rhineland, traced the roots of their culture to Apulia (southwest Italy through the heel of the boot) and to a mystical figure named Abu Aaron, who lived in the ninth century. Jewish communities stretched out along the Via Appia, which runs from Rome to Brindisi (in Apulia); this road was built by the ancient Romans and is still in use. There were numerous Jews in *Sicily. Southern Jewish communities were expelled in 1492, 1511, and (a remnant in Naples) in 1541; these areas were then under Spanish rule, and their fate was sealed by the expulsion order from *Spain of 1492. North of Rome, Jews are rarely mentioned until about the thirteenth century, when Jews were invited to open small loan banks, whose *condotta* (permits) required them to operate for periods of five to ten years. By the sixteenth century, Jewish communities were found throughout the north. Perhaps the best known northern community was in *Venice, where Jews settled formally only in 1516. The preexisting name of the island where Jews lived provided

the word "*ghetto," referring to an area restricted to Jewish habitation.

At the end of the sixteenth century, Jews were expelled from the Duchy of Lombardy (Milan), also a Spanish dependency, but important communities remained in Ferrara and Modena. The 1492 expulsion of Jews from Spain led to significant Jewish immigration to parts of Italy not under Spanish influence. Many of these Jews came to Italy after first stopping in the *Ottoman Empire. Ashkenazi Jews also emigrated from German-speaking Europe to northern Italy, beginning in the sixteenth century. Many who settled in Venice Italianized their names; for example, Lausitz became Luzzatti, Esslingen became Ottolenghi, and Marburg, Morpurgo.

Newer Jews seem to have integrated rapidly into the native Jewish population, certainly in Rome. Marriage between Jewish groups of differing ethnic backgrounds was frequent; religious laws, both Jewish and Christian, made marriage between Jews and Christians legally impossible. Sicilian Jews, for instance, who arrived in Rome after 1492, seem to have had an active strategy of marrying into Italian and *Sephardi families. Other groups emulated them. By 1571, the Burial Society instructed people to choose the *'edah* (ethnic identity group) with which they wished to be formally associated. In Venice, where the *'edah* division was more rigid, the ghetto itself was divided into ethnic districts, based on the time of their founding; thus, there is an old, new, and most recent ghetto, whose borders are still clearly marked. Similarly, the various ethnic Jewish communities in the Venetian ghetto each had their own *synagogues. In Rome, the actual dimensions of the historic ghetto are no longer known because 95% of its buildings and roads were demolished in the late nineteenth century. The site, where 3,000 to 4,000 people had been crowded into about two city blocks, was considered unsanitary.

In the early Middle Ages, Oria in Apulia hosted a flourishing talmudic culture, as testified to by the eleventh century liturgical poet Aḥimaaz ben Paltiel (see POETRY, LITURGICAL). Italian Jewish intellectual flowering came in waves, notably in Rome in the twelfth through fourteenth centuries and in places like Ferrara, Mantua, and Venice during the later Renaissance. Zerahiah Ḥen (thirteenth century), Hillel of Verona (ca. 1220-c.1295), and Judah Romano (c. 1293-after 1330) wrote philosophical and mystical works; Joseph ha-Kohen, Solomon ibn Verga (fifteenth and sixteenth centuries), and Azariah dei *Rossi (1513–1578) are known for their historical writings. Other important writers include Leon *Modena, the belle lettrist Immanuel of Rome (ca. 1261-ca.1328), and Simone Luzzatto (1583–1663). The baroque music of Salamone Rossi continues to be played today. During the later ghetto period, about the eighteenth century, intellectual life reached its nadir. So did the status of women, the various rights Jewish law accorded them having been reduced by the force of local Roman law, known as *ius commune*. Family size was generally small, with two to four surviving children.

Italian Jews, *loazim*, as they are known in Hebrew, are Italians, neither *Ashkenazim nor *Sephardim. Their culture has undergone successive modifications influenced by various immigrant waves. Special Italian synagogue music has a Sephardi influence, alongside that from Gregorian chant. The *shofar is blown in continuous undulating notes, and at the end of *Yom Kippur, the *Torah scrolls are removed from the ark, just as at *kol nidrei*. A *mizmarah*, an evening of song and study, is celebrated to honor the birth of daughters in lieu of the *circumcision party for the birth of a son. Roman Jews in the Middle Ages perfected Judeo-Italiano, a mode of Italian mixed with many Hebrew words. Centuries later, they developed Judeo-Romanesco, a more local meld of Roman speech and Hebrew. Neither of these two became a real language like *Yiddish. Jewish family names are often after small Italian towns, like di Segni and di Tivoli. These mostly distinctive names are easily recognized by all Italians.

The end of the Italian ghettos, which occurred at various moments during the nineteenth century depending on locale, signaled a rush to strong acculturation and assimilation, and sometimes baptism. Ironically, baptism rates were much higher than during the ghetto era, when the Catholic Church had applied significant conversionary pressures, virtually kidnapping potential converts. However, when racial laws were announced by Mussolini in 1938, few Christians protested. Later, Italian Fascists sometimes outdid the *Nazi SS in cruelty. This is not to lessen the importance of the enormous aid furnished by the many Italian Christians who hid or otherwise assisted Jews during the German occupation in 1943 and 1944. Of the approximately 50,000 Jews in Italy before the war, about 7,000 to 8,000 perished, mostly at *Auschwitz. While this is a high number, it is a low percentage compared to the devastation in countries like Holland (see AMSTERDAM; and HOLOCAUST). On October 16, 1943, the Germans raided the area of Jewish residence in Rome, mostly where the ghetto had stood, and arrested more than two thousand Jews. Despite continuing denials, the truth is that Pope Pius did little to save these people, who were detained in (what is still) the army's military college, which can be seen from the windows of the papal apartments in the nearby Vatican.

In the first decade of the twenty-first century, Italian Jewry numbers about 30,000, half of whom live in Rome; this community is mostly of Italian origin. The community in Milan, also large, has a large component of immigrants from the rest of Europe and also from *North Africa, *Iraq, and *Iran. Communities like Venice, Bologna, Pisa, Livorno (Leghorn), and Naples number in the hundreds or one or two thousand. As elsewhere in the West, *intermarriage is common.

For further reading, see D. Ruderman, *Essential Papers on Jewish Culture in Renaissance and Baroque Italy* (1992); idem, *Kabbalah, Magic, and Science: The Cultural Universe of a Sixteenth Century Jewish Physician* (1988); A. Stille, *Benevolence and Betrayal: Five Italian Families under Fascism*; and A. Sacerdoti, *The Guide to Jewish Italy* (2004). **Maps 4, 8, 10**

KENNETH STOW

Iyar is the second month of the Jewish calendar, equivalent to April and/or May of the Gregorian calendar. Special days in Iyar include Lag B'Omer (Iyar 18; see OMER) and *Yom Ha-Atzma'ut (Israel's Independence Day; Iyar 5). **see also CALENDAR; CALENDAR: MONTHS OF THE YEAR.**

J

Jacob (also known as Israel) is the younger son of *Isaac and *Rebekah and the father of sons who would become the eponymous founders of the *Israelite tribes. Jacob is a central character of *Genesis 25:19–35:29; he plays a smaller role in *Joseph's story, primarily with his deathbed testament (Gen 49). A subversive, trickster figure, Jacob struggles with his twin brother *Esau in their mother's womb, and God tells Rebekah that "the elder shall serve the younger"(25:23). At birth, Jacob attempts to supplant his older brother by gripping Esau's heel (Hebrew, *akev*, a folk etymology for *ya'akov*) and later dupes him into selling his birthright (Hebrew, *berakhah*). Rebekah helps Jacob trick his elderly father into offering him the blessing due to Esau. When a devastated Esau responds with anger, Jacob flees to Haran in *Mesopotomia. En route, Jacob encounters God in a vision of angels at a place he names *Beth El (28:10–22). In Haran, his relationship with his uncle Laban is characterized by duplicity and struggle. Jacob seeks to marry Laban's younger daughter *Rachel, but after seven years of labor, Laban tricks Jacob by sending his older daughter *Leah into Jacob's marital tent. Jacob marries Rachel shortly thereafter, but must pay for her with another seven years of labor. Jacob has seven children with Leah, two each with his wives' maidservants Bilhah and Zilpah, and two with Rachel after a long period of infertility. When Jacob and his family set out to return to his homeland, they spend a night at the Jabbok River, where Jacob wrestles with a "man" (in other traditions, an "angel"; cf. Hosea 12:5). In this climactic scene, literally a crossing, Jacob is transformed. He prevails through direct struggle, not trickery, and the man renames him "Israel" (perhaps, "one who strives with God"). Afterward, Jacob reunites with Esau and offers him not deception but a "gift" (Hebrew, *berakhah* [33:11]) as reconciliation.

Jacob's narrative is a structured literary creation that makes use of folkloric motifs but is not a folktale itself; it exhibits thematic and symbolic links with its literary context in Genesis and beyond. Thus Jacob's exile and return offer a microcosm of the entire *Pentateuch, indeed of the entire Hebrew *Bible. Further, Jacob's tale illustrates a significant motif in Genesis – the election of the younger son over the older – which is an indication of the divine role in human events (Abel over Cain, Isaac over Ishmael, Joseph over his brothers, Ephraim over Manasseh). The conflict between brothers stands in for the uneasy relationship between Israel and *Edom (cf. Gen 36). Most important, Jacob represents the familial unity of all Israel, particularly insofar as his narrative role as the father of twelve sons parallels his symbolic role as the parent of the twelve tribes (Gen 49). These dual roles are in evidence in the frequent references to Jacob outside of Genesis. In poetic texts (e.g., Deut 32 and *Psalms) and the *Prophets (most frequently Deutero-*Isaiah), the name "Jacob" (to the exclusion of the other two patriarchs) becomes a poetic term for the nation or people of Israel. For further reading, see S. Niditch, *A Prelude to Biblical Folklore:*

Underdogs and Tricksters (2nd ed., 2000); and M. Fishbane, *Text and Texture: Close Readings of Selected Biblical Texts* (1979).

SEAN BURT

Jacob ben Asher (ca. 1270–ca. 1340) was a halakhic authority. Born in *Germany, he accompanied his father,*Asher ben Jeḥiel (the Rosh), to Toledo, Spain (see SPAIN, CHRISTIAN), at the beginning of the fourteenth century. He is known as Baal ha-Turim (master of the rows) after his major halakhic work, *Arba'ah Turim* (The Four Rows). In this volume Jacob ben Asher arranged *halakhah and *customs pertinent to interpersonal relationships and communal conduct in four sections. *Oraḥ Ḥayyim* is concerned with blessings, prayers, the Sabbath, festivals, and fasts; *Yoreh De'ah* covers dietary and ritual slaughter laws, among others; *Even ha-Ezer* deals with family law; and *Ḥoshen Mishpat* addresses civil law and ethical prescriptions. The *Arba'ah Turim*, which includes Franco-German legal decisions along with those of Spain, was widely accepted throughout the *Diaspora and remains a standard code of Jewish law (see *Halakhah*). He was also the author/editor of a Torah commentary focusing on *peshat* interpretation (see BIBLICAL COMMENTARY: FROM THE MIDDLE AGES TO 1800); he left an *ethical will for his children, an excerpt of which appears in I. Abrahams' classic collection, *Hebrew Ethical Wills* (1926, 2006).

JUDITH R. BASKIN

Jamaica. When *Columbus arrived at the *Caribbean island of Jamaica in 1494, on his second voyage to the new world, his crew included at least three *conversos*: Marco, the surgeon; Luis de Torres, the interpreter; and Mestre Bernal, the physician. From 1594 to 1655 (when the island was conquered by *Britain), a few Jews of Iberian origin lived in Jamaica, calling themselves Portuguese merchants. Because Jamaica did not fall under the bishopric of Cuba, they were safe from the *Inquisition. After the British conquest, these Jews were permitted to stay; they built a *synagogue in Port Royal that was destroyed in the earthquake of 1692. The Jewish community then moved to Kingston and later to Spanish Town.

Jamaica's Jewish presence increased beginning in the 1660s; by 1769 Spanish Town's Jewish population included three hundred individuals, making it the third-largest Jewish community in the English-speaking world, exceeded only by London and Charleston, South Carolina. *Ashkenazim arrived in Jamaica by 1780, and they then built their own synagogues. There have been at least nine synagogues in Jamaica at various times and perhaps a tenth one in Port Royal, replacing the synagogue destroyed in 1692 (J. A. P. M. Andrade, *A Record of the Jews in Jamaica* [1941]); a number of cemeteries survive (R. D. Barnett and P. Wright, *The Jews of Jamaica – Tombstone Inscriptions 1663–1880* [1997]). Most Jamaican Jews were urban merchants who owned a few slaves; a few Jews played minor roles in the slave trade as consignees; that is, agents responsible for auctioning off newly arrived Africans and transporting them to their new masters (Faber).

In 1831, Jamaican Jews achieved full political rights, and all discriminatory laws and taxes were rescinded; over the next decades, significant numbers of Jews held political office. After emancipation in 1838, a shortage of labor and a decline in sugar production resulted in many Jews leaving the island. A major fire in Kingston in 1882 destroyed two newly built synagogues (one *Sephardic and the other Ashkenazic). An amalgamation of both congregations, henceforth known as the United Congregation of Israelites, occurred in 1921. The community's remaining synagogue, Shaarei Shalom, on Duke Street in Kingston, was originally built in 1885; that edifice was destroyed in the earthquake and fire of 1907 and rebuilt in 1912. At the beginning of the twenty-first century the community remains active with approximately two hundred members. It uses the Spanish/Portuguese ritual, although blessings recited before reading from the *Torah and the *birkhat kohanim* on the afternoon of *Yom Kippur follow Ashkenazic tradition. The orientation of the congregation has changed from *Orthodox to Liberal, and it is affiliated with the Liberal Jewish Congregations of the Caribbean and Latin America. The Torah scrolls and communal silver remain at the synagogue.

Jamaican Jews who have been active in the arts include the early-nineteenth-century artist, Isaac Mendes Belisario; musician Sir Frederic Hyman Cowen; and the nineteenth-century actor, Morton Tavares. For further reading, see E. Faber, *Jews, Slaves and the Slave Trade* (1998); M. Arbell, *The Portuguese Jews of Jamaica* (2000); and M. Delevante and A. Alberga, *The Island of One People: A History of the Jews in Jamaica* (2006).   ANTHONY MACFARLANE

Jeremiah is the second of the major prophetic books (see BIBLE: PROPHETS AND PROPHECY; PROPHETS [*NEVI'IM*]). According to Jeremiah 1:1–3, the prophet was active from the thirteenth year of the reign of *Josiah (627 BCE) until the fall of *Jerusalem in 587/586 BCE. References to Josiah in the book are scant, however, and the prophet's flourishing seems to have been subsequent to the king's death at Megiddo in 609 BCE until just after Nebuchadnezzar's conquest of Jerusalem. Jeremiah is also identified as descended from priests of Anathoth (1:1), a village in the northeastern environs of Jerusalem. Narrative passages recall his patronage by Jerusalemite scribes, particularly the house of Shaphan (26:24, 36:10–12), who were involved in the discovery of the *Deuteronomic code (2 Kgs 22). Jeremiah's mixed priestly and scribal background is reflected in his poetry where he appears conversant with priestly traditions (Jer 2:3/Lev 22:14–16; Jer 4:23–26/Gen 1), as well as with the poetic and legal corpora that were influential for the Deuteronomists (e.g., Jer 8:19/Deut 32:21; Jer 3:1/Deut 24:1–4).

The book contains *poetry purporting to be the words of Jeremiah himself, as well as prose stories and legends about the prophet. Several sections of poetry are organized topically. These include statements delivered on the occasion of a drought (14:1–15:9), an anthology of oracles related to the topic of kingship (21:11–23:8; see ISRAELITES: KINGSHIP), and various statements on prophecy (23:9–40). Chapters 46–51 are a discrete collection of oracles against foreign nations. Other subsections are more difficult to isolate. Jeremiah 2–6 has some internal cohesion, relating a sequence of prophecies of judgment against the kingdoms of *Israel and *Judah using the language of the *covenantal lawsuit (*rîv*). Chapters 30–31 are similarly cohesive, preserving a series of restoration oracles. Chapters 37–45 are predominantly biographical prose with brief poetic sections interspersed.

Other layers of the book are not so well integrated. Personal laments relating the prophet's emotional distress are distributed throughout Jeremiah 11–20 (11:18–23; 12:1–6; 15:10–14, 15–21; 17:14–18; 18:18–23; 20:7–13, 14–18). A loose collection of stories describing symbolic actions performed by the prophet or his proxy are also present (e.g., 13:1–11, 16:1–4, 18:1–12, 19:1–15, 27:1–28:17, 32:6–15, 35:1–19, 36:1–32, 43:8–13; cf. 51:59–64). Two epistles supposedly written by the prophet appear in Jeremiah 29 and 45, and Jeremiah 52 concludes the book with a historical appendix (ch. 52), which is duplicated in 2 *Kings 24:18–25:30.

Given this literary diversity, the book is best regarded as a compendium of materials by and about Jeremiah. Although Jeremiah 36 describes how the prophet's collected sayings were written down, the story has been influenced by important Deuteronomic texts such as 2 Kings 22 and Deuteronomy 17, and its historical value is suspect. Baruch ben Neriah is mentioned as a scribe attending the prophet (32:9–15, 36:4–19, 43:1–7, 45:1–5), but his role is controversial, and the texts mentioning him cannot be used as historical data. The presence of both thematic and terminological doublets (e.g., 7:3–15/ 26:2–6; 23:5–6/ 33:14–16) suggests the book's complex literary pre-history. Possibly, Judean refugees in *Egypt and *Babylon separately preserved recollections of Jeremiah, and their literary traditions were combined over a protracted period, in part under the influence of Deuteronomic thinkers.

Despite its complicated formation process and the unevenness of its contents, a clear and coherent voice speaks from the text. Jeremiah's poetic style favors concise, cadenced wordplays (1:10, 20:3, among others), often playing creatively on a single verb (2:5, 17:14). Such structures are frequently built into more elaborate oracles that suggest complex logical relationships (8:4–12). Jeremiah presents vivid images (4:3–4) and sometimes develops more elaborate poems around them (10:1–16, 20:7–12). A master rhetorician, he cites the positions of his interlocutors and attempts to answer the objections of his audience (e.g., 13:20–27). Only *Amos (ch. 3) compares to Jeremiah in his degree of intellectual engagement with his audience.

Jeremiah's literary style reflects his situation in the final days of the Judean monarchy, after the initial deportation of 597 BCE. He sought to prepare Judeans for a new way of living as a community without the mediating institutions of *Temple (3:16–18, 7:21–23) and palace (23:1–4). He drew on *Hosea's language (e.g., Hosea 2) to describe *God in patriarchal terms (Jer 2–3), even as he criticized traditional patriarchal authority (30:4–7, 31:18–22). In the process, Jeremiah overturned well-established ideas of collective guilt and trans-generational punishment (31:29–20; cf. Ezek 18:1–32). For Jeremiah each person was an ethically responsible individual. The prophet imagined a radically new sort of covenantal relationship between God and Israel that did not depend on written laws, but was realized as an internal ethical ideal within each person (31:31–34).

Jeremiah had a profound impact on Israelite cultural life and on the formation of the Hebrew *Bible. *Ezra 1:1 attributes to Jeremiah a prediction of restoration based on statements such as 25:11 and 29:10. The prophet's assurances that God would one day restore Israel and Judah (e.g., 31:7–14) were probably a source of comfort to Judean refugees in *Babylonian exile. This influence is evident in the development of Deutero-*Isaiah in which poems like Jeremiah 20:7–12 were adapted to give voice to the exiles' own suffering (e.g., Isa 50:4–9; cf., Jer 11:19/Isa 53:7–8). This community also preserved legends that Jeremiah had hidden the accoutrements of the Temple before Nebuchadnezzar's conquest (2 *Macc 2:1–8; cf. Jer 31:33). Further, the author of *Job drew extensively on Jeremiah's biography and his poetry to construct the figure of the righteous sufferer (see Job 3/Jer 20:14–18).

Important research includes W. L. Holladay, *Jeremiah 2: A Commentary on the Book of the Prophet Jeremiah, Chapters 26–52* (1989); B. D. Sommer, *A Prophet Reads Scripture: Allusion in Isaiah 40–66* (1998); and E. L. Greenstein, "Jeremiah as an Inspiration to the Poet of Job," in *Inspired Speech: Prophecy in the Ancient Near East*, ed. J. Kaltner and L. Stuhlman (2004), 98–110.   EDWARD SILVER

Jericho, located just north of the Dead Sea, is mentioned often in the Hebrew *Bible. Located on an ancient trade route, Jericho, which has abundant water and a temperate climate, is considered one of the oldest cities in the world, extending back at least ten thousand years. Archeologists have uncovered more than twenty settlement layers (see ARCHEOLOGY, LAND OF ISRAEL: ANCIENT TIMES TO PERSIAN PERIOD). Jericho figures in the biblical account of Israelite conquest and settlement. *Joshua's spies, who are sent to reconnoiter Jericho, are saved from capture by the harlot Rahab, who states her belief in the power and uniqueness of Israel's God (Josh 2). Joshua 6 describes the Israelite conquest of the city, in which all living creatures in Jericho, except for Rahab and her family, were destroyed (Josh 6). However, archeological evidence does not support the biblical account; the city walls appear to have been destroyed at some time around 1550 BCE, several centuries earlier than any likely Israelite settlement. Two *synagogues from the *Byzantine period have been found near Jericho, both with mosaic floors with Jewish symbols. Contemporary Jericho is a *Palestinian city on the occupied West Bank, with a population of 25,000. **Map 2**   KATE FRIEDMAN

Jeroboam challenged the leadership of *Rehoboam, the son of King *Solomon, at *Shechem after Solomon's death. When Rehoboam refused to lessen the heavy taxes that Solomon had imposed, Jeroboam led the secession of ten of the Israelite tribes from the *United Monarchy and founded the kingdom of *Israel (1 Kgs 12:4, 16–20; 2 Chron 10:4). Jeroboam went on to reign for twenty-two years, first from Shechem and then from Tirzah. According to biblical sources, Jeroboam established shrines at Dan and *Beth El where golden calves were worshiped (1 Kgs 12:28–29).

Jerusalem: Biblical and Rabbinic Sources. Biblical sources largely focus on Jerusalem's history from *David's time forward (ca. 1000 BCE). However, extrabiblical literary and archeological data, as well as a few biblical references, provide scattered details about the city's pre-Israelite history. Remnants of houses from the third millennium have been found, although even in the second millennium the city's population was not large. Situated on a mount atop two hills and surrounded by valleys, the city was well protected and long had defensive walls and secure access to water (through the Gihon Spring). This made it an attractive location even though it was not directly on major trade routes.

*Egyptian texts from the second millennium call the city "Rushalimum" or "Urusalim." These names may refer to the god Salem, suggesting that the name may have originally meant "city of Salem." Enigmatic biblical references support this identification: *Abraham met Melchizedek of Salem after a battle (Gen 14:18), and Psalm 76:2 links "Salem" with "Zion" (see later discussion). Although Jerusalem sounds like *ir-shalom*, Hebrew for "city of peace," this appealing association has no etymological basis.

The name "Jerusalem" does not appear in the *Torah, although forward-looking hints are found in *Deuteronomy 12:5. Biblical references first appear in *Joshua 10:1 and 15:8 and in *Judges 1:8. After David's capture of the city around 1000 BCE, he made it his capital (2 Sam 5), settling an area on the southeastern part of the mount as the "City of David" (alternately called "*Zion," a pre-Israelite name for the extant fortress). Jerusalem's central location, between the northern and southern *Israelite tribes, in the territory of the minor tribe Benjamin, made it a wise choice for a capital. David elevated its status by situating the *Ark of the Covenant there (2 Sam 6). His son *Solomon famously built the *Temple, which became a center for *Israelite religion and was meant to replace all the other holy places throughout the land (1 Kgs 5–8). As the location of the Temple and kingship (see ISRAELITES: KINGSHIP), Jerusalem's preeminence in subsequent Jewish thought was secured.

Jerusalem was only briefly the capital of all the Israelite tribes. With the division of the unified kingdom around 930 BCE, Jerusalem became the capital city of *Judah, the southern kingdom. The city was repeatedly attacked: by Egyptians around 925 (1 Kgs 14); Arameans in the late ninth century (2 Kgs 12); and even by *Israel, the northern kingdom, in the early eighth century (2 Kgs 14). Some attacks were repulsed through the payment of tribute, although an *Assyrian conquest in 701 under Sennacherib was only barely averted by a plague. To *Hezekiah, the king, and the residents of Jerusalem this was a miracle (2 Kgs 19; Isa 36–37). Despite these vicissitudes, throughout the First Temple period the city remained the center of religious and political life in the south. It grew in population and size, especially under Hezekiah in the late eighth century, who built up its defensive walls and famously constructed a tunnel (discovered in 1838) to bring water into the city (2 Kgs 20:20).

The Bible describes widespread religious syncretism in the First Temple period. *Prophets condemned the worship of foreign gods, with minimal success (Isa 10:11; Jer 44:17). The Deuteronomistic history indicts nearly all the kings for promoting child sacrifice (2 Kgs 23:10) and worship of *Baal and *Asherah in the city (1 Kgs 16:32–33). Even the Temple itself was filled with idolatrous statues (2 Kgs 23:4; Ezek 8:6). A few kings attempted to purify the Temple and city (2 Kgs 18:4, 23:4–20), but their reforms were short-lived. *Babylonian invaders in 586 BCE sacked the city, and the

Temple burnt to the ground; biblical authors explain this devastation as divine punishment for idolatry (2 Kgs 24–25; Lam 1–5).

After the city was sacked, the Jerusalem elite were taken into *exile in Babylonia, although most residents were left behind. Presumably, no sacrifices were made on the ruined Temple Mount during the half-century of exile. With the fall of Babylonia to the *Persians in 539 BCE, this policy of forced exile was reversed, and (descendants of) the exiles were allowed to return. After a few decades, a modest new Temple was erected on the mount (Haggai 2:3). Only with the arrival of *Nehemiah, in the mid-fifth century, did major reconstruction and reorganization begin (Neh 2–6).

Jerusalem submitted to *Alexander the Great in 332 BCE to avoid destruction. After his death, control of Judea and Jerusalem passed first to the *Ptolemies (323–198 BCE) and then the *Seleucids (198–ca. 164 BCE). Both were generally tolerant, interfering minimally in internal affairs of subject peoples. They empowered Zadokite priests for religious and political leadership, in conformity with a biblical model favored by Jews as well. After the ascension of Antiochus IV in 175 this stability was upset. A *Hellenized Jewish elite, eager to join in Greek culture, rejected traditional religious rituals. They also constructed a gymnasium, the classic Greek educational institution, in Jerusalem (1 Macc 1:13–15). Antiochus, perhaps with their encouragement, banned observance of the laws in the *Torah (1 Macc 1:44–64) and interfered with priestly appointments (1 Macc 7:5; 2 Macc 4:7). He then sacked the city, desecrated the Temple, and constructed a garrison for troops. The *Hasmonean family led a revolt and retook the Temple in 164, eventually gaining control over Judea, although foreign troops were not completely removed from Jerusalem until ca. 141 BCE. The Hasmoneans remained in power through 63 BCE, fortifying Jerusalem, extending its walls, and building a palace (the *Letter of *Aristeas* 83–120 may be a contemporary description).

Jewish sovereignty ended in 63 BCE, with the arrival of the *Romans under Pompey. To the dismay of the Jews, who permitted the High Priest alone to enter the Temple's Holy of Holies one day a year, Pompey freely walked in, vividly symbolizing Jerusalem's subjugation. The land was placed under Roman administrators, who also appointed puppet rulers, most famously *Herod the Great (reigned from 37–4 BCE); Herod dramatically increased the size and grandeur of the city, constructing a new palace, massive towers, and aqueducts. According to *Josephus, he replaced the existing Temple with a new structure of monumental proportions on an enlarged mount (*Jewish Antiquities* 15:380–425) and also constructed pools and tombs outside the city and theaters for pagan-style games, despite widespread Jewish opposition.

Not long after Herod's rebuilding project was finished, the city and Temple were razed during the First *Jewish War against Rome (66–70 CE). The Temple was leveled; only a retaining wall of the mount ("the Western Wall") remained. The destruction of the altar at the one authorized cult site meant that sacrifices could no longer be offered, a prohibition observed to this day. The three perimeter walls around the city were destroyed, and much of the city was burned down (*Josephus, *Jewish War* 6:149–266). Under Emperor Hadrian, a second revolt, led by *Bar Kokhba, broke out (132–35 CE), possibly fired by a desire to reconstruct the Temple. It, too, was ultimately repressed by Rome, with further destruction to the city. The city was renamed Aelia Capitolina, in honor of Hadrian (whose family name was Aelius) and the Capitoline gods. As punishment, Jews may have been banned from entering the city after the war for decades (Justin, *Dialogue* 16). The city was rebuilt in Roman style, with pagan temples, forums, baths, and a grid system of streets. Eventually, Jews trickled back into the city, and we learn from fourth-century *Christian sources of regular visitors and a few synagogues (Jerome; the Bordeaux pilgrim; see also JT *Pesaḥim* 7:11). The Temple was not rebuilt, and the mount remained in ruins until the advent of *Islam in the seventh century. The emerging rabbinic movement was mostly centered north of the city, in the *Galilee.

JERUSALEM IN JEWISH TRADITION: Veneration of Jerusalem goes back to its early association with David, as the "city of the great king" (Ps 48:2). Its political significance was augmented by the presence of the Temple, which made it the religious center as well. Although Jewish tradition never limited God's presence to any one place, Jerusalem nonetheless was unique, for it was there that "the glory of the Lord" (1 Kgs 8:11) and the "name" of God dwelled (Deut 12:5). It was a city "chosen" by God (Zech 3:2; Ps 132:13) and "the holy city" (Dan 9:24; Neh 11:1). Residents trusted that they would be protected from military and natural threats (Isa 31:5, 37:35). The faithful made regular pilgrimages to the city to offer sacrifices during the *festivals (Deut 16:16; cf. Luke 2:41). Many *psalms celebrate travel to Jerusalem. The "Psalms of Ascent" (120–134), likely recited by those entering the city, refer to the rituals of the *priests and the royal throne. Those living outside the land yearned to be in Jerusalem (Isa 27:13; Ps 137). *Diaspora Jews revered the city and Temple, sending regular contributions for its upkeep and making *pilgrimages (*Philo, *Gaius* 281; Acts 2:5–11).

Jews described Jerusalem in cosmic and fanciful language. It was the "navel of the earth," from which the world was created (Ezek 38:12; Jubilees 8:19; *Sibylline Oracles 5:247). Solomon's Temple is said to have been constructed on the same spot where *Abraham nearly sacrificed *Isaac (2 Chron 3:1). *Garden of Eden imagery is applied to the city (1 Enoch 26), and basic geography was ignored: Although Jerusalem was not the highest spot in the region, it was said to be "up in the heights" (Ps 68:19). Regardless of where one began one's voyage, when traveling to the city, one was said to "ascend" (Ezra 1:3). Although it was not the largest or most significant city in the region, Jerusalem was said to be "in the midst of nations, with countries round about her" (Ezek 5:5). It was in Jerusalem that the great events of the final days would occur and the dispersed would be gathered together in a city purged of idolatry and wrongdoing (Jer 31; Joel 4). *Ezekiel predicted a new Temple, of incomparably greater glory and size, to be built on the spot of the destroyed Temple (40–48). Not only Israel but all the nations would go up to Jerusalem to worship the one true *God (Isa 2:3; Zech 8:22, 14:16; Tobit 13:11; Sibylline Oracles 3:710–23).

Rabbinic views on Jerusalem reveal complex attitudes toward a revered city that had long been under foreign sovereignty and whose great Temple still lay in ruin. The Rabbis felt a deep, continuing attachment to the city, while also accommodating themselves to the loss of the Temple rituals, regular pilgrimages, and ancient institutions of priesthood and kingship. They vividly praised the city whose air was always fragrant and whose beauty surpassed all other cities (*Avot de Rabbi Natan* version A, ch. 28; BT *Yoma* 39b; BT *Bava Batra* 4a); the creation of the world began in Jerusalem (BT *Yoma* 53b–54b), and the city was of unequaled height (*Sifre Deuteronomy* 37). Rabbinic teachings recognized the need to mourn Jerusalem's destruction, but cautioned against excessive sadness (BT *Bava Batra* 60b). They prescribed rituals for visitors to the ruins (BT *Mo'ed Katan* 26a) and ordained fast days to commemorate the city's disasters (BT *Rosh Hashanah* 18a–19b). Through *worship, God's gracious acts in Jerusalem were recalled, and the hope that God would once again elevate a Davidic king over a rebuilt city was expressed. The Rabbis ordained the recitation of the laws of sacrifice, reenacting through *prayer rituals what could no longer literally be performed. Their devotion to Jerusalem was emphasized with the exclamation, "Next year in Jerusalem," that ended the *Passover *seder*. The halakhic regulations for the city and Temple (such as tithes, sacrifices, and pilgrimage) remained central to rabbinic study. In Jewish life and liturgy, evocation of Jerusalem brightened a diminished present as a symbol of a glorious past and a yearned for and idealized future.

For further reading, see A. Halkin, ed., *Zion in Jewish Literature* (1961); J. Levenson, *Sinai and Zion* (1985); L. Levine, ed., *Jerusalem: Its Sanctity and Centrality to Judaism, Christianity, and Islam* (1999); idem, *Jerusalem: Portrait of the City in the Second Temple Period* (2002); Y. Eliav, *God's Mountain* (2005); and **ARCHEOLOGY, LAND OF ISRAEL: ANCIENT TIMES TO PERSIAN PERIOD; and ARCHEOLOGY, LAND OF ISRAEL: SECOND TEMPLE PERIOD; Maps 1–5**   ADAM GREGERMAN

Jerusalem: 1948–1967. Between 1948 and 1967, Jerusalem was divided between Israel, which controlled the western portion of the city, and Jordan, which controlled the eastern portion. Contrary to UN General Assembly Resolution 181 of November 29, 1947, which still remains in force, both Israel and Jordan refused to accept the city as an international entity and instead preferred its partition. Jordan and Israel regarded this arrangement as a pragmatic alternative to an all-or-nothing approach. It is no coincidence that, except for odd days here and there, the administration of urban concerns shared by both parts of the city, such as water, sewage, pest control, and legal and illegal civilian movement, was undertaken in an atmosphere of calm and characterized by a degree of cooperation. A good example of such cooperation was the convoy of Israeli soldiers disguised as policemen (with Jordanian knowledge) that was escorted by the Jordanian Legion to the Israeli enclave of Mt. Scopus every two weeks. Tourists and Arabs (usually Christian) were also allowed to move between the two parts of the city via the Mandelbaum Gate. As time passed, the joint Israeli-Jordanian Ceasefire Committee also evolved into a civilian forum for city administration and the solving of problems that arose from time to time in a city where the border passed through residential neighborhoods and, in some places, private homes.

Notwithstanding this cooperation, Israel encouraged the construction of civilian residences in demilitarized zones and no-man's land, and Jordan prevented Israeli access to the holy places, even though all of these acts ran counter to the Israeli–Jordanian cease-fire agreement of April 1948. Such actions, and the fact that a border fence ran through the

heart of the city, detracted from the city's appearance and quality of life.

Although there was no weakening of the religious bond that many Israelis felt for the Jewish holy places, most of which were located in East Jerusalem (except for Mount Zion), Israel appeared to have come to terms with the partition of the city. This approach was based on a *Zionist tradition, passed down from *Herzl to *Weizmann to *Ben-Gurion, which was hesitant about the prospect of future Israeli control of Jerusalem's Christian and Muslim holy places. For this reason, Herzl viewed the holy places as an extraterritorial area, and it was actually the Jewish Agency that was responsible in 1937 for the idea of dividing the city. In response to the Peel Commission's plan to partition Palestine into Jewish and Arab states and to continue *British Mandate rule in Jerusalem, Jewish Agency leaders proposed separating the eastern section of the city, which would remain under Mandate rule, from the western portion of the city that was devoid of holy places and would serve as the capital of the Jewish state. This proposal was also based on demography; even before 1948 most Arabs lived in the eastern portion of the city, and most Jews lived in west Jerusalem.

After the partition of the city (which took place on the ground in May–June 1948, but only officially in April–May 1949) and the annexation of its western portion by Israel in December 1949, Israel began working to transform West Jerusalem into a capital city in its own right. Through a relatively quick process that lasted less than twenty years, Israel established three centers in West Jerusalem: a government center in Givat Ram (including a parliament, government offices, and subsequently the central bank and the Supreme Court); a national cultural center (including the Hebrew University and the Israel Museum), located adjacent to the government center; and on Mount Herzl, to the west of these centers, a national memorial center (including the national and military cemetery and the Holocaust memorial museum *Yad Vashem). These centers created a Jewish Zionist presence to counterbalance the inaccessible holy places located in East Jerusalem.

For their part, King Abdullah of Jordan and his successor, King Hussein, were certainly interested in maintaining the eastern portion of the city as primarily Palestinian. After all, it contained the holy places and most importantly the *al-Aqsa* mosque compound, which was centered around *Haram al-Sharif*. However, in contrast to Israel, Jordan failed to develop East Jerusalem, primarily because of the constant tension between the Hashemites and the Palestinian population of the city. In July 1951, King Abdullah was assassinated by a Palestinian near *Haram al-Sharif* in the Old City in East Jerusalem.

Jerusalem's location on the border of two countries without diplomatic relations and, in the case of Israel, at the end of a long and narrow geographical corridor, hampered the city's development. West Jerusalem became a city with a population composed mostly of government employees, academics, and Ultra-Orthodox Jews, with only a small percentage of merchants and small industrialists. East Jerusalem remained a medium-sized town. Nonetheless, both sides came to terms with the partition of the city, and neither side took any significant action to change the situation. That Israel also supported the status quo was evident in the fall of 1956, when the Sinai War created political and military conditions that could have allowed Israel to unite the city if it wished to do so. The Arab–Israeli war (Six Day War) of June 1967 in which Israel captured East Jerusalem surprised both parts of the city (See also ISRAEL, STATE OF: WARS [1956–1967]). **Maps 12, 13**

For further reading, see M. Golani, "Jerusalem's Hope Lies Only in Partition: Israeli Policy on the Jerusalem Question, 1948–67," *International Journal of Middle East Studies* 31 (1999): 577–604; M. Gilbert, *Jerusalem in the Twentieth Century* (1996); and B. Wasserstein, *Divided Jerusalem* (2001).

MOTTI GOLANI

Jerusalem: Since 1967. The Six Day War broke out on June 5, 1967 (see ISRAEL, STATE OF: WARS [1956–1967]). Despite Israeli warnings, the Jordanians joined the war, shelling along the city line and capturing the British governor's palace from the UN observers residing there. On June 7, once Israel had surrounded the Old City, Israeli paratroopers broke through the Lions' Gate and took over the walled part of the city. After two and a half days of fighting, the war ended with the entire city under Israeli control.

On June 27, 1967, the *Knesset passed the Law and Administration Ordinance (Amendment No. 11), authorizing the government to apply the law, jurisdiction, and administration of Israel to areas formerly part of Mandatory *Palestine. Similarly, the Municipal Ordinance was amended to permit the extension of the city's municipal boundaries. The following day the government issued an order to apply Israeli law to East Jerusalem, which was now included within the jurisdiction of the Jerusalem municipality, with Teddy Kollek at its head. The legal changes indicated the de facto annexation of East Jerusalem to the State of Israel. A law was also passed guaranteeing the safety of holy places and free access to them, an attempt to soften the anticipated international opposition to Israel's actions.

Many of the annexed areas of East Jerusalem had not been part of the Jordanian municipality. Approximately 70 square kilometers were added, including twenty-eight neighborhoods and villages that had either been independent or had been part of neighboring towns. Jerusalem became Israel's biggest city, now covering 126 square kilometers, three times its pre-war size. The new borders of the city were drawn hastily and according to political and military considerations. The aim was to annex as much territory as possible with as little Arab population as possible, thereby providing locations for numerous Jewish neighborhoods that would guarantee a Jewish majority within the city. There was also concern that the new city include many of the highest topographical ranges. The northern boundaries were set to enable the incorporation of Atarot (Kalandia) airport. The tombs of Rachel and Nebi Samuel were left outside the city limits (**Map 14**).

These principles and other political developments also dictated the location of the new Jewish residential areas, for which 50,023 dunams of land were expropriated from Jerusalem's new territory. During the first stage (1968–70), a series of contiguous Jewish neighborhoods reaching to Mount Scopus were built in the north. Within the Old City, work was begun to reconstruct the Jewish Quarter, which had been in ruins since 1948. In the second stage (1970–80), four huge new neighborhoods were built in the north, east,

and south of the city. In the largest new neighborhoods, Gilo and Ramot Alon, there are now around 30,000 residents, more than in an average Israeli town. During the late 1980s, the third stage focused on filling in the area between Neve Ya'akov and French Hill with the construction of Pisgat Ze'ev, which comprised 12,000 housing units. Ramat Shlomo was built along the Shoafat range, and the neighborhood of Har Homa was constructed south of the Mar Elias Monastery in the fourth stage, from the beginning of the 1990s. In addition, a number of Israeli governmental institutions were erected in the eastern parts of the city, including the small government center in Sheikh Jarach and the campuses of the Hebrew University and the Hadassah Hospital, which were rebuilt and expanded on Mt. Scopus.

The push for development that began in 1967 also affected the western part of the city: Older sections were expanded, and new neighborhoods were built there as well. Industrial areas (especially high-tech centers) were established. A large new shopping mall in Malcha even managed to erode the popularity of the traditional shopping district at "the triangle" in the center of town, and a new highway was paved in response to development needs.

In contrast to the great momentum for development in the Jewish sectors of the city, largely due to governmental initiatives, the lack of momentum for development of the Arab sector is striking. The Israeli establishment hardly initiated any public building for the Arab population and limited private building. There is also a gap between what is provided to the Jewish and to the Arab sectors in municipal services; basic services, such as sewage, roads, and garbage removal, are sorely deficient in Arab neighborhoods. These deficiencies are tied to the special anomalies that characterize the status of East Jerusalem's Arabs, who received the standing of permanent residents in Israel in 1967 (but not full citizenship). This status gave them rights and responsibilities similar to those of the country's citizens, apart from the right to elect members of the Israeli Parliament and the right to carry an Israeli passport. However, although East Jerusalem's Arabs have the right to receive Israeli citizenship if they request it, most have chosen not to do so and maintain Jordanian citizenship.

The gradual disassociation of Jordan from the West Bank and from East Jerusalem (in the late 1980s) and the creation of the Palestinian Authority as a result of the Oslo agreements in the 1990s brought about an increase in Palestinian involvement in East Jerusalem. Israel acknowledged the ties between the Palestinian residents and recognized their right to elect and be elected (under certain conditions) to the institutions of the Palestinian Authority. Israel also permitted significant Palestinian autonomy in certain areas, such as education. The decision of Arab residents of East Jerusalem not to take advantage of their right to vote in elections for the city council (as part of their unwillingness to recognize the legitimacy of Israeli rule) is one of the principal factors that explains the discrimination in municipal services.

Despite Israeli policy, the percentage of Arab residents as a proportion of the city's residents is growing; 2007 statistics show 245,000 Arab residents of Jerusalem, 34% of the city population of 720,000, as compared to 26% in 1967. The reality that one-third of the city's residents identify themselves, one way or another, with the Palestinian people and the growing influence of the Palestinian Authority in the city are among the main reasons why Jerusalem is a major point of contention in the ongoing peace process. A number of proposals for arrangements in the city, as well as the negotiations at Camp David (July 2000), have created a split in the Israeli consensus regarding Jerusalem as a united city under Israeli sovereignty. However, the outbreak of the Second *Intifada at the end of 2000, the violent events that followed, and the erection of the Separation Wall between East Jerusalem and the West Bank brought about a return by Jewish hawks to an unyielding position on the question of Jerusalem.

The growing tension within the Jewish sector between the nonreligious and the Ultra-Orthodox, the growing demographic strength of the Ultra-Orthodox (making up 30% of the Jewish population of Jerusalem), and economic and social factors (unemployment and the high cost of housing) have resulted in a growing outward migration of the economically strong nonreligious population. These frictions, combined with the difficulties in Arab–Jewish relations, have lowered the city's status and centrality in the Israeli consciousness, especially among the nonreligious. These complexities have had a major impact on Jerusalem's status as the capital of Israel and will pose continuing dilemmas and new challenges for Israeli society and its leaders.

For further reading, see M. Benvenisti, *City of Stone: The Hidden History of Jerusalem* (1998); M. J. Breger and O. Ahimeir, eds., *Jerusalem: A City and Its Future* (2002); M. Gilbert, *Jerusalem in the Twentieth Century* (1996); and B. Wasserstein, *Divided Jerusalem* (2001).   AMNON RAMON

Jerusalem Talmud. See TALMUD, JERUSALEM

Jesus: See CHRISTIANITY AND SECOND TEMPLE JUDAISM; NEW TESTAMENT

Jethro is a priest of Midian and the father-in-law of *Moses. Moses encounters and aids seven sisters at a well when he flees to Midian to escape Pharaoh's wrath. Their father, called Reuel in *Exodus 2:18, shelters Moses and gives him his daughter Zipporah in marriage. Moses' father-in-law is called Jethro in Exodus 3:1 and Exodus 18; in Exodus 4:18, he is Jether and Jethro. In Numbers 10:29, Moses invites Hobab, "son of Reuel the Midianite, Moses' father-in-law," to guide the Israelites in the wilderness. Judges 4:11 refers to a group known as the Kenites and describes them as "descendants of Hobab, father-in-law of Moses." There is no scholarly consensus on this variety of designations, apparently indicative of diverse Israelite traditions.

In Exodus 18, Jethro brings his daughter and two grandsons to Moses in the wilderness where he was encamped at the "mountain of God" (18:6). Jethro praises YHWH as "greater than all gods" (18:11). He also advises Moses to appoint judges to hear minor cases so that Moses could concentrate on important disputes (18:22). Moses follows this counsel, and the chapter ends with Jethro's return to Midian. The account of these judicial reforms in Deuteronomy 1:9–17 does not mention Jethro.

Rabbinic traditions linked Jethro to *Job and *Balaam as Pharaoh's counselors before the Exodus (BT *Sotah* 11a; *Exodus Rabbah* 27:6); appalled by Pharaoh's plan to murder Israelite infants, Jethro fled to Midian and converted to Judaism. Rabbinic championing of Jethro as a model proselyte also rests on his praise of God (Exod 18:11) and

biblical links between Israelites and Kenites, seen as Jethro's descendants (Judg 1:16; I Chron 2:55). To the four biblical names associated with Moses' father-in-law, the Rabbis added Keni, Heber, and Putiel (*Mekhilta Yitro* 1; *Sifre Numbers* 78) and expounded each to his credit. See J. R. Baskin, *Pharaoh's Counsellors: Job, Jethro, and Balaam in Rabbinic and Patristic Tradition* (1983).   JUDITH R. BASKIN

Jewish Agency: See BRITISH MANDATE OVER PALESTINE

Jewish Anti-Fascist Committee. In early 1942, Joseph Stalin created five anti-fascist committees: for women, scientists, young people, ethnic Slavs, and Jews. Each encouraged support in the West for the alliance between the Soviet Union and the western democracies. The Jewish Anti-Fascist Committee (JAC) was chaired by the *Yiddish* theater director and actor, Solomon Mikhoels; its members included the Yiddish writers Dovid Bergelson, Peretz Markish, and Itsik Fefer, along with the journalists Ilya *Ehrenburg and Vasily Grossman. Mikhoels and Fefer came to the United States in 1943 where they raised millions of dollars for the Soviet war effort. On July 8, fifty thousand people greeted them at the Polo Grounds in *New York City.

By the close of 1943, the Red Army was forcing the *Wehrmacht* out of Soviet territory, and it soon discovered massacre sites. Members of the JAC learned of the murder of many relatives. Deeply affected by the news, they looked for ways to help survivors and appealed for assistance to western Jewish organizations. Ehrenburg and Grossman compiled and edited *The Black Book: The Ruthless Murder of Jews by German-Fascist Invaders Throughout the Temporarily-Occupied Regions of the Soviet Union and in the Death Camps of Poland during the War 1941–1945*, also known as *The Black Book*, a collection of documents and testimony about the *Holocaust and Jewish resistance against the *Nazis (see HOLOCAUST DOCUMENTATION; and HOLOCAUST RESISTANCE). With the advent of the Cold War, contact with the West was virtually forbidden. The committee's wartime activities were held against it, and Mikhoels was killed in January 1948. In September, Golda *Meir came to Moscow as *Israel's first ambassador. She was greeted by crowds at the main *synagogue. The JAC was held responsible for organizing this outpouring of enthusiasm, and within a year, fifteen JAC members were targeted for a political trial and almost all "confessed" under torture to espionage, treason, and "bourgeois nationalism." Convicted in secret, thirteen of the fifteen defendants, including Yiddish writers and poets Dovid Bergelson, Itsik Fefer, David Hofshteyn, Leib Kvitko, and Peretz Markish, were executed on August 12, 1952, an event known as the "Night of the Murdered Poets" (see also, POETRY: YIDDISH). For recent research, see J. Rubenstein, *Stalin's Secret Pogrom: The Postwar Inquisition of the Jewish Anti-Fascist Committee* (2005).   JOSHUA RUBENSTEIN

Jewish Community Center: See UNITED STATES: COMMUNITY CENTER MOVEMENT

Jewish Publication Society. Founded in Philadelphia in 1888 as a membership organization and publisher, the nonprofit, nondenominational Jewish Publication Society (JPS) of America, as it was then called, marked American Jewry's third effort to establish a society for the publication of Jewish books. Earlier attempts in 1845 and 1871 ended in failure. The rapid growth of America's Jewish population, the desire to forge a new Jewish cultural center in the United States, and the hope that books would help bind together a fractured Jewish community underlay the society's establishment. JPS was one of a series of Jewish cultural and educational institutions, founded during an era of communal renaissance, that promoted Jewish unity, sought to counter *antisemitism, and aimed to "inspire our youth."

The JPS published its first book in 1890 and has since published well over 1,000 titles, covering every aspect of Jewish history and life. Its list includes books by the foremost scholars and writers of the times, all carefully vetted by an editorial (formerly "publications") committee charged with maintaining JPS standards. The committee, through the years, has tended to favor scholarly and timeless volumes over popular and timely ones, and books reflecting community consensus over controversial topics. The goal has been to publish and disseminate Jewish books, not to make money, and as a result the JPS has rarely enjoyed robust financial health.

Henrietta *Szold served as the first full-time salaried officer of JPS, its editor in everything but name. Under her leadership (1893–1916), it completed publication of Heinrich *Graetz's *History of the Jews,* translated from the German, which established its reputation as a publisher of the first rank. It also published numerous other works of cultural significance by such luminaries as Solomon *Schechter, Louis Ginzberg, and Israel *Zangwill. In 1917, it issued a new Jewish translation of the *Bible into English and launched the Schiff Library of Jewish Classics, a series designed to make available "in the original and in the vernacular" the best of post-biblical Jewish literature before the modern era. Together, these books did much to establish the United States as a cultural center for world Jewry.

Subsequently, JPS experienced ups and downs in response to competition, the vicissitudes of the book trade, world Jewish events, and its own business strategy. At different times, scholarly books, popular books, children's books, fiction, co-publications, and translations all moved in and out of favor. Books on the Bible proved perennially popular, and in the post-war years, the society undertook both a new translation of the Bible, completed with the publication of the JPS *Tanakh* in 1985, and a new Bible commentary. It also published *The Jewish Catalog* (1973), later expanded to three volumes, which helped define the Jewish counterculture of the 1970s.

Under the editorship of Ellen Frankel (1991–2010), JPS reshaped its business plan and mission. It altered its membership program and focused its publishing energies on Bible and Bible commentary, classic texts in translation, reference and resource books for adult Jewish learners and lay readers, books by women authors, and children's books. On the history of the first century of JPS, see J. D. Sarna, *JPS: The Americanization of Jewish Culture 1888–1988* (1989).

JONATHAN D. SARNA

Jewish Renewal Movement: See JUDAISM: JEWISH RENEWAL MOVEMENT

Jewish Science is a philosophy of Judaism that developed into a movement in 1922 with the establishment of the Society of Jewish Science in *New York City. The term was coined by Reform Rabbi Alfred Geiger Moses

of Mobile, Alabama, in his *Jewish Science: Divine Healing in Judaism* (1916). He sought to stem the tide of American Jewish attraction to Christian Science by labeling the latter's denial of the reality of sickness and death as irrational and by equating divine healing with the universally available power of autosuggestion. Although later formulators similarly acknowledged the significance of modern psychology, they viewed the theological insights of Jewish Science as most important.

To Reform Rabbi Morris Lichtenstein and his wife, Tehilla, leaders of the Society of Jewish Science, Jewish Science was grounded in belief in *God as a nonsupernatural power, or divine mind, on which one could draw to overcome physical and psychological ailments and to achieve happiness, health, calm, and other states of personal well-being. Drawing on Jewish literature and liturgy in their sermons and published writings, they made the Jewish context of Jewish Science clear. In addition to Sunday school classes and worship services in Manhattan, from 1956–77, the society held similar activities at its synagogue in Old Bethpage, Long Island.

Although Reform Rabbi Clifton Harby Levy, who helped establish and led the Manhattan-based Centre of Jewish Science from 1924 until his death in 1962, also focused on God as healer, he drew on more traditional images of divinity, describing prayer as a feeling of closeness to God rather than of one's own internal power. He helped popularize Jewish Science ideas within the Reform movement, created educational programs for use by Reform congregations, and kept alive issues concerning medical and religious cooperation within the Central Conference of American Rabbis. In 1937, thanks to the efforts of Levy and others, *Hebrew Union College offered as part of the rabbinical school curriculum its first elective course in pastoral psychology. A course in pastoral counseling has long since become a requirement in the rabbinic program of Hebrew Union College-Jewish Institute of Religion, and similar courses are now offered at other rabbinic institutions (see JUDAISM, REFORM: NORTH AMERICA).

The Society of Jewish Science, the largest of the Jewish Science groups, reached a membership peak of one thousand during Morris Lichtenstein's tenure as leader (1922–38). As of 2007 its membership was less than one hundred and fifty. Yet, although Jewish Science never grew significantly as a movement, the teachings of Moses, the Lichtensteins, and Levy had a direct impact on thousands of American Jews. The works of the Lichtensteins are particularly accessible. Pre-dating the current Jewish interest in spiritual healing by more than seventy years, Jewish Science's emphasis on the connection between the mind and the body; its belief that illness cannot be overcome by medicine alone; the use of visualization, affirmation, and meditation to discover and draw on one's inner divine powers; and its overriding message that to do well one must *be* well remain Jewish Science's greatest legacies.

ELLEN M. UMANSKY

Jewish Studies. Academic Jewish studies refers to the analytical study of the Jewish experience using modern research tools and methodologies. Scholars of academic Jewish studies use a range of disciplinary approaches from the humanities and social studies to investigate and teach aspects of Jewish religion, history, thought, and culture, as well as associated languages and literatures. Academic Jewish studies research and teaching are nondoctrinal, nonparochial, and nondenominational; they take place in secular institutions of higher education and at some seminaries, both Jewish and Christian, that offer graduate degrees in academic fields. Scholars specializing in Jewish studies in these settings are not necessarily Jews nor are they advocates for Jewish students or Jewish concerns. Similarly, their students fit no particular profile: Academic Jewish studies instruction offers access to a body of knowledge and potential for intellectual growth to all interested students, regardless of their religious or ethnic backgrounds.

The significant expansion of Jewish studies in American universities is a relatively recent phenomenon. Although the Hebrew language was included in the curriculum of several of the earliest colleges to be established on the North American continent in the seventeenth and eighteenth centuries, it was taught as part of a theologically oriented curriculum designed to assist potential Christian clergymen in understanding their own religious heritage. Some instructors of Hebrew, such as Judah Monis who taught at Harvard University between 1722 and 1760, were Jews or of Jewish heritage. Jewish studies at American universities were truly established in the 1890s under the influence of German Jewish scholarship, specifically the *Wissenschaft des Judentums* (Scientific Study of Judaism). In the late-nineteenth-century United States, academic Jewish learning was established at secular universities, most often with the active communal and financial support of members of the American Jewish community. In the early twentieth century, Jewish scholars held at least sixteen subsidized positions in Semitic studies at major universities. Many of the donors for these positions hoped that recognition of the centrality of Jewish knowledge and scholarship in the development of western thought would also hasten acceptance and appreciation of Jews in the United States. Certainly, the establishment of positions in Semitic languages and literatures played a role in legitimizing the Jewish and Judaic presence in the American university at a time when being a Jew could still disqualify a candidate for an academic post. Most of the courses in Semitics that these scholars offered appealed to advanced students, both Jewish and non-Jewish, in biblical and related subjects; the courses were generally beyond the interests and ability levels of most undergraduates. Still, their very existence delivered the message that the Jewish literary and cultural heritage belonged in the university curriculum.

In the second decade of the twentieth century, communal support for university positions diminished as Jewish philanthropists focused on the multiple needs of the large hosts of immigrants from *Eastern Europe. In the period between the world wars, American academic Jewish studies took a new direction as an emphasis on the breadth and diversity of the Jewish experience replaced the focus on Semitics. During this era several elite institutions, again with the financial support of generous endowments from American Jews and Jewish communities, established positions in areas such as Jewish history and Modern Hebrew language and literature. These institutions integrated the faculty members holding these positions into appropriate university departments, whether History, English, Near Eastern Languages, or Religious Studies, where their courses became part of the mainstream undergraduate academic curriculum. Such scholars include the historian Dr. Salo Baron at Columbia University.

A third phase in the development of academic Jewish studies in North American colleges and universities began in the last third of the twentieth century. The impact of the Six Day War in 1967 and the Yom Kippur War of 1973 (see ISRAEL, STATE OF: WARS), as well as increasing discussion of the *Holocaust, inspired many Jewish young people to learn more about their identities and heritage on the university level. The unprecedented number of Jewish "baby boomers" who descended on college campuses beginning in the mid-1960s, particularly in the Northeast, played a role as well, as did the expanding number of Jews in the professoriate. The emphasis in the 1960s and 1970s on concentrating Jewish learning in one academic program that transcended disciplinary agendas was a decisive move away from the earlier "cultural pluralism" approach that had encouraged the location of Jewish studies scholars within larger departments. The arguments for establishing separate Jewish studies units were similar to those for other particularistic area studies, such as African American studies and women's studies. For one thing, such academic endeavors were essentially interdisciplinary. For another, without dedicated outside funding it was unlikely that more traditional disciplines would direct limited and highly contested resources to what many faculty members regarded as marginal and intellectually problematic areas of discourse.

There are no absolute data on the number of positions, programs, and departments in Jewish studies. However, in 2010, the website of the Association of Jewish Studies (www.ajsnet.org) listed more than 230 endowed chairs in Jewish studies at 80 colleges and universities, including several in Israel, Canada, and Australia. Many other positions and programs in Jewish studies at North American institutions of higher learning and elsewhere are not dependent on outside funding.

A major change in Jewish studies in North America in the decades between 1975 and 2011 is the increased number of women who have entered the field and climbed the academic ladder from graduate students to professors in every area of Jewish studies scholarship. This sudden appearance of females in the world of academic Jewish scholarship is, of course, the result of the overwhelming changes in the domestic, religious, and communal roles of Jewish women in recent decades (see JUDAISM, FEMINIST). The presence of women has transformed the content and methodological approaches of Jewish studies teaching and research. At the end of the first decade of the twenty-first century, virtually all female and male academics involved in Jewish studies teaching and scholarship take for granted the importance of gender as an intellectual category of analysis and consider the constructions and consequences of gender in explicating many facets of the Jewish experience (see WOMEN entries).

The 1969 establishment of the Association for Jewish Studies (AJS) was a signal indication of the growth of academic Jewish studies in late-twentieth-century North America. Initially founded to facilitate communication among a relative handful of Jewish studies scholars, by 2009 the AJS had more than 1,800 members, most of whom were PhDs teaching in an institution of higher education. One-fifth of the membership consisted of graduate students, representing the future of Jewish studies in North America and abroad. The Women's Caucus of the AJS was founded in 1986; in 2009, more than 47% of AJS members were women as compared to just over 10% in the late 1970s. In 1985, the AJS became a constituent member of the American Council of Learned Societies. This acceptance, after several unsuccessful applications, served as final validation that the academic world recognized Jewish studies as "an important and well-populated field of study" with a "unique intellectual focus and interdisciplinary concerns." This acceptance was crucial in legitimizing the field in the larger scholarly arena, and it was also significant for the organization's continued professionalization. With offices at the *Center for Jewish History in *New York City, the AJS convenes an annual conference; administers several book prizes, publishing subsidies, and travel grants; and publishes an academic journal, *The AJS Review*, and a twice-yearly magazine, *AJS Perspectives*.

Jewish studies programs and departments in North America have consistently encouraged their students, undergraduate and graduate, to study in Israel. Many programs have also welcomed academic colleagues from Israel into their midst as speakers and visiting scholars. These ties have been strengthened for many by participation in the World Union of Jewish Studies (centered at Hebrew University), which holds conferences every four years in Jerusalem. Recent decades have also seen the growth of Jewish studies organizations in Western and Eastern Europe and the former *Soviet Union. Among these are the European Association for Jewish Studies (EAJS), founded in 1981, with offices in Oxford, UK, which encourages and supports the teaching of Jewish studies at the university level in Europe and furthers an understanding of the importance of Jewish culture and civilization and of the impact it has had on European cultures over many centuries. In Russia, SEFER, housed at the Moscow Center for University Teaching of Jewish Civilization, is an umbrella organization for university Jewish studies in the CIS (Commonwealth of Independent States) and the *Baltic states. It seems likely that, in the future, Jewish studies professionals from North America will play a growing role in an increasingly vibrant and active international community of students and scholars.

Changing demographics in the early-twenty-first century indicate that the absolute number of Jews in the larger population, including student populations, is in steady decline (see UNITED STATES: DEMOGRAPHY). The future of Jewish studies in North American universities will therefore depend on the field's continuing appeal to a larger constituency. Most Jewish studies programs design their curriculum and courses to appeal to the broadest possible student audiences; in part this is accomplished by ensuring that their courses fulfill university "general education" and "diversity" requirements. At the end of the twenty-first century, more and more students who take courses and choose undergraduate majors and graduate training in Jewish studies are non-Jews who have come to the field out of intellectual curiosity, not out of interest in their own religious or ethnic heritage. Similarly, many scholars and faculty members who work in Jewish studies in North America and abroad are not themselves Jews. This phenomenon is indicative of the increasing integration of Jewish studies into higher education. This "normalization" of Jewish studies within the university is desirable from a scholarly point of view but it also points to potential future conflicts between academic Jewish studies programs and the concerns of the Jewish communities and donors who have thus far been essential to the presence and success of Jewish studies at many North American institutions.

For further reading, see P. Ritterband and H. S. Wechsler, *Jewish Learning in American Universities: The First Century* (1994).
                                                    JUDITH R. BASKIN

Jewish Studies: France (Nineteenth Century). As a result of the *emancipation and reorganization of French Jewry, traditional talmudic studies in France ceased early in the nineteenth century. They were replaced by mid-century with the modern scientific study of Judaism under the leadership of scholars like Adolphe Franck (1809–1893) and Salomon Munk (1803–1867). Franck, the first Jew to pass the "*aggregation*" examination in philosophy in France (1832), was elected to the *Académie des Sciences Morales et Politiques* in 1844 and became the first Jewish professor at the Collège de France. At the same time he was president of the Central *Consistory, where he took an active role in the modernization of Judaism and the rabbinate. Franck was vigorously anti-atheist and wrote extensively on Judaism for the Jewish press. In 1843 he produced a scholarly study of the *Kabbalah that paved the way for the scientific study of Jewish *mysticism.

Munk, who was born in Germany, had known or studied with Leopold *Zunz and Eduard Gans, (1798–1839) as well as with Hegel, and Goethe. In Paris he became cataloguer of Hebrew, Chaldaic, Syriac, and Arabic manuscripts in the *Bibliothèque Nationale de Paris*. Later in life he was appointed professor of Hebrew at the Collège de France. Munk's scholarly work was devoted mainly to medieval *Judeo-Arabic literature, especially the works of *Maimonides. Between 1856 and 1856 he published a three volume edition of the Arabic text of Maimonides' Guide of the Perplexed *(Moreh Nebukim)* with French translation and annotations. In addition to his scholarship, Munk was active in the community as secretary of the Central Consistory, where he aided the effort to modernize the French rabbinate. He traveled with Moses *Montefiore and Adolphe Crémieux to Egypt in connection with the *Damascus Affair, and his knowledge of Arabic was critical to the enterprise. In *Egypt he promoted the establishment of schools modeled on European methods of instruction.

Other Jewish scholars, such as Arsène and James Darmesteter, Joseph and Hartwig Derenbourg, Théodore and Salomon Reinach, Joseph Halévy, Jules Oppert, and Moise Schwab, although often appointed to positions in non-Jewish subjects in the humanities in various institutions of higher education, all wrote extensively on Judaism and made important contributions to Jewish studies. It was in France that the first secular academic position in the world was created for the study of rabbinic culture, with Joseph Derenbourg appointed in 1877 to a post in rabbinical Hebrew at the *École Pratique des Hautes Études* in Paris. The same institution also created the first chair in Rabbinics in France in 1896, appointing Israël Lévi, who later became the Chief Rabbi of France. Isidore Loeb and Israël Lévi were the first of a series of scholars who directed the creation of the great Jewish research library of the *Alliance Israélite Universelle.

Beginning in the middle of the nineteenth century many Jewish university professors and scholars, including James

Darmesteter, Hartwig Derenbourg, Robert Hertz, Sylvain Lévi, and Salomon Reinach, made significant contributions in the developing field of Oriental studies. They produced works in the general fields of comparative linguistics, mythology, and ancient religions, laying foundations for the disciplines of religious studies and the sociology of religion. The founder of the field of sociology, Emile Durkheim, was the son of an Alsatian rabbi. By 1895 Jews were disproportionately represented in the *Institut de France*, constituting 7 of its 260 members. Among important Jewish philosophers were Henri Bergson (Nobel Prize for Literature, 1927), Léon Brunschwieg, and Lucien Lévy-Bruhl.

The *Société des Etudes Juives*, founded in 1880, largely under the impetus of Chief Rabbi of Paris, Zadoc Kahn (a future Chief Rabbi of France), with the help of Baron James Edouard de *Rothschild, Isidore Loeb, Arsène Darmesteter, and Charles Netter, published scientific books by scholars of Judaism and Jewish history. Its journal, *La Revue des Études Juives*, edited initially by Isidore Loeb and then by Israël Lévi, provided an ongoing forum for French Jewish scholarship. The French rabbinate, under the direction of Zadoc Kahn, produced a respected translation of the Bible. For more on this topic, see P. C. Albert, *The Modernization of French Jewry: Consistory and Community in the Nineteenth Century* (1977); J. R. Berkovitz, *Rites and Passages: The Beginnings of Modern Jewish Culture in France, 1650–1860* (2004); and I. Strenski, *Durkheim and the Jews of France* (1997).   PHYLLIS COHEN ALBERT

Jewish Theological Seminary of America (JTS) was established in *New York City in 1887 in response to the radical direction of American Reform Judaism (see JUDAISM, REFORM: NORTH AMERICA), outlined in its 1885 Pittsburgh Platform. Moderate Jewish communal leaders, principally Sabato Morais, Henry Pereira Mendes, Alexander Kohut, and Cyrus *Adler organized support for a rabbinical seminary more traditional than *Hebrew Union College, but also reflective of the nineteenth-century Positive-Historical school's conception of Judaism as an evolving religion. The JTS curriculum was modeled after that of the seminary in Breslau founded by Zacharias *Frankel; it stressed biblical, historical, and philosophical subjects in addition to the traditional focus on *rabbinic *literature and *Judaism.

Despite community outreach and organizing efforts, JTS did not successfully create a congregational base, leading to financial struggles during the school's first fifteen years. In 1902, when JTS was on the brink of closing, Solomon *Schechter was recruited from Cambridge University to assume the presidency. Schechter transformed JTS into a center of Jewish scholarship, significantly expanding the library, bringing scholars from Europe, and establishing a Teacher's Institute. It was Schechter who selected the school symbol – the burning bush that was not consumed – representing the reinvigoration of American Judaism at the seminary.

In 1929, the seminary opened its Museum of Jewish Ceremonial Objects; thanks to a bequest from Mrs. Felix Warburg (Frieda Schiff Warburg), it is now the Jewish Museum, located on Fifth Avenue in New York City. Under the leadership of Louis Finkelstein (d. 1991), the role of JTS was dramatically revised to include educating society at large about Judaism and its connections to democracy and religious toleration. In 1947, JTS founded Camp Ramah, the

first in a network of *summer camps of that name, and in recent decades has established a number of summer travel programs for young people.

In the latter half of the twentieth century, issues of religious observance, denominational unity, *feminism, and *homosexuality became sources of tension within the seminary. After much debate, JTS admitted women to rabbinic studies in 1983. A 2007 decision by the law committee permitted self-identified gay and lesbian individuals, given the assent of the faculty, to enter JTS and the Ziegler Rabbinical School in California, but not the Jerusalem-based Schechter Seminary.

In the first decade of the twenty-first century, JTS consists of five schools: List College (an undergraduate division offering dual degrees with Columbia University and Barnard College), the Rabbinical School, Cantors Institute, Graduate School, and the William Davidson Graduate School of Jewish Education. The most recent chancellor, Dr. Arnold M. Eisen, was installed in 2007.   RACHEL GORDAN

Jewish War, First. The First Jewish War against *Rome, sometimes referred to as the "Great Jewish Revolt," began in 66 CE and ended officially with the capture of *Jerusalem and the destruction of the Second *Temple in 70 CE. According to *Josephus, whose *Jewish War* is the major source of information, the war was sparked by a riot in Caesarea that began over a dispute between a synagogue congregation and the Gentile owner of the neighboring buildings. The riot triggered a series of events, culminating in the termination of the loyalty sacrifice offered in the Jerusalem Temple to the God of Israel on behalf of Caesar and Rome. According to Josephus, this affront "laid the foundation" for the revolt. However, it is clear from Josephus' writings and modern scholarship that the real causes were more complex.

The most obvious cause was the poor and sometimes corrupt administrations of the prefects and procurators appointed by Rome. These relatively low-level short-term officials frequently exercised poor judgment, offending the religious sensitivities of the Jews, particularly with regard to the Temple. After the death of *Herod the Great in 4 BCE, the Jewish leadership was equally ineffective. Another key factor was the highly factionalized nature of the country's population; religious sectarianism, socioeconomic divisions, and regionalism created a volatile environment, as did long-standing strife between Jews and non-Jews. Scholars have also pointed to economic downturn and power struggles among the elite as causes of the war (M. Goodman, *The Ruling Class of Judaea: The Origins of the Jewish Revolt against Rome A.D. 66–70* [1987]).

Although the war technically lasted four years, it was largely a one-sided fight. After a successful initial defense of Jerusalem, the Jews were unable to regain the upper hand. The war lasted so long partly because of the cautious military tactics of Vespasian, as well as the internal political turmoil of the Roman Empire after the suicide of Nero in 68; the rapid succession of general-emperors during the following year put the war on hold. By the time the war resumed, the Jewish forces had shrunk back to the capital city and a few strongholds in the Judean Desert, the most famous of which is *Masada. The siege of Jerusalem, led by Vespasian's son Titus in the year 70, marks the climax of the war. The rebels' factional infighting continued within the city walls during the siege. Although a unified front was finally achieved, Roman military power was overwhelming and in the ensuing battle the Jerusalem Temple was destroyed. The revolt's failure and the destruction of the Temple make this one of the most historically important and theologically significant events in Jewish history. With Jerusalem in ruins and the Temple destroyed, the Jews found themselves in a crisis since so much of public religious life had revolved around the Temple and the offering of sacrifices (see TEMPLE, SECOND; TEMPLE AND TEMPLE CULT). This theological dilemma would ultimately be resolved by the rise of rabbinic Judaism in the late ancient and medieval periods (see JUDAISM).   STEVEN H. WERLIN

Jewish War, Second. The second Jewish revolt against Rome, also known as the *Bar Kokhba Revolt, began in 132 CE and ended with the fall of Beitar in 136 CE. While the First *Jewish War was documented by *Josephus, no similar historical account exists for this rebellion. Therefore, scholars have had to rely on a variety of sources, some of them badly truncated and others much later in date than the events themselves. Some Roman sources mention isolated details about the course of the revolt; the fullest account is that of Dio Cassius in his history of Rome. However, the chapter that describes the events of the war seems to have been composed by the abridger of the book, Xiphilinus, an eleventh-century monk whose words are suffused with hatred for the Jews. Other Christian sources also have a negative tone. Important information comes from *archeological finds at the central sites of the revolt, such as Beitar, Tel Shalem, and underground hideouts; coins that were minted during its course; and papyri that include correspondence between the leader of the revolt and various rebels. These finds establish that the revolt was led by Simon bar Koseva (known by the messianic *Aramaic epithet, Bar Kokhba ["son of the star" based on *Balaam's prophecy in Num 24]; see MESSIANISM: BIBLICAL, SECOND TEMPLE ERAS).

The main question is why Jews would have revolted against Rome given the bitter defeats that had previously led to the destruction of the *Temple and the city of *Jerusalem in 70 CE. Perhaps economic distress among evicted farmers led to agitations against foreign rule. In response, Rome increased its military presence to two legions and auxiliary units that were encamped in a number of stations throughout the country. According to Dio Cassius, the Jews were goaded to revolt when the Emperor Hadrian set up the colony of Aelia Capitolina and built a temple to Jupiter during a visit to Jerusalem in 130 CE. In fact, it is unlikely that the founding of Aelia Capitolina was a significant factor. The Second War was not connected with Jerusalem; had the change in the city's status been a major concern, the rebels would probably have attempted to conquer the city. According to the "Life of Hadrian," included with other emperors' biographies in the Roman *Historia Augusta*, the cause of the war was a general prohibition against *circumcision imposed by Hadrian. This assumption is apparently supported by an edict published in 139 CE by Antoninus Pius, Hadrian's heir, which permitted circumcision for Jews only. However, the sources indicate that the decree against circumcision was not imposed before the revolt nor was it generally imposed against all Jews. Rather, most of the Jewish sources imply

that the circumcision decree was a punitive measure against rebels in the regions where the revolt had spread.

A final explanation attributes the cause to the pretensions of Bar Kokhba, the rebellion's leader, and those who supported him as fulfilling expectations of *messianic redemption, political independence, and freedom from Rome. Coins struck during the war indicate that Bar Kokhba was joined by a priest (*kohen*) called Eleazar, who may have filled the role of religious authority; the mottos "For Jerusalem" and "For the Freedom of Jerusalem" also appear on the coins. Some scholars have interpreted these inscriptions as evidence that the rebels conquered and controlled Jerusalem between 132 and 134 CE, when it was reconquered by the Romans. However, this seems unlikely because very few of these inscribed coins have been found in Jerusalem and there are no indications that the city was conquered and held by the rebels. Modern scholarship is divided on whether the war took place throughout the Land of Israel or if it was confined to the region of Judea. From archeological evidence it appears that the revolt was limited to regions around Hebron, Jerusalem, and Ramallah in the north; Beitar in the west; and the western shores of the Dead Sea in the east. Widespread evidence of coins from the rebellion and a system of hideouts and places of refuge have been found there, but not in other parts of the country.

The initial success of the revolt brought about a sharp reversal in Hadrian's original low-key response. In the spring of 134 CE, he dispatched senior officers to Judea, headed by Julius Severus, who gathered four legions and secondary units from six other legions. According to Dio Cassius, Severus razed 50 main forts and 985 villages. Although these numbers are probably exaggerated, Severus undoubtedly eradicated the main opposition. Some of the remaining rebels fled to cave refuges in the Judaean desert, where the Bar Kokhba letters were later found; others escaped to Beitar, which was beseiged by the Romans in the spring of 135 CE. The siege of Beitar, about 11 kilometers southwest of Jerusalem, ended the war. Well fortified by the rebels, Beitar was situated on a steep-sided mountain surrounded on three sides by valleys. The Romans constructed a dike 4,000 meters long around the town, including towers and artillery positions. They also filled in the moat that protected the southern side, set up battery ramps, and with the help of siege towers breached the walls of the city.

The fall of Beitar left a deep impression in Jewish sources, which also preserve various versions of the death of Bar Kokhba. Among the immediate results of the revolt's failure were loss of life, sale into slavery of captured rebels, and a decrease in the Jewish population in regions where the revolt occurred. The province of Judea was renamed Syria *Palestina, an indication that Jews were no longer the dominant factor in the population. One of the Romans' punitive acts was a prohibition not only of Jewish residence in Jerusalem but even of entry into the city, which then became a place of foreign residents.

After the revolt was suppressed, the Romans prohibited public Jewish ritual observances in an attempt to undermine the independent leadership of the Jewish people by preventing communal gatherings. Some Jews observed the commandments secretly, and others transgressed publicly to demonstrate that they were prepared to die as *martyrs for the sake of observing the commandments. Antoninus Pius later canceled the decrees. Another outcome of the revolt was that the center of Jewish life in the Land of Israel was transferred to the *Galilee, whose residents had not taken part in the rebellion. Many Jews resettled there, and the Jewish leadership institutions of the *Patriarchate and the *Sanhedrin were reinstated.

For further reading, see R. G. Marks, *The Image of Bar Kokhba in Traditional Jewish Literature: National Hero or False Messiah* (1994); Y. Yadin, *Bar-Kokhba: The Rediscovery of the Legendary Hero of the Last Jewish Revolt against Imperial Rome* (1971); and idem, *The Documents from the Bar Kokhba Period in the Cave of Letters*, with H. Cotton and J. Naveh (2002).

MENAHEM MOR

Jewish Welfare Board: See ADLER, CYRUS; ORGANIZATIONS: NORTH AMERICA; UNITED STATES: MILITARY CHAPLAINCY

Jezebel: See AHAB

Job is a book in the "*Writings" section of the Hebrew *Bible; it is usually found following *Proverbs, although in some manuscripts Job comes first. With Proverbs and *Ecclesiastes, it comprises the biblical wisdom literature. The book presents itself as the story of a wealthy and God-fearing man from the land of Uz who is made the subject of a wager between the Lord and a character known as "the *satan*"; that is, "the adversary." The *satan* is certain that Job's good fortune is the cause of his upright behavior; if this can be removed, Job will "bless" (euphemistically, curse) God to His face. God gives permission to the *satan* first to destroy Job's wealth and kill his children and then to afflict him physically, sparing only his life. Three friends come to comfort Job, and he sits silently with them for seven days and nights (a source for the Jewish mourning custom of *shivah*) before bursting out with a blistering curse – not against God, but against his own birth. With this, the prose, folktale-like beginning to the book is suspended, and the longest, most remarkable, and most difficult poetry in the Bible begins.

The long first section of this poem (Job 3–26) is a debate between Job and each of his three friends in turn about why Job's afflictions have come upon him. Job insists on his innocence while the friends argue that evil comes as a punishment for wrongdoing. This section is followed by an interlude (Job 27–31) in which Job insists angrily that he has not deserved his affliction; in the midst of this interlude comes chapter 28, which asks, "Where Can Wisdom Be Found?" This meditation functions as the eye at the center of the hurricane that is the book of Job.

In Job 32–37, a new character, Elihu, suddenly appears; he also tries but fails to convince Job of his misdeeds. All that Job himself wishes to do is to confront God to fight the charges against him. When God does at last appear out of a whirlwind in Job 38–42, there are no explanations. Rather, after an extraordinary and highly detailed excursus through the wonders of the natural world, God demands that Job prove himself of equal power or fall silent and accept what God has done. The book's final chapter returns to the folktale style of the beginning of the book, restoring Job's riches, giving him more children, and letting him die "old and contented." The key to whether this ending is meant to be satisfying or ironic lies in understanding Job's words in 42:6, but there is no agreement on the correct translation of this verse.

Job is also mentioned in Ezekiel 14:13–21, where he is linked with *Noah and *Daniel as one of the three most righteous men who ever lived. It seems likely, however, that the biblical Job (in the famous expression from BT *Bava Batra* 15a) *lo hayah ve-lo nivra*; that is, "he never existed at all." Rather he is a fictional character who is used to explore the problem that later *Judaism would refer to as *tzaddik ve-ra lo*, or why bad things happen to good people (see EVIL AND SUFFERING). Due to the book's difficult language and challenging theology, it plays a minor role in Jewish *worship. However, the morning blessings begin with a phrase from Job 38:36, praising God for "giving wisdom to the rooster"; in addition, a phrase taken from Job 25:2, describing God as "making peace in His heights," begins the last line of the full *kaddish* or prayer of sanctification. For further reading, see *The Book of Job*, translation, introduction, and notes by Raymond P. Scheindlin.

MICHAEL CARASIK

Job: Rabbinic Traditions. The Rabbis were fascinated and troubled by Job, as is evident in the large number of *aggadot* about him. A primary concern is when Job lived. Opinions expressed in BT *Bava Batra* 14b–16b include the time of *Abraham, the time of the tribes (when he is said to have married *Jacob's daughter *Dinah), the time of the *Exodus, the period of the *Judges, and the return of the exiles from *Babylon. He was said to have been contemporaneous with both the *Queen of Sheba and Ahasuerus (see ESTHER, BOOK OF). Some said Job never existed and his story is an allegory. The most widespread view was that Job lived in the time of *Moses and served as an advisor to Pharaoh (see later discussion).

A closely linked question is whether Job was a Jew or a Gentile. Although some Rabbis maintained that "he was an Israelite" and that *halakhah can be deduced from his words, the predominant rabbinic opinion teaches that Job was a righteous Gentile and "one of the seven Gentile prophets." The sages praised his positive qualities, including modesty and hospitality. Nevertheless, this admirable non-Jew is said to fall short in comparisons to Abraham (ADRN A 2, 7; BT *Bava Batra* 16a), since Abraham served God out of love, but Job served God only out of fear of losing his reward (JT *Berakhot* 14b), although others disagreed (M. *Sotah* 5:5 and JT *Sotah* 20c). Resolution is achieved in BT *Sotah* 31a, where a tradition attributed to R. Meir equated "fearing God" with "loving God" for both Abraham and Job.

Job's sufferings were explained variously. According to BT *Sotah* 11a, Job joined *Balaam and *Jethro in advising Pharaoh on how to deal with the enslaved children of Israel. Balaam, who advised slaying male children, was himself slain. Job, who remained silent, was sentenced to suffering. Jethro, who fled, became a proselyte to Judaism (similarly BT *Sanhedrin* 106a; *Exodus Rabbah* 27:3). Job was also accused of questioning divine justice in his heart, even before his actual afflictions began (BT *Bava Batra* 16a–b).

Rabbinic ambivalence toward Job was based not only on the difficulties of the book of Job itself, but also on the predominant identification of Job as a Gentile. Job's complaints during his suffering were frequently compared unfavorably to the endurance of the patriarchs, kings, and prophets of Israel who faced far greater trials (*Deuteronomy Rabbah* 2:4; *Pesikta Rabbati* 47). Some sages explained Job's restoration with the claim that "the Holy One doubled his reward in this world in order to banish him from the world to come" (BT *Bava Batra* 15b). Conversely, *Pesikta Rabbati* links Job's punishments and redemption with the chastisements and ultimate consolation of the Jewish people (26:7, 29/30).

There may be an element of anti-Christian polemic in rabbinic efforts to denigrate Job, or in contrast, to claim him as a Jew. Such approaches, already evident in tannaitic sources (see TANNA, TANNAIM), may be responding to Christian portrayals of Job as a patient sufferer and to Job's inclusion in Christian constructs of a preexistent community of Gentile priests outside the nation of Israel. Mention of disputes over Job's identity appears in one of the letters of the *Church Father Jerome, where he identifies Job as descended from *Esau and not Levi, "although the Hebrews declare the contrary" (Lt. 73). For more on this topic, see J. R. Baskin, *Pharaoh's Counsellors: Job, Jethro and Balaam in Rabbinic and Patristic Tradition* (1983).   JUDITH R. BASKIN

Joel is the second book of the twelve minor prophets (see BIBLE: PROPHETS AND PROPHECY; PROPHETS [*NEVI'IM*]). One of the few prophetic books without a date, Joel was probably written after the *Babylonian Exile. Its first two chapters describe a vague and terrifying threat to *Jerusalem (1:1–2:11) that culminates in a call to collective *repentance (2:12–17) and a divine response (2:18–32). Chapters 3 and 4 describe *God's intervention on *Judah's behalf, the restoration of its fortunes, and its engagement in a cosmic battle against national foes. Joel marks an important transition from the language of earlier prophecy to the *apocalyptic eschatological ideas that become prominent in post-biblical Judaism and early *Christianity.

Joel frequently refers to prior scripture, transforming its meaning in the process. For example, Joel 3:10 reverses the call to beat swords into plowshares found in *Micah 4:3 and *Isaiah 2:4. Joel also reimagines the "Day of YHWH," an important theological concept in early Israel. Originally, it referred to the belief in God's climactic intervention in history to defend the nation (Isaiah 34). *Amos had mocked naïve faith in YHWH's uncritical support of Israel, suggesting instead that the Day of YHWH meant judgment and not salvation (Amos 5:18–20). For Joel, the Day of YHWH retains this ambivalent character (1:15–18), but the conflict swiftly escalates from an earthly battle (2:1, 11) to a cosmic war (4:14–16). In this new understanding, the Day of YHWH also describes the nation's ultimate restoration (4:17–18).
          EDWARD SILVER

Joḥanan ben Zakkai was a Pharisaic leader at the time of the First *Jewish War (66–70 CE) against *Rome (see PHARISEES). In many ways the founder of rabbinic Judaism (see JUDAISM; RABBINIC LITERATURE entries), Joḥanan is said to have obtained permission from the Roman authorities to leave the besieged city of *Jerusalem with his followers and to establish a center of learning at Yavneh (Jabneh, Jamnia). He is also credited with urging the substitution of ethical behavior (acts of lovingkindness) for the sacrificial cult that was no longer possible after the destruction of the *Temple in 70 CE (**see JUDAISM; TANNAIM; TEMPLE AND TEMPLE CULT; WORSHIP**).

Joint Distribution Committee (full title: the American Jewish Joint Distribution Committee, also known as the JDC

or the Joint), is the largest Jewish relief and welfare organization granting assistance to Jews outside North America. It was founded in 1914, under the chairmanship of Felix M. Warburg, when American *Orthodox, *Reform, and socialist Jews joined forces to provide emergency aid to suffering Jewish populations in *Eastern Europe and *Palestine during World War I. JDC focused on child care and the distribution of food, clothes, and medical and sanitary aid. Beginning in 1923, JDC undertook rehabilitation and reconstruction of Jewish communities by founding a network of cooperative credit institutions for craftsmen and small businessmen, establishing courses for vocational training, and encouraging Jewish engagement in *agriculture throughout Eastern Europe. In 1924, in cooperation with the Soviet government, JDC launched a large-scale project for the agrarization of Soviet Jews left without a livelihood (Agro-Joint). As a result, more than 150,000 Jews settled on land in the Crimea and *Ukraine.

With Hitler's 1933 rise to power, through the *Holocaust period, JDC made efforts to provide relief and to rescue European Jews. Until December 1941, when the United States entered World War II, JDC legally supported the increasingly impoverished *German Jewish community and aided *Polish Jewish communal organizations. Subsequently, through its European headquarters in Lisbon, JDC supported illegal *Holocaust rescue and *resistance activities in German-occupied Europe, including armed resistance in *France and Poland. It sent parcels to Polish Jews in the *Soviet Union via Teheran, and it financially assisted Swedish diplomat Raoul Wallenberg's efforts to rescue tens of thousands of Jews in *Hungary (see HOLOCAUST RESCUERS).

During the first post-war years, JDC cared for more than 200,000 Jews in *displaced persons camps in Europe and supported the illegal movement of Jews from Europe to *Palestine. JDC also invested heavily in the reconstruction of European Jewish communities. After the founding of *Israel in 1948, JDC subsidized the immigration of hundreds of thousands of Jews, first from Europe, *North Africa, and the Middle East and later from *Romania, *Ethiopia, and the *Soviet Union. In cooperation with the Israeli government, JDC established and fostered institutional care and social services for aged, handicapped, and chronically ill people in Israel (MALBEN) and aided in creating community centers and programs for weak and disadvantaged populations, including children and youth at risk. In 1976 it established JDC-Israel, moving its headquarters from *Tel Aviv to *Jerusalem.

Beginning in the 1950s when JDC was unable to operate openly in the Eastern Bloc countries (except in Poland between 1957 and 1967, and Romania since 1967), it financially supported the massive dispatch of individual clothing and food parcels, *matzah* for *Passover observance, and financial remittances, directed mostly by the Israeli governmental organization Nativ. JDC renewed its operations in Hungary, *Czechoslovakia, and Poland in the early 1980s and in the USSR in 1988. Dedicated to reviving Jewish communal life in the Soviet Union and its successor countries, JDC has set up more than 170 welfare centers (*hasadim*), which provide elderly and needy Jewish survivors with food, medical assistance, home care, and cultural activities, and 180 Jewish libraries. JDC supports the local Jewish press and fosters religious and cultural activity; it also builds new Jewish community centers. In addition, JDC strengthens Jewish education throughout Europe, trains young community leadership, and supports the European Council of Jewish Communities.

JDC continues to be involved in emergency operations, as during the 2000 economic crisis in *Argentina, which affected the well-being of tens of thousands of Argentine Jews. It also provides nonsectarian emergency aid, for example, to Armenia (1989) and Georgia (1992) after earthquakes, and to the tsunami victims in South Asia in 2004. At present JDC operates in more than fifty countries.

MICHAEL BEIZER

Jonah, the fifth book of the minor prophets (see BIBLE: PROPHETS AND PROPHECY; PROPHETS [*NEVI'IM*]), differs from other prophetic writings in that it is a narrative containing only one short oracle: "yet five days and Nineveh will be overturned" [or "will turn"; the Hebrew *nehpakhet* is ambiguous] (3:4). At the outset, Jonah ben Amittai flees aboard a ship rather than obey *God's command to prophesy destruction against Nineveh. When God responds by blasting the sea with storms, blame falls on Jonah and he is thrown overboard by the sailors. The storm ceases, but God sends a large fish to swallow Jonah; inside the fish, Jonah recites a *psalm-like prayer. After three days, the fish vomits Jonah up on the land (ch. 2). God repeats the call to prophesy and Jonah obeys, travels to Nineveh, and utters his oracle. All the inhabitants of the city, human and animal, repent, and God relents (ch. 3). When Jonah is enraged that his prophecy was not fulfilled, God teaches him a lesson about divine compassion by sending a plant to shade Jonah and then killing the plant with a worm. When Jonah laments the destruction of the plant, which he had neither planted nor tended, God responds, "And should I not care about Nineveh...?" (4:11).

Some have understood the story as historical (a prophet of the same name appears in 1 Kgs 14:25). However, the book's fantastical, humorous, and exaggerated language has led most commentators to take it as a literary creation. Many read Jonah as a straightforwardly didactic narrative, although its fundamental playfulness and ambiguity stubbornly resist definitive interpretation. Presumably because of its emphasis on *repentance, Jonah has traditionally been the *haftarah (prophetic reading) during the afternoon service on *Yom Kippur, the Day of Atonement. Recent research includes Y. Sherwood, *A Biblical Text and Its Afterlives: The Survival of Jonah in Western Culture* (2000).

SEAN BURT

Jonah ben Abraham Gerondi (1200–1263) was a *Spanish rabbi, writer, and moralist who studied in *France and lived at various times in Gerona, Barcelona, and Toledo, where he died. As a young man, he joined his teacher Solomon ben Abraham in attacking the philosophical writings of *Maimonides; later in life he repented and studied Maimonides' writings. His most important contribution was in *ethics (*torat ha-musar*). In his writings and sermons he preached against disregard of the *commandments, sexual immorality, and neglect and exploitation of the poor; he demanded that Jews of all social levels take a role in communal leadership and responsibility, even if only at the level of regular prayer. His works included commentaries on

*Proverbs and M. *Avot*, a compilation on the laws of slaughter, and a number of other ethical and halakhic writings. Recent research includes, I. Ta-Shma, "Rabbi Yonah Girondi: Spirituality and Leadership," in M. Idel and M. Ostow, eds., *Jewish Mystical Leaders and Leadership in the Thirteenth Century* (1998).

Jonas, Regina (1902–1944), born in *Berlin, was the first woman to receive rabbinic ordination. Although she completed rabbinic studies at the *Hochschule für die Wissenschaft des Judentums*, her teachers refused her ordination to avoid conflict with the German *Orthodox community. Instead, she was ordained privately in Berlin in 1935 by Max Dienemann, a Liberal rabbi. Henceforth, her title was Fraülein Rabbiner Jonas. Jonas did not find a congregational pulpit, but served as a teacher and chaplain in Berlin. She published articles about Judaism and about her own experiences and lectured widely in Germany, taking on increasing communal responsibilities in Berlin when the *Nazi regime came to power. In November 1942, Jonas was deported to the ghetto of *Theresienstadt where she continued her pastoral and pedagogical work. Like other incarcerated Jewish leaders, she delivered many lectures for her fellow prisoners; five of these focused on the history of Jewish women. Jonas was sent to *Auschwitz where she was murdered on December 12, 1944. Recent scholarship includes K. Von Kellenbach, "'God Does Not Oppress Any Human Being': The Life and Thought of Rabbi Regina Jonas," *Leo Baeck Year Book* (1994); idem "Denial and Defiance in the Work of Rabbi Regina Jonas," in *In God's Name: Genocide and Religion in the 20th Century*, ed. P Mack and O. Bartov (2000); and E. Klapheck, *Fraülein Rabbiner Jonas: The Story of the First Woman Rabbi* (2004); **see also RABBINIC ORDINATION OF WOMEN**.

JUDITH R. BASKIN

Joseph (Gen 37, 39–50) is the eleventh son of *Jacob and firstborn son of *Rachel, father of Manasseh and Ephraim (ISRAELITES: TRIBES), and the central figure in an extended *narrative in *Genesis 37–50. Joseph is Jacob's favorite son for whom he made "a coat of many colors" (37:3). Joseph's envious brothers sell him to Midianite merchants (37:28), who in turn sell him to the Egyptian Potiphar (39:1). Potiphar's wife falsely accuses Joseph of attempted rape and Joseph is imprisoned (39:20). In prison, Joseph explains the dreams of other inmates, and when Pharaoh needs a dream interpreter Joseph is summoned (41:14). When Joseph explains Pharaoh's dreams as predictions of seven fertile years followed by seven years of famine, Pharaoh appoints Joseph to be his viceroy over *Egypt (41:40). Under Joseph's management, the Egyptians build grain depots to prepare for the lean years. When famine comes, Jacob's sons go to Egypt to buy grain and eventually encounter Joseph but do not recognize him. After a period of testing, Joseph forgives his brothers and explains that their actions had been part of the divine plan (45:5). Jacob and his family settle in Egypt where the Israelites stay until the Exodus. During their departure from Egypt, the Israelites take Joseph's bones with them, as they had promised (Exod 13:19). According to tradition, Joseph is buried in *Shechem, a city in the territory of the tribe of Manasseh. There is no tribe of Joseph; rather, Joseph's two sons each became the father of a half-tribe.

MOSHE RACHMUTH

Josephus, Flavius (37–ca. 100 CE), was a nobleman, *priest, general of Jewish troops in the *Galilee during the First *Jewish War against *Rome, and later a writer in Rome under the protection of the Flavian Dynasty. The importance of Josephus' works, all written in Greek, can hardly be overstated. Four complete works survive: *The Jewish War* (events of 66–73 CE, with a lengthy pre-history), *Jewish Antiquities* (from creation to the eve of war, with extensive biblical paraphrase), *Life of Josephus* (his brief career as a Galilean commander), and the work known as *Against Apion* (a vigorous defense of Jewish law and custom). These volumes tell us most of what we claim to know about Judean society in the later *Second Temple period, including the later *Hasmoneans, King *Herod and his descendants, Roman administration of Judea and the first revolt (66–73 CE), Galilean society, the high priesthood and the *Temple regimen, *Pharisees, *Sadducees, *Essenes, and other pietistic and insurgent groups.

The traditional scholarly approach to Josephus downplayed his importance as a writer and thinker – partly because of the presumed character flaws of this "general" who surrendered to the Roman enemy and lived the latter half of his life comfortably in Rome; partly because the Church preserved his works for Christian apologetic purposes; partly because he was thought to have strung together sources without much original input; and partly because, where his narratives overlap, contradictions abound. Scholars tended to evaluate his writings in terms of historical realities, which were increasingly being illuminated by *archeology. Because his descriptions of Judean sites proved generally correct, Josephus was often declared an accurate historian.

Since the 1980s, scholarship on both the literary and historical fronts has changed its assumptions and methods. On the one hand, new tools have facilitated careful investigation of Josephus' writings as artful compositions. This analysis, illustrated by several translation and commentary projects, has led to a new appreciation of his intelligence and skill. When we read Josephus' writings as structured narratives, against a Roman context in which the ruling Flavians were elaborately celebrating the recent defeat of the Judeans (81–96 CE), we recognize their power as coherent assertions of the Judean character. On the other hand, this very recognition of Josephus' artistry complicates the practice of co-opting passages thought to be "unbiased," as if they were neutral statements of fact. Josephus' biases, which color every phrase, turn out to be historically important, for they bring to life in abundant detail the situation of a Judean nobleman in post–70 Rome. For further reading, see P. Bilde, *Flavius Josephus between Jerusalem and Rome* (1988); and S. Mason, *Josephus, Judea, and Christian Origins: Methods and Categories* (2009).   STEVE MASON

Joshua is the book that inaugurates the *Prophets (*Nevi'im*), the middle section of the Hebrew *Bible. Joshua introduces a new era marked by the rise of a generation that did not know slavery in *Egypt, and it begins the story of the Israelites' return to their ancestral homeland. At the same time, Joshua emphasizes fidelity to the *God of Israel and adherence to the *Torah in the same language as *Deuteronomy. Scholars recognize the book of Joshua as part of a collection of historically oriented writings known

as the "Deuteronomistic History" that includes Deuteronomy, Joshua, *Judges, 1 and 2 *Samuel, and 1 and 2 *Kings. Joshua's leadership is contingent on the degree to which he resembles *Moses and upholds the *Torah.

The book of Joshua can be divided into two parts: Israel's battles of conquest and the redistricting of the land to accommodate the tribes of Israel. The book begins east of the Jordan River and describes the miraculous crossing: The river stops flowing when the feet of the *priests carrying the *Ark of the Covenant touch the water, and all Israel crosses on dry land (3–4). The ritual dimension of this event is emphasized when the men of Israel undergo mass *circumcision, the people celebrate *Passover, and Joshua encounters the Divine in the form of the captain of a heavenly army (5). In 8:30–35, after a victorious battle, the people of Israel stand between the mountains of Gerizim and Ebal as Joshua publicly recites the Torah to the people. Joshua 11 concludes with the declaration that "Joshua conquered all of the land."

The second portion of the book focuses on the territorial claims of individual *Israelite tribes. These boundary lists reflect the territorial divisions that existed in the period of the Divided Monarchy (ca. 931–722 BCE; see ISRAELITES: KINGSHIP) when regional and tribal affiliations coexisted with national and religious affiliations. Joshua 21 addresses the situation of the tribe of Levi that inherits sacred duties rather than territory; because they still require a place to live and to pasture their flocks, the other tribes must relinquish certain towns and fields to sustain them. The book concludes with Joshua's preparations for his death (23) and the renewal of the national *covenant at *Shechem (24). The importance of the Jordan crossing and conquest of the land in the larger narrative of Israel's founding, exile, and return has led some scholars to propose the idea of a Hexateuch, a six-book canon spanning *Genesis to Joshua, rather than a five-book *Pentateuch.

Although Joshua is represented as a focused general, he is something of a flat character, lacking the pathos associated with such figures as *Moses or *David. Some have suggested that Joshua is intended as a model of a good king whose attributes are reflected in the Judean kings *Hezekiah and *Josiah.

Jews and Christians have understood the book of Joshua as demonstrating the ideology that homeland entails warfare. Joshua espouses the notion of "holy war" insofar as battles and the displacement of resident populations are sanctioned by God and the spoils of war are placed under a ban called *herem*. Because of its explicit military theme, Joshua has also been subject to critical readings. The Rabbis who wrote and compiled the *Talmud and *midrash excised the notion of holy war from Judaism, in part by commenting very little on the book of Joshua. Contemporary readings have observed counter traditions, arguing that rather than exterminating their neighbors, the tribes of Israel lived alongside them (6:25, 9:26–27, 11:22, 13:13, 16:10, 17:11–13) and that "the Jebusites dwell with the people of Judah in Jerusalem until today" (15:63).

For further reading, see G. Mitchell, *Together in the Land: A Reading of the Book of Joshua* (1993); and M. Weinfeld, *The Promise of the Land: The Inheritance of the Land of Canaan by the Israelites* (1993); **see also BIBLE: REPRESENTATIONS OF WAR AND PEACE.**   RACHEL HAVRELOCK

Josiah, king of *Judah (687–608 BCE), is praised highly for his devotion to "the ways of his ancestor *David" (2 Kgs 22:1–2). During Josiah's thirty-three-year reign, a "book of teaching," probably *Deuteronomy, was "discovered" while the *Temple was being repaired (2 Kgs 22:8–10). On the basis of this scroll, whose authenticity was validated by the female *prophet Huldah (2 Kgs 22: 14–20; 2 Chron 34:22–28) and that was publicly read before the elders (2 Kgs 23:1–3; 2 Chron 34:29–33), Josiah reestablished the Mosaic *covenant with the people. He introduced success-ful, if short-lived, religious reforms that centralized wor-ship in the *Jerusalem Temple, eradicated pagan shrines and religious objects from the land (2 Kgs 23:4–20; 2 Chron 34:1–7), and returned the people to the commandments, injunctions, and laws of the "Lord, God of their fathers" (2 Chron 34: 31–33). Josiah was killed in battle against Neco, Pharaoh of *Egypt (2 Kgs 23:29–30), and succeeded by his son Jehoahaz.   KATE FRIEDMAN

Josippon, Book of (*Sefer Yosippon*). This *Hebrew book derives from the *Hegessipus,* a Latin manuscript based on *Josephus' *The Jewish War* and *Antiquities of the Jews.* Writ-ten in southern *Italy by an anonymous author in the tenth century CE, this work chronicles Jewish history from cre-ation to the end of the First *Jewish War against *Rome. The first printed edition was published in Mantua in 1480; an illustrated *Yiddish version was printed in Zurich in 1546. **See also MARTYRDOM.**

Journalism: Israel. A lack of formal training has character-ized journalism in Israel since the first *Hebrew newspaper in *Palestine, *Ha-Levanon,* appeared in 1863. Although the press has nurtured the growth of numerous political leaders and even produced recipients of the country's most presti-gious national award, the Israel Prize, Israel had no insti-tutionalized journalism education program until the begin-ning of the 1990s. In fact, the academic world and the media were often at loggerheads, expressing mutual alienation and mistrust.

The birth of Israel as a democratic state ostensibly guaran-teed freedom of the press, after many decades of tight offi-cial supervision during the *Ottoman era and the *British Mandate period. Since its establishment in 1963, the Israel Press Council has played an important role in protecting this freedom and the independence of journalists. The Press Council, whose members include representatives of the pub-lic (including the Council's president), publishers, editors, and members of the National Journalists' Union, has suc-ceeded in blocking legislative initiatives liable to dimin-ish press independence. The Press Council formulated the Code of Ethics that serves as a guideline for Israeli journal-ists. Local journalists' associations are active in Israel's three largest cities: in *Jerusalem since 1933 and in *Tel Aviv and Haifa since 1935; these are linked to the National Journalists' Union. For decades, the power of the national union, estab-lished in 1948, was derived from its status as the representa-tive organization in negotiations over wage agreements, all of which were collective. Over the years, the union's rep-resentative status has decreased considerably, primarily as the result of the shift from collective work agreements to individual contracts. As a result, many contemporary Israeli journalists are not members of the journalists' associations or the union.

The Israeli press originated from various sources. Dur-ing the nineteenth and early twentieth centuries, the first journalists arrived from Eastern and Western Europe. Some were influenced by the writing styles of Jewish periodicals published in *Poland and *Russia; others adhered to West-ern European press norms. Subsequently, Israeli journalists assigned to the United States returned with a clear pref-erence for American reporting styles and procedures. This covert struggle between East and West has characterized Israeli journalism for decades.

The Hebrew University of Jerusalem was the first to offer studies in communications, but the concentration was on theory, with no substantive professional training except for a few rather eclectic workshops. Other universities followed that pattern. The gap was partially filled by private enter-prises offering semi-professional courses. Many journalists began their careers by performing their compulsory military service in the Israeli Defense Forces media (a radio station and some periodicals). Others found their way to the pro-fession by chance or employee referral. Training itself took place primarily on the job. In the early 1990s some colleges began to offer journalism courses taught by experienced pro-fessionals as part of the communications curriculum. Nev-ertheless, at the end of the first decade of the twenty-first century no Israeli academic institution offers a degree in journalism. For further reading, see D. Caspi and Y. Limor, *The In/Outsiders: The Mass Media in Israel* (1999); and Y. Limor, "The Media in Israel," in *Trends in Israeli Society,* ed. E. Ya'ar and Z. Shavit (2003), 1017–1103.   YEHIEL LIMOR

Journalism, Ladino (Ottoman Empire). The *Ladino press in the *Ottoman Empire, the first and most influential genre of modern Ladino print culture, played a central role in westernizing Ottoman Jewry. It emerged in the aftermath of the *Damascus Affair (the *ritual murder accusation of 1840), which directed the attention of western Jews to the plight of their eastern co-religionists and demonstrated the importance of disseminating information for building inter-national Jewish solidarity. The first Ladino newspaper, *La Buena Esperansa* (The Good Hope), appeared in Izmir in 1842. Between 1842 and 1939, approximately 275 Ladino periodicals were published in the Ottoman Empire and its former territories, although only some survived. The major-ity appeared in Salonika (105), Istanbul (45), Sofia (30), and Izmir (23). The Ladino press consisted of annual, monthly, weekly, and daily publications (with some variations). The publications varied in format and length, ranging from four to more than thirty-two pages, and some had supplements.

These periodicals fundamentally transformed Ladino as a language and made print culture accessible to the masses. *Sephardic journalists achieved this transformation by replacing Hebrew and Turkish words with Romance equivalents often glossed in parentheses. Although the first Ladino newspapers presupposed a knowledge of Hebrew, thus addressing only educated men, by the 1870s most peri-odicals were intended for mass readerships of both sexes. There are no reliable figures for the circulation of Ladino periodicals. An analysis of available data suggests that even the most popular Ladino newspapers sold in the hundreds. Yet, their actual circulation significantly surpassed these numbers, because each issue was shared by relatives and neighbors and was read aloud to the illiterate. Thus one subscription sufficed for ten or more people. By the 1900s, both men and women could read newspapers in cafes and at the libraries of some clubs (e.g., the Salonikan *Kadima*).

Some Ladino periodicals were subsidized by *Zionist organizations, *B'nai B'rith, or rarely, the *Alliance Israélite Universelle; others fully depended on subscriptions, sales, and advertisements. To attract more readers, they published serialized novels, often sold later as chapbooks alongside other books produced by the same publisher. Many periodicals closed for lack of funds and others were understaffed and barely survived.

After 1878, all Ottoman publications were subject to censorship, which became especially severe in the 1890s. Official authorization was required to found a periodical, and all periodicals were obliged to defend Ottoman interests and discredit the sultan's enemies. Periodicals were prohibited from indicating their circulation, reporting on assassinations and rebellions, and using such words as "massacre," "dynamite," and "constitution." Thus, in July 1908, *El Tiempo* (Istanbul, 1872–1930) was closed by censorship for an "indefinite period." After the Young Turk revolution (1908) when censorship was abolished and Zionist organizations were legalized, the Sephardi press experienced an unprecedented boom that resulted in the appearance of dozens of new periodicals, particularly Zionist, socialist, and humoristic ones.

The founders of the early Ladino newspapers (e.g., Betzalel Saadi Halévy, Yehuda Nehama) were *maskilim* (adherents of the *Haskalah*) who had not received a secular education but shared liberal views and a concern for what they perceived as the ignorance and fanaticism of their coreligionists. Most of the journalists whose careers began in the 1880s and later (e.g., Elia Carmona, Alexander Ben Ghiat, Shmuel Saadi Halévy) were graduates of the Alliance Israélite Universelle schools, fluent in a few languages, and knowledgeable in Jewish history and tradition. Some (e.g., David Fresco, Joseph Romano, Abraham Galante) were persecuted and even excommunicated by rabbinical authorities, who felt threatened by their publications. Despite the differences in their ideological stances, all Ladino periodicals endeavoured to disseminate progressive ideas, offer objective coverage of local and international developments, enlighten their readers, and provide them with appropriate entertainment.

The impact of the Ladino press, which was both a tool and a product of westernization, on the Ottoman Jews exceeded the most ambitious aspirations of its creators. It connected generations of Sephardim to the larger world, increased literacy, developed reading habits of men and women, supported modern Ladino fiction, and created a sphere of public discussions inside and between Ottoman Jewish communities. For further reading, see G. Nassi, ed., *Jewish Journalism and Printing Houses in the Ottoman Empire and Modern Turkey* (2001); and S. A. Stein, *Making Jews Modern: The Yiddish and Ladino Press in the Russian and Ottoman Empires* (2003).

OLGA BOROVAYA

Journalism: United States (English Language).
The first significant journalist of Jewish origin in the United States was Mordecai M. Noah (1785–1851), an editor of partisan newspapers of the Early Republic such as the *National Advocate* and the *New York Evening Star*. A Democrat and a proto-*Zionist or "restorationist," Noah personified the slash-and-burn style of early American newspapers that would later be discredited by Adolph S. Ochs (1855–1935), the most important Jew in the history of U.S. journalism. In 1896, this young publisher of the *Chattanooga Times* purchased a financially failing daily, the *New York Times*. Without disavowing a preference for the Democratic Party, he upheld an ideal of objectivity that would become the twentieth-century standard against which the best of newspaper journalism was henceforth measured.

Ochs insisted on news gathering that would accumulate facts to be presented impartially in the *Times*. He was reluctant to interfere in the editorial decisions of the newspaper that he and his family owned, and he maintained strict separation between the news columns and the editorial page. Ochs' values were conveyed to his descendants as well. His son-in-law, Arthur Hays Sulzberger, published the *Times* from 1935 until 1961; another son-in-law, Orvil Dryfoos, from 1961 until 1963; and then Ochs' son Arthur Ochs (Punch) Sulzberger from 1963 until 1992. Punch Sulzberger's son, Arthur Ochs Sulzberger Jr., became the first non-Jew in the family to run the newspaper. The fidelity to the Ochs tradition is traced in S. E. Tifft and A. S. Jones's *The Trust* (1999).

In the tenacity with which editors and reporters pursued and presented stories, the *Times* dwarfed all other newspapers in the world. No other newspaper was ever so comprehensive; its news room covered 1.3 acres. Although the newspaper was generally deferential to Washington until the 1960s, the *Times* very often deserved its reputation for making a serious stab at impartiality. Its Jewish ownership was not irrelevant, however, to the history of the *Times*. Ochs' own admiration for German *Kultur* may have slowed the newspaper's recognition of Germany's descent into *Nazi barbarism. During World War II, coverage of the *Holocaust was shockingly inadequate (a failure that was hardly unique). The family's opposition to *Zionism was patent. Anxieties about *antisemitism also stunted the careers of some Jewish reporters and editors. Because the *Times* was known as a "Jewish newspaper," it was not until 1977 that a Jew (A. M. Rosenthal) become its executive editor; it was another seven years before Thomas L. Friedman became the first Jewish bureau chief assigned to cover *Israel and its neighbors.

Similar concerns haunted the career and the reputation of Walter Lippmann (1889–1974), the ablest intellectual of the twentieth century to work within the field of American journalism. He co-founded and co-edited the leading liberal weekly magazine, *The New Republic*, in 1914 and in the following decade presided over the editorial page of the Pulitzer family's fabled *New York World*. By the end of the 1920s, Lippmann had invented the syndicated column of political opinion, and from his perch at the *New York Herald-Tribune*, he was able to hover above the rest of the media and indeed above diplomacy. Until the 1960s, foreign governments were said to formally accredit their ambassadors to the president and by private letter to Lippmann. Ronald Steel's biography, *Walter Lippmann and the American Century* (1980), also exposes the private shame that this brilliant political analyst and gifted prose stylist harbored because of his Jewish origins, as well as his psychic struggle to sustain an Olympian stance of disinterestedness.

Lippmann's approach to journalism was interpretive. Yet if the gathering of news, rather than the formation of opinion, is what distinguished American journalism after Ochs, then no one more fully exemplified the pursuit of scoops than Herbert Bayard Swope (1882–1958). He won the first Pulitzer Prize for reporting (1917) and beat out all other reporters at the Versailles Peace Conference, getting a front-row seat by dressing as a diplomat. From a campaign speech by Franklin D. Roosevelt in 1932, Swope singled out the phrase "new deal"; fifteen years later, he coined the phrase "cold war."

Such figures as Lippmann and Swope did not alter the perception of daily journalism as devoid of prestige, at least in the first half of the twentieth century; the absence of snobbery gave vocational opportunities to the ambitious and the reckless. Ben Hecht (1894–1964) not only lived the myth of a flamboyant press but he also largely created that myth, especially in *The Front Page*, the 1928 play that he co-authored. Covering *Chicago during an era that was scandalous for the extent of its corruption, criminality, and raunchiness, Hecht more than anyone else drew the profile of the archetypal newspaperman: a cynical drunkard indifferent to the Victorian moral code and defiant of genteel notions of privacy. Nothing could have been less predictable than the political turn that Hecht took in the 1940s, when Nazism turned him into an ardent Jewish nationalist and the battle for *Palestine turned him into a right-wing Zionist, although by then he had abandoned his newspaper career for Hollywood (see FILM: UNITED STATES; ZIONISM).

The impact of Jews on American journalism has been so huge that bigots from Henry Ford (in *The International Jew*) to Richard Nixon (on the Oval Office tapes) took notice. Yet, Jewish ownership of newspapers has been statistically insignificant. Here the *Times* has loomed large, although it is quite atypical. What is striking about the chain begun by Samuel I. Newhouse (1895–1979) is the sheer variety of its media outlets, rather than any political or ethnic perspective that the family has sought to impose; the chief interest has been profit, not policy. Jews have certainly been prominent as editors, columnists, and pundits – especially in recent decades and when only three *television networks flourished. At one time or another, CBS, NBC and ABC each had Jewish presidents (appointed by boards of directors; see BROADCASTING INDUSTRY: RADIO AND TELEVISION). Yet, the polyvocal character of the American media mitigates against anything so simplistic as a clear and coherent Jewish interest, much less Jewish domination (see also PERIODICALS: CANADA; PERIODICALS: UNITED STATES [ENGLISH LANGUAGE]).

STEPHEN J. WHITFIELD

Journalism, Yiddish (Eastern Europe).

The *Yiddish press in *Eastern Europe before the 1880s was shaped by the ideology of the *Haskalah*, which typically held Yiddish in low esteem but used it to communicate with the largest number of Jewish readers. The first "Yiddish" newspaper was the *Warsaw weekly, *Der Beobakhter an der Weykhsel* (1823–24), which promoted the ideal of cultural integration into Polish society. However, it actually appeared in German transliterated into Hebrew letters with an admixture of Hebrew words. *Kol mevaser* (1862–73) reflected

the *Ukrainian Yiddish of its editor Alexander Zederbaum, despite bearing a Hebrew title for reasons of prestige. Ostensibly aimed at female readers, it began its career as a profit-generating supplement to the entrepreneur's Hebrew newspaper *Ha-Melitz*. It played a pioneering role in Yiddish journalism, helping bring news of events and ideas from the wider world to still largely traditional readers and popularizing the serialized works of a new generation of important Yiddish writers.

After the closing of *Dos yidishe folksblat* (1881–90), Zederbaum's second Yiddish newspaper, Russian officials routinely rejected tens of requests for concessions to found a new Yiddish newspaper on the grounds that censors were ignorant of *zhargon* and that the applicants were politically unreliable. The government was far more lenient in granting permission for Hebrew publications, possibly because it considered Hebrew a classical language whose audience was a relatively small and conservative elite and whose use did not conflict with the goal of linguistically Russifying Jews. The government nonetheless permitted the appearance of a number of Yiddish periodicals of significant literary and intellectual caliber, such as the annuals *Yudishe folksbibliotek* (Kiev, 1888 and 1889) and *Yudishe bibliotek* (1891, 1892, 1895) and the *Zionist *Der yud* (printed in Kraków but edited in *Warsaw, 1899–1903). Expressing an emerging Jewish nationalist sensibility, these journals printed essays of historical, sociological, and scientific character as well as works of belles lettres, helping standardize Yiddish and increasing its prestige as a literary language.

With a Yiddish daily press that was effectively illegal in tsarist *Russia, newspapers were legally imported from neighboring countries. Publications appearing in the politically more liberal *Habsburg *Galicia included the monthly *Tsaytung*, published in Lemberg during the revolutionary year 1848, the bimonthly *Der izraelit* (1869–72); and the daily *Togblat* (Lemberg, 1904–39). Until World War I, Yiddish newspaper publication in *Romania was concentrated in Jassy (*Koyroys hoitim*, weekly, 1855–56, 1867–71) and Bucharest (*Hayoets lebeys yisroel berumenye*, biweekly, 1874–1913, an early supporter of the *Hivat Tzion* movement). A number of clandestine Yiddish publications, the work of socialist and revolutionary parties such as the *Bund's *Der yidisher arbayter* (1896–97), were also either printed illegally in Russia or smuggled in from abroad. The first full-fledged Yiddish daily in Russia, *Der fraynd* (1903–13), appeared in *Saint Petersburg, far away from the millions of Yiddish speakers in the *Pale of Settlement and Congress Poland, until transferring its offices in late 1909 to Warsaw. The liberalization of tsarist press policies allowed for a virtual explosion of dailies around 1905. In the wake of the first Russian Revolution, Warsaw became the "metropolis of the Yiddish press" in Eastern Europe.

In independent *Poland, Yiddish periodicals and newspapers spanned the ideological and cultural spectrum, including sports, political satire, literature and criticism, scholarship, and children's interests. Among the most widely read dailies in the interwar period were the bitter rivals *Haynt* (left-leaning Zionist) and *Der moment* (nonpartisan and later Revisionist Zionist), the Warsaw Bundist organ *Folkstsaytung*, *Agudat Israel's *Der yud*, and the *Vilna *Tog*. As linguistic Polonization intensified in this period, however, Yiddish periodicals faced increasing competition from both the Polish and the growing Polish Jewish presses. Just as Hebrew writers and editors were often also active in Yiddish publishing, many of those active in Yiddish worked simultaneously for Polish Jewish publications.

In the *Soviet Union, where Yiddish was recognized as the national language of the Jews while Hebrew- and Russian-language Jewish presses were eliminated, the state-supported Yiddish press encouraged many new and amateur writers, often of inferior caliber. Conforming to the dictate, "socialist in content, national in form," it was constrained by official ideology and its Jewish content was generally weak; Jews often preferred to read the dominant Russian press instead. The largest dailies *Der emes* (Moscow, 1920–38, earlier called *Di varhayt*), *Der shtern* (Kharkov, 1925–41), and *Oktyaber* (Minsk, 1925–41) appeared alongside smaller local papers. However, many political, literary, and scholarly journals (among them *Di royte velt*, *Di yidishe shprakh*, and *Der prolit*) were often of excellent quality. Their numbers and frequency declined by the late 1930s because of the increasingly severe repression of Yiddish culture and growing linguistic assimilation.

The annexation of Bessarabia and Bukovina by Romania, areas with large numbers of unacculturated Jews, significantly increased its Jewish population and reinforced Yiddish cultural life in the interwar years. A variety of publications of an ideological, literary, and humorous character appeared, including the literary-political journal *Tshernovitser bleter* (1928–38). Severed from the larger Jewish communities of Poland and the USSR, Jews in the *Baltic states had difficulty sustaining a Yiddish press because of their limited numbers, but they managed to publish dailies in Lithuania and Latvia for much of this period. Although even traditional Jews in *Hungary tended to speak Hungarian, a Yiddish press also existed in Subcarpathian Ruthenia, which was Hungarian before World War I and Czechoslovakian thereafter.

After the *Holocaust, a number of weekly and semiweekly Yiddish publications representing different political views appeared between 1945 and 1949 in Poland. However, the post–WW II *communist regime permitted only a single Yiddish newspaper, *Di folks-shtime* (1945–91). It was considered more liberal than the Soviet Yiddish press and explored a greater number of Jewish issues after the period of liberalization in 1956. Little was published in Yiddish in the USSR after Stalin's suppression of Yiddish culture (1948–52), with the exception of the newspaper *Birobidzhaner shtern* (1930-present) in the Jewish autonomous region of *Birobidjan. The Moscow literary monthly *Sovetish heymland* (1961–91) appeared after Stalin's death, largely to appease voices in the West who complained about the suppression of Jewish culture and to disseminate Soviet propaganda at home and especially abroad. After the collapse of the Soviet Union, *Sovetish heymland* continued as *Di yidishe gas* (1993–97).

For further reading, see G. Estraikh, "The Yiddish-Language Communist Press," *Studies in Contemporary Jewry* 20 (2004): 62–82; A. Greenbaum, "Newspapers and Periodicals," in *The YIVO Encyclopedia of Jews in Eastern Europe* (2005); A. Orbach, *New Voices of Russian Jewry* (1980); and S. A. Stein, *Making Jews Modern: The Yiddish and Ladino Press in the Russian and Ottoman Empires* (2004).

KALMAN WEISER

Journalism, Yiddish (North America). The North American *Yiddish press first arose in the 1870s and 1880s at the start of the mass migration of Yiddish-speaking Jews from *Eastern Europe to the *United States. The immigrants brought with them no tradition of newspaper reading, so the American Yiddish press helped pioneer the development of modern Yiddish journalism. Thus, journalists played an important role in the emergence of Yiddish as a modern public language in which it was possible to discuss a wide range of political and cultural subjects. The Yiddish press cemented ethnic communal ties and brought news from the "old home," but it also Americanized the immigrants by translating the life of their new country into a language they understood.

In its heyday, the Yiddish press included hundreds of dailies, weeklies, monthlies, and quarterlies covering a wide spectrum of ideological outlooks and special interests. However, it started slowly, with the earliest publications, the *Yidishe tsaytung* and the *Yidishe post* (both 1870), culling much of their content from European Hebrew and German sources. Over the next three decades many publications came and went, often after just a few issues. Most were weeklies, with an occasional attempt to publish a daily newspaper. Kasriel Sarasohn (1835–1905), an immigrant from near Suwalki, Russian Poland, published the first Yiddish daily newspaper. He settled in *New York City in 1871 and, after one false start, began in 1874 to publish the weekly *Yidishe gazetn* (1874–1928), which became the first Yiddish daily for two brief stints in 1881 and 1883. In 1885, Sarasohn began to issue the *Yidishes tageblat*, a daily that was *Orthodox in religious orientation, conservative in politics, and sensationalistic in its approach to news. This proved a successful combination, and the *Tageblat* maintained its status as the most widely read Yiddish newspaper for two decades, until it was absorbed by the *Morgn zhurnal* in 1928.

The formula of combining high-mindedness with sensationalist reporting was perfected by Abraham Cahan (1860–1951), the long-time editor of the *Forverts* (Jewish Daily Forward). The *Forverts* was established in 1897 under Cahan's editorship as the organ of a dissident faction of the Socialist Labor Party (SLP). After several months at the helm of the *Forverts*, Cahan, who hailed from near *Vilna and who wrote in Yiddish, Russian, and English, joined the staff of the *Commercial Advertiser*. When he returned to the *Forverts* for good in 1901, he transformed it into a lively and popular newspaper. On any given day, the front page might include news of local murders and suicides along with stories on socialist advances in Europe or strikes in New York. Inside were didactic articles on socialist theory and drama criticism along with trashy serialized novels. Cahan's most famous innovations were the "Gallery of Missing Husbands," which featured photographs of men who had deserted their families, and the *Bintl brif* (Bundle of Letters), in which readers wrote to the editors seeking advice on personal problems. Soon, the *Forverts* overtook the *Tageblat* to become the most popular Yiddish daily in the world, as well as the most widely read socialist daily in the country.

By 1901, there were six Yiddish dailies in New York City: the *Tageblat*; the *Forverts*; the *Abenblat* (1894–1902), an organ of the SLP; the *Teglikher Herold* (1891–1904); the *Yidisher Abendpost* (1899–1905); and the *Morgn Zhurnal* (1901–53),

Plate 1. ASTARTE FIGURINES. Judah, Israelite period, 8th century–early 6th century BCE. The Israel Museum, Jerusalem. Accession numbers: 68.32.4, 64.67/3, 64.67/4 IAA 60–725, 80–2. Photo © The Israel Museum Jerusalem by Nahum Slapak. See ARCHEOLOGY, LAND OF ISRAEL: ANCIENT TIMES TO PERSIAN PERIOD; CANAAN, CANAANITES; ISRAELITES: MARRIAGE AND FAMILY; ISRAELITES: RELIGION; JUDAH, KINGDOM OF; and WOMEN, ANCIENT: BIBLICAL REPRESENTATIONS.

Plate 2. DEAD SEA SCROLL: The Community Rule (detail). Qumran, 1st century BCE–1st century CE. Parchment. The Shrine of the Book at the Israel Museum, Jerusalem. Accession number: 96.83/208A. Photo © The Israel Museum, Jerusalem. See ARCHEOLOGY, LAND OF ISRAEL: SECOND TEMPLE PERIOD; DEAD SEA SCROLLS; and QUMRAN.

Plate 3. SYNAGOGUE MOSAIC FLOOR (detail): The central shrine (possibly a Torah ark) and the menorahs, *shofars*, and incense shovels symbolize the Jerusalem Temple and expectation of messianic redemption. Beth Shean, Byzantine period, 6th century CE. The Israel Museum, Jerusalem. IAA Photo © The Israel Museum Jerusalem. See ART: LATE ANTIQUITY; BYZANTINE EMPIRE; DECAPOLIS CITIES; MENORAH; MESSIANISM: BIBLICAL AND SECOND TEMPLE ERAS; *SHOFAR*; and SYNAGOGUES, ANCIENT.

Plate 4. THE REGENSBURG PENTATEUCH: This depiction of Aaron the High Priest lighting the Tabernacle menorah, with Tabernacle implements, invokes a rebuilt Temple and future redemption. Regensburg, Bavaria, Germany, ca. 1300 CE. Pen and ink, tempera and gold leaf on vellum. The Israel Museum, Jerusalem. Accession number: B05.0009; 180/05. Photo © The Israel Museum Jerusalem by David Harris. See AARON; ART: MEDIEVAL MANUSCRIPT ILLUSTRATION; MENORAH; TABERNACLE; and TEMPLE AND TEMPLE CULT.

Plate 5. PASSOVER PLATE. Spain, ca. 1480. Earthenware. The Israel Museum, Jerusalem. Gift of Jakob Michael, New York, in memory of his wife, Erna Sondheimer-Michael. Accession number: B65.12.0483; 134/057. Photo © The Israel Museum Jerusalem by Nahum Slapak. See CEREMONIAL OBJECTS; PASSOVER; and SPAIN, CHRISTIAN.

Plate 6. BRIDAL CASKET (*cofanetto*) represents from right to left the three duties incumbent on Jewish women: *ḥallah* (putting aside a portion of the Sabbath dough); *niddah*; and *hadlakat ha-ner* (kindling Sabbath lights). North Italy, late 15th century. Cast and engraved silver, niello, partly gilt. The Israel Museum, Jerusalem. Gift of Astorre Mayer, Milan Accession number: B51.04.0207; 131/030. Photo © The Israel Museum Jerusalem. See *NIDDAH*; SABBATH; IMMERSION, RITUAL: WOMEN; MIKVEH; and WOMEN, ANCIENT: RABBINIC JUDAISM.

Plate 7. *MAḤZOR CORFU*: Elijah sounding a *shofar* while leading the Messiah into Jerusalem. Corfu, Greece, 1709. Courtesy of The Library of The Jewish Theological Seminary. See ELIJAH: BIBLICAL AND POST-BIBLICAL TRADITIONS; GREECE; MESSIANISM: EARLY MODERN; PRAYER BOOKS; *SHOFAR*; and WORSHIP.

Plate 8. TORAH FINIALS (*rimonim*). Cochin, India, 18th century–19th century. Gold: repoussé, cutout and engraved; tin backing. The Jewish Museum, New York City. Photo credit: The Jewish Museum, NY / Art Resource, NY ART64627. See CEREMONIAL OBJECTS; COCHIN JEWS; INDIA; and TORAH.

Plate 9. Israel Dov Rosenbaum, *MIZRAH* (an ornamental plaque on the wall of a synagogue or home indicating east [*mizrah*], the direction of prayer). Podkamen, Ukraine, 1877. Paint, ink, and pencil on cut-out paper. The Jewish Museum, New York City. Gift of Helen W. Finkel in memory of Israel Dov Rosenbaum and Bessie Rosenbaum Finkel. Photo credit: The Jewish Museum, NY / Art Resource, NYART312632. See SYNAGOGUES: NINETEENTH CENTURY; SYNAGOGUES, WOODEN; and WORSHIP.

Plate 10. ḤANUKKAH LAMP. Central Anti-Atlas Mountains (?) (Morocco), 19th–early 20th century. Copper alloy: cast and enameled. The Jewish Museum, New York City. Gift of Dr. Harry G. Friedman Photo credit: The Jewish Museum, NY / Art Resource, NY ART392475. See CEREMONIAL OBJECTS; CEREMONIAL OBJECTS: ISLAMIC LANDS; ḤANUKKAH; and NORTH AFRICA.

Plate 11. Ze'ev Raban (1890–1970), ḤANUKKAH LAMP. Bezalel School, Jerusalem, early 1920s. Copper alloy: die-stamped. The Jewish Museum, New York City. Gift of Dr. Harry G. Friedman, F 5455. Location: NY, U.S.A. Photo credit: The Jewish Museum, NY / Art Resource, NY ART392476. See ART: ISRAELI; CEREMONIAL OBJECTS; and ḤANUKKAH.

Plate 12. Isidor Kaufmann (1853–1921), FRIDAY EVENING, ca. 1920. Oil on canvas. The Jewish Museum, New York City. Gift of Mr. and Mrs. M. R. Schweitzer, JM 4–63. Photo: John Parnell. Photo credit: The Jewish Museum, NY / Art Resource, NY ART58316. See ART, EUROPE: NINETEENTH CENTURY; SABBATH; and WOMEN, MODERN: EASTERN EUROPE.

Plate 13. El (Eleazar) Lissitzky (1890–1941), ḤAD GADYA SUITE (Tale of a Goat): Depiction of "Father bought a kid for two *zuzim*," 1919. Lithograph on paper. The Jewish Museum, New York City. Gift of Leonard E. and Phyllis S. Greenberg, 1986–121c. Location: NY, U.S.A. © Photo credit: The Jewish Museum, NY / Art Resource, NY ART154902. See ART, EUROPE: TWENTIETH CENTURY; ART: ILLUSTRATED YIDDISH BOOKS: "Modern Era"; and PASSOVER.

Plate 14. Marc Chagall (1887–1985), WHITE CRUCIFIXION, 1938. Oil on canvas. The Art Institute of Chicago. Gift of Alfred S. Alschuler, 1946.925. Photography © The Art Institute of Chicago. See ART, EUROPE: TWENTIETH CENTURY; POGROM; RUSSIA; and HOLOCAUST REPRESENTATION: ART.

Plate 15. Jacques Lipchitz (1891–1973), THE SACRIFICE, 1949–57. Bronze. The Jewish Museum, New York City. Gift of Mr. and Mrs. Albert A. List, JM 16–65. Photo by Richard Goodbody, Inc. Photo credit: The Jewish Museum, NY / Art Resource, NY ART312382. See ART, EUROPE: TWENTIETH CENTURY; and HOLOCAUST REPRESENTATION: ART.

Plate 16. Max Weber (1881–1961), STILL LIFE WITH CHALLAH, ca. 1930. Oil on canvas. The Jewish Museum, New York City. Gift of Joy S. Weber, 1994–59. Photo Credit: The Jewish Museum, NY / Art Resource, NY Art392477. See ART, AMERICAN: BEFORE 1940; and SABBATH.

Plate 17. Lee Krasner (1908–1984), SELF-PORTRAIT, ca. 1930. Oil on linen. The Jewish Museum, New York City. Purchase: Esther Leah Ritz Bequest; B. Gerald Cantor, Lady Kathleen Epstein, and Louis E. and Rosalyn M. Schecter Gifts. Location: NY, U.S.A. Photo credit: The Jewish Museum, NY / Art Resource, NY ART379662. See ART, AMERICAN: SINCE 1940.

Plate 18. Ben Shahn (1898–1969), NEW YORK, 1947. Tempera on paper mounted on panel. The Jewish Museum, New York City. Purchase: Oscar and Regina Gruss Charitable and Educational Foundation Fund, 1996–23. Photo: John Parnell. Photo credit: The Jewish Museum, NY / Art Resource, NY ART132848. See ART, AMERICAN: BEFORE 1940; and ART, AMERICAN: SINCE 1940; and NEW YORK CITY.

Plate 19. Leonard Baskin (1922–2000), THE ALTAR, 1977. Lindenwood: carved and laminated. Location: The Jewish Museum, New York City. Photo credit: © Estate of the artist. See ART, AMERICAN: SINCE 1940; and HOLOCAUST REPRESENTATION: ART.

Plate 20. Deborah Kass (b. 1952), SIX BLUE BARBRAS (THE JEWISH JACKIE SERIES), 1992. Screen print and acrylic on canvas. The Jewish Museum, New York City. Gift of Seth Cohen, 2004–10. Photo by Richard Goodbody, Inc. Photo credit: The Jewish Museum, NY / Art Resource, NY ART334071. See ART, AMERICAN: SINCE 1940; and CELEBRITIES.

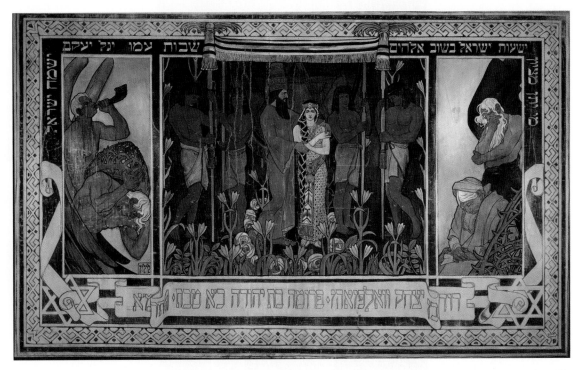

Plate 21. Ephraim Moses Lilien (1874–1925), SKETCH FOR A CARPET (triptych; dedicated to Mr. and Mrs. David Wolff-son): right: *GALUT* [exile], center: ALLEGORICAL WEDDING, left: LIBERATION, 1906. Oil and pencil on canvas. The Israel Museum, Jerusalem. Photo © The Israel Museum Jerusalem. Accession number: B88.0279. See ART, EUROPE: TWENTIETH CENTURY; and ART: ISRAELI.

Plate 22. Reuven Rubin, FIRST FRUITS (triptych): right: SERENITY (THE BEDOUINE); center: FRUIT OF THE LAND; left: THE SHEPHERD, 1923. Oil on canvas. Rubin Museum Collection, Tel Aviv. See ART: ISRAELI.

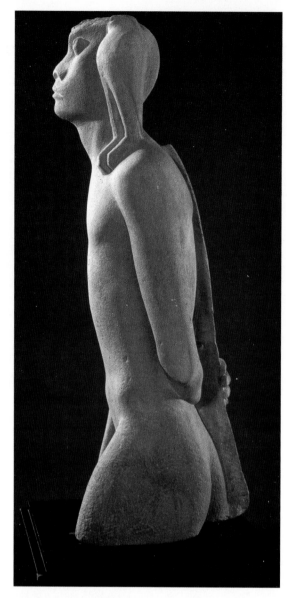

Plate 23. Itzhak Danziger (1916–1977), NIMROD, 1939.
Nubian sandstone. The Israel Museum, Jerusalem. Gift of
Dr. H. David Orgler, Zurich and Jerusalem. © Estate of the
artist. Accession number: B81.0600. Photo (c) The Israel
Museum Jerusalem by Nahum Salpak. See ART: ISRAELI.

Plate 24. Mordecai Ardon (1896–1992), AT THE GATES OF JERUSALEM (triptych): right: SIGN; center: LADDERS;
left: ROCK, 1967. Oil on canvas. The Israel Museum, Jerusalem. Gift of the artist in honor of Israel's twentieth anniversary and the reunification of Jerusalem. © Estate of the artist. Accession number: B67.0546. Photo (c) The Israel Museum
Jerusalem. See ART: ISRAELI.

a morning newspaper famous for its classifieds as well as its pro-Orthodox (see JUDAISM: ORTHODOX) and *Zionist views. Other important newspapers included the *Varhayt* (1905–18), begun by Louis Miller, a defector from the *Forverts*; the *Tog* (Day; 1914–53), a daily that aimed for a higher class of reader, had a liberal Zionist editorial line, and offered a wide range of columnists; and the communist *Frayhayt* (1922–88). The circulation of the Yiddish press peaked in 1916, with 717,146 readers daily.

The New York dailies were just the tip of the Yiddish journalistic iceberg. Not only did they publish local editions in a number of other cities but local newspapers also existed in places such as *Philadelphia, *Chicago, Cleveland, and Montreal. Moreover, weeklies and monthlies were published for a variety of constituencies and interests, including businessmen, women, members of fraternal orders and trade unions, people with common regional origins in the old country, theatergoers, health devotees, literary enthusiasts, and chess players. Among the most significant and long-lasting journals were the anarchist *Fraye arbeter shtime* (Free Voice of Labor; 1890–93, 1899–1977), which was known for its high literary standards; *Di Tsukunft* (The Future; 1892–present), which devoted itself to "science, literature, socialism"; the Labor Zionist *Der Yidisher kemfer* (The Jewish Fighter) first appeared in 1906. The most important humor magazine was *Groyser kundes* (The Big Wag; 1909–27).

In the 1920s, the Yiddish press was at the height of its journalistic prowess, but a decline in readership was already evident. Restrictive laws all but ended the mass immigration, and by 1930 a majority of American Jews were native born. The American-born generation preferred to read English newspapers and magazines, as did the immigrants in increasing numbers. The *Varhayt* had already closed, and in 1928 the *Tageblat* was absorbed by the *Morgn Zhurnal*. By 1927, daily circulation was down to 536,346. Still, the Yiddish press retained a mass readership and exerted significant influence, especially in New York. The decline accelerated after World War II. A small cohort of Yiddish-speaking *Holocaust survivors helped maintain circulations for a while, but they could not make up for the disappearance of the older immigrant readership. The *Tog* and the *Morgn Zhurnal* merged in 1953, and the combined newspaper folded in 1971. The *Frayhayt* closed up shop in 1988. The *Forverts* became a weekly in 1983. Most other magazines and journals also ceased publication. Only the *Hasidic community bucked the trend and founded new publications: The *Algemeyner Zhurnal* (1972–) was close to the Lubavitcher Hasidic community and represented the most continuity with the older Yiddish press, because its founder and editor, Gershon Jacobson (1933–2005), had worked for the *Tog-Morgn zhurnal* (see HABAD). Satmarer Hasidim published *Der Yid* (ca. 1951–) and the rival *Der Blat* (2000–). For further reading, see M. Rischin, *The Promised City: New York's Jews, 1870–1914* (1962); I. Howe, *World of Our Fathers* (1976); and I. Metzker, ed., *A Bintel Brief: Sixty Years of Letters From the Lower East Side to the Jewish Daily Forward* (1990).   DANIEL SOYER

Judah, Kingdom of. Judah was one of the twelve Israelite tribes (see TRIBES, TWELVE) and was also the name of the southern kingdom of the Divided Monarchy, established after the death of *Solomon. The tribe of Judah traced its ancestry to the fourth son of *Jacob and *Leah (Gen 29:35).

When *Joshua allocated the land of *Canaan, Judah was assigned a large region west of the Dead Sea containing Bethlehem and *Hebron. Jacob's blessing of Judah in Genesis 49:8–12, assigning the tribe preeminence and promising that "the scepter shall not depart from Judah," is a reflection of the tribal roots of the Davidic dynasty that succeeded King *Saul and provided more than a half-century of successful united rule of all the tribes under *David and *Solomon. In 930 BCE, with the accession of Solomon's son *Rehoboam, the northern tribes rejected the hegemony of Judah and formed the kingdom of *Israel. The tribes of Judah and Benjamin henceforth constituted the kingdom of Judah with *Jerusalem as its capital and religious center (see TEMPLE AND TEMPLE CULT). Judah was conquered by *Babylon in 586 BCE, and a significant part of the population was exiled to *Mesopotamia. **Map 2**   ELIZABETH SHULMAN

Judah ben Asher (1270–1349) was a rabbi and halakhic scholar. The son of *Asher ben Jehiel (the Rosh) and brother of *Jacob ben Asher, Judah was born in Cologne, *Germany, and immigrated to Toledo, *Spain, where his parents and brother later joined him. In 1321, he succeeded his father as Toledo's rabbi and then assumed the position as head of the Jewish *court (*beit din*) and Toledo *yeshivah* after his father's death in 1327. Judah had limited vision from an infection he acquired in childhood; he describes his treatment by a female eye specialist in his *ethical will (I. Abrahams, *Hebrew Ethical Wills* [1926, 2006]). Judah ben Asher maintained positive relations with the Castilian government, which apparently consulted him in some judicial cases involving non-Jews. His writings include *Zikhron Yehudah*, a collection of his responsa, as well as his ethical will.   KATE FRIEDMAN

Judah ha-Nasi (or Judah the *Patriarch) was a *Tanna of the late second and early third century CE and the leader of the rabbinic community. He is credited with compiling the *Mishnah around 200 CE; in the Mishnah, he is referred to simply as Rabbi.

Judah the Pious. See BAAL SHEM; MIDDLE AGES: HASIDEI ASHKENAZ.

Judaism in virtually all of its present-day forms has its origins in rabbinic Judaism (ca. 50–600 CE), an intellectual and religious movement that developed in the aftermath of the destruction of the Second *Temple in *Jerusalem in 70 CE. Through its most important literary achievement, the Babylonian *Talmud, the ongoing literary and legal endeavor (see HALAKHAH) of rabbinic Judaism shaped and determined virtually all forms of Jewish life and practice before 1800. Moreover, all contemporary forms of Judaism are built on its foundations. The destruction of the Temple, the cessation of sacrificial offerings, and the disempowerment of the hereditary priesthood ended Israelite religion, the religious practice that informs most biblical books (see ISRAELITES: RELIGION; TEMPLE AND TEMPLE CULT). Judaism as invented by the Rabbis represented a new and enduring development in the life of the Jewish people.

Even before the destruction of the Temple in 70 CE, the founders of the rabbinic movement, the *Pharisees, created a way of life that valued personal piety and devotion to *Torah study. Authority in this movement was based on depth of learning and obedience to divine *commandments, rather than on wealth and birth. When the Pharisee leader *Johanan ben Zakkai obtained permission from *Rome to leave the besieged city of Jerusalem with his students to establish a study center in Yavneh, the nascent rabbinic movement constructed a Judaism that could survive and flourish without the Temple cult. Rabbinic tradition relates that when Johanan contemplated the ruins of the Temple, he told his grieving students that the appropriate substitute for Temple sacrifices was acts of lovingkindness (*Avot de-Rabbi Natan* version A, ch. 11a; and *Avot de-Rabbi Natan* B, ch. 7), an indication that rabbinic Judaism, echoing many of the biblical prophets (see BIBLE: PROPHETS AND PROPHECY), placed ethical behavior at the center of the relationship between *God and human beings (see ETHICS entries).

Rabbinic Judaism evolved over a long sweep of time and reflects influences from a variety of cultural settings. It is distinguished by a focus on the role of multivocal interpretation of divine *revelation – the conviction that the divine will emerges through discussion and debate rather than prophetic pronouncement. The Oral *Torah that constitutes rabbinic literature is an expansion and adumbration of the Written Torah; in fact, for the Rabbis both sources of Torah were received at Sinai. Oral Torah is an extensive body of writings that encompass a range of competing interpretations and opinions; although majority views are privileged, minority opinions are preserved as well. All are honored as sincere efforts to understand Written Torah and apply its insights and commandments to the human condition. Jews believe that this effort, the rabbinic endeavor, is continuous and always evolving.

At the conclusion of one of his talmudic readings, the twentieth-century French philosopher Emmanuel *Levinas declared that the most glorious title for *God is "Parent of orphans and Champion of widows" (Ps 68:6). He suggested that the encounter with this exemplar of compassion is best achieved in engagement with divine revelation: "Consecration to God: his epiphany, beyond all theology and any visible image, however complete, is repeated in the daily Sinai of [human beings] sitting before an astonishing book, ever again in progress because of its very completeness" (1994, 108). In this statement Levinas encapsulates the essential rabbinic components of Judaism: the ongoing engagement with Torah in all of its diverse forms and the ethical treatment of the other as the way to human *redemption.

See E. Levinas, "The Nations and the Presence of Israel: From the Tractate *Pesahim* 118b," in *In the Time of the Nations*, ed. E. Levinas and M. Smith (1994), 108; **see also RABBINIC HERMENEUTICS; RABBINIC LITERATURE** entries.

JUDITH R. BASKIN

Judaism, Conservative. The seeds of the Conservative movement were planted in *Germany in the Positive-Historical approach to Judaism originated by Zacharias *Frankel in 1845. Adherents of this movement believed that *halakhah* had always undergone a process of development, and they used the critical study of texts in the academic manner of university scholarship. However, they rejected what they saw as radical and historically unjustified innovations of Reform Judaism (see JUDAISM, REFORM), including abrogation of *dietary laws, curtailment of traditional *Sabbath and *festival observances, and the removal of most Hebrew *prayers from *worship.

Leaders of the American Conservative movement, which began with the founding of the *Jewish Theological Seminary of America (JTS) in *New York City in 1887, proclaimed their belief in "the preservation in the United States of the knowledge and practice of historical Judaism, as ordained in the law of Moses and expounded by the Prophets and Sages of Israel in Biblical and Talmudical writings." This ethos was later reflected in the motto, "Tradition and Change." Thus, the platform of Conservative Judaism stressed fidelity to Jewish law and practice while at the same time acknowledging that Judaism had always been influenced by the societies within which Jews had lived. Although the movement's leaders developed a complex rationale for the positions taken by Conservative Judaism, for many decades most Conservative Jews simply saw themselves as taking a moderate middle position between Reform and Orthodox (see JUDAISM, ORTHODOX) adherents.

At the time of the establishment of JTS, Reform Judaism was the dominant affiliation among Jews in the United States; in 1880, 188 of 200 American synagogues identified as Reform. However, the immigration of several million Jews from *Eastern Europe to America between 1880 and 1920 drastically changed the Jewish religious landscape. JTS was founded by a coalition of German Reform and *Sephardic Jews to train Americanized rabbis to serve the new immigrants, most of whom had never been exposed to modernized forms of Judaism. Headed by Solomon *Schechter, who was brought from a British teaching post at Cambridge to lead the new seminary, the school combined the scientific study of Jewish texts with traditional practice. Graduates founded congregations where the language of prayer was *Hebrew and the liturgy was traditional, but the *sermon was delivered in English and often addressed events of the day as well as traditional explications of the *Torah and *Haftarah readings.

One deviation from tradition that characterized the Conservative movement almost from its inception was a somewhat more egalitarian approach to the status and role of *women. This approach was symbolized for many decades by the installation of mixed-gender seating for worship (known colloquially as family pews) in most Conservative synagogues, the inclusion of girls in afterschool and Sunday morning formal religious education, and the institution of the *confirmation ceremony. After World War II this egalitarianism was expressed in the broader inclusion of women in public organizational and liturgical roles and participation in *life-cycle rituals such as the *Bat Mitzvah.

By the middle of the twentieth century, Conservative Judaism had taken hold among the second and third generation of Eastern European Jewish immigrants, especially in the suburbs of big cities around the United States. Synagogue centers formed the core of the grassroots movement, along with youth, men's and women's *organizations, and overnight *summer camping. In 1975, more American Jews were affiliated with Conservative synagogues than with those of any other movement within Judaism. By the 1990s, however, there were a growing decline in the number of Conservative adherents and an aging of the population in Conservative synagogues. At the end of the first decade of the twenty-first century, the movement has a worldwide membership but is still overwhelmingly American in numbers and character. Today there are more than a million Conservative Jews in the United States and another 100,000 in *Canada, Europe, *Latin America, and *Israel (in the *Masorti [Hebrew for "traditional"] movement).

Fundamental to Conservative Judaism is fidelity to the rabbinic interpretation of Jewish law, which is assumed to have developed over time and continues to develop today. Only those who believe in the sanctity of tradition, adhere to its precepts, and are learned in *Halakhah are considered qualified to interpret these legal traditions. Conservative Jews accept the notion of *revelation without delineating a specific version that must be accepted. Thus, the *mitzvot* (*commandments) are binding, along with ethical precepts and practices including dietary laws (*kashrut*), observance of the Sabbath and festivals, and life-cycle rituals. Jewish peoplehood has always been a central tenet of Conservative Judaism along with a commitment to rebuilding a Jewish state in the land of *Israel ("*Emet veEmunah*": *Statement of Principles of Conservative Judaism* [1988]).

Rabbis are central to the functioning of the Conservative movement. A Committee on Jewish Law and Practice, which includes members from the faculty of JTS, the Rabbinical Assembly (the organization of Conservative rabbis), and some lay observers, rules on matters of Jewish law; only rabbis may submit queries. At the local level, the congregational rabbi is the *mara d'atra* (*Aramaic for teacher/decisor of this place). If the law committee has permitted a range of practice in a given area, then the rabbi of the individual congregation may choose any of the approved practices for her or his *synagogue. The only recourse of the congregation, if a significant number of members disagree with that choice, is not to renew the rabbi's contract. If the law committee has ruled unanimously on a topic (such as the prohibition on officiating at an interfaith marriage), then a Conservative rabbi who deviates from this practice may be asked to resign from the Rabbinical Assembly.

In addition to Solomon Schechter, all of the presidents and chancellors of JTS have been important shapers of the movement. Certain professors have also played central roles, including rabbinics scholars Louis Ginzberg and Saul Lieberman, historian Alexander Marx, and biblical scholar H. L. Ginzberg. Other influential faculty members have included Mordecai M. *Kaplan, founder of the *Reconstructionist movement, and the theologian Abraham Joshua *Heschel. The present chancellor, Dr. Arnold M. Eisen, was appointed in 2007.

The Conservative movement has three major organizational structures, with the Jewish Theological Seminary at the center. The United Synagogue of Conservative Judaism (USCJ) is the organization of the more than seven hundred synagogues. The Rabbinical Assembly (RA), the organization of Conservative rabbis, began as an alumni association of JTS, but currently has many members who were trained elsewhere and were later admitted to the RA. There is an international women's organization called the Women's League of Conservative Judaism, as well as the International Federation of Jewish Men's Clubs. The movement's youth organization, with 25,000 members, is called United Synagogue Youth. The movement also sponsors seven overnight Ramah summer camps and several day camps and organizes trips to Israel for youth and adults. During the last quarter of the twentieth century the Solomon Schechter Day School movement, particularly for the elementary grades,

grew rapidly to include more than seventy schools. In recent decades a growing number of Conservative high schools have been founded in the United States. There is a Conservative Zionist movement called Mercaz and a growing number of Masorti synagogues, as well as youth groups, summer camps, elementary and high schools, and a branch of JTS in Israel (see JUDAISM, ISRAELI FORMS OF).

The Conservative movement has faced many controversies. In the mid-twentieth century, controversial issues concerned driving to the synagogue in automobiles on the Sabbath and using the organ or other live *music in the synagogue on the Sabbath and festivals. Today the vast majority of Conservative synagogues do not have organs, but they all have parking lots, and most Conservative Jews drive to services on the Sabbath and festivals. *Gender equality was the most pervasive long-term controversial issue; it was settled in the mid-1980s, when the *ordination of women as rabbis and, subsequently, as *cantors was approved. At that time the prevailing movement slogan was "Traditional-Egalitarian."

In the late 1980s the institution of patrilineal descent was hotly debated. As the incidence of interfaith marriages among Jews and non-Jews rose in America to its present level of 47% of new marriages, the number of members of Conservative synagogues with grandchildren who were not born Jewish increased (see INTERMARRIAGE). This led to great pressure on the law committee to follow the Reform and Reconstructionist movements in approving patrilineal as well as matrilineal Jewish descent as the basis of Jewish identity. However, this change was resisted. Thus, by the 1990s, there were clear "lines in the sand" that differentiated Conservative from *Orthodox Jews (ordination of women) and Conservative and Orthodox Jews (who accepted only matrilineal descent) from Reform and Reconstructionist Judaism. These divisive decisions caused some Conservative Jews to leave the movement both from the right and the left, but they had the positive effect of more clearly defining the Conservative ideology for members.

The most controversial issue in the first decade of the twenty-first century was the status of openly identified gay and lesbian Jews as candidates for ordination. A 2007 decision by the law committee permitted such gay and lesbian individuals, given the assent of the faculty, to enter JTS and the Ziegler Rabbinical School in California, but not the Jerusalem-based Schechter Seminary.

For further reading, see M. Davis, *The Emergence of Conservative Judaism* (1963); D. J. Elazar and R. M. Geffen, *The Conservative Movement in Judaism: Challenges and Opportunities* (2000); and N. Gillman, *Conservative Judaism: The New Century* (1993).   RELA MINTZ GEFFEN

Judaism, Feminist. This term refers to the transformation of Jewish religious and communal life either through the incorporation of feminist perspectives, values, and practices into mainstream *synagogues and other Jewish organizations, or the creation of new formally or informally organized Jewish groups that self-identify as feminist. Although one might argue that patriarchy is too deeply embedded within Judaism and Jewish life to be ignored or overcome, many contemporary Jewish feminists, especially in North America, maintain that the creation of a feminist Judaism is both possible and imperative. It is possible because the central Jewish concept of *covenant is one that includes men and women, and it is imperative if Judaism is to remain an ongoing, meaningful religious tradition (see also LIFE-CYCLE RITUALS; PRAYER; WORSHIP).

Those attempting to create a feminist Judaism within existing Jewish institutions and organizations place major emphasis on creating inclusive communities that welcome heterosexual, gay, bisexual, and transgendered Jews; traditional and nontraditional Jewish families; Jews who are physically challenged and have other differences – and that provide rituals (such as gay commitment ceremonies performed by a leader of the congregation) that make each of its members feel at home. Egalitarian worship is often equated with feminist Judaism, but most feminists insist that egalitarianism, although important, is insufficient. Also needed are a more just distribution of power within the Jewish community and linguistic changes during public worship that make women's role as covenantal partners clear. These liturgical changes include a deemphasis or elimination of divine images of hierarchical domination, such as Lord and King, and the addition of other *gender-neutral ways of characterizing the deity. Suggestions for alternate terms include *Elah*, the grammatically feminine form of *El* (God), and *Shekhinah*, a grammatically feminine noun referring to God's indwelling presence that medieval Jewish mystics viewed as female by nature. Identifying *Shekhinah* as "She-Who-Dwells-Within," Rabbi Lynn Gottlieb envisions God as a being who connects all of life, expresses our longing for wholeness, and ultimately calls us to justice (*She Who Dwells Within: A Feminist Vision of a Renewed Judaism* [1995]).

In *Standing Again at Sinai: Judaism from a Feminist Perspective* (1990), feminist theologian Judith Plaskow proposes such anthropomorphic images of God as lover, companion, co-creator, and friend, while also endorsing the nonanthropomorphic "richly ambiguous" image of God as *makom* (place) – an image that points "to community as a special place of God's self-manifestation" (165). Poet and theologian Marcia Falk further suggests images composed of the basic elements of creation – earth, water, wind, and fire – such as *eyn ha-ḥayyim*, "wellspring or source of life"; *nishmat kol ḥai*, "breath of all living things"; and *nitzotzot ha-nefesh*, "sparks of the inner, unseen self" – to "help construct a theology of immanence that will both affirm the sanctity of the world and shatter the idolatrous reign of the lord/God/king" ("Toward a Feminist Jewish Reconstruction of Monotheism," *Tikkun* 4 [1989]: 53, 56).

Do such changes, however, in and of themselves constitute a feminist Judaism? For the theologians cited earlier, as well as for many others, the answer is "no." As Judith Plaskow has written, all three basic elements of Judaism – God, Torah, and Israel – need to be reenvisioned before a feminist Judaism can truly be created. This new vision includes constructing a new concept of Israel (or community) that recognizes women as fully Jewish while also taking women's experiences seriously, including the feminist experience of personal empowerment (*Standing Again at Sinai*, 86). Although Plaskow points to *halakhah* (rabbinic law) as negative when it "submerges women in the covenant community" (85), feminist ethicist and theologian Rachel Adler proposes the re-creation and renewal of liberal or progressive Judaism by reappropriating *halakhah* as a

source of meaning. Drawing on the work of ethicist Robert Cover, envisioning law as a bridge between what a community is and what it hopes to be, Adler advocates retaining traditional laws that are grounded in the practice of the progressive Jewish community while adding new laws, which are grounded in new stories, that reflect new communal practices (*Engendering Judaism: An Inclusive Theology and Ethics* [1998]).

The feminist Judaism that Gottlieb, Falk, and Adler envision is a transformed progressive Jewish community composed of women and men. Without rejecting the possibility of transforming mainstream progressive Jewish communities, Plaskow uses the term "feminist community" to refer to "women discovering in community [that] the power of our individual and collective voices... is connected to a greater [power] that grounds and sustains it" (*Standing Again at Sinai*, 86). Although she does not invoke the term "feminist Judaism," Reconstructionist Rabbi Rebecca Alpert attempts to transform Judaism according to a lesbian perspective that is clearly feminist. She seeks to create a balance between individual and communal needs by envisioning lesbian Jews as part of a broad coalition involved in the transformation of Jewish life. This coalition includes heterosexual feminists working with lesbians to change women's roles and places in Judaism; gay Jewish men with whom lesbian Jews have created "alternative structures for community and worship"; and heterosexual intermarried couples who, like lesbian Jews, are concerned "about the importance of differences in loving relationships, and about ways of making relationships across differences holy." It also includes progressive Jewish educators seeking to find ways of teaching children a Jewish history that includes the stories of lesbian Jews and Jews "discouraged by the values of some in the Jewish community" who, together with lesbian Jews, are trying to forge new coalitions "with other [non-Jewish] groups who want to bring justice and peace to a troubled world" (*Like Bread on the Seder Plate: Jewish Lesbians and the Transformation of Tradition* [1997], 165–66).

One must ask, however, whether a feminist Judaism necessitates the creation of a new, trans-denominational movement that views Judaism through the lens of women's experiences. Some would argue that the currently existing trans-denominational *Jewish Renewal movement, which includes a number of small autonomous Jewish groups affiliated with ALEPH (Alliance for Jewish Renewal), is *already* committed to the creation of a feminist Judaism. Others might claim that feminist rituals, such as women's celebration of *Rosh Ḥodesh (New Moon) and women's *Passover *seders*, which tell the story of Jewish women's oppression – as well as the use of new Passover *seder* ritual objects, including a "Miriam's Cup" filled with water and an orange added to the *seder* plate or decorated on *matzah* covers to symbolize the ever-expanding roles of women in Judaism – are indications that it is possible to create a feminist Judaism without abandoning mainstream communal affiliation. Susannah Heschel, however, has written that working for change within particular denominations may be a misdirection of feminist efforts; she suggests, "Judaism is not an edifice lying behind doors and guards and we should not have to go through a denomination to reach it" ("Introduction," *On Being a Jewish Feminist: A Reader*, ed. S. Heschel, [1983], xxiii).

The creation of a feminist Judaism need not imply female separatism.

Nonetheless, as Judith Plaskow maintains, it is the "crucial contradiction between the increased participation of women in all aspects of Jewish life and the *content* of the tradition that... provides the warrant and necessity for women-only spaces" ("The Continuing Value of Separatism," [2000], in *The Coming of Lilith: Essays on Feminism, Judaism, and Sexual Ethics, 1972–2003*, ed. with D. Berman [2005], 160). The size and nature of these spaces may differ. Yet what they share in common is the goal of creating Jewish communities that not only welcome and honor difference but also take seriously the lived experiences, voices, and visions of Jewish women.

ELLEN M. UMANSKY

Judaism, Humanistic. Humanistic Judaism maintains that Judaism is an ethnic culture created by the Jewish people and molded by Jewish experience. Established by Rabbi Sherwin Wine in 1963 in Detroit, Michigan, Humanistic Judaism eschews theological-religious terms and instead defines Jews as those who identify with the history, culture, and future of the Jewish people. The roots of Humanistic Judaism lie in the *Haskalah*, the secular nationalism of the past hundred years, the democratic revolution of modern times, and the *Holocaust experience, all of which have taught Humanistic Jews to value pluralism, ethics, and human responsibility. Humanistic Judaism was also developed as a solution to the problem of retaining Jewish identity among nonreligious secular North American Jews at a time when other forms of secular Jewish identity were declining.

According to Humanistic Judaism, *reason is the best method for the discovery of truth. Thus, people have the power to solve human problems, and ethical guidelines derive from the human quest for renewal, justice, and happiness. Because Humanistic Judaism's worldview centers around the autonomous human and not a god figure, god-language and *worship are inappropriate to a humanistic style of life, and neither the *shema* nor the *kaddish* prayers are recited.

Humanistic Jews study Jewish history and culture from a naturalistic perspective; they cultivate Jewish languages, celebrate holidays in a humanistic spirit, mark life-cycle events with secular poetry and music, respond ethically to personal needs and social issues, and organize communities in which goals are accomplished cooperatively. The *kibbutz movement in *Israel formulated an ideology, ethic, and practice based on humanistic values and Jewish cultural traditions, and Humanistic Judaism also shares much in common with Reconstructionist Judaism, with its emphasis on retaining Jewish identity while accepting a scientific worldview and a humanistic ethical outlook. However, Humanistic Judaism presents a more radical departure from traditional Judaism than does Reconstructionism, because it has created nontheistic rituals and ceremonies. Many Humanistic Jewish communities are served by certified leaders. In ascending order of training, the titles of these leaders are *madrikh* (guide), senior leader, and rabbi, all trained by the International Institute for Secular Humanistic Judaism.

RACHEL GORDAN

Judaism, Israeli Forms of. The practice of Judaism and the development of Jewish culture in Israel have been profoundly influenced by *Zionism's complicated attitude toward Jewish tradition. A secular movement of Jewish national revival, Zionism was an effort to renew Judaism and the Jewish people, in part through radical changes in the observance and practices of Jewish tradition.

For its proponents, Zionism served as a kind of ethno-national substitute for traditional Judaism, which was conceived as archaic, "exilic," and degenerative. Instead of this "old" Judaism, Zionist ideology constructed an image of the "new Jew," who was represented as embodying an authentic national Jewish identity rooted in the independent existence of a *Hebrew-speaking society in the Land of Israel. This transformation of Judaism and Jewishness allowed the Israeli Jew to identify Israeliness with Judaism/Jewishness. Indeed, many contemporary Israeli Jews, including those who do not identify themselves as "religious," continue to observe some traditional religious rituals, even though the dominant Zionist culture has been indifferent and sometimes hostile to such observance.

The creation of the State of Israel, along with the influx of new immigrants still closely tied to traditional practice, breathed new life into Jewish religious tradition. Jewish symbols were adapted to build and to strengthen national identity and loyalty. The first and second generations of native-born Israelis, whose Israeli identity was constructed under the inspiration of Zionist ideology, resolved the paradox of being a secular Jew by redefining Judaism in Israeli-Zionist terms. The civil religion of the state provided a coherent system of holidays, rituals, symbols, myths, values, and beliefs that were interpreted as Jewish without the stain of the *Diaspora, through an identification of Israeli-Zionist identity and Jewishness. Traditional rituals that did not embody these Zionist ideals were considered culturally trivial.

The most significant change in this regard in the last decades of the twentieth century has been the dramatic weakening of Zionism's grip on Israeli political culture. This process began with the Yom Kippur War (1973), when the basic beliefs on which Israeli-Zionist identity was built began to be questioned. Without the Zionist meta-narrative, Israeli Jews were left without an unmediated tie to Judaism and Jewishness and without a foundation for the Jewish component of their Israeli identity. At a cultural level, the dissociation of Judaism and Israeliness left Judaism as the property of the *Orthodox and the rabbinical establishment, allowing the latter a practical monopoly on the definition of Jewishness.

As the Zionist meta-narrative gradually lost its hold during the 1970s and 1980s, it was replaced, at least in the dominant realm of the public sphere, by a post-national narrative, built around the values of universalism and humanism. In the framework of this narrative, both Jewish-religious identity and Israeli-Zionist ethno-national identity (with its accompanying Jewish component) were perceived as anachronistic identities that only served to isolate Israelis from the rest of the world. The new narrative emphasized the motif of peace, and the consequences of peace contained messianic and eschatological elements. Indeed, some interpreted this approach as a reinterpretation of Jewish *messianism. There were also those who, under the cry for a "return to the Jewish book shelf," sought new interpretations of Judaism in which the values of universalism and humanism became the major values of the Jewish tradition. However, these voices were a minority among the wide range of voices that emphasized the ties among Judaism/Jewishness, religion, and the Orthodox establishment, which were often portrayed as obstacles to truth and peace. Indeed, for many Israelis, Judaism (or Orthodoxy) became a symbol of extremism, violence, and ultranationalism. In their private lives Jews continued to observe some Jewish ritual, and in their minds and hearts continued to harbor feelings of association with Jewishness and the Jewish people, but the public culture provided neither a language nor a symbol system for its expression. This is the paradox of religion in Israel: Although practically all surveys of Israeli Jews suggest that the overwhelming majority, even among those who do not define themselves as "religious," observe many Jewish rituals and report that Judaism and the Jewish people are important to them, Judaism and Jewishness play a decidedly secondary role in mainstream Israeli culture.

Common public discourse divides Israeli Jews into three categories of Jewish identity, based on level of observance: "secular" (*ḥiloni*), "traditionalist" (**masorti*), and "religious" (*dati*). These categories are usually further divided, as religious identification has developed into a socio-political mark of identity. According to the most recent surveys, people who identify as secular (or "not religious") constitute about half of Israeli Jews. Around one-third of Israeli Jews identify as "traditionalist," and one-fifth as "religious." Nevertheless, as research into the meaning associated with these labels shows, they tend to confuse more than explain. Thus, for example, although the term "secular" is usually understood to denote nonobservance, secular Israeli Jews report a rather high level of observance of Jewish rituals and practices. It seems instead that "secular" is used to denote a "neutral" religious identity that provides a "default" identity for those who do not wish to be identified by their observance.

Ethnicity – that is, country of origin – plays a decisive role in the practice of Jewish tradition in Israel. Mizraḥim, those born in Arabic-speaking or predominantly Muslim countries, or those whose parents came from such countries, tend to have a high level of observance and strong commitment to Jewish, as well as Israeli, identities. This is far less the case for **Ashkenazim*, those born in European or predominantly Christian countries, or those whose forebears were born in these countries. In addition, Mizraḥim tend to maintain a more moderate attitude toward Jewish tradition, identifying mostly as "traditionalists," whereas Ashkenazim tend to present more extreme attitudes and usually choose either "secular" or "religious" as the labels of their Jewish identity (see also various entries under ISRAEL, STATE OF).

Research on this topic includes C. S. Liebman and E. Don-Yehiya, *Civil Religion in Israel: Traditional Judaism and Political Culture in the Jewish State* (1983); S. Deshen, C. S. Liebman, and M. Shokeid, eds., *Israeli Judaism (Studies of Israeli Society vol. VII)* (1995); and C. S. Liebman and E. Katz, eds., *The Jewishness of Israelis: Responses to the Guttman Report* (1997).

YAACOV YADGAR

Judaism: Jewish Renewal Movement. This loosely defined movement within contemporary non-*Orthodox American Judaism emphasizes intense personal spirituality, serious and creative text study, and social justice. It also privileges

Jewish experiences that are intimate, participatory, and egalitarian, promoting the spiritual growth and healing of individuals, communities, and society as a whole. It draws heavily from *rabbinic teachings and *mysticism, as well as *Ḥasidic wisdom, combining them with the insights of contemporary *ecology, *feminism, and psychology. Jewish Renewal emerged in the 1980s and 1990s as a successor to the *ḥavurah* movement, which fostered small, mostly non-synagogue-based worship and study communities and alternative communal prayer groups (*minyanim*). In this sense, its most important intellectual "ancestor" would have been Abraham Joshua *Heschel, who as early as the 1950s noted a spiritual ache and lack of emotive warmth within postwar American Jewry. Although not anticlerical in the formal sense (it does, in fact, ordain its own rabbis), Jewish Renewal fosters a "do it yourself" Judaism that encourages the participant to "own" Judaism and to become an active worshiper, rather than being dependent on professionals. Therefore, it is not surprising to note that Jewish Renewal's unique *worship style embraces the use of "New Age" techniques, such as chant, meditation, and even yoga, as well as new artistic expressions, in its efforts to create a modern intensity in worship. It has reimagined the study and teaching of *Torah, preferring interactive techniques over "frontal" lectures and seminars. It has boldly reclaimed previously ignored or disinherited Jewish theological options by fostering interests in mysticism, angels, the *afterlife, and the healing potential of prayer. Jewish Renewal has a broad social vision. It is unstintingly egalitarian regarding issues of *gender, sexuality, and the family. Its politics are unfailingly liberal, even leftist. Its liberalism manifests itself in its openness to the teachings and influences of other religious traditions; this is most manifest in the Jewish Buddhist ("JuBu") phenomenon, but is also found in thoughtful encounters with Hinduism and Sufism (Muslim mysticism). Jewish Renewal often teaches the implicit message that all spiritual paths are similar and that all spiritual wisdom is interchangeable, even to the point of flirting with syncretism.

To be sure, Jewish Renewal struggles with critical issues. How does one construct a Jewish identity that is rooted in tradition and yet trumpets creativity (often radical) and individualism? How can a movement be authentically Jewish and yet be influenced by a plethora of non-Jewish intellectual and theological streams? And will this movement prove to be fertile, replicating itself into the next generation?

The principal exponents of Jewish Renewal have been "Reb Zalman" Schachter-Shalomi (born 1924, Poland), who first translated Jewish mysticism into a popular, practical idiom; Arthur Waskow (born 1933), who has combined leftist politics with Jewish spirituality; Arthur Green (born 1941), a scholar of Ḥasidism and mysticism; Lawrence Kushner (born 1943), a major popularizer of Jewish mystical texts; Michael Lerner (born 1943), editor of the leftist *TIKKUN* magazine and proponent of the "politics of meaning," the notion that politics and public life should speak to the inner anguish of the contemporary individual; and Rabbi Marcia Prager, a prayer leader, storyteller, and musician.

JEFFREY K. SALKIN

Judaism, Liberal. Liberal Judaism is one of the forms of Progressive Judaism in *Britain, together with Reform Judaism. Liberal Judaism is to the left of British Reform

Judaism and sees itself as similar in practice, attitudes, and definition to Reform Judaism in North America.

Judaism, Masorti. Because Israel has an official chief rabbinate that is *Orthodox, Conservative Judaism, as do other forms of non-Orthodox Judaism, suffers a number of limitations in Israel. This situation is particularly problematic because, by the end of the second decade of the twenty-first century, populations will likely have shifted such that for the first time more Jews will live in Israel than in the United States. Non-Orthodox rabbis are not recognized to officiate at *marriages or Jewish *divorce proceedings. The thorniest issue has been *conversion to Judaism, particularly in the case of tens of thousands of immigrants to Israel from the former *Soviet Union who want to convert to Judaism but do not want to become Orthodox. There have also been problems in obtaining land and funds to build synagogues and schools. Despite these obstacles, and particularly in the last twenty years, the Masorti movement has created and maintained institutions in Israel, trained native-born rabbis and teachers, and nurtured synagogues and a youth movement, Noar Masorti (NOAM). The growth of an Israeli brand of Masorti Judaism, as well as branches in Europe and *Latin America, will be important to watch in the coming decades. For further reading, see J. Ruskay and D. Szioni, eds., *Deepening the Commitment: Zionism and the Masorti Movement* (1990).
RELA MINTZ GEFFEN

Judaism, Neolog. Neolog Judaism is a moderate reform movement that developed in mid-nineteenth-century *Hungary. It modernized the style of Jewish worship and introduced organ music, but retained the traditional liturgy and gender separation. Orthodox Hungarian Jews, *Hasidim and non-Hasidim alike, denounced the Neolog movement as apostasy. In 1868 the Hungarian government sanctioned the division of Hungarian Jews into three separate communities: Neolog, Orthodox, and status quo ante (also Orthodox). In the peace agreements that followed World War I, Hungary lost significant territories and population, including almost half of its Jews. The most religious and least assimilated Jewish communities lived in the areas that were lost. After 1920, the majority of Hungary's remaining Jews, almost half of whom lived in Budapest, affiliated with Neolog. Neolog continues to be the most prominent form of Jewish practice in present-day Hungary.

Judaism, Orthodox: Modern Othodox refers to an interpretation of Orthodox Judaism that arose in the nineteenth century to affirm the authority of the intellectual and communal heritage of pre-modern rabbinic *Judaism and to oppose advocates of a conscious alteration or reform of Judaism "in the spirit of the times." Ideologically, many Modern Orthodox Jews see themselves in continuity with the teachings of such nineteenth-century Orthodox rabbis as Samson Raphael *Hirsch and Esriel Hildesheimer, who, in differing ways, advocated a stringent observance of *halakhah (the rabbinic legal system) coupled with a positive engagement with aspects of modern western culture. Overwhelmingly *Zionist and pro-Israel in their orientation, Modern Orthodox Jews tend to support ideologies of the Religious Zionist [*Mizrachi] movement as it developed in Israel and to connect with the teachings of Rabbi Abraham Isaac ha-Kohen *Kook. They often look to *Yeshiva

University for education and guidance, and many of them think of its long-time rabbinic leader, Rabbi Joseph Baer *Soloveitchik, as their intellectual and spiritual mentor. For the most part, Modern Orthodoxy flourishes in North America, although Modern Orthodox Jews constitute an important part of the anglophone immigrant community in Israel.

In North America, Modern Orthodoxy developed before World War II as a reaction to the Orthodoxy of the *Yiddish-speaking immigrant generation. A key dividing line between "immigrant" and "modern" Orthodoxy was use of the English language in sermons and publications. On the other side, a key concern was differentiating Modern Orthodoxy from *Conservative Judaism, whose right wing espoused positions that were often almost indistinguishable from those of the Modern Orthodox. In that era, the overwhelming majority of Modern Orthodox Jews sent their children to public schools, giving them a supplementary Judaic education.

In the latter half of the twentieth century, Modern Orthodox Jews have expressed themselves to a large extent in terms of their educational choices. Like nearly all contemporary Orthodox Jews, they overwhelmingly give their children an intensive Jewish education in day schools where they also receive their secular education and socialize with children from similar backgrounds. This day school education is commonly supplemented with a year or more of study in an Israeli *yeshivah or seminary. However, the Modern Orthodox differ from *Ultra-Orthodox (Ḥaredi) Jews in their attitude toward secular education and engagement with contemporary society as a whole. Whereas Ultra-Orthodox Jews seek to limit secular education to the minimum possible under the law, even at the cost of limiting their children's economic prospects, Modern Orthodox Jews see at least an instrumental value to secular studies in general, and to higher education in particular, in terms of making a living in contemporary society and engaging in the professions. Moreover, some Modern Orthodox Jews perceive a positive good to be derived from secular studies through the broadening and enriching of Torah study. In cases where the teachings of Torah seem to be in conflict with current scientific theory, such as the age of the universe, Modern Orthodox Jews are likelier than Ultra-Orthodox Jews to accept the findings of science and to reinterpret biblical and rabbinic sources accordingly.

Ultra-Orthodox Jews seek to minimize formal contact between their communities and those of non-Orthodox Jews and certainly do not wish to accord to non-Orthodox religious leaders or organizations any de jure recognition. Modern Orthodox Jews are somewhat divided on this issue: Some advocate organizational separation from non-Orthodox Jews, whereas others see positive results in Orthodox engagement with non-Orthodox organizations.

Sociologically, Modern Orthodox Jews have been often characterized by a reputation for laxness in halakhic observance. This has placed Modern Orthodoxy at a distinct disadvantage because the global trend within Orthodox Judaism in the last decades of the twentieth century and into the twenty-first century has been a move toward greater exactitude in halakhic observance, often characterized as a "shift to the right." This phenomenon has been facilitated by the trend among Modern Orthodox day schools to hire Ultra-Orthodox teachers, as well as the exposure to the viewpoint of right-wing Orthodoxy that is often part of the study experience in Israel.

Modern Orthodox Jews, in contrast to their Ultra-Orthodox counterparts, are not often characterized by firm and clear ideological stances. Indeed, it has been argued that the "modernity" of Modern Orthodox Jews is largely behavioral and not ideological. Thus, in contrast to Ultra-Orthodox Jews, who can point to a strong authority structure in the persons of the heads of major Ḥaredi *yeshivot* and Ḥasidic *rebbes*, Modern Orthodox Jews have no real functioning central authority. The authority of rabbis identified with Modern Orthodoxy, like Shlomo Riskin, is personal and does not begin to compare with that of prominent rabbis in the Ḥaredi communities. The former president of *Yeshiva University, Rabbi Norman Lamm, has suggested replacing the label "Modern Orthodoxy" with "Centrist Orthodoxy." In terms of publications, Modern Orthodox Jews have nothing to compare with the impact created by Artscroll and other anglophone Ḥaredi publishers and often use the books these publishers produce.

Ideological proponents of Modern Orthodoxy, led by Rabbi Saul Berman, organized themselves in 1999 in a group called *Edah*, with the slogan, "The Courage to Be Modern and Orthodox." Among other things, *Edah* articulated positions that affirmed the equality of women in Judaism while preserving the halakhic process. The demise of *Edah* in 2005 demonstrates the organizational weakness of ideological Modern Orthodoxy. The liberal Orthodox yeshiva *Chovevei Torah* has taken up some of the void left by *Edah*.

One of the pioneers of research into Modern Orthodoxy was Charles Liebman, whose 1966 study, *Orthodoxy in American Jewish Life*, was highly influential; also important are the articles of sociologist C. I. Waxman, especially "Dilemmas of Modern Orthodoxy: Sociological and Philosophical," *Judaism* (Winter, 1993). Also useful are S. C. Heilman and S. M. Cohen, *Cosmopolitans & Parochials: Modern Orthodox Jews in America* (1989); and Heilman, *Sliding to the Right: The Contest for the Future of American Jewish Orthodoxy* (2006).

IRA ROBINSON

Judaism, Orthodox: Ultra-Orthodox. This term refers to fervently religious Jews who adhere to the strictest interpretations of *halakhah (Jewish legal tradition), in particular those that prohibit compromises with modern culture and secular studies. Ultra-Orthodox Jews minimize social contact and intellectual engagement with those outside their community, except in cases of economic necessity. Members of these communities prefer the Hebrew designation Ḥaredim (literally "tremblers," from "those who tremble before God's word" [Isaiah 66:2 and also 66:5]).

This isolationist, anti-modernist ideology developed in late-eighteenth-century *Central Europe, where Jewish Orthodoxy emerged in response to the modernization agenda of the *Haskalah, or Jewish Enlightenment. As Orthodoxy coalesced into a distinct denomination of Judaism in direct opposition to the emergence of the *Reform movement, its proponents debated the appropriate attitude toward non-Jewish culture and the proper posture toward non-observant Jews. Orthodox Jews who advocated minimal contact with Gentile culture and prohibited secular studies became known as the Ultra-Orthodox.

An official Ultra-Orthodox community first emerged as one of three *Hungarian Jewish denominations at the Hungarian Jewish Congress of 1868–69. This convocation took place in response to Hungary's 1867 "Jewish Emancipation Law." The other two denominations were the *Neolog (Reform) and the Status Quo, which today might be called Modern Orthodox. In 1876, the Orthodox community in *Germany, where the Reform movement was the largest Jewish denomination, became bitterly split. Those favoring a modern form of traditionally observant Judaism that remained an integral part of the larger community were championed by Rabbi Dov Bamberger. Rabbi Isaac Breuer led those who insisted on complete separation from non-Orthodox Jews and Jewish movements, especially the Reformers and *Zionists. Breuer's influential work, *Der Neue Kusari,* articulated an uncompromising Ultra-Orthodox theology that even categorized collaboration with Reform Jews as a modern form of idolatry. His supporters advocated *Trennungsorthodoxie,* or separatist Orthodoxy, although Breuer and his followers did not ban all secular studies. They followed the prescription of Rabbi Samson Raphael *Hirsch, *"Torah im derekh eretz"* (Torah with worldly culture), which encouraged engagement with those aspects of German culture that did not directly threaten religious observance.

The most extreme form of Ultra-Orthodoxy, insisting on intellectual and cultural isolationism and rejecting any innovations in Jewish life, was found in southern Hungary and *Romania where Rabbi Moses Sofer of Pressburg (1762–1839) had established an extreme approach. Strictly Orthodox Jews in the *Russian Empire, including today's *Poland, *Ukraine, and *Baltic states, never developed an official theology of separation because the Reform movement, which had triggered such separatism in the West, was almost nonexistent in these regions. However, in response to secular Jewish ideologies, like *Zionism and *socialism, there was a discernible movement toward increased piety and religious conservatism among both *Ḥasidim and *mitnaggedim (non-Ḥasidic Orthodox) and within the major rabbinical academies (yeshivot), most of which banned the study of secular subjects, unless required to include them in their curricula by Russian law.

In addition, there was a discernible rise in vigilance regarding the observance of certain aspects of Jewish law; there was also a renewed emphasis on practices that had previously been treated with a certain degree of latitude, such as the use of traditional Jewish language, ethnic customs, appearance, and dress. For men this change involved an intensified rejection of western clothing, in favor of the traditional *kapotehs* or long black coats and black hats, and an insistence on not trimming beards or *peyot* (side curls). For women, there was a renewed emphasis on the laws of modesty including completely *covering the hair with hats, *tikhels* (head scarves), or *sheitels* (wigs) and wearing understated dresses that concealed the arms and legs. Because language was perceived as a conduit to social assimilation, Ultra-Orthodox Jews in northern Hungary, Romania, Poland, and Lithuania insisted on maintaining *Yiddish as the vernacular of Jewish daily life. Only in Germany and the large cities of central Hungary, such as Budapest, Szeged, and Miskolcz, did Ultra-Orthodox Jews speak German or Hungarian among themselves.

Ultra-Orthodoxy vehemently rejected Zionism, not only as a modern, secular nationalist ideology modeled after European nationalisms but also as a usurpation of the traditional insistence on passively awaiting the *messiah's appearance. Many of the leading rabbis of Central and Eastern Europe issued bans on any cooperation with Zionists, condemning them as heretics. At the same time, the *Agudat Israel party, founded at a conference in Kattowitz, Poland, in 1912, supported the renewal of immigration of Jews to Palestine but rejected Zionist ideology. Its neo-socialist branch, *Poalei Agudat Israel*, led by Isaac Breuer, established religious *moshavim* (collective farms) in *Palestine during the years of the *British Mandate (see ISRAEL, STATE OF: AGRICULTURAL SETTLEMENTS, 1878-1948). The emergence of *Agudat Israel* further divided the Ultra-Orthodox community because numerous Ḥasidic *rebbes*, most notably Ḥayyim Elazar Shapira of Munkatch, condemned the organization as a modern, neo-Zionist, and hence heretical political movement. This uncompromising opposition to even the slightest compromise with Zionism or any other modern political organizations was taken up after the *Holocaust by Rabbi Joel Teitelbaum, the Satmar rebbe, whose followers in New York constitute the largest Ḥasidic community outside of Israel, and by the Ultra-Orthodox group, *Neturei Karta*, in *Jerusalem.

The Ultra-Orthodox communities of Europe were entirely destroyed during the *Holocaust, along with more than 90% of their members. After *World War II, however, against most expectations, Ultra-Orthodoxy reconstituted itself, establishing communities, consisting mainly of Holocaust survivors, in Israel, the United States, *Belgium, *Canada, *Britain, and *France. These Ultra-Orthodox communities have experienced remarkable growth, unanticipated by the large majority of Jewish social scientists. In the first decade of the twenty-first century, they are the fastest growing segment of the Jewish community worldwide, a result of high birthrates and minute attrition. In large cities, such as Antwerp, B'nai B'rak, Brooklyn (New York), Jerusalem, Lakewood, (New Jersey), London, Los Angeles, Montreal, and Paris, Ultra-Orthodox Jews live apart from the non-Orthodox and maintain autonomous communal and religious institutions. In addition to *Agudat Israel*, which continues to operate as a worldwide federation representing the majority of Ḥaredi Jews (except the ardently anti-Zionist), the Ultra-Orthodox maintain their own rabbinical and community councils. In Israel, they are represented by the *Edah ha-Ḥaredit* as well as by several political parties, such as *Agudat Israel* and *Degel ha-Torah*. In North America, the rabbinic leadership group is Agudas ha-Rabonim of the United States and Canada. The highest and final arbitrator of political and halakhic issues of contention is the international tribunal, *Mo'etset Gedolay ha-Torah* (Council of Torah Sages).

An interesting recent development is the attraction of many *Sephardic Jews in Israel and the United States to the Ḥaredi ideology and way of life, including adoption of Eastern European Ḥaredi dress and halakhic stringencies that were entirely unknown in their Muslim lands of origin. Although there is little exact information, the number of Ultra-Orthodox Jews is estimated at 300,000 in North America, 500,000 in Israel, and another 75,000 in Canada, Europe, and *Latin America. For further reading, see J. Katz,

A House Divided: Orthodoxy and Schism in Nineteenth-Century Central European Jewry (1998); and A. Mittleman, *The Politics of Torah: The Jewish Political Tradition and the Founding of Agudat Israel* (1996).
ALLAN NADLER

Judaism, Progressive. Progressive Judaism refers to contemporary forms of Judaism that are rooted in the teachings of the biblical *prophets, particularly those that stress inwardness and a desire to enact the values of justice, equality, democracy, peace, personal fulfillment, and collective obligations. Although its practices are anchored in Jewish thought and tradition, Progressive Judaism grants full equality to all Jews in Jewish life and religious practice, regardless of *gender and sexual orientation. Moreover, the denominations that are part of the movement challenge laws and practices that are contrary to fundamental Jewish principles of justice and ethical behavior. **See WORLD UNION FOR PROGRESSIVE JUDAISM.**
RACHEL GORDAN

Judaism, Reconstructionist. This movement, which originated in the philosophy of Mordecai *Kaplan (1881–1983), is now considered the fourth religious denomination of American *Judaism, along with *Reform, *Conservative, and *Orthodox (see JUDAISM entries).

Kaplan defined Judaism as the evolving religious civilization of the Jewish people, and his main ideas are presented in his seminal 1934 work, *Judaism as a Civilization*. He understood Jewish civilization to encompass a way of life that includes not only beliefs but also values, language, law, literature, customs, art, food, and music. Kaplan espoused a utopian vision of an organic Jewish community that would function democratically. He was also an avid cultural *Zionist and believed that a Jewish state in *Palestine would be the center that would hold these organic communities together in a worldwide, democratic Jewish structure of governance.

THEOLOGY, OBSERVANCE, AND LITURGY: Kaplan was best known for his radical religious vision. He defined *God as "the Power that makes for salvation" and rejected anthropomorphic and supernatural views of God; rather, he understood God as an impersonal force that acts through and not beyond the natural world and inspires human beings to aspire to do good in the world. Although Kaplan's position has been thought by many to be atheistic, he was a passionate believer in the existence of this impersonal force. Kaplan also rejected the idea that the Jews were in any way chosen. A God that did not act in history could not single out one people for any special role. Kaplan taught that all peoples have a unique function to fulfill in the world and that each group could, through what he called "ethical nationhood," serve a divine purpose.

Kaplan did not approach Jewish observance from the perspective of *halakhah. Instead he encouraged observance of the *Sabbath and *dietary laws because they bind the Jewish people together. Kaplan expressed these new approaches through liturgical change. He published a *haggadah* in 1941 that told the *Passover story as the triumphs of Moses and Israel, rather than God. A Sabbath *prayer book, published in 1945, changed the wording of key prayers to eliminate the concept of *chosenness, reward and punishment, and references to *Temple sacrifice; it also removed special status for the descendants of *priests and *levites because that did not reflect a democratic vision. Orthodox rabbis publicly burned the Sabbath prayer book in 1945, and Kaplan was excommunicated.

THE SPREAD OF RECONSTRUCTIONISM: Kaplan hoped that his ideas would influence the leadership of the American Jewish community, but he did not wish to start a new movement. He was a rabbi of a synagogue that he founded in 1922, the Society for the Advancement of Judaism (SAJ), in *New York City. At the SAJ he carried out his experiments in liturgy. The SAJ is also famous as the location of the first modern *Bat Mitzvah, held rather unceremoniously for Kaplan's eldest daughter Judith in 1922.

Kaplan's primary vocation was as Professor of Homiletics at the *Jewish Theological Seminary, a position he held from 1909–63. There he influenced several generations of rabbis, some of whom were intent on turning his vision into a program. The task of movement building fell to Kaplan's son-in-law, Ira Eisenstein (1906–2001). Eisenstein slowly built an organizational structure that began with the Reconstructionist Foundation in 1940. In 1954 he organized the Reconstructionist Federation of Congregations. Through the next few decades these institutions grew gradually, adding a few dozen or more Reconstructionist groups around the United States and *Canada.

The slow growth of the movement can be attributed to several factors in addition to Kaplan's own reticence. Many of his followers were institutionally loyal to the Reform and Conservative movements. In addition, Kaplan's ideology was intellectually challenging and rigorous, attracting a small number of Jews who were dissatisfied with traditional *synagogue life. As sociologist Charles Liebman pointed out in an influential study in the 1970s, Reconstructionism functioned as the folk religion of American Jewry. Kaplan's work accurately depicted what American Jews believed and practiced, but not necessarily how they wanted Jewish institutions to look.

For Reconstructionism to grow as a movement, it was necessary to start a school for training rabbis. The *Reconstructionist Rabbinical College (RRC) was founded in 1968 in *Philadelphia. The school reflected the Reconstructionist ideology; thus, the *ordination of women followed Kaplan's belief in women's equality. The curriculum traced Jewish civilization through its historical stages. Living in two civilizations meant that graduates of the RRC would also obtain doctoral degrees in religious studies from a secular institution. The first graduates organized the Reconstructionist Rabbinical Association (RRA) in 1974. The RRA welcomed not only graduates of the RRC but also rabbis who were supportive of the Reconstructionist philosophy and movement. The addition of an organization of Reconstructionist rabbis enabled the Reconstructionist movement to mirror the tripartite organizational structure of the Reform and Conservative movements and gain legitimacy on the national level. Changes followed Kaplan's death and Eisenstein's retirement in the early 1980s. In 1981 Ira Silverman was chosen to succeed Eisenstein as president of the RRC, and Arthur Green, David Teutsch, and Dan Ehrenkrantz have served subsequently. Their leadership has emphasized peoplehood, community, democracy, women's equality, the creation of new rituals, and an informal style of *worship.

SHIFTS IN EMPHASIS: Ultimately Kaplan's theology and his unbridled enthusiasm for America would become a source of tension, as spirituality became a dominant feature of the next generation of Reconstructionism. Reconstructionist Judaism has followed the contemporary Jewish trend toward a focus on the human–divine encounter that is predicated on a more traditional view of God as a partner in conversation. Although Reconstructionist Jews in the early twenty-first century are not likely to believe that God responds directly to supplication or acts to reward or punish them in their lives, they are likely to seek a relationship with God through prayer and meditation.

The emphasis on inclusive community is the other defining characteristic of Reconstructionist Judaism. Reconstructionists welcome Jews who see themselves as unwelcome in the rest of the Jewish community, particularly gay men and lesbians and the intermarried. The Reconstructionist Rabbinical Association adopted patrilineal descent (accepting as Jews those who are the child of a Jewish father and a non-Jewish mother) and developed guidelines for welcoming intermarried couples in 1978. The Reconstructionist Rabbinical College was the first seminary to admit openly gay and lesbian students in 1984. Contemporary Reconstructionism is best described in R. Alpert and J. Staub's primer, *Exploring Judaism: A Reconstructionist Approach* (2nd ed., 2001).
    REBECCA T. ALPERT

Judaism, Reform: France. From early in the nineteenth century there were reform-minded French Jews, but unlike in Germany (see JUDAISM, REFORM: GERMANY), they were not rabbis, but well-educated and scholarly laymen. Michel Berr (the first Jewish lawyer in France) and Olry Terquem (a mathematician) were early exponents of radical reform; they advocated switching the Sabbath to Sunday, using French in prayers, and abbreviating the service. Although the *Consistories never accepted radical change, they gradually modernized *synagogue *worship through a number of measures that created an outwardly more decorous appearance.

Under pressure from lay members of the Consistories, a conference of chief rabbis was convened in Paris in May 1856 to suggest changes that would reduce defections from the synagogues. The rabbis at the conference decided to improve and modernize rabbinical education by transferring the rabbinical seminary, founded in 1829 in Metz, a city without a university, to Paris. The goal was to encourage rabbinic students to pursue a secular postsecondary education alongside their religious studies. The conference adopted a dress code for rabbis that resembled that of the Catholic clergy. In regard to synagogue services, the representatives approved shortening services, instituting more decorum, and making greater use of *sermons. They endorsed synagogue blessings for newborn girls and a ceremony of "religious initiation" (*confirmation) for both boys and girls, which would be based on an examination of the candidates' achievement in religious studies. The rabbis urged that funeral services be conducted with more pomp and ruled that organs were permitted to be used in synagogues on the *Sabbath and *festivals, provided that they were played by non-Jews.

Ceremonial changes were instituted unevenly. To avoid a breach within French Judaism, it had been agreed that implementation should be left to the discretion of individual rabbis, rather than forced on the more traditional communities. Paris had already taken the lead with the introduction in the Paris synagogue of four-part music as early as 1820 and a choir a decade later. In 1852 an organ was installed. The confirmation ceremony was introduced in Paris in 1840 and became almost universal by the 1850s. By that time, too, burial practices and *circumcision were modernized, and ritual ceremonies for newborn girls were in use. There were occasional attempts by small groups to create more radically reform synagogues, but the consistorial system had no provision for alternative synagogue movements, and therefore no Reform movement emerged. Only at the end of the century was a durable Reform congregation established, in response to the suggestion by Chief Rabbi Zadoc Kahn in 1896 that Sunday services might stem the tide of defections by making Judaism available to the many who were required to work on Saturdays. Kahn then instituted a series of popular Sunday lectures that included liturgical elements, and in 1899 his son-in-law, Rabbi Israel Lévi, took over the project.

With Kahn's blessing, a group of reform-minded Jews constituted itself under the name *L'Union Libérale Israélite* and used space in the main consistorial synagogue building for Sunday Reform services. The 1905 law on separation of religion and state made it possible for these reformers to disconnect from the Consistory and establish an independent congregation, which they did in 1907. Limited for a long time to one synagogue in Paris, it was only after World War II that additional Reform synagogues were established in France. For more on this topic, see P. C. Albert, *The Modernization of French Jewry: Consistory and Community in the Nineteenth Century* (1977); and P. E. Hyman, *The Jews of Modern France* (1998).   PHYLLIS COHEN ALBERT

Judaism, Reform: Germany. Although the first congregation with a revised ritual was established in *Amsterdam in 1797, the Reform movement in Judaism had its greatest European success in *Germany where, by the last decades of the nineteenth century, the majority of Jews adhered to a moderately reformed Liberal Judaism. Ritual reform first appeared in Germany during the period of French dominance in Westphalia (1808–14) and then briefly in Prussia until it was prohibited there during the period of Napoleonic reaction in 1823. It established itself permanently in Hamburg with the formation of the Hamburg Temple in 1817. Among early *worship reforms were use of the vernacular alongside *Hebrew, organ accompaniment, a weekly edifying *sermon in German, a higher degree of decorum, and the removal of passages from the liturgy that were vengeful or expressed hopes for return to *Zion and the reestablishment of the sacrificial *Temple cult. These changes aroused opposition on the part of traditionalists, but they did not succeed in stifling the movement.

By the mid-1840s, a new rabbinate had emerged in Germany that was university educated and committed to religious reform. Its members participated in rabbinical conferences (1844–46) that dealt with such matters as liturgical reform, the role of the Hebrew language, the observance of the *Sabbath under conditions of occupational integration, and the religious equality of *women. In Germany the Reform movement was closely related to the struggle of German Jews for political *emancipation and was dependent on the progress of political liberalism. However, leaders of the movement stressed repeatedly that they would not sacrifice their beliefs to gain political ends. By mid-century

the rabbinical leadership held a broad spectrum of opinions – from those like Zacharias *Frankel (1801–1875), who favored only a moderate reform based on Jewish law and the will of observant Jews, to Samuel Holdheim (1806–1860), who distinguished sharply between an eternal moral and theological essence and changeable forms that could be adjusted to contemporary circumstances. Holdheim became the rabbi of a radical independent congregation in *Berlin, which was unique in the German movement in that it called itself Reform rather than Liberal. Abraham *Geiger (1810–1874) occupied a position between Frankel and Holdheim; like the former, he stressed historical continuity, but like the latter, he based Judaism on *prophetic morality rather than Jewish law (*halakhah). During the second half of the nineteenth century the German Reform movement stagnated as idealism gave way to materialism. German Protestantism, which in some respects had served as a model for Reform, turned from liberalism to reaction. Only toward the end of the century did a new generation of liberal religious thinkers, especially Hermann *Cohen (1842–1918) and Leo Baeck (1873–1956), breathe new life into the movement.

Under the *Nazi regime, Liberal Judaism in Germany experienced a brief revival as the synagogue became an emotional refuge and Liberal rabbis like Baeck and Joachim Prinz (1902–1988) offered spiritual resistance in the face of degradation. In recent years Liberal Judaism has reappeared in Germany; a number of congregations have been established as well as a rabbinical seminary, the Abraham Geiger College, in Berlin.   MICHAEL A. MEYER

Judaism, Reform: North America. There are approximately 1.5 million Reform Jews belonging to slightly more than nine hundred Reform congregations in the *United States and *Canada. In addition, many others identify as Reform Jews without belonging to or participating in a Reform congregation. The Reform movement has grown dramatically relative to the other Jewish religious streams and in particular the *Conservative movement. Reform Jews form a plurality of those affiliated with one of the Jewish denominational groups in the United States, which in turn is less than half of all American Jews. The Reform movement has been regarded as the trendsetter among the large American Jewish denominations. Although the *Reconstructionist movement has frequently embraced various reforms slightly earlier and *Jewish Renewal and others have embraced spiritual innovations much more vigorously, the Reform movement has nevertheless been seen as the most influential progressive voice because of its numbers (see JUDAISM entries).

The earliest synagogues in colonial America were *Sephardic Orthodox, and the Reform movement began to develop in the United States in the 1820s and 1830s with the growing *immigration of Jews from *Central Europe. The first attempt at building a Reform temple in the United States began in 1824 in the Sephardic community of *Charleston, South Carolina, when forty-seven members of Congregation Beth Elohim signed a petition to the board of directors requesting that they consider a number of minor ritual reforms, including the introduction of a small number of prayers in English.

In the period between 1836 and 1881, American Reform Judaism grew steadily with the arrival of about 250,000 Jews from Central Europe, many of whom were already sympathetic to the movement. On the eve of the large-scale immigration of *Eastern European Jewry that began in the 1880s, the Reform movement dominated American Judaism. It appealed to people who wanted to maintain a Jewish identity and various Jewish practices without a system of compulsory ritual adherence. No longer obligated to observe all the laws and customs of Orthodox Judaism, members of Reform synagogues could maintain forms of practice that remained distinctive and meaningful in a modern Christian-dominated society and yet did not separate Jews significantly from their Christian neighbors.

The first leader of American Reform Judaism was Isaac Mayer *Wise (1819–1900), who arrived in the United States from Bohemia in 1846. He was the main influence behind the establishment of the Union of American Hebrew Congregations (UAHC) in 1873, and he founded the *Hebrew Union College (HUC) in Cincinnati, Ohio, in 1875 (the first seminary for rabbinic training in North America) and the Central Conference of American Rabbis (CCAR) in 1889. He was regarded as the leader of the moderate wing of the Reform movement, which battled with the radical reformers, most of whom lived along the East Coast. Led by David *Einhorn (1808–1879), the radical reformers eventually succeeded in creating a deritualized form of Liberal Judaism, which became known as Classical Reform. Classical Reform was defined by the 1885 *Declaration of Principles*, which became known as the Pittsburgh Platform. It minimized ritual and emphasized ethical behavior in a universalistic context as the central message of the biblical prophets.

An important feature of American Reform Judaism was its stated commitment to the equality of women; it was expressed in various ways, including mixed seating during worship. Family pews were first introduced in Albany, New York, in 1851, and then in 1854 in *New York City; by the 1870s, they were the norm in most American synagogues. Girls and boys were educated together, and American Reform congregations initially replaced *Bar Mitzvah with *confirmation, a group ceremony for young people in their mid-teens. *Ordination of women as rabbis and cantors, however, did not occur until late in the twentieth century. The first synagogue sisterhood groups emerged in the 1890s; these local groups were linked when the National Federation of Temple Sisterhoods (now Women of Reform Judaism [WRJ]; see SYNAGOGUE SISTERHOODS) was established in 1913. In 2005, WRJ had 75,000 members in five hundred local affiliates in the United States, Canada, and twelve other countries. Organization membership independently financed the publication of *The Torah: A Women's Commentary* (ed. T. Eshkenzi and A. Weiss [2008]), with contributions from more than 250 female scholars and rabbis.

Reform theologians were influenced by the modern biblical criticism of their time and were involved as well in the academic study of religion. They fostered a Reform Judaism that did not interpret the *Bible in a literal manner and saw no conflict between religion and science. Most believed that *God created the world in some form or manner and continued to be involved as part of an ongoing process of progressive *revelation. Late-nineteenth-century and early-twentieth-century reformers stressed the importance of ethical monotheism. They believed that the ethical message of Judaism derived from one beneficent creator God who exists as the source and goal of all humanity. Without the existence of God, any attempt to aspire to high ethical standards of behavior would be useless. The mission of Israel was to spread the concept of ethical monotheism, serving as God's messengers in an age without *prophets.

As a corollary to this idea of the mission of Israel in the *Diaspora, most but not all Reform leaders rejected *Zionism. Judaism was a portable sanctuary, and Jews could practice their religion wherever they lived. As Minister Gustavus Posnanski famously declared at the dedication of the new building of the newly Reform congregation in *Charleston, South Carolina, "this country is our Palestine, this city our Jerusalem, this house of God our Temple." These Reform leaders believed that because Jews were fully accepted as equal citizens in the United States of America, they had no need and no inclination to leave what they regarded as their homeland. Various American Reform statements of principles confirmed that they no longer believed in the religious concept of the ingathering of the exiles. For example, rabbinical leaders at the Philadelphia Conference of 1869 wrote, "The Messianic aim of Israel is not the restoration of the old Jewish state under a descendant of David, involving a second separation from the nations of the earth, but the union of all the children of God in the confession of the unity of God, so as to realize the unity of all rational creatures, and their call to moral sanctification."

Although a number of Reform rabbis, such as Max Heller and Bernhard Felsenthal, supported Zionism, the majority undoubtedly agreed with these words of the Pittsburgh Platform of 1885: "We consider ourselves no longer a nation, but a religious community; and we therefore expect neither a return to Palestine, nor a sacrificial worship under the sons of Aaron, nor the restoration of any of the laws concerning a Jewish state." This majority sentiment in the late nineteenth and very early twentieth century began to change after future Supreme Court Justice Louis Dembitz *Brandeis became a Zionist in 1912. After the *Nazi advent to power in Germany in 1933, increasing numbers of Reform Jews understood that, regardless of religious theory, there was a dire need for a place of refuge for European Jews. By the early 1940s, only a handful of Reform Jews remained staunchly anti-Zionist. They organized the American Council for Judaism, which exists in attenuated form to the present.

The American religious environment changed in the years immediately after *World War II, and the Reform movement adjusted accordingly. Jews of every persuasion were moving in ever larger numbers to the suburbs, and it was important for the religious denominations to organize new congregations that would in turn contribute to the development of their movements. Much of the credit for the relatively successful adaptation of Reform Judaism to the post–World War II environment goes to Maurice Eisendrath (1902–1973), who became executive director of the Union of American Hebrew Congregations (renamed the Union for Reform Judaism in 2003) in 1943 and its president in 1946. Eisendrath increased the profile of the movement by moving the national headquarters from Cincinnati to New York City in 1948. The "House of Living Judaism" was built on Fifth Avenue and 65th Street in Manhattan, next to the major New York City Reform synagogue, Temple Emanu-El. Although there had originally been one rabbinical seminary, the Hebrew Union College (HUC) in Cincinnati, by the end of the twentieth century, there were four separate centers. The 1950 merger of the Jewish Institute of Religion (JIR), which had been established by Rabbi Stephen Wise, with the Hebrew Union College provided a *New York City location. HUC-JIR then established additional campuses in *Los Angeles and *Jerusalem, making it the largest and most prestigious Reform rabbinical seminary in the world.

One of the central issues facing the Reform movement was how to provide its members with guidance on ceremonial observance without creating another legal structure. Any obligatory system of religious laws would have been anathema to most Reform Jews. Nevertheless, many religious leaders felt that Reform Judaism allowed too much freedom and that most lay people interpreted this freedom as meaning that they did not have to observe any ritual whatsoever. Reform "*covenant" theologians believed that one of the solutions to this problem was to reemphasize the centrality of the berit, the covenant between God and the children of Israel. The covenant was presented as an organic historical relationship that was reciprocal and continued from generation to generation. Emphasis on this covenant provided a liberal framework for helping people understand that incorporating religious practices into their lives could be an expression of commitment to this relationship with the divine.

The HUC-JIR began ordaining women in 1972; in recent decades, female rabbis have brought an energy and dynamism that have enlivened Reform worship and education. The first woman to be ordained was Sally Jane *Priesand. HUC-JIR established the Sally J. Priesand Visiting Professorship in her honor in the fall of 1999 at its New York campus. By the early twenty-first century, women rabbis, as well as cantors, synagogue presidents, and other religious leaders, have become increasingly numerous, not only in Reform Judaism but also in Reconstructionist and Conservative Judaism (see RABBINIC ORDINATION OF WOMEN).

Another area where Reform Judaism has changed dramatically is in the realm of *worship. The Union Prayer Book had been a ubiquitous presence since the closing years of the 1800s; by the 1960s, many younger people found its ponderous language excessively formal and its theological conceptions outdated. There was, however, no consensus on what a new prayer book might look like. The CCAR Liturgy Committee decided that it was not possible to create a single service that would be satisfactory to the different theological positions within the movement, and so they decided to include multiple services in the new prayer book, thus allowing for considerable theological diversity. When Gates of Prayer: The New Union Prayer Book was published in 1975, it included ten Sabbath evening and six Sabbath morning services that differed in theological focus. Unfortunately, Gates of Prayer was published in a non-gender-sensitive format and was also awkward to use. After many years of work and numerous drafts, the CCAR published a new prayer book, Mishkan T'filah (Tabernacle of Prayer) in 2007. This was the first Reform prayer book in memory to have a Hebrew name, and unlike previous prayer books published by the CCAR, it only opened from the Hebrew side. It incorporated many traditional elements that had been excised from the original Union Prayer Book, although there were still places where the liturgy differed from the Orthodox prayer book, either because of theological differences or for purposes of brevity (see PRAYER BOOKS: UNITED STATES).

Outreach was another revolutionary development in American Judaism that was pioneered by the Reform movement. In December 1978, UAHC President Alexander Schindler called for a sustained effort to reach out to the unaffiliated, particularly the growing number of Jews who had intermarried. Arguing against the norms of the times, Schindler said that *intermarriage did not necessarily mean that a couple was lost to the Jewish community. This call led to an extensive effort to welcome interfaith couples as well as converts, now referred to as "Jews by choice." As more intermarried couples began raising children, the question of how to treat the offspring of Jewish fathers and Gentile mothers became more acute. On March 15, 1983, the CCAR passed a resolution prepared by the CCAR Committee on Patrilineal Descent entitled "The Status of Children of Mixed Marriages." Jewish tradition had generally held to matrilineal descent, teaching that the religion of the mother determined the religion of her child. However, this resolution declared that the child of one Jewish parent, whether female or male, is presumed to be of Jewish descent; it went on to say: "This presumption of the Jewish status of the offspring of any mixed marriage is to be established through appropriate and timely public and formal acts of identification with the Jewish faith and people. The performance of these *mitzvot serves to commit those who participate in them, both parent and child, to Jewish life." This resolution generated a great deal of controversy, both before and after its adaptation. Some saw it as a radical and unwarranted departure from tradition, whereas others hailed it as a revolutionary breakthrough. The sheer numbers of children of such unions make patrilineal descent an essential element of Reform outreach, and many within the Conservative movement believe that they need to adopt a similar approach as soon as possible.

The Reform movement also moved toward the full acceptance of gays, lesbians, bisexuals, and transgendered individuals. In 1990, the Hebrew Union College began admitting openly gay and lesbian students to their rabbinic program. In 1996, the CCAR passed a resolution supporting the rights of homosexual couples to a civil marriage, and in 2002 it supported the rights of rabbis to officiate at same-sex commitment ceremonies (see also ETHICS, SEXUAL).

A new theological platform for Reform Judaism was approved in 1999 at the CCAR annual conference in Pittsburgh, where the original Classical Reform Pittsburgh Platform had been endorsed in 1885. The new platform reintroduced many traditional religious concepts and rituals. Although these were presented as options that could be evaluated rather than as *commandments that had to be observed, their inclusion was a clear indication of the Reform movement's increasing return to many traditional Jewish practices. Yet, the Reform movement has also accepted new definitions of Jewish identity and religious fidelity, such as patrilineal descent. In the first decade of the twenty-first century Reform Judaism is, as a number of observers have pointed out, moving in two directions at the same time.

For further reading, see M. A. Meyer, Response to Modernity: A History of the Reform Movement in Judaism (1988); A. M. Schindler, "Not by Birth Alone: The Case for a Missionary Judaism," in Contemporary Debates in American Reform Judaism: Conflicting Visions, ed. D. E. Kaplan (2001); R. N. Levy, A

Vision of Holiness: The Future of Reform Judaism (2005); M. Washofsky, *Jewish Living: A Guide to Contemporary Reform Practice* (2001); and D. E. Kaplan, *American Reform Judaism: An Introduction* (2003).   DANA EVAN KAPLAN

Judea was the Greek and Roman designation for the southern area of the *Land of Israel; it derived from *Yehud, the Persian name for the province including *Jerusalem and the surrounding region (see PERSIA, ANCIENT).

Judeo-Arabic Language and Literature. Judeo-Arabic is one of the spoken and written languages used by Jews in Arabic-speaking lands. Like other Jewish languages it is characterized by the use of Hebrew script and a large quantity of *Hebrew and *Aramaic vocabulary, as well as pronunciation, grammar, and idiomatic expressions that differ from the dominant language. Judeo-Arabic originated in the Arabic dialect spoken by Jews living in *Arabia in the pre-Islamic period. Unfortunately, no Judeo-Arabic written documents survive from that time. As *Islam expanded into the Middle East and *North Africa, Judeo-Arabic became the dominant language of medieval Jewish communities under Muslim rule. Important works written in Judeo-Arabic include *Saadia Gaon's (882–942) *Book of Doctrines and Opinions*, Judah *Halevi's (1086–1167) *Kuzari*, and *Maimonides' (1135–1204) *Guide of the Perplexed.*

After the fifteenth century, as a result of increased segregation of Jews and Muslims and the establishment of separate Jewish neighborhoods, Jewish knowledge of Classical Arabic diminished. At the same time the level of education throughout the Muslim world also declined, and written texts in both communities became more colloquialized. These changes can be seen in the genre of *ŝarḥ*, colloquial Judeo-Arabic translations of the Bible that were more accessible than Saadia Gaon's tenth-century translation. This genre also grew in importance with the eclipse of scientific writing in Arabic in general and in Judeo-Arabic in particular. After the 1492 expulsion from *Spain, Judeo-Arabic writing was devoted almost exclusively to Jewish subjects, including *ŝarḥ*, legal texts, liturgy, and poetry. Characterized by local dialects and regional literary forms, Judeo-Arabic had a broad geographic distribution, expanding from the Middle East to Europe, the Americas, India, and East Asia through Jewish immigrations to these areas from *North Africa, *Iraq, and *Yemen.

Secular themes returned in the second half of the nineteenth century with the establishment of Judeo-Arabic newspapers, particularly in Tunisia. This press functioned in the same way as its Yiddish and Ladino counterparts (see JOURNALISM entries) providing news of interest to the Jewish community. Judeo-Arabic periodicals served as an agent of modernization by informing their readers of developments in science and technology and translating world literature into the local dialects. However, with the establishment of the *Alliance Israélite Universelle network of schools in the Middle East and North Africa, Judeo-Arabic began to be eclipsed by French, and the Judeo-Arabic press disappeared. Judeo-Arabic did continue to flourish in the folklore and oral traditions of Jewish communities, even among the first generation of immigrants to *Israel. However, the children of immigrants were subject to the Israeli government's emphasis on Hebrew language, and as a result

Judeo-Arabic dialects began dying out. In the early twenty-first century, significant research is focused on documenting the language, literature, and oral traditions of these communities.

For further reading see J. Blau, *The Emergence and Linguistic Background of Judeo-Arabic: A Study of the Origins of Middle Arabic* (1965); and N. Stillman, *The Language and Culture of the Jews of Sefrou, Morocco: An Ethnolinguistic Study* (1988).
                    SHARON VANCE

Judeo-German: See YIDDISH

Judeo-Persian Language and Literature. Jews were living in *Iran (*Persia) for some two thousand years before the Arab Islamic conquest in the seventh century, but the cultural life of the community in those times is largely unknown. Some Jewish works date from the early centuries of Islamic Iran, but most surviving manuscripts date from later centuries. The literature of the Jews of Iran is written in the Judeo-Persian language, the classical Persian language using *Hebrew script. Old Jewish Persian texts have features of the local dialect (Farsi) of southern Iran just before and after the Islamic conquest. Works in Judeo-Persian include Bible translations and commentaries, religious and secular poetry, chronicles, rabbinical works, grammatical treatises, didactic poetry, historical texts, and translations of medieval Hebrew *poetry, as well as transcriptions of classical Persian poetry. For examples, see V. B. Moreen, ed., *In Queen Esther's Garden: An Anthology of Judeo-Persian Literature* (2000).

A demonstrably close connection exists between Jewish literary culture and classical Muslim Persian literature. Judeo-Persian poets incorporated stylistic devices, names, words, and expressions from Muslim Persian poetry. Shahin, a highly influential fourteenth-century Judeo-Persian poet, used Persian and Islamic elements to present biblical narratives in the Persian epic mode. Imrani of Shiraz (1454–1536) translated and poeticized a tractate of the *Mishnah using Persian motifs and a Persian setting. His 1523 versified *Fathnameh* (Book of Conquest) retells narratives from the books of *Joshua, *Ruth, and *Samuel. A seventeenth-century Judeo-Persian manuscript of this work, with colored illustrations in the Persian (Isfahan) style, now in the British Museum, exhibits the close connection between Judeo-Persian and Muslim Persian texts. Imrani's works combine Jewish and Muslim legends and elements from Persian poetry. His *Ganjnameh* (Book of Treasure), a versified discourse on religious topics composed in 1536, has Jewish content and Hebrew words and expressions, as well as ideas and expressions common to Muslim Persian poetry. Binyamin ben Misha'el (pen-name Amina), born in Kashan in 1672, wrote lyrical poems. Other Judeo-Persian writers used Persian motifs and settings, proverbs, and moral tales; there are also Judeo-Persian translations of the great secular classical poets of Iran, including Ferdowsi (tenth century), Sa'di (thirteenth century), and Hafez (fourteenth century). Siman Tov Melammed (d. 1823 or 1828) wrote a mystical-philosophical work that expressed Jewish concepts in Muslim mystical (Sufi) terminology.

The works of Judeo-Persian poets, especially those of Shahin, brought delight and comfort to Jewish audiences. These works figured in the everyday life of the community and were read and sung on the *Sabbath and other special occasions, using traditional Persian melodies. Jews could often recite from memory works by well-known Judeo-Persian and Muslim poets, which were copied into the Hebrew script. Muslim traditions and texts that have disappeared are often preserved in Judeo-Persian texts and oral traditions. However, few Judeo-Persian works have been translated into western languages, and the full extent of the Judeo-Persian cultural contribution remains largely unknown. Recent research includes G. Lazard, *The Origins of Literary Persian* (1993); and A. Netzer, "Persian Jewry and Literature. A Sociocultural View," in *Sephardi and Middle Eastern Jewries: History and Culture in the Modern Era*, ed. H. Goldberg (1996).   RIVANNE SANDLER

Judeo-Spanish: See LADINO

Judges, Book of. (Hebrew, *Shoftim*). Although the historical chronology is difficult to reconstruct, the book of Judges purports to document an intermediate period between the unity of Israel under the leadership of *Joshua (2:6–10) and the institution of a monarchy (see ISRAELITES: KINGSHIP). The book's narrators emphasize several problems during this era, beginning with the fact that the *Israelite tribes live among other nations, mix with them, and adopt their customs (2:10b–15, 3:5–8, 10:6). Furthermore, the Israelites repeatedly neglect their covenantal duties and are subsequently punished by *God (2:1–5, 3, 10:10–16). The Israelites also lack a king, and therefore "every person does as he sees fit" (17:6, 18:1, 19:1, 21:25). Although the book proposes both short- and long-term solutions to these problems, the conundrum of *covenant persists. Each time the Israelites neglect the fidelity due to God, they lose God's protection and are defeated by their enemies. The short-term solution is for a leader or "judge" (*shofet*) to arise, enlist God's support, and deliver Israel from oppression (2:16). If the leader further inspires Israelite repentance, then a halcyon period ensues. These judges or charismatic leaders, however, often preside over a specific tribe or cluster of tribes; thus, they promote factionalism rather than unity. In the most egregious example, the book of Judges ends with most of the other tribes attacking the tribe of Benjamin. The book's underlying message appears to be that Israel needs a king, yet the subsequent books of *Samuel and *Kings describe the shortcomings of kingship and hint at the superiority of *prophecy. Although adherence to the covenant appears to be the key to stability, Judges, like most biblical books, speaks to the impossibility of achieving flawless collective obedience to divine *commandments. This implies that the covenant is a constantly shifting relationship between Israel and God; like human relationships it presents challenges as well as security. Nevertheless, Judges conveys an enduring sense of the past (6:7–10); the covenant transcends human institutions and survives them.

The judges themselves display martial qualities rather than juridical ones and rescue Israel through force of arms. Several are described as heroes, *gibborim*, a word from the same Hebrew root as *gever* (man; 6:12, 11:1). Women's bodies often operate as symbols of the disunity or unity of the tribes (see chapters 19–21); foreign women ensnare Samson (13–16), and anxiety concerning mothers with low status permeates the stories of Abimelech (8:29–9:57) and Jephthah (11–12). The book's daughters, all of whom seem to lack mothers, suffer bleak fates (1:14–15, 11:34–40, 19, 21:20–24). *Deborah the prophetess, a "mother in Israel" (5:7), is an exception: She foresees and enables a battle (4:6–9) and memorializes it in a victory song. The stories of Jephthah's daughter (11:34–40), the woman raped and battered at Gibeah (19), and the young women apprehended at *Shiloh (21:20–24) suggest that national cohesion is built on the abuse of women, whereas the narratives about Deborah (4:9), Jael (4:17–21), and Delilah (16:4–20) show that women with insight into human character can have a strong impact on national events. For further reading, see S. Ackerman, *Warrior, Dancer, Seductress, Queen: Women in Judges and Biblical Israel* (1999); and M. Bal, *Death and Dissymmetry: The Politics of Coherence in the Book of Judges* (1988).
                                                              RACHEL HAVRELOCK

Jüdischer Frauenbund (JFB; League of Jewish Women) was an organization founded in Germany in 1904 by Bertha *Pappenheim. The JFB combined feminist and social welfare goals with a strong sense of Jewish identity. Among its concerns were fighting for women's suffrage, expanding women's roles in the Jewish community, providing women with career training, and fighting the traffic in women (see PROSTITUTION: MODERN TIMES).

Judith, Book of. See APOCRYPHA; HANUKKAH AND WOMEN

K

Kabbalah is the traditional appellation of the major Jewish esoteric-mystical group of schools that appeared in the late twelfth century and continue to this day. The term in Hebrew simply means "tradition." In this context, however, it refers to the "secret tradition" given to *Moses on Mount Sinai. Scores of kabbalistic circles have operated in Judaism during the past eight centuries, producing hundreds of original spiritual worldviews that differ considerably from each other. There is hardly any idea or trend in kabbalistic literature whose opposite cannot also be found in this vast treasury of esoteric speculations. In addition, there are very few elements that are common to most kabbalistic systems because each school and each writer had particular emphases and original ideas.

Although it is nearly impossible to present general characteristics of the whole vast range of kabbalistic spirituality, most kabbalists shared the view of a series of divine emanations, the *sefirot*, which serve as a ladder from the unreachable supreme godhead to the created universe. Many kabbalists tended to a dualistic worldview (see DUALISM), believing that the universe is a battleground between divine and satanic powers and that this struggle is reflected within every person. A significant number placed *messianic expectations, and sometimes messianic activity, at the center of their teachings. One of the unique characteristic of many kabbalistic systems, an element that separates the Kabbalah from other esoteric and mystical systems, is the belief in the cosmic consequences of individual actions. Fulfillment of *commandments and ethical behavior can have a positive impact on the divine powers while evil deeds can have a contrary effect. The term "theurgy" is often used to describe this phenomenon that insists that the divine presence in the world and the fate of the universe are actually decided by human actions, good and evil.

Some kabbalists were interested in *magic and included such elements in their works; others were not. Some kabbalists used *numerology extensively; many others did not. The Kabbalah, as such, is not mysticism but rather the opposite: It claims to be based on ancient tradition rather than on direct individual experience of the divine realm; yet some kabbalists like Abraham *Abulafia and Moses Ḥayyim *Luzzatto, among others, described such personal experiences of the divine.

HISTORICAL DEVELOPMENT: In the last decades of the twelfth century and the first part of the thirteenth, several circles of Jewish esoterics produced visions of the world that included a new concept. They suggested that within *God there are different layers of divine powers with different functions. Three such circles appeared in *Germany and northern *France: the circle of the Kalonymus family in the Rhineland; the Unique Cherub Circle, which based its traditions on a fictional *baraita attributed to Joseph ben Uziel; and the anonymous author of the *Sefer ha-Ḥayyim* (Book of Life). It seems that each of these groups produced its teachings independently. Three other groups existed in southern Europe: the *Iyyun* circle, named after its central text, *Sefer ha-Iyyun* (Book of Contemplation), which flourished in southern *France or northern *Spain in the late twelfth century and the beginning of the thirteenth; the *Bahir* (Book of Brilliance), which was identified by Gershom *Scholem as the earliest text of the Kabbalah; and the circle of kabbalists in Provence, headed by Isaac ben Abraham (known as *Isaac the Blind). The *Iyyun* circle presented a mostly independent system concerning the structure of the divine world. It is unclear whether there was any connection between the *Bahir* and the southern France circle. Scholem viewed the *Iyyun* circle as following the teachings of the *Bahir*, yet there are meaningful differences between them that are difficult to explain if they were in close connection.

The direct history of kabbalist schools begins with the *Iyyun* circle in southern France, which was the main inspiration for the center that emerged in the Catalan town of Gerona in the first half of the thirteenth century. Two kabbalists, Ezra ben Solomon and Azriel, produced their writings there, unifying and developing the teachings of the *Bahir* and their predecessors. The next generation of kabbalists in Gerona was headed by Moses ben Naḥman (*Naḥmanides), who was one of the most influential leaders of Spanish Jewry in that period; he and several members of this circle took part in the great controversy over the writings of *Maimonides that divided Spanish Jewry in 1232–35 and later. From the center in Gerona, the Kabbalah spread, and several circles were active in the second half of the thirteenth century. These included the Cohen brothers, Jacob and Isaac, in Castile, and Abraham Abulafia, a wandering teacher with his own unique mystical system. The Kabbalah reached *Italy at that time, but its main center was the Spanish school headed by Moses de *Leon and Joseph Gikatilla, who wrote numerous kabbalistic works in Hebrew. The *Zohar*, the most important and influential work of the Kabbalah, emerged from this circle at the end of the thirteenth century. This was the "golden age" of the medieval Kabbalah, but its teachings were known only to the few people interested in this esoteric tradition and had minimal impact on Jewish culture as a whole.

The age of the *Zohar* was followed by a period of relative decline when kabbalistic circles were few and far between; one probably flourished in *Byzantium in the fourteenth century, producing the works of *Sefer ha-Peliah* (The Wondrous Book) and *Sefer ha-Kanah* (The Book of the Kanah Family). In the last decades before the 1492 expulsion from Spain, there was a surge of kabbalistic writings, many of them expressing intense messianic expectations. After the expulsion, kabbalists spread to other countries, mainly Italy, as well as *Greece and Turkey in the flourishing *Ottoman Empire. In this era the Kabbalah emerged from esoteric circles and became increasingly a part of general Jewish intellectual discourse. The *Zohar* was quoted by many, especially in Italy, and was printed in the sixteenth century. Kabbalah replaced the tradition of Jewish rationalistic philosophy, which was discredited after the expulsion, because it was blamed for the mass conversion of Spanish Jewish intellectuals to Christianity (see *Spain, Christian).

In the late fifteenth century, the Kabbalah began to spread beyond the boundaries of Judaism when some humanists in Florence, led by Count Pico della Mirandola, became interested in its teachings. Pico – following in the path of his teacher, Marsilio Ficino, who had translated the Hermetic library from Greek to Latin – studied Hebrew, had Jewish teachers, and employed translators who knew Hebrew and Latin. Under Pico's direction, Flavius Mithredates, a Jewish convert to Christianity, translated several kabbalistic works into Latin. One of Pico's disciples, Johannes Reuchlin, a German, became expert in Hebrew and wrote several works; the most important among them is *De arte kabbalistica* (1517), a highly detailed exposition of Kabbalah. In the sixteenth century, Christian Kabbalah appeared in Germany, France, and later the Netherlands, becoming a part of European scholarly discourse for the next two hundred years. It was, however, a Christian phenomenon, addressing Christian theological problems. Pico declared that the veracity of Christianity is best demonstrated by the disciplines of magic and Kabbalah. The Kabbalah, interpreted as testimony to Christian concepts, proved the antiquity of the Christian message, as these humanists understood it (see CHRISTIAN HEBRAISM).

In the first decades of the sixteenth century, kabbalists began to congregate in the town of *Safed, in the *Galilee, attracted by the belief that the tomb of the talmudic sage, R. Simon bar Yoḥai, the supposed author of the *Zohar*, was located in the nearby town of Miron. These kabbalists included several scholars who were exiles from Spain. Prominent among them was Moses *Cordovero, the author of numerous kabbalistic treatises and a monumental commentary on the *Zohar* (*Or Yakar* [Precious Light]). His most influential work was *Pardes Rimonim* (Orchard of Pomegranates), a systematic presentation of the main subjects of classical Spanish Kabbalah. By the middle of the century Safed was a vibrant center of kabbalistic creativity.

In 1570 Isaac *Luria Ashkenazi, known by the acronym "Ari," returned to Safed (he was born there but had migrated to *Egypt) and began to present a new, revolutionary, and intensely mythological interpretation of kabbalistic tradition. His teachings were radically eschatological; like many other kabbalists in Safed he believed that the messianic era was imminent. Lurianic Kabbalah demanded that every Jew participate in a spiritual process of strengthening the powers of goodness and rejecting evil forces, thus speeding and enabling the coming of the *messiah. In fact, Lurianic Kabbalah may be regarded as a national ideology, uniting all Jews in the endeavor to bring forth *redemption. Luria died in 1572, in a plague, when he was thirty-eight years old. The group of disciples that had surrounded him continued to develop his teachings; they were led by Ḥayyim Vital, who wrote numerous volumes presenting Luria's Kabbalah. In the seventeenth century this new school gradually replaced all others, including Cordovero's, and became the dominant *theology of Judaism.

One of the adherents of Lurianic Kabbalah was Nathan, a young mystic from Gaza, who met the messianic pretender *Shabbatai Zevi in 1665 and became convinced that he was indeed the messiah. In many letters, pamphlets,

and treatises, Nathan presented himself as the prophet of the messiah, and his message spread quickly throughout *Turkey, the Middle East, and Europe. By the summer of 1666 it had engulfed almost all major Jewish communities, and thus began the greatest Jewish messianic movement since ancient times. Shabbatai Zevi ultimately converted to Islam at the order of the Ottoman Sultan, but the movement continued unabated, mostly in "underground" circles, until the beginning of the nineteenth century. A group of *Sabbateans converted to Islam following Shabbatai Zevi, and their descendants, known as the Dönmeh ("foreigners" in Turkish), survive as a sect to the present. Another group followed Jacob *Frank and converted to Christianity in *Poland in 1760; they remained a separate sect (Frankists) for two generations. Most Sabbateans, however, remained within Judaism, and some developed new kabbalistic-messianic systems. The most prominent example is Moses Ḥayyim *Luzzatto (Ramhal), who lived in Padua in the first half of the eighteenth century.

The founders of the *Ḥasidic movement in the middle and second half of the eighteenth century were kabbalistic preachers. The Kabbalah served as a theological foundation for the traditions and writings of the founder of Ḥasidism, the Besht (Israel *Baal Shem Tov), and his disciples, Jacob Joseph of Polonoi and *Dov Ber of Międzyrzecz, Some of the third-generation leaders of Ḥasidism, the disciples of Dov Ber, were prominent kabbalists, most notably Schneur *Zalman of Liady, the founder of *Ḥabad (Lubavitch) Ḥasidism, and *Naḥman of Bratzlav, a great-grandson of the Besht, who founded Bratzlav Ḥasidism. The opponents of Ḥasidism (*mitnaggedim, literally "opponents") were kabbalists as well. Elijah, the *Vilna Gaon, the leader of the opposition to Ḥasidism, was an authority on the Kabbalah. A kabbalistic center flourished in *Jerusalem in the eighteenth century, and kabbalists immigrated there, as well as to *Hebron and Safed in the nineteenth century. In the first half of the twentieth century Rav Judah Ashlag wrote an extensive, multivolume commentary on the *Zohar*, adapting it to conform to the Lurianic worldview.

In the last decades of the twentieth century and the first decade of the twenty-first, several groups in North America, Israel, and Europe have developed various integrations of some kabbalistic traditions with New Age ideas and trends, producing mixtures with astrology, *numerology, occultism, *magic, Buddhism, and other elements. These became very popular and attracted Jews and non-Jews alike. One of the most influential, the Center for the Study of Kabbalah, derived material from the teachings of Rav Ashlag and counted popular culture celebrities among its adherents. In Israel the term "kabbalist" has been adopted by various kinds of magicians and healers. The authentic Kabbalah survives in the early twenty-first century mainly in some Ḥasidic circles.

Among important studies are J. Dan, *Kabbalah: A Very Short Introduction* (2004); idem, *Jewish Mysticism*, vols. 1– 4 (1998–99); G. Scholem, *Major Trends in Jewish Mysticism* (1941); idem, *Kabbalah* (1974); M. Idel, *Kabbalah: New Perspectives* (1988); I. Tishby, *The Wisdom of the Zohar* (1989); D. Matt, *The Zohar*, Pritzker Edition, 5 vols. to date (2004–09).

JOSEPH DAN

Kabbalah, Lurianic is the mystical system devised by Isaac *Luria (1534–1572). The revolutionary aspect of Lurianic

*Kabbalah is the basic concept that perfection, even divine perfection, has never existed, even in the eternal godhead before creation, but will come into being in the future. The achievement of perfection is the reason for the existence of everything, including the divine realm. Thus, Luria addressed the problem of the purpose of existence in the most radical manner, one adopted by very few philosophers and theologians. According to Luria, creation was not a departure from divine perfection but rather a means for achieving it. A teleological backbone runs through Lurianic teaching and transforms the Kabbalah into a historically oriented concept, directing human participation in the achievement of the divine goal behind creation. Mysticism usually is ahistorical or even anti-historical, directing the mystic away from history and into the perfection of divine existence (which is usually in the past). The early Kabbalah was concerned mainly with the individual mystic's spiritual achievements. Lurianism teaches the community and its members their role in the historical achievement of redemption; it is therefore an intensely redemptive and probably messianic phenomenon (see REDEMPTION; MESSIANISM: EARLY MODERN).

Luria used an ancient Hebrew term, *tzimtzum, as a cornerstone for a vast theological mythology, in which the eternal godhead, *Ein Sof, contracted itself away from the space in which creation was to proceed to bring forward an "empty" space (tehiru). This process is conceived as a cathartic one, in which the Ein Sof separated itself from some potential elements within it that remained within the "empty" space as residues (reshimu). These elements incorporated the roots of what later developed into the powers of evil. According to this myth, God then proceeded to try and create the specific divine powers, the *sefirot as conceived in early Kabbalah, by pouring divine light in the form of a "straight line" into the tehiru. The sefirot comprised, according to previous formulations (mainly by Moses *Cordovero in *Safed) a duality of elements: the divine essence (atzmut) and the vessels in which it is contained (kelim). Lurianic myth describes the ensuing catastrophe, the *"breaking of the vessels" (shevirat ha-kelim), which occurred when the reshimu rebelled against its role in the construction of the vessels and caused them to shatter. If it were not for this catastrophe, the divine purpose would have been achieved by the transformation of the reshimu into a constructive element in creation. Instead, the shevirah established an independent realm of the broken vessels in the lower part of the tehiru, where many divine lights and sparks (nitzot) are held captive by the evil powers that derive their sustenance from them.

The process of creation that followed the shevirat ha-kelim was therefore an imperfect one. The unification of the divine realm and the overcoming of the evil element became the supreme purposes of existence. This "correction" underlies the most potent and influential Lurianic term, *tikkun olam ("mending" or "correcting the world"). All aspects of creation, human existence, and human deeds are directed toward the achievement of tikkun. All phases of history, from the creation of *Adam and his sin in the Garden of Eden to the theophany on Mount Sinai and the sin of the *golden calf (*Exod 32–34), were interpreted as failed attempts to achieve tikkun. Luria and his school were certain that they lived in the period when the final tikkun would be achieved. They believed it likely that 1575, the year shilo, according to

Genesis 49:10, would begin a messianic age in which Isaac Luria and his disciple Ḥayyim Vital would play a personal and central role.

Large sections of the Lurianic corpus are dedicated to the elaborate depiction of the way in which traditional Jewish rituals, prayers, and actions contribute to the achievement of tikkun. The "uplifting of the sparks" is the hidden meaning and purpose of every aspect of religious life. A detailed systematic psychology was developed, describing the origins of the various parts of the human soul and its functions in this process, and Luria and his disciples reedited the Jewish prayer book to include texts and "intentions" (*kavannot) that direct every word toward the achievement of this universal purpose. Lurianic Kabbalah also initiated several rituals and "customs," many of which are called tikkunim, dedicated to the fulfillment of this mythological endeavor. The idea of the tikkun gives a core to all Jewish precepts and demands, uniting them in the great effort of achieving the divine purpose of existence.

Some aspects of the Lurianic corpus are not directly related to this myth. One of the best-known works by Ḥayyim Vital, Sha'arei Kedushah (Gates of Holiness), is an ethical work teaching the reader, even a sinner and an ignoramus, how to achieve the highest mystical stage of "the holy spirit." This is a classical work of individual mystical direction, via mystica, which can be read independently of the vast Lurianic myth, even though the terminology used is clearly Lurianic (the fourth and last chapter of this work was not printed in the many traditional editions because it was regarded as too radically mystical).

Another intriguing aspect of Lurianic teachings is the new conception of the sefirot. They are no longer understood as divine entities with individual characteristics, as in the early Kabbalah, but as structural aspects of everything. Vital's works abound with descriptions of every entity, from the most highly divine to the basest material artifact, as comprised of elements reflecting the structure of the divine realm. Each sefirah itself comprises the ten sefirot (Luria preferred a system of five "faces" to that of the ten sefirot, but it is essentially the same structure; the six sefirot from four to nine are united in "the small face," ze'er anpin, reducing the number to five). Each such aspect also includes ten sefirot, and so on, ad infinitum. Previous kabbalists, in the fourteenth and fifteenth centuries, who followed some Zoharic statements, also used the concept of "sefirot within the sefirot," but in Vital's writings this idea has been developed into a central system encompassing the structure of everything within the human being, the universe, and the divine realms. It can be viewed as a scientific attitude, describing a principal structure that governs all existence. This is a conception very similar to that of harmonia mundi, the parallel structure of the divine realm, the created universe, and the soul of human beings, which dominated European scientific and theological thought in the sixteenth and seventeenth centuries.

Luria and his direct disciples, especially Ḥayyim Vital, insisted on keeping the Lurianic message a complete secret. The radical nature of this mythology was conceived as an esoteric truth, which should not be revealed to the public. Luria's early death was explained by some as a divine punishment for revealing these secrets to people on earth. Even Solomon Shlumil's letters, in the beginning of the seventeenth century, present no details of this myth. The fame of

Luria as a great and saintly person, based on the hagiographical stories of *Shivḥei ha-Ari* and *Toledot ha-Ari*, preceded the spreading of his ideas. Yet in the first half of the seventeenth century the central concepts spread via the works of Saruk, some writings of Vital, and ethical works that used Lurianic concepts, like the *Shnei Luḥot ha-Berit* (Two Tables of the Covenant) by Isaiah Halevi Horowitz and many others. The teachings of Luria gradually replaced those of *Cordovero.

Gershom *Scholem's studies presented Lurianic Kabbalah, both before its emergence in Safed and after its dissemination in the seventeenth century, in close connection with two major historical events in Judaism: the 1492 expulsion from *Spain and the messianic movement around *Shabbetai Zevi in the 1600s. Scholem saw in Luria's teachings an expression of the new awareness of exile that characterized Jewish perceptions of the community's fate after the expulsion. Luria placed the experience of exile within the godhead, in the *tzimtzum*, and in the captivity of the sparks; the redemption of God from its exile is the essence of the human endeavor for *redemption. The spreading of Lurianic concepts, even in a most basic form, paved the way for the *Sabbatean message, which used, especially in the writings of Nathan of Gaza, Shabbatai Zevi's "prophet," Lurianic symbolism to explain the role of the messiah in redeeming the last sparks and destroying the powers of evil. In various forms, Lurianic symbols continued to be among the most potent and influential elements of Jewish spirituality in *Ḥasidic and other Jewish sects and circles of the eighteenth and nineteenth centuries and in many respects even today. For further reading, see G. Scholem, *Major Trends in Jewish Mysticism* (1954), 244–86; and idem, *On the Kabbalah and Its Symbolism* (1965), 87–117.   JOSEPH DAN

Kaddish is an *Aramaic *prayer (with some Hebrew additions) expressing ten praises of the divine name; it may have originated as a doxology (a brief hymn praising *God) used to conclude study sessions in rabbinic times. This function is preserved because the *kaddish,* in one form or another, concludes each segment of communal *worship. The forms include the *kaddish shalem* (full *kaddish*), the *ḥatzi kaddish* (half *kaddish*), the mourners' *kaddish* (*kaddish yatom,* literally orphan's *kaddish*), and the *kaddish de-rabbanan* (Rabbis' *kaddish*). The *kaddish shalem* is recited after the *amidah* (see WORSHIP) by the leader of the *synagogue service, and the congregation responds at appropriate points. The *ḥatzi kaddish* contains only the first two major paragraphs of the *kaddish shalem* and is recited before the blessings of the *shema* (see WORSHIP) and at the end of certain sections of the service, such as the reading of the weekly *Torah portion. The *kaddish de-rabbanan* contains the *kaddish shalem* with an additional paragraph after the first two that consists of a prayer for students. It is recited after study sessions and may be read in the synagogue after passages from *rabbinic literature.

The origins of the mourners' *kaddish* are obscure; the practice of reciting it while mourning may have originated in thirteenth-century *Ashkenaz.

The mourner's *kaddish,* which includes the *kaddish shalem* with the exception of the third paragraph, is recited by mourners at the burial of a close relative (parent, sibling, spouse, child), at the graves of close relatives, and at the conclusion of each of the three daily synagogue services (see WORSHIP) during the first eleven months that follow the death of a parent or the thirty days following the death of another close family member (see DEATH AND MOURNING). Although the *kaddish* makes no explicit reference to death, it may have been deemed appropriate for mourners because of its emphasis on faith in divine justice and dominion over the universe and its request for present and future peace for all Israel. At some burials mourners recite a somewhat extended *kaddish shalem* that includes a reference to *resurrection and the rebuilding of the *Temple in Jerusalem in the first paragraph. The *kaddish* is always recited while standing and facing Jerusalem and only in the presence of a *minyan* (a quorum of ten, whose make-up will depend on how the worshiping community defines eligibility [see WORSHIP]). In some contemporary synagogue prayer, mourners rise and recite the mourners' *kaddish* together. For further reading, see R. L. Eisenberg, *The JPS Guide to Jewish Traditions (2004)*; and L. Wieseltier, *Kaddish* (2000).   ELIZABETH SHULMAN

Kafka, Franz (1883–1924), one of the most influential fiction writers of the twentieth century, was born in Bohemia into a middle-class, German-speaking Jewish family; he spent most of his life in *Prague. Kafka took a law degree from the Charles-Ferdinand University and afterward worked for an insurance company while devoting his free time to literature. Although he was also fluent in Czech, his major works were written in German. His novels include *The Trial* (1925), *The Castle* (1926), and *Amerika* (1927). Important short stories are "The Judgment" (1913), "The Metamorphosis" (1915), "A Country Doctor" (1919), "In the Penal Colony" (1920), and "A Hunger Artist" (1922). Kafka's writings, influenced by authors such as Kleist, Flaubert, and Dostoyevsky, are generally devoid of sentimentality and reflect the anxiety and alienation of modern human beings. His main characters tend to fail in their objectives because of anonymous opposing forces or are punished even before they have formally offended the law.

Kafka's diaries and letters shed light on the personal background and genesis of his literary oeuvre. They portray the writer's relationships with Felice Bauer, Milena Jesenská, and later on Dora Diamant, and they often address the question of his Jewish heritage. Although Kafka was not directly involved in Jewish religious life and never explicitly made it a theme in his literary texts, *Judaism nevertheless represents an important undercurrent in his work. After his encounter with *Ḥasidic culture, whose authenticity and spiritual depth he admired, he gradually began to consider the precariousness of western Jewish identity. During the last few years of his life he was increasingly drawn to *Zionism. After his death from tuberculosis, his friend and publisher Max Brod rescued most of his writings and edited and published them posthumously. These enigmatic, multilayered texts have fascinated generations of readers and continue to prompt an array of literary and philosophical interpretations and theories.

Recent research includes R. Robertson, *Kafka: Judaism, Politics and Literature* (1985); K.-E. Grözinger, S. Mosès, and H. D. Zimmermann, eds., *Franz Kafka und das Judentum* (1987); I. Bruce, *Kafka and Cultural Zionism: Dates in Palestine* (2007); M. Gelber, ed., *Kafka, Zionism and Beyond* (2004); and V. Liska: *When Kafka Says We: Uncommon Communities in*

German-Jewish Literature (2009); see also LITERATURE: CEN-
TRAL EUROPE.   VIVIAN LISKA AND ARVI SEPP

Kahal, Kehillah: See COMMUNAL ORGANIZATION: MEDIEVAL AND EARLY MODERN ERAS

Kallah Months (*yarḥei kallah*) were month-long intensive
study sessions convened twice each year by the Babylonian academies during the *amoraic and *geonic eras. They
took place during the agriculturally slack months of Adar
(February/March) and Elul (August/September) and were
open to interested individuals who were unable to commit themselves to year-long studies. Each month-long
period was apparently devoted to a specific tractate of the
*Mishnah. In contemporary times, this phrase refers to orga-
nized study sessions of specific length, generally convened
during vacation periods.   JUDITH R. BASKIN

Kaplan, Mordecai M. (1881–1983) is the founder
of the Reconstructionist trend in American *Judaism.
*Reconstructionism became a separate denomination in the
late 1960s, one of the few movements in modern Judaism
that resulted from the vision of a single personality. Born in
Svenciony, *Lithuania (then part of the Russian *Pale of Settlement), Kaplan was brought to the United States in 1889;
he graduated in 1900 from the City College of New York
and in 1902 received an M.A. from Columbia University and
rabbinic ordination from the *Jewish Theological Seminary
(JTS) of America. Kaplan served as rabbi of several Orthodox
synagogues before becoming a faculty member at JTS, head
of its Teachers Institute, and later Professor of Homiletics and
Philosophies of Religion. For many years he led the Society
for the Advancement of Judaism, a *synagogue on the Upper
West Side of Manhattan that he established in 1922 to exemplify his approach to the revitalization of American Judaism
(see JUDAISM: RECONSTRUCTIONIST).

Kaplan's first and seminal book, *Judaism as a Civilization:
Towards a Reconstruction of American Jewish Life* (1934), criticized all Jewish religious movements of his time for their
inability to grasp that Judaism was the "evolving religious
civilization" of the Jewish people. Informed by the findings of modern biblical and historical scholarship, Kaplan
emphasized the social nature of Jewish identity along with
the essential roles of Jewish ethical teachings and religious
practices in constructing group cohesion. In his many essays
and books he addressed a wide range of Jewish issues from
a perspective influenced by sociology and religious naturalism, drawing on the writings of Matthew Arnold, William
James, John Dewey, Emile Durkheim, and *Aḥad Ha-Am.
Kaplan understood religion as a collective phenomenon and
Judaism as far more than a "church." Early on he was associated with the Jewish Center movement that expanded
the program of synagogues to include social and artistic
activities in addition to formal worship and study. Supportive of cultural *Zionism, Kaplan saw Jews as an international people who should fully accept democratic forms of
government (see US: COMMUNITY CENTER MOVEMENT).

Kaplan's view of religion was pragmatic and functional,
rather than metaphysical or existential. Religion was a
form of group consciousness; suitably modernized, it made
possible a this-worldly form of salvation; that is, self-
fulfillment. He understood Jewish religious practice as an
agglomeration of folkways sanctified by tradition, rather

than *commandments (*mitzvot*) in the traditional sense.
Among his innovations were *Bat Mitzvah and changes in
*liturgy (the latter triggered his formal excommunication
[see ḤEREM] by a group of *Orthodox rabbis in 1945). One
of his most controversial views was the rejection of the
concept of the Jews as the "chosen people"; he believed
that every people could have a vocation to contribute special insights to humanity. Kaplan had a considerable, if
often unacknowledged influence on Reform and Conservative rabbis (see JUDAISM, REFORM: UNITED STATES; and
JUDAISM, CONSERVATIVE). Soon after his 1963 retirement from JTS, his supporters constituted Reconstructionism as a separate Jewish denomination. Kaplan's journals
from 1913 to 1934 were published as *Communings of the
Spirit*, ed. M. Scult (2002). Recent research includes R. M.
Seltzer, "Which *Wissenschaft*? Reconstructionism's Theological Appropriation of Sociology and Religious Naturalism," in
Modern Judaism and Historical Consciousness, ed. A. Gotzmann
and C. Wiese (2007), 415–44.   ROBERT M. SELTZER

Karaism, the longest surviving form of sectarian Judaism,
apparently took its name from the Hebrew word *mikra*
(scripture). Karaites rejected the rabbinic concept of an Oral
*Torah; they believed that the details of divine *revelation
could be found through close reading of the Written Torah
(Hebrew *Bible) alone. The Karaites' reading of the Bible,
conducted independently of *rabbinic literature, led to religious practices that distinguish their communities from
those of the majority of Jews (known, in the context of
Karaism, as *Rabbanites). Areas of Karaite difference include
(a) methods of calculating the *calendar (leading to the
observance of *Shavuot always on a Sunday and no observance of a second day of the holidays, even on *Rosh Ha-
Shanah); (b) *dietary laws: no blanket prohibition of meat
and milk together and different regulations concerning ritual
slaughter (*sheḥitah*); (c) *synagogue and *festival practices:
no *tefillin, no chairs in the synagogues, no blowing a *shofar
on *Rosh Ha-Shanah, and no observance of *Ḥanukkah; (d)
*prayer liturgy: based mainly on *Psalms; (e) different laws
of prohibited sexual relations; (f) *Sabbath practices: no hot
food or sexual relations, but the use of Sabbath lamps, without a blessing, since the fifteenth century; and (g) different
ritual *purity laws.

Karaite origins remain a mystery. The Rabbanites generally attribute the movement's founding to Anan ben David
(mid-eighth century CE), a disappointed candidate to be
*Exilarch (head of the Babylonian community) whose anger
caused him to secede from normative Judaism. Karaites
claim that their form of Judaism is the original one and
that the schism between the two groups of Jews has its origins in the *Second Temple period when, they assert, the
Rabbanite concept of the Oral Torah was invented. Modern
research has demonstrated that Anan was most certainly not
the founder of Karaism (he founded a group called Ananites;
only later was Anan appropriated by the Karaites). Opinion
remains divided as to how much, if any, connection there is
to Second Temple groups (such as the *Dead Sea covenan-
ters) or whether Karaism is purely a medieval movement.

No matter what their origins, by the tenth century
the Karaites were a well-organized alternative to rabbinic
Judaism. They enjoyed a "golden age" in the Land of
Israel between the tenth and eleventh centuries, creating

institutions parallel to those of rabbinic Judaism and developing their own form of law, exegesis, linguistic studies, polemics, and historiography. Their religiosity was characterized as well by "mourning for Zion," adopting ascetic practices in the hope of bringing the *messiah. Important early Karaites include Benjamin al-Nahawendi; Daniel al-Kumisi, who called for Jewish immigration to the Land of Israel; Jefet ben Eli, the chief Karaite exegete who composed commentaries on all books of the Bible (in *Judeo-Arabic, which was the literary language of most early Karaites); Abu'l Harun al-Faraj, grammarian; Joseph al-Basir, theologian and legalist; and Jeshua ben Judah, theologian and exegete. Jacob al-Kirkisani, one of the few Karaites of the period who lived outside the Land of Israel and was not a Mourner of Zion, was a legalist, theologian, and exegete.

In the tenth century, Karaites began making their way into *Byzantium, which became the center of Karaite creativity in the twelfth century after the demise of the community in the Land of Israel. Byzantine Karaites succeeded in adapting classical Karaism to the needs of the *Diaspora. The outstanding figures of this period were Judah Hadassi (fl. 1148), whose summa of law and lore serves as a digest of classical Karaism; Aaron ben Joseph (fl. 1294), exegete; Aaron ben Elijah (d. 1369), author of books of law, exegesis, and philosophy; and Elijah Bashyatchi (d. 1490), the final decisor of Karaite Judaism. The Byzantine period of Karaism is marked by constant Karaite attempts to narrow the differences between themselves and Rabbanite Jews.

Karaites had moved into the Crimea by the thirteenth century and into parts of *Eastern Europe by the fifteenth century. These communities were marked by increased intellectual rapprochement with Rabbanism, while, at the same time, the social distance between the groups grew. Unlike the communities in Arabic-speaking countries (such as *Egypt, which has had a continuous Karaite presence from the Middle Ages to the present), Karaites of Eastern Europe spoke a different language from the Rabbanites (a Turkic dialect usually called Karaim, rather than the Rabbanite *Yiddish), and intermarriage was rare. Yet, early modern Karaite intellectuals were very knowledgeable about Rabbanite literature, which was decisive in forming their worldview. One of the early modern Karaite thinkers was Isaac ben Abraham of Troki (d. 1594), best known for his anti-Christian polemic that was used extensively by Rabbanites; another notable figure was Simhah Isaac Lutski (d. 1760), the author of twenty-four books. The last well-known Karaite was Abraham Firkovitch (d. 1874), whose collections of manuscripts, held today in the Russian National Library of *Saint Petersburg, are a major resource for the study of Karaism and Rabbanism alike.

When tsarist expansionism in the late eighteenth century brought Eastern European Karaites under Russian control, the Karaites looked for ways to avoid the legal disabilities (e.g., taxes and conscription) legislated against Jews. They avoided these laws by convincing the Russian authorities that they were not Jews; by the early twentieth century, some Karaites theorized that they were of Turkish origin with no relation to the Jewish people. This identification was generally accepted by the *Nazis and led to the survival of most Karaites in World War II.

At the beginning of the twenty-first century there are approximately 30,000 Karaites worldwide; most are located in Israel, concentrated in the cities of Ramla, Ashdod, Ofakim, and Beer Sheva and the agricultural villages of Mazliah and Ranen. Small communities of Karaites also exist today in the San Francisco area of *California, Western Europe, *Turkey, *Lithuania, and Crimea. Israeli Karaites, most of whom immigrated from Egypt, have their own religious institutions that are generally accepted de facto, if not de jure, by Israeli law. Some Israeli rabbinical authorities permit intermarriage between Karaites and Rabbanites if the Karaite partner is willing to accept rabbinic Judaism. Maintaining their own separate Jewish identity and avoiding secularization and assimilation into the broader Jewish society are two of the major challenges facing contemporary Karaites.   DANIEL J. LASKER

Karo, Joseph Ben Ephraim (1488–1575) is best known today as the author of the last comprehensive code of Jewish law, the *Shulhan Arukh*. Karo was born, most probably, in Faro, on the southern coast of *Portugal. After the forced conversion of Portuguese Jewry in 1497, Karo and his family lived in various places in the eastern Mediterranean basin, including *Cairo and Adrianople (today Edirne, *Turkey). Subsequently, he lived in Nikopol, *Bulgaria, and, most probably at one point, Salonika (see BALKANS). In 1536, Karo moved to *Palestine and settled in *Safed, where he became a central spiritual and intellectual force in that famous community. Among his associates in Safed were his close friend, Solomon Alkabetz, a kabbalist and author of the *Sabbath poem, *"Lekha dodi"* ("Come, My Beloved"), and the charismatic messianic propagandist Solomon Molkho, whose meteoric career and execution at the stake profoundly affected Karo. Karo discusses Alkabetz and Molkho in a mystical diary, never intended for publication. The surviving portions, which have been analyzed by R. J. Z. Werblowsky in *Josef Karo, Lawyer and Mystic* (1977), reveal Karo as a deeply committed *kabbalist.

Karo's fame and influence rest on his *halakhic writings. He worked on the *Beit Yosef*, an encyclopedic work on Jewish law, for thirty-two years, and it assured him an international reputation. His code, the *Shulhan Arukh*, which was intended as a summary of conclusions of the *Beit Yosef* for popular use, became authoritative both in the *Sephardic world and, with modifications, in the *Ashkenazic world as well. Karo also composed a commentary on parts of *Maimonides' *Mishneh Torah*, called *Kesef Mishneh*, and wrote numerous *responsa, selections of which have survived in two published volumes. Also extant is a small work on talmudic methodology, *Kelalei ha-Talmud*.   SAMUEL MORELL

Kashrut: See DIETARY LAWS

Kavannah is the correct attitude or intention required to pray or perform a religious ritual with sincerity.

Kehillah: See COMMUNAL ORGANIZATION

Ketubbah refers to the *Aramaic contract presented by a husband to his wife at their *marriage; this contract delineates the legal and financial terms of their union. Among other requirements, a husband promises to provide his wife with food, appropriate clothing, and conjugal rights, and he pledges that her property will pass to her heirs. The *ketubbah*, which developed in *rabbinic times, protected a woman financially; should the marriage end through death or divorce, she would receive the dowry she brought into the marriage as well as an additional stipulated amount from her spouse. The *ketubbah* enhanced women's status, prevented rash divorces, and limited the numbers of indigent widows and divorcées dependent on community support. The medieval *ketubbah* could also contain added stipulations such as assurances that a husband would not take a second wife; that he would not beat his wife; and that before traveling he would prepare a conditional bill of *divorce and deposit his marriage gift so that his wife would be able to remarry if he perished on his journey. As dated legal documents identifying specific individuals and communities, *ketubbot* are an important historical source. Some *ketubbot* inventoried the contents of the dowry, an indication of local material culture, while decorated *ketubbot* reflect Jewish *art of various times and places. For further reading, see J. R. Baskin, "Medieval Jewish Models of Marriage," in *The Medieval Marriage Scene: Prudence, Passion, Policy*, ed. S. Roush and C. Baskins (2005), 1–22; and S. Sabar, *Ketubbah: The Art of the Jewish Marriage Contract* (2001). JUDITH R. BASKIN

Ketuvim: See BIBLE; and WRITINGS

Khazars. The Khazar Empire (ca. 630s/650s–ca. 965–969 CE) was the largest political entity of *Eastern Europe of its day, ruling over a variety of Turkic, Iranian, Slavic, Finno-Ugric, and north Caucasian peoples in an area extending from the borders of modern Kazakhstan and Uzbekistan in the east to Kiev in the west, and from the Middle Volga zone in the north to the north Caucasus and Crimea in the south. At the height of its power in the ninth century, Khazaria was a major element in international commerce (north–south and east–west) and derived considerable revenue from the tithe it took on goods passing through its realm.

The Khazars Empire derived from the Türk Empire (552–630, 682–742) – in eastern Inner Asia, 552–659; in western Inner Asia, ca. 690s–766. When Türk power faded, the Khazars emerged as an independent power. In the course of wars with the Arabs for control of the Caucasus (beginning in the mid-seventh century and slackening after 737), the Khazars continued the *entente* that the Türks had with *Byzantium, both sharing a common foe in the Arabian Caliphate. Khazaria was Constantinople's first line of defense against nomadic incursions from the steppe.

The Khazars had been typical Turkic shamanists. After an Arab invasion of Khazaria in 737, the ruler, the *Qaghan*, had been forced to convert to *Islam, which he soon abjured. During the reign of the 'Abbâsid Caliph Hârûn al-Rashîd (786–809), the *Qaghan*, increasingly a sacralized, ceremonial figure, or his deputy, the *Qaghan-Beg*, the de facto ruler, converted to *Judaism. This dating is confirmed by Khazar imitation Arab dirhams (units of currency) dating to 837/838, which substitute the statement *Mûsâ rasûl Allâh* ("Moses is the Messenger of God"), for the Muslim profession of faith. Thereafter, Judaism, in its *Rabbanite form, spread within the Khazar core tribes, and Khazaria attracted Jews fleeing persecution in *Byzantium and elsewhere. Khazar Hebrew sources dating from the mid-tenth century give several accounts of the conversion, presenting it as a return to an ancestral faith. Muslim sources also mention Khazar Judaism; the Byzantines are noticeably silent. The Khazaro-Byzantine alliance turned to open hostility in the tenth century.

Weakened by the shifting trade patterns favoring its vassal, Volga Bulgharia, and by growing difficulties with the Slavo-Scandinavian Rus' and the Turkic Pechenegs and Oghuz, the Khazar state succumbed to Rus' and Oghuz attacks in 965–69. The Khazar element in the shaping of Eastern European Jewry remains the subject of speculation.

For further reading, see P. B. Golden, "The Conversion of the Khazars to Judaism," in *The World of the Khazars: New Perspectives* (2007), ed. P. B. Golden, H. Ben-Shammai, and A. Róna-Tas, 123–62; D. M. Dunlop, *The History of the Jewish Khazars* (1954); and N. Golb and O. Pritsak, *Khazarian Hebrew Documents of the Tenth Century* (1982).

PETER B. GOLDEN

Kibbutz Movement: See ISRAEL, STATE OF: KIBBUTZ MOVEMENT

Kiddush, literally, "sanctification," is a blessing over wine recited in the home before the evening meal on the eve of the *Sabbath and *festivals (BT *Pesahim* 101a). The custom of also reciting the *kiddush* in the *synagogue at the end of Friday evening synagogue services developed in *Babylon in rabbinic times for the benefit of travelers (BT *Pesahim* 101a). A shorter *kiddush*, known as the *Kiddush Rabbah* (great *kiddush*) is recited before the afternoon meal on the Sabbath and festivals (BT *Pesahim* 106a). In contemporary times, this *kiddush* is usually recited in the synagogue after morning worship, as part of a light meal and social gathering. *Women are included in the obligation to hear or recite the *kiddush*, even though it is a time-bound positive commandment, because they are also obligated to "remember" (Exod 2:8) and "observe" (Deut 5:12) the Sabbath day (BT *Berakhot* 20b).

The Friday evening *kiddush* is introduced with readings from Genesis 1:31 and 2:1–3 that describe the culminating day of creation. The *kiddush* itself includes the short blessing over wine and a longer blessing sanctifying the Sabbath as Israel's inheritance as a commemoration of creation (Exod 20:11) and *redemption from slavery in *Egypt (Deut 5:15; see TEN COMMANDMENTS). It is generally customary to stand during the biblical introduction to the Friday evening *kiddush*; various communities have different customs regarding whether one should sit or stand for the entire prayer. The Friday evening *kiddush* may also be recited over grape juice or over the Sabbath loaves (*hallah*). The *Kiddush Rabbah* usually consists of the short blessing over wine and may be recited over grape juice, wine, or another alcoholic drink. The festival *kiddush* omits the introductory biblical passage and concludes with a reference to God, "who hallows Israel and the festive seasons." For further reading, see R. L. Eisenberg, *The JPS Guide to Jewish Traditions* (2004).

ELIZABETH SHULMAN

Kimḥi Family were influential Jewish *grammarians and Bible exegetes in Provence (see FRANCE, SOUTHERN) during the late twelfth and early thirteenth centuries. JOSEPH KIMḤI (ca. 1105–ca. 1170) immigrated to Narbonne from Muslim *Spain (ca. 1150) in the wake of *Almohad invasions. He and several other prominent Spanish émigrés, most notably Judah ibn Tibbon and Abraham *ibn Ezra, introduced the accomplishments of Spanish Jewry to Provence and other parts of Christian Europe. Joseph's *Sefer ha-Berit* (Book of the Covenant) was one of the first Jewish polemics against Christianity (see MIDDLE AGES: JEWISH–CHRISTIAN POLEMICS). His grammatical and exegetical works, as well as his translations and teachings, influenced his sons, Moses and David, and other students.

The writings of MOSES KIMḤI (d. c. 1190), known as Remak, were better preserved than those of his father, although his interests were narrower. His Hebrew grammatical work, *Mahalakh Shevilei ha-Da'at* (Journey on the Paths of Knowledge), was translated into Latin by Sebastian Muenster (d. 1552) as *Liber Viarum Linguae Sacrae* and was popular among sixteenth-century *Christian Hebraists. His commentaries on *Proverbs, *Ezra, and *Nehemiah, mistakenly attributed to Abraham ibn Ezra, were printed in rabbinic Bibles. Moses passed on their father's teachings to his younger brother, David, who was only ten years old when Joseph died.

DAVID KIMḤI (ca. 1160–1235), known by the acronym Radak and the most prominent family member, was strongly influenced by his father and brother. As a staunch defender of *Maimonides' *rationalism, he played a key role in the Maimonidean controversy. Radak's first work was a Hebrew philological treatise that reviewed and adapted the linguistic discoveries of the great Spanish Jewish grammarians. The grammatical and lexical parts of this treatise became known separately as *Sefer Mikhlol* (Book of Completeness) and *Sefer ha-Shorashim* (Book of Roots). Although he included a few of his own Hebrew grammatical discoveries, Radak realized that little creative work remained to be done in the field. His arrangement of the material was so successful that his linguistic works overshadowed the prior works they summarized, which were mostly written in Arabic.

Radak then wrote Hebrew commentaries on *Chronicles, *Psalms, Former and Latter *Prophets, and *Genesis (see BIBLICAL COMMENTARY: MIDDLE AGES TO 1800). His biblical exegesis synthesized the comments and explanatory approaches of his predecessors, arranging them in an exegetical context for the reader and supplementing them with many of his own incisive interpretations; their readable style obviated the need for supercommentaries. Although clearly a beneficiary of Spanish Jewish culture, Radak was profoundly influenced by Provençal and *midrashic traditions from northern France (see FRANCE: MIDDLE AGES), as is evident from his heavy reliance on rabbinic interpretation. His commentaries also included philosophical and polemical discussions; this tension between the Spanish and rabbinic modes of exegesis is a hallmark of Radak's commentaries and contributed to their popularity and relevance over the centuries. Both the commentaries and grammatical works survive in many manuscripts and editions. They also strongly influenced *Christian Hebraists from the sixteenth to nineteenth centuries. For further reading, see F. Talmage, *David Kimhi: The Man and the Commentaries* (1975).

NAOMI GRUNHAUS

Kindertransport (also known as the Refugee Children Movement). In the aftermath of the *Nazi *Kristallnacht* pogrom, the British Jewish Refugee Committee was successful in appeals to British political leaders to approve the admission to *Britain of unaccompanied children up to the age of seventeen from *Germany, *Austria, *Czechoslovakia, Danzig, and *Poland. The equivalent of $250 (50 pounds sterling) had to be guaranteed for each child to pay for their eventual return to their own countries. Members of a number of organizations, Jewish and non-Jewish, helped usher the children through Europe and found shelter for the refugees, who were mostly Jews, throughout the United Kingdom with private families, on farms, and in group homes, hostels, and boarding schools. Some older children were placed as domestics and agricultural workers, and more than one thousand served with British or Australian military forces. Between December 1938 and September 1939, the *Kindertransport* saved approximately ten thousand children. Although perhaps 20% were reunited with family members after the war, most found that their parents had not survived.

Film documentaries describing the *Kindertransport* experience include *My Knees Were Jumping: Remembering the Kindertransports*, directed by Melissa Hacker (1996), and *Into the Arms of Strangers: Stories of the Kindertransports*, directed by Mark Jonathan Harris (2000), which won the 2001 Academy Award for best documentary feature. Among many literary works are Lore Segal's autobiographical novel, *Other People's Houses* (1964); W. G. Sebald's novel, *Austerlitz* (2002); and Diane Samuels' 1993 play, *Kindertransport*. British poet and novelist Karen Gershon (born Käthe Löwenthal [1923–1993]), herself a *Kindertransport* child, published *We Came As Children* (1966), a collective biography of *Kindertransport* participants. **See also BRITAIN: EARLY MODERN AND MODERN; HOLOCAUST; HOLOCAUST RESCUERS; LITERATURE: BRITAIN.**   ELIZABETH SHULMAN

Kings, Books of. Kings 1 and 2 are biblical books in the *Prophets division of the Hebrew *Bible; contemporary scholars understand them as part of a larger work embracing *Deuteronomy through 2 Kings. This *biblical narrative was created in the seventh or sixth century BCE to explain the destruction of *Israel and *Judah by the *Mesopotamian powers of *Assyria and *Babylon and to offer hope for a revival of fortunes. This "Deuteronomistic History" (DH), as Martin Noth named it in 1943, has profoundly shaped our understanding of both the history of Israel and of history writing in general. The two books of Kings assumed separate identities because the entire DH could not fit on a single scroll. Early manuscripts of the *Septuagint name them *3–4 Reigns*, as separate works, but medieval Hebrew manuscripts such as Codex Leningrad treat 1–2 Kings as a single work. The *Dead Sea Scrolls include three fragmentary manuscripts of 1–2 Kings (4Q54, 5Q2, and 6Q4). The Septuagint (in the Lucianic recension) and Masoretic text differ widely, with the former repeating material and making several additions (e.g., 1 Kgs 2:35^{a-o} and 2:46^{a-l}).

Kings 1 and 2 recount the history of Israel and Judah from the mid-tenth to the early sixth centuries BCE. Beginning with the death of *David (1 Kgs 1–2), they report the reign of *Solomon (1 Kgs 3–11), including the building of the *Temple in *Jerusalem and his creation of the basic structures of a state. After the break-up of the so-called *United Monarchy, in the late tenth century BCE, the narrative alternates stories of kings of Israel and Judah and ends with the fall of *Samaria to Assyria in 722 BCE (1 Kgs 12–2 Kgs 17). The work concludes with a single narrative strand about the last kings of Judah (2 Kgs 18:1–25:26) and a brief epilogue about the release of the exiled king Jehoiachin ca. 562 BCE (2 Kgs 25:27–30). The basic historical framework of the books can be corroborated at several points, with the raid of Shishak/Shoshenk (1 Kgs 14:25–26) appearing in *Egyptian texts, and the reigns of Omri, *Ahab, Jehu, Ahaz, *Hezekiah, and *Josiah all being attested in Mesopotamian texts. Legendary material about both kings (see ISRAELITES: KINGSHIP) and prophets (see BIBLE: PROPHETS AND PROPHECY) appears in the books; both the sequence of kings and the stories about them from the mid-ninth century on seem to be relatively reliable.

The Deuteronomistic editor(s) of the books may have worked over a period of several decades. Some scholars have argued for a two-stage redactional history, with most of the material having been worked up during the reign of *Josiah (ca. 640–609 BCE) as a response to the religious reforms of that period. According to this approach, a more pessimistic reworking of the material occurred during the *Babylonian Exile, probably soon after the latest recorded event of the work (ca. 562–560 BCE). Others have posited a three-stage redactional history. More recent scholars have proposed even more elaborate models, with editing occurring well into the *Persian period (539–334 BCE). Those who assign a late date to the last layers run into the difficulty that, unlike 1 and 2 Chronicles, 1 and 2 Kings lack obvious anachronisms or late linguistic features, at least in the Masoretic text (see MASORETES).

However one understands the evolution of these books, two things are clear. First, those responsible for them used older material of widely varying provenances. These sources include royal chronicles, court legends, poems, tales of prophets (circulating in prophetic "schools"), and perhaps royal inscriptions. Second, the Deuteronomists imposed on this material a chronological order and theological aim that, while respecting traditional understandings, imparted a new coherence. The Deuteronomistic theology is most visible in Solomon's prayer in 1 Kings 8, the summaries at the end of each reign (which evaluate each king's relationship to the Jerusalem sanctuary and basic moral laws), and the summary of Israel's history in 2 Kings 17. In that summary the belief in divine retribution for injustice and idolatry, along with a conviction of God's readiness to forgive the penitent, comes to the fore. The Deuteronomists' unease with, though not rejection of, kingship also plays a prominent role throughout the work.

Although Mesopotamians invented historiography in the late third millennium, the Deuteronomists were innovators in both the scale and the aims of their work. Far from offering propaganda for a monarch or a mere listing of events, they sought to create a meaningful account of the past that would also serve the future. For further reading, see M. Cogan, *1 Kings* (2000); M. Cogan and H. Tadmor, *II Kings* (1988); and A. K. Grayson, *Assyrian and Babylonian Chronicles* (2000).   MARK W. HAMILTON

Kislev is the ninth month of the Jewish calendar, usually equivalent to November and/or December of the Gregorian calendar. The festival of *Hanukkah takes place from Kislev 25 to Tevet 2. **See also CALENDAR; CALENDAR: MONTHS OF THE YEAR.**

Kittel is a simple long-sleeved, belted, calf-length white robe traditionally worn by Jewish men on a number of

important ceremonial occasions. It may be made of linen, cotton, or silk. Although it is reminiscent of a shroud, it is worn during both joyous and solemn ritual moments. The kittel was traditionally donned by a groom on his wedding day and by married men on *Rosh Ha-Shanah (the Jewish New Year), *Yom Kippur (the Day of Atonement), and when leading the *Passover *seder*. The white color is a symbol of purity and solemnity and the style reflects simplicity, humility, and the equality of all human beings before *God.

RELA MINTZ GEFFEN

Knesset: Israel's parliament. **See ISRAEL, STATE OF: POLITICAL INSTITUTIONS.**

Kook, Rabbi Abraham Isaac (1865–1935) was born in Grieva, *Latvia, and immigrated to *Ottoman Empire *Palestine in 1904 where he served as the Chief Rabbi of Jaffa and its environs. He later became Palestine's first elected Chief Rabbi in 1921 and served in that role until his death in 1935. He was an inspirational and visionary leader, mystic, and halakhist (legal decisor) to generations of followers and admirers. His father was of Lithuanian descent, and his mother came from the *Hasidic lineage of Lubavitch. As a young man, Kook briefly served as the rabbi of Zamuel and Boisk before immigrating to Palestine.

During his tenure as Chief Rabbi, Kook wrote extensively, producing numerous volumes of *responsa (halakhic decisions), many of which were collected and published after his death by his son, Rabbi Zvi Yehuda Kook (1891–1982). Many of his speculative, mystical, and autobiographical musings were published posthumously by various disciples, in addition to his son, most prominently Rabbi David Cohen (known as the "Nazir"). Three of Kook's major works were published during his lifetime; *Arpelei Tohar* (1914), *Orot* (1920), and *Orot ha-Teshuvah* (1925). *Arpelei Tohar* was quite controversial as it presented a spiritual *Zionist vision from the Ultra-Orthodox (see JUDAISM, ORTHODOX: ULTRA-ORTHODOX) camp that affirmed the viability, and even necessity, of the secular Zionist project. His more personal writings were collected by the Nazir and published in the three-volume *Orot ha-Kodesh*, which reads like a mystical diary (see KABBALAH). *Orot* contains Kook's more nationalistic writings and was edited by his son Rabbi Zvi Yehuda, who later became the spiritual guide for the settler movement known as *Gush Emunim*. *Orot* and *Orot ha-Teshuvah* are both in English translation.

Arguably his most comprehensive works, *Orot* and *Orot ha-Kodesh* were often censored to soften the radical tendencies of this idiosyncratic and mystically inspired thinker. In 1999, uncensored versions of these and other texts were published in three volumes, *Shemoneh Kevatzim* (The Eight Notebooks), and a smaller volume *Haderav* (His Room; 1998, 2nd expanded ed., 2002), which also contains some previously unpublished material.

These new uncensored texts taken from Kook's original notebooks sparked a renewed interest in Kook as a religious thinker, although Kook's radical tendencies were well known in his lifetime. For example, his laudatory eulogy for the staunchly secular Theodor *Herzl, in which Kook referred to him as Messiah ben Joseph (a pre-Davidic *messiah in classical Judaism), was viewed by many in his traditional camp as offensive and even blasphemous. Kook's support of *Hebrew-language education in place of the

*Yiddish schools of the "old *Yishuv* (settlement)" community was another point of contention between him and many in his constituency.

The three major motifs of Kook's thinking are *repentance, light, and holiness. Kook posited that repentance is part of the nature of the cosmos – that the cosmos returns on itself and, in doing so, reveals the innate holiness of creation in nature, history, and culture. He believed that Israel's return to the Holy Land is part of a larger act of cosmic return, or "repentance," a sign of the impending disclosure of divine will and the light of *redemption. The secular Zionists who abandoned their homes in the *Diaspora to dwell in the land and build a Jewish society there were, in Kook's mind, unconsciously a part of this trajectory of cosmic return. Light is a theme that permeates all of Kook's writings. He was a highly optimistic thinker living in an optimistic time for the Jewish people, although his personal writings exhibit a surprisingly dark soul pained by feelings of alienation and anguish at being unable to express its love for God. Yet he firmly believed that the power of the holy, embedded in the human soul, could overcome the forces of evil and destruction and bring about redemption. Although an ultra-traditionalist in behavior and practice, Kook embraced a kind of cosmic positivism based on the conviction that history (in this case, the return of the Jewish people to their land) was a sign of progress and should be embraced as an act of divine will, even though it was being channeled though the profane nature of secularity.

Kook's writings, many of which have been filtered through his more activist and militant son Rabbi Zvi Yehuda, have become the major resource for *Gush Emunim* and the settler movement in contemporary Israel. They have also become a resource for Israel's liberal religious peace movement (see ISRAEL, STATE OF: PEACE MOVEMENT). The fact that these opposing sides could both claim Kook as their inspiration highlights the ambiguous and enigmatic nature of his writings (most of which were not meant for publication). Kook's thinking draws from the entire body of classical Judaism: the *Bible, *Talmud and *midrash, Maimonides, the *Zohar, Cordoverean (see CORDOVERO, MOSES) and *Lurianic *Kabbalah, *musar literature, and *Ḥasidism. His romantic perspective is reminiscent of thinkers such as Hegel, Tolstoy, and the secular Zionist ideologue Aharon David *Gordon. His larger-than-life persona and the radical, innovative, and often obscure message of his writings make him one of the most important, yet difficult, figures in twentieth-century Jewish *thought.   SHAUL MAGID

Kosher: Food that is fit for eating according to Jewish law (*halakhah). **See DIETARY LAWS.**

Kristallnacht ("crystal night" or "night of broken glass") refers to a series of *Nazi-sponsored *pogroms launched across *Germany on November 9–10, 1938, that destroyed or damaged 1,500 *synagogues and thousands of Jewish businesses and homes. Scores of Jews were murdered, and on November 16, the Gestapo rounded up 30,000 Jewish men and sent them to the *Dachau concentration camp outside of Munich. *Kristallnacht*, which was ostensibly prompted by the Paris murder of a low-level German diplomat, Ernst vom Rath, by a young Jew, Herschel Grynszpan, in early November, was controversial in and outside of Germany.

It infuriated some of Hitler's closest associates who were concerned about its impact on the German economy and the country's image abroad. Regardless, Nazi leaders were in agreement when it came to blaming Jews for the violence, and they required Germany's Jewish community to pay 1 billion *Reichsmarks* ($401 million) for the murder of vom Rath and the damages caused by the riot. *Kristallnacht* also represented a major turning point in German policy toward its Jews. Many Jews who still remained in Germany and *Austria were convinced by *Kristallnacht* that they should find any means possible to leave. On January 30, 1939, Hitler told the Reichstag that if Jewish financiers "once again" plunged Europe into war, the result would not be the bolshevization of the world, but the "annihilation of the Jewish race in Europe." **See HOLOCAUST; HOLOCAUST: ROLE OF GENDER**, etc.   DAVID M. CROWE

Krochmal, Nachman (1785–1840), was a self-taught philosopher, historian, and *Haskalah figure in *Habsburg *Galicia who brought a *Wissenschaft* sensibility to his theory of the history of Judaism. Born in Brody to a prosperous family, Krochmal received a good Jewish education and benefited from his father's contacts with Jewish intellectuals in Prussia. At fourteen, he married Sara Haberman, moved to Zolkiev, and was further supported in his studies by his father-in-law.

Krochmal studied Moses *Mendelssohn and Salomon *Maimon as well as *Maimonides (using Maimon's Hebrew commentary), *Ibn Ezra, and *Naḥmanides. He taught himself German, Latin, French, Arabic, and Syriac and then immersed himself in the works of Immanuel Kant. His intensive study brought on a physical breakdown in 1808, and he received medical treatment in Lemberg. On returning to Zolkiev he read Fichte, Schelling, and Hegel. He was particularly influenced by Hegelian Idealism and used it to create his own theories on the nature of *Judaism as a religion and Jewish history as an expression of a unique connection between *God and the Jews. After his in-laws' deaths in 1814, he became responsible for his family's financial welfare, and he worked first as a merchant and then as a bookkeeper.

Krochmal, a gifted teacher who preferred discussion and discourse, did not publish widely; however, his insistence on teaching *Haskalah* ideas and texts made him a potentially threatening intellectual force. A dispute with *Ḥasidim in Galicia about his relationship to a *Karaite community led to a debate by correspondence. At the urging of friends and students, he collected his ideas in writing, but illness and severe poverty kept him from completing a systematic book. In 1851, a decade after his death, Krochmal's most well-known work, *Moreh Nevukhei Ha-Zeman* (Guide of the Perplexed of the Time), was published posthumously by his friend Leopold *Zunz. Edited, organized, and titled by Zunz, the book outlines Krochmal's philosophies of religion and history, presents an analysis of *halakhah* and *aggadah*, and sketches his adaptation of Hegelian thought in a philosophy of Jewish history.

Krochmal followed Maimonides in elevating philosophy to the level of religion itself; his rejection of a competition between philosophical and theological knowledge allowed him to articulate a theory of creation emanating from the Absolute Spirit (synonymous with God). He presented

Judaism and Jewish history as occurring in a series of three stages (each corresponding directly with the relationship of Israel to God). By delineating a progressive and unique unfolding of Jewish experience and development that responded to the historical contexts in which Jews lived, Krochmal moved beyond both contemporary Jewish views of an eternal, unchanging Judaism and Hegel's relegation of Judaism to an archaic history. For further reading see Y. Amir, "The Perplexity of Our Time: Rabbi Nachman Krochmal and Modern Jewish Existence," *Modern Judaism* 23(3) (2003); and J. Harris, *Nachman Krochmal: Guiding the Perplexed of the Modern Age* (1991).   LEAH HOCHMAN

Kurdistan is a cultural-ethnic-geographic term referring to an area split among five states: *Turkey, *Iran, *Iraq, *Syria, and Armenia. Kurdish Jews were a tiny minority among several minorities who lived among the Kurdish majority, which itself was a minority in each state. The Jews lived in about two hundred villages and towns throughout Kurdistan, but mostly in Iraq and Iran. In 1950 their total number was estimated to be at most 25,000, a very small number relative to other Jewries. Kurdish Jews originally spoke *Aramaic; with the Islamic conquests in the seventh century, Aramaic was gradually superseded by *Arabic and survived only in the remote mountainous areas of Kurdistan. Judaism in Kurdistan was very rudimentary, based mostly on oral transmission of inherited Judaic practices, customs, and lore. Yet Kurdish Jews, like other conservative rural-farming societies, were quite traditional in practice. Practically all Jews kept *dietary laws very strictly (called *Halala*, from the Arabic *Halal*); men prayed in *synagogues twice daily, morning and evening; on *Sabbaths and *festivals, all men and boys, almost without exception, attended services. Yet, literacy or deep knowledge of Jewish sources was not common among men and almost nonexistent among women.

Amazingly, Kurdistan had one female rabbi, named Asnat Barzani, who headed a *yeshivah* ca. 1680. She explains that this came about because her father did not have any sons; therefore, he taught her to study and teach *Torah. Even when he gave her in *marriage, he made her husband take a pre-nuptial oath not to make her do any routine housework (U. Melammed and R. L. Melammed, "Rabbi Asenath: A Female Yeshiva Director in Kurdistan," [Hebrew] *Pe'amim* 82 [2000]: 163–78).

Jews were weavers, farmers, shopkeepers, shoemakers, tailors, dyers, and gold and silversmiths. Many were loggers who transported wood and other material by rafts on the river. In general, Kurdish Jews were intermediaries between the rural countryside and the larger urban areas. They would sell urban merchandise, such as tea, sugar, textiles, and buttons, to the villagers and, in return, sell village products, such as wool, furs, and wood for construction, to city people. There was a saying that these Jewish merchants never died in their own beds but rather on the road, whether through natural death or misadventure, by being robbed and killed by brigands.

There were several religious minorities in Kurdistan and a measure of pluralism, so Jews were not discriminated against in particular. Actually, other minorities suffered more because they had local political aspirations, whereas the Jews did not. Kurdish Jews were *Zionists in the traditional sense that they loved the Land of Israel and expressed this love in their prayers and customs. Many individuals immigrated to *Palestine after World War I. After 1948, practically all Kurdish Jews made *aliyah to Israel. On Kurdish Jewry, see Y. Sabar, *Folk Literature of Kurdistani Jews* (1982).

YONA SABAR

L

Lachish was a *Canaanite and later *Israelite city, destroyed by *Assyria in 701 BCE. The site of Lachish (Tell ed-Duweir) is strategically located in the lowlands (*shephelah*) at the juncture of the Judean hills, some 15 miles (24 km) west of *Hebron. It was a vital city in both the Bronze and Iron Ages. According to the *Bible, *Joshua and his troops completely destroyed Canaanite Lachish (Josh 10:31–32), after which the city was incorporated into the territory of *Judah (Josh 15:39). Later fortified by *Rehoboam, (2 Chron 11:5–12), Lachish was second in importance only to *Jerusalem.

The Assyrian destruction of Lachish is well documented through the excavation of the site. In addition, it is noted in the Bible (2 Kgs 18:13–14, 17; 19:8; cf. Isa 36:1–2, 37:8), represented in reliefs on the walls of Sennacherib's palace in Nineveh, now in the British Museum in London, and implied on Sennacherib's prism. Its subsequent destruction in the early sixth century BCE by *Babylon under Nebuchadnezzar has been revealed *archeologically (see ARCHEOLOGY, LAND OF ISRAEL: ANCIENT TIMES TO PERSIAN PERIOD). In addition, letters written in ink on clay ostraca, found at Lachish, support the story of the city's destruction as described by *Jeremiah (34:6–7). The site was reoccupied during the *Persian period (Neh 11:30), at which time new construction included an administrative building and a temple.   BETH ALPERT NAKHAI

Ladino, also commonly known as Judeo-Spanish or Judezmo, is the language used by the *Sephardic Jews expelled from Spain in 1492 (see SPAIN, CHRISTIAN) who subsequently settled throughout the *Ottoman Empire in the eastern Mediterranean. The Jews who settled in *North Africa spoke a variety of the language known as *hakitía*.

It is not entirely clear whether Ladino existed in Spain before the expulsion (see LITERATURE, LADINO). Dialectal variations of medieval Spanish were transferred to the various locations in which the exiled Jews settled. Over time, regional Ladino dialects began to unify as a result of constant communication among these various communities and close contact with local languages. The main centers of Ladino ultimately became Istanbul and Thessalonika (Salonika; see BALKANS; GREECE). It appears that Ladino only started to develop as a unique Jewish language with some dialectal variations at the beginning of the seventeenth century. Ladino was traditionally written in the Sephardic Hebrew alphabet, later known as Rashi script. Printed materials were written in either Rashi script or in square Hebrew letters. Ladino-speaking communities began using the Latin alphabet in the middle of the twentieth century.

Ladino uses the same grammar as Spanish with some variations that stem from substandard medieval Spanish. Verbs are conjugated similarly to Spanish with some modifications. The Ladino tense system is less elaborate than the Spanish equivalent, and compound verbs are frequently formed using the verb *tener*, "have, own," rather than *haber*, "have,"

(e.g., *tengo avlado*, "I have been talking"). The Spanish *ustedes* polite form of second-person address does not exist in Ladino. The diminutive in Ladino is *-iko/-ika* rather than the Spanish *-ito/-ita*. *Hebrew influence on the language can also be seen in syntactic structures. Ladino has retained much medieval Spanish vocabulary, and a considerable number of Hebrew-*Aramaic words have become fused and integrated into the language. Over the course of the centuries, many loanwords have also been added to the language from Turkish, Arabic, and Greek.

At the beginning of the twenty-first century, Ladino is fast becoming an endangered language because of the lack of new native speakers. The main reasons are the *Haskalah* movement in Europe, the dispersion of Sephardic Jews around the world, the murder of most Greek Jews during the *Holocaust, and the growing influences of secularism and modernism. Nevertheless, there is growing academic interest in the language and its literature, and several grammar books and dictionaries have recently been published for the use of both Ladino speakers and academic researchers, including E. Kohen and D. Kohen-Gordon, *Ladino-English, English-Ladino: Concise Encyclopedic Dictionary* (2000); **see also** LITERATURE: LADINO.

ORA RODRIGUE SCHWARZWALD

Lag B'Omer: See OMER

Lamentations, Book of ('*Eikha*). Consisting of five separate poems, this biblical book, found in the *Writings section of the *Bible, bewails the *Babylonian destruction of *Jerusalem and the obliteration of the First *Temple (586 BCE). Traditionally attributed to the prophet *Jeremiah, many of the laments directly contradict his prophecies, leading modern scholarship to question that attribution. One of the *Five Scrolls, Lamentations is read during worship for *Tisha B'Av, which commemorates the destruction of both of the Jerusalem Temples.

Each poem is structured on the Hebrew alphabet in a generalized acrostic form. No single poetic voice predominates; rather, the chapters reveal a variety of speakers. Whether the book was to be read as separate lament poems, one continuous poem, or as a related cycle of poems is unclear. The laments describe Jerusalem's ruin, focusing on the devastation of the Temple: "He has laid waste His dwelling like a garden; He has destroyed His place of meeting" (2:6). The destruction fulfills prophetic warnings against Israel's idolatry: "As He ordained long ago, He has demolished [Jerusalem] without pity; He has made the enemy rejoice over you, and exalted the might of your foes" (2:17). The people seek God's help, blame God for their suffering, and accuse God of hiding from Israel. However, unlike in the book of *Job, God never responds. The obvious questions – Is suffering part of God's divine economy? Is suffering something that humanity brings on itself? Or is suffering more powerful than God? – are mostly left unanswered (see EVIL AND SUFFERING).

Chapter 3, the theological heart of Lamentations, provides the closest thing to a response. The triumph of hope over suffering will provide sustenance to the exiled community: "Yet this I call to mind and therefore I have hope: Because of the Lord's great love we are not consumed, for his compassions never fail. They are new every morning; great is your faithfulness. I say to myself, 'The Lord is my portion; therefore I will wait for him'" (3:21–24). For further reading, see T. Linafelt, *Surviving Lamentations: Catastrophe, Lament, and Protest in the Afterlife of a Biblical Book* (2000); and F. W. Dobbs-Allsopp, *Weep, O Daughter of Zion: A Study of the City Lament Genre in the Hebrew Bible* (1993).

SANDRA COLLINS

Land of Israel: See ISRAEL, LAND OF

Landsmanschaftn: See UNITED STATES: FRATERNAL SOCIETIES

Lasker-Schüler, Else (1869–1945) came from a well-to-do assimilated family in the industrial city of Elberfeld in the Rhineland region of *Germany. After marrying the physician Berthold Lasker in 1894, she moved to *Berlin where she took art lessons and published her first poems in 1901. Her fascination with the countries and cultures of the Middle East, evident in the poems and prose of *Die Nächte Tino von Bagdads* (The Nights of Tino of Baghdad [Berlin, 1907]), was integrated into her life-long occupation with Jewish themes. It found its first expression in the powerful *"Hebräische Balladen"* (Hebrew Ballads [Berlin, 1912]). With her second husband Herwarth Walden, promoter of Expressionism in his journal *Der Sturm* (The Storm), she fought for the acceptance of modern art and literature. She described the Berlin bohème in *Mein Herz* (My Heart [Berlin, 1914]) a "novel in letters." In her drawings and writings she created an artistic realm, Thebes, ruled by her alter ego, Prince Jussuf.

*World War I, which she passionately opposed, destroyed her vision of a Europe, if not the world, united by art. A ten-volume edition of her works with her cover designs was published in 1919/20. Her play *Die Wupper*, named for the river of her home town, was first performed in 1919. After her second divorce she supported herself with her graphic art. Her only son Paul, a gifted artist himself, died in 1926 at the age of twenty-seven of tuberculosis. She responded to the rise of *antisemitism in the early 1930s with her 1932 play *Arthur Aronymus und seine Väter* (Arthur Aronymus and his Fathers), first performed in Zürich in 1936. The collection of essays and poems, *Konzert* (Concert [Berlin, 1932]), was published when she received the Kleist prize, the highest literary award at the time. Four months later she fled to Switzerland. After her first journey to *Palestine in 1934 she wrote *Hebräerland* (Land of the Hebrews [Zürich, 1937]). In 1939, unable to return to Europe, she remained in *Jerusalem. She founded a lecture circle, wrote a play, *Ichundich* (I and I), the sum of her life and times, and magnificent poems in *Mein blaues Klavier* (My Blue Piano [Jerusalem, 1943]). Her works and letters are published in an eleven-volume critical edition (Frankfurt am Main, 1996–2010). Recent research includes B. Falkenberg, *Else Lasker-Schüler. A Life* (2003); and S. Bauschinger, *Else Lasker-Schüler. Biographie* (2004). SIGRID BAUSCHINGER

Latin America. The beginnings of Jewish life in Latin America are difficult to trace. During the years that *Spain and *Portugal established their New World empires, all Spanish and Portuguese subjects were required to be Catholic. Spain, the stricter of the two, even forbade Jews who had converted to Christianity to immigrate to its colonies, although the ban proved impossible to enforce. No doubt some Spanish and Portuguese colonists maintained Jewish observances, aided by the proximity of Dutch and British colonies, such as Surinam and several *Caribbean islands, where Judaism was tolerated. The community in Recife, *Brazil, under Dutch control from 1630 to 1654, had a *synagogue and attracted Jewish immigrants from Europe. However, the clandestine nature of Jewish life in Spanish and Portuguese colonies makes it an elusive topic of study.

Some have argued that Monterrey, *Mexico, was founded as a crypto-Jewish refuge and that Cuba's mountains once sheltered villages of openly observant Jews (see CARIBBEAN). The *Inquisition had offices in Mexico City and Lima, and inquisitors' records provide written sources of information about hidden Jews during the colonial period. However, this documentation is flawed by the outlook of the inquisitors who were zealously determined to discover secret practitioners of Judaism. J. L. Elkin's survey of the shaky information on colonial-era Jews suggests that the true history of Jewish life in Latin America starts in the nineteenth century, not long after the end of the wars that established independence in Latin American countries (1810–24).

During the middle years of the nineteenth century, from the 1830s to the late 1880s, small numbers of openly Jewish immigrants arrived sporadically in Latin America. Many of the new arrivals were *Ashkenazic Jews from Western Europe, displaced by the Franco-Prussian wars. *Sephardic Jews from *North Africa also arrived, settling in Brazil and *Argentina. Venezuela, Colombia, and Costa Rica received Sephardic immigrants from Caribbean islands. In particular, Curação, the island off Venezuela colonized by the Dutch, had a long-established Jewish community that fostered communities on the mainland. *Jamaican Jews immigrated as well; Jorge Isaacs, the nineteenth-century Colombian writer, son of a Jewish Jamaican father, made this background a theme of his hugely popular 1867 novel *María*. Even after the Inquisition officially ended, the idea that everyone should be Catholic persisted; in many countries, only the Catholic Church performed marriages and registered births and deaths. Because of these obstacles and because the dispersed Jewish immigrants had difficulty forming communities, many individuals abandoned Jewish life.

Larger scale immigration, from the 1880s to the end of *World War I, created the modern Latin American Jewish communities. In this period, the bulk of the immigrants were *Eastern Europeans, fleeing *pogroms and regulations designed to crowd Jews into a restricted area where there were little means of livelihood. Certain Latin American countries, most notably Argentina and Brazil, sought European immigrants to accelerate growth and modernization. The Jewish Colonization Association, established by the philanthropist *Baron Maurice de Hirsch, recruited principally Eastern European Jews to settle in agricultural colonies in Argentina and, unsuccessfully, in Brazil. Other Jewish farming settlements were created in Uruguay, the Dominican Republic, and later in Bolivia. The settlement of Jewish immigrants on farms was intended not only to provide a safe home and a livelihood but also to promote Jewish self-renewal through working the soil, one theme of *Zionist thought. However, the colonies gradually lost population owing to the greater appeal of urban culture.

A massive *agricultural colonization effort accounts for the predominantly *Ashkenazic origin and size of today's Argentine Jewish population. By 1917, Argentina had some 110,000 Jews (the contemporary population is somewhat under 200,000 and declining). Some of the immigrants to Argentina moved on to Chile, whose Jewish population today is more than 20,000. Uruguay's Jewish population, currently around 20,000, grew quickly during the early twentieth century. Brazil, which also recruited immigrants, attracted a diverse Jewish population; currently there are just under 100,000 Jewish Brazilians. Mexico's Jewish population, now more than 40,000, grew gradually and continues to be divided into distinct communities by geographical origin. In 1938 the Central Committee of the Jewish Community of Mexico was formed to coordinate these communities. Cuba hosted a settled, mostly Sephardic, population and various Jewish groups in transit to other countries. Refugees from *Nazi persecution and post-war *displaced persons were admitted to various Latin American countries; some, like Bolivia and Paraguay, previously had few European immigrants. This was the last growth spurt for Latin American Jewish communities, many of which now face declining numbers owing to *intermarriage and emigration.

As the Jewish population increased, *antisemitism became more evident. The 1919 Tragic Week in Buenos Aires brought attacks on the Jewish neighborhood. Antisemitism has persisted, both the conservative variety, associated with traditional Catholicism and the military, and the anti-Jewish tendencies of some sectors of the left. Ex-*Nazis, including the hunted criminals Adolf Eichmann, Josef Mengele, and Klaus Barbie, were harbored by Argentina, Brazil, Bolivia, Chile, and Paraguay. In 1960, Israeli intelligence agents, without informing Argentine authorities, captured Adolf Eichmann in Buenos Aires and spirited him to *Israel for trial (see HOLOCAUST TRIALS). Accusations that Israel had violated Argentine sovereignty led to renewed expressions of antisemitism.

Even scattered communities created burial societies and relief services, but denser population allowed the formation of large and complex Jewish social and cultural associations. The best known in Latin America is the Buenos Aires AMIA (Asociación Mutual Israelita Argentina), an umbrella organization that provides social services, community affairs, educational programs, research archives, cultural events, and a publications program. The AMIA drew international attention when its building, since rebuilt, was destroyed in a 1994 terrorist bombing that caused significant loss of life. Other sizable organizations, such as the Comunidad Ashkenazí of Mexico City, also sponsor cultural activities and house research collections.

At the beginning of the twentieth century, the many Eastern European immigrants provided an audience for *Yiddish culture. Buenos Aires was home to Yiddish *theaters, the newspapers *Di Presse* and *Di Yidishe Zaitung*, and Yiddish writers such as José Rabinovich. Yiddish culture at one time thrived in Mexico City, home of the poet Jacobo Glantz. Although the first generation of Eastern Europeans maintained Yiddish, their descendants often did not. By the 1920s Spanish was increasingly favored as the language of

cultural activities. Jewish participation in national intellectual life also began early in the twentieth century. The Argentine Alberto Gerchunoff, best remembered for his 1910 novel *Los gauchos judíos* (The Jewish Gauchos of the Pampas), was the first Latin American Jewish intellectual to attain national visibility. Gerchunoff addressed a largely non-Jewish readership via the mainstream *La Nación* newspaper, there were also Spanish-language publications for a Jewish audience. The magazine *Judaica* (Buenos Aires) was perhaps the most noted of many publications featuring Jewish topics. Many Jewish immigrants and their children were in the publishing industry, where their knowledge of languages and of European literatures made them especially useful as editors and translators. By the mid-twentieth century, a number of Jewish creative writers had become well known, including the Argentines César Tiempo (real name, Israel Zeitlin), Samuel Eichelbaum, and Bernardo Verbitsky and the Brazilians Pedro Bloch and Clarice Lispector; Lispector would eventually earn international recognition and provoke debate over the "Jewishness" of her writing (see LITERATURE: LATIN AMERICA). The Lithuanian-born Brazilian painter Lasar Segall created images of immigrant life.

The military regimes of the 1970s and 1980s in Argentina, Chile, and Uruguay brought antisemitism to the fore. In his 1981 *Prisoner without a Name, Cell without a Number*, the Argentine newspaperman Jacobo Timerman recounts that, while he was detained and tortured by the military, he discovered that belief in a Jewish plan for world domination was widespread among his captors. Jewish Argentines were disproportionately represented among those "disappeared" by the armed forces. Consequently, many Jews left the country, accelerating the population decline of the community. Since the 1959 Cuban revolution, Cuba's Jewish population, estimated at 15,000 in 1950, has also declined; present-day estimates range from 600 to 1,500. Many Cuban Jews settled in Puerto Rico, and many others moved to the U.S. mainland. Cuban-born U.S. *anthropologist Ruth Behar discusses Jews remaining in Cuba in *An Island Called Home: Returning to Jewish Cuba* (2007). Recent research includes J. L. Elkin, *The Jews of Latin America* (rev. ed., 1998).

NAOMI LINDSTROM

Latvia: See BALTIC STATES

Law: Ancient *Near East and Hebrew *Bible. The law collections of the Hebrew Bible belong to an ancient Near Eastern legal tradition that includes the well-known Code of *Hammurabi (Babylonia, ca. 1750 BCE), discovered on a stele (stone monument) in 1901–02, as well as other important law collections discovered in the twentieth century, including the Laws of Ur-Nammu (Sumer, ca. 2100 BCE), Laws of Lipit-Ishtar (Sumer, ca. 1930 BCE), and Laws of Eshnunna (Sumer, ca. 1800 BCE); the Hittite Laws (ca. 1500 BCE); and the Middle Assyrian Laws (1075 BCE). Ancient Near Eastern law collections were often framed by a narrative prologue and epilogue that laud the greatness of the king and invoke his divine mandate. For example, the Code of Hammurabi declares that the gods have invested Hammurabi with the task of "bring[ing] about the rule of righteousness in the land, [and] destroy[ing] the wicked and the evil-doers." Depicted on the stele is an image of what appears to be Hammurabi receiving the laws from the sun god Shamash; beneath this bas-relief are inscribed the narrative prologue and more than 280 laws that comprise Hammurabi's collection.

The legal collections of the Bible are found in the Torah (*Pentateuch), embedded in the story of the Israelites' miraculous Exodus from *Egypt and the divine *revelation at Mount Sinai. Contrary to other ancient Near Eastern law codes, no human king is credited with responsibility for disseminating the law. According to *Deuteronomy (5:20–30), *God proclaimed some or all of the *Ten Commandments directly to the Israelites, but revealed the rest of the "laws and the ordinances" to *Moses who would act as an intermediary. The divine law was to be understood as the stipulations to the *covenant between God and Israel. The law, known in Hebrew simply as *torah* or "instruction," consists of the Ten Commandments (Exod 20:1–17 and Deut 5:6–21) and three legal collections: the Covenant Code (Exod 20:23–23:19), the Holiness Code (Lev 17–26), and the laws of Deuteronomy (Deut 12–28). Scholars debate the relative chronology of these codes but there seems to be general consensus that the Covenant Code is the oldest. In addition to these collections, many laws can be found scattered throughout the entirety of the Pentateuch, especially *Exodus through Deuteronomy. These biblical law codes contain much shared material, and many laws are repeated two or more times in the Bible. There are also significant differences among the biblical law codes that often reveal diverging social settings or distinct ideological assumptions.

In an influential essay, "The Origins of Israelite Law" (1967), Albrecht Alt distinguished between two forms of law found in the Hebrew Bible. "Apodictic" law issues its rules in absolute terms: "You shall not steal" (Exod 20:13). "Casuistic" law, in contrast, is expressed through the use of a hypothetical case and an "if / when . . . , then . . ." structure, as in, "When a man steals an ox or a sheep, and slaughters it or sells it, [then] he shall pay five oxen for the ox, and four sheep for the sheep" (Exod 21:37). The Ten Commandments are composed of apodictic law, whereas the other law collections predominantly contain casuistic law. Alt maintained that apodictic law was entirely native to Israel, although later scholarship has cast some doubt on this assertion. Casuistic law, however, is the main form of law used in all ancient Near Eastern law codes.

There is much overlap in content among biblical and ancient Near Eastern civil and criminal legislation. The *lex talionis*, or law of retaliation ("an eye for an eye"), is a common feature of the Code of Hammurabi, other ancient Near Eastern law codes, and biblical law. However, biblical law codes apply the *lex talionis* far more universally than other codes, which make numerous distinctions based on the social statuses of the injured and injuring parties. In addition, biblical law codes, unlike the ancient Near Eastern collections, do not allow for vicarious talionic punishment, as in the execution of the minor son of a free man who murdered the minor son of another free man. Although all ancient Near Eastern law calls for the death penalty for murder, biblical law codes allow for less flexibility in this regard. As opposed to many ancient Near Eastern law codes that give the victim's next-of-kin a choice between implementing the death penalty or accepting ransom from the murderer, biblical laws demand that no ransom be substituted for the life of the innocent victim. This divergence from other Near Eastern practice can be attributed either to the Israelite

notion that innocent blood "pollutes" the land, an impurity that can only be purged by shedding the blood of the murderer, or the notion that the crime of murder is an offense against God, who cannot be repaid monetarily. Finally, biblical law codes differ from the major ancient Near Eastern law codes in including cultic ("religious") law amid civil and criminal statutes.

The function of the ancient Near Eastern and biblical law codes is much debated. The term "code" is most probably a misnomer, because the law collections are not nearly comprehensive, organized, or practical enough to have functioned as an authoritative code of law for governing of a society. The law "collections," then, may have had one or more of several alternative purposes, as follows: (1) They may have provided a guide for judicial decision making, offering a judge a nonbinding list of precedents that he could consult; (2) they may have been used as pedagogical tools for training either citizens or jurists; or (3) they may have been promulgated primarily as royal public relations exercises, displaying the greatness and wisdom of the king / God as evidenced through his fair and perfect laws. Biblical and ancient Near Eastern law, as recorded and inscribed for perpetuity, ought to be seen on the whole as ideal norms toward which individuals, communities, and courts sought to strive.

For further reading, see M. Walzer, "The Legal Codes of Ancient Israel," *Yale Journal of Law and the Humanities* 335 (1992); and V. Matthews, B. Levinson, and T. Frymer-Kensky, eds., *Gender and Law in the Hebrew Bible and the Ancient Near East* (1998).   CHAYA T. HALBERSTAM

Leah (Gen 29–35) and her younger sister *Rachel are *Jacob's wives. Leah is the elder daughter of Laban, the brother of Jacob's mother *Rebekah. Leah marries Jacob through sororal polygyny (a system of marriage that allows a man to marry sisters, who are considered equal in status to each other in their relationship with their husband). Jacob only wanted to marry Rachel, but their father Laban argued that the younger Rachel could not marry before the elder Leah. In a social system where women validated their position in their husband's household through bearing children, particularly sons, Leah competed with Rachel, Rachel's slave (often translated "handmaid") Zilpah, and her own slave Bilhah. Leah bears six of Jacob's sons, who later become six of the *Israelite tribes – Reuben, Simeon, Levi, *Judah, Issachar, and Zebulun – and one daughter, *Dinah. No other daughters are named in the text. *Genesis 29:31 indicates that Leah was blessed with fecundity because she was unloved by Jacob.   NAOMI STEINBERG

Leeser, Isaac (1806–1868) was born in Prussia and emigrated to the *United States in 1824; he was a prolific author who served as the reader/*cantor of Mikve Israel Congregation in *Philadelphia. A traditionalist who pioneered English-language *sermons and founded a short-lived rabbinical seminary, Leeser published *The Occident and American Jewish Advocate*, the first important U.S. Jewish *periodical to achieve widespread circulation. In its pages he instructed American Jews about religious practices, advocated for charitable and religious endeavors, and provided a forum for spiritual writing by men and women. He also established a publishing company for Jewish works, translated the *Bible into English, and served as advisor to numerous Jewish ventures, including the first Jewish Sunday school (1838), led by Rebecca *Gratz. Recent research includes L. Sussman, *Isaac Leeser and the Making of American Judaism* (1995).

JUDITH R. BASKIN

Leibowitz, Yeshayahu: See EVIL AND SUFFERING; THOUGHT, MODERN

Leo Baeck Institute (LBI) is a research, exhibition, and lecture center that is devoted to the study, preservation, and comprehensive documentation of German-speaking Jewry from its origins to the post-war period. It was established by German Jews in 1955 and named after German rabbi, Jewish historian, and *Holocaust survivor Leo Baeck (1873–1956), who became the institute's first international president. The LBI is a constituent of the *Center for Jewish History in *New York City and also has centers in *Jerusalem and London (see *Britain). All the centers regularly hold local and international conferences on a variety of themes. Since 1956, the LBI has published a yearbook containing scholarship on the history and culture of the Jews of *Central Europe. The LBI archives contain items from nearly every phase of German Jewish history, including family papers, artwork, photographs, community histories, business and public records, and more than 1,500 memoirs (see MEMOIR AND LIFE WRITING); along with the LBI library, the archives are recognized as the most comprehensive collection of written works and works on paper documenting the Jewish community of *Germany.

ELIZABETH SHULMAN

Levi, Primo (1919–1987), writer and chemist, was born in Turin, *Italy; except for two brief periods, he resided in the same apartment in that city his whole life. Strongly linked to the Piedmont Jewish community, Levi's family was secular in its culture, as were most other members of Turin's Jewish upper middle class. Levi's interest in science began as a schoolboy, and in 1937 he enrolled in the chemistry faculty of the University of Turin. The 1938 racial laws forbidding Jews admission to universities posed difficulties even for students who were already enrolled, but Levi managed to complete his doctorate in 1942 and found work as a chemist. In October 1943, after Mussolini's deposal and reinstatement in the *Nazi-ruled Salo government, Levi joined a partisan group in the mountains. His group, however, was ill prepared for guerilla fighting. After two months it was betrayed, and Levi was captured by an Italian militia. Levi, who identified himself as a Jew rather than a partisan, was sent to the Fossoli camp from which, in a group of 650 Italian Jews, he was deported to *Auschwitz (a name then still unknown to him), arriving at the end of February 1944. Levi was among only twenty-four members of this group to survive the eleven months before Auschwitz's liberation by Soviet troops, and he repeatedly attributed his survival mainly to chance and luck. In the post-liberation chaos, Levi's return to Turin took nine months. Between 1945 and 1948, Levi married Lucia Morpurgo, with whom he had a son and daughter, found employment in a paint factory where he would work for thirty years as a chemist and administrator, and published his first book, *If This Is a Man* (American title: *Survival in Auschwitz*).

Levi viewed his experience of Auschwitz as initiating his literary career and transforming his Jewish identity (among other things, it brought his first encounter with *Eastern European Jews and *Yiddish). Few copies were published of his first book, but its reprinting in 1958 drew broader attention to Levi as both *Holocaust survivor and writer. In 1963, *The Truce*, recounting his homeward journey from Auschwitz, won immediate acclaim (American title, *The Reawakening*). After that, Levi pursued dual careers as chemist/administrator and writer, claiming that his memoirs and fiction reflected the discipline and inventive reach of science. *The Periodic Table* (1984) is an unusual synthesis of that training and the literary imagination. Other major works include *The Wrench* (1978), *If Not Now, When?* (1982), and his last completed book, *The Drowned and the Saved* (1986), in which, returning to the Holocaust, he identifies a "gray zone" of morality among both perpetrators and victims. Levi's reflective analysis of Nazi actions is sometimes interpreted as an expression of forgiveness, but he himself rejected that view. His many writings covered a wide range of subjects, but the Holocaust and the Jewish experience were never far removed. Levi, who had long suffered from bouts of depression, died in 1987, probably by suicide. His achievement as writer and thinker brought him international renown that has continued to grow.

BEREL LANG

Levi ben Gershon: See GERSONIDES

Levinas, Emmanuel (1906–1995) was a twentieth-century Jewish philosopher born in Kovno, *Lithuania (see THOUGHT, MODERN). In 1923, Levinas enrolled in the University of Strasbourg; during 1928–29 he studied in Freiburg with both Husserl and Heidegger. Levinas became a naturalized citizen of France in 1930 and also began his relationship of more than fifty years with the *Alliance Israélite Universelle du Bassin Méditerranéen. After *World War II, in which he served as a Russian translator and eventually was interned in a POW camp, Levinas worked for the Ecole Normale Israélite Orientale, a branch of the Alliance that trained male teachers; he was appointed director in 1947. Between 1947 and 1951 he studied Talmud with Mordecai Shoshani, whom Levinas referred to as "prestigious and merciless." In 1957 Levinas was a founding member of the Colloquia of the French Jewish Intellectuals, which met annually for the next three decades. He earned his Doctor of Letters in 1961; *Totality and Infinity* was his thesis. He held positions at the University of Poitiers, the University of Paris-Nanterre (1967), and the Sorbonne (1973).

Levinas's scholarly corpus falls into two categories: philosophical writings and writings on Judaism. Until recently, the philosophical community resisted the view that Levinas was a Jewish thinker, preferring to see him as a philosopher who was Jewish; his bodies of writing on Judaism were seen as parallel but not significantly connected. More recent scholarship assumes that Levinas's Jewish background was a powerful influence on his thought and that his Jewish writings reflected a philosophical emphasis.

Levinas's philosophical project is focused on the ethical response to the "other." In *Time and the Other* (1947) and *Totality and Infinity* (1961), he emphasized the characterization of subjectivity as ethical subjectivity. Significantly influenced by Franz *Rosenzweig's *The Star of Redemption*, Levinas radically altered the modern philosophical view that subjectivity is defined by freedom and *autonomy (i.e., the ability to make choices). Motivated by his own concern that western ontology was too "neutral" and that even Jewish philosophy, such as Martin *Buber's I–Thou structure was not radical enough as a foundation for an ethical system, Levinas reconceived subjectivity in terms of its relationship to an other. Subjectivity is founded on our asymmetrical and irrecusable ethical responsibility for the other.

This radical conception of subjectivity as essentially not free originated in Levinas's 1935 book, *De l'evasion*, translated and published in English as *On Escape* (2003), which developed the theme of his 1934 essay, "Philosophical reflections on Hitlerism." This early essay not only presciently foresaw the potential horror of Hitler's power but also traced the philosophical underpinnings of *Nazism, demonstrating an underlying logic to "Hitlerism." Although his interest in the other did not emerge until after World War II, these early writings revealed the ethical concerns that continued to characterize his philosophical and Jewish writings. Levinas's magnum opus, *Otherwise than Being, or beyond Essence* (1974), shifted the the earlier emphasis on a response to the other to a focus on the ethical subject. Notable in this later work is Levinas's exchange of *Torah citations for citations from the prophetic writings.

Levinas's talmudic readings emerged from his participation in the Colloquia of the French Jewish Intellectuals. These lectures aimed to draw French Jewish intellectuals back into Judaism and Jewish life by demonstrating the contemporary relevance of the Jewish sacred texts from which Levinas drew illustrations of the ethical responsibility to others. Translations of some of these readings include *Nine Talmudic Readings* (1994) and *New Talmudic Readings* (1999). Levinas's writings have influenced scholarship in aesthetics, education, feminist theory, Jewish studies, literary theory, philosophy, political science, and religious studies.

CLAIRE KATZ

Levinsohn, Isaac Baer (1788–1860). Born in Kremenets, *Russia, Levinsohn was a writer, a scholar, and a highly influential proponent of *Haskalah* in Russia; he is also known by the acronym Ribal. A brilliant *Talmud student, Levinsohn mastered Russian and other European languages and worked as a translator for Russian forces during the 1812 French invasion. Levinsohn subsequently spent some time in *Austro-Hungarian *Galicia, where he was influenced by various *Haskalah* figures including Nachman *Krochmal. Levinsohn returned to Kremenets in 1823 because of poor health. He devoted himself to writing and worked with the Russian government to mitigate various aspects of Jewish life.

Levinsohn was a polemicist for *Haskalah*; his writings satirized not only *Hasidism but also corrupt leaders of Jewish communities and those who condoned the kidnapping of Jewish children to meet Russian military quotas. His most influential work was *Teudah be-Yisrael* (Testimony in Israel), published in 1823 and strongly influenced by *Mendelssohn's *Jerusalem*. In it, Levinsohn champions *Hebrew as the language of the Jewish people, "the bond of religion and national survival"; scathingly criticizes traditional Jewish forms of education; and advocates that Jews study Russian and German. *Beit Yehudah* (House of Judah), which appeared in 1838 despite considerable rabbinic opposition, is presented as an explanation of Jewish beliefs, practices, and history to an educated Christian.

The book also sets out a program for how Jewish life in Russia should be reformed according to *Haskalah* values. *Efes Damim* (No Blood), a refutation of the *ritual murder accusation, appeared in 1837 and was later translated into English, German, and Russian in response to the *Damascus Affair of 1840. Levinsohn's recommendations in *Teudah be-Yisrael* that Jews return to a life of agricultural labor had an impact on early *Zionist groups and ideologies (**see GORDON, AHARON DAVID**).   KATE FRIEDMAN

Levirate Marriage: See MARRIAGE, LEVIRATE

Leviticus, Book of, in Hebrew *vayikra* ("and he [God] called," after the initial Hebrew word of the book), is the third book of the *Torah. The book is also known as *torat kohanim*, "Torah (instruction) of the priests," in *rabbinic literature. The name "Leviticus" is derived from the Greek title for the book, *Levitikon*, "pertaining to the Levites." Leviticus presents the basic laws of holy service, purity, ethics, and atonement for the levitical *priesthood. Young children in traditional Jewish circles customarily begin their study of the Torah with Leviticus because the pure should begin with the laws of *purity and *atonement.

Following the narratives concerning the construction of the *Tabernacle at Mount Sinai in Exodus 35–40, Leviticus focuses on the divine *revelation of Torah from the Tabernacle itself. It asserts the holy character of *God and calls on Israel to sanctify itself so that the nation will be able to relate to God and observe the divine will. Although the tribe of Levi (see ISRAELITES: TRIBES; TRIBES, TWELVE) is not formally designated as the priestly tribe until Numbers 17–18, Leviticus presumes that the Levites will serve as Israel's holy priests before God. Consequently, Leviticus focuses on the role of the priests in sanctifying the people.

The book includes three major literary units. Leviticus 1–7 presents instruction concerning the presentation of holy offerings in the sanctuary, including the *'olah*, "the whole burnt offering," presented regularly in the Temple; the *minhah*, "the gift or grain offering," which normally accompanies the *'olah*; the *zebah shelamim*, "the sacrifice of well-being," normally presented to give thanks to God; the *hata'at*, "the sin or purification offering," presented to atone for a transgression committed against divine Torah; and the *'asham*, "the guilt or reparation offering," presented when restitution is made for a transgression. Leviticus 8–10 describes the ordination of Aaron and his sons as the priests of the sanctuary; the deaths of Aaron's sons Nadab and Abihu (10:1–3) illustrate the importance of observing divine commandments when serving in the sanctuary. Leviticus 11–27 includes numerous ordinances concerning the sanctification of the people; these regulations concern the human consumption of meat, childbirth, skin diseases, bodily discharges, sanctification of the sanctuary, proper slaughter of animals and treatment of blood, improper sexual relations, ethical and ritual laws of holiness, improper religious practice, proper conduct and status of the priests, priestly handling of offerings, observance of sacred times, the burning of lamps and presentation of bread in the sanctuary, blasphemy, disposition of land, and the Temple tax, vows, and tithes (see COMMANDMENTS; and LAW: ANCIENT *NEAR EAST AND HEBREW *BIBLE).

Modern biblical scholarship (see BIBLE: MODERN SCHOLARSHIP) generally views Leviticus as part of the priestly stratum or source of the *Pentateuch, which was composed in the post-exilic period beginning in the late sixth century BCE when the *Jerusalem *Temple was rebuilt and the priesthood emerged as the leading body in ancient Judaism (see TEMPLE AND TEMPLE CULT). A number of scholars maintain, however, that the Priestly Code of Leviticus 1–16 may date as early as the reign of King *Hezekiah of *Judah (715–687 BCE), whereas the so-called Holiness Code of Leviticus 17–27 may date to the post-exilic era. Recent scholarship includes B. Schwartz, "Leviticus," in *The Jewish Study Bible*, ed. A. Berlin and M. Brettler (2003); B. A. Levine, *Leviticus: Jewish Publication Society Torah Commentary* (1989); and J. Milgrom, *Leviticus*, 3 vols. (1991–2001).

MARVIN A. SWEENEY

Libya: See NORTH AFRICA

Life-Cycle Rituals. Passages from one stage of life to another, and rites to mark them, are universal characteristics of human civilization. Public Jewish life-cycle rituals link participants to other Jews across space and time. The familiarity of the ritual enhances its power, infusing it with communal and historical meaning for the celebrants and reinforcing memories of similar moments in the lives of the onlookers. The Rabbis, who understood this ritual aspect of human nature, ordained that many of life's passages be marked in the presence of a quorum, the minimum definition of community. For this reason, *marriage and the recitation of *kaddish (the prayer for mourners) traditionally require the presence of a *minyan (ten male Jews over *Bar Mitzvah age in *Orthodox Jewish practice but ten adult Jews in most non-Orthodox forms of *Judaism).

The communal context of ritual performance is further reinforced through the prescription of a *seudah shel mitzvah* (commanded feast) at *circumcisions and *marriages; at these festive occasions, special introductions and interpolations are added to the *blessing after meals (*birkat ha-mazon*). Some life-cycle events such as birth, puberty, illness, and death are biologically determined, whereas others, including adolescence, marriage, divorce, and midlife, owe more of their identities to social construction. Over time these differentiations tended to blur and even disappear in Judaism, as social convention gained precedence over biological determinism. For example, the fact that the celebration of Bar and *Bat Mitzvah originally marked the onset of puberty has become irrelevant to their celebration in the present day. Yet, the celebrants are still within an age range close to puberty, maintaining the legal fiction of the biological connection.

As a result of a confluence of factors internal to Jewish life and community, and of contextual trends in American society more generally, rites of passage have become an important vehicle for exploring and evoking religious community, identity, and spirituality in contemporary American Judaism. One reason for this is the increased level of Jewish *education among American Jewish adults and their consequent familiarity with existing life-cycle rituals; this has led to a lessening of clericalism and the enfranchisement of the laity as ritual performers. Another factor is increased knowledge and acceptance of home rituals in Reform Judaism (see JUDAISM, REFORM: NORTH AMERICA), including increasing openness to such practices as the *dietary laws and *mikveh (ritual *immersion).

RITUALS FOR WOMEN: Jewish *feminist efforts to include women in traditional rituals and to create new ones marking moments of significance in women's lives have also promoted a growth in interest and innovation. Although the *Bat Mitzvah ceremony was created in the first half of the twentieth century, it was with the surge of the Jewish *feminist movement that more intensive reworking of life-cycle rituals began. The traditional liturgy has been expanded to include mothers' names in *circumcision and naming ceremonies and to create covenantal ceremonies to welcome baby girls to the world (*Simḥat Bat*, discussed in more detail later). Sometimes the focus was on bringing women into practices from which they had customarily been excluded, such as mourning rituals and especially the obligation to recite the *kaddish* prayer. In other instances (the creation of childbirth or menopause rituals), the aim was to enable women to give expression to their experience when Judaism had failed to recognize passages central to women's lives.

One of the first active steps taken by the burgeoning Jewish feminist movement in the mid-1970s was to write ceremonies to sanctify publicly the entry of Jewish baby girls into the *covenant. Male infants had benefited from multiple ceremonies for generations. These include the *ben* or *shalom zakhor* on the Friday night after birth – a party that included Torah study and special foods meant to protect the infant before his naming in the synagogue on *Sabbath morning; the actual covenantal circumcision ceremony, *berit milah*; and, for firstborn sons of mothers without priestly backgrounds, the rite of *pidyon ha-ben*, the *redemption of the firstborn son from sacred service, on the thirtieth day after birth. Over the last thirty years parents and rabbis have developed numerous versions of *Berit Bat* (the covenant of a daughter) or *Simḥat Bat* (the joy of a daughter) ceremonies for home and synagogue use.

The development of printed scripts for birth ceremonies for baby girls has had ramifications for other life-cycle rituals. These often homemade manuals serve as vehicles for innovation and as educational tools to enable assimilated Jews and the growing number of non-Jews who attend Jewish life-cycle events to understand and follow the ritual process. Booklets detailing ceremonies for baby girls have led to similar materials for the *berit milah* (circumcision) ritual. These, in turn, led to wedding manuals that explain the nuances of all aspects of the traditional Jewish wedding ceremony along with any special prayers or props unique to a particular wedding, as well as identifications of the participants. The personalized booklet is also now found frequently at Bar and Bat Mitzvah ceremonies. Finally, the first generations of booklets for funerals are now appearing.

MARRIAGE: The last quarter of the twentieth century saw the reinstitution of many traditional wedding rituals, albeit with an egalitarian emphasis (e.g., brides circled grooms, but then the grooms circled the brides). Brides and grooms from the more traditional and liberal movements in Judaism immersed themselves in the *mikveh (ritual bath), fasted, and read the confessional the morning before the wedding, all in a spirit of renewal before beginning a new life. Some couples wrote the words of their own marriage documents and spoke to each other under the *ḥuppah* (wedding canopy). In contrast to the traditional ceremony where the bride was passive, it has become normative for the bride and groom to exchange rings and for the ceremony to be more reciprocal. Finally, at some interfaith weddings and gay and lesbian commitment ceremonies, Jewish traditions were adapted to the new situations. Interfaith couples were wed under canopies and broke glasses at the close of the ceremony, often in syncretistic rites that included Christian clergy, ceremonial readings, and Jewish ritual objects.

MOURNING RITUALS: Jewish mourning customs are very compelling, even to those who do not practice many other rituals. The cycle of seven days of intense mourning at home (sitting *shivah*), within thirty days of semi-mourning (for parents, spouses, children, and siblings), and a full eleven months of saying the *kaddish* (special mourner's prayer) for parents, enables the bereaved to gradually return to normal life in a structured progression. Traditionally, women were not expected to participate in the recitation of the mourner's *kaddish* because they were not counted as members of the *minyan* required for communal prayer. However, women are part of the *minyan* in Reform, Reconstructionist, and most Conservative practice, and they recite the mourner's *kaddish* as a matter of course. At the beginning of the twenty-first century, many *Modern Orthodox women recite the *kaddish* (see DEATH AND MOURNING).

Valuable sources include R. L. Eisenberg, *The JPS Guide to Jewish Traditions* (2004); R. M. Geffen, *Celebration and Renewal: Rites of Passage in Judaism* (1993); H. E. Goldberg, *Jewish Passages: Cycles of Life* (2003); I. G. Marcus, *The Jewish Life Cycle: Rites of Passage from Biblical to Modern Times* (2004); R. L. Millen, *Women, Birth, and Death in Jewish Law and Practice* (2004); V. L. Ochs, *Inventing Jewish Ritual: New American Traditions* (2007); D. Sperber, *On Changes in Jewish Liturgy: Options and Limitations* (2010). RELA MINTZ GEFFEN

Lilienthal, Max (1815–1882), was an educator and rabbi, born and educated in Munich, *Germany. While serving as director of a Jewish school in Riga, *Latvia, Lilienthal became acquainted with S. S. Uvarov, *Russia's minister of education. In 1841, Uvarov enlisted him to draw up plans to persuade Russian Jews to accept state schools that would combine secular studies with a traditional Jewish education. His first audiences were the Orthodox leadership and chief proponents of *Haskalah* in the *Pale of Settlement. However, Lilienthal succeeded in alienating both groups who became distrustful of both the foreign envoy and the government's motives, suspecting a tsarist plan to convert Jews and jeopardize traditional Jewish education. Lilienthal tried again in 1843, after Uvarov appointed a Commission for the Education of the Jews, made up of Jewish leaders, to study government proposals for educational reform. Lilienthal visited a number of major Jewish centers and was successful in gaining some support. In 1844 the Russian law establishing state-run Jewish schools was enacted, accompanied by several anti-Jewish statues. These included the exclusion of *Talmud study from the curriculum.

Lilienthal immigrated to the *United States in 1845, apparently having come to believe that the Russian government intended to exploit the Jewish school network as a vehicle for conversion. In *New York City he ran a Jewish school and served as a rabbi. In 1855, Lilenthal became rabbi of Bene Israel, a Reform congregation in Cincinnati; he was a strong advocate for Reform Judaism (see JUDAISM,

REFORM: NORTH AMERICA) and a prominent civic leader who was particularly energetic in fighting for the exclusion of all religious education from public schools.

KATE FRIEDMAN

Lilith is a major figure in Jewish demonology with roots in ancient *Near Eastern folklore. Mentioned in *Isaiah among the wild beasts and demons who will devastate the world on the day of divine retribution (34:14), Lilith appears in *rabbinic literature as a female night spirit with a woman's face, long hair, and wings (BT *Eruvin* 100b, *Niddah* 24b, *Shabbat* 151b, and *Bava Batra* 73b). The medieval *Alphabet of Ben Sira*, a midrashic work of the *geonic period, conflated the demonic Lilith with rabbinic traditions about the "first *Eve," a being believed to have been created simultaneously with *Adam and subsequently rejected by him in favor of a more subservient partner (*Genesis Rabbah* 17:7, 18:4, and 22:7). This exegetical fiction reconciled the contradictions in the two biblical accounts of female creation (Gen 1 and Gen 2:4ff.). According to the *Alphabet*, Lilith was the "first Eve," who would not give up her equality with Adam, refused a subordinate position in sexual intercourse, and ultimately fled her husband, pronouncing the divine name and flying away. Despite being pursued and captured by angels, Lilith refused to return to Adam, asserting her demon status and her intention to harm women in childbirth and kill newborn infants. The *Alphabet* advises that Lilith is powerless to injure mothers and infants wearing protective amulets. Many Jewish amulets with preventive inscriptions against Lilith survive, indicating both the tenacity of this legend and the perils of childbirth before the modern era.

In the *Kabbalah, Lilith is said to rule over the world of evil (the *sitra ahra*) with her partner, *Samael. In this mystical construction of reality, Lilith mirrors the role of the *Shekhinah* ("Divine Presence") in the world of sanctity. Just as the *Shekhinah* is said to be the mother of the house of Israel, so Lilith is the mother of the unholy beings who constitute the "mixed multitude" (the *erev-rav*) of the world of impurity.

See J. Dan, "Samael, Lilith, and the Concept of Evil," *Association for Jewish Studies Review* 5 (1980): 17–40. A. Cantor, "The Lilith Question," in *On Being A Jewish Feminist: A Reader*, ed. Susannah Heschel (1983; rev. ed. 1995), offers a contemporary feminist reading of legends connected to Lilith; T. Schrire, *Hebrew Magic Amulets: Their Decipherment and Interpretation* (1966; rep. 1982) presents information about amulets used by Jewish women for protection against her.

JUDITH R. BASKIN

Literature: See also AGGADAH; BIBLE; BIBLE: POETRY, and other BIBLE entries; HOLOCAUST LITERATURE; HOLOCAUST LITERATURE: FICTION; HOLOCAUST LITERATURE: POETRY; HOLOCAUST REPRESENTATION: DRAMA; MEMOIR AND LIFE WRITING entries: POETRY entries; THEATER entries; and TRAVEL WRITING

Literature: Britain. Anglo-Jewish literature begins in the nineteenth century with sentimental domestic romances by middle-class Jewish women who wished to instill in their readers Victorian values and patriotism, while promoting the moral precepts of Judaism and identification with the plight of *Diaspora Jews under the *Inquisition or in tsarist

*Russia. Most of these women have passed into obscurity, but as Michael Galchinsky has written, they understood their choice of a dominant cultural form as an entry ticket into full cultural participation in the Victorian world. The best known of these Victorian writers is Grace Aguilar (1816–1847), daughter of a *Sephardic businessman, who wrote poetry and novels that ranged from historical to domestic romance, including *Vale of Cedars* (1831–35; published posthumously, 1850), *Home Influence* (1836), and its sequel, *A Mother's Recompense* (1837). In her religious and historical writings (including *Spirit of Judaism* [1842], *The Jewish Faith* [1845], and *Women of Israel* [1845]), as well as in her fiction, Aguilar extols the benefits of successful acculturation to English life and compares the spirit of Judaism with that of Christianity. At the same time, she combats conversionist arguments and assigns to women the role of transmitting in the domestic sphere the heritage of the exiled Jewish nation (see BRITAIN: EARLY MODERN AND MODERN).

The first Anglo-Jewish novel that can be said to be a full social critique of the Jewish community is *Reuben Sachs* (1889), by the poet Amy Levy (1861–1888), who committed suicide at twenty-seven. This novel is a study of the wealthy Jews of Bayswater, in West London, at a time when London's East End was teeming with penniless Jewish immigrants from *Eastern Europe. Another realist novel of revolt is *Dr Phillips: A Maida Vale Idyll* (1887) by Frank Danby (pseudonym of Julia Frankau, 1859–1916), a tale of a man who murders his German Jewish wife and elopes with a Christian mistress. Some scholars regard this work as a self-hating discourse of Jewish racial and cultural inferiority. By contrast, Benjamin Farjeon (1838–1903) was a prolific novelist who emulated Charles Dickens; in the few novels he devoted to Jewish subjects, such as *Solomon Isaacs* (1877), *Aaron the Jew* (1894), and *Pride of Race* (1901), he represents Jews as a valuable model of economic success.

Israel *Zangwill (1864–1926) is the acknowledged chronicler of East End Jewry. His *Children of the Ghetto* (1892) is a critical appraisal of the old ways lost to Anglicization, yet Zangwill senses a poetic idealism in these destitute paupers. His heroine, Esther Ansell, and other protagonists must choose between apostasy and a return to the *ghetto. Esther writes a novel under a pseudonym in which she castigates the hypocrisy of the wealthy assimilated community of her benefactors, who do not suspect the true identity of the author. The response of these benefactors, who regard themselves as having rescued Esther from the gutter, was to become a recurrent refrain of critics of the Anglo-Jewish novel: What will the Gentiles say? At the end of the novel, Esther sails to America, that melting pot in the title of Zangwill's play (1908), where, presumably, she will be better able to reconcile her yearnings for independence and her instinctive loyalty to the Jewish people. Zangwill promoted his brand of *Zionism through the Jewish Territorial Organization, which sought to settle Jews in Uganda and elsewhere, and was a sometimes controversial, misunderstood spokesman for English Jewry.

Zangwill's *The King of Schnorrers* (1894) is a picaresque satire that shows his comic talent but also internalizes antisemitic stereotypes. Two other collections of stories, *Ghetto Tragedies* (1893) and *Ghetto Comedies* (1907), also demonstrate his skillful depiction of his fellow Jews.

The Jewish readership in England, emancipated in 1858 and well on the way to assimilation and prosperity, generally preferred not to be reminded of the squalor of the East End that was depicted in Zangwill's *Children of the Ghetto* or Samuel Gordon's *Sons of the Covenant* (1900). Full assimilation was the hope of the interwar generation of Jewish writers, for whom the East End represented all they hated in their origins. Suburbanization took its toll on religious and ethnic affiliation, as we see in *Magnolia Street* (1932) by the popular novelist and essayist, Louis Golding (1895–1958). Set in Manchester (the fictional Doomington), Golding's novel attempts to bridge the Jewish and Gentile sides of the street, mainly through romance. A different, more polemical view of the Jew's assimilation in English society is presented by the novel, *The Five Books of Mr. Moses* (1929), by the Liverpool preacher and poet, Izak Goller (1891–1939).

After World War II, the disappearing Jewish East End became a source of bittersweet nostalgia in the plays of Arnold Wesker (b. 1932; knighted 2006), particularly *Chicken Soup with Barley* (1959), and of Bernard Kops (b. 1926), who adapts Shakespeare to a Jewish family situation in *The Hamlet of Stepney Green* (1957); the sentimental tales, *Make Me an Offer* (1952) and *A Kid for Two Farthings* (1953), by Wolf Mankowitz (1924–1998); and the historical novels of Emmanuel Litvinoff (b. 1915), as well as his autobiographical *Journey through a Small Planet* (1972). Beginning with *The Birthday Party* in 1957, Harold Pinter (1930–2008; Nobel Prize Laureate 2006) dealt in existential terms with questions of identity and language, but the unmistakable situation of the Jew after the *Holocaust is always present in his absurd comedy of menace. Because Pinter came from Hackney, a working-class district outside the East End, he had an ear for social displacement and alienation.

The new generation of Jews who became writers in the decade of the "Angry Young Men" owed little allegiance to the *synagogue and could write equally about Jewish and non-Jewish themes. Jews were now prominent in literature and the arts, and Jewish themes were no longer considered exotic or regional. The consciousness of living after the Holocaust was particularly strong in the writing of German Jewish refugees, such as Karen Gershon (born Käthe Löwenthal [1923–1993]), who came to Britain as a *Kindertransport child. Gershon's best known poem, "I Was Not There" (1966), sums up the feeling of abandonment by parents, as well as guilt for not being with the victims when they were deported to their deaths. Her novel, *The Bread of Exile* (1985), describes the humiliating refugee experience of the war years; in *The Fifth Generation* (1987), another *Kindertransport survivor, Barbara, marries a Gentile and adopts a child who may be a Holocaust victim or the son of Hitler. The return to *Germany in search of the lost home, family, and childhood is a claim to reparations that would somehow exorcise the haunting past that bequeaths the guilt of survival "to the fifth generation." Gershon also published a collective biography of the children who escaped to Britain on the *Kindertransport in 1938–39, *We Came As Children* (1966). The legacy of the refugee children is also the subject of a successful play by Diane Samuels (b. 1960), *Kindertransport* (1993). The Jew's status as a refugee is reflected, too, in some of the work of Eva Figes (b. 1932), herself a refugee from Germany; Anita Brookner (b. 1928); and Ruth Prawer Jhabvala (b. 1927), who also came to

Britain from Germany but left for India with her husband in 1951 and in the 1970s relocated to the United States.

In general, from the 1960s on, Jewish writers found themselves, to use the title of Efraim Sicher's study of Jewish writing in Britain, "beyond marginality." Rapid social mobilization had eased their way out of the poverty of the East End, and now Anglo-Jewry's disaffected young writers could critique the wall-to-wall carpeted superficiality of a complacent Jewish bourgeoisie who were as hypocritical as the Bayswater Jews in *Reuben Sachs*. In the category of what Anglo-Jewish novelist and *Jewish Chronicle* columnist Chaim Bermant (1929–1998) called the "Golders Green novel" may be included *The Bankrupts* (1958) by soccer columnist Brian Glanville (b. 1931); *The Crossing Point* (1960) by Gerda Charles (pseudonym of Edna Lipson, 1914–1996); *The Limits of Love* (1960) by American-born screenwriter Frederic Raphael (b. 1931); and Bermant's own *Jericho Sleep Alone* (1964). *The Elected Member* (U.S. title, *Chosen People*, 1969; Booker Prize, 1970) by Bernice Rubens (1928–2004) is another novel in this genre that brilliantly describes the disturbed mind of a young Jew overattached to his dead mother and addicted to hallucinogens.

The translator, poet, and biographer Elaine Feinstein (b. 1930) made her mark as an English novelist with *The Amberstone Exit* (1972) and *The Glass Alembic* (1973); her *The Shadow Master* (1978) reflects a historical reassessment of secular *Diaspora identity as *Israel became a focus of Jewish culture and solidarity after the *Six Day War. *The Shadow Master* spans the centuries and countries of Jewish dispersion in a plot that revolves around the seventeenth-century false messiah *Shabbetai Zevi. The precariousness of Jewish history in the Diaspora lurks behind the comfort of assimilation in several of Feinstein's novels (*Children of the Rose*, 1975; *The Survivors*, 1982; *The Border*, 1984). Feinstein's Russian Jewish parentage may explain her interest in such Russian poets as Marina Tsvetaeva and Anna Akhmatova, who have been formative influences on her work. Among the dead writers with whom she converses in her imagination in *Russian Jerusalem* (2008) is Isaac Babel (1894–1940; see LITERATURE: *RUSSIA AND *SOVIET UNION [IN RUSSIAN]).

The women's movement of the 1970s influenced *Guardian* columnist Linda Grant (b. 1951), who, like Eva Figes, has written important works on feminist issues. Grant's novel, *When I Lived in Modern Times* (2000), winner of the Orange Prize, is set in *Tel Aviv in the days before the 1948 War of Independence and the establishment of the State of Israel. It explores gender, sexuality, and identity in the retrospect of disillusioned idealism through the story of Evelyn Sert, a Jewish woman who escapes a vacuous post-war existence in England and becomes involved with a fighter in the Jewish underground. Grant's reportage, *The People on the Streets* (2006), is a ground-level view of Israelis coping with their complex political and security situation. The vantage point of a child of immigrants affords Grant an empathic position in *The Clothes on Their Backs* (2008), a novel about survival and betrayal, as well as about how clothes define personalities, whereas *Remind Me Who I Am Again* (1998) is an account of her mother's decline into dementia that explores the role of memory in forming family history. Grant's novel *Still Here* (2002) is also about repressed memory, set in her native Liverpool, in the debris of middle age after the sexual revolution.

The unembarrassed unearthing of a family's past is represented in a narrative about the discovery of a sealed room at 19 Princelet Street, in London's East End. Ian Sinclair and Rachel Lichtenstein's exploration of that lost Jewish history in *Rodinsky's Room* (2000) opens up a post-modern palimpsest of time and space, as Jewish memory enters a multicultural and multiethnic world inhabited by children of Asian immigrants. Jeremy Gavron (b. 1961) taps similar veins of fact, fantasy, and cultural archeology of the East End in his novel, *An Acre of Barren Ground* (2005), subtitled "The History of Everyone Who Ever Lived in Brick Lane."

Prominent in contemporary British Jewish writing are irreverent satires about a generation that is aware of its Jewish heritage and of antisemitism, but sees no contradiction in enjoying the hedonism of a promiscuous post-modernism. These types appear in the short-story collection *Hearts of Gold* (1979) and the novels *Bedbugs* (1982) and *Blood Libels* (1986) by Clive Sinclair (b. 1945), whose fantasies owe much to Isaac Bashevis Singer. They are also evident in the comic novels by Howard Jacobson (b. 1942), such as *The Mighty Walzer* (1999) or *Kalooki Nights* (2006), fictional memoirs of coming of age in Manchester. His satire of self-hating Jewish anti-Zionists, *The Finkler Question* (2010), won the prestigious Booker prize. Although he sees himself as a Jewish Jane Austen, Jacobson is more like a British Philip Roth who celebrates Jewish humor and the disputatious Jewish mind; he has offered his own zany view of Anglo-Jewry in *Roots Schmoots* (1993). Like Sinclair in *Blood Libels* and Jeremy Gavron in *The Book of Israel* (2002), Jacobson writes back to antisemitism, past and present, just as post-colonial authors write back to Empire.

Elena Lappin (born Moscow, 1954), sister of German Jewish humorist Max Biller (see LITERATURE: CONTEMPORARY EUROPE), has explored the comic situations of women who marry into the Anglo-Jewish community, as in the title piece of *Foreign Brides* (1999), in which an Israeli woman vents her frustration at her football crazy, outwardly religious husband by feeding the family meat that is not kosher and seducing the pork butcher. Lappin's novel *The Nose* (2001) is a satire of the Anglo-Jewish literary scene, based on her own experience as editor of *The Jewish Quarterly* (founded by Jacob Sonntag in 1953). Another insider's view is a controversial prize-winning first novel by Naomi Alderman (b. 1974), *Disobedience* (2006), about a lesbian daughter of a rabbi in the north London suburb of Hendon, whereas a third novel, *When We Were Bad* (2007) by Charlotte Mendelson (b. 1972), shows a north London Jewish family spiraling out of control. These novelists use unashamedly Jewish language and situations, and their voices blend into the multiethnic diversity of post-modern British fiction. Alderman's Orthodox feminist persona recalls American author Pearl Abrahams' *The Romance Reader*, and indeed, the preoccupation with sexual, spiritual, and personal identity in these novels is shared with a number of contemporary Jewish American authors.

For further reading, see B. Cheyette, ed., *Contemporary Jewish Writing in Britain and Ireland: An Anthology* (1998); M. Galchinsky, *The Origin of the Modern Jewish Woman Writer: Romance and Reform in Victorian England* (1996); and E. Sicher, *Beyond Marginality: Anglo-Jewish Writing after the Holocaust* (1985).

EFRAIM SICHER

Literature: Canada.

Literature: Canada. A. M. Klein (1909–1972), the founding father of Canadian Jewish literature, spent most of his life in Montreal, *Canada's cultural Jewish center throughout the twentieth century. In 1927 he published some of his early poetry in the *Menorah Journal, and in 1938 he became the editor of the *Canadian Jewish Chronicle*. An early collection of his poetry, *Hath Not a Jew* (1940), contains a preface by Ludwig Lewisohn, who describes Klein as "the first contributor of authentic Jewish poetry to the English language." From his traditional background, the poet draws on biblical and talmudic sources as well as medieval *Yiddish and *Hebrew *folktales. In a poem about *Spinoza, Klein identifies with the philosopher's skepticism: "From glass and dust of glass he brought to light, out of the pulver and the polished lens . . . and hence the infinitesimal and infinite."

The poet's transformational powers recur in a later poem, "Autobiographical," which begins "Out of the ghetto streets where a Jewboy / Dreamed pavement into pleasant Bibleland," and ends with the same "Jewboy" hearing "The Hebrew violins, / Delighting in the sobbed Oriental note." Klein appended this poem to his novel, *The Second Scroll* (1951), as "Gloss Aleph." (Other "glosses" include a polemical essay on the Sistine Chapel and a play that demonstrates the injustices of Muslim society toward Jews.) Loosely structured on the *Pentateuch, *The Second Scroll* follows the life of a messianic figure, Melech Davidson, from surviving the *Holocaust to his *aliyah (emigration) to the newly established State of Israel. His nameless nephew leaves Montreal to track Uncle Melech from Rome to Casablanca to Israel, but never succeeds in meeting his mysterious relative, either in the *Diaspora or in Zion. This failed encounter represents a motif not only in Klein's life and writing but also in the rest of Canadian Jewish literature. After *The Second Scroll* Klein became increasingly reclusive and spent his last years in silence.

As if responding to his mentor's withdrawal, Montreal poet Irving Layton (1912–2006) developed an outspoken persona. In the prophetic tradition, Layton excoriated *antisemitism in Canada and around the world, at the same time condemning his fellow Jews for their materialist, bourgeois values. In turn, Klein and Layton influenced Leonard Cohen (b. 1934), who assumed the mantle of prophet and priest in his poetry and fiction, beginning with *Let Us Compare Mythologies* (1956) and *The Spice-Box of Earth* (1961). The black romanticism of his third collection, *Flowers for Hitler* (1964), differs from Klein's satiric poem, "The Hitleriad" (1944). Whereas Klein was historically too close to his subject matter and flawed in his use of the neoclassical mock-epic form, Cohen seems more remote and his surrealist mode borders on the absurd. Cohen's two novels move from his autobiographical *The Favorite Game* (1963) to the mythological, post-modernist *Beautiful Losers* (1966). The former novel deals harshly with his affluent family in Montreal, whereas the latter explores the historical terrain of an Indian tribe that serves as a substitute for his own Jewish tribe.

Mordecai Richler (1931–2001) is by far the most significant novelist to capture Montreal's Jewish community. Most interesting among his many works are *The Apprenticeship of Duddy Kravitz* (1959), *St. Urbain's Horseman* (1971), and *Solomon Gursky Was Here* (1989). Predominantly a satirist railing against both the injustices done to Jews and the

follies within Jewish society, Richler used cinematic techniques to critique the newly rich. Duddy's apprenticeship represents the comic coming of age of Montreal's Jewry. *St. Urbain's Horseman* copies the quest motif in Klein's *The Second Scroll*, with Cousin Joey as a messianic *golem who roams the Diaspora to avenge Nazi crimes. *Solomon Gursky* is even more explicit in its backhanded tribute to Klein's close personal and professional relationship to the Bronfman family of Montreal, as Richler visits remote Canadian territories where the Gurskys interact with native peoples.

If Yiddish influences may be found in Montreal's literature from Klein to Richler, then the novels of Chava Rosenfarb (b. 1923) explore her *Polish heritage in the greatest detail, most notably her trilogy, *The Tree of Life* (1972), which chronicles the Łódź *ghetto.

Three francophone writers differentiate Montreal from other cities in North America. Naim Kattan (b. 1928) writes extensively about his *Iraqi past and his migration to North America, with *France as an intermediate stage. Biblical allusions fill his work, as they also inform the poetry and prose of Monique Bosco (b. 1927), who immigrated to Montreal after World War II. Her writing is marked by a *feminist critique of patriarchal patterns in *Judaism. A Yiddish and French sensibility informs the post-modern writing of Régine Robin, who relies on Jewish legends to invigorate contemporary Montreal and Paris. Robert Majzels (b. 1950), who writes in English, is the most experimental Jewish writer in Montreal: Like Robin and others, he employs post-modern pastiche and translation of languages to come to terms with post-Holocaust identity in his unique city.

If Montreal has been the primary center of Jewish Canadian literature, then Winnipeg is a second pole, combining its Yiddish-socialist ethos with a northern and western Canadian sensibility. Adele Wiseman (1928–1992), Miriam Waddington (1917–2004), and Jack Ludwig (b. 1922) constitute a troika of Winnipeg's Jewish writers. Wiseman's first novel, *The Sacrifice* (1956), charts three generations of an immigrant family, each member possessing a biblical name. A tragic novel in which Abraham the butcher commits murder, it depicts the hardships of this poor family's adjustment to the New World. By contrast, her second novel, *Crackpot* (1974), focuses on the comic aspects of its heroine Hoda, who transcends her immigrant roots. Indebted to A. M. Klein, Peretz, Mendele, and Sholem Aleichem (see LITERATURE, YIDDISH: 1800 TO TWENTY-FIRST CENTURY), Miriam Waddington's lyrical poetry demonstrates a strong social commitment. Jack Ludwig's novels show the influence of James Joyce, as his protagonists celebrate the joys of Jewish life across North America.

Further west, Henry Kreisel's (1922–1991) fiction also exhibits Klein's influence. In one of his short stories, "The Almost Meeting" (1981), Kreisel describes his failed encounter with Klein. Both of Kreisel's novels focus on the Holocaust: In *The Rich Man* (1947) the protagonist Jacob Grossman returns to *Vienna from Canada to visit his family just before World War II, and in *The Betrayal* (1964), the author examines the psychological dimensions of the Holocaust as it impinges on the lives of survivors in Edmonton.

Also on the prairies, and influenced by Klein, Eli Mandel (1922–1990) returns to his Jewish roots in a post-modern quest for meaning and identity among the Jewish graves in Estevan, Saskatchewan. He combines pastiche and palimpsests extensively in his long Holocaust poem, "On the 25th Anniversary of the Liberation of Auschwitz: Memorial Services, Toronto, January 25, 1970 YMHA Bloor & Spadina." Through running commentary he re-creates the tragic and eerie feeling of participating in the *Shoah. Similarly, J. J. Steinfeld's short stories are obsessed with the Shoah through the lens of a second-generation survivor. The short stories of Norman Levine (1923–2005) depict the isolated lives of Jewish characters from the immigrant district of Ottawa to down-and-out artists in rural England. Levine uses a minimalist painterly style in all of his naturalist writing.

In recent years Canada has witnessed a shift away from Jewish Montreal to Toronto, where Matt Cohen (1942–1999), Anne Michaels (b. 1958), and David Bezmozgis (b. 1973) exemplify a new sensibility embodying the changes from a conservative white Anglo-Saxon Protestant dominated Ontario to a multicultural metropolis in Toronto. Also noteworthy among the contemporary poets are Seymour Mayne (b. 1944) and Kenneth Sherman (b. 1950), the former for carrying on Klein's tradition in a *Zionist fashion, the latter for combining nostalgia, lyricism, and a subtle Jewish spirit that transcends ordinary experience. Yet another follower of Klein, Phyllis Gotlieb (b. 1926) yokes together children's verse, *Hasidism, and science fiction. In fiction, Lilian Nattel returns to Yiddish roots in historic novels, and Susan Glickman's *The Violin Lover* (2006) captures Jewish musical activities in London just before World War II. Aryeh Lev Stollman blends science and fantasy with Jewish learning in his fiction, Norman Ravvin grapples with a neo-Yiddish sensibility across the Canadian landscape, and Cary Fagan's (b. 1957) novels carry on where Matt Cohen's leave off. Edeet Ravel uses political allegory in her novels set in *Israel, whereas the leftist plays of Jason Sherman are critical of Israeli military policies. This polyphony of voices suggests that no single direction has clearly emerged for the future of Canadian Jewish literature, but the pull of the past informs all of this writing. MICHAEL GREENSTEIN

Literature: Central Europe. Numerous Central European Jewish writers who wrote in German, as well as other languages, have had a significant impact on western culture. Moreover, numerous aspects of the particular cultural milieu of *Central Europe are evident in the literary and artistic productivity of Jews who lived or live in this part of the world.

In 1929, literary critic and writer Walter *Benjamin wrote an article entitled "Jews in German Culture." In the first of two parts, Benjamin surveys the Jewish presence within German culture from Moses *Mendelssohn to Karl *Marx and Moses Hess, and from Hermann *Cohen to Otto Weininger and Sigmund *Freud. In the second section of his essay, Benjamin considers Jews as participants in creating German national literature, from the time of Süsskind von Trimberg, the thirteenth-century Jewish *Minnesänger* (troubadour), to the outstanding Jewish writers and Expressionist poets of the 1920s, including Franz *Kafka, Else *Lasker-Schüler, Alfred Döblin (1978–1957), Arnold Zweig (1887–1968), and Lion Feuchtwanger (1884–1958). Whereas Benjamin tends to view Jewish writers as being heavily dependent on German models, he also sometimes considers them as full and independent partners in the literary and cultural endeavors that comprised German

culture. For example, Benjamin credits Heinrich Heine (1797–1856) and Ludwig Börne (1786–1937) with importing the French *feuilleton* (topical supplement) into German literary journalism. Also, Benjamin cites Berthold Auerbach, Leopold Kompert, and Karl Emil Franzos as the initiators of the German literary genre known as "Ghetto Literature."

There is no overarching thesis in Benjamin's article about the relationship of the Jewish to the Germanic component in Central European Jewish literature and culture. If there is one unifying aspect to the productivity of the figures Benjamin presents, it is the implicit criterion of German-language productivity by Jews. However, this criterion is not necessarily applicable to Central European Jewish literature. A recent anthology, *Yale Companion to Jewish Writing and Thought in German Culture (1096–1996)*, edited by S. Gilman and J. Zipes (1997), includes, in addition to Central European writers who wrote in German, several Central European Jewish writers who produced texts in *Hebrew, Judeo-German (*Judendeutsch*), or *Yiddish. Jewish literary and cultural projects that were generated in languages other than German also fit within the purview of Central European Jewish literature if they were carried out or came to fruition within Central Europe. For example, Gilman and Zipes include commentary on *Glückel of Hameln's seventeenth- and early-eighteenth-century memoir written in Western Yiddish and on a seventeenth-century Yiddish *purimspil* (*Purim play) written in Leipzig (see entries under LITERATURE: YIDDISH). An essay on the Hebrew-language periodical *Ha-Me'assef* is also included in the compendium; among the centerpieces of the Jewish Enlightenment movement (*Haskalah*) in German-speaking lands from the 1790s, this periodical published odes in Hebrew in honor of political leaders like Frederick the Great of Prussia or Joseph II of Austria alongside Hebrew translations of important eighteenth-century German literature. The impact and adoption of German literary models such as the ode, as well as the Jewish fascination with Central European writers and political leaders, are important aspects of this Jewish literary production. Yiddish and Hebrew literature and culture, especially in *Berlin and *Vienna, but also elsewhere in Central Europe, were important aspects of Central European Jewish creative activity up through the twentieth century, until they were largely erased by *Nazism.

Walter Benjamin and others have viewed Moses *Mendelssohn's translation of the *Torah into German in the late eighteenth century as the gateway through which Central European Jewry entered German cultural space. In fact, mastering German was a revolutionary act within the Jewish community with far-reaching consequences regarding Jewish integration into German culture. Despite a scurrilous refrain in German *antisemitic writing defining Jews as "others" (that is, other than truly German) who were inherently incapable of writing "pure" or paradigmatic German, Jewish writers consistently refuted this claim by their stylistic virtuosity and significant literary achievements. In 1939, the popular German Jewish novelist and art critic Georg Hermann (1871–1943) claimed that it was precisely the German-language authors of Jewish origin who had become the towering figures in modern German literature. In this regard he mentioned Hugo von Hofmannsthal (1874–1929), Richard Beer-Hofmann (1866–1945), Arthur Schnitzler (1862–1931), Peter Altenberg (1859–1919), Rudolf

Borchardt (1957–1945), and others. He argued that the German literature that was renowned internationally was primarily produced by German and Austrian Jews, especially Schnitzler, Franz Werfel (1890–1945), Lion Feuchtwanger, Jakob Wassermann (1873–1934), Stefan Zweig (1881–1942), and Arnold Zweig. Hermann emphasized that Central European theater was deeply indebted to talented dramatists, directors, and actors of Jewish origin; theater criticism, especially, was dominated by Jews. According to Hermann, the same was true of literary scholarship and criticism.

This viewpoint was part of a famous and controversial debate about the Jewish role in German culture initiated by Moritz Goldstein (1880–1977) in a provocative polemic entitled "Deutsch-jüdischer Parnass" (German Jewish Parnassus, 1912). Goldstein claimed that the Jews in Germany had become the custodians and arbiters of the spiritual – specifically, the literary and cultural – treasures of German society, while German society denied Jews the right and the capability to fulfill this role. Goldstein cited the strong presence of Jews in the German press, and he celebrated their high visibility in the world of music and public concerts, also noting their important presence in German theater. He opined that, because many Jews were to be found among the ranks of Germany's best poets, writers, and academicians, Jews were on the verge of taking undisputed control of German literature and literary studies. This claim of a Jewish domination in Central European literary and cultural life appears to have established itself in diverse quarters. Stefan Zweig, the popular Austrian Jewish cultural mediator, translator, writer, and poet of the first half of the twentieth century, declared in his memoirs, written shortly before his suicide in exile in 1942, that "nine-tenths of what the world celebrated as Viennese culture … was either promoted, nourished, or even created by Viennese Jewry." Another important writer from this milieu was Joseph Roth (1894–1939), whose *Radetzky March* (1932) expressed the complex emotions Jews retained toward the *Habsburg Empire.

Goldstein's thesis that Central European literature and culture were largely Jewish, however, had little impact in stemming the various strains of antisemitic writings that continued to emphasize the supposedly unbridgeable incompatibility between Germanic and Jewish cultures. On the Jewish side, the growth of cultural *Zionism in the early twentieth century encouraged the idea of a German-language Jewish national literature and culture. Supporters of this "Jewish cultural renaissance" furthered a new cultural orientation in the German-language Zionist press and founded a Jewish national publishing company in Berlin, the Jüdischer Verlag, which sought to establish itself as the center of the Jewish national literary cultural enterprise in German. They also published a series of ambitiously conceived literary and artistic anthologies, like the *Jüdischer Almanach* (1902) or *Jüdische Kunstler* (1903), which attempted to delineate a Jewish national canon in literature and the arts, while focusing on German-language authors and emphasizing the role of Central European Jewry in Jewish national literary and artistic productions.

Dynamic intellectuals and artists, including Nathan Birnbaum (1864–1937), Martin *Buber, Berthold Feiwel (1875–1937), and Ephraim Moses Lilien (see ART, EUROPE: TWENTIETH CENTURY; ART: ISRAEL) spearheaded this movement, and a long list of German Jewish and Austrian Jewish writers and poets also were part of its orbit. The German cultural Zionists saw the production of significant Jewish literature and art in the German-speaking Diaspora as a prelude to the renaissance that would eventually take place in Hebrew in the Land of Israel. They encouraged literature and art that focused on Jewish figures and themes from the *Bible or *Talmud or gave expression to Jewish spiritual and religious experiences, as well as to Jewish identity concerns in the Diaspora. This movement, therefore, argued both explicitly and implicitly for Jewish difference and separateness from the Central European, Germanic cultural milieu. Some names not normally associated with a Jewish national literature in German or with Jewish art in Germany and Austria appear in cultural Zionist anthologies and related publications; they include Karl Wolfskehl (1869–1948), Efraim Frisch (1873–1942), Max Liebermann (1848–1935), and Stefan Zweig. It is fair to say that each changed his views over time concerning *Zionism and his own relationships to Jewish culture and to Central European culture. Eventually, they all experienced the rise of Nazism firsthand. Wolfskehl, Frisch, and Zweig sought to escape Europe. Liebermann, who served as president of the Prussian Academy of the Arts, had to resign from his position in 1933 after the Nazis came to power. He died in Berlin in 1935.

Central European Jewish literature and culture do not end with the Nazi period, despite the deep ruptures it caused. Whereas the majority of Jewish writers who managed to survive in exile continued to live and write (mostly in German) outside of Germany and Austria after World War II, some, including Alfred Döblin and Hilda Domin (1909–2006), returned to Central Europe. Some very prominent Jewish writers, including Arnold Zweig, Stephan Hermlin (1915–1997), and Anna Seghers (1900–1983), returned to communist East Germany or grew up there (Jurek Becker [1937–1997]; Chaim Noll [b. 1954]). Their writings and careers need to be evaluated in terms of how they provided continuity or commentary on Jewish-related issues in Central Europe after the war.

Some observers have claimed that a resurgence in German Jewish and Austrian Jewish letters has been under way at least since the 1990s. Writers, journalists, and cultural critics, such as Marcel Reich-Ranicki, Ralph Giordano, and Henryk Broder, have raised questions about the Jewish relationship to German culture and have encouraged younger Jewish writers in German to probe issues of Jewish identity in post-Holocaust Central Europe. German writers and poets, including Rafael Seligmann (b. 1947), Maxim Biller (b. 1960), and Barbara Honigmann (b. 1949), and an Austrian contingent composed of Robert Menasse (b. 1954), Robert Schindel (b. 1944), and Doron Rabinovici (b. 1961), may be considered to belong to this group. Recent immigrants to Central Europe from the former *Soviet Union who write in German, including Vladimir Vertlib (1966) and Vladimir Kaminer (b. 1967), are also part of this cohort. Their works suggest that Central Europe continues to provide an important location for Jewish identity construction in the German language and for dialogue about it, despite the *Holocaust and despite Zionism, or even in the face of both.

MARK H. GELBER

Literature: Contemporary Europe. European and Jewish identity and history are mutually and intimately intertwined. In the literary realm Jewish authors continue to be creative participants in an ongoing debate on the continent's past and future while also renegotiating relationships between Jewish and non-Jewish cultures. Despite the minority position of present-day European Jewish authors, a vigorous resurgence of Jewish culture can be observed as many Jewish writers have turned to their own origins, reflecting on their identity and position in a Gentile society.

Jewish authors express a variety of possible relationships to Judaism, as well as to the cultural, literary, and historical contexts of the countries where they are citizens. Although most contemporary Jewish writers did not personally experience the tragedy of the *Holocaust, its traces occupy a central position in their literature and play an important role in Jewish self-awareness. Their literary aesthetics reflects the secondary trauma of growing up within families shattered by the Holocaust, and their writing has been shaped by the legacy of the victims and the testimonies of the survivors.

Holocaust writing by first-generation survivors encompasses a variety of primarily semi-autobiographical genres like the memoir, the *bildungsroman*, and the family saga, in which history and fiction, testimony and poetry go hand in hand without excluding one another. The Hungarian Imre Kertész (b. 1929) was awarded the Nobel Prize for Literature in 2002 for works such as *Fateless* (1975) that draw on his experiences in *Auschwitz and Buchenwald. Autobiography is often the literary form chosen to render the history of the self after the catastrophe, paradigmatically adopted in Primo *Levi's memoir, *If This Is a Man* (1959; also published as *Survival in Auschwitz)*, or Elie *Wiesel's testimony, *Night* (1960).

The remembrance of the lost world of the *shtetl is an important element in much of the European Jewish literature written in the last half of the twentieth century. In the tradition of the Jewish Holocaust memorial books, *yizker bikher* (see YIZKOR BOOKS), many authors aim to preserve the lost communities of *Eastern Europe. Accordingly, the second and third generation give a concrete literary voice to the persecution and displacement of their forebears. This writing is generated by the need to re-create a picture of the past as experienced by their families. It illustrates the vicissitudes of the modern Jewish experience at large by rendering multigenerational stories that feature ancestors enjoying emancipation or struggling to achieve it, tempted by secularization, pressured into assimilation, displaced by *pogroms, haunted by persecution, or blinded by ideologies. In her novel *In Memory's Garden* (2002), the Polish author Joanna Olczak-Ronikier (b. 1934) reflects the imperative of *zakhor*, the Jewish command to remember, for many of her peers. However, even though a number of common dynamics can be identified, European Jewish literature displays a diversity that is embedded in various national contexts.

In Italy, Jewish writers often consider *italianità* and *ebreicità* to be components of one single identity. Apart from authors such as Primo *Levi and Giorgio Bassani (1916–2000), who transformed their personal experiences as Jews under *Nazism into literature, the Italian literary tradition shows very little interest in cultural particularism. Indeed, contemporary Italian Jewish writers, such as Clara Sereni (b. 1946; *Keeping House*, 2005), Stefano Jesurum (*Soltanto per amore* [Only for Love], 1996), and Giorgio Pressburger (b. 1937; *Teeth and Spies*, 1999; *Snow and Guilt*, 2000), demonstrate a spirit of universality and sense of being part of the Italian nation.

In Austria, Jewish authors such as Robert Schindel (b. 1944; *Born-Where*, 1995), Doron Rabinovici (b. 1961; *The Search for M.*, 2000), or Robert Menasse (b. 1954; *Meaningful Certainty*, 2000; *Vertreibung aus der Hölle* [Expulsion from Hell], 2001) reject a closed and unified concept of Jewish identity and distance themselves from the previous generation of Jewish writers like Paul Celan (see HOLOCAUST LITERATURE: POETRY). Conversely, contemporary German Jewish literature, while rejecting the shame of living in Germany as the country of Nazi perpetrators – a feeling predominant among the survivor generation – is more confrontational about the German past and more explicit and conscious of its Jewish heritage. After the student revolts at the end of the 1960s, Jewish writers in Germany participated in exposing the crimes of the previous generation of Germans or their attitude as indifferent bystanders. German novelists such as Barbara Honigmann (b. 1949; *A Love Made out of Nothing & Zohara's Journey*, 2003), Esther Dischereit (b. 1952, *Joëmis Tisch* [Joëmi's Table], 1988), Maxim Biller (b. 1960; *Land der Väter und Verräter* [Land of the Fathers and Betrayers], 1994), Ulla Berkéwicz (b. 1948; *Engel sind schwarz und weiß* [Angels are Black and White], 1992), and Rafael Seligmann (b. 1947; *Rubinsteins Versteigerung* [Rubinstein's Auction], 1989) are on the whole more explicitly and antagonistically Jewish than writers in other European Jewish literatures. Yet, Russian-born Vladimir Kaminer (b. 1967; *Russian Disco*, 2002), an important young author in the pop literature scene, observes German society as an immigrant outsider in present-day Berlin without consciously foregrounding his narrative position as a Jew.

In France, home to the largest Jewish community in Europe, a reversal of the assimilationist tendency began in the 1980s. Recent French Jewish literature, self-confidently and assertively articulating Jewish particularity, can roughly be divided into two major groups made up of *Sephardic and *Ashkenazi authors. On the one hand, immigrant Maghrebi (*North African) novelists display a cultural, national, historical, and linguistic distance from the geographic regions in which their parents grew up, but on the other, they relate to France as a former colonial power. Notions of exile and diasporic existence are particularly present in the writings of Marlène Amar (b. 1949; *Des gens infréquentables* [Bad Company], 1996), Ami Bouganim (*Le fils du serpent* [The Son of the Snake], 1981), Marcel Bénabou (b. 1939; *Jacob, Menahem and Mimoun*, 1998), and Gil Ben Aych (*Le livre d'Étoile* [Étoile's Book], 1986). In contrast, French-born Ashkenazi novelists, often writing family portraits, articulate the pain of their ancestors who faced discrimination and persecution or portray their country as a society that came to terms with its collaborationist past quite late. In this context, important authors include Eliette Abécassis (b. 1969; *L'or et la cendre* [Gold and Ashes], 1998), Annette Kahn (*Why My Father Died*, 1991), Alain Glückstein (*Nos grands Hommes* [Our Great Men], 1997), Myriam Anissimov (b. 1943; *Sa majesté la Mort* [Her Majesty, Death], 1999), Patrick Modiani (b. 1945; *Missing Person*, 2005), Georges Perec (1936–1982; *Ellis Island*, 1995), and Cécile Wajsbrot (b. 1954; *La trahison* [The Betrayal], 1997).

Similar to the situation in Italy, younger Jewish authors in the Netherlands are largely unconcerned with the traditions of Jewish literature in their country. This is because Dutch Jewish authors never explicitly considered themselves a minority group. They were part of mainstream culture and enjoyed a status free from the pressures of cultural assimilation or of self-justification. To a great extent, this is still the case. Leading figures of the younger generation include Arnon Grunberg (*Blue Mondays*, 1997), Marcel Möring (*In Babylon*, 2000), Leon de Winter (*Hoffman's Hunger*, 1995), Carl Friedman (*Nightfather*, 1995), Gerhard L. Durlacher (*The Search*, 1988), and Abel Herzberg (*Between Two Streams*, 1997).

In contrast to the situation in capitalist Western Europe before the 1989 fall of the Berlin Wall, in communist Eastern Europe the exploration of Jewish religious, cultural, or ethnic identity was discarded as a remnant of bourgeois ideology; this position fostered state censorship of Jewish authors, who were consequently forced to emigrate or publish abroad. Thus, for certain contemporary Jewish writers, primarily in Hungary, Poland, and Russia, Stalinist terror and Soviet tyranny play an important role in their conception of Europe as a space of democratic values. Jewish writing in today's Russia holds a decentered position not only at Europe's periphery but also between Jewish tradition and dominant Russian culture. As such it distances itself from Russia's highly centralized structure and its antisemitism, which is still present in large parts of society. In the works of present-day Russian authors, such as Alexandr Melikhov (*Ljubov' k otecheskim grobam* [Love with Fatherly Graves], 2001), Dina Rubina (*Here Comes the Messiah!*, 2000), Sergei Kaledin (*The Humble Cemetery* and *Gleb Bogdyshev Goes Moonlighting*, 1990), Asar Eppel (*The Grassy Street*, 1998), Ljudmila Ulitskaya (*The Funeral Party*, 2002), Semyon Lipkin (*Zapiski zhil'ca* [Notes of a Tenant], 1991), or Nobel Prize winner Joseph Brodsky (*To Urania* [1998]), explicit Jewish themes, like the representation of Jewish suffering during the Holocaust, are rarely central.

Jewish authors consider themselves to be part of European society, yet simultaneously, in varying degrees and different aspects, they are also distinct from it. In their respective mother tongues, they continue to create a complex and engaging body of literary texts that eloquently express the pressures between the past and the present and between mainstream and minority populations. Although the relationship of these writers to Judaism varies with each individual, from maintaining distance to passionate rediscovery and assertive commitment, the often uneasy, singular, and decentered position of Jews and Jewish culture in modern European nation-states lies at the heart of all of their narratives.

For further reading, see V. Liska and T. Nolden, eds., *Contemporary Jewish Writing in Europe: A Guide* (2007); D. C. Lorenz, ed., *Contemporary Jewish Writing in Austria: An Anthology* (1999); L. Morris and K. Remmler, eds., *Contemporary Jewish Writing in Germany: An Anthology* (2002); T. Nolden, *In Lieu of Memory: Contemporary Jewish Writing in France* (2006); idem and F. Malino, eds., *Voices of the Diaspora: Jewish Women Writing in Contemporary Europe* (2005); A. Polonsky and M. Adamczyk-Garbowska, eds., *Contemporary Jewish Writing in Poland: An Anthology* (2001); and S. Rubin Suleiman and

E. Forgacs, eds., *Contemporary Jewish Writing in Hungary: An Anthology* (2003).
VIVIAN LISKA and ARVI SEPP

Literature: France. Armand Lunel (1892–1977), prominent writer and historian of French Jewry, rightly suggested that the *Dreyfus Affair led to an awakening of Jewish consciousness in French letters, interrupting a long-standing commitment to acculturation that had affected literature as well. The authors who took decidedly Jewish positions, often expressing Zionist predilections, included Bernard Lazare (1865–1930); Edmond Fleg (1874–1964), whose seminal *Anthologie juive* appeared in 1923; André Spire (1868–1966); Jean-Richard Bloch (1884–1947); Max Jacob (1874–1944); and Henri Franck (1888–1912). The journal *La Revue juive*, edited in Geneva by the Corfu-born Albert Cohen (1895–1981), became a popular forum of discussion, critiquing positions that (à la Marcel Proust's) were now deemed lacking in Jewish self-awareness or self-assertiveness. Albert Cohen's own literary career was marked both at its beginning and its end with important examples of Jewish writing that spoke out against *antisemitism and racial prejudice.

The next phase of Jewish writing in France has been called a "literature of the *Shoah" (see HOLOCAUST LITERATURE) and encompasses authors such as Anna Langfus (1920–1966), Elie *Wiesel (b. 1928), Arnold Mandel (1913–87), Piotr Rawicz (1919–82), and André Schwarz-Bart (1928–2006). It is worth noting that many of them were émigrés from Eastern Europe whose native tongue was not French: Elie Wiesel, for example, was born in Sighet (now *Romania). The reception history of Wiesel's famed autobiographical narrative *La nuit* (Night [1958]) also shows the delay in the public reception of survivor memoirs, a genre that eventually would become part of world literature (see HOLOCAUST DIARIES; MEMOIR AND LIFE WRITING entries). Wiesel's memoir was based on a 900-page narrative originally written in *Yiddish and published in Buenos Aires, *Argentina, before it was condensed into the short version that appeared in French in 1958. Wiesel shared this kind of delayed acclaim with other authors who addressed the *Shoah: Schwarz-Bart won the prestigious *prix Goncourt* for his 1959 seminal family saga, *Le dernier des justes* (The Last of the Just), and Polish-born Anna Langfus received the award in 1962 for her novel *Les bagages de sable* (Bags of Sand), which is part of a series of works chronicling the persecution of a Jewish family from *Poland.

Of exceptional status among his peers is the *Vilna-born author and resistance fighter Romain Gary (1914–1980), whose enormous oeuvre (also published under the pseudonym Emile Ajar) includes biting satires (*La danse de Gengis Cohn*, 1967) and narrative accounts of post-war Europe (*Education européene*, 1945). In 2004 Jewish writer Myriam Anissimov published a perceptive biography of this prolific writer and diplomat (*Romain Gary, le caméléon*).

Albert Memmi (born in Tunisia in 1921 and trained at the Sorbonne) is one of the first representatives of the *Sephardic influence in French Jewish life and letters. His 1953 autobiographical novel *La statue de sel* (Pillar of Salt) created a format followed by many *Maghreb-born writers who began to publish in France in the wake of decolonialization. Memmi also became an influential advocate for the colonized subject, rather than limiting his critical analysis to the marginalized position of the Jew in a culturally homogeneous Christian society.

The critic Clara Lévy in her study *Ecritures de l'identité: Les ecrivains juifs apres la Shoah* (Writings of Identity: Jewish Writers After the Shoah;1998) suggested that the omnipresence of the past represents the crucial distinction of French survivor literature; the role of the past changes with the authors who began to write in the 1970s and 1980s and whose writings have been characterized as a literature "in lieu of memory" (Nolden). The arrival of *Sephardic Jews from France's former territories and colonies in the Maghreb (but also from *Egypt) added new thematic and stylistic features, whereas French-born authors of *Ashkenazic background began to turn away from Marxist denials of ethnic and religious identities and set out to rediscover their Jewish roots. In many of his works Georges Perec (1936–1982) addressed the situation of the Jew and the "l'univers concentrationnaire" (The Concentration Camp Universe; title of a 1946 book by David Rousset, b. 1912) in intriguingly post-modern fashion. Alain Finkielkraut (b. 1949), in his seminal 1980 essay *"Le Juif imaginaire"* ("The Imaginary Jew"), programmatically challenged members of his generation to find an appropriate voice through which to articulate their unique situation of having been born after the Shoah. Eschewing the literary practices of Jewish invisibility and acculturation, second- and third-generation writers like Henri Raczymow (b. 1948), Patrick Modiano (b. 1945), Myriam Anissimov (b. 1943), Antoine Spire, Norbert Czarny, and Cécile Wajsbrot, openly address French society's complicity in the persecution of French Jews during the so-called *années noires* (black years).

Some of these writers also render self-critical portrayals of Jewish life in present-day France by using literary forms ranging from conventional memoirs (Serge Koster, Claude Gutman, Anne Rabinovitch) and multigenerational genealogies (Anissimov) to avant-garde narratives (Patrick Modiano, Gérard Wajcman, Georges Perec) and sensationalist police thrillers (Eliette Abécassis, Clément Weill Raynal). Henri Raczymow has emerged as one of the literary historians of this contemporary era of French Jewish writing.

North African women writers like Katia Rubinstein, Nelcya Delanoë, Chochana Boukhobza, Paule Darmon, and Marlène Amar joined Annie Goldmann (*Les filles de Mardochée* [The Daughters of Mordechai], 1979) in her attempt to create a literary space suitable for negotiating a female identity as a post-colonial French Sephardic Jew without succumbing to the temptations of acculturation or of nostalgia for the lost world of North African Jewish life.

Their male counterparts as well, among them most prominently Marcel Bénabou, Jean Luc Allouche, Gil Ben Aych, and Marcos Koskas, have found unique ways of integrating the idioms of the *hallas* and *mellah*, the centers of Jewish life and learning in North Africa, into their narratives. The term "couscous literature" has been coined to point to the unique mixing of languages (among them *Arabic and *Ladino), literary styles, and narrative conventions that is characteristic of some of these authors' work. Eschewing traditional demands for concise and stylistically pure literary diction, they create a vivacious literature in which, however, a religious dimension is hardly present. For further reading, see T. Nolden, *In Lieu of Memory: Contemporary Jewish Writing in France* (2006).   THOMAS NOLDEN

Literature: Graphic Novels. The graphic novel, a genre that integrates complex literary narratives with continuous visual images characteristic of comic books, has received considerable attention as an explosive cultural phenomenon that effectively blurs the boundaries between popular culture and high art. Beginning in 1992 when Art Spiegelman won the Pulitzer Prize for *Maus*, this genre has attracted both critical acclaim and a rapidly expanding readership. Jewish writers and artists are a dynamic presence both in the origins and the latest trends in the graphic novel. Indeed, most scholars credit Will Eisner (1917–2005), the son of a Jewish Austrian immigrant to the United States, as the essential figure with which any discussion of the graphic novel's development (Jewish or otherwise) must begin.

Astonishingly, Eisner's career encompassed eight decades, from the "golden age" of the comic book to the critical and popular embrace of the graphic novel. Long recognized as a profound innovator in the development of visual narrative and the language of comics, Eisner created numerous comic icons such as "the Spirit." His narrative and visual style are consistently informed by a hard-edged realism, indelibly influenced by his early life in *New York City tenements. That perspective is especially visible in his four stories of struggling immigrants entitled *A Contract with God and Other Stories* (1978), widely acknowledged as the first graphic fiction. *To the Heart of the Storm* (1991), considered the most successful of Eisner's frequent ventures into autobiography, presents a series of compelling flashbacks, the peripatetic reveries of a young inductee on a troop train on his way to basic training in 1942. "Willie's" wide-ranging family history encompasses the settlement of his mother's family in 1880s America, his father's exploits in early-twentieth-century *Vienna, and *World War II. At times reminiscent of Studs Terkel's oral histories, this work counters the American myth of progress and opportunity by demonstrating the character's and his family's unending battles with *antisemitism.

Eisner always recognized that visual art could be a potent weapon in combating stereotypes of the Jew, just as it had once proven effective in circulating hostile images. Describing the process that influenced *Fagin the Jew* (2003), he remarks how, in "examining the illustrations of the original editions of Charles Dickens' 1838 novel *Oliver Twist*, I found an unquestionable example of visual defamation in classic literature. The memory of their awful use by the Nazis . . . one hundred years later, added evidence to the persistence of evil stereotyping. Combating it became an obsessive pursuit" (*Fagin the Jew*, 4). His final work, *The Plot*, completed just before his death, tells the story behind *The Protocols of the Elders of Zion*, the fraudulent antisemitic screed that describes the supposed Jewish plan for global influence and domination (see RUSSIA). Eisner also wrote the influential study, *Comics & Sequential Art* (1985). Michael Chabon's Pulitzer-prize-winning novel, *Kavalier and Clay* (2000), is based in part on Eisner's early years. In 2002, Eisner received a Lifetime Achievement Award from the National Federation for Jewish Culture (presented by Art Spiegelman). The highest recognition of achievement in the graphic novel, the Eisner Award, is named after him.

Despite Eisner's strong early efforts, it was not until the publication of Spiegelman's *Maus: A Survivor's Tale* (the first volume was published in 1986; earlier drafts appeared in

Spiegelman's self-published magazine, *Raw*) that the graphic novel's potential received critical appreciation. Originally published in two volumes (*My Father Bleeds History* and *Here My Troubles Began*), *Maus* juxtaposes Spiegelman's tumultuous relationship with his survivor father, Vladek, with a narrative based on the latter's harrowing recollections of his life before and during the *Holocaust. In "Art's" retelling of events, the reader is introduced to an analogous world of hatred and atrocity wherein Jews are translated as mice along with corresponding representations of Poles as pigs, Germans as cats, and Americans as dogs. Much of the remarkable power of *Maus* derives from its historical verisimilitude as well as its urgent force, exercised through both textual and illustrative clues, in demonstrating the limits and misuses of "identity."

Ultimately, *Maus* bears witness to the once-suppressed story of Anja, Art's mother, who killed herself without leaving a farewell note. Vladek destroyed Anja's journals, and her absence ensured that Art (who suffered a psychic breakdown) and Vladek would be forever connected through their shared incapacity to transcend Holocaust trauma and grief. Spiegelman's subsequent works include a complex political and personal response to the horror of 9/11: *In the Shadow of No Towers* (2004). Here Spiegelman (who still lives not far from Ground Zero), ingathers a range of famous ("Little Nemo in Slumberland") as well as obscure newspaper comic strips of the late nineteenth and early twentieth century to mediate between his family's intimate story and a critique of the Bush administration's disastrous exploitation of tragedy.

Spiegelman's success with *Maus* inspired other graphic memoirs and novels with Holocaust themes, including Joe Kubert's *Yossel, April 19, 1943* (2003), a "counter-history" of what might have been his family's fate had they remained in *Poland; Pascal Croci's *Auschwitz*, based on interviews with concentration camp survivors (2004); Bernice Eisenstein's second-generation memoir, *I Was the Child of Holocaust Survivors* (2006); and Miriam Katin's critically acclaimed account of her and her mother's flight from the Nazis, *We Are on Our Own* (2006). The recent emergence of these sophisticated works suggests that the creative possibilities for second-generation graphic forms of commemoration are far from exhausted.

In his series, *Julius Knipl: Real Estate Photographer* (1996), Brooklyn-born Ben Katchor (b. 1951) offers up what appears to be *New York City's Lower East Side as a *Yiddish landscape of wandering Jews nostalgic for the ephemeral artifacts of their (not necessarily reliable) memories. Katchor delights in converting the everyday and the known into the strange and unfamiliar (and the reverse). Although his city remains nameless, it is instantly recognizable in its intense strangeness and aching loneliness. Katchor's *The Jew of New York* (2000) is a complex exploration of ethnicity and belonging in early-nineteenth-century America; it is based on the utterly fantastical and yet entirely historical figure of Major Mordecai Noah who sought to create a Jewish homeland in upstate New York. Although often whimsical, this work's multiple story lines, uncanny characters, and striking imagery illuminate historical matters such as the racial obsession that the Native Americans were one of the Lost Tribes of Israel or the Jewish American community's reluctance to identify with a proto-Zionist movement that would effectively disavow their American identity. Katchor

began his career as a contributor to Art Spiegelman's legendary underground magazine *Raw* and has been the recipient of a Guggenheim and other prestigious awards. His reimagined Jewish pasts and interrogations of "authenticity" warrant careful consideration alongside other Jewish American voices such as Philip Roth and Michael Chabon.

In Europe, few emerging graphic novelists in recent years have generated more excitement than the staggeringly prolific Joann Sfar; his *Le Chat du rabbin* (The Rabbi's Cat, 2005) and *Klezmer* (2006) series portray the disparate histories and cultural worlds of *Sephardic and *Ashkenazic Jews with manic energy and astonishing invention. In *France, Sfar's works have frequently appeared on the best-selling lists compiled by *L'Express*. In *The Rabbi's Cat*, set in 1930s Algeria, the titular feline gains the power of speech and challenges his rabbinic master to instruct him in the Jewish faith so that he might have a proper *Bar Mitzvah. Sfar's exuberant imagery and absurdly humorous episodes present profoundly serious meditations on the complex relation between Jewish tradition and modernity, celebrating the rich contact zones of *North African and Ashkenazi Jewry (in *The Rabbi's Cat*) and the cultural exchanges of *gypsies, Jews, and others in early-twentieth-century *Ukraine (in *Klezmer*).

Italian cartoonist Vittorio Giardino bears witness to the darker aspects of the modern Jewish encounter with Europe through his elegantly drawn multivolume series, *A Jew in Communist Prague*, which many critics have praised as a masterpiece. Visually, Giardino's meticulously detailed full-color panels capture the atmosphere and architecture of post-war *Prague, while his narrative poignantly traces the precarious coming-of-age of the young protagonist, Jonas, during the years of his father's imprisonment – officially for being a "counterrevolutionary," although the narrative makes abundantly clear that he is the victim of unofficial state antisemitism.

In *Israel, the graphic novel has taken a little longer to catch on as a cultural phenomenon, but its artists and writers have long produced innovative and often startling work. The internationally acclaimed Actus Tragicus, a collective of five comic artists (Mira Friedmann, Yirmi Pinkus, Itzik Rennert, Rutu Modan, and Batia Kolton), have based many of the stories included in their annual collections on the irreverent fiction of Etgar Keret. Rutu Modan also created an Israel-based serial for the Sunday *New York Times* (2008), and her *Exit Wounds* (2007) is a gripping examination of the fraught nexus of terrorism and the quotidian in Israeli society. Eli Eshed's and Uri Fink's subversive approaches to *Zionist historiography and Israeli icons in *Ha-golem: Sipuro shel comics Israeli* (The Golem: The Story of an Israeli Comic) present an inventive recasting of the *golem figure as a troubling symbol of the excesses of Jewish power, whereas Ilana Zeffren's personal and political chronicle, *Sipur varod* (Pink Story), is a stirring examination of gay life in Israel. Another illuminating portrait of Israeli life is presented in Miriam Libicki's autobiographical comic *Jobnik* (2008), an acerbic and candid examination of her challenging years as an immigrant soldier. Libicki is also the author of "Towards a Hot Jew: The Israeli Soldier as a Fetish Object," a remarkable pictorial essay that interrogates the popular culture image of the Jewish body in the *Diaspora versus Israel. Most recently, Ari Folman transformed his *Waltz With Bashir: A*

Lebanon War Story (2008), a critically acclaimed animated film exploring Folman's long-suppressed recollections (and those of his fellow veterans) of serving in Israel's 1982 invasion of Lebanon, into an equally powerful graphic novel (2009). In addition to their surreal, hallucinogenic explorations of the unreliable nature of memory, both versions of *Bashir* are extraordinary works of wartime testimony, culminating in an unsparing portrayal of the Sabra and Shatila massacres.

At the end of the first decade of the twenty-first century, it is clear that the graphic novel has triumphantly emerged as a remarkable conduit for presenting the great narrative themes of the Jewish visual and textual imagination (mobility, flight, adaptation, transformation, disguise, metamorphosis), and it is even beginning to contribute to the ancient tradition of *midrashic interpretation. J. T. Waldman's *Megillat Esther* (2006), a visually opulent and voluptuous rendering of the book of *Esther (featuring the Hebrew text with an original English translation), has been praised by biblical scholars and aficionados of the graphic novel alike. Waldman's luminous black-and-white drawings, inspired by an eclectic range of influences including ancient Persian art, produce intriguing new layers of meaning.

Recent research addressing either the Jewish contribution to the graphic novel or the history and evolution of the comics includes S. Baskind and R. Omer-Sherman, eds., *The Jewish Graphic Novel: Critical Approaches* (2008); P. Buhle, *Jews and American Comics* (2008); D. Fingeroth, *Disguised as Clark Kent: Jews, Comics, and the Creation of the Superhero* (2007); D. Geis, ed., *Considering Maus: Approaches to Art Spiegelman's "Survivor's Tale" of the Holocaust* (2003); and A. Kaplan, *From Krakow To Krypton: A History of Jews in Comic Books* (2008).

R A N E N   O M E R - S H E R M A N

Literature, Hebrew: *Haskalah*.

The *Haskalah* ("enlightenment") was a Jewish literary, cultural, and social movement patterned after the European Enlightenment; it started in *Germany (Prussia) in the 1780s and moved first to *Galicia and *Russia, and then to *Lithuania and *Poland, lasting through the 1880s. Its initiators were young *maskilim* (followers of the *Haskalah*) in Königsberg and *Berlin who wished to emulate modern trends in European life and to introduce changes into Jewish society and Jewish culture.

Adhering to Enlightenment principles of humanism, tolerance, and freedom and prompted by medieval Jewish rationalists, especially *Maimonides, the *maskilim* envisioned a renewed form of Hebrew literature. They imagined that this literature would follow the trends of neoclassicism, adapting the poetics of contemporary European letters as well as the rediscovered aesthetics of the Hebrew *Bible. They also wished to revive the *Hebrew language as a medium for modern Hebrew letters. In contrast to the contemporary rabbinic linguistic practice of mixing Hebrew and *Aramaic and disregarding somewhat the proper use of Hebrew grammar, the *maskilim* insisted on using Biblical Hebrew (see HEBREW, BIBLICAL) for their creative writing, especially poetry. They studied the Hebrew language, grammar, and vocabulary in depth and published philological treatises and lexicons such as *Talmud Lashon Ivri* (Study of the Hebrew Language) and *Otzar ha-Shorashim* (Treasury of Roots) by the grammarian and biblical scholar Judah Leib ben Zeev (1764–1811)

An accompanying maskilic goal was to modernize Jewish education with a revised curriculum based on the formative texts of Judaism, starting with the Bible, together with secular disciplines, languages (especially Hebrew and German), and European customs and manners. Naphtali Herz Wessely (1725–1805) advocated these chages in his influential treatise on education, *Divrei Shalom ve-Emet* (Words of Peace and Truth), published between 1782 and 1785. *Maskilim* formed a society of Hebraists (*Ḥevrat Dorshei Leshon Ever* [Society for the Seekers of the Hebrew Language]) and launched a Hebrew journal, *Ha-Me'assef* (The Gatherer); published between 1783 and 1811, the journal was edited by the activist and author Isaac Euchel. Introducing various European literary genres, the *maskilim* published satire (*Ktav Yosher* [An Epistle of Righteousness] by Saul Berlin), biography and epistolary writings (*Toldot Rambeman: Lebensgeschichte Mos. Mendelssohns* [The Life Story of *Moses Mendelssohn] by Euchel), and dialogues of the dead (Aaron Wolfssohn). Concurrently, they also revived traditional Hebrew genres such as fables (Joel Brill), proverbs (Isaac Satanow), and polemics (Isaac Satanow). Thus, the Hebrew *Haskalah* continued previous phases of Hebrew literature and initiated new trends that broke with the past by fostering Modernism and *secularism.

The *maskilim* hoped to revive interest in the Hebrew Bible by continuing Moses Mendelssohn's *Bi'ur* project, the translation of the *Pentateuch into German (in Hebrew characters) with commentaries. Subsequently, they published translations and commentaries on other biblical books. Their poetry, which included idylls on nature and biblical epics such as *Shirei Tiferet* (Songs of Glory), on *Moses, by Wessely; *Nir David* (David's Lamp [light]), by Shalom Ha-Cohen, used biblical forms but was influenced by such German poets as Solomon Gessner and Frederick Klopstock. The *maskilim* also wrote sentimental poems and biblical dramas, such as *Melukhat Sha'ul* (The Reign of Saul) by Joseph Ha'efrati.

In the 1820s, *Haskalah* literary activities began in Austria and Galicia, with the publication in *Vienna of a second Hebrew journal, *Bikkurei ha-Itim* (The First Fruits of the Times; 1820–31); it was edited by Shalom ha-Cohen and others. The study of Judaism in Hebrew, known as *Ḥochmat Israel,* emerged at the same time in *Galicia and *Italy, following a similar trend in Germany (*Wissenschaft des Judentums*). Its Galician proponents were Nachman *Krochmal in his historiosophy of Judaism, *Moreh Nevukhei ha-Zeman* (The Guide to the Perplexed of the Time), and Solomon Judah Rapoport, who wrote essays on talmudic subjects and biographies of major Jewish figures. In *Italy, Samuel David *Luzzatto wrote studies of the Bible and of Judaism (*Mehkerei ha-Yahadut* [Studies of Judaism]) and explored medieval manuscripts. They and others, such as the Italian scholar Isaac Samuel Reggio, who asserted the compatibility between Judaism and philosophy in his *Ha-Torah veha-Philosophiah* (Torah and Philosophy), contributed learned articles to the third Hebrew journal, *Kerem Ḥemed* (Delightful Vineyard; 1831–56), edited by Samuel Leib Goldenberg and Shneur Sachs. These learned *maskilim* critically probed Jewish history, examined the dating and the authorship of some biblical books, and revisited the *Talmud, its sages, and their ways of studying the *halakhah. Galicia was the venue of a bitter clash between *Haskalah* and *Hasidism, which culminated in anti-Ḥasidic satire by Joseph Perl (*Megaleh Tmirin*

[Revealer of Secrets]; *Bohen Tzaddik* [Test of the Righteous]) and by Isaac Erter (*Ha-Tzofeh Leveit Yisra'el* [The Watchman of the House of Israel). Some *maskilim* also argued against the *Kabbalah and the authenticity of the *Zohar* and endeavored to eradicate superstitious customs and beliefs (Judah Leib Mises in *Kine'at ha-Emet* [The Zeal for Truth]).

There were various attempts between 1843 and 1845 to revive *Bikkurei ha-Itim* or to emulate its policy of combining belles lettres and timely, literary, and scholarly essays. Samuel Joseph Fünn founded and edited *Pirḥei Tzafon* (Flowers of the North) in *Vilna (1841, 1844); Mendel Stern launched a literary and scholarly quarterly, *Kokhvei Yitzḥak* (Stars of Isaac; 1845–69, 1873) in *Vienna; and Joshua Heschel Schorr founded and edited *He-Ḥalutz* (The Vanguard; 1852–89), an anti-rabbinic, scholarly, and polemical periodical published in Lwów and other places. Another scholarly and literary periodical, *Otzar Neḥmad* (Pleasing Treasury; 1856–63), was issued in Vienna by Isaac Blumenfeld.

The first of the popular weeklies, *Ha-Magid* (The Herald; 1856–1903), edited by Eliezer Silberman and others, was devoted to current events and to general interest articles; *Ha-Melitz* (The Advocate; 1860–1904), edited by Alexander Zederbaum and others, and *Ha-Tzefirah* (The Dawn; 1862–1931), edited by Ḥayyim Zelig Slonimsky, were launched first as weeklies and later published as dailies. Another important periodical was the weekly, turned monthly, *Ha-Karmel* (Carmel; 1860–71, 1871–80), edited by Fünn, in Vilna, which promoted moderate *Haskalah*; *Ha-Levanon* (Lebanon; 1863–86), launched first in *Jerusalem and then in Paris and other places, was edited by Jehiel Bril. *Ha-Shaḥar* (The Dawn; 1868–84), a literary monthly published in Vienna and edited by Peretz Smolenskin, included short stories, literary reviews, and essays on Judaism and contemporary issues by major writers. Abraham Baer Gottlober launched the literary monthly *Ha-Boker Or* (First Light of Morning; 1876–86) in Lemberg (Lvov) and *Warsaw. Overall, these periodicals served as vital instruments of mass communication, helping disseminate the *Haskalah*, its ideology, and Hebrew literature to a wider public in Eastern Europe and beyond.

The third *Haskalah* center – in Russia, Lithuania, and Poland – thrived in the second half of the nineteenth century; this phase of the *Haskalah* attempted to reach beyond the intellectuals to the masses. Thus, following the trend of romanticism, Abraham Mapu published the first Hebrew novel, *Ahavat Zion* (Love of Zion), in 1853. This historical romance, set in First *Temple times and written in Biblical Hebrew, evoked national images of the glorious past. Mapu's realistic 1857 novel, *Ayit Zavu'a* (The Hypocrite), exposed hypocritical characters in Jewish society, including some negative portrayals of *maskilim*, and advocated reorienting young Jews toward productive occupations such as agriculture.

In the 1860s and 1870s, two major autobiographies were published. Mordecai Aaron Günzburg published his life story, *Avi'ezer*, in 1863/4, and Moses Leib Lilienblum published his *Hatot Ne'urim* (Sins of Youth) in 1872. Both documented the failure of Jewish education and the struggles of young *maskilim* against obstacles raised by traditional Jewish society. Lilienblum, in *Orḥot ha-Talmud* (The Paths of the Talmud), and Judah Leib Gordon, in *Binah Leto'ei Ru'aḥ* (Insight to the Confused), were among radical *maskilim* who

carried on a continuous battle against religious authorities and argued that Jewish law could and should be modified to fit modern times and circumstances.

Adam Ha-Cohen Lebensohn (*Shirei Sfat Kodesh* [Songs of the Holy Tongue]) followed the old school of *Haskalah* poetry in his philosophical verses and flowery language; his son, Micah Joseph Lebensohn (*Shirei Bat Zion* [Songs of the Daughter of Zion], *Kinor Bat Zion* [The Harp of the Daughter of Zion]) wrote biblical epics and romantic and lyrical verses. The poet and translator Meir Ha-Levi Letteris published his translations and adaptations of European classical drama (*Geza Yishai* [The Stump of Jesse] after Racine's *Athalie*, and *Ben Abuya* after Goethe's *Faust*, based on the life of the rabbinic apostate *Elisha ben Abuya). Judah Leib Gordon published epics, fables, and poetry; in his timely poems he criticized the Jewish community and contemporary rabbis (*Kol Shirei Y. L. Gordon* [Complete Poems of Y. L. Gordon]).

A surge of works of literary criticism emerged in the 1860s, exemplified by the critical writings of Abraham Uri Kovner (*Heker Davar* [Probe of the Matter]), Abraham Jacob Papirna (*Kankan Ḥadash Malei Yashan* [A New Jar with Old Contents]), and Shalom Jacob Abramovich (*Mishpat Shalom* [Peaceful Judgment]; Abramovich later wrote under the pseudonym, Mendele Mokher Seforim [Mendele the Bookseller]). They criticized *Haskalah* poetry and prose for their use of *melitzah* (grandiloquence and bombastic phraseology) and for dealing with irrelevant subjects. This school of criticism, following contemporary trends in Russian criticism, declared the need for a more realistic and practical literature.

Among realist novelists in the last quarter of the nineteenth century were Peretz Smolenskin, who wrote *Hato'eh Bedarchei ha-Ḥayyim* (The Wanderer in the Paths of Life), a picaresque semi-autobiographical novel, and *Kevurat Ḥamor* (Donkey's Burial), a satiric criticism of Jewish society; Reuben Asher Braudes, whose novel *Ha-Dat ve-Ḥayyim* (Religion and Life) promoted religious reforms; and Abramovich who wrote *Ha-Avot veha-Banim* (Fathers and Sons), a love story depicting the clash between young *maskilim* and traditional society. Among those writing satiric short stories was Mordecai David Brandstädter, who highlighted conflicts between *maskilim* and traditionalists.

With the rise of Jewish nationalism in the last quarter of the nineteenth century, *Haskalah*, with its orientation toward European culture, lost favor, and the 1881 *pogroms in southern Russia signaled its demise.

For further reading see M. Pelli, *The Age of Haskalah: Studies in Hebrew Literature of the Enlightenment in Germany* (2006); idem, *In Search of Genres: Hebrew Enlightenment and Modernity: An Analytical Study of Literary Genres in 18th- and 19th-Century Hebrew Enlightenment* (2005); M. Waxman, *A History of Jewish Literature*, vols. 3, 4 (1936); and E. Silberschlag, *From Renaissance to Renaissance: Hebrew Literature from 1492–1970* (1973).

MOSHE PELLI

Literature, Hebrew: Israeli Fiction. The connections between narrative and nation-building, and the tensions between spiritual longing and material existence, are apparent in the parallel developments of Israel and Hebrew-language fiction in the twentieth and twenty-first centuries (see ISRAEL, STATE OF entries).

1940s: As Israeli literary critic Gershon Shaked (1929–2006) noted, Israel's native literary culture did not begin until the 1940s. S. Y. *Agnon's *Only Yesterday* (1945) stands as a milestone in the subversion and abandonment of the social realist *"Eretz Israel"* genre fiction of earlier writers. The novel signals a high-water mark for aesthetic accomplishment that contemporary writers still aspire to achieve. Agnon's masterpiece depicts the alienation of a Second *Aliyah (1904–1913) pioneer as he moves between the secular and religious worlds and between tradition and modernity. *Only Yesterday* touches on the central themes of Israeli literature: the collective versus the individual, the spiritual versus the material, and *Diaspora versus *Zion. It remains a powerful patchwork of the styles that have come to define Modern Hebrew literature: myth, epic, social realism, psychological realism, magical realism, and symbolic parable.

S. Yizhar (Yizhar Smilansky, 1916–2006) is far more representative of the 1940s. He initiated the style and substance of an Israeli-born literature, created by the so-called Native Generation, also known as the "Generation of 1948" or the "Palmakh Generation." With the *War of Independence (1947–49) barely ended, Yizhar penned his short story, "The Prisoner" (1949), which examines the interrogation and abuse of an *Arab shepherd by Israeli soldiers. Despite the military ethos of the time, Yizhar's story helped institute what have become substantial motifs in Israeli fiction: the (mis)treatment of its Arab citizens and neighbors and the tragic heroism of the Israeli (soldier or civilian) who must struggle to preserve dignity while wielding power. His 1949 novella, *The Story of Hirbet Hizah*, has similar themes (see ARABS: REPRESENTATIONS IN ISRAELI LITERATURE).

Even as the emerging Israeli state battled to set its borders and establish a stable economy, it sought to absorb hundreds of thousands of immigrants. The Native Generation had been raised on images of the stoic, strong, and brave "New Hebrew," but the *Holocaust survivors who arrived on Israel's shores were ravaged both physically and mentally. These survivors were often met with impatience, contempt, and silence by *sabras* (native-born Israelis), intolerant of vulnerability even as Israel faced an uncertain future. Yehudit Hendel's (b. 1926) story, "They Are Different People" (1949), may be one of the earliest works to confront the bewildering encounter between survivors and *sabras*. The encounter with *Mizrahi Jews from Muslim countries proved more reassuring. Israel's mass evacuation of *Yemen's Jewry during Operation Magic Carpet (1949) captivated the country with a display of its own heroism. This episode helped popularize the work of Mordecai Tabib (1910–1979), a writer born in Israel to Yemenite parents. He achieved early success with *As a Weed in the Field* (1948), his depiction of the Yemenite Jewish community in Israel. The neglect of Jews from Muslim lands remains a contentious issue in literary studies today (see MIZRAHI MIZRAHIM).

1950s: Agnon produced several outstanding works in the 1950s, including the novellas *Tehillah* (1950) and the enigmatic *Edo and Enam* (1950). In *Tehillah*, Agnon crafts a sophisticated allegory of *Jerusalem, whereas the mysterious and complex tale of passion in *Edo and Enam* underlies a symbolic account of the confrontation between tradition and modernity. Some point to Agnon as the spiritual inheritor of Franz *Kafka, but unlike Kafka's writings, Agnon's works clearly reveal their debt to the religious traditions, language, customs, and teachings of rabbinic *Judaism and therefore stand apart from many other works in the Israeli literary canon.

Yizhar's rich output during this decade explores the legacy of the War of Independence and the fate of displaced Arabs in ways that undermine the Zionist narrative of national rebirth. The title story in his collection *Midnight Convoy* (1950) describes a desperate effort to resupply a besieged settlement in lyric terms and incorporates eroticized images of the Israeli landscape. Yizhar refined his depiction of the extremes of war and sacrifice in his mammoth *The Days of Ziklag* (1958), a novel that depicts a week in the lives of fighters preparing for battle. Through the use of stream-of-consciousness techniques, this novel rewrote readers' expectations of wartime fiction. The short story "The Swimming Contest" (1952) by Benjamin Tammuz (1919–1989) similarly complicated the belief in the Israeli military's nobility. In this story, the longing for coexistence between Jews and Arabs in Israel is brutally shattered by the killing of an Arab combatant. Moshe Shamir (1921–2004), another influential Native Generation author, published a fictionalized biography of his fallen brother, *With His Own Hands* (1951). This seminal work helped enshrine the romantic image of the fighting pioneer Israeli as bold, resourceful, pure of intention, and pure in arms. Shamir's ideological fiction echoes the work of Haim Hazaz, a writer who achieved great popularity in the 1930s and 1940s for several celebrated stories. These were published in one volume of *Selected Stories* in 1952, renewing his stature among younger writers.

The late 1950s saw the emergence of A. B. *Yehoshua (b. 1936), who published groundbreaking stories that reveal traces of Agnon's influence and, indirectly, Kafka's. These stories include "The Yatir Evening Express" (1959) and "Death of the Old Man" (1957). The first tale treats an isolation that begets violence when villagers derail a train, whereas the second examines violence directed against an isolated, elderly tenant. Resentment over conformist pressures finds anxious expression at the end of the decade in the novel *Fortunes of a Fool* (1959) by Aharon Megged (b. 1920), in which the ineffective antihero evokes the rootless protagonists of diasporic Jewish fiction, pointedly rejecting the figure of the New Hebrew enshrined by Shamir and other contemporaries of the Native Generation.

1960s: After Adolf Eichmann's capture, trial, and eventual execution (1960–62; see HOLOCAUST TRIALS), the *Shoah became a central focus of much Israeli literature. A survivor himself, Aharon Appelfeld (b. 1932) has crafted some of the most sensitive post-Holocaust fiction in Hebrew, although typically without treating the horrors directly. Appelfeld's early novel, *Smoke* (1962), subtly treats the trauma endured by those who emerged from *Nazi-occupied Europe. A host of talented writers who had absorbed the Palmakh ethos, including Yehuda Amichai (1924–2000) in *Not of This Time, Not of This Place* (1963), Haim Gouri (b. 1923) in *The Chocolate Deal* (1965), and Yoram Kaniuk (b. 1930) in *Adam Resurrected* (1969), examined how the Shoah ruptured Jewish continuity and challenged the Zionist meta-narrative of Jewish rebirth in Israel. In the case of both Gouri and Kaniuk, the terrors of the Shoah receded only to expose an absurd, nonredemptive world in which detached irony gives way to black humor.

War, conquest, and grief receive complex treatment during this decade as Israeli society and its political borders profoundly changed. Kaniuk's *Himmo, King of Jerusalem* (1965) describes a morbid love affair between a beautiful nurse and her horribly disfigured and mortally wounded patient. As a kind of Israeli predecessor to *The English Patient*, Kaniuk's slim novel both solidifies and subverts the Israeli cult of sacrifice. Others who critically examined hero worship and sacrifice include Aharon Megged in *The Living and the Dead* (1965) and A. B. Yehoshua in his collection, *Facing the Forests* (1968). Megged measures the impotence of his contemporaries against the boldness of the earlier pioneers and finds both wanting. Yehoshua, especially in the much praised title story to his collection (first published 1963), contemplates the lassitude of a younger generation with a mixture of envy and contempt, while reserving no small measure of satire for the hubris of Israel's founding generation.

Amos Oz's (b. 1939) collection *Where the Jackals Howl* (1965), marked the appearance of Israel's most well-known literary talent and symbol of the "Statehood Generation" or "New Wave." This volume's best stories present allegorical and psychologically complex tales of the *kibbutz. For Oz, conflicts raging inside the kibbutz, the ideal socialist labor commune, become a cipher for the grim realities of an unattainable yet ever promised utopia. Oz's novel, *My Michael* (1968)] appeared shortly after Israel's sweeping victory in the Six Day War (1967). Often considered an Israeli revision of *Madame Bovary*, Oz's novel imagines the inner life of a woman who finds release from her stultifying married life in sexual fantasies involving Arab men.

1970s: The euphoria following the Six Day War gave way among many intellectuals to a recognition that Israel's military triumph had failed to alter the country's status in the Middle East. Border incursions, state-sponsored terrorism, and skirmishes with neighboring Arab states continued. Oz's two novellas *Unto Death* and *A Late Love* (1971) seem to have captured a sense of impending crisis: The former displaces conquest and its legacy to the era of the *Crusades; the latter depicts one man's apocalyptic paranoia. Yehoshua also treated the cycle of warfare, grief, and retribution in the long story, "In the Beginning of Summer 1970" (1971), in which a father is mistakenly informed that his son has been killed in the line of duty.

Published on the cusp of the previous decade, David Shahar's (1926–1997) search for the lost era of pre-state Palestine in *Summer in the Street of the Prophets* (1969) is the first book of his multivolume epic, *The Palace of Shattered Vessels* (1969–94). This spiritually inflected epic marks a turn toward the nostalgic that emerged prominently in the 1970s. Yaakov Shabtai's (1934–1981) bittersweet and carnivalesque stories of his youth in *Tel Aviv were collected in *Uncle Peretz Takes Flight* (1972), but Shabtai's masterpiece is the formally inventive *Past Continuous* (1977). This novel makes use of a breathless, headlong rush of prose with little punctuation to narrate the alienation between Israeli generations. The posthumous publication of Agnon's incomplete *A City and the Fullness Thereof* (1973) revealed a different retrospective take, focusing on the author's pre-war youth. Agnon, Hebrew literature's only Nobel Prize winner (1966), died in 1970, but he continued to cast a long shadow on the literary world in Israel.

The Yom Kippur War (1973) severely tested Israel's military might. Perhaps as a consequence of a renewed sense of vulnerability, a darkness of tone and subject matter found its way into much Hebrew literature. The bleakest expression appears in Amos Kenan's (b. 1927) *Shoah II* (1975), which suggests an apocalyptic end to Jewish existence brought on by occupation and an abandonment of principles. Appelfeld approached the Holocaust in an oblique way in his masterful novella *Badenheim 1939* (1979), which imagines a European resort narrowing into a ghetto. Yet, the disillusionment and crisis of the era were nowhere more strongly felt than in Yehoshua's *The Lover* (1977). Yehoshua's first novel reveals the influence of Faulkner in its use of multiple first-person narratives and fragmented chronology to tell the symbolically charged story of a disappearance that reveals the divides and ruptures within an Israeli family.

1980s: Israel emerged from the malaise of the 1970s only to deal with threats to its northern borders, the First Lebanon War, and a restive *Palestinian population. Internal social, ethnic, and economic divides continued unabated, notably characterized in the work of two Mizraḥi writers, Eli Amir (b. 1937) and Sami Michael (b. 1926). Amir's semi-autobiographical *Scapegoat* (1983) follows the acculturation of the child of Baghdadi Jewish professionals into Israel's *Ashkenazi-dominated society, whereas Michael's *Trumpet in the Wadi* (1987) treats the relationships among Christians, Jews, and Muslims on the eve of armed conflict. Self-described Israeli Palestinian novelist Anton Shammas (b. 1950) is the author of the novel *Arabesques* (1986), a stylistic and thematic triumph of Hebrew literature, which covers several generations of his family's life. For these writers who acknowledge a hybrid identity, the claims of the individual outweigh the claims of the collective. Although different in tone and subject matter, Yehoshua Kenaz's (b. 1937) *Infiltration* (1986) examines another collection of outsiders, army recruits in the 1950s who are sidelined from combat and hence relegated to the periphery of Israel's celebration of militarism.

The personal and the political are increasingly conflated during this era. A microcosm of Israeli society appears in Amos Oz's *Black Box* (1987), an epistolary novel written in multiple voices that describes both familial estrangement and the decline of a social consensus. *Blue Mountain* (1988) by Meir Shalev (b. 1949) treats the immigrant story with both pathos and whimsy. Savyon Liebrecht (b. 1948) approaches the political and the personal with a feminist slant in stories from her collections, *Apples from the Desert* (1986) and *Horses on the Geha Highway* (1988). The title story of her first collection describes a mother's quest to bring her daughter back into the religious community; another standout, "A Room on the Roof," conveys fumbling efforts at good will between Israelis and Palestinians, as well as mistrust and condescension.

The first novel to treat the occupation of Palestinians, David Grossman's (b. 1954) *Smile of the Lamb* (1983), portrays the ethical compromises made by Israeli civilians and soldiers, while not shying away from acknowledging Palestinian suffering. Later, Grossman's nonfiction classic, *The Yellow Wind* (1987), recorded simmering Palestinian resentment that would explode during the First Intifada (1987–1993). Grossman's novel, *See Under: Love* (1986), is a complex work that employs post-modern strategies to explore the legacy of the Shoah. His ambitious novel is indebted to the fiction of slain Polish Jewish writer Bruno Schulz.

1990s: This decade saw an increasingly violent Intifada, military clashes in southern Lebanon, the bombing of Israeli cities by Iraq during the first Gulf War (1991), the Oslo Peace Accords, the assassination of Prime Minister Yitzhak *Rabin (1995), a tremendous influx of Jews (and non-Jews) from the former *Soviet Union, and an encroaching Americanization. The stratification of Israeli society, its exhaustion by the security situation, and a longing for normalcy are reflected in the "different wave" (Avraham Balaban) or "post-national" (Hanan Hever) writers who came to the fore, including Orly Castel-Blum (b. 1960), whose darkly comic *Dolly City* (1992) imagines a grotesque and paranoid vision of a dystopic Israel. Her work shares similarities to that of Etgar Keret (b. 1967), who achieved popular and critical acclaim with his short stories collected in *Tsinorot* (1992) and *Missing Kissinger* (1994). These hyperrealist and often humorous tales incorporate slang and pop culture references to examine previously solemn subjects such as the occupation of Palestinians and the Holocaust.

Writers from the former Soviet Union are an emerging group in Israel, ably represented by Alona Kimhi (b. 1966), whose debut collection *Lunar Eclipse* (1996) features well-crafted stories of emotional estrangement. The title story presents a probing examination of a Russian immigrant family. Ronit Matalon (b. 1959) writes of an older immigrant community, but one still marginalized in Israeli society. Her collection *Strangers At Home* (1992) sensitively takes readers inside Mizrahi immigrant homes and workplaces. Matalon's novel *The One Facing Us* (1995) features a teenaged protagonist who seeks to retrace her family's lives, loves, and losses through photographs while she endures an exile in Cameroon. This post-modern *Bildungsroman* presents one family's chronicle against the backdrop of the Mizrahi *Diaspora.

Another family saga written by a Mizrahi writer who is at the center of the Modern Hebrew canon is Yehoshua's *Mr. Mani* (1990). One of the most important Israeli novels, *Mr. Mani* is a tour de force composed of five one-sided "conversations." Each conversation treats a progressively more distant historical era, beginning in 1982 and ending in 1848, cumulatively presenting roughly one hundred and forty years of Jewish history as a cosmic farce, rather than as governed by divine election. A more mainstream epic, Polish-born author Dan Tsalka's (b. 1936) sweeping *A Thousand Hearts* (1991), follows the fortunes and foolishness of the immigrants from the Third Aliyah (1919–23) who created modern-day Israel. Tsalka's novel, too, strives to demonstrate the origins of the enduring conflicts between East and West within Israel and without.

2000s: As the Second Intifada raged and as Israel embarked on the Second Lebanon War, the new millennium more and more resembled the old one. The *post-Zionism of the 1990s continued to exert its influence on society and on belles lettres. Castel-Blum's fun house of a novel, *Human Parts* (2002), powerfully evokes the terror of suicide bombing, while capturing the despair of a society riven by religious differences, ethnic strife, and economic injustice. Amir Gutfreund's (b. 1963) *Our Holocaust* (2000) plunges readers into an encounter with the history and memory of the Holocaust, while also daring to ponder whether Israeli

society teeters on the edge of catastrophe. The brutality of war is brought home by Ron Leshem (b. 1976) in *Beaufort* (2005), a vivid novel grounded in interviews with soldiers who manned the bloody borderlands of south Lebanon prior to the Israeli withdrawal (2000). David Grossman's *To the End of the Land* (2008) introduces the memorable figure of a woman who believes her son will be killed in battle; Scheherazade-like, she then embarks on a desperate journey to keep him alive by telling his story. Hailed as a masterpiece, Grossman's grief-fueled novel has captivated critics and readers in Israel and abroad. Another celebrated author and activist, Amos Oz, returned to form, publishing his profoundly moving *A Tale of Love and Darkness* (2002). This semi-autobiographical work recounts the author's coming of age during Israel's early years and amidst the idiosyncratic souls who populated his family. As a personal saga of sadness and joy, of violence and compassion, Oz's *memoir-novel serves as a fitting monument to the first six decades of Israel's tumultuous existence. **See also MEMOIR AND LIFE WRITING: HEBREW; MEMOIR AND LIFE WRITING: MIZRAHI.**

ADAM ROVNER

Literature, Hebrew: Medieval Spain. In addition to the well-known tradition of lyric poetry by authors such as Samuel ibn Naghrela ha-Nagid (*Samuel ha-Nagid), Solomon *ibn Gabirol, Moses *ibn Ezra, and Judah *Halevi (see POETRY, MEDIEVAL: MUSLIM WORLD), *Spain was also home to a tradition of rhyming prose narratives, known in Arabic as *maqamat* and in Hebrew as *mahberot*. The genre was adapted from Arabic authors such as Al-Hariri (1054–1122), whose proto-picaresque *maqamat* set the standard for rhetorical acrobatics and flowery narrative prose in the Muslim world. In the classical *maqama*, the narrator describes a series of deceptions that befall the protagonist at the hands of an eloquent and roguish antagonist, who dazzles his audiences and loosens their purse strings. The Castilian Judah al-Harizi (ca. 1165–1225) translated Al-Hariri's *maqamat* into Hebrew with the title *Mahbarot Itiel* (The *Maqamat* of Itiel). He then composed his own original *maqamat* in Hebrew, titled *Tahkemoni* (The Book of Tahkemoni: Jewish Tales from Medieval Spain, trans. D. S. Segal [2000]). His Barcelonan contemporary, the physician Joseph ibn Zabara (ca. 1140–1200), wrote *Sefer Sha`ashu`im* (The Book of Delight, trans. M. Hadas [1962]); this work broke somewhat with the conventional *maqama* genre in that it featured a continuous story line of the frame tale genre in which shorter stories and discourses are set within the context of a discussion between protagonist and antagonist, as in the Arabic classic *Kalila wa-Dimna* (Kalila and Dimna, ca. 750) by Abdallah ibn al-Muqaffa`.

There are two Hebrew translations of *Kalila wa-Dimna* by Spanish writers, a complete version by Jacob ben Elazar (fl. ca. 1220–40) and a partial one by a man known only as Joel. Ben Elazar was also the author of an innovative collection of stories, *Sefer Meshalim* (The Book of Tales), also known as *Sipurei Ahavah* (Love Stories), some of which combine Arabic and Hebrew literary techniques with those more characteristic of the French and Italian novellas of the times. Contemporary with ben Elazar's translation of *Kalila wa-Dimna* is the anonymous Hebrew translation of another Arabic frame tale, the *Mishle Sendabar* (Tales of Sendebar, trans. M. Epstein [1967]). Both of these originally Arabic works were also translated into Castilian by King Alfonso X "The Learned" (*Calila e Digna*, 1251) and his brother Don Fadrique (*Sendebar*, 1253).

The Castilian author Isaac ibn Sahula (b. 1244) produced the encyclopedic *Meshal Hakadmoni* (*Meshal Haqadmoni: Fables from the Distant Past*, trans. R. Loewe [2004]) during the reign of Alfonso X (1252–84) and his successor Sancho IV (1284–95). Unlike Al-Ḥarizi, who hewed to the classical structure of the *maqama*, Ibn Sahula adapted the frame tale structure from *Kalila wa-Dimna*; thus, *Meshal Hakadmoni* is an extended debate between two protagonists, the "Moralist" and the "Cynic," who embody the two main currents of intellectual thought in the Jewish community of Castile. Stories from *Meshal Hakadmoni* appear in later Spanish classics such as the 1343 *Libro de buen amor* (Book of Good Love) by Juan Ruiz and the 1340 *Conde Lucanor* (Count Lucanor) by Juan Manuel. Ibn Sahula, who wrote *kabbalistic treatises as well as a commentary on the *Song of Songs (see BIBLICAL COMMENTARY), was the first author to make specific reference to the *Zohar; he is thought to have been acquainted with its author, *Moses de Leon.

The only Spanish Jewish author of the Middle Ages to win renown among Christian readers and listeners was Shem Tov ben Isaac ibn Ardutiel of Carrión (d. ca. 1369), known in Castilian as "Sem Tob" or "Santob de Carrión." His Castilian work, the *Proverbios morales* (*Jewish Wisdom in Christian Spain: The Moral Proverbs of Shem Tov de Carrión*, trans. T. Perry [1987]), has become a classic of Spanish literature, but his Hebrew *maḥberot*, although artistically important, are largely overlooked. *Milḥemet ha-`Et veha-Misparayim* (The Debate between the Pen and the Scissors) is an enigmatic lampoon of the literary debates between pen and sword common to the Middle Ages. Critics are in disagreement as to its allegorical meaning, and it has been largely overshadowed by the better known, earlier *maqamat* of al-Ḥarizi and Ibn Zabara.

After Shem Tov, Hebrew poetry enjoyed a bit of a renaissance in the late fourteenth and early fifteenth centuries in Zaragoza, where there was a very active circle of Hebrew poets, among them Solomon Bonafed and Solomon ben Meshullam Da Piera. Although this scene produced little prose narrative of note, there is one exception. Vidal Benvenist wrote *Melitzat `Efer ve-Dina* (The Tale of Efer and Dina; M. Huss, *Melitzat `Efer ve-Dina le-Don Vidal Benvenesht* [2003]), a tragicomic farce of a novella narrating the misadventures of an older widower named Efer who misguidedly marries a very young girl named Dina. Efer's inability to satisfy his conjugal requirements leads him to fatally overdose on an aphrodisiac. In a lengthy epilogue, Benvenist explains that `Efer ve-Dina is a moral allegory, but the work's popularity suggests that the story stood on its own as entertainment.

Recent scholarship on the Spanish Hebrew *maqamat* includes J. Decter, *Jewish Iberian Literature: From al-Andalus to Christian Spain* (2007); D. A. Wacks, *Framing Iberia: Maqamat and Frametale Narratives in Medieval Spain* (2007); and M. Hamilton, *Representing Others in Medieval Iberia* (2007).

DAVID A. WACKS

Literature, Hebrew: Women Writers, 1882–2010.

The entry of women writers into the Modern Hebrew literary scene was slow and halting, accompanied by an equally uneasy and belated recognition from the critical community.

POETRY: The poetic standards established by the *Bialik School necessitated deep familiarity with traditional texts, which was an exclusively male domain within the traditional Jewish educational system. Women only began to write verse in Hebrew after World War I when the national-cultural revolution in the *Yishuv established a clear preference for spoken Hebrew in its everyday usage. Even then, the lyrical style and personal themes favored by female poets were at odds with the militant, macho-intoned *Zionist meta-narrative and its poetics of harnessing art to the collective nationalist effort. Further, the tendency of subsequent literary historians to view poetry as a series of male "anxieties of influence" helped eliminate women poets from the canon of Modern Hebrew writing. Nevertheless, some of the women poets who appeared in the 1920s received public attention despite being marginalized by the literary establishment. The most prominent among these were Rachel (pseudonym of Rachel Bluwstein), Esther Raab, Elisheva Bichovsky, Yocheved Bat-Miriam, and Anda Amir-Pinkerfeld.

Rachel (1890–1931) was raised in Poltava and arrived in *Palestine in 1909; planning for a life of farming, she died young of tuberculosis. Rachel rose to mythic proportions in the popular culture of the *Yishuv* because of her minimalist, lyrical, and nostalgic poems and her personal themes of loneliness, barrenness, and lost youth. Her verses, short and melodious, lent themselves to music; yet, although her poems were widely sung, they were deemed of no great poetic value by the critical establishment. Esther Raab (1894–1981), the first native-born female poet, also produced minimalist poetry, characterized by elliptical, irregular syntax and weighted with lustful energy and feminine rebelliousness. Leah Goldberg (1911–1970), who spent her childhood in *Russia and *Lithuania, arrived in *Tel Aviv in 1935, joining the circle of Modernist authors led by Abraham Shlonsky. Primarily a poet, Goldberg also excelled as prose writer, critic, editor, dramatist, and translator. Her poetry, initially avoiding the Jewish themes of her contemporaries, is characterized by a conversational style, using ordinary, familiar words and images and finding the lyrical in everyday experience. Elisheva Bichovsky (1888–1949), born to a Christian family in Russia, married Shimon Bichovsky and immigrated to Palestine in 1925. She started as a Russian poet before adopting Hebrew for her poetic expression, and her dreamy, romantic verses were received enthusiastically by the reading public but soon forgotten. Yocheved Bat-Miriam (1901–1980) left *Belorussia to settle in Palestine; she wrote Symbolist poetry, suggestive and musical, often mystical and romantic. Anda Amir-Pinkerfeld (1902–1981), who emigrated to Palestine from *Galicia, focused her poetry on the female experience and women's lives and was largely ignored at the time.

Among the most notable women poets after the establishment of Israel in 1948 are Zelda, Ayin Tur Malka, Dahlia Ravikovitch, Nurit Zarchi, Yona Wallach, Rachel Chalfi, and Rivka Miriam. Zelda (1914–1984), who came from Russia as a child, stands out as a poet from the *Ultra-Orthodox community who won critical acclaim across the ideological and religious spectrum. Her poetry is suffused with mystical and *kabbalist echoes and expresses human yearnings for the presence of the Divine. Dahlia Ravikovitch (1936–2005), native born, is considered one of the most important poets in Modern Hebrew literature. Her poetry is rich with biblical citations, expressing personal longings for distant worlds of beauty and freedom; she also published verses of political protest addressing current issues. Yona Wallach (1944–1985), born in Israel, became known early in life for her iconoclastic, offbeat poetry and fantastic, strikingly erotic imagery. She is considered a major avant-garde voice, and her popularity is still growing despite her untimely death.

FICTION: Women prose writers of the *Yishuv* narrated both their private lives and their encounter with the new land, but most were marginalized by literary historiographers because they did not conform to the poetics of epic deeds and heroic nation-building. Among the more important were Nechama Pukhachevsky, Hemdah Ben-Yehuda, and Devorah Baron, but only Baron attracted the interest of the literary establishment. Baron (1887–1956), born in Belorussia, the daughter of a village rabbi, settled in Palestine in 1911 and published stories on Jewish life in the small Eastern European *shtetl, chronicling both its bleakness and its wealth of culture. She mainly focused on women's circumstances such as *marriage, *infertility, *divorce, and poverty, describing her father's sensitivity to the plight of women.

Female writers who began to publish after the birth of Israel, such as Amalia Kahana-Carmon (b. 1926), Yehudit Hendel (b. 1926), Shulamit Hareven (1931–2003), Rachel Eytan (b. 1931), Shulamit Lapid (b. 1934), and Ruth Almog (b. 1936), were acutely conscious of the discrepancy between their inclinations to portray subjective emotions and intimate relationships and the cult of physical heroism that was favored by the male arbiters of culture. This conflict often triggered self-doubt and low self-esteem in women writers, as well as a tendency to present women as victims, prone to mental disintegration and even madness. Kahana-Carmon's lyrical prose works, mostly written in the Modernist technique of stream of consciousness, have been likened to Virginia Woolf's novels. Many of her female characters are mentally tenuous, craving an ideal romantic relationship. By contrast, Shulamit Hareven presents strong female personalities who voice feminist opinions. Among Ruth Almog's main themes are mental breakdowns suffered by women as well as the plight of second-generation *Holocaust survivors. Shulamit Lapid, in her widely popular novel *Gei 'Oni*, reconstructs a heroic chapter in *Zionist history, successfully inserting the female point of view.

These women writers and others began to feel empowered to seek a more private vision in the 1970s, when the trend to reassess the Zionist meta-narrative caused writers of both sexes to turn away from ideological and political themes. Women writers won both public and critical accolades and became integrated into the mainstream history of Modern Hebrew literature, with the canonical establishment finally according them critical appreciation for offering an alternative, rather than minor, poetics.

A more radical turning point occurred in the late 1980s when *gender issues, along with other social concerns, came to the fore in both Israeli public discourse and fiction, followed by an unquestioned openness to women writers on the part of the literary/critical establishment. Women felt freer to express themselves as fiction writers and to introduce the feminine dimension to the national culture,

unfettered by the sense of inferiority or estrangement that plagued the earlier generation. This also came about as a result of a new awareness in Israel of literary and cultural trends in the West, especially the modern women's movement in North America and Europe, which legitimized gender issues as worthy literary themes and validated women's stylistic preferences. Female writers were further emboldened to claim a central position by the general receptiveness in Israel to the post-modern spirit, which rejects any master narrative and prefers small "local" narratives of minorities of all sorts – ethnic, economic, or gender.

Women fiction writers born after the establishment of Israel – including Savyon Liebrecht (b. 1948 in Germany), Michal Govrin (b. 1950), Shifra Horn (b. 1951), Nava Semel (b. 1954), Zeruya Shalev (b. 1959), Ronit Matalon (b. 1959), Orly Castel-Bloom (b. 1960), and Yehudit Katzir (b. 1963) – revolutionized the literary scene. The country's critical establishment has placed them at the very core of current *post-Zionist, post-modern Israeli culture. While displaying a diversity of genres, styles, and themes, their feminine point of view has been accepted as a viable new form of literary poetics. Despite their artistic differences, these writers all transgress ideological, ethnic, and sexual boundaries, previously the domain of masculine literary experience. Their protagonists often feel the need to mend a ruptured reality or are presented as architects, intent on building new feminine models to replace the old male structures. Like the male writers of their generation, they express the agony of the second-generation *Holocaust survivor. They also reveal sympathy toward the *Arab minority and resentment of the macho culture still prevalent in Israel. Several of these writers cast their novels in the form of the hitherto male genre of the *Künstlerroman*, turning it into "the portrait of the artist as a young woman," thus asserting the validity of female artistic talent.

The most iconoclastic among these writers is Orly Castel-Bloom, whose dark, post-modernist, deconstructionist style envisions modern society in the image of depleted selves, grotesque actions, and broken-down social and familial structures. Savyon Liebrecht's realistic prose offers a sober look at central problems in current Israeli society such as the debate over the treatment of Palestinians, the psychological issues of children of Holocaust survivors, and the cult of machismo that still suffuses Israeli popular culture. Her writings intertwine social realism with feminist sensibility and major public issues with the private, feminine point of view. Zeruya Shalev's style is sexually bold and graphic, focusing on male-female relationships and blatantly oblivious to public matters. Michal Govrin's fiction, filled with a dense web of allusions to traditional Jewish texts, presents female protagonists who engage in crossing borders and opt for a non-Zionist view of modern Israel, such as Old World *mysticism or political activism on the far left, coupled with a romantic involvement with the ethnic taboo, an Arab man. Yehudit Katzir's works, mostly set in her home town, Haifa, are premised on a symbiotic relationship between the female protagonist and the city, employing the sensual feminine contours of the Haifa landscape as a semiotic marker of the female physical and mental condition. Her stories introduce multiple shades of love relationships, including a sexual affair between a schoolgirl and her female teacher; her protagonists are mostly imaginative and sensitive young girls, who grow up to become storytellers. Additionally, within the genre of the sophisticated thriller, Batya Gur (1947–2005) won international acclaim; indeed, Israeli best-seller lists of popular, less critically significant fiction prominently feature a good number of female writers.

Hebrew women writers have journeyed from marginality to mainstream, finally breaking into a previously male canon and validating female artistic visions and thematic concerns. These writers of the late twentieth and early twenty-first century have revolutionized Hebrew poetics by placing female existence and gender issues at the heart of literary expression; in the process they have also brought attention to their precursors, many of whom were deemed irrelevant in their own times.

For further reading in English, see N. Aschkenasy, *Feminine Images in Hebraic Literary Tradition* (1987); Y. Feldman, *No Room of Their Own: Gender and Nation in Israeli Women's Fiction* (1999); M. Gluzman, *The Politics of Canonicity: Lines of Resistance in Modernist Hebrew Poetry* (2003); S. E. Jelen and S. Pinsker, eds., *Hebrew, Gender, and Modernity: Critical Responses to Dvorah Baron's Fiction* (2007); W. Zierler, *And Rachel Stole the Idols: The Emergence of Modern Hebrew Women Writing* (2004); and "Foreword," in *The Defiant Muse: Hebrew Feminist Poems*, ed. S. Kaufman, G. Hasan-Rokem, and T. S. Hess (1999), 1–21.   NEHAMA ASCHKENASY

Literature, Hebrew: The *Yishuv*, 1880–1948. In the *Yishuv* (the Jewish settlement in *Palestine), literary expression was part of the *Hebrew revival. Initially, authors used imagery, landscapes, and ideas that reflected their European countries of origin, producing material of marginal literary quality. In the 1920s, when the center of Hebrew letters moved from Odessa to *Tel Aviv, literature began to evoke the local landscape and the daily experiences of the immigrant population. However, because Hebrew was still unfamiliar as a spoken language for many, writing of this era is often stilted and steeped in biblical style and phrases, or it echoes the Russo-Yiddish features and forms the writers knew from Europe. This is particularly pronounced in the case of Hebrew *theater. The *Habimah,* which was founded in Moscow in 1918 and transferred to Tel Aviv in 1926, brought Russo-Hebrew pronunciation as well as Russian acting and theatrical conventions. It was not until the 1960s that the *Cameri Theater* began to modernize the language and adopt Israeli cultural conventions (see THEATER: ISRAEL).

Native Jewish writers in the *Yishuv* descended from families that had come from Middle Eastern cities of the *Ottoman Empire, sometimes as much as three centuries earlier. Among the most well known is Yehuda Burla (1886–1969). These multilingual writers were engaged with the Arab culture around them and generally wrote short stories about daily life, tending to portray heroes at the center of romantic involvements. Shoshannah Shababo (1910–1992), Burla's student, wrote novels and many short stories, including a series of animal fables. Her work features colloquial language, contemporary usage, and representations of the diverse society of Christians, Muslims, and Jews in Palestine – rare qualities at that time. However, her teacher characterized her work as "trivial, melodramatic and sensational," which may account for the neglect of her work by later critics.

This Middle Eastern fiction is in marked contrast to writing by authors who arrived as part of the waves of immigration (see ISRAEL, STATE OF: JEWISH IMMIGRATION BEFORE 1948) to Palestine from *Eastern Europe. The Second Aliyah (1904–14) was particularly important, bringing idealists inspired by the efforts of Eliezer ben Yehuda (1858–1922) to revive the Hebrew language (see HEBREW: MODERN REVIVAL). These writers were responsible for establishing Tel Aviv as the center of Hebrew letters in the 1920s, and they were key in developing a Hebrew vernacular that used *Sephardi pronunciation. In contrast, contemporaneous Hebrew writers in Europe continued to work with Hebrew as a primarily textual language.

Women authors who immigrated to Palestine during the Second Aliyah include Hemdah Ben-Yehuda (1873–1951), Devorah Baron (1887–1956), and Rahel Yanait (Ben Zvi, 1886–1979). Ben-Yehuda and Yanait wrote about pioneering and the particular experiences and status of women during this period. Yanait often wrote about the large number of suicides among this wave of immigration. Baron, the most distinguished of these writers, had been taught Jewish law by her father, a rabbi; she was a realistic writer and wrote short stories about women's plight under the yoke of religious life. Like many Second Aliyah writers, Baron described the *shtetl* of her youth. Central to the literary scene in *British Mandate Palestine, Baron edited the literary section of *Ha-Po'el ha-Tzair,* the major literary organ of the time, which was edited by her husband until his death in 1937 (see also LITERATURE, HEBREW: WOMEN WRITERS [1882–2009]).

S. Y. *Agnon (1888–1970) is the most celebrated of the Second Aliyah writers, and in 1966 he shared the Nobel Prize for Literature with the European Jewish poet Nelly Sachs. Agnon is the only writer in Hebrew ever to have won this award. The first story he published in Palestine was "*Agunot*" (Forsaken Wives). His pen name "Agnon," which he adopted as his official surname in 1924, is derived from the title of this story. That same year a fire at his house destroyed his collection of rare books and manuscripts. Agnon moved to Talpiot near *Jerusalem with his family, but in 1929 his library was destroyed once more, this time during anti-Jewish riots. These two traumatic events became repeated themes in his stories, reflecting the destruction of the Jewish people and the need to rebuild. Agnon tells the story of the Second Aliyah immigrant experience in his novel *Tmol Shilshom* (Only Yesterday). His anti-hero Isaac Kumer follows the *Zionist dream to build the land, but when he arrives he soon discovers that he is ill suited to this task and he is outbid by cheaper Arab laborers. Finally he moves to Jerusalem and adopts a spiritually oriented lifestyle instead. In this work, Agnon portrays the disillusionment of his generation and the hardships that they faced in their encounter with the land they hoped to settle and work. Other important works by Agnon are *Shirah* (1971), *A Guest for the Night* (1939), and *A Simple Tale* (1935).

There are a number of representations of the Land of Israel as a site of hostility in the works of Second Aliyah writers, who recorded accounts of attacks on pioneers by marauding bandits and the ravages of illness such as malaria. However, in the main, early *Yishuv* literature portrayed historical narratives of the Jewish past far more often than the contemporary pioneer experience. Asher Barash (1889–1952), from Lopatin, *Galicia, began publishing in Hebrew in 1908 and immigrated to *Eretz Israel* in 1915. His story "Facing the Gates of Heaven" examines the self-immolation of the only Jewish survivor of an entire community that was destroyed in Cossack massacres.

Among the important contributors to the development of Hebrew literature in this period were Uri Nissan Gnessin (1879–1913) and Joseph Haim Brenner (1881–1921). Together they wrote and published a literary weekly in *Warsaw and then moved to London where they founded a Hebrew periodical. Although Gnessin spent several months in Palestine, he left and returned to Russia where he died of a heart-attack at thirty-four. Gnessin introduced psychologically oriented prose mainly through short stories, and his complete works run to three volumes in Hebrew. Brenner moved to Palestine in 1909 and stayed; he was killed in 1921 by Arab rioters in Tel Aviv. Born in southern Russia, he was influenced by Dostoevsky and Turgenev, and his main characters are maladjusted young men rebelling against their parents' generation. His Palestine writing depicts the alienation and isolation felt by the pioneer generation. He mocks Zionists who sentimentalized or romanticized the settlement enterprise; his pessimistic novel *Breakdown and Bereavement* (1920) conveys his generation's ethos. As a literary figure Brenner was extremely important; he developed the psychological novel in Hebrew, and along with Agnon, he was instrumental in the move of Hebrew letters to Palestine. Another important figure of this era was Aharon Reuveni (1886–1971).

According to critic Gershon Shaked, the Second Aliyah generation wrote about both the literal experience of immigration and their ideological commitment to settling the land. "Predominantly anti-genre," the literary style of these writers realistically presented the challenges faced by individuals and by the collective. In contrast, writers of the Third Aliyah (1919–23), although resembling their predecessors to some extent, "revived and revivified genre writing." Their subject matter "clearly defined heroes and enemies and unambiguous goals." They contrasted favorably the pioneer, the agricultural worker, and the ideologue with the urban dweller and merchant. This writing depicts the struggle of the hero against disease, political threats, and the inhospitable land.

Third Aliyah writers include Hayyim Hazaz (1898–1973) and Avigdor Hameiri (born Feuerstein; 1890–1970). Hazaz's fiction encompasses a wide variety of Jewish experience: He wrote about the *Yemenite Jewish community and other immigrants from Middle Eastern countries in both fiction and nonfiction, short stories, novels, and plays. His works include *The Gates of Bronze* (1923) and *The End of Days* (1950). Hameiri immigrated to Palestine in 1921, joined the staff of the daily newspaper *Ha'aretz*, edited several literary and cultural journals, and wrote more than thirty books.

As Hameiri's generation began to control the publishing apparatus in Palestine and as presses were established by the *kibbutz and Labor movements, European readers were no longer the main audience for material being written in Palestine. In the 1920s *Moznayim*, published by the Hebrew writers' society, and *Ketuvim* were among the literary journals that spread an interest in Hebrew literature. Yet, many of the prose writers of this period have been forgotten or neglected, because their literary productions were rarely

original and did not attain the canonical status of works of the previous generation. The most prevalent tropes and themes were those of the Hebrew warrior who was as forceful in his relations with women as he was in fighting Arabs. This figure was an antithesis to the hapless, helpless stereotype of the Eastern European immigrant. Often this character was a ḥalutz (pioneer) and *shomer* (guard), working the land by day and protecting it by night.

In its poetry, the Third Aliyah generation was more radical. Uri Zvi Greenberg (1896–1981), Abraham Shlonsky (1900–1973), Isaac Lamdan (1900–1954), and Sh. Shalom (Shalom Joseph Shapira, 1904–1990) had all fought in World War I in Europe. Their poetry reflects problems of adjustment in the *Yishuv,* as well as the wasteland environment of a post-war world. Isaac Lamdan's poem "Masada" became the anthem of a generation, representing Jewish sacrifice that reflected the increasingly tense political situation developing in the *Yishuv* after the 1920–21 and 1929 riots that culminated in the Palestinian uprising of 1933–36. Subsequently poetry moved away from the pioneering imagery of the landscape and became increasingly urbanized. This is evident in the works of Natan Alterman (1910–1970) and Leah Goldberg (1911–1970; see POETRY, MODERN HEBREW).

The fiction writer Moshe Smilansky (1874–1953) was rediscovered by members of a new generation who were publishing novels in the 1940s and 1950s. Smilansky first traveled to Palestine in the 1890s; he worked in agriculture and was a founder of the Jewish Farmers Association. He fervently supported physical work, believing in its redemptive powers. His series on Arab life and depictions of pastoral surroundings and the Palestine landscape were ahead of his generation, who were still depicting European geography, and he profoundly influenced the content and styles of the first generation of native Ashkenazi writers.

Beginning in the 1940s during World War II, and then in the early years of Israel, a new group of writers dominated the literary field. They were born in Palestine (or had migrated there as children), fought in the 1948 War of Independence (see ISRAEL, STATE OF: FOUNDING OF THE MODERN STATE; ISRAEL, STATE OF: WARS), and went on to serve in governmental roles or in leading literary/educational positions. This generation wrote epic novels about the complex personal struggles of the pioneering hero generation. Aharon Megged (b. 1920) was born in Poland and moved to Palestine when he was six, growing up within the *Yishuv*. He served as Israel's cultural attaché in London between 1968 and 1971. S. Yizhar (born Yizhar Smilansky; 1916–2006) was born in Rehovot into a Zionist pioneer intelligentsia family. He was a member of the *Knesset and is best known for his masterpiece *Days of Ziklag* (1958). Moshe Shamir (1921–2004), who was born in *Safed but lived mostly in Tel Aviv, served in the 1948 war and later the Knesset (1977–81). He became a voice of his generation with his novels, *The King of Flesh and Blood* (1958) and *With His Own Hands* (1970). Shamir's *He Walked Through the Fields* (1947) was the first play performed in the State of Israel in 1948 (see THEATER: ISRAEL).

Nevertheless, a counter-canonical trend is also evident during this period. In contrast to Shamir, Yizhar, and Megged with their Labor Zionist backgrounds, active revisionists such as Jonathan Ratosh (1908–1981), who were strongly influenced by an ancient, pre-biblical mythology and vocabulary, founded the Canaanite movement. Although this movement never had a significant number of adherents, its "emphasis on myth and its stylistic mannerisms had considerable impact on contemporary poetry" (Carmi, 139).

The search for an authentic literary identity expressed in Hebrew, whether in the style of the traditional Labor Zionist literary canon, with its complex psychological components, or in the Canaanite mode, which was devoted to stripping away modern trends to find an authentic mythical past, characterized the literature of the *Yishuv* in its final phase. On the eve of the establishment of Israel, it was these two trends that would influence literary development in the decades to come.

For further reading, see S. Halkin, *Modern Hebrew Literature* (1970); A. Alcalay, *Keys to the Garden: New Israeli Writing* (1996); E. Zakim, *Build and Be Built: Landscape, Literature, and the Construction of Zionist Identity* (2006); G. Shaked, *Modern Hebrew Fiction* (2000); and T. Carmi, ed., *The Penguin Book of Hebrew Verse* (1981).　　　　RACHEL S. HARRIS

Literature, Ladino, refers to written or oral verbal compositions in the language of *Sephardic Jewry. The written genres were mainly reserved for educated people, mostly men, whereas folkloristic oral genres were universally known and often used by all Sephardic community members. Some *Ladino literature is similar to the equivalent literary genres of Iberian Spanish (which was subsequently developed by Sephardic Jews [see LITERATURE, HEBREW: MEDIEVAL SPAIN]). Other genres are new, either autonomous of any prior tradition or developed under the influence of local literary forms. Although many of these genres are Jewish in nature, many others are Jewish only by virtue of the language in which they are written, their Hebrew orthography, and their source and target audience. The genres include translations into Ladino, rabbinical literature, drama, belles lettres, newspapers, other written publications, and popular folkloristic oral genres that have been written down in recent generations.

Very little literature before the 1492 expulsion from *Spain exists in Spanish written in Hebrew letters. Works that have survived include *Coplas de Yosef* (Verses of Joseph), by an anonymous writer; some *Kharjas* (the concluding Spanish verses of Hebrew poems); *Takannot Valladolid* (Regulations of Valladolid) for the communities in Castile formulated in 1432; instructions for conducting the *Passover *seder*; various contracts, written oaths, declarations, medical recipes, and agreements, most of them short and fragmented; and an entire manuscript of a women's Ladino *prayer book from the fifteenth century (published by Moshe Lazar in 1995). Texts written by Jews in Latin script in Spain were made either for Christian patrons or for Jews who had converted to Christianity; they were in contemporary Spanish and not Ladino. Most Ladino literature was published after the expulsion from Spain, especially between the eighteenth century and the middle of the twentieth century.

TRANSLATIONS: Ladino translations are word-for-word translations of Hebrew liturgical texts into the Judeo-Spanish vernacular. This process started as an oral tradition in the Middle Ages, with the translations appearing in printed form from the sixteenth century onward. The most well-known translations are the Ladino *Pentateuch from Constantinople in 1547 (written in Hebrew script) and the Ferrara Bible, 1553 (written in Latin script). Several *haftarot (e.g., for *Tisha B'Av) and the *Megillot* (*FIVE SCROLLS) were also published continually in different locations throughout the *Ottoman Empire. The daily *siddur* and the holiday maḥzor (see PRAYER BOOKS) were translated in full in Ferrara using Latin script in 1552. The first extant Ladino *siddur* in Hebrew script was published for women around 1550 in Thessalonika. Since the eighteenth century only certain passages of prayer books have been translated into Ladino using Hebrew script. The Passover *haggadah* and *Mishnah tractate *Avot (Ethics of the Fathers) were continually translated into Ladino and published either as part of the *maḥzor* or as separate booklets. Ladino translations published in Latin script in *Italy, *Amsterdam, and London were aimed at converted Jews (see CONVERSOS) who were returning to Judaism; these translations are slightly "Hispanized" compared to equivalent Ladino texts produced in the Ottoman Empire.

RABBINIC LITERATURE: Rabbinic literature includes Bible commentaries (see BIBLICAL COMMENTARY); the Mishnah, and the Passover *haggadah*; works relating to ethical behavior; Jewish legal works; *mystical writings; and *sermons. The most famous of these publications in Ladino in the sixteenth century are Moshe Almosnino's *Sefer Hanhagat ha-Ḥayyim: El regimiento de la vida* (The Management of Life) and *Crónica de los Reyes Otomanos* (The History of the Ottoman Kings; known to the Spanish world as *Extremos y grandezas de Constantinopla*). Also published contemporaneously were *Meza de la alma* (an edited translation of *Shulḥan ha-Panim* by Joseph *Karo); *El deber de los corazones* (translated by Zadiq Forman from *Baḥia ibn Pakuda's *Ḥovat Ha-Levavot* (Duties of the Heart); and *Dinim de sheḥitah i bedikah* (by an anonymous writer). From the eighteenth century many other similar books were published by Abraham ben Isaac Asa (who also wrote a new Ladino translation of the entire *Bible); Yehudah Eliezer Papo'; Yehuda ben Shlomo Hai; Alcalai' Shabetai ben Yaakov Vital; and others. (The most updated list can be found in Dov Cohen's *Bibliography of Ladino Books*, www.hebrew-bibliography.com).

Meam Loez, one of the most voluminous and important rabbinic works in Ladino, was started by Rabbi Jacob Khuli (1689?–1732). He assembled biblical commentaries, ethical rules, and literary, historical, midrashic, halakhic, and kabbalistic sources into one Ladino composition. He completed the commentaries on *Genesis and *Exodus (until chapter 27), and after his death other rabbis carried on the enterprise. This Ladino classic was eventually published in its unfinished form, and the work ran into several editions. Because of its educational value, the book has been translated with some adjustments and additions into Hebrew, English, and other languages.

DRAMA: Although Ladino drama has existed since immediately after the expulsion from Spain, there are no texts left from that period. Many new plays were produced from the middle of the nineteenth century and survive in both printed and manuscript form, but many others no longer exist. In addition to biblical and historical topics like *Esther, *Joseph and his brothers, and Jephthah and his daughter, plays used other themes, either religiously oriented or entirely secular. The plays were not necessarily original; for example, *La famía misterioza* (The Mysterious Family) by J. Behar and *Los Budžukes* (The Twins; based on Shakespeare's *Comedy of Errors*). Many of these plays were musicals or semi-musicals.

BELLES LETTRES: Biographies, novels, and stories were written in Ladino from the second half of the nineteenth century. Some novels were written about historical Jewish people or events, but most were devoted to matters of contemporary life, and many were adaptations or translations of literature written in other languages. Original Ladino poetry was also published from the nineteenth century onward (mostly in newspapers and pamphlets).

NEWSPAPERS: A Ladino newspaper, *La Buena Esperansa* (The Good Hope), was published in 1842 Izmir. Since then hundreds of newspapers have been published there and in other cities, mostly in Thessalonika and Istanbul (Constantinople). The contents of the newspapers varied greatly: political, satirical-humorist, Zionist, or political-national. In addition to news and editorial articles, the newspapers included stories, poems, and various other sections found in modern newspapers (see JOURNALISM: *LADINO [OTTOMAN EMPIRE]).

OTHER PUBLISHED GENRES: Sephardic communities produced books and pamphlets in Ladino on the following topics: history of the Jews, biographies of personalities, analyses of Jewish life in recent times, *Zionism and nationalism, Jewish humor, grammar, pedagogical textbooks, and calendars. Missionaries in the community published books in Ladino about *Christianity, Hebrew grammar books, and even a Ladino biblical dictionary.

POPULAR AND FOLKLORISTIC GENRES: These genres were primarily oral and have only been recorded in print since the end of the nineteenth century. They include poetic literature, proverbs, *folktales, riddles, and jokes. The rich Ladino poetic oral folkloristic tradition includes the following genres: *romansas* (or *romances*) or ballads; *coplas* (or *complas*), poems of educational origin in assorted narratives; and *cantigas* (or *canticas*), which are lyric songs, especially love songs. Most of the *coplas* are related to Jewish life, whereas most of the *romansas* are not. These three types of *poetry are very old, and their origins can be traced back to Spain. However, a careful analysis of these genres reveals that many are later innovations, either adapted from local non-Jewish traditions or written by creative writers as new works using norms taken from the old traditions.

Many Ladino proverbs can be traced back to Spain. Some proverbs of Hispanic origin seem not to have changed over the centuries, although the vocabulary used may not be exactly the same. Others are based on Hebrew sayings or on similar proverbs from neighboring languages. Folktales, riddles, fables, and jokes generally relate to a communal attribute and were transmitted orally, especially by women, whereas men wrote satirical stories, folktales, and riddles. Folkloristic verbal compositions reflect the vernacular language more than the other literary genres and need further research.

Very little creative Ladino literature has been written since the middle of the twentieth century, despite efforts to reinvigorate the language. Current publications in Ladino written using Latin script are few, and their target readership is gradually decreasing. Most of these publications appear in bi- or multilingual formats, with the exception of the periodical *Aki Yerushalaim: Revista Kulturala Djudeo-Espanyola* (Here in Jerusalem: Cultural Journal of Judeo-Spanish), founded in *Israel in 1979. Several poets still write Ladino poems, which appear in bilingual publications. The newspapers *Shalom* in *Turkey, *Los Muestros: La boz de los sefardim* (Los Muestros: The Voice of the Sephardim) in *Belgium, and *La Lettre Sepharade* in the *United States and *France include small Ladino sections. Ladino plays are produced from time to time in Israel and Turkey, but can only fill a theater for a couple of evenings. Articles are sometimes published in Ladino (e.g., in *Ladinar* at Bar-Ilan University and by the Gaon Center at Ben-Gurion University in Israel). There are also some Ladino internet forums.

Recent research includes D. M. Bunis, "The Language of the Sephardim: A Historical Overview," in *Moreshet Sepharad: The Sephardi Legacy*, ed. H. Beinart (1992); idem, "Distinctive Characteristics of Jewish Ibero-Romance, Circa 1492," *Hispania Judaica Bulletin* (2004); P. Díaz-Mas, *Sephardim: The Jews from Spain* (1992); and O. R. Schwarzwald, "Judeo-Spanish Studies," in *Oxford Handbook of Jewish Studies*, ed. M. Goodman (2002), 572–600.

ORA RODRIGUE SCHWARZWALD

Literature: Latin America. The earliest literary works by Jews in the Spanish- and Portuguese-speaking Americas date back to the colonial period and are connected with the expulsion of the Jews from *Spain in 1492. In his first voyage across the Atlantic, *Columbus's crew included crypto-Jews and *conversos, some of whom worked as interpreters with the indigenous population. Throughout the sixteenth century, the New World became a magnet for Spanish individuals and families escaping the *Inquisition. *Testimonios*, inquisitorial reports, and other personal chronicles survive, among them the autobiography, correspondence, and last will and testament of Luis de Carvajal the Younger, known as Joseph Lumbroso, a victim of one of the largest *autos-da-fe* in Mexico City (1596).

A number of prominent colonial authors were rumored to have "Jewish blood." In the Age of Independence, starting in 1810 and covering more than the first half of the nineteenth century, such rumors were widespread. Friar Miguel Hidalgo y Costilla, a leader of *Mexico's independence movement, was accused of being *judaizantes*. Writers born at the end of the nineteenth century, like Jorge Isaacs, author of the romantic novel *María* (1867), which was translated into English by Rollo Ogden (1890), did indeed have Jewish ancestry.

The arrival of *Ashkenazim from the European *Pale of Settlement in the last two decades of the nineteenth century and first three of the twentieth injected a new *weltanschauung* into Jewish life in the region. These immigrants to *Argentina, *Brazil, Mexico, Cuba, and other countries were impoverished *Yiddish speakers who, within a short period of time, embraced Spanish as their vehicle of communication. Alberto Gerchunoff, who died in 1950, is considered the grandfather of Latin American Jewish literature. His book *The Jewish Gauchos of the Pampas* (1910) consists of a series of vignettes about the interaction of Jews and Gauchos in the Argentine countryside. Gerchunoff dreamed of Argentina as a place where Jews would thrive. But a *pogrom in 1919, called *Semana trágica* (Tragic Week), destroyed his hopes; as he matured, he became an ardent

*Zionist. An immigrant from *Russia, Gerchunoff grew up reading Yiddish novels by Sh. Y. Abramovich, Sholem Aleichem, and I. L. Peretz (see LITERATURE, YIDDISH: 1800 TO TWENTY-FIRST CENTURY). On learning Spanish, he became infatuated with *Don Quixote of La Mancha*; *Jewish Gauchos of the Pampas* includes overt and tangential references to Cervantes' book. Gerchunoff wrote about Baruch *Spinoza, Heinrich Heine, and other Jewish rebels as well.

The three largest Jewish communities in Latin America, in order of size, are *Argentina, *Brazil, and *Mexico. Argentine writers, who either idealized or rebelled against Gerchunoff, include César Tiempo, Bernardo Verbitzky, and Germán Rozenmacher. The country's two most prominent twentieth-century Jewish authors are journalist Jacobo Timmerman (*Prisoner without a Name, Cell without a Number*) and statesman Marcos Aguinis (*Marrano*). Others include Isidoro Blainsten, Ricardo Feierstein, Mario Goloboff, Alicia Steimberg, Ana María Shúa, and Mario Szichman.

As in other countries in the region, Yiddish literature flourished in Brazil in the first decades of the twentieth century. A useful anthology showcasing provocative pieces is Alan Astro's *Yiddish South of the Border* (2003). However, it is in Portuguese that most Jewish authors in the country thrive. Samuel Rawet (*The Prophet*), Clarice Lispector (*The Hour of the Star*), and the prolific Moacyr Scliar (*The Centaur in the Garden*) offer, in their oeuvres, a complex picture of Jewish life in a religiously diverse, multiracial society. Lispector, who seldom wrote about her Jewish identity, is referred to as "the Virginia Woolf of Brazil." Scliar, who died in 2011, had a penchant for humor that brought him an international audience.

Through his poems, Yiddish writer Jacobo Glantz, a native of *Ukraine, established connections among Mexico, Eastern Europe, and *New York City. His daughter Margo Glantz (*The Family Tree* and *The Wake*) became an eminent novelist, critic, and scholar of women's literature, whose studies analyze figures like Sor Juana Inés de la Cruz. Equally significant is Angelina Muñiz-Huberman (*Enclosed Garden*), whose themes often address *Kabbalah and the Sephardic past.

Ilan Stavans (*On Borrowed Words, The Disappearance, Resurrecting Hebrew*), moved to the United States from Mexico at the age of twenty-five. For decades his writing has contextualized Latin American Jewish literature. Using a variety of media, Stavans' books, plays, and films focus on language and history. From 1996 to 2006 he edited the "Jewish Latin America" series at the University of New Mexico Press. It included translations into English of works by Gerchunoff, Scliar, and others.

Other countries in the region with important Jewish writers are Chile (Ariel Dorfman, Marjorie Agosín); Peru (Isaac Goldemberg); Cuba (José Kozer, Ruth Behar), Guatemala (Victor Perera, Alcina Lubitch Domecq); Costa Rica (Isaac Chocrón); Uruguay (Mauricio Rosencof, Teresa Porzecanski); and Venezuela (Alicia Freilich). Recurrent themes that manifest themselves in the tradition are *antisemitism, assimilation, and the connection between literature and politics. The Hispanic world is a stage for a particular type of antisemitism that developed in the period of Muslim rule, which was known as *La Convivencia* in medieval *Spain. Each country in the region has adapted it to its idiosyncratic needs. Consequently, Jewish authors of different nations present the theme differently.

This is also the case with assimilation: Jewish populations from Mexico to Argentine have been shrinking since the 1970s. Today most Latin American Jewish authors live abroad – in the United States, *Israel, Spain, and *France – and their connections with their native places have become increasingly tenuous. Frequently, their books are published abroad first (and in other languages) and only then at home, if at all. As for the connection between literature and politics, the economic and social disparities that characterize Latin America have turned authors into spokespersons for the voiceless. Jewish writers have generally been advocates of left-wing causes and movements; for instance, during Argentina's "Dirty War" and Chile's Pinochet dictatorial regime. They, like other Jews, have paid a disproportionate price through torture and becoming *desaparecidos*. They often emphasize the connection between these violent periods and the *Holocaust.

Another common theme, which is typical of Jewish *Diaspora literature in general, is the search for a genealogical tree. Although interest in the colonial period remains small, novels, stories, and poems point to *Poland, *Russia, *Lithuania, and other Eastern European nations in the quest for origins. Similarly of interest are the empathy between Jews and the indigenous population and the ambivalent liaison between Jews and the State of *Israel. Although Latin America has been a fertile ground for Zionist youth recruitment, the topic remains marginal in the region's literature. More prevalent is the theme of terrorism, especially since the attacks in Buenos Aires against the Israeli Embassy and the AMIA, the Jewish community center, in the early 1990s.

Finally, several non-Jewish writers from Latin America have injected Jewish content into their work. The most prominent is Jorge Luis Borges, whose stories ("Emma Zunz," "The Secret Miracle," "Death and the Compass," "The Aleph") and poems reflect on talmudic, kabbalistic, and historical themes. Other notable non-Jewish authors manifesting this interest include Julio Cortázar ("Press Clippings"), Carlos Fuentes (*A Change of Skin, The Hydra Head, Terra Nostra*), Mario Vargas Llosa (*The Story-Teller*), and, in a more tangential fashion, Roberto Bolaño (*Nazi Literature in the Americas*). Conversely, Jewish authors not from Latin America have set their plots in the Jewish communities of various Spanish-speaking countries of the Americas. Yiddish writers from Sholem Aleichem to Isaac Bashevis Singer published stories set in Argentina, Brazil, and Mexico. English-language novelists have done the same.

Among valuable resources are the following anthologies: I. Stavans, ed., *Tropical Synagogues* (1994); M. Agosin, ed., *The House of Memory* (1999); and S. A. Sadow, ed., *King David's Harp* (1999). In 1997, D. B. Lockhart compiled a dictionary, *Jewish Writers of Latin America*; **see also FILM: LATIN AMERICA; LATIN AMERICA.**   ILAN STAVANS

Literature: *Russia and *Soviet Union (In Russian).

The first Jewish contributions to Russian literature took place in the 1860s, when Russian literature itself was in the period of its greatest creative unfolding. Pushkin had died not long before; Gogol, Turgenev, Dostoyevsky, and Tolstoy were all producing masterworks. Such brilliance was unexpected a mere hundred years after the first intellectuals attempted to write Russian, a language of peasants, in a European style. Jewish writing followed a similar trajectory with similar astonishing results, but with the further complication that Jews in the Russian Empire had somehow to obtain a secular education. Moreover, all Jewish writers in Russia had to break to some extent with their religious communities, they had to contend with ethnic and religious discrimination, and they had to decide in which language to write. The choice of *Hebrew, *Yiddish, Polish, or Russian (among other possibilities) involved serious questions of identity, status, and politics.

Those who chose Russian were associating themselves with a major world literature and a large group of readers who were not necessarily well disposed toward Jews. Jewish writers responded to this situation by serving as both critics of Jewish life and apologists for it. Osip Rabinovich (1817–1869), the first Jew to publish in the Russian mainstream press, wrote about Jewish cantonists (forced recruits), emphasizing their suffering and their loyalty to Russia. In his novel *Goryachee vremia* (Seething Times), written against the backdrop of the Polish rebellion, Lev Levanda (1835–1888) examines the dilemma of young Jews, bent on assimilation but forced to choose between Poland and Russia. The memoirs of Grigory Bogrov (1825–1885) reflect the writer's ambivalence toward his Jewish background. Written a little later, the plays and novels of Semyon Yushkevich (1868–1927) expose the seamy underside of the Jewish bourgeoisie. Closer to the twentieth century came well-known writers whose works resonated with a larger public. The poet Semyon Frug (Shimen Frug in Yiddish; 1860–1916) wrote in Russian about Jewish suffering and Jewish identification with *Jerusalem; S. Ansky (the pseudonym of the once Russian radical and later Jewish ethnographer, Shloyme Zanvl/ Semyon Akimovich Rappoport [1863–1920]) is best known for his play *The Dybbuk*, which had both Russian and Yiddish variants. He also wrote stories in Russian about assimilating Jewish youth.

The next generation of writers came of age as Russian speakers, nurtured in Russian schools on Russian and European classics. Although highly conscious of, and hampered by, their Jewish backgrounds, they did not have Jewish educations. Among them are some of the greatest writers of the twentieth century. The extraordinary Osip Mandel'stam (1891–1938) was a complex poet who filtered the experience of modern upheaval through allusions to the Greek and Roman classics. Boris Pasternak (1890–1960) began as a futurist (a Modernist school associated with the Russian poet Vladimir Mayakovsky), but eventually renounced futurism in favor of simplicity and clarity. Pasternak is best known to non-Russians for his novel *Dr. Zhivago*, which includes a series of poems on the Russian Orthodox liturgical calendar. Both poets were drawn to Christianity: Mandel'stam in intellectual and cultural ways – his early baptism was perfunctory – and Pasternak profoundly. And both writers suffered from the *Soviet regime. Mandel'stam died in a transit camp on his way to the Gulag, whereas Pasternak had to renounce the Nobel Prize awarded to him in 1958.

With the revolutions of 1917 (the *Bolshevik revolution was the second of two), Jews gained civil rights and moved in droves to major Soviet cities, now legally open to them. Literature was a high priority for the Soviet state, and Jews participated on every level and in just about every competing literary group as poets, fiction writers, children's literature writers, and theorists. Ilya Il'f (1897–1937), with his non-Jewish co-author Yevgeny Petrov, wrote satires that defined an era and still loom large in the Russian imagination. Poet Eduard Bagritsky (1895–1934) was a revolutionary Modernist. The most famous of this group is Isaac Babel (1894–1940), whose precisely crafted stories reflect the deep ambivalence of the civil war period. Like Il'f and Bagritsky, Babel came from Odessa and understood Jewish life profoundly; his stories pit Cossacks against Jews and make unlikely heroes out of Odessa Jewish thugs. Il'f and Bagritsky both died young of tuberculosis; Babel, who had been fascinated by the transformation of the Soviet state and its excesses, was arrested and executed.

The Great Terror that claimed the lives of Babel and Mandel'stam was followed by World War II. Ilya *Ehrenburg (1891–1967), a famous satirist (and erstwhile Parisian expatriate), became, along with Vasily Grossman (1905–1964), Russia's best-loved war correspondent. Ehrenburg and Grossman responded not only to war but also to the *Holocaust. In the atmosphere of post-war state *antisemitism, this was neither easy nor safe. Both men sought unsuccessfully to document the Holocaust on Soviet territory. *Life and Fate,* Grossman's magisterial novel, is about the war as experienced by both Russians and Jews; because he called specific attention to Jewish lives and fates, the manuscript was confiscated. The fate of that novel is also a part of Russian Jewish literary history. A copy saved, at great personal risk, by the poet Semyon Lipkin (1911–2003), was smuggled out of the country in 1980 by the satirist Vladimir Voinovich (b. 1932) and prepared for publication in Switzerland by the scholar Simon Markish (1931–2003), son of the Yiddish writer Peretz Markish who had been executed by Stalin in 1952 (see JEWISH ANTI-FASCIST COMMITTEE).

The liberalization that followed Stalin's death in 1953 was named after Ehrenburg's 1954 novel *The Thaw*. As the dissident intelligentsia took hold in the decades that followed, Jewish and part-Jewish writers became prominent both as liberals who managed to get provocative works into print and as radicals who published illegally in the West or who circulated their works privately in typescript. Voinovich falls into these categories, along with Yuly Daniel' (1925–1988), the son of a Yiddish writer, who was put on trial for publishing his works abroad. Joseph Brodsky (1940–1996), the best known internationally of these Jewish dissident writers, had been tried and sentenced to five years in a labor camp for not having a job, although his real transgression, obvious at the trial, was being a poet outside of the state's literary bureaucracy. After his release, Brodsky moved to the United States; in 1987, he received the Nobel Prize.

As Russian-speaking Jewish and part-Jewish writers emigrated to *Israel, Europe, and the United States, literature moved with them. With the fall of the Soviet Union, these literatures became one. The American emigré Sergey Dovlatov (1941–1990) became a beloved figure for a new generation of Russian readers. Novelists like Vasily Aksenov (b. 1932), Dina Rubina (b. 1953)**,** and Lyudmila Ulitskaya (b. 1943); satirists like Igor' Guberman (b. 1936) and Mikhail Zhvanetsky (b. 1934); and poets like Lev Rubinshtein (b.1947) reach Russian readers across the globe.

ALICE NAKHIMOVSKY

Literature: Scandinavia. Jewish history in Scandinavia is comparatively short, and few scholars have devoted attention to the community's cultural contributions. The reasons for this lack of attention are both geographic and linguistic: Scandinavia itself lies in Western Europe's north-ernmost climes, and a relatively small population speaks the Scandinavian languages. Moreover, Jewish contributions to Scandinavian letters emerged only during the nineteenth century when notions of a national literature began to hold sway. Thus, it is not surprising that the achievements of a small, largely assimilated minority residing on Europe's geographical and linguistic periphery have gone relatively unnoticed. As the Danish Jew, Georg Brandes (1842–1927), wrote in his riposte to criticism about his lack of engagement in the then-emerging *Zionist movement, "To write in Danish is the same as writing in water" ("Zionismen," 1905).

Accordingly, works of Jewish authors writing in the Scandinavian languages have been generally inaccessible to the world beyond the region. Peter Stenberg aptly describes the domestic situation of Swedish Jewish authors in his introduction to the recently published volume, *Contemporary Jewish Writing in Sweden* (2004), where he reports on an unnamed Swedish colleague who remarked that "he could not think of a major Swedish writer who was Jewish. When I began to list the authors who had agreed to appear in the anthology, he admitted his surprise at his own ignorance of the ethnic background of such prominent colleagues."

Three general historical trends are evident in Jewish writing in Scandinavia. The earliest Jewish inhabitants of the region were considered alien by their neighbors and published no literature. Their nineteenth-century descendants struggled to forge an identity based more on nation than on creed, and they assimilated for the most part, contributing significantly to emerging national cultures. In recent years, a body of Scandinavian Jewish literature has emerged that confronts the loss of a particularly Jewish identity. The representation of Jews by Scandinavians follows a similar paradigm: The first literary references describe an absent other; the next phase addresses the issue of social inclusion or exclusion; and finally, the issue of Jewish particularity comes to the fore.

The first Scandinavian literary work to address Jewish subjects was the Icelandic saga, *Gyðinga saga* (The Saga of the Jews), which was a thirteenth-century translation of 1 *Maccabees and fragmented excerpts from the writings of Flavius *Josephus. By the eighteenth century, the plays of the Dano-Norwegian playwright and professor, Ludvig Holberg (1684–1754), openly depict the presence of Jews in the everyday life of Copenhagen. In 1742, wearing his scholarly cap, Holberg published the first history of the Jewish people in a Scandinavian language, *Den jødiske Historie fra Verdens Begyndelse, fortsat til disse Tider* (Jewish History from the Beginning of the World, Continued until Our Times).

The issue of active Jewish participation in Scandinavian life became a subject of literary debate in the early nineteenth century, and the trope of "*Moses" emerges. In 1814, when the Danish king granted Jews greater freedom, Thomas Thaarup (1749–1821) responded by penning the *antisemitic lyric, *Moses og Jesus*. An example of a philosemitic use of the same trope comes from Norway where Jewish residence was banned until the mid-nineteenth century. The Norwegian poet Henrik Wergeland (1808–1845) polemicized in favor of allowing Jewish immigration in his poems "*Jøden*" (The Jew) in 1842 and

"*Jødinden*" (The Jewess) in 1844. In "*Jøden*" he employed the motif of Moses at the border of the "Promised Land" to criticize the exclusion of Jews from Norway. The Swedish author August Strindberg's social satire, *Det nya riket* (The New Kingdom) appeared in bookstores in 1882. In a chapter entitled "Moses," Strindberg satirically savaged the new rising class of Jewish entrepreneurs, publishers, and patrons of the arts. Despite extensive Jewish contributions to the dissemination and explication of late-nineteenth-century Swedish writers such as Strindberg, he complained that, even though "Moses" devotes himself to Swedish literature like no other, his love has been unduly rewarded by his control of academic endeavors. In a similar vein, Strindberg's friend Ola Hansson, a Swedish author with a distinct pan-German bias, attacked Georg Brandes, questioning his authenticity as an interpreter of Scandinavian literature and claiming that he was split by his doubleness as a Jew and a Dane. Although this type of attack was not restricted to Scandinavian debates, it is interesting to note that Brandes, a secular Jew who was a leader of the progressive literary avant-garde, was criticized for impurity by a member of the next generation of avant-gardists, as anti-Jewish feeling turned to a discourse of racial antisemitism at the end of the nineteenth century.

The most interesting representations of Jews are less clear-cut. Hans Christian Andersen's (1805–1875) "*Jødepigen*" (The Jewish Maiden [1855]), is a tale about a poor and loyal Jewish servant who cares for her mistress through good times and bad. The story ends with her death. Because she was a Jew, she is buried outside of the churchyard, and the tale ends by commenting on how the Jewess deserves resurrection and will be saved by the "Holy Ghost." Thus, Andersen's Jewess assimilates in death if not in life.

Perhaps the most interesting depiction of a Jewish character, however, precedes "*Jødepigen*" by two decades. The Swedish polymath, Carl Love Jonas Almqvist (1793–1866), wrote *Drottningens Juvelsmycke* (The Queen's Diadem), which was published in 1834; the novel includes a relatively minor character named Benjamin Cohen, also known "the White Jew." Cohen's role in the action is quite interesting. On the one hand, he is a stereotype, a venal pawnbroker, who buys the titular symbol of sovereignty stolen from the palace on the night of the murder of Gustav III, the very king who had invited Jews to live in Sweden. Although Cohen speaks in the type of *Yiddish-inflected Dano-Swedish that would be the staple of antisemitic lampoons well into the next century, there is a twist to the tale as Cohen later claims that he is not a Jew at all, and the question of stolen sovereignty in relation to the Jewish people is ironically raised. Although Almqvist interrogates notions of identity in general, his depiction of Jewish identity as an unstable and mutable concept guided by stereotype illuminates the image of Jews in nineteenth-century Sweden.

German-born Aaron Isaac (1730–1817) was Sweden's first legal Jewish resident, and he wrote the oldest extant text about Jewish life in Scandinavia. Isaac wrote his memoirs in Western *Yiddish using Hebrew orthography. However, the text was not published until 1897. In 1932, the Swedish Jewish historians Hugo Valentin and Abraham Brody translated, edited, and reissued the memoirs under the title *Aaron Isaacs minnen: En Judisk kulturbild från gustaviansk tid* (Aaron Isaac's Memoirs: A Picture of Jewish

Culture from the Gustavian Age). Born Jewish, the prolific Danish poet and playwright Henrik Hertz (1798–1870) converted and did not address Jewish issues.

Thus, the history of published Scandinavian Jewish literature should begin with Meïr Aron Goldschmidt (1819–1887). Goldschmidt's novel *En Jøde* (A Jew) from 1845 is reputed to be the first depiction of a Jewish life from birth to death in Europe. The subject of Jewish assimilation is prominent in this novel as Goldschmidt depicts how sexual desire, patriotism, prejudice, and modernity inflect the particularities of identity. Early on in the novel, the young protagonist stabs a Christian Dane during the *pogrom of 1819, and the motif of blood between Jews and Christians looms large in his mind. Later, he serves as a mercenary and revolutionary abroad, hoping to impress the non-Jewish woman he loves. On his return home, he lends money to a Christian, and when he is rumored to be a usurer, he withdraws from Christian society, becoming the stereotype he had hoped to transcend. Although Goldschmidt's reputation has been colored by his satirical savagery of the philosopher, Søren Kierkegaard, he was one of the leading Danish novelists of the first part of the nineteenth century, and he continued to engage with issues of Jewish life and assimilation throughout his career (see also DENMARK).

The Jewish contribution to the emergence, dissemination, publication, and eventually the canonization of modern Scandinavian letters at the end of the nineteenth century was significant. Georg Brandes, raised in an assimilated and secular Jewish home in Copenhagen, was perhaps the most influential Scandinavian man of letters of this era. He championed Ibsen, coined the phrase "the modern breakthrough," and introduced French literary aesthetics, John Stuart Mill, and Friedrich Nietzsche to the larger reading public in Scandinavia. Brandes was the inspirational leader of a politically engaged literary avant-garde in the seventh and eighth decades of the nineteenth century. Later on he defended *Dreyfus in print and advocated for peace and scientific inquiry. Brandes, a generation younger than Goldschmidt, was critical of the older man's self-identification. After listening to a talk by the author of *En Jøde* in the 1860s, Brandes remarked that he identified himself neither as Jewish nor as Danish. However, Brandes' desire not to identify himself as Jewish did not stop others from doing so. In a letter to August Strindberg, he once remarked that he had long enjoyed the "odium of being the North's anti-Christ." Georg's brother Edvard (1847–1931) was a playwright and a politician.

In Sweden, the poet Oscar Levertin (1862–1906), who originally was inspired by Georg Brandes' call for a critically engaged form of literary realism with pan-European ambition, became part of a nationalistic countermovement. Levertin and another Jewish Swede, Henrik Schück (1855–1947), initiated work on a history of Swedish literature inflected by national romantic notions. At the end of his short life, Levertin's creative work addressed his Jewishness. In the prefatory verse to *Kung Salomo och Morolf* (1905), Levertin remarks, "Myself, I am west and eastern," an interesting trope considering the orientalist discourse of his time.

Henri Nathansen (1868–1944) was a Danish Jewish writer who engaged issues of Jewish assimilation directly. His most popular play *Indenfor Murene* (Inside the Walls [1912]) addressed the issue of *intermarriage and Jewish family life. Tragically, Nathansen committed suicide after fleeing *Denmark in 1944. A portion of his novel, *Mendel Philipsen og Søn* (1932) was adapted and filmed by Liv Ullman as *Sofie* in 1992 (see FILM: EUROPE [POST–WORLD WAR II]).

Contemporary Jewish literature in Scandinavia has been largely concerned with three subjects: the *Holocaust, Jewish identity, and *Israel. Exiled German writers such as Nobel Prize winner Nelly Sachs (1891–1970) and Peter Weiss (1916–1982) lived and wrote in Sweden. Other survivors of the *Shoah, such as Cordelia Edvardson (b. 1929), Zenia Larrson (b. 1922), and Hédi Fried (b. 1924), have written autobiographical works in Swedish. Georg Klein (b. 1925), Erland Josephson (b. 1923), and Per Wästberg (b.1933) are Swedish writers born before World War II. A younger generation of Swedish Jewish writers is concerned largely with the Jewish past and Israel, whereas in Denmark, an older generation of Jewish writers often revisits the experience of fleeing the German occupation in Denmark. The most prominent Danish Jewish writer is Suzanne Brøgger (b. 1944), who is a member of the Danish Academy. Her novel, *Jadekatten: en Slægtssaga* (The Jade Cat: A Family Saga [1997]), depicts the fate of a Jewish family during the *Nazi occupation. Pia Tafdrup (1952) is a Danish Jewish poet who is also a member of the Danish Academy. Morton Thing (b. 1945) has written several cultural histories about the Jewish experience in Denmark.

Norway has a shorter history of Jewish settlement than Sweden and Denmark and also a scant history of Jewish literary activity. Jewish cultural life blossomed in the period between World War I and II, but half of the Jewish population was murdered by the Nazis. Leo Eitinger (1912–1996), who fled to Norway in 1939 and was deported to *Auschwitz in 1942, was a psychiatrist by training and wrote several books about antisemitism and his experiences in Norway. Eva Scheer (b. 1915) has published both fiction and nonfiction about Jewish life, folktales, and migration history. Mona Levin (b. 1939), daughter of the pianist Robert Levin, has published a 1983 biography of her father entitled *Med livet i hendene* (With Life in His Hands). Øystein Wingaard Wolf (1958) is the most prominent Norwegian novelist with a Jewish background. His books focus on Eastern European Jewish culture. For further reading in addition to Stenberg, see K. H. Ober, *Meïr Goldschmidt* (1976).   MICHAEL STERN

Literature: United States (Since 1900). In 1977 Irving Howe rashly announced the end of the writing of American Jewish literature. The American subject, for Howe as for others, had been immigration and the turmoil of assimilation. With the amazingly successful integration of American Jews into American society, that subject seemed exhausted, irrelevant, and impertinent. What hardships, special exclusions, disadvantages, and discrimination might late-twentieth-century American Jews claim? Yet, even though Howe was correct concerning the themes of the major canon of Jewish American writers, he was incorrect in his prophecy for the future course of American Jewish literature. Like all great traditions, American Jewish literature was more than a single-subject literature.

At the end of the nineteenth century and into the early decades of the twentieth century, the major figure in American Jewish fiction was the refugee Jew in his (and sometimes her) new world. This is the subject of the short stories and novels of Abraham Cahan (1860–1951), Mary Antin (1881–1949), Anzia Yezierska (ca. 1885–1970), Ludwig Lewisohn (1882–1955), and Michael Gold (1893–1967). Typical works include Cahan's *Yekl: A Tale of the New York Ghetto* (1896) or his masterpiece, *The Rise of David Levinsky* (1917); Antin's aptly entitled, autobiographical *The Promised Land* (1912), which had to do with the promised land of the United States, and not the Jewish one; Yezierska's short stories and what was to become her most famous novel, *The Bread Givers* (1925); Lewisohn's autobiographical *Up Stream* (1922) and *The Island Within* (1928); and Gold's groundbreaking novel *Jews without Money* (1930), one of the earliest socially, indeed socialistically, informed Jewish American works. The most important early-twentieth-century writer about immigrant life was probably Henry Roth (1905–1995); his 1934 novel *Call It Sleep* burst on the American public with full force only in the 1960s when it came to be viewed as the great work of Jewish Modernism. All of these writers wrote primarily about the Jewish immigrant experience, often as that experience was lived among other ethnic and religious groups in American cities. Themes included the longings for the world left behind, the hopes and expectations of the new life in America, the disruptions of family and community relationships, and the budding realization that even the fulfillment of the American dream might not deliver the satisfactions seemingly promised by the *goldene medina*.

Indeed, this realization of the limitations of material wealth and individualist self-fulfillment, as Cahan so brilliantly portrayed it in *David Levinsky,* was in part what produced the amazing fit between Jewish authorship and the American literary tradition. As Jews began their integration into American life, the triumvirate of writers who dominated the canon in the mid-twentieth century became less concerned with the immigrant refugee experience and more with the existential, universal issues that the Jew in America might come to represent. Bernard Malamud (1914–1986), Saul Bellow (1915–2005), and Philip Roth (b. 1933) all wrote different kinds of fiction. So, too, did Cynthia Ozick (b. 1928), who was sometimes linked with Malamud, Bellow, and Roth as the one female Jewish writer of stature, and Isaac Bashevis Singer (1904–1991), the European-born *Yiddish writer and Nobel Laureate (1978) who began his career in America only in the 1940s.

Malamud, Bellow, and Roth readily found a place in mainstream American writing, as their inclusion in the major American anthologies of the 1960s and 1970s and in the university curriculum more than testifies. The Jewish subject of alienation, defamiliarization, and existential angst – the outsider struggling and not quite succeeding in finding a place within the dominant culture – was a quintessentially American subject, going back to the very origins of American fiction in the nineteenth century. In his 1976 novel, *The Ghost Writer*, Philip Roth introduces his lifelong protagonist and alter ego Nathan Zuckerman; it is no accident that this comic and yet deeply philosophical portrait of the artist as a young Jewish man takes place in the New England of Hawthorne, Melville, and Henry James where American literature itself had its inception. Roth is a great humorist of Jewish neuroses, the comedy of Jewish family life, and of the assimilated Jew whose Jewishness is still primary to his identity, even if it is the aspect of himself that he would most like to be free of. These themes are central to

Roth's first published fiction, *Goodbye, Columbus and Other Stories* (1959), and such other works as *Portnoy's Complaint* (1969) and *Sabbath's Theater* (1995), and they continue, as well, in the Zuckerman novels, up through *The Counterlife* (1987), *American Pastoral* (1997), and *The Human Stain* (2000). At the same time, a graver, more serious tone, which predominates in some of Roth's later novels, such as *The Plot against America* (2004), *The Human Stain*, *Everyman* (2006), and *Indignation* (2008) has also been present from the start.

Saul Bellow's writing is less wildly comic than Roth's, but his Jewish fiction is also characterized by irony, satire, and tremendous wit and precision. Bellow, who received the Nobel Prize for Literature in 1976, also focused on the American Jew (even where he is not Jewish, as in *Henderson, the Rain King* [1959]). In Bellow's case, the preferred protagonist is the Jewish intellectual everyman in an America dissolving at its seams, losing the integrity of the past (such as it was), and moving into a future even more valueless and chaotic than the present. From such early novels as *Seize the Day* (1956), *Herzog* (1964), and *Mr. Sammler's Planet* (1970), through more recent fictions like *Ravelstein* (2000), the great theme of Bellow's fiction is the struggle of the self to achieve itself, in the face of everything that opposes it, including the meaningless of success.

Malamud, Ozick, and Singer pursue the Jewish subject somewhat differently. For Malamud, the immigrant Yiddish-speaking Jew, in such novels and short-story collections as *The Assistant* (1957) and *The Magic Barrel* (1958), is less an American everyman than a suffering Christ. More deeply in touch with the literature of the European Jewish *shtetl and with the Yiddish culture of the early-twentieth-century Jewish immigrant than either Roth or Bellow, Malamud not only Americanizes but also Christianizes the Jewish subject, recalling the concluding image of Henry Roth's *Call It Sleep*, where its young child protagonist is virtually crucified on the railway tracks. Ozick's immersion in the *yiddishkeit* of Europe and the American ghetto is at least equal to Malamud's, but it remains more specifically, concretely Jewish (i.e., non-universalist or Christian). From the publication of her first collection of short stories, *The Pagan Rabbi* in 1971, through the appearance of her other story collections and novels, including *The Cannibal Galaxy* (1983), *The Messiah of Stockholm* (1987), *The Shawl* (1980, 1983, 1989), *The Puttermesser Papers* (1997), and *Heir to the Glimmering World* (2004), and in her many essay collections as well, Ozick engages Jewish history and the textual tradition to extend the canon, not only of American literature but also of Jewish literature. Singer, who initially wrote in Yiddish and whose fiction remained connected, like Ozick's, to the European Jewish experience and the tradition of Yiddish writing, preserved an idea of Yiddish for a post-*Holocaust, non-Yiddish-speaking modern world. Similarly, Ozick has preserved an idea of Jewish writing in English, as constituting an American Jewish tradition in literature. Her most recent novel is *Foreign Bodies* (2010).

Malamud, Ozick, and Singer – precisely because they stayed more rooted in Jewish history, traditions, and sources than other American Jewish writers – were the direct antecedents of writers who emerged in the last two decades of the twentieth century. These include Steve Stern (b. 1947), Art Spiegelman (b. 1948), Melvin Jules Bukiet (b. 1953), Rebecca Goldstein (b. 1950), Michael Chabon (b. 1963), Allegra Goodman (b. 1967), Nathan Englander

(b. 1970), and Aryeh Lev Stollman. These authors have undertaken an expansion of the American Jewish subject, not only by tackling the Holocaust (for example, in *Maus* [1986, 1991] by graphic novelist Spiegelman [see LITER-ATURE: GRAPHIC NOVELS]) but also by restoring Jewish textual traditions (religious and secular) that had persisted in writings of Malamud, Singer, and Ozick. Some of these writers came from traditional *Orthodox or near Orthodox Jewish backgrounds; those who did not have undertaken the task of reading extensively in Jewish texts and traditions, which play prominent roles in both the themes and structures of their fictions. Writers who have emerged in the first decade of the twenty-first century for whom Jewish themes are central include Jonathan Safran Foer (b. 1977), Myla Goldberg (b. 1972), Dara Horn (b. 1977), Nicole Kraus (b. 1974), and Tova Mirvis (**see also LITERATURE, UNITED STATES: POPULAR FICTION; LITERATURE: WOMEN WRITERS (EUROPE AND NORTH AMERICA)**).

EMILY BUDICK

Literature, United States: Popular Fiction. Two best-selling middlebrow novels of the 1950s signaled a new turn in Jewish writing within mainstream American literature. *Marjorie Morningstar* (1955) by Herman Wouk (b. 1915) and *Exodus* (1958) by Leon Uris (1924–2003) neatly illustrated the three Jewish experiences in the first part of the twentieth century that proved compelling to a mass American readership and exploitable to general publishers: the traumas of the *Holocaust, the struggle for Jewish *national and cultural self-determination, and the social and psychological hardships of acculturation. The success of both novels and of their *film adaptations rested on the ways they reflected and relieved Jewish anxieties about those experiences and satisfied Gentile curiosity about Jewish identity. They cast a long shadow over popular Jewish fiction and inevitably tied that fiction to the social novel, to Hollywood, and to American cultural productions in general. Over the next forty years, however, as writers, publishers, readers, and critics expanded definitions of "popular," a wider range of narratives developed, and a longer, multinational history of popular Jewish fiction became visible. Like popular fiction in general, this often-denigrated mode of Jewish writing fulfills readers' desire for instruction about and solutions to the confusions of the modern world and, in the right hands, is capable of an entertaining complexity.

At the beginning of the twentieth century what counted as "popular" Jewish literary work in America, as elsewhere, depended on the tastes and retail demands of an insular but still diverse Jewish readership. A 1906 magazine article on Jewish bookstores of the Lower East Side suggests that *Yiddish stories by Mendele Mokher Seforim (Sholem Abramovich [1835–1917]) and Jacob Dineson (1856–1919), plays by Jacob Gordin (1853–1909), and Yiddish translations of Shakespeare and Tolstoy were commercially fashionable. This reflected the situation of late-nineteenth- and early-twentieth-century Yiddish literature in both America and *Eastern Europe where the line between the literary and the popular was indistinct and readers were not yet categorized by their reading preferences.

It is not until the post–World War I expansion of publishing and mass-circulated newspapers that definitions of "popular" changed in relation to audience and content. In *Poland the emergence of a vigorous Yiddish tabloid press during the interwar years and its publication of serialized *shund* novels – "trashy" sensationalist novels written by anonymous hacks and established writers such as Yehoshua Perle (1888–1943), Yisroel Rabon (1900–1943), and Isaac *Bashevis Singer (1904–1991) – led to heated arguments about the dangers of pandering to working- and middle-class readers' taste for formulaic stories featuring mild eroticism and violence. In the United States, the post-war growth of American and American Jewish publishing, the creation of the influential Book-of-the-Month Club, and the hiring of Jews at mainstream publishing companies shifted the meaning of "popular" in relation to American Jewish writing to connote primarily middlebrow fiction and commensurately wider circulation among both Jewish and non-Jewish readers. Edna Ferber (1887–1968), Ben Hecht (1893–1964), and Irwin Shaw (1913–1984) met great success in this publishing environment.

Whereas Ferber, Hecht, and Shaw typified a new class of popular Jewish writers who wrote on a wide range of general subjects, Milton Steinberg (1903–1950) and Leo Rosten (1908–1997) created a new mode of popular Jewish fiction that defended Jewish particularity against the forces of acculturation. Both wrote commercially successful middlebrow novels during the interwar period. Rosten's comic novel, *The Education of H*Y*M*A*N K*AP*L*A*N* (1937), dramatizes an immigrant's attempt to learn the English language and its cultural connotations without the loss of his endearing, positive sense of Jewish self-worth. Steinberg's historical fiction, *As A Driven Leaf* (1939), dramatizes the life of *Elisha ben Abuya, the famous heretic of talmudic lore, whose attraction to Hellenistic philosophy reflected the wrangle among Steinberg's contemporaries between Judaism and secular American life and values. Both novels became staples in Jewish adult education programs, maintaining a kind of popularity even to the present.

The rise of a popular Jewish fiction defined by its appeal to a mass audience, however, is a result of the economic boom following *World War II and the explosion of mass-market publishing. In combination with greater social mobility among Jews, increased leisure time, and a wave of post-war Jewish writing in English that explained or celebrated the passage of Jews and their nostalgia into the American mainstream, mass-market publishing expanded opportunities and audiences for popular fiction, especially genre fiction, patterned on the Wouk and Uris model.

As those two writers continued to mine Jewish history, Chaim Potok (1929–2002) earned national acclaim by revealing the conflicts within and between the *Ḥasidic and *Modern Orthodox communities in Brooklyn. Novels like *The Chosen* (1967), *The Promise* (1969), and *My Name is Asher Lev* (1972), examine the strains that secular society, *Zionism, liberal Jewish *theology, western philosophy and art, and the Holocaust placed on Jews and Jewish practice in America. That Potok's social novels prominently feature educational settings – the *synagogue, the library, the *yeshivah*, the graduate seminary – helps explain their popularity with general readers who found in them, and in the 1981 film version of *The Chosen*, compelling explanations of Judaism and Judaic scholarship. At roughly the same time the best-selling detective novels of Harry Kemelman (1908–1996) investigated Jewish acculturation to the middle-class

American suburb and rendered it safe for Jewish family and congregational life. Over the course of twelve books from 1964 to 1996, Kemelman's protagonist, Rabbi David Small, defended his congregants and his faith, lecturing throughout on the meaning of Jewish religious practice and cultural mores for the benefit of non-Jews, and on how Jews ought to navigate the social mysteries of America for the benefit of his co-religionists.

Kemelman's work, and the short detective stories of James Yaffe (b. 1927) that appeared in the 1950s and '60s, paved the way for writers as varied as Marissa Piesman (b. 1956), Stuart Kaminsky (b. 1934), Kinky Friedman (b. 1944), Richard Zimler (b. 1956), Sharon Kahn (b. 1934), Ayelet Waldman (b. 1964), David Liss (b. 1966), Faye Kellerman (b. 1952), and Rochelle Krich (b. 1947). Kellerman's Peter Decker and Rina Lazarus mysteries and Krich's Jessica Drake mysteries, in particular, garnered wide readerships by featuring women detectives who inspect and defend Orthodox Judaism as an engine for contemporary American Jewish religious and cultural reawakening. The internationally distributed Israeli mysteries of Batya Gur (1947–2005), published in the United States between 1992 and 2006, also achieved mass-market success. Through Chief Superintendent Michael Ohayon of the *Jerusalem police, Gur conducted philosophical investigations into the frayed social fabric of the Jewish state just when America's political interests seemed to align more sharply with it. A similar dynamic is at work in the Gabriel Allon spy thrillers by Daniel Silva (b. 1960), a series that began with *The Kill Artist* (2000) and feature a morally conflicted Mossad assassin. These fictions by Kellerman, Krich, Gur, and Silva illustrate how religious revival and the challenges of Jewish national self-determination have eclipsed American Jewish acculturation as subject matter in mass-marketed Jewish mysteries and thrillers.

Popular Jewish fantasy and science fiction, a much smaller and still evolving genre, first reached a wide audience with *Wandering Stars: An Anthology of Jewish Fantasy and Science Fiction* (1974, 1998). Edited by Jack Dann (b. 1945), it identifies the apparent founders of the genre, writers already famous within science fiction such as Isaac Asimov (1920–1992), Harlan Ellison (b. 1934), William Tenn (Philip Klass [b. 1920]), and Robert Silverberg (b. 1935), all of whose most well-known work has no Jewish content. Their short stories in this collection, however, packaged with Isaac *Bashevis Singer's "Jachid and Jechida" and Bernard Malamud's "Jewbird," established an arguable tradition of speculative Jewish fiction about galactic *Diasporas, the supernatural, persecution, and the search for a Jewish home planet. A second volume, *More Wandering Stars* (1999), and works by Avram Davidson (1923–1993), Joel Rosenberg (b. 1954), Philip Graubart, Daniel (D. J.) Kessler, and Michael Burstein (b. 1970) carry on these themes of wandering and homecoming. In many ways, Marge Piercy's (b. 1936) speculative futurist novel *He, She and It* (1991) fits into this category as well.

In contrast, the popular Jewish romance developed energetically through a series of provocative innovations, the first initiated by Belva Plain (b. 1919). Her novel *Evergreen* (1978), adapted into a TV mini-series in 1985, chronicled the family saga of Polish Jewish immigrant Anna Friedman as she moved from the Lower East Side to arrival in the

suburbs; this novel helped cement a now classic narrative of American Jewish social and material success into the popular imagination. By yoking that narrative to the forbidden loves and marital compromises of romance fiction, Plain, along with Gloria Goldreich (b. 1934) and Maisie Mosco (b. 1939?) in *Britain, created a profitable formula for stories that explored a woman's perspective on Jewish family, identity, and desire. Anita Diamant (b. 1951) reshaped the genre still further in her international best seller *The Red Tent* (1997), which retells the biblical story of *Dinah from Dinah's point of view. The novel incited contentious debate, facilitated by book clubs and reading groups, about the role and contributions of women to Jewish and Christian theology and religiosity. A stream of novels revisiting and refiguring Jewish women in history and within Orthodox communities soon followed, from the historical romances of Maggie Anton (Margaret Antonofsky [b. 1958?]) and Dora Levy Mossanen (b. 1945), to the biblical romances of the Israeli academic Eva Etzioni-Halevy (b. 1934), to the middlebrow love stories of Tova Mirvis (b.1972) and Naomi Ragen (b. 1949) whose novels have replaced Chaim Potok's as mass-market primers on the esoteric worlds of Modern and Ultra-Orthodoxy (see JUDAISM, ORTHODOX entries).

This increasing reciprocity between contemporary popular Jewish fiction and historical or Orthodox subject matter illuminates current literary and social trends. The recent boom in graphic novels (see LITERATURE: GRAPHIC NOVELS), for example, brought overdue recognition to the Jewish writer/artists who helped develop the comic book medium and introduced American audiences to Israeli comics artists like Uri Fink (b. 1963) and the Actus Tragicus collective: Mira Friedmann (b. 1952), Yirmi Pinkus (b. 1966), Itzik Rennert (b. 1956), Rutu Modan (b. 1966), and Batia Kolton (b. 1967). Yet the commercial and critical success of Art Spiegelman's *Maus* (1986, 1991) and the fan-fueled celebrations of Will Eisner (1917–2005) and his portraits of immigrant and first-generation American Jews in *A Contract with God* (1978) underlined the enduring attraction of woeful Jewish pasts to general audiences and publishers. *The Jew of New York* (1998) by Ben Katchor (b. 1951), *Yossel* (2003) by Joe Kubert (b. 1926), and the Jewish graphic novels of James Sturm (b. 1965) and French Jewish writer/artist Joann Sfar (b. 1971) are all mainstream historical fictions about Jewish acculturation or the Holocaust.

Springing up alongside them, however, are comic books by JT Waldman (b. 1979?), Alan Oirich (b. 1957), Robert J. Avrech (b. 1950), and Eric Mahr (1955–2010) aimed at a specifically Jewish mass readership and distributed by Jewish publishers worldwide. They resemble popular Jewish romances in their concern to explain or defend a resurgent Judaism, Jewish religious figures, and Orthodox religious practice as guides for the perplexed. Yet, they are a reminder, too, that formulaic Orthodox fiction – marketed by many of the same publishers and written in English and Hebrew in the United States, United Kingdom, South Africa, and Israel by writers such as Chava Rosenberg, Libby Lazewnik, and Ruthie Pearlman (b. 1949) – is itself a burgeoning literary niche, one inhabited nearly exclusively by Orthodox and Ultra-Orthodox women. The reprinting by a number of these publishers of nineteenth- and twentieth-century middlebrow fiction by Orthodox apologists is also drawing critical attention to earlier popular and middlebrow writers such as Godchaux Weil (1806–1878) in France, Marcus Lehmann (1831–1890) in Germany, Nathan Mayer (1838–1912) in the United States, Alexander Ben Ghiat (1860?-1925?) in Turkey, Samuel Gordon (1871–1927) in the United Kingdom, and Mikhoel-Ber Sokolov (1902–1942) in Poland. Whether looking back at such writers or at those just starting out, the popular Jewish fiction they produced furnishes an important commentary on modern Jewish life and literacy.

LAURENCE ROTH

Literature: Women Writers (Europe and North America).

Any account of Jewish women's writing in Europe and North America must begin with the work of *Gluckel of Hameln (1646–1724), who, between 1690, when she was first widowed with fourteen children, and 1719, recorded in her *Judeo-German memoir an account of Jewish life in seventeenth-century *Germany that details her family relationships, business dealings, and personal faith. The memoir is intercalated with didactic parables and moral lessons, inspired by the vernacular printed material available to Jewish women of the day. These included books of *customs, *ethical literature, collections of *folktales, paraphrases of the *Torah, and *tkhines*, devotional literature written for and often by women that provides vernacular prayers for *synagogue worship and *life-cycle and domestic rituals (see PRAYER: WOMEN'S DEVOTIONAL; WOMEN: EARLY MODERN EUROPE).

Jewish women with literary aspirations in early-nineteenth-century *England, *France, *Germany, and the *United States confronted fictional stereotypes of themselves as "Jessicas" (Shylock's daughter in Shakespeare's *The Merchant of Venice*) who convert and marry Christians or as stalwart "Rebeccas" (the heroine of Walter Scott's *Ivanhoe* [1820]), who renounce romantic love for a Christian in favor of loyalty to their own heritage. One of the most influential answers to such depictions was the historical romance *The Vale of Cedars, or The Martyr* (1850) by Grace Aguilar (1816–1847). Aguilar, whose heritage was *Sephardic, was a staunch defender of Judaism; her theological and historical writings, such as *The Spirit of Judaism* (1842) and *The Women of Israel* (1845), were widely read and were influential for Jewish reform movements in England and in the United States. One enthusiast was Rebecca *Gratz, founder of the American Jewish Sunday School movement.

The first published collection of poems by a Jewish woman in the United States was *Fancy's Sketch Book* (1833) by Penina Moïse (1797–1880). Like Aguilar, she published in both Jewish and secular periodicals, also focusing on Jewish ritual reform, Jewish rights, assimilation, and resisting conversion. Emma *Lazarus (1849–1887), whose poem "The New Colossus" is inscribed on the pedestal of the Statue of Liberty, was a prolific essayist on a range of topics of public and Jewish interest.

Eugénie Foa (1796-??), a French writer of Sephardic background, began her career as a novelist with *La Juive* (The Jewess; 1835), a historical romance about a Jewish woman who renounces her Christian lover. The novel includes descriptions of "exotic" Jewish rituals and was clearly targeted at the same non-Jewish audience fascinated by a contemporaneous opera of the same title by Jacques Fromenthal Halévy and Eugène Scribe. Aguilar and Foa also produced fictions depicting contemporary Jewish communities

in England and France, respectively. "Rachel, or The Inheritance," Foa's opening story in a collection entitled *Rachel* (1833), purports to be the posthumously discovered memoirs of a Jewish woman writer who, after refusing marriage to her Christian lover, is abandoned by her Jewish husband (as was the case with Foa). Aguilar's novella, *The Perez Family* (1843), similarly addresses the issue of *intermarriage by depicting a failed marriage between a Jewish man and Christian woman.

In 1833 Germany, the letters of Rahel Levin Varnhagen (1771–1832), a well-known Jewish salon hostess and avid correspondent, were posthumously published as *Rahel: Ein Buch des Andenkens für ihre Freunde* (Rahel: A Remembrance Book for Her Friends). Varnhagen was part of a group of "Jewish" salon hostesses including Moses *Mendelssohn's daughter, Brendel, who became the translator and writer Dorothea Schlegel, most of whom ultimately converted and intermarried. The "Jessica" theme of conversion and intermarriage continued to do battle with the "Rebecca" model of dutiful renunciation and spinsterhood throughout nineteenth-century literature by Jewish women. Later examples include *Jenny* (1843) by Fanny Lewald (1811–1889) in Germany; *Reuben Sachs* (1889) by Amy Levy (1861–1889) in England; and *Other Things Being Equal* (1892) by Emma Wolf (1865–1932) of San Francisco.

The close of the nineteenth century brought waves of immigrants from Eastern Europe to Western Europe and North America. Some of these women immigrants wrote in *Yiddish; others began writing in Russian or Polish, but subsequently switched to Yiddish or English. Many of their writings have been translated for the first time in the groundbreaking collections, *Found Treasures* (1994) and *Arguing with the Storm* (2007). Two immigrant writers who wrote successfully in English are Mary Antin (1881–1949) who published her autobiography, *The Promised Land,* about her 1912 journey from Poland to the United States. Anzia Yezierska (1885?–1970), whose most famous novel is *The Bread Givers* (1925), also collaborated on film versions of her stories and books.

In the twentieth century increasing numbers of American Jewish women writers have appealed to wider audiences by addressing both specifically Jewish and universal themes. Tillie Olsen (1913–2007), Grace Paley (1922–2007), and Cynthia Ozick (b. 1928) all achieved widespread critical acclaim and popularity among general audiences primarily for their short stories or, in Ozick's case, also for her many novels and literary essays. Jo Sinclair (Ruth Seid [1913–1995]), whose novel *Wasteland* (1946) treats Jewish self-hatred and features a Jewish lesbian character and whose *The Changelings* (1955) deals with tensions between Jewish and *African American communities in the Midwest, merits mention with Olsen and Paley because all three focused on issues of social identity and difference in the mid-twentieth-century American setting.

Joanne Greenberg (b. 1932), a prolific novelist who is best known for *I Never Promised You a Rose Garden* (1964; written under the pseudonym Hannah Green), about a young Jewish woman's mental breakdown and successful recovery, has addressed similar themes of otherness and disability. (Her other works with Jewish themes and/or characters include *The King's Persons* [1963], about the massacre of the Jewish population of York in 1190; *A Season of Delight* [1981];

Age of Consent [1989]; and *Miri, Who Charms* [2009]). Greenberg's notable contemporary is Lynne Sharon Schwartz (b. 1939); her astonishing vision of growing up in McCarthy-era New York is a feature of *Leaving Brooklyn* (1989), about a girl with one blind eye.

In recent decades, American Jewish women writers who have achieved general acclaim include award-winning poets such as Muriel Rukeyser (1913–1980), Maxine Kumin (b. 1925), Adrienne Rich (b. 1929), Marge Piercy (b. 1936, also a prolific novelist), Irena Klepfisz (b. 1941), and Louise Glück (b.1943), and notable playwrights Wendy Wasserstein (1950–2006) and Joan Schenkar (b. 1951). Jewish women's contributions to contemporary fiction are particularly notable. *The Mind-Body Problem* (1983) by Rebecca Goldstein (b. 1950) focuses on an Orthodox girl's sexual and intellectual liberation. This book grew out of its historical context, cross-fertilized by writers such as Erica Jong and Betty Friedan, as well as, perhaps, Chaim Potok's *The Chosen* (1967). It helped found a still burgeoning subgenre of women's *Orthodox (or renounced Orthodox) novels by authors such as Pearl Abraham, Allegra Goodman (b. 1967), Ruchama King, Tova Mirvis, and Risa Miller.

Goldstein's more technically sophisticated work, *Mazel* (1995), harks back to the familiar family saga, found in precursors like British writer G. B. Stern's (1890–1973) *The Matriarch* (1924; originally published as *Tents of Israel* in Britain). Following in those generic footsteps are Canadian writer and poet Anne Michaels (b. 1958; *Fugitive Pieces* [1996]), British author Tamar Yellin (*The Genizah at the House of Shepher* [2005]), and American Dara Horn (*In the Image* [2002]; *The World to Come* [2006]; *All Other Nights* ([2009]). In *The Red Tent* (1997), Anita Diamant combines deeply researched historical fiction and a feminist reimagining of early Jewish women's lives in a popular revision of the biblical story of *Jacob's daughter *Dinah, beginning a trend in feminist historical fiction. For example, Eva Etzioni-Halevy (b. 1939), an Israeli author who publishes in English, is the author of the biblical romances *The Song of Hannah* (2005), *The Garden of Ruth* (2006), and *The Triumph of Deborah* (2008). The best of these historical fictions imagine the lives of women in historical eras for which there are few firsthand accounts of women's lives and thoughts. Maggie Anton self-published now-acclaimed trilogy called *Rashi's Daughters* (2005, 2007, 2009), exploring the lives of the three daughters of *Rashi, the renowned biblical and talmudic commentator who lived in twelfth-century France. Canadian author Lilian Nattel (b. 1956) explores the intertwined lives of the male and female dwellers in a fictional *shtetl* in 1880s *Poland in *The River Midnight* (1999) and in the Jewish immigrant underbelly of London in *The Singing Fire* (2004). British writer Linda Grant (b. 1951) offers the perspective of a Jewish immigrant from England and of Zionist rebels in British Mandate Palestine in *When I Lived in Modern Times* (2000). *The Family Orchard* (2000) by Nomi Eve (b. 1968) is a six-generation family saga that begins in Palestine in 1837.

Female authors from more recent Jewish immigrations to the United States include Gina Nahai, whose novels, *The Cry of the Peacock* (1992), *Moonlight on the Avenue of Faith* (1999), and *Caspian Rain* (2007), are about Jewish communities in Iran and Iranian Jewish communities in the Diaspora; Ruth Knafo Setton, whose novel *The Road to Fez* (2001) is about

Jewish Morocco; and Lara Vapnyar (b. 1971), who has written a short-story collection about Soviet Jewry, *There Are Jews in My House* (2002).

Memoirs, especially of the Holocaust, by Jewish women are numerous; some noteworthy European examples that appear in English include German Swedish Cordelia Edvardson's (b. 1929) *Burned Child Seeks the Fire* (1997); Hungarian American Magda Denes' (1934–1996) *Castles Burning* (1998); and Polish Italian Edith Brück's (b. 1932) *Letter to My Mother* (2006). Some North American Jewish women have chosen the lives of women during and after the Holocaust as a subject for fiction; for example, *Anya* (1974) by Susan Fromberg Schaeffer (b. 1941) and Cynthia Ozick's *The Shawl: A Story and a Novella* (1989). Depictions of Holocaust survivors and their children also appear in Anne Michaels' *Fugitive Pieces* (discussed earlier); Shira Nayman's *Awake in the Dark: Stories* (2006); and the autobiographical fiction cycle, *The Holocaust Kid* (2001), by Sonia Pilcer, who was born in a *displaced persons camp. Other authors who deal with the special trauma of survivors' children include Elisabeth Rosner (*The Speed of Light* [2001] and *Blue Nude* [2003]) and Linda Grant (*The Clothes on their Backs* [2008]). Pushing the very limits of what can be written about the Holocaust are Holocaust memoirs as graphic novels (after Art Spiegelman's *Maus*) and Holocaust satires. In the former group, there are *We Are On Our Own* (2006) by Miriam Katin (b. 1942) and I *Was a Child of Holocaust Survivors* (2006) by Bernice Eisenstein (b. 1949). In the latter, there are *My Holocaust* (2007) by Tova Reich, *The Empress of Weehawken* (2007) by Irene Dische (b. 1952), and "The Living," from the short-story collection *How is This Night Different?* (2006) by Elisa Albert.

Finally, samples of Jewish women's writing in English and in translation from Europe and elsewhere can be found in anthologies published by University of Nebraska Press in the series on Contemporary Jewish Writing; one should also note the critical works, *Keepers of the Motherland: German Texts by Jewish Women Writers* (1994), by Dagmar Lorenz; *Voices of the Diaspora: Jewish Women Writing in Contemporary Europe* (2006), an anthology edited by Thomas Nolden and Frances Malino; and *Contemporary Jewish Writing in Europe: A Guide* (2008) by Vivian Liska and Thomas Nolden. The last work includes a helpful double bibliography offering critical information and highlighting which authors' works are currently available in English translation.

For further reading, see E. Avery, ed., *Modern Jewish Women Writers in America* (2007); J. Burstein, *Telling Little Secrets: American Jewish Writing since the 1980s* (2006); T. Nolden, *In Lieu of Memory: Contemporary Jewish Writing in France* (2006); C. Tylee, ed., *"In the Open": Jewish Women Writers and British Culture* (2006); A. F. Roller, *The Literary Imagination of Ultra-Orthodox Jewish Women* (1999); and A. Shapiro, ed., *American Jewish Women Writers: A Bio-Bibliographical and Critical Sourcebook* (1994).   JUDITH LEWIN

Literature, Yiddish: Beginnings to 1700.

Literature, Yiddish: Beginnings to 1700. Yiddish developed as Jews moved into German-speaking territories in the course of the late first millennium CE and adapted the local language, as Jews had done in earlier migrations. Yiddish thus became the vernacular of *Ashkenaz and ultimately also a literary language that complemented *Hebrew literature over the course of a millennium. By the late Middle Ages, Yiddish literature spanned the same range of genres as did other European vernaculars of the period. Although a myth has grown over the centuries that Yiddish is "women's literature," because women rarely learned Hebrew, few of the genres discussed in this entry are inherently gender specific. In addition, there is clear evidence that the functional audience for early Yiddish literature comprised all of Yiddish-speaking Jewry, including the educated men who generally wrote, edited, published, distributed, sold, and indeed also bought and read early Yiddish books.

The earliest textual evidence of Yiddish appears in some thirty Yiddish glosses in *Rashi's *Bible and Talmud commentaries (see BIBLICAL COMMENTARIES), demonstrating the use of the language by Rashi (who had studied in the Rhineland) and his students. As the religious glossing tradition developed, so did *Bible translation, from fifteenth-century literal translations for students of Hebrew to seventeenth-century idiomatic versions for Yiddish readers. The *Tzene-rene* (Go Forth and Behold [Hanau, 1622]), a biblical paraphrase with traditional commentary, is the most influential book in the history of Yiddish and indeed Ashkenazic culture. It functioned as the Bible for male and female readers with little or no knowledge of Hebrew, appearing in more than two hundred editions over the course of four centuries. Beyond translation, poetic adaptations of biblical narratives and *midrashim* developed early in Yiddish, including dozens of texts from the earliest Yiddish anthology (Cairo *Genizah codex, 1382) to Moshe Esrim ve-Arba's *Shmuel-bukh* (Book of Samuel [Augsburg, 1544]), the great masterpiece of the tradition, combining both Jewish sacred and Germanic heroic traditions.

Although liturgy (see WORSHIP) remained strictly the domain of *Hebrew-*Aramaic, translations of the *prayer book appeared by the fifteenth century, making it comprehensible to those who knew little Hebrew. Yiddish also fulfilled important liturgical functions in domestic ritual: Bilingual *Passover hymns had appeared by the fifteenth century, and there were also many collections of *tkhines* (supplications) and *slikhes* (penitentials), the most important domains of Yiddish prayer. Similarly, although traditional legal textuality (*halakhah), like liturgy, remained staunchly Hebrew-Aramaic, Yiddish frequently appears as quoted testimony in rabbinical responses to legal queries (see RESPONSA).

Among the most important and statistically most widespread genres in Ashkenaz were writings that taught proper conduct according to locally defined usage, *minhogim* (Hebrew, *minhagim*; see CUSTOM), through books of customs and literature emphasizing proper morals and ethical behavior. Such *muser* (Hebrew, *musar*) writings, characterized by illustrative narratives, parables, and legends, include Isaac b. Eliakim of Posen's *Seyfer lev tov* (Book of the Good Heart) published in *Prague in 1620.

Because of its obvious Christian origin, it is quite remarkable to find the secular epic or romance among popular early Yiddish genres. *Dukus Horant* (Duke Horant [1382]), for example, narrates a typical royal bridal quest, whereas the fifteenth-century *Vidvilt* (As You Wish) is an Arthurian romance concerning Sir Gawain and his son; both are from German sources. The masterpieces of the genre are Elye Bokher (Elijah) Levita's rather conventional *Bovo d'Antona* (Bovo of Antona [1507]); and the consummate renaissance epic *Pariz un Viene* (Paris and Vienna [Verona, 1594]). These last two works are derived from Italian sources.

Although most narrative prose in Yiddish was translated from Hebrew, such as the popular quasi-historical *Yousifen* (*Josippon [Zurich, 1546]), there were also genuine original masterpieces among Yiddish compositions, such as the *Maase Briyo ve-Zimro* (Tale of Briyo and Zimro [ms., 1585]), a thriller of international intrigue and star-crossed lovers. The moral tale/ fable appeared in many forms, from an early lion fable (1382), to the often risqué *Ki-bukh* (Book of Cows [Verona, 1595]), to the masterful *Maase-Bukh* (Book of Tales [Basel, 1602]). An adaptive compilation of traditional Jewish and secular folktale sources and the period's most influential collection of tales, the *Maase-Bukh* was designed as a vernacular *aggadah* to teach ethical principles through pious exempla. The work by Glikl bas Leyb Pinkerle (*Glückel of Hameln; written 1691–1719) combines aspects of *muser, minhogim, maase*, historiography, and *memoir, giving profound insight into the period through the eyes of an intelligent and capable businesswoman. Additionally in prose there were treatises on hygiene, geography, accounting, mathematics, and medical practice (including magical charms and potions). The first Yiddish proto-newspaper *Dinstagishe-Fraytagishe Kurantn* (Tuesday-Friday Courier) appeared in 1686–87 in *Amsterdam, reporting on international events.

Jewish *theater arose from the holiday performance of *purimshpiln*. Although there is evidence for their prior existence, the earliest complete *Purim play extant is an *Akhashveyresh-shpil* (Ahasuerus-play [1697]), a bawdy burlesque based on the *Esther story. In the ensuing decades, Purim plays became sophisticated baroque dramas with orchestral accompaniment, branching out to include other biblical subjects. Yiddish drama did not venture beyond *purimshpiln* until the *Haskalah period, beginning in the eighteenth century.

Although early Yiddish literature did not possess a well-defined lyric genre, many lyric modes are present, the earliest of which is a rhymed blessing in the Worms *Maḥzor* (1272), followed by the aforementioned Passover hymns; rhymed penitential prayers, including *Torah songs (some composed by women); reflective philosophical poems such as Isaac Wallich's *memento mori* poem (ca. 1700); playful philosophical disputations, such as Zalmen Soyfer's debate between wine and water (1516); and biting Venetian satire, such as Elia Levita's "*Ha-mavdil lid*" (Ha-Mavdil Song [1514]), a drinking song of *yeshivah students ("*Pumay*" [Whoopee], ca. 1600), and a brief and hauntingly lyrical fourteenth- or fifteenth-century love song written on the fly-leaf of a Rashi manuscript ("*Vu zol ikh hin?*" [Where Should I Go?]).

Like other European literatures of the period, Yiddish also possessed historical narrative in poetic form, often commemorating recent events that affected the Jewish community, such as Elkhonon Hellen's *Megilas Vints* (Scroll of Vincent), on the Fettmilch insurrection in Frankfurt am Main in 1614–16 (Amsterdam, 1648); Joseph ben Eliezer Lipman Ashkenazi's *Kino al gezeyrous ha-kehilous de'k''k Ukraine* (Lament on the Destruction of the Ukrainian Communities [Prague, 1648]) on the *Chmelnitzki massacres; and Jacob Tousk's (Taussig) *Eyn sheyn nay lid fun meshiekh* (A Fine New Song about the Messiah [Amsterdam, 1666]), which expresses a pious believer's joy at *Shabbatai Zevi's supposed fulfillment of messianic prophecy. For further reading, see J. C. Frakes, ed., *Early Yiddish Texts, 1100–1750* (2004); and J. Baumgarten, *Introduction to Old Yiddish Literature*, rev. ed. (2005).

JEROLD C. FRAKES

Literature, Yiddish: 1800 to Twenty-First Century. Yiddish literature helped shape both the traditional culture and the gradual modernization of the Jews. Although some adherents of the Jewish Enlightenment (**Haskalah*) opposed the use of Yiddish, Yiddish authors contributed to education and secularization in several important ways. During the short period between 1860 and 1940, Yiddish literature recapitulated many aspects of European literary history and, at the same time, introduced Eastern European Jews to the modern world. Before its abrupt decline in the 1940s and 1950s, Yiddish was an influential medium of political and cultural activity.

Some of the earliest modern Yiddish writing arose among the **Hasidim and their antagonists, the **mitnaggedim*. Two forms of Hasidic writing made an especially deep impression: orally transmitted tales about Hasidic leaders, such as the **Baal Shem Tov, and stories told by the leaders themselves. The hagiographic collection *Shivhei ha-Besht* (In Praise of the Baal Shem Tov) appeared in Hebrew in 1815 and was soon followed by several popular Yiddish editions. In a very different mode, Nathan Sternharz published fantasy tales by his Hasidic master, R. **Nahman of Bratslav. When Nahman's *Sippurei ma`asiyot* was published in a bilingual Hebrew-Yiddish edition in 1815, it provided an important precedent for future Yiddish writing.

Other significant early-nineteenth-century Yiddish narratives, based on the writings of the German author J. H. Campe (d. 1818), were published by Haikl Hurwitz of Uman and by Mendel Lefin of Satanov. In 1817 Hurwitz, an enlightened acquaintance of Nahman of Bratslav and Nathan Sternharz, published a Yiddish translation of Campe's *Die Entdeckung von* Amerika (The Discovery of America). Lefin translated several of Campe's narratives of sea adventure, including a bilingual edition of *Onia so`ara* (Raging Ship; ca. 1815–20) in Hebrew and Yiddish. Influenced by the German Bible translations and commentaries of Moses **Mendelssohn and his followers, Lefin also translated the biblical book of **Proverbs into Yiddish (*Sefer mishlei Shlomo*; 1814); in so doing, he showed the inadequacy of the outmoded *Tsenerene*. In Tarnopol, Joseph Perl (1773–1839) founded a modern Jewish school and wrote powerful parodies of Hasidic writing in several Hebrew and Yiddish works. Most of his Yiddish writings were not published until the twentieth century, however, and his Yiddish translation of Fielding's *Tom Jones* remains in an unpublished manuscript. Although Perl was not known for his Yiddish texts and did not overtly contribute to the evolution of Yiddish style, his parodic Hebrew writing introduced an effective Yiddish-inflected Hebrew that, by caricaturing the Hebrew of Hasidic authors, surpassed the prevailing neobiblical style called *melitza*.

The beginnings of modern Yiddish fiction are usually traced to the Yiddish newspaper *Kol mevasser* (1862–73), a supplement to the Odessa-based Hebrew newspaper *Ha-Melitz* (see JOURNALISM: YIDDISH [EASTERN EUROPE]). In *Kol mevasser* of 1864–65, S. Y. Abramovich serialized his first Yiddish novel, *The Little Man*, creating his folksy persona

Mendele Mokher Seforim (Mendele the Bookseller; 1836–1917); the next year he printed *The Wishing-Ring* (first version, 1865). Previously known only as a young Hebrew-language essayist who had also written a Hebrew novella, Abramovich showed that it was possible to write serious and original fiction in Yiddish. In the subsequent decade he broke new ground with three seminal Yiddish novels: *Fishke the Lame* (first version, 1869), *The Nag* (1873), and *The Brief Travels of Benjamin the Third* (1878). In the spirit of Enlightenment literature, Abramovich used biting satire to attack the foibles of Jews (as well as Russians and Ukrainians, to a lesser extent) in the small towns of **Eastern Europe. After 1886 Abramovich revised and expanded his early fiction, sometimes dulling the satiric barbs, while making extensive contributions to Hebrew literature. H. N. **Bialik, who helped translate *Fishke the Lame* into Hebrew around 1900, proclaimed Abramovich "the creator of the *nusah*, the dominant style in the **Hebrew revival at the end of the nineteenth century.

Sholem Aleichem (the pen name of Solomon Rabinovitch; 1859–1916) was a self-proclaimed successor to S. Y. Abramovich, whom he dubbed "the grandfather." Sholem Aleichem began publishing stories and novels in Hebrew and Yiddish in the 1880s, and he strove to raise the general level of Yiddish writing by editing two volumes of *The Jewish Popular Library* (1888–89). He solicited Yiddish prose and poetry from the best living authors, including Abramovich, and he persuaded other Hebrew writers to try their hands at Yiddish.

In a mock trial of N. M. Shaykevitch called *Shomer's Trial* (1888), Sholem Aleichem attacked that author's trashy Yiddish works, which were then circulating widely. Among other criticisms, Sholem Aleichem accused Shomer of stealing his plots from contemporary French novels that were illsuited to Yiddish readers. In his own fiction, by contrast, Sholem Aleichem proved that it was possible to write Jewish novels that were not simply derivative of prior European authors. With his books *Stempeniu* and *Yosele the Nightingale* (1888–89), about a Jewish violinist and a Jewish singer, respectively, Sholem Aleichem presented a distinctive Jewish perspective in tsarist **Russia and provided a new impetus for Yiddish writing.

During his remarkably prolific career, Sholem Aleichem's greatest literary accomplishment may have been his creation and perfection of the genre of the oral-style Yiddish monologue. In dozens of original short stories written early in the twentieth century and later collected in the volumes *Monologues* and *Railroad Stories*, he showed that Yiddish was ideally suited to representing the diversity of male and female Jewish voices. His best-known creation is Tevye the Dairyman, a loquacious monologist who recounts sad episodes from his family life in a sequence of stories written between 1894 and 1916. Centering on Tevye's daughters' rebellion against his authority and the tradition of arranged **marriages, these tales aptly represent the decline of the traditional Jewish world and the rise of Jewish assimilation into western societies. Sholem Aleichem was the most popular Yiddish author in his own time, and he became a household name around the world after the appearance of the Broadway musical *Fiddler on the Roof* (1964) and its Hollywood film version (1971), based on his Tevye stories (see FILM, THEATER: UNITED STATES).

A contemporary rival of Sholem Aleichem was I. L. Peretz (1852–1915), the third "classic Yiddish author." Although he started writing in Hebrew during the 1870s, in 1888 he responded to Sholem Aleichem's call for submissions to *The Jewish Popular Library* and produced the ballad "Monish." Based in *Warsaw from 1889 until his death in 1915, Peretz excelled as a short-story writer in Yiddish and Hebrew. Unlike Abramovich and Sholem Aleichem, who were essentially nineteenth-century realist authors, Peretz was a Modernist who wrote for a somewhat more educated readership. He was influenced by contemporary Polish authors and in *"Der meshugener batlen"* (The Mad Talmudist; 1890) and "The Messenger," he experimented with the avant-garde literary forms of internal monologue and stream of consciousness.

Peretz influenced the neoromantic trend in modern Jewish culture by using Ḥasidic elements in a sequence of Yiddish and Hebrew stories published from 1889 to 1902. Although he initially had satiric intentions, gradually Peretz came to believe that the artistic revival of Ḥasidic traditions could help revive modern Jewish life. Even Martin *Buber was influenced by Peretz's neo-Ḥasidic stories, which led to his retellings of Ḥasidic tales in German from 1905 to 1908. The texts by Peretz and Buber introduced many western readers to the Ḥasidic world, albeit in portrayals that were sometimes distorted by sentimentalism. Toward the end of his life, striving to help rebuild traditional Jewish culture, Peretz turned to the popular genre of *folktales.

S. Ansky (also An-ski) the pseudonym of Solomon Rapoport (1863–1920), was an ethnographer and friend of I. L. Peretz. He extended the neoromantic movement into Yiddish theater with his play *The Dybbuk* (1916; first performed in 1919). Although the play was originally written in Russian for Stanislavski's Moscow Art Theater, it was subsequently translated into Hebrew by H. N. *Bialik and then into Yiddish by Ansky. *The Dybbuk*, which is infused with materials from Ḥasidic circles and from the author's ethnographic expeditions, quickly became a standard work in the repertoire of Yiddish and Hebrew theater troupes (see also *DYBBUK*).

Dovid Bergelson (1884–1952) was arguably the greatest twentieth-century Yiddish novelist. Living mainly in Kiev, he wrote a sequence of landmark novels that are at the aesthetic level of works by other leading European Modernists. Particularly memorable are his novels, *Arum vokzal* (At the Depot; 1909) and *Descent, Opgang* (Departing; 1920), and the novella *In a fargrebter shtot* (In a Backwoods Town; 1914). Bergelson's fiction is an outstanding instance of modernistic style, using dream sequences, internal monologues, nonlinear plots, and shifting narrative perspectives. At odds with more nostalgic portrayals, Bergelson conveys the gloom of the decaying *shtetl and suggests that, decades before the *Holocaust, the small Jewish towns of Eastern Europe were already doomed.

Lamed (Levi Joshua) Shapiro (1878–1948) was a fine prose stylist who described the final years of traditional European Jewish *yeshivah life in "Eating Days" and wrote searing portrayals of *antisemitism and *pogroms in stories like "White Challah" and "The Cross." Sholem Asch (1880–1957), like many other young Yiddish authors, was encouraged by I. L. Peretz in *Warsaw. In 1904, his portrayal of Jewish life in "The Shtetl" met with success. Asch achieved

notoriety when his play *God of Vengeance* (1907), set in a brothel, was performed, and his works were translated into Russian, Polish, German, and French. During World War II, he became the object of bitter criticism when he began publishing novels on Christian themes.

American Jewish writing had its origins in Yiddish works and in implicit translations from Yiddish. In the twentieth century Polish-born American Jews such as Yankev Glatshteyn (Jacob Glatstein; 1896–1971), A. Leyeles (Aaron Glanz; 1889–1966), and Y. L. Teller helped created modernistic Yiddish poetry. They called themselves "Introspectivists" (*Inzikhistn*) and wrote many memorable verses from 1919 until most of their prospective audience was eliminated by the *Nazi genocide, American assimilation, and Soviet repression. Other American Jewish authors such as Mary Antin (1881–1949) and Anzia Yezierska (ca. 1885–1970) explicitly or implicitly translated their earliest English works from Yiddish. The Yiddishized grammar of Yezierska's characters echoes in Henry Roth's (1905–1995) *Call It Sleep* (1934), Bernard Malamud's (1914–1986) *The Magic Barrel* (1958), and Grace Paley's "Goodbye and Good Luck" (in *The Little Disturbances of Man*, 1959; see LITERATURE: UNITED STATES; LITERATURE: WOMEN WRITERS [EUROPE AND NORTH AMERICA]).

Women writers have written many striking Yiddish poems and stories that express a distinctive perspective. For instance, Anna Margolin (pseudonym of Rosa Lebensboym, 1887–1952) was associated with the Introspectivists in New York and wrote beautiful lyrical poems such as "Slender Ships." Celia Dropkin (1888–1956) wrote poems and stories (e.g., "The Dancer") that were printed in leading publications. Kadya Molodowsky (1894–1975) published her first poetry under the influence of Dovid Bergelson and his circle (see POETRY, YIDDISH). Many other noteworthy Yiddish works by women authors, such as Fradel Schtok (1888–1952), Rachel Korn (1898–1982), Blume Lempel (1907–1999), Chava Rosenfarb (1923-2011), and Yente Serdatsky (1877–1962), are included in the volume *Found Treasures*. Irene Klepfisz (b. 1941) has achieved recognition for her innovative efforts to write poems on the border between English and Yiddish (*A Few Words in the Mother Tongue* [1991]).

Although the *Yishuv (see LITERATURE, YIDDISH: *Yishuv*) and Israel fostered Hebrew as the national language and did little to support Yiddish writing, a number of writers were active there in the twentieth century. Leading authors were Avraham Sutzkever (1913–2010), Leyb Rokhman (1918–1978), and Tsvi Kanar (1929–2009), notable for their Holocaust poetry and prose; Yosl Birshteyn (1920–2003), a humoristic author of *The Collector*; and the poets Rikuda Potash (1906–1965) and Lev Berinsky (b. ca. 1948).

In 1978 I. B. Singer (1904–1991), younger brother of the writer I. J. Singer (1893–1944), became the only Yiddish author to receive a Nobel Prize for Literature. After moving from Warsaw to *New York City in 1935, Singer began publishing widely in American Yiddish newspapers (see JOURNALISM: YIDDISH [NORTH AMERICA]). His breakthrough into English came when the story "Gimpel the Fool" was published in an outstanding translation by Saul Bellow and reprinted in the short-story collection, *Gimpel the Fool* (1957). Cynthia Ozick unforgettably satirized Singer's milieu of aging New York Yiddish writers in her story, "Envy; or,

Yiddish in America." With a thematic emphasis on sex and demons, Singer appealed to Americans' interest in what was perceived as an exotic foreign culture. Several of his works have been adapted to the stage and screen.

Since the Nazi genocide destroyed all of the European centers of Yiddish culture, the number of native speakers of Yiddish has dwindled, except among some *Ḥasidic communities. These Ultra-Orthodox (see JUDAISM, ORTHODOX) Jews seldom participate in secular literary culture, however, and they have produced few readers and writers of Yiddish literature. Nevertheless, a devoted group of secular Yiddishists continues to read, write, and speak about Yiddish literature. Courses on Yiddish language and literature are being taught at many universities around the world, and academic research is thriving. While Hebrew has been transformed from an ancient language into a language of everyday Israeli life, Yiddish literature is gradually being transformed from a part of Jewish popular culture into a classical literature (see also MEMOIR AND LIFE WRITING: YIDDISH; POETRY, YIDDISH; THEATER, YIDDISH).

Among recent translations are K. Frieden, ed., *Classic Yiddish Stories of S. Y. Abramovitsh, Sholem Aleichem, and I. L. Peretz* (2004); F. Forman et al., eds., *Found Treasures: Stories by Yiddish Women Writers* (1994); J. Neugroschel, ed., *No Star Too Beautiful: A Treasury of Yiddish Stories* (2004); R. Wisse, ed., *The I. L. Peretz Reader* (1990); L. Shapiro, ed., *The Cross and Other Jewish Stories* (2007); Sholem Aleichem, *Tevye the Dairyman and the Railroad Stories*, ed. Hillel Halkin (1987); and I. Howe and E. Greenberg, eds., *A Treasury of Yiddish Stories*, 2nd ed. (1990). Critical studies include K. Frieden, *Classic Yiddish Fiction: Abramovitsh, Sholem Aleichem, and Peretz* (1995); B. Harshav, *The Meaning of Yiddish* (1990); D. Miron, *A Traveler Disguised: The Rise of Modern Yiddish Fiction in the Nineteenth Century*, 2nd ed. (1996); idem, *The Image of the Shtetl and Other Studies of Modern Jewish Literary Imagination* (2000); N. Seidman, *A Marriage Made in Heaven: The Sexual Politics of Hebrew and Yiddish* (1997); and R. Wisse, *I. L. Peretz and the Making of Modern Jewish Culture* (1991).

KEN FRIEDEN

Literature, Yiddish: The *Yishuv*. Until the early twentieth century Yiddish literature in *Palestine was confined to religious works; in the 1920s, however, increasing numbers of immigrants from *Eastern Europe caused a major shift. Although *Zionist ideology proscribed Yiddish and its culture as epitomizing exilic existence, Yiddish writers who had been active in Europe continued writing in the *Yishuv, the Jewish community in Palestine – both for immigrants eager for materials in their native language and for a worldwide Yiddish audience. Some of these writers, many of whom followed Modernist trends, expressed views of Palestinian life that diverged from the Zionist mainstream ideal, perhaps empowered by writing in the forbidden language.

Between 1928 and 1946, the Yiddish Writers' and Journalists' Club in Palestine published twenty-six literary magazines featuring fiction, poetry, cultural criticism, and reviews. There is no information about the distribution of these magazines, yet their continued appearance is indicative of an ongoing demand. Numerous collections of locally written poetry and prose also appeared, both in Palestine and elsewhere. Because the Palestinian Yiddish writers were intimately connected with the European Yiddish culture of

their native lands, the *Holocaust and its effects became an increasing theme in their work as information about its scope emerged.

Prose writers include Zalmen Brokhes (1886–1977), who published stories of Palestinian life starting in 1910, as well as two collections of prose (1918, 1937). Implicit criticism of Zionist ideology underlies much of Brokhes' fiction, which often deals with the complex emotional dilemmas of rootless characters unaffiliated with any ideology who have come to their traditional homeland, yet feel estranged from it and from fellow Jews. Some of his stories are nuanced by an idealized orientalism, as they address problematics of identity; thus, Jewish characters admire those who have assimilated into the native Arab population and are hardly recognizable as Jews. The work of Avrom Rivess (1900–1963) appeared in most of the Yiddish magazines and was partly collected in a 1947 volume. Rivess deployed Expressionist techniques in his reevaluations of the idealized paradigm of the Zionist pioneer. Although a socialist like most other contemporaneous Palestinian Zionist writers, he lived in the developing city of *Tel Aviv and was concerned with urban issues. The Jewish characters whom Rivess describes struggle with themselves and the alien landscape, expressing doubt and dissatisfaction with the realization of the Zionist ideal. He also presents an unusual perspective on the Zionist project through the eyes of non-Jewish characters, such as a native Arab and an antisemitic Pole. Samuel Izban (1905–1995), who lived in Palestine between 1920 and 1938, published two volumes of Palestinian stories (1936, 1942). He depicted the effects of modernization on Palestinian Jews and on Jewish experiences in different areas of Palestine during the violent period of the Arab revolt (1936–39). Among his topics are the manifestations of middle-class European life that immigrants transplanted to Tel Aviv, the unique culture of Jewish minorities from Arabic-speaking countries, and the tiny group of *Karaite Jews in the Old City of *Jerusalem.

Most Yiddish poets active in Palestine expressed the mainstream socialist *Zionism ideology, although some were preoccupied with private issues. The most prominent was Aryeh Shamri (1907–1978), whose pre-1948 poetry expresses the inner conflicts experienced by many young Zionists who left their homes in Europe while also extolling the virtues and joys of *kibbutz life. Shamri published two volumes of poems before 1948 and edited collections of Yiddish writing. His major work, the long narrative poem "*Leyzer Tsipress*" (1936), charts the progress of a young pioneer who finds solace for his homesickness in the creation of a new kibbutz. The prolific poet Yosef Papiernikov (1899–1993), who published six collections of poetry between 1927 and 1947, wrote lyrical and political poetry anchored in Zionist idealism. Starting in 1937, his work addressed the rise of *Nazism and the Holocaust, linking the tragic events in Europe with the young Zionists who had left their families behind to create a new homeland. The poet and prose writer Rikuda Potash (1906–1965), author of two volumes of poetry (1951, 1960), began publishing in *Poland and continued to write Yiddish poetry and short prose in Palestine. Her idiosyncratic poetry is highly lyrical and incorporates ancient and modern Middle Eastern and European themes, combining allusions to prehistoric cave art with references to Modernist painters such as Marc Chagall and Chaim Soutine (see ART, EUROPE: TWENTIETH CENTURY). Her poems offer biblical rereadings that foreground characters that the *Bible portrays as minor or negative. Her work, like that of the other Yiddish writers in Palestine, offers a range of perspectives on the evolving Zionist community and the transplantation and transformation of Eastern European Jewish culture (see POETRY, YIDDISH).

For further reading, see Y. Chaver, *What Must Be Forgotten: The Survival of Yiddish in Zionist Palestine* (2004); and N. Seidman, *A Marriage Made in Heaven: The Sexual Politics of Hebrew and Yiddish* (1997); **see also LITERATURE, YIDDISH: FROM 1800**.

YAEL CHAVER

Lithuania: See BALTIC STATES; POLAND; COUNCIL OF FOUR LANDS AND COUNCIL OF LITHUANIA

Liturgy: See PRAYER; WORSHIP

Los Angeles, on the southern California coast, is home to the second largest Jewish population in the *United States after *New York City. Spread over a large metropolitan area, Los Angeles originated as a small satellite of Gold Rush *San Francisco. In the city's early decades, Jews, mainly from *Central Europe, along with native-born *Sephardim, helped establish urban life as merchants, bankers, and civic leaders; Emil Harris served as the city's police chief in the late 1870s. Families observed the *Sabbath and *festivals in their homes and formed associations. The Hebrew Benevolent Society, founded in 1854, established a cemetery and a traditional congregation. Using funds largely raised by the community's women, they constructed the long-lived B'nai B'rith congregation (now Wilshire Boulevard Temple).

By national standards, Los Angeles's Jewish community developed late; in 1900 the Jewish community numbered just 2,500. However, soon after the 1906 San Francisco earthquake and fire, the center of western Jewish life shifted to Los Angeles. From 1907 to 1927, during a time of peak Jewish migration, San Francisco's Jewish population rose by only 5,000, whereas Los Angeles saw 58,000 new Jewish settlers. New railroad routes, water sources, and the discovery of oil helped make growth viable. Attracted by the city's boosterism, mild climate, and economic potential, Jews of East European origin, including immigrants, eastern migrants, and those born in California moved to Los Angeles to work in the new movie industry (see FILM: UNITED STATES), start related businesses, and heal from illness. To provide for this "health rush," Jews established the City of Hope hospital for tuberculosis care in 1912.

During the 1920s Jewish organizations multiplied as Jewish life spread from the downtown area to new centers, especially in multiethnic Boyle Heights, where 80,000 Jews supported the Orthodox Breed Street Shul, as well as the Hebrew Sheltering Society, Talmud Torah, Modern Social Center, and the Kaspare Cohn Hospital (later part of Cedars-Sinai Medical Center). Nearby City Terrace became home to Yiddish secularists. Jews of Sephardic origin consecrated their first Los Angeles synagogue in 1932.

After *World War II booming industries, real estate development, and new universities brought Jewish veterans. As Los Angeles grew by leaps and bounds, Jews settled near Fairfax, in the western part of the city, and in its valleys. This increasing population, 519,000 by 1999, stimulated the growth of Jewish *community centers; Orthodox, Conservative, and Reform congregations (see JUDAISM entries);

a western branch of *Hebrew Union College, the University of Judaism (now the American Jewish University); the Skirball Jewish Center; the Museum of Tolerance; and the Brandeis-Bardin Institute. In recent years significant Persian and Israeli communities have increased the city's Jewish diversity and pushed the Jewish population toward 600,000.

For further reading, see E. Eisenberg, A. Kahn, and W. Toll, *Jews of the Pacific Coast: Reinventing Community on America's Edge* (2010); A. Kahn and M. Dollinger, *California Jews* (2004); and M. Vorspan and L. P. Gartner, *History of the Jews of Los Angeles* (1970); **see also UNITED STATES, WESTERN**.

AVA FRAN KAHN

Love. Teachings on human and divine love abound in Jewish sources. From the *Bible to the present, prophets, poets, and philosophers have contemplated love's virtues and perils. Perspectives and approaches include the romantic, *mystical, intellectual, and pragmatic. Love is understood in the Bible and the *Talmud not only as emotion but also as action benefiting the self and others. Human and divine love are both sometimes conceived as intense yearnings that cannot be fulfilled.

The Hebrew noun for love, *ahavah,* and the verb *ahv* occur more than two hundred times in biblical narratives and poetry, marking it as a primary and recurring motif in interhuman and human–divine relationships. Unlike Greek (and Christian) terms that distinguish between spiritual (*agape*) and physical (*eros*) love, *ahavah* ranges in meaning from the sensuous to the spiritual, conveying notions of attachment, passion, affection, preference, loyalty, and yearning. Whereas other biblical nouns and verbs refer to a particular type of love, such as *hesed,* which often designates kindness and loyalty, or *heshek,* which denotes desire or passion, the verbal root *ahv* is used in a wide variety of social, political, and spiritual contexts.

Biblical stories, poetry (see BIBLE: POETRY), and *commandments (*mitzvot*) address parental love, romantic love, marital love, friendship, love of neighbor, and love of *God. The first use of *ahv* refers to *Abraham's love for *Isaac when God commands Abraham to sacrifice his beloved son (Gen 22:2). Similar examples of parental love include *Jacob's love for *Joseph (Gen 37:3, 44:20), Isaac's love for *Esau, and *Rebekah's love for Jacob (Gen 25:28). The active participle *ohev* (literally "lover") signifies a deep bond of friendship. A primary example is the relationship between *David and Jonathan (2 Sam 1:26). In *Proverbs 18:24, a friend is called *ohev* and is praised as "more devoted than a brother."

Episodes of a man's passionate love for a woman often have tragic consequences. An example is David's attraction to *Bathsheba, which ends with David's orchestration of her husband's death. Another case is the revenge against a lover turned rapist, as in Amnon's love for his half-sister *Tamar; this love is turned into hate and results in Amnon's murder at the hands of Tamar's brother Absalom (2 Sam 2:8–4:12, 9–20; 1 Kgs 1–2). In most cases of marital love, men are depicted in the active role of lover, whereas women are described in passive terms as being loved. Exceptions include, "And Rebecca loved Jacob" (Gen 25:28) and "And Michal, daughter of Saul, loved him [David]" (1 Sam 18:28).

A prominent use of *ahv* is in the *mitzvot (commandments) to love God, the neighbor, and the stranger. All three commandments use the verbal form *ve-ahavta* ("and you shall love"). According to a number of medieval Jewish *Bible commentaries, *ahv* signifies not only an emotion but also action. This observation stems from the fact that the verb is followed by the preposition *le* ("for" or "to"); literally, you shall love to your neighbor as yourself. This commandment implies an action and could be articulated as "Do for your neighbor as you would do for yourself." Some commentaries suggest that loving our neighbor as ourselves is an ideal to strive for. The ideal is articulated as a sincere, unlimited concern for the well-being of others. Other interpretations emphasize that because this directive is listed among the commandments called *kedoshim* or "sanctified acts" (Lev 19–20), it must be expressed in concrete acts. The *Mishneh Torah* of Moses *Maimonides enumerates several examples of neighborly love, including visiting the sick, comforting mourners, joining a funeral procession, and providing a *bride and groom with all their needs.

Perhaps the most frequent context of love in the Bible is the intimate relationship between God and Israel. According to Deuteronomy 7:7–8, it is because of God's love (*meh-ahavat*) and the divine oath sworn "to your fathers" that God redeemed Israel from slavery. Divine love for Israel is dependent on Israel's love for God, which is seen as a religious obligation (Deut 10:12). This motif of reciprocal love appears in the range of interpretations of *Song of Songs. This biblical book is at once a celebration of human sexual love and, according to rabbinic and philosophic allegorical interpretations, an expression of the love between Israel and God. The eight chapters are permeated with depictions of the physical beauty of the lovers and of the Land of Israel. The mood and tone of the poems that comprise the Song of Songs exude erotic desire for union and consummation. The noun *ahava* and related verbs occur seventeen times in the Song, and numerous other verbs and nouns are used to convey the dynamics of the couple's mutual desire and love.

In Song of Songs, the woman's voice is prominent; this contrasts with other biblical books in which explicit references to women's desires are rare. The pain of separation is particularly acute for the woman, who refers to herself as "love sick" (2:5).

The last chapter contains one of the most profound reflections about the power of love in the history of literature: "Love is strong as death.... Many waters cannot quench love, neither can the floods drown it; if a man would give all the wealth of his house for love, he would be utterly scorned" (8:6–7).

Evaluating notions of love in talmudic writings yields an abundance of positions and perspectives that range from *halakhic discussions on fulfilling one's marital sexual obligation to meditations on love of neighbor and love of God. Among the numerous rabbinic personalities, the life and thought of the second-century-CE sage and martyr *Akiva stand out as a remarkable tribute to the exalted powers of human and divine love. Midrashic traditions about his marriage to Rachel, their mutual devotion, and his views of marriage are exemplary of the wisdom of love. He taught that "love thy neighbor as thyself" is the greatest principle in the Torah (*Sifra, Kedoshim* 2) because it is predicated on love of oneself, which provides a foundation for love of others. He also held that love between man and woman represents the highest level of holiness and that marital

harmony evokes the presence of the *Shekhinah* (divine presence). Thus, he taught that one must not marry without love, not only because of the likelihood that the marriage would fail but also because of the potential risk of hating a spouse, a fellow human being. Akiva implied that human love is a manifestation of divine love and that the Song of Songs is simultaneously a celebration of romantic love and a celebration of the special love of Israel and God. Thus, he argued for the inclusion of the Song of Songs in the Bible: "For the entire world was not worthy as the day on which the Song of Songs was given to Israel, for all of scripture is holy, and the Song of Songs is holy of holies!" (M. *Yadayim* 3:5).

The *Zohar*, the principal work of Jewish mystical theosophy, conceives of love and desire in terms of the individual, the community of Israel, and the unity within the godhead. On the one hand, loving God is the responsibility of the soul. As a particle of the divine, the soul seeks reunion with God. The righteous soul after death is depicted in God's "palace of love" where God fondles and caresses her, "even as a father treats his beloved daughter." Additionally, the *Zohar*'s description of the love between Israel and God is expressed within the erotic language of the Song of Songs. Furthermore, the *Zohar* conceives of the cosmic rupture that occurred within God as a separation between God and His creation, and between the "upper worlds" and "lower worlds." The birth of human souls is the result of God's joining with the *Shekhinah* (the feminine principle of the divinity representing God's immanence); this process provides a rationale for procreation, because the sexual union below affects the state of the upper worlds by bringing harmony to the male and female aspects of the divine. One who does not engage in procreation "diminishes the image that comprises all images" (*Zohar* I, 13a). Therefore, marital sexual union has cosmic redemptive value reflecting the union between God and the *Shekhinah*, or the upper and lower worlds, which is the reintegration of primordial unity.

The theme of love, especially love of God, pervades medieval Jewish *thought. Love of God is a religious duty, based on the commandment, "And thou shalt love the Lord thy God with all thy heart and with all thy soul and with all thy might" (Deut 6:5). According to Jewish philosophers such as *Saadia Gaon, Solomon *ibn Gabirol, *Baḥia ibn Pakuda, Abraham *ibn Ezra, and *Maimonides, love of God should be a rational love achieved by contemplation and studying philosophy and the sciences. In the tradition of Aristotle, philosophers such as Maimonides envisioned an intellectual love of God. Such love leads to the eternal life of the soul, because the eternity of the soul depends on the achievement of rational perfection. In contrast, thinkers such as Judah *Halevi rejected the rationalist approach as too sterile and instead insisted on the experience of faith, which creates an intimacy with the divine that leads to the overflow of love for God.

In the modern and contemporary period, the discourse of love of God is found most profoundly in the writings of *Ḥasidic masters. According to Shneur *Zalman of Liady (1745–1812), love is the inclination of the entire self and being toward the other. Love is "the cleaving of spirit unto spirit ... manifesting in all parts of the soul: the intellect and emotions, as well as their modes of expression: thought, speech, and action. All of these are cloven unto the beloved." The Ḥasidic masters elevated the experience of mystical love of God as the most sublime human experience by fusing mystical contemplation with daily prayer. They described and prescribed stages whereby the Ḥasid moves from the heart to the intellect in yearning for God until reaching a stage of transcendence: "There are times when the love of God burns so powerfully within your heart that…it is not yourself who speak[s]; rather it is through you that the words are spoken" (Green and Holtz, 62).

Franz *Rosenzweig theorized about love as a central theological motif in *The Star of Redemption*, in which he conceptualized *revelation – the encounter of the human and the divine – as the outpouring of divine love upon the soul. Using the Song of Songs as a template for conceiving the dialogical moment of God and the human soul, Rosenzweig claims, "It is not enough that God's relationship to man is explained by the simile of the lover and the beloved. God's word must contain the relationship of lover to beloved directly…and so we find it in the Song of Songs" (trans. W. W. Hallo [1971], 199). Love and speech become interchangeable in Rosenzweig's *midrashic interpretation of the Song, underscoring the erotic and dialogical nature of love. The intimacy and presentness of love in revelation transform the self to a compassionate posture toward the other, which is manifested as love of neighbor. The boundaries between the erotic and the spiritual, the human and the divine, blur in the face of the fecundity of love.

For further reading, see A. and C. Bloch, *The Song of Songs: A New Translation* (1995); M. Goshen-Gottstein, "Abraham – Lover or Beloved of God," in *Love and Death in the Ancient Near East: Essays in Honor of Marvin H. Pope*, ed. J. H. Marks and R. M. Good (1987), 101–04; A. Green and B. Holtz, eds., *Your Word Is Fire: The Hasidic Masters on Contemplative Prayer* (1987); L. Jacobs, "The Love of God," in idem, *A Jewish Theology* (1973); Y. Muffs, *Love and Joy: Law, Language, and Religion in Ancient Israel* (1992); J. Van Seters, "Love and Death in the Court History of David," in *Love and Death in the Ancient Near East*, ed. J. H. Marks and R. M. Good (1987), 121–24.

YUDIT KORNBERG GREENBERG

Luria, Isaac (1534–1572) was the greatest mystic in the kabbalist center of sixteenth-century *Safed. Known by his acronym *ha-Ari* ("the lion"; usually said to stand for "Our Master Rabbi Isaac," but often read as "the Divine Rabbi Isaac"), Luria was born in *Jerusalem in 1534; after his father's death, his mother brought him to her brother's house in *Egypt where he grew up. He settled in Safed in 1570, only two years before his death, where a small group of disciples congregated around him. Knowledge is incomplete concerning his life before that. It seems that he studied *Talmud and *halakhah under several teachers, most notably David ben Zimra and Bezalel Ashkenazi, and became known as a master of legal studies; he made his living in commerce. He married his uncle's daughter in Egypt and had several children. Many legends surround his early studies in *Kabbalah, some of which may have a basis in fact; certainly he wrote a commentary on a section of the *Zohar, influenced by the teachings of Moses *Cordovero. His arrival in Safed was seen as particularly meaningful. He may have studied for a time with Cordovero, who died in 1570.

When Luria died in a plague, one of his disciples eulogized him in the traditional manner, without expressing anything exceptional concerning his personality or teachings. The first document that presents him as a great teacher and revealer of mystical secrets is the agreement, prepared by his main disciple, Ḥayyim Vital (d. 1620), and signed by several disciples, in which they undertake not to study or transcribe Lurianic teachings in Vital's absence and to keep these teachings secret. Several years later, legends concerning Luria's great spiritual powers began to spread in Safed, and some versions of his teachings began to be known, especially in Italy; they were spread by Israel Saruk (or Sarug), who presented himself as a disciple of Luria. A group of letters written by a visitor from Poland, Shlomo Shlumil of Dreznitz, between 1609 and 1615, are the first presentation of Lurianic legends; these had an almost immediate impact in Europe. Three of them were printed as a separate treatise, known as *Shivḥei ha-Ari* (Praises of the Ari). Later, a hagiographical work, *Toledot ha-Ari* (History of the Ari), was assembled, including much miraculous material.

During the first thirty or forty years after his death, three of his disciples wrote down versions of his teachings: Ḥayyim Vital, in several volumes and editions; Joseph ibn Tabul (only a few remnants of his version remain, mostly within the Vital corpus); and Moshe Yona, whose version was discovered only recently. The relationships among these four versions (including Saruk's) has not yet been analyzed in a comprehensive, satisfactory way. Luria himself wrote only a few pages that survived, adding very little to the understanding of the core of his teachings.

According to a tradition preserved by his disciples, Luria claimed that when he tried to put his ideas on paper they would come in a rush like a great river and could not be recorded. There can be little doubt that his disciples heavily edited the extant texts. In the authentic layer of the Lurianic hagiography, he is presented as possessing unusual spiritual power that enabled him to see into the souls of people, recognize their sins, and predict their future behavior. He could identify the various parts of every soul and its previous wonderings in other bodies in previous generations. In his *Sefer ha-Ḥezyonot* (Book of Visions), Vital preserved his teacher's detailed description of the history of Vital's soul (which, Vital believed, was the soul of the *messiah). It seems that Luria told several of his disciples such histories of their souls, fragments of which are preserved in Vital's works on the subject of *gilgul* (transmigration of souls), an important aspect of the Lurianic worldview. For further reading, see L. Fine, *Physician of the Soul, Healer of the Cosmos: Isaac Luria and his Kabbalistic Fellowship* (2003); **see also KABBALAH, LURIANIC.**

JOSEPH DAN

Luzzatto, Moses Ḥayyim (1707–1747) was a messianic leader, playwright, *mystic, and ethical writer. Luzzato, who grew up in Padua, *Italy, was deeply immersed in the culture of his time; its influence is reflected in his poetry and especially his Hebrew plays, like *Migdal Oz* (The Fortress) and *La-Yesharim Tehillah* (Glory to the Righteous), written in the fashionable Italian allegorical manner. Several scholars designate Luzzatto as the first writer of Modern Hebrew literature, two generations before the emergence of the *Berlin school of Hebrew *Haskalah* (enlightenment) writers. In his youth, he also wrote *Leshon Limudim* (The Learned Tongue), a manual of rhetoric.

Luzzatto established a secret society that soon turned into a mystical-messianic sect. He claimed that a *maggid*, a messenger from the divine world, appeared to him in 1727, transmitting secrets, directing his actions, and instructing him in the composition of a new, messianic version of the *Zohar, reflecting the arrival of the messianic age. He believed that he was the new *Moses, the final redeemer, the supreme *messiah, and his friend and disciple, Rabbi David Valle, was the messiah, son of David. *Shabbatai Zevi, the failed messiah, was the messiah, son of Joseph. In 1731 Luzzatto married a woman named Zipporah (like the biblical Moses) and wrote a commentary on his own marriage contract portraying the marriage as the culmination of the messianic process.

Luzzatto's messianic activities aroused opposition, and he was ordered by rabbinic courts to stop publishing and preaching. He left Italy and settled in *Amsterdam in 1735, where he wrote several ethical treatises, among them *Messilat Yesharim* (The Path of the Righteous), the most popular and influential modern Jewish work in this genre. In 1743 he traveled to the Land of *Israel and settled in Acre (Acco), where he and his family perished in a plague in 1747. Despite the controversy surrounding him, his kabbalistic and ethical works had a profound influence on the modern movements of *Hasidism, as well as on the nineteenth-century *tenuat ha-musar* (*Musar* Movement) in *Eastern Europe. For further reading, see S. Ginzburg, *The Life and Works of Moses Hayyim Luzzatto* (1931).   JOSEPH DAN

Luzzatto, Samuel David (1800–1865), philologist, *Bible commentator (see BIBLICAL COMMENTARIES), prolific writer, translator, and *Haskalah* figure in *Italy, was often known by the acronym Shadal (or Shedal). Born in Trieste, Luzzatto displayed precocious critical faculties; even as a young boy he called attention to deficiencies in commentaries on the book of *Job. His early intellectual contributions included a Hebrew grammar in Italian and a translation of the life of Aesop into Hebrew; he also translated both the *Ashkenazic prayer book (1821–22) and the Italian rite (1829) into Italian. By age thirteen, Luzzatto had withdrawn from school to help support his family, returning only to attend lectures on *Talmud given by Abraham Eliezer ha-Levi, Chief Rabbi of Trieste. In 1829, Luzzatto was appointed professor at the rabbinical college of Padua, established in that same year by the Jewish communities of Lombardy-Venetia, where he taught Bible, philology, and Jewish *thought and history. He wrote both biblical commentaries and grammatical works on the Hebrew language, and he translated a number of biblical books into Italian; he also delivered a series of lectures on aspects of Jewish theology that were published in Italian. An admired Hebrew poet himself, Luzzato published editions of the poems of Judah *Halevi , with whose approach to Judaism he had considerable sympathy, as well as an influential anthology of medieval Hebrew *poetry (*Tal Orot*, 1881).

Luzzatto was a strong opponent of philosophical approaches to Judaism, and he also held negative views of Jewish *mysticism. Instead of rationalizing or spiritualizing the *commandments, he developed a positive system of Jewish life and practice grounded in *revelation, tradition, and the *election of Israel. He believed that Hebrew language and literature developed and enhanced the Jewish spirit. In a prolific literary career that spanned more than fifty years, he wrote in both Hebrew and Italian and left behind a voluminous correspondence; many of his writings still remain uncollected, and others are unpublished. Eighty-nine of Luzzato's letters, essentially treatises addressing liturgical, bibliographical, exegetical, grammatical, historical, philosophical, and theological themes, are collected in *Peninei Shedal* (The Pearls of Samuel David Luzzatto), published by his sons in 1883.   LISA RUBENSTEIN CALEVI

Maccabees, Books of are four works of Jewish historiography included in the *Septuagint. Although all four are in the Greek Orthodox canon and the first two are in the Catholic canon, Protestants relegate all four to the *Apocrypha. Because Jewish tradition ascribes them no significance at all, it has not preserved them. 1 Maccabees, originally written in *Hebrew, recounts the history of the *Hasmoneans from the beginnings of their rebellion against the *Seleucids in 168/7 BCE to the successful establishment of the dynasty. The books focuses first (ch. 2) on the founder of the dynasty, Mattathias, and then, successively, on each of his sons – Judah Maccabee (chs. 3–9), Jonathan (chs. 9–12), and Simon (chs. 13–16) – until Simon was succeeded by his own son, John Hyrcanus (ch. 16). The book, probably written in the late second century BCE, should be understood as a dynastic history justifying the new line of rulers. In contrast, 2 Maccabees, originally written in Greek, focuses on the history of *Jerusalem in the 170s and 160s. Despite the fact that it often overlaps 1 Maccabees, it is a work of the *Diaspora (originally based on a longer history by one Jason of Cyrene [2:23]) and, accordingly, much more religiously oriented. After first establishing that Gentile kings are generally benevolent to the Jews (ch. 3), it emphasizes the sinful nature of Jewish Hellenizing (ch. 4) and presents Antiochus Epiphanes' attack on Jerusalem and persecution of Judaism as a result of God's chastisements (chs. 5–6, following the theology of Deut 32). In this context, the book offers, in chapters 6 and 7, famous scenes of torture and *martyrdom that brought about *atonement and reconciled God with His people, thereby allowing for the victories of Judah Maccabee (chs. 8–15). The book is prefaced by two epistles sent by the Jews of Judea to those of *Egypt, asking them to participate in the celebration of the *Ḥanukkah festival in memory of the rededication of the *Temple; the dates in the first of these letters indicate that the book was written in the mid-to-late second century BCE. The title of 3 Maccabees is a misnomer, for the book has nothing to do with the Maccabees and little to do with the Land of Israel. Rather, the book reports a conflict between the Jews of Egypt and King *Ptolemy IV Philopator (221–205 BCE), who, after his failed attempt to enter the Jerusalem Temple (chs. 1–2), took his wrath out on the Jews of Egypt and attempted to annihilate them. Just in the nick of time, divine intervention foiled his attempt to have the Jews trampled by drunken elephants (ch. 6). This led to the king's repentance and the establishment of a festival (ch. 7), which the book was evidently meant to explain. In many ways, the book is reminiscent of *Esther. Written in Greek in the first century CE or later, 4 Maccabees is basically a philosophical treatise that uses the martyrdom stories of 2 Maccabees to establish the thesis that "devout reason is sovereign over the emotions."   Daniel R. Schwartz

Maghreb: See NORTH AFRICA

Magic refers to actions and rituals intended to transform reality for particular purposes. Magical behavior within a Jewish context, whether involving written incantations, talismanic objects, or specific actions, generally took place outside the ordained "official" realm of worship and practice. It is certainly the case that a range of activities that have magical intentions have always been a part of popular Jewish culture, despite the condemnation of magical practices in the *Bible and *rabbinic literature.

MAGIC IN THE HEBREW BIBLE: Although *Deuteronomy 18:10 forbids sorcery and divination, many biblical rituals and actions have magical elements. These include magical procedures related to agriculture, as in *Genesis 30:37–43 where *Jacob practices a type of talismanic breeding with goats, and the ritual trial of the woman accused of adultery (*sotah*) in *Numbers 5:11–31. The Bible portrays foreign sorcerers and Israelite *prophets who have magical powers, but their special abilities are generally understood to be subject to God's will. Thus, *Moses' "miracles" performed in contest with Pharaoh's magicians in *Exodus 7:8–12 derive from *God, and *Balaam's intended curses of the Israelites in the wilderness are turned into blessings through divine intervention (Num 23–24). The account of the witch of Endor in 1 *Samuel 28–3-25, who brings up the shade of the dead Samuel from Sheol at *Saul's request, preserves an obvious belief that the dead may be recalled to the land of the living but also makes clear that doing so is forbidden. A series of stories connected with the prophet *Elisha (2 Kgs 4:2–6, 16–17, 29–35, 38–41; 5:13–14, 25–27; 6:6) describe events that might be termed magical or miraculous.

SECOND TEMPLE AND RABBINIC SOURCES: *Second Temple era and rabbinic texts on magical themes discuss the transmission of magic from God through angels to humankind. These traditions also associate sorcery with traditions brought down by angels gone bad and with the introduction of technology (e.g., 1 Enoch 8:3). The book of Tobit, found in the *Apocrypha, has a number of magical elements, including a malevolent demon and the healing powers of the angel Raphael. Although significant Second Temple material remnants of magical praxis are lacking, numerous written traditions describe *Solomon as a wise magician who had control of demons and who used verbal remedies for healing and exorcism, who had mastered the "Book of Remedies" of *Hezekiah (since secreted away), and who created new modalities of magical/medical healing (*Josephus, *Antiquities* 8.2.5 §§45–49; Testament of Solomon). The *pseudepigraphical Testament of Solomon serves as a fundamental treatise on Jewish demonology. Recent scholarship on Second Temple Judaism indicates that invoking the divine "Name of Power" and appeals to specific angels who assist the magician were central elements of magic rituals. A major theme of this magic tradition is healing. In *Sefer ha-Razim* (The Book of Secrets), dated by most scholars to the later talmudic period or early medieval times (sixth to ninth centuries), magical knowledge is said to have been transmitted by the angel Raphael to Noah in the antediluvian period.

Rabbinic traditions indicate that magic could be performed by men of learning, piety, and virtue (BT *Sanhedrin* 65a–67b). This magic is not seen to be in contradiction to monotheism because it derives from *God and is divinely transmitted to Jewish holy men. Thus, in general, rabbinic literature accentuates the numinous magical power of priestly ornaments and the staff of *Moses (*Mekhilta, Beshallah*, ed. Weiss, 4.60; *Pirke de Rabbi Eliezer* 40; *Sefer ha-Yashar; Yalkut*, Exodus 168), and the *Talmud preserves stories about holy men who were able to invoke the "Name of Power" – that is, the Tetragrammaton – to heal allies and insiders or kill or wound enemies of Israel. *Torah scholars were said to be able to destroy ideological opponents of the Jews with one flash of an angry gaze (BT *Shabbat* 34a; BT *Bava Batra* 75a). Rabbis are described as fighting heretics and witches, not with rational arguments, but with spells and visual energy; an example is the tale of Simon ben Shetah and the witches of Ashkelon in JT *Hagigah* 2.2 (77d–78a) and the parallel story in JT *Sanhedrin* 6.9 (23c).

However, rabbinic literature also maintains a negative view of magical actions because they may "contradict (or damage) the heavenly hosts" (BT *Sanhedrin* 67b; *Hullin* 7b). Like the mixing of species (*kilayim*) or sex between humans and animals, witchcraft or sorcery destroys the cosmic fabric of energy, injuring God, as it were, and negatively affecting the world's balance. Thus, magicians are feared because they dangerously mix that which should remain separate, physically and metaphysically. The Rabbis in the Talmud discussed the prohibition, "One shall not allow a witch to live" (Exod 22:17), in the context of capital crimes and believed that men as well as women can be tried for sorcery.

Nevertheless, in rabbinical literature, women are particularly associated with witchcraft. Although the Rabbis took for granted that both men and women had the potential to manipulate the powerful forces operative in the cosmos by reciting efficacious spells, they assumed that only a few men dabbled in such activities. Moreover, the Rabbis connected women's supposed predilection for conjuration with the sexual unreliability and untrustworthiness that they also projected onto females. A statement attributed to the first-century-CE sage Hillel in M. *Avot* 2:7 warns, among other things, that "the more wives, the more witchcraft"; BT *Sanhedrin* 67a remarks that "most women are involved in witchcraft," and BT *'Eruvin* 64b notes in passing that present generations of the daughters of Israel indulge freely in witchcraft; BT *Pesahim* 111a warns, "When two women sit at a crossroad, one on one side of the road, and one on the other side of the road, facing each other, they are certainly engaged in witchcraft," and provides a spell that a male traveler can use for protection against them. BT *Gittin* 45a describes an accusation of witchcraft against two daughters of R. Nahman. Several rabbinic passages, such as BT *Pesahim* 110a, link sorceresses and human waste and offer formulas to use against them.

Although the Jerusalem Talmud contains several key sections devoted to the halakhic context of magical practice, it lacks the extensive demonology and the traditions of magical incantation and praxis found in the Babylonian Talmud, an indication that much of this material came into Jewish popular religion from Parthian and Sassanian culture. For example, Jewish magic was often characterized by verbal formulas designed to influence metaphysical entities such as angels, demons, and even God to act on the world in some specific way, ideally for the benefit of the practitioner or the client of the practitioner. Such adjurations have been found written on amulets and incantation bowls, as well as in handbooks for practitioners from late antiquity into the modern period. Although each text differed according to the specific situation, the language often contained quotations from Scripture invoking earlier actions of power and magic, such as the splitting of the Red Sea or *Elisha's miracles, in the context of the magical prescription. In this way, the practitioner assumed the role and efficacy, if not the identity, of the biblical hero, as he or she performed the magic. Incantation bowls from late ancient Babylonia seem to have been used to expel household demons and other malevolent entities and to combat disease and misfortunes attributed to witches.

GEONIC ERA: Jewish magical recipe books began to be compiled in late antiquity and by the *geonic period the scribalization of Jewish magic is evident in handbooks such as the *Sword of Moses, Sefer Ha-Razim,* and other books with magic content found in the Cairo *Genizah. Much work remains to be done in cataloguing Jewish magical texts from around the world; editing magic books, amulets, and bowls; and analyzing their use in later kabbalistic imagery and praxis (see MYSTICISM: *HEKHALOT* AND *MERKAVAH LITERATURE*; KABBALAH).

For further reading, see the extensive and comprehensive bibliography in the second edition of the *Encyclopedia Judaica*, s.v. "Magic" (2007); J. Naveh and S. Shaked, *Amulets and Magical Bowls* (1987); N. Janowitz, *Magic in the Roman World* (2001); G. Bohak, *Ancient Jewish Magic* (2008); J. Trachtenberg, *Jewish Magic and Superstition* (1939; devoted to medieval Jewish magic); L. Schiffman and M. Swartz, *Hebrew and Aramaic Incantation Texts from the Cairo Geniza* (1992); M. Swartz, *Scholastic Magic* (1996); and J. Seidel "Charming Criminals," in *Ancient Magic and Ritual Power*, ed. M. Meyer and P. Mirecki (1995).   JONATHAN SEIDEL

Magnes, Judah L. (1877–1948) was a prominent American rabbi, Jewish communal leader, and *Zionist. Born in Oakland, California, he earned ordination at *Hebrew Union College and a PhD from the University of Heidelberg. Between 1904 and 1912, he officiated at Temple Israel in Brooklyn and at Temple Emanu-El and B'nai Jeshurun Synagogue in Manhattan. He ultimately left the Reform rabbinate over issues regarding his support of traditional modes of Jewish worship (see JUDAISM, REFORM: NORTH AMERICA). From 1909 to 1922, Magnes served as chairman of the *New York City *Kehillah*, an organization founded to mediate community conflicts. During *World War I, Magnes emerged as a leading pacifist and important figure in the People's Council for Democracy and Peace; he and his family later moved to *Jerusalem in 1922, where he became involved in efforts to establish the Hebrew University in Jerusalem. He served as its first chancellor (1925–35) and first president (1935–48). In response to the 1929 riots, Magnes became committed to establishing Jewish–Arab cooperation. Throughout the remainder of his life he advocated tirelessly for the establishment of a binational state in *Palestine. His activities included the establishment of *Ihud* in 1942, an organization that promoted Jewish–Arab cooperation. For further reading see A. Goren, *Dissenter in Zion: From the Writings of Judah L. Magnes* (1982); and D. P. Kotzin, "Transporting the American Peace Movement to British Palestine: Judah L. Magnes, American Pacifist and Zionist," *Peace & Change* 29 (July 2004): 390–418.

DANIEL P. KOTZIN

Mahzor (pl. *mahzorim*) comes from the Hebrew for "cycle" and refers to *prayer books containing the liturgies for the *High Holidays and/or the *Festivals (see WORSHIP).

Maimon, Salomon (1753–1800) was a Polish-Lithuanian rationalist philosopher whose fame extended both from his self-promoting, reflective autobiography and the philosophical acumen that prompted Immanuel Kant to note that "none of my critics have understood me...as well as Herr Maimon." Born in Sukowiborg (near Mirz) as Solomon ben Joshua, Maimon changed his name in his thirties in homage to *Maimonides and as a way of participating in the Germanized world whose acknowledgment and support he desired.

Maimon received a traditional education and, by his own account, showed extraordinary promise in *Talmud study. At the age of eleven he received rabbinic ordination, married, and moved in with his wife's family. In his *Lebensgeschichte* (An Autobiography [trans., J. Clark Murray (2001)]), published in 1792, Maimon describes the abuse he suffered from his mother-in-law and the miserable conditions of Polish Jewish life; through his own intellectual devices, he read Maimonides, taught himself German (albeit imperfectly), and studied *Kabbalah. Looking for guidance, he sought out *Dov Ber of Miedzyrzecz, but was acutely disappointed; Maimon's sharp critique of *Hasidism, however, belies the deep intellectual influence of that encounter. To follow the demands of his philosophical awakening and escape his domestic life, Maimon took a position as a tutor. He abandoned *Poland altogether in 1776 and went to *Berlin, but was turned out of the city before making any serious contacts; he lived as a beggar before finding a sponsor in Posen. Back in Berlin by 1780, he read eclectically and voraciously and met Moses *Mendelssohn, who introduced him to other proponents of the *Haskalah*.

Maimon was intellectually astute but socially inept, and he never polished his language skills. Virtually unintelligible, unrepentantly *Spinozistic, and scathingly honest, Maimon was again expelled from Berlin. His peripatetic life led him to Breslau where his wife found him and demanded a divorce. He returned to Berlin by 1787 where he achieved some professional acclaim. Writing in German and Hebrew, Maimon contributed several articles to Enlightenment journals, published ten major philosophical studies (including *Versuch über die Transscendentalphilosophie mit einem Anhang über die symbolische Erkenntniß und Anmerkungen* [Essay on Transcendental Philosophy with an Appendix on Symbolic Knowledge and Notes], his major work on Kant's *Critique of Pure Reason*) and published *Giva'at Ha-Moreh* [The Hill of the Guide], a heavily edited Hebrew commentary on Maimonides' *Guide of the Perplexed*.

Maimon's philosophical sophistication was unparalleled: His grasp and critique of Kant's idea of the thing-in-itself exposed weaknesses in reigning notions of the limits of human experience, the finitude of human cognition, and the ability to theorize about God. He wrote on metaphysics, logic, ethics, legal theory, philosophy, and mathematics. Although influenced by Maimonides, he was independently modern in his commitment to freedom of thought. However, Maimon suffered from his poverty and low status. In 1795 Graf Heinrich Wilhelm Adolf Kalkreuth offered his patronage, and Maimon lived the remainder of his life in Nieder-Siegersdorf in Niederschlesien (Lower Silesia, now Poland).

Recent scholarship includes A. Socher, *The Radical Enlightenment of Solomon Maimon: Judaism, Heresy, and Philosophy* (2006); and M. Buzaglo, *Solomon Maimon: Monism, Skepticism and Mathematics* (2002).   LEAH HOCHMAN

Maimonides (MOSES BEN MAIMON, also known as Rambam) was born in Cordova, *Spain, in 1138, but he and his family were forced to flee in 1148 when the *Almohads, an extremist sect, invaded southern Spain and offered all non-Muslims the choice of conversion, death, or exile. Maimonides' family fled Spain and traveled through *North Africa, where, for some time, they lived incognito as Muslims. In 1166, Maimonides settled in Fustat, *Egypt (old Cairo), where he wrote most of his best-known works and served as court physician to the Sultan. He died in Fustat in 1204. Often regarded as the greatest Jewish philosopher of all time, Maimonides was also a talmudic expositor and renowned physician (see *HALAKHAH*; MEDICINE).

His first masterpiece, the *Commentary on the Mishnah*, published in 1168, is best known for its treatment of Chapter 10 of Tractate *Sanhedrin*. There, Maimonides lists thirteen principles he considers binding on every Jew: the existence of *God, the absolute unity of God, the incorporeality of God, the eternity of God, that God alone is to be worshiped, that God communicates to *prophets, that *Moses is the greatest prophet, that the *Torah was given by God, that the Torah is immutable, divine providence, that there is divine punishment and reward, that there will be a *messiah, and that the dead will be *resurrected. A Jew who accepts these principles, although he or she may commit every possible sin, is still accounted a Jew and has a share in *redemption. A Jew who denies even one removes him- or herself from the community of Israel and has no share in its destiny.

Maimonides' second masterpiece, the *Mishneh Torah*, finished in 1178, is a fourteen-volume code of Jewish law that systematizes all 613 original *commandments (*mitzvot*), explaining in simple and elegant Hebrew prose what they are and what purposes they are intended to serve. (Since the *Mishneh Torah* has fourteen parts and the Hebrew number fourteen spells out the word *yad*, or "hand," this code is often known in Jewish tradition as the *Yad* or *Yad Hazakah* [Strong Hand]). According to Maimonides, no commandment is given for the sake of obedience alone. Of special note is Book One, which sets forth the foundations of Jewish belief, a theory of moral traits or dispositions, the need for every Jew to study the Torah, and the importance of *repentance. Also of special importance is Book Fourteen, which ends by arguing that a messiah will come, restore sovereignty to Israel, establish peace with the other nations, and lead the world to the study of science and philosophy. Unlike some Jewish accounts of the coming of the messiah, Maimonides rejects the idea of a cataclysm, the performance of miracles, or abrogation of the *Torah, insisting that the world will follow its normal course.

Maimonides' philosophic reputation rests mainly on the *Guide of the Perplexed*, published in *Judeo-Arabic in 1190. Its overall theme is the conflict between secular and spiritual sources of knowledge or, as we might say, *reason and *revelation. If reason directs us to a God who is immaterial, unchanging, and devoid of emotion, on a literal reading, then revelation directs us to a God who has bodily parts, grows angry, and changes location. Maimonides argues that a literal reading of Scripture is unjustified, and thus the conflict is apparent rather than real.

According to Maimonides, all of Jewish law (*halakhah*) aims at two things: the improvement of the body and the improvement of the soul. The former is a means to the latter; the soul is improved by acquiring correct opinions and eventually knowledge. The basis of all knowledge is summed up in the first two commandments, which Maimonides takes as (1) belief in a timeless, changeless, immaterial God and (2) rejection of idolatry. Only by acquiring knowledge can a person fulfill the commandment to love God.

Therefore, a person who has a false conception of God, one based on a literal reading of Scripture, is not worshiping God, no matter how many other commandments he or she may perform. That is not to say that the other commandments can be dispensed with – Maimonides does not countenance liberalization of the law. Rather, it is to say that the purpose of the other commandments is to put us in a position where we can perfect our intellect. This purpose could only be achieved if we lived in an orderly society that promoted the health and well-being of its members. Still health and well-being are not enough: A perfect society must also look after spiritual and intellectual growth.

Two features characterize Maimonides' thinking. The first may be described as demystification. In almost everything he wrote, Maimonides sought to free Judaism of any taint of mythology or superstition. Beyond the rejection of literal interpretation, he is skeptical of miracles and anything else that defies rational explanation. The second feature may be described as intellectualism. Rather than comfort, merriment, or ethnic solidarity, the purpose of Judaism is to direct us to truth. Should Scripture appear to say something that reason can show is false, we have no choice but to reinterpret it to conform to reason so that truth is preserved.

Behind this claim is the view that reason is a God-given faculty that defines us as human beings. In his terms, "[Man's] ultimate perfection is to become rational in actuality; this would consist in his knowing everything concerning all beings that it is within the capacity of man to know" (*Guide of the Perplexed*, Book 3, chapter 27). Rather than impeding the human relationship with God, reason brings us closer to God. This does not mean that reason can answer every question put to it. Maimonides is clear that part of rationality consists in the recognition that reason has limits. Thus, he makes the qualification that reason can only lead to things "*that it is within the capacity of man to know.*" His basic point is that, when reason can answer a question, as in reason's affirmation of the existence of a timeless, changeless, immaterial God, we have a sacred obligation to trust it.

Despite his fame, Maimonides became the source of a long-standing controversy. To supporters, he restored Judaism to the intellectual rigor it was always supposed to have had. To detractors, he corrupted Judaism by assigning a larger role to Aristotle than to Moses. Whichever view one takes, there is no denying that, after the publication of Maimonides' works, Judaism was never the same. An old saying sums up his contribution well: "From Moses to Moses, there was none like Moses."

In addition to the primary sources mentioned earlier, for further reading, see I. Twersky, *A Maimonides Reader* (1972); D. Hartmann, *Maimonides: Torah and Philosophic Quest* (1976); R. L. Weiss, *Maimonides' Ethics* (1991); and K. Seeskin, ed., *The Cambridge Companion to Maimonides* (2005); **also see THOUGHT, MEDIEVAL.** KENNETH SEESKIN

Majdanek was a *Nazi forced labor camp and death camp in *Poland near Lublin. It opened in the summer of 1941 as the Waffen-SS POW Camp Lublin and later as the Waffen-SS Concentration Camp Lublin. More than 360,000 of its half-million prisoners would die there; 16% of those who died were Jews. Many perished from the camp's harsh living and working conditions, and the SS murdered many others on the camp's gallows, guillotine, or in one of Majdanek's four gas chambers. **See HOLOCAUST: CAMPS AND KILLING CENTERS.** DAVID M. CROWE

Malachi, Book of is the last book of the prophetic corpus and of the Minor Prophets of the Hebrew *Bible (see BIBLE: PROPHETS AND PROPHECY; PROPHETS [*NEVI'IM*]). The title of the book means "my messenger" and comes from 3:1, which mentions an eschatological or *messianic figure; it may be assumed that the author was anonymous. The author is particularly harsh in his criticism of the priests for corrupting the *Temple cult and offering incorrect teaching of the *Torah regarding *covenant laws (1:6–2:5). This criticism is surprising because the presumed date of composition is only about two generations after the rededication of the Second *Temple in 515 BCE. In calling the community to *repent (3:6–12), the author chastises those who do not and promises that those who do will be remembered for good (3:13–21). The book concludes on a positive note, linking the teaching of *Moses to the coming of the eschatological prophet, *Elijah, who will inaugurate the messianic era (3:22–24). By linking Mosaic teaching to prophetic eschatology, Malachi weds law and prophecy in a way that was to be identified with *rabbinic Judaism. ERIC MEYERS

Marrano is a derogatory term for a *converso* or "New Christian," a Jew who converted to Christianity under force in fourteenth- or fifteenth-century *Spain and *Portugal; some were crypto-Jews, practicing Jewish rituals in secret. **See INQUISITION, SPANISH; SPAIN, CHRISTIAN.**

Marriage and Marriage Customs. Nearly all Jewish texts praise marriage and hold it out as an ideal. The statement of Genesis 2:18, "It is not good for man to be alone," and the directive of Genesis 2:24 to "be fruitful and multiply," were understood in Jewish tradition as religious obligations. Rabbinic texts present marriage as a bulwark against sinful thoughts and behavior (see, for example, M. *Kiddushin* 4:12). So important is marriage that Jewish law rules that a man may sell a Torah scroll to obtain funds to marry (BT *Megillah* 27a; *Mishneh Torah, Hilkhot Sefer Torah* 10:2; *Shulḥan Arukh, Yoreh De'ah* 270:1, and *Even ha-Ezer* 1:2).

There is little evidence for what marriage ceremonies looked like in biblical times. From the rabbinic period onward, the legal core of Jewish marriage has been a two-step process. The first stage, *kiddushin* or *erusin*, is often translated in English as *"betrothal."* Although the couple does not yet live together, it is a form of unofficial marriage during which the laws of *adultery apply; a betrothal may only be dissolved by *divorce (or death of one of the parties). *Kiddushin* is created by the man presenting to the woman an item of minimal value (most commonly a ring is used) and stating, "You are betrothed to me according to the laws of Moses and Israel"; through this process, he "acquires" her as his wife. Rabbinic law also allows for *kiddushin* to be created by means of a document or an act of sexual intercourse (M. *Kiddushin* 1:1), but these fell out of Jewish practice early on.

The marriage is completed through *nissuin*, "nuptials," also known as bringing the *bride into the *ḥuppah*. In rabbinic times, the *ḥuppah* was a bridal chamber, and bringing the bride into it represented her entry into the husband's household. In modern practice, the *ḥuppah* is an open canopy under which the wedding takes place, although it continues to symbolize the new household being created. The *nissuin* is accompanied by seven blessings, the *sheva berakhot*. These blessings recall the creation of the world and human beings, the hope for the return to *Zion, and the joy of companionship and marriage; they are recited over a cup of wine, which the bride and groom then share. At one time *kiddushin* and *nissuin* could take place as much as a year or more apart but since approximately the twelfth century CE, the practice has been to combine both in one extended ceremony. The two parts may be separated by a reading of the marriage contract (see later) or by words to the couple from the officiant or another person chosen for the occasion. The ceremony is usually followed by *yiḥud*, a period of seclusion for the bride and groom, which symbolically and legally represents the consummation of the marriage.

Biblical and rabbinic law allow for polygyny, although its frequency is difficult to gauge. Polygyny was formally prohibited among *Ashkenazi Jews in a ruling attributed to the German scholar R. *Gershom ben Judah (960–1028) in his *"ḥerem de-Rabbenu Gershom."* Men of *Sephardi and *Mizraḥi descent, particularly those living in Islamic societies, did not consider themselves bound by the *ḥerem* and sometimes contracted plural marriages well into the twentieth century. The State of Israel formally outlawed polygamy in 1951, but allowed for already polygamous immigrant families to remain intact. Moreover, because taking a second wife is valid by biblical law, if a man does so in violation of the law the relationship must still be dissolved by *divorce; civil penalties such as imprisonment can also be brought to bear.

Weddings are prohibited during certain days and periods of the year. A wedding should not take place on the *Sabbath or on a *festival, for example, because of the rabbinic principle that one should not dilute the celebration of the holiday with the celebration of the wedding. Conversely, weddings traditionally do not take place during the period of the counting of the *Omer between *Passover and *Shavuot, or during the three weeks between the 17th of Tammuz and *Tisha B'Av, because both are considered to be periods of mourning.

In the post-talmudic period, it became customary to complete the wedding ceremony with the breaking underfoot of a glass or similar object by the groom. Various interpretations of this custom include frightening off evil spirits

and commemorating the destruction of *Jerusalem, even at the happiest moments. Other common customs include the *aufruf*: calling up the groom, or either or both members of the couple in egalitarian communities, to the *Torah on the *Sabbath before the wedding. Both *bride and groom may fast on the day of the wedding before the ceremony and say penitential prayers usually reserved for *Yom Kippur. Some couples also avoid seeing each other before the wedding, either for the day of the wedding itself or up to a week in advance. Immediately before the ceremony, the groom may place a veil over his bride's face in the *bedeken* ceremony; one common explanation is that it prevents a man from being deceived as to the identity of the woman he is marrying, as was the biblical figure *Jacob (Gen 29).

A Jewish marriage often includes the writing of a marriage contract (*ketubbah*) that is given by the groom to the bride. Originally, this document recorded the dowry and other property brought into the marriage and the conditions of its inheritance or return, as well as a deferred monetary pledge from the husband to the wife should he divorce or pre-decease her. It further spelled out obligations of the husband to the wife, such as providing financial maintenance, having regular sexual contact with her, and redeeming her if she was taken captive. Although a traditional version of the *ketubbah* is included in many Jewish marriages even to this day (particularly in Orthodox and Conservative practice [see JUDAISM, ORTHODOX; JUDAISM, CONSERVATIVE]), it is generally considered to be symbolic and unenforceable. In the more liberal movements, couples may write their own contracts with individualized and mutual/egalitarian promises and commitments.

Other modern innovations to the wedding ceremony have generally centered on making the bride a more active and equal participant in the ceremony, in contrast to the traditional ceremony, in which she need only passively accept the ring given to her by the groom. These innovations include the addition of words for the bride to say when accepting the ring, a mutual exchange of rings (and even mutual statements of setting aside the other in betrothal), and the inclusion of women as participants in reading the *ketubbah*, reciting blessings, or officiating over the wedding. Other modern adaptations of Jewish wedding customs include ceremonies for marriages between a Jewish and non-Jewish partner or ceremonies for the commitment of two Jewish same-sex partners to each other (see also LIFE-CYCLE RITUALS).

For further reading, see R. Biale, *Women and Jewish Law* (2nd ed., 1995); G. Labovitz, *Marriage and Metaphor: Constructions of Gender in Rabbinic Literature* (2009); and J. R. Baskin, "Medieval Jewish Models of Marriage," in *The Medieval Marriage Scene: Prudence, Passion, Policy*, ed. S. Roush and C. Baskins (2005), 1–22.   GAIL LABOVITZ

Marriage, Levirate, from the Latin *levir* (brother-in-law), refers to the mandated marriage of a widowed woman to her husband's brother. In *Israelite religion and *Judaism, levirate marriage applies to a childless widow, based on the ruling in Deuteronomy 25:6–8 that if a man dies and leaves no sons, his widow should not be married to a "stranger." Rather her husband's oldest brother is to perform the duty of the *levir* (in Hebrew, *yibbum*) and marry her. The first son that the woman bears to her new husband will be considered the heir of the deceased brother, "that his name may not be blotted out in Israel." (By rabbinic times, levirate marriage was considered obligatory only when the widow had no child of either sex [M. *Yevamot* 2:5; BT *Yevamot* 22b]). Should the brother-in-law refuse to perform this obligation, then he and his brother's widow had to perform a ceremony called *halitzah* (removal), which is described in Deuteronomy 25:9–10. The woman approaches the brother-in-law in the presence of the community elders, pulls his sandal from his foot, spits in his face, and declares, "Thus shall be done to the man who will not build up his brother's house!" Then the brother-in-law "shall go in Israel by the name of 'the family of the unsandaled one,'" and the released widow is now free to marry as she chooses.

The purpose of levirate marriage in Israelite religion was to preserve patriarchal patterns of inheritance; it also provided protection for widows in societies that offered single women few attractive options. Levirate marriage presupposed a polygynous society in which a man could have more than one wife. A man who refused the duty of the *levir* may have been concerned about his own potential economic loss in providing an heir for his brother's property, as well as the impact of adding another woman and her potential children to his household. It is interesting to note that in all other circumstances biblical law forbids a man to marry his brother's widow (Lev 18:16, 20:21). Levirate marriage appears in biblical narrative in the story of *Tamar, the daughter-in-law of *Jacob's son *Judah, in *Genesis 38. Although the events in the book of *Ruth bear similarities to levirate marriage, Boaz's agreement to marry his kinsman's widow, Ruth, reflects the institution of the *goel* (redeemer of clan property).

Rabbinic Judaism continued the practice of levirate marriage, although some rabbinic sages recommended *halitzah* in all cases (BT *Bekhorot* 13a and *Yevamot* 109a). A tractate of the Talmud, *Yevamot* (sisters-in-law), is devoted to the ramifications of this custom. During the medieval period, rabbinic authorities who lived in the Muslim world, where polygyny was a cultural norm, generally supported levirate marriage. However, levirate marriage was rendered virtually impossible among Jewish communities in Christian regions by the legal amendment (*takkanah*) against polygyny attributed to R. *Gershom ben Judah of Mainz ca. 1000. Nevertheless, the ceremony of *halitzah* had to be performed by the brother-in-law before the childless widow could remarry. A 1950 *takkanah* by the Chief Rabbinate of the State of Israel prohibited the practice of levirate marriage in Israel and made performance of *halitzah* obligatory.

In the contemporary era, Orthodox Judaism (see JUDAISM: ORTHODOX entries) requires a childless widow to undergo *halitzah* to be free to remarry. The ceremony takes place in the presence of a specially convened Jewish *court (*beit din*) of five ordained rabbis. The ritual "*halitzah*" shoe used is made entirely of leather. The widowed sister-in-law must remove this shoe from the right foot of the *levir* and spit on the ground; she then repeats in Hebrew the formula mandated in Deuteronomy 25:9–10. All present join her in reciting the final three words of this passage three times.

Sometimes, a *levir* refuses to participate in the *halitzah* ceremony out of hopes of extorting financial gain from the widow or her family or because of geographical distance, rejection of traditional Jewish ritual, or disabilities to which he is subject. Despite Israeli legislation and efforts

of Orthodox Jewish courts to intervene in individual cases, some women remain bound to a brother-in-law's whims and are unable to remarry. Such women are among those termed *agunot* (sing. *agunah*; "chained" or "anchored women"). This is one of the disturbing surviving remnants of women's secondary legal status in *halakhah* (Jewish law). Recent scholarship includes D. E. Weisberg, *Levirate Marriage and the Family in Ancient Judaism* (2009).   JUDITH R. BASKIN

Marshall, Louis (1856–1929) was a prominent attorney and one of the most influential Jewish communal leaders of his day. The son of German Jewish *immigrants, Marshall was born in Syracuse, New York; he later moved to *New York City where he played a crucial role in the reorganization of the *Jewish Theological Seminary of America and was a prominent supporter and leader of both the New York *Kehillah* and the *American Jewish Committee. He worked to combat *antisemitism and to improve conditions for immigrants on the Lower East Side, and he also opposed immigration restrictions that would have closed the *United States to Jewish refugees. Marshall was a supporter of the rights of all minority groups and fought for social justice; he was also a conservationist. Believing that Jews were not a separate nationality, Marshall did not embrace *Zionism, although he was a supporter of the *Balfour Declaration. For further reading, see H. Alpert, *Louis Marshall: 1856–1929* (2008); C. Reznikoff, ed., *Louis Marshall: Champion of Liberty*, 2 vols. (1957); and J. Sarna, "Two Jewish Lawyers Named Louis," *American Jewish History* 94(1–2) (2008).
                                        MICHAEL R. COHEN

Martyrdom, the act of submitting to death rather than compromising one's convictions, is generally believed to have emerged in Judaism in *Hellenistic times. This view is based mainly on 2 *Maccabees, which describes the executions of a scribe named Eleazar (ch. 6) and of seven anonymous brothers in the presence of their mother (ch. 7) for refusing to eat pork and to worship the *Seleucid king Antiochus IV. However, the unique stylistic, linguistic, and thematic features of these two stories, together with the plausibility that the final format of the book is the work of a mid-first-century-CE redactor, contest the stories' Hellenistic provenance.

Versions of these stories surfaced in 4 *Maccabees, from the first or second century CE, when martyrdom gained popularity in Jewish circles under *Roman-Christian influences. Internalizing the Roman ideal of "noble death," first-century writers *Philo of Alexandria, *Josephus Flavius, and the anonymous author of the *Assumption of Moses* (see PSEUDEPIGRAPHA) presented contemporaneous Jews as emulators of a long-standing Jewish martyrological tradition (although none of them mentioned the Maccabean martyrs). They describe Jews killed by Romans and threats by peaceful Jewish protestors to commit suicide and kill each other rather than see violations of Jewish laws. *Temple imagery (see TEMPLE AND TEMPLE CULT) of priests and ritual sacrifices helped these authors justify such exceptional forms of voluntary death. Yet Philo's and Josephus' peaceful protestors did not have to make good on their promises, because the Roman authorities abandoned their offensive decrees. Although these Jewish martyrological discourses endorsed the admired Roman ideal, they also reflected anxiety, because of the general biblical prohibition against taking human life and the absence of a martyrological doctrine in *Judaism.

Theologizing the concept of voluntary death became the task of the *Rabbis. Their rulings attempted to balance the Jewish commitment to the sanctity of life and the popular notion of voluntary death. A second-century rabbinic council at Lod allegedly set the basic rule: When forced to choose between transgressing the commandments (*mitzvot) and death, a Jew "should transgress rather than be killed," except in cases of idolatry, sexual misconduct, and homicide (BT *Sanhedrin* 74a–b, JT *Sanhedrin* 3:6, 21b). In contrast, Rabbi Ishmael argued that engaging in idolatrous worship was permitted to save one's life, because Leviticus 18:5 instructed that one was to live by the commandments, not die for them, but this minority position was challenged.

The Rabbis distinguished between forced idolatrous worship in private, which is permissible to save one's life, and in public (i.e., in the presence of at least ten men), which must be avoided. According to other talmudic views, in times of religious persecution Jews must let themselves be killed, even for a trivial commandment. However, if the demand to transgress benefits only the oppressor and does not aim at denigrating Judaism publicly, life should be chosen. All of these *halakhic (legal) discussions employ the verb "to be killed," stressing the passive nature of martyrdom. These rulings abandoned the Temple symbols and the images of active martyrdom found in first- and second-century-CE Jewish narratives.

Several martyrological accounts appear in the Talmud and various *midrash collections. They include a version of the anonymous mother and sons narrative from Maccabean times (BT *Gittin* 57b; *Lamentations Rabbah* 1:16, §50) and the story of four hundred girls and boys who drowned themselves in the sea en route to Rome to escape sexual slavery (BT *Gittin* 57b). More famous and detailed are the accounts about the Roman executions of ten Rabbis, including *Akiva, Hananiah ben Teradyon, and Judah ben Baba, during the second-century-CE Hadrianic persecutions (BT *Sanhedrin* 14a; BT *Avodah Zarah* 8b, 17b–18a; *Lamentations Rabbah* 2:2). These talmudic accounts lack a specific term for martyrdom. Only later did rabbinic discussion link the need to avoid a public transgression at all costs to the act of sanctifying God's name (*kiddush ha-Shem*). A post-talmudic text, called both *Midrash Eleh Ezkerah* (These I Shall Remember) and *Midrash 'Asarah Harugei Malkut* (The Ten Killed by the Royal Government), reworks individual talmudic tales into a legendary martyrology, known as the "Ten Martyrs." Excerpts from this midrash appear in a *selihah* (penitential prayer) recited on *Yom Kippur, also entitled *Eleh Ezkerah*. Similar content appears in a dirge for *Tisha B'Av entitled *Artzei ha-Levanon* (The Cedars of Lebanon).

No other period in history is more identified with Jewish martyrdom than the *Middle Ages. The first known case took place in Otranto in southern *Italy, a *Byzantine province at the time. A tenth-century epistle reports the self-sacrifice of two rabbis and their student. Equally important to the history of Jewish martyrdom is the liturgy and literature produced by Italian/Byzantine Jewry, especially the tenth-century *Sefer Yosippon* (Book of *Josippon). It retells the Maccabean stories of martyrdom and Josephus' accounts of events during the conflicts with Rome. Together with contemporary liturgical works, *Sefer Yosippon* restored to Jewish

memory the nonrabbinic martyrs of the past and the Temple cult symbols of the Roman period, especially the *korban* (sacrifice).

The Book of Josippon became part of the curriculum in Franco-German (*Ashkenazic) study centers like the one in Mainz headed by Rabbi *Gershom ben Judah, the Light of the Exile. The French rabbis – Joseph bar Solomon of Carcassonne, an eleventh-century liturgical poet (see POETRY: LITURGICAL [*PIYYUT*]), and *Rashi (d. 1105) – were also familiar with the book. By the early eleventh century martyrdom went beyond literature in France. A Hebrew account describes Jewish women drowning themselves in a river in response to King Robert's campaign of forced conversion, whereas others were "put under the sword." Latin accounts also ascribe suicide to these French Jews.

The First *Crusade initiated a significant chapter in the history of Jewish martyrdom. In the late spring and summer of 1096, bands of crusaders attacked European Jewish communities with the slogan, "death or conversion." Many were killed by crusaders, and others ritually killed their families and themselves to avoid forced conversion. Three Hebrew narratives describe these events and praise the martyrs, comparing them to the martyr-heroes of the past, including the anonymous Maccabean mother with her seven sons and the martyrs of the talmudic period. Also in the list are the biblical "martyrs" *Daniel and his three associates, as well as *Abraham and his son *Isaac. Medieval *midrashim* (legends) present Abraham's binding (*akedah) of Isaac on the altar (Gen 22) as an actual offering, followed by Isaac's miraculous revival, making the *akedah* synonymous with martyrdom (see S. Spiegel, *The Last Trial* [1967]).

Together with medieval liturgical poetry (*piyyutim*), the *midrashim*, and the memorial books (*Memorbücher*) of the dead, the reports of forced conversion and *kiddush ha-Shem* generated a distinctive Ashkenazic style of reporting and commemorating. The singing of the liturgy *Aleinu le-shabeah* (We should praise *God) and the meditation *Unetanneh tokef* (the title of a medieval liturgical poem that is recited on *Rosh Ha-Shanah and Yom Kippur) were ascribed to the martyrs themselves. Other responses to the events of 1096, including the poem *Av ha-Rahamim* (Merciful Father), the mourners' *Kaddish, and the *Yizkor memorial service, have all remained an integral part of Ashkenazic liturgy and worship.

Although the massacres during the so-called Shepherd's Crusade and the Black Death of the fourteenth century were far more devastating, it was the martyrologies of the crusading period that have left a lasting impression on the collective memory of Ashkenaz, and their style was used to describe the massacres of Jews by *Chmelnitzki and his Cossacks (1648–49) in *Poland and the *Ukraine (1768).

Yet, martyrdom, and especially the taking of others' lives, was not without controversy. Medieval rabbinic authorities like Rabbi Jacob ben Meir Tam (d. 1171 [see TOSAFISTS]) viewed self-destruction as a legitimate way of avoiding torture in cases of forced conversions, and Rabbi *Meir of Rothenburg (d. 1293) answered in the negative when a Jew inquired if he needed to do penance for having sacrificed his family during a massacre. Nevertheless these discussions and inquiries also reveal misgivings and perplexities. This is evident also from a medieval *Bible commentary that rejected acts of self-destruction and in which a certain rabbi labeled another a "murderer" for ritually taking the lives of others. Moses *Maimonides mocked another rabbi for recommending martyrdom. His *Epistle on Martyrdom* (c. 1165) rejects self-destruction when faced with the Muslim demand to convert, because he did not consider *Islam an idolatrous religion. Except for an early case of *kiddush ha-Shem* in 1148, it seems that Maimonides' ruling prevailed during the *Almohad regime in *North Africa and *Spain.

Martyrdom resurfaced in Christian *Spain at the close of the fourteen century. Ashkenazic-style reports describe acts of *kiddush ha-Shem* in reaction to mob violence. Among those involved were descendants of Franco-German rabbis like Rabbi *Asher ben Jeḥiel, who had established study centers in Spain. However, *kiddush ha-Shem* was less common in Spain. After the 1492 *expulsion, *Sephardim invoked the concept of *kiddush ha-Shem* to describe the hardship of exile and the struggle of crypto-Jews to remain loyal to Judaism.

Kiddush ha-Shem received additional meaning after the *Holocaust. Even though the *Nazis did not offer Jews a choice between life and death, the six million victims of the Holocaust are considered martyrs because the Nazis indiscriminately murdered them only for being Jews. Together with other martyrs, they are remembered in the *Yizkor* service as saints who sanctified God's name.

For further reading, see R. Chazan, *European Jewry and the First Crusade* (1987); J. Cohen, *Sanctifying the Name of God* (2004); and S. Shepkaru, *Jewish Martyrs in the Pagan and Christian Worlds* (2005).   SHMUEL SHEPKARU

Marx, Karl (1818–1883) was born in Trier in the Rhineland to parents from observant families who descended from a distinguished rabbinic line. His paternal grandfather, Meir Halevi Marx, was rabbi of Trier, a position Marx's uncle, Samuel Marx, later assumed. Marx's maternal grandfather, Issac Pressburg, had been rabbi of the Dutch city of Nijmegen. His father, Heschel Marx (1782–1838), trained in law. After the 1815 restoration of the Kingdom of Prussia, an edict barred Jews from practicing law, and Marx's father became a Lutheran, officially changing his name to Heinrich. Karl was baptized in 1824, at the age of six. His mother, Henrietta Pressburg, converted a year later, after the death of her father.

Marx received a secular education and studied history and philosophy at the universities of Bonn and Berlin. In 1841, Marx received his PhD from the university in Jena. Denied teaching posts because of his membership in the radical group, the Young Hegelians, Marx became editor of *Rheinische Zeitung* in 1842. There he expressed open aversion to organized religion. His co-editor, the German Jewish socialist, Moses Hess (1812–1875), commented that "Dr. Marx . . . will give medieval religion and politics their last blow." In 1843, Marx married Jenny von Westphalen, who was from a Prussian aristocratic family; they moved to Paris where Marx began a lifelong friendship and collaboration with Friedrich Engels. In Paris Engels gave Marx a copy of his first book, *The Conditions of the Working Class in England* (German, 1845).

Expelled from France in 1845, Marx moved to Belgium with Engels; he renounced his Prussian citizenship and became, for the rest of his life, stateless. In Belgium Marx formulated his theory of class struggle, arguing that history, beginning in the feudal era, could be reduced to the conflict between classes. He argued in *The Communist Manifesto* (1848) that the passage from feudalism to capitalism divided the bourgeoisie and proletariat into two hostile camps; after the inevitable overthrow of the former, the proletariat would eliminate social classes by abolishing private property.

Marx's attitude to Jews and Judaism has evoked accusations of antisemitism. In *On the Jewish Question* (1844), he associated Jewry with usury and finance capitalism, writing, "The social emancipation of the Jew is the emancipation of society from Judaism." In an 1843 letter, Marx wrote that "the Israelite faith is repugnant to me." Recent scholars, however, have situated Marx's views in the wider context of his revulsion for all organized religions; they point to his friendships with contemporary Jewish intellectuals like Moses Hess and Heinrich *Graetz (1817–1891) and note the complexity of his views on the "Jewish question." Marx unambiguously favored Jewish emancipation and full rights for Jews as Jews. When the French parliament called for a universal Sunday rest day, Marx opposed the bill because it legalized "the Sunday of the Christians"; he asked, "Should not the Jewish Sabbath have the same right?" Thus, Marx distinguished between the role Jews had played in the modern state, which he believed was negative, and the rights they were entitled to as individuals, which he absolutely supported. For further reading, see R. C. Tucker, ed., *The Marx-Engels Reader*, 2nd ed. (1978); S. Avineri, "Marx and Jewish Emancipation," *Journal of the History of Ideas*, 23(3) (1964): 445–50; and D. M. Snyder, *Freud, Einstein, and Marx: The Influence of Judaism on Their Works* (1998).   JOSHUA D. ZIMMERMAN

Masada is a mountain located on the southwestern shore of the Dead Sea in *Israel. The small plateau served as a royal citadel and desert palace for *Herod the Great and later as the final stronghold of rebels in the First *Jewish War against *Rome. In his *Jewish War* (7.280–303), the first-century-CE historian *Josephus describes the site's lavishly decorated palaces and remarkable feats of architectural engineering. The excavations carried out in 1963–65 largely confirmed Josephus' description of the impressive fortress (Y. Yadin, *Masada: Herod's Fortress and the Zealots' Last Stand* [1966, 1998]). Herod employed the latest Roman artistic and architectural techniques, including frescoed walls and mosaic floors, to construct his secluded palace and safe haven.

The Jewish rebels who took Masada at the time of the First Jewish War were a group known as the *Sicarii* (Daggermen). The rebels held the fortress for a number of years before the Romans surrounded them. After a three- to six-month siege, the Romans took the fortress in the spring of 73 or 74 CE. Josephus relates the famous story of the mass suicide of the 960 rebels (*Jewish War* 7.320–401). Archeological and literary evidence have been cited both to confirm and to deny the account, leaving a strong sense of doubt among many scholars that it actually occurred. **Map 3**   STEVEN H. WERLIN

***Masorah*; Masoretes.** *Masorah*, which means "transmission," refers to scribal traditions that evolved to preserve correct readings, performance, and reproduction of the biblical text. Although vowel signs were introduced into the biblical text by the sixth or seventh century, the Masoretes developed various systems of graphemes (written symbols) to facilitate accurate vocalization, accentuation, and cantillation (chanting). These *grammarians and *scribes lived in the Land of Israel, primarily in Tiberias in the *Galilee and *Jerusalem, and also in *Iraq; they were active between the seventh and eleventh centuries.

Masorah also refers to textual notes that the Masoretes added to the margins of manuscripts and the bottom of the pages of biblical codices to facilitate the correct reading and copying of the biblical text. The necessity for such annotations arose from the early practice of writing the biblical text in continuous script without breaks between words, sentences, or paragraphs. Although final forms of some Hebrew letters were introduced in late antiquity and the *Talmud alludes to paragraph divisions, marking the division of the text into verses was an early concern of the Masoretes.

Masoretic textual notes are typically divided into two categories. The *Masorah Parva* (minor *masorah*) most frequently indicates certain words that are to be read aloud differently from how they are written; it also identifies difficult words whose distinctive spelling was worthy of special attention by copyists. The *Masorah Magna* (greater *masorah*), preserves concordances of unique grammatical forms as well as mnemonic devices highlighting significant features of vocalization and cantillation of the text.

Rabbinic literature mentions the practice of liturgical recitation (*kerei*) diverging from written text (*ketiv*). This practice serves a number of purposes, including correcting archaic grammatical forms and textual errors preserved in the written text, as well as softening strong language in the written text that is nonetheless retained in oral recitation. In addition to the textual *masorah*, a numerical *masorah* developed to aid copyists. It indicates, for example, the number of verses in each biblical book and annotates key milestones, such as the midpoint of the number of verses in the *Torah.

No uniform tradition exists for the *masorah* as a whole: Each school of Masoretes employed a different set of graphemes to establish vocalization, accent, and cantillation, and their annotations differed as well. Thus, the Tiberian system uses eight signs to indicate seven vowels, whereas the older Palestinian system indicates only five vowels. The Tiberian school of Masoretes developed into two rival factions, that of Ben Asher and that of Ben Naphtali; the Ben Asher school eventually gained ascendancy. The tenth-century Aleppo Codex, considered the most authoritative masoretic document, represents the Ben Asher tradition.

As Tiberian vocalization marks do not indicate accent, a system of cantillation graphemes was also developed. For the prose books of the Bible, this system relies on dots and lines indicating either conjunctive or disjunctive accents, placed above or below a word to mark the accented syllable. Some of the names and symbols of these accents are reminiscent of hand movements, long used as prompts in public recitation and retained to this day by some communities. Accent placement follows structured rules that generally rely on the logic of the biblical verse but also take the verse's rhythm into account. The poetic books of *Psalms, *Proverbs, and *Job use a different system of accents. Because of their canonical status in public reading, masoretic notes were also appended to *Targum Onkelos, an *Aramaic Bible translation. For further reading, see J. R. Jacobson, *Chanting the Hebrew Bible: The Art of Cantillation* (2002), 360–94.

PHILLIP I. ACKERMAN-LIEBERMAN

Mathematics: See SCIENCE AND MATHEMATICS

Medicine. From the biblical period to modern times, there has been a strong connection between Judaism and medicine. Many of Judaism's most famous sages were also physicians, and Jews have looked favorably on medicine as a profession. This cultural affinity is based on economics and education. As a minority community, Jews were often barred from livelihoods in agriculture and in crafts. However, under Persian, Greek, Roman, Muslim, and Christian rule, the profession of medicine was consistently available to Jews. In addition, mastery of the corpus of Jewish religious literature requires a thorough knowledge of medicine and science. For example, slaughtering animals according to ritual norms (*shehitah*) entails substantial anatomical knowledge to detect blemishes and anatomical irregularities that might render the animal unfit for consumption; similarly, the laws pertinent to conjugal restrictions during women's menstrual cycles (*niddah*) necessitate significant gynecological specialization. Moreover, just as medicine, especially in its pre-modern forms, demanded familiarity with *astronomy, botany, zoology, and mathematics, so too mastery of *rabbinic Judaism called for encyclopedic learning. In the Renaissance, for example, educated Jews pursued the cultural ideal of *hakham kolel*, a Hebrew rendering of the Latin *homo universalis* or perhaps the Italian *uomo universale*, appellations that were accorded to a person of universal learning.

BIBLICAL PERIOD: Most of what we know about Jewish medicine in the biblical period comes from the Hebrew Bible itself (see ILLNESS AND DISEASE: BIBLE AND ANCIENT NEAR EAST). Common ailments were treated by means of preventive medicine such as ritual washing and dietary restrictions. More unusual diseases sometimes called for *magical treatments; according to BT *Pesahim* 56a, King *Hezekiah (2 Kings 18–20) prohibited the "Book of Cures," which purportedly contained remedies for all known diseases. Additionally, midwifery was a distinguished profession for Israelite women. The book of Exodus praises Shifrah and Puah for their bravery in defying the Egyptian king's order to kill male Jewish infants (Exod 1:15–17). Finally, it is important to note that, although ancient Jews practiced medicine, *God was considered the ultimate healer, and physicians only acted as God's instruments, as attested by Exodus 15:26: "I am the Lord that heals you." Above all, medicine in the Bible is chiefly concerned with hygiene, and some 213 of the 613 *commandments deal with preventing the transmission of contagious disease. Practices such as quarantine, the immersion of utensils and clothing in scalding water, and prescribed bathing all reflect this focus.

TALMUDIC PERIOD: Numerous talmudic dicta, such as "the saving of a life (*pikuah nefesh*) takes precedence over the observance of the *Sabbath" (BT *Yoma* 85a), illustrate the importance given to healing. At this time (200–600 CE), Jewish physicians were prized throughout the Greco-Roman world, as attested in the medical writings of Pliny the Younger, Aulus Cornelius Celsus, and Galen. Prominent Gentile rulers and religious leaders (such as the *Church Father Basil [fl. 300 CE]) retained Jewish physicians. Pedagogically, the study of medicine was closely linked to the religious curriculum of the time. Many of the talmudic sages, including Ishmael, Haninah ben Dosa, and Samuel ben Abba ha-Cohen, were practicing physicians. Modern physicians have detected precocious knowledge in talmudic medical references to embryology, as well as in other areas.

MIDDLE AGES: Medieval Jewish physicians played a major role in the transmission of ancient Greek medical knowledge; they often worked alongside Gentile scholars in translating Greek and Arabic medical texts, usually by way of Hebrew, into Latin and eventually the European vernaculars. Medieval Christian physicians such as Roger Bacon (thirteenth century) and Vesalius (sixteenth century) urged their students and readers to study Hebrew as a resource for medical knowledge and may have known Hebrew themselves. In *Byzantium especially, Jews played a crucial role in the transmission of Greek medical learning to European culture. The sixth-century physician Asaph ben Berekhiah, known more commonly as Asaph ha-Rophei (Asaph the Physician), wrote an encyclopedic medical work reflecting contemporary practices. Several centuries later, in Byzantine-ruled southern *Italy, Shabbetai Donnolo was closely associated with Salerno's famous medical school; he wrote a well-known medical work, *Sefer ha-Yakar* (E. Lieber, "Asaf's Book of Medicines," *Dumbarton Oaks Papers* 38 [1984], 233–49). In *Spain, where Jewish culture flourished under Muslim rule, a number of Jewish viziers, translators, and philosophers were also physicians. The eleventh-century linguist and *Court Jew Ḥasdai ibn Shaprut translated Dioscorides' *Materia medica*, a pharmacological handbook, into Arabic. Judah *Halevi (twelfth century), better known as a poet and author of the philosophical work *The Kuzari*, was also a practicing physician. Towering over all other scholars of the period was Moses *Maimonides (1135–1204). In addition to his myriad accomplishments as a community leader, halakhic codifier, and religious philosopher, he also wrote medical works, the most famous of which was *Pirkei Moshe* (Chapters of Moses; see H. Davidson, *Moses Maimonides: the Man and his Works* [2005]).

RENAISSANCE AND BAROQUE ERAS: After the 1492 expulsion of Jews from Spain (see SPAIN, CHRISTIAN), many Iberian Jewish doctors, some of whom were forced to convert to Christianity, took their talents elsewhere, most importantly to *North Africa, *Italy, the Low Countries, and the *Ottoman Empire. One such figure is Amatus Lusitanus (1511–1568), who published more than seven hundred Latin *consilia,* or medical case studies, which demonstrate deep medical learning and a refreshingly anecdotal nature. In fact, the practice of narrative medicine, endorsed by several contemporary physicians, has deep roots in the Renaissance period and especially in the works of *Sephardi Jews.

Jewish physicians abounded in early modern Italy. David de Pomis (1525–1593) served as Pope Pius IV's personal physician and wrote an apologetic work in Latin defending the legacy of Jewish doctors. Italian Jewish physicians were particularly celebrated for their integration of medical learning with traditional Jewish education and culture. Medical schools, including Padua, were among the first to offer admission to Jews, beginning in the early seventeenth century. Numerous Jews matriculated, and most were awarded the degree *artium ac medicinae doctor* (Doctor of Arts and Medicine). Joseph Zahalon (1630–1693), scion of a Spanish rabbinical dynasty, took his degree from the University of Rome and wrote a Hebrew medical encyclopedia intended for lay people entitled *Otzar ha-Ḥayyim* (Treasury of Life). In many ways it may be seen as a forerunner of modern efforts to popularize medical knowledge, such as Dr. Spock's child care books or www.webmd.com. Joseph Delmedigo (1591–1655), a graduate of Padua, studied with Galileo Galilei and wrote prolifically on a great variety of topics, including medicine.

MODERN PERIOD: In the wake of the French Revolution, Jews were gradually granted civic *emancipation in most of Western Europe. As a result, many barriers to attendance at European universities, most of which had not been as tolerant as those in Italy, and various other obstacles to professional advancement, were removed. Throughout the nineteenth and twentieth centuries, in Europe and North America, Jewish doctors and medical researchers were responsible for many important discoveries and developments. It is difficult to imagine the progress of modern medicine without the contributions of Sigmund *Freud (d. 1939) in psychology or Jonas Salk (d. 1995), who discovered a widely used polio vaccine, in infectious diseases.

In the early-twenty-first century, Jews are significantly involved in medicine and medical research. In *Israel, scientists continue to break new ground in all areas of medical research and treatment, and centers such as Hadassah Hospital and the Weizmann Institute of Science have achieved worldwide fame. In North America, Jewish physicians are ubiquitous to the extent of becoming a cultural fixture.

For further reading, see H. Friedenwald, *The Jews and Medicine* (1944); J. Preuss, *Biblical and Talmudic Medicine*, trans. F. Rosner (1993); R. Barkaï, "Le judaïsme espagnol du Moyen Âge et la médicine," in *Le Monde sépharade*, ed. S. I. Trigano (2006); J. Shatzmiller, *Jews, Medicine, and Medieval Society* (1995); D. Ruderman, *Jewish Thought and Scientific Discovery in Early Modern Europe* (1995); N. Berger, ed., *Jews and Medicine: Religion, Culture, Science* (1995); and "Medicine," *Encyclopedia Judaica*, 2nd ed. (2006); **see also NURSING: UNITED STATES.**   ANDREW BERNS

Megillah, Hebrew for "scroll," may refer specifically to the biblical book of *Esther, which is publicly read on the festival of *Purim, often from a specially designated and decorated scroll (see CEREMONIAL OBJECTS). Esther is one of five relatively brief biblical books that constitute the *Five Scrolls (*ḥamesh megillot*); the others are *Ecclesiastes, *Lamentations, *Ruth, and *Song of Songs. *Megillah* is also the name of a tractate in Order *Mo'ed* of the *Mishnah and *Talmud; it deals with the observance of the festival of *Purim and aspects of the book of Esther.

Megillat Ta'anit (Scroll of Fasting) is a document of a semi-historical character that originated among the sages of the *Second Temple era. It was apparently compiled between 41 and 70 CE. The scroll is essentially a list of about thirty-five dates drawn up in *Aramaic and arranged in *calendar order. Its goal, as stated in its opening sentence, is to forbid Jews to fast on these days that are defined in the Jerusalem *Talmud as "days on which miracles had been performed for Israel." The dates listed are, in the main, those of joyous events of various kinds during the Second Temple period, from the days of *Ezra and *Nehemiah to the times of the destruction of the *Temple. An explanatory commentary in *Hebrew, known as the "Scholion," was later appended to the scroll and has been transmitted in two versions. The most recent edition is V. Noam, *Megillat Ta'anit: Versions, Interpretation, History, with a Critical Edition* (2003).

VERED NOAM

Meḥitzah (literally, "partition") is a physical divider separating men and women during *synagogue *worship in Modern Orthodox and Ultra-Orthodox forms of *Judaism. Although there was a "women's court" (*ezrat nashim*) in the Second *Temple in Jerusalem, it was open to men and women; only at the joyous water-drawing ceremony on the harvest festival of *Sukkot were the sexes separated (BT *Sukkot* 51b–52). There may have been separate sections for women in ancient synagogues, but there is no definitive evidence for this; the *Talmud refers to efforts to separate men and women in synagogues during crowded festival worship (BT *Kiddushin* 81 a) to preserve propriety.

Separate worship sections or rooms for women only became widespread in the later Middle Ages. Men prayed together in the central part of the synagogue because they are obligated to participate in communal worship; women, who are not so obligated, were relegated behind a visual barrier of some kind, either in the back of the sanctuary or in an upstairs gallery. Placing women away from the center of worship and out of the sight of men may also have been an effort to preserve modest behavior between the sexes and to focus men's attention on prayer (because women's voices are said to be a sexual distraction to men [BT *Berakhot* 24a]). In some places, such as the German city of Worms, women prayed in a separate room with a small window that connected to the main synagogue so that they could hear the service.

In the twenty-first century, men and women are no longer separated during worship in liberal forms of Jewish practice. Reform Judaism eliminated the *meḥitzah* in the 1800s on the grounds that it had no biblical basis. Although men and women still prayed separately in Reform synagogues in Europe into the twentieth century, there was no longer a physical divider; family seating was usually the norm in Reform synagogues in the United States (see JUDAISM, REFORM entries). Traditional communities consider *meḥitzah* as a requirement during prayer, although they differ as to the height and nature of the partition. Thus, there are a variety of styles of *meḥitzot*, including balconies, fixed partitions, movable partitions, curtains, and in some cases entirely separate rooms. In some Modern Orthodox synagogues in the United States there are no visual barriers, and the *Torah scroll can be passed between the men's and women's sections, offering women more inclusion in public worship.

For further reading, see essays in S. Grossman and R. Haut, eds., *Daughters of the King: Women and the Synagogue* (1992).

JUDITH R. BASKIN

Meir Ben Barukh (Maharam) of Rothenburg (ca. 1215–1293) was the leading *Ashkenazic rabbinic authority in northern Europe during the second half of the thirteenth century. He studied with *Tosafists in both France (see FRANCE, MEDIEVAL) and *Germany, including Isaac ben Moses (known as the Or Zarua) in Würzburg, Jeḥiel ben Joseph of Paris, and Samuel ben Solomon of Falaise.

Meir wrote his liturgical elegy (*kinnah*) for the Talmud, "You who have been consumed by the fire, seek the well-being of your mourners," after he witnessed its burning in Paris in 1242. This event, and others in his native Germany, focused Meir's attention on the incipient decline of Ashkenazic Jewry; his *halakhic writings and methods reflect these developments in several ways. His admiration for *Maimonides' *Mishneh Torah* and for Isaac Alfasi's *Halakhot Rabbati*, for example, inspired several of his students – R. *Asher ben Jeḥiel (Rosh), Mordecai ben Hillel, and Meir ha-Kohen – to write works and commentaries that were linked to these great *Sephardic codes (see HALAKHAH). Meir wrote hundreds of *responsa, which, together with those of his predecessors, were preserved by his students. This ensured the survival of large amounts of Ashkenazic halakhic material in its original form.

In his *Sefer Tashbez*, Samson ben Zadok observed and recorded Meir's comportment in a variety of situations, emphasizing his practical halakhic applications and customs. This genre, which was not so much in vogue in Ashkenaz during the twelfth and thirteenth centuries, became a dominant form of rabbinic expression during the later Middle Ages. Although sometimes seen as stringent, Meir's halakhic rulings often managed to blend or combine opposing positions. This tendency, which may have come to Meir through the teachings of the *Ḥasidei Ashkenaz* (the German pietists; see MIDDLE AGES: *Ḥasidei Ashkenaz*), characterized his approach to communal government and monetary affairs, as well as his rulings in ritual matters. His affinity for German pietism can also be seen in his Torah commentary, which was based for the most part on masoretic details (see MASORAH; MASORETES), and in some of his many liturgical poems (see POETRY: LITURGICAL [*PIYYUT*]).

Meir was arrested in Lombardy in 1286 (perhaps while he was on the way to the Land of *Israel), and he was held in several locales in Germany for seven years until his death. During his imprisonment, Meir completed his *Tosafot* to Tractate *Yoma* and was able to consult with students and colleagues. No stranger to tragedy, Meir ruled that a father who had slain his family (in Koblenz in the 1260s) in anticipation of the imminent threat of conversionary efforts (and had then himself been spared) did not require any special expiation, because he had acted in accordance with earlier Ashkenazic halakhic practices (see MARTYRDOM). Based on a passage in *hekhalot* literature, Meir also wrote that once a person decided to undertake *martyrdom, he did not feel the pain of death. After his death in 1293, Meir's remains were held until 1307, when they were successfully ransomed by a Jew named Alexander Wimpfin. In accordance with his request, Alexander was ultimately buried next to Meir in the Jewish cemetery of Worms, where their graves (and tombstones) can still be seen.

EPHRAIM KANARFOGEL

Meir, Golda (1898–1978) was the fourth prime minister of the State of *Israel. Born Golda Mabovitch in Kiev in the *Russian Empire (modern-day *Ukraine), she emigrated with her family to Milwaukee, Wisconsin, in 1906 where she attended public schools. She attended what is now the University of Wisconsin–Milwaukee and worked at a Yiddish-speaking school before moving to Denver, Colorado, to live with her sister. There she became increasingly involved in the Labor Zionist movement (see ZIONISM) and also met Morris Meyerson whom she married at the age of nineteen. They immigrated to *Palestine in 1921 and joined Kibbutz Merhavia in the Jezreel valley; a natural leader, Golda left the kibbutz for *Tel Aviv in 1924 to become an official of the Histadrut Trade Union. She served as an emissary to the *United States between 1932 and 1936 and in 1946 became head of the Political Department of the Jewish Agency, the chief liaison with the *Palestine *British Mandate government. After Israel's creation, she became the new state's first ambassador to the *Soviet Union. In 1949 she was elected to the Knesset as a member of *Mapai* (see ISRAEL, STATE OF: POLITICAL PARTIES) and was appointed minister of labor; in 1956 she became foreign minister, the position she held until her retirement in 1965. When Prime Minister Levi Eshkol died in 1969, Meir was urged to return to politics and, with the support of the Labor Party, became Israel's first female prime minister. Major events during her time in office include the murders of Israeli athletes at the 1972 Munich Summer Olympics and the Yom Kippur War of 1973 (see ISRAEL, STATE OF: ARAB-ISRAELI CONFLICT). She resigned from office on April 11, 1974. In 1975, Golda Meir was awarded the Israel Prize for her contributions to the state and also published her autobiography, *My Life*.

ELIZABETH SHULMAN

Memoir and Life Writing: Hebrew (1780s to Present).

A key point of contention in the field of Jewish lifewriting in general, and Israeli lifewriting specifically, is whether Jewish history's collective emphasis stands in essential tension with the individual impulse at the heart of autobiographical writing. Israeli literary critic Gershon Shaked (2000) suggests that writers in Hebrew from the late nineteenth century onward have faced a choice between engaging with socioeconomic and political issues or retreating to the internal realms of confession, romance, or spirituality. This split between public and private continued to structure Hebrew literary output through the first decades of the State of *Israel and has had a significant impact on the production, cultural status, and social role of Israeli lifewriting in its many manifestations.

A survey of Israeli lifewriting – that is, memoirs written in Hebrew after the declaration of the State of *Israel in 1948 – must begin with its precedents in *Haskalah* (Jewish Enlightenment) and turn-of-the-century autobiographical literature (see LITERATURE, HEBREW: *HASKALAH*; for a seventeenth-century Hebrew autobiography, see MODENA, LEON). Scholars have examined how *Haskalah* authors absorbed or digressed from the influential paradigms set by Jean-Jacques Rousseau, whose *Confessions* (1782–89) addressed society rather than *God and emphasized the years of childhood as central to comprehending the adult. Salomon *Maimon's *Lebensgeschichte* (Life History; 1796) and Mordecai Aaron Günzberg's *Aviezer* (ca. 1828) both relied on the Rousseauian model; their focus on childhood and on education in *heder* (the traditional Jewish pedagogical system) and their critique of Jewish marital norms are particularly noteworthy. Among Hebrew memoirs from Eastern Europe, Moses Leib Lilienblum's *Hattot Neurim* (Sins of Youth; 1876) is generally considered the most important. Lilienblum's work in turn influenced the next generation of European Jewish intellectuals such as Micah Joseph Berdichevsky and Mordecai Ze'ev Feierberg.

During the *tehiyah* (see HEBREW: MODERN REVIVAL) of the late nineteenth and early twentieth centuries, fictional autobiographies often became a vehicle to express the personal crises of a generation of young Jews. Dubbed *telushim* (uprooted ones), these young men attempted to free themselves from the bonds of traditional Jewish life and join secular European society; the "apostasy narrative," describing their crises of faith, grounds their disguised tales. Feierberg's *Le'an* (Whither?; 1899) and Joseph Haim Brenner's *Ba-Horef* (In Winter; 1903) are outstanding examples of this genre's ripening at the turn of the century. Also from this period, although in a different vein, is *Safiah* (Aftergrowth; 1908–19) by the preeminent poet Hayyim Nahman *Bialik. This fragmentary collection of first-person prose sketches recalls the early childhood of a boy named Shmulik in his native village.

After this creative spurt, Hebrew fictional autobiography was a somewhat dormant genre until the 1970s. Meanwhile, in the decades immediately preceding and following the establishment of Israel, the national enterprise of settling the Jewish homeland dictated the focus of personal and public literature. Memoirs of the settlement movement and autobiographical works by Zionist leaders began to surface (see ZIONISM). Creative fiction was expected to adhere to the Zionist ideological agenda by supporting the collective striving toward national goals; such themes as the War of Independence and redeeming the land through agriculture prevailed. As Yael S. Feldman has written, saying "I" and expressing individuality were still difficult tasks for writers into the 1970s. Even when David Shahar (*The Palace of Shattered Vessels* series; 1969 onward) and Hanoch Bartov (*Shel mi atah yeled* [Whose Little Boy Are You?]; 1970) crafted fictional autobiographies, significant historical moments in the Israeli national narrative framed their recollections of childhood. This period also saw the publication of autobiographies by political icons such as Yigal Allon (1975), Golda *Meir (1975), Moshe Dayan (1976), and Yitzhak *Rabin (1979). Michael Keren has convincingly shown how these leaders' awareness of current events as well as their own mythological legacies led to narrative choices that enhanced particular aspects of their public identities.

This ideological emphasis militated against intensely personal, confessional works in mid-twentieth-century Israeli society. A notable exception was Pinhas Sadeh's *Ha-hayyim kemashal* (Life as a Parable; 1958). In Sadeh's paradigm-setting book he declares, "Since I cannot write, do not want to write, and it is impossible that I could write about anything apart from myself, all that I really need to know is myself." Although it was marginalized at first because of its combination of existential confessionalism and Christian theology, *Ha-hayyim kemashal* gradually won an audience and recognition of its innovations.

The past two decades have shown renewed interest in both Hebrew literary autobiography and the life writing of Israeli public figures. S. Yizhar's *Mikdamot* (Preliminaries; 1992), Haim Beer's *Havalim* (The Pure Element of Time; 1998), Nurit Zarchi's *Mishakei bedidut* (Games of Loneliness; 1999), and Amos Oz's *Sipur al ahavah vehoshekh* (A Tale of Love and Darkness; 2002) are examples of relatively unmasked attempts by acclaimed authors to create detailed, yet aesthetically innovative narratives about their lives. In *Sipur hayyim* (Story of a Life; 1999), Aharon Appelfeld continued his exploration of *Holocaust memories in the context of Israeli lifewriting. These and other recent publications point not only to the authors' desires to portray themselves in the context of their family, education, and young adult-hood but also to the receptiveness of the Hebrew-reading audience to such works.

Israeli historiography, like Israeli literary culture, did not immediately make space for the writing of individual lives. The reasons are similar: an initial adherence to collective ideological imperatives, followed by an expanded perspective. Where Zionist historiography might once have focused on nation, class, and the historical process as forces, it now increasingly recognizes the role of individuals in shaping history. Perhaps the relative stability of the nation-state, more than sixty years after its founding, has made possible this backward-looking stage of Israeli society and culture. Anita Shapira's biography of Berl Katznelson, *Berl: Biografiyah* (1980), is viewed as a watershed moment that opened up the field of academic biography in Israel. In a similar vein are works on David *Ben-Gurion by Shabtai Tevet (1976) and Michael Bar-Zohar (1980), as well as Yehuda Reinharz's study of Chaim *Weizmann (1987). Literary figures are also benefiting from the recent acceptance of Hebrew biography. Yehoshua Porat's biography of Yonatan Ratosh (1989), Ehud Ben-Ezer's biography of Esther Raab (1998), and Haim Beer's group portrait of Bialik, Brenner, and S. Y. *Agnon (1992) constitute examples of Hebrew literary criticism entering the age of biography. Taken together, these developments in Israeli lifewriting indicate that the once dominant discourse of the national narrative has given way to a more flexible and variegated texture of literary production (see also ISRAEL, STATE OF entries).

For further reading, see Y. Feldman, "Living on the Top Floor: The Arrested Autobiography in Israeli Fiction," *Modern Hebrew Literature* 1 (1988): 72–77; A. Mintz, *Banished from Their Father's Table: Loss of Faith and Hebrew Autobiography* (1989); G. Shaked, *Modern Hebrew Fiction* (2000); M. Keren, "National Icons and Personal Identities in Three Israeli Autobiographies," *Biography* 27(2) (2004): 357–83; M. Moseley, *Being for Myself Alone: Origins of Jewish Autobiography* (2006); and T. Hess, "The Confessions of a Bad Reader: Embodied Selves, Narrative Strategies, and Subversion in Israeli Women's Autobiography," *Prooftexts* 27 (2007): 151–87.　　　　　　　　　　　　HANNAH S. PRESSMAN

Memoir and Life Writing: Mizraḥi. The *Mizraḥi (Middle Eastern) memoir tells the personal story of Jewish life in Arab and Muslim lands, written for the most part after that life was no longer possible. In part, these memoirs are efforts to recover, preserve, and reclaim a lost heritage, either responding to the dominant *Ashkenazi culture or reformulating or reframing the Mizraḥi identity. The increasing popularity of the Mizraḥi memoir speaks to a growing interest in "ethnic" literature and the embrace of the personal narrative. Depending on their author and intended audience, these autobiographical works tend to emphasize either the fruitful links between Jews and Muslims before their disruption caused by the historical and cultural changes of the second half of the twentieth century, or the tragedy of the increasing inhospitality of the ancestral home.

These memoirs are written in Arabic by those who maintained it as their mother tongue; in French by those who studied at *Alliance Israélite Universelle schools; in Hebrew by those who immigrated to *Israel; and in English by those wishing to reach a larger – and western – audience. They re-create a life that no longer exists, often including rich details of the quotidian that evoke a time before electricity and nationalism, in which Jewish *festivals and traditional *customs were woven into the daily routine and the family sat at the center.

Most of these memoirs take place during times of intense societal changes, including increasing secularization, modernization, and urbanization. As traditional Muslim societies became more aware of the larger world and as ideas of political nationalism spread, the status of Jews changed. The memoirs portray these changes from the perspectives of individuals, depicting personal stories against tumultuous historical backdrops. The audiences for these works are the writers themselves and their peers, their children, and Jews from very different backgrounds. One of the earliest such works – Albert Memmi's 1953 autobiographical novel *La Statue de Sel* (Pillar of Salt), the story of a young Jewish boy growing up in French-colonized and *Nazi-occupied Tunisia – has become a classic (see NORTH AFRICA). Although nearly every community has its chronicler, a greater number of works are set in *Egypt, *Iran, and *Iraq.

A number of Egyptian-born writers have followed essayist Jacqueline Kahanoff's lead in writing about the Levantine dimension of their lives. Her *From East the Sun*, originally written in English, was first published in Aharon Amir's Hebrew translation *Memizraḥ ha-Shemesh* (1978). André Aciman (*Out of Egypt*; 1994), Gini Alhadeff (*The Sun at Midday: Tales of a Mediterranean Family*; 1997), and Lucette Lagnado (*The Man in the Sharkskin Suit*; 2007) also recall their origins in Egypt: They write of cosmopolitan families; eccentric relatives; the colorful confusion of languages, cultures, and identities; and the devastating impact of dislocation and exile.

Although Alexandria is the more Mediterranean of Egypt's major cities, Cairo is also a site of multiculturalism and of fluid identities. Cairo-born Claudia Roden develops the language of food, offering memories of her lost past through tracking down other displaced Middle Easterners to gather recipes and compile cookbooks. Her first cookbook, *A Book of Middle Eastern Food* (1974), intersperses stories and personal reminiscences with recipes. The book works on two levels: a sharing of memories with compatriots and a culinary introduction to the region for a western audience. The texts based in Egypt share a number of memories – the quail harvest, summers in Alexandria, street vendors, social stratification, shifting identities, and multilingualism: French for culture and education, Italian for assumed identity, *Ladino and/or Turkish from the past, and Arabic limited to the lower classes and thus the kitchen, with English as a language of the future.

In recent years a number of Jewish women have joined their non-Jewish counterparts in writing memoirs set in Iran. (For a variety of reasons these memoirs tend to be written in English.) Although the 1979 revolution is the catalyst for nearly all of them, the difference is that the Jewish writers do not tend to idealize pre-revolutionary Iran. Instead they show themselves chafing against the restrictions that limited them as girls and the hatred that threatens them as Jews. Examples include Roya Hakakian, *Journey from the Land of No: A Memoir of a Girlhood Caught in Revolutionary Iran* (2004); Farideh Goldin, *Wedding Song: Memoirs of an Iranian Jewish Woman* (2003); Dalia Sofer, *Septembers of Shiraz* (2007); and the autobiographical fiction of Gina Nahai

(*Moonlight on the Avenue of Faith*; 1999; *The Eye of the Peacock*; 2000, and *Caspian Rain*; 2008).

A number of writers have memorialized Iraq – and especially Baghdad – from before the great exodus of the Jewish community in the middle of the last century. These memoirs tend to portray the lively cultural exchange during the literary renaissance – the friendships among Arabs and Kurds, Muslims, Christians, and Jews that took place in the coffeehouses. Although Nissim Rejwan (*Last Jews in Baghdad*; 2004) describes a lower class background, Isaac bar Moshe (*Khuruj Min al-Iraq* [Leaving Iraq, 1975]; *Beit fi Baghdad* [A House in Baghdad], 1983) and Sasson Somekh (*Baghdad Etmol* [Baghdad Yesterday]; 2003) are from the comfortable middle class. Their memoirs, written in Arabic, recall overlapping social circles and intellectual development, but Bar Moshe details the unraveling of the community in far greater detail than other authors. In a novelized autobiography, Mona Yahia (*When the Gray Beetles Took over Baghdad*, 2000) further fleshes out the community's collapse. Earlier works in Arabic include *Kull Shay Hadi fi al-Iyadah* (All Quiet in the Surgery, 1981) by physician Salman Darwishe and *Qissat Hayati fi Wadi al-Rafidayn* (The Story of My Life in Mesopotamia, 1980) by poet Anwar Shaul. Violette Shamash (1918–2006) provides an overview of twentieth-century Jewish life and history in Iraq through events in the lives of her own family in *Memories of Eden: A Journey through Jewish Baghdad* (2008).

Recently, the children of those who grew up in Arab lands have begun to publish memoirs recovering their parents' histories; for example, Jack Marshall, *From Baghdad to Brooklyn: Growing up in a Jewish-Arabic Family in Midcentury America* (2005); Marina Benjamin, *The Last Days in Babylon: The History of a Family, the Story of a Nation* (2006); and Ariel Sabar, *My Father's Paradise: A Son's Search for His Family's Past* (2007). This last book documents the decline of the small Jewish community in *Kurdistan and its problematic resettlement in Israel.

Although the process of recovery is a common motif – and allows these books to qualify as memoirs – it is the Mizrahi past that captures the reader's interest. Together these narratives serve to complement the Ashkenazi memoir and to correct Jewish historiography. Ranging from nostalgic to tragic, the past is either a lost idyll, a series of tribulations, or, most commonly, a combination of the two: the story of a home becoming no longer home.

NANCY E. BERG

Memoir and Life Writing: Yiddish. With the exception of a few pre-modern Yiddish memoirs, most notably the memoirs of Glikl Hameln (1689–1719; published as *Zikhroynes* in 1896; see GLÜCKEL OF HAMELN), Yiddish lifewriting developed in the 1880s. The first biographical entries on Yiddish writers appeared in 1889 in Nahum Sokolov's *Sefer Zikaron le-Sofrei Yisrael ha-Khaim Itanu Kayom* (A Memoir Book of Contemporary Jewish Writers). *Shloyme Reb Khayims* (Shloyme, Hayyim's Son) by Mendele Mokher Seforim (the pseudonym of Sholem Jacob Abramovich), written between 1894–1914, is the first Yiddish autobiographical novel; the first part, *Petikhta*, was originally written in Hebrew and later reworked in Yiddish. This work is paradigmatic of the Yiddish autobiographical genre in its rejection of the confessional model that has characterized the genre in Hebrew. Instead, *Shloyme Reb Khayims* presents a fictionalized version

of the author's life narrative and embeds it within a larger Jewish context by foregrounding ethnographic and cultural historical phenomena. Sholem Aleichem's autobiographical *Funem Yarid* (From the Fair; 1913–16) was modeled on Abramovich's recollections and presents episodes from the author's childhood and early youth in novelized form. This is in contrast to I. L. Peretz's mature self-examination in *Mayne Zikhroynes* (My Memoirs; 1913–16; see LITERATURE, YIDDISH: FROM 1800 TO THE TWENTY-FIRST CENTURY).

In addition to literary autobiography, other subgenres of Yiddish life writing emerged in the twentieth century. Ezekiel Kotik's *Mayne Zikhroynes* (My Memoirs; 1913) exemplifies a Yiddish ethnographic memoir. Yiddish memoirs of Jewish political leaders and party members, cultural leaders, actors, painters, and other artists also proliferated. A prime example is Abraham Cahan's five-volume *Bleter fun mayn lebn* (Pages from My Life; 1926–36). One rich literary form was the autobiographical *poeme* or long narrative poem. Examples include Menahem Boreysho's *Der Geyer. Kapitln fun a Lebn* (The Walker: Chapters from a Life; 1943); and Y. Y. Schwartz, *Kentoki* (Kentucky; 1925) and *Yunge yorn* (Youth; 1952). A particularly important subgenre is the Yiddish *khurbn* or *Holocaust memoir, originally crafted as testimony and eyewitness accounts (see also HOLOCAUST DIARIES). These are exemplified by Mark Turkov's 176-volume series, *Dos Poylishe Yidntum* (Polish Jewry; published in Buenos Aires between 1946 and 1966), which includes Elie Wiesel's 1955 *Un di Velt hot Geshvign* (And the World Was Silent; later reworked in English as *Night*).

The artistically most accomplished Yiddish autobiographical novels are Jacob Glatstein's *Ven Yash iz Geforn* (When Yash Set Out; 1938]) and *Ven Yash iz Gekumen* (When Yash Arrived; 1940]; Jonah Rosenfeld's *Eyner Aleyn* (All Alone; 1940); Y. Y. Trunk's seven-volume *Poyln: Zikhroynes un Bilder* (Poland: Memoirs and Pictures; 1944–53); I. J. Singer, *Fun a Velt Vos iz Nishto Mer* (From a World That Is No More; 1946); Dovid Bergelson's *Bam Dnyepr* (On the Dnieper; 1932, 1940); and I. B. Singer's rich and diverse autobiographical œuvre, including *In mayn tatns bezdn-shtub* (1956; published in 1966 in English as *In My Father's Court*). More recent examples include Joseph Buloff's *Fun Altn Markplats* (From the Old Marketplace; 1995) and Boris Sandler's *Lamedvovnikes fun mayn zikorn* (Lamedvovniks from My Memory; serialized in *Forverts*, 2005).

Although women writers have produced few major novels in Yiddish, some, in addition to Glikl Hameln, have excelled as writers of autobiography. Examples include Bella *Chagall's *Brenendike Likht* (1945; published in English as *Burning Lights*, 1946); Esther Singer Kreitman's *Sheydim-Tants* (Demon's Dance, 1936; published in English as *Deborah*, 1983); Hinde Bergner, *In di lange vinternekht* (In the Long Winter Nights; 1946), and Puah Rakovsky, *Zikhroynes fun a yidisher revolutsyonerin* (Memoirs of a Jewish Woman Revolutionary, 1953; published in English as *My Life as a Radical Jewish Woman*, ed. P. E. Hyman [2001]).

Three recent critical studies of the Jewish autobiography provide the first systematic attempts in English to establish coherent theoretical and historical frameworks. Marcus Moseley's application of Rousseau's confessional paradigm situates the field in a historical context of publication data, critical reception, and textual influence. The only book-length study of Yiddish autobiographical writing to date is Jan Schwarz's *Imagining Lives,* which establishes a theoretical framework encompassing the diversity and variety of Yiddish life writing with particular focus on the autobiographical novel. The book provides close readings of eight autobiographical works by seven Yiddish writers highlighting ethnography, genre hybridity, and lack of self-examination. Schwarz also discusses the most influential exceptions – the confessional works of I. L. Peretz, I. B. Singer, and Jonah Rosenfeld – noting that "Yiddish writers became masters of comic relief, irony, meta-discourse and wordplay inscribed in a literary discourse that was highly ambivalent about modern concepts such as 'privacy,' 'inwardness' and 'self'" (160).

The more than eight hundred *Yizkor* books (memorial volumes) of Eastern European Jewish communities assembled and published by Holocaust survivors provide a treasure trove of Yiddish autobiographical material, much of which has never been translated (see HOLOCAUST DIARIES). A rich collection of autobiographies by young people, mostly in Yiddish, submitted to *YIVO competitions in the 1930s, has been edited by Jeffrey Shandler.

For further reading, see J. Shandler, ed., *Awakening Lives: Autobiographies of Jewish Youth in Poland before the Holocaust* (2002); M. Stanislawski, *Autobiographical Jews: Essays in Jewish Self-Fashioning* (2004); J. Schwarz, *Imagining Lives: Autobiographical Fiction of Yiddish Writers* (2005); M. Moseley, *Being for Myself Alone: Origins of Jewish Autobiography* (2006); D. Assaf, "Introduction," *Journey to a Nineteenth-Century Shtetl: The Memoirs of Yekhezkel Kotik* (2002); J. Kugelmass and J. Boyarin, eds., *From a Ruined Garden: The Memorial Books of Polish Jewry* (1998); and E. Lifschutz, *Bibliography of American and Canadian Jewish Memoirs and Autobiographies* (1970).

JAN SCHWARZ

Menasseh Ben Israel (1604–1657) was an *Amsterdam rabbi, author, and publisher who attempted to negotiate the readmission of Jews to *Britain. Born Manoel Dias Soeiro to *converso parents who had left *Portugal in 1603, he arrived in Amsterdam with his family as a child. A talented orator, he became rabbi of the Neveh Shalom congregation at age eighteen. In 1627 he founded Amsterdam's first Hebrew *printing press. One of his earliest writings, *El Conciliador,* which attempted to reconcile discrepancies in the Hebrew *Bible, won him recognition from Jews and Gentiles, and he began corresponding with prominent non-Jewish scholars. Ben Israel wrote several other treatises on Jewish doctrine, including *Nishmat Ḥayyim (*On the Immortality of the Soul), which discusses reincarnation of souls. In 1650 he published the *Hope of Israel* in Spanish, Hebrew, Latin, and English. This volume dealt with the claim of Aaron Levi Montezinos (Antonio de Montesinos) that the natives of the Andes are descendants of the ten lost tribes of Israel (see ISRAEL, KINGDOM OF; and TRIBES, TEN LOST), and in it Ben Israel argued that Jews have to reside in England (as well as all other parts of the world) for the messiah to come (see MESSIANISM: EARLY MODERN). In 1655 he traveled to England to promote the official recognition of Jews. Oliver Cromwell, who led England at that time, was open to Jewish readmission and called the Whitehall Conference in December 1655 to consider whether and under what conditions it was lawful to admit Jews. Although millennarians

supported readmission, merchants feared commercial competition and *antisemitic literature probably influenced public opinion against the proposal as well. Rather than have a negative decision on record, Cromwell dismissed the gathering. In 1656 Menasseh ben Israel published *Vindiciae Judaeorum* in defense of the Jews. He returned to Amsterdam in 1657 after being granted a pension from Cromwell and died later that year.

ELIZABETH SHULMAN

Mendelssohn, Moses (1729–1786) was a German Enlightenment thinker and writer and the central figure in the initial stages of the *Haskalah, the Jewish Enlightenment movement. Born in Dessau (Anhalt), the fourteen-year-old Moses Mendelssohn walked to *Berlin to continue learning with his mentor David Fraenkel, who had been named rabbi in Berlin. Fraenkel's introduced Mendelssohn to the *Haskalah, the religious enlightenment of Judaism in the eighteenth and nineteenth centuries that echoed the contemporaneous scientific and intellectual revolutions in European thought. In Berlin Mendelssohn befriended several Jews (including Aron Gumpertz and Israel Samoscz) who studied European and ancient languages, mathematics, *medicine, and natural *science along with more traditional Jewish subjects; under their guidance Mendelssohn immersed himself in contemporary theology, ancient philosophy, and classical literature. He earned a small livelihood, first through tutoring and then as a bookkeeper for a silk manufacturing company (one of the professions available to Jews in Prussia); later he became a partner and then inherited the business, working full time throughout his life. Mendelssohn married Fromet Guggenheim in 1762; together they had ten children – Sara, Brendel (later Dorothea von Schlegel), Chaim, Recha, Mendel, Joseph, Yente (later Henriette), Abraham, Sisa, and Nathan; five survived to adulthood.

Over the course of his successful intellectual career, Mendelssohn published widely (and often anonymously) in German (on aesthetics, belles lettres, metaphysics, mathematics, contract law, religious liberty, and *Judaism) and in Hebrew (on logic, *aesthetics, *literature, *halakhah, medieval theology, and *Bible commentary). With his close friends Gotthold Ephraim Lessing and Friedrich Nicolai, Mendelssohn co-edited the *Bibliothek der schönen Wissenschaften und der freyen Künste* (Library of the Fine Arts and the Arts of Freedom, 1757–58) and the *Briefe, die neueste Literatur betreffend* (Letters Concerning the Latest Literature, 1759–65), two of the main organs of the German Enlightenment in the eighteenth century. In his aesthetics, Mendelssohn introduced and greatly expanded the ideas of the sublime, the ugly, genius, tragedy, and the creative use of human imagination; his innovative theory of language took advantage of Enlightenment ideas about language formation, the transference of symbols, semiotic significance, and cultural development. His work in metaphysics, *Phaedo: or On the Immortality of the Soul, in Three Dialogues* (1767), brought him international attention and earned him the oft-quoted moniker, the "German Socrates"; even before its publication Mendelssohn's reputation as a philosopher was secured with his two prize-winning essays, "Pope, A Metaphysician!" (1755, co-written with Lessing) and "On Evidence in Metaphysical Sciences" (1763). Famous for his clear prose, philosophical acumen, and adherence to Judaism,

Mendelssohn's publications came to an abrupt halt after he suffered a severe breakdown brought about by the public appeal for his conversion to Christianity by Swiss pastor Johann Caspar Lavater in 1769–70 and the royal rejection of his admission to the Berlin Academy (despite unanimous nomination).

After a slow recovery, Mendelssohn turned his attention toward *Bible translation, including the *Psalms and *Ecclesiastes, before issuing a full translation of the *Torah (transliterated into German using Hebrew characters), accompanied by a commentary called the *Bi'ur* (1780–83). Many Jewish leaders reacted negatively to his endeavor. The sting of the epithet, "the Jewish Luther," was fully intended; both the translation and the *Bi'ur* were rejected by halakhic authorities in *Central Europe who saw the effort as a thinly veiled attempt to teach *Yiddish-speaking Jews the German language and thereby introduce them to the secularizing forces of European culture.

However, Mendelssohn's prominence allowed him to aid several Jewish communities threatened with expulsion, heavy taxation, or violence; he prevailed on powerful figures among his non-Jewish contacts to use their influence to help where and when they could. Mendelssohn interceded in a dispute about early burial in Mecklenburg-Schwerin; Pastor Lavater intervened at Mendelssohn's request on behalf of a Swiss Jewish community; and Mendelssohn's close acquaintance, Wilhelm von Dohm, helped when Jews in Alsace-Lorraine were endangered. Dohm's treatise advocating Jewish civil *emancipation, *On the Civil Improvement of the Jews* (1781), launched a public debate that lasted a century. The following year, Mendelssohn published a German translation of *Menasseh ben Israel's 1656 appeal to Oliver Cromwell, *Vindicae Judaerum*, to which he attached a lengthy preface that advocated Jewish civil acceptance on economic and humanitarian grounds.

That work prompted a second conversionary appeal from an anonymous author (later revealed as August Cranz). Unlike the Lavater affair, Mendelssohn used this opportunity to write a full-scale rational defense of Judaism, *Jerusalem, or On Ecclesiastical Power and Judaism* (1783), a work that begins with a discursive analysis of the need to separate church from state. In addition to his political and religious works, Mendelssohn continued to publish in philosophy, particularly with an eye toward education and edification; his *Morning Hours, or Lectures on the Existence of God* (1785) is a collection of a series of lectures delivered to his son and a close circle of friends. At the same time, Mendelssohn became involved in a controversy regarding Lessing's reputation as a natural philosopher (the so-called Pantheism Debate). Against the charge that his friend held closely guarded secrets about his true religiosity, Mendelssohn aggressively argued that Lessing had been theologically misunderstood. The exchange of letters and essays became so fierce that early in January 1786 Mendelssohn ran to his publisher without a coat, became quite ill very quickly, and died within a few days.

The public mourning on news of his death was international in scope, and plans began immediately to erect a monument to his memory. A rise in anti-Jewish sentiment thwarted that effort, but within the German Jewish community Mendelssohn became a model of the possibilities of Jewish Enlightenment, intellectual aptitude, and,

somewhat ironically, ecumenical dialogue. The Hebrew biographical eulogy written by Isaac Euchel, a leading figure in the *Haskalah*, made Mendelssohn a symbol of the potential within Jewish scholarship and solidified his place in the histories of modern philosophy, Jewish *thought, and Jewish *emancipation. In modern Judaism, Mendelssohn is alternately reviled (by those who blame him for liberal forms of Judaism and the organizational breakdown of traditional Judaism) and revered (by those who praise him for opening the *ghetto doors). In fact, his admirers included Samson Raphael *Hirsch and David *Friedländer, two very different Jewish thinkers whose influence on nineteenth-century German Jewry had widely distinct impacts. For further reading, see A. Altmann, *Moses Mendelssohn: A Biographical Study* (1973); and S. Feiner, *Moses Mendelssohn: Sage of Modernity* (2010).   LEAH HOCHMAN

Mendes-Nasi Family. The most prominent and best known figures of *Ottoman Jewry were the Portuguese *conversos, Gracia Mendes (ca. 1510–1569) and her nephew, Joseph Nasi (ca. 1524–1579). The Mendes-Nasi *banking house was renowned throughout Europe for its wide-ranging commercial activities and its list of prominent clients, which included the royal houses of *France and *Spain. In 1553, Gracia settled in Istanbul, and Joseph followed her in 1554. In Istanbul, they openly returned to *Judaism and became leading members of the Jewish community. They also became heavily engaged in tax farming and commercial enterprises. To manage their affairs in the *Ottoman Empire and Europe, Gracia and Joseph developed a broad network of agents, functionaries, and correspondents. Joseph's familiarity with European affairs, and his many informants, made him an invaluable advisor to the Ottoman court. Among various honors, he received an official appointment as governor of Naxos and the Cyclades archipelago.

Both Gracia and Joseph were deeply involved in philanthropic activities within the Jewish communities of Istanbul and Salonika, where they founded *synagogues and *yeshivot and supported scholars. Gracia and later Joseph, who became her son-in-law in 1553 when he married his cousin Reyna, secured from the sultan a concession to develop the *Galilee town of Tiberias, then in ruins, and its vicinity. They founded a *yeshivah* there and completed the reconstruction of the town's walls in 1565. Although Jews did settle in Tiberias and its community flourished for a while, the project encountered numerous difficulties and was abandoned in the seventeenth century. **See also, WOMEN, EARLY MODERN.**   AVIGDOR LEVY

Menorah. Menorah is the Hebrew word for a stand or repository for a lamp. This term generally designates the golden lamp stand of the wilderness *Tabernacle, as described in *Pentateuchal texts, and also the ten golden lamp stands of the First *Temple (1 Kgs 7:49). A cylindrical, unbranched menorah with a single lamp, probably seven-spouted, perhaps stood in a pre-monarchic tent shrine (see Lev 24:1; cf. 1 Sam 3:3). The First Temple lamp stands, also unbranched, held multi-spouted lamps (see Zech 4:2). The elaborate seven-branched menorah of the Second *Temple, as known from ancient art as well as *Josephus and *rabbinic literature, probably influenced the description (Exod 25:31–40; 37:17–24) of the Tabernacle menorah. With its branches and elaborate botanical decorations, it would have resembled a stylized tree and thus symbolized divine power as a source of fertility. Its lamps may have signified divine omniscience. Like the other sacred furnishings, the menorah contributed to the sense of divine presence in *God's earthly dwelling.   CAROL MEYERS

Menorah Association,

the intercollegiate national Jewish organization devoted to serving the needs of American Jewish undergraduates, came into being at a time when American Jewish college students were far and few between and campus life was inhospitable to expressions of Jewish collective identity. Established at Harvard in 1906, where, as one of its sayings would have it, young American Jews were encouraged to find themselves "as Jews in the modern world, without ghettoism and yet with a certain distinction," the Menorah Association spread to some eighty campuses by 1920, before losing ground to *Hillel at one end of the spectrum and Jewish *fraternities and sororities at the other. In the years before *World War I, the organization provided a public address for Jewish collegians – a place for intellectual give-and-take and socializing.

The Menorah Association went on to publish a sophisticated intellectual magazine known as *The Menorah Journal* (published in various forms between 1915–62), which intended, according to the editorial statement in the first issue, to be "a Jewish forum open to all sides, devoted first and last to bringing out the values of Jewish culture and ideals, of Hebraism and of Judaism and striving for their advancement." Its impact on American Jewish arts and letters was far reaching, especially during the interwar years. Within its "timely, vivacious, and readable" pages, contributors as varied as Salo Baron, Sidney Hook, Mordecai M. *Kaplan, Lewis Mumford, Solomon *Schechter, and Lionel Trilling reckoned with the challenges and possibilities of the modern Jewish experience.

JENNA WEISSMAN JOSELIT

Mesopotamia and Ancient Israel.

Mesopotamia ("between the rivers") refers to the geographical area on both sides of the Tigris and Euphrates Rivers extending northward from the Persian Gulf. Now constituted as *Iraq, this fertile area was one of the birthplaces of urban civilization and the development of a system of writing. With the nineteenth-century decipherment of cuneiform, which used wedge-shaped symbols to indicate words and syllables, hundreds of thousands of tablets and monumental inscriptions became available to modern scholars. These were written in a variety of languages, including Sumerian, Hittite, Hurrian, and Akkadian. Along with the discovery of this literary heritage of the ancient *Near East came the realization that certain sections of the *Pentateuch show a remarkable correspondence with Akkadian texts in particular. These correlations can be grouped into four categories.

MYTHOLOGICAL TEXTS AND GENESIS 1–11: *Genesis 1–11 tells the story of humankind from creation to *Abraham. Numerous aspects of this narrative demonstrate familiarity with Mesopotamian culture. Although Genesis 1 has several interesting parallels with the Babylonian epic of creation, called *Enuma Elish*, the *flood story of Genesis 6–9 provides the most striking parallels with Mesopotamian texts, particularly with the epics of Gilgamesh and Atrahasis.

Common to the *Bible and these texts are the following elements: the gods/God decide to send a flood; one man is chosen to build a boat and save himself, his family members, and creatures; the boat comes to rest on a mountain; the hero sends out birds to see if the land has dried sufficiently to disembark; the hero offers a sacrifice; and human history begins anew. The most notable contrasts between the Bible and the epic of Atrahasis concern the reasons for the flood and the measures taken to prevent future catastrophes. In the Mesopotamian myth, the gods bring the great flood because of the incessant noise caused by humankind, which is generally understood as a reference to overpopulation. Subsequently, in an effort to stem overpopulation, the gods introduce infertility, stillbirth, and women who are not allowed to reproduce. This stands in stark contrast with the Bible's assertion that humankind was wiped out because of their corrupt and violent nature. Similarly, in the aftermath of the flood, the Israelite God introduces capital punishment for homicide and repeatedly prescribes that *Noah's family "be fruitful and multiply" (Gen 9:1–7). The Bible's assertion that the ark came to rest on Mount Ararat in present-day Armenia, and not on a mountaintop in the vicinity of the Land of Israel, is also suggestive of the Mesopotamian origins of the biblical account. Further, the story of the Tower of Babel in Genesis 11 offers an obvious satire on Mesopotamian culture, because the tower is certainly a reference to a ziggurat, a tall pyramidal structure found in a typical Mesopotamian temple complex that was thought to provide a connecting link between heaven and earth. In the Torah, the tower represents humanity's rejection of God's command to "fill the earth" (9:1, 7) and thus results in their scattering and disunity. According to this tongue-in-cheek view of a characteristic Mesopotamian institution, "Babel," which in Akkadian means "gate of god," is equated with confused gibberish as God "confounds" (Hebrew, *balal*) human speech (Gen 11:9).

SOCIAL CUSTOMS AND THE ANCESTORS OF ISRAEL: The discovery of a large archive at Nuzi, in present-day northeastern Iraq, provides scholars with extensive family records offering details regarding *marriage, *adoption, and inheritance practices in the fifteenth century BCE. Although a previous generation of scholars may have exaggerated the parallels between the social customs of Nuzi and the ancestors of Israel, it is clear that the patriarchs and their families as represented in biblical narratives, were very much a part of the culture of the ancient Near East (see BIBLE: ANCESTRAL NARRATIVES). For example, just as Laban makes *Jacob swear that he will take no wives in addition to his daughters *Rachel and *Leah (Gen 31:50), so Nuzi marriage contracts include a clause prohibiting the husband's marriage to additional women in order to safeguard the status of the first wife. That the firstborn son is entitled to a greater or perhaps double portion of the inheritance is documented at Nuzi and in other ancient Near Eastern legal sources (see LAW: ANCIENT NEAR EAST and HEBREW BIBLE) and is assumed in the Genesis narratives (see Deut 21:17). The practice of an infertile wife providing her husband with a concubine or slave wife to bear children is found several times in Genesis (chapters 16, 30) and is well documented in ancient Near Eastern law codes.

BIBLICAL AND CUNEIFORM LAW: Collections of legal material from the ancient Near East generally pre-date the

*Torah, but the two legal bodies share several features in common. The Code of *Hammurabi, dated to the eighteenth century BCE, is the most famous law collection because it is the most extensive, consisting of a prologue, epilogue, and 282 laws. One element typical of these law collections is their "case law" or "if-then" phraseology; this casuistic style is also found in Exodus 21–22. In addition, the Torah incorporates several legal themes found in Mesopotamian law. Among these are the following: (1) The Goring Ox: Exodus 21 contains several stipulations regarding an ox that gores people or other oxen. If the ox had a previous history of goring and the owner neglected to take precautions, the penalty is more severe. This same distinction is made in the Laws of Hammurabi and the Laws of Eshnunna. Exodus 21:35 stipulates that, if an ox gores and kills another man's ox, both oxen, the dead and the live, are sold and the owners split the proceeds; the same is found in the Laws of Eshnunna 53; (2) Battery of a Pregnant Woman: Israelite and Mesopotamian laws both deal with the penalty for a man who hits a pregnant woman and causes her to lose her fetus or her life (Exod 21:21–22; Lipit Ishtar d–e–f; CH 209–214, Middle Assyrian Law 21, 51–52); and (3) "Eye for an Eye": the legal principle of exact retribution is found in the Torah and the Hammurabi code (Exod 21:24–24; Lev 24:20; LH 196–200), but in the latter it only applies to the upper class.

However, although there is overlap in style and subject matter, fundamental differences are obvious. Mesopotamian law takes the principle of exact retribution to an extreme and therefore prescribes vicarious punishment, so that according to Hammurabi's laws, a builder has to hand over his son for execution if his shoddy construction kills the son of the owner of a home he built. The Torah rejects this principle. In addition, Israel was unique in its belief that only God can promulgate law. Outside of the Bible, law functioned as the expression of the king's will, and the gods served only to inspire him with attributes of equity and justice. Modern scholars assume that the ordinances in these legal collections were never actually imposed on the people but rather functioned as royal propaganda to assert the king's legitimacy because he was seen as instituting justice. The extent to which the people of ancient Israel observed the laws of the Torah is unclear, but their explicit purpose was to serve as the stipulations of God's *covenant with Israel, with the purpose of producing a "holy nation" (Exod 19:6). Thus, unlike Mesopotamian law, the Torah includes legislation regarding rituals, religious festivals, and admonitions of a moral nature, such as the prohibition of mistreating vulnerable members of society and the commandment to "love one's fellow as oneself" (Lev 19:18).

COVENANT AND TREATY FORMS: Many of the texts recovered from the ancient Near East were found in royal archives so it is not surprising that treaties between kings, both of small city-states and vast empires, are available for comparison with biblical texts. The two major sources of these political texts are the *Hittite Empire (present-day Turkey in the period 1500–1400 BCE) and the Neo-Assyrian period (northern Iraq, 750–610 BCE). An analysis of the treaties and the covenant forms found in the Torah leads many scholars to conclude that Israelite authors borrowed a form used by other peoples to express political fealty to convey Israel's *covenant relationship with its God.

For example, the basic elements of the sixty-odd treaties found include the following: (1) an introduction of the speaker, the king or overlord, and the basis of his authority to proclaim a treaty; (2) the historical prologue, which recounts the previous relationship of the treaty partners; (3) the stipulations of the treaty, including nonaggression, payment of tribute, and the prohibition of making treaties with the overlord's enemies; (4) a statement concerning the disposition of the document and when it is read; (5) calling of the gods to witness the treaty-making; and (6) enumeration of blessings for those who observe the terms of the document and curses for those who transgress. These elements do not all occur in every treaty; however, the treaties as a whole exhibit a basic unity. In the Hebrew Bible, the texts that describe the covenant at Sinai (Exod 20–24, as well as the book of Deuteronomy), exhibit almost all of these elements, whereas Leviticus 26 preserves a catalogue of blessings and curses linked to Israel's adherence to the covenant. Thus, modern scholars assume that Israelite theologians adopted a contractual form known in ancient Near Eastern political life to express a vassal king's exclusive relationship with his overlord to express Israel's religious belief that its relationship with its God is also exclusive.

For further reading, see John H. Walton, *Ancient Israelite Literature in Its Cultural Context* (1994); A. Kuhrt, *The Ancient Near East 3000–330 BC* (1995); and J. B. Pritchard, ed., *Ancient Near Eastern Texts Relating to the Old Testament* (1969). **Map 1**
ELAINE GOODFRIEND

Messianism: Biblical and *Second Temple Eras. Messiah is an anglicized form of the Hebrew word for "an anointed one," *mashiah.* *Anointment with oil was a characteristic Hebrew ritual of initiation into a divinely sanctioned role, particularly as king. A few passages in the prophetic writings in the Hebrew *Bible express an expectation that at some future time God would establish an anointed king who would rule with justice and righteousness. Because several biblical statements promised that Israel would never fail to have a king of the seed of *David (*2 Sam 7), Jews naturally believed that this ruler would be a descendant of King David. The expected king is sometimes called the son of David (Isa 11; Ezek 35; Micah 5; Jer 33:14–16; Zech 9), or he is called the "branch," ostensibly a "new shoot of the Davidic family tree" (Jer 23). The messiah of the Hebrew Bible is a human being who will restore Israel to its former independence and prominence. As God's anointed, he is, according to Isaiah 11:3–4, the strong vindicator who will carry out divine vengeance against Israel's enemies.

Messianic expectations also appear in *apocalyptic and pseudepigraphical writings (see PSEUDEPIGRAPHA). In the pseudepigraphical Psalm of Solomon, dated variously to the first century BCE or CE, the theme of the victorious battles of the messiah is extended against all those Gentile nations who have harmed Jerusalem, and the messiah himself is seen as a blameless ruler (17:36–37a, 39–40). In the *Dead Sea Scrolls the generic term "messiah" describes an expected rule by two concurrent messiahs: a priestly messiah descended from *Aaron and an anointed descendant of David.

Messianism: Early Modern. Jews in the centuries between approximately 1400 and 1800 drew from a long tradition and a rich array of biblical, rabbinic, and medieval Jewish sources in thinking about the messiah and the end of days. Significant historical and social developments, such as the 1492 expulsion of the Jews from *Spain, fueled messianic conjecture. Early modern Jewish messianism was also closely connected to Christian and Islamic messianic speculation. Although generally discouraged by rabbinic authorities, some early modern Jews did attempt to calculate the beginning of the messianic era.

Jewish messianic views were rarely simple and not always uniform. For example, some Jews believed that the coming of the messiah would be accompanied by an *apocalyptic overturning of society through warfare, natural disaster, and cosmic changes. Others imagined a more peaceful transformation. In either event, messianism addressed the challenge of divine promise and current and historical suffering by positing a future reality that reestablished the position of Jews and Judaism. This was a comforting notion at times of persecution and marginalization; messianic anticipation could also serve as a catalyst for early modern Jews to repent for their own perceived shortcomings.

Throughout the Early Modern period, numerous Jews claimed to be harbingers of the messiah or the messiah himself. One example is the early-sixteenth-century figure Asher Lemlein of Ruetlingen, who circulated around *Germany and northern *Italy. Asher was reported to have claimed the title of *prophet and had some success gathering followers and believers in his doctrines and in his ascetic practices of fasting and flagellation. Other well-known messianic figures included David Reuveni, who approached the pope in the 1520s to obtain a letter to the Holy Roman Emperor and king of France in a quest to secure arms for his alleged state, and Solomon Molkho, who had some interactions with Reuveni and was viewed by some as a messianic prophet. Reuveni found support among Jews in Rome, especially among *conversos, some of whom believed he heralded the messiah. Molkho's parents were Portuguese conversos. He traveled extensively in Europe and the *Ottoman Empire, before being burned at the stake in 1538 in Mantua, Italy for refusing to return to *Christianity.

Jewish messianism took on mystical dimensions in sixteenth-century *Safed, where Isaac *Luria stood at the center of a colorful group of kabbalists and ascetics. Under Luria's teaching, the emphasis on human actions in bringing about the final *redemption reached new heights. Dramatic events and discoveries, especially those in the New World, further excited messianic speculation. The important *Amsterdam rabbinic leader *Menasseh ben Israel (1604–1657), who developed a host of relationships with Christian scholars and who advocated vociferously for the readmission of Jews to England, speculated about connections between North America natives and legendary accounts of the "Ten Lost Tribes" (see TRIBES, TEN LOST).

Popular legends during this period also told about warrior Jews, hiding in the mountains, waiting to usher in apocalyptic times. The myth of the "Red Jews" provided a powerful image for a Christian society expecting the apocalypse and fearing the very real westward spread of the Turks. It simultaneously reinforced anti-Jewish stereotypes and the fear that the Jews were plotting, this time with military assistance, the overthrow of Christianity and the establishment of Jewish dominion over the entire world.

Certainly the best known Jewish messianic figure of the Early Modern period was *Shabbatai Zevi. Zevi was born in the Ottoman city of Smyrna (Izmir) in 1626. After an extended period of semi-seclusion between 1642 and 1648, he publicly proclaimed himself the messiah. Later, in 1665 in an apparent trance, Nathan of Gaza (1644–1680), who would become something like Zevi's publicity agent, made several utterances, including referring to Zevi as the messiah and to himself as a prophet chosen by God. Zevi traveled to *Jerusalem, but was expelled by the rabbis there. Tales of his alleged miracles spread throughout Europe and the Islamic world; he was credited with *resurrection of the dead, among other wonders. Although many, including prominent lay people and rabbinic leaders, discounted Zevi and his accomplice, large numbers of Jews were apparently convinced that the messianic era was beginning. Poor economic conditions and the penitential aspects of his messianism may have added to Zevi's appeal (see also WOMEN: EARLY MODERN PERIOD).

In 1666 Zevi sailed to Constantinople from Smyrna, where he announced he would assume rule over the Ottoman state. In February of that year, he was arrested by Turkish authorities. After being imprisoned and given the choice between death and conversion to Islam, Zevi became a Muslim. He was eventually banished to Albania, where he died in 1676. Although many followers were quite naturally devastated, some held fast to their belief in the failed messiah, convinced by Nathan of Gaza that Zevi had to penetrate the world of Islam to elevate the remaining divine sparks and save the Muslims from evil, before ushering in the messianic era. Others supporters argued that Zevi was indeed the messiah, but was the Messiah son of Joseph, who would serve as a precursor to the Messiah son of David. Small pockets of believers endured long after Zevi's conversion and death, forming sectarian *Sabbatean groups. Such beliefs were frequently condemned; Sabbateans were excommunicated by the Polish *Council of Four Lands in 1669.

Among important studies on this topic, see A. H. Silver, *A History of Messianic Speculation in Israel: From the First through the Seventeenth Centuries* (1927; rep. 1959); M. Saperstein, ed., *Essential Papers on Messianic Movements and Personalities in Jewish History* (1992); M. Goldish, *The Sabbatean Prophets* (2004); A. Gow, *The Red Jews: Antisemitism in an Apocalyptic Age, 1200–1600* (1995); and D. B. Ruderman, "Hope against Hope: Jewish and Christian Messianic Expectations in the Late Middle Ages," in *Exile and Diaspora: Studies in the History of the Jewish People Presented to Professor Haim Beinart*, ed. A. Mirsky, A. Grossman, and Y. Kaplan (1991), 185–202.

DEAN PHILLIP BELL

Messianism: Modern Approaches. There are a number of approaches to the issue of messianism in twenty-first-century Judaism. One of the most prominent originates in attempts to explain why Jews do not consider Jesus to be the messiah. A frequent Jewish answer is that sources in the Hebrew *Bible and *Second Temple era texts pre-determined Jewish messianic expectation in the first century CE toward a figure who would win political independence from *Rome; the failure of Jesus of Nazareth to do this would naturally have led contemporaneous Jews to dismiss claims that he was the messiah (Segal).

This argument, although well grounded in traditional sources, is nevertheless problematic for three reasons. First, it fails to explain the existence of "Jewish Christians" among early Christianity's adherents, such as the author of the Gospel of Matthew (P. Schäfer). Second, this kind of argument is absent in the rabbinic literature of antiquity: When the Catalan rabbi Moses *Naḥmanides made such a claim at the Barcelona Disputation of 1263, he was among the first to do so. Most importantly, Jewish messianic views in late antiquity were not limited to a royal figure of the Davidic line. Although it is true that the term "messiah" (lit. "anointed") refers to the king of Israel who is likened to a son of God in *Psalms 2, we also find less politicized notions of "messiah" in the binary messianism of *priest and *king in *Zechariah 4 and various *Dead Sea Scroll texts. Similarly, Second Temple and *rabbinic literature gave messianic associations to the vision in *Daniel 7 of a heavenly figure described as "one like a son of man" (Collins).

Given the difficulty of precisely defining what does or does not count as a valid messianic ideology in Judaism, a more useful approach is to develop a historical typology of the various forms in which messianic expectation has been expressed in Jewish culture. The central piece of scholarship in this regard is Gershom *Scholem's 1959 essay, "Toward An Understanding of the Messianic Idea in Judaism." There Scholem analyzes classical Jewish texts, kabbalistic writings, and the documents of *Sabbatean and post-Sabbatean movements (see SHABBATAI ZEVI) to demonstrate that the messianic idea in Jewish tradition is primarily associated with *apocalypse and catastrophe. For Scholem, the "revolutionary, cataclysmic element in the transition from every historical present to the messianic future" was rooted in the utopian aspect of Jewish messianism, which sees the ideal as future. (This tendency always coexists with the anti-apocalyptic "restorative" aspect of the messianic idea, which sees the ideal as past, although the ratio between the two elements differs in various historical contexts.) Scholem argued that liberal Judaism's "bourgeois" association of the messianic idea with Enlightenment notions of progress ignored the apocalyptic aspect of Jewish tradition.

Messianic utopianism in Judaism, according to Scholem, requires an utter break between the future and the present: Present structures will be nullified and destroyed. Although he saw a great deal of potential in the ability of this anarchic element of the Jewish tradition to ground the revolutionary creativity in the *Zionism of his time, Scholem also saw dangers when the apocalyptic element in Jewish messianism was not in harmony with its more traditional restorative aspect. In Scholem's view, the *antinomian trends that began in *Lurianic Kabbalah in the sixteenth century led to the heightened antinomianism of the radical Sabbateans who believed *Shabbatai Zevi's conversion to Islam in 1666 to be necessary; in turn, antipathy to these trends grounded the break from Jewish history epitomized in post-Enlightenment liberal Judaism.

Scholem's typology allows us to categorize the differing twentieth-century religious responses to Zionism summarized by Aviezer Ravitzky. The support of the *Ultra-Orthodox Neturei Karta (Guardians of the City) for *Palestinian rights is in line with a perspective that insists that the messianic era must be effected by divine intervention; therefore, the socially destructive apocalyptic energies of messianism as a human phenomenon risk detaching God from Jewish history. Similarly, Rabbi Abraham Isaac *Kook's progressive notion of history, which led him to see the political successes of Zionism as a sign of imminent religious *redemption, is broadly utopian. The notion of the rate of progress as pre-determined, and the insistence that the present moment is on the cusp of redemption, led his son Rabbi Zvi Yehudah Kook (and, more broadly, the contemporary Israeli settler movement) to assert that "the State of Israel is divine." Here, anarchy shows itself in an abandonment of political realism.

Scholem also associated the restorative pole of the messianic idea with passivity and the anarchic-utopian pole with activity. These associations are no longer viable. When a group of anti-Zionist Ultra-Orthodox Jews demonstrates outside the Israeli consulate in *New York City, is this "passive"? When West Bank settlers are carried by Israeli police from their homes during the dismantling of settlements, is this "active"? The blurring of the boundary between the anarchist and the bourgeois, which seemed so clear for Scholem, may make it desirable to view expressions of the messianic idea – and not only in the contemporary period – as strategies by which a particular worldview is validated. In other words, a messianic ideology is one of many pragmatic strategies by which a religious Jewish community hopes to achieve or sustain power of one form or another.

This is true for the rabbis of antiquity who warned against hastening the end. It is true for Maimonides' rationalist approach to the messianic idea. It is true for Sabbateanists; it is true for Kook and Neturei Karta. It is true for the Ḥabad Ḥasidim who in the 1990s said that the messiah's arrival was imminent, and it is true for those *Ḥabad Ḥasidim who believed that their rebbe Menaḥem Mendel *Schneerson was himself the messiah, and for those among that group who believe that Schneerson remains invisibly present within their community after his death in 1994 (Berger). It is even true of the identification of the messiah with the ethically responsible self in the writings of the twentieth-century French Jewish philosopher Emmanuel *Levinas. Where all these views differ is not in viewing messianism as a strategy, but in their convictions of where essential power resides: Is it in the divine, in the community, or in the individual? In and through those self-definitions, the parameters of lives in the historical present are drawn – even if (and perhaps because) the messiah is not present.

For further reading, see A. F. Segal, Rebecca's Children (1986); P. Schäfer, Jesus in the Talmud (2007); J. J. Collins, The Scepter and the Star (1995); G. Scholem, The Messianic Idea in Judaism (1971); A. Ravitzky, Messianism, Zionism, and Jewish Religious Radicalism (1996); D. Berger, The Rebbe, The Messiah, and the Scandal of Orthodox Indifference (2001); E. Levinas, Difficult Freedom (1990); and M. Kavka, Jewish Messianism and the History of Philosophy (2004). MARTIN KAVKA

Metatron refers to one of the supreme powers in the divine realm in *talmudic, *midrashic, and *kabbalistic literature. Metatron is often associated with the term sar ha-panim (prince of the countenance), meaning an entity with the power of standing face to face with God (while others are to His left, right, or behind Him). Talmudic literature associates Metatron with Exodus 23:21, "for my name is in him"; the name should therefore be interpreted as deriving from Greek *tetra* ("four") and the *Tetragrammaton*, the divine name of four letters (although other explanations have been offered, based on references to Metatron as a "messenger"). According to BT Ḥagigah 15a, the sage *Elisha ben Abuya was declared a heretic when he observed Metatron sitting on a throne in the seventh heaven and judging the world, and he said, "Perhaps there are two powers in heaven." Metatron may also be associated with the *sar ha-olam* (prince of the world), an opaque midrashic reference, probably to a demiurgic power. He is frequently described in *hekhalot* mystical literature, and the most detailed description is found in the late *pseudepigraphical work, 3 Enoch (also called *The Hebrew Apocalypse of Enoch* and *Sefer Hekhalot* [Book of the Palaces]), which describes the gradual transformation of Enoch ben Jared (Gen 5:24) into the power Metatron (see ESCHATOLOGY; MYSTICISM: *HEKHALOT* AND *MERKAVAH* LITERATURE). The identification of Metatron with Enoch was probably motivated by the wish to sever any connection between Metatron and the creation, because there were tendencies to view him as a demiurgic power. In 3 Enoch, Metatron is called a *na'ar* (youth or servant), and the same appellation is found in *gnostic treatises. Gershom *Scholem identified him with Yahoel, an angel who appears in *The Apocalypse of Abraham*, a pseudepigraphical work of the first or second century CE. Medieval kabbalists often connected Metatron with different entities of the divine realms as described in the *Kabbalah, most often with the *Shekhinah* (G. Scholem, *Kabbalah* [1974], 377–81).

JOSEPH DAN

Mexico was probably the first European settlement in the Americas to receive Jews. A few came with *Columbus, probably escaping from the persecution of the *Inquisition in the Iberian Peninsula. Yet New Spain was not particularly welcoming to Jews, even *conversos*, because the reigning ideologies of *Spain were instituted on the new continent. Documents relating to *auto-de-fés* – the public ritual of penance in which those condemned as heretics or apostates (especially Jews) were sentenced and burned at the stake – provide evidence of the persecution that Jews endured in New Spain. Moreover, derogatory concepts about Jews fostered by the Inquisition took root, entering Mexico's culture and language and remaining unchallenged.

Mexico's contemporary Jewish community traces its roots to more recent immigrants who arrived during the second half of the nineteenth century. Although a few wealthy European Jews established large business enterprises, they were too few to constitute an organization of any sort. It was the subsequent male immigrants from *Turkey, *Syria (Aleppo and Damascus), and the *Balkans, all poor, who established organized communities. Early on, they brought a rabbi (*hakham*) to perform rites and lead the group. The importation of brides from the "Old Countries" enabled the communities to grow and maintain their culture and religion.

*Eastern Europeans who arrived in the second decade of the twentieth century followed a small group of Jews from the *United States who had settled in Mexico, for the most part to escape conscription during *World War I. Most Eastern Europeans arrived by ship in the port of Veracruz

and then traveled through the hinterland to reach Mexico City, where most settled. As the numbers of *Ashkenazim increased, Jewish communities formed along ethnic and linguistic lines. If Arabic, French, and *Ladino were the linguistic tools for the earlier groups, *Yiddish was central for the Eastern Europeans, who had also brought the different ideologies of their countries of origin. The Ashkenazim ultimately established a network of secular Jewish day schools and organizations that directed the communal life of Mexican Jews.

Although the first Ashkenazic immigrants made great strides into the business world by becoming small shopkeepers and eventually dealing in larger enterprises, their children took advantage of educational opportunities. Within a few decades, the peddlers and shopkeepers, the bakers, and the tailors of the immigrant generation were replaced by a generation of professionals who distinguished themselves in many walks of life. In the last decades of the twentieth century, Jews ventured into politics as well. By this time, *Yiddish had been supplanted by Spanish, the language in which almost all of the contemporary expression of the community is handled. Whether this trend represented a loss for the community or a welcome form of adaptation is still a matter of debate for some. After World War II, Mexico permitted only a few dozen Jews into the country; this was the state policy of most *Latin American countries. In the first decade of the twenty-first century, Mexico's Jewish community is stabilized at 40,000. More than 90% live in the capital, and there are smaller communities in Monterrey, Guadalajara, and Tampico and, of late, in Cancun, among other places. Currently, Jews of *Sephardi and *Mizrahi (Middle Eastern) origins hold most of the positions of authority within the various organizations; this is a significant change from previous decades when Ashkenazim were the major community leaders.

For further reading, see A. Cimet, *Ashkenazi Jews in Mexico: Ideologies in the Structuring of a Community* (1997); and A. Gojman de Backal, *Generaciones Judias en Mexico, 1922–1992* (1993).

ADINA CIMET

Mezuzah (literally, "doorpost") refers to a parchment, called a *klaf*, and its container that are traditionally nailed to the right side of the doorpost of a Jewish home at an angle, with the top tilted inward. Many Jews place a *mezuzah* on the main entrance within thirty days of moving into a new residence; some also affix one to each exterior and interior door (with the exception of the bathroom). The containers can be produced from a variety of materials and are often decorative. The parchment, which must be handwritten in a prescribed way with quill and ink by a trained scribe, contains Deuteronomy 6:4–9 (which begins with the *shema and ends with the *commandment to write "these words" on the doorpost of one's house) and Deuteronomy 11:13–21 (which contains the same commandment and promises of blessings for fulfilling it). The word *Shaddai* (usually translated as "Almighty") is written on the inside of the back of the *mezuzah* and is often visible through a small hole in the container. Although many superstitions about the protective and talismanic powers of the *mezuzah* have been part of Jewish popular religion over the centuries, mainstream tradition has been insistent that its purpose is to remind people during their daily routines of the unity of *God and to strengthen their love and worship of God (*Maimonides, *Mishneh Torah, Tefillin* 5:4, 6:13).   ELIZABETH SHULMAN

Micah is the sixth book of the Minor or Twelve *Prophets; it is dated to the middle and late eighth century BCE. The prophet Micah came from the town of Moreshet near Gath in southwest *Judah, a rural area that bordered on *Philistia. He was especially concerned with the plight of simple folk who were exploited by urban sophisticates. His prophecies present an intricate mix of weal and woe. He excoriates his audience and offers them comfort, predicting both a divine judgment that will lay the nation waste and a renewal that will follow for the now chastened nation. Micah shares with *Isaiah, his contemporary, a critique of economic and social developments in eighth-century society. His angry denunciations of the wealthy and powerful are the strongest found in the Hebrew *Bible (3:1–4). The prophetic emphasis on morality is central for Micah; he criticizes idolatry in only a few brief passages. Without rejecting the sacrificial cult at the center of *Israelite religion, he ridicules the quantity of offerings brought by the rich and stresses that justice, grace, and humility are more important than worship (6:6–8). He differs from Isaiah in predicting that God's punishment of Judah may lead to *Jerusalem's fall to a foreign enemy (3:12). Micah criticizes those who (like Isaiah) believe in Zion's inviolability (3:11).

False prophecy is a particular concern for Micah, but unlike *Jeremiah he does not regard the false prophets as complete fabricators; their failure is that they transmit God's message inaccurately (e.g., 3:5–8). His vision of the *eschaton* (day of judgment or last days) is less universal than Isaiah's; he predicts the punishment of Israel's foes but not the subsequent creation of a *covenant between them and God (5:4–8). Although he lived in the southern kingdom, he is concerned as well by the fate of *Israel, the northern kingdom. As a result, some scholars have speculated that chapters 6–7 stem from a northern prophet; however, earlier chapters, clearly of Judean origin, also discuss events in the north, making such speculation unnecessary. Micah's prophecies were recalled on the eve of Jerusalem's destruction in the late sixth century BCE and served as a precedent (and legal defense) for similar prophecies by *Jeremiah (Jer 26:18). Micah includes several obscure prophecies about the monarchy in the period of the *eschaton* (2:12–13, 5:1–4) that became especially influential in the later development of *messianic ideologies.   BENJAMIN D. SOMMER

Middle Ages: Childhood. Medieval Jewish communities in Christian countries felt under siege and under constant pressure to convert to Christianity. The threat was three-pronged: theological seduction, economic temptations, and forced coercion using violence. To withstand these temptations and pressures, Jewish communities developed a sophisticated socialization process. Already in the eleventh century Jews recognized that the main thrust of Christian *conversion efforts was directed at children. In descriptions written immediately after the First *Crusade (1096 and subsequent years), it is clear that the extreme behavior of parents in killing their children and in committing suicide themselves was based on the conviction that Christians wished

to convert Jewish children. Christian theological discussions on whether or not children of Jews could be taken and converted by force to the "true religion" do not appear until the end of the twelfth century and during the thirteenth century. However, when the community of Blois in the Rhine Valley in France in 1171 was annihilated following a *ritual murder accusation, surviving Jewish children were brought up as Christians. Thus, Jews took this threat seriously and defined childhood and youth as the time for intensive *education in Jewish practice, values, and identity to enable young people to resist Christianity and even the possibility of forced coercion to Christianity on pain of death (see MARTYRDOM).

The definition of the special character of "childhood" is evident in discussions on breastfeeding and in the Rabbis' ruling that infants should be nursed for twenty-four months. If a woman was divorced she could not remarry until the infant reached two years, for fear that the new "father" would demand that she stop breastfeeding. The manifold discussions in Jewish sources related to Christian wet nurses make it clear that there was an awareness that a suckling infant "knows who is breastfeeding him" and that changing a wet nurse should be assiduously avoided lest the child's health be jeopardized, even if the nurse did "bad things" (was deceitful or swore). It was believed that everything an infant ate would have an effect when he or she grew up; therefore it was stressed that the wet nurse must eat only kosher food. The wet nurse, whether she was Jewish or Christian, had to live in the parents' home where she would be under supervision.

When the infant was weaned, it reached the age of childhood. This was a distinct and special period in which attention had to be paid to "children's behavior" because the understanding of children is different from that of adults. During this time, children are more sensitive, both from a spiritual and a physical point of view; they are easily frightened and easily surprised, and it was desirable for parents to supervise them strictly. The quality of a child's early years was recognized as having an influence on his or her adult life. The physical closeness of parents and children – particularly the close relationship between the father and his small children – is expressed in sources that describe how the father holds his child close to him during meals and during the *blessings after meals, when he is with his books studying, and even when at prayer. The father is warned to watch if the child soils himself, but there is no advice or instruction to remove the small child. We find many descriptions of heartbreak, bitter weeping, and inconsolability following the death of children, as well as advice to adults not to kiss their children in front of bereaved parents and not to boast about them in their presence.

From the age of five and older, young boys started formal studies with a special ceremony on *Shavuot, although they continued, in most cases, to stay at home. Fathers hired teachers for their sons and, it would seem, included children of relatives or needy children in this home teaching arrangement. In this way the father could know what the teacher was teaching and also evaluate his quality. In the literature we find a regulation obliging a father to hire a teacher for his son (or to teach him himself); a father who was absent for long periods for business had to leave funds for his wife to hire a teacher. In the *responsa literature there are many instances of parents refusing to pay teachers their wages because, in their opinion, they had not taught properly, had missed lessons, or could not show that the children had made any progress. Home teaching also permitted girls to study occasionally or to pick up knowledge by hearing what was going on. The communal ḥeder (teaching room) was established towards the end of the medieval period and boys left the house at age five or six to go to their studies. The curriculum consisted of learning the Hebrew letters and starting to read them, followed by learning passages from the *Torah, then the *Mishnah, and later on the *Talmud. At an older age able boys went to study at a *yeshivah, but this was after the period defined as childhood.

During childhood, parents employed a complex and proven process of socialization to ensure the internalization of Jewish values. Special emphasis was placed on the level of each child's understanding. Thus, introduction to the world of mitzvot (divine *commandments) began in accordance with their apprehension and mental capacity, not according to chronological or biological age. The age of thirteen was regarded as the time when all boys were considered adults by virtue of their chronological age and not on account of their mental capability. The *Bar Mitzvah ceremony did not exist in the Middle Ages and only developed later, when communities began marking the capability of the boy according to his chronological age. In addition to his ceremonial initiation into learning at the age of five, a boy attended synagogue with his father and became socialized in *Sabbath and *festival *synagogue rituals and *customs. In contrast, girls were socialized into Judaism and Jewish identity through learning domestic practices and rituals from their mothers in the home (see EDUCATION, BOYS: MEDIEVAL AND EARLY MODERN; EDUCATION, GIRLS: MEDIEVAL AND EARLY MODERN).

For further reading, see E. Kanarfogel, *Jewish Education and Society in the High Middle Ages* (1992); I. G. Marcus, *Rituals of Childhood: Jewish Acculturation in Medieval Europe* (1996); E. Baumgarten, *Mothers and Children: Jewish Family Life in Medieval Europe* (2004); and S. Goldin, "Jewish Society under Pressure: The Concept of Childhood," in *Youth in the Middle Ages*, ed. P. J. Goldberg and F. Riddy (2004), 25–43.

SIMHA GOLDIN

Middle Ages: Crusades. Pope Urban II's proclamation of the First Crusade at the Council of Clermont, on November 27, 1095, set in motion an unprecedented movement that changed the Middle East and had significant repercussions on religious, economic, political, and social life in Western Europe. The crusader movement also dramatically affected the fate of Jewish communities in Europe and the Middle East. Urban II's call evoked an extraordinary response: Men and women throughout Europe, of all ages and social classes, set out to liberate *Jerusalem and the holy places from the Muslims. Theirs was a penitential war; the pope had promised remission of all sins for those taking the cross. Although reasons varied, this spiritual reward, granted in an age of religious revival, is considered to have been among the crusaders' main motivations.

The First Crusade embarked from Europe in three major waves between 1096 and 1101. Generally known as the People's Crusade or the Popular Crusade, the first wave consisted of independent bands of poor people as well as experienced knights, such as Emicho, count of Flonheim. They began their march in the spring of 1096, five months before the date set by the Pope (August 15) and without waiting to gather that year's harvest. In their march through northeastern *France, the Rhineland, Bavaria, and Bohemia, these crusading bands, together with local townspeople, ferociously attacked the Jewish communities they encountered. These assaults were the first of many violent acts perpetrated against Jewish communities by crusaders and would become a characteristic feature of the crusading movement.

Modern scholars debate the motives for these attacks. Although traditionally they have been attributed to the greed of poorly equipped and disorganized crusading bands, historians in recent years have focused on spiritual and ideological reasons. Looting and material gain were not the sole aim but a common means to supply badly equipped armies. The crusaders' principal purposes were to avenge the crucifixion of Christ, to convert Jews by forced baptism, and to create a uniform Christian society by eliminating the "other" by baptism or by death. These ideas are expressed in contemporary sources, both Jewish and Christian. A Hebrew narrative reports crusaders complaining about their long march to avenge those who had profaned the holy shrines, while "the Jews – they whose forefathers murdered and crucified him for no reason [were close at hand]. Let us first avenge ourselves on them and exterminate them from among the nations so that the name of Israel will no longer be remembered, or let them adopt our faith." Forced *conversion of non-Christians was against canon law, and the Church prohibited attacks on Jewish lives and property. However, crusader rhetoric and zeal aroused profound anti-Jewish sentiments and a high degree of violence, which local leaders, both lay and religious, were generally unable to prevent.

The attacks seem to have started in Rouen, shortly after the Council of Clermont. Contemporary sources refer to letters being sent by the Jews of France (see FRANCE, MEDIEVAL) to the *German communities of Trier and Mainz, warning them about the approaching threat and advising them to buy their safety by bribing leaders of the crusader bands. Yet Jewish communities in Trier and even in *Prague were nevertheless assaulted; the cruelest attacks were in the Rhineland – mainly in the towns of Speyer, Worms, Cologne, and Mainz – where the Jewish communities were almost totally destroyed. Some of these attacks were outbursts of spontaneous violence by crusaders and burghers; others, such as the annihilation of the Jewry of Mainz, were organized and premeditated. In May 1096, Count Emicho encamped outside Mainz, where he prepared his army to storm the city. Once the city gates were opened by townspeople, Emicho's army attacked the archbishop's palace, where many Jews had taken shelter. There, after Jewish defenders failed to fight back the crusader forces, many Jews were slaughtered; others chose to take their own lives and those of members of their families. The Jews of Mainz were not alone in choosing this recourse; it was shared by many others who were faced with forced baptism. *Martyrdom to sanctify God's name (mavet al kiddush ha-Shem) was the Jews' most remarkable response to the 1096 attacks.

The 1096 massacres are described in three unique Hebrew narrative sources: the so-called *Mainz Anonymous* or *The Narrative of the Old Persecution*; the *Solomon bar Simson Chronicle*; and the so-called *Eliezer bar Nathan Chronicle*. The first was written close to the events and the other two about a generation later. Jews also memorialized the victims in lists of martyrs and in poetry (see POETRY, MEDIEVAL: CHRISTIAN EUROPE). However, Christian sources on the First Crusade hardly mentioned these events. The most complete description is found in Albert of Aachen's *Historia Hierosolymitana*.

Although the 1096 assaults were the most devastating, anti-Jewish violence continued in subsequent crusades. As part of the call for the Second Crusade (1147–49), some crusader preachers, such as the Cistercian monk Ralph, called for attacks on Jews in towns in France and Germany. These acts of violence were reduced or prevented by the interventions of the Cistercian abbot Bernard of Clairvaux, one of the leading figures of the medieval church, and of Conrad III of Germany. Similarly, on the eve of the departure of the Third Crusade (1189–92), Emperor Frederick I Barbarossa took firm measures to protect the Jews in the Rhineland. The Third Crusade, however, did lead to deadly attacks on Jewish communities in *England. The attacks started in London, on the coronation day of Richard I (September 3, 1189), and spread to Norwich, King's Lynn, Stamford, Lincoln, Bury St. Edmunds, and York. In York, the Jewish population was annihilated: The city castle, where the Jews had taken refuge, was set on fire by the attackers. Many Jews took their own lives, whereas others, who were able to leave the castle after promising to accept baptism, were massacred outside its gates. Violence against Jews also occurred during the Shepherds' Crusade of 1320.

For further reading see S. Eidelberg, trans. and ed., *The Jews and the Crusaders: The Hebrew Chronicles of the First and Second Crusades* (1977); R. Chazan, *God, Humanity and History: The Hebrew First Crusade Narrative* (2000); J. Riley-Smith, "Christian Violence and the Crusades," in *Religious Violence between Christians and Jews: Medieval Roots, Modern Perspectives*, ed. A. Sapir Abulafia (2002), 3–21; J. Bronstein, "The Crusades and the Jews: Some Reflections on the 1096 Massacre," *History Compass* 5 (2007): 1268–79; R. C. Stacey, "Crusades, Martyrdoms, and the Jews of Norman England, 1096–1190," in *Juden und Christen zur Zeit der Kreuzzüge*, ed. A. Haverkamp (1999), 233–51; and D. Nirenberg, *Communities of Violence: Persecution of Minorities in the Middle Ages* (1996), 43–69. **Map 7**   JUDITH BRONSTEIN

Middle Ages: Demography.

For the first half of the Middle Ages (roughly the sixth through the tenth centuries), the overwhelming majority of Jews lived under Muslim domination, with a substantial number residing in eastern Christendom under *Byzantine rule. Western Christendom was a distant third in terms of the Jewish population it hosted and the power and creativity of that population. Even in Europe, the largest Jewish communities were in areas under Muslim control, such as most of the *Iberian Peninsula (*Spain) and southern sectors of *Italy (see also SICILY).

This distribution of world Jewry reflected the relative power of the three major power blocs during the first half of the Middle Ages: the dominant *Islamic bloc, the still potent Greek Christian bloc, and weak and backward Latin Christendom. Significant change in world Jewish demography largely resulted from alterations in the patterns of medieval economic, political, and military power. Beginning around the year 1000, Christian Europe unexpectedly surged forward in population, economy, military might, political organization, and cultural creativity. As western Christendom advanced, it became home to an increasingly large Jewish population.

Some of western Christendom's new Jews fell into the Christian orbit as a result of the expansion of Christian power and control. As Christian forces eliminated Muslim enclaves on the Italian and Iberian Peninsulas, the largest Jewish communities in Europe came under Christian domination. In addition, the accelerating vigor of western Christendom attracted enterprising Jews from nearby Islamic territories into the old areas of Jewish settlement across southern Europe. More strikingly, this new vigor enticed Jews from Islamic territories and the Christian sectors of southern Europe into areas of northern Europe in which Jewish communities had never taken hold. Arguably the most important development of the second half of the Middle Ages (roughly the eleventh through the fifteenth centuries) was a pronounced shift in the center of gravity in world Jewish population, power, and creativity. During this period, Jews began the process of becoming a predominantly European people, centered in Latin Christian areas of the western world.

With the passage of time, the varied areas of the Iberian Peninsula and southern France (see FRANCE, SOUTHERN) achieved increasing political coherence and economic progress. The Italian Peninsula was not able to reach the same level of political coherence, which stunted its economic development as well. By the early fourteenth century, southern French Jewry was expelled by the Capetian rulers of a unified France that stretched from the Mediterranean Sea into the northern areas of Western Europe. At the end of the fifteenth century, a similar fate befell the large Jewish communities of the Iberian Peninsula. Only Italian Jewry was able to preserve itself, although sectors of these Jews were uprooted from time to time. Curiously, Italy's failure to achieve political coherence worked to the Jews' advantage, enabling them to avoid the wholesale expulsions that afflicted their co-religionists further westward.

The lack of Jewish economic diversification in northern Europe created an obvious need for demographic mobility (see ENGLAND: MIDDLE AGES; FRANCE: MIDDLE AGES; GERMANY). As the Jewish population grew, urban centers could absorb only a finite number of Jews involved in limited economic activities. There was thus a constant pressure toward demographic movement. While Jews seem to have clustered initially in the major urban centers of northern France and *England, economic pressures constantly drove them out of these centers and into lesser urban areas. Likewise, limited economic opportunities influenced Jewish readiness to respond positively to invitations emanating from *Eastern Europe. Willingness to move into uncharted territories and to respond to economic opportunity brought Jews into areas of medieval Europe previously unfamiliar to them. Adaptation to limited economic circumstances and the willingness to strike out into new locales were a constant feature of Jewish life in Latin Christendom throughout the Middle Ages. For further reading, see R. Chazan, *The Jews* *of Medieval Western Christendom* (2006); and idem, *Fashioning Jewish Identity in Medieval Western Europe* (2009); **see also** COMMERCE, MEDIEVAL; **Map 7.**   ROBERT CHAZAN

Middle Ages: Ḥasidei Ashkenaz (the pious ones of Ashkenaz or the German pietists).

The *Ḥasidei Ashkenaz* were circles of *mystics and pietists that flourished mainly in the *Rhineland and in Regensburg (and to a lesser extent in northern France) from the second half of the twelfth century through the late thirteenth century. These schools were independent of each other and developed different theologies and worldviews. The most influential branch of *Ḥasidei Ashkenaz* was descended from the prominent Kalonymus rabbinic families in pre-crusade Mainz; it was founded by R. Samuel ben Kalonymus of Speyer (b. 1115), who was also known by the epithets *he-Ḥasid* (the pious), *ha-Kadosh* (the holy), and *ha-Navi* (the prophet). Some see the formation of this branch as closely linked to the religious notion of *martyrdom (*kiddush ha-Shem*) that became more prevalent in *Germany at the time of the First *Crusade in 1096. Samuel's son R. Judah he-Ḥasid (d. 1217) and Judah's student (and relative) Eleazar ben Judah (ben Kalonymus) of Worms (d. 1230 or 1237) subsequently headed this circle in the Rhineland, although Judah left for Regensburg in 1195.

The main exoteric work of this movement is *Sefer Ḥasidim* (Book of the Pious), which is attributed to Judah he-Ḥasid, but appears to contain material from all three of the movement's leaders. This lengthy treatise is suffused with ethical and prescriptive materials that were addressed both to the aspiring pietist and to the devoted nonpietist. A small number of passages in *Sefer Ḥasidim* (and elsewhere) intimate that the pietists may have constituted separate communities or should at least strive to do so, an instruction that was apparently never actualized. Indeed, Judah served (together with two nonpietist rabbinic scholars) as a member of the rabbinic court in Regensburg, and Eleazar sat on the rabbinic court in Worms and was also a signatory on the supercommunal ordinances promulgated for Speyer, Worms, and Mainz (the so-called *Takkanot Shu"m*) during the 1220s. *Sefer Ḥasidim* criticizes the prayers, educational methods, and religious mores of nonpietist rabbinic scholars (and laymen), even as it makes recommendations in these areas for the benefit of all Jews. Necromancy, the occult, and the world of the souls are vividly discussed within the exempla in this work, as are the behaviors of Christians that are worthy of emulation (such as decorum during prayer and the dedication of chivalrous knights to their principles) and those that are not.

The social theories of Judah he-Ḥasid in *Sefer Ḥasidim* and the more prolific Eleazar of Worms in his halakhic work, *Sefer Rokeaḥ* (Book of the Perfumer), and in several of his esoteric works (including his prayer commentary) differed significantly, as did the ways in which they instructed sinners to seek *repentance. Often their guidance had elements in common with surrounding Christian penitential practices.

Judah and Eleazar composed commentaries to the Torah (see BIBLICAL COMMENTARY) that ran the gamut from forms of *peshat* interpretation and simple *gematria* (see NUMEROLOGY) passages to more complex numerical and letter manipulations and esoteric constructs. It is possible to detect nascent *kabbalistic teachings, especially in the writings of Eleazar, together with prayer interpretations that revolve around a precise counting of the Hebrew words and letters in each prayer text, in addition to *midrashic and fully esoteric interpretations of the *liturgy. Eleazar of Worms was also a prodigious author of liturgical poems (*piyyutim*; see POETRY, LITURGICAL [*PIYYUT*]); Judah the Pious was not, although he is perhaps the author of the so-called *Shir ha-Kavod*. Eleazar's student, Abraham ben Azriel of Bohemia, produced an extensive commentary to the *piyyutim* entitled *Arugat ha-Bosem* (Bed of Spices [Song of Songs 3:15]). R. Moses ben Isaac of *Vienna (ca. 1200–1270) records a variety of teachings from both Judah and Eleazar (with whom he studied) in his halakhic compendium, *Sefer Or Zarua*. Judah's descendants continued his tradition of esoteric studies. Particularly noteworthy is his great-grandson, Moses ben Eliezer, who composed a mystical commentary on the *Shi'ur Komah*. Among the esoteric theories of this school, the divine *kavod*, which emanated from the godhead and served as the subject of *revelation (a concept that has its origins in the writings of *Saadia Gaon), became especially influential. Also of importance is the more exoteric notion that focused extreme devotion on every detail of the commandments and the imperative that sought to uncover the covert or hidden divine will (see also KABBALAH).

The Circle of the Unique Cherub (*Ḥug ha-Keruv ha-Meyuḥad*) is also associated with Ḥasidei Ashkenaz. This school based many of its mystical teachings on a pseudepigraphical treatise, *Baraita de Yosef ben Uziel*, the author of which was said to be descended from Ben Sira (see WISDOM OF BEN SIRA) and the prophet *Jeremiah. This circle also produced a commentary (that is attributed to Saadia Gaon) on the earlier mystical work *Sefer Yetzirah*, and additional commentaries to *Sefer Yetzirah* as well. One of the leading figures in this group was Elḥanan ben Jakar of London (who also lived for a time in northwest France and was the author of several works). This circle also produced a theological work entitled *Sod ha-Sodot* (Secret of Secrets).

A third branch of *Ḥasidei Ashkenaz* produced several anonymous mystical and ethical treatises. Among these is *Sefer Ḥayyim* (written at the turn of the twelfth century) that has been (incorrectly) attributed to the Tosafist student of R. Jacob Tam, R. Ḥayyim ha-Kohen. *Sefer ha-Navon*, a commentary to the *shema and *Shi'ur Komah* (composed c. 1230) has recently been attributed to a R. Neḥemiah ben Solomon, who may be the same person as R. Troestlin ha-Navi of Erfurt.

Modern scholarship initially posited a gap between the *Ḥasidei Ashkenaz* and the *Tosafists, who flourished in northern France and Germany at the same time and were the leading talmudists and halakhists of the day. More recently, however, it has been shown that these distinct groups of rabbinic scholars interacted productively on both intellectual and spiritual levels. Tosafists sometimes accepted the broader curriculum and the sharp focus on deciding matters of Jewish law (as opposed to unbridled theoretical study) that were stressed by the Rhineland pietists, even as the pietists participated to an extent in Tosafist talmudic study. R. Eleazar of Worms composed *Tosafot* to BT *Bava Kamma* that were based on the *Tosafot* of R. Isaac (Ri) of Dampierre, and *Sefer Ḥasidim* proclaims the virtue of possessing genuine *Tosafot* texts. Similarly, it is possible to point to Tosafists in both northern France and Germany who affected pietists' behaviors and regimens. These include R. Moses of Coucy and the brothers (R. Moses and R. Samuel) of Evreux in the mid-thirteenth century, as well as R. Isaac of Corbeil and R. *Meir ben Barukh of Rothenburg in the second half of that century. At the same time, however, only the *Ḥasidei Ashkenaz* were familiar with *Neoplatonic and other philosophical systems, which they joined with earlier Jewish *mystical texts (most notably *hekhalot* literature, which was more widely available in medieval Ashkenaz) to put forward theosophical and theurgic doctrines and formulations. A number of these doctrines made their way southward and were subsequently absorbed by the systems of kabbalistic teachings then developing elsewhere in medieval Europe.

For further reading, see J. R. Baskin, "Women and Sexual Ambivalence in *Sefer Hasidim*," *Jewish Quarterly Review* 96 (2006): 1–8; M. Idel, "Some Forlorn Writings of an Ashkenazi Prophet: R. Nehemiah ben Shlomo ha-Navi," *Jewish Quarterly Review* 95 (2005): 183–96; E. Kanarfogel, "R. Judah he-Hasid and the Rabbinic Scholars of Regensburg: Interactions, Influences and Implications," *Jewish Quarterly Review* 96 (2006): 17–37; I. Marcus, *Piety and Society* (1981); and H. Soloveitchik, "Three Themes in the *Sefer Hasidim*," *Association for Jewish Studies Review* 1 (1976): 311–57.

EPHRAIM KANARFOGEL

Middle Ages: Jewish–Christian Polemics.

Medieval Jewish polemicists against *Christianity inherited only a thin legacy of Jewish responses to Christian arguments in late antiquity. Nonetheless, under the impact of a challenging and often dangerous environment, Jews produced a rich and variegated polemical literature.

In the early Christian centuries, we find sporadic remarks in *rabbinic literature that respond to Christian claims and doctrines that Jews saw as theologically unacceptable, such as some degree of multiplicity in the deity. Various versions of a counter-gospel called *Toldot Yeshu* (The Biography of Jesus) began to circulate, providing generations of Jews with a hostile narrative of Jesus' illegitimate birth followed by a supposed career of sorcery, rebelliousness, and eventual hanging on a stalk of cabbage. The earliest full work containing sustained arguments against Christianity is a polemic of eastern provenance entitled *The Book of Nestor the Priest*. Although it is sketchy and poorly organized, it covers many points of contention between Jews and Christians, ranging from disputed interpretations of passages in the Hebrew *Bible to Jewish claims of inconsistencies in the *New Testament. This work exerted considerable influence on later Jewish authors in the heart of Christian Europe.

Sporadic philosophical arguments against Christian doctrines began to appear by the tenth century in works of Jewish thinkers like R. *Saadia Gaon, who lived in the Muslim orbit; similarly, biblical exegetes periodically refuted the Christological understanding of a few key verses in the Hebrew Bible. However, full-fledged polemical works by European Jews did not emerge until the third quarter of the twelfth century, when Jacob ben Reuben's *Milḥamot ha-Shem* (Wars of the Lord) and Joseph *Kimḥi's *Sefer ha-Berit* (Book of the Covenant) appeared almost simultaneously in southern France (see FRANCE: MIDDLE AGES; FRANCE, SOUTHERN: MIDDLE AGES).

Although the themes addressed in these and later polemics vary widely, this literature essentially consists of warring interpretations of biblical words, verses, and passages. Thus, Christians asserted that the plural form, "Let us make man," in *Genesis 1:26 refers to at least two of the persons in the triune God; conversely, Jews argued that it is a plural of majesty or that it describes God's inclusion of the angels or the lower elements in the divine decision. Christians translated the word *almah* in *Isaiah 7:14 as "virgin," whereas Jews understood it as "young woman," insisting that both context and philology ruled out the christological interpretation. Christians saw the servant in Isaiah 53 as the suffering Jesus, while Jews usually took the figure as a collective representation of the Jewish people in exile.

Beyond the Hebrew Bible, Jews had to address the painful argument that their suffering and exile proved their rejection by God; thus, contemporary circumstances entered the fray. This was a double-edged sword because Jewish polemicists were able to cite the failure of the Crusades (see MIDDLE AGES: CRUSADES) and what they saw as the evident moral inferiority of contemporary Christians to buttress their own position. Jews also brought critical literary approaches, sometimes incorporating historical analysis, to bear on the New Testament. These approaches ranged from a critique of contradictions and inconsistencies to sharply divergent assessments of Jesus; on the one hand, he was depicted as a sinner, even an idolater, but on the other he was portrayed as a fully committed, if sometimes foolish or megalomaniacal, adherent of the *Torah.

These themes are evident to a greater or lesser degree in the major thirteenth-century polemics, *Sefer Yosef ha-Mekanne* (The Book of Joseph the Zealot) and the *Nizzaḥon Vetus* (Old Book of Polemic) both from northern Europe, as well as in Meir of Narbonne's *Milḥemet Mitzvah* (Obligatory War). Although a critique of Matthew had already appeared in Jacob ben Reuben's work, Profiat Duran, a fourteenth-century Spanish Jew, constructed the most sophisticated analysis of the New Testament in his *Kelimat ha-Goyim* (Shame of the Gentiles).

The philosophical dimension of Jewish polemic was developed almost exclusively by *Sephardic Jews, although the *Ta'anot* (Arguments) of the Italian Moses ben Solomon of Salerno is the most impressive work of this genre before the fourteenth century. Ḥasdai *Crescas, a major philosopher, turned his attention to the Christian challenge, and his *Refutation of the Christian Principles* is the most technical and challenging philosophical polemic of the Middle Ages. While Christians usually took the offensive with respect to discussions of the Hebrew Scriptures, Jews generally initiated philosophical arguments regarding Christian doctrine. Thus, they maintained that the Trinity is a manifestly contradictory belief; that a God who is unlimited and unchangeable could not take on flesh; that transubstantiation, aside from its evident logical challenges, requires the body of Jesus to be present on several altars simultaneously; and that the preservation of Mary's virginity during childbirth requires two objects to take up the same space at the same time. All of this, they said, entails logical contradictions that cannot be overcome even by the miracles of an omnipotent God.

In the thirteenth century, Jews were challenged by a Christian assault on the *Talmud that posed multidimensional dangers. Although this attack originated earlier, it reached maturity in two public disputations: one in 1240 in Paris and the other in 1263 in Barcelona. In the first, Nicholas Donin, a Jewish convert to Christianity, asserted that the Talmud contained foolishness, theologically objectionable beliefs, laws and other dicta hostile to Gentiles, and blasphemous statements regarding Jesus and Mary. Moreover, Donin claimed that the Talmud constituted "another law" beyond the Hebrew Bible. Thus, he argued, the long-standing Christian perception, so important to the protected status of the Jews – that Jews observe the Hebrew Bible – needed to be radically rethought. R. Jeḥiel of Paris mounted a defense, arguing among other things that contemporary Christians are not subsumed under the discriminatory laws in the Talmud that were aimed at ancient pagans; that in light of an apparent anachronism, at least some talmudic passages about "Jesus" refer to someone other than the founder of Christianity; and that the Talmud is a necessary supplement to the Hebrew Bible without which many biblical laws would be impossible to apply.

In the 1263 Barcelona disputation, another convert, Pablo Christiani, argued that the Talmud contains manifold proofs of Christian doctrine. Moses *Naḥmanides replied that if this were so the Rabbis would have embraced Christianity. However, this argument did not prevent him and later Iberian Jews from having to confront a campaign of growing sophistication that reached its climax in the lengthy Tortosa disputation of 1413–14. Isaac *Abravanel, the last great figure produced by medieval Iberian Jewry, devoted an entire work, *Yeshu'ot Meshiḥo* (The Saving Acts of His Messiah), to providing an explication for Jews of rabbinic passages used by Christians in this sustained attack.

For further reading, see D. Berger, *The Jewish-Christian Debate in the High Middle Ages: A Critical Edition of the* Nizzahon Vetus *with an Introduction, Translation, and Commentary* (1979); S. Krauss and W. Horbury, *The Jewish-Christian Controversy: From the Earliest Times to 1789* (1995); and D. Lasker, *Jewish Philosophical Polemics against Christianity in the Middle Ages*, 2nd ed. (2007).   DAVID BERGER

Midrash: See *AGGADAH*; RABBINIC HERMENEUTICS; RABBINIC LITERATURE: MIDRASH

Mikdash: See TEMPLE AND TEMPLE CULT; TEMPLE, SECOND.

Mikveh (pl. *mikva'ot*; a ritual bath). A mikveh is "a place where [water] is accumulated" and refers to an artificial reservoir of water used for the ritual purification of persons and objects. Often, a mikveh includes two pools: one for the actual immersion, generally with broad steps leading into the water, and the other as a reservoir that collects rain water to be used in the main pool. The oldest known *mikva'ot* are from the *Hasmonean period, around 150 BCE.

Two millennia ago, a significant part of Jewish purity rituals was connected to the Second *Temple in *Jerusalem, including ritual *immersion before entering the Temple precincts. Archeologists have excavated more than forty *mikva'ot* of the Second Temple era on the Temple Mount. After the Temple's destruction in 70 CE, the majority of ritual purity laws became obsolete, and the use of ritual baths was mainly reserved for a specific domain of purity, the *niddah* laws related to women's menstrual cycle. In theory,

the Rabbis could have decreed that these laws were also irrelevant after the destruction of the Temple, but they decided otherwise.

Although women may ritually immerse in a natural body of water, doing so can be problematic and unreliable. Thus, each Jewish community generally built its own mikveh, sometimes even before building a *synagogue. The mikveh's basic physical structure is determined by Jewish law (*Mikva'ot*, sixth tractate of the Order *Tohorot* (Purities) of the *Mishnah and *Talmuds). The water volume should be about several hundred liters (the exact amount is a subject for debate, because of the various interpretations of the rabbinic volume of forty *se'ah*). For a mikveh to be valid, its water, or at least a portion of it, must be accumulated in a "natural" way; it should not be "drawn water." For this reason, many *mikva'ot* are located in places where water can be accumulated naturally. Since the Middle Ages, *mikva'ot* have often been built under or near *synagogues. Today, the vast majority of modern *mikva'ot* are heated, but before the Early Modern period, this was not the case.

A mikveh can be used for other Jewish ritual purposes, including the purification of certain utensils produced by non-Jews, the ritual immersion of *converts to Judaism, immersion by women before *marriage, and voluntary ritual immersion for men. This practice of male ritual immersion has existed since ancient times, but it has become especially common since the sixteenth century, with the rise of *kabbalistic and then *Ḥasidic circles. Although in theory the main purpose of such immersion is for purification after ejaculation, men's mikveh immersion is more often understood as a spiritual preparation for the *Sabbath and major *festivals. **See also IMMERSION, RITUAL: WOMEN; *NIDDAH*; PURITY AND IMPURITY.**   EVYATAR MARIENBERG

Minyan is a worship quorum, generally composed of ten adult Jewish males in traditional *Judaism and ten adult Jews in liberal forms of Jewish *worship. A *minyan* is required for communal *Torah reading and the recitation of certain communal prayers such as the *Kaddish*.

Miriam. One of the few biblical women not presented as someone's wife or mother, Miriam appears with her brothers *Aaron and *Moses as a leader of the *Israelites during the Exodus period (see Micah 6:4). She is mentioned in five biblical books, more than any other woman; unlike Moses, Miriam is called a *prophet in Exodus. Credited with helping her mother save the infant Moses (Exod 2), Miriam also figures prominently as composer and performer (with a cohort of women) of the song with which the Israelites celebrated their miraculous deliverance from the Egyptians at the Sea of Reeds (Exod 15:20–21 and also Exod 15: 1–20). This is one of the earliest poems in the *Bible and one of the earliest biblical proclamations of divine intervention in human affairs. Miriam's role as its composer gives her a primary place in the Bible's prophetic tradition. When Miriam is punished for criticizing Moses, her brother appeals to God on her behalf (Numb 12). **See also, EGYPT AND ANCIENT ISRAEL.**
                                        CAROL MEYERS

Mishkan: See TABERNACLE

Mishnah (ca. 200 CE) is an ancient book of case law containing traditions that pertain to ritual, civil, and criminal domains. The Mishnah is significant because it was the first literary work produced by the rabbinic movement (ca. 50–600 CE), a movement that shaped the scriptural, scholastic, and liturgical modes of religious expression characteristic of pre-modern *Judaism.

The project of collecting legal traditions into retrievable form is said to have begun shortly after the destruction of the Second *Temple in 70 CE. According to T. *Eduyot* 1:1, "When the sages entered the vineyard at Yavneh they said: 'The time is coming when people will seek a word from the teachings of the Torah, but will not find it, or [they will seek] a word from the teachings of the scribes, but will not find it.... They said: let us begin [by collecting the traditions of] *Hillel and Shammai.'" Traditions were passed on in a formal manner to stem the losses brought about by the destruction of the central cultic and scribal center. More than one-third of the legal teachings recorded in the Mishnah concern rituals practiced at the *Jerusalem *Temple.

Several features of the Mishnah's literary form seem particularly well designed to aid in the preservation and formal transmission of tradition. For example, legal traditions are often grouped in sets of three or five, a feature commonly associated with oral tradition. Likewise, the Mishnah employs parallel structures with extensive repetition of key elements. It also organizes its traditions topically, rather than by associatively linking them with biblical verses, enabling its students to recall teachings by subject matter or a sage's name. The broadest topical divisions in the Mishnah are known as orders (*sedarim*, pl.; *seder*, sing.), which are further subdivided into sixty-three tractates (*masekhtot*, pl.; *masekhet*, sing.). Each tractate is divided into chapters, and each chapter consists of individually numbered teachings – each of which is known as a *mishnah* (pl. *mishnayot*). The six orders of the Mishnah are laws of Agriculture (*Zera'im*), Holidays (*Mo'ed*), Women (*Nashim*), Civil Laws (*Nezikin*), Holy Things (*Kodashim*), and Purities (*Tohorot*). *Masekhet*, the Hebrew word for tractate, literally means "webbing" and alludes to the fact that the Mishnah's topical organization is a loose one, with the Mishnah often associatively shifting from topic to topic. An additional feature of the Mishnah that aids in the formal transmission of tradition is its condensed expression. Where parallels (especially in the *Tosefta) often preserve lengthy and spelled-out versions of tradition, the Mishnah is known for its laconic and telegraphic style.

Traditional accounts attribute the redaction of the Mishnah to R. Judah the *Patriarch (*Judah ha-Nasi, referred to in the Mishnah as Rabbi) in 200 CE (see BT *Bava Metzia* 86a: "The end of Mishnah is Rabbi and Rabbi Natan"). Earlier collections of legal traditions that were similarly arranged by topic and divorced from relevant biblical verses are said to have served as the prototype and basis for Rabbi's collection. Important earlier collections are said to have circulated in the name of R. Meir, and before that in the name of R. *Akiva; both were among the *Tannaim, sages active between 50 and 200 CE.

Scholars debate why legal traditions were collected in the Mishnah. One school of thought suggests that R. Judah the Patriarch edited the Mishnah to serve as an authoritative law code (Epstein, 1957). In this conception, R. Judah edited the Mishnah to codify his preferred legal positions. The major difficulty with this explanation is that the Mishnah contains numerous unresolved legal disputes. Later sages, especially the school associated with R. Joḥanan, developed a number of rules to determine practical law in the face of the numerous disputes (e.g., "when there is a dispute between X and Y, the law follows Y"; Zlotnick). The other leading theory suggests that the Mishnah was formulated to serve as a pedagogical tool in the training of rabbinic sages (Goldberg). The legal cases in the Mishnah would have exposed rabbinic disciples to key legal principles and provided the grounds for conceptual consideration of how different principles intersect (Alexander). Regardless of which theory is historically accurate, subsequent generations of sages used the Mishnah both as a resource for legal decision making and for academic training. More recent attention to the literary arrangement of traditions has led scholars to assert that the Mishnah presents conceptual distillations of religious *thought and philosophy.

Of all the genres of rabbinic literature collectively known as "Oral *Torah," the Mishnah shows the clearest signs of having been orally performed in antiquity. As noted earlier, many of the Mishnah's literary features seem designed to facilitate oral transmission. A subject of ongoing scholarly debate has been the question of when, how, and for what purposes was the Mishnah written down. Some scholars suggest that the official version of the Mishnah was available only in "oral" form, as memorized by official performers in the rabbinic academies (Lieberman). Others propose that an official written version of the Mishnah existed (Epstein, 2000). Recent scholarship has argued that oral and literary modes of text production, performance, and preservation were used in conjunction with each other (Jaffee).

Although it is true that the Mishnah distills and records early legal traditions for posterity, the Mishnah's historical significance is not limited to its relationship to the past. It is equally (if not more) important because it served as the springboard for oral study after it was redacted. In the centuries following its promulgation by R. Judah, the Mishnah became the central curricular document around which rabbinic learning was organized. Each of the Talmuds (the Jerusalem *Talmud, completed around 400 CE, and the Babylonian *Talmud, completed around 600 CE) is structured as a commentary to the Mishnah. In the Talmuds, the legal traditions of the Mishnah become the subject of extended conversation, debate, argument, and interpretation (see also RABBINIC LITERATURE: MISHNAH AND TALMUD).

Important research includes J. Neusner, *A History of the Mishnaic Law of Purities: The Redaction and Formulation of the Order of Purities in Mishnah and Tosefta* (1977); idem, *Judaism: The Evidence of the Mishnah* (1988); J. N. Epstein, *Introduction to Tannaitic Literature* (1957); idem, *Introduction to the Text of the Mishnah* (2000); D. Zlotnick, *The Iron Pillar – Mishnah* (1988); A. Goldberg, "The Mishnah – A Study Book of Halakhah," in *Literature of the Sages*, ed. S. Safrai (1987); E. S. Alexander, *Transmitting Mishnah* (2006); S. Lieberman, "The Oral Publication of the Mishnah," in *Hellenism in Jewish Palestine* (1994), ed. S. Lieberman; and M. Jaffee, *Torah in the Mouth* (2001).   ELIZABETH SHANKS ALEXANDER

Mishnah: Orders and Tractates

ZERA'IM (Seeds)	MO'ED (Seasons)	NASHIM (Women)	NEZIKIN (Damages)	KODASHIM (Holy Things)	TOHOROT (Ritual Purities)
Berakhot	Shabbat	Yevamot	Bava Metzia	Zevahim	Keilim
Pe'ah	Eruvin	Ketubbot	Bava Kamma	Menahot	Oholot
Demai	Pesahim	Nedarim	Bava Batra	Hullin	Nega'im
Kil'ayim	Shekalim	Nazir	Sanhedrin	Bekhorot	Parah
Shevi'it	Yoma	Sotah	Makkot	Arakhin	Tohorot
Terumot	Sukkah	Gittin	Shevu'ot	Temurah	Mikva'ot
Ma'aserot	Beitzah	Kiddushin	Eduyot	Keritot	Niddah
Ma'aser Sheni	Rosh Ha-Shanah		Avodah Zarah	Me'ilah	Makhshirin
Hallah	Ta'anit		Avot	Tamid	Zavim
Orlah	Megillah		Horayot	Middot	Tevul Yom
Bikkurim	Mo'ed Katan			Kinnim	Yadayim
	Hagigah				Uktzim

Mishneh Torah is Moses *Maimonides' fourteen-volume codification of Jewish law completed in 1190 in *Egypt.

Mitnaggedim (sing. *mitnagged*) were those Jews who opposed the Hasidic movment that began in eighteenth-century *Poland. **See HASIDISM: EUROPE; VILNA GAON, ELIJAH.**

Mitzvah (pl. *mitzvot*) is the Hebrew word for "commandment." In the Hebrew *Bible, the term is synonymous with *torah* (instruction), *mishpat* (ruling), *hukah* (statute), and *mishmeret* (observance). Yet, *mitzvah* encompasses all these definitions. Although *mitzvah* can refer to any kind of commandment, the word is usually used in reference to divine mandates. An additional meaning appears in *rabbinic literature where a *mitzvah* can be a laudatory, but not strictly required, religious act. For example, it is a greater *mitzvah* for a man to betroth his bride in person, rather than by proxy (BT *Kiddushin* 41a; see BETROTHAL). In the *Talmud, the word *mitzvah* can refer broadly to any religious observance and has an exclusively religious connotation. The Rabbis adopted the word *gezerah* (edict or decree) to refer to an order from a secular authority. The sages also categorized *mitzvot* into groups, including positive (those requiring one to perform an act) and negative (those prohibiting one from performing an act). Another rabbinic categorization separated *mitzvot d'oraita* (*Torah commandments), which are commandments considered to be from *God, whether or not explicitly stated in the *Pentateuch, from *mitzvot d'rabbanan* (commandments of our Rabbis), which are behaviors the sages considered to be either required or prohibited by rabbinic authority. The medieval halakhic tradition (see *HALAKHAH*), based on a statement in BT *Makkot* 23b, developed the notion that there were 613 divine *mitzvot*. Many attempts to list the 613 were made, but they all differed to some degree, and no list achieved authoritative status.

In *Yiddish, the word *mitzvah* came to mean any good deed, whether religious or secular in nature. This is still the meaning most commonly intended when *Ashkenazic Jews use the word. *Sephardic and Middle Eastern (*Mizrahi) Jews rarely use the word in this way. However, they do use the term to refer to a prestigious *synagogue ritual act, such as being called to recite the blessings before and after a portion of the day's Torah (see TORAH READING) or *Haftarah* readings. Ashkenazic Jews use the word *kibbud* (honor) to express that meaning. In Modern Hebrew, the term *mitzvah* is exclusively religious. Israelis use the word *pekudah* to refer to a secular command or directive.

MARCUS MORDECHAI SCHWARTZ

Mizrachi refers to the Religious Zionist movement founded in 1902 in *Vilna by Rabbi Isaac Jacob Reines. Mizrachi is allied with the Religious Zionist and Modern Orthodox movements in Israel and throughout the world (see JUDAISM, ORTHODOX: MODERN ORTHODOX; JUDAISM, ISRAELI FORMS OF). The Mizrachi youth movement Benei Akiva was founded in 1929; it is one of the largest organizations in Israel (see ISRAEL, STATE OF: YOUTH MOVEMENTS) and has many chapters throughout the world.

Mizrachi Women's Organization of America, known as AMIT since 1983, was founded in 1925. Initially a women's auxiliary to Mizrachi, the organization declared its autonomy in 1934. **See ORGANIZATIONS, WOMEN'S: NORTH AMERICA.**

MIZRAH refers to a decorative plaque hung on the eastern wall of a synagogue or home to indicate the direction of *prayer (see **Plate 9**).

Mizrahi (pl. Mizrahim) designates communities with long histories in the Middle East and North Africa. The term differentiates Mizrahi Jews from *Sephardim, who established themselves in these regions after the 1492 expulsion from *Spain. **See also, EGYPT; IRAN; IRAQ; KURDISTAN; NORTH AFRICA; and YEMEN.**

Moab is a region that extended east–west from the Dead Sea to the Syro-Arabian Desert. It was crossed toward the north by the Arnon River (Wadi Mujib), and its southern border was the Zered River (Wadi el-Hesa). The king's highway (Num 21:22) ran north–south through the country. Known from the Early Bronze Age, Moab appeared in *Egyptian texts in the Late Bronze Age IIB. Changing borders reflected international relations throughout the Iron Age II: Moab was intermittently ruled by foreign nations including

*Israel, Neo-*Assyria, and *Babylon. Moabite kings, some known from local, biblical, and Neo-Assyrian texts, ruled from the capital Dibon (Dhiban). The national god Chemosh was worshiped both in Moab and in *Jerusalem (by *Solomon's Moabite wives; 1 Kgs 11:7–8). The ninth-century-BCE Mesha Stele (Moabite Stone) attests to Moab's king Mesha regaining his freedom from Omri, king of *Israel (2 Kgs 3:4–5). Excavations at Dhiban, Madaba, Tall Hisban (Hesbon), `Ara`ir (Aroer), and other sites illuminate Moabite culture. Its economy combined agriculture and pastoralism.

Moab is mentioned often in the *Bible. It shares roots with the *Israelites (through *Abraham and Lot in *Gen 19:37; through *David in the book of *Ruth; and through Solomon in 1 Kgs 11:1, 7, 33). More frequently, relations with Israel are shown as hostile (Num 21:29–39, 22:1ff; Judg 3:12–30; 1 Sam 14: 47; 2 Sam 8:2–3; Ezra 9:1; Neh 13:1–2; various prophets). In the fourth to third centuries BCE, Moab became home to Nabateans moving north from their desert homeland. **Map 2**   BETH ALPERT NAKHAI

Modena, Leon (Judah Aryeh mi-Modena [1571–1648]) was a Venetian rabbi, *cantor, orator, teacher, author, and polemicist (see ITALY; VENICE). Both before and after his rabbinic ordination in 1609, Modena undertook a variety of occupations and activities to gain income and influence. He served as a legal clerk for the rabbis of Venice; taught students of all ages, including Christians; was a proofreader and publication expediter; wrote *poetry for books, weddings, and gravestones; was a popular preacher and a letter writer; translated Hebrew documents for the government; and served as *maestro di cappella* for Jewish musical groups, as a cantor, and as a rabbi outside of Venice. He was offered a chair in oriental languages in Paris that he refused. Often in his life, Modena turned to gambling, justifying this compulsion in a pastoral dialogue, *Sur mera* (1595), and in a responsum (see RESPONSA LITERATURE).

In his many published books, Modena demonstrated his skills as an author, teacher, and popularizer of rabbinic teachings. In *Sod Yesharim* (Secret of the Upright, 1594/5), he prefaced magic tricks, folk remedies, and riddles to a curriculum of biblical and rabbinic studies. In *Tzemah Tzaddik* (Flower of the Virtuous, 1600), he embellished a Hebrew translation of the popular *Fior di Virtù*, with citations from Jewish sources. In *Midbar Yehudah* (The Wilderness of Judah, 1602), he included Hebrew translations of his *sermons and "*Kinah Shemor*," a macaronic poem, sounding and meaning the same in Hebrew and Italian. Modena made the first complete Italian translation of the *Passover *haggadah* (1609). In *Galut Yehudah* (The Exile of Judah, 1612), he tried to overcome church laws against translating the Bible into Italian by providing a glossary of words, to which he later added one of rabbinic terms (1640). In *Lev Aryeh* (The Life of Judah, 1612), he presented a Hebrew system of memory improvement as a preface to a work on the 613 religious *commandments. Modena used current dramatic standards and Italian language to bring traditional rabbinic sources to the attention of Italian Jews in his play, *L'Ester* (1619), on the life of Queen *Esther. He contributed an index, *Beit lehem yehudah* (Bethlehem in Judah, 1625) to the anthology *Ein Yaakov*, the major source of rabbinic materials in *Italy (where the *Talmud was banned), as well as a supplementary collection of rabbinic teachings, *Beit Yehu-*

dah (The House of Judah, 1635). Modena's *Historia de' Riti Hebraici* (History of Jewish Rituals, 1637, 1638), written in Italian, provided the first vernacular description of *Judaism by a Jew for a non-Jewish audience.

Modena's important writings remained unpublished during his lifetime, as did his sermons, *poetry (*Shirei Yehudah* [The Poetry of Judah]), letters, *responsa (*Ziknei Yehudah* [The Elders of Judah]), testaments, *Bible commentaries, and autobiography (*Hayyei Yehudah* [The Life of Judah]). Topics addressed in his responsa reveal many aspects of Jewish life in seventeenth-century Italy: They include answers to questions about musical performances in *synagogues, men going about bareheaded, and Jews playing tennis or traveling by boat on the *Sabbath. His most significant writings were polemics against Jewish heresy, Christianity, and Jewish *mysticism; these included *Sha'agat Aryeh* (The Roar of the Lion, 1622) written against *Kol Sakhal* (The Voice of the Fool), a work that he claimed to have translated from Spanish; and *Diffesa* (Defense, 1626), a defense of the Talmud written in Italian (see also MIDDLE AGES: JEWISH–CHRISTIAN POLEMICS).

Modena was a critic of recent trends in Jewish mysticism, especially the spread of the new school of Lurianic Kabbalah (see KABBALAH, LURIANIC) and the influence of Christian Kabbalah on Jewish apostasy (see CHRISTIAN HEBRAISM). These efforts culminated in a trilogy of works: a tract against reincarnation, *Ben David* (The Son of David, 1636); a text challenging the authenticity of the *Kabbalah, *Ari Nohem* (The Lion Roars, 1639); and an attack on Christian Kabbalah, *Magen vaHerev* (Shield and Sword, 1645). In his autobiography, the first in Hebrew, Modena regularly recorded the details of his unhappy but productive life. It is testimony to Modena's candor about himself and his times. Living in the Venetian *ghetto in the midst of Christian society, and on the boundaries between Judaism and Christianity, between Hebrew and Italian, and between medieval and modern Jewry, Modena was a highly accomplished scholar, community leader, and writer, but also a complex and tormented individual.

For further reading, see *The Autobiography of a Seventeenth Century Venetian Rabbi: Leon Modena's Life of Judah*, trans. and ed. M. R. Cohen, with essays by M. R. Cohen, T. K. Rabb, H. E. Adelman, N. Z. Davis, and B. C. I. Ravid.

HOWARD TZVI ADELMAN

Modern Orthodox Judaism: See JUDAISM, ORTHODOX

Money Lending: Medieval and Early Modern Europe. Money lending, together with *commerce, was the chief livelihood of Jews in medieval and early modern Europe. There was also a substantial Jewish servant class, and many Jews, as were non-Jews, were active in more than one profession at the same time. Credit operations often went hand in hand with activities such as minting, money changing, the plate and bullion trade, and tax collection. Like money lending, these activities demanded capital, accounting and metallurgical skills, as well as close ties with the holders of political power. One of the earliest extant documents before the year 1000 portrays a Jew of southern *France busy "in the affairs of the archbishop of Narbonne, supplying his needs; . . . exchanging his gold and silver; investing in merchandise; contracting with a junior partner; and lending money for interest."

In medieval society, a variety of people extended credit in a range of situations. Informal arrangements for small credit needs were part of family and neighborhood networks in villages and towns. Christian merchants extended loans for business capital, as well as for political purposes, to colleagues, town governments, and kings. Ecclesiastical institutions were frequently involved in credit operations, usually camouflaged as charitable help. In some locations only Jews served as professional money lenders, in other regions foreign Christians – the so-called Lombards and Cahorsins – were also active. In *Italy, local merchants and professional money lenders, all of whom were Christians, largely met the credit needs; only in the fourteenth century did Jewish bankers arrive in parts of Italy from *Germany. England appears to be a special case, because there the credit business was the principal activity of Jews from the time of their arrival in the late eleventh century (see ENGLAND: MIDDLE AGES). Often, Jewish and Christian credit existed simultaneously, fulfilling different functions and serving different clienteles.

Jews were borrowers, as well as lenders. However, lending money to a fellow Jew transgressed the biblical prohibition, "To a foreigner you may lend upon interest, but to your brother you shall not lend upon interest" (Deut 23:20–21). In southern Europe, where Jews frequently owned property, mortgaging land was a frequent expedient in this situation. In northern *France and in *Germany, where Jewish ownership of agricultural property was much more circumscribed, the prohibition urgently called for a solution. Experts in religious law came to permit a number of exceptions, including the regular interest-bearing loan, provided the subterfuge of a pawn and a non-Jewish intermediary were employed.

In the early Middle Ages, in southern France (see FRANCE, SOUTHERN) and then in *Ashkenaz, Jewish money lending first appeared as a byproduct of trade operations, when the vendor consented to delayed payment for goods delivered. Effectively a loan, such postponement was granted to preferred customers (implied in the term, ma'arufiya) with whom a business relationship had long been established. Regular loans, typically granted to the nobility, also appear in the sources; once again this procedure was geared toward maintaining a business association. As in Jewish commercial enterprises in this period, the credit clientele in Ashkenaz was mostly from the upper classes; their financial needs did not stem from destitution. In contrast, there are signs of a low-end lending market involving Jews and their neighbors in rural areas of southern and central France. By the twelfth century the clientele in the north was still mainly made up of members of the elite, which now included both clergy (archbishops, bishops, abbots, priors, deacons, communities of monks, and cathedral priests) and laity (kings, dukes, princes, margraves and burgraves, counts, landed proprietors, and knights). Commoners were among the patrons in the thirteenth century, and by the early fourteenth century they made up a significant part of the clientele. The largest numbers of borrowers were burghers, who came from practically every major town and many smaller ones, as well as peasants. In the later Middle Ages, Christian financiers took over lending to the well-to-do, and Jews dealt with the most problematic and socially volatile clientele: the poor. This remained the situation in the Early Modern period as well. At the very end of the era

under consideration, a resurgence of Jewish involvement in high finance ultimately led to the establishment of banking houses of the *Rothschilds, Warburgs, and many other families in the nineteenth century (see BANKING AND BANKING HOUSES).

Surviving sources shed little direct light on personal motives for borrowing money. There is no mention of the expenses incurred by crusaders, an undertaking that many historians conjecture may have plunged people into debt and thus set the scene for the persecutions of the twelfth century. As for kings, princes, prelates, and town governments, it is safe to infer that many loans were motivated by political necessity. Thus, Vivelin "the Red" of Strasbourg, at the top echelon of Jewish bankers in early-fourteenth-century Germany, lent substantial sums to the Count Palatine of the Rhine and to the archbishop of Mainz. He also served as counselor to the archbishop of Trier, with whose Jewish and Christian officials he jointly carried out numerous financial deals. He was the principal in a complicated arrangement by which King Edward III of England, in dire need of cash for his military operations in France, raised the immense sum of 340,000 gold florins in 1338/9. As part of security for the loan, the English crown was pawned to the archbishop of Trier, who eventually turned it over to Vivelin.

Outside the elite, the demand for credit by significant numbers of commoners has usually been seen as tied to economic distress. However, in many documented cases this premise is clearly inapplicable. Peasants often took out loans in the fall after the harvest was in, when food was plentiful. Significantly, much of the information on credit in the countryside, indeed on early credit in general, comes from regions that specialized in viticulture. It has been recently suggested that wine growing and its recurring need for high money inputs provided the initial stimulus for Jews to move from trade to money lending (Soloveitchik). Recourse to the money lender for survival applies much more to the great number of borrowers from the urban lower classes who made up the bulk of clients in later medieval Germany and *Spain.

An integral part of the lending business, then as now, was the necessity for collateral: tangible assets to secure outstanding loans. Given the agricultural character of medieval society, it is not surprising that the earliest and, for a long time, the most important pawns were landed properties. With increasing legal elaboration came the development of additional forms, such as the written deed claimable in court or the warranty promise by a third party. There was also a curious medieval custom called in German Einlager (literally "depositing") and in Hebrew, "eating on someone as warranty." In case of failure to pay, the debtor agreed to lodge on his account a party in an inn, with their horses in the stable, to eat and drink merrily away until payment of the debt was effected. This custom was also practiced between Jews, apparently without the horses.

The use of pledges gave rise to serious and sometimes unbearable tensions. From early on, pawning ecclesiastical utensils to Jews was seen as sacrilegious. Even more fraught with difficulties was the privileged status that came to be granted to Jews (and to the Italian money lenders called Lombards) in regard to stolen goods. Civil authorities walked a thin line between the need to deter theft and the wish to promote the smooth performance of the marketplace. Thus, it became accepted practice to let the lender swear that such pawns had been accepted in good faith as security, rather than acquired as cheap goods of doubtful provenance. Conversely, an increasing range of objects were prohibited as pawns: ecclesiastical utensils; goods whose wet or bloody condition suggested theft or robbery; the weaponry and armor of the members of urban militias; the buckets, axes, and shovels kept at different locations throughout town in case of fire; and a whole range of tools and raw materials essential for the livelihood of artisans. Accepting pawns as security could and did easily develop into pawnbroking, a practice that aroused intense antagonism. However, daily practice might sometimes have been more relaxed, as has recently been suggested in a local study based on records from fourteenth-century Marseilles (Shatzmiller).

Interest rates were exorbitantly high, reaching sometimes more than 100% per year, but the rich usually borrowed more cheaply and for longer periods. Government authorities closely monitored money lending for control of interest rates, for taxation, and for the maintenance of social calm. The most elaborate system was the English "Exchequer of the Jews" and its local branches, the "Registries of Deeds." In return, Jewish bankers everywhere depended on the government, its agents, and its legal machinery to collect debts, recoup capital and interest, and foreclose on collateral when the lender failed. In short, to carry out their business, Jews depended on Christian rulers to employ the machinery of authority against the Christian borrower. Such assistance created anxieties for some especially pious monarchs, like the thirteenth-century French king Saint Louis, who felt significant guilt. Protecting Jewish lenders also left authorities open to criticism and heavy pressure, especially when combined with accusations of corruption and taking bribes from the Jews.

Altogether, money lending was a risky business, and things could go very wrong. Rabbi *Abraham ben David of Posquières (southern France, twelfth century) had some pertinent advice to investors in the lending business (Responsum no. 14):

> And do not lend without a good pledge of gold and silver; and put the money regularly beneath the earth to safeguard from fire and thieves without people knowing about this, so that it shall not be known to thieves and make them think of stealing; and when you receive a pledge of gold and silver conceal it in a secure place beneath the earth. And do not take pledges of gold and silver from great townsmen and violent men so that you shall not be forced to return them without security against your will.

The resentment surrounding lending money created an intense and enduring negative image of Jews in much of medieval Europe. These tensions remain visible in a variety of cultural forms, including Shakespeare's *Merchant of Venice*, written more than three hundred years after the last Jewish money lender had been expelled from England.

For further reading, see H. Soloveitchik, *Principles and Pressures: Jewish Trade in Gentile Wine in the Middle Ages* (2003); R. W. Emery, *The Jews of Perpignan in the 13th Century: An Economic Study Based on Notarial Records* (1959); J. Shatzmiller, *Shylock Reconsidered: Jews, Moneylenders and Medieval Society* (1990); and M. Toch, *The Economic History of Medieval European Jews*. vol. I: *The Early Middle Ages* (forthcoming).

MICHAEL TOCH

Monotheism, Ethical: See GOD; JUDAISM: REFORM entries; THEOLOGY

Montefiore, Moses Haim (1784–1885) was a British businessman, communal leader, and philanthropist who was revered for his interventions to assist Jewish communities in *Eastern Europe and Muslim lands. Although born in Livorno, Montefiore came from a family of Anglo-Italian merchants already well established in London. His cosmopolitan roots in the western *Sephardi Diaspora informed his Jewish activism and belie his popular image as the quintessential English Jew. Montefiore made a fortune on the stock exchange, thanks partly to his marriage to the wealthy, *Ashkenazi **JUDITH BARENT COHEN** (1784–1862), whose brother-in-law Nathan *Rothschild became a close associate. In later life the Rothschild connection added greatly to Montefiore's influence, but his fame as a humanitarian in the non-Jewish world owed much to business connections forged with evangelical and nonconformist Christians.

In his forties, Montefiore cut back his business activity before embarking for *Palestine with Judith in 1827. This life-changing pilgrimage inspired Montefiore's second career as a communal leader, as well as Judith's growing confidence as a pioneering Anglo-Jewish writer. In all, Montefiore made seven visits to Palestine; the last one was in 1875 when he was ninety. Montefiore devoted the 1830s to campaigning for Anglo-Jewish emancipation; to this end he served as Sheriff of the City of London, an office that brought him a knighthood. Although he served as president of the Board of Deputies for British Jews for some forty years (see BRITAIN: EARLY MODERN AND MODERN), his role in Jewish communal politics was controversial. He was widely blamed for the bitter divide that developed in Britain between *Reform and mainstream Judaism. Meanwhile, Montefiore's high-profile foreign missions (accompanied by Judith) brought the couple growing celebrity. The intersection between Jewish interests and British imperialism ensured that they had their greatest success in the Muslim world, where Montefiore's intervention in the *Damascus Affair (1840) and their mission to Morocco (1864) elicited formal commitments to protect local Jews. Missions to *Russia (1846), Rome (1859), and *Romania (1867) had less direct impact, but contributed to the globalization of modern Jewish consciousness.

Montefiore's long-standing commitment to Palestine also proved pivotal in this regard. His second visit (1839) has attracted particular attention because of Montefiore's precocious scheme to promote Jewish agricultural colonization, a project more influenced by contact with British antislavery activists than an explicitly nationalist agenda. Judith's account of the expedition (1844) became a central reference in debates about the introduction of productive industries in Palestine, although the scheme foundered as did later agricultural and industrial initiatives. Only the windmill and almshouses Montefiore built outside the Old City survived to become symbols of modern *Jerusalem.

All these activities were facilitated by Montefiore's innovative *philanthropy. Through the Holy Land Relief Fund (1855) and the Persian Famine Relief Fund (1872) he pioneered subscription fundraising in a global, Jewish context; however, he left nothing substantial to the early *Zionists who raised money in his name. The only charitable institution Montefiore founded was the Judith Lady Montefiore Theological College in Ramsgate, in memory of his wife. Their loving marriage had been marred by infertility. She found expression through publishing her travel diaries and compiling the first ever Jewish *cookbook (1846); rumours of illegitimate children suggest this profoundly religious man may have sought comfort in extramarital affairs. A recent study is A. Green, *Moses Montefiore: Jewish Liberator, Imperial Hero* (2010).   ABIGAIL GREEN

Months: See CALENDAR: MONTHS OF THE YEAR; NEW MOON

Montreal: See CANADA; LITERATURE: CANADA

Morocco: See NORTH AFRICA

Mortara Affair. This international cause célèbre involved the abduction and rearing of a Jewish Italian boy, Edgardo Mortara (1851–1940), as a ward of the Papal States after his involuntary baptism. When still a toddler Mortara became seriously ill. Worried that he might die and fearing for his soul, the family's teenaged servant, Anna Morisi, sprinkled Mortara with water. Four years later, after Morisi reported her crude baptism to a friend, the Inquisition of Bologna (a city then part of the Papal States) became aware of the incident. The Catholic Church swiftly applied canon law to affirm the inviolate nature of the baptismal act and insisted on its legal and moral obligation to rear and educate any baptized Jewish child. On June 23, 1858, civil authorities abducted Mortara, then six years old, from his parents' home. Pope Pius IX (Giovanni Mastai Ferretti, 1792–1878) adopted the child as his son, prompting an international scandal. The incident undermined and even hastened the end of the Vatican's temporal powers and had profound ramifications for the unification of *Italy.

Despite their repeated appeals, requests by Salomone Mortara and Marianna Padovani for the return of their son were denied. Church authorities maintained the validity of Edgardo's baptism and declared that the young boy would be returned only if his parents converted, which they refused to do. Although the seizure of an involuntarily baptized Jewish child in nineteenth-century Italy was not unheard of (a five-year-old girl secretly baptized by a domestic was removed from her home in Ferrara in 1817), this particular case attracted significant international attention. European leaders, including Count Camillo Cavour, architect of the Italian unification movement, and Napoleon III, protested the abduction. By late 1858, *The New York Times* had published more than twenty articles about the incident. The Mortara Affair also highlighted Jewish vulnerability and played a central role in the founding of the *Alliance Israélite Universelle. In 1870, the annexation of Rome to the kingdom of Italy successfully completed Italian unification and vindicated nationalist, liberal, and anticlerical ideologies. Mortara, nineteen years old at the time, moved to *France. There, he entered the Augustinian order and four years later was ordained a priest, adopting the spiritual name Pius. His missionary work would take him to Munich, Mainz, and Breslau. In 1912, he provided a written statement (which mentioned his abduction) in favor of the canonization of Pius IX. The beatification, which took place in September 2000 during the papacy of Pope John Paul II, was strongly protested by descendants of the Mortara family, among other groups. Mortara attended his mother's funeral, led by the rabbi of Bologna, in 1895. He died in Belgium at the age of eighty-eight, two months before the Nazi invasion of that country.

Edgardo's story has been dramatized and embellished by several playwrights, including Herman Moos in his 1860 play, *Mortara, or The Pope and His Inquisitors*. In 2002, Pulitzer-prize-winning playwright Alfred Uhry adapted David Kertzer's definitive book, *The Kidnapping of Edgardo Mortara* (1997), into the play *Edgardo Mine* (now *The Kidnapping of Edgardo Mortara*).   LISA RUBENSTEIN CALEVI

Moses is the Israelite leader whose story appears in the biblical books of *Exodus through *Deuteronomy. Born to a Levite family, he is placed in a basket and set afloat on the Nile by his mother to save him from the *Egyptian edict to kill all male Hebrew infants. Moses is rescued and adopted by the pharaoh's daughter (Exod 2:1–10) and comes of age in the Egyptian court. As a young man he flees to Midian after killing an abusive overseer (2:11–15); there he marries Zipporah, daughter of *Jethro, priest of Midian, and encounters *God in a burning bush (2:16–3:6). Countering all of Moses' protestations of inadequacy, God commands him to free the Hebrews from their Egyptian oppressors (3:7–4:17). Moses' entreaties to Pharaoh initiate a sequence of escalating confrontations that culminate in the unleashing of ten plagues (5–12). When Pharaoh relents, Moses instructs the people to institute the *Passover to commemorate their escape from servitude (12–13). When Moses leads the people out of Egypt, Pharaoh reconsiders his decision and gives chase. At the Red Sea (or "Reed Sea"; Hebrew, *yam suf*) the Egyptian army perishes after the Hebrews miraculously cross over on dry land (14–15).

Moses leads the people for forty years in the wilderness, the signature moment of which is the theophany at Sinai (or Horeb) and Moses' reception of the laws of the *covenant. At the end of the wilderness sojourn, Moses delivers a farewell address (Deut 32) and dies before the people enter the land of *Canaan.

The centrality of Moses as liberator, lawgiver, prophet, judge, and priest can hardly be overstated. A leader on the most intimate terms with God, yet humble (Num 12:3) and even reluctant, he came to represent, in many ways, an ideal personage. Several other characters in the monotheistic traditions can be said to be portrayed as varieties of a "second Moses": *Joshua, *Elijah, *Josiah, and *Ezra, as well as Jesus and Muhammed. Post-biblical Jewish interpreters represented Moses as a paragon of their own belief systems: For Hellenistic Jews he became a philosopher; for rabbinic Jews he was the author of the *Pentateuch and promulgator of the Oral *Torah.

For all that, something of Moses resists emulation. He is a man characterized by both a quick temper and passivity; other aspects of his story reveal a side that is enigmatic, even esoteric (the "bridegroom of blood" episode [Exod 4:24–26], the magicians' duels in Pharaoh's court [Exod 7], the bronze serpent [Num 21:4–9]). Moses is the people's intercessor, yet he is nevertheless removed from them. He requires *Aaron to speak for him (Exod 4:10–17, 27–31), and he wears a veil to obscure his glowing face (Exod 34:29–35). Deuteronomy explicitly describes his connection with God as unique and unsurpassed (Deut 34:10–12). In addition, his death outside of the land and his unknown grave (34:6) ensure that he belongs to a previous age; it is significant that Moses' descendants play no discernible role in biblical Israel's later history.

This inaccessibility is also reflected in the question of the historical Moses. No extrabiblical sources attest to him, and many aspects of his story echo episodes from other ancient texts. Nonetheless, some elements of the narrative, such as his name, do have an authentically Egyptian feel, and recent historical research plausibly allows for a modified, reduced version of the Exodus. However, the nature of the literature and the scanty historical evidence make any level of certainty highly unlikely. Recent scholarship includes B. Britt, *Rewriting Moses* (2004); W. H. C. Propp, *Exodus 1–18* (1999); and S. Weitzman, *Song and Story in Biblical Narrative* (1997).

SEAN BURT

Moses de Leon (ca. 1240–1305) was the principal author of the *Zohar*, the most important work of the *Kabbalah. He was born in Leon in *Spain, wandered among several communities in Castile, resided for many years in Guadalajara and then in Avila, and died in Arevalo. As a young man he studied Jewish *thought, especially the works of *Maimonides, but then dedicated himself to *mysticism, writing more than twenty treatises. In the 1270s he began to write the *Midrash ha-Ne'elam* (The Esoteric Midrash), which became the earliest stratum of the *Zohar*. According to Gershom *Scholem, Moses de Leon completed the *Zohar*, which was written in *Aramaic, in the early 1290s and then wrote many of his Hebrew works; Isaiah Tishby maintained that he continued to write sections of the *Zohar* until his death. He made a meager living selling portions of the *Zohar*; he claimed he had copied them from an ancient manuscript that originated with the second-century-CE *Tanna, Rabbi Simon bar Yoḥai. After de Leon's death, his destitute widow was offered a large sum of money for the original text of the *Zohar*. She denied its existence, claiming that her late husband "was writing from his mind."

The writings of Moses de Leon include Bible commentaries (see BIBLICAL COMMENTARY) and interpretations of *prayers and *commandments; most have never been printed. His best known treatises are *Sefer ha-Rimon* (Book of the Pomegranate) on the kabbalistic reasons for the commandments, *Or Zarua* (Spreading Light) on creation, *Ha-Nefesh ha-Ḥakhamah* (The Wise Soul), and *Shaarei Zedek* (Gates of Justice) on *Ecclesiastes. For further reading, see G. Scholem, *Kabbalah* (1974), 432–34; and I. Tishby, *Wisdom of the Zohar*, vol. 1 (1989). JOSEPH DAN

Musar Movement. The Hebrew term *musar*, usually translated as morals or *ethics, also bears the meaning of chastisement and method. In the teaching of the nineteenth-century *Musar* movement, all senses of *musar* combine, creating a powerful call for serious self-examination and correction of the religious life. Whereas *Hasidism emphasizes joyfulness and devotional feeling during religious activities, the *Musar* movement – associated with the *mitnaggedim (the "opponents," the rabbinical movement that stood in opposition to Hasidism) – stresses labor, duty, and seriousness as essential prerequisites for a genuine religious and moral life.

Proponents of the *Musar* movement locate its origins in the teachings of the *Vilna Gaon and his students, but the real founder was Rabbi Israel (Lifkin) Salanter (1810–1883). Salanter, who typified in his personality the religious duty of love and respect to other human beings, directed his students to work constantly on their moral virtues and to be sensitive to the needs and feelings of others. Salanter urged his followers to study traditional ethical and moral (*musar*) works, such as the famous *Mesillat Yesharim* (Path of the Just) by the eighteenth-century Italian *kabbalist Moses Ḥayyim *Luzzato and the eleventh-century ethical classic *Ḥovot ha-Levavot* (Duties of the Heart) by the Spanish pietist *Baḥia ibn Pakuda. Salanter taught that these books should be studied as a spiritual exercise arousing the deepest feelings of the soul. *Musar* study was to be undertaken loudly, with repetitions, to stimulate enthusiasm (*hitpalut*); the student of *musar* had to experience the religious weight of ideas such as "fear of Heaven," "rewards and punishment," "intention," and "virtues" and correct his or her life accordingly.

During his lifetime Salanter was recognized as one of the preeminent *Lithuanian rabbis and leaders. However, his social and religious group did not expand beyond several dozen faithful students and admirers. Initially Salanter hoped that his teaching would influence traditional-minded Lithuanian Jews, but the movement's very strict requirements were not attractive to the public. Salanter's students expanded the boundaries of the *Musar* movement after his death by opening *yeshivot* and other educational institutions that followed Salanter's teachings. With the movement's growing success, antagonism began to develop from different quarters. Followers of the *Haskalah criticized Salanter and his students as reactionary, and conservative *mitnaggedim considered his novel approach to be a break with the Lithuanian emphasis on speculative study of *Torah. After long and fierce debates the *Musar* movement prevailed, and most Lithuanian-style *yeshivot* added moral teachings to their curriculum. Most also created the position of *mashgiaḥ ruḥani* (spiritual supervisor) to guide the students' moral and religious behavior.

After Salanter's time, not only the size but also the ideas and methods of the *Musar* movement continued to develop, and various schools of thought emerged. The dominant approach was developed by Note Hirsh (Natan Tsevi) Finkel (1849–1927), known as the *Saba* (elder or grandfather) of Slobodka, the spiritual director of the central *Musar Yeshivah* in Slobodka. Finkel's most important educational principle was the greatness and responsibility of humankind, as created in God's image.

In the early twenty-first century, the most influential Lithuanian-style *yeshivot* in *Israel and the *United States continue to share a deep commitment to the teachings and practices of the *Musar* movement. Indeed, among nearly all present-day Orthodox Jews (see JUDAISM, ORTHODOX), and especially in the non-Ḥasidic branch of Ḥaredi (Ultra-Orthodox) Jews, its ideas are preserved in an emphasis on serious self-examination and correction in all aspects of life. For further reading, see I. Etkes, *Rabbi Israel Salanter and the Mussar Movement* (1993); and H. Goldberg, *Israel Salanter: Text, Structure, Idea* (1982). CHAIM MEIR NERIA

Museums. The first Jewish museums were established in Europe, the *United States, and *Palestine in the early twentieth century, and their history is integrally linked with the twentieth-century Jewish experience. Jewish museums acquire Jewish *art defined in its broadest sense to include antiquities, *ceremonial objects, ethnographic artifacts, historical documents and memorabilia, and fine and folk art. These artifacts reflect the 4,000-year history and heritage of the Jewish people as it evolved in many lands (see entries under ART and CEREMONIAL OBJECTS).

EUROPE: Jewish museums are the product of the modern age when major demographic shifts, increasing secularization, and the rise of nationalism radically altered patterns of Jewish life. Several factors led to the development of Jewish museums. One was the academic aspirations of the *Wissenschaft des Judentums, the scientific study of Judaism, which originated in *Germany in the 1820. An underlying political agenda of the Wissenschaft movement was to focus on Judaism's contributions to western civilization and thus dispel *antisemitic stereotypes. A society dedicated to the study of Jewish art was founded in *Vienna in 1895 and a museum was established in 1897. Similar developments took place in *Frankfurt (1901 and 1922) and in Budapest (1910 and 1916; see HUNGARY). A 1906 urban renewal project in the *Prague ghetto spurred a salvage effort and the creation of a museum. The rescue effort of Jewish artifacts was also extended across Bohemia and Moravia. In *Eastern Europe, the emigration of more than two million Jews motivated S. Ansky, author of The Dybbuk, to organize a regional expedition to document folkways and collect objects. A museum was established in *Saint Petersburg in 1913. A museum named for Ansky was formed in *Vilna in 1920; *YIVO was founded in 1925. In Lwów, the public museum first collected Judaica; a Jewish art society was founded in the 1920s and a museum established in 1931. The museum's holdings along with Maksymilian Goldstein's collection were transferred to the Municipal Museum in 1941. Museums in Danzig in 1904 and *Warsaw in 1910 grew from private collections. Collection, cataloguing, and study of Jewish art continued after World War I with new museums in Breslau, Kassel, Munich, Mainz, and Odessa; the Jewish Museum in *Berlin was dedicated in January 1933. Museums were opened in *Amsterdam and London (see *Britain) in 1932.

During the *Holocaust, European Jewish museums were either looted or completely destroyed. The Danzig collection was shipped to the Jewish Museum in *New York City for safekeeping. After the war, the Jewish Cultural Reconstruction (JCR), a consortium of American Jewish institutions, was authorized by the State Department to identify and distribute heirless and unclaimed Jewish property in the American Occupied Zone of Germany to Jewish communities in *Israel and worldwide; about three hundred objects were returned to *Holland. Part of YIVO's collection was recovered and sent to its new home in New York City. In the post–World War II era, a few Jewish museums, including those in London, Amsterdam, and Budapest, renewed their activities, and new museums were established in Paris, Belgrade, *Warsaw, and Kraków.

A remarkable phenomenon, beginning in the 1960s, has been the revival of European Jewish museums. Museums have been established or reopened in *Austria, *Belgium, *Denmark, *France (Paris and the Alsace region), *Germany, *Greece (Rhodes and Salonika), Ireland, *Italy, Morocco, Norway, *Portugal, *Spain, Sweden, Switzerland, and *Turkey.

Since the collapse of communism in the late 1980s, scores of Jewish museums have been created across the region in *Belarus, Bosnia-Herzegovina, *Bulgaria, Croatia, Czech Republic, Hungary, *Latvia, *Lithuania, *Poland, *Romania, Slovakia, and *Ukraine, where a collection was discovered in 1989 at the Historical Treasures Museum of the Ukraine in Kiev. The Ansky Collection, long hidden in storage, is displayed at the State Ethnographic Museum in Saint Petersburg, where there is also a Jewish museum. A museum is being built in Moscow as well. The Lwów collections in the Museum of Ethnography and Artistic Crafts were made public in the 1990s. After the reunification of Germany, numerous Jewish museums were built, the most prominent among them in Berlin in 2001 and Munich in 2007. Nearly one hundred *synagogues have been restored and many house museums. Thirty countries are members of the Association of European Jewish Museums (AEFM), which "seeks to promote the study of European Jewish history and works to protect and preserve Jewish sites and the Jewish cultural heritage in Europe." Efforts are ongoing to recover artifacts from pre-war European Jewish museum collections aided in part by provenance data now accessible on the internet.

ISRAEL: The Bezalel Art School for Arts and Crafts opened in *Jerusalem in 1906 and the Bezalel Museum soon afterward, also in Jerusalem (see ART: ISRAELI). The school was ideologically aligned with *Zionism, and the aim of its founder Boris Schatz was to create a new Jewish art influenced by those ideals. The establishment of the State of *Israel in 1948 led to tremendous growth in museums. The Bezalel Museum was incorporated into the Israel Museum, the national museum, which houses encyclopedic collections ranging from prehistory through contemporary art. Today there are some two hundred museums in Israel. A number of them, such as the Wolfson Museum and the Nahon Museum of Italian Jewish Art, both in Jerusalem, are similar to Jewish museums elsewhere in the world in their collections and exhibitions of Judaica and Jewish art. Others focus on Israeli history. The Eretz Israel Museum founded in Tel Aviv in 1953 is comprised of theme pavilions including *archeology, ethnography, and folklore. Independence Hall, where David *Ben-Gurion proclaimed the establishment of Israel, is located in the former home of Meir Dizengoff, *Tel Aviv's first mayor, which he donated in 1932 for the Tel Aviv Museum of Art. Israeli art is featured in many museums including Ein Harod, founded in 1933. Homes of luminaries in Israeli society, including artists, have been preserved as museums, and Theodor *Herzl's study from Vienna is reconstructed at the Herzl Museum in Jerusalem. Ethnic heritage is the focus of museums such as the World Center for the Heritage of North African Jewry, the Babylonian Jewry Heritage Center, and the Rosh Ha'ayin Museum of Yemenite Jewry. Beth Ha-Tefusoth on the campus of Tel Aviv University opened in 1978 to tell the story of the Jewish people in the *Diaspora. Thousands of archeological sites throughout Israel have been made accessible for visitors.

THE AMERICAS AND THE CARIBBEAN: In the United States, the Jewish Museum was launched at the *Jewish Theological Seminary (JTS) of America in New York City in 1904 and the Union Museum at *Hebrew Union College (now HUC-JIR) in Cincinnati, Ohio, in 1913. Early acquisitions included private collections, several of which had been primarily formed in Europe. For four decades, they were the only two Jewish museums in the United States, although some synagogues housed commemorative artifacts and ceremonial objects that later formed the basis of museum collections. The Jewish Museum has gained international stature in the art world and in the field of Jewish art; the JTS Library also maintains significant visual arts holdings. Parts of the HUC-JIR collection are housed at the Skirball Cultural Center in *Los Angeles, which became an HUC-JIR affiliate in 1996.

After the *Six Day War in 1967, there was a tremendous upsurge in interest in Jewish life and culture. This interest coincided with a general focus on ethnicity that has significantly affected American life. The Council of American Jewish Museums (CAJM) was founded in 1977 with seven members: B'nai B'rith Klutznick National Museum, Washington, D.C.; Jewish Museum, New York City; *Yeshiva University Museum, New York City; Magnes Museum, Berkeley, California; National Museum of American Jewish History, *Philadelphia; Spertus Museum, *Chicago; and Skirball Museum, Los Angeles. Today CAJM's seventy-five members include art and history museums, Jewish historic sites, archives, *Holocaust memorial and education centers, synagogue museums, children's museums, and galleries connected with Jewish Community Centers and universities. CAJM's mission is "to assist its members as they educate and inspire diverse audiences on all aspects of Jewish culture and history." A number focus on regional Jewish history, including those in Alaska, Maryland, Florida, Oregon, and the Museum of the Southern Jewish Experience in Mississippi. The *Center for Jewish History in New York is a unique partnership of five major institutions: American Jewish Historical Society, American Sephardi Federation, *Leo Baeck Institute, Yeshiva University Museum, and *YIVO.

In *Canada, a museum was created in 1964 at Beth Tzedec Congregation in Toronto with historian Cecil Roth's collection, formed over a fifty-year period. Museums were later founded in Winnipeg and Montreal, and Jewish historical societies have been formed in several cities, including Calgary, Vancouver, and St. John. In *Latin America, the Buenos Aires Jewish Museum was established in *Argentina in 1967. The Jewish Museum of Rio de Janeiro was formed in *Brazil in 1977. In Chile, museums in Santiago and Valparaiso both highlight the *Sephardic experience, as does the Jewish Museum in Caracas, Venezuela. The Jewish Museums in Paraguay and Mexico City house documentation on the *Holocaust. In the *Caribbean, historic synagogues in Curaçao, *Jamaica, and St. Thomas have museums featuring the history of these communities.

ASIA, AUSTRALIA, and SOUTH AFRICA: The effort to preserve local Jewish history has been a major impetus to conserve Jewish sites across the globe, often as museums. Some of these communities have a long history; others have emerged within the last two centuries. Sometimes the Jewish presence is dwindling or is no more. In *India, the Paradesi Synagogue in Cochin, India, which dates to 1568, and several synagogues in Mumbai are being maintained. In Shanghai, *China, the Ohel Rachel Synagogue is undergoing renovation.

The Jewish community in *Australia dates to the nineteenth century and grew with immigrants from Eastern Europe, refugees fleeing *Nazi Germany in the 1930s, and

survivors after the war. Jewish museums were established in Melbourne in 1982 and Sydney in 1992. The Jewish community in *South Africa also dates to the nineteenth century. The Jewish museum opened in Capetown in 2000, and a Holocaust Center is located nearby.

HOLOCAUST MUSEUMS AND MEMORIALS: Beginning in the 1970s, Holocaust museums and memorials have been established worldwide. The Association of Holocaust Organizations is a network of hundreds of institutions that "advance Holocaust programming, education, and research." Lohamei ha-Ghettaot, the Kibbutz of the Ghetto Fighters, organized a museum in 1949. *Yad Vashem in Jerusalem was founded in 1953 to serve as the international site of remembrance. For decades there were only a few memorials, among them the Anne *Frank House in Amsterdam. Several were at camps, including *Auschwitz, Bergen-Belsen, Buchenwald, Dachau, *Theresienstadt, and *Treblinka, and at the site of the *Warsaw ghetto. Memorials, monuments, and museums have now been built in Berlin, Copenhagen, Paris, and Rome and at many other locations across Europe and in places where Jews sought refuge, such as Shanghai. Israel has a number of Holocaust memorials and museums, including some that commemorate the heroic resistance of individuals, such as the Hannah Senesh House and Yad Mordecai, a tribute to Mordecai Anielewitz, the commander of the Warsaw ghetto uprising. Three major museums opened in the 1990s in the United States: the United States Holocaust Memorial Museum in Washington, D.C.; the Simon Wiesenthal Center in Los Angeles; and the Museum of Jewish Heritage in New York (see also HOLOCAUST MEMORIALS).

In 2010 there are nearly three hundred Jewish museums throughout the world, and their numbers continue to increase. They share a common mission both to preserve the Jewish heritage and to confront issues of contemporary Jewish identity and cultural renewal. Many museums have published catalogues about their history, collections, and of special exhibitions; for a survey, see G. C. Grossman, *Jewish Museums of the World* (2003). Other useful works include A. Sacerdoti, *The Guide to Jewish Italy* (2004); R. E. Gruber, *Jewish Heritage Travel: Guide to Eastern Europe* (2007); R. and B. Z. Dorfman, *Synagogues Without Jews* (2000); and J. E. Young, *The Texture of Memory: Holocaust Memorials and Meaning* (1993).   GRACE COHEN GROSSMAN

Music, Biblical Era: See BIBLE: MUSIC AND DANCE

Music, Folk. Musicologists typically designate the musical traditions of a given culture as religious, folk, and art. Folk music is part of the personal, communal, and celebratory lives of ordinary people. Although Jewish religious music has historically been performed by men, folk music is sung in the home by both men and women. Where art music is the product of an identified composer, folk music makes use of well-known traditional melodies whose authors are unknown.

In the modern period, these categories overlap in interesting ways. Both *Ashkenazic and *Sephardic Jews have venerable folk traditions. Major categories within Ashkenazic folk music include *Yiddish songs, *klezmer* music, and *Hasidic *niggunim* (wordless songs). In the Sephardic tradition, Judeo-Spanish (*Ladino) songs and *piyyutim* (see POETRY: LITURGICAL [*PIYYUT*]) are important categories.

In the second half of the twentieth century and into the twenty-first century, performers have collected, studied, and taken these Jewish folk traditions into new performance arenas.

Ashkenazic folk songs of *Central and *Eastern Europe were part of Jewish *life-cycle rituals and joyous *festival celebrations in the home. Many songs were in Yiddish, the spoken language of most Ashkenazic Jews. Their topics range from religious to secular themes; many Yiddish songs originated in the Yiddish *theater. In America, Jews who maintained an allegiance to a secular Yiddish culture particularly emphasized the preservation of this musical tradition. *Klezmer* (the Yiddish word derives from the Hebrew term for a musical instrument) refers to the instrumental accompaniments to Yiddish songs in the theater; *klezmer* music was also heard at Jewish weddings, *Bar Mitzvahs, and other life-cycle events. Many *klezmer* styles derive from Eastern European folk traditions. *Hasidic music may be both vocal and instrumental. Joyous and fervent singing characterizes the *niggunim*, the wordless songs sung in the *synagogue and at a *tisch* (literally "table," referring to a gathering with a *rebbe*, the spiritual leader of a Hasidic dynasty).

Each of these genres fits into a particular musical context, depending on its role in European Jewish life. Thus, *cantorial music is connected with the *synagogue; Yiddish songs are associated with daily life or the theater; *klezmer* music is heard during celebratory life-cycle events; Hasidic music is found in the synagogue and also as part of ritual life in the home; and art music is heard in the concert hall. Each genre is more easily defined through its use or context rather than through discrete musical definitions, nor can sharp lines be drawn among these various styles. *Cantors not only sang for the synagogue but they certainly also sang Yiddish songs. Some Yiddish songs depict a *hazzan* (cantor) and may even parody the emotional style of cantorial singing. The aesthetic of the virtuosic playing of a clarinet for a *klezmer* musician is said to follow the *geshrai*, or "wail," of the cantor. The interrelationship of the genres is also found within the very fabric of the music itself: *Nusakh* (the *liturgical tradition of the synagogue) is incorporated into Yiddish songs, *klezmer*, Hasidic melodies, and art music. When new songs were composed for each genre they were often written in the style of Jewish prayer modes.

The Judeo-Spanish (Ladino) traditions of Sephardic Jews have retained many aspects of medieval *Spanish and *Portuguese culture. This synthesis of Jewish and Spanish cultures has continued for the five hundred years since the 1492 expulsion of Spanish Jews, although the balance of preservation versus new influence has varied in different times and places. The Spanish tradition has been ongoing for Jews in Morocco (see NORTH AFRICA), whereas Jews in *Turkey and *Greece (and see BALKANS) have adopted some local Middle Eastern influences. Some historians hold that the venerable musical forms of these Sephardic Jews, namely the *ballad* and *romancero*, were time-honored traditions, untouched by new cultural influence and thus faithfully transmitted. Modern scholars, however, have been unable to validate this claim. Nevertheless, Judeo-Spanish (*Ladino) music has deep historic roots and, like other forms of Jewish music, is both perpetuated and innovatively revitalized by modern performers.

Women have long conserved Judeo-Spanish music: Many of the song texts of the *romancero* and *ballad* deal with women's experiences in life-cycle events, passionate or erotic courtly *poetry, and epic tales or stories. Dirges relating the deaths of individuals in untimely and other circumstances are known as *endechas*, while *coplas* are short holiday songs (see also LITERATURE, LADINO). The wedding context has been a particular rich source of music for Sephardic women. The preparation of the *bride for the *mikveh (ritual bath) before the wedding, a bride's dowry, and her relationship with her mother-in-law are among the subjects of these songs. Some Judeo-Spanish melodies are also incorporated into the prayer liturgy.

The practice of singing *piyyutim* is an important part of religious life; it started in the sixth century and has continued. In the past two hundred years Sephardi and *Mizrahi (Middle Eastern) communities have renewed this tradition; for example, in North Africa, *Turkey, Syria, and *Iraq. These texts are sung, some with elaborate melodies, on the *Sabbath in the synagogue between the portions of *Torah reading or at home as part of the festive Sabbath meal. They are also sung during *life-cycle rituals.

Songs connected to *Zionism and building a Jewish homeland in the Land of Israel comprise an additional Jewish folk music genre during the twentieth century; they were sung in a variety of languages including Yiddish, Judeo-Spanish, Russian, Polish, English, Arabic, and Hebrew. In the second half of the century, traditional Zionist songs as well as new compositions that came out of the State of *Israel, founded in 1948, were prominent in North American Jewish life in synagogues, classrooms, and youth groups and at social events and *summer camps.

For further reading, see I. J. Katz, "A Judeo-Spanish Romancero," *Ethnomusicology* 12(1) (1968): 72–85; E. Koskoff, *Music in Lubavitch Life* (2000); S. Rogovoy, *Essential Klezmer: A Music Lover's Guide to Jewish Roots and Soul Music, from the Old World to the Jazz Age to the Downtown Avant-Garde* (2000); R. Rubin, *Voices of a People: The Story of Yiddish Folksong* (1950); E. Seroussi, "New Directions in the Music of the Sephardic Jews," in *Modern Jews and Their Musical Agendas, Studies in Contemporary Jewry*, ed. E. Mendelsohn, 9 (1993), 61–77; and M. Slobin, *Tenement Songs: The Popular Music of the Jewish Immigrants* (1982).   MARK KLIGMAN

Music, Popular. Popular Jewish music encompasses the range of musical practices that address Jewish identity outside religious ritual and western art music composition. In this essay, the focus is on distinctive forms of music that Jews have enjoyed in social and recreational contexts. However, the very porousness of the borders between so-called popular, classical, and sacred music has always been a characteristic of Jewish music.

Although Jews undoubtedly used music in their daily lives before the late nineteenth century, what we know from that earlier time period amounts mainly to lyrics and fragmentary descriptions. By the end of the nineteenth century, however, the mass migration of millions of Jews from *Eastern Europe, the rise of *Zionism, and the development of music recording technologies led Jews to explore new ways to express, preserve, and distribute their ideas of Jewish sound. In the first half of the twentieth century the ability to record and replay musical performances through phonograph records, piano rolls, mass-produced sheet music, and radio *broadcasting allowed Jews and others to explore sounds beyond their local musical spheres. Although communities relied on live musicians to perform for their celebrations and *life-cycle events, they also found mass media a convenient and novel way to hear a wide range of Jewish musical artists and practices.

Musicians actively addressed these listening practices. Jewish wedding players (klezmorim) had developed a well-established presence in Eastern Europe by the nineteenth century, and their popularity crossed over to North America with *immigration. Each city with a significant Jewish population had its own network of musicians, who played for events both inside and outside the Jewish community. Many made recordings, and the most prominent musicians, such as clarinetists Naftule Brandwein (1884–1963) and Dave Tarras (1897–1989), became household names and important symbols of the Eastern European Jewish experience in America (see also MUSIC, FOLK).

*Synagogue singing also became a prominent form of Jewish popular expression, as *cantors became superstars alongside their opera counterparts. Many, including Mordechai Hershman (1888–1940), Moishe Oysher (1907–1958), and Yossele Rosenblatt (1882–1933), supplemented their synagogue positions with best-selling records, international concert tours, and *film appearances (Rosenblatt, for example, performed briefly in the film *The Jazz Singer* [1927]). A few "lady cantors," particularly Sophie Kurtzer (1896–1974), emerged on the scene as both performers and recording artists; because of their gender they were not permitted to sing in synagogues, but instead performed liturgical music on the vaudeville stage ("*Di Eybecke Mame*: Women in Yiddish Theater and Popular Song 1905–1929" [1993 CD]). The Yiddish *theater, which took root in numerous European and American cities around the turn of the twentieth century, also expanded into the *Yiddish recording and film industries. Musicals comprised an important popular component of the theater, and composers such as Sholom Secunda (1894–1974), who wrote "*Bei Mir Bistu Shayn*," and Joseph Rumshinsky (ca. 1881–1956) teamed with actor/singers such as Molly Picon (1898–1992) and Aaron Lebedeff (1873–1960) to create icons of popular song for Yiddish-speaking audiences. Their work crossed over into broader cultural realms of American culture as well, with Yiddish songs appearing in the jazz standards repertoire and hit parades by the 1930s (see FILM: YIDDISH-LANGUAGE).

In the Middle East and Mediterranean, meanwhile, different ideas of Jewish "popular" music emerged. Prominent Jewish music researcher Abraham Z. Idelsohn (1882–1938) attempted to fashion a new, "pure" repertoire of Hebrew folk songs that would prepare children for enculturation into a pre-Israeli, Hebrew-speaking society. Songwriters such as Mordecai Zeira (1905–1968) and singers such as Bracha Zefira (1911–1990) contributed in a similar spirit, through folk-like songs that combined Hebrew lyrics, socialist ideologies, pastoral imagery, easily sung melodies, youthful idealism, and promises of cultural integration. Such efforts at *Zionist music-making, some of which had roots in late-nineteenth-century Europe, became important parts of the Zionist project, both in *Palestine and internationally. Recording companies in *Turkey and *Greece also issued records of Jewish performers versed in Arabic and Mediterranean traditions, providing another current of popular music production important to Sephardic communities.

The rise of the *Nazi regime ironically gave an initial boost to Jewish popular music in *Central Europe by consolidating Jewish cultural production in the 1930s; after the start of the war, accounts show that Jews continued to write and exchange popular songs even as they were moved into *ghettos and concentration camps. The *Holocaust ultimately silenced Jewish music in most of Europe; after World War II, Palestine/Israel and the *United States became the central sites of training, recording, and popular musical consumption.

ISRAEL: In Israel, popular song became a means of nation-building and part of the government's central project for creating a unified Israeli culture. Already by Israeli statehood in 1948, the country had a significant body of songs from which it drew for local public singing sessions and national celebrations. Songwriters such as Naomi Shemer (1930–2004) later added to this repertoire with songs that extolled the land in poetic, biblically inspired terms. The Israeli *military, central to the country's security, also became an important source for new popular music through its entertainment troupes. Based on British practices, these troupes kept up the morale of soldiers while wittily addressing contemporary concerns. Their shows and songs often became sensations throughout Israel and started the careers of many Israeli popular musicians, including Arik Einstein (b. 1939), Danny Sanderson (b. 1950), Ehud Manor (1941–2005), and Yehoram Gaon (b. 1939).

Outside the army, attempts to create a specifically "Israeli" popular music in the 1960s took the form of national song contests, such as the Israel Song Festival, the Ḥasidic Song Festival, and the Mizraḥi Song Festival (and, later, the Pre-Eurovision Competition). Determined both through popular vote and "expert" panels, these competitions introduced such songs as "Abanibi" (1978) and "Jerusalem of Gold" (1967). Meanwhile the Ḥasidic Song Festival became an important platform for Shlomo Carlebach's music in the 1970s. The influence of rock music from Europe and the United States led to another transformation of the Israeli scene toward the end of the 1960s. Although groups simply covered English songs at first, eventually bands such as the Churchills and Kaveret began to combine rock aesthetics and Hebrew lyrics to reflect the Israeli experience. Artists such as Shlomo Artzi (b. 1949), T-Slam, Rami Kleinstein (b. 1962), Rita (b. 1962), and Aviv Geffen (b. 1973) became central figures between the 1970s and the turn of the twenty-first century, creating a culture of concerts alongside the popular public singing tradition.

The 1980s brought artists from the previously marginalized Middle Eastern (*Mizraḥi) Jewish communities into the public spotlight. Although singers such as Haim Moshe (b. 1955) and Zohar Argov (1955–1987) had achieved popularity earlier, they had fought to do so on their own terms. Now, figures such as Yemenite Jewish singer Ofra Haza (1957–2000) thrived in the flourishing world music scene in the mid-1980s with a successful blend of rock and Middle Eastern music. The group Ethnix followed in the late 1980s, using exotic imagery and sounds to build a following. A few years later, The Teapacks (Tipex) and Eyal Golan (b. 1971) continued to open doors to the mainstream industry. In doing so, Mizraḥi artists began to give Israel an ethnic sound that distinguished its music from that of other countries and helped define "Israeliness" in the international music market.

Rap and hip-hop styles also became important within Israeli popular music from the late 1990s, with artists such as Segol 59 (b. 1969) and Subliminal (b. 1979) outlining political positions through their songs, and novelist David Grossman writing the lyrics for Ha-Dag Nahash's biggest hit, "The Sticker Song" (*Shirat ha-Sticker*) in 2004.

UNITED STATES: In North America (and elsewhere), where Jews represented a tiny percentage of the population, popular music was used by different Jewish constituencies to forge a dialogue with the emerging youth culture scene.

Perhaps the most influential Jewish music of the postwar era came from the folk revival, which held an increasingly central position within young adult life in the 1950s, just as Jewish enrollment in college campuses rose and youth movements came to prominence. With Jewish wedding band music and the cantorial "star" system in decline, folk music became a key form of expression for young people and a means of empowerment for Jewish self-expression. Moving this agenda forward was *Orthodox rabbi Shlomo Carlebach (1925–1994). As one of *Ḥabad Lubavitch's first emissaries to college campuses in the 1950s, Carlebach took up the guitar to make his religious message attractive to young people. Although he left Ḥabad soon afterward, his songs and ministry propelled him into a legendary and sometimes controversial career. Carlebach became a fixture of the folk music scene in the 1960s, and he gave well-received concerts in such venues as Manhattan's Village Gate and the Berkeley Folk Festival. His more than twenty official albums (mostly live) and two songbooks brought him popularity throughout the Jewish world and provided a basis for what would become the Orthodox music industry. His near-constant touring exposed him to a wide fan base, and his three "homes" – the House of Love and Prayer in San Francisco, the "Carlebach Shul" in *New York City, and Moshav Modi'in in Israel – provided spaces for other musicians to follow in his footsteps.

Carlebach's success, the rise of a new generation of young Jews in the 1970s, and a renewed American fascination with ethnic identity led Jewish popular music to turn toward "revived" forms of expression. Musicians such as Joel Rubin, Zev Feldman, and Hankus Netsky researched the music of the *klezmorim* and formed their own ensembles, leading to a new genre known as "*klezmer* music." In Boston, a group called "Voice of the Turtle," influenced by the Early Music movement, performed music derived from Sephardic Jewish communities. In liberal Jewish movements, meanwhile, young musicians such as Michael Isaacson (b. 1946), Debbie Friedman (1952–2011), Jeffrey Klepper (b. 1954), and Daniel Freelander (b. 1952) began to present their own contemporary liturgical settings. Orthodox Jewish artists such as the Diaspora Yeshiva Band (centered in Israel, but composed largely of American Jews) and Avraham Fried (b. 1959) created musical settings of devotional texts in rock and bluegrass styles. All these approaches gained attention through public performances and internationally distributed albums.

The radical Jewish culture movement, outlined by jazz saxophonist John Zorn (b. 1953) in 1992, moved Jewish music into even edgier realms. The underground popularity of his and others' avant-garde musical efforts throughout the 1990s inspired bold rhetorical pairings of sound, performance, and Jewish symbolism. Related movements at the close of the twentieth century, often fueled by survivalist philanthropic efforts, led to an expansion of "radical" Jewish musical activity, including record labels JDub, Reboot Stereophonic, and OyHoo, as well as performance venues such as New York's Makor. Through these and other networks, including an expanding number of Jewish music festivals across North America, young Jewish musicians could explore and support new forms of musical expression such as (nonparody) Jewish hip-hop, reggae, punk, and a wide array of styles and fusions. Among the most prominent of these musicians was Matisyahu (b. Matthew Miller, 1979), a young *baal teshuvah* (an individual who recently "returned" to Orthodox Judaism). He was initially signed by JDub and his career as a Ḥasidic reggae performer led to mainstream recognition in 2005.

At the end of the first decade of the twenty-first century, Jewish popular music comprises a wide spectrum of activities, linked with any of a number of established musical genres. Orthodox popular music artists release dozens of albums per year, providing observant Jews with a culturally sanctioned space for enjoying popular music recreationally. Expanded *a cappella* offerings timed for the weeks between *Passover and *Shavuot, when some Jews do not listen to instrumental music, and the cultivation of female artists for female audiences highlight creativity in this area. Jewish composers and performers within *Reform Judaism and other liberal religious communities continue to find inspiration from acoustic/folk, country, and gospel artists and inspire a wide network of local song leaders. Downloading services (such as jTunes and OySongs) help music travel to ever wider audiences, and periodic efforts to establish a Jewish Grammy award emphasize the place some American Jews want "Jewish music" to occupy. These and other diverse efforts to reinvent the idea of Jewish music for new audiences continue to make popular Jewish music a vibrant, wide-ranging, and ever changing process linking identity with creativity.

For further reading, see S. Gilbert, *Music in the Holocaust: Confronting Life in the Nazi Ghettos and Camps* (2004); M. Kligman, "Contemporary Jewish Music in America," *American Jewish Yearbook* (2001); S. Rogovoy, *The Essential Klezmer* (2000); E. Seroussi and M. Regev, *Popular Music and National Culture in Israel* (2004); M. Slobin, ed., *American Klezmer: Its Roots and Offshoots* (2001); idem, *Chosen Voices: The Story of the American Cantorate* (2002 [1989]); and idem, *Fiddler on the Move* (2003).   JUDAH M. COHEN

Music, Religious. Music, both vocal and instrumental, has always played an important role in Jewish life; this is evident in biblical writings, such as the "Song at the Sea" in *Exodus 15. *David is described as a musician who plays the *kinnor*, a hand-held lyre (1 Sam 16:14–23); *prophets are also connected to musical activities (1 Sam 10:5; 2 Kgs 3:15). During First and Second *Temple times, music accompanied sacrifices and celebrations. Many of the *psalms were probably performed with singing and musical accompaniment (see BIBLE: MUSIC AND DANCE). After the destruction of the Second Temple in 70 CE, when the Rabbis prohibited musical instruments during *worship to indicate mourning, music was relegated to a subsidiary role. Over the next 2,000 years music increasingly returned to Jewish religious life, both in the *synagogue, in *life-cycle celebrations, and in other aspects of Jewish life (see also CANTOR, CANTORATE entries).

Jews have been strongly influenced by the prevalent musical styles in their diverse places of residence. *Ashkenazic Jews follow Western and Eastern European cultural aesthetics, whereas *Sephardi and *Mizraḥi Jews follow a range of musical practices, from the Andalusian styles of *Spain and *North Africa to Middle Eastern music from the Levant (*Turkey, *Syria, Lebanon, *Iraq, and *Egypt). Although liturgical texts are similar among Ashkenazic, Sephardi, and Mizraḥi Jews, the music that accompanies them conforms to regional traditions. Music has been and continues to be transmitted orally; written documentation is limited before 1750.

There are three genres of Jewish liturgical music: cantillation, chant, and liturgical song. The development of these three genres shows the changes and growth of music in Jewish religious life. Cantillation refers to the intonation of biblical and liturgical texts. Although scholars differ in their dating of cantillation, it has probably been practiced since Second Temple times. The Ben Asher Family in the *Galilee city of Tiberias in the early Middle Ages codified the system of *ta'amim*, the accent signs that indicate the tonal structure of a biblical sentence; these signs refer to a melodic formula, not an exact musical pitch. A. Z. Idelsohn, one of the first Jewish musicologists, believed the various twentieth-century practices of cantillation were survivals of ancient traditions. However, modern scholars are doubtful that modern practices faithfully maintain traditions that are more than two thousand years old (Shiloah; Seroussi).

Chant refers to the musical rendering of biblical texts and medieval liturgical writings found in the *siddur* (*prayer book). Practices include the chanting of *Psalm texts found in the *worship and in the various statutory *prayers (*shema and *amidah). Ashkenazic, Sephardi, and Mizraḥi communities have different rites; that is, different musical styles of chanting. The styles of liturgical song are also unique to each rite; this is the area that has shown the most growth and development in the modern era. *Piyyutim* (see POETRY: LITURGICAL [PIYYUT]) have been written throughout the past two thousand years and been sung using adaptations of melodies from various locales.

ASHKENAZIC MUSIC: The primary aspect of chant in the *Ashkenazic tradition is the practice of Jewish prayer modes or *nusakh*. The term *nusakh* also means liturgical rite. In this context it refers to prayer modes that operate like other musical modes that are defined by two parameters: scalar definition and a stock of melodies variously applied. The number of modes used in the Jewish tradition is a matter of scholarly debate. The generally accepted practice today, which is a part of the pedagogy in American cantorial schools, is the adoption of three prayer modes: *Ha-Shem Malakh*, *Magen Avot*, and *Ahavah Rabbah*. The name of each mode derives from the opening words of a liturgical passage that marks one of the first usages of that particular prayer mode in the *Sabbath liturgy. Hence, music and text are closely associated.

In most instances a Jewish prayer mode is defined by the four lowest notes (or tetrachord) that make each of the three primary modes unique. The *Ha-Shem Malakh* mode is similar intervalically to the western major scale with a lowered seventh (C-D-E-F-G-A-Bb-C). *Magen Avot* is equivalent to a western natural minor scale (C-D-Eb-F-G-Ab-Bb-C). *Ahavah Rabbah* has often been called the most "Jewish" of these modes because it is quite distinctive (C-Db-E-F-G-Ab-Bb-C) and without an equivalent in western music. Its essential feature is the augmented second interval between the second and third notes of the mode (D-flat to E-natural).

Ahavah Rabbah means "great love"; this designation aptly reflects the affective association of this mode, which expresses "great love" for God through a unique musical sound. The melancholy nature of the mode enhances its rich musical expression. *Ha-Shem Malakh* ("the Lord reigns") expresses God's majesty. *Magen Avot* ("shield of our fathers") does not have an affect and is used as a didactic mode to recite the text.

All three modes are used during Sabbath worship to convey various aspects of the text. Sabbath prayer on Friday night begins with the *Kabbalat Shabbat* psalms offering praises to God that are chanted in the *Ha-Shem Malach*. Likewise, this mode is appropriately used on the *High Holidays, particularly *Rosh Ha-Shanah. The *Ahavah Rabbah* mode is used on Shabbat morning for a contemplative section of the service before the *amidah prayer.

Liturgical melodies in Ashkenazic practice can be divided into two categories: *Mi-Sinai niggunim* (melodies from Mount Sinai) and metrical tunes. These two categories contain known melodies that are either sung by the *ḥazzan* (*cantor), the congregation, or both and are associated with particular liturgical sections at specific times during the calendar year. The *Mi-Sinai niggunim* represent the oldest body of melodies in the Ashkenazic tradition and encompass the recurrent melodies of the High Holidays and the three *festivals of *Sukkot, *Passover, and *Shavuot. Documentation for these traditions begins in the eighteenth century, but they were most likely used even earlier. They include High Holiday melodies like *kol nidrei* and the *aleinu. Mi-Sinai niggunim* comprise set tunes of greater length than Jewish prayer modes, which are shorter musical fragments. Both musical types are similar in that they flexibly apply the melody or melodic fragment to the text.

In addition to the recurring melodic phrases of the *Mi-Sinai niggunim*, the Ashkenazic tradition contains a vast array of metrical tunes. These melodies are characterized by their regular rhythms that facilitate congregational singing. The German liturgical tradition in particular made regular use of metrical tunes. *Adon Olam* and *Yigdal* are liturgical poems sung at the end of Sabbath prayer; there are many musical settings for these texts. Other melodies for specific holidays that were well established in the nineteenth century include *Adir Hu* for Passover, *Maoz Tzur* for *Ḥanukkah, and *Eli Tziyon* on *Tisha B'Av.

Specific practices in the synagogue inform Ashkenazic liturgical performance. In antiphonal singing, the cantor sings solo passages and the congregation responds. The cantor's portions consist of a few lines of the liturgical text that mark closure to a paragraph; this is known as a *ḥatimah*, a seal that ends the prayer. Some congregational responses are the utterance of a word, such as *amen*, or a phrase of text. One particular practice in the Ashkenazic tradition is worth noting. During the seventeenth and eighteenth centuries aesthetic beauty became a central goal of synagogue music.

The ḥazzan was assisted by two others, and together they became known as the *meshorerim.* One of the participants was a boy and referred to as the "singer," and the other was a man known as the "bass." Many musical manuscripts of this period indicate a melodic line to be sung by one of the three participants. Evidence for this practice is also taken from illustrations found in *prayer books (e.g., the *Leipzig Maḥzor*) showing the main singer and two assistants. The addition of more singers gradually led to choral singing in the forms of hymns, beginning in 1810, and four-part choral writing. Salomon Sulzer was among the first to develop choral music in an artistic style that became popular in nineteenth-century Western Europe.

During the era of the *Haskalah (Jewish Enlightenment) in *Central European cities, musical practitioners began incorporating external influences while, at the same time, retaining elements of traditional Jewish music, such as the *Mi-Sinai niggunim.* The most significant development in Central European cantorial and synagogue music resulted from the liturgical and aesthetic changes of the *Reform movement. Although changes in various Central European cities began in the late 1700s and early 1800s, reforms did not take shape in an established fashion until the mid-nineteenth century under the musical leadership of Salomon Sulzer (1804–1890). Sulzer began to officiate at the New Synagogue in *Vienna in 1826, and he elevated the office of cantor with his fine musicianship; Schubert and Liszt admired his singing. Sulzer's lasting contribution is his two-volume publication *Shir Zion,* a collection of his compositions and those by other composers that he commissioned; it was published in 1840 and 1866. Sulzer's goal was to take traditional Jewish melodies and "purify" them. He felt that ornate baroque musical elaborations did not befit the dignity of the service.

Another significant figure in Central European synagogue music was Louis Lewandowski (1821–1894). He served as a choral director and composer in *Berlin at the Old Synagogue in the Heidereutergasse, and after 1866 at the New Synagogue. His musical compositions appear in two publications, *Kol Rinah U'T'fillah* (A Voice of Joy and Prayer, 1871), for one and two voices, and *Todah W'Simrah* (Thanksgiving and Song, 1876–1882), for four voices and solos, with optional organ accompaniment. Lewandowski's musical compositions in *Kol Rinah U'T'fillah* contain simple choral responses designed for ease of use with congregations. Many of the *Todah W'Simrah* compositions include organ accompaniment that doubled the choral line or filled in the solo melodic line. The accompaniment adds a rich texture but the optional indication displays Lewandowski's recognition that not all congregations would want or be able to afford an organist.

The *Eastern European cantorial style remained traditional in focus. Few Eastern European synagogues incorporated the reforms commonly found in Central Europe. Adherence to traditional melodies and the Jewish prayer modes remained the norm, although some cantors came to *Vienna to study with Sulzer and incorporated his musical innovations in a style appropriate for their home communities. The hallmark of the Eastern European style was the use of recurring melodic fragments that convey a deep emotional feeling to the congregation. Ornate musical embellishments were used to transport the listener into a

spiritual realm. Word repetition was not uncommon. The nicely patterned phrases of Central Europe came to be known as *ḥazzanut ha-seder,* which means "orderly *cantorial style,*" whereas the free and ornate Eastern European style was known as *ḥazzanut ha-regesh,* or "emotional cantorial style." This latter approach became the foundation for the "golden age of the cantorate" in America during the first few decades of the twentieth century. Despite their stylistic differences, *ḥazzanut ha-seder* and *ḥazzanut ha-regesh* were also intermingled in the compositions of cantors from the Eastern European musical world who studied with cantors such as Sulzer.

Jewish religious music also includes a variety of *niggunim,* songs with and without words that are performed in various contexts in *Hasidic communities. These songs are sung to a variety of syllables like "Ay, yai, yai"; "Bum, bum, bum"; and "Tra, la, la." Some claim that the use of these different vocables, nonsense words, is significant. Melodies are often in the *Ahavah Rabbah* prayer mode. Types of *niggunim* include *stam niggun,* a regular tune with a clear rhythm; *devekut niggun,* ecstatic, usually slow, melodies sung on special occasions to reach a deep spiritual state; and *rebbe's niggun,* which is like a *devekut niggun* but is a special melody initiated by the *rebbe.* Jewish celebrations also included the singing of *Yiddish songs and *klezmer* music (see MUSIC, FOLK; MUSIC, POPULAR).

Jews from Central and Eastern Europe brought their synagogue music with them to America. Over time these two Ashkenazic styles merged into what has been called *minhag America* ("American *custom").

Between 1880 and 1930 cantorial music was extremely popular among American Jews, and Eastern European-born cantors recorded their liturgical music on 78 rpm recordings. The most prolific cantor was Yossele Rosenblatt; other major performers include Zavel Kwartin, Pierre Pinchik, Mordecai Hershman, Gershon Sirota, and Labele Waldman. By the 1930s, this "Old World" music began to lose appeal as congregations sought to develop a new aesthetic for the American synagogue. Composers such as A. W. Binder, Isadore Freed, and Herbert Fromm used a range of approaches during the 1930s, 1940s, and 1950s. One strategy was to use traditional melodies, but to add new harmonies and styles that were more contemporary. Another approach was to write new melodies in the style of older melodies or new melodies in a contemporary style. Directing their music at congregations seeking an identity as American Jews, these composers offered a musical style that combined aspects of European heritage with the more familiar sounds of American culture. In the 1950s through the 1970s, another generation of composers – some born in America, others in Europe – found new ways to write for the synagogue. Max Helfman, Max Janowski, Heinrich Schalit, and Frederik Piket wrote music for the synagogue that incorporated artistic uses of the organ and choir and some moments of traditional cantorial artistry.

By the 1970s American Jewish children and young people were attending Jewish *summer camps where they were exposed to a range of Jewish musical styles including *folk music. As they brought these new modes back to their congregations, clashes developed between accessible and singable music versus traditional cantorial styles. Certainly, by the early twenty-first century, the trend in American synagogue worship of all denominations is for participatory music as opposed to cantorial performance.

American Jews of all denominations have also been creating music for liturgical use that expresses their religious experiences and aspirations. Composers and performers include Debbie Friedman (1952–2011) and *Kol B'Seder* in the Reform movement and *Safam* and Craig Taubman in *Conservative Judaism. Among the vast array of performers in the *Orthodox community are Mordecai Ben David, Avraham Fried, *Regesh*, Miami Boys Choir, Dedi, and Yaakov Shweky. Other composers, including Michael Isaacson, Benjie Ellen Schiller, and Ami Aloni, have combined a range of music styles that tend to be accessible to congregations. The neo-Ḥasidic repertoire of Rabbi Shlomo Carlebach has also been an important resource for contemporary worship.

SEPHARDIC MUSIC: Cantillation and liturgical chant in Sephardi/Mizraḥi communities are significantly influenced by the music of the majority culture in any given location. Western Sephardic Jews (from communities in *England, *Amsterdam, and the Americas) use western musical scales and styles. Some of the liturgical chanting in this tradition is choral, an influence of neighboring Ashkenazic communities. Jews from the Levant, the most eastern end of the Mediterranean, closely follow the musical styles of their Arab surroundings – including the use of *maqamat,* Middle Eastern scales that include notes not found on fixed-pitch western instruments like a clarinet, trumpet, or piano. Like *nusakh* in the Ashkenazic tradition, *maqamat* are systematically applied to the liturgy. As with the recitation of the Qu'ran, cantillation and liturgical singing in the Levant are centered around one *maqam,* but once it is established the *ḥazzan* changes the *maqam,* an artistry demonstrating a unique synthesis of Jewish and Arab cultures. The North African tradition combines the western and Middle Eastern styles. Like western Sephardic music, North African liturgical music uses western scales, but like the Levant style, unique rhythms are found in the music (see NORTH AFRICA).

Piyyutim, which are created from pre-existing music, serve as an important genre of liturgical song. The process of adaptation begins with the selection of a pre-existing song that has a text, which can be in Arabic, Spanish, or Greek, and the selection of music in a Middle Eastern style. The second step is to create a Hebrew poem, a *piyyut.* The melody is then applied to the new text, and it is incorporated into the liturgy. At the end of the first decade of the twenty-first century singing and learning these songs are an active part of Sephardi/Mizraḥi religious culture in Israel. This music is heard not only in the synagogue but also on the radio, on recordings, and in concerts.

For further reading, see H. Avenary, "The Concept of Mode in European Synagogue Chant," *YUVAL* 2 (1971): 11–12; B. Cohon, "The Structure of Jewish Prayer Modes," *Journal of the American Musicological Society* (1950); M. Kligman, *Maqam and Liturgy* (2008); A. Z. Idelsohn, *Jewish Music in Its Historical Development* (1929); A. Shiloah, *Jewish Musical Traditions* (1992); and E. Seroussi et al., "Jewish Music," in *Grove Dictionary of Music and Musicians* (2001).

MARK KLIGMAN

Music, Synagogue. Just as the *synagogue itself was created as a substitute for the Jerusalem *Temple, synagogue music emerged in the shadow of the Temple. Synagogues could not wholly re-create the elaborate musical accompaniment provided by the choirs and orchestra of the Temple, but delegations of pious Israelites from around the country (called *anshei ma'amad* [men of standing]) were specially designated to represent their communities; they visited the Temple for one week at a time, observed the rituals there, and apparently brought home transferable aspects of the rite, including the music.

The destruction of the Jerusalem Temple in 70 CE forced dramatic changes in Jewish worship. The Rabbis now saw musical accompaniment as inappropriate for a nation that was mourning the loss of its spiritual center, and they understood the quotation in Hosea 9:1 ("Rejoice not, O Israel, as other peoples exult"; cf. BT *Gittin* 7a) to be a blanket indictment of virtually all musical activities, including those of the synagogue. The choral and instrumental performances that had distinguished the Temple rituals were discontinued.

The sole "musical" remnant of the Temple service to survive transplantation to the synagogue was the ritual chanting of portions of the *Torah. Instituted in the time of the Second Jerusalem Temple, this practice became the centerpiece of the new synagogue service, and by the third century CE, what had been a fairly simple act of declaiming the sacred text became an obligatory musical exercise (see BT *Megillah* 32a). The "oral transmission" of the tradition governing proper pronunciation and grammatical syntax of the biblical text gave way to a series of written systems whose symbols also acquired musical significance. Chanting of the scriptural passages became known as cantillation (see MUSIC, RELIGIOUS), and in addition to varying motives to articulate grammatical phrases, unique music evolved to distinguish the chanting of different scrolls. The music used to chant from the *Pentateuch was different from that used for *prophetic passages (see *HAFTARAH*) or for the scroll of *Esther (read on *Purim) or *Lamentations (read on *Tisha B'Av), or those read on the pilgrimage *festivals of *Passover, *Shavuot, and *Sukkot (the *Song of Songs, *Ruth, and *Ecclesiastes, respectively [see FIVE SCROLLS]).

As the liturgy became increasingly complex, with distinctive content for morning, afternoon, and evening *worship and with additional passages for *Sabbath and the festivals, the music used for chanting these texts underwent similar elaboration. The term *nusakh* emerged to refer both to the composition of specific liturgies and to the music used for rendering those selections. Morning and evening services would sound different from each other; weekday worship would differ from Sabbath prayers; and music for the pilgrimage festivals would be distinguished from *High Holiday melodies.

Describing the evolution of synagogue music might have remained a simple task, but for another important outcome of the destruction of the Temple: the concomitant dispersal of the Jewish people among the nations of the world. With memory of the historic Temple practices fading (in the absence of any form of written notation to preserve it), Jews living as small minorities among larger communities with their own rich musical traditions inevitably fell under the sway of the majority culture. *Nusakh* and cantillation continued to define synagogue musical practice but the actual development of each genre was complicated by the evolution of widely divergent "local" practices. Three broad divisions took shape: Middle Eastern or *Mizraḥi communities from what are now referred to as Muslim lands; *Sephardic Jews, representing the once-flourishing Spanish-Portuguese traditions (dispersed among a variety of Mediterranean and other locales after the expulsion of the Jews from *Spain and *Portugal in the late fifteenth century); and *Ashkenazim, Jews from Central and Eastern Europe. Within these three large divisions are infinite variations. Yet, despite the inevitable alterations that have resulted from centuries of oral transmission (and the vagaries of personal preference), each retains a commitment to its historic sense of "tradition."

The juxtaposition of European Jewish communities with the evolution of western culture has resulted in the development of synagogue musical models and forms that do not strictly conform to the time-honored practices of *nusakh* and cantillation. A 1605 responsum by Leon *Modena (1571–1648) paved the way for the introduction of unaccompanied choral music into some Sephardic synagogues; Leone and Salamone Rossi (ca. 1570–ca. 1628) were particularly prolific composers in this regard, but isolated compositions by both Christian and Jewish composers in *Italy, *France, and *Amsterdam point to a relatively limited receptivity to this type of music throughout the Sephardic *Diaspora.

New attitudes promulgated by the nineteenth-century *Reform movement produced fundamental alterations in Ashkenazic synagogue music. In their desire to modernize many aspects of the synagogue ritual, reformers abolished *nusakh* and cantillation and encouraged Reform *cantors to produce beautiful music like that written by Bach and other masters of church music. Unfortunately, the typical synagogue musician fell far short of this ideal. However, Salomon Sulzer (1804–1890), Louis Lewandowski (1821–1894), and others succeeded in composing well-received music for cantor, choir, and the organ, whose adoption signaled a rejection of the centuries-long mourning for the Temple.

To be sure, not all Ashkenazic communities adopted these radical musical innovations, and in time, even the Reform movement modified its stance in opposition to any traditional music. In particular, Salomon Sulzer respected the historic role of *nusakh* and sought to substitute a "new *nusakh*" that incorporated contemporary musical values for some of the traditional forms of the past. He and others also preserved a core of traditional melodies known as "*Mi-Sinai*" tunes, that, although not literally "from Sinai," had been a much beloved part of Ashkenazic tradition since the eleventh century. This notion of keeping the best of the past while incorporating new musical forms and models has, to a greater or lesser extent, informed all of Ashkenazic synagogue music ever since. In addition, the technological advances of the twenty-first century have made possible an increased sharing of "ethnic" melodies across denominational and cultural boundaries, resulting in new definitions of "tradition" and a richer heritage of new and historic musical materials from which future synagogue music will inevitably draw.   MARSHA BRYAN EDELMAN

Mysticism: See also; KABBALAH; KABBALAH, LURIANIC; MYSTICISM: *HEKHALOT* AND *MERKAVAH* LITERATURE; MYSTICISM, WOMEN AND, etc.

Mysticism: Ancient. Several concepts that developed within the normative culture of early rabbinic *Judaism in the first and second centuries CE provided the context for the emergence of Jewish mystical creativity in late antiquity. The most important concepts were esoteric speculations concerning the divine realm, described in the *Mishnah as "the work of the chariot" (*ma'aseh merkavah*), consisting of exegetical-homiletical discussions of the first chapter of *Ezekiel and related biblical texts, and "the work of creation" (*ma'aseh bereshit*), reflections on the biblical narratives of the creation. In addition, the emergence of the celestial power *Metatron, a demiurgic mythical figure, and the development of *Samael, a satanic figure, also provided important material for subsequent mystical speculation.

The term *ma'aseh bereshit* in M. Ḥagigah 2:1 refers to homiletical exegesis of the biblical chapters dedicated to the creation, mainly the first chapters of *Genesis. The *Talmuds, especially M. Ḥagigah 2, as well as the *Tosefta and *midrash, include a variety of homilies and stories interpreting the process of creation. The largest collection of these traditions is at the beginning of the midrash collection *Genesis Rabbah*, but such traditions also appear frequently in other classical and late *midrashim*. Although BT Ḥagigah prohibits dealing (at least in public) with "what is below and what is above, what is before and what is after" (a quote from the *apocryphal book, *Wisdom of Ben Sira), several treatises dedicated specifically to this subject were composed in the late talmudic and *geonic periods. They include the *Baraita de-Ma'aseh Bereshit*, *Midrash Konen*, and *Midrash Tadsheh*. *Sefer Yetzirah* also fits into the *ma'aseh bereshit* literature of late antiquity.

Medieval Jewish mystics and esoterics devoted much effort to the subject of creation, especially in the numerous commentaries on *Sefer Yetzirah* written by kabbalists and the *Hasidei Ashkenaz in the thirteenth century. In the *Kabbalah, *ma'aseh bereshit* acquired an intense mystical significance; the term sometimes denoted not only the creation of the universe but also the emanation of the divine hypostases, the *sefirot*. The detailed study of this process in the *Zohar and other kabbalistic works served not only to describe the past but also revealed a mystical purpose in the present. The knowledge of the secrets of Genesis could enable the mystic to ascend the same ladder in reverse and return to the primordial perfection of the divine world.

Ma'aseh merkavah, literally "the work of the chariot," is also a mishnaic term indicating the midrashic exposition of the celestial chariot described in Ezekiel 1 and 10 (M. Ḥagigah 2:1). In the same way as *ma'aseh bereshit* (the work of creation) refers to the midrashic expounding of Genesis 1–2, *ma'aseh merkavah* was extended to include any discussion or description of the celestial realms. At the end of the twelfth century, *Maimonides identified *ma'aseh merkavah* with metaphysics (and *ma'aseh bereshit* with physics); many other Jewish writers connected *ma'aseh merkavah* with mystical speculation and theosophy. Several treatises of *hekhalot and *merkavah* mysticism, the Jewish esoteric speculations of the talmudic and geonic periods, include the term *merkavah* in their titles and expound, in great detail, the descriptions in Ezekiel. *Reuyot Yeḥezkel*, for instance, is an ancient treatise describing the seven chariots Ezekiel saw when he looked into the waters of the river Kvar, when one firmament after another opened above him to reveal the chariot in each. The *merkavah* texts were also important in medieval Europe. Eleazar ben Judah of Worms (d. 1238) wrote a treatise called "The Secret of the Chariot"; Spanish and Provençal mystics, especially in *Sefer ha-*Bahir* and the *Iyyun* Circle, used *merkavah* terminology as a source for their mystical symbolism.

A distinction should be made between *ma'aseh merkavah*, which is essentially an intellectual activity of midrashic homiletics, and *yeridah le-merkavah*, "descending to the chariot," which is the actual mystical activity of ascension to the divine palaces (*hekhalot*), described in several ancient texts. The "descenders" used imagery from Ezekiel, but their main sources and symbols were taken from the *Song of Songs and other texts (**see KABBALAH**).   JOSEPH DAN

Mysticism: *Hekhalot* and *Merkavah* Literature.

These ancient Hebrew esoterical and mystical writings were composed between the third and the seventh centuries. This literature includes about two dozen treatises and deals with four broad subjects. *Merkavah* ("chariot") literature is concerned with homiletical interpretation of *Ezekiel 1 and other biblical descriptions of the celestial realms, with particular emphasis on the terminology of Ezekiel's vision of the divine chariot (*ma'aseh merkavah*). The second group comprises *magical works that delineate formulas by which angelic powers can be forced to serve human needs. These include *Sefer ha-Razim* (The Book of Secrets), "The Sword of Moses," and "*Havdalah* of Rabbi Akiva." A third category, the "work of creation," emphasizes cosmogony and cosmology (*ma'aseh bereshit*), is discussed throughout this literature (see also, MYSTICISM: ANCIENT). The *Hekhalot* ("palaces") texts detail the mystical ascent to the celestial palaces. This ancient library of esoteric texts, combined with *Sefer Yetzirah* and sections in the *Talmud and *midrash dealing with these subjects, together with the myths of *Metatron and *Samael, have served over the centuries as the basic sources of mystical terminology, imagery, and ideas concerning the celestial and divine realms.

The first clear appearance of a school of mystics in ancient Judaism is attested by the works of the self-described *yordei ha-merkavah*, "the descenders to the chariot." Their writings, integrated into *hekhalot* and *merkavah* literature, usually include a mixture of *magic, cosmogony and cosmology, and speculations concerning the chariot envisioned by Ezekiel. Some describe actual mystical activity, including ascension to the divine world and participation in celestial rituals. This mystical material is found mainly in five works. These are *Hekhalot Zutarti*, "the lesser book of *hekhalot*," the center of which is the description of the ascension of Rabbi *Akiva to the divine throne. *Hekhalot Rabbati*, the most elaborate extant work of its kind, is centered around the story of the ten martyrs (see MARTYRDOM) and the ascension of Rabbi Ishmael (described as a High Priest the son of a High Priest); this work imagines that the *Temple has not been destroyed. The remaining three are *Ma'aseh Merkavah*, an untitled collection of hymns and descriptions of mystical ascensions (published by Gershom *Scholem, who gave it its title); the *Shiur Komah* (Measurement of Height), the description of the divine figure of the Creator (*yotzer*) in anthropomorphic terms, listing the divine limbs, their mysterious names, and their measurements; and *Sefer Hekhalot*, known also as the *Third Book of Enoch* or the *Hebrew Apocalypse of Enoch*. The first part of this text relates the elevation of *Enoch and his transformation into the divine power of *Metatron, "the prince of the countenance"; the second part is a detailed, systematic

description of the divine realms and the powers that govern them. To these may be added another treatise, the *Sar Torah*, the "Prince of the Torah," describing the descent of the *Shekhinah to the Second Temple when it was being built by those who returned from *Babylonian exile.

These mystical treatises include several characteristics not found anywhere else. They are: 1) the term *hekhalot*, "palaces" or "temples," seven of which comprise the divine world; 2) the divine pleroma, constituted of several powers who are called "Lord God of Israel" in addition to their "angelic" names; 3) the image of God as the *shiur komah*; 4) a unique concept of history, completely disregarding talmudic tradition; 5) the terminology of ascent and descent to the chariot; 6) reliance on a new interpretation of the *Song of Songs as a self-description of God, in addition to an exegetical focus on Ezekiel and other visionary texts; and 7) the insistence that there is an individual way through which a human being can approach God, independent of halakhic and midrashic contexts. In this way, these treatises present a spiritual alternative to the "exoteric" Jewish way of life.

Hekhalot mysticism is different from medieval Jewish mysticism in its emphasis on the visionary and in its continuous references to direct, individual mystical experiences, rather than a reliance on textual exegesis. The *Shiur Komah* and the other works in this group contain the earliest Jewish descriptions of God and his pleroma, mainly using monarchic terminology and images. A significant part of this literature is instructions about how to overcome the grave dangers the mystic might encounter on his way (especially at the gate of the sixth palace). The many hymns include those sung by celestial powers and others by the mystics themselves; some of these were included in the *prayer book. The ultimate purpose of this mystical journey is to view "the king in his beauty" and to be integrated into the pleroma surrounding God. The description of the transformation of Enoch can be regarded as the earliest Hebrew example of *unio mystica* (mystical communion). Scholarly studies include J. Dan, *Jewish Mysticism* vol. I (1998); idem, *Ancient Jewish Mysticism* (1989); P. Schäfer, *The Hidden and Manifest God: Some Major Themes in Early Jewish Mysticism* (1992); and D. J. Halperin, *The Faces of the Chariot* (1988).   JOSEPH DAN

Mysticism, Women and.

Women have been conspicuously absent from Jewish mysticism from its earliest incarnation in *hekhalot* mysticism (see MYSTICISM: *HEKHALOT* AND *MERKAVAH*) through medieval *Kabbalah. Although feminine imagery abounds in Kabbalah, historical evidence for female mystics does not. This glaring absence has been noted by several scholars of medieval Jewish history and mysticism who offer varying explanations. Gershom *Scholem attributes women's absence to the association between women and the demonic in Jewish myth (37–38). Judith Baskin suggests that Kabbalah is a highly intellectual text-based enterprise, and few if any medieval or early modern Jewish women would have been able to attain the requisite expertise. Sharon Koren notes that late antique and medieval Jewish mystics were unique in their understanding of physical impurity as an insurmountable obstacle to divine communion. Close reading of mystical writings, from *hekhalot* through pre-expulsion Kabbalah, reveals that women were actively barred from mystical pursuits because of what was seen as their innate impurity (see PURITY).

Jewish practice, however, has never been monolithic or without variations. There is some evidence that Jewish women engaged in "alternate" forms of spirituality in the late ancient and early modern eras. There were women prophets in the Bible (see BIBLE: PROPHETS AND PROPHECY). Late antique *pseudepigraphical literature, such as The Testament of Job and Joseph and Asenath, describes women speaking with angels. *Philo reported that women participated in the spiritual exercises of the Therapeutae. Moreover, in the late ancient period, some women may have engaged in magical practices. Indeed, the rabbinic claim that "most women engage in sorcery" may refer to women's success as healers (see MAGIC).

In early modern *Safed, Ḥayyim Vital mentions in his mystical diary that spirits would possess certain women and speak through their agency. These women were not kabbalists; rather they served as vessels for dispossessed souls (often male). Women participated actively in the *Sabbatean movement, and some functioned as prophets. Eva Frank (1754–1816), daughter of the charismatic Sabbatean leader Jacob *Frank (1726–1791), played a major role in her father's *antinomian theology. Originally named Rachel, Eva is referred to in Frankist writings as the Lady, the Virgin, or Matronita, the Aramaic name for *Shekhinah, the feminine aspect of the Divine in kabbalistic thought. She became known as Eva after the conversion of her family to Christianity in 1760. Jacob Frank saw himself as the eternal *Messiah and told his followers that Eva-Rachel should be recognized as the Shekhinah who would lead them as a messianic redeemer while he was temporarily absent. Ultimately, Frank claimed, he would be reborn and united with his daughter in "the unity of Messiah and Shekhinah." Long after her death, many Frankist families continued to keep a miniature portrait of Eva Frank and honored her as a saintly woman who was falsely reviled.

In *Ḥasidism, some women, most famously Hannah Rochel *Verbermacher, also known as the Maid of Ludmir, functioned as spiritual leaders. Yet as many scholars have noted, the Maid of Ludmir was able to succeed only as long as she denied her femininity.

Women have turned to mystical traditions in the modern period. Recently, some feminists have reclaimed the symbol of the Shekhinah as a means of supplementing what they perceive to be the patriarchal bias of Jewish theology. Judith Plaskow urges that the "long suppressed femaleness of God, acknowledged in the mystical tradition, but even here shaped and articulated by men, must be reexplored and reintegrated into Israel." Toward that goal, many Jewish feminists have reinterpreted mystical themes and emphasize the symbol of the Shekhinah in innovative prayer rituals. Women figure prominently in the Jewish Renewal movement (see JUDAISM: JEWISH RENEWAL MOVEMENT) – a spiritual community described by David Wolfe-Blank as "Ḥasidism meets feminism." New adaptations of Kabbalah and greater educational opportunities may enable women to breach the boundaries of Jewish esotericism and actively participate in Jewish mysticism.

For further reading, see J. R. Baskin, "Dolce of Worms: Women Saints in Judaism," in Women Saints in World Religions, ed. A. Sharma (2000), 39, 42; J. H. Chajes, Between Worlds: Dybbuks, Exorcists, and Early Modern Judaism (2003); S. Fishbane, "'Most Women Engage in Sorcery': An Analysis of Sorceresses in the Babylonian Talmud," Jewish History 7 (2003): 27–42; S. Koren, "The Woman from Whom God Wanders," Ph.D. diss., Yale University, 1999; J. Plaskow, "The Right Question is Theological," in On Being a Jewish Feminist, ed. S. Heschel (1995); G. Scholem, Major Trends in Jewish Mysticism (1941); A. Rapoport-Albert, "On the Position of Women in Sabbatianism," in HaHalom VeShivro: The Sabbatean Movement and its Aftermath: Messianism Sabbatianism and Frankism, ed. R. Elior (2001), 279–94; and C. Weissler, "Meanings of the Shekhinah in the Jewish Renewal Movement," in Women Remaking American Judaism, ed. R. Prell and D. Weinberg (2007), 51–81; and see LILITH.

SHARON KOREN

N

Nagid is a title of biblical origin (I Sam 10:1) that was used to refer to Jewish notables and communal leaders in the lands of *Islam. Initially this title was an honorific bestowed by the *geonic academies (*yeshivot*) of *Babylonia and *Palestine; by the Mamluk period in *Egypt (1250–1517), *nagid* was the official designation of the head of the Jewish community, a position that had become hereditary. Documents from the Cairo *Genizah indicate that the use of *nagid* in this sense already appeared around 1065, when the office of head of the community was first established, but it did not become the normative title until the thirteenth century.

Before the thirteenth century, local Jewish notables who were close to Muslim authorities, many of whom were physicians (see MEDICINE) and had unimpeded access, would be granted the title *nagid* by one or more of the geonic academies. This title was in recognition of both their intermediary roles on behalf of the Jewish community and their support of the academies. Thus, the title, the equivalent of the Arabic *amīr*, recognized the authority of these notables rather than conferring it on them, and its use by the notables constituted deference to geonic leadership.

Jewish communal leaders in Tunisia (see NORTH AFRICA), *Spain, and *Egypt bore this title from the eleventh century, perhaps the most famous being the Granada physician and courtier Samuel ibn Naghrela (d. ca.1056), also known as *Samuel ha-Nagid; the title also appears periodically in the twelfth century in *Syria and *Yemen. One Zakkār ben 'Ammār was appointed *nagid* of the Jews of Palermo in 1069, but no other *nagid* of *Sicily is known; this suggests that the term was not yet attached to an established office of the headship of the Jews. However, in Egypt from the time of Abraham Maimonides (d. 1237), the title *nagid* and the hereditary headship of the Jewish community (*ra'īs al-yahūd*)were linked. The office seems to have disappeared from Egypt by the 1600s in favor of the honorific *hakham,* or chief rabbi, although it persisted in the Maghreb (North Africa) until the nineteenth century. For further reading, see S. D. Goitein, *A Mediterranean Society*, 2:23–40 (1967–93); and M. Cohen, *Jewish Self-Government in Medieval Egypt* (1980).   PHILLIP I. ACKERMAN-LIEBERMAN

Nahman Ben Simha of Bratzlav (1721–1810) was the

great-grandson of the founder of the *Hasidic movement, Israel *Baal Shem Tov (the Besht), whose daughter, Edel, was his grandmother. He was also the grandson of Rabbi Nahman of Horodenka, a prominent disciple-colleague of the Besht. Nahman was born in Medzibuz, *Ukraine; he lived some time in Husiatin and then moved to Medevdovka, where he began to assemble adherents and assume the role of a Hasidic *tzaddik. In 1798 he traveled to the Land of Israel, visiting Jaffa, Tiberias, *Safed, and Haifa. He was in Acre in 1799 when Napoleon besieged the town and he escaped on a Turkish ship. After many hardships, he reached Crete and then returned to Ukraine. He settled in Zlatopoli, but was attacked by the local *tzaddik,* the Sava

("grandfather") of Shpoli, who accused him of leaning toward heretical *Sabbatean ideas. He moved to Bratzlav, where he was joined by Nathan Sernhartz of Nemirov, who became his faithful disciple, biographer, and editor of his writings. He later settled in Uman, where he died, probably of tuberculosis.

Rabbi Nahman's teachings are presented in the two volumes of his collected sermons, *Likutei Moharan* (Lessons of Rabbi Nahman, printed in 1808 and 1811). In 1806, probably as the result of the death of his young son, he began to tell stories, presented as *folktales, but that were highly original and enigmatic. Rabbi Nahman combined Lurianic mystical teachings (see KABBALAH, LURIANIC) with intense personal perceptions. He emphasized the paradoxical (he used the Hebrew term *kushia*) nature of the Lurianic myth, turning it into a personal vision of his own messianic destiny. In his homilies, and especially in his narratives, he described in enigmatic terms the difficult journey of the *messiah toward the completion of his redemptive mission. The radical nature of his ideas and the controversy surrounding him contributed to the fact that he attracted only a small group of adherents while other Hasidic dynasties gathered thousands of followers.

When Rabbi Nahman died, his adherents did not appoint anyone to replace him. Because they were the only Hasidic group who followed a dead *tzaddik,* they were called the "dead Hasidim." (In the 1990s the Lubavitch Hasidism [*Habad] also became leaderless when Rabbi Menahem Mendel *Schneersohn died without an heir.) Bratzlav Hasidism had few resources and was very loosely organized; its main concern was to print and reprint the writings of Rabbi Nahman.

Nahman of Bratzlav became the best-known Hasidic leader among non-Hasidim, Jews and non-Jews. Martin *Buber's first work was a translation, or adaptation, into German of Rabbi Nahman's narratives. Because of its relaxed organization, Bratzlav Hasidim attracted many spiritualists and "New Age" adherents in the late twentieth century. The movement is open to every seeker of mystical and esoteric teachings (see KABBALAH), and its popularity continues to increase. For further reading, see D. Assaf, ed., *Bibliography of Bratzlav Hasidism* (2000).   JOSEPH DAN

Nahmanides (Moses Ben Nahman), also known as the

Ramban, was born in 1195 and died in 1270. He lived most of his life in the Catalonian city of Girona in the Crown of Aragon, emigrating to *Jerusalem in 1265. He is known for his participation in and narrative of the Barcelona disputation (1263), for his contribution to *mystical teachings, and for his *Bible and *Talmud commentaries.

Among Nahmanides' many surviving works, his systematic *Torah commentary is perhaps the most significant (see also BIBLICAL COMMENTARY). Written in *Jerusalem near the end of his life, it is simultaneously innovative and firmly rooted in the dominant scholarly traditions of his age. In his methodological introduction, he sets the scene for a unique reading of Scripture, presenting the Torah as a text whose innumerable layers of meaning reveal themselves differently depending on the reader. Naḥmanides cites interpretations of well-recognized authorities, principally *Rashi and Abraham *ibn Ezra, but also *Maimonides. He makes use of *midrash, sometimes to lend support to his own readings and sometimes as a rhetorical foil against which to project a new and unprecedented interpretation. In addition, he weaves references to mystical interpretations into his commentary (see KABBALAH), although he often stops short of developing them beyond the level of allusions or hints.

As a commentator and *halakhic innovator, Naḥmanides strove to synthesize or reconcile diverse approaches and views. In his Torah commentary, he brought together the *Tosafists' emphasis on the *peshat* (plain meaning of the text) with the philosophical and mystical preference for allegorical readings. His legal writing similarly advanced a synthetic approach that paid homage to varied authorities. Naḥmanides' "Letter to the French Rabbis," a response to their plea that he support a *ḥerem (ban of excommunication) placed on students of Maimonides' philosophy, is indicative of his broader approach to matters of halakhic interpretation. In this letter, Naḥmanides worked to reconcile the various parties by reviewing the legal precedents that either supported or contradicted the use of a ḥerem to achieve ideological ends.

Naḥmanides also examined the intersections between Jewish and Christian interpretations of the Hebrew Bible and history. Responses to Christian interpretations can be discerned in his biblical commentary, in his *Sefer ha-Geulah* (The Book of Redemption), and most directly in his account of the Barcelona disputation, *Sefer ha-Vikuaḥ* (The Book of the Disputation). The extant version of the *Vikuaḥ* (likely not the original, which Naḥmanides wrote at the behest of the bishop of Girona) uses Jewish and Christian sources to show that the Jewish *messiah was to be expected within the following century. Circulation of this work in Christian circles resulted in Naḥmanides' expulsion from the Crown of Aragon by order of Pope Clement IV.

Recent research includes N. Caputo, *Nahmanides in Medieval Catalonia: History, Community, and Exile* (2008). **See also MIDDLE AGES: JEWISH–CHRISTIAN POLEMICS; THOUGHT, MEDIEVAL.**   NINA CAPUTO

Nasi: See PATRIARCH

Nasi Family: See MENDES-NASI FAMILY; and WOMEN: EARLY MODERN EUROPE

National Council of Jewish Women: See ORGANIZATIONS, WOMEN'S: NORTH AMERICA.

Nazi Party. Nazi is an abbreviation for the National Socialist German Workers' Party (*Nationalsozialistische Deutsche Arbeiterpartei* [NSDAP]) that formed in *Germany in 1919 and achieved power in 1933, establishing the Third Reich. Under the leadership of Adolf Hitler, the NSDAP established a totalitarian regime in Germany that actively attempted to eliminate from German society political opponents, especially communists, as well as those deemed of insufficient "racial purity," including Jews and *Roma.

The Nazis also targeted homosexuals and individuals with physical or mental handicaps as unworthy to live. With its invasion of *Poland in September 1939, the Nazi leadership fomented what would become *World War II. This cataclysm, which concluded with Germany's defeat in 1945, resulted in millions of deaths, including the deliberate murder of as many as six million Jews, as well as of many political prisoners and others the Nazis deemed undesirable. See *EINSATZGRUPPEN*; GERMANY; HOLOCAUST entries; and entries on European countries.

Nazirite (from the Hebrew word *nazir*, "separated" or "dedicated"). According to Numbers 6:1–21, a man or woman who takes a vow of devotion to *God for at least thirty days assumes Nazirite obligations, including abstaining from grapes and all derivative products, leaving hair unshorn, and shunning contact with a corpse. At the conclusion of a nazirite vow, the Nazirite brings three specified sacrifices to the *Temple, following which the hair of the head is shaved and burned on the fire as a sacrifice of well-being. Some individuals, such as Samson and *Samuel (Judg 13:7; 1 Sam 1:21), were permanent Nazirites. *Halakhic regulations concerning the Nazirite are found in the *Mishnah and *Talmud in Tractate *Nazir* and are summarized in *Maimonides' *Mishneh Torah, Hafla'ah, Nazir*.   KATE FRIEDMAN

Near East, Ancient. This term refers to the geographical region in which ancient Near Eastern civilizations were located; it extends from *Iran in the east to *Egypt in the west, and from *Turkey in the north to *Arabia in the south. It is labeled the "Near East" from the perspective of Europe and in contrast to eastern Asia, the "Far East." Civilization began in the Near East with the domestication of cereal plants and flock animals around 8000 BCE, a development that allowed for a sharp rise in population, the growth of cities, and, by 3100 BCE, the advent of writing. After the conquests of *Alexander the Great in 332 BCE, the cultures of the region began to merge with that of ancient Greece, and this new *Hellenistic civilization largely marks the end of the ancient Near East.

The ancient Near East also provided the "cradle" of Jewish civilization, because the Land of *Israel, situated on the land bridge between *Egypt and *Mesopotamia, was heavily influenced by the cultures of these regions. When they find similarities between the Hebrew *Bible and ancient Near Eastern texts, modern scholars assume that the Mesopotamian or Egyptian sources influenced the Israelite version, because of the greater antiquity and cultural dominance of these civilizations. Fragments of Babylonian literary texts from Mesopotamia have been found in Israel, Egypt, and *Ugarit, on the Mediterranean coast of *Syria, indicating the broad extent of their cultural dissemination. The Israelites may also have absorbed aspects of ancient Near Eastern culture indirectly via the *Canaanites who lived in the land before their arrival. *Genesis records that *Abraham, *Jacob, and Jacob's twelve sons, the ancestors of the twelve *Israelite tribes, all lived for a time in both Mesopotamia and Egypt. According to *Exodus, Israel as a people came into existence in the land of Egypt and, after the conquest of the land of Canaan, settled among a variety of native peoples. The courts of the *United Monarchy, under *David and *Solomon, and later those of the kingdoms of

*Israel and *Judah may have employed scribes and administrators trained in the scribal schools and royal bureaucracies of other nations, and these individuals would have brought the intellectual traditions of their homelands. The dual kingdoms of *Israel and *Judah endured centuries of domination by the two great empires of Mesopotamia – *Assyria and *Babylonia. The 580s BCE exile of Judah's upper classes to Babylonia and *Persia exerted a particularly significant influence on later Jewish institutions. Considering all of the various cultural pressures imposed on the small nation of ancient Israel, what is truly remarkable was its ability to maintain such a distinctive sense of its *God and its unique role in world history. **Map 1**   ELAINE GOODFRIEND

Nehemiah, Book of: See EZRA and NEHEMIAH, BOOKS OF

Ner Tamid ("eternal flame" or "light"). In every *synagogue a light is always kept illuminated above or in front of the ark (*aron ha-kodesh*) in which the *Torah scrolls are stored. The *ner tamid* fulfills the *commandment in *Exodus 27:20–21 that a light is to be kept burning in the Tent of Meeting "from evening to morning before the Lord." It is also a remembrance of the *menorah that was always lit in the *Jerusalem *Temple and of the presence of *God who accompanied the *Israelites in the wilderness as a pillar of flame by night (Exod 13:21–22). Historically, these lights were fueled by oil; in the contemporary era, they tend to be electric, often with back-up systems in case of power failure. **See also** ḤANUKKAH.

Netherlands: See AMSTERDAM

Nevi'im: Literally "prophets," this term is the designation for the second of the three traditional divisions of the Hebrew Bible. **See PROPHETIC BOOKS (*NEVI'IM*).**

New Christians: See *CONVERSOS*; INQUISITION, SPANISH; SPAIN, CHRISTIAN

New Moon: See ROSH ḤODESH

New Testament refers to the Christian canonical Scriptures that consist of twenty-seven writings: the four Gospels (Mark, Matthew, Luke, and John), describing the mission and teaching, death, *resurrection, and exaltation to God's right hand of Jesus of Nazareth, whom Christians regard as the *messiah; the Acts of the Apostles, describing the beginnings of *Christianity as a messianic sect within *Second Temple Judaism; twenty-one letters of differing lengths attributed to leading figures from the first generation of Christianity, notably the apostle Paul; and an *apocalypse (the Revelation of John) somewhat similar to the book of *Daniel. The Gospels and the letters of Paul were widely recognized as authoritative by the Christian churches by the end of the second century, and the complete body of literature was designated canonical in the fourth century. It is important to note that as "canon" these writings define not only the features that unify Christianity but also the diversity that equally characterizes Christianity.

These writings are described as "the *New* Testament," both because the only sacred text recognized by the very first Christians was the Hebrew *Bible or *Septuagint, and because over the next two centuries these twenty-seven writings came to be regarded as a supplement or complement to the *Tanakh* (Hebrew Bible). The *Tanakh* was designated the *Old* Testament and included as a fundamental part of the Christian Bible. Therefore, the New Testament did not so much supersede the Old Testament as provide the lens through which Christians read the *Tanakh*. It was the key to the Christian interpretation of the Hebrew Scriptures. In fact, within Christianity the New Testament plays a role in relation to the *Tanakh* somewhat equivalent to the role of the *Mishnah in relation to the *Tanakh* within rabbinic *Judaism.

It is important, then, to appreciate that the New Testament writings are interrelated with the *Tanakh* by a host of assumptions, themes, concerns, language, quotations, and allusions. It is not possible to appreciate the writings of the New Testament without knowledge of and reference to the *Tanakh*. The New Testament on its own would have many gaps in the religion it inculcated; these gaps are the unspoken taken-for-granteds of the New Testament writers, and they can only be filled from the writings that the New Testament writers regarded as their Scripture.

It is also highly significant that almost all the New Testament writers were Jews. Because Christianity began within and as part of the rich diversity of late *Second Temple Judaism, it is not inappropriate to describe the New Testament as *Jewish literature*, which tells of a renewal movement within Second Temple Judaism that ultimately grew mostly beyond the boundaries of traditional Judaism and became Christianity.

Christian biblical scholarship has always depended on the help of interested or sympathetic rabbis. After centuries of suspicion and hostility, the latter half of the twentieth century saw an increase in Jewish and Christian scholars working together to achieve a better understanding of the circumstances that produced the New Testament. The Jewishness of the foundational inspirational figure, Jesus, is now taken for granted, and the Jewishness of his mission and message is widely accepted on all sides. More controversial is the character of the ex-*Pharisee and apostle to the Gentiles, Paul, whose own writings probably indicate an individual who saw his role as fulfilling or helping fulfill Israel's commission to be a light to the Gentiles.

Helpful readings include R. E. Brown, *An Introduction to the New Testament* (1997); J. D. G. Dunn, *Unity and Diversity in the New Testament: An Inquiry into the Character of Earliest Christianity*, 3rd ed. (2006); and S. McKnight and G. R. Osborne, *The Face of New Testament Studies: A Survey of Recent Research* (2004).   JAMES D. G. DUNN

New Year For Trees: See TU B'SHEVAT

New Years. Jewish tradition acknowledges four distinct new year observances throughout the conventional twelve-month cycle (M. *Rosh Ha-Shanah* 1:1), although the *Bible itself, in *Exodus 12:2, identifies only the first day of the spring month of Nissan (March–April) as the start of the year. Rabbinic Judaism, however, interprets this particular new year as the commemoration of the beginning of Jewish national *redemption, when the Israelite *tribes dedicated special offerings at the *Tabernacle. The Rabbis further identify a new year of trees, *Tu B'Shevat, or the fifteenth of the Hebrew month of Shevat (January–February), and a new year for tithing cattle on the first of Elul (August–September). The most commonly known Jewish new year is the first of Tishri (September–October), called *Rosh Ha-Shanah, literally the "Head of the Year." Rosh Ha-Shanah is one of the most observed and revered Jewish holidays, signifying spiritual renewal (see HIGH HOLIDAYS).

PAUL STEINBERG

New York City. Since 1654, when it was called New *Amsterdam, Jews have participated in the life of New York City, helping shape its distinctive attributes as the largest city in the *United States. Their presence increased the city's religious diversity and contributed to New York's initial prominence as a seaport and mercantile center and later as a city of light industry. Jews transformed the Lower East Side of Manhattan into a storied immigrant enclave and helped make New York the nation's intellectual, artistic, musical, theatrical, and cultural center. In return New York gave Jews opportunities for social and economic mobility, a free public educational system from kindergarten through college, and a headquarters for diverse national organizations, as well as freedom for political, religious, and ideological expression. Three hundred years after the first twenty-four Jews arrived, roughly two million Jews lived in New York City, more than 25% of its population.

Jews first came to New Amsterdam as refugees, fleeing the Portuguese conquest of *Brazil. Although they were not welcomed, Jews were permitted to live, trade, and practice their religion in private, provided they took care of their needy. The freedoms Jews won, including the right to stand guard and bear arms, endured under *British rule, and Jews integrated into New York's colonial culture and politics, working as merchants, craftsmen, and traders. They established the first *synagogue in North America, Shearith Israel (Remnant of Israel) in 1704, consecrated the first *cemetery, and opened the first Jewish school. By the time of the Revolutionary War (see UNITED STATES: AMERICAN REVOLUTION), community and congregation were largely co-extensive. Jews forged links with fellow New Yorkers as well as with Jews in other colonial cities and across the Atlantic as they struggled to balance commercial success with the requirements of religious observance.

In the wake of the American Revolution, Jewish life was democratized, including expanded opportunities for *women in the synagogue. After 1825, the city's Jewish population more than doubled in each succeeding decade, from 7,000 in 1840, to 40,000 in 1860, to 500,000 in 1900. At the beginning of the twentieth century, New York City, with 40% of American Jews, was the largest Jewish community in the United States; more Jews lived in New York than in any European city. Jewish immigrants from the *German states, *Habsburg Empire, *Ottoman Empire, and *Russian Empire established their own congregations; started alternative forms of Jewish fellowship, such as the fraternal order B'nai B'rith (Sons of the Covenant; see UNITED STATES: FRATERNAL SOCIETIES); introduced intellectual activities, including library associations and a Young Men's Hebrew Association; and developed philanthropic organizations, including a hospital. Jewish intellectuals, rabbis, writers, poets, political activists, and educators – along with garment manufacturers, bankers, printers, and publishers – came as immigrants. As the city entered a period of explosive growth after its 1898 consolidation with Brooklyn, Queens, and Staten Island, American-born Jews also found opportunities in New York.

By 1900, interlocking networks of New York Jews had transformed American Judaism. They experimented with forms of community such as the New York Kehillah (1908–22), types of organizational leadership such as the *American Jewish Committee (1906), women's organizations such as Hadassah (1912; see ORGANIZATIONS: NORTH AMERICA; ORGANIZATIONS, NORTH AMERICA: WOMEN'S), Jewish settlement houses such as the *Educational Alliance, institutions of higher education such as the *Jewish Theological Seminary (reorganized 1902) and *Yeshiva University, immigrant aid societies, *labor unions, socialist *fraternal orders, *Zionist organizations, as well as many varied philanthropies. New York Jews simultaneously built an expansive *Yiddish cultural infrastructure of newspapers (see JOURNALISM, YIDDISH), theaters (see THEATER, YIDDISH), schools, and publications, as well as fraternal organizations, congregations, and charities where Yiddish was the favored language. These immigrant worlds intersected with English-language cultural production in *art, *music, *theater, and publishing and were sustained by such light industries as food, clothing (see FASHION), cigar manufacturing, and construction. Jews occupied all rungs on the socioeconomic ladder from peddler and garment worker to salesman and civil servant to banker and lawyer.

The pace of immigration was halted first by *World War I and then by federal legislation. In the 1920s internal migration took Jews to apartment houses built by Jewish builders in middle-class neighborhoods of Brooklyn, upper Manhattan, and the Bronx. Jews embraced public education as a vehicle of socioeconomic mobility, taking advantage of the city's free educational system. They sought to develop a way of life that retained Jewish dimensions even as they pursued political involvement and economic opportunity in American society.

Conscious of increasing *antisemitism in American life between the world wars, especially restrictions on residence, education, and occupations, New York Jews accepted responsibility to alleviate Jewish suffering abroad. With more than a million Jews in the city and every form of Jewish religious and political expression from communist to Ultra-Orthodox, there was little consensus regarding how best to combat antisemitism, succor European Jews, and aid the small *Zionist community in *Palestine. Multiple organizations developed, each with its own program.

World War II brought refugees from *Nazism to New York City, including *Ḥasidim and other devoutly Orthodox Jews, as well as intellectuals, artists, and photographers from Europe's capital cities, many of whom further enhanced New York's role as producer of elite culture, even as popular culture, including *music, comics (see LITERATURE: GRAPHIC NOVELS), theater, *radio, and publishing continued to flourish. Similarly, the visible presence of diverse Orthodox groups in the city coexisted with liberal forms of *Judaism.

Immigrants helped sustain New York's Jewish working class; only in the 1970s did the city's Jewish occupational profile change dramatically as Jews moved into the middle and upper middle classes, out of manufacturing and into managerial and professional positions, finance, real estate, and education. Simultaneously, New York Jews left the city for the Sunbelt and suburbs, reducing the population to just over 1 million by 1980. The city's ethnic composition changed as well, as the increasing numbers of nonwhite residents made Jews a more prominent percentage of white New Yorkers. Since the 1980s, young Jews have returned to New York City, especially Manhattan and Brooklyn, as its fortunes have improved. Immigrants from the former *Soviet Union and Israelis have provided New York Jews with an ongoing foreign-born population whose presence has rejuvenated declining Jewish neighborhoods.

Sheer size has given New York's Jews tremendous psychological security, unusual for the twentieth century. In the interplay of overlapping communities, Jews discovered their own identities and experimented with alternative voices. Jews participated in New York's famous style – brash, ironic, fast-paced, and humane – and also helped build an urban politics that was socialist in sympathies, liberal in values, and democratic in ethos. For further reading see, M. Rischin, *The Promised City* (1963); D. D. Moore, *At Home in America* (1981); and E. Lederhendler, *New York Jews and the Decline of Urban Ethnicity* (2001).   DEBORAH DASH MOORE

New Zealand. Although several Jewish merchants and prospectors traded temporarily in New Zealand in the 1830s, a permanent Jewish community only formed a decade later with the settlement of Wellington. The community, mostly shopkeepers with familial and business connections with *Australia and *Britain, remained small and tenuous until the discovery of gold on the West Coast in 1864. The gold rush pushed the Jewish population over 1,200 in 1867. *Synagogues were established in the main towns. With the community's close ties with Britain, these and other institutions were modeled along Anglo-Jewish lines. Jews encountered little prejudice, and a number of successful businessmen made the leap from commerce to local politics. For example, Julius Vogel served as prime minister for two terms in the 1870s. New Zealand's geographical isolation ensured that it was almost entirely bypassed during the period of *Eastern European mass migration. The Jewish population only passed 2,500 in the 1930s, boosted by an influx of as many as 1,000 German Jewish refugees. During the postwar period, the community grew slowly to around 4,500 Jews in 1960 and about 7,000 in 2008. Although the size of New Zealand Jewry has been supplemented by immigration – Hungarians after 1956; Russians, Israelis, and South Africans over the last three decades – this influx has been somewhat offset by the departure of significant numbers of Jews for Australia. The bulk of the Jewish population is now clustered in Auckland and Wellington, which are served by day schools, *Reform and *Orthodox congregations, and an array of cultural and social organizations. For further reading, see L. M. Goldman, *The History of Jews in New Zealand* (1958); and S. Levine, *The New Zealand Jewish Community* (1999).   ADAM MENDELSOHN

Newport, Rhode Island. This Atlantic port city was founded in 1639. In 1658 fifteen Jewish families of *Sephardic origin arrived in Newport and established Jeshuat Israel (Salvation of Israel), the second Jewish congregation in what would become the *United States. The community purchased land and consecrated a *cemetery in 1677. Newport is known for the oldest standing *synagogue in North America, built by the preeminent colonial architect Peter Harrison and dedicated in 1763. It is known as the Touro Synagogue, in honor of the community's *Amsterdam-born *cantor, Isaac Touro. In 1790 President George Washington wrote a letter, "To the Hebrew Congregation in Newport," declaring that the United States would "give to bigotry no sanction, to persecution no assistance." The synagogue continues to serve an active Jewish congregation.   KATE FRIEDMAN

Niddah is the term used in Jewish tradition for a menstruating woman and, by extension, for menstruation, menstrual impurity, laws related to menstruation, and the like. In the Hebrew *Bible, *niddah* appears within the wider context of discussions of *purity and impurity. The word derives from a Hebrew root (ndd/ndh) that pertains to "wandering" or "exclusion," suggesting that a menstruating woman or others in a state of impurity should be excluded from the community.

The main biblical sources about menstruation are found in Leviticus 15:19–24, 18:19, and 20:18. In the first text, the menstruating woman and persons and objects with which she comes into contact are, or become, impure. There is no suggestion, however, that intimate relations with a woman during this period of seven days are forbidden. The two other texts formally warn against sexual relations and include the statement that both men and women who transgress the prohibition "shall be cut off from among their people." These texts were discussed and developed in various types of Jewish literature of the *Second Temple period, as well as in the *Mishnah and *Talmud.

The Rabbis read the three biblical texts, as well as the later part of Leviticus 15, which seems to speak about a woman who suffers from a long lasting and abnormal genital discharge, as complementing one another. They resolved at least some of the discrepancies among them by distinguishing between regular menstrual bleeding and protracted bleeding unrelated to menstruation. However, the Rabbis also instituted a major change in the laws of *niddah*, which continues to be observed in traditional communities. This was the addition of seven "clean" or "white" days following the cessation of bleeding before marital intimacy could be resumed (BT *Shabbat* 13a). The Rabbis also made *immersion in a *mikveh (ritual bath) mandatory in all cases at the conclusion of the *niddah* state and before resumption of sexual relations. The punishment of being "cut off from among the people" was generally understood to mean a premature death "by the hands of Heaven."

According to rabbinic tradition, a woman is in a state of *niddah* from the onset of her menstrual bleeding, if not a little earlier, until her ritual immersion. The immersion must be performed seven days after the end of the bleeding. During the Middle Ages it was decreed that the counting of these seven "clean" or "white" days" cannot begin before four or five days had passed from the onset of the bleeding. Thus, a woman who keeps these laws according to rabbinic/*Orthodox tradition will generally immerse in the mikveh around the twelfth day of her cycle. In addition to the basic prohibition of physical contact between a *niddah* and her husband, some domestic activities, considered by the Rabbis as possible triggers of intimacy between husband and wife, were declared forbidden as well. According to some traditions, which at times were sanctioned by the highest authorities, a *niddah* should also avoid entering *synagogues and *cemeteries. Observance of these rules is one of the three ritual obligations specifically incumbent on women – together with *ḥallah*, separating a part of the dough used to make *Sabbath loaves, and *hadlakah,* kindling Sabbath lights.

Although traditional Jewish communities have considered the *niddah* laws to be extremely important, some discomfort with those laws can be detected today, even in the most traditional circles. The many apologetic works explaining the purported benefits of observing these laws and the euphemism for these regulations– *taharat ha-mishpaḥah* (purity of the family) – are just two reflections of this discomfort. This expression, likely coined first in Germany, replaces the traditional expression *hilkhot niddah* (laws of *niddah*), reducing some of its negative connotations. Another example of the reshaping of these laws is the decision of *Conservative Judaism that couples should observe only the seven biblically ordained days of *niddah* separation without the "white days" added during the rabbinic era.

Recent books on this subject include C. Fonrobert, *Menstrual Purity: Rabbinic and Christian Reconstructions of Biblical Gender* (2000); and R. Wasserfall, ed., *Women and Water: Menstruation in Jewish Life and Law* (1999); **see also** BARAITA DE-NIDDAH.   EVYATAR MARIENBERG

Nissan is the first month of the Jewish calendar; it is equivalent to March and/or April on the Gregorian calendar. Its status as the beginning of the Jewish calendar year derives from Exodus 12:1–2. The festival of *Passover (Pesaḥ) takes place from Nissan 15–21, preceded by the Fast of the Firstborn (Nissan 14; see FAST DAYS). *Yom ha-Shoah is commemorated on or around 27 Nissan. **See also** CALENDAR; CALENDAR: MONTHS OF THE YEAR.

Noah: See FLOOD; GENESIS

North Africa. Northern Africa from the west of *Egypt to the Atlantic coast of Morocco, known as *al-Maghrib* in Arabic (referred to as the Maghreb or North Africa), has been an important region of Jewish life since ancient times. The origins of North African Jews are unknown; historical evidence demonstrates a scattering of Jewish communities across the Maghreb in *Roman times. During the late Roman period, the Maghreb was a place of active proselytism and heterodoxy, and there are traditions that there were converts to Judaism among the indigenous Berber (Amazigh, pl. Imazighen) population.

At the time of the Muslim conquest of North Africa in the seventh century CE (see ISLAM AND JUDAISM), Jewish communities were found on the Mediterranean and Atlantic coasts, as well as along the caravan trails of the interior regions north of the Sahara. From the tenth century, if not earlier, a major Jewish community, known for its rabbinical scholars and traders, was established in Sijilmasa, the most important city and center of trade in the southeastern Moroccan pre-Saharan region under an independent Kharijite dynasty. Jews were also found in Berber regions dominated by the Ibadi Islam, a branch of the Kharijite movement; some Jews have continued to live in Ibadite centers – including Jabal Nafusa in Libya, the southern Tunisian island

of Jerba, and the Mzab on the edge of the Sahara in central Algeria – until recent times.

The city of Fez in north central Morocco, founded in the late eighth century and developed as the capital of the Idrisid dynasty, became perhaps the largest Jewish community in the Maghreb in the early Islamic centuries. Jews quickly established themselves in other Muslim cities in what would today be Algeria and Tunisia, such as Tahert, Tlemcen, Kairouan, and Mahdiya. The Maghreb became an integral part of the Jewish world in the Muslim Mediterranean, with Fez and Kairouan developing into major centers of talmudic learning. At the same time *Karaism spread to North Africa, gaining strength in the pre-Saharan region of Ouargla in Algeria; over time it dwindled in importance, surviving only in some remote areas, such as in the High Atlas Mountains.

Two Berber dynasties, the *Amoravids, followed by the *Almohads, emerged in the eleventh and twelfth centuries. They ruled a vast empire including much of the Maghreb and *Spain from their capital of Marrakesh. Forced conversions under the exceptionally intolerant Almohad dynasty led to the disappearance or eclipse of numerous Jewish communities. Some Jews practiced *Judaism secretly, while others, including Moses *Maimonides and his family, went into exile. The Almohad persecutions, however, did not last beyond the first decades of the thirteenth century, and Jewish life again appeared in the Maghreb, under the Hafsids in Tunisia, the Zayyanids in Algeria, and the Marinids in Morocco. Jews lived in large numbers in interior cities such as Marrakesh, and they contributed to the growth of coastal cities such as Tetuan, Algiers, Oran, Gabes, Tunis, and Tripoli.

The mass influx of Jews to North Africa from the *Iberian Peninsula, after the persecutions of 1391 and especially the expulsion of 1492, changed the religious and cultural landscape of the Maghreb. Although the Iberian Peninsula and the Maghreb had originally been part of the same cultural and social network, Spanish Jews (see SPAIN, CHRISTIAN), who had become increasingly hispanicized in the centuries before the expulsion, brought important changes to North African Jewry, forming new communities or infusing the old with new customs and religious practices. In some places, the Spanish Jews, referred to in rabbinical sources as the exiles (*megorashim*), came into conflict with the native *toshavim* and sometimes took over religious or communal leadership. Over the centuries a degree of assimilation took place, especially in Morocco where a new kind of cultural synthesis occurred, with Spanish giving way to Arabic in most places (although Judeo-Spanish/*Ladino lingered in parts of the Mediterranean littoral). In the religious domain, the *Sephardi legal tradition remained strong, and until modern times legal documents still referred to the Castilian *minhag.* Spanish mystics also brought their traditions to North Africa, finding fertile ground throughout the Maghreb, especially in the southern regions of the Sous and Dra'a valleys of Morocco. Almost everywhere in the Maghreb, *mysticism fused with popular practices and customs. In recent centuries mystical elements were manifest in the popular veneration of holy men (Hebrew, *kedoshim* or *tzaddikim*) and *pilgrimages to their shrines on the anniversaries of their deaths (Hebrew, *hillula,* pl. *hillulot).* The Spanish tradition of Hebrew poetry spread, but adopted a Maghrebi style, evident in liturgical poetry (*piyyutim*; see POETRY, LITURGICAL [*PIYYUT*]). With the demise of Jewish life in Spain, the Andalusian traditions became an important component of the cultural identity of North African Jewry in their religious customs and practices, *music, and artistic expression.

The political transformation of the sixteenth-century Maghreb redefined Jewish communities in North Africa. The end of the Berber Marinid dynasty in Morocco gave rise to an Arab sharifian (Arabic *sharif*, pl. *shurafa*; claiming descent from the Prophet Muhammad) dynasty of the Sa'dis, followed by the emergence of the Alawids in the seventeenth century (still ruling in the twenty-first century). Jews were more numerous in Alawid territories than in any other part of the Muslim world, with hundreds of communities in both urban and rural areas. Already in the fifteenth century, with increased population pressures caused by the Iberian immigrants, the Marinids had created a separate quarter for the Jews in their capital city of Fez called the *mellah*. In the sixteenth century, the Sa'dis created a *mellah* for the Jews in their capital Marrakesh, and subsequently the Alawids created new *mellahs*. The term *mellah* came to connote the Moroccan Jewish quarter or even the Jewry of a given locale, whether or not Jews were actually confined to a designated neighborhood. The boundaries of the *mellah* were far more porous than the walls of the *ghettos of early modern Europe; Jews were usually able to circulate throughout the city, travel, and settle in other parts of Morocco.

In the sixteenth century, regions of North Africa east of Morocco came under the orbit of the *Ottoman Empire, which established what became known as the regencies of Tunis, Algiers, and Tripolitania. Although the Ottomans maintained nominal control, the local Turkish military corps had considerable autonomy; in some places they formed local dynasties, such as the Husaynids in Tunisia. Jews were an important component of the capital cities in Ottoman North Africa, and they were also numerous in various provincial towns and villages along the coast and in the interior. They formed part of a vast network of communities linked by traders and scholars who circulated throughout the Mediterranean. Italian Jews (see ITALY) from the Tuscan port of Livorno were important in Ottoman North Africa, especially in Algeria and Tunisia, where they maintained an identity distinctive from local Jews. They were engaged in the buying and selling of goods and captives for the corsairs, as well as the import and export trade, and many Livornese, as in Algiers, occupied leadership positions in the Jewish communities.

North African Jews held a range of economic roles, from large-scale merchants (Arabic, *tujjar*) who were closely connected to the Muslim rulers, to the traders involved in the regional and trans-Saharan caravan trade, to the ubiquitous Jewish peddlers and artisans who plied their wares in rural areas and served as important intermediaries between the town and the countryside. As elsewhere in the Islamic world before the modern period, Jews were considered to be "people of the book" (Arabic, *ahl al-kitab*), belonging to a legitimate yet inferior religion that was protected by the Islamic state. As protected subjects (Arabic, *dhimmis), Jews were allowed to practice their religion in exchange for the payment of an annual poll tax (Arabic, *jizya*) and the acceptance of certain disabilities indicating their inferiority to Muslims.

The Muslim authorities were responsible for ensuring the protection of the Jewish communities, and only in a few cases was this "contract" violated, most notably under the Almohads, and occasionally by local rulers, such as when the Jews in the Algerian Saharan region of Touat were massacred in the fifteenth century. With the disappearance of indigenous Christians from the Maghreb, probably in the Middle Ages, Jews became the only *dhimmis*, in contrast to the Middle East with its large and diverse Christian populations.

The growth of European power in the Maghreb challenged the status of the Jews. Already serving as important middlemen in the North African–European trade, Jews took advantage of new opportunities and were important instruments for European expansion into new markets. Some Jews obtained the protection of the foreign consulates and extraterritorial rights as brokers for foreign firms, based on the system of capitulations between the foreign powers and the Ottoman Empire, or through treaty relations with North African governments. This enabled them to escape the jurisdiction of the Muslim authorities and increased tensions between Muslims and Jews. The appearance of foreign Jewish organizations, especially after the foundation of the *Alliance Israélite Universelle in 1860 and its establishment of a network of schools, also precipitated changes in the Jewish communities of the Maghreb as these organizations pressed for changes in the status of the Jews and the modernization of their educational systems.

Pressured to implement the Tanzimat reforms of the Ottoman Empire, the Husaynid beys of Tunisia lifted the civil disabilities associated with *dhimmi* status in the "fundamental pact" (*'ahd al-aman*) of 1858, followed by the constitution of 1861. The constitution was suspended after a revolt in 1864, but the legal disabilities of the *dhimmi* were not reinstated in the period before the establishment of the French protectorate in 1881. In Libya, when direct Ottoman control after 1835 put an end to the hereditary Qaramanli dynasty, Jews were subject to the Tanzimat reforms that abolished the legal disabilities and special obligations associated with *dhimmi* status. Although Morocco was subject to outside pressures, and a growing number of Moroccan Jews became protégés of foreign powers, the Islamic *dhimma* system was maintained there through the nineteenth century until it fell into disuse after the establishment of the protectorate in 1912.

Colonial rule in the Maghreb hastened the transformation of the North African Jewish communities. From 1830, the French conquest of Algeria and the establishment of direct colonial rule led to the dismantling of the self-governing institutions of the Jewish community and the imposition of restrictions on rabbinic jurisdiction to religious matters that had no connection to French civil or criminal law (see FRANCE: 1789–1939). Algerian Jewry was integrated into the French Jewish *Consistory system by the establishment of three Consistories in Algeria, which were subordinate to the central Consistory in Paris (see FRANCE: CONSISTORIES, 1806-1939). In 1870, Algerian Jews were collectively naturalized as Frenchmen (except for the Jews of the Mzab region of the Algerian Sahara, which was still not firmly under French control) through the Crémieux Decree. In the 1880s, the enfranchisement of Algerian Jews met with considerable opposition from the French settler population amid a mood of growing *antisemitism; this hostility was aggravated during the time of the *Dreyfus Affair when anti-Jewish rioting occurred. While most Jews in Algeria maintained a close connection to their indigenous culture, receiving a modern French education and identification with France led to assimilation to French culture that continued, despite the suspension of the Crémieux Decree under the Vichy regime in *World War II. The mass emigration to France and, to a much lesser extent, to *Israel (about 100,000 out of 140,000 Jews were still in Algeria in 1950), during the revolution and especially from 1962–63 after Algerian independence, was a decisive turning point; the community rapidly dwindled in the 1970s, with the few remaining Jews becoming nearly invisible.

The virtual end to Libyan Jewry came even sooner. Under Italian rule, beginning in 1911, Jewish institutions were also made subservient to the colonial authorities, but the degree of Italianization was uneven depending on location and sectors of the Jewish population. Fascist colonial rule (from 1922) came to an end during World War II with the British occupation beginning in 1943. Arab rioting in Tripoli in November 1945, which spread to surrounding areas, was a major turning point; further rioting after the establishment of the State of Israel in 1948 caused the majority of Libyan Jews to emigrate. Most of the remaining Jews left with the end of the British administration and Libyan independence at the beginning of 1952, and the last few thousand emigrated as Jewish life became extremely difficult after the Six Day War of 1967 (see ISRAEL, STATE OF: WARS (1956–1967) and Mu'ammar Qadhafi's revolution of 1969. The majority of the approximately 36,000 Jews in Libya after World War II immigrated to Israel, and several thousand settled in Italy and other countries.

Unlike Algeria which was ruled by France as a direct colony, Tunisia was established as a French protectorate. This meant that France maintained the traditional institutions of the country, while also modernizing them. The self-governing institutions of the Jewish community continued to function in theory, but in reality efforts were made to reduce the authority of the rabbinical *courts and local Jewish leadership, while the Alliance Israélite Universelle accelerated its efforts to encourage Jewish identification with French culture. Although a significant number of Jews obtained French citizenship, there was no equivalent to the Crémieux Decree in Tunisia. Yet even without citizenship for all, Tunisian Jewry's political and social status was transformed, and new generations of Tunisian Jews were greatly influenced by French secular culture and education. When Tunisia achieved independence in 1956, there were about 105,000 thousand Jews in the country. By the 1960s, the majority had left for France or Israel. However, several hundred still remained at the beginning of the twenty-first century, primarily in Jerba and Tunis.

Morocco had the largest Jewish population of any country in the modern Islamic world, about 280,000 before the era of mass emigration, and it was one of the last areas subjected to foreign occupation. A protectorate was established in Morocco in 1912 (although the conquest of the country was completed only in the 1930s). The French claimed most of the territory, Spain ruled several regions in the north, and Tangier became an international zone. Rather than abolishing the Alawid dynasty, the colonial authorities

preserved the sharifian government as a symbolic entity, using the sultan to issue *dahirs* and legitimize foreign rule. Jews' *dhimmi* status was eliminated de facto (but never formally abolished), because they were no longer subject to the Islamic *shari'a* courts, but their status was left poorly formulated with no clear notion of nationality. Jewish internal autonomy, guaranteed to the *dhimmi* by the Islamic state, was also undermined by reducing the judicial autonomy of Jewish courts and placing the organizations of the Jewish community under the control and surveillance of the colonial regime. The Alliance Israélite Universelle network of schools in Morocco was greatly expanded during the colonial period and became the quasi-official Jewish educational system for Moroccan Jewry, with the approval of the protectorate authorities. Modernization and the growth of secular culture made inroads in traditional Jewish life, as did a massive process of urbanization, with the modern city of Casablanca growing to become the largest community in Morocco. However, modern trends coexisted with continued adherence to traditional Jewish religious practice. With the growth of the anticolonial movement in the 1950s and the uncertainties of the future in an independent state, the era of mass emigration began, especially in 1955, the year before Morocco's independence in 1956. After independence, *Zionism was banned, and emigration was organized clandestinely for several years. Although many Jews adjusted to life in independent Morocco, emigration continued in a steady stream over the next few decades. At the beginning of the twenty-first century, only a few thousand Jews remain. A far larger number of Moroccan Jews and their descendants live in Israel, France, North America, and in smaller numbers on other continents.

For further reading, see J. Gerber, *Jewish Society in Fez, 1450–1700: Studies in Communal and Economic Life* (1980); H. E. Goldberg, *Jewish Life in Muslim Libya: Rivals and Relatives* (1990); E. Gottreich, *The Mellah of Marrakesh: Jewish and Muslim Space in Morocco's Red City* (2007); H. Z. Hirschberg, *A History of the Jews in North Africa*, 2 vols. (1974–81); M. M. Laskier, *North African Jewry in the Twentieth Century: The Jews of Morocco, Tunisia and Algeria* (1994); D. J. Schroeter, *The Sultan's Jew: Morocco and the Sephardi World* (2002); idem, "Jewish Communities of Morocco: History and Identity," in *Morocco: Jews and Art in a Muslim Land*, ed. V. B. Mann (2000), 25–54; R. S. Simon, M. M. Laskier, and S. Reguer, eds., *The Jews of the Middle East and North Africa in Modern Times* (1993); N. A. Stillman, *The Jews of Arab Lands: A History and Source Book* (1979); and H. Zafrani, *Two Thousand Years of Jewish Life in Morocco* (2005). **Map 5**   DANIEL J. SCHROETER

Numbers, Book of, known in Hebrew as *běmidbar*, "in (the) wilderness (of)" (from the initial verse of the book), is the fourth book of the *Pentateuch. The book is also known as "the fifth of those who were counted" in rabbinic literature. The expression refers to Numbers as the book of the five books of the *Torah that refers to the censuses of Israel in the wilderness. The name Numbers is derived from the Greek title of the book, *Arithmoi* ("numbers"). The book narrates Israel's departure from Mount Sinai, its journey through the wilderness, and its arrival in the land of *Moab across the Jordan River from the Land of *Israel.

The book of Numbers is well integrated into the larger literary structure of the *Pentateuch. Indeed, the initial unit of the book, Numbers 1–2, concludes the narrative block concerning the *revelation of the Torah at Mount Sinai that began at Exodus 19. This final segment provides an account of Israel's census immediately before its departure from Sinai. The literary structure of Numbers 3–36 is governed by travel formulas that trace Israel's journey from slavery in *Egypt, through the wilderness, and on to *Moab and the Jordan River, prior to entering the promised land of Israel. The narrative emphasizes tensions in the relationship between *God and the people that require the establishment of the tribe of Levi as *priests who will serve as holy intermediaries between God and Israel.

Numbers 3–36 includes six major literary units defined by the stages of Israel's journey from Mount Sinai to Moab. Numbers 3:1–10:10 focuses on the sanctification of Israel under the leadership of the Levites; it is the Levites who will purify the people and the *Tabernacle in preparation for the journey through the wilderness. Numbers 10:11–19:22 narrates the journey from Sinai to the wilderness of Paran, including the organization of the tribes around the Tabernacle. During the journey, the people complain against God and Moses for various reasons, such as lack of food, questions of leadership, and fear of the *Canaanites, and God decrees that the wilderness generation will die without entering the Land of Israel. The tribe of Levi is selected to serve as priests, and the line of *Aaron is chosen to serve as the chief priests (*kohanim*) of Israel.

Numbers 20:1–20 recounts the journey from Paran to the wilderness of Zin or Kadesh; there, *Moses and Aaron are condemned for failing to sanctify God. Numbers 20:22–21:3 describes the trip from Zin/Kadesh to Mt. Hor where Aaron dies. In Numbers 21:4–35 the Israelites journey from Mt. Hor to Moab; these chapters include the defeat of Sihon and Og who tried to oppose Israel. Numbers 22–36 recounts Israel's arrival in Moab; these chapters include *Balaam's blessing of Israel, the grant of eternal priesthood to Phineas ben Elazar ben Aaron (ancestor of the Zadokite priestly line in *Jerusalem), a new census of the people, the selection of *Joshua to succeed Moses as leader of the Israelites, and questions concerning the distribution of the Land of Israel among the *Israelite tribes.

Modern biblical scholarship generally views Numbers as a product of the post-exilic Priestly stratum or source of the Pentateuch, although it includes much earlier material from the northern Israelite E stratum and the southern Judean J stratum (see BIBLE: MODERN SCHOLARSHIP).

For further discussion, see N. S. Fox, "Numbers," in *The Jewish Study Bible*, ed. A. Berlin and M. Brettler (2003); J. Milgrom, *Numbers: The Jewish Publication Society Torah Commentary* (1990); and B. A. Levine, *Numbers*, 2 vols. (1993; 2000).
                                                      MARVIN A. SWEENEY

Numerology (*Gematria*). As in Greek and Arabic (and partially in Latin), the letters of the Hebrew alphabet also represent numbers. (The first nine letters of the alphabet represent the numbers one through nine; the next ten represent the numbers ten through one hundred; and the final three letters represent two hundred, three hundred, and four hundred.) The concept of separate signs for numbers reached Hebrew only in the nineteenth century, several centuries after it was accepted in European languages. Jewish scholars, since late antiquity, have used this duality of the

meaning of the letters as a tool, mostly for homiletical and exegetical purposes. *Gematria*, the Hebrew term used to designate this practice, is derived from Greek, indicating *Hellenistic influence. The earliest Hebrew literary *gematria* is found in a Greek Christian text from the late first century CE. It is the reference to the "number of the Beast, 666," in the *New Testament book of Revelations: 666 is the numerical value of the Hebrew letters indicating the name, Nero Caesar (Rev 13:18). In the *Talmud and *Midrash only a few examples of *gematria* appear; it seems that the Rabbis avoided using it for *halakhic (legal) purposes, thus denying it any normative authority.

The concept of numerological analysis is often attributed to the ancient work of cosmology and cosmogony, the *Sefer Yetzirah* (Book of Creation), whose date of composition is unknown (probably third or fourth century CE). However, there is no basis for this attribution, because there is no use of *gematria* in that work. *Sefer Yetzirah* does attribute the process of creation to the power of the twenty-two letters of the alphabet and the ten *sefirot belimah*, a term that in the Middle Ages was explained as referring to the first ten numbers. However, *Sefer Yetzirah* itself does not say this and there is no further use of numerology in the book.

In medieval times the use of *gematria* expanded in Hebrew exegetical writings, in homiletical works, and especially in the writings of esoterics and mystics (see KABBALAH). The first systematic presentation of this system is found in the *Sefer ha-Ḥokhmah* (The Book of Wisdom) of Eleazar ben Judah of Worms, written in 1217. Rabbi Eleazar wrote a list of the seventy-three "gates of wisdom" (that number being the *gematria* of the word *ḥokhmah*, "wisdom"), a methodological directory indicating how every verse in the *Bible should be interpreted. About twenty of these "gates" are numerical in nature, focusing on the number of words in the verse, the number of letters, the number of times the name of *God is mentioned, the number of times a particular letter is used, and other numerical features, including *gematria* itself. This work constituted a formal acceptance of numerical values as normative methodologies for discovering and interpreting the secret meanings of biblical texts. Judah ben Samuel the Pious of Regensburg, the teacher of Rabbi Eleazar, used these methods to demonstrate the meaning of the *prayer book (see MIDDLE AGES; ḤASIDEI ASHKENAZ). He believed that there was an underlying numerical harmony designed by God that was reflected in all sacred texts as well as in universal phenomena. Several decades later the Spanish mystic Abraham *Abulafia developed a similar system, using *gematria* as a central tool in his writings and attributing its authority to the *Sefer Yetzirah*.

Many mystics in the Middle Ages and modern times used *gematria* in their exegetical speculations, although many others did not. In the first work of the *Kabbalah, the *Bahir, written at the end of the twelfth century, there is only occasional, nonsystematic use of *gematria*, and it is used only seldom in the vast, colorful, and dynamic homiletical discussions of the *Zohar. Ḥayyim Vital, who preserved the teachings of Isaac *Luria, the great kabbalist of sixteenth-century *Safed, made only marginal use of this method (see KABBALAH, LURIANIC). Other kabbalists, however, used it abundantly.

When kabbalistic works became known in Christian Europe, Christian Kabbalists, starting with the school of Pico della Mirandola in Florence at the end of the fifteenth century, and continuing in Johannes Reuchlin's *De arte kabbalistica* (1517), found *gematria* an intriguing new concept; they sometimes identified it with the Kabbalah as a whole (see CHRISTIAN HEBRAISM). This was the beginning of the tendency to view Jewish mysticism as based on numerology, a concept that is not supported by the characteristics of the Hebrew texts themselves.   JOSEPH DAN

Nursing: United States. Jewish precepts of "visiting the sick" and "performing acts of lovingkindness" may refer to ancient traditions of nursing. The modern profession of nursing developed in the mid-nineteenth century, based on the activity of volunteer caregivers, primarily women, in time of war. The professionalization of nursing and its acceptance as a "respectable" career for women are often attributed to the work done by Florence Nightingale during the Crimean War. In the *United States, the *Civil War was the central event in the development of the profession.

As part of their traditional communal responsibilities, Jewish women in nineteenth-century America created benevolent societies to care for the sick in cities and towns where they lived. During the Civil War, Jewish women, like their non-Jewish counterparts, voluntarily cared for sick and wounded soldiers. Most notable among these Jewish volunteer "nurses" were Phoebe Yates Pember (1861–1920), who served as the Matron of the Chimborazo Hospital in Richmond, Virginia, and Rosanna (Rosana) Osterman (1809–1866), who turned her home in Galveston, Texas, into a hospital, where she cared for the wounded of both the Confederate and Union fighting forces.

The remainder of the nineteenth century witnessed a rapid expansion and consolidation in the advancement of the nursing profession in the United States. By the early 1900s, the credibility of nursing had been established, hospitals were creating nursing schools, and knowledgeable,

trained nurses were very much in demand. Many women who were seeking a role in society beyond the home and family were attracted to this profession. Articles appeared in the Jewish press urging young Jewish immigrant women to take up nursing as a career; Jewish women who entered the profession often went into Jewish hospital training schools.

Jewish women were also active in establishing nursing programs in the community. Foremost among them was Lillian *Wald (1867–1940), who studied at the New York Hospital School of Nursing. With the support of Jewish philanthropists, notably Jacob Schiff, she set up the Henry Street Settlement and the Visiting Nurses of Henry Street. Wald coined the term "public health nursing"; her district nursing scheme inspired Henrietta *Szold, who recruited two American Jewish nurses, Rose Kaplan (1867–1917) and Rae Landy (1885–1952), to go to *Palestine in 1913 and set up a similar program. From this modest project grew the vast network of health services that continue to be sponsored by Hadassah, the *Zionist women's organization that Szold founded (see ORGANIZATIONS, WOMEN'S: NORTH AMERICA).

Throughout the twentieth century, Jewish nurses, including such notables as Margaret Arnstein (1904 -1972), Naomi Deutsch (1890–1983), Myra Levine (1920–1996), Blanche Pfefferkorn (1884-1961), and Mathilda Scheuer (1890–1974), have played a leading role nationally and internationally in the advancement of nursing education, public health nursing, and nursing administration. The profession of nursing in America has also continued to grow as an academic discipline, firmly placed within the nation's system of higher education. Early in the twenty-first century, nursing is experiencing a shortage of practitioners. Jewish women and men are drawn to this profession, which offers opportunities for fulfilling and rewarding careers in an area of endeavor that reflects and fulfills ancient Judaic benevolent precepts (**see also MEDICINE**).   EVELYN ROSE BENSON

O

Obadiah is the fourth book of the Minor or Twelve *Prophets; it consists of only twenty-one verses. This oracle against *Edom, the nation living southeast of *Judah, excoriates the Edomites for their glee when *Jerusalem was destroyed, predicts their ruin, and looks forward to a day when the Judean and Israelite exiles will return to reclaim lands taken away from them by Edomites and others. Oracles against other nations occur frequently in prophetic literature (see, e.g., Isa 14–23; Jer 46–51; Ezek 25–32), and oracles against Edom are especially common (Jer 49:7–22; Ezek 25:12–14; Isa 34).

Obadiah was likely written shortly after the *Babylonians destroyed the *Temple in 586 BCE. It shares with *Lamentations 4:21–22, *Psalm 137:7, and other exilic and post-exilic texts the view that the Edomites somehow abetted the Babylonians or joyfully watched Judah's discomfiture; verses 17–19 may imply that the Edomites occupied Judean territory after the Babylonian conquest. It is not clear to what extent these texts reflect genuine Edomite collusion against Judah and to what extent they are expressions of long-standing enmity between the nations. Already in the pre-exilic era Edomites had begun to settle in the Negev, to the west of their traditional territory, although much of this settlement in Judean territory may have been relatively peaceful. Obadiah verses 1–5 closely resemble *Jeremiah 49:9 and 49:14–16, probably because both of these texts use an older oracle against Edom. Rabbinic tradition identifies the author of this book with the character Obadiah in 1 Kings 18, who protected prophets of God from Queen Jezebel (BT *Sanhedrin* 39b). This would locate the author of this book in the ninth-century-BCE northern kingdom of Israel. In fact, the book reflects the fall of the southern kingdom in the late sixth century.

BENJAMIN D. SOMMER

Omer. The word *omer* refers to a measured offering of barley given on the second day of *Passover at the time of the *Temple. In that era, this offering was necessary before the grain from the new crop could be used. From the day that this offering was given, seven weeks were counted, at which point the holiday of *Shavuot was celebrated. In the second century CE, this period of time became a time of mourning. Tradition relates this tradition to the death by plague of 24,000 students who had been taught by Rabbi *Akiva. Some believe that this is a veiled reference to the Hadrianic persecutions that took a terrible toll on the Jews between 135 and 138 CE after the Second *Jewish War against *Rome. The *omer* period is forty-nine days long, of which thirty-three days are treated as days of semi-mourning. Various customs exist as to which thirty-three days should be commemorated in this way. On Lag B'Omer, the thirty-third day of the *omer* period, all the rules of mourning are lifted, and joyous events, such as weddings, can take place.

BARRY FREUNDEL

Omer, Counting of the (*sefirat ha-omer*). The *omer* is counted beginning on the second night of *Passover through the night before *Shavuot. This practice originates in the barley sacrifice offered in the *Temple on the second day of Passover (Lev 23:15–16). The counting is done after nightfall each day, and the requirement is to count both the days and the weeks. For example, one would say, "Today is the twenty-fifth day, which is three weeks and four days in the *omer*." A blessing is recited before counting, and the count is done standing. However, if one forgets to count at night, one counts during the day without a blessing. If one misses an entire day, the custom is to continue counting throughout the *omer* period, but without a blessing.

BARRY FREUNDEL

Oral Torah: See TORAH

Ordination: See RABBINIC ORDINATION; RABBINIC ORDINATION OF WOMEN

Organizations: North America. The organizational structure of the American Jewish community is informed by the singular pluralistic nature of American society, a model unique in Jewish history, in which multiple organizational "voices" express a range of views and ideological interests, even as they achieve consensus on core issues and concerns. The organizing principle of American Jewish communal structure is federalism: Institutions voluntarily and contractually link themselves to each other, thereby creating partnerships that benefit the Jewish community.

The beginning of an organized American Jewish community can be dated to 1859 with the establishment of the Board of Delegates of American Israelites. However, communal efforts at large-scale organization, in response to pressing national and local communal needs, developed as a result of the massive immigration from *Eastern Europe from 1880–1920. The earliest organizational response, the federation (see later discussion), addressed the needs of funding local social services. The *Boston Federation of Jewish Charities (1895) paved the way, and by the turn of the century federations of Jewish organizations representing different constituencies had been established in a number of communities. Historically important as well was B'nai B'rith, an international Jewish fraternal group with a substantial membership, founded in the United States in 1843 (see UNITED STATES: FRATERNAL SOCIETIES).

Contemporary American Jewish organizational structure is expressed, locally and nationally, in five arenas of activity: social services, religion, public affairs and community relations, Israel and other international concerns, and education and culture. In the social service sphere, the local federation is the key agency, organized by contractual agreement with its member social service agencies for the purposes of joint fundraising and allocations. Over the years federations have become responsible as well for communal and social planning and for coordination of social services within the community. The federations are organized under an umbrella or "roof" agency, the United Jewish Communities (UJC) of North America, successor to the highly effective Council of Jewish Federations and the United Jewish Appeal, which was a fundraising arm on behalf of *Israel. UJC represents 155 federations and more than 400 independent Jewish communities across North America.

Denominational groupings in American Jewish religious life include the Orthodox, Conservative, Reform, and Reconstructionist movements (see entries under JUDAISM), each with its own rabbinical association and congregational body (which also serves as the public affairs arm for its movement). The organizational structures for the various movements include the Rabbinical Council of America and the Union of Orthodox Jewish Congregations of America for the mainstream Orthodox community; the Rabbinical Assembly and the United Synagogue of Conservative Judaism; the Central Conference of American Rabbis and the Union for Reform Judaism (formerly the Union of American Hebrew Congregations, founded in 1873 as the first synagogue body in America); and the Reconstructionist Rabbinical Association and the Jewish Reconstructionist Federation.

The community relations sphere plays out on both the local and national levels. Eleven national organizations, each operating from a distinctive ideological base, are active in this arena. The three "defense" agencies – the American Jewish Committee (founded in 1906), the Anti-Defamation League (founded in 1913 by B'nai B'rith), and the American Jewish Congress (founded in 1918) – are the most visible. On the local level, more than a hundred Jewish community relations councils (JCRCs) monitor community activity and provide an active grassroots presence for advocacy on national issues.

Advocacy on behalf of Israel is a subset of the community relations sphere of activity, with the national agencies and the JCRCs doing the work, together with a highly effective lobbying group, the American Israel Public Affairs Committee (AIPAC), and the Conference of Presidents of Major American Jewish Organizations, which has the mandate of being a spokesperson to the administration on behalf of the American Jewish community on matters related to Israel. *Zionist organizations do not have the impact they once had, with the exception of Hadassah, the women's organization with a substantial grassroots membership and a multi-issue agenda (see ORGANIZATIONS, WOMEN'S: NORTH AMERICA; SZOLD, HENRIETTA).

Finally, *education and culture are relative newcomers to the Jewish organizational scene, with national agencies in each arena, such as the Jewish Educational Service of North America (JESNA), coming into being only over the last half-century or so. With the growing recognition since 1968 of the importance of Jewish education, and especially since 1990, emerging agencies in this arena have a significant communal voice. In recent decades, new organizations as well have appeared in all the spheres of activity. Special mention ought to be made of the impact of Jewish family foundations, which have made "donor-directed" giving a powerful force in American Jewish life.

For further reading, see J. A. Chanes, *A Primer on the American Jewish Community* (3rd ed., 2008); idem, "Who Does What? Jewish Advocacy and Jewish Interest," in *Jews in American Politics*, ed. L. S. Maisel and I. N. Forman (2004); and N. Linzer, J. A. Chanes, and D. Schnall, eds., *A Portrait of the American Jewish Community* (1998). Also useful is D. J. Elazar, *Community and Polity: The Organizational Dynamics of the American Jewish Community* (rev. ed., 1995); **see also UNITED STATES: FRATERNAL SOCIETIES; UNITED STATES: LABOR MOVEMENT; and ORGANIZATIONS, WOMEN'S: NORTH AMERICA.** JEROME A. CHANES

Organizations, Women's: North America. Jewish women have played significant roles in a multitude of causes, including the labor (see UNITED STATES: LABOR MOVEMENT), feminist (see JUDAISM: FEMINISM), and socialist movements. They have also banded together to meet various needs in the Jewish community. Most modern Jewish women's organizations trace their origins to small groups dedicated to service, philanthropic, and religious work. Many of these organizations began as auxiliaries to existing men's groups that then branched off to pursue their own agendas and to control the expenditure of their often prodigious fundraising. Despite varied interests and multiple ways of identifying as Jewish, these groups share a commitment to the continuation of Jewish life, the promotion of Jewish education, and the provision of social services and relief to Jewish communities locally and around the world, as well as a belief in women's potential to contribute significantly to public life.

Jewish women's organizations in the United States began with Rebecca *Gratz (1781–1869), a *Philadelphia native who established models and agendas that would be followed by the many groups that succeeded her. Concerned about evangelical overtones in other charities, Gratz created the Female Hebrew Benevolent Association in 1819. In 1838 she founded the first Hebrew Sunday School, serving both male and female students. By mid-century she had opened the Jewish Foster Home; it eventually became the Association for Jewish Children in Philadelphia.

A great increase in Jewish women's organizational activity occurred with the simultaneous influx of immigrants from *Eastern Europe and the rise of the "club women movement" in the late nineteenth century. By this time both middle-class Protestants and Jews had subscribed to the notion of "separate spheres," associating women with domestic and child-rearing responsibilities and men with the realms of business and politics. Women in both groups were perceived to be more closely associated with religion (although not religious leadership) than their male counterparts. *Sisterhoods of Personal Service, which were generally associated with Reform *synagogues, played a major role in these years. Formed throughout the nation, these organizations participated in immigrant aid and established settlement houses and religious schools. The National Federation of Temple Sisterhoods was formed in 1913 to coordinate their efforts. (In 1993 the group became Women of Reform Judaism-The Federation of Temple Sisterhoods.) In 1918 the Women's League for Conservative Judaism was founded. Both organizations sought to promote religious observance in the home as well as the synagogue; they assisted synagogue functioning and supported programs of Jewish education (see SYNAGOGUE SISTERHOODS).

The *National Council of Jewish Women was founded in 1893. This group, which emerged from the Parliament of Religions of the *Chicago World's Fair and maintained close ties to non-Jewish club women, sought to promote Jewish and American values. It consistently expanded its programming over the years, with notable attention paid to Jewish *education, immigrant aid and education, services to the blind, and Jews living in rural areas. Although initially reluctant to take stands on such then-controversial issues as *Zionism and women's suffrage, in the post–*World War II era the organization became actively involved in politics as a member of the Women's Joint Congressional Committee and, in the 1970s, as an advocate for the Equal Rights Amendment and as a supporter of *Israel.

Another organization established in these years was B'nai B'rith Women (1897), which started as an auxiliary of the men's organization. Although the men withheld formal recognition of these auxiliaries until 1953, they functioned independently, providing social outlets as well as philanthropic and political activism. The Young Women's Hebrew Association (YWHA) followed a similar trajectory, emerging from the Young Men's Hebrew Association (YMHA) in 1902. It continued the YMHA's interest in social and cultural endeavors, but had a stronger focus on Judaism than the men's group. Over time the YWHA expanded its services, becoming a model for the Jewish *Community Center movement later in the twentieth century (see SPORTS, UNITED STATES: WOMEN; UNITED STATES: FRATERNAL SOCIETIES).

Not all Jewish organizations of the period were associated with the middle class. Many working-class Jews were active in such labor groups as the *International Ladies Garment Workers Union and the *Workmen's Circle but few working-class groups composed solely of women emerged. However, Women's American ORT was one such organization. Founded in Russia in 1880, ORT (Organization for Rehabilitation through Training) provided vocational training for Jews and supported *agricultural colonies. Internationalized in 1921, the group gained the support of the international labor movement. Women's American ORT was founded in 1927; it underwrote vocational education in Eastern Europe and provided aid to refugees and *displaced persons in the World War II era. In recent decades, it has worked with ORT International to expand educational offerings in Israel, *Latin America, and the former *Soviet Union.

The Emma Lazarus Federation of Jewish Women's Clubs was founded in 1944 as the women's division of the Jewish People's Fraternal Order of the International Workers Order. This group provided relief to victims of World War II and in the post-war years maintained a commitment to progressive values such as combating *antisemitism and racism, even as many members distanced themselves from the Communist Party. Working-class women were also active in the Zionist movement. *Pioneer Women, known today as Na'amat, was founded in 1925 to support pioneer women in *Palestine. The organization placed great emphasis on *Yiddish and immigrant identity in its early years, although this identification changed over time as Jewish immigration to the United States from Eastern Europe declined. Na'amat has maintained an active role in Israel, working closely with the Labor Zionist movement (see ZIONISM).

Other Zionist women's organizations include *Mizrachi (AMIT), founded in 1925 as the Mizrachi Women's Organization of America. This organization was directed at *Orthodox Jewish women who supported Zionism, and it emerged from auxiliaries to male Mizrachi groups. Mizrachi women's activism has centered on Israel, including operating religious vocational schools for girls. The group is also known for assisting with the waves of immigration to Israel from the "Teheran children" of the 1940s to more recent arrivals.

The largest Jewish women's organization, in or outside the realm of Zionism, is Hadassah, the Women's Zionist Organization of America. Founded in 1912 by Henrietta *Szold (1860–1945), Hadassah quickly grew to become one of the major Jewish women's organizations in the United States. Hadassah engages in a wide range of activities at home and abroad, including establishing the American Zionist Medical Unit during World War I, providing social services and medical care in Palestine (see NURSING: UNITED STATES), promoting Jewish and Zionist education in the United States, playing a major role in the Youth Aliyah from Germany in the 1930s (see HOLOCAUST RESCUE), and opening the Hadassah Medical Center at Ein Kerem in *Jerusalem in 1952.

On women's organizations in Europe during this period, see BRITAIN; WOMEN, MODERN: CENTRAL EUROPE; WOMEN, MODERN: EASTERN EUROPE.

For additional information, see relevant entries in P. E. Hyman and D. D. Moore, eds., *Jewish Women in America* (1998); P. E. Hyman and D. Ofer, eds., *Jewish Women: A Comprehensive Historical Encyclopedia*, CD-ROM (2007); S. Reinharz and M. A. Raider, eds., *Jewish Women and the Zionist Enterprise* (2004); F. Rogow, *Gone to Another Meeting: The National Council of Jewish Women, 1893–1993* (1993); and E. B. Simmons, *Hadassah and the Zionist Project* (2006).

MARY MCCUNE

Ottoman Empire. The Ottoman Empire was founded by Osman I (d. 1324), who united the provinces of Turkish Anatolia. In the centuries to come, the empire expanded into the European *Balkans and conquered the remaining territories of the Christian *Byzantine Empire, including Constantinople, which fell in 1453. The Ottoman Empire was a reliable and welcoming haven for Jews throughout its history. Jews were a privileged minority who made important contributions to the development and expansion of the economy and administration, as well as to Ottoman science, *medicine, technology, culture, and entertainment. They experienced unprecedented levels of individual and religious freedom and long periods of prosperity and cultural efflorescence. The Ottoman Jews also knew periods of spiritual and material impoverishment, reflecting the general decline of Ottoman society, but they were never singled out for religious persecution or oppression.

OTTOMAN–JEWISH SYMBIOSIS: As Ottoman power increased in Anatolia and the Balkans, communities of Greek-speaking Jews, known as *Romaniotes, came under their control. The Jews were mostly urban, engaged in *commerce, crafts, and the professions. By contrast, the Ottoman Turks were primarily warriors, peasants, and nomadic herdsmen. Because the Turkish urban classes were small and Jews were regarded as politically more reliable than the local Christians, the Ottomans preferred to repopulate newly conquered towns with Jewish settlers. They encouraged Jews to settle in Bursa, their first important capital (since 1326), with the expectation that Jews would help in the city's reconstruction and economic development. Similarly, in 1361, when the Ottomans captured Adrianople (Edirne, in Turkish) and subsequently designated it as their new capital, they again settled considerable numbers of Jews in the city. Jewish settlers included not only local Romaniotes but also Jewish immigrants from abroad, mainly from *Hungary, *France, *Italy, and *Sicily.

A similar development, but on a far larger scale, took place after the 1453 conquest of Constantinople (Istanbul) and its transformation into the new Ottoman capital. Although Turks, Greeks, Armenians, and Slavs were also settled there to repopulate the nearly desolate city, no group was concentrated to a greater extent than the Jews, who were relocated near Istanbul's port, the hub of the city's economic activity. Jews in the Ottoman Empire as a whole constituted a small fraction of the entire population, but in Istanbul made up more than 10% of the residents and were the third largest group after Turks and Greeks.

Jews engaged in a wide range of crafts and professions, but their greatest contribution was developing Istanbul's domestic and international trade. By 1480, they dominated the city's commercial life, playing a major role in the operation and administration of the customhouses and the docks and forming partnerships to bid for tax-farming contracts and government monopolies. Jews were also heavily engaged in the minting of coins and in their distribution.

OTTOMAN EXPANSION AND JEWISH IMMIGRATION: Between 1450 and 1600, the Ottoman state was transformed into a world power. By the end of the sixteenth century, the sultans' domain extended from *Hungary and Transylvania in the north to *Yemen in the south, and from the borders of Morocco (see NORTH AFRICA) in the west to the *Iranian plateau in the east. The administration of such a vast empire created complex needs, as well as opportunities. The newly conquered territories required legions of bureaucrats and entrepreneurs to govern and administer them and to exploit their resources to meet the ever-increasing financial needs of the state. Additionally, by virtue of its new position and power, the Ottoman Empire played a leading role in international affairs and the world economy.

Ottoman expansion coincided with a period of severe persecution of Jews in Europe and their expulsions from *England (1290), most of *France (1306 and 1394), Austria (1421), and later from many of the *German lands; many *Ashkenazim resettled in the Ottoman Empire. In 1467, a new wave of massacres and attacks on Jews and *conversos was initiated in *Spain, culminating in the establishment of the *Inquisition in 1480. This resulted in the first significant immigration of Iberian Jews, *Sephardim, to the Ottoman Empire. The worst period of Jewish suffering occurred in the period 1492–1511, when Jews were expelled not only from *Spain (1492) and *Portugal (1497) but also from *Sicily and Savoy (1492), Navarre and Provence (1498), Marseilles (1507), the kingdom of Naples (1510–11), and other places. The diminishing possibilities for refuge in Europe and the establishment of successful patterns of immigration and settlement in the Ottoman Empire made it a preferred destination for increasing waves of Jewish refugees; these waves numbered in the tens of thousands and continued through the sixteenth and into the seventeenth century.

The Ottomans, who were pleased to provide the Jewish refugees with a safe haven, took an active role in directing Jewish immigrants to areas where they were most needed by offering incentives, such as exemptions from certain taxes. Although reliable figures are not available, it is likely that more Jews lived in the Ottoman Empire by 1600, than in any other state in the world. The European Jews, especially the *Sephardim, possessed the knowledge, experience, and skills suited to meet the new needs of the rising Ottoman Empire. Like the Romaniotes, many of the Iberian Jews had extensive expertise in banking, *commerce, tax farming, management of ports and customhouses, and the purveying of large quantities of foodstuffs, clothing, and arms for the government. Additionally, the Sephardim had also been prominent in international *banking and business. Ironically, their expulsion and dispersal across the Mediterranean lands, the Atlantic seaboard, and the New World presented them with opportunities to forge widely flung commercial and banking networks and propelled some to new heights of wealth and fortune. Within a short time of their arrival in the Ottoman Empire, European Jews were found in every major center of international trade. Salonika, which had a Jewish majority, was regarded, because of the activities of its Jewish merchants, as the most important commercial city in the eastern Mediterranean (see GREECE).

In addition to their entrepreneurial and managerial skills, European Jews brought knowledge of European sciences and *medicine. They introduced *printing and a range of new technologies and methods of production, which the Ottomans used in the exploitation of mineral resources and the manufacture of textiles, arms, munitions, and other products. Jewish entrepreneurs and laborers turned Salonika, Istanbul, and *Safed into major centers of textile production. Jews from Salonika managed the exploitation of the silver mines in Sidrekapsi, and in Rhodes they were engaged in mining sulfur. As administrators of ports and customhouses, Jews played an important role in the development of the Danube basin, an area of great economic and military importance. Jews were also instrumental in the revitalization and reorganization of the economies of Ottoman Syria, *Iraq, *Egypt, and *North Africa. In Egypt, for example, a Sephardic Jew, Abraham Castro, was appointed in 1520 to administer the local mint.

Many individual Jews rose to politically influential positions as advisors to ministers and governors, and even to the sultans themselves. The quickest paths to political prominence were careers in medicine or banking. One of the best-known and most influential Ottoman Jewish physicians was Moses Hamon (ca. l490–ca. 1554), who served as personal physician to the sultans Selim I (ruled 1512–20) and Suleiman the Magnificent (1520–1566). Moses used his political influence to promote Jewish interests, prevailing on Suleiman the Magnificent to issue an order protecting Jews against *ritual murder accusations (blood libels). He also interceded with the sultan to exert pressure on *Venice to permit the departure of the *Mendes-Nasi family, a renowned Marrano family, to safe haven in the Ottoman Empire. Moses was a patron of Jewish learning and scholarship who maintained a major *yeshivah* headed by the renowned scholar, Rabbi Joseph Taitazak.

COMMUNITY LIFE: Ottoman Jewry was very diverse, comprising several different ethnic groups, each with its own spoken language, culture, and religious customs and traditions. In the Balkans and Anatolia, the native, Greek-speaking Romaniotes and the immigrant, Spanish-speaking Sephardim were the dominant groups in the sixteenth century. Over time, most of the Romaniotes were assimilated into Sephardic culture. In the *Arabic-speaking Ottoman provinces of the Middle East and North Africa, most Jews spoke Arabic. In addition, numerous smaller groups of Ashkenazi and Italian Jews, who were spread across the empire, maintained their distinctive culture and organization into modern times.

In general, the Jews in the Ottoman Empire enjoyed a broad measure of autonomy and personal freedom to settle wherever they wished and to travel; they could engage in almost every occupation and profession; practice their religion; establish their own religious, judicial, educational, and social institutions; and organize community life with minimal government interference. Economic prosperity and freedom of worship facilitated the emergence of new major Jewish cultural centers, which attracted scholars from various parts of the Ottoman Empire and Europe and from which education and culture radiated to the smaller communities. Indeed, in the sixteenth century, Salonika, Istanbul, and Safed emerged as world centers of Jewish scholarship and intellectual and cultural creativity. Among the great luminaries of that period were the legal scholar, Joseph *Karo (ca. 1488–1575), and the mystic and poet, Solomon Alkabetz (ca. 1505–1584). **Map 9**

In the sixteenth century, because of the diversity of the Jewish population, community institutions tended to be decentralized. However, during the seventeenth century, with growing integration among the various groups, Jewish institutions became more centralized and communities began to appoint chief rabbis (rav ha-kolel). In the larger communities (Istanbul, Salonika, Izmir, Edirne), the chief rabbinate was usually held jointly by two or three chief rabbis, representing various interests within the community. As of 1835, the Ottoman authorities appointed an official chief rabbi (ḥakham bashi; haham başı, in Turkish spelling), first in Istanbul and later in other major cities. The authorities regarded the Ḥakham Bashi of Istanbul as representing all the Jews of the empire.

DECLINE AND REAWAKENING: In the seventeenth and eighteenth centuries, Ottoman Jewish communities, as did the empire generally, underwent a period of material and spiritual decline. Jews, and non-Jews alike suffered from the wars and disorder affecting many Ottoman provinces. In areas that remained firmly under government control, Jewish life and property were generally secure. Although Jews continued to play a significant role in Ottoman economic, political, and cultural life, they lost their primacy to other minority groups, especially Greeks and Armenians. In the nineteenth century, however, Jews greatly benefited from the reforms introduced by modernizing Ottoman rulers. Of all the Ottoman religious minorities, Jews were the only group that did not entertain separatist nationalist aspirations and remained loyal to the state, preferring to live in the multireligious and polyethnic Ottoman Empire, rather than in the newly established Balkan nation-states. In return, the Ottoman government took great care to ensure that Jewish representatives were appointed to the new state institutions, such as municipal, provincial, and state councils; the new secular law courts; and the first Ottoman parliament (1877–78). Jews were also encouraged to enroll in state schools, which enabled them to pursue careers in government service and politics.

In the second half of the nineteenth century, western Jewish philanthropic organizations also began to play a major role in modernizing Ottoman Jewish life. The most important was the *Alliance Israélite Universelle (AIU). Established in Paris in 1860, the AIU founded dozens of schools throughout the empire; using French as the language of instruction, these schools offered a European curriculum and brought significant segments of the Jewish population into modernity. By 1912, the AIU operated 115 schools in the Ottoman Empire, including schools for girls, with a total enrollment of some 19,000 students.

Modernization increased the cultural diversity of Ottoman Jewry and contributed to its politicization. During the empire's final decades, considerable numbers of Jews, like Moïse Cohen Tekinalp (1883–1961) and Emmanuel Carasso (Karasu; d. 1934), were enthusiastic supporters of the Young Turk movement and called for Jewish integration into Turkish society and culture. Others supported political *Zionism, which had become popular among the Jewish masses. Many Jews shared the views of Lucien Sciuto (1858–1947), editor of the Zionist paper L'Aurore, who believed that Ottoman patriotism and Zionism complemented one another and who advocated an Ottoman–Zionist alliance.

The Ottoman government, however, which already had considerable difficulties with separatist nationalist movements, was opposed to political *Zionism. Still, it regarded Zionism in a class by itself because Zionists used diplomacy, politics, and economic methods to advance their cause, rather than violence. Turkish leaders also recognized the economic benefits that the Zionist enterprise had brought to *Palestine and the empire as a whole, and they respected the political influence that Zionist leaders exercised internationally. Consequently, Turkish leaders were prepared to engage in dialogue. Although they unsuccessfully opposed Zionist settlement in Palestine, Turkish leaders continued to welcome Jewish immigration to other parts of the empire.

By 1908, the Ottoman Empire had lost most of its possessions in Europe and Africa, and its Jewish population was reduced to some 450,000. The Jews, together with the rest of the Ottoman population, suffered heavy losses during the Balkan Wars (1912–13) and World War I. After these two conflicts the empire lost almost all of its remaining territories in Europe and its Arab provinces with their significant Jewish communities. With this final disintegration, less than 100,000 Jews remained in the truncated Ottoman Empire, which in 1923 became the *Turkish Republic (see TURKEY).

For further reading, see E. Benbassa and A. Rodrigue, Sephardi Jewry: A History of the Judeo-Spanish Community, 14th–20th Centuries (2000); A. Levy, The Sephardim in the Ottoman Empire (1994); idem, ed., The Jews of the Ottoman Empire (1994); idem, ed., Jews, Turks, Ottomans: A Shared History, Fifteenth through the Twentieth Century (2002); A. Rodrigue, French Jews, Turkish Jews: The Alliance Israélite Universelle and the Politics of Jewish Schooling in Turkey, 1860–1925 (1990); M. Rozen, A History of the Jewish Community of Istanbul: The

Formative Years, 1453–1566 (2002); and N. Todorov, *The Balkan City, 1400–1900* (1983). ‌ᴀᴠɪɢᴅᴏʀ Lᴇᴠʏ

Oz, Amos (b. 1939). One of the most popular and widely translated Israeli writers (see LITERATURE, HEBREW: ISRAELI FICTION [1945–2009]), Amos Oz has achieved a powerful and enduring reputation for his evocative representations of the inner and outer landscapes of the Israeli people, his penetrating literary essays, and his unsparing political criticism of his country's policies vis-à-vis the Palestinians. Oz's works have been translated into more than thirty languages. His vision of the art of the novel has been equally informed by Hebrew Modernists such as S. Y. *Agnon and Russian novelists such as Tolstoy and Chekhov. These varied influences were present as early as his first collection of short stories, *Where the Jackals Howl* (1965), which was soon followed by his first novel, *Elsewhere Perhaps* (1966). The overwhelmingly positive critical reception of his second novel *My Michael* (1968) ensured his position in the vanguard of Israeli writers and launched his still expanding international reputation. In these works, Oz helped inaugurate a discursive tradition in contemporary Hebrew letters of artistically engaging not only with biblical precedents and archetypes in provocative ways but also with the landscape itself (particularly the desert), to illuminate the present conflicts and paradoxes that beset Israeli society.

Oz's first autobiographic work, *A Tale of Love and Darkness* (2004), is a complex novelistic memoir that reveals the sources of many of the author's most haunting images and even plots, particularly in the fraught realm of parent–child relations (see MEMOIR AND LIFE WRITING: HEBREW). Of Oz's numerous novels, short fiction, and essay collections, this epic work has received the greatest critical approbation, perhaps because this searing memoir sheds new light on many of the themes of his earlier novels.

Rᴀɴᴇɴ Oᴍᴇʀ-Sʜᴇʀᴍᴀɴ

P

Pale of Settlement refers to the area in the Russian Empire in which Jews were permitted to settle. This large swath of western *Russia, constituting just under 500,000 square miles, was officially called *cherta postoiannogo zhitel'stava evreev*. (The term "Pale" [an enclosure] was drawn from its use in depicting nineteenth-century Irish conditions.) The Russian Pale included fifteen provinces that were consolidated in imperial statutes from 1804 to 1835; these were subject to intermittent alterations until the Pale's effective abolition in 1915 and official dissolution with the Russian Revolution in February 1917. Jews made up some 12% of the population of the Pale; in many urban areas, especially in northern provinces in *Lithuania and *Belorussia, they made up the majority. **Map 11**

The Pale originated in 1792 after the first partition of *Poland in 1772. Merchants wary of competition and alleged Jewish economic mendacity protested the influx of Jews from Belorussia into Russia. Such sentiments had a continuing influence on the ongoing existence of the Pale; Russian officials who occasionally considered its abolition were persuaded that Jews would have a disruptive economic impact if permitted to settle more freely. The Pale restricted Jewish residence, roughly speaking, to those areas where they had lived before the Polish partitions (1772, 1793, 1795). Included also was New Russia, which had been acquired from the *Ottoman Empire; its largest city, a major Jewish center, was Odessa. However, Congress Poland (called the Vistula provinces after 1863) fell outside the boundaries of the Pale, despite the region's high concentration of Jews. Even within the fifteen provinces of the Pale, certain cities (Kiev, especially), peasant villages in some of the provinces, and an area of some fifty miles adjacent to the western borders of Russia prohibited Jewish settlement until the second half of the nineteenth century.

By the late 1850s and early 1860s some of these restrictions were lifted: Jewish merchants were permitted to settle outside the Pale, as were Jews who held academic degrees and, eventually, even Jewish craftsmen. During this era, the Jewish populations of Moscow and *Saint Petersburg began to grow in size. Contraction occurred after the pogroms of 1881–82 when the so-called May Laws limited Jewish residence in villages. At the same time actions were taken to remove Jews living outside the boundaries of the Pale; the most dramatic incident was the 1891 expulsion of large numbers of Moscow Jews. Even before the introduction of the May Laws, Jews living outside the original boundaries of the Pale were subjected to intermittent harassment, arrest, and expulsions.

By the late nineteenth century, Jews, western liberals, and others saw the existence of the Pale, along with the eruption of *pogroms in the 1880s and later, as the most egregious examples of anti-Jewish treatment in Russia. However, it is important to point out no resident of the Russian Empire enjoyed freedom of movement (even nobles enjoyed such freedom as a privilege, not a right), and the general restriction of Jewish settlement to the Pale was consistent with such presumptions. Certainly, the Pale was unique in its form, but its basic intent to restrict residence reflected an overarching principle of Russian governance. **Map 11**

Pale restrictions were temporarily suspended in 1916 during *World War I when large numbers of Jewish refugees, many exiled by the Russian army, moved into Russia's interior. With the February 1917 Russian Revolution, the Pale of Settlement was officially abolished. For further reading, see Hans Rogger, *Jewish Policies and Right-Wing Politics in Imperial Russia* (1986); **see also RUSSIA.**   STEVEN J. ZIPPERSTEIN

Palestine as a geographical designation has its origins in the second century CE after the unsuccessful Second *Jewish War, when *Rome joined the humbled province of Judea (which already included *Samaria) with *Galilee to form a new province called Syria Palestina. The name "Palestina" was a reference to the *Philistines, who had settled along the coast of the Land of Israel in biblical times. The Philistines came under *Assyrian rule in the mid-eighth century BCE and disappeared from history after their conquest and exile by the *Babylonians in 604 BCE.

Palestine passed from *Byzantine to *Muslim control in the 630s CE and was a province of various Muslim powers, including the Umayyad and Abassid Caliphates, the Fatimids, the Mamluks, and the *Ottoman Empire (see EGYPT; IRAQ; ISLAM). Parts of the region constituted a Christian *Crusader kingdom from 1099–1187 CE. During *World War I, the Ottoman Empire, which sided with the Central Powers, was driven from the region by British forces, which captured *Jerusalem in 1917. After the war, *Britain assumed a mandate over Palestine (affirmed by the League of Nations in 1922) and formally administered the region from 1920 to 1948 (see BRITISH MANDATE OVER PALESTINE). In 1947, the United Nations voted to partition Palestine into separate Jewish and Arab states (see ISRAEL, STATE OF: FOUNDING OF THE MODERN STATE); although this vote precipitated the British withdrawal in May 1948 and ultimately led to the establishment of the State of Israel, much of the territory that was to form a new Arab entity initially fell under the political control of Jordan and Egypt or became part of Israel. A significant proportion of the Arab population of Mandate Palestine became refugees living in camps in areas under Jordanian and Egyptian authority (see ISRAEL, STATE OF: WARS [1948] and **Maps 12, 13**).

Since 1967 (see ISRAEL, STATE OF: WARS [1956–1967]), efforts to form an independent Palestinian state have progressed haltingly. In 1988 the State of Palestine was formally declared and recognized by more than one hundred United Nations member states. The European Union and the United States have diplomatic ties with the Palestinian Authority, and a number of other countries recognize Palestine as a national entity. Substantive negotiations have taken place with Israel, particularly in 2000, but without ultimate success thus far, and substantial disagreements remain. At the end of the first decade of the twenty-first century, Palestinian leadership is divided and in conflict; Gaza is under the authority of Hamas, and the West Bank is governed by the Palestinian Authority. When or whether the elusive goal of a viable Palestinian state will be achieved – and if so, in what form – remains unclear.   JUDITH R. BASKIN

Palestine: UN Partition Plan, 1947: See BRITISH MANDATE OVER PALESTINE; ISRAEL, STATE OF: FOUNDING OF THE MODERN STATE; Map 12

Pappenheim, Bertha (1859–1936) was born in *Vienna, but lived most of her life in *Germany. A feminist leader, social worker, activist in the international campaign against "white slavery" (see PROSTITUTES, PROSTITUTION: MODERN ERA), author, and translator, she founded (1904) and led the German Jüdischer Frauenbund (League of Jewish Women) and co-founded the International Jewish Women's League (1914). A pioneer in modern Jewish social work, Pappenheim founded Women's Relief (1901, *Frankfurt), a women-led organization that served Jewish women and Eastern European Jewish immigrants and refugees, inspiring similar projects throughout *Central and *Eastern Europe. Pappenheim founded an innovative home for unwed mothers and at-risk girls and children (1907, Isenburg); she was instrumental in establishing the Central Welfare Agency of German Jews (1917), which coordinated the social service efforts of Jewish communities and private organizations across Germany. Late in life, she advised the administration of the Beth Jacob girls' schools in *Poland (see SCHENIRER, SARAH) and lectured at Franz *Rosenzweig's and Martin *Buber's Free Jewish House of Learning in Frankfurt. Pappenheim was also a prolific writer of speeches, travel accounts, plays, stories, prayers, and aphorisms, and she was the translator of Mary Wollstonecraft's *Vindication of the Rights of Women*, the *Memoirs of* *Glückel of Hameln (to whom she was distantly related), and other Old *Yiddish texts into German. She is also known for her role in the history of psychoanalysis as the subject of the case study "Anna O." in Josef Breuer and Sigmund *Freud's *Studies on Hysteria* (1895) and as having coined the phrase "talking cure." Recent scholarship includes E. Loentz, *Let Me Continue to Speak the Truth: Bertha Pappenheim as Author and Activist* (2007).   ELIZABETH LOENTZ

Passover (Pesaḥ [often Pesach] in Hebrew) is one of the three pilgrimage *festivals, beginning on the 15th of *Nissan (March or April). From an agricultural perspective, Passover is associated with the spring season and the beginning of the barley harvest. This aspect is remembered today with the counting of the *omer, beginning on the festival's second day. More significantly, Passover commemorates the events described in the book of *Exodus, wherein the *Israelites were enslaved and then freed from *Egypt through divine miracles and the leadership of *Moses.

The Hebrew name of the holiday, Pesaḥ, comes from the Hebrew three-letter root *peh/ samekh/ ḥet*, meaning "to pass over" or "to spare." During the last of the ten plagues, just before the Exodus, God "passed over" the houses of the Jews and killed only the firstborn of the Egyptians. The word *pesaḥ* also refers to the paschal sacrifice, which was an animal (a yearling sheep or goat) that was sacrificed at Passover in the *Temple in Jerusalem. As with most other Jewish

holidays, Passover has additional descriptive names: *Ḥag ha-Aviv* (the festival of spring), *Ḥag ha-Matzot* (the festival of unleavened breads), and *Zeman Ḥerutenu* (season of our freedom).

The *Bible instructs that Passover lasts seven days (Lev 23:5). The first and final days have greater significance than the intermediary days, *ḥol ha-mo'ed* (literally, "the mundane of the festival"). On the first and final days there are festival restrictions from work and also directives to perform certain rituals, such as holding a ceremonial meal, the *seder*, on the first day; there are also *customs, such as the recitation of *Yizkor, the memorial prayer, on the last day. Jews outside of Israel traditionally observe the diasporic two-day extension of sacred days (*yom tov sheni shel galuyot*) and therefore conduct a *seder* on each of the first two nights of Passover. *Diaspora Jews also add a second holy day at the end of Passover, making Passover last eight days. Jews in Israel keep one first day of Passover and thus hold only one *seder*, and they observe only one holy day at the end.

Traditional observance of Passover requires intense preparation, beginning with the elimination of any *ḥametz* from the home. *Ḥametz* is food that is made from any of five grains (wheat, barley, oats, spelt, or rye) and has been allowed to rise. Prohibited foods include items such as pasta, cereal, and beer, because they contain byproducts or derivatives of the principal forms of *ḥametz*. Expanding on the Torah's injunction, "and no leaven shall be found in your houses" (Exod 12:19), Jewish law stipulates that one must not only refrain from consuming *ḥametz* but it is also forbidden to own it or to derive benefit from it (e.g., making money in a *ḥametz*-related business venture or enjoying *ḥametz* in a social activity with non-Jews).

*Ashkenazic Jews also prohibit a group of foods called *kitniyot* (from the Hebrew adjective *katan* or "little"), in addition to *ḥametz*. These include rice, corn, millet, and legumes (beans, peas, lentils, seeds, and peanuts) and all their derivatives. This ban against eating *kitniyot* was likely an extra protective measure to make sure people would not accidentally cross the line from non-*ḥametz* into *ḥametz*. The Ashkenazic injunction concerns the act of consumption only (not the owning of *kitniyot*), and because *kitniyot* are not *ḥametz*, there is no obligation to destroy or sell these foods. *Sephardim do not adhere to this prohibition.

The removal of *ḥametz* can be especially painstaking because even the smallest amount of *ḥametz* in food renders it unacceptable for Passover, unlike other accidental mixing of prohibited foods (e.g., dairy and meat) that may be disregarded if it involves less than one-sixtieth of the sum. Therefore, Passover cleaning often entails serious scrubbing and wiping clear areas and appliances used for food, as well as exchanging dishes and cookware used all year for those reserved for Passover.

The cleaning efforts are formalized at sunset on the 14th of Nissan, the evening before the first *seder*, with *bedikat ḥametz*, the search for *ḥametz*, performed systematically to ensure that none is left in the house; *bi'ur ḥametz* (destruction of *ḥametz*), a ceremony wherein the *ḥametz* found is taken outside and burned the following morning; and *mekhirat ḥametz*, the sale of *ḥametz* to a non-Jewish friend, which technically fulfills the obligation not to "own" *ḥametz*, but stipulates that the original owner repurchases the *ḥametz* at the close of the festival.

The festival (15th of Nissan) commences with the *seder*. The original *seder*, as devised in the talmudic era, was based on the Roman version of a Greek symposium. The *seder* is not meant to be overly formal; rather participants are to act like free people and recline comfortably, and small children are welcome to play an active role. It follows a fourteen-part procedure that is set forth in a text called the *haggadah*. This book recalls and teaches the story of the Exodus through symbolic foods set on a large *seder* plate, the prescribed eating of *matzah* (unleavened bread), four questions, rabbinic teachings, and folksongs. In this way, the *seder* fulfills the biblical commandment, "And you shall explain to your son on that day, 'It is because of what the Almighty did for me when I went free from Egypt'" (Exod 13:8). Four cups of wine are consumed, each at a specific point during the *seder*, and a substantial meal is served at about the midpoint.

Hallel is recited on the first and last days of the festival, and a half-*hallel* is recited during the intermediary days. A special prayer (*tefillat tal* [the prayer of dew]) that officially marks the end of winter and the beginning of spring is chanted in synagogue on the first day. On the intermediary *Sabbath of Passover, Ashkenazic Jews read the *Song of Songs in *synagogue, as it expresses God's intimate relationship with the Jewish people, a central Passover theme.

The Christian holiday of Easter is related to Passover in that both are springtime observances that emphasize themes of rebirth. Christ is referred to as the paschal sacrifice in Christian liturgical language, and some say that the Last Supper was a Passover *seder*.

For further reading, see P. Steinberg, *Celebrating the Jewish Year: The Spring and Summer Holidays* (2009); P. Goodman, *The Passover Anthology* (1961); T. H. Gaster, *Festivals of the Jewish Year* (1952); I. Greenberg, *The Jewish Way: Living the Holidays* (1993); and I. Klein, *A Guide to Religious Jewish Practice* (1979).   PAUL STEINBERG

Patriarch (Hebrew, *nasi*). The Patriarchs were hereditary leaders of the Jewish community in the Land of *Israel in the first five or six centuries CE. They were descendants of the family of Gamaliel (I) mentioned in Acts 5:34 (see *NEW TESTAMENT) and his son Simon (e.g., *Josephus, *War* 4.159; *Life* 309), who were significant figures in pre-70 CE *Jerusalem. Simon's son Gamaliel II plays an important role in traditions about the early rabbinic movement. By a certain point in the third century – perhaps in connection with Judah the Patriarch (d. ca. 200 [*Judah ha-Nasi]), the editor of the *Mishnah – the Patriarch emerged as a major figure in local matters and claimed an inherited right to the office (descent from *David) and a role in the administration and exercise of justice, all without formal recognition from the *Roman government. At the end of the fourth century and for a brief period, however, Roman laws did recognize the status of the Patriarchs and assigned them the authority to appoint and depose community officials in the *Diaspora as well. See H. Lapin, "The Rabbinic Movement," in J. R. Baskin and K. Seeskin, eds., *The Cambridge Guide to Jewish History, Religion, and Culture* (2010), 58–84.

Pentateuch is the Greek term – five [*penta*] books [*teuchos*] – for the *Torah section of the Hebrew *Bible, also known as the Five Books of Moses. These biblical books are *Genesis, *Exodus, *Leviticus, *Numbers, and *Deuteronomy.

Periodicals: *Canada (English Language). The Canadian Jewish community is served by national and regional English-language periodicals. The most widely read periodicals are the weeklies sponsored by Jewish organizations. *The Canadian Jewish News* is published out of Toronto and Montreal by the Canadian Jewish Congress, an overarching comprehensive organization. *The Jewish Tribune*, sponsored by B'nai B'rith Canada, takes a somewhat more conservative approach. *Outlook*, a national magazine of opinion, published six times a year, describes itself as "independent" and "secular with a socialist humanist perspective." *Afterword* seeks to attract younger Canadian Jews. In 2008 regional/local periodicals were published in Ottawa, Edmonton, Calgary, Vancouver, Winnipeg, and Vancouver. Two cultural publications of note are *Parchment: The Journal of Canadian Jewish Writing* and *Canadian Jewish Studies*.   LIBBY K. WHITE

Periodicals: United States (English Language). In 2008, the website of the "Index to Jewish Periodicals" (*www.jewishperiodicals.com*) listed more than two hundred English-language publications of various kinds "devoted to Jewish affairs." Of these, the great majority are published in the *United States.

The English-language Jewish press in the United States originated in response to Christian missionary efforts. In 1823 Henry Jackson, a Jewish printer living in *New York City, refuted the claims of conversionists in *The Jew*. Isaac *Leeser (1806–1868) of *Philadelphia edited *The Occident and American Jewish Advocate* from 1843 until his death. This monthly journal contained articles on Jewish history, news from the American and international press, reports on American Jewish settlements, fiction, and poetry. *The Occident* attacked *antisemitism and *intermarriage, endorsed separation of church and state, and supported a Jewish state in *Palestine. Leeser focused on matters on which Jews could agree, such as the Edgar *Mortara case, General Ulysses Grant's Order 11 (see UNITED STATES: CIVIL WAR), Sunday closings, and Jewish chaplains in the army (see UNITED STATES: MILITARY CHAPLAINCY). *The Occident* supported benevolent societies, Jewish hospitals, and day schools. After Leeser's death, Mayer Sulzberger edited *The Occident* for one year and then it ceased publication.

Isaac Mayer *Wise (1819–1900) established *The Israelite* in 1854 as a weekly journal. Based in Cincinnati, Ohio, Wise was especially concerned to promote the practice of American Reform Judaism (see JUDAISM, REFORM: NORTH AMERICA) and to provide information for Jews in small towns throughout the United States who were at a distance from major Jewish population centers. *The Israelite* included sermons and editorials, news of the Jewish world, as well as fiction by Wise and others. It attacked the assumption that the United States was a Christian country and proclaimed the Reform tenet that Jews were a religious group, not a national entity. *The Israelite* became *The American Israelite* after 1876, and it continued to be published into the first decade of the twenty-first century.

The American Israelite was the first of the many periodicals published by denominational movements to communicate with their members and the public at large. In the early twenty-first century *The Jewish Observer* and *Tradition* represent Orthodox approaches. The Conservative movement publishes *Voices of Conservative/Masorti Judaism*, and

Conservative Judaism, whereas Reform publications include *Reform Judaism* and the *CCAR Journal*. *The Reconstructionist* and *Humanistic Judaism* are published by smaller denominations (see entries under JUDAISM).

Jewish nonsectarian organizations also publish periodicals for their members and for other interested readers. B'nai B'rith (see UNITED STATES: FRATERNAL SOCIETIES) began publication of its first magazine, *Menorah*, in 1886. Its twenty-first-century successor is *B'nai B'rith Magazine*. The *American Jewish Committee published the monthly magazine *Commentary* between 1945 and 2006. Initially a liberal center-left publication, *Commentary* became increasingly conservative in the 1970s under its editor Norman Podhoretz. Since 2007, *Commentary* has been published as an "independent journal of public opinion." The *American Jewish Congress publishes *Congress Monthly*, which focuses on civil liberties, racial equality, political liberalism, and *Zionism, as well as the more academic *Judaism: A Quarterly of Jewish Life and Thought*.

The first American *Zionist magazine was the *Maccabean*, which appeared in 1901; it is now *The American Zionist*. The Theodor Herzl Foundation of the American Zionist Foundation has published *Midstream Magazine* since the 1950s. The periodical describes itself as the leading intellectual Zionist journal in the world, "a medium of informed discussion and lively thinking." *Hadassah Magazine* began life as a modest "bulletin" for members of what is now *Hadassah: The Women's Zionist Organization of America. It has evolved into a stylish "Jewish feature and literary magazine" that emphasizes events in Israel and the Jewish world for a predominantly female audience.

The *Menorah Journal*, originally associated with the *Menorah Association, a group that sponsored Jewish organizations on college campuses, was published in different forms between 1915 and 1962. This sophisticated and intellectual periodical had a significant impact on American Jewish culture. Many contributors were well-known academics, and the journal's content included translations from *Yiddish, articles on Zionism, reports on cultural events, and art reproductions.

A number of American Jewish periodicals are independent. The largest, *Moment* magazine, founded in 1975 by Elie *Wiesel and Leonard Fein, comments on contemporary American Jewish society from disparate points of view. *Tikkun*, founded in 1986 and edited by Michael Lerner, is a Jewish critique of politics, culture, and society from a leftist perspective. *Lilith Magazine* (1976), and *Bridges: A Jewish Feminist Journal* (1989) are among independent periodicals directed at Jewish feminists (see JUDAISM, FEMINIST). *Heeb*, established in 2001, takes an iconoclastic and satiric approach geared to a college and post-college audience.

In the first decade of the twenty-first century, many American Jewish communities support English-language weekly or monthly newspapers. Although the existence of some of these periodicals is tenuous because of inadequate funding and lack of professional staffing, these local periodicals play an important communal role in providing international and national Jewish news. A major resource for these local and regional periodicals is the Jewish Telegraphic Agency, which describes itself as "the Global News Service of the Jewish People"; it was originally founded as the Jewish Correspondence Bureau by Jacob Landau in 1917. Local periodicals also report on a variety of Jewish events in their communities and regions and provide calendars of educational programs and upcoming activities. Many are affiliated with the American Jewish Press Association, founded in 1944 as "a voluntary not-for-profit professional association for the English-language Jewish press in North America." The English-language *Forward*, published weekly since 1990 as an independent and progressive source of news and opinion on Jewish affairs, is particularly renowned for its cultural pages.

A broad variety of academic journals focused on the Jewish experience are published in the United States. The oldest is the *Jewish Quarterly Review*, established in 1889. *American Jewish History*, published by the American Jewish Historical Society, the oldest national ethnic historical organization in the United States, was founded in 1892 as *Publications of the American Jewish Historical Society*. *Jewish Social Studies: History, Culture, and Society* appeared between 1939 and 1993; a new series of the journal began in 1994. Among other academic journals are the *AJS Review*, founded in 1976 as the scholarly publication of the Association for Jewish Studies; *Prooftexts: A Journal of Jewish Literary History*, published since 1980; *Shofar: An Interdisciplinary Journal for Jewish Studies*, established in 1981; *Nashim: A Journal of Jewish Women's Studies and Gender Issues*, co-founded by the Schechter Institute of Jewish Studies in *Jerusalem and the Hadassah-Brandeis Institute in 1998; and the *Journal of Jewish Communal Service*, published by the Jewish Communal Service Association for Jewish communal professionals.

For further reading, see L. Harap, *In the Mainstream: Jewish Presence in the Twentieth Century: American Literature 1950's–80's* (1989). See PERIODICALS: CANADA (ENGLISH LANGUAGE) and BRITAIN for information on other English-language periodicals of Jewish interest, and see entries under JOURNALISM.

　　　　　　　　　　　　　　　　　　LIBBY K. WHITE

Persia, Ancient. Cyrus the Great, part of the Achaemenid dynasty, became king of Persia in 557 BCE and reigned until 530 BCE. His father Cambyses I ruled over Anshan, in the heart of what is now *Iran. After defeating the *Babylonian King Nabonidus in 539, Cyrus ultimately assumed control over all of western Asia. In 538, Cyrus authorized the Jewish community in Babylonia to return to *Judah and rebuild the *Temple in *Jerusalem (Ezra 1). His son Cambyses II(reigned 530–522 BCE) extended the empire as far as *Egypt. Darius I (522–486 BCE) consolidated the empire, and his reign figures prominently in the chronological headings of the prophetic books of *Haggai (1:1, 15; 2:1; 10; 18; 20) and *Zechariah (1:7, 7:1). Although Darius succeeded in establishing Persian rule over a vast stretch of territory from Libya and Egypt in the west, Ionia and Lydia in the north, all the way to the Indus in the east, and the Persian Gulf and Arabian Sea to the south, much of the fifth century BCE was spent in wars with the Greeks. Despite many challenges to imperial rule, Persian control over this vast area lasted until the conquests of *Alexander the Great in 330 BCE. The rulers of the relatively tranquil Achaemenid dynasty allowed a measure of home rule in all their satrapies (provinces), along with religious freedom. In this era long-lasting and culturally important *Diaspora centers were established in Iran and *Iraq (see BABYLONIAN EXILE). The book of *Esther, although generally seen as fictional, is set in Persia and reflects a highly acculturated Jewish community.

During Achaemenid rule there was significant rebuilding of Jewish life in the Land of Israel, a province called *Yehud by the Persians. Jews returned to Yehud in 538 under the governor Sheshbazzar (Ezra 1:8, 5:14); in 520 BCE under the leadership of the Persian-appointed governor *Zerubbabel (Haggai 1:1, 14); and in the fifth century under the leadership of *Ezra and *Nehemiah. However, a far larger number remained in Babylon. Persian rule over the province of Yehud lasted from 539 to 332 BCE, when the *Hellenistic era began with the arrival of *Alexander the Great in western Asia. The rebuilding of the Jerusalem *Temple was undertaken during the years of Persian rule; the small amount of material evidence from this era indicates that most Jews were involved in farming and lived at a subsistence level (see ARCHEOLOGY, LAND OF ISRAEL: SECOND TEMPLE PERIOD).

There is very little information about the Jews who remained in central Mesopotamia during the Hellenistic (331–238 BCE) and Parthian (238 BCE–224 CE) periods. More information is available for era of the Persian Sassanian dynasty (224–651 CE). It was under its rule that the Babylonian academies of *Sura and *Pumbedita became the center of rabbinic culture, ultimately producing the Babylonian *Talmud. The Sassanian rulers, who championed the Zoroastrian religion, changed imperial culture toward a more consciously "Persian" aesthetic and identity. Zoroastrianism and Persian language and culture were quite visible, as the Talmud attests, in part because Ctesiphon, located on the Tigris River in Iraq, served as the Sassanian capital. However, forms of *Aramaic remained the general vernacular and were used as scholarly languages, at least among the Jewish and Christian communities.

Within this broad cultural and political context, Jews flourished in Mesopotamia. The Talmud refers to very few instances of state-sponsored religious restrictions or persecutions (see, e.g., BT *Yevamot* 63b; BT *Bava Metzia* 86b). Rabbinic tradition reveals that some Jews closely identified with Babylonia, claiming biblical-era origins for the Shaf V'yativ synagogue in Nehardea. In 651 CE, Muslim forces conquered the Sassanian Empire, introducing a new era for the Jews of western Asia (see ISLAM AND JUDAISM; IRAN; IRAQ; JUDEO-PERSIAN LANGUAGE AND LITERATURE). For further reading, see H. Lapin, "The Rabbinic Movement," in *The Cambridge Guide to Jewish History, Religion, and Culture*, ed. J. R. Baskin and K. Seeskin (2010).

Pesaḥ (or Pesach): See PASSOVER

Pharisees   (ca. mid-second century BCE–70 CE) were one of the Jewish groups to emerge in *Judea after the *Maccabean revolt. Although popularly known from hostile *New Testament accounts as punctilious and legalistic Jews, a more balanced portrait of Pharisees as scholars, teachers, and community leaders emerges from other sources. The term "Pharisees" (Hebrew, *perushim*; Greek: *pharisaioi*), appears to mean "separatists" in Hebrew, although it is doubtful whether it always referred to a specific group or was a self-chosen designation. What the Pharisees separated from is also unclear – perhaps from Jews less devoted to biblical *purity laws or *Torah study.

The main historical sources – *Josephus, rabbinic texts, and the New Testament – emphasize different aspects of the Pharisees. Josephus focuses on their political involvements and religious interests. The New Testament Gospels savage Pharisees as falsely pious and arrogant, but also reveal a competition between them and Jesus for popular support, thereby partially explaining the hostility. Scattered New Testament references, which are less hostile, confirm the Gospels' presentations of the Pharisees as zealously devoted to *Torah. Rabbinic texts post-date the Pharisees by at least a century and reveal mixed attitudes toward them, but generally confirm other descriptions of Pharisaic religious views.

Josephus provides the most information (*Jewish War* 2:162–66; *Jewish Antiquities* 13:288–98, 400–21; 17:42; 18:4–17). He describes the Pharisees' sporadic involvement in national affairs, typically through opposition to or alignment with more powerful leaders. They fell afoul of *Hasmonean rulers John Hyrcanus (reigned 134–04 BCE) and Alexander Jannaeus (reigned 103–76 BCE), who supported the rival *Sadducees, but found favor under Salome Alexandra (reigned 76–67 BCE), who allowed them to persecute their opponents. A few Pharisees opposed *Rome before the war in 66–70 CE. Rabbinic and New Testament texts hint at the Pharisees' limited involvement in politics. According to the New Testament, some Pharisees sit on councils (Acts 5:34) and are involved in palace intrigues (BT *Kiddushin* 66a), but notably, they play no role in the trial of Jesus.

Josephus focuses on the Pharisees' specific religious views: their belief in free will, an imperishable soul, and reward and punishment after death. He also highlights their fidelity to "traditions of their fathers," teachings that clarify, expand, and alter biblical law (see *HALAKHAH*) in an effort to make ancient *commandments relevant. These religious issues are confirmed by other sources (Mark 7:3; Acts 23:8; cf. M. *Avot* 1:1, 3:15). The New Testament and rabbinic writings emphasize piety based in the home and community that is separate from (although not opposed to) *Temple worship. Pharisees are said to observe commandments rigorously regarding the *Sabbath, purity, *marriage, and *dietary rules (provoking disputes with Jesus over competing interpretations; Matt 12:1, 15:2), and to revere Torah study. This strict observance made them popular with the masses, who appreciated their zeal and welcomed their guidance (Matt 23; M. *Toharot* 4:12; BT *Niddah* 33b).

The rabbinic movement has its roots in the Pharisaic movement, whose model of personal piety in daily life and devotion to Torah study was well suited for a world after 70 CE, when Jews no longer had a Temple or political power. For further reading, see E. Rivkin, *A Hidden Revolution* (1978); S. Mason, *Flavius Josephus on the Pharisees* (2001); and A. Saldarini, *Pharisees, Scribes, and Sadducees in Palestinian Society* (2001).   ADAM GREGERMAN

Philadelphia.   With a bustling tidewater port and tolerant attitude toward religious diversity, Philadelphia, Pennsylvania's largest city, attracted Jews early in the eighteenth century. Six Jews had traded in the merchant town by 1719, and New York merchants and brothers Nathan and Isaac Levy settled there with their families in 1737. Nathan's 1740 purchase of land for a Jewish cemetery laid the groundwork for Philadelphia's first Jewish communal institution.

By 1761, immigrants from *Central Europe increased the Jewish population, and a prayer group was functioning. This congregation, already serving three hundred Jews, incorporated in 1782 as Mikveh Israel (Hope of Israel), following *Sephardic ritual. Before the end of the century, a second congregation, Rodeph Shalom (Seeker of Peace), was established, the first in the *United States to follow *Ashkenazic customs.

Upheavals in Europe brought more Jews to North America throughout the nineteenth century, and newcomers to Philadelphia often required charitable services. By 1820, two independent benevolent societies existed; Rodeph Shalom congregants formed an additional larger association, the United Hebrew Beneficent Society, in 1829. These groups also enjoyed support from Jews in other states and from local Gentiles. Philadelphia Jews rose to national influence during the Jacksonian era when Isaac *Leeser (1806–1867) became prayer leader at Mikveh Israel. Leeser published *The Occident and American Jewish Advocate*, the first important Jewish *periodical to achieve widespread circulation. In its pages he instructed American Jews about religious practices, advocated for charitable and religious endeavors, and provided a forum for spiritual writing by men and women. Leeser also established a publishing company for Jewish works, translated the *Bible into English, established a short-lived rabbinical seminary, and served as advisor to numerous Jewish ventures. These included the first Jewish Sunday school (1838), led by Mikveh Israel's Rebecca *Gratz (1781–1869), and the Jews' Hospital (1866). Sabato Morais (1823–1897), his successor at Mikveh Israel, continued to advocate for an Americanized form of traditional Judaism and established the Young Men's Hebrew Association (see UNITED STATES: COMMUNITY CENTERS) and New York's *Jewish Theological Seminary (1887). Younger Philadelphians linked to Mikveh Israel helped organize the *Jewish Publication Society (1888), the American Jewish Historical Society (1892), and the *American Jewish Committee (1906). Beginning in 1906, Philadelphia rabbi Bernard Levinthal (1865–1952) played a role in the establishment of *Yeshiva University in *New York City. Increasing immigration led to the formation of many new congregations, some of which participated in the effort to streamline and simplify Jewish practice; Keneseth Israel (Assembly of Israel, 1847) became a nationally influential *Reform congregation in the later nineteenth century.

By 1905, Philadelphia's 75,000 Jews supported one hundred and fifty different Jewish associations, including a rabbinical *court and *kosher supervising agency. The *American Jewish Congress was founded in Philadelphia in 1916 to obtain "not charity but justice" for Europe's Jews, and in 1939 Maurice B. Fagin founded Philadelphia's Anti-Defamation Council, forerunner to *B'nai B'rith's Anti-Defamation League. In the 1970s, Philadelphia's active movement to aid Jews trapped in the *Soviet Union made it a national hub for tourists traveling to the USSR to assist Jews. By the end of the twentieth century Philadelphia's Jewish population of 260,000 included approximately 6,000 Soviet immigrants. For further reading, see D. Ashton, *Rebecca Gratz: Women and Judaism in Antebellum America* (1997); idem, *Jewish Life in Pennsylvania* (1998); and M. Friedman, *When Philadelphia Was the Capital of Jewish America* (1993).   DIANNE ASHTON

Philanthropy. There is no exactly analogous word for philanthropy or charity in the Jewish lexicon. The word "philanthropy," from the Greek, means love of humankind, whereas charity, from the Latin *caritas*, refers to an act of lovingkindness. *Tzedakah* is the operative Jewish value concept, and it is based in the root *tzedek*, which means righteousness or "doing the right thing." People should help those who are less fortunate because they are commanded to do so, whether or not they have any connection to the recipient. The twelfth-century Jewish philosopher Moses *Maimonides famously describes eight degrees of giving, noting that even one who is a beneficiary must donate to others as well. For Maimonides the highest levels of *tzedakah* were to give anonymously in such a way that the recipient would ultimately become independent (*Mishneh Torah*, "Laws of Gifts to the Poor" 10:7–14). Today, philanthropy is an imperative imbued in many Jews who may not observe other *commandments.   RELA MINTZ GEFFEN

Philistines. The Bible represents the Philistines as one of the bitter foes of the biblical *Israelites. Their area of habitation along the fertile coastal strip of southwestern *Canaan stretched from the border of *Egypt's Sinai Peninsula in the south to the banks of the Yarkon River in modern-day *Tel Aviv in the north, and from the Mediterranean Sea in the west to the *shephelah*, the low-lying Judean foothills in the east. According to Egyptian sources, they were one of a number of ethnic groups later termed "Sea Peoples," who were on the move during the transitional period between the Late Bronze and Early Iron Ages (ca. 1200–1150 BCE). By the reign of Pharaoh Ramses III in the early twelfth century, the Philistines were settled in the area traditionally associated with them. Hence, their rise in the land was more or less concurrent with the rise of the Israelites in the central hill country.

This situation is reflected in *Judges, in which the Philistines are among the peoples opposed to the nascent Israelites, and particularly in *Samuel, in which pressure from Philistine expansionism leads in part to the decision to institute kingship in Israel (see ISRAELITES: KINGSHIP). *Saul, the first king of Israel, dies in battle against the Philistines (1 Sam 31), but King *David's relationship with them is more complex. Although he is presented as a scourge of the Philistines, for example killing their champion Goliath (1 Sam 17), in a number of texts he is allied with them and even becomes a vassal of Achish, the king of Gath (1 Sam 27). After assuming kingship over all Israel, David turns against his erstwhile suzerains and effectively brings an end to Philistine expansionism (2 Sam 5:17–25; 8:1; 21:15–22; 23:9–17). From that time onward, they play a minor role in biblical narrative and prophetic texts and eventually pass from the scene.

This indistinct biblical portrait may be supplemented by both textual and material finds. Egyptian texts convey information regarding the period of Philistine settlement and *Assyrian and *Babylonian sources document the later phases of their history in the eighth and seventh centuries BCE. Archeological excavations in the 1960s in Philistia deepened our understanding of their history and material culture. *Archeological evidence indicates that the Philistines originated in the Aegean world, as reflected in their pottery, architecture, small finds, names, and faunal remains. Nonetheless, within a couple of generations they had more or less acculturated to their Canaanite environment, and during the latter centuries of their habitation, they exhibited many features of regional Canaanite culture, including its pantheon of deities and its script.

Whereas the Bible presents the Philistines as a united conglomeration of five cities (the "Pentapolis" consisting of Ashkelon, Ashdod, and Gaza along the coast, and Ekron and Gath farther inland), extrabiblical evidence points to a system of independent city-states, which engaged in a tightrope walk of shifting alliances with each other and with the major powers in Egypt and *Mesopotamia that had designs on their territory and trade. Coming under the control of Assyria at the time of Tiglath-Pileser's western campaigns (743–732 BCE), the Philistines disappeared from history after their conquest by the Babylonians under Nebuchadnezzar II in 604 BCE. Their memory lives on in the geographical designation "*Palestine." For further reading, see T. Dothan, *The Philistines and Their Material Culture* (1982); C. S. Ehrlich, *The Philistines in Transition* (1996); and A. E. Killebrew, *Biblical Peoples and Ethnicity* (2005). **Map 2**   CARL S. EHRLICH

Philo Judaeus of Alexandria (ca. 20 BCE to 50 CE), was a preeminent *Hellenistic Jewish thinker, biblical exegete, and delegate of the Jews to the Roman emperor Caligula. The two epithets for Philo, "Judaeus" and "of *Alexandria," highlight his importance as a writer who brought together Jewish tradition and Greek philosophy. Despite his great learning, we know little about his education. Philo came from a prominent family; according to *Josephus, his brother was the very wealthy Alexander the alabarch (an official under Roman rule), whose son Tiberius Julius Alexander turned away from Jewish practices and served under the Romans in several high posts. The most famous episode of Philo's life was his participation in a mission to Caligula in 39 or 40 CE after a violent uprising, whose causes scholars continue to debate, against the Jews in Alexandria in 38 CE. By his own account an attendee at sports and theatrical events, Philo appeared to have enjoyed many aspects of Hellenistic culture.

Philo, who wrote in Greek and probably knew little if any Hebrew, produced more than forty extant treatises; most are commentaries on the Greek *Pentateuch. They can be grouped into three series, each with apparently different aims and audiences. The "Allegorical Commentary," a verse-by-verse commentary on parts of *Genesis that is marked by long digressions and allegorical interpretations, seems directed toward Jews like Philo himself who were well educated in Jewish tradition and Greek thought. By contrast, in the "Exposition of the Law" and two companion works on *Moses, Philo evidently assumes that his readers have little or no familiarity with Jewish Scripture and practices; his favorable presentations may be addressed either toward Jews or non-Jews. In those works, which offer various interpretations including allegorical ones, he discusses the Bible in thematic treatises on creation, the patriarchs, the Decalogue (see TEN COMMANDMENTS), particular laws, virtues, and rewards and punishments. A third series, preserved primarily and incompletely in Armenian translation – *Questions and Answers on Genesis and Exodus* – contains questions and answers on individual verses. This series, probably directed toward Jews alone, includes both literal

and allegorical interpretations and may have been intended for *synagogue or school study or as preliminary notes for the "Allegorical Commentary." Philo also wrote several treatises on philosophical topics, including providence and the (non-) rationality of animals. In two treatises, *Against Flaccus* and *On the Embassy to Gaius*, he recounts in dramatic detail the recent anti-Jewish Alexandrian uprising and the legation to Caligula. In another work, he describes a contemporary group of ascetics (the Therapeutae) who lived by Lake Mareotis, close to Alexandria. These miscellaneous writings could have been written for both Jews and non-Jews. In the *Hypothetica*, Philo offers a sympathetic account, probably for a critical audience, of Jewish laws and discusses another Jewish group, the *Essenes. Several of his treatises have been lost.

Central to Philo's thought was his belief in the one, true *God. Although he speaks of a transcendent God far removed from the sensible, mortal world, Philo also refers to the soul as God's abode. Philo's God is both personal – the God of *Abraham, *Isaac, and *Jacob – and abstract: the Existent (in Greek, *to on*). Both concepts are supported by *Exodus 3:14–15 (Greek), in which the God of the patriarchs reveals His name as *ho ōn*, He who is. Discussing the interaction between God and creation, Philo mentions different intermediaries, most prominently the Logos and God's creative and kingly powers. For Philo, the height of human happiness was to "see God" – not what He is (impossible to know), but that He is (*On Rewards and Punishments* 44) – with the eyes not of the body but of the soul.

Deeply influenced by Platonic thought and Greek exegetical methods, Philo distinguished between body and soul and the sensible and intellectual worlds. Especially known for his allegorical interpretations of the *Bible, in which he presents Scripture's deeper meaning, Philo viewed Scripture as a symbolic account of the soul's quest to see God and the soul's battle against the passions. For example, Israel's exodus from Egypt symbolizes the soul leaving behind the "land" of the body, senses, and passions. The war among the kings in Genesis 14 represents the conflict between the four passions and five senses, which ends when reason, symbolized by *Abraham, intervenes. With its view of a universal, symbolic meaning underlying the particular biblical details, Philo's thought is marked by a tension between the universal and the particular. This tension is also reflected in his use of general Greek philosophy to explain particular Jewish traditions and his apparent openness to the wise and virtuous of all nations, on one hand, and his fervent loyalty to the Jews, on the other.

Although Philo is the most famous representative of Hellenistic Judaism, he had many predecessors who produced a rich Jewish literature in Greek based on the Greek Bible (the *Septuagint). Among these predecessors were Aristobulus, whose writings survive in fragments, and the author of the *Letter of *Aristeas, both of whom interpreted the Bible symbolically. Alexandria itself was home to a vibrant Jewish community for centuries under the rule of the *Ptolemies (323–30 BCE; see also PTOLEMIES: IMPACT ON JEWISH CULTURE AND THOUGHT). After the Romans took over in 30 BCE and later during Philo's lifetime, relations between Jews and their neighbors deteriorated, and Philo is our chief witness to the contemporary violence, which some scholars call the first *pogrom. Christians appreciated Philo's idea of the Logos; his symbolic approach to Scripture and his writings, preserved by the Church, had a stronger influence on *Christianity (see CHURCH FATHERS) than on Judaism. The Rabbis do not refer to Philo, perhaps more unintentionally than deliberately, because he wrote in Greek rather than Hebrew or *Aramaic and focused on philosophical instead of practical, legal issues. A probable contemporary of *Hillel and Jesus, the pre-rabbinic and nonrabbinic Philo was nonetheless deeply committed to the Jewish people, their beliefs, and their practices. In a well-known passage (*On the Migration of Abraham* 89–93), he declares it essential not only to recognize the symbolic value of the laws but also to follow these laws in practice. After *Josephus (37-ca. 100 CE), Philo was not mentioned again until 1573, in Azariah dei *Rossi's *The Light of the Eyes*. Despite this long neglect, in recent years Philo has gained more attention in Jewish studies.

The standard English translation of Philo's works is by F. C. Colson, G. H. Whitaker, and Ralph Marcus, trans., *Philo in Ten Volumes* (*and Two Supplementary Volumes*; 1929–62). For a general bibliography and for recent studies on Philo as a Jew, see E. Birnbaum, "Two Millennia Later: General Resources and Particular Perspectives on Philo the Jew," *Currents in Biblical Research* 4 (2006): 241–76.

ELLEN BIRNBAUM

Philosophy: See THOUGHT, MEDIEVAL; THOUGHT, EARLY MODERN; THOUGHT, MODERN

Phoenicia; Phoenicians. Phoenicians is the Greek name for the Semitic-language-speaking people who, beginning in the Iron Age, lived in the area of the eastern Mediterranean stretching from northern *Canaan to southern *Syria and inland to the mountains of Lebanon. Less a unified nation than a collection of independent city-states (the most prominent being Arwad, Byblos, Sidon, and Tyre), Phoenicia was most well known for its seafaring mercantile economy, and particularly for its trade in timber, luxury goods and crafts, and purple dye. The Phoenicians largely fell under the control of various regional powers from the mid-ninth to the early sixth century BCE, but experienced a renewal under the *Persians, who made extensive use of their fleets. During this era, the Phoenician colony city of Carthage in *North Africa was founded. An era of power struggles and relative decline followed, culminating in the complete loss of autonomy to *Rome in 64 BCE. 1 *Kings notes that *Solomon entered into economic and political alliances with Hiram of Tyre, leading most notably to Solomon's use of Tyrean goods and craftspeople for the construction of the first *Jerusalem *Temple (1 Kgs 5–7). Additionally, several prophetic oracles speak of and against the Phoenicians (e.g., Ezek 26–28; Isa 23). Their religion is not well understood, but it appears to have had similarities to *Canaanite practices. Its most infamous aspect was the widely reported practice of child sacrifice. Biblical and Greek polemics obscure the issue, but the discovery in Carthage of a *tophet*, or sacred precinct (cf. Jer 7), containing burned remains of infants and small children appears to verify the practice, even if the children sacrificed quite possibly were victims of the high infant mortality rates of the period. For further reading, see G. E. Markoe, *Phoenicians* (2000). **Map 2** SEAN BURT

Photography has influenced political, environmental, and social change at the same time as culture, environment,

and technology have shaped the development of photography. Technological innovations have transformed photography from early daguerreotypes on polished silver plates, to glass negatives, to film, and, most recently, to digital images on computers. Equipment has varied from large-view cameras on tripods, to tiny rangefinders such as the Leica, to the 35-mm single lens reflex with interchangeable lenses. At first, photography was considered a scientific process, but later artistic influences included the Pre-Raphaelites, the Arts and Crafts movement, the Impressionists, and the Surrealists.

From its beginnings, photography, which lacked a formal academic structure, was a venture open to anyone regardless of age, religion, or gender. From a Jewish perspective the field was open because *halakhic authorities did not consider a photograph a graven image. The rise of photography in the second half of the nineteenth century also paralleled a move toward secularism in Jewish life; most early Jewish photographers appear not to have incorporated Jewish subject matter into their work.

The daguerreotype was invented in France in 1839. This new technology quickly traveled across Europe and was brought to the *United States by Samuel F. B. Morse. The first Jewish American photographer, Solomon Carvalho (1815–1897), was born into a *Sephardic family in *Charleston, South Carolina. He studied the daguerreotype technique under Morse. Carvalho served as photographer on John Charles Fremont's expedition (1853–54) to find a route for the first transcontinental railroad (see also ART, AMERICAN: BEFORE 1940).

In Europe, Jewish photographers can be dated back to Hermann Gunther Biouw (1804–1850) and his sister Johanna Biouw in *Germany who made daguerreotype portraits. Johanna established her own clientele as a *Wanderdaguerreotypistin* (itinerant daguerreotypist) in 1848. Berthe Wehnert-Beckmann (1815–1901) had established herself as an itinerant daguerreotypist in southern Prussia by age twenty-eight, likely making her the world's first female Jewish professional photographer.

In a number of locales, such as the western provinces of *Russia, Jews operated photography studios and served Gentile as well as Jewish clients. As Jeffrey Shandler has noted, photography facilitated new cultural practices. The taking of pictures marked significant milestones in people's lives, and the photographs served as tokens of remembrance among an increasingly mobile population. In addition, posing for photographs enabled subjects to fashion new images of themselves, including fantasies realized through the use of the various props and backdrops available at photography studios.

Photographic images became increasingly important in shaping Jewish popular culture at the beginning of the twentieth century. New printing techniques facilitated the mass production of picture postcards, which became widely popular across Europe and in America. Among the vast array of images to appear on these cards were many hundreds related to Jewish life, from portraits of famous Jewish authors to the facades of synagogue buildings, as well as images of archetypal Jewish figures and biblical scenes. In addition to their use in correspondence and their appeal as collectibles, postcards engendered new kinds of cultural interactions (Shandler).

Jews also played a significant role in the shaping of the photographic image in the larger culture. The acceptance of photography as an art form in the early 1900s was due to the efforts of Alfred Stieglitz (1864–1946), particularly his work on behalf of artistic photographers and his guidance concerning the formation of the Photo-Secession, a group of American photographers supporting the creative use of the camera. With Stieglitz, Paul Strand (1890–1976), who helped found the Photo League in New York City, introduced Modernism into twentieth-century photography.

The general introduction of 35-mm film in the 1930s and the subsequent use of cameras with interchangeable lenses enabled a new generation of photographers to bring a faster, more informal style to photography. In Germany, the photojournalist Erich Salomon (1886–1944) was among the first to use a miniature camera, allowing him to quietly capture people unposed and unaware of the photograph being made. Based on his technique, *The London Graphic* coined the term "candid camera." Robert Capa (1913–1954), born André Friedmann in *Hungary, earned the title, "The Greatest Photographer in the World," for his derring-do during the Spanish Civil War. He was among the first wave of soldiers storming the beaches on D-Day, June 6, 1944. He and David (Chim) Seymour (1911–1956) established the photo agency Magnum. Capa served as president of Magnum for three years before he was killed by a landmine while covering the war in Indochina in 1954. Capa's brother, Cornell (1918–2008), established the International Center for Photography in *New York City. Arthur Fellig (1899–1968), better known as Weegee, gained distinction as the first photographer to respond to crime scenes with the aid of his police scanner.

Social documentary attracted many Jewish photographers whose concern for recording the human condition dominated their work. Arthur Rothstein (1915–1985) and Ben Shahn (1898–1969) worked for the Farm Security Administration during the 1930s to make visual records of the impact of the Great Depression and to expedite aid to stricken Americans. Roman Vishniac (1897–1990) photographed Jewish urban life and scenes from the doomed Jewish villages of *Eastern Europe before his immigration to America.

Other European photographers who came to the United States before *World War II include Alfred Eisenstaedt (1898–1995), who became a celebrated *Life Magazine* photographer famous for the photograph of the kiss in Times Square on V-J Day in 1945. Swiss-born Robert Frank (b. 1924) traveled across the United States in the 1950s and published *The Americans*, a cynical look at his adopted country that contributed to a new form of work often referred to as street photography. (Other Jewish photographers in this genre include Lee Friedlander [b. 1934], Garry Winogrand [1928–1984], William Klein [b. 1928], Helen Leavitt [b. 1913], and Walter Rosenblum [1919–2000]). Lotte Jacobi (1896–1990), a fourth-generation photographer whose photographic roots went back to the daguerreotype, was known for her psychologically acute portraits of famous artists, scientists, and politicians. Hungarian-born André Kertesz (1894–1985) is considered a seminal figure of photojournalism, the photo essay, and artistic photography. Man Ray (1890–1976), born Emmanuel Radnisky in Brooklyn, New York, moved to Paris where he sketched, painted, sculpted,

and established a photo studio. His experimentation resulted in the Rayograph – a form of camera-less photography.

Important photographers of the post–World War II era include Mary Ellen Mark (b. 1940), who photographs diverse cultures and people around the world for magazines, exhibitions, and books; Bruce Davidson (b. 1933), who created photographic explorations of the civil rights movement (see UNITED STATES: CIVIL RIGHTS MOVEMENT), the subterranean world of the New York subway system, and Spanish Harlem; and Joel Meyerowitz (b. 1938), known for his photographs of New York City and landscapes of *Italy and Massachusetts.

New York City produced many Jewish fashion photographers, including Lillian Bassman (b. 1917), Richard Avedon (1923–2004), and Irving Penn (1917–2009). Avedon created a large portfolio of portraits, employing a style where the subject stood facing the camera in front of a white background. Penn also favored a simple background, whereas Bassman brought drama to her prints. Diane Arbus (1923–1971) began her career as a fashion photographer, but became a central figure in contemporary documentary photography with her direct, confrontational human depictions. Elliott Erwitt (b. 1928) is known for the humor he finds while photographing candid, everyday settings.

Annie Liebowitz (b. 1949) became well known beginning in the 1980s when she was photographing celebrities for *Rolling Stone* magazine. During his sixty-year career Arnold Newman (1918–2006) photographed presidents, artists, actors, and writers. He is credited with popularizing the environmental portrait that demonstrated personality and character by placing the subject within his or her usual surroundings. Richard Misrach's (b. 1949) color landscapes explore human influences on the environment. Digital technology has allowed him to create large images, some as large as 6 × 10 feet. Arthur Ollman (b. 1947), who creates color landscapes at night, served as the first director of the Museum of Photographic Arts. For further reading, see G. Gilbert, *The Illustrated Worldwide Who's Who of Jews in Photography* (1996); and N. Rosenblum, *A World History of Photography* (1984); **see also ART, AMERICAN: SINCE 1940.**

CAROLE GLAUBER

Phylacteries: See TEFILLIN

Pidyon Ha-Ben: See FIRSTBORN SON, REDEMPTION OF

Pilgrimage *(aliyah la-regel)*. After the suppression of the *Bar Kokhba rebellion in 135 CE, Jews were forbidden by *Roman imperial decree to live in or even enter *Jerusalem. Late ancient *Christian sources suggest, however, that they were permitted to visit the city on the 9th of Av (*Tisha B'Av) to lament the destruction of the *Temple. *Karaite sources mention that under Roman-*Byzantine rule Jewish pilgrims were restricted to less significant sites in *Palestine, such as Tiberias in the *Galilee, Gaza, or Zoar (near the Dead Sea).

MEDIEVAL PERIOD: These limitations were removed during the Muslim period (638–1099), and many Jews made pilgrimages to Jerusalem. Some sources speak of people coming annually from as far as *Iraq, the coast of *North Africa, and *Italy. During the month of Tishri and especially during the festival of Tabernacles (*Sukkot), Jewish pilgrims from both Muslim regions and Christian Europe assembled on the Mount of Olives to pray and perform a ritual walk around the perimeter of the Temple mount, reciting prayers at each gate. The heads of the Jerusalem *yeshivah* and other Jewish dignitaries from Muslim countries attended this central pilgrimage event, which was used as an opportunity for public announcements, such as an annual reassertion of the rabbinic ban on Karaism (Gil).

Unlike pilgrimages to the *Temple in pre-exilic and Second Temple times that were made to fulfill a biblical decree (Deut 16:16), medieval Jewish pilgrimages were not focused on Jerusalem alone. Sahal ben Matzliah, a tenth-century Karaite writer, in a critique of rabbinic Jews and their practices, describes Jewish pilgrimages to the graves of deceased Jewish dignitaries in the *Galilee for healing purposes. This custom intensified after the establishment of the Latin Crusader Kingdom of Jerusalem in 1099, when Christian authorities prohibited the public ritual aspects of Jewish pilgrimage and pilgrimage became an individual matter. Because Jews were again banned from permanent settlement in Jerusalem, other cities like *Hebron, especially the Cave of the Patriarchs and Matriarchs (*me'arat ha-makhpelah*), became preferred pilgrimage destinations. Visits to the tombs of luminaries for personal supplication were common until at least the end of the Mamluk period in the early sixteenth century, and they remained an ongoing aspect of Jewish pilgrimage, especially in the Muslim world, well into the twentieth century.

Several medieval accounts of pilgrimages to the Land of Israel (and elsewhere) written by Jews have survived. The three most notable are those of the Iberian *Benjamin of Tudela and the German Petahiah of Regensburg, both of the twelfth century, and the thirteenth-century writings of Jacob ben Nethanel ha-Cohen, from southern *France. These *travel writings make clear that the motivations for pilgrimage were not only pietistic and religious; for medieval Jews, pilgrimage was also an opportunity for *tourism and adventure. Pilgrimage accounts indicate that medieval travelers frequented a number of Jewish sites in Palestine, both in Jerusalem and elsewhere. In a 1267 letter written from Jerusalem to his son, Moses *Nahmanides commented, "Continually people crowd into Jerusalem, men and women, from Damascus, Zobah [Aleppo], and from all parts of the country, to see the Sanctuary and to mourn there" (F. Kobler, ed., *Letters of Jews through the Ages* [1952], 1:226). Cairo *Genizah documents also reveal that women were among the Jews who visited holy shrines and made pilgrimages to Jerusalem and elsewhere; widows, in particular, had significant freedom of movement (S. D. Goitein, *A Mediterranean Society: The Family* [1978], 3:338). The identification of holy sites for pilgrimage served also as a polemical point of debate in the ongoing debate between medieval Jews and Christians (Reiner).

Jews also made pilgrimages in their respective countries of settlement. Some accounts from the Rhineland mention journeys to the grave site of Rabbi *Judah the Pious in Regensburg (see HASIDEI ASHKENAZ), as well as to the graves of the martyrs killed during the First *Crusade of 1096 (Shoham-Steiner). Tombs of holy men and of male and female martyrs were also popular pilgrimage sites in Middle Eastern countries (Zenner, Stillman).

MODERN PERIOD: Pilgrimages to tombs have remained an aspect of Jewish popular religion, particularly among men and women of *Mizrahi (Middle Eastern) and *Sephardic origins; many believe that such visits may prompt the deceased to intercede between the supplicant and *God. Similar beliefs and practices are held by the *Hasidim within *Ashkenazic Jewry, but generally not by other Ashkenazic Jews.

For further reading, see M. Gil, "The Aliya and Pilgrimage in the Early Arab Period," in *The Jerusalem Cathedra* 3, ed. L. Levine (1983), 163–73; E. Reiner, "Traditions of Holy Places in Medieval Palestine: Oral versus Written," in *Offerings from Jerusalem: Portrayals of Holy Places by Jewish Artists*, ed. R. Sarfati (2002), 9–19; E. Shoham-Steiner, "'For a Prayer in That Place Would Be Most Welcome': Jews, Holy Shrines and Miracles – A New Approach," *Viator* 37 (2006): 369–95; S. Sered, *Women as Ritual Experts* (1996); and W. P. Zenner, "Saints and Piecemeal Supernaturalism among the Jerusalem Sephardim," *Anthropological Quarterly* 38(4) (1965): 201–17; and see TRAVEL WRITING: MIDDLE AGES AND EARLY MODERN PERIOD.

EPHRAIM SHOHAM-STEINER

Pinsker, Leon (Lev, or Yehudah Leib; 1821–1891), a doctor and expert in pathology, emerged in the last decade of his life as the chair of the central committee of the proto-*Zionist organization, Hovevei Zion. He was born in Tomaszow and died in Odessa; his father was a Jewish educator in Odessa and a *Karaite specialist. Leon Pinsker's Jewish involvements were originally liberal and integrationist. The *pogroms of 1881–82, however, inspired him to write the anguished German-language pamphlet, *Autoemancipation* (1882). As the informal leader of Russia's Jewish nationalists before the 1884 formal establishment of *Hovevei Zion*, and then as its organizational head until his death, he sought to achieve formal governmental recognition of the body, to organize its fundraising, and to mediate between its religious and nonreligious members. Much to his frustration, none of these tasks was accomplished with unequivocal success.

Pinsker is best remembered for *Autoemancipation*, in which he described the Jews as a ghostlike people without the concrete trappings of nationhood; indestructible, they would continue to inspire unease until they found themselves a home. For further reading see David Vital, *The Origins of Zionism* (1975).

STEVEN J. ZIPPERSTEIN

Piyyut/Piyyutim: See POETRY, LITURGICAL (*PIYYUT*)

Poetry, Biblical: See BIBLE: POETRY

Poetry: Britain. Isaac Rosenberg (1890–1918) was the first Anglo-Jewish poet to write explicitly Jewish verse in English. Poems, such as "The Burning of the Temple," "The Destruction of Jerusalem by the Babylonian Hordes," and "Through These Pale Cold Days," reflect on Jewish history and a *Zionist future by "the pools of Hebron again." Rosenberg also wrote an unfinished play in verse, *Moses*, in which Hebrew slaves are inducted into "some newer nature, a consciousness/ Like naked light seizing the all-eyed soul." Despite these themes, Rosenberg is read mainly as a *World War I poet.

Rosenberg's Modernist emphasis is also found in the poems of John Rodker (1894–1955). Significantly, Rodker told Ezra Pound that he had "no history to speak of." Unlike Rosenberg, Rodker did not write explicitly about Jewishness. Rather, he wrote poems, plays, and novels as an outsider, someone who felt exilic as a Jew in England. In his autobiography, *Memoirs of Other Fronts* (1932), Rodker stated, "In Paris I feel English, in London a foreigner." His intense, often imagistic poems stress alienation and the elaborate masks that modernity compels people to wear. Pound believed that Rodker's poetic novel *Adolphe 1920* (1929) marked a notable "development" from James Joyce's *Ulysses* (1922). Other, less influential Anglo-Jewish poets at work between the wars include Lazarus Aaronson, A. Abrahams, Gilbert Frankau (son of the Victorian Anglo-Jewish novelist Julia Frankau), Louis Golding, Joseph Leftwich, Julius Lipton, James Singer, and Humbert Wolfe.

In the wake of *World War II, Anglo-Jewish poets became more assertive. After the *Holocaust, poets such as Jon Silkin (1930–1997), Philip Hobsbaum (1932–2005), and Elaine Feinstein (b. 1930) felt compelled to reconsider their English and Jewish identities. The Welsh poet Dannie Abse (b. 1923) expressed a widely held view when in "White Balloon," he wrote, "Dear love, Auschwitz made me/ more of a Jew than Moses did." Silkin wrote "A Prayer Cup," which features "wine," in a figure of Christian transubstantiation, changing to "three inches of the blood/ of six million." Meanwhile, Hobsbaum ironically recorded the lessons learned at the "University of Auschwitz" in his poem, "Professor Grottmann Explains Everything." Feinstein, too, wrote of feeling "like someone/ who has escaped too lightly/ from the great hell of the camps" and then added, "except that I don't altogether escape" ("Lisson Grove").

Beginning in the 1960s, several women added their voices to Anglo-Jewish verse. Elaine Feinstein harked back to an important Anglo-Jewish forebear in the eponymous "Amy Levy" (see LITERATURE: BRITAIN). The poem has Levy (1861–1889) question Feinstein in a dream: "Here, it is my name that makes me strange./ A hundred years on, is it still the same?" Thus, Feinstein pessimistically suggests that "a hundred years on" the situation of Anglo-Jewish women poets is, indeed, "the same." Among other contemporary women poets, Ruth Fainlight (b. 1931), Karen Gershon (1923–1993), Lotte Kramer (b. 1923), Gerda Mayer (b. 1927), Jenny Joseph (b. 1932), and Joanne Limburg (b. 1970) merit attention.

Gershon, Kramer, and Mayer share some history because all three poets were *Kindertransport refugees from continental Europe. Much of their poetry concerns this childhood flight from *Nazism; for example, Gershon's "The Children's Exodus," Kramer's "Dover Harbour," and Mayer's "The Emigration Game – Winter 1938/39." Fainlight stands in interesting contrast to Feinstein. Whereas the latter celebrates her exilic freedom (indeed, she has written three poems with the title and theme of "Exile"), Fainlight tends not to romanticize her Jewishness in this way. Rather, Fainlight presents Jewishness as unchosen displacement (see, for instance, "Vertical"), with poetry and other arts offering a safe aesthetic space where the pressure of dominant cultures may be provisionally eased and contained (see, for example, "With David in the Nimrud Galleries," "Paradise," and "Green"). Exile is also a concern of Jenny Joseph. Her poem "An Exile in Devon" is situated among "English country lanes," a locale in which the speaker feels "very lonely." Here the poem's persona cannot relate to her insular English friend who "never has known greater danger than/ All who watch tides and storms in a peaceful country." Yearning for a shared

emotional landscape, the speaker poignantly states, "I ache for the misery I fight against." By contrast, "Warning" is set "in the street," far from rural England. This poem celebrates difference and nonconformity: "When I am an old woman I shall wear purple/ With a red hat which doesn't go, and doesn't suit me." Here Joseph's persona exalts in *chutzpah* and personal freedom: She plans to "gobble up samples in shops" and leave her English friends "shocked and surprised." According to BBC polls, "Warning" remains a favorite poem of the English reading public. Like Joseph, Joanne Limburg brings humor to bear on her situation as an English Jew. Poems such as "Mother Chicken Soup" and "The Nose on My Face" tackle stereotypes surrounding the "Jewish mother" and Jewish women in England. The former poem concludes with the speaker's mother boiling herself in a pot of chicken soup. Her (suicide) note reads, "I don't expect gratitude -/ Only that you should do as much/ for your own children./ Turn me up to 150/ When you get in. Mum." Humorously, "The Nose on My Face" lists ways in which Jewish women are negatively portrayed in English culture and society and satirizes English hypocrisy about such stereotypes.

Among other poets deploying humor to evoke their sense of dislocation from mainstream Englishness are Daniel Weissbort (b. 1935), Bernard Kops (b. 1926), and Michael Rosen (b. 1946). For example, Weissbort's "So English," "The Name's Progress," and "My Country" wittily evoke childhood alienation in the midst of popular patriotism and expectations that British Jews should assimilate. Irony abounds in Weissbort's verse; for example, "With nostalgia, I remember/ 'Onward Christian Soldiers' and/ 'To be a Pilgrim'" ("Memories of War"). By contrast, Bernard Kops expresses earnest nostalgia for the lost London of the Jewish East End: "Belonging – we belonged./ Poverty came later,/ when most of us did well/ and moved away" ("Passover '38"). Kops' humor is informed by melancholy, together with memories of Hitler: "a madman on the radio, far away." Michael Rosen is probably best known as a children's writer; again, many of his poems concern childhood experiences. Regarding *antisemitism in English society ("New School") and literature ("English Literature"), Rosen is unflinchingly perceptive. However, it is Emanuel Litvinoff (b. 1915) who has probably written the most powerful poem about English literary antisemitism: "To T.S. Eliot."

Several acclaimed Anglo-Jewish poets are also translators, notably Michael Hamburger (b. 1924) of German, Richard Burns (b. 1943) of Serbian, and George Szirtes (b. 1948) of Hungarian verse. Other accomplished poets, such as Nobel Laureate Harold Pinter (1930–2008) and Michelene Wandor (b. 1940), are better known as playwrights (see LITERATURE: BRITAIN; THEATER: BRITAIN). Similarly, Jonathan Treitel (b. 1959) is an acclaimed novelist while also a respected poet.   PETER LAWSON

Poetry, Holocaust: See HOLOCAUST LITERATURE: POETRY

Poetry, Liturgical (*Piyyut*). *Piyyut* (pl. *piyyutim*) refers to a poem created to substitute for, adorn, or preface a passage from the Jewish *liturgy or a liturgical rite. The Hebrew term derives from the Greek ποιητής (something made, created), which is related to the English word "poetry."

The term *"piyyut"* first appears in Rabbinic Hebrew, indicating an awareness that these works differed in form and idiom from biblical poetry (see BIBLE: POETRY) and the biblicizing poetry of the *Second Temple period. The genre may have its roots within Hebrew literature, perhaps as an intensified form of *midrashic (prose) rhetoric; other elements, however, suggest a complicated relationship with contemporaneous Christian liturgical poetry. Unlike biblical poetry, *piyyutim* typically employ end-rhyme, quote explicitly from textual sources, allude to midrash, and consist of complicated multi-poem forms. *Piyyutim* display deep familiarity with rabbinic traditions of interpretation, and their many rhetorical features, such as metonymy, resemble *midrashic methods of reading. Originally, *piyyutim* occupied the place of statutory prayers; poems were interwoven with liturgical formulas, as well as allusions to the weekly *Torah reading and contemporary events. As the texts of the prayers became fixed, poems were used to frame the standardized wordings rather than replacing them.

The earliest *piyyutim* (ca. fourth and fifth centuries CE) were composed primarily for *Tisha B'Av and the *High Holidays; these poems embellished specific liturgical moments, such as the *shofar* or *avodah* services (see WORSHIP), or they developed topical themes such as penitence or mourning. In their classical period (fifth to seventh centuries CE), the majority of *piyyutim* adorned the blessings of the *Sabbath and *festival *amidah* (standing prayer). These poems assume the so-called triennial cycle of Torah readings typical in the Land of Israel and have proven critical in reconstructing the ancient lectionary, including the *haftarah* cycle. As the Babylonian (annual) lectionary became more widespread, and the text of the *amidah* became standardized, *piyyutim* embellishing the *shema (affirmation of divine unity) and its blessings became increasingly popular. Eventually, poets throughout the Jewish world were composing for almost all liturgical occasions, including *marriages and *circumcisions. As the liturgy became standardized, local selections of *piyyutim* often served to distinguish various rites from one another.

Although the Babylonian *Geonim initially resisted the liturgical variation and diversity introduced by *piyyutim*, over time they came to accommodate to their extremely popular use. In the Middle Ages, *piyyutim* developed along distinctive trajectories in medieval *Ashkenaz and *Sepharad. Ashkenazic poetry amplified the complex styles typical of the classical *piyyutim*, emphasizing ornate forms, opaque allusions to the *Bible and rabbinic traditions, and clever but artificial grammatical constructions. Medieval Sephardic poets rejected the conventions of classical *piyyut* in favor of a more lyrical aesthetic and innovated by introducing Arabic meter. In the later Middle Ages, *piyyutim* incorporating kabbalistic themes (see KABBALAH) became popular in both Sephardic and Ashkenazic *prayer books.

Piyyutim are not only beautiful literary works in their own right but they also shed light on numerous aspects of Jewish culture through the centuries. They reveal dramatic literary developments in Hebrew poetics and *aesthetics; indicate the complex development and experience of the Jewish prayer service; intersect in tantalizing ways with early *synagogue *art and early Christian hymnography; and suggest much about the creation and transmission of rabbinic *aggadah in the popular synagogue context in Jewish antiquity and the Middle Ages. For further reading, see L. S. Lieber, *Yannai on Genesis: An Invitation to Piyyut* (2010).   LAURA S. LIEBER

Poetry, Medieval: Christian Europe. In *Italy, Hebrew rhymes on lapidaries date from the late seventh to early eighth centuries. Southern Italian Jews had preserved liturgical poetry (see POETRY: LITURGICAL [*PIYYUT*]) by the sixth-century poet Eleazar ben Kallir and new compositions did not appear until the ninth century. Early *paytanim* (composers of *piyyutim*) include Shefatiah, his son Amitai, and Silano. By the mid-tenth century, *piyyutim* flourished in central and northern Italy, composed by poets such as Solomon ha-Bavli and Meshullam bar Kalonymos. Italian *paytanim* adhered to Palestinian exemplars, but they were also innovative, devising a new "word meter" that would become popular in later *Askenazic *piyyutim*. They composed *piyyutim* for sections of the *liturgy without Kallirian exemplars, chiefly the *Yotser* and *Ma'ariv*. These traditions traveled to the Rhineland of *Germany with Meshullam bar Kalonymos, who was purportedly enticed by Charlemagne to settle in Mainz.

Early Italian Jewish poets also used Hebrew for nonliturgical literature. The works of Shabbetai Donnolo, the ninth-century physician (see MEDICINE) and metaphysician, had a long life. A macaronic Italian and Hebrew song from the tenth century documents early Jewish participation in the Sicilian slave trade. Immanuel of Rome (ca. 1261–ca. 1332) introduced the sonnet to Hebrew soon after its appearance in Italian (1300), but disapproval of Immanuel's profane subject matter drove the Hebrew sonnet underground for another two centuries. By Immanuel's time, poets had abandoned the heavy aesthetic of Palestinian *piyyut* for the lighter elegance of Spanish Hebrew verse (see POETRY, MEDIEVAL: MUSLIM WORLD; SPAIN, MUSLIM). Immanuel also adapted the quantitative metrics of Spanish Hebrew, paving the way for the stress-syllabic meters that would characterize later Hebrew poetry in Europe. Other poets from this later period include Moses da Rieti (1388–after 1460), who introduced the *terza rima* into Hebrew and whose *Mikdash Me'at* (Little Sanctuary) was inspired by Dante's *Divine Comedy*. The lament of Moses Remos (ca. 1406–1430), a Majorcan-born physician living in *Sicily, was written just before his execution in Sicily on charges of poisoning a patient.

Italian Jewish poetry, with its Palestinian traditions, made its way into *Germany with the migration of southern Italian Jews in the mid-tenth century. This explains why German (*Ashkenazic) Jewish practice preserved Palestinian texts and customs that survived nowhere else in Europe. Early Ashkenaz *paytanim* include Meshullam bar Kalonymos, Simon bar Isaac bar Abun, *Gershom Meor ha-Golah of Mainz ("Light of the Exile"; ca. 960–1028), and Meir bar Isaac Shatz ("Nehorai"). Often linked to these poets is Joseph ben Samuel Tov Elem (= Bonfils) in Limoges, an indication of early Ashkenazic hegemony over the Jewish communities of France (see FRANCE: MIDDLE AGES). Ashkenazic reverence for Kallir and his early Italian successors inspired a unique genre, the *piyyut* commentary, a largely unpublished literature. Ashkenazic Jews, seeking new sites in the *liturgy to embellish poetically, produced a prolific corpus of the penitential genres known as *selihot* and *kinnot* (sing., *selihah*, *kinnah*). After the First Crusade attacks on Jewish

Rhineland communities (see MIDDLE AGES: CRUSADES), poetic laments commemorated the victims. The Ashkenazic *selihot* and *kinnot* that memorialize Jewish suicide-martyrs embody Jewish ideals of resistance and faith while embedding historical details in verse, a new development in European Hebrew poetry.

The evidence for secular poetry in Ashkenaz is virtually nonexistent, although songs, stories, and poems presumably had their place in communal life. Among surviving religious poetry are works associated with the *Hasidei Ashkenaz*, or German pietists. The great mystical poem, "*Shir ha-Yihud*" (Poem of [Divine] Union) is attributed to their founder, *Judah the Pious; Judah's grandson, Eleazar ben Judah of Worms, the Rokeah; ca. 1165–ca. 1230), composed a moving elegy describing the murder of his wife and daughters (see WOMEN: MIDDLE AGES).

Although scholars have largely considered French Jewry part of Ashkenaz, its poetic legacy is distinct. By the early twelfth century, Troyes, home to the renowned Solomon bar Isaac (*Rashi, d. 1105), was a magnet for Jewish scholars. Rashi and his grandsons, the *Tosafist exegetes Samuel ben Meir (the Rashbam, ca.1055–ca. 1174) and Jacob ben Meir (Rabbenu Tam, d. 1171), were also poets, although poetry did not figure centrally in their intellectual universe and was less emphasized as a mature occupation than it was among German Jews. Some French poets, like Rabbenu Tam, and some Ashkenazic poets who studied in France, like Ephraim of Regensburg or *Meir of Rothenberg, show an awareness of Spanish styles. Meir of Rothenberg (d.1293) was in Paris in the early 1240s when the Talmud was burned following its trial for blasphemy. His lament, "Ask, O You who have been burned in fire," which is still recited on *Tisha B'Av, was modeled on Judah *Halevi's beloved poem, "Zion, won't you ask about the fate of your captives?"

French rabbis also composed penitential *selihot* and *kinnot* with *martyrological themes; many commemorate incidents of judicial execution, reflecting the changing tenor of anti-Jewish violence during the thirteenth century. Judah bar Jacob composed a double set of *kinnot* in response to the burning of thirteen Jews in Troyes in 1288; one in Judeo-French attests to a largely lost tradition of vernacular composition. (A macaronic wedding song in Hebrew and Judeo-French also survives.) Yom Tov Joigny, who composed a lament for the martyrs of Blois (1171), was among the two hundred martyrs of York (1191 [see MARTYRDOM]). After the expulsion of 1306, traces of French Jewish poetry survive in Provence and Catalonia and, after the final expulsion of 1394, in northern Italy.

England was home to several thousand Jews from the mid-twelfth century until their expulsion in 1290 (see ENGLAND: MIDDLE AGES). Most of this community originated in Normandy and retained strong ties to French Jewish tradition. Although very little remains of their literature, at least two thirteenth-century poets are known: Meir ben Elias of Norwich and Jacob of London. Scholars debate whether Berekhiah ha-Nakdan, the author of a lively Hebrew collection of fox tales, a popular medieval genre of animal stories, was an English Jew.

Provence is usually treated as a cultural satellite of Spain. Languedoc became French in 1224, but Provence proper, south of the Rhone, was not annexed until the late fifteenth century. Twelfth-century Spanish refugees to Provence, like Joseph *Kimhi (ca. 1105–ca. 1170), brought with them a highly developed interest in biblical *grammar, exegesis, and elegant Hebrew verse. Kimhi's *Bible commentaries contain poetic prefaces, and he wrote didactic and liturgical poems. The late-thirteenth-century Gascon exile, Isaac ha-Gorni, has been called Provence's Hebrew "troubadour"; his extant lyrics depict his travels through the Jewish communities of Provence and his clashes with local notables and poets (see FRANCE, SOUTHERN: MIDDLE AGES).

The *piyyutim* of Isaac ha-Seniri (d. after 1229) and Zerahiah ha-Levi (ca. 1125–?) were beloved in Provence for centuries; others, by Solomon Melguerri and Reuben bar Isaac of Montpellier, were later transplanted by exiles to *North Africa. Abraham Bedersi (mid-thirteenth century to after 1290) and his son Jedaiah (ca. 1270–after 1306) wrote polemical, philosophical, and moralistic verse. Jedaiah, and perhaps his father, composed eccentric forms of alliterative verse; Jedaiah also authored a rhymed philosophical meditation, *Behinat 'Olam* (Examination of the World), one of the most popular medieval Hebrew books, as well as a unique Hebrew poetic treatise, *Sefer ha-Pardes* (The Book of the Orchard). Other unusual poetic works include the Hebrew and Judeo-Provençal Esther verse romances of Crescas (Israel) Caslari (d. after 1357) and the *Evel Rabbati* (The Great Mourning) of Jacob ben Solomon, which describes his daughter's death from plague in 1382.

In the mid-twelfth century, increasing areas of Muslim Spain returned to Christian rule. The bridge figure for this period is Abraham *ibn Ezra (ca. 1093–ca. 1167). With the Berber invasions of the Muslim South, he began his peregrinations through North Africa, Italy, Provence, France, and England. A stylist and grammarian, as well as a composer of sacred and secular verse, Ibn Ezra introduced the poetic forms and meters of Spanish Hebrew into Christian lands. The popular *maqama* evolved in Christian Spain to reflect the interests of the vernacular romance (see LITERATURE, HEBREW: MEDIEVAL SPAIN). Joseph ibn Zabara, Judah ibn Shabbetai, Judah al-Harizi (an émigré in Provence), Jacob ben Elazar, Shem Tov ibn Falaquera, and Isaac ibn Sahula all composed *maqamot* of enduring appeal. Christian Spain also produced kabbalistic poets, like the biblical exegete Moses ben Nahman (*Nahmanides or the Ramban; 1194–1270) and Meshullam Dapiera (early thirteenth century to after 1260; see KABBALAH). The visionary author of the *Sefer ha-Ot* (Book of the Letter), Abraham *Abulafia (1240–ca. 1291) wandered through Palestine, *Greece, and Italy; his legendary journey to Rome in 1288 to convert the Pope nearly ended in his death.

Among secular poets of later thirteenth-century Christian *Spain is Todros Abulafia (1247–after 1300), who belonged to the circle of poets, scholars, and translators at the court of Alfonso X (the Wise) of Castile. His poetry addresses an astonishing diversity of themes, including the romance topos of "spiritual love." Shem Tov Ardutiel, or Santob de Carrión (late thirteenth century to after 1345), wrote a Hebrew *maqama* (*Milhemet ha-Et ve-ha-Misparayim* [The Battle of the Pen and Scissors]) and the Spanish *Proverbios morales*. However, by the late fourteenth century, Hebrew poetry, like its authors, was under siege. Approximately two-thirds of Spanish Jewry converted after the 1391 *pogroms. The poets known as the *Adat Nognim* (Band of Singers) continued to write, some as Christians. Solomon Dapiera (1340s–after

1417) converted in 1413–14 after the Disputation of Tortosa; Vidal Benveniste, his student, remained a Jew. Solomon ha-Levi (baptized Pablo de Santa Maria, ca. 1351–1435), whose *Purim parody in verse was written from a London prison in 1389, converted after 1391. Solomon Bonafed (d. after 1445) remained a Jew. After 1492, the legacy of these poets was carried into exile. A few survivors, such as Judah Uziel of Fez and Naḥman Sanbel, a follower of the *messianic pretender, David *Reuveni, continued to write. Over the years, the memory of French and Provençal poetry was overshadowed by the Spanish. Nonetheless, in many Hebrew manuscripts, poems from these traditions await reclamation.

For further reading, see T. Carmi, ed. and trans., *Penguin Book of Hebrew Verse* (1981); B. Bar Tikvah, "Reciprocity between the Provençal School of *Piyyutim* and the Schools of Catalonia and Askenazi France," in *Rashi: 1040–1990: Hommage à Ephraim Urbach*, ed. G. Sed-Rajna (1993), 375–83; P. Cole, ed. and trans., *The Dream of the Poem: Hebrew Poetry from Muslim and Christian Spain 950–1492* (2007); S. L. Einbinder, "Meir b. Elijah of Norwich: Persecution and Poetry among Medieval English Jews," *Journal of Medieval History* 26(2) (2000): 145–62; idem, *Beautiful Death: Jewish Poetry and Martyrdom in Medieval France* (2002); and I. Ta-Shema, "Ashkenazi Jewry in the Eleventh Century: Life and Literature," in *Ashkenaz: The German Jewish Heritage*, ed. G. Hirschler (1987), 20–23.   SUSAN L. EINBINDER

Poetry, Medieval: Muslim World. Nearly all of the Hebrew verse composed during the first centuries of *Islam adhered in form and content to a religious poetic model going back to the traditional *piyyut* (see POETRY: LITURGICAL [*PIYYUT*]) of *Byzantine Palestine. It is only with *Saadia Gaon that Hebrew poetry in the Muslim world begins to reflect the Jews' encounter with Islamic civilization. Arabization of the Jewish communities of the Muslim world west of the Iranian plateau and the cosmopolitan intellectual and cultural environment in Baghdad prompted Saadia to create a multifaceted intellectual agenda for the Jewish communities under his guidance. This innovative cultural program placed Hebrew poetry in a position of prominence.

Saadia Gaon and likeminded religious intellectuals were aware that Muslim society held Arabic poetry and its classical language in very high esteem. It also attached great importance to the "inimitable wondrousness" of the Arabic Qur'an. These developments in Arabo-Islamic culture stimulated Jewish reconsideration of the Hebrew *Bible and its classical language, leading to renewal and innovation in Hebrew poetry. Under Saadia, Biblical *Hebrew replaced the decidedly aclassical and inventive Hebrew of the traditional *piyyut*. He compiled a poetic manual for Hebrew poets as well as a philosophical poem and other nonliturgical verse as part of his revamping of the Jewish higher curriculum. Nevertheless, it fell to the Jewish community in al-Andalus (present-day *Spain), on the western frontier of Islam, to develop Hebrew poetry most fully.

*Dunash ben Labrat, a Moroccan who had ventured eastward to become one of Saadia Gaon's disciples, returned to the Muslim West; in Umayyad Cordoba he developed a Hebrew prosody based on Arabic metrics. Ben Labrat also introduced Arabic-inspired social themes to his new style of Hebrew verse, alongside his ongoing production of liturgical poetry. By the end of the tenth century a more artistically sophisticated generation of Andalusi Hebrew poets had emerged, although several of them stuck firmly to the older liturgical poetic style. However, Andalusi Jewish elites swiftly embraced the new style of Hebrew poetry and supported a class of professional poets who, like their Arabic counterparts, sang the praises of their patrons.

Hebrew poetry was such a cornerstone of the Andalusi Jewish cultural scene that it rapidly became a vehicle for imaginative exercises on various themes, self-expression, and artistic experimentation and was never confined to professional poets. By the third generation, the Andalusi school of Hebrew verse came of age in the towering figure of *Samuel ha-Nagid (d. 1056), the first of the four greatest poets of the period, as well as a rabbinic scholar, communal leader, and high official in the Muslim state of Granada. Samuel mastered the metrical system that Dunash had devised, and he incorporated into Hebrew all of the major themes and genres (e.g., panegyric, wine, love, floral, meditative, lament, gnomic, martial) developed in Arabic poetry. Like Samuel ha-Nagid, each of the three most accomplished poets to follow mastered Andalusi rhetorical conventions and style while developing his own individual voice in a dialectical relationship with poetic tradition. Each poet also found new ways to incorporate language, images, and motifs drawn from social poetry (even including erotic elements that were used to explore the relationship between God and Israel) in his liturgical compositions.

Solomon *ibn Gabirol (d. ca. 1058) was a socially alienated, philosophically minded poet who incorporated Neoplatonic thought into much of his verse. He emphasized the inner spiritual life of the individual in his liturgical compositions, blurring the thematic lines between religious and nonreligious Hebrew poetry. Moses *ibn Ezra (d. ca. 1138), two of whose Arabic prose works about Andalusi Hebrew poetry and poetics have also come down to us, was deemed "the penitential poet" by tradition, on account of his large corpus of penitential poems. He is also regarded as the most "conservative" Hebrew poet because he closely followed Arabic verse in form and content. Although the creation of Hebrew poetry in Muslim Spain would not actually end until Saadia ibn Danaan at the end of the sixteenth century, Judah *Halevi (d.1141) was the last great Hebrew poet of the immediate period who was associated with the Arabic cultural environment. Halevi is almost universally regarded as the most artistically accomplished post-biblical Hebrew poet. His unique lyric sensibility is reflected in social and liturgical verse alike; he created an entirely new genre of Hebrew "sea poems" that serve as a brilliant poetic reflection of his inner turmoil and fervent hope in abandoning Iberia for the Land of Israel. Translations of these poets' work appear in T. Carmi, *The Penguin Book of Hebrew Verse* (1981), and P. Cole, *The Dream of the Poem* (2007).

In addition to the mono-rhymed Arabic-style Hebrew lyric designed for recitation, from the eleventh century on poets also composed metrically complex strophic poems (in Arabic, *muwashshah* [girdle poem]) that were sung to musical accompaniment. In their Hebrew incarnations, the piquant concluding segment of this type of poem could be in colloquial Arabic, a romance language, or Hebrew.

Some time after the Arabic literary form of elevated rhymed prose arrived in al-Andalus from the Muslim

East, various types of Hebrew rhymed prose narratives interspersed with short poems became popular forms of entertainment as much as vehicles for literary artistry. Judah al-Ḥarizi (thirteenth century), originally from Castile, left Iberia for the Muslim East and composed the *Book of Tahkemoni*, the classical Hebrew collection of the Arabic *maqama* genre (rhetorical anecdotes). Among others, the sixteenth-century Yemeni author Zechariah al-Dahiri modeled his own *maqama* collection after al-Ḥarizi (see also LITERATURE, HEBREW: MEDIEVAL SPAIN).

From al-Andalus, Hebrew poetry migrated south and east. Because of their renown and prestige, the poetry collections of the great Andalusi Jewish literary and religious intellectuals were quickly copied and absorbed by socially more conservative Jewish communities and their poets in *North Africa, *Egypt (the thirteenth-century *Rabbanite Joseph ben Tanḥum Yerushalmi and the *Karaite Moses Darʿi), *Yemen, *Iraq, and subsequently in other parts of the *Ottoman Empire. Although the social themes never attained as much popularity in the East as they had enjoyed in al-Andalus, the biblicizing style and arabicizing prosody of the Andalusian poets caught on and were employed in sacred compositions. From the sixteenth century on, Hebrew poetry in Muslim lands turned even more sharply to deeply pious yearnings for *redemption and to mystical themes (see KABBALAH). Among many important poets, Israel Najara (sixteenth-century *Palestine) and Shalem Shabazi (seventeenth-century Yemen) stand out for composing hundreds of liturgical poems.   Ross Brann

Poetry, Modern Hebrew.

Since its beginnings in the late nineteenth century, Modern *Hebrew poetry has been characterized by a tension between centuries of earlier Hebrew literary texts, with their rich metaphorical and literary allusions, and the colloquial Hebrew of the contemporary world, with its reliance on everyday speech and physical realities.

EARLY EXEMPLARS: Hayyim Nahman *Bialik (1873–1934), considered the father of Modern Hebrew poetry, wrote his first Hebrew poem, "*El ha-Tzippor*" (To the Bird), in Odessa in 1882. Reflecting his longing for a Jewish homeland, Bialik's poetry lamented the degeneration of the Jewish nation in exile and called for a new future. This focus made him the first Jewish national poet. Bialik was educated in Jewish tradition and Hebrew lore, and his rich poetic imagery drew on this heritage while also expressing the inner conflicts of modern individuals.

Saul Tchernikhovsky (1875–1943) came from a markedly different background. Secular by upbringing, Tchernikhovsky was interested in European literature; he translated works into Hebrew from more than fifteen languages. Profoundly influenced by the landscapes of his childhood – the fertile fields and the vast steppes of the Russian Crimea – his poetry is steeped in natural imagery. Tchernikhovsky coined many new terms for flora and fauna, providing a new Hebrew vocabulary for his verdant imagery. Alongside his contributions to Hebrew poetic form and linguistic tools was his thematic interest in depicting women and the female anatomy. Tchernikhovsky's revival of love themes in Hebrew poetry was deeply influenced by the writings of Immanuel of Rome (ca . 1261–ca. 1328), who wrote passionate Hebrew love sonnets based on Italian models (see POETRY, MEDIEVAL: CHRISTIAN EUROPE).

In their respective ways, Bialik and Tchernikhovsky developed a future for Hebrew poetry by introducing innovative forms and language. However, both men were working with a written Hebrew that lacked the vibrancy of living speech. In the 1920s, as the center of Hebrew poetry moved to *Palestine, with its preferred use of *Sephardic pronunciation, their intricate poetic cadences, rhythms, and rhymes, composed in the *Ashkenazi pronunciation of *Eastern Europe, soon lost favor. Difficult to read and trapped within Eastern European motifs, rather than the living landscape of *Palestine, these two poets were soon superseded by a new generation.

PALESTINIAN PERIOD (1920–47): In the era after World War I and before the establishment of the State of *Israel, poets first introduced the rhythms of the spoken language into Hebrew poetry, although their literary themes continued to be influenced by European movements, including Russian Futurism, Russian Symbolism, and German Expressionism. Among this generation were the poets Yehuda Karni (1884–1949), Uri Tzvi Greenberg (1896–1981), Isaac Lamdan (1899–1954), Abraham Shlonsky (1900–1973), S. Shalom (1904–1990), and Natan Alterman (1910–1970). These poets described the realities of life in the *Yishuv, the Jewish community in Palestine, capturing authentic experience. They secularized biblical imagery to represent the challenges and joys of settling the land, with poets like Abraham Shlonsky rebelling against Bialik's "classicism." Abba Kovner (1918–1987), Itamar Ya'oz Kest (b. 1934), and others also represented in poetic terms the starker truths of the daily struggle for survival in Palestine.

Lyrical poetry capturing the essence of the Palestine landscape was characteristic of this era. Esther Raab (1894–1981) and Rahel Bluwstein (1890–1931), known simply as Rahel, published elegiac, erotic, and sensual descriptions of the Land of Israel. Concurrently, Leah Goldberg (1911–1970) and Natan Alterman were depicting the growth of *Tel Aviv, Palestine's urban center. Alterman's importance as a national figure, occupying the status Bialik had once held, was assured through his weekly newspaper column that discussed current events in verse. His ironic and satirical wit introduced new dimensions of humor into Hebrew poetry. Although most Modern Hebrew poetry is secular, there were important exceptions in this period. Greenberg and Zelda (Zelda Shneurson Mishkowsky [1916–1984]) were steeped in *Hasidism and wrote poetry full of allusions to traditional *Judaism. Greenberg's religious poetry encapsulated his belief in the messianic vision of a Jewish return to the Land of Israel.

PALMAKH GENERATION (*DOR HA-PALMAKH*). These poets, who began publishing in the 1940s, included Natan Zach (b. 1930), Yehuda Amichai (1924–2000), Haim Gouri (b. 1923), Anadad Eldan (b. 1924), Amir Gilboa (1917–1984), and Ted Carmi (1925–1994). Born in Israel or immigrating there as children, they were raised within the material reality of *Zionist ideology in the 1920s and 1930s, with Hebrew as their dominant spoken language. Many of these men had served as soldiers in the Palmakh (pre-state Jewish defense forces) or British Army, and they became officers in the 1948 War of Independence. Turning from the European influences of previous generations, they looked to the Anglo-American literary traditions of late Modernism. Influenced by poets such as W. H. Auden and William

Carlos Williams, their poetry shaped biblical imagery into a colloquial discourse. Thematically, these writers expressed the premises of Zionist ideology, which they often challenged or questioned. Shying away from the bombastic literary traditions of their predecessors with its exalted language, they focused on personal details of intimate and private experiences. Their tone, reflecting existentialist sentiments, was deliberately understated and often focused on personal loss or grief.

Yehuda Amichai (1924–2000), whose early poetry reflects the thematics of this generation, came increasingly to represent the minutiae of daily life. His writings are characterized by gentle irony and tender depictions of love – whether sexual love, love for people, or love for Israel, particularly *Jerusalem. His discovery by British poet Ted Hughes in the 1960s and the subsequent translation of his work into more than thirty languages gave Amichai an international reputation and following. His complex integration of traditional religious figures and texts into profoundly secular poetry resonated with the Israeli public, and the simplicity of his language and modes of expression made his poetry accessible and popular.

NEW WAVE GENERATION: During the 1960s and 1970s the "New Wave" generation began to experiment with avant-garde poetry. This generation included Pinḥas Sadeh (1929–1994) Yonah Wallach (1944–1985), Yair Hurvitz (1941–1988), and Meir Wieseltier (b. 1941). Sometimes known as the *Dor ha-Medinah* (generation of the state), these writers experimented with language, producing radical and dissonant verse with sparse forms, fractured sentences, and disjointed images. Much of this poetry is hypersexualized or political in content, although it can convey equally well the fragmentation of the human being in the modern world.

OTHER APPROACHES: Despite these historical divisions it would be wrong to suggest that all Israeli poets were bound by such classifications. Dalia Rabikovitch (1936–2005) began by writing romantic poetry peopled with mythological and fantastical figures; her early works appeared in the 1950s in Avraham Shlonsky's journal *Orlion*. Her later poetry has a bitter and sarcastic tone; its free-flowing and discordant language is characteristic of the *Dor ha-Medinah* poets. She is best known in Israel for poetry that reflects her involvement with the *Israeli peace movement after the 1982 Lebanon War. Hebrew poetry that expressed the horrors of war and a longing for peace appeared as far back as Bialik's poem, "*Ba-Ir Ha-Harigah*" (In the City of Slaughter), about the 1905 Kishinev *pogrom in Moldova. Poets in the 1920s and 1930s frequently invoked their experiences of fighting in World War I in Europe, before their arrival in Palestine, or of the violence against Jews in Palestine, particularly in the riots of 1929. The *Dor ha-Palmakh* poets often portrayed images of soldiers, dead comrades, and the violence and perceived heroism of war. In addition to serving in the War of Independence, many, such as Haim Gouri, helped resettle refugees and *Holocaust survivors in Europe and Israel. Their use of military imagery is ambiguous, neither celebratory nor condemnatory. It was Hebrew poets from the 1970s and 1980s, such as Dalia Rabikovitch, Maya Bejerano (b. 1949), and Isaac Laor (b. 1948), who became increasingly critical of war and celebrated peace. A number of recent anthologies have appeared that gather writings of this kind from different historical periods in Israel. They include *No Rattling of Sabers: An Anthology of Israeli War Poetry* (ed. E. Raizen; 1996); *No Sign of Ceasefire: An Anthology of Contemporary Israeli Poetry* (ed. W. Bargad and S. Chyet; 2002); and *After the First Rain: Israeli Poems on War and Peace* (ed. M. Dor and B. Goldberg; 1998).

The publication of *Keys to the Garden: New Israeli Writing* (ed. A. Alcalay; 1996), an anthology of Mizraḥi poetry, heightened an awareness of voices that had been relegated to the margins of the Hebrew literary canon, which had historically been dominated by *Ashkenazi men. Featuring writers from the Levant, *Turkey, *Iran, *India, and the Arab world, this anthology offered poetry concerned with themes of cultural identity, race, class, gender, and political allegiances. Erez Biton (b. 1942), Amira Hess, Lev Hakak, Shlomo Avayou (b. 1939), Ronny Someck (b. 1951), Tikva Levi, and Sami Shalom Chetrit (b. 1960) are just a few of the writers whose concern with issues beyond the Zionist ideological narrative has begun to reshape the Israeli poetic map. Similarly, *The Defiant Muse: Hebrew Feminist Poems from Antiquity to the Present : A Bilingual Anthology* (ed. S. Kaufman, G. Hasan-Rokem, and T. Hess; 1999) made women's Hebrew poetry more readily available in translation than ever before.

Contemporary Hebrew poetry has experienced a resurgence in popularity since 2000. A proliferation of literary journals in Israel has made verse accessible to nontraditional readers of poetry, and poetry festivals held throughout the country have also renewed interest in the medium. A host of new poets are emerging whose subject matter is delineated by the themes of the journals in which the poems appear. Radical, political, and feminist poetry appears alongside experiments in literary forms. Isaac Laor has been among those senior poets working to encourage new poetic voices through his literary journal, *Mita'am: A Journal of Literature and Radical Thought*. Amir Or (b. 1956) has fostered the development of Hebrew poetry through the Helicon Society, which offers courses and workshops for Jewish and Arab poets to work together; he also publishes journals featuring these younger poets. Along with this support of innovative themes and styles, there is a renewed interest in the ballad and a return to more traditional poetic forms, advocated by journals such as *Ho!*.

A number of leading Hebrew poets have had their verses adopted or adapted as lyrics for popular *music. Natan Alterman wrote lyrics to several songs that became immensely popular, and Yona Wallach has written lyrics for rock bands. Even when particular poets appear to have been replaced by younger generations, musical versions of their poetry continue to be popular. Demonstrating the durability of great poetic verse, Bialik's love poem "*Hikhnisini Taḥat K'nafekh*" (Take Me under Your Wing), written in 1905, continues to be sung in a haunting, lilting rendition and is often heard on televised music competitions. A classic resource is T. Carmi, *Penguin Book of Hebrew Verse* (1981).   RACHEL S. HARRIS

Poetry: United States. Jewish poets in the *United States have produced a remarkably rich and diverse body of work since at least the late nineteenth century. Mid-twentieth-century Jewish poets such as Karl Shapiro (1913–2000) and Howard Nemerov (1920–1991) and, more recently, Alan Shapiro (b. 1952) and Robert Pinsky (b. 1940), have received academic acclaim as masters of traditional formalist verse, but Jews have been especially important figures in experimental strains of modern and contemporary poetics. Post–World War II poets Allen Ginsberg (1926–1997), Jerome Rothenberg (b. 1931), and Charles Bernstein (1950) became leaders in the countercultural movements of "Beat" poetry, "ethnopoetics," and "Language" poetry.

Among American Jewish poets are many women, including Emma Lazarus (1849–1887), whose "New Colossus" is etched on the base of the Statue of Liberty. Feminist poets Muriel Rukeyser (1913–1980) and Adrienne Rich (b. 1920) also have written on behalf of other aggrieved communities. For example, Rukeyser's 1938 Book of the Dead documents the disastrous exposure of hundreds of West Virginia tunnel workers to silica dust. The long poems of Charles Reznikoff (1894–1976) – Testimony, based on trial records concerning mistreatment of *African Americans, and Holocaust – blend historical documentation with the Modernist technique of Objectivism. The contemporary poet Irena Klepfisz (born 1941 in the *Warsaw *ghetto) sets *Yiddish beside English in her poetry, which often invokes the *Holocaust. Jewish Modernists such as Moyshe-Leyb Halpern (1886–1932) and Jacob Glatstein (1896–1971), writing in Yiddish in the first decades of the twentieth century, also made important contributions to the experimental and innovative strains of American poetry (see POETRY, YIDDISH).

Despite these accomplishments (and the fact that three recent American poet laureates – Louise Gluck [b. 1943], Pinsky, and Stanley Kunitz [1905–2006] – have been Jews), the study of Jewish American poetry remains in its infancy. In "The Sorrows of American Jewish Poetry" (in Figures of Capable Imagination [1976]), literary critic Harold Bloom infamously suggested that poetic practice is "alien to a Jewish sensibility." "The Jew," he argued, "cannot wholly commit himself to the 'pragmatic religion-of-poetry,' or hold a precursor poet in "god-like esteem" (251, 253). Bloom viewed as unconscionably transgressive the idea of the Jewish poet mixing allegiances and influences with a "gentile precursor." In 1994, novelist and essayist Cynthia Ozick suggested that Jewish American poetry has yet to come into its own because it "depends upon its ability to generate a shared vision of communal well being, grounded in a culturally distinct language, a 'new Yiddish'" ("America: Toward Yavneh," in What is Jewish Literature?, ed. H. Wirth-Nesher [1999]).

*Diaspora poetics – that is, the emphasis on a lost or erased origin that maintains its spectral power over the secular Jewish culture of America – and the acceptance of an unstable, linguistically oriented sense of self that exists in between clearly delineated spaces may be the signal characteristics of Jewish American poetry. Both are evident in the Yiddish Modernist poetry of Mikhl Likht (1893–1953). Born in the Ukraine, Likht became immersed in the *New York City Yiddish Modernist culture in the 1920s. A translator of Wallace Stevens, Ezra Pound, and Gertrude Stein, Likht was so committed to an introspectivist poetics and kaleidoscopic stylistics that even fellow Yiddish Modernists found him utterly incomprehensible. Becoming doubly inaccessible, Likht positioned himself as a Yiddish writer who eschewed proletarian themes and as an American Modernist who wrote in Yiddish, a language that none of his peers (Stevens, Mina Loy, Carl Sandberg) could have understood.

In contrast, Charles Reznikoff translated diasporism from a deficit state into a literary opportunity in which the possibility of redemption coexists with the face of loss. His contemporary, Louis Zukofsky (1904–1978), attempted to transform his alienation from traditional *Judaism and the situation of diasporism into the grounds for a radical humanistic ethics and a poetics that celebrates the sublimity of the particular things found in everyday life.

The diasporic poetics of Likht, Reznikoff, and Zukofsky is carried forward in the work of several important contemporary Jewish American poets, such as Alicia Ostriker (b. 1937), Norman Finkelstein (b. 1954), Rachel Blau DuPlessis (b. 1941), and Michael Heller (b. 1937). In "Remains of the Diaspora," poet and memoirist Heller, following H. N. *Bialik, argues that for the diasporic Jew "language replaces essence" and that the space of the "between" becomes an ironic foundation for poetic utterance. For Heller, as for other contemporary radical Jewish poets such as Finkelstein in Tracks, Armand Schwerner (1927–1999) in Tablets, and Ostriker in the Nakedness of the Fathers, the Hebrew *Bible and other religious texts remain important sources of inspiration, even as these texts no longer possess canonical authority or signify the poet's allegiance to Judaism as a religious practice.

In Ostriker's poetry, the gaps, silences, and omissions in the biblical text represent a literary opportunity, metaphorically, to give birth to the feminine and maternal aspects of Judaism. Ostriker argues that these impulses have been repressed in the patriarchal tradition, but, like the grandmother swallowed by the wolf in the fairy tale, await a return. Like Reznikoff, Ostriker also emphasizes a poetics of immanent spirituality, which she links to the *Shekhinah, or the feminine principal of a nontranscendent *God. Ostriker's project is to "encounter the physical selves of women," especially through attempts to reimagine the voice of the Jewish mother as something much more complex than the stereotypical smothering figure. In yet another way Ostriker's contemporary feminist *midrashic project dovetails with Reznikoff, whom she cites in her text. She imagines radicalism and her version of cultural Jewishness in a political context, as a call to social change. Both of these contemporary Jewish poets upend exclusionary ways of thinking about "sacred" and "secular" spaces, preferring to struggle to determine what Ostriker calls the "sacredness immanent within matter."

Several landmark publications have begun to rectify the lack of significant commentary on poetry by American Jews. These include the essay, "Jewish American Poetry," by M. Y. Schreiber in The Cambridge Companion to Jewish American Literature (ed. H. Wirth-Nesher and M. P. Kramer [2003]), and, most prominently, the Norton Anthology of Jewish American Literature (ed. J. Chametzky, J. Felstiner, H. Flanzbaum, and K. Hellerstein [2001]), which brought canonical status and a wide audience to previously underacknowledged poets. The anthology offers translations of Yiddish poets associated with experimental movements such as Introspectivism; Modernist poets writing in English (including the Objectivists – Reznikoff, George Oppen [1908–1984], and Carl Rakosi [1903–2004]); and Zukofsky, an unofficial student of Ezra Pound whose epic poem "A" was consciously written in response to Eliot's "The Waste Land"; as well as a range of contemporary voices (among them, Pinsky, Allen Grossman [b. 1932], Philip Levine [b. 1928], and Jacqueline Osherow [b. 1956]).

DANIEL MORRIS

Poetry, Yiddish. Despite the existence of fourteenth-century *Yiddish verse narratives, Yiddish poetry is best understood as *modern* poetry. That is, only with the possibilities of a secular culture, as well as the political and societal transformations associated with modernity in *Eastern Europe, could Yiddish writing emerge as a self-consciously literary phenomenon. The most significant cultural "moment" for Yiddish poetry occurred roughly from the 1880s through the 1920s.

It is an irony of Yiddish culture that a language castigated by the Jewish intelligentsia of the *Haskalah* as an ugly "jargon" and as secondary to *Hebrew could lend itself so well to the production of poetry. Yet it has been argued that the very properties that led to the denigration of Yiddish, such as its fusing of Germanic, Hebraic, and Slavic components and its relative porousness to other languages, offered poets an appealing latitude in diction and sensibility. In addition, the development of Yiddish over hundreds of years as the language of daily life, through which and into which *Ashkenazi Jews poured their sufferings, insights, and joys, also made the language a responsive medium for poetry. Yiddish writers drew on a rich vernacular repository of idioms, proverbs, *folklore, and *music. It is not surprising that many Yiddish poets wrote their first poems in other languages since their literary influences came from German and Russian, as well as from *Hebrew, which was part of Jewish traditional education. The exhilaration of Yiddish poets as they both discovered and enhanced the poetic power of their own language comes through in their periodic "manifestos" and essays, as well as in their poems.

Modern Yiddish poetry can be viewed as progressing through several "movements" involving loosely grouped writers in *New York City, Kiev, *Warsaw, and Moscow and progressing from "proletarian," labor-oriented verse into more sophisticated phases of romanticism and Modernism – all within a matter of decades.

"Sweatshop poetry," with its vivid calls to action and images filled with anger and pathos, appealed to the urban-centered working masses. Beginning in the 1880s, these poems flourished in New York City, where a vast number of Jewish immigrants fleeing strife in Eastern Europe were struggling to live. Published in Yiddish newspapers (see JOURNALISM, YIDDISH: NORTH AMERICA) and sung in the streets, this poetry became a source of political sustenance and cultural strength at a time when labor organizing (see UNITED STATES: LABOR MOVEMENT) and the writing of poetry seemed to go hand in hand. Significant labor poets included Dovid Edelstadt (1866–1892), whose poems, set to music, have titles such as *"In kampf"* (In Struggle) and *"Vakht uf*!" (Awake) and urge their audience to throw off their chains and demand their workers' rights; and Morris Rosenfeld (1862–1923), who gained a reputation as the voice of the sweatshop workers and whose poems were the first Yiddish poems to be translated into English.

The proletarian impulse in Yiddish poetry was cast aside in New York by the group *Di Yunge* (The Youth), the next generation of writers who emerged in 1907 with its own literary journal and gatherings in local cafes. These poets pursued an aesthetic of beauty and a poetry that spoke in the first person, rather than as, or for, a collective. Yet many of the poets themselves differed little from their readers in the work they did to survive: Proletarian aesthetes,

they were paperhangers, house painters, shop workers, and boot makers. Although poets such as Mani Leyb (1883–1953), Moyshe Leyb-Halpern (1886–1932), Zisha Landoy (or Landau; 1889–1937), Anna Margolin (1887–1952), and H. Leyvik (1888–1962) are associated in some way with *Di Yunge*, they had sharply different styles, each bringing something new and memorable into Yiddish poetry. Leyb and Leyb-Halpern represented two extremes: the former with a mellifluous "high" style, marking a preoccupation with beauty against harsh material life, and the latter with a satirical, at times grotesque, "low" style, enmeshed in everyday struggles. In recent years, Leyb-Halpern has found perhaps his most appreciative audience, due in part to contemporary critics' appreciation for his more Modernist style.

The years after *World War I brought forth new groupings of Modernist writers in New York, *Poland, and the *Soviet Union, each with its little magazines, café gathering places, and literary arguments against the writers who had so recently preceded them. It was a time of artistic ferment in all the arts, and because Yiddish poets were writing what literally could not have been dreamed of before in a traditional Jewish context, they identified with the international avant-garde. In New York, where immigrant poets were free to be as Jewish and as American as they chose, a group of writers formed the group *In zikh* (Inside the Self, or introspectivist), issuing a manifesto in 1919 that declared (among other things) their independence from the necessity of having Jewish content in their poems. In contrast to members of *Di Yunge*, who never fully felt at ease in America, these younger poets knew English well, and some had even attended college in New York. Most were attracted to the imagism and free verse of their Anglo-Modernist contemporaries; they regarded themselves as cosmopolitans who happened to write in Yiddish, rather than as representatives of a Jewish culture. Significant *In zikh* poets included A. Leyeles (born Aron Glaz; 1889–1966), N. B. Minkov, Yankev Glatshteyn (Jacob Glatstein; 1896–1971), and Mikhl Likht (1893–1953), with Tsilia (Celia) Dropkin (1887–1956) tangentially affiliated. Of these writers, Glatshteyn is the best known, most translated, and most valorized as a poet of international stature. Likht, the least translated, is deserving of twenty-first-century rediscovery because of his radical embrace of Modernist experimentation.

The *In zikh* assertion of the "kaleidoscopic" individual psyche as a filter for experience brought them close to the Expressionism of their colleague poets in *Eastern Europe. Yet where the New York writers wrote with excitement about the "chaos" of the city in which they found themselves, the Yiddish poets in interwar *Poland and the *Soviet Union actually lived in chaotic conditions that were dangerous as well as stimulating. In the new Polish state that emerged after *World War I, Jews were confronted with rising Polish nationalism and *antisemitism. A Modernist aesthetic could not be the sole concern for poets in this milieu. In Warsaw, a group of poets spearheaded by Peretz Markish (1895–1952) published its first journal in 1922, declaring themselves as young, happy explorers of their frightening, dark times. Dismissed by one critic as an anarchic "gang," these writers took the word as their banner and called themselves *Di Khalyastre*. Their fervor is reflected in poet Melekh Ravitsh's (1893–1976) comment, often cited by critics, that being a Yiddish writer in Warsaw then was "to feel the redemption at hand and to be at its center." Ravitsh edited his own journal that same year, *Di Vog* (The Scale) as did a third "gang member," Uri Tzvi Greenberg (*Albatros*). Just two years later, the group was shattered by ideological differences. Greenberg (1896–1981) emigrated to *Palestine and Markish sought to live out his revolutionary ideals by returning to the Soviet Union in 1926. Ravitsh left Warsaw in the 1930s, traveling widely in the service of Yiddish culture. Of the *Di Khalyastre* poets, it is Markish who has won particular critical appreciation.

The early 1920s were also the high point of Modernist and revolutionary fervor for Yiddish poets in the Soviet Union, boosted by the regime's brief period of support for Yiddish *secularism. In 1922, Kiev-based writers led by Dovid Hofshteyn (1889–1952) published their literary journal *Shtrom* (Stream), in Moscow. For a time, they managed to balance their loyalty to Yiddish and Jewish culture with support for the new political ideals. By the mid-1920s, however, the political climate in the Soviet Union had hardened to the point where writers had to alter their poetry to fit party demands. Significant Soviet poets include Hofshteyn, Izi Kharik (1898–1937), Leyb Kvitko (ca. 1890–1952), as well as Moyshe Kulbak (1896–1940), whose stylistic range has been admired by critics. Another important cohort of Yiddish poets were *Yung Vilne*, who were active writers and social activists in Polish *Vilna in the 1930s. Of this group, Avrom (Abraham) Sutzkever (1913–2010) represents a bridge to the other side of *World War II and the *Holocaust, because almost alone among his fellow poets he survived and had a long and fruitful career as a poet in *Israel.

There are numerous Yiddish poets who do not fit into the above categories. Significant among them are Avrom Reyzen (Abraham Reisen; 1876–1953), known for his gentle, folksy lyrics; Yehoash (Solomon Bloomgarden; 1872–1927), an early Modernist who translated the Hebrew *Bible into Yiddish; Itzik Manger (1901–1969), who fashioned whimsical poems around biblical characters; and Kadya Molodowsky (1894–1975), whose evocative poetry focusing on women has drawn the positive regard of feminist critics.

The genocide of Eastern European Jewry brought Yiddish poetry as a widely developing genre to a definitive end. In the Soviet Union, repression and worse overtook most Yiddish writers. Kulbak and Kharik disappeared into prison camps in the 1930s; Hofshteyn, Markish, Kvitko, Fefer, and other Yiddish writers were executed on August 12, 1952, as part of a general purge of Yiddish leaders and intelligentsia (see also JEWISH ANTI-FASCIST COMMITTEE). For North American writers, who could only look on with horror from afar, the murder of their colleagues and destruction of their home culture and collective past meant the disintegration of their own future prospects in Yiddish (already weakened by Jews' rapid assimilation into American life). In response, most of the *In zikh* poets rejected their cosmopolitanism. In Yankev Glatshteyn's 1938 poem, "*A gute nakht velt*" (Good Night, World), he stingingly rebukes "piggish German" and "hostile Polack" and proudly returns to his "four [ghetto] walls," again embracing traditional Jewish motifs in his poetry.

Yiddish poetry (as well as the language and culture itself) was long denigrated in Israel, in part because of a conscious privileging of Hebrew as the state language. However, Yiddish poets who arrived in Israel after the war were active in writing and publishing as members of the group *Yung Yisroel* (Young Israel). Significant writers included Moyshe Yungman (b. 1922), Rivke Bassman-Ben-Chaim, Rukhl Fishman (1935–1984), and Avrom Sutzkever, under whose leadership the internationally respected literary journal, *Di Goldene Keyt* (The Golden Chain), flourished for many years. The Yiddish newspaper, *The Forverts*, published weekly in New York, often publishes work by Yiddish poets in Israel, as well as contemporary poets in the United States and other countries. However diminished, Yiddish poetry is still being written and translated.

For further reading, see M. L. Bachman, *Recovering "Yiddishland": Threshold Moments in American Literature* (2008); M. Falk, *With Teeth in the Earth: Selected Poems of Malka Heifetz Tussman* (1992); A. Glaser and D. Weintraub, eds., *Proletpen: America's Rebel Yiddish Poets* (2005); *The Selected Poems of Jacob Glatstein*, trans. R. Whitman (1972); B. Zunoff, ed., *I Keep Recalling: The Holocaust Poems of Jacob Glatstein* (1993); B. Harshav and B. Harshav, eds., *American Yiddish Poetry, A Bilingual Anthology* (1986); idem, eds., *Sing, Stranger: A Century of American Yiddish Poetry: A Historical Anthology* (2006); I. Howe, R. R. Wisse, and K. Shmeruk, eds., *The Penguin Book of Modern Yiddish Verse*, (1987); R. H. Korn, *Paper Roses* (*Papirene Rozen*), trans. S. Levitan (1985); A. Kramer, ed., *A Century of Yiddish Poetry* (1989); R. R. Wisse, *A Little Love in Big Manhattan: Two Yiddish Poets* (1988); L. Wolf, ed. and trans., *The World According to Itzik: Selected Poetry and Prose by Itzik Manger* (2002); S. Kumove, ed. and trans., *Drunk from the Bitter Truth: The Poems of Anna Margolin* (2005); K. Hellerstein, ed. and trans., *Paprine Brikn: Paper Bridges, Selected Poems of Kadya Molodowsky*, (1999); I. J. Schwartz, *Kentucky* (*Kentoki*), trans. G. Dubrovsky (1990); Abraham Sutzkever, *The Fiddle Rose: Poems 1970–72*, trans. R. R. Wisse (1990); R. Whitman, ed. and trans., *An Anthology of Modern Yiddish Poetry* (1966); and S. Wolitz, "Di Khalyastre, the Yiddish Modernist Movement in Poland: An Overview," *Yiddish* 4(3) (1987): 5–19. **See also LITERATURE, YIDDISH; MEMOIR AND LIFE WRITING: YIDDISH; THEATER, YIDDISH; YIDDISH; AND YIDDISH DICTIONARIES.**

MERLE LYN BACHMAN

Pogrom, a Russian word meaning "destruction," entered foreign languages after the anti-Jewish riots of 1881–82 in the *Russian Empire; it is often used in connection with any mass anti-Jewish violence. Earlier pogroms in the Russian Empire occurred in 1821, 1859, and 1871 in Odessa, mainly perpetrated by Greeks. The first major pogrom wave began on Easter 1881, after the murder of Tsar Alexander II on March 1 and in response to rumors that the new tsar had ordered attacks on Jews. Starting in Elisavetgrad (now Kirovograd) on April 15, pogroms spread to major cities in Russia's southeastern and southern regions (now *Ukraine) and from there to surrounding towns and villages. Sporadic pogroms also erupted between 1882 and 1884. These pogroms were directed primarily against Jewish property, and there were relatively few casualties. The most striking feature of these pogroms was the hesitant response of the authorities, who usually ended the riots only on the third day. Russian authorities and newspapers blamed Jewish economic "exploitation" for causing outbursts of popular anger. As a result, Jews were forbidden to settle in rural areas. Among Jews, the pogroms undermined hopes of

Jewish integration into Russian society and increased emigration, as well as enthusiasm for expanding the Jewish presence in *Palestine.

After twenty years of relative calm, a terrible pogrom broke out on April 6–8, 1903 in Kishinev. Local authorities did not respond for three days while forty-seven Jews were killed, more than four hundred wounded, and seven hundred houses were burned; damage was estimated at three million rubles. Public opinion blamed the reactionary Interior Minister Viacheslav Pleve for organizing the massacre. The shock of Kishinev intensified an oppositional and revolutionary mood among Russian Jews, and young people began to organize armed self-defense squads. The pogrom that erupted on September 14–16, 1903, in Gomel turned into a battle in which *Zionist and *Bundist units repulsed the rioting mob. Ten Jews and eight Christians were killed; the authorities prosecuted both the rioters and members of the self-defense groups. The mobilization for the Russo-Japanese war in 1904 was accompanied by forty-three "mobilization" pogroms; similarly, the outbreak of the first Russian Revolution in 1905 was followed by as many as fifty pogroms between January and mid-October 1905. Some of these were successfully checked by self-defense units. The publication of the Imperial Manifest promising civil liberties and the establishment of a parliament on October 17, 1905, was followed by a massive outbreak of anti-Jewish violence. In late October and November 1905, almost 3,000 Jews perished in approximately six hundred pogroms, mostly in the Ukraine region. Russian troops were active participants in pogroms in Białystok (June 1–3, 1906; seventy killed) and Siedlce (August 26–29, 1906; thirty killed). A new wave of anti-Jewish violence erupted during *World War I, when Russian units, particularly Cossacks, undertook pogroms in Russian territory and in Austrian *Galicia. During the Civil War (1918–20), which started after the Russian Revolution of 1917, there were extremely bloody pogroms, especially in Ukraine, where all the fighting armies robbed and massacred Jews, who were alternately blamed for supporting the *Bolsheviks or for being bourgeoisie. Although the Bolsheviks struggled to quell anti-Jewish violence within the Red Army, the atrocities performed by the Whites, by the Ukrainian Directory army under S. Petlura, by the Polish army, and by numerous "Green" bands continued uncurbed. It is estimated that about 50,000 Jews lost their lives in the Civil War pogroms; the most destructive was a pogrom in Proskurov by a Ukrainian unit (February 15, 1919) in which approximately 1,600 Jews were killed.

There were also anti-Jewish attacks immediately after the end of *World War II in *Poland; the most notorious occurred in Kielce, where a mob murdered forty *Holocaust survivors on July 4, 1946.

For further reading, see Committee of the Jewish Delegations, *The Pogroms in the Ukraine under the Ukrainian Governments (1917–1920): Historical Survey with Documents and Photographs* (1927); J. D. Klier and S. Lambroza, eds., *Pogroms: Anti-Jewish Violence in Modern Jewish History* (1992); and I. M. Aronson, *Troubled Waters: The Origins of the 1881 Anti-Jewish Pogroms in Russia* (1990).   VLADIMIR LEVIN

Poland was home to one of Europe's largest and most important Jewish communities from the early sixteenth century through World War II. Significant religious, cultural, and political influences on contemporary Jewish life developed in Poland. Russian and Ukrainian Jews, as well as much of the Jewish population in the *United States and *Israel, can trace their origins to Polish Jewry.

Pre-modern Poland was far larger than the area within its contemporary borders. The first Polish state was established at the end of the tenth century. The sixteenth-century union between the kingdom of Poland and the Grand Duchy of *Lithuania formed the Polish-Lithuanian Commonwealth, making Poland one of the largest states of Europe, encompassing parts of present-day *Ukraine, *Belarus, and the *Baltic states. Yet at the end of the eighteenth century the country was partitioned by the surrounding *Russian, Prussian, and *Habsburg Empires. Poland was not reestablished as an independent state until after World War I.

Significant Jewish settlement in Poland began in the twelfth to fourteenth centuries with migration from Western Europe and especially from German-speaking lands, in the wake of persecutions during the *Crusades and black death. Early Jewish settlers in Poland also came from the Crimea and the Mediterranean, but by the fourteenth century most Jews in Poland were of *Ashkenazic origin. They brought with them communal institutions, religious traditions, and the Judeo-German language, which later developed into *Yiddish, the everyday language of most Polish Jews. Jewish migrants were also drawn by economic opportunity at a time of increased state consolidation. Polish kings encouraged Jewish settlement to develop the economy, but Jews were allowed to settle only in certain locations with specific permission granted by charter; they sometimes faced persecution from church authorities and townspeople, who considered Jews to be economic competitors.

In 1264 Bolesław the Pious of Kalisz granted the first charter allowing Jewish residence in Poland, and in 1334 a charter from Kazimierz the Great placed Jews under the jurisdiction of royal governors. Early Jewish population centers were Kraków, Kalisz, Gniezno, Sandomierz, and other princely capitals. Perhaps 18,000 Jews lived in Poland and 6,000 in the Grand Duchy of Lithuania in the early sixteenth century, about 0.5% of the population. With the establishment of the Polish-Lithuanian Commonwealth in 1569 and Poland's concomitant expansion when *Ukraine was transferred from Lithuania to Poland, Jewish settlement became increasingly characterized by residence in small towns owned by Polish nobility, *szlachta* in Polish. These magnates, who became dominant in Polish politics and the economy at the expense of the king, encouraged Jewish settlement as a means of developing their towns. The relationship between the *szlachta* and Jews characterized Polish Jewish life from the mid-sixteenth century until the eighteenth-century partitions and was the origin of Jewish residence in the small private town, the *shtetl* ("small town" in Yiddish). Numbering about 20,000 to 30,000 Jews at the end of the fifteenth century, Poland's Jewish population had increased to about 300,000 in the mid-seventeenth century.

More significant Jewish settlement in private towns took place from the late seventeenth through the eighteenth century, when Jewish residence was connected with economic reconstruction after Poland's mid-seventeenth-century wars with Sweden and the Muscovites. The occupations of Polish Jewry were more diversified than in many other locations in Europe; small-town economic development depended on

Jews as craftsmen, traders, and managers of the magnate estates. By the eighteenth century more than 70% of Polish Jewry lived in the eastern part of the country, mainly in towns.

The mid-seventeenth-century wars, especially the peasant revolt led by Bogdan *Chmelnitzki (also Chmielnicki) in Ukraine in 1648, disrupted Polish Jewish life. Devastation to Jewish communities was significant, although probably not as widespread as indicated by Nathan Hannover's chronicle, written in 1653. Perhaps one-fifth of the Jewish population was killed. Historians have also disagreed about the extent to which the uprising and wars left Polish Jewry in crisis. It is clear, however, that Poland-Lithuania emerged from the turmoil as a weaker state.

Until the mid-eighteenth century, medieval Polish Jewry enjoyed permanent, centralized communal autonomy to a greater degree than elsewhere in Europe in the form of the *Council of Four Lands, which met once or twice a year from the sixteenth century until its dissolution in 1764. Yet even in medieval Poland and increasingly in modernity, Jewish life was influenced by interactions with Poland and Polish society as Jews contributed to the development of the Polish state, its economy, and culture. Religious life flourished among medieval Polish Jewry, and *yeshivot* in Poland and Lithuania trained rabbis for communities throughout Europe. Yet the eighteenth century also witnessed consolidation of the Catholic Church's influence in the Polish state, and one historian argues that the worst religious persecution of Polish Jewry took place in the 1740s and 1750s.

The end of the eighteenth century saw the fragmentation of Poland and its Jewish population. Approximately 750,000 Jews lived in Poland-Lithuania in 1764–65; after three partitions of Poland (1772, 1793, 1795), approximately 150,000 came under Prussian rule, about 250,000 under *Habsburg rule, and the remainder found themselves under tsarist rule. Poland's Jewish population was subsequently subject to the varying rulings of the partitioning states. Poland continued to exist as a political entity under Russian control; it was called Congress Poland or the Polish kingdom, but had a largely diminishing degree of autonomy. Other territories of the former Polish-Lithuanian Commonwealth under tsarist control further east were incorporated directly into the *Russian Empire.

Even as the Polish state was disintegrating, Polish Jewish religious life was experiencing a major upheaval as *Hasidism developed and spread rapidly to most areas of the former Polish-Lithuanian Commonwealth. Early Hasidic circles multiplied throughout Ukraine beginning in the mid-eighteenth century. By the mid-nineteenth century Hasidism predominated in the Polish kingdom and had spread into present-day *Belarus, *Romania, and *Hungary. Hasidism attracted only a minority of the Jewish population in Lithuania. In the nineteenth century the *Haskalah also made inroads among a minority of Jews, prompting Hasidim and *mitnaggedim, opponents of Hasidism, to unite in opposition. An increasing minority of Jews, partly drawn from a small group of economic elites, became proponents of assimilation; by the mid-nineteenth century, they sought to transform Polish Jews into "Poles of the Mosaic faith." Polish Jews took part in the Kościuszko insurrection in 1794 and in both nineteenth-century Polish uprisings against Russian rule. *Emancipation of Jews in the Polish Kingdom in 1862 removed restrictions on Jewish settlement. Because Jews elsewhere in the Russian Empire did not yet enjoy these rights, the Polish Kingdom experienced an influx of Jews from the Russian interior.

Polish–Jewish relations deteriorated in the late 1860s, and in 1881–82 pogroms took place in the Polish Kingdom as elsewhere in the tsarist realm. The subsequent development of *Zionism, socialism, and their variants, together with the move from small town to large city as part of industrialization, led to significant shifts in Jewish life, particularly after 1905 when restrictions on political activity in the Russian Empire were eased. Polish independence after *World War I was accompanied by recognition of minority rights when Poland signed the Minorities' Treaty at Versailles, under pressure from the Allies. At the same time, hundreds of Jews were killed when they were caught in border conflicts between Poland and its eastern neighbors after World War I.

Interwar Polish Jewry comprised the largest Jewish community in Europe, second in the world only to the *United States. In 1921 Poland's population of 27.2 million included 2.86 million Jews; in 1931 Jews numbered 3.1 million out of a population of 31.9 million. Migration from small towns to large cities accelerated, and by the late 1930s nearly one-third of Polish Jews lived in the twelve largest cities. Jews were among the many ethnic minorities who accounted for more than 30% of Poland's population. The interwar Jewish economic structure continued to differ from that of the surrounding population. Whereas a majority of ethnic Poles were employed in agriculture, in 1931 about 96% of Polish Jews worked in nonfarm occupations, mainly as artisans, traders, or small shopkeepers. A small number were industrialists and other economic elites, and 56% percent of doctors and one-third of legal professionals were Jewish.

Interwar Jewish political and cultural life flourished. *Zionist parties were strongest in the early interwar years, whereas the *Bund garnered limited support until the second half of the 1930s, when its opposition to boycotts and anti-Jewish violence gave it the support of majorities in Łódź, *Warsaw, and elsewhere. Many Jews remained religious, and they formed *Agudat Israel in response to the secular Jewish parties. Yet as traditional religious life weakened and occupational prospects dimmed, youth groups affiliated with political parties nourished cultural as well as political interests. Interwar Jewish youth became increasingly Polonized as a majority attended Polish-language public elementary schools; however, many Polish-speaking Jewish young people identified with Zionism. The Polish-language Jewish press came into its own, including periodicals founded by journalists seeking to develop a modern Jewish national culture. The Yiddish press still had the largest circulation among Jews (see JOURNALISM: YIDDISH [EASTERN EUROPE]); although a Hebrew press developed it struggled for readers.

The economic depression of the 1930s hit Poland with particularly severity. Economic boycotts, anti-Jewish violence at universities, and quotas in some liberal professions resulted in a desperate situation for many Jews. No outright antisemitic legislation was enacted as it was elsewhere in Eastern Europe, but the Polish government did not oppose economic discrimination and passed legislation restricting *kosher slaughtering. In 1934 Poland renounced its obligations under the Minorities' Treaty, and in the second half of the 1930s economic boycotts escalated. *Pogroms occurred in Przytyk in 1936 and in other towns and continued until the first half of 1938, when the government began to clamp down on the violence.

With the outbreak of *World War II, Poland was partitioned between the *Soviet Union and *Nazi *Germany. Between 1 million and 1.2 million Jews lived in the eight provinces of eastern Poland that came under Soviet control. Another 300,000 Jews in Soviet-occupied Poland were refugees from Nazi-occupied areas. Under Soviet rule, Jewish institutions were dissolved or disbanded themselves in anticipation of Soviet authority. Jews, along with the non-Jewish population, suffered from Sovietization of the economy and from deportations to the Soviet interior. In Nazi-occupied Poland, terror against Jews began immediately. Nazi authorities appointed a Jewish Council, the *Judenrat*, in most Jewish communities to implement their orders; in larger cities, the *Judenrat* also oversaw formal and informal Jewish communal and social welfare efforts. Enclosed ghettos (see HOLOCAUST: GHETTOS) were established in large cities throughout Nazi-occupied Poland, whereas in smaller towns Jews were required to live in often unenclosed ghettos or were deported to ghettos in nearby cities. Death from starvation and disease was common.

After the outbreak of the Nazi–Soviet war on June 22, 1941, Jews living in what had been Soviet-occupied eastern Poland were among the first victims of mass shootings during the early stage of the Nazi genocide, as the German army advanced eastward (see *EINSATZGRUPPEN*; HOLOCAUST entries). Jews who survived these mass shootings were rounded up into ghettos, which often were liquidated in a few months. Pogroms carried out by surrounding non-Jewish populations in Polish territory that had been under Soviet control accompanied the Nazi invasion of the Soviet Union, particularly in the area that is presently northeastern Poland. The extent of Nazi supervision of this violence is still unclear.

Polish Jews were among the first victims of industrialized mass murder through gassing at Nazi camps beginning in December 1941. All six Nazi annihilation camps were located on Polish territory; three were established as part of Operation Reinhard specifically for the genocide of Polish Jewry (see HOLOCAUST: CAMPS AND KILLING CENTERS).

Approximately 50,000 Polish Jews survived the *Holocaust on Polish territory and an estimated 250,000 survived in the Soviet interior. After the war, Poland's prewar eastern territories became part of the Soviet Union, and returning Polish Jews were resettled in Poland's western territories newly acquired from Germany, particularly Lower Silesia. Jewish communities were also reestablished in Łódź, Warsaw, Kraków, Gdańsk, and other cities. Approximately 275,000 Jews lived in Poland in the early post-war years, a number that fluctuated with returns and departures. Post-war pogroms, culminating with the murder of 40 Jews in *Kielce in July 1946, contributed to mass Jewish emigration, and only an estimated 94,000 Jews remained in Poland by 1948. Poland's surviving Jewish population continued to be depleted by emigration waves from 1956 to 1960, which left around 36,800 Jews in Poland; a government antisemitic campaign in 1967–68 prompted the departure of at least an additional 13,000 Jews and the remaining Jewish population became increasingly assimilated.

By the end of communist rule in 1989, approximately 10,000 Jews were estimated to be living in Poland. Following the revival of Jewish religious and communal life in the two decades since then, population estimates have at least doubled. Only a fraction are members of Jewish communal institutions, but efforts to develop Jewish life have revived existing Jewish organizations and led to the establishment of new Jewish institutions.

For further reading, see A. Polonsky, *The Jews in Poland and Russia*, 3 vols. (2009, 2011); G. D. Hundert, *Jews in Poland-Lithuania in the Eighteenth Century* (2004); M. Opalski and I. Bartal, *Poles and Jews: A Failed Brotherhood* (1992); J. Gross, *Neighbors: The Destruction of the Jewish Community in Jedwabne, Poland* (2001); D. Engel, *In the Shadow of Auschwitz: The Polish Government-in-Exile and the Jews, 1939–1942* (1987); and J. Michlic, *Poland's Threatening Other: The Image of the Jew from 1880 to the Present* (2006). **Maps 8, 11**   KAREN AUERBACH

Portugal. Many Jews fled to Portugal at the time of the expulsion from *Spain in 1492, joining an ancient native community/ Seeking to retain these valuable immigrants, King Manoel I chose to ignore the troubled history of the Spanish *conversos and in 1497 forcibly converted all of the Jews in Portugal. Many of these Portuguese conversos retained a crypto-Jewish identity and a number left Portugal for various *Sephardic Diaspora centers in the *Ottoman Empire, *Amsterdam, *France, and the New World (see BRAZIL and CARIBBEAN) over the next few centuries. The *inquisition was established in Portugal in 1536 and remained in effect until 1821. **Map 6**

Some Jewish families of Portuguese origin from Morocco returned to Portugal in the nineteenth century and a synagogue was dedicated in Lisbon in 1904. During World War II, significant number of Jewish refugees were able to escape Nazi-occupied Europe through Portugal, which was officially neutral. The Jewish population at the beginning of the twenty-first century was approximately 1000.

Post-Zionism, like *Zionism, is best understood as a discourse, a body or assemblage of concepts and practices that position people to think and act in particular ways. Zionism has provided the dominant model through which Israelis and other Jews view Jewish history and Israeli national identity. This model is grounded in concepts such as homeland, return to Zion, ingathering of the exiles, redemption of the land, ascent (*aliyah) and descent (*yeridah*), together with related practices. Similar to other forms of nationalism, Zionism constructs a model of the good citizen who accepts and enacts the truths of Zionist discourse as "commonsensical." These truths include the following: The Land of *Israel belongs solely to the Jewish people; the State of *Israel is a Jewish state, the state of the Jewish people; it is incumbent on all Jews to live in the State of Israel; a full Jewish life can only be lived in Israel; and Israel should be ordered by Jewish concepts and practices derived from Zionism. The discourse and practices that embody and disseminate these truths set limits on the ways in which Jewish history, Jewish culture, and Jewish identity can be legitimately represented and discussed. Those positioned by Zionism regard Zionist concepts and practices to be "normal," and they view practices that depart from Zionism as problematic and abnormal.

Post-Zionism functions as a minoritarian discourse that brings to light and challenges the "unseen" or concealed power relations embodied in the dominant mode of thought. Rendering problematic what Zionists accept as truth, it strives to transform Israeli society and culture. One way in which it does this is by opening spaces for alternative Israeli discourses. Whereas Zionism designates the Land of Israel to be the possession of the Jewish people and inscribes that "truth" into legal, political, and social practices, post-Zionism challenges such assumptions and practices. From a post-Zionist perspective, the prevailing Zionist model of Israeliness marginalizes or excludes groups such as Jews from Middle Eastern countries (*Mizraḥim), *women, *Arab citizens of Israel, and gays, and lesbians. In contrast, post-Zionist writings seek to validate the position of such groups, while questioning the capacity of Zionism to address and resolve effectively the basic problems confronting a democratic state.

From a post-Zionist perspective, the dominant Israeli scholarship has been conscripted to the service of Zionist ideology that grounds accounts of Israeli history and society in Zionist "truths" or *doxa*. Disseminated through schools, universities, scholarly texts, the military, the media, state documents, laws, geographical sites, memorials, and the official calendar, these "truths" have shaped the prevailing conceptions of Israeli national identity and culture.

In its current usage, post-Zionism was first used to designate a group of scholarly writings that emerged in the 1980s. These writings challenged dominant Israeli historical narratives regarding the Zionist settlement of the land, the 1948 war, the 1948 Palestinian Arab flight, the history and reception of Jews from Middle Eastern countries, and Israeli efforts at peace (see relevant entries under ISRAEL, STATE OF). They also questioned prevailing representations of Israel as a society that accepted and treated equally all Jews and all citizens. Subsequent post-Zionist scholarship revealed the inequitable effects of the practices of defining boundaries and allocating space that are grounded in the Zionist concept of Israel as a Jewish state.

The scholars whose writings have been designated as post-Zionist are members of a generation that was born or grew to maturity in the decades after the 1948 establishment of Israel. Their perspectives were shaped by events such as the post-1967 Israeli occupation of the West Bank and Gaza, the near defeat of Israel in the 1973 Yom Kippur War, the 1982 invasion of Lebanon and its aftermath, the growing impact of Mizraḥi Jews, the emergence of a militant Israeli religious right, the growing power of Israeli settlers in the West Bank and Gaza, and the development of a powerful Palestinian national identity within the occupied territories and among Israel's Arab citizens. For a growing number of Israelis, such events rendered untenable previously dominant views of Israeli society and culture. Consequently, many scholars and critics felt the need for new ways of understanding Israel and its history.

The journal *Theory & Criticism*, founded in 1990, developed a theoretically informed post-Zionist critique and applied it to areas of society and culture not previously addressed by historians and sociologists. Drawing on the writings of French philosopher Michel Foucault, many contributors highlighted the power relations inherent in Israeli history and society. Applying concepts from feminist, post-structuralist, and post-colonial writings, they sought to render problematic the Zionist assumptions that informed prevailing concepts of Israeli national identity.

Challenging prevailing forms of Israeli national identity, post-Zionism has created spaces for imagining alternative, non-Zionist, pluralistic forms of Israeli national identity. Rather than viewing Israel as a Jewish state dominated by one ethnic group, many post-Zionists envision a democratic state marked by diversity and difference, in which all groups share equitably in the access to power. Insofar as post-Zionism creates spaces for alternative, more complex understandings of Israeli society and culture, it functions as a transformative force in Israeli national life. At the end of the first decade of the twenty-first century, post-Zionist views are increasingly evident within the academy and in areas of public culture such as *film, *literature, and television.

The ambiguous and conflicting meanings ascribed to the term "post-Zionism" mirror the ambiguity and conflicted meanings associated with the term "Zionism." Rather than engage in the futile task of either discovering or positing an essential meaning of the term, it is more useful to perceive it as a pragmatically useful label for a type of discourse that produces identifiable effects and to focus on how such discourse operates and what it does. Although many scholars so identified reject the label "post-Zionist," their writings nonetheless have helped shape an alternative, post-Zionist rethinking of Israeli society, politics, and history.

Post-Zionism also renders problematic the ways that many Jews worldwide understand Jewishness. Challenging Jews to reflect critically on previously unquestioned premises of Jewish identity, its proponents argue that post-Zionism opens new ways of conceptualizing Jewish and Israeli identity and Jewish *ethics. For further reading, see E. Nimni, ed., *The Challenges of Post-Zionism* (2003); L. J. Silberstein, *The Postzionist Debates: Knowledge and Power in Israeli Culture* (1999); and L. J. Silberstein, ed., *Postzionism: A Reader* (2008).

LAURENCE J. SILBERSTEIN

Prague is the cultural and political center of Bohemia and the Czech lands and the capital of the present-day Czech Republic (see also CZECHOSLOVAKIA). It is home to one of the oldest and, at times, most populous Jewish settlements north of the Alps. In 2009 the city's population was approximately 1.2 million, including an estimated several thousand Jews.

Jewish merchants are mentioned as present in the late tenth century; several sources testify to casualties in Prague during anti-Jewish rioting that accompanied the First *Crusade in 1096. The earliest permanent Jewish settlements were probably located in the two castle districts (under the *Pražský hrad* and *Vyšehrad*). By approximately the mid-twelfth century, the Jewish population began to shift to the Old Town (*Staré Město*), where the city's Jewish Quarter would remain throughout the later medieval and modern periods. Several *Tosafists lived in Prague. Isaac ben Moses of *Vienna (ca. 1200–1270), who studied there, included many glosses in old Czech in his *Or Zarua* (Spreading Light), a widely circulated book of *customs. The most infamous incident of medieval anti-Jewish violence, a massacre of Prague's Jews at the time of Passover and Easter in 1389, was memorialized by Avigdor Kara (d. 1439) in an elegy that became part of the local liturgy for *Yom Kippur. After the Hussite Wars (1419–37), which confirmed the complete break of several Bohemian Christian denominations from the Roman Catholic Church, Prague's Jews were among Europe's first to live in a setting of multiple Christianities.

In the sixteenth century, Prague Jews, particularly Gershon ben Solomon Cohen and his family, pioneered the *printing of Hebrew books in Central Europe. During this era, the economically diverse community suffered internal strife; in 1541 and again in 1559, Ferdinand I expelled the Jews from Bohemia, although several wealthy families were allowed to remain during each of these brief expulsions. In 1564 a burial society was founded, indicating renewed growth in the Jewish community. Burial society and *synagogue records show that a female leadership existed alongside the male, most likely responsible for matters having to do directly with women's roles in these institutions and the burial of women.

Jewish scholarship flourished in the cosmopolitan atmosphere fostered by Rudolf II (1576–1612). Rabbi Judah Loew ben Bezalel (the Maharal of Prague) served as chief rabbi from 1597 until his death in 1609. Scholars associated with his circle include Rabbi Yom-Tov Lipmann Heller (d. 1654) and the astronomer and historian David Gans (1541–1613; see also SCIENCE AND MATHEMATICS). Rivkah bas Meir Tiktiner (d. 1605), the first woman known to have published an entire Hebrew composition, *Meneket Rivkah* (Rebekah's Nurse), a guide to pious behavior for women, also lived for some time in Prague and is buried there. Medieval and early modern gravestone inscriptions single out at least a half-dozen additional women for their level of learning or because they preached to other women.

Rudolf's reign was followed by political disintegration and the outbreak of the Thirty Years War, and Prague's Jews marked decisive events in their liturgical calendar with annual days of commemoration recalling, for example, the second Defenestration of Prague (1618) and the Battle of White Mountain (1620). At first Jews gained materially from the seventeenth-century re-Catholicization of Prague; some purchased the homes of exiled Protestant nobles, greatly expanding the size of the Jewish Quarter. By the second half of the seventeenth century, however, the general deterioration of Bohemia's political and cultural situation affected Jewish life as well. Plague took thousands of lives during 1679–80, and a fire in 1689 leveled the Jewish Quarter. Homelessness forced Jews to rent accommodations in Christian homes, leading to calls for a permanent elimination, relocation, or reduction of the Jewish community. Nonetheless, the quarter was rebuilt in its original location.

Relative stability returned briefly during the tenure of David Oppenheim, appointed chief rabbi in 1702. Beila Horowitz and Rachel Raudnitz published a Yiddish tale of the Jewish community's origins. Pressures to reduce the Jewish population prevailed, however, with the 1726 enactment of the Familiants laws, which limited the number of Jewish families in the country. In 1744, Maria Theresa ordered the expulsion of Prague's Jews, arousing both strident opposition and international Jewish diplomatic efforts. Jews returned to the city by 1748, but in 1754 fire again devastated the Jewish Quarter.

Joseph II's Edicts of Tolerance (1781–82) opened new doors for Bohemia's Jews by removing many restrictions based on religion, but they also signaled the dismantling of Jewish autonomy. Chief Rabbi Ezekiel Landau (1754–1793), a prominent scholar, supported some reforms while fighting for the continuation of traditional Jewish practice against *Haskalah thinkers like Peter Beer (ca. 1758–1838) and Herz Homberg (1749–1841). Solomon Judah Rapoport (1790–1867), a prominent *maskil* (supporter of *Haskalah*) of the following generation, was also active in Prague.

Between 1896 and 1912, the now impoverished Jewish Quarter was completely cleared and rebuilt; six of the original synagogues, including the thirteenth-century Altneuschul, and the Jewish Town Hall remained standing. To save what he could of the old ghetto's material remains, Salomon Hugo Lieben established the Jewish Museum of Prague (see also MUSEUMS). Also around this time, a variety of *Zionist and other Jewish movements were active in Prague. A large circle of Jews often met in the salon run by Berta Fanta, which Albert *Einstein also visited.

After the *Nazi occupation of Czechoslovakia, Lieben, librarian Tobias Jakobovits, and their colleagues in the Jewish Museum reached an arrangement with the occupiers. They continued to collect and catalogue artifacts, many from Bohemian and Moravian Jewish communities effectively eliminated by deportations, for what the Nazis presumed would be a museum to the extinct race. Lieben died in Prague in 1942, and Jakobovits was eventually deported and perished in *Auschwitz. Thanks to their efforts and those of their staff, however, innumerable artifacts and documents were preserved, and the Jewish Museum in Prague still houses extensive collections of Judaica, including more than 11,000 textiles. During the communist era, Jewish property and institutions, including the museum, were nationalized. Most have been returned to the Jewish community since the 1989 Velvet Revolution. Today, the Jewish Museum collections are housed in several of the surviving synagogue buildings, and the city has a number of active synagogues and prayer groups of various denominations, a Jewish school, and kosher restaurants.

For further reading, see D. Altschuler, ed., *The Precious Legacy: Judaic Treasures from the Czechoslovak State Collection* (1983); P. Demetz, *Prague in Black and Gold: Scenes from the Life of a European City* (1997); H. J. Kieval, *Languages of Community: The Jewish Experience in the Czech Lands* (2000); and M. Vilímková, *The Prague Ghetto* (1990). **Map 8**

RACHEL L. GREENBLATT

Prayer: See BIBLE: PRAYER LANGUAGE; BLESSINGS; ISRAELITES: RELIGION; TEMPLE AND TEMPLE CULT; WORSHIP; and entries that follow

Prayer: Women's Devotional. Prayer in Judaism developed as private, individual supplication among men and women alike. Biblical prayers (see BIBLE: PRAYER LANGUAGE) are presented as spontaneous appeals to *God, with specific, direct requests. Examples of women who pray include the matriarchs *Sarah, *Rebekah, *Rachel, and *Leah. However, the Bible generally does not provide us with the texts of these prayers. One of the first private prayers whose actual wording is recorded is that of Moses, who beseeches God on behalf of his sister Miriam: "God – I pray You; please heal her" (Num 12:13). The first complete woman's prayer is the supplication of *Hannah (the mother of the prophet *Samuel) for a son. Later on, Hannah's heartfelt, intimate, whispered appeal to God was adopted as the paradigm for the individual prayer (*amidah) that is at the heart of every public worship service (see WORSHIP). Her contribution is commemorated in the introduction to prayer books used in many Jewish communities, with the words, "And Hannah prayed..."

The destruction of the Second *Temple led to the development of the public prayer service as a replacement for the daily sacrifices and ultimately to the development of written liturgy. Men, as participants in the formal *synagogue prayer quorum (*minyan), henceforth followed a set liturgical Hebrew text for public worship that was ultimately recorded in the *prayer book (*siddur). This public and communal orientation dictated the wording of the prayers, their subject matter, and their language. Still, when people felt that the prayer book failed to address their own private challenges and difficulties, they were entitled, even within the framework of the communal prayer service, to choose their own subjects for prayer, to use their own words, and to pray in their own way.

According to *halakhah, women are required to pray as individuals, but they are exempt from time-bound commandments that include participation in public prayer (M. Kiddushin 1:7). Thus, their connection with the synagogue and the formal prayer service has traditionally been far more tenuous than that of men. M. Berakhot 3:3 exempts women from mandatory participation in the recitation of the *shema, but requires them to participate in the grace after meals (see BLESSINGS: BEFORE AND AFTER MEALS) and "prayer." Medieval rabbis disagreed over whether this prayer is "the Prayer" (i.e., the amidah) or simply a requirement for daily prayerfulness. In addition, women were generally removed from the world of the religious study hall; they had little formal religious education and were generally unfamiliar with the Hebrew language. They spoke the language of their surroundings or its adaptation by the Jewish community (in Eastern Europe – *Yiddish; among Spanish exiles – *Ladino; in *Yemen and other Arab countries – *Judeo-Arabic). Halakhah permits a person to pray in the language with which he or she is most familiar. As Rabbi Abraham Danzig (Poland, 1748–1820) wrote in Hayyei Adam, his authoritative halakhic guide, "Those who do not understand the Holy Tongue, along with women, should rather pray in a language that they understand; only, they should pray wholeheartedly" (Rule 22:12). In some communities, a female "leader" (firzogerin) would recite the traditional (Hebrew) prayers in the local vernacular in the women's section of the medieval synagogue, and the other women gathered would repeat them after her. As early as the thirteenth century there is evidence of women "*cantors" who led other women in prayer (see WOMEN: MIDDLE AGES).

Women's lack of familiarity with Hebrew, along with the particular needs and difficulties of their lives, created an opportunity for liturgical creativity and for personal, private prayer. The rich tapestry of women's prayer customs, rituals, and formulas created over the course of Jewish history reflects different periods, different styles, and different languages. Many of these traditions were passed down from mother to daughter within the home, without ever being committed to writing. (Sometimes, as in the case of the Spanish and Portuguese *conversos, secrecy was of the utmost importance.) Some of the prayers that have been preserved in writing testify to extensive familiarity with religious texts. Examples of women liturgists include the medieval Rabbanit

Marcena of Gerona; the seventeenth-century Asnat Mizrahi of the Barzani rabbinical family, who eventually became the head of the yeshivah in Mosul, *Kurdistan; and the eighteenth-century Sarah Rebekah Rachel Leah Horowitz, learned author of Tkhine imohes (Supplication of the Matriarchs). Horowitz composed an *Aramaic prayer in rabbinic style, together with a Hebrew introduction and *Yiddish prose translation. Devorà *Ascarelli translated Hebrew liturgical poetry into rhymed Italian, presumably for use by female worshipers. Her Abitacolo degli oranti (Abode of the Supplicants) was completed in 1537 and published in 1601.

In *Central and *Eastern Europe, starting in the sixteenth century, a tradition developed among educated, religious women of reciting supplications, called tkhines in Yiddish, for female use in domestic rituals and in synagogue worship. Collections of such vernacular prayers, many written by men, began to appear in the sixteenth century; the invention of *printing facilitated their production and spread. Most books of tkhines were arranged in order of subject, with no mention of the names of their authors. Where names do appear, they are mostly figures about whom little is known. Sarah bas Tovim (early-eighteenth-century *Poland) was among the most beloved composers of tkhines. Her Shloyshe sheorim (The Three Gates) includes prayers for the three "women's commandments" (hallah [the *Sabbath loaves], *niddah, and hadlakah [kindling Sabbath lights]) as well as tkhines for the *High Holidays and Sabbath (see also WOMEN: EARLY MODERN EUROPE).

Another notable figure is Fanny Neuda, (d. 1894) who composed a book of prayers in German for women and girls that was published in *Prague in 1855. Her Stunden der Andacht (Hours of Devotion) went through twenty-eight editions by the 1920s and was also translated into English. Recent decades have witnessed a flourishing of women's prayers. Some communities have adopted certain prayers composed by women to be recited by the congregation as a whole; in some places it has become customary for women to recite prayers on significant occasions in their lives or as part of newly created rituals that highlight women's rites of passage.

For further reading, see A. Lavie, A Jewish Woman's Prayer Book (2008); E. Taitz, "Women Voices, Women's Prayers: Women in the European Synagogues of the Middle Ages," in Daughters of the King: Women and the Synagogue, ed. S. Grossman and R. Haut (1992); V. L. Ochs, Inventing Jewish Ritual (2007); E. M. Umansky and D. Ashton, eds., Four Centuries of Jewish Women's Spirituality: A Sourcebook, rev. ed. (2008); and C. Weissler, Voices of the Matriarchs: Listening to the Prayers of Early Modern Jewish Women (1999); **also see** BIBLE: PRAYER LANGUAGE; JUDAISM, FEMINIST; PRAYER BOOKS: UNITED STATES; WOMEN: EARLY MODERN EUROPE; WORSHIP. ALIZA LAVIE

Prayer Books (see also WORSHIP). The first formal Jewish prayer books (siddur; pl. siddurim, from seder, the Hebrew word for "order") originate during the period of the *Geonim (ca. 600–1038). The Seder Rav Amram Gaon (ca. 875) was the response of the Babylonian Gaon, Rav *Amram bar Sheshna, to a Spanish Jewish community's request for a detailing of the annual order of prayers (see RESPONSA LITERATURE). Subsequently, *Saadia Gaon produced the Kitāb Jāmi'al-Halawāt wa 'l-Tasābīh (The

Comprehensive Book of Prayers and Praises). These books contributed enormously toward the standardization of the liturgy. The earlier of the two, *Seder Rav Amram*, was sent to the Jews of Spain at their request around 860. It included all of the regular prayers according to the annual cycle for weekdays, *Sabbaths, *festivals, *New Moons, *fasts, and the holidays of *Ḥanukkah and *Purim. Each section of prayers was prefaced with the pertinent laws (see *HALAKHAH*), and at the end, there were special prayers and benedictions for use in daily life (e.g., blessings to be recited before partaking of specific foods or at grace after meals [see BLESSINGS: BEFORE AND AFTER MEALS) and for rites of passage in the *life cycle (e.g., *circumcision, *marriage, and burial). As a work of literature, Rav Amram's prayer book pales in comparison with Saadia's liturgical masterpiece, composed some time between 928 and 942. Saadia's prayer book went far beyond Rav Amram's and, for that matter, most later prayer books in that it was not merely an arranged compilation of existing prayers. The *Kitāb Jāmi ʿal-Ḥalawāt wa 'l-Tasābīḥ* offered the worshiper a complete and systematic introduction to the subject of liturgy, its historical evolution, significance, and rationale. It also provided helpful notes and comments to the service and to individual prayers, all in *Judeo-Arabic, rather than *Hebrew, for easy understanding by the lay person. In addition to the required prayers, Saadia included liturgical poems (*piyyutim*) by great poets of the past, such as Jose ben Jose, as well as his own poetical creations, which were highly regarded by later generations and served as thematic and linguistic models for liturgical poets of the golden age of Hebrew letters in Islamic Spain (see POETRY: LITURGICAL [*PIYYUT*]; POETRY, MEDIEVAL: MUSLIM WORLD; SPAIN, MUSLIM).

Local variations in prayer books were common until the development of *printing centralized the production of prayer books regionally. Iberian (*Sephardi) Jews, expelled from *Spain in 1492 and *Portugal in 1497, also imposed their own rite or prayer practices in their new communities, leading to the virtual disappearance of the local liturgies of *North Africa, the *Balkans, and the entire Middle East (except *Yemen). Printed prayer books according to the Sephardi rite, usually produced in *Italy, become standard in these countries.

Prayer Books: United States (see also WORSHIP). The

first prayer books (*siddurim*) edited in the *United States appeared in the second half of the nineteenth century. Like their Western European counterparts, these books were largely the work of individual, non-Orthodox rabbis who adapted, to varying degrees, the inherited rabbinic liturgy to conform to the rationalist temper of the age; to insights emerging from scientific inquiry, comparative religion, and biblical criticism; and to sensitivities resulting from the growing social and cultural integration of the Jewish community into American life. In these prayer books, references to *revelation of the Torah at Sinai, the physical *resurrection of the dead, a personal *messiah, the splitting of the Red Sea, biblical understandings of divine reward and punishment (see COVENANT), requests for the reinstitution of the sacrificial system (see TEMPLE AND TEMPLE CULT), the ingathering of the exiles (see ESCHATOLOGY), and assertions of Jewish *election were often replaced or, in deference to the text's antiquity, translated nonliterally.

*Reform Judaism's *Union Prayer Book* (see JUDAISM, REFORM: NORTH AMERICA), published in 1895 (with successive updated editions), was the first prayer book produced by a movement. It was followed by the Reconstructionist *Sabbath Prayer Book* (1945) and the Conservative *Sabbath and Festival Prayer Book* (1946; see JUDAISM, CONSERVATIVE; JUDAISM, RECONSTRUCTIONIST). *High Holiday and daily liturgies were also published by the Reform and Reconstructionist movements in the first half of the twentieth century. All of these *siddurim* reflected the sensitivities evident in the individually edited liturgies of the previous century.

Each of the liberal movements has revised its official liturgy in the last half-century, sometimes more than once. Reform Judaism published *Gates of Prayer* in 1975 and *Gates of Repentance* in 1978, and *Mishkan T'filah*, an entirely new *Sabbath, weekday, and *festival prayer book, in 2007. Conservative Judaism published *Siddur Sim Shalom: A Prayer Book for Shabbat, Festivals and Weekdays* in 1985; a significantly revised edition appeared in 1998. The Conservative movement's first High Holiday liturgy was released in 1972; a revised version, *Maḥzor Lev Shalem*, appeared in 2010. The Reconstructionist *Kol Haneshamah* prayer book series appeared between 1989 and 1999. As in the nineteenth century, liturgies have also been created by individuals, most notably by Sydney Greenberg and Jonathan D. Levine (*Likrat Shabbat* [1971]) and Marcia Falk (*The Book of Blessings* [1996]).

The many factors that have motivated this hunger for new liturgy include the feminist critique of traditional androcentric language used to address God (see JUDAISM, FEMINIST); issues surrounding the horrors of the *Holocaust and the founding of the State of *Israel; increased interest in mysticism (see KABBALAH) and spirituality; the growing informality of English usage; the thirst for novelty; renewed affirmation of liturgical forms that were previously rejected; and the growing number of Jews who lack *synagogue and Hebrew literacy, on the one hand, and those who wish to return more Hebrew to the liturgy, on the other.

The first American *Orthodox *siddurim* were reprints of traditional European prayer books. This changed in 1949 with the publication of Phillip Birnbaum's *Ha-Siddur ha-Shalem*, followed in 1960 by David de Sola Pool's *Traditional Prayer Book*. These *siddurim* did not revise the established liturgical texts but responded to modern sensitivities by including English readings, a contemporary commentary, and prayers for the State of Israel and the United States. English readings are omitted in the widely used *The Complete Artscroll Siddur* (1984), but the text includes an extensive rubric and a less formal English translation; one edition provides a complete transliteration of the Hebrew prayers. These changes reflect a community that has become ritually stringent in the last thirty years while attracting greater numbers of Jews not raised in observant households.

ERIC CAPLAN

Priesand, Sally Jane (b. 1946) was the first woman ordained a rabbi in North America (June 1972). As a teenager in Cleveland, Ohio, Priesand had little sense of the challenges she would face as a woman pioneering in a male-dominated profession. When she matriculated at Reform *Judaism's *Hebrew Union College-Jewish Institute of

Religion in 1968, she found herself in the media spotlight. She met faculty opposed to the ordination of any woman and synagogue members who viewed her as a curiosity.

In 1972, she became assistant rabbi at *New York City's Stephen Wise Free Synagogue (1972–79). From 1979 to 1981 she held part-time positions and in 1981 became rabbi at Monmouth Reform Temple in Tinton Falls, New Jersey. There, until her retirement in 2006, she acted on her conviction that a rabbi's primary task is to enable Jews to take responsibility for their Judaism. The author of *Judaism and the New Woman* (1975), Rabbi Priesand asked her congregants to share her passions for Judaism, social justice, women's equality, and *Israel. **See also JUDAISM: FEMINIST; RABBINIC ORDINATION OF WOMEN.**

PAMELA S. NADELL

Priests and Priesthood: See AARON; CANAAN, CANAAN-ITES; LEVITICUS, BOOK OF; ISRAELITES: RELIGION; TEMPLE AND TEMPLE CULT; WORSHIP

Printing. This entry surveys books printed with Hebrew type and includes not only books written in *Hebrew but also works in *Yiddish, *Ladino (Judeo-Spanish), *Aramaic, Judeo-Italian, *Judeo-Arabic, and Judeo-Greek that have been printed in Hebrew alphabets.

FIFTEENTH CENTURY: Hebrew incunabula (books printed before January 1501) appeared in *Italy, *Spain, *Portugal, and in the *Ottoman Empire (one edition only). According to modern research about one hundred and forty editions, printed on about forty presses, were printed in the incunable period. Many of these editions are rare; in all, about two thousand copies are preserved in public collections, and approximately one hundred are in private hands, dispersed around the globe.

The first dated Hebrew printed book was finished on February 17, 1475, in southern Italy by Abraham ben Garton. However, as early as 1469–72 a group of six undated books was printed in Rome. One of these editions mentions the names of Obadiah, Manasseh, and Benjamin of Rome. From a number of technical features it appears that the large Hebrew dictionary (*Sefer ha-Shorashim* [Book of Roots]) by David *Kimḥi was the first Hebrew book ever printed. In 1475 the press of Meshullam Cusi was active in northern *Italy, and between 1474 and 1477 Abraham Conat published attractive books. The first Jewish woman mentioned as associated with a printing press was Abraham Conat's wife Estellina. In 1482 Abraham ben Ḥayyim of Pesaro printed the first Hebrew *Pentateuch at Bologna. After 1483, members of the Soncino family became the leading printers of Hebrew books in Italy. Joshua Solomon began to publish separate treatises from the Babylonian *Talmud in the town of Soncino. Also working at Soncino were his nephews Gershom and Solomon. Under pressure from the Catholic Church, Joshua Solomon had to flee to Naples; Gershom became an itinerant printer who established presses at Brescia, Barco; later at Fano, Pesaro, Altona, Rimini, Ancona, and Cesena; and finally at Salonika and Constantinople. In 1494 Gershom published a vocalized Hebrew Bible in Brescia; it has become famous because Martin Luther used it as a source for his German translation of the Old Testament (see REFORMATION). The Soncino family published more than one-third of all the Hebrew incunabula ever printed. In Naples a second Hebrew press belonged to Joseph ben

Jacob Ashkenazi Gunzenhauser and his son Azriel. Probably as a result of the war between *France and the kingdom of Naples, the production of Hebrew books there came to an end in about 1492, after twenty books had been published.

Knowledge of the history of Hebrew book production in the Iberian Peninsula during the fifteenth century is limited, because much historical evidence was destroyed with the expulsion of the Jews from *Spain in 1492 and subsequent events in *Portugal in 1497. *Rashi's commentary on the Pentateuch from the press of Solomon ben Moses Alkabits Halevi at Guadalajara, probably dating from 1476, is the oldest known Spanish Hebrew printed book. Like the first dated Italian Hebrew book, which happens to be the same text, it is known from one copy only. Ten years later Eliezer Alantansi was active at Híjar. His books display a high degree of aesthetic quality. In Zamora, Samuel ben Musa printed another commentary on the Pentateuch by Rashi, probably in 1492, again known from one copy only.

The first Hebrew book to be printed in Portugal was an edition of the Pentateuch, issued in 1487 at Faro from the press of Samuel Giacon; only one copy is known. In Lisbon Eliezer Toledano published a number of very fine printed books. In Leiria Samuel Dortas owned a printing shop together with his sons. He published not only Hebrew books but also volumes in Latin and Spanish.

The first Hebrew press in the *Ottoman Empire was founded as early as 1493. The brothers Samuel and David ibn Naḥmias, who had escaped from Spain, published *Jacob ben Asher's popular *Arba'ah Turim* (The Four Orders of the Code Of Law) on December 13, 1493, in Constantinople. This was the first book in a long succession of more than eight hundred Hebrew and Ladino publications printed in that city up to the twentieth century.

SIXTEENTH CENTURY: After two centuries of expulsions (*England, *France, *Germany, and Spain), almost the whole of Europe, with the exception of northern Italy and the Papal States, was closed to Jews. The result was a radical shift eastward. At the same time, the spread of Hebrew printing continued throughout the sixteenth century; new Hebrew presses were established not only in France, Germany, Switzerland, *Poland, *Czechoslovakia, and the Low Countries but also in Morocco (see NORTH AFRICA), *Egypt, and the Land of *Israel.

Originally, Hebrew printing in Italy was dominated by Gershom Soncino. However, after Daniel Bomberg established his Hebrew press in *Venice, Soncino was surpassed. Bomberg invested large sums of money in his firm and published more than two hundred and twenty Hebrew works with the help of famous Jewish scholars. His large rabbinic bibles in three editions are famous all over the world. Thereafter, Venice became the center of Hebrew printing for a long period. The owners of the presses were Christians, like de Farri, Giustiniani, Bragadini, Zanetti, di Gara, Cavalli, and Grypho but the typesetters and correctors were mainly Jews. Outside Venice, Hebrew presses were active in Genoa, Mantua, Rome, and Bologna. The Venetian editions of the *Talmud were extremely important. However, a struggle between Giustiniani and Bragadini caused the confiscation and burning of thousands of Talmud volumes in 1554 by the Catholic Church, after which it was forbidden to print the Talmud in Italy. Important printing houses were established in the second half of the century in Cremona, Ferrara, Mantua, Riva di Trento, Sabbioneta, and Verona.

Outside Europe, Hebrew printing developed mainly in the Ottoman Empire. Many presses flourished in Constantinople/Istanbul. Closely associated were the Hebrew presses in Salonika. Short-lived presses were also established in Adrianople, Cairo, *Safed, and Fez.

In Eastern Europe a flourishing printing office was set up in *Prague by Gershom Cohen, the founder of a dynasty of printers. His *Passover *haggadah* of 1526 became widely famous as the first lavishly illustrated printed *Passover ritual. In Oels, Augsburg, Ichenhausen, and Heddernheim, both Hebrew and *Yiddish texts were published (including the medieval rhymed versions of the books of *Samuel and *Kings). In *Poland, the Helicz brothers were active in Kraków. Ḥayyim Shwarts and his son established a press in Lublin associated with Eliezer ben Isaac Ashkenazi, who moved in 1577 to Safed to publish the first book printed in the Holy Land. In 1562 Kalonymos ben Mordecai Jaffe set up a printing office in Lublin that was carried on by his heirs up to the end of the seventeenth century.

Christian printers of Hebrew books outside Italy include Martin Le Jeune and Chrétien Wechel in Paris; Robertus I Stephanus (Estienne) in Paris and Geneva; Froben and Petri in Basel; and Froschouer in Zürich. In Germany, Hebrew books appeared in Tübingen, Augsburg, Cologne, Mainz, Wittenberg, Leipzig, Solingen, and Isny. Christoph Plantin of Antwerp produced a number of editions of the Hebrew Bible. One of his most prestigious projects was the large polyglot *Biblia Regia*.

SEVENTEENTH AND EIGHTEENTH CENTURIES: At the end of the sixteenth century Sephardic Jews settled in *Amsterdam where the need for a Hebrew printing office was soon felt. On January 1, 1627, *Menasseh ben Israel, the well-known rabbi, printer, and diplomat, published a Hebrew *prayer book. Amsterdam now became the new international center of Hebrew printing. By 1655 Menasseh's press had published about fifty Hebrew books (and some Yiddish), in addition to works in Spanish, Portuguese, and Dutch. In 1640 Immanuel Benveniste established himself as a printer of Hebrew books in Amsterdam. In the next nineteen years he published almost every important text from Jewish literature. His uncensored edition of the Babylonian Talmud (1644–48) became famous. His employer Uri Feiwesh Halevi, grandson of the first rabbi in Amsterdam, became his successor in 1658. He published Hebrew and Yiddish books, especially for German and Polish Jews in the city; he also published the first newspaper in Yiddish, which appeared every Tuesday and Friday.

In 1654 Joseph Athias founded a printing office in Amsterdam. In addition to Hebrew books, he also published books in other languages. He published a Yiddish Bible in competition with Uri Feiwesh Halevi with poor results, but his Hebrew Bible met with much more success; the edition had to be reprinted in 1667, and he was rewarded by the Dutch authorities for this achievement. His Bible became the leading text edition well into the nineteenth century. His son Immanuel Athias continued the press until 1714. His monumental edition of *Maimonides' *Mishneh Torah* in 1702/3 is considered by specialists to be the most beautifully printed Hebrew book ever produced in Amsterdam. Another

member of the Athias family, Abraham, was a printer of Hebrew books from 1728 to 1746. David de Castro Tartas published important editions at the end of the seventeenth century. In addition to these large printing concerns, quite a number of smaller shops were active, including those of Jehudah ben Mordecai, Samuel ben Moses Halevi, Reuben ben Elyakim, Jacob and Isaac de Cordova, Moses Kosman Emerich, Moses Dias, Asher Anshel Shoḥet, Moses Mendes Coutinho, Joseph Dayan, Moses Frankfurt, Isaac Jehudah Leon Templo, and Naftali Hirz Levi Rofeh and his heirs (up to 1813). Most important during more than two centuries was the firm of Proops, which held a monopoly on the Hebrew book market until the economic crisis in the Netherlands at the end of the eighteenth century.

In Germany, many Hebrew presses were active, but Jews were hardly ever allowed to own a press. Very often, the owners were Christians, who left the actual printing to Jewish specialists. There were Hebrew presses at Fürth, Sulzbach and Wilhermsdorf; at Dessau, Dyhernfurth and Halle; at Altona, *Berlin, *Frankfurt on the Main and Frankfurt on the Oder, Gotha, Hamburg, Hanau, Jessnitz, Karlsruhe, Neuwied, Offenbach, and Wandsbeck.

NEW ERA: By 1760 the center of Hebrew printing had moved to *Eastern Europe. At the same time ecclesiastical and governmental censorship increased. Many local presses came into being, but were heavily supervised and produced books of inferior quality. In *Russia the first Hebrew book was published in 1760. More than thirty presses were established in the *Ukraine, *Belorussia, *Lithuania, and *Poland. *Vilna became a center, where the Romm family edited rabbinic texts. *Warsaw became more and more important, and by about 1800 *Vienna had a leading position. Influenced by the Mendelssohnian Enlightenment (*Haskalah), new Hebrew presses in Berlin, Königsberg, and Breslau were established. The first Hebrew journal, *Ha-Me'assef* (The Gatherer) was published in Berlin between 1783 and 1811 (see LITERATURE, HEBREW: *HASKALAH*). In *France, Hebrew presses became active in Metz (about 1760), Strasbourg (about 1770), and Paris (1806). Hebrew presses existed in *Britain in London and Edinburgh; in Italy, Livorno, Pisa, and Reggio Emilia had Hebrew printing offices. Jewish printers worked in the *United States, beginning in *New York City as early as 1825. At the end of the nineteenth century, Hebrew presses were established in every city in *Canada with a substantial Jewish community, including Toronto. Yiddish and Hebrew journals were also published in many locations (see JOURNALISM: YIDDISH; PERIODICALS: CANADA: PERIODICALS: UNITED STATES).

There was a short typographical renaissance between the world wars. E. Lissitzky designed splendid books in Moscow, Kiev, Odessa, and *Berlin (see ART: ILLUSTRATED YIDDISH BOOKS). The "Soncino Gesellschaft" in Berlin stimulated the love for fine printing; Jewish designers who became interested in the development of new Hebrew type faces included Rafael Frank with his Frank-Ruehl letter. Henri Friedländer developed a completely new type face, the Hadassah type. In Israel, E. Korén's new type face was used in the so-called *Korén-Bible*, a masterpiece of Modern Hebrew typography. After 1948, the State of Israel became a center of new developments in the printing and publishing of Hebrew books.

For further reading see "Printing, Hebrew," in *Encyclopaedia Judaica*, 2nd ed. (2007), 16: 529–40; S. Iakerson, *Catalogue of Hebrew Incunabula from the Collection of the Library of the Jewish Theological Seminary of America* (2004–05); *Catalogue of Books Printed in the XV*th *Century Now in the British Library: BMC Part XIII, Hebraica*, compiled by A. K. Offenberg (2004); M. J. Heller, *The Sixteenth Century Hebrew Book. An Abridged Thesaurus* (2004); L. Fuks and R. G. Fuks-Mansfeld, *Hebrew Typography in the Northern Netherlands 1585–1815* (1984, 1987); and H. Friedlaender, *The Making of Hadassah Hebrew* (1975); **see also WOMEN: EARLY MODERN EUROPE.**   ADRI K. OFFENBERG

Prophets (*Nevi'im*) is the second section of the three traditional divisions of the *Tanakh* (see also BIBLE, HEBREW; BIBLE: PROPHETS AND PROPHECY). The books in this division include the historical books of *Joshua through *Kings, which contain narratives about rulers and prophets (often known as Former Prophets), and books that collect the prophecies of specific individuals (often known as Latter Prophets). Three of these books in the Latter Prophets – Isaiah, Jeremiah, and Ezekiel – are generally designated as the Major Prophets, because of their considerable length. The other far shorter books in the Latter Prophets are known as the Minor Prophets and also as the Twelve Prophets. The books in the Prophets division of the *Tanakh* appear in the following order: *Joshua; *Judges; 1 and 2 *Samuel; 1 and 2 *Kings; and *Isaiah; *Jeremiah; *Ezekiel; *Hosea; *Joel; *Amos; *Obadiah; *Jonah; *Micah; *Nahum; *Habakkuk; *Zephaniah; *Haggai; *Zechariah; and *Malachi.

Prostitutes, Prostitution: Hebrew Bible Through Middle Ages. The Hebrew *Bible mentions many times the practice of offering sexual services in return for material compensation, both in its literal sense and as a metaphor for Israel's worship of other gods. The Hebrew term for prostitution, *zenut, zenunim*, also serves as a general term for sex outside of marriage in the Hebrew Bible and Jewish texts in general, so that it is occasionally uncertain which activity a text is addressing. In Hebrew, the prostitute is called a *zonah*, but perhaps also a *kedeshah*. References to prostitution by males are ambiguous (Deut 23:18–19; 1 Kgs 22:47). Legislation in the Torah attempts to outlaw prostitution, although it states no penalty, except for the daughter of a *priest who is to be burned (Deut 23:18; Lev 19:29, 21:9). A prostitute is forbidden to bring her wages to the sanctuary as payment for any vow (Deut 23:19), and a priest may not marry a prostitute (Lev 21:7, 14). In contrast, biblical narratives show a more benign attitude to the prostitute. Rahab, the prostitute of *Jericho, shows exemplary faith and foresight when she harbors Israelite spies (Josh 2, 6). *Tamar poses as a prostitute to seduce *Judah for a just cause and becomes the ancestor of *David and the line of the *Messiah (Gen 38). One of the unnamed prostitutes who come before King *Solomon for justice shows unselfish compassion (1 Kgs 3).

In addition to common prostitution, modern scholars have assumed the existence of "cultic" or "temple" prostitution both in Israel and its neighbors. In this case, a shrine or temple receives the payment for sexual relations, either because the prostitute was the employee of the temple or because an individual had sexual relations in fulfillment of a vow. The Hebrew term *kadesh/kedeshah* is associated with this form of prostitution in particular because of the association of the root *k-d-sh* with holiness (Gen 38; Deut 23:18, Hos 4:14; 1 Kgs 22:47). Biblical scholarship in recent years has expressed greater skepticism about the existence or prevalence of these practices.

Prostitution is frequently used in the Hebrew Bible as a metaphor for Israel's abandonment of its covenant and the worship of other gods. This is evident in the expression, "to whore after other gods" (Exod 34:15–16; Deut 31:16; Judg 2:17), and in the allegories found in prophetic books (Hos 1–3; Jer 2:20–25, 3; Ezek 16, 23).

In post-biblical Jewish texts, the introduction of prostitutes in the Jerusalem *Temple was considered an outrageous desecration of its holiness (2 Macc 6; BT *Gittin* 56b). To specify those who are off-limits for marriage to a priest, the *Talmud expands the definition of a prostitute, *zonah*, to include any woman who has sexual intercourse outside the context of *marriage; female converts to Judaism along with emancipated slave women are included in this category because it is assumed that they were previously promiscuous (BT *Yevamot* 61a). The Talmud imagines that professional prostitutes may be either Jewish or Gentile, but in either case, a Jewish man must stay at least four cubits from a prostitute's door (BT *Avodah Zarah* 17a). According to the Talmud, an extravagantly expensive Gentile prostitute converted to Judaism and married a Jew because his *tzitzit* (ritual *fringes) miraculously prevented him from having sexual relations with her (BT *Menaḥot* 44a).

Jewish texts from the medieval period attest to the existence of Jewish prostitutes and brothels in Jewish neighborhoods. Jewish authorities tolerated and on occasion even subsidized prostitution in Jewish communities because it was thought to serve a positive function in preventing the violation of virgins and married women, a notion adopted from Christian society.

For further reading, see E. A. Goodfriend, "Prostitution," *Anchor Bible Dictionary* (1992), 5:505–10; J. R. Baskin, "Prostitution: Not a Job for a Nice Jewish Girl," in *The Passionate Torah: Sex and Judaism*, ed. D. Ruttenberg (2009), 29–35; A. Grossman, *Pious and Rebellious: Jewish Women in Medieval Europe* (2004), 133–47; and Y. Assis, "Sexual Behavior in Medieval Hispano-Jewish Society," in *Jewish History*, ed. A. Rapoport-Albert and S. Zipperstein (1998), 25–59.
                                                                    ELAINE A. GOODFRIEND

Prostitutes, Prostitution: Modern Era. During the late nineteenth century, there was significant Jewish involvement in the "white slave trade," a euphemism for the trafficking of women across international borders for the purpose of prostitution. Impoverishment, social breakdown, and a high degree of geographic mobility in Eastern Europe enabled profiteers to induce or entrap Jewish women to travel abroad and serve as prostitutes. Young widows, abandoned wives (*agunot*), spinsters, or "ruined women" were offered an escape from poverty and shame and the promise of riches in distant lands. On arrival the women were usually placed in brothels where they had to work, initially without pay, to pay back all of the fees incurred through their travels. Some young women from poor families were tricked into "marriages" and then transported abroad to a life of prostitution. Others became prostitutes of their own volition to escape the drudgery of factory or domestic work or the grinding poverty of family life.

Jews neither controlled nor dominated the white slave trade, but they did oversee the large and lucrative traffic in Jewish women. By the turn of the twentieth century, Jewish criminal gangs managed a complex system of routes, personnel, brothels, and corrupted officials. Obtaining accurate statistics on Jewish prostitution is nearly impossible. Although prostitution was legal in most European states in the late nineteenth century, it carried a social stigma and legal consequences, such as the need to submit to regular medical examinations. Additionally, many women engaged in prostitution only on an occasional basis. Nonetheless it is estimated that the proportion of Jews among prostitutes was never, even at its height, greater than the proportion of Jews in the population.

Jewish women from Europe were sent as far as *South Africa and the Far East, with *Britain and Constantinople serving as major transit points; one of the main destinations was *Latin America. Latin American countries were eager to attract European immigrants and imported thousands of young men to serve in their growing economies. Open borders and underdeveloped law enforcement capacities led to rampant prostitution. In 1900, shortly after having been excluded from the Jewish cemetery by the local burial society, the Polish Jewish pimps of Buenos Aires chartered a mutual aid society and obtained their own cemetery (see *Argentina). The groups that came to be known as the Zwi Migdal Society later had a *synagogue as well. This was only the most infamous of a series of Jewish communal institutions established by and for criminal elements around the world.

North America was another destination of the white slave trade, as well as a recruiting ground. Crowded and poor immigrant neighborhoods in cities across the United States provided ideal conditions for prostitution.

Opposition to trafficking in women began in the 1880s. Sensational press stories about kidnappings of young girls raised general as well as Jewish opposition, and non-Jewish organizations began to form to combat the white slave trade. In 1899, Britain's fiery evangelical campaigner William Coote toured Europe trying to raise awareness about the need to regulate cross-border traffic and protect women. The *Rothschild family partly financed Coote's trip. Only several years previously, the formation of the Jewish Association for the Protection of Girls and Women had created a central agency for British Jewish action. In Germany, Bertha *Pappenheim tirelessly fought for the rights of women. Combating the trade in women was one of the central platforms of her Jüdischer Frauenbund, established in 1904. This and other voluntary associations across Europe established travelers aid stations at major terminals and worked to have laws changed to prevent the free movement of human traffic. Equally important, they established international communication lines. The National Council of Jewish Women in the United States undertook similar initiatives in the American immigrant community (see ORGANIZATIONS, WOMEN'S: NORTH AMERICA).

*World War I essentially put an end to the period of major Jewish involvement in prostitution. Jewish prostitution and small-scale procuring and trafficking continued, but the conditions were no longer ripe for large-scale activities as emigration slowed down and Jews in western countries increasingly moved up the economic ladder.

Prostitution once again came to the fore in Jewish communal concerns after the collapse of the *Soviet Union and the large-scale immigration of former Soviet citizens to *Israel in the 1990s. Among the many immigrants was a small minority of individuals involved in a variety of criminal activities, including trafficking and prostitution. The relatively open immigration policies contained in the Law of Return made Israel a useful hub for international criminal enterprise. Vulnerable women from every ethnic group in the former Soviet Union were brought into Israel either voluntarily or in some cases by deception to serve as prostitutes in Israel or to be shipped elsewhere. As the scope and size of the problem became clear, the Israeli government worked with internal nongovernmental organizations and women's groups as well as international bodies to craft appropriate policies on judicial and criminal matters, as well as issues of rehabilitation and repatriation. Although these efforts did not end the international traffic in women, by 2004 they had proven effective in increasing both the prosecution of leaders of criminal rings and the rehabilitation of their victims.

For further reading, see E. Bristow, *Prostitution and Prejudice: The Jewish Fight against White Slavery 1870–1939* (1983); R. Gershuni, "Trafficking in Persons for the Purpose of Prostitution: The Israeli Experience," *Mediterranean Quarterly* (Fall 2004): 133–46; N. Glickman, *The Jewish White Slave Trade and the Untold Story of Raquel Liberman* (2000); and R. Rosen, *The Lost Sisterhood: Prostitution in America, 1900–1918* (1982).   ELIYANA R. ADLER

Protestant Reformation: See REFORMATION

Provence: See FRANCE, SOUTHERN

Proverbs is part of the *Writings (*Ketuvim*), the third section of the Hebrew *Bible. It is usually found following *Psalms, although in some manuscripts *Job precedes it. With Job and *Ecclesiastes, Proverbs comprises biblical wisdom literature.

Proverbs is a collection of sayings intended to teach young men how to live prosperous, happy, and righteous lives. The book believes that wisdom is essential to achieve these goals and frames its purpose as an explication of "proverbs and maxims, the words of the wise and their riddles" (1:6). The Hebrew name of the book, *Mishlei*, is short for its first two words, *mishlei shelomo*, part of a title that identifies the contents of the book as "the proverbs of Solomon son of David, king of Israel." Later Jewish literature often quotes Proverbs by introducing it with the words, "Solomon said..."

Proverbs 1–9 present extended teachings in praise of wisdom, personified as a female character who sometimes speaks the teachings in praise of herself. In rabbinic tradition, "wisdom" in the book of Proverbs always refers to *Torah. The most well-known verses in the book are 3:17–18: "Her ways are ways of pleasantness, and all her paths are peace; she is a tree of life to those who hold fast to her, and all who take hold of her are happy." These verses are quoted (in reverse order) in the *synagogue liturgy as the Torah scroll is returned to the ark. Another passage from the book that continues to be a living part of Jewish tradition is 31:10–31, the alphabet acrostic in praise of "the capable woman," known from its first two words as *eshet ḥayil*. This has traditionally been recited at the dinner table on *Sabbath evening. In some households, the "capable woman" is understood literally as the woman of the house; in others, it refers to the Torah. In its biblical context, these words were probably meant to match the metaphoric description of "wisdom" as a woman in chapters 1–9, especially Proverbs 8. The bulk of Proverbs, however, is made up of the single-line proverbs that give the book its name. Despite many scholarly efforts to understand them in context, there is no apparent reason for their present arrangement (see also BIBLE: WISDOM LITERATURE).

According to a famous passage in BT *Shabbat* 30b, the Sages wished to exclude Proverbs from the Bible because of an apparent contradiction: Proverbs 26:4 advises, "Do not answer a dullard in accord with his folly," while the next verse gives the opposite advice: "Answer a dullard in accord with his folly." Because each alternative is sometimes appropriate, cooler heads prevailed. Although the book of Proverbs refers frequently to "the Lord," there is nothing else specifically Jewish about it except that it is written in Hebrew. Indeed, Proverbs 22:17–24:22 are apparently a Hebraized version of an *Egyptian text teaching similar principles. Nonetheless, the attribution of most of the book to *Solomon secured its solid place in the Bible.

MICHAEL CARASIK

Psalms. The Book of Psalms, in Hebrew *Tehillim*, is the first book of the third section of the Hebrew *Bible, *Ketuvim* or Writings. Its English title reflects the Greek translation of the Hebrew term *mizmor*, which opens many psalms, and means "a song sung to the accompaniment of a plucked instrument." *Tehillim* means "songs of praise," reflecting the most common genre of poetry (see BIBLE: POETRY) in Psalms.

Jewish tradition associates the book with King *David, assuming that he wrote all or most of the psalms that it contains. Approximately half of these psalms open with a superscription or title that contains the word *ledavid*; it is not clear, however, if this title is meant to ascribe authorship to him or may suggest that the psalm is written in the style of a Davidic composition. Rather than viewing the book of Psalms as composed by David and largely reflecting various prayers recited in response to events in his life, it should be viewed as a nonhaphazard collection of collections of different genres from various places and times, sharing many qualities of ancient *Near Eastern prayers (see BIBLE: PRAYER LANGUAGE).

Psalms has a broad structure: It opens with a psalm comparing the entire collection to the five-part *Torah; indeed, Psalms is divided into five parts or books (1–41, 42–72, 73–89, 90–106, and 107–150). It is not a random collection of prayers, but a structured book that should be studied as Torah. Many of the psalms in the early part of the book are laments or petitions, whereas toward the end, hymns that praise *God predominate: The book thus moves from requests to thanksgiving. There are also psalms commemorating God's role in history, psalms celebrating God as king, and others. Some are to be recited by individuals, others by the community. There are also some collections within Psalms, such as the Psalms of Ascent (120–134). Psalm 14 is duplicated in a slightly different form in Psalm 53, indicating the complex history of the book and its editing. Some Psalms have a very early origin, such as Psalm 29, which shows clear connections to pre-Israelite *poetry, whereas others are written later, such as Psalm 137, which opens, "By the rivers of Babylon, there we sat." Although many of the psalms

likely originated in the *Temple in Jerusalem, internal references suggest that some (e.g., Psalm 80) were composed in the northern kingdom of *Israel.

It is unclear how individual psalms were used in the Jerusalem Temple or exactly who composed them. A few psalms, such as 118:27, "bind the festal offering to the horns of the altar with cords," incorporate explicit hints of when they were recited. Most likely there were guilds of Levites such as the Asaphites (see Psalms 50, 73–83), who were in charge of composing and reciting psalms (see TEMPLE AND TEMPLE CULT). They were well versed in Israelite poetry and ancient Near Eastern prayers, which explains why Psalms shares so many motifs, techniques, and even phrases found in the poetry of Israel's neighbors. Yet Psalms should not be understood only in terms of its origin. It has had a lasting impact on *Judaism: More than half of the psalms are used as post-biblical liturgy (see WORSHIP), and very many verses from Psalms are recontextualized in Jewish prayer language and quoted in a broad range of Jewish literature.

MARC BRETTLER

Pseudepigrapha means "false writings"; more precisely, this term refers to texts attributed to authors who did not write them. Pseudepigrapha is also the designation for extracanonical Jewish texts composed in the (roughly) five centuries from *Alexander the Great to the end of the second century CE. However, this name is inaccurate on a literal level because only some of these diverse works are falsely attributed to known figures; the remainder are either unattributed or indicate something about their true author.

Jewish pseudepigrapha share essential traits that legitimate grouping them together: Like the canonical texts of Judaism – the Hebrew *Bible and *rabbinic literature – they were all composed by Jews, and they shaped and expressed a range of Jewish self-definitions. However, unlike the canonical texts, these writings did not achieve enduring authority in Judaism; instead, they fell from use and, in many cases, from memory as well. Many survive only because *Christians of late antiquity and the medieval period preserved them out of largely antiquarian interests; others were preserved in the *Apocrypha, in what became the Roman Catholic Old Testament (e.g., *Wisdom of Ben Sira, *Tobit, 1 *Maccabees, etc.). Most of these works survive in Greek, although in some cases they are certainly translations of Hebrew originals. Some pseudepigraphical writings are only extant in other languages of the early church, including Syriac, Coptic, Armenian, Ethiopic, and Georgian.

Surveys of the pseudepigrapha typically organize them by genre (e.g., Charlesworth). The chief difficulty with this approach is uncertainty regarding the genre of some pseudepigrapha. An alternative, historical approach surveys the literature by compositional history (e.g., Nickelsburg). It labors under an equally limiting impediment, namely the difficulty of dating works that are often preserved only secondarily. For simplicity of presentation and in spite of its evident deficiencies, this entry uses the genre approach.

APOCALYPTIC LITERATURE: Apocalyptic literature is generally defined as narrative literature in which an otherworldly being reveals heavenly secrets about a coming new age and place. A number of Jewish pseudepigrapha fit that definition, chief among them 1 Enoch and 4 Ezra (others include 2 Enoch, 3 Enoch, 2 Baruch, *Sibylline Oracles, and Apocalypse of Elijah; see also ESCHATOLOGY: SECOND TEMPLE).

1 Enoch is an anthology of apocalyptic texts ascribed to the biblical Enoch, whose privilege of having "walked with God . . . because God took him" (Gen 5:24) qualified him as a bearer of heavenly mysteries. The texts came into existence over the course of as much as two centuries and explain earthly evil as the consequence of a heavenly rebellion (1 Enoch 6–16; cf. Gen 6:1–4); they include Enoch's description of his heavenly tour (chs. 7–36) and an "Animal Apocalypse" that assigns animal identities to actors in a historical apocalypse (ch. 83–90). As a whole, 1 Enoch expresses the dissatisfaction of pious Jews with *Hellenistic rulers, "Hellenizing Jews," and perhaps even the *Maccabees.

4 Ezra records a sequence of conversations between a seer and an angel and an ensuing sequence of visions that, like parts of 1 Enoch, amount to an historical apocalypse. In the case of 4 Ezra, the apocalyptic vision is more targeted, addressing the sense of loss in the late 70s CE after the destruction of the *Temple by *Rome.

TESTAMENTS: Modeled on the valedictory speech of *Moses in *Deuteronomy 33 and similar works, the testamentary genre is well attested in Jewish pseudepigrapha. The exemplars of this genre generally relate the deathbed speech of a biblical hero in which he instructs and exhorts his children. The Testament of Job, composed some time after the Roman annexation of *Egypt in the late first century BCE, accomplishes the hortatory objective indirectly. In his deathbed speech, *Job tells his second set of children how he came to lose his first family as a result of his opposition to Satan's maintenance of a temple in Egypt, and that he knew his destruction of Satan's temple would bring such suffering on him. Yet, he also knew that, if he was patient in his suffering, God would doubly reward him for his perseverance. The work seems to argue for Jewish perseverance in the face of severely diminished prospects as a result of the transition from *Ptolemaic to Roman rule.

A second example, the Testament of Moses, composed some time in the first third of the first century CE, reports Moses' deathbed speech to *Joshua, who is apprehensive about having to assume leadership. Moses foretells the trials and triumphs of the people of Israel to the days of *Herod and beyond, showing that God's promises to Israel would prevail over any deficiencies in Joshua's leadership, as well as the sin and punishment of Israel. Indeed, the history Moses narrates ends with a certain Taxo being martyred, an event that seems to precipitate God's final judgment against evil, which is described in a hymn in near-apocalyptic terms. Before breaking off (only a single incomplete Latin manuscript of the testament is extant), Joshua expresses his abiding anxiety and Moses reassures him of God's steadfast commitment to keeping His promises.

The Testaments of the Twelve Patriarchs also has a strong anticipatory element: Each speech from the twelve sons of *Jacob recounts an event or events from the patriarch's life, his exhortation to hold to a virtue or avoid a vice evoked by his narrative, and a prophecy of his descendants' fate through history to the end of time. In its present form the Testaments is a Christian work, roughly datable to 200 CE. However, as evidenced by the use of Jewish source material in the speech by Levi and some other speeches

(see, for example, the *Aramaic Levi Document, attested in the *Dead Sea Scrolls and Cairo *Genizah fragments), most agree that the Christian composition relied on an earlier Jewish original.

Other testaments include the Testament of Solomon, Testament of Adam, and Testaments of the Three Patriarch (*Abraham, *Isaac, and Jacob).

THE BIBLE REWRITTEN, EXPANDED, AND EXPOUNDED: This broad category of texts comprises a range of multi-genre contributions to the literature of early Judaism. Jubilees is an example of the Bible rewritten. Dated some time in the middle of the second century BCE, it is framed as a revelation by the "angel of the presence" to Moses of events from Genesis 1 to Exodus 20. The history covered is divided into 49-year periods ("jubilees"), and it heavily rewrites the corresponding biblical account. It does so for several purposes, among which are assigning to the ancestral period the origin of the pure priesthood in Levi (especially 30–32) and the development of biblical and nonbiblical laws (e.g., the requirement of a 364-day solar calendar). It also aims to rehabilitate the stained reputations of the ancestors in the biblical record. Thus, Jacob's negative judgment of Levi and Simeon because of the incident involving *Dinah and *Shechem is erased; rather, their zeal is why the *priesthood was assigned to Levi (30:17–20; cf. Gen 34; 49:5–7). It also includes an "apocalypse" in ch. 23 that envisions justification for those who embrace the book's agenda. This indicates that Jubilees was probably intended as an expansive proposal for how early Judaism should define itself going forward in the *Hasmonean era.

The book, Joseph and Aseneth, exemplifies "the Bible expanded." This work explains how the devout Israelite *Joseph could have married the daughter of an Egyptian priest of On (Gen 41:45). The first half of the book reports how Aseneth, love-struck from the first moment she saw Joseph, was rejected because she was not an Israelite (8:5). After Aseneth undergoes a complex conversion process, she and Joseph marry (chs. 1–21). The second half reports that Pharaoh's son, jealous of Joseph, recruits Joseph's brothers – Dan, Gad, Naphtali, and Asher – to carry out his plot to steal Aseneth and murder Joseph; Simeon and Levi and other brothers save the married couple. In the process, Pharaoh's son is mortally wounded, Pharaoh dies of grief, and Joseph becomes Pharaoh of Egypt (chs. 22–29). The date of the work is contested (at least one scholar assigns it Christian authorship), but it was most likely written in Egypt around the turn of the Common Era.

The Letter of *Aristeas typifies what one might call the "Bible expounded." Works of this kind neither rewrite nor expand a single element of the Bible; rather they create completely new legends and accounts that build from a simple event or the name and memory of a biblical figure (e.g., Martyrdom and Ascension of Isaiah). The Letter of Aristeas recounts the creation of the *Septuagint at the behest of *Ptolemy II. Some other examples of this broad category of texts include Jannes and Jambres, 4 Baruch, Pseudo-Philo, the Aramaic Levi Document, the Life of Adam and Eve, and Lives of the Prophets.

WISDOM LITERATURE: Texts in this category are less a genre than exemplars of a literary strategy that argues for a particular worldview. These writings employ a variety of "wisdom subgenres" (e.g., diatribes, hortatory discourses, apothegms, parables, proverbs) to argue for particular visions of reality. The Wisdom of Solomon, an early Roman-era hortatory discourse by a Jew of *Alexandria, exemplifies this type of literature. Responding to the declining fortunes of Jews under Roman rule, the author calls his audience to a deeper appreciation of their own traditions and argues for the preeminence of God's wisdom as an organizing principle for the community's life. In 1:1–6:11 the author explains that possessing wisdom leads to righteousness, which in turn offers immortality. In 6:12–9:18 the authorial voice becomes that of *Solomon (although he is not named) who describes in alternating portions his search for wisdom and its extraordinary qualities. The remainder of the book, chs, 10–19, demonstrates from Israel's history (especially in Egypt in the days of Moses) how wisdom executes justice and mercy according to recipients' righteousness (with a special emphasis on idolatry).

Some of the other wisdom works from this era include *Wisdom of Ben Sira, Pseudo-Phocylides, 3 *Maccabees, and 4 Maccabees.

PRAYERS, PSALMS, AND HYMNS: This category of texts includes, among others, Prayer of Manasseh and Psalms of Solomon (see also Prayer of Joseph, Prayer of Jacob, Odes of Solomon). Prayer of Manasseh is an individual lament over past sins and purports to be the petition that Manasseh successfully used to be released from Babylonian captivity (2 Chron 33:12–13). It dates perhaps from just before the destruction of the Temple in 70 CE and focuses on the effectiveness of contrition and *repentance in evoking God's mercy.

Psalms of Solomon, dating perhaps from the first century CE, is similar in style and tone to the biblical *psalms, with the exception of its historical references (e.g., Pompey in Psalm 2) and its distinctive messianic hope (especially Psalm 18). It also captures the contrasting notions of God's justice apparent in the Torah, arguing at points that God deals strictly in retributive justice (8:9–14) and at others that God offers unilateral mercy (3:6–8; 4:6).

FRAGMENTARY WORKS: A number of texts from early Judaism are known only through their fragmentary reproduction in non-Jewish sources like the *Church Fathers Eusebius in *Ecclesiastical History* or Clement of Alexandria in *Stromateis*. Among these are also the writings of historians and chronographers like Demetrius and Eupolemus, the historical novelist Artapanus, the playwright Ezekiel the tragedian, and *Philo the epic poet. In various ways and by means of diverse genres they rewrote, expanded, and expounded the Bible and broader Jewish traditions of their day. For further reading, see James Charlesworth, *Old Testament Pseudepigrapha* (1983); and G. W. E. Nickelsburg, *Jewish Literature between the Bible and the Mishnah*, 2nd ed. (2005); and **PTOLEMIES: IMPACT ON JEWISH CULTURE AND THOUGHT**.

ROBERT KUGLER

Psychoanalysis is both a therapeutic technique and a global theory of human behavior, individual and collective. Although its scientific status remains in dispute, its vision of human experience as governed by powerful though largely unconscious drives continues to inform psychology in both theory and practice, and it plays a central role in the self-understanding of the West, especially in the social sciences, the humanities, and the arts.

Psychoanalysis originated with the clinical experiences of the Viennese Jewish physician Sigmund *Freud (1856–1939), who trained in neurology both in *Vienna and in Paris. Freud's early studies of hysterical symptoms convinced him that pathological behavior could be relieved even without hypnosis if the patient was permitted to speak freely about past traumas. This method (dubbed the "talking cure" by Bertha *Pappenheim) prompted the conclusion that "hysterics suffer mainly from reminiscences." From this clinical discovery there emerged a sophisticated theory of mental life applicable not only to hysterical patients but also to all human beings, both as individuals and in the collective. A key insight that animated the early psychoanalytic movement was that most if not all of human behavior is permeated with meanings derived from partly suppressed traumas that were originally sustained in the course of early childhood development. In *The Interpretation of Dreams* (1900), Freud took the unorthodox approach of using his own biographical material as clinical evidence and argued that dreams should be understood as the unconscious mind's creative attempt to realize desires disallowed by the conscious mind. Dreams were thus "wish fulfillments," and the analysis of dream symbolism was to serve as "the royal road to the unconscious." In *The Psychopathology of Everyday Life* (1901), Freud further claimed that normal or functional adult waking life exhibits various seemingly meaningless phenomena (e.g., jokes, slips, lapses in memory, etc.) that serve a similar function of wish fulfillment (hence the popular term, "Freudian slip"). The crucial principle for psychoanalytic technique is that the client must effect a "transference" to the analyst: Through this emotional bond earlier traumas are reenacted in the clinical setting under the analyst's guidance, so that the client can gain a more conscious understanding and acceptance of previously unconscious difficulties.

In his early work Freud proposed a "topography" of mind, distinguishing among conscious, unconscious, and preconscious processes. The later "meta-psychology" (developed after World War I) divides the individual psyche into three roles: "id," "ego," and "super-ego." The id (Latin for "it," and in Freud's German texts identified simply as *das Es* or "the it") is the seat of instinctual drive. Because the id's only goal is to satisfy its desires, Freud describes it as operating according to the "pleasure principle." However, external reality often frustrates the id's desires. The ego (Latin for "I," the self as empirical subject, and in Freud's German, *das Ich*) is the agency that acts on behalf of the id to realize its desires in light of the world's obstructions. The ego operates only in accordance with the "reality principle." The ego helps the id realize its desires, directly through sexuality, indirectly through aim-inhibited relations of friendship, or by diverting the drives into other nonsexual, physical, intellectual, and artistic-creative activities (a diversion Freud called "sublimation"). Freud's meta-psychology (see, e.g., *The Ego and the Id*, 1923) suggests that much of our psychic difficulty is due to "repression," the internal and unrelieved pressure that results when our drives find no route to realization.

Psychoanalysis pays strong attention to sexual feelings in early childhood because they are considered crucial to the development of normative adult psychology (see, e.g., Freud, *Three Essays on the Theory of Sexuality* [1905]). Freud was initially convinced that much childhood trauma was traceable to actual incidents of "seduction" (i.e., sexual abuse). However, early in his career he abandoned this theory and concluded instead that memories of seduction are wish-fulfillment fantasies. According to the classical Freudian theory of the "Oedipal Complex," the young (male) child's first romantic attachment is to his mother, whose breast is the primary object of desire. The father first appears as a threat to this symbiotic relation. The child can only overcome his anxiety over the possible loss of the mother's love and his fear of the father (defined as "castration anxiety") by identifying with and thereby internalizing his father's authority. The result is to install a new psychological structure, the super-ego, which functions as the inner voice of moral authority (popularly known as "conscience") and which represents the inner psychological projection of external social norms. It is the super-ego that frequently sets up powerful internal inhibitions on the realization of id drives, resulting in a psychological condition of drive suppression that Freud called "neurosis."

By the mid-1910s Freud had begun to apply the lessons of his meta-psychology and his technique for symptom interpretation to the behavior of whole groups and cultures (see, e.g., *Totem and Taboo* [1913]; *Group Psychology and the Analysis of the Ego* [1921]). The ultimate consequence of this turn was a speculative anthropology and full-blown theory of civilization. The brutality of World War I seemed to provide evidence of a second drive alongside the instinct for pleasure. This second, or "death drive" (first announced in *Beyond the Pleasure Principle* [1920]), represents the human organism's longing for destruction and ultimate stasis. Freud ultimately concluded that because this drive cannot be given full expression (either directly or through sublimation), modern societies must repress their instinctive longing for violence. In addition, because the super-ego condemns even the recognition of such violent desires, much of our guilt is thrust back into the unconscious. All of modern civilization is therefore neurotic, and irremediably so. The classic statement of this claim is *Civilization and its Discontents* (1930).

Freud's attitude toward religion was largely hostile. As a partisan of modern science, he tended to see religious belief as little more than a mass delusion and an infantile flight into fantasy (see, e.g., *The Future of an Illusion* [1927]). Yet even on this point Freud's views remained complex. His final book, *Moses and Monotheism*, published in 1939, speculates that *Moses was an Egyptian prince who introduced a primitive form of monotheistic sun worship to his Jewish followers; they then murdered their leader, whose memory was transformed into a divinity that become the supersensory object of veneration and fear. In Freud's account, *Judaism is thus created as the original Oedipal rebellion and stands as a paradigm for the birth of civilization. This controversial theory seems to suggest that Hebrew monotheism cannot be condemned as merely a mass delusion, because it provided western society with its earliest and most powerful explanation for the authority of its moral principles and its renunciation of instinct. It has even been argued that, notwithstanding his apparent hostility to religion, Freud saw psychoanalysis itself as the most advanced cultural manifestation of Judaism (see Y. H. Yerushalmi, *Freud's Moses: Judaism Terminable and Interminable* [1993]).

The scientific status and therapeutic efficacy of psychoanalysis remain much disputed. Freud himself suggested that psychoanalysis encountered "resistance" because it confronts us with facts about our own desires we do not wish to know, and like the discoveries of Copernicus and Darwin, it challenges the human being's feelings of dignity and uniqueness in the universe (see Freud's 1925 essay, "The Resistances to Psychoanalysis"). Yet the psychoanalytic movement is highly diverse and has itself thrived on criticism, spawning especially rich schools of feminist psychoanalysis, Lacanian structuralism, and object relations. Whatever their scientific status, psychoanalytic explanations are now commonplace, and they have inestimably enriched our understanding of human desire and meaning.

PETER E. GORDON

Ptolemies were the Macedonian rulers of *Egypt from the death of *Alexander the Great (323 BCE) to the annexation of Egypt by *Rome (30 BCE). Over the course of the dynasty, the Ptolemies maintained varying degrees of control over Egypt, the western Levant, and assorted other regions in and on the edges of the Mediterranean and the Aegean. Between the late fourth century and approximately 200 BCE, these territories included the Land of Israel. During the Fifth Syrian War (202–198), Antiochus III (reigned 223–187) took advantage of a period of weakness in Egypt and recovered the region for the *Seleucids.

Ptolemy I Soter (305–282) began as satrap of Egypt in the year of Alexander's death. When the struggles among Alexander's generals and successors (the *Diadochoi*) for control of his empire drew to a close, Ptolemy took the title of king in 305/304. Among his descendants were Ptolemy IV Philopator (221–204), who won the Fourth Syrian War at the battle of Raphia in 217 BCE, but only with the help of native Egyptian troops. Philopator's dependence on native Egyptians engendered renewed nationalism among Egyptians and opened the floodgates to rebellion against Macedonian rule that never completely abated. Ptolemy V Theos Epiphanes was a weak ruler and lost Ptolemaic holdings in the western Levant and throughout the Mediterranean and Aegean to the Seleucids in 200 (the Fifth Syrian War).

The subsequent history of the dynasty is a story of court intrigue, assassinations, disputed successions, and a diminishing empire. Beginning with Ptolemy IX Soter II (116–107), claimants to the throne made increasingly complicated overtures to Rome for assistance. Thus when Ptolemy XII left control of Egypt to Cleopatra VII in 51 BCE and she faced opposition, she turned to Rome for help, further involving the empire in Ptolemaic Egypt. Cleopatra curried favor first with Caesar, then with Mark Antony. When Octavian defeated Antony at the Battle of Actium, Cleopatra was without options and committed suicide in the same year (31). Ptolemy XV Caesar, a son Cleopatra claimed was fathered by Caesar, was assassinated by Octavian in 30, and the Ptolemaic dynasty came to an end.

Judeans living in Egypt flourished under the Ptolemies because of the empire's policy of permitting considerable opportunity and freedom to the many ethnicities gathered in Egypt. Having arrived in Egypt as early as the sixth century BCE under *Persian rule, Judeans were already well settled there by the time of the Ptolemies, and the vast documentary evidence from Egypt testifies to their even deeper integration with the land, its inhabitants, and its cultures under Macedonian rule. Among important texts about Jewish life in Ptolemaic Egypt are the *Letter of *Aristeas* and the

Jewish *Politeuma* Papyri from second-century Heracleopolis (**see EGYPT: HERACLEOPOLIS PAPYRI**). ROBERT KUGLER

Ptolemies: Impact on Jewish Culture and Thought.

Interactions with Greek political, social, and intellectual life under Ptolemaic rule had a transformative effect on Jewish culture and theology, both in the Land of *Israel and in *Diaspora communities. The Zenon Papyri attest to the appearance of Greeks and Hellenic institutions in *Syria and *Phoenicia in the third century BCE. At the same time as some Greeks resettled in the Jewish homeland, some Jews moved to other parts of the Mediterranean world where they adopted the Greek language and *Hellenistic customs. The diadochic wars and later civil strife brought many Jewish slaves to Egypt, but the vast majority willingly migrated there for social advancement and economic gain. Records reveal that Jews were fully integrated into the rhythms of Ptolemaic social and political life, occupying positions as soldiers, civil bureaucrats, and businessmen.

Jewish writers also benefited from the Ptolemaic interest in higher learning and *Alexandria's vibrant intellectual climate. The translation of the Hebrew *Bible into Greek (the *Septuagint), which the *Letter of *Aristeas* asserts took place during the reign of Ptolemy II (reigned 285–246 BCE), probably occurred over the course of two centuries (third to first centuries BCE). In addition, Jewish authors from this period readily incorporated Hellenistic literary techniques into their own works: Artapanus created a historical romance extolling *Abraham, *Joseph, and *Moses for their cultural achievements; the poet Philo's *On Jerusalem* and the playwright Ezekiel's *Exagoge* are examples of Greek-language Jewish poetry modeled on the Greek epic and classical tragedy, respectively; and the writings of Aristoboulus reconciled Jewish traditions with Hellenistic philosophy, ideas that he supposedly taught to Ptolemy VI (reigned 180–145 BCE).

DAVID M. REIS

Pumbedita was one of the most important centers of Jewish communal and cultural life in *Babylonia during the period when the *Talmud was being formed and in the subsequent era of the *Geonim. Its precise location is debated, but it was located at the northwest corner of the area of intensive Jewish settlement, near the junction of the Euphrates River and a major canal (near present-day Falluja). Pumbedita is best known as a major center of rabbinic learning. According to *Sherira Gaon, its talmudic academy was founded by Rav Judah in the mid-third century CE after Nehardea was devastated by Palmyrean raids. Despite some interruptions and temporary relocations, this academy retained its prominence for many centuries alongside competing centers, including *Sura. The Babylonian Talmud contrasts the versions of traditional materials preserved in these two centers on dozens of occasions. In the geonic period the Pumbedita academy, which could also be referred to as Nehardea, retained its central role alongside the academy of Sura. At the end of the ninth century it relocated to Baghdad, but continued to be known as the academy of Pumbedita until at least the middle of the eleventh century. **Map 5** ROBERT BRODY

Purim (literally, "lots") is a minor *festival, commemorating the events described in the book of *Esther found in the *Writings section (*Ketuvim*) of the Hebrew *Bible. Purim is

observed on the 14th of *Adar (the second month of Adar during a leap year [see CALENDAR]). In walled cities that have stood since the time of *Joshua (e.g., *Jerusalem), Purim is observed on the 15th of Adar and is known as *Shushan Purim*. The central observance of the festival is listening to the reading of the book of Esther from a parchment scroll or *megillah (see *FIVE SCROLLS*). The *megillah* is read both on the evening of the festival and in the morning, accompanied by *blessings. It is customary to sound *graggers* or noisemakers whenever the wicked Haman's name is mentioned. Another custom is giving gifts to the poor (*mattanot l'evyonim*), usually in the form of money, as well as sending gifts of at least two types of food to friends (*mishlo'aḥ manot*). In addition, a festive meal or *seudah* is held during the mid to late afternoon.

Purim is a day of frivolity, when costumes and role-playing are acceptable. Children and adults dress in costumes and masks, often portraying the characters in the biblical story. Purim *spiels* (plays and skits) have been popular since the medieval period. These plays generally include a satire of the rabbi or other esteemed communal figures. In addition, the *Talmud says that one should become intoxicated on Purim "until he is unable to distinguish (*ad delo yada*) between 'cursed be Haman' and 'blessed be Mordecai.'"

For further reading, see P. Steinberg, *Celebrating the Jewish Year: The Winter Holidays* (2009); T. H. Gaster, *Festivals of the Jewish Year* (1952); E. Ki Tov, *The Book of Our Heritage* (1979); and P. Goodman, *The Purim Anthology* (1973).

PAUL STEINBERG

Purity and Impurity, Ritual (Heb. *tohorah ve-tumah*). In Israelite religion, a ritually pure person or object was eligible to have contact with holy places, such as the wilderness *Tabernacle or the *Jerusalem *Temple and related holy objects, whereas an impure person or object was not. Biblical laws of ritual purity and impurity are found in priestly documents (see BIBLE: MODERN SCHOLARSHIP) in *Leviticus 11–17 and *Numbers 19; additional laws appear in Leviticus 5:2–3; Numbers 31:19–20, and *Deuteronomy 14:3–21; 23:10–15; 24:8; 26:14. The three main sources of impurity are corpses and certain animal carcasses; skin diseases in humans (*zara'at*) and fungal growths in fabrics and houses; and male and female genital discharges. Many scholars have noted that the physical substances and states labeled impure are characteristics of the physicality that separates created beings from *God. Human beings must cleanse themselves from sources of impurity such as death and procreation before approaching the *Tabernacle or *Jerusalem *Temple, because they are sites of holiness.

In the biblical system, all Israelites, including priests and ordinary Israelites, men and women, are subject to ritual impurity. Those in a state of ritual impurity can contaminate other people, objects, and spaces. However, ritual impurity is understood as impermanent. Methods of purification, specified in each case, generally involve a waiting period of some kind followed by *immersion in "living water" (*mayyim ḥayyim*; [Lev 15:13]); laundering of ritually impure garments and objects; and bringing a burnt offering and a purification offering (*ḥattat*) to the sanctuary at a prescribed time.

Biblical impurity regulations are systematized in great detail in *rabbinic literature. Twelve tractates in the

*Mishnah and the *Tosefta, comprising the order *Tohorot* (Ritual Purities), as well as many additional legal rulings in other tractates, legal *midrash collections, and the two *Talmuds, demonstrate the importance of ritual purity and impurity legislation in rabbinic *Judaism. As in the Bible, impurity is removed by sacrifices, *immersion in water (see MIKVEH), waiting periods of various lengths, and in some cases special cultic acts. According to rabbinic sources, priests in the *Second Temple era were especially strict about the purity of the Temple in Jerusalem itself and took precautions to protect sacred objects and the priests from impurity. No burials were permitted in Jerusalem, for exam-ple, and corpses were not allowed to be kept in the city overnight.

Most of the laws of impurity and purity are no longer operative in the contemporary era, mainly as a result of the destruction of the Jerusalem Temple. In traditional Jewish communities, the laws concerning a husband's separation from the *niddah* continue to be observed, as do strictures forbidding those of priestly descent from contact with corpses. Recent scholarship on this complex topic includes C. Hayes, *Gentile Impurities and Jewish Identities* (2002); and J. Klawans, *Impurity and Sin in Ancient Judaism* (2000).

JUDITH R. BASKIN

Q

Queen of Sheba. Monarch of a prosperous empire in what is now modern-day *Yemen or southwestern *Arabia, the Queen of Sheba is mentioned in 1 *Kings 10:-1–13 and 2 *Chronicles 9:1–12. According to these accounts, the Queen of Sheba, hearing of King *Solomon's fame, comes to test his *wisdom, bringing gifts of spices, gold, and precious stones. Impressed by Solomon's court and his answers to her questions, she offers blessings and praise to Solomon and his *God.

Later Jewish legends suggest that the queen and Solomon had a romantic relationship (*Alphabet of Ben Sira* 2). Ethiopian traditions identify Sheba with *Ethiopia; Ethiopian Jews, the Beta Israel, are said to be descendants of Israelite escorts who returned with Menelik, the supposed son of the union of Solomon and the Queen of Sheba and founder of the Ethiopian royal dynasty. On the Queen of Sheba in Jewish, Christian, Muslim, and Ethiopian traditions, see J. B. Pritchard, ed., *Solomon and Sheba* (1972); and J. Lassner, *Demonizing the Queen of Sheba: Boundaries of Gender and Culture in Postbiblical Judaism and Medieval Islam* (1993).

KATE FRIEDMAN

Qumran. Khirbet Qumran, a small site on a marl plateau overlooking the northwest shore of the Dead Sea, about twenty-two kilometers east of *Jerusalem, became famous after the discovery of hundreds of scrolls in the nearby caves that date to the late *Second Temple period. Later termed the *Dead Sea Scrolls, these documents are believed by most scholars to constitute the library of the inhabitants of Qumran. The site's name comes from the modern Arabic name for the adjacent dry river bed, Wadi Qumran. The etymology of the word "Qumran" is unknown, as is the site's ancient name.

Although nineteenth-century European explorers surveyed the ruins of Qumran, the site received little attention before the discovery of the scrolls in 1946/47. After Israel's War of Independence in 1948 (see ISRAEL, STATE OF: FOUNDING), the site fell under the jurisdiction of the Jordanian Department of Antiquities. In 1951, Roland de Vaux, a French biblical scholar at the École Biblique in Jerusalem, along with G. Lankester Harding, the chief inspector of antiquities in Jordan, began the first season of excavation at Qumran. Four additional seasons took place between 1953 and 1956.

Covering less than one-and-a-half acres, Qumran was thought to be a late *Roman fort before the discovery of the scrolls. The excavations, however, revealed that the buildings, constructed mostly of rough fieldstones, are unlike other Roman military installations. De Vaux verified Qumran's connection to the scrolls by noting that certain types of ceramic vessels such as cylindrical jars ("scroll jars") are found at the site and in the surrounding caves, but are rare or unattested at other sites in Judea.

Recent reexaminations of de Vaux's work have shown that the community associated with the Dead Sea Scrolls first occupied Qumran during the late *Hellenistic or *Hasmonean period, probably not long after 100 BCE. The site was destroyed by the earthquake of 31 BCE and rebuilt. After destruction by fire around 9/8 BCE, the settlement was abandoned for a few years and was reoccupied by the same community after 4 BCE. The site was inhabited until its destruction by the Romans in 68 CE, during the First *Jewish War (66–70 CE). A Roman garrison occupied the site for several years after the revolt (Magness).

The settlement of Qumran has several unusual features. For example, the lack of domestic structures inside the settlement suggests that the majority of inhabitants lived in tents and huts outside the site or in the surrounding caves. The community probably numbered between one and two hundred members at any given time. Because there are no sources of fresh water in the vicinity of Qumran, the inhabitants constructed an aqueduct that carried rainwater from flash floods in the wadi to the settlement. More than a dozen pools within the settlement would have been filled in a single flash flood, a natural phenomenon that typically occurs only once or twice per season in the region. Ten of the pools seem to have been used as Jewish ritual *immersion pools, or *mikva'ot* (see *MIKVEH). These pools have broad sets of steps that lead to the bottom, sometimes with ancillary features such as alternating deep and shallow treads and low partitions. Qumran boasts the highest density of *mikva'ot* per square foot of any site so far discovered. This concern with ritual *purity, together with evidence from the scrolls, indicates that the Qumran community considered the Jerusalem *Temple and its *priesthood polluted; the community therefore constituted their group as a substitute temple with every full member living as if he were a priest officiating in the Temple.

A large dining room with an adjacent pantry that contained more than one thousand dishes is evidence for communal meals, such as those described in the scrolls and by the ancient Jewish historian, *Josephus. Some of the Dead Sea Scrolls might have been written in a room that de Vaux identified as a *scriptorium*, or writing room; it was furnished with plastered mud-brick tables and benches and yielded a number of inkwells.

Many scholars have identified the inhabitants of Qumran and the authors of the scrolls as the Jewish sect known as the *Essenes, who are described by Josephus in his second book, *Jewish War*. Because archeological evidence both supports and refutes such an identification, the matter largely comes down to how one interprets the literary evidence of Josephus and the scrolls.

In the past two decades, some scholars have questioned de Vaux's interpretation of Qumran as a sectarian settlement, suggesting that the site was a villa, manor house, fort, or industrial center. Such alternative theories, however, ignore the connection between the scrolls and the site, established beyond doubt by the archeological finds. Therefore, most scholars still accept de Vaux's interpretation of Qumran as

a sectarian settlement associated with the Dead Sea Scrolls. For further reading, see R. de Vaux, *Archaeology and the Dead Sea Scrolls* (1973); and J. Magness, *The Archaeology of Qumran and the Dead Sea Scrolls* (2002).   STEVEN H. WERLIN

R

Rabbanites/Rabbinites was the name given by *Karaites to those who adhered to rabbinic *Judaism.

Rabbi refers to a Jewish teacher and religious authority (see RABBINIC ORDINATION; RABBINIC ORDINATION OF WOMEN). The word derives from *rav*, the Hebrew word for "great." The form "rabbi" is a combination of *rav* and a first-person possessive suffix; it has the sense of "my revered master" or "my revered teacher." After the destruction of the Second *Temple in 70 CE, the proponents of rabbinic Judaism came to be known as the Rabbis; the word first appears in the *Mishnah. The related term "Rabban" is associated with the *Patriarchs who served as leaders of the rabbinic community in post–70 CE *Palestine. **See also entries under JUDAISM.**

Rabbinic Hermeneutics (methods of interpreting Scripture) are grounded in the belief that the *Pentateuch was revealed in every detail by *God, who dictated its content to *Moses. Furthermore, the rabbinic approach to interpretation regards the *Torah as profoundly intentional: Every word and every letter have the potential to reveal insights into the meaning of the text. For the *Rabbis, there can be no simple repetitions or contradictions in a divinely composed work; every apparent contradiction or doubling of a word or story is seen as an opportunity for exegesis. Finally, the Rabbis read the Hebrew *Bible with the assumption that every part of it is connected to and therefore may shed light on every other part. For this reason, much of rabbinic hermeneutics relies on close and careful reading of the biblical text.

The early Rabbis employed various strategies when reading Scripture. The most famous are referred to as the "Thirteen Principles of Rabbi Ishmael," first set forth in the opening of the *midrash collection *Sifra*. The first principle, *kal vahomer*, utilizes logical inference. If there are two situations, one that is generally stricter and the other more lenient, a prohibition that applies to the more lenient case can also be applied to the stricter situation, even if there is no explicit textual reference linking that restriction to the latter. The remaining principles make assumptions about the relationship of words or phrases within Scripture. The most far-reaching principle is *gezerah shavah*, which allows one to apply a ruling explicit in one case to a second less obvious case when the two cases use identical language, even a single common word. Others, such as *kelal ufrat* and *binyan av*, allow the exegete to broaden or restrict the application of a rule based on the presence of specific and general terms within a verse, or to derive information about the scope of a law in one verse from information in an adjacent verse.

In addition to the principles associated with Rabbi Ishmael, rabbinic exegetes used other approaches. Rabbi *Akiva was known (and sometimes criticized by his colleagues) for deriving or basing rulings on a single letter, specifically the *vav* or *yod* used as *matres lectionis* (this term [Latin for "mothers of reading"] refers to the occasional use of certain consonants as vowels in Hebrew orthography to indicate particular forms of words when there might otherwise be ambiguity). In Biblical Hebrew the same word may be written in two ways (full or defective spelling); Akiva saw the additional letter, used only to indicate a certain vowel sound in an alphabet without vowels, as an invitation to expand the scope of the law. He also argued that the doubling of verbs (the infinitive absolute form), employed in Biblical Hebrew as an intensifier, provided the exegete an opportunity to expand the law's application.

One of the distinctions between other exegetical systems and rabbinic hermeneutics is that the latter lacks a consistent link between signifiers and that which is signified. Whereas in some interpretive approaches a certain number or color or animal will always signify the same thing, rabbinic hermeneutics allows for a word to convey one thing in one context and another meaning elsewhere. For example, the *gezerah shavah* principle allows the exegete to apply a meaning derived from one verse to another verse based on a common word, without reference to the meaning of that word. It is not the import of the word but simply its presence that signals to the exegete that one verse can be used to explain the other.

This fluidity of meaning or significance allows for significant exegetical flexibility and even playfulness but it can also make rabbinic exegesis seem imprecise and open-ended. In *aggadah*, this tendency could be given free rein, but in *halakhah*, such imprecision could potentially lead to anarchy. The Rabbis themselves were aware of the potential for chaos; they declared that a sage could not create a *gezerah shavah* on his own, but could only transmit one that he had learned from his teacher. The expansive nature of hermeneutics was apparently kept in check, particularly in the realm of legal exegesis, by the constraints of the rabbinic community's understanding of the limits of the law. Nonlegal exegesis was far less constrained, because it had no prescriptive bearing on daily life.

Despite their belief in divine *revelation of Torah and their use of shared exegetical principles, the Rabbis in no way display or insist on a monolithic view of Torah. In fact, the Rabbis celebrated the multivocality of Scripture, offering, validating, and preserving competing interpretations of words and verses, even when those opposing readings had an impact on law and practice. Although they proclaimed, "The law follows so-and-so," the Rabbis still insisted that opposing views could also be "the words of the living God."

Although most rabbinic exegesis focuses on the Hebrew Bible, the Rabbis sometimes applied similar strategies to earlier rabbinic texts. The Babylonian *Talmud may query the use of inclusive terms such as "all" or "every," asking, "What is this term meant to include?" The Talmud often argues that the *Mishnah's choice of words, its word order, and the ordering of rules are intentional decisions that can be used as the basis for interpretation.

Modern scholarship not only analyzes the rabbinic hermeneutics of the past but has also expanded the ways in which biblical and rabbinic texts are read. Like the classical Rabbis, contemporary scholars operate on the assumption that the wording of these texts is intentional and should be read carefully. The tools of literary criticism are now applied to ancient writings; word choice, voice, and motif are all important criteria for interpreting texts. Scholars may ask many of the same questions posed by ancient and medieval commentators, albeit with a willingness to consider radically different solutions. Modern readers might question the Rabbis' willingness to interpret a verse in *Genesis with the aid of a verse from *Psalms but they too employ intertextual interpretation to enrich understanding of the *Bible. Comparative studies, anthropology, folklore studies, feminist criticism, and other methodologies are all used to read the Hebrew Bible and rabbinic texts. Thus, the rabbinic dictum, "The Torah has seventy facets," has been adopted and expanded by modern scholarship.

For further reading, see D. Boyarin, *Intertextuality and the Reading of Midrash* (1990); M. Fishbane, *The Midrashic Imagination* (1993); and C. E. Fonrobert and M. S. Jaffee, eds., *The Cambridge Companion to the Talmud and Rabbinic Literature* (2007).   DVORA E. WEISBERG

Rabbinic Judaism: See JUDAISM

Rabbinic Literature: Midrash. Midrash, from the Hebrew root *d-r-š* – "to investigate, seek, search out, examine" – may refer generally to the interpretation of any text, sacred or secular, ancient or contemporary. In its strictest sense, however, midrash is the process of *Bible exegesis or commentary that characterizes classical rabbinic interpretation. It also refers to the vast and varied rabbinic compilations from the late antique and medieval periods that preserve what were originally oral exegetical traditions. Midrash, as both a process and the result of that process, grew out of the Rabbis' attempt to construct contemporary meaning out of biblical verses. Through midrash, rabbinic commentators made biblical ordinances relevant, taught moral lessons, told stories, and maintained the Jewish meta-narrative that has shaped and continues to sustain the Jewish people.

Midrash compilations, which were created between the fifth and thirteenth centuries, take several forms. Halakhic *midrashim*, the earliest midrashic collections, deal primarily with issues of *halakhah*, rabbinic law. They are exegetical works that provide word-by-word explications of verses in the books of *Exodus, *Leviticus, *Numbers, and *Deuteronomy. Halakhic compilations include *Mekhilta de Rabbi Ishmael*, a verse-by-verse exposition of Exodus 12:1–23:19, as well as Exodus 31:12–17 and 35:1–3; *Sifra*, a running commentary on Leviticus in its entirety; and *Sifre Numbers* and *Sifre Deuteronomy*. Redacted in the Land of Israel, these compilations are also known as tannaitic midrashim because they are written in Mishnaic *Hebrew and the sages mentioned are *Tannaim, Rabbis of the period from the beginning of the first to the third century CE, as well as the first generation of *Amoraim, Rabbis of the third and fourth centuries CE.

Aggadic compilations are also verse-by-verse exegeses of biblical books; in these instances the focus is on non-legal material, *aggadah*, rather than *halakhah*. The premier examples of aggadic exegetical compilations are *Genesis Rabbah* and *Lamentations Rabbah*. These two works are part of the larger compilation, *Midrash Rabbah*, which also includes midrashic compilations on the rest of the *Pentateuch and the other *Five *Megillot* (scrolls).

Homiletical midrash collections gather a series of *sermons based on a particular verse or group of verses. They include *Leviticus Rabbah*, *Deuteronomy Rabbah*, and *Numbers Rabbah*, as well as other compilations such as *Pesikta de Rav Kahana*, which collects selected passages or sections read in the *synagogue on special *Sabbaths or *festival days. In these works, chapters are constituted of homilies that cohere around a particular topic. The collections of homilies also share a structural arrangement: a series of proems (*petiḥtot*), the body (*gufa*) of the homily, and an eschatological conclusion or peroration. The *petiḥta* (proem) is usually a verse from the Writings section of the Hebrew *Bible, especially from *Psalms or the *wisdom literature, although also sometimes from the Prophets (see BIBLE: PROPHETS AND PROPHETIC LITERATURE). This proem is an earmark of all aggadic compilations, whether exegetical or homiletical. Through a chain of interpretations, the seemingly extraneous verse is connected to the verse under discussion. This structure exemplifies a fundamental aspect of midrash: the desire to unite the diverse parts of the tripartite canon – *Torah, *Prophets, and *Writings – into a harmonious, seamless whole that reflects the oneness of God's word.

Later compilations, which are more difficult to date, include the *Midrash on Psalms*; *Exodus Rabbah*; *Tanna de-be Eliyahu*, also known as *Seder Eliyahu*; and the *Tanḥuma-Yelamdenu* literature, which consists of a group of homiletic *midrashim* on the Torah. In addition to the aforementioned compilations, anthologies of *midrashim* were edited during the middle to late medieval period. Among them are the *Yalkut Shim'oni* (known simply as the *Yalkut*), *Yalkut ha-Makhiri*, and the *Midrash ha-Gadol*. The *Yalkut*, compiled from more than fifty works and covering the entire span of the Hebrew Bible (*Tanakh*), is one of the most well-known and comprehensive medieval collections.

Despite the broad designation of midrash compilations as either halakhic or aggadic, it is important to note that halakhic midrash collections contain aggadic material and vice versa. In addition, whether halakhic or aggadic, late antique or early medieval, the midrashic locus of exegesis is a biblical word or phrase. Punsters par excellence, the Rabbis were keen on making philological associations. They culled *Tanakh* for verbal affinities; they spun stories and drew connections to elucidate the word or verse at hand. Every letter of a word, every phrase, was open to interpretation; this was based on the conviction that the divine word was expressed in a certain way to teach or explain something. Nothing in Scripture is superfluous or repetitious; every word has many meanings, some more apparent than others. Indeed, one will often find contradictory statements from various Rabbis about the meaning of a word, and no one interpretation is privileged over another. This multiplicity of meaning does not challenge scriptural authority but rather reflects its infinitude.

*Rabbinic hermeneutics provided a range of exegetical strategies that are employed in halakhic and aggadic *midrashim*. The *kal vaḥomer* (literally "light and heavy") established an argument by means of a major or minor premise: "If this is true, how much more so is that true." This form of reasoning is found in both halakhic and aggadic *midrashim*. The *gezerah shavah* ("similar laws"), however, is more common to halakhic *midrashim*: By means of analogy, a particular detail of a biblical law in one verse is derived from the meaning of the word or phrase in the other. Other hermeneutical principles that characterize halakhic *midrashim* include the *binyan av*, through which a specific law in one verse may be applied to all other similar cases; *kelal ufrat, perat ukelal*, which applies rules of inference between general and specific statements and vice versa; and *hekkesh*, which establishes inference by analogy, whether explicit or implicit, between two subjects (but not words) within the same or similar contexts (see also RABBINIC HERMENEUTICS).

Nonlegal biblical passages are often explained by means of philological associations, including analogies based on the use of the same word in two different verses. Word play also takes the form of *gematria* (see NUMEROLOGY), whereby the arithmetical value of Hebrew letters is used to interpret a word or verse. In *notaricon* (shorthand writing) a Hebrew word becomes an acronym in which each letter stands for another word, which in turn forms a phrase or sentence.

In addition to word plays, midrashic literature contains scores of stories, maxims, and parables (*meshalim* [sing., *mashal*]). Parables about kings are one typical narrative form. Nearly all rabbinic *meshalim* have a bipartite structure: the fictional narrative, that is the *mashal* proper, and its application, the *nimshal*, which usually concludes with a biblical verse that serves as the *mashal*'s prooftext. Formulaic phrases mark the two parts: *mashal le*, "it is like," and *kakh*, "so, too, similarly."

Current studies in midrash reflect broad disciplinary trends in related humanities fields. This is most apparent in scholarship that addresses the literary and cultural aspects of rabbinic literature. Underlying this relatively recent trend in the study of midrash is the recognition that interpretive texts are themselves literary works and should be examined in light of literary motifs, themes, and structure. Moreover, as literature they reflect beliefs, values, and customs and also serve as cultural transmitters. Many contemporary scholars are no longer interested, for example, in how a story about a certain Rabbi may be used in constructing his historical biography. Instead, they analyze rabbinic narratives in terms of their literary quality. At the same time, these texts are also regarded as artifacts that function as conveyors and mediators of rabbinic culture. The historical import of narratives is therefore undiminished because they yield insight into the milieu of those who recorded, transmitted, and lived by them. Scholarship on midrash has advanced on the heels of other fields and it has in turn contributed to the study of the New Testament, patristic exegesis (see CHURCH FATHERS), the *Talmud, and late antique Judaism and has made its presence felt in areas such as literary theory.

This shift in how midrash is studied may be attributed to the fact that scholars of rabbinic literature are no longer trained solely within the confines of rabbinical seminaries. Advances in literary criticism, theory, and cultural studies have contributed to current interdisciplinary approaches to rabbinic literature, bringing a rich array of questions and a broad set of theoretical skills to the study of rabbinic texts, including the critical lenses of *gender, orality, and performance studies. Similarly, technological developments have facilitated the production of new critical editions of midrash collections. Whether scholars of rabbinic literature at the beginning of the twenty-first century address long-standing matters of concern or more novel issues, whether they support well-established positions or propose suggestive readings, they do so cognizant of broader contexts and alternative methodological frameworks, some of which are unique to the study of rabbinics and some of which are common to the study of ancient and medieval texts in general.

For further reading, see C. Bakhos, ed., *Current Trends in the Study of Midrash* (2006); J. R. Baskin, *Midrashic Women: Formations of the Feminine in Rabbinic Literature* (2002); D. Boyarin, *Intertextuality and the Reading of Midrash* (1990); S. Fraade, *From Tradition to Commentary: Torah and its Interpretation in the Midrash Sifre to Deuteronomy* (1991); G. Hartman and S. Budick, eds., *Midrash and Literature* (1986); G. Hasan-Rokem, *Web of Life: Folklore and Midrash in Rabbinic Literature* (2000); B. Visotzky, *Golden Bells and Pomegranates: Studies in Midrash Rabbah* (2005); and A. Yadin, *Scripture as Logos: Rabbi Ishmael and the Origins of Midrash* (2004).   CAROL BAKHOS

Rabbinic Literature: Mishnah and Talmuds. The rabbinic movement is often credited with the reinvention of Judaism in the wake of the *Roman destruction of the Second *Temple in *Jerusalem in 70 CE. The literature of this movement was produced orally by a network of Rabbis who lived roughly between the final years of the Second Temple and the Islamic (Umayyad) conquests of the seventh and eighth centuries CE. The earliest group of Rabbis, periodized as the *Tannaim (ca. 70–200 CE), engaged in study practices that produced two general types of text: *midrash and *mishnah*. Midrash is the creative interpretation of the *Tanakh, and *mishnah* is the formulation of statutes that clearly and unequivocally assert a legal requirement or theological principle. Individual *midrashim* or *mishnayot* attributed to their authors circulated orally in tannaitic Judea and formed the basis for discussions that transpired within disciple circles surrounding individual Rabbis.

Around the year 200 CE, the *Mishnah, a definitive collection of *mishnayot* arranged in six topical orders, divided into sixty-three topical tractates, with each tractate subdivided into chapters, was compiled by R. *Judah the Patriarch, a Rabbi with political authority in both the Jewish and Roman political arenas. The Mishnah combined preexisting *mishnayot* from different disciple circles, creating a legal code that canonized multivocal debate. However, the process of mishnaic redaction could not incorporate all prior *mishnah* traditions. The opinions held by Tannaim that were excluded from the Mishnah are called *baraitot*. Many of these traditions were collected in what is called the *Tosefta.

The Rabbis who were intellectually active in the period after the completion of the Mishnah in both Palestine and Babylonia are periodized as *Amoraim (ca. 200–ca. 500 CE). These Rabbis continued the practice of producing midrash and *mishnah*-type texts within small disciple circles. Over time, the intellectual conversations in rabbinic circles metamorphosed into a single intellectual discourse that incorporated both types of rabbinic traditions within a study practice characterized by intense debate and discussion. This discourse is occasionally referred to within rabbinic texts as *talmud*.

The two extant literary Talmuds, the *Jerusalem and Babylonian Talmuds, owe their general form and some content to the amoraic discourse of *talmud* that combined *mishnah* and midrash forms within an environment of successive generational interpretation and academic debate. Both Talmuds are structured around the Mishnah and can thus be described as commentaries to the Mishnah. However, despite their formal structure around the Mishnah, the Talmuds are not limited by the Mishnah's content. Rather they use the content of each individual *mishnah* as a conceptual starting point for a conversation that incorporates tannaitic *baraitot* (in both *mishnah* and midrash form), amoraic statements (in both *mishnah* and midrash form), and interpretations and debates about these statements conducted by named Rabbis of later generations and by the Talmud's anonymous voice. These conversations can also include biographical anecdotes about contemporaneous figures. An individual *mishnah* may generate several such conversations, or *sugyot* (sing., *sugyah*). Both Talmuds are anthological in the sense that they collect earlier materials from disparate Rabbis who lived in different geographic regions (in both Palestine and Babylonia), in different times (ca. 70–ca. 750 CE). Each Talmud can be described as a collage that juxtaposes different texts and even different genres of text, while explicitly attributing the voices in its conversation to a temporally and geographically diverse rabbinic population.

Concurrently with the production of the Talmuds and for some centuries beyond their completion, the rabbinic movement also compiled midrashic works that were based on expansions of biblical texts rather than explications of the Mishnah (for a discussion of these writings, see RABBINIC LITERATURE: MIDRASH; *AGGADAH*).

Since its composition, the Babylonian Talmud (BT; also known as the Bavli) has been the primary vocational curriculum of rabbinic scholars. The primacy of BT as a study text owes a great deal both to its literary merits as the definitive comprehensive work of rabbinic literature and to the political power of the Babylonian *Geonate that emerged as the leadership of world Jewry during the period of the Abbasid dynasty (750–1000 CE). The Geonim created large bureaucratic academies or *yeshivot* that trained hundreds of students in BT while conducting polemics with their Palestinian rabbinic peers. The geonic choice of BT as its primary literary text reflects its inherent value, its linguistic use of Babylonian (Eastern) *Aramaic, and the fact that it is the sole surviving literary patrimony of the Babylonian Rabbis.

As the primary text of scholars who have devoted their lives to study for more than a millennium, the Bavli has been the subject of many important commentaries. Chief among these is the commentary of *Rashi, remarkable for its combination of brevity and conceptual depth. Also of note are the writings of the French and German *Tosafists, who applied a dialectical style to BT that is reminiscent of the dialectic found within BT itself. Where BT is energized by its contrasts of tannaitic and amoraic sources that are apparently in disagreement, Tosafist commentary is characterized by its insistence that all of BT must cohere and by the dialectical distinctions that individual Tosafists offer to extract themselves from apparent inconsistencies. Within the history of theoretical Talmud study, this kind of reasoning has occasionally led to *pilpul*, a form of question-and-answer dialogue that can be described as more ritualistic than substantive.

The various codes of Jewish law that were compiled in the medieval period and in the Renaissance drew heavily on BT as the dominant work of rabbinic literature, and particularly of rabbinic law. BT so dominated Jewish legal study that each attempt to simplify Jewish law through the production of a code occasioned resistance among those who preferred the explicit multivocality of BT legal discourse. Even as codes have become the default descriptions of Jewish law for the masses, legal experts continue to return to BT to craft their own responses to new crises, often through *responsa literature. In this way, rabbinic literature continues to be a living and ever expanding endeavor. **See also** HALAKHAH; MISHNAH; TALMUD, BABYLONIAN; TALMUD, JERUSALEM.

BARRY WIMPFHEIMER

Rabbinic Ordination refers to the granting of the title "*rabbi." Processes leading to ordaining rabbis have varied widely. The rabbinic tradition viewed the transfer of leadership from *Moses to Joshua (Num 27:22, 23; Deut 34:9) as the first link in a long chain of ordinations continuing into their own times (M. *Avot 1:1). A rabbi with Mosaic ordination (*semikhah*, literally, "laying on of hands") had very broad powers, perhaps even a seat on the *Sanhedrin (Jewish *court and legislative body). Only granted in the Land of Israel, this ordination was discontinued in late antiquity, probably as a result of persecution. Various efforts were made in the medieval and early modern periods to revive the practice. The most famous effort was the 1538 attempt by Jacob Berab and Joseph *Karo in *Safed. In the early twenty-first century, rabbinic leader and scholar Adin Steinsaltz was involved in a similar undertaking.

In the *Middle Ages, the title "rabbi" was generally granted to an individual by *rashut* (a license) or *minnui* (an appointment). He then became the judge and leader of a particular community. The powers granted to such an appointee were much more restricted than those of the Mosaic ordainees. Originally granted only by the *Exilarch, the head of the Jewish community in *Iraq, this "appointment" likely evolved into the form of ordination that became most common from the thirteenth to the nineteenth centuries: *hattarat hora'ah*, literally, "a permit to instruct." The assignment of the written permit conferred recognition of Jewish halakhic competence and protection from claims of malpractice. Although no laying on of hands occurred in the grant of *hattarat hora'ah*, it also came to be known colloquially as *semikhah*.

In the nineteenth century, newly organized liberal movements of Judaism began to ordain rabbinic leaders graduating from modern, academically oriented seminaries. With a curriculum much broader than the merely legal (see HALAKHAH), these seminaries recognized that contemporary Jews were as much in need of pastors as of the legal experts required by medieval and early modern communities. Today, ordination from the seminaries of liberal movements and *hattarat hora'ah* exist side by side; both are popularly termed *semikhah*. Liberal rabbinic seminaries began ordaining woman in the 1970s and 1980s, and all non-Orthodox seminaries now do so. Most also ordain gays and lesbians (see entries under JUDAISM).

MARCUS MORDECHAI SCHWARTZ

Rabbinic Ordination of Women. Women's quest for rabbinical *ordination dates to the late nineteenth century in *Germany and the *United States; it was, in part, a natural consequence of *Reform Judaism's insistence on the religious equality of men and women. The ordination of women also emerged as part of a larger cultural debate about women's rights and their access to the learned professions. In the 1890s, the charismatic female Jewish preacher Ray Frank (1861–1948) was hailed in the press as "the girl Rabbi of the Golden West." In the decades that followed, a handful of individuals, among them Martha Neumark at Cincinnati's *Hebrew Union College and Irma Levy Lindheim, Dora Askowith, and Helen Levinthal at New York's Jewish Institute of Religion, unsuccessfully sought ordination. In 1935, Regina *Jonas (1902–1944) was privately ordained in Germany and became the first woman rabbi. Jonas used her position to offer solace to her persecuted co-religionists in *Nazi Germany; she was deported and murdered at *Auschwitz.

The question of women's ordination continued to be discussed in the United States in the 1950s and 1960s. In the 1950s the story of Paula Ackerman succeeding her late husband in the pulpit was so newsworthy that her picture appeared in *Time* magazine. In the 1960s, the topic gained greater urgency as the second wave of feminism gathered force. For many Americans and American Jews, female ordination became an important symbol of Judaism's commitment to gender equity.

In 1972, Sally *Priesand was ordained by the Hebrew Union College-Jewish Institute of Religion in Cincinnati, Ohio. Two years later the *Reconstructionist movement ordained Sandy Eisenberg Sasso and, in 1985, after a vociferous public debate that lasted slightly longer than a decade, the *Conservative movement ordained Amy Eilberg. Jacqueline Tabick, the first female rabbi in *Britain, was ordained in 1975 by Leo Baeck College, an institution under the joint sponsorship of the Reform Synagogues of Great Britain and the Union of Liberal and Progressive Synagogues. Even as the question of the permissibility of women's ordination was resolved in the liberal movements of American Judaism and the United Kingdom, and the first women were ordained in *Israel, some Orthodox Jews began to ask if there would be Orthodox female rabbis. By the early twenty-first century, a few Orthodox women, including Haviva Ner-David and Sara Hurwitz, had received private, not seminary, ordination. Hurwitz assumed the title of Rabba.

As the struggle for female ordination was achieved for many, the history of women in the rabbinate opened. It began with the challenges that the presence of women rabbis raised for their seminaries, their congregants, and their male colleagues. It continued with the difficulties these women faced as they sought to reconcile feminism with Judaism (see JUDAISM: FEMINIST) and demanded Judaism's embrace of women's voices and perspectives. The pioneering cluster of female rabbis had to convince congregations to hire them and then had to establish their authority in a hitherto exclusively male profession; they even had to fight for maternity leave. Yet, if these initial skirmishes were mostly fought by the first cohorts of women ordained, the larger issue of living within a tradition that had largely ignored female perspectives remains an ongoing challenge.

Female rabbis decry the exclusion of women's voices and views from the sacred texts of Jewish tradition, especially its liturgy and the giant corpus of *rabbinic literature. These rabbis have often rediscovered women from the Jewish past, reinterpreting their lives to cast them as role models and to teach lessons for Jews today. They have also turned a critical lens on the trajectory of women's lives, asking how Judaism could signify moments of change, of joy, of despair, and especially those intimately linked to the feminine. They seek to unite Judaism, through Jewish feminism, with the occasions, great and small, that rest at the core of women's lives, and they have created an array of new rituals to do so. They have also extended their feminist critique to include the challenges that face gays and lesbians (see ETHICS, SEXUAL).

At the beginning of the twenty-first century, several hundred women have been ordained as rabbis in North America, the United Kingdom, and Israel, and as many as half of rabbinical students in seminaries of liberal denominations of Judaism, including those of the Conservative/Masorti and Reconstructionist movements, are female (see entries under JUDAISM). The paths of rabbis who are women have not been free of obstacles. Many female clergy hold subordinate positions in larger *synagogues or work as educators or chaplains, rather than as senior leaders of congregations. These occupational patterns are a reflection not only of persistent cultural prejudices toward women as religious authority figures but also of many women's choices of rabbinic options that allow them time for the demands of home and family.

Recent books on women and ordination include E. Klapheck, *Fräulein Rabbiner Jonas: The Story of the First Woman Rabbi* (2004); P. S. Nadell, *Women Who Would Be Rabbis: A History of Women's Ordination, 1889–1985* (1998); H. Ner-David, *Life on the Fringes: A Feminist Journey toward Traditional Rabbinic Ordination* (2000); and S. Sheridan, ed., *Hear Our Voice: Women Rabbis Tell Their Stories* (1994) on women's ordination in Britain.

PAMELA S. NADELL

Rabin, Yitzhak (1922–1995), the fifth prime minister of *Israel, was born in *Jerusalem and grew up in *Tel Aviv where he attended agricultural school. In 1941, he joined the *Palmakh* branch of the Haganah (see ISRAEL, STATE OF: MILITARY AND PARAMILITARY BODIES) and assisted in the allied invasion of Lebanon. He rose to the position of Chief Operations Officer of the Palmakh in 1947. During the 1948 War of Independence he directed Israeli operations in Jerusalem (see ISRAEL, STATE OF: FOUNDING; ISRAEL, STATE OF: WARS). In 1964 he was appointed Chief of Staff of the Israeli Defense Forces (IDF). After the 1967 Six Day War, he retired from the IDF and became ambassador to the United States. He was appointed minister of labor in March 1974 by Golda *Meir and succeeded her as prime minister of Israel after her resignation the following month. The Sinai Interim Agreement was a major accomplishment of the early part of his term and a step toward peace between Israel and Egypt. Rabin resigned before new elections in May 1977, when it was revealed that his wife was maintaining a foreign currency bank account in contravention of Israeli law. In

1992 Rabin defeated Shimon Peres to become leader of the Labor Party (see ISRAEL, STATE OF: POLITICAL PARTIES). He played an important role in negotiating the Oslo Accords and a peace treaty with Jordan; in 1994 he was awarded the Nobel Peace Prize with Shimon Peres and Yasser Arafat. On November 4, 1995, Rabin was assassinated in Tel Aviv by Yigal Amir, an right-wing Israeli who was an opponent of the Oslo Accords.   ELIZABETH SHULMAN

Rachel and her older sister *Leah are *Jacob's wives; her story is told in *Genesis 29–35. Rachel is the younger daughter of Laban, the brother of Jacob's mother *Rebekah. Rachel first encounters Jacob at a well, where he falls in love with her. Although Jacob undertakes to work for Laban for seven years in order to marry Rachel, Laban substitutes her sister Leah for Rachel at the time of marriage. Jacob marries Rachel shortly thereafter, in return for another seven years of promised labor. The sisters' rivalry for Jacob's affection is magnified by Rachel's long period of childlessness (see INFERTILITY); nevertheless, she is always the beloved wife. Frustrated by her infertility, Rachel gives her slave Bilhah to Jacob as a surrogate mother, and Bilhah bears Dan and Naphtali. With divine help, Rachel is finally able to conceive. Her sons are *Joseph and Benjamin; she dies while giving birth to Benjamin and is buried on the road to Bethlehem (Gen 35:19–20). Although Rachel and Leah compete against each other as co-wives of Jacob, they are united in feeling that Laban has cheated them economically (31:14–15). Sharing in her family's trickster traditions, Rachel does not hesitate to deceive her father about her theft of his household gods as Jacob and his family prepare to return to *Canaan.   NAOMI STEINBERG

Radhanites (Arabic, *radhaniya*) were Jewish merchants who maintained trans-Eurasian trading routes in the early Muslim period, described in the *Kitab al-maslik wa'l-mamalik* (Book of Routes and Kingdoms) of Ibn Khurdadhbeh, overseer of the mail and information services in the mid-ninth-century Abbasid Empire. These merchants are also mentioned as *rahadaniya* in the *Kitab al-buldan* (Book of the Countries) by the early-tenth-century geographer, Ibn al-Faqih. Scholars have long debated the geographic origin of these multilingual traders whose land and sea routes traversed Europe, *India, and *China, as well as the Middle East and *North Africa. Their goods included furs, weapons, eunuchs, and slaves from northern and eastern Europe, and musk and perfume, fine fabrics, and spices such as cinnamon and camphor from China. The current consensus, based on the research of Moshe Gil ("The Radhanite Merchants and the Land of Radhan," *Journal of Economic and Social History of the Orient* 17 [1974]: 209–28), is that the Radhanites came from the region of Radhan, on the Tigris River in southern *Iraq, the area of origin of the Jewish population of Baghdad and an ancient mercantile center.   KATE FRIEDMAN

Radio: United States. From 1920 to 1953, radio was the single most powerful and popular medium in the *United States, dominating the cultural and political landscape. Radio *broadcasts entertained audiences during the Depression, became a key vehicle for President Franklin Delano Roosevelt to rally the support of the American public, and emerged as a vital source of mobilization, entertainment,

and news during *World War II. The 1930s and 1940s are often called radio's "Golden Age."

During those two decades, the United States was still absorbing the twenty-five million immigrants who arrived between 1881 and 1924, including some two and a half million *Yiddish-speaking Jews from *Eastern Europe. By 1930, American Jews made up about 3% of the American population, but they were overrepresented on radio. As with vaudeville and Hollywood *film (see ENTERTAINMENT), Jews played critical roles in the development of radio (see also BROADCASTING). Among the most influential figures were three children of Jewish immigrants: David Sarnoff (1891–1971), William Paley (1901–1990), and Gertrude Berg (1899–1966).

Sarnoff, who immigrated from Europe with his family at age nine, was instrumental in establishing the Radio Corporation of America (RCA), which owned the National Broadcasting Corporation (NBC); he assumed the presidency in 1930. William Paley entered the radio business in the mid-1920s, first as a program sponsor and two years later as the president of the Columbia Broadcasting System (CBS), which competed with Sarnoff's NBC for dominance of the young medium. Gertrude Berg was a writer, producer, and performer whose program, *The Goldbergs*, which debuted on NBC in 1929, made her one of the most popular and powerful women in radio throughout the 1930s and 1940s. Through *The Goldbergs*, Berg became one of the most recognizable figures in the medium, both for her Yiddish-accented portrayal of matriarch Molly Goldberg and for her strength and stature behind the scenes. Whereas Sarnoff and Paley cast long shadows over the development of network radio by virtue of their ownership of the two largest radio networks, Berg mined *The Goldbergs* for every audience, every outlet, and every possible story line. After seventeen years on radio, countless live performances, several books, guest appearances on other radio and television programs, innumerable magazine articles, six seasons on television, and a handful of live stage shows, she retired shortly before her death.

Berg was one of many popular Jewish radio performers. Others included Arthur Tracy (born Abba Tracousky), known as the "Street Singer," one of radio's first superstars, and Mel Blanc, the famous voice-over artist, who began his career on radio in Los Angeles. For other performers, like Al Jolson, Eddie Cantor, Fanny Brice, and Groucho Marx, radio became another venue for their already substantial success. Jack Benny, George Burns, and cartoonist Harry Hirschfeld were among radio's early luminaries and other performers used radio to supplement their careers off the air.

Berg's Molly Goldberg stands out as one of a handful of Jewish characters who became part of the popular culture pantheon, but other, lesser known but regular Jewish characters inhabited the radio landscape. Among them were Jack Benny's pals, Mr. Kitzel and Schlepperman; Izzy Finkelstein, who appeared on WMAQ's program *Kaltenmeyer's Kindergarten*; Papa David Solomon from *Life Can Be Beautiful*; and Mrs. Nussbaum from the *Fred Allen Show*. Other shows revolved around Jewish characters, like WBNX's comedy, *Bronx Marriage Bureau*. CBS debuted a program called *Meyer the Buyer* in 1932, and *Potash and Perlmutter* were the title characters of a series of popular short stories. *Mama Bloom's Brood*, a melodramatic saga of a Jewish family, also aired during the 1930s.

Following the success of *The Goldbergs* and the popularity of Eddie Cantor, NBC surveyed its audiences and found that people responded positively to characters "of a Jewish type." However, Jewish entertainers like Cantor and Benny were still far more popular than their more overtly Jewish counterparts. With the notable exception of *The Goldbergs*, performers who specialized in Yiddish accents generally remained minor stars in mainstream American broadcasting.

For the sizable audience of Jewish immigrants interested in Yiddish programming, local stations created a thriving and creative radio culture on the margins of the mainstream. Yiddish stations operated on a shoestring budget and struggled to stay on the air; nevertheless, they, their performers, and their sponsors created a relatively independent arena for broadcasting Jewishness and Jewish culture. Stations relied on "time brokers" to strike sponsorship deals with local businesses. As a result, Yiddish programs were often sponsored by businesses like Parmet Brothers' Furniture in New York, Harry Kandel's Appliances in Philadelphia, or the oddly named Chicago Pharmacy in Los Angeles. Thus, commercial radio became part of a delicate network of local businesses, theaters, performers, and even charities – all of which used radio to speak to and about the communities they served.

Most Jewish immigrants and their children listened to both Yiddish and English programs, and their tastes and preferences took shape around the interactions between the two. To Jewish immigrant listeners, programs like *Clara, Lu and Em*, or *The Shadow* may have sounded more foreign than familiar, while shows in Yiddish like *Bay tate mames tish* ('Round the Family Table) and *Der yidisher filosof* (The Jewish Philosopher) featured the sounds of fictionalized Jewish familial strife. In fact, the culture of Yiddish radio relied heavily on the direction of English radio: Yiddish-speaking audiences were listening to radio even before the first Yiddish broadcast was made, the Yiddish press reported on and carried listings for English radio programming, and Yiddish-speaking radio performers copied the successful formulas of their English-speaking counterparts. Yiddish radio and its audiences benefited from radio's multilingualism, which permitted its immigrant audience to navigate complementary relationships among their Jewish communities and their American contexts.

Even though *television came to replace radio as the primary medium of in-home entertainment during the early 1950s, Yiddish-language radio continued in large American cities like *New York, *Chicago, Detroit, Baltimore, *Philadelphia, and Los Angeles through the 1970s. Yiddish-language programs were also heard in smaller markets like Rochester, New York; Tuscaloosa, Alabama; and, in 1960, Honolulu. Yiddish programming in cities with significant Yiddish-speaking audiences like New York and Miami adapted to changes in radio more broadly, playing more records and reading more news, just as their English counterparts underwent similar changes. New York housed the majority of radio stations that carried Yiddish programs and produced more Yiddish-speaking performers than any other city. This was mainly thanks to WEVD, "the station that speaks your language," which dedicated most of its broadcast hours to programming in Yiddish. Local businesspeople owned and operated smaller stations, which featured Yiddish programs alongside shows in other immigrant languages.

For further reading, see J. Dunning, *On the Air: The Encyclopedia of Old-Time Radio* (1998); A. Y. Kelman, *Station Identification: A Cultural History of Yiddish Radio in the United States* (2009); J. Hoberman and J. Shandler, *Entertaining America* (2003); and for a good catalogue of programs and characters, see D. Siegel and S. Siegel, *Radio and the Jews* (2007).

ARI Y. KELMAN

Rashi, the acronym for Rabbi Solomon ben Isaac (1040–1105), who was born in Troyes in northern France (see FRANCE: MIDDLE AGES), was a universally revered and respected rabbi, teacher, author, and communal leader. At age eighteen, already married, he left for Mainz, where he spent six years at the *yeshivah* of R. *Gershom ben Judah of Mainz studying with Jacob ben Jakar. After the latter's death he moved to Worms, where he spent about four years studying with R. Isaac ha-Levi. At age thirty, he returned to Troyes, where he spent the rest of his life, apparently earning his living from engaging in commercial activities with Christians; he was probably not a vintner or wine merchant as some have suggested. Two of his three daughters were married to prominent scholars, Jochebed to Meir ben Samuel and Miriam to Judah ben Nathan. Jochebed's four sons were all great scholars; the most prominent were Samuel (Rashbam) and Jacob (Rabbenu Tam).

Shortly after his return to Troyes, Rashi founded a *yeshivah* where he cultivated an atmosphere of warmth, openness, creativity, critical thinking, and dedication to the truth. He encouraged his students to write, and they produced works in many fields, including biblical commentary, talmudic exegesis, *halakhah, *midrash, and *piyyut* (see POETRY, LITURGICAL [*PIYYUT*]) commentary. Among his most famous students were Shemaiah, who seems to have served as his personal secretary; Joseph Kara; and his grandsons Samuel and Jacob.

Rashi was soon recognized as the greatest scholar of his generation and assumed leadership of his community, exerting his influence throughout the region and beyond. Although modest in manner, he was not afraid to take a stand. He tended to be lenient in his halakhic decisions and opposed his teachers when he was convinced he was right. He encouraged peace and unity both within his own community and between other communities in the region. Rashi took a firm stance against certain local customs that he felt contravened the teachings of the Babylonian *Talmud, which he insisted took precedence. In general he had a very positive attitude to women; he particularly supported the right of women to refuse *yibbum* (see MARRIAGE, LEVIRATE). On the question of apostates (Jews who had converted to *Christianity) he was also lenient, preferring a welcoming approach that facilitated bringing them back into the community.

The most innovative and influential of Rashi's many works was his *Bible commentary (see BIBLICAL COMMENTARY). He was the first *Ashkenazi exegete to produce a running commentary on the entire Hebrew Bible (the sections on *Ezra-Nehemiah, *Chronicles, and from *Job 40:25 to the end have not survived). He combined midrashic sources with grammatical and linguistic comments and included observations on aspects of contemporary life. His *Torah commentary is particularly weighted with midrashic material: Only a quarter of the comments are original to him, whereas in the rest of the Bible commentary the figure is two-thirds. Yet the Torah commentary is not a mere anthology. Rashi carefully chose which comments to include and then edited them to suit his exegetical needs, usually avoiding traditions that diverged from the *peshat* or contextual meaning. Despite his declared intention to incorporate only *aggadot that properly explained the biblical text, he often cites *aggadot* for didactic or polemical reasons or sometimes simply out of his love for *aggadah* (see also RABBINIC LITERATURE: MIDRASH).

Rashi also wrote a commentary on most of the Babylonian *Talmud. This enterprise was not as innovative as his biblical commentary (there were precedents in *Germany) but it represented the culmination of Ashkenazi talmudic exegesis and superseded all those that preceded it. Aimed at a more advanced student, it became an enduring indispensable aid to Talmud study and has since been included in almost every printed edition of the Talmud, generally on the inner margin beside the binding.

In addition, Rashi wrote hundreds of *responsa. Most that survive are in the areas of religious ritual and conduct. Rashi was also an innovator in the field of Hebrew language, coining more than a thousand new words and inventing a new system of Hebrew grammar, although the latter did not have a lasting impact. His commentaries also preserve hundreds of glosses in Old French, the vernacular language of his milieu, many unattested in other sources (see FRANCE: MIDDLE AGES).

Rashi lived at a time of great intellectual and religious ferment. The so-called twelfth-century renaissance was already underway in France by the middle of the eleventh century, and many of its intellectual currents influenced his *yeshivah*. This was also a time of religious persecution. The First *Crusade of 1096 had a profound impact on Jewish communities in the Rhineland and surrounding areas. At the same time Christian clerics were beginning to press Jewish conversion to Christianity and coerce Jewish leaders to engage in religious disputations (see MIDDLE AGES: JEWISH–CHRISTIAN POLEMICS). In his biblical commentaries Rashi is consistently negative in his characterizations of Gentiles (e.g., *Esau, *Ishmael, and *Balaam in his Torah commentary), and in a number of his commentaries (*Isaiah, Minor Prophets, *Psalms, *Song of Songs) he openly polemicizes with Christian views. He also stresses at every turn the virtues of the Jewish people, the Land of Israel, and the special relationship between God and Israel. As a leader, he believed his duty was to defend his faith and provide encouragement and ammunition for his followers in the face of Christian hostility.

Rashi's influence was immense. His Torah commentary gained unprecedented acceptance throughout the Jewish world; it was the first Hebrew book printed (1470–75) and has been the subject of hundreds of supercommentaries and scholarly articles (see PRINTING). It was also studied intently by Christian scholars and translated into several languages. The halakhic ruling in the *Arba'ah Turim* (see JACOB BEN ASHER) and *Shulhan Arukh* (see HALAKHAH) that one may fulfill one's obligation of reviewing the weekly Torah portion with Rashi's commentary instead of *Targum Onkelos* has given it near-canonical status. It is the primary commentary that is studied in schools and *yeshivot*, and some circles take Rashi's comments as the only true interpretation. As someone known for his humility and as a man who made the pursuit of truth his credo, Rashi might have been puzzled and even appalled by this phenomenon. He was constantly revising his commentaries and expressed regret to his grandson, Rashbam, that he did not have time to incorporate the new insights being revealed by his students every day. Although much in Rashi's commentaries is timeless, portions were intended to give solace and support to a beleaguered community, weary of the exile, and these need to be understood in their proper context.

For further reading, see M. Banitt, *Rashi, Interpreter of the Biblical Letter* (1985); B. Gelles, *Peshat and Derash in the Exegesis of Rashi* (1981); M. Liber, *Rashi* (1906); C. Pearl, *Rashi* (1988); and E. Shereshevsky, *Rashi, the Man and His World* (1982).   BARRY DOV WALFISH

Reason. In most theological discussions, reason stands for what the human mind is capable of discovering on its own and is opposed to *revelation. According to Moses *Maimonides, reason can demonstrate the existence of *God without the aid of Scripture. By the same token, Judaism holds there are some *commandments (*mishpatim*) that even if God had not given them, we would be justified in giving to ourselves on the basis of reason; for example, the prohibitions against murder, stealing, and false testimony. Beyond this, it is often said that Judaism does not assert anything that reason can show to be absurd. Although Jewish beliefs often go *beyond* what reason can show (e.g., that the world was created), they never go *against* reason.

What then can reason show? A great deal of medieval *thought took on the question of what to do with biblical passages that suggest God has bodily parts, occupies space, and changes location. How can this be true if, as Judaism asserts, God is one? After all, anything that has parts or takes up space is divisible. The answer was that, because reason can show that God is immaterial, any passage that suggests otherwise cannot be read in a literal fashion. Thus, instead of saying that God walked with Noah, we would have to say that Noah was beloved of God. In this way, reason is needed to arrive at the true meaning of Scripture.

How far can reason extend? Maimonides did not think reason was capable of demonstrating that the world was created. Nor, in his opinion, could reason answer all the questions one might ask about prophecy (see BIBLE: PROPHETS AND PROPHECY) and providence. Similarly, a person could object that reason can show that murder, stealing, and lying are immoral, but it does not explain the details of how to pray or how to observe the *festivals and *life-cycle rituals. For that we have to turn to revelation, or at least revelation as interpreted by *rabbinic tradition. In the contemporary world, the ability of reason to demonstrate something as basic as the existence of God or the truths of geometry has been called into question as alternative conceptual schemes are articulated and defended.

The obvious conclusion is that reason and revelation must work together. According to Deuteronomy 4:6, the *Torah was intended to be a body of wisdom. Without reason to provide clarity and structure, the Torah would be confusing and misleading. Take the often-quoted line, "An eye for an eye, a tooth for a tooth" (Exod 21:23–27). Does this mean that God approves of dismemberment as a form of compensation? The answer is no. All that is being asserted is the principle of *lex talionis*: The severity of the punishment, whether assessed through imprisonment or financial compensation, should match the severity of the crime. By the same token, without the guidance of revelation, many of the questions people ask about life, *death, and the purpose of human existence would go unanswered. The success or failure of a religion may be judged on how well it balances the claims of one with those of the other.

For further study, see Maimonides, *Mishneh Torah*, Book 1, "Basic Principles of the Torah" (1178); Maimonides, *Guide of the Perplexed* (1190); H. Cohen, *Religion of Reason out of the Sources of Judaism* (1919); M. Buber, *Eclipse of God* (1952); L. Goodman, *God of Abraham* (1996); and K. Seeskin, *Searching for a Distant God* (2000).   KENNETH SEESKIN

Rebbetzin. This Jewish honorific term for a rabbi's wife derives from Yiddish and probably originated in medieval Europe. Although no such title exists in ancient Judaism, its emergence in the vernacular language of *Central and *East European Jewry indicates that rabbis' wives frequently assumed important if unofficial religious roles in Jewish communities. Rabbis tended to marry women from elite families whose daughters received Jewish educations far superior to those of most women. Many learned *rebbetzins* led prayers in the women's section of the synagogue (see WORSHIP) and undertook a variety of female community endeavors including bridal arrangements, burial preparations, and dispensing of charity (see WOMEN: MIDDLE AGES). Some *rebbetzins* were regarded as reliable witnesses of their husbands' rulings on ritual matters, particularly related to the *dietary laws, and might be consulted for legal opinions based on their knowledge of their husbands' practices. In a social context that honored scholarship above economic success, the *rebbetzin* frequently supported her family financially by running a business while her husband devoted himself to study. In East European communities the *rebbetzin* often had a monopoly on the sale of yeast; she might also cater refreshments following *life cycle events where her husband officiated.

In North America, the *rebbetzin* in all denominations of Judaism was expected to fulfill a number of social, communal, and educational functions within her husband's congregation. Before the introduction of female ordination in non-Orthodox forms of Judaism beginning in the 1970s (see RABBINIC ORDINATION OF WOMEN), some women who become *rebbetzins* built on their husbands' positions to achieve their own leadership roles as teachers and representatives of Jewish life within their communities and the larger non-Jewish world. With changing social mores and increased professional opportunities for Jewish women in many fields, including the rabbinate and cantorate (see entries on CANTORS; CANTORATE) it is less common for early-twenty-first century rabbis' spouses to follow these patterns. However, within the Orthodox Jewish community, most *rebbetzins* continue to fulfill traditional expectations, serving as domestic hostesses to their husbands' congregations and as teachers and counselors to female congregants (see JUDAISM: ORTHODOX entries).

For further reading, see I. Etkes, "Marriage and Torah Study among the *Lomdim* in Lithuania in the Nineteenth Century," in *The Jewish Family: Metaphor and Memory*, ed. D. Kraemer (1989), 153–78; and S. R. Schwartz, *The Rabbi's Wife: The Rebbetzin in American Jewish Life* (2006).
                                                                                                JUDITH R. BASKIN

Rebekah is the matriarch of the second generation of Israelite ancestors. She stands out for her relationship to her husband *Isaac and the dynamic quality of her actions. Like the other matriarchs, she overcomes *infertility (a motif that highlights the importance of offspring and the divine role in human events). She is the only matriarch who has a monogamous marriage, and she is the first whose husband is said to love her (Gen 24:67). Rebekah dominates the longest chapter in Genesis (24), in which she is identified as a suitable wife for Isaac through her actions at the well and is blessed by her brother, Laban, as the future ancestor of myriads (24:60; cf. 22:17 where God makes the same promise to *Abraham). When pregnant, Rebekah receives an oracle directly from God (25:23) indicating that the twins in her womb are the eponymous ancestors of two nations and that the younger will prevail. She subsequently tricks her husband (27) into blessing her favored second son *Jacob over his brother *Esau.   CAROL MEYERS

Reconstructionist Rabbinical College (RRC) was founded in 1968 in *Philadelphia by its first president, Ira Eisenstein. The establishment of this school put Reconstructionism (see JUDAISM, RECONSTRUCTIONIST) on the map as an independent denomination in the American Jewish community. The training program and curriculum reflect Reconstructionist ideology. Because of the movement's belief in women's equality, women were accepted as rabbinical students from its inception; in 1974 Sandy Eisenberg Sasso was the first woman to be ordained. The curriculum at RRC is constructed around seminars that focus on the evolving history and culture of the Jewish people. Today the school has both rabbinical and cantorial training programs (see entries under CANTOR, CANTORATE). It also supports centers that contribute to the understanding of Jewish views on women and gender studies, ethics, and aging. Many graduates assume leadership roles in Reconstructionist congregations, but others also serve Reform and Conservative congregations or undertake careers as Jewish communal service professionals, institutional chaplains, principals of day schools, or as chaplains on college campuses.   REBECCA ALPERT

Red Heifer. Numbers 19 describes the ritual of the red heifer that is slaughtered outside the camp and burned with its flesh, blood, and dung. When combined with spring water, the heifer's ashes produce a "water of lustration" (*mei ha-niddah*) that is efficacious in eliminating ritual impurity acquired from contact with or propinquity to a corpse, grave, or human bone. The red heifer used in this ritual has to be perfect and unblemished and could never have been yoked (Num 19:2). All involved in the slaughter, burning, and gathering of the heifer's ashes are rendered ritually unclean until the evening. M. *Parah*, part of the *Mishnah's order *Tohorot* (Purities), details the ritual of the red heifer; among other criteria, the presence of even two black hairs is said to invalidate an otherwise red animal. In fact, finding a heifer that fulfills all halakhic requirements is all but impossible; according to M. *Parah* 3:4, only eight such heifers were ever sacrificed. Later Jewish tradition characterized this law as a *ḥok*, a divine commandment beyond human reasoning.

KATE FRIEDMAN

Redemption. In Jewish tradition, redemption connotes the restoration or return to an original state from a position of difficulty. In the *Pentateuch, two terms describe acts of redemption: *go'el* and *padah*. *Go'el* refers to a kinsman who is obligated to help a near relative when that relative has either sold himself to a wealthy "stranger or sojourner" (Lev 25: 47–55) or has been forced to sell some of his property (25:23); the *go'el* must also avenge the blood of his nearest relative (Gen 9:5). According to levirate marriage (see MAR-RIAGE, LEVIRATE) legislation (see *HALAKHAH*), the *go'el* must marry the childless widow of his brother or, in some cases, near kinsman (Ruth 4:4). *Padah* refers to the redemption or ransom required to free an individual or group of people from bondage or ownership. The term is used specifically with respect to the deliverance of Israel from slavery (Deut 7:8). *Padah* is also used to refer to the deliverance of the firstborn son (Exod 13:13, 14: Lev 27:26; see REDEMP-TION OF FIRSTBORN SON [*PIDYON HA-BEN*]).

Both classical (*Isaiah and *Amos) and exilic (*Jeremiah) prophetic writings link the idea of redemption to the concept of *teshuvah* (*repentance or return). The statement, "Seek me and live" (Amos 5:4–6), links human responsibility for repentance to the accessibility of divine redemption. For Isaiah, human repentance is tied to the hope for an "end of days" or a time of universal liberation from war (2:2–4). The prophet Jeremiah understands redemption as the post-exilic restoration when "the remnant will be gathered up and restored" (23:2–4) and returned to the land (23:5–8, 33:14–26).

Rabbinic Judaism invokes the biblical *padah* and applies the notion of ransom buying to halakhic merit. Rabbi *Akiva, for example, attributes the parting of the Reed Sea to the merit of Jacob (*Mekhilta* 29b; *Exodus Rabbah* 21:8). Rabbinic Judaism also develops the prophetic link between *teshuvah* and redemption, conceptualizing redemption as a divine–human partnership of *atonement: God will forgive those who are truly repentant.

The medieval philosopher Moses *Maimonides (*The Guide of the Perplexed*) likened redemption to the full actualization of the human intellect that will take place in the world to come (*olam ha-ba*). This concept of redemption received further expansion in Jewish *mysticism in the idea of *tikkun* or repair. According to this conception, human beings can help restore divine unity through their halakhic deeds and observance (see KABBALAH).

By contrast, Hermann *Cohen identified Jewish redemption with autonomous ethical action (*The Religion of Reason: Out of the Sources of Judaism*). Both Martin *Buber and Franz *Rosenzweig challenged this strictly ethical understanding of redemption. For Buber, redemption reflected the individual's capacity to respond with the whole being to the divine encounter ("Faith of Judaism"). For Rosenzweig, Jewish redemption meant the community's ability to sustain itself through its liturgical *calendar and to anticipate the full redemption of all persons in a not-yet future (*The Star of Redemption*).

RANDI RASHKOVER

Redemption of Firstborn Son (*Pidyon Ha-Ben*). This ritual originated in the biblical period when firstborn sons were to be consecrated to God to serve as priests (Num 3:12). When the priesthood was assigned to the Levites (see ISRAELITES: RELIGION; TEMPLE AND TEMPLE CULT), firstborn sons in nonpriestly families were redeemed from the priesthood at the price of five shekels (Num 3:46–48). Biblical *commandments also required that firstborn unclean animals be redeemed and that firstborn clean animals be sacrificed (Num 18:15–17). Redemption of firstborn sons is also explained as a commemoration of the slaying of the firstborn sons of the *Egyptians before the exodus (Exod 13:15; Num 3:13). The redemption is to occur on the thirtieth day after birth, although it may be postponed if that day is a *Sabbath, * festival, or *fast day. The ritual includes the recitation of a *blessing followed by the *sheheheyanu* prayer of thanksgiving; the father redeems his infant by giving five silver coins of a specific minimum weight to a guest of high priestly descent (*kohen*). Often the coins are returned to the family as a gift. Redemption does not apply in case of cesarean section or a miscarriage or stillbirth after the first forty days of a previous pregnancy, since the commandment refers to the firstborn son's opening of the mother's womb (Num 3:12).

ELIZABETH SHULMAN

Reform Judaism: See JUDAISM, REFORM entries

Reformation. Between 1517 and 1620, the Protestant Reformation split European Christendom into competing confessional churches, including Anglican, Lutheran, Reformed, and Tridentine Catholic. It affected Jews most directly in the Holy Roman Empire of *Germany, and in *Italy and *Poland. Martin Luther made Jews a central image in his writings, symbolizing human rebellion against *God. This belief permeates his anti-Jewish polemical books, most notably *On the Jews and Their Lies* (1543). Traditional Catholics continued to believe that Jews sometimes committed *host desecration and *ritual murder. Apart from a few expulsions from cities or territories, the Reformation did not ultimately affect Jewish life in the Holy Roman Empire as much as did the shift toward princely absolutism in the later sixteenth and seventeenth centuries (see COURT JEWS).

Within the Italian states, Jews experienced the Reformation through a tightening of control over their lives. In 1553, the Catholic Church introduced censorship controls over Jewish *printing and books and banned the *Talmud. These measures forced Jewish communities to introduce their own form of pre-publication censorship. Pope Paul IV decreed in his bull *Cum nimis absurdum* (1555) that henceforth Jews would be tolerated in Catholic lands only under much stricter conditions. By the 1580s, a number of Italian towns and cities had forced their Jewish residents to live in small, densely populated, walled *"ghettos," giving them a visible yet isolated place within the community. The Catholic Church also made *conversions of Jews a higher priority than before, and a number of Jews became Catholic proselytes. Polish Jewry also experienced some elements of the Catholic Reformation, notably polemical attacks and limited press controls, although the community also benefited from increased German Jewish immigration by the end of the sixteenth century.

In both Italy and in the Holy Roman Empire, Jews responded to crises through appeals to the authorities, reliance on widespread family networks, and migration when necessary. The Reformation stimulated both Jewish hopes and fears, raising *messianic expectations among some, while others anticipated persecution and even the possibility of *martyrdom. Jews were also indirectly affected by internal Christian developments. *Christian Hebraism, a movement that was particularly strong in German-speaking Europe during the Reformation, would ultimately provide both Protestants and Catholics with a more realistic idea of Jews and their beliefs. The new biblicism among Protestants also awakened eschatological hopes, which traditionally included the mass conversion of the Jews. Such hopes encouraged some political leaders to support Jewish residence in *Britain (see *MENASSEH BEN ISRAEL).

For recent research, see D. P. Bell and S. G. Burnett, eds., *Jews, Judaism and the Reformation in Sixteenth Century Germany* (2006); A. Raz-Krakotzkin, *The Censor, the Editor, and the Text: The Catholic Church and the Shaping of the Jewish Canon in the Sixteenth Century* (2007); D. Ruderman, ed., *Essential Papers on Jewish Culture in Renaissance and Baroque Italy* (1992); K. R. Stow, *Catholic Thought and Papal Jewish Policy 1555–1593* (1977); and M. Teter, *Jews and Heretics in Catholic Poland* (2006).   STEPHEN G. BURNETT

Rehoboam   (ca. 928–911 BCE), son of *Solomon with Naamah, an *Ammonite (1 Kgs 14:21, 31), was king of *Judah for seventeen years. After his father's death, Rehoboam confronted the ten northern tribes, led by his rival Jeroboam, at *Shechem and considered their demand that he lighten the heavy taxation Solomon had imposed (1 Kgs 12:4; 2 Chron 10:4). Disregarding advice from Solomon's elders, the young Rehoboam listened to his contemporaries and declared that he would significantly increase his father's demands (l Kgs 12:13–14). This harsh response became the justification for the secession of *Israel from the *United Monarchy and its establishment as the kingdom of Israel under Jeroboam (1 Kgs 12:16–20). During the fifth year of Rehoboam's reign, Shishak of *Egypt conquered and sacked *Jerusalem and the *Temple and carried off Solomon's golden shields (1 Kgs 14:25–26).
                                                      KATE FRIEDMAN

Repentance. The Hebrew term for repentance is *teshuvah*, "returning," and generally refers to returning to *God and virtue. *Judaism acknowledges that humanity is created with an inclination toward evil (*yetzer ha-ra*) and that people will transgress. Yet it provides ample opportunity for Jews to engage in *teshuvah*, as the daily liturgy (see WORSHIP) identifies God as appealing for *teshuvah* (*ha-rotzeh b'teshuvah*).

Teshuvah is an important biblical theme, particularly in the prophetic writings (see BIBLE: PROPHETS AND PROPHECY). The book of *Jonah, read on the afternoon of *Yom Kippur, is the primary biblical text that has the power and importance of *teshuvah* as its central message. The story's moral, which is often repeated in liturgy (especially the *High Holiday *maḥzor), is that God prefers the wicked to repent and return to virtue and live, rather than be punished and destroyed.

After the destruction of the Second *Temple by *Rome in 70 CE, *teshuvah* and the role of related spiritual endeavors, such as prayer, became of utmost concern to the *Rabbis. *Atonement for sins was no longer possible through sacrifice (see TEMPLE AND TEMPLE CULT) so they attempted to demonstrate that nonsacrificial methods were equally effective. Thus, the most significant meditations on *teshuvah* are

not found in the *Bible, but in *rabbinic literature. Numerous, scattered statements throughout the *Talmud speak of the importance of *teshuvah* in a person's life, asserting that it will bring *redemption and longevity, as well as divert evil. Moreover, the Rabbis regard *teshuvah* as so fundamental to human existence that the Talmud lists it as one of the seven things created before God created the world (BT *Pesaḥim* 54b).

Later Jewish thinkers further elucidated the process of *teshuvah*. *Saadia Gaon (see THOUGHT, MEDIEVAL) claimed that there are four stages to *teshuvah*: renunciation of sin, feelings of remorse, pursuit of forgiveness, and the determination not to relapse into sin (*Emunot V'De'ot*, ch. 5). The first attempt to systemize the ideology of *teshuvah* in the Jewish tradition, however, is found in *Maimonides' *Mishneh Torah*, where he writes that repentance is always possible, even at the moment before death (*Hilkhot Teshuvah* 1–2).

Jewish thought asserts that *teshuvah* at any time is considered acceptable and meritorious. However, particular importance is associated with the *High Holidays, especially *Yom Kippur. Beginning with *Rosh Ha-Shanah and ending with Yom Kippur, Jews reflect on their actions in the past year, seek forgiveness from others, and attempt to make up for whatever wrongs they may have committed. According to the M. *Yoma* 8:9, however, only Yom Kippur, as the Day of Atonement, can effect pardon for offenses between an individual and God; therefore, one who confesses and atones on Yom Kippur can be forgiven for sins against God. Offenses against another person, such as assault, injury, or theft, are not forgiven until the perpetrator pays full restitution, begs for forgiveness, and does something to appease the victim. Maimonides explains that, if the victim still refuses forgiveness, the perpetrator should repeat the procedure a second and third time, if necessary. The Rabbis believed that *teshuvah* is something fundamentally important to do before death (*Avot* 2:10). Consequently, confessionals and opportunities to repent are included throughout daily (e.g., *tahanun*) and seasonal *worship (e.g., *seliḥot*).

In recent times, the term used to describe one who chooses to assume traditional Jewish ritual and moral observances is *baal teshuvah* or "one who repents."

For further reading, see L. Jacobs, *Judaism and Theology: Essays on the Jewish Religion* (2005); P. H. Peli, *Soloveitchik on Repentance* (1984); and M. Strassfeld, *A Book of Life: Embracing Judaism as a Spiritual Practice* (2006).   PAUL STEINBERG

Responsa Literature refers to a legal process through which individuals and communities send inquiries on legal issues (*she'elot*) to rabbinic authorities. These inquiries, together with the responses to them (*teshuvot*), constitute responsa literature. The responsum, the written answer to the question, is generally designed to clarify the law (see HALAKHAH) and provide a halakhic solution to an authentic dilemma. Responsa literature covers a wide range of topics, including economic, social, familial, and ethical issues; major emphases change with the concerns of succeeding generations.

In the introduction to his legal code, the *Mishneh Torah*, Moses *Maimonides describes the process of responsa literature as follows: "And the residents of every city would address halakhic questions to a contemporary *gaon* (leading talmudic scholar) concerning both religious and general concerns, depending often on proper explanation of difficult talmudic passages, and he would respond to them in his wisdom." In time the various responsa would find their way into literary collections. Although most responsa were written in *Hebrew with smatterings of *Aramaic, some were written in other languages. For example, a noticeable percentage of responsa from the geonic period, as well as medieval responsa written by Isaac Alfasi (also known as the Rif; 1013–1103), who lived in Morocco, and Maimonides, who lived in Egypt, were in *Judeo-Arabic (Arabic written in Hebrew letters).

Responsa literature, which originated in the period of the *Geonim, still continues today; thus, this genre covers a period of approximately 1,200 years. In every generation, prominent respondents (*poskim*) emerged who were accepted locally, regionally, and even internationally as Jewish legal authorities, even though they did not represent a formal judicial body. In early periods, responsa were given recognition as legal rulings, particularly in cases dealing with monetary issues. In later times, however, because of historical circumstances and changes in Jewish communal structure, they came to be viewed more as legal opinions than as rulings. Since responsa reflect an actual reality related to specific cases, they achieved a preferred status relative to other halakhic sources, particularly in comparison to legal codes that often seemed more theoretical than practical. As a result, when there was a contradiction between the two, the general tendency was to follow the responsum, although there are opinions that give preference to legal codes (see *HALAKHAH*). In addition to serving as instruments for halakhic rulings, the responsa are also an important source for documenting Jewish history and legal development.

Generally, the authors of the responsa responded to questions posed by both litigants and tended not to respond at the request of only one litigant. This was in accord with *Rashi's statement (*Responsa of Rashi*, Elfenbein edition, 74), "It is not our approach to make ourselves into advocates who respond decisively to a litigant." This statement is consistent with the dictum of Judah ben Tabbai in M. *Avot 1:8: "Do not act as an advocate." Occasionally, questions to authorities were posed by rabbinic judges before whom the litigants appeared, rather than by the litigants themselves.

In general, inquiries were sent to the halakhic centers of the time, both by locals and by individuals who lived further afield. In geonic times, the respondents were the highest judicial authorities, who had legal power that extended over the entire Jewish *Diaspora; indeed, the responsa literature of the Geonim contributed significantly to preserving a unified Jewish *halakhah*. In the wake of historical transformations in the later Middle Ages, both the nature and the scope of the questions posed underwent changes. Even during the geonic period, however, the unity of the *halakhah* was sometimes broken, as evidenced by contradictory responses to the same question. Infrequently, questioners turned to two authorities with a query so they could choose the preferred response; however, the Geonim strongly frowned on this practice.

During the geonic period, the most important respondents were Natronai, *Saadia, Samuel ben Hofni, Sherira, and *Hai; they were succeeded by Joseph ben Meir ibn Migash,

Isaac Alfasi (Rif), Maimonides, and *Nahmanides; and subsequently in *North Africa by the Ribash, the Tashbatz, and the Rashbash. *Gershom ben Judah of Mainz (Ragmah) and *Rashi stand out among respondents in medieval *France and *Germany; after them, important respondents include Jacob ben Meir Tam; *Meir ben Barukh of Rothenberg (Maharam); and *Asher ben Jehiel (Rosh), a student of the Maharam, who spent the later part of his life in *Spain.

The vast quantity of responsa collections, the large number of authors, and the diverse range of topics they address make it extremely difficult to navigate this literature. Beginning in the seventeenth century, there were attempts to reduce this difficulty by creating collections of responsa organized in a systematic fashion. However, these attempts were far from comprehensive. In recent years, the Institute for Research in Jewish Law of the Hebrew University has published an index of responsa literature, which can now be accessed through the Responsa Project software created by Bar-Ilan University. For further reading, see N. S. Hecht, B. S. Jackson, S. M. Passamaneck, D. Piattelli, and A. M. Rabello, eds., *An Introduction to the History and Sources of Jewish Law* (1996).   GIDEON LIBSON

Resurrection. *Daniel is the first book in the Hebrew *Bible to stress the concept of resurrection, together with the idea that those resurrected will ascend to heaven for astral immortality. This idea became central to other apocalyptic writers because it supported the belief that God would intervene in the lives of the persecuted to reestablish justice. The form of immortality that was envisioned may well have been angelic. The angels had been identified with the stars as early as the First *Temple period. Several strands of late *Hellenistic spirituality apparently involved the way in which astral immortality was gained. For instance, the books of Enoch (see PSEUDEPIGRAPHA) are obsessed with the notion of astral journey, as are the *hekhalot* texts of Jewish mysticism (see MYSTICISM: *HEKHALOT* AND *MERKAVAH* LITERATURE). Aramaic fragments of 1 Enoch were found at *Qumran, indicating that *Enoch writings were known to the *Dead Sea Scroll sectarians.

Talmudic texts hint that the earliest Rabbis occasionally practiced mystical ascension techniques and traditions. For instance, *Josephus reports that the *Essenes "immortalize" (*athanatizousin*) souls, which is almost the same term that appears in the Mithras liturgy (*Antiquities* 18.18). In another phrase that suggests the theme of the rivalry between angels and men over the approach of a mystic making a heavenly ascent, Josephus says that they "think the approach of the righteous to be much fought over." The Dead Sea Scrolls also report that the members of the Qumran groups are "together with the angels of the Most High and there is no need for an interpreter." The location for this meeting must be either heaven or the re-created ideal earth. The Qumran community probably believed its forebears to have ascended to heaven as angels after their deaths, as Daniel 12 implies.

The Qumran community held that the angels were their close companions. The "Scroll of the War of the Sons of Light against the Sons of Darkness" describes a military plan in which the angels of God descend to lead the numerically insignificant Qumran community to victory. Its priestly

preoccupation with ritual cleanliness is functional for a group that desired angelic company. Angels would not consent to enter an Essene camp unless the Qumranites were in an adequate state of ritual *purity, the same state recognized by the Rabbis as a necessary precondition for ascent to the heavenly Temple. For further reading, see A. F. Segal, *Life after Death: A History of the Afterlife in Western Religions* (2004); **see also AFTERLIFE: HEBREW BIBLE AND SECOND TEMPLE PERIOD.**
                                                        ALAN F. SEGAL

Revelation denotes either the appearance of the divine presence to human beings or the divine communication of teachings and commandments to human beings. The Hebrew *Bible recounts numerous instances of appearances or revelations of *God's presence (*gilui ha-shekhinah*) or manifestations by divine beings who are God's messengers to human beings. In these stories, an appearance of the divine may confer promises of future blessing, bring a human being into a covenantal relationship, provide warning, or give practical, moral, or religious instruction.

Revelation in a more specific sense refers to God's issuance of commandments to human beings. In the Hebrew Bible, God issues commandments *(*mitzvot*) in the framework of a *covenant (*berit*), in which the human party is obliged to observe the commandments in exchange for divine favor and blessing and on the pain of punishment. In the theophany at Mount Sinai (*ma'amad har Sinai* [Exod 19–20]), God appears to the assembled Israelites, appoints them as a holy people, and gives them the *Ten Commandments through the mediation of *Moses. This is the most significant example of divine revelation in the Hebrew *Bible, although the Hebrew Bible also relates several instances of such covenants between God and human partners; for example, *Noah (Gen 9), *Abraham (Gen 15, 17), and David (2 Sam 7). Late biblical and post-biblical Jewish thought assigned primacy to the Sinai revelation and claimed that the entire written text of the *Pentateuch was revealed to Moses at that time.

For rabbinic *Judaism, the revelation to Moses at Mount Sinai contains both the entire Written *Torah (*Torah she'bikhtav*) and also an Oral Torah (*Torah she'b'al peh*), which contains additional laws given to Moses at Sinai as well as resolutions to legal perplexities arising from interpretive problems in the Written Torah itself. The authority of the Rabbis rested not only on their expertise in interpreting and applying the Written Torah but also on their possession of this oral tradition that originated from Moses' encounter with God at Sinai (cf. M. *Avot* 1:1). This authority was challenged by the medieval *Karaite movement, which accepted the divine origin of the Written Torah but not of the Oral Torah. The belief that God revealed Torah from heaven (*torah min ha-shamayim*) was considered to be of such importance that the Rabbis declared that anyone who denied it would lose a place in the world to come (M. *Sanhedrin* 10:1). Because the Rabbis believed that the entire text of the Torah was a product of the divine mind, their interpretive method of *midrash could uncover both legal and nonlegal religious teachings that went beyond the plain sense meaning of the written text (see RABBINIC HERMENEUTICS).

Medieval Jewish thinkers treated the Written Torah as the supreme source of all religious and moral knowledge (see THOUGHT, MEDIEVAL). The medieval Jewish mystical

teachings of the *Kabbalah held that by correctly interpreting the Torah one could glean its secret mystical teachings about the inner life of the godhead. Medieval Jewish philosophers who had studied the philosophies of Plato, Aristotle, and their ancient and medieval successors argued that the claims about God's activity in the world were either consistent with or even superior to the metaphysical and scientific teachings of these philosophies. *Maimonides, for example, claimed that a proper reading of the Written Torah showed that Moses was not only the greatest prophet in human history but also possessed great scientific and philosophical knowledge.

Modern debates about the nature of divine revelation have been deeply affected by developments in modern biblical scholarship, in particular the documentary source hypothesis, which showed that the *Pentateuch was likely composed of several literary strands and only later redacted into a single canon (see BIBLE: MODERN SCHOLARSHIP). Most Orthodox Jews reject the conclusions of biblical scholarship or only accept those conclusions that are consistent with the traditional belief in the unity and divinity of the Pentateuch. However, for many Jews, the traditional notion of revelation of the entire Written Torah as a whole has become untenable. Nonetheless, many non-Orthodox Jewish thinkers maintain that a belief in divine revelation is central to Judaism, even if their conception of revelation does not conform to the traditional view. Such thinkers disagree about the extent to which a divine–human encounter involves a verbal communication from God and the extent to which the biblically ordained commandments and the rabbinic legal system (*halakhah*) remain binding on modern Jews. For example, Martin *Buber and Franz *Rosenzweig agreed that revelation consisted primarily in the revelation of the divine presence to Israel, and not the articulation of specific law. However, Buber held that every person had to interpret what God demanded of him or her individually, while Rosenzweig argued that observance of the concrete laws of both the Written and Oral Torah was the proper response to God's commanding presence (cf. F. Rosenzweig, *On Jewish Learning* [1955]). Many non-Orthodox thinkers view the biblical text as an interpretation, and not a recording of the event of revelation, or as Abraham Joshua *Heschel put it, a *midrash* on revelation (*God in Search of Man* [1959]). Liberal Jewish thinkers have also introduced the idea of *progressive revelation*: Because every generation is capable of contributing innovative moral and religious insights to Jewish life, the understanding of God's will unfolds and develops through history.

                                                    WILLIAM PLEVAN

Ringelblum, Emanuel (1900–1944) was an historian, social worker, and organizer of the *Oyneg Shabes* Project in the *Warsaw ghetto (see HOLOCAUST: GHETTOS). In 1939, Ringelblum formed a group of clandestine archivists who gathered significant documentation chronicling the horrific daily events of the Warsaw ghetto (including Jewish Council notices, personal testimonies, photographs, poetry, essays, announcements of cultural events, and underground newspapers) as well as information about deportations and death camps. The group buried the documentation in milk cans some of which were recovered after *World War II. The Ringelbum archive is one of the most valuable collections of primary source documentation about the Holocaust. For further reading, see S. Kassow, *Who Will Write Our History? Emanuel Ringelblum, the Warsaw Ghetto, and the Oyneg Shabes Archive* (2007); **see also HOLOCAUST DIARIES; HOLOCAUST DOCUMENTATION.**

Ritual Bath: See IMMERSION, RITUAL: WOMEN; MIKVEH; *NIDDAH*

Ritual Murder Accusation (also blood libel) is a myth that developed in medieval Christian Europe after the First Crusade (see MIDDLE AGES: CRUSADES), first as a false accusation of "ritual murder," according to which Jews were accused of capturing a Christian, usually a young male, and crucifying him around Easter/*Passover. Later, a blood motif was added, claiming that Jews collected Christian blood for ritual, "medical," or magical use. This version of the accusation became known as the "blood libel."

The first recorded accusation took place in Norwich, England (see ENGLAND: MIDDLE AGES) in 1144, when the mutilated body of an apprentice, William, was found around Easter. Efforts to implicate Jews failed because of royal protection provided by Henry II. In the twelfth century there were five more ritual murder accusations in England and France (see FRANCE: MIDDLE AGES) – Gloucester, 1168; Blois, 1171; Pontoise, 1179; Bury St. Edmunds, 1181; and Winchester 1192 – some of these accusations ended in the arrests and executions of Jews. It has been recently argued that the case of Richard of Pontoise led to the change in policies toward the Jews by Philip Augustus of France and their expulsion in 1181 from the Île de France. Ritual murder accusations turned into the blood libel in the thirteenth century, perhaps because of the increasing centrality of blood imagery in Christian ritual and worship. In 1236, Jews in Fulda, *Germany, were accused of killing several Christian children to collect their blood for medicinal purposes. Emperor Frederick II ordered an inquiry into the validity of such charges, focusing on whether or not Jews needed Christian blood. After scholars and prominent converts testified that no tenet of Jewish religion required blood, the accused Jews were exonerated. In the thirteenth century there were an estimated fifteen ritual murder accusations. One, in Valreas, France, in 1247, resulted in a papal intervention when Pope Innocent IV sent a letter to the Archbishop of Vienne, condemning blood accusations against Jews. The 1255 accusation that developed after the death of Hugh of Lincoln is evoked in the final stanza of the ritual murder narrative that constitutes "The Prioress's Tale" in Geoffrey Chaucer's fourteenth-century *Canterbury Tales.*

Extensive records have survived from a ritual murder accusation and the ensuing trial in Trent (Trento) in northern *Italy in 1475. On March 26, 1475, Easter Sunday, the body of a two-year-old boy, Simon, was found in the cellar of a Jewish home in Trent. On the instigation of Bishop Hinderbach of Trent, eighteen Jewish men and one Jewish woman were immediately arrested, interrogated under torture, and executed. Seeking canonization of Simon, Hinderbach did all he could to establish a local cult, promoting alleged miracles resulting from Simon's martyrdom. Pope Sixtus IV sent an emissary, Bishop Battista Dei Giudici of Ventimiglia, to investigate. Documentation was collected, and in the process, numerous broadsheets depicting the death of Simon were published, popularizing the imagery

of ritual murder. One of these images provided the basis for the depiction of Simon of Trent above the main city gate, the Brückenturm, in *Frankfurt. Despite initial papal opposition, a local cult in Trent developed and was legitimized in 1588. Although Simon was never canonized, his feast (on March 24) became part of the Catholic calendar. It was only suppressed in 1965 after the Second Vatican Council. As R. Po-Chia Hsia has shown, undoubtedly because of the publication of illustrated broadsheets about Trent, other accusations followed in northern *Italy and the Holy Roman Empire (Reggio, Mantua, 1478; Arena, 1479; Portobuffuola and Verona, 1480). The popularity of Simon's story also retroactively stimulated several local legends about child murders (e.g., Lienz, 1442, recorded 1475; Rinn, 1462).

The blood accusation was sometimes conflated with the libel that Jews *desecrated the host (the communion wafer believed to be the body of Christ). After the Protestant *Reformation, which challenged the Catholic doctrine of transubstantiation, accusations gradually diminished in Protestant areas. In Catholic areas, however, they continued.

Blood libels and host desecration accusations appeared in *Poland for the first time in the sixteenth century, at the height of the *Reformation, and continued through the end of the eighteenth century. A 1756 trial in Jampol led to a Jewish diplomatic mission to Pope Benedict XIV, who charged Cardinal Giovanni Ganganelli to write a report about blood accusations against Jews. The future Pope Clement XIV produced a forty-page report refuting the blood accusations. However, the accusations did not stop, enduring in early modern Poland until 1787.

The blood libels were not just a phenomenon of the premodern period. They continued through the twentieth century, albeit in a somewhat different form. Although the first nineteenth-century accusation surfaced in Damascus in 1840 (see DAMASCUS AFFAIR), Europe remained the main arena, in which a new wave of accusations and a new debate about their validity took place in the nineteenth and early twentieth century. The question of ritual murder or blood libel became a subject of dispute and a proxy in a broader struggle between Modernist and anti-Modernist Catholic intellectuals in Europe. Yet the question became real when new trials sprang up across Eastern and Central Europe.

Whereas the 1840 *Damascus Affair followed older patterns, including the acceptance of the ritual murder charge by officials and a mode of investigation that involved torture, it did not have the "modern" characteristics of the cases that took place in Europe in the latter part of the nineteenth century. European newspapers recorded hundreds of accusations against Jews in the last two decades of the nineteenth century, but not all of these cases became full-fledged trials. Six trials – Kutaisi in Georgia, 1871; Tiszaeszlar, Hungary, 1882–83; Xanten, Germany, 1891–92; Polna, Bohemia, 1899–1900; Konitz, West Prussia, 1900–01; and Kiev, *Russian Empire, 1911–13 (the famous Mendel *Beilis case) – drew wide international attention. That the timing of the trials coincided with the rise of political *antisemitism is not coincidental. As H. Kieval has argued, these trials employed modern methods of investigation, including forensics. Although actual trials may not have continued beyond the first decades of the twentieth century, the myth has not died. It appeared in *Nazi antisemitic rhetoric and still persists on antisemitic websites. Rumors of Jews killing Christian children were used to incite violence in Eastern Europe in the wake of *World War II, resulting in *pogroms against Jewish survivors returning home (e.g., Topolčany, Slovakia, 1945–46; Kielce, Poland, 1946).

For further reading, see J. Frankel, *The Damascus Affair: "Ritual Murder," Politics, and the Jews in 1840* (1997); R. Po-chia Hsia, *The Myth of Ritual Murder: Jews and Magic in Reformation Germany* (1988); idem, *Trent 1475: Stories of a Ritual Murder Trial* 1992); H. Kieval, *Blood Inscriptions: "The Ritual Murder" Trial in Modern Europe* (2008); M. Rubin, *Gentile Tales: The Narrative Assault on Late Medieval Jews* (2004); and K. R. Stow, *Jewish Dogs: An Image and Its Interpreters: Continuity in the Catholic-Jewish Encounter* (2006).   MAGDA TETER

Roma: See HOLOCAUST: ROMA

Romania. Archeological evidence (such as coins discovered in Banat and Hebrew inscriptions found at Sarmizegetusa, the former capital citadel of Dacia) date a Jewish presence in what is now Romania from as early as the second century CE, when Jewish soldiers in the legions of *Rome arrived (and perhaps settled) in the region, with the conquest of Dacia. The first documentary proof of the local population's contacts with Jews appears in the writings of *Benjamin of Tudela, the mid-twelfth-century Jewish traveler; he describes good relations between *Byzantine Jews and the Vlachs living south of the Danube (today the Aromanians). Benjamin's stories are confirmed by medieval documents (like commercial deeds and interfaith marriage certificates), which show that, by the thirteenth century, Jews were crossing *Bulgaria and the Danubian lands as the main traders between *Byzantium, *Russia, and *Poland. Jews were present in Transylvania from the eleventh or twelfth century (under King Ladislau I), but were not particularly welcome; they enjoyed more favorable treatment in the mid-thirteenth century when King Bela IV decided to encourage their settlement in this area.

During the fourteenth and fifteenth centuries, *Ashkenazi Jews from *Germany, Poland, *Austria, Moravia, Czechia, and *Ukraine, as well as *Sephardic Jews from the *Ottoman Empire and *Spain who were traveling through Moldova and Wallachia, started forming stable Jewish communities. Ashkenazi Jews settled mostly in Moldova, where they continued to play an important role in trade between the Ottoman Empire and Poland; Sephardic Jews preferred Wallachia and the southern commercial routes. The first Jewish quarter is mentioned at the beginning of the fourteenth century in Cetatea Albă (Bolgrad). By 1550 the first Sephardic community is mentioned in Bucharest. In the mid-sixteenth century an Ashkenazi Jewish community was established in Iassy.

Some Wallachian and Moldovan rulers, such as Dan I (late fourteenth century) and Stephen the Great (late fifteenth century), saw the benefits of a Jewish presence and provided various privileges to the new settlers. Dan I gave Jews the right to lease land by the year. Stephen the Great is known for using the diplomatic services of Isaac Beg, a Jewish physician accredited at his court as a representative of the Ottoman sultan Uzun Hassan in 1473–74. Other rulers (such as Peter Raresh of Moldova in the mid-sixteenth century) encouraged *money lending by borrowing from Galician,

German, and Ottoman Jews. Nevertheless, most of the settled Jews were rather poor, as mentioned in accounts from the late-sixteenth-century reign of Michael the Brave of Wallachia and Moldova. It was only in the seventeenth century that the Jewish communities started playing a role in the economy of the Danubian Principalities, as shown by the inclusion of provisions related to Jewish converts to Christianity in the "Govora Bill of Rights" (1640 Wallachia) and to the Jewish inhabitants in the "Romanian Book of Learning" (1646 Moldova). The visit to Iassy of prominent rabbis Elia del Medigo and Shlomo ben Arvay in the early seventeenth century demonstrates the cultural importance of the local community at that time. More Jewish communities were established in Moldova throughout the seventeenth century with the arrival of refugees from Ukraine after Bogdan *Chmelnitzki's Cossack uprising and *pogroms (Piatra Neamţ, Soroca, Ştefăneşti, Focşani, Roman, Kishinev). New communities were also recorded in Wallachia (Craiova, Târgovişte), as well as the first Jewish guild (at the turn of the eighteenth century, under Constantin Brâncoveanu).

In early-seventeenth-century Transylvania, Prince Gabriel Bethlen provided benefits to Ottoman Jewish merchants in an attempt to boost local trade; he gave them the right to settle, practice their religion, and travel freely. In many cases, however, these rights were not enforced. Still, they led to the emergence of new Jewish communities (Alba Iulia).

Jewish immigration to Moldova and Wallachia increased in the eighteenth century. Rulers recognized Jewish contributions to the emergence of internal markets, the flow of local commerce and its connection to the international economy, and the development of certain crafts and trades; they granted Jewish communities autonomy and rights. Jewish physicians and advisors served at their courts (Constantin Brâncoveanu, Nicholas Mavrocordat), and rulers encouraged new settlements (Oradea, Cluj, Dej, Sighet, Arad, under Joseph II). Still, this was also the time of a first *pogrom and destruction of a *synagogue (Bucharest, 1715, under Sherban Cantacuzino); the first official *ritual murder accusation (Oniţcani, Moldova, 1726, under Michael Racovitza); the imposition of excessive taxation against the Jews; and strict control of their community life (Transylvania, 1776, under Maria Theresa). This oscillation between privileges and restrictions continued in the first half of the nineteenth century and culminated with the enforcement of the "Organic Regulations" of both Moldova and Wallachia that labeled the Jews as aliens and stripped them of all political and civic rights (1831–32).

Despite these restrictions, Jewish immigration continued to increase in the nineteenth century, and a number of Jewish intellectuals joined Romanian national revolutionary movements. Jewish bankers Davicion Bally and Hillel Manoach and painters C. D. Rosenthal and Barbu Iscovescu provided active (including financial) support to the Revolution of 1848. However, even though the revolutionaries included Jewish *emancipation among their demands the new authorities refused to grant it. On his election as ruler of both Moldova and Wallachia (thus achieving the unification of the Danubian Principalities), Alexander John Cuza gave civil and political rights to the Jews in accordance with international provisions (1865). However, these rights were never realized, as he was forced to abdicate a few months later. Cuza was followed by German Prince Karl von

Hohenzollern Sigmaringen, who, under pressure from nationalist and xenophobic Romanian parliamentarians, promulgated a new constitution in which Article 7 denied any civil and political rights to the Jews. This made the "Jewish problem" in Romania official and happened about the time (1867) when the Jews of Transylvania were becoming *Hungarian citizens, enjoying full and equal civil and political rights. **Map 10**

Despite the fact they were not Romanian citizens, many Jews fought in Romania's Independence War of 1877–78. The Peace Congress of Berlin (1878) made emancipation of the Jews a condition of the international recognition of Romania's independence; the Romanian authorities revised the constitution, but only provided for the naturalization of individual Jews. Approximately 888 Jews who had fought in the Independence War were initially naturalized; by 1913, only 4,668 of the 231,038 Jews living in Romania were full citizens. Many Jews were expelled or left on their own.

About 23,000 Jews (mostly noncitizens) fought in the Romanian Unification War of 1916–18 (World War I); many were decorated for their service. The post-war unification of Wallachia, Moldova, and Transylvania, as well as Bessarabia and Bukovina, tripled the number of Romanian Jews. The Constitution of 1923 finally granted Jews full and equal civil and political rights. As a result, many Jews became involved in political life, assuming important positions. By 1930 the number of Jews in Romania exceeded 750,000. In addition to the traditional *Ashkenazi and *Sephardic communities, there were Neolog (see JUDAISM, NEOLOG) communities in Transylvania. The strong Orthodox community of Sighet is particularly well known. Important Ḥasidic dynasties that originated in Romania include the Satmar and Klausenberg communities (see also ḤASIDISM: EUROPE). **Map 10**

In 1937, with the coming into office of the Goga-Cuza government, *antisemitism became state policy; by 1938, 220,000 Jews were stripped of Romanian citizenship.

In 1940, after the occupation of Bessarabia and Bukovina by the Soviet Union, Jews were accused of having sided with the enemy, and a decree issued in August imposed a legal status on Jews that was based on the *Nazi Nuremberg Laws. At the same time, Hungary annexed northern Transylvania with its 150,000 Jews. These Jews were deported to Nazi death camps in the summer of 1944, and 85% perished. In 1941, Bessarabia and northern Bukovina were retaken by Romania; most Jewish residents of these regions were eventually deported to Nazi death camps in Transnistria. The Jews of Wallachia and Moldova were taken to forced labor battalions, evacuated, and abused, but most were not deported or exterminated. Between 280,000 and 380,000 Romanian Jews died in the *Holocaust. During the communist regime, most of Romania's remaining Jews emigrated, mainly to *Israel, under an agreement with the local authorities ("the ransom of the Jews"). Today only 8,000 Jews still live in Romania, most of them elderly people. About half live in Bucharest. Nevertheless, community life continues: there are a number of Ashkenazic Orthodox congregations; most of the Sephardic communities disappeared after World War II and those few remaining are now included in Orthodox communities), with a number of active synagogues, several museums, a *Yiddish theater, a publishing house, a newspaper, a research center, and youth clubs. Valuable studies of this community include V. Neumann, *The History of Romanian Jews*, 5 vols. (2002–04); C. Iancu et al., eds., *The Jews of Romania* (1866–1938), 3 vols. (1998–2006), and R. Ioanid, *The Ransom of the Jews* (2005). Felicia Waldman

Romaniote Jews are the "indigenous" Greek-speaking Jews of *Greece and the *Balkans who first came to the region in the Roman period, in the centuries before and after the start of the Common Era. They were known as *Benei Romania*, or Romaniote Jews, because Jews called Byzantium and other Greek-ruled lands *Romania*, the land of the Romans. The distinctive *customs of this community are known as "*minhag Romania*." **See also BYZANTINE EMPIRE; TURKEY. Map 9**

Rome; Roman Empire When Jews first came into contact with Rome in the second century BCE, their response was neutral. Thus, *Daniel 11:30, reinterpreting *Numbers 24:24, speaks of "ships of Kittim" who came against Antiochus IV and forced him to withdraw from *Egypt. As the *Septuagint and the *Targum make clear, the Kittim are the Romans. The treaty between Judah *Maccabee and Rome (1 Macc 8) offers high praise for the Romans, who are described as men of great valor and nobility, as faithful friends of their allies, and as being governed in full harmony by their Senate. They were also far enough away so that Judah did not transgress God's word when making a treaty with them (Deut 7:1–2, 20:15). Yet when Pompey conquered *Jerusalem in 63 BCE and desecrated the *Temple, Rome's image suddenly became absolutely negative: "Alien nations ascended your altar; they trampled it proudly with their sandals" (Psalms of Solomon 2:2 [see PSEUDEPIGRAPHA]); God is asked "to turn the pride of the dragon (i.e. Pompey) into dishonor," and before long, "God showed me the insolent one slain on the mountains of Egypt" (2:25–26). The *Dead Sea Scrolls frequently speak of the Romans as Kittim, "swift and powerful in battle," "with cunning and treachery they behave towards all the peoples…like an eagle, insatiable" (1QpHab II 12–13; III 5–6.11–12). The Roman Senate, once so praised, now becomes "the house of blame" (IV 11). The "Scroll of the War of the Sons of Light against the Sons of Darkness" foretells Rome's final destruction in the war between light and darkness, when the Kittim form the satanic "army of Belial" (1QM I 13).

After the destruction of Jerusalem and the Temple in 70 CE, *Josephus Flavius is alone in defending the Romans. He argues that without God's help they could never have built such a huge empire (*Jewish War* 2:390); God stands now on the side of Rome (5:367–8). Josephus extols Roman philanthropy and leniency in victory (5:341.372) and insists that Titus wanted to preserve the Temple, even against the will of the Jews (6:128). According to Josephus, Rome's actions should be understood as a fulfilment of God's plan. The contemporary book, Apocalypse of Ezra (see PSEUDEPIGRAPHA), sees Rome quite differently, describing it as the eagle coming up from the sea that reigns over the whole earth. It is the fourth beast of Daniel 7:7–8 that has wielded power over the world with terror and oppression, but its end has come; the earth shall be freed from its violence and be refreshed again (4 Ezra 11).

*Rabbinic literature is not uniform in its representations of Rome and of the Roman emperors. The image of Vespasian is mainly positive. However, Titus alone is fully blamed for the destruction and desecration of the Temple; he is

the godless ruler who consciously provokes God's wrath and is finally punished forever in hell (BT *Gittin* 56b–57a). Hadrian, who is praised by the *Sibylline Oracles early in his reign as "the best of all men" (5:48), receives very positive treatment in some rabbinic texts (e.g., *Leviticus Rabbah* 25:5); however, most rabbinic views are wholly negative because of his suppression of the Second *Jewish War led by *Bar Kokhba (JT *Taanit* 4, 68d–69a). An emperor interested in Judaism and in friendly contact with *Judah ha-Nasi is depicted in several anecdotes about "Antoninus and Rabbi" (e.g., BT '*Avodah Zarah* 10a–b); "Antoninus" is a conflation of several emperors, including Marcus Aurelius and Caracalla. Although in general the anecdotes are positive toward Antoninus, some texts are rather critical. The last emperor to be mentioned several times in rabbinic literature is Diocletian, whose image is between neutral and positive (e.g., JT *Berakhot* 3:1, 6a; JT *Avodah Zarah* 5:4, 44d).

Regarding Roman rule, most Rabbis tried to come to terms with reality and to restrain their fellow Jews from waging a new revolt. R. Judah praises Rome because "they organize markets, repair bridges, set up bathhouses," but R. Simon ben Yoḥai objects: "Whatever they set up, they set up only for their own convenience. Markets serve them for their whores, bathhouses to preen themselves in, and bridges to collect tolls" (BT *Shabbat* 33b). Many rabbinic texts conflate Rome with *Esau, Jacob's perennial rival and enemy, and with Esau's descendants, the *Edomites, who under the leadership of Amalek attacked the Israelite tribes at Rephidim (Exod 17). Rome is the "pig," an utterly impure animal. It is also the sinful empire or, more clearly, the fourth empire of Daniel 2, which comes after *Babylon, Media, and Greece and is the worst of all, but whose fall will lead to the final *redemption.

The Christianization of the empire in the fourth century did not change this negative image. When Christian Rome claimed to fulfill biblical prophecies and to be the true Israel, the Rabbis countered that the Oral *Torah was the true sign of God's *election (see also REVELATION).

In the political turmoil of the early seventh century when *Palestine was conquered by the *Persians, retaken by Rome, and finally taken over by the militant forces of *Islam, *apocalyptic hopes led to a much more aggressive and violent attitude toward Rome. This is documented in the apocalyptic *Sefer Zerubbabel* and some *piyyutim* (see POETRY: LITURGICAL [*PIYYUT*]) closely related with it. Yet when the situation calmed, Jewish attitudes toward Rome (in this case, the *Byzantine Empire) again became more moderate, accepting the status quo and even seeing Rome as an instrument in God's plan, although always full of hope that the fourth empire would soon come to an end and give way to God's rule. Recent research includes M. Hadas-Lebel, *Jerusalem against Rome* (2006); and M. Goodman, *Jews and Romans: The Clash of Ancient Civilizations* (2007). **Map 4**

GÜNTER STEMBERGER

Rosenzweig, Franz (1886–1929) was a German Jewish philosopher and theologian best known for his philosophical book, *The Star of Redemption*. Rosenzweig argued for a "new thinking," a new form of philosophy that recognized the actuality of divine *revelation. Throughout his writings, he aimed to demonstrate the capacity of the Jewish literary tradition to inflect and inform this new type of reflection and

to serve as the spiritual, social, and intellectual grounding for Jewish thought and community. A central figure among German Jewish intellectuals in the Wilhelmine and Weimar Jewish renaissance, he wrote on education, Jewish religious observance, translation and translational philosophy, biblical hermeneutics, and the theological divide between Judaism and Christianity.

Rosenzweig was born and raised in an assimilated bourgeois family in Kassel, *Germany. He studied philosophy with Heinrich Rickert and Friedrich Meinecke in Freiburg, completing a doctoral dissertation in 1913 entitled *Hegel and the State* (published in 1920). Rosenzweig's early advocacy of a neo-Hegelian revolution in philosophy and history developed in conversation with a close-knit group of friends, including assimilated Jews who had converted to Protestantism. However, passionate and formative dialogues on philosophy and theology with one member of this circle, Eugen Rosenstock (later, Rosenstock-Huessy, 1888–1973), convinced Rosenzweig of the need for a robust concept of revelation to anchor and orient human thought and action. His "conversion" from a secularized Hegelian philosophy to a belief in divine revelation generated a spiritual crisis. In 1913 Rosenzweig planned to be baptized, but he soon reversed himself and embraced Judaism instead. At this time he wrote that liberal Judaism and liberal Christianity had both overly accommodated the pernicious historicism and idealism of the day ("Atheistic Theology," [1914]); like the Christian dialectical theologians who emerged in this period, Rosenzweig argued that only a radical theism was adequate to address the failures of modern *thought. Over time, Rosenzweig came to argue that the Jewish concept of revelation uniquely posited an unmediated relationship between human beings and God (see *Judaism despite Christianity: The Letters on Christianity and Judaism between Eugen Rosenstock-Huessy and Franz Rosenzweig* [1969]).

Rosenzweig began studying Jewish texts and languages in 1914 with Hermann *Cohen (1842–1918) and others at the Institute for the Scientific Study of Judaism. During *World War I, he served in an anti-aircraft gun unit in Macedonia and began the outline for his best-known work ("The Germ Cell of the Star of Redemption" [1917]). He wrote *The Star of Redemption* (published in 1921) on postcards mailed home. *The Star* contrasts the Hegelian-influenced concept of a total synthesis between God's revelation and the historical process, and the conception of the human philosophical task that flows from it, with a view based on the acknowledgment of God's creation of the world. The book, which examines what Rosenzweig regards as the three irreducible constituent elements of the cosmos – God, the human being, the world – argues that God's revelation animates the world, the individual, and the collectives of the faithful. For Rosenzweig, these communities are constituted by the Jewish people and Christian believers; each asymmetrically ritualizes God's revelation in the world. Rosenzweig's interlocutors in *The Star* include Goethe, Schelling, and Fichte as well as the ever-present Hegel, but the unusual style derives as well from passages from the Hebrew *Bible and Jewish liturgy that are integrated into a more traditional philosophical presentation.

After the war, Rosenzweig decided against a university professorship and devoted himself to the recapitulation and fine-tuning of the philosophical insights of *The Star* of Redemption (The New Thinking [1925]; Understanding the Sick and the Healthy: A View of World, Man, and God [1953]); adult Jewish education; and translation of Hebrew texts into German. Rosenzweig's assumption of official leadership of the Freies Jüdisches Lehrhaus in 1920 allowed him to put ideas he had developed for Jewish educational innovation ("It is Time" [1917]) into the context of his commitment to furthering German Jewish engagement with the texts of the Jewish tradition ("Towards a Renaissance of Jewish Learning" [1920]). Rosenzweig's goal was to construct a new form of Jewish learning that would recognize the challenges of post-emancipation Jewish life. He imagined that adult Jewish learning should move from the periphery (acculturated Jewish identity and superficial understanding of Judaism) toward the center (profound engagement with the texts, languages, and central ideas of *Torah). This model for learning became influential and generated new interest in adult Jewish study, in Germany and elsewhere.

Rosenzweig translated the *blessing after meals and *Sabbath evening liturgy (1920), the liturgical poetry of Judah *Halevi (Sixty Poems and Hymns of Yehudah Halevi [1924; expanded edition, 1927]), and, in collaboration with Martin *Buber, the Hebrew *Bible (1925–29; see BIBLE: TRANSLATIONS AND TRANSLATORS). Rosenzweig's translations of these Hebrew texts into German reflected multiple and sometimes competing social and cultural identities; he focused on cultivating "hearers" rather than mere "readers" of liturgical and poetic Hebrew and its unique vocal and spiritual register. The Bible translation in particular (which Buber completed alone in 1961) was intended to stretch the German language and compel the attention of readers who had become immune to the Bible's audacious religious vision.

Rosenzweig's articulation of Jewish communal identity and praxis took a careful path that valued both individual *autonomy and communal ties cemented by biological membership and divine *election ("The Builders" [1924]). His personal politics defied easy classification because he distanced himself from both *Zionism and the major organizations of liberal German Jewry (see JUDAISM, REFORM: GERMANY). He profoundly influenced contemporaneous theologians, such as Buber, and later Jewish thinkers grappling with modern conceptions of *revelation and the ethical imperatives of Judaism, such as Arthur A. Cohen and Emmanuel *Levinas (see THOUGHT, MODERN).

In 1922 Rosenzweig was given a diagnosis of amyotrophic lateral sclerosis, and from then on he suffered increasingly from debilitating muscular degeneration. Thanks to the tremendous labors of his wife, Edith Hahn Rosenzweig, he remained productive despite his near-paralysis until his death, just shy of age 43, in 1929.   MARA H. BENJAMIN

Rosh Ha-Shanah: See HIGH HOLIDAYS; NEW YEARS

Rosh Ḥodesh, the New Moon, (literally, "head of the month") indicates the beginning of each Hebrew month. The Bible describes Rosh Ḥodesh as a semi-festival, celebrated with special sacrifices (Num 28:11–15) and the sounding of trumpets (Num 10:10). The dates of Rosh Ḥodesh were fixed in the fourth century CE under the *Patriarch (nasi) Hillel II. It is observed eleven times per year, because the 1st of Tishri is *Rosh Ha-Shanah. Observance of Rosh Ḥodesh begins the preceding *Sabbath, with a special *Blessing of the

Moon. Additional *liturgy is recited on Rosh Ḥodesh itself (e.g., *Hallel), representing its festive status, and mourning and fasting are prohibited. Months of thirty days require two days of Rosh Ḥodesh, and months of twenty-nine days require one day. Rosh Ḥodesh has long been considered a special day for *women; T. Rosh Ha-Shanah 23a describes it as a reward for Israelite women's righteousness. Some contemporary Jewish women and girls participate in Rosh Ḥodesh groups of various kinds. For further reading, see P. Adelman, Miriam's Well: Rituals for Jewish Women Around the Year (1996); and C. Diament, Moonbeams: A Hadassah Rosh Hodesh Guide (2000).   PAUL STEINBERG

Rossi, Azariah dei (1511–1578). Born in Mantua to an illustrious *Italian Jewish family, Azariah dei Rossi was an innovative Jewish historian and multilingual poet. Learned in Latin, Greek, and Italian, as well as Hebrew, and strongly influenced by Italian humanism, he conducted extensive critical and comparative historical research. In his magnum opus on Jewish history, Me'or Einaim (Light of the Eyes), he cited more than one hundred non-Jewish sources in his discussion of biblical and rabbinic history and literature. Many contemporaneous rabbinic authorities spurned Rossi's revolutionary historiography because of his reliance on non-Jewish historiography to align Jewish chronology and his skepticism toward *aggadic *midrash. However, nineteenth-century *Wissenschaft scholars praised Rossi as "the first true Jewish historian."

Rothschild, Baroness Betty de (1805–1886) grew up in *Frankfurt nurtured by the Orthodox traditions of the *ghetto while simultaneously tutored in the social skills appropriate to a modern European lady. At nineteen, she married her uncle James and moved to his ornate mansion in the heart of Paris where she presided over a salon famous for its opulence; there, financial leaders mingled with imperial ambassadors and leading artists. Betty became an intimate of Queen Marie-Amelie, she introduced Chopin to Paris and became his pupil, and Ingres painted her portrait. She educated her five children for leadership roles in French society and in Jewish *philanthropy. Betty championed vocational and moral education for young women, creating and presiding over the first modern Jewish women's philanthropic society for a half-century. In her will she left instructions for her children to value strong family ties and to remain loyal to their faith. Recent scholarship includes L. S. Schor, The Life and Legacy of Baroness Betty de Rothschild (2006).   LAURA S. SCHOR

Rothschild Family. In 1770, Mayer Amschel Rothschild (1744–1812), a twenty-six-year-old coin dealer, recently accorded the title of Court Agent to William, Prince of Hesse-Kassel, married Gudule Schnapper (d. 1849), the seventeen-year-old daughter of a prosperous family. Mayer and his bride both lived in the judengasse, the Jewish *ghetto of *Frankfurt. In partnership with his brother Kalman, Mayer used the dowry brought by Gudule to invest and trade, soon establishing himself as Frankfurt's leading coin and antiquities dealer.

During the next twenty-two years, Mayer and Gudule had nineteen children, ten of whom – five girls and five boys – survived to adulthood. Each of the children was put to work in the back room of the family house, which accommodated Mayer's growing business. By the 1790s the focus of the business had changed to *banking, and the Rothschilds had become one of the wealthiest families of the ghetto, conducting business all over *Germany as well as in *Amsterdam, Paris, London, and *Vienna. Clients included wealthy Christian firms as well as Jewish families of means. In the following years, each of the Rothschild children made a suitable marriage, deepening the relationship among the Rothschilds and other wealthy Jewish families in Frankfurt, Hamburg, and London. The daughters were given dowries and each son received a share of the business. **James Rothschild** (d. 1868), the youngest child, married his niece Betty, the first of many intrafamily weddings.

In 1810, Mayer Rothschild and his sons entered into a business agreement that codified the business philosophy articulated in the company motto: *Concordia, Industria, Integritas*. Each of his sons would become a partner, but only Mayer was permitted to withdraw capital, hire, and fire, and his sons could not marry without his consent. This agreement was modified in the coming decades, as leadership passed from one generation to the next, but the principles of family solidarity and financial prudence remained unchanged. During the Napoleonic wars, **Nathan Rothschild** (d. 1836) propelled the family to a new level of financial success by establishing a bank in London and developing ties with the British government. Soon after, James Rothschild started a bank in Paris, establishing ties with successive French governments. **Salomon Rothschild** (d. 1855) moved to Vienna and worked with the Austrian imperial government. **Carl (Kalman) Rothschild** (d. 1855) established a bank in Naples, working with Austria and establishing financial ties with the Vatican. The oldest son, **Amschel Mayer** (d. 1855), remained in Frankfurt. All five brothers were ennobled by Austrian Emperor Francis I (1816 and 1818), receiving the title of Baron; **Nathaniel Mayer Rothschild** (d. 1915), of the London branch of the family, received the British peerage title of Lord Rothschild in 1885. Four of the brothers had large families. In the next generation there were twelve sons who were educated to take over the growing family empire that now included railroads, mines, vineyards, race horses, and a variety of other investments extending beyond Europe to the Americas and Asia. **Lionel Rothschild** (d. 1879) of England became the first Jewish member of the House of Parliament, and **Alphonse Rothschild** (d. 1905) of France became the first Jewish member of the Bank of France.

Rothschild wealth attracted *antisemitic caricature, but the Rothschilds, unlike many of their wealthy coreligionists, resisted the temptation to convert. They used their high profile and connections to government leaders to protect Jews around the world. In the absence of world Jewish organizations, Jewish community leaders in the Muslim world and in *Eastern Europe began to turn to members of the family to solve their problems, both pecuniary and political.

In addition to responding to crises, the Rothschild family helped fellow Jews educate themselves for life in the modernizing world. Following the leadership of Mayer Amschel, who championed the effort to grant the Jews of Frankfurt citizenship rights and who later founded a modern school for poor Jewish children, the Rothschild families in *Britain and *France also established modern schools so that Jewish young people would be able to participate in the changing economies of their cities and towns while maintaining their Jewish identities. When they realized that hospital rooms were adorned with crucifixes and that dying patients were visited by Christian clergy, the Rothschilds began to build Jewish hospitals. Later, seeking to provide cleaner and healthier housing for the urban poor, they added subsidized housing to their roster of philanthropic projects. Rothschild *philanthropy was not limited to support of Jewish interests. Many members of the family developed individual philanthropic interests in the arts, in science and *medicine, and in social services for the chronically ill and for criminals.

Edmond de Rothschild (d. 1934), born a century after Mayer Amschel, turned his philanthropic energy to *Palestine, funding *agricultural settlements and supporting the Modern *Hebrew revival in the hope of creating a place for Jewish regeneration. His son **James** ("Jimmy"; d. 1957) bequeathed funds for the construction of *Israel's Knesset (parliament) in his memory; his daughter-in-law **Dorothy Pinto de Rothschild** (d. 1988) funded a new building for Israel's Supreme Court and additions to *Yad Vashem in Israel. For further reading, see N. Ferguson, *The World's Banker: The History of the House of Rothschild* (1998).

LAURA S. SCHOR

Rubenstein, Richard L. (b. 1924), the author of the provocative *After Auschwitz: History, Theology and Contemporary Judaism* (1966), was the first theologian (see THEOLOGY) to engage directly the theological challenges and psychological predicaments posed by the *Holocaust (see HOLOCAUST: THEOLOGICAL RESPONSES). Against the grain of classical and modern Jewish *thought, Rubenstein abandoned both the *God of history and Jewish *election. Preoccupied by the failure of theodicy – divine justice – he presented in its stead a type of Jewish paganism centered around a naturalized conception of the Jewish people, ritual practice, and of God, based on the cyclical rhythm of nature. He saw suffering (see EVIL AND SUFFERING) as part of the natural state, not the deserved punishment meted out by a just and loving deity (see COVENANT).

Rubenstein's thought shows a self-conscious shift away from the prophetic theology and ethics avowed by *Buber and *Heschel; rather, he tends toward the more archaic theological and cultural system represented by the priestly religion of *Leviticus. His innovations were bitterly contested when they first appeared. Ironically, however, most Jewish theologians who defended classical Jewish theology against Rubenstein have followed his rejection of theodicy in response to the problem of evil. Jewish feminism has been the only branch of Jewish theology and thought that has caught up with Rubenstein's emphasis on the body and other material constructs (see JUDAISM, FEMINIST).

ZACHARY BRAITERMAN

Russia. At the end of the nineteenth century some five or six million Jews lived in the Russian Empire. Another two million hugged its margins at the eastern edges of *Austria-Hungary and Prussia (see GERMANY); together they constituted two-thirds of the world's Jews. Despite pronounced regional differences, the Jews of Russia shared a reliance on *Yiddish, widespread religious piety, and employment in a narrow cluster of occupations. Russia was the site of the most vigorous religious trends in modern Jewish life (*Hasidism captured the allegiance of probably half of Russia's Jews), and the most influential political ideologies of Jewish modernity (*Zionism and Jewish socialism [see BUND]) were first formulated there.

Jews entered Russia in the late eighteenth and early nineteenth centuries as a byproduct of the partitions of *Poland (1772, 1793, 1795). Previously, the Russian Empire had prohibited Jewish residence because of religious bias. Perhaps as many as one million Jews lived in the region of Poland acquired by Russia through the partitions. Jews were also part of the population of New Russia, the region on the northern littoral of the Black and Azov Seas that was acquired by Russia from the *Ottoman Empire over the course of the eighteenth and early nineteenth centuries. During the nineteenth century Jews holding certain occupations (first merchants, later artisans) and those with higher education were allowed to move to Moscow, *Saint Petersburg, and elsewhere outside the *Pale of Settlement and historic Poland, where the vast majority of Russia's Jews resided. Jews made up some 12% of the population of southwestern Russia and Poland; in many urban areas they were often the majority, especially in northern provinces in *Lithuania and *Belorussia. Despite intermittent efforts to assimilate them, the Russian government believed in the essential separateness of Jewry, and there was little intervention into Jewish life until the reign of Nicholas I (1825–55). **Map 11**

On the whole, the only state-recognized bodies representing Russian Jewry were the local *kahals*. These Jewish *communal structures were charged with taxation and other aspects of internal administration; after the conscription reforms instituted under Nicholas I in 1827, they were also responsible for delivering draftees. *Kahal* electors and officeholders came from the wealthiest sector with a sprinkling of learned Jews. Jewish communal life also included *hevras*, or associations, the most prestigious of which was the *hevra kadisha*, the burial association. Eventually, *kahals* were implicated in the cantonist system, when Jews were forcibly recruited into the army, often at very young ages. This was one of the darkest chapters in Russian Jewish life, and it ended soon after the death of Nicholas I in 1855. Folksongs, many of them furious and among the most poignant artifacts of their kind produced by Russia's Jews, circulated for decades about the abuses of the rich protecting their own offspring from the draft at the expense of the children of the poor. Although *kahals* were officially abolished by the Russian government in 1844, they continued to function. Laws were instituted to ensure that rabbis had a command of either Russian or a European language, but were rarely enforced. Under the reign of Alexander II (1855–81) economic, juridical, and educational reforms were instituted that offered the promise that Russia, like other European countries, was moving toward better integrating its Jews.

In southern regions, *Ukraine, and New Russia, Jews were concentrated in commerce, mostly petty trade. In Lithuania and Belorussia, the majority earned their living in small workshops, primarily in clothing, leather, cigarette manufacturing, and the like. Over the course of the nineteenth century, petty merchants were undermined by the decline of fairs and the rise of permanent markets and also by the government's battle with smuggling. The industrial-

ization of Russia in the last quarter of the nineteenth century further weakened the economic standing of artisans, undermined their independence, and tied them to a larger, more complex market that made it harder to earn a profit. The building of railways marginalized some previously crucial commercial and banking centers (Berdichev, for example), but also enabled the rapid growth of southern ports like Odessa, and Kharkov. Jews were central in the commercial life of Odessa and in manufacturing circles in Białystok and Łódź; they had a major impact on the marketing of sugar and a crucial role in the building of railways. A small but highly visible sector of wealthy Jewish merchants emerged, most obviously in Saint Petersburg, but also in Odessa, *Warsaw, and other cities. A steady movement from small towns (often called a *shtetl*, the diminutive for *shtot*, "city" in Yiddish) to cities began in the middle of the nineteenth century. Increasing impoverishment and overpopulation characterized late-nineteenth-century Russian Jewry, whose population increased eightfold between 1800 and 1900.

Most Jews lived among Poles, Ukrainians, and Lithuanians and had little contact with Russians. Operating from an almost entirely Jewish frame of reference, they saw the regions in which they lived as subdivided along Jewish cultural lines, with variations in religious practice, Yiddish pronunciation, regional customs, legends, and food preferences and specialties. Until the 1860s, even most modernizing Jews did not see acquisition of the Russian language as desirous; those anxious for access to the larger world learned German or sometimes Polish.

Hasidism dominated much of religious Jewish life in the Russian Empire, with the exception of Lithuania. Rabbinic or mitnaggedic Judaism, the religious alternative to Hasidism, concentrated much of its effort on training talented male students in talmudic academies (*yeshivot*); the most important was in Volozhin, outside of *Vilna. The *mitnaggedim* sought to consolidate their values through the production of talmudic scholars who would fan out across Eastern Europe and influence the norms of Jews around them. Hasidim established countless separate prayer houses in places small and large where *tzaddiks*, *rebbes* with local and sometimes regional stature, exerted influence. By the late nineteenth century, the *Musar* movement, established by Israel Salanter (1810–1883), sought to co-opt Hasidism's emphasis on meditation and introspection for rabbinic Judaism while also hoping to win back some youth drawn to modern trends like the *Haskalah* (Jewish enlightenment).

The introduction of a spate of government-sponsored Jewish schools in the 1840s and 1850s and the liberalization of government policy under Alexander II (1855–81) excited Jewish hopes for the liberalization of Russia. These trends encouraged larger numbers of Jewish youth to acquire secular educations and bolstered the social and cultural foundations of the Jewish enlightenment movement in Russia. Its first significant intellectual leader was Isaac Baer *Levinsohn whose 1827 *Teudah be-Yisrael* (Testimony in Israel) set the tone for the *Haskalah* in Russia with his insistence that occupational, linguistic, and educational reforms among Jews were the trademarks of lasting change.

The *Haskalah* inspired Hebrew fiction; Abraham Mapu's biblically based novels created shockwaves for many eager, cloistered readers (see LITERATURE, HEBREW: *HASKALAH*). Beginning in the 1860s, the enlightenment movement reached more readers through Yiddish literature. Mendele Mokher Seforim (Sholem Jacob Abramovich), like so many other Yiddish writers, started in Hebrew and then switched to the more widely known and accessible Jewish vernacular (see LITERATURE, YIDDISH: 1800 TO . . .).

Jewish institutional life expanded considerably beginning in the 1860s with the publication of newspapers in Russian, Hebrew, and Yiddish (see JOURNALISM: YIDDISH [EASTERN EUROPE]; LITERATURE: RUSSIA AND SOVIET UNION [IN RUSSIAN]) and the creation of the *Society for the Promotion of Enlightenment among the Jews of Russia (OPE), based in Saint Petersburg with branches in Odessa and elsewhere. Those most closely associated with such *Haskalah* institutions were a cluster of wealthy Jews (most importantly the Günzburgs); professionals trained in Russian universities, typically as lawyers or doctors; a few modernized rabbis; writers; and a good many intellectuals who believed in the prospect for a Europeanized Russia. *Britain and, to a lesser extent, *France provided models of Jewish acculturation, as consolidated under the influence of Moses *Montefiore, whose blend of altruism and moderate piety and whose courageous efforts on behalf of the Russian and *Ottoman Empires and of other Jews left a deep impression.

Religious circles also incorporated modernizing changes: A spate of new *yeshivot* in Lithuania sought to battle modern trends by attracting the best minds to Torah study instead of the secular educations that were increasingly the destination of many talented Jews beginning in the 1860s and '70s. Slowly religious circles became alert to the need for systematic education for girls as well. Some Jewish women began to appear on the pages of Jewish periodicals; Maria Saker of Odessa, later an important Jewish pedagogue, was probably the first Jewish woman to publish articles in Russian in Jewish newspapers. Girls were exempt from the restrictions imposed on Jewish entry into Russian educational institutions that were imposed in the 1880s, and their numbers in Russian schools continued to rise considerably. Beginning in the late 1860s, young Jewish women and men were found in substantial numbers among Russian radicals. Their presence was made powerfully visible when Alexander II was assassinated in 1881 and it was discovered that one of the plotters, Hesia Helfman, was a Jew (see also SCHENIRER, SARAH, on education for girls).

The sudden and ferocious *pogroms of the 1880s that broke out in the immediate wake of the assassination, together with the widespread belief that they were fomented by government authorities, increased the numbers of Jewish immigrants headed westward. Many headed for Brody on Austria-Hungary's eastern border where they were aided by Jewish philanthropic institutions based in Paris or London. The Hebrew Immigrant Aid Society (HIAS) and other groups sought to protect immigrants from exploitation, to facilitate their movement across Europe, preferably to the *United States, or to help those who left Russia precipitously to return.

New political ideologies, most importantly Zionism and Jewish socialism, insisted that the pogroms of Russia were the work of the authorities. Such views, also shared by many western liberals, were bolstered by increasingly murderous waves of attacks against Jews in 1903, and especially

1905–06. The Kishinev pogrom of 1903, in which forty-seven Jews were killed, many were raped, and much property was destroyed, precipitated hundreds of public demonstrations worldwide. It was argued that the Russian government fomented such violence to press Jews to emigrate, or to deflect animosity that might otherwise be directed at it, or to punish Jews for their political radicalism.

Certainly, pogroms reinforced Russian Jewry's mounting sense of insecurity. However, the mass migration of some two million Jews from the empire (one-third of all Russian Jews) was mostly prompted by other reasons. This is clear because the trajectory of internal migration in those years was largely from poorer regions in the northern Pale of Settlement (where there were few pogroms) to the more economically vibrant southern provinces (where nearly all pogroms erupted). Proportionately as many Jews abandoned the economically depressed but mostly pogrom-free *Galicia, which was under Austrian rule and where Jews enjoyed equal civic rights, as left the Russian Empire.

Mass migration was a byproduct of poverty (especially in Lithuania and Belarus), overpopulation, post-1881 restrictions on residence, and also the sense that *antisemitism was gaining the upper hand. Moreover, the image of the United States as a land of opportunity was fanned by publicist literature in Yiddish, cheap steamship tickets, and reports of plentiful employment. The mass migration was mainly from the lower middle class. Most of the poorest Jews stayed behind, as did most of the richest and the most resolutely pious. No doubt, there were good reasons for Jews in Russia to believe that their future would deteriorate: The increase in anti-Jewish rhetoric and violence, the heightened prominence of antisemitism in Russian public life, and eventually the Mendel *Beilis affair of 1911–13 were all widely viewed as evidence of a dark, ever-encircling phenomenon. By the turn of the twentieth century, probably the best known Russian words in the West were tsar, vodka, and pogrom.

Those who sought to stem the migratory tide (and, of course, two-thirds of the Jewish community remained in Russia) fell into different camps. Many religious leaders attempted to dissuade immigration because it was viewed as disruptive and even disastrous to traditional norms. Some Jewish intellectuals continued to insist on the prospect for integration into Russia, although liberalism lost ground as the century waned. After the 1905 revolution, most great hopes for the newly established Russian parliament were disappointed. Among the most powerfully felt political options was Jewish socialism. The Jewish Socialist Labor *Bund, founded in 1897, attracted 33,000 members and was by far Russia's largest Marxist group. With various spurts and theoretical changes, Jewish socialism charted a subtle course between *Marxism and nationalism. It expanded at times of revolutionary turbulence and optimism (in 1905 especially) and contracted at others. Still, the heroism of Jewish revolutionaries, their work in organizing self-defense groups to protect Jews from pogroms, and their participation in philanthropic activities endeared them widely even to Jews without socialist convictions.

Zionism was built on institutional and ideological foundations that dated back to responses by intellectuals and others to the pogroms of 1881–82. Much of the movement's constituency was drawn from Russian Jews, under the leadership of Leon *Pinsker, the author of *Autoemancipation*

(1882). The most influential intellectual figure in the movement, even after the ascendancy of Theodor *Herzl, was the Odessa-based essayist *Aḥad Ha-Am (Asher Ginzberg), editor of the Hebrew journal, *Ha-Shiloaḥ*. He saw Zionism as the prime mechanism for Jews to absorb western culture without submerging their Jewish identity, and he stressed the cultural benefits of rebuilding Jewish *Palestine. Zionism had about 100,000 devotees, but most of them viewed it in philanthropic rather than avowedly political terms.

The 1905 revolution opened up new possibilities for Jewish public activity and, in turn, closed off others. Jews could now vote for members of the new Russian parliament, or *duma*, but changes in electoral laws marginalized Jews, liberals, and nearly all but the most conservative. After 1907, political parties like the Bund shrunk in size, but devotees threw much energy into educational and cultural activities, literary and ethnographic projects, and the launching of many hundreds of modernized Jewish schools and lending libraries. Restrictions were lifted on Yiddish publishing, which flourished in these years with dozens of periodicals. Brilliant writers (the most famous being Isaac Leib Peretz and Sholem Aleichem [Shalom Rabinowitz]) vied for recognition in a crowded, vibrant marketplace. To be sure, many felt that the Russian Jewish world around them was in the midst of decay; such themes figured prominently in Russian cultural and artistic life in general, and they are echoed in the ethnographic and belletristic work of Semyon Ansky (Shloyme Zanvl Rappoport), author of the most famous Yiddish play, *The Dybbuk* (see LITERATURE, YIDDISH: 1800 TO TWENTY-FIRST CENTURY; THEATER, YIDDISH). Ansky was also responsible for a major ethnographic expedition that toured hundreds of places in the Ukraine between 1912 and 1914 culling the artifacts, songs, and tales of a culture that he believed was on the verge of disappearance.

Late imperial Russia was more and more open to Jews of talent. Jewish-born artists, include El Lissitzky and Marc Chagall, occupied an increasingly visible role in cultural affairs along with newly emerging writers (see ART: EUROPE [TWENTIETH CENTURY]; ART: ILLUSTRATED YIDDISH BOOKS). Arguably, the finest of all Russian poets of the 1920s was Osip Mandelstam, and the best prose writer was Isaac Babel (see LITERATURE: RUSSIA AND SOVIET UNION [IN RUSSIAN]). In Odessa, despite a vociferously antisemitic municipal government at the end of the nineteenth century, Jews owned two of the city's three dailies; Jewish journalists, including the future Revisionist Zionist leader Vladimir Jabotinsky, wrote for all three of Odessa's liberal newspapers. The Jewish backgrounds of Marxists like Leon *Trotsky did not stand in the way of their political influence. The internationalist arm of Russian Marxism,

Menshevism, came to be dominated by ideological leaders of Jewish birth. Young Jews in small towns as well as cities now increasingly favored the Russian language (and to an extent also Polish).

At the same time, antisemitism emerged in the last years of the reign of Nicholas II (1896–1917) as a crucial, ever more prominent bulwark of reactionary ideology. In some circles, including those associated with the Russian-inspired forgery, *The Protocols of the Elders of Zion*, it constituted the centerpiece of a future, post-Romanov Russian identity. The ferocity of anti-Jewish hatred, erupting with such murderous results in the years immediately following the 1917 Russian Revolution, can be traced in some measure to the consolidation of such ideas. *World War I led to the mass evacuation in 1914–15 of hundreds of thousands of Jews, often under profoundly degrading conditions. With the Eastern front situated in Russian Jewry's demographic heartland, charges of Jewish disloyalty were widespread. When tsarism collapsed in February 1917 in the midst of the war, the imperial regime found few defenders. **Map 10**

For further reading, see I. Levitats, *The Jewish Community in Russia, 1772–1844* (1943); M. Stanislawski, *Tsar Nicholas I and the Jews* (1983); I. Etkes, *Israel Salanter and the Mussar Movement* (1993); S. J. Zipperstein, *The Jews of Odessa: A Cultural History, 1794–1881* (1985); B. Nathans, *Beyond the Pale: The Jewish Encounter with Late Imperial Russia* (2002); and J. Frankel, *Prophecy and Politics: Socialism, Nationalism, and the Jews in Russia, 1862–1917* (1981).   STEVEN J. ZIPPERSTEIN

Ruth, Book of, is a novella of four chapters in the *Writings section of the Hebrew *Bible. Although set "in the time of the *Judges" (Ruth 1:1), there is no scholarly consensus on when the book was composed. Some place it shortly after the reign of *David (ca. 900 BCE) because of the prominence given to David's genealogy (4:17–22) at the book's conclusion. Others suggest the book was written during the *Persian period (ca. 500 BCE), in opposition to *Ezra's and *Nehemiah's prohibitions of foreign marriages.

The book tells the story of Naomi, wife of Elimelekh of Bethlehem in *Judah, and her daughter-in-law Ruth, a Moabite; both are widowed in *Moab. While a second widowed daughter-in-law, Orpah, chooses to return to her own family, Ruth expresses loyalty to Naomi and Naomi's people (1:16–17) and returns with her to Bethlehem. There, thanks to Naomi's strategizing and Ruth's courageous assertiveness, Ruth is ultimately redeemed and acquired as a wife by Naomi's kinsman, Boaz (Ruth 3–4). The couple's great-grandson is King *David. The book of Ruth is one of the *Five Scrolls and is read in the synagogue on the festival of *Shavuot. **See also MARRIAGE, LEVIRATE; REDEMPTION.**

KATE FRIEDMAN

S

Saadia Ben Joseph Gaon (882–942) was the outstanding Jewish personality of the geonic period (eighth-eleventh centuries). His intellectual accomplishments cover the entire spectrum of Jewish endeavors: *Bible translation and *Bible commentary, *theology, *thought, liturgy, linguistics, chronology, calendation, *poetry, polemics, and more. Born in Fayyum, *Egypt, Saadia studied in the Land of Israel before moving to *Iraq. Given his foreign origins, Saadia would not have been a natural choice to become *Gaon, the head of the Babylonian talmudical academy of *Sura, but the strength of his personality and his multiple accomplishments could not be ignored. His tenure as the head of the academy was not untroubled, however, and his principled stances and combative personality made for clashes with the communal authorities.

Saadia's early career was marked by polemical defenses of Babylonian rabbinic hegemony in the following areas: (1) the Jewish *calendar (against Ben Meir, the Gaon of the Land of Israel); (2) the divine origin of the Bible (against the heretic Haywayhi of Balkh, usually known in Hebrew as Hivi ha-Balkhi); and (3) the truth of the Oral *Torah versus the *Karaites. It should be noted, however, that the traditional *Rabbanite view of Saadia as the victor over a major Karaite threat overemphasizes the status of Karaism in his day. Saadia's translation of the Bible into *Arabic and his rationalistic commentaries on most of its books set the standard for later Jewish understanding of Scripture. His *prayer book had a major impact on subsequent Jewish liturgy, and his linguistic studies and poetry expanded understanding of the Hebrew language (see POETRY, MEDIEVAL: MUSLIM WORLD). The form of *Judeo-Arabic that Saadia employed played a major role in the standardization of usage in that language.

Saadia is probably best remembered in the Jewish world for his theological/philosophical book, *The Book of Doctrines and Opinions*, because that is one of his few Judeo-Arabic compositions to have been translated into Hebrew in the Middle Ages. The structure of this book is similar to that of Islamic theological works known as *Kalam*: It begins by defending the use of *reason for religious reasons, proceeds to prove the existence of *God by demonstrating that the world was created and thus needs a Creator, continues by discussing the nature of divine unity, and concludes with a defense of divine justice. The book also discusses the reasons for the *commandments, free will, reward and punishment, *resurrection, the *messiah, and the *afterlife. Some of these philosophical ideas are also repeated in Saadia's *Commentary on *Sefer Yetzirah, a speculative text of unknown provenance. Although Saadia did not adopt all doctrines of the *Kalam*, such as the existence of atoms, his work is clearly indebted to the Islamic model, and it represents the integration of the Jewish tradition with the reigning form of rational speculation of his day. Although Jewish philosophers would later abandon Saadia's form of theological philosophy, especially under the decisive influence of *Maimonides'

Aristotelianism, his authoritative work set the pattern for subsequent rational defenses of Jewish tradition (see THOUGHT, MEDIEVAL).

In the past century, with the discovery of Saadia's original Judeo-Arabic works, many of them in the Cairo *Genizah, the breadth and depth of his intellectual accomplishments have attracted greater interest, and appreciation of his accomplishments has only been heightened.

DANIEL J. LASKER

Sabbateanism (*Ottoman Empire and *Turkey) denotes the *mystical, heterodox Judaism taught by *Shabbatai Zevi (1626–1676) and practiced by his followers (see KABBALAH, LURIANIC; MESSIANISM: EARLY MODERN). After his forced conversion to *Islam in 1666, Zevi's movement split, and some of its members returned to the Jewish fold. Others followed his lead into a nominal conversion to *Islam, while continuing to observe Zevi's teachings in secret, including a strict endogamy. Although most of this latter group settled in the *Ottoman port city of Salonika, other, smaller groups existed in Edirne and Izmir. Doctrinal and personal disputes over the following decades would eventually lead them to subdivide into (at least) three separate and mutually antagonistic groups, which became known (among other names) as the Yakubi, Kapanji, and Karakash. The subgroups continued to live in close proximity to one another, although with minimal social contact and no intermarriage. Although others, including the authorities, seem to have been aware of their existence, these groups' outward compliance to Islamic practice combined with the Ottomans' traditional religious tolerance ensured that they could continue to live largely unmolested for the next two centuries.

Ultimately, it was the increasing modernization and westernization of the Ottoman Empire in the second half of the nineteenth century that produced the greatest crisis for the group. A "revolt" among Sabbatean youth against their communities' backwardness led to a greater openness toward and participation in the surrounding Ottoman society, including contemporary revolutionary political movements. By virtue of this greater exposure to the West, several members played important roles in the Young Turk Revolution (1908–18). The Greek capture of Salonika (1912), the Great Fire in that city (1917), and the Greco-Turkish Population Exchange (1924) combined to destroy the Sabbateans' communal structure and inner cohesion; their members subsequently dispersed to the western cities of the Turkish Republic and, to a lesser extent, Europe and North America. Although a small remnant of Karakash reportedly continues to practice their religion, the majority of Sabbateans (or *Selânikli Dönme*) have assimilated into secular Turkish society, where they have excelled in business, politics, academia, and journalism. Despite their material success, they have increasingly become objects of hostility, as both individuals and as a perceived group, from the country's religious and ultra-nationalist right (and, increasingly, the left). Recent scholarship includes M. D. Baer, *The Dönme: Jewish Converts, Muslim Revolutionaries, and Secular Turks* (2009); and **see also ANTINOMIANISM; FRANK, JACOB AND FRANKISM.**   PAUL F. BESSEMER

Sabbath (Hebrew, *Shabbat*) is observed from sunset Friday evening until nightfall on Saturday. The word "Sabbath" is drawn from the Hebrew root *sh/v/t*, meaning "to cease"; this verb is used to describe God's rest from creation on the seventh day of the first week (Gen 2:2–3). The ordinance to observe the Sabbath is the fourth of the *Ten Commandments and the only ritual observance that is included. In the version that appears in Exodus 20:8–11, the *Israelites are to "remember" the Sabbath day and "keep it holy" because God has blessed and sanctified this day as a commemoration of divine rest. In the reiteration of the Ten Commandments in Deuteronomy 5:12–15, the Israelites are commanded to "observe" the Sabbath, and the day of rest is connected with the experience of slavery in *Egypt and divine *redemption. At the epiphany at Mount Sinai (Exod 31:13–14), the Sabbath is described as an eternal sign of God's sanctification of Israel and as a holy day to be observed throughout the generations as a remembrance of creation. Whoever profanes the Sabbath will be put to death (31:14, 15). Sabbath observance applies to all living beings within the Israelite community: men, women, children, servants, and non-Israelite visitors, as well as animals, a reminder of the inclusiveness of creation (Exod 20:10). Sabbath observance took on special resonance during the *Babylonian Exile because it offered a way to maintain Jewish religious distinctiveness in a foreign setting where there was no central shrine.

There are only a few biblical indications as to what was specifically forbidden on the Sabbath. However, rabbinic *halakhah developed an elaborate corpus of rules defining prohibited "work," based on the thirty-nine activities connected with the construction of the wilderness *Tabernacle (Exod 31). These prohibitions are listed in the *Mishnah in Tractate *Shabbat* and encompass actions linked to agricultural labor, textile manufacture, preparation of bread, slaughtering, working with leather and parchment, writing, building, transporting an object between private and public spaces, and lighting a fire. Theologians have suggested that one must cease from these and related activities because they all exemplify human efforts to master the world; on the Sabbath, human beings should remember that they were created and should exist in a state of harmony with the rest of the created world.

The Sabbath is in many ways the most holy of days on the Jewish calendar, rivaled only by *Yom Kippur, the Day of Atonement, which is termed "Sabbath of Sabbaths" in Leviticus 23. However, as in any instance where human life is endangered, everything possible must be done to save it, even if doing so requires doing actions that are ordinarily forbidden on the Sabbath. Over time, Jews have found creative solutions to observing the Sabbath without creating impossible burdens. These include the innovation of the *eruv, which enables carrying within a circumscribed area; employing a non-Jew to perform tasks forbidden to Jews; keeping the oven and burners at low heat to provide warm meals and hot water; and using technologies such as electronic timers to turn lights on and off. Various denominations of *Judaism differ in their classification of certain Sabbath prohibitions, such as whether the use of electricity and automobiles on Shabbat constitutes lighting a fire.

The Sabbath traditionally includes three festive meals: dinner on Friday evening, lunch on Saturday, and another meal before the conclusion of the Sabbath. The Friday evening meal is preceded by the kindling of Sabbath lights by a woman or women of the household and the recitation of a *blessing (a man may also kindle the lights and recite the blessing if no women are present); the recitation of *kiddush over a cup of wine, and the blessing of the special Sabbath bread (see *ḥallah*). It is the custom to have two loaves of *ḥallah* at each Sabbath meal as a reminder of the double portion of *manna* that God provided during Israel's wilderness wanderings on the day before the Sabbath (Exod 16:22–30). Many people sing Sabbath songs (*zemirot*) at meals to enhance the joyousness of the day.

Sabbath *synagogue ritual includes communal worship on Friday evening, Saturday morning, and, in traditional settings, on Saturday afternoon. Friday evening worship begins with the *Kabbalat Shabbat* service, which originated in the community of mystics in sixteenth-century *Safed. Central to *Kabbalat Shabbat* is the recitation of the hymn *Lekha dodi likrat kallah, penei shabbat nekabbelah* (Come, my beloved, to meet the bride, let us receive the presence of the Sabbath), which is attributed to Solomon ha-Levi Alkabetz (ca. 1500–1580). As in this hymn, the Sabbath is often characterized in female terms as a queen or *bride (*Genesis Rabbah* 11:9). Worship on Sabbath morning includes the reading of the weekly Torah portion (see TORAH READING) and *haftarah portion. During the afternoon service, a section of the following week's Torah reading is chanted (see WORSHIP). Saturday afternoons are often a time for personal or communal study. The Sabbath concludes with the *havdalah ritual, recited when three stars are visible on Saturday evening, to mark the separation between the holiness of the Sabbath and the ordinary days of the working week. An additional Saturday evening custom, *melaveh malkah* (accompanying the queen), includes a festive meal to mark the end of the Sabbath and to prolong its joyousness for a few more hours.

Jewish fast days, except *Yom Kippur, are moved forward a day if they fall on the Sabbath; mourning rituals are postponed, and in traditional communities weddings do not take place until after sunset on Saturday. Special Sabbaths precede or coincide with the observance of *Rosh Ha-Shanah, Yom Kippur, *Tu B'Shevat, *Purim, *Passover, *Tisha B'Av, and *Sukkot (see e.g., *SHABBAT HA-GADOL*).

For further reading, see R. L. Eisenberg, *The JPS Guide to Jewish Traditions* (2004); E. Ginsburg, *The Sabbath in the Classical Kabbalah* (1989); and A. J. Heschel, *The Sabbath* (1951; rep. 2005).   ELIZABETH SHULMAN

Saboraim are probably the least known link in the chain of rabbinic tradition (see JUDAISM; RABBINIC LITERATURE); they come after the *Amoraim and before the *Geonim (see also STAM, STAMMAIM). The title means approximately "opiners" and seems to imply that the dicta of these Rabbis are to be treated as "opinions," of lesser status than those of their predecessors, the Amoraim or "sayers." Our earliest and most important sources with regard to the Saboraim date to the geonic period, but even in geonic sources we find only a few scattered references and obscure remarks. An exception is the Epistle of Sherira *Gaon, written toward the end of this period in 986 CE, which provides the most extensive early discussion of the Saboraim; it is the most reliable source for this period, despite the centuries that elapsed between the last Saboraim and Sherira's time. Among other sources, Sherira had access to contemporary chronological lists, part of which he quoted verbatim. Later writers, including the historian *Abraham ibn Daud and medieval rabbinic authors, give at best derivative accounts of the Saboraim and their works, and their attributions of particular talmudic passages to the Saboraim are often conjectural. According to Sherira, the saboraic period was quite brief and confined to the early decades of the sixth century CE. It was followed by a period during which the major Babylonian academies were unable to function normally because of persecution by the Zoroastrian authorities; when they reopened toward the end of the century, the geonic period had begun.

According to Sherira and the somewhat earlier *Seder Tannaim ve-Amoraim*, the Saboraim played a relatively minor role in completing the redaction of the Babylonian *Talmud. The nature of their contribution is described in vague terms, such as "they settled all open questions" or, in contrast, "they innovated nothing." A very small number of specific opinions attributed to named Saboraim are found in the Talmud; in addition, Sherira attributes to them a long anonymous passage at the opening of Tractate *Kiddushin* "and others as well." This tantalizing remark has provided a springboard for recent generations of academic Talmud scholars, who have attempted to identify or characterize additional saboraic contributions among the anonymous portions of the Babylonian Talmud. Some scholars have gone so far as to attribute all anonymous portions of the Talmud to the Saboraim or have described them as "the designers and the real builders of the Talmud" (see TALMUD, BABYLONIAN). Others have attributed particular types of discussions or remarks to this shadowy group. The question of the saboraic contribution is of crucial importance for any theory of talmudic redaction, but it is unlikely that a consensus can be achieved in view of the dearth of ancient evidence and the problematic nature of some of what does exist. For further reading, see R. Brody, *The Geonim of Babylonia and the Shaping of Medieval Jewish Culture* (1998).   ROBERT BRODY

Sacrifice: See LEVITICUS; SECOND TEMPLE PERIOD; TEMPLE AND TEMPLE CULT; WORSHIP

Sadducees were a group of traditional, elite Jews in the last two centuries of the *Second Temple period. They came from wealthy and priestly classes and, although not large in number, sometimes had a significant influence on political and religious life in the period before 70 CE. Sadducees held prominent positions in the *Temple, with some serving as the High *Priest (Acts 5:17; *Jewish Antiquities* 20:199; BT *Yoma* 19b), and they rejected innovations that might weaken this central institution. Their general conservatism is reflected in their opposition to interpretations of the Written *Torah promulgated by the *Pharisees, especially the oral traditions taught by scribes outside the Temple. Politically, they endorsed collaboration with ruling authorities, Jewish and Gentile. A few may have supported the revolt against *Rome in 66 CE, but most opposed it, correctly judging that

*apocalyptic fervor and military adventurism threatened not just their positions but also Judean society as a whole.

Reconstruction of their views and history is difficult. No extant text can be attributed to a Sadducean author with certainty, and other sources such as *Josephus, the *New Testament, and *rabbinic literature mention them only occasionally. The origins of the group are murky. Although the name "Sadducees" (Hebrew, *zaddukim*; Greek, s*addoukkaioi*) is related to the Hebrew word for "righteous," it may also link them, in tradition if not in fact, with the High Priest Zadok under *David (2 Sam 8:17; 1 Kgs 1:32–39). From Zadok's line emerged priests entrusted with control of Temple ritual (Ezek 44:15). Only later, after the *Hasmonean revolt in the mid-second century BCE, do Sadducees appear as a discrete group. Josephus mentions them incidentally (*Jewish Antiquities* 13:173) in a section on the early Hasmonean period (160–42 BCE). However, they first appear to have played a role in public affairs under John Hyrcanus (134–104 BCE), who favored them over the *Pharisees after the latter opposed his usurping the position of High Priest (*Jewish Antiquities* 13:289–97; cf. BT *Kiddushin* 66a). A rabbinic statement (*Avot de Rabbi Nathan* A5/B10) that the Saducees emerged after a dispute over the *afterlife is too vague to be historically useful.

Sources typically show that the Sadducees engaged in conflicts over biblical interpretation (see BIBLICAL COMMENTARY), although they seldom provide social or historical context to the disputes. Scattered throughout *rabbinic literature are disagreements between Sadducees and others (often Pharisees) regarding *purity, the *Sabbath, Temple administration, and criminal law (M. *Yadayim* 4:6–7; M. *Niddah* 4:2; M. *Makkot* 1:6; BT *Ḥagigah* 23a). In the *New Testament, Sadducees argue with Jesus and his followers about *resurrection (Mark 12:18; Acts 4:1, 23:6). Josephus presents them as a small, combative group that denies resurrection, rejects the Pharisees' approach to biblical interpretation, and insists that humans have free will (*Jewish War* 2:164–66; *Jewish Antiquities* 18:16–17). Although these positions are generally consistent with biblical teachings, no source presents them favorably; in Josephus and rabbinic literature they are contrasted unfavorably with the popular Pharisees. With the Temple's destruction in 70 CE, the Sadducees disappeared from history.

For further reading, see G. Baumbach, "The Sadducees in Josephus," in *Josephus, the Bible, and History*, ed. L. H. Feldman and G. Hata (1989); and A. Saldarini, *Pharisees, Scribes, and Sadducees in Palestinian Society* (2001).

ADAM GREGERMAN

Safed (Tzfat in Hebrew) is a small town in the Upper *Galilee in northern Israel that served as a center for Jewish mystics (see KABBALAH) beginning in the sixteenth century. Many kabbalists among the Jews who were exiled from *Spain in 1492 assembled in this town, which was under *Ottoman rule. They were attracted by the tradition that the tomb of Simon bar Yoḥai, the second-century sage to whom the *Zohar, the main book of the *Kabbalah, is attributed, was located in nearby Miron. Among the important Safed figures of this period were Joseph *Karo, the great halakhist, mystic, and author of the *Shulḥan Arukh*, the major law code of modern Judaism (see *HALAKHAH*); Moses Alsheikh, a great sermonist; and Israel Najara, a significant liturgical poet (see POETRY: LITURGICAL [*PIYYUT*]). The Safed kabbalists included Solomon Alkabetz (to whom the hymn *Lekha Dodi*, welcoming the *Sabbath, is attributed); Moses *Cordovero; and especially Isaac *Luria, who revolutionized the Kabbalah with his disciples, particularly Ḥayyim Vital (see KABBALAH, LURIANIC). The community in Safed declined at the end of the 1500s, but was reinvigorated in the eighteenth century when *Ḥasidic leaders began to arrive. To this day the city remains a center for Ḥasidim and kabbalists; celebrations of the Lag B'Omer festival (see *Omer) in Miron honoring the memory of Simon bar Yoḥai attract hundreds of thousands of Israelis every year. For further reading, see L. Fine, *Safed Spirituality* (1984). **Map 9**   JOSEPH DAN

Saint Petersburg (also called Petrograd, 1914–24, and Leningrad, 1924–91) is an important Russian administrative, financial, industrial, scientific, and cultural city and a large Baltic seaport. It was founded in 1703 by Tsar Peter I and served as *Russia's capital until 1918. Individuals of Jewish origin, most of whom had been baptized, lived in Saint Petersburg in the city's early years. However, a Jewish community was not founded until 1802, and it was only in the 1860s that a few thousand Jews settled in the city, as a result of the reforms of Alexander II. A separate Jewish cemetery (Preobrazhensky) was opened in 1874, and the Great Synagogue was dedicated in 1893.

Because of the restrictive legislation on settlement, the pre-revolutionary Jewish community was comparatively better educated, more acquainted with Russian culture, and better off than the Jewish population as a whole. A dynasty of oligarchs, the Baron Günzburgs (Yevzel, Horace, and David), led the community from 1870 until 1910. The communal leaders often represented all of Russian Jewry before the central authorities whenever protection of Jewish interests was needed. In the second half of the nineteenth century, Saint Petersburg became a center of Jewish publishing (mostly in Russian) and of Jewish public, political, and cultural activity. A number of Jewish Russian-language public organizations were founded there, including the *Society for the Promotion of Enlightenment among the Jews of Russia (OPE, 1863); the Society for Crafts and Agricultural Labor among Jews in Russia (ORT, 1880); and the Society for Safeguarding the Health of the Jewish Population (OZE, 1912).

By 1897, the Jewish population had grown to 17,000, and it increased to 50,000 in 1917. As a result of the February 1917 anti-monarchist revolution, Grigory Shreider, a Jew and member of the Socialist-Revolutionary Party, was elected mayor of the city. In September 1917, Leon *Trotsky became the chairman of the Petrograd Soviet (Council) of Workers, Soldiers, and Peasants and played a decisive role in the *Bolshevik October Revolution. The 1920s and the beginning of the 1930s saw an influx of Jews to Leningrad from the former *Pale of Settlement; they sought education, employment, and integration into Soviet society. During the interwar period Jews became the largest minority in the city, constituting 201,000, or 6% of the city population in 1939; they were prominent as administrators, physicians, writers and journalists, artists and musicians, lawyers, and university faculty.

During the Stalinist era, individual Jews paid for their advances in Soviet society with the loss of any permitted form of Jewish identity. In Saint Petersburg, all synagogues

but one were closed, and *Zionist activity was eradicated. Communal leaders (Lev Gurevich), Jewish scholars (Israel Zinberg), and Hebrew writers (Ḥaim Lensky) were arrested; some were shot and others died in camps. On the eve of *World War II, Leningrad had no Jewish press, schools, clubs, performance groups, or any other Jewish organizations.

Leningrad was not occupied by the *Nazis, but the city was held under siege for almost three years (1941–44); during this time, up to a million people, including thousand of Jews, died from hunger, cold, and shelling. Many were evacuated to the east and returned to their homes after the war.

With the appearance of the post-war state and growing *antisemitism, the number of Jews and their roles in Leningrad life gradually declined. The Jewish population dwindled from 167,000 in 1959, to 108,000 in 1989, and to 36,000 in 2004, because of negative natural growth and subsequent emigrations. Between 1967 and 1989, Leningrad was a major center of the *Soviet Jewish movement for immigration to *Israel. In 1970, a group of Leningrad and Riga "refuseniks" unsuccessfully attempted to hijack a small plane to escape to Sweden and then to Israel. In the 1980s an underground *Leningrad Jewish Almanac* was published (see SOVIET UNION: JEWISH MOVEMENT, 1967–1989).

In the second decade of the twenty-first century, Saint Petersburg has the second largest Jewish community in Russia, numbering approximately 40,000. However, the community has a high median age, extremely low birth rate, and a high percentage of *intermarriages. It has a number of Jewish religious, charitable, and cultural organizations; the Grand Choral Synagogue, dedicated in 1893, was reconstructed and renovated between 2000 and 2005. For further reading, see M. Beizer, *The Jews of St. Petersburg: Excursions through a Noble Past* (1989). **Map 11**   MICHAEL BEIZER

Salonika: See BALKANS; GREECE, Map 9

Samael is one of the most common names in *rabbinic literature for an evil power in the divine realms; in the literature of medieval *Kabbalah, Samael is identified with the devil himself. The name, which was probably included in the list of the rebellious archangels in 1 Enoch (see ESCHATOLOGY: SECOND TEMPLE PERIOD; PSEUDEPIGRAPHA), is usually explained as "the blind one" (and so it appears in *gnostic literature). It is possible, however, that the name is derived from *semol*, the Hebrew word for "left," which is often identified with evil and the sinister ("Evil comes from the north" [Jer 1:14]). In talmudic literature, Samael is mentioned as a tempter (e.g., of *Abraham) or as Satan, the "prosecutor'" (*kategor*) in the divine world. His figure appears increasingly in late *midrashim* of the early medieval period. In *hekhalot* literature (especially in *Hekhalot Rabbati*), he is called the Prince of *Rome, who demands the death of ten sages, described in detail in the story of the martyrs (see MARTYRDOM). In all ancient sources, he is described as a servant of God, part of the hierarchy of the divine court. The first *midrashic source to depict him as evil is chapter 13 of *Pirkei de-Rabbi Eliezer* (seventh to eighth century CE), in which he is the head of a group of rebellious angels and is identified with the snake who tempted *Adam and *Eve. This chapter was incorporated into the *Bahir, the earliest text of the Kabbalah (late twelfth century).

A different role for Samael is first alluded to in the thirteenth century in *Naḥmanides' *Commentary on the Torah* (at Lev 16), which describes him as the "soul of the sphere of Mars," the source of bloodshed and evil. Samael has a central role in Isaac ha-Cohen's "Treatise on the Emanations on the Left" (first half of the thirteenth century), which describes him as the highest emanation of the divine system of evil powers; his counterpart is said to be *Lilith. The concept of the *sitra aḥra*, "the other (i.e., the left) side," in the *Zohar* is based on this treatise; subsequently Samael became the common reference to the devil in kabbalistic literature and popular literature based on the Kabbalah. Often he is referred to as the *samekh-mem*, the first two letters of his name, so as not to pronounce the name in full (see J. Dan, *Jewish Mysticism* [1999], 3: 253–82, 367–414).   JOSEPH DAN

Samaria (Hebrew, Shomron) is a city located 56 kilometers (35 miles) northwest of *Jerusalem, strategically situated astride important trade routes. According to the Bible, Samaria fell within the tribal territory of Manasseh (Josh 17). In the early ninth century BCE, Omri, king of *Israel, purchased the site and made it his capital (1 Kgs 16:23–24). He and especially his son *Ahab fortified the site and transformed it into a cosmopolitan city that looked to *Phoenicia for its architectural style and decorative elements. Its elegant palace was vilified in the kingdom of *Judah as a "house of ivory" (1 Kgs 22:39; Amos 3:15, 6:4). Excavated plaques of ivory and semi-precious stones attest to royal opulence and eighth-century *ostraca* (inscribed pot fragments) illuminate Samaria's economy.

Samaria was conquered, with the rest of the kingdom of Israel, by the *Assyrians in 721 BCE, and its population was deported (2 Kgs 17:1–6). Foreigners were resettled at the site of the destroyed capital (2 Kgs 17:24–33), after which the region fell under successive *Babylonian and *Persian control. Letters from the Jewish community of Elephantine in *Egypt indicate that during the Persian period Samaria still held a place of importance in the Jewish world (cf. Ezra 4:1–3). In the *Hellenistic period, it became a center of pagan culture. Late in the first century BCE, *Herod the Great renovated the city, renaming it Sebaste and building a great Roman temple there. **Map 2**   BETH ALPERT NAKHAI

Samaritans (Hebrew, *shomronim*; "keepers") constitute a religious community parallel to but distinct from *Judaism. Attempts to construct a definitive history of the Samaritans suffer from the problematic nature of the available sources, which are often fragmentary, late, and heavily colored by polemic. The Samaritan chronicles trace their origins to the eleventh century BCE, when the priest Eli abandoned *Shechem to establish a new shrine at *Shiloh. For the Samaritans, this schism divided Israel into the true people of God (the Samaritans consider themselves the "keepers" of the law) and deviant Jews. Jewish sources see the matter differently, tracing the history of the Samaritans back to the "Samarians" (also called "Cutheans"), foreigners whom the *Assyrians resettled in *Samaria after the destruction of the northern kingdom of *Israel (2 Kgs 17:5–6, 24–41). Later Jewish writers cite this biblical story as proof that the Samaritans possessed alien genealogical roots and practiced a syncretistic, and thus inauthentic, form of *Judaism.

After Jewish captives returned from the *Babylonian Exile, they clashed with those who had not experienced deportation. Areas of disagreement included who should have authority in rebuilding the *Temple, *intermarriage, and the reconstruction of *Jerusalem's walls (*Ezra 4:1–24, 9:1–4; *Neh 13:23–29; 1 Esdras 2:16–30 [see PSEUDEPIGRAPHA]). The leaders of the returning exiles sought to shape their new community by isolating it from the "people of the land." Yet at this stage their "opponents" were not yet organized into a definable religious sect, despite the later attempts of *Josephus and the Samaritan chronicles to portray these clashes as an instance of Jewish–Samaritan conflict.

It is during the *Hellenistic period that the contours of a distinct Samaritan religious tradition emerge. Their temple at Mount Gerizim, dating to the fourth century BCE, became a symbol for the Samaritan religion and an obvious rival to the Jerusalem *Temple. Later, the Samaritans refused to participate in the *Maccabean revolt, sensing that its religious interests were incompatible with their own. The differences between the groups were also apparent to the *Hasmoneans who captured Shechem, destroyed the Mount Gerizim sanctuary, and established Jewish control of the region of *Samaria during the reign of John Hyrcanus (134–104 BCE). The Samaritans experienced uneven fortunes in subsequent centuries, benefiting from the largesse of *Rome in the first century BCE but experiencing persecutions under Pontius Pilate (r. 26–36), Hadrian (r. 117–138), and the *Byzantine Empire.

The *New Testament and *rabbinic literature display an ambivalent attitude toward the Samaritans. Although Jesus forbids his apostles from missionizing to the Samaritans (Matt 10:5), Luke highlights their superior piety and faith (Luke 10:29–37, 17:11–19) and includes Samaria among the places receptive to apostolic preaching (Acts 1:8, 8:4–25). The *Talmud occasionally offers a positive evaluation of the Samaritans, but more often emphasizes their differences: The *Rabbis refuse to classify Samaritans as Israelites, prohibit marriage with them, and underscore distinctions in worship and ritual cleanliness practices (M. *Berakhot* 7:1; M. *Kiddushin* 4:3; M. *Nedarim* 3:10; M. *Niddah* 4:1).

At the beginning of the twenty-first century, a small Samaritan community of under a thousand remains in the Middle East; most live in the Israeli town of Holon and in Kiryat Luza on Mount Gerizim, on the West Bank near the city of Nablus.   DAVID M. REIS

Samuel, Books of. The three central institutions of ancient Israel – the monarchy (see ISRAELITES: KINGSHIP), the *priesthood (see TEMPLE AND TEMPLE CULT), and prophecy (see BIBLE: PROPHETS AND PROPHECY) – are at issue in the books of Samuel. They are depicted as developing simultaneously as interdependent branches of the state. Although the intrigues associated with the throne occupy the bulk of the narrative, the monarchy alone appears to be an insufficient vehicle of God's will for Israel. Thus, this account of the rise and fall of *Saul and the rise of *David and his house is not named after either monarch, but rather after the prophet Samuel, anointer of both kings.

Scholars have proposed numerous subdivisions for the book of Samuel beyond its now standard division into two books, 1 and 2 Samuel. The German scholar Leonhard Rost suggested that portions of 2 Samuel 6 through 1 Kings 2 are a cohesive unit, concerned with David's successor as king.

However, one need not detach these chapters from their context to identify succession as the central theme throughout the books of Samuel. Heredity figures as a problematic basis for succession in each of the three political spheres. The priest Eli who administers the shrine at *Shiloh has unworthy sons – Hophni and Phinehas die ignominious deaths – and therefore passes religious authority to Samuel (1 Sam 2:12–4:22). David later designates the house of Zadok to serve as priests (2 Sam 20:26), yet also attempts to place his own sons in a priestly role (2 Sam 8:18). Samuel positions his sons as his successors, but their corrupt tendencies lead to the people's demand for a king (1 Sam 8:1–5, 12:1–2). Other prophets, such as Nathan (2 Sam 7, 12) and Gad (1 Sam 22:5; 2 Sam 24:11–25), seem to arise spontaneously to both advise and harass the king. The problem of hereditary succession is most pronounced in regard to the throne. Saul, the first king of Israel, watches the kingdom slip and God withdraw from him during his lifetime. His surviving descendants become dependents, who live and die according to David's word. Even King David, to whom God promises "your throne will be established for eternity" (2 Sam 7:16), endures the rebellions of three of his sons before pronouncing *Solomon his successor from his deathbed.

Parallel to the stress that underlies the family structure is the tension between the northern tribes of *Israel and the southern tribe of *Judah that is sometimes concealed and sometimes exacerbated by the monarchy (see TRIBES, TWELVE). Those who initially question the legitimacy of Saul's rule (1 Sam 10:27) seem to be quieted by his military victories (11:12), but a rival state of Judah is established by the covert initiation of David (1 Sam 16:12–13; 2 Sam 2:1–4a). While David moves to centralize the state by establishing *Jerusalem as its capital (2 Sam 7) and by conducting a census (2 Sam 24), the northern tribes side with a pretender on three separate occasions (2 Sam 2:8–11, 15, 20:1–2). Despite the fact that the establishment of the monarchy benefits the kingdom in the international arena, it does not efface regional affiliations (see ISRAELITES: TRIBES).

Although subject to familial schism and tribal strife, the monarchy develops in response to external pressures. It is inaugurated to consolidate the military and stave off the *Philistine advance on Israel (1 Sam 9:16); the residents of particular regions rally behind the king based on his ability to defend them, and the king builds his reputation by expanding his treasury and his country's borders through conquest. In the early part of his career, David is able to finesse his alliances to strengthen his kingdom. However, biblical narrative makes clear that the glory and spoils of war do not belong to humans alone. Saul's downfall is precipitated by his failure to uphold the ban against Amalek and his acquisition of Amalekite property (1 Sam 15:4–35). The battle engineered to do away with *Bathsheba's cuckolded husband constitutes David's worst crime (2 Sam 11:14–12:14).

The political has a distinctly personal edge as intrigues and battles materialize amidst the complexity of human motivation. Scholars attribute 1 and 2 Samuel to the *Deuteronomistic History, a chronicle of early Israel that spans *Joshua to *Kings, yet the characterizations in Samuel display a particular interiority. As Samuel inveighs against the monarchy, we see a man disappointed in his people's lack of religious devotion and his own ability to rouse them. God's abandonment of Saul results in bouts of paranoia and depression that plague him until his final day. When facing the violent lust of her brother Amnon, *Tamar looks squarely at the bleak fate of a violated woman (2 Sam 13). Rizpah, Saul's concubine, illustrates that vengeance settles scores while opening fresh wounds as she watches over the dismembered corpses of her sons and other descendants of Saul until they receive proper burial (2 Sam 21:8–14). David is twice compelled to survive as a fugitive, first when he is pursued during his youth by Saul, a father figure, and later in life when he is threatened by his son Absalom.

RACHEL HAVRELOCK

Samuel ibn Naghrela Ha-Nagid (993–1056) was the chief minister and commanded the armies of the Berber kingdom of Granada (see SPAIN, MUSLIM). An outstanding talmudic scholar, he was also one of the greatest medieval Hebrew poets (see POETRY, MEDIEVAL: MUSLIM WORLD). As the title *nagid indicates, ibn Naghrela also led Granada's Jewish community. An exemplar of the Jewish courtier class of Muslim Spain, ibn Naghrela's success demonstrates the heights to which a Jew could rise in this milieu. However, his achievements also brought significant hostility from Muslims who did not believe that a *dhimmi should wield so much power. Ten years after Samuel's death, his son, Joseph ha-Nagid, who had succeeded his father as chief minister and whose opulent lifestyle had aroused resentment, was assassinated in a popular uprising. The Jewish quarter of Granada was destroyed, and its inhabitants were killed by an angry mob.   JUDITH R. BASKIN

San Francisco was founded during the tumultuous years of the California Gold Rush, and its Jewish community grew quickly. By 1851, American-born Jews, including *Sephardim, as well as immigrants from *Britain, *Poland, parts of *Germany, and *France, had created benevolent societies and congregations. In the 1870s the Jewish population of San Francisco reached 16,000, second only to *New York City. The thriving community established *synagogues, associations, schools, an orphan asylum, and several newspapers. Twentieth-century immigrants contributed to the growth of community organizations, settlement houses, and a Jewish hospital. After World War II, Jews created new institutions including day and high schools, museums, and a renowned film festival. Between 1986 and 2004 the Jewish population, including surrounding communities, doubled to 228,000. With little *antisemitism, many Jews achieved success in commerce and elected office. These include Adolph Sutro as mayor (1894–96), Julius Kahn (1899–1903, 1905–24) and Florence Prag Kahn (1925–37) in the U.S. House of Representatives, and Barbara Boxer and former mayor Diane Feinstein, both currently in the U.S. Senate. For further reading, see A. F. Kahn, *Jewish Voices of the California Gold Rush* (2002); F. Rosenbaum, *Cosmopolitans: A Social & Cultural History of the Jews of the San Francisco Bay Area* (2009); and E. Eisenberg, A. F. Kahn, and W. Toll, *Jews of the Pacific Coast: Reinventing Community on America's Edge* (2010); **see also UNITED STATES, WESTERN.**   AVA FRAN KAHN

Sanhedrin. The Sanhedrin developed in the *Second Temple period as a judicial and legislative body for the Jewish population in *Jerusalem; its name derives from the Greek designation (*synhedrion*) for advisory councils to *Hellenistic rulers. Historical sources give conflicting views of the San-hedrin and its functions, perhaps because the Sanhedrin took on a different character when it came under rabbinic leadership after the destruction of the Second *Temple in 70 CE. Before that time, the Sanhedrin represented more than one point of view. The two major parties were the *Pharisees and *Sadducees; according to *Josephus each party had periods of ascendancy and decline, at least in *Hasmonean times. The Sanhedrin is said to have had seventy-one members. The presiding officer was initially the high priest; in the second century BCE, power was transferred to a new hereditary office, the *Nasi* (or *Patriarch). The *Av* *Beit Din* (Head of the Court) presided over the Sanhedrin when it heard criminal cases. While the Temple stood, the Sanhedrin was said to have met daily (except on the *Sabbath and *festivals) in a special chamber, the "hall of hewn stones" (*lishkat ha-gazit*; *Sifra, Vayikra* 19a; BT *Sanhedrin* 88b).

Some scholars believe that, after the Temple's destruction, the Sanhedrin was reestablished as a center of rabbinic jurisprudence in Yavneh and later in other locations. Its final location was said to have been in Tiberias in the *Galilee (BT *Rosh Ha-Shanah* 31a, b).   JUDITH R. BASKIN

Sanhedrin, France: See FRANCE: CONSISTORIES, 1806–1939

Sarah, ancestral mother of the Jewish people, is the wife of *Abraham and the mother of *Isaac. Originally Sarai, her name is changed as part of God's *covenant with Abraham in *Genesis 17:15. Living in a society where a woman fulfilled her duty to her husband's household through child bearing, Sarah's *infertility (11:30) threatens her status as Abraham's primary wife. To alleviate this threat, Sarah tells Abraham to father a child through a surrogate, her Egyptian slave (often translated as maid or handmaid) *Hagar: "Consort with my maid; perhaps I shall have a son through her" (Gen 16:2). The child of Abraham and Hagar is *Ishmael, a name selected by God. However, when Sarah is ninety years old, she becomes pregnant through God's intervention and gives birth to Isaac. To protect her interests and those of her son, Sarah persuades Abraham to expel Hagar and Ishmael. This was possible because Sarah's interests, as Abraham's primary wife, took precedence over those of Hagar. Moreover, the marriage between Abraham and Sarah was based on patrilineal endogamy (i.e., both partners to the marriage were descended from the patrilineage of Terah, Abraham's father [Gen 20:12]), whereas the Egyptian Hagar had no genealogical ties to either Terah or Abraham. **See also BIBLE: ANCESTRAL NARRATIVES.**   NAOMI STEINBERG

Saul was the first king of the *United Monarchy of all the *Israelite *tribes. He reigned from about 1020–1000 BCE. His story begins in 1 *Samuel 9 where he is described as the son of Kish, a Benjaminite and "a man of substance." He is "an excellent young man; no one among the Israelites was handsomer than he; he was a head taller than any of the people" (9:1–2). According to 1 Samuel 10, Saul is chosen by God as king, anointed by Samuel, and supported by the people. Saul organizes an army and leads battle on behalf of all Israel against its regional enemies; of these the *Philistines are the most threatening.

Saul's fall from divine favor and his loss of Samuel's support are explained as a result of his impatience in making

a burnt offering before a battle in Gilgal (13:8–14) prior to Samuel's promised arrival. In his victory over Amalek, Saul increases God's anger when he does not obey Samuel's divine directive to annihilate all living creatures connected with the defeated nation. At this point, Samuel tells him that, because Saul has rejected God's command, "the Lord has rejected you as king over Israel" (15:26).

The rest of Saul's story details his descent into madness and his increasing envy of *David. In his final battle against the Philistines at Mount Gilboa, the defeated Saul loses all of his men, including his three sons Abinadab, Jonathan, and Malchi-shua; he commits suicide by falling on his sword rather than face the ignominy of falling into enemy hands (1 Sam 31:3). David's poetic elegy over Saul and Jonathan (2 Sam 2) laments, "How the mighty have fallen," and recalls Saul who clothed the daughters of Israel "in crimson and finery."   KATE FRIEDMAN

Schechter, Solomon (1847–1915), the important Anglo-American scholar and religious leader, was born in Focşani, *Romania, and died in *New York City. Reared in a Ḥasidic family, Schechter received a traditional Jewish education in Romania and *Poland. He studied in *Vienna and *Berlin at modern institutions that advocated the scientific study of Judaism (see *WISSENSCHAFT DES JUDENTUMS*) and at the University of Berlin. Beginning in 1890 he taught rabbinics at Cambridge University in *Britain, before becoming president, in 1902, of the *Jewish Theological Seminary of America (JTS) in New York City, which he led until his death.

Schechter's foremost scholarly success was his retrieval of more than 100,000 documents from the Cairo *Genizah, an achievement that revolutionized the study of rabbinic and medieval Jewish life. His greatest fame came as a public intellectual and institutional leader. Schechter reached a popular readership through his English-language essays on the literary, historical, and theological traditions of the Jewish people, published in three volumes as *Studies in Judaism* (1896, 1908, 1924); his theological writings were collected in *Some Aspects of Rabbinic Theology* (1909).

Schechter endeavored to make JTS the North American center for academic Judaic scholarship and believed that its achievements would raise the general level of American Jewish culture. Under his leadership, "Schechter's Seminary" and Conservative Judaism (see JUDAISM, CONSERVATIVE) were positioned as the vital center of American Jewish life, against Reform, which he criticized for its assimilationism, and Orthodoxy, which he deemed too rigid and backward to cope with modernity (see JUDAISM entries). At JTS, Schechter legitimized the modern rabbi and scholar as a public figure as well as a religious leader.

Schechter never fit easily into any modern form of Judaism or Jewish ideology; rather than serving as a partisan for any one position, he was interested in the spectrum of Jewish expression from *Ḥasidism to *Haskalah*. Schechter studied Judaism critically while simultaneously defending it against forces he deemed to be its foes. Thus, he embraced Judaism as a faith, with a history and tradition, but also argued that it grew organically, housed inside of a living people. Schechter used the term "Catholic Israel" to express his vision of a Judaism that would receive and re-create a living Jewish tradition, linking Jews together in time and space, as a people and as *covenantal partners with *God. He supported *Zionism, convinced that the creation of a physical and spiritual center for world Jewry would unify Jewish life and counter assimilation and *antisemitism.   DAVID STARR

Schenirer, Sarah (1883–1935) was the founder of the *Beit Yaakov (Bais Yaakov)* school network. A native of Kraków, Schenirer was educated in Polish schools, becoming a seamstress at fourteen to help support her family. Schenirer's vision of education for religious women found broad support from many Orthodox leaders in post-World War I *Central and *Eastern Europe who had come to believe that traditions against educating girls should be disregarded, given the rapidly changing social conditions and widespread assimilation. The *Agudat Yisrael* movement provided the *Beit Yaakov* network with financial assistance, logistical guidance, and a literary forum, the Yiddish-language *Beys-Yankev Zhurnal*. Schenirer's dedication was supplemented by the organizational professionalism of Dr. Leo Deutschlander and the female teachers he recruited from Germany who taught summer training courses and, later on, at the central teachers' seminary in Kraków that Schenirer founded. There were 227 Beit Yaakov schools in Poland by 1935, with more than 27,000 pupils. Schools were also established in *Austria, *Czechoslovakia, *Romania, *Lithuania, *Palestine, and the *United States. For further reading, see G. Bacon, "Schenirer, Sarah," *Encyclopedia Judaica*, 2nd ed. (2006).

Schindler, Oskar (1908–1974), a Czech rescuer of Jews during the *Holocaust, was made famous by Steven Spielberg's 1993 film, *Schindler's List*, based on the book by Thomas Keneally. In the late 1930s Schindler worked as a spy for *Abwehr*, the Germany military's counterintelligence branch, and was arrested and imprisoned in Czechoslovakia in 1938 for his activities; he was released following the Munich Agreement. Schindler arrived in Kraków, *Poland, in the fall of 1939 with the goal of making as much money as he could. He took over a Jewish-owned pots and pans factory, *Emalia*, which had gone bankrupt before the war broke out. He inherited the factory's Jewish managerial team and relied heavily on them to run the factory. The genius behind *Emalia's* operations was an Orthodox Jew, Abraham Bankier. It was Bankier who suggested that Schindler consider using Jewish workers as an inexpensive source of labor, knowing that work meant life for Jews in Nazi-occupied Poland. Over time, Schindler gained such a good reputation as a benevolent factory owner that he was invited to meet secretly in Budapest in late 1943 with representatives of *Palestine's Jewish Agency. They convinced him to act as a conduit for Jewish funds smuggled into Poland to help Jews in various forced labor and concentration camps (see HOLOCAUST: CAMPS AND KILLING CENTERS).

Schindler also built a sub-camp at *Emalia* for his Jewish workers. In July 1944, when Schindler was ordered to close his sub-camp and send his Jewish workers to Płaszów, he decided to open a new factory in Brünnlitz (Brnenec) in what is now the Czech Republic, which would employ a thousand Jewish workers. He invested a significant amount of time and resources to obtain the necessary SS and military permissions to open his new factory in Brünnlitz. Although he had little to do with making up the

semi-mythical "Schindler's list," he did everything possible to ensure the transfer of 1,000 Jewish workers from Kraków to his new factory. From October 1944 to May 1945, Schindler spent most of the wealth that he had made in Kraków to save the lives of 1,098 Jews. He and his wife Emilie are recognized at Yad Vashem in Israel as Righteous among the Nations for their efforts to save Jews.

For further reading, see D. M. Crowe, *Oskar Schindler: The Untold Account of His Life, Wartime Activities, and the True Story behind the List* (2004); and M. Pemper, *The Road to Rescue: The Untold Story of Schindler's List* (2008); **see also HOLOCAUST; HOLOCAUST RESCUERS**.   DAVID M. CROWE

Schneerson, Menachem Mendel (1902–1994), the seventh rebbe of the Lubavitcher *Ḥasidim (see ḤABAD), was born in Nikolayev, *Ukraine. His mother, *Rebbetzin* Chana Schneerson, hailed from an elite rabbinic family; his father, Rabbi Levi Yitzchak Schneerson, was a gifted scholar. In 1929, Schneerson married Chaya Mushka Schneersohn, a distant cousin, in *Warsaw. Chaya Mushka was a daughter of Rabbi Yosef Yitzchak Schneersohn, then the Lubavitcher Rebbe. Rabbi Menachem Mendel studied mathematics and science at the University of *Berlin and the Sorbonne in Paris. In 1941, he and his wife moved to *New York City; they had no children.

Rabbi Yosef Yitzchak died in 1950, and Rabbi Menachem Mendel became Rebbe the next year. He led Lubavitch for forty-four years, helping a small movement that was nearly destroyed during the *Holocaust burgeon into a worldwide community that has influenced Jews far beyond Ḥasidic and even *Orthodox circles (see JUDAISM, ORTHODOX). During the final years of Schneerson's life, a large percentage of his followers became convinced that he was the *messiah: They assumed he was immortal and would usher the world into a glorious messianic age. When he passed away, deep-seated political strife emerged around this issue, because many believe the messiah must come from the ranks of the living. Some Lubavitchers are convinced that Schneerson will not be the messiah, some are unsure, and a fair number believe strongly that he will indeed usher in the messianic age. This controversy and the lack of an obvious heir have meant that there is no universally recognized Lubavitch leader in the first decades of the twenty-first century.

Schneerson's true legacy lies in the extraordinary growth that Lubavitch enjoyed during his leadership. This expansion, which owes much to Schneerson's emphasis on outreach to Jews beyond the Lubavitch community, seems likely to continue. Lubavitch scholar Simon Jacobson estimates that Lubavitch has more than 200,000 followers around the world. Other scholars weigh in with lower estimates, but Schneerson clearly revolutionized Lubavitch in size, scope, and passion.   STEPHANIE WELLEN LEVINE

Scholem, Gershom Gerhard (1897–1982) was the founder of the scholarly study of Jewish *mysticism (see also KABBALAH), a towering figure in twentieth-century *Jewish studies, and a highly influential Jewish thinker. Born to an assimilated Jewish family in *Berlin, Scholem became committed to *Zionism as a young man; he associated with Martin *Buber and began to study Hebrew and *Talmud. His close friendship with Walter *Benjamin lasted until Benjamin's death in 1940 (G. Scholem, *Walter Benjamin: The Story of a Friendship* [1982]). Scholem decided to write his doctoral thesis on the *Bahir, which he identified as the earliest work of the Kabbalah. His first book was a translation of this work into German with a commentary (Leipzig [1923]).

Scholem immigrated to *Jerusalem in 1923 and worked in the Jewish National Library that had been established at that time; he wrote the library's index for Judaica, which is still in use (G. Scholem, *From Berlin to Jerusalem: Memories of My Youth* [1980]). In 1925 he delivered one of the opening lectures of the Institute of Jewish Studies in Jerusalem. The next year, together with the Institute of Chemistry (opening lecture given by Albert *Einstein), it became the core of the just founded Hebrew University of Jerusalem. Scholem taught scores of students about Jewish mysticism throughout his career at Hebrew University. He also participated in a small circle of Jerusalem intellectuals known as *Berit Shalom* (Pact of Peace), which was dedicated to fostering peaceful relations between Jews and Arabs. He assembled an exhaustive library on Kabbalah, which is now housed in a special reading room at the National and University Library in Jerusalem (*The Library of Gershom Scholem on Jewish Mysticism*, ed. J. Dan and E. Liebes, 2 vols. [1999]).

Scholem's best known work, *Major Trends in Jewish Mysticism* (1941, 1946; 2nd ed., 1954), was the first historical survey of Jewish mysticism. In 1957 he published (in Hebrew) his history of the messianic movement headed by *Shabbatai Zevi, which was translated into many languages. Other important books include *Jewish Gnosticism, Merkabah Mysticism, and Talmudic Tradition* (1960). His articles for the *Encyclopedia Judaica*, including a comprehensive article on the Kabbalah, appeared in book form as *Kabbalah* (1974). Scholem served as the president of the Israeli Academy of Arts and Sciences between 1968 and 1974. After his death, several volumes of his diaries and correspondence were published, including A. D. Skinner, ed., *A Life in Letters, 1914–1982* (2002); and idem, *Lamentations of Youth: The Diaries of Gershom Scholem, 1913–1919* (2008).

On Scholem's heritage, see J. Dan, *Gershom Scholem and the Mystical Dimension in Jewish History* (1987); idem, *Jewish Mysticism*, vol. 4 (1999); and P. Schaefer and J. Dan, eds., *Major Trends in Jewish Mysticism: Fifty Years After* (1993).

JOSEPH DAN

Science and Mathematics: Middle Ages and Early Modern Period.

According to an ancient myth, retold in differing versions by medieval Jews, Muslims, and Christians, science originated in ancient Israel, was mastered by *Solomon (who wrote hundreds of lost books on the sciences), and was stolen by or passed on to the other nations. Judah *Halevi's formulation asserted, "In truth, the roots and principles of all the sciences were transferred from us to the Chaldeans first, and then to the Persians and Medians, and then to the Greeks, and then the Romans" (*Kuzari* II, 66). This popular myth (cf. also *Maimonides, *Guide of the Perplexed* I, 71) reflected Jewish pride, but it also legitimized scientific study by Jews. Despite the conviction that all truth could be found in the Torah and in the face of rabbinic prohibitions against the study of Greek wisdom (e.g., BT *Sotah* 49b, *Bava Kamma* 82b; cf. *Menaḥot* 99b), learned medieval Jews, many of them leading rabbis, talmudists, and biblical commentators, studied the sciences. Some sought knowledge for its own sake; for others scientific study was a religious duty connected with the desire to know and draw near to *God (e.g., Maimonides, *Mishneh Torah*, Laws of Repentance X, 6). Some Jews used science to defend Judaism from subversive claims stemming from faulty or pseudo-science. Ḥasdai *Crescas wrote his pioneering critique of Aristotelian natural science as part of his efforts to strengthen Jewish commitment after forced conversions and massacres took place in Christian *Spain in 1391. Troubled by the dependence of Maimonides and his followers on "the words of the Greek [Aristotle]," which had weakened Jewish faith, Crescas sought to make known the "fallaciousness of his proofs and the fraudulence of his arguments" (Crescas, *Light of the Lord*, intro.)

Jewish scientists, like their Muslim predecessors, devoted effort to enumerating the sciences. Their listings indicate the range of scientific inquiry. Most followed the Aristotelian division of science into theoretical and practical, with logic being considered an instrument for scientific inquiry, but not a science. Theoretical science was divided into mathematics, natural science, and divine science and practical science was divided into *ethics, economics or governance of the household, and politics.

Mathematics (discussed later) was usually divided into the *quadrivium* of arithmetic, geometry, astronomy, and music. Sometimes, following Alfarabi, optics, mechanics, and engineering were included as well. The division of natural science generally followed Aristotle's books: *The Physics, On the Heavens, On Generation and Corruption, Meteorology, On Animals, On the Soul, Parva naturalia*, the pseudo-Aristotelian *On Plants*, and occasionally the pseudo-Aristotelian *On Minerals*. Some enumerations also added *medicine, as well as *astrology, alchemy, and other occult sciences. Jewish scientists who adhered to the Aristotelian tradition emphasized the importance of the orderly study of the sciences before approaching metaphysical questions. Maimonides cautioned the student for whom he wrote the *Guide* to study the sciences systematically, so that the "truth should be established in your mind according to the proper methods and that certainty should not come to you by accident" (*Guide*, epistle dedicatory [Pines trans., p. 4]). The first Hebrew translation of a work of Aristotelian science, *Meteorology* (translated by Samuel ibn Tibbon in 1210; ed. R. Fontaine [1995]), insists that students of natural science begin with the *Physics*, Aristotle's book on the principles of nature, and then proceed to *On the Heavens* and *On Generation and Corruption*, before turning to the various subjects of *Meteorology*.

Medieval Jewish science arose at the same time as medieval Islamic science; both were a direct result of the translation movements from Greek and Syriac into Arabic from the mid-eighth to the end of the tenth century. Except for certain very influential early Hebrew texts, such as *Sefer Yetzirah* and *Mishnat ha-Middot*, whose dating cannot be determined with certainty, Jewish and Muslim scientists relied on Arabic translations of the major works of Greek science and mathematics and the growing contributions of Arabic scholars in these fields. One of the first accounts of the beginnings of medieval Jewish science was provided in 1068 by the Islamic historian and scientist Sâ'id al-Andalusî in his *Book of the Categories of Nations*. Al-Andalusî lists Jewish scientists, physicians, and astrologers, from the East and the West, with special attention to contemporaries in al-Andalus (*Spain), noting their fields and their accomplishments. In fact, with a few major exceptions, such as the leading eighth-century astrologer, Mâshâ'allâh, Jewish scientists writing in Arabic made few contributions (see ASTROLOGY).

The first versatile and prolific Jewish scientists were two twelfth-century Spanish thinkers, *Abraham bar Ḥiyya (ca. 1065–1140) and Abraham *ibn Ezra (ca. 1089–1167); both wrote in Hebrew. Bar Ḥiyya wrote on mathematics, geometry, astronomy, astrology, and philosophy. He compiled the first Hebrew encyclopedia of science, *The Foundations of Intelligence and the Tower of Belief*; among other topics, it contains sections on logic, the *quadrivium* and optics, the natural sciences, and divine science. Ibn Ezra, best known for his *biblical commentaries, wrote about thirty scientific treatises, most of which treat astronomy and astrology. S. Sela has shown that, although ibn Ezra's scientific writings are for the most part reference works and textbooks for laymen, based on his Arabic sources, he does not hesitate to explicate his sources and criticize them sharply. Both bar Ḥiyya and ibn Ezra were pioneers in the development of a scientific Hebrew terminology.

Maimonides, who was learned and well read in all the sciences, wrote a bit on mathematics and astronomy and a great deal on *medicine; he rooted his theology in twenty-five premises he claimed were demonstrated by Aristotle in his books on natural science (*Guide* II, introduction). Although Maimonides declared that he did not intend to break new ground in science in his *Guide* (II, 2, preface), he may have influenced the course of Hebrew science with his recommendation in a letter to Samuel ibn Tibbon, the translator into Hebrew of the *Guide*, that the "books of Aristotle are the roots and principles of all the compositions on the sciences, but they cannot be understood without the commentaries on them by Alexander of Aphrodisias, Themistius, and Averroes." Perhaps this is why few works of Aristotle were translated from Arabic into Hebrew, but virtually all the commentaries on Aristotle's writings by Averroes were. Through these commentaries, Jews learned and mastered Aristotelian natural science in Hebrew. These translations were part of an impressive translation movement that in the century and one-half after Maimonides' death made available to Hebrew readers works on logic, natural science, and divine science, as well as more than fifty works of Greek and Arabic mathematics and astronomy and nearly one hundred medical and pharmacological writings (far more if one counts Latin-to-Hebrew translations).

Hebrew encyclopedias of science were another valuable source for scientific instruction, particularly in the thirteenth century. Some, such as Judah ben Solomon ha-Kohen's *Midrash ha-Ḥokhmah* (The Exposition of Wisdom), ranged over the various subjects of logic, geometry, astronomy and astrology, natural science, and divine science; others, like Shem-Tov Falaquera's *De'ot ha-Filosofim* (The Opinions of the Philosophers), went into greater depth, but limited the subject matter to natural and divine science. The many translations of Averroes' commentaries on natural science also gave rise to a tradition of supercommentaries on these texts, the most famous and significant of which were by *Gersonides (1288–1344). Gersonides carefully explicated Averroes, but did not hesitate to criticize him and Aristotle when he disagreed with their science; he also put forward novel interpretations of his own. Thus, his study of Aristotle's analysis of motion in the *Physics* resulted in an original non-Aristotelian understanding of the concept of force and of the

relation among force, resistance, and motion (R. Glasner, in *Studies in the History and Philosophy of Science*, 28 [1997]). Glasner has also shown how Gersonides dealt with one of the central problems of medieval science: the basic incompatibility between Ptolemaic astronomy, with its system of epicycles, and Aristotelian physics. Gersonides, like Averroes, rejected epicycles, but went on to propose his own planetary models, while modifying and adapting Aristotelian physics to fit his theories.

Ḥasdai *Crescas is another creative and influential figure in the history of science; his knowledge of Aristotelian science was based primarily on the Hebrew translations of Averroes. As part of his revolutionary critique of Aristotelian science, Crescas argued for the actual existence of the void and the infinite, in opposition to the Aristotelian science of his day, and he put forward bold new theories of space and time. Some have contended that, with the exception of Gersonides and Crescas, Jews writing in Hebrew contributed little originality to medieval scientific inquiry. However, recent studies have countered this generalization. For example, the medieval Jewish students and commentators on Averroes were not passive readers of the texts nor did they accept blindly the principles and claims of Aristotelian natural science. Their desire to understand and explicate inevitably gave rise to critique and innovation. The modern emphasis on creativity, however, can be misleading. What must be noted is that the hundreds of Hebrew translations, both from Arabic and from Latin, made it possible for Jews to master the sciences of their day and, in some instances, to contribute to the progress of science.

Jewish interest in science continued throughout the medieval period and was spurred on by the Italian Renaissance. In the early seventeenth century, Jews were at the center of scientific discovery. For example, David Gans worked in Tycho Brahe's observatory near *Prague and discussed scientific questions with Tycho and Johannes Kepler. The young Joseph Solomon Delmedigo was a student assisting Galileo in Padua. It has generally been thought that after Delmedigo there was little Jewish interest in science until the beginning of the eighteenth century, but recent scholarship has shown that this view is not quite accurate. Yet even those who point to "widespread interest in scientific endeavor" during this period admit that "only a handful of Jews contributed substantially to science, and even these were primarily active in the field of medicine" (D. B. Ruderman, *Jewish Thought and Scientific Discovery in Early Modern Europe* [1995], 12).

MATHEMATICS: In addition to early undated Hebrew mathematical compositions and the twelfth-century mathematical works of bar Ḥiyya and ibn Ezra, the Arabic-to-Hebrew translation movement of the thirteenth and fourteenth centuries made available an impressive list of Greek and Arabic works of the *quadrivium*. Among the Greek mathematicians translated into Hebrew were Archimedes, Autolycus, Euclid, Eutocius, Geminus, Menelaus, Nicomachus, Ptolemy, and Theodosius. Moreover, Arab mathematicians commented on the Arabic versions of many of these works, explicated them, and wrote their own independent treatises. Among the Arab mathematicians translated into Hebrew were Averroes, al-Bitrûjî, al-Farghânî, al-Hassâr, al-Khwârizmî, ibn Aflah, ibn al-Bannâ, ibn al-Muthannâ, Thabit ibn Qurra, and Zarqâllu. Through these translations medieval Jews could learn subjects such as arithmetic, geometry, algebra, optics, spherics, and astronomy. These translations gave rise to commentaries and independent treatises in Hebrew. The authors of these Hebrew works for the most part did not seek to advance mathematics, but rather to understand and explain it. One major exception is Gersonides, who made original contributions in the fields of mathematics and astronomy; he even invented observational instruments such as the Jacob Staff, for observing the distance between two stars, among other uses. Jews studied the mathematical sciences as part of the orderly curriculum of science referred to earlier. In particular, it was a prerequisite for the study of astronomy. There were also religious reasons for studying mathematics. For one, it was important for resolving *calendric matters, such as determining the time of the new moon (see ROSH HODESH) and of the *festivals. Bar Hiyya and ibn Ezra each wrote books entitled *Sefer ha-'Ibbur* (The Book of Intercalation).

For further reading, see S. Sela, *Abraham Ibn Ezra and the Rise of Medieval Hebrew Science* (2003); S. Harvey, *The Medieval Hebrew Encyclopedias of Science and Philosophy* (2000); W. Z. Harvey, *Physics and Metaphysics in Hasdai Crescas* (1998); and T. Lévy, "The Establishment of the Mathematical Bookshelf of the Medieval Hebrew Scholar: Translations and Translators," *Science in Context*, 10 (1997): 431–51.

STEVEN HARVEY

Second Temple Period is the era extending from the rebuilding of the *Jerusalem Temple in 515 BCE by exiles who had returned from *Babylon to the destruction of the Second *Temple in 70 CE during the First *Jewish War against *Rome. **See APOCRYPHA; ARCHEOLOGY, LAND OF ISRAEL: SECOND TEMPLE PERIOD; CHRISTIANITY AND SECOND TEMPLE JUDAISM; ESCHATOLOGY: SECOND TEMPLE PERIOD; HASMONEAN DYNASTY; HELLENISM; PSEUDEPIGRAPHA; WOMEN, ANCIENT: SECOND TEMPLE PERIOD and related entries**.

Secularism in the contemporary Jewish world is committed to the historical and cultural survival of Jews as an ethnic group, separate from the religious beliefs and practices of *Judaism. From a "secular" stance, particular distinctions among religious beliefs, practices, or feelings are irrelevant. The ideology of modern secularism calls for a life without recourse to scriptural authority, ecclesial property, or divine purpose.

Some have suggested that the first "secular Jew" was Benedict (Baruch) *Spinoza. In fact, the economic and social forces that have led to transformations of religious distinctions within Judaism have manifold causes. By the end of the eighteenth century, Jews like Berr Isaac Berr (writing in 1791) would voluntarily "divest" themselves from their "corporation in civil and political matters," unless otherwise commanded by "spiritual laws," in exchange for legal *emancipation. Similarly, the writer and poet Heinrich Heine (1797–1856) maintained that "the baptismal font is the ticket of admission to European culture." Many *Haskalah writers placed value in "the torah of man" before the "Torah of God," in the words of N. H. Wessely (1782). The Scientific Study of Judaism (*Wissenschaft des Judentums*, established 1819) provided scholarly documentation of the

diversity and ongoing change that have always characterized Jewish life. As a result, some urged a separation of the private realm of Jewish identity from the public realm of participation in the broader society; as Judah Leib Gordon's 1862 verse put it, "Be a man in the streets and a Jew at home." Others, like S. Tchernichowsky (1899), condemned exilic piety; he invoked "the God of gods, who took Canaan by storm/ Before they bound him in phylacteries." Before their destruction, *Central and *Eastern European Jewry had developed a range of Jewish secularisms in urban centers such as *Vienna, *Prague, Odessa (see RUSSIA), and *Warsaw that included political identities such as the *Bund and various approaches to *Zionism; Modernist endeavors in Yiddish and Hebrew *literature and *poetry (as well as literature in other languages); and the development of Yiddish and Hebrew *theater, *film, and *popular music. The degree of secularism among Middle Eastern Jewry varied geographically; by the mid-twentieth century, Jews in *Iran and *Iraq were overwhelmingly secular, but this was not the case in *Kurdistan and *Yemen.

Secular ideologies, which were generally held by the founders of the State of *Israel, pervade contemporary Israeli society in both extreme expressions ("the negation of *Diaspora") and moderate forms (*hiloni*, secularist). Modes of religious observance in Israel compromise in a range of ways with this pervasive secularism. Haredi or Ultra-Orthodox Jews (see JUDAISM, ORTHODOX: ULTRA-ORTHODOX) make only minimal compromises; for example, in regard to serving or not in the military (see JUDAISM, ISRAEI FORMS OF), whereas other groups show more flexibility.

It could be argued that all forms of North American Judaism are more or less secularized in their various accommodations to the modern secular world. Moreover, a majority of North American Jews maintain a secular ethnic identity without religious affiliation or significant religious practice. For further reading, see T. Deutscher, ed., *The Non-Jewish Jew and Other Essays* (1968); and M. Fox, "Judaism, Secularism, and Textual Interpretation," in idem, ed., *Modern Jewish Ethics* (1975).

GREGORY KAPLAN

Sefer Yetzirah (The Book of Creation), the most influential work to emerge from ancient speculations concerning creation, became one of the main sources of Hebrew *mystical terminology and imagery for many centuries. It was probably written (anonymously) in the third or fourth century, although the book itself does not contain any clear indication by which it can be dated. Various scholars have suggested dates of composition ranging from the first century CE, before the destruction of the Second *Temple in 70 CE, to the ninth century, just before the book's tenth-century commentaries were written. Many external influences have been suggested, including Neoplatonic, Neopythagorean, Zoroastrian, and Hindu, but no distinct parallels have yet been identified. The impact of *Sefer Yetzirah* was felt mainly from the tenth century and later, when it was adopted as a sacred text first by rationalist thinkers and *scientists and then (in the second half of the twelfth century) by esoterics and mystics (see KABBALAH). The work survives in three different versions, usually known as the "short," "long," and "Saadian" versions; each served as a basis for a tenth-century commentary by

Dunash ibn Tamim, Shabbatai Donolo, and *Saadia Gaon, respectively.

In brief and enigmatic sentences, *Sefer Yetzirah* presents a systematic view of the principles of the process of creation (*yetzirah*) and the laws governing nature and humans. In almost every respect, this system differs not only from the detailed discussions of the subject in the *Talmud and *midrash but also from the events presented in *Genesis 1. None of the actions and terms in the Genesis creation narrative is prominent in *Sefer Yetzirah*; indeed, even the term "creation" is not used in the most ancient versions. Rather, the world was "carved" (*ḥakak*). According to *Sefer Yetzirah*, the world came to be by "thirty-two paths of wondrous [divine] wisdom," which have been interpreted as the numbers from one to ten, plus the twenty-two letters of the Hebrew alphabet. This basic concept follows both the statement in the *Mishnah that the world was created by ten divine utterances (M. *Avot* 5:1) and the talmudic view that the world was created by the letters of the alphabet. *Sefer Yetzirah* systematizes these concepts, presenting a picture of the creation process that is largely independent of the version in Genesis 1.

The ten "numbers" (**sefirot*) are the ten directions, or five dimensions, of the universe: north, south, east, west, up, down (in space), beginning, end (in time), good, and evil; they also express the involvement of the three elements: air, water, and fire. Each letter of the alphabet is in charge of three realms – one in the universe (the stars), one in time (month, week, day), and one in the human being (an organ or a sense). The author invented a transcendent system of Hebrew grammar, seeing in the rules of language the source of the laws of nature. The grammatical distinction between masculine and feminine governs all existence. He viewed the difference between good and evil as a grammatical one, and as such both are present in the universe and in the human entity. The work does not deal with any religious or ethical subject. It does not mention *commandments, the people of Israel, the human soul, *prayer, or *redemption. The end of the book indicates that the understanding of these scientific laws brought *Abraham into a religious union with *God, and those who follow him in this may achieve the same mystical status.

Sefer Yetzirah is not mentioned in ancient Hebrew literature, and its terminology is original and unique (a reference to *hilkhot yetzirah* in Babylonian *Talmud Tractate *Sanhedrin* is probably unrelated to this work). Jewish rationalists and scientists in the tenth century "discovered" this book; Saadia Gaon and Dunash ibn Tamim wrote detailed commentaries in Arabic, and Shabbatai Donolo wrote a commentary in Hebrew. Many rationalistic, scientific commentaries followed until the twelfth century; of these, the most detailed was by Judah ben Barzilai of Barcelona. Late in the twelfth century the treatise became a major source for Jewish mystics and esoterics in Europe, kabbalists and non-kabbalists, many of whom derived their terminology from it. Since that time, Jews and Christians alike have regarded it as an ancient expression of Jewish mysticism. *Sefer Yetzirah* was first printed in Mantua in 1562 and has been reprinted scores of times since; it has also been translated into many languages. In 2004 Peter Hyman published a scholarly edition with a textual commentary, English translation, and detailed bibliography. Other studies include J. Dan, *Jewish Mysticism*, vol. I (1998); and G. Scholem, *The Origins of the Kabbalah* (1987).

JOSEPH DAN

Sefirot is an ancient cosmogonic Hebrew term that was adopted in the medieval *Kabbalah to describe the intrinsic structure of the divine world. It became the most recognizable kabbalistic term, and the system of ten *sefirot*, ten divine emanations or hypostases, became an identifying characteristic of the kabbalistic worldview.

The term *sefirot* originated in the ancient cosmogonic Hebrew work, **Sefer Yetzirah* (The Book of Creation). The first chapter of that work describes, in various, often conflicting ways, the ten *sefirot belimah* (numbers of nothingness?) that, together with the twenty-two letters of the Hebrew alphabet, constitute the thirty-two "secret paths of wisdom" by which God created the universe. Medieval commentators, like *Saadia Gaon, and modern scholars, like Gershom *Scholem, identified the *sefirot* with the ten primary numbers. The *Sefer Yetzirah* describes them as the ten directions of the universe: up, down, east, west, north, south, beginning, end, and good and evil. Another section of that work identifies them as archangels – the holy beasts of the *Ezekiel chariot (Ezek 1). Another section describes the first four *sefirot* as the stages in the evolution of the elements from which the universe was created. These elements consist of the spirit of God, from which air, water, and finally fire came forth (the fourth element, earth is not included in this system). The text states emphatically that the *sefirot* are ten in number: "ten and not nine, ten and not eleven."

During the tenth to twelfth centuries, philosophers and scientists in *Iraq, *Italy, and *Spain made several attempts to reconcile this ancient, opaque system with contemporary views of the world. By the end of the twelfth century, the system was adopted by esoterics and mystics in southern *France, *Spain, *Germany, and northern *France. Although writers in northern France and Germany retained the concept that the *sefirot* represented cosmological entities, kabbalists in southern France and Spain interpreted the term as indicating the intrinsic structure of the divine world. This is not evident in the first work of the Kabbalah, the **Bahir* (ca. 1190), but it is emphatically stated in the commentary on the *Sefer Yetzirah* written by *Isaac the Blind, the leader of the earliest circle of kabbalists in southern France, in the beginning of the thirteenth century. In the first half of the thirteenth century, the kabbalists in Gerona, Spain, adopted and developed the system of ten divine *sefirot*, and since then, with few exceptions (like Abraham *Abulafia in the second half of that century), it has become a prominent characteristic of Jewish *mysticism.

The Kabbalah transformed these emanations or hypostases, which likely have Neoplatonic origins, into a vast, colorful mythology. This system of *sefirot* dominates the complex, dynamic descriptions of the divine world of the *Zohar, and its main ideas became the "standard" kabbalistic description, although every kabbalist developed an individual system that diverged to some extent from that "standard."

The main outlines are as follows: The eternal God, the source of everything, called **Ein Sof*, is the origin of the flow of divine "light" from which all existence emerged. The "point" at which a divine will to create and evolve is identified is the first *sefirah*, usually called *keter* (crown). From *keter* the divine "plan" for all existence emerged; this is the second *sefirah, hokhmah* (the divine wisdom). The actual existence of divine beings begins with the third *sefirah, binah* (intelligence). These three *sefirot* represent, in the anthropomorphic terms of the Kabbalah, the head of the divine figure. From *binah* emerged the two arms: the fourth *sefirah, hesed* (charity) on the right, and the fifth, *din* (justice), on the left (also called *gevurah* [divine power]). The sixth *sefirah, tiferet* (grandeur, also called *rahamim* [mercy]), united the two ways of divine conduct of the world, representing the divine heart. The seventh and eighth *sefirot, nezah* (eternity) on the right and *hod* (glory) on the left, represent the two legs. Between them is the ninth *sefirah, yesod* (foundation) or *tzaddik* (righteousness), representing the male organ. The tenth *sefirah, malkhut* (kingdom) or *Shekhinah* (divine residence or presence), is a separate entity; it represents the female aspect of the divine world, the wife or the daughter, and it is the power that is dominant in the created worlds beneath it. It leads the hosts of angels and heavenly bodies, as well as the physical, human world. There is also a parallel system of *sefirot* – "the emanations on the left," the *sitra ahra* (the other side, meaning the left) – which represent the realm of evil, consisting of seven or ten *sefirot*, headed by *Samael and the feminine aspect, *Lilith.

The *sefirot* represent a dynamic, ever-changing realm. They thrive when divine flow is abundant, and the lower ones suffer when it is diminished by the sins of the people of Israel. The masculine and feminine powers come together in erotic union, and their joining increases the flow of divine goodness; however, when Israel's sins cause them to be separate, the powers of evil are strengthened. *Prayers, fulfillment of religious *commandments, and ethical deeds increase the good flow. In the *Zohar*, as well as in some other kabbalistic works, the imagery describing the *sefirot* is intensely mythological, attributing to the divine powers strong individual characteristics and relationships. At the same time, the detailed description of the emanation of the *sefirot* serves as a spiritual ladder that can be used by the mystic to uplift his or her soul, stage by stage, in the opposite direction – from the physical universe to the summit of the divine realms.

Lurianic Kabbalah (see KABBALAH, LURIANIC), which developed in sixteenth-century *Safed, while following the main contours of this system, transformed it into a structural theory: Everything in the universe is located according to this hierarchy, there is an infinite number of such groupings, and only its place in this cosmic ladder decides the particular characteristics of each entity. However, most kabbalists in the modern period did not accept this theory, and the concept of the *sefirot* as presented in the *Zohar* remained most prevalent. For further reading, see G. Scholem, *Kabbalah* (1974), 88–116; and I. Tishby, *The Wisdom of the Zohar*, (1989), vol. I.   JOSEPH DAN

Seleucids. After the death of *Alexander the Great in 323 BCE, his generals and other claimants scrambled to gain supremacy over the territory he had conquered. The wars of these "successors" (*Diadochi*) took place over a forty-two-year period (322–280). Within a few years, Ptolemy I (r. 305–283) and Seleucus I (r. 305–281) had claimed *Egypt and *Mesopotamia, respectively, and joined in an alliance against Antigonus, a rival general who had staked a claim to

Asia. In 312, after Ptolemy defeated the Antigonid forces at Gaza, Seleucus returned to *Babylon to secure his authority. Although ancient chronicles mark this year as the beginning of the Seleucid kingdom, it was not until 305 that Seleucus claimed the title "king." Three years later, Ptolemy and Seleucus joined Cassander and Lysimachus in an alliance against Antigonus, who was killed at the battle of Ipsus. Ipsus marked a pivotal moment in the history of *Palestine, for when the victorious generals divided Antigonus's land, Seleucus was awarded *Syria. Yet Ptolemy, whose armies had not participated in the fighting, claimed the southern region of Syria before Seleucus could secure it. For the next century, the *Ptolemies ruled the province that included the Land of Israel (called "Coele-Syria and *Phoenicia" by the Seleucids).

The geopolitical pendulum shifted during the Fifth Syrian War (202–198), when Antiochus III (r. 223–187) took advantage of a period of weakness in *Egypt and reconquered Palestine. His success was short-lived, however, for during the next decade the Romans repelled his advances into Greece and defeated him at Magnesia (190). Two years later, *Rome forced him to dismantle his army according to the provisions of the Treaty of Apamea (188). Seleucid prestige suffered further in 169, when Rome once again forced Antiochus IV (r. 175–164) to retreat unceremoniously from Egypt.

This humiliating defeat coincided with a rebellion in *Jerusalem that led Antiochus to institute a number of oppressive measures against the Jews: These events have been detailed in sources such as *Daniel, 1 and 2 *Maccabees, and *Josephus. During Antiochus's Egyptian campaign, Jerusalem fell into rebellion as Jason and Menelaus, rival claimants to the high *priesthood, jostled with one another for power. Antiochus responded by entering the city in 168 to quell the unrest by force. His relationship with the Jews apparently deteriorated, prompting him to station a garrison in the city as a show of force. Tensions mounted as Antiochus instituted a series of decrees that prevented the Jews from *worshiping, abolished their observance of the *Sabbath and *circumcision, and banned them from possessing the *Torah. He also dedicated the *Temple to Zeus Olympius (the "abomination of desolation") and compelled Jews to participate in Greek religious festivals. The ensuing Maccabean revolt culminated in the restoration of the Temple in 164 and the emergence of Jewish autonomy under the *Hasmonean dynasty (142–37).

Conflicts with the Parthians and Romans and internal dynastic struggles contributed to the contraction of the kingdom's territory in subsequent years. In 129 the Parthians conquered *Mesopotamia, leaving the Seleucids with little more than Syria. Thereafter, political factionalism accelerated the Seleucids' decline, culminating in Pompey's reorganization of Syria into a Roman province in 64 BCE.   DAVID M. REIS

Sepharad, Sephardim (adj. Sephardi, Sephardic). Sepharad is a biblical place name (Obadiah 20) that medieval Jews applied to their communities in the Iberian Peninsula (Spain and Portugal) and to the culture they created. After the expulsion of Spanish Jews in 1492 and the forced conversion of Portuguese Jews in 1497, Sephardim spread throughout the Mediterranean world, taking their distinctive traditions and vernacular language *Ladino with them. See *CONVERSOS*; SPAIN entries. **Maps 6, 9**

Septuagint is the translation of the Hebrew *Bible into Greek. *Septuaginta* means "seventy" in Latin (LXX), and this name derives from the tradition that the very first Greek translation of the *Torah (*Pentateuch) was said to have been translated by seventy-two elders, six from each tribe. This number was subsequently rounded off to seventy. The story of the miraculous creation of the translation (thirty-six pairs of translators working in separate cells yet producing identical renderings in seventy-two days) is first presented in the Jewish *Hellenistic *Letter of* *Aristeas* § 301–7 (second or first century BCE) and expanded in later sources, especially Epiphanius, *On Weights and Measures* (fourth century CE). The tradition preserved in *rabbinic literature, especially *Soferim* 1:5, of there being five translators of the Torah, one for each book, is more realistic than that of seventy-two (or seventy) translators.

NATURE AND CONTENT: The translation of the Torah into Greek was soon followed by translations of the other books of Hebrew Scripture. However, the first translation was so dominant that its name was ultimately attached to these other translations as well. The various translations differ greatly among themselves, and the name "LXX" ultimately came to designate a group of many translations of different natures that represent different approaches and were produced at different times. Most passages reflect the original Greek translations (the "Old Greek"), but some reflect later revisions.

The Septuagint contains Greek versions of all the books of Hebrew Scripture (the Hebrew canon). In addition, it contains Greek versions of Hebrew books such as Baruch and the *Wisdom of Ben Sira that were not included in the canon of Hebrew Scripture. It also includes writings originally written in Greek (e.g., 2–4 *Maccabees), so that the LXX is more than just a collection of translated works. All of these Greek books, most of them translations from *Hebrew and *Aramaic, were accepted as authoritative (sacred) by the Alexandrian Jewish community. Subsequently, all the books of Greek Scripture that are not included in the canon of the Hebrew Bible were rejected by traditional Judaism and are therefore traditionally named *sefarim hitzoniyim* (outside books) or *Apocrypha (the hidden books).

The books in the LXX are arranged differently from their position in the Hebrew Bible, in which the three large divisions are Torah, *Prophets, *Writings. In contrast, the books of Greek Scripture are arranged according to their content: Torah and historical books, books of poetry and wisdom, and prophetical books. Within each group, the sequence of the books differs from Hebrew Scripture. For example, in Greek Scripture, *Ruth (one of the *Five Scrolls, included among the Writings in Hebrew Scripture) follows the book of *Judges because its story took place "in the days of the Judges" (Ruth 1:1). Often the names of the books differ from their counterparts in Hebrew Scripture as well (e.g., 1 and 2 Samuel and 1 and 2 Kings are named 1–4 Kingdoms in the LXX).

DOCUMENTATION: The LXX is known from ancient leather and papyrus scrolls and codices, among them several early copies found among the *Dead Sea Scrolls. The most reliable complete texts of the LXX are the codices B (Vaticanus), A (Alexandrinus), and S (Sinaiticus), from the fourth to fifth centuries CE.

DATE: According to the *Letter of Aristeas*, *Ptolemy II Philadelphus (r. 285–246 BCE) initiated the translation of the Torah. This date is probably correct, whereas most other details in this document may be fictive. The translations of the Prophets and Writings were completed by the middle of the first century BCE. The grandson of Ben Sira knew the translation of the Prophets and part of the Writings in 132 or 116 BCE, according to different computations of the date of his Greek translation of the Wisdom of Ben Sira.

ORIGIN: The *Letter of Aristeas*, rabbinic literature, and various additional sources describe the Jewish origin of the LXX; its terminology and exegesis reflect its Jewish nature. However, the LXX often differs from the Hebrew text that was current in the Land of Israel from the second to first centuries BCE onward and that was later to become the *Masoretic text. These differences were not to the liking of the circles of the *Pharisees, and soon a trend developed to replace the LXX with new translations. These new translations adapted the Old Greek translation to the Hebrew text then current in the Land of Israel.

Jewish dislike of the LXX became stronger when the Greek writings of early *Christianity (the *New Testament [NT]) based themselves, quite naturally, on the LXX. The LXX influenced the NT at various levels. At an early stage, the belief developed that this translation was divinely inspired and hence the way was open for several *Church Fathers to claim that the LXX reflected the words of God more precisely than did the Hebrew Bible. Western Christianity held to the LXX as revealed scripture until it was replaced by the Vulgate translation produced by the Church Father Jerome (ca. 400 CE). In the Russian and Greek Orthodox churches, the LXX is still considered sacred.

BACKGROUND: Many renderings reflect the cultural environment of the translators, who came from both Palestinian and *Egyptian societies. When analyzing individual renderings, the translators' focus is on their linguistic and exegetical background and on the ideas behind them.

The translators often added their own religious convictions to verses in the Hebrew Bible. In several places, they interpreted the context as referring to the *messiah. In other instances, the translators avoided physical depictions of *God that were sometimes present in the Hebrew original. This phenomenon occurred especially in *Esther and *Proverbs. Probably the most characteristic feature of the book of Esther in the LXX is the addition of a religious background to a book that does not mention God's name in the original.

TEXTUAL AND LITERARY ANALYSIS OF HEBREW SCRIPTURE: The LXX was translated from a Hebrew text that differed, often greatly, from the Masoretic version. This is not surprising, because in antiquity many differing copies of the Hebrew Scripture text were in circulation. Some of these differences are minor, whereas others involve a whole paragraph, chapter, or even book. The contents of all these copies were considered "Scripture."   EMANUEL TOV

Serbia: See BALKANS

Sermons are a genre of oral discourse, usually within the context of the *worship service, in which the speaker crafts a message generally rooted in scriptural readings and bearing resonance to issues of contemporary concern. Although written texts are the best evidence for the sermon in the era before recordings and videotapes, they give little sense of what actual sermons were like. This is because rabbinic leaders in the pre-modern period delivered sermons in the vernacular spoken by their own Jewish communities, but recorded them for posterity in *Hebrew, usually after they had delivered the sermon.

The *New Testament and *rabbinic literature provide abundant evidence for sermons delivered as a regular part of *Sabbath worship. However, rabbinic writings preserve nothing comparable to the texts of sermons delivered by such *Church Fathers as Chrysostom, Augustine, and many other gifted Christian preachers, which were stenographically transcribed during delivery.

The earliest texts of Jewish sermons that were written by an individual preacher date from the thirteenth century. In form they reveal continuity with the homiletical *midrash: Beginning with a verse from the Writings section of the Hebrew *Bible, they discuss various interpretations of the verse before relating it to a verse in the weekly *Torah reading (*parashah*). Frequently a group of verses from the *parashah* are then interpreted so as to highlight a central theme. A new form for the Jewish sermon, influenced by Christian scholastic preaching, can be documented from the late fifteenth century. It begins with one verse from the *Torah reading, followed by a passage from the *Talmud or a *midrash. After an introduction, the body of the sermon usually focuses on a topic suggested by the opening verse. At some point, the rabbinic passage is shown to relate unexpectedly to the verse and the topic. This structure became dominant among the *Sephardic communities of the Mediterranean basin and later in northern Europe.

A different structure was common in the *Ashkenazi communities of northern and *Eastern Europe. Here, the sermon established a chain of connections in which one biblical verse or rabbinic passage led by association to another, which led to a third, and so forth. Here the goal often seemed more to demonstrate the knowledge and intellectual rigor of the preacher than to investigate a specific topic.

For Jewish preachers before the nineteenth century, commentary on biblical and rabbinic texts was paramount, and novelty of interpretation was highly valued. One striking homiletical technique was to problematize the classical text by raising a series of difficulties or "doubts" associated with it, before resolving all of the problems in an ingenious new way. Preachers influenced by philosophy interpreted the classical texts in accordance with their own intellectual commitments, often presenting familiar narratives as allegories of philosophical truths. As *festivals approached, sermons generally treated the legal and ritual requirements for proper observance, as well as the spiritual message of the occasions. The Sabbath preceding *Passover provided an opportunity for the preacher to review the complex laws of removing all inappropriate foods from the house; the sermon on the Sabbath before *Yom Kippur was devoted to a discussion of the complexities of *repentance and *atonement.

Sermons also accompanied *life-cycle events: *circumcision of a son, *marriage, and *death. Eulogies, an especially important preaching occasion, provide evidence for attitudes about death and the *afterlife (including reincarnation), as well as information about the individual being mourned. One role of the preacher was to rebuke the congregation for its religious failures, a tradition rooted in the biblical prophets (see BIBLE: PROPHETS AND PROPHECY). The challenge in the sermon of rebuke was to criticize the listeners in a manner that would not counterproductively turn them away from the preacher and his message.

The parable or exemplum, a fixture of Jewish discourse from biblical times, was an effective component of Jewish homiletics. Elaborate narratives from non-Jewish literature were occasionally mobilized for stunning rhetorical effect. Jacob Kranz (1741–1804), the Maggid of Dubno, was a preacher renowned for his ability to create parables to illustrate the most challenging points.

Beginning in the early nineteenth century, significant changes in the status of European Jewish communities and new movements within those communities resulted in a different style of Jewish preaching. Although the sermon was still usually anchored in a biblical text, the center of gravity shifted from exegesis to the elucidation of a religious theme.

With the greater integration of Jews into their surrounding society, new occasions for Jewish preaching arose, including the coronation or death of a monarch; government-proclaimed days of prayer or thanksgiving; the beginning of a war, a decisive battle, and the termination of conflict; and the passing of important new legislation. On some of these occasions Gentile dignitaries and other members of the non-Jewish community might be in attendance. Texts of these topical sermons were sometimes published in pamphlet form for wide distribution.

The late nineteenth and early twentieth centuries witnessed a flourishing of Jewish homiletical oratory. In many American congregations, Sunday morning weekday services and Friday evening Sabbath services became the primary preaching occasions, with the shorter liturgy allowing more time for the sermon. Jewish preachers frequently discussed controversial social issues both of specifically Jewish concern (*Judaism, Reform *Zionism) and of wider interest (rights of workers, capital punishment, war and peace). Many preachers attracted worshipers to the synagogue, and excellent preaching skills were considered a highly important qualification of an effective rabbi. The number of printed volumes of collected sermons expanded dramatically during this era.

In recent decades, the prestige of the sermon appears to have diminished significantly, with a preference for informal presentations inviting congregational response. Similarly, the time allotted to the sermon has diminished from generation to generation. Yet a new generation of women rabbis (see RABBINIC ORDINATION OF WOMEN) has breathed new life into the genre. It is unclear whether this will be sufficient to generate a renaissance of the sermon.

For surveys and representative examples of Jewish sermons from the High Middle Ages to the present, see M. Saperstein, *Jewish Preaching 1200–1800* (1989); idem, *"Your Voice Like a Ram's Horn": Themes and Texts in Traditional Jewish Preaching* (1996); idem, *Exile in Amsterdam: Saul Levi Morteira's Sermons to a Congregation of "New Jews"* (2003); and idem, *Jewish Preaching in Times of War: 1800–2001* (2008).

MARC SAPERSTEIN

Shabbat Ha-Gadol (GREAT SABBATH) refers to the *Sabbath directly preceding *Passover. One possible reason for its special designation is that the *haftarah* read on that day speaks of the "the awesome [*gadol*], fearful day of the Lord" (*Malachi 3:23) when the *messiah will appear. Another suggestion is that the Israelites fulfilled God's orders to have each Jewish household select a lamb (an animal worshiped by the Egyptians) to be used in the paschal sacrifice on the Sabbath before the exodus from *Egypt on the 14th of Nissan. The decision to make this sacrifice was the Israelites' first initiative as a liberated people. A third possibility is that in many communities the rabbi gives a lengthy sermon on *Shabbat ha-Gadol*, perhaps the grandest of the year, to discuss the many laws and practices of the *festival.

PAUL STEINBERG

Shabbetai Zevi (1626–1676) was the most notorious Jewish messianic claimant in the Early Modern period. Born in the bustling commercial city of Smyrna (present-day Izmir) on the western coast of the *Ottoman Empire (what is now *Turkey), he first declared himself the *messiah in 1648, shortly before his twenty-second birthday. However, only in the spring of 1665, when he was proclaimed messiah in Gaza by the brilliant young kabbalist Nathan Ashkenazi (also known as Nathan of Gaza), did people begin to pay attention.

Through the autumn and winter of 1665–66, the news of imminent *redemption swept the Jewish *Diaspora. From London to *Yemen, from *North Africa to *Poland, Jews of all ages and both sexes went into convulsions of penitence and "prophecy," saw visions of Shabbetai Zevi enthroned in heaven, sold their goods, and packed provisions for their voyage to the Holy Land. They recited public prayers for the newly revealed king; fasts mourning the destruction of the *Temple were abolished by rabbinic decree; and edition after edition of Nathan of Gaza's penitential liturgies rolled off the Hebrew presses. At the end of 1665, Zevi set sail for Constantinople, expecting to receive homage and a crown from the Ottoman sultan.

Instead, Shabbetai Zevi was arrested on landing. The authorities kept him for months in cushioned imprisonment in the fortress of Gallipoli where he comported himself as monarch, issuing proclamations and "decrees" and giving audiences to visitors from all over the Diaspora. In September 1666, he was abruptly summoned to Adrianople to appear before Sultan Mehmed IV. Presumably given the choice between conversion to *Islam or death, he chose Islam. He left the sultan's presence on September 16, wearing the turban that was Muslim headgear, his name changed to "Mehmed Effendi."

As news of his conversion spread, believers only slowly abandoned their faith. Many made excuses: They explained that "donning the turban" was not apostasy but assumption of royal power, or it was the messiah's destiny to become an apostate, thereby taking on himself the archaic sins of the Jewish people, or his apostasy was an act of *kabbalistic *tikkun* (mending), a descent into the regions of darkness to retrieve the divine "sparks" buried there (see KABBALAH, LURIANIC). Zevi himself, now a salaried functionary of the Ottoman court, continued to behave as the Jewish messiah, alternating Jewish rituals with Qur'anic recitations and proposing to convert the Jews to Islam through disputation

with his rabbinic followers. The sultan, growing tired at last of these interfaith antics, banished him at the beginning of 1673 to a remote spot on the Adriatic coast. There he died on *Yom Kippur, 1676.

The enigma of Shabbetai Zevi remains: How did this weak, self-absorbed, severely disturbed man – scholars like Gershom *Scholem have convincingly diagnosed him as suffering from bipolar (manic-depressive) disorder – command the allegiance and enthusiasm of otherwise sensible men and women from all over the Jewish world? There is probably no one key that will unlock this mystery. Yet part of his appeal certainly lay in his implied promise, made explicit in the sectarian activity that followed his death (see FRANK, JACOB AND FRANKISM; SABBATEANISM [OTTOMAN EMPIRE AND TURKEY]), to redeem Judaism not only from the yoke of Gentile rule but also from the shackles of its own religious law (see ANTINOMIANISM). Surely this man *must* be the messiah, argued Abraham Cardozo, one of his followers; if he were not, he would be too great a sinner for the world to endure.

The classic account is G. Scholem, *Sabbatai Sevi: The Mystical Messiah* (1973). Recent studies include M. Goldish, *The Sabbatian Prophets* (2004); and D. J. Halperin, *Sabbatai Zevi: Testimonies to a Fallen Messiah* (2007), who provides annotated translations of primary sources.

DAVID J. HALPERIN

Sharansky, Nathan (b. 1948 as Anatoly Borisovich Scharansky) was a human rights activist and a prisoner of conscience in the *Soviet Union and, as a resident of *Israel since 1986, was elected Chairman of the Executive of the Jewish Agency for Israel in June 2009.

A native of Donetsk, Soviet Union (now *Ukraine), Sharansky graduated from the Moscow Institute of Physics and Technology with a degree in computer science. After being denied a visa to Israel in 1973, he gained recognition as a spokesperson for Soviet Jewry and the Moscow Helsinki Watch Group. He was arrested in 1977, convicted in 1978 of treason and spying on behalf of the United States, and sentenced to thirteen years imprisonment and forced labor. His wife Avital organized a campaign for his release that gained international attention (see SOVIET UNION: JEWISH MOVEMENT, 1967–1989).

Sharansky was released in 1986 in exchange for two Soviet spies and immigrated to Israel. He was elected president of the Zionist Forum, an organization of former Soviet activist groups, in 1988. In 1995 he created *Yisrael B'Aliyah*, a political party devoted to helping Israel absorb Soviet immigrants. *Yisrael B'Aliyah* won seven Knesset seats in 1996, and Sharansky became minister of industry and trade. He served as minister of the interior from 1999 to 2000 and as minister of housing and construction and deputy prime minister from 2001 to 2003. In early 2003, his party merged with *Likud* (see ISRAEL, STATE OF: POLITICAL PARTIES), and Sharansky was given ministerial responsibilities for *Jerusalem and *Diaspora affairs. He resigned from government service in May 2005 in opposition to Ariel *Sharon's removal of Jewish settlements from Gaza. Since 2009, Sharansky has served as the Chairman of the Jewish Agency for Israel. Sharansky's books include the *memoir, *Fear No Evil* (1988); *The Case For Democracy: The Power of Freedom to Overcome Tyranny and Terror* (2006), co-written with Ron Dermer; and

Defending Identity: Its Indispensable Role in Protecting Democracy (2008).   ELIZABETH SHULMAN

Sharon, Ariel (b. Ariel Scheinermann in 1928) was the eleventh prime minister of the State of Israel, serving from March 2001 to April 2006. He suffered a severe stroke on January 4, 2006, from which he has never recovered.

Sharon spent more than thirty years in the Israeli military (see ISRAEL, STATE OF: MILITARY AND PARAMILITARY BODIES); he was appointed head of the Northern Command Staff in 1964, head of the Army Training Department in 1966, and head of the Southern Command Staff in 1969. During these years, he also earned a law degree from Hebrew University (1962). Sharon resigned from the army in 1972, but was recalled to service during the 1973 Yom Kippur War (see ISRAEL, ARAB-ISRAELI CONFLICT). Elected to the Knesset that same year, he resigned to serve as security advisor to Prime Minister Yitzhak *Rabin in 1975. Elected to the Knesset again in 1977, he served as minister of agriculture from 1977 to 1981 in Menahem *Begin's government. In 1981 he was appointed defense minister, but resigned in 1983 after Israel's Kahan Commission found him indirectly responsible for the massacres of Palestinians in the Sabra and Shatila refugee camps in Lebanon. His numerous governmental positions in the 1990s included minister of national infrastructure in 1996 and foreign minister in 1998. Sharon became Likud party leader after the resignation of Benjamin Netanyahu in 1999, and he was elected prime minister in a special election held on February 6, 2001. His disengagement plan, which called for Israeli troops and settlers to withdraw from the Gaza Strip, caused a rift in the Likud Party and prompted Sharon to leave Likud and form the Kadima party in November 2005 (see ISRAEL, STATE OF: POLITICAL PARTIES). The platform of the new party stressed peace with the Palestinians, security for Israel, and dismantling of terrorist groups.   ELIZABETH SHULMAN

Shaving. The *Bible prohibits shaving "the corners of one's beard" (Lev 19:27). However, *rabbinic literature sanctions the use of depilatories and cutting off the hair of the face with a scissor action as long as the blade does not touch the face. Nonetheless, throughout much of Jewish history, a beard was seen as a sign of authority and maturity. The image of the rabbi or scholar was always one that included a bearded face. In addition, not shaving is one of the requirements of the mourning process (see DEATH AND MOURNING). Therefore, after the loss of a close relative or during the parts of the *calendar that commemorate sad events in Jewish history, many men have the custom of not shaving.
                                                    BARRY FREUNDEL

Shavuot (literally, "Weeks") is one of the three pilgrimage *festivals. It falls on the 6th of *Sivan (May or June). The *Torah refers to Shavuot in three ways: *Hag Ha-Katzir* (Feast of the Harvest; Exod 23:16), a reminder of when two special loaves of bread made from the newly cut wheat would be offered at the *Temple; *Yom* (or *Hag*) *Ha-Bikkurim* (Feast of the First Fruits), when Israelites were to bring a Temple offering of new crops of any of the *shivat minim* (seven species; Num 28:26); and *Hag Ha-Shavuot* (Feast of Weeks; Deut 16:10), because Shavuot is the culmination of counting seven weeks after bringing the *omer* (an offering of sheaves of grain).

During the time of the Second *Temple, the *Sadducees and the *Pharisees debated the exact date to celebrate Shavuot. The argument concerned an ambiguity in Leviticus 23:15–16 about when to begin counting the *omer* (see OMER, COUNTING OF). The Sadducees argued that counting should begin the day after the Sunday after the first night of *Passover. The Pharisees, whose interpretation was ultimately accepted, contended that the counting should begin on the second day of Passover. Simultaneously, the Rabbis were debating exactly when the Torah was revealed. After centuries of discussion, the 6th of Sivan was celebrated as both Shavuot and the day on which the *Torah was given, *Zeman Matan Torateinu* (Season of the Giving of our Torah).

Shavuot observances follow those of festivals, including restrictions from work. Orthodox and Conservative Jews outside the Land of Israel traditionally observe the diasporic two-day extension of sacred days and therefore observe two days of Shavuot; Reform Jews observe Shavuot for one day (see entries under JUDAISM). The *Torah reading for the day is the *Ten Commandments. The book of *Ruth is also read in synagogue (on the second day in the *Diaspora) because it connects to themes of the harvest and accepting faith in Torah, and because Ruth is the great-grandmother of King *David whom, the Rabbis say, was born and died on Shavuot.

*Customs unique to Shavuot include decorating the home and *synagogue with flowers and greenery. This custom may originate from bringing *bikkurim* (first fruits) to the Temple as offerings or in remembrance of the lush description of Mount Sinai at the time the Torah was given (Exod 34:3). Another custom is *Tikkun Leil Shavuot* (Set Order of Study for the Night of Shavuot), which is an all-night study session developed by mystics (see KABBALAH). The *tikkun* is meant to inspire a sense of restless anticipation on the night preceding the giving of the Torah. Eating dairy products is also a Shavuot custom, likely as a demonstration of self-control, as manifested in Torah laws, especially the *dietary laws.

For further reading, see P. Steinberg, *Celebrating the Jewish Year: The Spring and Summer Holidays* (2009); I. Greenberg, *The Jewish Way: Living the Holidays* (1993); P. Goodman, *The Shavuot Anthology* (1992); and I. Klein, *A Guide to Religious Jewish Practice* (1979).   PAUL STEINBERG

Shechem (Tell Balâtah), a biblical city of refuge, is located in the Central Highlands within the territory of Ephraim (Josh 20:7, 21:21). It sits astride a major trade route between Mt. Ebal and Mt. Gerizim, 67 kilometers (40 miles) north of *Jerusalem. Its strategic location and proximity to fertile land ensured its importance throughout the Bronze Age. Shechem figures prominently in the *Genesis ancestral narratives. *Abraham (Gen 12:6–7) and *Jacob (Gen 33:18–20) both build altars there. Jacob's sons kill the male inhabitants of Shechem to avenge the rape of their sister *Dinah (Gen 44) by the eponymous prince of the city. There, *Joseph is buried (Josh 24:32). Later, the Shechemites are said to have first supported Gideon's son Abimelech, but later to have turned against him (Judg 9). The story of their revolt includes references to the Temple of El Berith/Baal Berith (also called the Tower of Shechem), undoubtedly the traditional *Canaanite temple that had long stood within the city. After *Solomon's death, his son *Rehoboam goes to Shechem to be acclaimed king (1 Kg 12:1), and soon after Jeroboam declares Shechem the first capital of the northern kingdom of *Israel (1 Kgs 12:25). Its destruction is attributed to the *Assyrians, who conquered Israel in the last quarter of the eighth century BCE. **Map 2**   BETH ALPERT NAKHAI

Sheḥitah. Ritual slaughter. **See** DIETARY LAWS.

Shekhinah. The *Rabbis use the term *Shekhinah* (dwelling or resting) to describe *God's presence or immanence in this world. Although this meaning is absent in the Hebrew *Bible, in *rabbinic literature the *Shekhinah* functions like the biblical *kavod* (glory) that accompanied the Israelites in the desert and rested on the *Tabernacle/ Tent of Meeting (*mishkan, ohel moed*). The Rabbis taught that the *Shekhinah* could be present when Jews behaved righteously, as when scholars studied (M. *Avot* 3:3), when a quorum of men prayed together (BT *Berakhot* 6a), or when husbands and wives engaged in licit sexual relations (BT *Sotah* 17a). The *Shekhinah* protects the weak (BT *Shabbat* 31a), cares for the sick (BT *Shabbat* 12b), and accompanies Israel in exile.

The Rabbis understood the *Shekhinah* as identical with God: the divine power manifest in the terrestrial realm. The *Shekhinah*, like sunshine, suffuses the earth with radiance, but is ontically identical with its guiding force. Some later rabbinic *midrashim*, however, personify the *Shekhinah*, describing it in ways that suggest *gender and ontic independence (among others, *Song of Songs Rabbah* 8:11; *Midrash Proverbs* to 22:28). Whatever the original rabbinic intentions might have been, medieval thinkers were uncomfortable with any intimation of anthropomorphism or of a compromised monotheism. *Philo, the first-century-CE Alexandrian Jewish philosopher, had already allegorized the *Shekhinah* as the *logos* of God. Nearly a millennium later, *Saadia ben Joseph Gaon (d. 942) propounded that God created the *Shekhinah* as a lower glory that would be visible to *prophets. This understanding was adopted by Abraham *ibn Ezra (d. 1167), Judah *Halevi (d. 1141), and *Maimonides (d. 1204).

By contrast, medieval *Kabbalah enlarged on the mythical possibilities inherent in Jewish tradition to articulate a theology of a feminine *Shekhinah*, the female aspect of a male God. These mystics believed that God is both hidden and manifest in our world. The hidden aspect, the *Ein Sof* (without end), lies beyond the realm of human cognition. Ten knowable attributes or *sefirot* flow from this eternal and infinite source. The feminine *Shekhinah* is the final emanation, mediating between heaven and earth and serving as the passive eye or door through which a mystic can achieve divine vision. The popularity of the *Shekhinah* in Kabbalah corresponds to the popularity of the cult of the Virgin Mary among contemporaneous Christians. The need for nurturing female images may be a response to similar theological needs and cultural stimuli.

In the kabbalistic vision, the *Shekhinah* is essential for cosmic homeostasis. Medieval kabbalists believed that all liturgical and ritual acts affect both the terrestrial and heavenly realms. Proper performance of the *commandments unites opposing *sefirot* and enables a divine union that is imagined in overtly sexual terms. Drawing on images from *Proverbs, *Song of Songs, rabbinic *midrashim*, and earlier

Jewish *mysticism, twelfth- and thirteenth-century kabbalists believed that the *Shekhinah* was the divine *bride who united with her spouse, the *sefirah Tiferet*, in a celestial bridal chamber. Halakhically sanctioned physical intercourse between a male mystic and his wife on earth, particularly on *Sabbath eve, was understood as a particularly effective means of fostering both divine and mystical union.

In sixteenth-century *Safed, mystics instituted the *Kabbalat Shabbat* ceremony welcoming the *Sabbath *bride. It was here that Solomon Alkabetz wrote the liturgical poem, *Lekha dodi likrat kallah* (Come my beloved to meet the bride), which has been associated with this ritual ever since. Isaac *Luria further enlarged on human marital union in his kabbalistic system as a means to effect *devekut* (divine union) between the masculine and feminine aspects of God (see KABBALAH, LURIANIC). Moreover, he and his students believed that it was necessary to perform each commandment with the intention (*kavannah*) of uniting God with the *Shekhinah*, as a way to achieve harmony in the cosmos (*tikkun olam*).

Although medieval Jewish mysticism conceived of the *Shekhinah* as feminine, it is important to note that medieval Jewish attitudes about the inferior position of women played a major role in her kabbalistic conceptualization. The *Zohar describes the *Shekhinah* as a passive vessel lacking any distinct personality (1:181a, among other references). Consequently, the *Shekhinah* is like a revolving sword with the potential for both good and evil (*Zohar* 1: 53b, 221b, 242a; 2:27b; 3:19b). When she is described in positive terms, she is often gendered as male, as the *sefirah Malkhut* or David; when she is under the sway of excessive judgment or the demonic "other side," she remains female (see LILITH; SAMAEL; *SEFIROT*).

The feminine *Shekhinah* remains a vibrant religious symbol among many contemporary Jews. *Hasidism adapted earlier mystical understandings of the *Shekhinah* into its theology and practices. Some Jewish feminists have incorporated the *Shekhinah* into Jewish liturgy (see JUDAISM, FEMINIST). The Jewish Renewal movement, founded on aspects of both Hasidism and feminism, emphasizes the role of the *Shekhinah* in *worship and ritual (see JUDAISM: JEWISH RENEWAL). In fact, the enduring symbol of the feminine *Shekhinah* has even crossed religious boundaries and been reconceived in New Age spirituality.

For further reading, see A. Green, "Bride, Spouse, Daughter: Images of the Feminine in Classical Jewish Sources," in *On Being a Jewish Feminist*, ed. S. Heschel (1983); idem, "*Shekhinah*, the Virgin Mary, and the Song of Songs: Reflections on a Kabbalistic Symbol in Its Historical Context," *AJS Review* 26 (2002): 1–52; M. Idel, "Sexual Metaphors and Praxis in the Kabbalah," in *The Jewish Family*, ed. D. Kraemer (1989); S. Koren, "Kabbalistic Physiology: Isaac the Blind, Nahmanides, and Moses de Leon on Menstruation," *AJS Review* 28 (2004): 317–39; idem, "*Shekhinah* as Female Symbol," *Encyclopedia Judaica*, 2nd ed. (2006); P. Schäfer, *Mirror of His Beauty: Feminine Images of God from the Bible to the Early Kabbalah* (2002); G. Scholem, "*Shekhinah*: The Feminine Element in Divinity," in *On the Mystical Shape of the Godhead*, ed. J. Chipman (1991); E. Wolfson, *Through a Speculum That Shines* (1994); and C. Weissler, "The Meanings of the *Shekhinah* in the Jewish Renewal Movement," *Nashim* 10 (2006): 53–83.

SHARON KOREN

Shema, "Hear!" or "Listen!" in Hebrew, refers to Judaism's fundamental profession of belief in and commitment to the unity and uniqueness of *God. The *shema,* often translated, "Hear, O Israel, the Lord our God, the Lord is one" (Deut 6:4), is recited twice daily in Jewish *worship and at other critical moments in a Jew's life.

Shemini Atzeret. This festival, whose name means "the eighth [day] of assembly," takes place on the 22nd of Tishri. It originates in the commandment in Leviticus 23:34 that after the seven days mandated for *Sukkot, "on the eighth day there shall be a holy convocation for you." Shemini Atzeret shares all of the characteristics of Sukkot, excluding the waving of the four species and dwelling in the *sukkah.* Many Jews in the *Diaspora celebrate Shemini Atzeret as the eighth day of Sukkot. In Israel and in Reform Judaism, Shemini Atzeret observance is merged with *Simḥat Torah.

Shevat, the eleventh month of the Jewish calendar, takes place in January and/or February of the Gregorian calendar. *Tu B'Shevat, the new year for trees, is celebrated on the 15th of this month.

Shiloh (Tell Seilûn), an important place of pilgrimage and *worship in the *Canaanite era, continued to serve as a sacred site during the period of *Israelite settlement (1 Sam 1:3). Centrally located in the territory of Ephraim, Shiloh was the place where the Israelites set up their *Tent of Meeting when they came into the promised land (*Josh 18:1). During the era of the *Judges, a sanctuary was constructed at Shiloh, and the *Ark of the Covenant was housed there (1 Sam 4:3–4). Priestly leaders and their families, including Phineas (Josh 22:12–13), Eli (1 Sam 1:10), and *Samuel (1 Sam 3:19–21), and their sons (1 Sam 2:12; 8:1–3) officiated at Shiloh. Israelites worshiped there during the vineyard festival (Judg 21:19–22) and at annual festivals (1 Sam 1:21). In addition, the sanctuary there served people in times of personal need (1 Sam 1:21–28). After *Solomon's construction of the *Jerusalem *Temple, the Shiloh sanctuary is rarely mentioned. However, the prophet Ahijah came from Shiloh to announce *Jeroboam's imminent ascent to *kingship of *Israel (1 Kgs 11:29–32), and mourners came from Shiloh to the site of Temple after its destruction by the *Babylonians (Jer 41:4–5).   BETH ALPERT NAKHAI

Shivah: See DEATH AND MOURNING

Shoah is a Hebrew word that means "sudden disaster" or "catastrophe"; it is often used instead of "*Holocaust" to designate the destruction of European Jewry in World War II. Because the word *shoah* has no ritual implications, it has none of the connotations of willing *martyrdom implicit in the word "holocaust," which in Greek means "a sacrifice (or offering) that is consumed by fire."

Shofar is a musical instrument that may be made from the horn of an antelope, gazelle, goat, or ram, but not from a cow's horn (BT *Rosh Ha-Shanah* 27a); a ram's horn is considered desirable because of its association with Genesis 22 (the *akedah* [binding of Isaac]; BT *Rosh Ha-Shanah* 16a). Biblical citations indicate that the *shofar* was sounded in religious, military, and ceremonial situations. Examples include the *revelation at Mount Sinai (Exod 19:16); the siege of *Jericho (Josh 6); proclamations of *festivals and new moons (see ROSH ḤODESH [Num 10:10; Ps 81:4]); celebrations praising *God (2 Sam 6:15; 1 Chron 15:28; Ps 98:6, 150:3); and the designation of a new king (1 Kgs 1:34).

Details of sounding the *shofar,* distinguishing between the use of long blasts (*tekiah*) and a series of short blasts (*teruah*), appear in Numbers 10:1–10; these blasts were expanded in rabbinic times with the addition of an undulating sound of three broken notes (*shevarim*). Isaiah 27:13 predicts that the sounding of the ram's horn will gather those dispersed in *Assyria and *Egypt and bring them to worship in *Jerusalem; midrashic legends associate the sound of the *shofar* with messianic *redemption and the *resurrection of the dead (see **Plate 7**).

In contemporary *worship, the *shofar* is sounded in the synagogue on *Rosh Ha-Shanah, "the first day of the seventh month" (Lev 23:24; Num 29:1), and at the end of the concluding *Ne'ilah* service on *Yom Kippur (Lev 25:9). The *shofar* is sounded only during the day and not on the *Sabbath.   ELIZABETH SHULMAN

Shtetl, the diminutive for *shtot,* "city" in *Yiddish, is a Jewish designation for towns in *Eastern Europe with significant Jewish populations. Although Jews often did not constitute the majority of the population in any given town, in Jewish minds, the *shtetl* was a distinctly Jewish entity. *Shtetls* (or *shtetlakh*), which ranged in size from a few hundred inhabitants to forty or fifty thousand, occupied a place between rural villages and cities. They were local economic centers whose markets drew peasants from the surrounding rural areas, as well as smaller numbers of Jewish farmers. Within the *shtetl,* Jews worked in a wide range of crafts and occupations; some Jews went out into the countryside to work in various capacities during the week, returning to the *shtetl* for the *Sabbath.

Shtetls developed in response to specific social, economic, and political circumstances in *Poland. In the late 1500s and early 1600s, Jews were encouraged to move from more central areas to underdeveloped areas in the east and south that Poland had gained in 1569 when it formed a union with *Lithuania. The powerful nobility owned vast estates and wished to profit from their natural resources. To foster economic development, they sought colonizers to whom they could entrust the management of these lands, and Jews, whose lack of political power meant they offered no potential threat, fit the bill. In exchange for taxes and fees, Jews received protection and were made managers and agents for absentee landlords. They served as tax collectors and leaseholders for all sources of income on these lands, such as tolls, mills, and fishing ponds. One major area of Jewish activity was in the manufacture and sale of alcohol, in which Jews played such a central role that the image of the Jew as tavern keeper became fixed in East European culture. The control Jews were granted over so many aspects of the lives of the peasantry contributed significantly to ethnic and religious tensions.

Jews in the *shtetls* were granted the right to self-rule, as long as the *kahal, their autonomous *community organization, paid the government the required taxes and filled conscription quotas. Running the *kahal* were wealthier members of the community; in this hierarchical society, women (see WOMEN: EASTERN EUROPE), the poor, single men, and the minimally literate had no political voice. The *kahal* ran the Jewish *court system, collected taxes, oversaw Jewish communal institutions, and hired people to fulfill the community's religious and administrative needs. Along with ritual slaughterers (see DIETARY LAWS), *cantors, and other functionaries, they hired a communal *rabbi. All the institutions needed for Jewish communal and religious life existed in the *shtetl*, including a *mikveh (ritual bath), *cemetery, *synagogue, and study house. Many social welfare organizations (*ḥevras*) engaged in providing for the needy – dowries for poor brides, helping the ill and their families, proper burial for the dead – while others served as settings for study and socializing.

Shtetls had mixed populations, but Jews generally constituted the majority. Some *shtetls*, such as mid-nineteenth-century Berdichev, were as much as 90% Jewish. Jews and non-Jews lived in separate areas of town, with Jews generally living close to the central marketplace. Jews and non-Jews interacted mainly, although not exclusively, through commercial dealings. Although linguistic barriers tended to limit interactions, the many Slavic words that worked their way into *Yiddish are an indication of the cross-cultural influences that developed. Some close personal relationships formed between Jews and non-Jews, but it was also not uncommon for violence to be directed at Jews, from small local attacks to large-scale *pogroms.

The number of *shtetls* in Poland increased significantly in the course of the seventeenth century and into the eighteenth century. By the second half of the eighteenth century, more than half of the Jewish population lived in hundreds of private towns owned by the Polish nobility. In the late 1700s, Poland was conquered and partitioned by its neighbors – Austria (see HABSBURG EMPIRE), Prussia (see GERMANY), and *Russia. Most *shtetls* were concentrated in a region that passed into the control of *Russia, which, for nearly three centuries, had forbidden Jewish residence within its boundaries. The tsars dealt with this new "Jewish problem" by establishing the *Pale of Settlement, restricting Jewish residence to these newly acquired "western borderlands." Although Jews would only be allowed to live outside of the Pale under specific circumstances until the time of the 1917 Russian Revolution, the *shtetls* themselves were not areas of confinement like the *ghettos of early modern Western Europe.

Many socioeconomic changes in the nineteenth century, including a growing Jewish movement to urban centers, began to erode *shtetl* life, particularly in former areas of Poland that were now part of the *Austro-Hungarian Empire and Germany. Although the Russian government abolished the *kahal* in 1844, Jewish communal self-government existed until the 1917 Russian Revolution. In the period after World War I, modernization changed *shtetl* life in many ways as new political movements, such as *Zionism, made inroads and as younger people left for cities. Nevertheless, much of the traditional *shtetl* world endured until it was effectively destroyed by the *Nazis during World War II.

A popular nostalgia for the traditional world of the *shtetl* began as early as the late nineteenth century, as modernization began to encroach on East European Jewish life in the many forms of the *Haskalah* (Jewish enlightenment movement). This nostalgia was expressed in Hebrew and Yiddish literature that was, itself, part of the change, such as the writings of Mendele Mokher Seforim and Sholem Aleichem

(see LITERATURE, YIDDISH). That nostalgia continues to color contemporary understandings of the *shtetl*, as seen in popular novels and in theatrical and film productions such as *Fiddler on the Roof* and *Yentl*.

Recent research includes M. Stanislawski, "Kahal," in *The YIVO Encyclopedia of Jews in Eastern Europe* (2008); D. Assaf, ed., *Journey to a 19th Century Shtetl: The Memoirs of Yekhezkel Kotik* (2008); I. Bartal, *The Jews of Eastern Europe, 1772–1881* (2006); Y. Eliach, *There Once Was a World: A 900-Year Chronicle of the Shtetl of Eishyshok* (1999); S. Kassow, "Shtetl," in *The YIVO Encyclopedia of Jews in Eastern Europe* (2008); G. D. Hundert, *The Jews in a Polish Private Town* (1992); and S. Zipperstein, *Imagining Russian Jewry* (1999).   LISA COHEN

Shulḥan Arukh (Set Table) is a codification of Jewish law prepared by Joseph *Karo in sixteenth-century *Safed. The *Shulḥan Arukh*, which was intended as a summary for popular use of Karo's *Beit Yosef*, an encyclopedic work on Jewish law, became authoritative both in the *Sephardic world and, with the additional notes provided by Moses *Isserles in his *Mappah* (Tablecloth), in the *Ashkenazic world as well. **See also HALAKHAH.**

Sibylline Oracles. The sibyl was a legendary Greek prophetess, known for prophecies of doom. Beginning in the second century BCE, Jews composed oracles in the name of the sibyl, praising *Judaism and predicting doom on their enemies. The standard collection contains twelve books. Part of Book 3 was composed in *Egypt in the second century BCE, under *Ptolemy VI Philometor. It predicts prosperity for the Jews in the reign of the seventh king of Egypt from the line of the Greeks. The fourth book, dated to the late first century CE, divides history into four kingdoms and ten generations and predicts cosmic destruction and *resurrection. It advocates baptism as a penitential ritual and is thought to come from *Syria. The fifth book, from Egypt, has bitter recriminations against *Rome for the destruction of the Second *Temple. There is also Jewish material in other books, but it has been reworked by *Christians. For further information, see J. J. Collins, "Sibylline Oracles," in *The Old Testament Pseudepigrapha*, ed. J. H. Charlesworth (1983), 1: 317–472; **see also PSEUDEPIGRAPHA.**   JOHN J. COLLINS

Sicily. Jews lived in Sicily for more than a millennium, for the most part in a state of *convivenza* (coexistence) with their Gentile neighbors, except toward the end, under Aragonese-*Spanish rule. The main cause for the change was the Catholic Church, chiefly the mendicant friars, whose conversionary sermons and rabble-rousing preaching resulted in persecution and massacre.

The early history and antecedents of the Jewish presence in Sicily, like that of most other Jewish settlements in Europe, are shrouded in myth and legend. It is generally assumed that Jews first settled on the island in the first century of the Christian era, but no hard documentary evidence has come to light so far to support this. The first piece of concrete and reliable evidence is a Latin epitaph on a tombstone in Catania, dated 383. Except for a few letters of Pope Gregory the Great, there is little information on the Jewish community until the Muslim conquest of the island in the ninth century (see ISLAM AND JUDAISM).

Sicilian Jewry became absorbed into the Muslim-Mediterranean world, which stretched from the Middle East and beyond to *Arabia and *India in the east, to *Spain in the west, and encompassing *North Africa from Morocco to *Egypt. The letters of Jewish traders in the Cairo *Genizah shed light on this chapter of Jewish history, providing information on shipping and ship movements in the Mediterranean and on trade with North Africa, Italy, Spain, and *Byzantium. Some of these merchants even ventured as far as Arabia, Aden, and *India.

With the Norman conquest of Sicily (1061–91), the island returned to Christian rule. However, it was not until the Aragonese conquest that the Jewish population was seriously affected. The Catholic Church undermined the position of the Jews in Sicily, and the Spanish rulers exported to Sicily some of their policies toward the Jews. All the same, relations between Jews and Christians appear to have been at times cordial and at other times at least tolerable. There existed no compulsory separate Jewish quarters, only voluntary ones such as the *Cassaro* in Palermo. Yet even in those areas, Christians lived intermingled with Jews.

Jews in Sicily were citizens and suffered from relatively few disabilities, particularly in the economic sphere where they engaged in agriculture and industry, trade, and *commerce, including international trade and shipping, as well as in most professions, which in turn enhanced their social status. There were an unusual number of craftsmen and physicians among the Jews. However, the majority were laborers, on the land and in town. In the fifteenth century the Sicilian Jewish population reached 25,000 or thereabouts, more than half of all Italian Jewry (see ITALY). All of this came to a sudden end with the expulsion order issued by Spain's monarchs in 1492 that affected the Jews of Sicily as well as those of the Iberian Peninsula (see SPAIN, CHRISTIAN). Some 80% of the Jews went into exile, whereas the remainder converted to Catholicism, only to be caught in the net of the Spanish *Inquisition.   SHLOMO SIMONSOHN

Siddur (pl. *siddurim*; also sometimes *seder/sedarim*) comes from the Hebrew for "order" and refers to a prayer book. Generally, although not always, the term refers to the order of prayers for weekdays and *Sabbaths. See also *MAHZOR*; PRAYER BOOKS; WORSHIP.

Silver, Abba Hillel (1893–1963) was a Lithuanian-born American *Zionist leader. Despite his *Orthodox background, Silver attended *Hebrew Union College in Cincinnati, Ohio, where he was ordained a Reform rabbi (see JUDAISM, REFORM: NORTH AMERICA) and received a doctorate. In 1917, with his appointment as rabbi of Tiferet Israel, an important Reform congregation in Cleveland, Ohio, he entered Jewish public life. He became chairman of the Zionist Emergency Committee and, in 1945, president of the Zionist Organization of America. As one of the three leaders of the Zionist movement after its 22nd Congress, he set forth the Zionist position during the discussions preceding the 1947 United Nations Partition Resolution (see ISRAEL, STATE OF: FOUNDING). Silver's rise to leadership in the 1940s and 1950s, a critical period for Jewish existence in modern times, constituted a significant change in American Zionism and the American Jewish community.

Silver created a new model for American ethnic politics. He welded broad sectors of American Jewry into a political force struggling to establish a Jewish state, and he himself made a critical contribution toward that goal. Contemporaries described Silver as a stubborn, charismatic, proud, and militant leader. He identified with the Republican Party, but opposed the Cold War; he struggled for individual rights, social justice, and freedom of speech and acted to combat unemployment and in support of workers' rights. With the 1948 establishment of the State of *Israel, Prime Minister David *Ben-Gurion, a long-standing rival, ousted Silver from most of his official positions in the Zionist movement and the Jewish Agency. Recent research includes a special issue of the *Journal of Israeli History* 17:1 (1996) and Z. Segev, "The Jewish State in Abba Hillel Silver's Overall World View," *American Jewish Archives* 56 (2004): 94–127.
                                                                                          ZOHAR SEGEV

Simhat Bat (joy of a daughter) is an evolving ritual to celebrate the birth of a daughter and her entry into the *covenant between God and the Jewish people. A *simhat bat*, like the *zeved ha-bat* (gift of a daughter) ritual performed in *Sephardic communities, is an opportunity to welcome, name, and bless a new daughter among family members and friends. Unlike the ritual *circumcision (*berit milah*) on the eighth day of life initiating male infants into the community, Judaism has not previously had a ritual to celebrate the birth of a daughter, and a variety of contemporary liturgies have been developed. These ceremonies may take place at home or in the synagogue. For further reading, see A. Diamant, *The New Jewish Baby Book* (2005); see also LIFE-CYCLE RITUALS.   JUDITH R. BASKIN

Simhat Torah (literally, joy of the Torah). This *festival is observed on the 23rd of Tishri, the day after *Shemini Atzeret, by many Jews in the *Diaspora. In most Reform congregations (see JUDAISM, REFORM: NORTH AMERICA) and in *Israel, Simhat Torah and Shemini Atzeret observances are combined and take place on the 22nd of Tishri, immediately following the conclusion of the seven days of *Sukkot. Simhat Torah celebrates the completion and recommencement of the yearly cycle of public *Torah reading. The festival is derived from *Deuteronomy's injunction to read portions of the *Torah publicly (31:9–13). The joyous celebration begins in the evening when the final Torah portion is read in the *synagogue; this reading is followed by seven *hakafot* (circuits) with Torah scrolls around the synagogue sanctuary accompanied by dancing and singing. The following morning, the final portion of Deuteronomy and the first portion of *Genesis are read; traditionally, the reader of the final section of the Torah is called *hatan Torah* (*bridegroom of the Torah), and the reader of the first section of Genesis is known as *hatan bereshit* (bridegroom of the beginning). Simhat Torah is also a time when some *synagogues offer a special welcome to children beginning their studies (see CONSECRATION). For further reading, see P. Steinberg, *Celebrating the Jewish Year: The Fall Holidays* (2009); and P. Goodman, *The Sukkot/Simchat Torah Anthology* (1988).   PAUL STEINBERG

Sisterhoods: See SYNAGOGUE SISTERHOODS

Sivan is the third month of the Jewish calendar; it is equivalent to May and/or June on the Gregorian calendar. The spring harvest festival of *Shavuot is celebrated on the 6th of Sivan.

Sobibór was a *Nazi death camp located about sixty-five miles northeast of Lublin. Like *Bełżec and *Treblinka, it was established following the 1941 *Aktion Reinhard* directive. The Nazis began the construction of Sobibór in the form of four small camps in March 1942 and opened it the following month. Sobibór III was the site of the three carbon monoxide asphyxiation chambers, mass graves, and the barracks for Jewish slave laborers. Commandant Franz Stangl and his staff murdered 250,000 Jews between April 1942 and September 1943 before transforming the site into a concentration camp. In September 1943 hundreds of Jewish inmates attacked their guards and escaped, although the SS subsequently captured about half of them. Himmler ordered Sobibór closed, and the site was turned into a farm. See HOLOCAUST; HOLOCAUST CAMPS AND KILLING CENTERS; HOLOCAUST RESISTANCE, etc.

DAVID M. CROWE

Social Work: United States. Before the 1880s, when institutionalized social work began to displace traditional modes of relief, American Jewish institutions offered social services to their own communities. The roots of this arrangement lay in American traditions of voluntarism and self-help, Jewish traditions of *philanthropy and mutual obligation, and the hostility and missionary tactics that often greeted Jews when they relied on non-Jewish social services.

The massive immigration of Jews from *Eastern Europe at the beginning of the twentieth century called into question the efficacy of these traditional arrangements; at the same time, charity organization societies and other institutions were emphasizing individualized service, interagency planning, and social reform. A new generation of pre-suffrage, college-educated women extended maternalist notions of women's duty into activist work on behalf of the new urban, immigrant, industrial workers. Among these were many Jewish women, including members of the National Council of Jewish Women (see ORGANIZATIONS, WOMEN'S: NORTH AMERICA), who worked specifically with Jewish immigrants, and *Lillian Wald, who opened the Henry Street Settlement House on *New York City's Lower East Side to provide health care to all local residents. Women and men worked to combat poverty and illness in sectarian and nonsectarian settings. They provided vocational guidance, small loans, direct relief, milk stations, *summer camps, mental health services, elderly care, and orphanages. These involvements often opened the door to other commitments, including public health and peace work, as well as campaigns for the rights of immigrants, labor (see UNITED STATES: LABOR MOVEMENT), women, and civil rights (see UNITED STATES: CIVIL RIGHTS MOVEMENT).

The diversity of the Jewish community in terms of nation of origin, social class, and ideology (including *Zionism) initially made the centralization of Jewish social services impossible. *New York City's Kehilla was a short-lived centralization experiment, which established the School for Jewish Communal Work (1916–19). By 1920, many American Jewish communities had federations, which raised and disbursed funds to various agencies and later led communities in social planning (see ORGANIZATIONS: NORTH AMERICA). Jewish social workers could choose to join Jewish professional societies and contribute to Jewish social work journals and conferences.

In and outside of Jewish social service agencies, American Jews were deeply involved in the transition of social work to a scientifically trained profession, as the field gradually came to rely on specialized experts trained in psychology and casework. During the Depression, a growing cadre of professionals with knowledge of social inequities laid the groundwork for shifting some social welfare responsibilities from religious and ethnic communities to city, state, and federally supported agencies.

Since 1914, overseas aid has also been an important focus of American Jewish social agencies' fundraising and energies. American Jews' experiences with immigration proved crucial to their assistance to displaced victims of *World War II. The Hebrew Immigrant Aid Society (founded in 1881 by East European Jews) and the American Jewish *Joint Distribution Committee (founded in 1914 by Jacob Schiff and other well-established German Jews) provided funds, trained workers, and helped rescue and resettle European Jews.

Within the United States, Jews have wrestled with the question of Jewish content in social work training. The Graduate School of Jewish Social Work, open from 1924–40, combined technical training with Jewish learning. Today, several Jewish-sponsored institutions sponsor social work training schools. Yeshiva University's Wurzweiler School of Social Work recently dropped the word "Jewish" from its *Jewish Social Work Forum* to attract a "more diverse pool of contributors," even as it retained its commitment to reflecting Jewish social work interests. Despite the *secularist pull, sectarian Jewish institutions, with their focus on intracommunal needs, family services, poverty, and refugees (abroad and at home), continue to serve as important focal points of Jewish affiliation and group identity for social workers, board members, donors, and volunteers.

MARJORIE N. FELD

Society for the Promotion of Enlightenment Among the Jews of Russia (OPE). From 1863 until 1929, the Society for the Promotion of Enlightenment Among the Jews of Russia was the only officially recognized, *secular Jewish educational institution in *Russia. During the 1860s, its leaders encouraged Jews to integrate into Russian society; after a dormant period, the movement became revitalized in the 1880s and 1890s, thanks to its expansive educational program. The *Bolsheviks closed it permanently in 1929.

The society was organized by Baron Horace Günzburg and Abram Brodskii, wealthy Jews who viewed themselves as representing the Jewish masses before the tsarist government. Their behind-the-scenes activity appeared to bear fruit during the reign of Alexander II (1856–81), when the government reversed several of the most heinous policies of Nicholas I, including the military recruitment of underaged boys. Alexander II extended new reforms to Jews considered "productive" or "useful," giving Jews of the First Merchant Guild, Jews with diplomas from a Russian institution of higher education, Jewish army veterans, and Jewish artisans with proper certification the right to leave the *Pale of Settlement and take up residence in Russia proper.

The OPE initially devoted most of its budget to scholarships for Jewish university students; it wished to support individuals fluent in Russian, cultivated in the arts and sciences, and therefore worthy of equal rights. The society also subsidized special supplements in the Hebrew newspaper, *ha-Zafirah*. Like many supporters of the *Haskalah* (Jewish enlightenment), early OPE leaders saw *Yiddish as one of the central reasons for the intellectual backwardness of Russia's Jews.

Approved in 1867, the Odessa OPE branch envisioned the total transformation of Jewish society. Eager to attain full integration and equal rights, they put their hopes in a translation of the Hebrew *Bible into Russian, which they hoped would have the same effect in Russia that Moses *Mendelssohn's *Bible translation had had in *Germany. At the same time the Odessa branch tried to satisfy the need for education among Jewish workers by offering unofficial courses. However, the Holy Synod refused to give permission for such a translation, and the government demanded that the branch stop giving instruction in Russian, maintaining that the courses spawned terrorism.

As a result of changes in the government after the attempt on Alexander II's life in 1866, the OPE entered a period of dormancy. Although the government did not shut down the organization entirely, despite Jacob Brafman's recommendation in his infamous *Book of the Kahal* (1868), the Odessa branch did close after the *pogroms in that city in 1871. However, during the 1870s, leaders in *Saint Petersburg kept a low profile, distributing the bulk of their small budget to scholarships.

In its later period, the OPE – active in Odessa, Moscow, Kiev, and Riga, in addition to Saint Petersburg – subsidized private Jewish schools where secular subjects were taught. Because boys attended religious schools, girls made up the majority of students; efforts to support schools with both Jewish and secular curricula were problematic. In 1906, Baron David Günzburg won the right to open a Jewish university, and the OPE opened a teachers' academy in Grodno in 1907; the society also moderated its policy on Yiddish in an effort to educate as many Jews as possible. The numbers of students in OPE schools and programs, although sizable, always remained lower than those in state-sponsored Jewish schools. In 1909, the OPE began publishing a journal devoted to issues of Jewish education in Russia, *The Messenger of the Society for the Promotion of Enlightenment*.

During and after World War I, OPE educated Jewish refugees with government and support from Jewish communities outside Russia. In Soviet times, facing Bolshevik opposition, the few remaining members congregated in the magnificent library in Saint Petersburg; Shaul Ginzburg and Israel Zinberg managed to publish several volumes of articles devoted to Jewish history. In 1929, the Bolsheviks closed the society and divided its archival treasures, giving part to a Jewish scholarly institute in Minsk and part to an institute in Kiev (see BOLSHEVISM: RUSSIAN EMPIRE AND SOVIET UNION).

Recent research on the OPE includes D. Fishman, *The Rise of Modern Yiddish Culture* (2005); B. Horowitz, "The Society for the Promotion of Enlightenment Among the Jews of Russia, and the Evolution of the St. Petersburg Russian-Jewish Intelligentsia, 1893–1905," *Studies in Contemporary Jewry* 19 (2004): 195–213; and S. Zipperstein, *Imagining Russian Jewry: Memory, History, Identity* (1999).   BRIAN HOROWITZ

Solomon is the son of *David and *Bathsheba (or Bathshua [1 Chron 3:5]) and the final king to rule over a *United Monarchy. The stories concerning Solomon are found in the books of *Kings and *Chronicles (the latter relies heavily on the former). Kings depicts Solomon, the tenth son of David, as an unlikely successor. Amidst the chaotic power struggles that characterize the end of David's reign, Solomon is represented as passive, chosen to be king rather than choosing to seek the throne. He attains his ascent, however, with the support of a powerful coalition, including his mother, the court prophet Nathan (see BIBLE: PROPHETS AND PROPHECY), and leaders of the priesthood and the military (1 Kgs 1), who obtain the blessing of the enfeebled David (only in Chronicles is Solomon elected by *God). As such, Solomon's succession may be seen as a coup over Adonijah, David's eldest remaining son.

The book of Kings describes Solomon's reign as Israel's golden age of prosperity. He creates an efficient bureaucracy and enters into political and economic agreements with neighboring nations (most notably *Egypt and *Phoenicia) that enrich Israel and expand its influence. He also embarks on a series of building projects, culminating in the construction of the *Temple in *Jerusalem. In addition, Solomon receives wisdom from God for which he becomes renowned worldwide (see especially 1 Kgs 3:16–28, 10).

Nonetheless, Solomon and his kingdom fall from their glorious heights, ultimately leading to the dissolution of the United Monarchy after his death. According to Kings, Solomon causes this fall by his introduction of illicit religious practices, brought by his many foreign wives. Chronicles, in contrast, scrupulously avoids criticism of him, although its emphasis on David's role in planning the Temple may be an implicit criticism of Solomon (Brueggemann).

Regarding the historicity of Solomon, the biblical texts appear to derive from some apparently authentic sources (for example, 1 Kgs 4:1–19; see also the citation of the "Book of the Acts of Solomon" in 1 Kgs 11:41). Other elements, such as the frequent use of symbolic numbers and the story of the *Queen of Sheba, reveal that the narrative had aims other than historical. Further, the extent and prosperity of the United Monarchy may be exaggerated. Despite the purported majesty of Solomon's kingdom, no extant extrabiblical sources of the tenth century mention him or an Israelite monarchy. Recent research additionally suggests that some building projects attributed to Solomon were instead ninth-century products of the northern kingdom of *Israel (Finkelstein and Silberman). Elsewhere in the Bible, Solomon stands for the pinnacle of human wisdom (outside of some critical traditions; see Neh 13:23–27 and perhaps Deut 17:14–20). *Ecclesiastes, *Song of Songs, parts of *Proverbs (see BIBLE: WISDOM LITERATURE), and the Wisdom of Solomon (see APOCRYPHA) are traditionally attributed to Solomon. Scholarly consensus, however, finds no credible historical connections between the king and these books. In post-biblical tradition, Solomon becomes a writer of psalms in the Psalms of Solomon (see PSEUDEPIGRAPHA). A noncanonical psalm found among the *Dead Sea Scrolls (11QPsAp[a]) additionally provides the earliest attestation of what became a vibrant complex of Solomonic traditions – namely Solomon as exorcist and practitioner of esoteric or *magical arts – which was further developed in the Testament of Solomon (see PSEUDEPIGRAPHA) and *Sefer ha-Razim* (Torijano; see MAGIC).

For further reading, see W. Brueggemann, *Israel's Ironic Icon of Human Achievement* (2005); I. Finkelstein and N. A.

Silberman, *David and Solomon: In Search of the Bible's Sacred Kings and the Roots of the Western Tradition* (2006); and P. Torijano, *Solomon the Esoteric King: From King to Magus, Development of a Tradition* (2002).   SEAN BURT

Soloveitchik, Joseph B. (1903–1993) was one of the greatest talmudists of the twentieth century, a prominent Jewish philosopher, and a leader of Orthodoxy (see JUDAISM, ORTHODOX: MODERN ORTHODOX), especially in North America. Born in Pruzhan, he taught *Talmud for more than four decades in *New York City at the Rabbi Isaac Elchanan Theological Seminary, affiliated with *Yeshiva University. He simultaneously served as the chief rabbinic figure in *Boston, commuting weekly between the two cities. A brilliant orator, "The Rav" influenced numerous leaders of American Orthodox Judaism. As a result of the *Holocaust, he broke from many traditionalist rabbis and family tradition and became a strong supporter of religious *Zionism, serving as honorary president of *Mizrachi, the religious Zionist movement.

Soloveitchik's talmudic method was that of the "Brisker" school, which implemented a mode of conceptual analysis pioneered by his grandfather, Rabbi Chaim Soloveitchik of Brisk (1853–1918). He held a PhD in philosophy from the University of *Berlin; in addition to his mastery of classic Jewish sources, he was broadly erudite in philosophy, Christian theology, science, and world literature. Soloveitchik especially engaged the writings of Karl Barth, Emil Brunner, Hermann *Cohen, Soren Kierkegaard, Rudolf Otto, and Max Scheler. His use of such material set him apart from many other Orthodox rabbinic authorities and greatly fortified a brand of Orthodoxy –generally known as "Modern" or "Centrist"– that embraces general culture. Soloveitchik's emphasis was on religious phenomenology and anthropology. Dominant themes in his work include dialectic, loneliness, suffering, and the power of *reason in the study of *halakhah. His two best known works are *Halakhic Man* (1944 [Hebrew]; trans. L. J. Kaplan, 1983), a depiction of the orientation of the halakhic scholar in neo-Kantian terms, and *The Lonely Man of Faith* (1965, 2006), an existentialist essay that depicts religious life as an oscillation between mastering nature and relating to *God in a *covenantal community.   DAVID SHATZ

Soloveitchik, Joseph B.: Religious Thought. Soloveitchik's view of Judaism emphasizes the centrality of normative action (*halakhah*) and its study. *Halakhic Man* offers a phenomenology of this ideal human type by comparing it to scientific "cognitive man" and mystical *homo religiosus*: It highlights the intellectual rigor, quantitative orientation, and this-worldliness that "halakhic man" shares with the former and contrasts it with the otherworldliness, qualitative orientation, and subjectivity characteristic of the latter. Despite the importance of *halakhah* and its study, recent scholarship has demonstrated that *Halakhic Man* is not a self-portrait; Soloveitchik himself allowed more room for "religious" yearnings than *Halakhic Man* would.

U-Vikkashtem mi-Sham (And You Shall Seek; published in Hebrew in 1978 but drafted in the 1940s) explores the human relationship with God. He emphasizes the interrelationship between how human beings seek God in a wide variety of inquiries and experiences and how God confronts human beings through *revelation and *commandment. At the primitive stage, revelation, which demands surrender to the divine will, collides with the human yearning for autonomous religious fulfillment. In the higher stages, imitation and cleaving to God provide modes of relationship to God that overcome the contradiction. Engagement in *halakhah* and its creative study plays an essential role in this process.

Halakhic Mind (written in the 1940s and published in 1984) adds an epistemological foundation to Soloveitchik's thought, arguing on the basis of contemporary physics and philosophy for pluralism and the methodological autonomy of religious knowledge. *Lonely Man of Faith* (1965), the best known of Soloveitchik's works composed in English, contrasts majestic man (the couple created in Genesis 1), whose technology and culture establish dominion over the world, with the man of faith (Adam and Eve of Genesis 2) who seeks personal relatedness; God ordains and endorses both of these aspects of the human personality. "Confrontation," written the year before, sketches a similar anthropology in setting guidelines for Jewish–Christian dialogue. Such dialogue was desirable in promoting ethical and social goals shared by the two religions, but not when the subject was the unique and incommensurable doctrines and experiences that distinguish each faith community.

Kol Dodi Dofek (The Voice of My Beloved Knocks [Song of Songs 5:2]), originally delivered as a lecture on Israel Independence Day 1956, is noteworthy for its rejection of traditional theodicy in favor of a halakhic orientation that stresses the practical imperative to respond to *evil. In this essay, Soloveitchik also proposes a theory of the dual nature of Jewish identity that encompasses the fate shared by all Jews and the sense of destiny defined by individual religious commitment.

Several important manuscripts, mainly from the 1950s, expand on these explorations of the human condition; they include *Family Redeemed, Worship of the Heart, Out of the Whirlwind,* and *Emergence of Ethical Man*. Other collections of essays and recorded material and unofficial sets of notes continue to appear.   SHALOM CARMY

Song of Songs, the book of (Hebrew, *Shir ha-Shirim*), also known as "The Song of Solomon" and "Canticles," is the fourth book of the *Writings section of the Hebrew *Bible, falling between the books of *Job and *Ruth. This book is one of the *Five Scrolls; it is traditionally recited in the *synagogue on the *Sabbath during *Passover.

The Song of Songs is an anthology of lyrical poems (see BIBLE: POETRY) of varying lengths, in which two lovers express their yearning for one another; they use bold metaphors and imagery from the worlds of nature and culture to create vivid emotional and sensual impressions. Unique among biblical books, the Song articulates the experience of erotic love between two humans; religious themes, the deity, and nationalism are altogether absent. Feminine voices are particularly prominent; the female lover has considerably more lines than her male beloved, and "the Daughters of Jerusalem" appear as a kind of recurring chorus.

Within the Bible, the erotic language and imagery of the Song resonate with charged passages from the prophets (see BIBLE: PROPHETS AND PROPHECY), notably *Hosea 2, *Jeremiah 2, and *Ezekiel 16, which use the language of romantic love to explore the nuances of the God–Israel relationship. Seen in the context of ancient literature, Song of Songs participates in a widespread ancient *Near Eastern and Mediterranean tradition of "secular" love lyrics, of which *Psalm 45 may also be an example. Passages from the Song resemble lyrics recovered from Sumer, *Babylonia, Ugarit (see CANAAN, CANAANITES), *Greece, and especially *Egypt. This book probably represents the finest surviving exemplar of what was once a widespread Israelite genre of writing.

Jewish (and Christian) tradition ascribes authorship of Song of Songs to King *Solomon, based on the invocation of his name in the first verse and a scattering of mentions in the text; most modern scholars, however, reject any Solomonic connection. Certain elements of the language are sufficiently archaic to support a pre-exilic dating and associations with the northern kingdom of *Israel, but other linguistic features, including Persian and Greek loanwords, typify late Biblical *Hebrew. The composite linguistic picture suggests that pre-exilic lyrics were redacted together into their current form during the *Babylonian Exile or post-exilic periods, with a resulting leveling of language.

Its nontheological and overtly erotic nature apparently led to controversy (genuine or rhetorical) over the Song's inclusion in the biblical canon, although the Greek, Latin, and *Dead Sea Scroll versions of the book are remarkably close to the *Masoretic text. However, by the early centuries of the Common Era, the Song of Songs had become prominent in *rabbinic and post-rabbinic exegesis. *Tannaitic sources indicate that Rabbi *Akiva (second century CE), the book's most vigorous champion, already understood the book to be an allegorical expression of God's love for Israel, arguing against others who may have regarded the book as no more than a collection of secular love songs (T. *Sanhedrin* 12.10). Far from being profane, the Song of Songs was, according to Rabbi Akiva, "the Holy of Holies" (M. *Yadayim* 3:5). Allegorical interpretation, in which the male lover is understood to be the deity and the female lover the community of Israel, transformed the Song into a powerful religious text while simultaneously giving Jewish *theology a deeply romantic, erotic vocabulary.

Over subsequent centuries, a rich and diverse exegetical tradition developed around the Song of Songs. As one of the Five Scrolls, the work has its own *midrashic anthologies (*Shir ha-Shirim Rabbah* and *Shir ha-Shirim Zuta*), produced by the Palestinian *Amoraim. The *Targum (*Aramaic paraphrase) of the Song, which was widely popular throughout the medieval Jewish world, retold the biblical book as a coded history of Israel from the time of Egyptian exile to the *messianic era. *Rashi's commentary likewise favors an historical interpretation, whereas Abraham *ibn Ezra composed a threefold commentary from philological, allegorical, and figurative perspectives. Synagogue poetry drew heavily on the Song; it became a central text for both Passover and *Shavuot liturgical poetry (see POETRY, LITURGICAL [PIYYUT]). Philosophical sources (particularly Neoplatonist) understood the woman to represent the soul of the individual. According to *kabbalistic interpretations, the feminine speaker in Song of Songs is identified with the *Shekhinah and her *sefirotic counterparts, such as the *Sabbath; the *Zohar itself opens with an exposition of Songs 2:2. Under the influence of medieval mystical practices, it became customary in many Jewish communities to recite the entire book or selected excerpts on Friday evenings as part of the *Kabbalat Shabbat* service (see SABBATH; SAFED). The romantic-erotic vocabulary of *Shir ha-Shirim* has exerted an enduring influence on the lexicon of Hebrew *poetry of all kinds to the present day.

LAURA S. LIEBER

Sororities: See FRATERNITIES AND SORORITIES: NORTH AMERICA

South Africa. Although the Dutch first claimed the Cape as a colony in 1652, using it as a strategic supply station on the sea route to *India, Jews only began to settle in southern Africa in the nineteenth century. Unlike its counterpart in the western hemisphere, the Dutch East India Company prohibited the settlement of those who were not Protestants. The legal basis for Jewish settlement was delayed until 1804 and only became ratified when *Britain captured the colony two years later. Over the next five decades, a trickle of Jews from Britain and the *German states settled in this distant colony. Because its economy was primarily agricultural, most Jews gravitated toward trade in the towns that spread from Cape Town into the hinterland. In the middle decades of the nineteenth century, they began to establish communal institutions, including the first *synagogue in Cape Town in 1841. The prospects of this small and tenuous anglicized community began to rise with the discovery of diamonds in 1867. Gold finds on the Witwatersrand two decades later completely transformed South African Jewry. Although only a small constituency in a vast Jewish migration out of *Eastern Europe, the 40,000 Jews who made their way to South Africa before the outbreak of *World War I were remarkably homogeneous, most hailing from the Kovno province in *Lithuania. Many settled in the new mining metropolis of Johannesburg, whereas others remained in Cape Town, their primary port of entry. In the countryside, Jews became a fixture in the rural economy, opening stores, operating as itinerant salesmen, supplying credit, and sending the harvest for sale to the cities. Although a minority of Jews became associated with organized crime in the unruly mining towns, the majority aspired to and attained respectability and middle-class status. They were aided in their upward mobility by their skin color: Jews were regarded as white and benefited from the advantages of racial privilege in an economy and society structured largely by race. Importantly for their political future, Jews gravitated toward the English-speaking population, which maintained a cultural and political affinity with Britain.

Clustered in the immigrant neighborhoods of Johannesburg and Cape Town, the new arrivals established their own synagogues, fraternal organizations, newspapers, cultural groups, and political organizations. They also brought an enthusiastic *Zionism that served as an important locus of communal identity and energy in an environment that encouraged ethnic nationalism and largely excluded Jews from mainstream political power. The South African Zionist Federation, established in 1898, also provided a vehicle to challenge the hold that the Anglo-Jewish elite continued to exercise on communal leadership. Despite some tensions between the Eastern European newcomers and the pre-existing community, the vast numerical preponderance of "Litvaks" and their economic success and rapid acculturation ensured that they soon took over the leadership of the key institutions of South African Jewry. Many of these institutions were modeled along British lines: South African Jews were officially represented by a Board of Deputies and ministered to by a chief rabbi. Although initially scornful of the lax and decorous Orthodoxy of their Anglo-Jewish counterparts, the Litvak community gradually adopted many of these same features. The Reform movement did not arrive in South Africa until 1933 and met substantial resistance (see JUDAISM: REFORM). In the first decade of the twenty-first century, it has still made only limited inroads into a community that is still overwhelmingly affiliated with *Orthodox congregations.

The decades between the world wars were deeply unsettling for South Africa and its Jewish community. Economic distress in the 1920s and 1930s led to a significant increase in vocal *antisemitism. The Quota Act of 1930 all but closed South Africa's doors to immigrants from Lithuania, although the act did enable the entry of about 6,000 German Jewish refugees between 1933 and 1939. Spurred on by a rag-tag assortment of organizations and extremists with fascist sympathies, the major Afrikaner political parties co-opted the "Jewish Question" as a central plank for political mobilization. Although the Jewish community enthusiastically supported the government's war effort, feelings about the Allied cause among the Afrikaner establishment were at best ambivalent and often hostile. Unsurprisingly the election victory of the leading Afrikaner political party in 1948 shocked South African Jewry. Although the National Party quickly abandoned its antisemitism and sought rapprochement, the Jewish community long remained nervous of the new government. This lingering apprehension underpinned the community's official neutrality to the government's policy of apartheid. The Board of Deputies strictly adhered to its traditional political neutrality into the 1980s.

For the most part, Jews limited their opposition to apartheid to support of rival political parties. Although the majority probably accepted the racial status quo, a significant minority became prominent in liberal and radical opposition politics. Heirs to an immigrant radical political tradition, they moved from trade union organization (and sometimes *Zionist youth movements) to the Communist Party. During the era of apartheid the broader Jewish community regarded this fringe minority with diffidence and concern.

The end of apartheid transformed the Jewish community's relationship with its radical fringe. A number of those exiled and imprisoned returned to prominent government posts. Since the 1990s, South Africa's embrace of multiculturalism has enhanced the standing of this prosperous community. A broad range of communal organizations and institutions continue to thrive. Johannesburg in particular has become the center of a Jewish religious revival, with fifty synagogues, seventeen small neighborhood prayer centers (*shtieblach*), and twelve Jewish day schools. However, the community's overall health is intimately intertwined with that of the broader society. Fears of crime and political and social instability continue to persuade many to emigrate. Since the early 1960s, emigration and a low birth rate have had a major demographic impact on the size and average age of the Jewish population. From a numerical peak of more than 120,000 in the early 1970s, the community, now heavily concentrated in Johannesburg and Cape Town, has declined to approximately 80,000 in the second decade

of the twenty-first century. Recent scholarship includes R. Mendelsohn and M. Shain, *The Jews in South Africa: An Illustrated History* (2008); and G. Shimoni, *Community and Conscience: The Jews in Apartheid South Africa* (2003).

ADAM MENDELSOHN

South America: See LATIN AMERICA

Soviet Union. The Soviet Union (Union of Soviet Socialist Republics [USSR]) was created in the former Russian Empire in 1922 after a period of civil war that followed the 1917 Bolshevik revolution. Its first leader, Vladimir Lenin (d. 1924), was succeeded by Joseph Stalin who maintained leadership until his death (d. 1954). The Soviet Union formally dissolved in 1991 and was succeeded by the Russian Federation. For relevant entries, **see BELORUSSIA; BIRO-BIDJAN; BOLSHEVISM; COMMUNISM; EHREN-BURG, ILYA; HOLOCAUST; JEWISH ANTI-FASCIST COMMITTEE; LITERATURE: RUSSIA AND SOVIET UNION; PALE OF SETTLEMENT; RUSSIA; SAINT PETERSBURG; SHARANSKY, NATHAN; SOCIETY FOR THE PROMOTION OF ENLIGHTENMENT AMONG THE JEWS OF RUSSIA (OPE); SOVIET UNION: JEWISH MOVEMENT, 1967–1989; TROTSKY, LEON; UKRAINE. Map 10**

Soviet Union: Jewish Movement, 1967–1989. The *Bolshevik leadership in the early years of the Soviet Union viewed the *Zionist movement as bourgeois and reactionary. Moreover, they never recognized de facto the natural right of Soviet citizens to emigrate. Therefore, after the 1917 October revolution the Zionist movement was gradually suppressed. The 1948 establishment of *Israel aroused enthusiasm among Soviet Jews, and many hoped they would be allowed to move to the Jewish state. However, the government launched an *antisemitic campaign of unprecedented severity instead, which continued until Stalin's death in 1953.

The post-Stalin "thaw" was marked, among other things, by the first trickles of Jewish emigration to Israel. The presence of a large Israeli delegation at the 1957 Festival of Youth and Students in Moscow created a great stir among Jews. However, dozens of those who made contacts with Israeli delegates or Israeli embassy staff were punished with imprisonment.

Israel's victory in June, 1967 over the united Arab armies in the Six Day War roused national pride among Soviet Jews, led to a variety of Zionist endeavors, and increased Jewish alienation from the Soviet state, which supported Israel's enemies. In Leningrad, an underground Zionist youth organization was formed. It had a committee, a charter of its own, a network of *ulpanim* to teach Hebrew, and connections with Zionist groups in other cities. In Moscow, initiatives usually came from veteran Zionists, who had returned from prison camps. The total membership of the Riga Zionist groups exceeded 150. In Odessa there were two Zionist groups.

On June 13, 1967, Moscow student Yaakov Kazakov publicly renounced his Soviet citizenship and demanded to be allowed to go to Israel. Jews began to address collective appeals to Soviet and international organizations, demanding the right to emigrate, as stipulated in the Universal Declaration of Human Rights. One appeal, to U Thant, Secretary General of the United Nations, was signed by 531

Georgian Jews. It ended with the words, "Israel or death!" A desperate demonstrative act of those refused exit visas was an attempt to hijack a small airplane and to fly it to Sweden. The operation was launched on June 15, 1970, by activists from Riga (see BALTIC STATES) and Leningrad (see SAINT PETERSBURG), and it was headed by ex-political prisoner Edward Kuznetsov and former military pilot Mark Dymshits. All the participants were arrested and sentenced to long prison terms, and Dymshits and Kuznetsov were sentenced to be executed. Only international protests led to the commutation of their death sentences to terms of fifteen years. Other trials followed, at which dozens of Zionists who had nothing to do with the hijacking were found guilty. After the hijacking attempt, the struggle for *aliyah emerged openly. On February 24, 1971, a large group of "refuseniks" from several cities held a demonstration in the reception room of the presidium of the Supreme Soviet of the USSR. This was followed by similar actions in *Lithuania, *Ukraine, *Belorussia, and Georgia. Some demonstrations attained their goals; others ended with arrests, as in the case of Moscow activist Ida Nudel who, on June 1, 1978, hung a placard from her balcony that said, "KGB, give me a visa to Israel."

Reacting to increased western support for Soviet Jews and hoping that the Zionist movement would be weakened if "troublemakers" were allowed to leave, the Soviet government sharply increased the number of exit permits. In 1971, 12,900 Jews left but only after a long bureaucratic process, severe humiliation, and surrender of their Soviet citizenship; a further 31,900 left in 1972. In 1972, a law was passed requiring the departing Jews to repay the Soviet Union for the costs of their educations. However, the government had to backtrack when the U.S. Congress adopted the Jackson-Vanik Amendment (December 1974), linking the provision of most-favored-nation trade status with the *United States to Soviet permission for emigration.

Between 1969 and 1971, a majority of the veterans of the Zionist movement left the USSR. Thereafter, the struggle for aliyah was led by a new group who included acculturated Soviet intelligentsia.

Increased emigration options enabled more Jews to go to the United States and other western countries. One factor behind this phenomenon, known as "dropping out" (neshirah in Hebrew), was fear about life in Israel in the wake of the Yom Kippur War of 1973. Another was the agreement of the United States to grant ex-Soviet Jews refugee status, which afforded them special rights. Propaganda in the Soviet mass media, which presented Zionism as the incarnation of universal evil, also made Israel appear less attractive to Soviet Jews.

The Jewish movement in the Soviet Union evolved within the context of a growing dissident movement that taught Jewish activists ways to struggle against the regime. Some Jewish dissidents believed that a common struggle waged by all opposition forces would be most effective. Others worried that cooperation with other dissidents would lead to increased repression against the Jewish movement. This happened in the case of Anatoly (Nathan) *Sharansky, who was one of the most visible Zionist activists and dissidents. In March 1977, he was arrested and sentenced to thirteen years in prison on the charge of espionage. The international campaign to release Sharansky made his name a household word. Finally, in 1986, Sharansky was freed in exchange for a Soviet spy who had been arrested by the Americans.

By the mid-1970s, some movement activists decided to elevate the national consciousness of the assimilated Jewish intelligentsia by increasing the amount of activities related to Jewish culture. In addition to teaching Hebrew, cultural activities included staging amateur plays, organizing song festivals, maintaining underground Jewish libraries, publishing samizdat journals (underground publications), and holding seminars on Jewish culture. Amateur purimshpils (*Purim plays, which updated the biblical history of Mordecai and *Esther to make fun of the Soviet regime and its persecution of Jews) enjoyed considerable popularity. There was even an attempt, in December 1976, to hold an international scientific symposium in Moscow on prospects for Jewish culture in the USSR. However, the Soviet authorities declared the symposium "a Zionist provocation" and forcibly prevented it from taking place.

As mentioned earlier, in the 1970s, Jewish samizdat began to appear in the form of periodicals; the first one was Iton (Riga). The most serious publications devoted to Jewish culture, history, and thought were Jews in the USSR (Moscow, 1972–79) and the Leningrad Jewish Almanac (1982–89). The most widespread form of Jewish cultural activity was the teaching of Hebrew. In the early 1980s, there were a hundred Hebrew teachers in Moscow alone, with more than 1,000 students. Yuli Kosharovsky organized summer seminar/camps for teachers of Hebrew, and Alexander Kholmyansky and Yuli Edelstein coordinated ulpanim throughout the country.

The movement for emigration entailed serious expense. Support was needed for "Prisoners of Zion," a designation for people who were fired from their jobs, as well as for reproducing samizdat, for providing kosher food for religious Jews, and for covering some of the expenses connected with emigration. To meet these needs, foreign aid, in the form of clothing packages, as well as money, was sent from abroad. The Israeli organization Nativ played a central role, distributing aid from the American *Joint Distribution Committee. Also involved were other foreign Jewish and non-Jewish organizations that fought for the rights of Soviet Jews. In North America, these organizations included the Student Struggle for Soviet Jewry, the Union of Councils for Soviet Jewry, the New York Conference on Soviet Jewry, the National Conference on Soviet Jewry, the Academic Committee for Soviet Jewry, the Ḥabad Lubavich Movement, and the Jewish Defense League. The Women's Campaign for Soviet Jewry, "35," was active in *Britain. All these organizations sent emissaries disguised as tourists who brought items that Soviet Jews could then sell. In response, the Soviet government used all means possible to halt foreign aid, including arresting tourists and confiscating items they were bringing to Soviet Jews.

1980–1989: The invasion of Afghanistan by the Soviet army in December 1979 resulted in the curtailment of Jewish emigration. A long period of mass refusal of emigration requests began. The majority of refuseniks waited seven to nine years to emigrate, but some were denied permission to leave for fifteen or more years. After an applicant was refused an exit visa, it was impossible to return to normal Soviet life. Many people lost their jobs and were deprived of their means of survival. Young Jewish male refuseniks faced the prospect of being conscripted after being expelled from university. Many lost the most productive years of their lives, and their professional qualifications were wasted. Nobody knew how long his or her refusal would last; making meaningful plans was impossible.

At this time, when the refuseniks numbered in the tens of thousands, the importance of Jewish cultural activity increased. Grigory Kanovich and Lev Utevsky ran an especially popular seminar on Jewish history and tradition, which was given in people's homes in Leningrad. In May 1981 the police broke into a seminar meeting, dispersed the gathering, arrested the mathematician Yevgeny Lein, and charged him with attacking a policeman. Seminars on Jewish culture took place also in Moscow, Kharkov, Kishinev, and Riga.

Some refuseniks turned to religion. A majority of the newly religious Jews were affiliated with Ḥabad *Hasidism, whereas others identified with the Lithuanian *mitnagged tradition. A Zionist-oriented religious movement known as Maḥanayim, a Hebrew word meaning "two camps," in reference to Moscow and *Jerusalem, was also established.

By the mid-1980s, the refuseniks had created the basis for an independent Jewish public, religious, and cultural life, which flourished during the 1990s. Although Mikhail Gorbachev proclaimed a new political course of glasnost (openness) in the spring of 1985, only in 1987 was aliyah renewed. By late 1989, almost all the long-term refuseniks and "Prisoners of Zion" had been allowed to emigrate. The government also legalized Jewish cultural, educational, and public organizations, although during the 1990s, the majority of Soviet Jews emigrated to Israel and the West.

Important studies include M. Azbel, Refusenik: Trapped in the Soviet Union (1981); H. Butman, From Leningrad to Jerusalem: The Gulag Way (1990); P. Buwalda, They Did Not Dwell Alone: Jewish Emigration from the Soviet Union 1967–1990 (1997); M. Gilbert, Jews of Hope (1984); E. Lein, Lest We Forget: The Refuseniks' Struggle and World Jewish Solidarity (1997); B. Morozov, Documents on Jewish Emigration (2002); and N. Sharansky, Fear No Evil (1988).　　　　　　MICHAEL BEIZER

Spain, Christian. From its earliest appearance under *Roman rule, Jewish society in the *Iberian Peninsula was marked by a high degree of cultural integration. In the early Middle Ages, Spain came under the control of the Visigoths, Christians of Germanic origin. Although Jews became the target of royal persecution and attempts at forced conversion, they nonetheless remained a prominent segment of Spanish society. The successful Muslim invasion in the early eighth century changed the situation of the Jews once again (see SPAIN, MUSLIM) and led to a significant cultural flowering. However, after several centuries of *Islamic hegemony, the balance of power in the peninsula shifted back to Christian dominance as the Reconquista (reconquest) effort pushed southward in the course of the twelfth and thirteenth centuries. At the same time, the intolerant rule of the *Almoravid Berbers in Muslim Spain led many Jews to move into Christian regions where they established communities in market towns, re-creating and extending many of the same roles as merchants, artisans, and civil servants that they had performed in Muslim al-Andalus.

The Jews of Christian Iberia were geographically and socially mobile, taking advantage of extensive royal protection and tax incentives, and establishing close ties with their Christian and Muslim neighbors. Despite Christian writings that caricatured Jews and attacked their religion, little effort was made to implement the segregation and legal restrictions suffered by Jews elsewhere in Europe. Wealthy *Sephardic merchants and courtiers imitated the postures of the Christian elite both in their dress and in their custom of taking Muslim concubines. This propensity toward social and cultural interaction with non-Jewish society provoked harsh condemnation from Jewish moral and spiritual leaders. The general permeability of social boundaries among Iberia's three religious groups also threatened to undermine the autonomy of Jewish *communal self-government. The willingness of many Jews to frequent Christian courts meant that their communal officials depended on royal intervention to buttress their control. These communities were often torn by internal strife that reflected and at times even exceeded that found in the dynamic and unruly frontier society in which they lived.

The reorientation of Iberian life away from *North Africa and the *Middle East toward the increasingly vibrant cultural orbit of Christian Europe also transformed Jewish religious culture. Jewish scholars continued to pursue an Andalusi educational curriculum with its strong emphasis on practical *halakhah, Greco-Arabic-oriented *thought (see SCIENCE AND MATHEMATICS: MIDDLE AGES AND EARLY MODERN; THOUGHT, MEDIEVAL), and Arabic literary (see LITERATURE, HEBREW: MEDIEVAL SPAIN) and *grammatical modes. Yet, beginning in the thirteenth century there was a distinct shift toward the cultural and intellectual trends of northern Europe. The Jewish centers of *France and *Germany had developed a strong tradition of *mysticism, ascetic pietism (see ḤASIDEI ASHKENAZ), and elaborate forms of talmudic exegesis (see TOSAFISTS). Increased interaction among scholars from both sides of the Pyrenees led to a considerable expansion of Sephardic intellectual interests. Catalan rabbis Moses ben Naḥman (*Naḥmanides) and Jonah Gerondi studied in these northern academies and became major vehicles for their mystical and penitential ideals, while thirteenth-century German scholars, such as Dan Ashkenazi and *Asher ben Yeḥiel, and his sons, helped bring northern European learning to Castile. Increasing interest in mysticism among Iberian Jews can be seen in the proliferation of kabbalistic study circles (see KABBALAH) and in the production of the Sefer ha-*Zohar (Book of Splendor) in the late thirteenth century. This overall shift in religious and intellectual approaches provoked a virulent and protracted debate over the suitability of the study of philosophical texts, particularly the writings of *Maimonides. In the end, the Sephardic tradition of accommodation and amplification won out, and Kabbalah took its place alongside philosophical and talmudic study in the Hispano-Jewish academies.

Throughout the thirteenth and fourteenth centuries, religious tensions between Jews and Christians manifested themselves in polemical literature, public disputations (see MIDDLE AGES: JEWISH–CHRISTIAN POLEMICS), and sporadic outbreaks of violence. Yet, such confrontation did little to alter the long-standing intercultural bonds and intracommunal factionalism that continued to characterize the daily life of most Jews. In 1391, however, this enduring paradigm of Iberian Jewish society suffered an unprecedented rupture. During the spring and summer of that year, Christian preachers helped ignite an outbreak of anti-Jewish riots that swept over the region. These attacks resulted in the murder of approximately one-third of Iberian Jewry and the forced conversion of another third. Intense missionary activity in the decades following the attacks augmented the numbers of these New Christians, or *conversos*, and permanently altered the relationship between Iberian Jews and Christians. No social or religious mechanisms existed to facilitate the integration of the *conversos* into Christian society or to prevent their contact with Iberian Jewry. As a result, the fate of the Jews became bound up with that of the *conversos* over the course of the fifteenth century. Municipal and regional councils' increasingly vigorous attempts to restrict Jewish rights were closely tied to the calumny that Jewish blood made the *conversos* resistant to true Christianization and to the growing sentiment that the Jews actively fostered heresy among the New Christians. This latter accusation was made official by the Spanish *Inquisition and motivated the decision of monarchs Ferdinand and Isabella to expel their Jews in 1492. In 1498 the Catholic monarchs successfully lobbied neighboring Navarre to expel its Jews as well, but their efforts to exert similar influence over *Portugal produced very different results. Seeking to retain this valuable new community, King Manoel I chose to ignore the troubled history of the Spanish New Christians and in 1497 forcibly converted all of the Jews in Portugal. This momentous decision extended the debate over the *conversos*' religious identity and further complicated their relationship to both the Christian and Jewish communities.

Despite the decline in political fortunes during the fifteenth century, Jewish intellectual life continued to flourish and to display strong signs of Christian influence. Jewish preachers and moralists followed closely the arguments and methodological developments of their Christian counterparts, noting with envy the respect and honor that they were able to command. The last generation of Jews born in Iberia boasted a number of significant poets, philosophers, kabbalists, and exegetes. Among these exiles, Joseph *Karo represents the continued vitality of Sephardic legal codification and theosophical *Kabbalah. His great legal compendium, *Beit Yosef*, and its more popular digest, the *Shulḥan Arukh* (see HALAKHAH), represent a culmination of the medieval Hispano-Jewish religious program. Karo's work became the rock on which much of Jewish society was established for centuries to come.

For further reading, see J. Ray, *The Sephardic Frontier: The Reconquista and the Jewish Community in Medieval Iberia* (2006); Y. Baer, *A History of the Jews in Christian Spain* (1961); and B. Gampel, "A Letter to a Wayward Teacher," in *Cultures of the Jews*, ed. David Biale (2002). **Maps 6, 7**   JONATHAN RAY

Spain, Muslim. Between 711 and 1492 Muslims ruled all or part of the *Iberian Peninsula. Muslim Spain (known as al-Andalus in Arabic and *Sepharad in Hebrew) represented a unique enclave in medieval Europe where Muslims, Christians, and Jews coexisted, sometimes peacefully, but more often in strife. The quality and nature of this coexistence, which was known as *convivencia*, have been the subject of some dispute among scholars. The coexistence of the three communities was fragile as Muslim and Christian kingdoms fought among themselves and with each other. Jews were subject populations under both Muslims and Christians, sometimes serving as cultural and political mediators between warring and competing dynasties and regimes. As a result of the diverse religious and ethnic mosaic that comprised Andalusia, a shared culture that was noted for its sophistication, originality, and brilliance emerged. So dazzling was the civilization of the Caliphate of Cordoba and its successor states that al-Andalus is frequently depicted as a lost paradise in Arabic as well as *Hebrew literature. As the Christian reconquest of Spain advanced in the twelfth century, both Jews and Muslims lamented the loss of Muslim Spain in romantic and nostalgic terms.

The Muslim invasion of Spain in 711 represented a welcome respite for the Jews after decades of persecution and forced conversion under Visigothic Christian kings. Jews who had fled to *North Africa returned and reverted to Judaism, finding the dynamic Umayyad dynasty of Cordoba eager to exploit the skills of its many minorities in its newly conquered province. By the ninth century, Muslim Spain formed an integral part of a vast medieval Muslim commercial nexus that extended from the Atlantic Ocean all the way to Central Asia and the Indian Ocean. Jews of far-flung communities across the Mediterranean were united by trade and shared values, as Muslim civilization, cemented by the Arabic language, spread through these far-flung territories.

Jewish cultural development in Spain drew its inspiration from at least two sources. On the one hand, medieval Andalusian Jews strengthened their cultural and economic ties with Jewish communities in neighboring *North Africa, Muslim *Sicily, *Palestine, *Egypt, and Babylonia (*Iraq). Through their correspondence with the ancient talmudic centers in Baghdad (*Sura and *Pumbedita) and their leaders (*Geonim), the Jews of Spain shared in the emergent rabbinic culture that would become the patrimony of much of world Jewry. At the same time, as the Jewish commercial and intellectual leadership came into contact with a worldly Arab elite, the Jews of Spain were profoundly influenced by local cultural developments. Arab culture was influenced by the courtly traditions of the court in Baghdad, which, in turn, drew heavily from older Persian models. At the same time, Arabic poetic models recalled the motifs of ancient pre-Islamic Arabian poetry. Andalusian Jews were exposed to both of these trends through their contacts in court circles, and they, too, were keenly interested in philology and linguistics, *poetry and *literature, and the ancient traditions of *philosophy and *science that now circulated in Arabic translation.

The *Judeo-Arabic tradition flourished until the mid-twelfth century. This tradition blended the special interests of Muslims, such as jurisprudence, philosophy, and theology, with Jewish *rabbinic and exegetical traditions (see BIBLICAL COMMENTARY). Adapting the forms and motifs of the courtly Arabic literary traditions that they imbibed in the cultural centers of Cordoba, Granada, and Seville, Jews fashioned a unique poetic corpus that was both secular and religious; it was written in a rare *Biblical Hebrew. This combination of the secular and religious, as well as the enormous range of interests and areas of inquiry, has been the hallmark of Sephardic civilization.

In the early tenth century, the ruling Umayyad prince 'Abd el-Rahman III announced his independence from the Abbasid Caliphate in Baghdad and declared himself Caliph of Cordoba. His dazzling court housed entertainers, scholars, experts in the sciences, artists, and architects, as well as a council of physicians, in which a learned Jew, Ḥasdai ibn Shaprut, soon came to the attention of the ruling monarch. An excellent physician who was gifted in languages, Ḥasdai performed vital fiscal and diplomatic services for the Muslim ruler. At the same time, Ḥasdai launched Spanish Jewry on an independent cultural and political course, surrounding himself with Hebrew poets and patronizing Judaic scholars. He also supported and defended beleaguered Jewish communities abroad, encouraged the emergence of a domestic school of rabbinic scholarship in Andalusia, and communicated with the Jewish king of the *Khazars in the Crimea. Ḥasdai is often credited with launching a renaissance in Jewish learning in Spain and of setting Andalusian Jewry on the path of cultural independence from the rabbinic center in Iraq. He is also invoked as the prototype of Sephardic leadership. Soon, several cities in Spain emerged as magnets for poets and scholars, and the Hebrew academy of Lucena rivaled the talmudic academy of Cordoba. Patrons included the poet-statesman-warrior *Samuel ibn Naghrela ha-Nagid.

By the mid-tenth century, Muslim Spain had emerged as the home of a new and exciting Hebrew poetry. Imitating their Muslim counterparts in both poetic form and content and drawing on the linguistic studies of their North African co-religionists, Hebrew poets in the employ of Jewish courtiers began to emerge from anonymity. Among their many themes were songs on wine, the wine party, and friendship (see POETRY, MEDIEVAL: MUSLIM WORLD). Philosophical musings and scientific observations were skillfully interwoven in their poetic verses. At the same time Hebrew poets wrote liturgical poetry that continues to adorn the Hebrew *prayer book and *High Holiday ritual (see POETRY, LITURGICAL [*PIYYUT*]). Among the most famous of the hundreds of poets were Solomon *ibn Gabirol, *Samuel ibn Naghrela (Samuel ha-Nagid), Moses *ibn Ezra, Abraham *ibn Ezra, and Judah *Halevi. The legacy of the Jews in Muslim Spain also extended into *science and philosophy, astronomy and *astrology, *grammar, and linguistics.

The golden era of Jewish life in Muslim Spain was short-lived. The Caliphate of Cordoba collapsed in 1006, and Andalusia was beset by devastating civil war. Jews fled Cordoba, hoping to find refuge and patronage in the small successor Berber kingdoms that flourished in eleventh-century Spain. The courts of the successor states (known as the *taifa* kingdoms) continued to pursue the earlier brilliant secular culture in Malaga, Badajoz, Saragossa, Granada, and more than a dozen other regional petty kingdoms. Yet the territory under Islamic rule on the peninsula was steadily contracting. After the fall of Toledo to Christian armies in 1085, Spanish Muslims hastily invited the *Almoravid Berbers of Morocco to assist in stemming the tide of Christian victories. In the atmosphere of mounting religious warfare and the First Crusade (see MIDDLE AGES: CRUSADES), the Almoravids introduced harsh discriminatory legislation against Christians and Jews in their kingdom. As a result, the exodus of the Jews from Muslim to Christian Spain commenced. The Almoravids, in turn, were replaced in the mid-twelfth century by the still more fervent and fundamentalist Muslims, known as the *Almohads, who invaded Spain in 1146–47. Their campaigns were based on a fierce and zeal-

ous Islamic fundamentalism that included a policy of forced conversion of Jews and Christians. In the unfolding atmosphere of religious persecution and *jihad*, Jews fled Muslim Spain into Christian Spain en masse. At this juncture, the great medieval thinker Moses *Maimonides and his family fled Cordoba, wandering in Spain for several years until they found temporary shelter in Morocco. Although he spent most of his adult life in *Egypt, Maimonides always regarded himself as a product of Andalusia/Sepharad.

By the end of the twelfth century, only a small remnant of Jews remained under Muslim rule in Spain. With the fall of Seville to the Christians in 1248, Muslim Spain was itself reduced to a small enclave in the south with its capital in Granada. The center of gravity of Jewish life shifted to Christian Toledo in the kingdom of Castile, to Barcelona in Catalonia, and to scores of towns and villages. Although the Jews continued to cultivate the Arabic language and their former poetic arts, also serving as translators of Arabic classics into Castilian or Latin, their political and cultural destiny was now tied to the broader trends of western Christendom. Demands for greater intellectual conformity as well as a reappraisal of the formerly accepted philosophic traditions began to clash with the former Iberian culture. Both Jews and Judaism were now under attack, and memories of Muslim Spain dimmed in the new and challenging realities of Christian *Spain. The Sephardic civilization that accompanied the Jewish exiles from Iberia in 1492 was a unique amalgam of the cultural richness created by Jews in both the Muslim and Christian realms.

Important research includes J. Gerber, *The Jews of Spain: A History of the Sephardic Experience* (1992); and S. D. Goitein, *A Mediterranean Society: The Jewish Communities of the Arab World as Portrayed in the Documents of the Cairo Genizah*, 6 vols. (1967–93). **Maps 5, 6**   JANE GERBER

Spinoza, Baruch (or Benedictus in Latin; 1632–1677), one of the major philosophical figures of early modern Europe, was born in *Amsterdam, the middle son in a prominent *Portuguese Jewish family of moderate means. As a student in the community's Talmud Torah (school), his intellectual gifts could not have gone unnoticed by the congregation's rabbis. However, he was forced to cut short his formal studies at age seventeen to help run his family's importing business, and he never progressed to the upper levels of the curriculum, which included advanced study of *Talmud.

On July 27, 1656, Spinoza was issued the harshest writ of *ḥerem, or excommunication, ever pronounced by the *Sephardic community of Amsterdam; this ban was never rescinded. Exactly what Spinoza's "monstrous deeds" and "abominable heresies" were alleged to have been remains unclear. Most likely, he was giving utterance to the radical ideas that would soon appear in his philosophical treatises.

To all appearances, Spinoza was content to leave Judaism and the community behind; he no longer harbored either faith or religious commitment. Within a few years, he left Amsterdam altogether. By the time his extant correspondence begins, in 1661, he is living in Rijnsburg, not far from Leiden. There, he worked on the *Treatise on the Emendation of the Intellect*, an essay on philosophical method, and the *Short Treatise on God, Man and His Well-Being*, an initial but aborted effort to lay out his metaphysical, epistemological, and moral views. His critical explanation of Descartes' *Principles of*

Philosophy, the only work he published under his own name in his lifetime and which earned him widespread renown as an expositor of Cartesian philosophy, was completed in 1663, after he had moved to Voorburg, outside The Hague. He was also working on what would eventually be called the *Ethics*, his philosophical masterpiece. However, when he saw the principles of toleration in Holland being threatened by reactionary forces, he put that work aside to complete his "scandalous" *Theological-Political Treatise*, published anonymously and to great alarm in 1670. When Spinoza died in The Hague, he was still at work on his *Political Treatise*; it was soon published by his friends along with his other unpublished writings, including a *Compendium to Hebrew Grammar*.

In the *Ethics*, Spinoza denies the traditional *God of Abrahamic religions as an anthropomorphic fiction. God, he insists, is not endowed with any of the psychological or moral characteristics necessary for a providential Being. God does not will, judge, or deliberate; nor is God good, wise, and just. For Spinoza, God is nothing but nature – *Deus sive Natura*, "God or Nature," in his famous phrase – the infinite, necessarily existing, eternal, and active substance of the universe. Everything else that exists is "in" God in the sense of being a part of nature (or a "mode" of the substance). There is nothing supernatural for Spinoza; whatever happens does so with an absolute necessity as a result of nature's laws and processes. Even human beings, including their states of mind, are determined by natural causality; there is no freedom of the will. With this metaphysics, Spinoza also rejects both the divine creation of the world, because nature (as God) is eternal, and the possibility of miracles, because there can be no supernaturally caused exceptions to the order of nature.

Spinoza, moreover, denies that human beings are endowed with an immortal soul. There is an eternal aspect of the human mind – namely, the adequate ideas or truths that the virtuous person pursuing knowledge acquires in this lifetime; because these ideas are eternal, they do not come to an end with the death of the person. Yet this eternity of the mind, which is enjoyed in this world, must not be confused with the personal immortality of the soul in some world-to-come. Such beliefs in personal immortality are a pernicious and superstitious doctrine that fosters the harmful passions of hope (for eternal reward) and fear (of eternal punishment). The life of freedom and happiness is an active one guided by reason and knowledge, within which the power of the passive affects (emotions) is diminished.

In the *Theological-Political Treatise*, Spinoza argues that the *Bible is not literally the work of God or even of *Moses. It is a compilation of human writings that were passed down through generations and finally edited in the *Second Temple period (most likely, he surmises, by *Ezra). Thus, Scripture is not a source of theological, scientific, philosophical, or historical knowledge, but only conveys the various ideas intended by its authors. Taking issue with *Maimonides' claim that the key to interpreting Scripture is *reason and demonstrable truth, Spinoza insists that its meaning should be investigated just as one investigates nature: through empirical study, inquiring into its authors, their language, and the historical, social, and political contexts in which they wrote. If there is a "divine" truth in Scripture, it is a simple moral one: Love your neighbor.

The ceremonial laws proclaimed in *Torah, Spinoza says, may have had a certain value and relevance in a particular historical period, as long as there was a *Temple. However, with the destruction of that central element of ancient *Israelite religion, the *commandments and the *halakhic structure that developed from them lost their *raison d'être*. Consequently, latter-day Jews are not obliged to observe them. Or, as one contemporary document describes Spinoza's views on this matter, "the Law is not true."

Finally, Spinoza denies that there is any metaphysically or morally interesting sense in which the Jews are God's chosen people (see ELECTION). There are no differences among human beings in which one group might take any special pride: All are equally a part of nature. The only sense in which the Jews, for a time, enjoyed a particular divine "vocation" was during the era of ancient *Israelite kingship, when they enjoyed the good fortune of a secure and well-ordered polity for an extended period of time. Yet, this polity was not the supernatural result of some special divine favor, but only the natural consequence of wise laws.

STEVEN NADLER

Sports and Americanization.

Sports and Americanization. The belief that Jews do not take part in American athletic pastimes was once widespread. Such stereotypes took on *antisemitic dimensions in less tolerant times, when supposed "cowardly" Jewish inactivity on the sports field was linked to their alleged absence from the battlefield. Early-twentieth-century opponents to immigration from *Eastern Europe connected presumed Jewish athletic inactivity to fears that these newcomers would not make the necessary cultural adjustments to become true Americans. To counter such inaccurate attitudes, historians of Jewish American involvement in athletics responded by identifying Jewish sports champions. This tradition continues among some eighteen Jewish sports halls of fame and several online archives, websites, and periodicals that chronicle Jewish athletic prowess.

The American Jewish encounter with sports, however, transcends competitive achievements. It is also a useful lens for the examination of Jewish acceptance, adjustment, and accommodation to American life. Involvement in athletic activities and allegiance to professional sports teams played central roles for Jews in becoming Americans, at least for Jewish males. Author Chaim Potok reflects this phenomenon in the opening chapter of *The Chosen*, his 1967 novel about *Modern Orthodox and *Ultra-Othodox youth in the 1940s, which is set at a baseball game between two *yeshivot*. Moreover, the entrepreneurial history of American Jews also plays a role, when Jewish team owners and boxing promoters and managers, particularly in the early decades of the twentieth century, are included in discussions of how immigrants and their children emerged from poverty through initiative in high-risk *entertainment industries (see SPORTS: UNITED STATES entries).

Contemporary Jewish union organizers and sports agents are likewise part of Jewish involvement in American sports. They have protected and enhanced the rights and salaries of athletes; their victories for their clients have transformed the economics of these popular attractions. As members of the media, Jews are also major players in the evolution of sports within American popular culture; their reporting, photography, and involvement in radio and television *sportscasting, commentary, and production have helped shape sports journalism and enhanced popular interest in these pastimes.

Those hostile to Jews have exploited the long-standing Jewish involvement in these off-the-field activities to allege Jewish control of American sports, and some have also resorted to more invidious characterizations of Jews as corruptors of athletics pastimes. Auto manufacturer Henry Ford articulated the most outrageous group censure when he blamed the infamous 1919 "Black Sox" baseball scandal on a Jewish conspiracy (see SPORTS, UNITED STATES: BASEBALL). In recent times, unfocused anger has often been directed at Jewish sports agents who are portrayed as controlling athletic labor unrest, even though they do not play the game.

Yet, the ever-increasing tolerance accorded Jews in contemporary America may also be reflected through the experience of sports. Most notable, perhaps, is the willingness of the majority of American sports fans to accept the *High Holidays as occasions when most Jewish athletes put their religion ahead of obligations to teammates.

Indeed, the conflicting demands of sports and religious practice are emblematic of Judaism's encounter with America. Of all the challenges to personal and religious identity that America posed to immigrant Jews and their children, none was more daunting than athletics. For most elders, sports and recreation remained a worthless frivolity, even if they offered health benefits. In contrast, the immigrants' children clearly understood that participation in athletics and some degree of knowledge about and enthusiasm for professional sports were fundamental American activities. Battles over the centrality of sports were a major source of intergenerational conflict. For many parents, practices and games on Friday nights, Saturdays, and Jewish *festivals, which lured children away from the *synagogue and the family table, were a particular crisis. Nonkosher (see DIETARY LAWS) training foods also undermined faith obligations. Sports forced youngsters to choose between Judaism and athletics, and generally, the secular pursuit won. Yet, forward-thinking rabbis also attempted to mitigate athletics' impact on their communities. From the Temple Center initiatives of Reform rabbis in the 1890s through the Synagogue Center efforts starting in the 1910s, and down to Jewish Community Centers of the present day (see UNITED STATES: COMMUNITY CENTERS), sports facilities have often been integrated into sacred spaces to indicate that Judaism and athletics are not inimical. These efforts are emblematic of a traditional faith's reconciliation with the modern world. No other modern Jewish community has used the "come to play, stay to pray" strategy as extensively as American Jews. For further reading, see J. S. Gurock, *Judaism's Encounter with American Sports* (2005).

JEFFREY S. GUROCK

Sports: Israel. Sports, which have been a major facet of Israeli life for more than a century, have both shaped and reflected individual and national aspirations. Positive attitudes toward competitive and recreational athletics overcame long-held cultural traditions and helped create a new Jewish physical self-image. Sports continue to serve as a unifying force for the young nation and embody Israel's ideals. Despite political rivalries, an arduous road to international acceptance, and an Olympic Games massacre, sports have become a passion, an industry, and a political force in Israeli society.

Although individual sporting activities took place in *Palestine for many years, organized sports emerged at the beginning of the twentieth century in physical education and self-defense classes in schools. In 1906, Russian *olim* (immigrants) formed the first sports associations: the Rishon Letzion (later renamed Maccabi, after the liberation fighters), Yaffo, and the Bar Giora Yerushalayim. Within a few years, there were ten branches of Maccabi, combining sports with Hebrew study and cultural activities. In 1910, a sports festival in Rehovot attracted more than a thousand participants. Soccer matches began to be held with Turkish and Arab students, and in 1912 regular soccer tournaments began to take place. After the establishment of the *British Mandate following World War I, the number and quality of sporting events increased. The Hapoel (the worker) and Beitar (named for the site of the last stand in the Second *Jewish War against *Rome) associations were formed in 1924. The desire to strengthen ties with *Diaspora Jews inspired the creation of the Jewish Olympics, the *Maccabiah, whose first games in 1932 (the 1,800-year anniversary of *Bar Kokhba's revolt) attracted 390 athletes representing fourteen nations and were enthusiastically embraced by the *Yishuv*.

Sporting competitions often became sites for expressions of anti-British sentiments and nationalistic rallies, as well as for internecine political rivalries. The importance of sports in demonstrating Israel's independence, place in the world of nations, pride, and integration of Jews from many parts of the world, was exemplified in September 1948, when a national soccer team toured the United States to raise funds and support, and in 1953, when Israel placed fifth at the European basketball championship in Moscow, in front of Jewish fans. In the ensuing years, sports increased in popularity, with regular classes and "sport badge" trials in schools; government-funded programs and facilities; the founding of the Wingate Institute for physical culture, teaching, and research; and some success in international competitions, mostly in the Asian games, and later at the Olympics. The Maccabiah games held every four years remained a popular event, although noted more for encouraging aliyah than for impressive results.

At the 1972 Munich Olympics, eleven members of the Israeli delegation were murdered by "Black September" terrorists. The atrocity, its mismanagement by German police, and the resumption of the games after only a day's hiatus all served to reinforce Israeli perceptions of world apathy and the need for self-reliance. It is a lingering wound.

As support for sports gradually increased, to the point where they became essential to Israeli society, the status of teams and players changed from amateur to professional. Sports, especially soccer, served as a harbinger and reflection of deep societal changes. These changes included the integration of non-Jews into national teams, the increasingly critical scrutiny from a greater number of media outlets, the passing of team ownership from political organizations to businesspeople and foreign oligarchs (to gain respectability and political legitimacy), the free transfer of players, and a widening gap between wealthy teams and the rest. In reaction, teams managed and owned by fans emerged, such as Hapoel Katamon FC (soccer) and Hapoel Ussishkin BC (basketball), which aimed once again to represent their communities.

Several unique historical circumstances and developments have shaped Israeli sports: a large military budget that leaves few funds for nonsecurity concerns; the universal draft, which has sometimes delayed the development of promising athletes; a poor organizational base; and the desire to create a "new Jew," strong in body and spirit. In the 1920s, religious authorities began voicing heated opposition (although some, including Rav *Kook, viewed sports favorably) and fought, sometimes physically, against holding sporting events on the *Sabbath.

Politics too has had a strong impact, as parties and ideological blocs battled on the playing field. Maccabi, Hapoel, Beitar, and Elitzur represented the liberal center, labor, the right, and religious *Zionism, respectively. From their inception, these associations often refused to compete against each other, and when they did, violence was common. Statehood in 1948 led to the formation of unified federations and leagues, but until the mid-1960s, under the "fifty-fifty system," all teams, delegations, and organizations were split equally between Maccabi and Hapoel. Several times the arrangement collapsed, and rival leagues were created until the courts intervened. With the rise of the right after the election of a Likud government in 1977, Beitar Jerusalem became the most popular soccer team, and its identification with *Mizraḥim (Jews of Middle Eastern origins) exemplified the changing power dynamics in the country.

Israel's relations with the Arab world have had a detrimental effect on its international sports activities. Until the mid-1940s, Jewish teams competed amicably with Arab counterparts in local leagues and with representatives of neighboring nations, including the Egyptian Army team. After independence, Israeli athletes and teams were tossed around and migrated among various European and Asian sports federations, sometimes being denied participation entirely. After the 1967 Six Day War (see ISRAEL, STATE OF: WARS), Muslim and Eastern European countries boycotted competition with Israeli sports teams, culminating in the country's 1982 expulsion from the Asian sports federations. For several years, with the exception of its basketball team, which remained in the Europe federation, Israeli teams were assigned to the Oceanic group – an anomaly that enabled Israel to advance, for the first and only time, to the World Cup, but inhibited progress because of a lack of competition. After the collapse of the Soviet bloc, Israel joined the Europe federation, where it faced stiffer competition but also a chance to improve. The 1993 Oslo peace process enabled limited but promising ties with Arab players and teams, but these prospects were dashed when bloodletting resumed.

Immigrants played a special role, often elevating the level of competition. In the 1930s, many Maccabiah participants chose to remain in the country rather than return to Europe, thus helping advance athletics, particularly soccer. In the early years of the state, *Eastern European world champions Agnes Keleti (gymnastics) and Angelica Rozeanu (table tennis) raised the bar, as did several gymnasts, high jumpers, and swimmers from the former USSR in the 1990s.

Israel first participated in the Olympic Games in 1952, when diver Yoav Ra'anan placed ninth, and has done so since, except for the 1980 Moscow games, when it joined a western boycott. For decades, results were poor but enthusiasm high. In the 1988 Seoul Olympics, Yoel Sela and Eldad Amir (sailing), who were headed for a certain medal but declined to sail on the last day of the competition because it coincided with *Yom Kippur, were hailed for upholding Jewish tradition over winning. After that, however, winning became a national obsession, and increased funding and training finally brought the desired results. Israel's first medals came in the 1992 Barcelona games, when Yael Arad and Oren Smadja won silver and bronze medals, respectively, in judo. Only one Israeli has ever won a gold medal: windsurfer Gal Friedman (whose first name means "wave") at the 2004 Athens games. Another windsurfer, Shahar Zubari, has won a bronze, as have kayaker Michael Kalganov and judoka Arik Ze'evi. These athletes also excelled at world and European championships, as did sailors Shimshon Brukman, Eytan Friedlander, Zefania Carmel, and Lydia Lazarov.

Tennis, too, has produced world-class performers: Shlomo Glickstein, Amos Mansdorf, Anna Smashnova, and Shahar Peer were ranked at various times since the 1980s among the world's top twenty players. In track and field, such achievements were rare, with the exception of sprinter David Tabak in the 1950s and Esther Roth-Sahamorov, who ruled Israeli track for two decades, starting in the late 1960s. Her finest moment came in the 1976 Montreal Olympics, where she placed sixth in the 100-meter hurdles, four years after her coach, Amitzur Shapira, was murdered at Munich. In the 1990s, pole vaulter Alex Averbuch shone.

Men's soccer, Israel's most popular sport, originated during late *Ottoman rule. The Palestine Football Association was established in 1928, and a league comprising British, Jewish, and Arab teams debuted in 1932. Although there was not yet a state, a national team was formed in 1934; its first games were pre-World Cup defeats to Egypt, 4–1 and 7–1. The 1956 pre-Olympic tournament with the *Soviet Union was a historic milestone for soccer and the nation. The games galvanized the identification of Soviet Jewry with the young state and were seen as both a call to open the gates to immigration and a part of the millennium-long battle against the *goyim* (nations), as expressed by popular poet Natan Alterman (see POETRY, MODERN HEBREW). The two losses did not alter these views. The national team's greatest successes came in a six-year span. It won the Asian Nations Cup (1964), reached the 1968 Olympic tournament's quarterfinals, and in the 1970 Mundial played to ties with Sweden and with Italy, the finalist. In the new millennium, the national team and the youth team have achieved respectable results, and Maccabi Haifa and Hapoel Tel Aviv have done well in European tournaments. Israel's top footballers have become cultural icons, with goalie Yaakov Chodorov, and Mordechai Spiegler, Eyal Berkovich, Chaim Revivo, and Yossi Benayoun (the latter three played well in the English and Spanish leagues) leading the way.

Basketball, second only to soccer in popularity, has been the most successful sport, with its greatest achievement the silver medal won in the 1979 European Championship of Nations. In Israel's first two decades, the league was ruled by the Hapoel and Maccabi teams of *Tel Aviv, but since the late 1960s, Maccabi has won all but two championships, at one point having twenty-three consecutive undefeated seasons. Bolstered by the best local players, new immigrants, and American players, Maccabi Tel Aviv became "the Nation's Team," winning the European champion title five times since 1977. Israel's greatest basketball stars – center Tanchum Cohen-Mintz and two dynamic guards, Tal Brody and Miki Berkovich – played for Maccabi. New Jersey-born Brody, an "All American" who immigrated in 1970 and immediately led his team and the nation to success, became known for his cry, "We are on the map," after defeating the Russian Army team in 1977, at a time when the USSR aided Israel's enemies. Berkovich, a superb clutch player, won nineteen championships and two European cups and led the national youth team to fourth place in the European championship.

Women athletes have kept pace with men, despite facing ongoing discrimination in funding, having fewer coaches and facilities, and receiving no more than 5% of all sports media coverage. Basketball is first in participation and popularity, with the leading teams being Elitzur Holon, Elitzur Ramla, and A. S. Ramat Ha-Sharon. Ramat Ha-Sharon, which is owned, run, and coached by women who are strong advocates for women's rights, reached the European Ronchetti Cup finals. Top national players included Anat Draigor, who led her Holon team to sixteen championships, and Limor Mizrachi and Shay Doron, who played briefly in the powerful WNBA league. Although a women's soccer league and a high school league have formed, and star Sylvie Jian has attained success abroad, female soccer players are still ignored or mocked. In response to legal challenges, Israel's Supreme Court determined that municipalities must increase funding for women's sports, but the national sports bodies, in which few women hold executive positions, still devote, on average, eight times more funding to men's teams.

Sports are popular in Arab communities, and Arab athletes represent the country in international competitions, with boxer Johar Abu Lashin winning the IPC world light heavyweight title. Rifat Turk, the first Arab footballer on the national team (and later deputy mayor of Tel Aviv), was followed by several others. Often they scored match-saving goals, but nonetheless were criticized for not joining in singing the national anthem. Teams representing Arab towns (with Muslim, Christian, and Jewish players who get along well) have reached the premier league, and Bnei Sakhnin won the State Cup in 2004; its elated fans waved Israeli and Palestinian flags. However, at times of heightened political tensions, anti-Arab feelings were expressed in stadiums and occasional fan violence erupted. Sports may help not only in establishing minority identity but also in serving as an "integrative enclave," with participants and fans identifying with the state. A number of projects have used sports to build bridges between Jews and Palestinians (Israeli citizens as well as those in the territories), with the Peres Center for Peace taking a leading role.

Israel excels in paraplegic sports; many athletes are former soldiers who were injured in battle. In this arena, Israelis have set many world records and won hundreds of Olympic medals, notably by basketball player and four-time Olympic table tennis champion Barukh Hagai and swimmer Karen Leibovitz.

In addition to competitive sports, *sport amami* (the peoples' sports) – including the three-day Jerusalem Hike, the Mount Tabor Run, and the swim across the Sea of Galilee –

are yearly events drawing thousands of participants of all ages and abilities. The popularity of sports is reflected in the establishment of a special government sports ministry and in the large number of cultural works devoted to it. Writers from *Bialik and Berdechevsky, through Pen and Shlonsky, and up to Gouri and Grossman, have described games and often participated in them (see LITERATURE, HEBREW entries; POETRY, MODERN HEBREW). Among a number of films that successfully blend sports, history, and art are *Cup Final*, which deals with soccer and the Lebanon War, and *Gloves*, about boxing in 1930s Tel Aviv.

In 1997, during the Maccabiah opening ceremonies in Tel Aviv, four Australian athletes marching on a bridge over the Yarkon River were killed and sixty-five others were injured when the bridge collapsed. The disaster was widely seen as a symptom of official mismanagement and a symbol of the failure of the Zionist dream, which the games embody. Yet, at the beginning of the twenty-first century, sports are more popular than ever in Israeli society.

For further reading, see Y. Galily and A. Ben-Porat, eds., "Sports, Politics and Society in the Land of Israel: Past and Present," *Israel Affairs* 13(3) (2007); H. Harif and Y. Galily, "Sports and Politics in Palestine: Football as a Mirror Reflecting the Relations between Jews and Britons," *Soccer and Society* 4(1) (2003): 41–56; H. Kaufman, "Jewish Sport in the Diaspora, Yishuv, and Israel: Between Nationalism and Politics," *Israel Studies* 10(2) (2005): 147–67; and T. Sorek, *Arab Sport in a Jewish State: The Integrative Enclave* (2007).

ALON RAAB

Sports, United States: Baseball. Baseball has been played by Jews since record keeping began after the *Civil War. Lipman "Lip" Pike, son of Dutch Jewish immigrants, was a power-hitting outfielder who played on some of the first professional barnstorming teams. A member of the St. Louis team in 1876, which was the inaugural season of the National League (NL), Pike established a Jewish presence from the beginnings of what is now known as Major League Baseball (MLB). Jacob Pike, his brother, was an umpire who officiated professionally in the 1870s. The number of Jewish players active during the formative period is unknown, as athletes commonly hid their identities to avoid *antisemitic reactions on the field and restrictions in public accommodations when traveling.

In 1919, Ty Cobb of the Detroit Tigers, an outspoken racist, ended the career of Jesse Baker (Michael Silverman) of the Washington Senators by spiking the rookie shortstop in the arm on learning he was Jewish. Among those who eventually revealed themselves as Jews were Klondike Kane (Harry Cohen), who pitched for three MLB teams before 1907, and Henry Bostwick (Lifschiftz) of the 1915 Boston Red Sox. Barney Pelty of Farmington, Missouri, pitched for the St. Louis Browns of the American League (AL) in 1903 and was known as "the Yiddish curver." George Stone, an outfielder from Lost Nation, Iowa, was the first Jew to win a MLB title, hitting .358 for the Browns in 1906. Pitcher Erskin Mayer, a Georgian, signed with Philadelphia in 1912 and won twenty-one games for the Phillies in their 1915 championship team. The Jewish presence in baseball was noted by Irving Berlin in a 1913 song, "Jake, Jake, the Yiddish Ballplayer." Songwriters Jack Norworth and Albert Von Tilzer (Gumbinski) composed "Take Me Out to the

Ballgame" (1908), which remains the game's unofficial anthem.

Among Jewish entrepreneurs active in organizing the sport were Aaron Stern, founding owner of the Cincinnati Reds, and Barney Dreyfuss, who bought the NL Pittsburgh Pirates in 1900. In 1903 Dreyfuss proposed what became the "World Series," launching the modern era of baseball; he was honored in 2008 with a special election to the Baseball Hall of Fame in Cooperstown, New York.

Jewish participation in baseball drew opposition, especially after the 1919 "Black Sox" scandal, in which eight Chicago White Sox were banned from MLB for "fixing" the World Series in return for bribes from gamblers, most prominently Arnold Rothstein. In 1923, *Collyer's Eye*, a sports magazine, reported that Sammy Bohne (Cohen) of the Reds conspired with gamblers to affect the outcomes of games. The Reds filed a libel suit, clearing Bohne's name. Henry Ford's *Dearborn Independent*, in a 1921 editorial, "The Jewish Degradation of Baseball," accused "the Jews" of turning "an American outdoor sport" into "vaudeville" for the sake of "money, money, money."

Charles Solomon "Buddy" Myer of the Washington Senators, son of an Ellisville, Mississippi, textile merchant, was the first Jewish MLB star. An infielder who played seventeen seasons (a standing career longevity record for Jewish players), Myer led the AL in stolen bases in 1928, won the batting title in 1935, and posted a .301 lifetime average. Morris "Moe" Berg, Myer's teammate for several years in Washington, was another of the relatively few college graduates then in MLB, completing a Princeton degree in languages and a Columbia law degree before signing with the White Sox in 1925. Berg had a long and undistinguished career as a catcher. In 1934, he was mysteriously named to a special team of superstars (including Babe Ruth and Jimmy Foxx) for an exhibition tour of Japan. It was later revealed that Berg had been recruited by the State Department to photograph Japanese military sites. Retiring from baseball in 1939, he took up espionage full-time, completing overseas missions during *World War II.

The first bona-fide Jewish baseball superstar was Henry Benjamin "Hank" Greenberg, the son of Romanian Jewish immigrants, who grew up in the Bronx (*New York City). Playing all but his final season with the Detroit Tigers, Greenberg hit 331 home runs (despite missing four seasons to serve in the wartime Pacific) and had a lifetime batting average of .313. He was the AL Most Valuable Player (MVP) in 1935 and 1940, leading the Tigers to World Series victories both seasons. Greenberg was harassed through much of his career with antisemitic taunts from players and fans. His refusal to play on *Yom Kippur was a model of behavior for future players, including Sandy Koufax and Shawn Green. Greenberg was the first Jewish player elected to the Hall of Fame (1956).

Sandy Koufax, a Brooklyn native, was the greatest Jewish pitcher (perhaps the greatest pitcher) to play the game; he joined the Brooklyn Dodgers in 1955, accompanying the team to Los Angeles in 1957. His impressive career statistics – four no-hitters (including a perfect game), a 2.76 lifetime Earned Run Average (ERA), and 2,396 strikeouts – do not do justice to the speed of his fastball or the intensity of his hero worship among Jewish baseball fans. He was the youngest player ever inducted into the Hall of Fame. Al Rosen, third

baseman for the Cleveland Indians (1947–56), led the AL in home runs twice and batted in more than a hundred runs for five consecutive seasons. A four-time All-star, he was the first player ever to be selected unanimously as AL MVP (1953). Hank Greenberg, then general manager of the Indians, mentored Rosen for a career as a baseball executive. Rosen eventually served as president of the Yankees (1979) and San Francisco Giants (1985–92).

Of the many Jewish executives and owners in MLB during the second half of the twentieth century, Allan H. "Bud" Selig was probably the most influential. He bought the Seattle Pilots in 1970 and transplanted them as the Milwaukee Brewers. In 1992, baseball owners appointed Selig as acting commissioner. In 1998, after selling the Brewers, Selig formally assumed office. He is the first Jewish baseball commissioner.

For further reading, see B. A. Boxerman and B. W. Boxerman, *Jews and Baseball* (2007); P. Levine, *Ellis Island to Ebbets Field: Sport and the American Jewish Experience* (1992); G. B. Kirsch, O. Harris, and C. E. Nolte, eds., *Encyclopedia of Ethnicity and Sports in the United States* (2000); and S. A. Riess, *Sports and the American Jew* (1998).   DAVID MARC

Sports, United States: Basketball. In 1891 Dr. James Naismith devised the game of basketball for the Young Men's Christian Association (YMCA) school in Springfield, Massachusetts, as an athletic indoor winter activity. Among the first known Jewish players was Frank Basloe (1887–1966), an immigrant from *Hungary, who grew up playing basketball in Herkimer, New York. Basloe made his mark on the sport as an organizer and promoter of professional barnstorming teams (1903–23) and later as an executive with several leagues. Beating the bushes for talent, Basloe raised teams that traveled the northeast quadrant of the country, challenging locals wherever Basloe could secure facilities and helping popularize the game. Basloe, who used basketball profits to capitalize a real estate business, endowed Herkimer's public library and helped found its synagogue.

Much Jewish basketball history took place in *New York City and *Philadelphia, where universities had eagerly adopted the sport because of its modest spatial demands at a time when Jewish enrollments were increasing. As with collegiate football, Jewish Ivy League students sometimes pursued basketball to counter *antisemitic stereotypes. The first known Jewish intercollegiate player, Henry Hart Elias at Columbia University (1901–03), was elected team captain as a senior. Another Columbia student, Samuel Melitzer, was the first Jewish player named to an All-American basketball team (1909). New York University, City College of New York, St. John's University, and Long Island University all became intercollegiate basketball powers with Jewish players on their rosters.

In Philadelphia, the University of Pennsylvania (Penn), Villanova University, and Temple University produced notable Jewish players and coaches. Michael Saxe starred on Penn's first Ivy League championship team in 1908 and became Villanova's first head coach (1921–26). Emanuel "Menchy" Goldblatt, a Penn All American in 1927, was a ball handler known for his stalling ability, an important element of the game before the introduction of the shot clock. Goldblatt was founding basketball coach and athletic director at Philadelphia Textile Institute (now Philadelphia University).

Mike Bloom, a 1938 All American, led Temple to its first National Invitational Tournament (NIT) championship and played professionally. Temple's Samuel Cozen (1929–30) began a distinguished Philadelphia coaching career at Overbrook High School, where he taught fundamentals to Wilt Chamberlain. As head coach at Drexel University (1953–68), he won eleven Mid-Atlantic Conference titles, with a career record of 230–94.

Harry Baum, an Austrian-born Jew who never played competitive basketball, was a pivotal figure in the sport's Jewish American history. A superb lacrosse player, Baum was a doctoral candidate in electrical engineering at Columbia when he began coaching immigrant Jewish boys at the University Settlement House. Beginning in 1906, Baum coached a youth team, the Bizzy Izzies, composed of Jewish boys who could not meet weight limits for public school teams. Baum designed an offensive strategy for the Izzies, while teaching fitness and proper nutrition; his team dominated the "midget" division of settlement house youth basketball and produced a half-dozen noteworthy basketball pioneers. Guards Barney Sedran (Sedransky) and Marty Friedman had long professional careers, sometimes playing for the same teams, including the New York Whirlwinds (1920–21), where they became known as the "Heavenly Twins." During *World War I, Friedman played for the U.S. Army's American Expeditionary Force team, which introduced basketball to Europeans. Sedran and Friedman were among the first in a tradition of star "Jewish guards," known for playmaking, ball control, and outside shooting. Both were inducted into the Basketball Hall of Fame. Another Izzie veteran, Lou Sugarman, was among the first Jewish students to win a collegiate athletic scholarship, accepting an offer from Syracuse University in 1908. Sugarman played professionally but, like many of his contemporaries, hedged his career options by earning a dental degree in the off-season. He was known to stop in the middle of a game to respond with his fists to an antisemitic remark from an opponent, fan, or teammate. Izzie veterans Ira Streusand and Jake Fuller (Furstman) played together for CCNY. Streusand, the school's first All American (1908), was so accurate from the foul line that he is sometimes cited as a factor leading to elimination of an early rule allowing a team to designate any player to shoot its free throws. Streusand and Fuller turned professional in 1911, joining Newburgh of the Hudson River League. Among their teammates was Joseph "Gid" Girsdansky, son of Max Girsdansky, a founder of the Socialist Party, U.S.A., and an NYU star who had helped the Violets to an undefeated record in 1908.

In 1919, Nat Holman, a twenty-three-year-old graduate of NYU, took over as basketball coach at CCNY, which subsequently emerged as a national basketball power, fielding a succession of Jewish All Americans: Louis Farer (1925), Pinky Match (1925), Moe Spahn (1932), Mo Goldman (1934), Bernard Fliegel (1938), Red Holzman (1942), and Irwin Dambrot (1950). The Beavers were the only team in collegiate basketball history to win both the NCAA and NIT post-season tournaments in a single season (1949–50), a feat that can never be repeated because of subsequent rule changes. Holman refused to adhere to racial exclusion agreements, which led segregation-state schools to avoid CCNY as an opponent. When the University of Kentucky was forced to play the Beavers in the 1949–50 NCAA championship game, Holman started his regular five, including two African Americans. After the CCNY victory, the Kentucky legislature ordered the state flag flown at half-staff.

Born and raised on the Lower East Side of Manhattan, Holman was team mascot for the Izzies at age eight, a college star for NYU, and a member of the Original Celtics (1922–30), one of the fabled teams of American sports. Holman, who was inducted into the Basketball Hall of Fame in 1964, helped organize the first U.S. Maccabiah Games team in 1932 and was widely known to Jewish fans across the country.

Professional basketball was an unstable business before World War II. With no "major league" in the sport, virtuoso teams were the pro game's only asset. The Philadelphia Sphas, a self-described "all-Jewish team," stands with the Original Celtics and Harlem Rens among the great pre-NBA teams. Organized in 1918 by Eddie Gottlieb, Harry Passon, and Hughie Black, with Jewish high school players, the team was originally sponsored by the Young Men's Hebrew Association (YMHA). In 1921, the South Philadelphia Hebrew Association (SPHA), a social club, agreed to back the team. The Sphas were successful at the box office; according to Harry Litwack, a Hall of Famer who coached at Temple for twenty-five years after retiring from the Sphas, there were certain antisemites who regularly attended, including a woman who sat in the front row and jabbed at Sphas players with a hat pin. After playing in several leagues that collapsed during the 1920s, the Sphas joined the American Basketball League (ABL) in 1933. Gottlieb, who had paid the franchise fee, became team owner and coach. With the Hebrew transliteration for "Spha" atop a Star of David emblazoned on their jerseys, the team played twelve seasons in the ABL, winning seven league championships. Standouts included Davey "Pretzel" Banks, a 5'5" guard who ranks thirteenth on the ABL's career scoring list; Temple All-American Mike Bloom; and Max Posnak, one of four Jewish starters on the 1929 St. John's University "Wonder Five" team.

In 1946, Gottlieb was offered the Philadelphia franchise in the new Basketball Association of America (BAA). However, BAA owners balked at the idea of the "all-Jewish team," and Gottlieb agreed to their terms, renaming his club the Philadelphia Warriors and taking some of the best players with him. The Sphas, still technically in existence, were left without a coach, home arena, or league. However, their legacy was still evident when the Warriors won the BAA championship in 1947 with three Jewish players on the team: Petey Rosenberg, a St. Joseph's star, and two NYU All Americans, Jerry Fleishman and Ralph Kaplowitz. Eventually, the Sphas were sold, and the once mighty "all-Jewish team" became the Washington Generals, who lost game after game, as per the script, to another team too "ethnic" for the new professional basketball league: the "all-black" Harlem Globetrotters, an exhibition team created by Abe Saperstein in *Chicago in 1926.

The National Basketball Association (NBA) came into existence in 1949 with the merger of the BAA and NBL. Maurice Podoloff, a Russian Jewish immigrant, served as president until 1961; he helped the NBA gain access to larger cities and better arenas, as pro basketball moved toward parity with baseball and football. The NBA's annual "most valuable player" award bears Podoloff's name, and its "rookie of the year" award is named for Gottlieb, acknowledging both as league founders. David Stern became the NBA's chief executive in 1984. Under his leadership, pro basketball has gained international prominence and a domestic marketing apparatus that is the envy of other sports.

Two Jewish NBA pioneers, a player and an owner-coach, both of whom would be inducted into the Basketball Hall of Fame, were crucial figures in the early success of the league. Adolph "Dolph" Schayes was perhaps the most accomplished Jewish player of the 1950s. A star at NYU (1944–48), he was drafted a year before the NBA consolidation by both the New York Knicks (BAA) and the Syracuse Nationals (NBL). Schayes stunned hometown fans by choosing Syracuse. During fifteen NBA seasons, he was a twelve-time East Division All-star and four-time all-NBA forward, and he led the league in free throws twice and rebounds once, scoring 18,434 career points and averaging 18.2 per game. In 1954–55, he gave Syracuse its only NBA championship, sinking two free throws in the final seconds of the final game against the Fort Wayne Pistons, who had led by 17 at the half. The team left Syracuse in 1963 for *Philadelphia, replacing the Warriors, which Gottlieb had moved to *San Francisco. Schayes became head coach of the new Philadelphia 76ers, winning NBA Coach of the Year honors in 1966. His son, Danny Schayes, an All American at Syracuse University, played in the NBA from 1981 to 1999. During that time, the number of Jewish players in the league declined. In 1986, when Ernie Grunfeld retired from the New York Knicks, Danny Schayes was the only Jewish player in the NBA. Others would follow, but no more than a handful.

Lester Harrison formed the NBL Rochester Royals in 1945, appointing himself coach. The Royals were NBL champions in their first two seasons and, after consolidation, won the 1951 NBA championship. Harrison racially integrated the NBL in 1946, signing two African American players: Pop Gates, who had played for the "all-black" Harlem Rens, and Dolly King (Long Island University). Among several Jewish players he signed were Jack "Dutch" Garfinkel, originator of the "look away" pass, and William "Red" Holzman, who later coached the New York Knicks to NBA championships in 1970 and 1973. Making their impact as coaches rather than players, Harrison and Holzman signaled the direction that Jewish involvement in the sport was taking.

Of the many Jewish NBA coaches, none was more successful than Arnold "Red" Auerbach, the Brooklyn-born son of Russian immigrants. A fair collegiate player, he never turned professional. However, as coach of the *Boston Celtics (1950–66), he built the NBA's greatest dynasty, winning nine league championships. Retiring from coaching with a record of 938–479, he remained the Celtics' general manager and president, shaping teams that added seven more league titles. Like Holman and Harrison, Auerbach opposed segregation in basketball, drafting and signing Chuck Cooper, the NBA's first African American player in 1950, and hiring Bill Russell, the NBA's first African American coach, in 1966.

For further reading, see F. Basloe (with D. G. Rohman), *I Grew up with Basketball: Twenty Years of Barnstorming with Cage Greats of Yesterday* (1952); P. Berger, *Heroes of Pro Basketball* (1968); P. Levine, *Ellis Island to Ebbets Field: Sport and the American Jewish Experience* (1992); G. B. Kirsch, O. Harris, and C. E. Nolte, eds. *Encyclopedia of Ethnicity and Sports in the United States* (2000); S. A. Riess, *Sports and the American*

Jew (1998); and J. Rosin, *Philly Hoops: The Sphas and Warriors* (2003).

DAVID MARC

Sports, United States: Football. American football was first played in the 1870s as an intercollegiate sport at elite colleges in the northeast and was gradually taken up by colleges across the country. Professional teams were formed by the turn of the century, but not systematically organized until the 1920s. Henry Moses Epstein, a member of the Columbia University team in 1870, is the first known Jewish student to play intercollegiate football. The first University of Pennsylvania football team, fielded in 1871, included Emil G. Hirsch, who went on to serve as rabbi for forty-two years at Sinai Synagogue, *Chicago's largest Reform congregation (see JUDAISM, REFORM: NORTH AMERICA). Lucius Littauer, heir to his family's glove-making fortune, played for Harvard (1875–78) and coached the Crimson team before serving five terms as a Republican congressman. Phil King, who quarterbacked at Princeton, was the first Jew named to an All-American football team, winning the honor three times (1891–93).

A total of nine Jewish students were selected as All Americans before 1920. Among them was Arthur "Bluey" Bluenthal (1911–12) of Princeton, believed to be the model for Robert Cohn, a character in Ernest Hemingway's *The Sun Also Rises*. Joseph Alexander of Syracuse University (1918–20) linked traditional collegiate football to the emerging National Football League (NFL). A practicing physician in 1925, he was the first player to sign a contract with the NFL's New York Giants and, as player-coach in 1926, the first Jewish head coach in the league. He returned to full-time medical practice in 1929.

Benny Friedman made the forward pass his principal offensive weapon, throwing a record twenty touchdown passes for the Giants in 1929. A successful head football coach at the City College of New York (CCNY) for nine years, Friedman became the first athletic director at Brandeis University. In the 1960s, Friedman spoke out on behalf of pension benefits for NFL pioneers, many of whom were suffering from chronic injuries that had impoverished them. As a result, he was effectively blacklisted from coaching and front-office positions and ignored by the Pro Football Hall of Fame. After a leg amputation necessitated by diabetes, Friedman committed suicide at age 76. He was inducted into the Hall of Fame posthumously in 2005.

John Alexander played only two pro seasons, but is acknowledged as an innovator in football defense. As a defensive tackle for the Milwaukee Badgers in 1922, he unveiled a new style of playing his position that included roaming between the line of scrimmage and the defensive backfield to achieve maximum flexibility in anticipating offensive strategy. Alexander credited the idea to his Milwaukee teammate Paul Robeson (the singer and political activist), whom he had also known while playing for Rutgers University in 1919. Brooklyn-born Sid Luckman had a distinguished college career as the quarterback of otherwise weak Columbia teams (1936–39). After a rough first professional season, Luckman took the Chicago Bears to the NFL title, defeating the Washington Redskins 73–0 in the championship game. In eleven seasons, Luckman passed for 14,683 yards and 137 touchdowns, bringing the Bears four league titles.

Among head coaches, Sid Gillman was known as one of football's great analysts and strategists. He is credited as the originator of the "West Coast offense," which places primary emphasis on deep forward passes, making use of the width as well as the length of the gridiron. Gilman, who had his greatest success with the San Diego Chargers, winning five division titles and an American Football League (AFL) championship, was an early advocate of using film review sessions for game preparation. Other important Jewish head coaches include Allie Sherman of the New York Giants (1961–68) and Marv Levy of the Montreal Alouettes (Canadian Football League, 1973–77), Kansas City Chiefs (1978–82), and Buffalo Bills (1986–97).

The first Jewish team owner was Nate Abrams, silent partner of the celebrated Earl "Curly" Lambeau of the Green Bay Packers. Another owner, Art Modell, was a New York advertising executive before buying the Cleveland Browns in 1961. When Cleveland city officials failed to meet his demands for stadium improvements in 1995, Modell moved the team to Baltimore. Modell made a lasting impact on the NFL behind the scenes, representing owners in television negotiations that led to increasingly lucrative contracts. Al Davis, owner of the Oakland Raiders, had served as an AFL commissioner in 1966. Under Davis, the Raiders became one of the most successful teams in professional sports, winning thirteen division championships, one AFL championship, and (after the merger with the NFL), three Super Bowls.

Although football referees are usually anonymous to the public, Jerry Markbreit, who officiated in high school, college, and professional football for forty-three years, achieved a degree of fame as the author of three books, including *Last Call: Memoirs of an NFL Referee* (with A. Steinberg, 2001), and as a columnist in the *Chicago Tribune* who answered questions on football rules. After ten seasons of officiating in the Big Ten Conference, Markbreit joined the NFL as a line judge in 1976 and was promoted to head referee after just one season. During his twenty-three years in the NFL, Markbreit was head referee in a record four Super Bowls.

Useful sources include B. Friedman. *The Passing Game* (1931); G. B. Kirsch, O. Harris, and C. E. Nolte, eds., *Encyclopedia of Ethnicity and Sports in the United States* (2000); P. Levine, *Ellis Island to Ebbets Field: Sport and the American Jewish Experience* (1992); B. Postal, J. Silver, and R. Silver, eds., *Encyclopedia of Jews in Sports* (1965); and S. A. Riess, *Sports and the American Jew* (1998).

DAVID MARC

Sports, United States: Women. American Jewish women have been active participants in American sports as athletes, administrators, and advocates. They have achieved national and international success in sports such as basketball, swimming, track and field, tennis, and golf.

Jewish women's involvement in athletics on a significant scale began at the end of the nineteenth century, first at Jewish settlement houses (see SOCIAL WORK: UNITED STATES) and then at Young Men's and Young Women's Hebrew Associations where immigrant Jewish women's participation in physical exercise and sport was encouraged as part of their Americanization process (see SPORTS AND AMERICANIZATION). While some Jewish women and girls engaged in sport for its health benefits, others became competitors. Women who challenged traditional gender and ethnic boundaries included Charlotte Epstein (1884–1938)

in competitive swimming and the Olympic Games, Lillian Copeland (1904–1964) as an Olympic track and field star, and Elaine Rosenthal (1896–2003) in competitive golf. Jewish women basketball players opened athletic prospects for other women.

In 1885 the Young Women's Union in *Philadelphia, the oldest Jewish settlement house in the United States, was established. It included a school for domestic instruction, classes in English and reading, and recreation and sports activities. Jewish women instructed young Jewish women and girls in calisthenics and gymnastics, and after a new building opened in 1900, both girls and boys used the gymnasium. Philanthropists who founded the Irene Kaufmann Settlement House in Pittsburgh in 1895 incorporated sport and physical education into its program; it offered women's volleyball, gymnastics, track, and other sports. *New York City's Educational Alliance and Hebrew Technical Institute for Girls, *Boston's Hebrew Industrial School, Detroit's Hannah Schloss Memorial Building, St. Louis's Jewish Educational Alliance, and other immigrant aid organizations integrated sport with educational programs for Jewish women and girls.

Chicago Hebrew Institute (CHI), the forerunner of today's Jewish *Community Centers, was organized in 1903 by a group of young men to promote the moral, physical, religious, and civic welfare of Jewish immigrants and residents in *Chicago, both male and female. In the report for 1913–14, the superintendent noted the success of the "Ladies of the English School for Foreigners Gymnasium Class." The opening of a new gymnasium and swimming pool at the CHI in 1915, with separate facilities for men and women, promoted women's athletic participation. Girls now had their own gym in which to develop their basketball ability and competitive spirit. The 1921 team compiled an impressive record and went undefeated in twenty-six games. They played teams from the Hull House settlement, the Illinois Athletic Club, church teams, and working-class girls' teams. In volleyball, too, these Jewish girls earned victories. At the Jewish People's Institute (the CHI changed its name in 1922), girls demonstrated prowess in swimming and won events in Chicago city competitions.

New York City's Young Women's Hebrew Association (YWHA), the oldest in the United States, offered physical culture to immigrant Jewish women at the beginning of the twentieth century. The large number of women using the facilities led to a campaign for a new building. In 1914 the impressive new YWHA facility opened with a comprehensive program in sports and physical culture training; it housed a synagogue as well. Jewish women and girls participated in the Young Women's Hebrew Athletic League, competing against other YWHAs and YWCAs.

Most YWHAs, however, had neither their own funding nor female staff trained in physical education and sports. During the early twentieth century, most YWHAs were affiliated with Young Men's Hebrew Association (YMHAs) and YMHA athletic spaces usually remained the male domain. Over time, however, with the aid of the National Jewish Welfare Board (JWB), several YMHA–YWHAs in various communities provided more athletic spaces for women. The JWB, which was organized in 1921 and became the national governing body for YMHAs and YWHAs and the National Council of Young Men's Hebrew and Kindred Associations, actively promoted the merger of YMHAs and YWHAs and sought to develop them into Jewish Community Centers (JCCs).

Basketball held wide appeal for women and girls at Jewish Ys. However, the women's basketball game differed from the men's version to accommodate concerns that basketball was too physically rough on women's bodies. Some medical commentators worried that too much physical exertion by women harmed their reproductive ability and that strenuous athletics promoted competition, rather than female cooperation. Jewish immigrant Senda Berenson became a leading physical educator of women and would become known as the "Mother of Women's Basketball." While attending the Boston Normal School for Gymnastics, she became interested in women's physical education. In 1892 Berenson became the Director of Physical Training at Smith College in Northampton, Massachusetts. After observing Dr. James Naismith's new basketball game at Springfield College, Berenson organized the first women's basketball game at Smith College in 1892, adapting the rules for women. Women's basketball gained popularity for Jews and Gentiles at colleges, schools, YWHAs and YWCAs, and in working-class leagues. To honor her vital role in basketball, Berenson was the first woman inducted into the Basketball Hall of Fame.

American women wanting to pursue competitive swimming benefited from the impressive leadership and reform activism of Charlotte Epstein. As an athlete and as an administrator promoting competitive aquatic sports for women in the Women's Swimming Association (WSA) and through her major involvement in the Olympic Games, the Maccabiah Games (the Jewish Olympics, begun in *Palestine in 1932 [see SPORTS: ISRAEL]), and YWHAs, Epstein changed the sporting culture for women. During the early twentieth century, male officials governing amateur athletics prohibited women swimmers from competing in sanctioned swim races, national championships, and the Olympic Games. They expressed concerns about young women and girls engaging in vigorous competitions and being watched by spectators. Epstein led the way to overcome gender restrictions in swimming for Jewish and non-Jewish swimmers alike. Gertrude Ederle, Olympian and the first woman to swim the English Channel (1926), learned to swim at Epstein's swimming club and credited Epstein and the WSA for launching the successful swimming careers of many early American swimming champions.

In several ways, Epstein campaigned to reform gender constraints in aquatic sports. She promoted the national and international success of WSA swimmers, including Olympians and national champions Aileen Riggin, Helen Meaney, Alice Lord, Eleanor Holm, as well as Gertrude Ederle. She also battled the U.S. Olympic Committee to enable American women swimmers and divers to go to the 1920 Olympics in Antwerp, Belgium, the first time females were allowed to compete in these sports at the Olympics. Epstein achieved the official position of Olympic team manager of the U.S. Women's Swimming Team for the 1920, 1924, and 1932 Games. She chaired the Swimming Committee in the 1935 Second Maccabiah Games held in *Tel Aviv, which included Jewish athletes from thirty countries. In 1936, however, Epstein refused to attend the *Berlin Olympic Games. As a Jew, she boycotted American participation in the "Nazi Olympics," and she withdrew from the American Olympic Committee (AOC) to protest *Nazi policies. Epstein's influential swimming career continued until her death in 1938. In 1939, in recognition of Epstein's distinguished service, the AOC issued a resolution to honor her; she was also inducted into the International Swimming Hall of Fame and the International Jewish Sports Hall of Fame.

American Jewish women also competed in track and field. In the 1920s Lillian Copeland attended the University of Southern California, where she became an outstanding track and field athlete, winning nine national titles and setting world records in the javelin throw and the discus throw. On the American women's Olympic team in the 1928 Olympics, she earned a silver medal in the discus. At the 1932 Los Angeles Olympic Games, Copeland won the gold medal in the discus throw, setting a world record. Sybil Koff, another track and field star in national competitions, contributed to American track and field victories at the 1932 and 1935 Maccabiah Games, winning a total of seven gold medals in these first two competitions. Although they both qualified for the 1936 American Olympic track team, Koff and Copeland boycotted the "Nazi Olympics."

Golf at Jewish country clubs drew the athletic interest of affluent Jewish women who had been excluded from Protestant country clubs. Elaine Rosenthal Reinhardt became one of the most prominent golfers in the early twentieth century, playing at Ravisloe Country Club, a Jewish club in Homewood, Illinois, outside Chicago. Her father, a successful businessman, was an active member of Ravisloe Country Club, and her mother and sister also played golf on the Ravisloe links. In 1914, at age 18, she reached the finals in the U.S. women's national golf championship in New York and in 1917 won the first of three Western Women's Golf Championships (also in 1918 and 1925), becoming the first woman to earn the "triple crown." During World War I, golf matches were halted, but Reinhardt was among elite golfers invited to participate in American Red Cross golf exhibition fundraisers with stars like Bobby Jones (Borish 2002, 84). At times, *antisemitic incidents occurred in the Western Women's Golf Association, as in 1923 when Jewish women golfers from six Jewish clubs in or near Chicago were barred from competing in the championship.

Outstanding tennis player Julie Heldman of Houston, Texas, won a gold, bronze, and silver medal in singles and doubles events at the 1968 Olympics in Mexico City, when tennis was an exhibition sport. She won three gold medals in the 1969 Maccabiah Games. Heldman was ranked as high as #2 in the United States in 1968–69 and #5 in the world in 1969. Her mother, Gladys Heldman (1922–2003), was the #1 amateur player in Texas and competed in the U.S. Open and Wimbledon; in 1953 she founded *World Tennis* magazine, which she sold in the 1970s. Gladys championed women's professional tennis, advancing its efforts to provide more prize money for women at a time when men dominated the sport. In 1970 Julie Heldman spearheaded the efforts of the best women players, like Billie Jean King and Rosie Casals, to form their own pro tour to battle gender discrimination and the lack of prize money. She played in the first Virginia Slims Circuit tournament, held in Houston in 1970; the Virginia Slims Circuit gained popularity and later merged with the U.S. Tennis Association. In honor of her achievements in sports Gladys Heldman was inducted into the International Tennis Hall of Fame in 1979 and the International Jewish Sports Hall of Fame in 1989; Julie Heldman was inducted into this Hall of Fame in 2001.

In the first decade of the twenty-first century, American Jewish women continue to play sports, participate in new opportunities in sports competitions, and pursue careers in sports industries like *sportscasting on *radio and *television. Contemporary Jewish women honored in 2003 at the Jewish Sports Hall of Fame included professional golf champion Amy Alcott, ESPN sportscaster Linda Cohn, Olympic world record swimmer and Maccabiah champion Marilyn Romanesky, and figure skaters Sarah Hughes, Olympic Gold Medal, 2002, and Alexandra (Sasha) Cohen, Olympic Silver Medal, 2006, among many others.

For further reading, see L. J. Borish, "American Jewish Women in Sports," in *Encyclopedia of American Jewish History*, ed. S. H. Norwood and E. G. Pollack (2008), 2:522–27; idem, "Women, Sports, and American Jewish Identity in the Late Nineteenth and Early Twentieth Centuries," in *With God on Their Side: Sport in the Service of Religion*, ed. T. Magdalinksi and T. J. L. Chandler (2002), 71–98; and S. A. Riess, eds., *Sports and the American Jew* (1998).   LINDA J. BORISH

Sportscasters. Broadcasts of sporting events began during the 1920s with the rise of commercial *radio. At first, staff announcers were assigned to cover these events, with little thought given to the need for specialized knowledge. Bill Stern, an actor and stage director who sometimes worked as a radio announcer, was among the first to specialize in sports broadcasting or sportscasting. After he lost a leg in an automobile accident in 1935, he gave up other pursuits to work full-time for National Broadcasting Corporation (NBC) radio sports, covering college football games, championship boxing, and other major events for the network as a play-by-play announcer. Between 1940 and 1952, Stern was NBC's first sports director. Marty Glickman, the Bronx-born son of Romanian Jewish immigrants, was instrumental in developing the art of play-by-play description. A track and football star at Syracuse University and member of the 1936 U.S. Olympic track team, Glickman joined the staff of New York radio station WHN as an unpaid office boy in 1939. Within a year he was broadcasting professional hockey games. In 1943, Glickman convinced WHN management to allow him to attempt a live broadcast of a charity all-star basketball game at Madison Square Garden, although basketball was then considered too fluid a game to describe coherently for radio audiences. Glickman addressed the problem by inventing a variety of descriptive terms, including "top of the key" and "set shot," which remain in common use. After World War II, Glickman became a ubiquitous radio and television voice in New York sports, serving as principal play-by-play announcer for many of the city's professional teams, including the Knicks (basketball), Rangers (hockey), and Giants and Jets (football). He was at the microphone for scores of events at every level of competition, from high school football to international track and field meets. However, Glickman was repeatedly overlooked for lucrative National Football League network television positions because of a voice characterized euphemistically by some executives as "too New York" for national audiences.

Johnny Most, whose unmistakably raspy voice announced Boston Celtics basketball games on radio and television from 1953 to 1990, was mentored by Glickman in the 1940s. The grandson of the German Jewish anarchist philosopher, Johann Most, Johnny Most developed into a quintessential home-team partisan, shamelessly rooting for the Celtics and denigrating opponents, a sportscasting style Glickman abhorred. In the 1960s, Glickman hired Marv Albert (Marvin Philip Aufrichtig) as his statistician and helped guide Albert to a career as a leading national play-by-play announcer in professional basketball and hockey.

Sam Balter, born in Detroit, was an All-American basketball player at UCLA (1927–29) and then a member of the Universal Pictures basketball team, which was selected to represent the United States at the *Berlin Olympic Games in 1936. The only Jewish American to win a gold medal at the *Nazi-hosted Olympics, Balter refused to appear at the awards ceremony with Adolph Hitler. Balter was the voice of southern California sports before the region had major league teams, serving as a play-by-play announcer for the Hollywood Stars and Los Angeles Angels baseball teams and the Los Angeles Stars basketball team, as well as for UCLA collegiate football and basketball (1945–52). He achieved a national following as host of *One for the Book*, the first radio sports commentary program, which aired on the Mutual network for eighteen years. Balter appeared in dozens of feature films and television programs as Hollywood's archetypal sportscaster.

Mel Allen (Melvin Allen Israel) was born in Birmingham, Alabama, the son of Russian immigrants. Admitted to the University of Alabama at fifteen, he began his career as a student, calling Crimson Tide football games on radio; he continued to cover football through much of his life, including fourteen Rose Bowl games. However, Allen was best known for his baseball work, serving as principal radio and television play-by-play announcer for the New York Yankees (1949–64) and for twenty-four All-star games and thirteen World Series. He also hosted the first baseball highlights program on television, *This Week in Baseball*. A master of understatement, Allen greeted even the most spectacular home run with his signature phrase, "Well, how about that?" In 1978, he received the Ford Frick Award, Major League Baseball's highest honor to a nonplayer.

Howard Cosell (Cohen) is remembered by many as a color commentator on American Broadcasting Corporation's (ABC) *Monday Night Football* telecasts during the 1970s. He was a brash, vociferous attorney-turned-broadcaster, and some thought the persona he projected bordered on stereotype. Earlier in his career, Cosell helped expand the role of the sportscaster from objective describer to advocacy journalist. This was especially true in boxing, the one sport in which Cosell served as a play-by-play announcer. He was alone among sportscasters in supporting Muhammad Ali when the boxing establishment stripped him of the heavyweight championship in response to political pressure, and Cosell did not hesitate to denounce poor officiating, something now expected of announcers. Suzyn Waldman, a former actress and singer, was one of the first female play-by-play announcers in Major League Baseball, joining the Yankees in 1994, and she has since become a color commentator. Waldman's readiness to show emotional responses

to events has made her a controversial figure among fans.
DAVID MARC

Stam, Stammaim. This term, which means "anonymous," refers to the editorial (stammaitic) layer of the Babylonian *Talmud, dating to the sixth century CE and possibly extending later. As the final authorities in the talmudic process, the anonymous Stammaim played a significant role in redacting tannaitic (see TANNAIM) and amoraic (see AMORAIM) texts into the form in which they appear today. See also SABORAIM.

Straus Family. This American Jewish family was prominent in business and politics. **Lazarus** Straus (d. 1898) was born in Otterburg, *Germany, and arrived in the *United States in 1854 after participating in the German revolutions of 1848. He worked as a peddler in the American South (see UNITED STATES, SOUTHERN), and after the *Civil War, he moved to *New York City, where he opened a crockery and glassware store with his two eldest sons.

Lazarus's youngest child, **Oscar** (1850–1926), was best known for his national and international political service, most notably serving as the secretary of commerce and labor (1906–09) for President Theodore Roosevelt; he was the first Jewish cabinet secretary. Oscar also represented the United States in Constantinople as minister (1887–89, 1898–99) and ambassador (1909–10); he worked with Woodrow Wilson to make the League of Nations part of the Versailles Treaty. In addition to his political prominence, Oscar Straus was also deeply involved in Jewish causes, serving on the boards of major Jewish organizations, raising money for Jews in *Eastern Europe, and helping found the American Jewish Historical Society.

Lazarus's youngest child **Isidor** (1845–1912) was a successful businessman who also entered politics. After the Civil War, he went into business with his father and his brother **Nathan**, and the two brothers subsequently became sole owners of R. H. Macy & Co. He later served New York in the House of Representatives and worked closely with President Grover Cleveland. Isidor was active in the Jewish community, serving on the boards of local and national religious institutions, and was president of the Educational Alliance. Isidor and his wife Ida died aboard the Titanic in 1912; their son **Jesse** (1872–1936) served as U.S. Ambassador to *France between 1933 and 1936.
MICHAEL R. COHEN

Strauss, Leo (1899–1973) was a German-born political theorist whose academic career unfolded mostly in the *United States. Although Strauss is best known for his interpretive studies of ancient and modern political philosophers, scholars have been increasingly attentive to his lifelong preoccupation with what he called the "theological-political problem," especially in its Jewish guise. His youthful essays on Jewish matters reflect his early commitment to political *Zionism, his awareness of its limitations, and his grappling with the avatars of modern Jewish thought (see THOUGHT, MODERN) from *Spinoza to *Rosenzweig (M. Zank ed., *Leo Strauss, The Early Writings: 1921–1932* [2002]). Strauss's first two books, *Spinoza's Critique of Religion* and *Philosophy and Law*, chart his path away from modern attempts to resolve the problem of Judaism toward an investigation of medieval Jewish philosophical efforts to reconcile the

heritage of *Jerusalem with that of the Greek philosophical tradition (see THOUGHT, MEDIEVAL). His subsequent studies of medieval Jewish thinkers such as Judah *Halevi and above all *Maimonides were marked by an emphasis on the esoteric character of their writing and the necessity of "reading between the lines" to arrive at their true intentions. In his own far from transparent writings on these thinkers, Strauss seems to have intimated that Maimonides may not have been at bottom a believing Jew at all, but a philosopher who upheld rabbinic *Judaism primarily for political reasons. Strauss's essays in *Persecution and the Art of Writing* and his introductory essay to Shlomo Pines' authoritative translation of the *Guide of the Perplexed* have sparked ongoing controversies over the nature of Maimonides' "secret teaching."

Strauss's own theological position has itself been a subject of much controversy. He made perfectly clear his belief that Jerusalem and Athens (Greek philosophy) present "incompatible claims" to our allegiance. Jerusalem's claim, he repeatedly stated, remains intact and eternally irrefutable even after the onslaught of the Enlightenment-bred criticism of religion. In a number of his later essays, he eloquently and admiringly reiterated the message emanating from Jerusalem as the call to live in "obedient love" of the Creator of the universe. He identified the creative tension between Jerusalem and Athens as the vital nerve of western civilization and recommended that "every one of us can be and ought to be either the one or the other, the philosopher open to the challenge of theology, or the theologian open to the challenge of philosophy" ("Progress or Return? The Contemporary Crisis in Western Civilization," *Modern Judaism* 1[1] [1981]: 17–45). None of these statements, however, have erased the suspicion that Strauss himself made his own personal decision in favor of Athens. Both his preponderant focus on the great thinkers of the western philosophical tradition and the testimony of some of his closest students have strengthened such suspicions. Yet the case is not closed. The very title of Kenneth Hart Green's study of Strauss's Jewish thought (*Jew and Philosopher: The Return to Maimonides in the Jewish Thought of Leo Strauss* [1993]) reflects the fact that Strauss can still be read as a thinker whose own fundamental allegiance was truly dual in nature.
ALLAN ARKUSH

Suffering: See EVIL AND SUFFERING

Sukkot (literally, "Booths"), also known as the Feast of Booths or the Feast of Tabernacles, is one of the three *pilgrimage *festivals, together with *Passover and *Shavuot. It takes place between the 15th and 21st of *Tishri. Many Jews in the *Diaspora observe an additional, eighth day (see later discussion and SHEMINI ATZERET). Sukkot was originally an agricultural celebration, marking the fall harvest (Deut 16:16). The agricultural nature of the holiday is underscored in Exodus 23:16 and 34:22 where it is described as *Hag Ha-Asif*, the Feast of Ingathering (of the fruits of the harvest).

Sukkot also plays a key role in the historical and spiritual identity of the Jewish people. The Israelites are instructed to live in booths during the seven-day holiday as a memorial to the exodus from *Egypt, "in order that future generations may know that I made the Israelite people live in booths when I brought them out of Egypt" (Lev 23:41–43). Sukkot's broad significance is likely why King *Solomon chose it as the day on which to dedicate the *Temple in *Jerusalem (1 Kgs 8:2) and why it is designated in the Bible as the holiday on which the *Torah is read publicly (Deut 31:10–12; Neh 8:1–18).

*Rabbinic Judaism emphasizes Sukkot's celebratory mood, referring to it as *zeman simḥateinu*, the time of our rejoicing. In fact, the Rabbis describe an elaborate, joyful ceremony called *Simḥat Beit ha-Sho'evah* (literally, "the rejoicing at the place of water drawing"), a ritual derived from Sukkot's association with the fall season and rainfall. Sukkot's observance involves two unique symbols: the *sukkah* itself and the four species. Each household is to construct a *sukkah* and dwell in it for the duration of the festival, conducting meals and even sleeping in it. This practice serves as a commemoration of the Israelites' experience in the desert. There are many rabbinic guidelines as to the building of the *sukkah*; for example, it must have a minimum of three walls and a roof of natural material (*sekhakh*). Talmudic Rabbis debated whether the *sukkah* is a representation of God's "clouds of glory" (*ananei kavod*) or God's sheltering presence, rather than of actual desert huts (BT *Sukkah* 11b). The four species – palm (*lulav*), citron (*etrog*), myrtle (*hadas*), and willow (*aravah*) – are bundled together and waved in every direction during parts of the synagogue service and paraded as symbols of joy and of the integral relationship among God, the Land of Israel, and the Jewish people.

Three other holy days have become incorporated into the observance of Sukkot; they deepen the holiday's meaning and add to its festivity. Hoshanah Rabbah (the seventh day of Sukkot, the 21st of Tishri) incorporates evocative rituals involving the four species; medieval *kabbalists deemed it the final day of annual judgment (*Zohar, Tzav* 31b). Shemini Atzeret, the 22nd of Tishri, which serves as both the eighth day of Sukkot in the Diaspora and a separate ordained festival, shares all of the characteristics of Sukkot, excluding the waving of the four species and dwelling in the *sukkah*. Finally, the joyous celebration of *Simḥat Torah has become appended to Sukkot; it is observed on the same day as Shemini Atzeret in *Israel and in many *Reform congregations (22nd of Tishri) and on the 23rd of Tishri by Conservative, Reconstructionist, and Orthodox Jews (see entries under JUDAISM) in the Diaspora.

For further reading, see P. Steinberg, *Celebrating the Jewish Year: The Fall Holidays* (2009); I. Greenberg, *The Jewish Way: Living the Holidays* (1993); P. Goodman, *The Sukkot/Simchat Torah Anthology* (1988); and I. Klein, *A Guide to Religious Jewish Practice* (1979).   PAUL STEINBERG

Sulam, Sarra Copia (ca. 1592–1641; also Sara Copia Sullam) was a Jewish writer, poet, and patron in early modern *Venice who cultivated a circle of Christian men of letters who gave her lessons in literature and philosophy in exchange for financial backing and intellectual camaraderie. She began a correspondence with the Genoese monk Ansaldo Cebà after reading his drama, *L'Ester*. She also maintained relations with Leon *Modena, who also wrote a play in Italian about *Esther and dedicated it to her. Gradually, Copia Sulam's Christian friends turned against her. Baldassare Bonifacio, a poet, priest, and legal scholar, published a treatise, "On the Immortality of the Soul," in which he claimed that Copia Sulam did not believe in this doctrine. She published a riposte, "The Manifesto of Sarra Copia Sulam, a Jewish Woman, in which She Refutes and Disavows the Opinion Denying Immortality of the Soul, Falsely Attributed to Her by Signor Baldassare Bonifacio." Two other members of her circle, the poets Numidio Paluzzi and Alessandro Berardelli, began to steal from her. She severed ties with them and brought charges against them. In revenge, in two publications, *Le Satire Sarreidi* and *Rime del Signor Numidio Paluzzi*, they accused her of stealing Paluzzi's writings and publishing them as her own.

As a Jewish woman writer who had both captivated and bested Christian clerics in public, Copia Sulam was an ideal target for accusations that would undermine her accomplishments as a woman and a Jew. An unidentified contemporary wrote a defense of Copia Sulam in the form of an imaginary trial before Apollo, in which some of history's greatest women writers defended her. Her Jewishness, which they mentioned frequently in their support of her, was not perceived as an obstacle to receiving a fair hearing. A recent compilation is D. Harran, ed. and trans., *Jewish Poet and Intellectual in Seventeenth-Century Venice: The Works of Sarra Copia Sulam in Verse and Prose along with Writings of Her Contemporaries in Her Praise, Condemnation, or Defense* (2009).

HOWARD TZVI ADELMAN

Summer Camping. Organized summer camping is a distinctly American phenomenon. Three periods of development in the history of Jewish summer camping in North America can be identified.

American Jewry's earliest encounters with the American camping movement were direct outgrowths of the Settlement, Fresh Air, and other social reform initiatives that arose during the last decade of the nineteenth century (see SOCIAL WORK: UNITED STATES). Camp Lehman (renamed Camp Isabella Freedman), established in 1893 by the Jewish Working Girls Vacation Society of *New York, may have been the first Jewish camp in the *United States. Jewish reformers wanted to establish settlement camps specifically for the children of Jewish immigrants. The Educational Alliance in New York founded a camp in 1901 that was incorporated as Surprise Lake Camp in 1902. In Cleveland, a committee of the United Jewish Charities established the first of many Fresh Air Camps in 1904. The *National Council of Jewish Women founded Camp Wise (1907) "for needy children, mothers, and babies." In addition to the Jewish camps that were sponsored by social welfare organizations, a host of privately owned camps cropped up during the first few decades of the twentieth century. Although these camps were privately owned, many of their founders were progressive thinkers who embraced the ideals that had inspired the pioneers of American camping.

The second phase was the emergence of educational camps or camps with an explicitly Jewish mission. In the early years of the twentieth century, many Jewish leaders began to contemplate new and innovative means to improve and strengthen Jewish *education in America and to counter assimilation. Efforts to acculturate and Americanize East European immigrants had been so effective that many Jews were drifting away from Jewish life and religious practice. Jewish educator Samson Benderly (1876–1944) insisted that a revitalized Jewish educational system could be effective in safeguarding the future of Jewish life in America if it focused less on "the amount of knowledge obtained... (and more on) the creation of a Jewish atmosphere." The camping environment emerged as an innovative vehicle for the promulgation of experiential Jewish learning. With the establishment of Camp Cejwin (1919), sponsored by the Central Jewish Institute, and Camp Boiberik (1919), a secular camp with an emphasis on *Yiddish language sponsored by the Sholem Aleichem Folk Institute, American Jews slowly began to recognize the educative potential of organized camping.

Some of the camps established during this period actively espoused a particular Jewish ideology, and their educational mission was to promote the camps' ideological point of view. Thus, camps were founded that promoted Yiddish language, *Zionism, *Hebrew learning, and *socialist ideals. A cadre of progressive Jewish educators, many of whom had either studied with or been directly influenced by the same progressive educators who inspired the trailblazers of the American camping movement, pioneered the development of camps with a specifically Jewish mission. Albert P. Schoolman (1894–1980), one of the progressive Jewish educators, took the helm of the newly established Camp Cejwin in 1923. A few years later, Jewish educators Isaac B. Berkson (1891–1975) and his wife, Libbie S. Berkson (1891–1970), collaborated with Alexander M. Dushkin (1890–1976) and his wife, Julia Dushkin (1895–1976), in the founding of Camp Modin (1922), which focused on Jewish learning and living. Samson Benderly also established a camp, Camp Achvah (1927), which emphasized the development of future Jewish educational leaders. Shlomo Bardin (1898–1976), a charismatic Zionist youth leader, founded a "Summer Camp Institute" (1941) under the sponsorship of the American Zionist Youth Commission, with financial backing from Supreme Court Justice Louis D. *Brandeis. The Institute was named for Brandeis after his death. Shlomo Shulsinger (1912–2004) established Camp Massad (1941), with an educational program that concentrated on Hebrew-language learning.

Jewish educational camping programs proved to be invaluable tools for the strengthening of Jewish life in mid-twentieth-century America. As American Jews left urban, immigrant neighborhoods and resettled in the suburbs, Jewish identity became ever more compartmentalized, and Jewish camping programs offered young people a chance to experience an all-encompassing Jewish environment.

During this post–World War II era, the establishment of camps associated with the religious movements of American Judaism marked the beginning of a third phase in Jewish camping. By the mid-1940s, some leaders of American Judaism's various religious streams began to recognize how organized camping programs could augment Jewish learning, develop leadership skills, and concomitantly strengthen ideological ties to their respective religious movements. Rabbi Moshe Davis (1916–1996), one of Camp Massad's founders in 1941, went on to play a central role in the establishment of Conservative *Judaism's Camp Ramah in 1947. Similarly, many of those who had been influenced by the first Jewish educational camps were instrumental in the development of the Hebrew program at Reform Judaism's first Union Institute (established in 1952). A number of large synagogues began to acquire camp sites of their own at this same time, and after the 1950s, camps associated

with the Orthodox and Ḥasidic movements also came into existence. During the last quarter of the twentieth century, both the Conservative and Reform movements continued to establish new camps in the United States and *Canada. In 2002 Camp JRF, the *Reconstructionist movement's first camp, opened, and Jewish camps in North America reflected the entire spectrum of Jewish religious practice and learning.

In the early decades of the twenty-first century, an estimated 50,000 young people annually attend nonprofit camps with Jewish affiliations and an additional 10,000 individuals serve as staff for these camps. These figures underscore the degree to which Jewish camping has become an established feature in the lives of many American Jews.

For further reading, see J. W. Joselit and K. S. Mittelman, eds., *A Worthy Use of Summer: Jewish Summer Camping in America* (1993); J. J. Goldberg and E. King, *Builders and Dreamers: Habonim Labor Zionist Youth in North America* (1993); W. Ackerman, "A World Apart: Hebrew Teachers Colleges and Hebrew-Speaking Camps," in *Hebrew in America*, ed. A. Mintz (1993), 105–28; and M. M. Lorge and G. P. Zola, eds., *A Place of Our Own: The Beginnings of Reform Jewish Camping in America* (2006).   GARY PHILLIP ZOLA

Sura was the original location of the preeminent Babylonian rabbinic academy (*yeshivah*) of the geonic era; it was founded by Rav, one of the two leaders of the first generation of Amoraim in Babylonia. The place name continued to be applied to the academy when it was relocated to Baghdad, sometime in the ninth century (see AMORAIM; GAON, GEONIM, GEONIC ACADEMIES; PUMBEDITA).

Synagogue is a place of Jewish worship and study. Its word derives from the Greek for "assembly"; its Hebrew equivalent is *beit kenesset* (house of assembly). Its origins are obscure and may go back to the *Babylonian Exile. Certainly, by the beginning of the first century CE, the synagogue was a well-established and essential Jewish institution in the *Land of Israel and the *Diaspora. Unlike the *Temple in *Jerusalem or other shrines in pre-exilic times, the synagogue was never a place in which sacrifices were offered, nor was it administered by priests (see TEMPLE AND TEMPLE CULT; WORSHIP). Beginning in the nineteenth century, some Jewish reformers began to call synagogues "temples" (see JUDAISM, REFORM), and since then this custom has become common among adherents of Reform, Conservative, and Reconstructionist Judaism. See other entries under SYNAGOGUES.

Synagogue Sisterhoods. Since the nineteenth century, North American Jewish women have formed organizations that promoted the good and welfare of their families, *synagogues, and the needy of the community (see ORGANIZATIONS, WOMEN'S: UNITED STATES). Even when there was sentiment against women earning money outside the home, there was never a norm that Jewish women's activities should be limited to the domestic realm. In fact, voluntary activity on behalf of the community was encouraged, particularly in arenas considered women's spheres in American society, such as *education, culture, and areas of religion apart from ritual. The predominant model in synagogues and elsewhere was separate men's and women's groups.

Synagogue sisterhoods gained in strength as the major American Jewish denominations became institutionalized in the late nineteenth and early twentieth centuries (see entries under JUDAISM). Sisterhoods offered Jewish women a place to gather as women and as Jews, to socialize, to study, to support important causes and, not least, to raise money for their synagogue and national movement institutions. During the interwar and post–World War II years when many hundreds of Reform and Conservative congregations were founded, both sisterhoods (and brotherhoods) were organized. Three major coordinating organizations brought local groups together for national efforts and support of movement institutions. The National Foundation of Temple Sisterhoods (NFTS), now Women of Reform Judaism, was founded in 1913; the Women's League of the United Synagogue (now Women's League for Conservative Judaism) was formed in 1918; and the Women's Branch of the Orthodox Union of Jewish Congregations was established in 1923.

As the Jewish feminist movement (see JUDAISM, FEMINIST) of the mid to late 1970s began to flourish, a sharp debate arose about the separation by gender of education, fundraising, and cultural support of synagogue life. Many sisterhoods had difficulty recruiting younger members, and as more women worked outside the home for pay and balanced the demands of dual-career families, they could not attend daytime meetings and had less energy for volunteer work. In a number of synagogues, men's clubs and sisterhoods began to institute jointly sponsored programming.

Assuming leadership roles in sisterhoods had historically provided an entry for some women into the broader power structure of the temple or synagogue. For many decades the only women on synagogue boards were revolving representatives of the sisterhood and parent-teachers association of the religious school. One of the few paths to female leadership in a Jewish organization was through regional and national sisterhood offices. During the last quarter of the twentieth century, this pattern changed somewhat as more and more women entered the mainstream of congregational and communal leadership. Nevertheless, synagogue sisterhoods continue to exist and play numerous important local and national roles. For example, the Women of Reform Judaism sponsored the publication of *The Torah: A Women's Commentary* (2008), which included contributions from more than two hundred female scholars. This volume, edited by T. C. Eskenazi and A. Weiss, won the 2008 National Jewish Book Council Everett Family Foundation Book of the Year designation.

Some sociologists have recently suggested that synagogue life, particularly in the liberal Jewish movements, has become "feminized," as has much of religious life in America in general. They argue that there is now an important role for single-gender groups, particularly the strengthening of men's clubs/brotherhoods and groups for teenage boys, to bring more men back into congregational life in an activist way.

Recent research includes S. B. Fishman and D. Parmer, *Matrilineal Ascent/Patrilineal Descent: The Gender Imbalance in American Jewish Life* (2008); and P. E. Hyman and D. Ofer, eds., *Jewish Women: A Comprehensive Historical Encyclopedia*, CD-ROM (2007).   RELA MINTZ GEFFEN

Synagogues, Ancient. Synagogues flourished throughout the *Land of Israel during the *Roman and *Byzantine periods, continuing well into *Islamic times. The centrality of local communities as sites of *Torah study and the development of private associations during the *Hellenistic period provide some context for this development.

By the first century CE at the latest, Jewish synagogues existed in the Land of Israel and the Roman *Diaspora. The clearest *archeological evidence for early synagogues is a monumental Greek inscription recovered in *Jerusalem that relates that a certain Theodotos, "son of Vettenos the priest and synagogue leader (*archisynagogos*), son of a synagogue leader, and grandson of a synagogue leader, built the synagogue for the reading of the Torah and studying of the commandments and as a hostel with chambers and water installations to provide for the needs of itinerants from abroad, which his fathers, the elders, and Simonides founded."

A number of buildings from the later part of the *Second Temple period in the Land of Israel have been identified as synagogues. These include structures uncovered at Gamla, *Masada, Herodium, and recently at Modi'in, Kiryat Sefer, and *Jericho. Each of the buildings at Gamla, Masada, and Herodium is a large meeting room surrounded by benches. *Philo of Alexandria describes the synagogues of the *Essenes as having such benches (*Every Good Man Is Free*, lines 81–82). The building at Gamla, constructed after 40 BCE, is a large, freestanding rectangular structure (16 × 20 meters) built on the city's western side next to the city wall. The main entrance was on the west, with an exedra and an open courtyard in front. The center of the hall was unpaved and surrounded (except for the main entrance) by stepped benches. The synagogue of Masada was built during the First *Jewish War of 66–74 CE. Located on the northwestern casement wall, the room is rectangular in shape (15 × 12 meters); benches with four tiers were built on three sides of the room. On the fourth side, at the northwestern end of the building was a large, protruding room (measuring 3.6 × 5.5 meters), within which fragments of the biblical books of *Deuteronomy and *Ezekiel were discovered. The room at Herodium was also fitted with benches during the First Jewish War. On the basis of the similarities between these benches and those at Masada, some scholars have identified this room as a synagogue.

Archeological evidence for synagogues during the two centuries following the destruction of *Jerusalem in 70 CE is sparse, although *rabbinic literature provides ample evidence for synagogues for this period. *Tannaitic writings, reflecting the late first through the early third centuries, provide information about synagogues within communities that were under rabbinic influence. M. *Megillah* 3:2 assumes that synagogue buildings were not so clearly distinguished that they could not be converted for use for another communal or industrial purpose. M. *Nedarim* 9:2 relates that a private house could be transformed into a synagogue, a parallel with Christian house synagogues, as well as the third-century *Dura Europos synagogue in Syria and synagogues elsewhere in the Diaspora. Sources discuss a synagogue in *Alexandria that bore similarities to the Jerusalem *Temple (T. *Sukkah* 4:6), whereas T. *Megillah* 3:21–23 suggests that the ideal synagogue, like the *Tabernacle/Temple, should be built "at the high point of the town," its doors open to the east. The interior of the synagogue was to be directed toward a scrolls box (*teva*) that was set on the wall aligned with Jerusalem. This literary testimony indicates that synagogues were a common feature on the Palestinian landscape by the third and fourth centuries CE.

More than one hundred synagogues from the fourth through eighth centuries are known from archeological evidence. Three basic "types" of synagogue buildings or basilicas have been discovered in the Land of Israel: the broadhouse, longhouse, and Galilean. The principle of sacred orientation may be observed in all three types, and platforms supporting Torah shrines were placed on the Jerusalem-aligned wall in the vast majority of cases. From the fifth century onward, longhouse basilicas often incorporated an apse. Broadhouse synagogues have been discovered at Khirbet Shema in the Upper *Galilee and at Eshtemoa and Khirbet Susiya in the Mount Hebron region of Judea. A Torah shrine was placed on the broad wall, aligned with Jerusalem.

Longhouse basilicas, generally dating to the fifth and sixth centuries, consisted of an atrium, sometimes a narthex, and a nave, the focal point of which was a Torah shrine set on a platform (*bimah*) on the Jerusalem-aligned wall. The Torah shrine (called an *aronah* or *beit aronah* in inscriptions and literary sources) was sometimes flanked by seven-branched *menorahs. These menorahs not only forged a connection between the synagogue and the Jerusalem Temple but they also provided illumination necessary for the reading of biblical scrolls and served to emphasize the ark platform. This arrangement is first reflected in the synagogue mosaic at Hammath Tiberias B, in level 2a. Many synagogues of the sixth century and later, including Na'aran and Beth Alpha, included an apse on the Jerusalem wall that housed the Torah shrine. This feature, together with the entire arrangement and many of the furnishings of the building, was borrowed from contemporary churches. The apse and *bimah* were sometimes separated from the nave by a screen.

The naves of many longhouse and apsidal basilicas and the hall of the broadhouse at Khirbet Susiya were paved with highly intricate mosaics. A number of mosaics included images of the Torah shrine area, the zodiac wheel, biblical imagery, and numerous dedicatory inscriptions in *Aramaic, Greek, and occasionally Hebrew. Images of the Torah shrine, flanked by two menorahs, appear at Hammath Tiberias, Sepphoris, Beth Alpha, Beth Shean A (which may actually be a *Samaritan synagogue), Na'aran, and Khirbet Susiya. These mosaic panels were laid in front of the *bimot* of these synagogues and were imprecise mirror images of them. The pediment of a Torah shrine very similar to the one at Beth Alpha was discovered at Nabratein (although at Nabratein the pediment is flanked by lions, and not birds, as at Beth Alpha). A large three-dimensional menorah was discovered at Hammath Tiberias A, and fragments of large menorahs were found at Maon (Judea), Khirbet Susiya, and Eshtemoa. A three-dimensional lion similar to those flanking the bottom of the ark in the Beth Alpha synagogue mosaic was discovered at Chorazin (see **Plate 3** for similar imagery).

The zodiac wheel mosaics within synagogues are clearly related to the course of the Jewish lunar–solar *calendar, as is made clear by the fifth-century mosaic from Sepphoris. The earliest zodiac wheel was found at Hammath Tiberias. There the signs of the zodiac are individually labeled in Hebrew, with the seasons personified in each corner. In the center is the sun god Helios. At Sepphoris, about a century later, the zodiac wheel includes both the signs and personifications of each month, clearly labeled with the Hebrew name of the month. The chariot of Helios appears, but Helios himself does not. At Ein Gedi the names of the months and zodiac signs appear in a long textual inscription, but they are not illustrated. These varying designs reflect the different attitudes held by various communities to possibly idolatrous imagery. The zodiac at Na'aran was defaced by iconoclasts (as were images at Khirbet Susiya and other sites) during the early Islamic period, reflecting changing Jewish attitudes toward visual representations, most likely in response to Muslim aniconism within mosques (see ISLAM AND JUDAISM). Biblical scenes that appear in synagogue mosaics include the binding of *Isaac (*akedah) at Beth Alpha and Sepphoris; the angels' visit to *Abraham and *Sarah and *Aaron before the *Tabernacle at Sepphoris; *Noah's ark at Gerasa; *Daniel in the lion's den at Na'aran, and perhaps Khirbet Susiya; and *David playing his harp at Gaza. All of these images appear in Christian art as well and seem to have been adopted for synagogue ornamentation from the larger cultural context. The similar scroll mosaics of the Maon (Nirim) synagogue near Gaza and of the nearby Shellal church reflect the close relationships between artisans and tastes across communal divides. Images of Aaron before the Tabernacle and assorted elements of the Jerusalem Temple sacrificial cult appear in the Sepphoris mosaic. Each of these biblical images parallels themes that are common in Jewish liturgical poetry and other literature from late antiquity (see POETRY, LITURGICAL [*PIYYUT*]). Particularly significant is a mosaic pavement from the narthex of the sixth-century synagogue at Rehov in the Beth Shean region. This twenty-nine-line inscription directly parallels texts that appear in rabbinic literature and is a copy of a fourth-century wall inscription from the same synagogue that is the earliest extant textual exemplar of *rabbinic literature.

Galilean-type basilicas, now generally dated from the fourth to sixth centuries, are found in the synagogues at Capernaum, Chorazin, Meiron, Nabratein, Kfar Baram, Umm al-Qantar, and Arbel. The synagogue at Meroth has some of these features. The emphasis on the decoration of the external facade of these buildings is closely related to church architecture in Syria. Typical of this group is the structure uncovered at Meiron, in which the triple facade faces southward toward Jerusalem. It is likely that the Torah shrine was placed between the portals of this structure, as at Meroth in the Upper Galilee and as has been conjectured at Capernaum and Chorazin.

DIASPORA SYNAGOGUES: Archeological and literary sources suggest that synagogues existed throughout the Roman and Sassanian (see PERSIA) Empires from the third century through the Islamic conquest. Diaspora synagogues were built according to the architectural norms of each locale. They are unified by the presence of a large Torah shrine, sometimes images of menorahs and Torah scrolls, and terminology found in dedicatory inscriptions. The synagogue uncovered at Dura Europos, a town in the Syrian desert, was a renovated private dwelling that was converted into a synagogue some time before 244/45 CE. The largest room had a large Torah shrine built on the western (Jerusalem-aligned) wall and benches around the walls. The façade of the Torah shrine was decorated with the image of the Jerusalem Temple, flanked on the right by the binding of Isaac (according to 2 Chron 3:1, this event took place on "Mount Moriah," the Temple Mount); on the left were representations of a seven-branched menorah, a palm frond (*lulav*), and a citron (*etrog*). In 244/5 CE the walls were completely covered with paintings representing biblical events read through the prism of Jewish biblical interpretation (*midrash). Sixty percent of the paintings have been preserved. The generally heroic themes include the discovery of *Moses by the daughter of Pharaoh, the crossing of the Red Sea, the tribes encamped around the Tabernacle, *Ezekiel's vision of the dry bones, and *Esther before King Ahashuerus. The paintings, inscriptions, and a unique prayer text on parchment parallel traditions preserved in rabbinic literature. **Map 4**

Impressive synagogues have been uncovered in Ostia Antica, the ancient port of Rome, and in Sardis in modern-day *Turkey. The Ostia synagogue building was originally constructed toward the end of the first century CE. It was renovated for use as a synagogue during the second and third centuries and was enlarged and partly rebuilt at the beginning of the fourth. The triple entrances in the facade of the second- to third-century basilica are aligned toward the east–southeast, perhaps in the direction of Jerusalem. A stepped podium stood on the wall opposite the main entrance. A Latin and Greek inscription from this construction phase mentions a shrine for the Torah. During the fourth century, the southernmost entrance portal on the eastern wall of the synagogue was sealed and replaced with a large free-standing Torah shrine. This Torah shrine is similar to images in wall paintings and gold glass discovered in the Jewish *catacombs of Rome and on oil lamps found in Ostia.

The Sardis synagogue is the largest synagogue yet uncovered, with its main hall measuring 54 × 18 meters. This impressive building, part of the southern side of the municipal center of Sardis, was taken over by the Jewish community and remodeled as a synagogue during the fourth century. The remodeling included the installation of two aediculae on stepped podia on the eastern wall of the synagogue and the construction of a podium in the center of the hall. The significance of these aediculae is made clear both by their prominence and by a nearby Greek inscription that reads, "Find, open, read, observe." Another Greek inscription refers to the Torah shrine as the *nomophylakion*, "the place that protects the Torah." Survey works on the history of the ancient synagogue include S. Fine, ed. *Sacred Realm: The Emergence of the Synagogue in the Ancient World* (1996); and L. I. Levine, *The Ancient Synagogue: The First Thousand Years* (1999).   STEPHEN FINE

Synagogues, Europe: Medieval to Eighteenth Century.
Few physical traces survive of medieval synagogues because Jews were expelled so often from their places of residence. Moreover, prohibitions against building new synagogues were intermittently in force throughout Christian Europe beginning in the fourth century. The most substantial synagogues were in *Spain, *Sicily, southern *Italy, and *Central Europe. Medieval synagogues were often located in or near the house or business of a wealthy community leader. A stone house in the medieval Italian town of Sermoneta may have housed such a synagogue; worshipers would have met in a large room on the first floor (above ground level).

A fifteenth-century Italian manuscript illustration shows a similar open room with a large decorated arch supported by Corinthian columns and a wooden coffered ceiling. A tall wooden ark (*aron ha-kodesh*, in which the Torah scroll or scrolls are stored) is set against one wall and a lower reader's table set before it; at either side are chests or desks for worshipers, facing the room's center. Later versions of domestic synagogues survive in Dubrovnik, Croatia, where a prayer room was created after 1532 on the third floor of a fourteenth-century house, and in Pfaffenhoffen, France, where a small house synagogue built in 1791 retains a medieval character.

More public "hall-type" synagogues include two examples in Trani, southern Italy, which were converted to churches in the fifteenth century, and fragments of two synagogues in Sopron (*Hungary) and one in Budapest. The partially reconstructed thirteenth-century synagogue of Sopron is set back from the street through a passageway between two houses. The sanctuary was a vaulted space with the small ark set permanently into the east wall and decorated with carved stonework; the women's prayer room had a separate entrance on the south. The synagogue complex included a caretaker's house, a fourteenth-century building to house travelers or the sick, and a *mikveh (ritual bath).

Vaulted stone synagogues were erected in larger towns with prosperous Jewish populations. Double-nave structures appear in Central Europe beginning in the twelfth century, including the synagogues at Worms (*Germany) and *Prague (Czech Republic). Other examples are known from Regensburg (Germany), *Vienna (Austria), and Maribor (Slovenia). The Worms synagogue was rebuilt after its destruction in World War II. The original structure built in 1034 was renovated between 1170 and 1200; the men's hall (1175) was divided by two columns on the east–west axis into parallel aisles of equal size. The ark stood at the east end; the *bimah* (elevated platform used for *Torah reading) was between the columns. A women's annex, at right angles to the men's section on the north side, was built in 1213. The so-called *Rashi chapel was added in 1624 at the short west end. In 1842, the women's annex was opened, and the wall separating it from the men's hall was broken by two large doorways with pointed arches.

The oldest synagogue in continuous use is Prague's thirteenth-century Altneushul (Old-New Synagogue). The Altneushul also has a double-nave plan, with two tall octagonal piers. The *bimah* is between the piers; its wrought iron enclosure with pointed arches probably dates from the fifteenth century. The women's section in the west annex, dated 1732, was later extended to the north side. Narrow windows about three feet above the floor level connect the women's annexes with the main hall.

The hundreds of synagogues that existed in medieval *Spain and *Portugal reflected Middle Eastern Jewish models and Muslim cultural influences. In Toledo, where there were at least nine synagogues and five *midrashim* (small chapels), two survive. The older, originally the Great Synagogue, is now commonly known as Santa Maria la Blanca, after the church into which it was transformed following the 1492 expulsion. Inside the modest exterior, four rows of thirty-two octagonal piers, which support horseshoe arches, articulate an impressive open space, and stucco ornaments in the clerestory windows convey a sense of opulence. There is no women's section or gallery. A similar synagogue in Segovia is now a church. The private Toledo synagogue of courtier Samuel Halevi Abulafia (1320–1360), known as El Transito, is very different. It was joined to his palace on the east side, and the large rectangular interior has rich stucco decoration with Hebrew inscriptions encircling the nave just below the high decorated ceiling. Some inscriptions praise King Pedro I, and others hail Abulafia as "prince among the princes of the tribe of Levi." A spacious gallery on the north side was possibly for women.

Between the sixteenth and eighteenth centuries, Italian Jewish communities built impressive synagogues. The finest were in Livorno, Ancona, Padua, and especially in the *Venice *ghetto, where five separate synagogues survive; each served a segment of Venice's diverse community. The Scuola Grande Tedesca (1528–29, rebuilt 1732–33) is located high up in a tall building in the Ghetto Nuovo. This location fulfilled the talmudic dictum that synagogues should be located at the highest point in town. The trapezoidal sanctuary is two stories high and has an elliptical gallery for women at the second level (a result of eighteenth-century remodeling); this gallery masks the room's irregularity and is reminiscent of contemporary theaters. Originally, the *bimah* was located in the center of the space. The Scuola Canton (1531–32; rebuilt with a new ark in 1736) is a small rectangular room filled with light, color, and delicate ornamentation reminiscent of Venetian patrician parlors or the meeting places of Christian confraternities. As in most Italian synagogues, the ark and *bimah* are set across from each other in a bipolar arrangement. Benches line the sides of the room, and congregants would follow the service by looking first left, then right. The richly carved and gilded wood ark is typical of Baroque-period Italian synagogues, but its size harmonizes with the intimate Renaissance space. The *bimah* (1780) is set in a raised niche protruding from the building and overhanging a canal. A little cupola provides light for the Torah reader; its columns are intricately carved with intertwined branches and twigs.

Two major synagogues were built in Venice's Ghetto Vecchio: the Scuola Levantina (built after 1589; remodeled in the seventeenth century) and the Scuola Spagnola (built after 1589; remodeled in the mid-seventeenth century). Grander than earlier synagogues, they employed workshops of prominent Christian architects, probably including Baldassare Longhena. The Scuola Grande Spagnola has a bipolar arrangement of ark and *bimah* set within a large rectangular space; an elliptical women's gallery is inserted high up in the tall room. The interior is sumptuously decorated with black and white marble, rich woods, and faux-marble wall painting. The exuberant ark design of rising classical elements culminates in a series of pediments and arches. Within this composition is the *Decalogue mounted on a frame of golden rays, a device used by Gian Lorenzo Bernini in St. Peter's Basilica in Rome.

Several eighteenth-century synagogues in Piedmont, such as Carmagnola, Cuneo, and Casale Monferatto, are unmarked on the outside, but richly adorned within. Most centrally placed *bimot* are octagonal, and ornate arks decorated with twisted columns refer to the Jerusalem *Temple. Two synagogues in southern France are similar: Carpentras (1367; remodeled in 1741 by Antoine d'Alemand) and Cavaillon (rebuilt in 1772 by Antoine and Pierre Armelin).

These *Sephardi synagogues present a taste of Versailles in their delicate frothy Rococo decoration.

A second arena of intensive synagogue building in the seventeenth and eighteenth centuries was in the new Dutch Republic and areas settled by Dutch traders. In 1670, the Portuguese Jewish community in *Amsterdam began building a grandiose place of worship with offices, a library, and schoolrooms on a plan by master-builder Elias Bouman. Similar to Bouman's design for the Ashkenazi Great Synagogue erected the year before, the synagogue is a restrained interpretation of the classical style: opulent but without the drama of the Italian Baroque. Dedicated in 1675, the Esnoga was at that time the largest synagogue in the world, seating 1,200 men with places in the galleries for more than 400 women and other visitors. Four giant Ionic columns on massive plinths on either side support the wooden barrel-vaulted ceiling. The columns on the east and west walls are engaged. Six smaller columns sustain the galleries, which run around three sides of the building. Part of the balcony accommodated women, the first instance of what would become standard practice in synagogue design. The great wooden ark is surmounted by pediments, crowns, and obelisks; above the central bay, in an aedicule beneath a crowned pediment is the *Decalogue. The seventy-two windows ensure bright light; in the evening, twenty-six magnificent chandeliers of various sizes and candlesticks on each bench light up the interior.

London's Sephardi Bevis Marks Synagogue (1701) recalls the red-brick exterior and interior plan (80 ft × 50 ft) of Amsterdam's Esnoga. London's Ashkenazim built their first synagogue in 1722, in Duke's Place, and another, the Hambro Synagogue, was erected in 1725; both are modeled on Bevis Marks. Inspired by the Amsterdam and London synagogues, Dutch and English Jews built similar structures in the New World. Amsterdam Jews who settled in Curaçao in 1659 erected a four-story synagogue in a tiled courtyard, reflecting the Esnoga and Spanish Baroque architecture. Other *Caribbean synagogues were erected in Surinam, Barbados, Nevis, St. Eustatius, and St. Thomas.

In Kraków, *Poland, legends date the Old Synagogue to the fourteenth century, but it was probably first erected in the late fifteenth century and then rebuilt by Italian architect Matteo Gucci in 1570. Many Polish synagogues of this era were designed by Italians, who adapted Italian architecture for Jewish use. The Old Synagogue retains the medieval double-nave plan, but incorporates many Renaissance features. The Remu Synagogue, built in 1557, was probably the first masonry Renaissance-style synagogue in Poland, replacing a 1553 wooden structure. This small rectilinear building with a single nave has round-headed windows set high in the walls and a Roman barrel vault; a separate room for women to the west was added in the nineteenth century. Built-in furnishings, including the ark and the poor-box, resemble sculpted wall tombs produced for the royal court and Polish churches. Similar "hall-type" synagogues, erected over the next century throughout Poland, included the famous, and now destroyed, 1582 Nachmanowiczes Synagogue (also known as TaZ Synagogue, or Golden Rose) in Lwów (now Lviv), *Ukraine. The Pinczow synagogue (ca. 1600) was one of the first Polish synagogues to include a women's section (situated over the vestibule). Deteriorated wall paintings from the second half of the eighteenth century, attributed to the Jewish painter Jehuda Leib, survive. The large barrel-vaulted Izaak Synagogue in Kraków (1638–44) also has a women's section at the west end, built over an entrance vestibule. The sanctuary recalls Baroque churches, but like other synagogues, much of its wall space was decorated with Hebrew liturgical texts.

Another important type of synagogue in late-sixteenth-century Poland is defined by its square or almost square plan and the presence of a large central *bimah*, surrounded by four corner columns or piers that rise to the ceiling vault. This "*bimah*-support synagogue" provided wider roof spans and larger uninterrupted interior spaces to better accommodate large crowds. The large space and the centrality of the reader's platform created a dramatic effect. The first such synagogue may have been the 1567 MaHaRSHal Synagogue in Lublin (rebuilt in 1656). Other examples in eastern Poland include Przemysl (1592–95), Zamosc, (ca. 1600), Tykocin, (1642), and Lancut (1761) and, in western *Ukraine, Satanov (eighteenth century) and Zhovkva (1692). The Lancut synagogue, which was sponsored by a local noble, has a simple plan: a vestibule, a room on the entrance side, and a main hall beyond. Women reached their gallery above the vestibule by an external stairway. The unusually light main prayer hall, several steps below the vestibule, is lit by large windows; the center *bimah*, comprised of four large thick columns set on square bases, supports the central vault. Painted images include zodiac signs, musical instruments mentioned in the *Psalms, and images of lions, unicorns, monkeys, grapes, birds, deer, and flowers. While expensive masonry synagogues were springing up throughout greater Poland, a parallel tradition developed of building synagogues in wood (see SYNAGOGUES, WOODEN).

In German urban centers, new synagogues were erected in fashionable styles. The *Berlin Heidereutergasse Synagogue (1712–14) resembled contemporary Protestant church architecture in detailing and spatial configuration. In Wörlitz, the Duke of Anhalt-Dessau sponsored a synagogue (1789–90) in an English garden setting that resembled an ancient round temple; the architect even called it the Temple of Vesta. This classical style can also be seen at Lunéville, France (1785–88) and frequently in the 1820s in *Vienna (1826, Seitenstettentempel); Wroclaw, Poland (1820s, White Stork Synagogue); Obuda, *Hungary (1821); and elsewhere.

SAMUEL D. GRUBER

Synagogues: France. Eighteenth-century synagogues of architectural significance in the former papal territories of Carpentras and Cavaillon are now considered French national historical treasures. A synagogue in Avignon from this era did not survive, but was completely rebuilt in 1846. The first large modern synagogue constructed after *emancipation (1790–91) was in Bordeaux in 1812. When it was destroyed by fire, it was replaced in 1882, with partial funding from the Pereire family; the new synagogue was the largest in Europe at that time.

Perhaps two hundred and fifty synagogues were built throughout France in the nineteenth century. The architectural challenge was to invent something that was the equivalent of monumental European churches, but still had some specifically Jewish features. The Romanesque style was repeatedly chosen and the Gothic rejected. Respected

architects were often involved, and they used styles and materials that were being introduced everywhere. The buildings themselves indicated the participation of Jews in French culture. The synagogue on the Rue des Tournelles in Paris, dedicated in 1876, was designed by a student of the great Victor Baltard (known for the market pavilions at Les Halles), and it benefited from the introduction of the metal-work methods of Gustave Eiffel. In the early twentieth century, immigrant Jews built a synagogue on the Rue Pavée in an Art Nouveau style designed by Hector Guimard, the architect known for his Paris Métro design.

PHYLLIS COHEN ALBERT

Synagogues: Nineteenth Century. Although traditional synagogue building in local forms, materials, and design continued with few alterations outside the European sphere of influence, significant innovations occurred in Europe, North America, and colonized areas. The opening of trades and educational opportunities to Jews allowed them to become building entrepreneurs, property owners, and sometimes architects and engineers, even in European countries where they lacked full civil rights. With gradual legal *emancipation, Jewish communities erected synagogues on public streets or outside traditional Jewish quarters. A municipal building inspector might determine the synagogue's site, size, and style, but Western and Central European Jews made architectural decisions on their own. Traditional Jewish districts survived, but educated and prosperous Jews often moved to new areas where they were generally permitted to construct new synagogues. Some governments promoted a single large synagogue in major cities to facilitate the supervision of Jews who had previously been dispersed in a number of small prayer houses. Large synagogues promoted greater prestige for their occupants and provided opportunities for impressive architecture; however, a single community synagogue forced those with differing ritual needs to worship privately in modest quarters. Synagogues also rose in towns where Jews had earlier been excluded by law or custom. Overall, the nineteenth century saw the construction of ampler, more orderly, and sturdier synagogues, especially in capitals and major commercial cities.

Other political changes in Europe affected synagogue design, particularly the growth of nationalism after the defeat of Napoleon in 1815. Throughout Europe, architects selected architectural styles from the past to express their distinctive national characters and histories. Italians often favored Roman-derived forms, whereas the French, inventors of Gothic architecture, promoted Gothic revival. However, the Jews, without their own European architectural heritage, spent the century trying to formulate a Jewish style. Thus, an Egyptian-style synagogue at Canterbury (1848, Hezekiah Marshall) evoked a country that had endured for millennia and that was close to the Jews' ancient homeland. Yet, because ancient Egyptians had persecuted the Israelites, that style soon lost favor.

Because Gothic architecture was specifically connected with Christian religious edifices, few Gothic synagogues were built, although several synagogues did include its slender, pointed-arched forms inside, where the congregation could privately enjoy the popular style. Only rarely and then among acculturated *Reform Jews did the Gothic style appear on the exterior (1888, Ceske Budejovice, Max Fleischer).

Greco-Roman architecture, with pagan associations, was usually considered unsuitable. Nevertheless, in the early nineteenth century, when Americans admired the Greek struggle for independence and associated the Greeks with their own revolutionaries, several U.S. congregations built synagogues in the Greek Revival mode (1841, *Charleston, Beth Elohim, Cyrus L. Warner and David L. Lopez). Occasionally, as in Warsaw (Tlomacka Street, l877, Leandro Marconi) and Moscow (Arkhipova Street, 1891, Ivan Shaposhnikov and Lev Bachman), a Roman facade was designed for Jews who prudently conformed to a style promoted by their repressive government. At the end of the century, when excavations uncovered ancient Roman-era synagogues, architects in *New York City (1897, Shearith Israel, Arnold Brunner) and *Chicago (1891, Kehillah Anshe Ma'ariv, Dankmar Adler and Louis Sullivan) devised synagogues meant to reflect an authentic Jewish past.

Islamic forms, connoting the Middle East, came to be seen as particularly suitable. After the construction of the synagogue at Dresden (l840, Gottfried Semper), where the interior supports, horseshoe arches, and ornamentation were inspired by the Alhambra palace in *Spain, this style was adopted in many cities, including Budapest (Dohány Street, l859, Ludwig von Förster); Cologne (Glockengasse, l861, Ernst Zwirner); and New York City (1868, Temple Emanu-El, Leopold Eidlitz). Spanish and *North African medieval (Moorish) architecture was as delicate and decorative as Gothic, so that it could be seen as "Jewish Gothic." Its potential for decorative elaboration recommended it to many congregations from Samara, Russia (end of the nineteenth century) to New York City's Eldridge Street synagogue (1887, Herter Brothers). This architectural style, however, did perpetuate views of European Jews as exotic and foreign.

Therefore, many Jewish architects favored versions of a sturdy and round-arched Romanesque style that was European in origin. This architectural style had preceded Gothic, just as Judaism had preceded Christianity, and was therefore considered conceptually appropriate. Examples include synagogues at Kassel (l843, Albert Rosengarten), Hannover (l870, Edwin Oppler), and Paris (Rue de la Victoire, l874, Alfred Aldrophe).

A compromise between Middle Eastern and native European styles called the Byzantine style appeared in synagogues; these buildings had central plans, domes, and, often, nonfigural mosaic decoration. Jews approved of the style's Middle Eastern origin and also its connotations of Roman imperial power, because Constantinople (modern Istanbul) was the capital of the *Byzantine or Eastern Roman Empire until 1453. Most of these structures, even if designed in the nineteenth century, were constructed in the early twentieth century.

A few exceptional synagogues defy stylistic classification. These include synagogues in Stockholm (1870, Vilhelm Scholander) and Turin (1889, Alessandro Antonelli), which has an elongated cupola. Most European Jews in Asia and South America imported European ideas about sacred architecture. Synagogues in colonial cities and in North America employed many European styles, but where there was no official state religion, as in the United States, the political connotations of style lost their European potency.

Changes generated by Jews themselves, rather than by governments, were also responsible for new synagogue designs. The Central European Reform movement (see JUDAISM, REFORM: GERMANY), starting with the synagogue in Seesen, Germany (l810), moved the *bimah* (elevated platform used for *Torah reading) eastward toward the *aron ha-kodesh* (Torah ark); placed seats in orderly pews instead of arranging individual chairs and reading desks in a U-shape around the *bimah*; and sometimes provided space for a male choir, a harmonium, or an organ in a loft. As women's literacy and attendance increased and as *sermons and *music became important within modernized services, a women's gallery on only one side of the interior no longer sufficed. Architects accommodated the overflow in galleries above the aisles of the principal interior space, an idea derived from Protestant churches. Tall screens no longer hid women entirely from the view of male worshipers, although decorative parapets provided both safety and a sense of separation. Many nineteenth-century synagogue forms persisted into the early twentieth century. For further reading, see C. H. Krinsky, *Synagogues of Europe: Architecture, History, Meaning* (1996).   CAROL HERSELLE KRINSKY

Synagogues: Twentieth Century. At the beginning of the twentieth century, most synagogues continued to be historicist in style. Some styles, like the Moorish style, were actually nineteenth-century pastiches of older motifs. However, in many of these buildings, new structural and mechanical technologies and new materials were enthusiastically embraced.

In the early twentieth century a few distinctive synagogue designs broke with tradition. These included the synagogue in Subotica, Serbia (Komor and Jakab, 1901), which combined Balkan, Hungarian, and Jewish folk and architectural traditions, and Hector Guimard's striking Art Nouveau Rue Pavée Synagogue in Paris (1911–13). After World War I there was a shift toward simpler forms. Traditional plan arrangements were often maintained, but Art Deco and Art Moderne styles reduced applied decoration and streamlined forms. Although exteriors were frequently treated monochromatically, many sanctuaries were brilliantly colored, with liturgical, functional, and even mechanical elements uniformly designed with Deco and Moderne motifs. A masterful example is Temple Beth El in Paterson, New Jersey, built in the Art Deco style (Frederick Wentworth, 1929).

In Europe, the developments of the Modernist movement were adapted for synagogues. In Zilina, Slovakia (1928–30), Peter Behrens created a stripped-down version of the domed synagogue popular in *Central Europe. Behrens placed a half-dome on a rectangular block; within, the dome rises on slender concrete piers from a square, set within the rectangular mass. Outside, the ground floor is faced in stone, and the rest of the structure is made of reinforced concrete. Despite the concrete, the building looks traditional because of its massing and the monumental entrance stairway. Like Zilina, the monumental Great Synagogue in *Tel Aviv (ca. 1930) combines traditional elements such as arched windows and a large central dome with the plain smooth wall surfaces and combined massing of block-like forms typical of early European Modernism. The Yeshurun Synagogue in *Jerusalem (Friedmann, Rubin, and Stolzer, 1934–35) eschews the hierarchical arrangement of multiple forms for a simple joining of two main masses – a rectangular block, entered on its long side, with a tall half-cylinder, housing the sanctuary, joined to the rear.

Experiments with Modernism in synagogue design in the 1920s and 1930s include the Dutch Cubist-style Jacob Obrechtplein Synagogue in *Amsterdam (1927–28), designed by Jewish architect Harry Elte; it also recalls Frank Lloyd Wright's Unity Temple near *Chicago. The Lekstraat Synagogue (A. Elzas, 1936–37), also in Amsterdam, is a plain stone box with simple square windows that emphasizes only the ark (aron ha-kodesh, in which the *Torah scroll or scrolls are stored) and the bimah (elevated platform used for *Torah reading). Elzas, who won a competition among nine Jewish architects for the commission, designed an unusually spare synagogue. The simple geometry and white concrete walls are offset slightly by the use of exterior stone and the introduction of abundant natural light through large windows. In London, Sir Evan Owen Williams designed a very open interior for the Dollis Hill Synagogue with galleries cantilevered from the wall, rather than supported by piers of columns. The walls and roof are made of corrugated concrete that strengthen the structure. Hexagonal and shield-shaped windows recall the Star of David.

Perhaps the most consistent modern synagogue form of the period was that built in Plauen, Germany (Fritz Landauer, 1930). It was conceived as a white box elevated on stilts at one end; the window arrangement differentiates discreet building functions, much as in contemporary industrial buildings. The Oberstrasse Synagogue in Hamburg (Felix Ascher and Robert Friedman, 1931) combines simple forms and an austere exterior with a symmetrical and hierarchical arrangement of space, the formality of which resembled contemporary civic buildings. Notable modern synagogues were also built in Brno, Czechoslovakia, and Athens, Greece.

After World War II and the *Holocaust, most synagogue construction took place in the United States, where Modernism quickly supplanted earlier styles as an expression of a new Judaism. Demand for suburban synagogues created a boom of modern-style synagogues that also served as educational and community centers. Eric Mendelsohn developed the full expansion of the sanctuary and multiple use of spaces – important concepts for modern synagogue design. He accentuated the sanctuary section within a larger complex using elevated and curvilinear forms; sliding partitions allowed spaces to serve diverse functions at different times. At B'nai Amoona (St. Louis, 1950) a dramatic parabolic roof rises from the ark wall to the entrance wall; the top is glazed, allowing light to pour over the congregation and onto the bimah and ark. Mendelsohn's sanctuary at the Park Synagogue in Cleveland is a hemispheric dome that rises almost straight from the ground.

Mendelsohn's designs formed the basis of most suburban synagogue architecture from the 1940s through the 1980s. Percival Goodman appreciated and implemented Mendelsohn's innovations. His many designs lacked Mendelsohn's drama, but they excelled in providing efficient, functional, and differentiated spatial arrangements, often highlighted with accents of modern art. His widely emulated work often applied sculpture to spaces, rather than sculpted space.

Influenced by Mendelsohn and Goodman, many architects transformed the sanctuary space with dynamic expressive forms, often of concrete and glass. Congregations frequently favored symbolic building profiles recalling mountains or tents. Frank Lloyd Wright expressed his intent for Beth Shalom Synagogue (Elkins Park, Pennsylvania, 1959), writing, "We want to create the kind of building that people... will feel as if they were resting in the very hands of God." At Congregation Israel in Glencoe, Illinois (Minoru Yamasaki, 1964), pre-cast concrete arches frame the building, but large gaps in the structure fill the sanctuary with filtered light. The interior is spacious, and the use of light, white walls, and little ornamentation create a cerebral space. The tall, thin gilded ark has been likened to a prayer shawl wrapping the Torah scrolls, but from the sanctuary entrance it also suggests a single flame – a burning bush or eternal light.

In post-War Europe, the primary element of the Ruhrallee Synagogue at Essen, Germany (Dieter Knoblauch and Heinz Heise, 1959), is a hemisphere that rises directly from the ground – with no visible substructure or drum. The unified shape may symbolize the monotheism of Judaism, but it also reflected current trends in architecture favoring pure geometric forms. Inside, the ark is a rectangle inscribed within a broad triangle, set into the shell of the hemispheric dome at the apex of which a Star of David is inscribed, within a series of small round windows that define the shape with light. German architect Alfred Jacoby has inherited these traditions. His designs – often bright, crisp, and comfortable, with a single defining expressive element – have been very popular in late-twentieth-century Germany. His synagogue in Park City, Utah, has brought the language of Mendelsohn and Goodman back to the United States.

The dramatic synagogue in Livorno, *Italy (Angelo di Castro, 1962), replaced the famous Renaissance synagogue destroyed in World War II. The expressive structure is defined by crooked concrete buttresses that, connected by concrete walls, appear to exert pressure to keep the building together; these buttresses allow a large unimpeded interior sanctuary that, like its predecessor, has rows of seats on three sides and the Torah ark on the fourth.

In *Israel, similar expressive tendencies are found. The synagogue in Beersheva (1961) nestles under a sweeping concrete vault that covers the sanctuary like a turtle shell. The vault is anchored in the ground on either side of the small prayer hall that is lit by a wall perforated from floor to ceiling by hexagonal openings. In contrast to Beersheva, the Israel Goldstein Synagogue on the Givat Ram campus of the Hebrew University (Heinz Rau and David Reznik, 1957) appears ready to float away. The windowless synagogue recalls a giant balloon, as its smooth white bulbous form seems to levitate off the ground; its lower level is pierced with wide arches that light the entire structure, including the sanctuary encased in the building's upper part. Perhaps the most inventive of modern synagogues is the one at the army officer training school at Mitzpeh Ramon (Zvi Hecker, 1969), set in dreary desert surroundings. The exterior of the small sanctuary is concrete that is faceted like crystal to create a complex arrangement of colored shapes and patterns.

Very different is the Cymbalista Synagogue at Tel Aviv University (Mario Botta, 1998), which creates within a unique sculptural form two sanctuaries that are equal in size. Each is a near-cube and they are bathed in natural light funneled from above. The shapes, volumes, and the use of light are indebted to unbuilt synagogue projects of Louis Kahn.

Toward the end of the twentieth century, the number of large synagogue projects has declined in Europe and North America, as resources shifted to the erection of large regional community centers and to Jewish museums and *Holocaust memorials. In a reaction to Modernism, some communities attempted to re-create the lost intimacy of Old World and inner city synagogues – often by erecting smaller chapels incorporating historical styles adjacent to big sanctuaries or including symbolic elements referring to the lost synagogue culture of the Old World. Another trend is the incorporation of "green" technologies into synagogue designs. Environmental concerns remain, however, mostly rhetorical, although a significant effort has been made to integrate synagogues more into natural settings and to include more *gardens and greenery in the synagogue experience. Windows onto gardens and wooded areas, as at the 1989 Jewish Center of the Hamptons by Norman Jaffe (East Hampton, New York), are increasingly common (see ECOLOGY).

In the first decades of the twenty-first century important new synagogues continue to be built that combine the traditions of rationalism and expressionism and also adapt the forms pioneered by the modern masters.

For further reading, see K. Elman and A. Giral, eds. *Percival Goodman: Architect, Planner, Teacher, Painter* (2001); S. D. Gruber, *American Synagogues: A Century of Architecture and Jewish Community* (2003); A. Kampf, *Contemporary Synagogue Art: Developments in the United States, 1945–1965* (1966); C. H. Krinsky, *Synagogues of Europe* (1985); R. Stephan, ed., *Eric Mendelsohn, Architect 1887–1953* (1999); and E. Van Voolen and A. Sachs, eds., *Contemporary Architecture and Jewish Identity* (2004).   SAMUEL D. GRUBER

Synagogues, Wooden. Wooden synagogues were constructed continuously in *Eastern Europe from the earliest period of Jewish settlement beginning in the fourteenth or fifteenth centuries until their almost complete destruction by the *Nazis beginning in 1939. Unlike the synagogues in almost every other country of the Jewish *Diaspora, which followed the existing forms of local and regional architecture, a distinctive type of wooden synagogue architecture emerged in the Jewish communities in the small towns or *shtetls of the Polish-Lithuanian Commonwealth.

The oldest documented wooden synagogues that survived into the twentieth century were built in the south central regions of present-day *Ukraine from the middle of the seventeenth century. Although there were once hundreds of wooden synagogues in small towns in what are now *Poland, Ukraine, *Belarus, and *Lithuania, the surviving documentation, primarily compiled by Polish architectural historians before *World War II, recorded only the largest and finest structures. One region of particular emphasis was present-day northwestern Poland and Lithuania where Jewish communities, such as Wolpa, Olkienniki, and Zabludow, had erected magnificent synagogues that are generally considered to be masterworks of Eastern European monumental wooden architecture. Late in the nineteenth century, Polish and European architectural historians began to photograph and study the wooden synagogues. The primary sources of documentation were compiled under the direction of the Polish art historian, Szymon Zajczyk, by students of the

Institute of Polish Architecture in Warsaw. It is this documentation that partially survived *Nazi destruction and was published by Maria and Kazimierz Piechotka in a series of landmark books beginning with *Wooden Synagogues* (1957 and 1959).

The construction system of most wooden synagogues combined a squared, stacked-log wall system of ancient Slavic origin with a technically advanced, early modern roof-trussing system that typically sheltered a unique, domed wooden cupola above the prayer hall. This curved, tent-like cupola was typically hung from the roof structure and, because of its technical and stylistic sophistication, was probably designed by regional architects employed by the Polish ruling class. This interior cupola combined Baroque styles related to monumental Polish civic buildings and churches with regional traditions of wood construction to produce the uniquely Jewish interior space of the small town synagogue. Surprisingly, this unique aspect of the wooden synagogues was not derivative of the masonry synagogues found in larger towns throughout these regions. The wooden synagogues were almost certainly built by non-Jewish craftsmen (Jews were generally excluded from the building trades) under the direction of regional master builders.

The interiors of these synagogues were dominated by an elaborate octagonal central *bimah* (elevated platform used for *Torah reading) and a monumental multitiered ark (*aron ha-kodesh*; storage cabinet for the *Torah scroll or scrolls) set along the western walls. Although directly related to wooden monumental architecture of the Baroque period, especially church altars, the ark and *bimah* followed distinctive Jewish stylistic models that had developed in the seventeenth and eighteenth centuries and were found throughout the *Ashkenazic Diaspora.

By the beginning of the eighteenth century, the prayer hall of the small town wooden synagogue was commonly built alongside a group of subordinate rooms and structures. Typically the auxiliary structures surrounding the prayer hall included an entrance hall, *beit midrash* (house of study), meeting rooms, a women's gallery, and possibly a school. Later in the nineteenth century, as the Jewish community grew, these functions were often transferred to neighboring buildings. A typical exterior expansion to the small town synagogue was the erection of a second-floor women's gallery above the entrance that replaced a first-floor gallery. This change in location may have reflected the influence of traditions from the larger towns. Such expansions can be recognized in exterior photographs by the presence of exterior stairs on the front of the synagogue that women used to attend services while men continued to use the main entrance to the prayer hall on the first floor.

Perhaps the most unusual aspect of the typical wooden synagogues from the seventeenth and eighteenth centuries was their common pattern of liturgical wall paintings. In synagogues from the oldest central Ukrainian regions, colorful, elaborate paintings covered the entire walls and ceiling of the prayer hall. The dominant visual elements of the paintings were large painted tablets with portions of daily prayer. Typically these prayers were painted with black Hebrew letters on brilliant white backgrounds and were surrounded by elaborately painted architectural surrounds with columns and arches following the precedent of book art and Hebrew illuminated manuscripts. The remaining surfaces of the interior were filled with ensembles of animal and vegetative motifs following highly stylized patterns typical of wooden synagogues throughout Eastern Europe.

Although early scholars sometimes attributed these paintings to the work or influence of local vernacular sources, the wooden synagogue paintings were actually the works of highly trained Jewish artists who occasionally signed and dated them. These artists probably worked in guild-like associations and produced a uniform liturgical art that was remarkably consistent in wooden synagogues throughout Eastern Europe. The most famous examples of wooden synagogue paintings to be photographed before their destruction were located in the towns of Gwozdziec, Chodorow, Jablonow, and Michalpol in the Podolia region of south central Ukraine. This regional style spread throughout Eastern Europe and was even imported to *Germany. In the 1730s, a well-documented artist from Brody in Ukraine, Eliezer Sussman, painted the walls of at least seven synagogues including, in 1735, the ceiling of the Horb Synagogue, which is preserved at the Israel Museum, *Jerusalem.

Although complex and exotic to a modern observer, these paintings actually followed consistent patterns of layout, motif, and liturgical reference. The paintings demonstrate the influence of sources outside of Poland, including *Sephardic/*Ottoman, Baroque, and Western European decorative arts motifs. They also reveal an older stratum of Ashkenazi Rhineland sources, particularly animal symbolism and architectural motifs of medieval origin. These paintings indicate a surprisingly multicultural and cosmopolitan development not usually associated with the small Polish/Ukrainian town or *shtetl*. See **Plate 9** for similar imagery. This artistic tradition flourished in the seventeenth and eighteenth centuries; the practice ended in the early nineteenth century, although the paintings were generally preserved. This change in the character of the small town synagogue is generally attributed to the changes in Jewish communities of Eastern Europe during the Early Modern period, such as the advent of the *Haskalah*, the rise of *Hasidism, and increasing industrialization and urbanization. Recent research includes T. C. Hubka, *Resplendent Synagogue: Architecture and Worship in an Eighteenth-Century Polish Community* (2003).   Thomas C. Hubka

Syria, Ancient. Located at the eastern end of the Mediterranean Sea, Syria is bordered by *Turkey, *Iraq, Jordan, Lebanon, and *Israel. In ancient times, Syria was an important trade center between *Mesopotamia and *Egypt; the city of Ebla, south of present-day Aleppo, was a major cultural and political power in the mid-third millennium BCE. Excavations at Ebla have yielded the earliest examples of a Semitic language, a form of Proto-Canaanite. The city of Ugarit, which flourished in the twelfth century BCE, is an important source of Canaanite literature, which was inscribed in an alphabetic cuneiform script on clay tablets (see CANAAN, CANAANITES; NEAR EAST, ANCIENT). Ugaritic, a northwest Semitic language, is closely related to Biblical *Hebrew; many of the writings from Ugarit offer important parallels to biblical writings, both prose and poetry, and have been valuable resources in translating difficult Hebrew words. They also illuminate the larger Canaanite context of which ancient Israel was a part (**Map 1**).

In the first millennium BCE, the *Phoenicians, who lived in an area stretching from northern Canaan to southern Syria and inland to the mountains of Lebanon, were the dominant ethnic group. Less a unified nation than a collection of independent city-states (Arwad, Byblos, Sidon, and Tyre), Phoenicia had a seafaring mercantile economy with trading connections throughout the region, including with the Israelite monarchies. In the *Hellenistic era, after the death of *Alexander the Great, Syria came under the rule of the *Seleucids, whose capital city was Antioch. In the mid-second century BCE, Seleucid Syria lost control of *Jerusalem and much of the Land of Israel to the *Hasmonean dynasty. After a century of decline, Syria was reorganized by Pompey into a *Roman province in 64 BCE, and it remained under Roman and *Byzantine rule until the *Muslim conquests of the seventh century CE. The Umayyad dynasty (661–750) established Damascus as its capital in 661. Significant numbers of Jews lived in Syria in Roman times, particularly in Damascus, and a sizable Jewish community lived there in the Muslim era as well. **Maps 4, 5**

Szold, Henrietta (1860–1945) was an editor and scholar, the guiding spirit and founder of Hadassah: The Women's Zionist Organization of America (see ORGANIZATIONS, WOMEN'S: NORTH AMERICA), and a political leader in pre-statehood *Palestine. Born in Baltimore, the oldest child of Rabbi Benjamin Szold and his wife Sophie (Schaar) Szold, Szold was highly educated by her father and at Western Female High School. For fifteen years, she taught adult classes at her father's *synagogue, Oheb Shalom, and taught French, German, botany, and mathematics at the Misses Adam's School. In 1889 she founded and became principal of one of the first immigrant night schools in America. Szold was a charter member of the Baltimore Zion Association and served on the executive committee of the newly founded Federation of American Zionists.

As executive secretary of the *Jewish Publication Society (JPS) from 1893–1916, Szold played a pioneering role in creating Jewish literary culture in the *United States, translating, editing, and overseeing the publication of dozens of significant works on Jewish history and religion, inaugurating the *American Jewish Year Book* series, and writing essays herself.

In 1902, Szold was accepted as a special student at the *Jewish Theological Seminary in *New York City after pledging that she would not pursue a rabbinic diploma. There she fell in love with the scholar Louis Ginzberg, whose works she translated and edited; she suffered a severe emotional crisis when Ginzberg married a younger woman. A turning point came after a trip to *Palestine with her mother in 1909. In 1912, with associates from her women's Zionist study circle, Szold formed "the daughters of Zion" and became its first president; in 1914, this group became Hadassah. Led by Szold, Hadassah established a nurses' settlement in Palestine; this program was followed by innovative contributions to the health and welfare of both Jews and Arabs, including clinics, dispensaries, hospitals, infant welfare stations, and other services oriented to women and children.

Szold went to live in Palestine in 1920; except for occasional visits to the United States, she remained there for the rest of her life. In 1927, she was appointed to the three-member Palestine Zionist Executive. In 1931, elected to the executive board of the Vaad Leumi (National Council), she established a comprehensive system of social welfare services including family welfare, child care, immigrant aid, and vocational schooling. Her most challenging task came two years later, when she became head of Youth Aliyah, organizing and supervising the rescue of thousands of children from *Nazi *Germany.

In her later life, Szold's support of Brit Shalom (Covenant of Peace) and subsequently, the Iḥud (Union) Association, which called for the creation of a binational state, drew criticism from some Zionist groups, including Hadassah. Yet her manifold contributions to the health, education, and welfare of the *Yishuv* and her moral and intellectual leadership of the American Zionist women's movement made her a beloved, even legendary, figure in her lifetime. At once a visionary and a practical administrator, Szold gave American Jewish women an enduring public role and public Jewish identity in *Zionism (see also, ISRAEL, STATE OF: PEACE MOVEMENT).

Recent research includes, B. R. Shargel, *Lost Love: The Untold Story of Henrietta Szold* (1997); B. Kessler, ed., *Daughter of Zion: Henrietta Szold and American Jewish Woman* (1995); and S. Reinharz and M. Raider, eds., *American Jewish Women and the Zionist Enterprise* (2005).   JOYCE ANTLER

T

Tabernacle (*mishkan* in Hebrew, literally "dwelling") refers to the portable shrine described in the *Pentateuch as accompanying the Israelites throughout their wilderness wanderings. The Tabernacle served as the center of sacrificial and cultic activity and was also the place where the *Ark of the Covenant was housed. According to Exodus 40:34, "the cloud covered the Tent of Meeting, and the Presence of the Lord filled the Tabernacle." Directions as to the construction of the Tabernacle and its component parts were revealed to Moses at Mount Sinai (Exod 25–27). It was to be erected facing eastward wherever the Israelites camped, and the tribes were to be arrayed around it in a prescribed pattern. Modern scholarship assigns the detailed traditions about building of the Tabernacle and the types of sacrifices to be offered there (Leviticus) to the Priestly strand of biblical authorship (see BIBLE: MODERN SCHOLARSHIP). According to these texts, the priests or *kohanim*, the descendants of *Aaron, brother of *Moses, officiated at the Tabernacle, while other members of the tribe of Levi, the "regular" Levites, had subservient roles (see PRIESTHOOD).

Many modern scholars question the historicity of the Tabernacle narratives described in the *Torah and suggest that Priestly writers of a later era projected their vision of a wilderness *mishkan* to reinforce the significance of the Jerusalem *Temple, "the place in which I will put my name" (Deut 12:5), to worshipers of their own time. Others suggest that stories about the Tabernacle reflect a shrine from the reign of King *David, which itself would have been based on shrines from the pre-monarchic period of Israelite life in the Land of Israel. **See also CANAAN, CANAANITES; EGYPT AND ANCIENT ISRAEL.**   ELIZABETH SHULMAN

Tallit (pl. *tallitot*) is a *prayer shawl, traditionally made of wool or silk, worn by adults during morning *worship, on *Tisha B'Av in the afternoon, and on *Yom Kippur at all services. Each of the prayer shawl's four corners has a fringe called *tzitzit* that is knotted in a particular way. These fringes are based on Numbers 15:38–40 and Deuteronomy 22:12, which ordain the making of twisted cords on the four corners of one's garment as a constant reminder of divine *commandments; Numbers 15:38–40 also specify that the fringes should include a blue thread, although this is no longer considered a requirement for the *tzitzit*. Until recently, only men wore *tallitot*; in the beginning of the twenty-first century, it is increasingly common for women to wear *tallitot* during worship, including in some Orthodox settings (JUDAISM, ORTHODOX: MODERN ORTHODOX). In some traditional communities, men wear a smaller, four-cornered garment called a *tallit katan* or *arba kanfot* under their clothing as a reminder throughout the day of the obligation to observe divine commandments.   ELIZABETH SHULMAN

Talmud, Babylonian. The Babylonian Talmud (abbreviated BT in this volume; also referred to as Bavli or Shas) is the literary pinnacle of *rabbinic *Judaism. From the time of its composition, it has been the work of literature most representative of Jewish ideas, values, laws, practices, rituals, and culture. The BT has served as both the primary study text in the rabbinic curriculum from the period of the *geonic academies to the present and the starting point for discussions of *halakhah* (Jewish law), both practical and theoretical.

The two extant literary Talmuds, the Jerusalem (JT) and Babylonian Talmuds, owe their general form and some content to the discourse of *talmud* ("study") undertaken by the *Amoraim, rabbinic scholars and teachers who were intellectually active in both *Palestine and *Babylonia from ca. 200–ca. 500 CE. The Amoraim, like their predecessors, the *Tannaim, produced two general types of texts: *midrash, the creative interpretation of the *Bible, and *mishnah*, the formulation of legal statutes and theological principles. The Talmuds include both approaches in their systematic discussions of the *Mishnah, the legal compilation completed in the Land of *Israel ca. 200 CE.

The Talmuds are structured as commentaries to the Mishnah; their expositions proceed order by order, tractate by tractate, and chapter to chapter, down to each individual *mishnah*. However, the Amoraim were not limited by the Mishnah's content; rather, they used the subject matter of each *mishnah* as a conceptual starting point for a conversation that incorporates tannaitic *beraitot* (traditions that do not appear in the Mishnah) in both *mishnah* and midrash form, amoraic statements (in both *mishnah* and midrash form), and interpretations and debates about these statements conducted by named Rabbis of later generations and by the Talmud's anonymous voice. These conversations can also include biographical anecdotes about contemporaneous figures. An individual *mishnah* may generate several such conversations, or *sugyot* (sing., *sugyah*). Redacted versions of these discussions, cumulatively termed *gemara* (study), were ultimately combined with the Mishnah to form the Talmud.

The BT is larger, less ambiguously composed, and more conceptually developed than its counterpart. While the JT was redacted in the fourth century CE, the BT remained a work in progress until the seventh century; even after its main redaction, the BT's text remained fluid enough to allow for interpolations and slight modifications until well into the period of the *Geonim. The two Talmuds are also the products of different political and cultural surroundings; the JT came together within a *Byzantine Roman environment populated by neighboring pagans and Christians, whereas the BT was redacted in the Sassanid Persian environment among neighboring Zoroastrians (see PERSIA).

Both Talmuds are anthological in the sense that they collect earlier materials from disparate Rabbis who lived in different geographic regions (in both Palestine and Babylonia), in different times (ca. 70–ca. 750 CE). Each Talmud can be described as a collage that juxtaposes different texts and even different genres of text, while explicitly attributing the voices in its conversation to a temporally and geographically diverse rabbinic population. That being said, each Talmud is the expression of a specific social group, and the ideas each contains reflect the weaknesses of that group as much as its strengths. In many ways, rabbinic literature is elitist and misogynistic, reflecting the limitations of its collective authors. Even within rabbinic literature, the BT reflects a particular suspicion of learned women. When earlier materials being used within a BT *sugyah* transmit the possibility of women of authority and knowledge, BT interpreters resist this presentation and rewrite their received sources to subjugate such women to rabbinic male authorities (see TALMUD STUDY: FEMINIST APPROACHES).

The energy of a talmudic *sugyah* is often dialectical, involved in resolving the apparent conflict of disagreeing canonical sources, be they biblical, tannaitic, or amoraic. A posed conflict can be resolved either by distinguishing the cases conceptually (dialectically) or by assigning two contradictory positions to named authorities of equal canonical weight. The issue of canonical weight emerges from the underlying assumption, shared by both Talmuds, that the periodization of Tannaim and Amoraim creates a line of authoritative division. According to this assumption, any *Tanna*, regardless of era, can argue with any other *Tanna*; similarly, any *Amora* can argue with any other *Amora*. However, an *Amora* may not argue with a *Tanna*, even if the time gap between the *Amora* and the *Tanna* is shorter than the gap between an earlier and later *Tanna* or an earlier and later *Amora*. Many talmudic *sugyot* have the feeling of bookkeeping exercises intended to preserve these assumptions about rabbinic canonical authority.

The traditional understanding of the Talmuds' composition is that both of the extant literary works are direct and accidental remnants of the intellectual discourse of *talmud*. Because scholars must have compiled an oral record of talmudic discourses to preserve the opinions of earlier Rabbis, the Talmuds that we have today, the thinking goes, are merely transcriptions of these oral records. This understanding of talmudic composition is still the scholarly consensus for the JT. Over the last forty years, however, scholars have reached a different understanding about the composition of the BT. Although the BT undoubtedly draws on the oral record of talmudic discourses in amoraic times, the BT's redacted text represents a more thorough and comprehensive redaction. This redaction (editing) is responsible both for the comparatively smooth organizational flow (relative to the JT) of the warp and woof of BT *sugyot* and for a significant portion of content that is unattributed to named Tannaim and Amoraim. The anonymous nature of the BT's redactors has earned them the name *Stammaim (anonymous ones).

In a given JT *sugyah*, the relationship between adjacent texts (for example a *mishnah*-style *baraita* and an amoraic *midrash*) is often ambiguous and left to the reader to determine, sometimes with great difficulty. Within a BT *sugyah*, by contrast, the relationship between collected texts is almost always expressly spelled out by the words of an anonymous stam, who notes that the two texts are mutually supportive, contradictory, or coincidentally overlapping. Additionally, a *sugyah* is often constructed linearly along historical lines, with tannaitic material followed by amoraic material followed by anonymous material. This creates the framework in which later authorities can comment on and interpret the opinions of their predecessors. As the latest authorities in this chain, the anonymous Stammaim play a significant role in interpreting tannaitic and amoraic texts, because all readers of the BT encounter the tannaitic and amoraic viewpoints through the lens of their stammaitic interpreters.

The importance of the Stammaim is not limited to a particular genre of talmudic composition. Within ethical or theological discussions, legal debates, or extensive narratives, the Stammaim shaped earlier materials and the evolution of ideas. Recent work has demonstrated the extent to which the Stammaim are responsible for some of the most famous BT narratives as well as for the abstract legal conceptualizations for which the BT is well known. In short, scholars now consider the Stammaim the authors of the BT as we know it.

Although the BT does not differentiate between *halakhah* (legal teachings) and *aggadah* (nonlegal traditions), geonic interests in consolidating legal authority led to a curriculum that was selectively oriented toward its legal portions. Some of the earliest geonic monographs are legal *codes whose prose is cut and pasted from the BT. The geonic *responsa, mostly legal rulings posted to distant Jewish communities, rely almost exclusively on the BT. Post-geonic responsa down to the present continue this practice of discussing legal issues within the framework of the BT *sugyot* in which they arise. Since the geonic period, vocational scholars have been more interested in the halakhic *sugyot* of the BT, even though the BT consists of roughly equal amounts of *halakhah* and *aggadah* and this material is not differentiated within the text.

Composed orally, the BT was studied orally into the geonic period, when it began to be transcribed. The earliest written text witness of the Bavli is an eighth- or ninth-century Cairo *Genizah fragment of a scroll containing Tractate Ḥullin. The BT survived in manuscript form until the dawn of printing. Among the surviving medieval manuscripts of the BT is Munich 95, a manuscript that records the BT in its entirety. Bavli tractates were printed in pre-expulsion Spain and by printers from the Soncino family in *Italy in the fifteenth century (see PRINTING). The first complete printed edition of the BT, the Bomberg Shas, was printed in *Venice between 1519 and 1523. The Vilna edition of 1880–86, printed by the "Press of the Widow and Romm Brothers" is a remarkable aesthetic achievement and has stood as the definitive edition of the BT ever since.

Two aggadic digests of BT, *Haggadot ha-Talmud* and *Ein Yaakov*, were printed in the sixteenth century. The latter volume was a popular text in the sixteenth through twentieth centuries and went through more than a hundred printings. In the last century, the entire BT has become a popular study text for nonvocational scholars, individuals who are not professionally involved with the Jewish community or academics in *Jewish studies, with the rise of *Daf Yomi*, a program that studies one two-sided page of BT every day and completes the BT in its entirety every seven and a half years. Recent celebrations to honor this completion have filled major arenas in the United States and Israel.

For further reading, see R. Kalmin, "The Formation and Character of the Babylonian Talmud," in *The Cambridge*

History of Judaism, vol. 4, ed. S. T. Katz (2006), 840–76; and C. E. Fonrobert and M. S. Jaffee, eds., *The Cambridge Companion to the Talmud and Rabbinic Literature* (2007).

BARRY WIMPFHEIMER

Talmud, Jerusalem (Yerushalmi, abbreviated in this volume as JT). This Talmud, also known as the Talmud of the Land of Israel or the Palestinian Talmud (and sometimes abbreviated at PT), is the commentary on the *Mishnah of the *Amoraim living in the Land of Israel. From the period of the *Geonim until early modernity, the JT was also known as *gemara d'vnei ma'arava* (the learning of the people of the West), *gemara d'vnei eretz Yisrael* (the learning of the people of the Land of Israel), as well as more briefly, *talmud eretz Yisrael* and *talmud d'ma'arava*.

The JT is organized according to the orders of the Mishnah and is divided into tractates, chapters, and *halakhot* (discussions of an individual *mishnah* or parts thereof). There is no JT to chapters 21–24 of Tractate *Shabbat*, chapter 3 of *Makkot*, Tractates *Avot and *Eduyyot*, all of order *Kodashim*, and most of order *Tohorot*, except for chapters 1–3 of *Niddah*. Scholars consider it unlikely that the JT ever included *Kodashim* and *Tohorot*, and attempts to reconstruct the missing portions of *Shabbat*, *Makkot*, and *Niddah* have proven flawed. Manuscript evidence suggests that even at an early stage the JT did not cover these mishnaic orders and chapters.

The JT explicates *mishnayot* and *beraitot*, presents *aggadah*, examines legal and conceptual issues ranging beyond the specific *mishnah* under discussion, and anthologizes material thematically related to the individual *mishnah*. One of the JT's noteworthy literary features is that of "transferred *sugyot*," which are often lengthy sequences of material that are repeated nearly verbatim in different JT tractates. These repetitions may be due to the redactors' desire either to use the transferred material to shed light on a discussion in another tractate or simply to include all relevant material within one tractate so that the tractate can be studied independently of the whole. Yet, the JT did not undergo the centuries of intensive scrutiny accorded the Babylonian *Talmud (BT) and was relatively neglected before the nineteenth century. Numerous textual problems render the JT a challenging subject of study; they were likely both cause and effect of its marginalization. Elucidating the text and establishing accurate readings in the JT are consequently important concerns of academic scholarship. Contemporary academic scholarship also studies the JT's literary features and *halakhah, as well as what it reveals about amoraic rabbinic culture in the Land of Israel.

The JT includes the teachings of five generations of Amoraim (ca. 220–360/370 CE), who were mainly active in Tiberias (the likely site of the JT's redaction), Lydda, Sepphoris, and Caesarea, all sites in the Land of Israel. Academic talmudists at one time believed that the end of the Palestinian *Patriarchate in 429 and/or a supposed climate of persecution in fifth-century Palestine served as the catalysts for the JT's redaction. Saul Lieberman also famously argued that the tractates *Bava Kamma*, *Bava Metzia*, and *Bava Batra* were edited in Caesarea approximately fifty years before the rest of the JT (ca. 350). His argument was based chiefly on these tractates' Caesarean focus, terser language, and the overwhelming presence in them of early Amoraim and the absence of major and especially late Amoraim.

Skepticism currently reigns about the arguments for a 429 date and about Lieberman's "Talmud of Caesarea" hypothesis (notwithstanding scholarly acknowledgment that those three tractates have distinctive features); the reasons for the JT's redaction remain unclear. It has very recently been suggested that the JT was redacted at the end of the Palestinian Amoraic period in ca. 360/370. Yet a ca. 400 date remains plausible because little in the JT's portrayal of the Amoraim suggests that they functioned as redactors. Moreover, an anonymous editorial layer, independent of the Amoraim, that arranges and comments on materials is clearly present.

The JT was first printed in *Venice in 1523 on the basis of a manuscript (the Leiden manuscript) copied by R. Jehiel ben R. Jekutiel in Rome in 1289. R. Jehiel described this manuscript as full of errors and stated that he had made corrections on his own authority. Later glossators also made changes to R. Jehiel's manuscript, and these changes, many of which were not based on solid knowledge of the JT or its Galilean *Aramaic dialect, made their way into the Venice edition, which is the basis of all subsequent printed editions. In 2001, the Academy of the Hebrew Language published a scholarly edition of the Leiden manuscript that, among other things, distinguishes the JT base text from the pre-1523 emendations. This new edition will facilitate scholarly research into the text of JT. The Leiden manuscript is the only manuscript of the entire JT, but partial manuscripts are also extant. These include the slightly older, incomplete Rome manuscript (which contains all of order *Zeraim* except for *Bikkurim*, and *Sotah*); the Escorial manuscript of the three *Bava* tractates (fifteenth century); and JT fragments from the Cairo *Genizah.

The JT contains Babylonian *sugyot* and teachings attributable to Babylonian Amoraim of the first three generations (ca. 220–350), but lacks teachings from the following four generations. The BT contains much Palestinian material, including traditions of the *nahotei* (those who descended), sages who transmitted rabbinic teachings between Babylonia and Palestine. Pre-modern and traditionalist scholarship inclined to the view that some traditions in the BT depended on teachings in the JT. Beginning in the nineteenth century, academic scholarship agreed that the BT knew nothing of the JT. This debate became more nuanced in the twentieth century, as some scholars argued that the inter-talmudic parallels are largely due to a layer of "early *talmud*" shared by the two rabbinic centers. This position has been further refined with the growing realization that some sages of the fourth and fifth Babylonian Amoraic generations (mid- to late-fourth century CE) were strongly influenced by Palestinian learning. This suggests that at least some intertalmudic parallels may be due to an influx of Palestinian materials into Babylonia toward the end of the Amoraic period in the Land of Israel. A recent study by Alyssa Gray argues that one BT tractate may have known and relied on its JT parallel.

For further reading, see J. Neusner, *The Talmud of the Land of Israel*, vol. 35 (1983); C. Hayes, *Between the Babylonian and Palestinian Talmuds* (1997); R. Kalmin, *The Sage in Jewish Society of Late Antiquity* (1999); idem, *Jewish Babylonia between Persia and Roman Palestine* (2006); B. Bokser, *Yerushalmi Pesachim*, ed. L. Schiffman (1994); and A. Gray, *A Talmud in Exile* (2005).

ALYSSA M. GRAY

Talmud Study: Feminist Approaches.

Feminist approaches to the Talmud are the direct result of Second Wave *feminism, an intellectual movement of the 1960s and '70s. Second Wave feminism investigated the origins of patriarchy and criticized patriarchal societies and religions that uphold and maintain women's inferior opportunities and secondary positions in most aspects of life. It identified monotheistic religions, among them *Christianity and *Judaism, as patriarchal religions; the feminist project of critiquing their foundational documents and holy canons began with the *Bible (both the Hebrew Scriptures and the *New Testament). Some feminist scholars also identified the *Talmud (particularly the Babylonian Talmud, which became in effect the second Jewish Scripture) as a site of patriarchal authority within Judaism.

Feminist studies in talmudic literature began with the rather naïve question of whether the Talmud should be seen as an improvement on the Hebrew Bible with regard to women or whether, on the contrary, it reinforced and increased women's secondary position and lesser status in Judaism. This approach arose from a similar Christian endeavor, in which Christian feminists were describing early Christianity as a reaction against the repressive attitude of Judaism to women, represented by the Rabbis who produced the Talmud. Elsewhere, I have defined this sort of assessment, in which scholars deem one patriarchal system as more friendly to women than another, as "comparative patriarchy," and I have questioned the usefulness of and motivations behind denigrating one system while praising another.

Since the mid-1980s, however, there has been a shift in emphasis in feminist studies of the Talmud. Increasingly, the Talmud itself and related documents (such as midrashic compositions of various eras) have become the focus of investigation and are studied as foundational Jewish patriarchal documents in their own right. Early scholars who engaged in feminist talmudic research tended to be women (foremost among them Judith Hauptman, Judith R. Baskin, and Judith R. Wegner), but as feminist (and women's) studies became a recognized discipline internationally (often in the process, changing its name to gender studies), many male scholars joined the project (Jacob Neusner and Daniel Boyarin have been especially influential in the talmudic realm). This change in emphasis arose not just because of an internal critique of earlier methods but also as a result of a paradigm shift evident in a broad range of fields. Feminist studies profited significantly from post-modern critiques of many academic disciplines, which deconstructed the way knowledge was created as a seat of power for the elite against the poor, the colonized, the dispossessed, and, among them, women. These critiques identified talmudic discourse as a prime example of a privileged male endeavor that participated in the disempowerment and silencing of female voices. Academic talmudic studies since the nineteenth-century *Wissenschaft des Judentums was seen as continuing these attitudes. Among the scholars who have been active in this newer feminist critique of rabbinic texts are Charlotte Fonrobert, Miriam Peskowitz, and Michael Satlow.

Most feminist studies of talmudic literature in the first decade of the twenty-first century tend to be focused on a specific issue (such as the talmudic construction of menstruation (*niddah), rabbinic attitudes to *marriage, or rabbinic formations of male–female division of labor) rather than on general analyses or overviews of rabbinic attitudes toward women. Many scholars are interested in how and why rabbinic literature constructed particular visions of women and of relations between the sexes. Some contemporary scholars have critiqued previous feminist endeavors for naiveté, a lack of attention to minority voices in rabbinic discourse, or insensitivity to nuance; some have described their own work as more sophisticated or rigorous than that of their predecessors. Perhaps, however, their work might best be described as a product of a new academic Zeitgeist.

At the end of the first decade of the twenty-first century, an innovative international project is underway. Its goal is to profit from all forms of feminist insight, to bring together scholars from the various approaches described earlier, and to draw on their collective energy to create a comprehensive feminist commentary on the Babylonian Talmud. The first volume, devoted to Tractate Taanit, appeared in 2008.

For further reading, see J. R. Baskin, "The Separation of Women in Rabbinic Literature," in Women, Religion and Social Change, ed. Y. Y. Haddad and E. B. Findly (1985); idem, Midrashic Women: Formations of the Feminine in Rabbinic Literature (2002); D. Boyarin, Carnal Israel: Reading Sex in Talmudic Culture (1993); C. E. Fonrobert, Menstrual Purity: Rabbinic and Christian Reconstructions of Biblical Gender (2000); J. Hauptman, "Women's Liberation in the Talmudic Period: An Assessment," Judaism 26(4) (1971–2): 22–28; idem, Rereading the Rabbis (1998); T. Ilan, "Jewish Women's Studies," in Oxford Handbook of Jewish Studies, ed. M. Goodman (2002), 770–96; idem, Massekhet Ta'anit (Feminist Commentary to the Babylonian Talmud), vol. II.9 (2008); J. Neusner, A History of the Mishnaic Law of Women IV (1980); M. Peskowitz, Spinning Fantasies: Rabbis, Gender, and History (1997); J. Plaskow, "Anti-Judaism in Feminist Christian Interpretation," in Searching the Scriptures. Volume One: A Feminist Commentary, ed. E. Schüssler Fiorenza (1994), 117–29; M. Satlow, Jewish Marriage in Antiquity (2001); and J. Romney Wegner, Chattel or Person: The Status of Women in the Mishnah (1988).

TAL ILAN

Talmud Study: Modern Approaches.

For many generations, the study and analysis of the talmudic corpus, especially the Babylonian *Talmud, was one of the most prestigious religious vocations in traditional Jewish societies. In nineteenth-century *Eastern Europe, influential forces, among them the *Hasidic movement and the *Haskalah (Jewish enlightenment), decentralized and weakened the position of Talmud study as the preeminent activity to which Jewish males, especially young Jewish boys, could aspire. In direct response to these challenges, the modern study of Talmud emerged and attracted new generations of scholars, outnumbering and possibly excelling previous generations.

The first modern *yeshivah (talmudic academy) was established by R. Chayim of Volozhin, the prominent disciple of the *Vilna Gaon, in Volozhin (now Valozhyn, *Belarus). Following the model and inspiration of his mentor, and in direct response to the theological challenges of Hasidism, R. Chayim of Volozhin developed a theology according to which scholars should undertake the study of *Torah in a contemplative manner, for the sake of the Torah itself (lishma), with little or no practical intent. The Volozhin

Yeshivah was therefore instituted as an absolutely independent institution, dedicated exclusively to the theoretical study of the Talmud. It was owned and administered by the *Rosh Yeshivah*, the dean, who was responsible for the spiritual development and material needs of his students. Methodological innovations were not visible or intended at first, but they soon developed in this rigorous environment.

Toward the end of the nineteenth century, Rav Chaim Soloveitchik, a brilliant scholar from Brisk, who taught for several years in the Volozhin Yeshivah, developed an original method of studying the Talmud. Rav Chaim Soloveitchik was not interested in the literal hermeneutics of the Talmud or in complex comparative and harmonistic studies of topics (*sugyot*) in the form of casuistic argument (*pilpul*). Instead, he preferred to take a single topic and to break it down into its basic analytical components to understand how these different elements interacted in constituting a specific *sugyah* and later giving rise to a single prescribed action or law. Although this method was not itself entirely unprecedented, the systematic way in which Rav Chaim Soloveitchik applied it and the technical language he created for it, such as *hakirah* (inquiry), *hiluk* (distinction), and *dinim* (underlying principles), were new. Rav Chaim Soloveitchik's method was further developed by his sons, Yitzhak Zev of Brisk and Moshe Soloveitchik, and by his grandsons, of whom the most famous was Joseph B. *Soloveitchik of *Boston, and by other more faithful disciples, such as Baruch Ber of Kaminitz (N. Solomon, *The Analytic Movement: Hayyim Soloveitchik and His Circle* [1993]). Although many challenged this new method, seeing it as far too synthetic an approach to the complexity of talmudic literature, it nonetheless spread quickly in the *yeshivah* world and paved the way for further methodological debates and modification. One such was promoted by Rabbi Shimon Shkop of Telz, who suggested that *sevarah* (natural and unaided logic), more than revelation, was the ground for monetary laws in Judaism.

During the twentieth century, the Talmud was studied in academic settings as well. The new generation of scholars – H. Albeck, J. N. Epstein, S. Lieberman, and E. A. Orbach – who came to academia after being exposed to the new and radical methods developed in the *yeshivot*, preferred a critical and historical approach to the Talmud. Previous generations of academic Talmud scholars had paid little if any attention to the rich and diverse manuscript tradition of the entire talmudic corpus or to how the historical process of redaction and editing shaped the tradition itself. In recent years, with the publication of a variety of critical editions, scholars are better able to identify different layers and previous forms of the various sections of the talmudic corpus; greater authority is now attached to the *Stammaim, the anonymous editors and redactors of the Babylonian Talmud (see TALMUD, BABYLONIAN). For contemporary approaches to academic Talmud study, see C. E. Fonrobert and M. S. Jaffee, eds., *The Cambridge Companion to the Talmud and Rabbinic Literature* (2007).   CHAIM MEIR NERIA

Tamar (Genesis 38) is the daughter-in-law of *Judah, one of *Jacob's sons. She first marries Er, who dies without offspring. Tamar is then married to Er's brother, Onan, in accordance with the Israelite principle of levirate marriage (see MARRIAGE, LEVIRATE), whereby a near male relative married a childless widow. Their first male child would

carry on the lineage of the deceased and inherit his property. Onan refuses to fulfill his levirate duty and is killed by God. Fearful that Tamar is the cause of his elder sons' deaths, Judah denies her his last son, Shelah. To obtain her rights, Tamar disguises herself as a *prostitute and becomes pregnant by Judah. Although Judah initially condemns Tamar for "playing the harlot," he ultimately acknowledges her righteousness. Tamar gives birth to twins, Perez and Zerah; through Perez, she is an ancestress of King *David (Ruth 4:12, 18–22; 1 Chron 2:4). Biblical tradition praises Tamar for her faithfulness to the principle of levirate marriage.

NAOMI STEINBERG

Tamar (2 Samuel) is the daughter of King *David (2 Sam 13). Although her mother is not directly identified, Tamar is said to be a full sister of Absalom, who was the son of Maacah (2 Sam 3:3). Tamar is also a half-sister of Amnon, David's firstborn son by his wife Ahinoam. Professing love for Tamar, Amnon uses a ruse to rape her and then immediately banishes her from his presence. Tamar's brother Absalom takes her into his house and advises her to remain quiet about this outrage and not to take it to heart; at this point, the forlorn Tamar disappears from the story. When Amnon's treatment of Tamar does not prompt David to take action, Absalom takes revenge against Amnon and kills him. This action advances Absalom's chances of becoming heir to the throne but also prompts his rebellion against his father that will lead to his own death. Thus, Tamar unwittingly plays a central role in the succession narrative that will ultimately result in *Solomon succeeding David as king.

In 2 Samuel 14:27, another Tamar is named as one of the four children and only daughter of Absalom; she is said to be beautiful, as was her father (14:25).   NAOMI STEINBERG

Tammuz is the fourth month of the Jewish calendar, usually falling in June and/or July according to the Gregorian calendar. **See also CALENDAR; CALENDAR: MONTHS OF THE YEAR.**

Tanakh is an acronym designating the Hebrew *Bible. It is formed from the Hebrew words ***T**orah (*Pentateuch/Five Books of Moses), **N**evi'im (*Prophets), and **K**etuvim (Writings).

Tannaim (sing. *Tanna*, from Aramaic *teni*, Hebrew *shanah*, "to repeat, learn, teach, recite") are the rabbinic teachers of the period of the *Mishnah, so called because their teachings are supposed to have been transmitted by continual oral repetition. Medieval authorities disagree about when the tannaitic period began. Most believed that the era began with *Hillel and Shammai (first century CE), but some saw Simon the Just, who lived two or three centuries earlier, as the first *Tanna* (e.g., Joseph ibn Aknin); others began with the destruction of the *Temple in 70 CE, regarding *Johanan ben Zakkai as the first *Tanna* (e.g., *Abraham ibn Daud in his *Sefer ha-Kabbalah*). The period of the Tannaim ends with *Judah ha-Nasi and his sons in the early third century (see MISHNAH). Since ibn Daud, the Tannaim have generally been counted as five generations, perhaps in conscious symmetry with the five "pairs" (*zugot*) leading up to Hillel and Shammai.

The most important Tannaim before 70 CE are Gamaliel the Elder and Simon ben Gamaliel; other scholars of the period are frequently mentioned collectively as the "houses" (or "schools"; *batei*) of Hillel and Shammai. Outstanding younger contemporaries of *Joḥanan ben Zakkai are Rabban Gamaliel II, Eliezer ben Hyrcanus, Joshua ben Ḥananiah, and Eleazar ben Azariah. R. Ishmael and R. *Akiva were the most important teachers before the Second *Jewish War against Rome (132–35 CE). The most outstanding members of the post-war generation were R. Meir, R. Nathan, R. Simon ben Yoḥai, R. Judah, and R. Neḥemiah. R. Ḥiyya, and Bar Kappara were younger contemporaries of Judah ha-Nasi.

All these Rabbis were active in *Palestine after the destruction of *Jerusalem, mostly at Yavneh (Jamnia) and Lod (Lydda) in *Judea; after *Bar Kokhba, the rabbinic center moved to the *Galilee, where at first Usha, then Beth Shearim, and finally Sepphoris were the major centers of the rabbinic movement. Many of the early Tannaim may have been *Pharisees before 70 CE, but this is explicitly attested only for Gamaliel the Elder in the *New Testament and for his son Simon ben Gamaliel by *Josephus. A number of early Rabbis were priests (see PRIESTHOOD); before 70, others may have been scribes. Older scholarship assumed that soon after the destruction of the Temple in 70, the Tannaim, under the leadership of the *Patriarch, took over the religious and perhaps also the political leadership of the Jewish people, continuing the old institution of the *Sanhedrin as the highest national authority. More recent studies question both the existence of a national Sanhedrin after 70 and the office of the Patriarch before Simon ben Gamaliel II or Judah ha-Nasi. Contemporary scholarship also minimizes the importance of the rabbinic movement in the tannaitic period and the influence of the Tannaim among the common people.

The teachings of the Tannaim are included in the Mishnah, *Tosefta, and halakhic *midrashim* on the books of *Exodus (*Mekhilta*), *Leviticus (*Sifra*), *Numbers (*Sifre on Numbers* and *Sifre Zuta*), and *Deuteronomy (*Sifre on Deuteronomy*), and in *Seder 'Olam Rabbah*, the rabbinic chronography attributed to Jose ben Ḥalafta. Other tannaitic teachings are found in both *Talmuds and other later rabbinic writings, introduced as *baraitot* ("external" teachings) with formulas such as *teno rabbanan* (our masters teach), *tanya* (it has been taught), or similar expressions containing the root *teni*. These teachings are considered to be especially authoritative, nearly at the same level as sayings in the Mishnah. Yet, many have been reworked or are outright pseudepigraphic.

Biographical anecdotes about some of the more famous Tannaim, such as Hillel, Akiva, or Meir, appear only in the Talmuds and later *midrashim* and cannot be taken at face value; many are hagiographic legends, incorporating and exemplifying the values of a much later period. The only Babylonian master coming close to the authority of the Palestinian Tannaim is Rav, also called Abba Arikha, "the Tall." He had studied in Palestine before returning to *Babylonia where he became the most important rabbinic teacher at *Sura on the Euphrates until his death in 247 (the date is given by Sherira *Gaon). The Babylonian Talmud states several times (e.g., BT *Sanhedrin* 83b), "He counts as a *Tanna* and may dispute (against the view adopted in the Mishnah)."

Another meaning of the term *tanna* is that of a coach who knew as much as possible of the rabbinic tradition by heart and passed on his knowledge to students by his continually repeated recitation. A kind of walking library, he was despised by many Rabbis because of his purely mechanical knowledge: "The magician mutters and does not know what he is saying. The *tanna* teaches and does not know what he is saying" (BT *Sotah* 22a). Despite such criticisms this office remained in existence until *geonic times because it was so closely connected with the rabbinic ritual of learning and the Oral *Torah.

For further reading, see J. Neusner, ed., *Dictionary of Ancient Rabbis. Selections from The Jewish Encyclopaedia* (2003); C. Hezser, *The Social Structure of the Rabbinic Movement in Roman Palestine* (1997); and G. Stemberger, *Introduction to the Talmud and Midrash* (1996).   GÜNTER STEMBERGER

Targum (pl. *targumim*) is the *Aramaic word for translation and refers especially to the Aramaic translations of the *Bible. During the *Second Temple period, Hebrew ceased to be the spoken language of the Jewish people; it was replaced by Greek (in the Hellenistic *Diaspora), Aramaic (in its various dialects in the *Land of Israel and *Babylonia), and Mishnaic Hebrew. There was thus a need for a translation that would accompany the public reading of sacred scriptures, thereby preventing them from becoming an incomprehensible and fossilized heritage of the past. This translation was especially needed after rabbinic preaching charged the biblical texts with new *aggadic and *halakhic interpretations that had to be transmitted to the masses. The need for this "mediator" between scriptures and the people was especially urgent in the *synagogues and in the schools in which the younger generation was educated. In addition to Greek translations of the Bible such as the *Septuagint, quite a few Aramaic texts preserve the synagogue activity of the *meturgemanim* (translators), which took place in the first seven centuries CE, until the Muslim conquest of the Middle East. The most famous translations are the translation of the *Pentateuch attributed to a certain Onkelos (who is believed to have lived in the Land of Israel in the first to second centuries CE) and the Targum to the *Prophets composed by his contemporary, Jonathan ben Uziel. These two *Targumim* were also used by the *Babylonian Rabbis and eventually were accepted as the authoritative translations of the biblical texts, thus achieving a great sanctity. Other *Targumim* that were created in the Land of Israel, such as the *Targum Yerushalmi* to the *Pentateuch, did not enjoy such a status, but they also testify to the ways in which the vitality of the sacred scriptures was maintained.

The *Targumim* incorporated many aggadic and halakhic traditions – words of rebuke or consolation, folk elements, and theological issues – into the biblical text, constructing new interpretations to suit the ears and needs of new generations. Often this meant that they drew away from the "simple" meaning of the text or inserted long additions that might sometimes overshadow the biblical source. The variegated traditions that were embedded in these translations frequently have a didactic tone; thus, they stress the importance of *Torah study or prayer, extol biblical ancestors, or vividly describe the end of days (see ESCHATOLOGY: SECOND TEMPLE PERIOD). They also emend apparent anthropomorphic descriptions of *God and publicize new rabbinic *halakhah* (legislation). From this perspective the *Targumim* should also be seen as "mediators" between the elite rabbinic class and ordinary Jews.

New languages spoken by the Jewish people from the seventh century onward, such as Arabic (see JUDEO-ARABIC) and later *Yiddish, displaced the Aramaic *Targumim*. Their use gradually declined but they continue to be used as aids for understanding the biblical text and a resource for scholarship. For further reading, see J. W. Bowker, *The Targums and Rabbinic Literature* (1969).   AVIGDOR SHINAN

Tefillin (also phylacteries), an *Aramaic word meaning "attachment," refers to small black leather boxes and straps worn on the head (between the eyes) and on the arm or hand (generally the left arm for a right-handed person and the right arm for a left-handed person [BT *Menahot* 37a]). The boxes contain parchments inscribed with four passages from the *Torah; the box for the forehead has four separate compartments, one for each parchment, and the box for the arm has a single compartment for one parchment on which all the passages are written. The passages (Exod 13:1–10, 13:11–16; Deut 6:4–9, 11:13–21) ordain that "these words" are to be worn as "a sign upon your hand and as frontlets between your eyes" as a reminder of *redemption from *Egypt and the *covenant between *God and the Israelites.

Men have traditionally worn *tefillin* during weekday morning *prayers (but not on the *Sabbath or *festivals) from the time of *Bar Mitzvah. Different communities wrap the *tefillin* around the arm in different ways. Many *Ashkenazim use a counterclockwise motion while *Sephardim and *Hasidim wind them clockwise. Jewish mystics (see KABBALAH) inscribed the word *Shaddai* (Almighty) on the *tefillin*, both in writing and in their modes of winding and knotting. Women are not obligated to put on ("lay") *tefillin*, but some have chosen to do so in various times and places according to rabbinic (BT *Eruvin* 96a) and medieval sources (Grossman). Some rabbinic authorities have permitted this practice (Solomon ben Aderet [Rashba]; Jacob ben Meir Tam [Rabbeinu Tam]) or allowed it with the stipulation that women should not recite the blessing since they are not obligated to observe this *commandment (*Maimonides); others have tried to discourage it (*Shulhan Arukh*; Moses Isserles [Rama]; see HALAKHAH). In the contemporary era, the practice is increasing among women, particularly in Conservative and Modern Orthodox forms of *Judaism. For further reading, see R. L. Eisenberg, *The JPS Guide to Jewish Traditions* (2004); and A. Grossman, *Pious and Rebellious: Jewish Women in Medieval Europe* (2004).

ELIZABETH SHULMAN

Tel Aviv is the second largest city in *Israel with a total population (with neighboring Jaffa) of nearly 400,000 and an area of twenty square miles (51.8 square kilometers). It is the economic center of Israel, as well as a popular tourist and cultural destination. Situated on Israel's Mediterranean coastline, Tel Aviv was founded in 1909 as a new Jewish city, north of the ancient port city of Jaffa, which had a predominantly Arab population. The name, which means "hill of spring," is derived from *Ezekiel 3:15: "And I came to the exiles at Tel Aviv"; it was also the title of the Hebrew translation by Nahum Sokolow of Theodor *Herzl's visionary novel about a Jewish state, *Altneuland*. Tel Aviv gained municipal status in 1934 and saw a dramatic increase in population during the 1929–39 Fifth Aliyah (see ISRAEL, STATE OF:

IMMIGRATION BEFORE 1948) which was constituted primarily of immigrants from *Nazi *Germany. In these years Tel Aviv's "White City" was developed by architects who had been trained in the International or Bauhaus style. These four thousand or more buildings within a concentrated area, the world's largest grouping of structures in this Modernist style, are characterized by asymmetry, functionality, and simplicity; the "White City" was named a UNESCO World Heritage Site in 2004.

Tel Aviv served as Israel's center of government until the end of 1949 when the capital was established in *Jerusalem. However, as of 2009, nearly all national embassies continue to be located in the Tel Aviv area. Much of Jaffa's Arab population (approximately 70,000 of a total population of 100,000 in 1948) left the city during the developing tensions at the end of the *British Mandate period and the conquest of the city by Haganah and Irgun forces on May 14, 1948 (see ISRAEL, STATE OF: MILITARY AND PARAMILITARY BODIES). The present Arab population of Jaffa is estimated at 10,000 out of a total population of 80,000. Tel Aviv and Jaffa were combined under one municipal government in 1950. For recent research, see the collected articles in *Israel Studies* 14(3) (2009). **Map 14**   ELIZABETH SHULMAN

Television: United States. Although Jews have been involved as executives, writers, and performers in the commercial television industry in the United States since its inception in 1939 (see BROADCASTING: RADIO AND TELEVISION), the medium has a conflicted history when it comes to the representation of Jewish characters and themes. As in other forms of entertainment such as *film, Jewish artists often found it necessary to minimize or erase the ethnic and religious specificity of their work. In television, which depends on reaching a broad audience and which is driven largely by commercial advertising, this tendency has been even more pronounced. Yet on those occasions when Jewish characters have been given leading roles, they have often proved extremely popular.

On January 17, 1949, just a few months after the start of prime-time network programming in the United States, the Columbia Broadcasting System (CBS) premiered *The Goldbergs*, the first television series to feature a Jewish family. Featuring Gertrude Berg (1898–1966), who was also the show's head writer, as Molly Goldberg, an immigrant wife and mother, this early situation comedy chronicled the struggles of a loving Jewish family and their Bronx neighbors as they sought to fit into modern American culture. Although *The Goldbergs*, which began as a radio series in 1929, seems like an historical anomaly – it would be nearly a quarter-century before another television series would be built around an explicitly Jewish family – the late 1940s actually saw a boom in ethnic-themed television series. In addition to *The Goldbergs*, viewers could tune in to programs such as *Life with Luigi* (Italian), *Amos and Andy* (African American), and *Life of Riley* (Irish). Most of these shows, including *The Goldbergs*, were adapted from the medium of radio, where ethnic dialects were both a steady source of humor and an effective way to differentiate one otherwise unremarkable comedy from another. Indeed, early episodes of *The Goldbergs* tended to rely heavily on Molly's misuse of English idiom for comic effect. Over the six-year life of the series (which included runs on the National Broadcasting

Corporation [NBC] and the short-lived DuMont network), however, the focus shifted to emphasize how Molly's traditional Jewish values could be reconciled with a growing American emphasis on consumerism and the nuclear family. In this sense *The Goldbergs* served to normalize the immigrant experience and to model a kind of post-war American citizenship. In the series' final season, the Goldberg family moved to the fictional suburb of Haverville, where they quickly learned to fit in with their Gentile neighbors.

After the cancellation of *The Goldbergs* in 1955, it would be nearly two decades before a television series featured an explicitly Jewish character as a central cast member. Throughout the late 1950s and 1960s, Jewish characters were scarce, and when they did appear it tended to be in supporting roles or one-episode guest appearances. Television historians attribute this disappearance of Jewish characters to self-policing by Jewish studio executives. Some writers who worked in the industry at the time report that there seemed to be quotas on how many Jewish characters would be approved by network executives. It is unclear whether this self-censorship was a response to the House Un-American Activities Committee (HUAC) hearings of the early 1950s, to real or perceived *antisemitism among the viewing public, or to these executives' own conflicted relationship to *Judaism. Regardless, television writers and producers of the 1950s and '60s learned to abide by the maxim (sometimes attributed to Neil Simon), "Write Yiddish; cast British." In the most infamous example of this phenomenon, a show called *Head of the Family*, written by and starring Jewish comedian Carl Reiner and based on his own experiences as a comedy writer for Sid Caesar's *Your Show of Shows* (1950–54), could not find a network willing to produce it until it was recast with different leading actors as *The Dick Van Dyke Show* (1961–66). Although Reiner himself did appear in the show, it was as the ethnically neutral Alan Brady (based on Caesar). Meanwhile, the only explicitly Jewish character in the show was a supporting role, Maurice "Buddy" Sorrell (Morey Amsterdam).

Although Jews were rarely depicted as lead characters in regular dramatic series, the 1950s and 1960s did see a number of important television movies featuring Jewish characters, often as stand-alone episodes of anthology-style series such as *Philco Television Playhouse*, *Matinee Theater*, and *Playhouse 90*. Many of these "teleplays" focused on the *Holocaust, including *Anne Frank: The Diary of a Young Girl* (1952) and *The Final Ingredient* (1959), both co-produced by the *Jewish Theological Seminary (see HOLOCAUST REPRESENTATION: TELEVISION). The most famous example of televised Holocaust drama during this period was *Judgment at Nuremberg* (1959, remade as a feature film in 1961), which dramatized the Nuremberg war crimes trials and included actual newsreel footage of the liberation of the Nazi concentration camps.

Bridget Loves Bernie, the show that reintroduced a Jewish leading character to prime-time series television in 1972, was not without controversy. A comedy built around the romance between a young Jewish cab driver, Bernie Steinberg (David Birney), and his Irish Catholic bride, Bridget Fitzgerald (Meredith Baxter), the show presented ethnic *intermarriage as not only acceptable but also as (arguably) a desirable remedy to the ethnic and racial divisiveness of 1970s culture. The show earned top ratings, but it was cancelled after only one season because of vocal protest from Jewish advocacy groups. Having drawn flak for a comic portrayal of Jews, the networks seemed to avoid overt representations of Jewish characters in sitcoms for most of the 1970s, with one notable exception. In 1974, the Jewish character Rhoda Morgenstern (Valerie Harper) went from a supporting character in *The Mary Tyler Moore Show* (1970–77) to star in her own spinoff, *Rhoda* (1974–79). Although Rhoda's Jewish identity was rarely central to the show's plot, it was nevertheless clearly marked. This stands in contrast to several other shows of the 1970s in which Jewish characters did not appear explicitly, but which nevertheless were (and continue to be) read as Jewish by viewers inclined to do so. Typically, these shows, which include *Barney Miller* (1975–83), *Welcome Back Kotter* (1975–79), and *Taxi* (1979–83), feature a Jewish actor in a leading role in which the character's religion or ethnicity is never specified, leaving open the possibility that he might be Jewish. Generally speaking, however, televised representations of Jewish characters in the 1970s were reserved for more serious fare, such as the Emmy-winning NBC mini-series, *Holocaust: The Story of the Family Weiss* (1978).

The 1980s saw two significant developments in network programming that helped open the door for more overt depictions of Jews. First was the popularity of ensemble-based dramas such as *Hill Street Blues* (1981–87) and *L.A. Law* (1986–94). With shows following more characters and more story lines simultaneously, producers seemed more willing to allow some of those characters and stories to be explicitly marked as Jewish. For example, a recurring story line in *thirtysomething* (1987–91) centered around Jewish ad man Michael Steadman (Ken Olin) and his struggles with how to maintain his connection to Judaism. Over the course of the show's four seasons, viewers saw Steadman's wedding to a non-Jewish woman, the couple's holiday observances, and their son's *circumcision ceremony. Yet because these episodes were embedded within the context of a multifocal ensemble series, *thirtysomething* was not thought of as a "Jewish show."

The other significant development in this period was the declining influence of the old-school television moguls. Increasingly, the networks were run by a younger generation of executives who were less reluctant to showcase explicitly Jewish characters. Thus, by the early 1990s there were several highly successful series built around Jewish characters, most notably *Seinfeld* (1989–98), *Northern Exposure* (1990–95), and *Brooklyn Bridge* (1991–93). Although these shows tended to portray Jews positively, the range of characters often seemed limited to the *schlemiel* stereotype made famous in American culture by Woody Allen. For example, *Newsweek* declared in 1992, "A new breed of leading man has swum into the television mainstream. He's funny, he's highly verbal and he's slightly neurotic. Oh, and Jewish." While Jewish leading men were becoming more common, fewer shows featured Jewish women. Those that did, such as *The Nanny* (1993–99) and *Will and Grace* (1998–2006), drew criticism for perpetuating stereotypes of the "Jewish American Princess."

With the expansion of cable and satellite television since the late 1990s, programmers have seemed more willing than ever before to depict a broad range of Jewish characters. This has led to some downright unflattering portrayals of

Jews, such as Larry David's character in *Curb Your Enthusiasm* (2000–present), as well as shows that have turned classic Jewish stereotypes inside out by embracing them, such as *The Daily Show with Jon Stewart* (1999–) and the Comedy Central movie *The Hebrew Hammer* (2003). Nevertheless, some portrayals of Jewish characters still periodically provoke controversy, and frank depiction of Jewish ritual observance is still extremely rare on America's airwaves.

Recent years have seen a significant surge in scholarly attention to images of Jews in television. Two especially valuable studies are D. Zurawik's *The Jews of Prime Time* (2003) and V. Brook's *Something Ain't Kosher Here: The Rise of the "Jewish" Sitcom* (2003). Although this scholarly attention reflects in part a growth in television studies in general, it also seems to indicate a greater awareness of the role that depictions of Jews on television play in defining Jewish American culture.   HENRY BIAL

Temple, Second. This term signifies both a concrete cultic, economic, and political institution that existed in *Jerusalem from ca. 515 BCE until 70 CE and a historiographic rubric for delineating the specific form(s) of Jewish religion, culture, and social organization that existed during that period. Despite significant transformations in the nature of *Judaism and Jewishness over the course of the Second Temple period, the Jerusalem Temple was a consistent source of stability and cohesion. Not only did this structure serve as the focal point for *worship, but regular *pilgrimage to the Jerusalem Temple and payment of the half-shekel tithe (instituted under *Hasmonean rule) also tied far-flung Jewish communities of the Mediterranean *Diaspora to their Judean homeland. At the same time, the very centrality of this institution and its personnel to the structure of Jewish society as the most concentrated locus of religious authority, social prestige, and political power guaranteed that it would remain a site of contestation, especially among the Judean elite.

The Second Temple and its sacrificial cult were reconstituted, in the face of significant delays, by Judean exiles returning from *Babylonia under the auspices of the Achaemenid (*Persian) Empire. It was built on the same sacred site in Jerusalem formerly occupied by the First Temple, which was constructed during the reign of *Solomon and destroyed by the Babylonians in 587/6 BCE (see TEMPLE AND TEMPLE CULT). From the time of the Second Temple's rededication in ca. 515 CE until its destruction in 70 CE by the *Romans, its leadership and operation were frequently disrupted. Most significantly, the *Seleucid military in 167 BCE desecrated the Temple and looted its treasury. These acts exacerbated existing tensions between the Judean population and their Syrian overlords, as well as among various sectors of Judean society. The ensuing revolt, led by the *Maccabee family of the provincial priestly clan of Hashman (*Hasmoneans), accomplished its primary aim of restoring the Jerusalem cult to its proper form, at least as this was understood by the rebels and their supporters. After the Temple's rededication in December 164 BCE (25 Kislev), the Hasmoneans gradually assumed control of the high *priesthood, formally displacing in 152 BCE the Zadokite family that had traditionally occupied the office. The Hasmoneans eventually used the Jerusalem Temple as

a base from which to consolidate political power in a quasi-independent Judean state. Likewise, a century later, *Herod the Great's massive remodeling project to transform the Second Temple from an obscure provincial sanctuary into a world-class shrine (completed in 19 BCE) was a major part of his concerted efforts to cement his standing within Jewish society, as well as to integrate Jerusalem into the emergent Roman imperial system. The Hasmonean usurpation of the high priesthood and its perquisites proved a profound ideological irritant that contributed decisively to the formation of a range of sectarian groups that competed for influence over Jewish religious practice in general and the sacrificial cult in particular. These sectarian movements, including the *Pharisees, *Sadducees, and the *Dead Sea Scrolls sect generally identified as the *Essenes, loom large in both ancient and modern accounts of the tensions that characterized Judean political and social life throughout the late Second Temple period.

The recurrent conflicts that mark the history of the Second Temple reflect its abiding centrality to the organization and functioning of Jewish society and religion. Equally significant, therefore, are the deep structural continuities in cultic practice, spatial arrangement, and ritual personnel. Throughout its history, the Second Temple was devoted to the worship of YHWH alone, and its priesthood became increasingly assertive in claiming that it was the sole authorized locus for sacrifice and its attendant rituals, notwithstanding the existence at various times during this period of other Yahwist shrines (i.e., the temples at Elephantine and Leontopolis in *Egypt as well as the *Samaritan temple on Mount Gerizim). Encompassing both preparatory purifications and a regular sequence of sacrificial actions, the elaborate system of vegetable and especially animal offerings enacted in the Temple was understood to maintain the presence of *God – and thus God's protection and blessing – within the Temple and its community.

The Temple was organized into concentric zones of increasing holiness, from the entrance and exit gates in the southern wall of the Temple platform to a series of courtyards (for Gentiles, women, ordinary Jews, and priests), to a holy place (*heikhal*), and finally to the "holy of holies" at the heart of the shrine itself (*devir*). Set off from each other by a complex system of barriers and screens, these spaces served distinctive functions in the operation of the cult; each was accessible to progressively restricted classes of people based on criteria of ethnicity (Jew/Gentile), gender (male/female), and caste (high priest/priest/laity). The Aaronite priesthood itself was divided into high priests (*kohanim*) and simple priests (Levites). As a source of great prestige and power, membership in the priesthood through genealogical descent was subject to intense scrutiny and often proved a matter of contentiousness. Thus, the Temple epitomized, in both symbolic and concrete ways, the hierarchical divisions internal to Jewish society as well as the relationship of Jews to the surrounding non-Jewish world.

For further reading, see J. R. Branham, "Penetrating the Sacred: Breaches and Barriers in the Jerusalem Temple," in *Thresholds of the Sacred*, ed. S. Gerstel (2006), 6–24; S. J. D. Cohen, "The Temple and the Synagogue," in *The Cambridge History of Judaism* 3: *The Early Roman Period*, ed. W. Horbury, W. D. Davies, and J. Sturdy (1999), 298–325; E. S. Gruen, *Diaspora: Jews Amidst Greeks and Romans* (2002);

M. Himmelfarb, *A Kingdom of Priests: Ancestry and Merit in Ancient Judaism* (2006); J. Klawans, *Purity, Sacrifice, and the Temple: Symbolism and Supersessionism in the Study of Ancient Judaism* (2006); and S. Schwartz, *Imperialism and Jewish Society, 200 BCE to 640 CE* (2001).   RA'ANAN BOUSTAN

Temple and Temple Cult.

The term "temple" generally relates to the Temple (*mikdash* or *bayit*) in *Jerusalem, built by King *Solomon in the mid-tenth century BCE (1 Kgs 5–8), although its development long pre-dated Solomon's reign. We encounter narratives in the *Pentateuch that depict the construction of the *Tabernacle (*mishkan*) during the period of the wilderness wanderings under the leadership of *Moses. Many scholars see in these traditions the hand of later Jerusalem *priests, projecting their own understanding of the Temple's role back into Israel's formative period, thereby reinforcing its significance to the worshipers of their own time. Others, however, see in the Tabernacle tales the depiction of a pre-Temple shrine that was constructed during the reign of King *David in *Jerusalem (ca. 1005–975 BCE), which would have drawn from earlier shrine models that had been a part of pre-monarchic tribal religion.

David's early tent-shrine in Jerusalem emulated that of the *Shiloh sanctuary. Shiloh was the most prominent pre-monarchic cult site that represented the traditional religious interests of the *Israelite tribes, with a priesthood that boasted descent from Moses. It was this tradition that dominated during David's reign in Jerusalem. This dominance was most evident when David installed Shiloh's most venerated icon, the *Ark of the Covenant, in Jerusalem to symbolize that city's role as the new center of national religion. It is this iconography that Solomon eventually incorporated into his much more ornate Temple, with a different priestly line and ritual fixtures.

In both cases, however, David's tent-shrine and Solomon's Temple were strongly influenced by even older traditions from Israel's neighbors. The tent-shrine had much in common with *Canaanite shrines to the deity El, and Solomon's Temple was patterned on other northwest Semitic temple structures in both *Phoenicia and further east in *Syria and *Mesopotamia. Thus, although the priesthoods associated with the earlier tent-shrine and the later Temple dedicated themselves to Israel's deity YHWH, their manner of religious expression was consistent with that of other ancient peoples of the region who worshiped their own deities in similar fashion.

During the monarchic period after Solomon's death, other religious centers existed in addition to Jerusalem. In the northern kingdom of *Israel, *Beth El constituted a major religious site with a full priesthood, liturgical traditions, and connections to northern royal circles much like the Jerusalem Temple in the southern kingdom of *Judah (see especially Amos 7:10–17). Unlike the Temple in Jerusalem (a former Canaanite city conquered only in David's day; see 2 Sam 5), Beth El had strong ties to ancestral tradition and was regarded by many Israelites as the more significant religious hub. Many scholars view Beth El as the locale where a number of important psalms and *biblical narrative traditions developed that were later preserved by scribes and priests in Jerusalem. Other religious sites also existed in the southern kingdom, such as the temple at the royal fortress of Arad; similar royally sponsored cult sites could be found throughout the Judean countryside. After the *Assyrian army destroyed the northern kingdom (721 BCE) and then devastated the Judean countryside in 701 BCE, only the Jerusalem Temple remained until its destruction at the hands of the Babylonians in 587 BCE. After the nearly fifty-year exile in *Babylonia, the Jerusalem Temple was rebuilt (the "Second *Temple," completed in 516 BCE) under the auspices of the *Persian rulers who succeeded the Babylonians. It once again became a central focus of religious life in the Land of Israel and a focus of *pilgrimage by *Diaspora Jews.

In all periods, the Jerusalem Temple cult consisted of a ritual system revolving around regular sacrifices (see WORSHIP) and the production of sacred literature. Both aspects were governed by the Jerusalem priesthood (*kohanim*) that claimed descent from *Aaron. They were assisted by the Levites, members of the tribe of Levi who were not direct descendants of Aaron. In the pre-exilic period, this priesthood remained largely sponsored by the royal Davidic family, similar to the Beth El priesthood in the north that was a client group of the northern kings. The Temple itself was a physical representation of the divine cosmos, and the Davidic king was its chief functionary, symbolizing his and YHWH's interconnected relationship as sovereigns of the heavens and earth (see also 2 Sam 7; Ps 2). The regular practice of sacrifice within the Temple's precincts maintained the devotional dialogue between the nation and its God, and many of the ritual texts in the book of *Leviticus (especially 1–16) provide some insight into how these sacrifices and related rituals were conducted. It was through the workings of the Temple cult that sin could be expiated, guilt forgiven, fertility and security maintained, and sacred doctrine taught.

Yet, the Temple cult was not universally accepted. The Israelite public (mostly the northern tribes, although likely some southerners as well) apparently denounced Solomon's Temple shortly after that king's death (1 Kgs 12:16), and many of the prophets express condemnation of its priesthood, systems of ritual, and mythic traditions (see BIBLE: PROPHETS AND PROPHECY; AMOS, etc.). In the late eighth century BCE, the prophet *Micah publicly declared that, because it supported injustice, the Temple mount in Jerusalem would be demolished (3:12), a threat remembered a century later when *Jeremiah condemned those who thought that the mere existence of the Temple and its ongoing cultic infrastructure would save them from the effects of their sins and transgressions (7:1–15, 26:17–9). This critique continued into the post-exilic period. Although some prophets supported the Temple and its functionaries (*Haggai; *Zechariah), others pointed out its flaws (*Isaiah 56–66; *Malachi), and this tension persisted between various Jewish sects well into the *Roman period. The final destruction of the Second Temple in 70 CE vindicated those critical of Temple-based groups, although the Temple and its practices remained an important ideological fixture in the later writings of *rabbinic Judaism, which fostered hopes of an eventual rebuilding of the Temple in the distant future.

For further reading, see I. Knohl, *The Sanctuary of Silence* (1995); J. Milgrom, *Leviticus 1–16* (1991); B. C. Ollenburger, *Zion, City of the Great King* (1987); and M. Fox et al., *Texts Temples and Traditions: A Tribute to Menahem Haran* (1996).   MARK LEUCHTER

Ten Commandments. The group of ordinances commonly referred to as the "Ten Commandments" or "Decalogue" are found twice in the *Torah: in *Exodus 20:2–14 and *Deuteronomy 5:6–18. Neither of these biblical passages uses the expression "ten commandments." The closest biblical parallel is in Exodus 34:28, where the phrase "ten words" (*aseret ha-devarim*; often translated as "ten commandments") appears in conjunction with "the words of the covenant" (*divrei ha-berit*) as what *Moses inscribed on the stone tablets that he was commanded to hew in preparation for his ascent of Mount Sinai (34:1).

There are numerous differences, some small, others more significant, between Exodus 20 and Deuteronomy 5. For example, in Exodus 20:8–11, the Israelites are to "remember" the *Sabbath day, and the commandment is related to the creation narrative in Genesis 1–2:4. The Sabbath imperative in Deuteronomy 5:12–15 is to "observe," and remembrance of the day is connected with the experience of slavery in *Egypt and divine *redemption. The prohibition against coveting in Exodus 20:14 includes the wife as one among many of the neighbor's possessions; in Deuteronomy 5:18, the neighbor's wife is a separate entity, mentioned apart from the neighbor's belongings. The order of the commandments is the same in both biblical books, but in the *Septuagint (the Greek translation produced by Alexandrian Jews in the early third century BCE) the command not to commit adultery comes before the prohibition against murder and directly after the imperative to honor one's parents.

The division of the verses into "ten commandments" is as old as Exodus 34, but there are several differing traditions about how to arrive at this number. For Jews, Exodus 20:2 (and Deut 5:6) is generally understood to comprise the first commandment, even though it contains no imperative. Further, Jews have typically imagined the commandments as written on two tablets of five each. With this configuration, the first five (including honoring of parents) reflect human obligations to God, whereas the latter five form a complementary grouping to regulate dealings with other human beings.

Biblical interpreters have also raised questions about the meaning or application of several of the commandments. What, for example, does it mean to take "God's name in vain"? Does "coveting" cover thought alone, or does it necessarily carry over to actions as well? Most scholars would agree that "murder" is a more accurate rendering than "kill," but there is still considerable disagreement over whether "having no other gods before me" was, in its biblical context, equivalent to "having no other gods *except* me," which would constitute an affirmation of *monotheism.

In form, the commandments are styled as apodictic: that is, they are direct imperatives with no "ifs, ands, or buts." This is a distinctively (although not uniquely) biblical way of expressing especially important laws. These commandments can be viewed as an essential component of the *covenant between God and Israel that was established, ratified, and renewed at several points in the Hebrew Bible. The overall structure of this covenant finds parallels elsewhere in the ancient *Near East (see LAW: ANCIENT NEAR EAST AND HEBREW BIBLE). In spite of the myriad difficulties in fully understanding the Ten Commandments and the differences in enumerating and ordering them, they stand somewhat apart from and above the rest of the laws of the Hebrew

*Bible. Nonetheless, it would not be correct to assert that they are inherently more important or of greater sanctity than any of the other *commandments given by God at Mount Sinai or on other occasions.

LEONARD GREENSPOON

Tevet, the tenth month of the Jewish calendar, is equivalent to December and/or January on the Gregorian calendar. See also CALENDAR; CALENDAR: MONTHS OF THE YEAR.

Theater: Britain. Plays by Jewish authors with Jewish themes did not gain prominence on the English stage until the late nineteenth century when Israel *Zangwill (1864–1926) dramatized his novel, *Children of the Ghetto* (1899). Set in London's East End, a center of Jewish immigration since the 1880s, the play depicts a conflict between Orthodox and secular worldviews, a recurrent theme in early Jewish theater. In *The Melting Pot* (1908), Zangwill imagines the disappearance of such dichotomies. Indeed, the play represents the *United States as the crucible in which Jewish and other ethnic minorities will melt into one new people. Such was the success of this drama that its title became a popular metaphor for the American *immigrant experience. Zangwill went on to adapt another of his novels into a successful comedy, *The King of Schnorrers* (1925), dramatizing the triumphs of the little man (here a *Sephardic beggar) in the face of the *Ashkenazic and Sephardic Jewish establishments.

After *World War II, a new generation of Jewish playwrights made its mark. The Nobel Laureate Harold Pinter (1930–2008) wrote several seminal pieces, including *The Birthday Party* (1957), *The Homecoming* (1964), and *Ashes to Ashes* (1996). In *The Birthday Party*, Goldberg and McCann interrogate Stanley, before taking him away to an unknown destination. As a Jew and an Irishman, the interrogators are marginal in English society. Most significantly, Stanley is a victim of circumstances beyond his control. As Pinter remarked at Jewish Book Week in London (2003), "My experience during the war and after the war was of a world which is extremely precarious, to put it mildly – fraught with anxiety and fear and dread of what was to come on the very next day." *The Homecoming* explores such precariousness within an implicitly Jewish family from London's East End. When Max's academic son visits with his American wife, his other son steals her. Meanwhile, Max presides over this terrain of shifting allegiances with patriarchal scorn. He derides both sons, who are correspondingly dismissive of him. Typically for Pinter, what is spoken frequently implies quite the opposite, and the recurrence of a stage-directed "Pause" leaves plenty of room for menace and paranoia to gestate. Like several of Pinter's later plays, such as *One for the Road* (1984) and *Mountain Language* (1988), *Ashes to Ashes* is more explicit about the issues of slave labor, torture, and totalitarian politics from a post-*Holocaust perspective of concern for the victims of inhumanity.

Arnold Wesker (b. 1932) also draws on working-class Jewish roots for his trilogy of plays first performed in 1958–60. These plays depict the socialist struggles of an East End Jewish family (*Chicken Soup with Barley, I'm Talking about Jerusalem*) and the stunted lives of Norfolk farm laborers (*Roots*). Often didactic, Wesker's drama diagnoses the situation shared by Jewish and Gentile members of the working class. He writes empathetically in the preface to the trilogy, "I am at one with these people: it is only that I am annoyed, with them and myself." In *Chicken Soup with Barley* and *I'm Talking about Jerusalem*, the politically engaged Kahn family members proclaim socialist ideals, but over the course of twenty years become gradually disillusioned as their political hopes fail to materialize. Like other Anglo-Jewish playwrights, Wesker has to reckon with the legacy of Shylock. Shakespeare's *The Merchant of Venice* (1598) casts a long shadow over representations of Jews on the English stage. In response, Wesker wrote *Shylock* (1980), originally titled *The Merchant*; this drama ambitiously rewrites Shakespeare's *antisemitic comedy from the perspective of the Venetian Jew. Wesker's Shylock shows generosity, gregariousness, and cultivation in marked contrast to the mean-minded and philistine Gentiles of *Venice.

Bernard Kops (b. 1926) brings another East End voice to English theater. His oeuvre began with *The Hamlet of Stepney Green* (1957). Here, as elsewhere, the poetry of the drama owes much both to Yiddish *folklore and biblical *prophecy. Kops has since written several successful plays with Jewish themes, including *Ezra* (1981) about the fascist poet Ezra Pound, *Dreams of Anne Frank* (1992), and *Green Rabbi* (1997).

Steven Berkoff (b. 1937) is also alive to the energies of the Jewish East End, as his Expressionistic drama *East* (1977) demonstrates. Jewish humor runs through both *Kvetch* (1986) and *Sit and Shiver* (2004). Interestingly, Berkoff turned to the Czech Jewish writer Franz *Kafka (1883–1924) for inspiration; his adaptations include *In the Penal Colony* (1968), *Metamorphosis* (1969), and *The Trial* (1971).

Jack Rosenthal (1931–2004) brought Anglo-Jewish drama to television audiences. In particular, *The Evacuees* (1975) follows the fortunes of two Jewish boys evacuated from Manchester to an outlying town during World War II; *Bar Mitzvah Boy* (1976) charts the embarrassments and eventual fulfillment of a Jewish boy's rite of passage. More recently, female playwrights have invigorated Anglo-Jewish drama. Julia Pascal (b. 1949) explores prejudice and tragedy in her *Holocaust Trilogy* (1990–92). She also celebrates *Yiddish theatrical culture in *The Yiddish Queen Lear* (1999) and presents perspectives from the *Arab–Israeli conflict in *Crossing Jerusalem* (2003–04).

Diane Samuels (b. 1960) has won acclaim with *Kindertransport* (1992). Her drama presents the Anglicization of a young female refugee from *Nazi *Germany. When Eva's mother arrives in *Britain to reclaim her daughter after the war, the ensuing emotional conflict suggests that fallout from the *Holocaust remains a disturbing presence in England.

Patrick Marber (b. 1964) is probably best known for his award-winning comedy *Closer* (1997), which was made into a Hollywood movie. His *Howard Katz* (2001) explores the conflict between Jewish values and the superficial world of *television in the life of a show-business agent. The play opens with Katz as a derelict and goes back in time to explore how he fell from success to catastrophic marginalization. Suffering a spiritual crisis, the *Job-like Katz rails against God while seeking some sort of *redemption.

Famous for screenplays and movies that are devoid of Jews, Mike Leigh (b. 1943) surprised critics with *Two Thousand Years* (2005), his drama about English Jews and *Israel. However, Leigh sees no disjuncture in his oeuvre, as he stated in a *Guardian* newspaper interview, "I don't think you can pull out any play or film from my canon that is not Jewish in its view of life and all its tragic-comic aspects."

PETER LAWSON

Theater: Europe. The participation of Jews in the creation of European drama and theater became significant with *emancipation and assimilation, beginning in the late eighteenth century. Jews became increasingly active as actors, directors, and theater managers, while also writing plays in the languages of their native countries. In nineteenth-century *France, Adolphe d'Ennery (1811–1899) wrote more than two hundred plays, vaudevilles, and melodramas; Ludovic Halévy (1834–1908), nephew of the composer Jacques Fromental Halévy, wrote comedies, farces, and libretti (mostly in collaboration with Henri Meilhac); and Catulle Mendès (1841–1909) penned verse-dramas and libretti. By and large, these works were in the popular style of their day, depicting the conventions and pleasures of bourgeois society. Occasionally they addressed Jewish concerns or featured Jewish characters, as in Mendès' *Les Mères ennemies* (1882). In the later nineteenth century, Albin Valabrègue (1853–1937) was a prolific French dramatist and dramatic critic, and Sarah Bernhardt (1844–1923) rose to international fame as the leading romantic French actress of her day, often called *"la belle juive."* She followed in the footsteps of Eliza Rachel Félix (1821–1858; known as Rachel), the leading classical actress of mid-nineteenth-century France. The most prominent theater personality of Jewish origin on the contemporary French scene is Arianne Mnouchkine (b. 1939), one of Europe's leading theater directors, who founded the Théâtre du soleil, a Parisian avant-garde ensemble, in 1964. Playwrights in French include the late Belgian-born René Kalisky (1936–1981), who unabashedly addressed Jewish themes, in particular the *Shoah Jean-Claude Grumberg (b. 1939), who wrote a number of *Holocaust plays, such as *L'atelier* (1979) and *Zone libre* (1990); and actor-dramatist Victor Haïm.

A similar growing involvement of Jews in drama and its production can be found in other European countries from the nineteenth century onward. In Holland, Herman Heijermans (1864–1924) wrote plays addressing problems of the lower middle class and Jewish themes (*Dora Kramer*, 1893; *Ghetto*, 1898). Louis Frederik Johannes Bouwmeester (1842–1925), born into an acting family, was known for his Shakespearean roles, not least as Shylock. In neighboring *Denmark, Henrik Hertz (1797–1870) wrote comedies, enjoying great success all over Europe with his lyrical drama, *Kong Renés Datter* (1845). Edvard (Cohen) Brandes (1847–1931) was highly influential as a dramaturge and theater critic, and his brother Georg Brandes (1842–1927) was one of the leading theater intellectuals of the day, promoting Scandinavian and German drama (see LITERATURE: SCANDINAVIA). Ferenc Molnár (1878–1952) was among the leading *Hungarian writers of the twentieth century, an author of popular plays that combine wit and romantic sentimentalism, such as *Liliom* (1909) and *The Swan* (1920). Bela Nagy was a much admired actress, and Oszkár Beregi (1876–1965) was famous for his Shakespearean roles. István Örkeny (1912–1979) was known for plays combining modern style with folkloristic elements. *Polish writer and critic Wilhelm Feldmann, author of *Sady Boze*, became a leading figure in Polish literature of the late nineteenth century.

Tadeusz Kantor (1915–1990) was a pivotal figure in Polish avant-garde theater, introducing "happening" and ritualistic elements in theater performance.

Yet nowhere in Europe was the participation of Jews in the theater arts as significant and enthusiastic as in *Germany and *Austria. Arnold Zweig provides an overview of their myriad activities in *Juden auf der deutschen Bühne* (Jews on the German Stage; 1928). Jacob Herzfeld (1769–1826), admired by Goethe and Schiller, was the first prominent Jewish actor in the late eighteenth century, followed in the nineteenth century by Ludwig Dessoir (1810–1874) and Bogumil Dawison (1818–1872), who was famous for his nuanced verisimilitude. The quality and quantity of Jewish performers were broadly noted in the nineteenth century, but Jews were equally active as directors and entrepreneurs. Adolph L'Arrogne (1838–1908) was prominent both as director and playwright; Ludwig Chronegk (1837–1890) acted as director of the famous Meiningen Court Theater; in Austria, Adolf von Sonnenthal (1834–1909), the uncontested star of the *Vienna Hofburg-theater, was appointed its director. Otto Brahm (1856–1912) championed social-oriented, naturalistic drama toward the end of the nineteenth century.

The late Wilhelmine Empire and the Weimar Republic were the heyday of Jewish participation in German theater life. Versatile director Max Reinhardt (1873–1943) introduced the new Modernist drama and created a theater of fantasy and spectacle, while his colleague Leopold Jessner (1878–1945), who became the first artistic director of the *Berlin State Theater in 1919, promoted Expressionistic and political drama. Jewish actors and directors were ubiquitous in the popular and revue theaters, particularly in Berlin and Vienna. A wide range of Jewish acting talents, including Ernst Deutsch, Fritz Kortner, Fritzi Massary, Max Pallenberg, Alexander Granach, Elizabeth Bergner, and Curt Bois, can still be seen in the cinema of the time. The list of Jewish dramaturges includes Felix Holländer, Arthur Kahane, and Heinz Liepmann. Ludwig Barnay, Oscar Blumenthal, and the brothers Anton and Donat Herrnfeld were well-known theater managers and producers.

Especially noteworthy is the successful activity of German and Austrian Jews as theater critics and theoreticians. Among the most prominent were Alfred Kerr, Siegfried Jacobsohn, Maximilian Harden, Karl Kraus, Alfred Polgar, Fritz Engel, Emil Faktor, Monty Jacobs, and Julius Bab. The famous Viennese playwright Arthur Schnitzler (1862–1931) depicted *fin-de-siècle* social and sexual decadence, and Richard Beer-Hofmann (1866–1945) wrote neo-romantic lyrical drama (*Jaákobs Traum*; 1918). Jewish dramatists such as Ernst Toller, Carl Sternheim, and Else *Lasker-Schüler played a prominent role in shaping Expressionist drama. Other Jewish authors who wrote for the stage include Lion Feuchtwanger (1884–1958) and Paul Kornfeld (1889–1942). Mention should also be made of Max Herrmann (1865–1942), who established theater/performance studies as an academic discipline. The rise of *National Socialism in the 1930s put an end to the remarkable impact of Jewish talent in German theater.

Although some prominent Jewish actors (Ernst Deutsch and Fritz Kortner) returned to the German-speaking stage after the Shoah, the persecution and murder of European Jewry by the Nazis marked the end of an amazing era of Jewish participation in German theater. Yet, many interesting productions in twenty-first-century Germany and Austria are the work of Jewish directors, who often address the Holocaust in their stagings. Some, such as Hungarian-born director and playwright George Tabori (1914–2007) or Peter Zadek (1926–2009), were born before the Holocaust; others such as Jossi Wieler and Arie Zinger were born afterward.

ANAT FEINBERG

Theater: Holocaust: See HOLOCAUST REPRESENTATION: DRAMA

Theater: Israel.
Israeli theater emerged with the establishment of the State of *Israel in May 1948. However, Israel's early cultural and theatrical activities must be understood in the contexts of theatrical performances in *Hebrew that took place in the pre-state period and of theatrical activities in Hebrew that took place outside of the Land of Israel, particularly in *Eastern Europe. Initially, Israeli theater was synonymous with theater performed in Hebrew, as opposed to *Yiddish theater or Jewish *theater in other languages. However, with the growing awareness of Israel's cultural diversity, beginning in the wake of the 1967 Six Day War and reaching a peak with the influx of immigration from the former *Soviet Union in the 1990s, theater in Russian and Arabic, as well as theater in Yiddish, Amharic (*Ethiopia), and Moroccan *Judeo-Arabic, also became part of Israel's cultural milieu. At the end of the first decade of the twenty-first century, *Arabic is the mother tongue of a little more than 20% of Israel's population (see DEMOGRAPHY).

The first Hebrew performances in the Land of Israel took place in schools, beginning in 1889, with pupils performing for their parents and teachers. These performances, which served as a tool for teaching the Hebrew language, were frequently steeped in the *Zionist ideology that provided the impetus for Jewish settlement and the establishment of a secular Jewish, later Israeli, culture. The theater in Israel has always served as a significant expression of this culture, as well as an extremely important form of entertainment.

Beginning in 1905, with an influx of immigrants with theater backgrounds or aspirations, a number of semi-professional theaters were established, primarily in Jaffa, but also in *Jerusalem and other places. These theaters performed Hebrew translations of plays from contemporaneous European repertoires (e.g., Ibsen, Chekhov, Hauptmann, and Molière). They also featured plays by Yiddish playwrights like Sholem Aleichem, Jacob Gordin, and Dovid Pinski, whose depictions of Jewish life in the *shtetl had a strong appeal for local audiences, most of whom had left this experience behind. However, these productions did not lead to a full professionalization of the Hebrew theater or to any significant production of Hebrew dramatic writing. During World War I, theatrical activities stopped, more or less completely. Although audiences yearned for theatrical depictions of life in the new country, such a repertoire did not develop for quite a long time.

The first fully professional theater performing in Hebrew was founded in Moscow in 1917 by a group of actors led by Menachem Gnessin (1882–1951), Hanna Rovina (1889–1980), and Nahum Zemah (1887–1952). Zemah, in particular, had already performed at one of the Zionist congresses before he successfully formed a Hebrew-language theater collective. The collective received professional training under Constantin Stanislavski, the leader of the famous Moscow Art Theater, and it was incorporated as the "Biblical Studio" within the network of "ethnic" theaters that had gained official support as a result of the *Bolshevik revolutionary spirit. The members of the collective referred to themselves as *Habimah*, Hebrew for "the stage." This term not only referred to the theatrical stage as such but also was the word for the elevated area in the *synagogue where *Torah reading traditionally took place. The first performance for which the *Habimah* theater became world famous was *The Dybbuk*, a play written in Yiddish by Ansky (see LITERATURE, YIDDISH; THEATER, YIDDISH) that was translated into Hebrew by the national poet Hayyim Nahman *Bialik. This production, which premiered in 1922, was directed by the Armenian-born director Jevgeni Vahtangov, and it remained in the *Habimah* repertoire until the mid-1960s. It is still considered an important Symbolist Expressionistic contribution to world theater.

During the 1920s, inspired by the success of *Habimah*, as well as the demands of the local population for a full theatrical culture, a number of Hebrew theaters were founded in the Land of Israel. The most successful were the *Eretz-Israel* Theater and the *Ohel* ("tent" or "tabernacle" in Hebrew) Theater. As a result of the growing pressures from the communist regime in the Soviet Union, beginning in the mid-1920s, the *Habimah* theater went on a world tour that ended with the troupe settling permanently in *Tel Aviv in 1931. *Habimah* received the official title of Israel's National Theater in 1958. Among the many theaters that were established during the pre-state period, the *Cameri* Theater, founded in 1944, remains the most vital; today it is the Tel Aviv Municipal Theater. Its premiere of a stage adaptation of the popular novel, *He Walked Through the Fields* by Moshe Shamir (1921–2004), depicting the Jewish struggle against *British Mandatory rule, took place a few days after the declaration of Israeli independence (see LITERATURE, HEBREW: *YISHUV* [1888–1948]).

By independence, there had already been several attempts to write Hebrew drama for the stage in response to the wish of the growing Jewish population to view their own reality mirrored theatrically. The Shamir play, adapted and directed by Josef Milo (1916–1997), who was among the group that founded the *Cameri* Theater, is not only technically the first Israeli play; it also became a model for a whole generation of playwrights depicting the first generation of young Israelis facing moral and personal dilemmas in the struggle for Israeli independence in the "Old-New" Jewish homeland. During this initial stage, Israeli drama and theater generally expressed the mainstream Zionist ideology on which Israeli society had been founded. An exception was the playwright Nissim Aloni (1926–1998), whose poetic-surrealistic dramas rebelled against this realist trend. Because established theaters were not eager to produce his lyrical, enigmatic texts, he founded his own short-lived theater, *Teatron Ha-Onot* (Theater of the Seasons).

In the wake of the 1967 Six Day War, and even more forcefully after the 1973 Yom Kippur (October) War (see ISRAEL, STATE OF: WARS), various playwrights began to question and criticize basic tenets of *Zionism, raising moral issues concerning the Israeli occupation of Palestinian land and Israeli expansionism and criticizing Israeli society for

its blindness to the suffering of others. The most prominent playwrights representing this trend are Hanoch Levin (1943–1999) and Joshua Sobol (b. 1939).

Levin began his career as writer and director (of his own plays) in the late 1960s with satirical revues; he gradually moved on to different genres of dramatic writing, developing a highly personal style that initially met with serious resistance from local audiences. After about a decade of writing and directing grotesque comedies of everyday life, Levin moved on to mythical plays such as *The Torments of Job* (1981), an improvisation based on the biblical *Job. In this performance and in many of his later fantastic spectacles of cruelty, Levin developed a distinct style of language and visual images; in his later work, he also became more poetic and compassionate. His constantly evolving originality, both as writer and a director, gradually earned him his well-deserved recognition. Levin's last performance, *Requiem* premiered at the *Cameri* Theater in 1999, a few months before his death; as of 2010, it was still in the repertoire of the theater.

Sobol began his playwriting career in the early 1970s, also with satirical writing, but established himself as an internationally performed dramatist with plays on historical subjects. His most frequently produced play, *Ghetto* (1984), presents the history of the theater company in the *Vilna *ghetto during the *Nazi occupation; it has been performed in more than twenty countries worldwide. *Ghetto* is the first part of a trilogy depicting Jewish life in the Vilna ghetto that problematizes the notion of survival. In *Shooting Magda (Palestinait)* (Palestinian Woman; 1985), he presents the complexities of Israeli–Palestinian cooperation as the characters attempt to make a television film about the life of the Israeli Palestinian woman Magda. These and many of Sobol's other plays were directed by Gedalia Besser at the Haifa Municipal Theater (which was founded in 1961 by Josef Milo). Sobol and Besser served as the theater's artistic directors between 1985 and 1988 until they were forced to resign because of strong reactions against Sobol's play, *The Jerusalem Syndrome*.

After Haifa had established its own municipal theater, *Jerusalem also opened its own local theater in 1968 at the Jerusalem Khan with a young group of actors led by British director Mike Alfreds and later by director Ilan Ronen (b. 1948), who subsequently served as the artistic director of the *Cameri* and after that of the *Habimah* National Theater. In 1973 the city of Beersheva opened its own municipal theater, completing the spread of established theaters to the peripheries of the country. In 2000 the Herzliya Ensemble was founded by Besser, further strengthening the hegemonic position of cultural activities in the Tel Aviv area. Given the economic difficulties faced by the established theaters, as well as a growing market economy approach to the arts in general and to the theater in particular, these established theaters frequently cooperate on major productions. This situation has led to a gradual decrease in the social and ideological content of the repertoire, because economic needs favor catering to an entertainment-hungry audience rather than a radical one, which had been the case in the 1980s and the first years of the 1990s.

With the big wave of immigration from the former Soviet Union beginning in 1990, a group of actors led by director Yevgeny Arye established a theater, *Gesher* (Bridge), performing in Russian. However, after a few performances, *Gesher* decided to present its performances in Hebrew for a much larger audience. Yet, the theater, now located in the southern part of Tel Aviv in Jaffa, has a distinct "Russian" performance style, reconnecting to the traditional style of the *Habimah* theater. The Arab-Hebrew Theatre of Jaffa, founded in 1998, is also located in Jaffa, which has mixed neighborhoods of Jews and Arabs. As its name indicates, it performs in both languages and for both communities, presenting experimental performances for adults as well as children's plays. The *Beit-Hagefen Theatre* in Haifa caters to the gradually growing Arabic-speaking population.

In addition to the expansion of established theaters, the frameworks for fringe theater have also gradually developed. The annual Acco Festival of Alternative Israeli Theater was established in 1980 by actor-director Oded Kotler (b. 1937); it takes place during the early fall *Sukkot holiday in the city of Acre, on the coast north of Haifa. Acre also has a mixed population of Arabs and Jews. This festival, which generally attracts a young audience, has had a crucial impact on the development of new forms of theater in Israel. Since its inception, the festival has encouraged socially and politically engaged theater. One outstanding example was the five-hour performance *Arbeit macht frei vom Toitland Europa* (Work Liberates from Deathland Europe) directed by Dudu Ma'ayan, depicting the daily life on the verge of madness of Selma, a *Holocaust survivor, and in particular her encounter with a local Palestinian, an Israeli Arab. The performance won the first prize at the 1991 festival.

Since the 1970s, and especially since the early 1990s, different genres of performance art have developed in Israel. Two of the more outstanding artists in this field are Tamar Raban and Ruth Kanner. The Zik group has added an interesting perspective to the art of performance by focusing on the processes that materials like clay and glass undergo in their formation. During this time there has also been a remarkable development of modern *dance in Israel, with choreographer Ohad Naharin at the Bat Sheva Dance Company and the Yasmin Goder Dance Ensemble as two of the more outstanding examples. They have added interesting forms of expression to the vital and steadily expanding Israeli performing arts culture.

For further reading, see the English-language journal, *Assaph: Studies in the Theatre* (published by Tel Aviv University since 1985); L. Ben-Zvi, ed., *Theatre in Israel* (1996); H. Levin, *The Labor of Life: Selected Plays*, trans. B. Harshav (2003); F. Rokem, *Performing History: Theatrical Representations of the Past in Contemporary Theatre* (2000); D. Urian, *The Arab in Israeli Drama and Theatre*, (1997); and idem, *Judaic Nature of Israeli Theatre: A Search for Identity* (2000).   FREDDIE ROKEM

Theater: United States. In the 1960s, British director Tyrone Guthrie noted that if Jews were to withdraw from the American theater, it "would collapse about next Thursday." Witticism aside, his remark accurately reflects the disproportionate presence of Jews in the theater, not only among audiences but also as writers, producers, directors, actors, and designers. It can be said that the story of the American theater, especially during the twentieth century, is partly a Jewish story and that Jewish sensibilities have had a significant impact on stage representations,

even when the subject matter has not been specifically Jewish.

BEGINNINGS: This presence goes back to the nineteenth century. Mordecai Manuel Noah (1785–1851), son of a Portuguese Jew, was one of the first playwrights to advocate for drama on national themes, frequently turning to recent history for his subject matter. He is most remembered for *She Would Be a Soldier* (1819). In terms of plays representing contemporary Jewish American life, a breakthrough figure is actor-manager M. B. Curtis (1852–1921); his appearance as the title character in *Sam'l of Posen* (1881) created the prototype of the fast-talking, wisecracking, immigrant traveling salesman. Two more "Sam'l" vehicles followed before Curtis's career fizzled in the 1890s. The plays, which appealed to both Jewish and non-Jewish audiences, helped create a vogue for comic stage Jews by the turn of the century, most notably David Warfield (1866–1951), who scored a big hit as the peddler Simon Levi in *The Auctioneer* (1901), directed by David Belasco (1853–1931). In contrast, knockabout comedians Joe Weber (1867–1942) and Lew Fields (1867–1941) were best known as stage Germans; between 1896 and 1903, their musical satires were the toast of New York.

Jewish entrepreneurs and managers, many of them of German or Central European backgrounds, also had established themselves by the turn of the century. Oscar Hammerstein I (1847–1919), who created everything from operas houses to vaudeville palaces, ultimately was the central force behind the move of *New York City theaters uptown to Times Square, thus helping define the "Broadway" of today. In 1895, seven Jewish theater owners formed the controversial "Theatrical Syndicate," which centralized booking practices. This group nearly monopolized American theatrical production and eliminated Victorian-era modes of theatrical organization. Manager Lee Shubert (1873?–1953) and his brothers, Sam and Jacob challenged the "Syndicate's" brief monopoly. Another fierce opponent was David Belasco, a multitalented playwright, director, producer, and career maker who brought new realism and artistic control to his meticulously designed productions, many of which enjoyed huge commercial success.

VAUDEVILLE: The vaudeville era featured numerous Jewish comics, many of whom used their ethnic identification as a fuel for comedy and eventually crossed over from vaudeville and revues to full-fledged musical comedies. Fanny Brice (1891–1951) became a sensation in 1909 with "Sadie Salome Go Home," and the next year joined the annual Ziegfeld revue, where she remained, on and off, until 1923, often doing comic turns with a homey, zany Jewish inflection. Sultry singer Sophie Tucker (1884–1966) made her debut with Ziegfeld in 1909 and was playing vaudeville's prestigious Palace Theater by 1914; her distinctive performance style brought a syncopated blues quality to American popular theater and cabaret. The exuberant Al Jolson (1886–1950) debuted at the Winter Garden in 1911 and was a headliner in shows and revues for two decades; his signatures were blackface routines. Another kinetic, sometime blackface comedian was the pop-eyed Eddie Cantor (1892–1964), who debuted with Ziegfeld in 1917 and went on to a number of Broadway successes in the following decade. The five Marx Brothers, a long-time vaudeville act, took Broadway by storm with *I'll Say She Is* (1924); although best remembered today for their later films, their stage work of the 1920s embodies the assertive comic energy that many first- and second-generation Jews were then bringing to the American stage.

MUSICALS: Perhaps in no theatrical genre was Jewish influence more profound than in the musical. A successful songwriter as early as 1905, Jerome Kern (1885–1945) laid the foundations for the American popular standard, eventually composing music for a series of musicals at the intimate Princess Theater (and similar venues) between 1915 and 1917. These fresh, urbane musicals are seen as pivotal to the genre. He also pioneered the "book musical" with his score for *Show Boat* (1927). Kern's work had an indelible influence on a young Richard Rodgers (1902–1979), whose long-time collaboration with lyricist Lorenz Hart (1895–1943) brought a smart, jazzy sophistication to the genre. Scoring their first success in 1925, the team peaked in popularity and influence in the late 1930s. Also of enduring popularity and cultural importance are the protean Irving Berlin (1888–1989) who, from 1907 on, contributed songs to every theatrical genre and the brothers George (1898–1937) and Ira (1896–1983) Gershwin who, as composer and lyricist, brought a brilliant, jazz-inflected energy to musical comedies of the 1920s. Later, George's score for *Porgy and Bess* (1935) pioneered a new type of folk opera. *The Cradle Will Rock* (1937), by Marc Blitzstein (1905–1964), controversially featured biting social commentary in a way never before seen in an American musical.

Cross-pollination among artists of Jewish background ultimately bore decisive musical fruit in 1943, when Kern's collaborator on *Showboat* and other operettas, Oscar Hammerstein II (1895–1960), teamed up with Rodgers for *Oklahoma!* Hammerstein's tender lyricism and scrupulous concern for dramatic integrity, when fused with Rodgers' arresting melodies and spirited pursuit of musical storytelling, resulted in a watershed "musical play" – a model to which many works aspired in the next generation. The collaboration lasted until Hammerstein's death and included such successes as *Carousel* (1945), *South Pacific* (1949), and *The King and I* (1951). The Rodgers and Hammerstein "musical play" mold was followed most successfully perhaps by Alan Jay Lerner (1918–1986) and Frederick Loewe (1904–1988) in *Brigadoon* (1947) and *My Fair Lady* (1956). Among creators of musical comedy in the 1940s and 1950s, leading Jews were Frank Loesser (1910–1969) and Adolph Green (1914–2002).

The 1950s, 1960s, and 1970s increasingly saw innovation in the musical theater. The legendary Jerome Robbins (1918–1998) combined the roles of director and choreographer with signature pieces such as *West Side Story* (1957) and *Fiddler on the Roof* (1964), forging a new model of director as auteur. The former featured a bold, colorful score by Leonard Bernstein (1918–1990), who was a frequent Broadway composer in the 1940s and 1950s. Stephen Sondheim (1930–) showed wit, feeling, and technical mastery as lyricist for both *West Side Story* and *Gypsy* (1959) before becoming a composer as well; writing both words and music, he explored new forms of musical storytelling through such works as *Company* (1970), *Follies* (1971), and *Sweeney Todd* (1979). He is widely seen as the foremost figure in American musical theater of the post–Rodgers-and-Hammerstein era. No recent producer-director of musicals has had more impact than Harold Prince (b. 1928) who, in works from

Cabaret (1966) to *Company* to *Evita* (1979), helped shape the "concept musical" production that depended heavily on the director as virtuosic auteur.

SOCIAL REALIST DRAMA: The Great Depression saw the emergence of a social realist drama, often with a leftist political agenda. The era's preeminent ensemble, which consisted predominantly of Jews of Eastern European origin, was the Group Theater, founded in 1931. Before it disbanded in 1940, it had staged such important works as *Awake and Sing!* (1935) and *Golden Boy* (1937), both by Clifford Odets (1906–63); it also staged *Johnny Johnson* (1936), featuring a score by Kurt Weill (1900–1950), a refugee from *Nazi Germany. Two of the Group Theater's co-founders, Harold Clurman (1901–1980) and Lee Strasberg (1901–1982), although frequently at odds, had a decisive impact on American actor training, with Strasberg eventually joining the influential Actors Studio in 1948. He is seen as a primary conduit for Stanislavsky's ideas to the American stage and for the resulting emergence of a more naturalistic, low-key "Method" acting style that was widespread by the 1950s.

PLAYWRIGHTS: Jews were among the country's leading playwrights. Starting in 1921, George S. Kaufman (1889–1961) was a prolific, commercially successful writer of wisecracking comedy. He is ultimately best remembered for his collaborations with Moss Hart (1904–1961), starting with *Once in a Lifetime* (1930). Hart later went on to further success as a director (*My Fair Lady*), theater memoirist (*Act One*; 1959), and producer. Elmer Rice (1892–1967) wrote perhaps the country's finest Expressionistic play, *The Adding Machine* (1923), before turning toward realism with *Street Scene* (1929), later adapted into an opera by Weill and Langston Hughes. Clifford Odets had fourteen plays produced between 1935 and 1954, enjoying his greatest success early on, when he was closely associated with the Group Theater; in addition to his tender portrayal of a working-class Jewish family in *Awake and Sing!*, his agit-prop *Waiting for Lefty* (1935) was a sensation for him and the Group Theater. Building on Odets' concern for domestic realism and social commentary was Arthur Miller (1915–2005), who towered over the American theater for three decades and is widely recognized as one of the greatest playwrights the country has produced. Miller scored major success with *All My Sons* (1947), *Death of a Salesman* (1949), and *The Crucible* (1953). He remained active into the 1990s, although his later work was received abroad more positively than in the United States (see also THEATER, UNITED STATES: PLAYWRIGHTS).

STAGE DESIGN: Stage design of the mid-twentieth century often aimed for "poetic" visual effects rather than the laborious literalism of the previous generation. Many of the leading exemplars of this new design were Jews, including Lee Simonson (1888–1967); Jo Mielziner (1901–1976), who had one Jewish parent, designed sets for *Death of a Salesman*, *South Pacific*, and *The King and I*, as well as for Tennessee Williams' *A Streetcar Named Desire* (1947). Boris Aronson (1900–1980) created memorable sets for many hit shows from the 1930s to the 1970s.

ALTERNATIVE THEATER: The 1960s alternative theater in New York was perhaps best represented by the work of Jewish artists. A key early influence was the Living Theater Company, created in 1946 by Julian Beck (1925–1985) and Judith Malina (b. 1926); a watershed moment was their 1959 production, *The Connection*, whose documentary-like, spontaneous quality explored new approaches to performance. In the 1960s, the group pioneered works based around improvisation and collective creation, working outside the United States for an extended period. Joseph Chaikin (1935–2003) founded the Open Theater in 1963, a company that explored new means of play creation and acting through a theater stripped of all but its essentials. In 1968, critic and practitioner Richard Schechner (b. 1934) defined these and other new companies as "environmental theater"; partly taking his cue from their work, he went on to shape the emerging field of Performance Studies.

ARTISTIC DIRECTORS: Although many Jews were instrumental in founding theaters in the post-war period, a few names stand out. In 1950 Zelda Fichandler (b. 1924) co-founded Arena Stage in Washington, D.C., and served as its artistic director for more than forty years, giving impetus to the nation's growing regional theater movement. In New York City, Joseph Papp (1921–1991) founded the Shakespearean Theater Festival in 1954, which eventually became the New York Shakespeare Festival, which in turn gave rise to the Public Theater, arguably the city's leading contemporary not-for-profit company and one with a long track record of creating important new work. Herbert Blau (b. 1926) co-founded both San Francisco's Actor's Workshop (1952) and New York's short-lived Repertory Theater of Lincoln Center (1965); as a director and theorist, he has been instrumental in bringing nonrealistic and avant-garde plays and practices to the American theater. Robert Brustein (b. 1927) is another leading figure in the regional theater scene, founding both Yale Repertory Theater (1966) and Cambridge's American Repertory Theater (1979). Emily Mann (b. 1952) is well known for her documentary theater pieces; she is also an accomplished director and, since 1990, artistic director of Princeton's McCarter Theater. Born and raised in Venezuela, playwright and director Moisés Kaufman (b. 1963) founded the Tectonic Theater Project; his documentary-style *Laramie Project* (2000) pushed boundaries of genres in exploring a hate crime in Wyoming. For further reading, see H. Erdman, *Staging the Jew: The Performance of an American Ethnicity, 1860–1920* (1997); **see also** ENTERTAINMENT.   HARLEY ERDMAN

Theater, United States: Playwrights.

American Jewish involvement in theatrical production was minimal before the late 1800s. When Jewish characters appeared on nineteenth-century American stages, they were likely to be hook-nosed, heavy-bearded, avaricious stereotypes in plays written and produced by Gentiles. Toward the end of the century, however, massive *immigration from *Eastern Europe gave Jews a more visible American presence. While Yiddish theater took root in Yiddish-speaking neighborhoods (see THEATER, YIDDISH), Jews also became active as theater owners and producers in the English-speaking theater. More gradually, English-speaking Jewish playwrights emerged; in most cases, they saw themselves as Americans who had no particular interest in writing about Jews.

Jewish writers were prominently involved in the great blossoming of American drama after *World War I. George S. Kaufman (1889–1961) was the leading American comic playwright of his time. With Moss Hart (1904–1961), also a Jew, he wrote *You Can't Take It with You* (1936) and *The Man Who Came to Dinner* (1939), among other plays; yet there are few Jewish characters or Jewish references in the forty-odd plays he wrote with various co-authors. Lillian Hellman (1905–1984), from a New Orleans Jewish family, based the villainous characters of *The Little Foxes* (1939) on her relatives, but expunged any suggestion of Jewishness.

No major American Jewish playwright has written exclusively about Jewish characters. However, over the course of the twentieth century, a canon of mainstream American plays by Jewish authors has emerged in which Jews take center stage and are confronted with issues facing them in real life. The great subject of this drama was the tension between Old World tradition and New World opportunity, a matter of urgent concern to members of all ethnic groups, in America and elsewhere.

This tension is dramatized explicitly, not to say blatantly, in *The Jazz Singer* (1925) by Samson Raphaelson (1894–1983), a Broadway hit starring George Jessel and later a famous movie starring Al Jolson, whose life story it parallels. The hero faces a stark choice: to be a *cantor like his father, who has thrown him out of the house for his "dirty music from the sidewalks," or a jazz-singing Broadway star. As so often happens in American Jewish drama, the conflict between heritage and opportunity is played out in an intensely emotional generational conflict (see also FILM: UNITED STATES). Elmer Rice (1892–1967) declared that his Jewish origin was "a matter to which I have paid no attention," but his *Street Scene* (1929) includes a Jewish family among the variegated residents of a New York tenement. In *Counsellor-at-Law* (1930), Rice once more depicts a teeming, multiethnic New York, but this time his protagonist (first played by Paul Muni, originally from the Yiddish theater) is a powerful Jewish lawyer, a hard-nosed immigrant boy who has worked his way up from poverty through native ability and unrelenting drive, only to be deserted by his fastidious wife and nearly destroyed by a malicious rival, both old-stock WASP Americans. Like so many characters in American Jewish plays, the protagonist of *Counsellor-at-Law* shows no interest whatever in Judaism as a religion; strikingly, American Jewish drama is almost entirely about secular Jews.

The Group Theater (1931–40), whose members left a permanent mark on American drama and *film, never defined itself as a Jewish institution, but there was something characteristically Jewish in its combination of left-wing idealism, endless disputation, and intense emotionalism on and off the stage. Two of its three directors were Jewish, as were many of its actors (including several Yiddish theater veterans) and a number of its playwrights, notably John Howard Lawson (1894–1977), author of *Success Story* (1932); Sidney Kingsley (1906–1995), who wrote *Men in White* (1933); and Clifford Odets (1906–1963). A minor actor with the company, Odets became the standard-bearer of Depression-era radical political theater when his one-act agit-prop play *Waiting for Lefty* (1935) galvanized its first audience into shouting "Strike! Strike!," along with the actors. *Lefty* was followed just weeks later by *Awake and Sing!*, the classic American Jewish family play; literary critic Alfred Kazin wrote joyfully of "watching my mother and father and uncles and aunts occupying the stage . . . by as much right as if they were Hamlet and Lear." Odets' play depicts the struggle between the two rival imperatives that competed to fill the vacuum left by the weakening of *Orthodox tradition. Bessie, the *mater familias*, stands for the Yankee dollar, for "success" for self and family; Jacob, her father, stands for the *Marxist revolution that seemed so bright with promise to so many Jews and to others at the time. Later plays by Odets include *Paradise Lost* (1935), a less successful Jewish family play full of Depression malaise, and *Golden Boy* (1937) about an Italian American youth (who might easily have been a Jew), who must choose between becoming a violinist or a prize fighter; it thus dramatizes another conflict between a higher calling and the lure of money and possessions. After the Group Theater dissolved, Odets, not himself immune to material success, spent most of his working life in Hollywood.

The most eminent of all Jewish playwrights is unquestionably Arthur Miller (1915–2005), although some critics reject him as an American Jewish writer. Miller wrote that early in life he struggled to identify himself "with mankind rather than one small tribal fraction of it," and certain critics have argued that in his masterpiece, *Death of a Salesman* (1949), he covered up the Jewishness of the Loman family in the interests of a false "universality." Only in his preface to the fiftieth-anniversary edition of *Salesman* did he acknowledge the Lomans as "Jews light-years away from religion or community that might have fostered Jewish identity." Miller's sense of himself as a Jew was complicated and changed over time. In *After the Fall* (1964), *Incident at Vichy* (1964), and *Playing for Time* (1985), he wrestles with the *Holocaust, which has cast a long shadow over American Jewish drama. In *The Price* (1968), he created his most charming comic character, an aged Jewish secondhand furniture dealer and dispenser of heavily accented wisdom. *Broken Glass*, written in 1994 but set in 1938, depicts a Brooklyn matron so traumatized by the news of Nazi horrors that she loses the ability to walk, while her husband eats himself up with his own ambivalence about his Jewishness. Written when Miller was seventy-eight, it was his first full-length play since his student days to focus on American Jews whose Jewish identities were explicitly at the center of their plight.

Neil Simon (b. 1927) wrote a succession of Broadway comedies that brought him immense popularity. His characters, in plays like *Barefoot in the Park* (1963) and *The Odd Couple* (1965) are fast-talking, wisecracking, middle-class New Yorkers – all characteristics frequently associated with Jews – but they are not explicitly Jewish. Like Miller, Simon seemed to be more at ease in confronting Jewish circumstances and responses directly as he grew older. The three semi-autobiographical plays of his Brighton Beach trilogy– *Brighton Beach Memoirs* (1982, 1983), *Biloxi Blues* (1984, 1985), and *Broadway Bound* (1986) – are about the escape of a young writer from the narrow limitations of his Jewish family into the wider world. *Lost in Yonkers* (1991) explores the indirect effects of Nazi tyranny on several generations of an American Jewish family.

In the first half of the twentieth century, American Jewish drama showed Jewish characters trying to establish themselves as Americans; after *World War II, however, a number of playwrights suggested that the unprecedented prosperity and acceptance that American Jews were enjoying entailed losses as well as gains. *The Tenth Man* (1959) by Paddy Chayefsky (1923–1981) focuses on a Jewish lawyer who is cured of "the *dybbuk of lovelessness" by a ritual exorcism in a shabby synagogue; in *Grown Ups* (1981) by Jules Feiffer

(b. 1929), a bright young Jewish reporter leaves his wife and quits his job at the *New York Times* in an explosion of futility. *Sight Unseen* (1991, 1992) by Donald Margulies (b. 1954) depicts a famous Jewish painter from Brooklyn who looks to a former Gentile lover to discover what is missing from his life. The heroes of all three plays are talented, "successful" young men who find themselves somehow adrift.

A different response to post-war middle-class Jewish prosperity was the embrace of nostalgia for an imagined past. Most of the leading composers of American musicals, including Irving Berlin, Jerome Kern, George Gershwin, Richard Rodgers, Leonard Bernstein, and Stephen Sondheim, were Jews who had little interest in explicitly Jewish themes. In the mid-1960s, however, Joseph Stein (1912–2010) wrote the book, Sheldon Harnick (b. 1924) wrote the lyrics, and Jerry Bock (1928–2010) composed the music for *Fiddler on the Roof* (1964), directed by Jerome Robbins (1918–1998). Adapted from stories of Eastern Europe *shtetl life by Yiddish writer Sholem Aleichem (see LITERATURE, YIDDISH: 1800 TO TWENTY-FIRST CENTURY), this enduringly successful musical reminded millions of Jews where their forebears had come from, and it provided the Gentile world with a sympathetic idea of what it meant to be a Jew. *The Producers* (2001), with book, lyrics, and music by Mel Brooks (b. 1926) (with an assist on the book by Thomas Meehan) completed the story, in a way, by gleefully reducing Hitler to a figure of fun.

In the last two decades of the twentieth century, American Jewish playwrights mainly expressed a rueful and comic acceptance of the complexity of middle-class American Jewish life. Alfred Uhry (b. 1936) wrote two shrewd plays, *Driving Miss Daisy* (1987) and *The Last Night of Ballyhoo* (1997), about well-established southern Jews of German descent. In contrast, Donald Margulies wrote several keenly perceptive plays about lower-middle-class Brooklyn Jews. After two whimsical hits, *A Thousand Clowns* (1965) and *I'm Not Rappaport* (1985), Herb Gardner (1934–2003) wrote the powerful *Conversations with My Father* (1992), about a saloonkeeper haunted by conflicting feelings about his Jewish identity. In *Isn't it Romantic?* (1981, 1983) and *The Sisters Rosensweig* (1992), Wendy Wasserstein (1950–2006) wrote empathically about Jewish women and their personal and generational struggles. Surprisingly, David Mamet (b. 1947), a major American playwright and a zestful polemicist on Jewish issues, has written only a few brief minor stage works on these issues, notably in the three one-act plays collectively entitled *The Old Neighborhood* (1997).

The most important American play of the 1990s was inarguably *Angels in America* (1991, 1992), subtitled "A Gay Fantasia on National Themes," a massive double-length drama by Tony Kushner (b. 1956). Several of its characters are Jews, including two historical figures, Roy Cohn and Ethel Rosenberg. In describing the play, Kushner said, "Judaism isn't what the play is about, but I'm Jewish and it took me by surprise that it wound up being all over the play." *Angels in America* begins with the funeral of an elderly immigrant Jewish woman. "You can never make the crossing that she made," says the rabbi to the congregation, but "In you that journey is." In the first decades of the twenty-first century, it seems safe to assume that some remnant of that journey will be part of the continuing psychic DNA of American Jewish drama.

For further reading, see H. Erdman, *Staging the Jew: The Performance of an American Ethnicity, 1860–1920* (1997); J. Novick, *Beyond the Golden Door: Jewish American Drama and Jewish American Experience* (2008); E. Schiff, ed., *Awake and Singing: New Edition: Six Great American Jewish Plays* (2004); and J. Shatzky and M. Taub, eds., *Contemporary Jewish-American Dramatists and Poets: A Bio-Critical Sourcebook* (1999).

JULIUS NOVICK

Theater, Yiddish. Long before scripted dramas were written and performed in *Yiddish, Yiddish speakers enjoyed performances of entertainers (*badkhonim*) at Jewish events, particularly weddings. Part of a wider fabric of medieval Jewish performers, including magicians who performed at fairs, wandering troubadours, and wedding musicians, *badkhonim* developed repertoires of wedding songs, riddles, parodies, and serious and comic songs. By the end of the sixteenth century, dramatic dialogues, primarily *purimshpiln* (*Purim plays), were performed publicly. The earliest extant manuscript of a *purimshpil* is an *Akhasheyresh-shpil* (Ahasuerus play) dating to 1697. These dramatizations were performed by men and boys, often students from *yeshivot* (religious seminaries). In a spirit of irreverence befitting the jovial mood of the Purim holiday, humor relied heavily on scatological and sexual jokes and puns, which often angered religious authorities.

Theatrical performances found a more regular place in Jewish life with the late-eighteenth-century advent of the *Haskalah or Jewish Enlightenment. The movement's proponents (*maskilim*) urged fellow Jews to become less insular, to integrate more fully into European society, and to benefit from secular thought. Despite fierce resistance from religious Jews, the *Haskalah* ultimately paved the way toward new forms of religious expression and a new orientation toward the non-Jewish world. Two *Berlin *maskilim* of the 1790s who took a strong interest in drama and wrote important Yiddish dramatic satires were Aaron Halle-Wolfssohn and Isaac Euchel. Euchel was the author of *Reb Henokh, oder vos tut men damit?* (Reb Henokh, or What Can Be Done with It?), and Wolfssohn wrote *Leichtsinn und Frömmelei* (Frivolity and False Piety). Important later maskilic plays include *Serkele* by Solomon Ettinger (1800–1856); Avrom Ber Gottlober's 1839 *Der dektukh* (The Bridal Veil); *Der ershter yidisher rekrut in rusland* (The First Jewish Recruit in Russia) by Israel Aksenfeld (1787–1866); and *Di takse* (The Tax) by S. Y. Abramovich (1836–1917), best known as Mendele Mokher Seforim (see LITERATURE, YIDDISH).

Soon after assembling his first troupe in Jassy, *Romania, in 1876, Avrom Goldfaden (1840–1908) began writing burlesques and full-length comedies, including *Di kishefmakherin* (The Sorceress) and *Der fanatic, oder di tsvey Kunileml* (The Fanatic, or the Two Kuni-Lemls), lampooning religious fanaticism. Before long, Goldfaden's company had rivals, one led by Joseph Lateiner (1853–1935) and the other by Moyshe Hurwitz (1844–1910). Other playwrights who would contribute to the foundation of the professional repertoire were Nokhem-Meyer ("Shomer") Shaykevitch (1849–1905) and Yoysef-Yude Lerner (1847–1907).

The *pogroms following the 1881 assassination of Tsar Alexander II helped spark a Jewish emigration from *Russia. As a result, Yiddish theater companies were created or expanded in Eastern European cities outside the Russian Empire, and new centers of Yiddish theater arose further west. However, the vast majority of Eastern European emigrants came to the *United States where *New York City emerged as a major center of Yiddish theater. There, the most popular plays from Eastern Europe were performed, as well as new works written largely in the same vein: that is, primarily melodramas, musicals, and broad comedies. Reviewers lamented the "low" taste of the Yiddish audience and hailed the early dramaturgical activity of Jacob Gordin (1853–1909). Gordin also deplored the existing repertoire and set out to reform Yiddish drama with such works as *Der yidisher kenig Lir* (The Jewish King Lear), *Mirele Efros*, and *Got, mentsh un tayvl* (God, Man, and Devil). Although Gordin was often praised in New York for breathing fresh life into Yiddish drama, European critics like I. L. Peretz (1852–1915) and Noyekh Prilutski (1882–1941) were less enthusiastic. Peretz regarded Gordin as little better than a *shund* (vulgar) playwright and felt that a different type of dramaturgy was needed to elevate the artistic level of Yiddish drama. Peretz wrote short plays influenced by naturalism, whereas his full-length verse-plays were symbolic (see also FILM: YIDDISH-LANGUAGE; LITERATURE, YIDDISH: FROM 1800 TO THE TWENTY-FIRST CENTURY).

Gordin created a following not just among American audiences and critics but also among a new generation of playwrights. Successful dramatists in New York at the turn of the twentieth century included Leon Kobrin, Zalmen Libin, Nokhem Rakov, and Isidore Zolotarevsky. However, the American Yiddish stage often belonged more to performers and composers than to playwrights. Audiences worshiped musical theater specialists like Boris and Bessie Thomashefsky, Sigmund and Dina Feinman, Clara Young, and Regina Prager; comedians like Berl Bernstein and Zelig Mogulesco; and character actors like Boaz Young and Bina Abramovitch. Because of the importance of *music in the Yiddish repertoire, its composers contributed as much to its success as its performers. Among the most important composers of music for the Yiddish theater were Arnold Perlmutter and Herman Wohl (who had many of their greatest successes as a team), Dovid Meyerovitch, Louis Friedsel, Joseph Rumshinsky, Abe Ellstein, Sholem Secunda, and Peretz Sandler.

As long as immigration continued, New York remained one of the world capitals of Yiddish theater, with a new generation of playwrights contributing to the maturation of Yiddish drama. Dovid Pinski (1872–1950) created biting satires, like *Der oytser* (The Treasure), but also wrote in a darker vein, in dramas like *Der eybiker yid* (The Eternal Jew) and *Di familye Tsvi* (The Family Tsvi). Peretz Hirschbein (1880–1948) is best known for his idylls of village life, such as *A farvorfn vinkl* (A Forsaken Nook) and *Grine felder* (Green Fields). Other accomplished dramatists working primarily in New York were Osip Dimov, H. Leivick, and Fishl Bimko, all of whom wrote for successful troupes. Foremost among these was Maurice Schwartz's Yiddish Art Theater, which performed western and Yiddish classics, new Yiddish dramas, and adaptations of *Yiddish literature, like Sholem Aleichem's *Tevye der milkhiker* (Tevye the Dairyman) and I. J. Singer's *Yoshe Kalb*, dramatized by Schwartz himself. For true ensemble acting, New York Yiddish audiences went to Artef (from the Yiddish acronym for Workers' Theater Collective). The company established itself as the avant-garde answer to commercial offerings with its innovative productions of classic and new Yiddish plays.

After the Russian Revolution (1917), state-sponsored Yiddish theaters were founded in a number of major cities of the *Soviet Union. Of the fourteen state Yiddish companies, by far the most celebrated was the Moscow State Yiddish Theater (best known by its Russian acronym, GOSET), which revolutionized Yiddish theater with avant-garde productions of Yiddish classics, new Yiddish plays, and works from the European repertoire. The company's founder, Alexander Granovsky, put his mark on Yiddish standards like Goldfaden's *Di kishefmakherin* (The Sorceress) and Sholem Aleichem's *Dos groyse gevins* (The Lottery). After Granovsky's 1928 defection to the West, actor Solomon Mikhoels (1890–1948) took over, focusing for a while on new works like *Boytre* by Moyshe Kulbak (1896–1940) and *Der toyber* (The Deaf Man) by Dovid Bergelson (1884–1952). When Soviet authorities used Kulbak's underworld drama as an excuse to crack down on the troupe (Kulbak was arrested and disappeared into the gulag), GOSET responded with politically correct versions of Goldfaden's *Shulamis* and *Bar Kokhba*.

Yiddish theater continued to thrive elsewhere in Eastern Europe in the first three decades of the twentieth century. Schwartz's Yiddish Art Theater, which formed just a couple of years after the *Vilna Troupe, found a lasting place on the world theatrical map with its 1920 production of S. Ansky's *Der dibek* (The *Dybbuk). The company's further successes included *Yoshke muzikant* (Yoshke the Musician) by Osip Dimov (born Joseph Perlman, 1878–1959) and *Kiddush ha-Shem* (Martyrdom) by Sholem Asch (1880–1957). The Vilna Troupe continued to perform until the *Holocaust, when its remaining members were trapped in the Vilna ghetto and liquidated along with their neighbors. Before then, however, interwar *Poland was fertile ground for new ventures in Yiddish theater. The 1920s brought the creation of such companies as VYKT (*Varshever yidisher kunst teater*, or Warsaw Yiddish Art Theater), founded in 1924 and led by Zygmunt Turkow (1896–1970) and his wife Ida Kaminska (1899–1980); VNYT (*Varshever nayer yidisher teater*, or Warsaw New Yiddish Theater), founded by Zygmunt's brother, Jonas Turkow (1892–1982), in 1929; and *Yung Teater* (Young Theater), established by Mikhl Weichert in 1932.

The annihilation of Polish Jewry by the *Nazis destroyed a particularly vibrant theatrical culture. Yet during the war, performers made valiant efforts to carry on their activities in the face of the gravest danger. *Warsaw *ghetto leader Emanuel *Ringelblum's diaries chronicle a variety of cultural undertakings, including musical and theatrical performance. As the Nazi ghettos were liquidated and the survivors were sent to concentration camps, they continued to perform even in the camps. After the war, surviving actors resumed theatrical activity, first in *displaced persons camps and then in the places where they settled.

Important secondary hubs of Yiddish theater include *Argentina; *South Africa, where Sarah Sylvia reigned as the leading star; *Australia, dominated by Polish immigrants Yankev Weislitz and Rochl Holzer; and Montreal (see CANADA), which had long served as a "provincial" theater on the North American circuit (along with *Chicago, *Philadelphia, Detroit, and Baltimore, among others). *Israel, home to countless native Yiddish speakers, was

problematic for Yiddish theater. The privileging of Hebrew over Yiddish in *British Mandate Palestine and later in the State of *Israel made it difficult to mount Yiddish theater productions. Nevertheless, Yiddish performances in Palestine began as early as the 1890s and continued into the early decades of the state. By the early twenty-first century, little regular activity remains, although Shmuel Atzmon's *Yiddishpil* company, based in *Tel Aviv, continues to carry the flame.

While Yiddish culture was all but destroyed by Hitler and Stalin, it also lost popularity in more comfortable venues. The Yiddish theater thrived in places like New York as long as there was a steady stream of new immigrants. That supply largely dried up after strict immigration quotas were imposed in the 1920s, and the American Yiddish theater began a steady decline. Nevertheless, Artef was important throughout the 1930s, as was the Yiddish Art Theater in the 1930s and 1940s. As of the early twenty-first century, the *Folksbine* is the only American company continuing to offer Yiddish performances on a fairly regular basis.

For further reading, see N. Sandrow, *Vagabond Stars* (1977; reprinted 1999); J. Berkowitz, ed., *Yiddish Theater: New Approaches* (2003); and J. Hoberman, *Bridge of Light* (1991), which focuses on Yiddish film. Memoirs include J. Adler, *A Life on the Stage* (1999); P. Burstein, *What a Life!* (2003); and H. Yablokoff, *Der Payatz* (1995). For English translations, see J. Berkowitz and J. Dauber, eds., *Landmark Yiddish Plays* (2006); and N. Sandrow, ed., *God, Man, and Devil* (1998).

JOEL BERKOWITZ

Theology. Judaism offers a rich theological tradition devoted to describing *God and how God functions within Jewish life.

BIBLICAL THEOLOGY: Covenantal theology, prophetic theology, Land of Israel/Temple theology, and wisdom theology are types of biblical theology. *Covenantal theology is based on the attributes of divine mercy and divine justice as they are exemplified in God's creation and ordering of the world and God's care for everything created (Gen 1). It also assumes that the divine–human relationship is predicated on divine promises and divine law. Both the Abrahamic and Mosaic covenants function according to the theo-logic of a God who issues both promises and *commandments. Obedience to these laws is the prerequisite to fulfillment of God's promises (Gen 17; Exod 19). Covenantal theology supports a theology of history in which acts of divine grace in the past are invoked to bring individuals into a present and future relationship with God.

Prophetic theology is expressed in the responses of *prophets like *Isaiah and *Jeremiah to historical challenges to covenantal theology such as war and exile (see BIBLE: PROPHETS AND PROPHECY). The prophets consider such events in light of a theology of reward and punishment according to which loss of divine favor is a result of human deviations from covenantal practice and obligation. Prophetic theology also develops expectations of divine *redemption and covenantal renewal at some future time (see ESCHATOLOGY: SECOND TEMPLE PERIOD). A related *Land of Israel/*Temple theology, or "theology of Zion," is expressed in the *Psalms and historical writings of the Hebrew *Bible. This theology identifies the Land of Israel and the *Jerusalem Temple as sacred meeting places between the divine and the human that provide access to divine reality and eternality. Wisdom writings, found in *Job, *Ecclesiastes, *Proverbs (see also BIBLE: WISDOM LITERATURE), and *Song of Songs, draw a connection between the divine order expressed within nature and the social norms incumbent on both Jews and Gentiles. Wisdom literature incorporates covenantal theology into this larger context of the divine order.

RABBINIC THEOLOGY: Rabbinic texts (*Mishnah, *Talmud, and *midrash) emphasize the two poles of divine reality: divine transcendence and divine immanence. According to the Rabbis, God transcends the created world, and the age of prophecy has come to an end: "The Holy One, blessed be He, is the Place of His world and His world is not His place" (*Rashi). Nonetheless, the Rabbis developed *halakhic and liturgical structures that presuppose God's concern for creation and in particular the ability of the individual to live according to divine law and engage in *repentance behaviors for the sake of *atonement and forgiveness. Rabbinic literature also wrestles with classic theological questions, including how and why God permits suffering (see EVIL AND SUFFERING); questions related to creation – was the world created at a particular moment in time?; and whether God speaks in the language of human beings.

MEDIEVAL THOUGHT: Like the wisdom tradition before it, Jewish *thought in the Middle Ages deepened the inquiry into the relationship between God's activity as revealer and God's activity as creator. However, medieval theology, as exemplified by the work of *Saadia Gaon (882–942) and Moses *Maimonides (1135–1204), used human *reason to inquire into the divine nature. The Book of Doctrines and Opinions, by Saadia Gaon offers one of the first systematic Jewish accounts of the link between a God available to analysis by human *reason and a God of tradition whose *revelation exceeds human understanding. Influenced by Aristotle, Maimonides' work presents a rigorous philosophico-theological investigation into the unity of God. In negative theology, an aspect of this inquiry, both positive and negative claims concerning God are declared beyond human understanding, while the true, unparalleled nature of God is continuously pointed to but never reduced to human propositions.

EARLY MODERN PERIOD: *Mysticism presented an altogether new set of paradigms for Jewish theology (see KABBALAH). The well-known kabbalist Isaac *Luria (1534–1572) described God as *Ein Sof (without end) – infinitely unknowable, on the one hand, and as generative of emanations or *sefirot through which this same God creates the world, on the other.

In the seventeenth century the work of Baruch *Spinoza (1632–1677) sent shock waves through Jewish intellectual circles. Spinoza challenged biblical and medieval claims concerning the transcendence of God over creation by positing an identity between God and substance (The Ethics). However, modern Jewish *thought has not sustained Spinoza's overturning of divine transcendence, and even thinkers as philosophically inclined as Moses *Mendelssohn (1729–1786) and Hermann *Cohen (1842–1918) reassert the Jewish commitment to the transcendence of God while maintaining the close connection between divine perfection and human theoretical and practical reason.

MODERN APPROACHES: Twentieth-century Jewish theology renewed the focus on the biblically-based model of covenantal theology. Whereas Martin *Buber's I and Thou recovers the biblical account of divine calling and human response, Franz *Rosenzweig's The Star of Redemption is alone in restoring the twofold emphasis on divine *love and command as the central elements in the divine–human relationship. Deeply concerned with tackling God's relationship to the suffering of the Jewish people during the *Shoah, post-Holocaust Jewish theologians like Eliezer *Berkovits and Elie *Wiesel use the covenantal model as their baseline for coming to terms with the depth of evil expressed in the *Holocaust (see also HOLOCAUST: THEOLOGICAL RESPONSES). Although some post-Holocaust theologians like Emil *Fackenheim and Richard *Rubenstein reject the validity of a covenantal theology in the wake of the Shoah, Jewish thinkers in America have enriched the covenantal account of Jewish theology. Both Abraham Joshua *Heschel (God in Search of Man) and Joseph B. *Soloveitchik (The Lonely Man of Faith) emphasize God's desire for the living response of the Jewish community to acts and expressions of divine love and divine command. More recently, David Novak has further developed Jewish covenantal theology and applied it to the challenge of contemporary multiculturalism.

Late-twentieth- and early-twenty-first-century Jewish theology has also been marked by the development of Jewish feminist theology (see JUDAISM, FEMINIST). Both Judith Plaskow (Standing again at Sinai) and Rachel Adler (Engendering Judaism) reconsider classic Jewish conceptions of God through the lens of women's narrative, secondary legal status, and liturgical experience.   RANDI RASHKOVER

Theresienstadt was a concentration camp north of Prague in the town of Terezín (Theresienstadt) in Czechoslovakia that was established in October 1941. It was initially a *ghetto for elderly and privileged Reich Jews, but Adolf Eichmann later transformed it into a special "show" camp to dispel rumors about the "Final Solution."

To maintain this façade, Eichmann, who kept an office at Theresienstadt, allowed the ghetto's large community of scholars, writers, musicians, and artists a certain amount of creative freedom to study, write, and compose. In 1944, Joseph Goebbels' propaganda office produced a film, Theresienstadt: Ein Dokumentarfilm aus dem jüdischen Siedlungsgebiet (Documentary Film of the Jewish Resettlement), that was later shown to a visiting Red Cross delegation. Fifteen thousand children passed through Theresienstadt on their way to death camps in occupied Poland. Some of their artwork and poems have been published in I Never Saw Another Butterfly, edited by Hana Volavkova. More than 33,000 Jews died in Theresienstadt and more than 87,000 were sent on to death camps. **See CZECHOSLOVAKIA; HOLOCAUST; HOLOCAUST: CAMPS AND KILLING CENTERS.**

DAVID M. CROWE

Thought, Early Modern (1500–1750). Jewish thought in the Early Modern period covers a broad spectrum, including philosophical and theological works as well as scientific, ethical, and homiletical writings.

After 1492, the rationalist approaches that were prevalent in the medieval period (see THOUGHT, MEDIEVAL) declined in prominence, and Jewish thinkers who upheld the eternality of the universe, the lack of personal providence, and Averroes' double truth became increasingly rare. Most sixteenth-century Jewish thinkers were conservative, claiming the superiority of *revelation over *reason; they produced homiletical and theological treatises that made use of philosophical language and style without substantive philosophical content. As a result, concepts and terminology acquired new meanings, entirely different from their original connotations.

Spanish exiles enriched the Mediterranean basin with their spiritual creativity and their organizational talents – gathering writings into "public libraries," broadening the scope of study and teaching, and so forth. Their rational style also influenced *Ashkenazic thought. Philosophical trends persisted into the sixteenth century, but they encountered conservative opposition. For instance, a sharp dispute erupted in the early sixteenth century around Shem Tov ibn Shem Tov's *Sefer ha-Emunot* (Book of Religious Beliefs) written at the end of the fourteenth century), which is a major attack on philosophy. Moses Alashkar adopted a classic rationalistic stance in this controversy, countering Shem Tov's arguments thoroughly in his *Hassagot* (Critical Notes), first printed in 1553. The wanderings of this sage from *Spain to *North Africa, *Greece, *Egypt, and *Jerusalem point to the hardships that exiled rationalists endured.

A unique type of philosophical literature emerged in countries that were part of the *Ottoman Empire. Joseph Taitatsak, who left Spain in 1492 and became a rabbi in Salonika (see BALKANS), adopted conservative approaches that medieval rationalists had rejected; these included the claim that the soul had been created directly by *God without intermediate hypostases. For proofs, Taitatsak relied on scholastic Christian literature and particularly on Thomas Aquinas's commentary on Aristotle, highlighting the Neoplatonic aspects of Aquinas's thought. Taitatsak also wrote a number of scholarly biblical exegeses.

In Salonika, Moses Almosnino (ca. 1515–ca. 1580) used a rationalist style, pervaded with philosophical terminology, to claim that the *Torah is superior to reason. Contrary to medieval rationalists, Almosnino claimed that the foundations of *science and wisdom are in the Torah and that knowledge is acquired through the study of Torah. At the same time, he continued to pursue serious philosophical studies and translated philosophical and scientific texts. Although Almosnino was not a kabbalist (see KABBALAH), his views parallel mystical claims that the Torah is a receptacle of supernal truths. This approach is also typical of other thinkers active in Almosnino's surroundings, whose ideas and conservatism drew them into the kabbalists' camp.

*Italy, too, was a center for thinkers hostile to philosophy and its authority. Isaac *Abravanel, Jeḥiel of Pisa (d. ca. 1574), and Judah Moscato (d. ca. 1593), who wrote a comprehensive commentary on Judah *Halevi's *The Kuzari*, attacked philosophers and disparaged their achievements. Nevertheless, Judah Abravanel, Isaac's son, also known as Leone Ebreo, wrote the *Dialoghi d'Amore* (Dialogues of Love), a treatise with definite philosophical traces. This sixteenth-century work is built as a dialogue between Sophia, who presents rational thought as the supreme value and the source of cosmic processes, and Philo, for whom the driving cosmic force is love. The philosophical stance is based

on Aristotle and on Averroes' commentary, and even Abravanel's description of love adopts a philosophical style.

Samuel Saul Siriro (d. 1655), a disciple of Saadia ibn Danan, who was active in Morocco (see NORTH AFRICA), wrote a book of homilies that combines a literal interpretation of *aggadah* and medieval thought. Siriro argued that miracles were meant to strengthen the faith of the masses, but perfect individuals do not need miracles because they attain knowledge of God through study. However, Siriro did not advocate the detailed curriculum carefully specified by medieval philosophers that included the study of logic, the life sciences, physics, and so forth. Rather, he depended on rabbinical homilies, emptying them of their philosophical contents while preserving their frame and style. Siriro painstakingly explained his perception of miracles, offering extensive support for the view that the perfect individual can bring them about. Contrary to Abraham *ibn Ezra, who said that miracles can only occur through the individual's conjunction with the supernal worlds, Siriro claimed that the image of God within human beings endows them with the ability to perform miracles. Siriro's homilies also make superficial use of the narrative-midrashic contents of the *Zohar, but not its kabbalistic teachings. Siriro cited philosophical texts, from *Maimonides' *Guide of the Perplexed* through *Gersonides' commentary on the Torah, and also alluded to fifteenth-century scholarly literature, such as Abraham Bibago's *Derekh Emunah* (The Path of Faith). Thus, Siriro's homilies point to a detachment from the content of medieval philosophy while preserving its style.

In Ashkenaz, Judah *Loew, the Maharal of *Prague (d. 1609), deliberately used a semi-philosophical scholarly style in his prose, giving readers the impression of confronting a rationalist body of work that required such terminology, although its contents were unswervingly opposed to rationalism. For instance, a central claim in the essay *Tiferet Israel* (The Splendor of Israel), which is devoted to the superiority of the Torah, is that technical and practical action are essentially preferable to abstract thinking. Loew devoted many discussions to the seemingly rational argument that the practice of the commandments is superior to any intellectual pursuit, insisting that the order of the world rests on spiritual rules and laws. Thus, cosmic laws demonstrate that religious practice, rather than intellectual study, leads to perfection.

Moses *Isserles, known as the Rema (d. 1572), wrote a long essay on the reasons for the *commandments in general and for the *Temple service in particular. He relied on medieval rationalist works, particularly on Maimonidean and post-Maimonidean treatises such as Albo's *Sefer ha-Ikkarim* (Book of the Principles of Faith). Although Isserles was an extremely conservative thinker, the prominent Ashkenazi sage Solomon Luria still attacked him for his exaggerated recourse to rationalism. Like Loew, Isserles also drew on the kabbalistic corpus and offered scholarly formulations of mystical approaches.

By the seventeenth century, the philosophical content and style of the Middle Ages, still present in sixteenth-century writings, had disappeared almost entirely. Exceptions were still evident in Italy, including the work of Leon (Judah Aryeh) *Modena, who was critical of Kabbalah. *Ma'aseh Tuviah*, a medical compendium by Tuviah Ha-Cohen (d. 1729), who grew up in Metz and Kraków, was well known in Ashkenaz. In this treatise, elementary theological approaches are presented as backed by philosophical claims.

In the *Ottoman Empire some homilists with a philosophical background, such as Joshua Benveniste (d. ca. 1668) and Solomon Amarilio (d. 1722), dissociated themselves from kabbalistic sources. Nissim ibn Shangi mingled homiletics, exegesis, and halakhic discussions in his writings. In contrast to the many homiletical works of this era, philosophical monographs are rare. A few important examples still appeared, however, defending the Oral Law. In seventeenth-century *Venice, Immanuel Aboab (d. 1628) wrote *Nomologia* or *Halakhic Homilies*. In this treatise, Aboab dealt with such theological and philosophical issues as the divine attributes, the reasons for the *commandments, and psychology. Aviad Sar Shalom Basilea (d. ca. 1743), who also wrote a book in defense of rabbinic tradition entitled *Emunat Ḥakhamim* (Faith of the Wise), attested that he is not a kabbalist but wished to defend the honor of tradition in all its manifestations, including Kabbalah.

Another essay on the same subject was written by the celebrated rabbi of the eighteenth-century *Sephardi community in London, David Nieto (d. 1728), originally from Italy. Nieto was involved in a serious polemic over a fundamentally philosophical issue. Preaching in London's Spanish-Portuguese synagogue in 1703, Nieto claimed that God and nature are one. When he was accused of conceptual associations with *Spinoza, a controversy erupted that abated only when Zvi Hirsch Ashkenazi and his Hamburg court cleared Nieto of any blame. Nieto wrote the book *Matteh Dan* (The Staff of Dan), which was called "the second *Kuzari*" because it followed the format of a dialogue between the Khazar king and a rabbi that Judah Halevi had used for his *Kuzari* This treatise, which was also intended to defend the eternity and holiness of *rabbinic tradition (the Oral *Torah), is suffused with philosophical scholarship from the Middle Ages and the Early Modern period. Nieto published several essays as well as *sermons, many marked by a philosophical orientation.

In more remote areas, unaffected by the Spanish exiles and their culture, medieval philosophical monographs were still popular. In seventeenth century *Iran, Judah ben Elazar published a comprehensive philosophical essay, *Hovot Yehudah* (The Duties of Judah). This book deals with four realms of Jewish thought: the existence of God, prophecy (see BIBLE: PROPHETS AND PROPHECY), *revelation, and *messianism. The book ends with a discussion on the soul and other topics that Jewish philosophy considered esoteric. Philosophical monographs of this kind were still produced in *Yemen as well.

For further reading, see R. Bonfil, *Rabbis and Jewish Communities in Renaissance Italy* (1993); B. D. Cooperman, ed., *Jewish Thought in the Sixteenth Century* (1983); and I. Twersky and B. Septimus, eds., *Jewish Thought in the Seventeenth Century* (1987).   DOV SCHWARTZ

Thought, Medieval. Medieval Jewish thinkers reread the *Bible and *rabbinic literature using philosophical language and ideas of classical Greece. However, the philosophy they produced was discontinuous with those earlier texts in form and focus. Rather, their writings defined aspects of medieval Judaism at the same time as they helped transmit religious thought from the Muslim world to medieval Christian culture.

*Israelite religion placed emphasis on the obligations of *covenant, not expressions of creed. *Rabbinic Judaism structured Jewish life into a coherent spiritual and social whole, organized around the *mitzvot, commandments mandated by God; after the destruction of the *Temple, the focus was on ritual and interpersonal ethics. Just as the Rabbis of the *Talmud developed, amplified, and reinterpreted biblical ideas about God, prophecy, creation, miracles, providence, human felicity, and more, the Jewish philosophers of the Middle Ages provided a new approach to encountering and knowing *God (see also THEOLOGY). Philosophical ideas were the subject of extended essays; they also were applied to biblical texts and penetrated traditional *Bible commentaries, legal discussions, and popular *sermons.

By the late eighth century CE, Jews in Muslim-dominated *Mesopotamia, *Spain, and *North Africa were coming into extended contact with the ideas of Greek philosophy as mediated through Arabic translations and the integration of philosophical ideas into *Islam. A similar development took place within Judaism beginning in the mid-800s. As intellectual intermediaries between Islamic thought and the Christian world, Jews, especially in Spain, were translators, commentators, and original thinkers who provided the multicultural and transnational bridges needed for intellectual discourse.

Medieval philosophy was dominated by internal and external religious disputes as well as by an extended dialogue between *reason (which included *science) and *revelation (which referred to the beliefs of religious traditions). The apologetic and polemical activity of medieval Jewish philosophy gave Jews an arena of intellectual equality with the more dominant religions of Islam and *Christianity. Jewish philosophers were particularly challenged by the contrast between the methodology of philosophy and that of the Bible and Talmud. As they shifted from narrative theology to a systematic exposition of ideas, these thinkers also reflected on the truth value of human reason and inquiry in relation to divine revelation. The understanding of God that religious philosophers adapted from Greek thinkers led them to reconsider the use of anthropomorphic language in the *Bible and *Talmud.

Jewish philosophers often contended that philosophy was actually the wisdom alluded to in *Proverbs and other traditional texts – that is, philosophy was initially developed by Jews but then lost because of the "tribulations of the exile." Jewish philosophers justified their activity by contending that they were recovering and restoring the original tradition that had been subsequently distorted by the Greeks. The claim that philosophy was native to Judaism and not a foreign import was augmented by the idea that philosophical endeavors helped fulfill commandments such as "knowing God."

Jewish thinkers included *Kalam* theologians, Neoplatonists, Aristotelians, and those who had qualified reservations about (or completely rejected) Aristotelian philosophy. The subject matter of medieval Jewish philosophy comprised physics and other sciences, metaphysics, ethics, and politics. Jewish philosophy was shaped by and affected Islamic philosophy, influenced the development of *Kabbalah, and played a role in Jewish–Christian dialogue and polemic (see MIDDLE AGES: JEWISH–CHRISTIAN POLEMICS).

*Saadia ben Joseph Gaon (*Egypt and *Iraq, 892–942) was the most prominent figure to use the rhetorical and rational approach of *Kalam*, a system of thought originating in Islam that sought to explain scripture in a manner congruent with reason. Saadia justifies the use of reason, seeing it as a complementary (but ultimately subsidiary) source of knowledge to revelation. In his *Book of Traditional Doctrines and Rational Opinions*, Saadia provides the first systematic exposition of many critical areas of Jewish belief and develops a model for understanding the commandments by distinguishing between those that are universal-rational and those that are ritual-traditional. Using the dialectical argumentation characteristic of Mutazilite *Kalam*, Saadia offers arguments for creation *ex nihilo* and, based on that principle, then articulates reasons for the existence, unity, and incorporeality of God. He proceeds to discuss divine providence and justice, human freedom, and the intellectual afterlife of the soul. Another rabbinic exponent of *Kalam* was Da'ud ibn Marwan (often called David al-Mukammis). *Kalam* theologians were also found among the *Karaites; the most prominent are Jacob al-Kirkisani, Japheth ben Eli ha-Levi , and Joseph al-Basir.

The physician Isaac ben Solomon Israeli (*North Africa, 850–ca. 932), the poet Solomon *ibn Gabirol (Spain, 1021–ca. 1058), and the jurist *Baḥia ibn Pakuda (Spain, late 1000s) are the three Jewish thinkers most closely identified with Neoplatonism. Although Israeli corresponded with Saadia and was known to *Maimonides, his works were primarily known in Latin and did not influence other Jewish thinkers. Gabirol's major work, *Fountain of Life*, was known exclusively in its Latin version, *Fons Vitae*; it too had little effect on Jewish thinkers. In contrast, his ethical work, *The Improvement of Moral Qualities*, and his liturgical poem, *The Sovereign Crown*, are still studied and recited. Baḥia's work, *Guide to the Duties of the Heart*, was translated from *Judeo-Arabic into Hebrew and had a significant impact on Jewish ethics and spiritual development. Ibn Gabirol's *Crown* reprises many of the ideas of *Fountain of Life* and articulates a deep yearning for spiritual purification and ascent to the divine. The ideas of ethical improvement and a spiritual ascent toward God are evident in ibn Gabirol's *Improvement* and in Baḥia's *Duties*. The intent of Baḥia's work is to alert Jews who are focused on external commandments to the inner spiritual experience. Baḥia leads the reader from the unity of God to a union with the divine. The Neoplatonic emphasis on the spiritual ascent is also found in various expressions of Jewish *mysticism.

The initial period of Jewish Aristotelianism extended from the ninth to the end of the twelfth century and was related to Arabic translations of Aristotle and Islamic commentary on that literature. Beginning in the thirteenth century, the Jewish intellectual center moved to Christian countries, and the language of discourse and translation shifted from Arabic to Hebrew. Jewish Aristotelians distinguished between philosophical and theological works and focused on disparities between their received tradition and the scientific-philosophical ideas derived from Aristotle. For example, biblical and rabbinic assumptions about creation and miracles did not accord with the physics of an eternal cosmic order and the regular patterning of natural phenomena. The metaphysical conception of a transcendent, unmoved mover was at variance with the biblical presentation of a "most moved mover," who had knowledge of and concern for individuals. The biblical portrayal of a *covenantal community serving God though adherence to specific commandments was not easily reconciled with a universal virtue-based ethics and claims that human felicity (*eudaemia*) could be attained through the intellectual apprehension of abstract knowledge. Aristotelian emphasis on reason led to a view of faith as cognitive and propositional, rather than an expression of loyalty to and relationship with God. Moreover, the notion of the attainment of individual intellectual excellence led to the conclusion that the *afterlife related to the perfection of the human soul, rather than to physical *resurrection and the politics of national restoration.

*Abraham ibn Daud (Spain, 1110–1180), the author of an essay about the transmission of the Jewish tradition, *Sefer Ha-Kabbalah* (Book of Tradition), also composed the first Aristotelian work, *Emunah Rabbah* (Exalted Faith), written by a Jew. Ibn Daud critiques the theological inadequacies of both Saadia and Ibn Gabirol and presents the bases of natural science in order to end confusion about the imagined disagreement between religion and philosophy. He writes of the healing of the soul through moral conduct, but gives preeminence to theoretical knowledge. In the quest for felicity, ibn Daud claims that ritual commandments and moral acts have value, although metaphysical philosophy seems to have greater significance. Following the Arab philosopher ibn Sina (Avicenna), he develops arguments for an incorporeal, necessarily existent God whose attributes cannot be discussed in a positive way, but who nonetheless has a relationship with this world.

The dominant figure in medieval Jewish thought is Moses ben Maimon, also known as Moses *Maimonides (Spain, North Africa, Egypt, 1135–1204). His three most significant works are the *Commentary to the Mishnah*, a survey of the oral tradition of Judaism; *Mishneh Torah*, a comprehensive legal code detailing the obligations of all Jews; and *Guide for the Perplexed*, the preeminent statement of medieval Jewish philosophy. He also wrote works of *medicine, logic, and legal *responsa. Maimonides is a pivotal figure, representing the apex of the Judeo-Arabic philosophical tradition. Except for the *Mishneh Torah*, which was written in Hebrew, all of Maimonides' works were composed in Arabic; the Hebrew translation of the *Guide* established the philosophical framework for Jews in Christian lands. His work affects all subsequent Jewish thought, influences key Christian thinkers, and is the starting point for *Spinoza's critique of religion.

Debates over Maimonides began in medieval times and continue in contemporary academic scholarship. One perspective has Maimonides offering a comprehensive demonstration of the coherence of Torah and philosophy. Another approach argues that Maimonides subtly introduced contradictions into the *Guide* to conceal his true, more radical, opinions. This method enabled Maimonides to bifurcate between *halakhic (legal) writings, which served as an exposition of revealed *theology for the masses, and speculative work that discussed and identified a more mature philosophical truth for the intellectual elite (see STRAUSS, LEO). How one understands Maimonides' views on virtually every major philosophical question depends on whether one sees a unified, coherent body of work infused by philosophy or an exoteric and esoteric division between legal theology and philosophy.

All agree that a major focus of Maimonides' philosophical project involves a philosophical hermeneutic of the Bible and rabbinic literature centered on a vigorous repudiation of idolatry, understood as false ideas about God (in addition to the worship of other deities). The *Guide* may be understood as a major rereading of scripture; it reinterprets any terms that might be understood to describe God or the actions of God in anthropomorphic ways. Maimonides also held that no positive attributes can be predicated of God, for such descriptions might impinge on the unity of God. To preserve this central idea, all positive terms, such as existence, life, power, will, and knowledge, had to be avoided when speaking of divinity. Maimonides contends that identical language may be used in relation to God and human beings, but the similarity is exclusively verbal, not essential. Negative attributes imply a philosophical agnosticism: Nothing can be known concerning the true being of God. The question of the predication of attributes to divinity was a distinctive and central issue in medieval Jewish philosophy.

The Aristotelian tradition continued in *Yemen, North Africa, Spain, and, particularly, in *Italy and southern *France. The Provence region of southern France became a center for biblical studies, talmudic exegesis, mathematics, and philosophy. During the eleventh and twelfth centuries, the translation project of the *ibn Tibbon family led to the dissemination of philosophical works in Hebrew and created the technical vocabulary needed to pursue philosophy in Hebrew. Over time, the major works of Jewish and Muslim thinkers became available in Hebrew. Along with the work of Maimonides, the writings of the Spanish-Islamic philosopher, Averroes, had a significant influence on subsequent thinkers. The philosophical agenda was defended and carried on in Provence in the thirteenth and fourteenth centuries by Shem Tov ibn Joseph Falaquera, Isaac Albalag, Jedaiah Berdisi ha-Penini, Nissim ben Moses of Marseille, and Levi ben Gershon (*Gersonides). In this period as well, a series of confrontations developed over the legitimacy of philosophy and the role of Maimonides in the canon of Jewish studies. Philosophical ideas also began to appear within *biblical commentaries and *sermons, bringing these ideas to a broader public. One response was to attribute religious laxity to the philosophical allegorization of biblical texts.

The most significant early critics of philosophy were Judah *Halevi (Spain, ca. 1070–1141) and Moses ben Naḥman (*Naḥmanides, Spain, 1194–1270). Halevi wrote in a dialogical style, and Naḥmanides' opinions are found scattered through his many works. During a later stage of Aristotelian criticism, Ḥasdai *Crescas (Spain, ca. 1340–1410) stands out for his rigorous philosophical argumentation. Although each thinker was influential in defense of a traditional expression of Judaism, their methodologies and their relationship to Aristotelianism differed from one another.

Naḥmanides was a physician, biblical commentator, talmudist, legal scholar, and kabbalist who defended the Rabbis of the *Mishnah and *Talmud, as well as the legal and theological positions of his predecessors, the *Geonim. Naḥmanides is often critical of philosophy, singling out Aristotle for opprobrium. In his *Torat ha-Adam*, which deals with illness, *death, and rituals of *mourning, Naḥmanides disparages philosophers who imagine that human beings should transcend pain and be indifferent to loss. Yet, throughout his writings, Naḥmanides adopts positions that join reason and revelation. Considered one of the significant figures in the development of Kabbalah, Naḥmanides occasionally incorporates philosophical concepts into what he accepts as the mystical teachings of antiquity. Although identified as a critic of Maimonides, their relationship is actually complex. In an effort to moderate the developing criticism of Maimonides, Naḥmanides counseled the rabbis of Provence to revoke their ban on the philosophical portions of the *Mishneh Torah* and only to prohibit study of the *Guide*. One of his key teachings is that divine providence is evidenced through hidden miracles performed for the pious (differing from Maimonides' focus on the intellectual elite). Naḥmanides also accepts that necessary processes dominate the natural world and apply to Gentiles, unexceptional Jews, and even to the Jewish people as a whole.

During the last century of Spanish Jewish life, an intellectually sophisticated and theologically conservative group of thinkers, led by Ḥasdai Crescas, offered a sustained critique of the naturalism and intellectual elitism of earlier Jewish Aristotelians. After the anti-Jewish riots of 1391, subsequent large-scale conversions to Christianity, lax observance of commandments, and a tendency to see Judaism as an expression of universal philosophical ideas, Jewish thinkers articulated an approach to Judaism that would reclaim its distinctiveness, assert the particular significance of the commandments, and affirm the importance of Jewish peoplehood. They also were influenced by Christian theologians who rejected philosophical naturalism, reasserted the importance of faith over intellect, and claimed that willful decisions for God were more religiously significant than rational reflection about the divine. Avner of Burgos (Spain, ca. 1270–ca. 1347), who converted to Christianity at a mature age, was another determinist thinker.

Crescas' primary student was Joseph Albo (d. 1444); his *Sefer ha-Ikkarim* (Book of the Principles of Faith) also explores the dogmas of Judaism. Albo limits the essential Jewish principles of faith to three: the existence of God, revelation, and divine justice (linked to the idea of immortality). All this was part of an effort by the intellectual leaders and members of the community to articulate a set of beliefs and behaviors that would provide spiritual strength, security, and solidarity for a beleaguered people.

The influence of Crescas extended through Abraham Bibago (d. ca. 1489), Abraham Shalom (d. 1492), and Isaac *Arama (ca. 1420–1494), all of whom sought to reinvigorate Judaism by emphasizing faith as a willful act extending beyond the limitations of reason. They stressed spiritual closeness with the divine and ultimate salvation through the practice of the commandments. The translation of Aristotle's *Ethics* into Hebrew led to a growing respect for philosophical *ethics. The increased influence of Kabbalah is also felt during this period, with philosophers respectfully introducing some mystical ideas into their writings. They all argued against dissident Jewish intellectuals and disputed core Christian beliefs while speaking respectfully of the culture of Christian faithfulness.

Isaac *Abravanel (1437–1508) was a prolific commentator and author who also should be considered among this group of medieval thinkers. In addition to his extended commentary to the Bible, he composed works on cosmology, providence, and messianic redemption. In his *Rosh Amanah* (Head of Faith), Abravanel contends that were Judaism to require a set of creedal propositions, Maimonides' principles would be sufficient. However, the entire body of 613 *mitzvot*, rather than any set of propositions, was essential for a Jewish future.

Medieval Jewish philosophy exhibited a subtle interplay of ideas brought from Greek thought with biblical and rabbinic texts and beliefs. The religious technique of close and strong reading of biblical texts enabled Jewish philosophers to bring new ideas into harmony with classical religious language. Efforts to establish correlations among *science, philosophy, and classical Judaism were not always successful, but even when the results of rational speculation were rejected, the creative interchange added much to Judaism, developed cultural bridges among the three Abrahamic religions, and forged a conduit between the *Hellenic heritage and modern thought.

For further reading, see D. Frank and O. Leaman, eds., *The Cambridge Companion to Medieval Jewish Philosophy* (2003); D. Frank, ed., *The Jewish Philosophy Reader* (2002); K. Seeskin, ed., *The Cambridge Companion to Maimonides* (2005); and H. Tirosh-Samuelson, *Happiness in Premodern Judaism: Virtue, Knowledge, and Well-Being* (2003).

BARUCH FRYDMAN-KOHL

Thought, Modern. Jewish thought embraces all serious forms of intellectual engagement with the Jewish heritage, ranging from sacred texts and their commentaries, to systematic examinations of the ethical and metaphysical implications of Jewish belief, to reflections on the meaning of the Jewish past, to works of fiction and poetry that reflect on distinctive Jewish themes, memories, and experiences. "Modern" is a problematic term covering multiple and contradictory phenomena because modernity is a series of responses to continuous economic, social, political, scientific, technological, and cultural changes. Jewish modernity partakes of these dynamic and contradictory elements.

For purposes of this brief summary, modern Jewish thought can be divided into three phases: from the late eighteenth century to around 1881, from around 1881 to 1948, and since 1945. These periods overlap, but they convey the shifting focus of modern Jewish thought. The first era was dominated by political *emancipation and rationalist ways of conveying the essence of *Judaism; the second by responses to *antisemitism and the development of *Zionism; and the third by the shock of the *Holocaust, the desire to reconnect with tradition, and intellectual efforts to render Judaism more egalitarian and inclusive.

The eighteenth-century *Enlightenment's espousal of universal rational values led to viewing the Jews as human beings first and foremost. Moses *Mendelssohn (1729–1786), a notable figure of the German Enlightenment, is usually considered to be the first major Jewish thinker thoroughly in the modern mode. Unlike Baruch/Benedict *Spinoza (1632–1677), who was profoundly affected by the early phases of the scientific and philosophical revolutions of early modern Europe but found himself outside Judaism, Mendelssohn remained a devoted Jew all his life. His treatise *Jerusalem* presented Judaism as a religion of *reason. Judaism's *revelation was a divinely inspired set of behaviors ("revealed legislation") that sustain the Jews as a holy people. Mendelssohn launched a Jewish Enlightenment movement, the *Haskalah*.

The *Berlin *Haskalah* founded by Mendelssohn was succeeded by the *Haskalah* in Austrian *Poland (*Galicia) in the 1820s and in parts of the *Russian *Pale of Settlement (*Vilna and elsewhere) soon after. The outstanding figure of the Galician *Haskalah* is Naḥman *Krochmal (1785–1840), who created an original philosophy of the cycles of Jewish history. The Russian *maskilim* defended the integrity of Judaism and brought scenes from the biblical past to life in their novels and other works. They were also critical of the backwardness of Jewish education and the rigidity of traditional rabbis. Major figures included Isaac Baer *Levinsohn (1788–1860), Abraham Mapu (1808–1867), Judah Leib Gordon (1830–1892), Moses Leib Lilienblum (1843–1910), and Peretz Smolenskin (1842–1885; see also LITERATURE, HEBREW: *HASKALAH*).

In German-speaking lands, the Berlin *Haskalah* found its continuation in efforts to modernize the liturgy, the most direct expression of Jewish faith and hope (see WORSHIP). Universalistic and utopian dimensions were to be emphasized, whereas prayers that called for the ingathering to the Holy Land in the days of the *messiah, reestablishment of the Davidic dynasty, and rebuilding of the Jerusalem *Temple were downplayed as contradictory to the aims of emancipation. In the 1820s the *Wissenschaft des Judentums*, the movement for the scientific study of Judaism, began to develop under the leadership of Leopold *Zunz (1794–1886). Modern historical knowledge of Judaism was to be the basis for a conception of historical progress that would demonstrate that Judaism was a thoroughly up-to-date religious option. Research uncovered lost works of Jewish literature and philosophy, leading to a great appreciation of what came to be called the "golden age" of medieval *Sephardic Jewry, a model of a sophisticated Judaism that German Jewry could emulate. The new historiography led to sweeping accounts of the saga of the Jewish people through many centuries, epitomized by the writings of Heinrich *Graetz (1817–1891) and even one early espousal of Jewish national revival – *Rome and Jerusalem* (1861) by Moses Hess (1812–1875).

During the first half of the nineteenth century, a range of views developed as to how much Judaism needed to be changed to fit "the spirit of the times." Samson Raphael *Hirsch (1808–1888), the founder of what is called Neo-Orthodox Judaism (see JUDAISM, ORTHODOX: MODERN ORTHODOX), agreed that Jews should modernize their secular way of life, but insisted on loyalty to the Torah and the commandments as supernatural revelation. Rabbinic synods in the 1840s brought together German rabbis who felt that some changes were necessary but disagreed as to exactly what they should be. The exponent of the reform position in his scholarly work was Abraham *Geiger (1810–1874); Samuel Holdheim (1806–1860) was one of the more extreme reformers (see JUDAISM, REFORM: GERMANY). Zacharias *Frankel (1801–1875) advocated a "Positive-Historical Judaism" that preserved traditional modes of worship and upheld continuity of the *halakhah* with respect for *Wissenschaft des Judentums* (see JUDAISM, CONSERVATIVE). Underlying specific issues was a drastic change in attitude according to which Judaism was subject to deliberate, conscious human choice, rather than a more passive consequence of obedience to the divine. This assertiveness would reappear in a different guise in *Zionism.

Thus, nineteenth-century Jewish thinkers attempted to define the tradition in relation to a new Jewish political status as well as in response to developments in science and historiography. Ethical monotheism was held to be the core of what had to be retained in a fully modern religion. For some Modernists, Judaism seemed to be congruent with the philosophy of Immanuel Kant, who postulated the idea of God as the necessary ground for the "moral law" as integral to a purified Judaism. Jewish thought was also influenced by post-Enlightenment Romantic aspirations toward the sublime and an appreciation of national cultures. The German philosopher G. W. F. Hegel conceived of the unfolding self-consciousness of *Geist* (Spirit, Mind) as being attained through the dialectic of ideas reacting against each other toward synthesis on an ever higher level. This conception supported the view of Jewish understandings of *Torah evolving over time as Jews adapted to changing circumstances and advanced to new stages of development.

In the mid-nineteenth-century *United States, many Jews found Reform Judaism an attractive alternative to more traditional forms of Jewish practice. The most assertive sector of the Reform rabbinate drafted a statement of principles in Pittsburgh in 1885 that expressed a willingness to drop whatever was anachronistically unsuited to the mores of modern society. It affirmed the openness of Judaism to the scientific worldview and a commitment to speak out on social issues (see JUDAISM, REFORM: NORTH AMERICA). Rabbis who felt that Reform had gone too far in instituting drastic change looked to Positive-Historical Judaism as precedent for preserving halakhic continuity with due respect for historical research; in the United States this approach became known as Conservative Judaism. Those who felt that this trend did not adhere closely enough to traditional *halakhah* coalesced into what became Modern Orthodoxy (see JUDAISM entries).

In Europe, the rise of modern *antisemitism, beginning in the 1870s, and the upsurge of mass socialist and nationalist movements presented new challenges for modern Jewish thought. Jewish movements emerged that offered completely secular interpretations of what was meaningful in Jewish history and culture. Spiritual (i.e., cultural) Zionists, such as *Ahad Ha-Am (Asher Ginzberg, 1856–1927) saw in the *Hebrew-language and literature revival, along with Jewish ethnicity and values, evidence that the ancient tradition could be adapted to secular life. Political Zionists like Leon *Pinsker (1821–1891) and Theodor *Herzl (1860–1904) emphasized the urgent need for a Jewish homeland ("self-emancipation") in view of the failure of emancipation in the *Diaspora to bring about the acceptance of Jews. For the Jewish Workers *Bund of Russia, Poland, and Lithuania, *Yiddish was the language of the Jewish masses and participation in the revolutionary struggle the primary goal. Left-wing movements, Zionist and non-Zionist alike, found support for their collectivist utopianism in the words of the biblical prophets and in the traditional communal structures of Jewish life.

The prestige of Darwinian biology played a notable role in late-nineteenth-century Jewish thought. Ideologists such as Ahad Ha-Am and Simon *Dubnow (1860–1941) explained the course of Jewish history as demonstrating the strength of a Jewish collective "will to survive" that had enabled the Jewish people to adapt to different environments and epochs. Jewish peoplehood was said to offer a sense of participation that provided identity to the individual Jew, together with a vision of a better world. Secular Jewish writers from Y. L. Peretz (1852–1915) to Martin *Buber (1878–1965) drew on *Hasidism and the traditional Jewish world to portray the emotional strength of the old Jewish way of life and tensions within it.

Modern Jewish religious historical scholarship opened up a new appreciation of rabbinic Judaism. Influential works included *Some Aspects of Rabbinic Theology* (1909) and *Studies in Judaism* by Solomon *Schechter (1847–1915) and *Jewish Theology, Systematically and Historically Considered* (1918) by Kaufmann Kohler (1843–1926). Responding to the claims of liberal Christianity that it had superseded Judaism, Jewish thinkers like Leo Baeck (1873–1956) defended the ethical and rational essence of Judaism. Jewish philosophy reached a high level of professional sophistication in the Jewish writings of Hermann *Cohen (1842–1918). Cohen combined an appreciation of prophetic ethics, democratic socialism, and the continued relevance of the philosophy of Immanuel Kant in a series of philosophical works and essays culminating in *Religion of Reason out of the Sources of Judaism* (1919). His concept of the "correlation" of the ideas of God and humankind was particularly influential. Jewish scholars inspired by cultural Zionism, such as Martin Buber and Gershom *Scholem (1897–1982), played an influential role in twentieth-century Jewish thought, as did Hermann Cohen's student, Franz *Rosenzweig (1886–1929).

In the 1920s and 1930s the *Reconstructionist position advocated by Mordecai M. *Kaplan (1881–1983), a dissident faculty member of the Conservative *Jewish Theological Seminary in *New York City, captured the attention of quite a few Reform and Conservative rabbis. Kaplan drew on sociological theory, progressive social values, and theories of religious naturalism to emphasize the evolving nature of Jewish civilization, the need for modern Judaism to come to terms with democracy and modern science, and a "transnatural" (but not supernatural) God that sustained human efforts to achieve self-realization. By the 1930s some prominent Reform rabbis took up the cause of Zionism and social reform in the Columbus Platform, which referred positively to *klal Yisrael* (the whole of the Jewish people) and Jewish practices that had previously been set aside by most Reform Jews.

In post–World War I Europe, however, expressions of cultural pessimism were moving theology in new directions. Yehezkel Kaufmann (1889–1963) applied a methodology derived from the sociology of religion in his 1930 analysis of Jewish history, *Golah ve-Nekhar* (Exile and Estrangement). His *History of the Religion of Israel* (1960) offered a conception of the uniqueness of *Israelite religion; his work reveals a growing presence of Jewish scholars in *Bible scholarship. *Religionswissenschaft* (the academic study of religion as such) was concerned with the varieties of experiencing the holy. Philosophical idealism gave way to phenomenology and what was later called existentialism. The writings of Franz Rosenzweig avoided philosophical reductionism, advocating what he called a "new thinking," based on open-minded reading of Jewish texts and selective appropriation of Jewish practices. Along with Martin Buber he began to publish a German translation of the Bible that sought to recapture the immediate effects of the Hebrew original. Buber himself was religiously unobservant, but appreciative of the inner religious impulse; his *I and Thou* focused on the intersubjective encounter in the here-and-now with others, including *God as the Eternal Thou.

The most recent phase of modern Jewish thought took shape after World War II. A central issue was the implications of the *Holocaust. Some reiterated that the suffering of the innocent has been a theme of Jewish thought at least since the biblical book of *Job and the *midrash (Michael Wyschogrod [b. 1928], Eliezer *Berkovits [1908–1992], and Emil *Fackenheim [1916–2003]), whereas others argued that the religious implications of the Holocaust mandated new theologies (Richard *Rubenstein [b. 1924], Irving Greenberg [b. 1933]).

Contemporary Jewish thought has moved in different directions. The academic study of Judaism and of the Jewish experience has achieved a high level of recognition that the proponents of *Wissenschaft des Judentums* only dreamed of, and a new generation of scholars has produced meticulous studies in almost every aspect of Jewish life. So far, few philosophies of Judaism have taken up the reconciliation of religious faith with modern science and historiography (to be sure, that is the case with general philosophy as well). The predominant tendency has been a reappraisal of elements of Judaism that Jewish Modernists had previously neglected. Emmanuel *Levinas (1906–1995), the most internationally recognized Jewish philosopher of the last decades of the twentieth century, made the primacy of *ethics the starting point of his philosophy, but kept his phenomenology separate from his readings of talmudic texts.

An increasing appreciation of traditional Judaism is heralded in a series of works of poetic power by Abraham Joshua *Heschel (1907–1972), who evoked the spirituality of the lost world of pious East European Jewry and the pathos of a *God who cared passionately about human life. As a result of the scholarship of Gershom Scholem and others, Jewish *mystical writings found a new respectability and have been examined for complex ideas of divine creativity. Thinkers who have found spiritual insight in the Ḥasidic masters include Martin Buber and Arthur Green. Contemporary Jewish thinkers have also drawn on midrashic and halakhic literature for insights on social and technological change, including challenges in bioethics and *environmental concerns (see ETHICS entries).

Against this neo-traditionalism has been the effort to confront and expunge sexist features of Judaism. Feminist Jewish thinkers, including Judith Plaskow (b. 1947), Susanna Heschel (b. 1952), Rachel Adler (b. 1943), and Hava Tirosh-Samuelson (b. 1950), have outlined a sweeping reorientation of Jewish spirituality to overcome ingrained patriarchal bias (see JUDAISM, FEMINIST). Similar reconsiderations have occurred with respect to *homosexuality.

By the end of the first decade of the twenty-first century, modern Jewish thought has become more pluralistic than ever. The lines among the liberal denominations have become attenuated while Orthodox Jewish thought in America and Israel (Joseph B. *Soloveitchik [1903–1993]; David Hartman [b. 1931]) has gained self-confidence. Humanistic Judaism espouses an anti-theistic religious reading of Judaism, whereas Jewish Renewal emphasizes immediate spiritual experience (see entries under JUDAISM). Overall, the tendency in recent Jewish thought by writers such as Arthur Green, Eugene B. Borowitz (b. 1924), and Neil Gillman (b. 1933) has been to affirm that Judaism can be a guide to life and that meanings applicable to contemporary concerns can be extracted from a range of Jewish texts.

ROBERT M. SELTZER

Tiberias: See GALILEE

Tikkun Olam (mending or correcting the world) is the most potent operative term in Lurianic Kabbalah (see KABBALAH, LURIANIC); it has expressed the messianic endeavor of believers in the kabbalistic worldview from the seventeenth century to the present (see MESSIANISM entries). Its source is the talmudic term *tikkun ha-olam*, a reference to deeds that enable the world to function correctly (used scores of times in the *Talmuds, especially in BT *Gittin* 3b). In the Lurianic myth, it represents the third and final phase in the cosmic-historical myth of creation. The first is the *tzimtzum*, the divine contraction within itself to create empty space in which emanation and creation could take place; the second phase is the *shevirah*, "*breaking of the vessels," the catastrophe in which the divine plan broke down. The third phase will be *tikkun*, which will correct that catastrophe and subsequent disasters and achieve the messianic *redemption of the divine and earthly realms.

Human beings advance the process of *tikkun* through fulfilling divine *commandments, observing ethical norms, and being spiritually devoted to *God. In terms of the Lurianic myth, each good deed frees a divine spark imprisoned by the powers of evil, strengthening the positive forces in the cosmic struggle between good and evil; conversely, each sin has the opposite effect. When all sparks are returned to their rightful place, *tikkun* will be complete and redemption achieved. The concept has been universally accepted by Orthodox Jewish thinkers in the last four centuries. The theologians of the heretical *Sabbatean movement in the seventeenth and eighteenth centuries, who were followers of *Shabbatai Zevi, assigned a central role in this process to the messiah. Modern *Hasidic sects believe that their leaders devote their mystical powers to this goal. For further reading, see G. Scholem, *Major Trends in Jewish Mysticism* (1954); and idem, *On the Kabbalah and Its Symbolism* (1960).

JOSEPH DAN

***Tikkun Olam*: Contemporary Understandings.** In the early twenty-first century, many Jews have interpreted *tikkun olam* as a Jewish imperative to work for ethical harmony, social justice, and *ecological practices, arguing that repairing the world is closely linked to Jewish values of righteousness and lovingkindness. See, for example, N. J. Diament, ed., *Tikkun Olam: Social Responsibility in Jewish Thought and Law* (1997); and E. N. Dorff, *The Way into Tikkun Olam: Repairing the World* (2007).

JUDITH R. BASKIN

Tisha B'Av, the 9th of *Av, is a major *fast day on the Jewish *calendar. When it falls on the *Sabbath it is deferred to the next day. According to tradition, this is the day on which both the First and Second *Temples were destroyed, and it is also associated with other disasters in Jewish history. Observances include communal reading of *Lamentations and other laments (*kinnot*); the book of *Job is customarily read in *Sephardic communities. Like Yom Kippur, Tisha B'Av has traditionally been a day of abstention from eating, drinking, bathing, engaging in sexual relations, and wearing leather shoes.

Tishri, the seventh month of the Jewish calendar, usually occurs in September and/or October according to the Gregorian calendar. The *High Holidays of Rosh Ha-Shanah (1st and 2nd) and Yom Kippur (10th) take place in Tishri, as does the festival of *Sukkot (15th to 21st) and the associated days of Hoshanah Rabbah (21st), *Shemini Atzeret (22nd), and *Simḥat Torah (22nd or 23rd depending on location and practice). **See also CALENDAR; CALENDAR: MONTHS OF THE YEAR.**

Tkhines is the Yiddish term for "supplicatory prayers" (Hebrew, *teḥinnot*). They are often associated with women's synagogue and domestic vernacular devotions in early modern Europe. See PRAYER: WOMEN'S DEVOTIONAL; and WOMEN: EARLY MODERN EUROPE.

Tobiads were a high-ranking Israelite family in *Second Temple times whose members were active from the fifth to the second century BCE. Their estate at Araq el Emir between Amman and the Jordan River was considered *Ammonite in biblical times. However, the Tobiads were habitually involved in the affairs of *Jerusalem.

Tobiah I, the first known Tobiad, had a hostile relationship with *Nehemiah. He was well connected and highly regarded in Jerusalem, and both he and his son married into aristocratic families. The high priest, Eliashib, allocated a chamber for him in the *Temple. However, Nehemiah removed Tobiah from the Temple and had his chamber purified. He also called Tobiah an "Ammonite servant" (Neh 2:19), suggesting that Jews were to shun his company.

A Tobiah II, thought to have been active ca. 300 BCE, is attested by two *Aramaic inscriptions from Araq el Emir. Tobiah III appears in the Zenon papyri. In 257, he sent letters to *Ptolemy Philadelphus and his finance minister, Apollonius, referring to presents sent to the king and his minister. Another papyrus (259) attests that Tobiah was the commander of a Ptolemaic military fort at Araq el Emir (V. A. Tcherikover, *Corpus Papyrorum Judaicarum* I [1957], 115–29). Some of his soldiers were Greek, and others were Jewish. Affinity with the Ptolemies is also evident in the tale about Joseph, son of Tobiah, and his son Hyrcanus in the writings of *Josephus (*Antiquities* 12.156–222, 228–236). These must be the son and grandson of Tobiah III; not only is Joseph's father's name identical with that of Tobiah III but also the careers of Joseph and Hyrcanus, covering the years ca. 230–175, are a chronological fit. The activities of Hyrcanus in Trans-Jordan seem apt, and the description of his fort resembles the archeological remains of Araq el Emir.

The tale makes its heroes the rulers of *Palestine's non-Jewish elements; Joseph is the country's tax farmer, and his son levies tribute from the Trans-Jordan barbarians. Both treat their non-Jewish taxpayers harshly, and both are depicted as extremely loyal to King Ptolemy, to the extent that Hyrcanus is portrayed as hostile to *Seleucus IV. The main points of this story are untrustworthy; if Hyrcanus had not accommodated himself to his new Seleucid masters, he would not have placed his money in the Temple while Seleucus IV was king. Moreover, the author of 2 *Maccabees, who mentions the Hyrcanus treasure to dissuade a Seleucid minister from sacking the sanctuary

(3:10–11), clearly considered Hyrcanus to be a respected partisan of Seleucus.

When internal strife plagued Jerusalem in 169 BCE, "the sons of Tobiah" sided with Menelaus and Antiochus IV. According to Josephus, they demonstrated loyalty to Antiochus by championing *Hellenism (*Jewish War* 1.31–32; *Antiquities* 12.239–241). These hellenizing tendencies were not new; Tobiah III used the greeting formula, "many thanks to the gods," in a letter to Apollonius, and statues of animals were found at Araq el Emir. However, in 163 when the enemies of the *Hasmoneans captured the family stronghold, some of the Tobiad soldiers were away fighting in Judea in support of the Jewish cause. Some of these combatants probably survived, but they, like their Tobiad commanders, are not mentioned after 163. For further reading, see E. Will and F. Larché, eds., *Iraq al-Amir* (1991); and D. Gera, *Judaea and Mediterranean Politics, 219 to 161 B.C.E.* (1998), 36–58.

DOV GERA

Tobit, Book of: See APOCRYPHA

Torah. The word *torah* can be understood broadly as "teaching" or "instruction." Torah sometimes designates the first of the three divisions of the Hebrew *Bible, also known as the Five Books of Moses or the *Pentateuch. The Torah contains the books of *Genesis, *Exodus, *Leviticus, *Numbers, and *Deuteronomy.

Yet Jews have also used the word "Torah" to refer to the entire body of Hebrew scriptures as God's *revelation to the people of Israel. It is in this context that "Written Torah" refers to the entire *Bible and "Oral Torah" designates the voluminous *rabbinic literature that grew up around the Written Torah. This Oral Torah (see BIBLICAL COMMENTARY: FROM THE MIDDLE AGES TO 1800; RABBINIC LITERATURE: MISHNAH AND TALMUDS), which was decisive for Jewish life, came to assume the sanctity and inviolability of the written word. The Rabbis taught that both components of divine revelation were delivered to the people of Israel at Mount Sinai through the mediation of *Moses and subsequently passed down through later prophets and other recognized authoritative figures (M. *Avot 1). Rabbinic *Judaism understands these two sources of divine instruction to be coexistent and equally essential.

Torah also refers to the Torah scroll, the handwritten, rolled parchment document used in *synagogue ritual, on which the Five Books of Moses are inscribed. As the symbolic representation of divine revelation, the Torah scroll is treated with the utmost respect and veneration (**see CEREMONIAL OBJECTS; TORAH READING**).

JUDITH R. BASKIN

Torah Reading. The center of liturgical activity in the *synagogue on the *Sabbath and *festivals is the communal reading from the Hebrew *Bible. This reading comprises a portion from the *Pentateuch, which is read continuously in a fixed cycle on Sabbaths and in a segmented way on the festivals and other specific days, such as days of *fasting or the first days of the Hebrew months (*Rosh Ḥodesh). On the Sabbath and festivals, selected chapters from the *Prophets (see BIBLE: PROPHETS AND PROPHECY; PROPHETS [*NEVI'IM*]) attuned to the *Torah readings are added (*Haftarah). On Sabbath afternoons, on Mondays, and on Thursdays, the first part of the following weekly unit is read. This custom dates to the *Second Temple period (according to some traditions it can be traced to the book of *Nehemiah, chapter 8), an era when divinely revealed scriptures began to be perceived as the most important channel of communication between human beings and God. In that era, sacrifices, prophecy, and dreams– the three most important venues of communication in the biblical period – ceased to play as important a role in Judaism. Instead, gathering for reading God's words, explaining them, and looking for their relevance to the ever-changing circumstances of life took place in the newly established institution of that time, the synagogue.

Our knowledge about Torah reading comes mainly from *rabbinic literature, in which the *Mishnah and other sources deal at length with various aspects of this custom. Although reading from the Torah on the festivals became fixed at a very early stage (because the reading was connected to the liturgical content of each specific holiday, such as reading the story of the exodus on *Passover), Sabbath readings took different forms. In the *Land of Israel, the Torah was read continuously in anything between 137 and 175 weeks, depending on local customs. These customs were flexible enough to allow the community to read at least the minimum of twenty-one verses (as ascribed by M. *Megillah* 4) and up to the average reading of forty verses as attested in various sources. It seems that different communities saw no harm in reading the Torah in the so-called, if imprecise, triennial cycle (137 weeks are always less than three years, while 175 weeks are more than three years). In these cycles the Torah was read at a moderate pace, without having a fixed date on which to start the new cycle of reading. As opposed to this custom, the Jews of *Babylon adopted an annual cycle of reading, which began every year on the first Sabbath after the holiday of *Sukkot. In this fixed cycle the Torah was divided into fifty-four units (each called a *parasha*; pl. *parashot*) that were read simultaneously in all synagogues (the last was read on the ninth day of *Sukkot). Only a few Jewish leap years have more than fifty-three Sabbaths; in all other years two *parashot* are joined and read together according to fixed rules. This fixed cycle became standard in the post-rabbinic period, both in the communities of the east and those of the west, thanks to the authority of the Babylonian *Talmud and its impact on Jewish religious life. In liberal forms of contemporary *Judaism, some attempts have been made to revert to variations of the ancient triennial reading but only time will tell if these modifications will prevail. In any case, the Torah reading remains the central core of Sabbath and festival *worship.

It should be noted that reading from the Torah was always accompanied in antiquity by a translation into the vernacular (see *TARGUM*) and almost invariably by a *sermon that expanded the biblical text in various directions. For further reading, see C. Perrot, "The Reading of the Bible in the Ancient Synagogue," in *Mikra: Text, Translation, Reading and Interpretation of the Hebrew Bible in Ancient Judaism and Early Christianity*, ed. M. J. Mulder and H. Sysling (1998), 137–59.

AVIGDOR SHINAN

Tosafists were rabbinic scholars in northern *France and *Germany during the twelfth and thirteenth centuries. They are best known for *Tosafot* (lit. "addenda"), glosses to the Babylonian *Talmud that are printed in the standard editions of the Talmud along with the commentary of *Rashi (Solomon ben Isaac [d. 1105]).

The earliest Tosafists were Rashi's family members or students, including his son-in-law Meir ben Samuel (ca. 1060–ca. 1135) and Isaac ben Asher, who later settled in Speyer. Rashi's grandson, Jacob ben Meir (Rabbeinu Tam [1100–1171]) of Ramerupt, and his great-grandson (and student of Rabbeinu Tam), Isaac ben Samuel (Ri) of Dampierre, influenced the method and style of the *Tosafot*. Students of Rabbeinu Tam were active in France, *England, the Rhineland, southern Germany, Bohemia, *Hungary, and beyond. Ri was responsible in large measure for the written formulations of Rabbeinu Tam's teachings. In turn, Ri's *Tosafot* were collected and edited by his student, Samson ben Abraham of Sens. The so-called *Tosafot Sens* are among the most authoritative extant collections. Ri's work was also continued by his son Elḥanan (who died a martyr's death during his father's lifetime), by Barukh ben Isaac (author of the halakhic treatise, *Sefer ha-Terumah*), and in the thirteenth century by Judah ben Isaac (Sirleon) of Paris. Students of Ri transmitted tosafist materials to *Provence and northern *Spain, where they were important for *Jonah ben Abraham of Gerona, *Naḥmanides, and other thirteenth-century Spanish scholars.

The tosafist method was based on close readings of the talmudic text and Rashi's commentary. The Tosafists raised internal linguistic questions and called attention to inconsistencies (along with verifications of the correct text of the Talmud itself), followed by an analysis of parallel passages in the Babylonian Talmud and a wide range of other *halakhic and *aggadic sources. They resolved contradictions by use of the dialectical method and according to fixed methodological principles. In addition, they also considered the implications of apparent inconsistencies for Jewish law and custom. Because the Talmud was the source of halakhic decision making (see *HALAKHAH*), it was necessary to resolve all forms of contradictions or inconsistencies, conceptual or linguistic, within the talmudic corpus, so that the Talmud could remain the ultimate arbiter of Jewish law and life.

Thirteenth-century French Tosafists also produced halakhic works and rulings. Moses of Coucy's *Sefer Mizvot Gadol* and the *pesakim* (decisions) of Jeḥiel of Paris are two examples of this shift. Nonetheless, the tosafist study hall at Evreux (in Normandy) continued to issue different forms of *Tosafot* comments, including the *Tosafot Shitah*, a presentation of the talmudic *sugya* with various explanations and tosafist discussions. Some scholars have suggested that this format was in response to the trial (and burning) of the Talmud around 1242 in Paris, after which the need to preserve remaining texts of the Talmud (and Rashi's commentary) became more acute. Others see this development as an effort (inspired perhaps by the teachings of the German Pietists [see MIDDLE AGES: ḤASIDEI ASHKENAZ]) to tone down the complex dialectic of the twelfth century in order to focus on the simple meaning of the talmudic text and its relevance for Jewish law (*halakhah*).

Although northern French Tosafists typically produced glosses to the text of the Talmud and to Rashi, twelfth-century German Tosafists, such as Eliezer ben Nathan (Raban) of Mainz and his grandson, Eliezer ben Joel ha-Levi (Rabiah), composed free-standing works presenting both talmudic comments and legal decisions and rulings. German

Tosafists tended to preserve their written *responsa, and German dialectic was more muted than its French counterpart. These divergences may have resulted from differing leadership roles: Northern French Tosafists saw themselves principally as academy heads (*roshei yeshivah*) and considered the interpretation of the underlying talmudic texts to be most important. In contrast, although many German Tosafists were also academy heads, their principal role was as communal judges (*dayyanim*).

These differences continued throughout the late twelfth and early thirteenth centuries, when there was relatively little contact between French and German centers. Several large legal works composed by German Tosafists during this period have been lost; two examples of such lost books are Ephraim ben Isaac of Regensburg's *Arba'ah Rashim* (The Four Heads) and *Sefer Ha-Ḥokhmah* (Book of Wisdom) of Barukh ben Samuel of Mainz. Although the *Tosafot* form ultimately became attached (via *printing) to the text of the Talmud, these larger and free-standing German works were not as easily retained. Isaac ben Moses of Vienna's thirteenth-century *Sefer Or Zarua*, which represented a renewed joining of German and northern French traditions (as well as those from *Austria and *Italy), contains *Tosafot* comments as well as more independent halakhic formulations, in addition to responsa and other rulings. It was not printed until 1862.

The availability of *Tosafot* texts was aided by late-thirteenth-century compilations directed by Perez of Corbeil, Eliezer of Touques (whose place of residence and study has been debated) and *Asher ben Jeḥiel (Rosh), who fled to Toledo, *Spain, in 1305 to escape persecution in Germany. Asher's teacher, *Meir ben Barukh of Rothenburg, and some of his students amalgamated German and French tosafist methods and compositions with the major pillars of *Sephardic *halakhah*. This combination reflects, in part, the general decline of *Ashkenazic Jewry, especially apparent in the second half of the thirteenth century.

Some have noted similarities between tosafist methods and Christian scholastics. Although there were direct scholarly contacts between twelfth-century Jewish and Christian biblical exegetes, there is no similar evidence with respect to legal literature. Perhaps social or economic interactions between Christian and Jewish scholars introduced Jews to general tendencies in contemporary Christian dialectic, if not the specific texts and literary formulations that supported it. Institutional shifts between pre-Crusade and tosafist academies and the twelfth-century change in the nature of authorship parallel the slightly earlier shift from monasteries to cathedral schools in the Christian educational system.

Recent research suggests that a number of Tosafists were keenly interested in biblical exegesis (see BIBLICAL COMMENTARY: FROM THE MIDDLE AGES TO 1800). Samuel ben Meir (Rashbam) and Joseph ben Isaac of Orleans (Bekhor Shor), both from the twelfth century, are known for their *peshat* exegesis. Yom Tov of Joigny, Jacob of Orleans, Isaiah di Trani (who studied in Germany with Simḥah of Speyer and came into contact with materials by Rabbeinu Tam and his students), and Moses of Coucy sought to develop Rashi's exegetical methods further. German and northern French Tosafists composed liturgical poems throughout the twelfth and thirteenth centuries, favoring genres that had not been fully used previously (see POETRY, MEDIEVAL: CHRISTIAN EUROPE). A number of Tosafists were also interested in Jewish *magic and *mysticism, especially *hekhalot* literature (see MYSTICISM: *HEKHALOT* AND *MERKAVAH* LITERATURE). Much of the data for tosafist involvement in these and other disciplines are found in manuscripts and will become clearer and better known as these texts are studied and published. For further reading, see E. Kanarfogel, *Peering through the Lattices: Mystical, Magical, and Pietistic Dimensions in the Tosafist Period* (1992).

EPHRAIM KANARFOGEL

Tosefta ("supplement"; *Aramaic for Hebrew *tosefet*) is the largest collection of teachings outside of the *Mishnah that are attributed to the *Tannaim (ca. 70–220 CE), the foundational layer of rabbinic sages in Roman *Palestine. The six-part structure of the Tosefta is very similar to that of the Mishnah. It contains all but four of the Mishnah's tractates, but it is between three and four times longer. Its compilation has been dated anywhere from the third to the fifth centuries, and perhaps even later. Its language is mostly Middle Hebrew, like that of the Mishnah. The best medieval manuscript in terms of completeness and accuracy, ms. Vienna, probably derives from fourteenth-century *Spain. It served as the basis for the leading scholarly edition by Saul Lieberman (1955–92). An older, inferior *Ashkenazi manuscript, ms. Erfurt, contains only the first four orders; it served as the basis of Moses Samuel Zuckermandel's edition (1880, 1882; reprinted with supplement by S. Lieberman, 1970). A now lost manuscript was the basis for the first printed edition (Venice, 1521–22). The only complete English translation was produced by Jacob Neusner and his students (6 vols., 1977–86; reprinted 2 vols., 2002).

The relationship between the Tosefta and the more authoritative Mishnah is a central and still vexing research question. Traditional scholarship characterized the Tosefta as a supplement to the Mishnah. Various medieval sources, including Rav Sherira *Gaon in his famous letter to the Jews of Kairouan, as well as *Rashi and *Maimonides, identified different Rabbis as the Tosefta's redactor. They included one of Rabbi *Akiva's last students, Rabbi Neḥemiah, based on a tradition attributed to Rabbi Joḥanan in BT *Sanhedrin* 86a. In fact, however, Rabbi Neḥemiah's attributed statements sometimes contradict the Tosefta's anonymous positions. A medieval authority, Rabbi Samson of Chinon, famously noted that "Tosefta" in the Talmud "is not what we call Tosefta." Other prominent candidates for the Tosefta's redactor proposed by medieval authorities include *Judah Ha-Nasi's colleague, Rabbi Ḥiyya; his student, R. Hoshayah (or Oshayah); and Bar Kappara. The academic consensus today is that "our" Tosefta's redactors cannot be identified.

The traditional characterization of the Tosefta as a supplement to the Mishnah stemmed from factors in addition to its name ("Supplement") and the various traditions regarding its editor: its larger volume, its reliance on late *Tannaim, its frequent identifications of the authors of parallel teachings cited anonymously in the Mishnah, its propensity to incorporate more scriptural exegesis than the Mishnah, and its greater quantity of *aggadah*. Another puzzle is the fact that it contains material in common with, at variance with, and independent of the Mishnah. The consensus today is that the Tosefta and the Mishnah were derived from earlier tannaitic collections and that the Tosefta seems to contain tannaitic traditions that pre-date the editing of the Mishnah. Recent studies have shown that the Tosefta as an edited collection appears not to have been available to the redactors of either the Jerusalem or the Babylonian *Talmuds. The Tosefta may provide evidence of changes to the Babylonian Talmud's versions of ostensibly tannaitic traditions, or *beraitot. Tosef-tan material was studied in the Babylonian academies of the *Geonim, perhaps in collections generically known as tosefata (plural for tosefta). For these and other reasons, the Tosefta's research value is tremendous, notwithstanding its complex transmissional and editorial history.

For further reading, see P. Mandel, "The Tosefta," in *The Cambridge History of Judaism: Volume 4: The Late Roman-Rabbinic Period*, ed. S. T. Katz (2006), 316–35; "The Tosefta," in *Introduction to the Talmud and Midrash*, ed. H. L. Strack and G. Stemberger (1992), 167–81.   ROBERT DAUM

Tourism refers to short-term, nonessential visits made to sites of interest. As a leisure activity away from home, Jewish tourism reflects and highlights social values present but often submerged in daily life. Such travel may also embody models and values designed to transform the participants' outlook, because both tours and sites may be crafted by various Jewish constituencies to promote particular points of view. Hence, Jewish tourism frequently expresses a relationship with the past while outlining a program for the future.

*PILGRIMAGE: Although modern tourism is often seen as originating in the eighteenth-century Grand Tour, it bears some continuity with traditions of religious pilgrimage. The *Torah commands thrice-yearly pilgrimages to the *Jerusalem *Temple (Exod 22:17; Deut 16:16). In the late *Second Temple period, pilgrimage to the Temple was one of the most widespread religiously motivated contemporary movements of people, and it profoundly shaped the nature of Jerusalem. The existential experience of oneness created in the gathering and common worship of Jews from all over the Near East made the Temple a unique site of social and spiritual convergence. In the centuries following the Temple's destruction in 70 CE, Jews and Jewish groups made pilgrimages to its ruins. Pilgrimages to tombs of tzaddikim (righteous sages) received new impetus through the practices of sixteenth-century *kabbalists in *Safed. Later, *Hasidic leaders encouraged mass pilgrimages of their followers to visit rebbes during the *festivals. Hilulot (celebrations) at cemeteries, which commemorate the anniversary of the deaths (ascent of the souls) of the righteous, were common, especially in *North Africa; these mass gatherings were also important times for cementing communal ties.

JEWISH RESORTS AND EXCURSIONS: The mass migrations of Jews to Western Europe, the *United States, and *Israel in the nineteenth and twentieth centuries; the intensive *urbanization of Jewish populations; the increase in leisure time and disposable income; the institution of paid vacations; and the greater ease of international travel created new tourism practices. These included visits to spas, ski resorts, or summer retreats that became ethnic vacation enclaves. Hotels and restaurants were built that catered to the religious or cultural needs of Jewish publics by supplying *kosher food, *synagogues, and, occasionally, *ritual baths, as well as *Passover seders and Jewish-oriented lectures and entertainment. The best known of these North

American vacation locations are the "Borsht Belt" in the Catskill mountains of New York State, the Laurentian mountains (north of Montreal), and Miami Beach (see UNITED STATES: SOUTH FLORIDA); others existed and some continue to exist in many European countries. With the decline of religious observance and the weakening of traditional social structures and strictures, these resorts became not only centers for Jewish family vacations but also meeting places for Jewish singles. Yet, these same forces eventually led to the decline of many of the resort centers catering exclusively to Jews.

HERITAGE AND GENEALOGICAL TOURS: Following the mass global Jewish migrations of the twentieth century, and once Jews were comfortably settled in their new homes – in *Israel or in the West – many returned to the "Old Country" to meet remaining family, immerse themselves temporarily in a nostalgic past, and display the prosperity achieved in their new places of residence. With growing cultural and temporal distance from the home country, such tours became sites of imagination of a mythic communal Jewish past, rather than of memories of a lived personal experience. This imagined past became more vivid when compared to a more fragmented, alienated present identity (as a result of acculturation in the West or the decline of commitment to *Zionism in Israel). In some cases, especially in contemporary Jewish tourism to *Eastern Europe, these voyages are often linked to genealogical research done on the *internet; in the case of North African Jewish immigrants, Old Country tourism is often combined with pilgrimages to saints' tombs, visits to ancestral homes and to tombs of family members, and sightseeing and shopping. These visits are an important source of capital, both economic and social, for small remaining local Jewish communities. Such tourism also supports certain threatened cultural forms, such as Andalusian *music, which is less popular among contemporary Moroccan Muslims. Through such tours, perceptions of center and periphery, *Diaspora and homeland, may be altered, sometimes in ways not foreseen by organizers or travelers. Thus, Israeli travelers seeking their North African roots in Morocco may come to find that they are far more Israeli than they thought (A. Levy, "Homecoming to the Diaspora: Nation and State in Visits of Israelis to Morocco," in *Homecomings: Unsettling Paths of Return*, ed. F. Markowitz and A. H. Stefansson [2004], 91–108).

For those seeking their ancient heritage, such as golden age Jewish *Spain or the *ghetto of *Venice, memory is replaced by culture and history. In such places, the small local Jewish communities play little role in the development or narration of Jewish tourist sites. Tours also take place to sites of first Jewish immigration, such as in visits to Ellis Island or the Lower East Side in *New York City. Here, the narratives told at the sites may adapt themselves to tourist expectations, while the present surroundings are likely to disappoint those seeking a frozen past painted in nostalgic hues. Jewish tour sites are promoted by a substantial literature, ranging from tourist bureau pamphlets to Jewish travel guides to large coffee-table books. Media products, such as *Fiddler on the Roof* or *Schindler's List*, are also instrumental in shaping the Jewish tourist map and visitors' expectations of heritage sites (see FILM: UNITED STATES).

Another destination is "exotic" Jewish communities, which combine the lure of the other with the connection to an imagined common tradition. This type of tourism includes visits to what many secular Jews see as representative of a more traditional "past," such as the Ultra-Orthodox (see JUDAISM, ORTHODOX: ULTRA-ORTHODOX) quarter of Meah Shearim in *Jerusalem. Other ethnically exotic tour destinations include Kai-feng in *China and *Cochin in *India. In some cases, visits become "missions" that combine tourism with financial or volunteer aid to a local Jewish community; such ventures are increasingly popular in *Latin America and parts of the former *Soviet Union.

In addition, the thirst for Jewish heritage may be satisfied through day trips to Jewish *museums, as well as the integration of Jewish museums (and old *synagogues) into broader vacation itineraries. These museums range from one-room synagogue annexes promoting local Jewish history to broadly conceived cultural centers (Jewish Museum in New York), to museums erected by state governments to introduce non-Jews to the basics of Judaism and glorify the Jewish history of the country (Jewish Museum in *Berlin). Jewish history and heritage museums, including museums that address the *Holocaust, define and authorize a variety of cultural messages ranging from Zionism to Jewish–Gentile symbiosis, from religious observance to the preservation of American freedoms and the need for tolerance among varying racial, ethnic, and religious groups (B. Kirshenblatt-Gimblett, "Exhibiting Jews," in *Destination Culture: Tourism, Museums, and Heritage* [2001], 83–131).

HOLOCAUST TOURS: Since the 1980s, visits to Holocaust sites in *Poland have become increasingly popular on both the Israeli and the *Diaspora agenda. Many culminate in the "March of the Living," during which thousands of Israeli and Diaspora Jewish youth walk in a flag-waving procession from *Auschwitz to Birkenau. On such tours, the abandoned Jewish sites become markers of destruction rather than nostalgic venues of past life. Poland is depicted as a Jewish cemetery and the Holocaust as the inevitable end to life there. The ideological agenda is to reaffirm the precariousness of Jewish life in the Diaspora and the immanent dangers of *antisemitism; strengthened commitment to Israel's security and opposition to assimilation are presented as necessary responses to the Holocaust (J. Feldman, *Above the Death-pits, Beneath the Flag: Youth Voyages to Holocaust Poland and the Performance of Israeli Identity* [2008]).

In recent years, several European countries whose Jewish communities were destroyed by the Holocaust have created entire Jewish landscapes, now devoid of living Jews. These include festivals of Jewish culture, restaurants offering "Jewish" food, restorations of abandoned Jewish synagogues and cemeteries, and revivals of art forms like klezmer *music. Many of these sites are promoted by national governments and local entrepreneurs in order to attract income from Jewish tourists; in some cases, developing Jewish heritage sites may broadcast a distancing from past antisemitism to a larger constituency. Alternatively, these sites may seek to recast the country's past as more tolerant or multicultural than it actually was, providing present groups fostering such values with a greater historical authority. Thus, local actors come to reshape their own heritage through touristic representations of Jews and Judaism (see R. E. Gruber, *Virtually Jewish: Reinventing Jewish Culture in Europe* [2002]).

TRAVEL TO ISRAEL: Among the most important contemporary Jewish touristic practices are visits to Israel by Jews from the Diaspora; these make up more than 20% of Israel's incoming tourism. Although individuals and families often spend substantial time visiting family members, group tours sponsored by synagogues, Jewish *Community Centers, or philanthropic organizations emphasize the integrity of local communities and the strengthening of their commitments to the State of Israel. A number of synagogues, Jewish day schools, and other organizations sponsor *Bar/Bat Mitzvah tours, thus integrating Israel into a family-focused rite of passage. These tours also tend to integrate and foster other practices that link Diaspora communities with Israel, including *philanthropy (mission tours), political support (solidarity tours), and *immigration (aliyah) orientation tours).

Many Jewish youth organizations, as well as Jewish day schools and synagogues, promote summer programs to Israel, some combining touring with study, archeological excavation, short-term volunteer service, or paramilitary training. Although the theme of "Jewish peoplehood" is prominent in almost all youth programs, no less important is the creation of an all-Jewish Diaspora social environment to strengthen future commitment to the community back home. Perhaps the most prominent project of the late twentieth and early twenty-first centuries has been Birthright Israel/*Taglit*, which offers free trips to Israel for Jewish university students and young people in their twenties. These trips are geared to strengthen Jewish identity, particularly for less affiliated Jewish youth, as well as increase support for Israel on college campuses (B. Chazan, ed., *The Israel Experience: Studies in Jewish Identity and Youth Culture* [2001]; see also, ISRAEL, STATE OF entries).

Almost all Jewish tour groups to Israel visit *Masada, pray at the Western Wall, and spend the *Sabbath in Jerusalem; many include speeches by Israeli politicians, rabbis, or educators. For most tourists, however, the contact with Israeli peers is minimal because such tours reinforce a monolithic mythic image of Israel over meaningful contact with the variety of modern Israeli cultures. On the margins of the map are tours focused on particular social or religious issues or with orientations critical of Israeli government positions ("alternative" tours).

In the present global culture, which presents Jews with a wide, often bewildering variety of options for being Jewish and a decline in traditional modes of expressing and performing "Jewishness," the experiential, short-term, sensory immersion offered by tourism will make it an increasingly important practice in the formation of Jewish identity.

JACKIE FELDMAN

Travel Writing: Middle Ages and Early Modern Period.

Spanning ages and cultures, travel has served as an almost universal literary subject, expressed in a variety of genres and forms. Pre-modern Jewish travel writing encompasses a disparate corpus of mostly *Hebrew texts that originate between the twelfth and eighteenth centuries. It includes travel guides; travelogues, diaries, and letters (sometimes in combination); and poems in which the travel motif may be used as a metaphor for a spiritual journey. The emergence of Jewish travel writing appears to be associated with the Crusades (see MIDDLE AGES: CRUSADES), when the growth of sea traffic from Western Europe to the Levant (eastern Mediterranean) also brought Jewish pilgrims and merchants to the Middle East and beyond. Just as medieval Jewish *pilgrimage to the *Land of Israel/*Palestine echoes certain patterns of Christian pilgrimage to the same region, the earliest Hebrew travel writings resemble the Latin (or vernacular) *itinerarium* (travel log). These documents range from brief notations of distances covered and places visited to more elaborate narratives. There are about a dozen Hebrew "itineraries," apparently from the twelfth and thirteenth centuries; all originate in Christian Europe, the region where most Jewish travel writers lived. Most of these itineraries record journeys to the Levant, but a few extend as far as *Iraq and *Iran.

In some of these itineraries, the narrator may be the traveler himself (no instance of a pre-modern Jewish woman travel writer is known), writing after having completed his peregrinations and addressing an audience at home; in others, the travels are told through a third person. Some works are actually fictional compilations of passages from earlier examples of the genre. In certain cases, as with Benjamin of Tudela's "Travel Book" (see later discussion), the characterization of the work as an "itinerary" seems questionable; the sequence of loosely connected topographic entries may be better described as a popular anthology of foreign places. Passages that border on ethnographic or historiographic commentary tend to go hand in hand with curiosity for the exotic and grotesque. Some of these works include journeys into the legendary realm of the "*Ten Lost Tribes" living at the River Sambation and tales about marvels and miracles (see ELDAD HA-DANI).

The most famous medieval Jewish traveler is *Benjamin of Tudela. The only information we have about him comes from his literary work. As the introduction to his *Sefer Massa'ot* (Book of Travels) suggests, he came from the city of Tudela in northern *Spain. He returned there in 1173, the only firm date that can be assigned to Benjamin and his journeys. The reader of the book gains an impression of a more or less contiguous land and sea route from Navarre, through southern France (see FRANCE, SOUTHERN), *Italy, and *Greece to *Syria, Palestine, Iraq, and eastern Iran. To what extent the account should be considered an authentic record of Benjamin's personal journeys is, however, open to debate. At the least, the references to *Arabia, *India, and *China are certainly based on hearsay. Benjamin's book has been transmitted in several manuscript versions and early printed editions, as well as numerous translations, reflecting the fact that it became a favorite among Jewish (and subsequently Christian) readers. These different versions reveal that the text underwent a process of editing; additional material attached by later generations makes it impossible to reconstruct Benjamin's original text.

A few decades after Benjamin, an *Ashkenazi rabbi, Petahiah of Regensburg, set out on a journey from Bohemia to the Middle East. However his *Sivvuv* (Circuit) appears to have been haphazardly assembled, without any effort at establishing a geographical or narrative sequence. It seems likely that *Sivvuv* was not written by the traveler himself, but was based on his oral reports.

From the fifteenth century onward, there are a number of extant Hebrew letters that were written by Italian Jewish merchants, pilgrims, and immigrants who traveled to the Land of Israel. Although their immediate addressees were often family members, friends, or business partners back home, these epistles were also intended for broader distribu-tion. Among them are the letters of the famous rabbi (and *Mishnah commentator) Obadiah of Bertinoro (1488) and the travel account of Meshullam of Volterra (1481), a Tuscan businessman. Obadiah offers a notably unbiased depiction of Muslim, Jewish, and other religious communities in *Egypt and Palestine; Meshullam, however, shares many of the cultural prejudices and stereotypes of his Christian countrymen vis-à-vis the East. A particular gem is the pilgrimage account by another Italian Jew, Rabbi Moses Basola, which begins with his ship's departure from *Venice in 1521 and concludes with his embarkation from Beirut in 1523. Moreover, the author includes extensive advice for future travelers on the same route.

Moses Almosnino, a *Sephardic rabbi from Salonika, left a Judeo-Spanish (*Ladino) account of his mission to Constantinople in 1566 that has certain similarities to contemporary Italian ambassadorial reports. It includes a description of the coronation parade of Sultan Selim II and a detailed portrait of the city of Constantinople. With some rearrangement and omissions, it was later printed in Latin script as *Extremos y grandezas de Constantinopla* (Madrid, 1638).

Eighteenth-century Hebrew literature includes new forms of travel writing, such as *Ma'agal Tov* (Good Circuit), the travel diary of Hayyim Joseph Azulai (Hida). This work offers the rare example of an *Ottoman Jew who, as an emissary on behalf of the Jewish community in Palestine, traveled to Western Europe, including a visit to Versailles. The description of travels in *Morocco by Samuel Romanelli, a Mantuan Jew (*Massa' ba-'rav* [Vision of an Arab Land]; cf. Isa 21:13) provides a fascinating amalgam of a traditional Hebrew travelogue infused by Enlightenment thought.

For more information on these writings, see E. N. Adler, ed., *Jewish Travellers* (1930); J. Prawer, *The History of the Jews in the Latin Kingdom of Jerusalem* (1988), 169–250; M. N. Adler, ed. and trans., *The Itinerary of Benjamin of Tudela* (1907); A. David, ed., *In Zion and Jerusalem: The Itinerary of Rabbi Moses Basola (1521–1523)* (1999); M. B. Lehmann, "Levantinos and Other Jews: Reading H.Y.D. Azulai's Travel Diary," *Journal of Jewish Studies* 13(3) (2007): 1–34; and M. Pelli, "The Literary Genre of the Travelogue in Hebrew Haskalah Literature: Shmuel Romanelli's *Masa Ba'rav*," *Modern Judaism* 11 (1991): 241–60.   MARTIN JACOBS

Treblinka, located in a remote area northeast of *Warsaw, was the deadliest of the *Nazi *Aktion Reinhard* death camps. From July 1942 until early August 1943, the Germans murdered 874,000 Jews and several thousand Roma there (see HOLOCAUST: ROMA). Treblinka I opened in the summer of 1941 as a forced labor camp, followed by Treblinka II, the death camp, a year later. Franz Stangl, Treblinka's commandant, did everything he could to disguise the entrance of the death camp and hide its real purpose from arriving victims. Treblinka was shut down after an uprising on August 2, 1943. Although the SS shot many of the camp's remaining prisoners during the escape, the rebels were able to destroy part of the camp. Unfortunately, the brick gas chambers remained intact and were used for several more weeks before Treblinka was closed and totally demolished. **See HOLOCAUST; HOLOCAUST: CAMPS AND KILLING CENTERS; HOLOCAUST RESISTANCE**, etc.

DAVID M. CROWE

Tribes, Ten Lost. Claims of descent from the "Ten Lost Tribes" are ancient and have proceeded from hundreds, if not thousands, of groups throughout the world. According to the Bible, the *Assyrians conquered the northern kingdom of *Israel in the eighth century BCE; the ten tribes (Reuben, Simeon, Issachar, Zebulun, Manasseh, Ephraim, Dan, Naphtali, Gad and Asher) that made up the population were exiled "in Halah, and in Habor by the river of Gozan and in the cities of the Medes" (2 Kgs 17:6). Their fate has always been something of an enigma. Although it was generally assumed that they had assimilated into the local population, biblical passages documented their place of exile (1 Chron 5:26), and prophetic proclamations (Isa 11:11–12; Ezek 37:21–23) suggested that they continued to live on and would be "ingathered" in latter days. Hopes of discovering the location of these ten tribes and belief in the possibility of their ultimate return were kept alive throughout the ages.

The *Mishnah and *Talmud discuss the fate of the ten tribes. Rabbi *Akiva believed that they had disappeared, whereas Rabbi Eliezer argued that they would eventually return (M. *Sanhedrin* 10:3). Some suggested that the tribes lived beyond the impassable Sambatyon River, which flowed six days of the week and stopped on the *Sabbath, when Israelites were forbidden to travel. References to this theme appear in Jewish classical texts (*Genesis Rabbah* 73:6; M. *Sanhedrin* 10:6; BT *Sanhedrin* 29b), as well as in *Josephus (*Wars* 7:96–97) and Pliny the Elder (*Historia Naturalis* 31:24).

The legend also became popular among members of Christian denominations, who sought out "Israelites" among Jews and Gentiles, whom they could convert to Christianity to hasten the arrival of the millennium. In the sixteenth century, Bishop Las Casas worked among Native Americans in order to "save" "Lost Israelites." In the nineteenth century, Rev. Joseph Wolff, a missionary for the London Society for Promoting Christianity among the Jews, became convinced that the Jews of Bukhara, as well as other non-Jewish tribes in the Hindu Kush area, were descendants of the tribes of Naphtali and Zebulun. In the nineteenth century, Dr. Francis Mason, of the American Baptist Foreign Mission Society in Burma, suggested that the worship of the indigenous Karen and their belief in a monotheistic eternal god called Y-wa were similar to that of the ancient Israelites. Others have noted that the Pathans, the largest single tribe in the world (fifteen million people), inhabiting an extensive area from Afghanistan through Pakistan to Kashmir in *India, are divided into distinct local tribes reminiscent of the ten tribes: Rabbani may be Reuben, Shinwari may be Shimon; Daftani may be a corruption of Naftali, Jajani – Gad, Afridi – Ephraim, and Yusufzai – the sons of Joseph.

In recent years, groups in Africa and in Asia have claimed "Lost Tribes" status, on the basis of which they wish to convert to Judaism and migrate to the State of Israel. Notable among these are the Shinlung from Mizoram and Manipur states in northeast *India, who have recently been designated "Bnei Menashe" (Children of Manasseh).

Important studies include A. Godbey, *The Lost Tribes: A Myth* (1930); T. Parfitt and E. T. Semi, *Judaising Movements: Studies in the Margins of Judaism* (2002); S. Weil, *Beyond the Sambatyon: The Myth of the Ten Lost Tribes* (1991); and idem, "Lost Israelites from North-East India: Re-Traditionalisation and Conversion among the Shinlung from the Indo-Burmese Borderlands," *The Anthropologist* 6(3) (2004): 219–33.

SHALVA WEIL

Tribes, Twelve. According to the *Torah, the twelve tribes of Israel stem from *Jacob's twelve sons: Reuben, Simeon, Levi, Judah, Dan, Naphtali, Gad, Asher, Issachar, Zebulun, Joseph, and Benjamin. The fact that the twelve are conceived amidst a competition between two sisters, *Rachel and *Leah, works etiologically to explain why conflict sometimes arises among them. Leah gives birth to Reuben, Simeon, Levi, Judah, Issachar, and Zebulun, as well as to a daughter, *Dinah. Leah also claims Gad and Asher, the sons of Zilpah, her servant and surrogate, as her descendants. Rachel similarly absorbs Dan and Naphtali, born to her servant Bilhah. After contending with prolonged barrenness, Rachel gives birth to Joseph and Benjamin. A dozen sons and one daughter may not, however, be the extent of Jacob's family because he is recorded immigrating to *Egypt with sons and daughters (Gen 46:7, 15). There is no tribe of Joseph; rather each of his two sons, Manasseh and Ephraim, became the father of an eponymous half-tribe. See also ISRAELITES: TRIBES.

Trotsky, Leon (1879–1940), a leader of the *Bolshevik Revolution, was born Lev Davidovich Bronstein in one of the Jewish farm colonies in southern *Ukraine. He became active in movements against the tsar and was first arrested in 1898. Exiled to Siberia, he escaped to London in 1903 with a false passport under the name Trotsky, which he had adopted from the name of a prison guard. In London, he met Vladimir Lenin and other leading Bolsheviks. Trotsky returned to *Russia in 1905 and helped lead the *Saint Petersburg Soviet (or Council of Workers) during the revolutionary upheaval. Arrested, tried, and sentenced to Siberian exile for life, he again escaped to Western Europe. After the abdication of Tsar Nicholas II, Trotsky returned to Russia in the spring of 1917. Together with Lenin, he led the Bolshevik seizure of power in October. During the ensuing Civil War, Trotsky organized the Red Army and successfully defended the revolution against White forces.

In spite of his prestige and skills as a military commander, an orator, and a writer, Trotsky was outmaneuvered by Joseph Stalin in the struggle for power after the death of Lenin in January 1924. Stripped of his party membership, Trotsky was exiled to *Turkey in 1929. Over the next decade, while living in Turkey, *France, and Norway, he led a campaign of opposition to Stalin. He wrote a history of the revolution, a memoir, and host of other books and articles, all to justify his role in the revolution. He also witnessed the rise of Hitler in *Germany and predicted annihilation for the Jews in the event of a new war. Hounded out of Europe, he was able to find refuge in *Mexico in 1937, where he was killed by a Stalinist agent in August 1940.

JOSHUA RUBENSTEIN

Tu B'Shevat (literally, "15th of Shevat") is known as *Rosh Ha-Shanah la-Ilanot*, or the new year for trees (see NEW YEARS). Rabbinic *Judaism identifies it as the boundary for determining a tree's first year for tithing purposes. A holiday of little religious significance with no mandated observances, Tu B'Shevat remained largely dormant until sixteenth- and seventeenth-century *Kabbalists endowed it with great mystical importance (see KABBALAH). They created a Tu B'Shevat *seder* that parallels the traditional *Passover *seder*, including an order of eating fruits, reciting blessings, and drinking four cups of wine. Early *Zionists enhanced the significance of Tu B'Shevat, associating it with restoring the Land of *Israel and planting trees. Today, Tu B'Shevat inspires a cross-pollination of religious, mystical, ecological (see ETHICS, ENVIRONMENTAL; ISRAEL, STATE OF: ECOLOGY), and Zionist currents, including kabbalistic rituals, tree planting, expressions of environmental concern and welfare, and pride in Israel. For further reading, see P. Steinberg, *Celebrating the Jewish Year: The Winter Holidays* (2009); and A. Elon, N. M. Hyman, and A. Waskow, eds., *Trees, Earth, and Torah: A Tu B'Shvat Anthology* (1999); **see also Ecology**.   PAUL STEINBERG

Tunisia: See NORTH AFRICA

Turkey. In the fourteenth century, when the *Ottoman state was in its early formative stages, Jews were already settled in Anatolia and the *Balkans, where they had lived for many centuries. Most of them were Greek-speaking because their traditions and culture had been formed under *Byzantine rule. They were known as *Benei Romania*, or *Romaniote Jews, because Byzantium and other Greek-ruled lands were known by the Jews as *Romania*, the land of the Romans, and they developed customs now known as "*minhag Romania*" (see GREECE). The first Ottoman Jews were thus the continuation of the sizable Greek-speaking Jewish communities in pre-Ottoman Asia Minor. Archeological evidence (found in Ephesus, Pergamon, Smyrna, and Sardis) shows that the first signs of Jewish life in Asia Minor date to the fourth century BCE, which makes the Jewish community of Turkey one of the oldest in the world.

The first Jewish colony to be mentioned in Turkish history proper was in Bursa, a city located in a province that has been the cradle of a number of civilizations and religions, from the pre-Christian era to the present. After his conquest of the city in 1324, Orhan, the second sultan of the newly founded Ottoman state, permitted the Jews to build their first synagogue, Etz ha-Hayyim, which has been in use ever since. Before that, under Byzantine rule, Jews had not been allowed to exercise their religion freely. Encouraged by more tolerant rule, many Jews migrated to the Ottoman lands toward the end of the fourteenth century and throughout the fifteenth century; *Karaites, as well as Jews expelled from *Hungary, *France, *Sicily, Venetian-ruled Salonika, and Bavaria, found refuge there.

In the mid-fifteenth century, after taking Constantinople (1453), Sultan Mehmet II issued an official invitation for Jews to settle in the empire. A great influx of Jews arrived during the reign of Mehmet's successor, Beyazid II (1481–1512), after the 1492 expulsion from *Spain. The Spanish Jews settled chiefly in Constantinople, Salonika, Adrianople, Nicopolis, *Jerusalem, *Safed, Damascus, and *Egypt and in Bursa, Tokat, and Amasya in Anatolia. Jews did not settle in Izmir until the mid-sixteenth century. Soon after their arrival at the end of the fifteenth century, *Sephardic Jews became the largest Jewish community in Ottoman lands. They outnumbered both the Romaniote Jews and the *Ashkenazi Jews coming from the *Habsburg Empire, who had constituted most of the Jewish communities in Ottoman lands until that time. The chief center of the Sephardic Jews

was Salonika, which became virtually a Spanish Jewish city as the Spanish Jews soon outnumbered their co-religionists of other nationalities and even the original native inhabitants. *Ladino became the ruling tongue, and its purity was maintained for about a century. In the middle of the sixteenth century, another wave of European Jewish refugees, expelled from *Italy and Bohemia, arrived in the Ottoman Empire. Moreover, in 1556 Sultan Suleiman the Magnificent saved the Ancona *conversos from papal persecution by declaring them Ottoman subjects.

Jews introduced various arts and industries into the country, including *printing; Sephardim David and Samuel ibn Nahmias established the first Hebrew printing press in Istanbul in 1493. Jews distinguished themselves in *medicine and served as interpreters and diplomatic agents at the Ottoman courts. In Muslim Constantinople many owned beautiful houses and gardens on the shores of the Bosphorus.

The Ottoman Empire at this time was a classic example of a pluralistic society. Although the Ottoman state was established as a Turkoman principality, it soon expanded to the Rumelia region and established control over Central and Eastern Anatolia, the Middle East, and North Africa, uniting dense Muslim and Christian populations under its administration. When the Sephardic Jews who migrated from Spain are added to this diversity, the extent of religious and ethnic pluralism in the Ottoman state is evident. Legal enforcement of pluralism played a considerable role in the success of the Ottoman experience. The general principle in Islamic-Ottoman law was the application of the same regulations to all individuals in a Muslim society (including non-Muslims). In addition, Christians, Jews, and followers of other religions were also given an opportunity to implement their own laws in certain areas. Non-Muslims were vested with the right to apply to their religious courts in personal status matters as well as the right to apply to Ottoman courts. Jews were on a par with Christians in exercising this judicial right. The Ottoman world was a medley of peoples in a diverse society, with different sections of the community living side by side, but separately, within the same political unit. Christian and Jewish communities in the Ottoman Empire lived under what has been called the *millet* system. *Millet*, which originally meant a religious community, came to mean "nation" in the nineteenth century. The system provided, on the one hand, a degree of religious, cultural, and ethnic continuity within these communities, while on the other it permitted their incorporation into the Ottoman administrative, economic, and political system.

In this relaxed atmosphere, Jewish culture flourished. The sixteenth century witnessed the rise of important thinkers like the *kabbalists of *Safed (Joseph *Karo, Moses *Cordovero, Isaac *Luria, Hayyim Vital); the seventeenth century was marked by the messianic movement of *Shabbatai Zevi, which ended with the emergence of the Dönmeh, pseudo-converts to Islam who maintained Jewish identity and traditions in secret (see SABBATEANISM: OTTOMAN EMPIRE AND TURKEY).

During the Crimean War (1853–56), Jews who were fleeing the war zone took refuge in the Ottoman Empire. Throughout the nineteenth century, and especially after 1875, as the empire was contracting, giving rise to new nation-states in the Balkans, considerable numbers of Jews, together with even larger numbers of Muslims, migrated from the newly independent states to the remaining Ottoman territories. The Balkan Jews were joined by many Russian Jews who were also seeking refuge in the Ottoman Empire. These immigrants were generally well received and even assisted by the Ottoman authorities and the local Jewish communities. However, in ensuing decades, many of these immigrants moved again, mainly to Western Europe, the Americas, and several African countries. This outward movement also swept with it established Ottoman Jews, who were attracted by economic opportunity in the West. The modern education and Western languages that many of them had recently acquired further facilitated this movement. However, those who stayed in the Ottoman lands continued to prosper and felt like a protected minority.

The new Republic of 1923 was certainly different from the empire in mentality and organization. The Jews, who were once a recognized autonomous community of the Ottoman state, became "equal citizens'" of Turkey, and all their institutions came under "state control." In 1933, after Hitler's ascension to power, Ataturk invited Jews to leave *Nazi Germany and settle in Turkey. During *World War II, Turkey, as a neutral country, not only protected its Jews but also facilitated the safe land and sea passage of thousands of European Jewish refugees, mostly to *Palestine and the Americas. Across Europe, Turkish diplomats provided documents and visas to fleeing Jews, and many Jewish agencies managed to help the war victims from their headquarters in Istanbul.

Today there are approximately 26,000 Jews living in Turkey. The vast majority are in Istanbul, with a community of about 2,500 in Izmir and smaller groups located in Adana, Ankara, Bursa, Çanakkale, Iskenderun, and Kırklareli. Sephardic Jews make up 96% of the community, with Ashkenazi Jews accounting for the rest. There are about one hundred Karaites, an independent group that does not accept the authority of the chief rabbi. Turkish Jews are legally represented, as they have been for many centuries, by the *Hakham Başı*, a chief rabbi, who is assisted by a religious council made up of a Rosh *Beit Din* (head of the Jewish *court) and three *Hakhamim*. Thirty-five lay counselors look after the secular affairs of the community, and an executive committee of fourteen, the president of which must be elected from among the lay counselors, runs daily affairs. In the early twenty-first century, sixteen *synagogues are operating in Istanbul; they are classified as religious foundations (*Vakifs*). The community's newspaper, *Shalom*, is printed in Turkish and Ladino. The Jewish community also maintains a primary school for nearly 300 pupils and a secondary school for 250 students in Istanbul, plus an elementary school for 140 children in Izmir. Turkish is the language of instruction, and Hebrew is taught as well. Two Jewish hospitals (in Istanbul and Izmir) serve the community. Both cities have homes for the aged (*Moshav Zekinim*) and

several welfare associations to assist the poor, the sick, needy children, and orphans. Social clubs containing libraries, cultural and sports facilities, and discotheques give young people opportunities to meet. There are several Jewish professors teaching at the universities of Istanbul and Ankara, and many Turkish Jews are prominent in business, industry, and the liberal professions.

Important studies of this community include B. Braude, *Christians and Jews in the Ottoman Empire* (1982); H. Inalcik, "The Ottoman Decline and its Effects upon Reaya," *Aspects of the Balkans: Continuity and Change. Contributions to the International Balkan Conference*, ed. H. Bimbaum and S. Vryonis Jr. (1972); A. Levy, *The Jews of the Ottoman Empire* (1994); S. Shaw, *The Jews of the Ottoman Empire and the Turkish Republic* (1991); and W. F. Weiker, *Ottomans, Turks and the Jewish Polity: A History of the Jews of Turkey* (1992).   BÜLENT ŞENAY

Twelve Tribes: See TRIBES, TWELVE

***Tzaddik:* See ḤASIDISM: EUROPE**

***Tzedakah:* See PHILANTHROPY**

Tzimtzum (divine contraction) is one of the most profound and influential terms in Lurianic Kabbalah (see KABBALAH, LURIANIC). The concept is already present in *midrashic literature, in the esoteric teachings of the medieval *Hasidei Ashkenaz (especially the *Baraita of Joseph ben Uzziel*), and in the works of several early kabbalists, usually denoting the divine contraction into universal existence. The origin of *tzimtzum* appears to be in the midrashic description of the *Shekhinah being "contracted" into the space between the cherubim in the Holy of Holies in the *Jerusalem *Temple (*Tanhuma Vayakhel* 7).

In Lurianic Kabbalah, however, *tzimtzum* denotes the first step leading from the infinity of the eternal godhead (*Ein Sof*) to the emanation of the divine powers and the earthly world. According to Luria, the *tzimtzum* is a negative process. It signifies the contraction of the infinite divine into itself, to create an empty space (*tehiru*) into which the divine light can flow and shape the *sefirot. In the original Lurianic myth this was a cathartic process through which potentially evil elements were purged from the godhead; they remained in the *tehiru*, later to evolve into the satanic powers. Later Lurianic kabbalists gave different interpretations, some of them describing the *tzimtzum* as a benevolent act, limiting the infinity of God to enable divine communication with creation. The term, in different interpretations, was used by Christian kabbalists (see CHRISTIAN HEBRAISM) and European esoterics in the seventeenth and eighteenth centuries. For further reading, see G. Scholem, *Major Trends in Jewish Mysticism* (1954); idem, *Kabbalah* (1974); **see also LURIA, ISAAC.**   JOSEPH DAN

U

Ugarit: See CANAAN, CANAANITES; SYRIA, ANCIENT

Ukraine. According to archeological evidence from Greek colonies in Crimea, Jews appeared in what is now Ukraine in the last centuries BCE. In the seventh to ninth centuries CE, the steppe part of contemporary Ukraine was under the control of the *Khazar state. The Khazars had accepted Judaism as their official religion and gave refuge to Jews from *Islamic and *Byzantine regions. Jews were present in the medieval towns of Kievan Rus'; a letter from Kiev Jews dated to the first third of the tenth century was found in the Cairo *Genizah, and a *pogrom in Kiev in 1113 is mentioned in the *Russian Primary Chronicle*.

*Ashkenazi Jews began to settle in Ukraine in the thirteenth and fourteenth centuries, in territories belonging to the Polish kingdom and the Great Duchy of *Lithuania; Ashkenazi immigration continued until the mid-seventeenth century. Jews settled in towns under royal protection where they engaged in local and international trade, served as tax collectors, and established industries. After the Lublin Union of 1569, when *Poland and Lithuania became one state, Polish colonization of the eastern Ukraine began. Lands were distributed among Polish magnates who established private towns and villages and invited Jews to fulfill various managerial functions. Jews administered large landholdings and villages, collected taxes from the Ukrainian peasantry, leased inns and mills, and produced and sold alcohol. The close connections between Jews and the Polish landlords proved especially harmful during the *Chmelnitzki uprising of 1648–49, when much of the Jewish population of the eastern and central Ukraine was killed or fled. Jewish settlements in right-bank Ukraine (west of the Dnieper River) were revived relatively quickly but left-bank Ukraine, under the control of *Russia, remained closed to Jews until the end of the eighteenth century.

Jewish economic roles continued unchanged during the eighteenth century, although their prosperity diminished significantly. Jews were often targets of the *haidamak* anti-Polish bands, which destroyed many communities; especially notorious was the slaughter in Uman in 1768. In the first half of the 1700s, there were clandestine groups of adherents of *Shabbatai Zevi; the area became the center of the *Frankist movement in the mid-eighteenth century. *Hasidism originated in right-bank Ukraine where the movement's founders, Israel *Baal Shem Tov (Międzybóż in Podolia) and Dov *Ber the Maggid of Międzyrzecz (Volhynia), and their followers resided.

In the first partition of Poland in 1772, the areas of Ruś Czerwona were annexed by *Habsburg Austria and became known as eastern *Galicia. The Russian Empire annexed right-bank Ukraine in the second partition of 1793. According to the 1764 census, there were approximately 120,000 Jews in the Ukrainian lands annexed by Austria and around 130,000 in the Ukrainian lands annexed by Russia. Thus, both empires acquired large numbers of Jews who were deeply involved in the feudal agricultural economy and constituted a significant part of the urban population. In 1794, the Russian government allowed Jewish settlement in left-bank Ukraine and in southern regions of contemporary Ukraine newly acquired from the *Ottoman Empire. With the annexation of the Crimea in 1783, local Jews (*krymchaks*) and *Karaites, who had continued to live in the peninsula under the Tatar khans, also came under Russian rule.

In Galicia, the Austrian government immediately began to implement measures for "improvement" and "productivization" of Jews, to reorganize Jewish communities, to establish state Jewish schools, and to support the *Haskalah movement. However, Galician Jewry remained highly traditional into the early twentieth century; Hasidism had an extremely strong influence there (the first Orthodox political organization, *Maḥzikei ha-Dat* [Strengtheners of the Faith], was established in Galicia in 1878). Jews were emancipated in 1867, but Galicia, as well as Transcarpathia and Bukovina, remained the most underdeveloped areas of the Habsburg Empire. The acculturation of Jews in Galicia gravitated first toward German and after 1867 toward Polish culture; in Bukovina and Transcarpathia, the influence of German and Hungarian cultures, respectively, on the educated strata of Jews was very strong. In 1890, there were approximately 811,000 Jews in eastern Galicia, 90,000 in Bukovina, and 100,000 in Transcarpathia.

In the Russian Empire, during the nineteenth century, Jewish settlement was spread through left-bank and southern Ukraine. During this period of rapid demographic growth, thousands of Jews were attracted to new urban and commercial centers like Odessa, Ekaterinoslav (now Dnepropetrovsk), and Nikolaiev; at the same time Jewish *agricultural colonies were established in the steppe regions. Jews in the Russian Empire did not have civil equality, and after 1881 their settlement in rural areas was prohibited. Ukraine was the major location of pogroms in 1881–82 and 1905. According to the census of 1897, there were 1,893,000 Jews in Russian Ukraine, constituting 9.9% of the total population.

On the eve of World War I, Jews in the Russian Empire, including those in Ukraine, were diverse. Traditional communities on the right bank of the Dnieper were dominated by Hasidim, mostly of the Sadigora and Chernobyl' dynasties; Jews lived in small towns (*shtetls* or *stetlakh*) where they made up about half of the population. Left-bank areas had been settled by immigrants from Lithuania and *Belorussia; Hasidim in these communities belonged to *Habad. In the multinational and vibrant urban centers in the south, Jews were modernized and highly acculturated; they constituted 30% of town and city dwellers. *Zionism had a significant influence, especially in the south, whereas Jewish socialist parties (the *Bund and Poalei-Zion, among others) were relatively weak.

When the Russian Empire collapsed in 1917, an independent Ukrainian state was established with its capital in Kiev; Jews were granted national autonomy, and a ministry for Jewish affairs was created in the Ukrainian government. However, the autonomy was short-lived, and the Civil War of 1918–20 that took place on Ukrainian territory brought with it an extremely high level of anti-Jewish violence. All the fighting armies – but especially the White army of General Anton Denikin, the Simon Petlura army of the Ukrainian People's Republic, and numerous "Green" bands of various *atamans* (Cossack leaders) – perpetrated perhaps as many as 1,500 pogroms in which approximately 50,000 Jews were murdered.

Between 1919 and 1939 the western part of contemporary Ukraine (Galicia and parts of Volhynia) was part of Poland, whereas the rest became the Ukrainian Soviet Socialist Republic of the USSR. Jewish social and economic life in the Polish territories remained unchanged, and Jewish religious communities were officially recognized. Although Jews had full citizenship rights, the Polish regime grew increasingly discriminatory, aiming to minimize the Jewish role in the economy and to restrict the numbers of Jews in universities and in the state service. At the same time, Jewish culture as well as Jewish politics of various kinds (Zionist, socialist, Orthodox) flourished.

In Soviet Ukraine the Soviet authorities deliberately destroyed the traditional Jewish socioeconomic structure and religious institutions, while rapid urbanization and significant upward mobility took place. In the 1920s, left-wing Jewish culture blossomed in Ukraine, but it was liquidated by the authorities toward the end of the 1930s. Until the late 1930s the authorities supported *Yiddish as the national language of Jews: in 1931 there were more than one hundred Jewish local soviets (governing councils) operating in Yiddish, Yiddish state schools, and courts of justice with Yiddish-language procedures. Three Jewish national regions – Kalinendorf, Novozlatopol', and Stalindorf – existed in 1930. There were one hundred and sixty-two agricultural colonies in these regions involving 200,000 Jews. Because of emigration to major Soviet centers, the Jewish population in Ukraine declined from 1,750,000 in 1926 to 1,533,000 in 1939.

With the outbreak of World War II, the USSR annexed western Ukraine from Poland in 1939 and northern Bukovina from *Romania in 1940, thus acquiring large Jewish populations (1,056,000 and 282,000, respectively) and important Jewish centers such as Lwów and Czernowitz, which had never previously been under Russian rule. Soviet authorities nationalized private property and prohibited Jewish political, religious, and cultural activities. *Nazi Germany occupied Ukraine in the summer and autumn of 1941 and its easternmost regions in the summer of 1942. Even before the arrival of German units, Ukrainian nationalists in eastern Ukraine began the mass murder of Jews. The advancing German army and *Einsatzgruppen C and D murdered the majority of Jews in eastern Ukraine by the end of 1941 (the well-known mass murder of 35,000 Jews took place in Babi Yar near Kiev on September 29–30, 1941). In western Ukraine, Jews were concentrated in ghettos and sent to death camps during 1942 (see HOLOCAUST: CAMPS AND KILLING CENTERS; HOLOCAUST: GHETTOS). Only in the zone occupied by Romania (Transnistria), especially in its northern part, did significant numbers of Jews remain alive. More then 1.5 million Ukrainian Jews (approximately 60%) perished during the *Holocaust.

After World War II, many Jews who had been evacuated to eastern regions of Russia returned to Ukraine, whereas those from the former Polish and Romanian territories were allowed to leave the USSR. The Ukrainian Soviet authorities displayed the highest level of *antisemitismof any Soviet republic, especially in the decade following the war. Nonetheless, in the areas annexed in 1939 (eastern Galicia, northern Bukovina) and in 1945 (Transcarpathia, annexed from *Czechoslovakia), as well as in former Romanian-occupied areas, vestiges of Jewish culture and religion continued to exist until the end of the twentieth century. The number of Jews in Ukraine decreased from 840,000 (2% of the total population) in 1959 to 487,000 (1%) in 1989. Twenty-six of the forty-one legal *synagogues were closed between 1959 and 1962; however, in many places illegal prayer groups gathered in private homes. The authorities persecuted those who engaged in Jewish religious or cultural activities and allowed publication of antisemitic literature.

The revival of Jewish life in Ukraine started in the late 1980s, at the time of *perestroika*. At the same time, however, in the late 1980s and early 1990s, about three-quarters of Ukrainian Jews emigrated to *Israel and the *United States. In the independent Ukraine, established in 1991, extensive Jewish cultural, educational, social, and religious activities have developed. In the mid-1990s, there were about 250 Jewish organizations and religious communities; 106 Jewish newspapers were published in 2000–03.

For further reading, see H. Abramson, *A Prayer for the Government: Ukrainians and Jews in Revolutionary Times, 1917–1920* (1999); H. Aster and P. J. Potichnyj, eds., *Ukrainian-Jewish Relations in Historical Perspective* (1990); I. Bartal, *The Jews of Eastern Europe, 1772–1881* (2005); Z. Gitelman, *Jewish Nationality and Soviet Politics: The Jewish Sections of the CPSU, 1917–1930* (1972); and V. Khanin, ed., *Documents on Ukrainian-Jewish Identity and Emigration, 1944–1990* (2003). **Map 11**

VLADIMIR LEVIN

United Monarchy refers to the period from approximately 1030 to 930 BCE when the twelve Israelite *tribes were united under one ruler. The first king, *Saul, from the tribe of Benjamin, reigned from ca. 1030 to 1010 BCE. He was followed by *David (ca. 1008–970 BCE), from the tribe of Judah, who was succeeded by his son *Solomon (ca. 970–931 BCE). The United Monarchy broke down early in the reign of Solomon's son *Rehoboam when ten of the tribes were led in secession by *Jeroboam and founded the northern kingdom of *Israel. Rehoboam and his dynastic successors continued to rule the southern kingdom of *Judah until its defeat by *Babylon in 586 BCE. **See also ISRAELITES: KINGSHIP; KINGS and SAMUEL, BOOKS OF; Map 2.**

United States: African American–Jewish Relations. For much of American history, geographic and demographic factors limited interactions between African Americans and Jews. Jewish communities were small and predominantly urban, and although allusions to the *Bible in slave spirituals suggest a sense of kinship with Jewish experience, in reality the everyday interaction between slaves and Jews was very limited. Few Jews lived in the south (see UNITED STATES: CIVIL WAR; UNITED STATES, SOUTHERN), and those who did rarely owned plantations. Nevertheless, roughly one in four southern Jews were slaveholders, and Jews participated in the slave economy as investors and traders. For example, Aaron Lopez (1731–1782), a Newport, Rhode Island, merchant, brought twenty-one boatloads of slaves from Africa during his lifetime. Jews spoke both for and against abolitionism. Judah P. Benjamin (1811–1884) defended slavery before the Senate in 1858, before serving in the Confederate cabinet.Rabbi David *Einhorn (1809–1879) fled Baltimore in 1861 after preaching against slavery. For the most part Jews shared the racial attitudes of their neighbors. After the Civil War, Jewish peddlers expanded their routes through the south, selling merchandise to former slaves and their families in the new rural economy. Some stayed to open stores and were often more willing to serve black customers than were their white Gentile counterparts.

The concurrent mass migrations of Jews from *Eastern Europe to the United States and of African Americans from the south to northern industrial cities from the 1880s onward fundamentally altered the preexisting pattern of African American–Jewish relations. In their new urban environments, Jews and blacks came into close contact. This was not, however, a relationship of equals. Jews were free from the restrictions of racial segregation (although they were victims of social exclusion) and for the most part did not compete directly with African Americans for industrial jobs. Nonetheless, their relationship entailed both conflict and collaboration. Many Jews were storekeepers and landlords within black neighborhoods, selling to black customers and competing with local black businessmen. Jewish and African American cultural, political, and intellectual leaders often found kinship and common cause. The *Yiddish press criticized episodes of lynching in the south, Jewish-led socialist trade unions aggressively recruited black members, and the *Communist Party and National Association for the Advancement of Colored People (NAACP), respectively, provided a welcoming home for radicals and liberals of both communities. However, this cooperation did not extend far beyond community elites.

This political collaboration climaxed in the decades immediately after *World War II, the apex of the fabled "black-Jewish alliance" during the civil rights struggle (see UNITED STATES: CIVIL RIGHTS MOVEMENT) when Jewish defense agencies, including the American Jewish Committee, American Jewish Congress, and Anti-Defamation League of B'nai B'rith, worked in tandem with the NAACP (see ORGANIZATIONS: NORTH AMERICA). This cooperation was mutually beneficial. Jewish groups believed that *antisemitism and racism had common roots and that advancing African American civil rights through legislation enforcing fair standards in hiring and housing would ultimately benefit Jews. The Jewish defense agencies and the NAACP pursued their struggle through the courts and legislative chambers. Jewish students and political activists preferred direct action in the streets, joining and participating in the marches and sit-ins organized by the Student Nonviolent Coordinating Committee and the Congress of Racial Equality.

Jews, both men and women, formed a disproportionately large percentage of Freedom Riders and participants in the Mississippi Freedom Summer. The murders of civil rights activists Michael Schwerner, Andrew Goodman, and James Chaney – two Jews and an African American – in rural Mississippi in 1964 demonstrate this outsized involvement. The prominence of Jews, including a number of rabbis, among the "outside agitators" in the south was of concern to local Jews, who worried that Jews and blacks would be inexorably linked in the minds of often violent segregationist extremists.

As the civil rights struggle fragmented and was radicalized in the late 1960s, the close alliance between Jewish and African American political activists soured. Memories of close cooperation during the 1950s and 1960s heightened the sense of disappointment and disenchantment felt by many Jews when some civil rights organizations adopted separatist and anti-Zionist platforms. Moreover, Jewish landlords and storekeepers who owned property and stores within African American neighborhoods were particularly hard hit during the race riots of the late 1960s and by campaigns for black economic self-reliance. At much the same time, Jewish inner-city neighborhoods were being emptied by white flight. The public relationship between Jews and African Americans deteriorated further in the last few decades of the twentieth century as a series of acrimonious episodes exposed the raw nerves of both communities. These included the 1979 forced resignation of Andrew Young, a black civil rights hero, as America's chief delegate at the United Nations for making secret contacts with the Palestinian Liberation Organization; the rise of the crudely antisemitic Louis Farrakhan and the Nation of Islam; and the 1991 rioting in Crown Heights, which followed the accidental killing of an African American boy by a *Hasidic funeral motorcade. These incidents almost uniformly ended in the trading of accusations of antisemitism and racism. Although Jews and African Americans remain united in their loyalty to the Democratic Party and adherence to liberal politics in the first decade of the twenty-first century, there is evidence that their interests have diverged on a number of key issues, including affirmative action. In the 2008 presidential election, however, successful candidate Barack Obama received overwhelming Jewish support; figures based on exit polling data suggest that 78% of Jewish voters supported Obama, and some have suggested that his election has restored links between Jews and African Americans.

Recent studies include H. Diner, *In the Almost Promised Land: American Jews and Blacks, 1915–1935* (1995); M. Adams and J. Bracey, eds., *Strangers and Neighbors: Relations between Blacks and Jews in the United States* (1999); and C. Greenberg, *Troubling the Waters: Black-Jewish Relations in the American Century* (2006).   ADAM MENDELSOHN

United States: Agricultural Settlements. Between 1881 and 1910, Jews from *Eastern Europe established approximately seventy planned farming settlements in the United States. A major impetus came from *Am Olam* (Eternal People), a Russian Jewish organization that aimed to solve the "Jewish problem" through establishment of socialist, agrarian colonies in North America. Members believed that an "abnormal" Jewish occupational profile fueled *antisemitism, that a "return" to farming would "normalize" Jewish life, and that colonies would demonstrate the value of communal living and the Jewish capacity for productive labor. Although these colonies were short-lived, they played a key role in opening rural areas to Jewish settlement.

Between 1881 and 1884, approximately twenty-four colonies, some consisting of only a few dozen individuals and others with sixty or more families, were founded in locations including Louisiana, the Dakotas, Oregon, Colorado, Arkansas, Kansas, and New Jersey. Many were sponsored by established American Jews, eager to divert immigrants from settling in northeastern cities, and *Am Olam* chapters founded a few as well. Others were settled by groups espousing similar philosophies, but whose connections to *Am Olam* are unclear. Although some were strictly communal, others divided land into private holdings. Many group leaders were intellectuals and students, but colonists also brought experience in trade and, in some cases, farming. Most colonists were drawn from the southern *Pale of Settlement in *Russia, where Jewish farming settlements existed in the nineteenth century.

Economic activity was largely agrarian. There was a heavy emphasis on intellectual and cultural development, with several colonies creating disciplined educational regimes. Religious life was notably lacking, as many leaders had rejected traditional Judaism while still in Russia. Although there is evidence of religious observance at some colonies, in others tradition was ignored or even flouted by such practices as raising pigs.

Most colonies lasted five years or less, with some succumbing to floods, grasshoppers, blizzards, and hailstorms. Others were torn apart by disagreements, as at New Odessa, Oregon. Colonies were also derailed by disputes between settlers and sponsors, including misunderstandings over whether aid was intended as a gift or a loan. The settlements that lasted the longest were in central New Jersey. Proximity to *New York City and *Philadelphia made them attractive to newcomers and enabled sponsors to exercise oversight. Sponsors transformed these colonies by establishing factories to attract additional settlers; in 1891, for example, Woodbine was founded as a mixed agricultural-industrial settlement in southern New Jersey. The New Jersey colonies reached their peak population in the mid-1910s. Yet, growth altered their character, as industrial settlers did not share the ideologies and backgrounds of earlier colonists. Over time, these communities became distinctive for their rural location rather than their ideological orientation.

Although settlements similar to the *Am Olam* colonies, like Clarion, Utah, were founded as late as 1911, by the early 1890s tensions with settlers as well as the high rate of failure led sponsors to turn their support to individual farmers, rather than colonies. In contrast to Clarion and the earlier colonies, the rich cultural life and cooperative economic enterprises that characterized settlements of socialist-oriented Jewish chicken farmers in northern New Jersey and Petaluma, California, which developed in the 1920s, resulted from a cluster of individual farmers, rather than a planned, collective settlement.

Despite their short duration, agricultural colonies established migration streams that brought other Jewish migrants to rural America. In North Dakota, independent Jewish farm families replaced colonists, and Jewish merchants followed, settling in towns. Painted Woods Colony had dwindled to three families by 1900, but there were two hundred and fifty Jewish farm families in the region by 1912. Of the eight hundred Jewish homesteaders in North Dakota, about half were members of organized colonies. These early pioneers often

became Jewish community leaders in these remote areas and in the larger cities of second settlement. For example, Portland, Oregon, attracted colony veterans whose experience and relative acculturation propelled them into leadership positions.

For further reading, see E. Eisenberg, *Jewish Agricultural Colonies in New Jersey* (1995); idem, "From Cooperative Farming to Urban Leadership," in *Jewish Life in the American West*, ed. A. Kahn (2002); R. A. Goldberg, *Back to the Soil* (1986); and K. Kann, *Comrades and Chicken Farmers* (1993); **see also, BARON DE HIRSCH FUND.**   ELLEN EISENBERG

United States: American Revolution.

In 1776, about 2,000 Jews, constituting less than one-tenth of 1% of the population, lived in the thirteen North American colonies that were poised to rebel against British rule. Most of these Jews, many of Sephardic descent (see UNITED STATES: SEPHARDIM), were involved in merchant activities and tended to oppose British trade restrictions, although some supported the British side. Jewish merchants were among those who signed the Non-Importation Resolution of 1765, as well as the Agreement of 1769, pledging not to deal in British goods.

Jews fought in militias against the British; the first Jew to die of battle wounds was Francis Salvador, who had arrived in South Carolina in 1773 and been elected to its General Assembly. The thirty Jewish men who joined the patriot cause in South Carolina formed their own "Jews' Company." Two Pennsylvanian Jews, Solomon Bush and David Salisbury Franks, attained the rank of lieutenant colonel. Other Jews provided financial support. Polish immigrant Haym Salomon (1740–1785), who settled in *New York City in 1775 and worked as a financial broker for overseas merchants, became an advocate of the revolutionary cause. Like many Jews, he fled to *Philadelphia when the British occupied New York. Salomon negotiated significant loans, without commission, from *France and Holland for the war effort and is said to have provided funds to individual members of the Continental Congress during their stays in Philadelphia. Similarly, the brothers Michael and Barnard Gratz, who had immigrated to Philadelphia from Prussia, became suppliers of arms and clothing to the American army.

Despite Jewish military and financial support for the Revolution, discriminatory legislation of various kinds persisted in most states, in some cases into the 1820s. It was only with the 1791 adoption of the First Amendment to the Constitution (part of the Bill of Rights), proclaiming that "Congress shall make no law respecting an establishment of religion or prohibiting the free exercise thereof," that the separation of religion and government in the new United States of America was affirmed and the way was opened to equal rights for all citizens regardless of religious beliefs. For further reading, see H. Diner, *The Jews of the United States: 1654–2000* (2004).

ELIZABETH SHULMAN

United States: Civil Rights Movement.

*African Americans consider two triumphant moments as centerpieces of the American civil rights movement: the March on Washington for Jobs and Freedom in August, 1963, and the protest march from Selma to Birmingham, Alabama, in February, 1965. These events are scarcely less iconic for the American Jewish community. Rabbi Joachim Prinz, who had fled *Nazi

*Germany in 1937, preceded Dr. Martin Luther King Jr. to the podium in Washington, speaking shortly before King delivered his famous "I have a Dream" speech. Abraham Joshua *Heschel interlocked arms with King, Ralph Bunche, and Ralph Abernathy in the front row of marchers in Selma. This intermeshing of African American and Jewish memory is not accidental. Instead it speaks to a long and dedicated involvement by Jews in the American civil rights movement.

This Jewish engagement with civil rights for African Americans began early. Joel Spingarn, one of the founders of the National Association for the Advancement of Colored People (NAACP) in 1909, was the first of many Jews to become involved in the leadership of the organization. Others provided financial support for the NAACP Legal Defense Fund. Julius Rosenwald, part owner of Sears, Roebuck, provided a different kind of philanthropic aid, working with Booker T. Wasington to dramatically improve education for black children in the south. At the ideological fringe of both communities, black and Jewish radicals found common cause within the Communist Party. Support for civil rights extended beyond the elites: there is evidence of Jewish working class sympathy for black civil rights from the 1920s onwards. A sense of identification, kinship, and shared victimhood with African Americans persisted well after most Jews had entered the middle class.

In the decades following the Second World War, the Jewish defense agencies – the American Jewish Committee, American Jewish Congress, and Anti-Defamation League of *B'nai B'rith (ADL), collaborated closely with the NAACP. There were benefits to cooperation since both groups sought federal legislation that would enforce fair standards in housing and employment. Jewish defense agencies believed that racism and antisemitism were twin phenomena; advancing black civil rights would undermine lingering prejudices and restrictions that also affected Jews. Both Jewish and black organizations shared common tactical approaches, relying on a combination of educational efforts (particularly the distribution of literature), legal challenges, and lobbying for legislation. The ADL, for example, filed an *amicus curiae* brief in Brown v. Board of Education, provided legal aid to the NAACP, and used its southern field offices to distribute school textbooks that promoted desegregation.

Rabbis and college students also flocked to the banner of the civil rights struggle. The *Reform, *Conservative, and *Orthodox movements all publicly declared their support for the Brown decision in favor of school desegregation. Members of the Reform Central Conference of American Rabbis (CCAR) and the Conservative Rabbinical Assembly, activated by a sense of moral imperative and prophetic impulse, formed delegations to join sit-ins and marched in solidarity in southern states. Some students also credited Jewish values as their inspiration for joining the civil rights movement. In the early 1960s, the Student Nonviolent Coordinating Committee (SNCC) and the Congress of Racial Equality (CORE) provided a welcoming ideological home for young Jewish radicals. Jews, both men and women, formed a disproportionately large cohort among Freedom Riders and participants in the Mississippi Freedom Summer. This prominence was tragically reflected in the murders of Michael Schwerner, Andrew Goodman, and James Chaney, an African American and two Jewish civil rights activists, in rural Mississippi in 1964.

These public demonstrations of support for the civil rights movement by rabbis and students created tensions within southern Jewry. Although a small number of southern rabbis spoke and acted against segregation, most southern Jews preferred to maintain a safe silence on the topic. Many feared that the rabbis and Jewish activists who flocked southwards would lead ardent segregationists to associate their small and vulnerable Jewish communities with "outside agitators." These fears were magnified by the wave of bombings at *synagogues and *community centers, including six in 1958 alone.

While the NAACP and Jewish groups continued to cooperate into the 1970s and 1980s, albeit at a lower level of intensity, the close partnership between Jewish and black political activists soured as the the civil rights movement itself fragmented and radicalized. In the late 1960s, student organizations such as SNCC embraced an agenda based on separatism, eventually expelling their white members. SNCC's adoption of an anti-*Zionist platform following the Six Day War (see ISRAEL, STATE OF: WARS [1956–1967]) compounded the sense of betrayal among longtime Jewish supporters. The rift was the first in a series of episodes that fomented distrust between Jewish and African American groups and often produced countervailing charges of antisemitism and racism. Incidents in the late 1960s and 1970s, including race riots in a number of northern cities, the struggle for control over the predominantly African American Ocean-Brownsville school district in New York City, and the rise of Louis Farrakhan and the Nation of Islam, narrowed the once broad support that the civil rights movement had enjoyed within the Jewish community. Black and Jewish groups could still find common cause in the 1980s and 1990s, but on a number of key issues, such as affirmative action, their interests increasingly diverged.

For further reading, see C. Greenberg, *Troubling the Waters: Black-Jewish Relations in the American Century* (2006); and M. Adams and J. Bracey, eds., *Strangers and Neighbors: Relations between Blacks and Jews in the United States* (1999); and UNITED STATES: AFRICAN AMERICAN-JEWISH RELATIONS.   ADAM MENDELSOHN

United States: Civil War. In 1861, about 125,000 Jews, mostly recent *immigrants, lived in northern states and supported the Union; 25,000 Jews lived in southern states and supported the Confederacy. Jews ultimately fought on both sides of the American Civil War (1861–65). They composed prayers for the Union and for the Confederacy and in some cases literally battled against their own relatives. All told, about 8,000–10,000 Jews donned uniforms, and at least fifty rose through the ranks to become officers. Judah P. Benjamin (1811–1884) of Louisiana, one of the most accomplished Jews of his day, served at different times as the Confederacy's Attorney General, Secretary of War, and Secretary of State.

On the issue of slavery, Jews resembled their neighbors, owning slaves where it was legal to do so and expressing a full spectrum of views from pro-slavery to abolitionist. A well-publicized address by Rabbi Morris Raphall of *New York City, delivered on the National Fast Day (January 4, 1861) just before the war, concluded that slaveholding as such was "no sin." Other Jewish leaders condemned such views.

During the war, Jewish supporters of the Union cause waged a political battle to amend the military chaplaincy law, passed in 1861, that stipulated that a regimental chaplain be "a regular ordained minister of some Christian denomination." At least two Jewish chaplains (one of whom was not "regularly ordained") were rejected on account of the discriminatory law, thereby disadvantaging Jewish soldiers and delegitimizing the Jewish faith. One of the rejected chaplains, Rev. Arnold Fischel, came to Washington to lobby personally on behalf of a change in the chaplaincy law, and President Abraham Lincoln promised him support. A revised bill that legalized non-Christian chaplains, a landmark in the legal recognition of America's non-Christian faiths, became law on July 17, 1862 (see also UNITED STATES: MILITARY CHAPLAINCY).

Exactly five months later, on December 17, 1862, an even greater challenge confronted Jews when General Ulysses S. Grant expelled "Jews as a class" from his war zone in an attempt to end the smuggling and cotton speculation in which Jews and non-Jews alike engaged. Because they were easily identifiable and stigmatized by age-old stereotypes, Jews came to symbolize for Grant *all* wartime profiteers. When informed of the order by Jewish victims who had been forced from their homes, President Lincoln had it countermanded on January 4, 1863. The episode reminded Jews of their vulnerability but also empowered them with the knowledge that they could fight back against bigotry and win.

A dramatic upsurge in many forms of anti-Jewish intolerance, in the north as well as in the south, characterized the Civil War era. Wartime tensions victimized Jews, much as they did Catholics and African Americans. Some Jews read special significance into the fact that the war ended on the eve of *Passover. Southern Jews continued to memorialize their wartime victims long after the war ended, creating a Jewish counterpart to the south's "religion of the lost cause." For further reading, see B. W. Korn, *American Jewry and the Civil War* (1951); **see also UNITED STATES, SOUTHERN.**
JONATHAN D. SARNA

United States: Community Centers.
Jewish Community Centers (JCCs) are an example of an American Jewish institution that has reinvented itself in response to changing communal needs. Founded in the 1850s as social clubs for German Jewish *immigrants, they were first known as Young Men's and Young Women's Hebrew Associations (YM/YWHAs). Strongly influenced by the YMCA movement, they aimed to counteract assimilatory forces by providing a comfortable space within which young adult Jews could mingle. By the 1880s there were YM/YWHAs in *New York City, *Chicago, and St. Louis. Their programs encompassed athletics, literary societies, social events, religious services, holiday celebrations, and some limited social services.

Social welfare functions became central between 1880 and 1920 when the Y's were transformed from social clubs to settlement houses that helped support and Americanize tens of thousands of Jewish immigrants from *East Europe. Similar to Jane Adams' Hull House in Chicago, centers such as the Henry Street Settlement on the Lower East Side of Manhattan held English-language and citizenship classes as well as lessons in deportment, *fashion, and cooking. By the middle of the twentieth century when the post–*World War II move to the suburbs accelerated along with the baby boom, the newly renamed Jewish Community Centers (JCCs) were refashioned into hubs of *sports, recreation, and cultural activities, as well as a range of programs for children. A few, epitomized by the 92nd Street Y in New York City and later on by the DCJCC in the heart of the nation's capital, specialized in educational and cultural events.

A recurring debate in communal leadership circles concerned the role that the maintenance of Jewish identity should play in JCC programming. There was also ongoing competition with local *synagogues whose lay and professional leadership felt that some Jews affiliated with JCCs instead of with synagogues. Such notables as Oscar Janowsky and Rabbi Mordecai *Kaplan wrote harsh critiques of the role of JCCs. Kaplan was credited with inventing the Synagogue Center movement based on his conception of a "synagogue center" combining religious, social, and communal activities. Subsequently, many *Conservative synagogues founded by his students between 1945 and 1975 had "Jewish Center" as part of their name. The "shul with a pool" phenomenon emerged, with the Forest Hills Jewish Center in New York City leading the way.

At the beginning of the twenty-first century, the JCC movement has expanded in several important ways. Although individual JCCs are generally autonomous and receive significant support from local Jewish federations, the national organization (JCCA) has grown in importance, raising major grant money and providing trips to Israel and American-based training for staff in Judaic and social work skills. The umbrella organization has also set standards for child care, prepared curricula, and initiated grants to train camp directors (see SUMMER CAMPING). The JCCA supports a large network of infant care and nursery schools, teen programming, summer day camps, and some overnight camps. Many JCCs house senior day care programs as well as athletic facilities. They also provide the venue for children's competitive sports teams that do not meet on the *Sabbath and other services aimed primarily at the *Orthodox community, such as swimming pool hours separated by gender. For further reading, see D. Kaufman, *Shul with a Pool: The Synagogue-Center in American Jewish History* (1998).
RELA MINTZ GEFFEN

United States: Demography.
From the beginning of Jewish settlement in the mid-seventeenth century in what is today the United States until the late twentieth century, the number of Jews has risen steadily. Changes in the size of the American Jewish population were determined mostly by the interplay between natural increase on the one hand and the migratory balance on the other; primary relationships with non-Jews in mixed families did not directly cause quantitative gains or losses because only the assignment of religious identity to their offspring had this effect. Jewish demographic evolution was not evenly spread throughout the period; what mainly affected the pace of increase was the number of new immigrants. Immigration also played a significant role in the sub-ethnic composition of *Sephardic and *Ashkenazic Jews, as well as in the nativity structure of foreign-born versus American-born Jews.

Any assessment of the demography of American Jews is dependent on the nature and quality of information sources, and it is further affected by the definition of group identity.

Hence, even very basic demographic data should be regarded as estimates. For the colonial period, the statistical information has heavily relied on documentation of *synagogue membership and Jewish communities. Since 1776, the United States has rigorously separated church and state, forbidding the census or any other official ongoing or temporary registration from inquiring into matters of creed. This has prevented any separate classification of religious groups. The single exception was the 1957 Current Population Survey that was voluntary and included a question on religion. For specific eras, such as the mass immigration at the turn of the nineteenth century, censuses can be used to study, at least partially, the demography of the Jews by defining them according to country of birth (*Russia) and mother tongue (*Yiddish).

Noncensus proxy indicators, especially valid in periods of ethno-religious segregation and strong Jewish identity, are death certificates and cemetery of internment, the number of pupils absent from school on *Yom Kippur, and distinguishable Jewish names. Since the mid-twentieth century there has been a growth in communal and nationwide surveys that allocate Jews by a single or a combination of methods, including master lists, distinctive Jewish names, and random samples. Informal surveys, conducted by private research groups, often introduce a question on religion. However, given the small proportion of Jews in the total American population, these samples are inadequate for quantitative analyses of the Jewish population.

In past eras, given strong religious identity and almost universal endogamy, the definition of "who is a Jew" was unequivocal. However, more recently, as successful acculturation has increased familial relationships with non-Jews, this definition has gained in complexity. This difficulty has been further enhanced by the ambiguity of "Jewishness," which is viewed as both a religion and an ethnicity. In the United States, where religious affiliation is not anchored by legal provision, people can informally switch from one religious group to another, and changes in religious affiliation are reversible. There may also be multiple bases of identity. Most demographic research relies on subjective self-declaration and considers as Jews all those who define themselves as such, whether they see themselves as belonging to a religious, ethnic, cultural, or other group. This designation may also include people with no religion (or a religion theologically compatible with Judaism) who do not consider themselves Jewish but have a Jewish mother and/or father.

Despite the many methodological and conceptual limitations, there is a rich and comprehensive documentation of the evolution of the American Jewish population and its demographic characteristics. The beginning of the community dates to 1654 with the permanent settlement in New Amsterdam, later *New York City, of twenty-three Jewish refugees of *Sephardic origin from Recife, *Brazil. Over the next few decades the number of Jews increased slowly to about 300 in 1700, 2,500 in the revolutionary year of 1776, and up to roughly 3,000 Jews in 1820. With this growth, the Jewish community also became more diverse, including people from many countries in Europe. By 1730, Jews from *Central Europe already outnumbered their Sephardic counterparts in America, and over the next two centuries the percentage of *Ashkenazic Jews in the American Jewish population continued to grow. Although Jewish immigration never stopped, by the early nineteenth century the proportion of native-born Jews had increased substantially (see UNITED STATES: IMMIGRATION).

The Jewish population was 15,000 in 1840, 150,000 in 1860, and approximately one-quarter of a million in 1880. This rate of increase was 15% higher than that of the American population as a whole, with most of the growth being attributable to large-scale immigration from German-speaking (Central) Europe. Although the new arrivals settled disproportionately in New York, these years were characterized also by spatial dispersion throughout the continent. The paramount reasons for this internal movement were economic in nature and included the establishment of new markets and the search to exploit new opportunities. In the process, Judaism also spread to become a nationwide religion, and the foundations for Jewish institutions and organized activities were laid.

No doubt the most meaningful demographic change for American Jews was the mass immigration of two million *East European Jews who entered the country between 1881 and the outbreak of *World War I. Accompanied by internal demographic development, the number of Jews had climbed to 3.4 million by 1920. Since the overwhelming majority of the new immigrants had arrived from a single defined area, the composition of the American Jewish community came to be dominated by Jews of Eastern European provenance. Such a large immigration over such a relatively short span of time also increased the share of Jews in the total American population from approximately 0.5% at the beginning of the period to more than 3% in 1914. Likewise, in light of the geopolitical changes in Europe, especially the dismantling of large empires into smaller sovereign countries, the United States came to have the largest concentration of Jews in the world, and it maintained this demographic seniority throughout the twentieth century. Because the immigrants tended to stay in cities that were ports of entry, the percentage of Jews in these locations was far higher than elsewhere, and the northeast became home to as many as two-thirds of America's Jews.

The new immigrants came mostly from the poorer strata of Eastern European Jewry. After a short period of hard work in physical jobs, they began to move up the socioeconomic ladder. This trend was accelerated between the two world wars and especially by the immigrants' American-born children, who by the 1930s had become a majority among the Jewish population. Restrictions on entry to the United States, despite some flexibility after the rise of the *Nazi party in *Germany and immediately following the end of *World War II, substantially diminished the number of Jewish immigrants. Overall, between 1933 and 1950 some 300,000 Jewish refugees, survivors, and *displaced persons from Europe settled in the United States. Given that the American Jewish population had increased to five million by 1950, these low numbers indicate the declining importance of immigration as a component in the demographic development of American Jewry.

The second half of the twentieth century was characterized by the full acceptance of Jews into the social and economic American mainstream and by their unprecedented achievements in education, occupational mobility, and income, as well as in the public and political arenas. Jews began to spread geographically from city centers to the suburbs, and on the national level many moved to southern and western states, distributing the Jewish population almost equally among the Sunbelt regions and the Northeast and Midwest. However, their successful integration affected the demographic patterns of the Jews, slowing their demographic evolution. By 1990, the Jewish population had slightly increased to an all-time high of 5.5 million. However, after that, it began to diminish for the first time in its history and in 2005 numbered 5.3 million. These numbers reflect wide social processes of marriage postponement, increased divorce rates, frequent interfaith marriage, which now comprise half of all new marriages involving at least one Jewish partner, and low fertility. Since the majority of the children of mixed couples are not raised within the Jewish faith, actual Jewish fertility has dropped deeper below the required threshold for intergenerational replacement. These patterns have resulted in the aging of the Jewish population and in a larger number of deaths than births; eventually they will lead to negative natural movement. Even a positive international migration balance from countries including *Israel and the former *Soviet Union has not offset the internal demographic losses (see DEMOGRAPHY).

Accordingly, Jews in 2010 comprised less than 2% of total American population. From a worldwide Jewish perspective, the United States no longer has the largest concentration of Jews; rather it shares this position with Israel. With due caution, barring possible changes in the demographic patterns as a result of general socioeconomic and cultural processes or particularistic Jewish circumstances, the number of American Jews is anticipated to diminish somewhat further.

UZI REBHUN

United States: Economic Life. At the turn of the twenty-first century, about 44% of all American Jewish men worked in professional occupations, and another 23% earned their living in management positions. Moreover, 40% of the married men in these two occupational categories had wives who also worked in professional or managerial occupations. As a consequence, some two-thirds of American Jewish families had occupations that placed them comfortably in the upper middle class, and only 2% lived in households below the poverty line. Young Jewish adults are entering these same occupations at about the same rate as their parents, suggesting that this level of economic security is likely to persist for some decades into the future.

The economic life of American Jewry was not always this prosperous. At the turn of the twentieth century, in the middle of the period of mass Jewish migration from *Eastern Europe and *Russia, most American Jewish men – more than 80% – were in blue-collar occupations; about a quarter of these blue-collar employees worked in crafts occupations and the rest as operatives and unskilled laborers. Their earnings were correspondingly low, mainly because these occupations were at the low end of the wage distribution but also because the American economy had yet to experience the large increase in worker productivity that would characterize the twentieth century. Jewish women from these poor families typically worked until marriage and sometimes afterward as well, but most withdrew from the labor force once they began having children.

The transformation of the male Jewish labor force from one dominated by low-paid blue-collar workers to one with

a majority of well-paid professionals and managers was largely achieved by 1950 and has been relatively stable for the last half-century. This remarkable phenomenon was achieved largely because of the heavy emphasis that Jewish immigrants placed on taking advantage of American educational opportunities for their children. Seeing education as a route to social assimilation – or, as they would have put it, Americanization – as well as economic advancement, Jewish parents were willing to make sacrifices in their own consumption levels to keep their children out of the workplace and in school. Among Jewish men born during the interwar period (1925–40), most of whom were the sons of blue-collar immigrants, fully one-quarter pursued higher education beyond college and earned an advanced degree. Although opportunities for higher education were expanding dramatically for all Americans, only 12% of non-Jewish men in this age cohort earned advanced degrees. Thus, despite a clear pattern of anti-Jewish discrimination in many colleges and universities, Jewish men were able to earn high-level degrees at more than twice the rate as their non-Jewish counterparts.

Jewish families educated their daughters as well as their sons, although labor market opportunities for women would lag behind those for men for several decades. Jewish women not only finished high school but often college as well, and among those born during the interwar period some 15–20% would go on to earn advanced degrees. As was the case for their brothers, this was markedly higher than the 5–7% of non-Jewish women in this cohort who earned advanced degrees. Many of these Jewish women entered the professions as public schoolteachers and social workers, whereas others worked in Jewish communal institutions on a volunteer basis. It was also common for the wife of a self-employed man to help in her husband's business, for example as a bookkeeper or receptionist, perhaps part-time or on a seasonal basis.

As soon as their income position improved, American Jewish immigrants or their adult children moved to middle-class housing in more attractive neighborhoods than the crowded tenements in which they had initially settled. By the 1950s they would move again into even more pleasant suburban neighborhoods. Recognizing that their own improved income status derived from educational achievements, Jewish parents continued to emphasize the importance of education for their children. With higher incomes than their immigrant parents, they could afford to live in neighborhoods with high-quality public schools and to finance higher education for their children. Most third-generation American Jewish youth would go to college. Among those born during and after *World War II (1941–75), about 40% of the Jewish men and 30% of the Jewish women would continue their education and earn advanced degrees. These rates were at least three times higher than the rates at which their non-Jewish counterparts were earning advanced degrees, resulting in a disproportionate presence of Jews on many university campuses. They would go on to be disproportionately represented in a number of professions as well, although Jews would always remain a small minority in each occupation because they are such a small fraction (about 2%) of the American population.

One of the most significant economic decisions made by immigrant Jews at the turn of the twentieth century was to limit their number of children. Jewish fertility rates in Russia and Eastern Europe had been very high, and most immigrant Jews came from large families, in which eight, ten, or even more siblings would not have been remarkable. Yet, low-income American Jews understood that they could not provide many advantages for so many children. Statistical data for the year 2000 are available for married Jewish women born since 1925. In every age group, these women have borne between 2 and 2.5 children on average. This low fertility rate began much earlier than most people realize, and it enabled the relatively large investments that even low-income immigrants made in the health and education of their children. Each generation of Jewish women tended to be better educated than their non-Jewish counterparts and thus more likely to improve their children's educational opportunities. Jewish families avoided the pattern of other immigrant groups where the mother worked and the older daughters cared for young siblings. Instead, Jewish mothers typically withdrew from the labor force to care for young children and often reentered when the children were older. Even as later decades saw young families with higher incomes, Jewish parents chose not to have more children but rather to invest even more heavily in the education and health of each child.

The prevalence of high-level graduate education and professional training among young Jewish men and women affects not only their future income prospects but also their family lives. Since young adults tend not to think of marriage until they can see the shape of their future careers, the typical age at marriage is several years older than that of earlier generations, especially for women. Increasing numbers of people earning graduate and professional degrees mean that single adults become a rising proportion of the Jewish population, and their parents, the so-called empty nesters, become correspondingly more numerous as well. Jews tend to have higher rates of marriage than non-Jews, yet the proportion of women who never marry has been rising, and couples who marry later are more likely to remain childless. Jewish fertility rates have been falling well below replacement levels because of the high incidence of unmarried women, but young Jewish families still have 2–2.5 children on average and emphasize the importance of health and education for both sons and daughters. Jewish communal institutions seem to be adapting to the needs of two-career couples with high expectations. It is likely, therefore, that the economic life of American Jews has stabilized at its current level, well above that of the general U.S. population, and, at least in its large outlines, will persist for several generations to come.

For further reading, see C. U. Chiswick, *Economics of American Judaism* (2008); B. R. Chiswick, "The Occupational Attainment and Earnings of American Jewry, 1890–1990," *Contemporary Jewry* 20 (1999): 68–98; idem, "The Occupational Attainment of American Jewry: 1990–2000," *Contemporary Jewry* 27 (2007): 80–111; and *2000/01 National Jewish Population Survey*, available at *www.jewishdatabank.org*.

CARMEL U. CHISWICK

United States: Fraternal Societies.

United States: Fraternal Societies. When Jewish fraternal associations first emerged in the mid-nineteenth century, they were based on other fraternal societies such as the Freemasons. These groups helped new *immigrants maintain their Jewish identities while integrating into American society; they emphasized education, English-language skills, and American ideals, while fostering either a religious or ethnically Jewish consciousness. By 1917, there were almost 3,000 lodges with nearly 500,000 members.

The first and most prominent Jewish fraternal society was B'nai B'rith, founded in 1843 by a group of German immigrants, many of whom were also members of the Masons and Odd Fellows (see also ORGANIZATIONS: NORTH AMERICA). B'nai B'rith, translated as "Sons of the Covenant," lived by its motto of "Benevolence, Brotherly Love, and Harmony," providing sick benefits to members and support for widows and orphans. Its emphasis on an American Jewish identity based more on Jewish peoplehood than religion provided a *secular alternative to the *synagogue. Although B'nai B'rith was not anti-religious – some of its members were national religious leaders – it consciously avoided any mention of potentially divisive religious controversies to maintain unity. After its founding generation had successfully integrated into American society, B'nai B'rith discarded Americanization rituals and began to emphasize Jewish social service. A similar organization, the United Order of True Sisters, was founded in 1846 with comparable goals for women, but it did not achieve the success of B'nai B'rith (see ORGANIZATIONS, WOMEN'S: NORTH AMERICA).

Whereas B'nai B'rith focused on the generation of German Jewish immigrants, new fraternal societies emerged after 1880 as East European Jews began to arrive in America in greater numbers. The *Arbeter Ring (*Workmen's Circle), one of the most prominent fraternal groups, held educational lectures and discussions, as well as picnics, dinners, and dances, and also served as a mutual aid society for its members. The *Arbeter Ring* differed from many other fraternal societies in its admission of women. By 1906, more than 30% of its members were women, many of whom played an important role in local branches. Another difference was that a major focus of the *Arbeter Ring* was advocacy for radical socialist politics; not surprisingly, many of its early members were avowed socialists. After 1900 the society began to expand its membership, and by 1906, it boasted 8,000 members. It continued to grow rapidly, gaining 19,000 new members in 1909 alone. Many of these new members were not as politically inclined, but the *Arbeter Ring* continued to focus on socialist causes.

The *Arbeter Ring* was one of many fraternal societies for East European immigrants, some of which included *landsmanschaftn* (groups of immigrants from the same hometown). The Independent Order B'rith Abraham fraternal society was an umbrella organization for groups of new immigrants. More than 120 of its 354 New York branches were *landsmanshaftn*, which helped it become the largest American Jewish fraternal society by *World War I. *Landsmanshaft* organizations joined larger fraternal societies for financial reasons and to enhance their benefits, as well as for social prestige and networking opportunities. Many *landsmanshaftn* also had ladies auxiliaries. Finally, whereas *landsmanshaftn* helped maintain Old World ties, joining a fraternal society helped integrate the immigrants into the American milieu by exposing them to rituals that emphasized a hybrid American Jewish identity.

After the precipitous decline of Jewish *immigration after World War I, the need for Americanization declined, and so, too, did the prominence of Jewish fraternal societies. However, many *landsmanschaftn* continued to function into the twenty-first century through the maintenance of cemetery plots and burial services for the descendants of original members.

For further reading, see D. Soyer, *Jewish Immigrant Associations and American Identity in New York, 1880–1939* (1997); D. D. Moore, *B'nai B'rith and the Challenge of Ethnic Leadership* (1981); J. Sarna, *American Judaism* (2004); and C. Wilhelm, "The Independent Order of True Sisters," *American Jewish Archives* 54(1) (2002): 37–63.   MICHAEL R. COHEN

United States: Higher Education.

The Jewish encounter with American higher education is an important barometer of the Jewish position in American society. In the early years of the United States, the denominational bent of the nine colonial American colleges limited Jewish contact to an occasional student matriculation. This situation remained unchanged until the final decades of the nineteenth century, when some universities began to view a Jewish faculty and student presence as evidence of their broader missions of research and community service. This academic receptivity led American Jews to view the nation's colleges and universities as vehicles for educational, cultural, and social acceptance and advancement, and the numbers of Jewish students seeking higher education increased steadily. By 1910, the City College of New York was a predominantly Jewish institution. Similarly, a small but significant number of Jewish faculty appeared on college and university rosters around the country. Finally, Jewish philanthropists, perceiving institutional receptivity and hospitality, increasingly supported institutional initiatives.

In the early twentieth century, the rise of campus *antisemitism reflected the general social antisemitism in response to the large Eastern European Jewish migrations. Academic appointments became increasingly difficult to obtain, especially in the humanities. The social life of Jewish college students became more segregated, the rapid increase in Jewish fraternities being one indicator (see FRATERNITIES AND SORORITIES: NORTH AMERICA). After World War I, institutions hitherto viewed as open to all of merit and character began to impose admissions restrictions. Jews continued to attend college during the 1920s and 1930s, although not always the ones they regarded as most desirable. Graduate school acceptances were more difficult to obtain, particularly at medical and engineering schools. After World War II, although some restrictions on student admissions and faculty appointments persisted, most Jews seeking access to higher education found opportunities. The growth of public higher education, the lessening of antisemitic attitudes, a renewed emphasis on scholarship, passage of anti-discrimination legislation, and increased competition for competent faculty in the 1950s and early 1960s had overcome most remaining prejudices.

FACULTY: Most colleges in the nineteenth century stressed the inculcation of Christian discipline and piety, and many applied informal or explicit religious tests to prospective faculty. Only toward the end of the century, when American colleges and nascent universities relinquished their explicitly Christian orientation in favor of research

and subject mastery, did career opportunities emerge for Jews. Although prejudice persisted, possibilities for academic careers were better for Jews in late-nineteenth-century America than in England or Germany.

Receptivity to Jewish faculty was often linked to Jewish philanthropy. Under President Seth Low (1889–1901), Columbia University accepted many endowments and contributions from New York's Jewish community. Low emphasized Columbia's public role, including the provision of impartial access to all positions and facilities. Although Columbia's trustees did not invite a Jew to membership for another third of a century, Low appointed or reappointed several Jewish faculty. The *Jewish Encyclopedia* (1901–05) contained an entry for most of the major American universities, each indicating the Jewish representation on the faculty. From three to seven names were listed for most institutions; a significant number of these professors (about sixteen) taught in Semitics departments (see JEWISH STUDIES); the rest were spread over a large number of disciplines. The University of California at Berkeley appointed one of the first female Jewish professors, economist Jessica Blanche Peixotto in 1904; she became a full professor in 1918, the first woman to achieve that rank in the University of California system. Jews had the most difficulty obtaining appointments in fields that interpreted past and present Christian culture, such as history, religion, English literature, and art. Franz Boas's leadership in *anthropology assured continued Jewish representation in that field, and Jews secured appointment to prominent posts in other "newer" disciplines. This pattern persisted through the 1960s when Jews, by then well represented in the social sciences and professions, remained underrepresented in the humanities. Jewish women also remained underrepresented at that time.

Academic antisemitism flourished in the early twentieth century as the Eastern European Jewish migrations increased in size and visibility and as more Eastern European students appeared at elite institutions. The occasional Jewish student who obtained admission to graduate school seldom went on to a significant academic career. Jewish representation on European university faculties slightly increased early in the century as the Jewish numbers in American institutions declined. Factors that ultimately reversed this pervasive discrimination included the appointment to university faculties of significant numbers of scholars fleeing *Nazism, including many Jews; the general liberalization of attitudes that occurred during and after World War II; and changing demographic and economic conditions. American colleges played a significant role in the war effort, and Jews capitalized on opportunities when stationed at colleges where their potential for admission or employment would previously have been restricted. There was no turning back once the war had privileged intellectual over social considerations in faculty appointments.

Knowledge of the results of European antisemitism further silenced objections to Jewish appointments. Once Jews became part of a college or university hierarchy, their views on subsequent appointment and promotion decisions had to be considered. Finally, the rapid growth in undergraduate enrollments, due first to the G.I. Bill and then to the rising birth rate and the increase in the number of women attending college, created a severe faculty shortage. By the first decade of the twenty-first century, Jews comprised more than 10% of the American professoriate, although they were only 2% of the American population. The proportion of Jewish academics approached 40% and higher at certain "elite" institutions.

STUDENTS: Schools and universities began to attract American Jewish students and their parents in the late nineteenth century as it became clear that economic advancement required secular education. Universities, when opening or incorporating extant professional schools, raised their entrance requirements to include a bachelor's degree. Increased economic security among Jews made a longer period of post-secondary education feasible. The American Jewish student population exhibited rapid growth, high visibility, and strong geographic, institutional, and disciplinary concentrations.

Jewish students soon found themselves blamed for their own success. Initial concern about the increasing size of the Jewish student body was moderate: From its start in the late nineteenth century through *World War I, the gradual Jewish influx involved, for the most part, assimilated students. The movement toward liberalized access to American colleges that occurred between 1890 and 1910 discouraged any proclivity toward admissions restrictions. These factors continued to influence admissions policies after World War I. However, the balance soon shifted. With a college education now imperative to social advancement, officials feared that the growing Jewish presence might reduce higher education's attractiveness to the Gentile constituency. Fear of the foreigner and racial categorization had become commonplace by the 1920s, and Jews had attained enough upward mobility to translate an abstract "threat" into a present reality.

Discrimination in college admissions and the enactment of immigration restrictions occurred simultaneously. Admissions restrictions most frequently were imposed at or near major Jewish population centers. Universities devised two restrictive devices: selective admission and quotas. Created and elaborated at Columbia University after World War I, *selective admissions* postulated that the individual characteristics of *some* Jewish students created a "problem" and that mechanisms existed to distinguish between "desirable" and "undesirable" students. Application forms eliciting social characteristics, "psychological" (intelligence or aptitude) tests, photographs, character references, and personal interviews were near simultaneous innovations designed to facilitate such distinctions. Viewing "desirability" as an individual property, Columbia University authorities concluded that, given adequate information about each candidate and a large enough applicant pool, one could compose a freshman class containing an acceptable academic and social mix. This usually meant excluding most Jews of Eastern European origins. Harvard president Abbott Lawrence Lowell (1910–33) viewed the presence of Jews as a group as problematic apart from any member's personal characteristics. All interests, therefore, would be best satisfied by placing a quota (a strict limitation) on the number of Jewish students – even if all who applied appeared individually desirable.

Advocates of selective admissions viewed the expanded dossier as a way of evaluating social desirability while retaining the focus of admissions decisions on the individual student. The result was a Jewish enrollment at the desired level. The cost for these institutions was a laborious and subjective admissions procedure; the gains consisted of an "acceptable" student body, according to the administration's narrow definition. The use of selective admissions deflected much criticism precisely because it singled out no single status as "key." To the contrary, quota establishment remained indefensible (a university was not, after all, a social club or summer resort). Consequently, it was a covert, although common, practice.

Although private institutions had nearly free rein to change their admissions policies, the U.S. Constitution's Fourteenth Amendment meant that public colleges concerned about a Jewish presence and lacking an indigenous Jewish population were confined to restricting out-of-state matriculations. The existence of restricted boarding houses at state schools with dormitory shortages also proved effective. Even if legally prohibited from the invidious use of selective admissions, college officials retained broad discretion over admissions. After World War II, many colleges confronted litigation and antidiscrimination legislation (such as the 1948 Fair Education Practices Act in New York State). These colleges still managed to save the selective admissions process (and its subjective and discretionary methods), while having to cease all discrimination on the grounds of race, creed, color, or national origin. Title VI of the 1964 Civil Rights Act, although primarily aimed at equal treatment for blacks and Hispanics, also assured equal treatment for Jews. Today, few selective institutions are accused of anti-Jewish discrimination, although it is not clear precisely when discriminatory practices ended at a number of colleges.

Jewish students received little help from college officials when confronted with social ostracism. However, they occasionally obtained the support of Jewish philanthropists to "neutralize" their fellow students' antisemitism. Jacob Schiff, the financier, anonymously endowed the student center at Barnard College to counter the self-selecting student culture. Centrally located, its facilities would be open to all. Jewish students responded to social exclusion either by focusing on their academic work (thereby earning the reputation of "grinds") or by establishing predominantly Jewish academic and social organizations. At Harvard College in 1906, a group of Jewish undergraduates organized the first *Menorah Society, which had as its purpose "the promotion in American colleges and universities of the study of Jewish history, culture and problems, and the advancement of Jewish ideals." Other students did not aspire to inclusion in either the Gentile or Jewish student cultures. In traveling a difficult road, some relied on their Jewishness for strength; others sublimated their frustrations into some creative endeavor. Some perhaps never fully recovered from the negative status that their Gentile counterparts attached to them.

Jewish students moved into the mainstream after World War II; their transition was eased in the 1960s by the decline of fraternities and sororities as mainstays of student culture. Some identifiably Jewish organizations, such as Menorah, declined; others, such as *Hillel Foundations, grew. Academically, Jewish students opted for a broader spectrum of institutions as overt and covert discrimination declined and as public higher education increased in size to absorb the baby boom. As discrimination declined in professions dominated by firms (e.g., engineering) rather than by individual practice (e.g., medicine), they chose majors leading to a larger number of occupations. In this climate, assimilation (and, less openly, a fear of *intermarriage) replaced inclusion as the main problem perceived by the concerned Jewish community.

For further reading, see L. S. Feuer, "The Stages in the Social History of Jewish Professors in American Colleges and Universities," *American Jewish History* 71 (June 1982): 432–65; D. Oren, *Joining the Club: A History of Jews and Yale* (1986, reprinted 2001); M. Synnott, *The Half-Opened Door: Discrimination and Admissions at Harvard, Yale, and Princeton, 1900–1970* (1979, reprinted 2010); and H. S. Wechsler, "Academe," in *Jewish American History and Culture: An Encyclopedia*, ed. J. Fischel and S. Pinsker (1992), 3–13.

HAROLD S. WECHSLER

United States: Immigration. Since the 1980s, scholars of Jewish immigration have shifted their emphasis from political and social motivations that might seem unique to Jews, like generalized persecution or specific *pogroms, to a more nuanced view that integrates Jewish population movements into the general social evolution of Europe. Explanations for the immigration of Jews to North America still acknowledge their respective niches in the economies and moral imagination of European states, but Jewish immigration is no longer depicted as a mass exodus divided into distinctive ethnic eras – *Sephardic, *German, and *East European. Instead it is seen as part of the much larger migration of people away from Europe and as a sequence of strategies devised to sustain families in response to the continuing evolution of European capitalism.

The first Jewish settlers in the Americas were indeed Sephardim, members of former Portuguese *converso families who had re-created themselves as Jews in seventeenth-century *Amsterdam. "Jews of the Portuguese Nation" adjusted to the expansion of the Dutch trading empire by moving around it in disproportionate numbers. For example, after the Dutch captured Recife, *Brazil, from *Portugal in 1630, half of the civilian population of about 3,000 consisted of Sephardic Jews. When the Portuguese recaptured the area in 1654, Jews either relocated to Curacao, the Dutch free port off the coast of Spanish Venezuela, or returned to Amsterdam. Curacao remained the largest Jewish enclave in the Americas, at about 1,500, through the American Revolution (see CARIBBEAN). In 1654, a fugitive group of twenty-three refugees from Recife were part of the passenger contingent that landed in New Amsterdam. To resist Governor Stuyvesant's attempts to evict them, they used their influence with relatives who owned stock in the Dutch West India Company. Few stayed beyond a year or two. When the English captured the port in 1664 and renamed it *New York, the Jews were able to remain; more Jews also arrived from England, because Oliver Cromwell, England's ruler in the 1650s, had authorized the reentry to his realm of a modest group of Sephardic merchants from Amsterdam (see BRITAIN: EARLY MODERN AND MODERN).

Among the Jews who formed a congregation in New York in the 1690s were Sephardim from London and *Ashkenazim from the Rhineland or the *Baltic. Sephardim and Ashkenazim in London and Amsterdam sustained separate institutions, but in the North American colonies, the members of the two small groups blended to support synagogues, cemeteries, and benevolent societies. By the 1740s,

Jews in New York supplied the British Army with goods of various kinds and some went with the troops on the attempted conquest of *Canada in 1756–58. A few of these Jews became the nucleus of a tiny Jewish community in Montreal. By the outbreak of the *American Revolution, Jewish mercantile enclaves in *Charleston, *Philadelphia, and New York numbered in total about 2,000 to 2,500 persons. Their isolation from further immigration during the generation spanning the French Revolution (1789) and the end of the Napoleonic Wars (1815) enabled them to see themselves as an elite enclave in the new nation.

Between 1820 and *World War I, Jews participated in the massive population transfer from Europe to the Americas. The spread of industrial capitalism, intensified *urbanization, and the accompanying transformation of agriculture led millions of rural young people to work in the mines, along the docks, and in the factories of European cities. Jews who had lived among them as peddlers and produce dealers found their customers leaving and their economic functions becoming obsolete. Steadily through the nineteenth century, young Jews left rural areas for cities like Hamburg and *Berlin. A few thousand young Jewish men in the 1820s moved to the English Midlands, where relatives in Manchester or Birmingham might supply them with items to peddle in the countryside. By the early 1840s, as the United States recovered from a severe depression and as German farm families populated its Midwest, America became the key destination for emigrating Jews.

Jews left the German lands in disproportionate numbers; although they constituted only 1.1% of the German population, they were 4% of the emigrants. By 1860, the Jewish population of the United States was estimated at 150,000, as tens of thousands of young men followed family chains of migration to join relatives and bring others, including wives, in their wake. By 1860, there were 40,000 Jews in New York and 8,000 in both Baltimore and Philadelphia. Other young men began their careers as peddlers, following the new canal and railroad networks deep into the interior of the still sparsely populated country. Supplied with goods by relatives, they traveled into the cotton country of the South (see UNITED STATES, SOUTHERN), with its transportation hub of New Orleans. In 1860 about 4,000 Jews lived in that city, many from Alsace. Other Jewish peddlers proceeded from St. Louis to follow the Santa Fe Trail to New Mexico.

With the discovery of gold in California in 1848, Jewish young men came to *San Francisco; by 1870, the city's Jewish population was 17,000, the second largest community in the nation (see SAN FRANCISCO; UNITED STATES, WESTERN). On the Pacific slope, including Victoria, British Columbia, Jews created a mercantile network between the 1850s and 1880s, bringing dry goods and credit to mining and farming towns and exporting gold dust, hides, and farm commodities through relatives and partners in the hub city of San Francisco. Throughout the unsettled region, Jewish merchants gained exceptional civic status as pillars of stability. Although Jewish emigration after 1880 is dominated by an unprecedented stream of people from *Eastern Europe, another 100,000 new immigrants from Germany reached America between 1872 and 1914.

As railroad networks extended into *Poland and *Ukraine, as the Jewish population grew through natural increase far faster than the local peasantry, and as Russian state policy limited Jewish opportunities, Jews left their towns and villages in larger numbers. Some migrated to the Black Sea port of Odessa, where they dominated the grain trade to the Mediterranean. However, far larger numbers resettled in northern cities like *Warsaw, *Vilna, and Minsk where many found work in the new mass-production clothing factories, most owned by Jews. Pogroms, primarily in Moldavia and Ukraine between 1903 and 1906, induced many more Jews to emigrate, but economic upheavals underlay the political horrors. Between 1881 and 1924, with a lengthy hiatus during World War I, perhaps 2.3 million Jews from Eastern Europe arrived in the United States, comprising about 10% of the total foreign influx. About 75% of Jewish immigrants arrived from *Russia, 4% from *Romania, and approximately 19% from the lands of the *Habsburg Austro-Hungarian Empire, especially *Galicia. Unlike their predecessors from German lands, Jews were the largest group to leave Russia, followed by Poles and Finns.

In addition, from 1880 through 1914, about 90,000 Jews arrived in *Canada, and the trickle continued at 4,000 annually throughout World War I. Most settled in Ontario, especially Toronto, but several thousand moved to the prairie hub of Winnipeg. Between 1892 and 1914, 90,000 Jews also arrived in *Argentina. The *Baron Maurice de Hirsch Fund and its affiliates, as well as the Argentine government, subsidized twenty thousand or more so they might be located on cooperative farms. Some managed to acquire their own land, but most relocated to Buenos Aires. Unlike in Canada or the United States, however, more than 40% of these immigrants left the country, most for North America, perhaps because of the instability of an economy that depended on agricultural exports.

The migration from *Central Europe in the mid-nineteenth century had consisted primarily of single people but the mass exodus from Eastern Europe was mainly made up of young families, usually linked through brothers, sisters, and in-laws. The need to accommodate traditional religious values and to be near places of industrial employment led East European Jews to settle in congested urban enclaves. There, distinctive Jewish neighborhoods permitted the establishment of a culture that featured both observance of *Orthodox Judaism and *Bundist socialism. New York City in the 1890s became the capital of *Yiddish theater and Yiddish publishing (see JOURNALISM, YIDDISH: NORTH AMERICA) and by 1930 held more than two million Jews, a number unprecedented in history. Smaller groups, still in the hundreds of thousands, settled in industrial cities like *Philadelphia and *Chicago, whose Jewish communities were as large as those of Odessa or Vienna. Enclaves of 500 to 1,000 Jews, mostly small storekeepers and their families, were established in small cities throughout the Midwest. Contingents of 3,000 or more Jews, including Sephardim from Rhodes and the Sea of Marmora, settled along the Pacific Slope in Seattle, Portland, and *Los Angeles.

In 1924 the U.S. government drastically curtailed legal immigration through the imposition of national origins quotas. Jews who still desired to immigrate, if permitted to do so by their country of origin, had to wait until the number assigned them by American consuls became eligible. During the *Nazi years and the severe Depression in the United States, thousands desiring to enter were unable to do so.

Starting in 1965, when the United States began to liberalize its immigration laws, Jews again became a small proportion of millions of newcomers. Thousands of young Israelis, some with professional skills, organized a family-based transit between the two countries, a migration that persists. In the immediate aftermath of the *Iranian Revolution of 1979, more than 300,000 persons, including more than 30,000 Jews in family groups, fled to the United States. After the collapse of the *Soviet Union, at least 100,000 Jews emigrated from Russia. Although the Russians settled primarily in the New York area, most of the Iranians and many of the Israelis felt more comfortable in the salubrious climate of southern California. These communities play distinctive roles in cultural and political life in *Los Angeles, which is now American Jewry's second city.

Relevant studies include J. Bodnar, *The Transplanted: A History of Immigrants in Urban America* (1985); W. Nugent, *Crossings: The Great Transatlantic Migrations, 1870–1914* (1992); D. M. Swetschinski, *Reluctant Cosmopolitans: The Portuguese Jews of Seventeenth Century Amsterdam* (2000); A. Barkai, *Branching Out: German-Jewish Immigration to the United States, 1820–1914* (1994); M. Rischin, *The Promised City: New York's Jews, 1870–1914* (1962); G. Tulchinsky, *Taking Root: The Origins of the Canadian Jewish Community* (1993); H. Avni, *Argentina and the Jews: A History of Jewish Immigration* (1991); S. Feher, "From the Rivers of Babylon to the Valleys of Los Angeles: The Exodus and Adaptation of Iranian Jews," in *Gatherings in Diaspora: Religious Communities and the New Immigration*, ed. R. S. Warner and J. G. Wittner (1998); and S. J. Gold, *The Israeli Diaspora* (2002).   WILLIAM TOLL

United States: Labor Movement. Encompassing trade unions and union federations, newspapers, political parties, fraternal societies (see UNITED STATES: FRATERNAL SOCIETIES), theater groups, educational institutions, housing cooperatives, vacation resorts, and even a bank, the Jewish labor movement sought to raise the consciousness and skills of workers to empower them to fight for their rights and prepare them to take charge of society. Through its many activities and institutions, the movement's programs also tried to infuse a bit of its socialist vision of justice and equality into the present world. Although the Jewish labor movement faded as American Jews moved into the middle class, it left a legacy of liberalism that still exists today.

The Jewish labor movement arose with the mass *immigration of *Yiddish-speaking Jews from *Eastern Europe to the United States in the last quarter of the nineteenth century. Despite a number of large strikes, the movement's early years were marked by instability. The radical intellectuals who assumed leadership of the movement found that Jewish workers made willing strikers, but that once the moment of crisis was past the unions would melt away along with the gains achieved in the strikes. Nevertheless, the United Hebrew Trades (UHT), a federation of predominantly Jewish unions, was established in 1888.

The garment industry was home to the greatest concentration of Jewish workers. By 1900, the year the International Ladies' Garment Workers' Union (ILGWU) was founded, Jews made up a majority of its workers and employers. A decade later, two dramatic strikes greatly expanded the union's membership and influence. The first came in 1909–10 as 20,000 shirtwaist makers, mostly young women, walked off the job. Although the strike ended without official union recognition, it won higher wages and improved conditions and established a precedent for collective bargaining. A few months later, 60,000 cloak makers struck, leading to the establishment of the "Protocol of Peace," a pioneering agreement that set up a structure for mediating disputes in the industry. Between 1910 and 1914, furriers, millinery workers, and men's tailors also engaged in large strikes that strengthened their unions. In 1914 the Amalgamated Clothing Workers of America (the ACWA) was founded as a militant alternative to the United Garment Workers, which had been formed in 1891 for workers in the men's ready made clothing industry, and soon outstripped the older union in size and importance.

A number of other institutions contributed to the success of the labor movement. The *Forverts* (Jewish Daily Forward) appeared in 1897 and within a decade became the most widely read Yiddish daily newspaper in the world and the largest socialist daily in the country (see JOURNALISM, YIDDISH: NORTH AMERICA). Not only did it serve as the most prominent voice of the Jewish labor movement but it also offered material support to unions and striking workers. Founded as a radical workers' mutual aid society in 1892, the *Workmen's Circle (*Arbeter Ring) reorganized itself as a multibranch fraternal order in 1900. Led by socialists, it provided its members with medical and death benefits, a venue for social interaction, and a forum for cultural development. It also supported members when they were on strike and provided material aid to striking unions. By the 1920s, it sponsored a network of Yiddish children's schools and summer camps, a theater group, a tuberculosis sanatorium, and other institutions (see US: FRATERNAL SOCIETIES).

The success of the Jewish labor movement, in turn, contributed to the success of the Socialist Party in the 1910s. In 1914 the Lower East Side sent socialist labor lawyer Meyer London to Congress. Other socialists represented working-class Jewish districts on the New York City Board of Aldermen, in the New York State legislature, and on the municipal bench. In the 1920s, factional fighting between *Communist Party members and noncommunists (mainly socialists and anarchists) nearly wrecked the ILGWU, especially in the wake of a disastrous communist-led cloak makers' strike in 1926. The ACWA fared better, beginning its experiments in "new unionism" by taking a leading role in regulating conditions in the men's clothing industry, building a cooperative housing project, and establishing a bank.

In the 1930s, the labor movement emerged stronger than ever, even as it drew closer to the American mainstream. The ILGWU, under noncommunist leadership, took advantage of the New Deal's pro-labor policies after 1933. By the end of the decade, it and the ACWA each claimed hundreds of thousands of members, making their leaders, David Dubinsky (1892–1982) and Sidney Hillman (1887–1946), two of the most powerful labor leaders in the country. The rejuvenated ILGWU followed the example of the ACWA in providing services for members, including a summer resort. It even sponsored *Pins and Needles* (1937), a commercially successful musical revue. Both unions helped form the Congress of Industrial Organizations (CIO), but the ILGWU soon returned to the American Federation of Labor (AFL). Seeking a path to political respectability, many of the Jewish unions and labor leaders helped establish the

American Labor Party (ALP), which played an important role in the electoral successes of progressive politicians in New York State. In 1934, the Jewish unions, the Workmen's Circle, and other groups formed the Jewish Labor Committee (JLC) to wage propaganda campaigns against the *Nazi regime in *Germany and help socialist and labor leaders escape Europe for the United States.

Even as the movement reached new heights of membership and influence, however, it was beginning to lose momentum. Few American-born Jews followed their immigrant parents into the needle trades, instead choosing white-collar careers, a trend that accelerated after *World War II. Although many individual Jews remained active in the labor movement as leaders and staffers, Jewish union members now tended to concentrate in teacher, public employee, and other white-collar unions. In the early twenty-first century, both the Jewish Labor Committee and the Workmen's Circle remain active, although their memberships are small. Outside of the remnants of its core institutions, the abiding influence of the Jewish labor movement is evident in the relative liberalism of the Jewish community, in the institutions of the general labor movement, in the cooperative housing projects that dot New York City, and in other surviving social programs of the New Deal. On this topic, see M. Epstein, *Jewish Labor in the USA*, 2 vols. (1950, 1953); H. Kosak, *Cultures of Opposition: Jewish Immigrant Workers, New York City, 1881–1905* (2000); and T. Michels, *A Fire in Their Hearts: Yiddish Socialists in New York* (2005).   DANIEL SOYER

United States: Military Chaplaincy. The rabbinical chaplaincy of the U.S. armed forces is one of the most significant examples of pan-denominational cooperation in American Jewish history. It demonstrates American Jewry's full participation and acculturation into American society, while also illustrating American Jewry's perpetuation of cultural and religious distinctiveness within a largely Christian society.

Although the American military chaplaincy dates to the *Revolutionary War, the first official rabbinical chaplain was not appointed until the *Civil War. Before that, American law required that chaplains be ordained by a "Christian denomination." With congressional support and following American Jewish advocacy, the legislation was amended to state that chaplains possess ordination from "some denomination." In 1862, President Abraham Lincoln appointed Rabbi Jacob Frankel as the first of three rabbis to serve as Civil War chaplains. Like their Christian counterparts, the rabbi-chaplains were tasked with facilitating ritual observance and *worship, teaching wartime moral conduct, and boosting morale. The modern American Jewish chaplaincy emerged in 1917, during preparations for the American entry into *World War I, when the *Jewish Welfare Board (JWB) was established to serve the religious needs of the 250,000 Jews then in the U.S. armed forces. Composed of the Young Men's Hebrew and Kindred Associations and other national Jewish organizations – most significantly the Reform movement's Central Conference of American Rabbis and Union of American Hebrew Congregations, the Conservative movement's United Synagogue of America, and the Union of Orthodox Congregations and *Agudas ha-Rabbanim*, the Orthodox rabbinical organization (see entries under JUDAISM) – the JWB was led by Cyrus *Adler. Rabbi Elkan C. Voorsanger became the first rabbi commissioned as a chaplain and officer in 1917; he was followed by twenty-four others serving in the Army and Navy. Along with distributing ritual items including Bibles and *mezzuzot*, the rabbis created a uniquely multidenominational JWB prayer book.

In 1941, in response to the military build-up preceding *World War II, the rabbinically led Committee on Army Navy Religious Affairs (CANRA) was established as a distinct organization within the JWB and was later expanded to include Orthodox and Conservative rabbinical organizations. The CANRA, chaired by Orthodox Rabbi David de Sola Pool, commissioned more than three hundred rabbi-chaplains. Across the United States and in every theater of war from Europe to the Pacific, they served the 500,000 Jews in the armed forces during World War II. Perhaps the CANRA's greatest challenge was responding to Jewish religious diversity. Although most servicemen were traditional in background, the majority of chaplains were Reform. However, despite profound differences over ritual practice and ideology, liturgy (see WORSHIP) and *halakhah* were adapted to wartime realities and divergent needs. In addition to providing ritual items, including revised *prayer books, the chaplains also endeavored to enable a modicum of accommodation to Jewish *dietary laws (*kashrut*) for Jewish servicemen. Although never again on the same scale as during World War II, the rabbinical chaplaincy has continued since then, meeting the needs of Jews in the armed services and fostering American religious ecumenism. For further reading, see B. W. Korn, *American Jewry and the Civil War* (2001); A. I. Slomovitz, *The Fighting Rabbis* (1998); and P. S. Bernstein, *Rabbis at War* (1971).   DANIEL M. BRONSTEIN

United States: Political Involvement.

Except for the colonial period and the early years of the Republic, when Jewish voting rights were restricted and Jews could not hold office, Jews in the United States have enjoyed full political rights. In the early nineteenth century, Jews, concentrated in Atlantic port cities, generally supported the party of Thomas Jefferson and the Democratic Republicans.

The Jewish percentage of the population remained small until the arrival of immigrants from Central Europe in the mid-nineteenth century (see UNITED STATES: IMMIGRATION). Subsequently Jewish involvement in civic affairs was active, but tended to be at the local level, especially in small towns in the west, where many Jews were merchants (see UNITED STATES, WESTERN). On the eve of the Civil War (see UNITED STATES: CIVIL WAR), sectionalism typically dictated Jewish partisan identification. In the south, Jews were Democrats, and they supported the Confederacy (see UNITED STATES, SOUTHERN). In the north, they affiliated with the Whig Party and later the new Republican Party. In their quest for acceptance, southern Jews generally supported slavery. Although the majority of northern Jews were not abolitionists, some were fervent critics of slavery. Judah P. Benjamin (1811–1884) was the first Jewish senator, elected from Louisiana in 1853. An ardent states' rights advocate and defender of slavery, Benjamin served the Confederacy as Attorney General, Secretary of War, and Secretary of State. When the Confederacy surrendered, he fled to England.

The stresses of the Civil War provoked *antisemitism, generally expressed in allegations of treachery and charges of profiteering. In Kentucky, Union General Ulysses S. Grant accused Jews of smuggling and speculation and ordered them expelled. Jewish activists organized protest rallies in several northern cities. Under this political pressure, President Abraham Lincoln revoked the order. From this episode, Jews learned that, although antisemitism existed in America, they could fight back against such discrimination. For the next half-century, Jews generally voted Republican, the party of Lincoln, although they had not yet emerged as an identifiable political bloc.

In the nineteenth century, Jews exhibited an interest in politics that would come to exemplify their political behavior. Central European and later Eastern European Jewish immigrants at the local level worked as election workers and ward bosses in urban political machines. A few, such as Abe Reuf in *San Francisco, would lead citywide machines.

The vast numbers of Eastern European Jews who emigrated to the United States beginning in the 1880s expanded the Jewish impact and involvement in politics. Those immigrants, emigrating from industrial cities, had prior political experience with the Russian *Bund, which promoted a progressive agenda for the advancement of rights for workers. Many Jews were already imbued with the *Marxist philosophy apparent in the Socialist Labor Party. While Jews, especially in major urban centers such as *New York City, were politically liberal, most were not socialists or communists. However, a disproportionate and vocal percentage of the leaders of leftist and radical organizations in this era were Jews.

Many Jews were employed in the garment industry in New York City, an example for many radicals of the worst characteristics of industrial capitalism. The Jewish labor movement (see UNITED STATES: LABOR MOVEMENT), created and led by these radicals, also served as a political forum and movement, providing a foundation for Jewish political identity and action. Although women would not gain the right to vote until 1920, Eastern European Jewish women garment workers were in the forefront of the crusade for structural reforms and improved working conditions, efforts that often coincided with the Progressive movement. Some would join the fight for female suffrage, setting a precedent for the preponderance of Jewish involvement in the Second Wave of feminism in the 1960s (see later). Others were more radical. Rose Schneiderman (1882–1972), Pauline Newman (1889–1986), and Clara Lemlich Shavelson (1886–1982) were labor and women's rights advocates who devoted themselves to improving the conditions of working women. Anarchists, the political extreme among Eastern European Jews, were best epitomized by Emma Goldman (1869–1940), a polemicist, labor organizer, enemy of capitalism and militarism, and crusader for social and economic justice, who was deported to Russia in 1919.

In the early twentieth century, Eastern European Jews comprised nearly 40% of those who voted for Socialist Party candidates. One was Meyer London (1871–1926), elected to represent the Lower East Side of New York City in Congress in 1914. Beginning with the election of Woodrow Wilson in 1912 and continuing through the 1920s, this voting behavior would begin to change as urban Jews voted increasingly for Democratic Party candidates. In 1928, they gave an unprecedented percentage of their votes to Al Smith, the party nominee. Others would continue voting socialist until 1932, when their support for Franklin D. Roosevelt marked the beginning of overwhelming Jewish support for the Democratic Party. Jewish radicals, influenced by the despair of the Great Depression, would continue to comprise 40% of the membership in the American Communist Party in the 1930s. Ultimately, however, pragmatists among radical leaders recognized that progressive reforms were more appealing to Jewish voters than the goal of restructuring society. Jewish defections from the Communist Party began with the antisemitic persecutions and imprisonments in the Soviet Union during the Stalinist era. Desertions from the party accelerated with the Nazi-Soviet Pact of 1939, and Jewish support of communism generally ended with the persecution of leftists in the anti-communist crusade of the early Cold War years.

In the aftermath of *World War II, amid revelations of the *Holocaust and the recognition that American Jews had been unable to persuade President Roosevelt to do more to help European Jewry, Jews became active political advocates for U.S. recognition of the State of *Israel. Although President Harry S. Truman did not send arms shipments to the new nation, the importance of the Jewish vote, among other issues, persuaded him to recognize Israel. For many Jews, the American relationship with Israel remains the primary factor influencing their political behavior. This collective voice, along with the lobbying effectiveness of the American Israel Political Action Committee (AIPAC), has ensured American support for Israel (see ORGANIZATIONS: NORTH AMERICA).

Throughout the twentieth century, Jews held leadership positions in national civil rights organizations (see UNITED STATES: CIVIL RIGHTS MOVEMENT). Jews formed a significant segment of the white, northern civil rights activists working in the south for voting rights and against segregation in the 1950s and 1960s. In creating a more just society, many Jewish activists believed they would help ensure a society that was welcoming to Jews. In the 1960s, many among the New Left were of Jewish background. On university campuses, Jews constituted nearly half of the national membership of the Students for a Democratic Society; similarly, Jews made up a disproportionate share of those who protested the Vietnam War.

In the 1950s and 1960s, Jewish women, liberal and well educated, played an important leadership role in the second wave of the feminist movement. They demanded equality, an end to discrimination, and control over their own bodies, among other issues. Betty Friedan (1921–2006), author of *The Feminine Mystique* (1963) and co-founder of the National Organization for Women, advocated for expanded public roles for women. Jewish feminists involved in the women's rights movement would also address the role of women within Judaism (see JUDAISM, FEMINIST). Jewish women serving in the U.S. Congress, such as Congresswoman Bella Abzug (1920–1998; D-New York) and Senator Barbara Boxer (D-California), have worked to advance issues relevant to all women.

In recent years, the neoconservative movement has attracted prominent Jewish proponents. Some were former Marxist intellectuals who shifted to the right in response to the social ferment of the 1960s. By the 1980s, many supported the Cold War policies of President Ronald Reagan. In the early twenty-first century, neoconservatives were important figures in the construction of an activist American foreign policy and a strong national defense.

Nevertheless, except for 1980, when Jews turned against President Jimmy Carter on issues related to his policies toward Israel, the economy, and the Iranian hostage crisis, Jews have voted overwhelmingly Democratic in all presidential elections since 1932, and they have become an influential and key constituency group within the party. Only in local and statewide elections, on specific financial or public policy issues, have significant numbers of Jews cast votes for centrist Republican candidates. Despite economic advancement, social acceptance, and suburbanization, American Jews, more than any other religious and ethnic group, remain consistently liberal. They vote for Democratic candidates in national elections on questions of civil liberties, civil rights, and social justice for the disadvantaged. Except for those who are religiously traditional, a group that is increasing in size and influence, Jews strongly support the separation of church and state, public education, and *abortion rights. They continue to be disproportionately involved in politics as generous campaign contributors, political fundraisers, and informed and frequent voters; in large urban states, they form a critical group within the electorate. In recent decades, Jews have been elected to state and national office in increasing numbers. In 2000, Senator Joseph Lieberman (D-.Connecticut) was the vice-presidential candidate on the Democratic presidential ticket.

For further reading, see M. Dollinger, *Quest for Inclusion: Jews and Liberalism in Modern America* (2000); L. S. Maisel, *Jews in American Politics: Essays* (2003); and M. E. Staub, *Torn at the Roots: The Crisis of American Liberalism in Postwar America* (2002).   ARLENE LAZAROWITZ

United States Presidents. From the first years of the Republic, American Jews looked to American presidents to support their right to practice *Judaism and to guarantee their inclusion in the body politic. Several *synagogues sent letters to the first president, expressing uncertainty about their status in the new nation. In an often quoted letter, President George Washington assured "the children of the Stock of Abraham" they would be safe to practice Judaism (see NEWPORT, RHODE ISLAND). Thomas Jefferson championed equal political rights for Jews, not because of his particular respect for Judaism, but because he respected the rights of all to hold disparate religious beliefs.

Until the mid-nineteenth century, very few American Jews were named to federal positions. An exception was the appointment in 1813 by President James Madison of Mordecai Noah as ambassador to Tunis, the first diplomatic post awarded to a Jew. Given American difficulties with Barbary pirates, this was an important position. However, the State Department recalled Noah two years later because of protests from Muslim Tunisia over the appointment of a Jew. Although anti-Jewish sentiments may have deterred other appointments, this is the only case when overtly antisemitic reasons were cited in rescinding a Jewish presidential appointment.

The upheavals of the *Civil War also exposed antisemitic feelings. By this time, immigration from *Central Europe had augmented the Jewish population. When General Ulysses Grant issued Order Number 11, expelling Jews from areas of Kentucky for alleged profiteering, Jews appealed to President Abraham Lincoln, who revoked the order (see UNITED STATES: CIVIL WAR). When Grant was elected president after the Civil War, he maintained good relations with American Jews.

The vast immigration of *Eastern European Jews in the late nineteenth and early twentieth centuries gave Jews increased political influence. President Theodore Roosevelt selected Oscar Straus (see STRAUS FAMILY) for his cabinet, the first such appointment of a Jew. President Woodrow Wilson took the political risk of appointing Louis *Brandeis, an outspoken reformer, to the Supreme Court. Brandeis played an important role in persuading Wilson to support the *Balfour Declaration, a British statement of support for an eventual Jewish homeland in *Palestine, despite opposition from the State Department and his other advisors. In response, in 1916, a substantial number of Jews, who had generally voted Republican, the party of Lincoln, voted for Wilson.

The striking shift in Jewish voting behavior would occur during the Great Depression, when Jews overwhelmingly supported Franklin D. Roosevelt. Roosevelt's New Deal programs benefited Jews, and the New Deal also granted Jews leadership roles in government agencies and as advisors. As the size of the federal bureaucracy increased, Roosevelt appointed more Jews to government positions than all prior presidents combined. Roosevelt's response to the *Holocaust and American reluctance to admit significant numbers of European Jews to the United States remain controversial. Many question whether Roosevelt did as much as he could to assist Jewish refugees. Under pressure to address the Jewish refugee crisis, he convened a conference of world leaders at Evian-les-Bains, France in 1938, but it did not offer any solutions. Throughout the war, the State Department actively obstructed Jewish immigration, even though the government was well informed about *Nazi plans to exterminate European Jews. Roosevelt did not establish the War Refugee Board until 1944. More recently, Robert Rosen has maintained that the climate of the times explains Roosevelt's cautious approach. Antisemitic feelings were pervasive in the 1930s and many Americans blamed Jews for the Depression. The anti-immigrant sentiment that led to the 1924 legislation that restricted immigration to the United States from Eastern and Southern Europe remained high, and there was popular feeling that Jews were pressuring the United States into war with *Germany (see HOLOCAUST: UNITED STATES JEWISH RESPONSE).

After *World War II, Jewish political efforts, combined with the shock of revelations about the Holocaust, persuaded President Harry S. Truman to recognize *Israel in 1948, despite opposition from the State Department. When war broke out between Israel and the Arab states, however, Truman embargoed any arms sales to Israel.

Since 1948, Israel has dominated the relationship between Jews and American presidents. The Eisenhower administration generally sided with Arabs in the region. President John F. Kennedy departed from this policy when he sold Hawk anti-aircraft defensive missiles to Israel. President Lyndon B. Johnson had good relations with American Jews, who had become adept at lobbying for Israel. In the period before and after the 1967 Six Day War, Johnson developed a special patron–client relationship between the United States and

Israel, an unwritten security guarantee that identified Israel as a critical strategic Cold War asset in the Middle East.

Few Jews voted for President Richard M. Nixon, whose aversion to Jews is evident in the antisemitic comments on the tapes of his White House conversations. Nevertheless, Nixon appointed Henry Kissinger, a Jew, as his national security advisor and later as Secretary of State. After the 1973 surprise Arab attack on Israel, Nixon sent weaponry that made a critical difference in Israel's ability to turn the tide.

President Jimmy Carter alienated important segments of the Jewish population. The praise he received in 1978 for his instrumental role in reaching a peace agreement between Israel and Egypt was eclipsed by his support for a Palestinian homeland. In his failed 1980 reelection bid, Carter received only 45% of the Jewish vote, which had been consistently Democratic since 1928. President Ronald Reagan, Carter's Republican successor, strengthened relations with Israel and had generally good relations with Jews. President Bill Clinton appointed Jews to his Cabinet, the Supreme Court, and ambassadorships; Jewish support for his administration was strong. Despite his often unquestioning support for the policies of the Israeli government, President George W. Bush did not have wide support among most American Jews. Aside from traditionally religious Jews, most did not share his conservative social agenda. According to exit poll data, 78% of Jewish voters supported Barack Obama in the 2008 presidential election.

For further reading, see D. G. Dalin and A. J. Kolatch, *The Presidents of the United States and the Jews* (2000); F. Hirschfeld, *George Washington and the Jews* (2005); and R. Rosen et al., *Franklin D. Roosevelt and the Jews* (2007).

ARLENE LAZAROWITZ

United States: Sephardim. *Sephardic Jews, descendants of those who had been expelled from *Spain or who had become *conversos in Spain or *Portugal, were the first Jews to arrive in the Americas. Fearing the *Inquisition, these Sephardic Jews had learned to practice crypto-Judaism, shedding all outward signs of Jewishness while creating new forms of Jewish practice that were invisible to the outside world. They took these traditions with them as they scattered to new locations where they were often welcomed because they were involved in international trade.

The road to Sephardic Jewish settlement in North America ran through Recife, *Brazil. In an effort to attract Jewish merchants to their colonies in Brazil, the Dutch government promised them the right to practice Judaism. Within a decade, the Jewish community had grown to between 1,000 and 1,450. When the Portuguese recaptured Brazil, however, Jews were given three months to leave. Although most went to *Amsterdam and the *Caribbean, in 1654 a small group of twenty-three arrived in New Amsterdam (which became *New York when the settlement was ultimately ceded to *Britain in 1674), marking the first Jewish settlement in what would become the United States.

These first American Jews were allowed to settle because of their economic networks. For example, New York's Jewish merchants traded goods as diverse as cotton, rum, bricks, and onions in the North American colonies, the Caribbean world, Europe, and beyond. One colonial Jew owned a fleet of ships and dealt in rum, textiles, lumber, and ginger throughout the world. Other merchants shipped goods like corn and lumber to *England and in turn imported English products. With such mercantile backgrounds, it is not surprising that these Sephardic Jews settled primarily in major port cities such as *Newport, Rhode Island; New York City; *Philadelphia; *Charleston, South Carolina; and Savannah, Georgia – all of which were somewhat tolerant of outsiders. They avoided other port cities, however, such as *Boston, which was particularly homogeneous and rather unwelcoming to immigrants, and New Orleans, which officially barred Jews from settlement. These Sephardic Jews also settled based on mercantile and familial ties.

Despite the importance of their trade, most Sephardic Jewish port city communities developed slowly, remaining small in size on the eve of the *American Revolution. The first twenty-three Jewish settlers in New York, for example, had grown to only about three hundred by the mid-eighteenth century. Similarly, Newport, the northernmost Sephardic Jewish community, which emerged in 1658 with fifteen families, had only approximately thirty families before 1776. Philadelphia's Jewish community did not begin to grow until the 1740s and 1750s; by 1770, it numbered only about a hundred. Charleston's Jewish community emerged in 1697 and by the second half of the eighteenth century had just fifty Jewish families. Jews also settled in Savannah beginning in 1733, but significant growth did not begin until the 1790s.

With a heritage of practicing Judaism either discreetly or clandestinely, Sephardic Jews in America sought to maintain the duality between their public and private religious lives. They were free to practice Judaism openly within their homes, so many kept *kosher kitchens and observed such rituals as kindling *Sabbath lights. Jews were also permitted to build *synagogues, so *worship was a key component of American Judaism. Yet, as they practiced Judaism in the private sphere, they also tried valiantly to shield Judaism from the public eye. For example, their synagogue buildings, although awe inspiring and beautiful on the inside, were very plain on the outside, hardly distinguishable from ordinary buildings. Moreover, the portraits of themselves that they commissioned showed virtually no outward signs of their Jewish heritage.

Although Sephardic Jews hoped to shield Judaism from the public eye, they soon discovered that such neat compartmentalization was impossible. They especially found conflicts with *dietary laws and Sabbath and *festival observance because the rhythms of daily life in America did not follow the Jewish calendar. Should an individual observe the Sabbath, turning away business on Saturdays while Christian neighbors could earn money? It was relatively easy to maintain dietary observances within one's own home, but should a Jew spurn the opportunity to break bread in the home of a Christian neighbor? Sephardic Jews were the first to face what would soon become the quintessential American Jewish dilemma – how to balance Judaism with the American environment.

After 1776, the dominance of the Sephardic Jews waned considerably. Old trade networks collapsed, the peddler replaced the merchant as the primary Jewish businessperson, and German Jewish immigration, and later East European Jewish immigration, overwhelmed the Sephardic community and its leadership (see UNITED STATES:

IMMIGRATION). Since then, Sephardim have been a significant minority of American Jews.

For further reading, see A. Ben-Ur, *Sephardic Jews in America* (2009); E. Faber, *A Time for Planting: The First Migration, 1654–1820* (1992); J. Sarna, *American Judaism* (2004); and R. Brilliant and E. Smith, eds., *Facing the New World: Jewish Portraits in Colonial and Federal America* (1997).

MICHAEL R. COHEN

United States: South Florida.

The 555,000 Jews in south Florida, including 255,000 in Palm Beach County, 186,000 in Broward County, and 113,000 in Miami, represent about 10% of the population of south Florida and the third highest percentage of Jews in any major U.S. metropolitan area; they also constitute almost 10% of Jews in the United States.

Jewish settlement began in the late 1890s when twenty-two Jews migrated to Miami from other U.S. locations; soon, twelve of the sixteen merchants in downtown Miami were Jewish. *Antisemitism severely restricted the residential options of south Florida's Jews in the 1920s and 1930s. However, by the early 1930s, a Jew served on the Miami Beach City Council, and by the early 1940s a Jew was elected mayor. Significant Jewish population growth occurred between 1950 and 1975, and Miami Beach, a place where Jews once faced significant discrimination, is now known as an important Jewish area throughout the world. In 2008, the Jewish population of Miami was 113,000, a significant decrease from a peak of more than 200,000 in 1975.

In the early 1900s, some Jewish merchants moved northwards into Broward County, and opened department stores. By 1923, however, there were still only seven Jewish families in the county. The first religious service was held in 1926, and the first *synagogue was built in 1937. Explosive growth in the Jewish population occurred in the 1970s and 1980s, but the Jewish population began a slow decline during the early 1990s, a decline that accelerated with the loss of 55,000 Jews from 1997–2008.

The first Jews settled in Palm Beach County in the 1890s, opening retail stores. In 1923, Temple Israel, a Reform congregation, was formed, and a Jew became mayor of the city of West Palm Beach that same year. The largest increases in south Florida's Jewish population occurred after *World War II, when Jews from the Northeast and Midwest moved in large numbers to Florida. In Palm Beach County, for example, more than half of the Jewish households derive from New York or New Jersey. In the late 1950s, thousands of Cuban Jews found refuge in south Florida. Problems in *Argentina, Columbia, Venezuela, and other *Latin American countries in the late 1990s bolstered the adult Hispanic Jewish population of south Florida to more than 15,000 persons. South Florida is also home to more than 22,000 *Israeli adults.

Three Jewish entrepreneurs started the first Century Village development in West Palm Beach in 1967, developing the concept of the large planned retirement community that has since spread throughout south Florida and attracted many Jewish full or part-time residents. About 275,000 elderly Jews live in the area. "Snowbirds," who spend three to seven months in Florida and the remainder of the year in the northeast or midwest, form more than 10% of the population. Explosive growth in the Jewish population occurred in the 1980s and 1990s. Much of the growth in the 2000s is occurring in Boynton Beach, which now has more Jews than St. Louis, Missouri. Miami Beach, North Miami Beach, and Boca Raton have significant concentrations of Orthodox Jews (see JUDAISM, ORTHODOX). A recent collection of scholarly studies is A. Greenbaum, ed., *Jews of South Florida* (2005).   IRA M. SHESKIN

United States, Southern.

Jews settled early and extensively in the American south, although rarely in large numbers. Generally welcomed, Jews influenced the south's society and economy beyond their numbers.

In colonial days, Jews settled on the southern coast as early as 1585, and communities formed in fledgling port cities. Trading networks linked Jewish traders to *Newport, Rhode Island, and to *New York City, to the *Caribbean, and to London (see BRITAIN: EARLY MODERN AND MODERN). In 1733, London's Bevis Marks congregation sponsored the immigration of forty-two poor, mostly *Sephardic Jews to Savannah; these settlers organized a *synagogue, Mickve Israel, in 1735. Jews had arrived in *Charleston in 1695, and in 1749 founded Kahal Kadosh (holy congregation) Beth Elohim. Baltimore had a Jewish cemetery by 1786, and Richmond Jews organized Beth Shalome congregation in 1789. Charleston's Jewish community of seven hundred was the nation's largest in 1820.

Although Maryland and North Carolina included religious requirements for citizenship in their state constitutions, Jews gained acceptance in those states. In 1775 Francis Salvador became the first American Jew elected to public office when he took a seat in the South Carolina Provincial Congress. David Emmanuel served as governor of Georgia in 1801. In 1845 David Yulee became Florida's first senator, and Judah P. Benjamin was elected to the Senate from Louisiana in 1852. Philanthropist Judah Touro (1775–1854) resided in New Orleans.

Jews followed the nation's expansion into the southern heartland. With the German immigration in the mid-nineteenth century (see UNITED STATES: IMMIGRATION), Jewish peddlers and merchants created commercial networks from Baltimore and Cincinnati along rivers, canals, roads, and railways. By 1860, cities like Louisville and New Orleans had Jewish populations of 2,000, and the Baltimore community had grown to 8,000. Alsatian and Bavarian Jews migrated up the Mississippi from New Orleans.

German Jews arrived as the south was developing a distinct regional identity in response to abolitionism. Jews owned and traded slaves, but not significantly. Their slaveholding was typical of their class and place as an urban people. When the Civil War came (see UNITED STATES: CIVIL WAR), several thousand Jews fought for the Confederacy, and rabbis sermonized in support of states' rights. Judah P. Benjamin served in the Confederate cabinet.

In forming congregations, southern Jews followed tradition, first organizing benevolent societies and purchasing burial grounds. Charleston's Hebra [ḥevrah] Gemilut Hasadim Society of 1784 and its Hebrew Orphan Society of 1801 were the first such societies in America. As communities grew and prospered, these societies evolved into congregations. The Gemilath Chesed of Atlanta, founded in 1860, became the Hebrew Benevolent Congregation, later known as The Temple. Memphis dedicated a cemetery in 1847,

followed by a benevolent society in 1850 and a congregation in 1853.

Southern Jews lived distant from communal and rabbinic authority. Reform Judaism (see JUDAISM, REFORM: UNITED STATES) in America began in Charleston in 1824 when twenty-four young Jews, led by playwright Isaac Harby, organized the Reformed Society of Israelites that sought to rationalize theology and introduce Protestant decorum into worship. In 1840, Abraham Rice, the first ordained American rabbi, arrived in Baltimore, but his Orthodoxy was countered by German-born Rabbi David *Einhorn, who advocated radical Reform. When Isaac Mayer *Wise of Cincinnati convened a Union of American Hebrew Congregations in 1873, nearly half the delegates were southerners. The Conference of Rabbis of Southern Congregations, founded in 1885, endorsed the Pittsburgh Platform that espoused classical Reform Judaism. By 1900 almost three-quarters of the South's Jewish communities had a Reform temple. Rabbi Edward B. M. Browne published a newspaper, *The Jewish South* (1877–ca. 1881), which reported from 177 communities in thirteen states. An 1878 census listed 290 southern towns with Jewish populations, comprising nearly one-fifth of America's Jews.

From the 1880s to 1920s, some two million East European Jews immigrated to America; of these, a small but persistent number headed south. The Galveston Plan directed 10,000 immigrants to Texas after 1907 (see also ZANGWILL, ISRAEL). Levantine Jews settled in Mobile and Atlanta. East European Jews spread across the region, and by 1927 fourteen southern cities claimed more than 1,000 Jews. Atlanta's Rabbi Tobias Geffen, a Lithuanian immigrant, served as religious arbiter for Orthodox Jewry in the south.

Jewish peddlers, merchants, and capitalists were instrumental in helping create an urban and commercial New South after the Civil War. The Burdine, Godchaux, Hecht, Maas, Rich, and Thalhimer families became department store magnates in urban centers. Jewish industrialists like the Cone brothers of Greensboro, North Carolina, built textile mills that transformed the region. With the New South came a new color line that reordered racial and social relations. In Louisiana and Mississippi mobs of angry farmers burned the stores of Jewish merchants who held crop liens. In 1913 a Jewish factory manager in Atlanta, Leo Frank, was wrongly convicted of murdering a child laborer, a girl from a farm family. Two years later, after the Georgia governor overturned the unjust verdict, a mob lynched Frank. In the 1920s, a revived Ku Klux Klan often mixed *antisemitism into its racist, anti-Catholic rhetoric.

Yet, Jews, as white people, met wide acceptance. Southern universities were less inclined to impose quotas than some of their northern counterparts (see UNITED STATES: HIGHER EDUCATION). During *World War II Jews flocked to growing cities and camp towns as the Roosevelt administration built military bases and industrial installations in the south. In the post-war years, southern Jews, like Jews nationally, prospered, and the region saw new Jewish institution building.

However, Jewish comfort as acculturated southerners was challenged by the *civil rights movement. A few Jews were prominent segregationists, but others, like attorney Morris Abrams and journalist Harry Golden, forthrightly advocated integration. While national Jewish defense agencies endorsed desegregation and northern Jews were disproportionate among white activists, southern Jews spoke quietly, fearing a white backlash. In the 1950s, racial extremists bombed synagogues, most notably The Temple in Atlanta.

Southern Jews remained linked to global Jewry through affiliates of B'nai B'rith and the National Council of Jewish Women (see ORGANIZATIONS: NORTH AMERICA; ORGANIZATIONS, WOMEN'S: NORTH AMERICA). With its German and Reform heritage, the south is often described as non- or anti-Zionist, but important *Zionist leaders, including Louis *Brandeis of Louisville and Henrietta *Szold of Baltimore, emerged from the region. Zionist societies were established in six southern states by 1900, and *Hadassah counted twenty-four chapters in 1933. By 1913, Atlanta, Baltimore, Dallas, Little Rock, Memphis, and New Orleans had organized Jewish federations. In the early twenty-first century, the Jewish Federations of North America has fifty-six affiliates in the south.

Whether southern Jewry reflects a unique culture that differs from the American Jewish mainstream is a contentious topic. Eli Evans in *The Provincials: A Personal History of Jews in the South* (rev. ed., 2005) and Alfred Uhry in his play, *Driving Miss Daisy*, portray a culturally distinct people. Local and regional Jewish heritage societies have proliferated, and Jewish museums featuring local history can be found in a half-dozen cities. In 1976, a Southern Jewish Historical Society was organized, and an Institute for Southern Jewish Life located near Jackson, Mississippi, serves regional communities. Day schools, high schools, summer camps, Jewish Community Centers, and academic Jewish studies programs have proliferated.

As a region once noted for its racial and economic backwardness was transformed into the prosperous Sunbelt, Jews, like other Americans headed southward. Communities in Sunbelt cities have grown exponentially, while those in agrarian small towns have languished. Almost one-quarter of America's Jews now reside in the south. Atlanta holds some 100,000 Jews, and the south Florida communities of Miami and Boca Raton-West Palm Beach rank among the nation's largest, although they are culturally northern (see UNITED STATES: SOUTH FLORIDA). A core of self-identifying southern Jews with generational roots in the region persists, but the larger number comprises relative newcomers who migrated to the south to retire, to enjoy the lifestyle, or to find economic opportunity. For further reading, see M. I. Goldberg and M. Ferris, eds., *Jewish Roots in Southern Soil: A New History* (2006).　LEONARD ROGOFF

United States, Western. Providing the catalyst for western settlement, the California Gold Rush of 1849 coincided with heightened Jewish *immigration to the United States. The growing economy drew both men and women from the eastern United States, *Poland, *Britain, *Central Europe, and *France. All joined in creating diverse Jewish communities in the west. Like the well-known Levi Strauss, who arrived in California in 1853, many Jews became merchants, selling necessities to miners and settlers. By the 1870s, California's Jewish population numbered more than 20,000, more than any other state outside of New York. These first settlers established a strong, diverse community that provided the framework for all that followed. After the rush, Jewish immigration slowed, but never stopped; at the end

of the first decade of the twenty-first century, the second largest Jewish urban population in the United States is in *Los Angeles and its environs.

In contrast to Jewish immigrants in the eastern United States, most Jews who settled in the west were already acculturated to American life because many had already gained English-language skills and citizenship. In the west, where all were newcomers and there was no Protestant hegemony, Jews participated in civil leadership, becoming mayors, judges, and educators, even while they were founding Jewish community life. *San Francisco, the major port and an instant city, became the nineteenth-century center for western Jewry. With a population that had reached 3,000 by 1855, San Francisco's Jews built a complex community life, including social, religious, educational, and fraternal organizations. Often, chain migration brought brothers, sisters, and cousins to the area as well. It was common for one family member to remain in San Francisco while others established stores in other parts of the region; relying on extended families, western Jews built regional businesses and social networks. In San Francisco, men bought merchandise, made social and business connections, and frequently found wives. Before the twentieth century, the majority of the observant settled in San Francisco, where they could take advantage of *synagogues, kosher butchers, and community organizations. San Francisco's Jewish newspapers, including *The Gleaner*, and *The Hebrew*, informed the region and beyond about western life. To serve their community, San Francisco Jews organized an orphan asylum (1871) and a Jewish hospital (1887).

Jews traveled readily among western cities. By 1868, a transcontinental rail terminus sat in Oakland, just across the bay from San Francisco. Some who chose to leave San Francisco settled in the mining towns and river cities that dotted the region, establishing shops and participating in establishing local governments, and also organizing Jewish institutions such as benevolent societies and a few congregations. Others settled in the burgeoning urban centers, including San Diego, Los Angeles, Portland, and Seattle. When these cities grew and prospered, so did their Jewish communities.

Many western communities organized benevolent and burial societies, soon followed by congregations. The history of these early congregations illustrates the distinguishing features of western cities. San Francisco's Emanu-El started as an Orthodox congregation in 1851; a little more than a decade later, it began to introduce reforms. Seating became family style, rather than gender segregated, and the *Torah was read in three-year rather than yearly cycles. Many of Emanu-El's merchant founders gained success in the community, moving from dry goods stores to nationally known companies. The founders of the Alaska Commercial Company and Levi Strauss, the manufacturer of denim jeans, all joined Emanu-El. Successful financially, they became philanthropists, funding the orphan asylum, the hospital, and settlement houses. Its members supported the theaters, museums, and music venues. Although the members of other congregations played important roles in community development, the names of Emanu-El's members mark the prominent parks, buildings, and cultural institutions of the city. However, the community has always been diverse. Today, a multiplicity of Reform, Reconstructionist, Conservative, Orthodox, gay, and Renewal congregations (see JUDAISM entries), and Jewish *community centers serve the city's multifaceted Jewry.

In Los Angeles, Congregation B'nai B'rith (known as Wilshire Boulevard Temple), for many years defined that city's Jewry for the outside world. Founded as Orthodox in 1862, it soon became more liberal. With connections to founding families as well as members of the film elite, B'nai B'rith was an influential place. This status was reinforced by the 1915 hiring of the flamboyant Edgar Magnin, who served as the congregation's rabbi for more than 60 years. Magnin, a western native with an outgoing style, became the embodiment of Los Angeles Jewry for Angelinos. However, although it was the most visible, B'nai B'rith was only one of many congregations. Continued immigration from the eastern United States, Europe, *Iran, and *Israel led to the establishment of a wide variety of synagogues, organizations, and institutions representing all elements of Jewry, including *Sephardic, *Ḥabad, and *secularist. Los Angeles became the center of western Jewish life in the twentieth century and is home to premier institutions, among them *Hebrew Union College, the American Jewish University, the Simon Wiesenthal Center, and the Skirball Cultural Center (see MUSEUMS).

Reflecting the interconnections among western communities, the Jews of Portland, Oregon, maintained close ties with San Francisco Jewry. Reform congregation Beth Israel, founded in Portland in 1858, even adopted Emanu-El's constitution. Later congregations mirrored the origins of their founders from Posen, Russia, and Sephardic communities. Eastern European immigrants built a significant community in south Portland, with stores and institutions that catered to the early-twentieth-century immigrants. Jewish Seattle also formed commercial and social networks with Jews in other western cities. In addition to its *Central European founders, Seattle became home to a Sephardic community from Rhodes and Marmara, as well as to Eastern European Jews. As a port city, Seattle attracted immigrants who formed their own community organizations and synagogues. Unlike those in other western cities, Seattle's first Jewish house of worship was Reform, while Orthodox and Sephardic congregations developed later and built ethnic communities.

Although Jews settled predominantly in cities, exceptions did exist. Some lived in small towns and others in agricultural communities, most notably in New Odessa, Oregon, and in Petaluma, California (see UNITED STATES: AGRICULTURAL SETTLEMENTS).

Scholars have noted that Jewish innovation often starts in the west and moves eastward. Florence Prag Kahn (1866–1948), the first Jewish congresswoman, hailed from San Francisco. In 1890 the charismatic female Jewish journalist, Rachel (Ray) Frank (1861–1948), a San Francisco native, preached a High Holiday sermon in Spokane, Washington; she was hailed in the press as "the girl Rabbi of the Golden West" (see RABBINIC ORDINATION OF WOMEN). Jewish adventurers and nonconformists helped build western communities. The open west, with little antisemitism, facilitated Jewish success in commercial, philanthropic, and political spheres and fostered Jewish diversity as well.

For further reading, see A. F. Kahn, *Jewish Voices of the California Gold Rush: A Documentary History, 1849–1880* (2002); idem, E. Eisenberg, and W. Toll, *Jews of the Pacific Coast:*

Reinventing Community on America's Edge (2010); and W. Toll, *The Making of an Ethnic Middle Class: Portland Jewry over Four Generations* (1982).   AVA FRAN KAHN

Urban Life. No aspect of human activity has been as significant in the shaping of modern Jewish history as urban life. In the relatively free and open atmosphere of the modern cities that emerged in Europe and America in the nineteenth and twentieth centuries, Jews were strongly influenced by and influenced the currents of political, social, economic, and cultural change that arose in the wake of the French and Industrial Revolutions.

Jewish communities could already be found in the developing cities of medieval Europe. In the early modern era, Jews played an important role in the economic growth of cities, although they were generally restricted in their mobility, their professions, and their places of residence. With their *emancipation in Western and *Central Europe in the nineteenth century, individual Jews found new opportunities for individual advancement in major capitals like *Berlin, Paris (see FRANCE: 1789–1939), London (see BRITAIN: EARLY MODERN AND MODERN), and *Vienna.

Urban Jews tended to gravitate toward those businesses and professions that were increasingly in demand among the growing European middle class, such as ready-made clothing and retailing and the liberal professions of law, education, and *medicine. They were also active in movements of political change and in the Modernist cultural movements that flourished in cities. Although most governments no longer placed restrictions on where they could live, Jews in urban areas continued in large part to socialize with and live among other Jews.

As Jews slowly integrated into Western and Central European society, the relative openness of urban life led to changes in both individual and collective thought and behavior. Traditional Jewish observance loosened its hold on young men and women, and movements of religious reform arose that sought to find a balance between commitment to Judaism and participation in the larger world. Influenced by *secularizing tendencies that were increasingly evident in European cities, some Jews created new forms of collective identity that rested on cultural and ethnic ties rather than religious observance. As a result, Jewish communities became increasingly pluralistic and decentralized.

In *Eastern Europe, the pace of Jewish urbanization in the nineteenth century was far slower, due in large part to the many restrictions placed on Jews by tsarist regimes. Nevertheless, small circles of young intellectuals who had managed to escape the Russian *Pale of Settlement took advantage of the opportunities offered them in cities like Odessa, *Vilna, and *Saint Petersburg to create a modern Hebrew and later Yiddish *literature. The outbreak of the Russian Revolution in 1917 lifted many of the limits that had previously been placed on Jews and allowed significant numbers to participate in the modernization of Soviet society in urban settings.

In North America, Jews settled in major port cities during the colonial era. The arrival of hundreds of thousands of *immigrants from *Germany and later from Eastern Europe in the nineteenth century strengthened Jewish urban life in the *United States. Beginning in the 1880s, Polish and Russian Jews congregated in areas like the Lower East Side of

*New York City, where they developed their own distinctive social, economic, and cultural life. After *World War II, the lure of new economic opportunities, affordable housing, and quality education for their children led American Jews to move to the suburbs. By the 1970s, American Jews were migrating beyond the suburbs to the "exurbs," as well as to new urban and suburban communities in western, southwestern, and southeastern states (see UNITED STATES, SOUTHERN; UNITED STATES, WESTERN).

Jewish urban concentration led to a backlash in the late nineteenth and twentieth centuries. In Germany and France, the association of Jews with urban life was a central theme of a new and virulent *antisemitism, especially among more traditional elements of the lower middle class who viewed the modern city as a center of moral corruption and decay. Within the Jewish community, newly created *Zionist movements condemned what they regarded as the parasitic and physically debilitating nature of urban Jewish life and preached the virtues of agricultural labor in communal farms in *Palestine. Yet the attractions of the city continued to draw Jews. It is not coincidental that the State of *Israel has one of the most highly concentrated urban populations in the world.

At the end of the first decade of the twenty-first century, the cities of Europe and America no longer have the magnetic appeal they once had for Jews. Jews have largely abandoned the "inner city"; their apartments, stores, and houses of worship have been taken over by newer immigrants from Africa and Asia. Those who remain represent differing and contrasting populations including *Ultra-Orthodox communities, newer immigrants from the former *Soviet Union, young professionals, and growing numbers of retirees.

For further reading, see E. Lederhendler, *New York Jews and the Decline of Urban Ethnicity, 1950–1970* (2001); D. D. Moore, *To the Golden Cities: Pursuing the American Jewish Dream in Miami and L.A.* (1994); and "People of the City: Jews and the Urban Challenge," *Studies in Contemporary Jewry* 15 (1999).

DAVID WEINBERG

V

Venice. While there is evidence from as early as the tenth century that Jewish merchants did business in the Italian city of Venice, the first Jewish settlements were not established until the thirteenth century. They were located on the island of Spinalonga (later called the Giudecca), away from the main part of the city. The first group of Jews allowed to live within central Venice were money lenders, who had been granted a charter in 1382. However, they left Venice in 1397 when their charter was not renewed. Any Jew who entered Venice was required to wear a yellow circle on his outer clothing; this was changed to a yellow head-covering in 1496.

In 1509, after numerous Jews living on the Venetian mainland fled across the lagoon to Venice in the face of invading armies, the government realized that allowing them to stay in the city would be doubly beneficial. They could provide the hard-pressed treasury with annual payments, and their pawnbroking services were convenient for the urban poor. Consequently, in 1513 the Venetian government granted the Jews a charter allowing them to lend money; that permission was periodically renewed until the end of the Venetian Republic in 1797 (see MONEY LENDING: MEDIEVAL AND EARLY MODERN EUROPE).

However, many Venetians, especially clerics, objected to Jews residing throughout the city, so in 1516 the Senate required all Jews to move to the island known as the *Ghetto Nuovo* (new ghetto), which was walled up and provided with two gates that were locked from sunset to sunrise. The word "*ghetto," which is of Venetian origin, initially referred to a municipal copper foundry (*il geto*) that ceased operation in the mid-fifteenth century. The area where it had been located became known as the *Ghetto Vecchio* (old ghetto); the foundry dumping grounds across the canal was called the *Ghetto Nuovo*. The word "ghetto" then became the common designation for the many compulsory, segregated, and enclosed Jewish quarters established throughout Catholic *Reformation *Italy.

In 1541, visiting Levantine Jewish merchants complained to the Venetian government that they did not have sufficient space in the *Ghetto Nuovo*. Because of their importance in trade with the East, the government assigned them the *Ghetto Vecchio*, which was also walled up with a gate at each end. In the following decades, many New Christians (*conversos*) who had left *Spain and *Portugal settled in Venice. The government usually did not concern itself with the origin and background of those New Christians as long as they resided as Jews in the ghetto. In 1589, in response to the serious decline in Venetian maritime commerce, the government issued a ten-year safe-conduct charter allowing both Levantine Jewish merchants and New Christian merchants from the *Iberian Peninsula to settle in Venice as Venetian subjects. Euphemistically referring to the New Christian merchants as Ponentine, meaning "western" Jews, rather than as New Christians, the government required them to reside in the ghetto and wear the special Jewish head covering.

Venice became a vibrant center of Jewish culture. Several *synagogues using the Italian, *Sephardi, and Levantine rites were established, and the community maintained a cemetery, established in 1386, on the Lido. Among well-known rabbis was the prolific Leon *Modena (1571–1648). His numerous works include a remarkably frank autobiography written in Hebrew that recorded the everyday life, practices, and values of the Jews in early modern Venice, including their extensive relationships with their Christian neighbors on all levels, from intellectual exchanges to joint participation in alchemy experiments and gambling. Venice also became a major center of Jewish *printing, especially in Hebrew.

By the eighteenth century, Venice had declined economically, and the financial condition of the Jewish community declined accordingly. In 1722, the Venetian government, concerned because it needed the Jewish community to provide loans, established the *Inquisitorato sopra l'Università degli Ebrei* to restore and maintain the Jewish community's financial solvency and to promote the smooth functioning of its money-lending operations.

The French occupation of Venice in May 1797 led to the abolition of the restrictions on the Jews, the destruction of the ghetto gates, and freedom from wearing the special head covering. When *Habsburg Austria took control of Venice later that same year, it reinstituted some restrictions, but not the ghetto. In 1805, when Venice became a part of the Napoleonic kingdom of Italy, the rights of the Jews were restored. The Austrians returned in 1814 and so did many restrictions against Jews. The Republic of Venice led by Daniele Manin, who was of Jewish descent and appointed two Jewish ministers, briefly restored Jewish rights during the Revolution of 1848–49. Yet it was only after Venice became a part of the emerging kingdom of *Italy in 1866 that the Jews received complete *emancipation. In the following decades, the size of the Jewish community decreased because of emigration and intermarriage. Deportations during the *Holocaust further reduced the population. Today, Venice has an active Jewish community of around 500 members. It holds services in the old synagogues and sponsors a Jewish museum and bookstore in the ghetto.

For further reading, see B. Ravid, "The Venetian Government and the Jews," in *The Jews of Early Modern Venice*, ed. R. C. Davis and B. Ravid (2001), 3–30; idem, *Studies on the Jews of Venice, 1382–1797* (2003); and U. Fortis, *The Ghetto on the Lagoon*, rev. ed. (2000); **see also SYNAGOGUES, EUROPE: MEDIEVAL TO EIGTHTEENTH CENTURY. Map 8**
BENJAMIN RAVID

Verbermacher, Hannah Rachel (ca. 1815–1895), known in *Ḥasidism as "the Holy Maid of Ludomir," is one of the few *women who achieved a position of religious leadership in any form of Judaism before the twentieth century. The only child of a wealthy merchant, Hannah was unusually well educated and demonstrated exceptional piety, studying holy texts and adopting religious practices ordinarily reserved for men. After she had a mystical vision, the young Hannah broke off her engagement and devoted herself to learning and prayer. When her father died, she used her sizable inheritance to build a study house with an attached dwelling in Ludomir, where she lived in complete solitude. She soon acquired a reputation for saintliness and miracle working, attracting both men and women to her "court," where she delivered learned lectures on the *Sabbath from behind a door.

Verbermacher's achievements reflect a profound spirituality that found communal expression despite a lack of leadership, contemplative, or ascetic options for women in her society. Her success was facilitated by her personal wealth and the cultural influences of a larger Christian environment familiar with "holy maidens" and female saints, but it certainly did not go unopposed. Hannah's rejection of a conventional female role presented a direct affront to the Ḥasidic leaders of her region, who believed that Jewish women should serve as enablers of their husbands' religious activities. Ultimately Hannah acceded to rabbinic pressure and entered into two brief and unsuccessful marriages. Although apparently unconsummated, these marriages had the intended result of ending her religious leadership. Hannah spent the latter part of her life in the Land of Israel where she was involved with mystical and messianic circles and continued to attract followers; nothing she may have written survives. A recent study is N. Deutsch, *The Maiden of Ludmir: A Jewish Holy Woman and Her World* (2003).

JUDITH R. BASKIN

Vienna, the capital of the *Habsburg Monarchy until 1918 and of the Austrian Republic afterward, contained one of the largest and most creative European Jewish communities in the late nineteenth and early twentieth centuries. The site of a Jewish community in the late Middle Ages and again in the Early Modern period, Vienna expelled its Jews in 1670 and thereafter refused to allow Jewish settlement in the city. Despite this ban, wealthy Jews could purchase residence rights. In the 1820s, 135 Jews possessed the right of "toleration"; including their families, servants, and employees, Vienna's Jewish population numbered 2,000–4,000. The community grew substantially after the Revolution of 1848, when restrictions on Jewish movement and residence in Vienna were lifted. Jews migrated to Vienna from the Habsburg provinces of Bohemia and Moravia (today's *Czech Republic); from *Hungary, especially from western Hungary and western Slovakia; and, beginning in the 1890s, from *Galicia, the region of southern *Poland that Austria annexed at the end of the eighteenth century. In 1910, 175,318 Jews lived in Vienna, forming 8% of the total population. During World War I, tens of thousands of Jewish refugees fled to Vienna when the Russian army invaded Galicia. In the interwar years, about 200,000 Jews resided in the city.

All restrictions against Jews ended in the 1860s, culminating in *emancipation in 1867. Jews entered all branches of *commerce, and some became industrialists, mostly in textiles, clothing, and furniture manufacture. Many became commercial employees – clerks, salesmen, and managers – and some entered the professions, especially *medicine and law. Jews attended the public schools, including the elite secondary schools and the university, in very large numbers. They adopted an identity as German Austrians, loyal to the Habsburg Monarchy and devoted to German culture. A very large percentage of Vienna's writers, journalists, intellectuals, and composers, including Arthur Schnitzler, Stefan Zweig, Sigmund *Freud, Gustav Mahler, and Arnold Schoenberg, were Jews or of Jewish origin (see LITERATURE: CENTRAL EUROPE).

Although some Jews attempted to assimilate utterly, even converting to Christianity, most remained Jews. Despite a decline in the level of Jewish religious observance, Jewish religious life flourished, both in the modernized traditionalism of the community's *synagogues and in the small synagogues that catered to religiously observant Jews. Most Jews lived in three contiguous districts, one of which, the Leopoldstadt, was affectionately called *Die Mazzesinsel* (the island of *matzah*) because so many Jews lived there. Jews also created many charitable, social, and political organizations in which they could articulate various forms of Jewish identity and socialize primarily with other Jews.

Vienna was the birthplace of Jewish nationalism. In 1883, a group of Jewish university students led by Nathan Birnbaum created Kadimah, the first Jewish nationalist dueling fraternity. Vienna was also the home of Theodor *Herzl, founder of political *Zionism. Although Zionism was a minority movement during Herzl's lifetime, it nevertheless attracted many young Jews. By 1932, Zionists formed the majority on the board of the Jewish community of Vienna.

Zionism flourished in Vienna because of the model provided by other national movements in the Habsburg Monarchy and also in reaction to *antisemitism in local politics. Led by Karl Lueger, Vienna's Christian Social Party, which catered to the resentments of lower-middle-class artisans, shopkeepers, and low-level civil servants, won a majority of seats on the Vienna City Council in 1895; it held a majority until 1919. Lueger served as mayor of Vienna from 1897 until his death in 1910. Although the city government did not enact any anti-Jewish measures, antisemitic rhetoric permeated political life and made Jews nervous about their place in Viennese society.

In the interwar period, the situation deteriorated as Jews confronted rising antisemitism in the rump Austrian Republic and, after 1933, the threat of a *Nazi takeover. Ultimately, the Christian Social government of Austria, which opposed the Nazis, proved incapable of preventing Austrian Nazis and their German allies from arranging the union (*Anschluss*) of Austria with *Germany in March 1938. Immediately afterward, the Nazis imposed the anti-Jewish measures that were already in place in Germany, pushing Jews out of culture, public life, and the economy. Adolf Eichmann, the head of the Jewish section of the Gestapo, came to Vienna to organize Jewish emigration. Many Jews managed to get visas for *Palestine, *Britain, and the *United States, but at least half could not do so. In 1942, the remaining Jews in Vienna were deported to the death camps, often via *Theresienstadt or a ghetto in *Poland (see HOLOCAUST; HOLOCAUST: CAMPS AND KILLING CENTERS; HOLOCAUST: GHETTOS).

A small Jewish community formed in Vienna after World War II, comprised of people who had successfully hidden or returned from the camps, as well as survivors from *Eastern Europe. Later arrivals included refugees from *Hungary in 1956 and the *Soviet Union in the 1970s. By 2000, the approximately 8,000 Jews in Vienna maintained all the institutions of a flourishing Jewish community. For further reading, see M. L. Rozenblit, *The Jews of Vienna, 1867–1914: Assimilation and Identity* (1983); and H. P. Freidenreich, *Jewish Politics in Vienna, 1918–1938* (1991).

MARSHA L. ROZENBLIT

Vilna (Wilno in Polish, Vilnius in Lithuanian) was the capital of the Grand Duchy of Lithuania from 1325 and of the Lithuanian Soviet Socialist Republic from 1940–91; it has been the capital of independent Lithuania since 1991 (see BALTIC STATES). Jewish Vilna was celebrated for its scholarship, its *Hebrew and *Yiddish literature and press, its religious creativity, and its political activism.

An organized Jewish community existed in Vilna by 1568, and by the late eighteenth century, the city was a hub of Torah study. The rabbinic leader Elijah ben Solomon Zalman, known as the *Vilna Gaon, and his followers influenced developments in both *halakhah* and *Kabbalah. The Gaon's *Ḥasidic opponents also maintained a strong presence in the city. In the 1800s, Vilna was simultaneously a center of the *Haskalah* (the Jewish Enlightenment) and of traditional *yeshivot*, including one established by the *Musar* movement. Despite this vibrant Jewish activity, *antisemitism was a constant reality. **Maps 8, 11**

In the late nineteenth century, a census found more than 60,000 Jews in Vilna, more than 40% of the city's population. Local authorities and *Russian imperial rulers discouraged Jewish participation in government; overcrowding and lack of economic opportunities led to high *immigration, mainly to the *United States and *South Africa. Many Jews who remained were involved in Jewish political movements; the Jewish socialist *Bund was founded in Vilna, and the city was also a headquarters of political *Zionism. The Historical Ethnographic Society, led by Semyon Ansky, and the *YIVO Research Institute for Yiddish Language and Culture were established in Vilna. In the interwar years, Vilna became the world center of secular Yiddish culture. However, the community's economic situation declined after Vilna became part of *Poland in 1922 and antisemitism intensified.

The 1941 *Nazi invasion doomed Jewish Vilna. In the first days of the occupation, much of Vilna's estimated Jewish population of up to 80,000 was murdered in the Ponary woods. A fighting organization was set up in the Vilna ghetto; one of its commanders was Abba Kovner, later a well-known poet in *Israel (see POETRY, MODERN HEBREW). After the Russian liberation of Vilna in July 1944, 6,000 survivors attempted to set up a community. The liberators suppressed manifestations of Judaism, and under Soviet rule specifically Jewish *Holocaust losses were ignored. Independent Lithuania has been slow to return confiscated communal property and to face up to charges of Lithuanian collaboration with the German invaders during World War II.

For further reading, see Y. Arad, *Ghetto in Flames: The Struggle and Destruction in the Holocaust of the Jews in Vilna* (1980); L. S. Davidowicz, *From that Place and Time: A Memoir, 1938–47* (1989); and D. Katz, *Lithuanian Jewish Culture* (2004).

LIBBY K. WHITE

Vilna Gaon, Elijah (1720–1797). Elijah, the son of Solomon Zalman, is known as the *Gaon (genius) of Vilna. He was the most accomplished rabbinic figure and *Talmud scholar produced by Eastern European Jewry. Living an ascetic life and holding no public office, the Gaon of Vilna dedicated himself entirely to the intensive study of all layers and areas of biblical, rabbinical, and mystical writings, achieving an unprecedented mastery of this literature. Armed with new methods, vast knowledge, and a towering reputation, he changed the intellectual focus and curriculum of Lithuanian Jewry and helped reinvigorate and expand the study of *Torah as the ideal way of life. The Gaon is accurately described as the founding father of the *mitnaggedim*, the movement that stood in opposition to *Hasidism. He carried on the fight against Hasidism personally and exercised all his power and authority to put an end to it, although without success.

The Vilna Gaon was also the most important rabbinic forerunner of the Eastern European *Haskalah*. Most of his influence spread through his disciples, themselves rabbinical scholars of the highest stature, such as R. Chayim of Volozhin, the founder of the first modern *yeshivah*, and R. Yisroel of Shkelov, the leader of a group of the Gaon's students who emigrated together to the Land of *Israel, in anticipation of the coming *redemption. Recent research includes I. Etkes, *The Gaon of Vilna: The Man and His Image* (2002).

CHAIM MEIR NERIA

W

Wald, Lillian D. (1867–1940), nurse, social worker, and political reformer, was born in Ohio to parents of Polish and German origins (see NURSING: UNITED STATES; SOCIAL WORK: UNITED STATES). Her prosperous family subsequently moved to Rochester, New York, where Lillian attended a private French-language boarding school. Wald graduated from the New York Hospital School of Nursing in 1891 and then attended the Women's Medical College. While teaching home nursing classes to immigrants on *New York City's Lower East Side, she first witnessed urban poverty and the lack of health services for the poor. In 1893, Wald and a colleague established residence in an immigrant neighborhood and founded the Nurses' Settlement. Relying on her nursing and settlement movement connections, Wald enlisted the funding and friendship of financier and philanthropist Jacob Schiff, who introduced her to the city's elite networks.

Wald's institution grew into the Henry Street Settlement House, which offered visiting nursing, as well as citizenship classes and amateur theater. She campaigned for parks, playgrounds, and school lunch programs and pioneered public school nursing and classes for disabled students. Completely *secular and at times criticized for the lack of Jewish content in her work, Wald contributed to the increasing secularization and professionalization of social work and nursing. Alongside other political progressives, she linked her local efforts to broader reform campaigns for labor (see UNITED STATES: LABOR MOVEMENT), women's, immigrant, and civil rights (see UNITED STATES: CIVIL RIGHTS; for global anti-militarism; and for public health. Her intimate relationships with women continued to sustain her after her retirement in 1933. The two institutions she founded, Henry Street Settlement House and the Visiting Nurse Service of New York, continue to serve the needs of all New Yorkers.

MARJORIE N. FELD

Wannsee Conference was a meeting arranged by *Nazi security chief Reinhard Heydrich at an SS villa in Wannsee, a suburb outside of *Berlin, to ensure coordination among various government and party agencies involved in aspects of the deportation and murder of European Jewry. Initially planned for December 9, 1941, the Wannsee Conference was postponed after the Japanese attack on Pearl Harbor two days earlier and took place instead on January 20, 1942. By that time, plans for the implementation of the "Final Solution" were almost complete. **See HOLOCAUST; HOLOCAUST: CAMPS AND KILLING CENTERS.**

DAVID M. CROWE

Warsaw, which became the capital of *Poland in the sixteenth century, was a major center of Jewish life in the nineteenth and early twentieth centuries. Warsaw's earliest known Jewish community, established in the late fourteenth or early fifteenth century, probably consisted of no more than fifteen families. In 1527 Warsaw prohibited Jewish settlement, but Jews lived in private enclaves of noblemen and others, called *jurydyki*, and for a payment were allowed to live and trade elsewhere in the city when the Polish Diet (parliament) convened. Jews also settled in right-bank Praga as early as the mid-seventeenth century, and an authorized community was established there in 1775.

Only after the late-eighteenth-century partitions of Poland, when Warsaw initially came under Prussian rule, was the prohibition against permanent Jewish settlement lifted and a *kehillah* (see COMMUNAL ORGANIZATION) established. The Jewish population and its institutions grew; a *cemetery was founded in 1806 (a Jewish burial ground already existed in right-bank Praga). Under *Russian rule after the Napoleonic wars, the Jewish population increased from 12,000 (17% of Warsaw's population) in 1805 to 72,000 (32%) in 1864. The number of Jews doubled again by 1887 and had reached 301,268 by 1911, constituting 38% of Warsaw's population.

Warsaw developed into Europe's largest Jewish center after the 1862 *emancipation of Jews in the Russian-controlled, semi-autonomous Polish kingdom. A mix of *Ḥasidim, *mitnaggedim*, and *maskilim* (see HASKALAH) at the outset of the 1800s became a largely Ḥasidic population as the century progressed, with an increasing minority of Polonized (acculturated) Jews. This latter group controlled the *kehillah*, the communal government, in the last decades of the century. Beginning in 1868, an influx of Jews from the Russian interior, so-called Litvaks, deepened internal Jewish divisions.

Polish–Jewish relations fluctuated with political and economic conditions. Anti-Jewish riots occurred in 1790 and 1805, but Warsaw Jews also took part in the 1794 Kościuszko insurrection and in nineteenth-century Polish uprisings against Russian rule. The city was the center of a "Polish-Jewish brotherhood" beginning in 1861, yet relations deteriorated in the late 1860s and 1870s and two Jews were killed in a *pogrom that began on Christmas Day, 1881. The industrializing city subsequently became a center of Jewish politics, particularly between 1905 and 1914. Warsaw became a *Yiddish literary center in the 1880s and was the heart of the Yiddish literary world by the mid-1890s (see LITERATURE, YIDDISH). Five-sixths of Warsaw Jews reported Yiddish as their native language at the beginning of the twentieth century. **Map 11**

During World War I, 80,000 Jewish refugees arrived in Warsaw, even as Jews confronted worsening economic conditions. Interwar Warsaw Jewry, numbering 333,300 in 1931, experienced increased *antisemitism and impoverishment in the 1930s. However, Jewish cultural and political life flourished in the capital of newly independent Poland with two mass-circulation Yiddish *journals, Polish- and Hebrew-language periodicals, and a vibrant Yiddish theater (see THEATER, YIDDISH). By 1926 more than four hundred *synagogues and prayer houses operated, including the Great Synagogue, built in 1876–78 by Polonized Jews.

On the eve of World War II, approximately 60% of Warsaw Jews lived in the northwest Muranów district, adjacent Grzybów, and nearby areas, which had been predominantly Jewish since the late nineteenth century. Another 8% lived in right-bank Praga, whereas a small number of Jewish bankers and industrialists lived in Warsaw's most prestigious districts.

Persecution of Jews began soon after the 1939 *Nazi invasion that began World War II. In November 1940, the Nazis established a *ghetto in which as many as 445,000 Jews, including small-town refugees, were confined. Beginning July 22, 1942, 265,000 ghetto residents were sent to *Treblinka and killed, leaving behind about 70,000 Jews. The Warsaw ghetto uprising broke out on Passover 1943, after which the Nazis destroyed the ghetto and deported the surviving Jews (see HOLOCAUST; HOLOCAUST: GHETTOS; HOLOCAUST: RESISTANCE).

After the Holocaust, an estimated 18,000 Jews lived in Warsaw, but the population decreased as a result of postwar emigration waves. Early-twenty-first-century Warsaw has seen a small-scale revival of Jewish communal life, centered on the Nożyk synagogue, two congregations, and Jewish cultural and academic institutions.

For further reading, see W. T. Bartoszewski and A. Polonsky, eds., *The Jews in Warsaw: A History* (1991); G. S. Paulsson, *Secret City: The Hidden Jews of Warsaw, 1940–1945* (2002); and M. Shore, *Caviar and Ashes: A Warsaw Generation's Life and Death in Marxism, 1918–1968* (2006).   KAREN AUERBACH

Weizmann, Chaim (1874–1952), along with Theodor *Herzl and David *Ben-Gurion, is one of the three men most responsible for achieving the aspirations of political *Zionism. He was born in *Russia and trained in biochemistry in Switzerland and *Germany. Weizmann became involved in Zionism while a student in Switzerland. He settled in *Britain in 1904 and taught in the Chemistry Department at the University of Manchester. His research led to a process for producing acetone from corn that proved essential to Britain in the production of artillery shells during World War I.

Weizmann, who was a highly effective public speaker and an accomplished diplomat, is credited with facilitating the *Balfour Declaration of 1917, which expressed British support for a Jewish "National Home" in *Palestine. He was president of the World Zionist Organization between 1920 and 1931 and 1935 to 1946. As the center of Zionist leadership shifted to Palestine, Weizmann was somewhat marginalized by Ben-Gurion and his supporters. However, he continued to be a crucial advocate for the establishment of the State of *Israel, both in Britain and with the U.S. president Harry Truman. In 1949, Weizmann was named president of the State of Israel, a mainly ceremonial position. The garden of his home in Rehovot, where he is buried, is now part of Israel's Weizmann Institute of Science.

Wengeroff, Pauline Epstein (1833–1916), whose autobiography, *Memoiren einer Grossmutter* (Memoirs of a Grandmother), is an important source on Jewish life in nineteenth-century *Russia, was born in Bobruisk into the upper economic echelon of *Russian Jewry; her

entrepreneurial grandfather and father served as contractors to the Russian government, and her husband, Ḥonon Wengeroff, became a successful banker. The Epsteins were strict in their religious observance; they were *mitnaggedim, upholders of traditional rabbinic Judaism and opponents of Ḥasidism. Pauline's father was an early enthusiast of the *Haskalah (Jewish Enlightenment) in *Eastern Europe and encouraged his daughters in their study of German, the language Pauline chose decades later for her memoir. The first edition of *Memoiren einer Grossmutter*, published in 1913 when Pauline was in her seventies, depicted the life of a privileged and pious Jewish family in the 1840s. It describes in detail the observance of the Jewish holy days and *festivals in her parental home. After this volume's unexpected success, Wengeroff expanded her portrait of traditional Jewish family life into a far more substantive and complex autobiography detailing her problematic marriage and her bitterness over her children's conversions. It was published in 1919 as the second edition of *Memoiren*. Translations include *Memoirs of a Grandmother: Scenes from the Cultural History of the Jews of Russia in the Nineteenth Century*, Vol. One, trans., intro., S. Magnus (2010); and B. D. Cooperman, ed. and introduction, *Rememberings: The World of a Russian-Jewish Woman in the Nineteenth Century* (2000). **See also WOMEN, MODERN: EASTERN EUROPE.**   JUDITH R. BASKIN

White Paper, 1939. In May 1939, *Britain issued a White Paper (a policy document) on British policy in *Palestine, then under *British Mandate authority. It stated that Britain's objective was "the establishment within ten years of an independent Palestine state." To accomplish this objective, Arabs were to be given "an increasing part in the government of their country," and between 1939 and 1944 Jewish immigration into Palestine was to be limited to 75,000 persons. After that date, "no further Jewish immigration will be permitted unless the Arabs of Palestine are prepared to acquiesce in it." Finally, the Palestine government would be granted "powers to prohibit and regulate [further private] transfer of land [from Palestinian Arabs to Palestinian Jews]." These restrictions on Jewish immigration and land purchase were strictly enforced throughout World War II, despite the *Nazi persecution and murder of European Jewry, and remained in effect until the end of the *British Mandate in 1948. **See also ISRAEL, STATE OF: FOUNDING.**

White Russia: See BELORUSSIA

Wiesel, Elie (b. 1928), thinker and author of more than forty books, was born in Sighet in the Carpathian Mountains of Transylvania, then part of *Hungary and now in *Romania. In 1944 he was deported with his family to *Auschwitz, where his mother and younger sister were murdered. He and his father were later taken to *Buchenwald, where his father was killed. After the war Wiesel was moved to *France with other orphans. There, he studied philosophy and literature at the Sorbonne and Jewish texts with a private tutor and mentor. His writing reflects an amalgamation of secular and religious traditions. In 1956, he moved to *New York City.

In 1956, Wiesel published a memoir of his wartime experiences written in *Yiddish, *Un de velt hot geshvign* (And the World Was Silent). Although he continued to publish essays and stories in Yiddish, his major works were written in

French. *Night* (1958) presents Auschwitz through the memory of a religious young man's struggle not simply for physical survival, but with a *God whose silence ruptures his faith in the Jewish *covenant and continuity. The first of a trilogy, *Night*, was followed by *Dawn* (1960) and *The Accident* (1961), which contemplate the ethics of violence and the will to live in the aftermath of the *Holocaust. In *The Town beyond the Wall* (1962) a Holocaust survivor who returns to his native town confronts the disturbing indifference to the deportation of Jews; *The Gates of the Forest* (1964) and *A Beggar in Jerusalem* (1970) expand on topics introduced in *Night* through the reflections of a Jewish child survivor whose experiences have damaged his capacity for communion with God and with other people.

In Wiesel's oeuvre, mystical and mysterious storytellers help negotiate the gap between despair and faith. He also retells stories about biblical characters (*Messengers of God* [1975], *Five Biblical Portraits* [1981]), the Talmud and other classic Jewish texts (*Sages and Dreamers* [1991]), along with *Hasidic rebbes and mystical figures (*Souls on Fire* [1972]; *Four Hassidic Masters* [1982]; *Somewhere a Master* [1982]). Several themes run through all of Wiesel's writing, regardless of genre: the nature of God and faith, the human and the Jewish relationship with God, the place of *evil in human existence, and the possibility of *ethics and human good in a post-Holocaust world. In the late 1990s, Wiesel published two volumes of memoirs, *All the Rivers Run to the Sea* (1994) and *And the Sea Is Never Full* (1996).

Wiesel has been active against persecution and genocide globally, speaking out on behalf of *Soviet Jewry in the 1960s and 1970s, and later on behalf of blacks in apartheid *South Africa, the victims of the Cambodian and Rwandan genocides, and other oppressed peoples. In 1986 he was awarded the Nobel Peace Prize.   SARA R. HOROWITZ

Wisdom of Ben Sira, also known as Ecclesiasticus, is a sapiential instruction that was written, according to Sira 50:27, in *Jerusalem in the second century BCE by a Jewish scribe named Jeshua ben Eleazar ben Sira (see also APOCRYPHA; BIBLE: WISDOM LITERATURE). Wisdom of Ben Sira is not canonical in *Judaism, but is cited more than eighty times in *rabbinic literature (e.g., *BT Sanhedrin* 100b; *Genesis Rabbah* 91:3). In Catholic tradition it is a book of the Old Testament while Protestant denominations consider it part of the Apocrypha.

Hebrew manuscripts of Ben Sira came to light in 1896 among Cairo *Genizah documents. Additional Hebrew scrolls of the book have been discovered among the *Dead Sea Scrolls and at *Masada. To date, approximately 64% of the text is available in Hebrew. A Greek translation was written in *Alexandria by a grandson of Ben Sira in 132 BCE, according to the prologue of the composition. This date, along with the book's silence regarding Antiochus IV and the *Maccabean revolt (175–164 BCE), suggests it was written before this crisis, around 180 BCE.

A lengthy work of instruction, Wisdom of Ben Sira comprises fifty-one chapters; the last contains hymns that were probably added to the book at a later time. The text contains proverbs, sayings, and longer units of poetry and instruction. Its author, a scribe and member of the retainer class, encouraged students to acquire wisdom from him (24:34). In chapter 51, apparently by a secondary author, people are urged

to study at a "house of instruction" (*beit midrash*; 51:23). Ben Sira praises the profession of scribe as superior to menial professions (38:24–39:11). It is likely that his students were wealthy; he urges them to lend money and to help the poor (29:1–20). He is loyal to the aristocratic *priests of Jerusalem (7:29–31), and the poem ends with a paean to the High Priest Simon (probably Simon II, 219–196 BCE; 50:1–24).

The book's themes are wisdom, Torah, and piety. Pursuing and cultivating wisdom, which signifies the ability to understand the world and live an ethical life, should be defining and ongoing personal endeavors (6:18–37; cf. 1:1–10, 4:11–19, 14:20–15:10). The personification of wisdom as a woman is adapted from *Proverbs 8 (ch. 24), and *Torah is portrayed as a major source of wisdom (24:23; 15:1). Ben Sira teaches his students to venerate the law and follow its *commandments (1:26), to cultivate "fear of the Lord," and to maintain an attitude of reverence and humility before God, the "crown" and "root" of wisdom (1:18, 20; cf. Proverbs 1:7). Two lengthy hymns praise God and the work of creation, which reflects divine grandeur and wisdom (39:12–15, 42:15–33). The history of Israel is also a major topic of instruction, especially in chapters 44–49, a section known as "the Praise of the Fathers." In addition, Wisdom of Ben Sira contains teachings on various spheres of ordinary life, such as *marriage (25:13–26:27), filial piety (3:1–16), and table manners (31:12–32:13).

MATTHEW GOFF

Wise, Isaac Mayer (1819–1900) was the first leader of American Reform Judaism. He arrived in the United States from Bohemia in 1846. He was the main influence behind the establishment of the Union of American Hebrew Congregations (UAHC) in 1873; the Hebrew Union College (HUC) in Cincinnati, Ohio, in 1875 (the first seminary for rabbinic training in North America); and the Central Conference of American Rabbis (CCAR) in 1889. He was regarded as the leader of the moderate wing of the Reform movement, which battled with more radical reformers (**see JUDAISM, REFORM: NORTH AMERICA**).

Wissenschaft Des Judentums (Scientific Study of Judaism) is a post-Enlightenment European Jewish movement dedicated to promoting the rational, scientific, and critical study of Jewish religion, history, and culture. Originating in mid-nineteenth-century *Germany, *Wissenschaft des Judentums* reshaped Jewish learning into an academic endeavor that was compatible with the scientific methodologies of the German university while arguing that the Jewish experience had a place in higher education and scholarship. Although pervasive *antisemitism tended to deny Jewish Studies a secure place in the European university curriculum, the *Wissenschaft* approach, furthered by nineteenth-century scholars like Leopold *Zunz, Abraham *Geiger, and Heinrich *Graetz, found an institutional home in the academic rabbinic seminaries of Central Europe. **See also JEWISH STUDIES.**

Women, Ancient: Biblical Representations. The Hebrew *Bible is a document produced mainly by male elites, including priests, prophets, sages, and courtiers, and its contents were directed largely toward adult males of ancient Israel and *Yehud, the post-exilic community in the Land of *Israel (see BABYLONIAN EXILE). Its gender language thus reflects the orientation of the text toward the male heads of the corporate households that comprised Israelite society and does not necessarily reflect the way women were regarded in social reality. As a literary work, therefore, the Bible is not a comprehensive source of information about women in Israelite history or society. Female figures in the Bible are best understood in relation to their position and role in the canon, rather than as exemplars of actual women in Israelite antiquity (for what is known about Israelite women's actual lives, see WOMEN, ANCIENT: ISRAELITE; and ISRAELITES: MARRIAGE AND FAMILY LIFE).

NAMED WOMEN: The names of 137 women appear in the Hebrew Bible; they represent 8% of all named individuals. The relatively small number of named women is an indication of the overall male orientation of the shapers of the canon. It also reflects the biblical focus on political events and national institutions (*Temple, *priesthood, the military, and kings and kingship [see ISRAELITES: KINGSHIP]), which were almost always the domains of men rather than women. In addition, this paucity of named females highlights the way the text reinforces the patrilineages, which were the decisive factors in property allocations and ownership and which, in turn, determined the economic viability of families and their place in the social order. For example, large groups of male names in the extensive genealogies of *Genesis, *Numbers, and 1 *Chronicles represent male lineages reflecting ancient Israel's male-based kinship structures. Even so, among the hundreds of male names in 1 Chronicles 1–9 are also the names of forty-seven women. Their presence serves to highlight the men with whom they are linked; however, occasionally it is a function of their own importance, as is the case for Zeruiah and Abigail, sisters of *David who are themselves progenitors of lineages (1 Chron 2:16–17), and the Ephraimite woman She'erah who built three cities, one of which bore her name (1 Chron 7:24).

The distribution of named women is fairly even across the three sections of the Hebrew Bible: forty-five are in the *Pentateuch, forty-nine in *Prophets, and forty-one in *Writings. Most women appear only once, and fleetingly. However, nearly a third (forty-seven) are mentioned in several biblical books: Thirty-three appear twice; eight are in three books; three – Michal (daughter of *Saul and wife of *David), Serah (daughter of Asher and granddaughter of *Jacob), and the *Tamar of Genesis – are found in four books; and one, *Miriam, is found in five different books. Miriam reappears most often because of her prominence in the Exodus account, and Tamar and Michal are also important narrative figures. However, the recurrence of Serah and of most women mentioned twice is a function of their relationship to a significant male figure, usually a king.

Unlike named biblical men, who are identified by their patrilineages, the named women are identified relationally, typically as someone's wife, secondary wife, or concubine. Occasionally, a named woman is said to be the daughter of a certain man, usually for a significant narrative reason. Examples are the tragic story of Jacob's daughter *Dinah (Gen 34), the account of Caleb's daughter Achsah and her acquisition of property (Josh 15:16–17; Judg 1:12–15), the five daughters of Zelophehad (Hogah, Mahlah, Milcah, Noah, and Tirzah) who also acquire property (Num 27:1–11; 36), and the daughters of leading monarchic figures (Saul's daughters Merab and Michal, David's daughter *Tamar,

*Solomon's daughters Basemath and Taphath, Jehoram's daughter Jehosheba, and *Ahab's daughter Athaliah). Similarly, a few women are identified as the sister of an important figure such as David, who also is the only male for whom a niece (Abihail) and a granddaughter (another Tamar) are named. Indeed, the clustering of named women around key male figures highlights the prominence of those men.

Many wives are also identified as mothers, especially in genealogies. The mothers of virtually every Judean king and of several Israelite kings are mentioned; a few bear the title "queen mother" (gᵉbîrâ), which probably denotes a female court function, not simply parentage. In only four instances are the identities of named women provided without direct reference to a man: *Rebekah's nurse Deborah (Gen 35:8); the two midwives, Puah and Shifrah (Exod 1); and Rahab, the harlot of *Jericho (Josh 2). *Deborah the judge may be a fifth instance if the name "Lappidoth" associated with her (Judg 4:4) is a town, rather than a spouse.

Of the named women, thirty are pre-Israelite or foreign women; only eight of these play sustained narrative roles. *Eve is preeminent in this respect as the "mother of all the living" (Gen 3:20). The others include strong female figures: the Egyptian slave-wife *Hagar, who bears *Abraham's first son (Gen 16, 21:9–21, 25:12); the Midianite woman Zipporah, who marries *Moses and saves him from death (Exod 2:21–22, 4:20–26, 18:2–6); the *Canaanite *prostitute Rahab of Jericho, who protects Joshua's spies (Josh 2:1–21; 6:17, 22–25); the Kenite woman *Jael, who slays the Canaanite general Sisera (Judg 4:17–21, 5:24–27); and the infamous *Phoenician princess Jezebel, who became Ahab's wife and co-ruler (1 Kgs 16:31, 18, 19:1–2, 21; 2 Kgs 9). In addition, foreign women are significant narrative figures in the two biblical books bearing women's names: Ruth and Orpah, both Moabites, in *Ruth, and Vashti, a Persian, in *Esther.

Of the one hundred and seven named Hebrew or Israelite women, thirty-three have an active role in a biblical story. All appear in prose accounts; only one woman, the wayward Gomer (in *Hosea 1–3, much of which is prose), appears in the largely poetic prophetic books. A significant concentration of female narrative figures appear in the family stories of Genesis, which account for the origins of the Israelite lineages; these stories include the matriarchs and handmaids of Genesis – *Sarah, Rebekah, *Rachel, *Leah, Bilhah, and Zilpah – along with Dinah and Tamar. Several more with sustained narrative roles – namely Miriam, Deborah, Delilah, and *Hannah – appear in accounts of the pre-monarchic era and may attest to prominent community roles for women in pre-national life. Additional narrative figures appear in the accounts of the royal families of *Israel and *Judah: *Bathsheba, Michal, the Abigail who is David's second wife, the Tamar who is David's daughter, Athaliah who reigned as queen (2 Kgs 11), and Huldah the prophet (2 Kgs 22:14–20). As with the women of Genesis, the interest in lineage accounts for most of the attention to female figures of the monarchic period; still, in both instances, the narratives provide a glimpse into the lives of women in privileged contexts. Finally, Naomi (see RUTH) and *Esther have commanding and perhaps heroic roles in biblical novellas.

UNNAMED WOMEN: In addition to the named women, unnamed female figures as individuals or as groups are mentioned more than eight hundred times in the Hebrew

Bible. Of these, about two hundred are part of gender pairs (and are discussed later, along with common-gender terms). Most of the other six hundred citations are representatives of the female gender in legal texts, where issues of sexuality relating to patrilineality or *purity predominate, and in the figurative language of poetic texts. Indeed, their frequent appearance in poetic imagery means that 39% of the unnamed female figures appear in Prophets, especially in the poetry of the Latter Prophets (although five prophetic books – *Obadiah, *Jonah, *Habakkuk, *Zephaniah, and *Haggai – do not mention any women; see BIBLE: PROPHETS AND PROPHECY), whereas 32% are in the Pentateuch and 29% in *Writings.

The focus of the Bible on kinship relationships is evident in the identity of these unnamed women. Well more than half are mentioned by familial designations: Wives appear most often (some one hundred and fifteen times); daughters and daughters-in-law occur eighty-four times; mothers, stepmothers, and mothers-in-law are specified forty-five times; and others (granddaughters, sisters, sisters-in-law, concubines, widows, divorcées, and aunts) account for the rest. Another 22% of the unnamed women are generic figures, called variously women, young women, or maidens; miscellaneous others, including about twenty designated foreign women and twenty labeled servants, account for 8%.

The other 12% of the unnamed women – seventy-two in all – are those whose sole or primary identification is related to seventeen different occupational or public roles. These include sixteen prostitutes, fourteen royal figures, and other occupations appearing six or fewer times (nurses, midwives, bakers, perfumers, cooks, skilled or weaving women, cult servants, wizards or sorcerers, mediums, lamenters, wise women, heralds, and prophets). More than half of these women are found in Prophets, especially in the narratives of Former Prophets, with the others about equally distributed between the Pentateuch and Writings.

Unnamed female figures have noteworthy narrative roles in only twenty-eight passages. Women in pairs or groups figure rather briefly in eight texts: Lot's two daughters in Genesis; Zipporah's six sisters in Exodus; the two prostitutes of 1 *Kings; the two mothers of 2 Kings; the women in *Jeremiah who worship the Queen of Heaven; also in Jeremiah the women who seek refuge in Egypt; the daughters of Jerusalem who are foils to the Shulammite throughout the *Song of Songs; and the prophesying women in *Ezekiel. Thirteen of the other twenty unnamed women are featured in extended narratives in Former Prophets: in *Judges the daughter of Jephthah, Samson's mother, the mother of Micah, and the unfortunate concubine of the Levite; in 1 *Samuel the medium of Endor; in 2 Samuel the wise woman of Tekoa and the wise woman of Abel of Beth-Maacah; and in the books of *Kings the *Queen of Sheba, the widow of Zarephath, and the Shunammite. The remaining seven (such as the woman of Thebez in Judges) have briefer but no less important narrative roles. In addition, three women – Lemuel's sagacious mother, the valorous woman of *Proverbs 31, and the sensuous Shulammite of the *Song of Songs – are important poetic figures.

WOMEN IN GENDER PAIRS AND COMMON-GENDER TERMS: In two other kinds of references, women are linked with males as equivalent persons. One is the set of about two hundred gender pairs – instances in which female figures are paired with their male counterparts to indicate the totality of that category. Again, family relationships predominate: daughter–son in seventy-nine instances, mother–father thirty-one times, *bride–groom in five texts, and sister–brother in three passages. In some thirty-five instances, the pair is simply woman–man or female–male; in fourteen cases, opposing age groups (old women–old men; maiden–youth) form pairs. Finally, some six texts use women–men–children to indicate a sizable group.

Several concentrations of these gender pairs are notable. More than half, especially the daughter–son pairs, appear in Major Prophets, where they serve to focus and intensify the meaning of parallel poetic lines; the dozen mother–father pairs in Proverbs serve a similar function. That another twenty-eight are found in Genesis can be attributed to the general family context as well as to the unusual presence of daughters along with sons in the genealogies of Genesis 5 and 11.

Women also appear indirectly in many common-gender Hebrew nouns, which have only one form but can refer to both genders either collectively or in reference to individuals. Examples are 'ādām (humankind), ʿam (people), ʿēdâh (community), banim (offspring), gôy (nation), nepeš (person), kāhāl (community, congregation), and zeraʿ (seed, offspring). Many of these terms have a wide semantic range and are not always gender inclusive; thus, each usage must be evaluated according to its context. Doing so indicates that women offer sacrifices, participate in community events, and are involved in a variety of other group experiences.

PERSONIFIED OR METAPHORIC AND DIVINE WOMEN: Female figures appear in the Hebrew Bible in several other ways. One is the personification of women as polities (cities, villages, or countries), especially in poetic passages and usually using family relationships. "Daughter" appears some eighty-four times, representing eight different countries or peoples (including *Judah) and five different cities (especially *Jerusalem/*Zion, which is represented some thirty-four times). The most frequently personified place is Jerusalem, which also appears as a whore, princess, queen, mother, wife, bride, maid, and woman. Jerusalem and *Samaria are called sisters named Oholibah and Oholah in the extended marital metaphor of Ezekiel 23 (cf. chap. 16); marriage imagery also figures in the four epithets for Jerusalem – Azubah (Forsaken), Shemamah (Desolate), Hephzibah (I delight in her), and Beulah (Espoused) – in Isaiah 62:4.

Women are also personified as abstract qualities, mainly in *Proverbs, where Wisdom along with Folly, Strange Woman, and Adulteress are recurring images; Wickedness is a woman in Zechariah 5:8. Finally, notably but not exclusively in Former Prophets, a number of female deities (*Asherah, Anath, Astarte, Ashimah, *Lilith) are mentioned by name; the designation "Queen of Heaven" appears five times in *Jeremiah (see CANAAN, CANAANITES; NEAR EAST, ANCIENT).

Recent scholarship includes C. Meyers, T. Craven, and R. S. Kraemer, eds., *Women in Scripture: A Dictionary of Named and Unnamed Women in the Hebrew Bible, the Apocryphal/Deuterocanonical Books, and the New Testament* (2000); and C. A. Newsome and S. H. Ringe, eds., *Women's Bible Commentary*, expanded edition (1998).   CAROL MEYERS

Women, Ancient: Israelite. Most Israelite women (and men) lived in agrarian settlements; their daily existence centered on the myriad tasks required for survival in a world in which virtually all of a family's foodstuffs, clothing, and other basic commodities were produced in the household. Women's lives were thus embedded in the economic functions of their self-sufficient households, and their religious and social lives were also integrally related to family life. Indeed, senior women in a family held managerial roles, organizing and supervising the labors of children and other family members. Elite women, including female relatives of the royal, priestly, and military bureaucracies and wives of well-to-do landowners, had the assistance of servants or slaves. Yet, the roles of most women as wives, mothers, and daughters were subsumed into the productive activities of their households.

Some Israelite women also engaged in "professional" activities. Unlike household life, which is largely invisible in the Hebrew *Bible, many (but perhaps not all) extra-household community functions for women are known from biblical texts. The one mentioned most frequently is that of *prostitute, a profession occurring in virtually every culture. Biblical texts discourage sex-for-hire in several ways, such as not allowing the earnings of a prostitute to be used for a *Temple donation (Deut 23:18) and by forbidding fathers to exploit their daughters by profiting from their sexuality (Lev 19:29). In addition, *priests, but not others, are forbidden from marrying prostitutes (Lev 21:7, 14). However, the Bible never explicitly proscribes prostitution, and two biblical heroes, *Tamar (Gen 38) and Rahab (Josh 2), act as prostitutes and are not condemned.

Women also practiced crafts or trades that were often outgrowths of their household activities. Groups of women weave fabrics for the *Tabernacle (Exod 35:26). Young women are conscripted to work in the royal precincts as bakers, cooks, and perfumers (1 Sam 8:13). The well-to-do woman of *Proverbs 31 markets garments she produces (31:13, 24); the discovery of seals (used in commercial transactions) inscribed with women's names further suggests the presence of Israelite businesswomen. Women are even said to have been construction workers in the post-exilic period (Neh 3:12).

Community service included leadership roles. *Deborah is prominent among the judges, perhaps the only one of these military heroes who also adjudicates (Judg 4:4–5). Also on the national level are royal women (e.g., Jezebel and Athaliah) who, by virtue of their class, exercise political power. A few (*Solomon's mother *Bathsheba and Asa's mother Maacah) are designated "queen mother" ($g^e b\hat{\imath} r\hat{a}$), probably the title of a female court functionary. Unnamed but no less significant are the two "wise women" whose sagacity, knowledge of traditional sayings, and psychological acumen play a national role (2 Sam 14:1–20, 20:14–22); other such women likely existed but go unmentioned.

Communications in biblical days were carried out by couriers, such as the servant girl bearing messages between Jonathan and *David (2 Sam 17:17). However, people usually dispatched messengers of the same gender, such as the girls conveying dinner invitations for Woman Wisdom (Prov 9:3–4). These messengers were important personnel, responsible for conveying the exact words of their employers and then returning with an accurate response. The female

heralds who made announcements to a wider audience (Isa 40:9; Ps 68:12) played a similar message-bearing role.

Several community religious roles for women also appear in the Hebrew Bible. The enigmatic women stationed at the entrance to the Tent of Meeting (Exod 38:8; cf. 1 Sam 2:22; see TABERNACLE) were likely menial laborers in the national shrine. More prominent are the female prophetic figures who communicated God's will to the people (see BIBLE: PROPHETS AND PROPHECY); several are significant actors in biblical narrative (*Miriam, Deborah, Huldah [2 Kgs 22], and Noadiah [Neh 6:14]), and others are unnamed and referred to only briefly (Isa 8:3; Ezek 13:17–23; Joel 3:1). Also mentioned are female sorcerers, wizards, and necromancers who apparently used special divinatory powers to help their clients (see MAGIC). Despite the negative biblical perspective on these women (Exod 22:17; Lev 20:27), they were skilled in the occult arts; moreover, the medium of Endor helps King *Saul without narrative censure (1 Sam 28:7–14). Indeed, those women provided a valuable service in assisting with what would be considered medical problems today (see ILLNESS AND DISEASE: BIBLE AND ANCIENT NEAR EAST; MEDICINE). A more explicitly medical practitioner, the midwife (Gen 35:17, 38:28; Exod 1:15–21), also had a religious role, for reciting chants and prayers was likely part of midwifery. However, women called "nurses" (Gen 24:59, 35:8; 2 Kg 11:2–3) were wet nurses and not medical attendants; they appear infrequently, usually as a sign of status for the women said to employ them.

Finally, women were active in the cultural realm. *Biblical poems with important religious messages are attributed to women (the songs of Miriam [Exod 15], Deborah [Judg 5], and Hannah [1 Sam 2]), and some or all of the love poetry in the *Song of Songs is probably a woman's composition. Women performed with frame drums (Ps 68:26), sometimes while also dancing and singing in victory celebrations (Exod 15:20–21; 1 Sam 18:6–7; Jer 31:4). They likely played other musical instruments, and they were vocalists in secular (2 Sam 19:36; Eccles 2:8; Ezra 2:65; Neh 7:67) and perhaps religious (1 Chron 25:5–6) contexts. Women were also experts in a specialized vocal performance, namely, singing laments for the dead (Jer 9:16–19; Ezek 32:16; cf. 2 Chron 35:25; see also BIBLE: MUSIC AND DANCE).

Although not attested in the Hebrew Bible, evidence from ethnography or ancient Near Eastern texts suggests that some women were vintners and others produced many kinds of artifacts, including ceramic vessels, terracotta figurines, amulets, baskets, textile implements, and even ground stone tools, that have been recovered from Iron Age sites. Because at least some elite women apparently could write (1 Kgs 21:8–9; Esther 9:29), Israelite women, like their sisters elsewhere, may have served as scribes.

Overall, the relative infrequency with which women with activities beyond the household appear in the Hebrew Bible is a function of the agendas of the text and should not be taken as a sign that those women lacked importance in Israelite life. As for the women themselves, the significance of having professional or community roles lay partly in the prestige and satisfaction of serving a general constituency. In addition, professions involving technical skills or group performance gave those with expertise the opportunity to mentor others and experience concomitant status. Moreover, such work provided women with the opportunity for creativity, self-expression, and the positive regard of those they served.

Scholarship on this topic includes A. Brenner, *The Israelite Woman: Social Role and Literary Type in Biblical Narrative* (1985); M. I. Gruber, "Women in the Ancient Levant," in *Women's Roles in Ancient Civilizations: A Reference Guide*, ed. B. Vivante (1999), 115–52; and C. Meyers, T. Craven, and R. S. Kraemer, eds., *Women in Scripture: A Dictionary of Named and Unnamed Women in the Hebrew Bible, the Apocrypha/Deuterocanonical Books, and the New Testament* (2000); see also ISRAELITES: MARRIAGE AND FAMILY LIFE; WOMEN, ANCIENT: BIBLICAL REPRESENTATONS.

CAROL MEYERS

Women, Ancient: Rabbinic Judaism. Jewish women in the late ancient period lived not only in *Palestine but also in *Babylonia, as well as in Jewish *Diaspora communities throughout the *Hellenistic world; their lives were regulated by the norms of a "common Judaism" of which we know next to nothing. The vast body of *rabbinic literature, which was composed by Jews in the first five or six centuries of the Common Era, formulated new approaches to Jewish women's lives and behavior. The foremost rabbinic composition is the *Mishnah, which was published in Palestine ca. 200 CE. It became an authoritative text in subsequent eras, not least because it served as the thematic framework and provided the content for discussion and expansion in both the Jerusalem and Babylonian *Talmuds. The Mishnah is divided into six orders, one of which is called "Women" (*Nashim*). The existence of a separate order devoted to women (with no parallel division devoted to men) indicates the androcentric character of the document. The Mishnah is about Jewish men and, as Jacob Neusner has shown, the ways in which they must act to assert their Jewishness. Authority over women – and their orderly transfer from one male authority figure to another – is one of these areas of male concern.

The order *Nashim* is divided into seven tractates: *Yevamot* (Levirate Widows [see MARRIAGE, LEVIRATE]), *Ketubbot* (*Marriage Contracts), *Nedarim* (Vows), *Nazir* (Nazirite Vows), *Sotah* (*Adultery), *Gittin* (*Divorce Documents) and *Kiddushin* (*Betrothals). At least two of these tractates (*Nedarim* and *Nazir*) are not devoted to women at all. Jacob Neusner has suggested that *Nashim* is not really about women but rather about their relations to men and about how the latter exert control over them. Judith Romney Wegner's work supports his conclusions, which are further substantiated by the existence of another tractate in the Mishnah, *Niddah*, that is devoted to a uniquely feminine topic – menstruation. This tractate is not found in *Nashim*, but is situated in the order *Tohorot* (Purities), probably because its main themes are the ways in which a menstruating woman can transmit a state of ritual impurity to a man (see PURITY).

The entire order of *Nashim* and Tractate *Niddah* have complementary tractates in the *Tosefta, as well as commentaries in the Jerusalem and Babylonian *Talmuds. There are no commentaries on the other tractates in *Tohorot* in either Talmud, likely because most issues relevant to ritual purity in Judaism ceased to be operative after the destruction of the Second *Temple, but the belief that a menstruating woman could impart ritual impurity never lost its potency in Jewish life and thought. Feminist scholars such as Tirzah Meacham and Charlotte Fonrobert have suggested another reason for the existence of commentaries to *Niddah*: Men used menstruation regulations to control women and limit their autonomy, even over their own bodies.

The parallel traditions to *Nashim* in the Tosefta indicate that certain issues that were debated by the Rabbis were then eliminated or reworked to fit the ideology of the Mishnah. The status of women is a prime example of this sort of transformation. As amply demonstrated by Judith Hauptman, the Tosefta includes many lenient references to women that were then reworked or completely eliminated from the Mishnah, which maintains a more stringent approach to women's opportunities. Studies carried out by other scholars, including Gail Labovitz, Ishay Rosen-Zvi, and myself, substantiate Hauptman's conclusions. The most likely explanation for this phenomenon is that, as the Rabbis gained ascendancy in Jewish society in the centuries following the destruction of the Second *Temple, they felt an increasing need to control women's lives, because they viewed them as inherently unruly and dangerous.

Subsequent studies have demonstrated that a similar trend to reduce women's public obligations and independence can be observed in other layers of rabbinic literature. Thus, major segments of the Mishnah and the Tosefta are dedicated to disputes between two "houses" or schools of rabbinic opinion: *Beit* Shammai and *Beit* *Hillel. Rabbinic literature declared *Beit* Hillel as the authoritative voice that Jews should follow. A comparison of their rulings about women indicates a consistent tendency of *Beit* Shammai to treat women as possessing personhood and agency. Thus, the wholesale rejection of the rulings of *Beit* Shammai did much to diminish women's status.

A similar picture emerges from the halakhic *midrashim*, compositions dating to the time of the Mishnah. Scholars divide these *midrashim* into two schools – that of Rabbi *Akiva and that of Rabbi Ishmael. Rabbi Akiva is by far the more prominent of these two rabbis, and the Mishnah is a product of his school. A comparison of the two corpora demonstrates that the school of Rabbi Ishmael far more often than the school of Rabbi Akiva sought to include women in its interpretation of biblical verses where no women are mentioned.

This tendency, found in the early strata of rabbinic literature, changes somewhat in the exegesis of these texts found in the Talmuds. As Hauptman shows, many leniencies that were rejected by the Mishnah and are only found in the Tosefta are reintroduced in *baraitot* in the Talmuds. Thus the *halakhah* that emerges from the Talmuds is often less harsh toward women than that of the Mishnah. Yet a tendency of denigration is also found in the Talmuds. These compositions give ample attention to the literary genre of *aggadah*, which preserves many stories about women and their daily lives. As Judith Baskin has demonstrated, however, many of these narratives are used to reinforce patriarchal control of women. In this genre, too, a development for the worse can be seen. Stories about women in the earlier Jerusalem Talmud are subsequently retold much less favorably in the Babylonian Talmud. Yet, because the genre of *aggadah* is more suited than *halakhah* to portray actual events and situations, women often come through in a more human light. Later rabbinic *midrashim*, such as *Genesis Rabbah*, *Leviticus Rabbah*, and *Lamentations Rabbah*, and even significantly late documents such as the *Tanḥuma* are, as Galit Hasan-Rokem has demonstrated, an excellent resource for the portrayal and reflection of real women and their exploits and achievements.

For further reading, see J. R. Baskin, *Midrashic Women: Formations of the Feminine in Rabbinic Literature* (2002); C. Fonrobert, *Menstrual Purity: Rabbinic and Christian Reconstructions of Biblical Gender* (2000); G. Hasan-Rokem, *Tales of the Neighborhood: Jewish Narrative Dialogue in Late Antiquity* (2003); J. Hauptman, *Rereading the Rabbis: A Woman's Voice* (1997); T. Ilan, *Integrating Women into Second Temple History* (2001); idem, *Silencing the Queen: The Literary Histories of Shelamzion and Other Jewish Women* (2006); G. Labovitz, "'These are the Labors': Constructions of the Woman Nursing Her Child in the Mishnah and Tosefta," *Nashim* 3 (2000): 15–42; T. Meacham, "An Abbreviated History of the Development of the Jewish Menstrual Laws," in *Woman and Water: Menstruation in Jewish Life and Law*, ed. R. Wasserfall (1999), 23–39; J. Neusner, *A History of the Mishnaic Law of Women* IV (1980); I. Rosen-Zvi, "Measure for Measure as a Hermeneutical Tool in Early Rabbinic Literature: The Case of Tosefta Sotah," *Journal of Jewish Studies* 57 (2006): 269–86; and J. R. Wegner, *Chattel or Person: The Status of Women in the Mishnah* (1988).

TAL ILAN

Women, Ancient: *Second Temple Period.

Women, Ancient: *Second Temple Period. Important sources on women for this era (530 BCE–70 CE) include *Josephus and *Philo of Alexandria, as well as the *Apocrypha, the *Pseudepigrapha, and the *Dead Sea Scrolls. The *New Testament gospels, which represent the Jesus movement – a Jewish Second *Temple sect – are also a valuable resource. In addition, documentary collections of inscriptions and papyri demonstrate the changing status of women in *marriage, *divorce, and other aspects of Jewish life.

The marriage contract (*ketubbah*), which regulates the financial relationship between husband and wife, emerged during the Second Temple period, as indicated both by a group of Persian-period Jewish papyri from Elephantine, *Egypt, and the apocryphal book of Tobit (7:13). Thereafter, the marriage contract, which is not mentioned in the Hebrew *Bible, is attested both by documentary evidence and the *Mishnah (see M. *Ketubbot* and also T. *Ketubbot* 12:1; JT *Ketubbot* 8:11, 32b–c; BT *Ketubbot* 82b).

Although the Hebrew Bible allows a husband to divorce his wife, this issue was apparently hotly debated in the Second Temple period. The Dead Sea Scrolls recognize divorce, but not remarriage thereafter (for both partners; CD IV 20–1; 4Q271). Jesus rejected the concept of divorce altogether (e.g., Mark 10:11–12), but a modified version of this opposition is found in Matthew (5:32; 19:9), which allows divorce in cases of *adultery. According to the New Testament (Mark 10:2–3), the *Pharisees recognized a liberal interpretation of divorce, albeit unilateral divorce – that is, it could be only initiated by the husband. Yet at least one reference in the writings of Josephus (*Antiquities* 15.259–60) and at least one document (*XHev/Se* 13) from the early second century CE suggest that Judaism also knew of wife-initiated divorce.

Incest regulations were also debated during this era. Although the incest laws enumerated in the Bible (Lev 18) are quite detailed, they do not mention some relationships.

For example, a man is not forbidden to marry his niece. The Pharisees apparently condoned such a marriage, whereas the Dead Sea sect condemned it (CD V 9–11).

Josephus also specifically states that women may not serve as witnesses or judges in Jewish law *courts (*Ant.* 4:219). This assertion was carried over to rabbinic *halakhah, in sources including M. *Rosh Ha-Shanah* 1:8 and the *midrash collection *Sifre Deuteronomy* 17.

Little is known about women's participation in Temple rituals and observances. The Temple was an all-male institution, and there are few sources describing its functions. The late Mishnah informs us that women wove the Temple curtain (M. *Shekalim* 2:6) and participated in Temple celebrations of *Sukkot (M. *Middot* 2:5; T. *Sukkah* 4:1) and *Passover (M. *Pesaḥim* 8:1); it also relates that Queen Helene of Adiabene, a convert to Judaism, donated money to adorn the Temple (M. *Yoma* 3:10). However, these sources may be anachronistic and unreliable.

Yet, religious and national expressions were not restricted to the Temple. Important religious concepts such as *martyrdom (sacrifice of oneself for spiritual ideals) and zealotry (active personal participation in the destruction of the enemy) were developed and became dominant in this era. Various sources describe women acting in both these capacities. The fictional book of Judith, in the *Apocrypha, tells of a woman who assassinates the enemy's general in an act of personal zealotry. In 2 *Maccabees 6:12–17, a mother witnesses the deaths of her seven sons, and she herself dies as a martyr rather than transgress the Jewish *commandments (see ḤANUKKAH AND WOMEN).

Second Temple Jewish politics was characterized by religious splintering that led to the creation of many sects. Women were probably present and active in most of these religious/political groups. Philo relates the active membership of women in a local Jewish sect, the Therapeutai, who retreated from the world to engage in contemplation and worship (*De Vita Contemplativa* [The Contemplative Life]). The New Testament reports the presence of women in the group that followed Jesus and assigns them a vital role in the founding of *Christianity after the crucifixion (e.g., Matt 28:1–10; Luke 23:55–24:11). It is now generally accepted that the Dead Sea sect also counted females among its members, and it is likely that even the Pharisees and the *Zealots welcomed women. It was during this period that the reign of the only legitimate queen in Jewish history, Shelomzion (Salome) Alexandra (ruled ca. 76–67 BCE), occurred. She succeeded her husband, the *Hasmonean ruler Alexander Jannaeus, and sources suggest that her reign was one of peace and prosperity.

For further reading, see T. Ilan, *Integrating Women into Second Temple History* (2001); idem, *Jewish Women in Greco-Roman Palestine: An Inquiry into Image and Status* (1994); idem, *Silencing the Queen: The Literary Histories of Shelamzion and Other Jewish Women* (2006); J. E. Taylor, *Jewish Women Philosophers of First Century Alexandria: Philo's 'Therapeutae' Reconsidered* (2003); and C. Wassen, *Women in the Damascus Document* (2005).

TAL ILAN

Women: Early Modern Europe.

Women: Early Modern Europe. During the years between 1492 and 1750, the Jews of Europe underwent significant social, religious, and demographic changes that had an impact on women's lives in a number of locations.

SEPHARDI DIASPORA: Benvenida *Abravanel (ca. 1473– after 1560), niece of the statesman-philosopher Isaac *Abravanel, married her first cousin Samuel. The couple left *Spain in 1492 for *Italy where Don Samuel became head of the Jewish community in Naples. Benvenida was an educated woman who established a good relationship with the Duchess of Tuscany. When the Jews of southern Italy were threatened with expulsion in 1541, Benvenida used her influence to negotiate a postponement of the decree. After her husband's death in 1547, she took over his business concerns and attained important trade privileges. Benvenida also gained renown as a pious and charitable woman, much given to fasting, whose home was a center of study and culture. In 1524–25, Benvenida became an enthusiastic supporter of the messianic pretender David Reuveni (d. 1538). She is said to have sent him financial support, a silk banner with the *Ten Commandments written in gold on both sides, and a Turkish gown of gold cloth (see MESSIANISM: EARLY MODERN).

Gracia Nasi (see also MENDES-NASI FAMILY) was born a *conversa and was baptized as Beatriz de Luna in *Portugal. Her husband Francisco, whom she married in 1528, left her half of his property when he died in 1536. Once the *Inquisition was established in that same year, Doña Gracia resolved to move elsewhere, taking care to move slowly to preserve the maximum amount of their fortune. Ultimately, the family ended up in Constantinople (see OTTOMAN EMPIRE) where Doña Gracia supported numerous scholars and rabbis and aided in the publication of scholarly works. Because of her connections, wealth, mobility, and foresight, Doña Gracia managed to escape the reach of the Inquisition. However, many other crypto-Jewish women were not so fortunate.

As the Spanish and Portuguese Inquisitions became obsessed with discovering unfaithful New Christians, women were particularly at risk, because they played a crucial role in perpetuating Judaism in this period. Without communal institutions or leadership, the home became the sole source of Jewish continuity, and women were central in preserving Jewish domestic rituals, especially the *dietary laws and *Sabbath observance. Such practices were always dangerous, because servants often testified to the Inquisition about their employers' judaizing activities. Numerous crypto-Jewish women were arrested and tortured, and many sacrificed their lives as martyrs for their faith in the course of the fifteenth and sixteenth centuries.

ITALY, 1600–1800: At least two Jewish women in seventeenth-century Italy became distinguished published writers in Italian. Devorà *Ascarelli translated Hebrew liturgical poetry into rhymed Italian, presumably for use by female worshipers. Her *Abitacolo degli oranti* (The Abode of the Supplicants), completed in 1537 and published in 1601, may be the earliest published Jewish literary work written by a woman. The most accomplished Jewish woman of this period in terms of education and literary productivity was the writer and poet Sarra Copia *Sulam (1592–1641). A member of a wealthy and prominent family in *Venice, she married Jacob Sulam, a local Jewish leader. She formed a salon of mostly Christian men of letters for whom she provided financial support, as well as intellectual friendships that later soured. Another talented woman of this period was the professional singer known as Madama Europa

Rossi, a highly accomplished performer in the court of the Gonzaga family in late-sixteenth- and early-seventeenth-century Mantua and the sister of the composer and musician Salamone Rossi (see MUSIC, SYNAGOGUE).

As early as the thirteenth century in Italy, certain rabbis allowed girls to receive a Jewish education. Most young women learned to read and write Italian at school or at home, and some learned Hebrew as well. Many of the teachers of girls were women, and those who taught Hebrew were known as *rabbit* or *rabbanit*. Other women, often widows, offered instruction in domestic skills. Two women of this period exceptional for their learning were sisters, Fioretta (Bat Sheva) Modena and Diana Rieti. According to the Venetian rabbi Leon *Modena (1571–1648), who was Fioretta's nephew, the women had mastered Torah, Mishnah, Talmud, midrash, Jewish law, and Kabbalah (Modena, Ḥayyei, fol. 15b). At the age of seventy-five, after the death of her husband Solomon da Modena, Fioretta set out to live in *Safed, a city known for its many mystics.

An interesting feature of the early modern Italian Jewish community is the licensing of specific women to act as ritual slaughterers and porgers of meat (*nikkur* or *treibern* [remove veins and sinews]). This contrasts with efforts by rabbis elsewhere in Christian Europe to limit women's rights to be involved in kosher slaughtering and porging. The probable reason for this liberality was to enable women to provide food for their families in isolated locations, such as summer houses in the mountains, or in distressed circumstances (see DIETARY LAWS).

CENTRAL EUROPE: The invention of *printing in the fifteenth century, which made the dissemination of popular literature practicable and inexpensive, played an important role in expanding Jewish women's religious lives and increasing their piety in *Central and *Eastern Europe in the Early Modern period. Access to reading matter in the vernacular had a transformative effect on many women, deepening their knowledge of Judaism and Jewish traditions; it even empowered a few women to become writers themselves. Rabbinic injunctions against women's learning were believed to apply to Talmud study, but not to the Bible or legal rulings necessary for women's everyday activities. Although Jewish women were generally ignorant of Hebrew, most were literate in Jewish vernaculars (Judeo-German [Western Yiddish] in Central Europe and *Yiddish in Eastern Europe, written in Hebrew characters), which had long been essential to women's economic activities. Translations of the Hebrew *Bible, the first books to be printed in the Jewish vernacular, gave women, as well as less learned men, access to Judaism's holy texts. Particularly popular were the *Taytsh-khumesh* (Vernacular Five Books [of Moses]), first published by Sheftl Hurwitz in Prague in 1608 or 1610, and the *Tzene-rene* (the title is derived from Song of Songs 3:11: "Go out and See [Daughters of Zion"]), by Jankev ben Isaac Ashkenazi (ca. 1590–1618), both of which included homilies on the weekly biblical readings from the *Torah and *Prophets, as well as stories, legends, and parables drawn from rabbinic literature; the *Zohar and other mystical texts; and histories and travel accounts. Also available to female readers was *musar literature: ethical treatises that discussed proper conduct, a woman's religious obligations, and her relations with her husband, such as the *Brantshpigl* (Burning Mirror) by Moses ben Henoch

Altschuler (1596) and the *Meneket Rivkah* (Rebecca's Nurse) of Rebecca bas Meir Tiktiner of *Prague (d. 1550; posthumously published in the early seventeenth century). These vernacular books intended for women were also read by Jewish men, many of whom did not possess significant Jewish scholarship; they were printed in a special typeface, *vayber taytsh* ("women's vernacular") based on the cursive Hebrew handwriting that women were taught for business contracts, marriage agreements, and correspondence.

Although all the Hebrew and Aramaic prayers of the standard liturgy were translated into Judeo-German/Yiddish, they were never as central to women as *tkhines*, supplicatory prayers that were intended for female use in Jewish rituals and in worship, both in the synagogue and at home. Collections of such prayers began to appear in the sixteenth century. Chava Weissler has pointed out that, although much of this literature was written by men for women and represents men's conceptions of women's religious lives, *tkhines* do demonstrate what women prayed about and offer insight into how they understood the meanings of their religious acts. Sarah Rebecca Rachel Leah Horowitz (ca. 1720–ca. 1800), the highly educated author of the *Tkhine imohes* (*Tkhine* of the Matriarchs), emphasizes the power and importance of women's prayer. In the *Shloyse sheorim* (Three Gates), Sarah bas Tovim (probably eighteenth century) makes use of rabbinic and mystical texts in Yiddish to construct a new vision of women's religious lives in which women's prayer was as significant as men's (see also PRAYER: WOMEN'S DEVOTIONAL).

COURT JEWS: One early modern woman who wrote in her own voice was *Glückel of Hameln; (also Glikl bas Judah Leib; 1646–1724). Born into the prosperous *Court Jew milieu of Central Europe, Glückel was well read in Judeo-German literature and had some knowledge of Hebrew and German as well; her memorial notice characterizes her as "a learned woman" (*melumedet*), unusual praise in her time and place. Betrothed at twelve, married at fourteen, and the mother of fourteen children, Glückel was active in business and pious in religious observance, including regular synagogue attendance. Glückel was at the threshold of modernity, both as a woman and as a Jew, and her business activities reflect the growing economic participation of Jews in the non-Jewish world, whereas her religious and secular educations speak to the broader horizons and new educational opportunities available to some seventeenth-century Jews – including women.

Esther Schulhoff Aaron *Liebmann (ca. 1645–1714) came from the same milieu as Glückel. Married first to Israel Aaron (d. 1673), supplier to the Brandenburg court and founder of the *Berlin Jewish community, Esther subsequently wed Jost Leibmann. Liebmann's first wife, Malka, was Glückel's niece, and Liebmann himself learned the jewelry business from Glückel's husband, Hayyim Hameln. Esther and her husband were the court jewelers to Frederick I of Prussia and the leading family in the Berlin Jewish community. Esther worked actively alongside her husband and successfully carried on their business after her husband's death. Like many Court Jews, Liebmann's fortunes depended on the favor of the ruler. After the death of Frederick I and the accession of Frederick William I in 1713, Esther Liebmann was put under house arrest and released only after she had paid the king a substantial fine.

MYSTICISM AND MESSIANIC MOVEMENTS: Women are connected with both mysticism (see also MYSTICISM: WOMEN) and the messianic movements that are a significant feature of Jewish history in early modern Europe. This phenomenon first appeared among crypto-Jewish women in Spain. As R. Melammed has written, *conversas*, observing secretly in the hope of salvation, were likely candidates to have a mystical or messianic penchant. During the post-expulsion period, several women and girls experienced visions and delivered messianic prophecies, particularly in the La Mancha and Extremadura regions of Castile. From 1499 to 1502, Mari Gómez of Chillón and Inés, a twelve-year-old from Herrera, inspired a renewal of Jewish observance, with special emphasis on fasting, based on their predicting of the imminent arrival of *Elijah, heralding messianic *redemption in the Land of Israel. The Inquisition quickly extinguished this movement: Inés was burned at the stake in 1500, and Mari Gómez escaped to Portugal.

Rachel Aberlin (fourth quarter of the sixteenth century, lead of *Israel) was active in Safed, Jerusalem, and Damascus. She figures as a mystic in *Sefer ha-Hezionot* (The Book of Visions), the memoir of her contemporary, Hayyim Vital. Vital, the most prominent disciple of the greatest sixteenth-century kabbalist, Isaac *Luria, refers to "Rachel Aberlin" and "Rachel ha-Ashkenaziah" frequently in entries that provide rare insight into the mystical religiosity of early modern Jewish women in the period preceding *Sabbateanism. Aberlin is portrayed in *Sefer ha-Hezionot* as a woman who regularly experienced mystical visions, from pillars of fire to Elijah the prophet. She is said to have been "accustomed to seeing visions, demons, souls, and angels." Aberlin seems to have been an important figure to other women in her community, who regarded her as a spiritual leader.

Sarah, one of the wives of the preeminent messianic figure of the Early Modern period, *Shabbetai Zevi (1626–1676), continues to be an enigma to historians. Apparently a survivor of the 1648 *Chmelnitzki pogroms in *Poland who had been brought up as a Christian, Sarah attracted attention with her beauty and her claims that she was destined to marry the messiah. According to some reports, Sarah was an erstwhile prostitute, who had traveled from Poland to *Amsterdam and then to Italy, where she worked as a servant for various Jewish families and institutions. Exactly how she and Shabbetai Zevi were brought together is unknown. However, the couple was married in Cairo in March 1664. At least one source reports that Shabbetai married her because of her ill repute, so as to fulfill the words of the Prophet Hosea: "Take yourself a wife of whoredom" (1:2). Sarah, who subsequently gave birth to a son and a daughter, converted to *Islam shortly after her husband's conversion in 1666. In 1671, Shabbetai divorced Sarah, even though she was pregnant, and arranged a marriage with another woman. He then changed his mind and took Sarah back. She died in 1674.

An interesting facet of Shabbetai Zevi's messianic claims was his promise to ameliorate the secondary status of women in Judaism. He allowed women in synagogues he visited in Constantinople, Smyrna, and Salonika to be called up to the *Torah. According to Gershom *Scholem, Shabbetai is reported to have promised in 1665 that he would lift the "curse of Eve" from women and added, "Blessed are you, for I have come to make you free and happy like your husbands, for I have come to take away Adam's sin." Scholem has suggested that Shabbetai may have been attracted by "the audacity of Sarah, the reputed harlot, because he cherished the dream of the reparation of Adam's sin and of the consequent restoration of woman to her original freedom" (405). Scholem goes on to argue that the idea that the *messiah would repair *Adam's sin was current in Lurianic mystical writings, but Shabbetai seems to have been the first to make the connection in terms of the emancipation of women.

Eva Frank (1754–1816), daughter of the charismatic Sabbatean leader Jacob *Frank (1726–1791), played a major role in the messianic and *antinomian Frankist movement. Originally named Rachel, she is referred to in Frankist writings as the Lady, the Virgin, or *Matronita*, the Aramaic name of the mystical female entity, the *Shekhinah*. She became known as Eva after the conversion of her family to Christianity in 1760. Jacob Frank saw himself as the eternal messiah and told his followers to recognize Eva-Rachel as the mystical royal figure of the *Shekhinah*, who would lead them as a messianic redeemer in his temporary absence. Ultimately, Frank claimed, he would be reborn and united with his daughter in "the unity of Messiah and *Shekhinah*." After Jacob Frank's death in 1791, Eva led the Frankist community in its hopes of imminent messianic redemption. Even after she died, many Frankist families continued to keep her portrait and honored her as a saintly woman who was falsely reviled.

For further reading, see H. Adelman. "Finding Women's Voices in Italian Jewish Literature," in *Women of the Word: Jewish Women and Jewish Writing*, ed. J. R. Baskin (1994), 50–69; idem; "Italian Jewish Women," in *Jewish Women in Historical Perspective*, ed. J. R. Baskin (1998), 150–68; J. R. Baskin, "Jewish Women's Piety and the Impact of Printing in Early Modern Europe," in *Culture and Change: Attending to Early Modern Women*, ed. M. Mikesell and A. Seeff (2003), 221–40; R. L. Melammed, *Heretics or Daughters of Israel? The Crypto-Jewish Women of Castile* (1999); M. Keil. "Public Roles of Jewish Women in Fourteenth and Fifteenth-Centuries Ashkenaz," in *The Jews of Europe in the Middle Ages (Tenth to Fifteenth Centuries)*, ed. C. Cluse (2004), 317–30; G. Scholem. *Sabbatai Sevi* (1973); and C. Weissler, *Voices of the Matriarchs: Listening to the Prayers of Early Modern Jewish Women* (1998).

JUDITH R. BASKIN

Women: Middle Ages. In medieval times most Jews lived in the *Diaspora. Significant Jewish populations were in the Muslim worlds of *North Africa, *Iraq, and *Spain (*Sepharad), and there were far smaller numbers of Jews in Christian Europe (*Ashkenaz). All Jewish communities governed themselves by the Babylonian *Talmud; halakhic sources confirm that medieval Judaism continued rabbinic patterns in ordaining separate gender roles and religious obligations for men and women and in relegating females to secondary, enabling positions (see WOMEN, ANCIENT: RABBINIC JUDAISM). However, norms and customs of local environments were also factors in how Jewish social life developed, because Jews assumed the language, dress, and many of the mores of their Gentile neighbors, including cultural attitudes toward appropriate female behavior. Virtually no documents written by medieval Jewish women, beyond personal correspondence, survive

(see also EDUCATION, GIRLS: MEDIEVAL AND EARLY MODERN).

Jewish social life in the Muslim realm was strongly influenced by *Islamic customs and polygyny was not uncommon. Although Jewish women of prosperous families were not literally isolated in women's quarters, community norms dictated that women remain out of the public eye. The observation of the preeminent sage of medieval Judaism, Moses *Maimonides (ll35–l204), who lived much of his life in *Egypt – "There is nothing more beautiful for a wife than sitting in the corner of her house" – reflects the high degree of Jewish acculturation to their environment. As accounts of marital disputes in Cairo *Genizah documents indicate, however, Jewish women had significant freedom of movement for visits to the *synagogue and bathhouse, social and condolence calls, and business activities, such as the buying and selling of flax. Women, who were married quite young, frequently to considerably older men and often to relatives, were often protected by social safeguards written into the marriage contract (*ketubbah); these altered Jewish laws and practices unfavorable to women, particularly in instances of desertion and *divorce. Such additions to the standard contract attempted to provide security against many of the known pitfalls of married life; some *ketubbot* included guarantees that, in case of separation, a divorce document (*get*) freeing the wife would be produced by her husband without delay and that the husband would not marry another wife, not beat his wife, not separate her against her will from her parents, nor travel anywhere without her consent. Quite frequently, the contract also stipulated that the husband would write a conditional bill of divorce before setting out on a journey so that his wife would be free to remarry should he fail to return after a specified length of time. Following biblical custom, Jewish grooms in the Muslim milieu also contributed a marriage gift (*mohar*), part of which was payable to the bride's father at the time of the wedding, with a portion reserved for the bride in the event of a divorce or her husband's death. Similarly the bride brought property into the marriage in the form of her dowry and trousseau. This dowry, which was also to be returned to the wife in case of divorce or her husband's death, was generally far more valuable than the husband's marriage gift; it gave a wealthy family significant leverage in finding a suitable match for their daughter and ensuring her proper treatment.

The small Jewish communities of medieval Christian Europe lived in an atmosphere of religious suspicion and legal disability. After the Crusades (see MIDDLE AGES: CRUSADES), Jews were prohibited from virtually any source of livelihood but *money lending and were often compelled to wear distinctive clothing and badges. By the end of the medieval period, Jews had been expelled from areas where they had long lived (including England in 1290 and Spain in 1492) or were forced to live in crowded *ghettos (see ITALY). Despite their political insecurity, Jews enjoyed a high standard of living and were significantly acculturated. Jewish women participated in the family economy; as Jews prospered in trade and money lending, particularly between 1100 and 1300, women played an increasingly vital and often autonomous part in their family's economic lives, both as merchants and as financial brokers. Indeed, Jewish women's influential position and activities during the High Middle Ages parallel those of Christian women within the upper bourgeoisie, as both groups of women achieved literacy, had financial skills, and ran their households and economic affairs effectively during their husbands' absences, whether on mercantile or military endeavors. Indications of the high status of Jewish women in *Ashkenaz include large dowries, significant freedom of movement, and the eleventh-century rabbinic ruling (takkanah) attributed to Rabbi *Gershom ben Judah of Mainz, forbidding polygyny for Jews in Christian countries; he also ruled that no woman could be divorced against her will. It was also the custom in Ashkenaz for husbands to leave their wives with a conditional divorce document when they set out on journeys so that their wives would be free to remarry should they fail to return after a specified length of time. Otherwise, a woman whose husband disappeared with no witness to his fate would become an *agunah and would be forbidden from marrying another man.

Women's high status and economic success in Ashkenaz are attested as well by their increased involvement in Jewish religious life, including the voluntary assumption of religious practices from which they were exempt in rabbinic Judaism. A. Grossman has connected women's insertion of themselves into areas of Jewish practice that were previously exclusively male not only to their economic success but also to contemporaneous religious revivals in which Christian women took part in reshaping prayers and religious worship in the church. One example is the insistence of prominent women in serving as godmother (sandeka'it) at the *circumcision of a son or grandson. R. *Meir of Rothenburg, a major rabbinic leader of the fourteenth century, attempted to abolish this practice because he believed the presence of perfumed and well-dressed women in the synagogue among men was immodest. His failure to eliminate this custom, which continued until the beginning of the fifteenth century, indicates women's social power. Yet, it is important to note that, as the political and economic situation of European Jewish communities worsened beginning in the mid-fourteenth century and traditional authority was reasserted, most of the privileges that Jewish women had achieved were gradually curtailed.

Jews in Christian *Spain retained significant Islamic cultural influences, as in the attitude that women should remain at home, a feature of Sephardic life well into the Early Modern period, even when Jews lived in very different places after the 1492 expulsion. The Muslim practice of polygyny also had a significant impact on Spanish Jewry, who never wholly accepted Rabbi Gershom's ban. Even under Christian rulers, Spanish Jews who wished to take second wives, usually because of fertility problems or unhappy relationships with their first spouse, could obtain special royal permission by paying a fee. Although second marriages were more frequent among the wealthy, who could most easily afford the expenses of an expanded household, their prevalence indicates the lower status of the Sephardic woman as compared to Jewish women in the rest of Europe.

However, this lower status was not true in all areas. Under halakhah, widows do not inherit their husband's property, but instead either receive back their dowry or are supported by the estate of their deceased spouse. Widows who chose to remarry generally had to give up custody of their minor children to their late husband's family. However, during the late medieval period, some Jewish men in Spain filed Latin wills with Christian courts to ensure that their wives could inherit their property and maintain custody of their children. This is an example of the Jewish willingness to circumvent the disadvantages for women inherent in halakhah when it conflicted with personal circumstances and the norms of the majority culture. Widows, especially those who benefited from their husbands' recourse to the generous inheritance laws of Christian Spain, were often in control of significant resources.

Positive Jewish attitudes toward marriage and sexuality were at odds with medieval Christian teachings, which enjoined celibacy on the representatives of the church, frowned on second marriages, forbade divorce, and taught that the only purpose of marital sexuality should be procreation. Influence from the Christian environment may account for the ambivalence toward sexuality characteristic of the German Jewish pietists of the twelfth and thirteenth centuries, the *Ḥasidei Ashkenaz, whose writings, such as *Sefer Ḥasidim (Book of the Pious), express not only an obsessive concern with the ubiquity of extramarital sexual temptations but also a profound ambivalence about the joys of marital sexuality. Although a happy marital relationship lessened the likelihood of involvement in illicit sexual temptation or activity outside marriage and was, therefore, a good thing, the Ḥasidei Ashkenaz were concerned that connubial pleasure might distract a man from God, who should be the focus of his greatest and most intense devotion.

Although celibacy and monastic living allowed a significant number of Christian women and, to a certain extent, some Muslim women to cross gender boundaries and secure a place alongside men as scholars, saints, and mystics in both Christianity and Islam, rabbinic insistence on universal marriage forbade any access to such life alternatives for Jewish women. Formal Judaism offered no adult avenues through which Jewish women could express their spiritual aspirations beyond marital devotion, maternal solicitude, observance of domestic Jewish rituals, and acts of charity to others. As A. Rapaport-Albert has observed, despite a Jewish ambivalence toward asceticism in general, Jewish mystical circles sanctioned ritualistic practices for men, which could include prolonged periods of sexual abstinence. Conversely, religious leaders criticized women who adopted such ascetic practices as fasting, prayer, and acts of personal deprivation. These signs of single-minded devotion to God were seen as a dereliction of a woman's primary duties to her husband and family and were suspect even in the unmarried girl and the widow (cf. BT Sotah 22a). Given these prohibitions, it is not surprising that medieval Jewish *mysticism was an essentially male endeavor.

A great deal is known about one medieval Jewish woman's activities from a poetic elegy written by Eleazar ben Judah of Worms for his wife Dolce, who was murdered along with her two daughters by intruders in their home in 1196. Dolce was the economic support for an extensive household, including children, students, and teachers. Her husband praises her needlework, recounting that she prepared thread and gut to sew together books, Torah scrolls, and other religious objects. He writes that the pious Dolce taught other women and led them in prayer; she prepared brides for their marriages and bathed the dead and sewed their shrouds, meritorious endeavors in Jewish tradition.

More than anything, R. Eleazar reveres his wife for facilitating the spiritual activities of the men of her household; the reward he invokes for Dolce at the conclusion of his lament (based on Proverbs 31:10–31) is to be wrapped in the eternal life of Paradise, a tribute to her deeds on which so many depended.

For further reading, see J. R. Baskin, "Dolce of Worms: The Lives and Deaths of an Exemplary Medieval Jewish Woman and Her Daughters," in *Judaism in Practice*, ed. L. Fine (2001), 429–37; E. Baumgarten, *Mothers and Children: Jewish Family Life in Medieval Ashkenaz* (2007); S. D. Goitein, *A Mediterranean Society*. 5 vols. (1978–88); A. Grossman, *Pious and Rebellious: Jewish Women in Medieval Europe* (2001; trans. 2004); R. L. Melammed, "Sephardi Women in the Medieval and Early Modern Periods," in *Jewish Women in Historical Perspective*, ed. J. R. Baskin (1998); E. Taitz, S. Henry, C. Tallan, *The JPS Guide to Jewish Women* (2003).   JUDITH R. BASKIN

Women, Modern: Britain and North America.

As many European and American Jews entered the middle class in the course of the 1800s, Judaism's preferred positioning of women in the domestic realm, which conformed well to nineteenth-century Christian bourgeois models of female domesticity, was preserved. Jewish literature and the Jewish press of the late nineteenth century, both in *Britain and the *United States, described the Jewish woman as the "guardian angel of the house," "mother in Israel," and "priestess of the Jewish ideal" and assigned her primary responsibility for the Jewish identity and education of her children. Women were encouraged to express their spirituality in domestic activities such as traditional Jewish cooking and home-based observance of the *Sabbath and *festivals. However, making women rather than men responsible for inculcating Jewish identity and practices in children led from praise to criticism, as commentators began to blame mothers for their children's increasing acculturation to the larger non-Jewish culture.

In England a significant number of Jewish women worked in the public domain to hasten the Jewish Enlightenment and *emancipation and to further religious reform. These women included social activists and advocates of liberal Judaism like Lily Montagu (1873–1963), as well as writers of both fiction and non-fiction with Jewish themes directed to Jewish and Gentile audiences, such as Grace Aguilar (d. 1847), and Marion and Celia Moss (1840s). In her popular book, *The Women of Israel*, Aguilar described the exalted position of women in Judaism, highlighting what she saw as women's traditional role in hastening *redemption through instructing children and through other domestic activities (see LITERATURE: BRITAIN). Despite these uplifting messages, Jewish women's success in the world of literature was upsetting to the men of their milieu; although male Jewish reformers in England supported a degree of female emancipation in principle, they tended to limit and undermine women's writing and influence in the public sphere.

Nineteenth- and early-twentieth-century male leaders also discouraged efforts by women to work with men for Jewish communal goals, but they did not object to women banding together for various public purposes that benefited the Jewish community. In emulation of bourgeois Christian models of female *philanthropy and religious activism, middle-class Jewish women established service and social welfare organizations in Germany, England, and North America, including the Jüdischer Frauenbund in Germany (founded in 1904), the Union of Jewish Women in Great Britain (founded in 1902), and the National Council of Jewish Women in the United States (founded in 1893). For many Jewish women, whose synagogue roles remained limited, organizational involvement became a spiritual undertaking (see ORGANIZATIONS, WOMEN'S: NORTH AMERICA). These groups cooperated in the international campaign against coercion of poor women into *prostitution, worked for female suffrage, instituted social welfare services (see SOCIAL WORK: UNITED STATES), and argued for greater recognition of women within their respective Jewish communities. In the process, as women acquired administrative expertise and assumed authoritative and responsible public roles, they blurred the boundaries between traditional male and female spheres of action. In North America, Jewish women's organizations included *synagogue sisterhoods, which devoted themselves to the domestic management of the *synagogue – decorating the sanctuary for festivals, catering synagogue events, and performing many other housekeeping functions. National organizations of sisterhoods, separated by denomination, encouraged local groups in their activities and provided a forum for public female leadership. Sisterhoods of all denominations, however, recognized that females had to be Jewishly educated to strengthen Jewish observance at home and instill Jewish values in their children, and they encouraged expanded educational opportunities for women of all ages. Similarly, American Jewish women played a central role in establishing, supervising, and teaching in synagogue religious schools (see GRATZ, REBECCA).

The first generation of Jewish immigrants from *Eastern Europe who arrived in the United States between 1880 and 1914 were not, on the whole, middle class. Of these immigrants, 43% were women, a far higher proportion than among other immigrant groups. The values these immigrants brought with them, even as they were gradually transformed by America, permitted women to play a complex role in helping their families adjust to their new environment. Thus, most women contributed to the family income in one way or another. A significant number sought the benefits of higher education, whereas others took advantage of a variety of public secular activities. Young Jewish immigrant women were influenced by the world of work where they were exposed to union issues and socialist ideas; many were ardent participants and leaders in labor activism (see UNITED STATES: LABOR MOVEMENT). Even after they married, Jewish women continued their public roles through leading rent strikes, organizing the 1902 kosher meat boycott, and agitating for the availability of birth control information and support for women's suffrage. In the period after *World War II, Eastern European Jewish immigrants and their children became increasingly successful economically and began to enter the middle class. They tended to follow the educational, occupational, residential, and religious patterns of previous waves of Jewish settlers in North America, including affiliation with Conservative and Reform synagogues (see JUDAISM entries) and a preference that women should not work outside the home. Many women now had leisure for volunteer activities and became members of the national Jewish women's organizations founded earlier in the American Jewish experience or became involved in synagogue sisterhood activities.

CONTEMPORARY REALITIES: In the early twenty-first century, women's roles in Jewish organizational life are in a period of significant transformation. In this more egalitarian era, where women are often highly educated and hold professional jobs, it is not unusual to see women leaders in synagogues and in other Jewish communal groups that are not limited to women. This integration of the sexes in general communal leadership has called into question the continued existence of same-sex organizations such as synagogue sisterhoods and brotherhoods. Moreover, at a time when many women are employed outside the home, it is far more difficult for middle-class women to spare the hours they once devoted to volunteer activities; this may also affect the continued existence of Jewish women's organizations.

In the last three decades of the twentieth century and in the first decade of the twenty-first, Jewish women's religious and educational opportunities and roles in Judaism and the Jewish community have expanded in a number of ways, such as the ordination of women as rabbis in the liberal wings of Judaism (see RABBINIC ORDINATION OF WOMEN), women becoming *cantors, the transformations of synagogue liturgy to include women as worshipers and to incorporate gender-neutral language about God (see JUDAISM, FEMINIST; WORSHIP), and the development of new *life-cycle rituals. Many women who did not receive substantial Jewish educations in childhood are taking advantage of adult education opportunities (see EDUCATION, NORTH AMERICA: ADULT), and a number participate in adult *Bat Mitzvah ceremonies.

Rabbinic ordination for women is still far from imminent in Orthodox communities (see JUDAISM, ORTHODOX), although educational opportunities for women have expanded impressively in traditional Judaism in the past hundred years. The first religiously oriented schools for Jewish girls from Orthodox families were established in 1918 in Eastern Europe under the leadership of Sarah *Schenirer (1883–1935). Although the *Bais Yaakov* school network that Schenirer inspired emphasized modesty and humility more than rigorous study, it set a precedent for female education in Orthodox Judaism that has endured. In the present day, the secular opportunities that have transformed women's educational and vocational expectations in the wider world have had a decided impact on some sectors of the traditional community as well. Orthodox girls and women now have many options for serious study of traditional Jewish texts, and some have also become authors on Jewish topics of all kinds. In the early twenty-first century, halakhically knowledgeable women serve as rabbinic assistants in a number of Modern Orthodox synagogues in North America and are trained to act as expert advocates on legal issues connected with women's status in *Israel.

Contemporaneous and in many ways linked with the growth and development of Jewish feminism is the visibility of identified gay and lesbian Jews, as well as of single Jews regardless of sexual orientation, as active participants within the Jewish community. Although Jewish domestic life has historically been centered around family units consisting of male and female parents and their children, the delayed age of marriage and the growing numbers of unmarried Jews, as well as contemporary openness regarding

homosexuality, have changed the demographic make-up of many Jewish communities. Most liberal approaches to Judaism agree that Jewish ethical teachings and the future of the Jewish people require communal institutions to welcome and value formerly marginalized individuals and groups who do not conform to traditional family models (see ETHICS, SEXUAL).

For further reading, see M. Galchinsky, *The Origin of the Modern Jewish Woman Writer: Romance and Reform in Victorian England* (1996); E. M. Umansky, *Lily Montagu and the Advancement of Liberal Judaism: From Vision to Vocation* (1983); P. E. Hyman, *Gender and Assimilation in Modern Jewish History: The Roles and Representation of Women* (1995); L. G. Kuzmack, *Women's Cause: The Jewish Woman's Movement in England and the United States, 1881–1933* (1990); S. B. Fishman, *A Breath of Life: Feminism in the American Jewish Community* (1993); D. Orenstein, ed., *Lifecycles: Jewish Women on Life Passages and Personal Milestones* (1994); and V. L. Ochs, *Inventing Jewish Ritual* (2007).
                                                          JUDITH R. BASKIN

Women, Modern: Central Europe. Before 1750, the lives of Jewish women in the various *German states and the *Habsburg Empire did not differ greatly from those of other *Yiddish-speaking *Ashkenazi women within *Poland or the *Russian Empire, but thereafter their paths diverged considerably. Growing up in towns or villages with small, traditional Jewish communities, Jewish women before 1750 generally married in their late teens or early twenties and raised fairly large families, while helping their husbands run a business at home or in the marketplace. Young Jewish girls learned household and economic skills from their mothers; most could read *Yiddish and some learned *Hebrew or secular subjects with tutors in the home, but usually they received little formal instruction.

The first Central European Jewish woman we know about from her own writings is Glikl bas Judah Leib (1747–1824), often referred to as *Glückel of Hameln, who wrote a memoir (see also LITERATURE: WOMEN WRITERS (EUROPE AND NORTH AMERICA): LITERATURE, YIDDISH: BEGINNINGS TO 1800; MEMOIR AND LIFE WRITING; WOMEN: EARLY MODERN EUROPE). Her family belonged to the elite group of wealthy *Court Jews involved in international trading of jewels and other goods. Married at fourteen and the mother of twelve children who survived to adulthood, she was very actively involved in her husband's business, especially when he was traveling. She was also greatly preoccupied with arranging suitable *marriages for her children and providing her daughters with dowries. Glückel was knowledgeable about Jewish ritual and values; she maintained a traditional Jewish home, strictly observing *dietary laws and the laws of *niddah. As a widow, she often attended *synagogue, sitting in a separate women's gallery curtained off from the men (see also FAMILY AND MARRIAGE: EARLY MODERN PERIOD).

By the end of the eighteenth century, however, some wealthy and well-educated Jewish women began to distance themselves from their traditional roles and to interact with non-Jews in social settings. Some of these women ultimately left the Jewish community. In early nineteenth century *Berlin, a small group of "salon women" entertained leading German intellectuals and noblemen in their homes; some of these women, including *Moses Mendelssohn's daughter Dorothea Veit von Schlegel ([born Brendel] 1764–1839), divorced their Jewish husbands and converted to Christianity so they could marry non-Jewish men. Another woman of this circle was Rahel Levin Varnhagen, (1771–1833), a woman of letters who converted and married a Christian diplomat, Karl August Varnhagen von Ense. Although *divorce and *intermarriage remained quite rare in Germany and Austria-Hungary before World War I, baptism was generally a prerequisite for a Jewish woman to marry a Christian. The vast majority of Jewish women, however, married Jewish men and raised their children as Jews.

During the course of the nineteenth century, German Jewish women became increasingly urbanized and adopted a more middle-class lifestyle. Gradually, they abandoned their significant economic role in the family business and focused their attention on their household and on child rearing. M. Kaplan has shown that women became responsible for preserving Jewish tradition in the home, especially through preparing *Sabbath eve and *festival family dinners and creating what has become known as "domestic (or gastronomic) Judaism," while at the same time inculcating German language and culture (Bildung) in their children. Jewish women also became involved in voluntary philanthropic activities and formed Jewish women's clubs.

Yet, women did not take part in the leadership of the organized Jewish community (or Gemeinde), nor did they engage in the study of Jewish texts. As the Reform movement developed in nineteenth-century Central Europe, synagogue worship became more accessible for women: German *sermons became the norm, prayer services were conducted in the vernacular, and *confirmation ceremonies were introduced for both girls and boys (see JUDAISM, REFORM: GERMANY). Married women often frequented synagogues, sometimes outnumbering the men, but separate seating for men and women continued to prevail in Central European synagogues. As B. M. Baader has pointed out, German Jewish women did not become as learned as Jewish men had been, but instead Jewish men became less knowledgeable about *Torah and *Talmud and more like the women in their level of Jewish education.

In Central Europe, Jewish girls were more highly educated than Christian girls; they attended Jewish communal and public coed elementary schools and also private secondary schools for girls. In the early twentieth century, Jewish women began attending university in disproportionately large numbers, following the examples of their fathers and brothers. Both unmarried and married Jewish women were discouraged from working outside the home for pay, but single women, including widows and divorcées, often sought employment in commerce, teaching, social work, and other professions to support themselves and their families, especially after World War I.

Jewish women played a very prominent role in the late-nineteenth-century German women's movement and in 1904 created the Jüdischer Frauenbund (League of Jewish Women), led by Bertha *Pappenheim. They were in the forefront of the establishment of modern kindergartens, the fight against the coercion of women into *prostitution, the struggle for women's suffrage, and the promotion of birth control. Some also became quite visible in Central European politics, especially within the Social Democratic and *Communist Parties.

By the twentieth century, Jewish women in Central Europe were marrying in their mid- to late twenties, and some never married, whether by choice or because of a lack of suitable partners. Arranged marriages were no longer common, dowries played less of a role, and most marriages had at least the appearance of being love matches. After World War I, *intermarriage increased, while the number of Jewish marriages declined; more Jewish men married outside the faith than Jewish women. German Jewish women were among the pioneers in family planning in Central Europe; the Jewish birth rate began to decline about a generation earlier than the overall German birth rate. By the interwar years, having two or three children was becoming the norm in Jewish families.

Jewish women were highly acculturated into middle-class German society and often served as patrons of the arts and the theater; for the most part, they identified both as Germans (or Austrians) and as Jews. However, they were all aware of *antisemitism and tended to socialize primarily with other Jews. After the *Nazis assumed power, Jewish women were more willing than Jewish men to leave Central Europe; however, proportionately more women than men remained when World War II began, whether because they felt less threatened personally, because they were elderly, or because they chose to remain with elderly parents. Even during the Nazi era, women continued to take care of their families and to work on behalf of others in the Jewish community as long as this was possible (see also HOLOCAUST: ROLE OF GENDER).

For further reading, see D. Hertz, *Jewish High Society in Old Regime Berlin* (1988); M. Kaplan, *The Making of the Jewish Middle Class* (1991); idem, *Between Dignity and Despair: Jewish Life in Nazi Germany* (1999); B. M. Baader, *Gender, Judaism, and Bourgeois Culture in Germany* (2006); and H. P. Friedenreich, *Female, Jewish and Educated: The Lives of Central European University Women* (2002). HARRIET PASS FREIDENREICH

Women, Modern: Eastern Europe.

The domestic and communal roles, religious lives, and educations of the Jews of Eastern Europe were highly gendered. This traditional model prevailed well into the nineteenth century, when new ideologies and economic factors led to the opening of unprecedented opportunities for Eastern European Jewish women.

In traditional Jewish life, women were absent from communal leadership, study, and worship. Just as women were not able to hold public office in non-Jewish society, so, too, they could hold no office within the structure of the kahal or kehillah, the local Jewish self-government (see COMMUNAL ORGANIZATION). However, women could serve as members of certain communal organizations (ḥevrot), such as the burial society (ḥevra kadishah). Their activity within these groups increased significantly in the later nineteenth century. However, women remained excluded from traditional communal religious life, which maintained its dominance until the late nineteenth century. Sitting in a separate section of the *synagogue, they could attend public worship, but were not religiously obligated to do so. For the benefit of those women who did not know the prayers and perhaps could not read, a literate woman might recite the service aloud, whether in *Hebrew or *Yiddish, in the women's section (see WORSHIP).

Women's major religious activities were home-based, rather than centered on the synagogue or study house. They were expected to observe those *commandments that applied especially to them, to run their homes according to Jewish norms, and to raise and ensure the education of their children. Most girls did not receive any formal education, although some did spend a few years at ḥeder, the traditional primary school. Female education was primarily of a practical, domestic nature, transmitted from mother to daughter. If women were literate, it was likely to be in Yiddish, not Hebrew. In their home rituals and practices, they were able to express their spirituality through *tkhines, personal supplications in Yiddish that were specifically written for women (see PRAYER: WOMEN'S DEVOTIONAL). As an informal religious-social activity, women often met together on *Sabbath afternoons to read devotional literature, particularly the Tzene-rene, a Yiddish retelling of the weekly *Torah portion with moralistic and narrative elaborations (see LITERATURE: YIDDISH [BEGINNINGS TO 1700]). The *Ḥasidic movement, which spread rapidly from the early 1800s on, did not improve women's position. Not only did *Ḥasidism retain traditional gender roles but it also encouraged men to leave their families to spend holidays and other extended periods in the courts of their rebbes, leaving women and children home alone (see also ḤASIDISM, EUROPE: WOMEN; VERBERMACHER, HANNAH RACHEL).

As the nineteenth century unfolded, however, formal educational opportunities expanded, at least for some women. Although males were safeguarded from secular subjects, particularly foreign languages, which were seen as the gateway to non-Jewish ideas and society, girls were often allowed and even encouraged to learn other languages. Women in the lower classes needed these skills to enhance their earning opportunities; for Jewish woman in the middle and upper classes, linguistic facility was a sign of their family's culture and prosperity and also had economic benefits as well.

As the nineteenth century progressed, the division between women's and men's roles widened because of demographic and socioeconomic factors. While the population grew rapidly, economic circumstances worsened, and more men devoted their time to study. Traditional Jewish society placed a high value on this activity because it provided a meaningful occupation and reduced the competition for employment. Many women became the breadwinners, earning religious merit vicariously by enabling their men to participate in a life of piety.

Leading figures of the *Haskalah, the Jewish Enlightenment, such as Judah Leib Gordon, championed the cause of women, underscoring what they viewed as their victimization by traditional rabbinic culture. Proponents of the Jewish Enlightenment (maskilim) attacked arranged *marriages, early marriages, men who did not support their families, and women working outside the home. The maskilic vision was not of a world of gender equality; rather they sought to remake Eastern European Jewish society on the model of western middle-class (bourgeois) society in which women were homemakers, nurturing the next generation. To educate and shape the future molders of the Jewish people, maskilim established schools for Jewish girls. Given the traditional value system, modern education for girls was not

controversial. However, efforts to reform traditional modes of education for boys were strongly opposed.

As nineteenth-century Jewish women were increasingly exposed to new ideas through education and the growing availability of popular Yiddish novels, a small number of women became writers themselves. This minority of educated Jewish women, such as Miriam Markel-Mosessohn and Pauline Epstein *Wengeroff, served as "agents of acculturation" (Balin). Jewish women wrote in Russian, Polish, and German, as well as in Yiddish. However, many Jewish women found that their literary aspirations led to estrangement from a Jewish society that was not accepting of female encroachment into what were considered male realms of achievement.

The *Russian government severely limited opportunities for higher education for women in general; only an elite minority obtained higher education through special courses for women. When educational opportunities for girls opened at the time of the Russian Revolution (1917), Jews availed themselves of these new options. Some also went to Western Europe for professional training. In reaction to the increasing number of Jewish girls gaining a secular education in the interwar period, a network of Orthodox schools for girls, the Bais Yaakov schools, was founded to offer an education steeped in traditional values that would keep girls within the fold (see SCHENIRER, SARAH).

For the most part, women worked by helping their husbands in their work. Some also had market stalls or ran inns. The primary route to financial and economic independence was through widowhood. Along with educational opportunities, however, employment opportunities for Jewish women in both *Poland and Russia increased over the course of the nineteenth and into the twentieth century. Women also obtained professional training in occupations that were considered less prestigious, more poorly compensated, and less desirable for men, such as pharmacy and dentistry.

*Marriage ages underwent a shift in the course of the nineteenth century. Initially, Jewish society still valued early arranged marriages: boys at thirteen and girls at twelve (although only the wealthy could afford to marry their children off so early). By the late nineteenth century, marriages more often took place at a later age, and although they were still arranged, the young people involved were sometimes allowed to have input into the choice. The primary criteria employed in the matchmaking process for elite families were family wealth and lineage, in addition to "the state of health, appearance, talents, and temperaments of the candidates for marriage" (Etkes). Major considerations were the prospective groom's level of learning and facility for study. It was considered meritorious, if one could afford it, to obtain a bridegroom for one's daughter who would devote himself to full-time study.

Because the couple was often very young and the groom was usually studying and not earning a living, the couple often lived with the bride's parents for a few years. Their marriage document specified the number of years the couple would live with and be supported by the bride's parents. Sometimes a husband would travel and spend prolonged periods in other cities to pursue his Torah studies, leaving his wife behind. If the couple already had children, the wife had to raise the children alone, while also supporting the family. In a typical home, there was no shared responsibility for caring for children, educating children, or any household business. A Jewish woman was expected to fulfill these roles happily, as her part in supporting a scholar, although sources indicate that marital tensions often developed because of this gendered division of labor. Yet, the number of Jewish men who devoted themselves to scholarship was always relatively small. Jews at the lower end of the social ladder, possessing neither financial resources nor learning, would often make their own matches. Young women might work as household servants, seamstresses, or laundresses to earn their own dowries so that they could arrange a marriage for themselves.

Women became active members in the various types of political organizations that emerged in the second half of the nineteenth century. They participated in disproportionate numbers in the general revolutionary movements in tsarist Russia, as well as in the *Zionist movement and the *Bund, the Jewish labor movement. Examples include Puah Rakovsky and Anna Rozental, respectively. It was only in the Bund, however, that women had significant opportunities to hold positions of leadership.

Recent research includes E. R. Adler, *In Her Hands: The Education of Jewish Girls in Tsarist Russia* (2010); C. B. Balin, *To Reveal Our Hearts: Jewish Women Writers in Tsarist Russia* (2000); I. Etkes, "Marriage and Torah Study among the *Lomdim* in Lithuania in the Nineteenth Century," in *The Jewish Family: Metaphor and Memory*, ed. D. Kraemer (1989); C. R. Freeze, *Jewish Marriage and Divorce in Imperial Russia* (2002); P. E. Hyman, "Gender," *The YIVO Encyclopedia of Jews in Eastern Europe* (2008); P. Rakovska, *My Life as a Radical Jewish Woman: Memoirs of a Zionist Feminist in Poland*, ed. P. E. Hyman (2003); S. Stampfer, "Gender Differentiation and Education of the Jewish Woman in Nineteenth-Century Eastern Europe," *Polin* 7 (1992); and C. Weissler, *Voices of the Matriarchs: Listening to the Prayers of Early Modern Jewish Women* (1999).   LISA COHEN

Women: Pre- and Post-State Israel. The pioneers of the First *Aliyah (1882–1903) and Second Aliyah (1904–18) included both men and women (see ISRAEL, STATE OF: JEWISH IMMIGRATION BEFORE 1948). Most of the women of the First Aliyah accompanied their husbands and settled into domestic roles in agricultural settlements or urban environments. The women of this immigration wave, most of whom were deeply committed to their new lives in *Palestine, achieved little public recognition or participation. Many of the idealistic young people of the Second Aliyah, inspired by Labor *Zionism, had been trained to work the land in *Russia in Zionist training schools that stressed the equality of women and men. On arriving in *Palestine, most young single women, a significant minority among the second wave of immigrants (17–18%), found their options limited and their choices narrowed, simply as a result of their gender. Unmarried women were virtually unemployable as agricultural workers and were forced to survive by providing men with kitchen and laundry services. Denied membership as single women in most collective settlements and refused employment as agricultural workers, a few women founded successful female agricultural and urban collectives.

In the years after World War I, the majority of single women in the *Yishuv* ended up working in cities as cooks or laundresses, seamstresses or clerks, or maids in private homes. Under the immigration regulations imposed by the *British Mandate on the Third Aliyah (1919–23), women were allowed to enter Palestine as dependents, wives, and elderly mothers, but only a few could enter as prospective workers and receive a labor immigration permit. Fewer women than men immigrated to Palestine (36% were women) and two-thirds to 90% of all women came as dependents, as compared to 10–20% of all men. Labor permits were allocated to more than 50% of all men and to only 10% of immigrant women. In the *Yishuv*, traditional gendered divisions of labor and patterns of authority tended to be preserved, and these patterns continued after 1948 as well.

The kibbutz (collective agricultural settlement) movement provided an alternative for the relatively few single women who were accepted into these communities. Many *kibbutzim* were dedicated to bold social restructurings of the family to create a society in which each individual would achieve economic independence. In such a setting, wives would not be dependent on their husbands and would no longer be subservient to them. The family was to be renewed in such a way that men and women would be equal and independent partners sharing common goals, and women would be emancipated from domestic demands to work with men in building the land. Yet even on the kibbutz, women mainly worked in kitchens and laundries, and their role in child care was difficult since children were often raised collectively in children's houses under the care of nurses and teachers. Parents only saw their children for an hour or two each day. In this way, mothers were freed to function as independent members of the collective, and children were to benefit from feeling that all the adults were concerned for their welfare. Yet, there is a general acknowledgment now that collective child rearing was problematic for both children and parents. In the twenty-first century, the kibbutz children's house is a thing of the past (see STATE OF ISRAEL: KIBBUTZ MOVEMENT).

Modern Israel continues to be far from progressive where the status of women is concerned. At the beginning of the twenty-first century, it is more conservative than most other western democracies on women's issues. Despite significant achievements and a high level of education, Israeli women continue to earn less than their male counterparts, are less visible and influential in the political arena, do not share equal responsibilities or privileges in the military, have unequal rights and freedoms in family life, and are secondary in shaping the nation's cultural orientation. This inequality is a result of entrenched attitudes towards women in Jewish tradition in general, as well as the impact of highly conservative Middle Eastern cultures on many Israelis from Muslim countries.

Although women are eligible for military service, most women in the army are assigned to education, clerical work, and training. Fewer than half of all eligible women are actually conscripted because they are not really needed in the military, although army technology is beginning to create more equal tasks for the Israeli woman soldier and in recent years women's opportunities in the military have been expanding. Given the historical pattern of secondary roles, however, women remain poorly represented in the upper echelons of the military, as they are in public and political life, in the civil service, and in academia. Because a military background has come to be a necessary prerequisite for public office, women have found it very difficult to break into politics. One consequence of the emphasis on national security is that what are seen as women's issues, particularly in areas like health, education, and welfare, have received low priority.

The Committee for the Advancement of the Status of Women and individual female members of the Knesset (Israeli parliament) are attempting to advance women's status through legislative initiatives addressing equality at work, violence against women, and welfare, health, and fertility concerns. The growing awareness of the unequal status of women in the early-twenty-first century has led to an increasing presence of women in managerial and decision-making positions. In recent decades, Israel's growing feminist movement has begun to bring cases to Israel's Supreme Court on issues as diverse as access to *abortion, women's right to be elected to and hold seats on municipal religious councils, and the ability of women's prayer groups to hold services at the Western Wall (see also ISRAEL, STATE OF: PEACE MOVEMENT).

This increased feminist activity, influenced by the women's movement throughout the western world, has illuminated the gender and religious tensions that characterize modern Israeli society. Although legal advocacy and political activities constitute alternative approaches to combating women's unequal roles, fundamental transformations in Israel's governmental structure are necessary if gender equality is to be realized. Similarly, true change for women will only come when the adjudication of family law and personal status issues is removed from the sole control of the Orthodox rabbinate, which has been inflexible in easing the discriminations against women inherent in halakhic tradition.

Important scholarship includes D. Bernstein, ed., *Pioneers and Homemakers: Jewish Women in Pre-State Israel* (1992); idem, *The Struggle for Equality: Urban Women Workers in Prestate Israeli Society* (1986); E. Fuchs, ed., *Israeli Women's Studies: A Reader* (2005); M. Palgi et al., *Sexual Equality: The Israeli Kibbutz Tests the Theories* (1983); and K. Misra and M. Rich, eds., *Jewish Feminism in Israel: Some Contemporary Perspectives* (2000).   JUDITH R. BASKIN

Workmen's Circle (*Arbeter Ring*). Founded by *Eastern European Jewish immigrants in *New York City in the late 1890s, this fraternal society (see UNITED STATES: FRATERNAL SOCIETIES) offered its members mutual aid, health and death benefits, and educational and cultural activities. The order supported international labor and socialist movements (see UNITED STATES: LABOR MOVEMENT) and championed *Yiddish as the Jewish language. In the first decade of the twenty-first century, the group highlights its Jewish identity, but originally it did not espouse explicitly Jewish goals.

In 1900, the Workmen's Circle became a national organization and grew rapidly. Members played a significant role in the development of the trade union movement, and the organization provided a range of social, educational, and health services, including a tuberculosis sanatorium that operated from 1910 to 1955. In 1916 it founded a network of secular supplementary schools for children that stressed the

study of Yiddish language and Jewish history. The Workmen's Circle also maintained summer camps (see SUMMER CAMPING), choruses, and dramatic societies and sponsored lectures. The years 1920–26 marked the high point for membership, followed by a subsequent decline as a result of restrictive U.S. immigration laws. Despite efforts to avoid a rift over *communism, thousands of pro-communist members left the order and created a rival group, the International Workers Order, in 1929.

*World War II brought change as many young Jews reared in a Workmen Circle milieu entered the military and gradually became estranged from the order's socialist ideals. Reflecting this reality, the post-war Workmen's Circle began adopting positions that were liberal and allied with the Democratic Party.

In the first decade of the twenty-first century, with a membership composed primarily of American-born Jews, the order operates a summer camp for children, a summer resort for adults, and several homes for the elderly; it also works on behalf of liberal and leftist positions. Although membership has declined, branches operate in several American Jewish communities.   RACHEL GORDAN

World Union for Progressive Judaism was founded in London (see BRITAIN: EARLY MODERN AND MODERN) in 1926 as the international body of Reform, Liberal, Progressive, and Reconstructionist Jews (see JUDAISM entries). Since 1973 its international headquarters has been in *Jerusalem. The World Union membership encompasses more than one and a half million Jews in more than thirty countries. In *Israel, the World Union for Progressive Judaism has established synagogue-community centers, settlements, schools, and a World Education Center in Jerusalem. The newest centers of activity are in *Eastern and *Central Europe. In the former *Soviet Union, many new congregations and leadership training programs have been established. The World Union publishes *prayer books and liturgical and educational materials, helps recruit rabbinic and professional leaders, and assists new congregations throughout the world.   RACHEL GORDAN

World War I: Impact on American Jews. American Jews were deeply divided about World War I (1914–18) until late in the conflict. Only by confronting a series of dramatic events overseas and the demands of wartime life could the nation's three million Jews unite in their support for the Allies, a turbulent process that underscored their changing identities in the *United States.

American Jewish opinion rested most heavily on the fate of the Jewish *Pale of Settlement and the *Russian Empire. During the war's first three years, a majority of the Jewish population, *immigrants from *Eastern Europe, wished above all for the end of tsarist rule and its notorious *antisemitism. Thus, there was strong American Jewish sentiment in favor of a German victory. With the Russian Revolution of February 1917 and the entry of the United States into the war that April, many were able to shift their support to the Allies. Initially the opposition to the American war effort from the Jewish left was one of the largest sources of dissent in the country. Yet, the Treaty of Brest-Litovsk signed by *Germany and the new *Bolshevik government in Russia soon reversed this remaining opposition. Under that agreement, Germany occupied much of Eastern Europe in early 1918, placing millions of Jews under military rule. In stark contrast, Woodrow Wilson's championing of national self-determination and Anglo-American approval of a Jewish homeland in *Palestine (in the *Balfour Declaration of 1917) made Allied war aims acceptable across the diverse political spectrum of American Jewry.

This consensus mirrored Jewish cooperation on a variety of war-related activities, most urgently on efforts to aid Jewish refugees along the Eastern Front and in *Palestine. Displaying remarkable unity, the Eastern European and Central European communities, together with Jewish labor, formed the American Jewish *Joint Distribution Committee, which between 1914 and 1924 administered more than $60 million in critical services to 750,000 Jews in Eastern Europe alone. Unprecedented Jewish cooperation also strengthened the American war effort. Approximately 200,000 Jews served in the U.S. armed forces. To meet their cultural needs, a diverse group of Jewish religious bodies created the Jewish Welfare Board, providing military locations worldwide with rabbis, social workers, and recreational activities (see UNITED STATES: MILITARY CHAPLAINCY). Jews also served in homefront agencies and contributed millions of dollars to the nation's Liberty Loan and Red Cross campaigns.

American Jewish opinion converged most dramatically in the desire to secure a haven for the world's oppressed Jews. Before 1914, *Zionism had few American advocates, but the war's devastation made the goal of a Jewish homeland both critical and realistic. By November 1918, membership in American Zionist organizations totaled 200,000, and a nationally elected *American Jewish Congress prepared to attend the Versailles peace negotiations.

As a result of World War I, American Jews further distanced themselves from their European pasts, increased their attachment to life in the United States, and became a powerful influence in international Jewish affairs. Despite the tragedy of Versailles and the rise of American antisemitism during the 1920s, the war years produced enduring sources of strength and unity in American Jewish life.

For further reading, see C. M. Sterba, *Good Americans: Italian and Jewish Immigrants during the First World War* (2003); G. Sorin, *A Time for Building: The Third Migration, 1880–1920* (1992); and A. Gal, "The Mission Motif in American Zionism, 1898–1948," *American Jewish History* 75(4) (1980): 363–85.   CHRISTOPHER M. STERBA

World War II: Impact on American Jews. American Jews had been watching the spread of *antisemitism in Europe since Hitler's rise to power in 1933. Unlike the situation of divided loyalties during *World War I, American Jews were united in their opposition to *Nazism, although they differed on how best to oppose Germany. These differences evolved over the course of the war's six years, colored by ideologies that ranged from fervent communism to deeply pious Orthodoxy, with most American Jews positioned as strong proponents of the New Deal. American Jews voted overwhelmingly to support President Franklin Delano Roosevelt for an unprecedented third term in 1940 and a fourth term in 1944. They believed in the four freedoms: freedom of speech and religion and freedom from want and fear. The Jewish commitment to defeating Hitler contributed to their enthusiastic embrace of military service once the United States entered the conflict after the bombing of Pearl Harbor on December

7, 1941. More than a half-million Jews served in all branches of the armed forces, roughly one-half of those eligible for the draft.

Jews also sought to rescue European Jews, especially during the years when the United States was not at war. Here, too, American Jews differed on the best ways to respond to escalating Nazi persecution, detention in concentration camps, ghettoization of Polish Jews, reports of mass murders of hundreds of thousands of Jewish civilians after the German invasion of the Soviet Union in June 1941, and, finally, extermination of millions in death camps (see HOLOCAUST and related entries). This final devastating news reached American Jews late in 1942, during the first year of American participation in the war, which had been filled with defeats inflicted by Japan. The unfolding of the *Shoah, coupled with extensive military service, transformed American Jews. They emerged from the war as the largest, most prosperous, politically engaged Jewish community in the world, eager to build a different world for their children.

Sharp disagreements divided American Jews regarding how to rescue European Jews. These intracommunal conflicts erupted as *antisemitism flourished in the United States, finding expression on the floors of Congress, in boardrooms and clubrooms, in popular culture, and within many Christian churches. Often accused of exercising too much power in the United States and of goading the nation to war, Jews discovered how little influence they possessed to loosen restrictive *immigration quotas or persuade President Roosevelt to challenge British policy limiting Jewish immigration to Palestine (see WHITE PAPER, 1939). Even within such ideological groups as *Zionists or left-wing radicals, Jews proposed alternative solutions designed to advance their goals. These included opening a second front, supporting the Allies in their efforts to win the war, advocating for a Jewish army, bombing *Auschwitz, ransoming *Hungarian Jews, and admitting refugees into camps in the United States. Each Jewish group raised funds, agitated in the press, lobbied Congress and the executive branch, staged rallies, petitioned, and protested.

Liberation of the death camps in 1945 revealed how their efforts had been unsuccessful in stopping or even slowing the murder of European Jews. Historians continue to debate whether American Jews could have done more and whether the failure stemmed from a lack of determination, flawed policies, lack of power, or from antisemitic individuals in the Roosevelt administration (see also HOLOCAUST: UNITED STATES JEWISH RESPONSE).

Although most American Jews watched the war unfold from the security of the homefront, almost all of them also worried about a relative in uniform who was fighting. Military service introduced young Jews who had grown up in big cities to a country they had never seen. They encountered fellow citizens who had never met Jews, as well as Jews from American small towns and from parts of the world considered exotic, like *North Africa and *India. Jews in uniform learned how to fight the enemies of the United States as well as the prejudices of their fellow soldiers. Jews in the military met all challenges to prove their bravery and manhood. They sustained substantial losses and casualties, fighting in all theaters of war. They also discovered that their Jewishness was integral to their identities, as integral as their American patriotism.

The armed forces propagated the concept of an American Judeo-Christian tradition: Judaism was represented as one of the three fighting faiths of democracy, symbolized in the sacrificial heroism of the four chaplains on the USAT *Dorchester* (two Protestants, a Catholic, and a Jew), who gave up their life preservers that other men might live when the ship was torpedoed in February 1943. Jewish GIs learned to pray together with Protestant and Catholic soldiers, especially at memorial services. The 311 Jewish chaplains who served during the war not only ministered to men of all faiths and championed the fatherhood of God and brotherhood of man, central tenets of the emerging Judeo-Christian tradition, but also established a Jewish ecumenism among Orthodox, Conservative, and Reform Jews (see JUDAISM entries), expressed in the joint *prayer book they developed and used during the war (see also UNITED STATES: MILITARY CHAPLAINCY). These experiences dramatically changed perceptions of Jews and Judaism in the United States after the war and encouraged cooperation among diverse American Jewish rabbis, as well as non-Jewish clergy (see INTERFAITH DIALOGUE: UNITED STATES).

The end of the European war in May 1945 revealed the staggering losses that world Jews had sustained and embittered the taste of victory. Liberating the death camps sickened and angered even combat-hardened veterans; the Third Reich was worse than they had ever imagined. Although the war did not end until the Japanese surrender in August, images of the stacks of emaciated bodies, mounds of hair and eyeglasses, and pitiful stares of living skeletons endured as the ultimate horrors of World War II for American Jews, rather than the agonies of the bombing of Hiroshima and Nagasaki.

When the United States entered World War II, American Jews expected the war would change the world. They did not realize how the war would change them. Secure in their American identity in the post-war era, they accepted their new position as leaders of the most powerful community of the Jewish *Diaspora. As they extended their hands in support of Jews struggling for a Jewish state, they also addressed the unfinished business of rectifying the injustices of American democracy. They recognized that the fight against antisemitism involved preserving and defending democracy and seeking full equality for all Americans in a free society. For further reading, see D. D. Moore, *GI Jews* (2004); Y. Bauer, *American Jewry and the Holocaust* (1981); and H. Feingold, *Bearing Witness* (1995).   DEBORAH DASH MOORE

Worship. BIBLICAL PERIOD: Israelites, like the peoples in surrounding cultures, worshiped through sacrifices. The Hebrew *Bible presents Israelite worship (as opposed to individual devotional acts) as beginning after the revelation of the *Torah at Mount Sinai and the erection of the desert *Tabernacle (*mishkan*) that housed the *ark containing the *Ten Commandments. There were also secondary places of worship. King *David brought the ark to *Jerusalem (2 Sam 6), and his son, King *Solomon, built the magnificent First *Temple to house it (1 Kgs 6–8). When the kingdom split after Solomon's death, Jeroboam built new temples in his northern kingdom of *Israel, explicitly to discourage pilgrimage to Jerusalem, now capital of the southern kingdom of *Judah (1 Kgs 12:28ff). Centralization of Israelite religion in Jerusalem followed the fall of the northern kingdom to the

*Assyrians in 722 BCE. The First Temple was destroyed by the *Babylonians in 586 BCE. In 516 BCE, two decades after the *Persians permitted Jewish leaders to return to Judah and Jerusalem, construction of the Second Temple began. This Temple, rebuilt and expanded over the years, stood until its destruction during the First *Jewish War against *Rome in 70 CE.

Temple worship on behalf of the entire nation revolved around morning and evening offerings by the priests of a sheep or goat, the *tamid*, accompanied by a meal offering and a libation. An additional or *musaf* offering of the same sort, as well as other animal offerings specific to the day, marked most holidays. The priests (*kohanim*), descendants of Moses' brother *Aaron, were assisted by Levites, also members of the tribe of Levi. Jewish households, both in the Land of Israel and the *Diaspora, paid annual taxes to support sacrificial worship. Generally, portions of sacrificed animals fed the priests or formed the heart of a communal meal for those making offerings. Individuals also brought occasional sacrifices according to their means to cleanse themselves from sin or impurity or as a special mark of thanksgiving. Daily offerings included wine, fine flour, and agricultural products. Male Jews were expected to attend the Temple for the three *pilgrimage *festivals: *Passover, *Shavuot (Weeks), and *Sukkot; most, however, attended infrequently (see also TEMPLE AND TEMPLE CULT).

By the late *Second Temple period, the *synagogue (Greek for "gathering place"; Hebrew, *beit kenesset*, with the same meaning) emerged as the center of local Jewish communal life, both in the Land of Israel and the Diaspora. Similar institutions, often called associations or colleges, were normal parts of the social, political, and religious structure of Greco-Roman society.

RABBINIC PRAYER: The Rabbis, the leaders of *rabbinic Judaism, shaped the foundations of contemporary Jewish liturgy. Their fundamental prayer structures appear in the *Mishnah, the earliest rabbinic text (ca. 200 CE), although there is almost no evidence for widespread participation in rabbinic worship practices until the third or fourth centuries. After the Temple's destruction, R.*Johanan ben Zakkai issued decrees adapting non-sacrificial Temple rituals for use outside of the Temple (M. *Rosh Ha-Shanah* 4:1–4). His successor, Gamaliel, decreed that "every day, each person must recite (the) eighteen benedictions" (M. *Berakhot* 4:3). Rabbinic texts refer to these benedictions as "The Prayer" (*ha-tefillah*); later, Jews commonly called it the *shemoneh esrei* (eighteen) or the *amidah (standing), for the posture in which it is recited. The *amidah* was recited facing Jerusalem, and its times of recitation were correlated to the times for the Temple's perpetual offerings (BT *Berakhot* 26a–b; JT *Berakhot* 4:1, 7b); in the absence of the Temple it now functioned as Israel's covenantal worship of God.

The separate paragraphs of this prayer were recited in order and, ideally, in *Hebrew. When at least ten adult male Jews (a *minyan*) were present, one person could serve as the community's representative before God, reciting the prayers aloud while the others fulfilled their obligations by responding "amen." The *amidah* begins with three benedictions of praise, establishing the worshiper's relationship with the monarch/God; only then is it appropriate to voice personal petitions, followed by three final blessings offering thanksgiving before leaving the monarch's presence. The weekday petitions collectively call on God to fulfill the messianic promise of restoring Jewish sovereignty in the Land of Israel, complete with a Davidic monarch and a rebuilt Temple in Jerusalem. The Talmud teaches that Rabban Gamliel called for adding another petition, a nineteenth benediction, known as the *birkat ha-minim*, the malediction of the sectarians (BT *Berakhot* 28b–29a).

Less is known about the origins of the rest of rabbinic liturgy. At some point, the pre-rabbinic synagogue's reading of scripture became a cyclical reading of the entire *Torah (*Pentateuch/Five Books of Moses), accompanied by thematically appropriate prophetic passages (*haftarah). Housing for the Torah scroll, required for the liturgical proclamation of the text, became an architectural feature of the Jerusalem-facing wall of the synagogue. By the late first millennium, elaborate Torah scroll processions and liturgies for moving it from the ark to the reading desk and back became standard. The Torah has come to embody or channel divine holiness, accessible in every synagogue and not just in the Jerusalem Temple. Consequently, prayers requesting divine blessings for healing, the well-being of the community, local rulers, and the deceased, are recited near the scroll. Medieval mystics understood the opened scroll and the opened ark to be gateways to Heaven (see KABBALAH).

The *shema* and its blessings are also a rabbinic liturgical element. These consist of three biblical passages (Deut 6:4–9, 11:13–21; Num 15:37–41) surrounded by rabbinic blessings. The *shema* is an affirmation of divine unity; its name is simply the first word of the first verse, "Hear!" Recitation of the *shema* twice daily follows the command, in Deuteronomy 6:7, to speak these words "when you lie down and when you rise up"; it was probably originally a home ritual, recited at bedtime and on arising. Deuteronomy 6:8 commands that these words should be bound on one's person – on one's arm and between the eyes (*tefillin) – and Deuteronomy 6:9 commands their writing on the doorposts and gates of one's house (*mezuzah). According to Numbers 15:38–40, Jewish males are commanded to tie fringes (*tzitzit*) on the corners of their garments as a constant reminder of their relationship with God. Traditional Jews wear this fringed *tallit all day as an undergarment and in shawl form for morning prayers. Two blessings precede the *shema*, and one follows it in the morning; two follow it in the evening. The prior blessings speak of God as creator of the world who expresses love for Israel by revealing Torah. The subsequent blessing evokes God's work in redeeming Israel from *Egypt. Later thinkers recognized these three themes of divine creation, *revelation, and *redemption as the core of Jewish *theology. The fourth evening blessing speaks of God's protection through the night. The *shema* and its blessings gradually merged with the *amidah* into a single rabbinic prayer service that takes place three times each weekday: *shaḥarit* (morning), *minḥah* (afternoon), and *ma'ariv* or *arvit* (evening); the afternoon service consists primarily of the *amidah*.

MEDIEVAL DEVELOPMENTS: Rabbinic leaders, especially in Babylonia, but also in the Land of *Israel, began to ensure that their liturgical systems were standardized during the period of the *Geonim (ca. 600–1038). The first formal Jewish *prayer book (*siddur*; pl. *siddurim*, from *seder*, the Hebrew word for "order") – the *Seder Rav Amram Gaon* (ca. 875) – was the response of the Babylonian Gaon, Rav *Amram bar Sheshna, to a Spanish Jewish community's request that he detail the annual order of prayers (see RESPONSA). Local variations were common until the development of *printing centralized the production of prayer books regionally. Iberian (*Sephardi) Jews, expelled from *Spain in 1492 and *Portugal in 1497, also imposed their own rite or prayer practices in their new communities, leading to the virtual disappearance of the local liturgies of *North Africa, the *Balkans, and the entire Middle East (except *Yemen). Printed Sephardi-rite prayer books, usually produced in *Italy, become standard in these regions.

Today most Jews pray either according to the Sephardi rite (*minhag sefarad*), often in a version deeply influenced by mystical teachings, or according to the Ashkenazi rite of *Central and *Eastern Europe (*minhag *Ashkenaz). Ashkenazi liturgy contains a subgroup of rites adopted by the eighteenth-century *Ḥasidic movements in imitation of the sixteenth-century *Safed mystic, Isaac *Luria; these rites have Sephardi elements (*nusakh sefarad*). Yemenite and some Italian Jews also preserve their historical rites.

IMPACT OF MODERNITY: Reform Judaism, which began in early-nineteenth-century *Germany (see entries for JUDAISM, REFORM), initiated a variety of liturgical changes; Reform Jews tended to discard ritual garb like the *tallit and *tefillin and, in America, men's head coverings. In America, family seating also became the norm. Various prayers were reworded for both theological and political reasons, virtually eliminating the Temple-centered cluster of ideas that had driven the liturgy's initial construction.

Responses to Reform in Western Europe and North America established the map of Jewish liturgies persisting today. Those rejecting change froze their practice, including elements that were purely customary; others compromised to varying degrees. Modern Orthodoxy (see JUDAISM, ORTHODOX: MODERN ORTHODOX) eliminated poetic additions to the service except for on the *High Holidays and adopted the vernacular *sermon, but maintained all other prayers. Conservative Judaism (see JUDAISM, CONSERVATIVE) retained most traditional prayers, but made subtle changes, usually based on some historical precedent. Thus, references to Temple sacrifices became memories of the past and not prayers for the future; some prayers for peace voiced universal hopes. Some Conservative congregations added instrumental music to Sabbath services and occasional vernacular prayers.

The rise of political *Zionism, the destruction of European Jewry in the *Holocaust, and the founding of the State of *Israel created a new reality to which all Jews needed to adapt liturgically. Since the 1950s, very few at the liberal end of the spectrum still consider references to the Land of Israel to be irrelevant, although most continue to emphasize universal redemption rather than the personal *messiah or a restoration of the Temple cult. The eschatological meaning of the modern State of Israel also generated liturgical issues for traditional Jews. According to some, this state lacks messianic qualities and cannot be accepted as a fulfillment of millennia-long prayers and dreams. According to others, it is "the beginning of the sprouting of our redemption."

Demand for greater "spirituality" beginning in the 1960s generated selective retrievals of liturgical traditions, including in Reform Judaism, and encouraged less formal worshiping communities. Synagogue *music (see MUSIC, RELIGIOUS; MUSIC, SYNAGOGUE) became less formal, encouraging congregational participation. In some twenty-first-century settings, leading the service is once again the responsibility of the community as a whole and not of its paid clergy. In the last three decades of the twentieth century the feminist movement changed the face of the synagogue and elements of its worship texts (see JUDAISM, FEMINIST). With the *ordination of women as rabbis and *cantors in Reform, Conservative, and Reconstructionist Judaism (see JUDAISM, RECONSTRUCTIONIST), women achieved full liturgical participation in non-Orthodox synagogues as prayer leaders, Torah readers, speakers, and congregational leaders. Feminist challenges to gendered language about humans and God prompted liturgical changes, first in the English translations in the American liberal prayer books, and then more limited changes to the Hebrew texts. Modern Orthodox women, too, have become more present in the synagogue, engaged in Jewish learning, worship, and communal leadership; the traditional liturgy itself, however, remains virtually unchanged.

For further reading, see R. Langer, *To Worship God Properly: Tensions between Liturgical Custom and Halakhah in Judaism* (1998); L. A. Hoffman, *The Canonization of the Synagogue Service* (1979); S. C. Reif, *Judaism and Hebrew Prayer: New Perspectives on Jewish Liturgical History* (1993); and J. Tabory, "The Piety of Politics: Jewish Prayers for the State of Israel," in *Liturgy in the Life of the Synagogue: Studies in the History of Jewish Prayer*, ed. R. Langer and S. Fine, 225–46 (2005); **see also BIBLE: PRAYER LANGUAGE; ISRAELITES: RELIGION; PRAYER: WOMEN'S DEVOTIONAL; TEMPLE AND TEMPLE CULT.**   RUTH LANGER

Writings (*Ketuvim*) is the third section of the *Tanakh* (see BIBLE). The thirteen books of this division, in the order in which they now appear, are *Psalms, *Proverbs, *Job, *Song of Songs, *Ruth, *Lamentations, *Ecclesiastes, *Esther, *Daniel, *Ezra, *Nehemiah, and 1 and 2 *Chronicles.

Y

Yad Vashem, the Holocaust Martyrs' and Heroes' Remembrance Authority, was founded in *Jerusalem by the Israeli government in 1953. It is now an extensive center for documentation, research, education, and commemoration of the *Holocaust. It takes its name from Isaiah 56:5: "And to them will I give in my house and within my walls a memorial and a name (*yad va-shem*) . . . that shall not be cut off." **See also HOLOCAUST DOCUMENTATION; HOLOCAUST MEMORIALS; MUSEUMS.**

Yahrzeit (also *yortsayt*). This *Yiddish word (literally "anniversary") refers to the yearly commemoration (according to the Hebrew date) of the death of a close family member (see DEATH AND MOURNING). Among observances associated with *yahrzeit* are kindling a twenty-four-hour candle on the evening before the date of death, visiting the cemetery, making a donation to a worthy cause, and studying *Torah. Parents, children, siblings, and the spouse of the deceased traditionally recite the *kaddish* sanctification during one or more *synagogue services, either on the date of death or the preceding *Sabbath. Fasting on the anniversary of the death of a parent was customary during talmudic times (BT *Nedarim* 12a; BT *Shevuot* 20a), and some individuals continue this practice. In the first year after a death, *yahrzeit* takes place on the anniversary of the funeral. In subsequent years, it is observed on the actual date of death. Modern *yahrzeit* rituals originated in fifteenth-century *Germany, and the word has its origins in the German *Jarhzeit*, which had similar associations in Christian practice. In *Sephardic communities, *yahrzeit* may be called *naḥalah* (inheritance) or *meldado* (study session).

ELIZABETH SHULMAN

Yehoshua, A. B. (b. 1936), a major Israeli writer, was born in *Jerusalem to a *Sephardic family that had lived in the city for five generations. After studying Hebrew literature and philosophy at the Hebrew University of Jerusalem, he taught for many years at the University of Haifa. Yehoshua's widely translated and numerous novels, short fiction, plays, and polemics have been awarded many literary prizes in Israel and abroad. Many critics regard him as Israel's boldest and most politically erudite writer; his art has influenced generations of average Israelis who grew up reading works such as *The Lover* (1977) in high school. A Faulknerian work that examines the interiority of a dysfunctional Jewish family and those who come into their lives, *The Lover* established Yehoshua's genius for approaching issues of national importance through the foibles of private individuals whose neuroses often serve as an urgent allegory of Israel's maladies. Even Yehoshua's earliest works have enjoyed an unwavering reputation. His frequent engagement with the entwined destinies of Jews and Arabs in Israel began with his 1963 story, *Mul ha-Ya`arot* (Facing the Forests), and figures significantly in later novels such as *The Liberated Bride* (2004) and *Friendly Fire* (2008). Other highly acclaimed novels include

Mr. Mani (1992), an epistolary story of several generations of Sephardic Jews living in the Land of Israel and the Mediterranean, and *A Journey to the End of the Millennium* (1999), a subtle examination of the contrasting communities of Sephardic and *Ashkenazi Jews in the medieval world that also manages to wink slyly at Israel's religious and social tensions in the present. A sometimes controversial figure, Yehoshua is well known for his consistent disavowal of Jewish identity in the *Diaspora as well as for his staunch opposition to Israel's occupation of *Palestinian territories.

RANEN OMER-SHERMAN

Yehud is the *Aramaic term for the tribal territory of *Judah that was applied by *Persia after its conquest of the *Babylonian Empire in the 530s BCE. From this word came the Greek, Latin, and English words for the area, Judea. An inhabitant of this region was known as *Yehudi*, a Judean. The English designations "Jew" and "Jewish" derive from this word.

Yemen. Yemenite Jews trace their origins to the period of the *Babylonia Exile (587 BCE). Until modern times, the community was mainly known through *Maimonides' "Epistle to Yemen" (ca. 1172; see A. S. Halkin, *Moses Maimonides' Epistle to Yemen* [1952]), which addressed a period of persecution in the life of Yemenite Jews, and the *Bustan al-`Ukul*, a twelfth-century ethical, philosophical, and theological work by Natanel ibn Fayyumi. **Map 5**

There was little knowledge about Yemenite Jews because the Jews of Yemen were cut off both from the outside world and from the mainstream of Jewish culture with the rise of the Zaydi regime in the early tenth century (see "al-Zaidiya," *Encyclopedia of Islam* 4:1196–98). As a result of this isolation, they developed specific cultural traits and peculiarities; they also preserved an archive of documents and literary works that would otherwise have been lost. Yemenite Jewry was "rediscovered" by Rabbi Jacob Saphir (1822–1886), an extensive traveler, who visited this long-secluded Jewish community in 1859. He recorded his travels and experiences in Yemen in a book entitled *Even Sappir* (2 vols., 1866, 1874), in which he characterized the Yemenite Jews as "the most authentic Jews in the world" (2: 68). Saphir described several customs related to family life, including very early marriages. He wrote that it was not unusual to see a twelve-year-old Yemenite girl who was already a mother. He also indicated that it was customary for Yemenite men to have two or three wives. Locusts, which were rampant in Yemen and are considered kosher, were a popular source of food (see Lev 11:22). Like their Arab neighbors, Yemenite Jews were fond of chewing the leaves of the *kat* (*catha edulis*), a mildly narcotic shrub.

The discovery of the Cairo *Genizah documents has significantly enhanced scholarly knowledge of the Jews of Yemen between the tenth and thirteenth centuries, shedding light on multifaceted relationships and merchant alliances (particularly in Aden) with Jewish communities in *Iraq, *Egypt, and elsewhere. Jewish Yemenite writings about their own history are scant, perhaps due in part to the scarcity of writing materials. The resulting shortage of books apparently accounts for the marvelous ability of some Yemenite Jews to read a book from all possible angles, a capability that developed when several children seated around one single copy of a book learned to read the Hebrew *Bible and other sacred writings.

Yemenite Jewry did not generate scholars and writers of universal renown. Their writings focused mainly on the pervasive atmosphere of hostility and contempt and the occasional outbreaks of violence they experienced. They also wrote religious poetry (see POETRY, LITURGICAL [*PIYYUT*]) and *midrash (homilies based on biblical passages). Particularly noteworthy is *Midrash ha-Gadol*, compiled by Rabbi David ben Amram ha-Adani in the thirteenth century. The greatest and most famous Yemenite poet was Rabbi Shalom Shabazi (1619-after 1679) who was venerated as a poet and saint. Many of his poems continue to be chanted by Yemenite Jews on various occasions.

In 1949, about fifty thousand Yemenite Jews, virtually the entire community, were flown to *Israel in a gigantic operation known as "On Eagles' Wings" (very often referred to as "Operation Magic Carpet"). Many Israelis viewed this exotic, religious people with their dangling earlocks as "prophets stepping out of the Bible" (S. Barer, *The Magic Carpet* [1952], ix). Their rich repertory of *dance, *music, and *folklore, which seemed to reflect ancient Hebrew culture, made them an object of emulation and source of inspiration for the newly developing Israeli culture. Despite the relatively small numbers of Yemenite Jews in the general Israeli population, they have made significant contributions to contemporary Israeli life. A valuable compendium on this community is R. S. Simon, M. M. Laskier, and S. Regeur, eds., *The Jews of the Middle East and North Africa in Modern Times* (2003).

REUBEN AHARONI

Yerushalmi: See TALMUD, JERUSALEM

Yeshiva University

Yeshiva University (YU), a research university in *New York City whose motto is *Torah uMadah* (Torah together with secular studies), has graduate schools in business, *education, *social work, *medicine, law, and other fields. Students combine Jewish studies with the arts and sciences, and men may also pursue *rabbinic ordination, sometimes while also earning advanced degrees in secular subjects.

YU began as the Rabbi Isaac Elhanan Theological Seminary (RIETS), founded in 1896–97 as the rabbinical school of the Union of Orthodox Rabbis of the United States and Canada (UOR) and named for Rabbi Isaac Elhanan Spektor. The school trained rabbis according to the educational practices of the great Lithuanian *yeshivot*. In 1915 Rabbi Bernard Revel (d. 1940) became leader of the institution; he aspired to make traditional Jewish study meaningful in America, harmonizing the best of modern culture with the learning and spirit of the *Torah and traditional *Judaism.

As RIETS graduates competed for rabbinical positions with graduates of the *Jewish Theological Seminary (JTS), which was still considered an Orthodox school in the early twentieth century, they found themselves at a disadvantage because, unlike JTS, RIETS did not teach practical rabbinics, homiletics, and related subjects. Student strikes demanding

instruction in these subjects resulted in their eventual implementation at RIETS.

In 1928, YU established Yeshiva College, a degree-granting undergraduate institution integrating Jewish subjects and secular studies. At that time, YU left its Lower East Side site and moved to Washington Heights in upper Manhattan. In 1936, the school established its first graduate school (in Jewish studies), while Revel worked to bring faculty from Europe. Revel was succeeded by Rabbi Samuel Belkin (d. 1975); under his leadership, YU expanded rapidly, obtaining university status in 1945. Over the years new schools were opened, including Stern College for women (1954), as well as secular, nonsectarian divisions, including the Albert Einstein Medical School, the Benjamin N. Cardozo School of Law, and the Wurzweiler School of Social Work. Richard M. Joel, a legal scholar, became Yeshiva University's fourth president in 2003, succeeding Dr. Norman Lamm.

RACHEL GORDAN

Yeshivah (pl. *yeshivot*), from the Hebrew root *y/sh/v* meaning to "sit," is a school or academy devoted to the advanced study of classical Jewish texts.

Yiddish is a Germanic-based vernacular Jewish language written in Hebrew script. It developed in German-speaking *Central Europe in the *Middle Ages and became the primary language of most Jews living in *Eastern Europe in early modern and modern times; it is also known in its western forms as Judeo-German. See LITERATURE, YIDDISH: FROM ITS BEGINNINGS TO 1700; LITERATURE, YIDDISH: FROM 1800 TO THE TWENTY-FIRST CENTURY; LITERATURE, YIDDISH: *YISHUV*; as well as relevant entries under JOURNALISM, POETRY, and THEATER.

Yiddish Dictionaries. Dictionaries reflecting modern *Eastern European Yiddish first appeared in the nineteenth century. Y. M. Lifshits based his *Rusish-yudisher verter bikh* (1869) and his *Yudesh-rusisher verter bikh* (1876) largely on the Ukrainian dialect. Alexander Harkavy compiled his 1928 *Yiddish-English-Hebrew Dictionary*, which strongly reflected Lithuanian and literary Yiddish, while an immigrant in *New York City. Later, a number of dictionaries paired literary Yiddish with Hebrew, Russian, Belorussian, Ukrainian, Polish, English, Spanish, French, German, Japanese and Esperanto. Before World War II and shortly thereafter, dictionaries mainly helped Yiddish speakers learn other languages. In recent decades, they more often serve the needs of students of the language and propagate the norms of Standard Yiddish. The most significant dictionaries include Harkavy (1928); Uriel Weinreich, *Modern Yiddish-English English-Yiddish Dictionary* (1969); the Yiddish-Yiddish *Groyser verterbukh fun der yidisher shprakh* (ed. Yudel Mark [1961–80], as yet incomplete); the *Russko-evreiskyi (idish) slovar'* (ed. M. A. Shapiro [1984]); and the *Dictionnaire Yiddish-Français* (ed. Y. Niborski [2002]). Dictionaries of specialized terminologies, rhyming and spelling dictionaries, and lexicons of Yiddish's Semitic component also exist.   KALMAN WEISER

Yishuv, from the Hebrew word for "settlement," refers to the Jewish community in *Palestine from the late nineteenth century to the founding of the State of *Israel in 1948.

Yivo Institute for Jewish Research (YIVO) was founded as the Yiddish Scientific Institute in *Vilna, *Poland (now

Vilnius, Lithuania) in 1925. Its headquarters were relocated to *New York City in 1940. In 2000, YIVO became one of the constituent members of the *Center for Jewish History. Dedicated to the history and culture of *Ashkenazi Jewry and to its influence in the Americas, YIVO is a resource center for East European Jewish Studies; *Yiddish language, literature and folklore; and the American Jewish immigrant experience. The YIVO library holds over 385,000 volumes in twelve languages, and the archives contains more than 24,000,000 items, including manuscripts, documents, photographs, sound recordings, art works, films, posters, sheet music, and other artifacts. Among the Institute's publications are *Yidishe shprakh*, a Yiddish linguistics journal; *YIVO-bleter*, a Yiddish-language scholarly journal; and the English language *YIVO Annual of Jewish Social Science*. Recently published books (both 2008) include a revised edition, now with a translation of the complete text and notes, of M. Weinreich, *History of the Yiddish Language*, and G. D. Hundert, ed., *The YIVO Encyclopedia of Jews in Eastern Europe*.

ELIZABETH SHULMAN

Yizkor (Hebrew, "May [God] remember") is a communal *synagogue memorial service that takes place four times a year. Originally only recited on *Yom Kippur, *Yizkor* services are now also traditionally held in *Diaspora synagogues after the *Torah and *Haftarah* readings on *Shemini Atzeret, the eighth day of *Sukkot; the eighth day of *Passover; and the second day of *Shavuot. In *Israel and in Reform congregations (see JUDAISM, REFORM), *Yizkor* takes places on the combined day of Shemini Atzeret/Simḥat Torah; the seventh day of Passover; and the single day of Shavuot. *Yizkor* services include both communal readings and prayers and silent devotions during which mourners can recall their loved ones. The *cantor chants *El Malei Raḥamim* (God, Full of Compassion), the memorial prayer that is also voiced at a funeral. The last prayer in the *Yizkor* services, *Av ha-Raḥamim* (Compassionate Father), recalls all Jewish *martyrs throughout the ages. The *Kaddish* sanctification is not a traditional component of *Yizkor*, but many congregations choose to recite it. In some communities it is customary for those whose parents are still alive to leave the sanctuary while *Yizkor* is being recited and to return for the final prayer.

ELIZABETH SHULMAN

Yizkor Books (memorial books) are a special category of books devoted to the commemoration of particular Jewish communities destroyed in the *Holocaust. Most appear under one of three names: *yizker bukh* (*Yiddish), *sefer zikaron* (*Hebrew), or *pinkas* (chronicle). These works commemorate cities, towns, and regions in *Eastern Europe – especially in *Poland, *Ukraine, and *Belarus – by bringing together personal *memoirs and testimonies, historical narratives, biographical sketches, original documents, literary works, statistical analyses, maps, photographs, and paintings. Varying in length and format, most share a similar structure, presenting the history of the local Jewish community from its beginning until the Holocaust; discussing important sites, prominent families and leaders, renowned *synagogues, religious life, and educational, political, and cultural institutions and organizations; and describing the destruction of the community, with accounts of survival and resistance (see HOLOCAUST RESISTANCE). Some include descriptions of post-war visits and reports on the activities of the town's

*fraternal societies (*landsmanshaftn*), organizations formed by immigrants from the same town or region. Most volumes include a list of local Jews murdered during the Holocaust. Although some of these books are written by a single author (and at times closely resemble a memoir or a local history), most result from collaborations among former residents who formed a special book committee, collected materials over a period of time, and sometimes employed an editor or commissioned a historian. Some historians, such as N. M. Gelber and N. Blumenthal, were regularly involved in these initiatives. Although *Pinkas ha-kehillot* (Encyclopedia of Jewish Communities), published by *Yad Vashem, is devoted to whole countries or regions, most memorial books commemorate smaller areas, usually individual cities or towns and their immediate vicinity. In some cases, more than one book dedicated to a certain community was created, usually as a result of geographic, linguistic, or ideological divisions among former inhabitants.

A book about Łódź was published as early as 1943 and a few others appeared in the immediate aftermath of the war, but the majority of *yizkor* books were published in the 1950s and 1960s, with numerous volumes added in the subsequent two decades. Most were published in *Israel or in *New York City. New books sometimes take innovative forms, such as community reconstructions or websites. Although the exact number of memorial books depends on their precise definition, there are estimated to be more than six hundred titles.

Large collections of memorial books can be found in research libraries in the United States and Israel. The Dorot Jewish Division of the New York Public Library has digitized its entire collection and provides online access on its website. A bibliography by Z. M. Baker is included in *From a Ruined Garden: The Memorial Books of Polish Jewry*, ed. J. Kugelmass, J. Boyarin, and Z. M. Baker (2nd ed., 1998). Other lists of books can be found online at various websites, especially those dedicated to Jewish genealogy. The bulk of memorial books are written in Hebrew and Yiddish with sections or summaries in English; a few are written in other languages. Although the editors of the books frequently declared their aim as preserving and transmitting the knowledge of their community to future generations, their format and language target a relatively narrow audience. Attempts to make the books more accessible have led to several translation projects, most notably a JewishGen initiative launched in 1994. In addition to translations into English, it also coordinates translations into other languages; for example, Polish. Because of the collective character and commemorative function of *yizkor* books, as well as the often idealized, romanticized, or reconciliatory images they present, some historians warn against using them uncritically. Further analysis of this genre can be gleaned from the comprehensive introduction to *From a Ruined Garden*.

NATALIA ALEKSIUN-MADRZAK

Yom Ha-Atzma'ut (Independence Day) is the Israeli national and religious holiday celebrating the proclamation of the establishment of the State of *Israel on May 14, 1948. It is observed according to the corresponding date on the Jewish *calendar, the 5th of Iyar. In Israel, Yom Ha-Atzma'ut events include an official evening ceremony on Mount Herzl in *Jerusalem; related events include the International Bible Contest for Jewish Youth, the Hebrew Song

Festival, and the awarding of the Israel Prize. The day before Yom Ha-Atzma'ut is Yom Ha-Zikaron (Day of Remembrance) in memory of Israeli soldiers who died in battle. Rituals and liturgy to commemorate Yom Ha-Atzma'ut are still being shaped; no formulations have yet achieved universal acceptance.   ELIZABETH SHULMAN

Yom Ha-Shoah or **Yom Ha-Shoah Veha-Gevurah** (Holocaust and Heroism Remembrance Day) is a day of commemoration for Jews who were murdered during the *Holocaust and for those who resisted *Nazi persecution (see HOLOCAUST RESISTANCE). In *Israel it is observed on the 27th of Nissan, the anniversary of the *Warsaw ghetto uprising (see HOLOCAUST: GHETTOS). In 1951, Prime Minister David *Ben-Gurion and President Yitzhak Ben-Zvi instituted Yom Ha-Shoah in Israel. It begins at sundown with a ceremony at *Yad Vashem in *Jerusalem. At ten o'clock the next morning, sirens sound for two minutes and people throughout Israel stand in silence.

Many *Diaspora communities observe Yom Ha-Shoah with *synagogue worship and special communal programs and vigils. Ritual and liturgy to address the specific theological and historical resonances of the Holocaust are still being formed; one custom is to light a twenty-four-hour *yahrzeit candle. Some Orthodox Jews choose to commemorate the victims of *Nazi genocide on traditional mourning days, such as *Tisha B'Av and the 10th of Tevet, rather than on Yom Ha-Shoah.   ELIZABETH SHULMAN

Yom Kippur (Day of Atonement): See HIGH HOLIDAYS

Z

Zalman, Schneur Ben Baruch, of Liady (1745–1813) was the founder of the *Ḥasidic Lubavitch community (*Ḥabad). Rabbi Zalman was a disciple of the Maggid, Rabbi Dov *Ber of Miedzyrzecz, the heir of the founder of Ḥasidism, Rabbi Israel *Baal Shem Tov. His two closest colleagues, Menachem Mendel of Vitebsk and Abraham of Kalisk, immigrated to *Safed in 1777, and he assumed the leadership of the community in southern *Russia and provided support for Ḥasidic groups in the Holy Land. His influence grew, and thousands flocked to his court. He tried to resolve the conflict between the Ḥasidim and the *mitnaggedim ("opponents" of Ḥasidism) by arranging a meeting with Rabbi Elijah, the *Vilna Gaon, in 1774, but was unsuccessful. He was arrested by the Russian police on suspicion of making foreign contacts; to this day, Lubavitch Ḥasidim celebrate the day he was released, the 19th of Kislev in 1798.

Zalman's exoteric spiritual work, usually known as the *Tanya* (It Was Taught; 1st ed., 1787, definitive ed., 1814) is held sacred by the Ḥabad Ḥasidim; his teachings, including esoteric ones, are presented in his sermons collected in *Torah Or* (The Light of the Torah; 1837) and *Likutei Torah* (Selections of the Torah; 1848). He taught an intense *mystical doctrine, holding all existence as an illusion and advocating identification with *ayin*, the absence of all worldly elements, which brings the worshiper to communion with *God. For further reading, see N. Loewenthal, *Communicating the Infinite: The Emergence of the Habad School* (1990); and R. Elior, *The Paradoxical Theology of Habad* (1996).

JOSEPH DAN

Zangwill, Israel (1864–1926) was an Anglo-Jewish writer and founder of the Jewish Territorial Organization (JTO). Born to Jewish immigrants in London, Zangwill attended the Jews' Free School and graduated in 1884, with honors, from the University of London (see BRITAIN: EARLY MODERN AND MODERN). At first a journalist and humorist, he gained fame with his 1892 novel, *Children of the Ghetto*, a trenchant study of Jewish life in Britain. The comic *King of Schnorrers* followed in 1894, and throughout the 1890s Zangwill published stories on Jewish themes and other fiction not specifically Jewish. As one of the "Wanderers of Kilburn," Zangwill associated with Solomon *Schechter, Joseph Jacobs, and other prominent Jews who went on to found the Jewish Historical Society of England. His friends included other notable men and women, both Jews and Christians, in the arts, literature, and theater. Zangwill became a leading English *Zionist in 1895 after Max Nordau introduced him to Theodor *Herzl.

In 1903 Zangwill married writer and feminist Edith Ayrton and became active in the British women's suffrage movement. He translated the *mahzor* (High Holiday *prayer book) with Arthur Davis, Nina Davis Salomon, and others (1904–09) and the religious poetry of Solomon *ibn Gabirol (1923). Among numerous contributions to *theater in this period, *The Melting Pot* (1908) has been the most enduring (see THEATER: BRITAIN). In 1905, Zangwill split with the mainstream Zionist movement and formed the JTO, the goal of which was to establish a Jewish homeland wherever one could be found; the organization was best known for its advocacy of East Africa, although it considered many locations. Ultimately its greatest success was in working with Jacob Schiff's Galveston Plan to settle 10,000 immigrants in Texas and other western regions of the *United States (1907–14; see UNITED STATES, SOUTHERN).

Zangwill briefly returned to the Zionist fold at the time of the *Balfour Declaration. He warned, however, that Jews needed a homeland with autonomy, not just a place of refuge under British or other rule. Recognizing the difficulty of the Arab presence in *Palestine, Zangwill criticized Zionist leadership in a major 1923 address and alienated many Jews. At his death, however, the Jewish world mourned the loss of a prominent literary interpreter, defender, and public figure. For further reading, see M. Rochelson, *A Jew in the Public Arena: The Career of Israel Zangwill* (2008); and J. H. Udelson, *Dreamer of the Ghetto: The Life and Works of Israel Zangwill* (1990); **see also LITERATURE: BRITAIN.**

MERI-JANE ROCHELSON

Zealots. *The Jewish War* (JW) by *Josephus is the only source of information on a group called "Zealots" and their activities during the First *Jewish War against *Rome (66–73 CE). According to Josephus (*JW* 4.128–140), the Zealots emerged as an alliance of armed groups that fled the countryside and converged on *Jerusalem in the winter of 67–68 CE in an attempt to escape the advance of Roman troops. There is no explicit evidence that the Zealots existed as a distinctly identifiable political and military force before that time, even though some of their leaders such as Eleazar, son of Simon, were active at earlier stages of the uprising and probably belonged to Jerusalem's priestly elite (*JW* 2.564–65; 4.225; 5.5). While in Jerusalem, the Zealots launched a series of purges against scions of the old *Herodian aristocracy, seized control of the *Temple, and challenged established high priestly authority by electing a new High Priest by lot (*JW* 4.139–57). The Zealots' actions provoked a military backlash spearheaded by Jerusalem's aristocracy. The initial success of the aristocratic party, however, was short-lived as some of its members (John of Gischala), as well as forces that arrived from the Idumean countryside, helped the Zealots break out of the Temple and effectively take control of Jerusalem. In the ensuing bloodbath, the Zealots took revenge on their opponents (*JW* 4.158–388). When the alliance broke down, the Zealots, under Eleazar, son of Simon, were cornered in the inner court of the Temple; eventually, John of Gischala managed to take full control of the Temple and tricked the Zealots into surrendering (*JW* 4.389–97, 577–84; 5.98–105). Afterward they effectively disappeared from the scene as a distinct group, probably sharing in the final defense of Jerusalem against Roman troops and perishing in the process (*JW* 6.92, 148; 7.215).

Research on the Zealots has been to a large degree shaped by M. Smith ("Zealots and Sicarii, Their Origins and Relation," *Harvard Theological Review* 64 [1971]: 1–19; and "The Troublemakers," in *The Cambridge History of Judaism*, ed. W. Horbury et al. [1999], 3:501–68).

Rejecting earlier conceptualizations of the "Zealots" as an umbrella term for groups and movements that had resisted Roman rule in Judea on religious grounds after Herod's death in 4 BCE (see M. Hengel, *The Zealots: Investigations into the Jewish Freedom Movement in the Period from Herod I until 70 A.D.* [1989]), Smith suggested that the Zealots were a specific and relatively short-lived group of rebels from the countryside that emerged in Jerusalem in the winter of 67–68 CE. R. Horsley developed Smith's argument by portraying the Zealots as a peasant revolutionary movement ("The Zealots: Their Origin, Relationships and Importance in the Jewish Revolt," *Novum Testamentum* 28 [1986]: 159–92). In contrast, M. Goodman noted the organizing role of the Jerusalem aristocracy in the formation of the Zealots (*The Ruling Class of Judaea: The Origins of the Jewish Revolt against Rome A.D. 66–70* [1987]). Although most scholars have embraced Smith's historical assessment, his apparent neglect of a religious component within Zealot ideology remains problematic (see D. Rhoads, *Israel in Revolution* [1976] on possible priestly influences).   ALEXEI SIVERTSEV

Zechariah is a post-exilic biblical book that is part of the twelve Minor Prophets (see BIBLE: PROPHETS AND PROPHECY; PROPHETS [*NEVI'IM*]). Zechariah 1–8 (First Zechariah) reflects the period just before the rededication of the *Jerusalem *Temple in 515 BCE; it is separate and distinct from Zechariah 9–14 (Second or Deutero-Zechariah), which dates at least to the middle of the fifth century.

The core of First Zechariah's message is conveyed in a series of visions in chapters 1–6 that are amplified and clarified in the oracles that surround them; chapters 7 and 8 conclude with a series of individual oracles. Zechariah 3 is set in the heavenly court where Satan unsuccessfully challenges Joshua the High Priest before God; God reaffirms the *covenant through a symbolic cleansing of Joshua's garments and pledges to remove iniquity from the land. Chapter 4 depicts the Temple symbolically by a golden lamp stand (*menorah) flanked by two messianic figures. Second Zechariah consists of a series of oracles including chapter 9 in which *God is depicted as Divine Warrior. Although the character of these chapters is decidedly *apocalyptic, many of the themes are carried forward from First Zechariah. The dramatic end-of-time battles depicted in Zechariah 12–14 culminate in an image of pilgrims going up to Jerusalem to celebrate the *pilgrimage *festival of *Sukkot, the Feast of Booths (14:16–19), when the land will become pure and there will be peace in Jerusalem (14:20–21).   ERIC MEYERS

Zephaniah, Book of. This biblical book appears ninth among the twelve Minor Prophets (see PROPHETS [*NEVI'IM*]). Zephaniah is identified in a detailed genealogical superscription (1:1) as living in the days of *Josiah, king of *Judah (640–609 BCE), the same era in which *Jeremiah was also active. He is said to be a descendant of *Hezekiah, presumably a reference to the Judean king who died in 687 BCE. This short book of three chapters denounces the people of Judah and *Jerusalem for their self-satisfaction and shamelessness and for their participation in the worship of *Baal. Drawing on language from *Genesis, Zephaniah warns that God, in a reversal of creation, will destroy "mankind from the face of the earth" (1:3), a reference that also evokes the *flood. The prophet goes on to excoriate other nations of the region, warning them of the day of anger that will soon overtake them for their haughtiness, "for insulting and jeering at the people of the Lord of Hosts" (2:10). The book ends on a note of consolation (3:8–19) for the "remnant of Israel" who seek God and obey God's commandments and who "need fear misfortune no more" (3:15). *Repentance will annul the divine judgment, and God "will soothe with his love those long disconsolate" (3:17); the prophet promises, "At that time I will gather you/And at that time I will bring you [home]" (3:20). Then, Judah will be "renowned and famous/Among all the peoples on earth/When I restore your fortunes/Before their eyes" (3:20).

Scholars are divided as to when this book was written. Many believe that the concluding prophecy of consolation was written after the *Babylonian Exile, but that earlier sections may have originated in *Josiah's reign, before his religious reforms that occurred ca. 622 BCE. For further reading, see A. Berlin, *Zephaniah: A New Translation with Introduction and Commentary* (1994); and M. A. Sweeney, *Zephaniah: A Commentary* (2003); **see also BIBLE: PROPHETS AND PROPHECY.**   JUDITH R. BASKIN

Zerubbabel was governor of the *Persian province of *Yehud during the first wave of Judean restoration, ca. 520–510 BCE. Serving jointly with the High Priest Joshua ben Johazadak, he was instrumental in persuading the Judean population to rebuild the *Jerusalem *Temple. His name is a common east Semitic *Babylonian name, and he was apparently raised in the *Persian court. Because Zerubbabel was a descendant of King *David, his appointment by the Persian government aroused expectations that the Davidic kingdom would be reestablished. The book of *Zechariah, however, makes it quite clear that his role in the newly established province of Yehud was to be more limited and that hopes for the reestablishment of a Davidic kingship would have to be delayed to the distant future (4:6–10).   ERIC MEYERS

Zion (Hebrew, *Tziyyon*) was the pre-Israelite name for the central fortress in the Jebusite city of *Jerusalem that was conquered by King *David. It became a synonym in biblical and later Jewish tradition for the city of Jerusalem, for the site of the *Temple, and for the Land of *Israel in general. Signal examples include Psalms 137 and 147. Zion is mentioned frequently in biblical poetry as the holy mountain on which God has founded a divine city (e.g., Psalms 46, 76, 78, 87) and in prophetic writings as the source of divine teachings, as in Isaiah 2:3, "For out of Zion shall go forth the law and the word of the Lord from Jerusalem." Since medieval times, Mount Zion has designated a hill south of the walled city of Jerusalem, not the area of the Temple Mount. **See also JERUSALEM: BIBLICAL AND RABBINIC SOURCES.**

Zionism, a term coined in the 1890s by the *Vienna-born intellectual Nathan Birnbaum (1804–1937), betokens the modern Jewish nationalist movement that is characterized by a complicated if not contradictory relationship to the

Jewish past. Zionism echoes the age-old *messianic expectation of a restoration of the Jews to the Land of *Israel, but departs from tradition by affirming that the Jews can emancipate themselves from exile without awaiting explicit and manifest support from God for the launching of such an operation. It likewise replaces the eschatological vision of a Jewish kingdom governed in accordance with divine law with the effort to construct a state along fully modern lines. Dismissing these innovations as heresies, the very man who named the movement turned wholly against it after his return to Orthodox Judaism (see JUDAISM, ORTHODOX). Yet an important segment of religious Jewry has also played a part in the political Zionist movement from its beginnings to the present, and many *secular forces within the movement remain thoroughly imbued with quasi-messianic aspirations.

Although there were some resourceful nineteenth-century Orthodox thinkers who endeavored to undermine traditional quietism from within and can justly be regarded as precursors of Zionism, the true parents of the movement were secularized, more or less assimilated intellectuals who were activated not by a fresh understanding of God's wishes but by a new conception of the Jewish people's needs. The increasingly desperate situation of the Jewish masses in *Eastern Europe and the reemergence of *antisemitism in the west convinced Leon *Pinsker, Theodor *Herzl, and many others that "the Jewish problem" could be solved only through the reconstitution of the Jews as a normal nation in a territory of their own: Herzl expressed this idea in *The Jewish State* (1896). For most proponents of this belief, the optimum location for the fulfillment of such an endeavor was their ancestral homeland.

Zionism before Herzl, known as "Palestinophilism" and led by the Russian physician Pinsker, achieved only very limited success. At the first congress of the World Zionist Organization in 1897, convened by Herzl and held in the Swiss city of Basel, the new organization prudently refrained from declaring its intention of creating a state and called only for the establishment of "a home for the Jewish people in *Palestine secured under public law." How that goal was to be attained and what kind of a home was to be built became the primary questions over which Zionists differed in ensuing decades.

Differences between "practical" Zionists, who focused on concrete efforts to establish a growing Jewish presence in *Ottoman *Palestine, and "political" Zionists, who gave priority to diplomatic endeavors to obtain effective control of the entire land, diminished in the aftermath of Herzl's death in 1904. Chaim *Weizmann and others developed a "synthetic Zionism" that stressed the importance of both paths. They fostered the development of Jewish Palestine (the *Yishuv) in the years before World War I and achieved a crucial success in 1917, with the British issuance of the *Balfour Declaration recognizing the right of Jews to establish their national home there. Only the Revisionists, established in 1925 and led by Vladimir Jabotinsky (1880–1940), found the League of Nations-sanctioned *British Mandate over Palestine to be essentially unsatisfactory. They continued to demand the rapid creation of a Jewish state that would include not only the territory demarcated in the early 1920s as Palestine but also what became known as Trans-Jordan (present-day Jordan) – by force, if necessary.

Political Zionists envisioned a Jewish state modeled on the best achievements and dreams of the modern West, a state that would lack any peculiarly Jewish characteristics. Cultural Zionists, inspired by the Russian-born thinker Asher Ginzberg, who styled himself "*Ahad Ha-Am" (One of the People), deplored the alienation of Herzl and his followers from Jewish tradition; they hoped to resolve the "problem of *Judaism," not the "Jewish problem." What was of the highest importance and was actually attainable, they argued, was the creation of a spiritual and cultural center in Palestine that could serve as the base for a modern, secular, but still deeply Jewish culture that would bind together the world's Jews and prevent their assimilation.

This program was anathema to the small minority of Orthodox Jews who found ample support in Jewish tradition for a pre-messianic return to the Holy Land and established within the Zionist movement the *Mizrachi organization, which was dedicated to reconstructing "the Land of Israel for the people of Israel according to the Torah of Israel." This camp was able to form a tactical alliance with political Zionists, who showed respect for their religious beliefs and strove to cooperate with them, but it regarded the cultural Zionists as ideological adversaries. Ahad Ha-Am and his followers also faced comparably strong criticism from a different direction. Intellectuals like Micah Joseph Berdichevsky (1865–1921) chastised them for their half-measures; they repudiated the legacy of rabbinic *Judaism in its entirety and utterly "negated the Exile." For them, the goal of Zionism was to create a "new Hebrew" who would represent a revivification of the noblest exemplars of biblical heroism.

Their deep-seated differences notwithstanding, all of these Zionists and others (apart from the Revisionists, who created a rival organization of their own) were able to collaborate on the central task of building a Jewish community in Palestine, even as they pursued their disparate aims within a variety of institutional frameworks. They did so increasingly under the leadership of socialist Zionists and in conflict with the country's *Arab residents.

Blending Zionism with socialism was not difficult in principle; however, formulating a *Marxist version of Zionism required considerable ingenuity. The Russian Ber Borokhov (1881–1917) was endowed with just enough Marxism to compose a corpus of writings that "scientifically" demonstrated the inevitability of the transference of the Jewish people's class struggle to Palestine and the ultimate success of the relocated Jewish proletariat in installing socialism in their own country. In the course of their first decades in Palestine, however, the Marxist Zionists largely outgrew their contorted dogmatism and joined together with non-Marxists to formulate a "constructivist socialism" that relied on the worldwide Jewish bourgeoisie for financial support and was flexible enough to live fairly harmoniously with out-and-out capitalists in Palestine itself. By the mid-1930s, the proponents of this new ideology, the socialist Mapai Party (the party of the workers of the Land of Israel), constituted the dominant force in the Zionist movement.

As Zionism developed, it became a divided but cohesive movement. Nevertheless, its considerable worldwide support represented, at least at first, only a minority of the world's Jews. In the indigenous population of Palestine, Zionism found an intransigent enemy that disputed its claim to the land and struggled to prevent its realization. Most

Zionists, for their part, justified what they considered to be their superior right to the Land of Israel on the basis of one or more of the following considerations: divine authority, international law, the Jews' unbroken historical ties to the land, their pressing need for a physical and cultural homeland, and the Zionists' investment of labor and material. However, a few acknowledged that the local Arabs possessed a right to Palestine that was not inferior to that of the Jews, that the land belonged to two different peoples in equal measure, and that future political arrangements had to reflect this situation. Ready to compromise and circumscribe Zionism's domain, these irenic forces lacked any Arab counterparts and were soon confined to the margins of their movement (see ISRAEL, STATE OF: PEACE MOVEMENT).

Most other Zionists continued to profess that their movement would ultimately prove beneficial to the Arabs of Palestine, but simultaneously devoted their best efforts to constructing an entity that would be powerful and prosperous enough to take control of the country once the Jews constituted the large majority of the population. When Zionist growth inevitably provoked Arab hostility, the mainstream of the movement reluctantly began to develop a combative attitude and a military capacity. The development of this force eventually made it possible for the Zionist movement, with the support of most of the world's Jews, to attain its fundamental end goal (see ISRAEL, STATE OF: MILITARY AND PARAMILITARY BODIES). The United Nations-authorized establishment of the State of *Israel in 1948 in part of what had been *British Mandate Palestine marked the fulfillment of the wishes of Herzl and the political Zionists, even if it failed to achieve all of the mutually incompatible aims of cultural, religious, and socialist Zionists (see ISRAEL, STATE OF: FOUNDING).

In subsequent years, even some of the movement's most noteworthy leaders have declared that Zionism, having accomplished its purpose, has become obsolete. Many of the children of Zionist pioneers developed the habit of enclosing the term in parentheses and pronouncing it sarcastically. The World Zionist Organization has survived, however, and the term "Zionism" has been largely redefined to mean support for the State of Israel. The persistence and intensification of opposition to the state's very existence have left Zionist spokespersons with a task to perform. They continue to defend their movement and the state it has produced as forces that enabled the Jewish people to implement its right of self-determination and to provide a refuge for the victims of persecution.

In recent years Zionists have faced the new challenge of a tendency styled *post-Zionism. Some of its proponents, within and outside Israel, have acknowledged that Zionism once represented a legitimate expression of Jewish nationalism. Others, however, describe Zionism as a movement rooted in an unfortunate and contrived redefinition of an ancient religious group as a modern nation and tainted from the outset by colonialist aims. Both groups have focused not so much on debating the original legitimacy of the Zionist idea as on deploring the way in which the entanglement of Zionist and Israeli identities has generated unjustifiable violations of liberal values and accorded second-class citizenship to Israel's non-Jewish citizens. The remedy post-Zionists propose is the transformation of the Jewish state into "a state of all its citizens." In response to their criticisms and proposals and to mounting anti-Zionist calls for the creation of a binational state in all of what was once Mandate Palestine, Zionists in Israel and elsewhere have risen to defend their movement. Some have done so by seeking primarily to discredit post-Zionists. Others have sought to restate and revitalize their ideological principles and to justify the continued existence of Israel as a Jewish state while simultaneously addressing what they take to be the valid concerns of the post-Zionists (R. Gavison, "The Jews' Right to Statehood: A Defense," *Azure* 15 [2003]: 71–109).

In other respects, too, those still committed to Zionism remain, as always, at odds with each other. As the Israeli writer Amos *Oz has frequently declared, Zionism has always been "not a first name but a surname, a family name and this family is divided, feuding over the question of a 'master plan' for the enterprise" (*In the Land of Israel* [1982]). Over the years, the feud has evolved, and some of the more prominent participants in it have disappeared. For instance, the socialists are all but gone. Between the secular Zionists and the religious camp, however, there is an unending *kulturkampf*, a struggle over the proper relationship between *Judaism and the Jewish state, which seems to lend itself more readily to resolution on paper than in the streets of Israel (see JUDAISM, FORMS OF ISRAELI).

For more on this topic, see A. Ravitzky, *Messianism, Zionism and Religious Radicalism* (1996); C. S. Liebman and E. Don-Yehiya, *Religion and Politics in Israel* (1984); J. Myers, *Seeking Zion: Modernity and Messianic Activism in the Writings of Tsevi Hirsch Kalischer* (2003); D. Vital, *The Origins of Zionism* (1975); idem, *Zionism: The Formative Years* (1982); idem, *Zionism: The Crucial Phase* (1987); W. Laqueur, *A History of Zionism* (1972); S. Zipperstein, *Elusive Prophet: Ahad Ha'am and the Origins of Zionism* (1993); E. Luz, *Parallels Meet: Religion and Nationalism in the Early Zionist Movement: 1882–1904* (1988); J. Frankel, *Prophecy and Politics: Socialism, Nationalism and the Russian Jews, 1862–1927* (1982); G. Shimoni, *The Zionist Ideology* (1995); P. Mendes-Flohr, ed., *A Land of Two Peoples: Martin Buber on Jews and Arabs* (1983); A. Shapira, *Land and Power: The Zionist Resort to Force, 1881–1948* (1992); R. Wistrich, ed., *Anti-Zionism and Antisemitism in the Contemporary World* (1990); L. Silberstein, *The Postzionism Debates: Knowledge and Power in Israeli Culture* (1999); and Y. Hazony, *The Jewish State: The Struggle for Israel's Soul* (2000).

ALLAN ARKUSH

Zionism: France. Between 1789 and 1939, French Jews were more deeply engaged with *Palestine than with other places of Jewish settlement (see FRANCE: 1789–1939). The Holy Land not only represented a religious center and place of historic origin but also retained its potential as a future homeland. As early as 1801, Michel Berr suggested that a revival of Jewish nationalism could provide an alternative to the possible failure of *emancipation. Rather than live in slavery in the *Diaspora, he said, Jews could revive their nationality by taking up arms and recapturing their ancient land. It is possible that Berr had been influenced by a proclamation attributed to Napoleon during his siege of Acre in 1799 when he is said to have called on Jews to join his army and reestablish themselves in Palestine. This story continued to circulate long after Napoleon's time and may have influenced others to consider the possibility of reestablishing a Jewish nation.

Mid-nineteenth-century French republicans supported the national liberation of many peoples, including Poles, Italians, and Greeks. L. M. Lambert, the chief rabbi of Metz, endorsed Jewish nationalism in the 1840s, arguing that Jews have as much right to their own nation as the Greeks and Poles; he argued that the potential for Jews to leave France and reenter their ancient homeland in no way created a conflict with French patriotism. In the same decade, Jan Czynski, a Polish exile of Jewish ancestry living in Paris, published a journal, *Réveil d'Israël*, whose sole purpose was to call on Jews (whom he described as the oldest nation) to reclaim their homeland.

Ernest Laharanne, a minor official of the regime of Emperor Napoleon III, revived the idea in his 1860 *La Nouvelle Question d'Orient*. At that time France had troops in Syria and Lebanon, and imperialist motives were likely behind the suggestion that Jews reestablish their nation. Laharanne suggested that Jews might "serve as the intermediary between Europe and East Asia." By the 1860s all the major Jewish journals of the period gave space and credence to those who argued for Jewish national restoration. Lazare Lévy Bing, a member of the Jewish school committee in Nancy, and later of the Paris Consistory, stressed the importance of Jewish children learning the Hebrew language by predicting its role in a future unification of the world, with *Jerusalem as its center.

In 1897, however, when Theodor *Herzl founded the *World Zionist Organization and sought international support for the creation of a state, the French Jewish establishment opted for *emancipation, rather than Zionism, as a goal for world Jewry, although some prominent French Jews did join the movement. Nor did the French Jewish establishment support political Zionism at the end of World War I. Sylvain Lévi, president of the *Alliance Israelite Universelle, went so far as to advise the Foreign Ministry to prevent representatives of French Zionism from speaking at the 1919 peace conference. Claiming that French Zionism was not French at all, but reflected only the views of foreign Jews in France, he argued that a Jewish national homeland would endanger the status of Jews elsewhere by raising the notion of dual loyalty. In that year, the Central Consistory (see FRANCE: CONSISTORIES, 1806–1939) even determined to make a "declaration of war against Zionism."

The Jewish press, in contrast, responded positively to the 1917 *Balfour Declaration, and French Jews were more influenced by Zionism than the stance of its official institutions might suggest. By the 1930s the Consistories recognized the power of Zionism to encourage Jewish identity and so minimized their opposition. Eventually, with the growing refugee problem, it became more acceptable for Consistory members and rabbis to support Zionist activity. For more on this topic, see P. E. Hyman, *The Jews of Modern France* (1998).

PHYLLIS COHEN ALBERT

Zionism: United States. As a movement dedicated to reestablishing a Jewish homeland in *Palestine, *Zionism needed to engage the interest and support of American Jews uninterested in moving to Palestine. After the establishment of Ḥibbat Zion (Love of Zion), a proto-Zionist group formed in 1880s *Russia in response to *pogroms, small chapters emerged in American cities. When Theodor *Herzl took over the reins of world Zionism, these chapters debated his ideas

and raised money for the *Yishuv* (Jewish settlement) in Palestine. However, Zionism did not capture the imagination of many American Jews before the second decade of the twentieth century because many Jews, particularly of *Central European descent, believed that support of Zionism jeopardized their status as American citizens. This question of dual loyalty required resolution before Zionism could appeal to American Jews.

A watershed moment in Zionist history occurred when Louis *Brandeis became chairman of the Federation of American Zionists (FAZ) in 1914. Brandeis called on Zionists to stop debating ideas and to start recruiting new members and raising funds. FAZ membership grew, and by 1918 chapters had formed in every major American Jewish community. American Zionism was also strengthened through the work of Zionist organizations affiliated with FAZ such as *Hadassah, socialist Zionists, and religious Zionists (*Mizrachi).

Brandeis finally resolved the conflict between Zionism and American identity by arguing that Palestine offered an opportunity to create an egalitarian, democratic society along the model of Jeffersonian ideals. All Americans had dual loyalties, Brandeis argued, and this was only a problem if these loyalties conflicted, which was not the case for American Zionists. Brandeis's focus on the practical – on helping European Jews settle Palestine – provided a clear purpose for American Zionists who had no desire to leave their country. Brandeis himself seemed to embody the idea that one could be both a good American and a Zionist when President Wilson appointed him to the Supreme Court in 1916.

Eventually, Brandeis's indifference to the religious aspects of Zionism left a void that was filled by Chaim *Weizmann, his successor in the Zionist Organization of America (ZOA). Weizmann's support came from Jews of Eastern European background who saw him as the embodiment of *yiddishkeit* (Jewishness). Although the 1920s and 1930s were not a good time for Zionism, as *Britain weakened its commitment to the *Balfour Declaration and Hitler rose to power, World War II and subsequent post-war prosperity galvanized America Zionism as a new and more militant leadership took over. With European Zionism destroyed, America and Palestine became the centers of world Zionism.

In post-war America, the ZOA under Rabbi Abba Hillel *Silver became the greatest ally of the *Yishuv* in its fight for independence. American Zionists also played a central role in helping convince President Harry S. Truman to recognize Israel when it declared independence in 1948. Ironically, this moment also marked the beginning of the decline of American Zionism as the new state began to speak for itself and most American Jews continued to evince little interest in moving to Israel. Still, support for Israel has continued to serve as a rallying point for many of the diverse segments of American Jewry (see ORGANIZATIONS: NORTH AMERICA). For further reading, see M. Urofsky, *American Zionism from Herzl to the Holocaust* (1975); and M. Raider, *The Emergence of American Zionism* (1998).

RACHEL GORDAN

Zohar (splendor or brightness) is the most important and influential work of the *Kabbalah. It was written in northern *Spain in the last decades of the thirteenth century, but has traditionally been regarded as expressing ancient esoteric teachings, given to *Moses on Mount Sinai. Many Jews place it alongside the *Bible and the *Talmud as the third source of divine wisdom given by *God to Israel. In fact, the principal author of the *Zohar* was the kabbalist *Moses de Leon (d. 1305), who may have collaborated with his colleague, Joseph Gikatilla, and possibly some other kabbalists of that period. The earliest quotations from the *Zohar* appear in 1291, and soon after that it dominated other works of Jewish *mysticism, both in the Middle Ages and in modern times. The *Zohar* was printed twice in *Italy in the sixteenth century: in one volume in Cremona (1559) and in three volumes in Mantua (1558–60). The latter became the standard edition of the work. Two more volumes were added to the *Zohar* library: *Zohar Ḥadash* (The New *Zohar*) first printed in Salonika in 1597, which is a collection of segments of the work taken from many manuscripts, and *Tikkunei Zohar* (Emendations of the *Zohar*), first printed in Mantua in 1558. This is a separate work, written by an early-fourteenth-century kabbalist who imitated the language and style of the *Zohar*.

The *Zohar* is written in a unique version of *Aramaic, many aspects of which were created by its author. The body of the work is a series of homiletical commentaries on the weekly *Torah readings in the order in which they are read in the *synagogue throughout the year. These commentaries are attributed to *Tannaim, the rabbinic sages associated with the production of the *Mishnah in the second century CE. Their leader, according to the *Zohar* narratives, was R. *Simon bar Yoḥai, assisted by his son Eleazar. According to talmudic legend, R. Simon and his son hid from the *Romans in a cave for seven years. The *Zohar* embellishes this narrative, adding to it other talmudic legends, and presents a fictional framework within which its homiletical interpretations are interwoven. Additional characters include a wondrous old man and a brilliant child (*yenuka*), who reveal celestial secrets.

Other treatises are also included in the *Zohar*. One is the *Midrash Ha-Ne'elam* (The Esoteric Midrash), written partly in Hebrew; this seems to be the earliest part of the work. Another is the *Sava de-Mishpatim* (The Old Man in the Torah Portion of *Mishpatim*). Two highly esoteric sections are the *Idra Rabba* (The Great Assembly) and *Idra Zuta* (The Small Assembly). The first includes a complex presentation of the secrets of the divine world as reflected in the anthropomorphic structure of that realm. In the second, there is a description of the mystical ceremony surrounding R. Simon's death. Another highly esoteric section is *Sifra de-Zeniuta* (Book of Concealment), dealing with the secrets of the cosmogonic process (an explanation of the origins of the cosmos). In several sections of the *Zohar* another treatise is preserved: the *Ra'aya Mehemna* (The Faithful Shepherd). This text about *Moses was written by a later kabbalist, the author of the *Tikkunei Zohar*.

Moses de Leon distributed copies of sections of the *Zohar*, claiming that they originated from an ancient manuscript. After his death, however, his widow denied the existence of such a document. Thus, the belief in the antiquity of the *Zohar* became a test of Jewish orthodoxy; doubting it, as some Jewish scholars have done since the end of the fifteenth century, continues to be regarded as heresy in some circles.

For good English translations, see the anthology, I. Tishby, ed., *The Wisdom of the Zohar*, 3 vols. (1989), arranged by subject, with detailed introductions and commentaries; and the *Pritzker Zohar*, translation and commentary by D. Matt (2004–09); five volumes have thus far appeared. Also useful is A. Green, *A Guide to the Zohar* (2004).

JOSEPH DAN

Zunz, Leopold (Yom Tov Lipmann), born in Detmold in 1794 and died in *Berlin in 1886, was the founder and an important representative of Jewish academic scholarship (*Wissenschaft des Judentums*) in nineteenth-century *Germany. Zunz was educated at the Samsonsche Freischule in Wolfenbuettel, which during his attendance was profoundly reformed by Samuel Meyer Ehrenberg. After completing his studies at a local high school Zunz taught at the Samsonsche Freischule between 1810 and 1815. In 1815 he began his studies at the recently established University of Berlin, where his most influential teachers were the classicists Friedrich August Wolf and August Boeckh. They inspired his interest in philology, the main area of his future research. His ground-breaking essay of 1818, "*Etwas über die rabbinische Litteratur*" (On Rabbinic Literature), can be seen as an outline for the future discipline of *Jewish Studies. In 1819, Zunz was among the co-founders of the Verein für Cultur und Wissenschaft der Juden (Association for the Culture and Science of Judaism), and he edited the short-lived journal of the association (1822). Zunz initially favored religious reforms and served for a brief time as a preacher in the Berlin Reform congregation (see JUDAISM, REFORM: GERMANY) and later in *Prague (1835–36). He earned his living as editor of a Berlin newspaper, director of the primary school of the Jewish community, and director of a Jewish teachers' seminary. His attempts to establish a chair for Jewish Studies at the University of Berlin failed. Zunz was an active supporter of the aborted Revolution of 1848. In *Namen der Juden* (1837) Zunz tried to combat the Prussian government's restriction on the names Jews could bear. In his most important scholarly works, Zunz analyzed medieval religious *poetry and the history of Jewish *worship (*Die synagogale Poesie des Mittelalters* [1855] and *Der Ritus des synagogalen Gottesdienstes* [1859]). His edition of Nachman *Krochmal's *Moreh nevukhei ha-zeman* (Guide of the Perplexed of the Time) appeared in 1851.

MICHAEL BRENNER

INDEX OF NAMES

*indicates that there is an entry for this individual

0 1341 1366922 7